THE

RHS

PLANT FINDER 1997-98

THE RHS PLANT FINDER 1997-98

DEVISED BY CHRIS PHILIP

COMPILED BY THE
ROYAL HORTICULTURAL SOCIETY

EDITED BY TONY LORD
WITH THE BOTANISTS
OF THE RHS GARDEN, WISLEY

DORLING KINDERSLEY
LONDON • NEW YORK • SYDNEY • MOSCOW

A DORLING KINDERSLEY BOOK

Published by
Dorling Kindersley Ltd
9 Henrietta Street
LONDON WC2E 8PS
Visit us on the World Wide Web at http://www.dk.com

First edition April 1987
Eleventh edition April 1997

British Library Cataloguing Publication Data.
A Catalogue record for this book is available from the British Library.

ISBN 0 7513 1082 4
ISSN 0961-2599

Compiled by
The Royal Horticultural Society
80 Vincent Square
London
SW1P 2PE
Registered charity no: 222879
Visit us on the World Wide Web at http://www.rhs.org.uk

Maps by Alan Cooper

Printed by
Unwin Brothers, Woking, Surrey

Front cover photographs clockwise from top right: *Meconopsis betonicifolia, Convolvulus cneorum, Allium cristophii, Arisaema candidissimum, Cotinus* 'Flame', *Phlox divaricata* subsp. *laphamii* 'Chattahoochee', *Euphorbia characias* subsp. *characias, Magnolia grandiflora* 'Exmouth', *Penstemon* 'Rubicundus', *Brugmansia* × *candida* 'Grand Marnier'

Back cover photographs clockwise from top right: *Corydalis solida* f. *transsylvanica* 'George Baker', *Tecophilaea cyanocrocus* 'Leichtlinii', *Arbutus unedo, Asplenium nidus, Convolvulus sabatius, Paeonia lactiflora* 'Bowl of Beauty', *Roscoea cautleyoides, Gentiana septemfida, Cercis siliquastrum, Agapetes serpens*

CONTENTS

SYMBOLS AND ABBREVIATIONS

Symbols appearing to the left of the name

*	Name not validated. Not listed in the appropriate International Registration Authority checklist nor in works cited in the Bibliography. For fuller discussion see Nomenclature on page 10
I	Invalid name. See *International Code of Botanical Nomenclature* 1994 and *International Code of Nomenclature for Cultivated Plants* 1995. For fuller discussion see Nomenclature on page 10
N	Refer to Nomenclature Notes on page 15
¶	New plant entry in this year's Edition (or reinstated from list of previously deleted plants)
◆	New or amended synonym or cross-reference included for the first time this year
§	Plant listed elsewhere in the PLANT DIRECTORY under a synonym
×	Hybrid genus
+	Graft hybrid genus

Symbols appearing to the right of the name

=	National Council for the Conservation of Plants and Gardens (NCCPG) Collection exists for all or part of this genus
🏆	The Royal Horticultural Society's Award of Garden Merit
®	Registered Trade Mark
™	Trade Mark
(d)	double-flowered
(f)	female
(m)	male
(v)	variegated plant

For abbreviations relating to individual genera see **Classification of Genera** page 24.

For **Collectors' References** see page 29.

Symbols and Abbreviations used as part of the name

×	hybrid species
aff.	affinis (allied to)
cl.	clone
cv(s)	cultivar(s)
f.	forma (botanical form)
g.	grex
sp.	species
subsp.	subspecies
subvar.	subvarietas (botanical subvariety)
var.	varietas (botanical variety)

IMPORTANT NOTE TO USERS

To avoid disappointment, we suggest that you always:

Check with the nursery before visiting or ordering and always use the current edition of the book.

The RHS Plant Finder exists to put gardeners in touch with nurserymen. It does *not* offer value judgements on the nurseries or the plants it lists nor intend any reflection on any other nursery or plant *not* listed.

In addition ***The RHS Plant Finder*** tries to cross-reference plant names to their correct *valid* name, although in some cases it is all too easy to understand why British nurserymen have preferred a more immediately comprehensible English name! *Every* name, apart from 'common' names, that has been shown in a catalogue has been listed, which is why there are so many cross-references. It is, clearly, the nursery's responsibility to ensure that its stock is accurately named both in its catalogue and on the plant when it is sold.

The Compiler and Editors of ***The RHS Plant Finder*** have taken every care, in the time available, to check all the information supplied to them by the nurseries concerned. Nevertheless, in a work of this kind, containing as it does hundreds of thousands of separate computer encodings, errors and omissions will, inevitably, occur. Neither the Royal Horticultural Society, the Publisher nor the Editors can accept responsibility for any consequences that may arise from such errors.

If you find mistakes we hope that you will let us know so that the matter can be corrected in the next edition.

PREFACE

IT IS MY PLEASURE to welcome readers to the 1997-98 edition of *The RHS Plant Finder*, which this year has been compiled for the first time by the Royal Horticultural Society.

This is also the eleventh edition of a book that has become something of a landmark in horticultural publishing. That it is so, is due to Chris Philip's invaluable work over the last 10 years which has done much to establish a firm foundation for more stable plant nomenclature. As well as this, he has developed over the years an unrivalled guide to the rich variety of plants available from specialist nurseries all over the country.

We are very grateful to all these nurseries, for only with their co-operation and help is it possible to produce this very comprehensive book.

There has also been a great deal of input from many botanists and horticulturists, including the Society's Advisory Panel on Nomenclature and Taxonomy. All of these people are working towards the goal of achieving a stable and consistent nomenclature for cultivated plants. *The RHS Plant Finder* is now compiled from our horticultural database, *BG-BASE*™, which provides a core resource of information on plant names for the Society.

While we have made no change to the structure of the book, there are a number of differences in the way the plant names are presented and I would encourage all readers to start with the section on how to use this book, where the changes are highlighted (please see p 8).

Every year hundreds of comments and queries concerning nomenclature are received. Regretfully it is impossible for Dr Tony Lord or the Society to reply to all these individually, but we do assure nurseries that all their queries are considered.

As plant nomenclature and taxonomy is constantly changing, no horticultural book or record can ever be totally up to date. Each edition of *The RHS Plant Finder* is therefore, by definition, a snapshot at that point in time. Changes in names will have taken place between the time this edition goes to print and the time it is bought, which is just a matter of weeks. But the research continues as part of the Society's work both in trials at Wisley and on the part of individual botanists.

Chris Philip continues to play an active role through the production of the electronic version of the *Plant Finder Reference Library* on CD-Rom.

I hope that this new edition of *The RHS Plant Finder* will continue to be a helpful source of information and an invaluable guide to successful plant hunting.

Gordon Rae
Director General
The Royal Horticultural Society

HOW TO USE THE DIRECTORY

Look up the plant you require in the alphabetical **Plant Directory**. Against each plant you will find a four-letter Code, or Codes, for example ECha SLan, each Code representing one nursery offering that plant. The first letter of each Code indicates the main area of the country in which the nursery is situated, based on their county:

HOW TO FIND YOUR PLANT

Geographical Key to Nursery Codes

[C] = **South West England**
Avon, Devon, Dorset, Channel Isles, Cornwall, Isles of Scilly, Somerset & Wiltshire.

[E] = **Eastern England**
Cambridgeshire, Essex, Lincolnshire, Norfolk & Suffolk.

[G] = **Scotland**
Borders, Central, Dumfries & Galloway, Fife, Grampian, Highlands, Inverness, Strathclyde.

[I] = **Northern Ireland & Republic of Ireland**.

[L] = **London area**
Bedfordshire, Berkshire, Buckinghamshire, Hertfordshire, London, Middlesex, Surrey.

[M] = **Midlands**
Cheshire, Derbyshire, Isle of Man, Leicestershire, Northamptonshire, Nottinghamshire, Oxfordshire, Staffordshire, Warwickshire, West Midlands.

[N] = **Northern England**
Cleveland, Cumbria, Durham, East Yorkshire, Greater Manchester, Humberside, Lancashire, Merseyside, Northumberland, North Yorkshire, South Yorkshire, Tyne & Wear, West Yorkshire.

[S] = **Southern England**
East Sussex, Hampshire, Isle of Wight, Kent, West Sussex.

[W] = **Wales and Western England**
All Welsh counties, Gloucestershire, Herefordshire, Shropshire and Worcestershire.

Turn to the **Code-Nursery Index** on page 711 where, in alphabetical order of Codes, you will find details of each nursery which offers the plant in question. If you wish to visit any of these nurseries you can find its *approximate* location on one of the maps at the back. Those few nurseries which sell *only* by Mail Order are not shown on the maps. ***Always check that the nursery you select has the plant in stock before you set out.***

Changes in this Edition

● Cultivars marked ® in previous editions have mostly been re-styled as trade designations (selling names). For a full discussion, see page 9.

● The way in which cultivars of certain genera are listed has been altered for clarity and consistency, notably in the genus *Rhododendron* which is no longer divided between azaleas and hybrids. Climbing roses are also listed differently in this edition. For example, *Rosa* 'Allgold, Climbing' will appear as *Rosa* 'Climbing Allgold', using the correct form of cultivar name.

● Family names follow modern classifications, including for example the splits of the family Liliaceae. They all now conform to the -aceae ending. For example, Compositae becomes Asteraceae.

● Abbreviations in the cross-references have been expanded for clarity throughout the book.

● Synonym references have been increased for selected large genera to help you find your plant.

● For descriptive terms which appear after the main part of the name, a smaller font has been introduced to distinguish name parts that are authors, common names, collectors' codes and other descriptive terms. For example, *Acaena anserinifolia* Druce, *Cyclamen coum* Blanchard's form pink-flowered.

● A Fruit and Vegetable Index has been introduced to cross-refer readers from the common to the botanical name. The index is on page 829.

Widely Available Plants

In some cases, against the plant name you will see the term 'Widely available' instead of a Nursery Code. Clearly, if we were to include every plant listed by all nurseries, ***The RHS Plant Finder*** would become unmanageably bulky. We have therefore had to ask nurseries to restrict their entries to only those plants that are not already well represented. As a result, if more than 30 nurseries offer any plant the Directory gives no Code and the plant is listed as 'Widely available'. You should have little difficulty in finding these in local nurseries or Garden Centres. However, if any readers do have difficulty in finding such plants, we will be pleased to send them a full list of all the nurseries that we have on file as stockists. This could include anything from 31 to a maximum of 50. Please write to:

The Administrator, The RHS Plant Finder, RHS Garden, Wisley, Woking, Surrey GU23 6QB

All such enquiries *must* include the full name of the plant being sought, as shown in ***The RHS Plant Finder***, together with a *stamped addressed envelope*.

Nursery-Code Index
For convenience, a reverse **Nursery-Code Index** is included on page 703. This gives the names of the nurseries listed in the **Plant Directory** in alphabetical order of nursery names together with their relevant Codes.

Additional Nursery Index
There is also an **Additional Nursery Index**, on page 808, containing brief details of other nurseries that have not been included in the **Plant Directory**. They may be listed in this Index for a number of reasons, for example, their stock is small and changes too quickly for them to be able to issue a viable catalogue, or the major part of their stock would have to be listed as 'Widely available', or simply because their latest Catalogue was not received in time for inclusion. Again, their catalogues may either give mainly English names, (and this particularly applies to herb nurseries) or Latin names which do not provide sufficient information to establish easily the genus or species of the plant concerned. The location of these nurseries on the maps is marked by their listed numbers.

If you have difficulty finding your plant
If you cannot immediately find the plant you seek, look through the various species of the genus. **<u>You may be using an incomplete name</u>**. The problem is most likely to arise in very large genera such as *Phlox* where there are a number of possible species, each with a large number of cultivars. A search through the whole genus may well bring success.

If the plant you seek is not listed in the **Plant Directory**, it is possible that a nursery in the **Additional Nursery Index** which specialises in similar plants may be able to offer it. In addition to the plants listed in their catalogues, many nurseries are often able to supply other plants of the same general type that they specialise in. They may not list them if they only have a few available. In some cases they can arrange to propagate special items from their stock plants.

It may be that the plant name you seek is a synonym. Our intention is to list Nursery Codes only against the correct botanical name; where you look up a synonym you will be cross-referred to the correct name. **Major new cross-references** and synonyms have been marked with a ◆. This sign has only been used when the genus, species or cultivar name has been altered, but not where there have been merely minor typographic or orthographic changes.

If a cross-reference appears to go nowhere, check if the entry appears in **Plant Deletions**.

SUPPORTING INFORMATION ABOUT PLANTS

Classification of Genera
Genera including a large number of species or with many cultivars are often subdivided into groups, each based on a particular characteristic or combination of characteristics. Colour of flower or fruit and shape of flower are common examples, and with fruit, whether a cultivar is grown for culinary or dessert purposes. How such groups are named differs from genus to genus.

To help users of ***The RHS Plant Finder*** find exactly the plants they want, the majority of classifications used within cultivated genera are listed with codes, and each species or cultivar is marked with the appropriate code in brackets after its name in the **Plant Directory**. This year, the codes relating to edible fruits have been listed with the more specialised classifications; these apply across several genera. To find the explanation of each code, simply look up the code under the genus concerned in the **Classification of Genera** on page 24

Trade Designations (Selling Names) and Plant Breeders' Rights
Plants granted protection under Plant Breeders' Rights (PBR) legislation are often given a code or nonsense name for registration purposes. Under the rules of the *International Code of Nomenclature for Cultivated Plants 1995* (ICNCP), such a name, established by a legal process, has to be regarded as the correct cultivar name for the plant. Unfortunately, the names are often unpronounceable and usually meaningless so the plants are given other names designed to attract sales when they are released. These are often referred to as selling names but are officially termed trade designations. Also, when a cultivar name is translated into a language

other than that in which it was published, the translation is regarded as a trade designation in the same way as a PBR selling name. The name in its original language is the correct cultivar name.

While PBRs remain active it is a legal requirement for both names to appear on a label at point-of-sale. The reason for this may not appear obvious until it is realised that there is potentially no limit to the number of trade designations for any one plant. In reality, most plants are sold under only one trade designation, but some, especially roses, are sold under a number of names, particularly when cultivars are introduced to other countries. Usually, the registered or original cultivar name is the only way to ensure that the same plant is not bought unwittingly under two or more different trade designations.

Although the use of trade designations goes against the principle that a cultivar should have only one correct name, the ICNCP has had to accommodate them, and from this year ***The RHS Plant Finder*** follows its recommendations. These are always to quote the cultivar name and trade designation together and to style the trade designation in a different typeface, without single quotation marks.

Example in *Rosa*:

The Cheshire Regiment 'Fryzebedee' (HT) =	MFry
The Cheshire Regiment	See ***R***. The Cheshire Regiment = **'Fryzebedee'**

The first of these names will be found alphabetically under the first letter of the cultivar name ('Fryzebedee'); the second name by the first letter of the trade designation (The).

In the **Plant Directory**, plants are listed in alphabetical order of cultivar name, including names with trade designations attached. Such entries may appear to be out of sequence until this explanation is taken into account.

We often receive queries as to whether certain varieties are the subject of Plant Breeders' Rights. Up to date information on all matters concerning PBR in the UK can be obtained from Mrs J G H Lee at the Plant Variety Rights Office, White House Lane, Huntingdon Road, Cambridge CB3 0LF. Telephone (01223) 342350, Fax (01223) 342386.

For details of plants which may be covered by Community Rights contact the Community Plant Variety Office (CPVO), 102 Rue de la Loi, 1st Floor Office 1/11, B-1040, Brussels, Belgium. Telephone +32 2 299 1944, Fax +32 2 299 1946.

Variegated Plants
Following a suggestion from the Variegated Plant Group of the Hardy Plant Society, we have added a (v) to those plants which are 'variegated' although this may not be apparent from their name. Plants named 'Variegata' or 'Marginata' (in combination) are not coded as all except *Iris variegata, Rosa* 'Variegata di Bologna' and *R.* 'Centifolia Variegata' have variegated leaves rather than flowers. The dividing line between variegation and less distinct colour marking is necessarily arbitrary and plants with light veins, pale, silver or dark zones or leaves flushed in paler colours are not shown as being variegated unless there is an absolutely sharp distinction between paler and darker zones.

For further details of the Variegated Plant Group, please write to: Stephen Taffler, 18 Hayes End Manor, South Petherton, Somerset TA13 5BE.

Following the **Plant Directory** and the **Nursery Indexes**, towards the end of the book, are several further indexes. These include:

Reverse Synonyms
It is likely that users of this book will come across names in certain genera which they did not expect to find. This may be because species have been transferred from another genus (or genera). In the list of **Reverse Synonyms** on page 830, the left-hand name of each pair is that of an accepted genus to which species have been transferred from the genus on the right. Sometimes all species will have been transferred, but in many cases only a few will be affected. Consulting **Reverse Synonyms** enables users to find the genera from which species have been transferred. If the right-hand genus is then found in the **Plant Directory**, the movements of species become clear through the cross-references in the nursery-code column.

Plant Deletions
The **Plant Deletions Index** contains plant names that were listed in one or other of the 10 previous editions of ***The RHS Plant Finder***, but are now no longer represented. As a result there are a few instances where a genus exists in the main **Plant Directory** but with no apparent entries for either species or cultivars. These will be found in the **Plant Deletions Index** on page 834. It is also possible that some cross-references may not apparently refer to an entry in the main Directory. Again this is because the plant in question had a supplier or suppliers but is now in the **Plant Deletions Index**. These references are deliberately kept so as to provide an historic record of synonyms and plant availability and to aid those who wish to try and find any of these 'deleted' plants.

These deletions arise, not only because the

nursery that supplied the plants may have gone out of business, but also because some nurseries who were included previously have not responded to our latest questionnaire and have thus had to be deleted. Such plants may well be still available but we have no current knowledge of their whereabouts. Furthermore, some items may have been misnamed by nurseries in previous editions, but are now appearing under their correct name.

For those who wish to try and find previously listed plants, back editions of ***The RHS Plant Finder*** are still available at £6.00 (incl. p&p) from **The Administrator, *The RHS Plant Finder*, RHS Garden, Wisley, Woking, Surrey GU23 6QB. Cheques should be made payable to RHS Enterprises Ltd.**

Hardy Plant Society Search List

During the last few years the Hardy Plant Society has published a search list of scarce and desirable plants that might not be available in the British Isles. As a result, numerous new plants have been brought into cultivation and many old cultivars have been reintroduced. The HPS has built up a list of about 1,000 plants about which it is keen to obtain further information. See page 900.

Supporting Information about Nurseries

The details given for each nursery (listed in the relevant Index at the back) have been compiled from information supplied to us in answer to a questionnaire. In some cases, because of constraints of space, the entries have been slightly abbreviated and blanks have been left where no information has been provided.

Opening Times

The word 'daily' implies every day including Sunday and Bank Holidays. Although opening times have been published as submitted and where applicable, it is *always* advisable, especially if travelling a long distance, to check with the nursery first.

Mail Order - UK & EC

Many nurseries provide a Mail Order service which, in many cases, now extends to all members of the European Community. Where it is shown that there is 'No minimum charge' (Nmc) it should be realised that to send even one plant may involve the nursery in substantial postage and packing costs. Even so, some nurseries may not be prepared to send tender or bulky plants. Nurseries that are prepared to undertake Mail Order to both UK and EC destinations are shown in **bold** type in the **Code-Nursery Index**.

Catalogue Cost

Some nurseries offer their catalogue free, or for a few stamps (the odd value quoted can usually be made up from a combination of first or second class stamps), but a *large*, at least (A5) stamped addressed envelope is always appreciated as well. Overseas customers should use an equivalent number of International Reply Coupons (IRCs) in place of stamps.

Wholesale or Retail

The main trading method is indicated, but it should be stressed that some wholesalers do have retail outlets and many retailers also have a wholesale trade and would frequently be prepared to offer discounts for large single orders.

Export - (Outside the EC)

Nurseries that are prepared to consider exporting are indicated. However, there is usually a substantial minimum charge and, in addition, all the additional costs of Phytosanitary Certificates and Customs would have to be met by the purchaser.

Deleted Nurseries

Every year a few nurseries ask to be deleted. This may be because they are about to move or close, or they are changing the way in which they trade. About three per cent do not reply so we have no information concerning them and they are therefore deleted.

Please, never use an old edition.

New Nursery Entries

Nurseries that are appearing in ***The RHS Plant Finder*** for the first time this year are printed in **bold type** in the **Nursery-Code Index** starting on page 703.

If any other nursery wishes to be considered for inclusion in the next edition of ***The RHS Plant Finder*** (1998-99), please write for details to:

The Administrator
The RHS Plant Finder
RHS Garden
Wisley
Woking
Surrey
GU23 6QB

The closing date for new entries will be 31 January 1998.

Nomenclature

'The question of nomenclature is always a vexed one. The only thing certain is, that it is impossible to please everyone.'

W J Bean - Preface to First Edition of *Trees & Shrubs Hardy in the British Isles*.

This eleventh edition is the first to be generated from *BG-BASE*™, the database software now used by the RHS to maintain its records, both the plant records of its living collections and of the dried specimens in the Wisley Herbarium. Written by Dr Kerry Walter and Michael O'Neal for the management of botanic gardens, *BG-BASE*™ has been further developed to tackle the complexities of cultivated plant nomenclature (such as cultivar-group names, trade designations etc), as well as to generate ***The RHS Plant Finder***, in which nursery codes are annually attached to each name.

The transition from the simple but effective database used by Chris Philip to the much more extensive *BG-BASE*™ has not been easy; with many more fields for the separate parts of plant names and for information about the plants, a great deal of restructuring of information transferred from Chris Philip has been necessary. Ultimately, with the addition of the Society's International Registers and Trials records, we hope the RHS horticultural database will be the most comprehensive and thoroughly-checked of its kind in the world, a foundation stone for the generation of authoritative and reliable publications and lists and a token of the Society's commitment to the dissemination of accurate information about garden plants.

Following the acquisition of ***The Plant Finder*** by the Royal Horticultural Society, the Society's Advisory Panel on Nomenclature and Taxonomy was set up to try to establish the agreed list of plant names now held on the RHS horticultural database and used in this and other RHS publications. The panel looks at all recent and current proposals to change or correct names and strives for a balance between the stability of well-known names and botanical and taxonomic correctness according to the codes of nomenclature.

The panel reports to the Society's Science and Horticultural Advice Committee. Unlike the independent Horticultural Taxonomy Group (Hortax), its aim is to consider individual problems of plant nomenclature rather than general principles. Chaired by Chris Brickell, the panel includes Susyn Andrews (Kew), Dr Stephen Jury (University of Reading), Sabina Knees (Edinburgh), Dr Alan Leslie (RHS), Tony Lord, Dr Simon Thornton-Wood (RHS), Piers Trehane (Index Hortensis) and Adrian Whiteley (RHS).

Once again, the panel has considered a great many proposals to change or correct names during the last year. Inevitably, it will take some time to reach consensus on some of the more problematic names and we have yet to decide which of the changes to Crassulaceae and Rosaceae suggested in *European Garden Flora* Volume 4, or to wisterias in Peter Valder's recent book, to adopt. We feel it is important not to make any changes until we are sure they are absolutely justified: few things annoy gardeners more than changes to plant names that are subsequently shown to be ill-founded and have to be reversed. Under the aegis of Reading University, work continues on the eternally contentious ivies. We have enlisted the help of the British Pteridological Society in establishing agreed names for fern cultivars and cultivar-groups and hope to have reached consensus on these in time for our next edition. With the help of Mrs Margaret Easter, some study on thymes has been initiated, one of the most vexing genera in which almost half the cultivars clearly do not belong to the species to which they are usually ascribed.

Many name changes proposed by nurseries and Plant Finder users over the past year have been adopted but others have yet to be considered and approved by the Panel: we hope that all those who have generously told us about wrong names will be patient if the corrections they suggest are not immediately made: all such opinions are much valued but the volume of information is great and must be thoroughly checked before we make changes.

Families and genera used in ***The RHS Plant Finder*** are almost always those given in Brummitt's *Vascular Plant Families and Genera*. Thus, for the third year, there are no major changes to genera in this edition. For spellings and genders of generic names, Greuter's *Names in Current Use* is being followed; there are rare cases in which this disagrees with some prominent recent publications such as its use of the spelling *Diplarrhena* as opposed to *Diplarrena* in the current *Flora of Australia*. However, the general effect will be to keep names in exactly the same form as they are already known to gardeners.

In some cases the panel feels that the conflicting views about the naming of some groups of plants will not be easily resolved. Our policy is to wait until an absolutely clear consensus is reached, not to rush to rename plants only to have to change names a second time when opinions have shifted yet again.

As in last years, this edition contains few major changes to plant names. Many proposals to make further changes have been resisted until the panel has had time to study them more fully. If nomenclatural arguments are finely balanced, we will retain old names in the interests of stability. This does not alter the fact that all involved in the publication of ***The RHS Plant Finder*** remain committed to the use of plant names that are as correct as possible. As before, gardeners and nurserymen may still choose to differ and use what names they want, many preferring a more conservative and a few a more radical approach to naming. Except for those names in which we have made corrections of a couple of letters to bring them in line with the codes of nomenclature, we are responsible for *none* of the name changes in this or any other edition of ***The RHS Plant Finder***.

Rules of Nomenclature

Throughout ***The RHS Plant Finder*** we try to follow the rules of nomenclature set out in the *International Code of Botanical Nomenclature 1994* (ICBN) and the *International Code of Nomenclature for Cultivated Plants 1995* (ICNCP). Cultivar names which are clearly not permissible under this code and for which there seems to be no valid alternative are marked **I** (for invalid). The commonest sorts of invalid names seem to be those that are wholly or partly in Latin (not permissible since 1959, eg 'Pixie Alba', 'Superba', 'Variegata') and those which use a Latin generic name as a cultivar name (eg *Rosa* 'Corylus', *Viola* 'Gazania'). If no prior valid name exists, an enterprising nurseryman may publish a new valid name for any such plant. This would be considered validly published if it appeared in a dated catalogue with a clear description of the plant; the originator, if still alive, must be willing to accept the new name.

Apart from being discourteous to the plants' originators and their countries, the translating of foreign plant names into English is a bad and insular practice that is likely to cause confusion; it is also contrary to Article 28 of the 1995 ICNCP. In this edition, this and other Articles of the new code are applied more strictly than before. The Code requires that such translations be considered trade designations and not cultivar names and so should be presented in a different font (here sans serif) and not in quotes. These and other epithets that are not strictly cultivar names, including trade marks and registered trade marks, have previously all been annotated ® as a simplistic catch-all designation; we hope to give a more precise indication of the status of all such names and in this edition ® is only used for true registered trade marks. It may be years yet before we make sense of the host of German names and apparent English translations for a genus such as *Coreopsis*, many of which must be synonyms. Throughout ***The RHS Plant Finder***, we have tried to give preference to the original name in every case, although English translations are also given as trade designations where they are in general use.

The substitution of slick selling names by nurseries which do not like, or have not bothered to find out, the correct names of the plants they sell is sharp practice not expected of any reputable nursery; it is also a probable breach of the Trades Description Act.

The publication of the ICNCP has done a great deal to clarify nomenclature without generally introducing rules that cause destabilising name changes. However, it significantly alters the sort of plant names that are allowed since 1 January 1996: nurseries who name plants are strongly urged to check that the names they want to use are acceptable under the new code.

One Article of the Code that comes into play with this edition particularly, because it affects names published since 1995, is Art. 17.13, dealing in part with the use of botanical or common generic names within a cultivar or group name. This bans names in which the last word of the cultivar name is the common or botanical name of a genus. Two sorts of such names are commonly found: those based on colours (ending Lilac, Lavender, Rose, Rosa, Mauve (French for *Malva*)) and those based on personal names (Rosemary, Hazel). These will be marked **I** in ***The RHS Plant Finder*** if known to have been published after 1995 or marked with an asterisk if their date of publication is unknown. This rule does not preclude cultivar epithets ending with common names which apply to only part of a genus such as Apricot, Cerise, Cherry, Lemon, Lime, Orange, Peach, Pink, or Violet.

Another Article of the new Code which the Panel has considered in the last year is Art. 17.11, banning cultivar names consisting of solely adjectival words in a modern language, unless one of these words may be considered a substantive or unless the epithet is the recognized name of a colour. As this rule is retroactive, applying to all cultivar names whenever they were published, if applied strictly it could require rejection of several hundred cultivar names in ***The RHS Plant Finder***, many of them very well known and widely used. Furthermore, it is difficult to apply: many adjectives also have substantive meanings, albeit sometimes obscure ones, that might or might not justify acceptance of the names; it is not easy to decide which names of colours are accepted and which are not. Our Panel's judgement is that, as currently worded, this Article is unintentionally restrictive and potentially destabilizing; a future edition of the Code is unlikely to be so proscriptive. So for the time being we will not use this Article as a basis for making changes, nor for declaring already established names unacceptable.

Orthography

The ruling on orthography (i.e. correct spelling) of commemorative names, re-stated in the 1994 *International Code of Botanical Nomenclature*, has aroused a great deal of debate at Panel meetings. This subject is discussed in the supplement to Bean's *Trees and Shrubs Hardy in the British Isles* (1988) and is given in ICBN Article 60 and the subsequent recommendations 60C.I. The meaning of Article 60.7 Example 10 (which tells us that the epithet *billardierii*, derived from the part-Latinization Billardierius, is unacceptable and must be corrected to *billardierei*) is not absolutely clear. However, my reading of it is that except for full-scale Latinizations of names (e.g. *brunonius* for Brown, thus *Rosa brunonii*), the name of the person commemorated should remain in its original form. Names ending in -er (e.g. Solander, Faber) may be become *solandri* (as in pure Latin, because -er is a usual Latin termination) or *solanderi*, if the specific name was originally spelt in this way. If this interpretation is correct, names such as *backhousiana, catesbaei, glazoviana, manescavii* and *bureavii* are not allowed and must be corrected to *backhouseana, catesbyi, glaziouana, manescaui* and *bureaui* respectively. However, not all of the several authors of the Code share the same interpretation; I have been reluctant to make further corrections in this edition until there is greater consensus on the true meaning of all the parts of the Code relating to orthography.

If my reading of the Code's rulings on orthography is correct, botanical epithets commemorating someone whose name has been transliterated from script other than Roman (e.g. Cyrillic or Japanese) present problems. Though ICNCP tells us which system of transliteration should be used, it is sometimes difficult to apply orthographic corrections to these: botanists whose names were originally in Cyrillic often had a preferred transliteration of their own name, often based on old French systems in the case of pre-Revolutionary names, and it is hard to justify rejecting these; it is therefore difficult to be dogmatic about the orthography of, for instance, Russian commemorative names. However, implementation of this rule has been assisted by another new publication from Kew, *Authors of Plant Names*, which is particularly helpful in giving acceptable transliterations of names that were originally in Cyrillic.

Verification of names

Although we find that many nurseries have greatly improved the accuracy of their plant names, plants which are new entries often appear in their catalogues under a bewildering variety of wrong names and misspellings. This is partly a reflection on the rarity of the plants and nurserymen are not to be blamed for not finding correct names for plants that do not appear in recent authoritative garden literature. Some plants are simply too new for valid names and descriptions yet to have appeared in print.

Although we try to verify every name which appears in these pages, the amount of time which can be allotted to checking each of over 70,000 entries must be limited. There is always a proportion which do not appear in any of the reference sources used (i.e. those listed in the Bibliography) and those unverified names for which there may be scope for error are marked with an asterisk. Such errors may occur with species we cannot find listed (possibly synonyms for more recent and better known names) or may include misspellings (particularly of names transliterated from Japanese or Chinese, or commemorating a person). We are especially circumspect about names not known to the International Registrar for a particular genus. We are always grateful to receive information about the naming and origin of any asterisked plant and once we feel reassured about the plant's pedigree, the asterisk will be removed. Of course, many such names will prove to be absolutely correct and buyers can be reassured if they know that the selling nursery takes great care with the naming of its plants. However, although we are able to check that names are valid, correctly styled and spelt, we have no means of checking that nurseries are applying them to the right plant; *caveat emptor!*

We have great sympathy for gardeners who want to find a particular cultivar but are not sure to which species it belongs. The problem is acute for genera such as *Juniperus* and readers must search through all the entries to find their plants; even nurseries seem uncertain of the species of 'Skyrocket'. Because gardeners generally do not know (or disagree) to which species cultivars of bougainvilleas, hostas and saxifrages should be ascribed, these have been listed by cultivar first, giving the species in parentheses.

Adjectival names

Latin adjectival names, whether for species, subspecies, cultivar etc., must agree in gender with the genus, *not* with the specific name if the latter is a noun (as for *Styrax obassia, Lonicera caprifolium* etc.). Thus azaleas have to agree with *Rhododendron*, their true genus (neuter), rather than *Azalea* (feminine). For French cultivar names, adjectives should agree with whatever is being described; for roses, this is almost always *la rose* (feminine) but on rare occasions *le rosier* (when describing vegetative characteristics such as climbing forms), *l'oeillet* or *le pompon* (all masculine).

It is often the case that gardeners consider two plants to be distinct but botanists, who know of a whole range of intermediates linking the two, consider them to be the same species. The most notable example is for the rhododendrons, many species of which were 'sunk' in Cullen and Chamberlain's recent revision. In such cases we have always tried to provide names that retain important horticultural entities, even if not botanically distinct, often by calling the sunk species by a Group name, such as *Rhododendron rubiginosum* Desquamatum Group. Group names are also used for swarms of hybrids with the same parentage. These were formerly treated as grex names, a term now only used for orchids; thus grex names for lilies, bromeliads and begonias are now styled as Groups. A single clone from the Group may be given the same cultivar name, e.g. 'Polar Bear'. In many cases nursery catalogues do not specify whether the named clone is being offered or other selections from the hybrid swarm and entries are therefore given as e.g. *Rhododendron* Polar Bear Group & cl.

One new requirement of the new ICNCP is that cultivar-group names used after 1 January 1996 must have been validly published with a description or reference to a previously published description. Such publication is beyond the scope and purpose of ***The RHS Plant Finder***. As editor, I may not style the more variable taxa that appear in this and subsequent editions as cultivar-groups unless they have been published elsewhere as Groups. Nevertheless, I still feel it is helpful to gardeners and other plant users to use cultivar names only for those plants that fulfil the Code's definition of a cultivar ('distinct, uniform and stable') in its narrow sense. This applies particularly to mixtures and races of seed-raised plants that embrace significant variation and may be changed in character from year to year: any new entries that are of this nature are here styled neither as cultivars nor as cultivar-groups but simply as epithets or descriptions, without quotation marks and thus beyond the scope of the new Code. This applies especially to plants described as 'strains' or 'hybrids', though the latter term is sometimes merely a provenance rather than a sign of common parentage. Thus plants here appearing as cultivars with their names in quotes have, as far as I can tell, uniform and predictable characteristics. There are a few cases in which it is difficult to tell whether a 'sunk' species remains horticulturally distinct enough to merit a group name, as for many of the rhododendrons; we would be grateful if users would let us know of any plants that we have 'sunk' in synonymy but which still need to be distinguished by a separate name. In many cases, the plants gardeners grow will be the most extreme variants of a species; although one 'end' of the species will seem to be quite a different plant from the other 'end' to the gardener, the botanist will see them as the outer limits of a continuous range of variation and will give them the same species name. We often hear gardeners complain 'How can these two plants have the same name? They are different!'. In such cases, although the botanist may have to 'lump' them under the same name, we will always try to provide an acceptable name to distinguish an important horticultural entity, even if it is not botanically distinct.

Taxonomic rank

In this edition, subspecies, varietas and forma are shown as subsp., var. and f. respectively. Each of these ranks indicates a successively less significant change in the characteristics of the plant from the original type on which the species was based; in general terms, a subspecies may be expected to be more markedly different from the type of a species than a forma which may differ in only one characteristic such as flower colour, hairiness of leaf or habit.

The ICBN requires the rank of each infraspecific botanical epithet to be given. In many cases, it is not at all clear whether a colour form shown as, say, alba is a true botanical forma or a cultivar of garden origin. Our inclination here is not to treat such plants as cultivars if they are recorded as being naturally occurring, nor if they embrace considerable variation: forma *alba* would be preferred if a valid publication is recorded, otherwise a previously-published Group name or a simple description. In the absence of conclusive evidence we will leave such names styled as they are at present and so some ranks remain to be added in future editions. In many cases, *alba* is assumed without any proof to be the correct name for a white-flowered variant though research often shows that the validly published name is something quite different such as f. *albiflora, leucantha* or *nivea*.

Author citations

In many cases the same species name has been used by two or more authors for quite different plants. Thus *Bloomingthingia grandiflora* of Linnaeus might be an altogether different species from *B. grandiflora* of gardeners (*B. grandiflora* hort.). In such circumstances it becomes necessary to define whose *Bloomingthingia* we are considering by quoting the author of the name directly after the species name. Generally the more recent name will be invalid and may be cross-referenced to the plant's first validly published name. Author's names appear directly after the species name and if abbreviated follow Brummitt and Powell's *Authors of Plant Names*; abbreviations are also listed in e.g. Mabberley's *The Plant-Book.* Such names appear in a smaller typeface, and neither in quotes nor in sans serif font so should not be confused with cultivar names or trade designations. In this edition we have uncovered yet more muddles resulting from two or more plants being known by the same name; we have, we hoped, resolved these by clearer cross-referencing.

Hyphenation

Some items of the ICBN have been 'more honour'd in the breach than in the observance'. One such is the ruling on hyphenation (Article 60.9) which forbids the use of hyphens after a 'compounding form' (i.e. *albo, pseudo, aureo, neo*). Hyphens are still permitted to divide separate words such as *novae-angliae* or *uva-crispa* and following the Tokyo Congress, after a vowel terminating a compounding form when followed by the same vowel (e.g. *Gaultheria semi-infera, Gentiana sino-ornata*).

Terminations of commemorative names

Another item of the code which is often ignored is that covering terminations of commemorative names (Article 60.11, referring to Recommendation 60C). A botanical epithet commemorating Helena must be styled *helenae* whereas one commemorating Helen may be styled either *heleniae* or, following Helena as an established Latin form of the same name or, quite frequently, of Ellen, *helenae*; in such cases when either spelling could be legitimate, the original is followed. When there is no accepted Latin alternative, the *-iae* ending is used and this seems to be more correct for *murieliae* and *edithiae*. The genitive form of names ending in *-a* is always *-ae*, even if a man is being commemorated (as for *Picea koyamae*). It is this same article which requires that the well known *Crocosmia* be spelt *masoniorum* and not *masonorum* and that *Rosa wichurana* be spelt thus and not *wichuraiana*.

The RHS Plant Finder is useful not only as a directory of plant sources but as a 'menu' of plants grown by British gardeners. Such a list is of great value not only to private gardeners; landscapers can use it to check the range of plants they can incorporate in designs; gardeners in countries of the European Union can check which plants they can import by Mail Order; botanists can discover the species grown in Britain, some of them from recorded natural sources; nurserymen can use it to select for propagation first-rate plants that are still not readily available; horticultural authors, who often only want to write about plants the public are able to buy, will find it invaluable. For all such users, ***The RHS Plant Finder*** can be recommended as a source of standard, up-to-date and reliable nomenclature.

Tony Lord
April 1997

Nomenclature Notes

These notes refer to plants in the main PLANT DIRECTORY that are marked with a 'N'.

'Bean Supplement' refers to W J Bean *Trees & Shrubs Hardy in the British Isles* (Supplement to the 8th edition) edited by D L Clarke 1988.

Acer palmatum* var. *coreanum
This is not synonymous with *A. palmatum* 'Koreanum'.

***Acer palmatum* 'Sango-kaku'/ 'Senkaki'**
Two or more clones are offered under these names. *A. palmatum* 'Eddisbury' is similar with brighter coral stems.

***Acer pseudoplatanus* 'Leopoldii'**
True 'Leopoldii' has leaves stained with yellowish pink and purple. Plants are often *A. pseudoplatanus* f. *variegatum*.

***Acer pseudoplatanus* 'Spaethii'**
Has large leaves with light yellow specks.

Aconitum autumnale
A synonym of *A. napellus* and *A. carmichaelii* Wilsonii Group.

***Achillea ptarmica* The Pearl Group**
Refers to variable seed-raised double-flowered plants. The cultivar names 'The Pearl' and 'Boule de Neige' apply only to plants propagated vegetatively from the originals.

***Acorus gramineus* 'Oborozuki' & 'Ogon'**
Although these seem to be the same clone in British gardens, 'Oborozuki' is a distinct brighter yellow cultivar in the USA.

Alchemilla alpina
The true species is very rare in cultivation. Plants under this name are usually *A. plicatula* or *A. conjuncta*.

Alchemilla splendens
The true species is probably not in cultivation in the British Isles.

***Alopecurus pratensis* 'Aureus'**
Name applies only to plants with all gold leaves, not to green and gold striped forms.

Anemone magellanica
According to *European Garden Flora*, this is a form of the very variable *A. multifida*.

***Anemone nemorosa* 'Alba Plena'**
This name is used for several double white forms including *A. nemorosa* 'Flore Pleno' and *A. nemorosa* 'Vestal'.

***Anthemis tinctoria* 'Grallach Gold'**
The true cultivar of this name has golden yellow flowers. Plants with orange yellow flowers are *A. tinctoria* 'Beauty of Grallach'.

***Artemisia* 'Faith Raven' & 'Powis Castle'**
Most plants labelled 'Faith Raven' are identical with 'Powis Castle'.

***Artemisia granatensis* hort.**
Possibly a variant of *A. absinthium.*

***Artemisia ludoviciana* 'Silver Queen'**
Two cultivars are grown under this name, one with cut leaves, the other with entire leaves.

***Artemisia ludoviciana* var. *latiloba* / *A. ludoviciana* 'Valerie Finnis'**
Leaves of the former are glabrous at maturity, those of the latter are not.

***Artemisia stelleriana* 'Boughton Silver'**
This is the first validly published name for this plant. 'Silver Brocade' seems to have been published earlier but in an undated publication; it is not therefore validly published.

***Aster amellus* Violet Queen**
It is probable that more than one cultivar is sold under this name.

Aster dumosus
Many of the asters listed under *A. novi-belgii* contain varying amounts of *A. dumosus* blood in their parentage. It is not possible to allocate these to one species or the other and they are therefore listed under *A. novi-belgii.*

***Aster* ×*frikartii* 'Mönch'**
The true plant is very rare in British gardens. Most plants are another form of *A.* ×*frikartii*, usually 'Wunder von Stäfa'.

Aster novi-belgii
See note under *A. dumosus*. *A. laevis* is also involved in the parentage of most cultivars.

Aster turbinellus
Two hybrids are available from nurseries under this name, one of them the holder of an AGM. The pure species does not seem to be in cultivation.

Azara paraguayensis
This is an unpublished name for what seems to be a hybrid between *A. serrata* and *A lanceolata*.

Berberis aristata
Plants so named may be either *B. chitria* or *B. floribunda*.

***Berberis buxifolia* 'Nana'/ 'Pygmaea'**
See explanation in Bean Supplement.

***Berberis* × *ottawensis* f. *purpurea* / 'Superba'**
'Superba' is a clonal selection from f. *purpurea*.
***Berberis* × *ottawensis* 'Superba'**
See note in Bean Supplement, p 109.
***Berberis stenophylla* 'Lemon Queen'**
This sport from 'Pink Pearl' was first named in 1982. The same mutation occurred again and was named 'Cream Showers'. The older name has priority.
***Bergenia* Ballawley hybrids**
The name 'Ballawley' refers only to plants vegetatively propagated from the original clone. Seed-raised plants, which may differ considerably, should be called Ballawley hybrids.
***Betula pendula* 'Dalecarlica'**
The true plant of this name is rare in cultivation in the British Isles and is probably not available from nurseries.
Betula utilis* var. *jacquemontii
Plants are often the clone 'Inverleith' which may or may not be a form of *B. utilis*.
Brachyscome
Originally published as *Brachyscome* by Cassini who later revised his spelling to *Brachycome*. The original spelling has been internationally adopted.
Brachyglottis greyi* and *laxifolia
Both these species are extremely rare in cultivation, plants under these names usually being *B.* 'Sunshine'.
***Buddleja davidii* Petite Indigo™, Petite Plum™ 'Nanho Blue', 'Nanho Purple'**
These cultivars or hybrids of *B. davidii* var. *nanhoensis* are claimed by some to be synonyms while others claim the 'Nanho' plants were raised in Holland and the 'Petite' plants in the USA. We are not yet certain whether these names are synonyms and if so which have priority.
Buddleja fallowiana
Many plants in cultivation are not the true species but the hybrid 'West Hill'.
***Calamagrostis* × *acutiflora* 'Karl Foerster'**
C. × *acutiflora* 'Stricta' differs in being 15cm taller, 10-15 days earlier flowering with a less fluffy inflorescence.
Caltha polypetala
This name is often applied to a large-flowered variant of C. *palustris*. The true species has more (7-10) petals.
***Camassia leichtlinii* 'Alba'**
The true cultivar is a blueish-white flowered selection of C. *leichtlinii* subsp. *suksdorfii*.
***Camassia leichtlinii* 'Plena'**
This has starry, transparent green-white flowers; creamy-white 'Semiplena' is sometimes offered under this name.
***Camellia* 'Campbellii'**
This name is used for five cultivars including 'Margherita Coleoni' but applies correctly to Guichard's 1894 cultivar, single to semi-double full rose pink.
***Camellia* 'Cleopatra'**
There are three cultivars with this name.
***Camellia* 'Perfecta'**
There are three cultivars of this name. 'Perfecta' of Jury is the plant usually offered by nurseries in the British Isles.
Campanula persicifolia
Plants under "cup and saucer white" are not definitely ascribed to a particular cultivar. 'White Cup and Saucer' is a cultivar named by Margery Fish.
***Carex morrowii* 'Variegata'**
C. hachijoensis 'Evergold' is sometimes sold under this name.
Carya illinoinensis
The correct spelling of this name is discussed in *Baileya*, **10(1)**, 1962.
Cassinia retorta
Now included within *C. leptophylla*. A valid infra-specific epithet has yet to be published.
***Cedrus deodara* 'Prostrata'**
The true plant is extremely rare if not lost to cultivation. Most plants under this name are *C. deodara* 'Pendula'.
***Ceanothus* 'Italian Skies'**
Many plants under this name are not true to name.
***Chamaecyparis lawsoniana* 'Columnaris Glauca'**
Plants under this name might be *C. lawsoniana* 'Columnaris' or a new invalidly named cultivar.
***Chamaecyparis lawsoniana* 'Elegantissima'**
This name has been applied to two cultivars, 'Elegantissima' of Schelle and subsequently (invalidly) 'Elegantissima' of Hillier.
***Chamaecyparis lawsoniana* 'Smithii'**
Plants offered under this name might include some which are *C. lawsoniana* 'Darleyensis'.
***Chamaecyparis pisifera* 'Squarrosa Argentea'**
There are two plants of this name, one (valid) with variegated foliage, the other (invalid) with silvery foliage.
***Cistus ladanifer* Linnaeus**
Plants offered are usually *C.* × *cyprius*.
Cistus* × *loretii
Plants in cultivation under this name are usually forms of *C.* × *dansereaui*.
Cistus* × *obtusifolius
C. × *nigricans* is sometimes offered under this name.
Cistus* × *purpureus
The cultivar 'Betty Taudevin' does not appear to be distinct from this hybrid.
***Cistus* 'Silver Pink'**
Plants under this name are not usually true to type. *C.* 'Grayswood Pink', *C.* 'Peggy

Sammons' and *C.* × *skanbergii* are often offered under this name.

Clematis chrysocoma
The true *C. chrysocoma* is a non-climbing erect plant with dense yellow down on the young growth, still uncommon in cultivation.

***Clematis heracleifolia* 'Campanile'**
Might be *C.* × *bonstedtii* 'Campanile'.

***Clematis heracleifolia* 'Côte d'Azur'**
Might be *C.* × *bonstedtii* 'Côte d'Azur'

***Clematis* 'Jackmanii Superba'**
Plants under this name are usually *C.* 'Gipsy Queen'.

Clematis montana
This name should refer to the white-flowered form only. Pink-flowered forms are referable to *C. montana* var. *rubens*.

***Clematis* 'Victoria'**
There is also a Latvian cultivar of this name with petals with a central white bar.

Colchicum 'Autumn Queen'
Entries here might refer to the slightly different *C.* 'Prinses Astrid'.

***Cornus* 'Norman Hadden'**
See note in Bean Supplement, p 184.

Cotoneaster dammeri
Plants sold under this name are usually *C. dammeri* 'Major'.

Crataegus coccinea
Plants might be *C. intricata*, *C. pedicellata* or *C. biltmoreana*.

***Crocosmia* × *crocosmiiflora* 'Citronella'**
The true plant of this name has a dark eye and grows at Wisley. The plant usually offered may be more correctly *C.* 'Golden Fleece'.

***Crocosmia* × *crocosmiiflora* 'Honey Angels'**
Also wrongly referred to as 'Citronella'.

***Crocosmia* × *crocosmiiflora* 'James Coey'**
Has large tomato-red flowers. A smaller flowered plant similar to *C.* × *crocosmiiflora* 'Carmin Brillant' is sometimes sold under this name.

***Crocosmia* × *crocosmiiflora* 'Queen Alexandra'**
As many as 20 different clones are grown under this name. It is not clear which is correct.

***Crocosmia* × *crocosmiiflora* 'Solfaterre'**
This is the oldest version of this name that can positively be linked to the plant grown today. Lemoine's 'Solfatare', though an older name, is described as being 65cm high and having large outward-facing flowers and perhaps relates to a different plant.

***Crocus cartwrightianus* 'Albus'**
The plant offered is the true cultivar and not *C. hadriaticus.*

***Dendranthema* 'Anastasia Variegated'**
Despite its name, this seems to be derived from 'Mei-kyo' not 'Anastasia'.

***Dianthus* 'Musgrave's Pink' (p)**
This is the registered name of this white-flowered cultivar.

***Diascia* 'Apricot'**
Plants under this name are either *D. barberae* 'Hopleys Apricot' or *D. barberae* 'Blackthorn Apricot'.

Dryopteris affinis polydactyla
This name covers at least three different clones.

Elymus magellanicus
Although this is a valid name, Mr Roger Grounds has suggested that many plants might belong to a different, perhaps unnamed species.

***Epilobium glabellum* hort.**
Plants under this name are not *E. glabellum* but are close to *E. wilsonii* Petrie or perhaps a hybrid of it.

Erigeron salsuginosus
A synonym of *Aster sibiricus* but plants in cultivation under this name may be *E. peregrinus callianthemus*

Erodium cheilanthifolium
Most plants under this name are hybrids.

Erodium glandulosum
Plants under this name are often hybrids.

Erodium guttatum
Doubtfully in commerce; plants under this name are usually *E. heteradenum*, *E. cheilanthifolium* or hybrids.

Erodium petraeum
Many are hybrids, often *E.* 'Merstham Pink'.

***Erysimum cheiri* 'Baden-Powell'**
Plant of uncertain origin differing from *E. cheiri* 'Harpur Crewe' only in its shorter stature.

***Erysimum* 'Variegatum'**
This name might refer to any of the variegated cultivars of *Erysimum.*

***Eucryphia* 'Penwith'**
The cultivar name 'Penwith' was originally given to a hybrid of *E. cordifolia* × *E. lucida*, not *E.* × *hillieri.*

***Fagus sylvatica* Cuprea Group/Atropurpurea Group**
It is desirable to provide a name, Cuprea Group, for less richly coloured forms, used in historic landscapes before the purple clones appeared.

***Fagus sylvatica* 'Pendula'**
This name refers to the Knap Hill clone, the most common weeping form in English gardens. Other clones occur, particularly in Cornwall and Ireland.

***Forsythia* 'Beatrix Farrand'**
The true plant might not be in cultivation.

***Fragaria chiloensis* 'Variegata', *F. vesca* 'Variegata'**
Most, possibly all, plants under these names are *F.* × *ananassa* 'Variegata'.

Fuchsia
All names marked 'N', except the following, refer to more than one cultivar or species.

Fuchsia decussata
A hybrid of *F. magellanica* is also offered under this name.

Fuchsia loxensis
For a comparison of the true species with the hybrids 'Speciosa' and 'Loxensis' commonly grown under this name, see Boullemier's Check List (2nd ed.) p 268.

Fuchsia minimiflora
Some plants under this name might be *F. × bacillaris.*

***Fuchsia* 'Pumila'**
Plants under this name might be *F. magellanica* var. *pumila.*

Gentiana cachemirica
Most plants sold are not true to type.

***Geum* 'Borisii'**
This name refers to cultivars of *G. coccineum* Sibthorp & Smith, especially *G.* 'Werner Arends' and not to *G. × borisii* Kelleper.

Halimium alyssoides* and *H. halimifolium
Plants under these names are sometimes *H. × pauanum* or *H. × santae.*

***Hebe* 'Amy'**
Might include entries which refer to *H.* 'Purple Queen'.

***Hebe* 'C.P. Raffill'**
See note in Bean Supplement, p 265.

***Hebe* 'Carl Teschner'**
See note in Bean Supplement, p 264.

***Hebe* 'Glaucophylla'**
This plant is a green reversion of the hybrid *H.* 'Glaucophylla Variegata'.

***Hedera helix* 'Caenwoodiana'/ 'Pedata'**
Some authorities consider these to be distinct cultivars while others think them different morphological forms of the same unstable clone.

***Hedera helix* 'Oro di Bogliasco'**
Priority between this name and 'Jubiläum Goldherz' and 'Goldheart' has yet to be finally resolved.

Helleborus orientalis
Plants under this name are almost invariably hybrids and have been named *H. × hybridus.*

***Hemerocallis fulva* 'Kwanso', 'Kwanso Variegata', 'Flore Pleno' and 'Green Kwanso'**
For a discussion of these plants see *The Plantsman*, **7(2)**.

***Heuchera micrantha* var. *diversifolia* 'Palace Purple'**
This cultivar name refers only to plants with deep purple-red foliage. Seed-raised plants of inferior colouring should not be offered under this name.

***Hosta* 'Marginata Alba'**
This name is wrongly used both for *H. crispula* and, more commonly, for *H. fortunei* 'Albomarginata'.

Hosta montana
This name refers only to plants long grown in Europe, which differ from *H. elata.*

Hypericum fragile
The true *H. fragile* is probably not available from British nurseries.

***Hypericum* 'Gemo'**
Either a selection of *H. prolificum* or *H. prolificum × H. densiflorum.*

Ilex × altaclerensis
The argument for this spelling is given by Susyn Andrews, *The Plantsman*, **5(2)** and is not superceded by the more recent comments in the Supplement to Bean's Trees and Shrubs.

***Ilex verticillata* dwarf male/late male**
See note by Susyn Andrews, *The Garden* **119(2)**: 581-82.

Iris
Apart from those noted below, cultivar names marked 'N' are not registered. The majority of those marked 'I' have been previously used for a different cultivar.

***Iris histrioides* 'Major'**
Two clones are offered under this name, the true one pale blue with darker spotting on the falls, the incorrect one violet-blue with almost horizontal falls.

***Iris pallida* 'Variegata'**
The white-variegated *I. pallida* 'Argentea Variegata' is sometimes wrongly supplied under this name, which refers only to the gold-variegated cultivar.

Juniperus × media
This name is illegitimate if applied to hybrids of *J. chinensis × J. sabina*, having been previously used for a different hybrid (P.A. Schmidt, *IDS Yearbook* 1993, 47-48). Because of its importance to gardeners, a proposal to conserve its present use was tabled but subsequently rejected.

***Lamium maculatum* 'Chequers'**
This name refers to two plants; the first, validly named, is a large and vigorous form of *L. maculatum* with a stripe down the centre of the leaf; the second is silver-leaved and very similar to *L. maculatum* 'Beacon Silver'.

***Lavandula* 'Alba'**
Might be either *L. angustifolia* 'Alba' or *L. × intermedia* 'Alba'

***Lavandula angustifolia* 'Lavender Lady'/ *L.* 'Cambridge Lady'**
Might be synonyms of *L. angustifolia* 'Lady'.

***Lavandula × intermedia* 'Arabian Night'**

Plants under this name might be *L.* × *intermedia* 'Impress Purple'.

Lavandula spica
This name is classed as a name to be rejected (*nomen rejiciendum*) by the *International Code of Botanical Nomenclature*.

***Lavandula* 'Twickel Purple'**
Two cultivars are sold under this name, one a form of *L.* × *intermedia*, the other of *L. angustifolia*.

Lavatera olbia* and *L. thuringiaca
Although *L. olbia* is usually shrubby and *L. thuringiaca* usually herbaceous, both species are very variable. Cultivars formally ascribed to one species or the other are quite possibly hybrids and are listed by cultivar name alone pending the results of further research.

Leptospermum flavescens
This name is usually applied to plants correctly named *L. glaucescens*.

***Lobelia* 'Russian Princess'**
This has green, not purple, leaves and rich pink, not purple, flowers.

Lonicera* × *americana
Most plants offered by nurseries under this name are correctly *L.* × *italica*. The true *L.* × *americana* is still widely grown but is slow to propagate. See *The Plantsman*, **12(2)**.

***Lonicera* × *brownii* 'Fuchsioides'**
Plants under this name are usually *L.* × *brownii* 'Dropmore Scarlet'.

***Lonicera* × *heckrotii* 'Gold Flame'**
This name applies to the original clone. Many plants under this name are a different clone for which the name 'American Beauty' has been proposed.

***Lonicera periclymenum* 'Belgica'**
L. × *italica* is sometimes offered under this name.

***Lonicera periclymenum* 'Serotina'**
See note in Bean Supplement, p 315.

Lonicera sempervirens* f. *sulphurea
Plants in the British Isles usually a yellow-flowered form of *L. periclymenum*.

Macleaya cordata
Most, if not all, plants offered are *M.* × *kewensis*.

***Magnolia* × *highdownensis*.**
Believed to fall within the range of variation of *M. wilsonii*.

Magnolia obovata
This name refers to either *M. hypoleuca* or *M. officinalis*. The former is more common in cultivation.

***Magnolia* × *soulangeana* 'Burgundy'**
Most plants under this name are *M.* × *soulangeana* 'Purpliana'

Mahonia pinnata
Most plants in cultivation under this name are believed to be *M.* × *wagneri* 'Pinnacle'.

***Malus domestica* 'Dumeller's Seedling'**
The phonetic spelling 'Dumelow's Seedling' contravenes the ICBN ruling on orthography, i.e. that commemorative names should retain the original spelling of the person's name (Article 60.11).

***Melissa officinalis* 'Variegata'**
The true cultivar of this name was striped with white.

Nemesia caerulea
The lavender blue clone 'Joan Wilder', described and illustrated in *The Hardy Plant*, **14(1)**, 11-14, does not come true from seed; it may only be propagated from cuttings.

***Osmanthus heterophyllus* 'Gulftide'**
Probably correctly *O.* × *fortunei* 'Gulftide'.

***Papaver orientale* 'Flore Pleno'**
P. 'Fireball' is sometimes offered under this name.

Passiflora antioquiensis
According to National Colection holder John Vanderplank, the true species is not in cultivation in the British Isles. Plants under this name are likely to be clones of *P.* × *exoniensis*.

***Pelargonium* 'Beauty of Eastbourne'**
This should not be confused with *P.* 'Eastbourne Beauty', a different cultivar.

***Pelargonium* 'Lass o'Gowrie'**
The American plant of this name has pointed, not rounded leaf lobes.

Pelargonium quercifolium
Plants under this name are mainly hybrids. The true species has pointed, not rounded leaf lobes.

***Penstemon* 'Taoensis'**
This name for a small-flowered cultivar or hybrid of *P. isophyllus* originally appeared as 'Taoense' but must be corrected to agree in gender with *Penstemon* (masculine). Presumably an invalid name (published in Latin form since 1958), it is not synonymous with *P. crandallii* subsp. *glabrescens* var. *taosensis*.

Pernettya
Botanists now consider that *Pernettya* (fruit a berry) is not separable from *Gaultheria* (fruit a capsule) because in some species the fruit is intermediate between a berry and a capsule. For a fuller explanation see D Middleton *The Plantsman*, **12(3)**.

***Picea pungens* 'Glauca Pendula'**
This name is used for several different glaucous cultivars.

Pinus aristata
Might include plants referable to *P. longaeva*.

Pinus ayacahuite
P. ayacahuite var. *veitchii* (syn. *P. veitchii)* is

occasionally sold under this name.

Pinus montezumae
Plants propagated from mature trees in British gardens are mostly an un-named long-needled variety of *P. rudis*.

***Pinus nigra* 'Cebennensis Nana'**
A doubtful and invalid name, probably a synonym for *P. nigra* 'Nana'.

Polemonium archibaldiae
Usually sterile with lavender-blue flowers. A self-fertile white-flowered plant is sometimes sold under this name.

***Polygonatum odoratum* var. *pluriflorum* 'Variegatum'**
Plants under this name might be *P.* × *falcatum* 'Variegatum'.

***Polystichum setiferum* 'Wollaston'**
Incomplete name which may refer to either of two cultivars.

Populus nigra* var. *italica
See note in Bean Supplement, p 393.

***Prunus cerasifera* 'Nigra'**
Plants under this name may be referrable to *P. cerasifera* 'Woodii'.

***Prunus laurocerasus* 'Castlewellan'**
We are grateful to Dr Charles Nelson for informing us that the name 'Marbled White' is not valid because although it has priority of publication it does not have the approval of the originator who asked for it to be called 'Castlewellan'.

***Prunus laurocerasus* 'Variegata'**
The true 'Variegata', (marginal variegation), dates from 1811 but this name is also used for the relatively recent cultivar *P. laurocerasus* 'Castlewellan'.

Prunus serrulata* var. *pubescens
See note in Bean Supplement, p 398.

***Prunus* × *subhirtella* 'Rosea'**
Might be *P. pendula* var. *ascendens* 'Rosea', *P. pendula* 'Pendula Rosea', or *P.* × *subhirtella* 'Autumnalis Rosea'.

Rheum* × *cultorum
The name *R.* × *cultorum* was published without adequate description and must be abandoned in favour of the validly published *R.* × *hybridum*.

***Rhododendron* (azaleas)**
All names marked 'N', except for the following, refer to more than one cultivar.

***Rhododendron* 'Hino-mayo'**
This name is based on a faulty transliteration (should be 'Hinamoyo') but the spelling 'Hino-mayo' is retained in the interests of stability.

***Rhododendron* Loderi Group/Kewense Group**
The name Kewense has priority of 13 years over the name Loderi for hybrids of *R. griffithianum* × *R. fortunei* subsp. *fortunei* and would, under normal circumstances be considered correct. However, the RHS as IRA for *Rhododendron* has conserved the name Loderi because it is more widely used by gardeners.

Rhus typhina
Linnaeus published both *R. typhina* and *R. hirta* as names for the same species. Though *R. hirta* has priority, it has been proposed that the name *R. typhina* should be conserved.

***Robinia hispida* 'Rosea'**
This name is applied to *R. hispida* (young shoots with bristles), *R. elliottii* (young shoots with grey down) and *R. boyntonii* (young shoot with neither bristles nor down).

Rosa
Coded cultivar names, the first three letters of which normally derive from the name of the breeder, are not listed separately for *Rosa*. These are usually sold under trade designations (no quotes, sans serif font). Roses often known by common names, e.g. Rosa Mundi and Hume's Blush, are referred to botanical names as given in Bean.

***Rosa* × *damascena* 'Trigintipetala'**
The true cultivar of this name is probably not in cultivation in the Britsh Isles.

Rosa gentiliana
Plants might be *R. multiflora* 'Wilsonii', *R. multiflora* var. *cathayensis, R. henryi* or a hybrid.

***Rosa* 'Gros Choux de Hollande' (Bb)**
It is doubtful if this name is correctly applied.

***Rosa* 'Maiden's Blush'**
R. 'Great Maiden's Blush' may be supplied under this name.

***Rosa* 'Marchesa Boccella'**
For a discussion on the correct identity of this rose see *Heritage Rose Foundation News*, Oct. 1989 & Jan. 1990.

***Rosa* 'Professeur Emile Perrot'**
For a discussion on the correct identity of this rose see *Heritage Roses,* Nov. 1991.

Rosa Sweetheart
This is not the same as the Sweetheart Rose, a common name for *R.* 'Cécile Brunner'.

Rosa wichurana
This is the correct spelling according to the ICBN 1994 Article 60.11 (which enforces Recommendation 60C.1c) and not *wichuraiana* for this rose commemorating Max Wichura.

***Salix alba* 'Tristis'**
This cultivar should not be confused with *S. tristis*, which is now correctly *S. humilis*. Although this cultivar is distinct in European gardens, most plants under this name in the British Isles are *S.* × *sepulcralis* var.

chrysocoma.

Salvia microphylla* var. *neurepia
The type of this variety is referableto the typical variety, *S. microphylla* var. *microphylla*.

***Salvia officinalis* 'Aurea'**
S. officinalis var. *aurea* is a rare variant of the common sage with leaves entirely of gold. It is represented in cultivation by the cultivar 'Kew Gold'. The plant usually offered as *S. officinalis* 'Aurea' is the gold variegated sage *S. officinalis* 'Icterina'.

Salvia sclarea* var. *turkestanica
Plants in gardens under this name are not *S. sclarea* var. *turkistaniana* of Mottet.

***Sambucus nigra* 'Aurea'**
Plants under this name are usually not *S. nigra*.

Sedum nevii
The true species is not in cultivation. Plants under this name are usually either *S. glaucophyllum* or occasionally *S. beyrichianum*.

Sempervivum arachnoideum* subsp. *tomentosum
Entries here might include plants classified as *S.* 'Hookeri'.

Senna corymbosa
See notes under *Cassia corymbosa* in Bean Supplement, p 148.

***Skimmia japonica* 'Foremanii'**
The true cultivar, which belongs to *S. japonica* Rogersii Group, is believed to be lost to cultivation. Plants offered under this name are usually *S. japonica* 'Veitchii'.

Sophora prostrata
The hybrid *S.* 'Little Baby' is sometimes offered under this name.

***Spiraea japonica* 'Shirobana'**
Shirobana-shimotsuke is the common name for *S. japonica* var. *albiflora*. Shirobana means white-flowered and does not apply to the two-coloured form.

Staphylea holocarpa* var. *rosea
This botanical variety has woolly leaves. The cultivar 'Rosea', with which it is often confused, does not.

***Stewartia ovata* var. *grandiflora*.**
Most, possibly all, plants available from British nurseries under this name are not true to name but are derived from the improved Nymans form.

***Thymus serpyllum* cultivars**
Most cultivars are probably correctly cultivars of *T. polytrichus* or hybrids though they will remain listed under *T. serpyllum* pending further research.

Thymus serpyllum* var. *albus
This name covers two different clones apparently of *T. polytrichus* subsp. *britannicus*.

***Thymus* 'Silver Posie'**
The cultivar name 'Silver Posie' is applied to several different plants, not all of them *T. vulgaris*.

***Tricyrtis* Hototogisu**
This is the common name applied generally to all Japanese *Tricyrtis* and specifically to *T. hirta*.

Tricyrtis macropoda
This name has been used for at least five different species.

Uncinia rubra
This name is loosely applied to *U. egmontiana* and *U. uncinata*.

***Verbena* 'Kemerton'**
Origin unknown, not from Kemerton.

***Viburnum opulus* 'Fructu Luteo'**
See note below.

***Viburnum opulus* 'Xanthocarpum'**
Some entries under this name might be the less compact *V. opulus* 'Fructu Luteo'.

Viburnum plicatum
Entries may include the 'snowball' form, *V. plicatum* 'Sterile'.

Viola labradorica
See Note in *The Garden*, **110(2)**: 96.

Classification of Genera

ACTINIDIA

(s-p)	Self-pollinating

BEGONIA

(C)	Cane
(R)	Rex
(S)	Semperflorens
(T)	× *tuberhybrida* (Tuberous)

CHRYSANTHEMUM see DENDRANTHEMA

CLEMATIS

(A)	Alpina Group (Section Atragene)
(D)	Diversifolia Group
(Fl)	Florida Group (double-flowered)
(Fo)	Fosteri Group
(I)	Integrifolia Group
(J)	Jackmanii Group
(L)	Lanuginosa Group
(P)	Patens Group
(T)	Texensis Group
(Ta)	Tangutica Group
(Vt)	Viticella Group

DAHLIA

(By The National Dahlia Society with corresponding numerical classification according to the Royal Horticultural Society's International Register)

(Sin)	1 Single
(Anem)	2 Anemone-flowered
(Col)	3 Collerette
(LWL)	4B Waterlily, Large
(MWL)	4C Waterlily, Medium
(SWL)	4D Waterlily, Small
(MinWL)	4E Waterlily, Miniature
(GD)	5A Decorative, Giant
(LD)	5B Decorative, Large
(MD)	5C Decorative, Medium
(SD)	5D Decorative, Small
(MinD)	5E Decorative, Miniature
(SBa)	6A Small Ball
(MinBa)	6B Miniature Ball
(Pom)	7 Pompon
(GC)	8A Cactus, Giant
(LC)	8B Cactus, Large
(MC)	8C Cactus, Medium
(SC)	8D Cactus, Small
(MinC)	8E Cactus, Miniature
(S-c)	9 Semi-cactus (unassigned)
(GS-c)	9A Semi-cactus, Giant
(LS-c)	9B Semi-cactus, Large
(MS-c)	9C Semi-cactus, Medium
(SS-c)	9D Semi-cactus, Small
(MinS-c)	9E Semi-cactus, Miniature
(Misc)	10 Miscellaneous
(O)	Orchid-flowering (in combination)
(B)	Botanical (in combination)
(DwB)	Dwarf Bedding (in combination)
(Fim)	Fimbriated (in combination)
(Lil)	Lilliput (in combination)

DENDRANTHEMA

(By the National Chrysanthemum Society)

(1)	Indoor Large (Exhibition)
(2)	Indoor Medium (Exhibition)
(3a)	Indoor Incurved: Large-flowered
(3b)	Indoor Incurved: Medium-flowered
(3c)	Indoor Incurved: Small-flowered
(4a)	Indoor Reflexed: Large-flowered
(4b)	Indoor Reflexed: Medium-flowered
(4c)	Indoor Reflexed: Small-flowered
(5a)	Indoor Intermediate: Large-flowered
(5b)	Indoor Intermediate: Medium-flowered
(5c)	Indoor Intermediate: Small-flowered
(6a)	Indoor Anemone: Large-flowered
(6b)	Indoor Anemone: Medium-flowered
(6c)	Indoor Anemone: Small-flowered
(7a)	Indoor Single: Large-flowered
(7b)	Indoor Single: Medium-flowered
(7c)	Indoor Single: Small-flowered
(8a)	Indoor True Pompon
(8b)	Indoor Semi-pompon
(9a)	Indoor Spray: Anemone
(9b)	Indoor Spray: Pompon
(9c)	Indoor Spray: Reflexed
(9d)	Indoor Spray: Single
(9e)	Indoor Spray: Intermediate
(9f)	Indoor Spray: Spider, Quill, Spoon or Any Other Type
(10a)	Indoor, Spider
(10b)	Indoor, Quill
(10c)	Indoor, Spoon
(11)	Any Other Indoor Type
(12a)	Indoor, Charm
(12b)	Indoor, Cascade
(13a)	October-flowering Incurved: Large-flowered
(13b)	October-flowering Incurved: Medium-flowered
(13c)	October-flowering Incurved: Small-flowered
(14a)	October-flowering Reflexed: Large-flowered

(14b) October-flowering Reflexed: Medium-flowered
(14c) October-flowering Reflexed: Small-flowered
(15a) October-flowering Intermediate: Large-flowered
(15b) October-flowering Intermediate: Medium-flowered
(15c) October-flowering Intermediate: Small-flowered
(16) October-flowering Large
(17a) October-flowering Single: Large-flowered
(17b) October-flowering Single: Medium-flowered
(17c) October-flowering Single: Small-flowered
(18a) October-flowering Pompon: True Pompon
(18b) October-flowering Pompon: Semi-pompon
(19a) October-flowering Spray: Anemone
(19b) October-flowering Spray: Pompon
(19c) October-flowering Spray: Reflexed
(19d) October-flowering Spray: Single
(19e) October-flowering Spray: Intermediate
(19f) October-flowering Spray: Spider, Quill, Spoon or Any Other Type
(20) Any Other October-flowering Type
(22) Charm
(23a) Early flowering Outdoor Incurved: Large-flowered
(23b) Early flowering Outdoor Incurved: Medium-flowered
(23c) Early flowering Outdoor Incurved: Small-flowered
(24a) Early flowering Outdoor Reflexed: Large-flowered
(24b) Early flowering Outdoor Reflexed: Medium-flowered
(24c) Early flowering Outdoor Reflexed: Small-flowered
(25a) Early flowering Outdoor Intermediate: Large-flowered
(25b) Early flowering Outdoor Intermediate: Medium-flowered
(25c) Early flowering Outdoor Intermediate: Small-flowered
(26a) Early flowering Outdoor Anemone: Large-flowered
(26b) Early flowering Outdoor Anemone: Medium-flowered
(27a) Early-flowering Outdoor Single: Large-flowered
(27b) Early-flowering Outdoor Single: Medium-flowered
(28a) Early-flowering Outdoor Pompon: True Pompon
(28b) Early-flowering Outdoor Pompon: Semi-pompon
(29a) Early-flowering Outdoor Spray: Anemone
(29b) Early-flowering Outdoor Spray: Pompon
(29c) Early-flowering Outdoor Spray: Reflexed
(29d) Early-flowering Outdoor Spray: Single
(29e) Early-flowering Outdoor Spray: Intermediate
(29f) Early-flowering Outdoor Spray: Spider, Quill, Spoon or Any Other Type
(29K) Early-flowering Outdoor Spray: Korean
(29Rub) Early-flowering Outdoor Spray: Rubellum
(30) Any Other Early-flowering Outdoor Type

DIANTHUS
(By the Royal Horticultural Society)
(p) Pink
(p,a) Annual Pink
(pf) Perpetual-flowering Carnation
(b) Border Carnation
(M) Malmaison Carnation

FRUIT
(B) Black (*Vitis*)
(C) Culinary (*Malus, Prunus, Pyrus, Ribes*)
(Cider) Cider (*Malus*)
(D) Dessert (*Malus, Prunus, Pyrus, Ribes*)
(F) Fruit
(G) Glasshouse (*Vitis*)
(O) Outdoor (*Vitis*)
(P) Pinkcurrant (*Ribes*)
(Perry) Perry (*Pyrus*)
(R) Red (*Vitis*), Redcurrant (*Ribes*)
(W) White (*Vitis*), Whitecurrant (*Ribes*)

GLADIOLUS
(B) Butterfly
(Colv) Colvillei
(G) Giant
(L) Large
(M) Medium
(Min) Miniature
(N) Nanus
(P) Primulinus
(S) Small
(Tub) Tubergenii

HYDRANGEA macrophylla
(H) Hortensia
(L) Lacecap

IRIS
(By the American Iris Society)
(AB) Arilbred
(BB) Border Bearded
(Cal-Sib) Series *Californicae* × Series *Sibiricae*
(CH) Californian Hybrid

(DB) Dwarf Bearded (not assigned)
(Dut) Dutch
(IB) Intermediate Bearded
(La) Louisiana Hybrid
(MDB) Miniature Dwarf Bearded
(MTB) Miniature Tall Bearded
(SDB) Standard Dwarf Bearded
(Sp) Spuria
(TB) Tall Bearded

LILIUM
(Classification according to *The International Lily Register* (ed. 3, 1982) with amendments from Supp. 10 (1992), Royal Horticultural Society)
(I) Hybrids derived from *L. amabile, L. bulbiferum, L. cernuum, L. concolor, L. davidii, L. × hollandicum, L. lancifolium, L. leichtlinii, L. × maculatum* and *L. pumilum*
(Ia) Early flowering with upright flowers, single or in an umbel
(Ib) Outward-facing flowers
(Ic) Pendant flowers
(II) Hybrids of Martagon type, one parent having been a form of *L. hansonii* or *L. martagon*
(III) Hybrids from *L. candidum, L. chalcedonicum* and other related European species (excluding *L. martagon*)
(IV) Hybrids of American species
(V) Hybrids derived from *L. formosanum* & *L. longiflorum*
(VI) Hybrid Trumpet Lilies & Aurelian hybrids from Asiatic species, including *L. henryi* but excluding those from *L. auratum, L. japonicum, L. rubellum and L. speciosum.*
(VIa) Plants with trumpet-shaped flowers
(VIb) Plants with bowl-shaped flowers
(VIc) Plants with flat flowers (or only the tips recurved)
(VId) Plants with recurved flowers
(VII) Hybrids of Far Eastern species as *L auratum, L. japonicum, L. rubellum* and *L. speciosum,*
(VIIa) Plants with trumpet-shaped flowers
(VIIb) Plants with bowl-shaped flowers
(VIIc) Plants with flat flowers
(VIId) Plants with recurved flowers
(VIII) All hybrids not in another division
(IX) All species and their varieties and forms

MALUS See FRUIT

NARCISSUS
(By The Royal Horticultural Society, revised 1977)
(1) Trumpet
(2) Large-cupped
(3) Small-cupped
(4) Double
(5) Triandrus
(6) Cyclamineus
(7) Jonquilla
(8) Tazetta
(9) Poeticus
(10) Species and wild forms and hybrids
(11) Split-corona
(12) Miscellaneous

NYMPHAEA
(H) Hardy
(D) Day-blooming
(N) Night-blooming
(T) Tropical

PAEONIA
(S) Shrubby

PELARGONIUM
(A) Angel
(C) Coloured Foliage (in combination)
(Ca) Cactus (in combination)
(d) Double (in combination)
(Dec) Decorative
(Dw) Dwarf
(DwI) Dwarf Ivy-leaved
(Fr) Frutetorum
(I) Ivy-leaved
(Min) Miniature
(MinI) Miniature Ivy-leaved
(R) Regal
(Sc) Scented-leaved
(St) Stellar (in combination)
(T) Tulip (in combination)
(U) Unique
(Z) Zonal

PRIMULA
(Classification as per W W Smith & Forrest (1928) and W W Smith & Fletcher (1941-49))
(1) Amethystina
(2) Auricula
(3) Bullatae
(4) Candelabra
(5) Capitatae
(6) Carolinella
(7) Cortusoides
(8) Cuneifolia
(9) Denticulata
(10) Dryadifolia
(11) Farinosae
(12) Floribundae
(13) Grandis
(14) Malacoides
(15) Malvacea
(16) Minutissimae
(17) Muscarioides
(18) Nivales
(19) Obconica

(20) Parryi
(21) Petiolares
(22) Pinnatae
(23) Pycnoloba
(24) Reinii
(25) Rotundifolia
(26) Sikkimensis
(27) Sinenses
(28) Soldanelloideae
(29) Souliei
(30) Vernales
(A) Alpine Auricula
(B) Border Auricula
(D) Double
(Poly) Polyanthus
(Prim) Primrose
(S) Show Auricula

PRUNUS See FRUIT

PYRUS See FRUIT

RHODODENDRON
(A) Azalea (deciduous, species or unclassified hybrid)
(Ad) Azaleodendron
(EA) Evergreen azalea
(G) Ghent azalea (deciduous)
(K) Knap Hill or Exbury azalea (deciduous)
(M) Mollis azalea (deciduous)
(O) Occidentalis azalea (deciduous)
(R) Rustica azalea (deciduous)
(V) Vireya rhododendron
(Vs) Viscosa azalea (deciduous)

RIBES See FRUIT

ROSA
(A) Alba
(Bb) Bourbon
(Bs) Boursault
(Ce) Centifolia
(Ch) China
(Cl) Climbing (in combination)
(D) Damask
(DPo) Damask Portland
(F) Floribunda or Cluster-flowered
(G) Gallica
(Ga) Garnette
(GC) Ground Cover
(HM) Hybrid Musk
(HP) Hybrid Perpetual
(HT) Hybrid Tea or Large-flowered
(Min) Miniature
(Mo) Moss (in combination)
(N) Noisette
(Patio) Patio, Miniature Floribunda or Dwarf Cluster-flowered
(Poly) Polyantha
(PiH) Pimpinellifolia hybrid (Hybrid Scots Briar)
(Ra) Rambler
(RH) Rubiginosa hybrid (Hybrid Sweet Briar)
(Ru) Rugosa
(S) Shrub
(T) Tea

SAXIFRAGA
(Classification from Hegi, G (revd. ed. 1975). *Illustrierte Flora von Mitteleuropa*
(1) Micranthes
(2) Hirculus
(3) Gymnopera
(4) Diptera
(5) Trachyphyllum
(6) Xanthizoon
(7) Aizoonia
(8) Porophyllum
(9) Porophyrion
(10) Miscopetalum
(11) Saxifraga
(12) Trachyphylloides
(13) Cymbalaria
(14) Discogyne

TULIPA
(Classification from *Classified List and International Register of Tulip Names* by Koninklijke Algemeene Vereening voor Bloembollenculture 1996)
(1) Single Early Group
(2) Double Early Group
(3) Triumph Group
(4) Darwinhybrid Group
(5) Single Late Group (including Darwin Group and Cottage Group)
(6) Lily-Flowered Group
(7) Fringed Group
(8) Viridiflora Group
(9) Rembrandt Group
(10) Parrot Group
(11) Double Late Group
(12) Kaufmanniana Group
(13) Fosteriana Group
(14) Greigii Group
(15) Miscellaneous

VIOLA
(C) Cornuta Hybrid
(dVt) Double Violet
(ExVa) Exhibition Viola
(FP) Fancy Pansy
(PVt) Parma Violet
(SP) Show Pansy
(T) Tricolor
(Va) Viola
(Vt) Violet
(Vtta) Violetta

VITIS See FRUIT

ACKNOWLEDGEMENTS

The task of preparing *BG-BASE*™ has required a great deal of work from all involved. This has been accomplished over a three year period by Dr Kerry Walter of BG-BASE Inc. and Niki Simpson, Database Administrator, assisted by Kate Haywood and Emma Cox (Plant Records staff). Dr Andrew Sier, Senior Database Administrator, has kept the database operational and assisted with name editing. Plant Finder Administrator Clare Burgh has taken over from Chris Philip in the compilation and dissemination of information to and from nurseries and, assisted by Maureen Morgan, has added many more nursery codes than has been possible in previous years. I continue to check names in the Plant Finder, especially each year's new entries, and all of our efforts are supervised by the RHS's Head of Botany, Dr Simon Thornton-Wood.

For the compilation of this edition, I am especially indebted to my colleagues on the RHS Advisory Panel on Nomenclature and Taxonomy: Chris Brickell, Susyn Andrews, Stephen Jury, Sabina Knees, Alan Leslie, Simon Thornton-Wood, Piers Trehane and Adrian Whiteley, along with Mike Grant and Diana Miller, all of whom have provided much valuable guidance during the past year. Scores of nurseries have sent helpful information about asterisked plants which has proved immensely helpful in verifying some of the most obscure names. I am grateful, too, to our regular correspondents, particularly Jennifer Hewitt for so thoroughly checking iris entries and to the RHS's International Registrars. Our thanks also go to Mike Grindley for checking transliterations and translations of Chinese names.

Artemisia	Dr J D Twibell ('94)
Bamboos	D McClintock ('90-'94)
Bougainvillea	S Read ('94)
Camellia	T J Savige, International Registrar, NSW ('93 & '96)
Cimicifuga	J Compton ('94)
Conifers	J Lewis, International Registrar, RHS Wisley ('93) H J Welch, World Conifer Data Pool ('90-'93) P Trehane, International Registrar, RHS Wisley ('94)
Cotoneaster	Jeanette Fryer, NCCPG Collection Holder ('91-'92)
Cyclamen	Dr C Grey-Wilson ('94)
Dahlia	R Hedge, RHS Wisley ('96 & '97)
Delphinium	Dr A C Leslie, International Registrar, RHS Wisley ('93 & '97)
Dianthus	Dr A C Leslie, International Registrar, RHS Wisley ('91-'97)
Gesneriaceae	J D Dates, International Registrar ('94)
Gladiolus	F N Franks ('92)
Heathers	D McClintock ('92)
Hebe	Mrs J Hewitt ('94-'97)
Hedera	P Q Rose & Mrs H Key ('91 & '93) Alison Rutherford ('92-'94)
Hypericum	Dr N K B Robson ('94-'97)
Ilex	Ms S Andrews ('92-'97)
Iris	Mrs J Hewitt ('95-'97)
Jovibarba & *Sempervivum*	P J Mitchell, International Registrar, Sempervivum Society ('91-'93)
Juniperus	J Lewis, International Registrar ('94)
Lavandula	Ms S Andrews ('92-'97)
Lilium	Dr A C Leslie, International Registrar, RHS Wisley ('91-'97)
Narcissus	Mrs S Kington, International Registrar, RHS ('91-'97)
Pelargonium	Mrs H Key ('91-'95)
Pelargonium spp.	Mrs D Miller ('93)
Polemonium	Mrs D Allison ('94)
Rhododendron	Dr A C Leslie, International Registrar, RHS Wisley ('91-'97)
Salix	Dr R D Meikle ('93)
Salvia	J Compton ('92 & '94)
Zauschneria	P Trehane ('94)

To all these, as well as the many readers and nurseries who have also made comments and suggestions, we are, once again, sincerely grateful.

Tony Lord

Collectors' References

Note: Collectors' numbers which do not appear to relate to the species listed are given an asterisk after the number.

A&JW	Anita & John Watson, S America
A&L	Ala & Lancaster expedition, N Iran 1972
AB&S	Archibald, Blanchard & Salmon, Morocco 1980's
AC&H	Apold, Cox & Hutchinson, 1962, NE Turkey
AC&W	Albury, Cheese & Watson
ACE	Alpine Garden Society expedition, China, 1994
ACL	A C Leslie
AGS/ES	Alpine Garden Society expedition, Sikkim
AGSJ	Alpine Garden Society expedition, Japan
Akagi	Akagi Botanical Garden
AL&JS	Sharman & Leslie, Yugoslavia, 1990
B	Len Beer
B&L	Brickell & Leslie, China
B&M	Chris Brickell & Brian Mathew
B&S	Peter Bird & Mike Salmon
B&SWJ	Bleddyn & Sue Wynn-Jones, Far East, 1993
BB	B Bartholomew
BC	Bill Chudziak, Kanchenjunga, 1993
BC&W	Beckett, Cheese & Watson
BL&M	Beer, Lancaster & Morris, NE Nepal, 1971
BM	Brian Mathew
BM&W	Binns, Mason & Wright
BSBE	Bowles Scholarship Botanical Expedition
Bu	S Bubert
C&Cu	K Cox & J Cuby
C&H	P Cox & P Hutchison, Assam, NE Frontier & N Bengal, 1965
C&K	Chamberlain & Knott
C&R	Christian & Roderick, California, Oregon, Washington
C&S	A Clark & I Sinclair
C&W	Cheese & Watson
CC	Chris Chadwell
CC&H	Chamberlain, Cox & Hutchison
CC&McK	Chadwell & McKelvie, Nepal, West Himalaya, 1990-92
CC&MR	Chris Chadwell & Magnus Ramsey, Kashmir, 1985; Himachal Pradesh & W Himalaya, 1989
CD&R	Compton, D'Arcy & Rix, China, Drakensburg, Mexico & Korea
CDB	C D Brickell
CE&H	Christian, Elliott & Hoog, Yugoslavia & Greece, 1982
CEE	Chengdu Edinburgh Expedition, 1991
CH&M	P Cox, P Hutchinson & MacDonald
CHP&W	Chadwell, Howard, Powell & Wright, Kashmir, 1983
CL	Dr C Lovell
CLD	Kew, Edinburgh & RHS, Zhongdian (Chungtien), Lijiang & Dali, China, 1990
CM&W	M Cheese, J Mitchel & J Watson
Cooper	Roland Edgar Cooper (1890-1962)
CT	Carla Teune
DF	Derek Fox
DS&T	Drake, Sharman & Thompson, Turkey, 1989
EGM	E G Millais
EKB	E K Balls
EM	East Malling Research Station clonal selection scheme
EMAK	Edinburgh Makalu Expedition
EMR	E Martyn Rix
ETE	Edinburgh Expedition, Taiwan
ETOT	M Flanagan & T Kirkham, Taiwan, 1992
F	George Forrest (1873-1932)
F&W	Anita Flores & John Watson, Chile, 1992
Farrer	Reginald Farrer (1880-1920)
FK	Fergus Kinimount, China & Nepal
FMB	F M Bailey
G	M F Gardner
G&K	M F Gardner & S G Knees
G&P	M F Gardner & C Page, Chile, 1992
GG	George Gusman
G-W&P	Grey-Wilson & Phillips
GS	George Sherriff (1898-1967)
Guitt	G G Guittonneau
Guiz	Guizhou Expedition, 1985
H	Paul Huggins. Oxford University Expedition, Tehri-Garwhal, Central Himalaya
H&B	O Hilliard & B L Burtt

H&W	Hedge & Wendelbo, Afghanistan, 1969
Harry Smith	Karl August Harald Smith (1889-1971)
HH&K	Sheilah & Spencer Hannay & Noël Kingsbury, Bulgaria, Sept. 1995
HM&S	Halliwell, Mason & Smallcombe
Hummel	D Hummel, China, 1950
HW&E	Hedge, Wendelbo & Ekberg, Afghanistan, 1982
HWEL	J M Hirst & D Webster, Lesotho
HWJCM	Crûg Heronswood expedition, Eastern Nepal, 1995
J&JA	Jim & Jenny Archibald
JCA	J C Archibald
JJH	Josef Halda Collection
JLS	J L Sharman, USA, 1988
JMT	Jim Mann Taylor
JR	J Russell
JRM	John Marr, Greece & Turkey, 1975
JW	J Watson
K	G Kirkpatrick
K&E	Kew & Edinburgh, China, 1989
K&LG	K & L Gillanders, Ecuador, 1994; Yunnan, 1993, 1994, 1996; Vietnam, 1992; Tibet, 1995
K&Mc	George Kirkpatrick and Ron McBeath.
KEKE	Kew/Edinburgh Kanchenjunga Expedition, 1989
KGB	Kunming-Gothenburg Expedition, NW Yunnan, 1993
KR	Keith Rushforth
KW	Frank Kingdon-Ward (1885-1958)
L	Roy Lancaster
L&S	F Ludlow (1885-1972) & G Sherriff
LA	Long Ashton Research Station clonal selection scheme.
LS&E	F Ludlow, G Sherriff & C Elliott
LS&H	F Ludlow, G Sherriff & Hicks, Bhutan, 1949
LS&T	F Ludlow, G Sherriff & G Taylor, SE Tibet, 1938
M&T	B Mathew & J Tomlinson
Mac&W	MacPhail & Watson
McB	Ron McBeath
McLaren	Henry McLaren, 2nd Baron Aberconway (1879-1953)
MS	Mike Salmon
MSF	M S Fillan, Tenerife, 1988; South Korea, 1989
MS&CL	Mike Salmon & Dr Chris Lovell
NNS	Northern Native Seeds (Ron Ratko), Seattle.
NS	Nick Turland (Northside Seeds)
Og	Mikinori Ogisu
P&C	D S Paterson & S Clarke
P&W	Polastri & Watson
PB	Peter Bird
PC&H	Graham Pattison, Peter Catt & Michael Hickson, Mexico, 1994
PD	Peter Davis
PF	Paul Furse
PJC	P J Christian
PJC&AH	P J Christian & A Hoog, Greece & Yugoslavia, 1985
Pras	Milan Prasil
PS&W	Polunin, Sykes & Williams, W Nepal, 1952
PW	Peter Wharton
R	J F C Rock (1884-1962)
RB	Ray Brown (Plant World, Devon), Chile, 1994
RH	R Hancock
RS	Reinhart Suckow
RV	Richard Valder
S&B	Mike Salmon & John Blanchard
S&F	Salmon & Fillan, Spain & Morocco
S&L	I Sinclair & D Long
S&SH	Sheilah & Spencer Hannay, Lesotho, NE Cape Province, 1989 & '91; C Nepal, 1993
SB&L	Salmon, Bird & Lovell, Jordan & Morocco
SBEC	Sino-British expedition, Cangshan, SW China, 1981
SBEL	Sino-British expedition, Lijiang, China
SD	Sashal Dayal
Sch	A D Schilling
SEP	Swedish expedition to Pakistan
SF	P Forde (Seaforde Gardens), Bhutan, Oct. 1990
SH	Spencer Hannay
Sich	Sichuan expedition, China, 1988
SS&W	Stainton, Sykes & Williams, Central Nepal, 1954
SSNY	Sino-Scottish Expedition, North West Yunnan
T	Nigel P Taylor
T&K	Nigel P Taylor & Sabina Knees
TS&BC	Terry Smythe & Bob Cherry, Yunnan, China, 1994
TSS	T Spring-Smyth
TW	Tony Weston (with A D Schilling), Nepal, 1985; (with K Rushforth) SW Yunnan, 1993
USDAPI	US Dept of Agriculture Plant Index Number
USDAPQ	US Dept of Agriculture Plant Quarantine Number
USNA	United States National Arboretum
VHH	Vernon H Heywood
W	E H Wilson (1876-1930)
W A	E H Wilson, for Arnold Arboretum, 1906-1919
W V	E H Wilson, for Veitch, 1899-1905
WM	Will McLewin
Wr	David & Anke Wraight
Yu	Tse Tsun Yu (1908-1986)

PLANT DIRECTORY

ABELIA † (Caprifoliaceae)

§ ***chinensis*** CB&S CChu CPle EHic SMer SPer SSta WFar WHCG WPat WRTC WSHC WWat
§ Confetti = 'Conti' (v) MAsh SPer
'Edward Goucher' ♀ CB&S CDoC CPle CWit EAst EBre ECro ELan LFis LPan MAll MGos NFla SEND SPer SPla WAbe WFar WGwG WPat WPyg WRTC WWat WWeb
engleriana CKni CPle CSam EBee ECtt EHic EPla MPla SBid SEas SHBN WWat
floribunda ♀ CB&S CBot CChu CDoC CFil CLan CPle CSam CTrw EBre ELan LHop MRav SEas SPer WAbe WWat
graebneriana CPle WWat
§ × ***grandiflora*** ♀ Widely available
– 'Aurea' See ***A. × grandiflora* 'Goldsport'**
¶ – 'Compacta' CEnd CSte
§ – 'Francis Mason' (v) ♀ Widely available
– 'Gold Strike' See ***A. × grandiflora* 'Goldsport'**
§ – 'Goldsport' CB&S CBlo CDoC EBee IOrc LHop MAll MPla MWat SAga SBod SEas SOWG WPat WPyg WRTC WWat
¶ – 'Prostrata' EHic
I – 'Variegata' See ***A. × grandiflora* 'Francis Mason'**
rupestris hort. See ***A. × grandiflora***
– Lindley See ***A. chinensis***
schumannii CAbP CB&S CBot CChu CFil CMCN CMHG CPle CSam EBre ELan ENot LHop MAll MAsh SDry SEas SHBN SPer SPla SSta WAbe WFar WHCG WPat WPyg WRTC WSHC WWat
spathulata CPle WWat
triflora CAbP CBot CDoC CFil CHan CKni CPle EHic LFis LHop SPla SSta WFar WPat WRTC WSHC WWat
zanderi CPle CTrw GQui

ABELIOPHYLLUM (Oleaceae)

distichum Widely available
– Roseum Group CB&S CFil CPMA CSam EBre EHic ELan GBuc LHop MAsh MBlu MPla MUlv SAga SEND SHBN SPer SSpi

ABELMOSCHUS (Malvaceae)

§ ***manihot*** LChe

ABIES † (Pinaceae)

alba LCon MBar
– 'Compacta' CKen
– 'King's Dwarf' CKen
– 'Microphylla' CKen
¶ – 'Schwarzwald' CKen
– 'Tortuosa' CKen
amabilis WFro
¶ – 'Spreading Star' ECho
balsamea f. ***balsamea*** WFro
– f. ***hudsonia*** ♀ CKen CMac CSte EHul ENHC GDra IOrc LCon LLin MBar MGos MOne NHar NHed NMen NWCA SLim SSmi WDin
– 'Nana' CKen EBre EHul ELan EOrn LBee LCon MAsh MBri MPla NHar SRms WDin WStI
– 'Piccolo' CKen
– 'Prostrata' CBlo ECho
¶ ***borisii-regis*** LCon
– 'Pendula' CKen
bornmuelleriana 'Archer' CKen
brachyphylla dwarf See ***A. homolepis* 'Prostrata'**
bracteata ETen LCon
cephalonica ETen LCon
§ – 'Meyer's Dwarf' EBre LCon LLin MAsh MBar
I – 'Nana' See ***A. cephalonica* 'Meyer's Dwarf'**
concolor ♀ CB&S CBlo CDoC GRei IOrc ISea LCon LPan MBal MBar NWea SPer WDin WFro WMou
– 'Archer's Dwarf' CKen LCon MGos
– 'Blue Spreader' CKen MGos
– 'Candicans' See ***A. concolor* 'Argentea'**
§ – 'Compacta' ♀ CDoC CKen EBre LCon LLin MAsh MBar MGos NHol SLim SSta
– 'Fagerhult' CKen
– 'Gable's Weeping' CKen NHol
– 'Glauca' See ***A. concolor* 'Violacea'**
– 'Glauca Compacta' See ***A. concolor* 'Compacta'**
– 'Hillier Broom' See ***A. concolor* 'Hillier's Dwarf'**
§ – 'Hillier's Dwarf' CKen
– 'Husky Pup' CKen
– var. ***lowiana*** 'Creamy' CKen
– 'Masonic Broom' CKen
– 'Piggelmee' CKen
– 'Swift's Silver' WFro
§ – 'Violacea' LCon MAsh MBar MGos SSta
– 'Violacea Prostrata' CBlo
– 'Wattezii' CKen LLin
delavayi var. ***delavayi*** IOrc
– – Fabri Group See ***A. fabri***
– 'Major Neishe' CKen
– 'Nana Headfort' See ***A. fargesii* 'Headfort'**
¶ – SF 656 ISea
ernesti See ***A. recurvata* var. *ernestii***
§ ***fabri*** LCon
§ ***fargesii*** 'Headfort' CBlo LCon MBar NHol
forrestii See ***A. delavayi* var. *smithii***
fraseri LCon MBal WFro WMou
– 'Kline's Nest' CKen
¶ ***georgei*** SF 519 ISea
grandis ♀ CB&S ENot GAri GRei IOrc LCon MBar NWea SHBN WDin WMou
– 'Compacta' CKen
holophylla LCon
homolepis ISea LCon MBlu
§ – 'Prostrata' CKen
kawakamii CFil
koreana Widely available
– 'Aurea' See ***A. koreana* 'Flava'**
– 'Blaue Zwo' CKen
– 'Cis' CKen
– 'Compact Dwarf' LCon LLin MBar MGos SSta WAbe
§ – 'Flava' CBlo CDoC CKen GAri LCon MBar NHol
¶ – 'Golden Dream' CKen
– 'Golden Wonder' COtt
– 'Inverleith' CKen
¶ – 'Luminetta' CKen
– 'Nisbet' CKen LCon
– 'Piccolo' CKen

– 'Pinocchio'	CKen
– 'Prostrate Beauty'	LCon
– 'Silberkugel'	CKen
– 'Silberlocke' 🏆	CDoC CKen EBre GAri IOrc LBee LCon LLin LPan MAsh MBar MBlu MBri MGos MPla NHol SLim SPer SSta
– 'Silberperl'	CKen
– 'Silver Show'	CKen
– 'Starker's Dwarf'	CKen
* – 'Threave'	CKen
lasiocarpa var. ***arizonica***	CLnd ETen LCon SIng SSta
– 'Arizonica Compacta' 🏆	CDoC CKen CMac EBre EHul IOrc LBee LCon LLin LPan MAsh MBar MBri MGos NHol SLim SMad SSta WDin
– 'Glauca'	See ***A. concolor*** **'Violacea'**
– 'Green Globe'	CBlo CKen LCon NHol
– 'Kenwith Blue'	CKen
– 'Witch's Broom'	CKen
magnifica	LCon LPan WFro
I – 'Nana'	CKen
marocana	See ***A. pinsapo*** var. ***marocana***
nobilis	See ***A. procera***
nordmanniana 🏆	CDoC CMCN EBee EHul LBuc LCon LPan MBal MBar MGos NWea SLim WDin WFro WGwG
– 'Barabits' Spreader'	CKen
– 'Golden Spreader' 🏆	CDoC CKen EBre EOrn LBee LCon LLin MAsh MBar MGos SLim SPer SSta
I – 'Pendula'	LPan
numidica	LCon LPan
– 'Pendula'	CKen LCon
* – 'Prostrata'	LPan
pindrow	CDoC CLnd CMCN EHal ETen
pinsapo	CFil LCon LPan MBar SEND WPGP
– 'Aurea'	CKen LBuc
– 'Aurea Nana'	CKen
– 'Glauca' 🏆	CDoC CKen ELan IOrc LCon LPan MBar MBlu NHol WDin
– 'Hamondii'	CKen
I – 'Horstmann'	CKen NHol WAbe
– 'Kelleriis'	LCon
§ – var. ***marocana***	WCoo
§ ***procera*** 🏆	CDoC EHul GAri GRei LCon MBal MBar NRoo NWea STre WDin WGwG WMou
– 'Blaue Hexe'	CKen
– 'Compacta'	See ***A. procera*** **'Prostrata'**
– Glauca Group	CDoC CMac EBre IOrc LCon LLin LPan MBar MBri MGos SLim WWes
– 'Glauca Prostrata'	EBre ENHC GAri IOrc LBee LPan MBar MGos SSta WDin WFar
– 'Mount Hood'	CKen
religiosa	GAri
squamata	LCon
sutchuenensis	See ***A. fargesii***
veitchii 🏆	IOrc LCon MBar
– 'Hedergott'	CKen
– 'Heine'	CKen

ABROMEITIELLA (Bromeliaceae)

brevifolia 🏆	CFil EOas

ABROTANELLA (Asteraceae)

¶ sp.	ECho

ABRUS (Papilionaceae)

¶ ***cantoniensis***	MSal
precatorius	MSal

ABUTILON † (Malvaceae)

'Alpha Glory'	ERom
'Amsterdam'	ERea
'Ashford Red' 🏆	CBot CCan IOrc LBlm LCns SLMG SMrm SOWG SRms WOMN
'Bloomsbury Can-can'	LBlm
'Bloomsbury Rose'	LBlm
'Boule de Neige'	CBot CBrk ERea LCns LHil MBri SLMG SOWG
'Canary Bird' 🏆	CB&S CBot CBrk CGre CHal CPle CSev ELan ERea ERom LBlm LCns LHil LHop MBri MLan SHBN SLMG WOMN
'Cannington Carol' (v) 🏆	CBrk CCan ERea LBlm SBid
'Cannington Peter' (v) 🏆	CBrk CCan CHal LBlm
'Cannington Sonia' (v)	ERea
'Cerise Queen'	CCan CSev
'Cloth of Gold'	LCns SOWG
Feuerglocke = 'Firebell'	CBrk CSev LHop SMrm
'Frances Elizabeth'	SOWG
'Glenroy Snowdrift'	MBal
globosum	See ***A. × hybridum***
'Golden Fleece'	CKni ERea GCal IBlr LCns
'Heather Bennington'	SOWG
'Henry Makepeace'	SOWG
'Hinton Seedling'	CBrk CFil EMil SBid SLMG
§ × ***hybridum***	MBri
◆ – 'Savitzii'	See ***A.*** **'Savitzii'**
'Kentish Belle' 🏆	CAbb CB&S CBot CFil CHal CMHG CPle CSev EBre ECot ENot IOrc MGrG NTow SBra SHBN SLMG SPer WWye
'Louis Marignac'	CBrk CCan ERea ERom LBlm
'Marion'	LCns SOWG
'Master Michael'	CKni EMil ERea SBid
megapotamicum 🏆	CB&S CBot CCan CMHG CPlN CPle ECha ELan ENot ERea GCra GQui MBal MGos MGrG MRav SAxl SBra SDix SHBN SLMG SOWG SPer WBod WHar WRTC WSHC WWat WWye
– 'Variegatum'	CAbb CB&S CBot CBrk CFil CWit ECtt ELan GOrc GQui IBlr IOrc LBlm LHil MBri MGrG NPer SBod SBra SEas SHBN SLMG SOWG SPer SRms WFar WHar
– 'Wisley Red'	EPfP WLRN
× ***milleri*** 🏆	CB&S ELan ERea IOrc SBra SHBN SMrm SVen WSHC
– 'Variegatum'	CB&S CBrk CCan CMHG CPle SEND SHBN SLMG
'Nabob' 🏆	CBrk CCan CFil CGre CHal CWit ERea LBlm LCns LHil MBri SBid SLMG SOWG
'Orange King'	CB&S
otocarpum	MSto
'Patrick Synge'	CBrk CFil CMHG CPle ERav ERea LBlm LCns LGre SLMG SMrm SOWG SVen
'Peaches and Cream'	CBrk
§ ***pictum***	ERea LBlm MBri
– 'Thompsonii' (v)	CBot CBrk CHal ERea LBlm LCns LHil NPer SLMG
'Pink Lady'	CB&S EMil ERea GQui MGrG SBra

'Red Bells'	CB&S GQui
'Red Goblin'	GCra
'Rotterdam'	CBrk LCns LHil SBid
§ 'Savitzii' (v)	CB&S CBot CBrk CHal ERea LHil SOWG SRms SVen
sellowianum var. ***marmoratum***	ERea SLMG
'Silver Belle'	LBlm
'Souvenir de Bonn' (v) 🏆	CBrk CSpe ERea IBlr LBlm LCns NCut SBid SMrm
striatum hort.	See ***A. pictum***
× ***suntense***	CB&S CHEx CMHG CPle CTrC EBre ELan ERea LHop MBal MSto NPer SHBN SLMG SPer SSta WEas
– 'Jermyns' 🏆	CDoC CEnd ECtt EOrc GCra LGre MMil SMad SMrm SSta WFar WPyg WWat
– 'Ralph Gould'	ECGP LHop
– 'Violetta'	CEnd SSpi
theophrasti	MSal
vitifolium	CB&S CBot CFil ECot ERea IOrc ISea LHop NEgg SChu SPer WOMN WPri WWat WWin WWye
– var. ***album***	CAbb CB&S CMHG EAst ECha ELan ERav LHop MGrG MLan SChu SEND SPer SSpi SSta WFar WWat WWye
– 'Ice Blue'	CBot
– 'Tennant's White' 🏆	CAbP CBot CCan CEnd CGre ERea LGre MBri SHBN SMad SPer WCot WCru
– 'Veronica Tennant' 🏆	CEnd EHal ERea GOrc LGre MBri SMrm WPyg

ACACIA † (Mimosaceae)

¶ ***acinacea***	CPle
alpina	WCel
armata	See ***A. paradoxa***
baileyana 🏆	CB&S CBrP CDoC CTrC ECon ECot ELan EMil ERea GQui LCns SBid
– 'Purpurea' 🏆	CAbb CB&S CDoC CGre CWit EBee EMil ERea GQui LHop MAll MBlu MLan SBid SPer
¶ ***caffra***	CTrC
¶ ***catechu***	MSal
cultriformis	ERea LCns
cyanophylla	See ***A. saligna***
dealbata 🏆	Widely available
– 'Gaulois Astier'	ERea
– 'Mirandole'	ERea
– 'Rêve d'Or'	ERea
– ***subalpina***	LPan
¶ ***decurrens***	CBrP
¶ ***erioloba***	CTrC
Exeter Hybrid	CGre
farnesiana	CPle
filicifolia	LPan WCel
floribunda 'Lisette'	ELan ERea LCns MAll
frigescens	MAll WCel
julibrissin	See ***Albizia julibrissin***
juniperina	See ***A. ulicifolia***
karroo	CArn CTbh CTrC
kybeanensis	WCel
longifolia	CAbb CB&S CBrP CHEx CTrC EOas LHil NPSI SMrm SRms
¶ ***maidenii***	NGno
mearnsii	CGre CTbh CTrC WCel
melanoxylon	CB&S ISea LHil MAll WCel
motteana	ECot ERea LCns
¶ ***mucronata***	CB&S
obliquinervia	WCel
¶ ***obtusifolia***	NGno
§ ***paradoxa***	CPle ERea LHop MAll MBlu
– var. ***angustifolia***	LBlm
podalyriifolia	CBrP CFil CTrC
polybotrya hort.	See ***A. glaucocarpa***
pravissima	CB&S CChu CDoC CFil CGre CHEx CMHG CPle CTbh CTrC CWit ERea GQui ISea LHop LPan MAll MBal SArc SBid WCel WNor
¶ ***pycnantha***	CBrP
retinodes 🏆	CAbb CB&S CBrP CDoC CGre CPle ELan EOas ERea GQui IDee LCns MAll SEND SRms
riceana	CB&S CDoC CTrC GQui
rivalis	ERea
¶ ***rotundifolia***	CPle
rubida	CTbh CTrC LPan MAll
salicina	MAll
§ ***saligna***	CAbb MCCP SMrm
sentis	See ***A. victoriae***
¶ ***sophorae***	MAll
¶ ***tortilis***	CTrC
* ***trinervis***	ERea
§ ***ulicifolia***	CGre CPle CWit
verniciflua	MAll
verticillata	CB&S CGre CPle EWes MAll
§ ***victoriae***	ERea

ACAENA (Rosaceae)

adscendens 'Glauca'	EMan LHop MBel NBir NNor
– hort.	See ***A. magellanica*** subsp. ***magellanica***
– Margery Fish	See ***A. affinis***
– Vahl	See ***A. magellanica*** subsp. ***laevigata***
§ ***affinis***	ECha SDix
§ ***anserinifolia*** Druce	ECha GLil MAll NHol WPer WWin
– hort.	See ***A. novae-zelandiae***
buchananii	CShe CTri EPot GIsl GMaP GTou MAll MBar MBri NBro NMGW NNor SAlw SIng SSmi WByw WDav WFar WHoo WMer WPbr WPer WPyg WWhi WWye
caerulea	See ***A. caesiiglauca***
§ ***caesiiglauca***	CBar CNic CRow CTri ECoo ECro GAbr GGar GTou MAll MWat NNor NSti SBla WEas WPer WWhi
– CC 451	MRPP
fissistipula	EHoe GAri GGar WHer WPer
glabra	GIsl
glaucophylla	See ***A. magellanica*** subsp. ***magellanica***
'Greencourt Hybrid'	CLyd
inermis	CLyd EGar ELan EPot GIsl GTou LCom MAll SIng SSmi WPer
§ ***magellanica*** subsp. ***laevigata***	EGoo EHoe GAri GGar GIsl GTou WWin
§ – subsp. ***magellanica***	ELan GTou MAll WMer
microphylla 🏆	EBre ECha ELan ESis GGar GIsl LBee MAll MBar MBri MWat NGre NMen NRoo SAlw SHFr SPer SSmi WByw WCer WCla WEas WPer WTyr
◆ – Copper Carpet	See ***A. microphylla*** **'Kupferteppich'**

– 'Glauca' — See *A. caesiiglauca*
§ – 'Kupferteppich' — CLTr CRow EGoo EHoe EPPr GAbr GAri GGar GMaP MBri MBro MCLN MRav NBro NCat NVic SIng WPat WPbr WPyg
– var. ***pallideolivacea*** — CRow
– 'Pewter Carpet' — EPPr SIng
– 'Pulchella' — EBre ECha EMan SChu
¶ ***minor*** — SAlw
myriophylla — EDAr WDav WNdy WPer
§ ***novae-zelandiae*** — CRow CTri EJud GIsl GTou SDix SIng SWat WPer
ovalifolia — CLyd CNic CRow GTou SLod WPer
'Pewter' — See *A. saccaticupula* **'Blue Haze'**
pinnatifida — ELan GTou NBro WPer
profundeincisa — See *A. anserinifolia* **Druce**
'Purple Carpet' — See *A. microphylla* **'Kupferteppich'**
¶ ***saccaticupula*** — MAll
§ – 'Blue Haze' — CGle CLTr CLyd CSam CShe ECha ELan EPot GCHN GTou MBar MTis NPer SDix SIng SPer WFar WHoo WPer WWhi
sanguisorbae Linnaeus f. — See *A. anserinifolia* **Druce**
sericea — WPer
viridior — See *A. anserinifolia* **Druce**

ACALYPHA (Euphorbiaceae)

hispida 🏆 — MBri
– 'Hispaniola' — CBrk ERea
pendula — See *A. reptans*

ACANTHOCALYX See MORINA

ACANTHOLIMON (Plumbaginaceae)

androsaceum — See *A. ulicinum*
¶ ***armenum*** — NMen
glumaceum — EPot MDHE NHol NMen NNrd WPat
hohenackeri — EPot SIng
§ ***ulicinum*** — EPot NWCA

ACANTHOPANAX See ELEUTHEROCOCCUS

ACANTHUS † (Acanthaceae)

balcanicus — See *A. hungaricus*
caroli-alexandri — WCot
dioscoridis var. ***perringii*** — CGle CHan SBla WCot
hirsutus — EMar EMon SCro WCot
– JCA 109.700 — SBla
– subsp. ***syriacus*** JCA 106.500 — CGle CLon LGre SBla
§ ***hungaricus*** — CArc CArn CGle CLon ECED EHal ELan EMan EMar EMon EPla GCal LFis MSte SBla SDix SPer SSoC SUsu SWat WCot WRus
– AL&JS 90097YU — EMon
longifolius — See *A. hungaricus*
mollis — Widely available
– 'Fielding Gold' — GCal
– 'Hollard's Gold' — CRDP SWat WCot
– Latifolius Group — EBee EBre EFou EGar EMon EPla MRav MUlv NHol NRai SChu SPer WGwG WWat
spinosus 🏆 — Widely available
¶ – 'Lady Moore' — IBlr
– Spinosissimus Group — CGle ECha EGar EMan EPla MUlv SMad SWat WCru WFar
syriacus — EMan GCal

ACCA (Myrtaceae)

sellowiana (F) — CArn CB&S CGre CHan CMHG CPle CSam ELan EPla ERea ESim GQui LHop LPan MSal MUlv SOWG SSta WPat WRTC WSHC
– 'Apollo' (F) — ERea
– 'Coolidge' (F) — ERea
– 'Mammoth' (F) — ERea
– 'Triumph' (F) — ERea
– 'Variegata' (F) — CGre

ACER † (Aceraceae)

acuminatum — CMCN WNor
albopurpurascens — CMCN
amplum — CMCN
argutum — CMCN WNor
barbinerve — WNor
buergerianum — CDoC CDul CEnd CGre CLnd CMCN CPMA GAri SSpi STre WNor WWat
– 'Goshiki-kaede' (v) — CPMA LNet
♦ – 'Integrifolium' — See *A. buergerianum* **'Subintegrum'**
¶ – 'Naruto' — CMCN
§ – 'Subintegrum' — CMCN
– 'Tanchô' — LNet
* – 'Variegatum' — CMCN
caesium — EPfP
campbellii — CMCN LNet
§ – subsp. ***flabellatum*** — CGre CMCN
– – var. ***yunnanense*** — CMCN
¶ – – – SF 533 — ISea
♦ – subsp. ***sinense*** — See *A. sinense*
♦ – subsp. ***wilsonii*** — See *A. wilsonii*
campestre 🏆 — CDoC CDul CKin CLnd CMCN CPer EBre ENot GRei IOrc LBuc LHyr LPan MBar MBri MGos NBee NRoo NWea SHBN SPer SSta WDin WMou WNor WOrn WPyg
– 'Carnival' — CB&S CEnd CMCN CPMA ELan LNet MBlu MBri MGos NHol SHBN SMad SSoC WMou WWeb
– 'Elsrijk' — CLnd
– 'Pendulum' — CBlo CDoC CEnd CTho
– 'Postelense' — CEnd CMCN LNet MBlu SSpi WMou
– 'Pulverulentum' (v) — CBlo CDoC CEnd CMCN LNet SMad SPer SSta
– 'Red Shine' — EBee MGos
– 'Royal Ruby' — CB&S CMCN CTho LNet MAsh MBlu SSta
* – 'Ruby Glow' — CBlo CDoC CEnd SPer
– 'Schwerinii' — CMCN
– 'William Caldwell' — CTho
capillipes 🏆 — CB&S CDul CMCN CSam CTho ELan ENot EPla IOrc LPan MAsh MBar MBri MGos SIgm SPer SSpi SSta STre WDin WGer WNor WPyg WWat
* – 'Variegatum' — CEnd
cappadocicum — CMCN WCoo WDin WNor WWes
– 'Aureum' 🏆 — CAbP CB&S CDoC CDul CEnd CLnd CMCN ELan ENot IOrc LNet LPan MBlu MBri MGos NBea SHBN SMad SPer SSpi WDin WMou WPyg

– var. ***mono***	See ***A. mono***
– 'Rubrum' 🏆	CBlo CDoC CDul CGre CLnd CMCN ENot IHos IOrc LPan MAsh MBlu MGos SPer SSpi WDin
– subsp. ***sinicum***	CMCN EPfP WCoo
carnea 'Variegatum'	CMCN
carpinifolium	CDoC CLnd CMCN LNet SSpi WGer WWes WWoo
catalpifolium	See ***A. longipes*** subsp. ***catalpifolium***
§ ***caudatifolium***	CMCN CTho
§ aff. – CC 1744	WHCr
§ aff. – CC 1927	WHCr
caudatum subsp. ***ukurunduense***	WNor
cinerascens	CMCN
cinnamomifolium	See ***A. coriaceifolium***
circinatum 🏆	CB&S CDul CMCN CSam CTho LBuc LNet MUlv SSpi SSta WDin WFro WGwG WHut WNor WWat
– 'Little Gem'	LNet
– 'Monroe'	LNet
cissifolium	CB&S CDoC CFil CMCN WNor
x ***conspicuum*** 'Elephant's Ear'	CPMA
– 'Phoenix'	CPMA LNet MBlu
◆– 'Silver Cardinal'	See ***A.* 'Silver Cardinal'**
§ ***cordatum***	CMCN
§ ***coriaceifolium***	CMCN WCoo
crataegifolium	CMCN WNor
– 'Veitchii' (v)	CMCN CPMA EPfP LNet SSta
creticum	See ***A. sempervirens***
dasycarpum	See ***A. saccharinum***
davidii	CAbP CB&S CDoC CMCN CMHG ENot IOrc ISea MAsh MBal MBar MGos MRav MWat SHBN SPer WDin WFro WNor
– 'Ernest Wilson'	CB&S CBlo CDul CMCN COtt ELan
– 'George Forrest' 🏆	CB&S CBlo CMCN CTho EBee EBre EPfP LPan MAsh MUlv SEND SSpi SSta WDin WOrn
– 'Karmen'	MGos
¶ – 'Rosalie'	MBlu
– 'Serpentine' 🏆	CB&S CMCN CPMA MAsh MBlu MBri NBee SSpi
diabolicum	CMCN
divergens	CMCN
elegantulum	CGre CMCN WFro WNor
erianthum	CDul CLnd SSpi SSta WNor
fabri	CMCN
◆***flabellatum***	See ***A. campbellii*** subsp. ***flabellatum***
§ ***forrestii***	CDul CMCN EPfP WNor
– 'Alice'	CB&S CMCN CPMA LNet MGos
franchetii	CMCN
x ***freemanii*** 'Autumn Blaze'	CDoC IOrc
– 'Autumn Fantasy'	MBlu
fulvescens	See ***A. longipes***
ginnala	See ***A. tataricum*** subsp. ***ginnala***
giraldii	CMCN
glabrum	CLnd CMCN WNor
– subsp. ***douglasii***	CMCN
globosum	See ***A. platanoides* 'Globosum'**
grandidentatum	See ***A. saccharum*** subsp. ***grandidentatum***
griseum 🏆	Widely available
grosseri	CMCN CTri NEgg WFro WLRN
– var. ***hersii*** 🏆	CDoC CDul CLnd CTho ELan ENot MAsh MBal MBri MRav MUlv NWea SPer SSta WDin WGer WNor WOrn WPyg WWat
heldreichii	CLnd CMCN MBlu
henryi	CGre CLnd CMCN ENot LNet SSpi WNor WWes WWoo
x ***hillieri***	CMCN
hookeri	CMCN
hyrcanum	CMCN
japonicum	CDul CMCN LNet MBal MBar SSta WAbe WDin WNor WWat
§ – 'Aconitifolium' 🏆	CAlt CDul CEnd CMCN CPMA CShe EJap ELan ENot IHos IOrc LNet LPan MAsh MBar MBlu MBri MGos MMor NPal SHBN SPer SReu SSpi SSta WDin WNor WPat WWat
¶ – 'Attaryi'	CMCN
– 'Aureum'	See ***A. shirasawanum* 'Aureum'**
– 'Ezo-no-momiji'	See ***A. shirasawanum* 'Ezo-no-momiji'**
– 'Filicifolium'	See ***A. japonicum* 'Aconitifolium'**
– 'Green Cascade'	CAlt CEnd CMCN CPMA WPat WWes
* – 'King Copse'	SMur
– 'Laciniatum'	See ***A. japonicum* 'Aconitifolium'**
– f. ***microphyllum***	See ***A. shirasawanum* 'Microphyllum'**
– 'Ogurayama'	See ***A. shirasawanum* 'Ogurayama'**
– 'O-isami'	CMCN LNet
– 'O-taki'	WWes
– 'Vitifolium' 🏆	CAlt CBlo CDoC CEnd CMCN CPMA ELan EPfP IOrc LNet LPan MBlu SReu SSpi SSta WDin
kawakamii	See ***A. caudatifolium***
laevigatum	CMCN
lanceolatum	CMCN
laxiflorum	CLnd CMCN SSpi
lobelii Bunge	See ***A. turkestanicum***
– Tenore	CLnd CMCN ENot SSpi
§ ***longipes***	CMCN
§ – subsp. ***catalpifolium***	CMCN
macrophyllum	CDoC CDul CFil CMCN EPfP LHyd MBlu
– 'Kimballiae'	CMCN
¶ – NJM 94040	WPGP
– 'Seattle Sentinel'	CMCN
* – 'Variegatum'	CMCN
¶ ***mandshuricum***	WWoo
§ ***maximowiczianum***	CB&S CDoC CEnd CLnd CMCN CSam ELan IOrc MBal SPer SSpi SSta WNor WWat WWes
maximowiczii	CMCN WNor
§ ***metcalfii***	WNor
micranthum 🏆	CMCN EPfP WCoo WNor WWes
§ ***mono***	CMCN
– 'Hoshiyadori' (v)	CMCN
– 'Shufu-nishiki'	CMCN
– var. ***tricuspis***	See ***A. cappadocicum*** subsp. ***sinicum*** var. ***tricaudatum***
monspessulanum	CFil CMCN
morrisonense	See ***A. caudatifolium***

negundo	CDul CLnd CMCN ENot NWea WNor
– 'Argenteovariegatum'	See ***A. negundo* 'Variegatum'**
– 'Auratum'	CBlo CMCN MBar WDin WPat
– 'Aureovariegatum'	CB&S CWLN MBar MUlv SHBN
§ – 'Elegans' (v)	CBlo CDoC CLnd CMCN COtt EBee EBre ELan ENot LPan MAsh NHol SHBN SPer
– 'Elegantissimum'	See ***A. negundo* 'Elegans'**
– 'Flamingo' (v) 🏆	CB&S CDul CEnd CLnd CMCN CWLN EBre ELan IOrc LBuc LHop LNet LPan MAsh MBar MBri MGos MMor NBee NHol SHBN SMad SPer SReu SSoC SSta WDin WPat WPyg
– 'Kelly's Gold'	CB&S CWLN
§ – 'Variegatum'	CB&S CLnd CWLN EBee ENot LPan MGos NBee SPer WDin
– var. ***violaceum*** 🏆	CB&S CMCN EPla
nikoense	See ***A. maximowiczianum***
oblongum	CMCN
§ ***obtusifolium***	CMCN
okamotoanum	CMCN
oliverianum	CMCN WCoo WNor
opalus	CDul CMCN
orientale	See ***A. sempervirens***
palmatum	CDul CLan CMCN CMHG ENot ESis GAbr LNet MBal MBar MMor NBee NFla SHBN SPer SSpi SSta STre WAbe WCoo WFro WNor WOrn WPat WWat
– 'Aka Shigitatsusawa'	CMCN EJap LNet
– 'Akaji-nishiki'	See ***A. truncatum* 'Akaji-nishiki'**
– 'Akegarasu'	CMCN
¶ – 'Aoba-jo'	CPMA
– 'Aoshime-no-uchi'	See ***A. palmatum* 'Shinobugaoka'**
– 'Aoyagi'	CMCN CPMA EJap LNet MAsh WWes
§ – 'Arakawa'	CMCN GAri LNet
– 'Aratama'	CMCN
– 'Asahi-zuru' (v)	CBlo CMCN CPMA LNet MGos MMor SSta WNor WWes
¶ – 'Atrolineare'	COtt
– f. ***atropurpureum***	CAlt CB&S CDul CShe EBre EJap ELan ENot GRei LHyd LNet MBal MBar MGos MMor NBee NWea SBod SHBN SPer SReu WBod WDin WOrn WPat WStI WWat
¶ – 'Atropurpureum'	NFla
– 'Atropurpureum Superbum'	CBlo CMCN MBri
– 'Aureum'	CAlt CBlo CFil CMCN CPMA ELan LNet MBri SBod SSpi WFar WPGP WRus
– Autumn Glory Group	CPMA SSpi WWes
* – 'Autumn Red'	LPan
* – 'Autumn Showers'	CEnd
– 'Azuma-murasaki'	CMCN
– 'Beni-kagami'	CDul CEnd CMCN COtt CPMA LNet
– 'Beni-kawa'	LNet
– 'Beni-komachi'	CB&S CFil CMCN CPMA LNet WNor WPGP WPat
– 'Beni-maiko'	CBlo CFil CMCN CPMA LNet WNor WPGP WPat WWeb WWes
– 'Beni-otake'	CB&S LNet
– 'Beni-schichihenge' (v)	CB&S CBlo CEnd CMCN CPMA ELan LNet MAsh NHol SSta WNor WPat
– 'Beni-shidare Variegated'	CMCN CPMA LNet
– 'Beni-tsukasa' (v)	CBlo CEnd CPMA LNet LPan SSpi WPat WWes
– 'Bloodgood' 🏆	Widely available
– 'Bonfire'	See ***A. truncatum* 'Akaji-nishiki'**
– 'Brocade'	CMCN WPat
– 'Burgundy Lace' 🏆	CAlt CB&S CBlo CEnd CMCN COtt CPMA EJap IOrc LNet MGos NHol WPat WPyg
– 'Butterfly' (v) 🏆	CAlt CB&S CEnd CFil CMCN CPMA EBre EJap ELan IOrc LNet LPan MAsh MBal MBar MBri MGos NHol SBod SPer SReu SSta WNor WPGP WPat WPyg WStI
– 'Carminium'	See ***A. palmatum* 'Corallinum'**
– 'Chirimen-nishiki' (v)	CMCN LNet
– 'Chishio'	See ***A. palmatum* 'Shishio'**
– 'Chishio Improved'	See ***A. palmatum* 'Shishio Improved'**
– 'Chitoseyama' 🏆	CAlt CBlo CDul CEnd CMCN COtt CPMA CTho ELan LNet MBar MBri MGos MMor SSpi SSta WNor WPat WWeb
– 'Coonara Pygmy'	CMCN CPMA LNet WPat WWes
– 'Coral Pink'	CPMA
§ – 'Corallinum'	CBlo CEnd CMCN COtt CPMA LNet LPan LRHS SSpi WPat
N – var. ***coreanum***	CMCN CSam WNor
– 'Deshôjô'	CB&S CBlo CMCN LNet LPan MAsh MBar MBlu MGos NHol WPat
– var. ***dissectum*** 🏆	CDoC CEnd CTho ENot IOrc LHyd MBar MBri MGos MLan NBee NHol NWea SHBN SReu SSoC WDin WFro WNor WPat WPyg WStI WWat
– – 'Crimson Queen' 🏆	CAlt CB&S CDoC CDul CEnd CMCN CPMA EJap IOrc LNet LPan MAsh MBal MBri MGos MMor NFla SPer WFar WNor WPat WPyg
– – Dissectum Atropurpureum Group	CAlt CB&S CPMA EBre ELan LHyd LNet LPan MBal MGos NWea SHBN SPer SReu SSpi SSta WBod WDin WPat WWat
– – 'Dissectum Flavescens'	CEnd CMCN CPMA ISea
§ – – 'Dissectum Nigrum'	CAlt CBlo CPMA CTri LNet MAsh MGos WLRN WPat
– – 'Dissectum Palmatifidum'	ISea LNet
¶ – – 'Dissectum Rubrifolium'	CMCN
§ – – 'Dissectum Variegatum'	COtt CPMA LNet MAsh SMur SSta
– – Dissectum Viride Group	CAlt CB&S CDul CMCN CPMA EJap ELan GRei ISea LNet MAsh MMor SPer SPla SSta WBod
– – 'Green Globe'	LPan
– – 'Inaba-shidare' 🏆	CB&S CDoC CEnd CMCN COtt CPMA EJap GRei LNet LPan MAsh MBar MBri MGos MMor NHol SPer SReu SSta WPyg
– – 'Lionheart'	CPMA
¶ – – 'Orangeola'	LNet WPat

– – 'Ornatum'	CDoC CMCN COtt CTri EJap MBri MGos SPer SSoC WFar
– 'Eddisbury'	MMor SSta WPat
– 'Effegi'	See ***A. palmatum*** **'Fireglow'**
– 'Elegans'	MAsh
– 'Ever Red'	See ***A. palmatum*** var. ***dissectum*** **'Dissectum Nigrum'**
– 'Filigree'	CAlt CBlo CFil CMCN CPMA EJap ISea LNet MAsh MBri MGos SSpi WPGP WPat
* – 'Fior d'Arangio'	CEnd COtt
§ – 'Fireglow'	CBlo CMCN COtt CPMA LPan WPat WWes
– 'Frederici Guglielmi'	See ***A. palmatum*** var. ***dissectum*** **'Dissectum Variegatum'**
– 'Garnet' 🏆	CEnd CMCN CPMA CSam CTho EBre EJap ELan IHos ISea LPan MAsh MBal MBar MBlu MBri MMor NBea NBee NHol SMad SPer SSpi SSta WDin WPat WPyg WStI WWat
– 'Goshiki-kotohime' (v)	CMCN CPMA
– 'Goshiki-shidare' (v)	CMCN LNet
– 'Green Trompenburg'	CMCN LNet
§ – 'Hagoromo'	CPMA LNet SPer
– 'Hanami-nishiki'	CMCN CPMA
– 'Harusame' (v)	CMCN LNet
– 'Hazeroino' (v)	CMCN
– var. ***heptalobum***	CMCN
§ – 'Heptalobum Elegans'	CBlo CMCN CPMA LRHS SHBN SSpi
– 'Heptalobum Elegans Purpureum'	See ***A. palmatum*** **'Hessei'**
§ – 'Hessei'	CEnd CMCN LNet WPat
– 'Higasayama' (v)	CB&S CBlo CFil CMCN COtt CPMA EJap ISea LNet NHol SSta WNor WPGP WPat WWes
– 'Hôgyoku'	CMCN EJap
– 'Ichigyôji'	CDul CEnd CMCN EJap MAsh
– 'Improved Shishio'	See ***A. palmatum*** **'Shishio Improved'**
– 'Inazuma'	CB&S CMCN EJap
– 'Jirô-shidare'	LNet SMur WWeb
– 'Junihitoe'	See ***A. shirasawanum*** **'Junihitoe'**
– 'Kagero' (v)	CPMA
§ – 'Kagiri-nishiki' (v)	CBlo CMCN CPMA EJap LNet MAsh MGos SPer SSta WNor
– 'Kamagata'	CEnd CMCN CPMA MAsh SSta WNor WPat WWeb
– 'Karaori-nishiki' (v)	EJap LNet LPan
– 'Karasugawa' (v)	CAlt CMCN CPMA LNet
– 'Kasagiyama'	CAlt CEnd CMCN COtt CPMA EJap LRHS WPat
¶ – 'Kasen-nishiki'	CPMA
– 'Kashima'	CDul CMCN CPMA EJap WNor
– 'Katsura'	CB&S CEnd CFil CMCN COtt CPMA EJap ELan ISea MAsh MBri NHol SPer SPla SSpi SSta WNor WPGP WPat
– 'Ki-hachijô'	CMCN EJap
– 'Kinran'	CMCN LNet WPat WWeb
– 'Kinshi'	CMCN CPMA LRHS SSta WWeb WWes
– 'Kiri-nishiki'	CMCN WPat
– 'Kiyohime'	CDoC CMCN
– 'Koshibori-nishiki'	CPMA
– 'Kotohime'	CMCN CPMA
– 'Koto-no-ito'	CMCN
– 'Kurui-jishi'	LNet
– 'Linearilobum' 🏆	CAlt CMCN EJap LHyd LNet MBlu NHol WNor WPat
– 'Linearilobum Atropurpureum'	EPfP WNor
– 'Little Princess'	See ***A. palmatum*** **'Mapi-no-machihime'**
¶ – 'Lutescens'	CMCN CPMA
– 'Maiko'	CDul CMCN
– 'Mama'	CMCN
§ – 'Mapi-no-machihime'	CMCN ELan LNet MAsh NHol SSta WPat WWat
– 'Masukagami' (v)	CEnd COtt
– 'Matsukaze'	CMCN COtt CPMA EJap WWes
¶ – 'Mikawa-yatsubusa'	CMCN
– 'Mirte'	LNet
– 'Moonfire'	CMCN CSte EJap LNet WWeb
– 'Murasaki-kyohim'	CMCN CPMA WPat
– 'Mure-hibari'	CMCN
– 'Murogawa'	CMCN
– 'Nicholsonii'	CMCN CTri LPan
– 'Nigrum'	CMCN WPat
§ – 'Nishiki-gawa'	CMCN CPMA
– 'Nomurishidare'	See ***A. palmatum*** **'Shôjô-shidare'**
– 'Nuresagi'	CMCN CPMA LNet
– 'O-kagami'	CMCN CPMA LNet MBri
– 'Okukuji-nishiki'	CPMA LNet
– 'Okushimo'	CFil CMCN CPMA LNet MAsh NHol SSta WNor WPGP WPat
– 'Omato'	LNet
– 'Omurayama'	CMCN CPMA EJap LNet LRHS MAsh SSta WNor WWeb WWes
§ – 'O-nishiki'	CMCN EJap LNet
– 'Orange Dream'	CMCN CPMA LPan MBri WWes
– 'Oridono-nishiki' (v)	CEnd CMCN COtt CPMA ELan EPfP LNet MBlu MGos NBee NPal SCoo SSta WNor
– 'Osakazuki' 🏆	Widely available
– 'Oshû-beni'	CMCN
– 'Oshû-shidare'	CMCN CPMA
– 'Otome-zakura'	CMCN
– 'Pendulum Julian'	CMCN WPat
– 'Pine Bark Maple'	See ***A. palmatum*** **'Nishiki-gawa'**
¶ – 'Pixie'	CMCN
– 'Red Dragon'	CB&S CPMA LNet
– 'Red Filigree Lace'	CAlt CEnd CMCN CPMA CSte ISea LNet MAsh
– 'Red Flash'	LPan
– 'Red Pygmy' 🏆	CAlt CB&S CBlo CDoC CEnd CMCN COtt CPMA EJap LNet MBar MBlu MBri MGos NHol SPer SSta WPat
– 'Reticulatum'	See ***A. palmatum*** **'Shigitatsu-sawa'**
– 'Ribesifolium'	See ***A. palmatum*** **'Shishigashira'**
– 'Roseomarginatum'	See ***A. palmatum*** **'Kagiri-nishiki'**
– 'Rough Bark Maple'	See ***A. palmatum*** **'Arakawa'**
– 'Rubrum'	CMCN EJap MBal WFar
– 'Rufescens'	CMCN
– 'Ryuzu'	CPMA
– 'Sagara-nishiki' (v)	CMCN CPMA
– 'Samidare'	CMCN EJap
N – 'Sango-kaku' 🏆	CAlt CB&S CDoC CEnd CFil CGre CMCN CPMA CSam ELan IHos IOrc ISea LHyd LNet MBal MBar MBri MGos NHol SBod SHBN SPer SPla SReu SSta WDin WNor WPat WWat
– 'Saoshika'	CDul CMCN
– 'Sazanami'	CMCN EJap WNor

¶ – 'Scolopendriifolium'	WPat
– 'Seigen'	CMCN WPat
– 'Seiryû' 🏆	CAbP CAlt CB&S CEnd CMCN COtt CPMA EJap ELan LNet LPan MBar MBri MGos MMor NHol SPer SSpi SSta WDin WFar WNor WPat
– 'Sekimori'	CMCN CPMA WWes
¶ – 'Sekka-yatsubusa'	CMCN
– 'Senkaki'	See ***A. palmatum* 'Sango-kaku'**
– 'Septemlobum Elegans'	See ***A. palmatum* 'Heptalobum Elegans'**
– 'Septemlobum Purpureum'	See ***A. palmatum* 'Hessei'**
– 'Sessilifolium' dwarf	See ***A. palmatum* 'Hagoromo'**
– 'Sessilifolium' tall	See ***A. palmatum* 'Koshimino'**
– 'Shaina'	CMCN COtt CPMA LPan WPat WWeb
– 'Sherwood Flame'	CBlo CMCN CPMA EJap LNet MBlu MBri MGos WPat
§ – 'Shigitatsu-sawa' (v)	CB&S CMCN CPMA LPan MAsh SSta
– 'Shigure-bato'	CMCN
¶ – 'Shikageori-nishiki'	MAsh
– 'Shime-no-uchi'	CMCN LNet
– 'Shindeshôjô'	CBlo CEnd CMCN COtt CPMA EJap ELan LNet LPan MAsh MBri SBod SHBN SPer SPla SReu SSta WFoF WNor WPGP WPat
§ – 'Shinobugaoka'	CBlo CMCN CPMA LNet
– 'Shinonome'	CMCN COtt
§ – 'Shishigashira'	CMCN COtt LPan MBar MBri MGos MMor SSta WFar WPat
§ – 'Shishio'	CBlo CMCN COtt LHyd LNet SSpi
§ – 'Shishio Improved'	CAlt CFil CMCN CPMA LNet MBlu MGos MMor SSta WNor WPGP
¶ – 'Shôjô'	CMCN
– 'Shôjô-nomura'	CEnd CMCN COtt
§ – 'Shôjô-shidare'	CEnd COtt LRHS MAsh SSpi
– 'Stella Rossa'	CBlo CMCN COtt CPMA WPat WWes
– 'Suminagashi'	CDoC CMCN COtt LNet SMur
– 'Takinogawa'	SMur WWeb
– 'Tamahime'	CMCN EJap WNor
– 'Tamukeyama'	CMCN CPMA
– 'Tana'	CMCN EJap WNor WPat
– 'Trompenburg'	CB&S CBlo CEnd CMCN COtt CPMA CTho EJap ELan LNet LPan MAsh MBri MBro MGos MMor NHol NPal SPer SPla SSpi SSta WNor WPat WPyg
– 'Tsuchigumo'	CMCN
– 'Tsukubane'	CMCN
– 'Tsukushigata'	CMCN
– 'Tsuma-beni'	CMCN CPMA CSte ELan LNet WPat WWeb
– 'Tsuma-gaki'	CMCN CPMA
– 'Ukigumo' (v)	CAlt CB&S CEnd CMCN CPMA EJap ELan LNet MAsh MGos NHol SPer SSta WPat
– 'Ukon'	CMCN WNor
– 'Umegae'	CMCN
– 'Utsu-semi'	CMCN LNet
– 'Versicolor' (v)	CMCN EJap LNet
– 'Villa Taranto'	CEnd CMCN CPMA EJap LNet LRHS MBlu MGos NPal
– 'Volubile'	CMCN MAsh
– 'Wabito'	CDul CMCN
¶ – 'Wakehurst Pink' (v)	CMCN

– 'Waterfall'	CBlo CMCN CPMA EJap LNet MGos
– 'Wilson's Pink Dwarf'	CMCN LNet
– 'Wou-nishiki'	See ***A. palmatum* 'O-nishiki'**
– 'Yûgure'	MGos
papilio	See ***A. caudatum***
paxii	CMCN
pectinatum subsp. ***forrestii***	See ***A. forrestii***
– 'Sirene'	CPMA MGos
pensylvanicum 🏆	CB&S CDoC CMCN CSam CTho ELan EPfP LPan MGos MRav NBee NHol NWea SHBN SPer SSpi WDin WNor WOrn WWat WWeb
– 'Erythrocladum' 🏆	CBlo CEnd CMCN CPMA LNet MBlu NHol SMad SSpi
pentaphyllum	CMCN LNet
pictum	See ***A. mono***
¶ ***pilosum*** var. ***stenolobum***	WWoo
platanoides 🏆	CKin CLnd CMCN CPer ENot GRei LBuc LHyr LPan MGos NRoo NWea SPer WDin WMou WNor
– 'Cleveland'	CB&S ENot
– 'Columnare'	CDoC CMCN ENot IOrc LPan WOrn
– 'Crimson King' 🏆	CB&S CDul CMCN CSam CTho CWLN EBre ELan GRei LBuc LHyr LNet LPan MAsh MBar MWat NBee NWea SChu SHBN SPer SSta WDin WJas WOrn
– 'Crimson Sentry'	CBlo CDul CEnd CLnd CMCN COtt CWLN EBee EBre IHos LBuc LNet MAsh MBri MGos WJas WLRN WOrn
– 'Cucullatum'	CMCN CTho
– 'Deborah'	CDoC CDul CLnd CTho LPan SHBN
¶ – 'Dissectum'	CTho
– 'Drummondii' (v) 🏆	CB&S CDul CLnd CMCN CTho CWLN EBre ELan ENot GRei LBuc LHyr LNet LPan MBar MBri MGos MWat NBee NWea SChu SHBN SPer SSta WDin WJas WOrn WStI
– 'Emerald Queen'	CDoC CLnd CMCN ENot SHBN WOrn
¶ – 'Faassen's Black'	LPan
§ – 'Globosum'	CLnd CMCN CWLN EBee ENot LPan MGos
– 'Goldsworth Purple'	CLnd CMCN
– 'Laciniatum'	CEnd CMCN ENot SLPl SPer
– 'Lorbergii'	See ***A. platanoides* 'Palmatifidum'**
– 'Olmsted'	ENot LNet
§ – 'Palmatifidum'	CSam
¶ – 'Princeton Gold'	LPan
¶ – 'Pyramidale Nanum'	CTho
– 'Royal Red'	CMCN CSte CWLN ENot MGos SHhN
– 'Schwedleri' 🏆	CBlo CDul CLnd CMCN CWLN EBee MGos NWea WDin
– 'Summershade'	CMCN CSte
pseudoplatanus	CB&S CDul CKin CLnd CMCN CPer CTri ENot GRei LBuc LHyr LPan MBar MGos NWea WDin WMou
§ – 'Atropurpureum' (v) 🏆	CBlo CDoC CLnd CTho ENot IOrc MSto NBee NWea

– 'Brilliantissimum' 🏆	CB&S CDul CLnd CMCN CWLN EBre ELan LHyr LNet LPan MAsh MBar MBri MGos MHlr MWat NBee NHol NWea SHBN SMad SPer SSta WDin WOrn WPat
– 'Constant P.'	ENot
– 'Corstorphinense'	CMCN
– 'Erectum'	EBee ENot WOrn
– 'Erythrocarpum'	CMCN
N– 'Leopoldii' (v) 🏆	CB&S CDoC CDul CLnd CMCN COtt CTho CWLN ELan ENot IOrc LPan MBar SHBN SPer WDin WOrn
– 'Negenia'	CMCN
– 'Nizetii' (v)	LRHS MBri WWeb
– 'Prinz Handjéry'	CB&S CBlo CDoC CDul CEnd CMCN CTri LNet LPan MAsh MBar MGos NWea SHBN SPer SSpi
– 'Simon-Louis Frères' (v)	CBar CBlo CDoC CDul CEnd CLnd CMCN LNet LPan MAsh MBri MGos MWat WFoF
N– 'Spaethii' hort.	See ***A. pseudoplatanus* 'Atropurpureum'**
– f. ***variegatum***	MSto WCot
– 'Worley' 🏆	CB&S CBlo CDoC CDul CLnd CMCN COtt CWLN ECtt ENot IOrc MLan NWea SHBN SPer WDin WJas WOrn
pseudosieboldianum	CFil CMCN CPMA SSpi WFro WNor WWoo
¶ – MSF 861	WPGP
¶ ***pubipalmatum***	WNor
pycnanthum	CMCN
regelii	See ***A. pentapotamicum***
rubescens	CSam
rubrum	CAgr CB&S CBlo CDoC CDul CGre CLnd CMCN CTri GCHN LHyr MAsh MGos MLan MWat NWea SPer WDin WNor WWat
¶ – 'Armstrong'	LPan
– 'Bowhall'	CMCN
– 'Morgan'	CEnd
– October Glory 🏆	CDoC CDul CEnd CMCN CMHG CSam CTho CTri IOrc LPan MAsh MBlu MBri MUlv SMad SSpi SSta WWeb
– Red Sunset	CMCN EBee MBlu MBri
– Scanlon 🏆	CDul CEnd CMCN LPan
– 'Schlesingeri'	CEnd CMCN MBlu
§ ***rufinerve*** 🏆	CB&S CDoC CDul CLnd CMCN CMHG CTho CTri ENot EPfP IOrc LPan MBri NBee NWea SPer SSpi STre WDin WGer WHCr WNor WOrn WPyg WStI
– 'Albolimbatum'	See ***A. rufinerve* 'Hatsuyuki'**
– 'Albomarginatum'	See ***A. rufinerve* 'Hatsuyuki'**
§ – 'Hatsuyuki' (v)	CBlo CEnd CMCN CPMA ELan NHol
§ ***saccharinum*** 🏆	CB&S CDul CLnd CMCN ELan ENot LHyr MGos MWat NWea SPer SSpi WDin WFar WHut WNor
– 'Elegans'	See ***A. ×freemanii* 'Elegant'**
– 'Fastigiatum'	See ***A. saccharinum* f. *pyramidale***
– f. ***laciniatum***	CMCN CWLN ENot MBlu MGos WDin
– 'Laciniatum Wieri'	CLnd CMCN CTho NBee WLRN WWes

– f. ***lutescens***	CMCN CTho ENot MBlu
§ – f. ***pyramidale***	CDoC CLnd CMCN CWLN ENot IOrc LPan
saccharum	CAgr CDoC CDul CLnd CMCN EBee NWea STre WNor
– ***barbatum***	CMCN
§ – subsp. ***grandidentatum***	CMCN
– subsp. ***leucoderme***	CMCN
– subsp. ***nigrum***	CMCN
¶ – subsp. ***skutchii***	CMCN
– 'Temple's Upright'	CMCN LNet WWes
§ ***sempervirens***	CMCN
serrulatum	CMCN
– CC 1891	WHCr
§ ***shirasawanum***	CDul CMCN WNor
§ – 'Aureum' 🏆	CAlt CBlo CEnd CMCN CPMA EJap ELan ENot LHyd LNet LPan MAsh MBar MBri MGos MMor NBee NFla NHol SMad SPer SSpi SSta WPat WPyg WStI WWat
§ – 'Ezo-no-momiji'	CMCN
§ – 'Microphyllum'	CMCN LNet WNor
§ – 'Ogurayama'	LNet
– 'Palmatifolium'	CBlo CMCN CPMA MGos WStI
sieboldianum	CLnd CMCN CTri SSpi WDin WNor
– 'Sode-no-uchi'	CMCN
sikkimense subsp. ***metcalfii***	See ***A. metcalfii***
§ 'Silver Cardinal' (v)	CEnd CPMA WWes
'Silver Vein'	CMCN CPMA EBee EBre LNet MBlu MBri SSpi
§ ***sinense***	CMCN WNor WWoo
¶ – var. ***pubinerve***	CGre
sp. CC 1648	WHCr
spicatum	CDul CMCN EPfP WNor
stachyophyllum	See ***A. tetramerum***
§ ***sterculiaceum***	CMCN
syriacum	See ***A. obtusifolium***
taronense	CMCN
tataricum	CAgr CMCN MSto SSpi
§ – subsp. ***ginnala*** 🏆	CAgr CB&S CDul CLnd CMCN CMHG CTho EBar ELan ENot IOrc MBal MGos SHBN WNor WWat
* – – 'Fire'	LNet
– – 'Flame'	CBlo CDoC CDul CLnd CPMA WWoo
– subsp. ***semenowii***	CMCN
tegmentosum	CMCN WCoo WNor WWoo
– subsp. ***glaucorufinerve***	See ***A. rufinerve***
tenellum	WCoo
tenuifolium	CMCN
thomsonii	CMCN
trautvetteri	CMCN CSam SSpi WNor
triflorum	CMCN EPfP SSpi WWat WWes WWoo
truncatum	CAgr CMCN EBee WNor WWoo
– 'Akikaze-nishiki' (v)	CPMA LNet
tschonoskii	CMCN GQui WWes
¶ – subsp. ***koreanum***	WNor
§ ***turkestanicum***	CMCN
ukurunduense	CMCN WNor
velutinum	CMCN
villosum	See ***A. sterculiaceum***
§ ***wilsonii***	CMCN WNor
× ***zoeschense***	CMCN
– 'Annae'	IOrc

ACERIPHYLLUM See MUKDENIA

× ACHICODONIA (Gesneriaceae)

§ 'Cornell Gem' NMos

ACHILLEA † (Asteraceae)

abrotanoides	EGoo ELan NGre
ageratifolia ♀	ECha LBee MBro MHig MTho NHol NMen NNor NWCA SSca SSmi WByw WLRN
– subsp. ***ageratifolia***	MRPP
§ – subsp. ***aizoon***	EGar WPer
§ ***ageratum***	CArn CSev EAst ELau GBar GPoy LHol MChe MSal SIde WHer WJek WPer WSel WWye
– 'W.B. Childs'	CArc CBos CChu CGle CSpe ECha ELan GBuc LCom LGre MArl MCLN MNrw MSte WAbb WCot WEas
'Alabaster'	CRDP EFou EMon GBuc LRHS MBel NPla SOkh
§ Anthea = 'Anblo'	CHad CWit EBee EBre EMan LFis MBel MBri MCLN MGrG MUlv NLak NRoo SCro SMad SWat WHow
◆ Anthea	See ***A.* Anthea = 'Anblo'**
§ 'Apfelblüte'	CMGP EAst EBre ECha ECtt ELan EMan EOrc GCra LCom LFis LHop MBri MCLN MGrG MRav MTis SPer SSpe SUsu SWat WMer
◆ Appleblossom	See ***A.* 'Apfelblüte'**
argentea hort.	See ***A. clavennae***
– Lamarck	See ***Tanacetum argenteum***
aurea	See ***A. chrysocoma***
'Bahama'	GBuc MLan NFai
'Bloodstone'	GMac
¶ ***brachyphylla***	EPot
cartilaginea	CArc EAst EFou EGar LHop MCLN MUlv WCot
– 'Silver Spray'	WWhi
chamaemelifolia	WHil
§ ***chrysocoma***	ELan EPPr ESis MWat NMen NRya NTow SSmi
– 'Grandiflora'	CHad MGrG NCat SMrm WLRN
§ ***clavennae***	CGle CShe EHoe GCHN GMac MHig MPla MWat NMen NRoo NTow SBla SMer SRms WAbe WCot
clypeolata	NFla SRms
coarctata	CArc CHan NBir WPer
'Coronation Gold' ♀	CDoC CShe CWit EBre ECED EFou ELan ENot EPfP MBri MWat SPer WEas
'Credo'	CGle CHad CMil CRDP CSev EAst EBee ECGP EFou EMan EMon EPPr GBuc MBel MCLN MHlr MUlv NCat SWat WCot WDav WWhi
* 'Crimson King'	LFis
'Croftway'	SCro
decolorans	See ***A. ageratum***
erba-rotta subsp. ***rupestris***	ESis MDHE MHig SMer WPer
§ 'Fanal'	CHor CMGP COtt CSpe CWit EBre ECha EHal ELan EMar EOrc LHop MBel MCLN MNrw MRav NHol NPla NVic SChu SCro SPer SUsu SWat WTyr WWin
'Feuerland'	CWit ECha EMon EPPr LFis MAvo MLLN NPla SMad SSpe WCot WFar WHoo WPer WWhi
filipendulina	MHew SWat
– 'Cloth of Gold'	CB&S CDoC CHor EBar EBre ECED ECtt GCHN GMaP MBri MRav NFai NMir NNor NRoo SEas SPla WBea WByw WGwG WHoo WPLl WPer WWtk
– 'Gold Plate' ♀	CDec CHad CLyd CShe EBre ECha ECtt EFou ELan EMon EPPr MBel MCLN MLan NOrc NTow SCro SPer WCot WEas WHil
– 'Parker's Variety'	EGar EJud GBuc MLan NOak
◆ Flowers of Sulphur	See ***A.* 'Schwefelblüte'**
'Forncett Beauty'	EFou
'Forncett Candy'	EFou
'Forncett Fletton'	EFou SCro SHel SUsu WCot
'Forncett Ivory'	EFou NCat
fraasii	WPer
glaberrima	WPer
grandifolia	CBre CChu CHan CMil CPou EGle EMan EMon EOrc EPad GCal LGan LGre MSte MTol MUlv NBro NCat SMad SPer SSvw WBea WCot WHer WWye
'Great Expectations'	See ***A.* 'Hoffnung'**
'Hartington White'	EMon GBuc MSte
'Hella Glashoff'	LGre WCot
§ 'Hoffnung'	CMGP EBre ECtt EFou EMan EOrc LHop SCro SPer SSpe WBro WLRN WPer WWin
holosericea NS 747	MRPP NWCA
'Huteri'	CInt CLyd CMHG CNic CPea ECtt ELan EMNN EPot ESis GCHN GMaP LBee MBro MHig NCat NMen NNor NNrd NTow SChu SSmi WAbe WEas WHil WPer WWin
'Inca Gold'	EBee ECha EPPr SUsu SWat
× ***jaborneggii***	GCHN
'Jambo'	CB&S
'James Chapman'	LCom
× ***kellereri***	ELan MBro MHig SAsh SSmi
× ***kolbiana***	EMan LHop MHig MWat NMen NNrd NRoo SSmi WHoo WPat WWin
§ – 'Weston'	CMHG MHig NRoo NTow
§ 'Lachsschönheit'	Widely available
× ***lewisii***	NMen
– 'King Edward' ♀	CInt CMea CSam EBre ECha EFou ELan ESis LBee MTho NBir NHol NMGW NRoo NTow SBla SChu SSmi SWat WPer
'Libella'	GBuc NFai
'Lusaka'	CB&S
'Martina'	EBee EFou EHal EMon EPPr GBuc NTow SCro
'McVities'	MAvo WCot
millefolium	CArn CGle ECWi EEls EJud EPar EWFC GBar GPoy LHol MGam MGra MHew NHex NLan NMir SIde WByw WHer WOak WSel WWye
– 'Burgundy'	EOrc

– 'Cerise Queen'	CB&S CHor CNic CShe EBre ECha ECro EFou ELan EMon EPar GCHN LHop MHFP MWat NFai NNor NNrd SPer SSoC SSpe SWat WBea WGwG WOve WPer WTyr WWye
– 'Colorado'	CChr CM&M CPou WHil
¶ – 'Fire King'	CHal
– 'Lansdorferglut'	EPPr LRHS MBri MCLN MUlv
– 'Lavender Beauty'	See *A. millefolium* **'Lilac Beauty'**
§ – 'Lilac Beauty'	CB&S CBos CDec CGle ECha EFou EMan EOrc EPPr GCra GLil MAvo MBel MBri WCot WHal WMer WPbr
* – 'Lilac Queen'	CMGP MArl MBri NFai
– 'Melanie'	WMer
– 'Paprika'	CDec CDoC CRDP EBar EBre EPar GBuc LCom MBri MCLN MCli MGrG NCat SMad WByw WRus WTyr WWhi
– 'Prospero'	LFis MSte
– 'Red Beauty'	EPar GCra MTis NCat SRms WOve
– f. ***rosea***	EJud MBal NRoo SRms WOMN
– 'Sammetriese'	CWan EFou ELan EMon EPPr GBuc MAvo MCLN MHFP MSte WCot WHoo WMaN WPyg WRHF
– 'Sweet Harmony'	LBuc
– 'White Queen'	EPfP LBuc WMer WPer
'Moonshine' ♀	Widely available
'Moonwalker'	CBlo EAst SIde WPer
'Nakuru'	NCat
nobilis subsp. ***neilreichii***	CArc CMea CRDP EGoo EMon EPPr LFis MHlr WCot WHal WOve
'Peter Davis'	See ***Hippolytia herderi***
¶ ***pindicola*** subsp. ***integrifolia***	CLyd EWes NHol
ptarmica	CArn CKin ECWi ELau EWFC GBar LHol MChe MHew MSal NMir SIde SPer WGwy WWye
* – 'Ballerina'	NCat NFla WRHF
◆ – Innocence	See *A. ptarmica* **'Unschuld'**
– 'Major'	EFou
– 'Nana Compacta'	CArc ECha EPPr MRav NNor SMrm SUsu WCot WPbr
– 'Perry's White'	CBre EMon GCal GLil MBri MHlr NCat WByw WCot WMer
– 'Stephanie Cohen'	WCot
– (The Pearl Group) 'Boule de Neige' (clonal) (d)	CBlo CHal LRHS MBri MCLN NPer SPer SPla WGwG WLRN WRHF WRTC
N – The Pearl Group seed-raised (d)	CB&S CGle EBre ECha EFou ELan GCHN LHop MFir MWat NCGP NFai NMir NNor NRoo NVic SHel SWat WBea WHil WMaN WOld WOve WPer WWin
§ – 'Unschuld'	NBir
pumila	See *A. distans* subsp. *tanacetifolia*
◆ Salmon Beauty	See *A.* **'Lachsschönheit'**
'Sandstone'	See *A.* **'Wesersandstein'**
§ 'Schwefelblüte'	ELan LFis MCLN NBir WCot
'Schwellenburg'	EFou EGle EPPr SCro
sibirica	CArc WElm WNdy WPri
– AGS 1241	CNic
– 'Kiku-san'	EMon
'Smiling Queen'	LCom NFai
Summer Pastels Group	CBot CM&M ECro EMan EMil GCHN MCLN MFir MSte NBus NFla NMir NOak NRoo SEas SHel SWat WLRN WOve WRha WTyr WWhi WWtk
'Summerwine'	CArc ECha EGoo EMon MBri SWat
I 'Taygetea'	CBot CGle CLyd CSam EBre ECha EFou ELan LBlm MBri MUlv MWat NSti SChu SDix SPer SUsu SWat WByw WCot WFar WKif WOve WRus WSHC
'Terracotta'	CArc CElw CRDP EFou EMon GBuc LFis MAvo MSte NBir NCat NHaw SOkh WCot WElm WHal WHoo WMaN WOve
'The Beacon'	See *A.* **'Fanal'**
tomentosa ♀	CHan CTri ECha ECtt ELan LHop MBal NNrd SWat WRHF
§ – 'Aurea'	ECtt ELan LHol MLan MOne NBro NNor NNrd SIde WHen WHil WPer WWin
– 'Maynard's Gold'	See *A. tomentosa* **'Aurea'**
§ ***umbellata***	NTow SAlw
– NS 390	NWCA
– 'Weston'	See *A.* × *kolbiana* **'Weston'**
'Walther Funcke'	CHad CRDP LFis LGre SMrm WCot
§ 'Wesersandstein'	CB&S EBee EFou EMon EPPr MBri WElm WOve
'Wilczekii'	NCat NChi SBod SRms

× ACHIMENANTHA (Gesneriaceae)

'Cerulean Mink'	See × *Smithicodonia* **'Cerulean Mink'**
'Dutch Treat'	NMos
'Ginger Peachy'	NMos
'Inferno'	NMos WDib
* 'Rose Bouquet'	NMos
'Royal'	NMos

ACHIMENES (Gesneriaceae)

'Adelaide'	NMos
'Adèle Delahaute'	NMos
'Adonis Blue'	NMos
'Almandine'	NMos
'Ambleside'	NMos
'Ambroise Verschaffelt'	LAma NMos
'Ami Van Houtte'	NMos
'Ann Marie'	NMos
'Apricot Glow'	NMos
'Aquamarine'	NMos
* 'Aries'	EOHP
'Bassenthwaite'	NMos
'Bea'	NMos
bella	See ***Eucodonia verticillata***
'Bernice'	NMos
'Blauer Planet'	NMos
'Bloodstone'	NMos
'Blue Gown'	NMos
'Brilliant'	NMos
'Butterfield Bronze'	NMos
'Buttermere'	NMos
'Camberwell Beauty'	NMos
'Cameo Rose'	NMos
'Cameo Triumph'	NMos
'Camille Brozzoni'	NMos
candida	NMos
'Carmine Queen'	NMos
'Cascade Cockade'	NMos
'Cascade Evening Glow'	NMos

'Cascade Fairy Pink' NMos
'Cascade Fashionable Pink' NMos
'Cascade Rosy Red' NMos
'Cascade Violet Night' NMos
'Cattleya' LAma NMos
'Chalkhill Blue' NMos
'Charm' LAma NMos
'Clouded Yellow' NMos
'Compact Great Rosy Red' NMos
'Coniston Water' NMos
'Copeland Boy' NMos
'Copeland Girl' NMos
'Coral Sunset' NMos
'Cornell Favourite 'A'' NMos
'Cornell Favourite 'B'' NMos
'Crimson Beauty' NMos
'Crimson Glory' NMos
'Crimson Tiger' NMos
'Crummock Water' NMos
'Cupido' NMos
'Dentoniana' NMos
'Derwentwater' NMos
'Dorothy' NMos
'Dot' NMos
dulcis NMos
'Early Arnold' NMos
ehrenbergii See ***Eucodonia ehrenbergii***
'Elke Michelssen' NMos
'English Waltz' NMos
erecta WDib
'Escheriana' NMos
'Flamenco' NMos
'Flamingo' SDeJ
flava NMos
'Fritz Michelssen' NMos
'Gary John' NMos
'Gary/Jennifer' NMos
'Grape Wine' NMos
'Grasmere' NMos
'Harry Williams' LAma
§ 'Harveyi' NMos
'Haweswater' NMos
'Hilda Michelssen' NMos WDib
'Honey Gold' NMos
'Ida Michelssen' NMos
'India' NMos
§ 'Jaureguia Maxima' NMos
'Jennifer Goode' NMos
'Jewell Blue' NMos
'Johanna Michelssen' NMos
'Jubilee Gem' NMos
'Lakeland Lady' NMos
'Lavender Fancy' NMos
'Little Beauty' LAma NMos
'Little Red Tiger' NMos
longiflora NMos
– 'Alba' See ***A.* 'Jaureguia Maxima'**
– 'Major' NMos
'Magnificent' NMos
'Marie' NMos
'Masterpiece' NMos
'Maxima' LAma
'Menuett '80' NMos
'Milton' NMos
misera NMos
'Moonstone' NMos
'Old Rose Pink' LAma NMos
'Orange Queen' NMos
'Pally' NMos
'Panic Pink' NMos
'Patens Major' NMos
'Patricia' NMos
'Paul Arnold' NMos
'Peach Blossom' LAma NMos
'Peach Glow' NMos
'Peacock' NMos
'Pearly Queen' NMos
'Pendant Blue' NMos
'Pendant Purple' NMos
'Petticoat Pink' NMos
'Pink Beauty' NMos
'Pinocchio' NMos
'Prima Donna' EOHP NMos
'Pulcherrima' LAma
'Purple King' NMos
'Queen of Sheba' NMos
'Quickstep' NMos
'Rachael' NMos
'Red Admiral' NMos
'Red Giant' NMos
'Red Imp' NMos
'Red Top Hybrid' NMos
'Robin' NMos
'Rosenelfe' NMos
'Rosy Doll' NMos
'Rosy Frost' NMos
'Rydal Water' NMos
'Scafell' NMos
* ***selloana*** EOHP
'Shirley Dwarf White' NMos
'Shirley Fireglow' See ***A.* 'Harveyi'**
'Show-off' NMos
'Silver Wedding' NMos
'Snow Princess' SDeJ
◆ Snow White See ***A.* 'Schneewittchen'**
'Sparkle' NMos
'Stan's Delight' EOHP NMos WDib
'Sue' NMos
'Tango' NMos
'Tantivvy' NMos
'Tarantella' NMos
'Teresa' NMos
'Tiny Blue' NMos
'Topsy' NMos
'Troutbeck' NMos
'Ullswater' NMos
'Vanessa' NMos
'Viola Michelssen' NMos
'Violacea Semiplena' NMos
'Vivid' LAma NMos
'Warren' NMos
'Wastwater' NMos
'Wetterflow's Triumph' NMos
'White Admiral' NMos
'White Rajah' NMos
'Wilma' NMos
'Windermere' NMos

ACHLYS (Berberidaceae)
japonica WCru

ACHNATHERUM See STIPA

ACIDANTHERA See GLADIOLUS

ACINOS (Lamiaceae)
§ ***alpinus*** CShe NMen NNrd SBla SChu
– subsp. ***meridionalis*** EGle NHol NTow
§ ***arvensis*** CArn LHol MBri MSal
§ ***corsicus*** ESis LFis NMen SIde WJek WPat WWin

ACIPHYLLA (Apiaceae)

aurea CDoC GAbr GCal MBal NHar SIgm SMad
- CC 464 LKoh
¶ *colensoi* GAbr GCLN
* – *major* GCLN
¶ *crosby-smithii* GCLN
¶ *dobsonii* GCLN
glaucescens GDra MBal NHar
hectoris EBee EPot GCLN GDra
horrida SIgm
¶ *kirkii* GCLN
'Lomond' GCLN SIgm
lyallii NTow
monroi EPot GCLN GDra
montana EBee EPot GCLN SIgm
pinnatifida EPot GCLN GCrs NHar
scott-thomsonii ECou ETen GCal
¶ *simplex* GCLN
squarrosa EBee ECou GCal SIgm WCot
subflabellata ECou GCal NHar NTow SIgm

ACNISTUS (Solanaceae)

australis See ***Dunalia australis***

ACOELORRHAPHE (Arecaceae)

See Plant Deletions

ACOKANTHERA (Apocynaceae)

spectabilis See ***A. oblongifolia***

ACONITUM (Ranunculaceae)

¶ *alboviolaceum* GCal
anglicum See ***A. napellus*** subsp. ***napellus* Anglicum Group**
N *autumnale* NBir
bartlettii B&SWJ 337 WCru
'Blue Sceptre' EBre NRoo SRms
'Bressingham Spire' 🏆 CDoC CMGP CShe EBre ECtt EFou EPla GAbr GMaP MBel MBri MRav MWat NDea NOrc NPer NRoo SChu SPer
× *cammarum* 'Bicolor' 🏆 CDoC CGle CHad CMHG CSpe EBre EFou ELan EOrc GBri GCHN GCal GCra GMaP MBel MBri MCLN MWat NBro NPer NRoo SPer SSoC SWat WByw WEas WFar WHil WHow WOld
– 'Grandiflorum Album' EBre LGre NRoo
§ *carmichaelii* CArn CBot CGle CLon CMil EBar EBre ECED ECro EFou EMan GAbr IBlr MBro MHlr MRav NFla NNor NOrc NRoo SCro WBea WDav WHoo WRTC WRus
– 'Arendsii' CMGP CMHG EBre ECha ECro ECtt EOrc GMaP LFis MBri MBro MGrG MRav MSte NDea NRoo NTow SChu SPer SPla SSoC WCot WEas WFar WWye
– Wilsonii Group CHad CHan ECro GCra GGar MBri MLsm MSte MTol NTow SAga SChu SSoC WPer WWye
§ – – 'Barker's Variety' CPou CRow ECED EFou GBuc MFir MUlv NDea NHol NSti WMer WRus
– – 'Kelmscott' 🏆 EGle MUlv SAga SBla SDix WByw WFar WRHF
cilicicum See ***Eranthis hyemalis* Cilicica Group**
compactum See ***A. napellus*** subsp. ***vulgare***
deflexum MSto
'Eleonara' EFou EPfP LRHS MBri MRav MUlv WFar
elwesii GCal GGar
episcopale EBee
aff. – CLD 1426 WCot WFar
fischeri hort. See ***A. carmichaelii***
gymnandrum EMon
§ *hemsleyanum* Widely available
– dark blue CMea
– *latisectum* IBlr
heterophyllum MSto WCot
◆ *hyemale* See ***Eranthis hyemalis***
'Ivorine' Widely available
japonicum MSto
lamarckii See ***A. lycoctonum*** subsp. ***neapolitanum***
lycoctonum CDoC SSoC WRHF
– 'Dark Eyes' WCot
§ – subsp. *lycoctonum* EAst ECED MSal SRms
– subsp. *moldavicum* GBin
§ – subsp. *neapolitanum* CBlo CLon ELan EMil EPfP GCal LGan NSti WRus
§ – subsp. *vulparia* CArn ECha ECtt EFou GCal GPoy LHol MAvo MSal NDea NRoo WByw WCot WEas
napellus CArn CBlo CShe CSpe ECtt EFou EWFC GAbr GPoy LGan LHol MBro MCLN MWat NFla NNor SIde SSoC SWat WHil WHoo WOld WRTC WShi WWat WWhi WWye
◆ – 'Albiflorus' See ***A. napellus*** subsp. ***vulgare* 'Albidum'**
– 'Blue Valley' EBee EPfP
◆ – 'Carneum' See ***A. napellus*** subsp. ***vulgare* 'Carneum'**
§ – subsp. *napellus* Anglicum Group CRow CSev GBuc IBlr MHlr MSal MSte NSti WCot WPen WUnd
– 'Rubellum' CHan CSpe LBuc MCli NPri
– 'Sphere's Variety' NOrc WPyg
– subsp. *tauricum* WCot
§ – subsp. *vulgare* 'Albidum' CBot CMGP CSev EBee EFou EMan ETen LBuc NCat NHol NPri NSti SCro SPer WByw WHil WHow WLRN WRus
§ – – 'Carneum' EBre ECha EFou GCra GMac MRav NRoo NSti WByw WCot WDav WEas WHal WHer WKif WWin
neapolitanum See ***A. lycoctonum*** subsp. ***neapolitanum***
'Newry Blue' CHad EHal ELan GBuc MBri MUlv NHol WFar WHil WMer WPer WRHF
orientale hort. See ***A. lycoctonum*** subsp. ***vulparia***
paniculatum 'Roseum' CSpe CWan LRHS
pyrenaicum See ***A. lycoctonum*** subsp. ***neapolitanum***
ranunculifolius See ***A. lycoctonum*** subsp. ***neapolitanum***
¶ *sczukinii* EMon
septentrionale See ***A. lycoctonum*** subsp. ***lycoctonum***

'Spark's Variety' ♀	CBre CDoC CHan EAst EBar EBre ECED EFou ELan GBri GMaP GMac LFis LGre MBri MCLN MHlr MRav MTis NRoo SChu SCro SDix SHig SMad SSoC WFar
'Stainless Steel'	EFou LRHS MBri WFar
stapfianum B&L 12038	WThi
x ***tubergenii***	See ***Eranthis hyemalis*** **Tubergenii Group**
volubile hort.	See ***A. hemsleyanum***
vulparia	See ***A. lycoctonum*** subsp. ***vulparia***

ACONOGONON See PERSICARIA

ACORUS (Araceae)

calamus	CArn CBen CRow CWGN CWat EHon ELau GPoy LPBA MHew MSta NDea NGno SHig SWat SWyc WChe WHer WMAq
– 'Purpureus'	WChe
– 'Variegatus'	CB&S CBen CRow CWGN CWat EBre ECha ECtt EHon EMFW GAbr GCal LHil LPBA LWak MBal MSta NDea SHig SPer SWat SWyc WChe WHil WMAq WWye
gramineus	CRow EMFW LGan LPBA MBel MLan SWat WHer WPri WRHF WWye
¶ – 'Hakuro-nishiki' (v)	EPPr
I – 'Licorice'	WCot
– 'Masamune'	EPPr GCal WCot WHil WLeb
N – 'Oborozuki'	CRow EGle EPla LHop
N – 'Ogon' (v)	Widely available
– 'Pusillus'	CRow EPPr EPla ESOG LHil NBro
– 'Variegatus'	Widely available
– 'Yodo-no-yuki'	CRow EPPr EPla

ACRADENIA (Rutaceae)

frankliniae	CAbb CB&S CBrd CChu CFil CMHG CPle IBlr IDee ISea MAll SArc SBid WBod WSHC

ACRIDOCARPUS (Malpighiaceae)

¶ ***natalitius***	CPlN

ACROCLADIUM See CALLIERGON

ACTAEA (Ranunculaceae)

§ ***alba*** ♀	CBrd CHan CLyd CPou CRow ECha GPoy GTou IBlr LGre MFir MSal NSti SHig WMer WOMN WWat WWye
asiatica B&SWJ 616	WCru
§ ***erythrocarpa*** Fischer	CHan CRDP GDra GPoy MSte WEas WOMN WWin
pachypoda	See ***A. alba***
§ ***rubra*** ♀	CBro CLyd CMHG CRow ECha EPar GAbr GCal IBlr MSCN NHol NSti SMad WByw WCra WCru WMer WWat
– ***alba***	See ***A. rubra*** **f.** ***neglecta***
§ – f. ***neglecta***	CHan GBuc WWat
§ ***spicata***	GLil GPoy MBro MSCN MSal MSte NSti NWoo WCru WDav
– var. ***alba***	See ***A. spicata***
– var. ***rubra***	See ***A. erythrocarpa*** **Fischer**

ACTINELLA (Asteraceae)

scaposa	See ***Tetraneuris scaposa***

ACTINIDIA † (Actinidiaceae)

arguta	CAgr CB&S CDoC CFil CPlN MSto WPGP
– B&SWJ 569	WCru
– 'Issai' (s-p)	CB&S EBee ERea ESim LBuc MGos
– (m)	CB&S SHBN
¶ ***callosa***	CPlN
– var. ***formosana*** B&SWJ 1790	WCru
chinensis hort.	See ***A. deliciosa***
§ ***deliciosa***	CGre CMac CWit ELan EMil ERom LHol MGos WSHC WStI
– 'Atlas'	MBri
– 'Blake' (s-p/F)	LBuc
– (f/F)	SHBN SPer WDin
– 'Hayward' (f/F)	CB&S CDoC CMac COtt CPlN EBre ELan EMil EMui ERea IOrc ISea MBri MGos MMor MWat NPal SBra SDea SHBN SSta WGwG WStI
– 'Jenny' (s-p/F)	LRHS MGos NDal SDea
– (m)	SDea SPer WDin
– 'Tomuri' (m)	CB&S CDoC CMac COtt CPlN CWLN EBre ELan EMil EMui ERea IOrc MWat NPal SBra SHBN SSta WStI
kolomikta ♀	Widely available
¶ ***melanandra***	CAgr CPlN
pilosula	CFil CPlN GCal GOrc WCru WPGP WSHC
polygama (F)	CPlN MSto WCru
¶ ***purpurea***	CPlN WCru

ACTINOTUS (Apiaceae)

See Plant Deletions

ADELOCARYUM See LINDELOFIA

ADENOCARPUS (Papilionaceae)

See Plant Deletions

ADENOPHORA † (Campanulaceae)

aurita	CB&S CChu CDoC CFir CKni EOrc GAbr MBri MLan MTis NSti NWoo SOkh SWat WAbe WCot WWat
axilliflora	EPad
bulleyana	CHan CPea CSev EAst ELan EPad EPot GAbr GBuc IBlr MAvo NBro NLak NPri SEND SSca SWat WFar WPLl WPen WPer
* ***campanulata***	WPer
confusa	CArc EAst EGar GAbr GCal MAvo MLLN SMac WCot
coronopifolia	EPad
divaricata	EPad
forrestii	CHan EBee EPad SBla WMaN
himalayana	ECro EGle EPad GBri GMac MAvo MNrw WCot WHil WPer WRHF
khasiana	CBlo CFir CPea EBee EPad GAbr MAvo NSti SOkh WCot WWin
koreana	EBee MAvo
latifolia Fischer	GBri
– hort.	See ***A. pereskiifolia***

liliifolia	CDec CRDP ECro ECtt EEls ELan EMar EPad GAbr GCal GMac MCLN NBro NCat NPer NSti SAxl SCro SMrm SSvw SWat WCot WHoo WPer WPyg WRTC
§ ***nikoensis***	EPad MHig WAbe
* – ***alba***	CGra
§ – var. ***stenophylla***	EPad MHig
nipponica	See ***A. nikoensis*** var. ***stenophylla***
§ ***pereskiifolia***	EAst EBee ECro EGar EPad GCal GMac LIck MAvo MHlr MSto MTol NBus WCot WPbr WPer
– 'Alba'	WCot
– var. ***heterotricha***	EPad
pereskiifolia uryuensis	EPad
polyantha	CHan CPea ECro EPad GBuc MAvo MTol SSca WByw
polymorpha	See ***A. nikoensis***
potaninii	CArc CDoC CFir ECro EFol EGle EPad GBuc LCom MAvo MGrG MNrw NBro SBla SSvw WHer WPer WPri WRHF WWhi
– 'Alba'	WPer
– lilac	WPer
remotiflora	ECro EPad
sp. Yunnan	EPad
stricta	EHal LRHS MAvo MLan WWeb
– subsp. ***sessilifolia***	EPad
sublata	EGar WFar
takedae	EPad WHil
– var. ***howozana***	EPad NSti
tashiroi	CElw CHan CLyd CNic EPad GAbr GBri GBuc MBro MNrw MTol NBro SCro SHel SIgm SMac SWat WHil WHoo WRTC WRus
triphylla	EPad WFar
¶ – var. ***hakusanensis***	MAvo NChi
– var. ***japonica***	EPad
– var. ***puellaris***	EPad
uehatae	EPad
– B&SWJ 126	WCru

ADENOSTYLES (Asteraceae)

alpina	See ***Cacalia glabra***

ADIANTUM † (Adiantaceae)

aleuticum	See ***A. pedatum*** var. ***subpumilum***
capillus-veneris	CHEx SRms
– 'Banksianum'	NMar
– 'Cornubiense'	WRic
– 'Mairisii'	See ***A.*** × ***mairisii***
– 'Pointonii'	NMar
concinnum	NMar
cuneatum	See ***A. raddianum***
diaphanum	NMar
edgeworthii	NMar
formosum	NMar
henslowianum	NMar
jordanii	CFil
§ × ***mairisii***	NMar WRic
* ***monocolor***	MBri
pedatum 🏆	CFil CGle CHEx CRDP EBre ECha EFer EFol EFou ELan EMon LWoo MBal MBri MHlr MRPP NFla NHol NOrc SAlw SApp SChu SPer SSpi SWat WAbe WHil WPGP WRic
– var. ***aleuticum***	See ***A. pedatum*** var. ***subpumilum***
– Asiatic form	See ***A. pedatum* 'Japonicum'**
– 'Imbricatum'	ECha ETen NHar NHol NMar SBla SRms
§ – 'Japonicum'	CFil CMil CRDP CWGN ELan MBri NBir NHol SEas SRms SSpi WCot WCru WRic
– 'Laciniatum'	CFil SRms
– var. ***minus***	See ***A. pedatum*** var. ***subpumilum***
– 'Miss Sharples'	NMar SRms WRic
– 'Roseum'	See ***A. pedatum* 'Japonicum'**
§ – var. ***subpumilum***	CFil CRDP EFer ELan EPfP IOrc NBro NHar NHol NMar SBla WFar WPGP WRic WWat
– – f. ***minimum***	NMar
peruvianum	MBri
pubescens	MBri NMar
§ ***raddianum***	CFil CHal NMar
– 'Brilliantelse'	MBri NMar
– 'Crested Majus'	NMar
– 'Crested Micropinnulum'	NMar
– 'Deflexum'	NMar
– 'Elegans'	NMar
– 'Feltham Beauty'	NMar
– 'Fragrans'	See ***A. raddianum* 'Fragrantissimum'**
§ – 'Fragrantissimum'	MBri NMar
– 'Fritz Luthi'	CHal MBri NMar
– 'Gracilis'	See ***A. raddianum* 'Gracillimum'**
§ – 'Gracillimum'	NMar
– 'Grandiceps'	NMar
– 'Gympie Gold'	NMar
– 'Kensington Gem' 🏆	NMar
– 'Legrand Morgan'	NMar
– 'Legrandii'	NMar
– 'Micropinnulum'	NMar
– 'Pacific Maid'	NMar
– 'Pacottii'	NMar
– 'Triumph'	NMar
– 'Tuffy Tips'	NMar
¶ – 'Variegated Pacottii'	NMar
– 'Variegated Tessellate'	EMon NMar
– 'Victoria's Elegans'	NMar
– 'Weigandii'	NMar
venustum 🏆	CDec CDoC CFil CGle CRDP EFer EHyt ELan EMon EPot GCal LWoo MBal NGar NHed NMar SBla SDix SRms SSpi SWat WAbe WCot WEas WFib WOMN WPGP WRic

ADLUMIA (Papaveraceae)

fungosa	CGle CPlN CSpe EBee EGoo EMar MEas WCru WOMN

ADONIS (Ranunculaceae)

aestivalis	ECWi
amurensis	CRDP EBre ELan EPar LAma NMen WCot
– 'Flore Pleno'	EBre EPar MBri SPer SRms WCot WFar
– 'Fukujukai'	EBre ECha LRHS NMGW WFar

annua	EWFC MGra MHew
brevistyla	NTow WAbe
vernalis	GPoy

ADOXA (Adoxaceae)

moschatellina	CKin CNat EWFC MTho WHer WShi WWye

AECHMEA † (Bromeliaceae)

caerulea	See ***A. lueddemanniana***
fasciata 🏆	MBri
Foster's Favorite Group 🏆	SLMG
¶ ***gamosepala***	WAbe

AEGLE (Rutaceae)

sepiaria	See ***Poncirus trifoliata***

AEGOPODIUM (Apiaceae)

podagraria 'Dangerous' (v)	CNat WCHb
– 'Hullavington' (v)	CNat
– 'Variegatum'	Widely available

AEONIUM (Crassulaceae)

arboreum 🏆	CAbb CHEx SLMG WHal WWhi
* – 'Arnold Schwarzkopff'	CAbb ERea GCra
– 'Atropurpureum' 🏆	CBrk CHEx ERea IBlr LHil MBri MLan NPer SEND SLMG WEas WWhi
¶ – 'Variegatum'	LHil
balsamiferum	CHEx CTrC LHil
canariense	CHEx LHil
§ – var. ***subplanum***	CTrC
cuneatum	CHEx CTbh CTrC SArc
x ***domesticum***	See ***Aichryson*** x ***domesticum***
haworthii 🏆	CHEx CHal CTrC GAri LHil
– 'Variegatum'	CHEx
holochrysum	IBlr
nobile	CHEx
percarneum	SLMG
simsii	CHEx
♦ ***subplanum***	See ***A. canariense*** var. ***subplanum***
tabuliforme 🏆	CHEx SLMG
undulatum 🏆	CHEx
'Zwartkop' 🏆	CHEx CTbh EGar EOas WEas WHal

AESCHYNANTHUS (Gesneriaceae)

'Big Apple'	WDib
Black Pagoda Group	WDib
'Fire Wheel'	WDib
hildebrandii	WDib
'Hot Flash'	WDib
lobbianus	See ***A. radicans***
longicalyx	WDib
§ ***longicaulis*** 🏆	MBri WDib
marmoratus	See ***A. longicaulis***
'Mira'	MBri
'Mona'	MBri
parvifolius	See ***A. radicans***
I 'Pulobbia'	MBri
'Purple Star'	MBri
§ ***radicans***	EBak MBri
radicans lobbianus	See ***A. radicans***
'Rigel'	MBri
* ***rigidus***	SLMG
speciosus 🏆	CHal
* ***speciosus rubens***	MBri
'Topaz'	MBri

AESCULUS † (Hippocastanaceae)

♦ ***arguta***	See ***A. glabra*** var. ***arguta***
x ***arnoldiana***	CDul CFil CMCN MBlu WPGP
¶ ***assamica***	WPGP
§ x ***bushii***	CFil EBee WPGP
californica	CFil CMCN CTho CTrw SMad WPGP
x ***carnea***	CDoC CDul ELan GRei ISea MBal MBar SHhN SSpi
– 'Aureomarginata'	MAsh SMad
– 'Briotii' 🏆	CB&S CDoC CDul CEnd CLnd COtt CTho EBre ELan ENot IHos IOrc LBuc LHyr LPan MAsh MBri MGos MWat NBee NWea SHBN SPer SSta WDin WOrn WStI
– 'Plantierensis'	CDul CTho ENot MBlu SSpi
chinensis	CEnd
'Dallimorei' (graft chimaera)	EBee SMad
discolor 'Koehnei'	MBri
§ ***flava*** 🏆	CFil CMCN CTho EBee ENot MMea SPer SSta WCoo WPGP
– f. ***vestita***	CDoC CDul MBlu
georgiana	See ***A. sylvatica***
glabra	CDul CFil CLnd CMCN CPMA CTho WPGP
§ – var. ***arguta***	CFil CMCN WPGP
– 'October Red'	CFil WPGP
glaucescens	CDul CMCN
hippocastanum 🏆	CB&S CDul CKin CLnd CPer CTho ELan ENot GRei IOrc ISea LBuc LHyr LPan MAsh MBal MBar MBri MGos NBee NWea SHBN SPer WDin WFar WMou WOrn WStI
§ – 'Baumannii' (d) 🏆	CDoC CDul CLnd COtt CSte ENot LPan MBlu MBri MGos NWea SHBN SPer WDin WStI
– 'Digitata'	CDul
– 'Flore Pleno'	See ***A. hippocastanum*** **'Baumannii'**
– 'Hampton Court Gold'	CEnd CMCN CTho
– 'Honiton Gold'	CTho
– 'Laciniata'	CDul CMCN MBlu SMad
– 'Wisselink'	CDul CMCN MBlu SMad
x ***hybrida***	CFil WPGP
indica 🏆	CDul CHEx CLnd CMCN CSam CTho CTrw ELan ENot EOas IHos IOrc ISea MBlu MBri SLPl SPer SSpi WDin WMou WPGP
– 'Sydney Pearce'	CEnd CFil CMCN EBee IOrc MBlu MMea SMad SPer SSpi WPGP
x ***marylandica***	CPMA
x ***mississippiensis***	See ***A.*** x ***bushii***
x ***mutabilis*** 'Harbisonii'	SMad
– 'Induta'	CFil MBlu MBri SMad SSpi WPGP WWes
§ – 'Penduliflora'	CDul CEnd CFil CTho MBlu SMad WPGP
x ***neglecta***	CLnd CMCN
– 'Erythroblastos' 🏆	CFil CLnd CMCN CPMA CTho LNet MBlu SHBN SMad SSpi WMou WPGP WPat
parviflora 🏆	CB&S CDul CFil CGre CMCN COtt CTho ELan EMil ENot ERav LNet LPan MBal MBlu MGos MUlv SMad SPer SSpi WDin WPGP WWat

§ ***pavia*** 🏆	CB&S CChu CDul CFil CMCN CTho ISea MBlu WPGP WWoo
– 'Atrosanguinea'	CBlo CDoC CDul CEnd CFil CMCN CPMA MAsh MBri NPal SMad WPGP
– var. ***discolor*** 'Koehnei'	SMad WAbe
– 'Penduliflora'	See ***A.*** × ***mutabilis*** **'Penduliflora'**
– 'Rosea Nana'	CMCN MBlu
splendens	See ***A. pavia***
§ ***sylvatica***	CFil WPGP
turbinata	CLnd CMCN ISea MBlu SMad SSpi WPGP
¶ ***wilsonii***	CB&S

AETHIONEMA (Brassicaceae)

armenum	ESis LFis LIck MLan NGre
coridifolium	NBus WPer
§ ***euonomioides***	NTow
graecum	See ***A. saxatile***
grandiflorum 🏆	CMHG CShe NBro NTow NWCA SHFr SSca WPer
– Pulchellum Group 🏆	CLyd CNic EPot LHop MBro NMen NPri SIng WAbe WWin
iberideum	MWat SRms WDav
oppositifolium	CLyd EHyt GTou MBro MRPP MWat NHol NMen NNrd NWCA WHoo WPyg
schistosum	NMen
'Warley Rose' 🏆	CShe EFou ELan EPot LHop MHig MTho MWat NGre NHed NHol NMen NNor NNrd NRya SIng SRms WHoo WPat WPyg WRus WWin
'Warley Ruber'	CLyd MHig NBir WAbe

AEXTOXICON (Aextoxicaceae)

punctatum	CGre

AFROCARPUS (Podocarpaceae)

¶ ***falcatus***	GCal

AGAPANTHUS † (Alliaceae)

'Accebt'	WWeb
§ ***africanus*** 🏆	EBee IBlr NRog SArc SLMG SWat WPer WWat
* – 'Albus' 🏆	CB&S CHad EMan EPfP IBlr LFis SEND SLMG WPer
'Albatross'	ECha
* ***alboroseus***	WThi
Ardernei Hybrid	CBot CFil ECha GCal IBlr LGre MUlv SSpi WCot
'Bethlehem Star'	ERav
'Bleuet'	WWeb
'Blue Baby'	CB&S CDoC CKni CLyd LRHS
'Blue Giant'	CBro CKni EBre EFou MUlv NCut SPla SWat WFar WMer WPyg
'Blue Imp'	ECtt EHic NHol
'Blue Moon'	CBro CHad ECha IBlr SEND SLod
'Blue Skies'	CB&S CTrC LRHS
'Blue Triumphator'	CBlo EBee EPfP EWll LBow LFis NCut SSte WHil WMer
'Bressingham Blue'	CBlo CBro EBre EFou GCal IBlr MSte SSpe
'Bressingham Bounty'	EBre
'Bressingham White'	CGle CSte CTri EBre ECtt EFol GCHN MBri MRav MUlv NRoo SSpe SWat WRus WWat
¶ 'Buckingham Palace'	IBlr
§ ***campanulatus***	CGle CMon CRDP EBee EBre ELan ERav GDra ISea MHlr SCro SWat WLRN
– var. ***albidus***	CBos CMGP CRDP CSev EBee EBre ECha EFou ELan GCra IBlr LHop MSte NFla NHol NRoo NSti NVic SChu SHig SPer WFar WWhi
– 'Albovittatus'	CRow LGre
* – 'Albus Nanus'	CBlo
– bright blue	GCal
– 'Cobalt Blue'	ECha
– 'Isis'	CBro CFir EBre ECha EGol GCHN IBlr MRav MUlv NRoo SPer WWeb
– Oxford blue	IBlr
– subsp. ***patens*** 🏆	EBre GBuc SHig SWat
¶ – – deep blue form	IBlr
* – 'Premier'	IBlr
– 'Profusion'	ECha IBlr
– 'Rosewarne'	CB&S GQui
– 'Slieve Donard Variety'	IBlr
* – 'Spokes'	IBlr
– variegated	EBee ECha EPPr WCot
– Wedgwood blue	IBlr
– 'Wendy'	IBlr
* – 'White Hope'	IBlr
'Castle of Mey'	CFil IBlr LGre LHyd MTho MUlv SAxl
caulescens 🏆	IBlr
¶ – subsp. ***caulescens***	SWat
'Cedric Morris'	ERav IBlr
comptonii	CMon IBlr
¶ – subsp. ***comptonii***	SWat
– forms	SLMG
¶ – subsp. ***longitubus***	SWat
♦ Danube	See ***A.*** **'Donau'**
§ 'Donau'	MUlv
¶ ***dyeri***	IBlr
'Evening Star'	ERav
¶ 'Findlay's Blue'	WCot
'Golden Rule' (v)	CRow IBlr LGre LHil SHig WCot
§ Headbourne hybrids	Widely available
'Holbrook'	CSam
'Hydon Mist'	LHyd
inapertus	CBlo CMon SAxl SBla SHig SWat
– subsp. ***hollandii***	CAvo CChu GCal IBlr SWat
¶ – subsp. ***inapertus***	SWat
– subsp. ***intermedius***	GCal IBlr SWat
¶ – subsp. ***pendulus***	CRow IBlr
'Kalmthout Blue'	EBee
'Kingston Blue'	ECha IBlr SWas
'Lady Moore'	IBlr SWas
'Lilliput'	CB&S CBro CChu CDoC CMHG CRDP CRow CSpe CVer EBre ECtt EFou EGol ELan EOrc GCHN GMaP MBri MGrG MRav NHol NOrc NRoo WRus WWat WWin
'Loch Hope' 🏆	CFil EBre
'Midnight Blue'	CGle ECha ELan GCal IBlr MBel SHig SWas WWeb
'Midnight Star'	ERav MSte
'Molly Howick'	SAxl
'Mooreanus'	GCal IBlr SAxl
'Morning Star'	ERav
¶ 'Norman Hadden'	IBlr
nutans 'Albus'	GCal
pale form	SApp
Palmer's Hybrids	See ***A.*** **Headbourne hybrids**

'Peter Pan' CB&S CDoC CMil CRow CSWP CSpe EBee GBuc LGre LHop NCut SAxl SPla WPyg WRHF WWat WWeb WWoo
'Phantom' IBlr
'Pinocchio' CAbb CSte WWoo
'Plas Merdyn Blue' IBlr
'Plas Merdyn White' IBlr
'Polar Ice' CFir EFou EGol EHic NCut WMer WPyg
praecox CDoC IBlr LWoo
– 'Flore Pleno' CLyd ECha EMon IBlr LGre
¶ – subsp. ***floribundus*** SWat
– – 'Saint Ivel' WHil
– subsp. ***maximus*** 'Albus' IBlr SHig
– 'Miniature Blue' SWat
– subsp. ***minimus*** IBlr SWat
¶ – – 'Adelaide' SWat
¶ – Mount Stewart form IBlr
§ – subsp. ***orientalis*** CBlo CHEx CHan ERea GAri IBlr NPal SMad SWat
– – var. ***albiflorus*** CBro CDoC ETub LBow NPal
¶ – subsp. ***praecox*** IBlr
¶ – – azure SWat
¶ – Slieve Donard form IBlr
– 'Storms River' SWat
– 'Variegatus' 🏆 SLMG
– 'Vittatus' (v) CHan WCot WFar
'Profusion' CBro SHig
'Purple Cloud' CB&S CDoC CRos CTrC LRHS SMad SPla
'Rhône' EFou
'Royal Blue' EBee ECtt EHic NHol
'San Gabriel' (v) EMon SAxl
'Sandringham' CChu CFil IBlr
'Sapphire' CB&S IBlr
'Snowball' CB&S
'Snowy Baby' CDoC CRos LRHS
'Snowy Owl' LWoo MUlv
'Storm Cloud' (d) ERea
'Streamline' CDoC EBee EMil LRHS SAxl
'Tinkerbell' CAbb CB&S CBro CDoC CHid CMil CRDP CRos CRow CSWP EFol EMan EMil ERav LRHS MDun MTho SAxl SMad SPer SPla WMer
'Torbay' SApp SBla SHig
umbellatus See ***A. praecox*** subsp. ***orientalis***
'Underway' CMon GCal SHig
'White Christmas' ERea
'White Dwarf' CHan ECha EFou EGol GCra LRHS MBri WFar WTre WWat
'White Ice' CB&S EBee EMil GQui SMad
'White Superior' CSpe
'White Umbrella' EOrc WWat
¶ 'Windsor Castle' IBlr
'Windsor Grey' IBlr
'Wolga' CAbb EFou
'Zella Thomas' LHyd

AGAPETES (Ericaceae)

buxifolia WBod
'Ludgvan Cross' CB&S CGre MBal
serpens 🏆 CGre MBal
– 'Nepal Cream' CGre MBal
– 'Scarlet Elf' SBid

AGARISTA (Ericaceae)

§ ***populifolia*** WWat

AGASTACHE (Lamiaceae)

anethiodora See ***A. foeniculum***
anisata See ***A. foeniculum***
barberi LGre
* – 'Tutti-frutti' CElw ECGP ECha EMan
'Blue Fortune' EBee GBri WWeb
§ ***cana*** CGle ECoo EOHP LGre MUlv WCot WFar WPbr
– 'Cinnabar Rose' WCot WFar
'Firebird' CArc CBot CBrk CChu CDoC CGle CLon CMil CRDP EBee EGar GCal GMac LGre LHop MNrw NBir NHaw NPla SAga SBla SOkh SUsu SWas SWat WCot WFar WWeb
§ ***foeniculum*** CArn CGle CHan CSev ECha EFou ELan ELau EMar EOHP GCHN GPoy LHol LHop MBri MChe MGam MGra MHew NFai NNor NSti NTow SIde WPer WWye
– 'Alabaster' CChu CGle CHan ECha ECro EFou EGoo ELau EMon WRha WWye
– 'Alba' CBlo CBot LCot MEas MLLN MSCN NTow SHDw SIde WFar WRha
§ ***mexicana*** CDoC CGle CSam CSev ECro ELan GAul GMac LHop LIck MChe MHar NPla NTow NWoo WWye
– 'Carille Carmine' CLTr WPer
– 'Champagne' CGle EGar EWll MCCP MCli SWat WPLI WPer
– 'Mauve Beauty' GBri LHop SMrm WPer
aff. – PC&H 153 CPle
– 'Rosea' See ***A. cana***
nepetoides CArn MHew MSal WWye
pringlei EBee GCal LGre SWat WCot
rugosa CArn CFir CSev EMan EOHP GBar GPoy MGra MHew MSal NCGP NPla SWat WCot WCru WJek WPbr WPer WSel WWye
– B&SWJ 735 EGoo
rupestris CPou CRDP LGre SMad WCot WKif
¶ – JCA 1.025.050 CMil
scrophulariifolia EBee
urticifolia CArn CPea EPfP MSal
– 'Alba' EGar EHal EPfP EWll SWat WEas WPer
I – 'Liquorice' CSam
– 'Liquorice Blue' EBee EMan EMar LRHS MLan SCro SPer SSte SWat WPer
– 'Liquorice White' CRDP CSam EBee EGar EMan SCro SPer SWat WOve
wrightii EBee

AGATHAEA See FELICIA

AGATHIS (Araucariaceae)

australis CFil

AGATHOSMA (Rutaceae)

ovata 'Kleitijies Kraal' CSpe

AGAVE (Agavaceae)

affinis See ***A. sobria***
americana CAbb CB&S CDoC CGre CHEx CTrC CWSG ECha ELau EOas GCra GQui IBlr LCns LHil LPal LPan MBro SArc SLMG SMad
– 'Marginata' CGre CHal CInt IBlr LHop

– 'Mediopicta'	CKni CTbh SArc SIgm SLMG
– 'Variegata'	CAbb CB&S CDoC CHEx CMdw CTbh CTrC CWSG ECha EWes GQui LCns NPer SArc SLMG SSoC
angustifolia	SLMG
attenuata	CTrC SArc
avellanidens	See ***A. sebastiana***
§ ***celsii***	CHEx CTbh SArc
cerulata	See ***A. sobria***
¶ ***chrysantha***	EOas
coarctata	See ***A. mitriformis***
¶ ***ferox***	CB&S CTbh
filifera	CHEx
gigantea	See ***Furcraea foetida***
mitis	See ***A. celsii***
neomexicana	SIgm
¶ ***palmeri***	EOas
parryi	CGre CHEx EGar EOas GCal SIgm
– var. ***couesii***	See ***A. parryi*** var. ***parryi***
– var. ***huachucensis***	CFir
§ – var. ***parryi***	CTbh
potatorum var. ***verschaffeltii***	CTbh
salmiana var. ***ferox***	CHEx SArc SLMG
¶ ***schidigera***	CBrP
schottii	CTbh
utahensis	EOas SIgm
– var. ***discreta***	CTbh
victoriae-reginae	CTbh EGar
xylonacantha	CHEx

AGERATINA See EUPATORIUM

AGLAONEMA (Araceae)

§ ***crispum***	MBri
* – 'Marie'	MBri
'Malay Beauty'	MBri
roebelinii	See ***A. crispum***
'Silver Queen' ♀	MBri

AGRIMONIA (Rosaceae)

eupatoria	CArn CKin ECWi EOHP EWFC GPoy MChe MGam MGra MHew NMir SIde SWat WCHb WCla WHer WOak WWye
* ***odorata***	WUnd
– Miller	See ***A. repens***
§ ***repens***	GBar MHew MSal WCHb

AGROPYRON (Poaceae)

glaucum	See ***Elymus hispidus***
magellanicum	See ***Elymus magellanicus***
pubiflorum	See ***Elymus magellanicus***
scabrum	See ***Elymus scabrus***

AGROSTEMMA (Caryophyllaceae)

coronaria	See ***Lychnis coronaria***
githago	CJew ECWi EWFC MGam MHew MSal WCla WCot WHer WJek WOak

AGROSTIS (Poaceae)

calamagrostis	See ***Calamagrostis epigejos***
canina 'Silver Needles' (v)	CBre CCuc CHor CInt EGle EHoe EJud EMon EPPr EPot ESOG ETPC EWes GBin GCal MMil WHal WHil WLeb
karsensis	See ***A. stolonifera***
nebulosa	GBin
§ ***stolonifera***	ETPC

AGROSTOCRINUM (Phormiaceae)

See Plant Deletions

AICHRYSON (Crassulaceae)

§ × ***domesticum***	CHEx CHal
– 'Variegatum' ♀	CHal EBak SLMG

AILANTHUS (Simaroubaceae)

§ ***altissima*** ♀	CB&S CHEx CLnd CTho EBre EMil ENot IOrc LPan MBlu MGos NBee SArc SPer WCoo WDin WNor WStI
glandulosa	See ***A. altissima***

AINSLIAEA (Asteraceae)

See Plant Deletions

AIPHANES (Arecaceae)

See Plant Deletions

AJANIA (Asteraceae)

§ ***pacifica***	CFis ECtt EFol ELan EMan EMar ERav GCal LHop MFir MHar NFai SUsu WGwG WHer WHil
tibetica JJH 9308103	NWCA
* ***xylorhiza*** JJH 95095	EPot

AJUGA (Lamiaceae)

'Arctic Fox'	WGle
¶ 'Brockbankii'	CHal
genevensis 'Alba'	LWoo
– 'Tottenham'	MCli WMer
metallica	See ***A. pyramidalis***
'Monmotaro San'	EGar
§ ***pyramidalis***	CFee ECha EGar EGol LWak NBrk SCro WHer
– 'Metallica Crispa'	CArc CRDP CShe NHar NNrd WHil WMer
reptans	CJew CKin ECWi ECtt EWFC GPoy LGro LHol LPBA MChe MHew MSal NBrk NFla NMir WChe WGwy WRHF
– 'Alba'	CArc CArn CCot CNic CRow CWGN ECha EFou GCal GMac MCLN MNrw MRav NBro NPla SSvw WBon WByw WCHb WFar WMer WPer WWye
♦ – 'Argentea'	See ***A. reptans 'Variegata'***
§ – 'Atropurpurea' ♀	CB&S CRow CWGN ECha EFol ELan ENot EPar LGro LPBA LSyl MWat NEgg NFai NHol NNor NRoo NSti SMad SPer WEas WWin
– 'Braunherz' ♀	Widely available
– 'Burgundy Glow' (v) ♀	Widely available
* – 'Burgundy Red'	GDra
– 'Carol'	CSte
§ – 'Catlin's Giant' ♀	CArc CBot CRDP CRow EBre ECha ECtt EFol EGol EHoe ELan EMon ERav GAbr GCal LHop NBir NHol NSti SAxl SMad SPer WCHb WEas WHal WHen WHil WHoo WPer
– 'Delight' (v)	ECot ELan EMon EPot MHar NNrd SBod WCHb WCer WEas
– 'Grey Lady'	EMon SMrm SUsu
– 'Harlequin' (v)	WMer

– 'Julia' EGoo EMon EPPr LWak
– 'Jumbo' See *A. reptans* **'Jungle Beauty'**
§ – 'Jungle Beauty' CRDP CRow CWGN EBre ECha ECtt EFou EGol EOrc EPar EPla GBar GCal LHop NFai NHol NRar SAxl SHel SPer WCer WHen WHer
– 'Macrophylla' See *A. reptans* **'Catlin's Giant'**
– 'Multicolor' (v) CArn CWGN ECha EFol EFou ELan EPar EPot GAbr GDra LGro LSyl LWak MBar MCLN MWat NFai NGre NNor NNrd SBod SPer SSmi WCer WCra WPer
– 'Palisander' CSte EBre NSti WLRN
I – 'Pat's Selection' CSte
– 'Pink Elf' CArc CB&S CLyd CNic CRow EBur ELan EMan EWes LHop NBro NNor NOak SHel SUsu SWat WBea WCer WFar WHoo WPer WPyg
– 'Pink Splendour' CBre CTri LCom NChi WCer
– 'Pink Surprise' CRow EBre EFou EGol EHoe EMar EMon EPla EPri GBar LRHS MCLN MMil NGre NHol NRya SSvw WCHb WPbr WTyr
– 'Purple Torch' ECha EGar ESis MBal MCli SLod WCHb WCer WEas WMer
– 'Purpurea' See *A. reptans* **'Atropurpurea'**
– 'Rosea' CHal WHil
– 'Schneekerze' MCli
– 'Silver Shadow' CBre NLak NPro WCHb
§ – 'Variegata' CArc CB&S EBre ECha ECtt EFou ELan GDra LBuc LGan LGro LHop MBar MBri MCLN MHig NEgg NRoo SAlw SBod SPer SSmi SWat SWyc WBea WHil WPbr

AKEBIA (Lardizabalaceae)

× ***pentaphylla*** CPlN CRHN CSte EMil EPfP ERea GQui MAsh SBra SPer
quinata Widely available
trifoliata CB&S CBlo CChu CPlN CSte EHic

ALANGIUM (Alangiaceae)

chinense CB&S CChu CFil CMCN WPGP
platanifolium CBot CFil CMCN EPla MBlu WBod WPGP

ALBIZIA (Mimosaceae)

distachya See ***Paraserianthes lophantha***
§ ***julibrissin*** CFil CHan CTho GOrc ISea MSal MWat SPer
– f. ***rosea*** ♀ CB&S CGre CHEx CMCN CPle CTrC ELan GQui LPan MUlv NPSI SArc SDry SMad SOWG WBod WNor WSHC
lophantha See ***Paraserianthes lophantha***

ALBUCA (Hyacinthaceae)

canadensis NRog
caudata CMon
humilis EPot ESis MHig MSto NRog NTow SIng WAbe WHil WOMN
juncifolia CMon
nelsonii CAvo CMon NRog
shawii SBla WAbe
tortuosa S&SH 53 CHan
wakefieldii CMon

ALCEA (Malvaceae)

'Arabian Nights' WHer
'Blackcurrant Whirl' WHer
ficifolia CGle EWes MEas MSto NBus NChi NFai SSvw
¶ ***pallida*** EMan
– HH&K 284 CHan
§ ***rosea*** CGle EJud MBri WEas WFar
– Chater's Double Group CHad EBre ECtt EMan MBri MCLN MLsm NNor SCoo SRms WOve WRHF
– double apricot SMad
– forms LCot NRoo SPer WLRN
– 'Lemon Light' CMdw MLsm WLRN WRHF
– Majorette Group ECtt
* – 'Negrite' MRav
– 'Nigra' CArn CGle CHad CJew CMGP CMil EBar EFou GCra MHlr MLsm MNrw MSte NNor NPri NRai NRoo SMad SPer SSoC SSvw WOve
– single EGoo
– single pink LCot
– Summer Carnival Group EMan NRoo SRms WGor WRHF
– yellow LCot
§ ***rugosa*** CGle CHad CMil CSam ECha ELan EMan LGan MSte SDix WCot WEas WKif WOMN WOld WRus
¶ ***rugosa alba*** SHam

ALCHEMILLA † (Rosaceae)

§ ***abyssinica*** CDoC CGle CHid CRow EHal GAbr GBuc MBel NWes WBro WCot WHen
N ***alpina*** CBro CFee CRow EFol ELan EPar EWFC GMac GTou LBee MHig MTho NBrk NEgg NMir NNor NRoo SIng WCla WFar WOld WPbr WPer WRus WTyr WWin
arvensis See ***Aphanes arvensis***
conjuncta CGle CHan CNic ECha ECro EFou EGol ELan ERav GAbr GCHN LHop MBel MGrG MTho NBrk NBro NChi NHol NOak NPla NRya NWCA SOkh SPer WBea WByw WEas WRTC WWye
elisabethae EMon EPPr MGrG NBrk WCHb
ellenbeckii CFee CLyd CMHG EBre ELan GCHN LBee LFis MBar NNor NNrd NRoo NSti NWCA WByw WCHb WEas WFar WPer
erythropoda ♀ Widely available
faeroensis CArc CHid CWan EGle LBee MDHE NChi NNor WHil WPer WWat
– var. ***pumila*** CLyd EBee LHop MSto SAlw
filicaulis 'Minima' CNat
§ × ***fulgens*** CArn CBlo EPPr GAri LFis NRoo SMac WAbe
glaucescens CNat
◆ ***hoppeana*** hort. See ***A. plicatula***

lapeyrousei CHid EMon EPPr MSto NChi SIng WPer
mollis ♀ CArn CB&S CHad CMHG CMea CRow CShe EBre ECha EGol ELan ENot GCHN LGro LHop LLWP NFla NHol NNor NRoo NSti SIng SMad SPer WEas WHil WOak WOld WRus WWin
* – 'Robusta' EBee ECha ECro MTho NBrk SApp SEND SWat
* – 'Senior' GCal
¶ – 'Variegata' IBlr
'Mr Poland's Variety' See ***A. venosa***
pedata See ***A. abyssinica***
pentaphylla EBee
pumila ECro MGrG
saxatilis EMan GAul
* ***siranines*** ERav
speciosa EBee EBre SHel
splendens See ***A. ×fulgens***
§ ***venosa*** SCro SLod SPer WWat
vulgaris hort. See ***A. xanthochlora***
§ ***xanthochlora*** ECro EGol GGar GPoy MHew MSal MTol NMir WHer WPer

ALECTRYON (Sapindaceae)
excelsus CHEx

ALETRIS (Melanthiaceae)
See Plant Deletions

ALISMA (Alismataceae)
lanceolatum WChe
plantago-aquatica CBen CKin CRow CWGN ECWi EHon EMFW GBar LPBA MHew MSta NDea SHig SWat WChe WMAq WWye
– var. ***parviflorum*** CBen CWGN EMFW LPBA MSta NDea SHig SRms SWat WChe

ALKANNA (Boraginaceae)
¶ ***aucheriana*** WDav
orientalis WCru
tinctoria MChe

ALLAMANDA (Apocynaceae)
cathartica CPlN ECon ERea LChe MBri
– 'Birthe' MBri
* – 'Chocolate Swirl' LChe
¶ – 'Grandiflora' CPlN
¶ – 'Williamsii' LChe
neriifolia See ***A. schottii***
schottii ♀ CPlN
violacea See ***A. blanchetii***

ALLARDIA (Asteraceae)
glabra See ***A. tridactylites***

ALLIARIA (Brassicaceae)
petiolata CArn CKin CSev CTiv ECWi EWFC WHer

ALLIUM † (Alliaceae)
§ ***acuminatum*** EHyt GCHN MFos NBir NGar WChr WCot
aflatunense hort. See ***A. hollandicum***
akaka GCrs MFos MSto
albidum See ***A. denudatum***
albopilosum See ***A. cristophii***
altissimum EBee LBow LRHS NRog WChr
amabile See ***A. mairei*** var. ***amabile***
ambiguum See ***A. roseum*** var. ***carneum***
ampeloprasum CFil ECha WHer WPGP
– var. ***babingtonii*** CNat WHer
amplectens GDra NRog WChr
anceps MFos
§ ***angulosum*** GAul MMil MSto WCot
atropurpureum ECha EMon EPar LBow NRog WCot
¶ ***aucheri*** LWoo
azureum See ***A. caeruleum***
'Beau Regard' LAma LBow NRog
beesianum hort. See ***A. cyaneum***
– W.W. Smith ♀ CGle CLyd EBre EBur ESis EWes MBal MBro MHig NBir NRya NWCA WCot
bulgaricum See ***Nectaroscordum siculum*** subsp. ***bulgaricum***
§ ***caeruleum*** ♀ CArn CAvo CBro CMil ELan EMon EPot ETub LAma LBow MBri MSto MWat NBir NRog NRya NSti SChu SUsu WBro WCHb WCot WPer WRHF
– ***azureum*** See ***A. caeruleum***
caesium EHyt
callimischon CAvo CBro CMon NRog WChr
¶ – subsp. ***callimischon*** MFos
– subsp. ***haemostictum*** EHyt EPot LBow NRog SBla SIng SWas WChr
campanulatum MSto
canadense CSam MTol
cardiostemon MBel
§ ***carinatum*** EBee GCHN
§ – subsp. ***pulchellum*** ♀ CArn CAvo CBro CHad CHan CMil CNic ECha EFou EPot LAma LBow LHop LLWP MBal MBro MNrw MTho MWat NNor NRog NSti NTow SAlw SHFr SIng SSvw SUsu WPer WWye
– – f. ***album*** CAvo CBro CMon CSWP ECha EFou EMon EPar EPot ETub LBow LFis MBal MNrw NRog NSti NTow SUsu WCot WPer WWin
– – 'Tubergen' ETub
carolinianum MSto
cepa ♀ CJew CMil GBar
– Aggregatum Group ELau WHil
– 'Perutile' CArn GBar GPoy ILis LHol SIde WSel
– Proliferum Group CArn CSev EJud GAbr GBar GPoy ILis LHol MChe NWoo SIde WApp WCHb WCer WHer WOak WSel
* – 'White Flower' WCot
cernuum ♀ Widely available
– ***album*** WHil
–'Hidcote' ♀ EMon NPla WCot
– ***roseum*** CLyd
chamaemoly littorale AB&S 4387 CMon
cirrhosum See ***A. carinatum*** subsp. ***pulchellum***
cowanii See ***A. neapolitanum* Cowanii Group**
crenulatum MSto

§ ***cristophii*** ♀	CArn CAvo CBro CGle CLon EBre ECha EFou ELan EMon EOrc EPot ERav ETub GAbr GBuc LAma LBow MBri MGrG MNrw NBir NBrk NRog SChu SSpi SUsu WCHb WFar WHoo
cupanii	CMon
– subsp. ***hirtovaginatum***	EHic
¶ ***cupuliferum***	MSto
§ ***cyaneum*** ♀	CArc CArn CAvo CGle CGra CLyd EFol EHyt LBee LBow LGan MHig NMen NNrd NRya NTow SSca WRus
cyathophorum	CBlo GCrs NRog
§ – var. ***farreri***	CArn CAvo CBro CMon CNic EHyt ELan EPot ERos ESis GAbr GCHN LBow LLWP MBal MHig NMen NNor NNrd NRya SAlw WAbe WHil WOMN
§ ***denudatum***	LBow
dichlamydeum	CBro LBow NRog WChr WDav
¶ – JCA 11765	LWoo
§ ***drummondii***	EBre ECha
elatum	See ***A. macleanii***
ericetorum	EBee ERos MSto
falcifolium	NTow WChr
¶ – JCA 11625	LWoo
farreri	See ***A. cyathophorum*** var. ***farreri***
fimbriatum var. ***abramsii***	WDav
'Firmament'	LBow
fistulosum	CArn CJew EJud ELan EPla GBar GPoy ILis MChe MGra NBrk NNor SIde WApp WCHb WCer WOak WPer WSel WTyr WWye
– 'Streaker'	WCot
flavum ♀	CArn CAvo CBro CGle CHan CLyd CMon EBar ECha EFol EFou ELan LBow LGan LHop LLWP MHig NMen NRog NSti SAlw SChu SHBN SIng WCla WGor WHil WPer
§ – 'Blue Leaf'	EBar EPot ERos
– 'Glaucum'	See ***A. flavum* 'Blue Leaf'**
– 'Golden Showers'	EBar WRHF
– var. ***minus***	CNic EHyt ELan EPot MTho NWCA
– var. ***nanum***	EPot NTow
– subsp. ***tauricum***	CMon
geyeri	WCot WDav
giganteum	CArn CB&S CBot CMea ELan EMan EMon EOrc EPar EPot ETub GCra LAma LBow MBri MRav NNor NOrc NRog SRms WCra WFar
'Gladiator'	CAvo LAma LBow NRog
glaucum	See ***A. senescens*** subsp. ***montanum*** var. ***glaucum***
'Globemaster'	EBee ETub LAma LBow
'Globus'	EPot LRHS
griffithianum	See ***A. rubellum***
haematochiton	LBow
heldreichii	EBee
hierochuntinum S&L 79	CMon
'His Excellency'	CAvo CBlo LBow LRHS
§ ***hollandicum*** ♀	CBro CGle CMon ECha EFou EMan LAma LBow MSto MWat NRog NSti SChu WPer WRHF

– 'Purple Sensation' ♀	CAvo CBro CGle CHad CSWP ECha EFou EMon EPar EPot ETub LAma LBow MBel MGrG MHlr MWat NBir NRog WBro WFar WHoo WPer WPyg WRHF
– 'Purple Surprise'	LRHS
humile	MSto
hyalinum	CMon EHyt NRog WChr
§ ***insubricum*** ♀	CHad CMea ERos MS&S MSto NBir SWas
jajlae	See ***A. rotundum*** subsp. ***jajlae***
jepsonii	WChr
kansuense	See ***A. sikkimense***
karataviense ♀	CArn CAvo CBos CBro CGle CRDP ECha EFou ELan EMon EOrc EPot ETub LAma LBow MBri MSto MTho MWat NBir NNrd NRog NSti SAlw WCra WHil WPat WPer
kharputense	LAma
libani	MSto WPer WWye
loratum	EPar
'Lucy Ball'	ETub LAma LBow NRog
§ ***macleanii***	CArn CMil EMon EPar LAma LBow MSto NRog
macranthum	CLyd EBee GCHN MSte MSto NSti WDav
macrochaetum	LAma
mairei	CFee CInt EPot ERos EWes GCHN MBar MDHE NBus NRya
§ – var. ***amabile***	CArc MBal MHig NRya NTow WOMN
– – pink	NBir
'Mars'	LBow LRHS
maximowiczii	EWes WThi
moly ♀	CArn CBro CGle CNic ELan ETub GBuc LAma LBow MBri MHig MRav MWat NMen NRog NRya NSti SAlw SIng WCHb WCla WCot WPer WShi WWin
– 'Jeannine' ♀	CBro CMea EBee EPot LBow NBrk
'Mount Everest'	CAvo LBow LRHS
multibulbosum	See ***A. nigrum***
◆ ***murrayanum*** hort.	See ***A. unifolium***
narcissiflorum hort.	See ***A. insubricum***
§ – Villars	CLyd MSto NMGW NMen NSla NSti NWCA SIng
neapolitanum	CAgr CArn CGle CLTr EGar ELan EPar LAma LBow MBri MBro NRog NSti WCot WPer
§ – Cowanii Group	CBro CSWP WDav WPer
– 'Grandiflorum'	EPla NRog
§ ***nigrum***	EFou EGar EMan EPar LAma LBow MHlr NBir NRog SChu WBro WCot WHal
nutans	EBee LBow MSto
nuttallii	See ***A. drummondii***
§ ***obliquum***	CAvo CHan ECha MSto WCot WPbr
odorum Linnaeus	See ***A. ramosum* Linnaeus**
olympicum	EHyt MBro
§ ***oreophilum*** ♀	CArn CAvo CBro ECha ECtt EHyt LAma LBow MFos MHig NMGW NRog SRms WCla WCot WPer WWye
– 'Agalik'	LRHS
– 'Zwanenburg' ♀	CBro CMea EPot NMen NRog
orientale	EPot LAma

ostrowskianum	See ***A. oreophilum***
pallens	CBre EFol ERav LBow MTho NBir
§ ***paniculatum***	CAvo CMea ECha EHic MMil NRog SChu
– subsp. ***fuscum***	EHic
paradoxum	LRHS NBir NRog
– var. ***normale***	EMon
– PF 5085	CMon
pedemontanum	See ***A. narcissiflorum* Villars**
peninsulare	WChr
perdulce	MSto
polyastrum	GCHN
porrum 'Saint Victor'	MHlr
pulchellum	See ***A. carinatum*** subsp. ***pulchellum***
pyrenaicum Costa & Vayreda	CAvo EBee ELan EMan
– hort.	See ***A. angulosum***
ramosum Jacquin	See ***A. obliquum***
§ – Linnaeus	LAma MSto WPer
'Rien Poortvliet'	CArn LAma LBow NRog
rosenbachianum	CArn CBro EHyt EMan EPar EPot LAma NCat NRog WRHF
– 'Album'	CMil EPar EPot LAma NRog WCot
– 'Michael Hoog'	EPot LRHS
– 'Purple King'	EPot LRHS
– 'Shing'	LRHS
roseum	CArc CArn CAvo CElw CLTr EBee ECtt ELau EMon LAma LBow NRog SAlw SChu WPer
– ***album***	LRHS
– B&S 396	CMon
§ – var. ***bulbiferum***	WCot
– 'Grandiflorum'	See ***A. roseum*** var. ***bulbiferum***
§ ***rotundum*** subsp. ***jajlae***	EBee EJud EWes NMen WPer
rubens	EBee
sarawschanicum	LRHS
sativum	CArn CWan EEls EJud ELau EOHP SIde WJek WOak WSel WWye
* – ***aureum***	GPoy
– var. ***ophioscorodon***	GPoy ILis
scabriscapum	CMon
schoenoprasum	CArn CJew CSev ECha ELau GAbr GCHN GPoy LBlm LHol MBal MBar MBel MBri MBro MChe MGra MHew MRav NCat NFai NNor SIde WBea WHil WJek WOak WPLI WPer WWye
– 'Black Isle Blush' 🏆	GPoy
– 'Corsican White'	EMon
– fine-leaved	CWan WRha
– 'Forescate'	EBee EBre ECha EFou EJud EWes GCHN LHol MBal MBri MUlv NHol SSpe WCHb WCot WLRN WPbr
– 'Pink Perfection' 🏆	GPoy
– 'Polyphant'	CBre CJew WCHb WNdy WRha
– ***roseum***	GBar
– var. ***sibiricum***	EJud GBar GPoy MBri MGra SDix SIde WSel
– 'Silver Chimes'	MRav
– 'Wallington White'	EMon MBro
– white	CHad CSWP ECha GBar LGre MBro MSte NBir SIde SSvw WBea WBon WCHb WCot WHer WRha WWye

schubertii	CArn CAvo CBro EMon EPar EPot ETub LAma LBow MBri MNrw NCat NRog
¶ ***scorodoprasum***	WCHb
– subsp. ***jajlae***	See ***A. rotundum*** subsp. ***jajlae***
¶ – subsp. ***rotundum***	LBow
scorzonerifolium var. ***xericiense***	CMon
senescens	CArn CTri ECro ELan EPar ERos GCHN LBow NChi NMen SRms SSpe SSvw WHil
§ – subsp. ***montanum***	EBee EGar ELan EPot ERav LWoo MBro NMen SDix SIng WAbe WCot
§ – – var. ***glaucum***	CHad CHan CLyd CMea CPBP EBre ECha EMan EPla ESis GCHN LBow MBel MHig MHlr MSto MTol NTow WCot WHer WPbr WPer WWye
– subsp. ***senescens***	EMon
sibthorpianum	See ***A. paniculatum***
siculum	See ***Nectaroscordum siculum***
§ ***sikkimense***	CMea EBee EBre EHyt GDra LFis MBro MSto NFai NMen NNrd NSla NTow NWCA SBla WCot WLRN WOMN WPer
¶ – ACE 1363	EBee
siskiyouense	MSto
sphaerocephalon	CArn CAvo CBro CHad ECha ELan EPar ETub LAma LBow LHop LLWP MNrw MTol MWat NOak NRog SUsu WCHb WEas WHil WOMN WPer WRHF WShi
stellatum	CArc EHyt SSpi
stellerianum	GCHN LBow WPer WPri
– var. ***kurilense***	CNic
§ ***stipitatum***	LAma LBow NRog WCot
– 'Album'	CBro EMon ETub LAma LBow NRog
¶ ***strictum***	WHil
szovitsii	MSto
tanguticum	EBee GCHN MTol
textile	MSto
thunbergii	CAvo EBee LBow NBir WChr
tibeticum	See ***A. sikkimense***
togashii	MSto
tricoccum	MSto
triquetrum	CAvo CGle CLTr EFol ELan ERav GBar GGar IBlr ILis LAma LBow NBir NMen NRog SIng WCHb WCru WHer WPer WShi WWin
tuberosum	CArn CAvo CLyd CSev ECha EFou EJud ELau ERos GPoy ILis LHol MBri MChe MGra MHew SIde WBea WCHb WCer WCot WOak WPer WWye
¶ – blue-flowered	SHDw
§ ***unifolium***	CAvo CBro CGle CHad CMon EPot ETub GAul LAma LBow LLWP MBri NBir NCat NRog SSpi WBro WCla WPer
ursinum	CArn CAvo CKin ETub EWFC GPoy LAma NMir NRog WGwy WHen WShi WWye
validum	MSto
victorialis	MSto
vineale	CArn CTiv WHer WPer
violaceum	See ***A. carinatum***
virgunculae	LBow SBla SWas WCot

wallichii	CLyd EBar EMon LAma NBir WCot
– B 445	WDav
zaprjagaevii	EBee
zebdanense	LAma LBow MNrw MSto

ALLOCASUARINA (Casuarinaceae)

§ ***littoralis***	CGre
monilifera	ECou
§ ***verticillata***	MAll

ALNUS † (Betulaceae)

cordata ♀	CAgr CB&S CDoC CKin CLnd CPer ELan ENot EPfP IOrc LBuc LHyr NBee NRog NWea SHBN SPer SSta WDin WFar WMou WOrn WStI
– wild origin	CSto
crispa	See ***A. viridis*** subsp. ***crispa***
firma	CMCN
– var. ***multinervis***	See ***A. pendula***
– var. ***sieboldiana***	See ***A. sieboldiana***
glutinosa	CB&S CDoC CKin CLnd CPer CSam CSto ENot GRei IOrc LBuc LHyr MGos NBee NRog NRoo NWea SHBN SHFr SPer WDin WMou WOrn WStI
– 'Aurea'	CEnd CTho EBee MBlu SSpi WWat
– 'Imperialis' ♀	CEnd CLnd CPMA CTho EBee ELan ENot EPfP MAsh MBri NBee SPer SSpi WDin WWat
– f. ***incisa***	ELan
– 'Laciniata'	CDoC CLnd CTho IOrc MBlu
– 'Pyramidalis'	CTho
hirsuta	CMCN
incana	CDoC CKin CLnd CMCN CPer CSto EBee ENot GRei IOrc LBuc MBar NRog NWea SHBN WDin WHut WMou WOrn
– 'Aurea'	CB&S CLnd COtt CTho ELan ENot IOrc LPan MBar MBlu MBri SHBN SPer WDin
– 'Laciniata'	CTho ENot WDin
– 'Pendula'	CMCN WMou
japonica	CSto
maritima	CSto
maximowiczii	CMCN CSto
– AGSJ 334	SSta
¶ ***nepalensis***	WFro
¶ ***nitida***	CMCN
oregona	See ***A. rubra***
rhombifolia	CSto
§ ***rubra***	CDoC CKin CLnd CMCN CPer CSto CTho ELan ENot GAri GRei IOrc LBuc NWea WDin WHut WMou
§ ***rugosa***	CMCN
serrulata	See ***A. rugosa***
§ ***sieboldiana***	CGre CSto
sinuata	CAgr CMCN MBlu
× ***spaethii*** ♀	CTho
subcordata	CLnd
viridis	CAgr CMCN GAri NWea
– subsp. ***crispa*** var. ***mollis***	CMCN

ALOCASIA (Araceae)

× ***amazonica*** ♀	MBri

ALOE (Aloeaceae)

arborescens	CAbb CHEx CTrC MBro
aristata	CHEx EOas EWes LBlm MBri MBro SArc SLMG
barbadensis	See ***A. vera***
brevifolia	CHEx CTbh EOas
¶ ***broomii***	CTrC
camperi 'Maculata'	MBri
ciliaris	CHEx ERea SLMG
¶ ***cooperi***	WHer
¶ ***dichotoma***	GBin
¶ ***erinacea***	CTrC
¶ ***ferox***	CTrC
humilis	IBlr
karasbergensis	LHil
¶ ***parvibracteata***	CTrC
¶ ***plicatilis***	CTrC
¶ ***pratensis***	CFir CTrC
saponaria	SLMG
striata	CHEx
striatula	CFil CTrC EOas IBlr SBid
– var. ***caesia***	IBlr
§ ***vera*** ♀	CArn ECon ELau EOHP ERea GPoy ILis LChe LHol MGra MSal NPer SIde SLMG WHer WOak
'Walmsley's Blue'	MBri

ALOINOPSIS (Aizoaceae)

¶ ***lueckhoffii***	CTrC

ALONSOA (Scrophulariaceae)

acutifolia	LHil
– coral	EAst LIck WLRN
linearis	LCot LHil
meridionalis	CElw WOve
* – 'Salmon Beauty'	CMdw
'Pink Beauty'	CMdw ELan GBri GMac
warscewiczii ♀	CSpe ELan ERea IBlr LGan LHil SAga WWin
– pale form	See ***A. warscewiczii*** **'Peachy-keen'**
§ – 'Peachy-keen'	CSpe EMan ERea GBri NLak SAga WWin

ALOPECURUS (Poaceae)

alpinus	CCuc CInt EHoe EMon ETPC
– subsp. ***glaucus***	EHoe ESOG ETen
lanatus	CInt NRya
pratensis	CKin
– 'Aureovariegatus'	Widely available
N – 'Aureus'	CMGP CNic ECha EFou EPot GAbr GBin MBal NBro NHol NSti NVic WByw WPer WRHF WWin

ALOPHIA (Iridaceae)

lahue	See ***Herbertia lahue***

ALOYSIA (Verbenaceae)

chamaedrifolia	CGre CPle
citriodora	See ***A. triphylla***
§ ***triphylla***	CArn CBot CPle CSam CSev CShe CTbh CTrw ECha ELan ERav ERea GPoy IOrc ISea LHol MBri NNor NRog NWoo SDix SIde SPer WCHb WEas WOak WWat WWye

ALPINIA (Zingiberaceae)

japonica	MSal
luteocarpa	LChe
speciosa	See ***A. zerumbet***

ALSOBIA See EPISCIA

ALSTROEMERIA † (Alstroemeriaceae)

angustifolia P&W 6574	MSto
'Apollo' 🏆	COtt LRHS SBai
aurantiaca	See *A. aurea*
§ *aurea*	CGle CGre ELan EMar EWoo LBlm MHlr MRav MUlv NCat NCut NMGW NSti WCot
– 'Cally Fire'	GCal
– 'Dover Orange'	CB&S CGle CTri EBee SMrm WCot
– 'Orange King'	CBlo CDoC EHic MUlv NCut SCoo SDeJ SRms
♦ Beatrix	**See *A.* Princess Beatrix = 'Stadoran'**
brasiliensis	CChu CGle CMil GCal MSto
'Charm'	EBee LIck LRHS SBai
'Dayspring Delight' (v)	CRDP
Diana	**See *A.* H.R.H. the Princess Alexandra = 'Stablaco'**
diluta subsp. *diluta*	MSto
Doctor Salter's Hybrids	EFou SRms
exserens JCA 14415	MSto
'Fortune'	MBri
Frederika	**See *A.* Princess Frederika = 'Stabronza'**
garaventae	MSto
Grace	**See *A.* Princess Grace = 'Starodo'**
♦ H.R.H. the Princess Alexandra	**See *A.* H.R.H. the Princess Alexandra = 'Stablaco'**
haemantha	MSto
I 'Hatch Hybrid'	GCal
'Hawera'	WCot
hookeri	MSto MTho SIgm SWas
Ileana	**See *A.* Rita = 'Zelido'**
Inca Hybrids	CB&S
King Cardinal	**See *A.* Princess Grace = 'Starodo'**
ligtu hybrids 🏆	CAvo CB&S CDoC CGle CHor CMea CPou CShe CTri EAst ECha ELan EMan EPfP ERav ETub LHop NNor NPer SDeJ SDix SPer SRms SWas WRus
¶ *ligtu* var. *ligtu*	LGre
'Little Eleanor'	COtt SBai SPla
magnifica RB 94012	MSto
Manon™	**See *A.* Princess Marie-Louise = 'Zelanon'**
Marie-Louise	**See *A.* Princess Marie-Louise = 'Zelanon'**
'Marina'	EBee LRHS MBri SBai
'Mars'	COtt LRHS SBai
Meyer Hybrids	MTho
♦ Mona Lisa	**See *A.* H.R.H. the Princess Alexandra = 'Stablaco'**
'Orange Gem' 🏆	COtt LRHS SBai
'Orange Glory' 🏆	COtt EBee LRHS SBai SPla
¶ *pallida*	CBro SSpi
– F&W 7241	SIgm
– JCA 12407	MSto
– JCA 14335	MSto SBla
patagonica P&W 6226	MFos NTow
§ *paupercula*	MSto
pelegrina	CMon MTho WCot
– 'Alba'	ELan
– 'Rosea'	ELan
'Pink Perfection'	COtt EBee LRHS MBri SBai SPla
presliana subsp. *australis* JCA 12590	MSto SSpi
– subsp. *presliana*	MSto SBla
– RB 94103	MSto WCot
♦ Princess Alice	**See *A.* Princess Alice = 'Staverpi'**
Princess Angela	LIck SSmt
♦ Princess Beatrix	**See *A.* Princess Beatrix = 'Stadoran'**
♦ Princess Carmina	**See *A.* Princess Carmina = 'Stasilva'**
♦ Princess Caroline	**See *A.* Princess Caroline = 'Staroko'**
Princess Charlotte	SSmt
♦ Princess Elizabeth	**See *A.* Queen Elizabeth The Queen Mother = 'Stamoli'**
♦ Princess Frederika	**See *A.* Princess Frederika = 'Stabronza'**
♦ Princess Grace	**See *A.* Princess Grace = 'Starodo'**
♦ Princess Marie-Louise	**See *A.* Princess Marie-Louise = 'Zelanon'**
♦ Princess Mira	**See *A.* Princess Mira = 'Stapripur'**
Princess Monica	LIck SSmt
Princess Ragna	SSmt
♦ Princess Sarah	**See *A.* Princess Sarah = 'Stalicamp'**
Princess Sissi	LIck SSmt
♦ Princess Sophia	**See *A.* Princess Sophia = 'Stajello'**
♦ Princess Victoria	**See *A.* Princess Victoria = 'Regina'**
Princess Zsa Zsa	LIck
pseudospathulata	MSto
¶ – RB 94010	WCot
§ *psittacina*	CBro CChu CGle CHad CHan CRDP CSpe ECro ELan EPar ERav EWoo GCal LHil LHop MSte NPSI NTow SLMG SSoC SSpi WFar WPGP WRus WSHC
– variegated	CRDP CSpe EGar ELan EMon EPPr NPla WCot
pulchella Sims	See *A. psittacina*
pulchra	SIgm
– BC&W 4751	CMon
– BC&W 4762	MSto SBla
pygmaea	EDAr EHyt MSto MTho SWas
♦ Queen Elizabeth the Queen Mother	**See *A.* Queen Elizabeth the Queen Mother = 'Stamoli'**
'Red Beauty'	LIck NBir SBai
'Red Elf'	COtt SBai
§ Princess Victoria = 'Regina'	SSmt
revoluta JCA 14378	CPou MSto
Sarah	**See *A.* Princess Sarah = 'Stalicamp'**
'Selina'	SBai
short purple	WCot
'Solent Arrow'	SBai
'Solent Candy'	MBri SBai WFar
'Solent Crest' 🏆	SBai
'Solent Dawn'	SBai
'Solent Glow'	SBai
'Solent Haze'	SBai
'Solent Mist'	SBai
'Solent Rose' 🏆	SBai
'Solent Wings'	MBri SBai
Sophia	**See *A.* Princess Sophia = 'Stajello'**
¶ *spathulata* RB 94015	WCot
'Spring Delight'	WCot
§ H.R.H. the Princess Alexandra = 'Stablaco'	SSmt

§ Princess Frederika = 'Stabronza' SSmt
§ Princess Beatrix = 'Stadoran' SSmt
§ Princess Sophia = 'Stajello' SSmt
§ Princess Sarah = 'Stalicamp' SSmt
§ Queen Elizabeth the Queen Mother = 'Stamoli' ♀ SPla SSmt
§ Princess Mira = 'Stapripur' ♀ SSmt
§ Princess Grace = 'Starodo' SSmt
§ Princess Caroline = 'Staroko' ♀ SSmt
§ Princess Carmina = 'Stasilva' ♀ SPla SSmt
§ Princess Alice = 'Staverpi' SSmt
'Sunstar' COtt SBai
¶ ***umbellata*** F&W 8497 SSpi
– JCA 14348 MSto
'Verona' COtt EBee SBai SPla
Victoria See **A. Princess Victoria = 'Regina'**
violacea See ***A. paupercula***
'White Apollo' EBee MBri SPla
'Yellow Friendship' ♀ COtt EBee LRHS MBri SBai SPla
Yellow King See **A. Princess Sophia = 'Stajello'**
§ Princess Marie-Louise = 'Zelanon' SPla SSmt

ALTHAEA (Malvaceae)
armeniaca EEls EMon GBuc GCal NCat
cannabina CRDP GBri GCal MAvo MFir MHlr MUlv NNor SOkh WCot WHoo WRus
officinalis CArn CHan CKin CSev ECoo ELan ELau EWFC GBar GPoy ILis LHol LHop MCLN MChe MGra MHew MMil MSal NDea NFai SIde SMad WApp WOak WPer WWye
officinalis alba MCLN NRai WHer WSan WWhi
§ –'Romney Marsh' GCal MRav MTol SAxl WCot WSHC
rosea See ***Alcea rosea***
rugosostellulata See ***Alcea rugosa***

ALTINGIA (Hamamelidaceae)
chinensis CMCN

ALYOGYNE (Malvaceae)
hakeifolia CSpe ERea LHil
§ ***huegelii*** CAbb CBrk EDAr EMan LCns LHil
– 'Santa Cruz' CB&S CSpe EOrc ERea LHop SMad SMrm SOWG SSoC

ALYSSOIDES (Brassicaceae)
utriculata CDoC CHor CMHG CNic EBar ELan LIck NBro NPri WBea WOve WPer WWin
– var. ***graeca*** MSte

ALYSSUM (Brassicaceae)
argenteum hort. See ***A. murale***
caespitosum NWCA
corymbosum See ***Aurinia corymbosa***
cuneifolium NMen WAbe
– var. ***pirinicum*** CLyd NGre
gemonense See ***Aurinia petraea***
idaeum LBee WThi
markgrafii CLyd LFlo WCot
montanum CArn ECha EGar ELan GAbr MWat SChu SRms
§ – 'Berggold' CB&S CTri EMan GAul GMaP LBee MLan NPri NRoo NVic SIde WLRN
♦ – Mountain Gold See ***A. montanum* 'Berggold'**
§ ***murale*** EGar NPri
oxycarpum EPot EWes LBee MFos SBla WAbe
petraeum See ***Aurinia petraea***
propinquum NWCA
pulvinare NGre WAbe
¶ ***purpureum*** EHyt
pyrenaicum NMen NWCA
repens NGre
saxatile See ***Aurinia saxatilis***
serpyllifolium CLyd MHig NWCA WIvy
spinosum CMea MBro MTho WAbe WFar
§ – 'Roseum' ♀ CMHG CShe ECha EHyt ELan EPot ESis LBee LHop MPla MWat NGre NMen NRoo NTow NWCA SBla WAbe WPat WPer WWin
stribrnyi NMen WIvy
tortuosum CLyd NMen WAbe
wulfenianum CMHG NPri NTow NWCA SIng

AMANA See **TULIPA**

× AMARCRINUM (Amaryllidaceae)
memoria-corsii CFil
– 'Howardii' CFil NRog

× AMARINE (Amaryllidaceae)
'Fletcheri' CMon
tubergenii LWoo NRog
– 'Zwanenburg' CAvo NRog

× AMARYGIA (Amaryllidaceae)
parkeri CFil NRog
§ – 'Alba' CAvo NRog

AMARYLLIS (Amaryllidaceae)
§ ***belladonna*** CB&S CBro CFil CHEx CMon CSpe EPar ERav ETub IHos LAma LBow MBri MUlv NRog SDeJ SSpi WCot
– 'Johannesburg' CAvo EMon ETub NRog
– 'Kimberley' EMon NRog
– 'Major' CAvo
♦ – 'Pallida' See ***A. belladonna* 'Elata'**
– 'Parkeri Alba' See **× *Amarygia parkeri* 'Alba'**
¶ – 'Purpurea' ETub

AMBROSIA (Asteraceae)
mexicana SIde

AMBROSINA (Araceae)
bassii S&L 315 CMon

AMELANCHIER † (Rosaceae)

alnifolia	CAgr CPle EPla ESim GAul WWat
arborea	WNor
bartramiana	SSta
canadensis	CLnd CPle CTho EBre ELan EMil GOrc GRei ISea LHop LHyr LNet MBar NHol NRog NRoo NWea SHBN SPer SSta WDin WFar WHCG WNor WPat WRTC WStI WWat
– 'Micropetala'	MUlv NHol
florida	See ***A. alnifolia*** var. ***semi-integrifolia***
× ***grandiflora*** 'Autumn Brilliance'	CEnd
– 'Ballerina' ♀	CB&S CDoC CEnd CMCN CPMA CSPN EBre ELan ESim LNet LPan MAsh MBri MGos MWat NBee NHol SHBN SPer SPla SSta WDin WHCG WPat WWat
¶ – 'Robin Hill'	LPan SMad
– 'Rubescens'	CEnd CPMA
laevis	CB&S CBlo CChu MBal NNor SPer
lamarckii ♀	CAgr CB&S CChu CDoC CEnd CPMA CSpe EBre ELan ENot IHos IOrc LBuc LHyr MAsh MGos NFla NSti NWea SHBN SPer SReu SSpi SSta WDin WOrn WPyg WStI WWat
I ***ovalis*** 'Edelweiss'	CBlo CEnd COtt CPMA LRHS SBid SMur SSta
pumila	CB&S CBlo CPle GAul GBin GDra LHop MBal MPla MSte NHol NTow WAbe WNor
rotundifolia 'Helvetia'	CEnd
'Snowflake'	CBlo CEnd CPMA LRHS SBid SSta
¶ ***spicata***	CBlo

AMICIA (Papilionaceae)

zygomeris	CAbb CBot CPle GBuc GCal GCra LHil SBid SMrm SSoC WEas WWye

AMMI (Apiaceae)

majus	CArn MSal
visnaga	MSal

AMMOCHARIS (Amaryllidaceae)

coranica	WChr

AMMOPHILA (Poaceae)

arenaria	ECWi GQui

AMOMUM (Zingiberaceae)

cardamomum	See ***A. compactum***

AMOMYRTUS (Myrtaceae)

§ ***luma***	CGre CLan CMHG CPle CTrw EPfP ISea MAll SArc WBod WWat

AMORPHA (Papilionaceae)

canescens	CB&S CBlo CFai CPle EBee EPfP NPSI NRog NSti SBid SEND SHhN SIng
fruticosa	CAgr CB&S CPle IOrc NRog SHFr

AMORPHOPHALLUS (Araceae)

bulbifer	LAma WCru
kiusianus	CFil

AMPELODESMOS (Poaceae)

mauritanicus	EHoe ETPC GBin MCCP NHol WChe WLRN

AMPELOPSIS † (Vitaceae)

aconitifolia	CPlN CWan
¶ ***arborea***	CPlN
¶ ***bodinieri***	CPlN
◆ ***brevipedunculata***	See ***A. glandulosa*** var. ***brevipedunculata***
¶ ***chaffanjonii***	CPlN SMur
§ ***glandulosa*** var. ***brevipedunculata***	CB&S GAri SIgm SPer WCru WDin WOMN
§ – – 'Elegans' (v)	CB&S CMac CPlN EBre ECtt ELan EPla LHol LHop LNet MBar MGos MRav NHol NRog SAga SBra SEas SHBN SPer SPla SSta WDin WFar WPat WRTC WSHC WStI
– – 'Tricolor'	See ***A. glandulosa*** var. ***brevipedunculata*** **'Elegans'**
– var. ***hancei*** B&SWJ 1793	WCru
– var. ***heterophylla*** B&SWJ 667	WCru
* – var. ***maximowiczii***	CPlN
henryana	See ***Parthenocissus henryana***
megalophylla	CB&S CBot CChu CGre CPlN EPla ETen GBin WCru WHCr WWat
¶ ***orientalis***	CPlN
sempervirens hort.	See ***Cissus striata***
sinica	WCru
sp. Taiwan B&SWJ 1173	WCru
¶ ***thunbergii***	CPlN
– B&SWJ 1863	WCru
tricuspidata 'Veitchii'	See ***Parthenocissus tricuspidata*** **'Veitchii'**

AMPHICOME See INCARVILLEA

AMSONIA (Apocynaceae)

ciliata	CFir LFis LGre SMrm SSvw WCot WFar WMer WPer
illustris	EBee EMon MSte WCot
§ ***orientalis*** ♀	CDec CHad CMil CVer ECha EPar ERea LHop MRav SAxl SCro SMrm SVen SWas WFar WOld WWin
tabernaemontana	CFir CHan CLyd EBar EBre ECro ELan EMan EMil EMon GBuc MMil MNrw SAga SHel SRms SWas WCot WFar
– var. ***salicifolia***	CShe EBre ECha ECro

AMYGDALUS See PRUNUS

ANACAMPTIS (Orchidaceae)

¶ ***pyramidalis***	SWes

ANACYCLUS (Asteraceae)

pyrethrum	GPoy
– var. ***depressus***	CGle EBre EHyt ELan EMNN ESis GAbr GMaP GTou LHop MHig NGre NMen NNor NVic NWCA SBla SIng WAbe WFar WHoo WOMN WPer WWin
– – 'Golden Gnome'	EBar LFis WRHF

– – 'Silberkissen' WDav WHil

ANAGALLIS (Primulaceae)

alternifolia var. *repens* CLyd SSca
arvensis ECWi EWFC MHew MSal WEas
– var. *caerulea* EWFC
foemina ECWi MSal
linifolia See *A. monellii* subsp. *linifolia*
§ *monellii* ♀ ELan EPot SBla SMrm SRms SUsu WCla WOMN WWin
§ – subsp. *linifolia* EHyt
– 'Sunrise' CPBP MHig MTho SUsu WOMN
'Skylover' EMan WLRN
tenella ECWi EWFC LFis NHar SIng
– 'Studland' ♀ CInt EPot NMen NNrd NWCA SBla SIng SSca WAbe WFar WOMN

ANANAS (Bromeliaceae)

comosus var. *variegatus* MBri

ANAPHALIS (Asteraceae)

alpicola EPot NCat NMen NTow
margaritacea CBot ECtt EFou GBin GCHN GMaP MBri NBro NCGP NOak NSti SIde SRms SSca SSpe WBea WByw WCot WFar
§ – var. *cinnamomea* CGle CHan ECED ELan EMon NHol SCro WEas
§ – 'Neuschnee' CTri LFis NHol NMir NPri NRoo SPla SSca WBea WMaN WPer WRHF
♦ – New Snow See *A. margaritacea* 'Neuschnee'
§ – var. *yedoensis* ♀ CBre CTri EBee ECha ECoo ECot EGle EPar MWat SDix SPer WHil WLRN WRHF
nepalensis B&SWJ 1634 GCra
§ – var. *monocephala* CGle ELan EMon MWat NSti
– – CC&McK 550 GCHN
nubigena See *A. nepalensis* var. *monocephala*
sinica subsp. *morii* ECha LBuc
triplinervis ♀ CBre CGle CShe EAst EBre EFol EFou ELan ESiP GDra GMaP MRav NBro NFla NHol NNor NVic SCro SSpe SWat WByw WEas WFar WHoo WOld WRus WTyr WWin
– var. *intermedia* See *A. nepalensis*
§ – 'Sommerschnee' ♀ CHor EBre ECha ECot ECtt EHal EOrc MBri MCLN MHFP MTis NCat NNor SAga SPer WBea WElm WGwG WPer
♦ – Summer Snow See *A. triplinervis* 'Sommerschnee'
yedoensis See *A. margaritacea* var. *yedoensis*

ANARRHINUM (Scrophulariaceae)

bellidifolium CMdw GAul MGrG NCGP NPri WPer

ANCHUSA (Boraginaceae)

angustissima See *A. leptophylla* subsp. *incana*
arvensis EWFC MHew
§ *azurea* NCut NOrc WPer
– 'Blue Angel' CBlo EMan EWll WLRN
– 'Dropmore' CBlo CDoC CMdw NBus NOrc NPer SIde SRms SWat WBea WOve WPer WRus WWhi
– 'Feltham Pride' CBot GMaP MLan NPer NRoo WFar WHoo WPer WPyg
– 'Little John' CSWP EBre ECot GLil SPer SRms SWat WMer
– 'Loddon Royalist' ♀ CArc CB&S CDoC CGle CShe CSpe EBre ECED EFou ELan LHop MBri MWat NFla NRoo SChu SPer SWat WCra WHow WMer WOve WRus WWin
– 'Morning Glory' CBlo LFis
– 'Opal' CArc CBlo CGle EBee ECot EFou EMan GCal LHop MMil MWat NRoo SChu SMrm SPla WLRN
– 'Royal Blue' CPou MLan WMer
barrelieri WPer
caespitosa hort. See *A. leptophylla* subsp. *incana*
capensis WPer
cespitosa Lamarck ♀ EHyt ELan EPot EWes LCom LHop SBla
italica See *A. azurea*
laxiflora See *Borago pygmaea*
§ *leptophylla* subsp. *incana* CRDP GBri NChi WCot
myosotidiflora See *Brunnera macrophylla*
officinalis CArn CJew CWan EJud EWFC LHol MHew MSal SHDw SIde
sempervirens See *Pentaglottis sempervirens*
undulata SIgm

ANDROCYMBIUM (Colchicaceae)

europaeum MS 510 CMon
gramineum SB&L 26 CMon
punicum S&L 325 CMon
¶ *rechingeri* CMon

ANDROMEDA (Ericaceae)

glaucophylla CMHG IOrc MBar
polifolia CMHG CSam EBre EMil IOrc WBod WFar
– 'Alba' EBre EDen ELan MAsh MBal MBar MBlu MDun MGos MHig MPla NHar SBod SPer SSta WDav WPat WPyg
– 'Blue Ice' LRHS
– 'Compacta' ♀ CHor EBre ELan EMil EPot GCHN MAsh MBal MBar MBri MGos MPla NHar NHol NMen SChu SPer SReu WPat WPyg WSHC WWin
– 'Grandiflora' CSte ELan ITim MBal MDun MGos SBod
– 'Kirigamine' CSte ELan MAsh MBal MBri MGos MHig NHol WPat WPyg NHar
– 'Macrophylla' ♀ EPot GDra ITim MBal MDun MHig NHar NHed NHol SIng SSta WAbe WPat WPyg
– 'Major' MBal
– 'Minima' MBal
– 'Nana' ELan EPot LNet MAsh MGos MHig SPer STre WLRN WStI WWat WWeb
– 'Nikko' CBlo EBar GBuc MBal MGos MHig NHar NHol SPer WPat WPyg
– 'Red Winter' CBlo CNic CRos CSte
– 'Shibutsu' GAri MGos MPla SSta

ANDROPOGON (Poaceae)

gerardii	EBee EHoe EMon ETPC WPer
◆ *ischaemum*	See ***Bothriochloa ischaemum***
saccharoides	ETPC
scoparius	See ***Schizachyrium scoparium***

ANDROSACE (Primulaceae)

albana	CLyd EWes NWCA WHil
armeniaca var. *macrantha*	NWCA
barbulata	GCHN
cantabrica	EHyt
carnea	CLyd CMea GCHN MTho NHar NHol NMen SAlw WCla WHil
carnea alba	LBee MBro NGre NHar WHoo
carnea 'Andorra'	EHyt WAbe
– subsp. *brigantiaca*	CLyd GTou NGre NHar NMen NRya NSla NWCA WAbe
– var. *halleri*	See ***A. carnea*** subsp. ***rosea***
– subsp. *laggeri* 🏆	EMNN EPot GTou NHar NSla WPat
– x *pyrenaica*	CGra EHyt EPot GCHN GDra NHar NMen NWCA WAbe WPat
§ – subsp. *rosea* 🏆	CPBP GDra NTow NWCA SIng WCla
ciliata	CGra GTou MRPP NMen NTow WAbe
cylindrica	CGra GCHN GDra GTou NGre NHar NMen SBla WFar
– x *hirtella*	GDra GTou NGre NHar NWCA SIng WAbe
delavayi	NWCA
¶ *foliosa*	EHyt
geraniifolia	ECha GCHN SAlw WAbe WCru
globifera	EHyt NHar
hausmannii	CGra GCHN GTou NGre
hedraeantha	CMea EPot NGre WAbe
x *heeri*	EPot
– 'Alba'	EHyt EPot GCHN GCLN ITim
himalaica	EHyt
hirtella	CPBP GCHN GTou MRPP NGre NHar NTow
jacquemontii	See ***A. villosa*** var. ***jacquemontii***
lactea	GCHN GTou NGre
§ *lactiflora*	WHil
§ *laevigata*	GCLN
– var. *ciliolata*	GTou NWCA
¶ – – NNS 94-38	MRPP
§ – var. *laevigata* 'Packwood'	CGra
lanuginosa 🏆	CLyd CMHG CPBP CShe EHyt ELan EPot LBee MHig MWat NGre NMen NWCA SBla WWin
– compact form	EPot
– 'Leichtlinii'	EHic
– 'Wisley Variety'	SIgm
limprichtii	See ***A. sarmentosa*** var. ***watkinsii***
mathildae	CGra GTou NNrd NTow NWCA
– x *carnea*	NMen
microphylla	See ***A. mucronifolia* Watt**
mollis	See ***A. sarmentosa*** var. ***yunnanensis***
§ *montana*	CGra MFos NWCA
mucronifolia CHP&W 296	NWCA
– hort.	See ***A. sempervivoides***
– x *sempervivoides*	EHyt EPot
§ – Watt	EPot GTou ITim NGre
muscoidea	GCLN NTow NWCA WAbe
– C&R 188	GTou
¶ – var. *longiscapa*	NWCA
¶ – var. *muscoidea*	CGra
– Schacht's form	CPBP EHyt
– SEP 132	EHyt
§ *nivalis*	MFos NTow
primuloides Duby	NCat
– hort.	See ***A. sarmentosa***
pubescens	CGra EPot GCHN GDra NHar SBla SIng WAbe
pyrenaica	CGra GCHN GCLN GTou ITim NGre NHar NTow NWCA SBla WAbe
rigida ACE 2336	EPot
¶ – KGB 168	EPot
robusta var. *breviscapa*	CGra MHig NWCA
rotundifolia	GCHN GTou WCru WRHF
salicifolia	See ***A. lactiflora***
§ *sarmentosa* 🏆	EHyt ELan GTou ITim LBee MBro MFir MHig MWat NGre NMen NNrd SChu SOkh SSmi WAbe WCla WEas WHoo WPyg
– 'Brilliant'	CNic
– CC 407	MRPP
– 'Chumbyi'	ESis MBro MOne MRPP NHol NTow NWCA SBla SIng SRms WHil WPat WPer
§ – 'Salmon's Variety'	CMea CTri NTow SIgm
– 'Sherriff's'	CMHG CShe CTri GCHN MBro NHar NTow SBla SIgm SIng SRms WDav
§ – var. *watkinsii*	EPot NHar NMen NNrd SIng WDav
§ – var. *yunnanensis*	CPBP MBro MHig SIgm SIng
§ *sempervivoides* 🏆	CLyd ECha EHyt ELan EPot GCHN GDra LBee MBro MHig NGre NHar NHed NHol NMen NWCA SAlw SBod SIgm SIng SSmi WAbe WDav WHil WHoo WOMN WPat WPyg WWin
– scented form	MBro
sericea	NWCA
spinulifera	SIng
studiosorum	GCHN
* *studiosorum album*	EHyt
vandellii	CGra EHyt GBin GCHN GTou MHig NGre NHar NWCA WAbe WDav
villosa	LRHS MHig WAbe WHil
– var. *arachnoidea* 'Superba'	EPot NMen
§ – var. *jacquemontii*	EHyt MNrw NHar NMen NNrd NTow SBla SIgm
¶ – – lilac form	EPot
– – pink	EPot
villosa taurica	CLyd EPot
vitaliana	See ***Vitaliana primuliflora***
watkinsii	See ***A. sarmentosa*** var. ***watkinsii***
¶ *yargongensis* ACE 1722	EPot NHar

ANDRYALA (Asteraceae)

agardhii	NMen NTow NWCA SSca WOMN
lanata	See ***Hieracium lanatum***

ANEMARRHENA (Asphodelaceae)

asphodeloides	EBee MSal WCot

ANEMIA (Schizaeaceae)

phyllitidis	NMar

ANEMONE † (Ranunculaceae)

altaica	GAbr MEas MSal NRoo SRms WHil WOld
'Andrea Atkinson'	EBee EGar LBuc MNFA NHol NSti WHoo WLRN
apennina 🏆	EPar SCro
– var. ***albiflora***	WChr
– 'Petrovac' CE&H 538	EPot WChr
baicalensis	EHic GLil
baldensis	CGle CPou LBee LHop NMen NOak SRms WOMN
biarmiensis	See ***A. narcissiflora*** subsp. ***biarmiensis***
blanda 🏆	EOrc LAma LHop MBri MBro MCLN MHig NFla NNrd NRog SChu WCot WFar WPat WPer
– blue	CAvo CBro CMea CTri ELan EPot ETub GAbr LAma MBri MBro MHlr MNFA NGar WPat
– 'Charmer'	CMil EBar EPar EPot NMen WPat
– 'Ingramii' 🏆	EMan EPar LAma LFis MBal MBro NNrd NRog WPat WRHF
– 'Ingramii' CE&H 626	WChr
– 'Pink Star'	CBro EBar EPot LAma NBir NRog WRus
– 'Radar' 🏆	CBro CMea CTri EPar EPot LAma NBir NRog
– var. ***rosea*** 🏆	CAvo ELan LAma WPer
– 'Violet Star'	CBro EPot MNFA
– 'White Splendour' 🏆	CAvo CBro CGle CMea ECha ELan EOrc EPar EPot ETub GAbr LAma LFis MBro MCLN MNFA MNrw NGar NMen NNrd NRog SChu WHil WPat WPer WRus
'Bodnant Burgundy'	LRHS
canadensis	CElw CNic CRDP CSpe MNrw NWoo WCot
caroliniana	CGle EBre EPot ESis GBuc NRoo
¶ ***coronaria***	EPot
– 'Craegh Castle'	LIck
– De Caen Group	CRDP CSut LAma WFar
– – forms	NRog
§ – – 'Die Braut'	CGle CRDP NRog
– – 'His Excellency'	See ***A. coronaria* (De Caen Group) 'Hollandia'**
§ – – 'Hollandia'	CRDP EPot ETub SUsu
– – 'Mister Fokker'	CRDP EPot ETub LAma NRog
♦ – – The Bride	See ***A. coronaria* (De Caen Group) 'Die Braut'**
– – 'The Governor'	GSki NCat NRog SUsu
– (Mona Lisa Group) 'Sylphide'	CRDP EPot NRog
– MS 783	CMon
– MS&CL 613	CMon
– Saint Brigid Group	CSut ETub LAma MBri NRog SDeJ
– – 'Lord Lieutenant'	NBir NCat NRog SUsu
– – 'Mount Everest'	NBir NCat
– – 'The Admiral'	ETub MNrw NBir NCat NRog
– Saint Piran Group	SDeJ
crinita	SMrm WDav WThi
cylindrica	CFir CGle CMHG CSWP EMon MNrw
decapetala	GCal WCot
demissa	NRya WHil
drummondii	MCli MHig WCla
¶ ***elongata*** B&SWJ 2975	WCru
fasciculata	See ***A. narcissiflora***

flaccida	CBro CRDP LGre LHop SIng WCot WCru WFar
× ***fulgens***	ECha NWCA SAlw
– 'Annulata Grandiflora'	CMon
– 'Multipetala'	NRog
– Saint Bavo Group	CBro ECGP
globosa	See ***A. multifida***
'Guernica'	GBuc WHil
hepatica	See ***Hepatica nobilis***
§ ***hortensis***	CMon SBla SMad SMrm WWat
hortensis alba	CMon
hortensis subsp. ***heldreichii***	WThi
– MS 958	CMon
§ ***hupehensis***	CBlo CBot LFis NOrc WCot
§ – 'Bowles' Pink'	CBlo CMil CRDP LGan MBri MWat SAxl SSca SWas WCot WCru WHoo
– 'Crispa'	CRDP WPbr
– 'Eugenie'	CGle CMil
– 'Hadspen Abundance' 🏆	Widely available
§ – var. ***japonica***	CBos CGle CPou EAst EGar GCal NMir NNor NPla SPer SSpi WCru WEas
§ – – 'Bressingham Glow'	CMHG CShe EBre ECtt ELan EOrc EPot LHop MBri MNFA MRav NHol NOrc NRoo NVic SPer WAbb WFar WGwG WOld
♦ – – Prince Henry	See ***A. hupehensis*** var. ***japonica* 'Prinz Heinrich'**
§ – – 'Prinz Heinrich' 🏆	CB&S CHad CMil EBar ECha EFou EJap EPfP LGre LHop MBel MBri MBro MCLN MRav MTis NCut NRoo SAxl SPer SPla SSpi WFar WHal WHoo WOld
– 'Praecox'	CMea EFou EGol GBri LHop MBri MCLN MCli NHol NRoo NSti SChu SCro SLod WAbb WCru WGwG WHal WWin
– 'Rosenschale'	GCal MBal MBri NRoo WFar
– 'September Charm' 🏆	CB&S CDoC ECha EFou ELan EOrc EPfP LHop MBri MCli MNFA MNrw NSti NTow SPer SSoC SWat WCra WCru WGwG WPyg
– 'Splendens'	CBlo EAst EBee EFou EMan MBri NCut WAbb WBro WFar WHal WPyg WRHF
§ × ***hybrida***	CAvo CGle IHos MBro NOak SChu SPla WCru WHil WHoo WOld WRHF
– 'Alba' hort. (UK)	See ***A.* × *hybrida* 'Honorine Jobert'**
♦ – 'Alba' hort. (USA)	See ***A.* × *hybrida* 'Lady Ardilaun'**
– 'Bowles' Pink'	See ***A. hupehensis* 'Bowles' Pink'**
– 'Bressingham Glow'	See ***A. hupehensis*** var. ***japonica* 'Bressingham Glow'**
– 'Coupe d'Argent'	EGar NRoo
– 'Elegans'	EFou EGar MCli MRav SWat
§ – 'Géante des Blanches' 🏆	CBlo CLon ECtt EGar GCal NRoo WHow
§ – 'Honorine Jobert' 🏆	Widely available
§ – 'Königin Charlotte' 🏆	CB&S CGle CMHG CMea CSte ECha EFou EGol ELan LHop MBel MBri MTis NBir NHol NMir NRoo SBla SChu SEas SMad SPer SSpi WHil WHoo WRus WWat WWeb

– 'Kriemhilde'	EJap GCal WCru
– 'Lady Gilmour'	See **A.** × ***hybrida* 'Margarete'**
– 'Loreley'	CBlo CMea EBee GCal NTow SPer WCot
– 'Luise Uhink'	CBlo CDoC CGle CHor CPou EBre NBir SSpi WEas
§ – 'Margarete'	CBlo CDec CPou ECtt EGol EJap EOrc GCal MWat NBir SChu SCro SLod WHoo
– 'Max Vogel'	CDoC WBcn WCot
– 'Monterosa'	CBos CGle CMil CPou EBre ELan GCal MBal NBir NCut WCot WCru WKif
– 'Pamina'	CAvo CBos CGle CMil CRDP EBee EBre EFou EGar EGol GCal LFis LGre MBri MBro MHlr NPri NTow SAxl SHar WCot WCru WElm WFar WHil WHoo WOld WPyg WRus
◆ – Prince Henry	See **A. *hupehensis*** var. ***japonica* 'Prinz Heinrich'**
– 'Prinz Heinrich'	See **A. *hupehensis*** var. ***japonica* 'Prinz Heinrich'**
– 'Profusion'	MHlr NCut SAxl SHBN WCot WOld WPyg WRus
◆ – Queen Charlotte	See **A.** × ***hybrida* 'Königin Charlotte'**
– 'Richard Ahrends'	EBee EGle EGol EMan LHop MBel MBri MCli MMil MNFA NCat NHol NRoo SAxl SCro SMad SMrm SWas SWat WAbe WCru WGer WGwG WHow
– 'Rosenschale'	CBos WCru WOld
– 'Rotkäppchen'	CLon GCal LBuc NBrk SAxl
§ – 'Superba'	SBla WKif
* – 'Thomas Ahrens'	CLon
§ – 'Whirlwind'	Widely available
– 'White Queen'	See **A.** × ***hybrida* 'Géante des Blanches'**
◆ – Wirbelwind	See **A.** × ***hybrida* 'Whirlwind'**
japonica	See **A.** × ***hybrida***
× ***lesseri***	CGle CLyd CNic EBre ECha ELan EPri GAbr GMac LHop MBri MBro NNrd NSti NWoo SAlw SBla SPer WAbe WCru WHil WHoo WWin
leveillei	CRDP CSpe EBre EGar ELan GLil MFir MHar NRoo SIgm WCot WCru WSan
§ × ***lipsiensis***	CAvo CBro CHad CLon CRDP EBre ECha EFol EHyt EPar EPot GCHN LGre MHig MNFA MTho NGar NTow NWCA SWas WAbe WCru
– 'Pallida'	CRDP MNFA WAbe WCot
N ***magellanica*** hort.	See **A. *multifida***
§ ***multifida***	CGle CMea EBar EBre ECha EEls EFol ELan EPot GTou LGan LHop MBal MBro MNrw NGre NNor NOak NRoo SIng WEas WHil WHoo WPat WPbr WWhi WWin
– var. ***globosa***	WWhi
– 'Major'	CFir CLon CLyd CNic CRDP GAbr LGan MBro NHol NWCA SBla
– red	CFir NNor NRoo NSla WHil
§ ***narcissiflora***	GSki LSyl NHar NRoo WHil
nemorosa ♀	CBro CElw CGle CKin EBre ECWi EPar EPot ETub EWFC LAma LBow LGan LSyl MBal MSal NGar NHar NHol SIng SSpi WFar WHil WMer WShi
N – 'Alba Plena'	CAvo CBro CSWP ECha EPot ERos ETub GMac MHig MTho NCat NMGW NNrd NRar NTow SIng SUsu WAbb WChr WCru WEas WIvy WRus
– 'Allenii' ♀	CBro ECha EHyt EPot ERos GMac LGre LWoo MBal MNFA NGar NHar NMen NRya NTow SIng SSpi SWas WAbe WChr WCot WCru
– 'Amy Doncaster'	WCot
– 'Atrocaerulea'	EPar EPot GBuc IBlr MNFA NGar NHol
– 'Blue Beauty'	EPot IBlr LWoo MBal NGar NHol NMen NNrd WAbe WCru
– 'Blue Bonnet'	CElw GBuc WCot
– 'Blue Queen'	EPot
– 'Bowles' Purple'	EPar EPot NGar NHar NRya NTow WAbe WChr WCru WFar WIvy
– 'Bracteata Pleniflora'	ECha EPot LHop MBal NGar NRya NWoo SBla WAbe
– 'Caerulea'	EPot
– 'Cedric's Pink'	SBla
– 'Danica'	MBal WAbe
– 'Dee Day'	GBuc LWoo SBla SWas
– double with a blue eye	LWoo
– 'Flore Pleno'	EBre EHic EHyt EOrc EPar MBal MBro NGar WAbe WMaN
– forms	CMon
– 'Green Fingers'	EPot LGre MTho NGar WChr WCru
– 'Hannah Gubbay'	EBee EPar IBlr LWoo MBal SIng WAbe
– 'Hilda'	EPar EPot LWoo MBal NNrd NRya NTow WAbe
– 'Knightshayes Vestal' (d)	WCot
– 'Lady Doneraile'	ECha LWoo NTow
– 'Leeds' Variety' ♀	CRDP EPot LGre MTho NGar NHar NHol SBla WChr
– 'Lychette'	CAvo EPar EPot IBlr LGre MBal NTow
– 'Monstrosa'	EBee EPar EPot WCot
– 'Pentre Pink'	IBlr MTho WAbe WChr WIvy
– pink	LGre
– × ***ranunculoïdes***	See **A.** × ***lipsiensis***
– 'Robinsoniana' ♀	Widely available
– 'Rosea'	CGle EPot LAma NHol WChr
– 'Royal Blue'	CNic CRDP ECha EPot GBuc LAma LWoo NHol SBla WAbe WCru WFar
– 'Vestal' ♀	CElw CGle CRDP EBre EMon EPot ERos GBuc LGre LWoo MNFA NFla NGar NMGW NMen NRya SBar SBla WBon
– 'Virescens'	NGar
– 'Viridiflora'	CRDP LGre MBri MTho WChr WCot WCru
– 'Wilks' Giant'	WCot
– 'Wilks' White'	EBee EPar EPot MBal
– 'Wyatt's Pink'	CAvo LGre LWoo WAbe
obtusiloba	CRDP GDra GTou MTho NHar SBla SWas WAbe WCot
obtusiloba alba	CRDP GDra NHar NHol NMen SBla

palmata	EBee NSla WCru
– 'Alba'	CMon
– MS 413	CMon
parviflora	SAlw
patens	See ***Pulsatilla patens***
pavonina	ERos MTho SWas WThi
polyanthes	GTou WThi
pulsatilla	See ***Pulsatilla vulgaris***
ranunculoides ♀	Widely available
– 'Pleniflora'	CAvo CRDP ECha EPar EPot LWoo MHlr NGar SBla WCot
rivularis	CAvo CBro CElw CGle CHan CRDP EBre ECha EMon EPot GMac LFlo LHop MBro MNrw NHar NHol NNor NOak NRoo SAxl SSpi SUsu SWas WAbe WDav WHoo WKif WOld WThi
¶ – CLD 573	WDav
rupicola	GCra NBir
× ***seemannii***	See ***A.*** × ***lipsiensis***
* ***sherriffii***	WCru
stellata	See ***A. hortensis***
sulphurea	See ***Pulsatilla alpina*** subsp. ***apiifolia***
sylvestris	Widely available
§ – 'Elise Fellmann' (d)	CRDP EFou WCot
– 'Flore Pleno'	See ***A. sylvestris* 'Elise Fellmann'**
– 'Macrantha'	CRDP EBee LWoo MHlr
tetrasepala	GCra SSca
§ ***tomentosa***	CGle CMGP ECha GLil MSte NHol NRoo SCro SMrm SRms SWat WBea WCot WEas WGwG WHow WWhi
– 'Robustissima'	CDoC CGle EFou EHic GMaP LHop MBri MBro MCli MNFA MOne MRav MTis SHBN SPer SPla WAbb WMer
trifolia	CRDP ECha EPot MBal NMen SUsu
trullifolia	CRDP EDAr NHar SBla
trullifolia alba	GTou LWoo
trullifolia blue form	GTou
– SBEC 797	NHol NTow
vernalis	See ***Pulsatilla vernalis***
virginiana	CFir EBee GBin GLil MSte WCot WCru WOve
§ ***vitifolia*** De Candolle	CBos
– B&SWJ 1452	WCru
– B&SWJ 2320	WCru
– CC&McK 43	CGle
– hort.	See ***A. tomentosa***

ANEMONELLA (Ranunculaceae)

thalictroides	CFir CGra CRDP CSpe EBee EFEx EPar LAma LWoo NGar NHar NHol NMen NRog NTow SBla SWas WAbe WChr WFar WIvy
¶ – 'Alba Plena'	NHar
– 'Cameo'	EFEx GCrs MFos MS&S
– 'Double Green'	EFEx
¶ – double pink	NHar
– 'Full Double White'	EFEx
– 'Green Hurricane'	EFEx
¶ – 'Oscar Schoaf' (d)	NHar
– pink	CBos CRDP EHyt LWoo NRog
– semi-double white	CRDP EHyt LWoo SBla WIvy

ANEMONOPSIS (Ranunculaceae)

macrophylla	CBro CPou CRDP EBre ECha GCra LGre MTho NTow SBla SHel WCot WCru WEas WOMN

ANEMOPAEGMA (Bignoniaceae)

chamberlaynii	CPlN

ANEMOPSIS (Saururaceae)

¶ ***californica***	CRDP

ANETHUM (Apiaceae)

graveolens	CArn EOHP GPoy LHol MChe MGra MHew SIde WCer WPer WSel WWye
– 'Dukat'	CJew CSev ELau GPoy MChe
– 'Fern Leaved'	WJek
– 'Sowa'	EOHP

ANGELICA (Apiaceae)

acutiloba	SIgm
archangelica	CArn CGle CSev ECha EEls EFou ELan EMar GAbr GPoy LHol MBri MChe MGra MHew NBro NFai NRoo SChu SIde SWat WOak WOve WPer WWhi WWye
– 'Corinne Tremaine'	WHer
atropurpurea	CBot EGar MSal SWat WCHb
curtisii	See ***A. triquinata***
gigas	CArc CBos CBot CBre CGle CHad CRDP CSpe ECha EFou IBlr LGre LHol MHlr MSte SIgm SSoC SWat WCHb WHal WHer WHil WPer WSan WWye
* ***hispanica***	CRDP
montana	See ***A. sylvestris***
pachycarpa	SDix SIgm SWat WCot
§ ***sylvestris***	CAgr CArn CKin CTiv EWFC GBar LHol MSal SWat WGwy WHer
* – 'Purpurea'	CMea SApp
taiwaniana	SWat
'Vicar's Mead'	IBlr

ANIGOZANTHOS (Haemodoraceae)

'Bush Ranger'	CB&S
flavidus	CHan CTrC MBri SOWG WCot WOMN
– red	ERav SSoC
– yellow	LHil
* ***humilis*** ♀	MSto
manglesii ♀	CSev CTrC MLan SVen WPer WRha
– 'Bush Dawn'	CB&S

ANISODONTEA (Malvaceae)

§ ***capensis***	CB&S CBar CBrk CSpe ELan ERea IBlr LHil LHop NBir NBrk SChu SMrm SOWG SVen WBod WEas WWin
elegans	CSpe LHil
huegelii	See ***Alyogyne huegelii***
× ***hypomadara*** hort.	See ***A. capensis***
§ – (Sprague) Bates	CMHG CSev ECtt EOrc LBlm LPan NPer NTow SEas SMad SRms WOMN WOld WPer WRus
julii	CSpe LHil MCCP NRai SMad WSan

malvastroides CBrk CSev EWoo LHil LHop
scabrosa CAbb CChe CChu EMil SAga SBid

ANISOTOME (Apiaceae)
¶ *haastii* SIgm
imbricata GDra
¶ *latifolia* CTrC

ANNONA (Annonaceae)
¶ *muricata* (F) LBlo
¶ *squamosa* (F) LBlo

ANODA (Malvaceae)
cristata 'Opal Cup' EBar EMon WBea

ANOIGANTHUS See CYRTANTHUS

ANOMATHECA (Iridaceae)
cruenta See ***A. laxa***
§ *laxa* CFee CMHG CNic CSpe CVer ECha ELan EPot ERos ETub LBee LGre MNrw MTho NMen SBar SDix SSca SSpi WAbe WCla WFar WHil WOMN WPat WPer WWin
– var. *alba* CSpe ELan EPot ERos LBee LBlm LGre MHar MTho NMen SSpi WAbe WHoo WOMN WWeb
– *alba-maculata* CMHG
– 'Joan Evans' EPot ERos SRms WAbe
– redspot SSpi
viridis CAvo CMon CPou LBow MNrw NMGW

ANOPTERUS (Escalloniaceae)
glandulosus CHEx IBlr WCru

ANREDERA (Basellaceae)
§ *cordifolia* CPlN LBow WCot WPer

ANTENNARIA (Asteraceae)
aprica See ***A. parvifolia***
dioica CTri ECro ELan GCHN GPoy LHol MBro MFir NBus SRms WCla WFar WHil WPyg WWye
– 'Alba' EHoe GAbr NRya WFar
– 'Alex Duguid' GTou SBla
– 'Aprica' See ***A. parvifolia***
§ – var. ***hyperborea*** LGro SSmi WAbe
– 'Minima' EPot GDra MHig MPla MWat NBro NHar NMen NNrd SIng WAbe
– 'Nyewoods Variety' CNic EPot GDra MHig NTow
– red SIng
– var. ***rosea*** See ***A. microphylla***
* – 'Rubra' CTri ECha EPPr ESis GAri GLil NMen NNrd SBla SHel SSmi WAbe WHen
dioica tomentosa See ***A. dioica*** var. ***hyperborea***
macrophylla hort. See ***A. microphylla***
§ *microphylla* 🏆 CMHG ELan EMNN LGro MBar MFir NHar NMen NRya NWCA SBod SIng SRms SSmi WBea WEas WPat WPer
– 'Plena' SRms
* – var. ***rosea*** WWhi
neglecta var. ***gaspensis*** SIng
§ *parvifolia* CLyd CNic CTri EPot ESis GCHN GDra LBee LFis MBar MPla NHar NNrd SBod SIng WAbe WCla WHil WPer WWin
– var. ***rosea*** See ***A. microphylla***
¶ *plantaginifolia* WCot
¶ *rosea* 🏆 NVic

ANTHEMIS (Asteraceae)
aizoon See ***Achillea ageratifolia*** subsp. ***aizoon***
arvensis ECWi
biebersteinii See ***A. marschalliana***
carpatica CGle GCHN NBro NWoo SIgm
– 'Karpatenschnee' CM&M MCli
cretica CBlo
¶ – subsp. ***cretica*** NS 754 NWCA
'Eva' LGan NCat WEas WOld
frutescens See ***Argyranthemum frutescens***
§ *marschalliana* CShe ECha ELan EPot ESis LBee NOak SIgm SSmi WAbe WPer
montana See ***A. cretica*** subsp. ***cretica***
nobilis See ***Chamaemelum nobile***
punctata subsp. ***cupaniana*** 🏆 Widely available
– – 'Nana' NPer
rudolphiana See ***A. marschalliana***
sancti-johannis CGle EBar EBre EMon GCra MBri NOak NPer NVic SMad SPer WBea WFar WPer
'Susanna Mitchell' EBre SHel
'Tetworth' EBar EBee ECha ELan EMar EMon EPPr GBuc LHop MAvo MCLN MHlr MMil MSte NChi NLak NTow SChu SMrm WCot WFar
tinctoria CArn CGle ECED EJud ELan ELau EMon EWFC GMac GPoy LHol MCLN MChe MGam MGra MHew NEgg NNor NPer SIde WAbe WApp WBea WByw WJek WOak WWin WWye
– 'Alba' CGle EAst EBee ECha EFol EMar EMon GCal LFis LGre MAvo NRoo NWoo SChu SHar WAbe WCot WFar WHen WLRN WPer
* – 'Compacta' EFou EOrc SMrm
– 'E.C. Buxton' Widely available
– 'Gold Mound' CShe
N– 'Grallach Gold' CGle CMil CRDP EBee ECha EGar EMon EOrc EWes LHop MBri MWat NCat NFla NHol NPer SCro SMrm WBea WEas WFar WMer WOld
– 'Kelwayi' CGle CHor CKel EAst EBar ECtt GCHN MCLN MFir MTis NBro NFai NMir NPer NTow SHel SPla WBea WHen WOve WPer
– 'Pride of Grallach' GCal GCra GMac LFis MAvo MHlr NCat NRoo WCot WTyr
– 'Sauce Hollandaise' Widely available
– 'Wargrave' CElw CGle CSam CSev ECha ECtt EFol EFou ELan EMon GAbr GMac LFis MCLN MUlv MWat NBro NFai NHol NPer NRoo SChu SDix SHel SMer SSvw WEas WFar WRus
triumfettii NPer

tuberculata	EBre LCom NChi SBla SIng

ANTHERICUM (Anthericaceae)

algeriense	See ***A. liliago*** var. ***major***
baeticum	CMon
* ***bovei***	SSpi
liliago ♀	CBro CFil CGle CRDP EBre ECED ELan EMan EPot ERos ESis GCal GDra LBee LGan LHop MCli MSte MTis NLak NRoo NTow SRms WCla WHow WPGP WPer
§ – var. ***major***	CAvo ECha GDra IBlr LGre WCot WDav
ramosum	CMon CSpe EBee ECha EFol ELan EPot ERos EWes GAul GBin GDra LGre MBro NWCA SHel SMrm SWas WAbe WCla WPbr WPer
– JCA 166.300	CAvo WDav
ramosum plumosum	See ***Trichopetalum plumosum***

ANTHOCERCIS (Solanaceae)

See Plant Deletions

ANTHOLYZA (Iridaceae)

coccinea	See ***Crocosmia paniculata***
♦ ***crocosmioides***	See ***Crocosmia latifolia***
paniculata	See ***Crocosmia paniculata***

ANTHOXANTHUM (Poaceae)

odoratum	CArn CJew CKin ETPC GBar GBin GPoy

ANTHRISCUS (Apiaceae)

cerefolium	CArn CJew CSev EOHP GPoy ILis LHol MChe MGra MHew SIde WJek WOak WPer WSel WWye
sylvestris	CNat ECWi
– 'Hullavington' (v)	CNat
– 'Moonlit Night'	EHoe
– 'Ravenswing'	Widely available

ANTHURIUM (Araceae)

amazonicum	MBri
andraeanum	MBri
andreanum 'Acropolis'	MBri
– 'Rose'	See ***A.*** × ***ferrierense*** **'Roseum'**
cordatum	See ***A. leuconeurum***
'Flamingo'	MBri
scherzerianum	MBri
– 'Rosemarie'	MBri

ANTHYLLIS (Papilionaceae)

hermanniae	CHan CMHG MAll MBro MHig WAbe WFar
– 'Compacta'	See ***A. hermanniae*** **'Minor'**
§ – 'Minor'	EPot NMen NSla SIng WDav
montana	ELan
– subsp. ***atropurpurea***	LRHS
– 'Rubra' ♀	CInt ECho EGle EPot LBee NMen NNor WWin
vulneraria	CKin ECWi EWFC GTou MChe MHew NMir NPri SUsu WApp WBea WCla WHer WPer WWtk
– var. ***coccinea***	CLyd CMHG CNic CSpe EGar MNrw MSte MSto MTho NGre NHol NNrd NSla NTow NWCA SAlw SUsu WAbe WHil WHoo
– var. ***iberica***	CHan
* – 'Peach'	CSpe

ANTIGONON (Polygonaceae)

leptopus	CPlN LChe SLMG
¶ – 'Album'	CPlN

ANTIRRHINUM (Scrophulariaceae)

asarina	See ***Asarina procumbens***
braun-blanquetii	CPea EBre ECro ELan EMan EMar GGar MTol SAga SIde SMad WBea WHoo WPLI WPri WWin
glutinosum	See ***A. hispanicum*** subsp. ***hispanicum***
§ ***hispanicum***	CGle EPri NBir SBla WCla WHer WOMN WPen
– 'Avalanche'	CHal CSpe EMan EMar MLan NPri SCoo WLRN
§ – subsp. ***hispanicum roseum***	CMea CSam CSpe CVer EDAr ELan NTow WCot WKif WOld
majus 'Black Prince'	CHad CWan MRav NRai SAga
– subsp. ***linkianum***	ECro LHop MAvo MSto WOMN WOld
¶ – subsp. ***majus***	SSpi
– 'Taff's White' (v)	CPou LGre MTho SAga SUsu WCot WLRN WRus
molle	CBot CHan CSpe ELan EOrc GCal MSte MSto MTho NBir NMen NPer NTow NWCA SUsu WCru WHoo WOMN WPyg WRus
– pink	CLyd CSWP EMar EOrc GCal MSte MTho SOkh WCru
'Powys Pride' (v)	CHar EMar MCLN MHlr SAga WCot WLRN WSan
pulverulentum	CSam ESis LGre LHop MArl MSto WKif
sempervirens	EPad ESis MSto SHFr SMad SOkh WOMN
¶ ***siculum***	MSto
'White Monarch'	NRai

APHANES (Rosaceae)

§ ***arvensis***	MSal NHex WWye

APHELANDRA (Acanthaceae)

alexandri	SLMG
squarrosa	CHal MBri
– 'Dania' (v)	MBri

APHYLLANTHES (Aphyllanthaceae)

monspeliensis	CFee MHig SBla WOMN

APIOS (Papilionaceae)

§ ***americana***	CPlN EMon WCru WSHC
tuberosa	See ***A. americana***

APIUM (Apiaceae)

graveolens	EJud EOHP EWFC GPoy MSal SIde WJek
nodiflorum	ECWi
¶ ***prostratum***	EOHP

APOCYNUM (Apocynaceae)

androsaemifolium	MSal
cannabinum	CArn GPoy MSal

APONOGETON (Aponogetonaceae)
distachyos CBen CHEx CRDP CRow CWGN CWat EBre EHon ELan EMFW LPBA MBal MSta NDea SHig SWat SWyc WChe
krausseanus See *A. desertorum*

APTENIA (Aizoaceae)
cordifolia CHEx CSev CTrC NPer SHFr
– 'Variegata' LHil MRav SHFr

AQUILEGIA † (Ranunculaceae)
akitensis hort. See *A. flabellata* var. *pumila*
alpina CBot CMea CShe ECtt ELan GAbr GCHN GTou MLan MSCN NFla NHol NNor NPSI SHel SPer WCla WFar WHen WOve WPer WSan WStI WWin
– 'Alba' CBlo NOak
– 'Hensol Harebell' See *A.* **'Hensol Harebell'**
'Alpine Blue' SIde
amaliae See *A. ottonis* subsp. *amaliae*
aragonensis See *A. pyrenaica*
§ *atrata* CGle CMea CPou EMan GCHN LCom LHop MHig MSte NOak WHal WPbr WPer
aurea CLTr CLon LWoo MSto NChi
baicalensis See *A. vulgaris* **Baicalensis Group**
'Ballerina' CMil EBee MSCN NCut NFai WSan
barnebyi CMea CMil CPBP CPou GAbr GBin GCra MBel MSto NWCA SIgm WSan
¶ *bernardii* NOak
bertolonii ♀ CFee CGle EHyt EMNN EPot GTou LHop MBro NHar NMen NNrd NOak NRoo NRya SAlw SBla SSmi WHoo WPat WPyg
bertolonii alba EWes NWCA
Biedermeier Group CM&M EBar GAbr GMac LFis MTol NOrc WPer
'Blue Berry' CLyd ESis MBro MPla NHar WOMN WPat
'Blue Bonnet' LBuc
¶ *brevicalcarata* LCom LLew
buergeriana CLTr CPou GAbr GBin GCra SAlw WBea WPer
– f. *flavescens* MLsm NLak WDav
♦ – var. *oxysepala* See *A. oxysepala*
caerulea ♀ CGle EMan GCHN GDra NCat SIgm SRms WPen
– 'Mrs Nicholls' MBri WMer
– var. *ochroleuca* GCHN
¶ – var. *pinetorum* GCal
canadensis ♀ CGle CLon EBar EBre ELan EPad GCal GDra MBal MNrw NBir NBro NGre NOak SIng WBea WOMN WOve WPer
– 'Corbett' GBuc
– 'Nana' CInt CSam EPot GAri GBuc MHar MSte MSto
cazorlensis See *A. pyrenaica* subsp. *cazorlensis*
'Celestial Blue' ELan
chaplinei GAbr NGre
chrysantha EBre EPad GBin GCHN GCra LFis LWoo MHlr NBus NHar NOak NPri SBla SChu SPla SRms WBea WCot WCru WOve WPLl WPbr WPer WRus
– var. *chaplinei* CBot GCal NBir
– 'Yellow Queen' CHid EFou EPfP GCal MAvo WElm WHil
clematiflora See *A. vulgaris* var. *stellata*
'Crimson Star' CBlo EBre EPfP NBus NPSI SPer
desertorum ESis NHar NHol NTow WDav
discolor CMea GDra GTou LHop MBro NGre NHed NMen NRoo NTow NWCA SIng WHil WOMN WPat WPer
'Dorothy' LHop
'Double Quilled Purple' WWhi
Double Rubies MBel MNrw SCro
¶ Dragonfly GAbr GMaP
I 'Dragonfly' CB&S CM&M EGoo GAri LWak MBri NFla NMir NOak SPer WFar WPer WRHF
'Dwarf Fairyland' CWan
'Eastgrove' WEas
ecalcarata See *Semiaquilegia ecalcarata*
einseleana CBot WHer
elegantula CWan GAbr GDra LCom MSto NGre NRoo WHal WOMN WPer
– JJA 11390 SIgm
'Firewheel' CMil EBee LCom WWhi
§ *flabellata* ♀ CGle CTri GAri GCHN MBro NMen WPat WPer
§ – f. *alba* CBot CTri ELan GCHN GGar LFlo NGre NWCA WEas WHil
– 'Blue Angel' CB&S CSte NPSI WHil WPer WWeb
– 'Jewel' ECho LFis NPro WHil
– 'Ministar' CHor CM&M CNic EBar EBre EFou ESis MBro MRav MTis NBro NMen NMir NNrd NOak NPSI NRoo WBea WFar WHil WHoo WPer WPyg WWin
– 'Nana Alba' See *A. flabellata* var. *pumila* f. *alba*
§ – var. *pumila* ♀ CShe ECha GAbr GCal GDra GTou LHop MBal MHig MNrw MRPP MTho NNrd NOak NRoo SBla SHel SIng WAbe WCla WCru WHil WPer
§ – – f. *alba* ♀ CBot CGle CMHG EBar EBre ECha EHyt ESis GAbr GCal GDra LHop MBal MHig MSte NBus NNrd NPSI NRoo SHel SIng SMac WCru WHil WRus WWin
– – f. *kurilensis* CGle EHyt GDra LBlm MSte WCla
– – 'Silver Edge' CArc CMil CPla EBee NFai NPro WBea WCot WSan
* – – 'Snowflakes' CMil
¶ – soft pink WHil
* – 'White Angel' CSev CSte EFou MLan NPSI NPro WPer WWeb
flavescens WPer
formosa CArc CBot CLon GBuc GCHN GGar GMac NBro NPri NRoo NWCA SAlw SBla SUsu WBea WCru WHal WOMN WPer
– var. *formosa* MSto
– var. *truncata* CGle CRDP GBin GBuc GCra WCru
§ *fragrans* CArn CChr CGle CInt CLon CNic CPou GAbr GBin GCHN LFlo LGan LSyl MCLN MTho NLak NOak NWes SBla WCra WHoo WOMN WRha WSan

– ex CC&MR 96 LKoh
– ex KBE 48 LKoh
glandulosa CSam GCra GDra ITim LCom LLew NRoo WEas
glauca See ***A. fragrans***
'Graeme's Green' NFai
grata CLon CMil GCHN LGre NRai SChu WCot
§ 'Hensol Harebell' ♀ CGle CHan CPou CSWP EBee LGan MBro MNrw NBus WBea WHoo WPyg WRus
hinckleyana See ***A. chrysantha*** var. ***hinckleyana***
hirsutissima See ***A. viscosa*** subsp. ***hirsutissima***
'Irish Elegance' CMHG NRai WNdy WRHF
japonica See ***A. flabellata*** var. ***pumila***
Jewel Hybrids EMNN MOne NRoo WHil WPer
jonesii CGra GCLN WAbe
– × ***saximontana*** MFos
'Koralle' CLTr CSte
'Kristall' EPri NOak SMrm WMer WPen
laramiensis CGra CPBP MFos NTow NWCA WOMN
longissima CArc CGle CHad CHar CLon CMea CMil CSam EBre EHic GAbr GBri MCLN MTho NMir NSti SBla WBea WCla WEas WHal WHil WHoo
– 'Alba' WEas
'Magpie' CLTr CM&M EWll NOak SChu SIde SIng SVen WSel
McKana Group CShe EAst EBre ECED ELan ENot GAbr GCHN GMaP LHop MWat NNor NOak NVic SCro SPer WBea WPer WTyr WWtk
* 'Mellow Yellow' CArc CKel CPla EBar ECGP GBuc MSCN NCut WBea WPer
micrantha ESis GCHN GCal
¶ aff. – JCA 1.061.350 CMil WPGP
moorcroftiana CPBP CPou EBee NLak
– CC 1371 LKoh MRPP
– CC 1414 LKoh
Mrs Scott-Elliot Hybrids CBlo EBee EMan GAbr LIck LWak MBri MLan SPer WFar
Music Series ♀ CHor NOak NPri NRoo SMrm SRms WByw
nevadensis See ***A. vulgaris*** subsp. ***nevadensis***
nigricans See ***A. atrata***
nivalis CPBP NGre SBla WOMN
§ ***olympica*** CPou EBre EMan EWes GAbr LGre NPri WCot WPer
'Orange Flaming Red' LHop
ottonis LHop
§ – subsp. ***amaliae*** MRPP WAbe
§ ***oxysepala*** CChu CGle CHar GCal GCra LFlo MSto NBus NRar SAga WCot WHal WSan
'Phyll's Bonnet' GCal
'Pink Bonnet' GCal
pubescens MSto WDav
pubiflora GCHN GCra
– CC&MR 96 WDav
§ ***pyrenaica*** CLTr CMea CTri LCom NHar NTow WCla WOMN
§ – subsp. ***cazorlensis*** CMea GCHN LCom MHar
'Quilled Violets' CMil EBee NWes
'Red Hobbit' CB&S CHan GBin GMaP NOrc NPSI WWeb
rockii CLD 0437 EBee
¶ – KGB 176 LWoo
'Roman Bronze' CPla GBin MCCP NCut WSan WWhi
* 'Rose Red' CChr
saximontana GCHN GTou LCom MSto NHol NMen NTow NWCA WOMN WPer
§ 'Schneekönigin' ELan GCHN NOak NWes WEas WHen WHil WPer
scopulorum CLyd MFos MSto NWCA SAlw WPer
– subsp. ***perplexans*** MSto
* ***secundiflora*** MSto
shockleyi CPou GBuc MLan NTow WHil WPer
sibirica WRus
'Silver Queen' WRus
skinneri CLon CMil EBee GAbr GBin LGre MCLN MNrw NBro NBus NLak NRai SCro WBea WCru WHal WHil WSan
◆ Snow Queen See ***A. 'Schneekönigin'***
Songbird Series CDoC EWll MLLN NPri SWat WLRN
stellata See ***A. vulgaris*** var. ***stellata***
'Sweet Lemon Drops' CPla LLew
thalictrifolia GBuc LGre SBla WCot
– JCA 174.400 WDav
transsilvanica EBar MNrw
triternata CMil GCal LLew NCut NTow SIgm
viridiflora Widely available
vulgaris CArn CWGN ECWi GAbr GPoy LHol LLWP MChe MHew NBro NMir SIde WApp WBon WOak WPer WShi WTyr WUnd WWye
– 'Adelaide Addison' CGle ECha ELan EMar GBri MNrw NFai NRoo NWes SWas WEas WFar WMer WRha WRus
– var. ***alba*** CArn CLTr CMea EMan GMac LLWP SEND WByw
– 'Aureovariegata' See ***A. vulgaris* Vervaeneana Group**
§ – Baicalensis Group GCHN WHil
– 'Bicolor Barlow' GCal
– 'Black Barlow' GCal NPSI
– 'Blue Barlow' GCal NPSI
– 'Blue Star' EBee ECtt EFou GCHN GCal NCat WPer
* – 'Cap de Rossiter' CRow
– 'Christa Barlow' NPSI
vulgaris clematiflora See ***A. vulgaris*** var. ***stellata***
vulgaris 'Dove' MRav NRoo SWat
– var. ***flore-pleno*** CLTr EFol EHic LLWP NChi WByw WPer
– – black CSWP WCot
– – blue SWas WCot
– – 'Burgundy' CMil
– – pink EBee
– – purple NSti
– – red GCra
– – white LGre NOak SApp SWas
* – 'Gold Finch' CBot NRoo
– golden-leaved CMea ECho EFou
– 'Grandmother's Garden' EWll WHil
– 'Granny's Gold' MBri
– 'Heidi' CBot EWll LBuc WPer
– f. ***inversa*** WBea
– 'Jane Hollow' CArc CPou CRow LGre

– 'Magpie'	See *A. vulgaris* **'William Guiness'**
* – 'Mathew Strominger'	GAul MTol NPri WPer
– 'Miss Coventry'	SWas
◆ – Munstead White	See *A. vulgaris* **'Nivea'**
§ – 'Nivea' ♀	CArc CBot CGle CHad CHan CMil CPou ECha ELan EMon GAbr LBlm LFis MCLN MNrw NFai NRoo SBla SHig SIde WBea WCla WHer WHil WHoo WRus
– 'Nora Barlow' ♀	CArn CB&S CGle CHad CHan CKel CRow EBar EBee ECha ELan EOrc GCHN GCal GMac LHop MBal MBri MRav NBro NGre NNor NRoo SIng SPer WCla WEas WHil WRus WWin
– Olympica Group	See *A. olympica*
– 'Patricia Zavros'	CLTr
– 'Pink Spurless'	See *A. vulgaris* var. *stellata* **pink**
¶ – 'Pom Pom Crimson'	GBin
– 'Pom Pom Rose'	WWhi
¶ – Pom Pom Series	CMil MCCP
– 'Red Star'	EBee ECtt EFou GCHN LCom NBus NCat NOak WHil WPer WRus
– 'Robin'	CBot NRoo SMrm SWat
– 'Rose Barlow'	GCal NPSI
– 'Ruby Port'	EHic GCal GMaP GMac LBuc MTis NBus NCat NChi NPSI NVic SLod SPla WPbr WWhi
– 'Silver Edge'	CMil ELan WBea WRha
– 'Snowdust'	EHoe
§ – var. *stellata*	CBot CGle EBar ELan GCHN GCra GMaP MTol NBro NFai NNrd NPer WBea WHal WPer WWhi WWin
– – 'Greenapples'	CLTr CMil EBee LCom LFlo WCot WSan WWhi
§ – – pink	GBin
– – red	LLWP
§ – – white	CGle CLTr GCHN LFis LHop NBro WFar WHal
– 'Sunlight White'	CMil SWat WMaN WPer WSan
– 'The Bride'	CBlo EBee MBro
– variegated foliage	See *A. vulgaris* **Vervaeneana Group**
N – – (v)	Widely available
¶ – Vervaeneana Group double white	EMon
– – 'Graeme Iddon'	GCra LGre MBri NBrk NFai NMGW WPbr WRus
◆ – – 'Woodside'	See *A. vulgaris* **Vervaeneana Group**
– – 'Woodside Blue'	WWhi
¶ – 'Violet Pom Pom'	CMil
– 'Westfaeld'	NOak NPri
– 'White Barlow'	GCal
– 'White Bonnets'	EBre SRos
– 'White Spurless'	See *A. vulgaris* var. *stellata* **white**
– 'White Star'	ECtt EFou GAbr GCHN LSyl MTis NBus NCat SPer WHil WPLl WPer
§ – 'William Guiness'	Widely available
– 'Wishy Washy'	NChi
yabeana	EBee EMon
'Yellow Star'	CM&M EWll WRHF

ARABIS † (Brassicaceae)

albida	See *A. alpina* subsp. *caucasica*
alpina	CB&S NMen
§ – subsp. ***caucasica***	MBar
– – 'Corfe Castle'	EDAr
§ – – 'Flore Pleno' ♀	CHad CNic CShe CTri EBre ECha ECtt ELan EOrc GAbr LGro LHop MFir MTho NFla NRoo NVic SAlw SBar SBod WByw WEas WFar WOMN WWin
¶ – – 'Goldsplash' (v)	NPro
– – 'Pink Pearl'	LRHS NPri
– – 'Pinkie'	EMNN NTay
* – subsp. ***caucasica rosea***	CHal MRav NBir SRms WFar WWtk
§ – subsp. ***caucasica*** 'Schneehaube' ♀	CHor EBar ECtt EMNN MBar NCGP NMir NOrc NRoo SIde SRms WLRN
◆ – – Snowcap	See *A. alpina* subsp. *caucasica* **'Schneehaube'**
– – 'Snowdrop'	LRHS MRav NPri SMer WFar
– – 'Variegata'	CBot CShe ECha EFol EHoe ELan EPot LBee LHop MBri MRav MTho NNor NRoo WByw WEas WFar WPat WPbr WWin
androsacea	EPot GMaP GTou MHig MPla MRPP NHed NMen NTow SAlw WLRN
x ***arendsii*** 'Compinkie'	ECtt NRoo SIde SRms WLRN WWtk
– 'La Fraicheur'	WMer
– 'Rosabella' (v)	ECha LHop
– 'Rose Frost'	SIde
aubrietoides	CLyd
blepharophylla	GAbr NTow WCot WOMN
§ – 'Frühlingszauber' ♀	CB&S CInt CPea CTri GDra MOne NGre NNrd NRoo SIde SRms WFar WGor WOve
◆ – Spring Charm	See *A. blepharophylla* **'Frühlingszauber'**
bryoides	EPot GTou LBee LRHS MDHE NTow
bryoides olympica	SIng
caucasica	See *A. alpina* subsp. *caucasica*
* 'Cloth of Gold'	CMHG
ferdinandi-coburgi	EGar EPot MPla NBro NBus SBod SRms WCla WEas WWin
– 'Aureovariegata'	CMHG CTri EHoe LGro NGre
– 'Old Gold'	CNic ECGP EFol EPot ESis LBee LHop MBar MHig MPla NEgg NHar NNrd NRoo SAlw SBla SBod SChu SHel SIng SSmi WCla WEas WHoo WPat WPbr WWin
– 'Variegata'	See *A. procurrens* **'Variegata'**
glabra	WPer
¶ x ***kellereri***	NMen
muralis	See *A. collina*
§ ***procurrens*** 'Variegata' ♀	ECGP ECha EFol ELan ESis EWes GTou LBee LHop MBal MBar MHig MTho MWat NGre NHar NHol NNor NRoo NWCA SBla SHFr SIng SSmi WCla
rosea	See *A. collina*
§ ***scabra***	CNat
◆ Snow Cap	See *A. alpina* subsp. *caucasica* **'Schneehaube'**
soyeri subsp. ***jacquinii***	See *A. soyeri* subsp. *coriacea*
stricta	See *A. scabra*
x ***sturii***	NTow
x ***suendermannii***	MPla

ARACHNIODES (Dryopteridaceae)

¶ *simplicior*	WCot
¶ *standishii*	WRic

ARAIOSTEGIA (Davalliaceae)

pseudocystopteris	CFil SSpi

ARALIA † (Araliaceae)

bipinnata	CDoC CFil
cachemirica	CHad GCal SDix
californica	GCal GPoy LGre MSal SIgm SMrm
chinensis	CB&S CMCN CSam EBar MSal NHol SPer
– hort.	See *A. elata*
continentalis	CHan GCal
¶ – CC 1035	WHCr
cordata	CPle GCal
§ *elata* 🏆	CAgr CDoC CHEx CHad CHan CLnd CPle CWSG EBre ELan ENot EOas IOrc LNet LPan MBal MBlu NBee NFla NNor SArc SEas SMad SPer SSpi WDin WNor
– 'Albomarginata'	See ***A. elata* 'Variegata'**
– 'Aureovariegata'	CB&S CDoC CSte ELan ENot IOrc LNet MAsh MBri NPal WDin WPat WPyg
§ – 'Variegata' 🏆	CB&S CBot CDoC CSte ELan EMil ENot IOrc LNet MBlu MBri NFla NPal SHBN SMad WDin WPat WPyg
racemosa	GCal GPoy MSal MSte SRms
sieboldii hort.	See ***Fatsia japonica***
spinosa	EBee WHer

ARAUCARIA (Araucariaceae)

angustifolia	CHEx
§ *araucana*	CAgr CB&S CDoC CHEx EBre EHul ELan ENot EOrn GRei IOrc LCon LLin LNet LPan MBal MBar MBri MGos NBee SArc SHBN SLim SMad SPer WDin WGwG WNor WPyg
cookii	See *A. columnaris*
excelsa	See *A. heterophylla*
§ *heterophylla* 🏆	EBre MBri WNor
imbricata	See *A. araucana*

ARAUJIA (Asclepiadaceae)

grandiflora	SLMG
¶ *graveolens*	CPlN
sericifera	CB&S CChr CDoC CGre CMHG CPlN CRHN CSpe CSte CTrw EMil ERea GQui LHop MGos

ARBUTUS † (Ericaceae)

¶ *andrachne*	CFil ISea
× *andrachnoides* 🏆	CAbP CB&S CBot CChu CDoC CFil CGre CMHG CPMA ELan IOrc LHop LNet LPan MBal MBlu SArc SBid SHBN SPer SReu SSpi SSta WHCG WPat WWat
glandulosa	See ***Arctostaphylos glandulosa***
marina	CAbP CFil CPMA CRos CSam CSte EBre ELan MAsh MBlu MBri SBid SMad SReu SSpi SSta
menziesii 🏆	CChu CFil CMCN EOas ISea LNet MBal SMad WCru WWat
unedo 🏆	CB&S CBot CMCN CPle CTrC CTrw EBre ELan ENot ERom IHos LHop LHyr LPan MBal MBri MGos MWat SHBN SMad SPer SReu SSpi SSta WAbe WBod WDin WHCG WPat WWin
– 'Compacta'	CB&S CChu CDoC EBre LPan MBlu MGos SHBN
– 'Elfin King'	ELan LRHS SSpi
– 'Quercifolia'	MBal SSta WPat WPyg
– f. *rubra* 🏆	CB&S CChu CDoC CMHG CTrC EBre EHal ELan IOrc LHop LNet MBal MBri MGos MHlr SPer SReu SSpi SSta WFar WPat WPyg WRHF
xalapensis	CSam

ARCHONTOPHOENIX (Arecaceae)
See Plant Deletions

ARCTANTHEMUM (Asteraceae)

§ *arcticum*	EBee EFou MSte NBrk
– 'Schwefelglanz'	ECha EFou

ARCTERICA See PIERIS

ARCTIUM (Asteraceae)

lappa	CArn CKin EJud EWFC GPoy MChe MGra MSal NHex SIde WHer
minus	CKin CTiv ECWi EWFC MHew MSal
pubens	CKin

ARCTOSTAPHYLOS (Ericaceae)

* *californica*	MBal
§ *glandulosa*	SArc
× *media* 'Snow Camp'	MBal
– 'Wood's Red'	MBal MBar MGos WFar
myrtifolia	GAri MBar
nevadensis	MBal MBar SReu SSta SSto
* – var. *coloradensis*	GGGa
nummularia	MBal
stanfordiana C&H 105	GGGa
uva-ursi	CAgr CArn CBlo ENot GPoy IOrc MBal MBar MBel MGos MHig MPla NNor SBod SEas SHBN SPer SSta
– 'Massachusetts'	CKni CSte ELan GQui MAsh SMur SReu SSta
– 'Snowcap'	MAsh
– 'Vancouver Jade'	CEnd CKni CSte EDen EPfP MAsh MBar MGos SReu SSta

ARCTOTIS (Asteraceae)

× *hybrida* 'African Sunrise'	CBrk SMrm SVen
– 'Apricot'	CBrk LHop MSte SAxl SMer SMrm SUsu WEas WRus
– 'Bacchus'	CBrk
– 'China Rose'	SAxl SMrm SUsu
– 'Flame'	CBar CBrk CHad CSpe LHil LHop MLan MMil MSte SAga SChu SMrm SUsu
* – 'Mahogany'	MSte SAxl SUsu WRus
– 'Midday Sun'	WLRN
– 'Pink'	SChu
* – 'Raspberry'	LBlm

– 'Red Devil'	CSpe SMrm WLRN
– 'Rosita'	CBrk
– 'Tangerine'	CSpe
– 'Terracotta'	MSte
– 'Torch'	CBrk SVen
– 'Wine'	CBar CBrk CHad LHil LHop MSte WEas WLRN
– 'Yellow'	CBrk
'Prostrate Raspberry'	CSpe
'Red Magic'	CBrk

ARDISIA (Myrsinaceae)

crenata	CHan MBri

ARECA (Arecaceae)

catechu	MBri

ARECASTRUM See SYAGRUS

ARENARIA (Caryophyllaceae)

alfacarensis	See *A. lithops*
balearica	CInt CLyd CNic ELan EPar GCHN LBee MFir MRPP MTho NGre SBod SIng SRms
bertolonii	LBee LRHS
caespitosa	See *Minuartia verna* subsp. *caespitosa*
festucoides	EWes GCHN GCLN GTou WLRN
grandiflora	ESis
hookeri	NWCA
¶ – var. *desertorum* NNS 93-53	MRPP
kingii	GLil WHil
ledebouriana	MWat NWCA WAbe
magellanica	See *Colobanthus quitensis*
montana 🏆	CGle ECha ECtt EHyt ELan EMNN GCHN GMaP MHar MHig MHlr MTho NMen NNor NRoo NVic WAbe WEas WFar WHil WPat WPbr WPer WWhi WWin
nevadensis	SIgm WAbe
norvegica	CNat
– subsp. *anglica*	WOMN
obtusiloba	See *Minuartia obtusiloba*
pinifolia	See *Minuartia circassica*
procera subsp. *glabra*	NMen
pseudacantholimon	NGre
pulvinata	See *A. lithops*
¶ *pungens*	WDav
purpurascens	CInt CLyd ECtt EHyt ELan EMNN EPot ESis MHig NMen NRoo NSla NWCA SAlw SIde SRms WHoo WPat
– 'Elliott's Variety'	NGre
◆ *recurva*	See *Minuartia recurva*
¶ *rubella*	NTow
tetraquetra	CTri EGle EHyt EPad GDra MTho MWat NMen NWCA
§ – subsp. *amabilis*	CLyd EHyt EPPr EPot LBee MHig MRPP NGre NHar NNrd NSla NTow SIng WHil
– var. *granatensis*	See *A. tetraquetra* subsp. *amabilis*
tmolea	LHop NNrd
verna	See *Minuartia verna*

ARENGA (Arecaceae)
See Plant Deletions

ARGEMONE (Papaveraceae)

grandiflora	EJud ELan
mexicana	CArc CMea ELan MSCN WHer WOMN WWin

ARGYLIA (Bignoniaceae)

¶ *adscendens*	WDav

ARGYRANTHEMUM † (Asteraceae)

'Apricot Surprise'	See ***A.* 'Peach Cheeks'**
'Beauty of Nice'	WEas
§ 'Blizzard' (d)	CB&S CBrk CLit EPri LIck LLWP MArl SMer SSte WLRN
'Bofinger'	LIck
broussonetii	CCan LIck NSty
'Butterfly'	LIck
§ *callichrysum* 'Etoile d'Or'	CBrk EBre IHos LHop LIck
– 'Penny'	CBrk
– 'Prado'	CB&S ECtt GCal LIck WLRN
◆ – Yellow Star	See ***A. callichrysum* 'Etoile d'Or'**
canariense hort.	See *A. frutescens* subsp. *canariae*
'Cheek's Peach'	See ***A.* 'Peach Cheeks'**
'Chelsea Princess'	EOrc
'Comtesse du Chambord'	LHil
'Cornish Gold' 🏆	CSpe LFis LIck MMil SMrm
coronopifolium	CCan LIck
double cream	CCan LHil LIck
double white	CHal LIck NHaw SCro
'Edelweiss' (d)	CBrk CCan CSev EBar ECtt LHil LIck MAvo WEas WHen
'Flamingo'	See *Rhodanthemum gayanum*
§ *foeniculaceum* hort.	CCan CHad CSev CTri ECha ELan GMac LBlm NPer NSty SIgm WEas WHen WKif WOMN
– pink	See ***A.* 'Petite Pink'**
§ – Webb 'Royal Haze' 🏆	CCan CLTr CSev EBar GCal LIck NPer SMer SSte SUsu
§ *frutescens*	CDoC CHEx CLit EBre ECha ECtt ELan EMan EOrc ERea LBlm LHil NFai WEas
* – 'Album Plenum'	EOrc SEND
§ – subsp. *canariae* 🏆	CBrk CHal
§ – subsp. *frutescens*	CCan
– subsp. *succulentum* 'Margaret Lynch'	CBrk CCan LIck
'George'	CLit
'Gill's Pink'	CBrk CElw CHid CLTr ECtt LHil LLWP NPla SSte
§ *gracile*	CSev LHil WEas
– 'Chelsea Girl' 🏆	CB&S CBrk CCan CInt CLTr CLit EAst ECtt EMan GMaP LIck MArl MSte SIgm SRms
'Hopleys Double Yellow'	LHil NSty
§ 'Jamaica Primrose' 🏆	CB&S CBar CBot CBrk CCan CHad CLit CSev CSpe EBre ELan EOrc ERea GMaP GMac IHos LHil LHop LIck NHaw NSty SCro SHFr WEas WOMN WPnn
* 'Jamaica Snowstorm'	CB&S CBar CLit EAst EBar LIck NFai NHaw NPla WHer
* 'Lemon Meringue'	CBrk CHal ECtt LIck NHaw SMer
'Levada Cream' 🏆	LIck
'Leyton Treasure'	CBrk
'Lilliput'	LIck

§ *maderense* ♀	CBrk CCan CElw CLTr CLit EOrc GCal IBlr LBlm LHil LHop LIck MSte NSty SUsu WEas WOMN WPer
– pale form	LIck NPla
'Mary Cheek' (d) ♀	CBrk CCan LHil LIck
'Mary Wootton' (d)	CBrk CCan CLit CSev ECtt ELan EOrc GMaP GMac LHil LIck MAvo NSty
mawii	See ***Rhodanthemum gayanum***
'Mini-snowflake'	See ***A.* 'Blizzard'**
'Mini-star Yellow'	WLRN
'Mrs F. Sander' (d)	CBrk ECtt NSty
'Nevada Cream'	See ***A.* 'Qinta White'**
ochroleucum	See ***A. maderense***
§ 'Peach Cheeks' (d)	CB&S CBrk CKni ELan EMan LIck MSte NFai NHaw SAga SCro SIgm SRms
§ 'Petite Pink' ♀	CB&S CBrk CHad EAst ECtt EGar EMan EOrc EPri GCal LIck MSte NHaw NPer SIgm SMer SRms WEas WHen
'Pink Australian'	CBrk CLTr EBar LHil LIck
'Pink Break'	CCan CHal
'Pink Delight'	See ***A.* 'Petite Pink'**
'Powder Puff' (d)	CBrk CCan CLTr CLit ECtt EOrc LIck MRav MSte NFai NHaw SCro
§ 'Qinta White' (d) ♀	CBrk CCan CLit ECtt LHil LHop LIck NPla NSty WEas
'Rollason's Red'	CBrk CCan ECtt EOrc LIck
'Royal Haze'	See ***A. foeniculaceum* 'Royal Haze' Webb**
'Royal Yellow'	LIck
¶ 'Silver Leaf'	WLRN
'Silver Queen'	See ***A. foeniculaceum* hort.**
single pink	CLTr CLit LHil LIck NSty
'Snowflake' (d)	CBrk CCan CHEx CSev ECtt EOrc IHos LHil MSte NPer WHen
'Sugar Baby'	CHal SMrm WLRN
'Sugar 'n' Ice'	WLRN
'Summer Pink'	SMrm WLRN
'Tenerife'	LIck MSte
'Tony Holmes'	CCan LIck
'Vancouver' (d) ♀	CB&S CBot CBrk CCan CInt CSpe EBar EBre ECha ELan EOrc GCal GMaP GMac IHos LHil LHop LIck NHaw NSty SChu SCro SDix SRms WEas WOMN
* 'Vera'	IHos LIck
'Wellwood Park'	CBrk CCan CLit EBre ECtt LIck
'White Spider'	LHil LIck NPla
'Yellow Australia'	LIck SCro

ARGYREIA (Convolvulaceae)

nervosa	CPlN

ARGYROCYTISUS See CYTISUS

ARISAEMA (Araceae)

amurense	CFil CFir EPot GDra LWoo NHar NHol NRog SSpi WChr WCot WCru WFar WPGP
candidissimum ♀	CAvo CBro CChu CFil CFir CRDP EBre EHyt EMan EPar EPot GCal LAma LWoo NHar NRog SBar SBla SHig SSpi SWas WChr WCot WCru WFox WHal WIvy WPbr
ciliatum	CDoC MHlr SSpi WCot
– CT 369	SWas WCru
concinnum	NRog WChr WCot WCru
consanguineum	CBro CChu CFil CGle LAma NRog WCru WPGP
– CLD 1519	WChr
costatum	CFil GBuc NRog WChr WCru WPGP
dracontium	EPot LAma LWoo MSal NRog WCru
erubescens	NRog WChr WCru
exappendiculatum	CFil CMon EPar WChr WCot WCru WPGP
flavum	CBro CFil EHyt EPot GCal LWoo NNrd NRog SBla SIng WCot WCru WPGP
¶ – CC 1782	LFis
¶ – subsp. *intermedium*	WChr
formosanum B&SWJ 280	WCru
fraternum	WChr
galeatum	LAma WChr WCru
griffithii	EPot GCra LAma NHol NRog SMad SSpi WChr WCru
helleborifolium	See ***A. tortuosum***
heterophyllum B&SWJ 280	WCru
intermedium	NRog WChr WCru
¶ – var. *biflagellatum*	CMon
jacquemontii	CAvo CBro EHyt EPot GBuc GCLN GDra LAma LWoo NRog WCru
– form	WCru
japonicum	See ***A. serratum***
kiushianum	EFEx WCru
§ *nepenthoides*	CBro EPot GCra LAma NRog WChr WCot WCru
ochraceum	See ***A. nepenthoides***
propinquum	EPot LAma NRog WCru
quinatum	NRog
* *quinatum pusillum*	NRog
* *quinatum zebrinum*	NRog
ringens hort.	See ***A. robustum***
– (Thunberg) Schott	EFEx LAma NHol WChr WCot WCru
§ *robustum*	CFil WPGP
sazensoo	See ***A. sikokianum***
§ *serratum*	CFil LAma SBla WCru WPGP
– GG 89394	NHol
– GG 89399	NHol
– GG 89404	NHol
§ *sikokianum*	EFEx EHyt EPot LAma NRog WChr WCru
sp. CLD 12482*	EEls
speciosum	ELan LAma NHol WChr WCru
taiwanense	CFil
– B&SWJ 269	WCru
ternatipartitum	WCru
¶ *thunbergii*	EFEx
– subsp. *urashima*	EFEx LAma LWoo NRog WChr WCru
* *tiliatum*	MHlr
§ *tortuosum*	CFil CMon ECha EHyt EPar LAma LWoo MBal NHol NRog NTow WChr WCot WCru
triphyllum	CFil EPar EPot LAma LWoo MSal NRog NWCA SAxl SLod SWas WChr WCru WPGP
verrucosum	LAma WCru
* *vulgare* var. *typicum*	WCot

ARISARUM (Araceae)

proboscideum	Widely available
– MS 958	CMon EMar

vulgare CRDP
– subsp. ***simorrhinum*** SF 396/347 CMon
– subsp. ***vulgare*** JRM 1396 CMon

ARISTEA (Iridaceae)

¶ ***africana*** SWat
¶ ***confusa*** SWat
ecklonii CFee CFil CHan CPou LFis SAxl SLod SWat WCot WPer
ensifolia ELan EMon SWat WThi
– S&SH 88 CHan
grandis WCot
¶ ***lugens*** SWat
¶ ***macrocarpa*** SWat
major CTrC ELan GSki SWat
– pink CGre
spiralis SWat
¶ ***woodii*** SWat

ARISTIDA (Poaceae)

purpurea ETPC

ARISTOLOCHIA (Aristolochiaceae)

baetica CPlN WCru
californica CPlN MSto
¶ ***chrysops*** CPlN
clematitis CArn CHan CPlN GPoy MHew MSal NHex WCru WPer WWye
¶ ***debilis*** CPlN
durior See ***A. macrophylla***
elegans See ***A. littoralis***
fimbriata CPlN MSto
gigantea CPlN LChe
grandiflora CPlN
¶ ***kaempferi*** CPlN
¶ – B&SWJ 293 WCru
§ ***labiata*** CPlN
§ ***littoralis*** 🏆 CPlN MSto SLMG SOWG
§ ***macrophylla*** CB&S CBot CHEx CPlN EBee ELan EPla ETen NFla NPal SBra SHBN SSoC WCru
¶ ***manshuriensis*** CPlN
– B&SWJ 962 WCru
paucinervis SF 235 MSto
peruviana CPlN
¶ ***pistolochia*** CPlN
◆ ***ringens*** Link & Otto See ***A. labiata***
¶ – Vahl CPlN
¶ ***rotunda*** CPlN
sempervirens CPlN
sipho See ***A. macrophylla***
¶ ***tagala*** CPlN
tomentosa CFil CPlN SSta
trilobata CPlN
¶ ***watsonii*** CPlN

ARISTOTELIA (Elaeocarpaceae)

§ ***chilensis*** CPle MAll MNes
– 'Variegata' CAbb CB&S CHan CPle CTre EMil EPla GOrc MMil WEas WLRN WPat WPyg WRTC
fruticosa CPle
– (f) ECou MAll
– (m) ECou MAll
macqui See ***A. chilensis***
¶ ***peduncularis*** LLew
serrata ECou

ARMERIA (Plumbaginaceae)

§ ***alliacea*** ECha GBar WPer
– f. ***leucantha*** CBot CWan NBro
§ ***alpina*** NHol
'Bee's Ruby' 🏆 ECED MBri WMer WPer WWye
caespitosa See ***A. juniperifolia***
Formosa Hybrids CTri ELan EMan IBlr LFis MNrw NCat NMir NOak SIde WRha
§ ***girardii*** EPot LBuc NHed
§ ***juniperifolia*** 🏆 CMHG EBre ECtt ELan EMNN ESis LBee LHop MPla MTho NGre NMen NNrd NRoo NTow NVic NWCA SBla WCla WWin
– 'Alba' ELan EPot LBee MHig MPla NGre NHar NMen NNrd NRoo NRya WWin
– 'Beechwood' LBee SBla SSmi
– 'Bevan's Variety' 🏆 CMHG CShe EBre ECha ELan EPot MBro MHig MNrw MWat NHar NHol NMen NNrd NRoo NRya SIng SSmi WAbe WHoo WPat WPyg
– dark form EWes GDra WAbe
– rose EPot
– spiny dwarf form EPot
§ ***maritima*** CArn CKin CMHG CRow EBre ECWi EPPr LBee LHol MBar MRav NCat NMen NNor SAlw SIde WApp WBea WOak WTyr
– 'Alba' CArn CB&S CLTr ECha ELan EPot ESis LBee MBal MBar MBri MCLN NMir NNor NNrd NRoo NRya SSvw WAbe WApp WBea WHen WPer WWhi WWin WWye
– subsp. ***alpina*** See ***A. alpina***
– 'Bloodstone' CB&S CShe CTri ECot ELan EPot LBee MWat
– 'Corsica' CMea CTri ECha MHar MOne NBir NRya SMer
◆ – Düsseldorf Pride See ***A. maritima* 'Düsseldorfer Stolz'**
§ – 'Düsseldorfer Stolz' CMHG CShe EBre ECha ELan MBri MBro NHar NHol NMen NNrd NRoo WHen WPat WWye
– 'Glory of Holland' EPot
– 'Laucheana' CBod NOak WHoo WPyg
* – 'Pink Lusitanica' WPer
– 'Ruby Glow' CNic CTri GAri LBuc NMen NOak
– 'Snowball' NOak
– 'Splendens' EMNN EMil ESis GCHN LFis MLan MOne MPla NHar NMir NRya WFar WPer WWin WWtk
– 'Vindictive' 🏆 CB&S CTri EGoo EPfP LGro MBal SRms
'Nifty Thrifty' (v) SCoo WCot WWeb
'Ornament' ECtt NRoo WCot WFar WHen
plantaginea See ***A. alliacea***
pseudarmeria EBee ELan MLan MNrw WEas
rumelica EBee
setacea See ***A. girardii***
sp. from Patagonia EPot WHil
tweedyi CLyd EPPr EWes GTou NGre NNor NRoo
vulgaris See ***A. maritima***
welwitschii CMHG SRms

ARMORACIA (Brassicaceae)

§ ***rusticana*** CArn CSev ELau GAbr GPoy ILis LHol MBri MGra MSal NPri SIde WCer WGwy WHer WJek WOak WSel WTyr WWye
– 'Variegata' CSev EFol EMar EMon EOrc GBar GCal LFis LHol LHop NSti NWes SMad SPla WCHb WCot WLRN

ARNEBIA (Boraginaceae)

¶ ***densiflora*** WDav
echioides See ***A. pulchra***
§ ***pulchra*** ECED NGar

ARNICA (Asteraceae)

angustifolia subsp. ***iljinii*** EBee NBir
chamissonis CSev CWan EBee GBar GGar LHol MHew MNrw MSal NWCA SIde WJek WPer WRha WWye
cordifolia MSto
montana CArn CJew EOHP GAul GPoy GTou LHol MChe MGra MSal NCGP SWat WBea WJek WPer WRHF WWye
– yellow MLan
nevadensis EBee
sachalinensis EBee

ARONIA (Rosaceae)

arbutifolia CB&S CGre CPle CTri EPfP EPla GBin IOrc MBal SBid SHBN SMac WAbe WDin WWat
– 'Erecta' CKni EBre EHic ELan EPfP LHop SAga SRms WWat
* ***flexuosa*** SOWG
melanocarpa CB&S CMCN CMHG CSam EBre EHic ELan EPla GWht MBar MBlu MRav NHol SBid SPer WDin WHCG WWat
– 'Autumn Magic' CFai CSam
– 'Viking' EBee EHal LBuc MUlv WLRN WWes
× ***prunifolia*** CB&S CDoC CMHG CPle EPla NHol SBid SPer WHCG WWat
– 'Brilliant' CDoC COtt EBar MAsh MMor MUlv SPer WBcn WWat

ARRHENATHERUM (Poaceae)

elatius subsp. ***bulbosum*** 'Variegatum' CArc CCuc CNic EAst EHoe ELan EMon EPla EPot ESOG ETPC GBin NCat NEgg NHol NOrc NSti NVic SAxl WEas WHil WPat WPer WRus

ARTEMISIA † (Asteraceae)

§ ***abrotanum*** ♀ CArn CB&S CFee CGle CSev ECha EEls ELan GPoy LFis LHol LHop LLWP MBal MBar MBri MChe MGra NFai NHol NNor NRoo NSti SDix SIde SMad SPer WEas WOak WWin
* – 'Variegata' EBee
absinthium CArn CSev EEls EMon EWFC GPoy LHol MBar MBri MChe MGam MGra NNor NSti SIde SPer SWat WApp WCer WOak WPer WWye
– 'Huntingdon' CHad
¶ – 'Lambrook Giant' EMan
– 'Lambrook Mist' COtt CSev ELan EPPr EPfP GBri LBuc MBel NRoo NSti SWat WHow WLRN WRus WWeb
– 'Lambrook Silver' ♀ Widely available
– 'Silver Ghost' EEls
* – 'Variegata' WJek
afra EEls
§ ***alba*** CSWP CSev EEls EMan EMon GBar GPoy ILis LHol NSti SIde SMad WCer WPer WTyr WWye
§ – 'Canescens' ♀ CGle CHan CLTr CSev CShe EBre ECha EEls EFou EOrc MBri MGra MNrw MTis NTow SBla SChu SDix SMrm SPer SSvw WHCG WHow WMer WPer WWat
annua EEls MSal SIde WWye
arborescens CArn CGle CMHG CTri ECha EEls ELan NFai NSti SDry SMad SPer WDin WHer
– 'Brass Band' See ***A. 'Powis Castle'***
– 'Faith Raven' CArn CShe EEls GBuc MBri NFai NNor WHer WMer WRus
– 'Porquerolles' EEls LHop MRav
arctica EEls
argyi EEls
§ ***armeniaca*** EEls WWin
assoana See ***A. caucasica***
atrata EEls
brachyloba EEls NPla WCHb
caerulescens See ***Seriphidium caerulescens***
¶ ***californica*** EEls
campestris subsp. ***borealis*** CJew EEls LHol MChe WCer WRha WSel
– subsp. ***campestris*** EEls
– subsp. ***maritima*** EEls
¶ – – Welsh form EEls
camphorata See ***A. alba***
cana See ***Seriphidium canum***
canariensis See ***A. thuscula***
canescens hort. See ***A. alba* 'Canescens'**
– Willdenow See ***A. armeniaca***
capillaris EEls SMad SMrm
§ ***caucasica*** ♀ CGle CPBP CShe EBre EEls EFol ESiP EWes GCHN LGro MTol NNrd SIng WCHb WEas WHer WHil WPer WWat
caucasica caucasica EEls WFar
chamaemelifolia CArn EEls EGar GBar LHol SIde WPer WSel WWye
cretacea See ***Seriphidium nutans***
discolor See ***A. ludoviciana*** var. ***incompta***
douglasiana EEls
– 'Valerie Finnis' See ***A. ludoviciana* 'Valerie Finnis'**
dracunculus CArn CGle CHad CSev ECha EEls ELan ELau GAbr GBar GPoy LHol MBar MChe MGra MRav NCGP NNor NRoo SDix SIde WCer WEas WOak WPer WWye
dracunculus dracunculoides CWan EEls EJud GBar NPri
eriantha EEls
ferganensis See ***Seriphidium ferganense***
¶ ***filifolia*** EEls
frigida ♀ EBre EEls EOrc GBar ILis MGra WEas WHCG WWhi WWin

glacialis	ECha EEls EGar WDav
gmelinii	EEls
gnaphalodes	See ***A. ludoviciana***
gracilis	See ***A. scoparia***
N ***granatensis*** hort.	MSte
kawakamii B&SWJ 088	MAvo WCru
kitadakensis	EEls
– 'Guizhou'	See ***A. lactiflora* Guizhou Group**
laciniata	EEls
lactiflora ♀	CGle CHad CHan ECED ECha ECtt EEls EFou ELan EPar GCal NNor NSti SCro SDix SPer WWye
– dark form	See ***A. lactiflora* Guizhou Group**
§ – Guizhou Group	Widely available
lactiflora purpurea	See ***A. lactiflora* Guizhou Group**
lactiflora 'Variegata'	See ***A. vulgaris* 'Variegata'**
¶ ***lagocephala***	GCal
lanata Willdenow	See ***A. caucasica***
laxa	See ***A. umbelliformis***
§ ***ludoviciana***	CGle CHan CM&M CShe ECED EEls ELan ESiP GOrc LBlm MGra MWat NNor NOak NOrc SIde WHil WOve WRHF WWhi WWin WWye
§ – var. ***incompta***	ECha EEls EFol NFai WHer
– var. ***latifolia***	See ***A. ludoviciana*** var. ***latiloba***
§ – var. ***latiloba*** ♀	CHad CHor EEls EFol EHoe EOrc GBuc LBlm LHop MBro MRav MTol NBro NOak NRoo WByw WCot WHoo WMer WPbr WPer
– 'Silver Queen' ♀	Widely available
§ – 'Valerie Finnis' ♀	CArc CHad CMGP CSam EBee ECha EEls EFou EGar GAbr GCal LRHS MCLN NRoo SMer SOkh SPer WCra WEas WFar WLRN WPbr WPer WRha WTyr
maritima	See ***Seriphidium maritimum***
molinieri	CSev EEls
mutellina	See ***A. umbelliformis***
niitakayamensis	EEls GBar WWat
¶ ***nitida***	EEls
nutans	See ***Seriphidium nutans***
palmeri A. Gray	See ***Seriphidium palmeri***
palmeri hort.	See ***A. ludoviciana***
pamirica	EEls
pedemontana	See ***A. caucasica***
pontica ♀	Widely available
N 'Powis Castle' ♀	Widely available
princeps	EEls
procera	See ***A. abrotanum***
purshiana	See ***A. ludoviciana***
pycnocephala 'David's Choice'	EEls
rutifolia	EEls
schmidtiana ♀	ECha ECot EEls EFou EMan EPot LHop MWat NCGP SOkh SPer WOve
– 'Nana' ♀	CB&S CGle CMea EBre EEls ELan EOrc EPri ESis GCra MBal MBar MBri MCLN MHar MTho NFla NNor NNrd NRoo NSti NVic SDix WAbe WMer WPbr WPyg WRus WWat WWin
§ ***scoparia***	EEls
sieberi	EEls
sp. Guiz 137	See ***A. lactiflora* Guizhou Group**
splendens hort.	See ***A. alba* 'Canescens'**
– Willdenow	CMHG CShe EBre EFol ELan MTol NSti WEas
stelleriana	CBrk CGle CShe EBre ECha ESiP GMaP LFis LHop MTho NBro NFla NMir NNor NSti SHel SPer WCot WEas WHoo WPer WRus
§ – 'Boughton Silver'	Widely available
N – 'Mori'	See ***A. stelleriana* 'Boughton Silver'**
– 'Nana'	ECha EEls EMan
– 'Prostata'	See ***A. stelleriana* 'Boughton Silver'**
– 'Silver Brocade'	See ***A. stelleriana* 'Boughton Silver'**
¶ ***taurica***	EEls
§ ***thuscula***	EEls
tridentata	See ***Seriphidium tridentatum***
§ ***umbelliformis***	EEls GBar SIde
vallesiaca	See ***Seriphidium vallesiacum***
verlotiorum	EEls GBar
* ***versicolor***	NNor
vulgaris	CArn CJew EEls EWFC GPoy LHol MChe MHew NCGP NNor SIde WHer WOak WWye
– 'Cragg-Barber Eye' (v)	CNat MAvo WAlt WCHb WHer WNdy WPbr
– 'Crispa'	ELau EMon SIde
– 'Peddar's Gold' (v)	EWes
§ – 'Variegata'	CArc CLTr CRDP CWit EBee EEls EFol EMon ERav GBar GLil LFis MAvo SLod SMad WCHb WFar WHer WHil WPbr WPer WRha
* x ***wurzellii***	EEls

ARTHROPODIUM (Anthericaceae)

candidum	CBot CHan CMea CRow CSpe EBar ECha ECou EFol EPPr EPla EPot MHlr NCat NWCA SHBN SUsu SVen WHal
candidum maculatum	CInt
candidum purpureum	CAbb CMea CRDP EAst EHoe ELan EMon EPPr GCal LHil NPSI SPla SSoC WCot WCru WFar WWin
cirratum	CAbb CAvo CSpe CTbh CTrC ECou EPPr LHil SVen WHal
– 'Matapouri Bay'	CB&S
milleflorum	ECou SAlw

ARUM (Araceae)

§ ***besserianum***	EPot WChr
§ ***concinnatum***	CFil CMon EPot SSpi WChr WCot WPGP
conophalloides	See ***A. rupicola*** var. ***rupicola***
cornutum	See ***Sauromatum venosum***
creticum	CBot CBro CFil CFir CHan CMon CSWP ECha EHyt EMan EPar EPot IBlr MMil MTho NRog NTow SAga SSpi WCot
– FCC form	LWoo WChr WCot
– yellow	NBir SDix
cyrenaicum	CMon GCra WChr
detruncatum var. ***detruncatum***	See ***A. rupicola*** var. ***rupicola***
§ ***dioscoridis***	CMon EBee MFos MTho NRog WChr WCot
– var. ***liepoldtii***	See ***A. dioscoridis***

– var. ***smithii*** See ***A. dioscoridis***
dracunculus See ***Dracunculus vulgaris***
elongatum EPot WChr
hygrophilum WChr
¶ ***idaeum*** SSpi
italicum CGle CTri EOrc ETub LAma MBri MTho NNrd NRog SEND SWat WAbe WByw WFar WOMN WOak WShi
– subsp. ***albispathum*** CFil CMon EFou EMon EPot LAma NRog WChr WCot WPGP
– black spotted form EHyt
– 'Green Marble' SBla
– subsp. ***italicum*** EPla SAWi
– – 'Bill Baker' EMon
§ – – 'Marmoratum' 🏆 Widely available
§ – – 'White Winter' CRDP EMon GBuc WCot WRus
italicum 'Nancy Lindsay' EMon
– subsp. ***neglectum*** 'Chameleon' CDec CHad CRDP EMon SMad WCot WWeb
– NL 1234 CMon
– 'Pictum' See ***A. italicum*** subsp. ***italicum* 'Marmoratum'**
korolkowii EPot NRog WChr
maculatum CKin ECWi EPar EPot EWFC GDra GPoy LAma MSal NHex WHer WShi WWye
– 'Painted Lady' EMon WCot
– 'Pleddel' WCot
* – 'Variegatum' GPoy
nickelii See ***A. concinnatum***
§ ***nigrum*** EMon
orientale EPot LWoo NTow
– subsp. ***alpinum*** CFil WPGP
– subsp. ***besserianum*** See ***A. besserianum***
– subsp. ***sintenisii*** WChr
palaestinum CAvo WCot
petteri hort. See ***A. nigrum***
N ***pictum*** CAvo CRDP EPot LAma NRog WChr WCot
– ACL 321/78 EMon
– CL 28 CMon
– 'Taff's Form' See ***A. italicum*** subsp. ***italicum* 'White Winter'**
purpureospathum CMon LWoo
* ***sintenisii*** WChr

ARUNCUS (Rosaceae)

aethusifolius CDoC CMHG CRow EBar ECha EFou EGol ELan EMon EOrc EPla GAbr LFis MBro MRav MUlv NBro NHar NHol NNor NOak NOrc WDav WEas WFar WHoo WPer WRus WWat WWin
◆ ***dioicus*** Child of Two Worlds See ***A. dioicus* 'Zweiweltenkind'**
– 'Glasnevin' CChu CRow CSev EBre ECha ECtt EGol EMan EPla LFis MBri MUlv NHol SChu SMac WMer
– var. ***kamtschaticus*** CChu NHol
– – AGSJ 238 NHol
– 'Kneiffii' Widely available
§ – (m) 🏆 CGle CHor CRow EBar EBre ECha EGol ELan ENot EPla GLil LGan MBal MCLN MRav NBro NDea NHol NNor SMad SPer SSpi SWat WFar WOld WOve WPer
§ – 'Zweiweltenkind' EBre MCli NHol WMer WPer
plumosus See ***A. dioicus* (m)**
sp. AGSJ 214 NHol
sylvestris See ***A. dioicus* (m)**

ARUNDINARIA † (Poaceae - Bambusoideae)

amabilis See ***Pseudosasa amabilis***
anceps See ***Yushania anceps***
angustifolia See ***Pleioblastus chino* f. *angustifolius***
auricoma See ***Pleioblastus auricomus***
chino See ***Pleioblastus chino***
disticha See ***Pleioblastus pygmaeus*** var. ***distichus***
falconeri See ***Himalayacalamus falconeri***
fangiana EPla
fargesii See ***Bashania fargesii***
fastuosa See ***Semiarundinaria fastuosa***
fortunei See ***Pleioblastus variegatus***
funghomii See ***Schizostachyum funghomii***
gigantea EPla SBam SDry WJun
hindsii See ***Pleioblastus hindsii* hort.**
hookeriana hort. See ***Himalayacalamus falconeri* 'Damarapa'**
– Munro See ***Himalayacalamus hookerianus***
humilis See ***Pleioblastus humilis***
japonica See ***Pseudosasa japonica***
jaunsarensis See ***Yushania anceps***
maling See ***Yushania maling***
marmorea See ***Chimonobambusa marmorea***
murieliae See ***Fargesia murieliae***
nitida See ***Fargesia nitida***
oedogonata See ***Clavinodum oedogonatum***
palmata See ***Sasa palmata***
pumila See ***Pleioblastus humilis*** var. ***pumilus***
pygmaea See ***Pleioblastus pygmaeus***
quadrangularis See ***Chimonobambusa quadrangularis***
simonii See ***Pleioblastus simonii***
spathiflora See ***Thamnocalamus spathiflorus***
§ ***tecta*** SDry
tessellata See ***Thamnocalamus tessellatus***
vagans See ***Sasaella ramosa***
variegata See ***Pleioblastus variegatus***
veitchii See ***Sasa veitchii***
viridistriata See ***Pleioblastus auricomus***
'Wang Tsai' See ***Bambusa multiplex* 'Fernleaf'**

ARUNDO (Poaceae)

donax CBen CFil CHEx CRow ECha EFul EPla EWes GAri LBlm LPBA LPan MBlu MUlv SArc SDix SMad SSoC
– 'Macrophylla' CKni CRow
– 'Variegata' See ***A. donax*** var. ***versicolor***
§ – var. ***versicolor*** (v) CB&S CBen CBot CBrk CHEx CRDP CRow ECha EFol EFul EPla EWes GCal LHil LHop LPan MSta MSte MUlv SArc SMad SPer SSoC WCot
pliniana CRow EPla

ASARINA (Scrophulariaceae)

antirrhiniflora See ***Maurandella antirrhiniflora***
barclayana See ***Maurandya barclayana***
erubescens See ***Lophospermum erubescens***
hispanica See ***Antirrhinum hispanicum***

lophantha	See ***Lophospermum erubescens***
lophospermum	See ***Lophospermum erubescens***
§ *procumbens*	CGle CMHG CShe CSpe ECha ELan GAbr GDra GTou LBlm MBal MTho NHex NNor NWCA SAlw SHFr SHel SLod SSpi WCla WHer WOMN WPer WPri WWin WWye
– 'Alba'	SRms
purpusii	See ***Maurandya purpusii***
scandens	See ***Maurandya scandens***
'Victoria Falls'	SLod

ASARUM † (Aristolochiaceae)

albomaculatum B&SWJ 1726	WCru
arifolium	EPar LWoo
canadense	CArn GPoy MSal WCru
caudatum	CHan CRow EBee EGar EPla LHop LWoo MBri MSal NBro NWCA SAxl SRms SSvw WCru WFar WHal
¶ *caudigerum* B&SWJ 1517	WCru
¶ *caulescens*	LWoo
europaeum	CHEx CHan CTri ECha EFol EFou ELan EMar EMon EPla GPoy LHop LWoo MFir MGrG MSal MWat NBro NGar NHex NSti SAxl SBar WCru WEas WFar WHer WWye
hartwegii	CRDP EHyt EPar EPot ERos LWoo MSal MSto WCru
infrapurpureum B&SWJ 1994	WCru
lemmonii	EGar
leptophyllum B&SWJ 1983	WCru
macranthum B&SWJ 1691	WCru
shuttleworthii	LWoo WCot WCru
¶ – 'Callaway'	WCot
¶ *taipingshanianum* B&SWJ 1688	WCru

ASCLEPIAS (Asclepiadaceae)

'Cinderella'	EBee LBuc SIgm WHil WOve
curassavica	CHal CSev EBar ELan LHil SHFr SLMG
§ *fascicularis*	SHFr SIgm
◆ *fasciculata*	See ***A. fascicularis***
fruticosa	See ***Gomphocarpus fruticosus***
incarnata	CHan CInt CSev EBee ECED ECro ELan GLil LFis MRav MSal MUlv SAxl SPer WPer
– 'Ice Ballet'	CSev EBee EFou EMan EWll LBuc MMil MTis SHam SIgm SWat
¶ – 'White Superior'	WHil
physocarpa	See ***Gomphocarpus physocarpus***
purpurascens	EWoo
syriaca	CArn CPea ECro MRav MSte WPer
tuberosa	CArn CB&S CDoC CM&M EBar EBee ECED ECro EMan GPoy MNrw MRav MSal NCut NLak WGwG WPer WWin
– Gay Butterflies Group	CInt MLan

ASIMINA (Annonaceae)

triloba	CAgr LBlo WWoo

ASPARAGUS (Asparagaceae)

asparagoides ♀	CPlN ERea
§ – 'Myrtifolius'	CHal
densiflorus 'Myersii' ♀	CHal ERea MBri SRms
– Sprengeri Group ♀	CHal MBri SRms
falcatus	ERea MBri SEND
officinalis ♀	CHEx ERea
pseudoscaber 'Spitzenschleier'	WCot
setaceus ♀	CHal MBri
– 'Pyramidalis'	MBri SRms
sp. B&SWJ 871	WCru
verticillatus	GCal MCCP SRms

ASPERULA (Rubiaceae)

§ *arcadiensis* ♀	EBre EHyt ELan MTho NMen SIng WOMN
– JCA 210.100	CPBP NTow
aristata subsp. *scabra*	ECha ELan EMar EMon
– subsp. *thessala*	See ***A. sintenisii***
cyanchica	MHew
daphneola	ECho EHyt EWes SBla
gussonei	CPBP EDAr EMNN EPot ESis GDra LBee MBro MHig MWat NHed NHol NMen NWCA SBla SSmi WAbe WPat
hexaphylla	ECED
hirta	CMea EHyt MHig
§ *lilaciflora*	MHig NWCA SRms SSmi
– var. *caespitosa*	See ***A. lilaciflora*** subsp. ***lilaciflora***
§ – subsp. *lilaciflora*	CMHG CPBP EBre ELan EPot MTho NMen NNrd WWin
nitida	ELan MTho NNrd
– subsp. *puberula*	See ***A. sintenisii***
odorata	See ***Galium odoratum***
§ *sintenisii* ♀	CPBP EPot LBee MBro NHar NMen NTow NWCA SBla SIng SSmi WAbe WHoo
taurina subsp. *caucasica*	EMon MBro NSti SAxl WCHb WCot WHal
taygetea NS 723	NWCA
tinctoria	CArn ELau GBar GPoy LHol MChe MHew MSal SIde SRms WCHb

ASPHODELINE (Asphodelaceae)

§ *brevicaulis*	SWas
liburnica	CMon ECGP ECha ELan EMan EMar GAbr MBel MBro MWat NBro SAga SDix SEND SSpi WCot WPer
§ *lutea*	Widely available
§ – 'Gelbkerze'	EMan WLRN
◆ – Yellow Candle	See ***A. lutea* 'Gelbkerze'**
taurica	GCal WDav WPer

ASPHODELUS (Asphodelaceae)

acaulis	ECha EWoo LWoo SWas WPGP
– SF 37	CFil CMon
§ *aestivus*	EBee SWat WPer
albus	CArn CBlo CBot CLon CMil CSpe EBee ECha LGre NPri NRai SAxl SPla SRms WCot WPer
– subsp. *albus*	CHan
brevicaulis	See ***Asphodeline brevicaulis***
cerasiferus	See ***A. ramosus***
fistulosus	CAvo CBlo CMil ELan NBir NBro SAga WCot WPer WWin WWye
lusitanicus	See ***A. ramosus***
luteus	See ***Asphodeline lutea***

microcarpus	See ***A. aestivus***
§ *ramosus*	CMon ECGP EMan GAul MTho WCot WPer

ASPIDISTRA (Convallariaceae)

elatior 🏆	CHEx CHal EBak ERav IBlr LHil MBri MHlr NRog SAxl SMad SRms WCot WOak
– 'Milky Way'	WCot
– 'Variegata' 🏆	CHal CRDP GCal IBlr LBlm MTho NBir SRms WCot
¶ *lurida*	IBlr
– 'Irish Mist'	EMon IBlr

ASPLENIUM † (Aspleniaceae)

adiantum-nigrum	NHar SRms
§ *aethiopicum*	EBee EFou
alternans	See ***A. dalhousieae***
bulbiferum 🏆	ECon LCns LHil NMar
canariense	NMar
§ *ceterach*	EFer SRms
dareoides	GDra
flabellifolium	NMar
fontanum	MBri NHar WAbe
forisiense	SMad
furcatum Thunberg	See ***A. aethiopicum***
nidus 🏆	MBri
¶ *oblongifolium*	NMar
platyneuron	CFil
ruta-muraria	SRms
§ *scolopendrium* 🏆	Widely available
– var. ***americanum***	WRic
– 'Angustatum'	CBar CBlo CMil EFou NHar SMad SPla SSoC
* – 'Circinatum'	CFil CRow WPGP
– 'Conglomeratum'	SRms
– Crispum Group	CCuc CFil CRDP CRow EBre ECha EFer ELan EMon EPla MBri MHlr NHar NHol SRms WAbe WFib WPGP
– – 'Golden Queen'	CRow
¶ – 'Crispum Bolton's Nobile'	WFib
* – Crispum Cristatum Group	EMon
– Crispum Fimbriatum Group	GQui
– 'Crispum Nobile'	CFil NBro NMar WEas WPGP WRic
– Cristatum Group	CDoC CFil CRDP CRow EBee ELan EMon IOrc MBal MBri MRav NHar NHed NHol NMar SMad SPer SRms SSoC SWat WFib WGor WRic
– Fimbriatum Group	MBri WRic
– 'Furcatum'	SMad WHil
– 'Kaye's Lacerated'	CRow EFer EGol ELan EMon MBri NHar NHed NHol NMar SChu WFib WRic
– Laceratum Group	SRms
– Marginatum Group	CFil CWGN NMar SWat WPGP
– – 'Irregulare'	CRDP NHar NHol SChu SRms WFib
– 'Muricatum'	CRDP NMar SChu WFib
– 'Ramocristatum'	CRow NMar WRic
– Ramomarginatum Group	CWGN EFer ELan EMon SRms WFar WRic
– 'Sagittatocristatum'	CFil WPGP
– 'Spirale'	NMar
– Undulatum Cristatum Group	MBri NHed WRic
– Undulatum Group	CBar EGol EPla GGar NHar NMar SRms SSpi SWat WRic
septentrionale	SRms
¶ *terrestre*	SRms
trichomanes	CCuc CDoC CFil EBee EBre EFer EFou ELan EMon GGar MBal MBri MLan MRPP NHar NHed NHol NMar SHam SRms WFib WPGP WRic
¶ – Cristatum Group	SRms
– Incisum Group	IOrc NHar NOrc SMad WCot WFib
– 'Incisum Moule'	WRic
viride	SRms

ASTARTEA (Myrtaceae)

fascicularis	ECon SOWG

ASTELIA (Asteliaceae)

banksii	CAbb CB&S CTrC EMil LHil
§ *chathamica*	CAbb CB&S CDoC CFee CFil CHEx CSWP CSpe EBee EBre EHic ERea GCal LHop SApp SArc SDry SMad WCru
– 'Silver Spear'	See ***A. chathamica***
cunninghamii	See ***A. solandri***
fragrans	CFil ECou LLew
graminea	ECou EHyt
¶ *grandis*	IBlr
nervosa	CAbb CFil CHEx ECou IBlr LHil SArc SMad WPGP
¶ *nivicola*	IBlr
¶ – 'Red Gem'	CBos IBlr
§ *solandri*	CFil CHEx LHil

ASTER † (Asteraceae)

acris	See ***A. sedifolius***
ageratoides	See ***A. trinervius*** subsp. ***ageratoides***
§ *albescens*	CGre CPle GOrc ISea MBal WSHC
alpigenus	WOMN
alpinus 🏆	CWGN EBar EBre EHyt EMNN GCHN MNrw MPla NHol NMen NNrd SBla SIng WFar WOMN WOld WPer WStI WWin
– var. ***albus***	CNic GBuc GCHN MLsm MPla NHol NPri SIng WPer
♦ – Dark Beauty	See ***A. alpinus* 'Dunkle Schöne'**
§ – 'Dunkle Schöne'	EFou NFai NOak WPer
– 'Happy End'	EMil NFai NHol NOak NPri NRoo
– 'Trimix'	ESis LFis NBir NMir NRoo NVic SRms WFar WHil
– violet	NPri WPer
– 'White Beauty'	EFou NFai SIde
amelloides	See ***Felicia amelloides***
amellus	NNor
– 'Blue King'	EFou LFis MBri NFai SPer WCot
– 'Breslau'	MBri WOld
– 'Brilliant'	CMGP EBee EBre ECtt EFou EMan EOrc EPPr MBri MWat NRoo SMer SMrm SPer WByw WCot WMer WOld WWin
– 'Butzemann'	EFou
– 'Doktor Otto Petschek'	WCra WFar WMer
♦ – Empress	See ***A. amellus* 'Glücksfund'**
– 'Framfieldii' 🏆	WOld
– 'Grunder'	EFou WOld

– 'Jacqueline Genebrier' ♀	CMil EPPr SAxl SChu SMrm SPla WOld
– 'King George' ♀	CKel EBre ECED EFou ELan EOrc EPPr ERav ERou MBel MWat NRoo SChu SPer SPla SWat WAbe WCot WEas WGwG WHoo WOld
– 'Kobold'	WFar WOld
– 'Lac de Genève'	CShe EMil WCra WOld
– 'Lady Hindlip'	MRav MUlv WEas
* – 'Mary Ann Neil'	LFis
– 'Moerheim Gem'	WEas WOld
– 'Mrs Ralph Woods'	WOld
– 'Nocturne'	ECED EPPr ERou LFis NBrk SMrm WByw WOld
– 'Peach Blossom'	CDoC WCot WOld
– 'Pink Pearl'	WOld
◆ – Pink Zenith	See *A. amellus* **'Rosa Erfüllung'**
§ – 'Rosa Erfüllung'	CShe EBre ECtt EFou ELan EOrc ERou GMaP MBri MRav NFla NNor NRoo NVic SBla SChu SPer SPla SSpe WAbe WCra WEas WHoo WOld WPer WRus
– 'Rudolph Goethe'	CSte EFou EMil EPri LIck MRav MUlv NFla NPri NVic SHBN SHel SSea WCot WEas WMer WOld
– 'Schöne von Ronsdorf'	LBuc
– 'September Glow'	ECha EGle EHal EOrc SPla
– 'Sonia'	ECED ECha EFou EGle LFis MBri NFla WCra WMer WOld
– 'Sonora'	LGre WOld
– 'Sternkugel'	CShe NBrk WOld
– 'Ultramarine'	WFar
– 'Vanity'	GBuc WOld
§ – 'Veilchenkönigin' ♀	CGle EBar EBre ECha ECtt EFou ELan EPPr ERou LFis MBri MBro MRav MTis NHaw NPla NTow SBla SChu SDix SUsu SWas WAbe WEas WFar WHoo WOld
N – Violet Queen	See *A. amellus* **'Veilchenkönigin'**
– 'Weltfriede'	WOld
asper	See *A. bakerianus*
§ *bakerianus*	CMGP NOak SBla SHel WFar WPer
'Barbara Worl'	SAsh
'Blue Star'	See *A. ericoides* 'Blue Star'
capensis 'Variegatus'	See *Felicia amelloides* **variegated**
§ *carolinianus*	WCot
'Cha-Cha'	CB&S
'Climax'	CBre ECha GBuc GCal GMac LBlm MNFA MRav MUlv NSti SAxl SHig SPer WOld
coelestis	See *Felicia amelloides*
'Coombe Fishacre' ♀	CGle EFou ERou GCal LFis LGre MBel MBri MMil MTol MUlv NCat NFai SAga SAxl SBla SHel SPla WByw WCot WEas WFar WOld
cordifolius	WFar
¶ – 'Aldebaran'	NBrk SAxl
– 'Chieftain' ♀	MWat WOld
– 'Elegans'	CDoC EFou EGar NSti SHig WOld
– 'Ideal'	CDoC WOld WPer
– 'Little Carlow'	See *A.* **'Little Carlow'** **(*cordifolius* hybrid)**
– 'Little Dorrit'	See *A.* **'Little Dorrit'** **(*cordifolius* hybrid)**
– 'Photograph'	See *A.* **'Photograph'**
– 'Silver Queen'	EOrc WOld
– 'Silver Spray'	CDoC EFou EHic EMan ERou GMaP MBri MBro MWat NBro WEas WHoo WMer WOld WPer WPyg
– 'Sweet Lavender' ♀	ERou GMac LFis NBrk WOld
corymbosus	See *A. divaricatus*
'Deep Pink Star'	WOld
delavayi	SUsu
– CLD 0494	NHol
diffusus	See *A. lateriflorus*
diplostephioides	CMil SSpi
§ *divaricatus*	Widely available
N *dumosus*	SHel WPer
eatonii	EBee
ericoides	CGle CSam EFou ERav SChu SIng WWin
– 'Blue Star' ♀	EFou EGar GBuc MBel NBrk NFai NSti SChu SHel WCot WOld
– 'Blue Wonder'	CGle MNFA NBrk
– 'Brimstone' ♀	CBre EOrc EPPr MNFA MRav SHel WOld
– 'Cinderella'	CArc CHor CVer EGar EHal EOrc EPPr GBuc GMac MNFA NFla NRoo NSti SPla WCot WOld
– 'Constance'	NBrk SHel WOld
* – 'Dainty'	CRDP
– 'Enchantress'	ERou
– 'Erlkönig'	CMGP EBee EFou EHic EPPr GAbr LHop MBri MMil MNFA MSte SChu SSpe SWat WOld WPer WWin
– 'Esther'	CGle ECha EGle ELan EMou EOrc EPri ERou LFis MNFA MSte NBrk SDix WOld
– 'Golden Spray' ♀	CBre EBee EFou MNFA NFai NSti SHel WMer WOld
– 'Herbstmyrte'	GBuc
– 'Hon. Edith Gibbs'	EOrc GMac
– 'Hon. Vicary Gibbs'	See *A.* **'Hon. Vicary Gibbs'** **(*ericoides* hybrid)**
– 'Kaytie Fisher'	LFis
– 'Maidenhood'	WBcn WOld
– 'Monte Cassino'	See *A. pringlei* **'Monte Cassino'**
– 'Pink Cloud' ♀	Widely available
– f. *prostratus*	EFol EMon ERav SCro
– 'Rosy Veil'	GMac NBrk WByw WIvy WOld
– 'Schneegitter'	EHic ESiP MBri MSte
– 'Sulphurea'	MWat
– 'White Heather'	CArc CBre CMea CVer EGar GMac LFis MBro MHlr NFai SAxl SPla WByw WCot WEas WHoo WIvy WOld WPyg
– 'Yvette Richardson'	MSte SHel WOld
farreri	NBro WPbr
¶ *foliaceus*	NTow
foliaceus var. *cusickii*	EMon
× *frikartii*	CMea EAst EBre EFou ELan ENot EOrc EPar ERou GCHN LHop MRav NFla SBla SChu SHBN SHel SPer SSoC WByw WEas WOld WPer WTyr WWin
– 'Eiger'	NBrk WOld
– 'Flora's Delight'	EBre EFou EOrc ERou MRav NRoo WOld
– 'Jungfrau'	MUlv NCut WOld
N – 'Mönch' ♀	Widely available

◆ – Wonder of Stafa	See *A.* × *frikartii* **'Wunder von Stäfa'**
§ – 'Wunder von Stäfa' ♀	EAst EBee EMan EOrc GMaP LFis LHop MBri MLsm MUlv NLak NSti SChu SHel WFar WLRN WOld
'Herfstweelde'	CMil EFou EGar EMon GBuc MSte SBla SHel SLod SWas
× ***herveyi***	EMan EMon EPPr WOld
himalaicus	GCHN GCra GTou
– CC&McK 145	GCHN MRPP NWCA
'Hittlemaar'	EPPr
§ 'Hon. Vicary Gibbs' ericoides hybrid	CBre EBee EOrc LFis MNFA MSte NBrk WCot WOld
hybridus luteus	See **× *Solidaster luteus***
§ 'Kylie' ♀	CBre EFou EMon LFis MSte NBrk SCro WCot WOld
laevis	MSte SHel SWas WCot
– 'Arcturus'	CDoC CFir CLTr EGar LBlm MBri NSti SSvw
– 'Blauhügel'	GCal
– 'Calliope'	CArc CHan EBar ECha GCal MSte SMrm SUsu SWas WCot WFar WIvy WKif WOld
lanceolatus 'Edwin Beckett'	LFis MNFA NBrk WOld
§ ***lateriflorus***	CGle CMea EJud EOrc ERav MNes MWat WHow WMaN WOld WPer
– 'Bleke Bet'	WCot
– 'Buck's Fizz'	CAbb ELan SPla
– 'Daisy Bush'	WCot
– 'Delight'	MUlv WCot
– 'Horizontalis' ♀	Widely available
– 'Lady in Black'	CBot SMrm WCot
– 'Lovely'	LFis MLLN WOld
– 'Prince'	CBos CGle CHad CMea CMil EBee ECha EFol EFou EHal ELan EMan EMon EPla ESiP EWes LFis LGre MHlr MSte NBir SHel SMad SPla SSpe SWas WCot
likiangensis	See ***A. asteroides***
§ ***linosyris***	LFis MSte SPer WCot WMer WOld
– 'Goldilocks'	See ***A. linosyris***
§ 'Little Carlow' (*cordifolius* hybrid) ♀	CBre CGle CVer EFou EHal EJud EOrc ERou GCal GMaP LFis LGre MBel MMil MNFA MRav MWat NFai NSti SAxl SBla SWas WCot WEas WNdy WOld WOve WPer WWat
§ 'Little Dorrit' (*cordifolius* hybrid)	GMac NWes WCot WOld
¶ ***maackii***	GCal
macrophyllus	CBlo CFee CPou EBee EBre EFol ELan EMon ERav MBel NSti SPer WOld
– 'Albus'	EMon EPPr WOld
– 'Twilight'	CGle EBee EGle EMan GCal GMac MSte SHel SWas WCot WFar WOld
mongolicus	See ***Kalimeris mongolica***
natalensis	See ***Felicia rosulata***
novae-angliae 'Andenken an Alma Pötschke' ♀	Widely available
– 'Andenken an Paul Gerbe'	EMon WMer
◆ – Autumn Snow	See ***A. novae-angliae*** **'Herbstschnee'**
– 'Barr's Blue'	EFou EMon MRav MSte MUlv MWat NCut SChu WMer WOld
– 'Barr's Pink'	CBre EFou EJud EMon LFis MRav MWat NFla SHel WEas WFar WMer WOld WPer WPyg
– 'Barr's Violet'	NCat NNor SAxl SRms WCot WOld WPer
– 'Christopher Harbutt'	ERou WOld
– 'Crimson Beauty'	EGar MWat WOld
– 'Festival'	CBlo LFis
– 'Forncett Jewel'	EFou
– 'Harrington's Pink' ♀	CBre CGle CMea ECED EFou ELan EMon EOrc ERou LHop MNFA MRav MWat NFai NNor NRoo NSti SChu SCro SHel SPer WByw WCra WEas WFar WHil WHow WOld WPyg WWin
§ – 'Herbstschnee'	CGle CShe EBre EFou EMon EOrc ERou GCHN GMac MBel MNFA MWat NFai NFla NHol NNor NRoo NSti SChu SEas SHel SPer SSpe WOld WPer
– 'Lachsglut'	EFou
¶ – 'Lou Williams'	WOld
– 'Lye End Beauty'	CBre CPou EMon EOrc MFir MNFA MRav MSte MUlv MWat NNor SChu WCot WOld
– 'Mrs S.T. Wright'	EFou EGar EMon ERou ESiP WByw WOld
* – 'Mrs S.W. Stern'	WOld
– 'Pink Parfait'	WCot
– 'Pink Victor'	CTri EFou EPPr NFai SEND
– 'Purple Cloud'	EMon EPPr ERou LHop MUlv
– 'Purple Dome'	CArc EBre EFou ELan EMon MBri SEND SSpe WCot WFar WOld
– 'Quinton Menzies'	EMon EOrc MUlv WOld
– 'Red Cloud'	EFou NFai
– 'Rosa Sieger'	EBre EMon SChu WMer WOld
– 'Rose Williams'	WOld
– 'Roter Stern'	EFou
– 'Rubinschatz'	WOld
– 'Rudelsburg'	EMon
– 'Sayer's Croft'	EGle WCot WOld
◆ – September Ruby	See ***A. novae-angliae*** **'Septemberrubin'**
§ – 'Septemberrubin'	CBlo CMea ECED ECtt EMon ERou LHop MRav MSte MUlv NFai SChu WByw WCot WEas WFar WOld WPyg WWin
– 'Treasure'	CBre EFou EMon WOld
– 'Violetta'	EMon MSte NFai WOld
– 'W. Bowman'	EMon
novi-belgii	SEas WHer
N – 'Ada Ballard'	CBlo CMGP CVer EBee ECED EMan ERou GCHN MBel SPer WGwG WLRN WOld
– 'Albanian'	CElw EJud WOld
– 'Alderman Vokes'	ERou WOld
– 'Alex Norman'	ERou WOld
– 'Algar's Pride'	ERou MUlv WOld
– 'Alice Haslam'	CBlo CMGP ECle ECtt EFou EPPr GBri MBri MFir MRav NOrc NPri SIde SSpe WByw WHil WLRN WOld WOve WPer WRHF WTyr
– 'Alpenglow'	WOld
– 'Anita Ballard'	WOld
– 'Anita Webb'	ERou GBri NBir WOld WPer
– 'Anneke'	EPfP WGor
◆ – Antwerp Pearl	See ***A. novi-belgii*** **'Antwerpse Parel'**
– 'Apollo'	CB&S MBri NBus NPri

– 'Apple Blossom'	SHel WOld
– 'Arctic'	ERou WBcn WOld
– 'Audrey'	CMGP EBar ECED ECtt EFou ERou GCHN GMaP MBri MLLN MNFA NBro NLak NOrc SChu SEas SMer SUsu WByw WCot WGwG WMer WOld
– 'Autumn Beauty'	WOld
– 'Autumn Days'	WOld
– 'Autumn Glory'	ERou WOld
– 'Autumn Rose'	WOld
– 'Baby Climax'	WOld
– 'Beauty of Colwall'	WOld
– 'Beechwood Challenger'	CDoC ERou MOne WMer WOld
– 'Beechwood Charm'	MNFA WOld
– 'Beechwood Rival'	WMer
– 'Beechwood Supreme'	ERou WOld
– 'Bewunderung'	EFou WOld
– 'Blandie'	CBlo CDoC CTri ECED EFou ERou LGan MSte MWat NBro SHel WLRN WOld
– 'Blauglut'	EFou WOld
– 'Blue Baby'	LHop MRav WPer
– 'Blue Bouquet'	CDoC ECED ERou SRms WByw WOld
– 'Blue Boy'	WOld
– 'Blue Danube'	WOld
– 'Blue Eyes'	ERou LGre WOld
– 'Blue Gown'	EGar ERou GCal MUlv WOld
– Blaue Lagune = 'Blue Lagoon'	CBlo NCut WOld
– 'Blue Patrol'	ERou WOld
– 'Blue Radiance'	MNFA WOld
– 'Blue Whirl'	ERou WOld
– 'Bonanza'	WOld
– 'Boningale Blue'	MUlv WOld
– 'Boningale White'	ERou WOld
– 'Bridesmaid'	SHel WOld
– 'Brightest and Best'	NBrk WOld
¶ – 'Caborn Pink'	LLWP
– 'Cameo'	WOld
– 'Cantab'	WBcn WOld
– 'Carlingcott'	ERou WOld
– 'Carnival'	CBlo CKel CM&M CMGP EBee EFou ERou LFis MBri MUlv NHaw NOrc SHel SPer SSpe WHow WOld
– 'Cecily'	WOld
– 'Charles Wilson'	WOld
– 'Chatterbox'	CDoC ECtt MRav MWat SChu SRms WOld
– 'Chelwood'	WOld
– 'Chequers'	CBlo CM&M EBee ECED ECot EMan ERou NNor WGor WHow WLRN WOld
– 'Christina'	See ***A. novi-belgii* 'Kristina'**
– 'Christine Soanes'	EFou WOld
– 'Cliff Lewis'	CShe ERou WOld
– 'Climax Albus'	See ***A.* 'White Climax'**
– 'Cloudy Blue'	CElw WOld
– 'Colonel F.R. Durham'	ERou WMer
– 'Coombe Delight'	ERou
– 'Coombe Gladys'	ERou WOld
– 'Coombe Joy'	ERou WOld
– 'Coombe Margaret'	MLLN WOld
– 'Coombe Pink'	ERou
– 'Coombe Queen'	WOld
– 'Coombe Radiance'	ERou WOld
– 'Coombe Ronald'	ERou MWat WOld
– 'Coombe Rosemary'	CDec EBre ECtt EPPr ERou MUlv WByw WCot WOld WRHF
– 'Coombe Violet'	LGre MWat NCat WOld
– 'Countess of Dudley'	WOld WPer
– 'Court Herald'	NCat WOld
– 'Crimson Brocade'	CDoC CTri ECED ELan ENot EPfP ERou MWat SHel SPer WMer WOld WWhi
– 'Dandy'	CBlo CKel COtt ECot EFou ELan MMil SChu SEas WByw WGwG WOld WSan
– 'Daniela'	EFou WOld
– 'Daphne Anne'	WOld
– 'Dauerblau'	EFou WOld
– 'Davey's True Blue'	CTri EFou EMan ERou WGwG WLRN WOld
– 'David Murray'	WOld
– 'Dazzler'	WOld
– 'Destiny'	WOld
– 'Diana'	CNic ERou WOld
– 'Diana Watts'	ERou WOld
– 'Dietgard'	WBcn WOld
– 'Dolly'	NBir WOld
– 'Dusky Maid'	SHel WOld
– 'Elizabeth'	CElw WOld
– 'Elizabeth Bright'	WOld
– 'Elizabeth Hutton'	WOld
– 'Elsie Dale'	WOld
– 'Elta'	WOld
– 'Erica'	CElw MWat WCot WOld
– 'Ernest Ballard'	ERou MRav WOld
– 'Eva'	WOld
– 'Eventide'	CB&S CElw CTri ECED EFou ENot ERou SPer WOld WRHF
– 'F.M. Simpson'	ERou
– 'Fair Lady'	ERou MWat WOld
– 'Faith'	WOld
– 'Farrington'	WOld
– 'Fellowship'	CB&S CElw CFir CKel CMGP EBre ECED EFou ERou GCHN MHlr MNFA MUlv MWat SEas SPer SRms WCot WEas WGwG WOld
– 'Fontaine'	WOld
– 'Freda Ballard'	EBee ECED ERou GCHN GMaP MRav MUlv MWat WGwG WLRN WOld
– 'Fuldatal'	EFou SHel WOld
– 'Gayborder Royal'	CFir ECED ERou SHel WOld
– 'Gayborder Splendour'	WOld
– 'Glory of Colwall'	WOld
– 'Goliath'	WOld
– 'Guardsman'	ERou MBri MUlv WOld
– 'Gulliver'	WOld
– 'Gurney Slade'	EJud ERou MBri NCut WOld
– 'Guy Ballard'	ERou
– 'Harrison's Blue'	ERou WOld WPer
– 'Heinz Richard'	CBlo CM&M EBee ECha EFou LHop MBri MUlv NBir SBla SChu WCot WLRN WOld
– 'Helen'	WOld
– 'Helen Ballard'	ERou NBrk WOld
– 'Herbstpurzel'	WGor WMer
– 'Hilda Ballard'	ERou WOld
– 'Ilse Brensell'	EFou WOld
– 'Irene'	WOld
– 'Isabel Allen'	WOld
– 'Janet McMullen'	EJud
– 'Janet Watts'	ERou WOld
– 'Jean'	MUlv MWat SChu SHel WOld
– 'Jean Gyte'	WOld

– 'Jenny' EBre ECED ECtt EFou ERav GCHN GMaP LHop MBri MBro MRav MWat NBir SHBN SPer WByw WEas WHil WHoo WOld WPer WTyr
– 'Jollity' WOld
– 'Judith' MUlv WOld
– 'Julia' WOld
– 'Karminkuppel' EFou WOld
– 'King of the Belgians' WOld
– 'King's College' CElw MBri WOld
§ – 'Kristina' EBre ECha ECtt EFol EFou ERou LLWP MCLN MOne MRav MUlv NBrk SChu SSpe SUsu WCot WHow WOld WRHF
– 'Lady Evelyn Drummond' WOld
– 'Lady Frances' WOld
– 'Lady in Blue' CElw EBre ECtt EFou ELan ENot GCHN IHos MBro MRav MWat NMir NVic SBla SEas SPer SSpe SUsu SWat WByw WFar WGwG WHil WHoo WOld WPer WTyr WWin
– 'Lady Paget' WOld
– 'Lassie' ERou LFis MLLN MWat WOld
– 'Lavender Dream' WOld
– 'Lawrence Chiswell' SHel WOld
– 'Lilac Time' WByw WOld
– 'Lisa Dawn' WOld
– 'Little Boy Blue' CB&S CDoC ERou NBus SHBN WByw WMer WOld
– 'Little Man in Blue' WOld
– 'Little Pink Beauty' EBar EBre ECtt EFou ELan ERou GCHN IHos LHop MBri MBro MRav NFai NMir NVic SAga SEas SHel SPer SSpe SWat WGwG WHoo WOld WTyr WWin
– 'Little Pink Lady' ECED ERou WOld
– 'Little Pink Pyramid' LLWP SRms
– 'Little Red Boy' CB&S CBlo ERou MBel MTol WOld
– 'Little Treasure' WOld
– 'Lucy' WOld
– 'Mabel Reeves' CShe
– 'Madge Cato' WOld
– 'Malvern Castle' ERou
– 'Mammoth' WOld
– 'Margaret Rose' NOrc NPla WOld
– 'Margery Bennett' ERou GBri WOld
– 'Marie Ballard' CB&S CElw CShe CTri EBre ECED ENot ERou GMaP MBri MFir MRav MWat NBro NNor NOrc SChu SEas SHBN SHel SPer SRms WEas WHow WOld WPer
– 'Marie's Pretty Please' WOld
– 'Marjorie' SEas WOld
– 'Marjory Ballard' WOld
– 'Martonie' WOld WPer
– 'Mary Ann Neil' WOld
– 'Mary Deane' WOld WPer
– 'Melbourne Belle' MUlv WOld
– 'Melbourne Magnet' ERou WOld
– 'Michael Watts' ERou WOld
– 'Mistress Quickly' CPou CTri ERou MBel SHel WOld
– 'Mount Everest' CDoC ERou WMer WOld WPer
– 'Mrs Leo Hunter' WOld
– 'Newton's Pink' CTri
– 'Niobe' ELan WMer WOMN
– 'Nobilis' WOld
– 'Norman's Jubilee' ERou MUlv NBir WOld
– 'Norton Fayre' CShe
– 'Nursteed Charm' WOld
– 'Oktoberschneekuppel' ERou MBri
– 'Orlando' ERou WCot WOld
– 'Pacific Amarant' SRos
– 'Pamela' ERou WOld
– 'Patricia Ballard' CBlo CMGP CShe CTri ECED ERou LFis MFir MRav MWat NBro NLak NNor SMer SPer SSpe WLRN WOld WPer
– 'Peace' WOld
– 'Percy Thrower' EFou ERou WEas WLRN WOld
– 'Peter Chiswell' MTol WOld
– 'Peter Harrison' GMaP GMac MOne NBir NBrk NBro WOld WPer
– 'Peter Pan' NBus WOld
– 'Picture' WOld
– 'Pink Gown' WOld
– 'Pink Lace' EBar ERou MLLN NPla WByw WOld WPer
– 'Pink Pyramid' EJud WOld
– 'Plenty' ERou MBri NCut WOld
– 'Pride of Colwall' ERou MUlv MWat
– 'Priory Blush' ERou GMac NBrk WOld
– 'Professor Anton Kippenberg' CBlo CShe EBee EFou EJud EMan EPPr ERav ERou GCHN GMaP GMac LBlm MBri MBro MRav NFai NPri SPer WOld
– 'Prosperity' ERou WOld
* – 'Prunella' ERou WOld
– 'Purple Dome' EBre ECha WBcn WOld
– 'Queen Mary' ERou WMer WOld
– 'Queen of Colwall' WOld
– 'Ralph Picton' WOld
– 'Raspberry Ripple' CBlo ECot ERou EWes NPla SEas WLRN WOld WSan
– 'Red Robin' MWat
– 'Red Sunset' CB&S ERou SRms WOld
* – 'Reitlinstal' WLRN
– 'Remembrance' EFou MBri WOld WWhi
– 'Reverend Vincent Dale' WOld
– 'Richness' ERou LGre SHel WOld
– 'Robin Adair' WOld
– 'Roland Smith' WOld
– 'Rose Bonnet' CKel CMGP EFou ENot IHos MMil MTol MWat SChu SHBN WLRN
– 'Rose Bouquet' WOld
– 'Rosebud' CBlo ELan SEas WEas WOld
– 'Rosemarie Sallmann' EFou
– 'Rosenwichtel' EFou EMar GAri MBri MCLN SAga WLRN WOld
– 'Royal Blue' WMer
– 'Royal Ruby' ECtt WBcn WOld
– 'Royal Velvet' ECED ENot ERou WOld
– 'Rozika' EFou WOld
– 'Rufus' ERou WOld
– 'Sailor Boy' CBre EFou ERou LFis MUlv WLRN WOld
– 'Saint Egwyn' WOld
– 'Sam Banham' ERou
– 'Sandford White Swan' EJud ERou LLWP MBel MBri MTol MUlv WPer
– 'Sandford's Purple' CVer
– 'Sarah Ballard' ERou MUlv MWat WOld

§ – 'Schneekissen'	EBre ECtt EGoo EHal EMan GMaP LHop MBri MBro NMir NPri NTow SAga SBla SEND SMer SPer WGwG WHil WLRN WOld
– 'Schöne von Dietlikon'	CDoC EFou MUlv WMer WOld
– 'Schoolgirl'	CShe ERou MBri MUlv WOld
– 'Sheena'	ERou MBri MUlv WCot WOld
◆– Snow Cushion	See *A. novi-belgii* **'Schneekissen'**
– 'Snowdrift'	WOld
– 'Snowsprite'	CB&S ECED ELan EMan MWat NBro NOrc SWat WByw WCot WGwG WHoo WOld
– 'Sonata'	EBee EFou EJud ERou GMaP NNor SPer WOld
– 'Sophia'	ERou NCut WOld
– 'Starlight'	ENot ERou WOld WRHF
– 'Steinebrück'	EFou WOld
– 'Sterling Silver'	CShe ERou WByw WOld
– 'Storm Clouds'	EFou LFis
– 'Sunset'	WOld
– 'Sweet Briar'	WOld
– 'Tapestry'	CDoC WBcn WOld
– 'Terry's Pride'	WOld
– 'The Archbishop'	WOld
– 'The Bishop'	ERou WOld
– 'The Cardinal'	ECED ERou LFis WOld
– 'The Choristers'	CShe CVer WOld
– 'The Dean'	ERou NHaw WOld
– 'The Rector'	WOld
– 'The Sexton'	ERou WOld
– 'Thundercloud'	SHel WOld
– 'Timsbury'	WOld
– 'Tony'	WOld
– 'Tosca'	LFis
– 'Tovarich'	GMac NBrk WOld
– 'Triumph'	LFis
– 'Trudi Ann'	EFou LFis NBir WOld
– 'Twinkle'	EFou LFis WOld
– 'Victor'	MBal WOld
– 'Violet Lady'	ERou WOld
– 'Violetta'	CB&S
– 'Waterperry'	MWat
– 'Weisse Wunder'	EFou WOld
– 'White Ladies'	CBlo EBee ECtt EFou ERou GAri GMaP LLWP MUlv MWat NNor NOrc SMer SPer WGwG WLRN
– 'White Swan'	CBre CPou EMon EPPr NOak WEas WOld
– 'White Wings'	WCot WOld
– 'Winston S. Churchill'	CRDP CTri ECED EFol ELan ENot ERou GMaP MHFP MNFA MTol MWat NNor NOrc NSti SEas SHBN SHel SPer SSea SSpe WOld
'Ochtendgloren' (*pringlei* hybrid) 🏆	EBre EFou EGle EMon EPPr GBuc MSte MUlv WCot WOld
pappei	See ***Felicia amoena***
'Pearl Star'	WOld
petiolatus	See ***Felicia petiolata***
§ 'Photograph' 🏆	EFou EGar MNFA MWat NBrk WOld
§ ***pilosus*** var. ***demotus*** 🏆	EGar EPPr MRav MSte SCro SHel SMrm SPla WFar
¶ 'Pink Cassino'	CB&S WRus
'Pink Star'	CMil EFou GMac MHlr NPri NSti NWoo SUsu WCot WOld
'Plowden's Pink'	WOld
¶ 'Poollicht'	EFou
§ ***pringlei*** 'Monte Cassino' 🏆	CGle COtt EBre ECha EFou EHal ERou LGre LHop MBel MRav MUlv MWat NBrk NFai NRoo NSti SDix SHel SPer SPla SUsu SWas WCot WHil WOld WRus WWat
I – 'Phoebe'	WCot
– 'Pink Cushion'	WCot
§ ***ptarmicoides***	CBlo CFee EFou EMon WCot WEas WOld WPer
pyrenaeus 'Lutetia'	EBee ECha EFou EGar EMan EPPr GCal GMac MMil MNFA MUlv NSti SHel WCot WFar WOld WOve
radula	CDoC EGar EMon EPPr GCal NBrk NSti WCot WOld
'Ringdove' (*ericoides* hybrid) 🏆	CMGP EBee ECED EGar ERou MMil MNFA MWat NSti SAxl SPla WCot WEas WLRN WOld WPen
'Rosa Star'	SHel WOld
rotundifolius 'Variegatus'	See ***Felicia amelloides variegated***
* ***sativus atrocaeruleus***	EBre ECro EPPr
scandens	See ***A. carolinianus***
schreberi	WCot
§ ***sedifolius***	EJud ELan EMan EMon LFis MNFA MSte MTol MWat SDix SUsu WCot WEas WFar WOld WPer WWhi
– 'Nanus'	CHan ECED ECha EFol EFou ERou LFis MBri NBir NFai NSti SMrm WByw WCot WFar WHow WOld
'Snow Flurry'	ECha EJud MHlr NSti WCot WOld
'Snow Star'	SHel WOld
spathulifolius	EBee
spectabilis	CChu CLyd GAbr WOld
stracheyi	NTow
subspicatus	EBee WPer
tataricus 'Jindai'	WCot
thomsonii 'Nanus'	CGle CLyd CSam EBre ECha EFou EMon GCHN LFis LGre MRav NNrd NRoo SBla SPer SUsu SWas WEas WHoo WHow WMer WOld WSHC
tibeticus	See ***A. flaccidus***
§ ***tongolensis***	CBlo SAga SEas SIgm WFar WOMN WWin
– 'Berggarten'	CMil EBre LFis MBri MCli MMil MRav NHaw NRoo SBla SCro SUsu WAbe WFar WMer
– 'Dunkleviolette'	GBuc NBro
– 'Lavender Star'	CBlo EFou GBuc NMir SRms
– 'Leuchtenburg'	ERou
– 'Napsbury'	CBlo ECha ERou GCal LFis MCli NPri NSti
– 'Sternschnuppe'	MCli
◆– Summer Greeting	See ***A. tongolensis*** **'Sommergrüss'**
– 'Wartburgstern'	EBee EGar EMan EPfP LFis MCli NPri SHel SPla WGwG WLRN WPer
tradescantii hort.	See ***A. pilosus*** var. ***demotus***
– Linnaeus	CGle CLTr EBar EBee ECha EFou ELan EMan MFir MNFA MRav MUlv NOak NSti SHel SMad SSvw WEas WOld
tripolium	CKin WHer WOld

N ***turbinellus*** hort. ♀	EFou EMon GBuc MHlr MNFA NBrk NTow SChu SMrm WCot WFar WHer WOld
umbellatus	CBre CLTr EMon EOrc EPPr SRms WCot WOld
vahlii	ECou GAbr WPer
vimineus Lamarck	See ***A. lateriflorus***
– 'Ptarmicoides'	See ***A. ptarmicoides***
§ 'White Climax'	EFou MUlv SHig WCot WOld
'Yvonne'	CBre

ASTERANTHERA (Gesneriaceae)

ovata	CAbb CChu CFil CGre CPlN GGGa GGar GOrc MBal SArc SBid SBra WAbe WBod WCru WGwG WSHC WWat

ASTERISCUS (Asteraceae)

'Gold Coin'	See ***A. maritimus***
§ ***maritimus***	EHic IHos LHil LIck MLan NPri SHFr

ASTEROMOEA (Asteraceae)

mongolica	See ***Kalimeris mongolica***

ASTILBE † (Saxifragaceae)

'Aphrodite' (*simplicifolia* hybrid)	CCuc EAst EBar EBee EGol EPGN GAbr LFis MBri NFla NHol NMir NOrc NPro SChu SPla SSpi WAbe WGor WSan WTyr
× ***arendsii***	CPea MBro NNor WPer
– 'Amethyst'	CBlo CCuc CHor CMGP CMHG CTri EBee EBre EGol EPGN MCli NFai NRoo SEas SHig SMer SPer
– 'Anita Pfeifer'	CMHG LBuc LRHS MBri WMer
– 'Bergkristall'	CCuc CMHG EMil
§ – 'Brautschleier' ♀	CB&S CMHG CTri ECtt EFou EGol ENot EPla GCHN MWat NCut NFai SMer
– 'Bressingham Beauty'	CCuc CMHG CShe EBre ECtt EHon ELan ENot EPGN EPar GCHN GMaP LSyl MBri MCLN MRav NBee NFla NHol NRoo SChu SCro SHig SPer
◆ – Bridal Veil	See *A.* × ***arendsii*** **'Brautschleier'**
– 'Bumalda'	CDoC CFir CMHG COtt EPGN GCHN MBri MCli MSte MUlv NBee SApp SHel WWat
– 'Cattleya'	CCuc CMHG EFou EPla WFar WGor
* – 'Cattleya Dunkel'	CMHG
– 'Ceres'	CCuc CDoC CMHG MWat NHol
§ – 'Diamant'	CDoC CHor CMHG LFis MBri SEas WFar
◆ – Diamond	See *A.* × ***arendsii*** **'Diamant'**
– 'Drayton Glory'	See *A.* × ***rosea*** **'Peach Blossom'**
– 'Elizabeth Bloom'	CKni EBre EPGN GCHN GSki MBri
– 'Ellie'	CCuc CSte MBri
– 'Erica'	CBlo CHor CMHG CTri GGar MBri MRav
– 'Fanal' ♀	Widely available
– 'Federsee'	CB&S CMGP CMHG ECha ELan EPGN LHop SCro SHig SPer WFar WLRN
§ – 'Feuer'	CB&S CCuc CMGP CMHG CSam CShe EBre ECha ELan GCHN GGar NHol NVic SPer SPla
◆ – Fire	See *A.* × ***arendsii*** **'Feuer'**
– 'Gertrud Brix'	CB&S CCuc EPar WMer WRus
– 'Gladstone'	CMea GDTE WGor WWeb
– 'Gloria'	CCuc CMHG CTri EBee MBri NCut
– 'Gloria Purpurea'	CBlo CCuc CHor CKni CMHG LRHS MBri MUlv NHol
◆ – Glow	See *A.* × ***arendsii*** **'Glut'**
§ – 'Glut'	CMHG MBri SCro SRms WFar
– 'Granat'	CCuc CDoC CHor CMHG EPGN MBal MCli NHol WLRN WWin
– 'Grete Püngel'	EGol EMil LRHS MBri WMer
– 'Harmony'	CMHG
◆ – Hyacinth	See *A.* × ***arendsii*** **'Hyazinth'**
§ – 'Hyazinth'	CMHG EBee EGol ELan EPGN GAbr MCli NBee NFai NHol NOrc SCro WGwG WTyr
– 'Irrlicht'	CB&S CCuc CGle CMHG CShe EBre ECha EHon ELan EPla LHop MBal NDea NFla NHol NRoo SChu SCro SPer SWat
– 'Kvele'	CMHG EBee EPGN MBri WFar
§ – 'Lachskönigin'	CMHG MWat
¶ – 'Mont Blanc'	CMHG
– 'Obergärtner Jürgens'	EPGN
– 'Paul Gaärder'	CMHG
– 'Pink Curtsy'	EBre
◆ – Pink Pearl	See *A.* × ***arendsii*** **'Rosa Perle'**
– 'Queen of Holland'	CMHG GLil MCli
◆ – Red Light	See *A.* × ***arendsii*** **'Rotlicht'**
§ – 'Rosa Perle'	CCuc CMHG ECha NHol
§ – 'Rotlicht'	MBri
◆ – Salmon Queen	See *A.* × ***arendsii*** **'Lachskönigin'**
– 'Snowdrift'	CCuc CMHG EBar EBre ECha EFou EGol EPGN EPla ERav GAri MCli MUlv NMir NNor NOak NOrc SHel SWat
¶ – 'Solferino'	CMHG
– 'Spartan'	CCuc CMHG EBee ECot EHic EPGN MBri NPro WFar WGor WLRN
– 'Spinell'	CBlo GLil MWat
– 'Venus'	CCuc CMHG CSam CShe ECED ECha ECtt EFou EGol MBel NHol NOrc NVic SChu SPer SWat WFar WTyr
¶ – 'Walküre'	CMHG
– 'Washington'	MCli WMer
§ – 'Weisse Gloria'	CCuc CMHG EBee EBre ECha EPar NMGW NPla NSti SPla WDav
– 'Weisse Perle'	CMHG
◆ – White Gloria	See *A.* × ***arendsii*** **'Weisse Gloria'**
– 'White Queen'	NHol NWoo
– 'William Reeves'	CCuc CKni CMHG MFir NHol
¶ – 'Zuster Theresa'	MBri
astilboides	CHan NHol WCot
'Atrorosea' (*simplicifolia* hybrid)	ECha MBri
'Betsy Cuperus' (*thunbergii* hybrid)	CMHG EFou MCli
'Bonn' (*japonica* hybrid)	CB&S EPar SRms WRus

§ 'Bronce Elegans' (*simplicifolia* hybrid) 🏆	CB&S COtt EBar EBre ECha EFou EPar GLil MBal MGrG NHar NHol NMir NOrc SChu SCro SPer WAbe WCot WFar WTyr
* 'Carmine King'	LFis
'Carnea' (*simplicifolia* hybrid)	EGol
'Catherine Deneuve'	EBre
'Cherry Ripe'	See ***A.*** × ***arendsii*** **'Feuer'**
chinensis	CMHG IBlr NCut
– var. ***davidii***	CMHG
– 'Finale'	CCuc EGle EPGN GLil NHol NOrc SPer WEas WFar
– 'Frankentroll'	CMHG
– 'Intermezzo'	EBee EPGN GMaP
§ – var. ***pumila*** 🏆	CB&S CCuc CGle CMHG CRow CTri ECha EFou ELan EMNN GAbr MBal MBar MBri NCat NCut NDea NFai NHar NHol NRoo NSti SApp SPer WAbe WEas WHoo WPer
chinensis pumila 'Serenade'	CCuc SHig WFar
chinensis 'Purple Glory'	CMHG
– 'Spätsommer'	CMHG
◆ – var. ***taquetii*** Purple Lance	See ***A. chinensis*** var. ***taquetii*** **'Purpurlanze'**
§ – – 'Purpurlanze'	CMHG EBre ECha GCHN MBri MRav MUlv NBir NCat NOrc WCot WFar WMer WTyr WWin
§ ***chinensis*** var. ***taquetii*** 'Superba' 🏆	CCuc CGle CMHG CRow EBre ECha ECoo ELan GCHN MNrw MSte NCut NDea NFai NHol NNor NSti NTow SDix SHig SPer WEas WOld WSan
– 'Veronica Klose'	CMHG EGol EPGN MBri NPro
– 'Visions'	CCuc CSte MBri
◆ Cologne	See ***A.*** **'Köln' (japonica hybrid)**
* 'Crimson Feather'	ECha
× ***crispa***	GAbr IBlr
– 'Gnom'	NHar
– 'Lilliput'	CB&S CMGP EPPr MBri NHar
– 'Perkeo' 🏆	CB&S CCuc CMHG CMea COtt CRow EBre ECha ECtt EGle EPGN GCHN GDra GGar LHop MBel MBri MBro MCli NBir NHar NHol NMen NOak NRoo SRms WCot
– 'Peter Pan'	NSla
– 'Snow Queen'	NHar NMen NPro WFar
'Darwin's Dream'	MBri
'Darwin's Surprise'	CSte
'Deutschland' (*japonica* hybrid)	CB&S CMHG EBre ECED EGol ELan EPGN GAbr GCHN LSyl MBri MCLN MGrG MRav NBir NHol NNor SApp SCro SMad SPer SPla SSoC SSpi SWat WAbe WEas WGwG WHoo WWin
'Dunkellachs' (*simplicifolia* hybrid)	CBlo CCuc CM&M EBee EBre ECha EGol EPGN MBri SHig SPla WAbe WMer
'Düsseldorf' (*japonica* hybrid)	CCuc CMHG GGar MBri SPer SSea WRus
'Emden' (*japonica* hybrid)	MWat
'Etna' (*japonica* hybrid)	CB&S CCuc CDoC CMHG EGle GBri GDTE MBal NCut SCro WRus WWeb

'Europa' (*japonica* hybrid)	CBlo CCuc CSte EAst EBee EMil MBal NCut NOak SMad SSoC WWeb
glaberrima	EPPr EPar NGre
– var. ***saxatilis*** 🏆	CCuc CRow ELan GAri GCHN MBal MBro NOak NRoo NRya NSla NTow NWoo SChu WAbe WHal
◆ ***glaberrima saxosa***	See ***A.*** **'Saxosa'**
* ***glaberrima saxosa minor***	NNrd
'Glenroy Elf'	MBal
grandis	CMHG EPGN GBur SHhN SSca
'Hennie Graafland' (*simplicifolia* hybrid)	CB&S CMHG EBee EGol WCra
'Inshriach Pink' (*simplicifolia* hybrid)	CBro CCuc CMHG EBre EGol ELan EPGN EPla GDra MBri MUlv NBir NHar NHol NMen NNrd NOak WHal
'Jo Ophorst' (*davidii* hybrid)	CCuc CMHG EBre ECha ECtt GCHN MBel MCLN MRav NDea SPer WGwG WLRN
'Koblenz' (*japonica* hybrid)	CCuc CMHG EPGN MBri
§ 'Köln' (*japonica* hybrid)	CMHG EMil
'Mainz' (*japonica* hybrid)	CMHG EGol
microphylla	CCuc CMHG NHol
– pink	CMHG NHol
'Moerheimi' (*thunbergii* hybrid)	CMHG
'Montgomery' (*pitardii* × *japonica*)	CCuc CHor EBre ECha EPGN MBri NFai NHol
◆ Ostrich Plume	See ***A.*** **'Straussenfeder' (*thunbergii* hybrid)**
'Peaches and Cream'	MRav
'Peter Barrow' (*glaberrima* hybrid)	SRms
'Professor van der Wielen' (*thunbergii* hybrid)	CCuc CGle CMHG EBre EGle EMan EPGN GCHN GCal GGar MCli MSte SMer SPer SRms WWat
pumila	See ***A. chinensis*** var. ***pumila***
* 'Red Admiral'	NNor
'Red Sentinel' (*japonica* hybrid)	CB&S CCuc EBre EFou EPar EPla GCHN MCli NBee NHar NHol NOrc SPla
'Rheinland' (*japonica* hybrid) 🏆	CCuc CMHG EGol EPfP GCHN MBri SSea WEas WHoo WRus
rivularis	CFil CMHG SDix WPGP
§ × ***rosea*** 'Peach Blossom'	CB&S CCuc CDoC CM&M CMHG EPGN EPar GCHN MBal MBro MGrG NBir NFai NHol NSti SEas SHel WFar WHoo WMer
– 'Queen Alexandra'	LFis
'Rosea' (*simplicifolia* hybrid)	CCuc NHol WFar
'Rosemary Bloom'	EBee EBre EPGN
§ 'Saxosa'	EPot ESis NMGW
* 'Saxosa' × ***glaberrima***	MFos
* 'Showstar'	SHam
simplicifolia 🏆	CGle CRow NHar NMen WCot WEas WFar
– 'Alba'	EFou GGar NHol
◆ – Bronze Elegance	See ***A.*** **'Bronce Elegans' (*simplicifolia* hybrid)**
– 'Darwin's Snow Sprite'	CSte MBri
– × ***glaberrima***	GDra NHar
* – 'Nana Alba'	NPro
– 'Praecox Alba'	CBlo CCuc EBre ECha MCli NFla NHol
sp. CLD 1559	NHol

'Sprite' (*simplicifolia* hybrid) 🏆	Widely available
§ 'Straussenfeder' (*thunbergii* hybrid) 🏆	CCuc CMGP CTri EBee EBre EFou EPla GCHN GCal GDTE GMaP MCli NHol SChu SHig WLRN WTyr
◆ 'Superba'	See *A. chinensis* var. *taquetii* **'Superba'**
¶ ***thunbergii***	WWat
'Vesuvius' (*japonica* hybrid)	CB&S CBlo CCuc CHor EPla LSyl MBel MGrG NCut NFai NSti
'W.E. Gladstone' (*japonica* hybrid)	CBlo CDoC CMHG EAst MSte NHol WMer
'Willie Buchanan' (*simplicifolia* hybrid)	Widely available
'Yakushima'	GCHN SRms

ASTILBOIDES (Saxifragaceae)

§ ***tabularis***	CGle CHEx CHad CHan CRow CWGN EBre ECha EFol EFou EGol ELan EOas GAbr MBro MCli NDea NSti SPer SSoC SWat WHoo WWat WWhi

ASTRAGALUS (Papilionaceae)

alopecuroides	EBee WCot
arnotianus	MSto
arnottii JCA 14169	CPBP WDav
cicer	MSto
¶ ***danicus***	WUnd
falcatus	EBee
glycyphyllos	CAgr EMan MSal WWye
§ ***massiliensis***	NTow
membranaceus	MSal
odoratus	EBee
tragacantha hort.	See ***A. massiliensis***
* ***whitneyi*** var. ***lenophyllus*** NNS 93-98	MRPP

ASTRANTHIUM (Asteraceae)

beamanii	CHan

ASTRANTIA (Apiaceae)

carniolica major	See ***A. major***
carniolica var. ***rubra***	CB&S CBot CBro CFee CKel CRow CSam CSpe EAst EBre ECED ECro EFou GLil LLWP MFir NDea NFai NFla SIng SPer SPla WAbe WByw WOMN WPyg WTyr WWat
– 'Variegata'	See *A. major* **'Sunningdale Variegated'**
helleborifolia hort.	See ***A. maxima***
§ ***major***	Widely available
major alba	CMHG CRow ECha EFol EFou EGol EMon LLWP NBir NCat NNor NPer WWeb
major subsp. ***biebersteinii***	NBir
– 'Buckland'	GBuc MHFP MTho SSpe SWas WFar WPbr
– 'Canneman'	CLon EMon WCot
– 'Claret'	CRDP EPPr LGre MHFP SWas WCot WFar
– 'Hadspen Blood'	CElw CHad CMil CSev EGol EMan GBri LGan MBel MBri MHFP MSta NNor NPro SApp SAxl SCro WBea WCot WFar WGle WMer WPbr WWeb
– 'Hillview Red'	WHil WPbr
– subsp. ***involucrata***	CDec CLon GCHN MBro NHol NVic SWat WFar WHow
– – 'Barrister'	CFil CSam GBuc MUlv WPGP
– – 'Margery Fish'	See ***A. major*** subsp. ***involucrata*** **'Shaggy'**
– – 'Moira Reid'	CArc LGan SMad WRus
§ – – 'Shaggy' 🏆	CMHG CShe EBre ECro GBri LGre MCLN MGrG NDea NNor NOak NWes SCro SPer SSpe SSvw WBea WByw WCru WEas WRus WWat
– 'Lars'	CBot CSte EAst EBee EFou EGol EMan EPPr MAvo NPri SMad SPla SSoC WCra WFar WRus WWeb
¶ – 'Maureen'	NOak
– 'Primadonna'	CSam EGol EOrc MSte MTis WFar WHil WHoo WPer WWat
major rosea	CBre CElw CGle CHan EBre ECro EFou EGol EMan EMil EMon LHop MCLN MCli MRav NBee NFla NHol NSti SChu SPer SSca WTyr
major 'Rosensinfonie'	EBee GLil MCli NCut WPyg
§ ***major rubra***	Widely available
major 'Ruby Wedding'	CBlo CGle CLon EBre EMon GBri MTho NNor NRai SBla SPer SWas WCot WFar WHoo WPbr WRus
§ – 'Sunningdale Variegated' 🏆	Widely available
– 'Titoki Point'	WCot
– 'Variegata'	See ***A. major*** **'Sunningdale Variegated'**
§ ***maxima*** 🏆	Widely available
– 'Mark Fenwick'	NBir
minor	NTow WCru
'Rainbow'	SAxl WHil
rubra	See ***A. major rubra***

ASYNEUMA (Campanulaceae)

canescens	CArc EPad NFai WCot WPen WWin
limonifolium subsp. ***pestalozzae***	EBee WBea
¶ ***lobelioides***	EHyt
pulvinatum	CPBP EHyt LBee SIng WAbe
– Mac&W 5880	EPot NNrd

ASYSTASIA (Acanthaceae)

bella	See ***Mackaya bella***
§ ***gangetica***	CSev LHil SLMG
violacea	See ***A. gangetica***

ATHAMANTA (Apiaceae)

turbith	SIgm
– subsp. ***haynaldii***	NTow

ATHEROSPERMA (Monimiaceae)

moschatum	CB&S CGre CLan CPle WSHC

ATHROTAXIS (Taxodiaceae)

cupressoides	CDoC GAri MBar
× ***laxifolia***	CDoC EBre LCon MBar MBri

ATHYRIUM † (Athyriaceae)

filix-femina ♀	CBar CCuc CFil CRow EBre ECha EFer EFou ELan EMon MBal MBri MSta NBro NEgg NFla NHed NHol NMar NOrc NPSI SPer SWat WBon WFib WHil WPGP WShi
* ***filix-femina congestum cristatum***	WFib
filix-femina 'Corymbiferum'	GQui NHar NMar SRms
– Cristatum Group	CCuc CWGN EFer ELan EMon NHol SWat WFib WRic
§ – Cruciatum Group	CRDP CRow EFer EGol ELan EMon GAri NHar NHol SAxl SRms WAbe WFar WFib WRic
– 'Fieldii'	CCuc CRow EFou NHar NHol SChu SRms WFib
– 'Frizelliae'	CBar CCuc CDoC CHan CMil CRDP CWGN EBre EFer EFou ELan EMon IOrc MBri MLan NHar NHed NHol NMar NOrc NPSI SChu SMad SPla SRms WFib WGor WHal WRic WWat
– 'Frizelliae Capitatum'	CCuc CRow SRms WFib
– 'Grandiceps'	NHar NMar SRms
– 'Minutissimum'	CCuc CDec CFil CRDP CWGN ECha EFou EGol EHon ELan EMon GCHN NMar SAxl WFib WPGP
– 'Plumosum Axminster'	CFil CRDP SAxl
– 'Plumosum Cristatum'	NMar
– Plumosum Group	CFil GQui NMar SChu WFib
– 'Plumosum Percristatum'	GQui NMar
– Ramocristatum Group	NMar
– 'Rotstiel'	LBuc
– 'Setigerum Cristatum'	NMar
* ***filix-femina superbum*** 'Druery'	WFib
filix-femina Vernoniae Group	EFer ELan EMon MBri WRic
– 'Vernoniae Cristatum'	EBee EBre EMon GBin MBal NHar NHol NMar WFib
– Victoriae Group & cl.	See ***A. filix-femina*** **Cruciatum Group**
goeringianum 'Pictum'	See ***A. niponicum*** **var.** ***pictum***
niponicum	CCuc WAbe
– crested	ELan
– f. ***metallicum***	See ***A. niponicum*** **var.** ***pictum***
§ – var. ***pictum*** ♀	Widely available
* – 'Pictum Cristatoflabellatum'	EMon
nipponicum var. ***pictum*** crested	MBri
otophorum	CRDP EBee EMon NHol NMar SChu SRms WRic
– var. ***okanum***	CFil EBre EFer ELan MBri NHar NPSI SAxl SMrm WAbe WCot
vidalii	CFil WRic

ATRACTYLODES (Asteraceae)

¶ ***japonica***	EFEx
¶ ***macrocephala***	EFEx

ATRAGENE See CLEMATIS

ATRAPHAXIS (Polygonaceae)
See Plant Deletions

ATRIPLEX (Chenopodiaceae)

canescens	CAgr WDin
halimus	CAgr CB&S CBot CGle CHad CHan CPle CShe EHoe ENot GOrc LHil NBir NBrk SPer SWat WCot WDin WHCG WHer WPat
hortensis	MChe WWye
– gold-leaved	MLan WCot
– var. ***rubra***	CArn CGle CHad CRDP EFol ELan EOHP LHol MChe MGra MHew NWes SIde WCHb WEas WHer WJek WKif WOak WWye
portulacoides	See ***Halimione portulacoides***

ATROPA (Solanaceae)

bella-donna	CArn ECWi GBar GPoy MSal WWye
bella-donna lutea	MSal
mandragora	See ***Mandragora officinarum***

ATROPANTHE (Solanaceae)

§ ***sinensis***	MSal

AUBRIETA † (Brassicaceae)

albomarginata	See ***A.*** **'Argenteovariegata'**
'Alix Brett'	CPBP CTri EBre ECtt EDAr ELan ESis LBee NEgg NHar NPer SAga
'April Joy'	CMHG ECot EDAr ELan MPla SRms
§ 'Argenteovariegata'	ELan LHop NHol NRoo SAga SBla SIgm WAbe WPyg WWeb
'Astolat' (v)	ELan GCHN LBee MOne NHar NHol NSla SAga SBla WAbe WEas WHil WPat WRHF
§ 'Aureovariegata'	EBre EFol EGle ELan MPla NPer NRoo SAlw SBla SIng WAbe WFar
'Belisha Beacon'	ECtt EMNN LBee LRHS MBri
Bengal Hybrids	GAbr
♦ Blaue Schönheit	See ***A.*** **'Blue Beauty'**
'Blue Cascade'	ECtt EPfP MPla WGor
'Blue Emperor'	WMer
¶ 'Blue Gown'	NEgg
'Blue King'	WMer
* 'Blue Mist'	GMaP MOne
§ 'Bob Saunders' (d)	CMHG CMea CTri EBre ELan LBee LHop NVic
* 'Bonsul'	CShe
'Bordeaux'	WMer
'Bressingham Pink' (d)	CMea CTri EBre ECtt ELan LHop MHig NHol
'Bressingham Red'	EBre WMer
canescens	MSto NTow
'Carnival'	See ***A.*** **'Hartswood Purple'**
§ ***columnae macrostyla***	MSto
* ***deltoidea*** 'Gloria'	WPat
– 'Nana Variegata'	CPBP EPot MPla MTho WGor
deltoidea rosea	MHig
deltoidea 'Tauricola'	WMer WPyg
– 'Tauricola Variegata'	CShe
– Variegata Group	CShe ECtt EFol EPot ESis LHop MFir MTho NMen NSla SIng WFar WPat
'Doctor Mules' ♀	CDoC CTri EBre ECtt IHos LBee MHig NEgg SIng SMer SRms WPat
'Doctor Mules Variegata'	LGro MHig NEgg NHol NPri WHil

'Dream'	ECtt SIng
'Elsa Lancaster'	EHyt EMNN EPot EWes MHig MTho NMen NSla SAlw
'Fire King'	WMer
§ 'Frühlingszauber'	SRms WGor
◆ Spring Charm = 'Frühlingszauber'	See *A.* **'Frühlingszauber'**
'Gloriosa'	CMHG NEgg SIng
'Godstone'	ESis EWes
'Golden Carpet'	NHol SIng
'Golden King'	See *A.* **'Aureovariegata'**
¶ ***gracilis***	MSto
– subsp. ***scardica***	NTow
* 'Graeca'	WHil
'Graeca Superba'	NPri
'Greencourt Purple'	CMHG EBre ELan EMNN GAbr GMaP MHig MOne SIng SMrm WHil
'Gurgedyke'	ECho ELan MHig NHol SIng SRms
'Hartswood'	SIng
§ 'Hartswood Purple'	CShe
'Hendersonii'	SRms
'Ina den Ouden'	WMer
'J.S. Baker'	SRms
'Joan Allen'	CMHG NHar WHil
'Joy' (d)	EMNN SIng
'Lavender Gem'	CMHG
'Leichtlinii'	NNrd NPri WPyg
'Lemon and Lime'	LBee LRHS
◆ ***libanotica***	See ***A. columnae macrostyla***
'Lilac Cascade'	LRHS
'Little Gem'	MHig
'Lodge Crave'	SIng
macedonica	EPot MSto
'Magician'	ECtt NHol
'Mars'	ECho ELan SRms
'Mary Poppins'	MHig
'Maurice Prichard'	ECtt EMNN
'Mrs Lloyd Edwards'	ECtt
'Mrs Rodewald'	CMHG CMea EMNN NEgg SRms
'Novalis Blue' ♀	SRms WLRN
'Oakington Lavender'	ECho ELan IHos LHop NHol
parviflora	MSto
'Pennine Glory'	CShe
'Pennine Heather'	CShe
'Pike's Variegated'	EDAr EWes SRms
pinardii	EHyt MSto
'Prichard's A1'	WMer WPyg
'Purity'	NPri SCoo SHam
'Purple Cascade'	ECtt EMNN GCHN MOne MPla SCoo SRms WFar WGor
'Purple Charm'	SRms
'Red Carpet'	CMHG EBre ELan EMNN EPot IHos LGro MFir MHig MPla NEgg SChu SIng WEas WWin
'Red Carpet Variegated'	LRHS
'Red Cascade'	ECtt EMNN GAbr GCHN MPla SCoo
'Red Dyke'	NHol SIng
'Riverslea'	NHol SIng
'Rosanna Miles'	SIng
'Rose Queen'	CMea LBee SMrm
'Rosea Splendens'	MPla
'Royal Blue'	NNrd NRoo SHam
'Royal Red'	NPri NRoo SHam SRms WFar WGor WHil
'Royal Violet'	NPri NRoo
'Schloss Eckberg'	WMer
'Schofield's Double'	See *A.* **'Bob Saunders'**
'Silberrand'	ECha ECtt EDAr NSla SAxl
thessala	MSto NTow
¶ 'Toby Saunders'	ECho
'Triumphante'	CTri
'Wanda'	ECho ELan IHos SIng
'Whitewell Gem'	SRms

AUCUBA † (Cornaceae)

japonica (f)	SPer
– (m)	CB&S CBlo CChu CDoC CHEx ELan SReu
– 'Crassifolia' (m)	CBlo CHig MBal MRav SArc
– 'Crotonifolia' (f/v) ♀	CB&S CDoC CHEx EBre ENot EPla LPan MBal MBar MBri MGos NFla NWea SDix SHBN SPer WDin WHar WStI
– 'Gold Dust' (f/v)	CLan WWeb
– 'Gold Splash'	CBlo
– 'Golden King' (m/v)	CB&S CBlo CDoC CTrw CWLN EBee EHic EPla LNet MGos MUlv MWat SPla
– 'Golden Spangles' (v)	CB&S CBlo CKni ECot MBal MPla WRHF
– 'Goldstrike' (v)	CBlo CDoC EHoe LNet
– 'Hillieri' (f)	CLan
– 'Lance Leaf' (m/v)	MUlv
– f. ***longifolia*** ♀	CBlo CHig SArc SDix
– 'Maculata'	See ***A. japonica*** **'Variegata'**
– 'Nana Rotundifolia' (f)	EPla MUlv
– 'Picturata' (m/v)	CB&S CDoC CWLN EBre EFol ENot MBal MBri MGos NHol SAga SBid SHBN SPer WFar
– 'Rozannie' (f/m)	CB&S CDoC CWLN EAst ENot EPla MAsh MBal MBlu MBri MGos MLan MUlv MWat NBee NFla SAga SPan SPer SPla SReu WDin WStI
– 'Salicifolia' (f)	CBlo ENot EPla MAsh MBri MUlv SMad SPer
– 'Speckles'	GSki
– 'Sulphurea Marginata' (f/v)	CB&S EFol EHic EPla MAsh MBri MUlv SAga SBid SPer WGwG
§ – 'Variegata' (f/v)	CChe CWLN ELan ENot GRei LBuc MBal MBar MBri MGos MRav MWat NBee NBir NFla NNor NWea SHBN SPer SReu WAbe WBod WDin WFar WGwG WHar WStI
– Windsor form	EPla LRHS
– 'Wykehurst' (v)	LRHS

AULAX (Proteaceae)

¶ ***cancellata***	CTrC

AURINIA (Brassicaceae)

§ ***corymbosa***	CHar NRai WBea
§ ***saxatilis*** ♀	CShe EBre GAbr GDra LWak MBar NPSI SIng WFar WWin
– 'Citrina' ♀	CShe ECha ECtt EGar GMaP MPla MWat SAlw SDix SRms WPyg
– 'Compacta'	CTri EBre ECtt ENot NMir NNor WHoo
– 'Dudley Nevill'	CShe EFol EMan GAbr MCLN MPla MSCN MWat SBla SChu WFar WFoF
– 'Dudley Nevill Variegated'	EBre ECED EGar EWes GAbr MCLN NBir NRoo WFar
– 'Flore Pleno'	NRoo SBla WEas
◆ – Gold Ball	See ***A. saxatilis*** **'Goldkugel'**
– 'Gold Dust'	ECtt LGro MOne SRms WCot

– 'Golden Queen'	CDoC ECtt
§ – 'Goldkugel'	ELan EMNN GAul LBee NVic SRms WLRN WWtk
– 'Silver Queen'	ELan NRoo WEas
– 'Variegata'	SBla

AUSTROCEDRUS (Cupressaceae)

§ ***chilensis***	CDoC CGre CKen CMCN LCon MBal

AVENA (Poaceae)

candida	See ***Helictotrichon sempervirens***

AVENULA See HELICTOTRICHON

AVERRHOA (Geraniaceae)

¶ ***carambola*** (F)	LBlo

AYAPANA See EUPATORIUM

AZARA † (Flacourtiaceae)

¶ ***alpina*** SF 4583	ISea
dentata	CB&S CFil CGre CMCN CMac CPle CTrw CWLN ERea MBal WPGP WSHC
– 'Variegata'	CMac ERea LRHS SBid
¶ ***integrifolia***	CFil
– 'Variegata'	CB&S CFil CGre CPle
lanceolata	CB&S CFil CPle CTri CTrw EPfP IOrc ISea SPer WBod WWat
microphylla ♀	CB&S CFee CFil CGre CMCN CMHG CPle CShe CWLN EPla IOrc ISea MBal NSti SArc SBra SDry SPer SSpi WBod WPGP WRTC WSHC
– 'Variegata'	CAbb CB&S CDoC CFil CMac CPle EBre EHoe EPfP GQui IOrc ISea LHop MBal MBel MLan SArc SBid SBra SPan SSpi WAbe WCru WFar WGer WPGP WSHC WWat
N ***paraguayensis***	CPle GAri ISea
* ***patagonica***	ISea
petiolaris	CFil CGre CHan CPle NFla WGer
serrata	CBot CFil CGre CHEx CHan CLTr CMCN CPle EPla GOrc ISea MSCN NTow SBra SDix SMad SPer SRms WCru WDin WFar WGer WHar WPyg WRTC WWat
sp. from Chile	CGre
uruguayensis	CFil CGre

AZOLLA (Azollaceae)

caroliniana auct. non Willdenow	See ***A. mexicana***
– Willdenow	See ***A. filiculoides***
§ ***filiculoides***	CBen CHEx CRow CWGN ECoo EHon EMFW LPBA MSta SCoo SRms SWat SWyc WStI
§ ***mexicana***	SWat

AZORELLA (Apiaceae)

filamentosa	ECou LLew
glebaria A Gray	See ***Bolax gummifera***
– hort.	See ***A. trifurcata***
gummifera	See ***Bolax gummifera***
lycopodioides	ECou GCHN
§ ***trifurcata***	CTri ELan EPot GAbr GAri GDra GTou MBro NRoo SRms SSmi WAbe WByw WPer
– 'Nana'	CNic GGar MBro MHig MTho MWat NGre NHol NMen NNrd SSmi WPat

AZORINA (Campanulaceae)

§ ***vidalii***	CBot CPle CPou CSpe EPad ERea SVen WPer
– 'Rosea'	EPad

BABIANA (Iridaceae)

ambigua	NRog
angustifolia	NRog
'Blue Gem'	LBow NRog
cedarbergensis	NRog
disticha	See ***B. plicata***
dregei	NRog
ecklonii	NRog
hybrids	LBow
'Laura'	NRog
nana	NRog
odorata	NRog
§ ***plicata***	NRog
pulchra	CFee LBow NRog
pygmaea	NRog
rubrocyanea	NRog
scabrifolia	NRog
secunda	NRog
striata	NRog
stricta	NRog
– 'Purple Star'	NRog
– 'Tubergen's Blue'	NRog
tubulosa	NRog
villosa	LBow NRog
villosula	NRog
'White King'	NRog
'Zwanenburg's Glory'	NRog

BACCHARIS (Asteraceae)

genistelloides	EPla
¶ ***glomeruliflora***	CPle
halimifolia	CPle GQui MAll SEND
– 'Twin Peaks'	SDry
magellanica	ECou
patagonica	CBlo CPle LHop MAll SAga SArc SDry WBod WCru WPen

BAECKEA (Myrtaceae)
See Plant Deletions

BAHIA (Asteraceae)

¶ ***ambrosioides***	SVen

BAILLONIA (Verbenaceae)

juncea	CPle WSHC

BALDELLIA (Alismataceae)

ranunculoides	CRow
– f. ***repens***	CRDP

BALLOTA (Lamiaceae)

acetabulosa	CHan ECha EFou EGoo EHal EMan EMar MBel SDix SDry WCot
'All Hallows Green'	CGle CSam EAst EBee EBre ECtt EFou EGoo EMar EOrc GCal LHop MBel MCLN SChu WOve WWat
hirsuta	CGle CHan EBee

nigra	CArn EBee MChe MHew MSal NCGP NLak NNor SIde WHer WWye
§ – 'Archer's Variegated' (v)	CArc CHan EBar EGar EJud EMar EWes MBel NLak SAga SIde WCot WHer WRus WSan
– 'Intakes White'	MInt
– 'Variegata'	See ***B. nigra* 'Archer's Variegated'**
– 'Zanzibar' (v)	CArc EMon MBel
pseudodictamnus ♀	CB&S CBot CGle CHan CKel EBre ECha EFol EGoo ELan LHop MBal MWat NBro NFai NNor NPer NSti SDix SHBN SPer SSpe WDin WEas WHil WOve WRTC WSHC WWat WWin

BALSAMITA See TANACETUM

BALSAMORHIZA (Asteraceae)

sagittata	EMan

BAMBUSA † (Poaceae - Bambusoideae)

* ***eutuldoides***	CB&S
glaucescens	See ***B. multiplex***
* ***gracilis***	CTrC
* ***gracillima***	CB&S COtt SBam WJun
§ ***multiplex***	EFul SBam WJun
– 'Alphonse Karr'	CB&S CDoC COtt EFul EPla SBam SDry WJun
– 'Chinese Goddess'	See ***B. multiplex* var. *riviereorum***
§ – 'Fernleaf'	CB&S COtt CTrC EFul SBam SDry WJun
– 'Wang Tsai'	See ***B. multiplex* 'Fernleaf'**
oldhamii	SBam
pubescens	See ***Dendrocalamus strictus***
textilis	WJun
tuldoides	WJun
ventricosa	SBam SDry WJun
vulgaris	SBam
– 'Vittata'	SBam
– 'Wamin'	SBam

BANISTERIOPSIS (Malpighiaceae)

¶ ***caapi***	NGno

BANKSIA (Proteaceae)

aspleniifolia	MAll
¶ ***burdettii***	CTrC
¶ ***caleyi***	CTrC
¶ ***ericifolia***	CTrC SOWG
¶ ***grandis***	SOWG
integrifolia	CB&S CTrC GQui LPan MAll WDin
marginata	CTrC ECou MAll
media	CTrC MAll
quercifolia	CGre
¶ ***robur***	CTrC
serrata	LPan SOWG
¶ ***speciosa***	CTrC
¶ ***spinulosa* var. *collina***	MAll
¶ – var. ***spinulosa***	MAll

BAPTISIA (Papilionaceae)

arachnifera	WCot
australis ♀	Widely available
– dark blue form	EFou
– 'Exaltata'	EBre ELan EMan GBuc LHop
§ ***bracteata***	ECro MSal SIgm
§ ***lactea***	CBot CMdw CPle EBee ECro ELan LFis MSal NBir SPla WCot
leucantha	See ***B. lactea***
leucophaea	See ***B. bracteata***
megacarpa	EBre WCot
pendula	EMan SIgm WCot
tinctoria	CPle CWan EMon MBro MHlr MSal WCot WHoo WPyg WThi

BARBAREA (Brassicaceae)

praecox	See ***B. verna***
rupicola	WPer
§ ***verna***	CArn GPoy SIde WApp WHer WWye
vulgaris 'Variegata'	CGle CHal ECha ECro EFol EHoe ELan ERav GAbr MFir MSCN NBro NHex NOak NVic SWat WBea WByw WCHb WOve WPbr WPer WSan WWin WWye

BARLERIA (Acanthaceae)

¶ ***cristata***	ECon
* ***cristata rosea***	ECon
greenii	CSpe
obtusa	CSpe ECon
– pink	CSpe
repens	ECon
– 'Blue Prince'	CSpe
– 'Rosea'	CSpe
suberecta	See ***Dicliptera suberecta***

BARTLETTINA See EUPATORIUM

BARTSIA (Scrophulariaceae)
See Plant Deletions

BASHANIA (Poaceae - Bambusoideae)

§ ***fargesii***	EPla ISta WJun

BASSIA (Chenopodiaceae)

scoparia	MSal

BAUERA (Cunoniaceae)
See Plant Deletions

BAUHINIA (Papilionaceae)

¶ ***corymbosa***	CPlN
galpinii	CPlN CTrC MSto
¶ ***glabra***	CPlN
natalensis	CSpe
¶ ***vahlii***	CPlN

BAUMEA (Cyperaceae)

* ***rubiginosa*** 'Variegata'	MSta

BEAUCARNEA (Agavaceae) See NOLINA

BEAUFORTIA (Myrtaceae)

micrantha	SOWG
orbifolia	SOWG
sparsa	CTrC MAll SOWG

BEAUMONTIA (Apocynaceae)

grandiflora	CPlN LChe

BEAUVERDIA See TRISTAGMA, IPHEION, LEUCOCORYNE

BECKMANNIA (Poaceae)

eruciformis	ETPC

BEDFORDIA (Asteraceae)

salicina	ECou MAll

BEGONIA † (Begoniaceae)

'Abel Carrière'	ER&R
acerifolia	See ***B. vitifolia***
aconitifolia	ER&R
acutifolia	ER&R
albopicta (C)	CHal EBak ER&R
– 'Rosea'	CHal WDib
'Allan Langdon' (T)	CBla
'Alleryi' (C)	ER&R
alnifolia	ER&R
'Alto Scharff'	ER&R
'Alzasco' (C)	ER&R
'Amy' (T)	CBla
angularis	See ***B. stipulacea***
'Anita Roseanna' (C)	ER&R
'Anna Christine' (C)	ER&R
'Anniversary' (T)	CBla
'Apollo' (T)	CBla
'Apricot Delight' (T)	CBla
'Aquarius'	ER&R
'Argentea' (R)	EBak MBri
x ***argenteoguttata*** (C)	CHal ER&R
'Aries'	ER&R
'Arthur Mallet'	ER&R
'Aruba'	ER&R
'Autumn Glow' (T)	ER&R
'Baby Perfection'	WDib
'Barbara Ann' (C)	ER&R
'Barclay Griffiths'	ER&R
'Beatrice Haddrell'	CHal ER&R WDib
'Bernat Klein' (T)	CBla
'Bess'	ER&R
'Bessie Buxton'	ER&R
'Bethlehem Star'	ER&R WDib
'Bettina Rothschild'	ER&R
'Beverly Jean'	ER&R
'Billie Langdon' (T)	CBla
'Black Knight'	CHal
'Bokit'	ER&R WDib
'Bonaire'	CHal
'Boomer' (C)	ER&R
'Bouton de Rose' (T)	NRog SDeJ
bowerae	CHal ER&R
§ – var. ***nigramarga***	ER&R
bracteosa	ER&R
brevirimosa	ER&R
¶ 'Brown Twist'	WDib
'Bunchii'	ER&R
'Burgundy Velvet'	ER&R
'Burle Marx'	ER&R LChe WDib
'Bush Baby'	CHal
'Buttermilk' (T)	CBla
'Calico Kew'	ER&R
'Calla Queen' (S)	ER&R
'Camelliiflora' (T)	NRog
'Can-can'	See ***B.*** **'Herzog van Sagan'**
'Carol Mac'	ER&R
'Carol Wilkins of Ballarat' (T)	CBla
'Carolina Moon' (R)	ER&R
carolineifolia	LHil
carrieae	ER&R
§ x ***carrierei***	MBri
x ***carrierei flore-pleno***	CHal
'Cathedral'	ER&R WDib
'Chantilly Lace'	CHal ER&R
'Charles Jaros'	ER&R
¶ 'Charm' (S)	WDib
'Christmas Candy'	ER&R WDib
'Chumash'	ER&R
'Clara' (R)	MBri
'Cleopatra'	CHal ER&R MRav SLMG WDib
'Clifton'	ER&R
coccinea (C)	ER&R WDib
compta	See ***B. stipulacea***
conchifolia var. ***rubrimacula***	ER&R
'Concord'	ER&R
convolvulacea	ER&R
* 'Coppelia'	CBla
x ***corallina***	EBak
§ – 'Lucerna' (C)	CHal EBak ER&R
– 'Lucerna Amazon' (C)	CHal IBlr
'Corbeille de Feu'	CHal ER&R
'Cowardly Lion' (R)	ER&R
'Crestabruchii'	ER&R
'Crimson Cascade'	CBla
* 'Crystal Cascade'	CBla
cubensis	ER&R
cucullata	CHal ER&R
'Curly Locks' (S)	CHal
'Dancing Girl'	ER&R
'Dannebo'	MBri
'D'Artagnan'	ER&R
'Dawnal Meyer' (C)	ER&R WDib
'Decker's Select'	ER&R
decora	ER&R
deliciosa	ER&R
'Dewdrop' (R)	ER&R WDib
diadema	ER&R
'Di-anna' (C)	ER&R
dichotoma	ER&R
dichroa (C)	ER&R
'Di-erna'	ER&R
dietrichiana	See ***B. echinosepala*** **'Dietrichiana'**
– Irmsch.	ER&R
'Digswelliana'	ER&R
discolor	See ***B. grandis*** subsp. ***evansiana***
dregei (T)	ER&R
'Druryi'	ER&R SLMG
'Dwarf Houghtonii'	ER&R
* 'Ebony' (C)	CHal ER&R
echinosepala	ER&R
'Edinburgh Brevirimosa'	ER&R
egregia	ER&R
'Elaine'	ER&R
§ 'Elaine Wilkerson'	ER&R
'Elaine's Baby'	See ***B.*** **'Elaine Wilkerson'**
'Elda'	ER&R
'Elda Haring' (R)	ER&R
'Elizabeth Hayden'	ER&R
'Elsie M. Frey'	ER&R
'Emerald Giant' (R)	ER&R WDib
'Emma Watson'	CHal ER&R
'Enchantment'	ER&R
'Enech'	ER&R
'English Knight'	ER&R
'English Lace'	ER&R
epipsila	ER&R
x ***erythrophylla*** 'Bunchii'	ER&R SLMG
§ – 'Helix'	CHal ER&R
'Essie Hunt'	ER&R
'Esther Albertine' (C)	ER&R
'Evening Star'	ER&R
'Exotica'	ER&R
'Fairy'	ER&R

'Fairylight' (T)	CBla
feastii 'Helix'	See ***B.*** × ***erythrophylla* 'Helix'**
fernando-costae	ER&R
'Festiva' (T)	CBla
'Filigree'	ER&R
'Fire Flush' (R)	CHal ER&R WDib
'Firedance' (T)	CBla
'Fireworks' (R)	ER&R WDib
'Five and Dime'	ER&R
'Flamingo'	ER&R
'Flo'Belle Moseley' (C)	ER&R WDib
'Florence Carrell'	ER&R
'Florence Rita' (C)	ER&R
foliosa	ER&R WDib
– var. ***amplifolia***	CHal ER&R
§ – var. ***miniata*** 'Rosea'	CHal
'Fred Bedson'	ER&R
friburgensis	ER&R
'Frosty Fairyland'	ER&R
'Fuchsifoliosa'	ER&R
fuchsioides ♀	ER&R GCra LIck MArl NPri SMrm WDib WEas
– 'Rosea'	See ***B. foliosa*** var. ***miniata* 'Rosea'**
'Full Moon' (T)	CBla
'Fuscomaculata'	ER&R
gehrtii	ER&R
glabra	ER&R
glaucophylla	See ***B. radicans***
'Gloire de Sceaux'	ER&R
goegoensis	ER&R
'Gold Cascade'	CBla
'Gold Doubloon' (T)	CBla
'Goldilocks' (T)	CBla
'Good 'n' Plenty'	ER&R
§ ***grandis*** subsp. ***evansiana***	CDec CGle CHEx CHal EBee ELan EOas ER&R GCal LHil LHop MSte MTho NPla SBar SChu SDix SMad SSpi WCot WCru
– – var. ***alba***	CHal EMon ER&R GCal LBlm LHil MSte MTho SMad SSpi WCot
– – 'Claret Jug'	CHan
¶ – 'Maria'	GCal
– 'Simsii'	CHan WFar
'Grey Feather'	ER&R
griffithii	See ***B. annulata***
'Gustav Lind' (S)	CBrk CHal ER&R GCra SSad
'Guy Savard' (C)	WDib
'Gypsy Maiden' (T)	CBla
haageana	See ***B. scharffii***
hatacoa	ER&R
– 'Silver'	ER&R
– 'Spotted'	ER&R
'Helen Teupel' (R)	ER&R
'Her Majesty' (R)	ER&R
§ 'Herzog van Sagan' (T)	CBla ER&R
hispida var. ***cucullifera***	ER&R
'Holmes Chapel'	ER&R
homonyma (T)	ER&R
'Honeysuckle' (C)	ER&R
hydrocotylifolia	ER&R
hypolipara	ER&R
incarnata (C)	ER&R
– 'Metallica'	SLMG
'Ingramii'	ER&R
'Interlaken' (C)	ER&R
'Irene Nuss' (C) ♀	ER&R
'Ivy Ever'	ER&R
'Jean Blair' (T)	CBla
'Jelly Roll Morton'	ER&R
'Joe Hayden'	ER&R SLMG
'Kagaribi' (C)	ER&R
kellermanii (C)	ER&R
kenworthyae	ER&R
* 'Krakatoa'	CBla
'La Paloma' (C)	WDib
'Lady Carol'	CHal
'Lady Clare'	ER&R
* 'Lady France'	ER&R MBri
'Lady Snow'	CHal
'Lawrence H. Fewkes'	ER&R
leathermaniae (C)	ER&R
'Lenore Olivier' (C)	ER&R
'Leopard'	ER&R MBri
'Lexington'	ER&R
'Libor' (C)	ER&R
'Lime Swirl'	ER&R
limmingheana	See ***B. radicans***
'Linda Harley'	ER&R
'Linda Myatt'	ER&R
lindeniana	CHal ER&R
listada	CHal ER&R MBri WDib
'Lithuania'	ER&R
'Little Brother Montgomery'	ER&R WDib
'Little Darling'	ER&R
'Lois Burks' (C)	ER&R WDib
'Loma Alta'	ER&R
'Looking Glass' (C)	ER&R WDib
'Lospe-tu'	ER&R
'Lou Anne'	CBla
'Lubbergei' (C)	ER&R
'Lucerna'	See ***B.*** × ***corallina* 'Lucerna'**
'Lulu Bower' (C)	ER&R
luxurians	ER&R
– 'Ziesenhenn'	ER&R
'Mabel Corwin'	ER&R
macdougallii var. ***purpurea***	CHal
macrocarpa	ER&R
'Mac's Gold'	ER&R
maculata 'Wightii' (C)	CHal CSpe ER&R
'Mad Hatter'	ER&R
'Madame Butterfly' (C)	ER&R
'Magic Carpet'	ER&R
'Magic Lace'	ER&R
'Majesty' (T)	CBla
manicata	ER&R WDib
'Maphil'	MBri
'Margaritae'	ER&R
'Marmaduke'	WDib
'Marmorata' (T)	NRog
'Martha Floro' (C)	ER&R
'Martin's Mystery'	ER&R
masoniana ♀	CHal ER&R ERea WDib
I 'Matador' (T)	CBla
mazae	ER&R
'Medora' (C)	ER&R
* 'Melissa' (T)	CBla
'Merry Christmas' (R) ♀	ER&R
metachroa	ER&R
metallica	CHal ER&R
'Midnight Sun'	ER&R
'Midnight Twister'	ER&R
'Mikado' (R)	ER&R
'Mirage'	ER&R
mollicaulis	ER&R
'Moon Maid'	ER&R
* 'Moulin Rouge'	CBla
'Mr Steve' (T)	CBla
'Mrs Hashimoto' (C)	ER&R
multinervia	ER&R

'Munchkin' ♀	ER&R WDib
'Mystique'	ER&R
natalensis (T)	ER&R
'Nell Gwynne' (T)	CBla
'Nelly Bly'	ER&R
nelumbifolia	ER&R
nigramarga	See ***B. bowerae*** var. ***nigramarga***
'Nokomis' (C)	ER&R
'Norah Bedson'	ER&R
'Northern Lights' (S)	ER&R
obscura	ER&R
'Obsession'	ER&R
'Odorata Alba'	ER&R
olbia Kerchove	ER&R
'Old Gold' (T)	ER&R
'Oliver Twist'	ER&R
'Ophelia' (T)	CBla
'Orange Cascade' (T)	CBla
'Orange Dainty'	ER&R
'Orange Rubra' (C)	CHal ER&R
'Orpha C. Fox' (C)	ER&R
'Orrell' (C)	ER&R
'Panasoffkee'	ER&R
'Panther'	ER&R
'Papillon' (T)	ER&R
partita	ER&R
'Passing Storm'	ER&R
'Patricia Ogdon'	ER&R
'Paul Harley'	ER&R
'Paul-bee'	ER&R
paulensis	ER&R
'Peggy Stevens' (C)	ER&R
'Persephone' (T)	CBla
'Piccolo'	ER&R
'Pickobeth' (C)	ER&R
'Picotee' (T)	CSut NRog
'Pinafore' (C)	ER&R
¶ 'Pink Champagne' (R)	CBla
'Pink Nacre'	ER&R
'Pink Parade' (C)	ER&R
'Pink Spot Lucerne' (C)	ER&R
polyantha	ER&R
'Président Carnot' (C)	ER&R SLMG
'Preussen'	ER&R
'Primrose' (T)	CBla
'Princess of Hanover' (R)	ER&R
procumbens	See ***B. radicans***
pustulata 'Argentea'	ER&R
'Queen Olympus'	ER&R WDib
'Quinebaug'	ER&R
§ ***radicans***	CHal ER&R MBri
'Raquel Wood'	ER&R
'Raspberry Swirl' (R)	CHal ER&R WDib
'Raymond George Nelson'	ER&R
'Red Berry' (R)	ER&R
'Red Planet'	ER&R WDib
'Red Reign'	ER&R
'Red Spider'	ER&R
'Regalia'	ER&R
rex	MBri
'Richard Robinson'	ER&R
'Richmondensis'	ER&R
'Ricinifolia'	ER&R
'Ricky Minter'	ER&R SLMG
roxburghii	ER&R
'Roy Hartley' (T)	CBla
'Royal Lustre'	ER&R
'Royalty' (T)	CBla
'Saber Dance' (R)	ER&R
'Sachsen'	ER&R
salicifolia (C)	ER&R
sanguinea	ER&R

'Scarlet Pimpernel' (T)	CBla
'Scarlett O'Hara' (T)	CBla ER&R
'Sceptre' (T)	CBla
scharffiana	ER&R
§ ***scharffii***	CHal EBak ER&R LChe
'Scherzo'	CHal ER&R
'Sea Coral' (T)	CBla
semperflorens hort.	See ***B.*** × ***carrierei***
'Serlis'	ER&R
serratipetala	CHal EBak ER&R MBri
* ***sheperdii***	WDib
'Silver Cloud'	ER&R WDib
'Silver Jewell'	WDib
'Silver Mist' (C)	ER&R
'Silver Points'	ER&R
'Silver Sweet' (R)	ER&R
'Silver Wings'	ER&R
'Sir John Falstaff'	ER&R
Skeezar Group	ER&R
– 'Brown Lake'	ER&R
'Snowcap' (S)	ER&R
solananthera	CHal ER&R LCns WDib
sonderiana	ERea
'Sophie Cecile' (C)	CHal ER&R
'Speculata' (R)	ER&R
'Spellbound'	ER&R WDib
'Spindrift'	ER&R
'Spotches'	ER&R
§ ***stipulacea***	CHal ER&R
§ – 'Bat Wings'	SLMG
subvillosa (S)	ER&R
'Sugar Candy' (T)	CBla
sutherlandii ♀	CAvo CHal EBak ER&R ERea LCns LHil MBri NBir NPer SAxl SDix SLMG SMrm SSad WCot WHer
¶ – 'Papaya'	CSpe
'Swan Song'	ER&R
'Sweet Dreams' (T)	CBla
'Sweet Magic'	CHal ER&R
'Swirly Top' (C)	ER&R
'Switzerland' (T)	LAma
'Sylvan Triumph' (C)	ER&R
'Tahiti' (T)	CBla
'Tapestry' (R)	ER&R
'Tea Rose'	ER&R
teuscheri (C)	ER&R
'Texastar'	ER&R
thelmae	ER&R
'Thrush' (R)	SLMG
'Thunderclap'	CHal ER&R
'Thurstonii'	CHal ER&R
'Tiger Paws'	CHal ER&R MBri
'Tingley Mallet' (C)	ER&R
'Tiny Bright' (R)	ER&R
'Tiny Gem'	ER&R
'Tom Ment' (C)	ER&R
'Tom Ment II' (C)	ER&R
'Tondelayo' (R)	ER&R
tripartita (T)	ER&R
'Trout' (C)	SLMG
'Two Face'	ER&R WDib
ulmifolia	ER&R
undulata (C)	ER&R
'Universe'	ER&R
venosa	ER&R
'Venus'	CHal ER&R
× ***verschaffeltii***	ER&R
'Vesuvius'	WDib
'Viaudii'	ER&R
'Viau-Scharff'	ER&R
§ ***vitifolia***	ER&R

'Weltoniensis' ER&R
'Weltoniensis Alba' (T) ER&R
'Witch Craft' (R) ER&R
'Withlacoochee' ER&R WDib
wollnyi ER&R
'Wood Nymph' (R) ER&R
'Yellow Sweety' (T) CBla
'Zuensis' ER&R
'Zulu' (T) CBla

BELAMCANDA (Iridaceae)
chinensis CBot CBro CHan EBar EBre EMan GAul GPoy LHop MSal NTow SCro SLMG SPla SVen WHal WHoo WPer WWye
– 'Dwarf Orange' CWan
– 'Hello Yellow' MSte
* – 'Yellow Bird' WCot

BELLEVALIA (Hyacinthaceae)
brevipedicellata MS 746 CMon
dubia CMon
forniculata GTou
hackelii MS 439 CMon
maura SF 387 CMon
nivalis CL 101 CMon
§ ***paradoxa*** EHyt ERos NRog WCot
pycnantha hort. See ***B. paradoxa***
romana EHyt MTho NRog
– JCA 523 CMon
sessiliflora CMon
sp. PD 20493 WOMN

BELLIS (Asteraceae)
perennis CKin CTiv ECWi EWFC MHew
– 'Alba Plena' ECho ELan
– 'Alice' CGle CLTr NSti WSan
– 'Annie' CGle
– 'Dawn Raider' EMon
– 'Dresden China' ♀ CHid CLyd ELan GAbr MTho NPro WAlt WRus
* – (Habanera Series) 'Lipstick' NBrk
◆ – Hen and Chicken See ***B. perennis* 'Prolifera'**
– 'Miss Mason' CGle GAbr NPro WRus
¶ – 'Monstrosa' NVic
– 'Odd Bod' CBos
– 'Parkinson's Great White' GAbr
– 'Pomponette' ♀ NVic
§ – 'Prolifera' CCot CElw GAbr NSti WAlt
– 'Rob Roy' ♀ CBos CGle
– 'Robert' GAbr
– 'Single Blue' See ***B. rotundifolia* 'Caerulescens'**
– 'Stafford Pink' CLTr GAbr
– 'Super Enorma' CNat
rotundifolia CElw CInt
§ – 'Caerulescens' CDec CMHG CNic CSev ELan GAbr MTho NBir NBro NMGW NMen NNrd WEas WOMN WRus

BELLIUM (Asteraceae)
bellidioides NHol WAbe
crassifolium canescens WPer
minutum CNic ESis LCom MHig MMil MTho NGre NTow

BELOPERONE See JUSTICIA

BENSONIELLA (Saxifragaceae)
oregona EBee EMon EPPr LRHS

BERBERIDOPSIS (Flacourtiaceae)
corallina CAbb CB&S CDoC CGre CMac CPlN CSam CWSG EBre ELan EMil EPla GQui IOrc LHol LHop MBal MBri SArc SBra SOWG SPer SSpi SSta WAbe WBod WDin WSHC WWat

BERBERIS † (Berberidaceae)
aggregata CAgr GAul MBal MNrw NBir SEas SPer SRms WDin WRTC
¶ ***amurensis*** 'Flamboyant' WBcn
x ***antoniana*** MBri NNor SHhN
aquifolium See ***Mahonia aquifolium***
– 'Fascicularis' See ***Mahonia* x *wagneri* 'Pinnacle'**
N ***aristata*** CAgr CArn CMCN EHal SMur
¶ ***atrocarpa*** CPle
bealei See ***Mahonia japonica* Bealei Group**
bergmanniae CPle SLPl
brevipedunculata Bean See ***B. prattii***
x ***bristolensis*** MBri SPla SRms
buxifolia CBlo CPle MBal WFar
– 'Nana' hort. See ***B. buxifolia* 'Pygmaea'**
N – 'Pygmaea' CAbP CPle CTri ELan EMil ENot MBal MBar MBri MPla MRav NHol NRoo SPer STre WFar WPyg WStI
calliantha ♀ CBlo CChe CChu SLPl WWat
candidula CSam EBee EBre ENot IOrc MBal MBar MWat NFla NHol NNor SBod SPer WDin WGwG WRTC WStI WWat
– 'Jytte' See ***B.* 'Jytte'**
x ***carminea*** 'Barbarossa' CBlo
– 'Buccaneer' CBlo ENot EPfP SBod SPer
– 'Pirate King' CBlo CShe EBee EMil ENot MBal MRav SEas SPer WRHF
¶ ***chitria*** CAgr
chrysosphaera CChu WWat
§ ***concinna*** GCrs
– B&SWJ 2124 WCru
congestiflora CPle SLPl
coryi See ***B. wilsoniae*** var. ***subcaulialata***
coxii CPle EPla MAll NTow SSpi
darwinii ♀ CB&S CLan CSam CShe CWLN EBre ELan ENot GRei LBuc MBal MBar MBri MGos MWat NNor NRoo NWea SHBN SMad SPer SReu SSta WBod WDin WHCG WPat WWin
dictyophylla ♀ CB&S CBot CFil CPMA CPle ELan MBri MGos SMad SSpi SSta WSHC
dulcis 'Nana' See ***B. buxifolia* 'Pygmaea'**
empetrifolia CPle NNor SIng
erythroclada See ***B. concinna***
x ***frikartii*** 'Amstelveen' ♀ CBlo CSam EBar EBee EBre EHic ELan ENot GAul WFar WGor
– 'Telstar' ♀ EBee EHic ENot LBuc MBal MBri MRav WStI
gagnepainii 'Fernspray' MBri MRav SBod SRms
– hort. See ***B. gagnepainii*** var. ***lanceifolia***

§ – var. ***lanceifolia***	CB&S CPle CTri EBee ENot EPla IOrc MBar MGos MWat NNor NWea SPer WFar WGwG WHCG
– 'Purpure'	See ***B.*** × ***interposita* 'Wallich's Purple'**
'Georgei'	CMHG CPle WBcn
glaucocarpa	ELan LRHS SSpi
'Goldilocks' ♀	CAbP CDoC CMHG CPMA EPfP MBlu MBri WGer
hookeri var. ***latifolia***	See ***B. manipurana***
× ***hybridogagnepainii*** 'Chenaultii'	CBlo ELan NFla SPer
hypokerina	CDoC CLan
§ × ***interposita*** 'Wallich's Purple'	CBlo EBee EHic ENot GAul MBal MBar SPer WGor WLRN WStI
jamesiana	CPle
julianae	CB&S CDoC EBre ELan ENot IOrc MBal MBar MBri MGos MRav NBee NFla NNor NWea SHBN SHFr SLPl SPer WDin WFar WHCG WHar WRTC WSHC
– 'Mary Poppins'	MBri MUlv
§ 'Jytte'	CDoC EBee
kawakamii	SLPl
knightii	See ***B. manipurana***
koreana	CMCN CSam ECtt EPla NFla WWes
lempergiana	CMCN CPle
linearifolia	WPat
– 'Orange King'	CAbP CB&S CDoC ELan ENot MAsh MGos NBee NHol SHBN SPer WDin WHar WPat WPyg WStI
'Little Favourite'	See ***B. thunbergii* 'Atropurpurea Nana'**
× ***lologensis***	IOrc MGos WDin WFar
– 'Apricot Queen' ♀	CAbP CB&S CDoC EBre MAsh MBal MBri NBee NEgg NFla SHBN SPer WDin WPyg WStI WWeb
– 'Mystery Fire'	CAbP CBlo CBot CDoC CKni COtt ECtt IOrc MAsh MBar MBlu MBri MGos MUlv NBee NEgg SCoo SPla WFar WHar
– 'Stapehill'	CB&S EBee ELan ENot EPfP MAsh MBri MUlv WFar
lycium	CAgr CPle EHal WHCr
§ ***manipurana***	CBlo CGre CPle EBee ENot
♦ × ***media*** Park Jewel	See ***B.*** × ***media* 'Parkjuweel'**
§ – 'Parkjuweel' ♀	CB&S CBlo EBee EHal EHic MAsh MRav SPer WFar WLRN WWeb
– 'Red Jewel' ♀	CBlo CChe CDoC EBre EPla MBri MGos MWat SEas SPer WAbe WFar WGwG WWeb
morrisonensis	CFil WPGP
× ***ottawensis***	CChe GRei WStI
– 'Auricoma'	MGos WWeb
– 'Decora'	SPer
N – f. ***purpurea***	EBee MBri NCut NFla SBod WDin WHar WRHF
§ – 'Silver Mile' (v)	CBot COtt CPle EHoe ELan EPfP LHop LNet MBel MBri MRav WFar WPat
N – 'Superba' ♀	CB&S CBlo CChe CDoC CPle CShe CTri ELan ENot GOrc LHop MBal MBar MGos NBee NHol NNor NRoo SPer SPla SSoC WDin WFar WHar
§ ***panlanensis***	EBee ENot MBar
patagonica	NNor
polyantha Hemsley	CBlo
– hort.	See ***B. prattii***
§ ***prattii***	CMHG MBri
pruinosa	CPle SLPl
'Red Tears'	CBlo CDoC CPMA CSam EHic LRHS MBlu MBri MGos MLan WHCG WWes
replicata	EPla SLPl
'Rubrostilla' ♀	EBee ENot EPla MBri NNor
* × ***rubrostilla*** 'Wisley'	LRHS
sanguinea hort.	See ***B. panlanensis***
sargentiana	CPle ENot NNor SLPl WWat
sherriffii	CPle
sieboldii	WPat WPyg WWat
sp.	EPla
¶ sp. ACE 2237	EPot
sp. C&S 1571	NMun
sp. C&S 1651	NMun
× ***stenophylla*** ♀	CB&S CChe CShe CWLN ELan GRei ISea LBuc MBar MBri MGos MLan MWat NBee NHed NHol NNor NRoo NWea SPer WDin WHCG WHar WWin
– 'Autumnalis'	CBlo
– 'Claret Cascade'	CBlo ECle EHal EHic ELan MAsh MBri MGos SPer WFar WRHF WWeb
– 'Coccinea'	EPla MGos
– 'Corallina Compacta' ♀	EHyt ELan EPot ESis LHop MAsh MBal MBlu MBro MGos MPla NHar NHol SChu SIng SPla SRms WAbe WPat WPyg
– 'Cornish Cream'	See ***B.*** × ***stenophylla* 'Lemon Queen'**
– 'Crawley Gem'	CBlo CMHG COtt LNet MAsh MBar MBri MGos MPla NBee NHol SPer WFar WLRN WStI WWin
– Cream Showers™	See ***B.*** × ***stenophylla* 'Lemon Queen'**
– 'Etna'	MAsh
– 'Irwinii'	CBlo CMHG CShe CTri ENot EPla IOrc MBar MBri MGos MWat NHol SPer WDin WFar WWeb
N – 'Lemon Queen'	NHol SPer
– 'Nana'	EPla SRms
– 'Pink Pearl'	CMHG CShe LBuc LRHS MGos SHBN
taliensis	CPle
temolaica	CFil CPMA CPle ELan MAsh MBlu MBri SLPl SPla SSpi SSta WPat WWat
thunbergii ♀	CBlo CDoC CTri ENot GRei LBuc MBal NWea SMer SPer WDin WFar WRTC WStI
– f. ***atropurpurea***	CB&S CPle CSam CWLN EBre ENot GRei LBuc MBal MBar MBri MGos MWat NNor NRoo NWea SPer WBod WDin WFar WWin
§ – 'Atropurpurea Nana' ♀	CB&S CShe EBre ECtt EHoe ENot ERom GRei LGro LHop MBal MBar MGos MPla MWat NHol NRoo SHBN SPer SReu SSta WDin WFar WPat WWat WWin
– 'Atropurpurea Superba'	See ***B.*** × ***ottawensis* 'Superba'**

– 'Aurea' CB&S CBot CMHG CSam CWLN EBre ELan ENot EPot LGro LHop LNet MAsh MBal MBar MBri MGos MWat NHed NHol NRoo SHBN SIgm SPer SSpi WDin WFar WHCG WPat WSHC
– 'Bagatelle' 🏆 CBlo COtt EBre ECtt ELan EMil ENot EPot ESis IOrc MAsh MBar MBri MGos MPla MRav MTis NBee NHar NRoo SPer WAbe WDin WPat WPyg
– 'Bonanza Gold' CAbP CSte ELan LRHS MAsh SMur
– 'Carpetbagger' IOrc WHar
– 'Crimson Pygmy' See ***B. thunbergii* 'Atropurpurea Nana'**
– 'Dart's Purple' CBlo ENot MBri WFar WWeb
– 'Dart's Red Lady' CBlo CBot CPMA EBre ECtt EHal ELan EMil ENot EPla GAul IOrc MAsh MBri MPla MRav NRoo SPer SPla WPat
– 'Erecta' CTri EMil ENot MBar MGos MRav NCut SPer WDin
– 'Golden Ring' CChe CPle CWLN EBar ECtt EHoe ELan EMil EPla GOrc LHop MBar MBri MGos MWat NRoo SChu SEND SPer SPla WDin WHCG WHar WPat WPyg WRTC WSHC
– 'Green Carpet' CBlo EBre EHic ENot IOrc MBal MBar MBlu SHhN SPer
– 'Green Mantle' See ***B. thunbergii* 'Kelleriis'**
– 'Green Marble' See ***B. thunbergii* 'Kelleriis'**
– 'Green Ornament' MWat NCut SPer
– 'Harlequin' CB&S CChe CPle CWLN EBre ECtt EHoe ELan EMil ENot IOrc MAsh MBal MBri MGos NBee SPer SPla WDin WFar WGwG WHar WPat WPyg WStI
– 'Helmond Pillar' CMHG CWLN EBre EHoe ELan EMil ENot EPla IOrc MBar MBlu MBri MGos MPla MRav MTis NBee NRoo SMad SPer WPat WPyg WSHC
§ – 'Kelleriis' CBlo CChe CDoC EBee EFol EHic EPla GOrc MBar SBod WStI WWeb
– 'Kobold' CBlo ENot ESis MAsh MBar MBri MGos MPla NBee NRoo SEas SPer WFar WLRN WPat WPyg
¶ – 'Pink Attraction' CBlo
– 'Pink Queen' (v) CBlo CWLN EBee MAsh MGos WHar WWeb
– 'Pow-wow' CB&S MGos SMur WBcn
– 'Red Chief' 🏆 CMHG CShe CWLN EBre ECtt ELan ENot LHop MBal MGos MRav MWat NRoo SChu SPer SPla SReu WAbe WDin WFar WHCG WHar WRTC WStI
– 'Red King' MRav WDin
– 'Red Pillar' CB&S CBlo CLan CPle EBre EHoe ELan MAsh MBal MBar MBlu MBri MGos MWat NBee NHol SHBN SPla WAbe WDin WFar WStI WWeb
– 'Red Rocket' EMil MAsh MGos
– 'Rose Glow' (v) 🏆 CB&S CMHG CShe CWLN ELan ENot GRei ISea LHop MBal MBar MBri MGos MPla MWat NHol NNor NRoo SHBN SMad SPer SReu SSpi WAbe WBod WDin WFar WHCG WPat
– 'Silver Beauty' (v) CB&S CBlo CDoC CMHG CPle EBee EHal ELan MGos MPla SBod WHCG WWeb
– 'Silver Mile' See ***B.* × *ottawensis* 'Silver Mile'**
* – 'Silver Queen' CBlo CHor
– 'Somerset' WWat
* – 'Tricolor' (v) CBlo EHic EHoe MUlv WFar WPat WPyg WSHC WWeb
tsangpoensis SLPl
valdiviana CB&S EBee
veitchii SLPl
verruculosa 🏆 CB&S CLan EAst ENot LHop MBal MBar MGos MPla NNor NWea SPer SPla WBod WDin WFar WGwG WRTC WWat WWeb
vulgaris CAgr CArn MSal
– 'Atropurpurea' CAgr
wallichiana B&SWJ 2432 WCru
wardii CB&S SLPl
wilsoniae 🏆 CB&S CBlo CFil CLan CPle CSam EBre ELan EMon ENot IOrc MBar MPla MWat NWea SHBN SLPl SPer WDin WFar WRTC
– blue LRHS MBri WGer
– 'Graciella' LRHS MBri
– var. ***guhtzunica*** EPla EWes
¶ – var. ***parvifolia*** CPle

BERCHEMIA (Rhamnaceae)

racemosa CPlN SBra SPer WSHC
¶ ***scandens*** CPlN

BERGENIA † (Saxifragaceae)

'Abendglocken' CMil EBee ECha EHic EPla LFis LGro MBri MTis NHol NSti SChu SPla WWoo
§ 'Abendglut' Widely available
acanthifolia See ***B.* × *spathulata***
'Admiral' ECha EGle MUlv
'Apple Court White' CDec
'Baby Doll' CDec COtt EBre ECha EFou EGol EPla GCal LHop MBri MUlv NBir NHol NMir NOrc NPer NRoo NTow SPla WBro WCot WRus
N Ballawley Hybrids CB&S CBot CMGP CMHG CShe EBre EGol EPar ERav LGro MUlv NHol SDix SPer SWat WCot WHil WWoo
'Bartók' MUlv SSpi
beesiana See ***B. purpurascens***
'Beethoven' EBre ECha EGle EPPr EPla NBir SSpi SWat WCot
◆ Bell Tower See ***B.* 'Glockenturm'**
'Bizet' SApp SSpi
'Brahms' CMil
'Bressingham Bountiful' CBlo MUlv SPer
'Bressingham Ruby' CDec COtt EBre EFol EGar EPla ERav GAri MHlr MUlv NBir NRoo SHBN WCot

'Bressingham Salmon'	CFee CMil EBre ELan ERav GAbr GMaP MHlr MMil MRav NHol NMir SHBN SPer WCot WMer
'Bressingham White' ♀	CBot CMHG EBre ECha ECtt EGol ELan EOrc ERav MBri MRav MUlv NCat NDea NFai NHol NRoo SPer WCot WRus WWin
'Britten'	CMil MBal
ciliata	CFee CHEx CHad CHan CMil ECha EPla GCal GCra MBal MRav NBir NSti SDix SPer WCot WCru WEas WKif WPer
– x ***crassifolia***	See ***B.*** x ***schmidtii***
ciliata ficifolia	EPla
ciliata f. ***ligulata***	ECha EPla NBir NSti NVic WHil WPer
cordifolia	CB&S CGle CHEx CKel CMHG EBre EHon ELan ENot EOrc ERav GAbr GCal MBal MFir NDea NFai NNor SHel SPer WCot WFar WPer WStI WTyr
– 'Purpurea' ♀	CB&S CShe EBre ECha ELan ENot EPla LBuc LGro MBri MCLN MRav NBir NFla SDix SHBN SHig SPer WGwG
– 'Redstart'	CBlo NMir NOak SPla
– 'Tubby Andrews' (v)	NRar
crassifolia	CB&S CGle CWGN EPla SHig SRms SSca WByw
– 'Autumn Red'	ECha EPla
– DF 90028	EMon
– 'Orbicularis'	See ***B.*** x ***schmidtii***
– var. ***pacifica***	CFil WPGP WWoo
delavayi	See ***B. purpurascens*** var. ***delavayi***
'Delbees'	See ***B. purpurascens* 'Ballawley'**
¶ ***emeiensis***	SBla
'Eric Smith'	ECha EPar EPla GAbr GCal LWoo
'Eric's Best'	GCra
'Evening Glow'	See ***B.* 'Abendglut'**
§ 'Glockenturm'	ECha EPla GCal MUlv
'Jo Watanabe'	ECha EPla
'Lambrook'	See ***B.* 'Margery Fish'**
§ 'Margery Fish'	CMil CShe ECha EPla SPer SPla
milesii	See ***B. stracheyi***
§ 'Morgenröte' ♀	CB&S CDoC CMGP COtt CShe EBar ECha EPla GCra MBri NDea NHol SAga SHBN SPer SPla SRms SWat
◆ Morning Red	See ***B.* 'Morgenröte'**
'Mrs Crawford'	ECha EPla
'Opal'	ECha EPla
'Profusion'	SPer
'Pugsley's Pink'	CArc CBlo CMil ECha EPla GCra LHop NCat SHBN WLRN
'Pugsley's Purple'	EBre
§ ***purpurascens*** ♀	CDec CMHG EBre EPla ERav GDra MBal MBro NHol SDix SPer WByw WCot WHoo WPyg WWin
§ – 'Ballawley'	EBee ECha EPla IBlr MUlv NDea NSti SSpi SWat
– var. ***delavayi*** CLD 1366	SRms WPer
– hybrid	SApp
'Purpurglocken'	ECha EPla GCal
'Red Beauty'	CBlo
'Rosette'	NFai
'Rosi Klose'	CGle ECha EPPr EPla EWes GCal NRoo NTow WCot
'Rotblum'	CSte ECtt GBin GMaP LFis LWak NCut WFar WPer
§ x ***schmidtii*** ♀	EWll NBir NFla SDix SHig WCot
'Schneekissen'	EGle LRHS MRav WLRN
§ 'Schneekönigin'	CGle ECha EPla NCat WGer
§ 'Silberlicht' ♀	CB&S CWGN EAst EBre ECha EFou ELan EOrc EPla GAbr GCra MBal MCLN NFai NFla NMir NRoo NSti SDix SHBN SHig SPer SSpi WByw WEas WFar WHoo WTyr
◆ Silverlight	See ***B.* 'Silberlicht'**
◆ Snow Queen	See ***B.* 'Schneekönigin'**
'Snowblush'	MBal SSpi
§ ***stracheyi***	CBot CFee ECha EFol EGol EGoo EPla GCra MHig SApp SDix SHig WPyg
– Alba Group	CArc CChu CGle CRDP ECha EMan GCal LHop NDea NGre NSti NWoo SApp SWas WLRN
– KBE 151	NHol
– KBE 209	EPla NHol
'Sunningdale'	CB&S CMGP EBee EBre ECha ELan EMan EPPr EPar EPla GCra GMaP MRav MTol NBir NFla NSti SChu SHig SPer SPla SSpi WMer
'Wintermärchen'	CM&M CMGP CMHG ECha ECtt EFou EGol ELan EPPr EPfP EPla ERav LGro MBri MCli MSte MUlv NHol NOrc NSti SAga SPla SSea WRus WWeb
'Winterzauber'	MUlv

BERKHEYA (Asteraceae)

macrocephala	NCat WCot WMer
¶ ***maritima***	GCra

BERLANDIERA (Asteraceae)

lyrata	CArn GCal NRai WCot

BERULA (Apiaceae)

erecta	EHon

BERZELIA (Bruniaceae)

¶ ***lanuginosa***	CTrC

BESCHORNERIA (Agavaceae)

tubiflora	CHEx
yuccoides ♀	CB&S CFil CHEx CHan CTbh CTrC EOas GCal IBlr LHil MSte SArc SSpi

BESSERA (Alliaceae)

elegans	ETub WChr

BESSEYA (Scrophulariaceae)

See Plant Deletions

BETA (Chenopodiaceae)

trigyna	EMon
vulgaris	WHer

BETONICA See STACHYS

BETULA † (Betulaceae)

alba Linnaeus	See ***B. pendula***
albosinensis ♀	CB&S CGre CMCN ELan GAri WCoo WDin WFro WNor WOrn
– 'Bowling Green'	CTho
– 'Chinese Garden'	CTho
– Clone F	CTho
– 'Conyngham'	CTho WWat
– F 19505	CEnd CSto
– var. ***septentrionalis*** ♀	CDoC CLnd CTho EBee ELan ENot GAri LNet MAsh MBlu MBri SPer SSpi SSta WWat
– W 4106	CSto
§ ***alleghaniensis***	CDoC CGre CLnd CMCN CSam CSto IOrc MBal NWea
apoiensis	CGre SSta
§ × ***caerulea***	CTho WWat
caerulea-grandis	See ***B.*** × ***caerulea***
celtiberica	See ***B. pubescens*** subsp. ***celtiberica***
chichibuensis	WAbe
¶ ***chinensis***	SMad
cordifolia	CSto MNes
costata Trautvetter	CDoC CLnd CMCN COtt CSam CTho CWLN ELan ENot NWea WDin WFro WOrn
davurica	CBlo CLnd CMCN WWoo
– 'Maurice Foster'	CEnd
delavayi B&L 12260	WHCr
ermanii	CB&S CDul CGre CLnd CMCN CMHG COtt CSam CSto CTho EBee ELan ENot IOrc LPan MAsh MBal MBlu MBri MGos NWea SPer SSpi STre WCoo WDin WNor WOrn
–var. ***saitoana*** subvar. ***genuina***	CFil
§ – 'Grayswood Hill' ♀	CEnd CSto CTho EBee MBal MGos SPer SSta WWat
– 'Hakkoda Orange'	CTho
'Fetisowii'	CDul CLnd CTho MBlu SPer SSta
§ ***fontinalis***	WHCr
forrestii Yu 10561	CEnd
fruticosa	See ***B. humilis***
glandulifera	CLnd CSto
glandulosa	MFos NSla
globispica	MNes
grossa	CLnd CMCN GAri
'Hergest'	CBlo CFil EPfP MAsh WHCr
§ ***humilis***	CDoC CLnd
'Inverleith'	CEnd EBee MBri SSpi WWat
jacquemontii	See ***B. utilis*** var. ***jacquemontii***
¶ ***kamtschatica***	GQui
lenta	CFil CLnd CMCN MBal
litvinovii	CMCN
¶ ***luminifera***	CBrd
lutea	See ***B. alleghaniensis***
maximowicziana	CB&S CDoC CLnd CMCN CTho GAri MBal SSta WFro WNor
medwedewii ♀	CDul CGre CLnd CMCN CTho EBee GAri SSta WAbe WWat
– from Winkworth	CTho
– 'Gold Bark'	MBlu
megrelica	CGre
michauxii	EHyt NHol WAbe WPat WPyg WRTC
× ***minor***	CSto

nana	CBlo ELan EMil ESis IOrc MBal MBar MBro MPla NSla SIng SMac SRms SSta STre WPer
– 'Glengarry'	EPot GAri GBin WDin
nigra ♀	CB&S CBlo CDoC CDul CGre CLnd CMCN CTho ENot IHos IOrc LMer LPan MAsh MBal NWea SMad SPer SSta WDin WFro WNor
– 'Heritage'	CDul CSte EBee ENot LPan MBlu SSta
occidentalis	See ***B. fontinalis***
papyrifera	CB&S CDul CLnd CMCN CSto ELan ENot IOrc LBuc LPan MBal MBar MGos NBee NWea SHBN SPer SSta WDin WNor WOrn WWat
– var. ***commutata***	SLPl
– var. ***kenaica***	CDoC CTho
– 'Saint George'	CTho WWat
– 'Vancouver'	CTho
§ ***pendula*** ♀	CB&S CDul CKin CLnd CPer CSto EBre ELan ENot GRei IOrc LBuc LHyr LPan MBal MBar MBri MGos MWat NBee NWea SHFr SPer WDin WMou WOrn
– f. *crispa*	See ***B. pendula* 'Laciniata'**
N– 'Dalecarlica' hort.	See ***B. pendula* 'Laciniata'**
– 'Fastigiata'	CBlo CDul CEnd CLnd CTho CWLN EBee EBre ELan ENot LPan MAsh MGos SPer WOrn
– 'Golden Cloud'	CB&S CBlo CLnd IOrc MAsh
– 'Gracilis'	EMil LPan
§ – 'Laciniata' ♀	CBlo CDul CLnd CTho ENot IOrc LPan MAsh MBar MBri MGos NBee NWea SHBN SPer SSta WDin WMou WPyg WWes
– 'Purpurea'	CLnd CTho CWSG EBre EFol ELan ENot IOrc LPan MBal MBar MBlu MGos NBee NWea SHBN SPer SSpi WDin
– 'Tristis' ♀	CB&S CDoC CDul CEnd CLnd CTho CTri EMil ENot GRei IOrc LPan MBal MBar NWea SPer SSpi SSta WDin WFar WMou WOrn WPyg
– 'Youngii' ♀	CB&S CDul CEnd CLnd EBre ELan ENot GRei LBuc LHyr LNet LPan MAsh MBal MBar MBri MGos MWat NBee NWea SHBN SPer SSta WDin WFar WOrn
platyphylla	CMCN GAri WFro
– var. ***japonica***	CLnd EBee WFro WNor WWoo
– – 'Whitespire'	SBir
– – 'Whitespire Senior'	CDoC ELan MBlu
* ***platyphylla kamtschatica***	WNor
populifolia	CMCN CSto GAri
potaninii	CMHG
§ ***pubescens***	CDul CKin CLnd CPer CSto IOrc ISea LHyr LNet LPan MBal NWea WDin WHut WMou
– 'Arnold Brembo'	CTho
§ – subsp. ***celtiberica***	CMHG
pumila	CSto
¶ ***raddeana***	WNor WPGP
resinifera Britton	See ***B. neoalaskana***
saposhnikovii	WNor

'Snow Queen'	CBlo CDul CEnd COtt CSte GRei LBuc MBri MGos SCoo SMer WHCr
szechuanica	CDoC CMCN CSto WAbe
– 'Liuba White'	CTho
tatewakiana	See ***B. ovalifolia***
tianschanica	LMer WNor
'Trost's Dwarf'	CB&S CBlo EHal GQui IOrc ISea MGos MPla NHar SPer WFar WPyg WWat
uber	CMCN
x ***utahensis***	CSto
utilis	CLnd CMCN CMHG CTho ELan EMil ENot LNet MAsh MBal MBar MRav NBee NHol SPer SSta WDin WFro WNor WOrn
– BL&M 100	CTho
– CC 1409	WHCr
– DB 319	GCra
¶ – F 19505	CTho
– 'Gregory Birch'	CEnd
N – var. ***jacquemontii*** ♀	CB&S CDul CEnd CLnd CMCN CSam EBre ELan IOrc LBuc LHyr LPan MAsh MBal MBlu MBri MGos MRav MWat NWea SHBN SPer SSta WDin WGer WMou WWat
– – 'Doorenbos' ♀	CLnd NBee NEgg SSta
– – 'Grayswood Ghost'	CBlo CEnd CTho EBee SSpi SSta
– – 'Jermyns' ♀	CLnd CTho ECot LNet MBlu SPer SSta WWat
– – 'Silver Shadow' ♀	CLnd CTho SPer SSta
– – wild origin	CSto
– 'Knightshayes'	CTho
¶ – McB 1257	CTho
– var. ***occidentalis*** 'Kyelang'	CTho
– var. ***prattii***	CEnd CGre CTho
– 'Ramdang River'	CTho
– S&L 5380	WHCr
– 'Schilling'	CEnd
– SF 48	ISea
– 'Silver Queen'	SSpi
verrucosa	See ***B. pendula***

BIARUM (Araceae)

arundanum	CMon
bovei S&L 132	CMon
carduchorum	GCrs
carratracense SF 233	CMon
davisii	EHyt GCrs LAma LRHS LWoo MFos
– subsp. ***davisii*** MS 785/735	CMon
– subsp. ***marmarisense***	CMon WChr
dispar AB&S 4455	CMon
– S&L 295	CMon
ditschianum	WChr
eximium FF 1024	CMon
– PD 26644	CMon
ochridense M&T 4629	CMon
pyrami PB	CMon
– S&L 584	CMon
spruneri S&L 229	CMon
tenuifolium	CMon EPot LAma LWoo SSpi
– AB&S 4356	CMon
– subsp. ***idomenaeum*** MS 758	CMon

BIDENS (Asteraceae)

atrosanguinea	See ***Cosmos atrosanguineus***
aurea	CGle ECtt EMan LIck MSte NFai SAga SCoo
cernua	MHew MSal
ferulifolia ♀	CBrk CLTr CSev ECtt ERea GMac LHil LHop MFir NPer SChu SHel SMer SMrm WEas WOMN
* 'Goldie'	CSpe NPri
heterophylla	CHan SBla SLod SUsu SWas
– CD&R 1230	CHan
– cream	CHan
– 'Hannay's Lemon Drop'	CHan
humilis	See ***B. triplinervia*** var. ***macrantha***
integrifolia	WCot
ostruthioides	CBrk
¶ ***pilosa***	CBre
* ***polyepsis***	ELan
sp. CD&R 1515	CGle CHan LWoo
tripartita	EWFC MSal

BIGNONIA (Bignoniaceae)

capreolata	CPlN EMil EPfP GOrc LPan SBra SSta WCru WSHC
lindleyana	See ***Clytostoma callistegioides***
unguis-cati	See ***Macfadyena unguis-cati***

BILDERDYKIA See FALLOPIA

BILLARDIERA (Pittosporaceae)

bicolor	CPlN
* ***cordata***	MSto
¶ ***cymosa***	SOWG
erubescens	MSto
longiflora	Widely available
– 'Cherry Berry'	CPlN CSte ECou ELan ICrw LHop SBra
longiflora fructu-albo	CGre CPlN CPle CSte ELan EWes LRHS MBal SBra
longiflora red berried	CPle CSam
scandens	CPlN ECou

BILLBERGIA (Bromeliaceae)

nutans	CHEx CHal CMdw EBak ELan EOas GAul GBin IBlr LBlm LCns MBri SArc SLMG SRms
* – 'Variegata'	LHil
pyramidalis var. ***striata*** (v)	SLMG
saundersii	See ***B. chlorosticta***
x ***windii*** ♀	CHal EBak ECon LCns SLMG SRms

BISCUTELLA (Brassicaceae)

frutescens	WWin

BISTORTA See PERSICARIA

BIXA (Bixaceae)

orellana	MSal

BLACKSTONIA (Gentianaceae)

See Plant Deletions

BLANDFORDIA (Blandfordiaceae)

See Plant Deletions

BLECHNUM (Blechnaceae)

alpinum	See ***B. penna-marina*** subsp. ***alpinum***

cartilagineum	CFil CRDP WPGP
chilense	See ***B. tabulare***
¶ *discolor*	WRic
gibbum	MBri
§ *glandulosum*	NMar
magellanicum	See ***B. tabulare***
¶ *minus*	WRic
moorei	NMar
nudum	CDoC CFil CRDP CTrC SHam
occidentale nanum	See ***B. glandulosum***
¶ *patersonii*	WRic
penna-marina	CBro CCuc CFil EBre ECou EMon EPar GGar MBal NGar NHar NMar NVic SChu SDix SMad SRms SSpi WAbe WEas WOMN WPGP WRic
§ – subsp. *alpinum*	CFil NMar WPGP
– 'Cristatum'	CCuc CFil EBre EMon GDra MBal NHar WPGP WRic
spicant 𝕻	CCuc CFil CKin EBre EFer EPfP GGar GQui IOrc LSyl MBal NBro NFla NHar NHed NMar NOrc SArc SPer SPla SRms WPGP WShi
– 'Cristatum'	NMar
– *incisum*	See ***B. spicant* 'Rickard's Serrate'**
§ – 'Rickard's Serrate'	NHar WRic
– Serratum Group	CFil
§ *tabulare* 𝕻	CCuc CFil CHEx CRow EMon EOas IBlr LSyl MBal SArc SAxl SChu SDix SHig SLod SSpi WPGP WRic
¶ *vulcanicum*	WRic

BLETILLA † (Orchidaceae)

g. **Brigantes**	EEve SWes WChr
* – 'Moonlight'	EEve SWes
g. **Coritani**	EEve LAma SWes WChr
formosana	EEve EFEx LAma SWes WChr
* – *alba*	EEve SWes WChr
hyacinthina	See ***B. striata***
ochracea	EEve EFEx LAma SWes WChr WCot
g. **Penway Dragon**	EEve SWes
* g. **Penway Imperial**	EEve SWes
g. **Penway Paris**	EEve SWes
g. **Penway Princess**	EEve SWes
* g. **Penway Rose**	EEve SWes
g. **Penway Sunset**	EEve SWes
§ *striata*	CTrC EBre EFEx ERea ERos IBlr LAma LHop MBri MCli MSal NHol NRog SWes WChr WCot WFar
– *alba*	See ***B. striata* f. *gebina***
– 'Albostriata'	CBot EFEx ELan IBlr LAma NHol NRog SWes WChr WCot
§ – f. *gebina*	CBot IBlr LAma NHol NNrd NRog SSpi SWes WChr WCot WFar
– var. *japonica*	EEve
– – f. *gebina*	SWes
– – – variegated	SWes
szetschuanica	EEve LAma SWes WChr
'Yokohama'	EEve EFEx LAma SWes WChr

BLOOMERIA (Alliaceae)

See Plant Deletions

BOCCONIA (Papaveraceae)

cordata	See ***Macleaya cordata***
microcarpa	See ***Macleaya microcarpa***

BOEHMERIA (Urticaceae)

¶ *biloba*	WCot

BOENNINGHAUSENIA (Rutaceae)

albiflora B&SWJ 1479	WCru
– S&SH 108	CHan

BOISDUVALIA (Onagraceae)

See Plant Deletions

BOLAX (Apiaceae)

glebaria	See ***Azorella trifurcata***
§ *gummifera*	EPot GCLN ITim

BOLTONIA (Asteraceae)

asteroides	CBlo CFee CGle CHan CSev ECoo EHal EMon GMac LCom NBrk NSti SWat WRHF
– var. *latisquama*	CBre CGle CHan CVer ECha ECro EFou EHic EMon ESiP GMaP GMac LRHS MAvo MBel MSte MTol MWat SMad SSvw WCot WFar
– – 'Nana'	CArc CBre CSev ECha EMan EPPr GBuc MRav NBrk NFai NPri WPer
– 'Snowbank'	EBre EFol ELan MBel MCli MUlv
incisa	See ***Kalimeris incisa***

BOLUSANTHUS (Papilionaceae)

¶ *speciosus*	CTrC

BOMAREA (Alstroemeriaceae)

caldasii 𝕻	CHEx CPlN CRHN ERea SBla WCot
edulis	ERea
¶ *hirtella*	CPlN
ovata	ERea
¶ *patacocensis*	CPle

BONGARDIA (Berberidaceae)

chrysogonum	EHyt LAma NRog

BOOPHONE (Amaryllidaceae)

disticha	WChr
guttata	WChr

BORAGO † (Boraginaceae)

alba	CJew EOHP LHol MChe WCHb
laxiflora	See ***B. pygmaea***
officinalis	CArn CSev EWFC GPoy LHol MBri MChe MGra MHew NFai NRai NVic SIde WHer WOak WPer WSel WWye
– 'Alba'	CBre CGle CSev EMon MGra NChi NHex SChu WCHb WHer WJek
* – 'Bill Archer' (v)	CNat
§ *pygmaea*	CArc CSev CSpe EBre ELan EMon ERav LHop MFir MHew MTho NSti NTow SAlw SChu SSvw SWat WCHb WHal WOMN WOak WPbr WWin WWye

BORNMUELLERA (Brassicaceae)

tymphaea	SIgm

BORONIA (Rutaceae)

'Heaven Scent'	CB&S EMil
heterophylla	CB&S CMHG ECon ERea LBlm LCns LHop MAll SAga SMrm
megastigma	CB&S EMil MAll
– brown	EMil
¶ – 'Brown Meg'	CB&S
'Southern Star'	CB&S

BOSCIA (Capparaceae)
See Plant Deletions

BOTHRIOCHLOA (Poaceae)

§ ***bladhii***	CHan EPPr ETPC
caucasica	See ***B. bladhii***
§ ***ischaemum***	CInt EGar EHoe MCCP

BOTRYOSTEGE See ELLIOTTIA

BOUGAINVILLEA (Nyctaginaceae)

'Afterglow'	CWDa ERea
'Ailsa Lambe'	See ***B.* (Spectoperuviana Group) 'Mary Palmer'**
* 'Alabama Sunset'	CWDa
'Alexandra'	LChe MBri SLMG
'Amethyst'	ERea MBri SLMG
'Apple Blossom'	See ***B.* × *buttiana* 'Audrey Grey'**
'Asia'	ERea
◆ 'Audrey Grey' (× *buttiana*)	See ***B.* × *buttiana* 'Audrey Grey'**
* ***aurantiaca***	CB&S
'Barbara Karst'	CWDa ERea
'Begum Sikander'	CWDa ERea
'Betty Lavers'	ERea
'Blondie'	CWDa
'Brasiliensis'	See ***B. spectabilis* 'Lateritia'**
'Bridal Bouquet'	See ***B.* × *buttiana* 'Mahara Off-white'**
'Brilliance'	CWDa ERea
'Brilliant'	See ***B.* 'Raspberry Ice'**
§ × ***buttiana*** 'Audrey Grey'	CB&S ERea
§ – 'Golden Glow'	ECon ERea
– 'Golden MacLean'	CWDa
§ – 'Jamaica Red'	ERea
§ – 'Lady Mary Baring'	EFlo ERea LCns SOWG
§ – 'Mahara Double Red' (d)	CWDa ERea SOWG
§ – 'Mahara Off-white' (d)	CWDa ERea SLMG
§ – 'Mahara Orange' (d)	ERea
§ – 'Mahara Pink' (d)	CWDa ERea
§ – 'Mardi Gras' (v)	CWDa ERea
§ – 'Mrs Butt' ♀	CWDa ERea
§ – 'Mrs Helen McLean'	ERea SLMG
§ – 'Poultonii'	ERea
§ – 'Poulton's Special' ♀	ERea LChe SLMG
§ – 'Rainbow Gold'	ERea
§ – Texas Dawn	ERea
'California Gold'	See ***B.* × *buttiana* 'Golden Glow'**
§ Camarillo Fiesta™ (*spectabilis* hybrid)	CWDa ERea SLMG
'Captain Caisy'	CWDa ERea
'Carson's Gold' (d)	CWDa
'Cherry Blossom'	See ***B.* × *buttiana* 'Mahara Off-white'**
§ 'Chiang Mai Beauty'	ERea
'Coconut Ice' (v)	CWDa EFlo LCns SOWG
'Crimson Lake'	See ***B.* × *buttiana* 'Mrs Butt'**
'Dania'	MBri
'Danica Rouge'	SLMG
'Daphne Mason'	ERea
'Dauphine'	See ***B.* × *buttiana* 'Mahara Pink'**
'David Lemmer'	CWDa ERea
'Dixie'	ERea
◆ 'Doctor David Barry' (*glabra*)	See ***B. glabra* 'Doctor David Barry'**
'Donyo'	CWDa ECon ERea LCns
'Durban'	See ***B. glabra* 'Jane Snook'**
◆ 'Elizabeth Angus' (*glabra*)	See ***B. glabra* 'Elizabeth Angus'**
'Elizabeth' (*spectabilis* hybrid)	ERea
* 'Elsbet'	CWDa
'Enchantment'	See ***B.* 'Mary Palmer's Enchantment'**
'Flamingo Pink'	See ***B.* 'Chiang Mai Beauty'**
¶ ***floribunda***	CWDa
'Gillian Greensmith'	ERea
glabra ♀	CB&S CPlN ERea LCns MBri
– A	ERea
§ – 'Doctor David Barry'	CWDa ERea
§ – 'Elizabeth Angus'	CWDa EFlo ERea
§ – 'Harrissii' (v)	CWDa ERea MBri
§ – 'Jane Snook'	CWDa ERea
§ – 'Jennifer Fernie'	ERea SLMG
§ – 'Magnifica'	ERea
§ – 'Pride of Singapore'	ERea
§ – 'Sanderiana'	ERea LPan NRog SLMG
– 'Variegata'	See ***B. glabra* 'Harrissii'**
'Gladys Hepburn'	ERea
'Gloucester Royal'	CWDa
* 'Glowing Flame'	CWDa
'Golden Dubloon'	See ***B.* × *buttiana* 'Mahara Orange'**
◆ 'Golden Glow' (× *buttiana*)	See ***B.* × *buttiana* 'Golden Glow'**
¶ 'Golden MacLean' (× *buttiana*)	See ***B.* × *buttiana* 'Golden Maclean'**
* 'Golden Tango'	CWDa
* 'Granada'	LChe
'Harlequin'	See ***B.* (Spectoperuviana Group) 'Thimma'**
◆ 'Harrissii' (*glabra*)	See ***B. glabra* 'Harrissii'**
'Hawaiian Scarlet'	See ***B.* 'Scarlett O'Hara'**
'Helen Johnson'	See ***B.* 'Temple Fire'**
◆ 'Indian Flame'	See ***B.* 'Partha'**
'Isobel Greensmith'	CWDa ERea LCns
* 'Jamaica Gold'	LChe
'Jamaica Orange'	CWDa ERea
◆ 'Jamaica Red' (× *buttiana*)	See ***B.* × *buttiana* 'Jamaica Red'**
'James Walker'	ERea
◆ 'Jane Snook' (*glabra*)	See ***B. glabra* 'Jane Snook'**
◆ 'Jennifer Fernie' (*glabra*)	See ***B. glabra* 'Jennifer Fernie'**
'Juanita Hatten'	CWDa ERea
'Kauai Royal'	See ***B. glabra* 'Elizabeth Angus'**
'Killie Campbell' ♀	ERea LChe MBri SLMG
'Klong Fire'	See ***B.* × *buttiana* 'Mahara Double Red'**
'La Jolla'	ERea
◆ 'Lady Mary Baring' (× *buttiana*)	See ***B.* × *buttiana* 'Lady Mary Baring'**
'Lavender Girl'	CWDa ERea
◆ 'Lemmer's Special'	See ***B.* 'Partha'**
'Limberlost Beauty'	See ***B.* × *buttiana* 'Mahara Off-white'**
¶ 'Little Caroline'	CWDa
§ 'Lord Willingdon'	ERea
◆ 'Los Banos Beauty'	See ***B.* × *buttiana* 'Mahara Pink'**
§ 'Louis Wathen'	CWDa LCns
◆ 'Magnifica' (*glabra*)	See ***B. glabra* 'Magnifica'**
'Magnifica Traillii'	See ***B. glabra* 'Magnifica'**
◆ 'Mahara Double Red' (× *buttiana*)	See ***B.* × *buttiana* 'Mahara Double Red'**
◆ 'Mahara Off-white' (× *buttiana*)	See ***B.* × *buttiana* 'Mahara Off-white'**

◆ 'Mahara Orange' (X *buttiana*)	See ***B.* X *buttiana* 'Mahara Orange'**
◆ 'Mahara Pink' (X *buttiana*)	See ***B.* X *buttiana* 'Mahara Pink'**
◆ 'Mahara White'	See ***B.* X *buttiana* 'Mahara Off-white'**
'Mahatma Gandhi'	See ***B.* (Spectroperuviana Group) 'Mrs H.C. Buck'**
◆ 'Mardi Gras' (X *buttiana*)	See ***B.* X *buttiana* 'Mardi Gras'**
§ 'Mary Palmer's Enchantment'	CWDa ERea
'Meriol Fitzpatrick'	ERea SLMG
* 'Michael Lemmer'	CWDa
'Mini-Thai'	See ***B.* 'Lord Willingdon'**
* 'Mischief'	CWDa
§ 'Miss Manila'	CWDa ERea
◆ 'Mrs Butt' (X *buttiana*)	See ***B.* X *buttiana* 'Mrs Butt'**
◆ 'Mrs Butt Variegated' (X *buttiana*)	See ***B.* X *buttiana* 'Mrs Butt Variegated'**
◆ 'Mrs Helen McLean' (X *buttiana*)	See ***B.* X *buttiana* 'Mrs Helen McLean'**
◆ 'Mrs McLean' (X *buttiana*)	See ***B.* X *buttiana* 'Mrs McClean'**
Natalii Group	CWDa ERea
'Nina Mitton'	CWDa ERea
'Ninja Turtle' (v)	ERea
* 'Orange Cotton'	LCns
'Orange Glow'	See ***B.* Camarillo Fiesta (spectabilis hybrid)**
'Orange King'	See ***B.* 'Louis Wathen'**
'Orange Stripe' (v)	ERea
'Pagoda Pink'	See ***B.* X *buttiana* 'Mahara Pink'**
§ 'Partha'	CWDa
'Pearl'	ERea
◆ 'Penelope'	See ***B.* 'Mary Palmer's Enchantment'**
'Pink Champagne'	See ***B.* X *buttiana* 'Mahara Pink'**
'Pink Clusters'	CWDa ERea
'Pink Pixie'	See ***B.* 'Lord Willingdon'**
◆ 'Poultonii' (X *buttiana*)	See ***B.* X *buttiana* 'Poultonii'**
◆ 'Poultonii Special' (X *buttiana*)	See ***B.* X *buttiana* 'Poulton's Special'**
'Poultonii Variegata'	ERea
◆ 'Pride of Singapore' (*glabra*)	See ***B. glabra* 'Pride of Singapore'**
◆ 'Princess Mahara'	See ***B.* X *buttiana* 'Mahara Double Red'**
'Purple Robe'	CWDa ERea
◆ 'Rainbow Gold' (X *buttiana*)	See ***B.* X *buttiana* 'Rainbow Gold'**
* 'Ralph Saunders'	LCns
§ 'Raspberry Ice' (v)	ERea SOWG
'Ratana Orange'	ERea
'Ratana Red'	ERea
'Red Diamond'	ERea SLMG
'Red Fantasy' (v)	ERea
'Red Glory'	CWDa ERea
* 'Reggae Gold'	CWDa
'Robyn's Glory'	See ***B.* X *buttiana* Texas Dawn**
'Rose Parme'	ERea
'Rosenka'	CWDa ERea
'Royal Purple'	CWDa ERea
'Rubyana'	CWDa ERea LChe LCns SOWG
'San Diego Red'	See ***B.* 'Scarlett O'Hara'**
◆ 'Sanderiana' (*glabra*)	See ***B. glabra* 'Sanderiana'**
'Sanderiana Variegata'	See ***B. glabra* 'Harrissii'**
'Scarlet Glory'	ERea
§ 'Scarlett O'Hara'	CB&S ECon ERea GQui SLMG SOWG
'Singapore Pink'	See ***B. glabra* 'Doctor David Barry'**
'Singapore White'	CWDa ERea
'Smartipants'	See ***B.* 'Lord Willingdon'**
'Snow Cap'	See ***B.* (Spectoperuviana Group) 'Mary Palmer'**
§ *spectabilis* 'Variegata'	CRHN
¶ – 'Wallflower'	CWDa
§ Spectoperuviana Group	ERea
§ – (v)	ERea
§ – 'Mary Palmer'	CWDa
– 'Mrs H.C. Buck'	CWDa ECon ERea LCns
– 'Makris'	ERea
¶ 'Summer Snow'	CWDa
Surprise	See ***B.* (Spectoperuviana Group) 'Mary Palmer'**
'Tango'	See ***B.* 'Miss Manila'**
* 'Tango Supreme'	CWDa
§ 'Temple Fire'	ERea SOWG
'Thai Gold'	See ***B.* X *buttiana* 'Mahara Orange'**
* 'Tom Thumb'	CWDa
* 'Tropical Bouquet'	CWDa
'Tropical Rainbow'	See ***B.* 'Raspberry Ice'**
* 'Turkish Delight'	CWDa ECon LChe LCns
◆ 'Variegata' (*glabra*)	See ***B. glabra* 'Harrissii'**
◆ 'Variegata' (*spectabilis*)	See ***B. spectabilis* 'Variegata'**
'Vera Blakeman'	CWDa ECon ERea LCns
'Vicky'	See ***B.* (Spectoperuviana Group) 'Thimma'**
¶ 'Wac Campbell' (d)	CWDa
'Weeping Beauty'	ERea
* 'White Cascade'	CWDa

BOUSSINGAULTIA (Basellaceae)

baselloides	See ***Anredera cordifolia***

BOUTELOUA (Poaceae)

curtipendula	EMon ETPC GBin MAvo
§ ***gracilis***	CCuc CInt CPea EBee ECha EFou ESOG ETPC MAvo MMil NBro NSti SAxl SLod SUsu WCot WPer

BOUVARDIA (Rubiaceae)

longiflora	LChe
triphylla	See ***B. ternifolia***

BOWENIA (Boweniaceae)

serrulata	CBrP LPal

BOWIEA (Hyacinthaceae)

volubilis	CHal CPlN

BOWKERIA (Scrophulariaceae)

citrina	CGre CPle
gerrardiana	CGre

BOYKINIA (Saxifragaceae)

aconitifolia	EBee EBre ECro ELan EMon GBin GTou LFis MGrG MRav NWoo WCot WCru
elata	See ***B. occidentalis***
heucheriformis	See ***B. jamesii***
§ ***jamesii***	CGra LBee MHig NNrd NTow NWCA WOMN WRHF
§ ***occidentalis***	EBee GGar
rotundifolia	ELan GBin GBuc NSti WCru
– JLS 86269LACA	EMon
tellimoides	See ***Peltoboykinia tellimoides***

BRACHYCHILUM See HEDYCHIUM

BRACHYCHITON (Sterculiaceae)
¶ *acerifolius* CTrC
populneus EPfP

BRACHYGLOTTIS † (Asteraceae)
§ *bidwillii* CChu MHig SDry SSta WAbe WCru
§ *buchananii* MAll SDry WCru WSHC
§ *compacta* EBee ECha ECou MAll MAsh MPla SDry SPer WEas
'Drysdale' EPfP MAll MAsh MRav SDry WCru
§ (Dunedin Group) 'Moira Reid' (v) CPle EBee EFol EGoo ELan EMon LHop MAll MBal MUlv SDry SPan WEas WSHC
§ – 'Sunshine' ♀ CChe EAst ELan ENot IBlr LGro LHop MBal MBri MGos NPer SPer SPla SRms WAbe WFar WHen WWat
§ *elaeagnifolia* ISea MAll
N *greyi* CLan CPle CShe EBee GIsl GRei ISea MAll MBar NNor NRoo WEas WWin
§ *huntii* CPle MAll WCru
§ *kirkii* CSev ERav
N *laxifolia* CLan NNor SIng
§ 'Leonard Cockayne' CHEx SPer
§ *monroi* ♀ CPle CSam EAst ECou EHoe ELan IBlr IOrc LHop MBal MBar MRav NNor SCoo SMer SPan SPer WAbe WEas WRTC WWat
– 'Clarence' ECou
repanda CHEx CPle
– × *greyi* CPle LHil MAll SArc
§ *rotundifolia* CAbb CDoC CGre CPle EGoo IBlr MAll MBlu WCru WEas
§ *spedenii* CFee GTou WCru
'Sunshine Variegated' See ***B.* (Dunedin Group) 'Moira Reid'**

BRACHYLAENA (Asteraceae)
¶ *discolor* CTrC

BRACHYPODIUM (Asteraceae)
phoenicoides ETPC
pinnatum EHoe EPPr ESOG ETPC
sylvaticum CKin ECWi ETPC WPer

BRACHYSCOME (Asteraceae)
'Blue Mist' LHil WLRN
'Harmony' IHos LHil
iberidifolia ELan
'Lemon Mist' LHil LHop WLRN
melanocarpa CSpe
multifida CSpe EMan IHos MBri
nivalis var. *alpina* See ***B. tadgellii***
'Pink Mist' LHil LHop
rigidula ECou NMen NTow
* 'Strawberry Mousse' LHil WLRN
§ *tadgellii* WPer
'Tinkerbell' CBar IHos WLRN

BRACHYSTACHYUM (Poaceae - Bambusoideae)
densiflorum SDry

BRACTEANTHA (Asteraceae)
acuminata De Candolle See ***B. subundulata***
bracteata 'Dargan Hill Monarch' CBrk CMHG CSev LHil LHop SRms WEas
– 'Skynet' CBrk GMac LHil LHop
§ 'Coco' MHlr WCot WEas

BRAHEA (Arecaceae)
armata CBrP CTbh CTrC LPal NPal SArc
brandegeei LPal
edulis CTrC LPal

BRASSAIA See SCHEFFLERA

BRASSICA (Brassicaceae)
japonica See ***B. juncea* var. *crispifolia***
§ *juncea* var. *crispifolia* CArn WJek
* *rapa* var. *japonica* WJek
* – var. *purpurea* WJek

BRAVOA (Agavaceae)
geminiflora See ***Polianthes geminiflora***

BRAYA (Brassicaceae)
See Plant Deletions

BREYNIA (Euphorbiaceae)
See Plant Deletions

× **BRIGANDRA** (Gesneriaceae)
calliantha NTow

BRIGGSIA (Gesneriaceae)
muscicola NTow

BRIMEURA (Hyacinthaceae)
§ *amethystina* CAvo ERos MHig
– 'Alba' CAvo ERos MHig NMen NRog WHil
§ *fastigiata* CMon

BRIZA (Poaceae)
maxima CJew EBre EJud EPla NSti WByw WHal WHer WWye
media CInt CKin EBar EBre ECWi EFou EHoe ELan EMan EOrc EPla ESOG ETPC EWFC GAbr GCHN GCal LHop MGra NHol NMir SLod SPer SPla WHal WStI
– Elatior Group ETPC
– 'Limouzi' EMon EPPr ESOG ETPC
triloba ETPC

BROCCHINIA (Bromeliaceae)
See Plant Deletions

BRODIAEA (Alliaceae)
§ *californica* CMon CNic LWoo WChr
– var. *leptandra* LWoo
capitata See ***Dichelostemma pulchellum***
coronaria subsp. *rosea* CMon
elegans CMon EMar WChr
ida-maia See ***Dichelostemma ida-maia***
jolonensis WChr
laxa See ***Triteleia laxa***
leptandra WChr
§ *minor* WChr
peduncularis See ***Triteleia peduncularis***
purdyi See ***B. minor***
stellaris WChr
terrestris WChr
volubilis WChr

BROMUS (Poaceae)
catharticus See ***B. unioloides***
inermis 'Skinner's Gold' (v) EBre EHoe EPPr ESOG EWes
macrostachys See ***B. lanceolatus***
morrisonensis B&SWJ 294 WCru
ramosus CKin EHoe EPPr ETPC GBin
§ *unioloides* ETPC

BROUSSONETIA (Moraceae)
papyrifera CB&S CBot CFil CHEx CMCN CPle ELan LPan SMad WPGP WWat
¶ – 'Laciniata' SMad

BROWALLIA (Solanaceae)
speciosa 'Major' MBri
– 'Silver Bells' MBri

BRUCKENTHALIA (Ericaceae)
spiculifolia ♀ EPot MBal MBar NHol
– 'Balkan Rose' GCal

BRUGMANSIA (Solanaceae)
§ *arborea* CArn CHEx LLew NPal SLMG SRms
aurea 'Golden Queen' CBrk ERea LLew
× *candida* EBak ERea LLew
– × *aurea* LLew
– 'Blush' ERea
§ – 'Grand Marnier' ♀ CBot ECon ECot ELan ERea LHil LLew MBri SLMG SOWG SSoC SVen WEas WKif
§ – 'Knightii' (d) ♀ CBot CBrk CHEx CSev EBak ECon ELan ERea LLew SOWG
– pink LLew
– 'Plena' See ***B.*** × ***candida* 'Knightii'**
– 'Primrose' ERea
× *flava* LLew
* × *insignis* 'Orange' LBlm
§ – pink CHEx LHil
meteloides See ***Datura inoxia***
'Panache' CBot
* pink LIck
rosei See ***B. sanguinea*** subsp. ***sanguinea* 'Flava'**
§ *sanguinea* ♀ CBrk CHEx CSev EBak ERea LHil LLew MBri SLMG SOWG SSoC SVen WHer
– 'Rosea' See ***B.*** × ***insignis* pink**
§ – subsp. *sanguinea* 'Flava' CHEx LLew MBri
§ *suaveolens* ♀ CHEx ELan ERea ISea LLew NPal
* – hybrid pink LLew
* – hybrid white LLew
suaveolens rosea See ***B.*** × ***insignis* pink**
suaveolens 'Variegata' ERea
– × *versicolor* See ***B.*** × ***insignis***
* 'Variegata Sunset' ERea
♦ *versicolor* hort. See ***B. arborea***
§ – Lagerheim CBrk ERea LBlm LPan SLMG SOWG
¶ yellow LIck

BRUNFELSIA (Solanaceae)
americana ECon LChe SLMG
calycina See ***B. pauciflora***
eximia See ***B. pauciflora***
¶ *jamaicensis* CSpe
¶ *latifolia* ECon
§ *pauciflora* ♀ ELan MBri SLMG
– 'Floribunda' LChe LCns SOWG
– 'Macrantha' LCns SLMG SOWG
undulata LChe SLMG

BRUNIA (Bruniaceae)
¶ *albiflora* CTrC

BRUNNERA (Boraginaceae)
§ *macrophylla* ♀ Widely available
– 'Alba' See ***B. macrophylla* 'Betty Bowring'**
§ – 'Betty Bowring' CBos CElw CHad CRow LWoo WFar WHal
§ – 'Dawson's White' (v) CBot CGle CHEx CRow EBre ECha EGol ELan EOrc EPla GCal LHop MBri MCLN MNes MRav MTho NHol NRoo SPer SSpi WCot WHil WPbr WRus
– 'Hadspen Cream' (v) ♀ Widely available
– Aluminium Spot = 'Langtrees' Widely available
– 'Variegata' See ***B. macrophylla* 'Dawson's White'**

× BRUNSCRINUM (Amaryllidaceae)
'Dorothy Hannibel' CMon

BRUNSVIGIA (Amaryllidaceae)
grandiflora WChr
gregaria WChr
multiflora See ***B. orientalis***
§ *orientalis* CMon NRog WChr
rosea 'Minor' See ***Amaryllis belladonna***

BRYANTHUS (Ericaceae)
See Plant Deletions

BRYONIA (Cucurbitaceae)
dioica EWFC GPoy MHew MSal

BRYOPHYLLUM See KALANCHOE

BRYUM (Sphagnaceae)
See Plant Deletions

BUCHLOE (Poaceae)
dactyloides ETPC

BUDDLEJA † (Buddlejaceae)
agathosma CBot CFil CHan CPle WEas WHar WPen WSHC
alternifolia ♀ Widely available
– 'Argentea' CBot CDoC CPMA CPle CSam EBar ELan EPla ERea MBro MHar MRav NFla NSti SHBN SPer SPla SSpi WCot WHCG WPat WSHC WWat
asiatica ♀ CBot CPlN CPle ECon ERea LCns SBid
auriculata CAbb CB&S CBlo CBot CHan CLTr CMCN CPle CWit ERea GQui LBlm LHil NSti SBid SDix SOWG SPer WCot WCru WHCG WWeb
australis CGre CPle
brevifolia See ***B. abbreviata***
* 'Butterfly Ball' LHop WBcn WPer
caryopteridifolia ENot SBid WWes

colvilei	CAbb CB&S CFil CHEx CHan CPle CTrw CWit MBal NSti SPer WCru WEas WPGP
– C&S 1577	NMun
– 'Kewensis'	CBot CGre CSam IBlr MBlu WCru WPGP WSHC
cordata	CPle
coriacea	CPle
§ ***crispa***	CBot CPle ECha ELan ERav LBlm SBid SBra SDry SHBN SOWG SPer SSpi SSta WCru WHCG WKif WPGP WPri WSHC WWat
– L 1544	NHex WPGP
crotonoides amplexicaulis	CPle
davidii	CArn CKin MBro NWea SHFr STre WDin WWye
– 'African Queen'	CSte CWLN EHic SPer
– var. ***alba***	CBlo SHBN
– 'Black Knight' ♀	CB&S CBot CShe CWLN EBre ELan ENot GOrc GRei LHop MBal MBar MBel MBri MGos MPla MWat NFla NNor NRoo NWea SHBN SMad SPer SSoC WBea WDin WEas WHCG
– 'Blue Horizon'	CPle GCHN MHar MHlr SEND WCot WRHF
– 'Border Beauty'	EHic SEas SPer SPla WRHF WWeb
– 'Dartmoor' ♀	CBot CMHG CPle CRow EBre ECtt ELan ENot LHop MAsh MGrG MMil NBrk NPer SDix SHBN SMad SMer SPer SPla SSta WBea WEas WHCG WPyg WSHC WWat WWeb
– 'Dart's Blue Butterfly'	MBri MUlv
– 'Dart's Ornamental White'	CBlo EBee MBri MUlv
– 'Dart's Papillon Blue'	SLPl
– 'Dart's Purple Rain'	CBlo MBri MUlv
– 'Empire Blue' ♀	CB&S CShe EBre ECtt ELan ENot GOrc MAsh MBal MUlv MWat NBee NFla NPer NWea SHBN SPer WDin WPyg WStI WTyr WWeb
– 'Fascinating'	CBlo CTri MAsh NPer SBod WTyr
– 'Flaming Violet'	CBlo
¶ – 'Fortune'	NNor
– 'Glasnevin'	CPle CTri SDix SHBN SPer
– 'Golden Sunset'	ECot
– 'Gonglepod'	ELan
– 'Harlequin' (v)	CB&S CLan CMHG CTrw CWLN EBre ELan ENot ISea LFis LHop MBal MBar MBel MBri MGos NNor NRoo SBod SPer SReu WDin WEas WHCG WPbr WPri WWat WWin
– 'Ile de France'	CB&S CBlo CWan EHic MGos MWat NWea SRms WWeb
– 'Les Kneale'	CPle MBal
– 'Masquerade'	CBlo CKni EHic ENot MGos MGrG NRoo WLRN WStI WWes
§ – 'Nanho Blue'	CB&S CDoC CPle EBre ECtt ELan ENot EPla IOrc LBuc LHop MAsh MBar MGos NFla NNor SBod SEas SHBN SPla WDin WHCG WHar WRTC WSHC
– 'Nanho Petite Indigo'	See ***B. davidii*** **'Nanho Blue'**
– 'Nanho Petite Purple'	See ***B. davidii*** **'Nanho Purple'**
§ – 'Nanho Purple'	CChe CDoC CWLN EBre ELan ENot GAri MAsh MBar MBel MBri NRoo SPer WHar WSHC WStI
– var. ***nanhoensis***	CBlo CHan CMHG CPle EBee MWat SEND SIde SPer WHCG
– var. ***nanhoensis alba***	CBar CBlo CChe EHal ELan LHop MLan MMil SPer SPla SRms WWat
– var. ***nanhoensis*** blue	CShe LHil MBri SPer WEas WTyr WWat
– 'Orchid Beauty'	CBlo EBar MLan NCut
– 'Peace'	CChe CTri EHic ENot NPer SPer
♦ – Petite Indigo®	See ***B. davidii*** **'Nanho Blue'**
♦ – Petite Plum®	See ***B. davidii*** **'Nanho Purple'**
– 'Pink Beauty'	CLTr SHBN SHFr WHCG WWat
– 'Pink Charming'	See ***B. davidii*** **'Charming'**
* – 'Pixie Blue'	NCut
¶ – 'Pixie Red'	NCut
* – 'Pixie White'	NCut
– 'Purple Prince'	CB&S EHic NCut WRHF
– 'Purple Rain'	SLPl
– 'Royal Purple'	MGos
– 'Royal Red' ♀	CB&S CShe CWLN ELan ENot GOrc GRei LHop MBal MBar MBri MGos MUlv MWat NFla NNor NPer NWea SBod SHBN SPer SReu SSoC WAbe WBod WDin WHCG WRTC WWin
– 'Summer Beauty'	CBlo CPle MGos WPat WWeb
– 'Variegated Royal Red'	CBlo SHBN
– 'White Bouquet'	CBlo EAst EBee GRei MBal MBel MPla MRav MWat NRoo NWea SBod SEND SEas SMer SPer SReu WAbe WLRN WWeb
– 'White Butterfly'	ELan
– 'White Cloud'	EPar GQui IOrc SRms WPri
– 'White Harlequin' (v)	CLTr CPle CRow EMon LHop WCot WEas WWat
– 'White Perfection'	CWLN
– 'White Profusion' ♀	CB&S CSam CShe ECtt ELan GCHN MBal MBar MGos MHlr NBee NBrk NFla NNor NWea SHBN WBea WDin WEas WFar WHCG WHar WPri WPyg WStI WWin
§ ***delavayi***	CMil CPle ERea WCru
N ***fallowiana***	CB&S CPle MSto NNor SReu
– var. ***alba*** ♀	CBot CDoC CPle ELan ENot LHop MBel NNor NSti SBid SHBN SPer SPla SSpi SSta WAbe WCru WPGP WSHC WWat
farreri	CBot CPle EWes MSte SOWG WBod
forrestii	CBot CHEx CPle WCru
globosa ♀	Widely available
– 'Cannington Gold'	CBlo MUlv
– 'Lemon Ball'	CB&S SMad
heliophila	See ***B. delavayi***
japonica	CPle
* 'Lady Curzon'	WRHF
x ***lewisiana***	CPle
– 'Margaret Pike'	CBot CFil SOWG WPGP

lindleyana	CAbb CB&S CBot CChu CFil CGre CHan CMCN CPle ELan EPla ERea MBel MRav NSti SBar SBid SChu SOWG SPan SPer SPla SSpi SUsu WCru WFar WHCG WSHC
'Lochinch' ♀	Widely available
loricata	CAbb CBot CGre CHan CPle ERea GQui MSte SOWG
– CD&R 190	EPla
macrostachya	CFil CPle
– SBEC 360	NHex WPGP
§ ***madagascariensis***	CB&S CHEx CPlN CPle CTbh LBlm SOWG WWat
myriantha	CPle GQui
nicodemia	See ***B. madagascariensis***
nivea	CAbb CBot CGre CMCN CPle EHic ELan MHar SBid SOWG
– var. ***yunnanensis***	CPle MSte
officinalis	CBot CDoC CPle ERea
paniculata	CPle
§ x ***pikei*** 'Hever'	CHal CPle GQui
'Pink Delight' ♀	Widely available
pterocaulis	CGre CPle
saligna	CGre CPle CTrC
salviifolia	CAbb CBot CFil CGre CPle CSWP CTbh EGar ELan SBid SDry SPan SPer WCot WLRN
sp. ACE 2522	CPle
sp. TS&BC 94062	CPle
sp. TS&BC 94287	CPle
sp. TS&BC 94408	CPle
stenostachya	CPle
sterniana	See ***B. crispa***
tibetica	See ***B. crispa***
tubiflora	CBot CPle ERea SOWG
venenifera B&SWJ 895	WCru
x ***weyeriana***	CBlo CLTr CSam ECtt EPar EPla GOrc LBlm MNrw MTis MWat NBir SBod SEas WBea WEas WFar WHCG WPri WPyg WSHC
* – 'Flight's Fancy'	EWes
– 'Golden Glow'	CB&S CBlo CChe CDoC CTri EBee EBre EHic GCHN MBri MPla NNor SHel WPyg WRTC WSel WWin
– 'Lady de Ramsey'	CWan SEND WNdy WPer
– 'Moonlight'	CPle CRow EAst EPla WSel
– 'Sungold' ♀	CB&S CPle ELan IOrc MBal MBel MBlu MGos NBee NFla SHBN SPer WCot WFar WHar WTyr
– 'Trewithen'	CB&S

BUGLOSSOIDES (Boraginaceae)

§ ***purpurocaerulea***	CKin CMHG CRDP ECha EEls ELan EMan EMar GCal MBro MHew MSal MSte SAxl SOkh WCot WCru WEas WOld WRHF WWin WWye

BULBINE (Asphodelaceae)

bulbosa	SAga WCot
caulescens	See ***B. frutescens***
§ ***frutescens***	CPea CSev EMar WBea WHal WWin WWye
– yellow	LHil
semibarbata	EGar NBro WPer

BULBINELLA (Asphodelaceae)

¶ ***angustifolia***	WCot
¶ ***cauda-felis***	WCot
floribunda	ETub
hookeri	CRDP ECou EPPr GAbr GDra GGar ITim LBee MFir MTho NGre NHar NHed WCot WPer
nutans var. ***nutans***	EEls
rossii	GDra

BULBINOPSIS See BULBINE

BULBOCODIUM (Colchicaceae)

vernum	CAvo EBre EHyt EPot ERos ETub LAma MBri NRog WAbe WHil

BUPHTHALMUM (Asteraceae)

§ ***salicifolium***	CInt CSam CSev EBre ELan EMon EPfP GMaP MBri MCli NBro NFla NNor NOrc NTow SPer SRms SWat WBea WMer WPer
– 'Alpengold'	ECha SIgm
– 'Dora'	EBee EMan NLak SUsu WGwG
♦ – Golden Beauty	See ***B. salicifolium* 'Golden Wonder'**
speciosum	See ***Telekia speciosa***

BUPLEURUM (Apiaceae)

angulosum	CFil CLon CLyd CRDP SIgm SMrm SWas WCru
– copper	See ***B. longifolium***
barceloi	SIgm
falcatum	CArc CGle CLTr CLyd EBee ECGP ECha MBro NBro NFla NSti SChu SMrm WCru WFar WWat
fruticosum	CB&S CBot CChu CFil CHad CHan CPle ECGP ELan ICrw MAll MHar SAxl SBid SBla SChu SIgm SSpi SSta WCru WEas WPat WSHC WWat
* ***griffithii***	MSal
¶ ***komarovianum***	GCal
§ ***longifolium***	CHan CRDP ECha GBin GGar NSti SWas WCot WCru
longiradiatum B&SWJ 729	WCru
¶ ***ranunculoides***	SMrm
rotundifolium	EWFC MSal WCot WCru
¶ ***salicifolium***	SIgm
spinosum	SIgm WCru
stellatum	GAri LBee
¶ ***tenue*** B&SWJ 2973	WCru

BURCHARDIA (Colchicaceae)

umbellata	CMon

BURSARIA (Pittosporaceae)

spinosa	CGre CPle ECou GQui LLew

BUTIA (Arecaceae)

capitata	CBrP CHEx CTbh CTrC EOas LPal NPal SArc SEND

BUTOMUS (Butomaceae)

umbellatus ♀	CBen CRow CWGN CWat ECha ECoo ECtt EHon EMFW LPBA MHew MSta NDea NVic SHig SRms SWat SWyc WChe WFar WMAq WShi
– 'Rosenrot'	CRow SBla SWyc

– 'Schneeweisschen'	CRow SWyc

BUXUS † (Buxaceae)

aurea 'Marginata'	See ***B. sempervirens* 'Marginata'**
balearica	CGre CPle EPla SDry SLan WSHC WWat
bodinieri	EPla SLan WWat
* 'David's Gold'	WSHC
* 'Golden Frimley'	LHop
'Green Gem'	CMil EHic NHar NHol SLan
'Green Mountain'	SLan
'Green Velvet'	EFol EHic NHol SLan WWeb
harlandii hort.	EPla GAri SIng SLan
– Hance 'Richard'	SLan STre
japonica 'Nana'	See ***B. microphylla***
macowanii	SLan
◆ ***macrophylla*** 'Asiatic Winter'	See ***B. microphylla* 'Winter Gem'**
§ ***microphylla***	CBlo CSWP EHic GDra LHol NHol SIde SIng SLan STre
– 'Compacta'	CFil SLan WPGP WPat
– 'Curly Locks'	EPla GAri NHol SLan
– 'Faulkner'	CDoC CSte ERea LHop MBlu MUlv NFla NHol SLan WLRN WWeb
– 'Grace Hendrick Phillips'	SLan
– 'Green Pillow'	SLan
– 'Helen Whiting'	SLan
– var. ***insularis***	See ***B. sinica*** var. ***insularis***
– var. ***japonica***	SLan
– – 'Aurea'	CWan
microphylla var. ***japonica*** 'Green Jade'	SLan
– 'Morris Dwarf'	SLan
– 'Morris Midget'	EHic NHol SLan
– 'National'	SLan
– 'Variegata'	CMHG
microphylla 'John Baldwin'	SLan
– var. ***koreana***	See ***B. sinica*** var. ***insularis***
– var. ***riparia***	See ***B. riparia***
– var. ***sinica***	See ***B. sinica***
§ – 'Winter Gem'	EHic SLPl
'Newport Blue'	MUlv
§ ***riparia***	SLan
* ***rugulosa*** var. ***intermedia***	SLan
sempervirens ♈	Widely available
§ – 'Angustifolia'	SLan SMad
– 'Argentea'	See ***B. sempervirens* 'Argenteovariegata'**
§ – 'Argenteovariegata'	CBlo EPfP MBal MRav SHig SLan WFar WSHC
– 'Aurea'	See ***B. sempervirens* 'Aureovariegata'**
– 'Aurea Maculata'	See ***B. sempervirens* 'Aureovariegata'**
– 'Aurea Marginata'	See ***B. sempervirens* 'Marginata'**
– 'Aurea Pendula' (v)	CMil EPla GAbr SLan SMad WWye
§ – 'Aureovariegata'	CArn CB&S EBee EBre EHic EPfP GAbr ISea MBar MGos MRav MWat NCut NHol SChu SIng SLan SPer WDin WFar WJek WLRN WWeb WWye
– 'Blauer Heinz'	CSev SLan SPer
§ – 'Blue Cone'	EHic GBin NHol
– 'Blue Spire'	See ***B. sempervirens* 'Blue Cone'**
§ – 'Elegantissima' (v) ♈	Widely available
– 'Gold Tip'	See ***B. sempervirens* 'Notata'**
– 'Greenpeace'	EBre EHic SLan
– 'Handsworthiensis'	EMil SEND SLan SPer
– 'Handsworthii'	CBlo CTri ERea NWea SRms
– subsp. ***hyrcana***	SLan
– 'Ickworth Giant'	SLan
– 'Inverewe'	SLan
– 'Kensington Gardens'	SLan
– 'Kingsville'	WCot
– 'Lace'	EBee NHol NSti
§ – 'Langley Beauty'	MHlr SLan
I – 'Langley Pendula'	See ***B. sempervirens* 'Langley Beauty'**
– 'Latifolia'	See ***B. sempervirens* 'Bullata'**
– 'Latifolia Macrophylla' ♈	EBee GAbr SEas SLan WLRN
§ – 'Latifolia Maculata' ♈	CAbP CChe EFol EPla GDra MBal MHlr MPla NHol NRoo SEas SLan STre WOak
– 'Longifolia'	See ***B. sempervirens* 'Angustifolia'**
§ – 'Marginata'	ECtt GCHN LHop MRav NHol NSti SHBN SHFr SLan WStI
– 'Memorial'	EHic GAbr LGre NHol SLan
– 'Myosotidifolia'	CFil CMHG EPla NHar SLan WWat
– 'Myrtifolia'	CBot NHar NHol SLan
§ – 'Notata' (v)	CBlo CDec CSWP ERea GAbr MAsh WGor WGwG
– 'Pendula'	CGre EHic SLan SMad
I – 'Pendula Esveld'	MHlr
– 'Prostrata'	EHic MHlr NHol SLan
– 'Pyramidalis'	EBee EHic GAbr NBee SLan
– 'Rosmarinifolia'	SLan
– 'Rotundifolia'	CLnd EBee LHol NFla SHhN SIde SLan WDin
– 'Salicifolia Elata'	SLan
– 'Silver Beauty' (v)	CB&S EMil MGos
– 'Silver Variegated'	See ***B. sempervirens* 'Elegantissima'**
– 'Suffruticosa' ♈	Widely available
– 'Suffruticosa Variegata'	CB&S EBee EOHP ERea SRms
– 'Vardar Valley'	EHic NHar SLan
* – 'Variegata'	EPfP
¶ – 'Waterfall'	SLan
§ ***sinica***	SLan
– 'Filigree'	NHol SLan
§ – var. ***insularis***	EPla
– – 'Justin Brouwers'	CSev SLan
– – 'Pincushion'	SLan
– – 'Tide Hill'	SLan
– – 'Winter Beauty'	MUlv
wallichiana	CFil SLan WPGP WWat

CACALIA (Asteraceae)

See Plant Deletions

CAESALPINIA (Caesalpiniaceae)

gilliesii	CBot CFai CGre CHEx EMil NPSI SEND SOWG
¶ ***pulcherrima***	LChe
¶ – f. ***flava***	LChe

CAIOPHORA (Loasaceae)

acuminata	MSto
coronata	MSto
prietea	MSto

CALADENIA (Orchidaceae)

g. **Fairy Floss**	SWes

CALADIUM (Araceae)

§ ***bicolor*** (v)	MBri
x ***hortulanum***	See ***C. bicolor***

§ *lindenii* (v) MBri

CALAMAGROSTIS (Poaceae)

N× *acutiflora* 'Karl Foerster' CArc CDoC CLon EBee EBre ECha EGar EHoe EPPr EPla ESOG ETPC GAbr GCal SAxl SDix SMer SPer WChe
– 'Overdam' (v) CArc CCuc CElw CInt CMea CSWP EBee EBre ECha EGar EHoe EMon EPPr EPla ESOG ESiP ETPC LHil LRHS MBri NHol NSti SApp SAsh SAxl SUsu WBro WChe WLRN
§ *epigejos* EPPr ETPC
¶ – CLD 1325 EPla

CALAMINTHA † (Lamiaceae)

alpina See ***Acinos alpinus***
clinopodium See ***Clinopodium vulgare***
cretica CLyd CMea EMon GBar LHol LHop MHew MTho NTow WDav WPbr WPer WWye
cretica variegata WEas
§ *grandiflora* CArn CBre CGle CLon CSev EBar EBre ECha ECoo EEls ELan EMon GMac GPoy LHol MBri MGrG NPer SAxl SUsu WBea WByw WCot WFar WHal WHoo WPbr WPer WRus WWye
– 'Variegata' CArc CDec CGle CMil EEls EFol ELan EMan EMon LFis LHop MBro MCLN MGrG NCGP NPer SCro SWat WByw WCHb WFar WHer WHoo WMaN WPbr WRus WSan
§ *nepeta* CArn CLon CMGP ECha ECoo EEls EWFC LGan LGre MCLN MFir MGrG MGra MRav MSte NBir NBro SBla SWat WEas WFar WHal WOve WPbr WPer WWin WWye
– subsp. *glandulosa* EMon WHoo
ACL 1050/90
– – 'White Cloud' CArc CGle CSpe EBre ECha EFou EMon GBuc GMac LGre LHol MBri MBro MCLN MSte NTow SChu SLod WHoo WMaN WPbr WRus
§ – subsp. *nepeta* CGle CHan CSev CShe EFou ELan EMon GBar GMac LHol LHop MBri MPla MTho NOak SCro SIde SPer SUsu WCHb WHoo WMer WRus WSHC WWat WWhi
– – 'Blue Cloud' CArc CGle CHan CHor CMil ECha EFou LGre LHol MBri MRav NTow SLod SUsu SWat WMaN WRus WWye
nepetoides See ***C. nepeta*** subsp. ***nepeta***
§ *sylvatica* CNat LHol WCla
– subsp. *ascendens* MHew WPbr
vulgaris See ***Clinopodium vulgare***

CALAMOVILFA (Poaceae)

longifolia ETPC

CALANDRINIA (Portulacaceae)

caespitosa CGra NGre NWCA
grandiflora CSpe EBar ELan LHop SAga WWin WWye
megarhiza See ***Claytonia megarhiza***
sericea CGra CPBP EHyt
sibirica See ***Claytonia sibirica***
umbellata EBar NPri NWCA SBla WPer WWin WWye
* *umbellata amarantha* WOMN

CALANTHE (Orchidaceae)

¶ *amamiana* EFEx
arisanenesis EFEx
aristulifera EFEx LAma NRog SWes WChr
bicolor See ***C. discolor*** var. ***flava***
¶ *biloba* LAma
¶ *brevicornu* LAma
caudatilabella EFEx
¶ *chloroleuca* LAma
discolor EFEx LAma NRog SWes WChr
§ – var. *flava* LAma NRar
¶ *hamata* EFEx
¶ *herbacea* LAma
g. **Hizen** SWes
g. **Ishi-zuchi** SWes
japonica EFEx
g. **Kozu** SWes
¶ *mannii* EFEx LAma
¶ *masuca* LAma
nipponica EFEx
¶ *puberula* LAma
reflexa EFEx LAma NRog SWes WChr
g. **Satsuma** SWes
§ *sieboldii* EFEx LAma NRog SWes WChr
striata See ***C. sieboldii***
¶ *tokunoshimensis* EFEx
tricarinata EFEx LAma SWes WChr

CALATHEA † (Marantaceae)

albertii MBri
albicans See ***C. micans***
crocata MBri
'Exotica' MBri
'Greystar' MBri
kegeljanii See ***C. bella***
lietzei MBri
– 'Greenstar' MBri
§ *majestica* MBri
makoyana ♀ CHal MBri
* 'Mavi Queen' MBri
metallica MBri
* 'Misto' MBri
oppenheimiana See ***Ctenanthe oppenheimiana***
orbiculata See ***C. truncata***
ornata See ***C. majestica***
picturata 'Argentea' MBri
– 'Vandenheckei' MBri
roseopicta MBri
§ *truncata* MBri
veitchiana MBri
warscewiczii MBri
'Wavestar' MBri
zebrina ♀ MBri

CALCEOLARIA † (Scrophulariaceae)

acutifolia See ***C. polyrhiza***
alba CPla GBri NRai
arachnoidea GCra MSto NWoo WWhi
× *banksii* GQui LBlm MFir
bicolor GCal GCra WCot
§ *biflora* CLyd CMea CNic ELan EPot GCHN GDra GTou MBal NWoo SAlw WWin
– 'Goldcrest Amber' EMNN GCra NMen SRms WPer

'Camden Hero' CBrk CKni GCra WWat
chelidonioides MTho
× ***clibranii*** CBrk
crenatiflora GCra MSto NWoo
cymbiflora MSto
darwinii CGra GCra GTou MSto NMen
ericoides WCot
– JCA 13818 MSto
falklandica ECtt ELan NCGP NWCA SHFr SRms SSca WPer WWin WWtk
filicaulis EPot MSto
fothergillii MSto NMen NTow
'Goldcrest' EPfP GCHN NPri
helianthemoides JCA 13911 MSto
'Hort's Variety' MTho
hyssopifolia JCA 13648 MSto
§ ***integrifolia*** ♀ CB&S CDec ELan EMar ERav LBlm MBal MFir NRog SAga SChu SPer SRms WOMN WWat WWye
– var. ***angustifolia*** ♀ SDry
– bronze SPer WAbe
'John Innes' EBur ELan ESis GBur NMen NWCA SIng WCot WHil
'Kentish Hero' CBot CBrk CDec CElw ELan EOrc ERav LBlm LHil NPer SChu WCot WWye
lagunae-blancae MSto
lanigera ELan EWes MSto WSan
mendocina MSto
mexicana MSto SHFr
nivalis JCA 13888 MSto
¶ aff. ***pavonii*** LHil
perfoliata JCA 13736 MSto
plantaginea See ***C. biflora***
§ ***polyrhiza*** ELan MBal MSto NMen NNrd NRoo NRya NWCA WCla
purpurea MSto
rugosa See ***C. integrifolia***
scabiosifolia See ***C. tripartita***
sp. ex P&W 6276 MRPP
sp. JCA 14128 MSto
sp. JCA 14172 MSto
'Stamford Park' CBrk
tenella ECtt ELan EPot ESis GDra MSto NHar NTow NWCA WAbe WPat
§ ***tripartita*** MSto
volckmannii MSto
'Walter Shrimpton' ELan EPot EWes NNrd

CALDCLUVIA (Cunoniaceae)
paniculata ISea

CALEA (Asteraceae)
¶ ***zacatechichi*** NGno

CALENDULA (Asteraceae)
officinalis CArn CJew ELau GPoy LHol MChe MGra MHew MSal SIde WHer WJek WOak WRha WSel WWye
– Fiesta Gitana WJek
– 'Prolifera' WBea WHer
– 'Variegata' MSal

CALLA (Araceae)
aethiopica See ***Zantedeschia aethiopica***
palustris CBen CHEx CRow CWGN CWat EBre ECoo EHon GAri GGar LPBA MSta NDea SHig SWat SWyc WChe WMAq

CALLIANDRA (Mimosaceae)
brevipes See ***C. selloi***
emarginata minima LCns

CALLIANTHEMUM (Ranunculaceae)
anemonoides NHar
coriandrifolium GDra

CALLICARPA (Verbenaceae)
americana var. ***lactea*** CPle
bodinieri NBir
– var. ***giraldii*** CDec CShe GBin MAsh MHlr MRav NFla SSta WDin WFar WRHF WRTC WWat WWeb
– – 'Profusion' ♀ CB&S CPle CWSG EBre ELan ENot GOrc IOrc LHop LNet LPan MBal MBel MBri MGos MPla NHol SHBN SPer SReu SSpi SSta WBod WHCG WHar WPat WStI WWat
cathayana CMCN
dichotoma CPle GSki MNes WSHC WWat WWin
japonica CPle WCoo
– 'Leucocarpa' CB&S CPle EHic EPfP LRHS SBid SPer WWat

CALLICOMA (Cunoniaceae)
¶ ***serratifolia*** MAll

CALLIERGON (Sphagnaceae)
See Plant Deletions

CALLIRHOE (Malvaceae)
involucrata EBee EMan NWCA

CALLISIA (Commelinaceae)
elegans ♀ CHal
§ ***navicularis*** CHal
repens CHal MBri

CALLISTEMON (Myrtaceae)
brachyandrus MAll
'Burning Bush' CB&S LBlm MAll SOWG
chisholmii SOWG
citrinus CLTr CPle CShe CTrC ECot ECou ERav ERom GOrc ISea MAll NPer SLMG SMac SOWG SPer WGwG WHar WWin
– 'Albus' See ***C. citrinus* 'White Anzac'**
– 'Canberra' SOWG
– 'Firebrand' CKni CSte LRHS WWeb
– 'Mauve Mist' CB&S CKni CSte CTrC LBlm LRHS MAll NPal SSta
– 'Perth Pink' See ***C.* 'Perth Pink'**
– 'Splendens' ♀ CB&S CDoC CHEx CSam EBre ELan EMil GQui IOrc MAll NPal SAga SBra SDry SHBN SHFr SOWG SReu SSta WBod WRTC WStI WWat
§ – 'White Anzac' CGre GCHN
– 'Yellow Queen' CB&S MAll
¶ ***coccineus*** CGre
¶ ***comboynensis*** SOWG
flavescens SOWG
flavovirens MAll SOWG

glaucus	See ***C. speciosus***
¶ 'King's Park Special'	SOWG
* *laevis*	ECon
¶ *lanceolatus*	CGre
linearifolius	MAll
linearis 🏆	CBlo CHan CMac CTrC CTri ECou EHic ELan EMil IOrc MAll MBal SLMG SOWG SRms SSpi WNor WRTC
macropunctatus	CGre MAll SOWG
pachyphyllus	MAll SOWG
pallidus	CB&S CChu CMHG CMac CPle CWit EGoo ELan EPfP MAll SOWG SSta
paludosus	See ***C. sieberi***
* *pearsonii*	SOWG
'Perth Pink'	CB&S CFee CTrC GSki MAll SBid SOWG
phoeniceus	MAll SOWG
pinifolius	MAll SOWG
– green form	LLew
pityoides	CGre ECou MAll SOWG WAbe
– alpine form	MAll
¶ – from Brown's Swamp, Australia	ECou MAll
polandii	SOWG
recurvus	MAll
'Red Clusters'	CB&S CSte ECon ELan ERea GSki LRHS MAll SOWG
rigidus	CB&S CBlo CChe CDoC CHEx CLan CMHG CTri CTrw EBre ELan EMil ISea MAll MBlu MGos MLan MUlv SLMG SOWG SSoC WCru WDin WWeb
'Royal Sceptre'	MAll
rugulosus	MAll SOWG
salignus 🏆	CChu CHEx CMHG CPlN CSam CTrC CTri IOrc ISea MAll MBal MCCP MUlv SAxl SLod SOWG SPer SSoC WRTC WSHC
– 'Ruber'	MAll
§ *sieberi* 🏆	CChu CGre CMHG CTrC ECou EPfP ISea MAll NBir SOWG WWat
§ *speciosus*	CTrC MAll SMur SOWG WAbe WLRN
subulatus	CMHG ECou MAll MBal MCCP NCut SArc SOWG
teretifolius	SOWG
viminalis	CTrC EHic MAll SOWG
– 'Captain Cook' 🏆	CB&S CChu CTrC ECou ERea LCns LRHS SOWG
– 'Hannah Ray'	MAll SOWG
– 'Little John'	CB&S CWSG LRHS MAll SBid SOWG
– 'Malawi Giant'	SOWG
'Violaceus'	CHan CPle MAll
viridiflorus	CChu CGre CPle CTrC ECou GQui IBlr MAll MCCP SOWG WHil WSan

CALLITRICHE (Callitrichaceae)

autumnalis	See ***C. hermaphroditica***
§ *hermaphroditica*	EMFW SAWi
§ *palustris*	CBen ECoo EHon SWyc
verna	See ***C. palustris***

CALLITRIS (Cupressaceae)

oblonga	CGre ECou
rhomboidea	CGre ECou

CALLUNA † (Ericaceae)

vulgaris	CKin ECWi MGos SRms
– 'Adrie'	EDen
– 'Alba Argentea'	EDen ENHC
– 'Alba Aurea'	ECho EDen ENHC MBar
– 'Alba Carlton'	EDen
– 'Alba Dumosa'	EDen ENHC
– 'Alba Elata'	CNCN ECho EDen ENHC MBar NYor
– 'Alba Elegans'	EDen
– 'Alba Elongata'	See ***C. vulgaris* 'Mair's Variety'**
– 'Alba Erecta'	EDen
– 'Alba Jae'	EDen MBar
– 'Alba Minor'	EDen
– 'Alba Multiflora'	EDen
– 'Alba Pilosa'	EDen
– 'Alba Plena' (d)	CB&S CMac CNCN EDen ENHC GSpe MBar SBod WStI
– 'Alba Praecox'	EDen
– 'Alba Pumila'	EDen MBar
§ – 'Alba Rigida'	CMac CNCN EDen ENHC MBar NYor SIng
– 'Alec Martin' (d)	EDen
– 'Alex Warwick'	EDen
– 'Alexandra'	EDen NHol NRoo SCoo WGre
– 'Alieke'	EDen
– 'Alison Yates'	EDen MBar
– 'Allegretto'	EDen
– 'Allegro' 🏆	CMac CNCN CWLN EDen ENHC GAri MBar MOke NHol NYor SBod WStI
– 'Alportii'	CWLN EDen ENHC GDra GSpe MBar MOke NYor SBod WStI
– 'Alportii Praecox'	CNCN ECho EDen ENHC MBar SBod
– 'Alys Sutcliffe'	EDen
– 'Amanda Wain'	ECho EDen
– 'Amethyst'	EDen
– 'Amilto'	CNCN EDen WGre
– 'Amy'	EDen
– 'Andrew Proudley'	EDen ENHC MBar NRoo
– 'Anette'	EDen SCoo
– 'Angela Wain'	ECho EDen NRoo
– 'Anna'	EDen
– 'Annabel' (d)	EDen
– 'Anne Dobbin'	EDen
– 'Anneke'	EDen
– 'Annemarie' (d) 🏆	CNCN CWLN EBre EDen MGos NHol SBod SCoo WGre
– 'Anthony Davis' 🏆	CNCN CWLN EDen ENHC MBar MGos MOke NHol NYor SBod WGre
– 'Anthony Wain'	EDen MGos
– 'Anton'	EDen
– 'Apollo'	EDen
– 'Applecross' (d)	CNCN EDen SHBN
– 'Arabella'	EDen
– 'Argentea'	EDen MBar
– 'Ariadne'	EDen
– 'Arina'	CNCN CWLN ECho EDen MBri MOke
– 'Arran Gold'	CNCN EDen ENHC GSpe MBar NYor WGre
– 'Ashgarth Amber'	EDen
– 'Ashgarth Amethyst'	EDen
– 'Asterix'	EDen
– 'Atalanta'	EDen
¶ – 'Athole Gold'	EDen

– 'August Beauty'	CNCN ECho EDen ENHC MOke
– 'Aurea'	CNCN ECho EDen ENHC GSpe
– 'Autumn Glow'	EDen
– 'Baby Ben'	CNCN EDen
– 'Barbara Fleur'	EDen SBod
– 'Barja'	EDen
– 'Barnett Anley'	CNCN CWLN ECho EDen ENHC GSpe
– 'Battle of Arnhem' 🏆	CNCN EDen MBar WGre
– 'Beechwood Crimson'	CNCN EDen ENHC
– 'Ben Nevis'	EDen
– 'Beoley Crimson'	CB&S CNCN EDen ENHC GAri GDra MBar MGos SBod
– 'Beoley Gold' 🏆	CB&S CNCN EBre EDen ENHC GSpe MBar MBri MGos MOke NHol NRoo NYor SBod SHBN WGre WStI
– 'Beoley Silver'	CNCN EDen NRoo WGre
– 'Bernadette'	EDen
– 'Betty Baum'	EDen
– 'Blazeaway'	CMac CNCN CWLN EDen ENHC GDra GSpe MBar MBri NHar NHol NRoo SBod SHBN WGre WStI
– 'Blueness'	EDen
– 'Bognie'	CNCN EDen ENHC WGre
– 'Bonfire Brilliance'	CNCN EDen MBar NHar NYor SBod
– 'Boreray'	CNCN EDen
– 'Boskoop'	CNCN CWLN EBre EDen ENHC MBar MBri NHol NRoo NYor SBod WGre
¶ – 'Bradford'	EDen
– 'Braemar'	CNCN EDen
– 'Braeriach'	EDen
– 'Branchy Anne'	EDen
– 'Bray Head'	CNCN EDen MBar SBod WGre
– 'Brightness'	EDen
– 'Brita Elisabeth' (d)	EDen
– 'Bud Lyle'	EDen WGre
– 'Bunsall'	CMac CNCN EDen
– 'Buxton Snowdrift'	EDen
– 'C.W. Nix'	CNCN ECho EDen ENHC GSpe MBar
– 'Caerketton White'	ECho EDen ENHC GSpe
– 'Caleb Threlkeld'	EDen
– 'Calf of Man'	EDen ENHC
– 'Californian Midge'	CNCN EDen ENHC GAri GSpe MBar MGos NHol NYor WGre
– 'Carl Röders' (d)	EDen
– 'Carmen'	ECho EDen NYor
– 'Carn Gold'	EDen
– 'Carole Chapman'	EDen ENHC MBar MGos SBod SHBN
– 'Carolyn'	EDen
– 'Catherine Anne'	EDen
– 'Celtic Gold'	EDen
– 'Chindit'	EDen
– 'Christina'	EDen
– 'Cilcennin Common'	EDen WGre
– 'Citronella'	EDen
– 'Clare Carpet'	EDen
– 'Coby'	EDen
– 'Coccinea'	CMac ECho EDen ENHC MBar SBod
– 'Colette'	EDen
– 'Con Brio'	CNCN EDen LRHS WGre
– 'Copper Glow'	EDen
– 'Coral Island'	EDen MBar MGos
– 'Cottswood Gold'	EDen
– 'County Wicklow' (D) 🏆	CNCN EBre EDen ENHC GSpe MBar MBri MGos MOke NHar NHol NRoo NYor SBod SHBN WGre
– 'Craig Rossie'	EDen
– 'Crail Orange'	EDen
– 'Cramond' (d)	CNCN ECho EDen ENHC GDra MBar
– 'Cream Steving'	EDen
– 'Crimson Glory'	CNCN EDen GSpe MBar NYor WGre WStI
– 'Crimson Sunset'	CNCN EDen SBod WStI
– 'Crowborough Beacon'	EDen
– 'Cuprea'	CNCN CWLN EDen ENHC GDra GSpe MBar MBri MOke NHol NRoo SBod WGre WStI
– 'Cuprea Select'	EDen
– 'Dainty Bess'	CNCN EDen MBar NYor SBod WGre WStI
– 'Dark Beauty' (d)	CNCN EBre EDen MGos NHol NRoo WStI
– 'Dark Star' (d) 🏆	CNCN CWLN EBre EDen GSpe MBar MGos MOke NHar NHol NRoo SCoo
– 'Darkness' 🏆	CB&S CNCN CWLN EDen ENHC GSpe MBar MBri MGos MOke NHar NHol NYor SBod SCoo SHBN WGre WStI
– 'Darleyensis'	EDen
– 'Dart's Amethyst'	EDen
– 'Dart's Beauty'	EDen
– 'Dart's Brilliant'	EDen
– 'Dart's Flamboyant'	CNCN EDen
– 'Dart's Gold'	EDen MBar NHar NRoo
– 'Dart's Hedgehog'	EDen WGre
– 'Dart's Parakeet'	CNCN EDen
– 'Dart's Parrot'	ECho EDen NHar
– 'Dart's Silver Rocket'	EDen NRoo
– 'Dart's Squirrel'	EDen
– 'David Eason'	CNCN ECho EDen ENHC
– 'David Hagenaars'	EDen
– 'David Hutton'	EDen MBar
– 'David Platt' (d)	EDen
– 'Denny Pratt'	EDen
– 'Desiree'	EDen
– 'Devon' (d)	EDen
– 'Diana'	EDen
– 'Dickson's Blazes'	EDen GSpe
– 'Dirry'	CNCN EDen GSpe
– 'Doctor Murray's White'	See ***C. vulgaris* 'Mullardoch'**
– 'Doris Rushworth'	EDen
– 'Drum-ra'	EDen ENHC GDra GSpe MBar NYor SBod SRms WGre
– 'Dunkeld White'	EDen
– 'Dunnet Lime'	EDen NYor
– 'Dunnydeer'	EDen ENHC
– 'Dunwood'	EDen MBar
§ – 'Durfordii'	EDen
– 'E. Hoare'	EDen MBar
– 'E.F. Brown'	CNCN EDen ENHC
– 'Easter-bonfire'	CNCN EDen NHol WGre
– 'Eckart Miessner'	EDen
– 'Edith Godbolt'	CNCN EDen ENHC
– 'Elaine'	EDen
– 'Elegant Pearl'	EDen MBar SBod
– 'Elegantissima'	CNCN CWLN EDen ENHC GSpe MOke WGre
– 'Elegantissima Lilac'	EDen
– 'Elegantissima Walter Ingwersen'	See ***C. vulgaris* 'Walter Ingwersen'**

– 'Elkstone'	CNCN EDen ENHC MBar SBod
– 'Ellen'	EDen
– 'Else Frye' (d)	EDen
– 'Elsie Purnell' (d) 🏆	CNCN CWLN EDen ENHC GSpe MBar MGos MOke NHol NYor SBod WGre WStI
– 'Emerald Jock'	EDen SBod
– 'Emma Louise Tuke'	ECho EDen
– 'Eric Easton'	EDen
¶ – 'Eskdale Gold'	EDen
– 'Fairy'	CMac CNCN EDen MOke NYor
– 'Falling Star'	EDen
– 'Feuerwerk'	EDen
§ – 'Finale' 🏆	CNCN EDen ENHC MBar WGre
– 'Findling'	EDen
– 'Fire King'	EDen MBar
– 'Firebreak'	EDen MBar WGre
– 'Firefly' 🏆	CMac CNCN CWLN EBre EDen ENHC GSpe MBar MBri MOke NHar NRoo SBod SHBN WGre WStI
– 'Firestar'	EDen
– 'Flamingo'	CNCN EBre EDen MBar MBri MOke NHar NHol NRoo WGre
– 'Flatling'	EDen
– 'Flore Pleno' (d)	EDen ENHC MBar
– 'Floriferous'	EDen
– 'Florrie Spicer'	EDen
– 'Fokko' (d)	EDen
– 'Fortyniner Gold'	EDen
– 'Foxhollow Wanderer'	CNCN EDen ENHC GSpe MBar MOke SBod
– 'Foxii'	EDen
– 'Foxii Floribunda'	ECho EDen ENHC GSpe MBar
– 'Foxii Lett's Form'	See ***C. vulgaris* 'Velvet Dome'**
– 'Foxii Nana'	CNCN EDen ENHC GSpe MBar NHar NHol SBod WGre
– 'Foya'	EDen
– 'Fred J. Chapple'	CNCN CWLN EDen ENHC GDra MBar MBri MOke SBod WGre WStI
– 'Fréjus'	EDen
– 'French Grey'	CNCN EDen
– 'Fritz Kircher'	EDen
– 'Gerda'	EDen
– 'Ginkels Glorie'	EDen
– 'Glasa'	EDen
– 'Glen Mashie'	EDen
– 'Glencoe' (d)	EDen ENHC GSpe MBar MBri MGos MOke NHar NYor WGre
– 'Glendoick Silver'	EDen
– 'Glenfiddich'	CNCN EDen MBar
– 'Glenlivet'	EDen MBar
– 'Glenmorangie'	EDen MBar
– 'Gnome Pink'	EDen
– 'Gold Charm'	EDen
– 'Gold Finch'	EDen
– 'Gold Flame'	CWLN EDen LRHS MBar SBod
– 'Gold Hamilton' (d)	ECho EDen
– 'Gold Haze' 🏆	CB&S CMac CNCN CWLN EBre EDen ENHC GSpe MBar MBri MOke NHol NRoo SBod SCoo WGre WStI
– 'Gold Knight'	ECho EDen LRHS MBar SBod
– 'Gold Kup'	EDen MBar
– 'Gold Mist'	ECho EDen LRHS
– 'Gold Spronk'	EDen
– 'Goldcarmen'	EDen
– 'Golden Carpet'	CB&S CNCN CWLN EDen ENHC GDra MBar MBri MGos MOke NHar NHol NYor SRms WGre WStI
– 'Golden Dew'	EDen
– 'Golden Dream' (d)	EDen
– 'Golden Feather'	CB&S CNCN EDen ENHC MBar MGos NYor SBod SHBN WGre
– 'Golden Fleece'	CNCN EDen
– 'Golden Max'	EDen NHar
– 'Golden Rivulet'	EDen ENHC LRHS MBar
– 'Golden Turret'	CNCN ECho EDen ENHC NRoo
– 'Golden Wonder' (d)	EDen
– 'Goldsworth Crimson'	ECho EDen ENHC
– 'Goldsworth Crimson Variegated'	CNCN EDen ENHC MBar SBod
– 'Grasmeriensis'	EDen MBar
– 'Great Comp'	EDen MBar
– 'Grey Carpet'	CNCN EDen MBar SBod
– 'Grijsje'	EDen
– 'Grizzly'	EDen
– 'Grönsinka'	EDen
– 'Guinea Gold'	CNCN ECho EDen MBar MBri NRoo WGre
§ – 'H.E. Beale' (d)	CB&S CNCN CWLN EBre EDen ENHC GDra GSpe MBar MBri MGos MOke NHar NHol NYor SBod SHBN WGre
– 'Hamlet Green'	CNCN CWLN EDen MBar
– 'Hammondii'	CNCN EDen NYor SBod WGre WStI
– 'Hammondii Aureifolia'	CNCN CWLN EBre EDen GAri MBar MBri MOke
– 'Hammondii Rubrifolia'	CNCN EDen MBar MBri MOke NHar
– 'Harlekin'	EDen NYor
– 'Harry Gibbon' (d)	EDen
– 'Harten's Findling'	EDen
– 'Hatjes Herbstfeuer' (d)	EDen
– 'Hayesensis'	EDen
– 'Heideberg'	EDen
– 'Heidepracht'	EDen
– 'Heidesinfonie'	EDen
– 'Heideteppich'	EDen
– 'Heidezwerg'	EDen
– 'Herbert Mitchell'	EDen
– 'Hester'	EDen
– 'Hetty'	EDen
– 'Hibernica'	EDen MBar WGre
– 'Hiemalis'	EDen ENHC MBar NYor
– 'Hiemalis Southcote'	See ***C. vulgaris* 'Durfordii'**
– 'Highland Cream'	CNCN
– 'Highland Rose'	CNCN EDen WGre
– 'Hilda Turberfield'	EDen
– 'Hillbrook Orange'	EDen MBar WGre
– 'Hillbrook Sparkler'	EDen
¶ – 'Hinton White'	EDen
– f. ***hirsuta***	WGre
– 'Hirsuta Albiflora'	EDen MBar
– 'Hirsuta Typica'	CNCN ECho EDen WGre
– 'Hirta'	CNCN EDen MBar SBod WGre
– 'Hollandia'	EDen
– 'Holstein'	EDen
– 'Hookstone'	EDen MBar WGre
– 'Hoyerhagen'	EDen
§ – 'Hugh Nicholson'	CNCN EDen ENHC NHar
– 'Humpty Dumpty'	ECho EDen ENHC NHol NYor
– 'Hypnoides'	EDen
– 'Ide's Double' (d)	EDen SBod
– 'Inchcolm'	EDen

– 'Ineke'	CNCN EDen ENHC MBar
– 'Ingrid Bouter' (d)	EDen
– 'Inshriach Bronze'	CNCN EDen ENHC GDra GSpe MBar SBod WGre
– 'Iris van Leyen'	CNCN EDen LRHS
– 'Islay Mist'	EDen
– 'Isobel Frye'	EDen MBar
– 'Isobel Hughes' (d)	EDen MBar
– 'J.H. Hamilton' (d) ♀	CNCN EDen ENHC GDra GSpe MBar MBri MGos NHol SBod SRms WGre WStI
– 'Jan'	CWLN EDen
– 'Jan Dekker'	CNCN EDen LRHS NHol SBod WGre
– 'Janice Chapman'	ECho EDen MBar WGre
– 'Japanese White'	EDen
– 'Jenny'	EDen
– 'Jill'	EDen
– 'Jimmy Dyce' (d) ♀	EDen SBod
– 'Joan Sparkes' (d)	CNCN EDen ENHC MBar WGre WStI
– 'John F. Letts'	CNCN EDen ENHC GSpe MBar MGos SBod SHBN SRms WGre WStI
– 'Johnson's Variety'	CNCN ECho EDen MBar WGre
– 'Josefine'	EDen
– 'Joseph's Coat'	EDen
– 'Joy Vanstone' ♀	CMac CNCN CWLN EDen ENHC MBar MBri MGos MOke NHol NRoo SHBN WGre
– 'Julia'	CNCN EDen
¶ – 'Julie Ann Platt'	EDen
– 'Julie Gill'	EDen
– 'Karin Blum'	EDen
– 'Kermit'	EDen
– 'Kerstin'	CNCN EDen LRHS WGre
– 'Kinlochruel' (d) ♀	CMac CNCN CWLN EDen ENHC GDra GSpe MBar MBri MGos MOke NHar NHol NRoo NYor SBod SHBN SRms WGre
– 'Kirby White'	CNCN CWLN EDen MBar MBri NHol NYor
– 'Kirsty Anderson'	EDen MOke
– 'Kit Hill'	EDen MBar
– 'Kuphaldtii'	EDen MBar
– 'Kuppendorf'	EDen
– 'Kynance'	CNCN EDen ENHC MBar
– 'Lady Maithe'	EDen
– 'Lambstails'	EDen MBar MGos
– 'L'Ancresse'	EDen
– 'Late Crimson Gold'	EDen
– 'Lemon Gem'	EDen
– 'Lemon Queen'	EDen
– 'Leprechaun'	EDen
– 'Leslie Slinger'	CNCN EDen ENHC LRHS MBar
– 'Lewis Lilac'	EDen WGre
– 'Liebestraum'	EDen
– 'Lime Glade'	CNCN ECho EDen
– 'Limelight'	EDen
– 'Llanbedrog Pride' (d)	CNCN EDen MBar
– 'Loch Turret'	CNCN EDen ENHC GSpe MBar MBri MOke NRoo
– 'Loch-na-Seil'	EDen MBar
– 'London Pride'	EDen
– 'Long White'	CNCN ECho EDen GSpe MBar
– 'Lyle's Late White'	CNCN EDen
– 'Lyle's Surprise'	EDen MBar
– 'Lyndon Proudley'	EDen ENHC
– 'Lüneberg Heath'	EDen
§ – 'Mair's Variety' ♀	CNCN EDen ENHC GDra GSpe MBar NYor SBod
– 'Mallard'	EDen
– 'Manitoba'	EDen
– 'Marie'	EDen
– 'Marion Blum'	EDen MBar
– 'Marleen'	CNCN EDen MBar NHol SBod
– 'Marlies'	EDen
– 'Martha Hermann'	EDen
– 'Masquerade'	EDen MBar
– 'Matita'	EDen
– 'Mauvelyn'	EDen
– 'Mazurka'	EDen
– 'Melanie'	EDen NHol
– 'Mies'	EDen
– 'Minima'	EDen MBar SBod
– 'Minima Smith's Variety'	EDen ENHC MBar
– 'Mini-öxabäck'	EDen
– 'Minty'	EDen
– 'Mirelle'	CNCN EDen
– 'Miss Muffet'	NHol
– 'Molecule'	EDen MBar
– 'Monika' (d)	EDen
– 'Moon Glow'	EDen
§ – 'Mousehole'	CNCN EDen ENHC GSpe MBar MGos MOke NHol WGre
– 'Mousehole Compact'	See *C. vulgaris* **'Mousehole'**
– 'Mrs Alf'	EDen
– 'Mrs E. Wilson' (d)	EDen
– 'Mrs Neil Collins'	EDen
– 'Mrs Pat'	CNCN EDen ENHC GAri MBar MOke NHol WGre
– 'Mrs Ronald Gray'	CMac CNCN CWLN EDen MBar WGre
– 'Mullach Mor'	EDen
§ – 'Mullardoch'	EDen MBar
– 'Mullion' ♀	CNCN EDen ENHC MBar MOke
– 'Multicolor'	CB&S CNCN EDen ENHC GDra GSpe MBar MOke NHol NYor SBod SRms
– 'Murielle Dobson'	EDen MBar
§ – 'My Dream' (d)	CNCN EBre EDen ENHC GSpe MBar NHol NRoo NYor SCoo WGre
– 'Nana'	ENHC
– 'Nana Compacta'	CMac CNCN EDen GSpe MBar MOke NYor SRms
– 'Natasja'	EDen
– 'Naturpark'	EDen ENHC MBar
– 'Nico'	EDen
– 'Nordlicht'	EDen
– 'October White'	CNCN EDen ENHC WGre
– 'Oiseval'	EDen
– 'Old Rose'	EDen
– 'Olive Turner'	EDen
– 'Olympic Gold'	EDen
¶ – 'Orange and Gold'	ECho EDen
– 'Orange Carpet'	EDen
– 'Orange Max'	EDen
– 'Orange Queen' ♀	CNCN EDen ENHC GSpe MBar NYor SBod
– 'Oxabäck'	MBar
– 'Oxshott Common'	CNCN EDen ENHC GQui MBar SBod WGre
– 'Pallida'	EDen
– 'Parsons' Gold'	EDen
– 'Parsons' Grey Selected'	EDen
– 'Pat's Gold'	EDen
– 'Peace'	EDen
– 'Pearl Drop'	EDen MBar

– 'Penhale' EDen
– 'Penny Bun' EDen
– 'Pepper and Salt' See *C. vulgaris* **'Hugh Nicholson'**
– 'Perestrojka' EDen
– 'Peter Sparkes' (d) CB&S CMac CNCN CWLN EDen ENHC GDra GSpe MBar MBri MGos MOke NHar NHol NYor SBod SRms WGre
– 'Petra' EDen
– 'Pewter Plate' EDen MBar
– 'Pink Beale' See *C. vulgaris* **'H.E. Beale'**
– 'Pink Dream' (d) EDen
– 'Pink Gown' CNCN EDen NYor
– 'Plantarium' EDen
– 'Platt's Surprise' (d) EDen
– 'Prizewinner' CNCN EDen
– 'Prostrata Flagelliformis' EDen
– 'Prostrate Orange' CNCN EDen GSpe MBar
– 'Punch's Dessert' EDen
– 'Pygmaea' EDen ENHC MBar
– 'Pyramidalis' ECho EDen ENHC
– 'Pyrenaica' EDen MBar
– 'R.A. McEwan' EDen
– 'Radnor' (d) ♀ CNCN EDen ENHC GSpe MBar MGos MOke NHar NYor SBod WGre
– 'Radnor Gold' (d) EDen MBar
– 'Ralph Purnell' CNCN EDen ENHC MBar NHar SBod
– 'Ralph Purnell Select' EDen
– 'Ralph's Pearl' EDen
– 'Ralph's Red' EDen
– 'Randall's Crimson' EDen
– 'Rannoch' EDen
– 'Red Carpet' CNCN EDen MBar MOke WGre
– 'Red Favorit' (d) CNCN EDen LRHS SBod WGre
– 'Red Fred' EDen MGos SCoo WGre
– 'Red Haze' CMac CNCN EDen ENHC MBar MOke NHol NRoo NYor SBod WGre WStI
– 'Red Max' EDen
♦– Red October See *C. vulgaris* **'Rote Oktober'**
– 'Red Pimpernel' CNCN EDen GSpe NYor
– 'Red Rug' EDen
– 'Red Star' (d) ♀ CNCN EDen GSpe LRHS MBar MOke NHol WGre
– 'Red Wings' EDen
– 'Redbud' CNCN EDen
– 'Reini' CNCN EDen WGre
– 'Rica' EDen
– 'Richard Cooper' EDen MBar
– 'Rigida Prostrata' See *C. vulgaris* **'Alba Rigida'**
– 'Rivington' EDen
– 'Robber Knight' EDen WGre
– 'Robert Chapman' ♀ CB&S CMac CNCN CWLN EBre EDen ENHC GDra GSpe MBar MBri MGos MOke NHar NHol NYor SBod WGre
¶– 'Rock Spray' EDen
– 'Roland Haagen' ♀ EDen MBar MOke NHar WGre
– 'Roma' ECho EDen ENHC MBar
– 'Romina' CNCN EDen NHol
– 'Ronas Hill' CNCN GDra
– 'Roodkapje' EDen
– 'Rosalind' CNCN GSpe MBar MOke NHol NYor WGre
– 'Rosalind, Underwood's' LRHS
– 'Ross Hutton' EDen
– 'Rotfuchs' EDen
– 'Ruby Slinger' CNCN CWLN EBre EDen MBar NYor SBod WGre
– 'Rusty Triumph' EDen SBod
– 'Ruth Sparkes' (d) CMac CNCN EDen ENHC MBar MOke NHol SBod
– Saint Kilda Group GSpe
– 'Saint Nick' CNCN EDen ENHC MBar
– 'Salland' EDen
– 'Sally Anne Proudley' CNCN EDen ENHC MBar SBod WGre
– 'Salmon Leap' CNCN EDen GSpe MBar NHol
– 'Sam Hewitt' EDen
– 'Sampford Sunset' CSam
– 'Sandhammaren' EDen
– 'Sandwood Bay' EDen
– 'Sarah Platt' (d) EDen
– 'Scaynes Hill' EDen
– 'Schurig's Sensation' (d) CNCN EBre EDen GAri GSpe MBar MBri MOke NHar NYor SBod
– 'Scotch Mist' EDen
– 'Sedloňov' EDen
– 'September Pink' EDen
– 'Serlei' EDen ENHC MBar MOke SBod
– 'Serlei Aurea' ♀ CNCN EDen ENHC GSpe MBar NYor SBod
– 'Serlei Grandiflora' EDen MBar
I – 'Serlei Lavender' EDen WGre
– 'Serlei Purpurea' EDen
– 'Serlei Rubra' EDen
– 'Sesam' EDen
– 'Shirley' CMac EDen MBar
– 'Silver Cloud' CNCN EDen MBar
– 'Silver Fox' ECho EDen
– 'Silver King' CNCN EDen MBar
– 'Silver Knight' CMac CNCN CWLN EBre EDen ENHC GDra GSpe MBar MBri MGos MOke NHar NHol NRoo NYor SBod SHBN WGre WStI
– 'Silver Queen' ♀ CMac CNCN CWLN EBre EDen ENHC GSpe MBar MBri MOke NHar NHol NRoo NYor SBod SRms WGre
– 'Silver Rose' ♀ CNCN EDen ENHC GSpe MBar NYor WGre
– 'Silver Sandra' EDen
– 'Silver Spire' CNCN EDen ENHC MBar
– 'Silver Stream' EDen ENHC MBar SBod
– 'Sir Anthony Hopkins' EDen
– 'Sir John Charrington' ♀ CMac CNCN EBre EDen ENHC GDra GSpe MBar MBri MGos MOke NHol NYor SBod SHBN WGre WStI
– 'Sirsson' CWLN EDen MBar MBri WGre
– 'Sister Anne' ♀ CNCN CWLN EBre EDen ENHC GDra MBri MGos MOke NHol SBod SHBN SRms
– 'Skipper' EDen MBar WGre
– 'Snowball' See *C. vulgaris* **'My Dream'**
– 'Snowflake' EDen
– 'Soay' EDen MBar SBod
– 'Sonja' (d) CNCN EDen
– 'Sonning' (d) EDen
– 'Sonny Boy' EDen
– 'Spicata' EDen
– 'Spicata Aurea' CNCN EDen MBar
– 'Spitfire' CNCN CWLN EDen ENHC GSpe MBar NHol WGre WStI
– 'Spook' EDen

– 'Spring Cream' 🏆	CNCN CWLN EBre EDen ENHC GSpe MBar MBri MGos MOke NHar NHol NYor SBod WGre WStI
– 'Spring Glow'	CMac CNCN CWLN EDen MBar MBri MOke NHar NYor SBod
– 'Spring Torch'	CB&S CNCN EBre EDen ENHC GDra GSpe MBar MBri MGos MOke NHar NHol NRoo NYor SBod SCoo SHBN WGre WStI
– 'Springbank'	EDen MBar
– 'Stag's Horn'	EDen
– 'Stefanie'	EDen
– 'Stranger'	EDen
– 'Strawberry Delight' (d)	EDen
– 'Summer Elegance'	EDen
– 'Summer Orange'	CNCN EDen MBar NHol
– 'Sunningdale'	See ***C. vulgaris* 'Finale'**
– 'Sunrise'	CNCN EDen ENHC MBar MGos MOke NHol SBod WGre WStI
– 'Sunset' 🏆	CB&S CNCN CWLN EBre EDen ENHC GDra GSpe MBar NHol NYor SBod SRms WGre WStI
– 'Sunset Glow'	EDen
– 'Talisker'	EDen
– 'Tenella'	EDen
– 'Tenuis'	CNCN ECho EDen ENHC MBar
– 'Terrick's Orange'	EDen
– 'The Pygmy'	EDen
– 'Tib' (d) 🏆	CMac CNCN CWLN EDen ENHC GSpe MBar MBri MOke NRoo NYor SBod SRms WGre WStI
– 'Tino'	EDen
– 'Tom Thumb'	EDen MBar
– 'Tomentosa Alba'	EDen
– 'Tom's Fancy'	EDen
– 'Torogay'	EDen
– 'Torulosa'	EDen ENHC
– 'Tremans'	EDen
– 'Tricolorifolia'	CNCN CWLN EDen ENHC GDra NHol SBod
– 'Underwoodii' 🏆	ECho EDen ENHC MBar
§ – 'Velvet Dome'	EDen MBar SBod
– 'Velvet Fascination'	CNCN ECho EDen LRHS MBar
– 'Violet Bamford'	EDen
– 'Visser's Fancy'	EDen WGre
§ – 'Walter Ingwersen'	EDen
– 'Westerlee Gold'	EDen
– 'Westerlee Green'	EDen
– 'Westphalia'	EDen
– 'White Carpet'	EDen MBar
– 'White Coral' (d)	EDen
– 'White Gold'	EDen
– 'White Gown'	EDen ENHC GDra
– 'White Lawn' 🏆	CNCN EDen MBar MGos NHol SHBN SRms
– 'White Mite'	ECho EDen ENHC MBar
– 'White Princess'	See ***C. vulgaris* 'White Queen'**
§ – 'White Queen'	EDen MBar
– 'White Star' (d)	EDen LRHS
– 'Whiteness'	CNCN EDen WGre
– 'Wickwar Flame' 🏆	CB&S CMac CNCN CWLN EBre EDen ENHC GDra MBar MBri MGos MOke NHar NHol NRoo NYor SBod WGre WStI
– 'Wingates Gem'	EDen
– 'Wingates Gold'	EDen
– 'Winter Chocolate'	CNCN CWLN EDen ENHC MBar MBri MGos MOke NHol NRoo NYor SBod WGre WStI
– 'Winter Fire'	EDen
– 'Winter Red'	EDen
– 'Wood Close'	EDen
– 'Yellow Basket'	EDen
– 'Yellow Dome'	CNCN
– 'Yellow One'	EDen
– 'Yvette's Gold'	EDen
– 'Yvette's Silver'	EDen
– 'Yvonne Clare'	EDen

CALOCEDRUS (Cupressaceae)

§ ***decurrens*** 🏆	CB&S CDoC CMac EBre EHul ENot EPfP IOrc LCon LPan MBal MBar MBlu MBri NWea SLim SPer WFro WMou WWat
– 'Aureovariegata'	CBlo CDoC CKen IOrc LCon LLin LNet LPan MAsh MBar MBlu MBri NHol SLim WDin
– 'Berrima Gold'	CKen
§ – 'Depressa'	CKen
– 'Intricata'	CKen
– 'Nana'	See ***C. decurrens* 'Depressa'**
– 'Pillar'	LRHS MBri

CALOCEPHALUS (Asteraceae)

brownii	See ***Leucophyta brownii***

CALOCHORTUS (Liliaceae)

albus	EPot WChr
– var. ***rubellus***	EPot GCrs LAma
amabilis	EPot WChr
amoenus	WChr
* ***argillosus***	EPot
barbatus	EHyt EPot MFos WOMN
– var. ***chihuahuaensis***	WChr
clavatus	EPot WChr
* ***clavatus avius***	EPot
¶ ***concolor***	EPot
eurycarpus	See ***C. nitidus***
¶ ***excavatus***	EPot
kennedyi	EPot
¶ ***leichtlinii***	EPot
luteus	EHyt EPot LAma WChr
macrocarpus	EPot
monophyllus	EPot WChr
§ ***nitidus***	EPot WChr
¶ ***obispoensis***	EPot
¶ ***pulchellus***	EPot
splendens	EPot LAma
¶ ***striatus***	EPot
¶ – JA 93-21	EHyt
superbus	EPot GCrs WChr
tolmiei	EPot
umbellatus	EPot WChr
uniflorus	EHyt EPot WChr WOMN
venustus	EHyt EPot LAma WChr
vestae	EHyt EPot WChr

CALOMERIA (Asteraceae)

§ ***amaranthoides***	LHol WJek

CALONYCTION See IPOMOEA

CALOPHACA (Papilionaceae)

¶ ***grandiflora***	CB&S

CALOPOGON (Orchidaceae)
See Plant Deletions

CALOSCORDUM (Alliaceae)
§ ***neriniflorum*** EBur EHyt SWas WAbe

CALOTHAMNUS (Myrtaceae)
blepharospermus SOWG
gilesii SOWG
homolophyllus SOWG
quadrifidus SOWG
rupestris SOWG
sanguineus SOWG
validus SOWG

CALOTROPIS (Asclepiadaceae)
¶ ***gigantea*** MSal

CALPURNIA (Papilionaceae)
¶ ***aurea*** CTrC

CALTHA † (Ranunculaceae)
'Auenwald' CRDP CRow LWoo
'Honeydew' CRDP CRow GBuc LWoo
introloba SWat
laeta See ***C. palustris*** var. ***palustris***
leptosepala CRow EBre LWoo NGre SRms
¶ – NNS 9420 EPot
natans CRDP CRow
palustris ♀ Widely available
– var. ***alba*** CBen CDec CHad CRow CWGN CWat EBre ECha EHon ELan EPot GDra LPBA MBal MBri MSta NBro NDea NHar NNor NSti SPer SWat SWyc WByw WChe WMAq WMer WOMN
¶ – 'Flore Pleno' ♀ NNor
– var. ***himalensis*** NGre
– 'Marilyn' CRDP
¶ – var. ***minor*** GCrs
– 'Multiplex' NCut
§ – var. ***palustris*** CBen CBre CRDP CRow CWGN EBre ECha EHon ELan EMFW EPar GAri GGar LPBA MSta NDea SHig SPer SSpi SWat WChe
– – 'Plena' CRow CWat EMil EPfP WCot WMAq
– var. ***radicans*** CRow EMFW
– – 'Flore Pleno' ♀ CBen CGle CRow CWGN EBre ECha EHon ELan GDra LHop LPBA MBal MBri MSta NDea NFai NHar NSti SHig SPer SWat SWyc WByw WChe
– 'Stagnalis' CRow SWyc
– 'Tyermannii' CRow
– 'Wheatfen' CNat
polypetala hort. See ***C. palustris*** var. ***palustris***
sagittata CRow
'Susan' CRow

CALYCANTHUS (Calycanthaceae)
fertilis CBot EBee EBre GOrc LBuc MBlu MUlv SPer SSta WSHC
– 'Purpureus' MBlu
floridus CArn CB&S CBot CChu CMCN CPMA CPle EBar ELan ENot IOrc LHol MBlu WLRN WWat WWin
– var. ***laevigatus*** See ***C. floridus*** var. ***glaucus***
occidentalis CB&S CMCN CPle ELan EMil LLew MBlu

CALYDOREA (Iridaceae)
speciosa See ***C. xiphioides***

CALYPSO (Orchidaceae)
¶ ***bulbosa*** SWes

CALYPTRIDIUM (Portulacaceae)
umbellatum See ***Spraguea umbellata***

CALYSTEGIA (Convolvulaceae)
§ ***hederacea*** 'Flore Pleno' CBos CPlN CSpe EBre ECha ELan EMon EOrc EPar LFis LHop MSCN MTho NSti SMad WCot WHer WWin
japonica 'Flore Pleno' See ***C. hederacea* 'Flore Pleno'**
¶ ***pulchra*** WCru
silvatica 'Incarnata' EBee EMon
tuguriorum ECou

CALYTRIX (Myrtaceae)
See Plant Deletions

CAMASSIA † (Hyacinthaceae)
cusickii CAvo CBro CMea EBre ECha ELan EMan EMon EPar LAma LBow MBri MTho NBir NFai NRog WCot
esculenta See ***C. quamash***
fraseri See ***C. scilloides***
leichtlinii 'Alba' hort. See ***C. leichtlinii*** subsp. ***leichtlinii***
* – 'Alba Plena' CMon
◆ – 'Blauwe Donau' See ***C. leichtlinii*** subsp. ***suksdorfii* 'Blauwe Donau'**
I – Blue Danube See ***C. leichtlinii*** subsp. ***suksdorfii* 'Blauwe Donau'**
– 'Electra' ECha SWas WFar
◆ – hort. See ***C. leichtlinii*** subsp. ***suksdorfii***
§ – subsp. ***leichtlinii*** ♀ CAvo CBro CMea EFou ELan EMan EMon EOrc ISea LAma LWoo MRav NCat WShi
N – 'Plena' ECED ECha WCot WFar
– 'Semiplena' CAvo CBro CFai CMea CRDP EMon EPar LWoo
§ – subsp. ***suksdorfii*** CAvo EBee ECha EFou EPar ETub GBuc LBow MUlv NCat SAga
§ – – 'Blauwe Donau' LAma LBow LRHS
– – Caerulea Group CBro CHad CMea CMil CRDP ELan EMan EMon EPar ISea LAma MUlv NRog WAbb
§ ***quamash*** CAvo CBro CElw CMea ECha ELan EMon EPar ETub LAma LBow LWoo MBri MRav MTho MTol NBir NRog SRms WByw WFar WShi
– 'Blue Melody' CBro CMea LRHS
– subsp. ***linearis*** NHol
– 'Orion' CBro CMea CSWP EMon GBuc LWoo WCot
§ ***scilloides*** EBee GCal MBri

CAMELLIA † (Theaceae)
'Auburn White' See ***C. japonica* 'Mrs Bertha A. Harms'**
'Baby Face' See ***C. reticulata* 'Tongzimian'**

'Barbara Clark' (*saluenensis* X *reticulata*)	MGos
'Barbara Hillier' (*reticulata* X *japonica*)	CTre
'Barchi'	See ***C. japonica* 'Contessa Samailoff'**
'Bertha Harms Blush'	See ***C. japonica* 'Mrs Bertha A. Harms'**
'Black Lace' (*reticulata* X *williamsii*)	CTrh EBee MAsh MBal SCog SExb SPer WLRN
'Bonnie Marie' (hybrid)	CGre CTre CWLN
'China Lady' (*reticulata* X *granthamiana*)	SCog
chrysantha	See ***C. nitidissima* var. *nitidissima***
'Contessa Lavinia Maggi'	See ***C. japonica* 'Lavinia Maggi'**
'Cornish Clay'	ISea
'Cornish Snow' (*japonica* X *cuspidata*) 🏆	CB&S CGre COtt CSam CTre CTrh CWLN GGGa IOrc ISea LNet MBal SHBN SMad SPer SReu SSpi SSta WWat
'Cornish Spring' (*japonica* X *cuspidata*) 🏆	CB&S CDoC COtt CTre CTrh EPfP WBcn WLRN WWat
'Corsica'	SHBN
crapnelliana	CGre
cuspidata	CGre CTre CTrh SSpi
'Czar'	See ***C. japonica* 'The Czar'**
'Dawn'	See ***C.* X *vernalis* 'Ginryû'**
'Delia Williams'	See ***C.* X *williamsii* 'Citation'**
'Diamond Head' (*japonica* X *reticulata*)	CB&S
'Doctor Clifford Parks' (*reticulata* X *japonica*) 🏆	CTre SCog
'Donckelaeri'	See ***C. japonica* 'Masayoshi'**
'Eclipsis'	See ***C. japonica* 'Press's Eclipse'**
'El Dorado' (*pitardii* X *japonica*)	CTrh SCog
'Extravaganza' (*japonica* hybrid)	CTrh SBod SCog
'Faustina Lechi'	See ***C. japonica* 'Faustina'**
'Felice Harris' (*sasanqua* X *reticulata*)	SCog
'First Flush' (*cuspidata* X *saluenensis*)	SCog
* 'Fishtail White'	SCog
'Forty-niner' (*reticulata* X *japonica*) 🏆	CB&S SCog
'Fragrant Pink' (*rusticana* X *lutchuensis*)	CTrh
'Francie L' (*saluenensis* X *reticulata*)	CGre CTre CTrh CWLN SCog SSta
'Frau Minna Seidel'	See ***C. japonica* 'Otome'**
'Freedom Bell' 🏆	CB&S CTre CTrh GGGa ISea MAsh SCog
¶ 'Gay Baby'	MGos
granthamiana	CGre
grijsii	CTrh
***hiemalis* 'Chansonette'**	SCog SPla
– 'Dazzler'	CTre CTrh SCog
'Hiemalis Hiryû'	See ***C. hiemalis* 'Kanjirô'**
§ ***hiemalis* 'Kanjirô'**	CTrh SCog
– 'Shôwa-no-sakae'	SCog
– 'Sparkling Burgundy'	CB&S CTre LHyd SCog
'Howard Asper' (*reticulata* X *japonica*)	SCog
'Imbricata Rubra'	See ***C. japonica* 'Imbricata'**
'Innovation' (X *williamsii* X *reticulata*)	CB&S CTre ISea MGos SCog
'Inspiration' (*reticulata* X *saluenensis*) 🏆	CB&S CGre CMac CSam CTre CTrh CWLN GGGa GWht ISea LHyd MBri MGos SBod SCog SHBN SSpi WBod

***japonica* 'Aaron's Ruby'**	CB&S COtt CTre
– 'Ada Pieper'	CTrh
– 'Adelina Patti'	CB&S CTre SCog
– 'Adolphe Audusson' 🏆	CB&S CMac CTre CTrh CTrw CWLN EBre ELan ENot EPfP IOrc LHyd LNet MAsh MBal MBri MGos SBod SCog SHBN SMad SPer SReu SSta WBod WStI
– 'Adolphe Audusson Special'	CB&S SCog
§ – 'Akashigata' 🏆	CTre CTrw EBee ENot IHos SCog SMad SPla SReu SSta WWat
§ – 'Akebono'	CTrw
– 'Alba Plena'	CDoC CGre CMac CTre CWLN EBee ENot IHos IOrc LNet MGos SBod SCog SPer WFox
– 'Alba Simplex'	CB&S CGre CMac CTre ELan EOHP EPfP IOrc LNet MBal SBod SCog SHBN SPer SSta WStI
– 'Alexander Hunter' 🏆	CTre CWLN MAsh SBod
¶ – 'Alice Wood'	CB&S
§ – 'Althaeiflora'	CB&S CGre CMac CTre SCog
– 'Ama-no-gawa'	SCog
– 'Anemoniflora'	CB&S CTre EBee ELan IHos SBod SPer
– 'Angel'	CB&S CTre CWLN SCog
– 'Ann Sothern'	CTrh
– 'Annie Wylam'	CTrh SCog
§ – 'Apollo'	CB&S CDoC CSam CTrh CWLN IHos MAsh MGos SHBN SPer WBcn
§ – 'Apple Blossom' 🏆	CGre CMac ELan MBal
– 'Arabella'	SCog
* – 'Augustine Supreme'	CMac
– 'Augusto Leal de Gouveia Pinto'	CB&S CTre SCog
– 'Ave Maria'	CTrh SCog
– 'Azurea'	CGre
¶ – 'Baby Sis'	CB&S
– 'Ballet Dancer' 🏆	SCog SPla WBcn
– 'Barbara Woodroof'	SCog
– 'Baron Gomer'	See ***C. japonica* 'Comte de Gomer'**
– 'Benten'	CTrw
– 'Berenice Boddy' 🏆	CB&S CTrh
– 'Berenice Perfection'	SCog
– 'Betty Foy Sanders'	CTrh
– 'Betty Sheffield'	CGre COtt CTre ECle MAsh MGos SBod SCog SHBN WBod
¶ – 'Betty Sheffield Blush'	CBlo
– 'Betty Sheffield Coral'	SCog
– 'Betty Sheffield Supreme'	CB&S CDoC CGre CMac SCog SPer
– 'Betty Sheffield White'	SCog
– 'Bienville'	SCog
– 'Blackburnia'	See ***C. japonica* 'Althaeiflora'**
– 'Blaze of Glory'	CDoC CGre CTrh SCog
§ – 'Blood of China'	CB&S CDoC CMac COtt MAsh SBod SCog SExb SPer WBod
– 'Bob Hope' 🏆	CB&S CGre CTre CTrh SCog
– 'Bob's Tinsie' 🏆	CGre CTre CTrh CTrw MBri SCog
§ – 'Bokuhan'	CGre CTre CTrh
– 'Brushfield's Yellow'	CB&S CDoC CGre MBal MGos SPer SSta
– 'Bush Hill Beauty'	See ***C. japonica* 'Lady de Saumarez'**

§ – 'C.M. Hovey' 🏆	CMHG CMac CTrh EPfP MAsh MBal MNes SCog SHBN WBcn WBod WFar
– 'C.M. Wilson' 🏆	CMac CTre SCog
N – 'Campbellii'	CMac
– 'Campsii Alba'	WStI
– 'Can Can'	CB&S SCog
– 'Cara Mia'	CB&S CTre
– 'Cardinal's Cap'	CGre
– 'Carolyn Tuttle'	CWLN
– 'Carter's Sunburst' 🏆	CB&S CDoC CTrh EPfP
– 'Cécile Brunazzi'	CMac SCog
– 'Chandleri Elegans'	See *C. japonica* **'Elegans'**
– 'Charlotte de Rothschild'	CTrh CTri
– 'Charming Betty'	See *C. japonica* **'Funny Face Betty'**
– 'Cheerio'	SCog
– 'Cheryll Lynn'	CTrh SCog WBod
– 'Cinderella'	CTre SCog
– 'Clarise Carleton'	CTre CTrh SCog
– 'Colonel Firey'	See *C. japonica* **'C.M. Hovey'**
– 'Colonial Dame'	MBri
– 'Commander Mulroy'	CTrh WBcn
– 'Compton's Brow'	See *C. japonica* **'Gauntlettii'**
§ – 'Comte de Gomer'	CGre ELan EPfP MBri SSta WBcn
– 'Conrad Hilton'	SCog
– 'Conspicua'	CB&S
§ – 'Coquettii' 🏆	CB&S CTre CWLN
– 'Countess of Orkney'	CTre
– 'Daikagura'	SCog
– 'Dainty'	CB&S
– 'Daitairin'	See *C. japonica* **'Dewatairin'**
– 'Dear Jenny'	CB&S CTre SCog
– 'Debutante'	CB&S CGre CMac CTre CTrh LHyd MAsh MBri SCog SHBN WBcn
– 'Desire'	CB&S CMHG CTrh SCog SPer
– 'Devonia'	CB&S CGre EPfP LHyd MBal MBri
§ – 'Dewatairin'	MNes SCog
– 'Dixie Knight'	SSta
– 'Dobreei'	CMac WGer WGwG
– 'Doctor Burnside'	CB&S CMHG CTrh SCog
– 'Doctor Tinsley' 🏆	CBlo CGre CTrh MAsh SCog WBcn
– 'Dona Herzilia de Freitas Magalhaes'	CB&S CTre SCog SSta
– 'Donnan's Dream'	CTrh
– 'Double Rose'	SCog
– 'Doutor Balthazar de Mello'	CMHG
– 'Drama Girl' 🏆	CB&S CGre CTre CTrw IOrc MBal SBod SCog
– 'Duc de Bretagne'	SCog
– 'Duchesse Decazes'	CB&S COtt CTre CWLN MGos
– 'Effendee'	See *C. sasanqua* **'Rosea Plena'**
– 'Eleanor Hagood'	CB&S CGre WBcn
§ – 'Elegans' 🏆	CB&S CGre CHig CMac CTre CWLN ECle ENot IHos IOrc LHyd MBal SBod SCog SHBN SPer SReu SSta WBcn WBod
– 'Elegans Champagne'	CTrh MAsh SCog WBcn
– 'Elegans Splendor'	CTre WBcn
– 'Elegans Supreme'	CGre CTre SCog
– 'Elisabeth'	SCog
– 'Elizabeth Arden'	CBlo CTre WBod
– 'Elizabeth Dowd'	CB&S SCog
– 'Elizabeth Hawkins'	CTre
– 'Ella Drayton'	SCog
– 'Emperor of Russia'	CB&S ELan WBod

– 'Erin Farmer'	CB&S SCog
– 'Faith'	SCog
– 'Fatima'	CTre
§ – 'Faustina'	SCog
– 'Fimbriata Alba'	See *C. japonica* **'Fimbriata'**
– 'Finlandia Variegated'	SCog
– 'Fire Dance'	CTrh
– 'Fire Falls'	CMHG
– 'Flame'	CB&S
§ – 'Fleur Dipater'	WBod
– 'Flowerwood'	SCog
– 'Forest Green'	ELan MAsh SCog
– 'Frosty Morn'	CB&S SCog
§ – 'Gauntlettii'	SCog
– 'Giardino Franchetti'	CGre
§ – 'Gigantea'	SCog
§ – 'Gigantea Red'	IOrc
– 'Gladys Wannamaker'	SCog
– 'Glen 40'	See *C. japonica* **'Coquettii'**
– 'Gloire de Nantes' 🏆	CB&S CGre CTrh MNes SCog WBod
* – 'Golden Wedding'	MAsh
– 'Grace Bunton'	SCog
– 'Granada'	SCog
– 'Grand Prix' 🏆	CMHG CTrh CTrw SCog SSta
– 'Grand Slam' 🏆	CB&S CMHG CMac COtt CTre CTrh EHic ISea MAsh SCog WBcn
– 'Guest of Honor'	CB&S COtt SCog WStI
– 'Guilio Nuccio' 🏆	CB&S CDoC CTre CWLN EBee EBre MGos SCog SExb SPer
– 'Gwenneth Morey'	CB&S CMHG CTre EPfP
§ – 'Hagoromo' 🏆	CBlo CGre ELan ENot EPfP IHos MBal SHBN WFox WWat
– 'Hakurakuten' 🏆	CBlo CTre CTrh ISea SBod SCog
– 'Hanafûki'	CTre SCog
– 'Hanatachibana'	CBlo SExb WBcn
– 'Hassaku'	See *C. japonica* **'Hassaku-shibori'**
– 'Hatsuzakura'	See *C. japonica* **'Dewatairin'**
– 'Hawaii'	CB&S CMac CTre CTrh SCog WFox
◆ – Herme	See *C. japonica* **'Hikarugenji'**
– 'High Hat'	CB&S LHyd SCog
– 'Hinomaru'	CMac
§ – 'Imbricata'	CBlo CDoC CTre CWLN EBee ENot IHos MGos SCog SExb
– 'Imbricata Alba'	SCog SSta
– 'In the Pink'	CMHG
– 'Italiana Vera'	MAsh
– 'J.J. Whitfield'	CMac
– 'Jack Jones Scented'	CMHG SCog
– 'Janet Waterhouse'	CB&S SCog WWat
– 'Jean Clere'	MGos WBcn
– 'Jean Lyne'	SCog
– 'Jingle Bells'	SCog
– 'Joseph Pfingstl'	CBlo CGre CMHG CTre WBod
– 'Joshua E. Youtz'	LHyd SCog
– 'Jovey Carlyon' (hybrid)	SCog
– 'Joy Sander'	See *C. japonica* **'Apple Blossom'**
– 'Julia France'	CB&S SCog
– 'Juno'	CB&S SCog
– 'Jupiter' 🏆	CB&S CDoC CMac CTre CTrh CTri CTrw CWLN EBee EHic EPfP ISea LHyd LNet MAsh MBal MGos SHBN SMad WBod
– 'K. Sawada'	SCog
– 'Katie'	SCog

– 'Kellingtoniana' See *C. japonica* **'Gigantea'**
– 'Kenny' CB&S
– 'Kewpie Doll' CTrh SCog
– 'Kick-off' CB&S CTrh SCog
– 'Kimberley' CB&S EPfP WBcn WLRN
– 'King's Ransom' CMac
§ – 'Kingyo-tsubaki' SSta WBod
– 'Kitty' SBid SCog
§ – 'Konronkoku' ♀ SCog WBcn
– 'Kouron-jura' See *C. japonica* **'Konronkoku'**
– 'Kramer's Beauty' SCog SPer
– 'Kramer's Supreme' CB&S CGre CMac LNet MBal MGos SBod SCog SExb WLRN WStI
– 'Lady Campbell' CWLN WBcn
◆ – Lady Clare See *C. japonica* **'Akashigata'**
§ – 'Lady de Saumarez' ♀ CMac LNet SBod SCog WFar
– 'Lady de Saumarez' white CGre
¶ – 'Lady Erma' CB&S
– 'Lady Loch' CTre CTrh MGos SCog
– 'Lady Marion' See *C. japonica* **'Kumasaka'**
– 'Lady McCulloch' SCog
– 'Lady Vansittart' CB&S CMac CSam CTre CWLN ELan ENot IHos ISea LHyd LNet MAsh MBal SBod SCog SPer WBcn WBod
§ – 'Lady Vansittart Pink' CMac MGos SBod SHBN
– 'Lady Vansittart Red' See *C. japonica* **'Lady Vansittart Pink'**
– 'Lanarth' CTre
– 'Latifolia' CTre
– 'Laurie Bray' CGre SCog
§ – 'Lavinia Maggi' ♀ CGre CTre CTrh ELan GAri IHos IOrc LHyd MAsh MBri MGos SBod SCog SHBN SPer SReu SRms SSta
– 'Lavinia Maggi Rosea' SCog
– 'L'Avvenire' CMac SCog
§ – 'Le Lys' SCog
– 'Lemon Drop' CTrh
– 'Lily Pons' CTrh SCog
– 'Little Bit' CB&S CTrh SPer SSta
– 'Little Bo Peep' CTrh
¶ – 'Little Red Riding Hood' CB&S COtt
¶ – 'Little Slam' CB&S
– 'Look-away' SCog
I – 'Lotus' See *C. japonica* **'Gauntlettii'**
– 'Lovelight' CTrh
– 'Lucy Hester' CTre MBal
– 'Lulu Belle' SCog
– 'Ma Belle' CMHG SCog
– 'Madame Charles Blard' SCog
– 'Madame de Strekaloff' CMac
– 'Madame Lebois' CB&S
– 'Madame Lourmand' WBod
– 'Madame Martin Cachet' CMHG SCog
– 'Madge Miller' CTre ELan
– 'Magic City' SCog
– 'Magnoliiflora' See *C. japonica* **'Hagoromo'**
◆ – 'Magnoliiflora Alba' See *C. japonica* **'Miyakodori'**
– 'Maiden's Blush' CMac SCog
– 'Man Size' SCog
– 'Margaret Davis Picotee' CB&S CGre CMHG CTrh CTrw MGos SCog SPla SSta WBcn
– 'Margarete Hertrich' SCog
– 'Margherita Coleoni' CB&S SBod SHBN WBcn WBod
– 'Marguérite Gouillon' ISea SCog
– 'Mariana' CTrh SSta
¶ – 'Marie Bracey' CB&S
– 'Marinka' CB&S
– 'Mariottii Rubra' CMac
– 'Marjorie Magnificent' WFar
– 'Mark Alan' CTrh
– 'Maroon and Gold' SCog
– 'Mars' ♀ CB&S CTre CWLN EHic WBod
– 'Mary Costa' CB&S CGre CTrh
– 'Mary J. Wheeler' CTrw
§ – 'Masayoshi' ♀ CGre CWLN IOrc LNet
§ – 'Mathotiana' CTrw MBal WBod
– 'Mathotiana Alba' ♀ CB&S MBal SBid SCog SPer SReu SSta
– 'Mathotiana Purple King' See *C. japonica* **'Julia Drayton'**
§ – 'Mathotiana Rosea' CB&S CDoC CMac CTre CWLN LNet SBod SCog SHBN SPer
– 'Mathotiana Supreme' CDoC SCog
– 'Matterhorn' CTrh WBcn
– 'Mattie Cole' CGre CTre SCog
– 'Mattie O'Reilly' CTre
– 'Melody Lane' SCog
– 'Mercury' ♀ CB&S CBlo CDoC CMac COtt GGGa SHBN SPer WBod
– 'Mercury Variegated' CMHG
– 'Midnight' CB&S CGre CMHG SCog WStI
– 'Midnight Serenade' CTrh
– 'Midsummer's Day' CB&S
§ – 'Mikenjaku' CBlo ENot LNet
– 'Miss Charleston' ♀ CB&S SCog
– 'Miss Universe' CGre CTrh SCog
§ – 'Miyakodori' EPfP
– 'Momiji-gari' CTrh
¶ – 'Monsieur Faucillon' CB&S
– 'Monstruosa Rubra' See *C. japonica* **'Gigantea Red'**
– 'Monte Carlo' SCog WBod
– 'Moonlight Bay' SCog
– 'Moshe Dayan' CDoC EBee
§ – 'Mrs Bertha A. Harms' CGre
– 'Mrs D.W. Davis' ♀ CB&S CGre CTrw SCog
* – 'Mutabilis' WBcn
– 'Nagasaki' See *C. japonica* **'Mikenjaku'**
– 'Nigra' See *C. japonica* **'Konronkoku'**
– 'Nobilissima' CB&S CDoC CMac CTre CTri CWLN EBee IHos ISea MAsh SBid SBod SCog SHBN SPer SPla SSta WBcn WWeb
– 'Nuccio's Cameo' CTrh
– 'Nuccio's Gem' ♀ CTrh ELan MBri SCog SSta
– 'Nuccio's Jewel' ♀ COtt CTre CTrh MAsh MGos SCog SExb SPer
– 'Nuccio's Pearl' CB&S MAsh SCog WBcn WFar
– 'Onetia Holland' CB&S CTre CTrw CWLN SCog
§ – 'O-niji' MBal SCog SPer
– 'Optima Rosea' CB&S EBee
– 'Painted Lady' CMac
– 'Paolina' SCog
– 'Paolina Maggi' SCog
– 'Patricia Ann' CTrh
– 'Pauline Winchester' SCog
– 'Paul's Apollo' See *C. japonica* **'Apollo'**
– 'Peachblossom' See *C. japonica* **'Fleur Dipater'**
– 'Pensacola Red' SCog
– 'Pink Champagne' CTre SBod SCog
– 'Pink Clouds' SCog
– 'Pink Pagoda' SCog
– 'Pink Perfection' See *C. japonica* **'Otome'**
– 'Pirate's Gold' (v) SCog
– 'Pompone' SCog

– 'Pope Pius IX'	See ***C. japonica* 'Prince Eugène Napoléon'**
– 'Powder Puff'	CTre
– 'Preston Rose'	CB&S CMac CTre CWLN ISea MBal WBcn WWat
– 'Pride of Descanso'	See ***C. japonica* 'Yukibotan'**
– 'Primavera'	CTrh SCog
¶ – 'Princess Baciocchi'	CB&S
* – 'Princess du Mahe'	CMac
– 'Professor Sargent'	SCog
– 'Purity'	See ***C. japonica* 'Shiragiku'**
– 'Purple Emperor'	See ***C. japonica* 'Julia Drayton'**
– 'R.L. Wheeler' ♀	CB&S CDoC CGre CTre CTrw CWLN MBal SCog
¶ – 'Rafia'	SSta
– 'Rainbow'	See ***C. japonica* 'O-niji'**
– 'Red Dandy'	CDoC SCog
– 'Red Ensign'	SCog
– 'Reg Ragland'	SCog
– 'Roger Hall'	SCog SPer
– 'Rôgetsu'	CB&S CGre
– 'Roman Soldier'	CB&S
– 'Rubescens Major' ♀	CB&S CGre CWLN ISea LHyd SCog
– 'Ruddigore'	CTrh
– 'Sabrina'	SCog
– 'Saint André'	CMac WLRN
– 'San Dimas'	CTrh SCog WBcn
– 'Saturnia'	COtt EBee SCog
– 'Scented Red'	WWat
– 'Scentsation' ♀	CMHG COtt CTre SCog
– 'Sea Gull'	CTrh
– 'Seiji'	CMac
– 'Serenade'	CMHG SCog
– 'Shin-akebono'	See ***C. japonica* 'Akebono'**
– 'Shirobotan'	GQui SCog SPla WBod
– 'Sierra Spring'	SCog
– 'Silver Anniversary'	CB&S CMHG ELan GQui MAsh MGos SBod SCog SReu SSta
– 'Silver Waves'	SCog
– 'Snow Goose'	SCog
– 'Souvenir de Bahuaud-Litou' ♀	CB&S CBlo CGre CTre SBid SCog WBod WWat
– 'Spencer's Pink'	CB&S CTre CTrw
– 'Spring Sonnet'	SCog
– 'Strawberry Swirl'	SCog
¶ – 'Sylva'	GGGa
– 'Sylvia'	CMac WBod
– 'Tammia'	CB&S COtt SCog
– 'Temple Incense'	CB&S
– 'Teresa Ragland'	SCog
– 'Teringa'	CTre
§ – 'The Czar'	CB&S CTre CTrw CWLN ISea SCog WBod
– 'The Mikado'	CGre CTre
– 'The Pilgrim'	SCog
– 'Thomas Cornelius Cole'	CTre
– 'Tickled Pink'	SCog
– 'Tiffany'	CB&S CDoC CTre LHyd LNet SCog SHBN SPla SSta
– 'Tinker Bell'	CGre SCog
– 'Tinker Toy'	CTrh
– 'Tom Thumb'	CMHG CTrh SRms
– 'Tomorrow'	CB&S CMac CTre CTrh CTrw MAsh SCog WBod WFox
– 'Tomorrow Park Hill'	SCog
§ – 'Tomorrow Variegated'	SCog
– 'Tomorrow's Dawn'	CB&S SCog
– 'Tregye'	CB&S
– 'Trewithen White'	CSam
§ – 'Tricolor' ♀	CB&S CDoC CGre CMac CTrh ENot IHos IOrc MAsh SCog SExb SHBN SPer WBod
– 'Tricolor Red'	See ***C. japonica* 'Lady de Saumarez'**
– 'Tricolor Superba'	WBod
– 'Twilight'	SCog
– 'Valtevareda'	CGre WFar
§ 'Japonica Variegata'	CGre WBcn
japonica 'Victor de Bisschop'	See ***C. japonica* 'Le Lys'**
– 'Victor Emmanuel'	See ***C. japonica* 'Blood of China'**
– 'Ville de Nantes'	CB&S SSta WBcn
– 'Virginia Carlyon'	CB&S CTre CWLN
– 'Vittorio Emanuele II'	CTrh WLRN
– 'Warrior'	COtt CTre CWLN
– 'White Nun'	SCog
– 'White Swan'	CB&S CMac COtt CTre CWLN EBee
– 'White Tulip'	CGre
– 'Wilamina'	CTrh
– 'Wildfire'	SCog
– 'William Bartlett'	CTrh
– 'William Honey'	CTrh SCog
– 'Woodville Red'	CTre
– 'Yoibijin'	See ***C. japonica* 'Suibijin'**
– 'Yours Truly'	CB&S CMac CTre CTrh CWLN LHyd SBod SCog
§ – 'Yukibotan'	SCog
– 'Yukimi-guruma'	WBod
§ – 'Yukishiro'	CTrw
– 'Zoraide Vanzi'	WBod
'Jury's Charity'	See ***C.* × *williamsii* 'Charity'**
kissi	CGre CTrh
'Lasca Beauty' (*reticulata* × *japonica*) ♀	SCog
'Leonard Messel' (*reticulata* × *williamsii*) ♀	CB&S CDoC CGre CMHG CTre CTrh ENot GGGa IHos ISea LHyd MBal MGos SBod SCog SExb SHBN SMad SPer SReu WBod WStI
'Lila Naff' (*reticulata* hybrid)	CTre SCog
'Madame Victor de Bisschop'	See ***C. japonica* 'Le Lys'**
'Magnolia Queen'	See ***C. japonica* 'Priscilla Brooks'**
§ ***maliflora*** (d)	CB&S WWat
'Nijinski' (*reticulata* hybrid)	ISea
§ ***nitidissima*** var. ***nitidissima***	CGre
oleifera	CSam CTre CTrh WWat
'Pink Spangles'	See ***C. japonica* 'Mathotiana Rosea'**
'Portuense'	See ***C.* 'Japonica Variegata'**
'Quintessence' (*japonica* × *lutchuensis*)	SCog
reticulata	CGre CTre
– 'Captain Rawes' ♀	CB&S CMac CTre
– 'Flore Pleno'	See ***C. reticulata* 'Songzilin'**
– 'Ming Temple'	CTre
¶ – 'Nuccio's Ruby'	WBcn
– 'William Hertrich'	CB&S CGre CTre
'Robert Fortune'	See ***C. reticulata* 'Songzilin'**
rosiflora	CTre CTrh
'Royalty' (*japonica* × *reticulata*)	CB&S CTre SCog
rusticana 'Arajishi'	CB&S CMac COtt CTre EBee SCog SCoo WBod WGwG
– 'Shiro-daikagura'	SCog WBod
'Salonica'	See ***C.* × *williamsii* 'Shimna'**
saluenensis	CGre CTre CTrh

– 'Apple Blossom'	See ***C.* 'Shôwa-wabisuke' (Wabisuke)**
– 'Baronesa de Soutelinho'	SCog
– 'Exbury Trumpet'	CTre
– x ***japonica***	See ***C.* x *williamsii***
– 'Trewithen Red'	CTrw
'Salutation' (*saluenensis* x *reticulata*)	CB&S CGre CSam CTre ISea SCog
sasanqua	CSam ISea
– 'Ben'	SCog
– 'Bettie Patricia'	SCog
– 'Crimson King' 🏆	CGre GQui MBal SBod SCog SHBN WStI
– 'Flamingo'	See ***C. sasanqua* 'Fukuzutsumi'**
– 'Flore Pleno'	See ***C. maliflora***
– 'Fuji-no-mine'	CTrh
§ – 'Fukuzutsumi'	CB&S COtt CWLN SBod
– 'Gay Sue'	CTrh
– 'Hugh Evans'	CB&S CDoC COtt CTre CTrh CWLN LHyd SCog SSta WFox
– 'Jean May'	CB&S CDoC COtt CTre SBod SCog
– 'Kenkyô'	SCog SPla SSta
– 'Little Liane'	SCog
– 'Little Pearl'	CTrh
– 'Lucinda'	SCog
– 'Mignonne'	CTrh
– 'Mine-no-yuki'	SCog
– 'Narumigata' 🏆	CB&S CDoC CMac COtt CTrw LHyd MBal MBlu SBod SCog SSta WSHC
– 'Nodami-ushiro'	CTrh
– 'Nyewoods'	CMac
– 'Paradise Blush'	SCog
– 'Paradise Glow'	SCog
– 'Paradise Hilda'	SCog
– 'Paradise Pearl'	SCog
– 'Paradise Petite'	SCog
– 'Paradise Venessa'	SCog
– 'Peach Blossom'	CB&S
– 'Plantation Pink'	ECle SCog SPer
¶ – 'Rainbow'	SSta
¶ – 'Rosea'	SSta
§ – 'Rosea Plena'	CB&S CMac CTre CTrw
I 'Sasanqua Rubra'	CMac
I ***sasanqua*** 'Sasanqua Variegata'	SSta WWat
– 'Shishigashira'	CTrh
– 'Snowflake'	CTrh SSta
– 'Tanya'	CTrh
'Satan's Robe' (*reticulata* hybrid) 🏆	CMHG CTre SCog
'Scentuous' (*japonica* x *lutchuensis*)	CTrh SCog WBcn
'Show Girl' (*sasanqua* x *reticulata*)	CTre CTrh SBod SCog WBod
§ ***sinensis***	CGre CTre
'Splendens'	See ***C. japonica* 'Coccinea'**
'Spring Festival' (*cuspidata* hybrid) 🏆	CHig CMHG CTrh
'Spring Mist' (*japonica* x *lutchuensis*)	CMHG CTrh
'Stella Polare'	See ***C. japonica* 'Etoile Polaire'**
'Strawberry Parfait'	SCog
'Swan Lake' (hybrid)	SCog
taliensis	CGre CTre
thea	See ***C. sinensis***
'Tinsie'	See ***C. japonica* 'Bokuhan'**
'Tôkô'	See ***C. sasanqua* 'Azuma-beni'**
'Tom Knudsen' (*reticulata* x *japonica*)	CMHG CTre CTrh EPfP
'Tomorrow Supreme'	See ***C. japonica* 'Tomorrow Variegated'**
transnokoensis	CTre
'Tricolor Sieboldii'	See ***C. japonica* 'Tricolor'**
'Tristrem Carlyon' (*reticulata* hybrid)	CB&S CBlo CTre CWLN WBod WFox
tsaii 🏆	CGre CTrh
'Usu-ôtome'	See ***C. japonica* 'Otome'**
'Valley Knudsen' (*saluenensis* x *reticulata*)	SCog
vernalis 'Hiryû'	SCog
– 'Kyô-nishiki'	SCog
– 'Yuletide'	SCog
'Waterloo'	See ***C. japonica* 'Etherington White'**
§ x ***williamsii***	CGre
– 'Anemone Frill'	CTrh
– 'Anticipation' 🏆	CB&S CGre CMHG CSam CTre CTrh CTrw CWLN EBre EPfP GGGa GWht IOrc ISea LHyd MAsh MBri MGos SBod SCog SExb SHBN SPer SSpi WBcn
– 'Anticipation Variegated'	SCog
– 'Ballet Queen'	CB&S MGos SPer
– 'Ballet Queen Variegated'	CDoC SCog SSta
– 'Bartley Number Five'	CMac
– 'Beatrice Michael'	CB&S CMac CTre SCog
– 'Bow Bells'	CGre CMac CTre CTrh LHyd SCog WWat
– 'Bowen Bryant' 🏆	CGre CTre CTrh CTrw GGGa SCog
– 'Bridal Gown'	CTrh SCog
– 'Brigadoon' 🏆	CTre CTrh CTri CTrw GGGa GWht IOrc ISea LHyd MAsh MBal MGos SCog SExb WGwG
– 'Burncoose'	CB&S
– 'Burncoose Apple Blossom'	CB&S
– 'C.F. Coates'	CTre MNes SSta
– 'Caerhays'	CB&S CTre
– 'Carolyn Williams'	CB&S
– 'Celebration'	CB&S
§ – 'Charity'	CTrh
– 'Charlean'	SCog
– 'Charles Colbert'	CTrh SCog
– 'Charles Michael'	CB&S CGre
– 'China Clay' 🏆	CB&S CDoC CSam CTre CWLN EBee LHyd SBod SCog WGwG
§ – 'Citation'	CB&S CGre CMac CTrw SCog WBod
– 'Clarrie Fawcett'	CTre
– 'Contribution'	CTrh
– 'Crinkles'	CGre
– 'Daintiness' 🏆	CB&S CDoC CTre CTrh SCog SPer
– 'Dark Nite'	CMHG
– 'Debbie' 🏆	CB&S CGre CMac CSam CTre CTrh CTrw CWLN EBre ELan GWht IOrc LHyd MAsh MBal MBri MGos MRav SBod SCog SExb SHBN SPer SSpi SSta WBcn WBod
– 'Debbie's Carnation'	CMHG SCog
– 'Donation' 🏆	Widely available
– 'Dream Boat'	CB&S CTrh

– 'E.G. Waterhouse'	CB&S CGre CMHG CTrh CTri CTrw EHic EPfP GWht MAsh MBal SBod SCog SSta WBcn WBod WWeb
– 'E.T.R. Carlyon' 🏆	CB&S CTre CWLN EPfP MAsh MBal SCog WFox
– 'Elegant Beauty'	CB&S CGre CTre CTrh CTrw CWLN IHos MBal SBod SCog SExb SPer WBcn
– 'Elizabeth Anderson'	CTrh
– 'Ellamine'	CB&S
– 'Elsie Jury' 🏆	CB&S CDoC CGre CMac CSam CTri CTrw CWLN GQui IHos IOrc LHyd MAsh MBal MGos SBod SCog SExb SPer WBcn WBod WGwG
¶ – 'Empire Rose'	SPer
– 'Exaltation'	CB&S SCog
– 'Francis Hanger'	CB&S CMac CSam CTre CTrh CTrw IOrc MBal SBod SCog SSpi WGwG
– 'Galaxie' 🏆	CB&S CTrh EPfP ISea
– 'Garden Glory'	CTre CTrh
– 'Gay Time'	CTre MAsh
– 'George Blandford' 🏆	CB&S CMHG CMac CTre
– 'Glenn's Orbit' 🏆	CB&S CGre CTre CTrw CWLN WBcn
– 'Golden Spangles' (v)	CB&S CGre CTre CTrh ELan EOHP IOrc LHyd MBal MBri MGos MNes SPer SPla SReu SSta WBcn
– 'Grand Jury'	CB&S CTre CWLN MGos
– 'Gwavas'	CB&S CTre CWLN
– 'Hilo'	CTrw
– 'Hiraethlyn' 🏆	CTre WBod
– 'Hope'	CTrh SCog
– 'J.C. Williams' 🏆	CB&S CGre CMac CSam CTre CTrw IHos IOrc ISea LHyd MBal MBri MRav SBod SCog SPer SSpi WBod
– 'Jenefer Carlyon' 🏆	CB&S CTre CWLN
– 'Jill Totty'	CTrh
– 'Joan Trehane' 🏆	CMHG CTrw CWLN
– 'Joyful Bells'	CTrh
– 'Jubilation'	SCog SPer
– 'Julia Hamiter' 🏆	CB&S CGre CTrw
– 'Jury's Yellow'	CB&S CTrh CTrw ECle ELan GQui IOrc MAsh MBri MGos SBod SCog SHBN SPer WWat
– 'Laura Boscawen'	CTrh
– 'Les Jury'	SCog
– 'Margaret Waterhouse'	CDoC COtt CTre SCog
– 'Mary Christian' 🏆	CB&S COtt CTre LBuc LHyd MRav WBod
– 'Mary Jobson'	CB&S CTre WWat
– 'Mary Larcom'	CTre
– 'Mary Phoebe Taylor'	CB&S CDoC CTre CTrh CTrw SBod SCog SHBN WBod WFox
– 'Mildred Veitch'	CGre CTre
– 'Mirage'	CTrh
– 'Mona Jury'	CMHG SCog
– 'Monica Dance'	CB&S
– 'Muskoka' 🏆	CB&S CTrh ISea
– 'New Venture'	CB&S
– 'November Pink'	CB&S CTre CWLN
– 'Opal Princess'	SCog
– 'Parkside'	CTre
– 'Phillippa Forward'	CMac
– 'Rendezvous'	CDoC SPla
– 'Rose Court'	WBod
– 'Rose Parade' 🏆	CTrh SCog
– 'Rosemary Williams'	CB&S CTre CTrw
– 'Ruby Bells'	CMHG
– 'Ruby Wedding'	GQui SCog SPer
– 'Saint Ewe' 🏆	CB&S CDoC CGre CMac CTre CTrh CTri CTrw CWLN MBal MBri MGos MRav SBod SCog SHBN SPer WBod
– 'Saint Michael' 🏆	CB&S
– 'Sayonara'	CTre CTrh CWLN
– 'Senorita'	CTrh LHyd
– 'Taylor's Perfection'	CDoC CTrw
I – 'The Duchess of Cornwall'	CTre
– 'Tiptoe' 🏆	CTrh SCog
– 'Tregrehan'	COtt
– 'Water Lily' 🏆	CB&S CDoC CTre CTrh CTrw EPfP MGos WBcn
– 'Wilber Foss'	CB&S CGre CTre CTrh CTrw
– 'William Carylon'	CB&S CTre MBal
– 'Wood Nymph'	COtt CTre ISea MBal
– 'Yesterday'	CTre MAsh SMur
'Winton' (*cuspidata* × *saluenensis*)	CB&S
'Yukihaki'	See ***C. japonica*** **'Yukishiro'**

CAMPANULA × SYMPHYANDRA (Campanulaceae)

C. punctata × ***S. ossetica***	CPou EPad NCat

CAMPANULA † (Campanulaceae)

¶ ***adsurgens***	EPad
aizoides	EPad
alaskana	See ***C. rotundifolia*** var. ***alaskana***
§ ***alliariifolia***	Widely available
– 'Ivory Bells'	See ***C. alliariifolia***
allionii	See ***C. alpestris***
§ ***alpestris***	EPad GCLN GTou MBro WDav
– 'Grandiflora'	EPad EPot
– JCA 250500	SBla
alpina	EPad GDra NNrd
– subsp. ***orbelica***	See ***C. orbelica***
americana	EPad
anchusiflora	EPad NWCA
andrewsii	EPad
– subsp. ***andrewsii***	EPad
argyrotricha	EPad
– CC&McK 477	GCHN NTow
arvatica 🏆	CLyd EPad EPot GCHN LBee MBro MHig MRPP NGre NHar NHol NNrd NRya NTow SSmi WAbe WDav
– 'Alba'	CLyd EPad EPot LBee MHig NTow
atlantis	EPad
aucheri	EBur EPad EPot GCLN GDra NSla
autraniana	EPad
'Avalon'	EPad SAsh
§ 'Balchiniana' (v)	EPad ERav NChi WEas
barbata	CNic ELan EPad GCHN GDra GTou LHop MSte MSto NMen NWCA SAlw WCla WPer
– var. ***alba***	ELan LCom
baumgartenii	EPad
bellidifolia	CMHG EPad GDra NBir
bertolae	EPad
§ ***betulifolia*** 🏆	CGra CSam ECtt EHyt EPad GCHN GDra MBro MFos NGre NHar NMGW NNor NNrd NTow WPat
– JCA 252.005	SBla

– x *trogerae*	EPad
biebersteiniana	EPad
'Birch Hybrid' 🏆	CMHG ECtt ELan EMNN EPad ESis GCHN GDra GMac LBee MBal MBro MTis NHar NMen NNrd NRoo SCro SIng WCra WFar WPyg
bononiensis	EMon EPad NBrk SOkh SRms WOld WPer
bornmuelleri	EPad
'Burghaltii' 🏆	Widely available
§ ***buseri***	EPad
caespitosa	EPad
calaminthifolia	EPad WMaN WOMN
§ ***carnica***	EPad MSte NNrd
carpatha	EPad MRPP
carpatica 🏆	CBos CGle CShe GAri GDra MBar MBri MHig NBro NNor SAlw SRms SWat WHoo WWin
– f. ***alba***	CGle CShe MBro NNor SIng SWat WHoo WMaN
§ – 'Blaue Clips'	CDoC EAst ECtt ELan EMNN EPad EPar ESis GTou MPla NFla NGre NMen NRoo SPer SPla SRms WFar WPer
◆ – Blue Clips	See ***C. carpatica* 'Blaue Clips'**
– 'Blue Moonlight'	EBre EPad LCom NNrd SMer
– 'Bressingham White'	CBlo EBre EPad GAri GCHN GDra SBla WHoo
– 'Caerulea'	CB&S
– 'Chewton Joy'	CLyd EBre EPPr EPad GAri GCHN LCom MBro
– 'Ditton Blue'	EPad GDra
– dwarf form	EPot
– 'Harvest Moon'	EPad
– 'Karpatenkrone'	CRDP EBee SHam
– 'Kathy'	CRDP GBuc SAlw SAsh
– 'Lavender'	WHil
– 'Maureen Haddon'	EBre EPad GAri GCHN GMac LCom NNrd NWCA
– 'Molly Pinsent'	CShe EPad NNrd NTow
¶ – 'Mrs V. Frère'	EPad
– 'Queen of Somerville'	EPad NNrd NWoo
– 'Riverslea'	EPad
– 'Snowdrift'	ELan EPad
– 'Suzie'	EWes LCom SBla
– var. ***turbinata***	GDra MTho NGre NSla WPer
– – f. ***alba***	NNrd
– – 'Craven Bells'	EPad
– – 'Georg Arends'	CLyd SAsh
– – 'Hannah'	EBre EPad GCHN GDra
– – 'Isabel'	EPad GCHN LRHS
– – 'Jewel'	EPad LBee LRHS SIng SSmi
– – 'Karl Foerster'	CTri EBre EPad GBuc GCHN GMac LCom MAvo MTho NNrd NRoo SMer WHoo WPer
– – 'Pallida'	GDra SSmi
– – 'Snowsprite'	LRHS
– – 'Wheatley Violet'	CLyd EPad GCHN LBee MRPP NMen NNrd SBla WPer
§ – 'Weisse Clips'	CRDP EAst ECtt ELan EMNN EPad EPar ESis GTou LHop MPla NFla NGre NMen NRoo SPer SPla SRms WFar WPer
◆ – White Clips	See ***C. carpatica* 'Weisse Clips'**
§ ***cashmeriana***	CGra EBur EPad GCHN GCra ITim NTow NWCA WOMN
celsii	EPad
cenisia	EPad
cephallenica	See ***C. garganica*** subsp. ***cephallenica***
cervicaria	EPad

cespitosa	EPad
§ ***chamissonis***	EHyt EPad GBuc NNrd NSla
§ – 'Major'	CPBP EMNN EPad EPot EWes NMGW SIng
– 'Oyobeni'	EPad MOne NHar SUsu WDav
§ – 'Superba' 🏆	CRDP EGle ELan GDra MBal MFos MTho NGre NMen NNrd NSla NTow SSmi WHil
¶ ***choruhensis***	EHyt EPad
§ ***cochleariifolia*** 🏆	Widely available
– var. ***alba***	CMea CShe CVer EMNN EPad EPot GCHN MBal MBro MHig MWat NGre NHar NMen NNrd NRya SAlw SBla SSmi WAbe WCla WHoo WMaN WPer
– 'Bavaria Blue'	NHar
– 'Bavaria White'	NHar
– 'Blue Tit'	EPad EPot GBuc
– 'Cambridge Blue'	EBre EPad GCHN NMen NNrd SSmi WAbe
– 'Elizabeth Oliver' (d)	CMea CPBP CRDP EBre EFol ELan EPad EPot ESis GCal GMac LFis LHop MBri MHig MPla MRPP MTho NBus NGre NHar NHol NNrd NPer NRoo NWCA SBla WEas WPat
– 'Flore Pleno'	ECtt EPad NHol NMen NNrd WRHF
– 'Miss Willmott'	CBrd EBur EPad MTho NBir NTow WRHF
– 'Oakington Blue'	CTri EPad NHol NNrd
– var. ***pallida***	SRms
– – 'Miranda'	CNic EPad MHig NNrd WIvy
– 'R.B. Loder' (D)	EPad LCom
– 'Silver Chimes'	EPad MBro NNrd WMaN
– 'Temple Bells'	NNrd WPer
– 'Tubby'	CInt CLyd CMea CRDP EPad GCHN LCom MTho NNrd SAga SRms
– 'Warleyensis'	See ***C.* x *haylodgensis* 'Warley White'**
– 'White Baby'	NPri
collina	CTri EPad GBri MBro NHar NPri SCro WAbe WHoo WPer WPyg
'Constellation'	EPad MDHE NCat NNrd
coriacea JCA 253.800	EPad
'Covadonga'	CLyd CPBP EPad LBee MBro MDHE
crispa JCA 253.901	EPad
dasyantha	See ***C. chamissonis***
divaricata	EPad
'E.K. Toogood'	CElw CPBP ECtt EFol EMNN EPad GMac LCom MAvo MDHE MWat NBro NFai NHar NHol NMen NNrd SBla SCro SMac SRms WAbe WHil WRHF
elatines	EPad NNrd NOak
– var. ***elatinoides***	EPad MHar
– – JCA 254.300	SBla
§ 'Elizabeth'	Widely available
ephesia	CMdw EPad
erinus	EPad
eriocarpa	See ***C. latifolia* 'Eriocarpa'**
excisa	EPad LBee NPri NTow
'Faichem'	EGar EPad GCra WPer WSan
fenestrellata	EPad MDHE MTho NBro SRms SSmi WPer
– subsp. ***fenestrellata***	EPad
– subsp. ***istriaca***	EPad
finitima	See ***C. betulifolia***

foliosa	EPad WCot
formanekiana ♀	CSam EBur EDAr EPad MFos NWCA WHil
fragilis	EBur ELan EPad NNrd WPer
– subsp. *cavolinii*	EHyt EPad
– 'Hirsuta'	EPad WHil
'G.F. Wilson' ♀	EBur EGle EPad MBal NNrd
garganica ♀	CSpe EFol ELan EOrc EPad ESis GAbr MBro MFir MRav NFla NHar NMen NNor NNrd NRoo SAlw SIde SIng WByw WFar WHoo WMaN WPer
– 'Aurea'	See ***C. garganica* 'Dickson's Gold'**
– 'Blue Diamond'	ELan EMNN EPad ESis LHop MOne NNrd SAga SCro SIng WAbe WLRN
§ – subsp. *cephallenica*	CLyd EMNN EPad MDHE NBro NHol NNrd
§ – 'Dickson's Gold'	Widely available
– 'Hirsuta'	SRms
– 'Major'	CWan
– 'W.H. Paine' ♀	CInt CLyd EBee EBre ECho EFol ELan EPad NCat NHol NNrd NSla
gieseckiana	EPad
§ 'Glandore'	EPad NCat
glomerata	CB&S CBot CKin CShe EBar EOrc EPad GTou MBal MFir MGam MHew NBro NFai NMir NRya NSti SOkh SSoC SUsu WBea WByw WFar WHil WWin
– var. *acaulis*	CDoC CNic EBar EBre EMNN EPad GCHN MBro NMen NOak NRoo NTow SEas SPla WFar WHil WHoo WPer WPyg WWin
– var. *alba*	CB&S CSev EBre EFol ELan EMon EPad GMaP LWak MBal MBri MBro MCLN MNrw MUlv NBro NFai SChu SPer SPla SSvw SWat WFar WHil WHoo WMaN WPer
– 'Alba Nana'	CLyd EPad NPro
– 'Caroline'	CSte EBee MRav SCro SPer WHil
♦ – Crown of Snow	See ***C. glomerata* 'Schneekrone'**
– var. *dahurica*	CHan CTri EPad LGan MCLN NNrd NOak WBea WEas WPer
– 'Joan Elliott'	CSev EBre ECha EPad GBuc LCom MRav MWat NBrk NCat SChu WCot WFar WLRN
– 'Purple Pixie'	EBre ECtt EPad
§ – 'Schneekrone'	EBre ECha EFou EPad MCli MGrG MRav NBrk NNor NOak NRoo WBea WFar WRHF WRus
– 'Superba' ♀	Widely available
– 'White Barn'	ECha GCra MRav NBrk NOak
grossekii	EPad GBuc MBel MSto
¶ *hagielia*	EPad
× *hallii*	CNic EPad EPot ESis MBro MPla MRPP NGre NRoo NWCA WPat
hawkinsiana	CPBP EPad
× *haylodgensis*	See ***C.* × *haylodgensis* 'Plena'**
§ – 'Plena'	CElw CShe CSpe ELan EPad EPot ESis GMac IHos LBee LHop MBal MBro MHig NBro NHar NPla NRoo SBla SIng SSmi WAbe WEas WHoo WKif WPyg
§ – 'Warley White' (d)	CSpe EBur ELan EPad EPot GDra NNrd
hemschinica	EPad
'Hemswell Starlight'	CLyd NMen NPro
hercegovina	EPad NTow
– 'Nana'	CGra CPBP NGre NNrd WAbe
herminii	EPad
heterophylla	EPad
hierosolymitana	EPad
¶ *iconia*	EPad
§ *incurva*	CBot CFir CGle CMHG CPou EBur EGar ELan EPad GBuc MMil MNrw MRPP MTho NBrk NBro NHol NLak NOak NSti SAlw SMrm WPer
incurva alba	ELan
incurva 'Blue Ice'	WWin
– JCA 256.800	MBro
× *innesii*	See ***C.* 'John Innes'**
isophylla ♀	EPad ERav MBri SIng SLMG WEas WOMN
– 'Alba' ♀	EPad SIng SLMG WEas WOMN
– 'Flore Pleno'	EBur EPad WOMN
– 'Mayi' (v) ♀	CSpe
– 'Variegata'	See ***C.* 'Balchiniana'**
jaubertiana	CGra EHyt EPad MFos
'Joe Elliott' ♀	CGra EPad LRHS MHig SWas
§ 'John Innes'	CLyd CShe EPad
justiniana	EPad
kemulariae	EPad ESis GCHN MAvo MBro NNrd WHil WPer
kemulariae alba	EPad MAvo
'Kent Belle'	Widely available
kladniana	EPad
kolenatiana	EPad GCHN
laciniata	CFir EPad
lactiflora	Widely available
lactiflora alba	See ***C. lactiflora* white**
lactiflora 'Blue Avalanche'	SMrm
– 'Blue Cross'	COtt EFou EPad LCom NRoo WCot
– 'Loddon Anna' ♀	Widely available
– 'Pouffe'	CDoC EBre ECha EFol EFou ELan EOrc EPad LGan MBro MGrG MRav NBro NFla NRoo SCro SPer SPla SWat WHil WHoo WOld WPyg WRus WWin
– 'Prichard's Variety' ♀	Widely available
– 'Violet'	EBee SWat WPer
§ – white ♀	CBot EBre ECha EFou EOrc EPad MBro MCLN NBir NBrk SPer SPla WHoo WOld WPer
– 'White Pouffe'	EBre EFou EHal ELan EOrc EPad ERav GAbr GMaP GMac MBro MRav SMer SOkh SPer SPla SWat WByw WCot WFar WHil WHoo WPyg WRus
lanata	CFir CSpe EBar EPad LCom SMad WBea
lasiocarpa	CPBP EBur EPad WFar

§ ***latifolia***	CAgr CArn CKin CSev ECWi ECha EFou EPad GAbr LGan MCLN MLsm NFla NMir NNor NOrc NTow SPer WCer WCla WEas WFar
– 'Brantwood'	CGle CInt CMil COtt EBre EMan EMar EPad MBel MFir MSte NBrk NHol NOak SChu SCro SMer SPer WBea WCot WWin
§ – 'Eriocarpa'	CHan
– 'Gloaming'	CSte EBee MCLN WCot
– var. ***macrantha***	EBre EEls EFou EPad GAbr GAul GLil LHop MCLN MCli MNrw MRav MSCN MSte NSti SIgm SSvw WCot WHil WHoo WOld WPer WRus WWat WWye
– var. ***macrantha alba***	CChu CDoC CM&M CMil ECtt EMan EPri GAul LCom LGre LHop NPri SCro SPla WCot WPer WPyg WWat
– 'Roger Wood'	EPad
– white	CGle CHan CMHG EBre ECha EOrc EPad MBro MCLN MSte NNor NTow SPer SSpi WEas WHoo WRus
– 'White Ladies'	EBre EFou EPad
§ ***latiloba***	CBre CGle CMHG EBre EGar EMon EPad LGro MBro MFir WByw WCot WEas WHoo WRHF WWin
latiloba alba 🏆	CBre CChu CElw CGle CVer EBee EBre EFou EHal EPad GAbr GCal GMac LFis LGan LHil MRav SCro WAbe WEas WHer WMaN
latiloba 'Hidcote Amethyst' 🏆	Widely available
– 'Highcliffe Variety' 🏆	CMGP EBee ECha EFou EJud EMan EPad EPfP LFis MBel MBri MCLN SPla SSpi WCot WEas WKif WLRN WOld WPbr WPer WRHF WRus
* – 'Highdown'	MAvo WFar
– 'Percy Piper' 🏆	CSam ECED EFou EHal ELan EPad GMac MBel MBri MNrw MRav MSCN NBrk NBro NNor NVic SCro SHel WByw WDav WFar WPbr WRHF
ledebouriana pulvinata 🏆	EPad
lingulata	EPad
linifolia	See ***C. carnica***
longestyla	EPad
'Lynchmere'	EPad EWes NNrd NTow
lyrata	EPad WGwy
makaschvilii	EBee EPad GCLN
'Marion Fisher'	CGra EPad
¶ ***medium*** 'Calycanthema'	EPad
mirabilis	EPad
'Mist Maiden'	CFee CLyd CMHG CPBP CShe EPad EPot LBee NNrd NTow WFar
moesiaca	EPad LCom
mollis	EPad SSca
– var. ***gibraltarica***	EPad NTow
muralis	See ***C. portenschlagiana***
nitida	See ***C. persicifolia*** var. ***planiflora***
– var. ***planiflora***	See ***C. persicifolia*** var. ***planiflora***

'Norman Grove'	CLyd EGle EPad EPot LBee MHig NNrd SAlw
¶ ***oblongifolioides***	EPad
ochroleuca	CMea CRDP EAst EBre EGar EPad GCal MAvo MCLN NLak SWat WBea WBro WHal
olympica Boissier	EPad GCra
– hort.	See ***C. rotundifolia* 'Olympica'**
§ ***orbelica***	EPad
oreadum	CGra EPad
orphanidea	EPad
ossetica	See ***Symphyandra ossetica***
pallida	EPad
– subsp. ***tibetica***	See ***C. cashmeriana***
parryi	EPad
patula	EPad LCom MHew WCla
– subsp. ***abietina***	EPad
'Paul Furse'	CMea EHic EPPr MAvo NSti WDav WHal WHil WWin
¶ ***peregrina***	EPad
persicifolia	CAgr CB&S CGle CNic CSev CShe EBre EFou EHon EPad GCHN GMac LHop MFir NBro NFai NHol NMir NNor NRoo NSti SDix SEas SPer SSvw WMaN WPer WRus WWat WWin
persicifolia alba	Widely available
§ ***persicifolia*** 'Alba Coronata' (d)	CDec CFir CMil EBre EMon EPPr EPad MAvo MBal MBro NBir NBrk NRoo SPer WEas WFar WRus
– 'Alba Plena'	See ***C. persicifolia* 'Alba Coronata'**
– 'Bennett's Blue'	EOrc EPad LFis
– blue	EMan EOrc NCut WEas WFar WPbr
– 'Blue Bell'	CBlo WBro
– 'Blue Bloomers' (d)	EMon GBri MAvo
– blue cup-in-cup	CMil CSpe WPbr WRus
– 'Boule de Neige' (d)	CDec CHan CLon CMil EBre ECha EMon EPad GCra GMac LFis MBel NBrk NMGW NOak NRya WCot WEas WHil WPbr
– 'Caerulea Coronata'	See ***C. persicifolia* 'Coronata'**
* – 'Caerulea Plena'	EBar EFol ELan WEas WPbr
– 'Capel Ulo' (v)	WHer
– 'Carillon'	EPad GBri NBrk WCot
§ – 'Chettle Charm'	Widely available
§ – 'Coronata' (d)	EFou MRav WRHF
N – cup & saucer white	CElw CLyd ELan MUlv NBrk WByw WHil WPbr WPer WRHF
– double blue	CLon CSWP EGar EOrc MBal MBel MCLN NBro NFai SBar SUsu SWas WByw WCot WEas WFar WPbr WRHF WRus WWhi
– double white	EBee ELan NChi WByw WRus
– 'Eastgrove Blue'	NWes
– 'Fleur de Neige' (d) 🏆	CGle CMea CSam EBre LCom MBel MBri MBro MUlv NOak NPro NRoo NTow SWat WHoo WPyg WRus WSel
– 'Flore Pleno'	CHan EPad NBir
– 'Frances'	EMon GBri MAvo MRav SWat WDav WMaN WPbr
– 'Frank Lawley'	EBre EFou EPad MUlv WPbr
– 'Gawen' (d)	CElw CGle GBri GMac LCom LGre MHlr WCot WPen WRHF WWoo

– 'George Chiswell'	See *C. persicifolia* **'Chettle Charm'**
– 'Grandiflora Alba'	GBuc SCro
– 'Grandiflora Caerulea'	SCro WHil
§ – 'Hampstead White' (d)	CArc CDec CHan CLon CMil EBee ECha EEls EFou EPad LFis MBel MBri MCLN NBir NBro SBla SChu SUsu WCot WEas WHoo
– 'Hetty'	See *C. persicifolia* **'Hampstead White'**
– Irish double white	EMon
– 'Moerheimii' (d)	EOrc EPad EPar MBel NBir WIvy WPbr
– var. ***nitida***	See *C. persicifolia* var. ***planiflora***
* – 'Peach Bells'	EBar NOak
– 'Perry's Boy Blue'	NTow NPer
– 'Pike's Supremo'	LHop NBir SCro
§ – var. ***planiflora***	CPBP CSpe EPad EPri GTou NHar WAbe WOMN
§ – – f. ***alba***	EPad WAbe WOMN WSan WWin
– 'Pride of Exmouth' (d)	CGle CPou CSam ELan EMon EPad GMac LHop LLWP MArl MBel MBro NNor NOak NVic WCot WDav WFar WHil WHoo WMaN WPbr WSan
– subsp. ***sessiliflora***	See ***C. latiloba***
– 'Snowdrift'	EBee
– 'Telham Beauty'	CDoC CKel COtt ECED EFou ELan EOrc EPri LHop MCLN MFir MRav SAga SMad SMer SMrm SPer WCra WHil WPbr WPer WRus WWat
– 'Wedgwood'	MBal
N– 'White Cup and Saucer' (d)	GMac NBrk NCat WFar WIvy WRus WWhi
– 'White Queen' (d)	CMGP EBee EFou EPad NCat NFai NVic WEas WTyr
– 'Wortham Belle' (d)	CGle CRDP CSev EBee EBre EFou EMan EPad EPri GCal LFis LHop MBel MCLN MMil NCat NHol NRoo SChu SCoo SPer SSpi SWat WGle WGwG WLRN WOve WRus WWoo
petraea	EPad
petrophila	CLyd NSla WAbe
pilosa	See ***C. chamissonis***
piperi	CGra CPBP EPad GCLN MFos NWCA SBla WAbe
– 'Townsend Ridge'	CGra
planiflora	See *C. persicifolia* var. ***planiflora***
§ ***portenschlagiana*** 🏆	CAgr CElw ELan EPad GAbr LGro MHar MHig MWat NBro NFla NGre NRoo NRya NVic SBla SDix SPer SRms SSmi WAbe WCot WEas WPyg WWin
– 'Lieslelotte'	GBuc MDHE
– 'Major'	CShe LIck SIng SRms WFar
– 'Resholdt's Variety'	CMea CNic CSam CShe EBre EFol EFou ELan EPad EPla GCHN LBee MUlv NCat NNrd WLRN WPer
poscharskyana	Widely available
– 'Blauranke'	EBee EBre EFol EPad EWes GAri GCHN MDHE NRoo
– 'Blue Gown'	GMaP WWeb
– 'E.H. Frost'	CBre CShe ECtt EMNN EPad ESis LBlm LHop LWak MBro MHig MPla MWat NBro NCat NHol NMGW NMen NNrd NRya SCro SIng SSmi WPer WWin
– 'Glandore'	See ***C. 'Glandore'***
– 'Lilacina'	EPPr EPad SCro SHel SIng WThi
– 'Lisduggan'	CBre CChr CGle CNic EBre EBur EFol EPad ESis EWes GAbr LCom MBal MBro MWat NBro NCat NNrd SBla WAbe WPer WPyg WWin
– 'Stella'	CShe EBre EMNN EPPr EPad ESis GCHN MRav NBro NCat NMen NNrd NRoo NVic SChu SDix SIng WPyg
– variegated	EHoe IBlr
primulifolia	CArc CInt CPou CSpe EBee EBre ECoo EGar ELan EPad GBuc GCra LFis MBro MMil MNrw NFai SAlw SSca WFar WHow WPer WPyg WSan WWin
× ***pseudoraineri***	EHyt ELan EPad EWes LCom NGre NNrd NSla SSmi
pulla	CLyd CMea CRDP EBur EHyt ELan EMNN EPad EPot ESis MBro MHig MTho NFla NGre NHar NMGW NMen NNrd SSmi WAbe WFar WPat WPer WPnn
pulla alba	CInt CPBP CRDP EHyt ELan EMNN EPad LBee NHar NMGW NNrd WPat
× ***pulloides***	CLyd EBre EPad LBee LCom NMen NNrd SSmi
punctata	CBot CMHG CMil CSpe EAst ECoo ECro EFou EPad GCHN LFis LGan LLWP MBel MBro MFir MRav NBrk NBro NGre NHar NSti SBla WCla WEas WFar WHil WPer WWin
– f. ***albiflora***	CHan EPad GMac LGan LHop MBri MBro MCCP MCLN NMen SCro WPbr WSan WWin
– var. ***hondoensis***	ECro EPad MBel NSti WBea
– f. ***impunctata***	EPad
* – 'Nana'	WHil
– 'Nana Alba'	CLon CMil CSpe EHyt GBin GCal GMac NRai SAlw WCot
– 'Pallida'	EPad
– 'Rosea'	CGle CMea LRHS MBri NNrd SRms WHil WSan
– 'Rubriflora'	Widely available
* 'Purple Dwarf'	NGre
pusilla	See ***C. cochleariifolia***
pyramidalis	CBot CMGP EFou EPad LIck MSCN NNor NOrc WByw WPer
pyramidalis alba	CM&M EFou EPad SIde SSca WPer
× ***pyraversi***	EPad
raddeana	CNic CRDP CTri EPad GCHN MBro NBus NGre NHar NMen NNrd NTow SCro SSmi WFar WRHF
raineri 🏆	CFee CGra CPBP EHyt EPad EPot LBee MBro MRPP NMen NOak NWCA SBla WAbe WPat WPyg

* – ***alba***	EPad
– 'Nettleton Gold'	EPot
¶ ***ramosissima***	EPad
§ ***rapunculoides***	CAgr CArc EPad LCom MCLN MCli MEas NPri SBla SSvw SWat WHer WPer
– 'Alba'	EMon EPad LCom
rapunculus	EPad ILis LCom
* 'Rearsby Belle'	WPbr
recurva	See ***C. incurva***
¶ ***reiseri***	EPad
¶ ***retrorsa***	EPad
◆ ***rhomboidalis*** Gorter	See ***C. rapunculoides***
rigidipila	EPad NNrd
rotundifolia	CArn CKin CNic ECWi EPad MGam MGra MHew NMir NNrd NRoo NSti SAlw SRms SSvw WBea WCla WGwy WJek WOak WOve WPer
§ – var. ***alaskana***	EPad NWCA
– var. ***alba***	EPad MBro NChi WHoo WPer WPyg
¶ – subsp. ***arctica*** 'Mount Jotunheimen'	CGra
– 'Caerulea Plena'	See ***C. rotundifolia* 'Flore Pleno'**
– forms	MBro
§ – 'Olympica'	CInt CShe EBar EBee EPad GAbr GCHN LFis MHar NPri SEas WFar WHil
– 'Superba'	SCro
rupestris	CBot CPBP EBur EPad MFos
rupicola	EPad
– JCA 262.400	SBla
samarkandensis	EPad
sarmatica	CGle EMon EPad GAbr GBuc LCom MSCN NNrd NOak NPri NRoo NSti SRms WPer
sartorii	CPBP ELan EPad LCom SAlw WSan WWin
saxatilis ♀	EPad
– subsp. ***saxatilis*** ♀	EPad
saxifraga	CGra EBur EHyt EPad GCHN NWCA
scabrella	CGra EHyt MFos
* ***scardica***	EPad
scheuchzeri	EPad NNrd
¶ ***sclerotricha***	EPad
scouleri	EPad GCLN NWCA
serrata	EPad
shetleri	CGra CPBP
sibirica	EPad NPri WPer
– subsp. ***taurica***	EPad
siegizmundii	EPad
'Southern Seedling'	EPad
¶ sp. from Morocco	CGra
sp. JCA 6872	EPad
sp. JCA 8363	EPad
sp. JJH 918638	EPad
¶ ***sparsa***	EPad
spathulata	EPad
– subsp. ***spathulata***	NNrd
– subsp. ***spruneriana***	EPad
speciosa	EPad WSan
spicata	EPad WHil
sporadum	EWoo MFos
'Stansfieldii'	CPBP EPad EPot NNrd NTow
stevenii subsp. ***beauverdiana***	EPad
sulphurea	EPad
takesimana	Widely available
* ***takesimana alba***	MAvo SMad WNdy WRus

takesimana dark form	LFis
– 'Elizabeth'	See ***C.* 'Elizabeth'**
thessala	CSWP EPad MSto
thyrsoides	CArc EFol EPad GDra GTou MNrw NBro NGre NNrd NWCA WCla WHal WPer
– subsp. ***carniolica***	EPad NChi
tommasiniana	EHyt EPad LBee NHar SAsh WOMN
topaliana	EPad WDav
– subsp. ***cordifolia***	EPad
trachelium	CGle CKin EBar ECWi ECoo EGar EJud EOrc EPad GMac LHop MHew MNrw MRav NHaw SSca WApp WByw WCla WFar WHer WPbr WPer
– var. ***alba***	CGle CPea EBre EFol EPad LCom LFis MCLN MFir MNrw NGre NNor SSca WCot WEas WFar WGwG WPer WWhi
– 'Alba Flore Pleno'	CFir CGle CPou ECha EFou ELan EMan EMon EPad LHop MBel SAxl SMac SOkh WByw WCot WFar WGle WHoo WPbr WRus WSan
– 'Bernice' (d)	Widely available
* – 'Faichem Lilac'	MAvo MTis
– lilac-blue	CBlo NCut NOrc
transsilvanica	EPad
¶ ***trautvetteri***	EPad
¶ ***trichocalycina***	EPad
tridentata	EPad NTow WPer
troegerae	CPBP EPad LBee LRHS SBla
tubulosa	See ***C. buseri***
'Tymonsii'	CPBP EBur ECho EHyt ELan EPad ESis LBee MHig NBir NTow
uniflora	EPad
'Van-Houttei'	CElw CHan CMil EMan EMon EPad GCal LCom LGre MAvo MSte NBrk WCot WFar WPbr WPer
versicolor	EPad WOMN WPer
– G&K 3347	EMon
– NS 745	MRPP NWCA
vidalii	See ***Azorina vidalii***
waldsteiniana	CPBP EPad EPot LBee NTow SSmi WFar WOMN WPer
– JCA 266.000	MBro
'Warley White'	See ***C. × haylodgensis* 'Warley White'**
'Warleyensis'	See ***C. × haylodgensis* 'Warley White'**
× ***wockei***	See ***C. × wockei* 'Puck'**
§ – 'Puck'	CPBP EBur EHyt EPad EPot ESis GDra LBee MBro NHar NMen NNrd NSla SIng SSmi WAbe WPat
xylocarpa	EPad
* 'Yvonne'	CRDP EDAr NNrd NPri SIng WLRN WPer
zoysii	CGra EHyt EPad LRHS MHig

CAMPANUMOEA (Campanulaceae)

javanica	See ***Codonopsis javanica* B&SWJ 380**

CAMPHOROSMA (Chenopodiaceae)

See Plant Deletions

CAMPSIS (Bignoniaceae)

grandiflora	CB&S CGre CPlN EBre EHic ELan ENot EPla LPan NPal
radicans	CArn CB&S CBot CDoC CHEx CMac CPlN CRHN ELan EPla GQui LPan MGrG MHlr MNrw MWat NFla SHBN SPer WDin
– 'Flamenco'	CB&S CPlN CSte EBee EBre EHic GQui IOrc LHop NPal SBra WBro WCru
§ – f. ***flava*** 🏆	CDoC CMac CPlN CSam EBee ELan IHos IOrc LHol LHop MBri MWat NPal NSti SBra SPer SSoC SSta WBro WFar WSHC
– 'Yellow Trumpet'	See ***C. radicans* f. *flava***
× ***tagliabuana*** 'Madame Galen' 🏆	CB&S CChu CMac CPlN EBre EMil EOrc EPla IOrc LHol LHop LPan MBlu MBri MGos MLan MWat NSti SBra SHBN SPer SReu SSpi SSta WFar WWeb

CAMPTOSORUS See ASPLENIUM

CAMPYLOTROPIS (Papilionaceae)
See Plant Deletions

CANARINA (Campanulaceae)

canariensis 🏆	CPlN WOMN

CANDOLLEA See HIBBERTIA

CANNA † (Cannaceae)

'Angele Martin'	CBrk
'Assaut'	CBrk
'Australia'	CBrk
'Black Knight'	CBrk GBuc LAma
brasiliensis 'Rosea'	CBrk
'Champion'	CBrk
'Chinese Coral'	LHil
'Cleopatra'	CBrk
coccinea	CBrk
Crozy Hybrids	MHlr
¶ 'Délibáb'	NCat
'Di Bartolo'	CBrk
'Durban' (v)	CBrk EOas LHil WCot
edulis	See ***C. indica***
× ***ehemanii***	CGre CHEx
'En Avant'	CBrk
'Endeavour'	CBrk LLew MSta
'Erebus'	CBrk MSta
'Etoile du Feu'	CBrk
'Extase'	CBrk
♦ Firebird	See ***C.* 'Oiseau de Feu'**
'Fireside'	CBrk LHil SAga
'General Eisenhower'	CBrk
× ***generalis***	CB&S CHEx
glauca	CBrk CMon SDix
'Gnom'	CBrk
'Golden Lucifer'	LAma MBri MRav SAga
'Hercule'	CBrk
hybrids	LBow
§ ***indica***	CB&S CBrk CHEx CMon CSev ERav GCra LBlm SArc SLMG
– 'Purpurea'	CBrk CMon ECha ERav LBlm SDix
iridiflora	CBrk CChu CMon CSev ECha EOas SArc SDix
'Jivago'	CBrk
'King Hakon'	CBrk
♦ King Humbert	See ***C.* 'Roi Humbert'**
'King Midas'	CBrk
'Königin Charlotte'	CBrk
'La Gloire'	CBrk
'Libération'	CBrk
'Louis Cayeux'	CBrk
'Lucifer'	CBrk EBee EOas LHil SLMG
lutea	LBlm WCot
malawiensis 'Variegata'	CSpe LHil
'Meyerbeer'	CBrk
'Mrs Tim Taylor'	CBrk
musifolia	CBrk LBlo LHil SDix
§ 'Oiseau de Feu'	MBri
'Oiseau d'Or'	CBrk LHil
'Orange Perfection'	CBrk
'Orchid'	CBrk CDoC LAma MBri
'Panache'	CBrk
'Perkeo'	CBrk
'Picadore'	CBrk
'Picasso'	CBrk LAma
* 'Pink Sunburst'	WCot
'President'	LAma MBri
'Pretoria' (v)	WCot
'Primrose Yellow'	EBee
'Professor Lorentz'	CBrk
'Ra'	CBrk LLew MSta
'Richard Wallace'	CBrk
§ 'Roi Humbert'	CBrk SLMG
'Roi Soleil'	CBrk
'Rosemond Coles'	CBrk EOas SLMG
'Saladin'	CBrk
'Salmon'	EBar
'Sémaphore'	CBrk
'Shenandoah'	CBrk
'Singapore Girl'	CBrk
'Strasbourg'	CBrk
'Striata'	CBrk CSev EOas MSta
'Striped Beauty'	CBrk
'Talisman'	CBrk
'Taney'	MSta
'Taroudant'	CBrk LHil
¶ 'Tashkent Red'	LHil
'Tirol'	CBrk
'Tropical Rose'	CLTr CSpe
'Verdi'	CBrk
warscewiczii	CBos CBrk LBlo SLMG
'Wyoming'	CBrk CDoC EOas LAma LHil LLew NPSI
'Yellow Humbert'	CDoC CSev EBar LAma

CANTUA (Polemoniaceae)

buxifolia	CB&S CFee CFil CGre CPle GQui LCns LHil SIgm SLMG SMad SOWG

CAPPARIS (Capparaceae)
See Plant Deletions

CAPSICUM (Solanaceae)

annuum	MBri
* – 'Janne'	MBri

CARAGANA (Papilionaceae)

arborescens	CAgr ENot IOrc MBar WDin WFro WStI WWat
– 'Lorbergii' 🏆	CDoC CEnd CLnd IOrc LPan MBlu MUlv NFla SEas SPer WAbe WDin WFoF
– 'Pendula'	CLnd EBre ELan GRei MAsh MBar MBlu MUlv NBee NEgg SPer WDin WStI

– 'Walker'	CB&S CBlo CDoC COtt EBee EBre EMil IOrc LPan MAsh MBar MBlu MBri MGos MUlv SMad SPer WStI
aurantiaca	MBar
brevispina	CPle SRms
franchetiana	CLnd
frutex 'Globosa'	SPer
jubata	MBlu

CARDAMINE † (Brassicaceae)

alba	WEas
asarifolia hort.	See ***Pachyphragma macrophyllum***
– Linnaeus	CArc EBre WCru
bulbifera	CHan CRDP LGan NWoo SIng WCru WUnd
enneaphyllos	ECha IBlr NGar SSpi WCru WFar
§ ***heptaphylla***	EBee ELan EPar GBri IBlr MBri MRav SWat WCru WHoo
¶ – Guincho form	IBlr
– white	WCot
§ ***kitaibelii***	EBee EPar NGar SSpi WCru
laciniata	SWat WCot
latifolia Vahl	See ***C. raphanifolia***
macrophylla	COtt SWas SWat WCot WCru
§ ***microphylla***	EHyt
× ***paxiana***	NGar
§ ***pentaphyllos***	CGle CLon CMea CWGN EBre ECha ELan EPar EPla ERos GAbr MBri MRav NGar NSti SIgm SSpi WCot WCru WFar WOMN
¶ – bright pink form	LWoo
pratensis	CArn CKin CRow CWGN ECWi EMan EWFC MEas NDea NMir SWat WCla WHer WOak WShi
– 'Edith' (d)	CGle CHid CMil CRow EMon GAri GBuc LRHS LWoo SAxl SWat WCot WHil
– 'Flore Pleno' ♀	CArc CBre CFee CGle CHid CNic CRow CSpe CVer CWGN ECha GAbr LRHS MCLN MNrw MSta MTho NBro SBla SWat WByw WChe WCla WEas WHoo WOMN WRus
– 'William' (d)	CGle CMea CVer EMon GBuc LRHS WCot WFar WHil
quinquefolia	CGle CMea EPar NCat SWas WCru WFar WHal
§ ***raphanifolia***	CBre CGle CRow CVer CWGN EBee ECha EMon GAbr GBuc GCal GGar MFir NBro NCat NChi NVic SWat WCru WFar
trifolia	CGle CRDP CWGN ECha ERos GAbr GCal LBee LGan MBar MHig MRav NBro NGar NNor NRya NTow SBar SBla SWat WByw WCru WFar WHal WHer WHil
* ***trifolia digitata***	EBre MTho WCot
waldsteinii	EGle NGar SWas WCot WCru WHal

CARDIANDRA (Hydrangeaceae)

¶ ***formosana*** B&SWJ 2005	WCru

CARDIOCRINUM (Liliaceae)

cordatum	MSto
– var. ***glehnii***	CFil MSto WPGP
giganteum ♀	CAvo CB&S CBot CBro CChu CFil CHEx EPar GGGa IBlr LAma LSyl MBal MBlu MGrG NRog SAga SMad SPer SSoC SSpi WChr WCot WCru WHer
– var. ***yunnanense***	GGGa IBlr SSpi WCru

CARDIOSPERMUM (Sapindaceae)

grandiflorum	CPlN

CARDUNCELLUS (Asteraceae)

See Plant Deletions

CARDUUS (Asteraceae)

benedictus	See ***Cnicus benedictus***

CAREX (Cyperaceae)

acutiformis	ECWi ETPC
albida	CCuc CInt EBee EGle EHoe EMon EPPr EPla ESOG ETPC EWes GFre MBal MLLN
appressa	ETPC GCal
arenaria	ECWi ETPC
atrata	CCuc ECoo EGar EHoe EMon EPPr EPla ESOG ESis ETPC
aurea	ETPC
baccans	GCal
berggrenii	CCuc CGle CLyd CPea CRow ECou EFou EHoe EPGN EPla EPot ESOG ESis GAbr GCHN MRPP NCat NGre NHar NHol NMen NMir NSti NWCA SWat WHal WPer WWin WWye
¶ ***binervis***	GBin
boottiana	GGar
¶ ***brunnea***	EHoe EPPr ESOG
– 'Variegata'	CCuc EHoe GGar WCot
buchananii	Widely available
– 'Viridis'	CB&S EGol ELan EPPr EPla ESOG ETPC WHer WPbr
caryophyllea 'The Beatles'	CArc CCuc EHoe EPPr EPla ESOG ETPC NHar NHol
comans	CCuc CKel CMea EBee EFol EGol EHoe ELan EMon EPPr EPar EPla ESOG GCHN GCal GFre GGar IBlr LHil MBal NBro NHol NOak SHel SIng
– bronze	Widely available
* – 'Small Red'	GFre
§ ***conica***	LCom LHil LHop MBri
– 'Hime-kan-suge'	See ***C. conica*** **'Snowline'**
§ – 'Snowline' (v)	Widely available
crinata	ETPC
crus-corvi	EPPr ETPC
dallii	ECou EWes
demissa	CArc CCuc CInt EHoe EPPr EPla ESOG WWye
depauperata	CCuc EHoe EMon EPla ESOG ETPC WWye
digitata	WWye
dipsacea	CElw CRow EBre ECou EHoe EMon EOrc EPla ESOG ETPC GCal GFre MBro NHed NWCA WChe WHal WPer WWye
¶ ***dissita***	CInt
divulsa subsp. ***leersii***	ETPC
dolichostachya 'Kaga-nishiki' (v)	ESOG WCot WHil
§ ***elata*** 'Aurea' (v) ♀	Widely available
– 'Knightshayes' (v)	EMon WCot
* 'Everbright' (v)	CB&S

◆ 'Evergold'	See ***C. hachijoensis* 'Evergold'**
firma	MHig NNrd
– 'Variegata'	CLyd EHyt EPPr EPar MAsh MDHE MTho NHar NMen NTow NWCA SChu WRus
§ ***flacca***	CArc EHoe ESOG GBin SApp
– 'Bias' (v)	CArc CKin CNat EMon EPPr ESOG NSti
* ***flagellaris*** 'Cyperacea'	CInt
flagellifera	CB&S CHad CMHG CRow CTrC CTri EBre ECou EGol EHoe EMon EPar EPla ESOG ESiP ETPC GBin GFre LGan NHol NPSI SUsu WEas WPer
– 'Rapunzel'	ETPC
flava	EHoe ESOG ETPC
forsteri	See ***C. pseudocyperus***
fortunei 'Variegata'	See ***C. morrowii* 'Variegata'**
'Frosted Curls'	Widely available
fuscula	ETPC
¶ ***glauca*** Bosc. ex Boott	ESOG
◆ – Scopoli	See ***C. flacca***
grayi	CHan EBre EGar EHoe EMon EPla ESOG ETPC GCal MSCN MTho WChe WCot WPer WWye
§ ***hachijoensis***	EPPr EPla ESOG
§ – 'Evergold' (v) 🏆	Widely available
'Hime-kan-suge'	See ***C. conica***
hirta	CKin EPPr
hispida	ETPC
hordeistichos	ETPC
humilis 'Hexe'	ETPC
kaloides	ECou EHoe EPPr EWes
'Little Red'	SApp
lurida	ETPC GBin MCCP
macloviana	EPPr ESOG ETPC
montana	EPPr
morrowii Boott	EBre EOrc IBlr MDHE NSti WPyg
◆ – 'Evergold'	See ***C. hachijoensis* 'Evergold'**
– 'Fisher's Form' (v)	CBrd CCuc CFil CHan CInt CSte CTrC EFol EFou EGol EHoe EOrc EPPr EPla ESOG ETPC GCHN LHil LHop MBri MUlv NHar NMir SApp WCot WPer WWye
– 'Gilt'	EMon EPPr ESOG
– hort.	See ***C. oshimensis***
– 'Nana Variegata'	NBir NWoo
N – 'Variegata'	CCuc CFil CGle CHan CMHG CRow EAst EFol EHoe ELan EMon EPPr EPla ESOG ETPC MBal MBar MRav NEgg NHed NHol NNor NSti SApp SHFr SPer WBea WWat
muricata	CKin
muskingumensis	CB&S CCuc EBee EBre EGar EHoe EMon EPPr EPla ESOG ETPC GBin LHil MBri NBro NFai NHol SApp SDix SMad SPan WPbr WPer WWye
– 'Oehme'	WCot
¶ – 'Small Red'	EMil
– 'Wachtposten'	ETPC GCal MFir
nigra	CKin EHon ETPC GAbr
– subsp. ***tornata***	SIng
¶ – variegated	WCot
ornithopoda	EPot LGan
– 'Aurea'	See ***C. ornithopoda* 'Variegata'**
§ – 'Variegata'	CCuc CKel CNic EBre ECtt EGol EHoe EPla ESiP ETPC GCHN GFre LHil MBal MBro NBro NGre NHar NHol SSmi WAbe WFar WHal WRus WWat WWye
§ ***oshimensis***	IBlr
– 'Evergold'	See ***C. hachijoensis* 'Evergold'**
– 'Variegata'	NBir SApp WCot
otrubae	CKin ETPC
ovalis	CKin
pallescens	GBin WWye
– 'Wood's Edge' (v)	CNat
panicea	ECWi EHoe EPPr ESOG ETPC
paniculata	ETPC
pendula	Widely available
– 'Moonraker'	CBot
petriei	CCuc CSam CVer CWSG EAst EBar ECha ECoo EHoe ELan EMon EPPr EPot ETPC GAbr GAri GFre LHil LLWP MHlr NHed NPSI NVic SPla SSoC WCot WFar WLeb WPer
phyllocephala 'Sparkler' (v)	WCot
pilulifera 'Tinney's Princess' (v)	CCuc EBee EHoe EPot IBlr MBri MCCP
plantaginea	CHan EFol EGar EHoe EMon EPPr EPla ESOG ETPC WCot WFar WPbr
§ ***pseudocyperus***	CInt CKin EGar EHoe EHon EPPr EPla ESOG ETPC EWFC GBin GCHN MSCN MSta SRms SWyc WPer WWye
pulicaris	CKin
remota	CKin EPPr ESOG ETPC GBin WWye
riparia	EMFW EPPr WShi
– 'Variegata'	CBen CCuc CGle CMGP CRow CWGN EBre ECha ECoo EFol EHoe EHon EMFW EMon EPPr EPla ESOG ESiP ETPC GCHN GCal LHil MBri MUlv NBro NFai SCro WAbb WByw WHil
secta	ECou EHoe EPPr ETPC GFre
– var. ***tenuiculmis***	EHoe EMon EPPr ESOG ETPC GBin NHol
siderosticha	CCuc EPot GAri WPer
– 'Variegata'	Widely available
'Silver Sceptre'	CMil EBee EMon NPSI SMrm WCot
sp. from Uganda	EPla GCal
¶ sp. from Wellington, New Zealand	EWes
stricta Goodenough	See ***C. elata***
– 'Bowles' Golden'	See ***C. elata* 'Aurea'**
stricta Lamarck	EPPr ETPC
sylvatica	CKin ECWi ESiP ETPC WWye
testacea	Widely available
– 'Old Gold'	SMer
trifida	ECou EFol EHoe EPla ESOG ETPC GAbr GCHN GCal NCat SPla WChe WCot WWye
uncifolia	ECou EPPr ESOG
vulpina	CKin EPPr ETPC

CARICA (Caricaceae)

See Plant Deletions

CARISSA (Apocynaceae)

bispinosa	SLMG

grandiflora	See ***C. macrocarpa***
§ ***macrocarpa*** (F)	CGre ERea

CARLINA (Asteraceae)

acanthifolia	GCal MAvo SIgm WGle
acaulis	CM&M CSpe ECro ELan LFis NBro NSti SRms SSpi WEas WOak WPer WPyg
– bronze	EMan GCal LHol NChi SIgm SMrm
acaulis caulescens	See ***C. acaulis*** subsp. ***simplex***
§ ***acaulis*** subsp. ***simplex***	CDec CSpe EBee ECGP ECha GBuc MHar MHlr NPri NRoo WCot WFar WHoo WPer
¶ – – bronze	MAvo
¶ ***corymbosa***	GCal
vulgaris	CKin EWFC WPer

CARMICHAELIA (Papilionaceae)

aligera	CPle ECou MAll
angustata	ECou MAll
appressa	ECou
§ ***arborea***	MAll WBod
arenaria	CPle ECou MAll
astonii	ECou
australis	See ***C. arborea***
cunninghamii	ECou
curta	ECou
enysii	CTri
¶ – AGS 27	MRPP
– var. ***ambigua***	ECou
– 'Pringle'	ECou
exsul	ECou
fieldii	ECou MAll
flagelliformis	CPle ECou
glabrata	CPle ECou MAll MBlu
grandiflora	MAll
kirkii	ECou
– × ***astonii***	ECou
– hybrid	SIgm
monroi	ECou MAll MHig
nigrans	ECou MAll
odorata	ECou MAll SVen
orbiculata	ECou MAll
ovata	ECou MAll
'Parson's Tiny'	ECou MAll
petriei	ECou MAll
rivulata	ECou MAll
robusta	ECou MAll
solandri	ECou
suteri	ECou
uniflora	ECou
violacea	ECou
virgata	ECou
williamsii	ECou

× CARMISPARTIUM (Papilionaceae)

astens	See × ***C. hutchinsii***
§ ***hutchinsii***	ECou
– 'County Park'	ECou MAll

CARPENTERIA (Hydrangeaceae)

californica ♀	CBot CPMA ELan EPfP ERea GQui IOrc LHop LNet MBri MGos NPal SBra SHBN SPer SReu SSpi SSta WAbe WDin WHCG WHar WPat WSHC WWat
– 'Ladhams' Variety'	CB&S SBra

CARPINUS † (Corylaceae)

betulus ♀	CB&S CDoC CKin CLnd CPer EBre ELan ENot GRei IHos IOrc LBuc LHyr LPan MBri NBee NWea SPer STre WDin WMou WNor WOrn WStI
– 'Columnaris'	CLnd CTho
* – 'Columnaris Nana'	CMCN
§ – 'Fastigiata' ♀	CB&S CBlo CDoC CLnd CMCN CTho EBre ELan ENot EPfP IOrc LHyr LPan MAsh MBar MBlu MGos NBee NWea WDin WMou WOrn WPyg
– 'Frans Fontaine'	CMCN CTho IOrc MBlu SHhN SSta
¶ – 'Horizontalis'	CMCN
– 'Incisa'	GAri
– 'Pendula'	CTho EBee EBre GAri
– 'Purpurea'	ENot MBlu
– 'Pyramidalis'	See ***C. betulus* 'Fastigiata'**
caroliniana	CLnd CMCN GAri ISea WNor WWoo
caucasica	CMCN
¶ ***cordata***	WDin
coreana	CMCN ISea WNor WWoo
fargesii	See ***C. laxiflora*** var. ***macrostachya***
¶ ***henryana***	WDin
japonica	CEnd CMCN EPfP SMad WWoo
laxiflora	CMCN GAri ISea SSpi WCoo WNor
§ – var. ***macrostachya***	CBlo CDoC CEnd
¶ ***mollicoma***	WWoo
¶ ***omeiensis***	WWoo
orientalis	CMCN GAri WNor
¶ ***polyneura***	WNor
× ***schuschaensis***	WNor
turczaninowii	CMCN ISea WDin WNor WWoo
viminea	WNor

CARPOBROTUS (Aizoaceae)

§ ***edulis***	CAgr CHEx CTrC EGoo EOas IBlr MCCP SArc SEND SLMG WHer
¶ ***muirii***	CTrC
¶ ***sauerae***	CTrC

CARPODETUS (Escalloniaceae)

serratus	CPle

CARTHAMUS (Asteraceae)

tinctorius	MChe MSal SIde

CARUM (Apiaceae)

carvi	CArn CJew GPoy LHol MChe MGra MHew NVic SIde WHer WJek WOak WPer WSel WWye
¶ ***copticum***	MSal
petroselinum	See ***Petroselinum crispum***

CARYA † (Juglandaceae)

cordiformis ♀	CMCN WWes
glabra	CAgr CMCN
N ***illinoinensis***	CMCN
myristiciformis	CMCN
ovata ♀	CAgr CMCN SSpi WCoo WWes
tomentosa	WWes

CARYOPTERIS † (Verbenaceae)

× *clandonensis*	CB&S CBot CPle CTrw ELan ENot GRei LHop MWat NBir NNor WBod WDin WFar WHCG WHar WSHC WStI WWat WWin WWye
– 'Arthur Simmonds'	CBlo ECha EHal EHic LFis LHop MBal MBri SPer WGor
– 'Ferndown'	CArn CChe CDoC EBee EBre ELan EMil LFis LHop MAsh SPer SPla SReu SSpi SWas WDin WFar WRTC WSHC WWeb
– 'First Choice'	EFou ELan LRHS MAsh SPer WRus
– 'Heavenly Blue' ♀	Widely available
– 'Kew Blue'	CB&S CBot CDoC CLTr CShe CSpe EAst EBre ELan EMil ENot MGos NFla SEas SHBN SPer SPla SSta WHar WOMN WPyg WSHC WWat WWeb WWye
¶ – 'Longwood Blue'	GCal LRHS
* – 'Pershore'	LRHS MTis
– 'Worcester Gold'	Widely available
divaricata	CFil CPle EBee EMon WPGP
§ ***incana***	CDoC CPle CShe EBre ELan ERav LFis LHop MSte SPer SPla WCot WSHC
¶ – pink form	LRHS
– weeping form	EHic GBuc GCal SBid SMrm
mastacanthus	See ***C. incana***
odorata	CPle

CARYOTA (Arecaceae)

mitis	LPal

CASSANDRA See CHAMAEDAPHNE

CASSIA (Caesalpiniaceae)

◆ ***corymbosa*** Lam.	See ***Senna corymbosa* Lam.**
◆ ***obtusifolia***	See ***Senna obtusifolia***

CASSINIA (Asteraceae)

leptophylla	CPle MAll SPer
– subsp. ***fulvida***	CB&S CPle ECou EHoe EMil EPla GOrc GTou IOrc MBar MBlu MPla NNor SAga SPer STre WDin
– subsp. ***vauvilliersii***	MAll NNor
– – var. ***albida***	CB&S CHan MAll SPer WBod WGer
– – 'Silberschmelze'	SOWG
N ***retorta***	CDoC ECou MAll NNor
– yellow	MAll
'Ward Silver'	CBot ECou EWes GSki MAll NNor SPan

CASSINIA × HELICHRYSUM (Asteraceae)

* ***Cassinia* × *Helichrysum***	WKif WPen WSHC

CASSIOPE † (Ericaceae)

'Askival'	GTou ITim
'Badenoch'	EPot GAri GDra LRHS MBal NHar
'Bearsden'	GAri GDra MBal MBar NHar WPat WPyg
'Edinburgh' ♀	CMHG EPot GAbr GDra MBal MBar NHar NHol NMen WAbe WDin WPat WPyg
'George Taylor'	WAbe
'Kathleen Dryden'	GDra MBal
lycopodioides ♀	EPot GDra GTou MBal MBar MGos NHar NHol WAbe WFar
– 'Beatrice Lilley'	ELan EPot EWes GAri GTou MBal MBar MHig NHar NHed NHol WAbe WPat WPyg
– 'Rokujô'	EPot NHol
'Medusa'	GDra GTou LRHS MBal MHig NHar NHol WPat WPyg
mertensiana	GTou GWht MBal MBar NHed NMen
– 'California Pink'	MHig
– dwarf form	MBal
– var. ***gracilis***	CMHG ELan LRHS MDun MGos MHig NHar NHol
¶ – – dwarf form	EPot
'Muirhead' ♀	EPot GDra GTou MBal MBar MHig NHar NHed NHol NMen SRms WAbe WDin WPat WPyg
'Randle Cooke' ♀	ELan EPot EWes GDra GTou MBal MBar MBro MHig NHar NHed NHol SRms WAbe WPat WPyg
selaginoides LS&E 13284	GAri
§ ***stelleriana***	SSta
tetragona	GTou LRHS MBal MBar SRms
– var. ***saximontana***	EPot GGGa MBal NHol
wardii	WAbe
– × ***fastigiata*** 'Askival Strain'	WAbe

CASTANEA † (Fagaceae)

'Layeroka' (F)	CAgr
* 'Marigoule'	MBlu
mollissima	CMCN GAri WWoo
¶ × ***neglecta***	CTho
sativa ♀	CB&S CDoC CHEx CKin CLnd CPer ENot GRei IOrc LBuc LHyr LPan MAsh MBar MBri MWat NBee NRog NWea SHBN SPer WDin WFar WMou WOrn WStI WWes
§ – 'Albomarginata'	CBlo CDoC CSte EBee EBre MBlu MBri MGos NBee SMad SPer SSpi SSta WDin WMou WWeb WWes
– 'Anny's Red'	MBlu
– 'Anny's Summer Red'	CDul SMad
– 'Argenteovariegata'	See ***C. sativa* 'Albomarginata'**
– 'Aspleniifolia'	CFil WPGP
– 'Aureomarginata'	See ***C. sativa* 'Variegata'**
– 'Bournette' (F)	ESim
* – 'Corkscrew'	CSte
* – 'Doré de Lyon'	MBlu
– 'Marron de Lyon' (F)	CTho ESim MBlu WMou
§ – 'Variegata'	CAbP CB&S CFil CMCN COtt CTho ELan EPfP LPan MAsh
– 'Vincent van Gogh'	SMad
'Simpson'	CAgr

CASTANOPSIS (Fagaceae)

cuspidata	CMCN

CASUARINA (Casuarinaceae)

cunninghamiana	CTrC
equisetifolia	CGre SMad
littoralis	See ***Allocasuarina littoralis***
stricta	See ***Allocasuarina verticillata***

CATALPA † (Bignoniaceae)

bignonioides ♀	CB&S CBot CDoC CHEx CLnd CMCN CTho ELan ENot IOrc LHyr LPan MBri MBro MWat NBee NPal NWea SPer WBod WDin WNor
– 'Aurea' ♀	Widely available
¶ – 'Nana'	CSte
– 'Purpurea'	See *C.* x ***erubescens*** **'Purpurea'**
– 'Variegata'	LNet SSta WPat WPyg
bungei	LPan
– 'Purpurea'	ELan
¶ x *erubescens*	LPan
§ – 'Purpurea' ♀	CB&S CBlo CBot CDoC CEnd CHEx CLnd EBre EMil IOrc MAsh MBlu SHBN SMad SPer SSoC WPat WPyg
fargesii	CChu CFil CLnd
ovata	CAgr CBlo CEnd CGre CHEx CMCN
speciosa	CB&S CHEx CLnd CMCN LRHS SPer WMou
– 'Pulverulenta'	CEnd CMCN

CATANANCHE (Asteraceae)

caerulea	CChr CDoC CHan CHor CMea CSev EBre ECha EFou MBri MCLN MRav NBro NFai NNor NRoo NSti NVic SChu SIgm SPer SSvw SUsu WHil WOld WPer WWhi WWin WWye
– 'Alba'	CGle CKel CPou EAst ECha EFou LIck MCLN MUlv NBir NNor NOak NPri SChu SIgm SPer SSvw SUsu WFar WPLI WPer WWhi
– 'Bicolor'	CArc CBre CM&M CSev EMan EMar GBur GCal LFis MCLN MHFP NFai NNor SAxl SMad WElm WGwG WHer WMaN
– 'Major' ♀	CShe ENot GCal MBri MWat SRms WEas
* – 'Stargazer'	WRHF
¶ *caespitosa*	EHyt

CATAPODIUM (Poaceae)

§ *rigidum*	ETPC

CATHA (Celastraceae)

¶ *edulis*	NGno

CATHARANTHUS (Apocynaceae)

roseus ♀	MBri
– Ocellatus Group	MBri

CAULOPHYLLUM (Berberidaceae)

thalictroides	CRDP MSal NGar WCot WThi

CAUTLEYA (Zingiberaceae)

¶ *gracilis*	CB&S
lutea	See ***C. gracilis***
spicata	CB&S CHEx CWit IBlr WCru
– 'Robusta'	CKni CRDP EMan SMad SSoC

CAYRATIA (Vitaceae)

¶ *japonica*	CPlN
– B&SWJ 570	WCru

CEANOTHUS † (Rhamnaceae)

'A.T. Johnson'	CBlo CKno CMac CPle CWLN ENot LNet NFai SHBN SPer SReu SRms SSoC WAbe WBod WGwG WHCG WRTC WWeb
americanus	CArn CPle LHol MSal NCGP WWye
– 'Fincham'	CKno
arboreus	SArc
– 'Owlswood Blue'	CKno CWLN LRHS
– 'Trewithen Blue' ♀	CB&S CChe CGre CHad CKno CLan CMHG CMac CPle CSam CTrw CWLN EBre ELan EMil IOrc ISea LHop LNet MRav NSti SAga SPer WAbe WFar WSHC WStI WWat WWeb
'Autumnal Blue' ♀	CB&S CKno CLTr CMHG CMac CPle EAst EHal ELan EMil ENot ISea LHop MBri MGos MHlr MPla MWat NFai NNor SHBN SPer SReu SSta WDin WEas WFar WPyg WWat WWin
azureus	See ***C. coeruleus***
'Basil Fox'	LRHS
'Blue Boy'	CKni
'Blue Buttons'	CKno CSte LRHS
'Blue Cushion'	CB&S CBlo CDoC CKno CLan CPle CWLN ECtt EHic LHop MAsh MGos MRav MWat WFar WWeb
'Blue Jeans'	CAbP CBlo CKni CKno CPle CSte CWLN MAsh MBri SBid
'Blue Mist'	CKno
* 'Blue Moon'	CKni CSte
'Blue Mound' ♀	CDoC CGre CKno CLTr CLan CMHG CPle CShe CTrw CWLN EBre EMil MGos MRav NHol NNor SMad SPer SPla SReu SSpi WGwG WSHC WWat WWeb
* 'Blue Star'	LHop
'Burkwoodii' ♀	CB&S CDoC CKno CMac CPle CSam EBre GRei IOrc MAsh MBal MBri MGos NNor SHBN SPer SReu WFar WGwG
'Burtonensis'	CKno WRHF
'Cascade' ♀	CB&S CKno CLan CMHG CSam CShe CWLN EAst ELan ENot IOrc LNet MBri MGos MWat NFla NNor SPer WAbe WBod WHCG WSHC WStI
'Concha'	Widely available
¶ *crassifolius* var. *planus*	LRHS
* – 'Plenus'	SBid
cyaneus	CGre CPle
'Cynthia Postan'	CKno CPle CSam CSte CWSG EBre LRHS MAsh MBlu SPan
'Dark Star'	CChe CKno CSte CTbh CWLN CWSG EPfP EWll LRHS MAsh SAga SOWG SReu SSta
'Delight' ♀	CBlo CKno EBee ELan EPla IOrc NFla NNor SBid SMad SPer SSoC WAbe WBod WFar WWat
x *delileanus* 'Gloire de Versailles' ♀	CB&S CBot CChe CKno CMac CPle CSam CShe ELan ENot IOrc ISea MBri MGos MWat NBee NBrk SHBN SPer SReu SSta WAbe WDin WFar WPyg WSHC WWeb WWin

– 'Henri Desfossé'	CBlo CKno CPle ELan MAsh SBid SOWG SPer WDin WFar WKif WStI
– 'Indigo'	CKno NFla
– 'Topaze' 🏆	CB&S CBlo CKno CPle CShe ELan EMil ENot NSti SAga SBid SOWG WHar WKif
dentatus Torrey & A Gray	CMac CPle CSam CWLN ELan ENot GRei IOrc MAsh MBal MGos NNor SChu SPer WBod WPyg
– var. ***floribundus***	EBee ELan
– 'Prostratus'	MBal
* – 'Superbus'	EBee WWeb
dentatus hort.	See ***C.*** × ***lobbianus***
'Dignity'	CKno CLan WWeb
divergens	CMac CPle MAll SBid WBod
'Edinburgh' 🏆	CBlo CKno CMHG CMac CPle CWLN MBri NCut SBid SPan WBod WWeb
'Edward Stevens'	CKno
* 'Elan'	EBee
'Eleanor Taylor'	CKni CKno CPle CWLN LRHS
'Fallen Skies'	LRHS
* 'Filden Park'	LRHS
foliosus	CGre CPle
– var. ***austromontanus***	CB&S CLTr CLan CPle CTrw EHic
'Frosty Blue'	CKno CPle MSta
'Gentian Plume'	CKno SMad
* 'Gloire Porrectus'	MBlu
gloriosus	CDoC CPle CSam EWes IOrc MAll SAga SBid SDry SPan WRTC WSHC WWat
– 'Anchor Bay'	CKni CKno CPle CSte ELan EPfP MAsh SOWG
– 'Emily Brown'	CB&S CKno
griseus var. ***horizontalis*** 'Hurricane Point'	CB&S CKno WFar
– – 'Yankee Point'	CB&S CChe CMHG CMac CPle ECtt EHal EMil ISea LHop LNet MBel MBri MRav NFai SHBN SPer WAbe WDin WFar WWeb
– 'Santa Ana'	CKno
hearstiorum	CPle LRHS
impressus	CB&S CDoC CGre CLan CMHG CPle CShe CWLN ELan EMil ENot GOrc MAsh MBal MRav SEas SPer SPla SSoC WAbe WBod WEas WFar WPyg WWeb
integerrimus macrothyrsus	CPle
N 'Italian Skies' 🏆	CB&S CDoC CKno CLan CMHG CMac CSam CWLN EHal ELan EMil LHop MAsh MBri MGos MRav SAga SEas SPer SPla WBod WWeb
'Joyce Coulter'	CB&S CKno EMil
'Julia Phelps'	CKno CMHG CSte CWSG WEas
'Ken Taylor'	CRos CWLN LRHS MAsh
§ × ***lobbianus***	CB&S CTri WLRN WRTC
– 'Russellianus'	CAbP CBlo CKno SHBN WBod
maritimus 'Point Sierra'	CKno
'Mary Lake'	CKno
× ***mendocinensis***	CPle
oliganthus	CPle
¶ × ***pallidus***	WBcn
– 'Golden Elan'	CPle
– 'Marie Simon'	CB&S CBlo CBot CKno CPle CWLN ELan EMil EPfP GOrc LHop MBri MRav NFla NNor SEas SMad SPer SRms WASP WFar WKif WPyg WSHC WTyr WWeb
– 'Perle Rose'	CB&S CBlo CBot CChe CKno CMac CPle CSam CSte IOrc MTis SHBN SOWG SPer SPla WKif WSHC
papillosus	CGre CMac CPle SBid
– var. ***roweanus***	CMac CPle CWLN GAri SDry WEas WWat
'Percy Picton'	CKno
¶ 'Pershore Zanzibar' (v)	LRHS SCoo
'Picnic Day'	CKno
'Pin Cushion'	CKno CSte CWSG LRHS SPla WFoF WPat WWat
'Point Millerton'	CBlo CWLN MAsh MBlu SPla SSta
prostratus	CDoC GSki LBuc MAsh SDry SHBN WAbe WEas WWeb WWin
'Puget Blue' 🏆	CB&S CBlo CHad CKno CLan CMHG CMac CPle CSam CTbh CWLN EBre ELan EMil GAbr LHop MAsh MBri MGos MPla MWat SDix SPer SReu SSpi SSta WBod WDin WKif WSHC
purpureus	CPle EBee EHic LBuc MAll WWeb
ramulosus	LRHS
'Ray Hartman'	CKno SMad SSoC WBcn
repens	See ***C. thyrsiflorus*** var. ***repens***
rigidus	CPle EBee SBid SDry SPla SRms WAbe WBod WSHC
– 'Snowball'	CKno ELan EPfP GSki MAsh WBcn
'Sierra Blue'	CKno WBod WFar
'Snow Flurries'	CB&S CKno CPle EBee EHal EHic EMil MBel MSta WFar WWat WWeb
sorediatus	CPle
'Southmead' 🏆	CBlo CKno CMac CTri CWLN EAst EBee EHic EMil GBuc IOrc ISea MAsh MBri MGos NCut NFla WAbe WBod WHCG WPat WWat
spinosus	CPle
'Thundercloud'	CKno
thyrsiflorus	CB&S CBlo CMac CPle CTri ELan LNet MAsh MBal MBri MTis NFai NHol SArc SHBN SRms WAbe WDin WFar WHar WRHF
– 'Millerton Point'	CKni CKno CPle CSte CWSG ELan SBid WPat
§ – var. ***repens*** 🏆	Widely available
– 'Skylark'	CBlo CDoC CKno CPle CRos CSam CSte CTbh CWLN EBee EHic ELan LHop MAsh MBri SBid SBra SDix SReu SSta WFar WWeb
'Tilden Park'	CKno
* 'Underway'	WWat
× ***veitchianus***	CB&S CBlo CMac CSam CShe CWLN EBre ELan ENot LNet MAsh MBar MWat NHol NPer SBid SEas SPer SSta WBod WRHF WRTC WWeb
verrucosus	CPle
'White Cascade'	CKno MAll MSta SPan WRTC

CEDRELA (Meliaceae)

sinensis	See ***Toona sinensis***

CEDRONELLA (Lamiaceae)

§ *canariensis*	CArn CGle CInt CSev GCal GPoy IBlr ILis LHol MChe MGra MHew MSal NHex SIde SOWG SWat WApp WCer WHer WOMN WOak WPer WWye
mexicana	See ***Agastache mexicana***
triphylla	See ***C. canariensis***

CEDRUS (Pinaceae)

atlantica	See ***C. libani*** subsp. ***atlantica***
brevifolia	See ***C. libani*** subsp. ***brevifolia***
deodara ♀	CChu CDoC CMac EHul ENHC ENot GRei IOrc ISea LBee LCon LHyr MBal MBar MBri MGos NBee NWea SHBN SLim SPer SReu STre WAbe WDin WMou WPyg WWat
– 'Albospica' (v)	MAsh
– 'Argentea'	MBar MGos NHol
– 'Aurea' ♀	CDoC EHul EOrn ISea LBee LCon LLin LPan MAsh MBar MBri SLim SReu SSta WDin WFar WFro WOrn
I – 'Aurea Pendula'	ENHC
– 'Blue Dwarf'	CKen LCon LLin MAsh NHol
– 'Blue Triumph'	LPan
– 'Cream Puff'	LCon LLin MBar MGos
– 'Feelin' Blue'	CDoC CKen COtt EBre LBee LCon LLin LPan MAsh MBar MBri MGos MRPP SCoo SLim WDin
– 'Gold Cone'	MGos
– 'Gold Mound'	CKen GAri
– 'Golden Horizon'	CDoC CKen CMac EBre EHul ENHC EOrn IOrc LBee LCon LLin LPan MAsh MBar MBri MGos NBee NHol SHBN SLim SPer SSta WDin WPyg
– 'Karl Fuchs'	EBre ETen LCon LRHS MAsh MBri WGor
– 'Kashmir'	MBri
– 'Klondyke'	MAsh
– 'Lime Glow'	CKen
¶ – 'Mountain Beauty'	CKen
– 'Nana'	CKen
– 'Nivea'	CKen
– 'Pendula'	EHul LPan MBar MGos MWat WGor WStI
– 'Pygmy'	CKen
– 'Roman Candle'	EOrn ISea SHBN
– 'Scott'	CKen
¶ – 'Silver Mist'	CKen
– 'Verticillata Glauca'	CDoC
libani	CMCN CTri LRHS MAsh NBee WPGP
§ – subsp. ***atlantica***	CDoC CGre EHul GAri LCon MBar NWea SLim WDin WGwG WMou
– – 'Aurea'	CDoC CMac LCon LLin LPan MAsh MBar MGos SSta WDin
– – 'Fastigiata'	CDoC CMac EHul LCon LPan MBar MBri SLim
– – 'Glauca Fastigiata'	CKen SMad
– – Glauca Group ♀	CDoC CKen CMac EBre EHul ELan ENHC ENot GRei LCon LLin LNet MBar MBri MGos MWat NBee NWea SHBN SLim SMad SPer SReu SSta WDin WMou WWat
– – 'Glauca Pendula'	CDoC CKen EHul EOrn IOrc LCon LNet LPan MBar MBri MGos NBee SLim SMad SSta WGer WOrn WWes
– – 'Pendula'	CMac GAri NBee
§ – subsp. ***brevifolia*** ♀	GAri ISea LCon MBar MBlu MBri SSta
– – 'Epstein'	LCon MBar
– – 'Hillier Compact'	CKen
– – 'Kenwith'	CKen
* – 'Home Park'	CKen
– subsp. ***libani*** ♀	CDoC CMac EHul ENot IOrc LCon MBar MBri MLan NWea SHBN SPer STre WDin WFro WMou WNor WWat
– – 'Comte de Dijon'	EHul LCon LLin SLim
– – Nana Group	CKen LCon MAsh
– – 'Sargentii'	CDoC CKen CMac EBre EHul EOrn ISea LCon LLin MAsh MBal MBar MBri MGos SLim SSta
– – 'Taurus'	MBar NHol

CELASTRUS (Celastraceae)

¶ ***angulatus***	CPlN
orbiculatus	CB&S CMCN CPlN EBee ELan EMil GBin MPla MRav NHol NPSI NPal NSti SPan SPer SReu SSta WBod WFar WSHC
– 'Diana' (f)	ELan
– 'Hercules' (m)	ELan
– Hermaphrodite Group ♀	CSam EHic EPla GAul GOrc GSki NHol SBra SDix WGer WWat
– JLS 88018WI	EMon
scandens	CB&S CMac CPlN ELan EOvi MSal SMur

CELMISIA † (Asteraceae)

¶ ***adamsii***	IBlr
allanii	GCLN IBlr
alpina	GAbr IBlr WCru
– large form	IBlr
angustifolia	EPot GCLN GCrs IBlr
¶ – silver form	IBlr
argentea	EPot EWes GCHN GTou NHar NHed
asteliifolia	IBlr
¶ Ballyrogan hybrids	IBlr
bellidioides	EMNN EPot GDra IBlr NHar NHol NMen NWCA WAbe
bonplandii	GCLN GTou IBlr SIgm
brevifolia	GCLN IBlr
coriacea	GCal GCra IBlr NHar NNor
– 'Harry Brice'	IBlr
dallii	EPot IBlr
densiflora	GDra IBlr SIgm
discolor	IBlr
dureitzii	IBlr
'Edrom'	GTou
glandulosa	IBlr
gracilenta	IBlr
– CC 563	NWCA
– forms	IBlr
graminifolia	IBlr
hectorii	EPot GTou IBlr ITim MHig

holosericea	IBlr SIgm
hookeri	GCal GCrs
incana	IBlr
Inshriach Hybrids	MBal
¶ Jury Hybrids	IBlr
¶ ***lindsayi***	GCrs
longifolia	GCLN GDra
– large form	IBlr
– small form	IBlr
mackaui	IBlr
monroi	IBlr
morganii	IBlr
prorepens	IBlr
♦ ***ramulosa***	See ***C. ramulosa*** var. ***tuberculata***
§ – var. ***tuberculata***	GTou IBlr ITim MHig WAbe
saxifraga	EPot IBlr
semicordata	GBri NHar
– 'David Shackleton'	IBlr
– subsp. ***stricta***	IBlr
* ***sericifolia***	IBlr
sericophylla	IBlr
¶ – large form	IBlr
sessiliflora	EPot GAri GTou IBlr ITim
– 'Mount Potts'	IBlr
spectabilis	IBlr MDun NEgg NGar NHar
– var. ***angustifolia***	IBlr
¶ – subsp. ***magnifica***	GAri IBlr
traversii	EPot IBlr NHar WAbe
verbascifolia	GCLN IBlr
viscosa	CFee IBlr NSla
§ ***walkeri***	GCrs GTou IBlr
webbiana	See ***C. walkeri***

CELOSIA (Amaranthaceae)

argentea var. ***cristata***	MBri
– – Plumosa Group	MBri

CELSIA See VERBASCUM

CELSIOVERBASCUM See VERBASCUM

CELTIS (Ulmaceae)

africana	CGre
aurantiaca	CMCN
australis	CB&S CMCN LPan SSpi SSta
caucasica	CMCN
laevigata	CMCN
occidentalis	CPle ELan EPfP LRHS
– var. ***pumila***	CMCN
¶ ***sinensis***	CMCN
tournefortii	CMCN

CENOLOPHIUM (Apiaceae)

denudatum	SIgm

CENTAUREA (Asteraceae)

argentea	CBot
¶ ***atropurpurea***	EMon
bella	CBot CChu CGle CHad CSam CSev EBre EFou EHal ELan EMar EOrc GCal LFis LHop MBri MGrG MHig NBro NNor NNrd NRoo NSti SHel SMrm SUsu
benoistii	CHad CHan EJud EMar WCot
'Blue Dreams'	EMon MAvo MGrG WPbr
cana	See ***C. triumfettii*** subsp. ***cana***
candidissima hort.	See ***C. cineraria***
– Lamarck	See ***C. rutifolia***
cheiranthifolia	EBee ECha WFar WPbr
§ – var. ***purpurascens***	EMon
§ ***cineraria*** ♀	CBrk SRms WEas
cyanus	CJew ECWi EWFC MHew WFar WJek
cynaroides	See ***Leuzea centauroides***
dealbata	CBot CKel CLon EBar ECtt GAbr LGan MCLN MFir NBro NFai NMir NOak NOrc NRoo SCro SHel WByw WFar WHoo WOve WPer WWin
– 'Steenbergii'	CGle CHor CMGP CPou CRDP EBre ECED EFol ELan GCal MBel MBri MCLN MRav NMGW NOak NPer NSti SHel SOkh SPer WAbb WByw WCot WFar
debeauxii subsp. ***nemoralis***	CKin
drabifolia	NTow
fischeri	See ***C. cheiranthifolia*** var. ***purpurascens***
glastifolia	EMon GCal MAvo WCot WPbr
* 'Gold Bullion'	EGar WBcn
gymnocarpa	See ***C. cineraria***
hypoleuca 'John Coutts'	Widely available
macrocephala	Widely available
montana	Widely available
montana alba	Widely available
§ ***montana carnea***	CArc CBre CElw CMea ECha MAvo NChi NFla WBon WHal WPbr WRus WWin
montana 'Grandiflora'	GCal MBri
* – 'Lady Flora Hastings'	CBot
– 'Ochroleuca'	CElw EMon SOkh SWat WPbr
– 'Parham'	CMGP CPou CSev EBee EMan GCal LBlm LFis MBel MBro MCLN MUlv NPla NRoo NSti SChu SMrm SOkh SPer SWat WLRN WPbr
montana rosea	See ***C. montana carnea***
* ***montana violacea***	IBlr
montana 'Violetta'	CPou NBir
nigra	CArn CKin CTiv ECWi EWFC MGam MHew NLan NMir WCla WJek
– var. ***alba***	CArn WNdy
– subsp. ***rivularis***	ECha WPbr
orientalis	ECha SIgm WPbr WPer
¶ ***ornata***	WCot
parilica NS 699	NWCA
phrygia	GBuc
pulcherrima	CBot ECha EFol EGle EMon MAvo MHar MLLN MTis NOak SIgm WCot WPbr WPer
'Pulchra Major'	See ***Leuzea centauroides***
rhapontica	See ***Leuzea rhapontica***
rigidifolia	LFis SMer
ruthenica	CHad ECha SIgm WCot WPbr
§ ***rutifolia***	WCot
salonitana	EMon MAvo WCot
scabiosa	CArn CKin CPea ECWi ECoo EHal EWFC MChe MHew MTol NCGP NLan SIde WApp WCla WGwy WJek WPer
scabiosa alba	CNat EBee EFou EMan NRoo NSti WNdy
scabiosa 'Nell Hill'	CNat WAlt
¶ ***seridis*** subsp. ***maritima***	WCot

simplicicaulis CGra CHan CInt CMea CNic CRDP EBre GAbr LFis LGan MBel MBro MFir MHlr MRav MTho MTol NRoo SAlw SRms WCot WEas WHil WHoo WOMN WPer
§ ***triumfettii*** subsp. ***cana*** 'Rosea' CNic CPea CRDP EFol EFou NNrd WWin
– subsp. ***stricta*** ECoo EMar EMon EPPr GBuc MAvo MSte NMGW NTow WOMN WPbr
– – from Macedonia LFis
uniflora subsp. ***nervosa*** CSam EMan MSto NBro WBea WPer

CENTAURIUM (Gentianaceae)

chloodes See *C. confertum*
§ ***confertum*** MNrw
erythraea CArn ECWi EWFC GPoy MChe MHew MSal SIde WCla WWye
scilloides CInt MBro MPla MTho NGre NMen NNor NNrd NTow NWCA SAlw SRms WCla WHoo WOMN WWin

CENTELLA (Apiaceae)

§ ***asiatica*** CArn EOHP MSal

CENTRADENIA (Melastomataceae)

inaequilateralis 'Cascade' CHal CInt CLTr ECtt EMan LHil MBri NFai WLRN
rosea See *C. inaequilateralis*

CENTRANTHUS (Valerianaceae)

§ ***ruber*** Widely available
§ ***ruber albus*** CB&S CBot CDoC CGle CHad CKin EBre ECha ECro EFol EFou ELan ERav MCLN NBir NBro NFai NNor NOrc SApp SPer SSvw WByw WEas WHen WHer WHil WPer
ruber atrococcineus ECha SPer WPer
ruber var. ***coccineus*** CB&S CDoC CLTr EBee EGoo ELan EPfP GAbr GBri MWat NFai NPri SEND SMrm WHil WTyr

CEPHALANTHERA (Orchidaceae)

¶ ***falcata*** EFEx
¶ ***longibracteata*** EFEx

CEPHALANTHUS (Rubiaceae)

occidentalis CB&S CBlo CPMA CPle CSte EBar EHic ELan EMil ERav LFis MBlu MPla SPer SSta WPat WRTC

CEPHALARIA (Dipsacaceae)

§ ***alpina*** CElw CGle ECha EMan ESis GCHN MBel MNrw NGre NHed NPri NTow SMer SOkh SRms SWat WFar WPer WRHF
– 'Nana' CMil CShe NWCA WPat WPyg
ambrosioides GAul MLLN
dipsacoides CArc
¶ ***flava*** EFou
§ ***gigantea*** Widely available
leucantha GAbr GBuc MBel MEas SIde SIgm WBea WWhi
litvinovii EMon
¶ ***natalensis*** CArc
radiata EBee
tatarica See *C. gigantea*

CEPHALOTAXUS (Cephalotaxaceae)

fortunei CGre
harringtonia LLin MRav SMur
– var. ***drupacea*** CMCN LCon WWat
– 'Fastigiata' CB&S CChu CDoC CKen EHul EOrn ETen LCon LPan MBar MBri SLim SMad SSmi WGer
– 'Gimborn's Pillow' MBar
– 'Korean Gold' CKen

CEPHALOTUS (Cephalotaceae)

follicularis EEls GTro MHel WMEx

CERASTIUM (Caryophyllaceae)

alpinum CMea ELan SRms WThi
– var. ***lanatum*** CPBP EWes MHig NGre NNrd NTow NWCA WCru WHil WPer
candidissimum EWes
theophrasti WPat
tomentosum CHal CTri EFer ELan GBur LGro NCGP NNor NPri NVic WBea WCer WFar WLRN WPer WWtk
– var. ***columnae*** CBlo EBre ECha ECho EHoe EPfP EWes MHar MHlr SRms WCot WHoo
– 'Silberteppich' EGoo LFis LRHS

CERATONIA (Caesalpiniaceae)

siliqua MSal

CERATOPHYLLUM (Ceratophyllaceae)

demersum CBen CRow EHon EMFW NDea SAWi SWat SWyc WChe

CERATOSTIGMA † (Plumbaginaceae)

abyssinicum ELan ERav LBlm
griffithii CB&S CBot CChe CHan CPle EBar EBre ECtt ELan ERav GOrc IOrc MPla NSti SEas SPer SSta WAbe WDin WFar WOld WPer WSHC WStI
– SF 149/150 ISea
minus CKni
§ ***plumbaginoides*** 🏆 Widely available
ulicinum LHop
willmottianum 🏆 Widely available
– 'Forest Blue' CKni CSte ELan LRHS MAsh SCoo SPer SPla SReu SSta WWeb

CERATOTHECA (Pedaliaceae)

triloba SWat

CERCIDIPHYLLUM † (Cercidiphyllaceae)

japonicum 🏆 Widely available
– var. ***magnificum*** 🏆 CEnd CFil CMCN MBlu MGos
– f. ***pendulum*** CBlo CEnd CFil CPMA CSte EBee ELan MBlu MBri SPer WWes
* – 'Red Fox' CMCN LRHS WFar WGer
– 'Rotfuchs' CEnd CPMA MBlu SMad SSpi
– 'Ruby' CB&S CPMA

CERCIS (Caesalpiniaceae)

canadensis CAgr CB&S CBot CMCN EMil MCCP MGos NPal SPer WNor WPat WWes
– 'Forest Pansy' ♀ CB&S CEnd CMCN COtt CPMA CSpe ELan EMil LHop LNet LPan MBlu MBri MGos SCoo SMad SPer SSta WPat WWes
chinensis CChu CLnd NPSI SPer WWoo
– f. ***alba*** ELan
– 'Avondale' CEnd CPMA LNet MBlu
¶ ***occidentalis*** SOWG
reniformis 'Texas White' CPMA
siliquastrum ♀ Widely available
– f. ***albida*** CB&S CBlo CBot CChu CDoC CLnd CTho LPan MBlu MSta SMad SPer WBod

CERCOCARPUS (Rosaceae)

breviflorus See ***C. montanus*** var. ***paucidentatus***

CERINTHE (Boraginaceae)

glabra CBos CHad CPea NRai WWye
'Kiwi Blue' NRai
major WEas WPri WSan
– 'Purpurascens' CElw CHad CMdw CMea CPea CRDP CSpe EJud EWoo LIck MCLN MEas MFir MHar NRai SHam SMad SMrm SSoC WBea WCot WPen WSan WWhi

CEROPEGIA (Asclepiadaceae)

¶ ***africana*** CPlN
¶ ***ampliata*** CPlN
barklyi CHal
lanceolata See ***C. longifolia***
linearis subsp. ***woodii*** ♀ CHal IBlr MBri SLMG SRms
§ ***longifolia*** SLMG
pubescens B&SWJ 2531 WCru
radicans CPlN SLMG
stapeliiformis ♀ SLMG

CEROXYLON (Arecaceae)

alpinum LPal
quindiuense LPal
utile LPal

CESTRUM (Solanaceae)

aurantiacum CPlN CPle ECon ERea IBlr LHil MNrw SLMG
§ ***elegans*** ♀ CBot CBrk CHal CPle IBlr LCns LHil SLMG SOWG WHar
fasciculatum CB&S CPle GQui IBlr LHil SLMG SOWG
'Newellii' ♀ CAbb CB&S CHEx CHan CPle CSev CTbh ELan ERea ERom GQui IBlr ISea LCns MBal NPSI SCog SLMG SMrm SOWG WOMN WSHC
nocturnum CB&S CPlN CPle ECon ELan ERea LBlm LHil LLew MSal SLMG
parqui ♀ CAbb CBot CChu CDec CGre CMHG CPle ECha ERea IBlr LHil LHop SDix SUsu WKif WOld WSHC
* – 'Cretian Purple' CPle
psittacinum CGre CPle SLMG
purpureum See ***C. elegans***
roseum 'Ilnacullin' CB&S CGre CPle ERea IBlr
* ***splendens*** SOWG
§ ***violaceum*** CB&S ERea LBlm LHil LLew
– pale blue LHil
¶ – 'Woodcote White' LHil

CETERACH See ASPLENIUM

CHAENACTIS (Asteraceae)

See Plant Deletions

CHAENOMELES (Rosaceae)

× ***californica*** CAgr
– 'Enchantress' CShe
cathayensis CPou EPla SSpi
– var. ***wilsonii*** CTho
§ ***japonica*** CAgr ENot GOrc GRei MBal MBar NNor SEND WDin WWeb
– f. ***alba*** CShe
– var. ***alpina*** MPla
– 'Orange Beauty' CDoC
– 'Sargentii' CB&S CBlo COtt CShe EHic NBee
lagenaria See ***C. speciosa***
maulei See ***C. japonica***
sinensis See ***Pseudocydonia sinensis***
§ ***speciosa*** CSam ISea MBal MBar NFla NNor NWea WNor
– 'Apple Blossom' See ***C. speciosa* 'Moerloosei'**
– 'Aurora' LRHS MBri
– 'Cardinalis' CGre
– 'Choshan' See ***C. × superba* 'Yaegaki'**
¶ – 'Contorta' CB&S EPfP
– 'Falconnet Charlet' CShe WGwG
– 'Geisha Girl' CB&S CBlo CChe CDoC CEnd CHar EBre ECtt ESis GAbr LHop MAsh MBri MGos MRav MUlv NPSI NTow SAga SHBN SPer SPla WPyg WWat WWeb
– 'Knap Hill Radiance' CBlo CShe
§ – 'Moerloosei' ♀ CChu CPMA CSam CShe EAst ELan MBri MPla MRav NPSI NSti SHBN SPer SPla SSta WDin WGwG WWat WWeb
– 'Nivalis' CB&S CBot CShe EAst EBre ELan ENot GRei IOrc LHop MBar MBri MGos MHlr MPla MRav NHol NSti SChu SHBN SPer SReu SSta WBod WDin WFar WGwG WPyg WWat
* – 'Port Eliot' CGre CWLN MBal WWeb
– 'Rosea Plena' CShe
– 'Rosemoor Seedling' GAri
– 'Rubra Grandiflora' CBlo CShe
– 'Simonii' CB&S CBlo CChu ENot ISea MBal MBri MGos NBee NFla NWea SEND SPer WWat
– 'Snow' CSam ISea MBal MPla MWat SEas WLRN WStI
– 'Tortuosa' CBlo CPMA EHic SMad WWat
– 'Umbilicata' ENot NHol SPer SRms
¶ × ***superba*** NNor
– 'Boule de Feu' CTri ECtt
– 'Cameo' (d) CAbP CBot CChe CDec EAst MBri SEas SLPl WLRN WWat
– 'Clementine' CBlo
– 'Coral Sea' CShe NNor

– 'Crimson and Gold' ♀	CBlo EBre ELan ENot GOrc IOrc LHop MBal MBar MBri MGos MRav MWat NBee NFla NPSI NPer SEas SHBN SPer SReu WDin WFar WGwG WHar WStI WWeb
– 'Elly Mossel'	CB&S CBlo NHol WLRN
– 'Etna'	CBlo EHic NCut
– 'Fire Dance'	CBlo EBee ECtt ENot GAul MAsh SEas SPer WLRN
– 'Hever Castle'	CBlo CShe MPla
– 'Hollandia'	CBlo CShe MGos NEgg WRHF
– 'Issai White'	LRHS MBri MUlv
– 'Jet Trail'	CB&S CBlo CDoC EAst EBee EBre EHic ELan ENot MBri MGos MRav SLPl SPla
– 'Knap Hill Scarlet' ♀	CBlo CShe EBre ECot EPfP IOrc LHop MAsh MHlr SEND SHBN SPer SPla SRms STre WBod WDin WStI WWat
– 'Lemon and Lime'	CDoC CPMA EBee ELan ENot MCCP MRav NSti SPer WWat
– 'Nicoline' ♀	CB&S CBlo CDoC EHic ENot GRei MBri MWat SBra WDin WFar WStI WWeb
– 'Ohio Red'	CWLN WBod
– 'Pink Lady' ♀	CB&S CBot CSam CShe EBre ELan ENot ESis GOrc GRei LHop MBal MBar MBri MGos MHlr MRav MWat NBee NEgg NFla NNor NSti SPer SReu SSta WFar WHar WPyg
– 'Rowallane' ♀	CBlo EBee ENot GAri MBal MRav MWat NFla SEas SHBN SPer WLRN
– 'Texas Scarlet'	MBri
§ – 'Yaegaki'	CShe
* 'Tosa Simonii'	EHic

CHAENORHINUM (Scrophulariaceae)

glareosum	CNic WCla
§ ***origanifolium***	CPBP CSpe ESis GAul LBee LRHS NWCA WCru WHil WWin
– 'Blue Dream'	CArc CMdw CSpe EBee EMan GBri LRHS MDHE NPri SAlw SCro SMrm WFar WGwG WLRN WPer

CHAEROPHYLLUM (Apiaceae)

hirsutum	CRow ELan NBrk
– 'Roseum'	CBot CBre CGle CHan CHar CLTr ECGP ECha ECoo EFol EFou EMar GCal MCLN MFir MRav MUlv NRoo NSti SBla SMrm SPer SSpi WAbb WByw WEas WFar WHal WSHC

CHAETACANTHUS (Acanthaceae)

See Plant Deletions

CHAMAEBATIARIA (Rosaceae)

See Plant Deletions

CHAMAECRISTA (Caesalpiniaceae)

See Plant Deletions

CHAMAECYPARIS † (Cupressaceae)

formosensis	CKen
funebris	See ***Cupressus funebris***
lawsoniana	EHul GAri GRei ISea MBar NWea WDin WMou
– 'Albospica' (v)	CMac EHul MBal MBar MWat SBod WFar
– 'Albospica Nana'	See ***C. lawsoniana* 'Nana Albospica'**
– 'Albovariegata'	ECho EHul EOrn LBee MBar SRms
– 'Albrechii'	ENot
– 'Allumii Aurea'	See ***C. lawsoniana* 'Alumigold'**
– 'Allumii Magnificent'	CB&S MAsh NBee WWeb
§ – 'Alumigold'	CB&S CDoC CKen CTri ENHC LCon MAsh MBal MBar MGos MWat SBod SLim SPer WDin WGwG WStI WWeb
– 'Alumii'	CChe CDoC CMac CTri EHul ENot GRei MBal MBar MGos NWea SLim SMer SPer WDin WStI WWeb
– 'Argentea'	See ***C. lawsoniana* 'Argenteovariegata'**
§ – 'Argenteovariegata'	CMac LCon SLim
I – 'Aurea Compacta'	ECho
– 'Aurea Densa' ♀	CBlo CKen CMac CTri CWLN EBar EHul EOrn GAri LCon MAsh MBar MGos SBod SSmi STre
– 'Aureovariegata'	MBal MBar
§ – 'Barabits' Globe'	MBar MWat
§ – 'Bleu Nantais'	CChe CKen CMac CTri EHul ENHC EOrn LBee LCon LLin LNet MAsh MBal MBar MGos MPla MWat NBee SBod SHBN SLim SSmi WGwG
– 'Blom'	CKen EHul LRHS MBri
– 'Blue Gem'	LBee NHol
§ – 'Blue Gown'	CBlo CTri EHul GRei LBee MBar MGos SRms WWeb
§ – 'Blue Jacket'	MBar
– 'Blue Nantais'	See ***C. lawsoniana* 'Bleu Nantais'**
– 'Blue Surprise'	CKen CWLN EBee EHoe EHul EOrn EPla LCon LLin MAsh MBal MBar MBri MOne MPla WFar WGwG
– 'Bowleri'	LCon
– 'Bregeon'	CKen
– 'Broomhill Gold'	CDoC CMac EBre EHul ENot LCon LNet MAsh MBal MBar MBri MGos MPla MWat NHol SBod SLim SPer WDin WGwG WWeb
– 'Buckland Gem'	WLRN
* – 'Burkwood's Blue'	MBar
– 'Caudata'	CKen MBar WBcn
– 'Chantry Gold'	CBlo CKen EBee EHul SLim
§ – 'Chilworth Silver' ♀	CChe CDoC CKen CMHG EBre EHul ENHC EOrn EPot LBee MBar MBri MGos MPla MWat NRoo SBod SHBN SIng SLim SPer WDin WFar WGwG WStI WWeb
– 'Chingii'	EHul
– 'Columnaris'	CB&S CDoC CMac EBre ENHC ENot EPfP GRei IHos IOrc ISea LBee MBal MBar MBri MGos MOke NBee NWea SHBN SLim WFar
– 'Columnaris Aurea'	See ***C. lawsoniana* 'Golden Spire'**

N – 'Columnaris Glauca'	CTri EBre EHul EOrn LCon LPan MAsh MGos MPla MWat SBod SPer WDin WFar WStI WWeb
I – 'Cream Crackers'	EHul
– 'Croftway'	EHul SRms
– 'Delorme'	CBlo
– 'Dik's Weeping'	SMad
– 'Drummondii'	EHul
– 'Duncanii'	EHul LCon MBal
– 'Dutch Gold'	CBlo EHul GAri MAsh
– 'Dwarf Blue'	See ***C. lawsoniana*** **'Pick's Dwarf Blue'**
– 'Eclipse'	CKen
N – 'Elegantissima'	CKen CMac
– 'Ellwoodii' ♀	CB&S CChe CMac EBre EHul ENHC ENot EPfP EPot GDra GRei LCon LLin MBal MBar MGos MPla MWat NEgg NRoo NWea SBod SLim SPer WDin WFar
– 'Ellwood's Empire'	MBri
– 'Ellwood's Gold' ♀	Widely available
– 'Ellwood's Gold Pillar'	CDoC EOrn LBee LLin MBri MGos NHol SLim SSmi WPat
§ – 'Ellwood's Nymph'	CKen EBee EOrn EPot MBar MBri NRya SHBN SLim WGor
– Ellwood's Pillar	CChe CDoC CKen CMac EBre EHul ENHC EOrn EPot LBee LCon LLin MAsh MBar MBri MGos MPla MWat NBee NHol SBod SLim SSmi WDin WFar WGwG
– 'Ellwood's Pygmy'	CMac ECho EPot MBar NHol
– 'Ellwood's Silver'	MAsh WFar WGor
– 'Ellwood's Variegata'	See ***C. lawsoniana*** **'Ellwood's White'**
§ – 'Ellwood's White' (v)	CKen CMac EHul EOrn MBal MBar MBri SHBN SSmi WFar
I – 'Emerald'	CKen MBar MBri NHol
– 'Emerald Spire'	CBlo CDoC CMac CTri MAsh
– 'Empire'	CBlo
– 'Erecta'	See ***C. lawsoniana*** **'Erecta Viridis'**
– 'Erecta Aurea'	ECho EHul LBee SBod
– 'Erecta Filiformis'	MBar MBri
§ – 'Erecta Viridis'	CB&S CDoC CMac CTri GRei LCon MBal MBar MPla MWat NEgg NWea SBod SLim WDin WFar WWeb
– 'Ericoides'	EHul SHhN
– 'Erika'	MBar
– 'Fantail'	CBlo
– 'Filiformis Compacta'	ECho EHul
– 'Fleckellwood'	EHul LBee LLin MAsh MBar MGos MPla SBod SLim SMer WGwG WLRN WStI
– 'Fletcheri' ♀	CB&S CMac EHul ENHC ENot LBee LCon MAsh MBar MGos MPla NBee NWea SBod SHBN SLim SPer WDin WFar WStI
– 'Fletcheri Aurea'	See ***C. lawsoniana*** **'Yellow Transparent'**
– 'Fletcheri Nana'	CBlo
– 'Fletcher's White'	ECho EHul MBar
– 'Forsteckensis'	CKen CMac CNic EBar EHul ENHC EOrn ESis ISea LLin MBar MGos MOne MWat NWea SLim SSmi WFar WGwG
I – 'Forsteckensis Aurea'	CBlo
– 'Fraseri'	CMac ENHC LCon MBar NWea WDin

– 'Gail's Gold'	CKen
– 'Gilt Edge'	CKen
– 'Gimbornii' ♀	CDoC CMac EBar EBre EHul ENHC EOrn LBee LCon LLin MAsh MBar MBri MPla NBee SBod SLim SRms WAbe
– 'Glauca Spek'	See ***C. lawsoniana*** **'Spek'**
– 'Globus'	See ***C. lawsoniana*** **'Barabits' Globe'**
– 'Gnome'	CChe CDoC CMac CNic EHul ENHC EOrn EPot ESis GAri LCon MBal MBar MGos MPla NHar NHol SBod SLim SPer
– 'Gold Flake'	CBlo MBar MBri MGos
– 'Gold Splash'	CKen ECho MBar
– 'Golden Guinea'	WGor
– 'Golden King'	MBar SRms
§ – 'Golden Pot'	CDoC CKen CMac CWLN EHul EOrn LBee LCon MBar MGos MOke MPla MWat NRoo SBod SMer WAbe WFar WGwG
§ – 'Golden Queen'	CKen CMHG EBee EHul
– 'Golden Showers'	CKen EHul
§ – 'Golden Spire'	LRHS MBar SBod
– 'Golden Triumph'	CBlo EHul
– 'Golden Wonder'	CDoC CMHG CMac EHul IOrc LBee LBuc LCon LNet MBal MBar MGos NWea SRms WFar WStI
– 'Goldfinger'	CDoC CKen NHol
– 'Grant's Gold'	EHul
– 'Grayswood Feather'	CDoC CKen CMac CTri EHul LBee LCon MAsh MBar MGos MPla SLim SMer WWeb
– 'Grayswood Gold'	CBlo CDoC CKen CWLN EBee EHul EOrn GAul LBee MBar MPla
– 'Grayswood Pillar' ♀	CBlo CKen CMac EHul EOrn LBee LCon MBal MBar MGos
– 'Green Globe'	CKen CNic EBre EHul EOrn EPot LBee LCon LLin MAsh MBar MBri MPla NHar NHol SBod WAbe WDin
§ – 'Green Hedger' ♀	CMac EHul ENot GRei LBuc MBar SBod SRms
§ – 'Green Pillar'	CChe CKen CTri GAri GWht IOrc LBee LPan MAsh MBal MBar MGos MWat SHBN WStI WWeb
– 'Green Spire'	See ***C. lawsoniana*** **'Green Pillar'**
– 'Green Wall'	EHul
– 'Grey Cone'	CKen LBee
– 'Hillieri'	MBar
– 'Hogger's Blue Gown'	See ***C. lawsoniana*** **'Blue Gown'**
* – 'Hogger's Gold'	CBlo EHul WGor
– 'Howarth's Gold'	GAri MBri
I – 'Imbricata Pendula'	CKen SMad
– 'Intertexta' ♀	CMHG EHul
¶ – 'Ivonne'	MGos
– 'Jackman's Green Hedger'	See ***C. lawsoniana*** **'Green Hedger'**
– 'Jackman's Variety'	See ***C. lawsoniana*** **'Green Pillar'**
– 'Kelleriis Gold'	EHul LPan
– 'Killiney Gold'	CMac
– 'Kilmacurragh' ♀	CMac ENHC ENot GRei MBal MBar MGos NWea SPer
– 'Kilworth Column'	CBlo MGos
– 'Knowefieldensis'	CMHG CMac EBee EHul LLin WWeb

§	– 'Lane' 🏆	CDoC CMHG CMac EBre EHul ENot EPfP LCon MAsh MBal MBar MGos NWea WAbe
	– 'Lanei'	See *C. lawsoniana* **'Lane'**
	– 'Lanei Aurea'	See *C. lawsoniana* **'Lane'**
	– 'Lemon Flame'	NHol
	– 'Lemon Queen'	CBlo EHul LBee LCon LRHS NBee SSte
	– 'Limelight'	CKen EHul EPot
	– 'Little Spire'	CDoC CMHG CTri EBre EOrn EPla LBee LCon LLin MBar MBri MGos MPla NHar NHol SLim WGor WGwG
	– 'Lombartsii'	CTri EHul LCon
	– 'Lutea' 🏆	CMac EHul LCon MBal MGos SBod SIng SPer
§	– 'Lutea Nana' 🏆	CBlo CKen CMac CWLN EBee EHul MBar MOne WLRN WWeb
	– 'Luteocompacta'	CKen LBee LRHS SHBN
	– 'Lycopodioides'	EHul MBar SSmi
*	– 'MacPenny's Gold'	CMac
	– 'Magnifica Aurea'	ENHC
	– 'Milford Blue Jacket'	See *C. lawsoniana* **'Blue Jacket'**
§	– 'Minima'	MBar SRms
	– 'Minima Aurea' 🏆	Widely available
I	– 'Minima Densa'	See *C. lawsoniana* **'Minima'**
	– 'Minima Glauca' 🏆	CMac EBar EBre EHul ENHC ENot EPfP EPot GRei LCon LLin MBal MBar MBri MGos MOke MPla NEgg NHol NWea SBod SHBN SLim SPer WDin
	– 'Moonlight'	CBlo MBar MGos MPla
	– 'Nana'	CMac MBar
§	– 'Nana Albospica' (v)	CKen EHul ENHC EOrn LBee LCon LLin MAsh MBal MBar MGos MPla NBee NPro SLim SPla WGwG
	– 'Nana Argentea'	CKen ECho EHul WGor
	– 'Nana Lutea'	See *C. lawsoniana* **'Lutea Nana'**
§	– 'Nana Rogersii'	EOrn MBar SRms WFar
	– 'New Silver'	CBlo
	– 'Nidiformis'	CBlo EHul LBee MBal MBar NWea SLim SRms
	– 'Nyewoods'	See *C. lawsoniana* **'Chilworth Silver'**
	– 'Nymph'	See *C. lawsoniana* **'Ellwood's Nymph'**
	– 'Pearl Nova'	CBlo
§	– 'Pelt's Blue' 🏆	CDoC CKen EHul LBee LCon LPan MGos NBee SHBN SLim SMer WLRN
	– 'Pembury Blue' 🏆	CDoC CKen CMHG CMac EBre EHul ENHC ENot EOrn EPfP LBee LCon MAsh MBar MGos MPla MWat NBee NWea SBod SHBN SLim SPer WDin WFar
	– 'Pendula'	MBar
§	– 'Pick's Dwarf Blue'	CBlo EHul MBar MBri NHol
	– Pot of Gold®	See *C. lawsoniana* **'Golden Pot'**
	– 'Pottenii'	CChe CDoC CMac EHul ENHC IOrc LBee LCon MAsh MBal MBar MGos MPla MWat NBee NWea SBod SHBN SPer WDin WFar WStI
	– 'Pygmaea Argentea' (v) 🏆	CKen CMac EBar EBre EHul ENHC EOrn EPfP EPla ESis LBee LCon LLin MAsh MBal MBar MBri MPla MWat SBod SLim SPer SPla SSmi WAbe WDin WFar WGwG
	– 'Pygmy'	CBlo CNic EBee EHul ESis GAri MBar MOne MPla SLim WLRN
	– 'Pyramidalis Lutea'	CKen
I	– 'Reid's Own Number One'	GRei
	– 'Rijnhof'	EHul GAri
	– 'Roger's Gold'	CBlo
	– 'Rogersii'	See *C. lawsoniana* **'Nana Rogersii'**
I	– 'Romana'	ENot MBri
	– 'Royal Gold'	ECho EHul EOrn
	– 'Silver Queen' (v)	CKen GRei MBal MBar NWea
	– 'Silver Threads' (v)	CKen CMac EBre EHul ENot EOrn EPla LBee LCon LLin MAsh MBar MBri MGos MPla MWat SBod SLim WStI WWeb
	– 'Silver Tip'	EHul SLim
I	– 'Slocockiana'	EHul SHBN
N	– 'Smithii'	CBlo CMHG EHul MBar NWea
	– 'Snow Flurry' (v)	EHul LBee
	– 'Snow White' (v)	CDoC EBre EHul EOrn EPla LBee LCon LLin MAsh MBar MBri MGos MPla NHol SLim SPla WGor WWeb
	– 'Somerset'	CBlo CMac LCon MBar WWeb
§	– 'Spek'	CB&S
	– 'Springtime'	CBlo EOrn MBri WGor WWeb
	– 'Stardust' 🏆	CChe CDoC CKen CMac EHul ENHC ENot GRei GWht IHos IOrc LCon MAsh MBal MBar MBri MGos MPla MWat NHol NRoo SBod SHBN SLim SPer WDin
	– 'Stewartii'	CMac CTri EBee EOHP MBal MBar MGos MPla NBee NWea SBod SHBN SMer SPer WStI
	– 'Stewartii Erecta'	CBlo ENot
	– 'Stilton Cheese'	MBar
*	– 'Summer Cream'	EHul
	– 'Summer Snow'	CB&S CChe CDoC CMHG CMac EHoe EHul ENot IOrc LBee LCon LLin MAsh MBal MBar MBri MGos MPla SBod SLim SPla WFar WGwG WStI WWeb
	– 'Sunkist'	CKen MAsh WFar
	– 'Tamariscifolia'	CDoC EHul ENHC EOrn LCon MBal MBar SBod WDin WFar WGwG WStI
	– 'Temple's White'	CKen
	– 'Tharandtensis Caesia'	EOrn LCon MBar WFar
	– 'Tilford'	EHul
	– 'Treasure' (v)	CDoC CKen CNic EBee EBre EHoe EHul EOrn LBee LCon LLin MAsh MBar MBri MGos NHol SLim WGor
	– 'Triomf van Boskoop'	EHul MBar
	– 'Van Pelt's Blue'	See *C. lawsoniana* **'Pelt's Blue'**
	– 'Versicolor' (v)	MBar
	– 'Westermannii'	CMac EHul LCon MBal SBod SLim SPer
	– 'White Spot' (v)	CDoC CKen EBre EHul ENHC LBee LCon MBal MBar MBri SLim WGwG WStI

– 'Winston Churchill'	CBlo LCon MBar MGos MPla SBod SLim SPer
– 'Wisselii' 🏆	CDoC CKen CMac CTri EHul ENHC ENot EOrn ISea LBee LCon LLin MAsh MBar NWea SBod SPer SRms WDin
– 'Wisselii Nana'	CKen EHul
– 'Wissel's Saguaro'	LRHS MBri
– 'Witzeliana'	CBlo ECho EOrn MBar MBri MGos WGer
– 'Wyevale Silver'	MBar WGor
– 'Yellow Cascade'	ECho EHul MOne
– 'Yellow Queen'	See *C. lawsoniana* **'Golden Queen'**
– 'Yellow Success'	See *C. lawsoniana* **'Golden Queen'**
§ – 'Yellow Transparent'	CMac CTri LCon MBar MGos SBod SHBN SLim SPer WGor
– 'Yvonne'	CBlo EPla LRHS MBar MBri NHol SLim SPla WWeb
leylandii	See ***x Cupressocyparis leylandii***
nootkatensis	MBar SMer WDin
– 'Aureovariegata'	EHul SIng
– 'Compacta'	CBlo CTri MBar
– 'Glauca'	ENHC MBar
– 'Gracilis'	EHul
– 'Jubilee'	SMad
– 'Lutea'	CMHG CMac CTri LCon MBal MBar NWea
– 'Nidifera'	MBar
– 'Pendula' 🏆	CDoC EBre EFol ENHC ENot EOrn IOrc LCon LLin LNet LPan MBal MBar MBri MGos NBee NWea SLim SMad SPer WDin WFar WGer
– 'Variegata'	LCon MBar SLim
obtusa 'Albospica'	ECho EHul
– 'Albovariegata'	CKen
– 'Aurea'	CDoC
I – 'Aureovariegata'	See *C. obtusa* **'Opaal'**
– 'Aurora'	CKen EOrn LCon
* – 'Autumn Gold'	MBar
– 'Bambi'	CKen EOrn MGos
– 'Bartley'	CKen EPot
– 'Bassett'	CKen
– 'Bess'	CKen
– 'Caespitosa'	CKen EPot
– 'Chabo-yadori'	CDoC CMHG CWLN EHul EOrn EPot LCon LLin MBal MBar MGos NHar NHol SBod SLim
– 'Chilworth'	CKen LCon MBar MBri
– 'Chima-anihiba'	See *C. obtusa* **'Pygmaea Densa'**
– 'Confucius'	EHul MAsh
– 'Contorta'	EOrn EPot LCon MBar MBri
– 'Coralliformis'	ECho EOrn LLin MBal MBar NHol SLim SMur
§ – 'Crippsii' 🏆	CB&S CKen CMac EHul ENot EOrn EPot LCon MBal MBar MGos NHol SBod SLim SPla WGer
– 'Crippsii Aurea'	See *C. obtusa* **'Crippsii'**
– 'Dainty Doll'	CKen EOrn
– 'Densa'	See *C. obtusa* **'Nana Densa'**
– 'Draht'	CBlo CDoC MBar
I – 'Ellie B'	CKen EOrn
– 'Ericoides'	CKen ECho EOrn
– 'Erika'	CBlo ECho MPla WBcn
– 'Fernspray Gold'	CDoC CKen CMHG CMac CTri CWLN EBee EHul ENot EOrn LCon LLin MAsh MBar MBri MPla NHar NHol SBod SLim WWeb
– 'Flabelliformis'	CKen EOrn
– 'Gimborn Beauty'	LCon
– 'Golden Fairy'	CKen EBre EOrn
– 'Golden Filament'	CKen
– 'Golden Nymph'	CKen EOrn LCon MAsh MBri
– 'Golden Sprite'	EBre EPot LCon MAsh MBri
– 'Goldilocks'	ECho EHul LCon
– 'Gracilis Aurea'	CKen
– 'Graciosa'	See *C. obtusa* **'Loenik'**
– 'Hage'	CKen EOrn EPot LCon MAsh MBri MPla
– 'Hypnoides Nana'	CKen EOrn
– 'Intermedia'	CKen EOrn EPot
– 'Juniperoides'	CKen EOrn WAbe
– 'Juniperoides Compacta'	CKen EPot WAbe
– 'Kamarachiba'	CKen
– 'Kanaamihiba'	EBre LCon MAsh MBar
– 'Konijn'	EOrn WLRN
– 'Kosteri'	CDoC CKen CMac EBre EHul ENHC EOrn EPot ESis LBee LCon LLin MBar MGos MPla NHar NHed SHBN SIng SLim
– 'Laxa'	LCon
– 'Little Markey'	CKen EOrn
§ – 'Loenik'	ENHC MBar NHol
– 'Lycopodioides'	EBre EOrn EPot
– 'Marian'	CKen
§ – 'Mariesii' (v)	CKen EBre EOrn LCon MAsh MBri SHBN
– 'Minima'	CKen EPot LCon
– 'Nana' 🏆	CKen CMHG CMac EPot GAri LBee LCon MBar MBri MGos MPla NHol SIng SLim SSmi
– 'Nana Albospica'	ECho
– 'Nana Aurea' 🏆	CDoC CMac CNic EBre EHul ENHC EPot LLin MBar MBri MWat NHol NWea SHBN SIgm SIng SMer WStI WWeb
– 'Nana Compacta'	LCon MBri
§ – 'Nana Densa'	CKen CMac
– 'Nana Gracilis' 🏆	CDoC CKen CWLN EBre EHul ENHC ENot EPfP EPot GRei ITim LBee LCon LLin LNet MBal MBar MBri MGos MWat NHar NHed NHol NWea SBod SHBN SLim SPer WDin
I – 'Nana Gracilis Aurea'	EHul SMur WFar
I – 'Nana Lutea'	CKen EBre EHul ENHC EOrn EPfP EPla EPot ESis LBee LCon LLin MAsh MBar MBri MPla NHol NRoo SBod SLim SPla SSmi WGer
– 'Nana Pyramidalis'	CBlo ECho EHul
– 'Nana Rigida'	See *C. obtusa* **'Rigid Dwarf'**
– 'Nana Variegata'	See *C. obtusa* **'Mariesii'**
§ – 'Opaal'	EPot LCon MBar WBcn
– 'Pygmaea'	CDoC EBre EHul ENHC ENot EOrn EPot ESis LCon LLin MBal MBar MPla NHar SBod SLim SPla WGwG
– 'Pygmaea Aurescens'	ENHC MBar SIng
§ – 'Pygmaea Densa'	CKen
– 'Reis Dwarf'	EPla
– 'Repens'	EOrn MOne
§ – 'Rigid Dwarf'	CKen EHul EOrn EPot LBee LCon LRHS MBar MBri WLRN

* – 'Saint Andrew'	CKen
¶ – 'Snowflake' (v)	CKen
– 'Snowkist' (v)	CKen
– 'Spiralis'	CKen EPla MBar
– 'Stoneham'	CKen LCon MBar
– 'Tempelhof'	CDoC CKen EHul EOrn EPot LCon LLin MAsh MBar MBri MGos MPla NHar NHed SBod SLim SMer SPla WWeb
– 'Tetragona Aurea' 𝕐	CB&S EHul ENHC EOrn EPot LCon MBar MGos SBod SLim WGer
– 'Tonia' (v)	CKen EHul EOrn ESis MOne WLRN WWeb
– 'Watchi'	LCon
– 'Wissel'	CKen EOrn
– 'Yellowtip' (v)	CKen EHul LCon MBar MGos
pisifera	GAri LMer WPLl
– 'Aurea Nana'	See ***C. pisifera* 'Strathmore'**
– 'Avenue'	CBlo CChe EHul LCon MPla NHol SPla WWeb
– 'Blue Tower'	CBlo
– 'Boulevard' 𝕐	CB&S CMHG CMac EBre EHul ENHC ENot EPfP EPot GDra GRei LBee LCon LLin MBal MBar MBri MGos MPla MWat NRoo NWea SBod SLim SPer SSmi WBod WDin WFar
– 'Compacta'	ECho EOrn MLan NHed WFar
– 'Compacta Variegata'	ECho EHul EOrn MBar NHed
¶ – 'Curly Tops'	CKen MGos
– 'Devon Cream'	CWLN LCon LLin MBar MPla NHol SBod WWeb
– 'Filifera'	CBlo CMac EBre MBal MBar SBod SIng SLim WBod WFar
– 'Filifera Aurea' 𝕐	CGre CKen CMHG CMac EBre EHul ENHC EOrn LCon LLin LNet MBal MBar MBri NBee NWea SBod WDin WFar
– 'Filifera Aureomarginata'	CMac EBre EPla GAri MBal MBar SLim
– 'Filifera Nana'	CDoC EBre EHul ENHC EOrn LCon MBal MBar MBri MOne MWat NHed SPer STre WDin WFar
I – 'Filifera Sungold'	See ***C. pisifera* 'Sungold'**
I – 'Filifera Variegata'	EHul LLin
* – 'Gold Cascade'	MGos
– 'Gold Cushion'	CKen
– 'Gold Dust'	See ***C. pisifera* 'Plumosa Aurea'**
– 'Gold Spangle'	CMHG EHul MBar MGos SBod WFar
* – 'Golden Dwarf'	SPla WLRN
– 'Golden Mop' 𝕐	CKen EHul LCon MAsh
– 'Hime-himuro'	CKen
– 'Hime-sawara'	CKen EOrn
– 'Nana'	CKen EBre EHul EPfP GAri IOrc LLin MAsh MBal MBar MBri MOne MWat NHed NHol SBod SMer SSmi WFar
I – 'Nana Albovariegata'	CBlo CDoC CNic LBee MBar MBri NPro SBod SSmi
– 'Nana Aurea'	See ***C. pisifera* 'Strathmore'**
§ – 'Nana Aureovariegata'	CDoC CMac EHul EPot ESis IOrc LCon MAsh MBal MBar MBri MPla MWat NHed NHol SBod SIng SPer SSmi WFar WGwG
I – 'Nana Compacta'	CMac SRms
– 'Nana Variegata'	ECho MBar
I – 'Parslorii'	CKen
– 'Pici'	CKen

– 'Plumosa'	MBal SRms
– 'Plumosa Albopicta'	ENHC MBal MBar SBod SIng
§ – 'Plumosa Aurea'	CKen EHul ENHC MAsh MBal MBar NWea WDin WFar WWeb
– 'Plumosa Aurea Compacta'	CBlo CKen CMHG CMac GAri LCon MPla NHed
I – 'Plumosa Aurea Compacta Variegata'	CMac
– 'Plumosa Aurea Nana'	CBlo CDoC ENot GAul MBal MBar MGos MPla NBee NHed WGwG
I – 'Plumosa Aurea Nana Compacta'	CMac SBod
– 'Plumosa Aurescens'	CBlo CMac
§ – 'Plumosa Compressa'	CDoC CKen CNic CWLN EHul ESis LBee LCon MBar MBri MGos NHed SIng SLim WGor
* – 'Plumosa Densa'	See ***C. pisifera* 'Plumosa Compressa'**
– 'Plumosa Flavescens'	CChe CDoC CMac CWLN EHul LLin MBar MPla MWat NHed
I – 'Plumosa Juniperoides'	CKen CWLN EBre EHul EOrn GAul ITim LCon MAsh MBar MOne MPla
– 'Plumosa Purple Dome'	See ***C. pisifera* 'Purple Dome'**
I – 'Plumosa Pygmaea'	ECho MGos MLan WGor
§ – 'Plumosa Rogersii'	CDoC EHul ENHC MBar MGos MPla SBod
§ – 'Purple Dome'	EHul MBar MGos MOne SBod WLRN
– 'Rogersii'	See ***C. pisifera* 'Plumosa Rogersii'**
– 'Silver and Gold' (v)	EHul MBar MOne
– 'Silver Lode' (v)	CKen EOrn
– 'Snow' (v)	CKen CMac EOrn EPot GAri MBal MBar MPla SBod SMer WDin
– 'Snowflake'	CKen EHul
§ – 'Squarrosa'	GAri GWht MBal MBar NWea SIng WDin WFar WGor
N – 'Squarrosa Argentea'	MBal
I – 'Squarrosa Blue Globe'	CKen
– 'Squarrosa Dumosa'	CKen EHul MBar
– 'Squarrosa Intermedia'	EHul LLin MBar MGos
I – 'Squarrosa Lombarts'	CMac EBre EHul ENHC EOrn LCon LLin MAsh MBar MPla MWat NHed NPro SBod SSmi
– 'Squarrosa Lutea'	MAsh MBar
– 'Squarrosa Sulphurea'	CMHG CMac EBre EHul EOrn EPfP EPot LBee LCon LLin MAsh MBal MBar MPla MWat NBee SBod SLim SPer WDin WFar WGwG WWeb
– 'Squarrosa Veitchii'	See ***C. pisifera* 'Squarrosa'**
§ – 'Strathmore'	CKen EHul LLin MBar NHol WGwG
§ – 'Sungold'	CDoC CKen CMHG CTri EHul ENot LBee LCon LLin MAsh MBar MBri MPla SBod SLim
– 'Tama-himuro'	CKen EPot LLin MGos SLim
– 'White Beauty'	CKen
* – 'White Brocade'	CMac
– 'White Pygmy'	EOrn EPot LCon MAsh
thyoides 'Andelyensis' 𝕐	CBlo CDoC CMac CNic CWLN EHul ENHC EOrn GAri LLin MBal MBar MPla NHol SIng WAbe
– 'Andelyensis Nana' 𝕐	CKen WPyg
– 'Aurea'	EHul MBar WBcn
– 'Conica'	CKen MAsh

– 'Ericoides' ♀	CChe CDoC CKen CMac CSam CTri CWLN EHul ENHC LBee LLin MAsh MBal MBar MWat NHed SBod SPer WDin WFar WGwG WPyg
§ – 'Glauca'	EOrn
– 'Kewensis'	See ***C. thyoides* 'Glauca'**
– 'Purple Heather'	LRHS SMur
– 'Red Star'	See ***C. thyoides* 'Rubicon'**
§ – 'Rubicon'	CDoC CKen CMac CWLN EBre EHul EOrn EPla ESis LBee LCon LLin MAsh MBar MGos MPla NHed SBod SLim SPla WFar WGer
– 'Schumaker's Blue Dwarf'	EPla WBcn
– 'Top Point'	CKen LCon SLim
– 'Variegata'	ECho EHul MBar

CHAMAECYTISUS (Papilionaceae)

§ ***albus***	ECtt ENot GQui NNor SDix SPer WDin WStI
glaber	CPle
§ ***hirsutus***	CFil CHan SBid WDav WPGP
§ ***hirsutus demissus*** ♀	EPot GDra MHar MHig WDav
proliferus	MAll
§ ***purpureus***	CAbP EBre ELan IOrc LHop MBal MBar MBri MGos MPla SHBN SPer WAbe WDin WFar WOMN WPat WWin
– f. ***albus***	EPfP MBar MPla SHBN SPer WAbe WOMN
§ – 'Atropurpureus' ♀	ENot MPla NFla NHol SPer
– 'Incarnatus'	See ***C. purpureus* 'Atropurpureus'**
pygmaeus C&W 3818	WOMN
§ ***supinus***	EBee LHop SHFr SRms

CHAMAEDAPHNE (Ericaceae)

§ ***calyculata***	CB&S CPle SPer WSHC
– 'Nana'	EHic MBal MBar MGos MPla SPer

CHAMAEDOREA (Arecaceae)

costaricana	LPal
elegans ♀	LPal MBri
erumpens ♀	NPal
metallica Cook ♀	LPal
– hort.	See ***C. microspadix***
seifrizii ♀	LPal

CHAMAELIRIUM (Melanthiaceae)

luteum	WCot WThi

CHAMAEMELUM (Asteraceae)

§ ***nobile***	CArn CSev ELau GBar GPoy LHol MBar MBri MGra NNrd NRoo SIde WApp WJek WOak WPLl WPer WSel WWye
– 'Flore Pleno'	CGle CHan CMea CSev CShe ECha ELan GMac GPoy LHol MBri MGra NBro NCat NRoo NSti SChu SIde SSvw WAbe WApp WBea WEas WFar WHal WJek WOak WOve WPer WWhi
– 'Treneague'	CArn CBre CSev CShe ELan ELau GAbr GPoy LHol LMor MBri MGra NHol NNor NRoo NSti SIde SIng WAbe WFar WHal WHer WJek WOak WPer WPri WWye

CHAMAENERION See EPILOBIUM

CHAMAEPERICLYMENUM See CORNUS

CHAMAEROPS (Arecaceae)

excelsa hort.	See ***Trachycarpus fortunei***
– Thunberg	See ***Rhapis excelsa***
humilis ♀	CAbb CBrP CFil CHEx CTbh CTrC EOas GAri IOrc LHil LPal NPal NRog SArc SDry SEND WGer
– 'Cerifera'	LPal

CHAMAESPARTIUM See GENISTA

CHAMELAUCIUM (Myrtaceae)

¶ ***uncinatum***	ECon

CHAMOMILLA See MATRICARIA

CHARA (Charophyceae)

vulgaris	SAWi

CHASMANTHE (Iridaceae)

aethiopica	CHan LHop MBel NRog
bicolor	CMon
floribunda	CFee NRog
– var. ***duckittii***	NRog

CHASMANTHIUM (Poaceae)

§ ***latifolium***	CDoC EBee ECha EFou EHoe ELan EPPr EPla ESOG ESiP ETPC GBin LHil NHar NPSI NSti SDix SMad WFar WHal WRus WWat

CHEILANTHES (Adiantaceae)

eatonii	WRic
lanosa	SIgm SRms
§ ***nivea***	WRic
tomentosa	WRic

CHEIRANTHUS See ERYSIMUM

CHELIDONIUM (Papaveraceae)

japonicum	EBre NCat SAlw WFar WPer
majus	CChr CJew CKin CRow ECWi EWFC GPoy MChe MHew MSal NHex SIde WCHb WHer WRHF WShi WWye
– 'Flore Pleno'	CArc CBre CGle CRow CWGN ECoo ELan GBar GCHN GCal MGam NBrk NBro NSti WCHb WHer WOve
– var. ***laciniatum***	EMon GBar WRha
– 'Laciniatum Flore Pleno'	CArc CGre CRow EJud EMar GCal IBlr NChi WCot WPer

CHELONE (Scrophulariaceae)

barbata	See ***Penstemon barbatus***

§ ***glabra***	CArn CHan ECha ECro EFol EFou EGol ELan ELau GCal GPoy LFis LHop MBel MHew MSal MUlv NBro NHol SChu SCro SPer WFar WMer WOld WPer WRus WWat WWye
lyonii	ETen MSCN NCut SHFr
obliqua	Widely available
– var. ***alba***	See ***C. glabra***

CHELONOPSIS (Lamiaceae)

moschata	EBee ECha

CHENOPODIUM (Chenopodiaceae)

ambrosioides	CSev
bonus-henricus	CArn CSev EJud ELau GAbr GBar GPoy ILis LHol MChe MGra NCGP SIde WApp WCHb WHer WOak WPer WSel WWye
botrys	MSal

CHEVREULIA (Asteraceae)

See Plant Deletions

CHIASTOPHYLLUM (Crassulaceae)

§ ***oppositifolium*** ♀	CGle CInt CShe ECha ELan ESis GCHN MBal MBar MBro MFir MHig NGre NRoo NWCA SAlw SHel SMer SSmi WAbe WEas WFar WHil WHoo WWin WWye
– 'Frosted Jade'	See ***C. oppositifolium* 'Jim's Pride'**
§ – 'Jim's Pride' (v)	CArc CBos CElw CRow EAst ECha EMon EPla EWes LBee LBlm LHop MHig MHlr NGre NPer SLod SMad SRms WAbe WCot WHil WRus WWin WWye
simplicifolium	See ***C. oppositifolium***

CHILIOTRICHUM (Asteraceae)

diffusum	CGre CPle ECou EHic GDra GOrc GSki IDee MAll MBlu SMad SPer

CHILOPSIS (Bignoniaceae)

linearis	MSto

CHIMAPHILA (Pyrolaceae)

¶ ***maculata***	WCot
¶ ***umbellata***	CSte

CHIMONANTHUS (Calycanthaceae)

fragrans	See ***C. praecox***
nitens	CMCN CPle
§ ***praecox***	CB&S CBot CPle EBre ELan ENot ERea IOrc LHol LHop LPan MBal MBar MBri MWat NPSI NSti NWea SDix SHBN SPer SReu SSta WBod WCoo WDin WHCG WNor WWat
– 'Grandiflorus' ♀	CEnd ENot
¶ – var. ***luteus*** Loudon	CB&S CBlo CEnd CPMA LRHS MBlu WWat WWeb
– 'Trenython'	CEnd CPMA
¶ ***yunnanensis***	EPfP

CHIMONOBAMBUSA (Poaceae - Bambusoideae)

falcata	See ***Drepanostachyum falcatum***
hookeriana hort.	See ***Himalayacalamus falconeri* 'Damarapa'**
macrophylla f. ***intermedia***	EPla SDry
§ ***marmorea***	CWLN EPla SBam SDry WJun
– 'Variegata'	EFul EPla SBam SDry WJun
§ ***microphylla***	SBam SDry
§ ***quadrangularis***	CWLN EFul EPla GAri SBam SDry WJun
– 'Svow' (v)	SDry
§ ***tumidissinoda***	EPla ISta SBam SDry

CHIOGENES See GAULTHERIA

CHIONANTHUS (Oleaceae)

retusus	CMCN EPfP WWat
virginicus	CB&S CBlo CEnd CFil CMCN CPMA ELan EPfP IOrc MBlu MPla NFla SMad SSta WDin WHCG WWat

CHIONOCHLOA (Poaceae)

conspicua	CB&S CElw CFil ETPC GAbr GAri MBal MFir NBir WLRN
– 'Rubra'	See ***C. rubra***
flavescens	GBin GSki
§ ***rubra***	CElw EBre EFol EHoe EMon EPPr EPla ETPC SHBN

CHIONODOXA † (Hyacinthaceae)

cretica	See ***C. nana***
§ ***forbesii***	CBro CMon EPot WPer WShi
– 'Alba'	EPar LAma NRog
– 'Blue Giant'	LRHS
– 'Pink Giant'	CAvo CBro CMea EBar ELan EPot ETub LAma NEgg WCra
– 'Rosea'	EPar LAma NRog
§ – Siehei Group ♀	CBro
gigantea	See ***C. luciliae* Gigantea Group**
luciliae Boissier ♀	CAvo CBro EPar EPot ETub LAma MBal MBri NMen NRog
§ – Gigantea Group	ELan EPot ETub LAma NEgg NRog
¶ – – 'Alba'	EPot
– hort.	See ***C. forbesii***
* ***mariesii***	LAma
§ ***nana***	CAvo CMon EHyt
sardensis ♀	CAvo CBro EBar EPar ETub LAma MBal NEgg NRog WCra WPer
siehei	See ***C. forbesii* Siehei Group**
tmolusi	See ***C. forbesii* 'Tmoli'**

CHIONOGRAPHIS (Liliaceae)

¶ ***japonica***	EFEx

CHIONOHEBE (Scrophulariaceae)

armstrongii	EPot ITim
densifolia	ECou EPot MHig NHed WPat
pulvinaris	CPBP ECou GCLN ITim NHar NHol NSla

× CHIONOSCILLA (Hyacinthaceae)

§ ***allenii***	CMon LAma WChr

CHIRITA (Gesneriaceae)

sinensis ♀	CHal WDib

CHIRONIA (Gentianaceae)

baccifera	CSpe

CHLIDANTHUS (Amaryllidaceae)

fragrans	NRog WChr

CHLOROPHYTUM (Anthericaceae)

comosum 'Mandaianum' (v)	CHal
– 'Variegatum' 🏆	CHal LChe MBri SRms
– 'Vittatum' (v) 🏆	SRms
* *laxum* 'Variegatum'	WCot
§ *majus*	WCot
nepalense B&SWJ 2393	WCru

CHOISYA (Rutaceae)

'Aztec Pearl' 🏆	Widely available
dumosa var. *arizonica*	SDry
ternata 🏆	Widely available
§ – Sundance = 'Lich' 🏆	Widely available
◆ – Moonsleeper	See *C. ternata* **Sundance = 'Lich'**
◆ – Sundance	See *C. ternata* **Sundance = 'Lich'**

CHONDROPETALUM (Restionaceae)

¶ *tectorum*	CTrC

CHONDROSUM (Poaceae)

gracile	See ***Bouteloua gracilis***

CHORDOSPARTIUM (Papilionaceae)

muritai	ECou MAll
stevensonii	CHEx CPle ECou EPfP MAll SBid WHer
– 'Duncan'	ECou
– 'Kiwi'	ECou
– 'Miller'	ECou

CHORISIA (Bombacaceae)
See Plant Deletions

CHORIZEMA (Papilionaceae)

cordatum 🏆	CPlN CPle MSto
diversifolium	CPlN ERea
ilicifolium	CAbb CB&S CPlN CSPN CSpe CSte CWSG ERea GQui MSto SBid

CHRYSALIDOCARPUS (Arecaceae)

lutescens 🏆	LPal MBri

CHRYSANTHEMOPSIS See RHODANTHEMUM

CHRYSANTHEMUM (Asteraceae)

alpinum	See ***Leucanthemopsis alpina***
arcticum Linnaeus	See ***Arctanthemum arcticum***
argenteum	See ***Tanacetum argenteum***
balsamita	See ***Tanacetum balsamita***
cinerariifolium	See ***Tanacetum cinerariifolium***
clusii	See ***Tanacetum corymbosum*** subsp. ***clusii***
coccineum	See ***Tanacetum coccineum***
coronarium	CArn EEls WJek
corymbosum	See ***Tanacetum corymbosum***
foeniculaceum	See ***Argyranthemum foeniculaceum* Webb**
frutescens	See ***Argyranthemum frutescens***
haradjanii	See ***Tanacetum haradjanii***
hosmariense	See ***Rhodanthemum hosmariense***
leucanthemum	See ***Leucanthemum vulgare***
macrophyllum	See ***Tanacetum macrophyllum***
mawii	See ***Rhodanthemum gayanum***
maximum hort.	See ***Leucanthemum* × *superbum***
– Ramond	See ***Leucanthemum maximum***
nankingense	See ***Dendranthema nankingense***
nipponicum	See ***Nipponanthemum nipponicum***
pacificum	See ***Ajania pacifica***
parthenium	See ***Tanacetum parthenium***
praeteritium	See ***Tanacetum praeteritum***
ptarmiciflorum	See ***Tanacetum ptarmiciflorum***
roseum	See ***Tanacetum coccineum***
rubellum	See ***Dendranthema zawadskii***
§ *segetum*	ECWi EWFC MHew NMir WHer WOak
uliginosum	See ***Leucanthemella serotina***
welwitschii	See ***C. segetum***
weyrichii	See ***Dendranthema weyrichii***
yezoense	See ***Dendranthema yezoense***

CHRYSOCOMA (Asteraceae)

ciliata JJH 9401633	NWCA
¶ *coma-aurea*	CTrC LHil

CHRYSOGONUM (Asteraceae)

australe	LCom
virginianum	CArc CHal CMea CRDP EBre ECha EFol MRav SPer WFar WPbr WRHF

CHRYSOLEPIS (Fagaceae)
See Plant Deletions

CHRYSOPOGON (Poaceae)

gryllus	EMon ETPC

CHRYSOPSIS (Asteraceae)

villosa	See ***Heterotheca villosa***

CHRYSOSPLENIUM (Saxifragaceae)

davidianum	CArc CBre CGle EBee ECha EMan EPar EPot MHar NBir SBar SMac SOkh WCot WCru WGer WWat
– SBEC 231	NHol NWoo
oppositifolium	EMNN GAri GDra GGar WCla WHer

CHRYSOTHAMNUS (Asteraceae)
See Plant Deletions

CHRYSOTHEMIS (Gesneriaceae)

pulchella 🏆	CHal

CHUNIOPHOENIX (Arecaceae)
See Plant Deletions

CHUQUIRAGA (Asteraceae)
See Plant Deletions

CHUSQUEA † (Poaceae - Bambusoideae)

¶ *argentina*	ISta
culeou 🏆	CDoC CFil CHEx EFul EOas EPla IOrc MNes SBam SDry SSta WJun WNor WPer
– 'Breviglumis'	See ***C. culeou* 'Tenuis'**
§ – 'Tenuis'	EPla SBam SDry

liebmannii	WJun
montana	ISta SBam
¶ ***nigricans***	ISta
quila	EPla ISta SBam SDry
ramosissima	SBam SDry
¶ ***valdiviensis***	ISta

CIBOTIUM (Dicksoniaceae)

See Plant Deletions

CICERBITA (Asteraceae)

§ ***alpina***	GAbr MTol NHex
¶ ***macrorhiza*** B&SWJ 2970	WCru
plumieri	MAvo WCot
– 'Blott'	WCot

CICHORIUM (Asteraceae)

intybus	CGle CHan CKin EAst EBre ECoo ECro EWFC GAbr GMaP LHol LHop MChe MGra MHew MHlr MSte NMir SIde SPer WApp WCHb WFar WGwG WHer WJek WOak WPer WWye
intybus album	CArc CGle CPou CRDP EBee ECha ECoo ECro EMan EMon LCom LHol LHop MSte NCat SApp SChu SWat WCHb
intybus roseum	CArc CGle CJew CPou CRDP EBee ECGP ECha ECoo ECot ECro ELan EMan EMon GBri LHol LHop MRav NRoo SChu SMrm SPer SWat WCHb WGwG WHow WWin
spinosum	ELan

CICUTA (Apiaceae)

See Plant Deletions

CIMICIFUGA † (Ranunculaceae)

acerina	See ***C. japonica***
§ ***americana***	GAul MSal SRms
cordifolia Pursh	See ***C. americana***
– Torrey & A Gray	See ***C. rubifolia***
dahurica	CHan CTri GAbr GCal LBuc MCli MSal SWat WCru
foetida	GPoy
§ ***japonica***	CHan CHid CRow CSte EBee EBre GAbr GCal LFis LGre WRus
racemosa 🏆	CArn CChu CRow EBre EGol ELan GAul GCal GPoy LFis LGan LHol MBal MSal NDea NHol NSti NWoo SPer WByw WFar
– var. ***cordifolia***	See ***C. rubifolia***
* – 'Purple Torch'	WEas
– 'Purpurea'	See ***C. simplex*** var. ***simplex*** **Atropurpurea Group**
ramosa	See ***C. simplex*** var. ***simplex*** **'Prichard's Giant'**
§ ***rubifolia***	CHan EBre GMaP LGre MSal WCru
simplex	CBot CFil CMea LHol MBri MHlr NPri SPer SWat WWat
– var. ***matsumurae*** 'Elstead' 🏆	CFil CHan CRow ECha EPar GCal LGre SSpi
– – 'Frau Herms'	ECha LGre
– – 'White Pearl'	CB&S CChu CDoC CHan CRow EAst EBre ECha EFou EGol ELan GMaP LFis LGre LHop MBri NCat NDea NFla NRoo NSti NTow SCro SMrm SPer SPla SSpi WCra WHoo WPbr
– 'Silver Axe'	GCal
§ – var. ***simplex***	Widely available
Atropurpurea Group	
– – 'Brunette'	SWat
§ – – 'Prichard's Giant'	CHan CSte GAri GBuc LGre MBri NHol SPla WPen
sp. B&SWJ 343	CPou

CINERARIA (Asteraceae)

maritima	See ***Senecio cineraria***

CINNAMOMUM (Lauraceae)

camphora	CB&S CChu CFil CHEx ERea GQui

CIONURA (Asclepiadaceae)

§ ***erecta***	CPlN
oreophila	CChu CPlN GCal SMur

CIRCAEA (Onagraceae)

lutetiana	CKin ECWi EWFC MHew MSal WHer WShi
– 'Caveat Emptor' (v)	EMon WCot

CIRSIUM (Asteraceae)

acaule	CKin ECro
diacantha	See ***Ptilostemon diacantha***
dissectum	CKin ECWi
eriophorum	CKin NMir
helenioides	See ***C. heterophyllum***
§ ***heterophyllum***	CKin ECro EMon WCot
* ***japonicum*** 'Pink Beauty'	WFar
– 'Rose Beauty'	ELan MBri MCLN NMir WFar
oleraceum	ECro
palustre	CKin
rivulare 'Atropurpureum'	CElw CGle CSev ELan MAvo MUlv NBir NTow SPer SSpi WByw WCHb WCot WEas WHal WMer WWye
vulgare	CKin CTiv

CISSUS (Vitaceae)

¶ ***adenopoda***	CPlN
antarctica 🏆	MBri
discolor	CHal
rhombifolia 🏆	MBri
– 'Ellen Danica' 🏆	CHal MBri
§ ***striata***	CB&S CHEx CPlN CSPN EMil SBra WCot WCru WWat

CISTUS † (Cistaceae)

x ***aguilarii***	CTri MAll SIgm SMrm WGer WOve WSHC
– 'Maculatus' 🏆	CB&S CBot CDoC CLTr CLon EBre ELan LGre MBri NFai SDry SEas SLMG SPer SPla WAbe WGer WHCG WKif WWeb WWin
albanicus	See ***C. sintenisii***
albidus	EBee NTow SDry SPan WCot WCru WHer
algarvensis	See ***Halimium ocymoides***
¶ 'Ann Baker'	SPan

'Anne Palmer'	CChu CHor CSev NBrk SAxl SIgm WAbe
atriplicifolius	See Halimium atriplicifolium
'Barnsley Pink'	See C. 'Grayswood Pink'
'Blanche'	LRHS SEND SIgm WKif
x canescens	WAbe
– 'Albus'	CB&S CMHG CShe LGre MBri NSti SIgm WAbe WHCG
'Chelsea Bonnet'	EBar EHic SBid SPan SUsu SVen WAbe WPen
§ clusii	CHar MAsh SAxl
coeris	See C. x hybridus
x corbariensis	See C. x hybridus
§ creticus subsp. incanus	LGre MNrw SIde SSte WHCG
§ – subsp. creticus	CMHG EBar EBee EGoo ELan ERav GBin LGre MAll MSte NNor SPer WAbe WGer WWin
crispus hort.	See C. x pulverulentus
§ – Linnaeus	CHan ECha GAbr LGre NNor SIgm SPan WAbe WCru WEas WGer WWeb
– 'Prostratus'	See C. crispus Linnaeus
– 'Sunset'	See C. x pulverulentus 'Sunset'
§ x cyprius 𝕐	CAlt CMHG CShe CSpe EAst ECtt ELan ENot LHop MBel MBri MGos MWat NBrk NSti SDix SEND SHBN SMad SPer SRms WBod WDin WGer WPnn WWeb
– 'Albiflorus'	WBcn
– 'Tania Compton'	SPan
§ x dansereaui	CHan CMHG CSam EBee ELan EMan ENot IOrc NSti SHBN SLMG SPer WAbe WPat WPyg WWat
– 'Decumbens' 𝕐	CB&S CLon CMHG EBar EBre ELan ESis LHol MAsh MBal MBel MBri NFai NNor SHBN SIgm SPer SPla SSoC WAbe WCru WDin WGer WHCG WPyg WRTC WWat WWeb
'Elma' 𝕐	CMHG CSpe ERav LGre MBri SAxl SDix SDry SIgm SPan WAbe WCru WHCG WWat
§ x florentinus	CLTr EBee IOrc MAll MMil NCut NNor SChu WSHC
formosus	See Halimium lasianthum
¶ 'Golden Treasure' (v)	ECle LRHS
§ 'Grayswood Pink'	CDoC CMHG ELan EPla ERav GCal MBri MSte NSti SCoo SEND SIgm SMrm SOkh SPla SRms SSoC SVen WAbe WGer WHCG
halimifolius	See Halimium halimifolium
hirsutus	EBee NWoo SDry SEND WHar
N – var. psilosepalus	EBar EEls WAbe WHer
§ x hybridus 𝕐	CChe CMHG CShe ECha ELan ENot GRei IOrc LHol LHop MGos MPla MWat NFai NNor NSti SDix SHBN SLPl SPer SSta SUsu WAbe WBod WDin WEas WHCG WOMN WWat WWin
incanus	See C. creticus subsp. incanus
§ – subsp. creticus	See C. creticus subsp. creticus
– subsp. incanus	See C. creticus subsp. incanus
ingwerseniana	See x Halimiocistus 'Ingwersenii'
ladinifer hort.	See C. x cyprius

ladinifer Linnaeus 𝕐	CB&S CSte ECha ELan IOrc MBal MLan MRav NNor NSti NTow SChu SPer SPla WCru WEas WFar WHar WSHC WWye
– var. albiflorus	CB&S SPan
– 'Pat'	CGre CSte
§ – Palhinhae Group 𝕐	See C. ladanifer var. sulcatus
– var. sulcatus	CLTr LGre MSte SDry SMac SVen WAbe WCot
lasianthus	See Halimium lasianthum
laurifolius 𝕐	CSte EBre ENot ESis LHol MBal MGos MLan NSti SLPl SPer WEas WGwG WHar WWat
x laxus 'Snow Queen'	See C. x laxus 'Snow White'
§ – 'Snow White'	CBlo CDoC CHan CKni ELan LGre LHop MBri MSte NPer NSti SAga SAxl SChu SPan SPer WKif WWeb
libanotis	CKni CSam CSte ELan NNor
'Little Gem'	MAsh MBri
x loretii hort.	See C. x dansereaui
N – Rouy & Fouc.	LGre WFar WKif
x lusitanicus Maund.	See C. x dansereaui
'Merrist Wood Cream'	See x Halimiocistus wintonensis 'Merrist Wood Cream'
monspeliensis	CHan CPle CWan GOrc MAll MAsh SAxl SDry SPer SPla SSpi SVen
¶ x nigricans	SPan
x obtusifolius	CHan CInt EBre EFol EHic ELan EPfP ESiP EWes MAll MBel MBri SLPl SMer
ocymoides	See Halimium ocymoides
¶ osbeckiifolius	SSpi
¶ 'Paladin'	WAbe
palhinhae	See C. ladanifer var. sulcatus
parviflorus hort.	See C. 'Grayswood Pink'
– Lamarck	CBot CSte ECha LGre LHol LHop MAll NSti SChu SPer WSHC
'Peggy Sammons' 𝕐	CBot CDoC CLTr CLon CSev CShe EBre ECha ELan ERav IOrc LHop MBri NBrk NSti SAxl SIgm SPer SSoC WBod WHCG WHar WPyg WSHC WWat
¶ x platysepalus	SVen
populifolius	CChe CFis CMHG ECha EHic NCat SPer SSta WAbe
– var. lasiocalyx 𝕐	See C. populifolius subsp. major
– subsp. major	CChu CPle EPfP ERav IOrc LGre SBid SMrm SVen
¶ psilosepalus	CPle WHer
§ x pulverulentus 𝕐	CHan CTri MAll SChu SCro WDin WLRN WSHC
§ – 'Sunset'	CB&S CChe EBre EFol ELan ENot GMac IOrc LHop MBri MGos MWat NBrk NSti SDix SEas SHBN SPer SPla SReu SSta SUsu WAbe WBod WDin WFar WHCG WRTC
– 'Warley Rose'	See C. 'Warley Rose'

N × ***purpureus*** ♈	CB&S CLan CMHG CSam EBre ECha ELan ENot GMac GOrc GRei IOrc LGre LHop MBri MGos MLan MPla NCat NCut NFla NHed SDix SHBN SLMG SMad SPer SReu SSoC SUsu SWas WAbe WCru WEas WFar WHCG WHar WRTC WSHC
– 'Alan Fradd'	CBlo CKni EBee EHic GMac LHol MGrG NBrk NHaw SAga SAxl SCoo SCro SEND SLod SMrm SPan SPla WCot WGwG WPen
– 'Betty Taudevin'	See ***C. × purpureus***
rosmarinifolius	See ***C. clusii***
sahucii	See ***× Halimiocistus sahucii***
salviifolius	CB&S CHan CSam EBee ERav MAll NChi SPan SSpi WHCG WLRN
– 'Avalanche'	WAbe
– × ***monspeliensis***	See ***C. × florentinus***
– 'Prostratus'	CMHG ELan LGre LRHS NPro WCru WWeb
'Silver Pink'	Widely available
§ ***sintenisii***	GCHN NSla
× ***skanbergii*** ♈	CB&S CLTr CMHG CSam ELan ENot ERav LFis LHop MGos MWat NBir NBrk NFai NSti SArc SAxl SDix SEas SHBN SPer WEas WGwG WPri WRTC WWat WWin
'Snow Fire'	CSte LRHS SLPl
'Snowflake'	See ***C.* 'Snow Fire'**
* 'Stripey'	SVen
symphytifolius	WFar WLRN
'Tania Compton'	See ***C. × cyprius* 'Tania Compton'**
'Thornfield White'	SAxl
tomentosus	See ***Helianthemum nummularium*** subsp. ***tomentosum***
× ***verguinii***	LGre LHop MBri SDix SIgm SPan
– var. ***albiflorus***	See ***C. × dansereaui* 'Portmeirion'**
villosus	See ***C. creticus***
'Warley Rose'	CLon CSam CShe EBar EGoo MBri NSti SAxl SHBN SIgm SPan WAbe
wintonensis	See ***× Halimiocistus wintonensis***

CITHAREXYLUM (Verbenaceae)

quadrangulare Jacquin	See ***C. spinosum***
§ ***spinosum***	CGre CPle

× CITROFORTUNELLA (Rutaceae)

floridana 'Eustis' (F)	ECon ERea SCit
– 'Lakeland' (F)	ERea
Lemonquat (F)	SCit
Limequat	See ***× C. floridana***
§ ***microcarpa*** (F) ♈	CGOG ERea LCns MBri SCit
§ – 'Tiger' (v/F)	CB&S ECon ERea LCns SCit
– 'Variegata'	See ***× C. microcarpa* 'Tiger'**
mitis	See ***× C. microcarpa***
Procimequat (F)	SCit
reticulata (F)	SCit
swinglei 'Tavares' (F)	ERea

× CITRONCIRUS (Rutaceae)

paradisi 'Swingle' (F)	SCit
webberi 'Benton'	SCit
– 'Carrizo'	CAgr SCit
– 'Rusk'	CAgr SCit
– 'Troyer'	CAgr

CITRONELLA (Icacinaceae)

§ ***gongonha***	CAbb CPle
mucronata	See ***C. gongonha***

CITRUS † (Rutaceae)

aurantiifolia (F)	SCit
– 'Indian Lime' × ***limon*** (F)	ERea
– 'La Valette' × ***limon*** (F)	ECon ERea
¶ ***aurantium*** (F)	SCit
– 'Aber's Narrowleaf' (F)	SCit
– 'Bigaradier Apepu'	SCit
– 'Bittersweet' (F)	SCit
– 'Bouquet de Fleurs'	ERea SCit
¶ – 'Bouquetier de Nice'	LChe
– 'Bouquetier de Nice à Fleurs Doubles'	SCit
– 'Gou-tou Cheng' (F)	SCit
– var. ***myrtifolia*** 'Chinotto' (F)	ERea SCit
– 'Sauvage' (F)	SCit
– 'Seville' (F)	CGOG ERea
– 'Smooth Flat Seville' (F)	SCit
– 'Willowleaf' (F)	SCit
bergamia	ERea
– 'Fantastico'	SCit
Calamondin	See ***× Citrofortunella microcarpa***
deliciosa	See ***C. × nobilis***
ichangensis (F)	SCit
jambhiri 'Milam'	SCit
– Red Rough Lemon (F)	SCit
– Rough Lemon (F)	SCit
– Schaub Rough Lemon (F)	SCit
japonica	See ***Fortunella japonica***
junos	CAgr
kinokuni	SCit
Kumquat	See ***Fortunella margarita***
latifolia 'Bearss' (F)	CGOG ERea
– 'Tahiti' (F)	ECon ERea LChe
* × ***latipes***	CAgr
limettoides (F)	SCit
limon (F)	LPan
– 'Eureka Variegated' (F)	CGOG SCit
– 'Fino' (F)	CGOG SCit
§ – 'Garey's Eureka' (F)	ERea LCns
– 'Imperial' (F)	ERea
– 'Lemonade' (F)	ERea SCit
– 'Lisbon' (F)	ERea
– 'Quatre Saisons'	See ***C. limon* 'Garey's Eureka'**
– × ***sinensis***	See ***C. × meyeri***
– 'Variegata' (F)	ERea
– 'Verna' (F)	CGOG SCit
– 'Villa Franca' (F)	ERea
– 'Yen Ben' (F)	SCit
× ***limonia*** 'Rangpur' (F)	ERea
macrophylla	SCit
maxima (F)	ERea SCit
medica (F)	SCit
– 'Ethrog' (F)	ECon ERea SCit
– var. ***sarcodactylis*** (F)	ERea SCit
× ***meyeri*** 'Meyer' (F)	CAgr CB&S CGOG ECon ERea GTwe LCns LHop SCit SLMG SPer
mitis	See ***× Citrofortunella microcarpa***
natsudaidai	SCit
§ × ***nobilis*** (F)	LPan

– 'Blida' (F)	ERea SCit
– 'Ellendale' (F)	SCit
– 'Murcott' (F)	ERea SCit
– Ortanique Group (F)	ECon SCit
– 'Silver Hill Owari' (F)	ERea
– Tangor Group (F)	ERea
× ***paradisi*** (F)	LPan
– 'Foster' (F)	ERea
– 'Golden Special' (F)	CTrC ERea
– 'Navel' (F)	SCit
– 'Red Blush' (F)	CGOG
– 'Star Ruby' (F)	ECon ERea SCit
– 'Wheeny' (F)	SCit
pennivesiculata (F)	SCit
'Ponderosa' (F)	ERea LChe SCit
reshni Cleopatra Mandarin (F)	SCit
reticulata 'Dancy' (F)	SCit
– 'Fina' (F)	SCit
– 'Hernandina' (F)	SCit
– (Mandarin Group) 'Clementine' (F)	ERea LCns
– – 'Comun' (F)	CGOG
– – 'De Nules' (F)	CGOG ECon SCit
– – 'Encore' (F)	ERea
– – 'Fortune' (F)	CGOG ECon SCit
– – 'Tomatera' (F)	CGOG
– 'Marisol' (F)	SCit
– 'Nour' (F)	SCit
§ – 'Nova' (F)	CGOG SCit
– × ***paradisi***	See ***C.*** × ***tangelo***
– Satsuma Group	See ***C. unshiu***
– – 'Clausellina' (F)	CGOG ECon ERea
– – 'Okitsu' (F)	CGOG SCit
– – 'Owari' (F)	CGOG SCit
– 'Suntina'	See ***C. reticulata* 'Nova'**
sinensis (F)	ERea LPan SArc
– 'Egg' (F)	ERea
– 'Embiguo' (F)	ERea
– 'Harwood Late' (F)	ERea
– 'Jaffa'	See ***C. sinensis* 'Shamouti'**
– 'Lane Late' (F)	SCit
– 'Malta Blood' (F)	ECon ERea
– 'Midknight' (F)	ERea
– 'Moro Blood' (F)	ERea LChe SCit
– 'Navelate' (F)	SCit
– 'Navelina' (F)	CGOG ECon ERea SCit
– 'Newhall' (F)	CGOG LChe SCit
– 'Parson Brown' (F)	ERea
– 'Prata' (F)	ERea
– 'Ruby' (F)	ERea
– 'Saint Michael' (F)	ERea
– 'Salustiana' (F)	CGOG SCit
– 'Sanguinelli' (F)	CGOG ERea LChe SCit
§ – 'Shamouti' (F)	ERea
– 'Succari' (F)	SCit
– 'Tarocco' (F)	SCit
– 'Thomson' (F)	ERea
– 'Valencia' (F)	ECot ERea
– 'Valencia Late' (F)	CGOG ECon ERea LChe SCit
– 'Washington' (F)	CGOG CTrC ERea GTwe SCit
tachibana	SCit
× ***tangelo*** 'Minneola' (F)	SCit
– 'Nocatee' (F)	SCit
– 'Orlando' (F)	SCit
– 'Samson' (F)	SCit
– 'Seminole' (F)	ERea
– 'Ugli' (F)	SCit
§ ***unshiu*** (F)	ERea
– 'Hashimoto' (F)	SCit
volkameriana	ERea SCit

CLADIUM (Cyperaceae)

mariscus	WChe

CLADOTHAMNUS (Ericaceae)

¶ ***pyroliflorus***	SSta

CLADOTHAMNUS See ELLIOTTIA

CLADRASTIS (Papilionaceae)

lutea ♈	CArn CB&S CChu CLnd CMCN CPle ELan LPan MBlu NPal WDin WNor WWat

CLARKIA (Onagraceae)

concinna	WOMN
* ***repens***	CSpe

CLAVINODUM (Poaceae - Bambusoideae)

§ ***oedogonatum***	EPla SDry

CLAYTONIA (Portulacaceae)

alsinoides	See ***C. sibirica***
australasica	See ***Neopaxia australasica***
caespitosa	NWCA
caroliniana	LAma NRog
§ ***megarhiza*** var. ***nivalis***	GDra MAsh NGre NTow NWCA
§ ***nevadensis***	EMar
parvifolia	See ***Naiocrene parvifolia***
§ ***perfoliata***	CArn EWFC GPoy ILis WCHb WHer WWye
§ ***sibirica***	CNic CRow CSpe ECoo EEls LGan LWak NBus NGre WFox WHen WPer WRHF WWye
– 'Alba'	WCot
virginica	LAma MBro NRog

CLEMATIS † (Ranunculaceae)

'Abundance' (Vt)	CDoC CPev CRHN CSCl CSPN EOvi ESCh ETho IOrc LHol LPri MBri MCad NBea NHol NTay SBra SChu SDix SHBN SPer SPla WSHC WTre
'Ada Sari' (L)	MCad
addisonii	CSCl EOvi MSto WOMN WTre
aethusifolia	CB&S CPlN CSCl CSPN EBee EOvi ETen ETho LPri MBri NTay SBra WCot WTre
afoliata	CPev ECou EOvi ETho MSto WCot WHil
'Akaishi'	MCad
akebioides	CHan CPlN CSCl MCad NBrk SBra SHBN SPer WFar
'Akemi' (L)	MCad
'Akeshina'	MCad
'Alabast' (Fl)	CBlo ERob ESCh MCad NTay WTre
'Alba Luxurians' (Vt) ♈	Widely available
albicoma	CSCl
'Albiflora'	CBlo CSPN MCad
I 'Albina Plena' (A/d)	ETho NBrk SPla
'Alice Fisk' (P)	CBlo CSCl EBee EOvi ESCh LPri MCad NBea NHaw SBra SHBN WGor
'Aljonushka'	CSCl ELan EOvi ESCh ETho LRHS MCad MGos NBea NBrk NTay SBra SPer SPla WSHC WTre
'Allanah' (J)	CRHN CSCl EBee ELan EOvi ESCh ETho LPri MCad MGos NBea NTay SBra SEas WTre

§ ***alpina*** ♀ (A)	CMac CPev CSCl GDra GMac GSki IOrc MBal MBar MCad NEgg NMen NPer NRoo SHBN WAbe WFar WStI WWat
– 'Burford White' (A)	CSCl EBee EOvi LPri MCad NBea NBrk
– 'Columbine' (A)	CPev EBee EOrc EOvi ETho LPri MBar MCad NBea NTay SBra SDix SPer WTre
– 'Columbine White' (A)	See ***C. alpina* 'White Columbine'**
– 'Constance' (A)	CBlo CSPN CSte EBee EOrc ESCh ETho NSti NTay SBra SRms WTre
– 'Foxy' (A)	CBlo ESCh ETho NTay
– 'Frances Rivis' ♀ (A)	Widely available
– 'Frankie' (A)	CDoC CSPN CSte EBre ECle ELan EOrc EOvi ESCh ETho NTay SBra WGor WTre
– 'Helsingborg' (A) ♀	CB&S CSCl CSPN CSte EBre ELan EOrc EOvi ESCh ETho LPri MBri MCad NBea NHol NSti NTay SBra SPla WFar WTre WWes
– 'Jacqueline du Pré' (A)	CHad CPev CSCl CSPN IHar MCad MGos NBrk SBra SPer WTre
– 'Jan Lindmark' (A)	See ***C. macropetala* 'Jan Lindmark'**
¶ – 'Odorata' (A)	ERob
§ – 'Pamela Jackman' (A)	CDoC CSCl CSPN EBre ELan EOvi ESCh IHar IOrc LFis LPri MCad MGos NBea NHol NRoo NTay SBra SDix SHFr SPer WFar WTre
– 'Pink Flamingo' (A)	CBlo CSPN EBre ELan ESCh ETho MBri NEgg NSti NTay SBra
– 'Rosy Pagoda' (A)	CSPN CSte EBee EBre ELan EOvi LPri MCad NBea NBir NRoo SSta WTre WWat
– 'Ruby' (A)	CMac CPev CSCl ELan EOrc EOvi ESCh ETho LHol LPri MBri MCad MGos NBea NEgg NHol NSti SBra SChu SDix SHBN SPer SReu SSta WTre WWat
§ – subsp. ***sibirica*** (A)	CPev EOvi MCad MSto NBea
§ – – 'White Moth' (A)	CBlo CMac CSCl CSPN EBre EHGC ELan EOvi ETho IHar LPri MBri MCad NBea NBrk NHol NRoo NTay SBra SPer SRms WSHC WTre
– 'Tage Lundell' (A)	See ***C.* 'Tage Lundell'**
§ – 'White Columbine' ♀ (A)	CBlo CRHN CSCl CSPN EBee EOvi ESCh ETho MBri MCad NBea SBra SPla
– 'Willy' (A)	CPev CSCl CSPN EBre ELan EOrc EOvi ESCh ETho IOrc LHol LPri MBar MBri MCad MGos NBea NHol NSti NTay SBod SBra SChu SDix SPer SPla WSHC WTre
¶ 'Ametistina' (A)	ERob
'André Devillers' (P)	MCad
I 'Andromeda'	ERob ESCh WTre
'Anita' (Ta)	ERob MCad SPer
'Anna' (P)	CBlo CSCl CSPN EOvi ERob MCad NTay
'Anna Louise' (P)	CSCl CSPN EBee ESCh ETho LRHS MBri MCad NTay WTre
'Annabel' (P)	ERob MCad NBea WTre
¶ 'Annamieke' (Ta)	CSCl ERob SBra SPer
* 'Anniversary'	LPri
apiifolia	CPev EOvi ERob ESCh SBra WTre
'Arabella' (D)	CHan CPev CPou CSCl CSPN EOvi ESCh ETho MBri MCad NBea NBrk SBra SPla WSHC WTre WWeb
'Arctic Queen'	CB&S CBlo CSCl CSPN EBre EHGC ESCh ETho MBri NBea WLRN WWeb WWes
aristata	CPlN ECou MCad MSto
armandii	CB&S CBot CHad CPev CSCl CSPN CShe EBre ELan EOvi ESCh ETho IOrc LHol MBri NPal NSti NTay SArc SBra SDix SHBN SPer SSoC WSHC WTre
– 'Apple Blossom'	CB&S CHan CPev CSCl CSPN EOvi GQui IHar IOrc LPri MBri MCad MGos NBea NTay SBra SHBN SPer SReu SSoC SSta WTre
– var. ***biondiana***	CMac EOvi ERob MNes SBla
– 'Bowl of Beauty'	ERob MCad
– 'Jeffries'	CSPN LRHS
– 'Meyeniana'	ERob
– 'Snowdrift'	CB&S CPev CSCl CSam EOvi ESCh LPri MCad MGos NTay SEas SPer SReu SRms WTre
x ***aromatica***	EOvi ERob ESCh ETho LFis MCad NBea SBra WTre
'Asagasumi' (L)	MCad
'Asao' (P)	CRHN CSCl CSPN CSte EBre ELan EOvi ESCh ETho LPri MCad NBea NTay SBra SPer SSoC WTre WWat WWeb
'Ascotiensis' (J) ♀	CPev CSCl CSPN EBee EBre EOvi ESCh ETho LPri MCad NBea NTay SBra SDix SPer WTre
'Ashitaka'	MCad
§ 'Aureolin' (Ta) ♀	CDoC CSte EBre MBar MBri MCad MGos NHol SBra WTre
'Aurora Borealis'	MCad
australis	MSto WAbe
'Bagatelle' (P)	MCad
'Barbara Dibley' (P)	CMac CPev CSCl CTri EOvi ESCh LPri MBri MCad NBea NTay SBod SBra SDix WBod WTre
'Barbara Jackman' (P)	CPev CSCl CSPN CSam ENot EOvi ETho LPri MBar MBri MCad MRav NBea NTay SBra SDix SPer WFar WStI WTre
barbellata (A)	EOvi ERob GDra LRHS MCad
– 'Pruinina'	See ***C.* 'Pruinina'**
'Beata' (L)	MCad
'Beauty of Richmond' (L)	CBlo EBee EOvi ESCh MCad NBea NNor SBra SDix SPer WTre
'Beauty of Worcester' (Fl/L)	CPev CSCl CSPN EBre ELan EOvi ESCh ETho LPri MAsh MBar MCad NBea NEgg NHaw NTay SBra SDix SPer WMer WTre
'Bees' Jubilee' (P) ♀	CB&S CMac CPev CSCl CSPN EBre ELan ENot EOvi ESCh ETho IHar IHos LPri MBar MBri MCad MGos NBea NRoo NTay SBra SDix SPer WBod WFar WTre

'Bella' (J)	MCad
'Belle Nantaise' (L)	CBlo CPev CSCl CSPN EBre EOvi ESCh ETho LPri MCad NBea NTay
'Belle of Woking' (Fl/P)	CPev CRHN CSCl CSPN EBre ELan EOvi ESCh ETho LPri MBar MBri MCad NBea NTay SBra SDix SHBN SPer WTre
'Benedictus' (P)	EOvi
'Bessie Watkinson'	MCad
¶ 'Betina' (A)	WTre
'Betty Corning' (VtxT)	CSCl CSPN EBre EMil EOrc EOvi ESCh ETho LFis LPri MBri MCad NBrk SBra WTre
'Betty Risdon'	NBea
§ 'Bill MacKenzie' (Ta) 🏆	CMHG CMac CPev CSCl CSam CShe EBre ELan EOvi ESCh ETho LPri MBal MBar MBri MCad MGos MWat NBea NHol NNor SBra SDix SHBN SPer SSta WSHC WTre WWat
'Black Prince'	ELan ERob ESCh WTre
§ 'Blekitny Anioł' (J/Vt)	CBlo EPfP ERob ESCh ETho LPri MCad NBrk NTay SBra WTre
◆ Blue Angel	See ***C.* 'Blekitny Anioł'**
'Blue Belle' (Vt)	CBar CPou CSCl CSPN ELan EOvi ESCh LPri MBri MCad NBea NBrk NSti NTay SBra
'Blue Bird' (A/d)	CBlo CMac CRHN CSCl EBee EOrc EOvi IOrc LPri MCad NBea NHol SBod SBra SPer WTre
'Blue Boy' (D)	See ***C.* × *eriostemon* 'Blue Boy'**
'Blue Boy' (LxP)	See ***C.* 'Elsa Späth'**
'Blue Dancer' (A)	CAbP CBlo CSCl EHGC ESCh LRHS MBal MWat NEgg NTay WWes
'Blue Gem' (L)	CBlo EOvi ERob ESCh MCad NBrk SBra WTre
'Blue Ravine' (P)	ESCh ETho NTay WTre
¶ × ***bonstedtii***	ESCh
– 'Côte d'Azur'	NCut WTre
– 'Crépuscule'	ERob NCut SRms WCot WTre
'Boskoop Beauty' (PxL)	EOvi MCad NBrk
'Bracebridge Star' (L/P)	CSCl EOvi ERob ESCh NBea SBra
brachiata	CSCl EOvi NBea SBra SDix
brachyura	ERob
'Brunette'	ERob MCad MGos SBra
buchananiana Finet & Gagnepain	See ***C. rehderiana***
'Burford Variety' (Ta)	EOrc ERob ESCh LPri MBri MCad NBea WTre
'Burma Star' (P)	CPev MCad
'C.W. Dowman' (P)	ERob SBra
'Caerulea Luxurians'	EOvi
* ***calanthe***	WCot
calycina	See ***C. cirrhosa***
campaniflora	CBot CHan CLon CNic CPev CPlN CSCl CSPN EHGC ELan EOrc EOvi ESCh ETho MBri MCad MSto NBea NBrk NSti SBra SDix WTre
– 'Lisboa'	EOrc ERob ESCh ETho NBrk
'Candy Stripe'	CSCl ERob NBrk
'Capitaine Thuilleaux'	See ***C.* 'Souvenir du Capitaine Thuilleaux'**
'Cardinal Wyszynski'	See ***C.* 'Kardynał Wyszyński'**
'Carmencita'	EOvi NBrk

'Carnaby' (L)	CB&S CSCl CSPN EBre ELan EOvi ESCh ETho LPri MBar MBri MCad MRav NBea NTay SBod SBra WTre WWeb
'Carnival Queen'	ERob WTre
'Caroline' (J)	CPev CSCl ETho MCad NBrk
× ***cartmanii*** (Fo)	ECou SBla
– 'Joe' (Fo)	CB&S CSCl EBre EHyt ESCh ETho EWes LPri MBri MCad MGos MLan NBea NHar NHol SAga SMad WAbe WTre
– 'Moonbeam' (Fo)	MGos NBrk
'Cassiopeia' (PxL)	EOvi
'Centre Attraction'	MCad
'Chalcedony' (FlxL)	CPev CSCl EOvi ESCh ETho MCad MGos NBrk WMer
'Charissima' (P)	CMac CPev CSCl EOvi ESCh ETho IHar LPri MBri MCad NBea
chiisanensis	EMar EOvi ERob MCad MSto SBra
chinensis Retz	CSPN ERob MCad
'Christian Steven' (J)	MCad WMer
chrysantha	EOvi
– var. ***paucidentata***	See ***C. hilariae***
chrysocoma B&L 12237	NBea SWas WTre
N – Franchet	CHan CPev CSCl EBar ELan EOvi ETho GMac LPri MBar MCad MRav NHol SBla SBra SDix WCru WTre WWat
– – hybrid	CSCl ERob
– hort.	See ***C. montana* var. *sericea***
§ ***cirrhosa***	CBlo CBot CPev CSCl EBre ELan EOvi ESCh GSki LPri MCad SPer WTre
– var. ***balearica*** 🏆	CB&S CBot CHan CMac CPev CSCl CSPN CSam EBre ELan ERav ESCh ETho GOrc IOrc LHol LHop LPri MBri MCad NBea NHol SBra SDix SHBN SPer SSta WTre WWat
– – forms	CPev MCad WCru
– 'Freckles' 🏆	Widely available
– 'Jingle Bells'	CBlo ERob ESCh ETho LFis WTre
– 'Wisley Cream'	CB&S CSCl CSPN EBre ECtt ELan EOrc ESCh ETho LPri MAsh MCad MHlr NBea NHol NSti NTay SBra SPer SPla WSHC WTre WWeb
coactilis	CSCl
'Colette Deville' (J)	ERob ESCh MCad NBrk SBra
columbiana	CSCl LFis MSto
– var. ***columbiana***	MSto
'Comtesse de Bouchaud' (J) 🏆	CMac CPev CSCl CSPN EBre ELan ENot EOvi ETho GRei IHos LPri MBar MBri MCad NBea NEgg NHaw NRoo SBra SDix SHBN SPer WTre
connata	CBot CPlN ERob ESCh MSto NBrk SBra WCru
'Corona' (PxL)	CBlo CPev CSPN EBee ELan EOvi LPri MBar MCad NBea NTay WTre
'Corry' (Ta)	ERob ESCh MCad NBea NBrk
'Countess of Lovelace' (P)	CB&S CMac CSCl CSPN EBre ELan EOvi ESCh ETho ICrw LPri MBar MCad MGos MHlr NBea NTay SBod SBra SDix SPer WTre
County Park Group (Fo)	ECou

'Crimson King' (L) CBlo CTri EOvi ESCh MAsh MCad SBod SBra WGor WTre
§ ***crispa*** CPlN CPou CSCl EOvi MCad MSto NBea SBra WTre
§ – 'Cylindrica' CBlo CSCl MCad MSto NBrk
I – 'Rosea' See ***C. crispa* 'Cylindrica'**
cunninghamii See ***C. parviflora***
¶ 'Cyanea' CBlo ESCh ETho NTay
x ***cylindrica*** CSCl CSPN EBee EOrc EOvi ESCh MCad NBrk SBra WTre
'Daniel Deronda' (P) ♈ CPev CSCl CSPN EBre ELan EOvi ESCh ETho LPri MBri MCad NBea NTay SBod SBra SDix SPer WGwG WTre
'Dawn' (L/P) CPev CSCl CSPN EBre EOvi ESCh ETho LPri MCad NBea NTay SBra SPer WGwG WStI WTre
'Debutante' ETho
'Denny's Double' ERob MCad NBrk
denticulata WCru
dioscoreifolia See ***C. terniflora***
'Doctor Ruppel' (P) ♈ CMac CPev CSCl CSPN EBre ELan EOvi ESCh ETho LPri MBar MBri MCad MGos NBea NNor NRoo SBod SBra SDix SHBN SPer WSHC
'Dorothy Tolver' ERob ESCh ETho
'Dorothy Walton' (J) CBlo CSCl CSPN EOvi ESCh ETho LPri MCad NBea NTay SBra
douglasii See ***C. hirsutissima***
'Duchess of Albany' (T) ♈ CHad CPev CRHN CSCl CSPN EBre ELan EOrc EOvi ESCh ETho LPri MBar MBri MCad NBea NHol NSti NTay SBra SChu SDix SHBN SPer SSoC WMer WSHC WTre WWat
'Duchess of Edinburgh' (Fl) CB&S CMac CPev CSCl CSPN EBre ELan EOvi ESCh ETho LPri MBar MBri MCad MGos NBea NTay SBra SChu SDix SHBN SPer SSoC SSta WSHC WTre WWat
'Duchess of Sutherland' (Vt/d) CPev CSCl CSPN EOvi ESCh ETho LPri MAsh MCad NBea NTay SBra SDix WSHC WTre
x ***durandii*** (D) ♈ CB&S CBot CHad CPev CRHN CSCl CSPN EBre ELan EOrc EOvi ESCh ETho LPri MBar MBri MCad NBea NHol NSti SBra SChu SDix SPer SPla WFar WSHC WTre
'Ebba' MCad
'Edith' (L) ♈ CBlo CSPN EBre EOvi ESCh ETho LPri MAsh MBri MCad NBea NBrk NTay SBra WGor WWat
'Edomurasaki' (L) CBlo CSCl CSPN EBee ESCh LPri LRHS NTay WTre
'Edouard Desfossé' (P) CBlo ESCh LRHS NTay
'Edward Prichard' EOvi ERob ESCh NBea NBrk NTay SBra SDix
'Ellenbank White' GMac
§ 'Elsa Späth' (L/P) ♈ CB&S CPev CSCl CSPN EBre ELan ENot EOvi ESCh ETho LPri MBar MBri MCad MGos MRav NBea SBra SDix SPer WMer WTre
'Elvan' (Vt) CHan CPev CSCl EOvi ESCh GMac MCad NBea NTay WSHC WTre
'Emajögi' (L) EOvi
'Emilia Plater' (Vt) ERob ETho MCad SBra
'Empress of India' (P) CBlo EBre EOvi ERob ESCh LPri MCad NBea WTre
§ x ***eriostemon*** (D) CSCl CSPN EMar EOvi ESCh LFis MCad NBrk NHaw NHol NSti SBra SChu SPer WTre
§ – 'Blue Boy' (D) EPfP ERob ESCh LFis MBri MCad NBrk NHaw SBra WTre
§ – 'Hendersonii' (D) CHan CLon CPev EAst EBre EHGC ELan EOrc EOvi ESCh ETho LHop MCad MRav MUlv NBea NBir NHol NTay SAxl SBra SCro SDix SPer SWat WGwG WOMN WSHC WTre
'Ernest Markham' (J/V) ♈ CB&S CMac CPev CSCl CSPN EBre ELan ENot EOvi ETho LPri MBar MBri MCad MGos NBea NHaw NRoo SBra SDix SHBN SPer SReu WFar WTre
'Esperanto' (J) EOvi MCad
'Etoile de Malicorne' (P) CBlo EBee EHGC EOvi ESCh ETho MBri MCad NBea SBra WGor WSHC WTre
'Etoile de Paris' (P) CBlo EHGC EOvi ERob ESCh ETho LRHS NTay SBra WTre
'Etoile Rose' (T) CHad CHan CPev CRHN CSCl CSPN EBre ELan EOrc EOvi ESCh ETho IOrc LFis LPri MCad NBea NTay SBra SChu SPer WFar WSHC WTre
'Etoile Violette' (Vt) ♈ CBar CHad CMac CSCl CSPN ELan ENot EOrc EOvi ESCh ETho LPri MBar MBri MCad MHlr NBea NSti SBod SBra SChu SDix SHBN SPer SSta WSHC WTre WWat
'Fair Rosamond' (L/P) CPev CSCl CSPN EOvi ESCh ETho LPri MBri MCad NBea NTay SBod SBra SDix WTre
'Fairy Queen' (L) CSCl EOvi ESCh ETho LPri MCad NBea SBra
fargesii See ***C. potaninii***
x ***fargesioides*** See ***C.* 'Paul Farges'**
fasciculiflora CBot CGre CMHG CPlN CSCl ETen MCad SBra SSpi WCru
– L 657 SBla
finetiana L. SDix
'Firefly' NTay
'Fireworks' (P) ♈ COtt CSPN EBee EBre EOvi ESCh ETho MBri MCad NBea NTay SBra WFoF WGor WTre WWeb
* ***fisca coreana*** CSCl
'Flamingo' (L) EOvi MCad
flammula CBot CHad CPev CPlN CRHN CSCl CSPN EBre ELan ESCh ETho LHol LHop LPri MCad NBea NSti SBra SDix SHBN SLPl SPer SSpi SSta WCru WTre WWat WWye
* ***flammula rotundiflora*** CSCl
***flammula* 'Rubra Marginata'** See ***C.* x *triternata* 'Rubromarginata'**
'Floralia' (A/d) CSCl CSPN CSte ELan EOvi ESCh LRHS MBri MCad ETho
florida ETho
– 'Bicolor' See ***C. florida* 'Sieboldii'**
– 'Flore Pleno' CPev CSCl CSPN EBre ELan EOrc EOvi ESCh ETho MCad NBea NHol NTay SBra SHBN SMad SPer SPla SSoC WTre

§ – 'Sieboldii'	CB&S CBot CPev CPlN CSCl CSPN EBre ELan EOrc ESCh ETho ICrw LPri MBri MCad NBea NHol NSti NTay SBod SBra SHBN SMad SPer SPla SSoC SSta WTre
foetida	ECou EHyt MSto
forrestii	See ***C. napaulensis***
§ ***forsteri***	CB&S CPlN CSCl CSPN CSam ESCh GSki LPri MCad NBrk SBod SBra WCru WOMN WSHC WTre WWat
– x ***indivisa***	WCru
'Four Star' (L)	LPri MCad NTay
'Fuji-musume' (L)	EOvi ERob LPri MCad WMer
fusca hort.	See ***C. japonica***
fusca Turczaninow	MCad MSto WTre
– dwarf form	MSto
§ – subsp. ***fusca***	CSCl ESCh
– var. ***kamtschatica***	See ***C. fusca*** subsp. ***fusca*** **Turczaninow**
– var. ***mandshurica***	CSCl
§ – var. ***violacea***	CSCl ESCh ETho MCad MSto NBea SBra WTre
'G. Steffner' (A)	EOvi ESCh
'Gabriëlle' (P)	ERob MCad WMer
'Général Sikorski' (L) 🏆	CMac CRHN CSCl CSPN CSam EBre ELan EOvi ESCh ETho LPri MBri MCad MGos NBea NHaw NTay SBra SDix SPer WTre WWat
gentianoides	CSPN ERob GCHN MCad
'Georg' (A/d)	EOvi
'Gillian Blades' (P) 🏆	CSCl CSPN EBre ELan EOvi ESCh ETho MBri MCad NBea NBrk NTay SBra SSoC WTre
'Gipsy Queen' (J) 🏆	CB&S CMac CPev CRHN CSCl CSPN EBre ELan ENot EOvi ESCh ETho LPri MBar MBri MCad NBea NTay SBod SBra SDix SHBN SPer WFar WTre WWat
'Gladys Picard' (P)	ERob ESCh MCad NBea
glauca hort.	See ***C. intricata***
glaucophylla	CSCl
glycinoides	MSto
'Glynderek' (L)	ERob MCad NTay WTre
¶ 'Golden Harvest' (Ta)	ERob WTre
'Golden Tiara' (Ta)	CSte ESCh ETho MAsh MCad MGos NBea SPer WCot WLRN WTre WWeb
gouriana	ERob ESCh SBra WTre
gracilifolia	ELan EOvi ERob ESCh LRHS WTre
'Grandiflora Sanguinea' Johnson (Vt)	See ***C. 'Södertälje'***
grata CC 1895	WHCr
– hort.	See ***C.*** x ***jouiniana***
– Wallich	CPev MCad NBrk WCru
'Gravetye Beauty' (T)	CHad CPev CSCl CSPN EBre ELan EOrc EOvi ESCh ETho LFis LHol LPri MBri MCad NBea NRoo SBra SDix SHBN SMad SPer SPla SReu SSta WMer WSHC WTre WWat
'Gravetye Seedling' (T)	EOvi
'Green Velvet' (Fo)	CSCl ECou
'Guernsey Cream' (P)	CBlo CSCl CSPN EBre ECle EHGC EMil ESCh ETho LPri MBri MCad NBea NTay SBra WLRN WWeb WWes
'Guiding Star'	ERob ESCh MCad NTay SBra
'H.F. Young' (L/P) 🏆	CPev CRHN CSCl CSPN EBre ELan EOvi ESCh ETho LPri MBar MBri MCad MGos NBea NTay SBod SBra SDix SHBN SPer SSta WTre WWin
'Hagley Hybrid' (J)	CMac CPev CSCl CSPN EBre ELan ENot EOvi ESCh ETho IHos LPri MBar MBri MCad MGos NBea NHaw NRoo SBod SBra SDix SPer SSta WBod WTre WWin
'Haku-ôkan' (L)	CPev CSCl CSPN EBee EBre EOvi ESCh ETho LPri MAsh MCad NBea NTay SBod SBra WTre
'Hanaguruma' (P)	ESCh MCad WMer
'Haru-no-hoshi'	EOvi
'Haruyama'	MCad
Havering Hybrids (Fo)	ECou
'Helen Cropper' (P)	ERob ETho MCad NBrk
'Helios' (Ta)	CSCl ESCh ETho IHar MBri MCad MGos NBrk SBra WCot
hendersonii Koch	See ***C.*** x ***eriostemon*** **'Hendersonii'**
– Standley	See ***C.*** x ***eriostemon***
'Henryi' 🏆	CPev CSCl CSPN EBre ELan EOvi ESCh ETho IOrc LPri MBar MBri MCad MLan NBea NTay SBra SDix SPer SPla WSHC WTre
¶ ***henryi*** var. ***morii*** B&SWJ 1668	WCru
heracleifolia	CBot CPou CSCl ESCh GCra GSki MCad NPri NRoo
N– 'Campanile'	CPev CSCl EOvi ESCh LPri MCad NBea NBir SDix
N– 'Côte d'Azur'	CBot EBre EFol EOvi ESCh MCad NBea
– var. ***davidiana***	CPev ELan EOvi ESCh NHol SRms
– – 'Wyevale' 🏆	CBot CHan CPev CSCl CSPN EBre ELan ESCh ETho IHos LHop LPri MBri MCad MUlv NBea NRoo SBra SCro SDix SPer SSoC WEas WFar WHil WTre WWye
– 'Jaggards'	CBot
¶ – 'Roundway Blue Bird'	CBot
'Herbert Johnson' (P)	CMac CPev EOvi ESCh ETho MCad SBra WTre
hexapetala	CSCl ERob
– De Candolle	See ***C. forsteri***
– hort.	See ***C. recta*** subsp. ***recta*** var. ***lasiosepala***
'Hidcote Purple' (L)	MCad
'Hikarugenji'	ERob MCad
§ ***hilariae***	CSCl EBee ERob ESCh SBra WTre
§ ***hirsutissima***	CSCl MSto NOak
– var. ***scottii***	WOMN
'Honora' (P)	ESCh MCad WTre
hookeriana	GCLN MSto WCot
'Horn of Plenty' (L/P) 🏆	CSCl CSPN EOvi ESCh ETho MBri MCad NBea NTay SBra SDix WTre
'Huldine' (Vt)	CB&S CGle CHad CPev CRHN CSCl CSPN EBre ELan EOvi ESCh ETho LHol LPri MBar MBri MCad NBea NSti SBra SChu SDix SPer SPla WSHC WTre WWat

§ 'Hybrida Sieboldii' (L)	CMac CSCl CSPN EOvi ESCh LPri MCad NBea NBrk NTay SBra SPer WTre
'Hythe Egret'	EHyt
ianthina	See ***C. fusca*** var. ***violacea*** **Turczaninow**
'Ilka' (P)	EOvi
¶ 'Imperial' (P/d)	ERob
§ ***indivisa***	CPev CSCl ECou LPri MCad WCot
– (f)	MCad
– 'Fairy' (Fo)	ECou
– var. ***lobata***	CSCl
– (m)	MCad
integrifolia	CPou CSCl EOrc ESCh LFis LGan LHop LPri MBri MBro MCad MGos MTho NHol NPer NRoo NSti SPer SSoC WCra WCru WFar WPer WTre
¶ – 'Alba'	CBot CSCl WSHC
§ – var. ***albiflora***	CHad EBee EOvi ESCh ETho LPri MBel MBri MCad NBea NBir NBrk NRoo SBra WCru WTre
– 'Amy'	ERob
* – 'Cascade'	CSCl
* – 'Finnis Form'	SChu
I – 'Hendersonii' hort.	ETho
– 'Hendersonii' Koch	See ***C.*** × ***eriostemon*** **'Hendersonii'**
– 'Lauren'	ERob
– 'Olgae'	CDoC CHad CPev CSCl CSPN EBee EOvi ESCh ETho LPri MCad NBea NBrk NTay SBra SDix
– 'Pangbourne Pink'	CHad ESCh ETho GBuc LRHS MCad NBea NBrk NHaw SBra WCot WCru WSHC WTre
– 'Pastel Blue'	CPev ERob ESCh MCad NBea
– 'Pastel Pink'	CPev ERob ESCh ETho MCad
– 'Rosea' 🏆	CBot CDoC CLon CPev CSCl CSPN EHGC EOvi ESCh ETho LGan LPri MBri MCad MTho NBea NBrk NTay SPer SSoC WCru WTre
– 'Tapestry'	CPev CSCl ERob ESCh MCad SBra WTre
– white	See ***C. integrifolia*** var. ***albiflora***
§ ***intricata***	CSCl CSPN ETen MCad MSto NSti WCot WTre WWat
'Ishobel' (P)	CSCl EOvi ERob ESCh LPri MCad NBrk WTre
ispahanica	See ***C. orientalis*** **Linnaeus**
'Ivan Olsson' (PxL)	ERob LPri
'Jackmanii' 🏆	CB&S CMac CRHN CSCl CTri EBre ENot EOvi ESCh ETho GRei IHar IHos MCad NBea NEgg NRoo NWea SBod SBra SPer SSoC WTre WWeb
'Jackmanii Alba' (J)	CPev CSCl CSPN EBre ELan EOvi ESCh ETho LPri MBar MBri MCad NBea NBrk SBra SDix SPer WTre
'Jackmanii Rubra' (J)	CPev CRHN CSCl EOvi ESCh LPri MAsh MCad NBea SBra WLRN WTre
N 'Jackmanii Superba' (J)	CMac CPev CSCl CSPN EBre ELan EOvi ETho LPri MBar MBri MCad MGos NBea SBra SDix SHBN SPer SReu SSta WBod WTre
'James Mason'	CBlo CPev CSCl CSPN ESCh ETho LRHS MCad NTay WMer
§ 'Jan Pawel II' (J)	CBlo CSCl CSPN EBee EBre ELan EOvi ESCh ETho IHar LPri MCad NBea NTay SBra SPer WTre
§ ***japonica***	CBlo CPev CSCl EOvi ETho MCad MSto NBea NBrk
'Jashio'	MCad
'Jenny Caddick'	MCad
'Jim Hollis' (Fl)	EOvi ERob ESCh MCad NTay WTre
'Joan Picton' (P)	CSCl EOvi ESCh LPri MAsh MCad NBea NTay SBra WTre
'Joanna' (Fo)	ECou
'John Gould Veitch' (Fl)	EOvi MCad
* 'John Gudmunsson'	ESCh
'John Huxtable' (J)	CDoC CPev CSCl EOvi ESCh ETho LPri MCad NBea NBrk NHaw NTay SBra SDix WGor WTre
◆ John Paul II	See ***C.*** **'Jan Pawel II'**
'John Warren' (L)	CSCl EOvi ESCh ETho LPri MCad NBea NTay SBod SBra SDix SPer WTre
'Jorma' (J)	MCad
§ × ***jouiniana***	EBee EOvi ESCh GBuc GOrc MBal MBlu MCad MUlv SPer WSHC
§ – 'Mrs Robert Brydon'	CShe ELan MCad NBea NBrk NTay SBra SPer WCot WTre
– 'Praecox' 🏆	CPev CRHN CSCl CSte EFol EFou EHal ELan EOrc EPla ESCh ETho GMac LPri MBar MBri MCad NBea NBir NHol SBra SChu SDix SPer WTre
'Jubileinyi 70'	EOvi ESCh
'Kacper' (L)	CSCl EOvi LPri MCad
§ 'Kakio' (P)	CSCl EBee ELan EOvi ESCh ETho LPri MCad NBea SBra SPer WLRN WTre
'Kaleidoscope'	MCad
§ 'Kardynał Wyszyński' (J)	CBlo CRHN CSCl EBee EBre EOvi ESCh LPri MCad MGos NBea SBra WTre
'Kasugayama' (L)	ERob MCad
'Katherine'	MCad WMer
'Kathleen Dunford' (Fl)	CBlo CSCl CSte EOvi ESCh LPri MAsh MCad NBea NTay SBra WMer WTre
'Kathleen Wheeler' (P)	CBlo CMac CPev EBre EOvi ESCh ETho LPri MCad NBea NTay SBra SDix WTre
'Keith Richardson' (P)	CPev CSCl EOvi LPri MCad NBea NBrk SBra WTre
'Ken Donson' (L) 🏆	CBlo CMac EBee EHGC EOvi ESCh ETho MCad NBrk NTay SBod SBra
'Kermesina' (Vt)	CHad CMac CPev CRHN CSam EBre ELan EOvi ESCh ETho IHar LHol LPri MBri MCad MRav NBea NHol NSti NTay SBra SDix SPer SSta WSHC WTre WWat
'King Edward VII' (L)	CSPN EOvi ESCh ETho LPri NBea NBrk SBra WGor
'King George V' (L)	EOvi ERob ESCh NBrk NTay SBra
'Kiri Te Kanawa'	CPev CSCl ESCh ETho MCad NBrk
kirilovii	CSCl ERob GSki
'Königskind' (P)	ERob ESCh MCad

koreana	CSCl EOvi MCad MSto NBea SBra
* ***koreana citra***	ESCh
koreana var. ***fragrans***	CSCl EOvi
– f. ***lutea***	CSCl EOvi MCad MSto
'Kosmiczeskaja Melodija' (J)	MCad
ladakhiana	CHan CPev CSCl EBee EOvi ESCh ETho MCad MSto NBea NBir NTay SBra WCru
'Lady Betty Balfour' (J/Vt)	CMac CPev CSCl CSPN EBar EBre ELan EOvi ESCh LPri MBri MCad NBea NHaw NTay SBra SDix WFar WGwG WStI WTre
'Lady Caroline Nevill' (L)	CPev CSCl EOvi ESCh ETho LPri MCad NBea NTay SBra WTre
'Lady in Red'	LPri
'Lady Londesborough' (P)	CPev CSCl CSPN ELan EOvi ESCh ETho LPri MCad NBea NBrk NTay SBra SDix WLRN WTre
'Lady Northcliffe' (L)	CMac CPev CSCl CTri ELan EOvi EPfP ESCh LPri MAsh MCad NBea NTay SBra SDix SPer WTre
'Ladybird Johnson' (T)	CPev CSCl EOvi ERob ESCh MCad NBrk
lanuginosa 'Candida'	MCad
lasiandra	ERob WTre
lasiantha	ESCh MSto
'Lasurstern' (P) 🏆	CB&S CMac CPev CSCl CSPN EBre ELan ENot EOvi ESCh ETho LPri MBar MBri MCad MLan NBea NHaw SBod SBra SDix SPer SSoC WFar WSHC WTre
'Laura' (L)	MCad
'Laura Denny' (P)	CSCl EOvi MCad NBrk
'Lavender Lace'	EBre MCad WTre
'Lawsoniana' (L)	CMac CSCl CSPN CWLN ESCh ETho LPri MAsh MBar MCad NBea NBrk NTay SBra WStI WTre
'Lemon Chiffon' (P)	CSCl ERob MCad NBrk SBra
'Liberation'	EBee ERob ESCh ETho LRHS NTay WTre
§ ***ligusticifolia***	CSCl EBee ERob MSto
'Lilacina Floribunda' (L)	CSCl CSPN ELan EOvi ESCh LPri MBar MCad NBea NBrk NTay SBra WSHC WTre
'Lilactime'	CBlo ERob ESCh LPri NBea
'Lincoln Star' (P)	CPev CSCl CSPN CSam EBre ELan EOvi ESCh ETho LPri MBar MCad MRav NBea NBrk NTay SBra SDix SPer WTre
'Lincolnshire Lady'	WPen
'Little Joe'	EHyt
'Little Nell' (Vt)	CHad CPev CRHN CSCl CSPN EBre ELan EOvi ESCh ETho LHol LPri MBri MCad MHlr NBea NBrk NHol NSti NTay SBod SBra SDix SPer SReu SSta WFar WSHC WTre
'Lord Nevill' (P) 🏆	CPev CRHN CSCl EBre EOvi ESCh IHar LPri MBri MCad NTay SBod SBra SDix WStI WTre
'Louise Rowe' (Fl)	CSCl EBee EBre EHGC ELan EOvi ESCh ETho IHar LPri MCad NBea NTay SBra WTre
'Lucie' (P)	ESCh MCad
'Lunar Lass' (Fo)	ECho EHyt EPot ETho LBee MCad WAbe
'Lunar Lass' × ***foetida***	EBee ECou GCHN
'Luther Burbank' (J)	EOvi ERob ESCh MCad
macropetala (A/d)	CB&S CPev CSCl CShe ELan ENot EOrc EOvi ESCh GDra LHol LPri MBal MBar MCad MGos MWat NBea NEgg NHol SBod SDix WBod WTre WWat WWin
– 'Alborosea' (A/d)	EOvi
– 'Anders' (A/d)	EOvi
– 'Ballerina' (A/d)	MCad
– 'Ballet Skirt' (A/d)	EHGC EOvi ERob ESCh MCad MGos
– 'Blue Lagoon' (A/d)	See ***C. macropetala* 'Lagoon'**
– forms (A/d)	CPev
– 'Harry Smith' (A/d)	CBlo ERob ESCh NBrk NTay
§ – 'Jan Lindmark' (A/d)	CSPN EBee EBre EHGC EOvi ESCh ETho MCad MGos NBea NBir NTay SBra SPla WFar WGor WTre
§ – 'Lagoon' (A/d)	CSte ETho LRHS NBrk SBra SMur WTre
– 'Maidwell Hall' hort. (A/d) 🏆	CDoC CMac CSCl EBre ECha EOvi ESCh ETho LFis LPri MBri MCad MGos NBea NBrk NHol NRoo SBra SChu SHBN SPer SPla WSHC WStI WTre
– 'Markham's Pink' (A/d) 🏆	CBot CMac CPev CSCl CSPN CSam EBre ELan EOrc EOvi ESCh ETho LHol LPri MBar MBri MCad NBea NHol NSti SBra SDix SHBN SPer SReu SSta WSHC WTre
– 'Pauline' (A/d)	EHGC ERob SBra
– 'Rosea' (A/d)	EOvi
– 'Salmonea' (A/d)	ECle EOvi ESCh
– 'Snowbird' (A/d)	CBlo CPev EOvi ETho NBea NHol SBra SPla WTre
– 'Vicky' (A/d)	CSCl
– 'Westleton' (A/d)	ERob ETho NHol WTre
¶ – 'White Lady' (A/d)	ERob
– 'White Moth'	See ***C. alpina*** **subsp.** ***sibirica*** **'White Moth'**
– 'White Swan'	See **C. 'White Swan'**
'Madame Baron Veillard' (J)	CPev CSCl CSPN EBre EOvi ESCh ETho IHar LPri MBar MCad MHlr NBea NBrk NTay SBra SDix WTre
'Madame Edouard André' (J) 🏆	CDoC CMac CPev CSCl CTri EOvi ESCh ETho LPri MCad NBea NTay SBra SDix WTre
'Madame Grangé' (J) 🏆	CPev CSPN EOvi ESCh ETho LPri MCad NBea NBrk NHaw NTay SBod SBra SDix WTre
'Madame Julia Correvon' (Vt) 🏆	CBar CHad CMac CSPN EBre ELan EOrc EOvi ETho IHar LPri MBar MBri MCad MGos NBea NBir NHaw NSti NTay SBra SDix SPer SSta WSHC WTre WWat
'Madame le Coultre'	See **C. 'Marie Boisselot'**
'Madame van Houtte' (L)	MCad
¶ 'Majojo' (Fo)	CB&S
¶ 'Mammut' (P)	ERob
§ ***mandschurica***	CSCl ERob MCad MSto
marata	GCLN MSto
– 'Temple Prince' (m)	ECou
– 'Temple Queen' (f)	ECou

'Marcel Moser' (P)	CPev EOvi ESCh MCad NBrk SBra SDix WFar WTre
'Margaret Hunt' (J)	CBlo CSCl CSPN EBee ELan EOvi ESCh ETho LPri MCad NBea NBrk NTay SBra SPla WTre
'Margaret Wood' (P)	ERob ESCh MCad
'Margot Koster' (Vt)	CBlo CDoC CRHN CSCl EBre EOvi ESCh LPri MBri MCad NBea NHaw NTay SBra WSHC WTre
§ 'Marie Boisselot' (L) 🏆	CB&S CGle CMac CPev CRHN CSCl CSPN CSam ELan ENot EOvi ETho LPri MBar MBri MCad MGos NBea NHaw NSti SBod SBra SChu SDix SHBN SPer WSHC WTre WWat
'Marie Louise Jensen' (J)	EOvi ESCh MCad NTay
marmoraria 🏆	CSCl ECou EPot MCad NHar NSla SBla WAbe WCot WFar WHil
– hybrid	LBee LRHS NHar WAbe
– x ***cartmanii*** 'Joe'	NHar
– x ***petriei*** (f)	CSCl
§ 'Maskarad' (Vt)	CBlo CSPN EBre EHGC ERob ESCh ETho LRHS NBrk SBra WLRN WTre
◆ Masquerade (Vt)	See ***C.* 'Maskarad'**
§ 'Matka Teresa'	MCad
'Matthais' (PxL)	EOvi
'Maureen' (L)	CPev CSCl CSPN EBee EOvi ESCh ETho LPri MCad NBea SBra SDix WTre
maximowicziana	See ***C. terniflora***
'Meeli' (J)	MCad
microphylla	ECou MCad MSto
¶ 'Miikla' (J)	ERob
'Minister' (P)	EOvi MCad
'Minuet' (Vt) 🏆	CHad CRHN CSCl CSPN EBre ELan EOvi ESCh ETho IOrc LPri MBri MCad NBea NHol NRoo NTay SBra SChu SDix SEas SPer WSHC WTre
'Miriam Markham' (J)	CBlo CPev ERob MCad NBea WTre
'Miss Bateman' (P) 🏆	CMac CPev CSCl CSPN EBre ELan EOvi ESCh ETho LPri MBar MBri MCad MPla NBea NRoo SBod SBra SDix SPer WSHC WTre
'Miss Crawshay' (P)	CBlo CPev CSCl EBee EOvi ESCh MCad NBea NTay SBra WTre
N ***montana***	CB&S CPev CSam CShe CTrw ENot EOvi ESCh GRei IHos LPri MBal MBar MCad MGos MWat NBea NEgg NRoo SBod SBra SDix SHBN SSta WTre
montana alba	See ***C. montana***
montana 'Alexander'	CBlo CDoC CPou CSCl CSPN EHGC EOvi ESCh LPri MCad MGos NTay SBra WCru WTre
* – 'Boughton Beauty'	NBrk WTre WWeb
– 'Broughton Star' (d)	CBlo CHad CPou CRHN CSCl CSPN EOvi ESCh ETho LFis LPri MBri MCad MGos NBea SBra WCot WTre
– 'Continuity'	EOvi MCad NBea SBra WSHC
– 'Elizabeth' 🏆	Widely available
– 'Fragrant Spring'	ERob ESCh MCad MGos NBea SBra
– 'Freda' 🏆	CRHN CSCl EBre EOvi ESCh ETho IHar LPri MBri MCad MGos NBea NHol NRoo NSti SBra SDix SHBN SMad SPer SPla WCru WTre
– 'Gothenburg'	CBlo ETho NBea SBra WWes
– f. ***grandiflora*** 🏆	CHad CMac EBre ECtt ELan EOvi ESCh ETho GMac GOrc ISea LBuc LPri MBri MCad MGos NBea NTay SBra SPer SReu WSHC WTre WWat WWeb
* – 'Lilacina'	CBlo WTre
– 'Marjorie' (d)	CB&S CDoC CSCl CSPN EBre ECtt ELan EOvi ESCh ETho GMac IHar LHol LPri MBal MBri MCad MRav NBea NHol NRoo NSti NTay SBra SChu SHBN SPer SPla WSHC WTre
– 'Mayleen'	CBlo CHad CPou CSCl CSte EBee EBre EHGC EOvi ESCh ETho LPri MBri MCad MGos NBea NTay SBra SHBN SPer SPla WPen WTre WWeb
– 'Mrs Margaret Jones' (d)	EOvi ERob ESCh ETho NBrk SBra WTre
– 'New Dawn'	ERob ESCh MCad NBea SBra
– 'Odorata'	CBlo CDoC CSCl ELan EOvi ETho GSki MCad MGos NTay SBra SPla WGor WWat
* – 'Olga'	ESCh
– 'Peveril'	CPev CSCl ERob ETho IHar MCad NBea NBrk SBra
– 'Picton's Variety'	CDoC CPev CSCl EBre EOrc EOvi ETho LPri MCad NBea NHol SBra SHBN SPer WTre
– 'Pink Perfection'	CDoC CSCl EBre ELan EOvi ESCh ETho GOrc LPri MCad NBea NBrk NHaw NHol NTay SBra SPer WTre WWeb
– 'Pleniflora'	MCad MGos SBra
– var. ***rubens*** 🏆	CMac CSCl CTrw EBre ELan ENot EOvi ESCh ETho GRei IHos ISea LPri MBal MBar MBri MCad NBea NHaw NHol NNor NWea SBod SBra SDix SPer SReu WBod WTre
¶ – – 'Rubens Odorata'	ESCh WTre
– 'Rubens Superba'	See ***C. montana* 'Superba'**
§ – var. ***sericea*** 🏆	CBot CHan CPev CSte CTri EOvi ESCh GMac LPri MCad NBea NBrk SBra SRms WCru WFoF WTre WWat WWeb
– 'Snow'	EOvi
– 'Spooneri'	See ***C. montana* var. *sericea***
§ – 'Superba'	CBlo EBee ECtt SHBN
– 'Tetrarose' 🏆	Widely available
– 'Veitch's Form'	CBot
– 'Vera'	CSPN EBee EHGC EOvi ESCh ETho MCad NBea NBir NBrk NTay SBra WCru
– 'Warwickshire Rose'	CHan ETho GMac MCad MGos NBea NBrk NHol SBra WCot WTre WWeb
– var. ***wilsonii***	CBot CLan CPev CSCl CSPN CSam CSte EBre ELan EOvi ESCh ETho LHol LPri MBar MCad MRav MWat NBea NTay SBra SDix SPer WSHC WTre
'Monte Cassino' (J)	CSCl ERob ESCh MCad NBrk WTre

§ 'Moonlight' (P)	CPev CSCl EBee EOvi ESCh ETho MCad NBea NBrk SBra SPer WTre
'Moonman' (Fo)	EHyt ETho
* 'Morning Cloud'	MCad
'Mother Theresa'	See **C. 'Matka Teresa'**
'Mrs Bush' (L)	CBlo EOvi ESCh LRHS MCad NBea NTay WTre WWes
'Mrs Cholmondeley' (L) 🏆	CMac CPev CSCl CSPN CSam EBre ELan ENot EOvi ESCh ETho LPri MBar MBri MCad MGos NBea NRoo SBra SDix SPer WFar WSHC WTre
'Mrs George Jackman' (P) 🏆	CPev EOvi ESCh ETho LPri MCad NBea NBrk SBra SDix WTre
'Mrs Hope' (L)	CPev EOvi ESCh MAsh MCad NBea NBrk SBra SDix
'Mrs James Mason'	CPev CSCl EOvi ESCh ETho MCad NBea SBra WTre
'Mrs N. Thompson' (P)	CMac CPev CSCl CSPN EBre ELan EOvi ESCh ETho IHar LPri MBar MBri MCad NBea NHaw NTay SBod SBra SDix SHBN SPla SSoC SSta WStI WTre
'Mrs P.B. Truax' (P)	CBlo CSCl CSPN EBee EOvi ESCh LPri MCad NBea NRoo NTay SBra SDix WLRN WTre
'Mrs Robert Brydon'	See **C. × *jouiniana* 'Mrs Robert Brydon'**
'Mrs Spencer Castle' (Vt)	CPev CSCl EBee EOvi ESCh LPri MAsh MCad NBea WTre
'Mrs T. Lundell'	EOvi ESCh ETho MCad NBrk
'Mukle'	MCad
'Multi Blue'	CB&S CSCl CSPN CTri EBre ELan EOvi ESCh ETho IHar LPri MCad MGos NBea SBra SMad SSoC WTre
'Muly'	MCad
'Musa China' (L)	MCad
'Myôjô' (P)	CSCl CSPN EOvi ESCh ETho LPri MCad NTay WMer WTre
'Myôkô' (L)	CBlo MCad WMer
§ ***napaulensis***	CB&S CPev CPlN CSCl EOvi EPot ESCh IBlr LPri MCad MSto NBea SBra SHFr WCru WLRN
'Natacha' (P)	ERob ESCh MCad
'Negritjanka' (J)	EOvi ERob WTre
'Nelly Moser' (L/P) 🏆	CB&S CMac CPev CSCl CSPN EBre ELan ENot EOvi ETho GRei IHos LPri MBal MBar MBri MCad MGos NBea NEgg NRoo SBra SDix SHBN SPer SSta WBod WTre WWin
New Zealand Hybrids	ECou
'Nikolai Rubtsov'	EOvi ERob MCad
'Niobe' (J) 🏆	CHad CMac CPev CSCl CSPN EBre ELan ENot EOvi ESCh ETho LPri MBar MBri MCad MGos NBea NHol NRoo NSti NTay SBra SChu SDix SPer WBod WFar WSHC WTre
'North Star'	See **C. 'Pôhjanael'**
'Nuit de Chine'	MCad
obscura	CSCl
occidentalis	MSto
¶ – var. ***dissecta***	ERob SSpi
– subsp. ***occidentalis***	CSCl
ochotensis	MSto
ochroleuca	MSto
'Olimpiada-80' (L)	ESCh SPla WTre
* 'Opaline'	MCad
orientalis 'Bill MacKenzie'	See **C. 'Bill MacKenzie'**
– hort.	See **C. *tibetana*** subsp. ***vernayi***
– 'Orange Peel'	See **C. *tibetana*** subsp. ***vernayi* 'Orange Peel'**
– 'Sherriffii'	See **C. *tibetana*** subsp. ***vernayi* LS&E 13342**
§ – Linnaeus	EBee ELan ESCh GSki MCad MSto NHol SBod SBra SReu WTre
– – var. ***daurica***	CHan
¶ – – var. ***orientalis***	ETho
* – 'Rubromarginata'	CPev
– var. ***tenuifolia***	ERob ESCh
'Otto Froebel' (L)	ETho MCad NTay
'Paddington'	ETho
'Pagoda' (P×Vt)	CDoC CPev CRHN CSCl CSPN EOvi ESCh ETho ICrw LFis MCad NBea SBra SPer SPla SRms WSHC WTre WWat
'Pamela Jackman'	See **C. *alpina* 'Pamela Jackman'**
paniculata Gmelin	See **C. *indivisa***
– Thunberg	See **C. *terniflora***
* 'Paola'	MCad
'Parasol'	ERob WTre
§ ***parviflora***	MSto
– × ***forsteri***	ESCh
* 'Pastel Princess'	MCad
patens	CBlo CSPN EOvi NBrk SBra
– Chinese form	ERob ESCh
– Japanese form	ERob ESCh
§ 'Paul Farges'	CSPN EHGC ERob ETho LFis MCad NBrk SBra WTre
'Pennell's Purity' (L)	MCad
'Percy Picton' (P)	MAsh WTre
'Perle d'Azur' (J) 🏆	CB&S CHad CMac CPev CSCl CSPN CSam EBre ELan EOrc EOvi ESCh ETho LPri MBri MCad NBea NHaw NRoo SBra SChu SDix SHBN SPer SSta WFar WSHC WTre
'Perrin's Pride' (Vt)	CSCl CSPN EHGC ERob ESCh ETho LRHS MCad NBrk NTay WFar WMer WTre
'Petit Faucon'	CBlo CSCl EBre EOrc ETho LRHS MBri WTre
petriei	ECou EHyt EOvi EPot ESCh WTre
– × ***foetida***	ECou
– × ***forsteri***	ECou
– 'Limelight' (m)	CSCl ECou
– × ***marmoraria***	GCHN
– × ***parviflora***	ECou
– 'Princess' (f)	CSCl ECou
'Peveril Pearl' (P)	CBlo CPev CSCl CSPN EBee EHGC ERob ESCh ETho LPri MCad NBrk NTay
¶ ***phlebantha***	CPlN
pierotii	ERob
'Pink Champagne'	See **C. 'Kakio'**
'Pink Fantasy' (J)	CMac CPev CSCl CSPN CTri EBee EBre EOvi ESCh ETho IHar LPri MAsh MBar MCad NBea NBrk NTay SBra WTre
'Pink Pearl'	EOvi MCad NBea NBrk
§ ***pitcheri***	CHan CPev CPlN CSCl ELan EOrc EOvi ESCh MBri MCad MSto NBea NBrk NSti NTay SSpi WSHC WTre
* – 'Phil Mason'	CSCl

* 'Pixie'	MGos
§ 'Pôhjanael' (J)	ERob MCad WTre
'Polish Spirit' (Vt) 🏆	CBar CDoC CRHN CSCl CSPN CTri EBre ELan EOrc EOvi ESCh ETho LHol MBri MCad NBea NHaw NHol NSti NTay SBra SPer SSta WFar WGor WTre
§ ***potaninii***	CSCl EBee ELan EOvi MBri MCad NBea SBra
§ – var. ***potaninii***	CGle CHan CPev EHyt ETen MBri MCad NBea SBra SDix
– var. ***souliei***	See ***C. potaninii*** var. ***potaninii***
'Prince Charles' (J)	CHad CPou CSCl EBee EBre EHGC ELan EOvi ESCh ETho LPri MCad NBea NBir NHaw NRoo NTay SBra SDix SPla WSHC WTre
¶ 'Prince Philip' (P)	ERob ESCh
§ 'Princess Diana' (T)	CBlo CPev ERob ESCh ETho
'Princess of Wales' (L)	CHan CSCl EOvi ESCh LPri MCad NBea SBra WSHC
'Prins Hendrik' (L/P)	CBlo CMac CSCl EHGC EOvi ESCh MCad WGor
'Proteus' (Fl)	CPev CRHN CSCl CSPN EBre ELan EOvi ESCh ETho IHar LPri MCad NBea NTay SBra SDix SPer SPla WTre
quadribracteolata	ECou EHyt EOvi
'Queen Alexandra'	ERob MCad
'Ramona'	See ***C.* 'Hybrida Sieboldii'**
ranunculoides KGB 111	MSto
recta	CFee CHad CHan CPev CSPN ELan EOvi LHol LPri MBri MBro MCad NBea NOak NRoo NWCA SPer WByw WHil WHoo WPer WPyg WTre WWye
– 'Grandiflora'	CSCl EBre NHol
– 'Peveril'	CPev ERob NBrk
– 'Purpurea'	Widely available
§ – subsp. ***recta*** var. ***lasiosepala***	WWat
* – 'Velvet Night'	MMil WTre
'Red Cooler'	MCad
§ ***rehderiana*** 🏆	CBot CGre CHad CPev CPlN CSCl CSPN CSam EBre ELan EOvi ESCh ETho LPri MBri MCad NBea NHol NTay SBra SChu SDix SHBN SPer SSpi WAbe WSHC WTre WWat
'Rhapsody'	CPev ERob IHar MCad NBrk WSHC WTre
'Richard Pennell' (P) 🏆	CMac CPev CSCl CSPN EBee EOvi ESCh ETho LPri MBri MCad NBea NBrk SBra SDix WTre
'Romantika' (J)	SBra SPer SPla
'Rose Supreme'	MCad
'Rosie O'Grady' (A)	CSPN EBre ELan EOrc EOvi ESCh ETho IHar LPri MBar MBri MCad MGos NBea NHol NSti SBra SPer WTre
* 'Rosugyana'	MCad
'Rouge Cardinal' (J)	CMac CPev CRHN CSCl CSPN EBre ELan EOvi ESCh ETho LPri MBar MBri MCad NBea SBod SBra SDix SHBN SPer SReu SSta WBod WTre
'Royal Velours' (Vt) 🏆	CDoC CHad CHan CPev CRHN CSCl CSPN EBre ELan EOvi ESCh ETho IOrc LFis LPri MCad NBea NHaw NHol SBod SBra SChu SDix SHBN SPer WFar WTre WWat
'Royal Velvet'	CB&S CSCl CSPN EHGC ESCh ETho MBri MCad NTay WTre WWeb
'Royalty' (LxP) 🏆	CB&S CSCl CSPN EBre ELan EOvi ESCh ETho LPri MBri MCad NBea NBir NTay SBra SDix WBod WTre
'Ruby Anniversary'	MCad
'Ruby Glow' (L)	CBlo CSPN EHGC EOvi ERob ESCh MCad NTay SBra WLRN
'Ruby Lady'	LPri
'Rüütel' (J)	MCad
'Sally Cadge' (P)	MCad
'Samantha Denny'	NBea WTre
'Saruga'	MCad
'Satsukibare'	ERob MCad
'Saturn' (Vt)	EBee ERob ESCh MCad NBea SBra SPla
'Scartho Gem' (P)	CMac CPev CSCl EBee EHGC EOvi ESCh MCad NBea NTay SBra
'Schneeglanz' (P)	MCad
'Sealand Gem' (L)	CBlo CPev CSCl CSPN EBee EOvi ESCh ETho MCad NBea NHaw NTay SBod SBra
'Serebrjannyj Ruczejok'	MCad
'Serenata' (J)	CSCl EOvi ETho LPri MCad NBea NTay SBra
serratifolia	CHan CLon CPev CSCl CSPN ELan EOvi ESCh ETho LPri MCad NBea NSti SBra SDix SPer WTre
'Sheila Thacker'	ETho
'Shogun'	MCad
sibirica	See ***C. alpina*** subsp. ***sibirica***
'Signe' (Vt)	ERob ESCh MCad
'Silver Lining'	MCad
'Silver Moon' (L) 🏆	CBlo CSCl CSPN ECle EOvi ESCh ETho LPri MAsh MCad NBea NTay SBra WFar WMer WTre
'Simi'	MCad
◆ ***simsii*** Britt. & A.Br.	See ***C. pitcheri***
◆ – Sweet	See ***C. crispa***
'Sir Garnet Wolseley' (P)	CBlo EHGC EOvi ESCh NBrk NTay SBod SBra SDix WTre
'Sir Trevor Lawrence' (T)	CPev CSCl CSPN EBre EOrc EOvi ESCh ETho LFis LPri MCad NBea NTay SBod SBra SDix SPer SSta WTre WWat
'Sizaja Ptitsa' (I)	EOvi
smilacifolia subsp. ***andersonii***	MSto
'Snow Queen'	CB&S CBlo CSCl CSPN EBre EOvi ESCh ETho LPri MBri MCad NBea NTay SBra WTre
'Södertälje'	CBlo CRHN CSCl CSPN EBre ELan EOvi ERob ESCh MCad NTay WLRN WTre MCad SBra
songarica	CBlo CSCl CSPN EBee EOvi LFis MCad MSto NBea NBrk NHol NSti SBra WCru WSHC
– var. ***songarica***	ERob
'Souvenir de J.L. Delbard' (P)	ERob NBea NBrk SBra

§ 'Souvenir du Capitaine Thuilleaux' (P)	CPev EOvi ESCh ETho LPri MBri MCad NBea SBra SPer WTre
sp. B&SWJ 1243	WCru
'Special Occasions'	ESCh ETho WWeb
spooneri	See ***C. montana*** var. ***sericea***
– 'Rosea'	See ***C.*** × ***vedrariensis* 'Rosea'**
'Sputnik' (J)	ERob MGos WTre
stans	CMdw CPou ERob ESCh LRHS SIng WCru WPri WTre
– 'Rusalka'	ERob
'Star Fish' (L)	ERob ESCh
'Star of India' (P/J) ♀	CBlo CPev CRHN CSCl EBee EBre ELan EOvi ESCh ETho IHar LPri MBri MCad NBea NTay SBra SDix WTre
'Strawberry Roan' (P)	EOvi NTay
'Sugar Candy' (P)	CB&S CBlo CSPN EBre EHGC ESCh MAsh NTay WTre WWeb WWes
'Summer Snow'	See ***C.* 'Paul Farges'**
'Sunset' (J)	CSPN ELan ESCh ETho MAsh MBri MCad NTay SBra WLRN
'Susan Allsop' (L)	CPev EOvi ESCh MCad
'Sylvia Denny' (Fl)	CSPN EBre ELan EOvi ESCh ETho IHar LPri MBar MBri MCad NBea NTay SBod SBra SPer WTre
'Sympathia' (L)	CSCl ERob MCad
§ 'Tage Lundell' (A)	CSPN EHGC EOrc EOvi ERob GMac MCad NBea NBrk NTay WTre
'Tango' (T)	CSCl ERob ESCh ETho MCad NBrk
tangutica	CBot CMHG CNic CPev CSCl CSPN ELan ENot EOvi ESCh GDra LHol LPri MBal MBar MCad NEgg NHar NHol NRoo SBod SBra SDix SPer SReu SSta WBod WTre
– 'Aureolin'	See ***C.* 'Aureolin'**
– 'Bill MacKenzie'	See ***C.* 'Bill MacKenzie'**
– 'Gravetye Variety'	CBlo CSCl ERob ESCh NHol
– 'Lambton Park'	EBee EOvi EPfP ESCh ETho LPri MCad NBea NBrk NTay SBra SPla WTre
– var. ***obtusiuscula***	MSto
– 'Radar Love'	CMdw SSte
¶ ***tashiroi*** B&SWJ 1423	WCru
'Tateshina' (P)	ERob MCad
¶ ***tenuiloba***	MSto
§ ***terniflora***	CPev CSCl EBee ESCh LPri MCad MSto NBea NBrk NTay SBra SPer
– Caddick's form	CHan
– var. ***mandshurica***	See ***C. mandschurica***
– var. ***robusta***	See ***C. terniflora*** var. ***terniflora***
§ – var. ***terniflora***	ERob ESCh
'Teshio' (Fl)	ERob ESCh LPri MCad SBra
'Tevia'	MCad
texensis	CSCl CSPN EOvi MCad MSto NBea SReu WFar
'The Bride' (J)	CSCl ERob MCad NBrk NTay
'The Comet'	LPri
* 'The First Lady'	MCad
'The President' (P) ♀	CB&S CMac CPev CRHN CSCl CSPN EBre ELan ENot EOvi ETho IHos LPri MBar MBri MCad MGos NBea NHaw NRoo SBod SBra SDix SHBN SPer SSoC WBod WTre
◆ 'The Princess of Wales'	See ***C.* 'Princess Diana'**
'The Vagabond' (P)	CBlo CSCl ELan LPri MCad NBea NBrk NTay WLRN WTre
thunbergii hort.	See ***C. terniflora***
– Steudel	See ***C. hirsuta***
§ ***tibetana***	CLon CMac CPev CSCl CSPN ELan ETho MBal MBar MCad MNrw MSto NNor SPer WWat
§ – subsp. ***vernayi*** ♀	CMHG CSCl EBee EOvi MCad MPla NBea SBra SPer WWat WWin
– – CC&McK 193	NWCA
– – var. ***laciniifolia***	ERob ESCh NHol WCru WTre
§ – – LS&E 13342	CPev CSCl EOrc EOvi ESCh MBri MCad NBea NBrk NHol SBra SDix SPer WTre
§ – – 'Orange Peel'	EBar EBee ENot EPot ESCh IOrc LBuc MCad MGos
'Titania' (P×L)	ERob
'Trianon' (P)	CSCl ERob MCad NBrk
§ × ***triternata*** 'Rubromarginata' ♀	CDoC CPev CRHN CSCl CSPN ELan EOrc ESCh ETho LFis LPri MCad NBea NHol NRoo SBod SBra SDix SPer SPla WCru WSHC WTre
* 'Tsuzuki'	ERob ESCh
'Tuczka' (J)	EOvi NBrk
'Twilight' (J)	CSPN ECle EOvi ESCh ETho MAsh MCad NBea NTay SBra SChu SPer WTre
'Ulrique' (P)	EBee ESCh LRHS NTay
uncinata	CPev EOvi
'Valge Daam' (L)	MCad
'Vanilla Cream'	ECou
× ***vedrariensis***	MCad SPer
– 'Dovedale'	CPev
– 'Highdown'	CBlo CSCl ERob LPri MCad NBea NHol SBra SPer
§ – 'Rosea'	CTrw MCad WSHC
¶ ***veitchiana***	ERob
'Venosa Violacea' (Vt) ♀	CRHN CSCl CSPN EHGC ELan EOrc EOvi ESCh ETho LPri MBri MCad NBea NSti SBra SChu SDix SPer WFar WSHC WTre
'Veronica's Choice' (L)	CPev CRHN CSCl EBee EBre ELan EOvi ESCh ETho MBri MCad MGos NBea NTay SBra
versicolor	CSCl EOvi ERob MSto
N 'Victoria' (J)	CPev CSCl EBre ELan EOvi ESCh ETho LPri MCad NBea NTay SBra SDix WTre
'Ville de Lyon' (Vt)	CB&S CMac CPev CSCl CSPN EBre ELan ENot EOvi ESCh ETho GRei IHos LPri MBar MBri MCad MGos NBea NEgg SBod SBra SDix SHBN SPer WSHC WTre WWin
'Vino' (J)	CBlo CSPN EBee EOvi ESCh ETho IHar MCad NBea NBrk NTay WTre
* 'Viola' (J)	ERob MCad WTre
'Violet Charm' (L)	CBlo CSPN ERob ESCh NTay WTre
'Violet Elizabeth' (P)	CSCl ESCh MCad NBrk SBra WTre
viorna	CPlN CSCl ERob LPri MSto NBea
virginiana Hooker	See ***C. ligusticifolia***
– hort.	See ***C. vitalba***
§ ***vitalba***	CArn CJew CKin CPev CSCl EBee ECWi ERob ESCh MBar MCad WGwy WHer

viticella	CPev CSCl EBee EOvi ESCh ETho LHol LPri MCad NBea SBra SDix WSHC WStI WTre WWat
* – 'Foxtrot'	WTre
– 'Mary Rose' (d)	CPev CSCl EOvi ERob ETho SBra
– 'Purpurea Plena Elegans' 🏆	CGle CHad CPev CRHN CSCl EBre ELan EOrc EOvi ESCh ETho LFis LHol LPri MBri MCad NBea NHol NRoo NSti SBra SDix SHBN SPer SReu SSoC SSta WSHC WTre
'Viticella Rubra' (Vt)	ETho NBrk
'Vivienne Lawson'	WTre
'Voluceau' (Vt)	CPou CRHN CSCl CSPN CWLN EBee ELan EOvi ESCh MCad NBea NTay SBra SPer WStI
¶ 'Vostok' (J)	ERob
'Vyvyan Pennell' (Fl/P) 🏆	CB&S CMac CPev CSCl CSPN EBre ELan EOvi ESCh ETho IHos LPri MBal MBar MBri MCad MGos NBea NEgg NHaw NTay SBra SDix SHBN SPer SReu SSta WTre
'W.E. Gladstone' (L)	CPev CSCl EBee EOvi ESCh ETho LPri MCad NBea NTay SBra SDix SPer WTre
'W.S. Callick' (P)	ERob ESCh MCad WTre
'Wada's Primrose' (P)	CDoC CSCl CSPN EBre EHGC ELan EOvi ESCh ETho IHar LPri MBri MCad MRav NBea NEgg NRoo NTay SBra SPer SPla WSHC WTre
'Walenburg' (Vt)	SBra
'Walter Pennell' (Fl/P)	CBlo CMac CPev EOvi ESCh ETho LPri MCad NBea SBra WGor WTre
'Warszawska Nike' (J)	CRHN CSCl ELan EOvi ESCh ETho IHar LPri MCad MGos NBea NTay SBra WTre
¶ 'Western Virgin'	ERob
§ 'White Swan' (A)	CBlo CSCl CSPN ESCh ETho LHol LPri MBri MCad MGos NBea NHol NRoo NSti SBra SChu SPer SPla SSoC WFoF
'White Tokyo' (A)	MGos
'Wilhelmina Tull' (L)	CSCl EOvi ERob MCad NBrk
'Will Goodwin' (L) 🏆	CB&S CSCl CSPN EBre ELan EOvi ESCh ETho LPri MBri MCad NBea NBrk SBra WTre
'William Kennett' (L)	CMac CPev CRHN CSCl CSPN EBar ELan EOvi ESCh ETho LPri MBar MBri MCad MGos MRav NBea SBod SBra SDix SPer WTre
¶ 'Wistaria Purple' (A)	NBrk
'Wolga' (P)	MCad
'Xerxes'	See *C.* **'Elsa Späth'**
'Yellow Queen'	See *C.* **'Moonlight'**
'Yorkshire Pride'	MCad
'Yukikomachi' (LxJ)	MCad
'Yvette Houry' (L)	ERob ESCh MCad WMer

CLEMATOPSIS (Ranunculaceae)

See Plant Deletions

CLEOME (Capparaceae)

arborea	CHan
§ ***hassleriana***	MLan SMrm SWat
spinosa hort.	See ***C. hassleriana***

CLERODENDRUM (Verbenaceae)

bungei 🏆	CAbb CB&S CBlo CBot CChu CGre CHEx CHad CPle CWit ELan EPar EPla ERea MBlu NPal SDix SLMG SMad SPer SSpi SSta WBod WGwG WOMN WWat
chinense 'Pleniflorum'	ERea
fragrans var. ***pleniflorum***	See ***C. chinense*** **'Pleniflorum'**
myricoides 'Ugandense'	CPlN CSpe ECon ELan ERea LChe LCns LHil SLMG SOWG SSad
§ ***philippinum*** (d)	See ***C. chinense*** **'Pleniflorum'**
¶ ***speciossissimum***	LChe
× ***speciosum***	CPlN LChe LCns
splendens 🏆	SLMG SOWG
thomsoniae 🏆	CPlN LChe MBri
trichotomum	CB&S CChu CEnd CGre CHEx CTrw CWit EBre EMil ENot EPla ERom GSki IOrc SPer SReu SSpi SSta WBod WCoo WDin WGer
– var. ***fargesii*** 🏆	CAbb CB&S CBlo CChu CPMA CPle EBar ELan GWht IOrc LHol LHop MBlu MGos NFla SHBN SMrm SPer SSpi WCot WEas WHar WPat WPyg WRTC WWat
* – – 'Variegatum'	CPMA LRHS SPer

CLETHRA (Clethraceae)

¶ ***acuminata***	CB&S WWoo
alnifolia	CB&S CBlo CBot CChu CGre CMHG CSam CWSG ECro ELan EMil IOrc MBar MBel SPer SRms SSpi WDin WWin WWye
– 'Alba'	EMil
* – 'Hummingbird'	LRHS
– 'Paniculata' 🏆	CDoC EHic WWat
– 'Pink Spire'	CB&S CDoC CKni EHic ELan MPla MRav MUlv SCoo SPer WFar WLRN WPyg WStI
– 'Rosea'	CBot CChu EMil GAul IOrc MBal MBar MBel MBlu MGos SHBN SPer WSHC WWat
* – 'Ruby Spice'	LRHS
arborea	CB&S CChu CFil CHEx CPle CTre
barbinervis 🏆	CAgr CB&S CFai CMCN CWSG GGGa SPer WCoo WSHC WWat
delavayi 🏆	GGGa GQui MBal
¶ – C&H 7067	GGGa
fargesii	MGos
monostachya	GGGa

CLEYERA (Theaceae)

fortunei	See ***C. japonica*** **'Fortunei'**
– 'Variegata'	See ***C. japonica*** **'Fortunei'**
§ ***japonica*** 'Fortunei' (v)	CFil WWat
– var. ***japonica***	MBal

CLIANTHUS (Papilionaceae)

§ ***puniceus*** 🏆	CAbb CB&S CBot CHEx CHan CMac CPlN CPle CTrw ECou ELan EMil ERea IHos LCns LHop MBal SArc SBid SHFr SLMG SOWG SPer SSoC WAbe WCru WDin WPat

§ – 'Albus' 🏆	CBot CDoC CPle CTrw ELan EMil ERea IHos IOrc LCns LHop MAll NPSI SBid SDry SLMG SOWG SPer SSoC
– 'Flamingo'	See ***C. puniceus* 'Roseus'**
– 'Red Admiral'	See ***C. puniceus***
– 'Red Cardinal'	See ***C. puniceus***
§ – 'Roseus'	ELan EMil ERea IHos LHop
– 'White Heron'	See ***C. puniceus* 'Albus'**

CLINOPODIUM (Lamiaceae)

acinos	See ***Acinos arvensis***
ascendens	See ***Calamintha sylvatica***
calamintha	See ***Calamintha nepeta***
grandiflorum	See ***Calamintha grandiflora***
§ *vulgare*	CArn CKin ECWi ECoo EOHP EWFC GBar LHol MHew NMir SIde WCla WHer WOve

CLINTONIA (Convallariaceae)

andrewsiana	CBro CFil GDra GGGa SSpi WChr WCru WThi
borealis	SWas WCru
¶ *udensis*	WCru
umbellulata	WCru
uniflora	WChr WCru

CLITORIA (Papilionaceae)

See Plant Deletions

CLIVIA (Amaryllidaceae)

gardenii	ERea WChr
miniata 🏆	CB&S CHal CTrC SRms
¶ – var. *citrina*	WChr
– – 'New Dawn'	ERea
– hybrids	ERea LAma LHil MBri NPal SEND
– 'Striata'	ERea
nobilis	ERea WChr

CLUSIA (Clusiaceae)

rosea	See ***C. major***

CLYTOSTOMA (Bignoniaceae)

§ *callistegioides*	CPlN ECon ERea

CNEORUM (Cneoraceae)

tricoccon	CFil WOMN

CNICUS (Asteraceae)

§ *benedictus*	CArn GPoy LHol MSal SIde WFar WHer WWye
diacantha	SCro

COBAEA (Cobaeaceae)

scandens 🏆	CPlN IBlr NFai NRai SMrm WGor WHal WPen
– f. *alba* 🏆	IBlr NRai WPen
sp. CD&R 1323	CHan
trianea	CPlN ERea

COCCULUS (Menispermaceae)

¶ *carolinus*	CPlN
§ *orbiculatus*	CPlN WCru
trilobus	See ***C. orbiculatus***

COCHLEARIA (Brassicaceae)

armoracia	See ***Armoracia rusticana***
glastifolia	EMon MSal
officinalis	MSal WHer

COCOS (Arecaceae)

plumosa	See ***Syagrus romanzoffiana***
weddelliana	See ***Lytocaryum weddellianum***

CODIAEUM † (Euphorbiaceae)

variegatum var. *pictum*	MBri
'Gold Moon' (v)	
– – 'Gold Sun' (v)	MBri
– – 'Goldfinger' (v)	MBri
– – 'Juliette' (v)	MBri
– – 'Louise' (v)	MBri
– – 'Mrs Iceton' (v)	MBri
– – 'Petra' (v)	MBri
– – 'Sunny Star' (v)	MBri

CODONANTHE (Gesneriaceae)

gracilis	EBak WDib
paula	WDib

× CODONATANTHUS (Gesneriaceae)

'Sunset'	WDib
'Tambourine'	MBri WDib

CODONOPSIS (Campanulaceae)

bhutanica	CNic EBee EPad MSto
bulleyana	EBee GCra NMen
cardiophylla	EPad GDra MNrw MSto
clematidea	Widely available
convolvulacea 🏆	CArc CBlo CChu CPlN CSpe EPad GBuc GDra MNrw MTho NHar NSla SDix WCru WHoo
– 'Alba'	See ***C. grey-wilsonii* 'Himal Snow'**
– Forrest's form	See ***C. forrestii* Diels**
dicentrifolia	EPad
§ *forrestii* Diels	CNic EBee EHyt EPad GCra NChi NHar NTow WCru
– hort.	See ***C. grey-wilsonii***
§ *grey-wilsonii*	LWoo NChi
§ – 'Himal Snow'	EPot GCrs GDra LWoo MSto NChi NHar SWas
handeliana	See ***C. tubulosa***
§ *javanica* B&SWJ 380	WCru
kawakamii	EPad
– B&SWJ 1592	WCru
§ *lanceolata*	CFir CPlN CRDP EPad GCra MSto NChi NHar SCro WCru
meleagris	CArc EBee EPad GCra GDra NChi NHar SAlw
¶ – hybrid	NChi
mollis	CBlo EBee EPad MSto MTis
obtusa	MSto NChi
ovata	CBot CFir CGle ELan EPad EPot EPri GBuc GCra GDra LGan LHop MSto MTho NBro NChi NWCA SBla SRms WEas
pilosula	EBee EPad GCra MNrw MSto MTho NChi WCru
rotundifolia	CPlN EBee
– var. *angustifolia*	MSto NChi
silvestris	EPad
sp. ACE 1687	EBee
subsimplex	CNic EBee EPad GCra MSto NChi
tangshen	CArn CChu CGre CPlN EBee EPad GBuc GCra GPoy MNrw MSal MSto MTho NBro NChi SAlw SBla WCru
§ *tubulosa*	EBee EPad MSto
ussuriensis	See ***C. lanceolata***

vinciflora	CFir CNic EPad GCra GDra MSto NChi NHol SBla WCru
viridiflora	CLyd EPad MHar NRoo WPer
viridis	EPad
– S&L 4962	GCra

COELOGLOSSUM See × DACTYLOGLOSSUM

COFFEA (Rubiaceae)

arabica	ECon

COIX (Poaceae)

lacryma-jobi	MSal

COLCHICUM † (Colchicaceae)

agrippinum 🏆	CAvo CBro CFee CMon ECha EHyt EMon EPar EPot LAma MBal MRav NBir NGar NMGW NRog WAbe WChr
algeriense AB&S 4353	CMon
'Antares'	LAma
atropurpureum	CBro EPot LAma
'Attlee'	EPot LAma LRHS NGar
'Autumn Herald'	LAma LRHS NGar
N 'Autumn Queen' 🏆	CBro LAma LRHS
§ ***autumnale***	CArn CAvo CBro CFee EPot ETub GPoy LAma MBal NMGW NRya WAbe WShi
* – 'Albopilosum'	NBir
§ – 'Alboplenum'	CBro CSWP EPot ETub LAma NMGW WChr
– 'Album'	CAvo CBro CSWP ECha EHyt EPar ETub GDra LAma MBal NBir
– var. ***major***	See ***C. byzantinum***
– var. ***minor***	See ***C. autumnale***
autumnale minor album plenum	See ***C. autumnale* 'Alboplenum'**
¶ ***autumnale*** 'Nancy Lindsay'	CBro NGar
§ – 'Pleniflorum'	CBro EPar LAma
– 'Roseum Plenum'	See ***C. autumnale* 'Pleniflorum'**
baytopiorum	EHyt LAma NGar WChr
– PB 224	CMon
'Beaconsfield'	NGar
§ ***bivonae***	CBro ECha EPot LAma NGar NMGW SMad
§ ***boissieri***	CMon EHyt NGar
– S&L 468	CMon
bornmuelleri Freyn	CAvo CBro EPar EPot LAma
– hort.	See ***C. speciosum*** var. ***bornmuelleri* hort.**
bowlesianum	See ***C. bivonae***
§ ***byzantinum*** 🏆	CAvo CBro CMon EMon EPar EPot LAma MBri NGar NRog WCot
byzantinum album	CBro ETub NGar
chalcedonicum	NGar
cilicicum	CBro CMon EPot ETub LAma NGar WAbe WChr
– Bowles' form	NGar
– 'Purpureum'	EPot LAma NGar WChr
'Conquest'	See ***C.* 'Glory of Heemstede'**
corsicum	CMon EHyt EPar LAma WChr
cupanii	EHyt EPot LAma
* – var. ***cousturieri***	EHyt
– Glossophyllum Group	CMon EPot
– MS 977	CMon
'Daendels'	EPot LAma LRHS NGar
deserti-syriaci SB&L 155	CMon
'Dick Trotter'	EPot LAma LRHS NGar
'Disraeli'	CBro LRHS
doerfleri	See ***C. hungaricum***
'E.A. Bowles'	EPot LAma NGar
fasciculare	LAma
§ ***giganteum***	EPot LAma NGar
§ 'Glory of Heemstede'	ECha LAma NGar
hierosolymitanum	LAma
§ ***hungaricum***	CBro EHyt LAma NGar WChr
– f. ***albiflorum***	EHyt
'Huxley'	NGar
illyricum	See ***C. giganteum***
kesselringii	LWoo WChr
kotschyi	LAma
laetum hort.	See ***C. parnassicum***
'Lilac Wonder'	CBro ECha EHyt EMan EPot ETub LAma MBri NMGW NNrd NRog WCot
lingulatum	LAma NRog
– S&L 217	CMon
'Little Woods'	NGar
§ ***longiflorum***	LAma
lusitanicum	LAma
– HC 2273	CMon
luteum	LAma NGar NRog WChr
macrophyllum	LAma
– S&L 578	CMon
micranthum	LAma
¶ – ABS 4522	EHyt
neapolitanum	See ***C. longiflorum***
* ***neapolitanum macranthum***	CMon
parlatoris Rix 2127	CMon
§ ***parnassicum***	CMon ECha
'Pink Goblet'	CBro EHyt EMon EPot LAma NGar
polyphyllum	LAma
'Prinses Astrid'	CAvo LAma NGar
procurrens	See ***C. boissieri***
psaridis S&L 198	CMon
pusillum MS 803/833	CMon
'Rosy Dawn'	CBro ECha EMon EPot LAma NGar WChr
sibthorpii	See ***C. bivonae***
speciosum 🏆	CAvo CBro CMon EBre EMon EPot ETub LAma MBal MHlr NBir NGar WCot
– 'Album' 🏆	CAvo CBro CFee EBre ECha EHyt EPar LAma MBri NBir NGar NMGW WChr
– 'Atrorubens'	ECha GDra LAma NGar
§ – var. ***bornmuelleri*** hort.	CMon EMon
– var. ***illyricum***	See ***C. giganteum***
– 'Maximum'	LAma NGar
stevenii SB&L 120	CMon
tenorei	LAma NBir
'The Giant'	CAvo CBro ECha EPot ETub LAma NNrd NRog
troodii 🏆	CMon LAma
turcicum	LAma
umbrosum	CMon
variegatum	CBro LAma
– S&L 594	CMon
'Violet Queen'	CBro CFee EPot LAma
'Waterlily'	CAvo CBro CLyd EBre ECha EMon EPar EPot ETub GAbr LAma MBal MBri NBir NMGW NRog WAbe WCot
'William Dykes'	EPot LAma NGar
'Zephyr'	LAma LRHS

COLEONEMA (Rutaceae)

album	CSpe SAga
pulchrum	CSpe CTrC LHop MAll

COLEUS See SOLENOSTEMON, PLECTRANTHUS

COLLETIA (Rhamnaceae)

armata	See ***C. hystrix***
cruciata	See ***C. paradoxa***
ferox	SMad
§ ***hystrix***	CB&S CPle MAll SArc SMad WCru WDin
– 'Rosea'	CAbb CGre CPle CWLN MBlu SArc SMur WAbe WSHC
§ ***paradoxa***	CB&S CGre CHEx CPle CTre CTri EPla MAll SArc SMad
– × ***spinosa***	SMad

COLLINSIA (Scrophulariaceae)

♦ ***bicolor*** Benth.	See ***C. heterophylla***
§ ***heterophylla***	MSto

COLLINSONIA (Lamiaceae)

canadensis	CArn EBee ELan MSal

COLLOMIA (Polemoniaceae)

biflora	MFos
debilis	NWCA
– var. ***larsenii***	GTou
¶ ***grandiflora***	CSpe LCot

COLOBANTHUS (Caryophyllaceae)

apetalus	NHol
¶ – var. ***alpinus***	EPot
buchananii	ECou
canaliculatus	CPBP ECou
muelleri	NTow
sp. CC 465	NWCA

COLOCASIA (Araceae)

antiquorum	See ***C. esculenta***
§ ***esculenta*** ♡	CHEx EOas
¶ – 'Illustris'	WCot

COLQUHOUNIA (Lamiaceae)

coccinea ♡	CArn CHal CHan CTrC EMil MAll MBal MRav NTow SDry WBod WSHC
– var. ***mollis***	See ***C. coccinea*** var. ***vestita***
§ – var. ***vestita***	CB&S CFai CFil CGre CPle CSte EBee EOrc NPSI SEND WPat

COLUMNEA (Gesneriaceae)

'Aladdin's Lamp'	CHal NMos WDib
'Apollo'	WDib
× ***banksii***	CHal MBri WDib
'Bold Venture'	WDib
* 'Bonfire'	WDib
§ 'Broget Stavanger' (v)	WDib
'Chanticleer' ♡	CHal MBri WDib
'Gavin Brown'	WDib
gloriosa	EBak
'Heidi'	MBri
hirta ♡	MBri WDib
– 'Variegata'	See ***C. 'Light Prince'***
'Inferno'	WDib
'Katsura'	MBri WDib
I 'Kewensis Variegata' ♡	MBri
§ 'Light Prince' (v)	MBri WDib
'Merkur'	WDib
microphylla 'Variegata'	MBri
I 'Midnight Lantern'	WDib
'Rising Sun'	WDib
'Robin'	WDib
schiedeana	CHal MBri WDib
'Starburst'	NMos
'Stavanger' ♡	CHal EBak MBri WDib
'Stavanger Variegated'	See ***C. 'Broget Stavanger'***
'Winifred Brown'	WDib
Yellow Dragon Group	CHal

COLUTEA (Papilionaceae)

arborescens	CAgr CArn CB&S EBre ELan EMil ENot IBlr IOrc MBlu MGos MSal NNor NWea SHBN SPer WDin WHer WOve WWin
× ***media***	CHad EMil MBel MBlu
– 'Copper Beauty'	CB&S ELan MGos SPer WPat
orientalis	CDoC
persica	SOWG

COLUTEOCARPUS (Brassicaceae)
See Plant Deletions

COMARUM See POTENTILLA

COMBRETUM (Combretaceae)

erythrophyllum	CGre CTrC
paniculatum	CPlN MSto

COMMELINA (Commelinaceae)

coelestis	See ***C. tuberosa*** **Coelestis Group**
dianthifolia	CFee CGra CInt CRDP EFol EMon GBuc GCal MSte MTho NTow SLMG SSad WCot WPer
* – 'Sapphirino'	EMon
tuberosa	CAvo CMdw EHic ELan GBuc MAvo MLan NSti SAlw SLod
– 'Alba'	ELan EMon GCal MSte NBro NTow SCro SUsu WHer WPer WWye
§ – Coelestis Group	CHan CInt CSev ECha EMon ETub GCal NBro NFai SCro SLMG SUsu WFar WHal WHer WOMN WPer WWin WWye
– 'Snowmelt'	MGrG
virginica hort.	See ***C. erecta***
– Linnaeus	IBlr

COMPTONIA (Myricaceae)
See Plant Deletions

CONANTHERA (Tecophilaeaceae)

campanulata	CMon

CONIOGRAMME (Adiantaceae)

¶ ***intermedia***	NMar

CONIOSELINUM (Apiaceae)

morrisonense B&SWJ 173	WCru

CONIUM (Apiaceae)

maculatum 'Golden Nemesis'	EMon

CONOCEPHALUM (Conocephalaceae)
See Plant Deletions

CONOPODIUM (Apiaceae)

majus	CKin WShi

CONRADINA (Lamiaceae)

verticillata	CFee CGra SBla

CONSOLIDA (Ranunculaceae)

§ ***ajacis***	EWFC MHew MSal
ambigua	See ***C. ajacis***
¶ ***regalis***	ECoo

CONVALLARIA † (Convallariaceae)

japonica	See ***Ophiopogon jaburan***
¶ ***keiskei***	LWoo
majalis ♀	Widely available
§ – 'Albostriata'	CChu CFil CRDP CRow ECha ELan EPar LWoo MTho NBir NGar NRar SAxl WCHb WCot WCru WEas WFox WHer
– 'Flore Pleno'	CSte EBee WCot WFox
– 'Fortin's Giant'	CAvo CBro CRDP CRow ECro EGar ELan EMan EMon EPar EPla ERav LHop LWoo MRav NBrk WCot
* – 'Haldon Grange'	EMon LWoo
– 'Hardwick Hall' (v)	CAvo CRDP CRow EFol EHoe LWoo WCot WFox
– 'Hofheim' (v)	CRow
– 'Prolificans'	CAvo CBro CRDP CRow EGar EMon EPar EPot LWoo NGar SSvw WPbr
– var. ***rosea***	CAvo CBro CRDP CRow CShe CSte EFou EGar ELan EMon EOHP EPar EPot ERav ERos LHol LHop LWoo MTho NBir NGar NHol NRar NSti SIng SPer WEas WGle WHil WOak
– 'Variegata'	CAvo CBlo CRow EFol EGar ERav SMac SMad WChr
– 'Vic Pawlowski's Gold' (v)	CRow WCHb
montana	LRHS NGar WChr WThi
transcaucasica	WHer

CONVOLVULUS (Convolvulaceae)

althaeoides	CBot CChr CFil CHad CMil CPle CSam ECGP ECha MNes MTho MTol SAga SAlw SBar SBla SChu SCro SHFr SMad SWas WAbb WCru WEas WHal WOld WWin
§ – subsp. ***tenuissimus***	CGle CSWP CSpe EBee EWes GCal LHop MSto NTow SAsh SAxl SUsu WCot
¶ ***arvensis***	CTiv
§ ***boissieri***	EHyt MTho SBla WAbe
cantabricus	MSto
chilensis RB 94080	MSto
cneorum ♀	Widely available
elegantissimus	See ***C. althaeoides*** subsp. ***tenuissimus***
incanus	WCru
lineatus	CPBP EHyt ELan ESis LBee MRPP MSto MTho NHar NMen NNrd NWCA SBla WAbe
mauritanicus	See ***C. sabatius***
nitidus	See ***C. boissieri***
remotus	MSto
§ ***sabatius*** ♀	Widely available
– dark form	CBrk CMHG CSpe ELan EMan GCal LFis LHil LHop LIck MSte SMrm SUsu

COOPERANTHES See ZEPHYRANTHES

COOPERIA See ZEPHYRANTHES

COPROSMA † (Rubiaceae)

acerosa	See ***C. brunnea***
areolata	ECou
atropurpurea (m)	ECou ITim MAll
baueri	See ***C. repens***
'Beatson's Gold' (f/v)	CAbb CB&S CBlo CBot CBrk CDec CGre CHan CLTr CMHG CPle CTrw EMil ERea GOrc GQui IOrc ISea MAll MPla NFai SChu STre WBod WHen WSHC
billardierei	See ***C. quadrifida***
'Blue Pearls' (f)	ECou
'Brunette' (f)	ECou
§ ***brunnea***	ECou MHig
– (m) × ***kirkii***	ECou
cheesemanii (f)	ECou
– (m)	ECou
– 'Mack'	MAll
– 'Red Mack'	MAll
'Chocolate Soldier' (m)	ECou
'Coppershine'	ERea MAll
crassifolia (m) × ***repens***	ECou
× ***cunninghamii*** (f)	ECou MAll
depressa	ECou
foetidissima Forster	ECou
'Green Girl' (f)	ECou MAll
'Hinerua' (f)	ECou
'Indigo Lustre' (f)	ECou
'Jewel' (f)	ECou
× ***kirkii*** 'Kirkii' (f)	CFee CInt ECou ERea STre
– 'Kirkii Variegata' (f)	CB&S CBot CGre CPle CTrC ECou EHoe EMil ERea GQui LHop MAll SEas SOWG STre WSHC
'Kiwi-gold' (v)	CB&S ECou ERea
'Lemon Drops' (f)	ECou
linariifolia	ECou
lucida (f)	ECou
– (m)	ECou
macrocarpa (f)	ECou
– (m)	ECou
nitida (f)	ECou
– (m)	ECou
parviflora (m)	ECou
'Pearl's Sister' (f)	ECou
'Pearly Queen' (f)	EBar ECou MAll
petriei	CLTr CNic ECou MHig NTow SIng WAbe
– 'Don' (m)	ECou
– 'Lyn' (f)	ECou
propinqua	EPla SDry WSHC
– (f)	ECou
– (m)	ECou
'Prostrata' (m)	ECou
pumila	ECou
§ ***repens***	LHil
– 'Apricot Flush' (f)	ECou
– 'Brownie' (f)	ECou
– 'County Park Purple' (f)	ECou ERea MAll
– 'Exotica' (f/v)	ECou LHop
§ – (f)	CHEx ECou
– (m)	CB&S ECou SEND
– 'Marble King' (m/v)	ECou
– 'Marble Queen' (m/v)	ECou LHil LHop MAll SEND SLMG WLRN
– 'Orangeade' (f)	ECou
– 'Painter's Palette'	CB&S LHil MAll
– 'Picturata' (m/v)	ECou ERea

– 'Pink Splendour' (m/v) CB&S CDoC CSpe ERea LHop MAll SEND
– 'Silver Queen' (m/v) ECou
– 'Variegata' (m) ECou LHil MAll
rhamnoides ECou
¶ ***rigida*** ECou MAll
robusta ECou MAll SDry
– 'Williamsii Variegata' (f/m) LHop
rotundifolia ECou
'Roy's Red' ECou
rugosa (f) ECou
tenuifolia (m) ECou
'Tuffet' (f) MUlv
'Violet Drops' (f) ECou MAll
virescens ECou MAll
'Walter Brockie' CChu CGre CHal CLTr LHil
'White Lady' (f) ECou MAll

COPTIS (Ranunculaceae)

quinquefolia WCru

CORALLOSPARTIUM (Papilionaceae)

crassicaule ECou

CORALLOSPARTIUM × CARMICHAELIA

Corallospartium crassicaule* x *Carmichaelia kirkii ECou MAll
Corallospartium 'County Park' x ***Carmichaelia*** ECou
Corallospartium 'Essex' x ***Carmichaelia*** ECou
Corallospartium 'Havering' x ***Carmichaelia*** ECou

CORDYLINE † (Agavaceae)

australis ♀ Widely available
– 'Albertii' (v) CB&S CHEx CTrC EHic ERea GQui IOrc LNet MBri NCut SArc WCot
* – 'Atropurpurea' CB&S
* – 'Black Tower' CB&S SSto
* – 'Coffee Cream' CSte CTor CTrC EBee ISea MBlu NPSI SSto WGer
– 'Pink Strip' CAbb CDoC MAsh SPla WWeb
– Purpurea Group CAbb CB&S CBot CHEx CSte EBre ENot ERea GQui IOrc ISea NCut SEND SHBN SMad SPer WFar WGer WStI WWeb
– 'Red Star' CAbb CB&S CBlo CDoC COtt CSpe CSte CTor EBee ECle EHic MAll MLan NHaw SMer WLRN WWeb WWes
– 'Sundance' CAbb CB&S CBlo CTor CTrC CWit EBee IOrc ISea MBri NCut NHaw SMer SPla SWat WPat WPyg WStI WWeb WWes
– 'Torbay Dazzler' (v) CAbb CB&S CDoC CHEx COtt CTor CWit EBre ELan IOrc ISea LPan MAsh MBal MBlu MBri NPal SEND SHBN SPer SPla WGer WPat WStI WWeb
– 'Torbay Green' CTor
* – 'Torbay Razzle Dazzle' CTor
– 'Torbay Red' CAbb CB&S COtt CSam CTor CTrC EBee ELan IOrc LPan MAsh MBlu MBri SPla WPat WWeb
– 'Torbay Sunset' CAbb CDoC COtt CTor ELan IOrc SSto WBod WLRN
– 'Torbay Surprise' CAbb CTor WLRN
– 'Variegata' CBot CHEx
* ***autumn*** CTrC NCut
banksii ECou EWes MAll
¶ ***baueri*** CTrC
fruticosa 'Atom' MBri
– 'Baby Ti' MBri
– 'Calypso Queen' MBri
– 'Kiwi' MBri
– 'Orange Prince' MBri
– 'Red Edge' MBri
– 'Yellow King' MBri
'Green Goddess' CB&S CTrC WWeb
§ ***indivisa*** CB&S CBrP CHEx CTrC EBak MAll MBri SArc
kaspar CHEx SArc
parryi 'Purpurea' NPal
* 'Pink Stripe' CB&S COtt CSte CTor CTrC SSto
'Purple Tower' CB&S CBlo CDoC COtt CTor CTrC EHic EMil IOrc WBod WFar WLRN WPat WWeb
§ ***stricta*** CHEx MBri
terminalis See ***C. fruticosa***
* 'Torbay Coffee Cream' EHic

COREOPSIS † (Asteraceae)

◆ ***auriculata*** Cutting Gold See ***C. auriculata* 'Schnittgold'**
§ – 'Schnittgold' CBlo CM&M CSam EWll LFis MWat NCut NRoo SHel WCot WPLl WPer
– 'Superba' EBre LFis
◆ Baby Sun See ***C.* 'Sonnenkind'**
'Goldfink' CTri EBre ECED ECha LCom MNrw MRav SIng SRms
grandiflora EHal SWat WOld WWeb WWtk
¶ – 'Astolat' CRDP
– 'Badengold' CB&S CDoC EMil WCot
– 'Domino' NOak WHil
– 'Early Sunrise' CDoC CSam EAst EBee ECtt GMaP NFai NMir NPer SMer WBea WHen WHil WHoo WPer WPyg WRHF
– 'Mayfield Giant' CBlo EBee EFou EMan EWll MBel MGrG MWat NFla NPri NVic SMer SPer SRms SWat WBea WFar
§ – 'Rotkehlchen' ECha
◆ – Ruby Throat See ***C. grandiflora* 'Rotkehlchen'**
¶ – variegated WCot
integrifolia EMon WCot WHil
lanceolata MLLN WCot
– 'Lichtstad' MBri
– 'Sterntaler' CFir EBee EFou EMil EPar MBri NOrc NPri NRoo NTow WHil WPer
maximilianii See ***Helianthus maximilianii***
palmata EBee
rosea CMea EGar EPla ERav MBel NPro WCot WHil WOld
– 'American Dream' Widely available
– 'Nana' SPla
§ 'Sonnenkind' CMea ECtt EPar GMaP LFis MBri MHig NBro NMen
◆ Sun Child See ***C.* 'Sonnenkind'**
'Sunburst' CBlo COtt ELan EOHP NFai NOak WOve WPer WWtk

'Sunray'	CB&S ECtt EPar MBri MFir MGrG MNrw NFai NNor NOak NOrc NRoo NVic SIde SSea WCot WGwG WPer WRHF WWeb WWye
tinctoria	MSal SIde
– var. ***atkinsoniana***	WPer
tripteris	EMon SMrm WCot WFar
verticillata	CChr CMea CShe CSpe ECha ENot EOrc ESiP LFis MBal MCLN MFir MWat NFai NPer SAxl SDix SRms SSpe SWat WAbe WEas WHal WOld WPyg
– 'Golden Gain'	EBee EBre EMan GBri LHop MArl MLLN MMil NCat NHol WGwG
– 'Golden Shower'	See *C. verticillata* **'Grandiflora'**
§ – 'Grandiflora' 🏆	CB&S CHor COtt CSev EBre EFou ELan GMaP MBri MCLN NCat NHol NNor NOak NVic SChu SMad SPer SPla SSpe WGwG WPbr WWin
– 'Moonbeam'	Widely available
– 'Zagreb'	COtt CSev EBre ECtt EFol EMil EPar EPla LFis MBri MCLN MSCN MUlv NHol NRoo NTay NTow SPla WFar WHil WMer WPbr WTyr

CORETHROGYNE (Asteraceae)

See Plant Deletions

CORIANDRUM (Apiaceae)

sativum	CArn EOHP GPoy ILis LHol MChe MGra MHew SIde WOak WPer WSel WWye
– 'Cilantro'	CJew CSev GAbr WHer
– 'Leisure'	CSev
– 'Santo'	ELau GPoy WJek

CORIARIA † (Coriariaceae)

intermedia B&SWJ 019	WCru
japonica	SDry WCru WWat
kingiana	ECou WCru
§ ***microphylla***	SDry WCru
myrtifolia	CB&S CFil CPle GSki SDry WCru
nepalensis	CPle GCal WCru
¶ ***ruscifolia***	WCru
* ***terminalis fructu-rubro***	CB&S
terminalis var. ***xanthocarpa***	ECha GBuc GCal IBlr MBal MNrw NHol SBar SIng WCot WCru
thymifolia	See *C. microphylla*

CORIS (Primulaceae)

See Plant Deletions

CORNUS † (Cornaceae)

alba	CDoC CKin CLnd CPer CTri ENot IHos IOrc MBar MBri NWea SRms WDin WMou WStI WWtk
* – 'Albovariegata'	ENot
– 'Argenteovariegata'	See *C. alba* **'Variegata'**
– 'Aurea' 🏆	CB&S CMCN EBre ECtt EHoe ELan EPla IOrc MAsh MBar MBri MRav NBee SEas SHBN SPer WAbe WDin WFar WPat WRTC
– 'Elegantissima' (v) 🏆	CB&S CLnd CMCN CShe CWLN EBre EHoe ELan ENot GRei LBuc LHop MBal MBar MBri MGos MWat NNor NWea SHBN SMad SPer SReu SSta WDin WWat
– 'Gouchaultii' (v)	CB&S CBlo CDoC CWLN CWan EBee EHic LPan MBar NPla SRms WDin
– 'Kesselringii'	CAbP CB&S EBre EHoe EMil ENot EPla GAul IOrc MBar MBri MWat NHol SEas SMad SPer SPla SSta WDin WFar WLeb
– 'Siberian Pearls'	CB&S COtt EBee ELan MBlu NEgg
§ – 'Sibirica' 🏆	CB&S CLnd CSpe EBre ELan ENot EPla GOrc GRei IOrc LBuc MBal MBar MBri MGos MWat NBee NFla NHol NNor NWea SHBN SMad SPer WAbe WDin WHCG WHar WWin
– 'Sibirica Variegata'	CChu CDoC CPMA EBee EBre EPla GOrc IOrc LPan MAsh MBlu MBri MGos NBee NEgg SHBN SSpi WFar WPat WPyg
– 'Spaethii' (v) 🏆	CB&S CBot CShe EBre EHoe ELan ENot EPla GOrc GRei IOrc LHop MBal MBar MGos MWat NBee NFla NNor NWea SHBN SMad SPer SSta WHar WRTC WWin
§ – 'Variegata'	CB&S CBlo EBee SPer WGwG WWin
– 'Westonbirt'	See *C. alba* **'Sibirica'**
alternifolia	CBlo CMHG COtt CPMA ELan IOrc LPan SPer SSpi WWat
§ – 'Argentea' (v) 🏆	CChu CDoC CFil CPMA CRos CShe CTho EBre EFol ELan EMil ICrw LHop LPan MAsh MGos MMor MWat NHol SHBN SMad SPer SReu SSpi SSta WHCG WPat WWat
– 'Variegata'	See *C. alternifolia* **'Argentea'**
amomum	CB&S CChu EPla NHol WWat
angustifolia	See *C. linifolia*
§ 'Ascona'	CPMA CRos ELan MBlu MBri SPer SSpi SSta WWes
australis	EPla
baileyi	See *C. stolonifera* **'Baileyi'**
§ ***canadensis*** 🏆	CAgr CB&S CFee CHEx CWGN ELan ENot IOrc ISea LBuc LNet MBar MBlu MBri NGre NHar NHed NHol NNor SHBN SPer SReu SSta WAbe WFar WPat WRus WWat
candidissima	See *C. racemosa*
capitata	CAgr CB&S CBar CChu CGre CHan CPMA CPle CTbh CTri CWLN IOrc SEND SSpi WAbe WCoo
chinensis	LPan
controversa	CAbP CB&S CDoC CFee CMCN CPMA CSam CTho ELan EMil IOrc LPan MBar MBlu NHed NWea SHBN SLPl SPer SReu SSpi SSta WCoo WDin WHar WWat
– 'Pagoda'	CBlo CEnd CPMA CSte MBlu SMad SMur SSpi
¶ – 'Variegata' 🏆	CTho MGos

– 'Variegata' Frans type	CB&S CBot CEnd CPMA CRos EBre EFol ELan EMil ERom IOrc LNet LPan MBlu MBri MMor MPla MSta MWat NHol SHBN SMad SPer SReu SSta WDin WHCG WPat WSHC WWat
'Eddie's White Wonder' 🏆	CB&S CEnd CFil CPMA CRos CTho ELan ICrw IOrc LNet LPan MBal MBlu MBri MGos SBid SHBN SPer SReu SSpi SSta WDin WPat WPyg
florida	CBlo EBre EHic ELan IOrc SPer SReu SSta WCoo WLRN WNor
– 'Alba Plena'	CBlo CPMA
– 'Apple Blossom'	CPMA
– 'Cherokee Chief' 🏆	CAbP CB&S CBlo CEnd COtt CPMA LPan MGos SMad
– 'Cherokee Princess'	CBlo CPMA CRos ELan LPan LRHS SMur
– 'Clear Moon'	LPan
– 'Cloud Nine'	CB&S COtt CPMA LPan LRHS MBal MGos SSpi
* – 'Daniela'	LPan
– 'Daybreak' (v)	CB&S CEnd COtt CPMA LPan MGos SPer WWeb
– 'First Lady'	CB&S CBlo CEnd CPMA LPan SPer
– 'Fragrant Cloud'	LPan
– 'G.H. Ford' (v)	CPMA
– 'Golden Nugget'	CPMA
– 'Green Glow' (v)	CPMA
– 'Junior Miss Variegated' (v)	CPMA
– 'Moonglow'	CPMA
– 'Pendula'	CPMA
– 'Pink Flame' (v)	CPMA
– 'Purple Glory'	CPMA
– 'Rainbow' (v)	CAbP CB&S CDoC COtt CPMA CRos ELan LPan MAsh MBri MGos SHBN SPer SSta WDin
– 'Red Giant'	CBlo CPMA CRos ELan LRHS MGos SMur SSpi
– 'Royal Red'	CPMA
– f. ***rubra***	CB&S CBlo CDoC CTho ELan EPfP LPan LRHS MGos NEgg SSta WNor WPyg
– 'Spring Song'	CPMA MBri
– 'Stoke's Pink'	CBlo CEnd COtt CPMA LNet
– 'Sunset' (v)	CBlo CEnd COtt CPMA MBlu MGos SPer WWeb
– 'Sweetwater'	CPMA
– 'Tricolor'	See *C. florida* **'Welchii'**
§ – 'Welchii' (v)	CEnd CPMA
– 'White Cloud'	CPMA CRos LPan
foemina	See ***C. stricta***
hemsleyi	EPla
§ ***hessei***	EBee ELan EPla NHol WPat WPyg
'Kelsey's Dwarf'	See *C. stolonifera* **'Kelseyi'**
kousa	CB&S CDoC CMCN ELan EMil ERom ISea LNet MBal MBar MWat NFla NNor SHBN SPer WAbe WCoo WDin WFar WHCG WHar WStI WWat
* ***kousa angustata***	CBlo MBal SPer
* ***kousa angustifolia***	SSta
kousa 'Bonfire' (v)	CPMA
– var. ***chinensis*** 🏆	CAgr CChu CGre CMCN CMHG CPMA CRos CSam EBre ECtt ELan IOrc MBri MGos NBee NEgg NHol SLPl SPer SReu SSta WAbe WDin WFar WHCG WNor WPat WSHC WWat
– – 'Bodnant Form'	CBlo CEnd CPMA SPer
– – 'China Girl'	CAbP CBlo CEnd COtt CPMA CRos CSte ELan LPan MAsh MBlu MBri MGos SHBN SMad SSta WPyg
– – 'Milky Way'	CBlo CPMA LPan SPer SSpi
– – Spinners form	CPMA
– 'Gold Star' (v)	CAbP CB&S CBlo CEnd COtt CPMA CTho ELan IOrc LPan MAsh MBri MGos SHBN SPer SPla
– 'Greta's Gold' (v)	CPMA
– 'Madame Butterfly'	CEnd CPMA ELan SSpi
* – 'Nicole'	LPan
– 'Radiant Rose'	CPMA
– 'Rosea'	CPMA
– 'Satomi' 🏆	CB&S CEnd CFil COtt CPMA ELan LNet LPan MAsh MBri SPer SReu SSpi SSta WDin
– 'Snowboy' (v)	CB&S CBlo CEnd COtt CPMA LRHS NEgg SPer
– 'Sunsplash' (v)	CPMA
– 'Temple Jewel' (v)	CPMA
– 'Weaver's Weeping'	CB&S COtt CPMA NEgg
macrophylla	CMCN
mas 🏆	CAgr CB&S CFee CPMA CPle EBre ELan ENot MBal MBar MBri MGos MWat NHol NNor NWea SHBN SPer SSta WCoo WDin WHCG WMou WPat WWat
– 'Aurea' (v)	CPMA EBee EBre ELan EMil MAsh MBri SHBN SPer SSpi SSta WDin WPat WRTC WWat
§ – 'Aureoelegantissima' (v)	CBlo CFil CPMA CSte ELan LNet MBri SPer SSta WPat
– 'Elegantissima'	See ***C. mas* 'Aureoelegantissima'**
– 'Golden Glory'	CB&S CPMA
– 'Variegata' 🏆	CB&S CBot CPMA ELan EMil IOrc LNet LPan MAsh MBri MGos NEgg NPal SHBN SPer SSpi WFar WPat WWat
N 'Norman Hadden' 🏆	CBar CPMA CRos CSam CTho MAsh MBlu SBid SHBN SHFr SMad SPer SSpi SSta WPat WWat
nuttallii	CB&S CSam CSte ELan EMil LPan MBal SHBN SSta WDin WNor WWat
– 'Ascona'	See ***C.* 'Ascona'**
– 'Colrigo Giant'	CPMA SSpi
– 'Gold Spot' (v)	CB&S CBlo CPMA IOrc MGos SPer WWes
– 'Monarch'	CB&S CBlo CPMA LPan SPer WWes
– 'North Star'	CPMA CRos SPer
– 'Portlemouth'	CEnd CPMA SPer
obliqua	CFil EPla WPGP
§ ***occidentalis***	EPla
officinalis	CMCN LPan SSta WWat
'Ormonde'	CPMA SPer SSpi WWes
'Pink Blush'	CPMA
pubescens	See ***C. occidentalis***
pumila	NHol WDin
§ ***racemosa***	WWat

I × ***rutgersiensis*** 'Aurora'	CPMA
– 'Ruth Ellen'	CPMA
– 'Stellar Pink'	CPMA
sanguinea	CBlo CKin CLnd CPer CTri EBre ENot LBuc NNor NWea WDin WHar
– 'Compressa'	See ***C. hessei***
– 'Midwinter Fire'	CB&S CBlo CDoC COtt EBee EBre ECle EPla EWll LBuc LPan MBar MGos MWat NBee SMad SPla SRms WFar WLRN
§ – 'Winter Beauty'	CDoC EMil IOrc LHop SCoo SEas WPat WPyg WWat
– 'Winter Flame'	See ***C. sanguinea* 'Winter Beauty'**
sp. CLD 613	EPla
stolonifera	CArn MGos
– 'Flaviramea' ♈	CB&S CLnd EBre ELan ENot GRei IOrc ISea LBuc MBar MBri MGos MWat NBee NNor NWea SHBN SPer SReu SSta WDin WHCG WHar WLeb WRTC WWat WWin
– 'Kelsey Gold'	MAsh SCoo
§ – 'Kelseyi'	CB&S CBlo CWit EBar EBee EPla ESis IOrc MBar NBee SLPl SPer WLRN WWat
§ – 'White Gold' (v)	CAbP CPMA EBee ENot EPla IOrc MBri MGos WWeb
– 'White Spot'	See ***C. stolonifera* 'White Gold'**
§ ***stricta***	CLnd
× ***unalaschkensis***	NHar
walteri	CMCN

COROKIA (Escalloniaceae)

buddlejoides	CAbb CMHG CPle ECou MAll MGrG SOWG WBod WCru
– var. ***linearis***	CPle
'Coppershine'	CB&S CMHG GOrc
cotoneaster	CAbP CHor CLan CPle CTrw ECou ELan ENot EPot MBlu MUlv NHol SDry SPer SReu SSta WFar WPat WSHC WStI WWat WWes
– 'Little Prince'	CB&S ELan
– 'Ohau Scarlet'	ECou
– 'Ohau Yellow'	ECou
– 'Swale Stream'	ECou
– 'Wanaka'	ECou
macrocarpa	CDoC CPle ISea MAll SDix SPer WSHC
× ***virgata***	CAbP CB&S CDec CHan CMHG CPle ECou ELan EMil IOrc ISea MAll MBlu MUlv SArc SPer WGwG WSHC WStI
– 'Bronze King'	CDoC CPle CWit SPer
¶ – 'Bronze Knight'	MHar
– 'Bronze Lady'	MAll MBal
– 'Cheesemanii'	ECou
– 'County Park Lemon'	ECou MAll SOWG
– 'County Park Purple'	ECou
* – 'Dartonii'	MBlu
* – 'Frosted Chocolate'	CB&S
– 'Havering'	ECou
* × ***virgata purpurea***	MAll
× ***virgata*** 'Red Wonder'	CBlo CMHG EBee EHal ERea MAll SAga SDry SEND SOWG
* – 'Sunsplash'	CB&S
– 'Virgata'	CChe ECou
– 'Yellow Wonder'	CB&S CMHG ECot ECou MAll SAga

CORONILLA (Papilionaceae)

cappadocica	See ***C. orientalis***
comosa	See ***Hippocrepis comosa***
emerus	See ***Hippocrepis emerus***
glauca	See ***C. valentina*** subsp. ***glauca***
globosa	SUsu
minima	NTow SBla WOMN
§ ***orientalis***	NWCA WWin
¶ – var. ***orientalis***	EHyt
valentina	CDoC CMac CSPN CSam ECha EMil LHop MHlr SBra SDix SVen WCot WFar WRHF
§ – subsp. ***glauca*** ♈	CB&S CBot CFee CGle CMac CPle CSam CTri ECha ELan ENot ERea IOrc MBal MSCN NTow SPer WAbe WHCG
– – 'Citrina' ♈	CAbb CB&S CBot CChu CDec CDoC CSam ECha ELan ERav LGre LHop MLan NPer SChu SPer SVen WAbe WHCG WKif WRus WSHC
* – – 'Pygmaea'	WCot
– – 'Variegata'	CAbb CB&S CBot CGle CHan CLTr CMac CPle CSPN CSam EBre ECha ELan EMil ERav ERea LHop SBra SDix SPer SSta WAbe WEas WFar WSHC
§ ***varia***	ECWi NPri WCot

CORREA (Rutaceae)

alba	CGre CSev ECou ERea MAll SMur
– 'Pinkie'	ECou ERea LHop MAll SOWG
backhouseana ♈	CAbb CB&S CHan CPle CSam CTri ERea GCal GQui IBlr IOrc ISea LCns LHop MAll SAga SLMG SOWG WBod WSHC
bauerlenii	MAll SOWG
calycina	ERea
decumbens	CPle ECon ECou GSki IDee LCns MAll SMur SOWG WSHC
'Dusky Bells'	CHan CPle CSWP ECon ECou LHop MAll SOWG SVen
'Dusky Maid'	CAbb MAll WAbe WLRN
'Harrisii'	See ***C.* 'Mannii'**
lawrenceana	CAbb CB&S GQui IBlr LHil MAll SBid WAbe WLRN
lawrenceana rosea	CMHG
§ 'Mannii' ♈	CBot CHan CLTr CSam CSev ECou ERea IOrc LHop MAll MNes SLMG SOWG WAbe WSHC WWat
'Marian's Marvel'	CAbb CB&S CMHG ERea GQui LCns SOWG SVen WAbe WLRN
pulchella	CB&S CGre CMHG CPle CTri ERea GQui LBlm MAll MNes SAga SOWG
§ ***reflexa***	CMHG CPle ECou LBlm MAll SOWG
reflexa virens	WEas
reflexa 'Yanakie'	CPle
speciosa	See ***C. reflexa***

CORTADERIA † (Poaceae - Bambusoideae)

argentea	See ***C. selloana***
§ ***fulvida***	CCuc EBre EGar EPla IBlr SMad

§ ***richardii*** (Endlicher) Zotov	CAbb CHEx CHan EFou EGar EHoe ELan ETPC GAri GGar IBlr MBal SArc
– hort.	See ***C. fulvida***
§ ***selloana***	CB&S CHEx CTri CWGN EBre ELan EOHP LNet MBar NBee NNor SArc WStI
§ – 'Albolineata' (v)	CMil EHoe EPla SEND SMad
§ – 'Aureolineata' (v) 🏆	CB&S EBre EGol EHoe ELan ENot EPla IHos MBal MBri MGos MUlv SAxl SEas SHBN SPer WPat
– 'Gold Band'	See ***C. selloana* 'Aureolineata'**
– 'Monstrosa'	SMad
– 'Pink Feather'	CBlo EBar NEgg SHBN SRms WFar WLRN WPyg WStI WWtk
– 'Pumila' 🏆	CB&S CCuc CDoC EBar EBee EBre ECtt EGol EHoe ELan ENot EPla GAbr MBal MBri MGos MUlv NEgg NFai SDix SEas SHBN SMad SPer SPla WLeb WStI
– 'Rendatleri'	CB&S CDoC EHoe ELan MAsh MBal MUlv SEND SEas SMad WLRN
¶ – 'Roi des Roses'	CBlo
– 'Rosea'	CHEx CSte EBee GSki MBal MBar MBri
¶ – 'Silver Comet'	WWoo
– 'Silver Fountain'	EGar ELan MAsh SPer
– 'Silver Stripe'	See ***C. selloana* 'Albolineata'**
– 'Sunningdale Silver' 🏆	CB&S CBlo EBre ECtt EGol EHoe ELan ENot EOrc IHos MBal MBri MGos MUlv MWat SEas SHBN SMad SPer WLeb WPyg
– 'White Feather'	CBlo CHEx CLan ECtt LFis SIde SPer WFar WHil WLRN
Toe Toe	See ***C. richardii* (Endlicher) Zotov**

CORTUSA (Primulaceae)

¶ ***altaica***	GCal
brotheri	NWCA
matthioli	CGle CSpe GTou LBee LGan MBal MFir NGre NMGW NMen NRya NTow NWCA WFar WWhi
– 'Alba'	EPPr GCal LBee MBal NHar NWCA SSca
– var. ***congesta***	EBee GBin
– subsp. ***pekinensis***	CFir GCra GDra GSki LBee NHar NRoo SIng
– var. ***yezoensis***	EHyt GCal

CORYDALIS (Papaveraceae)

¶ ***alexeenkoana***	EPot
¶ – subsp. ***vittae***	EHyt
ambigua Chamisso & Schlecht.	ETub
– hort.	See ***C. fumariifolia***
angustifolia	EPot NHar WChr
'Blue Panda'	CBos EBee EHyt EPPr SSoC SSpi SWas
bracteata	GCrs LRHS WChr
bracteata alba	WChr
bulbosa auct. non DC	See ***C. cava***
– De Candolle	See ***C. solida***
buschii	GCrs WChr
cashmeriana	EBre EHyt EPot GCra GTou NHar SBar SBla WAbe WHal
– 'Kailash'	GBuc
caucasica	EPot GDra LAma NTow WChr
– var. ***alba***	See ***C. malkensis***
§ ***cava*** 🏆	CGle CMil EPar EPot LAma LFis WChr
cava albiflora	EPar EPot
cheilanthifolia	CAvo CLTr CMea CNic CRow ECha ELan EPot EPri GCHN LBlm LHil MBri MBro MFir MRPP MRav NBro NNrd NPSI NWCA SPer SWat WCot WEas WFar WKif WOMN WPnn
¶ ***chionophila***	MSto
¶ ***conorhiza***	EPot
decipiens	EHyt EPot MHig MTho WChr WCot
elata	CAvo CMil CRDP CSev CSpe CVer EPPr EPla EPot IBlr LHop LWoo MAvo MTho NHar SAga SSoC SSpi SWas SWat WAbe WCot WCru WDav WFar WHal
– 'Blue Summit'	SBla
¶ ***erdelii***	GCrs
firouzii	EPot
flexuosa	Widely available
– CD&R 528	CAvo CGle EHyt LGre MBro MRav NHar NRar NRya SAga SIng WCot WCru WOMN WRHF
– 'China Blue' CD&R 528c	Widely available
– 'Nightshade'	MAvo SAxl SWat WCot
– 'Père David' CD&R 528b	Widely available
– 'Purple Leaf' CD&R 528a	Widely available
§ ***fumariifolia***	EPot LAma MTho NRog WChr
glauca	See ***C. sempervirens***
glaucescens	CMdw EPot WChr
henrikii	EHyt EPot GCrs
integra	GCrs WChr
intermedia	EPot NHar WChr
* ***itacifolia***	WCot
kashgarica	WChr
ledebouriana	WChr
linstowiana	CElw CLon CSpe EDAr EHyt EMon IBlr MSto WCot
¶ – CD&R 605	LWoo
¶ ***ludlowii***	NNrd
§ ***lutea***	ECro EGoo ELan EMar GBuc IBlr LGro MTol MUlv NFai NPer NPri NRoo NVic SEND SRms WBea WBon WCot WHen WRha
macrocentra	WChr
§ ***malkensis*** 🏆	EHyt EPot LWoo NBir NHar
nevskii	WChr
nobilis	EPot MSto
¶ ***nudicaulis***	GCrs
ochotensis	GCal MSto NRai
§ ***ochroleuca***	CAvo CRow EMan EMar EPot ESis GCra LFis MTho MTis NChi WBro WCru WFar WHal WRha
ophiocarpa	CGle ELan EMar EPPr GAri GCal GGar IBlr MBel MFos WBea WCot WFoF WOve
paczoskii	EHyt EPot LRHS WAbe WChr
¶ ***parnassica***	EHyt
paschei	EHyt
popovii	NHar WChr
pseudofumaria alba	See ***C. ochroleuca***
pumila	EPot LRHS NTow WChr
pumila alba	EPot

rosea	GBuc IBlr
ruksansii	EPot GCrs WChr
rupestris	MRPP
§ ***saxicola***	EBar EPot MSto
* ***scandens***	CPlN
schanginii	EPot WChr
¶ – subsp. ***ainii***	EPot GCrs
scouleri	CChr NBir WBea
§ ***sempervirens***	CHid MLan NFai NRai WCru WHer WPat WSan WWin
sempervirens alba	CHid ELan EMar WFoF WSan
sempervirens 'Rock Harlequin'	EJud
shanginii subsp. ***ainii***	WChr
smithiana	EDAr
– ACE 154	CPBP EHyt EPot GBuc MRPP NMen
aff. – CLD 385	WCot
§ ***solida*** 🏆	CBro CElw CGle CMea CRDP EHyt EPar EPot ETub IBlr LAma MHlr MRPP NGar NHar NMen NNrd NRog NRya WAbe WCot WFar WHil WShi WWeb WWhi
– 'Beth Evans' 🏆	CBro EHyt NHar SWas WCot
– 'Blushing Girl'	GCrs WChr
– BM 8499	NHol
– subsp. ***densiflora***	EHyt
– forms	EPot
– 'Harkov'	GCrs LRHS
– 'Highland Mist'	NHar
– subsp. ***incisa***	EPot LRHS
– MS 881	CMon
* – 'Prasil Sunset'	EHyt
* – 'Smokey Blue'	EHyt
– 'Snowstorm'	LWoo WChr
– f. ***transsylvanica***	CMon EHyt EPot LWoo NBir NHar NRya SWat WChr WOMN
– – 'George Baker' 🏆	CAvo CBro EHyt MTho NGar NHar NHol SBar SWas WAbe WChr WCot
– – 'Lahovice'	LWoo WChr
– – 'Nettleton Pink'	EPot
– 'White King'	WChr
sp. ACE 2443	EPot
speciosa	WChr
thalictrifolia Franchet	See ***C. saxicola***
tomentella	EPot MSto SBla WAbe
wendelboi	EPot GCrs WCot
wilsonii	CBot CLyd GCHN GCal GDra IBlr MTho NBro NMen NNrd NTow NWCA SBla WEas WHil WOMN
¶ ***zetterlundii***	GCrs

CORYLOPSIS † (Hamamelidaceae)

§ ***glabrescens***	CDoC CPMA EBre MBal SMur WNor
– var. ***gotoana***	CPMA ELan EPfP MAsh SMur SPer SSpi WWat
himalayana KR 990	WAbe
pauciflora 🏆	CB&S CPMA EBre ELan EMil ENot IOrc MBal MBar MBri MGos MPla NBee SBar SHBN SPer SReu SSta WBod WGwG WWat
platypetala	See ***C. sinensis*** var. ***calvescens***
– var. ***laevis***	See ***C. sinensis*** var. ***calvescens***
sinensis	EMil SSta WFar
§ – var. ***calvescens***	CBlo CPMA MBal
§ – – f. ***veitchiana*** 🏆	CBlo CPMA MBal SMur
§ – var. ***sinensis*** 🏆	CDoC CPMA CWit EHic MBal MGos SReu SSta WAbe WWat
– – 'Spring Purple'	CAbP CDoC CPMA EBre EPfP LHop MAsh MBlu MBri SMad SPer SPla SSpi SSta WWat
sp. from Chollipo, South Korea	ELan
spicata	CB&S CBlo CDoC CPMA ELan ENot IHos MBal MBlu MHlr MPla SCoo SPer WCot WHCG
veitchiana	See ***C. sinensis*** var. ***calvescens*** **f. *veitchiana***
willmottiae	See ***C. sinensis*** var. ***sinensis***

CORYLUS † (Corylaceae)

avellana (F)	CKin CLnd CPer EBre ENot ERea GRei IOrc LBuc LHyr MBal MBar MBri NBee NRog NRoo NWea SKee WDin WHar WMou WStI
– 'Aurea'	CBlo CDoC CEnd COtt CTho ELan MBlu MGos MWat SPer SPla SSta WDin WMou WPyg
– 'Bollwylle'	See ***C. maxima*** **'Halle'sche Riesennuss'**
– 'Contorta' 🏆	Widely available
– 'Cosford Cob' (F)	CBlo CDoC CTho CTri EBre ERea ESim GTwe LBuc MBlu MBri MGos NRog SDea SKee SPer WGwG
§ – 'Fuscorubra' (F)	CMac IOrc MRav
§ – 'Heterophylla'	CEnd CTho WMou
– 'Laciniata'	See ***C. avellana*** **'Heterophylla'**
♦ – 'Merveille de Bollwyller'	See ***C. maxima*** **'Halle'sche Riesennuss'**
– 'Nottingham Prolific'	See ***C. avellana*** **'Pearson's Prolific'**
§ – 'Pearson's Prolific' (F)	ERea ESim GTwe LBuc SDea
– 'Pendula'	MBlu WMou
– 'Purpurea'	See ***C. avellana*** **'Fuscorubra'**
– 'Webb's Prize Cob' (F)	ERea IOrc LHol NRog SDea WMou
colurna 🏆	CBlo CFil CLnd CMCN CTho ENot ESim IOrc LHyr MGos NBee NWea SKee SLPl SMad SPer WDin WMou WOrn
– x ***avellana***	See ***C.*** x ***colurnoides***
* – 'Te Terra Red'	CEnd CMCN MBlu SMad WMou
§ x ***colurnoides***	ESim
maxima (F)	CLnd GTwe NWea SDea WDin
* – 'Annise Summer Red'	MBlu
– 'Butler' (F)	CBlo ERea GTwe SKee WPyg
– 'Ennis' (F)	ERea GTwe SKee
– 'Fertile de Coutard'	See ***C. maxima*** **'White Filbert'**
– 'Frizzled Filbert' (F)	ERea
– 'Frühe van Frauendorf'	See ***C. maxima*** **'Red Filbert'**
– 'Grote Lambertsnoot'	See ***C. maxima*** **'Kentish Cob'**
– 'Gunslehert' (F)	CBlo ERea GTwe SKee WPyg
♦ – Halle Giant	See ***C. maxima*** **'Halle'sche Riesennuss'**
§ – 'Halle'sche Riesennuss' (F)	ERea GTwe LHol SDea SKee
§ – 'Kentish Cob' (F)	CBlo CDoC CSam CTho EBre ERea ESim GTwe IOrc LBuc MBlu MGos NRog SDea SFam SKee SPer SRms WHar WPyg WWeb
– 'Lambert's Filbert'	See ***C. maxima*** **'Kentish Cob'**
– 'Longue d'Espagne'	See ***C. maxima*** **'Kentish Cob'**

– 'Monsieur de Bouweller'	See *C. maxima* **'Halle'sche Riesennuss'**
◆– New Giant	See *C. maxima* **'Neue Riesennuss'**
– 'Purple Filbert'	See *C. maxima* **'Purpurea'**
§ – 'Purpurea' (F) 🏆	CTho EBre ELan ENot ERea LBuc MBal MBar MBri MGos MWat NBee NFla NWea SHBN SPer SSta WDin WHar WMou WPat WRTC WStI WTyr WWat WWin
§ – 'Red Filbert' (F)	CBlo CEnd ERea EWar GTwe IOrc MBlu MBri NRog SKee
– 'Red Zellernut'	See *C. maxima* **'Red Filbert'**
– 'Spanish White'	See *C. maxima* **'White Filbert'**
– 'Tonne de Giffon' (F)	SKee
§ – 'White Filbert' (F)	ERea GTwe NRog SKee WHar
– 'White Spanish Filbert'	See *C. maxima* **'White Filbert'**
– 'Witpit Lambertsnoot'	See *C. maxima* **'White Filbert'**
× ***vilmorinii***	WMou

CORYMBIUM (Asteraceae)

See Plant Deletions

CORYNEPHORUS (Poaceae)

canescens	EBee EBre EHoe ETPC GBin MCCP SMrm

CORYNOCARPUS (Corynocarpaceae)

laevigata	CHEx ECou MBri
laevigatus 'Picturatus'	CHEx
– 'Variegatus'	CB&S CHEx

COSMOS (Asteraceae)

§ ***atrosanguineus***	CAbb CArn CBot CChu CGle CHad CRDP CRow CSam CSev CSte EBre EFou EGol ELan EOrc GCHN GCal LHol LHop MBri MSta NHol NRoo NSti SBla SMad SPer WHoo WRus

COSTUS (Zingiberaceae)

§ ***cuspidatus***	LChe
igneus	See *C.* ***cuspidatus***
malortieanus	LChe
speciosus	NRog
¶ – tetraploid	LChe
spiralis	LChe

COTINUS † (Anacardiaceae)

americanus	See *C.* ***obovatus***
§ ***coggygria*** 🏆	CDoC CMCN EAst EBre ELan ENot IOrc LHop MBar MBri MWat NBee NNor SDix SHBN SPer WDin WFar WHCG WHar WWat WWes
– 'Foliis Purpureis'	See *C. coggygria* **Rubrifolius Group**
– 'Notcutt's Variety'	CBlo EBee EBre ELan ENot SPer SPla WWes
– 'Pink Champagne'	CPMA
– Purpureus Group	ENot
– 'Red Beauty'	COtt LRHS MBri
– 'Royal Purple' 🏆	CBot CLan CMHG CPle CShe EBee EBre EHoe ELan ENot GRei LHop MBal MBar MBri MGos MWat NHed NRoo SHBN SMad SPer SPla SReu SSta WBod WDin WHCG WPat WWat
§ – Rubrifolius Group	CWan EBee MBal NNor SChu SDix SPer SPla WHCG WWeb
– 'Velvet Cloak'	CPMA CSam ELan MAsh MGos SPer SPla SReu SSta WHCG WPat WPyg WWat
'Flame' 🏆	CBlo CPMA CShe EBre IOrc MAsh SPer SPla WPat WWeb
'Grace' 🏆	CAbP CB&S CChu CFil CMCN COtt CPMA CRos CSam CWSG EBre ELan LHop MAsh MBel MBri MGos SMad SPer SPla SReu SSta WDin WFar WHCG WPat WPyg WStI WWes
§ ***obovatus*** 🏆	CBlo CChu CGre CKni CMCN CMHG CPMA CPle ELan ENot SHBN SPer SSta WWat WWes

COTONEASTER † (Rosaceae)

acuminatus	SRms WPGP
adpressus 🏆	CBlo CDoC EPla GDra MGos NCut NHar NNor NWea
§ – 'Little Gem'	GAri MAsh MBri MPla NMen SRms WFar
– var. ***praecox***	See *C.* ***nanshan***
– 'Tom Thumb'	See *C. adpressus* **'Little Gem'**
affinis	SRms
afghanicus CC 738	WLRN
altaicus	SRms
ambiguus	SRms
amoenus	SLPl SRms
apiculatus	CSWP
armenus	SRms
§ ***ascendens***	SRms
assadii	SRms
assamensis	SRms
§ ***astrophoros***	CBlo MBlu SRms
atropurpureus	SRms
§ – 'Variegatus' 🏆	CBot EHoe ELan ENot EPot GRei IOrc LHop MBal MBar MBri MGos NBee NHol SHBN SPer SRms WAbe WGwG WSHC WWat WWin
bacillaris	SRms
boisianus	SRms
bradyi	SRms
§ ***bullatus*** 🏆	ELan ENot GAul GRei MGos NNor NTow SEND SPer SRms WRTC WSHC WWat
– 'Firebird'	CBlo SPer SRms
– f. ***floribundus***	See *C.* ***bullatus***
– var. ***macrophyllus***	See *C.* ***rehderi***
buxifoius blue-leaved	See *C.* ***lidjiangensis***
buxifolius f. ***vellaeus***	See *C.* ***astrophoros***
– Wallich ex Lindley	EBee EHic ESis SRms
calocarpus	SRms
cambricus	CNat SRms
canescens	SRms
cashmiriensis 🏆	EPfP LMer SRms
cavei	EPla SRms
chailaricus	SRms
chengkangensis	SRms
cinerascens	SRms
§ ***cochleatus*** 🏆	CChe EPot ESis GAri GDra LFis MBal MBar MGos MPla NFla NMen SReu SRms WCot WEas WRHF WWat
§ ***congestus***	CFee EBre IOrc MBal MBar MBri MBro MGos MRav MWat NNor NRoo SBla SPer SRms WAbe WHar WWat WWin

– 'Nanus'	CDoC CLyd CMHG CWLN ELan EMil EOrn ESis MAsh MOne MPla NNrd SIng SPla SRms WHCG WPat WPyg WWat WWeb
conspicuus	CSam SRms
– 'Decorus' 🏆	CMHG ELan ENot GDra GOrc GRei IOrc MBar MGos MRav NHol NNor NRoo NWea SEas SPer WDin WPyg WStI WWes
– 'Flameburst'	MBal MBri SHBN
– 'Red Alert'	SRms
– 'Red Glory'	SRms
* – 'Winter Jewel'	CBlo
crispii	SRms
cuspidatus	SRms
N ***dammeri*** 🏆	CChe CMHG EBre ELan ENot GRei ISea LBuc MAsh MBal MBar MGos NBee NNor NWea SIng SPer SRms WDin WHCG WHar WWat WWin
¶ – 'Major'	NFla
– 'Oakwood'	See ***C. radicans* 'Eichholz'**
– var. ***radicans*** hort.	CBlo CShe EBee SPla
– – Schneider	See ***C. radicans***
– 'Streibs Findling'	See ***C. procumbens***
dielsianus	NWea SRms
– 'Rubens'	SRms
discolor	SRms
distichus	See ***C. nitidus***
– var. ***tongolensis***	See ***C. splendens***
divaricatus	ENot GRei SPer SRms WFar WWat
duthieanus	SRms
elegans	SRms
ellipticus	SRms
'Erlinda' (v)	CEnd COtt CPMA ELan MBar MGos SMad SRms
fangianus	SRms
floccosus	CBlo EHal GOrc GRei MBri NWea SPer SRms WLRN WWat
forrestii	SRms
franchetii	CB&S CChe CMHG EBre ELan EMil ERom GCHN IOrc LBuc LPan MBal MGos MRav MWat NBee NWea SHBN SPer SPla SRms WDin WFar WHar WRTC WStI WTyr
frigidus	CBlo GAri NWea SRms
§ – 'Cornubia' 🏆	CBlo CLnd EBre ELan ENot GCHN GOrc LHop LNet LPan MAsh MBar MBri MGos MLan MRav MWat NWea SEas SHBN SPer SRms WDin WStI WWat
– 'Fructu Luteo'	IBlr
– 'Notcutt's Variety'	EBee ELan ENot WWes
¶ – 'Saint Monica'	MBlu
– 'Sherpa'	LMer
froebelii	SRms
gamblei	SRms
giraldii	SRms
glabratus	SLPl SRms
glacialis	SRms
glaucophyllus	SEND SRms
– TW 332	GWht
§ ***glomerulatus***	ESis MBar SRms
goloskokovii	SRms
gracilis	SRms
griffithii	SRms
harrovianus	SLPl SRms
harrysmithii	SRms

hebephyllus	SRms
henryanus	CDoC SRms
¶ – 'Anne Cornwallis'	WBcn
§ 'Herbstfeuer'	CBlo EBee ECtt MBal MGos MRav MWat NNor SPla SRms WAbe
hessei	SRms
'Highlight' (aff. *sheriffii*)	ECtt SRms
hissaricus	SRms
§ ***hjelmqvistii***	LBuc SRms WFar WRHF
– 'Robustus'	See ***C. hjelmqvistii***
– 'Rotundifolius'	See ***C. hjelmqvistii***
horizontalis 🏆	CLan CMHG CShe ELan ENot GOrc GRei IOrc ISea LGro MBal MBar MBri MGos MWat NBee NFla NNor NWea SDix SHBN SPer SReu SRms WAbe WBod WDin WWat WWin
– 'Tangstedt'	ENot
– 'Variegatus'	See ***C. atropurpureus* 'Variegatus'**
– var. ***wilsonii***	See ***C. ascendens***
humifusus	See ***C. dammeri***
hummelii	SRms
'Hybridus Pendulus'	See ***C. salicifolius* 'Pendulus'**
hylmoei	SLPl SRms
ignavus	EHal SLPl SRms
induratus	SRms
insculptus	SRms
insolitus	SRms
integerrimus	NHol SRms
§ ***integrifolius***	CMHG EHic ELan EPla ESis LNet MBal MBar MBri NHol NRoo SRms STre WWat WWin
juranus	SRms
kitiabelii	SRms
kweitschoviensis	SRms
lacteus 🏆	CBlo CSam CShe CTri ELan ENot EPla IOrc LBuc LPan MGos MRav SEND SHBN SPer SPla SRms WDin WFar WRHF WWat
– 'Golden Gate'	EFol
laxiflorus	SRms
§ ***lidjiangensis***	EBee MUlv SRms WCot
linearifolius	SRms
lucidus	SRms
ludlowii	SRms
§ ***mairei***	SRms
– Yu 14144	MBal
marginatus	SRms
marquandii	EPla NNor SRms
megalocarpus	SRms
meiophyllus 🏆	SRms
melanocarpus	SRms
melanotrichus	See ***C. cochleatus***
microphyllus 'Donard Gem'	See ***C. astrophoros***
– 'Teulon Porter'	See ***C. astrophoros***
– var. ***thymifolius***	See ***C. integrifolius***
– Wallich ex Lindley 🏆	CChe CLan EBre EFol ELan ENot GRei IOrc ISea MBar MBri MGos MLan NBee NNor NPSI NWea SDix SHBN SPer SRms STre WBod WDin WFar WGwG
miniatus	SRms
monopyrenus	SRms
* 'Mooncreeper'	CChe CDoC WRHF
morrisonensis	SRms
moupinensis	SRms
mucronatus	SRms

multiflorus Bunge	CBlo NWea SRms
§ ***nanshan***	GRei NWea SRms
– 'Boer'	MBri SRms WRHF
nepalensis	SRms
newryensis	SRms
niger	MSto SRms
nitens	SRms
nitidifolius	See ***C. glomerulatus***
§ ***nitidus***	SRms
nummularius	SRms
obscurus	SRms
oliganthus	SRms
¶ ***otto-schwarzii*** SF 636	ISea
pannosus	SLPl SRms WWat
paradoxus	SRms
parkeri	SRms
permutatus	SRms
perpusillus	GAri MBri SRms WFar
poluninii	SRms
polyanthemus	SRms
§ ***procumbens***	EPla ESis GAri MAsh NRoo SRms WCot
– 'Queen of Carpets'	CBlo EBre ECtt EHic MBri MGos SHhN SRms
– 'Seattle'	SRms
prostratus	SRms
– 'Arnold Forster'	SRms
pseudoambiguus	SRms
pyrenaicus	See ***C. congestus***
racemiflorus	SRms
§ ***radicans***	SRms
§ – 'Eichholz'	EBee ECtt EMil ENot MBri MGos WWeb
§ ***rehderi***	SRms
rokujdaisanensis	SRms
roseus	SRms
rotundifolius	SRms
'Royal Beauty'	See ***C.* × *suecicus* 'Coral Beauty'**
rugosus	SRms
salicifolius	CBlo CLnd GAul NBee NNor SRms WDin WFar
♦ – Autumn Fire	See ***C.* 'Herbstfeuer'**
– 'Avonbank'	CBlo CEnd EBee MAsh WLRN
– 'Elstead'	SPer
– 'Exburyensis'	CBlo CSam CTrw EBre LNet MAsh MBri MGos MWat NSti SHBN SPer SRms WDin WFar WHCG WRHF WWat WWeb WWin
– 'Fructu Luteo'	MBri WWes
– 'Gnom'	CBlo EPla GAul GOrc LNet MAsh MBal MBar MBlu MBri MGos NNor NRoo SPer SRms WWat
– 'Merriott Weeper'	CDoC WWat
♦ – Park Carpet	See ***C. salicifolius* 'Parkteppich'**
§ – 'Parkteppich'	CBlo NWea SPer
§ – 'Pendulus'	EBre ELan GRei IOrc LNet LPan MBal MBar MBri MGos MRav MWat NWea SHBN SPer SRms WHCG WHar WStI
¶ – 'Red Flare'	SPer
– 'Repens'	CBlo CChe CShe EHic GAul MBal MTis NNor NRoo NWea SPer SRms WFar
– 'Rothschildianus' 🏆	CLan CShe CTri EAst EBee EBre ECtt ELan EMil ENot GOrc LHop MBal MBar MRav SEas SPer SPla
– 'Scarlet Leader'	MBri
salwinensis	SLPl SRms
sandakphuensis	SRms
saxatilis	MSto SRms
scandinavicus	SRms
schantungensis	SRms
schlechtendalii 'Blazovice'	SRms
– 'Brno'	SRms
serotinus 🏆	EPla SLPl SRms
shansiensis	SRms
sikangensis	EPla SRms
simonsii 🏆	CChe CPer CTri EBre ELan IOrc LBuc MAsh MBar MBri MGos NBee NWea SPer SRms WDin WFar WHar WStI
soczavianus	SRms
§ ***splendens*** 🏆	ELan SRms WWat
– 'Sabrina'	See ***C. splendens***
staintonii	SRms
sternianus 🏆	CShe ENot EPfP MBar MBri SLPl SRms
– ACE 2200	EPot
suavis	SRms
subadpressus	SRms
§ × ***suecicus*** 'Coral Beauty'	CChe EBre ENot GRei IOrc LBuc LGro MBal MBar MBri MGos NBee NHol NNor SPer SRms WDin WFar WGwG WPyg WStI WWeb
– 'Skogholm'	CTri EBee EFol LPan MBal MBar MGos MWat NWea SPer SRms WDin WHar WStI WWin
talgaricus	SRms
tengyuehensis	SRms
tomentellus	SRms
tomentosus	SRms
transens	SRms
tripyrenus	SRms
turbinatus	SRms
turcomanicus	SRms
veitchii	SRms
vernae	SRms
vestitus	SRms
villosulus	SRms
wardii hort.	See ***C. mairei***
– W. W. Smith	CBlo CDoC IOrc NBee NWea
× ***watereri***	CLnd CWLN EBee ELan EPla LNet MAsh MGos NWea SPla WDin WWeb
– 'Cornubia'	See ***C. frigidus* 'Cornubia'**
– 'Goscote'	MGos
– 'John Waterer' 🏆	SRms WBod
– 'Pendulus'	See ***C. salicifolius* 'Pendulus'**
– 'Pink Champagne'	EHal MBri SPer
wilsonii	SRms
zabelii	SRms
– 'Magyar'	SRms

COTULA (Asteraceae)

atrata	See ***Leptinella atrata***
– var. ***dendyi***	See ***Leptinella dendyi***
coronopifolia	CBen CSev CWGN CWat LPBA MSta NDea SWat SWyc WChe
goyenii	See ***Leptinella goyenii***
hispida	Widely available
lineariloba	CPBP ECha EWes LBee WLRN
minor	See ***Leptinella minor***
pectinata	See ***Leptinella pectinata***
perpusilla	See ***Leptinella pusilla***
potentilloides	See ***Leptinella potentillina***
pyrethrifolia	See ***Leptinella pyrethrifolia***
reptans	See ***Leptinella scariosa***
rotundata	See ***Leptinella rotundata***

scariosa	See ***Leptinella scariosa***
sericea	See ***Leptinella albida***
serrulata	See ***Leptinella serrulata***
sp. C&H 452	MRPP NWCA
squalida	See ***Leptinella squalida***

COTYLEDON (Crassulaceae)

chrysantha	See ***Rosularia chrysantha***
gibbiflora var. *metallica*	See ***Echeveria gibbiflora*** var. ***metallica***
oppositifolia	See ***Chiastophyllum oppositifolium***
¶ *orbiculata*	CTrC
– S&SH 40	NGre
* *pomedosa*	MBri
* – 'Variegata'	MBri
simplicifolia	See ***Chiastophyllum oppositifolium***
undulata	WEas

COWANIA (Rosaceae)

stanburyana	CMdw

CRAIBIODENDRON (Ericaceae)

yunnanense	CPle MBal

CRAMBE (Brassicaceae)

abyssinica	WHil
cordifolia ♀	Widely available
koktebelica	ECha
maritima	CGle CSev ECGP ECha ECoo EMan EMar ERav GPoy MAvo MSal NNor NSti SSoC SWat WCot WCru WHer WHoo WPer
– 'Lilywhite'	ILis
orientalis	ECha MAvo
tataria	CArn EGar EMan MAvo WPer

CRASPEDIA (Asteraceae)

lanata var. *elongata*	GCLN
richea	See ***C. glauca***
uniflora	GCLN

CRASSULA (Crassulaceae)

anomala	NGre
arborescens	GAri SLMG SRms STre
argentea	See ***C. ovata***
coccinea	CHEx EDAr SLMG
dejecta × *coccinea*	CHEx
falcata ♀	IBlr MBri WCot
* *galanthea*	SLMG
§ *helmsii*	EHon EMFW NDea WChe WMAq
justi-corderoyi	CHal
§ *milfordiae*	CNic CTri EHyt ELan MBar MRPP NBir NGre NHar NNrd NSla SBod SSmi WPer
monstrosa	SLMG
¶ *muscosa*	STre
– 'Variegata'	SLMG
§ *ovata* ♀	CHal EBak GBin MBri NPer SLMG
– 'Basutoland'	MPla
¶ – 'Blue Bird'	GBin
* – 'Coral'	GBin
– 'Hummel's Sunset' (v) ♀	CHal SLMG
* *ovata nana*	STre
* *ovata* 'Riversii'	SLMG
– 'Variegata'	CHal EBak SLMG
pellucida subsp. *marginalis*	CHal
peploides	NGre
perforata	CHal SLMG
– 'Variegata'	CHal
portulacea	See ***C. ovata***
recurva	See ***C. helmsii***
rupestris ♀	MBri
rupicola	GAri
§ *sarcocaulis*	CHal CShe CTri ELan EOas EPot ESis GTou ITim MHar MPla MRPP MTho NGre NHar NMen NVic NWCA SBod SIng SRms SSmi STre WAbe WEas WPat WPer WSHC WWin
sarcocaulis alba	CHal ELan NGre NNrd SEND SHFr SIng STre WAbe WPer
sarcocaulis 'Ken Aslet'	NGre SIng STre
schmidtii	CHal MBri
sedifolia	See ***C. milfordiae***
sediformis	See ***C. milfordiae***
socialis	CHal
tetragona	SLMG

+ CRATAEGOMESPILUS (Rosaceae)

See Plant Deletions

CRATAEGUS (Rosaceae)

arnoldiana	CEnd CLnd CTho SEND SLPl
'Autumn Glory'	CBlo CEnd CLnd EBee EBre MGos
azarolus	CAgr WMou
– 'White Italian' (F)	ESim
champlainensis	CTho
N *coccinea*	NWea
cordata	See ***C. phaenopyrum***
crus-galli hort.	See ***C. persimilis* 'Prunifolia'**
– Linnaeus	CB&S CBlo CDoC CLnd CMCN CTho LBuc SPer WDin WHut WJas WMou
– – var. *pyracanthifolia*	CTho
× *durobrivensis*	CLnd CTho WWat
eriocarpa	CLnd
flabellata	CEnd SSpi
gemmosa	CEnd CTho
× *grignonensis*	CB&S CLnd ENot LBuc SPer WJas WPyg
§ *laciniata*	CEnd CLnd CMCN EBee EPfP SHBN SSpi STre WJas WMou
§ *laevigata*	WMou
– 'Coccinea Plena'	See ***C. laevigata* 'Paul's Scarlet'**
– 'Crimson Cloud'	CBlo CEnd CLnd EBee ENot EPfP MAsh MBri SCoo SPer WJas WOrn WPyg
– 'Mutabilis'	CSte CTho SHBN
§ – 'Paul's Scarlet' (d) ♀	CB&S CDoC CLnd CTho EBre ELan ENot GRei IOrc LBuc LPan MAsh MBar MBri MGos MRav MWat NBee NWea SHBN SPer WDin WFar WJas WMou WOrn WStI
– 'Pink Corkscrew'	CTho GAri
– 'Plena'	CB&S CBlo CDoC EBee IHos LPan MAsh MBri NWea SHBN SPer WMou WOrn
– 'Punicea'	CBlo
– 'Rosea Flore Pleno' ♀	CB&S CBlo CDoC CLnd CTho EBre ELan ENot GRei LBuc LPan MAsh MBar MBri MGos MWat NWea SHBN SPer WDin WJas WMou WStI

× *lavalleei* CBlo CLnd CTri ENot MAsh SPer WDin WHut WOrn
– 'Carrierei' ♀ CBlo CDoC CSam CTho EPfP IOrc LPan MBri NWea
× *media* 'Gireoudii' (v) CPMA EFol EPla LNet MBlu MGos WMou WPat
mexicana See ***C. pubescens* f. *stipulacea***
mollis CAgr
monogyna CB&S CDoC CKin CLnd CPer EBre ELan ENot EPfP GRei LBuc LHyr MBar MBri MGos NBee NWea SPer WDin WMou
– 'Biflora' CTho MAsh WMou
– 'Compacta' MBlu
¶ – 'Ferox' CTho
– 'Flexuosa' LNet
– 'Stricta' CLnd CTho EBee ENot SHhN WOrn
– 'Variegata' LNet WBcn WMou
× *mordenensis* 'Toba' (d) CBlo CDoC CLnd CTho ENot
orientalis See ***C. laciniata***
oxyacantha See ***C. laevigata***
pedicellata CLnd CTho LPan
§ *persimilis* 'Prunifolia' ♀ CB&S CDoC CSam CTho CTri EBre ELan ENot IHos LHyr MBar MBri MGos NWea SHBN SPer WDin WFar WMou WOrn WPyg
§ *phaenopyrum* CLnd CMCN CNat CTho SLPl SSpi WAbe WMou WWat
¶ *pinnatifida* WMou
– var. *major* CBlo CEnd ESim
* 'Praecox' CBlo WHut
prunifolia See ***C. persimilis* 'Prunifolia'**
§ *pubescens* f. *stipulacea* CMCN
punctata SLPl
schraderiana CTho WJas
succulenta var. *macracantha* CMCN
tanacetifolia CLnd CTho MBlu SSpi WMou
wattiana CLnd CTho

× CRATAEMESPILUS (Rosaceae)
grandiflora CNat CTho

CRAWFURDIA (Gentianaceae)
speciosa LLew

CREMANTHODIUM (Asteraceae)
See Plant Deletions

CRENULARIA See AETHIONEMA

CREPIS (Asteraceae)
aurea ECha EPar GAbr GAri GGar IBlr NHol SIng WPri
incana ♀ CFee CGle CMea EBre ECha EMan EPar GBri LHop MAvo MTho NHaw NSla SDix WAbe WCot WFar WWin

CRINITARIA See ASTER

CRINODENDRON (Elaeocarpaceae)
§ *hookerianum* ♀ Widely available
patagua CAbb CB&S CBot CEnd CGre CLTr CPle CSam EPfP EPla GQui LHop MAll MBal SBar SPer WAbe WSHC

CRINUM (Amaryllidaceae)
amoenum NRog WCot
aquaticum See ***C. campanulatum***
§ *bulbispermum* ELan WCot
– 'Album' ECha
capense See ***C. bulbispermum***
moorei ETub NRog
§ × *powellii* ♀ CAvo CB&S CMil CMon CSev CSpe EBak ECha ELan ETub LAma LBow LHop MBal MBri MSta MUlv NRog SDix SLMG SMer SPer SSpi WCru WHow
– 'Album' CAvo CHEx CHan CMon ECha ELan EMan ERav ETub EWes LAma LBow MUlv NRog SLMG SSpi WCru
– 'Longifolium' See ***C. bulbispermum***
– 'Roseum' See ***C.* × *powellii***
yemense CMon

CRIOGENES See CYPRIPEDIUM

CRISTARIA (Malvaceae)
See Plant Deletions

CRITHMUM (Apiaceae)
maritimum CArn GPoy MSal SIgm WWye

CROCOSMIA † (Iridaceae)
'Amberglow' CElw CGle EWoo IBlr MBri WCot WMer WPri
aurea var. *aurea* GCal IBlr
– hort. See ***C.* × *crocosmiiflora* 'George Davison' Davison**
– var. *maculata* IBlr
– var. *pauciflora* IBlr
* 'Baby Barnaby' CSte
'Bressingham Beacon' CKni CSte EBre MUlv SAxl SLod SWat
'Bressingham Blaze' CMHG EBre EGar GCal IBlr MBri NCat NOak NTay WCot
¶ 'Carnival' IBlr
× *crocosmiiflora* CLTr CTri ECha EGoo EPla IBlr MBel MCli NCut NOrc NTay SWat WCHb WCot WShi
¶ – 'Babylon' IBlr
– 'Canary Bird' CBlo CBro CRow EGar GAbr GCHN GCal IBlr NRoo
– 'Carmin Brillant' CBro CFil CLTr CRos CRow CSev CSte EBre EGar GCal IBlr IBro LAma LRHS MBri NHol NTay SPla WCot
¶ – 'Comet' IBlr IBro MBri
– 'Constance' CBre ETub IBlr WCHb WWoo
§ – 'Croesus' EGar GBri IBlr IBro MBel NRoo SWas WCot
¶ – 'Custard Cream' GBri IBlr IBro MBri WCot
¶ – 'Dusky Maiden' CHad CSte EAst EHic IBlr MCLN MMil NWes WCot
§ – 'E.A. Bowles' IBlr MUlv NRoo WCot
– 'Eastern Promise' CBre IBlr
– 'Elegans' CElw IBlr
§ – 'Emily McKenzie' Widely available
¶ – 'Firebrand' IBlr MBri WCot
¶ – 'Flamethrower' IBlr WCot
§ – 'George Davison' Davison CDec CGle CPou CRow CSev ECha EMan GCal IBlr MRav NHol WGle
§ – 'Gerbe d'Or' CRow ECGP EGar GBri IBlr IBro NRoo SWas WCot
– 'Gloria' IBlr

§ – 'Golden Glory'	EPar IBlr WCot
¶ – 'Golden Sheaf'	EGar GBri IBlr
– 'Goldfinch'	IBlr IBro
– 'Hades'	IBlr
¶ – 'Highlight'	IBlr
– 'His Majesty'	CAvo CGle CLTr CMil CRDP CRow CSam EBre EGar IBlr IBro LGre LRHS MBri NHol SAga WCot WGer WPer
§ – 'Jackanapes'	CAvo CBro CMil CRDP CRow EBre EGar EPPr EWoo GCal IBlr MBri NHol NRoo NTow SAxl SUsu WCot WCru WHal
§ – 'James Coey' J E Fitt	CBro CFee CFil CHad CRow CSte ECha EFou GCal IBlr LAma LHop MBel MCLN NCat NHol NOrc NRog SPer SSea WCot WFar WHil
* – 'Jesse van Dyke'	CRow IBlr
§ – 'Jessie'	IBlr MBri WCot WPer
¶ – 'Kiatschou'	CFil EBee ECha EGar IBlr SAxl SLod
– 'Lady Hamilton'	CAvo CBos CBro CChu CFee CFil CFir CMHG CRDP CRow EBre EGar GBuc GCal IBlr IBro LGre LHop MBri NRoo NTow SAga SAxl SChu SUsu SWas WFar WMer WRus
– 'Lady McKenzie'	See ***C.*** × ***crocosmiiflora* 'Emily McKenzie'**
– 'Lady Oxford'	CFil ECha EGar IBlr IBro WCot
¶ – 'Lutea'	EGar IBlr
– 'Marjorie'	CAvo WCot
¶ – 'Mephistopheles'	IBlr
¶ – 'Morning Light'	IBlr WCot WPri
§ – 'Mrs Geoffrey Howard'	CGle CRow CSam EGar GBri IBlr IBro SUsu SWas WCot
– 'Mrs Morrison'	See ***C.*** × ***crocosmiiflora* 'Mrs Geoffrey Howard'**
– Newry seedling	See ***C.*** × ***crocosmiiflora* 'Prometheus'**
– 'Nimbus'	GBri IBlr
§ – 'Norwich Canary'	Widely available
– 'Princess'	See ***C.*** × ***crocosmiiflora* 'Red Knight'**
¶ – 'Princess Alexandra'	IBlr WCHb WWoo
¶ – 'Prolificans'	IBlr
§ – 'Prometheus'	IBlr
N – 'Queen Alexandra' J.E. Fitt	CFir EBee ECha EGar EHal IBlr IBro LAma LHop MLan MUlv NCut SPla SWas SWat WCot WDav WHal
– 'Queen Charlotte'	IBlr
– 'Queen Mary II'	CSte EBee IBlr
¶ – 'Queen of Spain'	CRos EGar IBlr LRHS MBri NTay NWes WCot WMer
– 'Red King'	IBlr
§ – 'Red Knight'	EBee IBlr WCot WHil
– 'Rheingold'	See ***C.*** × ***crocosmiiflora* 'Golden Glory'**
¶ – 'Saracen'	EGar IBlr MBri WCot WFar WPer
– 'Sir Matthew Wilson'	EGar GBri IBlr
N – 'Solfaterre' 🏆	Widely available
– 'Solfaterre Coleton Fishacre'	See ***C.*** × ***crocosmiiflora* 'Gerbe d'Or'**
¶ – 'Star of the East'	Widely available
§ – 'Sulphurea'	CBos CBot CChu CPou CRos CRow CSam EBee EFou EOrc GCal GGar IBlr LAma LGre LHop MBel MBri MCLN NHol NRoo NWes SDix SOkh SPer WAbe WEas WHal WPer
¶ – 'Sultan'	CGle EGar IBlr WCot WFar
– 'Venus'	EGar IBlr
– 'Vesuvius' W. Pfitzer	IBlr MBri
'Darkleaf Apricot'	See ***C.*** × ***crocosmiiflora* 'Gerbe d'Or'**
'Debutante'	WCot
'Eldorado'	See ***C.*** × ***crocosmiiflora* 'E.A. Bowles'**
'Emberglow'	CBro CChu CMHG CRow CSam EBre EGar GCHN GCal IBlr LAma MBal MBri NHol NRoo SMer SPer SWat WAbb WHal WPer
'Fire King' hort.	See ***C.*** × ***crocosmiiflora* 'Jackanapes'**
'Firebird'	CBlo EBre ECha IBlr MUlv NHol NRoo SMer
'Fireglow'	IBlr WPer
'George Davison' hort.	See ***C.*** × ***crocosmiiflora* 'Golden Glory', 'Sulphurea'**
◆ Golden Fleece Lemoine	See ***C.*** × ***crocosmiiflora* 'Gerbe d'Or'**
N 'Honey Angels'	CSte EGar EWoo MBel MLan NTow SUsu WCot WPer
¶ 'Jackanapes'	WGer
'Jenny Bloom'	CAvo CBro CFil CSte EBre EGar GCal MUlv NBir NRoo NTay
§ 'Jupiter'	CAvo CBlo CWan EBee EBre EFou EGar EMil GAbr IBlr MMil NHol WHal
¶ 'Kiaora'	IBlr
'Lady Wilson' hort.	See ***C.*** × ***crocosmiiflora* 'Norwich Canary'**
'Lana de Savary'	CRow EGar GBri IBlr WCot
'Late Cornish'	See ***C.*** × ***crocosmiiflora* 'Queen Alexandra' J.E. Fitt**
'Late Lucifer'	SDix
§ ***latifolia***	IBlr
– 'Castle Ward Late'	CRow EGar GCal IBlr MSte WCot
¶ – 'Vulcan'	IBlr
* 'Lord Nelson'	CBos
'Lucifer' 🏆	Widely available
'Marcotijn'	CSam CSte EGar EWoo GCal IBlr IBro NTow SPla
'Mars'	CMil CSte EBee EBre EGar EHal GBuc GCal IBlr IBro LWak NCut NFai NHol NTay SUsu WBro WCHb WCot WFar WGer WPer WWoo
§ ***masoniorum*** 🏆	CB&S CHEx CHan CRow CShe ECha EFou ELan EOrc EWoo GAbr GBuc IBlr LAma LFis MWat NFla NHol NNor NRog SPer SWat WAbb WByw WCot WPer
– 'Dixter Flame'	IBlr SDix
– 'Fern Hill'	IBlr
– 'Flamenco'	CShe IBlr LRHS MBri MUlv WCot
– red	IBlr
¶ – 'Rowallane'	EBre GBri GCHN IBlr LRHS MBri MUlv NHol NRoo
– Rowallane orange	IBlr
mathewsiana	IBlr

¶ 'Mistral'	IBlr
'Mount Stewart'	See *C.* × ***crocosmiiflora* 'Jessie'**
'Mount Usher'	CAvo ECha EGar IBlr LRHS MBri
'Mr Bedford'	See *C.* × ***crocosmiiflora* 'Croesus'**
'Orangeade'	GBri IBlr
¶ aff. ***paniculata***	IBlr
§ –	CAvo CB&S CPou EMar GAbr IBlr MBal MUlv NHol NOrc NTow SArc SAxl SChu WCot WHoo WPyg
– 'Major'	CTri SPer
¶ – red	IBlr
¶ ***pearsei***	IBlr
pottsii	CFee CRow EBee EGar EPla GBin IBlr MUlv SLod WCot WFar
¶ – CD&R 109	CPou
– 'Culzean Pink'	IBlr
¶ – deep pink	IBlr
– 'Grandiflora'	IBlr
'Red Star'	NFai
rosea	See ***Tritonia disticha*** subsp. ***rubrolucens***
'Rowden Bronze'	See *C.* × ***crocosmiiflora* 'Gerbe d'Or'**
'Rowden Chrome'	See *C.* × ***crocosmiiflora* 'George Davison' Davison**
'Saturn'	See *C.* **'Jupiter'**
'Severn Sunrise'	CAvo CMil CRDP EBee EBre EFou EGar EMan EPPr EPla GBri IBlr LRHS MAvo MBel MGrG MHlr MMil NCat NHol NRoo NWes SApp SLod SWat WCot WFar WGle WMer
'Short Red'	WCot
'Sonate'	CWan NCut NWes WPer
'Spitfire'	CAvo CBot CBre CMil CRow CSam EBee EBre ECha EGar GBuc IBlr MBri MRav MSta NRoo SChu SWat WByw WEas WFar WLRN
'Tangerine Queen'	IBlr
* 'Voyager'	WWoo
'Vulcan'	CMil EBre EOrc EWoo IBlr MBri WFar
'Zeal Giant'	IBlr
'Zeal Tan'	CChu IBlr
¶ Zeal unnamed	IBlr

CROCUS † (Iridaceae)

abantensis	CAvo EHyt ERos LAma WChr
¶ ***adanensis***	EHyt
'Advance'	CAvo CBro EPar EPot EWal LAma NRog
§ ***aerius***	LAma
– 'Cambridge'	EHyt WChr
alatavicus	CBro EHyt EPot
albiflorus	See *C.* ***vernus*** subsp. ***albiflorus***
§ ***ancyrensis***	CAvo CBro EPar EPot ETub LAma NRog WShi
§ ***angustifolius*** ♀	CAvo CBro EBar EBre EPot LAma NRog
– 'Minor'	EPot LAma WChr
¶ ***antalyensis***	EPot
asturicus	See *C.* ***serotinus*** subsp. ***salzmannii***
asumaniae	EHyt ERos LRHS
aureus	See *C.* ***flavus*** subsp. ***flavus***
banaticus ♀	CBro EHyt EPot ERos LAma NGar NHol WChr WCot
banaticus albus	EHyt EPot
baytopiorum	EPot LAma WChr
biflorus	CBro LAma NRog
– subsp. ***adamii***	LAma LWoo MPhe WChr
– subsp. ***alexandri***	CBro EPot LAma MRPP NRog WChr
– 'Argenteus'	See *C.* ***biflorus*** subsp. ***biflorus***
§ – subsp. ***biflorus***	CMon ERos LAma
– – MS 984/957	CMon
– subsp. ***crewei***	ERos LAma
– subsp. ***isauricus***	LRHS WChr
– subsp. ***melantherus*** S&L 226	CMon
– 'Miss Vain'	CAvo LAma
– var. ***parkinsonii***	See *C.* ***biflorus*** subsp. ***biflorus***
– subsp. ***pulchricolor***	LAma WChr
– subsp. ***tauri***	WChr
¶ – subsp. ***weldenii***	MPhe
– – 'Albus'	LAma LRHS
– – 'Fairy'	CAvo CBro EPot LAma
biliottii	See *C.* ***aerius***
boryi ♀	CAvo EHyt EPot LRHS MSto
– CEH 582	WChr
– PJC 168	CMon
– VHH 1546	CMon
cambessedesii	CMon EHyt LWoo
¶ – PB 91	CMon
§ ***cancellatus*** subsp. ***cancellatus***	CBro EHyt ERos LAma
– var. ***cilicicus***	See *C.* ***cancellatus*** subsp. ***cancellatus***
– subsp. ***mazziaricus***	CNic EHyt ERos MPhe MSto
– subsp. ***pamphylicus***	LRHS
candidus var. ***subflavus***	See *C.* ***olivieri*** subsp. ***olivieri***
§ ***cartwrightianus*** ♀	CAvo CBro EHyt LAma MSto
N – 'Albus' ♀	CMon EHyt EPot ERos LWoo MNrw
– CE&H 613	WChr
– S&L 484	CMon
chrysanthus 'Ard Schenk'	EBar EPot LAma
– 'Blue Bird'	EPar EPot EWal LAma
– 'Blue Giant'	LAma
– 'Blue Pearl' ♀	CAvo CBro EHyt EPar EPot ETub LAma MBri NBir NRog WShi
– 'Blue Peter'	CBro LAma
– 'Brass Band'	LAma LRHS
– 'Canary Bird'	NRog
– 'Cream Beauty' ♀	CAvo CBro EBre EHyt EPar EPot ETub EWal LAma MBri NBir NRog WShi
– 'Dorothy'	EPot LAma NRog
– 'E.A. Bowles' ♀	LAma
– 'E.P. Bowles'	CBro EPot LAma MBri NRog
– 'Elegance'	CBro EPot LAma
– 'Eye-catcher'	EPot ETub LAma
– var. ***fuscotinctus***	CBro EPot ETub LAma MBri NRog WShi
– 'Gipsy Girl'	CBro EPot LAma MBri NRog
– 'Gladstone'	LAma
– 'Goldilocks'	CBro EPot ETub LAma
– 'Herald'	EPot LAma
– 'Ladykiller' ♀	CBro EBre EPar EPot LAma MBri NRog
– 'Moonlight'	CBro EPot LAma NRog
– 'Prins Claus'	CAvo EPot ETub LAma WShi
– 'Prinses Beatrix'	EPot LAma NRog
– 'Romance'	EPot LAma
– 'Saturnus'	LAma NRog
– 'Sky Blue'	LAma
– 'Skyline'	CBro EPot

– 'Snow Bunting' 🏆	CAvo CBro EHyt EPar EWal LAma NBir NRog
– 'Spring Pearl'	CBro LAma
– 'Sunkist'	LAma
¶ – 'Uschak Orange'	EPot
– 'Warley'	NRog
– 'White Beauty'	LAma
– 'White Triumphator'	EPot ETub LAma NBir NRog
– 'Zenith'	LAma LRHS
– 'Zwanenburg Bronze' 🏆	CAvo EBre EHyt EPar EPot EWal LAma NRog
'Cloth of Gold'	See ***C. angustifolius***
clusii	See ***C. serotinus*** subsp. ***clusii***
corsicus 🏆	EPar EPot ERos LAma WChr
cvijicii	EPot
cyprius	WChr
dalmaticus	EPot LAma WChr
'Dutch Yellow'	See ***C.*** × ***luteus* 'Golden Yellow'**
etruscus 🏆	CAvo
– B&S 334	CMon
* – 'Rosalind'	EPot
– 'Zwanenburg'	EPot LAma
flavus	See ***C. flavus*** subsp. ***flavus***
§ – subsp. ***flavus*** 🏆	EPot LAma WChr
– M&T 4578	CMon
fleischeri	EPot ERos LAma NMen WChr
gargaricus	EPot ERos GCLN LRHS
– subsp. ***herbertii***	WChr
'Golden Mammoth'	See ***C.*** × ***luteus* 'Golden Yellow'**
goulimyi 🏆	CAvo CBro EHyt EPar EPot ERos LAma MRPP WChr WCot WThi
– 'Albus'	See ***C. goulimyi* 'Mani White'**
¶ – deep colour form	EHyt
– var. ***leucanthus***	EHyt
§ – 'Mani White' 🏆	CAvo EHyt WChr
– S&L 197	CMon
'Haarlem Gem'	LAma WCot
§ ***hadriaticus*** 🏆	CAvo EHyt EPot LAma LWoo MSto WChr
– B&M 8039	WChr
– BM 8124	CMon
– var. ***chrysobelonicus***	See ***C. hadriaticus***
¶ – f. ***lilacinus***	EPot
hermoneus LB 1	CMon
hyemalis S&L 50	CMon
imperati subsp. ***imperati*** 'De Jager'	CAvo EPot ETub LAma WCot
– – MS 965	CMon
– subsp. ***suaveolens***	LRHS
– – MS 962	CMon
× ***jessoppiae***	WChr
karduchorum	CBro LAma NRog
korolkowii	EHyt EPar EPot ERos ETub LAma
– 'Agalik'	WChr
– 'Dytiscus'	WChr
– 'Golden Nugget'	EPot WChr
– 'Kiss of Spring'	EPot WChr
– 'Mountain Glory'	WChr
– 'Varzob'	WChr
– 'Yellow Princess'	EPot
– 'Yellow Tiger'	WChr
kosaninii	MPhe
kotschyanus 🏆	CAvo EHyt MSto
– 'Albus'	EPot SRms WChr
¶ – subsp. ***cappadocicus*** 🏆	EHyt
– CM&W 2720	CMon
§ – subsp. ***kotschyanus*** 🏆	CBro EPot LAma LWoo NRog WCot
– var. ***leucopharynx***	CMon ECha EPot
laevigatus 🏆	LWoo

– CE&H 612	CMon WChr
– 'Fontenayi'	CAvo CBro EHyt EPot ETub LAma WChr
– form	LAma
¶ – from Crete	EHyt
'Large Yellow'	See ***C.*** × ***luteus* 'Golden Yellow'**
lazicus	See ***C. scharojanii***
longiflorus 🏆	CAvo CBro EPot WChr
– MS 968/974/967	CMon
§ × ***luteus*** 'Golden Yellow' 🏆	EPot LAma MHlr
§ – 'Stellaris'	CMon EHyt EPot
malyi 🏆	CMon EPot GCrs LWoo MPhe
– CE&H 519	WChr
'Mammoth Yellow'	See ***C.*** × ***luteus* 'Golden Yellow'**
medius 🏆	CBro CMon ECha EPot ERos LAma NMGW NMen NRog
minimus	CBro CMea EHyt EPar EPot ERos LAma
niveus	CAvo CBro EHyt EPot LAma LWoo WCot
– blue	WChr
– PJC 164	WChr
– S&L 194	CMon
nudiflorus	CAvo CBro EPot ERos LAma LWoo NHol WChr
– MS 872	CMon
ochroleucus 🏆	CBro EBre EHyt EPot ERos LAma NRog
olivieri	EHyt EPar EPot ERos LAma MPhe
– subsp. ***balansae***	WChr
¶ – – 'Zwanenburg'	EPot
§ – subsp. ***olivieri***	CMon LAma WChr
oreocreticus	EHyt MSto
– PB 137	CMon
pallasii	EPot LAma MPhe
¶ ***pelistericus***	EHyt EPot
pestalozzae	EHyt EPot ERos
– var. ***caeruleus***	EPot WChr
pulchellus 🏆	EPot ETub LAma
pulchellus albus	WChr
pulchellus CE&H 558	WChr
– M&T 4584	CMon
'Purpureus'	See ***C. vernus* 'Purpureus Grandiflorus'**
reticulatus	EHyt LWoo MPhe WChr
– subsp. ***reticulatus***	EPot
robertianus 🏆	EHyt LRHS WChr
¶ ***rujanensis***	MPhe
sativus	CArn CAvo CBro ELan EPot GPoy LAma LHol MBri MHew MSal NRog SIde
– var. ***cartwrightianus***	See ***C. cartwrightianus***
– var. ***cashmirianus***	CMon ETub
scardicus	EHyt EPot NHar WChr
scepusiensis	See ***C. vernus*** subsp. ***vernus*** var. ***scepusiensis***
§ ***scharojanii***	EPot LRHS WChr
– var. ***flavus***	LRHS WChr
§ ***serotinus*** subsp. ***clusii*** 🏆	CBro EHyt EPot LAma WChr
§ – subsp. ***salzmannii***	CBro ECha EHyt ERos LAma MSto
– – AB&S 4326	CMon
– – 'Albus'	WChr
– – MS 343	CMon
– – SF 218	CMon
sibiricus	See ***C. sieberi***
§ ***sieberi*** 🏆	EHyt EPot ERos LAma
§ – 'Albus' 🏆	CAvo CBro EBar EPot LAma
– subsp. ***atticus***	EPot LAma
– 'Bowles' White'	See ***C. sieberi* 'Albus'**

– 'Firefly'	CBro EPot LAma NRog
– 'Hubert Edelsten' 🏆	CBro EPot ERos LAma
– f. ***pallidus***	CMon
– subsp. ***sublimis*** 'Tricolor' 🏆	CBro EPot ERos ETub LAma WChr
– 'Violet Queen'	CBro ETub LAma MBri NRog
speciosus 🏆	CAvo CBro EBre EPar ETub GCHN LAma NHol NMGW NRog WShi
– 'Aitchisonii'	CBro EPot LAma
– 'Albus' 🏆	CBro CMon ECha EPar EPot
– 'Artabir'	CAvo CBro EPot MRPP
– 'Cassiope'	EPot LAma
– 'Conqueror'	CBro ETub LAma
– 'Oxonian'	EMon EPot LAma
¶ – 'Big Boy' (*C. speciosus* × *pulchellus*)	EHyt
× ***stellaris***	See ***C.*** × ***luteus*** **'Stellaris'**
susianus	See ***C. angustifolius***
suterianus	See ***C. olivieri*** subsp. ***olivieri***
thomasii B&S 364	CMon
– MS 978/982	CMon
tommasinianus 🏆	CAvo CBro EPar EPot ETub LAma MBri NGar NMGW WShi
– f. ***albus***	CBro EHyt EPot LAma NGar
– 'Barr's Purple'	LAma
– 'Bobbo'	EHyt
– 'Eric Smith'	CAvo WChr
– 'Lilac Beauty'	EPot LAma
– PF 6584	CMon
– var. ***pictus***	CAvo EHyt LAma NGar WChr
¶ – purple tips	EHyt
– var. ***roseus***	CBro EHyt EPot LAma MRPP NGar WChr
– 'Ruby Giant'	CAvo CBro CNic EPar EPot ETub LAma NGar NRog WShi
– 'Whitewell Purple'	CAvo CBro EPot LAma MBri MHlr NGar NMGW NRog
tournefortii 🏆	CAvo CBro CMon EHyt EPot LAma LWoo
vallicola	MSto
veluchensis	EPot MPhe
– JCA 354.002	LWoo
veneris PB 198	CMon
§ ***vernus*** subsp. ***albiflorus***	EPot ERos LAma MSto
– 'Enchantress'	EPot ETub LAma
– 'Flower Record'	EPot NBir
– 'Graecus'	EHyt EPot
– 'Grand Maître'	LAma NRog
– 'Jeanne d'Arc'	CBro EPot ETub LAma NBir NRog
– 'King of the Blues'	LAma NRog
– 'Paulus Potter'	NRog
– 'Peter Pan'	NRog
– 'Pickwick'	EPot ETub LAma NBir NRog
§ – 'Purpureus Grandiflorus'	CBro EPot ETub LAma NRog
– 'Queen of the Blues'	CBro EPot NRog
– 'Remembrance'	EPot LAma NBir NRog
– 'Sky Blue'	NRog
– 'Snowstorm'	LAma
– 'Striped Beauty'	LAma NRog
– 'Vanguard'	CBro EPot ETub LAma NRog
– subsp. ***vernus*** 'Grandiflorus'	See ***C. vernus*** **'Purpureus Grandiflorus'**
§ – – Heuffelianus Group	EHyt EPot NGar
* – subsp. ***vernus napolitanus***	ERos
§ – subsp. ***vernus*** var. ***scepusiensis***	EHyt EPot ERos MRPP
– 'Victor Hugo'	NRog
¶ – WM 9615 from E Slovenia	MPhe
versicolor	MSto
– 'Picturatus'	EBre EPot ERos ETub LAma
'Yellow Mammoth'	See ***C.*** × ***luteus*** **'Golden Yellow'**
'Zephyr' 🏆	CBro EPot ETub GCLN ITim LAma
zonatus	See ***C. kotschyanus*** subsp. ***kotschyanus***

CROSSANDRA (Acanthaceae)

infundibuliformis	MBri

CROTALARIA (Papilionaceae)

¶ ***capensis***	CTrC

CROWEA (Rutaceae)

See Plant Deletions

CRUCIANELLA (Rubiaceae)

stylosa	See ***Phuopsis stylosa***

CRUCIATA (Rubiaceae)

§ ***laevipes***	CKin EWFC NMir

CRYPTANTHA (Boraginaceae)

See Plant Deletions

CRYPTANTHUS (Bromeliaceae)

bivittatus 🏆	CHal
– 'Pink Starlight' (v) 🏆	MBri
– 'Roseus Pictus'	CHal
bromelioides	MBri
* 'Red Starlight' (v)	MBri
× ***roseus*** 'Le Rey'	MBri
– 'Marian Oppenheimer'	MBri

× CRYPTBERGIA (Bromeliaceae)

See Plant Deletions

CRYPTOCARYA (Lauraceae)

alba	CGre

CRYPTOGRAMMA (Cryptogrammaceae)

crispa	CCuc SRms

CRYPTOMERIA (Taxodiaceae)

fortunei	See ***C. japonica*** var. ***sinensis***
japonica 🏆	CDoC GAri GAul IOrc ISea LCon MBar MLan STre WFro WNor
§ – 'Araucarioides'	ECho EHul
– 'Aritaki'	LCon
– 'Bandai-sugi' 🏆	CBlo CDoC CKen CMac EBar EHul EOrn LCon LLin MBar MGos MOne NHed SCoo SLim SSmi STre WStI
¶ – 'Barabits Gold'	MGos
– 'Compressa'	CBlo CKen CSam EBar EHul EPla LBee LCon LLin MBar MBri MOne MPla NHar SLim SSmi WLRN
§ – 'Cristata'	CDoC CMac ELan LCon LLin MBal MBar SIng WWeb
* – 'Cristata Compacta'	EOrn
– 'Elegans'	CB&S CDoC CHig CMac CWLN EHul ELan ENHC ENot EOrn GRei IOrc LCon LLin LNet LPan MBal MBar MWat SBod SHBN SLim SPer WDin WFar WPyg WWin

– 'Elegans Aurea'	CDoC CGre CTri CWLN EHul LCon LLin MBal MBar MPla SBod SRms STre WDin WPyg
– 'Elegans Compacta' ♀	CB&S CDoC EBar EBee EHul LBee LCon MBar MPla SLim
– 'Elegans Nana'	CBlo LBee SLim SRms
– 'Elegans Viridis'	CBlo SLim
– 'Enko-sugi'	See *C. japonica* **'Araucarioides'**
– 'Globosa'	CDoC EOrn SRms
– 'Globosa Nana'	EHul LBee LCon LLin LPan MBar NHed SHBN SLim WGor
– 'Gracilis'	LCon
– 'Jindai-sugi'	CMac MBal MBar MPla NHed
– 'Kilmacurragh'	CKen EHul MBar SLim
– 'Kohui Yatsubusa'	CKen
– 'Koshiji-yatsubusa'	EOrn MBar MBri
– 'Koshyi'	CKen
– 'Little Diamond'	CKen
– 'Lobbii Nana'	See *C. japonica* **'Nana'**
§ – 'Mankichi-sugi'	CBlo
– 'Midare-sugi'	See *C. japonica* **'Viridis'**
– 'Monstrosa'	CMHG MBar
– 'Monstrosa Nana'	See *C. japonica* **'Mankichi-sugi'**
§ – 'Nana'	CDoC CMac CTri EBre EHul ENHC LLin MBal MPla SBod SPer WLRN
– 'Pygmaea'	CBlo CWLN LCon MBar SRms
– 'Rasen-sugi'	COtt GAri LCon LPan NPal SLim SMad
– 'Sekkan-sugi'	CB&S EBre EHul EOrn EPla GAri LBee LCon LLin MAsh MBar MBri MGos MPla SAga SLim SMad WPyg
– 'Sekka-sugi'	See *C. japonica* **'Cristata'**
§ – var. ***sinensis***	CMCN LCon
* – – 'Vilmoriniana Compacta'	EOrn
§ – 'Spiralis'	CDoC CGre CKen CMHG CMac EHul EOrn EPfP IOrc LBee LCon LLin MBal MBar MBri MGos NHed SLim SPer SSmi WWeb
§ – 'Spiraliter Falcata'	CBlo CDoC MBar
– 'Tenzan-sugi'	CKen
– 'Tilford Gold'	EHul LLin MBar NHed WAbe
– 'Vilmorin Gold'	CKen EOrn
– 'Vilmorin Variegated'	EPla
– 'Vilmoriniana' ♀	CDoC CKen CMHG CWLN EBre EHul ENHC ENot EPfP EPot IOrc LBee LCon LLin MBal MBar MGos MWat NHar NHed NHol SBod SHBN SIng SLim SPer SPla SSmi SSta WDin
– 'Viminalis'	NHol
– 'Winter Bronze'	CKen
– 'Wogon'	See *C. japonica* **'Aurea'**
– 'Yatsubasa'	See *C. japonica* **'Tansu'**
– 'Yokohama'	CBlo EHul EOrn LCon MAsh MBar NHar NHol SLim
– 'Yore-sugi'	See *C. japonica* **'Spiralis'**
– 'Yoshino'	CKen
♦ ***sinensis***	See *C. japonica* var. ***sinensis***

CRYPTOSTEGIA (Asclepiadaceae)
See Plant Deletions

CRYPTOTAENIA (Apiaceae)

canadensis	MRav
japonica	CPou EOHP LFis WHer WJek
– f. ***atropurpurea***	CBos CElw CGle CRDP CVer EBre ECha ECoo ECro EFol EHoe EMan EMon GCal MNrw NPer NWes WCot WEas WPbr

CTENANTHE (Marantaceae)

§ ***amabilis*** ♀	CHal MBri
* 'Greystar'	MBri
lubbersiana ♀	CHal MBri
§ ***oppenheimiana***	MBri
setosa	MBri
'Stripe Star'	MBri

CUCUBALUS (Caryophyllaceae)

baccifer	EMon

CUCUMIS (Cucurbitaceae)

metulifer (F)	MSto

CUCURBITA (Cucurbitaceae)

'Cerrano'	MSto
ficifolia	MSto

CUDRANIA (Moraceae)

tricuspidata	CAgr

CUMINUM (Apiaceae)

cyminum	CArn SIde WSel

CUNILA (Lamiaceae)
See Plant Deletions

CUNNINGHAMIA (Taxodiaceae)

§ ***lanceolata***	CB&S CBlo CGre CMCN EFol ELan LCon LLin MDun MPla SLim SSta WNor
§ – 'Bánó'	CChu EPla MPla
– 'Compacta'	See *C. lanceolata* **'Bánó'**
* – 'Coolwijn's Compact'	CKen
– 'Little Leo'	CKen
– Ogisu 911101	CChu
sinensis	See ***C. lanceolata***
unicaniculata	See ***C. lanceolata***

CUNONIA (Cunoniaceae)

¶ ***capensis***	CTrC

CUPHEA (Lythraceae)

caeciliae	CBrk CHal CLTr
cyanaea	CAbb CBrk CHan CMHG CSev GMac LHil LHop SDix SIgm SVen WFar
cyanaea hirtella	CBrk EBee LHop
hyssopifolia ♀	CBrk CFee CHal CPle CTre EMil ERea GQui IBlr MBri SRms STre
– 'Alba'	CBrk CLTr CPle ERea LIck MLan NCut STre
– 'Riverdene Gold'	CBrk CHal CLTr
– 'Rob's Mauve'	CB&S
– 'Rosea'	LIck NCut
§ ***ignea*** ♀	CBrk CHal CLTr ELan IBlr LCns LHil MBri NPri SLMG SOWG SRms SUsu
– 'Variegata'	CBrk CHal IBlr LCns LHil SLod SOWG
llavea	See ***C.*** × ***purpurea***
macrophylla	CBrk
miniata hort.	See ***C.*** × ***purpurea***
platycentra	See ***C. ignea***

× CUPRESSOCYPARIS † (Cupressaceae)

§ ***leylandii*** CB&S CChe CDoC CMac EBre EHul ENHC ENot IOrc ISea LBuc LCon LHyr LPan MBal MBar MBri MGos SBod SLim SPer WHar WMou WStI
§ – 'Castlewellan' CB&S CDoC CMac EBre EHul ENHC ENot EPot ERom IOrc ISea LBuc LCon LHyr LPan MBal MBar MBri MGos MWat SBod SLim SPer WAbe WHar WMou
– 'Galway Gold' See **× *C. leylandii* 'Castlewellan'**
– 'Golconda' EBre
– 'Gold Rider' ♀ CDoC EHul IOrc LBee LPan MAsh MBar MBri MGos SLim SPer WHar WLRN WStI
§ – 'Harlequin' (v) CMHG LCon MBar WHar WWeb
– 'Hyde Hall' CTri EOrn EPla LBee LCon SBod SSto WAbe WLRN
– 'Michellii' MBar
– 'Naylor's Blue' CMac
– 'New Ornament' SMad
– 'Olive Green' COtt CSte IOrc LCon LPan SCoo WHar WWeb
– 'Robinson's Gold' ♀ CMac EHul GAri GQui ISea LBee LCon MAsh MBal MBar NWea SBod SLim WHar WStI
– 'Silver Dust' (v) MBri NEgg SRms WAbe WFar
– 'Variegata' See **× *C. leylandii* 'Harlequin'**
ovensii EHul

CUPRESSUS (Cupressaceae)

N ***arizonica*** var. ***arizonica*** MBal
– – 'Arctic' LRHS MBri WFar
◆ – var. ***bonita*** See ***C. arizonica*** var. ***arizonica***
– 'Conica Glauca' ENot MBar
– var. ***glabra*** 'Aurea' CBlo EBee EFol EHul LCon MBar SLim
– – 'Blue Ice' CB&S CDoC CKen CMHG EBee EHul LCon LLin MBar MBri MGos SLim
– – 'Compacta' CKen
– – 'Conica' CKen SBod WWat
I – – 'Fastigiata' CB&S EHul LCon LPan MBar MBri
– 'Pyramidalis' ♀ CMac SHhN SLim SPer
I – 'Sulfurea' CBlo CKen WWeb
bakeri CMHG ISea
cashmeriana See ***C. torulosa* 'Cashmeriana'**
chengiana CMCN
duclouxiana CMHG
§ ***funebris*** GAri ISea
glabra See ***C. arizonica*** var. ***glabra***
goveniana GAri MBar
guadalupensis CMHG
lusitanica 'Glauca Pendula' CKen CPMA LCon MBri
– 'Pygmy' CKen
macrocarpa CDoC CMCN EHul SEND WHCr
– 'Barnham Gold' SBod SRms
I – 'Compacta' CKen CMac
– 'Donard Gold' ♀ CMac CTri EOrn LCon MBal MBar
– 'Gold Cone' CKen
– 'Gold Spread' ♀ CDoC EHul EOrn LCon SLim
– 'Goldcrest' ♀ CB&S CDoC CMac EHul ENot EOrn IOrc LBee LCon LLin LPan MBal MBar MBri MGos MPla SBod SLim SPer WAbe WDin WPyg
– 'Golden Cone' CMac MBal
– 'Golden Pillar' CDoC CMac EHul LBee LCon LLin MAsh MBar MWat SLim SPla WDin WLRN WPyg
– 'Greenstead Magnificent' MAsh
– 'Horizontalis Aurea' CTri EBee EHul MBar
– 'Lohbrunner' CKen
– 'Lutea' CB&S CDoC CMac EHul MWat
– 'Pygmaea' CKen
– 'Sulphur Cushion' CKen
– 'Sulphurea' See ***C. macrocarpa* 'Crippsii'**
– 'Wilma' EBee EHul LCon WWeb
– 'Woking' CKen
sempervirens CB&S EHul LLin
– 'Green Pencil' See ***C. sempervirens* 'Green Spire'**
– 'Pyramidalis' See ***C. sempervirens* 'Stricta'**
– var. ***sempervirens*** See ***C. sempervirens* 'Stricta'**
§ – 'Stricta' ♀ CArn CSWP CSam EHul EPfP GAri LBee LCon LPan SArc SLPl
– 'Swane's Gold' ♀ CB&S CKen CMHG EHul LBee LCon LLin MPla SLim
– 'Totem Pole' CBlo EHul MGos SEND SLim WWeb
§ ***torulosa*** 'Cashmeriana' ♀ CDoC CHEx ERea MBri SLim WNor

CURCUMA (Zingiberaceae)

¶ ***petiolata*** WCot
¶ ***zedoaria*** LAma

CURTONUS See CROCOSMIA

CUSSONIA (Araliaceae)

¶ ***paniculata*** CTrC SIgm
¶ ***spicata*** CTrC

CYANANTHUS (Campanulaceae)

incanus EPad
inflatus GCra
integer hort. See ***C. microphyllus***
– 'Sherriff's Variety' GDra NHar NHol WAbe WDav
– Wallich WAbe
lobatus ♀ CMea EHyt EPad GBuc LBee NGre NSla SBla SRms WCru
– 'Albus' EPot EWes NHar SBla SWas
– 'Dark Beauty' EDAr NHar SChu
¶ – dark form EWes GDra WDav
– giant form GDra GTou NHar SBla WCru
– var. ***insignis*** EPad WThi
– × ***microphyllus*** NWCA WCru
longiflorus ACE 1963 NHar
§ ***microphyllus*** ♀ EPad GDra LBee NGre NSla SBla WCru
sherriffii WThi
spathulifolius EPad
– CLD 1492 NHar

CYANELLA (Tecophilaeaceae)

capensis See ***C. hyacinthoides***
orchidiformis CMon LBow

CYANOTIS (Commelinaceae)

somaliensis 🏆	CHal

CYATHEA (Cyatheaceae)

* *albifrons*	WRic
australis	CTrC EOas GQui WRic
¶ *brownii*	WRic
¶ *celebica*	WRic
cooperi	CB&S LCns WRic
* – 'Brentwood'	WRic
¶ *cunninghamii*	WRic
dealbata	CAbb CB&S CHEx GQui WRic
* *intermedia*	WRic
* 'Marleyi'	WRic
medullaris	CB&S CHEx WRic
¶ *rebeccae*	WRic
¶ *robertsiana*	WRic
smithii	CHEx WRic
tomentosissima	WRic
¶ *woollsiana*	WRic

CYATHODES (Epacridaceae)

§ *colensoi*	CChu CMHG ECou EPot GCal MBal MBar MBri MPla NHar SPer SSpi WAbe WBod WPat WWat
fasciculata	See ***Leucopogon fasciculatus***
fraseri	See ***Leucopogon fraseri***
juniperina	ECou
§ *parviflora*	ECou

CYBISTETES (Amaryllidaceae)

longifolia	NRog WChr

CYCAS (Cycadaceae)

cairnsiana	LPal
circinalis	LPal
kennedyana	See ***C. papuana***
media	LPal
§ *papuana*	LPal
revoluta 🏆	CAbb CBrP CHEx CTrC LCns LPal LPan MBri NPal SArc SEND WNor
§ *rumphii*	LPal
thouarsii	See ***C. rumphii***

CYCLAMEN † (Primulaceae)

africanum	CBro CElm CLCN CMon EBre EJWh EPot LAma MAsh NTow STil WAbe WIvy
balearicum	CAvo CBro CElm CLCN CMon EBre EHyt EJWh EPot LAma LCTD MAsh MBal SAlw SBla STil WCot
cilicium 🏆	Widely available
– f. *album*	CAvo CBro CElm CLCN EBre EHyt EJWh LAma LCTD MAsh SIng STil WChr
§ *coum* 🏆	Widely available
– var. *abchasicum*	See ***C. coum*** subsp. ***caucasicum***
* – Blanchard's form pink-flowered	EJWh
– 'Blush'	LCTD STil
– 'Broadleigh Silver'	LCTD
– BS 8927	LCTD
– BSBE	STil
§ – subsp. *caucasicum*	EPot LAma STil
– subsp. *coum*	CBro MBal
– – f. *albissimum*	LCTD
– – *album*	CAvo CBot CElm EHyt EPot LAma MAsh MSto NGre NHol NRoo SDeJ STil WAbe WChr WHoo WNor
– – *album* patterned leaved	LCTD STil
– – 'Atkinsii'	CBro MBro
– – 'Nymans' ex EKB 371	EPot LCTD SBla
– – Pewter Group 🏆	CMil MAsh MTho NGar NRoo SSpi WIvy WPyg
* – – – bicoloured	EJWh
– – – red	CLCN LAma LCTD SWas WChr WPat
– – – white	WChr
– – *roseum*	CAvo CElm LAma LBow SDeJ STil WAbe WChr
– – plain-leaved red	STil
¶ – – Silver Group	CBro LRHS
– – – bicolor	CElm LCTD
– – – red	CAvo EBre EPot LCTD MTho NHar STil WAbe WHoo
– 'Crimson King'	SDeJ
– dark pink	CAvo LCTD
– 'Dusky Maid'	LCTD
– forms	LAma LCTD MBro MS&S WWat
* – 'Heavy Metal'	LCTD
– *ibericum album*	See ***C. coum*** subsp. ***caucasicum album***
– 'Linnett Jewel'	LCTD
– 'Linnett Rose'	LCTD
– M&T 4051	CMon
¶ – marbled leaf	WHoo
– 'Maurice Dryden'	CAvo CBro CGle CLCN LAma LCTD MAsh MHig STil WIvy
– 'Meaden's Crimson'	LCTD
– *merymana*	CElm
– plain-leaved	CElm EPot LCTD
– red	WAbe WChr
– scented	CElm
– 'Silver Star'	LCTD
– 'Sterling Silver'	LCTD
– 'Tile Barn Elizabeth'	EHyt MAsh STil
¶ – TK form	ERos
– 'Turkish Princess'	LCTD
– 'Urfa'	EPot
creticum	CBro CLCN CMon EJWh LAma MAsh STil
– × *repandum*	CBro
cyprium	CAvo CBro CElm CLCN EBre EHyt EJWh EPot LAma MAsh MHig NGar NGre SBla STil WChr WCot WIvy
– 'E.S.'	CElm LCTD MAsh STil
europaeum	See ***C. purpurascens***
fatrense	See ***C. purpurascens*** subsp. ***purpurascens***
graecum	CBro CElm CFil CLCN EJWh EPot LAma MAsh SIng SSpi STil WIvy
– f. *album*	CAvo CBro EHyt EJWh LAma LRHS MAsh STil WChr
§ *hederifolium* 🏆	Widely available
– *albissimum albissimum*	LCTD
– f. *album*	CAvo CBro CElm CLCN CSWP EPot ERos ETub GPoy LAma LBow MBar MBri MBro MFos MSto NHar NHol NRog NTow SBla SIng SSpi STil SWas WAbe WCla WHoo WOMN WWat
– arrow-head form	LCTD

– 'Bowles' Apollo' CElm CSWP LCTD LWoo MAsh SBla SSpi STil
– 'Coquette' LCTD
– 'Fairy Rings' LCTD MAsh
– forms CElm LAma LCTD MS&S
– 'Green Elf' LCTD
– 'Nettleton Silver' EPot
– 'Perlenteppich' GMaP LCTD NHol
– red WPyg
– 'Rosenteppich' GMaP LCTD NHol
– Ruby strain LCTD
– scented CLCN LCTD SBla STil
– 'Silver Cloud' CBro CLCN LCTD LWoo MAsh STil
¶ – 'Silver Leaf' WIvy
– silver leaved CAvo CElm CMil EPot LCTD MAsh STil
– 'Silver Shield' LCTD
– 'White Bowles' Apollo' CLCN CMil LCTD
* – 'White Cloud' STil
ibericum See ***C. coum*** subsp. ***caucasicum***
intaminatum CAvo CBro CLCN CPBP CSWP EDAr EHyt EJWh EPot ERos LAma MAsh NGar NHol NTow SBla STil WAbe WIvy
– EKB 628 EPot
– patterned-leaved CElm EJWh LCTD NGre STil
– plain-leaved CElm NGre STil
latifolium See ***C. persicum***
libanoticum 🏆 CAvo CBro CElm CLCN EBre EHyt EJWh EPot LAma LCTD MAsh MBal NGre SAlw SBla STil WChr WCot
mirabile 🏆 CAvo CBro CFee CLCN EBre EJWh EPot LAma MAsh MHig MS&S NGar NGre SBla STil WAbe WChr WIvy
¶ – 'Tilebarn Anne' STil
¶ – 'Tilebarn Jan' STil
– 'Tilebarn Nicholas' STil
neapolitanum See ***C. hederifolium***
orbiculatum See ***C. coum***
parviflorum CBro CLCN EJWh EPot LAma STil
§ ***persicum*** CBro CElm CFil CLCN EJWh LAma MAsh STil
– RRL N8/65 CMon
– S&L 55 CMon
pseudibericum 🏆 CAvo CBro CLCN CMon EBre EHyt EJWh EPot LAma LCTD MAsh SBla STil WChr WIvy
– 'Roseum' CLCN EHyt LCTD MAsh STil
– scented form LCTD
§ ***purpurascens*** 🏆 CBro CElm CFil CLCN EBre EJWh EPot GDra LAma MAsh MFos MS&S NRoo SBla SSpi STil WChr WIvy WPat WWat
– var. ***fatrense*** See ***C. purpurascens*** subsp. ***purpurascens***
– 'Lake Garda' CFil MAsh SSpi WPGP
– Limone form SBla SSpi
§ – subsp. ***purpurascens*** EPot NGre STil
– silver-leaved LCTD
¶ – white-flowered SBla
repandum 🏆 CBro CElm CFil CLCN EBre EDAr EHyt EJWh EPot LAma LCTD MAsh MBal NGre NRoo SBla SSpi STil SWas WChr
– 'Album' CLCN EHyt EJWh EPot MAsh SBla STil
– × ***balearicum*** CLCN EJWh
¶ – JCA 5157 SSpi
¶ – subsp. ***peloponnesiacum*** 🏆 EJWh MAsh
§ – – f. ***peloponnesiacum*** 🏆 CBro CElm CLCN LCTD NGre SSpi STil
¶ – – f. ***vividum*** STil
– 'Pelops' See ***C. repandum*** subsp. ***peloponnesiacum* f. *peloponnesiacum***
– subsp. ***rhodense*** CLCN LAma LCTD MAsh SSpi STil
rohlfsianum CBro CFil CLCN CMon EJWh EPot MAsh NGre STil WChr
'Super Puppet' EOHP
trochopteranthum CAvo CBro CElm CLCN EHyt EJWh EPot LAma LCTD MAsh NHol NRog SBla STil WAbe WChr WIvy
– 'Pink Swirl' LCTD
– 'Red Devil' LCTD
× ***wellensiekii*** STil

CYCLANTHERA (Cucurbitaceae)

pedata CPlN MSto

CYCLOSORUS (Thelypteridaceae)

See Plant Deletions

CYDISTA (Bignoniaceae)

aequinoctialis CPlN

CYDONIA (Rosaceae)

* 'Isfahan' SKee
japonica See ***Chaenomeles speciosa***
oblonga (F) ESim LHol
– 'Bereczcki' See ***C. oblonga* 'Vranja'**
– 'Champion' (F) GTwe WJas
– 'Early Prolific' SKee
– 'Le Bourgeaut' (F) GTwe
* – 'Lescovacz' MGos WJas
– 'Ludovic' GTwe WJas
– Portugal = 'Lusitanica' (F) CBlo GTwe NRog SIgm WJas
– 'Meech's Prolific' (F) CDoC CSam CTho EMui ERea ESim GTwe MBlu MWat NDal SDea SFam SIgm SKee
– pear shaped CBlo CTri NRog
– 'Seibosa' (F) SKee
§ – 'Vranja' (F) 🏆 CBar CDoC CMac CTho EBre ERea EWar GTwe LBuc MBri MGos MMor NRog SDea SFam SIgm SKee SPer WDin WJas WMou

CYMBALARIA (Scrophulariaceae)

aequitriloba WAbe
– 'Alba' GGar
§ ***hepaticifolia*** EDAr EPot LBee MTol NGre NNrd SRms WCot WCru WPer
– 'Alba' CNic
§ ***muralis*** CArn CKin EBar ECWi EWFC GAbr MBar MTol NCGP NMir NPri SIde WGor WHer WTyr
– 'Albiflora' See ***C. muralis* 'Pallidior'**
§ – 'Globosa Alba' CHal EDAr EPot MDHE
– 'Globosa Rosea' NNrd WCla
– 'Nana Alba' CPea ELan EPPr GAbr MDHE MLan NNrd NPri NWCA WPer
§ – 'Pallidior' CMea ESis MBar NHar WHil WOMN WWin

§ *pallida* CMea LBee NHar NSla SBla WBea WByw WCla WCru WFar WHil WPer
§ *pilosa* ECtt EMNN GAbr NGre NNrd NSti WLRN
– 'Alba' NGre

CYMBIDIUM † (Orchidaceae)
¶ *ensifolium* var. *rubrigemmum* SWes
* *goeringii* var. *formosanum* SWes
¶ *kanran* SWes
¶ *sinense* SWes
* – var. *album* SWes

CYMBOPOGON (Poaceae)
citratus CArn CJew CSev ELau EOHP GPoy MChe MGra MSal NPri SHDw SIde WHer WJek WOak WWye
martinii EOHP GPoy MSal
nardus GPoy MSal

CYMOPHYLLUS (Cyperaceae)
fraseri EPla WCot

CYMOPTERUS (Apiaceae)
See Plant Deletions

CYNANCHUM (Asclepiadaceae)
* *acuminatifolium* GCal
sp. B&SWJ 1924 WCru

CYNARA (Asteraceae)
§ *baetica* subsp. *maroccana* ECha LGre WCot WHal
§ *cardunculus* ♀ CDoC CFee CHad CMea CSev ECha EFou ELan EOrc ERav GCal ILis MBel MBri MUlv NNor NPer SArc SDix SIgm SMad SPer SPla WCHb WCot WEas WHer WWin WWye
– ACL 380/78 EMon
– 'Cardy' CBot EGoo EMan MLLN WWhi
– dwarf form SDix
– Scolymus Group CB&S CHad CJew EBre ERav GCal GPoy ILis LHol MBri SMrm WByw WHer WOak
– – 'Green Globe' CBod CBot CSev ECoo NPSI NPer
– – 'Gros Camus de Bretagne' WCot
– – 'Gros Vert de Lâon' WCot
– – 'Purple Globe' CArn NPSI
– – 'Violetto di Chioggia' WHer
hystrix See *C. baetica* subsp. *maroccana*

CYNOGLOSSUM (Boraginaceae)
amabile ♀ EBar ELan SRms
¶ – 'Firmament' WCot
– f. *roseum* SCro WFar
dioscoridis CBot CGle WPer
grande CArc SCro
hungaricum EBee
nervosum CBot CGle EAst EBre ECED ECGP ECha ECtt EFou ELan EMar EMil EPar MRav MTol NMir NSti SPer SRms SWat WCHb WWhi WWin
officinale ECWi EWFC GBar MChe MHew MSal NMir SIde WCHb WCer WHer
zeylanicum CBot EMar WOMN

CYNOSURUS (Poaceae)
cristatus CKin

CYPELLA (Iridaceae)
aquatilis MSta
§ *coelestis* EGar WPer
herbertii CGle CMon LAma MHig
plumbea See *C. coelestis*

CYPERUS (Cyperaceae)
§ *albostriatus* CHal ETPC MBri
alternifolius hort. See *C. involucratus*
§ *cyperoides* MBri
diffusus hort. See *C. albostriatus*
§ *eragrostis* CCuc CDec CHal CRow EBee ECha EGar EHoe EPPr EPla ESOG ETPC SDix SWat WAbb
esculentus IBlr
fuscus CCuc EPPr WHal
haspan hort. See *C. papyrus* 'Nanus'
§ *involucratus* ♀ CBen CHEx CHal CKni CWGN EBak EMFW EOas EPla ERea ETPC LBlm LCns MBri MSta SArc SWat SWyc WChe WFar WWye
– 'Gracilis' EBak MBri
– 'Nanus' EPla
longus CBen CCuc CHan CRow CWGN CWat EBre EHoe EHon EMFW EPPr EPla ESOG ETPC LPBA MHew MSta NDea SMad SSoC SWat SWyc WChe WMAq
nanus CHEx
papyrus CHEx CTrC ERea ETPC LPan MBri MSta SSoC
§ – 'Nanus' CInt CRDP CTrC ERea WHal
sumula hort. See *C. cyperoides*
ustulatus ETPC
vegetus See *C. eragrostis*

CYPHANTHERA (Solanaceae)
See Plant Deletions

CYPHOMANDRA (Solanaceae)
betacea (F) LBlo LHil
– 'Goldmine' (F) ERea
– 'Oratia Red' (F) ERea

CYPRIPEDIUM (Orchidaceae)
acaule EFEx LAma
calceolus WChr
– var. *parviflorum* WChr
– var. *pubescens* WChr
debile EFEx LAma
* g. **Emil** SWes
¶ *flavum* SWes
¶ – red unspotted form EFEx
* – var. *speciosum* SWes
¶ – yellow spotted form EFEx
formosanum EFEx LAma SSpi
franchetii SWes
guttatum var. *guttatum* WChr
¶ – var. *yatabeanum* EFEx
¶ g. **Hank Small** SWes
¶ *henryi* EFEx SWes

japonicum EFEx LAma
¶ – var. *formosanum* SWes
¶ – var. *japonicum* SWes
kentuckiense WChr
macranthum EFEx SWes WChr
* – var. *album* SWes
¶ – dark pink form from Wou-long, China SWes
¶ – green-flowered EFEx
– var. *hotei-atsumorianum* EFEx SWes
¶ – light pink form from Man-chou, China SWes
¶ – var. *rebunense* EFEx
¶ – var. *speciosum* EFEx SWes
¶ *margaritaceum* EFEx SWes
¶ *passerinum* LAma SWes
reginae LAma WChr
¶ *segawae* EFEx SWes
¶ *tibeticum* SWes

CYRILLA (Cyrillaceae)

racemiflora CPle SSpi

CYRTANTHUS (Amaryllidaceae)

§ *brachyscyphus* EHic WChr WCot
breviflorus WChr
clavatus WChr
§ *elatus* ♀ CAvo CBro CHal CSev CSpe ERea ETub LAma LBow MBri NChi NRog SRms WChr
– 'Delicatus' ETub LBow WChr
falcatus CMon MLan WChr
luteus SMrm SWas
mackenii NGar NRog WChr
– var. *cooperi* LBow WChr
montanus WChr
obliquus WChr
obrienii SSca
parviflorus See *C. brachyscyphus*
* 'Pink Diamond' CBro
purpureus See *C. elatus*
sanguineus CMon WChr
smithiae WChr
speciosus See *C. elatus*
spiralis WChr
staadensis WChr

CYRTOMIUM (Aspidiaceae)

§ *caryotideum* GQui NMar SMad WRic
§ *falcatum* ♀ CCuc CHEx CHal CHid CRDP EBee EHic EMon MBri NOrc NPSI SArc SAxl SVen WHil WOMN WRic WWat
¶ – 'Butterfieldii' EMon
– 'Rochfordianum' CRow WFib
§ *fortunei* CFil CHal CHid EBee EBre EFer EFou EHic GBin IOrc NHar NHed NHol NMar NPSI SChu SRms WCot WFib WRic
– var. *clivicola* CBar EBre NHar NHed WRic
lonchitoides WRic
macrophyllum NMar WRic

CYRTOSPERMA (Araceae)

See Plant Deletions

CYSTOPTERIS † (Athyriaceae)

alpina SAxl
bulbifera CCuc CFil EFer GQui NMar NVic WEas
diaphana WRic
dickieana CFil GAri NHar NMar NVic SRms WFib
fragilis CCuc CFil EBre EFer EMon GQui MBal NBro NHed NMar SRms WFib WRic
¶ – 'Cristata' EMon
– var. *sempervirens* WRic

CYTISOPHYLLUM (Papilionaceae)

§ *sessilifolium* ESis

CYTISUS † (Papilionaceae)

albus Hacq. See *Chamaecytisus albus*
◆ – hort. See *C. multiflorus*
'Andreanus' See *C. scoparius* f. *andreanus*
ardoinoi ♀ GDra MBal MBro MHig MPla NHar NHol NRoo WDav
battandieri ♀ Widely available
– 'Yellow Tail' CDoC CEnd LRHS MBri MGos
x *beanii* ♀ CMHG ELan ENot ESis GDra GOrc MAll MAsh MBal MBar MPla MWat NHol NNor SAlw SPer SRms WDin WWat WWeb
'Boskoop Glory' CBlo SPer
'Boskoop Ruby' ♀ CBlo EBee GSki SSoC WLRN
'Burkwoodii' ♀ CB&S EBee EHic ENot GCHN MAll MBlu NFla SEND SPla WPyg WStI
'Butterfly' CB&S
canariensis See *Genista canariensis*
'Compact Crimson' EBre MAsh WRHF
'Cottage' CBlo EPot GDra MAll MBro MPla NHar NHol WAbe WBod WDav
'Cottage Gold' EHic GSki MPla
'Criterion' MAll NCut
'Dainty' MAll
'Dainty Maid' CEnd
'Daisy Hill' CBlo
§ *decumbens* CBlo CDoC EBee IOrc MAsh MBro NHar NHol WDav WWin
demissus See *Chamaecytisus hirsutus demissus*
'Dorothy Walpole' CBlo CMHG
'Dragonfly' CBlo ELan IOrc
'Dukaat' EBre MAsh SHBN WLRN
'Eastern Queen' CWan WWeb
'Firefly' CBlo MBal
'Fulgens' CBlo CDoC ELan MAsh MBar SPer WLRN WWeb
'Golden Cascade' CB&S CBlo ELan MWat WLRN WWeb
'Golden Showers' MBal
'Golden Sunlight' CBlo EBee ELan ENot SHBN WStI
'Goldfinch' CB&S CBlo CChe CDoC CWLN EBee ENot MBri MWat SMer WAbe WWeb
hirsutus See *Chamaecytisus hirsutus*
'Hollandia' ♀ CB&S CMHG EBre GCHN MAll MBar MGos NFla SHBN SPan SPer WDin WStI WWeb WWin
x *kewensis* ♀ CSam EBre ELan ENot EPot GDra GOrc GRei LGro LHop MBal MBar MBri MGos MPla MWat NBee NNor SHBN SPer SReu SRms SSta WDin WPat WRTC WWat WWin
– 'Niki' MAsh MBri MGos MPla SHBN WGer

'Killiney Red'	CChe CWLN EBee ENot IOrc MAll MBal MBri MLan SHBN WRHF
'Killiney Salmon'	EBee EHic ENot MAll MAsh MGos MPla SPan SSoC
'La Coquette'	CBlo CDoC CMHG MBar WLRN
'Lena' 🏆	CMHG CWLN EBee EBre GAri GOrc MAll MAsh MBar MBri MGos MPla MTis NRoo SPan WBod WStI WWeb
leucanthus	See ***Chamaecytisus albus***
'Lord Lambourne'	CBlo CChe NCut
maderensis	See ***Genista maderensis***
'Maria Burkwood'	CBlo EPfP SHBN
'Minstead' 🏆	EAst EBre ELan MAll MBal SPer WAbe
monspessulanus	See ***Genista monspessulana***
'Moonlight'	MAll SPer WGwG
'Moyclare Pink'	CMHG
'Muldean'	WWeb
§ ***multiflorus*** 🏆	MBal SPer SRms
– 'White Bouquet'	MBri
nigrescens	See ***C. nigricans***
§ ***nigricans***	CFil CPle ENot SPer WPGP
– 'Cyni'	ELan MAsh NFla SPer SReu SSpi SSta
nubigenus	See ***C. supranubius***
'Palette'	ELan SPer
'Porlock' 🏆	CDoC CLan CSPN CTre CWSG CWit ELan MTis SEND SPla WWeb
× ***praecox***	See ***C.*** × ***praecox* 'Warminster'**
– 'Albus'	EAst EBre ELan ENot GCHN GRei IOrc MAsh MBar MBri MGos MWat NRoo SEND SHBN SPan SPer SPla WAbe WGwG WHCG WWat
– 'Allgold' 🏆	CB&S CChe CMHG CSam EBre ENot GRei MAsh MBar MBri MPla MRav NHol NRoo SHBN SPer SPla SReu SSta WAbe WBod WDin WGwG
– 'Canary Bird'	See ***C.*** × ***praecox* 'Goldspeer'**
– 'Frisia'	CB&S GAri MBar NFla WFar
§ – 'Goldspeer'	CBlo EBee ENot SEND SPer WWeb
§ – 'Warminster' 🏆	EAst ELan ENot GCHN GDra GRei LHop MBal MBar MBri MGos MPla MWat NHol NRoo NWea SHBN SPer WAbe WWat WWin
'Princess'	MBri MPla WBcn
procumbens	LHop MBal WWat
purgans	CBlo CDoC CPle MAll MBal NNor WBod
purpureus	See ***Chamaecytisus purpureus***
racemosus	See ***Genista*** × ***spachiana***
♦ Red Favourite	See ***C.* 'Roter Favorit'**
'Red Wings'	CWLN GCHN GDra MGos SPer WAbe WStI
§ 'Roter Favorit'	MBar WGor
scoparius	CAgr CKin EBee ENot EWFC GRei NWea WDin WRha WWye
§ – f. ***andreanus*** 🏆	EBee ENot GRei MAll MGos NNor SPer
– – 'Splendens'	CB&S WStI
– 'Cornish Cream' 🏆	CB&S ECot EPfP MBri SPer WBod
§ – subsp. ***maritimus***	GSki MAll MBri SLPl WBod WGer
– 'Pastel Delight'	CB&S
– var. ***prostratus***	See ***C. scoparius*** subsp. ***maritimus***
♦ ***sessilifolius***	See ***Cytisophyllum sessilifolium***
supinus	See ***Chamaecytisus supinus***
'Windlesham Ruby'	CChe CWLN EAst EBee EHic ELan EPfP GRei MAsh MBar MPla SHBN SMer SPer WDin WPyg WWeb
'Zeelandia' 🏆	CB&S CWLN EBee EHic ENot MBar MPla MRav SEND SMer SPla SSoC WAbe WRHF WRTC WWeb WWtk

DABOECIA † (Ericaceae)

§ ***cantabrica***	GAri MBal
§ – f. ***alba***	CB&S CMac CNCN COCH EBre ENHC ENot GDra GSpe MBal MBar MBri MOke NHol SBod SHBN WStI
– 'Alba Globosa'	EDen ENHC MBar NYor WGre
* – 'Arielle'	EDen
– 'Atropurpurea'	CNCN COCH EBre EDen ENHC ENot GSpe MBal MGos MOke NHol NYor WBod WStI
– 'Barbara Phillips'	EDen MBar
– 'Bicolor' 🏆	CNCN COCH CWLN EDen ENHC GSpe MBal MGos MOke NHar WGre
– 'Blueless'	COCH EDen
– f. ***blumii*** 'Pink Blum'	EDen
– – 'White Blum'	CNCN COCH ECho EDen WGre
– 'Celtic Star'	EDen
– 'Charles Nelson' (d)	EDen MBar MOke
– 'Cherub'	EDen
– 'Cinderella'	CNCN EDen GSpe MBar
– 'Cleggan'	EDen
– 'Covadonga'	CNCN COCH EDen ENHC MBar
– 'Creeping White'	EDen
– 'Cupido'	CNCN COCH EDen MGos
– 'David Moss' 🏆	CNCN EDen MBal MBar NYor SBod WGre
– 'Donard Pink'	See ***D. cantabrica* 'Pink'**
– 'Early Bride'	COCH EDen ENHC
– 'Eskdale Baron'	EDen ENHC
– 'Eskdale Blea'	EDen
– 'Eskdale Blonde'	EDen
¶ – 'Glamour'	EDen
– 'Globosa Pink'	EDen
– 'Harlequin'	EDen
– 'Heather Yates'	CWLN EDen ENHC MOke NYor
– 'Hookstone Purple'	COCH CWLN EDen ENHC MBar MGos MOke NHol NYor WGre
– 'Lilacina'	CWLN EDen ENHC MBar
§ – 'Pink'	COCH EDen MBar NMen SRms
– 'Pink Lady'	EDen MBar
– 'Polifolia'	CB&S CNCN EDen GDra MOke SBod SHBN SRms
– 'Porter's Variety'	CWLN ECho EDen MBar MOke NHar
– 'Praegerae'	CB&S CMac CNCN EDen ENHC GSpe MBal MBar MGos NHol NYor SBod WGre
– 'Purpurea'	ECho EDen MBar
– 'Rainbow'	CDec CNCN EDen MBar
– 'Rodeo'	EDen

– 'Rosea'	EDen MBar
– subsp. ***scotica*** 'Bearsden'	EDen MBar
– –'Ben'	EDen
– –'Cora'	CNCN EDen ENHC GSpe MBar
– –'Goscote'	EDen MGos
– –'Jack Drake' ♀	CNCN EDen ENHC GDra GSpe MBal MBar MBri MOke WGre
– –'Red Imp'	EDen
– –'Robin'	EDen
– –'Silverwells' ♀	CNCN EDen MBar MBri MGos NHar NYor
– –'Tabramhill'	CNCN EDen MBar
§ – –'William Buchanan' ♀	CMac CNCN CWLN EDen ENHC GDra GSpe MBal MBar MBri MGos MOke NHar NHol NMen NYor SBod WGre
– –'William Buchanan Gold'	CNCN CWLN EDen MBar MBri
– 'Snowdrift'	EDen MBar
¶ – 'Tinkerbell'	ECho
– 'Waley's Red' ♀	COCH EDen ENHC GQui MBar NYor WGre
– 'White Carpet'	EDen
– 'Wijnie'	EDen
– 'William Buchanan'	See ***D. cantabrica* subsp. *scotica* 'William Buchanan'**
× ***scotica***	See ***D. cantabrica* subsp. *scotica***

DACRYCARPUS (Podocarpaceae)

§ ***dacrydioides***	ECou
– 'Dark Delight'	ECou

DACRYDIUM (Podocarpaceae)

bidwillii	See ***Halocarpus bidwillii***
cupressinum	ECou
franklinii	See ***Lagarostrobos franklinii***
laxifolium	See ***Lepidothamnus laxifolius***

DACTYLIS (Poaceae)

glomerata 'Variegata'	CCuc EGle EMan EMon EPPr ETPC IBlr NBro NCat NMir NSti

× DACTYLOGLOSSUM (Orchidaceae)

See Plant Deletions

DACTYLORHIZA (Orchidaceae)

aristata	EFEx
– × ***fuchsii***	EFEx
* ***aristata punctata***	EFEx
¶ × ***braunii***	IBlr
§ ***elata*** ♀	EPar IBlr SSpi WChr
* ***elata variegata***	IBlr
* g. **Florina**	SWes
§ ***foliosa*** ♀	CBro CEnd GCLN IBlr MBri MTho NHar NNrd WAbe WChr WCru WFar
§ ***fuchsii***	EPot ERos NGar NHar NRya SSpi WChe WChr WCru WHer WShi
* ***fuchsii alba***	SWes WChr
fuchsii 'Cruickshank'	NHar
♦ – × ***purpurella***	See ***D.* × *venusta***
¶ × ***grandis***	SWes
incarnata	LAma SWes WChr
¶ – subsp. ***cruenta***	SWes
* ***larissa*** × ***purpurella***	SWes
§ ***maculata***	CHid EPar IBlr LAma MSta NRog SWyc WChe WCru WHer WShi
– subsp. ***ericetorum***	WChr
maderensis	See ***D. foliosa***
§ ***majalis***	LAma SSpi SWes WChr WCru
– subsp. ***praetermissa***	See ***D. praetermissa***
– × ***sambucina***	See ***D.* 'Madonna'**
mascula	See ***Orchis mascula***
§ ***praetermissa***	SSpi
¶ ***purpurella***	SSpi WChr
'Tinney's Spotted'	NHar
* ***triphylla***	SWes

DAHLIA † (Asteraceae)

¶ 'Abridge Natalie' (SWL)	LAyl
'Alloway Cottage' (MD)	LAyl NHal
'Alltami Cherry' (SBa)	NHal
'Alltami Classic' (MD)	NHal
'Alltami Corsair' (MS-c)	LAyl NHal
'Alltami Cosmic' (LD)	NHal
'Almand's Climax' (GD) ♀	GDTE LBut
'Alstergruss' (Col)	NRog
¶ 'Alva's Doris' (SS-c) ♀	LAyl
'Alva's Supreme' (GD)	LBut NHal
'Amaran Candyfloss' (SD)	NHal
'Amaran Relish' (LD)	NHal
'Amaran Royale' (MinD)	NHal
'Amberglow' (MinBa)	LAyl NHal
'American Copper' (LD)	NHal
'Amgard Delicate' (LD)	NHal
* 'Anaïs'	CSut
* 'Anatol' (LD)	CSut
'Andrew Magson' (SS-c) ♀	NHal
'Andrew Mitchell' (MS-c)	NHal
* 'Andries Amber' (MinS-c)	LBut
'Andries' Orange' (MinS-c)	LBut
'Anglian Water' (MinD)	NHal
* 'Anniversary Ball' (MinBa)	LAyl
¶ 'Apricot Jewel' (SD)	LAyl
'Arabian Night' (SD)	CHad EBee LAma NRog SDeJ WPen
'Athalie' (SC)	GDTE NHal
'Autumn Lustre' (SWL) ♀	LAyl
'B.J. Beauty' (MD)	GDTE LAyl NHal
'Barbarry Ball' (SBa)	NHal
'Barbarry Banker' (MinD)	LAyl NHal
'Barbarry Flag' (MinD)	NHal
'Barbarry Gaiety' (MinD)	NHal
'Barbarry Gateway' (MinD)	NHal
'Barbarry Majestic' (SBa)	NHal
'Barbarry Pinky' (SD)	NHal
'Barbarry Snowball' (MinBa)	LAyl NHal
'Baret Joy' (LS-c)	NHal
'Bednall Beauty' (DwB)	CBos CBrk CDec CGle CHad CLTr CRDP CSpe EBee LHil LHop MHlr SMrm WCot
'Berwick Wood' (MD)	NHal
'Biddenham Fire' (SD)	LAyl SMrm
¶ 'Biddenham Strawberry' (SD)	LAyl
¶ 'Biddenham Sunset' (MS-c)	LAyl
'Bill Homberg' (GD)	NHal

'Bishop of Llandaff' (Misc)	CAvo CB&S CBot CBrk CDec CGle CHad CRDP CWit ECtt ELan ETub GCal LAyl LFis LHil LHop MBri NHal SChu SCro SHig SMad SMrm SPer SPla SUsu WCru WEas WHil
'Black Diamond' (Ba)	CHad
'Black Fire' (SD)	LAyl SMrm
'Black Monarch' (GD)	NHal
'Bloom's Amy' (MinD)	NHal
'Bonaventure' (GD)	NHal
¶ 'Bonne Esperance' (Sin/Lil)	CInt LBut
'Border Princess' (SC)	SDeJ
'Bracken Ballerina' (SWL)	LAyl LBut NHal
'Brackenhill Flame' (SD)	NHal
'Brandaris' (MS-c)	LAyl SMrm
¶ 'Brandysnap' (SD) 🏆	LAyl
¶ Burnished Bronze (Misc) 🏆	NRai
¶ 'Butterball' (MinD) 🏆	LAyl
'Calgary' (SD)	CSut
'Cameo' (WL)	NHal
'Candy Cupid' (MinBa)	GDTE LBut LIck NHal
'Candy Keene' (LS-c)	GDTE NHal
'Carolina Moon' (SD)	LAyl NHal
'Carstone Cobblers' (SBa)	NHal
'Charlie Two' (MD)	GDTE LAyl LBut NHal
¶ 'Cherry Wine' (SD)	LAyl
'Cheyenne' (SS-c)	LAyl NHal
¶ 'Chimborazo' (Col)	LAyl
'Christmas Carol' (Col)	NHal
¶ 'Christopher Nickerson' (MS-c)	LAyl
'Christopher Taylor' (SWL)	LAyl NHal SMrm
'Clair de Lune' (Col)	LBut NHal
'Clarion' (MS-c)	SDeJ
coccinea	CAvo CBos CFil CGle CMon CPou GCal WCot WPGP
– hybrids	GCal
'Connie Bartlam' (MD)	NHal
¶ 'Conway' (SS-c) 🏆	LAyl
'Corona' (SS-c/DwB)	LAyl NHal
'Corton Bess' (SD)	SMrm
'Cream Beauty' (SWL)	LBut
'Cream Delight' (SS-c)	NHal
'Cryfield Bryn' (SS-c)	NHal
'Cryfield Keene' (LS-c)	NHal
'Crystal Ann' (MS-c)	NHal
'Curiosity' (Col)	LBut NHal
'Czardas'	GCal
¶ 'Daddy's Choice' (SS-c)	LAyl
'Dad's Delight' (MinD)	LBut
'Daleko Jupiter' (GS-c)	GDTE LAyl NHal
'Dana Iris' (SS-c) 🏆	GDTE LAyl
¶ 'Dancing Queen' (S-c)	LBut
◆ 'Dandy'	See ***D.* 'Harvest Dandy'**
'Danjo Doc' (SD)	NHal
¶ 'Dark Splendour' (MC)	LAyl
¶ 'Davenport Anita' (MinD)	LAyl
'Davenport Honey' (MinD)	NHal
'Davenport Lesley' (MinD)	SMrm
¶ 'Davenport Sunlight' (MS-c)	LAyl
'David Digweed' (SD)	NHal
'David Howard' (MinD)	CGle CHad EBee EBre ECle ELan EPfP GCal MMil MOne NHal NHaw NHol SBid SPla WCot WHil WLRN
'Daytona' (SD)	CSut
¶ 'Dazzler' (MinD/DwB)	LAyl
'Deborah's Kiwi' (SC)	NHal
'Debra Anne Craven' (GS-c)	NHal
'Doris Day' (SC)	LAma LBut NHal NRog
'Doris Knight' (SC)	LBut
¶ 'Downham Royal' (MinBa)	CSut
'Duet' (MD)	LAma NRog
'Dusky Harmony' (SWL)	LBut
'Earl Marc' (SC)	LBut
¶ 'East Anglian' (SD)	LAyl
'East Court' (Sin)	SMrm
'Easter Sunday' (Col)	LAyl SMrm
'Eastwood Moonlight' (MS-c)	NHal
'Edinburgh' (SD)	LAma NRog WRha
'Elizabeth Hammett' (MinD)	NHal
'Ellen Houston' (DwB) 🏆	CHad MBri NHal WHil
'Elma E' (LD)	LAyl NHal
¶ 'Elmbrook Chieftain' (GD)	LAyl
'Emory Paul' (LD)	CSut
¶ 'Ernie Pitt' (SD)	LAyl
'Eveline' (SD)	ETub SDeJ
'Evelyn Foster' (MD)	NHal
¶ 'Exotic Dwarf' (Sin/Lil)	NHal
'Explosion' (SS-c)	LBut NHal
'Ezau' (GD)	CSut
'Fascination' 🏆	LAyl MHlr WCot
'Fashion Monger' (Col)	LAyl NHal
'Fermain' (MinD)	NHal
* 'Fernhill Suprise' (SD)	LBut
* 'Figaro White'	NRai
'Figurine' (SWL)	LAyl NHal
'Finchcocks' (SWL) 🏆	LAyl
'Fiona Stewart' (SBa)	GDTE
◆ 'Firebird' (MS-c)	See ***D.* 'Vuurvogel'**
'Firebird' (Sin)	NRog
¶ 'Flutterby' (SWL)	LAyl
* 'Fluttering'	SMrm
¶ 'Foreman's Jubilee' (GS-c)	LAyl
'Formby Supreme' (MD)	LAyl NHal
'Forncett Furnace' (B)	GCal
¶ 'Freya's Thalia' (Sin)	LBut
* 'Friquolet'	LAma
'Fusion' (MD)	CSut
¶ 'Gaiety' (SD/DwB)	LAyl
¶ 'Garden Festival' (SWL)	LAyl
'Garden Party' (MC) 🏆	LAyl
'Gateshead Festival' (SD)	LAyl NHal
'Gay Mini' (MinD)	LBut
¶ 'Gay Princess' (SWL)	LAyl
§ 'Geerling's Indian Summer' (MS-c) 🏆	NHal
'Gerrie Hoek' (SWL)	LAma LAyl LBut NRog
'Glorie van Heemstede' (SWL) 🏆	LAma LAyl LBut NHal NRog SMrm
'Go American' (GD)	NHal
'Gold Crown' (LS-c)	NRog
'Golden Emblem' (MD)	SDeJ
'Golden Impact' (MS-c)	NHal
'Good Earth' (MC)	LAma
¶ 'Good Hope' (MinD)	LIck
'Grenadier' (SWL)	MHlr WCot

'Grenidor Pastelle' (MS-c)	GDTE LAyl LBut NHal
¶ 'Gypsy Boy' (LD)	LAyl
'Hamari Accord' (LS-c) 🏆	LAyl NHal
¶ 'Hamari Bride' (MS-c) 🏆	LAyl
'Hamari Girl' (GD)	NHal
'Hamari Gold' (GD) 🏆	NHal
'Hamari Katrina' (LS-c)	LAyl
'Hamari Rosé' (MinBa) 🏆	LAyl NHal
¶ 'Hans Ricken' (SD)	LAyl
* 'Haresbrook'	WCot
* 'Hartenaas' (Col/DwB)	NRog
¶ 'Harvest Amanda' (Sin/Lil)	LBut
¶ 'Harvest Brownie' (Sin/Lil)	LBut
§ 'Harvest Dandy' (Sin/Lil)	LBut
§ 'Harvest Imp' (Sin/Lil)	LBut
§ 'Harvest Inflammation' (Sin/Lil) 🏆	LBut
§ 'Harvest Red Dwarf' (Sin/Lil)	LBut
§ 'Harvest Samantha' (DwB) 🏆	LBut
§ 'Harvest Tiny Tot' (Misc/Lil) 🏆	LBut
'Hayley Jayne' (SC)	NHal
'Hazard' (MS-c)	LAma NRog
I 'Hazel' (Sin/Lil)	LBut
'Henriette' (MC)	CSut
¶ 'Highgate Gold' (MS-c)	LAyl
'Hilda Clare' (Col)	LBut
'Hillcrest Albino' (SS-c) 🏆	LAyl NHal
'Hillcrest Desire' (SC)	NHal
'Hillcrest Hillton' (LS-c)	NHal
'Hillcrest Royal' (MC) 🏆	LAyl NHal
'Hillcrest Suffusion' (SD)	LBut NHal
'Hillcrest Ultra' (SD)	LAyl
'Hit Parade' (MS-c)	CSut LAma NRog
'Honey' (Anem/DwB)	CInt NRog
'Honeymoon Dress' (SD)	LAyl LBut NHal
'House of Orange' (MD)	SDeJ
¶ 'Hugh Mather' (MWL)	LAyl
◆ 'Imp'	See ***D.* 'Harvest Imp'**
imperialis	CMon GCal
'Inca Dambuster' (GS-c)	LBut NHal
◆ 'Inflammation'	See ***D.* 'Harvest Inflammation'**
'Iris' (Pom)	LBut NHal
'Jane Horton' (Col)	LBut
'Jean Fairs' (MinWL)	LBut
'Jean McMillan' (SC)	NHal
'Jeanette Carter' (MinD) 🏆	LAyl NHal
'Jescot Jess' (MinD)	LBut
'Jescot Julie' (O)	LAyl LBut
'Jessica' (S-c)	CSut NHal
'Jessie G' (SBa)	NHal
¶ 'Jessie Ross' (MinD/DwB)	LAyl
'Jill Day' (SC)	LBut
* 'Jill's Blush' (MS-c)	LAyl
'Jill's Delight' (MD) 🏆	LAyl
'Jim Branigan' (LS-c)	LAyl NHal
¶ 'Joan Beecham' (SWL)	LAyl
'Jocondo' (GD)	LAyl NHal
'Johann' (Pom)	LBut NHal
'John Prior' (SD)	LAyl NHal
'John Street' (SWL) 🏆	LAyl LBut
'Jo's Choice' (MinD)	LBut
'Karenglen' (MinD) 🏆	LBut NHal
'Kathleen's Alliance' (SC) 🏆	LAyl NHal
'Kathryn's Cupid' (MinBa)	GDTE LAyl NHal
'Keith's Choice' (MD)	NHal
'Kenn Emerland' (MS-c)	LAma
'Kenora Challenger' (LS-c)	LAyl NHal
'Kenora Fireball' (MinBa)	NHal
'Kenora Moonbeam' (MD)	NHal
'Kenora Petite' (MinS-c)	LBut
'Kenora Superb' (GS-c)	LAyl NHal
'Ken's Coral' (SWL)	NHal
'Kidd's Climax' (GD)	GDTE LBut NHal
'Kimi' (O)	LBut
'Kim's Marc' (SC)	GDTE LBut
'Kiwi Gloria' (SC)	GDTE LAyl NHal
'Klankstad Kerkrade' (SC)	LAyl NHal
'Klondike' (LS-c)	NHal
'Kochelsee' (MinD)	LAma
'Kym Willo' (Pom)	LBut
* 'Kyoto'	CSut
'La Cierva' (Col)	LBut NHal
'La Corbière' (DwBa)	NHal
'Lady Kerkrade' (SC)	NHal
'Lady Linda' (SD)	GDTE LAyl LBut NHal
¶ 'Lady Sunshine' (SS-c)	LAyl
'L'Ancresse' (MinBa)	LAyl NHal
* 'Laura's Choice' (SD)	LAyl
¶ 'Lavender Athalie' (SC)	LAyl
'Lemon Elegans' (SS-c)	GDTE LAyl LBut NHal
'Lilac Shadow' (S-c)	CSut
'Lilac Time' (MD)	SDeJ
'Lilianne Ballego' (MinD)	NHal
'Linda's Chester' (SC)	LBut NHal
'Lismore Willie' (SWL)	LAyl LBut
'Little Dorrit' (Sin/Lil) 🏆	LBut
'Little Dream' (S-c)	SDeJ
'Little Sally' (Pom)	LAyl LBut
'Little Tiger'	NRog
'Madame Vera' (SD)	LBut
¶ 'Maelstrom' (SD)	LAyl
¶ 'Majestic Kerkrade' (SC)	LAyl
'Majuba' (MD)	LAma NRog SDeJ
'Margaret Ann' (MinD)	LAyl LBut
'Mariner's Light' (SS-c) 🏆	LAyl
'Mark Damp' (LS-c)	NHal
'Mark Hardwick' (GD)	LAyl NHal
'Marlene Joy' (MS-c)	NHal
'Martin's Yellow' (Pom)	NHal
'Mary Layton' (Col)	NHal
'Mary Pitt' (MinD)	LAyl NHal
'Maxine Bailey' (SD)	NHal
merckii	CBot CBrk CGle CGre CHad CSpe ECha GCal MNrw MTho NBro NSti SMad SUsu WCru WPer WRus WWhi WWin
merckii alba	CFil CHad CSpe EBee ECha MTho WPer WRus
merckii compact	CBos CFil WPGP
'Meredith's Marion Smith' (SD)	NHal
'Mi Wong' (Pom)	GDTE LAyl NHal
'Mini' (Sin/Lil)	LBut
'Minley Carol' (Pom)	NHal
'Minley Iris' (Pom)	LBut
'Minley Linda' (Pom)	LAyl LBut NHal
'Monk Marc' (SC)	LBut
'Monkstown Diane' (SC)	LAyl NHal
'Moonfire' (Misc)	CBrk CFir EBee EBre ECle GCal LAyl LHop MMil MOne MTis NHal NHaw SSea WCot WHer WMer
'Moonlight' (SD)	LAyl MBri SBid

'Moor Place' (Pom)	LAyl NHal WCot
'Morning Dew' (SC)	SDeJ
'Morning Kiss' (LSD)	SDeJ
'Mount Noddy' (Sin)	SMrm
'Mrs McDonald Quill' (LD)	NHal
¶ 'Murdoch'	WCot
'Murillo'	NRog
'My Love' (SS-c)	LAma NRog
'Nargold' (MS-c)	NHal
'Neal Gillson' (MD)	LAyl NHal
'Nepos' (SWL)	LAyl NHal
'New Baby' (MinBa)	NRog
'Nina Chester' (SD)	LAyl NHal
'Noreen' (Pom)	LAyl NHal
¶ 'Oakwood Diamond' (SBa)	LBut
'Omo' (Sin/Lil) 🏆	LBut
'Orange Keith's Choice' (MD)	NHal
'Orange Mullet' (MinD) 🏆	LAyl
'Orfeo' (MC)	LAma NRog
I 'Orion' (MD)	CSut
'Ornamental Rays' (SC)	LBut
* 'Park Fever'	LAyl
'Park Princess' (DwB/SC)	LAma NHal SDeJ
'Paul Chester' (SC)	NHal
'Peach Cupid' (MinBa)	LBut NHal
'Peachette' (Misc/Lil) 🏆	LBut
'Pearl of Heemstede' (SD) 🏆	LAyl NHal
'Periton' (MinBa)	LAyl NHal
'Pink Jupiter' (GS-c)	LAyl NHal
'Pink Pastelle' (MS-c) 🏆	LAyl NHal
'Pink Sensation' (SC)	LBut
¶ 'Pink Shirley Alliance' (SC)	LAyl
* 'Pink Silvia'	CSut
'Pink Surprise' (LS-c)	SDeJ
¶ 'Pink Symbol' (MS-c)	LAyl
pinnata soft yellow	CDec CGle
¶ 'Piper's Pink' (SS-c/DwB) 🏆	LAyl
I 'Pippa' (MinWL)	LBut
'Plum Surprise' (Pom)	NHal
'Polventon' (SD)	LBut
'Pomponnette' (Anem)	CSut
¶ 'Pontiac' (SC)	LAyl
'Pop Willo' (Pom)	GDTE LBut NHal
'Porcelain' (SWL)	LBut NHal
'Potgieter' (MinBa)	NRog
'Preference' (SS-c)	LAma
'Preston Park' (Sin/DwB) 🏆	LAyl NHal
'Pride of Berlin'	See ***D.* 'Stolze von Berlin'**
'Primrose Diane' (SD)	NHal
'Promotion' (MC)	SDeJ
'Purple Gem'	NRog
* 'Quantum Leap'	SMrm WCot WWeb
'Radfo' (SS-c)	GDTE NHal
¶ 'Raffles' (SD)	LAyl
'Raiser's Pride' (MC)	NHal
'Rebecca Lynn' (MinD)	NHal
'Red Diamond' (MD)	NHal
◆ 'Red Dwarf'	See ***D.* 'Harvest Red Dwarf'**
'Red Velvet' (SWL)	LAyl NHal
I 'Reedley' (SWL)	LBut
'Reginald Keene' (LS-c)	GDTE NHal
'Rhonda' (Pom)	LBut NHal
'Rhonda Suzanne' (Pom)	LBut
'Richard Marc' (SC)	LBut
'Risca Miner' (SBa)	GDTE LBut
'Rose Jupiter' (LS-c)	LAyl NHal
¶ 'Rothesay Herald' (SD/DwB)	LAyl
¶ 'Rothesay Reveller' (MD)	LAyl
'Rotterdam' (MS-c)	SDeJ
I 'Roxy'	EBee EBre WCot WPen WWeb
¶ 'Royal Blush' (MinD)	LIck
'Ruby Wedding' (MinD)	NHal
¶ 'Ruskin Belle' (MS-c)	LAyl
'Ruskin Diana' (SD)	LBut NHal
* 'Ruskin Tangerine' (SBa)	LBut
'Ryedale Rebecca' (GS-c)	NHal
'Safe Shot' (MD)	NRog
¶ 'Saint Moritz' (SS-c)	CSut
¶ 'Salmon Athalie' (SC)	LAyl
'Salmon Beauty' (D)	SDeJ
'Salmon Keene' (LS-c)	NHal
'Salsa' (Pom) 🏆	NHal
◆ 'Samantha'	See ***D.* 'Harvest Samantha'**
'Satellite' (MS-c)	SDeJ
'Scarlet Kokarde' (MinD)	GDTE
'Scottish Rhapsody' (MS-c)	NHal
'Senzoe Ursula' (SD)	GDTE LAyl NHal
'Shandy' (SS-c)	LAyl NHal
sherffii	CBrk CFir CHal CMon GCal MCCP WRha
– x ***coccinea***	CHad
'Sherwood Standard' (MD)	NHal
¶ 'Sherwood Titan' (GS-c)	LAyl
¶ 'Shirley Alliance' (SC)	LAyl
'Shooting Star' (LS-c)	CSut
* 'Show and Tell'	CSut
'Siemen Doorenbos' (Anem)	NRog
'Silver City' (LD)	CSut NHal
'Small World' (Pom)	GDTE LAyl LBut NHal
'Snowstorm' (MD)	LAma SDeJ
¶ 'So Dainty' (MinS-c) 🏆	LAyl
'Sonia'	CSut
* 'Spacemaker'	SDeJ
§ 'Stolze von Berlin' (MinBa)	NRog
'Stoneleigh Cherry' (Pom)	LBut
'Suffolk Punch' (MD)	CSut LAyl LBut SMrm
'Suitzus Julie' (DwB)	NHal
'Summer Night' (MC)	CHad CSut
'Superfine' (SC)	LAyl NHal
'Swanvale' (SD)	NHal
'Sweet Sensation' (MS-c)	NHal
¶ 'Sweetheart' (SD)	CInt LBut
'Tally-ho' (WL)	LHil MBri WCot WWeb
'Thomas A. Edison' (MD)	CSut LAma
◆ 'Tiny Tot'	See ***D.* 'Harvest Tiny Tot'**
'Tommy Doc' (SS-c)	NHal
'Top Choice' (GS-c)	SDeJ
'Trendy' (SD)	SDeJ
'Trengrove Jill' (MD)	LAyl NHal
'Trengrove Tauranga' (MD)	LAyl
'Tui Orange' (SS-c)	NHal
'Vaguely Noble' (SBa)	NHal
¶ 'Vazon Bay' (MinBa)	CSut
'Vera's Elma' (LD)	NHal
'Veritable' (MS-c)	SDeJ
'Vicky Crutchfield' (SWL)	LAyl LBut
¶ 'Walter James' (SD)	LIck
'Wanda's Capella' (GD)	GDTE LAyl NHal
'Warkdon Willo' (Pom)	NHal
'Wendy's Place' (Pom)	NHal

'White Alva's' (GD) LAyl NHal
'White Ballet' (SD) ♀ LBut NHal
'White Kerkrade' (SC) NHal
¶ 'White Klankstad' (SC) LAyl
'White Linda' (SD) LAyl NHal
'White Moonlight' (MS-c) LBut NHal
'White Perfection' (GD) SDeJ
'White Swallow' (SS-c) NHal
'Willo's Surprise' (Pom) NHal
'Winston Churchill' (MinD) LBut
'Wittemans Superba' (SS-c) ♀ LAyl NHal
'Wootton Cupid' (MinBa) ♀ LAyl LBut NHal
'Wootton Impact' (MS-c) ♀ LBut NHal
'Worton Bluestreak' (SS-c) LBut
'Yellow Cheer' (SD/DwB) SDeJ
'Yellow Hammer' (Sin/DwB) ♀ LAyl NHal SChu SMrm WCot WHil
'Yellow Impact' (MS-c) NHal
¶ 'Yellow Spiky' (MS-c) LAyl
¶ 'Yellow Star' (MC) CSut
'Yellow Symbol' (MS-c) LBut
¶ 'Yelno Enchantment' (SWL) LAyl
'Yelno Harmony' (SD) ♀ LBut
¶ 'Yelno Velvena' (SWL) LAyl
I 'Yvonne' (MWL) NHal
'Zorro' (GD) ♀ LAyl LBut NHal

DAIS (Thymelaeaceae)

¶ ***cotinifolia*** CTrC

DAISWA See PARIS

DALEA (Papilionaceae)

¶ ***purpurea*** EMan

DAMPIERA (Goodeniaceae)

diversifolia CSpe

DANAE (Ruscaceae)

§ ***racemosa*** ♀ CFil EBre ECro EPla GCal IHos NRoo NTow SArc SBid SDry SPer SRms SSpi SSta

DAPHNE † (Thymelaeaceae)

acutiloba CPMA EB&P EPot ERea LRHS MPla SPer SSta WCru WWes
albowiana CPMA MPla WCru WPGP WWes
alpina CPMA EPot NNrd NRya SBla WOMN WPat
altaica CPMA
'Anton Fahndrich' SBla
arbuscula ♀ CPMA EPot SBla SIgm WPat
¶ – subsp. ***arbuscula*** f. ***albiflora*** SBla
'Beauworth' CPMA SBla
bholua CChu EB&P ERea LHop NSti SBid SReu SSta WCru WWat
I – 'Alba' CB&S CChu CPMA LRHS SBla SPer SSta WCru
– 'Damon Ridge' CPMA
– Darjeeling form CChu CFil CPMA CPle CSam EB&P ELan EPfP SBid SBla SPla SSpi WCru WPat WWat
– var. ***glacialis*** 'Gurkha' ♀ CPMA MPla SPer SPla
– 'Jacqueline Postill' ♀ CPMA LRHS MBri MPla SBla SMur WCru
– Waterhurst form CPMA
blagayana CPMA EB&P EPot LHop MBal MGrG MHig MPla NGar NSti SBla SIgm SPla SRms WCru WPat WWat
'Bramdean' SBla
× ***burkwoodii*** ♀ CB&S CBot CSam EAst EHyt EPot IOrc MBal MHig SHBN SPla WCru WDin WRHF WWat
– 'Albert Burkwood' CPMA NWea SBla
– 'Astrid' (v) CB&S COtt CPMA ELan LHop LNet MBlu MGos SCoo SSta WDin WPyg WWes
§ – 'Carol Mackie' (v) CBot CPMA EB&P GAbr LHop SBla SIgm SPer WWat
– 'G.K. Argles' CBlo CPMA LRHS SBid SBla SPer SPla WCru WPat WWes
– 'Gold Strike' (v) CPMA
– 'Lavenirei' CPMA
* – 'Moonlight' LRHS
– 'Somerset' CB&S CPMA CShe ELan ENot IOrc LHop LNet MBar MBlu MGos MPla NBee SAga SBla SEas SHBN SPer SReu SSoC SSta WDin WPyg WSHC
§ – 'Somerset Gold Edge' (v) CPMA SPer WCru
– 'Variegata' broad cream edge See ***D.* × *burkwoodii* 'Somerset Variegated'**
– 'Variegata' broad gold edge See ***D.* × *burkwoodii* 'Somerset Gold Edge'**
– 'Variegata' narrow gold edge See ***D.* × *burkwoodii* 'Carol Mackie'**
caucasica CPMA SBla
'Cheriton' SBla
cneorum CB&S CPMA MBal MBar NBee SReu SSoC SSta WDin WWat WWin
– f. ***alba*** SBla
– 'Eximia' ♀ CAlt CPMA EB&P EPot IOrc LNet MAsh MGos MGrG SHBN SPer SPla WAbe WCru
* – 'Poszta' CPMA SBla SPer
– var. ***pygmaea*** CPMA SBla WPat
– – 'Alba' WPat
– 'Rose Glow' CPMA
– 'Variegata' CPMA EB&P EPot LHop MBar MMil MPla NRya NWCA SAlw SBla SPer SPla SReu SSta WAbe WCru WSHC WWat
collina See ***D. sericea* Collina Group**
'Fragrant Cloud' (aff. *acutiloba*) SBla
genkwa CPMA CSte SPer
giraldii CBot CPMA EHyt EPot MGrG SIgm SSpi WCru
× ***hendersonii*** CPMA
– 'Appleblossom' SBla
¶ – CDB 11660 SBla
– 'Ernst Hauser' SBla
– 'Fritz Kummert' SBla
– 'Rosebud' SBla
× ***houtteana*** CBot CPMA EB&P LRHS MPla NBir NSti SSta WCru
× ***hybrida*** CPMA SBla
japonica 'Striata' See ***D. odora* 'Aureomarginata'**
jasminea CPMA GCrs SBla WPat
¶ – AM form EHyt

jezoensis	CPMA SBla SSta
juliae	SBla
'Kilmeston'	CPMA EHyt SBla
laureola	CPMA CSWP GPoy MBro MGos MPla NPer SPan SPer WWat WWye
– var. *cantabrica*	SChu
– subsp. *philippi*	CPMA CShe CSte EB&P LHop LRHS MPla SChu SHBN SPer SSto WAbe WCru WWat
'Leila Haines' x *arbuscula*	SBla
longilobata	WCru
– 'Peter Moore'	CPMA
x *mantensiana*	WPat
– 'Manten'	CPMA
'Meon'	SBla
mezereum	CBot CShe ENot EWFC GAbr GDra GPoy GRei MBal MBar MBri MGrG MPla NNor NNrd NPSI NRoo NWea SAlw SHBN SPer SReu SSoC SSta WDin WOMN WPat WWat
– f. *alba*	CShe GAbr IOrc LHop MBar MGrG MPla NNrd SEas SHBN SPer SReu SSta WAbe WCru WPat WPyg WWat
– 'Bowles' Variety'	CBot CPMA EPot SPer
– 'Grandiflora'	See ***D. mezereum*** var. ***autumnalis***
– 'Rosea'	MGos SRms
– var. *rubra*	CB&S CPMA ELan IOrc LNet NBee NFla SPer SReu WAbe WCru WDin WWeb
– 'Variegata'	LHop
x *napolitana* 🏆	CPMA EB&P LNet LRHS MGos SIng SSta WWat
odora	CChe CPMA CPle EB&P ERea LHol MGos SChu SRms SSta WCru WSel
§ – f. *alba*	CPMA CSte EB&P ERea MGos MPla NSti
§ – 'Aureomarginata'	Widely available
– 'Banana Split'	LRHS
– 'Clotted Cream'	CPMA
– var. *leucantha*	See ***D. odora* f. *alba***
– 'Marginata'	See ***D. odora* 'Aureomarginata'**
– var. *rubra*	CPMA CSte EB&P LHol LRHS NPSI
– 'Sakiwaka'	CPMA
– 'Walberton' (v)	EB&P LRHS
oleoides	GAbr LNet SBla
petraea	SBla
– 'Alba'	See ***D. petraea* 'Tremalzo'**
– 'Grandiflora' 🏆	EPot SBla WPat
§ – 'Tremalzo'	SBla
pontica 🏆	CPMA CPle EHyt ELan EOHP GAbr LHop MBro MPla SAxl SDix SMad SPer SSpi WCru WPat WRTC WWat
retusa	See ***D. tangutica* Retusa Group**
'Richard's Choice'	CPMA
x *rollsdorfii* 'Arnold Cihlarz'	SBla
'Rosy Wave'	SBla
§ *sericea* 🏆	CFil CPMA SBla SIgm WCru
§ – Collina Group	CAlt CPMA SMur SRms SSpi SSta WAbe WWat
x *suendermannii*	SBla
tangutica 🏆	CAlt CB&S CEnd CMHG EB&P ELan EPot IOrc LNet MBal MBar MBro MGrG MHig MPla MTho NHar NHol NPSI SDix SHBN SPer SSta WGwG WHCG WPat WPyg WWat
§ – Retusa Group 🏆	CB&S CPMA CShe EB&P ECha EHyt GAbr GDra LHop MAsh MBri MPla NRoo NSti SHBN SMac SReu SSta WAbe WPat WPyg
x *thauma*	SBla
– 'Aymon Correvon'	SBla
'Tichborne'	SBla

DAPHNIPHYLLUM (Daphniphyllaceae)

himalense var. *macropodum*	CChu CFil CHEx CPle EPfP SArc SBid SPer WPGP
– – B&SWJ 581	WCru

DARLINGTONIA (Sarraceniaceae)

californica 🏆	CFil EEls EFEx GTro MHel WMEx

DARMERA (Saxifragaceae)

§ *peltata* 🏆	CChu CHad CRDP CRow CSpe CWGN ECha EGol EHon ELan GAbr GMaP LHop LPBA MBri MFir MSta MUlv NBro NDea NSti SAxl SHig SMad SPer SSpi WCru WGer WWat
– 'Nana'	EBre ECha NHol WOld

DASYLIRION (Agavaceae)

§ *acrotrichum*	CHEx SArc
¶ *glaucophyllum*	CTrC
gracile Planchon	See ***D. acrotrichum***
longissimum	CAbb
wheeleri	CAbb CTrC EOas

DASYPHYLLUM (Asteraceae)

diacanthoides	CGre

DASYPYRUM (Poaceae)

See Plant Deletions

DATISCA (Datiscaceae)

cannabina	GCal

DATURA (Solanaceae)

arborea	See ***Brugmansia arborea***
chlorantha	See ***Brugmansia chlorantha***
cornigera	See ***Brugmansia arborea***
§ *inoxia*	EBak ERea MSal MSto SOWG SRms
metel	ERea
¶ – black	NRai
* – 'Cherub'	GQui
* – 'La Fleur Lilas'	WHer
meteloides	See ***D. inoxia***
rosea	See ***Brugmansia* x *insignis* pink**
rosei	See ***Brugmansia sanguinea***
sanguinea	See ***Brugmansia sanguinea***
stramonium	CArn EWFC MHew MSal WHer WWye
– Tatula Group	MSal
suaveolens	See ***Brugmansia suaveolens***
versicolor	See ***Brugmansia versicolor* Lagerheim**
◆ – 'Grand Marnier'	See ***Brugmansia* x *candida* 'Grand Marnier'**

DAUCUS (Apiaceae)

carota CArn CKin CTiv ECWi EWFC GAul MHew WHer

DAVALLIA † (Davalliaceae)

bullata See ***D. mariesii***
canariensis ♀ CFil CGre
fejeenis MBri
§ *mariesii* ♀ EOas MBri SDix
– var. *stenolepis* NMar SDix
pyxidata NMar
trichomanoides NMar
– var. *lorrainei* NMar
tyermannii NMar

DAVIDIA (Davidiaceae)

involucrata ♀ CChu CDoC CFil CHan CMCN CTho CWSG EBre ENot IOrc ISea LPan MAsh MBlu MBri MDun NWea SHBN SPer SReu SSpi WCru WDin WNor WStI WWat
– var. *vilmoriniana* ♀ CGre CSte ELan EPfP LNet LRHS MAsh MGos MWat NBee NFla SHhN SPer SSta WCoo

DEBREGEASIA (Urticaceae)

longifolia CAbb CPle

DECAISNEA (Lardizabalaceae)

fargesii CBrd CChu CGre CMHG CPle ELan EMil ENot LPan MBlu MCCP MDun MGos NHol NPal NTow SMad SPer SSta WCoo WDin WRTC WWat
– 'Harlequin' (v) CBot

DECODON (Lythraceae)

verticillatus CHan EHon

DECUMARIA (Saxifragaceae)

barbara CBot CChu CFil CGre CHEx CMac CPlN EMil EOvi EPfP EPla SBra SHBN SPer WCru WSHC WThi WWat
sinensis CGre CHEx CPlN EPfP SArc SSpi SSta WSHC

DEGENIA (Brassicaceae)

velebitica EPot GCLN NTow WDav

DEINANTHE (Hydrangeaceae)

bifida EBre WCru
caerulea WCru

DELAIREA (Asteraceae)

§ *odorata* CHEx CPle

DELONIX (Caesalpiniaceae)

regia LBlo SOWG

DELOSPERMA (Aizoaceae)

§ *aberdeenense* CHEx WCot WOMN
* *album* CHEx
ashtonii SIgm WPer
'Basutoland' See ***D. nubigenum***
¶ *congestum* WCot
cooperi CFai CTrC EOas MHig NGre NMen NSla NTow WCot WPat WPer WPyg WWoo
lineare NBir
lydenburgense IBlr
* *macei* WCot
macellum NGre
¶ *mariae* WCot
§ *nubigenum* CMHG CTrC EDAr ELan EOas EPot GGar LBee MFos NGre NNrd SBod SIng SSmi WHil WHoo WOMN WPer WPyg WWin
sutherlandii EDAr NGre NMen NSla WCot WPyg

DELPHINIUM † (Ranunculaceae)

'Agnes Brookes' ERou
alabamicum MSto
'Alice Artindale' CBos CDec CHad EGle LGre SMrm WCot WSan
ambiguum See ***Consolida ajacis***
andesicola MSto
'Ann Woodfield' MWoo
'Anne Page' ERou
Astolat Group CB&S CBot CDoC EBre ECED ELan GAbr LBlm MBri MRav MWat NFla NNor NPri NRoo SPer SSoC SUsu WSan
Avon strain EBar MWoo
'Barbara Nason' SOgg
barbeyi MSto
'Basil Clitheroe' EBre
Belladonna Group ELan
– 'Andenken an August Koeneman' See **D. (Belladonna Group) 'Wendy'**
– 'Atlantis' ECha EFou LGre MBri
– 'Balkleid' EFou MBri
– 'Blue Shadow' EFou
– 'Capri' EFou
– 'Casa Blanca' CBlo CDoC CGle EBee EBre EFou MAvo MTis WHow WLRN
– 'Cliveden Beauty' CDoC CGle EBee EBre EFou GBri LFis MAvo NRoo SMrm SPla WHow WLRN WMer
– 'Kleine Nachtmusik' EFou
– 'Moerheimii' CBlo EFou SPla WMer
– 'Peace' CSte EBre
– 'Piccolo' ECha EFou MBri SPla
– 'Pink Sensation' See ***D. × ruysii* 'Pink Sensation'**
– 'Völkerfrieden' EBee EBre EFou MBri MUlv NPri NPro SPla WMer WRus
× *bellamosum* CBlo CBot EBee EFou GAul GBri MAvo MTis SMrm SPla WHow WLRN
¶ 'Berghimmel' EFou
'Beryl Burton' ERou SOgg
'Betty Baseley' ERou
bicolor MSto
Black Knight Group CB&S CDoC EBre ECtt ELan GAbr MBri MRav MWat NFla NMir NNor NPri NRoo NVic SPer SSoC WBro WRus
'Blauwal' EFou
Blue Bird Group CB&S CDoC ELan GAbr MBri MRav NFla NMir NNor NPri NRoo NVic SHam SPer WPLl
'Blue Butterfly' See ***D. grandiflorum* 'Blue Butterfly'**
'Blue Dawn' ♀ CBla ERou SOgg

Blue Fountains Group	ELan EMan LHop MBri MTis NBee NFla NOak SPer WStI
Blue Heaven Group	WElm
Blue Jade Group	CBla ERou NNor SOgg
'Blue Jay'	CB&S CDoC CMGP EBre ENot LCom NBir NPri SPer WLRN
'Blue Lagoon'	CBla SOgg
'Blue Nile' 🏆	CBla ERou MWoo SOgg
Blue Springs Group	NOrc
'Blue Tit'	CBla ERou MWat SOgg
'Blue Triumph'	WPyg
¶ 'Blue Triumphator'	EFou
'Browne's Lavender'	SOgg
'Bruce' 🏆	ERou MWoo SOgg
brunonianum	CLyd MSto SBla SIng WOMN
bulleyanum	MSto
'Butterball'	CBla SOgg
californicum	MSto WWin
Cameliard Group	CB&S CMGP EBre ECtt ELan EMan GAbr NCut NFla NPri SPer WLRN
'Can-can'	ERou
cardinale	CBot CPou GCra MSto WHil WOMN
'Carl Topping'	ERou
carolinianum	MSto
cashmerianum	CBot CHan CPou ELan EWes MFos MSto MTho NTow WOMN
– 'Gladys Hull'	EWes
'Cassius' 🏆	CBla ERou MWoo SOgg
caucasicum	See ***D. speciosum***
¶ 'Celebration'	SOgg
ceratophorum	MSto
'Chelsea Star'	CBla ERou SOgg
'Cherub'	CBla ERou MWoo SOgg
chinense	See ***D. grandiflorum***
'Christel'	EFou
'Circe'	ERou
'Clack's Choice'	ERou
¶ 'Claire'	MWoo SOgg
'Clifford Lass'	MWoo SOgg
'Clifford Pink'	CBla MWoo SOgg
'Clifford Sky'	MWoo SOgg
Connecticut Yankees Group	CBlo CChr NNor NOak
'Conspicuous' 🏆	CBla ERou MWoo SOgg
'Constance Rivett'	ERou
'Cressida'	ERou
'Cristella'	ERou
'Crown Jewel'	CBla EFou ERou SOgg
'Cupid'	CBla ERou SOgg
'Daily Express'	ERou SOgg
'Darling Sue'	SOgg
'David's Magnificent'	WEas
decorum	MSto
delavayi	LFis MSto
'Demavand'	ERou
'Dolly Bird'	CBla ERou SOgg
'Dora Larkan'	SOgg
'Dreaming Spires'	LCom
'Duchess of Portland'	ERou
'Eamonn Andrews'	ERou SOgg
elatum	CBrd GCal SMrm SRms
'Elmfreude'	EBre
'Emily Hawkins' 🏆	ERou MWoo SOgg
'Eva Gower'	ERou
exaltatum	MSto
'F.W. Smith'	EFou WMer WPyg
'Fanfare' 🏆	CBla ERou LRHS SOgg
'Father Thames'	ERou

'Faust' 🏆	CBla EFou ERou LRHS MWat MWoo SOgg
'Fenella' 🏆	CBla LRHS MWoo
'Finsteraarhorn'	EFou
'Foxhill Nina'	SOgg
'Fred Yule'	ERou
Galahad Group	CB&S CDoC EBre ECED EFou ELan ENot GAbr LBlm LGre MBri MRav MWat NBir NFla NMir NNor NPri NRoo NVic SPer
'Garden Party'	CBla
'Gemma'	MWoo
geraniifolium	MSto NTow
'Gillian Dallas' 🏆	CBla ERou LRHS MWoo SOgg
¶ ***glareosum***	EHyt MSto WDav
glaucum	MSto
'Gordon Forsyth'	CBla ERou MWoo SOgg
'Gossamer'	EFou
§ ***grandiflorum***	ESis MSto NPla SMrm
§ – 'Blauer Zwerg'	CGle LCom WRus
§ – 'Blue Butterfly'	CBot CMea CSpe EBre EBur EFou EMar LHop NHar NLak NOrc SAga SBla SCoo WWhi WWin
♦ – Blue Dwarf	See ***D. grandiflorum* 'Blauer Zwerg'**
Guinevere Group	CB&S CMGP EBre ECtt EMan GAbr MBri MWat NBir NFla NNor NPri NRoo SPer WRHF
'Guy Langdon'	ERou
'Harlekijn'	EFou
'Harmony'	ERou
himalayae	MSto
¶ 'Honey Bee'	SOgg
hotulae	EBee
hybridum	MSto
¶ 'Icecap'	SOgg
Ivory Towers Group	ECtt
'James Nuttall'	ECha
'Joyce Roffey'	ERou
'Judy Knight'	ERou
'Kathleen Cooke'	SOgg
'Kestrel'	ERou
King Arthur Group	CB&S CDoC EBre ECtt ELan ENot GAbr MBri MRav MWat NFla NNor NPri
'Lady Guinevere'	ERou WPyg
'Lady Hambleden'	See ***D.* 'Patricia, Lady Hambleden'**
'Leonora'	ERou SOgg
likiangense	EBee EPot MSto
* 'Lilac Arrow'	EFou
'Lilian Bassett'	ERou MWoo SOgg
'Loch Leven' 🏆	CBla ERou MWoo SOgg
'Loch Nevis'	SOgg
'Lord Butler' 🏆	CBla LRHS SOgg
'Lorna'	ERou SOgg
§ ***luteum***	GCra MSto
Magic Fountains Series	EBre EFou GAbr NCut NPri NRoo SIde WGor WHil WRHF
I 'Magic Fountains Sky Blue'	EFou
'Margaret Farrand'	ERou
'Marie Broan'	ERou
'Max Euwe'	EFou
menziesii	EBee LBee MSto NWCA
'Michael Ayres'	CBla ERou MWoo SOgg
'Micky'	EFou
'Mighty Atom' 🏆	CBla EFou ERou MWoo SOgg WFar
'Min'	ERou MWoo SOgg

'Molly Buchanan' CBla ERou SOgg
montanum MSto
'Moonbeam' CBla SOgg
'Morning Cloud' ERou
'Mother Teresa' ERou
'Mrs Newton Lees' EBre EFou ERou WPyg
'Mrs T. Carlile' ERou
multiplex MSto
muscosum MSto
* 'Mystique' CBla ERou SOgg
'Nar' EFou
¶ ***nelsonii*** MSto
New Century Hybrids CB&S EBre
'Nicholas Woodfield' MWoo SOgg
'Nimrod' CBla ERou
'Nobility' CBla ERou SOgg
nudicaule CBot EBar ELan ESis GBuc GDra MSto NCGP NRoo NWCA WHil WOMN
– var. ***luteum*** See ***D. luteum***
nuttallianum MSto
occidentale MSto
'Olive Poppleton' CBla MWoo SOgg
'Oliver' ERou MWoo
* ***orfordii*** MSto
'Our Deb' 🏆 MWoo SOgg
oxysepalum MSto
Pacific Hybrids EBre ENot NOak SRms WByw
parryi MSto
'Patricia Johnson' ERou SOgg
'Pericles' CBla SOgg
Pink Dream Group 🏆 LCom
'Pink Ruffles' CBla ERou SOgg
pogonanthum MSto
'Polar Sun' ERou
'Princess Caroline' LRHS
przewalskii EPot MSto
'Purity' ERou
'Purple Ruffles' ERou
'Purple Sky' EFou
'Purple Triumph' ERou
'Purple Velvet' CBla
pylzowii CLyd GAul GCra MSto NNrd SSte
pyramidatum MSto
'Pyramus' ERou SOgg
¶ 'Red Rocket' EFou
requienii CBot CFee CLon ERav GBur GCra MSto MTho NBir WEas WHer
– variegated WHil WSan
'Rona' SOgg
'Rosemary Brock' 🏆 ERou MWoo SOgg
¶ Round Table Mixture SIde
'Royal Copenhagen' EBre
'Royal Flush' 🏆 CBla LRHS MWoo SOgg
¶ 'Royal Velvet' SOgg
'Ruby' CBla
§ × ***ruysii*** 'Pink Sensation' CBot CSte EBee EBre EFou ERou GBri LFis MUlv NCat NPri WHil WMer WPyg WRus
'Sabrina' CBla ERou
'Samantha' ERou
'Sandpiper' 🏆 SOgg
¶ 'Sarah Edwards' SOgg
scaposum MSto
¶ 'Schildknappe' EFou
¶ 'Schönbuch' EFou
scopulorum MSto
§ ***semibarbatum*** CBot NPri NRai SIgm WSan
'Sentinel' ERou
'Shimmer' CBla ERou SOgg
'Silver Jubilee' ERou
'Silver Moon' ERou SOgg
¶ 'Sky Beauty' EFou
* 'Sky Fantasie' EFou
'Skyline' CBla ERou SOgg
Snow White Group NBir NOak SRms
¶ 'Snowdon' SOgg
'Solomon' ERou
Southern Aristocrats Group MBro WGle WHoo WPyg
Southern Consort Group CBlo WGle WHoo WPyg
Southern Countess Group 🏆 WGle
Southern Debutante Group CBlo WGle WHoo WPyg
Southern Jesters Group CBlo WGle WHoo WPyg
Southern Ladies Group MBro WHoo WPyg
Southern Maidens Group 🏆 WGle
Southern Minstrels Group WGle
Southern Royals Group CBlo MBro WGle WHoo WPyg
¶ sp. ACW EWes
sp. CLD 349 MSto
§ ***speciosum*** MSto
'Spindrift' 🏆 SOgg
staphisagria EOHP MHew MSal WWye
* – 'Variegatum' WCot
'Strawberry Fair' CBla EFou ERou MWat SOgg
suave MSto
'Summer Haze' ERou
Summer Skies Group CB&S CMGP ECtt EFou EMan MBri MWat NBir NFla NNor NPri NRoo SPer SSoC WRus
'Summerfield Miranda' 🏆 MWoo SOgg
¶ 'Summerfield Oberon' MWoo
¶ 'Summerfield Viking' MWoo
'Sungleam' 🏆 CBla COtt EFou ERou LRHS MWat SOgg
'Sunkissed' MWoo SOgg
'Swan Lake' ERou
tatsienense CLyd CMdw EHyt GDra LHop MBro MSto MTho NChi NWCA SAlw SSca WHoo WOMN WPyg
– 'Album' EWes MSto WOMN
'Tessa' ERou
'Thundercloud' ERou SOgg
'Tiddles' 🏆 CBla LRHS SOgg
'Titania' CBla SOgg
trichophorum MSto
tricorne MFos MSto WCot
'Turkish Delight' CBla ERou SOgg
uliginosum MSto
'Vespers' CBla ERou SOgg
¶ ***vestitum*** GCan
virescens subsp. ***wootonii*** MSto
'Walton Beauty' MWoo
'Walton Gemstone' 🏆 CBla MWoo SOgg
'Watkin Samuel' ERou
'White Ruffles' CBla SOgg
yunnanense GDra
¶ 'Yvonne' EFou
zalil See ***D. semibarbatum***

DENDRANTHEMA † (Asteraceae)

'Adorn' (22d) MCol
'Agnes Ann' (29K) MCol
'Aimee Jane' (24b) WRil
'Alan Rowe' (5a) NHal
'Albert Broadhurst' (24b) NHal
'Albert's Yellow' (29Rub) MCol MMil
'Alexis' (5a) WRil

'Aline' (29K)	EHMN
'Alison' (29c)	EHMN LRHS
'Alison Kirk' (23b)	MCol NHal
'Allouise' (25b) 🏆	MCol NHal
'Allure' (22d)	WRil
'Amber Enbee Wedding' (29d)	WRil
¶ 'American Beauty' (5b)	MCol
'Amy Shoesmith' (15a)	MCol
'Anastasia' (28)	CArc CLTr ECtt EFol EMan EPPr GMac LHop LIck MCol MMil MRav NBrk NFai SCro SEas SPla SRms SUsu WEas WPer WRHF WWin
N 'Anastasia Variegated' (28)	CSam ECED EFol EMon MBel WCot WHer WRHF
'Anastasia White'	WCot
'Angelic' (28)	MCol
'Angora' (25b)	MCol
'Anja's Bouquet'	EBee EMan
'Ann Brook' (23b)	MCol
'Anna Marie' (18c) 🏆	EHMN MCol
'Annapurna' (3b)	WWol
'Anne' (29K)	EHMN
'Anne, Lady Brocket'	CMil EFou EMon GBuc MBel NBrk NBro WMaN
'Apollo'	EFou EMon EWll LRHS MAvo SMer
'Apricot' (29Rub)	EBre ECtt EFou EPPr MFir MMil MRav SMad SSoC SSvw WCot
'Apricot Alexis' (5a)	WRil
'Apricot Chessington' (25a)	NHal WRil
'Apricot Chivenor' (9c)	MCol NHal
'Apricot Courtier' (24a)	NHal WRil WWol
'Apricot Margaret' (29c) 🏆	LBut MCol
'Arctic' (9c)	MCol
'Audrey Shoesmith' (3a)	NHal
'Aunt Millicent' (29K)	MCol
'Autumn Days' (25b)	MCol NHal
'Autumn Sonata'	EBre
'Babs'	MMil
'Baden Locke' (24b)	WWol
'Bagley Cream' (3b)	MCol
'Balcombe Perfection' (5a)	MCol NHal WRil WWol
'Barbara' (22)	MCol NHal WLRN WRil
'Beacon' (5a)	NHal WRil
'Belair' (9c)	MCol
'Belle' (29K)	EHMN LRHS
'Beppie' (29e)	MCol
'Bertos'	EHMN
'Bessie Rowe' (25a)	MCol
'Betty' (29K)	MCol
'Betty Wiggins' (25b)	MCol
'Bill Bye' (1)	NHal
'Bill Wade' (25a)	MCol NHal WRil
'Black Magic' (24b)	MCol
'Bob Dear' (25a)	MCol
'Bonnie Jean' (9d)	MCol
'Bo-peep' (28)	EMon MCol
'Bravo'	MCol WLRN
* 'Breitner's Supreme'	WCot
'Brenda Rowe' (5a)	MCol
'Brietner' (24b)	MCol
'Bright Eye' (28)	MCol WPer
'Bright Golden Princess Anne' (4b)	NHal
'Brightness' (29K)	EHMN NFai SChu SHel SUsu WEas
'Broadacre' (7a)	MCol
'Broadway Mandy' (29c)	NHal WRil
'Bronze Belair' (9c)	MCol
'Bronze Bornholm' (14b)	MCol
'Bronze Cassandra' (5b)	NHal
'Bronze Dee Gem' (29c)	NHal
'Bronze Elegance' (28)	CLTr CM&M CMil EFou ELan EMan EMon ERav SIng SPer SPla SRms SUsu WAbe WByw WEas WMaN WRus WWat
'Bronze Elite' (29d)	EHMN
'Bronze Enbee Wedding' (29d)	NHal
'Bronze Fairy' (28a)	MCol
'Bronze John Wingfield' (24b)	WRil
'Bronze Margaret' (29c) 🏆	LBut MCol NHal SHel WRil
'Bronze Maria' (18a)	MCol
'Bronze Matlock' (24b)	NHal WRil WWol
'Bronze Max Riley' (23b)	NHal WRil
'Bronze Mayford Perfection' (5a) 🏆	MCol NHal
'Bronze Mei-kyo' (28)	CSam
'Bronze Yvonne Arnau' (24b)	MCol
'Bronzetti'	EHMN
'Brown Eyes' (29K)	EHMN WWin
'Bruera' (24a)	NHal
'Bryan Kirk' (4b)	NHal WWol
§ 'Buff Margaret' (29c)	SHel
'Buff Peter Rowe' (23b)	NHal
'Bullfinch' (12a)	EHMN WWol
'Bunty' (28)	EBee LRHS MRav NFai
'Butter Milk' (25c)	MCol
'Cameo' (28a)	MCol
'Candid' (15b)	MCol
'Candlewick Limelight' (29d)	WRil
'Candylite' (14b)	MCol
'Carlene Welby' (25b)	NHal WRil
'Carmine Blush'	WCot WDav
* 'Cassandra' (5b)	NHal
¶ 'Challenger' (25b)	WRil
'Charles Tandy' (5a)	WRil
'Charles Wood' (25a)	NHal
'Cheddar' (13a)	MCol
'Cherry Chessington' (25a)	WRil
'Cherry Enbee Wedding' (29d)	WRil
'Cherry Margaret' (29c)	NHal WRil
'Chessington' (25a)	MCol NHal WRil
'Chester Globe' (23b)	NHal
'Chestnut Talbot Parade' (29c) 🏆	NHal
'Chivenor' (9c)	MCol NHal
'Christine Hall' (25a)	MCol
'Christopher Lawson' (24a)	NHal WWol
I 'Citrus' (29K)	EFou
'Clara Curtis' (29Rub)	CGle CKel ECha EFou EHMN ELan EMon GMac LHop MBel MBri MCol MFir MRav NBir NBrk NHol NPer SChu SEas SPer SPla SUsu WEas WHoo WMaN WPer WRus WWin
'Clare Dobson' (25b)	WWol
'Clare Louise' (24b)	WRil
'Claudia' (24c)	EHMN MCol
'Colossus' (24a)	NHal WRil
'Columbine' (29K)	EHMN
'Cooper Nob' (29K)	EHMN

'Copper Margaret' (29c) LBut SHel
'Cornetto' (25b) MCol NHal WRil
'Corngold' (5b) NHal
'Cossack' (2) WWol
'Cottage Apricot' EBar EWoo GMac LHop NGar SMrm WRHF
'Cottage Pink' See ***D.* 'Emperor of China'**
'Cottingham' (25a) MCol
'Courtier' (24a) NHal
'Cream Elegance' (9c) NHal
'Cream John Hughes' (3b) NHal WRil
'Cream Margaret' (29c) NHal
'Cream Pauline White' (15a) WRil
'Cream West Bromwich' (14a) WRil
'Creamist' (25b) MCol WWol
'Cricket' (25b) MCol
'Crimson Yvonne Arnaud' (24b) 🏆 MCol
'Dana' (25b) 🏆 NHal
'Daniel Cooper' (29Rub) MCol
'Danielle' (29d) MCol
* 'Daphne' EHMN
'Dark Triumph' WLRN
'David Shoesmith' (25a) MCol
'Deane Dainty' (9f) MCol
'Debbie' (29K) EHMN
'Debonair' 🏆 MCol NHal WLRN WRil
'Dee Candy' (29c) NHal
'Dee Crimson' (29c) NHal
'Dee Gem' (29c) 🏆 NHal
'Dee Pink' (29c) MCol
'Denise' (28) 🏆 MCol WLRN
'Dennis Fletcher' (25a) WRil
'Derek Bircumshaw' (28a) MCol
'Deva Glow' (25a) MCol NHal
§ 'Doctor Tom Parr' (28) CGle EFou ELan EMon EPPr LGre MBel MFir NBrk
'Donna' (22f) MCol
'Doreen Burton' (25b) MCol
'Doreen Hall' (15a) MCol WRil
'Doreen Statham' (4b) NHal WWol
'Doris' (29K) EHMN
'Dorothy Stone' (25b) NHal
'Dorridge Beauty' (24a) NHal WWol
'Dorridge Bolero' WWol
'Dorridge Celebration' (3b) WWol
'Dorridge Crystal' (24a) NHal WRil WWol
'Dorridge Flair' (3b) NHal
'Dorridge King' (4b) WWol
'Dorridge Velvet' (4b) NHal
'Dorridge Vulcan' WWol
'Dragon' (9c) NHal
'Duchess of Edinburgh' (29Rub) CDec CGle CSam EBre ECED ECtt ELan EMon GMac LGre MBri MCol MFir MRav SEas SSvw WEas WMaN WPyg WRus
'Dulverton' (24c) MCol
'Early Bird' (24b) MCol
'Ed Hodgson' (25a) MCol NHal WRil
'Edelgard' WMaN
'Edelweiss' (29K) EFou LHop
'Egret' (23b) WRil
'Elegance' (9c) MCol NHal
'Elizabeth Lawson' (3a) NHal
'Elizabeth Shoesmith' (1) NHal
'Ellen' (29c) LBut NHal
'Emily' (22) 🏆 MCol
'Emily Peace' (25a) NHal
'Emma Lou' (23a) MCol NHal
§ 'Emperor of China' (29Rub) CDec CGle CMil ECha EFou EMar EMon GCal GCra GMac LGre MBel MCol MRav MSte MUlv NBrk NFai NNor SChu SHig SMad SSvw SUsu WEas WFar WHoo WMaN WRus
'Enbee Dell' (29d) MCol
'Enbee Frill' (29d) MCol
'Enbee Sunray' (29d) EFou
'Enbee Wedding' (29d) 🏆 MCol NHal WRil
'Encore' LFis
'Ermine' (23a) MCol NHal
'Evelyn Bush' (25a) MCol
'Eye Level' (5a) NHal WRil
'Fairway' (15a) NHal
'Fairweather' (3b) MCol WRil
'Fairy' (28) MCol
'Fairy Rose' (4b) LRHS MCol
'Fellbachar Wein' EFou
'Feu de l'Automne' EFou
'Fieldfare' (22) NHal
'Fiery Barbara' WLRN
'Flame Enbee Wedding' (29d) WRil
'Flamingo' (9f) MCol
§ 'Fleet Margaret' (29c) 🏆 LBut WRil
¶ 'Flying Saucer' (6a) MCol
'Foxdown' (25b) MCol
'Foxy Valerie' LFis WLRN
'Fred Shoesmith' (5a) MCol WRil
'Fresha' (25a) WRil
'Frolic' (25b) MCol WLRN
'Gala Princess' (24b) WWol
'Galaxy' (9d) 🏆 MCol NHal
'Gambit' (24a) MCol NHal
¶ 'Gary Scothern' (25b) MCol
'Gay Anne' (4b) NHal
'Gazelle' (23a) MCol
'Geordie' (25b) WRil
'George Griffiths' (24b) 🏆 NHal
'Gertrude' (19c) MCol
'Gigantic' (1) NHal
* 'Ginger' (30) WLRN
'Gingernut' (5b) MCol NHal WRil
'Gladys' (24b) EBee ELan EWoo
'Gloria' (25a) EHMN
'Gloria' (29K) MCol
'Glowing Lynn' WLRN
'Gold Chessington' (25a) WRil
'Gold Enbee Frill' WRil
'Gold Enbee Wedding' (29d) 🏆 NHal WRil
'Gold Foil' (5a) NHal WRil
'Gold Margaret' See ***D.* 'Golden Margaret'**
'Golden Anemone' EHMN
'Golden Angora' (25b) MCol
'Golden Cassandra' (5b) NHal
'Golden Courtier' (24a) NHal
'Golden Creamist' (25b) 🏆 MCol
'Golden Elegance' (5a) WWol
'Golden Honeyball' (15b) MCol
'Golden Ivy Garland' (5b) MCol
§ 'Golden Margaret' (29c) 🏆 LBut MCol NHal SHel WRil
'Golden Mayford Perfection' (5a) 🏆 MCol NHal
'Golden Pamela' (29c) NHal
'Golden Pixton' (25b) MCol
'Golden Plover' (22) NHal
'Golden Saskia' (7b) MCol

'Golden Seal' (7b)	EMon GBuc MCol NBrk
'Golden Taffeta' (9c)	NHal
'Golden Treasure' (28a)	MCol WWol
'Golden Wedding' (29K)	MCol
'Goldengreenheart'	WCot
'Goodlife Sombrero' (29a) 🏆	NHal
'Grace Riley' (24a)	MCol
'Grandchild' (29c)	EHMN LRHS MCol
§ ***grandiflorum***	MNrw SRms
'Green Satin' (5b)	WWol
¶ 'Grenadier' (24b)	MCol
'Grenadine' (22c) 🏆	NHal WRil
'Halloween' (4b)	NHal
'Handford Pink' (29K)	MCol
'Happy Geel'	EHMN
'Harry Wilson' (3b)	NHal
'Harry Woolman' (3b)	NHal
'Harvest Emily'	MCol
'Harvey' (29K)	MCol
'Hayley Griffin' (25a)	NHal
* 'Hazel' (29K)	EHMN LRHS
'Hazel Macintosh' (5a)	NHal
'Hazy Days' (25b)	MCol NHal
* 'Heather' (15a)	WLRN
'Heather James' (3b)	MCol NHal
'Hedgerow' (7b)	MCol
'Heide' (29c) 🏆	MCol NHal
'Hekla' (30)	MCol
'Helen' (29K)	EHMN WLRN
* 'Holly' (22b)	WLRN WRil
'Honey' (25b)	EHMN LRHS SMer
'Honeyball' (25b)	MCol
¶ 'Horace Martin'	LRHS
'Horningsea Pink'	ECGP EPPr
'Ian' (29K)	EHMN
'Imp' (28)	MCol
'Innocence' (29Rub)	CArc CGle CSam EBee EFou EHal ELan EMon GMac MAvo MBel MRav MUlv NFai SEas SMad SPla WEas
'Irene' (29K)	EHMN
'Ivy Garland' (5b)	MCol
'James Kelway'	EWll NBir
'Janice' (7a)	WLRN
¶ 'Janice Shreeve' (24a)	MCol
'Jante Wells' (28)	EMon MBel MCol MFir WEas
'Jennifer'	WLRN
'Jessica' (29c)	WLRN
◆ 'Jessie Cooper'	See ***D.* 'Mrs Jessie Cooper'**
'Jimmy Motram' (1)	NHal
'Joan' (25b)	EHMN LRHS
'John Cory' (3b)	NHal
'John Harrison' (25b)	MCol NHal
'John Hughes' (3b)	MCol NHal WRil
'John Lewis' (24b)	WWol
'John Riley' (14a)	WRil
'John Wingfield' (14b)	NHal WRil WWol
'Jules la Graveur'	EFou EMon GBuc MAvo MBel WByw
'Julia'	EFou
'June Rose' (24b)	NHal
'June Wakley' (25b)	MCol
'Karen Riley' (25a)	WRil
'Keystone' (25b)	MCol
'Kimberley Marie' (15b)	NHal
x ***koreanum***	See ***D. grandiflorum***
'Lady in Pink' (29Rub)	GBuc MAvo
'Lakelanders' (3b)	NHal WWol
¶ 'Laser' (24b)	WRil
'Laurie'	WLRN
'Leading Lady' (25b)	WWol
'Legend' (22)	NHal
'Lemon Margaret' (29c) 🏆	NHal SHel WRil
'Lilian Hoek' (29c)	EHMN
'Lilian Jackson' (7b)	MCol
'Lilian Shoesmith' (5b)	WRil
'Linda'	MCol WLRN WRil
'Lindy'	EFou
'L'Innocence' (29K)	GCal WMaN
'Lisa'	MCol WLRN
'Little Dorrit' (29K)	EHMN LRHS MCol
'Liverpool Festival' (23b)	MCol
'Long Island Beauty' (6b) 🏆	MCol
'Long Life' (25b)	MCol
'Lorna Wood' (13b)	NHal
'Louise' (25b)	EHMN LRHS
'Lucy Simpson' (29K)	MCol MMil WMaN
'Lundy' (2)	NHal
'Lyndale' (25b)	MCol
'Lynmal's Choice' (13b)	MCol
'Lynn' (22)	NHal WLRN
'Mac's Delight' (25b)	MCol
'Madeleine' (29c) 🏆	EBre LBut
'Malcolm Perkins' (25a)	NHal WRil
'Mandarin'	CGle EFou
'Margaret' (29c) 🏆	LBut MCol NHal SHel WRil
'Maria' (28a)	MCol
'Mariann' (12a)	WWol
'Marie Brunton' (15a)	NHal
'Marion' (25a)	EHMN LBut
'Martha'	LRHS
'Martin Riley' (23b)	MCol
'Mary' (29K)	EHMN MCol WMaN
'Mary Stevenson' (25b)	MCol
'Mary Stoker' (29Rub)	CGle CKel CMea CSam EBre ECha ECtt EFou EHal ELan EMon GBri GMac MBel MBri MBro MCol MNrw MRav NBro NFai SEas SPer WEas WHoo WMaN WPyg WRus
'Mason's Bronze' (7b)	MCol
'Matlock' (24b)	MCol NHal WRil
'Matthew Woolman' (4a)	WWol
'Maureen' (29K)	EHMN
'Mauve Gem' (29K)	EHMN
'Mavis' (28a)	MCol
'Max Riley' (23b) 🏆	NHal WRil
'May Shoesmith' (5a)	MCol NHal
'Mayford Perfection' (5a) 🏆	MCol NHal
'Megan'	WLRN WRil
'Megan Woolman' (3b)	WWol
'Mei-kyo' (28)	CGle CM&M CMea CMil ECtt EFou ELan EMon ERav MBel MRav NFai NHol SIng SPer SPla SRms SSea SSvw WAbe WEas WRus WWat
'Membury' (24b)	MCol NHal
'Minaret' (3b)	WWol
'Minstrel Boy' (3b)	MCol NHal WRil
'Mirage' (22b) 🏆	MCol
¶ 'Miss Prim' (24b)	WRil
'Moira' (29K)	EHMN LRHS
'Molly Lambert' (5a)	NHal
'Moonlight' (29K)	EHMN
'Morning Star' (12a)	WWol
'Mottram Barleycorn' (29d)	MCol
'Mottram Minstrel' (29d)	MCol
'Mottram Sentinel' (29d)	MCol
'Mottram Twotone' (29d)	MCol

§ 'Mrs Jessie Cooper' (29Rub)	EBee ECGP EFou ELan EMon NBrk SChu SEas WCot WHoo
'Music' (23b)	MCol NHal
'My Love' (7a)	MCol
'Myss Madi' (29c)	NHal
'Myss Rosie' (29c)	NHal
naktongense	See ***D. zawadskii*** var. ***latilobum***
'Nancy Perry' (29Rub)	CElw CSam ELan EMon LGan MCol SChu SEas
§ ***nankingense***	EMon
'Nantyderry Sunshine'	EFou MAvo SIng SMrm SPla SUsu WAbe WCot WEas WMaN WPen WPer WRus WWat
'Naomi' (22f)	WRil
'National Celebration' (25a)	NHal WRil
'Nell Gwyn' (29Rub)	MCol
'Nicole' (22c)	MCol NHal WLRN WRil
'Nu Dazzler' (9d)	MCol
'Nu Robin' (9d)	MCol
'Nu-Rosemary' (9d) ♀	NHal
'Old Cottage Yellow'	NFai
'Orange Allouise' (25b)	NHal
'Orange Enbee Wedding' (29d)	NHal
'Orange Fairway' (15b)	NHal
'Orange Margaret'	See ***D.*** **'Fleet Margaret'**
'Orangeade' (24b)	MCol
pacificum	See ***Ajania pacifica***
'Packwell' (24b)	MCol
'Pamela' (29c)	NHal
'Panache' (5a)	MCol
'Patricia Millar' (14b)	NHal
'Paul Boissier' (29Rub)	CArc CGle CMil EFou ELan EMon LGre MBel MHlr SUsu WByw WCot WEas
'Pauline White' (15a)	NHal WRil
'Payton Blaze' (29c)	MCol
'Payton Dale' (29c)	MCol NHal
'Payton Lady' (29c)	MCol
'Payton Pixie' (29c)	MCol
'Payton Snow' (29c)	MCol
'Peach Allouise' (25b) ♀	NHal
'Peach Courtier' (24a)	NHal
'Peach Enbee Wedding' (29d) ♀	LBut
'Peach Margaret'	See ***D.*** **'Salmon Margaret'**
'Peachy Lynn'	WLRN
'Pearl Celebration' (24a)	NHal WRil WWol
'Peggy' (28a)	EHMN
'Pelsall Imperial' (3a)	MCol
'Pennine Canary' (29c) ♀	LBut
'Pennine Cheer' (29c)	NHal WRil
'Pennine Club' (29d) ♀	NHal WRil
¶ 'Pennine Coffee' (29c)	WRil
'Pennine Crystal' (29c)	MCol
'Pennine Dancer' (29d)	LBut
'Pennine Dell' (29d)	MCol
'Pennine Digger' (29c)	WRil
'Pennine Eagle' (29c)	NHal
'Pennine Fizz' (29d)	WRil
'Pennine Gift' (29c)	NHal WRil
'Pennine Ginger' (29c) ♀	NHal WRil
¶ 'Pennine Gipsy' (29c)	WRil
'Pennine Glory'	NHal WRil
'Pennine Goal' (29c) ♀	NHal WRil
'Pennine Hannah' (29d)	NHal
'Pennine Hayley' (29d)	WRil
'Pennine Jade' (29d) ♀	LBut NHal
'Pennine Jessie' (29d)	NHal WRil
'Pennine Magnet' (29a) ♀	NHal WRil
'Pennine Marie' (29a)	NHal
'Pennine Oriel' (29a)	MCol NHal WRil
'Pennine Pageant' (29d)	WRil
¶ 'Pennine Panda' (29d)	WRil
'Pennine Polo' (29d)	NHal
'Pennine Posy' (29f)	WRil
'Pennine Pride' (29d)	WRil
'Pennine Punch' (29a)	MCol
'Pennine Purple' (29c)	EHMN MCol
'Pennine Ranger' (29d)	NHal WRil
'Pennine Ray' (29d)	WRil
'Pennine Ritz' (29d)	WRil
'Pennine Romeo'	WRil
'Pennine Saffron' (29c)	NHal WRil
'Pennine Sally' (29c)	WRil
'Pennine Ski' (29c)	MCol
'Pennine Slumber' (29c)	WRil
'Pennine Soldier' (29d) ♀	LBut NHal
'Pennine Sparkle' (29f)	WRil
¶ 'Pennine Splash' (29d)	WRil
'Pennine Sprite' (29d)	WRil
'Pennine Swan' (29c)	NHal WRil
'Pennine Swing' (29d)	NHal WRil
'Percy Salter' (24b)	MCol
'Perry's Peach'	NPer
'Peter Fraser' (14b)	WWol
'Peter Rowe' (23b)	MCol NHal
'Peter Sare'	EBre GMac
'Peter White' (23a)	MCol
'Peterkin'	EBre ECtt EMar EMon GMac LGre MUlv WRus
'Phil Houghton' (1)	WWol
'Piecas'	EHMN
¶ 'Pink Champagne' (4b)	MCol
'Pink Duke' (1)	NHal
'Pink Favorite' (5b)	MCol
'Pink Ice' (5b)	MCol
'Pink John Wingfield' (24b)	NHal WRil
'Pink Margaret' (29c)	NHal
'Pink Nu Rosemary' (9d)	MCol
'Pink Overture' (15b)	MCol
'Pink Pennine Cheer' (29c)	WRil
'Pink Progression'	ECED ECtt GMac NBir NBrk
'Pink World of Sport' (25a)	WRil
'Pixton' (25b)	MCol
'Playmate' (29K)	MCol
'Polar Gem' (3a)	MCol NHal
'Polaris' (9c)	EBre
'Pot Black' (14b)	WRil
'Primrose Alison Kirk' (23b)	MCol NHal
'Primrose Allouise' (24b)	NHal
'Primrose Anemone' (29K)	EHMN
'Primrose Angora' (25b)	MCol
'Primrose Bill Wade' (25a)	NHal WRil
'Primrose Chessington' (25a)	NHal WRil
'Primrose Courtier'	See ***D.*** **'Yellow Courtier'**
'Primrose Cricket' (25b)	MCol
'Primrose Dorothy Stone' (25b)	NHal WRil
'Primrose Enbee Wedding' (29d)	NHal
'Primrose Ermine' (23a)	NHal
'Primrose John Hughes' (3b)	NHal WRil
'Primrose Margaret'	See ***D.*** **'Buff Margaret'**

'Primrose Mayford Perfection' (5a) 🏆	MCol NHal
'Primrose Pennine Oriel' (29a)	WRil
'Primrose West Bromwich' (14a)	NHal WRil
'Princess' (29K)	EHMN LRHS MCol
'Princess Anne' (4b)	MCol NHal
'Promise' (25a)	MCol NHal
'Purleigh White'	EFou MAvo SIng SPla WAbe WMaN WRus
'Purple Fairie' (28b)	MCol
'Purple Glow' (5a)	NHal
'Purple Margaret' (29c)	LBut NHal SHel
'Purple Wessex Charm' (29d)	MCol
'Queenswood' (5b)	MCol
'Rachel Knowles' (25a)	MCol NHal WRil
'Radiant Lynn'	MCol WLRN
'Raquel' (29K)	MCol WLRN WRil
'Rayonnante' (11)	MCol
'Red Balcombe Perfection' (5a)	NHal WWol
'Red Carlene Welby' (25b)	WRil
'Red Chempak Rose' (14b)	WRil
'Red Claudia' (29c)	EHMN
'Red Early Bird' (24b)	MCol
'Red Eye Level' (5a)	WRil
'Red Formcast' (24a)	NHal
'Red Gambit' (24a)	NHal
'Red Mayford Perfection' (5a)	MCol
'Red Pamela' (29c)	NHal
'Red Payton Dale' (29c)	WRil
'Red Pheasant'	CArc EHMN
'Red Rosita' (29c)	MCol
'Red Shirley Model' (3a)	NHal
'Red Shoesmith Salmon' (4a)	MCol
'Red Wendy' (29c) 🏆	LBut MCol NHal
'Redall' (4c)	MCol
¶ 'Regal Mist' (25b)	MCol
'Regalia' (24b) 🏆	MCol
'Remarkable' (30)	MCol NHal WLRN
'Riley's Dynasty' (14a)	NHal
'Robeam' (9c)	WWol
'Robin' (22)	NHal WLRN WRil
'Robinson's Red'	WRus
'Romano Mauve'	EHMN
'Romantika'	EFou
'Romany' (2)	WEas
'Rose Broadway Mandy'	WRil
'Rose Enbee Wedding' (29d)	MCol NHal WWol
'Rose Mayford Perfection' (5a) 🏆	MCol NHal
'Rose Pink Debonair' (22)	WLRN
'Rosita' (28b)	MCol
'Roy Coopland' (5b)	WRil
'Royal Cardinal' (9c)	MCol
'Royal Command' (29Rub)	EMon MAvo NBro
'Royal Lynn'	MCol WLRN
'Rozette'	EHMN
rubellum	See ***D. zawadskii***
'Ruby Enbee Wedding' (29d)	NHal WRil
'Ruby Mound' (29K)	CRDP EFou EHMN LFis LGre MCol WEas
'Ruby Raynor' (29Rub)	MCol
'Rumpelstilzchen'	EBee EBre EMan EMar EPPr WPer
'Rybronze' (9d)	NHal
'Ryfinch' (9d)	MCol
'Ryflare' (9c)	WWol
'Ryflash' (9d)	MCol
'Rylands Gem' (24b)	MCol
'Rylands Victor' (23c)	MCol
'Rynoon' (9d)	MCol
'Rytorch' (9d)	MCol
'Salmon Cassandra' (5b)	NHal
'Salmon Enbee Wedding' (29d) 🏆	NHal WRil
'Salmon Fairie' (28)	MCol
§ 'Salmon Margaret' (29c) 🏆	LBut MCol SHel WRil
'Salmon Pauline White' (15a)	WRil
'Salmon Rylands Gem' (24b)	MCol
'Salmon Susan Rowe' (24b)	MCol
'Salmon Venice' (24b)	WRil
'Salurose'	EHMN
'Sam Vinter' (5a)	NHal WRil
'Sandy' (30)	MCol
'Sarah'	WLRN WRil
'Sarah's Yellow'	CSam
'Saskia' (7b)	MCol
'Scottie' (24b)	WRil
'Sea Urchin' (29c)	MCol
'Seashell' (28b)	MCol
'Setron'	EBee EHMN
'Sheila' (29K)	EHMN
'Shelley'	WLRN
'Shining Light' (29K)	EHMN MCol
'Shirley' (25b)	NHal WWol
'Simon Mills' (2)	NHal
'Snowbound' (29K)	MCol
'Soft Lynn'	NHal WLRN
'Solarama' (9e)	NHal
'Sonnenschein'	LHop WHen
'Sonya' (29K)	EHMN
'Sophia'	WLRN
'Southway Sanguine' (29d)	NHal
'Southway Sure' (29d)	LBut NHal
'Spartan Glory' (25b)	WWol
'Spartan Magic' (29d)	WWol
'Spartan Moon' (25b)	NVic WWol
'Spartan Rose' (29c)	WWol
'Spartan Torch'	WWol
'Spartan White' (29c)	WWol
'Spencer's Cottage' (13b)	MCol
* 'Spoons'	SCro SHel
'Stan's Choice' (29K)	MCol
'Starlet' (29K)	EHMN LRHS MCol
'Stockton' (3b)	NHal
'Stoke Festival' (25b)	MCol
'Stuart Jackson' (25a)	WRil
'Stunning Lynn'	WLRN
'Sun Spider' (29K)	EHMN
'Sun Valley' (5a)	MCol
'Sunbeam' (25a)	EBre ECtt EFou
'Suncharm Bronze' (22a)	WWol
'Suncharm Pink' (22a)	WWol
'Suncharm Red' (22a)	WWol
'Suncharm Yellow' (22a)	WWol
'Sundora' (22d)	NHal WLRN WRil
'Sunflight' (25b)	MCol
'Sunny Denise'	WLRN
'Sunny Linda'	WLRN WRil
'Susan Rowe' (24b)	MCol

'Sutton White' (25a) WRil
'Suzanne Marie' (14a) WRil
'Taffeta' (9c) MCol NHal
'Talbot Bolero' (29c) MCol NHal
'Talbot Parade' (29c) ♀ NHal
'Tang' (12a) WWol
'Tapestry Rose' CGle CMil EMon GMac MMil NBrk
'Tapis Blanc' EHMN
'Target' (24b) MCol NHal WLRN WRil
'The Favourite' (5b) MCol
'Tickled Pink' (29K) EHMN
'Toledo' (25a) WWol
'Tom Blackshaw' (25b) MCol NHal
'Tom Parr' See ***D.* 'Doctor Tom Parr'**
'Tom Snowball' (3b) NHal
'Tommy Trout' (28) MCol
'Tone Gambol' (29a) MCol
'Tone Sail' (29a) MCol
'Topsy' (29K) EHMN
'Tracy Waller' (24b) NHal
'Triumph' (22) NHal
'Tundra' (4a) NHal
'Universiade' (25a) NHal
'Vagabond Prince' CSam WHoo
'Valerie' (10) LFis WLRN
'Vanity Pink' (7b) MCol
'Vanity Primrose' (7b) MCol
'Venice' (24b) NHal WRil
'Venus' (29K) CBlo CWan MBro
'Vera Smith' (3b) MCol
'Veria' EHMN
'Virginia' (29K) EHMN
'Vrenelli' EFou
'Wedding Day' CLTr EMan EMon GBuc MAvo MFir MHlr MMil NNor SHel SRms SUsu WCot WHoo WMaN WRus
'Wedding Sunshine' EHMN LRHS MAvo MMil
'Wembley' (24b) WRil
'Wendy' (29c) ♀ LBut MCol NHal
'Wendy Tench' (29d) MCol
'Wessex Eclipse' (29c) MCol NHal
'Wessex Ivory' (29d) MCol
'Wessex Sunshine' (29d) MCol
'West Bromwich' (14a) NHal WRil
§ ***weyrichii*** CNic EBre EFol ELan LFis LHop MHig MTho NGre NHol NMen NNrd NWCA SBla SBod SHel SIng SSmi WAbe WHil WOMN
'White Allouise' (25b) ♀ NHal
'White Beppie' (29e) MCol
'White Bouquet' (28) MCol WWol
'White Cassandra' (5b) NHal
'White Enbee Wedding' (29d) WRil
'White Fairweather' (3b) WRil
'White Gem' (25b) EHMN
'White Gloss' (29K) EHMN LRHS SMer
'White Margaret' (29c) ♀ LBut MCol NHal SHel WRil WWol
'White Nu Rosemary' (9d) NHal
'White Rachel Knowles' (25a) MCol NHal WRil
'White Rayonnante' (11) MCol
'White Sands' (9d) MCol
'White Skylark' (22) NHal
'White Sonja' (29c) MCol
'White Spider' (10) MCol
'White Taffeta' (9c) MCol NHal
'White Tower' EPPr
'Win' (9c) NHal
'Windermere' (24a) NHal
'Winnie Bramley' (23a) WRil WWol
'Winning's Red' (29Rub) MAvo NBro SMad WWin
¶ 'Winter Queen' (5b) NHal
'Woolley Globe' (25b) WRil
'Woolman's Perfecta' (3a) NHal
'Woolman's Prince' (3a) WWol
'Woolman's Star' (3a) NHal
'World of Sport' (25a) WRil
'Yellow Alfreton Cream' (5b) WRil
'Yellow Allison Kirk' (23b) NHal
'Yellow Allouise' (25b) NHal
'Yellow Beppie' (29e) MCol
§ 'Yellow Courtier' (24a) NHal WRil
'Yellow Danielle' (29d) MCol
'Yellow Ellen' (29c) NHal
'Yellow Flying Saucer' (6a) MCol
'Yellow Fred Shoesmith' (5a) WWol
'Yellow Galaxy' (9d) ♀ MCol
'Yellow Gingernut' (25b) MCol NHal WRil
'Yellow Hammer' EHMN
'Yellow Hazy Days' (25b) NHal
'Yellow Heather James' (3b) MCol
'Yellow Heide' (29c) ♀ MCol NHal
'Yellow John Hughes' (3b) MCol NHal WRil
'Yellow John Wingfield' (14b) MCol NHal WRil
'Yellow Lilian Hoek' (29c) EHMN MCol
'Yellow Margaret' (29c) ♀ LBut MCol NHal WRil
'Yellow May Shoesmith' (5a) NHal
'Yellow Mayford Perfection' (5a) ♀ MCol NHal
'Yellow Megan Woolman' (3b) WWol
'Yellow Pennine Oriel' (29a) MCol NHal WRil
'Yellow Percy Salter' (24b) MCol
'Yellow Phil Houghton' (1) WWol
'Yellow Plover' (22) NHal
* 'Yellow Pom' LRHS
'Yellow Sands' (9d) MCol
'Yellow Spider' (10) MCol
'Yellow Starlet' (29K) EHMN MCol
'Yellow Taffeta' (9c) MCol
'Yellow Talbot Parade' WRil
'Yellow Triumph' (24a) WLRN
'Yellow Whitby' (5b) MCol
§ ***yezoense*** ♀ EBee EFou ELan EMan EMon MBel NFai SPla WCot WEas WRus
– 'Roseum' MBel NHol NSti WRus
'Yvonne Arnaud' (24b) MCol
§ ***zawadskii*** WHer WPyg WRus
'Zesty Barbara' WLRN

DENDRIOPOTERIUM See SANGUISORBA

DENDROBENTHAMIA See CORNUS

DENDROBIUM † (Orchidaceae)

¶ ***moniliforme*** SWes

DENDROCALAMUS (Poaceae - Bambusoideae)

giganteus	SBam
§ ***strictus***	SBam

DENDROMECON (Papaveraceae)

rigida	CB&S CChu CFil CPle EPfP LRHS SBid SMad SSoC SSta WPen

DENDROSERIS (Asteraceae)

littoralis	CHEx

DENTARIA (Brassicaceae)

californica	EPar
digitata	See ***Cardamine pentaphyllos***
diphylla	EPar
microphylla	See ***Cardamine microphylla***
pinnata	See ***Cardamine heptaphylla***
polyphylla	See ***Cardamine kitaibelii***

DERMATOBOTRYS (Scrophulariaceae)

See Plant Deletions

DERRIS (Papilionaceae)

¶ ***elliptica***	CPlN

DERWENTIA See PARAHEBE

DESCHAMPSIA (Poaceae)

cespitosa	CKin CNat CWGN EGar EPPr ESiP ETPC GFre GMaP MBar NHol WPer
– subsp. ***alpina***	EHoe EMon EPPr
◆ – Bronze Veil	See ***D. cespitosa* 'Bronzeschleier'**
§ – 'Bronzeschleier'	CHan EBre ECoo EFou EHoe EPla ESOG ETPC GBri GCHN GCal IBlr LGre MCLN MSte NHar NHol SMrm SPer WCot WRus WWat
– 'Fairy's Joke'	See ***D. cespitosa*** var. ***vivipara***
◆ – Gold Dust	See ***D. cespitosa* 'Goldstaub'**
◆ – Golden Dew	See ***D. cespitosa* 'Goldtau'**
◆ – Golden Pendant	See ***D. cespitosa* 'Goldgehänge'**
– 'Golden Shower'	CMil ECtt EMan NHol SLPl
◆ – Golden Veil	See ***D. cespitosa* 'Goldschleier'**
§ – 'Goldgehänge'	CCuc EGar EHoe EMon EPPr EPla ESOG ETPC GCal IBlr NSti
§ – 'Goldschleier'	CVer CWGN EBee EBre ECha EFou EHoe EMon EPPr EPla ESOG ETPC GAri GBuc GCHN IBlr NHar SApp
§ – 'Goldstaub'	EFou EPla ETPC GCal WCot
§ – 'Goldtau'	CSte EBre ECha EFol EHoe EMon EPGN EPPr EPla ESOG ESis ETPC GCHN LHil MCLN NEgg NHar NHol NOrc
– var. ***parviflora***	ETPC
¶ – subsp. ***paludosa***	EMon EPPr
§ – var. ***vivipara***	EBee ECtt EHoe EMon EPPr EPla ESOG ETPC GAul LHil NBro NHol NSti SLPl WFox
flexuosa	CCuc CPea EHoe EMon EPPr EPla ETPC MBri WPer
– 'Tatra Gold'	Widely available
media	ETPC
– bronze	ETPC
* 'Morning Dew'	ECoo
setacea bronze	ETPC

DESFONTAINIA (Loganiaceae)

§ ***spinosa*** 🏆	CAbb CB&S CLan CMHG CTrw CWSG ELan GOrc GRei GWht ISea LHop MBal MBar MBri MPla NPSI NPal SArc SDry SHBN SPer SReu SSta WAbe WCru WDin WSHC WWat
– 'Harold Comber'	MBal WBod WCru
spinosa hookeri	See ***D. spinosa***

DESMAZERIA (Poaceae)

rigida	See ***Catapodium rigidum***

DESMODIUM (Papilionaceae)

callianthum	CPle CTrC MAll
§ ***elegans***	CChu CFil CGre CPle CWSG EHal ELan LHil MTis WBod WFar WSHC
¶ ***podocarpum*** B&SWJ 1269	WCru
praestans	See ***D. yunnanense***
¶ ***styracifolium***	MSal
tiliifolium	See ***D. elegans***
§ ***yunnanense***	CPle EPfP LRHS SBid WCru WSHC

DESMOSCHOENUS (Cyperaceae)

See Plant Deletions

DEUTZIA † (Hydrangeaceae)

chunii	See ***D. ningpoensis***
compacta	CFil CHan CHar WBod WPGP WWat
– 'Lavender Time'	CPle ECle EHic GSki MPla NHol SEas SPan WPat WRHF
corymbosa	CFil
crenata 'Flore Pleno'	See ***D. scabra* 'Plena'**
– var. ***nakaiana***	CPBP SIng
– – 'Nikko'	CB&S CPBP CPle CTri EBre EFol EPla ESis EWes GOrc LHop MAsh MBar MGos MHig MPla NNrd WHCG WOMN WSHC WWeb WWin
× ***elegantissima***	CMHG CShe EBee MRav SReu SRms
– 'Fasciculata'	EHic SMad SPer WWin
– 'Rosealind' 🏆	CB&S EBre ECtt ELan ENot IOrc LHop MBri MGrG MPla NBee NCut NFla SEas SPer SPla SReu SSpi SSta WAbe WBod WKif WPat WPyg WSHC
glomeruliflora	CFil
gracilis	CTri MBal MBar MBel MPla MRav MWat NBee SEas SLod SPer WDin WGwG WHCG WStI WWat
– 'Carminea'	See ***D.* × *rosea* 'Carminea'**
§ – 'Marmorata'	CPMA ECro WHCG
– 'Variegata'	See ***D. gracilis* 'Marmorata'**
hookeriana	GGGa ISea WWat
× ***hybrida*** 'Contraste'	CDoC SPer
– 'Joconde'	ECtt EHic GSki NHol SMad WKif
– 'Magicien'	CHar CMHG CSam CShe EBre ECtt ELan ENot EPla MBal MRav NFla SEas SHBN SPer SSta WFar WHCG WHar WPat WPGP

– 'Mont Rose' 🏆	CB&S CShe EBre ELan ENot GRei LBuc MAsh MBal MBar MGos MPla MRav NBee NRoo SEas SPer SReu SSta WDin WHCG WSHC WStI WWin
– 'Perle Rose'	WLRN
× ***kalmiiflora***	CB&S EBre EPla MBar MBri MGos MGrG MRav NNor SLPl SPer SRms SWas WAbe WDin WRus
¶ × ***lemoinei***	CBot
longifolia 'Veitchii' 🏆	CPle GQui MRav
× ***magnifica***	CDoC ELan IOrc MRav NFla SPan SRms WHCG WHar WStI WWeb WWin
– 'Rubra'	See ***D.*** **'Strawberry Fields'**
monbeigii	ENot WWat
§ ***ningpoensis***	CEnd CWSG EBee EHic GAbr GAul NHol NSti SLPl SPer SSta
'Pink Pompon'	See ***D.*** **'Rosea Plena'**
pulchra	CFil CHan CHar CPle CShe CWLN ECle EHal EHic GOrc NPro NSti SBid SEND SMac SPer WHCG WWat
purpurascens	WPyg
× ***rosea***	CTrw EBre ECro ENot GRei MBar MPla MWat SHBN SMer SRms WHCG WKif WStI WTyr WWin
– 'Campanulata'	EBee ENot GSki
§ – 'Carminea' 🏆	CB&S CShe ELan MBal MHlr MTis SDix SEND SPer SRms SSta WDin WPyg
– 'Floribunda'	ELan
§ 'Rosea Plena'	EHic GSki MGrG MPla SMac SSta WWeb
scabra	NPro WCru
§ – 'Candidissima'	CBlo CMHG GQui MBri MRav SMer SPer WBod
– 'Codsall Pink'	EBee MGos MRav
§ – 'Plena'	CB&S CChe CPle EBee ECro ECtt ELan EPfP NNor SEND SHBN SPer WGwG WPyg
– 'Pride of Rochester'	CDoC EBre EHal EHic ENot GAul MBar MRav SPla WDin WHar WLRN
– 'Punctata' (v)	CMHG EFol EHoe SRms WLRN
– 'Variegata'	EPla NPro NSti WPGP
¶ ***schneideriana***	LRHS
setchuenensis	EPfP EPla GGGa GQui MAsh SBid SSpi SSta WSHC
– var. ***corymbiflora*** 🏆	CBot CFil WKif WPGP WWat
¶ sp. CC 1231	WHCr
§ 'Strawberry Fields' 🏆	CEnd CLTr LRHS MBlu MBri MTis WKif WLRN
taiwanensis	CFil WPGP
× ***wellsii***	See ***D. scabra*** **'Candidissima'**
× ***wilsonii***	SRms

DIANELLA † (Phormiaceae)

caerulea	ECou ELan GBuc LHil SHel SUsu WThi
– var. ***petasmatodes***	LHil
– 'Variegata'	See ***D. tasmanica*** **'Variegata'**
intermedia	IBlr WCot WWat
– 'Variegata'	EPPr WCot
nigra	CElw CFil ECou GCal LBlm
* – 'Variegata'	WCot
revoluta	ECou IBlr WCot
tasmanica	CChu CElw CFee CFir CGle CHan CMon CRow ECou EMar EPla GBuc GCal GGar IBlr LBlm MUlv NOrc SAga SArc SIgm SLod SSpi WWat
§ – 'Variegata'	CAbb CChu CFir CKni CRDP CRow CSam CSpe ECou EHoe ELan EPPr EWes GQui IBlr LHop NPSI WCot WOld WWat

DIANTHUS † (Caryophyllaceae)

'ACW 2116'	LBee LRHS NHar WPer
¶ 'Ada Florence'	MWoo
'Admiral Crompton' (pf)	NPin SHay
'Admiral Lord Anson' (b)	SSvw
'Admiration' (b)	SHay
'Afton Water' (b)	SHay
¶ 'Alan Hardy' (pf)	MWoo
'Alan Titchmarsh' (p)	NSti SBai
'Albatross' (p)	SChu
'Albert Portman' (p)	NCra
'Aldridge Yellow' (b)	SAll
'Alice' (p)	CThr EPfP SAll SHay
'Alice Forbes' (b)	SAll SHay
'Allen's Ballerina' (p)	NCra
§ 'Allen's Huntsman' (p)	CBlo
§ 'Allen's Maria' (p)	CBlo CThr NCra NPla SRms
'Alloway Star' (p)	CWan EMFP WPer
'Allspice' (p)	CLTr CLyd CThr EGar EMFP GAbr MBro NCra SChu SMrm SSvw WHoo WPer WPyg WWhi WWye
Allwoodii Alpinus Group (p,a)	CNic
'Allwood's Crimson' (pf)	SHay
alpinus 🏆	CGle CLyd EMFP GDra GTou LBee MBal NGre NHol NMen NNrd SBla SIgm SIng SRms WHen WPer
– 'Adonis'	GCLN
– 'Albus'	EHyt LBee MHig SBla
§ – 'Joan's Blood' 🏆	CLon CMea ECha EPot ESis GAbr LHop NHar NMen NRoo SAga SAlw SBla WAbe WHoo WLRN WPyg
– 'Millstream Salmon'	EPot
– 'Rax Alpe'	EPot NNrd
'Alyson' (p)	SAll
* 'Amalfi'	SAll
'Amarinth' (p)	CWan EGar EMar MNrw WPer
amurensis	CChr EBre GCal NBro SUsu WCla WPer
anatolicus	CInt CLyd CTri EGle EHic ELan LBee MHig NHol SBla SSmi WLRN WPer
'Andrew' (p)	SHay
¶ 'Angelo' (b)	SAll
'Ann Franklin' (pf)	MWoo NPin SBai
'Ann Unitt' (pf)	MWoo
'Annabelle' (p)	CLyd EMFP GMaP MDHE MHig SChu
'Annie Claybourne' (pf)	MWoo NPin
'Anniversay' (p)	LRHS NPin SBai
anomala	SIng
'Apricot Sue' (pf)	SHay
'Archfield'	CShe
arenarius	CMea CNic EMFP GAul GCHN MTol NPri SAlw SHel WPer WRHF WWin
'Argus'	CMil SSvw WPer
¶ Arizona (pf)	SAll
* 'Arlene'	SAll

armeria ♀	CKin EWFC MGra WHer WPer
¶ – Deptford pink	ELan
¶ 'Arnhem Spirit' (pf)	MWoo
arpadianus	GCLN MPla NGre NHol
'Arthur' (p)	EMFP
'Arthur Leslie' (b)	SAll
§ × ***arvernensis*** (p) ♀	CLyd CNic CSam ECha GAbr GDra MBro MHig MPla NGre NHar NMen NRoo WPat
¶ 'Ashley' (p)	SAll
atrorubens	See ***D. carthusianorum* Atrorubens Group**
'Audrey Robinson' (pf)	MWoo
'Aurora' (b)	SHay
'Autumn Tints' (b)	SAll
'Auvergne'	See ***D.* × *arvernensis***
'Avon Dasset'	LBuc LRHS
'Baby Treasure' (p)	CLyd GAbr NHol
'Badenia' (p)	CLon CLyd MHig SBla SChu SIgm
'Bailey's Apricot' (pf)	SHay
¶ 'Bailey's Yellow Delight' (p)	SBai
'Ballerina' (p)	EBre SHay
¶ ***barbatus***	GCal
– Nigrescens Group (p,a) ♀	CBre CHad CHan CSpe LBlm LFis MEas MHlr WCot
I – 'Sooty'	NRai WHer WWhi
– 'Wee Willie'	LHop
'Barleyfield Rose' (p)	CGra CLyd EWes MDHE NHar WAbe
'Barlow' (pf)	SHay
basuticus	MHig
§ 'Bat's Double Red' (p)	CCot EGar EMFP LBlm NCra SHig SSvw WPer
'Beauty of Cambridge' (b)	SAll
'Beauty of Healey' (p)	CLTr EMFP
'Becka Falls' (p)	CThr EBre NCra SHay SRms
'Becky Robinson' (p) ♀	CThr ELan EMFP SAga SAll SHay SSvw WWhi
'Bella'	CPBP
¶ 'Belle of Bookham' (b)	SAll
'Berlin Snow'	EPot MFos
'Bet Gilroy' (b)	SHay
'Betty Buckle' (p)	SChu
'Betty Day' (b)	SHay
'Betty Dee' (pf)	NPin
'Betty Norton' (p)	CLyd CShe EBee MBro MHig MOne NBus NCra NHaw SAlw SBla SMrm SSvw WHoo WKif WLRN WPer WPyg
'Betty Tucker' (b)	SHay
'Betty's Choice' (pf)	NPin
'Bibby's Cerise' (pf)	SHay
'Bill Smith' (pf)	NPin
'Binsey Red' (p)	EMFP SSvw
* 'Blue Carpet'	WPer
'Blue Hedgehog'	SMrm
'Blue Hills' (p)	CLyd ECho ELan LBee MWat SChu SIng
'Blue Ice' (b)	SAll SHay
'Blush'	See ***D.* 'Souvenir de la Malmaison'**
'Bobby' (p)	SAll
'Bobby Ames' (b)	SHay
'Bob's Highlight' (pf)	NPin
'Bombardier' (p)	EBre NCra NRoo
'Bookham Fancy' (b)	SAll SHay
'Bookham Grand' (b)	SHay
'Bookham Lad' (b)	SAll
'Bookham Lass' (b)	SHay
'Bookham Perfume' (b)	SBai SHay

'Bookham Sprite' (b)	SAll SHay
'Bourboule'	See ***D.* 'La Bourboule'**
'Bovey Belle' (p) ♀	CLTr CSam CThr EBre ECot EGoo NCra NPin NPla SBai SMer
'Boydii' (p)	CLyd NCra NRoo NTow WWoo
'Bransgore' (p)	MBro WHoo WPyg
§ Dona = 'Brecas' (pf)	SAll SBai
brevicaulis	NTow NWCA
brevicaulis brevicaulis	CGra
brevicaulis Mac&W 5849	WOMN
¶ 'Brian Tumbler' (b)	SAll
'Bridal Veil' (p)	CLon CThr EMFP GAbr NCra SChu SSvw
'Brigadier' (p)	MHar SRms WPer
'Brilliant'	See ***D. deltoides* 'Brilliant'**
'Brimstone' (b)	SHay
¶ 'Bruce Parker' (p)	SBai
'Brympton Red' (p)	CLon CLyd CThr ECha EFou EGar EMFP NCra NSti SBla SChu SMrm SSvw WEas WKif
§ 'Caesar's Mantle' (p)	NGre SSvw
caesius	See ***D. gratianopolitanus***
– 'Compactus'	See ***D. gratianopolitanus* 'Compactus Eydangeri'**
callizonus	CLyd CPBP ESis LBee NWCA WHil WOMN
'Calypso' (pf)	SHay
'Camelford' (p)	NCra WPer
'Camilla' (b)	CLyd CThr EBee EMFP SSvw
'Can-can' (pf)	SHay
'Candy' (p)	See ***D.* 'Sway Candy'**
'Candy Clove' (b)	SAll SHay
'Cannup's Pride' (pf)	SHay
'Carinda' (p)	SHay
'Carlotta' (p)	SHay
'Carmen' (b)	SHay
'Carmine Letitia Wyatt' (p)	EBee NRoo WLRN
'Caroline Bone' (b)	SHay
'Caroline Clove' (b)	SHay
'Carolyn Hardy' (pf)	MWoo
carthusianorum	CHad EGar EMFP GSki MNrw WPer
¶ – subsp. ***vaginatus***	GCLN
caryophyllus	CArn CJew MGra SIde WOak
* 'Casper' (pf)	SAll
'Casser's Pink' (p)	GBuc MTho
'Catherine Glover' (b)	SAll SHay
* 'Catherine Tucker'	WEas
'Catherine's Choice'	See ***D.* 'Rhian's Choice'**
¶ 'Cecil Wyatt' (p)	CMea CThr WLRN
§ 'Cedric's Oldest' (p)	SChu
¶ 'Champagne' (pf)	SAll
¶ 'Charity' (p)	CMHG
'Charles' (p)	SAll
¶ 'Charles Edward' (p)	SAll
'Charles Musgrave'	See ***D.* 'Musgrave's Pink'**
¶ 'Charlotte'	SAll SBai
'Charm' (b)	SHay
'Chastity' (p)	EMFP GAbr MBro NHol SBla SChu SSvw WDav WHoo WPyg
Cheddar pink	See ***D. gratianopolitanus***
'Cherry Clove' (b)	SAll
'Cherryripe' (p)	SHay
'Cheryl'	See ***D.* 'Houndspool Cheryl'**
'Chetwyn Doris' (p)	NPin SBai
chinensis (p,a)	MBri
'Chris Crew' (b) ♀	SBai
'Christine Hough' (b)	SAll
'Christopher' (p)	CBlo EBre GCHN SAll SHay
cinnabarinus	See ***D. biflorus***

'Circular Saw' (p)	CInt SChu
'Clara' (pf)	MWoo NPin SHay
'Clara's Flame' (pf)	SHay
'Clara's Lass' (pf)	MWoo NPin SHay
'Clare' (p)	SAll SHay
'Claret Joy' (p)	CThr EBre ELan EMFP NCra NPin SBai
'Clarinda' (b)	SAll
'Clunie' (b)	SAll SHay
§ 'Cockenzie Pink' (p)	CLTr CMil CThr EBee EMFP GAbr NChi SAll SSvw WEas
'Cocomo Sim' (pf)	SHay
'Colin's Shot Salmon' (pf)	NPin
'Constance' (p)	CBlo EBee EMFP SAll
'Constance Finnis'	See ***D.* 'Fair Folly'**
'Consul' (b)	SAll
'Copperhead' (b)	SHay
'Coronation Ruby' 🏆	LRHS NPin SBai
'Coste Budde' (p)	CLyd ECha EMFP SMrm WEas
'Cranmere Pool' (p) 🏆	CMea CThr EBee EBre ELan EMan LIck MWat NCra NPin NRoo SBai SHay SMrm
'Cream Sue' (pf)	MWoo NPin SHay
'Crimson Ace' (p)	SHay
'Crimson Chance'	NSla
¶ 'Crimson Tempo' (pf)	SBai
'Crimson Velvet' (b)	SHay
¶ ***crinitus***	SAlw SHFr
'Crompton Bride' (pf)	NPin
'Crompton Classic' (pf)	NPin
'Crompton Princess' (pf)	MWoo NPin
'Crompton Wizard' (pf)	NPin
'Crossways' (p)	CLyd EGle MHig NHar
'Crowley's Pink Sim' (pf)	SHay
* 'D.D.R.'	LBee LRHS
'Dad's Choice' (p)	LRHS SBai
'Dad's Favourite' (p)	CGle CLon CSam CThr ECha ELan EMFP LBlm NCra SAll SBai SHay SRms WEas WHoo WWhi
'Daily Mail' (p)	NCra SBai SChu SMer WWhi
'Dainty Clove' (b)	SHay
'Dainty Dame' (p)	CInt CKel CMea CTri EBee ESis LBee LIck LRHS MOne NBus NCra NHol NRoo SBla SChu SMrm WLRN WWoo
'Dainty Lady' (b)	SBai
'Damask Superb' (p)	CLyd EMFP SSvw WPer
¶ 'Daphne' (p)	SAll
¶ 'Dark Tempo' (pf)	SBai
¶ 'Darling' (b)	SAll
'Dartington Double' (p)	ELan NHol
'Dartington Laced'	CMil
'Dartmoor Forest' (p)	SBla
'David' (p)	SAll SHay
'David Saunders' (b) 🏆	SBai
'Dawlish Charm' (p)	CThr
¶ 'Dawlish Joy' (p)	CThr
'Dawn' (b)	SAll SHay
* 'Dazzler'	MPla
'Debi's Choice' (p)	NCra
'Deep Purple' (pf)	SHay
¶ 'Delphi' (pf)	SBai
deltoides 🏆	CArn CKin CSev CShe ECha ELan EMan EWFC LGro LHol MGra MOne MPla SAlw SRms WApp WCla WJek WOak WUnd
– 'Albus'	CChr CLyd ECha EMFP GSki MBar MPla MTol NNrd NOak SAlw SRms SWat WByw WCla WPer
¶ – 'Bright Eyes'	CChr
§ – 'Brilliant'	CSev GTou MNrw NNrd NOak SRms SWat WGor WOve
– 'Broughty Blaze'	GDra
– 'Dark Eyes'	EWes
deltoides degenii	EHyt
deltoides 'Erectus'	ELan SIde
◆ – Flashing Light	See ***D. deltoides* 'Leuchtfunk'**
§ – 'Leuchtfunk'	EBre EMNN EPPr GAul GDra GTou MOne MTis NFla NHar NMir NNrd NVic SAlw SRms SWat WEas WHen WPer WRHF
¶ – maiden pink	EPfP
– 'Microchip'	NHar NOak SRms SSca
* – 'Red Eye'	MNrw
¶ ***deltoides splendens***	EPfP
'Denis' (p)	CLyd EBre ELan NCra NPin NPla SAll SBai SRms
'Desert Song' (b)	SAll
¶ 'Desmond'	WRus
'Devon Blush' (p)	EBee EBre WWoo
'Devon Cream' (p)	CThr EBee EBre EMFP NRoo SRms WLRN
'Devon Dove' (p) 🏆	CMea CThr EBee EBre EMan EPfP GMaP NRoo WWoo
'Devon General' (p)	CThr CTri EBre WWoo
'Devon Glow' (p) 🏆	CLTr CThr EBre EMFP EPfP GMaP LFis LIck WLRN WWeb WWoo
¶ 'Devon Joy' (p)	CMea CThr
'Devon Magic' (p)	CBlo EBee LIck WWoo
'Devon Maid' (p) 🏆	CThr EBre
'Devon Pearl' (p)	CBlo CThr EBee NCra NRoo
'Devon Pride' (p)	EBre EMFP NCra
'Devon Wizard' (p)	EMFP NCra NRoo WLRN WWeb
'Dewdrop' (p)	CInt CLyd CMea CSWP CTri CWan EBee EBre ESis GCHN LBee LBuc MOne NBir NCra NHar NMen NRoo SAll SChu SMer SMrm SSvw WAbe WHil WLRN WPer
'Diana'	See ***D.* Dona = 'Brecas'**
'Diane' (p)	CLyd CShe CThr EBre ELan EMFP LHop NCra NPin SAll SBai SHay SMrm WEas WGwG WPer
* 'Diane Cape'	SAll
¶ 'Dick Portman' (p)	SBai
'Diplomat' (b)	SAll
'Doctor Archie Cameron' (b)	SHay
'Doctor Ramsey'	CLyd MHig
Dona	See ***D.* Dona = 'Brecas'**
'Dora'	MDHE
'Doris' (p) 🏆	CMea CShe CThr EBre ECha ELan EMFP ENot GCHN GMaP LFis LHop MWat NBro NCra NPin NRoo SAll SBai SHay SMrm SSvw WEas WWin
'Doris Allwood' (pf)	MWoo NPin
'Doris Elite' (p)	SAll
¶ 'Doris Galbally' (b)	SBai
'Doris Majestic' (p)	SAll
'Doris Ruby'	See ***D.* 'Houndspool Ruby'**
'Doris Supreme' (p)	SAll
'Double Irish'	See ***D.* 'Irish Pink'**
'Downs Cerise' (b)	SHay
§ 'Dubarry' (p)	CLyd CTri EWes LBee LRHS MHig SBla WGor WPer

'Duchess of Westminster' (M)	WMal
* 'Duet'	SAll
'Dunkirk' (b)	MWoo
'Dunkirk Spirit' (pf) 🏆	NPin SBai
'Dusky' (p)	NCra
'E.J. Baldry' (b)	SHay
'Earl of Essex' (p)	CCot CMil CThr CWan EMFP NCra SAll SHay WPer WWhi
'Ebor II' (b)	SAll SHay
'Edenside Scarlet' (b)	SHay
¶ 'Edenside White' (b)	SAll
'Edna' (p)	SAll
* 'Eilat'	SAll
¶ 'Eileen' (p)	SAll
¶ 'Eileen O'Connor' (b) 🏆	SBai
'Elizabeth' (p)	CElw CFee CGle CThr LHop
'Elizabeth Jane' (p)	EMFP
'Elizabeth Pink'	SMrm
¶ 'Elizabethan' (p)	CSam
* 'Elizabethan Pink'	CNic EGar SSvw WRha
'Ember Rose'	See ***D.* 'Le Rêve'**
'Emile Paré' (p)	MTho SChu SSvw
'Emperor'	See ***D.* 'Bat's Double Red'**
'Enid Anderson' (p)	SChu SSvw
erinaceus	EMNN EPot ESis GAul GCHN GTou ITim LBee MBro MOne MPla NHar NMen NRoo NTow NWCA WPer WWin
– var. ***alpinus***	CLyd EPot SIng
'Erycina' (b)	SAll SHay
'Ethel Hurford'	WHoo
'Eudoxia' (b)	SAll
'Eva Humphries' (b)	SAll SBai SHay
'Excelsior' (p)	CBlo CThr NNor NSti
'Exquisite' (b)	SAll SHay
§ 'Fair Folly' (p)	CThr EBee ELan EMFP NBus NRoo SChu SMrm SSvw WEas WPer
¶ 'Fair Lady' (p)	CMHG
'Fanal' (p)	CLyd CShe NBir
* 'Fancy Magic' (pf)	CBlo SAll
'Farnham Rose' (p)	CLTr SChu
'Fenbow Nutmeg Clove' (b)	NChi SChu
'Fettes Mount' (p)	CHid CLTr EMon GAbr LCot NChi NSti SSvw
'Fiery Cross' (b)	SAll SHay
'Fimbriatus' (p)	WHoo WPyg
'Fingo Clove' (b)	SAll
'Fiona' (p)	SAll
'Firecrest Rose'	CCot
'First Lady' (b)	SAll
'Flame' (p)	SHay
'Flame Sim' (pf)	SHay
'Fleur' (p)	SAll
¶ 'Forest Edge' (b)	SBai
'Forest Glow' (b)	SAll
'Forest Sprite' (b)	SAll SBai
'Forest Treasure' (b)	SAll SBai
'Forest Violet' (b)	SAll
'Fortuna' (p)	SAll
'Fountain's Abbey' (p)	EMFP NChi
'Fragrant Ann' (pf) 🏆	MWoo NPin SHay
¶ 'Fragrant Phyllis' (pf)	NPin
'Fragrant Rose' (pf)	SHay
* ***fragrantissimus***	LRHS
'Frances Isabel' (p) 🏆	NCra SAll
¶ 'Frances King' (pf)	MWoo
'Frances Sellars' (b)	SHay
'Frank's Frilly' (p)	CThr EMFP SSvw
'Freckles' (p)	CThr SBai SHay
'Freda' (p)	SAll
'Freeland Crimson Clove' (b)	SHay
'French'	CShe
freynii	CLyd EHyt EPPr EWes MOne NGre NHed NMen WAbe
* 'Frilly'	CMHG
N Fringed Pink	See ***D. superbus***
furcatus	MSto NWCA
'Fusilier' (p)	CLyd CMea CSpe EBre EPPr ESis LBee MBar MOne MRPP NCra NHol NPri NRoo SAll SChu SMrm WHoo WPer
'G.J. Sim' (pf)	SHay
'G.W. Hayward' (b)	SHay
'Gail Tilsey' (b)	SHay
'Galil' (pf)	SAll
'Garland' (p)	CLyd CMea CTri NHar NNrd NRoo WGor
'Garnet' (p)	EFol SChu
¶ 'Gaydena' (b)	SAll
'George Allwood' (pf)	NPin
giganteus	EMFP IBlr MNrw MSto WCot
'Gingham Gown' (p)	NBir NBrk NCat SAlw
'Gipsy Clove' (b)	SHay
glacialis	GTou LBee NHar NHol NRya
– subsp. ***gelidus***	CGra NGre NMen NTow
'Glebe Cottage White'	CGle CLTr CVer
'Glorious' (p)	SHay
'Golden Cross' (b)	SBai
'Golden Rain' (pf)	SHay
¶ 'Grandma Calvert' (p)	SAll
graniticus	WPer
'Gran's Favourite' (p) 🏆	CKel CLTr EBre ELan EMFP GMaP LFis MTho MWat NPin NRoo SBai SChu SHay WEas WPer WWye
§ ***gratianopolitanus*** 🏆	CArn CLyd CSev CTri GCHN GTou LBee LHol MGra MHig MNrw NMen NOak SIde SRms SSpi WAbe WOMN WPer WWye
¶ – 'Corinne Tremaine'	WPbr
¶ – 'Emmen' (p)	CInt
¶ – 'Fellerhexe' (p)	WEas
– 'Flore Pleno'	CLyd EMFP MInt SSvw
* – 'Karlik'	CLyd NWCA
§ – 'Princess Charming'	MHig
– red	GAbr
– 'Rosenfeder'	WPer
– 'Splendens'	WPer
§ – 'Tiny Rubies'	CLyd ECho WAbe WFar
'Gravetye Gem' (p)	NCra
'Gravetye Gem' (b)	CLyd NRoo SRms WPyg
'Grenadier' (p)	ECho ELan
¶ 'Greytown' (b)	GCal
'Gwendolen Read' (p)	SHay
haematocalyx	CNic EHyt NHol NWCA WAbe WPer
– 'Alpinus'	See ***D. haematocalyx*** subsp. ***pindicola***
§ – subsp. ***pindicola***	EMFP MFos NSla WOMN WPat
'Hannah Louise' (b)	SBai
'Harlequin' (p)	EBee ECtt EMFP NCra NRoo WPer
'Harmony' (b)	SAll SHay
¶ 'Harry Wilcock' (pf)	MWoo NPin
¶ 'Havana' (pf)	SBai
'Haytor'	See ***D.* 'Haytor White'**
'Haytor Rock' (p)	CThr EBee EBre EPfP NCra SHay WPer

§ 'Haytor White' (p) 🏆	CSam CThr EBre EMFP EMan ERav GCHN MHlr NCra NPin SBai SChu SHay SRms SSvw WEas WWhi
'Hazel Ruth' (b) 🏆	SBai
'Heidi' (p)	SRms
'Helen' (p)	CThr SAll SHay WEas
'Helena Hitchcock' (p)	CThr NPin
'Herbert's Pink' (p)	EMFP SIng
'Hidcote' (p)	CLyd CNic CShe ELan EMFP LIck MHig MWat NBus NMen NRoo SBla WLRN WWin
¶ 'Hidcote Red'	ECho
* Highgates Hybrid	CLyd
'Highland Fraser' (p)	GAbr MBro MHig SAll SRms WEas WHoo WKif WPat WWin
'Highland Queen' (p)	SAsh
'Hilda Scholes' (p)	NCra
* 'Hi-lite'	SAll
hispanicus	See ***D. pungens***
'Hope' (p)	CLyd CWan EBee EMFP SChu SSvw WPer
'Horsa' (b)	SHay
§ 'Houndspool Cheryl' (p) 🏆	CMea ELan EMFP ERav GAbr GMaP NPin SHam WWeb
§ 'Houndspool Ruby' (p) 🏆	CLyd CSam CThr EMFP MWat NOak NPin SBai SMer WEas WWeb
'Howard Hitchcock' (b) 🏆	SBai
'Huntsman'	See ***D.* 'Allen's Huntsman'**
'Ian' (p)	CLTr CThr CWan EPPr NPin SAll SBai SHay
'Ibis' (b)	SHay
'Icomb' (p)	CLyd CSam CTri CWan SRms WHoo WPer WPyg WWin
¶ 'Impulse' (pf)	SBai
'Ina' (p)	GDra SRms
¶ 'Incas' (pf)	SBai
'Inchmery' (p)	CCot CLTr CLyd CMil CThr EBre ECED EMFP NCra NNor NTow SAll SChu SHay SSvw WEas WHoo WMaN WWhi
'Indios' (pf)	SBai
'Inga Bowen' (p)	CThr
'Inglestone' (p)	CSam CTri NHar SBla WDav WPer
'Inshriach Dazzler' (p) 🏆	CInt CMea EBre GAbr GCHN GDra ITim LBee LHop NCra NHar NHed NHol NNrd NRoo SAlw SBla WDav WHal
'Inshriach Startler' (p)	CFee CMea GDra NRoo
'Irene Della-Torré' (b) 🏆	SBai
¶ 'Ivonne Orange' (pf)	SBai
'J.M. Bibby' (pf)	SHay
'Jacqueline Ann' (pf) 🏆	MWoo SHay
'Jane Austen' (p)	CLTr EBee NBrk NCra SChu WPer WWye
'Jane Coffey' (b)	SHay
¶ 'Janelle Welch' (pf)	MWoo
¶ 'Janet Walker' (p)	GMaP
japonicus	LCot
* 'Jenny Spillers'	ECha
'Jenny Wyatt' (p)	EBre NCra SHay
'Jess Hewins' (pf)	MWoo NPin SHay
'Jessica' (pf)	SAll
'Joan Randal' (pf)	SBai
¶ 'Joan Siminson' (p)	WWhi
'Joanne' (pf)	MWoo NPin SHay
'Joanne's Highlight' (pf)	NPin SHay
'Joan's Blood'	See ***D. alpinus* 'Joan's Blood'**
'Joe Vernon' (pf)	MWoo NPin
'John Ball' (p)	CLTr EMFP
'John Faulkner' (pf) 🏆	MWoo
'John Gray' (p)	CMil
¶ 'John Partridge' (p)	SBai
'Joker' (pf)	SHay
'Joy' (p)	CThr EBee EBre EMFP EMan NCra NPin SBai SHay SRms
'Judy' (p)	CLyd
¶ 'Julian' (p)	SAll
¶ 'Kathleen Hitchcock' (b)	SBai
'Kesteven Chambery' (p)	CLyd WPer
'Kesteven Chamonix' (p)	WPer
'Kesteven Kirkstead' 🏆	CSWP
'Kestor' (p)	NCra
¶ 'King of the Blacks' (p,a)	ELan MRav
kitaibelii	See ***D. petraeus* subsp. *petraeus***
'Kiwi Pretty' (p)	CThr
knappii	CLon CLyd CPea CPou EGar EGoo ELan EPPr GCHN LGan LIck MHar MNrw NChi NOak NPri SAga SAlw SIde SSca WCla WPer WRha WWin WWye
¶ 'Kosalamana' (pf)	SBai
§ 'La Bourboule' (p) 🏆	CSam ELan EMNN EPot GAbr GDra LBee MBar MBro MHig MPla MWat NMen NNrd NRoo SAlw SBla SIng SRms WDav WPat WPer WWin
'La Bourboule Albus' (p)	CTri EPot MHig NMen NRoo SBla WAbe WPer WWin
'Laced Hero' (p)	CElw CMil NChi SChu WPer
laced hybrids	WCla
'Laced Joy' (p)	CThr CWan MAvo SAll SChu SHay SMer WPer
'Laced Monarch' (p)	CThr EBee EBre EMFP GCHN MAvo MBro NBro NPin SAll SBai SChu SRms SSvw WPer
¶ 'Laced Mrs Sinkins' (p)	SBai
'Laced Prudence'	See ***D.* 'Prudence'**
'Laced Romeo' (p)	CCot EMFP SAll SChu SHay WEas
'Laced Treasure' (p)	CLTr CThr SAll
'Lady Granville' (p)	CMil MAvo SSvw
'Lady Salisbury' (p)	CMil EMFP
§ 'Lady Wharncliffe' (p)	CLTr CMil EMFP NChi SSvw WPer
¶ 'L'Amour' (b)	SAll
* 'Lancing'	EGoo EMon MAvo
'Lancing Lady' (b)	SAll
'Lancing Monarch' (b)	SAll SHay
langeanus	SIng
– NS 255	NWCA
'Laura' (p)	SAll SHay
'Lavender Clove' (b)	SAll SBai SHay
'Lavender Lady' (pf)	NPin
'Leiden' (b)	SAll SBai
'Lemsii' (p)	EMFP MBal NHar NMen NVic WHoo WPer WPyg WTyr WWye
'Lena Sim' (pf)	SHay
'Leslie Rennison' (b)	SAll SHay
'Letitia Wyatt' (p)	CMea CThr EBee LFis NCra NRoo
'Leuchtkugel'	WAbe
¶ 'Liberty'	SBai
'Lightning' (pf)	SAll
'Lilac Clove' (b)	SHay
¶ 'Lior' (pf)	SAll
'Little Diane' (p)	MWoo

'Little Jock' (p)	CInt CShe EBre ELan EMNN EPot GCHN LBee LHop MBal MBar MHig MWat NCra NEgg NFla NGre NHar NHol NNrd NRoo SAll SBla SSmi WEas WHoo WWin
'Little Miss Muffet' (p)	CLyd
'Little Old Lady'	See ***D.* 'Chelsea Pink'**
'Liz Rigby' (b)	SHay
'London Brocade' (p)	NBrk NCra
'London Delight' (p)	CCot CThr EBee NCra SHay WPer
'London Glow' (p)	CLTr CThr SAll
* 'London Joy'	WEas
'London Lovely' (p)	CLTr CThr NCra SAll SSvw
'London Poppet' (p)	CCot CThr SAll WHoo
'Loveliness' (p)	CBre MEas
lumnitzeri	EPot MSto WPer
¶ ***lusitanicus***	SSpi
'Lustre' (b)	SAll SHay
'Madame Dubarry'	See ***D.* 'Dubarry'**
'Madonna' (p)	CThr EBee SHay SSvw
¶ 'Malaga' (pf)	NPin SAll SBai
¶ 'Mambo' (pf)	SAll SBai
'Mandy' (p)	SAll
'Manningtree Pink'	See ***D.* 'Cedric's Oldest'**
'Manon' (pf)	SBai
¶ 'Marcato' (pf)	SBai
'Marg's Choice' (p) 🏆	EMFP
'Maria'	See ***D.* 'Allen's Maria'**
'Marmion' (M)	WMal
'Mars' (p)	ELan GAbr NBus NHed NMen NRoo SAll SChu WAbe WDav WWye
'Marshwood Melody' (p)	CThr NCra SBai
'Marshwood Mystery' (p)	CThr
'Mary Jane Birrel' (pf)	MWoo
'Mary Simister' (b)	SAll SHay
* 'Mary's Gilliflower'	EBee EMFP
'Master Stuart' (b)	SBai
'Matador' (b)	SHay
'Maudie Hinds' (b)	SBai
¶ 'Maureen Lambert' (pf)	MWoo
'Maybole' (b)	SAll SHay
'Maythorne' (p)	SRms
'Mendip Hills' (b)	SAll SHay
'Mendlesham Maid' (p)	EMFP
'Mercury' (p)	SAll
'Merlin Clove' (b)	SBai SHay
'Messines Pink' (p)	SAll
'Michael Saunders' (b)	SBai
¶ 'Michelangelo' (pf)	LIck
microlepis	ITim NMen NWCA WAbe
– f. ***albus***	NSla WAbe
¶ – ED 791562	EHyt
– 'Leuchtkugel'	EHyt
– var. ***musalae***	CMea EHyt EPot NHar
'Mida'	See ***D.* 'Melody'**
* 'Misty Morn'	MDHE
* 'Molly Blake'	WDav
* 'Momoko' (pf)	SAll
¶ 'Monarch' (pf)	SHam
'Mondriaan' (pf)	CInt EBee ELan LIck WLRN
'Monica Wyatt' (p) 🏆	CThr EBee EBre LFis NCra NPin NRoo SBai SChu SRms
monspessulanus	GAul NCGP NWCA WPer
'Montrose Pink'	See ***D.* 'Cockenzie Pink'**
'Mrs Clark'	See ***D.* 'Nellie Clark'**
'Mrs Elmhurst' (p)	NCra
¶ 'Mrs Holt' (p)	EMFP
'Mrs Jackson' (p)	CLyd GBin SAsh SBla
'Mrs Macbride' (p)	SSvw
'Mrs N. Clark'	See ***D.* 'Nellie Clark'**
'Mrs Perkins' (b)	SAll
'Mrs Shaw' (p)	NCra
'Mrs Sinkins' (p)	CGle CHad CKel CSam CShe CThr EAst EBre ECha ELan GAbr GCHN GMaP LBlm MBal MGra MHig MWat NFla NPin SAll SBai SHay SMer SSvw WEas WGwG WWhi WWye
'Munot'	EPfP
'Murcia' (pf)	SBai
'Murray's Laced Pink' (p)	SSvw
N 'Musgrave's Pink' (p)	CGle CLTr CLon CShe CThr EBee ECha ELan EMFP GAbr LHop NCra NHol SAll SChu SSvw WEas WHoo WPer
'Musgrave's White'	See ***D.* 'Musgrave's Pink'**
myrtinervius	CBar CInt CLTr EHyt ITim MOne MRPP NRoo NWCA WCla WOMN WPer
¶ 'Mystery' (pf)	SAll
'N.M. Goodall' (p)	LHop
'Nan Bailey' (p)	NCra SBai
* 'Napoleon'	SAll
'Napoleon III' (p)	WKif
nardiformis	CLyd NChi WPer
¶ 'Natalie Saunders' (b)	SBai
'Nautilus' (b)	SAll SHay
neglectus	See ***D. pavonius***
§ 'Nellie Clark' (p)	CShe MBal NMen SChu
¶ 'New Tempo' (pf)	SBai
¶ 'Nichola Ann' (b)	SAll
¶ 'Nicol' (pf)	SBai
nitidus	EHic MRPP NBir NGre WOMN WPer
nivalis	NMen
noeanus	See ***D. petraeus*** subsp. ***noeanus***
'Nonsuch' (p)	CMil EMFP NBrk
'Northland' (pf)	NPin
'Nyewoods Cream' (p)	CInt CLyd CTri EBre EMFP EPot ESis GAbr LBee MBar MBro MHig MPla MRav NCra NGre NHar NHol NMen NRoo SAlw SIng WPat WPer WTyr
§ 'Oakington' (p)	CSam CTri EBre EMNN GCHN MBal MWat NCra NMen SChu SMer
'Oakington Rose'	See ***D.* 'Oakington'**
'Oakwood Erin Mitchell' (p)	NPin
¶ 'Oakwood Gillian Garforth' (p)	SBai
'Oakwood Romance' (p)	NPin SBai
'Oakwood Rose Parker' (p)	LRHS NPin SBai
'Oakwood Splendour' (p)	NPin SBai
* 'Odino'	SAll
'Old Blush'	See ***D.* 'Souvenir de la Malmaison'**
'Old Clove Red' (b)	LFis
'Old Crimson Clove' (b)	NChi
'Old Dutch Pink' (p)	CLTr CMil NCra SChu SSvw
'Old Fringed White' (p)	CLTr EMFP SSvw
'Old Mother Hubbard' (p) 🏆	CFee
§ 'Old Square Eyes' (p)	CInt CLyd MNrw SAga SAll SBla SSvw WEas
'Old Velvet' (p)	CLTr CThr EFou GAbr GCal NCat SChu WMaN
'Oliver' (p)	SAll
* 'Olivia' (pf)	SAll

'Omagio' (pf)	SAll
* 'Ondina' (pf)	SAll
* 'Opera'	SAll
* 'Orange Magic' (pf)	SAll
'Orange Maid' (b)	SAll
'Orchid Beauty' (pf)	SHay
'Oscar' (b)	SAll
'Osprey' (b)	SHay
'Paddington' (p)	CThr NCra SChu
'Painted Beauty' (p)	CLTr CThr EMFP NBir
'Painted Lady' (p)	CMil CThr EMon MAvo MBro NHol SAll SChu
'Paisley Gem' (p)	CLTr CLon CThr NCra SChu WKif
'Patchwork'	SAsh
'Patricia' (b)	SHay
'Patricia Bell'	See ***D. turkestanicus* 'Patricia Bell'**
'Paul' (p)	EBre SBai
'Paul Hayward' (p)	SHay
§ ***pavonius*** ♀	CSam EHyt EWes GBin GTou NWCA SBla SIng WOMN WPer WWin
pavonius roysii	See ***D.* 'Roysii'**
I 'Pax' (pf)	SAll SBai
'Peach' (p)	SHay
'Pearl'	SAll
'Perfect Clove' (b)	SHay
§ ***petraeus***	EPPr EWes LRHS NCra NHol
§ – subsp. ***noeanus***	CPBP ESis SAlw WHal WPer
§ – subsp. ***petraeus***	NOak WPer
'Petticoat Lace' (p)	EMFP SHay
'Phantom' (b)	SHay
'Pheasant's Eye' (p)	CLTr CLyd EGoo EMFP NCra WPer
'Philip Archer' (b)	SHay
* 'Picton's Propeller' (p)	GBuc
'Pierrot'	See ***D.* 'Kobusa'**
'Pike's Pink' (p) ♀	Widely available
pindicola	See ***D. haematocalyx*** subsp. ***pindicola***
pinifolius	MSto
'Pink Bizarre' (b)	SHay
'Pink Calypso'	See ***D.* 'Truly Yours'**
'Pink Damask' (p)	GAbr WPer
* 'Pink Dona' (pf)	SAll
'Pink Doris' (pf)	NPin
* 'Pink Fringe'	NSla
'Pink Jewel' (p)	CInt CLyd CMea CTri ECha ESis LBee MHig MOne NHol NMen NRoo SAll SChu SIng WEas
'Pink Mist Sim' (pf)	SHay
'Pink Monica Wyatt' (p)	CThr
'Pink Mrs Sinkins' (p)	CLTr ECha EMFP GAri SAll SBai SChu WHoo
'Pink Pearl' (p)	CBlo CThr EBee SAll WLRN
'Pink Sim' (pf)	SAll
'Pixie' (b)	CLyd EPot NHol
plumarius	EBee NMir SRms SSvw WByw WGor WPLl WPer
– 'Albiflorus'	NOrc WPer
pontederae	MSto WPer
'Portsdown Fancy' (b)	SHay
'Portsdown Lass' (b)	SHay
'Portsdown Perfume' (b)	SHay
* 'Prado' (pf)	SAll SBai
preobrazhenskii	MSto NChi
'Pretty'	LHop
'Pretty Lady' (p)	LRHS MDHE NRoo
'Prince Charming' (p)	CGra CSam ELan EMNN GAbr GMaP ITim NMen NNrd NRoo SAga SBla SHel SIng WLRN WPer
'Princess Charming'	See ***D. gratianopolitanus* 'Princess Charming'**
'Princess of Wales' (M)	WMal
'Priory Pink' (p)	SAll
§ 'Prudence' (p)	CThr NCra SAll SBai WHoo
¶ 'Pudsey Prize' (p)	EHyt
'Purley King' (p)	CThr
'Purple Frosted' (pf)	SHay
'Purple Jenny' (p)	SAll
¶ 'Purple Pierrot' (pf)	SBai
¶ 'Purple Rendez-vous' (pf)	SAll SBai
pygmaeus	NBro
– B&SWJ 1510	WCru
'Queen of Hearts' (p)	CLyd EBre ESis LIck MOne NBus NChi SMrm WPer WWoo WWye
§ 'Queen of Henri' (p)	CLyd CMea EBee ERav GMaP LBee LFis MMil NCra NHaw NHol NNrd NPri NRoo SAlw SBla SChu WBro WHil
'Queen of Sheba' (p)	CThr EBee EMFP NChi NCra SChu SSvw
'Raby Castle'	See ***D.* 'Lord Chatham'**
'Rachel' (p)	CLyd EBre NRoo WAbe
'Raeden Pink' (p)	SSvw
'Raggio di Sole' (pf)	SAll SBai
'Rainbow Loveliness' (p,a)	NBir SAll SSca WCla WHil
¶ 'Ralph Gould' (p)	ECho
¶ 'Ramona'	SBai
'Red and White' (p)	WPer
'Red Emperor' (p)	WPer
'Red Penny' (p)	MBro NBro NCat NRoo SAsh WWin
* 'Red Rimon' (pf)	SAll
'Red Velvet'	CLyd CSWP LRHS SAsh SMrm
'Red-edged Skyline' (pf)	SHay
'Reiko' (pf)	SAll
'Reine de Henri'	See ***D.* 'Queen of Henri'**
'Rembrandt' (p)	WLRN
¶ 'Rendez-vous' (pf)	SAll SBai
'Renoir' (b)	SAll SHay
'Revell's Lady Wharncliffe'	See ***D.* 'Lady Wharncliffe'**
'Riccardo' (b) ♀	SBai
'Richard Gibbs' (p)	MHig NRoo WWin
'Rimon' (pf)	SAll
'Rivendell' (p)	CGra EHyt EPot NHar NSla WAbe
'Robert' (p)	SAll
'Robert Baden-Powell' (b)	SHay
'Roberta' (pf)	SAll
* 'Robin Ritchie'	WHoo
'Robin Thain' (b)	SAll SBai SHay
¶ 'Rodrigo' (pf)	SBai
'Ron's Joanne' (pf)	NPin SHay
'Roodkapje' (p)	SSvw
'Rosalind Linda' (pf)	MWoo
'Rose de Mai' (p)	CBre CLTr CMil CSam EBee EBre EMFP EMon LBlm NChi NCra SAll SChu SMer SSvw WEas WHoo
'Rose Joy' (p) ♀	CThr EBee EMFP NCra NPin SBai SHay SRms
'Rose Monica Wyatt' (p)	CThr
'Rose Perfection' (pf)	SHay
'Rosealie' (p)	SHay
'Royal Scot' (pf)	MWoo
'Royalty' (p)	SHay

§ 'Roysii' (p)	CLyd MPla WPer
'Rubin' (pf)	WEas
'Ruby'	See ***D.* 'Houndspool Ruby'**
'Ruby Doris'	See ***D.* 'Houndspool Ruby'**
rupicola	CNic
'Russling Robin'	See ***D.* 'Fair Maid of Kent'**
¶ 'Sahara' (pf)	SAll
'Saint Nicholas' (p)	EMFP NCra
'Sally Anne Hayward' (b)	SHay
'Salmon Clove' (b)	SHay
'Sam Barlow' (p)	CLTr CMil CThr EMFP GMaP NCra SAll SChu SHay SSvw WWin WWye
Sammy	CGra
¶ 'Samuel Doby' (p)	NCat
'Sandra Neal' (b) 🏆	SBai
'Santa Claus' (b)	SAll SHay
'Sappho' (b)	SHay
'Scania' (pf)	SHay
scardicus	EHyt
'Scarlet Fragrance' (b)	SHay
'Scarlet Joanne' (pf)	GBur MWoo NPin SHay
scopulorum perplexans	NTow
seguieri	GCra GSki MNrw WPer
serotinus	MSto
'Shaston' (b)	SHay
'Shaston Scarletta' (b)	SHay
'Shaston Superstar' (b)	SHay
'Shot Silk' (pf)	NPin
'Show Aristocrat' (p)	SAll
'Show Portrait' (p)	NNor
simulans	EHyt WOMN
'Sir Arthur Sim' (pf)	SHay
'Sir Cedric Morris'	See ***D.* 'Cedric's Oldest'**
'Sir David Scott' (p)	SSvw
* 'Six Hills'	CLyd MBro WPat
'Snow Clove' (b)	SHay
¶ 'Snowbird' (pf)	SAll
'Snowfire'	SChu
'Snowshill Mano' (p)	WPer
* 'Sofia' (pf)	SAll
'Solomon' (p)	CThr
¶ 'Solway Hannah Scholes' (pf)	NPin
¶ 'Solway Splash' (pf)	NPin
'Solway Sunset' (pf)	NPin
'Solway Surprise' (pf)	NPin
'Solway Susan' (pf)	NPin
¶ 'Solway Sweetheart' (pf)	NPin
'Sops-in-wine' (p)	CLTr CLon CSam CThr ECha EGar EMFP GCal LWak MNrw NCra SAll SChu SHay SSvw WEas WPbr
'Southmead' (p)	MHig
§ 'Souvenir de la Malmaison' (M)	CMil WMal
sp. B&SWJ 1414	GCra
sp. J Watson	MFos
'Spangle' (b)	SAll
'Spencer Bickham' (p)	EMFP EPot MNrw
'Spetchley'	WPer
'Spring Beauty' (p)	NBir
'Square Eyes'	See ***D.* 'Old Square Eyes'**
squarrosus	EGar EPot LBee MHar MHig NGre NWCA
* ***squarrosus alpinus***	ECho
squarrosus 'Nanus'	CLyd ELan EWes
'Squeeks' (p)	SChu
¶ 'Staccato' (pf)	SBai
'Stan Stroud' (b)	SHay
'Startler' (p)	SHay
¶ ***sternbergii***	GCrs
– JJH 931078	NWCA
'Storm' (pf)	SBai
'Strathspey' (b)	SAll SHay
'Strawberries and Cream' (p)	CThr EBee EBre EMFP EMan LHop NOrc NPin SBai SHay SMer
strictus var. ***brachyanthus***	See ***D. integer*** subsp. ***minutiflorus***
* ***strictus pulchellus***	EHyt
§ ***subacaulis***	EPot GAbr MMil NHar NWCA
suendermannii	See ***D. petraeus***
* 'Sullom Voe'	NRoo
'Sunray' (b)	SAll SHay
'Sunstar' (b)	SAll SHay
§ ***superbus***	EWes GCra MTho WCla WPer WWhi WWin WWye
– 'Crimsonia'	WPer
superbus longicalycinus	MNrw
I ***superbus*** 'Primadonna'	WPer
* – 'Rose'	WPer
– 'Snowdonia'	WPer
'Susan' (p)	EBee EMFP SAll
'Susannah' (p)	SAll
* 'Susan's Seedling'	SAll
'Swanlake' (p)	SHay
'Swansdown' (p)	NNor
'Sway Belle' (p)	CThr EBee NCra NPla SBai
§ 'Sway Candy' (p)	CThr NCra SBai
'Sway Gem' (p)	SBai
'Sway Joy' (p)	NCra SBai
'Sway Mist' (p)	NCra
'Sway Pearl' (p)	LRHS NCra NPin SBai
¶ 'Sway Ripple' (p)	SBai
'Sweet Sue' (b)	SAll SHay
'Sweetheart Abbey' (p)	CCot CLon CLyd CMil CThr EBee EMFP NCra SChu SMer SSvw WLRN
sylvestris	EPot
– 'Uniflorus'	MHig
'Tangerine Sim' (pf)	SHay
* 'Tasty' (pf)	SAll
'Tayside Red' (M)	WMal
'Telstar' (pf)	SHay
¶ 'Tempo' (pf)	SBai
* ***tenerifa***	MBri
¶ 'Terra' (pf)	SBai
'Terry Sutcliffe' (p)	CWan WPer
¶ 'Texas' (pf)	SAll
The Bloodie Pink	See ***D.* 'Caesar's Mantle'**
¶ 'Theo' (pf)	SAll
'Thomas' (p)	EFou NVic SAll SChu WEas
'Thomas Lee' (b)	SAll
'Thora' (M)	WMal
'Tinnington Secret Garden'	CLyd
'Tiny Rubies'	See ***D. gratianopolitanus* 'Tiny Rubies'**
'Toledo' (p)	EMFP
¶ 'Tom Portman' (p)	SBai
'Torino' (pf)	SAll
'Tracy Barlow' (b)	SHay
¶ 'Tracy Jardine' (pf)	MWoo
'Treasure' (p)	SHay
'Trevor' (p)	SAll
¶ 'Tundra' (pf)	SBai
turkestanicus	CLyd MSto NBir SSte
§ – 'Patricia Bell'	CSam SBla
* 'Tyrolean Trailing Carnations'	SAll
'Uncle Teddy' (b) 🏆	SBai
uniflorus	MHig
'Unique' (p)	CLon EMFP SBla SSvw

'Ursula Le Grove' (p)	CLTr EBee EMFP SSvw WHoo
¶ 'V.E. Jubilation' (pf)	MWoo
'Valda Wyatt' (p) ♀	CThr ELan EMFP EMan GCHN LHop NCra NPin NRoo SAll SBai SChu SRms WWhi
'Valencia' (pf)	SBai
¶ Van Gogh® (pf)	WLRN
'Velvet and Lace'	NRai
'Vera Woodfield' (pf)	MWoo NPin SHay
¶ 'Vermeer'	WLRN
'Violet Clove' (b)	SHay
'Visa' (pf)	SAll
'W.A. Musgrave'	See ***D.* 'Musgrave's Pink'**
'W.H. Brooks' (b)	SAll
'Waithman Beauty' (p)	CCot CLyd CTri ECha GAbr MBar MBro MHar MHig MPla NCra NRoo SAll SSvw WEas WHoo WPer WPyg WWye
'Waithman's Jubilee' (p)	CCot GCHN NBrk NCat SMrm SRms WPer
'Warden Hybrid' (p)	CMea CTri EMNN ESis GAbr MHig MOne NCra NHol NRoo SBla WAbe WLRN WWoo
'Warrior' (b)	CBlo SHay
'Weetwood Double' (p)	CSam WPer
'Welcome' (b)	SHay
weyrichii	EHyt NMen NNrd SIng WAbe WOMN WPer
'Whatfield Anona' (p)	CLyd EGle ELan SAll SMrm
'Whatfield Beauty'	ECho ELan EPot MDHE SAll
§ 'Whatfield Brilliant'	CLyd LBee LRHS
'Whatfield Can-can'	CInt CLyd CPBP EMFP ESis LIck MDHE MOne NCra NHol NRoo SAll WAbe WWeb WWoo
'Whatfield Cyclops'	CLyd ESis EWes MOne NCra NRoo SAll SChu WLRN WWoo
'Whatfield Dawn'	ECho ELan MDHE SAll
'Whatfield Dorothy Mann' (p)	CLyd ECho ELan MDHE SAll
'Whatfield Fuchsia' (p)	SAll
'Whatfield Gem' (p)	CInt CKel CLyd EBre EHyt ELan EMFP ESis GCal LIck MOne NCra NHol NMen NRoo SAll SMrm WPer WTyr
'Whatfield Joy' (p)	CLyd EHyt ELan EPot ESis GAbr LBee MOne MRPP NCra NHol NMen NPri NRoo NTow SAll SAlw
'Whatfield Magenta' (p)	CLyd CPBP EGle ELan EPot ESis GAbr LBee LRHS MOne NCra NHol NNrd NRoo SAll SBla SChu WAbe WEas
'Whatfield Mini' (p)	CLyd CSam SAll SBla WPer
'Whatfield Miss' (p)	SAll
¶ 'Whatfield Misty Morn' (p)	ECho ELan
'Whatfield Peach' (p)	SAll
¶ Whatfield pinks (p)	WHil
'Whatfield Pom Pom' (p)	CLyd
'Whatfield Pretty Lady' (p)	ECho ELan MDHE SAll
'Whatfield Rose' (p)	ECho MDHE SAll
'Whatfield Ruby' (p)	CLyd EGle EHyt ELan EMFP LBee LRHS MDHE SAll WPer
'Whatfield Supergem'	CLyd ECho ELan EPot MDHE SAll
'Whatfield White' (p)	CLyd ECho ELan LRHS MDHE SAll SIng
¶ 'Whatfield White Moon' (p)	ECho
'Whatfield Wink'	EGle
'Whatfield Wisp' (p)	CLyd CPBP CTri EGle EHyt ELan EPPr NBir NMen WLRN
'White Barn' (p)	ECha
'White Joy' (p)	EMFP
'White Ladies' (p)	CLyd CThr ELan ENot NChi SAll
'White Lightning' (pf)	SAll
'White Sim' (pf)	SHay
'Whitecliff' (b)	SAll SHay
'Whitehill' (p) ♀	CShe EPot NHol NMen NNrd NWCA NWoo WPat WWin
¶ 'Whitesmith' (b) ♀	SAll
'Widecombe Fair' (p)	CLTr CThr CTri EBee EBre EMan ERav LIck NCra NPla SAll
* 'Wild Velvet' (p)	SSvw
'William Brownhill' (p)	CMil EMFP SChu SMer SSvw
'William Sim' (pf)	SHay
'Winsome' (p)	SHay
'Woodfield's Jewel' (p)	MWoo
'Yellow Dusty Sim' (pf)	SHay
'Yorkshireman' (b)	SAll SHay
'Zebra' (b)	SAll SBai SHay
zederbaueri	NWCA SIng
'Zodiac' (pf)	SAll

DIAPENSIA (Diapensiaceae)

lapponica* var. *obovata	WAbe

DIARRHENA (Poaceae)

japonica	ETPC

DIASCIA † (Scrophulariaceae)

anastrepta	CVer EGar GCal LLWP MSCN SChu WPer WRus WWye
'Appleby Appleblossom'	SChu CSam CRDP CSpe EOrc EPot NHar SSoC SWas WPbr
'Appleby Apricot'	CBrk CSpe EMar EPot MAvo MOne MSCN MTho SWas WHoo
'Apricot' hort.	See ***D. barberae* 'Hopleys Apricot'**
'April Fool'	EOrc LLWP MAvo
* 'Aquarius'	SChu
barberae	CInt EBre EHic ELan GAri GCal LHop SEas WOve
§ – 'Blackthorn Apricot'	Widely available
§ – 'Fisher's Flora' ♀	LFis
§ – 'Hopleys Apricot'	CBrk CLTr ELan EOrc LHop NBrk NSti WCot WPbr
§ – 'Ruby Field' ♀	CB&S CElw CGle CKel CShe EBar ECha EFou ELan EMNN EOrc GCHN GCal GMac LHop MBri NBro NEgg NHaw SAxl SBla SIgm SIng SPer SVen WEas WHoo WOld WPat WRha
'Bloomsbury Ice'	LBlm
'Blush'	CSpe LHil
* 'Chalgrave Beauty'	EMan
'Coral Belle'	CBrk CPBP CRDP CSpe EMan EOrc EPot EWes LHil LLWP MAvo MDHE MMil NHar NLak NPla NWes SChu SHFr SHel SMac SSoC SWas WLRN WPbr WPen WPer WRus
§ ***cordata***	CGle CMHG CShe CSpe EMon EOrc EPot GDra IHos MBal MSCN NBro NHar NMen SHel WOve WPer WWin WWye
– hort.	See ***D. barberae* 'Fisher's Flora'**
– x 'Lilac Belle'	SCoo SHFr

cordifolia See *D. barberae* **'Fisher's Flora'**
'Cotswold Beauty' LFis
'Crûg Variegated' MAvo WCru WPbr WPer WWeb
'Dainty Duet' CBrk EOrc GMaP SChu WPer
'Dark Eyes' LHil
elegans See *D. vigilis*
'Elizabeth' ♀ LFis NFai NHar WPen
'Emma' CLon CSpe EBar LHop LLWP NHar NPla SIng
felthamii See *D. fetcaniensis*
§ *fetcaniensis* CBrk CHan CLon CMHG CMea CSam EMon LBlm LFis LGre LHop MBal MHig MTho NHaw NPer NSti SChu SCro SIgm SIng SPer WHal WPbr WPer WTyr WWin
* 'Fiona' LHil
flanaganii See *D. stachyoides*
'Frilly' CRDP CSpe ECtt MHig
'Hector Harrison' See *D.* **'Salmon Supreme'**
'Hector's Hardy' ♀ CSpe
§ *integerrima* CBot CBrk CDoC CHan CMHG CSam CSpe EBar ECha ELan EMon EOrc GCal LFis LGre LHil LLWP MBro MFir SAxl SChu SIgm SMrm SPla WEas WPer
* *integerrima alba* EMan EMar NHar
integerrima 'Harry Hay' CGle
integrifolia See *D. integerrima*
'Jackpot' EPot
'Jacqueline's Joy' CBrk CElw CGle CLyd CNic CRDP CSpe EMan NHar NHaw NPer NPla NTay SAga SChu SMrm SSoC SUsu WCru
'Joyce's Choice' Widely available
'Kate' CBrk CSpe LHil SChu SIng SMrm WCru
'Lady Valerie' CBrk CLTr CRDP CSpe EOrc LHil LHop LLWP MBri NHar NHaw NWes SLod SWas
'Lavender Bell' EOrc
'Lilac Belle' Widely available
'Lilac Dream' LHop LLWP
'Lilac Lace' (v) CSpe LLWP NHar WPbr
'Lilac Mist' CBrk CLTr CMil CSpe EOrc LGre LLWP NHar NPla SAxl SChu SDix SLod SSoC SUsu WPen
'Lilac Queen' WEas
lilacina CLTr CLyd CMHG ECtt EMan EOrc GAri GBuc MBel SUsu WPer WPri WWye
'Louise' CSpe EOrc EPot GBuc NHar SMrm
'Lucy' CRDP EPot LLWP NHar WPri
megathura GCal
mollis CSpe GCal LHil LLWP SIng
'Orangeade' EOrc LLWP
'Pale Face' CLon CSpe NHar
patens CBrk CDoC CLyd EOrc MAvo MTho SAga WPen
'Paula' LHil LHop
personata CBot LLWP
'Pink Queen' GCal
'Pink Spires' MAvo
'Pink Spot' SAga SIng
* 'Pisces' SChu
* 'Pitlochrie Pink' NEgg
'Red Start' EHic EOrc GMaP LHop LLWP MMil NHar NLak SChu SMrm WLRN WWoo
rigescens ♀ Widely available
– 'Anne Rennies' EOrc
– × *integerrima* SUsu WLRN
– × *lilacina* EBee EHic EMan EMar MArl MCLN NCat NHaw NHol NLak SIgm WPbr
¶ – pale form CSpe
◆ 'Ruby Field' See *D. barberae* **'Ruby Field'**
'Ruby's Pink' EOrc
'Rupert Lambert' CBrk CLTr EMon GBuc GCal GMac LHop LLWP MBel MBro NHar NSti SChu SCro SLod SUsu WDav WHoo WPer WPyg
§ 'Salmon Supreme' Widely available
'Selina's Choice' EOrc EPot GBuc
§ *stachyoides* EBar EBre EHal ELan LBlm LHop NHaw NPer WPbr WPer WRus WWhi
'Stella' LHop
* 'Strawberry Sundae' SCoo
'Super Salmon' EPot
'Sydney Olympics' CSpe EHic EPot LHil MAvo NHar SWas WCru WLRN
tugelensis CGle CLon SUsu
'Twinkle' CBrk CLyd CPBP CRDP CSpe CWan EHyt EMar EPot EWes GCal LHil LLWP MAvo NFai NHar NNrd NPri NTay SAga SChu SSea WAbe WCru WOMN WPer WWin
* 'Twins Gully' GCal
§ *vigilis* ♀ CBot CFee CHad CHan CLon CMHG CSam EBre EFou ELan EOrc GCHN GCal GMac LFis LGre LHil LHop MRPP NBro NCat NEgg NSti SChu SDix SPer WDav WEas WPer
– 'Jack Elliott' ex JE 8955 CB&S CLTr CSev CSpe CWan EBre EHic EWes LHop NHaw NHol NSti SHel SIde SUsu SWas WLRN WPer
'Wendy' EOrc LHop MAvo NFai NNrd
'Woodcote' LHil LLWP NLak

DIASCIA × LINARIA See NEMESIA caerulea

DICENTRA † (Papaveraceae)

'Adrian Bloom' CDoC EBar EBre GBur MCLN MCli MTho NCat NOak NSti SAxl SPer SPla WBro
'Bacchanal' CFil CHad CMHG CRow CWGN CWit EBre ECoo ECtt EFol EFou EPla LGre MBri MRav MTho NBir NNrd NOak NRoo NSti SChu SUsu WPbr WRus WSHC WWin
'Boothman's Variety' See *D.* **'Stuart Boothman'**
'Bountiful' CGle CMHG CRow EBee ECED EGol GMaP LHop MBro MCLN MTho NNor NRoo NSti SPer WRHF
'Brownie' CWGN EMon GBuc MBel MCLN NCat NSti SOkh WEas WPbr
canadensis EPot MSal MTho WCot WThi
'Catforth Filigree' NCat
chrysantha SCoo
'Coldham' CArc SBar WCru

cucullaria	CBos CGra CRDP CRow CSWP EHyt EPot LGre MTho NGar NHar NMen NRya NSti NTow NWCA SIng SWas WAbe WCru WDav WThi
– 'Pittsburg'	EBee SWas
* 'Dark Stuart Boothman'	NOak
eximia 'Alba'	See ***D. eximia* 'Snowdrift'**
– hort.	See ***D. formosa***
– (Ker-Gawler) Torrey	MTho MWat NSti SWat
§ – 'Snowdrift'	CM&M CSpe EAst EBee ELan LWoo MHFP MTho SRms SSpi WWat WWeb
§ ***formosa***	CGle CRow CWGN ECha EGol ELan EOrc LAma MBal MBro MCLN MTho NBro NNor NOak NOrc NPri NRoo SChu SSea WByw WEas WGwG WHoo WWin
§ ***formosa alba***	CBot CGle CHad CRow ECha ELan EOrc LGre MCLN NBir NNor NOak NRoo NVic SChu SPer WAbe WByw WFar WPbr WRus
* ***formosa*** 'Aurora'	EFou
– 'Furse's Form'	NOak SOkh
– subsp. ***oregona***	CMea CRow CWGN EPar GCal LWoo MBal MFos NCat NOak NPro NRoo NSti NTay WAbb WAbe WByw WCru WWin
– – 'Rosea'	NChi
'Langtrees' ♀	Widely available
'Luxuriant' ♀	CB&S CGle CRow CShe EBre ECtt EGol ELan EOrc EPar EPri GAbr GBur LGan MBri MCLN MGrG NFla NOak NPSI NRoo NSti SPer SWat WAbe WBea WHoo
macrantha	CAvo CBos CFil CGle CHad CHan CRDP CRow ECha LGre MTho SSpi WCru WOMN
macrocapnos	CB&S CFir CHan CPlN CRow EBre GQui MSto MTho NSti SMrm WCot WCru WSHC
'Pearl Drops'	CDec CRow EBre EFol EGol ELan EOrc GBuc GBur GMaP MBri MSte NOak NRoo SMac SOkh SPer SSoC WAbb WAbe WEas WHoo WMer WPbr WPyg WRus WWhi WWin
peregrina	GTou
§ ***scandens***	CBot CChu CGle CMea CMil CPlN CRHN CRow CSpe ELan EPfP GBin GCal MCCP MTho WCru WPbr WSHC WWhi
– B&SWJ 2427	WCru
* – 'Snowflakes'	GAbr
'Silver Smith'	CFil WPGP
'Snowflakes'	CDoC COtt EBre EFol GCHN NRoo SPer WCer
spectabilis ♀	Widely available
– 'Alba' ♀	Widely available
– 'Goldheart'	CHad
'Spring Morning'	CElw CGle CMHG CMil CRow ECha EGle IBlr SChu SSpi WEas WPbr WRHF WRus
§ 'Stuart Boothman' ♀	Widely available
thalictrifolia	See ***D. scandens***

DICHELOSTEMMA (Alliaceae)

congestum	CAvo LBow MNrw WCot
§ ***ida-maia***	CAvo
multiflorum	WChr
§ ***pulchellum***	NTow WChr
volubile	CPlN WChr

DICHORISANDRA (Commelinaceae)

See Plant Deletions

DICHOTOMANTHES (Rosaceae)

tristaniicarpa	CFil SRms

DICHROA (Hydrangeaceae)

febrifuga	CAbb CB&S CChu CFil CGre CHan GQui LBlm LCns LHil LHop SBid SOWG WCru
versicolor	CPle

DICHROMENA (Cyperaceae)

* ***colorata***	CRow

DICKSONIA † (Dicksoniaceae)

antarctica ♀	CAbb CB&S CDoC CFil CHEx COtt CRDP CTbh CTrC CTre CTrw CWLN EOas EWes ISea LHil LPal LPan NHol NPal SArc WFib WGer WNor WRic WWeb
¶ ***brackenridgei***	WRic
* ***conjugata***	WRic
fibrosa	CB&S CHEx WRic
* ***juxtaposita***	WRic
* ***neorosthornii***	WRic
squarrosa	CB&S CTrC ERea ISea SArc WRic

DICLIPTERA (Acanthaceae)

§ ***suberecta***	CBot CHal ERea LBlm Lhop SIgm

DICOMA (Asteraceae)

See Plant Deletions

DICRANOSTIGMA (Papaveraceae)

lactucoides	CPou

DICTAMNUS (Rutaceae)

albus ♀	CArn CChu CSpe EBre ECha EFou ELan GCal LFis LGre LHop MBel MBri MLan MUlv NHol NSti SBla SChu SPer WHoo WMer WOMN WWye
§ – var. ***purpureus*** ♀	CBot CChu EBre ECha EFou ELan ENot GCal GPoy LGre LHop MBel MBri MUlv NCut NHol NSti NWCA SAxl SBla SChu SEas SPer WHoo WOMN WOld
fraxinella	See ***D. albus* var. *purpureus***

DICTYOLIMON (Plumbaginaceae)

macrorrhabdos	NWCA

DICTYOSPERMA (Arecaceae)

album	MBri

DIDYMOCHLAENA (Aspidiaceae)

lunulata	See ***D. truncatula***
§ ***truncatula***	CHal MBri

DIDYMOSPERMA (Arecaceae)

caudatum	See ***Arenga caudata***

DIEFFENBACHIA (Araceae)

See Plant Deletions

DIERAMA (Iridaceae)

'Ariel'	IBlr
'Blush'	IBlr
cooperi	CHan IBlr
* 'Donard Legacy'	IBlr
§ *dracomontanum*	CAvo CBro CGle CHan CLon CPou CRDP CRow CVer GCal IBlr LGre MHar NBir NRoo SBla SWat WCot WOMN
– dwarf lilac	GCal
– dwarf pale pink	GCal
– dwarf pink	GCal
ensifolium	See ***D. pendulum***
grandiflorum	IBlr
igneum	CFai CFir CLon CMil ECGP ELan IBlr MNrw SIng SMad SSca WAbe WCot
– CD&R 278	CHan CRDP
jucundum	CHan GBuc
latifolium	CHan GCal IBlr
¶ *medium*	CLon GSki MHlr WCot
'Milkmaid'	IBlr
pauciflorum	CFir CHan CHid CLon CMil CRDP CVer LGre WAbe
§ *pendulum*	CAvo CBot CFee CLon CMGP EBre EFou ELan IBlr MBri MFir MHar NHol NRoo SPer SWat WAbe WByw WGwG WRus
– var. ***pumilum***	See ***D. dracomontanum***
'Puck'	ECha GCal GCra IBlr MRav NCat
pulcherrimum	Widely available
– var. ***album***	GBuc WCot
– 'Blackbird'	IBlr SSoC
– x ***dracomontanum***	SMad
– dwarf forms	GCal GSki WWhi
– forms	CRDP CRow IBlr NRoo WSan
– Slieve Donard Hybrids	GCal LHop MUlv WCot
reynoldsii	IBlr
robustum	CHan CLon IBlr
– white S&SH 18	CHan
* 'Snowbells'	WWhi
¶ sp. from Lesotho	GCal
sp. SH 20	CHan
sp. SH 49	CHan
sp. SH 63	CHan
sp. SH 85	CHan
'Titania'	IBlr
¶ *trichorhizum*	CHan
'Violet Ice'	IBlr
'Westminster Chimes'	IBlr

DIERVILLA † (Caprifoliaceae)

lonicera	CPle MTis SMac SPan WFar WWat
middendorffiana	See ***Weigela middendorffiana***
¶ *rivularis*	CPle
sessilifolia	CB&S CHan CPle EPar GOrc IOrc MBel MHlr SChu SLPl WBod WCot WHCG WRTC WRus WSHC WTyr WWin
x ***splendens***	CDoC CMHG CPMA CPle EBar EBre ECha EHoe ELan EMil EPla IOrc LHop MBar MPla MRav MUlv NHol SEas SLPl SPer SSta WAbe WDin WStI

DIETES (Iridaceae)

bicolor	CTrC ERea
grandiflora	CMon CTrC ERea
§ *iridioides*	CGle CSWP LBow MSte WPer

DIGITALIS † (Scrophulariaceae)

ambigua	See ***D. grandiflora***
apricot hybrids	See ***D. purpurea* 'Sutton's Apricot'**
'Butterfingers'	WCot
ciliata	CChr CFir EBar EBee ELan GAbr GCra MSto NLak NOak SSte WSel
davisiana	CBot CElw CLon ECha GCra LFlo MSto NLak NOak WHil WPer
dubia	CBot CM&M CMea ECtt LFlo NBir NPri WBro WCHb WGor WNdy
eriostachya	See ***D. lutea***
ferruginea	Widely available
– 'Gelber Herold'	CBot EBee EMan EPfP GMaP LGre SMrm WGor WWhi
– 'Gigantea'	CBot CPou EBee GCal SAxl SCro SMrm SSoC
– var. ***schischkinii***	EBee GCal
fontanesii	GCra
'Frosty'	LCom
x ***fulva***	MSto NBir WSel
'Glory of Roundway'	CBot NLak SWat WBro WCot WSan
§ *grandiflora* ♀	CBot CElw CGle CHad CHan CMdw CMea EBee EBre ECha EFou EGol ELan EOrc GAbr GMac LGan LHol MBri NMir NRoo NSti SBla SMer SPer WEas WOld WRus
– 'Carillon'	ECle ECro EMar MHar NLak NPro SSca WBro WGor WHoo WPer
– 'Dropmore Yellow'	NChi
* – 'Dwarf Carillon'	ETen
– 'Temple Bells'	EHic EMar LCom MBro MRav NLak SWat WHoo WHow WPer
heywoodii	See ***D. purpurea* subsp. *heywoodii***
'John Innes Tetra'	CHad CLon CMil EBar ECoo GBur LFlo LRHS MCLN NRoo SWat WElm WHil WHoo WPer WWin
kishinskyi	See ***D. parviflora***
laevigata	CAbb CBot CHad CSam EAst ECro EFou GAbr LFlo LGre MSCN MSte MSto NBro SBla SIgm SSoC SUsu WCHb WHer WPer
– subsp. ***graeca***	CMdw ECro SSoC
lamarckii hort.	See ***D. lanata***
– Ivanina	SIgm WPer
§ *lanata* ♀	Widely available
§ *lutea*	Widely available
– Brickell's form	MOne MSte
– 'Yellow Medley'	WCot

× ***mertonensis*** 🏆	CB&S CBot CChu CGle CHad CHan CSam CSev EBre ECha EFou EGol ELan EOrc LFis LHol LHop MTho NMir NOrc SIgm SPer SUsu WCru WEas WHil WPbr
'Molten Ore'	GCra
obscura	CBot CFir CGle CLon ECtt ELan GAbr GCra LFlo LGan LHop NOak NPri SBla SSoC WCHb WGor WHer WHil WPer WSel
orientalis	See ***D. grandiflora***
§ ***parviflora***	CArc CBot CHad EBar ECha EFol EFou EPad EPla GAbr LFlo LGan MFir MSCN MSto NBro NOak SSoC SSvw WBro WCHb WHil WMer WPer WPri
purpurea	CArn CKin EBre ECWi EFou ENot EWFC GPoy LHol NLan NMir NNor NPri SIde WCla WOak WPer WRHF WWye
– f. ***albiflora*** 🏆	CArn CB&S CBot CGle CHad EBre ECha EFou ELan EMon GAbr GBuc LFis LHop MRav MSCN MWat NFai NOrc NRoo SPer SSvw WCla WEas WHal WHoo WPbr WPer WRus WWye
– 'Chedglow' (v)	CNat WCHb
* – 'Danby Lodge'	WAlt
* – 'Dwarf Red'	ECoo
¶ – Excelsior Group	CB&S CBot CKel CSam CTri EBre EGoo EMan MBri MWat NFai NMir NNor NVic SPer SRms WGor WHil
– Excelsior Group White	CKni
– Foxy Group	CBot EBar NFai NRoo SRms SWat WHen WPer
– Giant Spotted Group	CMGP COtt EWll LBuc NTay SCoo WPer WRus
– Glittering Prizes Group	ECoo SWat
¶ – Gloxinioides Group	EPfP MRav
– – 'The Shirley' 🏆	ECtt EFou GCra SMrm WGor
§ – subsp. ***heywoodii***	CM&M CSam CSpe EBee ECro ELan EMar GBuc WBea WCHb WCru WElm WLRN WPer
– 'Isabelina'	CBot EBee NTay WPer
– subsp. ***mariana***	GCra
– subsp. ***nevadensis***	CBot
¶ – peloric	WHer
§ – 'Sutton's Apricot' 🏆	CB&S CBot CHad CHan CMil CSpe ECoo EFou ELan EMar GAbr LHop MCLN NBir NBrk NPri NRoo SMrm SPer SSvw WCra WHen WHil WPer WRus
* – 'Sutton's Giant Primrose'	CBot
* 'Roundway Gold'	CBot
sibirica	CChr GAbr GBuc GCra LGan MSto WHer WPer
thapsi	CBot CDec EBar EBee EMon LFlo MLsm MSto NChi NLak SBla SSca WBro WCHb WHil WPer WSel
– JCA 410.000	MBro
trojana	CLon CSpe GAbr GBuc LFis MSto NLak NPri NRoo SEND SLod SUsu WEas WHer WHil WPer WWin
Vesuvius Hybrids	CBot
viridiflora	CArn CChr CHar EBar ECro ECtt EGol ERav GAbr GAul GCra MSto NBro NPri SHel SSoC WBro WCHb WHer WHil WPbr WPer WWhi WWin

DIONAEA (Droseraceae)

muscipula	MHel WMEx

DIONYSIA (Primulaceae)

¶ ***archibaldii***	EHyt
aretioides 🏆	EHyt EPot WAbe
– 'Gravetye'	ECho MRPP
¶ – 'Paul Furse'	CGra
– 'Phyllis Carter'	CPBP ECho EPot MRPP NMen
¶ ***curviflora*** × ***tapetodes*** MK 2	EHyt
involucrata	CGra EHyt
* 'Nan Watson'	CGra
tapetodes	CGra EHyt SIgm
* – EGW no. 1	CGra
¶ – farinose form	ECho

DIOON (Zamiaceae)

edule	CBrP LPal NPal
mejiae	LPal
spinulosum	CBrP LPal

DIOSCOREA (Dioscoreaceae)

batatas	MSal
deltoidea	WCru
¶ ***dregeana***	CPlN
elephantipes	CPlN
quinqueloba	WCru
villosa	MSal

DIOSMA (Rutaceae)

ericoides	CPle EDen EPla LBuc SRms
– 'Sunset Gold'	CInt LBuc

DIOSPHAERA (Campanulaceae)

asperuloides	See ***Trachelium asperuloides***

DIOSPYROS (Ebenaceae)

duclouxii	CFil SBid WPGP
kaki (F)	CGre CMCN LPan SSpi
lotus	CAgr CB&S CFil CMCN LPan SSpi WPGP
virginiana (F)	CAgr CMCN ICrw SSpi

DIPCADI (Hyacinthaceae)

lividum SF 1	CMon
serotinum	WChr

DIPELTA (Caprifoliaceae)

floribunda	CBot CFil CPMA CPle LRHS MBlu WPGP
ventricosa	CFil LRHS SSta WPGP WWat
yunnanensis	CFil LRHS

DIPHYLLEIA (Berberidaceae)

cymosa	CChu CRDP ECha EPar MSal WCot WCru

DIPIDAX See ONIXOTIS

DIPLACUS See MIMULUS

DIPLADENIA See MANDEVILLA

DIPLARRHENA (Iridaceae)
§ ***latifolia*** CAvo LBee MHig SWas WAbe
moraea CChu CDoC CHan CHid ECha ECou GCal GGar IBlr ILis LFis MHig MTho SAxl SBar SBla SSpi WAbe WHal WOld WWin
moraea minor SWas
moraea West Coast form See ***D. latifolia***

DIPLAZIUM (Athyriaceae)
See Plant Deletions

DIPLOTAXIS (Brassicaceae)
¶ ***tenuifolia*** WUnd

DIPOGON (Papilionaceae)
§ ***lignosus*** CPlN CTrC MSto

DIPSACUS (Dipsacaceae)
§ ***fullonum*** CArn CHal CKin CLTr CWGN ECWi EJud EWFC GCHN MChe MGra MHew NBro NLan NMir SIde SSvw WApp WBea WByw WCer WHer WOak WPer WWye
– subsp. ***fullonum*** WJek
inermis CHan GCal GCan WFar
– CC&McK 567 GCHN
pilosus CKin EWFC
sativus NHex
sylvestris See ***D. fullonum***

DIPTERACANTHUS See RUELLIA

DIPTERONIA (Aceraceae)
sinensis CB&S CFil CMCN CSam SSpi WNor

DISA (Orchidaceae)
¶ × ***kewensis*** GCrs
'Kirstenbosch Pride' GCrs
tripetaloides GCrs
¶ ***uniflora*** GCrs

DISANTHUS (Hamamelidaceae)
cercidifolius 🏆 CAbP CChu CPMA CSte ELan ICrw MBlu MBri MGos SPer SReu SSpi SSta WDin WWat

DISCARIA (Rhamnaceae)
See Plant Deletions

DISELMA (Cupressaceae)
archeri CBlo CKen CNic LCon MBar

DISPOROPSIS (Convallariaceae)
arisanensis B&SWJ 1490 WCru
§ ***pernyi*** CAvo CChu CLon CRDP EBee ECha EPar LGre LWoo MBel NHar SAxl SBla SLod SWas WCot WCru WFar WHal

DISPORUM (Convallariaceae)
¶ ***cantoniense*** WCot
flavens CChu CRDP EBre EPar SWas WCot WPbr
hookeri WChr WCru
– var. ***oreganum*** CBro CRow GTou IBlr WCru
kawakamii B&SWJ 350 WCru
lanuginosum CBro WChr WThi
¶ ***lutescens*** WCru
maculatum CRDP LGre SMac
¶ ***nantauense*** B&SWJ 359 WCru
sessile 'Variegatum' CAvo CBro CChu CFil CHan CRDP CRow EBre ECha ELan EMan EPar EPla EPot NTow SAxl SBla SSpi SUsu SWas WCru WFar WHal WPbr WWin
shimadae B&SWJ 399 WCru
¶ ***smilacinum*** WCru
smithii CFil CHan CRDP EBee EPar EPot ERos GAbr NBir NHar NMen NTow WChr WCru WWat
sp. B&SWJ 872 WCru
taiwanense B&SWJ 1513 WCru
¶ ***uniflorum*** WCru

DISSOTIS (Melastomataceae)
canescens CSpe

DISTICTIS (Bignoniaceae)
buccinatoria CPlN ECon
¶ 'Mrs Rivers' CPlN

DISTYLIUM (Hamamelidaceae)
myricoides CMCN EPfP
racemosum CShe CTre ELan GSki SHBN SReu SSta WSHC WWat

DIURANTHERA See CHLOROPHYTUM

DIURIS (Orchidaceae)
corymbosa from South Australia SWes
– from West Australia SWes
drummondii 'Buttery' SWes
punctata 'Old Vic' SWes
sulphurea 'Golden Dragon' SWes

DIZYGOTHECA See SCHEFFLERA

DOBINEA (Podoaceae)
vulgaris B&SWJ 2532 WCru

DODECADENIA (Lauraceae)
See Plant Deletions

DODECATHEON † (Primulaceae)
alpinum CGra NHar NRoo NRya WThi
– JCA 11744 SBla
amethystinum See ***D. pulchellum***
clevelandii NTow NWoo
– subsp. ***insulare*** CNic LRHS MPhe NWCA SBla
– subsp. ***patulum*** LRHS
conjugens NTow
– JCA 11133 CNic
cusickii See ***D. pulchellum*** subsp. ***cusickii***
dentatum 🏆 CElw CVer EPar GLil LBee MBal MBro MPhe MTho NMen NNrd NSla NTow WAbe WThi
– subsp. ***ellisiae*** EHyt GCrs NGre NRya
frigidum WAbe
hendersonii 🏆 CBro EPar MBal MPhe SAlw SBla
* – var. ***parviflorum*** GCLN
integrifolium NNrd

§ ***jeffreyi*** — EMil EPot MBro MPhe NHar NMen NWCA SAlw SBla WAbe WCla
– 'Rotlicht' — NHar SMrm SRms
§ ***meadia*** ♀ — Widely available
* – 'Alba' — CSWP
– f. ***album*** ♀ — CB&S CBro CLon ECha EFou ELan EOrc EPar GDra LAma LHop MTho NRoo NRya NSti NTow SPer SRms WWat
– Cedar County form — WAbe
* – 'Goliath' — WHil
– membranaceous — WAbe
– 'Millard's Clone' — EPar
¶ – red shades — WHil
◆ ***pauciflorum*** (Dur.)E. Greene — See ***D. meadia***
◆ – hort. — See ***D. pulchellum***
poeticum — EHic MBro NHar NTow
§ ***pulchellum*** ♀ — CNic EPar EPot GDra LBee MBal MBro NHar NMen NRya SBla WAbe
¶ ***pulchellum album*** — WDav
§ ***pulchellum*** subsp. ***cusickii*** — LBee NWCA SRms
– subsp. ***pulchellum*** 'Red Wings' — CLon CMea CVer EBar EBre EPot GDra MBro NTow SAlw WHoo WPyg WRus
pulchellum radicatum — See ***D. pulchellum***
radicatum — See ***D. pulchellum***
redolens — WAbe
tetrandrum — See ***D. jeffreyi***

DODONAEA (Sapindaceae)

humilis (f) — ECou
– (m) — ECou
viscosa — ECou IBlr
– subsp. ***angustifolia*** — CPle CTrC
– subsp. ***cuneata*** — MAll
– subsp. ***linearis*** — MAll
– 'Purpurea' — CAbb CB&S CGre CPle ECou EHic ERea LHop MAll MUlv

DOLICHOS (Papilionaceae)

lablab — See ***Lablab purpureus***
lignosus — See ***Dipogon lignosus***

DOLICHOTHRIX (Asteraceae)

§ ***ericoides*** — WHer

DOMBEYA (Sterculiaceae)

burgessiae — IDee SOWG

DONDIA See HACQUETIA

DOODIA (Blechnaceae)

aspera — GQui NMar
caudata — NMar
heterophylla — NMar
media — GQui NMar SHam WRic
mollis — NMar
* ***rubra*** — NMar

DORONICUM † (Asteraceae)

austriacum — CArc CMGP EPri MSCN NCat WPer
carpetanum — CSam EJud
caucasicum — See ***D. orientale***
§ ***columnae*** — GDra
cordatum — See ***D. columnae***
§ × ***excelsum*** 'Harpur Crewe' — CDec CGle ECED EFou ELan MHlr NPer NTow NVic WCot WEas
'Finesse' — CBlo EBee EPfP NOak SOkh SRms WHil
§ 'Frühlingspracht' (d) — CRDP EBre ELan GDra NFla SPer SRms WCot
'Miss Mason' ♀ — CDoC CShe MBri MCLN NBro SPer
§ ***orientale*** — CBlo CSte GAbr GLil MOne MSCN NPla SEND SWat WByw WOve WTyr
– 'Goldcut' — EBee EWll NRoo SPla WLRN
– 'Magnificum' — EAst EBre EMan GAul GMaP MFir MWat NFai NFla NMir NOak SMer SRms WBea WFar WGwG WHil WPer WPyg WWin WWtk
pardalianches — CMea ECha GCra MHew WByw WCot WPer WRHF
plantagineum 'Excelsum' — See ***D. × excelsum* 'Harpur Crewe'**
'Riedels Goldkranz' — GBuc MBri NBro
◆ Spring Beauty — See ***D.* 'Frühlingspracht'**

DORYANTHES (Agavaceae)

palmeri — CHEx MSto

DORYCNIUM See LOTUS

DORYOPTERIS (Sinopteridaceae)

pedata — MBri

DOUGLASIA (Primulaceae)

◆ ***laevigata*** — See ***Androsace laevigata***
◆ ***montana*** — See ***Androsace montana***
◆ ***nivalis*** — See ***Androsace nivalis***
vitaliana — See ***Vitaliana primuliflora***

DOXANTHA See MACFADYENA

DRABA (Brassicaceae)

acaulis — WDav
aizoides — EBre ECha ELan GCHN GDra MHig MOne MPla NGre NMen NNrd NRya SRms WCla WHil WWin
– 'Compacta' — ELan
aizoon — See ***D. lasiocarpa***
alticola JJH 119.94 — EPot
§ ***aspera*** — GDra
bertolonii Boissier — See ***D. loeseleurii***
– Nyman — See ***D. aspera***
– Thell. — See ***D. brachystemon***
bruniifolia — EBre EBur EGle EWes MHig MTho NWCA SSmi WPer
– subsp. ***bruniifolia*** — CGra
bryoides — See ***D. rigida*** var. ***bryoides***
cappadocica — EHyt GBin GCLN MFos
¶ ***cinerea*** — GBin
compacta — See ***D. lasiocarpa* Compacta Group**
cretica — GBin NMen
cusickii — CGra CPBP
cuspidata — EPot
daurica — See ***D. glabella***
dedeana — EWes GBin WPer WWin
– subsp. ***mawii*** — NTow
densifolia — GCLN MFos MHig NGre NHol NTow WDav
– JJA 11826 — NWCA

¶ *dubia*	GBin
glacialis var. *pectinata*	NTow
haynaldii	NMen
hispanica	GBin NMen NWCA
¶ – subsp. *lebrunii*	MRPP
hoppeana	NWCA
imbricata	See *D. rigida* var. *imbricata*
§ *incana*	NNrd WPyg WWin
§ – Stylaris Group	MHig WPat
kitadakensis	GCHN
§ *lasiocarpa*	MRPP NRoo
§ *loeseleurii*	NPri WPer
lonchocarpa	MHig
longisiliqua ♀	CGra CLyd EHyt MHig NWCA SBla WHil
– EMR 2551	EPot
magellanica	CPBP MDHE
mollissima	CGra EHyt EPot GTou MHig NMen NWCA WAbe WDav
oligosperma	MFos NWCA
¶ *oreades* CC&McK 804	MRPP
parnassica	GCHN
paysonii	CLyd
– var. *treleasei*	MFos WAbe
polytricha	GDra GTou NSla WAbe
repens	See *D. sibirica*
rigida	CMea MLan MTho SIng SSmi
§ – var. *bryoides*	CGra EHyt GDra MBro NGre NHar NWCA WAbe
§ – var. *imbricata*	CPBP MBro NGre NHar NHol SSmi
– – f. *compacta*	EPot
rosularis	EPot GDra
rupestris	See *D. norvegica*
sakuraii	CMea NGre WPer WWin
x *salomonii*	EPot
sauteri	GCHN
scardica	See *D. lasiocarpa*
¶ sp. F&W 8173 from Peru	EHyt
streptocarpa	MFos
stylaris	See *D. incana* **Stylaris Group**
talassica	EPot
* *thymbriphyrestus*	CGra
ussuriensis	WPer
ventosa	GTou MHig NGre NTow SIng
yunnanensis ex JJH 90856	WDav

DRACAENA † (Agavaceae)

congesta	See *Cordyline stricta*
fragrans	MBri
– (Compacta Group) 'Compacta Purpurea'	MBri
– – 'Compacta Variegata'	MBri
– – 'Janet Craig' (v)	MBri
– (Deremensis Group) 'Lemon Lime' (v)	MBri
– – 'Warneckei' (v) ♀	MBri SRms
– – 'Yellow Stripe' (v)	MBri
* *fragrans glauca*	MBri
fragrans 'Massangeana' (v) ♀	MBri
indivisa	See *Cordyline indivisa*
marginata ♀ (v)	MBri
– 'Colorama' (v)	MBri
sanderiana ♀ (v)	MBri
* *schrijveriana*	MBri
steudneri	MBri
stricta	See *Cordyline stricta*

DRACOCEPHALUM (Lamiaceae)

altaiense	See *D. imberbe*
argunense	CRDP EBee GBuc LBee LFis LGre LRHS MHig NGre NMen SAxl SBla SCro SRms SSoC WPen WPer WWin
botryoides	CPBP NWCA
calophyllum ACE 1611	EBee
– var. *smithianum*	NGre
canescens	See *Lallemantia canescens*
forrestii	CLyd EPot ESis SBla SMac
grandiflorum	EBee MHig NGre
¶ *hemsleyanum*	SAlw WPat
§ *imberbe*	EFou
mairei	See *D. renatii*
moldavica	MSal SIde WWye
nutans	EBee NRai
aff. *paulsenii* JJH 9209334	EPot
prattii	See *Nepeta prattii*
§ *renatii*	MSal
ruyschianum	ELan EMan EMon GBuc MBro NWCA NWoo WCot WPer
sibiricum	See *Nepeta sibirica*
virginicum	See *Physostegia virginiana*
wendelboi	CPea GBri MLLN NBus WPbr WPer WWin

DRACOPHYLLUM (Epacridaceae)

See Plant Deletions

DRACUNCULUS (Araceae)

canariensis	GCra SWat
– MS 934	CMon
§ *vulgaris*	CGle CHEx EMon EPar EPot MRav NPSI SDix SEND SSoC SWat WCot WCru WHal

DRAPETES (Thymelaeaceae)

dieffenbachii	GDra
lyallii	GDra

DREGEA (Asclepiadaceae)

§ *sinensis*	CBot CChu CGre CMac CPlN CSam EBee ELan ERav ERea GQui NPal SBra SHBN SOWG SPer WCot WSHC WWat

DREPANOSTACHYUM (Poaceae - Bambusoideae)

§ *falcatum*	WJun
falconeri hort.	See *Himalayacalamus falconeri* **'Damarapa'**
hookerianum	See *Himalayacalamus hookerianus*
microphyllum	ISta WJun
* *scandens*	ISta

DRIMIOPSIS (Hyacinthaceae)

maculata	CMon

DRIMYS (Winteraceae)

aromatica	See *D. lanceolata*
colorata	See *Pseudowintera colorata*
§ *lanceolata*	CAbb CGre CHan CMHG CPle CTrw ECou ELan EMil GCal IOrc ISea LHop MBal MBel MBlu SDry SPer SReu SSta WAbe WBod WCru WSHC WWat
– (f)	ECou
– (m)	ECou

winteri	CAbb CAgr CB&S CDoC CFil CGre CHEx CPle CTrw EPfP IOrc ISea MUlv SArc SHBN SMad SPer WCru WDin WSHC WWat
– var. ***andina***	CChu CSam GGGa SBid SSpi
§ – var. ***chilensis***	CGre CHEx CLan ISea MBal WCru
– 'Fastigiata'	CChu LBlm
– Latifolia Group	See *D. winteri* var. *chilensis*

DROSANTHEMUM (Aizoaceae)

¶ ***bicolor***	CTrC
floribundum	CHEx WEas
hispidum	CHEx CHal EBre ELan EOas EPot LHop MHig MTho NGre NMen NNrd NTow NWCA SBod SIng WPat WPyg

DROSERA (Droseraceae)

adelae	MHel WMEx
aliciae	MHel WMEx
andersoniana	EFEx
anglica	WMEx
× ***badgerupii*** 'Lake Badgerup'	WMEx
'Beermullah'	WMEx
binata	GTro MHel WMEx
§ – subsp. ***dichotoma***	MHel
– 'Extremis'	WMEx
– 'Multifida'	MHel WMEx
browiana	EFEx
bulbigena	EFEx
¶ ***bulbosa***	WMEx
– subsp. ***bulbosa***	EFEx
bulbosa major	EFEx
× ***californica*** 'Californian Sunset'	WMEx
capensis	GTro MHel WMEx
capensis alba	GTro MHel WMEx
capensis narrow-leaved	WMEx
capillaris	WMEx
cuneifolia	WMEx
dichotoma	See *D. binata* subsp. *dichotoma*
dielsiana	WMEx
¶ ***erythrorrhiza***	WMEx
– subsp. ***collina***	EFEx WMEx
– subsp. ***erythrorrhiza***	EFEx
erythrorrhiza imbecilia	EFEx
erythrorrhiza subsp. ***magna***	EFEx
– subsp. ***squamosa***	EFEx
filiformis subsp. ***filiformis***	WMEx
– subsp. ***tracyi***	WMEx
gigantea	EFEx WMEx
graniticola	EFEx
hamiltonii	WMEx
heterophylla	EFEx WMEx
intermedia	WMEx
– × ***rotundifolia***	See *D.* × *beleziana*
loureirii	EFEx
macrantha	EFEx WMEx
– subsp. ***macrantha***	EFEx
macrophylla macrophylla	EFEx
macrophylla prophylla	EFEx
'Marston Dragon'	WMEx
¶ ***menziesii***	WMEx
– subsp. ***basifolia***	EFEx
– subsp. ***menziesii***	EFEx
– subsp. ***thysanosepala***	EFEx
modesta	EFEx
* ***multifida***	GTro
orbiculata	EFEx WMEx
peltata	EFEx MHel WMEx
– subsp. ***auriculata***	MHel
platypoda	EFEx WMEx
pulchella	WMEx
– giant form	WMEx
– × ***nitidula***	MHel WMEx
ramellosa	EFEx
rosulata	EFEx WMEx
rotundifolia	GBar WMEx
salina	EFEx
slackii	MHel WMEx
spathulata	WMEx
– Kansai	WMEx
– Kanto	WMEx
* ***spathulata lovelliae***	WMEx
¶ ***stolonifera***	WMEx
– subsp. ***compacta***	EFEx
– subsp. ***humilis***	EFEx
– subsp. ***porrecta***	EFEx
– subsp. ***rupicola***	EFEx
– subsp. ***stolonifera***	EFEx
¶ ***strictcaulis***	WMEx
tubaestylus	EFEx WMEx
¶ ***villosa***	WMEx
zonaria	EFEx WMEx

DRYANDRA (Proteaceae)

¶ ***formosa***	CTrC
¶ ***nivea***	CTrC
¶ ***nobilis***	CTrC
¶ ***praemorsa***	CTrC

DRYAS (Rosaceae)

drummondii	SBla WAbe
– 'Grandiflora'	GDra
* – 'Grandiflora E.B. Anderson'	NHar
grandis	NSla
§ ***integrifolia***	EPot GAri GDra NHar NMGW WAbe WWin
lanata	See *D. octopetala* var. *argentea*
octopetala 🏆	CAgr CBar CGle CSam ECha ELan ESis GDra GTou LHop MBal MBro MHig MWat NHar NHol NNor NNrd NVic SBla SIng WAbe WEas WFar WHoo WUnd WWin
– 'Minor' 🏆	LBee MBlu MBro MHig NMen NWoo WAbe WHoo WPat WPyg
× ***suendermannii*** 🏆	CMHG EBre ELan GAri GTou MBro NHol NNrd NRoo NWCA WAbe WHoo WPat WPyg
tenella	See *D. integrifolia*

DRYOPTERIS † (Aspidiaceae)

aemula	SRms
§ ***affinis*** 🏆	CCuc CFil CRow ECha EFou EHic EPar GGar MBal NHol NMar SRms WCru WFib WRic
§ – subsp. ***borreri***	EFer
¶ – 'Congesta'	WFib
– 'Congesta Cristata'	EBre NHar NHol
§ – 'Crispa Congesta'	CBar CCuc CDoC CMil EBee EFer ELan MBri NBir NLak SAxl SPer SPla SRms SWas WAbe WFib
– 'Crispa Gracilis'	EMon WRic
– Crispa Group	GBin IOrc

– 'Cristata Angustata' CMil EFer ELan EMon GBin IOrc MBri NHol NLak NMar SRms WFib WRic
– 'Cristata Grandiceps Askew' NCat NMar WFib
– Cristata Group CMil CRow NMar SChu SPla WFib WHer
– 'Cristata The King' CBar CCuc CDoC CRDP EBre EFer EGol ELan EMon GMaP GQui IOrc LSyl MBri NBro NCat NHar NHol NMar NOrc NVic SMer SRms WAbe WRic
– 'Linearis Cristata' SApp
– 'Pinderi' EFou ELan MBri NOrc WGor WRic
N – Polydactyla Group GQui NMar
* – 'Polydactyla Mapplebeck' EMon SRms
– 'Stableri' GQui WFib
atrata hort. See ***D. cycadina***
austriaca hort. See ***D. dilatata***
blandfordii CFil WCru
borreri See ***D. affinis*** subsp. ***borreri***
carthusiana CBar CBlo CFil NHar NMar SAxl SRms WRic
– 'Cristata' NVic
clintoniana WRic
x ***complexa*** 'Stablerae' NMar WRic
crassirhizoma WRic
crispifolia WFib
§ ***cycadina*** CCuc CDoC CFil CRDP CWGN EBee EFer ELan EMon IOrc MBri MHlr NHol NMar SMad SPla WFib WGor WRic WWat
darjeelingensis WCru
§ ***dilatata*** CBar CCuc CKin EBee ECha EFer ELan EMon MBal NHol NMar SPer SRms WFib WRic
– 'Crispa Whiteside' CFil EFer ELan EMon MBri NHar NHol SAxl SHam WAbe WFib WRic WWoo
– 'Grandiceps' CRDP CRow EFer MBri NHar NHol NVic SChu WFib WRic
– 'Lepidota Cristata' CCuc CMil CRDP CWGN ELan EMon IOrc NHar NHol NMar SPer SRms WFib WRic
– 'Lepidota Grandiceps' NMar
erythrosora ♀ Widely available
* ***erythrosora prolifera*** CDoC CMil CRDP CSpe EFer EMon GMaP MBri NBir NHar NHol NMar SHam WAbe WFib WRic
expansa EMon
¶ ***filix-mas*** LHil MGra WHil WShi
– 'Barnesii' CBlo CCuc EFer NHar NHed NMar WRic
– 'Bollandiae' WRic
* – 'Corymbifera Crispa' EFer
– 'Crispa' EHon NHol WFib
– 'Crispa Congesta' See ***D. affinis* 'Crispa Congesta'**
– 'Crispa Cristata' CCuc CRDP EBre EGol ELan EMon LHop MBri NHed NHol NMar SChu SMer SPla SRms SWat WFib WGor WRic
– 'Crispatissima' CCuc
– Cristata ♀ CBar CCuc CFil CKin CRow CWGN EBre ECha EFer EFou EHon ELan IOrc LHol MBal MBri MCLN MSta NHol NMar NOrc SChu SPer SWat WFib WRic WWye
* – 'Cristata Grandiceps' EFer
– Cristata Group EFer NHol NMar SPer WFib WRic
– – 'Fred Jackson' MLan NHol WFib
– 'Cristata Martindale' CRDP CRow GQui NHol NMar SRms WFib
– 'Depauperata' CFil CRDP SChu WFib WPGP
– 'Fluctuosa' SRms
– 'Grandiceps Wills' CRow EMon NHol NMar SChu WFib WRic
– 'Linearis' CBar CRow EBre EFer EHon ELan EMon IOrc MBri SRms
– 'Linearis Congesta' CFil WPGP
– 'Linearis Cristata' EBre NMar WRic
– 'Linearis Polydactyla' EHic NHar NLak NMar SPla WHil
– 'Mapplebeck' CCuc CKni CRDP CRow NHol
– 'Multicristata' NMar
– 'Polydactyla Dadds' IOrc MBri MLan WFib
– Polydactyla Group GAri NMar SPer WFib
* ***fructosa*** WRic
goldieana EFer GBin GMaP LSyl NHar NMar WFib WRic
guanchica CFil
hirtipes See ***D. cycadina***
hondoensis CFil
lacera NHar
marginalis NMar WRic
§ ***nigropalcacea*** NHar
odontoloma See ***D. nigropalcacea***
oreades NHar SRms
¶ ***paleacea*** WHil
pallida CFil
pseudomas See ***D. affinis***
x ***remota*** NMar SRms
shiroumensis NMar
sieboldii CCuc CFil ELan EMon NHar NMar SChu WFib WRic
stewartii NHar WRic
x ***tavelii*** IOrc
tokyoensis NHar WFib WRic
x ***uliginosa*** WRic
¶ ***uniformis*** EFer
wallichiana ♀ CBar CFil CKni ECha EFer EFou ELan EMon GBin GBuc MBri NHar NMar NOrc NPSI SAxl SBla SChu SRms WAbe WFib WHal WRic

DRYPIS (Caryophyllaceae)
See Plant Deletions

DUCHESNEA (Rosaceae)
chrysantha See ***D. indica***
§ ***indica*** CAgr CSWP ECro EHic EMan GAbr IBlr MRav NHol NPri NSti SRms SSca WCer WHil WOak
– 'Dingle Variegated' EFol
§ – 'Harlequin' (v) EFol EMon EPPr EPla GBar GBuc MCCP MNrw MTho NSti WBea WRha
– 'Variegata' See ***D. indica* 'Harlequin'**

DUDLEYA (Crassulaceae)
cymosa subsp. ***pumila*** CGra MFos
farinosa CHEx IBlr
¶ ***pulverulenta*** WDav

DUMORTIERA (Weisnerellaceae)
See Plant Deletions

DUNALIA (Solanaceae)

§ ***australis***	CGre CHan CPlN CPle LHil LLew SMad SOWG
– blue	EWll WHer
¶ – large-flowered form	LHil
– white	CBot

DURANTA (Verbenaceae)

§ ***erecta***	CPle CSpe SLMG
– 'Variegata'	CPle
plumieri	See ***D. erecta***
repens	See ***D. erecta***
* ***stenostophylla***	CSpe

DYCKIA (Bromeliaceae)

argentea	See ***Hechtia argentea***

DYMONDIA (Asteraceae)

margaretae	LRHS

DYSCHORISTE (Acanthaceae)

See Plant Deletions

EBENUS (Papilionaceae)

cretica	CPle

ECBALLIUM (Cucurbitaceae)

elaterium	MHew MSal WHer

ECCREMOCARPUS (Bignoniaceae)

ruber	See ***E. scaber* f. *carmineus***
scaber ♀	CB&S CChr CPlN CRHN CSev ELan EMil ENot GAbr GCHN LIck MBri MNrw NBro NPer SPer WFar WHoo WOve WPri WWye
– f. ***aureus***	CB&S CMHG ELan SHFr WHoo
§ – f. ***carmineus***	CB&S CMHG EBar EBee ELan GCHN MHar WCru WHoo WPyg
– f. ***roseus***	CBot CGle ELan WOMN

ECHEVERIA † (Crassulaceae)

affinis	MBri
agavoides ♀	MRav
* – 'Metallica'	MBri
* 'Black Knight'	LHil SLMG
* 'Black Prince'	NPer
derenbergii ♀	CHEx SLMG
* 'Duchess of Nuremberg'	SLMG
elegans ♀	CHEx CHal LHil MBri SArc
§ ***gibbiflora*** var. ***metallica*** ♀	WEas
◆ ***glauca*** Bak.	See ***E. secunda* var. *glauca***
harmsii ♀	CSWP LHil WEas WOMN
'Imbricata'	CHEx
'Paul Bunyon'	CHal
pulvinata ♀	CHal
§ ***secunda*** var. ***glauca***	GBur IBlr NBir SLMG
* – – 'Gigantea'	NPer
setosa ♀	CHEx SLMG
'Warfield Wonder' ♀	WEas

ECHINACEA (Asteraceae)

angustifolia	CArn GPoy MSal WWye
pallida	CBot CMil CWan EAst EBee EGar ELan LFis LHol MSal NCGP NCut SEND SMad SOkh SSoC SUsu WCot
paradoxa	CPou EMan MSal WCot
§ ***purpurea***	Widely available
– Bressingham Hybrids	EBre ELan SPer
– 'Leuchtstern'	CMdw CSte EBee GSki LGan NCut SMrm SPla WHil WPer WTre
– 'Magnus'	CBot CGle CSte EBre LHop MBel MNrw MSCN MTis MUlv NRoo SCro SMad SOkh WCra WHen WHil WHoo WPer WPyg
– 'Robert Bloom'	ECED LFis LHop WCot
– 'The King'	WRus
– 'White Lustre'	EBee EBre ECha EGar MUlv SPla WCot WMer
– 'White Swan'	CDoC CHan CKel CSte EBar EFou ELan EPot LGan LHop MBel MGrG MNrw MSte NFai NMir NOrc SEND SOkh SPer SSvw SUsu WByw WEas WHer WHil WHoo WOve WRus WWye
simulata	MSal

ECHINOPS (Asteraceae)

albus	See ***E.* 'Nivalis'**
* ***bannaticus*** 'Albus'	EAst EPfP
§ – 'Blue Globe'	EBee EHic EMan GAul GCal LCom LFis NCat SCoo SMrm SSca WGwG WHil WLRN WMer WPer WWhi
– 'Taplow Blue' ♀	CB&S CSev EBee EBre ECro EFou ELan GAbr GCal LHop MCLN MUlv MWat NCut NFla NPer SCro SEND SPer WLRN WMer
exaltatus	NBir
maracandicus	GCal
microcephalus	EGar EMon
– HH&K 285	CHan
§ 'Nivalis'	CBre EBee ECha ECro EHic ELan GAbr GCal NSti SEND SPer WLRN
* ***perringii***	GCal
ritro hort.	See ***E. bannaticus***
– Linnaeus ♀	CB&S CHan ECha ECtt ELan ENot GCHN MArl MCLN MHlr NBrk NBro NCut NFai NNor NRoo NVic SEND SPer SSvw WBea WEas WFar WOve WPLl WPer WWin
– subsp. ***ruthenicus***	ELan EMon MRav NTow WBro WCot
– 'Veitch's Blue'	CDoC EBee EBre GCal GLil MBri MCLN MCli NCat NCut NLak WLRN WMer
sp. HH&K 235	CHan
sphaerocephalus	CHan ECha ECro ELan EMan EMon GAul IBlr MEas MTol MUlv SSca WByw WCot WPer
tournefortii	EGar

ECHINOSPARTUM See GENISTA

ECHIUM (Boraginaceae)

§ ***candicans***	CAbb LHil SArc SVen
fastuosum	See ***E. candicans***
* ***nebrum***	GBri NPri
§ ***pininana***	CAbb CArc CGre CHEx CTbh CTrC ECoo ELan EOas EWes ISea SArc WHer WWhi
pinnifolium	See ***E. pininana***
russicum	CFir LGre SIgm WCot

¶ × *scilloniense*	CTrC
¶ *simplex*	CTrC
vulgare	CArn CKin ECWi EEls ELan EOHP EWFC LHol MChe MGra MHew MSal NCGP NMir SIde WHer WJek WWye
webbii	CGre CHan
wildpretii	CAbb CBot CHEx CPle CTrC SArc SIgm SMrm SVen WHal WHer

EDGEWORTHIA (Thymelaeaceae)

§ *chrysantha*	CB&S CPMA LPan WSHC
– B&SWJ 1048	WCru
– 'Rubra'	CPMA
papyrifera	See ***E. chrysantha***

EDRAIANTHUS (Campanulaceae)

dalmaticus	EPad SBla
dinaricus	NSla
graminifolius 🏆	ECtt EPad GDra LBee NHar NMen NWCA WFar WPer WWin
graminifolius albus	See ***E. graminifolius*** subsp. ***niveus***
parnassicus	EPad
§ *pumilio* 🏆	CGra EPad EPot NGre NHar NHed NMen NTow SBla SRms WAbe WDav
serbicus	NBir
§ *serpyllifolius*	CPea EPad

EGERIA (Hydrocharitaceae)

§ *densa*	CBen SWyc

EHRETIA (Boraginaceae)

§ *acuminata* var. *obovata*	CGre
ovalifolia	See ***E. acuminata*** var. ***obovata***
thyrsiflora	See ***E. acuminata*** var. ***obovata***

EICHHORNIA (Pontederiaceae)

'Azure'	MSta
crassipes	CBen CHEx CWGN CWat EMFW LPBA MSta NDea
– 'Major'	SAWi

ELAEAGNUS † (Elaeagnaceae)

angustifolia 🏆	CAgr CB&S CBot CPle MBlu MRav NSti SEND SHBN SLPl SPer SRms WDin WWat
– Caspica Group	See ***E.* 'Quicksilver'**
argentea	See ***E. commutata***
§ *commutata*	CAgr CBot CDoC CMCN CPle EHoe ENot EPar IOrc LHop MBlu NNor NRoo SLPl SMad SPer SSta WHCG WRus WStI WWat
× *ebbingei*	CB&S CHEx CShe EBre ELan ENot GOrc GRei IOrc LBuc MBal MGos MWat SHBN SPer SPla SReu SSta WBod WDin WFar WHCG WWat WWin
I – 'Aurea'	LPan
– 'Coastal Gold'	CBlo CDoC COtt CSte EBee EMil ENot LBuc MAsh MGos MUlv SReu SSta WWes
– 'Forest Gold'	CSte ELan LRHS MAsh
– 'Gilt Edge' (v) 🏆	CB&S CDoC CLan CMHG EBre EHoe ELan ENot IOrc LHop LPan MBal MBri MGos MPla MWat SHBN SPer SPla SReu SSta WAbe WHCG WHar WPat WRTC WStI
– 'Limelight' (v)	CB&S CShe EBre EFol EGol ELan ENot IOrc LBuc LHop LNet LPan MBal MBri MGos MPla NHol SHBN SPer SPla SReu SSta WAbe WDin WHCG WHar WPat WRTC WWat
– 'Salcombe Seedling'	LHop MBri MUlv WAbe
– 'Southern Seedling'	CHEx
glabra 'Reflexa'	See ***E.* × *reflexa***
macrophylla	CChu CLan CSam ENot NNor SDry
multiflora	CAgr CChu LBuc MBlu SPer
– 'Gigantea'	ELan
parvifolia 🏆	CChu EBee ENot SPan WWes
pungens	CPle ERom NBir
– 'Argenteovariegata'	See ***E. pungens* 'Variegata'**
– 'Aureovariegata'	See ***E. pungens* 'Maculata'**
– 'Dicksonii' (v)	CDoC LNet SPer SPla SRms SSpi WHCG
– 'Frederici' (v)	CB&S CDoC CMHG EHoe ELan ERav MAsh MBal MBri MPla MSta NHol SHBN SPer SSpi WDin WHCG WPat WRTC WWat
– 'Goldrim' (v)	COtt CSam GOrc MBri MGos NFla SHBN WDin
§ – 'Maculata' (v) 🏆	CB&S CShe EBre EGol ELan ENot GRei LHop LNet MBal MBar MBri MGos MPla MWat NHol NSti SHBN SPer SReu SSta WBod WDin WHCG WPat WWat
§ – 'Variegata'	CB&S CDoC EBee IOrc MBal MBri NBir SHBN SPer WAbe WHCG WLRN
§ 'Quicksilver' 🏆	CChu CFil CHad CKni CPMA ECha EGol ELan LGre MPla SPer SPla SSta WCru WEas WHCG WSHC WWat
§ × *reflexa*	CFil CPle WWat
umbellata	CAgr CPle EBee MBlu SPer WHCG WWat
umbellata borealis	CFil

ELAEOCARPUS (Elaeocarpaceae)

See Plant Deletions

ELATOSTEMA (Urticaceae)

◆ *daveauanum*	See ***E. repens*** var. ***repens***
¶ *repens* var. *pulchrum*	CHal MBri
§ – var. *repens* 🏆	CHal

ELEGIA (Restionaceae)

¶ *capensis*	CFee CTrC

ELEOCHARIS (Cyperaceae)

acicularis	CBen ELan EMFW NDea SWyc WChe
palustris	EMFW MSta SWyc

ELEPHANTOPUS (Asteraceae)

tomentosus	EBee

ELETTARIA (Zingiberaceae)
cardamomum CPle GPoy LBlm MBri MSal WCot WJek

ELEUTHEROCOCCUS (Araliaceae)
pictus See ***Kalopanax septemlobus***
senticosus GPoy
septemlobus See ***Kalopanax septemlobus***
§ *sieboldianus* MRav
– 'Aureomarginatus' CB&S
§ – 'Variegatus' CBot ELan IOrc LHop LPan MBlu MGos NPal WHer WSHC

ELINGAMITA (Myrsinaceae)
johnsonii CHEx

ELISENA (Amaryllidaceae)
longipetala See ***Hymenocallis longipetala***

ELLIOTTIA (Ericaceae)
bracteata See ***Tripetaleia bracteata***
pyroliflorus See ***Cladothamnus pyroliflorus***

ELLISIOPHYLLUM (Scrophulariaceae)
pinnatum B&SWJ 197 WCru

ELMERA (Saxifragaceae)
See Plant Deletions

ELODEA (Hydrocharitaceae)
canadensis CBen EHon EMFW SAWi SWat SWyc WChe
crispa See ***Lagarosiphon major***
densa See ***Egeria densa***

ELSHOLTZIA (Lamiaceae)
fruticosa CArn CPle WWye
stauntonii CArn CB&S CBot CDoC CFee ECha EMan EPri GPoy MTis SBid SEND SLPl SMad WSHC WWye
– 'Alba' CBot

ELYMUS (Poaceae)
arenarius See ***Leymus arenarius***
canadensis CCuc EHoe EPla ETPC NPSI
¶ – f. *glaucifolius* GCal
¶ *farctus* EPPr
giganteus See ***Leymus racemosus***
glaucus hort. See ***E. hispidus***
§ *hispidus* CArc CCuc CHan CInt CMil EBee ECoo EHoe EPPr ESOG ESis ETPC LHop MBri MNrw MUlv SAxl SBla SOkh SPer SUsu WHil
N *magellanicus* CElw CGle CInt CRow CSam CSpe EBre ECot EFol EHoe ELan EOrc ESOG ETPC GAbr GAul GCHN GCal MNrw NCat NFai NPSI NSti SBar SEND WAbb WEas WHil WPer WPri
§ *scabrus* EPla ESOG ETPC SMrm
tenuis CCuc CInt EBee EJud
villosus var. *arkansanus* EBee ESOG

ELYTROPUS (Apocynaceae)
See Plant Deletions

EMBOTHRIUM † (Proteaceae)
coccineum CB&S CHEx ELan EMil GOrc IOrc SDry SReu WCot WNor WPat WPyg
– Lanceolatum Group CGre CSte ELan LRHS MBal SArc SBid SHBN SPer SSpi SSta
– – 'Inca Flame' CAbP CFai COtt CPMA CSte CWSG ISea LRHS NHed SMur SSpi SSta WPat WWat
* – – 'Inca King' LRHS
– – 'Ñorquinco' ♀ CB&S IOrc LRHS MBal MBri WBod WCru WPyg
– Longifolium Group CB&S CEnd IBlr IOrc ISea

EMILIA (Asteraceae)
javanica hort. See ***E. coccinea***

EMINIUM (Araceae)
albertii LAma

EMMENOPTERYS (Rubiaceae)
See Plant Deletions

EMPETRUM (Empetraceae)
luteum MBar
nigrum GAri GPoy MBal MBar MHig SMur WPat
– 'Bernstein' EDen
* – 'Gold' CMHG
– var. *japonicum* GDra GTou
– 'Lucia' MGos

ENCEPHALARTOS (Zamiaceae)
natalensis LPal

ENDYMION See HYACINTHOIDES

ENGELMANNIA (Asteraceae)
See Plant Deletions

ENKIANTHUS † (Ericaceae)
campanulatus ♀ CB&S CFee CLan CMHG EBre ELan ENot GGGa GOrc GRei GWht LHyd LNet MBal MBar MBel MBri MGos NBee NHol SHBN SPer SReu SSta WBod WDin WHCG WNor WWat
– f. *albiflorus* CSte CWSG ELan GGGa MBal MBri SMur SPer
– var. *palibinii* CGre GAri GGGa LRHS MAsh MBal MGos WNor WWat
– 'Red Bells' CBlo COtt CPMA CSte CWSG EPfP LRHS MBri NHed SSta WWeb
– var. *sikokianus* GAri GGGa
* – 'Variegatus' LRHS
cernuus var. *matsudae* GAri
– f. *rubens* ♀ CB&S GAri GGGa MAsh MBal MBri SSpi SSta WDin WNor WWat
chinensis CSte EBre ELan EPfP GAri GCHN GGGa MAsh MBar SBar SPer WNor WWat
deflexus CFil CKni CSte LRHS SSta WPGP
perulatus ♀ CFil CSte EMil GAri LRHS MBar WWes

ENSETE (Musaceae)

§ *ventricosum*	CAbb CBot CHEx EOas LCns LPal SArc
* – 'Rubrum'	LCns

ENTELEA (Tiliaceae)

arborescens	CHEx ECou

EOMECON (Papaveraceae)

chionantha	CBot CHEx CHan CHid CSam CWGN EBre ECha EFer EMar ERos GAbr GCal IBlr MUlv NGre NSti SAxl SMad SSpi SUsu WCot WCru WFar WHer WWin WWye

EPACRIS (Epacridaceae)

¶ *paludosa*	GCrs GGGa
¶ *petrophila*	GGGa
– Baw Baw form	MHig

EPHEDRA (Ephedraceae)

alte	WCot
americana var. *andina*	SArc
distachya	GPoy NNor WWye
equisetina	EBee
– JJH 920912	EMon
– JJH 9308135	NWCA
fedtschenkoi	EBee
fragilis	EPla SDry
gerardiana	CNic NHex
– var. *sikkimensis*	EGar EPla SDry
§ *major*	SDry WHer
minima	NWCA
monosperma	EBee
nebrodensis	See ***E. major***
nevadensis	CArn GBin GPoy MSal
przewalskii	EBee
sinica	MSal
viridis	CArn GBin MSal

EPIDENDRUM (Orchidaceae)

criniferum	SLMG
radicans	See ***E. ibaguense***

EPIGAEA (Ericaceae)

asiatica	MBal
gaultherioides	GGGa MBal
repens	MBal

EPILOBIUM (Onagraceae)

§ *angustifolium*	CGle CKin ECWi GBar NNrd SWat WHer
§ *angustifolium album*	Widely available
angustifolium 'Isobel'	CArc LFis MAvo MRav NHex WAbb WCot
– f. *leucanthum*	See ***E. angustifolium album***
– 'Stahl Rose'	CArc CBot EMon EPPr EWes GCal MAvo NHex SMrm SWat WCot WSHC
californicum Haussknecht	See ***Zauschneria californica*** subsp. ***angustifolia***
– hort.	See ***Zauschneria californica***
canum	See ***Zauschneria californica*** subsp. ***cana***
§ *chlorifolium*	WOMN
– var. *kaikourense*	See ***E. chlorifolium***
crassum	CPBP EBar EHic GBuc NMen NWoo WWin
§ *dodonaei*	CGle EBee EMan LFis LHol MTho WCot WMaN WOMN WSHC WWin
fleischeri	CLyd EDAr MTho SAga SUsu WSHC
garrettii	See ***Zauschneria californica*** subsp. ***garrettii***
N *glabellum*	CArc CGle CMea CSpe ECha ELan EOrc GMac LBee LGre LHop MBel NBir NMen SAga SPer SUsu WAbe WEas WOMN WOve WPat WPer WWin
– 'Sulphureum'	CNic EBee GCra GMaP NChi
hirsutum	CKin CTiv ECWi SWat WCla
hirsutum album	NSti WAlt
hirsutum roseum	WRha
hirsutum 'Well Creek' (v)	CElw ECha EPPr LFis MAvo MCLN SWat WCot WPer
latifolium	NGre
luteum	WCla
microphyllum	See ***Zauschneria californica*** subsp. ***cana***
montanum	CKin CTiv
– variegated	CNat WAlt
obcordatum	CLTr LHop NWCA SBla
rosmarinifolium	See ***E. dodonaei***
* *spathulifolium*	LHop
¶ *tasmanicum*	SAlw WHer
¶ *tetragonum*	CTiv
villosum	See ***Zauschneria californica*** subsp. ***mexicana***
wilsonii hort.	See ***E. chlorifolium***

EPIMEDIUM † (Berberidaceae)

acuminatum	CElw CFil EFEx GLil LGre LWoo SChu WAbe WPGP
– L 575	CChu CLon SBla SSpi
alpinum	CMGP EPar GBuc MBal NHol SAlw SAxl SPer WPbr
Asiatic Hybrids	SChu SWas WPbr
'Beni-chidori'	GLil
'Beni-kujaku'	GLil
× *cantabrigiense*	EBre ECro ECtt EOrc EPla GCHN GDra GMaP MBal MBri MBro MRav NHol NRoo SMac SPer WCru WHow WPbr
cremeum	See ***E. grandiflorum*** subsp. ***koreanum***
davidii	CChu CRDP ECha GBri MBro SAxl SSpi SWas WAbe WHal WPbr
– EMR 4125	CElw LWoo SAga SBla
diphyllum	CChu CRDP EMon LGre SAga SBla SWas WHal WPbr
– dwarf white	GLil
dolichostemon	SWas
elongatum	WAbe
'Enchantress'	ECha GBuc NRoo SSpi WHal WPbr
fangii Og 81.997	SBla
¶ *franchetii* 'Brimstone Butterfly' Og 87.001	SBla
§ *grandiflorum* 🏆	CFir CHan CLTr CTri ECha EGar EHal ELan EPar GAbr GDra GMaP MBal MBri NBir NHar NMen SAga SBla SPer SWas WCru WPbr WRus
– 'Album'	LWoo
– var. *coelestre*	GLil
– 'Crimson Beauty'	CBos CChu ECha LGre LWoo SAga SChu WCot WCru WHal

– 'Elfenkönigin'	LRHS
¶ – 'Frohnleiten'	GAbr
– 'Koji'	WPbr
§ – subsp. ***koreanum***	CFil CLon CRDP EFEx GLil LGre LWoo MBro NHar SAxl SBla WAbe
– lilac seedling	CRDP LGre SAxl SWas WFar
– 'Lilafee'	CMil CRDP CSte EBee ECha EGar EMil GBri GMaP LGre NHar NPri SAga SAxl SOkh SWas WAbe WCru WPbr WRus
– 'Mount Kitadake'	SSpi SWas
– 'Nanum' ♀	CChu CMil CRDP EHyt LGre NHar NTow SBla SChu SWas WAbe WCru
– 'Rose Queen' ♀	CLTr CM&M CMil CSte EBre EHyt EPPr EPar EPla GGar LFis LGre NRoo SAxl SBla SChu SMac SSpi SWas
§ – 'Roseum'	EBre GBri LWoo NTow SPla
– 'Shikinomai'	SWas WPbr
– f. ***violaceum***	CFir CLTr LWoo SBla SChu SWas WAbe
– 'White Queen' ♀	CBos CFir CLon CRDP GLil LGre NOak SBla SSpi SWas WAbe WPbr
'Kaguyahime'	SBla
leptorrhizum	CBos CChu EMon NBrk SBla WAbe
– Og Y 44	CRDP EHyt SAga SSpi SWas
macranthum	See ***E. grandiflorum***
membranaceum	SWas WPbr
¶ ***ogisui*** Og 91.001	SBla
x ***omeiense***	SBla
¶ ***pauciflorum*** Og 92.123	SBla
x ***perralchicum*** ♀	CBro GBuc GMaP MBal MBel NRoo SChu SLPl WFox WRus WSHC
– 'Frohnleiten'	CVer EBre ECha ECtt EOrc EPar EPla EPot EPri ERav ERos GCHN LWoo MBri MCLN MHig MRav MSte MTol MUlv NBrk NRoo SMac SMad SPer SSpe WAbe WPbr
– 'Wisley'	MBro MUlv SAlw SBla
perralderianum	CFil CSam CWGN EBre EFou ELan LGan LGro MBal MBro MFir MRav NFla NHar SBla SCro SHig SOkh SPer SRms SSpi SSvw WAbe WCru WHen WHow WPbr WWin
– 'Weihenstephan'	SWas
pinnatum	CChu CDoC GMaP MSta WHal
§ – subsp. ***colchicum*** ♀	CFil CVer EBee EBre ELan EPot ERav LSyl LWoo MBal MBro NFla NRoo NRya SAga SDix SMac SPer SSpi WAbe WCru WHoo WPbr WRus
– – L 321	SBla
pinnatum elegans	See ***E. pinnatum*** subsp. ***colchicum***
¶ ***pubescens*** Og 91.003	SBla
pubigerum	EBee ECha EGar EGle EPla GAbr MBal WPbr
x ***rubrum*** ♀	Widely available
sagittatum	EFEx GLil WPbr
'Sasaki'	GLil
setosum	CChu CElw CFil ECha SAxl SBla SMac SWas WAbe WPbr
stellulatum 'Wudang Star' L 1193	SBla
'Sunset'	GLil
'Tamabotan'	GLil
x ***versicolor***	MBal WFox
– 'Cupreum'	SAxl SMac SSpi
– 'Neosulphureum'	CBro LWoo MTol SMac SSpi WHil
– 'Sulphureum' ♀	Widely available
– 'Versicolor'	LGre NHar SBla SWas
x ***warleyense***	CBos CChu CElw ECha ECro EFou EHyt ELan EPla EPot GCHN LFis LGan LGre MArl MBal MBro NHar SAga SBla SOkh SWas WAbe WCra WHal WPbr WRus WWin
– 'Orangekönigin'	CSte EBee LBuc MBel MMil SPla SWas WHil WPbr
x ***youngianum***	CB&S EGle SBla
– 'Lilacinum'	See ***E. x youngianum* 'Roseum'**
– 'Merlin'	CChu CFir ECha EHyt GLil SAxl SBla SChu SWas WAbe WSan
– 'Niveum' ♀	Widely available
§ – 'Roseum'	CBos CLon CRDP EFou EHyt EMan EMil EPar ERos GAbr MBal MBri MTol MUlv NHar NPri NSti NTow SBla SMac SMad SOkh SPer WPbr WRus
– 'Typicum'	CChu CLon SAxl WAbe
– white seedling	EHyt

EPIPACTIS (Orchidaceae)

gigantea	CAvo CBro CFee CFil ECha EHyt ELan EPar EPot ERos MBal MHig MS&S MTho NGar NHar SBla SWes WAbe WChe WChr WCot WCru
¶ – 'Enchantment'	SWes
– x ***palustris***	WChr
* – 'Serpentine Night'	IBlr
– x ***veratrifolia***	WChr
¶ ***helleborine***	SSpi WUnd
* g. **Lowland Legacy** 'Edelstein'	SWes
* – 'Frankfurt'	SWes
palustris	CAvo EDAr NGar NHar SWes WChe WHer
* g. **Sabine** 'Frankfurt'	SWes
thunbergii	EFEx
* ***veratrifolia*** 'Jerusalem'	SWes

EPIPREMNUM (Araceae)

§ ***aureum*** ♀	CHal EBak MBri
– 'Marble Queen' (v)	CHal
§ ***pinnatum***	MBri

EPISCIA (Gesneriaceae)

§ ***dianthiflora***	CHal MBri SRms WDib
* 'Iris August'	MBri
* ***primeria***	MBri
* 'San Miguel'	CHal MBri WDib

EQUISETUM † (Equisetaceae)

arvense	MSal
'Bandit'	EMon
camtschatcense	SMad WHil
¶ ***giganteum***	CNat
hyemale	CHEx CNat EBre MCCP WChe
§ – var. ***affine***	EBee ELan EPla WPbr
– var. ***robustum***	See ***E. hyemale*** var. ***affine***
japonicum	MCCP WChe
scirpoides	EBre EMFW MCCP WMAq
sylvaticum	CNat

ERAGROSTIS (Poaceae)

chloromelas	CMHG ETPC
curvula	ECha EHoe EMon EPPr ESOG ETPC GBin SApp WCot
– S&SH 10	CArc CHan NLak
trichodes	ETPC GBin WPer

ERANTHIS (Ranunculaceae)

§ ***hyemalis*** 🏆	CAvo CBro CMea ELan EMon EPar EPot ETub EWFC LAma MBri MBro MHew MHlr NGar NRog SAlw WHil WOMN WRHF WShi
§ – Cilicica Group	CBro CMea EPar EPot LAma NMen NRog WHil
§ – Tubergenii Group	EPot
– – 'Guinea Gold' 🏆	EHyt WChr

ERCILLA (Phytolaccaceae)

volubilis	CAbb CChu CFee CGre CPlN CPle CSam ERav ETen GOrc LHop WCru WSHC

EREMAEA (Myrtaceae)

¶ ***beaufortioides***	SOWG
pauciflora	SOWG

EREMURUS (Asphodelaceae)

§ ***aitchisonii***	LAma
* 'Brutus'	CMea
bungei	See ***E. stenophyllus*** subsp. ***stenophyllus***
elwesii	See ***E. aitchisonii***
himalaicus	CBot CSpe ELan EPar ETub LAma LBow MDun NEgg SAga SCoo SMad SPer WCra WPyg
x ***isabellinus*** 'Cleopatra'	CBot CSWP LAma LBow LRHS NPSI WCra
– 'Pinokkio'	ETub LAma NPSI WCra WPyg
– Ruiter Hybrids	CSWP EBee ECot ELan EMan EOrc EPar LAma NPSI SPer
– Shelford Hybrids	CB&S ELan LAma LBow MNrw NOak SDeJ
'Moneymaker'	LAma
¶ 'Oase'	ELan NPSI
'Obelisk'	CMea LRHS
robustus	CB&S CBot CHEx CSpe EPar ETub LAma LBow LFis MDun NRog SIgm SMad SPer WCot WCra WPyg
stenophyllus	CBro CSte NFai
– subsp. ***aurantiacus***	LFis
§ – subsp. ***stenophyllus***	ELan EOrc EPar ETub LAma LBow MNrw NEgg NNor NOak NRog SMad SPer WCot WPyg

ERIANTHUS See SACCHARUM

ERICA † (Ericaceae)

arborea	CNCN MBal SArc SHBN
§ – 'Albert's Gold' 🏆	CB&S CNCN CTrC CWLN EBre EDen ELan ENHC EPfP IOrc MAsh MBal MBar MBri MOke NHol SAga SBod SPla WGre
– var. ***alpina*** 🏆	CMac CNCN EDen ENHC ENot IOrc MBal MBar MGos NHar SBod SPer SReu SSta WGre WWat
– 'Arbora Gold'	See ***E. arborea* 'Albert's Gold'**
– 'Arnold's Gold'	See ***E. arborea* 'Albert's Gold'**
– 'Estrella Gold' 🏆	CDoC CNCN CWLN EBre EDen ELan ENHC GAul MAsh MBal MBar NHar NHol SBod SPer SPla SSta WGre WStI
– 'Spring Smile'	EDen
australis 🏆	CB&S ELan MBar SHBN SPer
– 'Castellar Blush'	CNCN EDen MAsh NHol
– 'Holehird'	EDen
– 'Mr Robert' 🏆	CNCN EDen ELan EPfP LRHS MBar SBod WGre
– 'Riverslea' 🏆	CNCN EDen ENHC GAri IOrc MAsh MBal MBar MOke NHol SBod WGre
bauera	EDen
canaliculata	CB&S CGre EDen EPfP MBal
carnea 'Accent'	EDen
– 'Adrienne Duncan' 🏆	CNCN COCH CWLN EDen ENHC MBar MBri MOke NHol NRoo SBod WGre
– 'Alan Coates'	CMac CNCN COCH EDen ENHC MBar WGre
– 'Alba'	COCH EDen
– 'Altadena'	CNCN COCH EDen MBar
– 'Amy Doncaster'	See ***E. carnea* 'Treasure Trove'**
– 'Ann Sparkes' 🏆	CMac CNCN COCH CWLN EBre EDen ENHC LGro MBar MBri MGos MOke MWat NHol NYor SBod SPla WGre
– 'Atrorubra'	CMac CNCN COCH EDen ENHC MBar NHol NYor
– 'Aurea'	CB&S CMac CNCN COCH EDen ENHC LGro MBar MBri MOke MPla NHol SBod WGre
– 'Barry Sellers'	COCH EDen LRHS
– 'Bell's Extra Special'	COCH EDen
– 'Beoley Pink'	CNCN COCH EDen SBod
– 'C.J. Backhouse'	COCH EDen ENHC
– 'Carnea'	CNCN COCH EDen ENHC MBar MOke NHol NYor WGre
– 'Catherine'	EDen
– 'Cecilia M. Beale'	CNCN COCH EDen ENHC MBar NHol
– 'Challenger' 🏆	CNCN COCH EBre EDen MBar MBri MGos NHol NRoo SBod WGre
– 'Christine Fletcher'	COCH EDen WGre
– 'Clare Wilkinson'	CNCN COCH EDen
– 'David's Seedling'	COCH EDen
– 'December Red'	CB&S CMac CNCN COCH CWLN EBre EDen ENHC MBar MBri MOke MWat NHol NYor SBod SPla WGre
– 'Dommesmoen'	EDen
– 'Early Red'	COCH EDen
– 'Eileen Porter'	CMac CNCN CWLN EDen ENHC GDra MBar
– 'Foxhollow' 🏆	CMac CNCN COCH CWLN EBre EDen ENHC ENot GDra GSpe LGro MBar MBri MGos MOke MPla MWat NHar NHol NRoo NYor SBod SHBN WGre
– 'Foxhollow Fairy'	CB&S CNCN COCH EDen ENHC MBar SRms WGre
– 'Gelber's Findling'	COCH
– 'Golden Starlet' 🏆	CNCN COCH EBre EDen MBar NHol SPla WGre
– 'Gracilis'	ECho EDen ENHC MBar NHol WGre
– 'Heathwood'	CB&S CNCN COCH CWLN EDen ENHC ENot MBar NHol SBod SRms
– 'Hilletje'	CNCN COCH EDen

– 'Ice Princess' CNCN COCH EDen WGre
– 'Isabell' CNCN EDen LRHS
– 'Jack Stitt' COCH EDen MBar WGre
– 'James Backhouse' CMac CNCN CWLN ECho EDen NHol
– 'January Sun' COCH EDen
– 'Jason Attwater' EDen
– 'Jean' CNCN EDen LRHS NHol
– 'Jennifer Anne' CNCN COCH EDen ENHC MBar NYor
– 'John Kampa' CNCN COCH EBre EDen ENHC MBar NHol NRoo NYor WGre
– 'John Pook' MGos
– 'King George' CMac CNCN COCH EBre EDen GSpe MBar MGos MWat NHar NHol NRoo NYor SBod SHBN SPla WGre
– 'Lake Garda' COCH EDen SPla
– 'Late Pink' COCH EDen
– 'Lesley Sparkes' COCH EDen ENHC MBar NYor WGre
– 'Little Peter' COCH EDen
– 'Lohse's Rubin' COCH ECho EDen WGre
– 'Loughrigg' ♀ CMac CNCN COCH EDen ENHC GDra GSpe MBar MGos MOke NHol NRoo NYor SBod WGre WStI
– 'March Seedling' CB&S CNCN COCH EBre EDen ENHC GDra GSpe MBar MBri MGos MOke MPla NHol NYor SBod SPla WGre WStI
– 'Margery Frearson' EDen
– 'Martin' COCH EDen
– 'Mrs Sam Doncaster' CNCN COCH ECho EDen MBar SBod
– 'Myretoun Ruby' ♀ CB&S CMac CNCN COCH EBre EDen ENHC ENot GDra GSpe LGro MBar MBri MGos MOke MPla MWat NHar NHol NRoo NYor SBod SHBN WGre
– 'Nathalie' CNCN EDen LRHS
– 'Orient' COCH EDen NHol
– 'Pallida' COCH EDen
– 'Pink Beauty' See ***E. carnea* 'Pink Pearl'**
– 'Pink Cloud' CNCN COCH EDen
– 'Pink Mist' COCH EDen LRHS
§ – 'Pink Pearl' CNCN COCH EDen MBar WGre
– 'Pink Spangles' ♀ CB&S CMac CNCN COCH EBre EDen ENHC GDra LGro MBar MBri MGos MOke MPla NHol NRoo NYor SBod WGre
– 'Pirbright Rose' CNCN COCH ECho EDen ENHC MPla SBod
– 'Polden Pride' COCH EDen
– 'Porter's Red' COCH ECho EDen LRHS MBar
– 'Praecox Rubra' ♀ CB&S CNCN COCH EDen ENHC GDra LGro MBar MGos MOke NHol NYor
– 'Prince of Wales' CNCN COCH ECho EDen ENHC NHol
– 'Queen Mary' CNCN ECho EDen ENHC SBod
– 'Queen of Spain' CNCN COCH EDen ENHC MBri MOke
– 'R.B. Cooke' ♀ CNCN COCH EDen ENHC LGro MBar MBri NYor SBod WGre
– 'Red Rover' COCH EDen
– 'Robert Jan' EDen
– 'Rosalie' CNCN EDen LRHS WGre
– 'Rosalinde Schorn' COCH EDen WGre
– 'Rosantha' CNCN EDen
– 'Rosea' ECho EDen
– 'Rosy Gem' CNCN ECho EDen MBar
– 'Rosy Morn' COCH EDen
– 'Rotes Juwel' CNCN EDen LRHS
– 'Rubinteppich' CNCN COCH EDen SBod
– 'Rubra' EDen
– 'Ruby Glow' CB&S CNCN COCH EDen ENHC ENot GSpe MBar MOke NHol NYor
– 'Scatterley' EDen
– 'Schatzalp' EDen
– 'Schneekuppe' CNCN COCH EDen
– 'Schneesturm' COCH EDen
§ – 'Sherwood Creeping' EDen ENHC MBar
– 'Sherwoodii' See ***E. carnea* 'Sherwood Creeping'**
– 'Smart's Heath' CNCN COCH ECho EDen ENHC
– 'Snow Queen' CNCN COCH EDen ENHC MBar NRoo SBod WGre
– 'Spring Cottage Crimson' COCH EDen MBar
– 'Spring Day' EDen
– 'Springwood Pink' CMac CNCN COCH EDen ENHC GDra GSpe LGro MBar MBri MGos MOke MPla MWat NHol NYor SBod SHBN WGre
– 'Springwood White' ♀ CB&S CMac CNCN COCH EBre EDen ENHC ENot GDra GSpe LGro MBar MBri MGos MOke MPla MWat NHar NHol NYor SBod SHBN WGre
– 'Startler' COCH EDen ENHC LRHS MBar NHol SBod SPla
– 'Sunshine Rambler' ♀ CNCN COCH EDen MBar MGos NHol WGre
– 'Thomas Kingscote' CNCN COCH EDen ENHC MBar WGre
§ – 'Treasure Trove' COCH EDen
– 'Tybesta Gold' CNCN COCH EDen
– 'Urville' See ***E. carnea* 'Vivellii'**
– 'Viking' CNCN COCH EDen NHol NRoo
§ – 'Vivellii' ♀ CMac CNCN COCH EBre EDen ENHC ENot GDra GSpe MBar MBri MOke MPla MWat NHar NHol NYor SBod WGre
– 'Vivellii Aurea' COCH EDen WGre
– 'Walter Reisert' CNCN COCH EDen
– 'Wanda' COCH EDen MBar
– 'Wentwood Red' COCH EDen
– 'Westwood Yellow' ♀ CNCN COCH EBre EDen ENHC LGro MBar MBri NHar NHol NYor SBod SPla WGre
¶ – 'White Glow' ECho
– 'White March Seedling' EDen
– 'Whitehall' EDen LRHS NHol
– 'Winter Beauty' CNCN COCH EDen MOke MPla NHol WGre
– 'Winter Gold' COCH EDen
– 'Winter Melody' EDen
– 'Winter Snow' EDen LGro
– 'Winterfreunde' EDen
– 'Wintersonne' EDen LGro
ciliaris alba EDen
***ciliaris* 'Aurea'** CMac CNCN EDen ENHC MBar SRms WGre
– 'Camla' EDen ENHC MBar

– 'Corfe Castle' 𝕐	CNCN CWLN EDen ENHC MBar SBod WGre
– 'David McClintock' 𝕐	CMac CNCN EDen ENHC MBar MGos WGre
– 'Globosa'	ECho EDen ENHC WGre
– 'Maweana'	EDen
– 'Mrs C.H. Gill' 𝕐	CMac CNCN EDen ENHC WGre
– 'Ram'	EDen
– 'Rotundiflora'	EDen
– 'Stapehill'	EDen
– 'Stoborough' 𝕐	CNCN CWLN EDen ENHC MBar
– 'White Wings'	CNCN EDen ENHC
– 'Wych'	EDen
cinerea* f. *alba	CMac
– 'Alba Major'	CNCN ECho EDen MBar
– 'Alba Minor' 𝕐	CNCN CWLN EBre EDen GSpe MBar MBri MOke NHar NHol SBod WGre
– 'Alette'	EDen
– 'Alfred Bowerman'	EDen
– 'Alice Anne Davies'	EDen
– 'Angarrack'	EDen
– 'Anja Blum'	EDen
– 'Ann Berry'	CNCN EDen ENHC MBar SBod WGre
– 'Apple Blossom'	EDen
– 'Apricot Charm'	CNCN EDen MBar SBod WGre
– 'Aquarel'	EDen
– 'Ashdown Forest'	EDen
– 'Ashgarth Garnet'	EDen MBar WGre
– 'Atrococcinea'	CB&S
– 'Atropurpurea'	CNCN ECho EDen MBar
– 'Atrorubens'	EDen ENHC GSpe MBar NHar SRms
– 'Atrorubens, Daisy Hill'	EDen
– 'Atrosanguinea'	CNCN ENHC GSpe MBar MGos SBod WGre
– 'Atrosanguinea Reuthe's Variety'	ECho EDen
– 'Atrosanguinea Smith's Variety'	ECho EDen
– 'Baylay's Variety'	EDen MBar
– 'Blossom Time'	EDen MBar
– 'Brick'	EDen
– 'Bucklebury Red'	EDen
– 'C.D. Eason' 𝕐	CNCN EBre EDen ENHC GDra GSpe MBar MBri MGos MOke NHol NYor SBod WGre
§ – 'C.G. Best' 𝕐	CMac CNCN EDen ENHC MBar WGre
– 'Cairn Valley'	EDen GSpe
– 'Caldy Island'	EDen MBar
– 'Carnea'	EDen
– 'Carnea Underwood's Variety'	EDen
– 'Celebration'	EDen WDav
– 'Cevennes' 𝕐	CNCN CWLN EDen ENHC GSpe MBar MGos MOke SBod WGre
– 'Champs Hill'	EDen
– 'Cindy' 𝕐	CNCN EDen ENHC GSpe MBar MOke NHol NYor
– 'Coccinea'	CNCN ECho EDen ENHC WGre
– 'Colligan Bridge'	EDen MBar
– 'Constance'	EDen ENHC MBar
– 'Contrast'	EDen GSpe LRHS MBar WGre
– 'Daphne Maginess'	CNCN
– 'Discovery'	EDen
– 'Doctor Small's Seedling'	EDen
– 'Domino'	CB&S CNCN CWLN EDen ENHC MBar MGos MOke NYor
– 'Duncan Fraser'	CNCN ECho EDen ENHC GSpe MBar
– 'Dunwood Sport'	EDen MBar
– 'Eden Valley' 𝕐	CMac CNCN EDen ENHC GSpe MBar MGos NHol SBod SRms WGre
– 'England'	ECho EDen ENHC
– 'Felthorpe'	EDen
– 'Fiddler's Gold' 𝕐	CNCN CWLN EDen ENHC GAri MBar MBri MOke NHar NHol
– 'Flamingo'	EDen
– 'Foxhollow Mahogany'	EDen ENHC GSpe MBal MBar NYor WGre
– 'Frances'	EDen ENHC
– 'Fred Corston'	EDen
– 'G. Osmond'	EDen ENHC MBar MOke
– 'Glasnevin Red'	EDen MBar NHar WGre
– 'Glencairn'	CWLN EDen MBar NHol
– 'Godrevy'	EDen SBod
– 'Golden Charm'	CNCN CWLN ECho EDen NHol
– 'Golden Drop'	CNCN EDen ENHC GSpe MBar MBri MGos MOke NHol NYor SBod WGre
– 'Golden Hue' 𝕐	CB&S CNCN CWLN EDen ENHC GSpe MBar MOke NHol WGre
– 'Golden Sport'	CWLN ECho EDen MGos NHar
– 'Golden Tee'	EDen
– 'Graham Thomas'	See ***E. cinerea* 'C.G. Best'**
– 'Grandiflora'	EDen MBar
– 'Guernsey Lime'	EDen ENHC MBar
– 'Guernsey Pink'	EDen
– 'Guernsey Plum'	EDen
– 'Guernsey Purple'	EDen
– 'Hardwick's Rose'	CNCN EDen MBar
– 'Harry Fulcher'	CNCN CWLN EDen ENHC MBri MOke NYor
– 'Heatherbank'	EDen
– 'Heathfield'	EDen
– 'Heidebrand'	EDen MBar
– 'Hermann Dijkhuizen'	EDen
– 'Honeymoon'	EDen ENHC GSpe MBar
– 'Hookstone Lavender'	EDen ENHC GSpe
– 'Hookstone White' 𝕐	CNCN EBre EDen ENHC GDra MBar WGre
– 'Hutton's Seedling'	EDen
– 'Iberian Beauty'	EDen
– 'Jack London'	CNCN EDen
– 'Janet'	ECho EDen ENHC MBar MGos WGre
– 'Jersey Wonder'	EDen
– 'Jim Hardy'	EDen
– 'John Ardron'	EDen SBod WGre
– 'John Eason'	EDen ENHC NHol
– 'Joseph Murphy'	CNCN EDen GSpe MBar NYor WGre
– 'Joseph Rock'	EDen
– 'Josephine Ross'	EDen GSpe MBar WGre
– 'Joyce Burfitt'	CNCN EDen ENHC
– 'Katinka'	CNCN EDen ENHC MBar NHol NYor WGre
– 'Kerry Cherry'	EDen
– 'Knap Hill Pink' 𝕐	CNCN ECho EDen ENHC MBar NYor

– 'Lady Skelton'	EDen MBar
– 'Lavender Lady'	EDen
– 'Lilac Time'	ECho EDen ENHC GSpe MBar
– 'Lilacina'	ECho EDen ENHC GSpe MBar MOke
– 'Lime Soda'	CNCN EDen ENHC MBri
– 'Lorna Anne Hutton'	EDen
– 'Maginess Pink'	CNCN
– 'Marina'	EDen
– 'Michael Hugo'	CNCN EDen
– 'Miss Waters'	EDen MBar NYor
– 'Mrs Dill'	ECho EDen ENHC MBar
– 'Mrs E.A. Mitchell'	CNCN CWLN EDen LRHS MGos MOke
– 'Mrs Ford'	EDen ENHC MBar
– 'My Love'	CNCN CWLN EDen ENHC MBar MBri MOke NYor
– 'Nell'	EDen MBar
– 'Nellie Dawson'	EDen
– 'Newick Lilac'	EDen MBar MOke
– 'Novar'	EDen
– 'Old Rose'	EDen
– 'P.S. Patrick' ♀	CNCN EDen ENHC GSpe MBar MGos
– 'Pallas'	EDen GSpe
– 'Pallida'	EDen
– 'Patricia Maginess'	CNCN
– 'Peñaz'	EDen
– 'Pentreath' ♀	CNCN CWLN EDen ENHC MBar MBri MOke NYor
– 'Pink Foam'	EDen MBar
– 'Pink Ice' ♀	CB&S CMac CNCN CWLN EBre EDen ENHC GDra GSpe MBar MBri MGos MOke NHar NHol SBod WGre
– 'Plummer's Seedling'	EDen GSpe MBar
– 'Prostrate Lavender'	EDen ENHC
– 'Providence'	EDen LRHS
– 'Purple Beauty'	CB&S CNCN CWLN EDen ENHC GSpe MBar MGos MOke NHol NYor WGre
– 'Purple Robe'	ECho EDen ENHC LRHS
– 'Purple Spreader'	EDen
– 'Purpurea'	EDen
– 'Pygmaea'	EDen MBar
– 'Red Pentreath'	EDen
– 'Rijneveld'	EDen
– 'Robert Michael'	EDen
– 'Rock Pool'	EDen GSpe MBar NHol WGre
– 'Rock Ruth'	EDen
– 'Romiley'	EDen ENHC MBar MBri MOke
– 'Rosabella'	CNCN EDen ENHC MBar NYor
– 'Rose Queen'	ECho EDen GSpe WGre
– 'Rosea'	EDen ENHC GSpe WGre
* – 'Rosea Splendens'	EDen
– 'Rozanne Waterer'	EDen
– 'Ruby'	CMac CNCN EDen ENHC GSpe MBar NYor
– 'Sandpit Hill'	EDen MBar WGre
– 'Schizopetala'	CNCN EDen MBar
– 'Sea Foam'	CNCN EDen ENHC MBar
– 'Sherry'	CNCN EDen ENHC GSpe MBar WGre
– 'Smith's Lawn'	EDen
– 'Snow Cream'	EDen MBar
– 'Son of Cevennes'	MGos
– 'Spicata'	EDen
– 'Splendens'	CNCN EDen ENHC
– 'Startler'	CB&S CWLN EDen ENHC GSpe MBri MOke
– 'Stephen Davis' ♀	CNCN CWLN EBre EDen ENHC GSpe MBar MBri MOke NHol NYor SBod WGre
* – 'Strawberry'	EDen
– 'Sue Lloyd'	EDen WGre
– 'Summer Gold'	CNCN EBre ECho EDen LRHS WDav
– 'Tilford'	EDen ENHC
– 'Tom Waterer'	EDen MBar
– 'Uschie Ziehmann'	EDen
– 'Velvet Night' ♀	CB&S CMac CNCN CWLN EDen ENHC GSpe MBar MBri MOke NHar NHol NYor SBod SRms WGre
– 'Victoria'	EDen MBar WGre
– 'Violetta'	CNCN EDen
– 'Vivienne Patricia'	EDen ENHC GSpe MBar NYor
– 'W.G. Notley'	EDen ENHC
– 'West End'	EDen
– 'White Dale'	ECho EDen MBar NYor WGre
– 'Windlebrooke' ♀	CNCN EDen ENHC MBar NHol NYor SBod WGre
– 'Wine'	EDen
– 'Yvonne'	ECho EDen
cruenta	EDen
curviflora	EDen
x ***darleyensis*** 'Ada S. Collings'	CNCN COCH EBre EDen ENHC MBar MPla NRoo NYor SBod SHBN SPla
– 'Alba'	See ***E.* x *darleyensis* 'Silberschmelze'**
– 'Archie Graham'	COCH EDen
§ – 'Arthur Johnson' ♀	CB&S CNCN COCH CWLN EBre EDen ENHC GSpe MBar MBri MGos MOke MPla NHol NYor SBod SHBN SPla SRms WGre
– 'Cherry Stevens'	See ***E.* x *darleyensis* 'Furzey'**
§ – 'Darley Dale'	CMac CNCN COCH CWLN EBre EDen ENHC GSpe MBar MBri MOke MPla NHol SBod WGre
– 'Dunreggan'	COCH EDen
– 'Dunwood Splendour'	See ***E.* x *darleyensis* 'Arthur Johnson'**
– 'Epe'	COCH EDen
– 'Erecta'	COCH EDen
§ – 'Furzey' ♀	CB&S CMac CNCN COCH EDen ENHC GSpe MBar MBri MGos MOke MPla NHar NHol NRoo NYor SBod SHBN SPla SRms WGre
– 'George Rendall'	CB&S CMac CNCN COCH CWLN EDen ENHC GDra GSpe MPla NHol SPla WGre
– 'Ghost Hills' ♀	CNCN COCH CWLN EBre EDen ENHC GDra MBar MOke MPla NHol NYor SBod SHBN WGre
– 'J.W. Porter' ♀	CNCN COCH CWLN EDen ENHC MBar MOke SPla WGre
§ – 'Jack H. Brummage'	CB&S CMac CNCN COCH CWLN EBre EDen ENHC MBar MBri MGos MOke MPla NHar NHol NYor SBod SHBN SPla WGre
– 'James Smith'	COCH EDen ENHC MBar
– 'Jenny Porter' ♀	CMac CNCN COCH CWLN EDen ENHC MBar MBri MOke WGre

- 'Kramer's Rote' ♀ CNCN COCH EBre EDen MBar MBri MGos MOke NHol NRoo SPla WGre
- 'Margaret Porter' CB&S CNCN COCH CWLN EDen ENHC MPla SBod WGre
- 'Mary Helen' CNCN COCH EDen LRHS NHol WGre
◆- Molten Silver See *E.* × ***darleyensis*** **'Silberschmelze'**
- 'Mrs Parris' Red' EDen
- 'Norman R. Webster' CNCN COCH EDen NRoo
- 'Pink Perfection' See *E.* × ***darleyensis*** **'Darley Dale'**
§ - 'Silberschmelze' CB&S CNCN COCH CWLN EBre EDen ENHC GDra GSpe MBar MBri MGos MOke MPla NHol SBod SHBN WGre
- 'Spring Surprise' EDen
- 'W.G. Pine' COCH EDen
- 'White Glow' CNCN COCH CWLN EDen ENHC NHol NYor WGre
- 'White Perfection' ♀ CNCN COCH CWLN EBre EDen MBar MBri NHol NRoo SPla WGre

discolor CGre
doliiformis EDen
§ ***erigena*** ELan SHBN
- 'Alba' CMac COCH EDen ENHC MBar
- 'Alba Compacta' EDen
- 'Brian Proudley' ♀ CNCN COCH EDen ENHC MBar SBod
- 'Brightness' CB&S CNCN COCH CWLN EBre EDen ENHC MBar MBri MOke NHar NHol NYor SBod
- 'Coccinea' COCH EDen ENHC
- 'Ewan Jones' CNCN COCH EDen ENHC IOrc MBar
- 'Glauca' COCH EDen ENHC SEND
- 'Golden Lady' ♀ CMac CNCN COCH CWLN EBre EDen ENHC MBar MBri MGos MOke NHol NYor SBod SPla WGre
- 'Hibernica' EDen
- 'Hibernica Alba' EDen MBar
- 'Irish Dusk' ♀ CNCN COCH CWLN EBre EDen ENHC MBar MBri MGos MOke NHar NHol NYor SBod SPla SRms WGre
- 'Irish Salmon' ♀ CB&S CMac CNCN COCH EDen MBar NYor SEND
- 'Irish Silver' COCH EDen MBar MBri
- 'Ivory' COCH EDen
- 'Mrs Parris' Lavender' EDen
- 'Mrs Parris' White' EDen
- 'Nana' EDen
- 'Nana Alba' CNCN COCH EDen MBar
- 'Rosea' ECho EDen ENHC MBar
- 'Rosslare' EDen
- 'Rubra' ECho EDen
- 'Rubra Compacta' ENHC
- 'Superba' CMac CNCN COCH EDen ENHC MBar MGos MOke SBod WGre
- 'W.T. Rackliff' ♀ CB&S CNCN COCH CWLN EBre EDen ENHC ENot MBar MBri MGos MOke NHol NYor SHBN SPla SRms WGre
- 'W.T. Rackliff Variegated' ENHC

fontana EDen
¶***formosa*** CGre
¶***glomiflora*** CGre
gracilis CGre ECho EDen
hibernica See ***E. erigena***
¶ × ***hiemalis*** EDen
¶***laeta*** CGre
lusitanica ♀ CB&S CMac CNCN COCH EDen ELan MAsh MBar SBod
- 'George Hunt' CDoC CNCN EBre EDen ELan ENHC MAsh NHol SBar SBod SPer
* - 'Sheffield Park' SPer
mackayana subsp. ***andevalensis*** EDen
- 'Ann D. Frearson' (d) CNCN EDen
- 'Doctor Ronald Gray' CNCN EDen ENHC MBar MBri MOke NYor SBod WGre
- 'Donegal' EDen
- 'Errigal Dusk' EDen
- 'Galicia' CNCN EDen
- 'Lawsoniana' EDen ENHC
- 'Maura' (d) ♀ EDen ENHC
- 'Plena' (d) CNCN EDen ENHC MBar MOke WGre
- 'Shining Light' ♀ EDen
- 'William M'Calla' EDen ENHC

mammosa EDen
manipuliflora CDoC EDen MBar
- 'Corfu' COCH EDen
- 'Don Richards' COCH EDen
- 'Elegant Spike' EDen
- 'Heaven Scent' ♀ CNCN COCH LRHS
- 'Ian Cooper' COCH EDen
- 'Korcula' COCH EDen
- 'Aldburgh' CNCN
- × ***vagans*** 'Valerie Griffiths' COCH EDen LRHS MBar SPla WGre

mediterranea See ***E. erigena***
× ***oldenburgensis*** 'Ammerland' EDen
- 'Oldenburg' EDen
pageana EDen
patersonia EDen
¶***plukenetii*** CGre
× ***praegeri*** See *E.* × ***stuartii***
scoparia subsp. ***azorica*** EDen
¶ - subsp. ***maderincola*** 'Madeira Gold' EDen
§ - subsp. ***scoparia*** 'Minima' EDen ENHC MBar
- - 'Pumila' See ***E. scoparia*** subsp. ***scoparia*** **'Minima'**
¶***sparsa*** CGre
speciosa EDen
¶***sphaeroidea*** CGre
§ × ***stuartii*** CWLN ENHC MBar SBod
- 'Charles Stuart' See *E.* × ***stuartii*** **'Stuartii'**
- 'Connemara' EDen
- 'Irish Lemon' ♀ CNCN EBre EDen ENHC GDra GSpe MBar NHar NHol SBod WGre
- 'Irish Orange' CNCN EDen ENHC GSpe MBar NHol SBod WGre
- 'Nacung' EDen
- 'Pat Turpin' EDen
§ - 'Stuartii' CNCN EDen

§ ***terminalis*** ♀ CNCN COCH EDen ENHC ENot IOrc MBar SBod SEND SPer SRms
terminalis stricta See ***E. terminalis***
terminalis 'Thelma Woolner' CMac CNCN COCH EDen ENHC MBar WGre
tetralix CKin ECWi SRms WCla

– 'Afternoon'	EDen
– 'Alba'	EDen
– 'Alba Mollis' 🏆	CMac CNCN CWLN EDen ENHC ENot GSpe MBar MBri MOke NHar NHol SBod WGre
– 'Alba Praecox'	EDen
– 'Allendale Pink'	EDen
– 'Ardy'	EDen ENHC
– 'Bala'	CNCN EDen
– 'Bartinney'	EDen MBar
– 'Con Underwood' 🏆	CMac CNCN CWLN EBre EDen ENHC GSpe MBar MBri MOke NHol NYor SBod SRms WGre
– 'Curled Roundstone'	EDen
– 'Dänemark'	EDen
– 'Daphne Underwood'	EDen WGre
– 'Darleyensis'	EDen
– 'Dee'	EDen
– 'Delta'	EDen ENHC MBar
– 'Foxhome'	EDen ENHC MBar
¶ – 'George Frazer'	EDen
– 'Hailstones'	EDen ENHC MBar NYor
– 'Helma'	EDen ENHC NYor
– 'Hookstone Pink'	CNCN EDen ENHC MOke NHar SBod SHBN WGre
– 'Humoresque'	EDen
– 'Ken Underwood'	CNCN EDen ENHC MBar SHBN WGre
– 'L.E. Underwood'	EDen ENHC MBar NHol WGre
– 'Mary Grace'	EDen
– 'Melbury White'	CNCN EDen ENHC MBar
– 'Morning Glow'	See ***E.*** × ***watsonii* 'F. White'**
– 'Pink Glow'	EDen
– 'Pink Pepper'	EDen
– 'Pink Star' 🏆	CMac CNCN EBre EDen ENHC GSpe MBar NHol WGre
– 'Rosea'	EDen
– 'Rubra'	EDen
§ – 'Ruby's Variety'	EDen MBar
– 'Ruby's Velvet'	See ***E. tetralix* 'Ruby's Variety'**
– 'Ruth's Gold'	CNCN CWLN EDen MBar NHol WGre
– 'Salmon Seedling'	EDen
– 'Silver Bells'	EDen ENHC MBar WGre
– 'Stardome'	EDen
– 'Swedish Yellow'	EDen
– 'Terschelling'	EDen
– 'Tina'	CNCN EDen
– 'Trixie'	EDen
– 'White House'	EDen
umbellata	CNCN EDen ENHC MBar WAbe WGre
vagans 'Alba Nana'	See ***E. vagans* 'Nana'**
– 'Birch Glow' 🏆	CNCN EDen ENHC NRoo NYor SBod WGre
– 'Carnea'	EDen
– 'Charm'	EDen
– 'Cornish Cream' 🏆	CNCN CWLN EDen ENHC GAri MBar NHol
– 'Cream'	CNCN EDen ENHC MOke NHar
– 'Diana Hornibrook'	CNCN CWLN EDen ENHC GSpe MBar MOke NHar SHBN WGre
– 'Diana's Gold'	EDen
– 'Fiddlestone' 🏆	CNCN EDen ENHC GSpe MBar NYor SBod WGre
– 'French White'	CNCN EDen MBar SBod
– 'George Underwood'	EDen ENHC MBar WGre
– 'Golden Triumph'	EDen MBar

– 'Grandiflora'	CNCN EDen MBar WGre
– 'Holden Pink'	CNCN EDen MOke NHar SBod
– 'Hookstone Rosea'	EDen MBar
– 'Ida M. Britten'	EDen MBar
– 'J.C. Fletcher'	EDen
– 'Kevernensis Alba' 🏆	EDen ENHC MBar SBod SRms
– 'Leucantha'	EDen
– 'Lilacina'	CMac CNCN EDen GSpe MBar
– 'Lyonesse' 🏆	CB&S CMac CNCN EBre EDen ENHC ENot GSpe MBar MBri MGos MOke NHol NRoo NYor SBod SRms WGre
– 'Miss Waterer'	EDen MBar
– 'Mrs D.F. Maxwell' 🏆	CB&S CMac CNCN EBre EDen ENHC GSpe MBar MBri MGos MOke NHar NHol NRoo NYor SBod SRms WGre
– 'Mrs Donaldson'	EDen
§ – 'Nana'	ECho EDen MBar
– 'Pallida'	CNCN EDen ENHC
– 'Peach Blossom'	EDen MBar
– 'Pyrenees Pink'	CMac CNCN EDen MBar MOke NHar WGre
– 'Rosea'	ECho EDen
– 'Rubra'	CNCN ECho EDen MBal MBar
– 'Rubra Grandiflora'	ENHC
– 'Saint Keverne'	CB&S CMac CNCN CWLN EDen ENHC MBal MBar MGos MOke NHar NHol NRoo SBod WGre
– 'Summertime'	CNCN EDen MBar
– 'Valerie Proudley' 🏆	CB&S CMac CNCN CWLN EBre EDen ENHC GDra GSpe MBar MBri MGos MOke MWat NHar NHol NYor SBod SHBN SPla SRms WGre
– 'Valerie Smith'	EDen
– 'Viridiflora'	CNCN EDen MBar
– 'White Giant'	EDen
– 'White Lady'	ECho EDen ENHC MBar
– 'White Rocket'	CNCN CWLN EDen MBar
– 'White Spire'	EDen
– 'Yellow John'	CNCN ECho EDen
× ***veitchii***	MBal
– 'Exeter' 🏆	CNCN COCH EDen EPfP GAri MAsh MBar WGre
– 'Gold Tips' 🏆	CNCN CTrC EDen ENHC MAsh MBal MBar MBri MGos MOke NHar WGre
– 'Pink Joy'	CNCN EDen ENHC GAri MAsh MBal MBri MOke NHar WGre
¶ ***versicolor***	CGre
verticillata	EDen
viridescens	CGre EDen
× ***watsonii*** 'Cherry Turpin'	EDen WGre
– 'Ciliaris Hybrida'	EDen
– 'Dawn' 🏆	CNCN CWLN EDen GDra GSpe MBar MBri NHar NRoo SBod SHBN WGre
– 'Dorothy Metheny'	EDen
§ – 'F. White'	EDen ENHC MBar
– 'Gwen'	CNCN EDen MBar
– 'H. Maxwell'	CNCN EDen GSpe MBal
– 'Mary'	EDen
– 'Pink Pacific'	EDen
– 'Rachel'	EDen MBal
– 'Truro'	EDen
× ***williamsii*** 'Cow-y-Jack'	EDen
– 'David Coombe'	EDen
– 'Golden Button'	WGre

– 'Gwavas'	CNCN CWLN EDen MBar SBod
– 'Ken Wilson'	EDen
– 'P.D. Williams' 🏆	CNCN CWLN ECho EDen MBal MBar WGre

ERIGERON † (Asteraceae)

acer	CKin EWFC MHew WCla WHer
¶ – var. ***debilis***	MFos
'Adria'	GBuc MAvo NLak SPer WHow
§ ***alpinus***	CNic GCHN GTou LBee MOne NGre
'Amity'	EBre EFou GCHN LCom SMer
aphanactis NNS 93-249	NWCA
¶ ***argentatus***	EHyt
atticus	MHig
aurantiacus	CM&M CSam EBar GAul LHop MCCP NBro NOak SEas SIng WBea WPLl WPer
§ ***aureus***	MDHE NMen NSla WAbe WOMN
§ – 'Canary Bird'	EGle EHyt EWes MDHE MSta NBir NHar SPla WAbe WDav
* 'Azure Beauty'	EPfP NPro
◆ Azure Fairy	See ***E. 'Azurfee'***
§ 'Azurfee'	CSam EBar ELan GAbr GMaP MCLN NFai NFla NMir NOak NRoo SEas SHel SMer SPer SPla WBea WHen WHil WMer WPer WWhi WWin
◆ Black Sea	See ***E. 'Schwarzes Meer'***
bloomeri	MFos
– NNS 92-108	NWCA
'Blue Beauty'	SRms
borealis	CSam GCHN
'Charity'	CGle CMGP EFou EGar WLRN
chrysopsidis 'Grand Ridge' 🏆	CPBP EBre EHyt NHar NWCA SIng WAbe
compactus consimilis	CGra
– NNS 93-252	MFos MRPP
compositus	CGra ELan GAbr GCHN NGre NWCA SAlw SRms WPer
§ – var. ***discoideus***	CNic EBur EHyt NMen WPer
¶ – var. ***glabratus***	MFos
– 'Rocky'	MSCN NPri
* ***daicus***	WHil
◆ Darkest of All	See ***E. 'Dunkelste Aller'***
'Dignity'	CShe EBee EFou EJud ELan GCHN LFis MWat NTow NVic SEas SMer SPer SSpe WCot WEas
'Dimity'	CGle ECha EFou EHic EPPr GMac LCom MBri WAbe WCot WWin
§ 'Dunkelste Aller' 🏆	CGle CRDP CSev EAst EBre ECED EFou EGar ELan EMan ENot GCHN MBri MRav MTis NFla NRoo NSti SHel SPer SPla SRms WMer WOld WTyr WWin
* ***epiroctícus***	SAlw
* – NS 462	NWCA
'Felicity'	CElw CShe EFou MBel MMil SRms
flettii	GCHN WPer WWin
'Foersters Liebling' 🏆	CSev EBee EFou ENot LFis MBri MHlr MNrw MWat NFla NPla NRoo SPla WByw WCot WMer
formosissimus	EBee

'Four Winds'	CShe ECtt ELan EMan EMon EPad EWes GAbr LHop MRav NMen WMer WPer
¶ from Big Horns	CGra
glaucus	CInt CWan EJud NCat NVic SMrm SSte WBro WCot WLRN
– 'Albus'	CSev LBee LHop MDHE SMad WPer WTyr
– 'Elstead Pink'	CElw CSev CShe CTri NFai SPla WByw WEas
* – 'Roger Raiche'	SMrm
– 'Roseus'	CB&S CHal
howellii	ECha
§ ***karvinskianus*** 🏆	CChr CGle CHad CHan CMea CNic ECha ELan EMar LGan LHop MHlr MNrw MWat NSti SAxl SDix SIng SMad SPer SPla SUsu WAbe WCla WEas WHil WRus WWhi
kennedyi alpigenum NS 93-276	MFos
leiomerus	CLyd CNic EPot LBee LCom MHig NTow NWCA SAlw WOMN
linearis	CGra MFos NWCA
'Mrs F.H. Beale'	LCom SCro
mucronatus	See ***E. karvinskianus***
multiradiatus	LLew NLak WPer
nanus	CGra CLyd NWCA WPat WPer WPyg
peregrinus	WPer
peregrinus callianthemus	CGra
philadelphicus	CElw CGle CMil EHic EMan NBir NBro SOkh
◆ Pink Jewel	See ***E. 'Rosa Juwel'***
◆ Pink Triumph	See ***E. 'Rosa Triumph'***
pinnatisectus	CWan LBee NNrd NWCA WPer
polymorphus	WAbe
'Prosperity'	CGle CShe EFou LCom MFos
pygmaeus	MFos
pyrenaicus hort.	See ***E. alpinus***
– Rouy	See ***Aster pyrenaeus***
'Quakeress'	CArc CElw CGle CRDP CSam EBre EFou EMan EMon GCHN LGan MBel MRav MTis NBro NCat NRoo SHel SMer SMrm SSpe SUsu WCot WRHF
§ 'Rosa Juwel'	CM&M CSam EBar EFou GAbr GCHN LCom LHop NBir NBro NFla NMir NOak NRoo SEND SEas SHel SMer SPer SPla SRms WBea WHen WPLl WPbr WPer WTyr
§ 'Rosa Triumph'	EFou SPla
'Rosenballett'	EBre NBrk WFar
roseus	ECha
'Rotes Meer'	ELan MBri NTow SEas
rotundifolius	See ***Bellis rotundifolia***
'Caerulescens'	**'Caerulescens'**
N ***salsuginosus***	NOak
§ 'Schneewittchen'	CGle CMGP CRDP EAst EBee EFou EGar ELan EMan LHop LRHS MWat NRoo NSti NVic SCro SPla WLRN WTyr
'Schöne Blaue'	NBro NPri NRoo
§ 'Schwarzes Meer'	EFou EHal LHop NRoo SPla WMer
scopulinis	EHyt LBee
'Serenity'	NCat
simplex	EHic LLew MDHE MWat NGre NMen NNrd NSla NTow

◆ Snow White	See *E.* **'Schneewittchen'**
'Sommerabend'	MUlv
'Sommerneuschnee'	CDoC ECha NPri SHel
sp. from Bald Mountains	NWCA
speciosus	SMer
'Strahlenmeer'	EBee LCom LRHS NCat WBea WCot WLRN
* ***strictus*** from Ireland	WNdy
trifidus	See *E.* ***compositus*** var. ***discoideus***
tweedyi	NBro NPri
uncialis conjugans	CGra
uniflorus	GBin NNrd
'Unity'	MWat
vagus	CSam WWin
– JCA 8911	MFos
'White Quakeress'	CBos CElw CRDP EJud GBuc LHil MAvo MCLN SLod SUsu WCot WRHF
'Wuppertal'	CBlo EBee EGar EMan LFis LRHS MMil NCat WLRN
yukonensis	CLyd

ERINACEA (Papilionaceae)

§ ***anthyllis*** ♀	MAll SIng
pungens	See *E.* ***anthyllis***

ERINUS (Scrophulariaceae)

alpinus ♀	CMea ELan ESis EWFC GTou MBal MBro MPla MRPP MWat NBro NGre NHol NNor NNrd NRoo SAlw SIng WAbe WCla WEas WFar WHil WPer WPyg WWin
– var. ***albus***	CBot CLyd CNic GTou MBro MPla NMen NNrd NWCA SAlw SRms WAbe WCla WDav WHoo WPer WPyg
– 'Dr Hähnle'	CNic EBre MHig NMen SAlw SRms WHoo WPyg
– 'Mrs Charles Boyle' ♀	GDra MBro WHoo WOld WPyg
* ***olivana***	WHil

ERIOBOTRYA (Rosaceae)

deflexa	CPle EMil
japonica (F) ♀	CAbb CB&S CBot CGre CHEx CHan CSte CTrC CWit EMil EPla ERea ERom ESim GQui LPan SArc SDea SDry SSta WHer WNor WWat
– 'Benlehr' (F)	ESim
– 'Mrs Cookson' (F)	ESim

ERIOCAPITELLA See ANEMONE

ERIOCEPHALUS (Asteraceae)

¶ ***africanus***	WJek

ERIOGONUM (Polygonaceae)

brevicaule var. ***nanum***	NWCA
caespitosum	CPBP NTow NWCA SIgm
§ – subsp. ***douglasii***	MFos NTow WDav
– – NNS 95-238	MRPP
croceum	SIgm
douglasii	See *E.* ***caespitosum*** subsp. ***douglasii***
flavum	WPer
heracleoides minus	MFos
jamesii	MHig WPat WPyg
kennedyi subsp. ***alpigenum***	WDav
– subsp. ***austromontanum***	NTow
¶ ***libertini***	WDav
¶ ***ochrocephalum***	WDav
ovalifolium	GCLN NTow NWCA SIgm
panguicense alpestre	NHol
¶ ***pauciflorum*** subsp. ***nebraskense***	WDav
rosense	EHyt
siskiyouense	NTow
thymoides	CGra
umbellatum	CHan ECha EPot MFir NHol NTow SIng
– var. ***humistratum***	NHol
– var. ***porteri***	NWCA
– var. ***subalpinum***	MHig
– var. ***torreyanum***	MBro MHig NHol WPat
– subsp. ***umbellatum***	LBee
¶ ***ursinum***	WDav

ERIOPHORUM (Cyperaceae)

angustifolium	CBen CWat ECWi EHoe EHon EMFW EPGN EPPr EPla ESOG ETPC GCHN GFre LPBA MSta NDea SWat WChe WHer WMAq WPer
latifolium	LPBA MSta WChe
vaginatum	See ***Scirpus fauriei*** var. ***vaginatus***

ERIOPHYLLUM (Asteraceae)

lanatum	CSam EBar ECha EMon GAbr LGan NCat NGre NTow NVic SBla SChu WEas WFar WOve WWin WWye
* – 'Pointe'	GSki

ERIOSTEMON (Rutaceae)

¶ ***myoporoides***	ECon LCns

ERITRICHIUM (Boraginaceae)

§ ***canum***	NTow WDav
nanum	CGra
rupestre	See *E.* ***canum***
– var. ***pectinatum***	NWCA
* ***sibiricum***	CSpe
strictum	See *E.* ***canum***

ERODIUM † (Geraniaceae)

absinthioides var. ***amanum***	GCHN
absinthoides	GCHN LCom LRHS WThi
– blue	GCHN
§ ***acaule***	GCHN NGre NRog NRoo NTow
alnifolium	GCHN
balearicum	See *E.* × ***variabile*** **'Album'**
battandierianum	GCHN
boissieri	GCHN
¶ ***botrys***	SCou
brachycarpum	GCHN
carvifolium	CBos CElw CFir GBur GCHN MBri
§ ***castellanum***	CSpe ESis GCHN MTis NBro NRog NRoo NSti SAlw SBla SCou SCro
chamaedryoides	See *E.* ***reichardii***
§ ***cheilanthifolium***	CSam EPot GCHN GGar LCom NLak WMaN
¶ – 'Bidderi'	MDHE

chrysanthum	Widely available
– pink	CGle EPPr LCom LGre SMrm SWas
chrysanthum sulphureum	WPnn
¶ *ciconium*	SCou
cicutarium	EWFC SCou
§ – subsp. *cicutarium*	GCHN
corsicum	CGle EBur EHyt ELan MDHE MTho NCat NRog WAbe
– 'Album'	CSam GCHN MDHE MMil WAbe
'County Park'	CElw ECou EDAr EWes NChi SChu WRus
crinitum	GCHN
¶ *danicum*	SCou
daucoides hort.	See *E. castellanum*
'Eileen Emmett'	GCHN MDHE
* 'Elizabeth'	GCHN
foetidum	GCHN MDHE NRog
* 'Frans Choice'	MDHE
N *glandulosum* ♀	CMea CShe ELan GCHN GCal LHop MBro NRog SAga SBla SRms SWas WBea WEas WKif WPat WPer WThi
gruinum	CMdw EFol GCHN MTol NRai WPnn WSan
guicciardii	EDAr
N *guttatum*	CGle EMan MPla MWat NBee NMen NTow SAga SRms WAbe WHal WPer WSHC
'Helen'	GCHN
heteradenum	See *E. petraeum*
¶ *hirtum*	SCou
× *hybridum*	EGle ELan EPar EWes NRoo WAbe WHal
– hort.	See *E.* **'Sara Francesca'**
hymenodes hort.	See *E. trifolium*
jahandiezianum	GCHN
'Julie Ritchie'	WHoo
'Katherine Joy'	MDHE NChi NHed NRog
× *kolbianum*	MDHE WHoo WPnn WPyg
– 'Natasha'	ECha ELan EMan EPot EPri EWes GCHN LBee MDHE NHol NMGW NMen NRog SChu SMrm SWat WFar WKif
'Las Meninas'	GCHN
× *lindavicum* 'Charter House'	GCHN
macradenum	See *E. glandulosum*
malacoides	GCHN SCou
manescaui	Widely available
¶ – dwarf form	CSpe
'Merstham Pink'	CMea ECha EPPr GCHN MDHE MMil MOne NHed NHol NRog NRoo SAga SAxl SBla SIng SMrm SUsu WKif
¶ *moschatum*	SCou
– Guitt 88041904	GCHN
munbyanum	GCHN
neuradifolium Guitt 86040601	GCHN
'Nunwood Pink'	GCHN MDHE
pelargoniiflorum	CArc CBot CGle CMea CRDP EFol ESis EWes GCHN LFis MTho NBro NMen SAga SAxl SCou SRms SWas WCra WEas WHil WOMN WPbr WPnn WPyg WRus WWin
N *petraeum*	EGle LFis NMen NSla WAbe WCot WOld
– subsp. *crispum*	See *E. cheilanthifolium*
– subsp. *glandulosum*	See *E. glandulosum*
– 'Pallidum'	CHal CSam
– 'Roseum'	EMan GCal SBla WAbe WPer WRus
'Pickering Pink'	GCHN MDHE NMen NRog SWat
pimpinellifolium	GCHN
'Princesse Marion'	GCHN
'Rachel'	GCHN MDHE
recorderi	GCHN
§ *reichardii*	CElw ESis LBee MFos MPla MTho NGre NHol NRog NRoo SBla SIng SRms SUsu SWat WBea WCla WOMN WPnn
– cultivars	See *E.* × *variabile*
– 'Derek'	ECho
¶ – JR 961	GCHN
¶ – JR 962	GCHN
¶ – JR 963	GCHN
¶ – JR 964	GCHN
¶ *rodiei*	GCHN MDHE
romanum	See *E. acaule*
§ *rupestre*	CBot CMea ECho ECtt GCHN MDHE NHed
salzmannii	See *E. cicutarium* subsp. *cicutarium*
§ 'Sara Francesca'	MDHE NSla
saxatile	GCHN
× *sebaceum* 'Polly'	GCHN
'Stephanie'	CElw CInt EGle GCHN LBee MDHE NChi NHol NRoo SAsh
supracanum	See *E. rupestre*
tordylioides	GCHN WHal
trichomanifolium De Candolle	EWes LCom SAsh SMrm WPnn
– hort.	See *E. valentinum*
§ *trifolium*	ELan MMil NChi NRoo NSti SIng SSpi SUsu WCru WHal WHoo
– Guitt 85051701	GCHN
– var. *montanum*	GCHN
§ *valentinum*	CElw GCHN NNrd NRog SWas
– 'Alicante'	MDHE
§ × *variabile*	EHyt
§ – 'Album'	CShe ELan EMNN EPot GBuc GBur GMac LBee MBar MPla MTho NCat NHar NMen NRoo NWCA SBla SMrm SUsu WAbe WCla WEas WHil WOMN WOld WPat WPer WPnn WWin
– 'Bishop's Form'	CShe ECtt EMNN EPot ESis GBur GMac LFis MBar MBro MHig MPla NBro NGre NHar NHol NMen NNrd NRog NRoo NTow SBla WHoo WPat
– 'Flore Pleno'	EAst ECtt EDAr EHyt ELan EWes MHig MPla NCat NGre NRog SHFr SIng WAbe WOld WPer
– 'Roseum' ♀	CBot ECho ELan EPar MHig NGre NRog NWCA SAlw SIng SRms WAbe WBro WOld WPer WWin
× *wilkommianum*	EDAr NRog

ERPETION See VIOLA

ERUCA (Brassicaceae)

vesicaria subsp. *sativa*	CArn CBod CJew ELau GPoy LHol MChe MGra SIde WHer WJek WOak WSel WWye

ERYNGIUM † (Apiaceae)

§ ***agavifolium***	Widely available
alpinum ♀	CB&S CChu CElw CGle EBre ECha EFou ELan EPar GDra GLil MBal MBro MCLN MTho NBir SPer SWat WEas WHal WHoo WOve
– 'Amethyst'	CRDP ELan GBuc MBri MCli MUlv NTow WMer
– 'Blue Star'	CBot EBee ELan EOrc GCal GCra LGre LHop MTis NCat NRoo NWes SPla SSpi WHoo WPer
– 'Holden Blue'	GCal
– 'Opal'	CShe LRHS MBri
– 'Slieve Donard'	EAst EBee IBlr LBuc LFis LRHS
– 'Superbum'	CBot CRDP GSki NRoo SBla SMad
amethystinum	CBot ECGP ECha EMan LGre MBri MSto NChi NLak SIgm WCot WLRN
biebersteinianum	See ***E. caucasicum***
– from Kashmir	LKoh
bourgatii	CArc CBot CGle CMea CSev CShe ECha ECtt EFou ELan EMon GTou LHop MBal MCLN MTho NHar NMen NNor NRoo NSti SBla SMad SPer SWat WHal WOld WPer WSHC
– 'Forncett Ultra'	EFou EMon
– 'Oxford Blue' ♀	CHan CLon CMil CRDP EPar LGre NTow SMrm SSoC SWas WEas
– 'Picos'	CGle WFar
bromeliifolium hort.	See ***E. agavifolium***
caeruleum	EMon EWes GAul MNrw NFai NLak SIng SMad
campestre	CBot EMon SIgm SMad WPer
§ ***caucasicum***	EBee GBuc LLew NLak
creticum	NBir NBro
decaisneanum	See ***E. pandanifolium***
♦ Delaroux	See ***E. proteiflorum***
dichotomum	EMon LGre
– Caeruleum Group	ECro
ebracteatum	CLon GCal SIgm
– var. ***poterioides***	SMad
§ ***eburneum***	CArc CBot CDoC EBre ECha EMon GBuc MSCN NBro NChi NLak
§ ***giganteum*** ♀	CDec CGle CHad CHan CMHG CMea CShe EBar ECha EFou ELan ERav LFis LGan LHil LHop MBal MHlr MTho MWat NBro NRoo NSti NWoo SBla SDix SUsu WEas WHal WOld
– 'Silver Ghost'	EFou EGle SDix SMrm
glaciale	CFil GCLN NLak WThi
– JJA 461.000	NWCA SBla
horridum	CArc CKel CLon EBee EBre ELan EWes GCra LFis MFir MNrw NBro NLak NSti SArc SIgm SMad WWhi WWin
maritimum	CArn CBot CPou CRDP EBee ECWi ECha ECoo GPoy LGre SIde SIgm SSpi SWas WSel
Miss Willmott's Ghost	See ***E. giganteum***
x ***oliverianum*** ♀	CRDP CSam ECGP EFou ELan EMan GAbr GBuc MBri MBro MCli NRoo SDix SMad SPer WByw WMer
§ ***pandanifolium***	CGre CKel CLon CMea EFou EGle ETen EWes GCal IBlr LHil NLak SArc SDix WCot WWhi
paniculatum	See ***E. eburneum***
planum	CGle CSam EAst EBar EBee EBre ECha ECtt ELan GBuc GCHN GMac LFis LHop MFir NFai NHar NMir NNor NRoo NWes SIgm SPer WByw WEas WPer WWye
– 'Bethlehem'	CLon CSte GCal WCot WMer WPyg
§ – 'Blauer Zwerg'	CLon CSte EFou GLil SCoo SMad SPla WCot WMer WPyg
– 'Blaukappe'	CBot CFir EBee ECGP EFou LGre NHol WHoo WOve WPyg
♦ – Blue Dwarf	See ***E. planum* 'Blauer Zwerg'**
– 'Blue Ribbon'	CRDP CSte SSte
– 'Flüela'	CChu CGle CLon EBee ECro EMan EWes GCal GMaP LFis MCLN NCat NLak NRai SApp SAxl SChu SPla SWat WGwG
– 'Seven Seas'	CFir EBee EMar GMaP LCom LFis LHop LRHS NCat NLak NRoo SAxl SChu SPla SWat WCot WLRN WPer
– 'Silverstone'	GCal
– 'Tetra Petra'	EFou MCCP NPSI WHil WPer
– violet blue	GCal
§ ***proteiflorum***	CChu CRDP CSev EBee ECha EMan EOas GCal LHop NLak SPla SRms SSpi SWat WBro WCot WGle
serra	CArc WCot
sp. CD&R	EWes
spinalba	CBot GCal GSki NLak NSla WPer
tricuspidatum	CBlo EBee LRHS MAvo WPer
x ***tripartitum*** ♀	CB&S CGle CSev CShe ECha EFou ELan GBuc GMac LHop MBri MFir MUlv MWat NBro NPSI NSti NTow NWes SChu SCro SDix SIgm SMad SPer SWat WDav WEas WOld WWin
– 'Variegatum'	EMon
* ***umbelliferum***	WCot
variifolium	CArc CArn CB&S CElw CGle CSev EBre ECha EFou EGol ELan EOrc GCHN GDra GMac LHop MBri MBro MWat NHol NMir NOrc NRoo NSti SMad SPer WEas WHil WPbr WRus
yuccifolium	CArn CChu CFir CSte ECoo EGar EMan EOas EWes GCal LHil MSCN NLak NPSI NSti SIgm SMad WHil
x ***zabelii***	CRDP ECGP ECha ELan GCal MFir MHlr MLan NBir NTow WCot
– 'Donard Variety'	CLon GCal MAvo
– 'Jewel'	CLon MUlv WPGP
– 'Violetta'	CGle CLon ELan GBuc MBri MUlv SWat WHoo

ERYSIMUM † (Brassicaceae)

alpestre	NBro
alpinum hort.	See ***E. hieraciifolium***
¶ ***amoenum***	WOMN
'Anne Marie'	CArc CKni ELan MRav SMrm SOkh
arenicola var. ***torulosum***	See ***E. torulosum***

◆ ***arkansanum***	See ***E. helveticum***
§ ***asperum***	NTow
'Aunt May'	CElw SMrm WRus
'Bowles' Mauve' 🏆	Widely available
'Bowles Yellow'	EHic GBuc SMer
'Bredon' 🏆	CKni ECoo ELan EOrc GAbr GCHN MAsh MRav NBro NCat NPer NSti NTow SAga SAxl SUsu WFar WKif WRus
'Butterscotch'	CArc CChr CDoC CElw CFee CGle CLTr CMHG CMil CSam MHig MRav NHaw SAxl SHel SSvw SUsu WMer WWhi
capitatum	CLyd MDHE NMen
'Cheerfulness'	EGar MArl MBri MRav SPla
cheiri	CJew EWFC IBlr LHol SIde WEas WHer
N – 'Baden-Powell' (d)	CMil EGar ELan EOrc
– 'Bloody Warrior' (d)	CArc CBot CCot CElw CHan ELan GBuc GCal GCra MPla MTho NPer
– 'Deben'	CBot
– 'Harpur Crewe' (d) 🏆	CB&S CBot CFee CGle CMHG CSev CShe EBre EFou ELan EPot LHop MBal MBri MTho NBro NFai NPer NSti SBla SChu SUsu WAbe WEas WHoo WPat WPyg WRus WWin
– 'Jane's Derision'	CNat
'Chelsea Jacket' 🏆	CMil ECGP EFou EHic GAbr MRav NChi SAga WMaN WOve WPen WRus
'Chequers'	ELan WMer WPer WRus
cheiri 'Helen Louise'	CWan
* 'Clent Calcutt'	WHil
concinnum	See ***E. suffrutescens***
'Constant Cheer' 🏆	CArc CCot CElw CSam CShe CSpe EMar GAbr GBuc GMac MCLN NCut NFai NPer SAga SUsu WBea WCra WEas WHil WKif WMer WOMN WPat WPer WRha WRus
¶ ***cuspidatum***	SSte
'Devon Gold'	See ***E.* 'Plant World Gold'**
'Devon Sunset'	CArc CElw CGle CHan CLyd CPla CSam CSpe LFlo MCLN MSte NHaw SAga SLod SUsu WEas WHil WOMN WPen WRus
'Dorothy Elmhirst'	See ***E.* 'Mrs L.K. Elmhirst'**
'Ellen Willmott'	WCot
* 'Gingernut'	NPer
'Glowing Embers'	CKni CRos ELan MAsh MBri SOkh SPla SUsu
'Gold Flame'	MWat
'Golden Gem'	EHic MDHE NHed WPen WPer WWtk
'Golden Jubilee'	CHal ECho NTow
§ ***helveticum***	CNic EPfP EPot ESis GCra GTou NPri NTow SRms SSca
§ ***hieraciifolium***	CSam MBal NBro SIde WLRN
¶ ***humile***	WCot
'Jacob's Jacket'	CCot CFee CGle CLTr CMil EBar EFou GAbr GCHN MSCN NPer NRoo SAga SChu WBea WEas WMer WRus WWin
'John Codrington'	CChr CGle CHan CMHG CMil CSam GBuc NBro NFai NPer NSti SAga SAxl SBla SChu SHBN SUsu WEas WHoo WKif
'Joseph's Coat'	CCot CElw
'Jubilee Gold'	ELan NCat SIng
'Julian Orchard'	CArc CMil LFlo SAxl WBea
kotschyanum	CLyd EPot LBee MDHE MHig NMen NPro NRoo NSla NTow NWCA WAbe
'Lady Roborough'	CMil GBuc SChu SMrm
* 'Lewis Hart'	MAvo WCot
linifolium	CPea EBur LWak MDHE NPri NWCA SRms WGor
§ – 'Variegatum'	CArc CBar CGle CSam EFol ELan EOrc EPot LHil LHop MAsh MSCN NBro NPer SAga SCro SPer WAbe WEas WHil WHoo WPer
'Mayflower'	GAbr
'Miss Hopton'	CCot NPer NTow WDav WEas WHil
'Moonlight'	CArc CCot CElw CMHG CSam CSpe EOrc GBuc GCHN LBee LWak MRav MSCN MTho NBrk NBro NNor NSti SChu SHel SPer SUsu WEas WHil WMaN WOve WPer WRus
§ 'Mrs L.K. Elmhirst'	CElw CHan MBri MGrG MRav NPer SHel WCot
mutabile	CArc CB&S CCot CInt CLTr CMHG CShe EOrc GCHN MFir MRav NBir NBro NCat NSti SMrm SSvw SUsu SVen WEas
– 'Variegatum'	CBot CElw CFis LHop WEas WHoo
'Onslow Seedling'	GCHN
'Orange Flame'	CMHG CNic CSam ECha EFol ELan EPad EPot GAbr LBee LHop MHig MPla MRav NBro NPer NPri NRoo NTow SChu WPer
perofskianum	WEas
¶ Perry's hybrid	NPer
'Perry's Peculiar'	NPer
'Perry's Pumpkin'	MGrG NPer
§ 'Plant World Gold'	COtt CPla SCoo
'Plantworld Lemon'	COtt CPla EPri SCoo
'Primrose'	GAbr GCHN LHop MHlr WCot WPer
§ ***pulchellum***	SUsu WEas WPat WPyg
– ***aurantiacum***	NPla
¶ aff. – JJH 9309143	NWCA
– 'Variegatum'	CSte NCut NFla NPri
pumilum De Candolle	See ***E. helveticum***
'Rosemoor'	EGar MRav SMrm
'Rufus'	CCot CMHG CSam EBee ELan EOrc GCHN MAvo SAga WEas
rupestre	See ***E. pulchellum***
§ ***scoparium***	CChr CSpe ECGP EHic LHop MAvo MCCP NBro NLak NRai NTow SIng
'Scorpio'	NCut
semperflorens	SMrm
'Sissinghurst Variegated'	See ***E. linifolium* 'Variegatum'**
'Sprite'	CLyd CMHG CMea CShe CTri EOrc EPot MPla NCat NChi NGre NNrd NPer WHil
§ ***suffrutescens***	CPle ESis LHop MAvo NBro NPer
'Sunbright'	NCat NRoo
'Sunshine'	ELan
§ ***torulosum***	EPad NPer
'Valerie Finnis'	EBar WMaN
N 'Variegatum'	CB&S SHBN WRus WWin

'Wenlock Beauty' 🏆	CCot CMHG CSam CSev ELan GCHN MSCN MTho NBro NFai NPer SAga SAxl SChu SRms SUsu WBea WMaN WMer WPer WRus WWhi
¶ 'Wenlock Beauty Variegated'	CArc CMil
wheeleri	CSpe EMar NMGW NPer NRai WCot WOMN
witmannii	CWan WPer

ERYTHRAEA See CENTAURIUM

ERYTHRINA (Papilionaceae)

crista-galli 🏆	CAbb CB&S CBot CGre CHEx ELan EMil ERea GQui LLew MLan SBid SOWG SSoC SUsu
– 'Compacta'	SMad
§ ***humeana***	CGre
indica	See ***E. variegata***
latissima	CTrC
lysistemon	CGre SOWG
princeps	See ***E. humeana***
§ ***variegata***	LLew
vespertilio	LLew SOWG

ERYTHRONIUM † (Liliaceae)

albidum	CSte LAma LWoo NRog
americanum	CArn CBro CRDP ECha EPot GDra LAma LBow LWoo MS&S MSal NRog SSpi SWas WAbe WCru
californicum 🏆	CAvo LWoo MPhe MS&S NRog SWas WChr
§ – 'White Beauty' 🏆	CAvo CBos CBro CWGN EBre ECha EHyt ELan EPot ETub ITim LAma LBow LWoo MBal MDun MHig MTho NGar NHar NHol NNrd SIng SSpi WAbe WChr WCru WKif
caucasicum	LBow NRog WChr
citrinum	MPhe WChr
'Citronella'	CBro EBar EPar ERos LAma LBow LWoo NEgg NHar NRog WChr WCru WPen
cliftonii	See ***E. multiscapoideum* Cliftonii Group**
dens-canis 🏆	CAvo CMea CRDP ECha EHyt ELan EPot ERos ETub LAma LBow LSyl MBal MBri MHig MNrw MS&S MTho NFai NGar NHol NRog NRoo NRya SSpi WAbe WHil WPat WShi
– 'Charmer'	EPot LRHS WChr
– 'Frans Hals'	EPar EPot ERos LAma MTho NRog WChr WCru
– from Serbia, white	MPhe
¶ – JCA 470.001	LWoo
– 'Lilac Wonder'	EPar EPot LAma MTho NRog WChr
– var. ***niveum***	EPot LAma WChr
– 'Old Aberdeen'	LRHS WChr
– 'Pink Perfection'	EPar EPot ERos LAma NHar NRog WChr WCru
– 'Purple King'	EPot ERos LAma NHar NRog SPla WChr WCru
– 'Rose Queen'	CBro EPar EPot ERos ETub LAma MTho NHar NHol NRog NSla SAxl WAbe WChr WPen
– from Slavenia	LWoo
– 'Snowflake'	CBos CRDP ECha EHyt EPar EPot ERos LAma LWoo NHar NHol NRog SSpi WAbe WChr WCru
– 'White Splendour'	CBro NEgg WChr
¶ – WM 9615 from E Slovenia	MPhe
elegans	CFil WPGP
grandiflorum	MPhe MS&S NHar WChr
helenae	CFil LWoo MPhe WPGP
hendersonii	LAma LWoo MPhe MS&S WChr
¶ – J&JA 12945	SSpi
¶ – JCA 11116	LWoo
howellii	CFil MPhe WChr WPGP
japonicum	CBro CWGN EBee EPar EPot LAma LBow NFai NPri NRog WAbe WCru
'Jeannine'	LAma NGar WChr WCru
'Joanna'	LAma
'Kondo'	CMGP EBee EHyt EMon EPot ERos LAma MHig MS&S MTho NGar NHar NRog NRoo WAbe WCru WPat
'Minnehaha' 🏆	WChr
* ***moerheimii***	LRHS
* – 'Semiplena'	EPot
§ ***multiscapoideum***	LWoo MPhe WChr
§ – Cliftonii Group	MPhe
oregonum	EPar LWoo MPhe MS&S NGar WAbe
– subsp. ***leucandrum***	LWoo MPhe
– – J&JA 13494	SSpi
'Pagoda' 🏆	CAvo CB&S CBro CLon CMea CMon CRDP CWGN ECha EHyt ELan EOrc EPot ETub LAma LBow MDun MS&S MUlv NEgg NGar NHar NNrd NRog NRoo NWCA WAbe WChr WPat
purdyi	See ***E. multiscapoideum***
revolutum 🏆	CBro CFil GGar IBlr LBow MS&S NGar NWoo SSpi WCru
– Johnsonii Group	CFil MBal NHar WChr WCru WPGP
– 'Knightshayes Pink'	CKni
¶ – 'Pink Beauty'	WNor
♦ – 'White Beauty'	See ***E. californicum* 'White Beauty'**
sibiricum	GCrs LRHS WChr
'Sundisc'	ECha EPot MTho NGar NRog WChr
tuolumnense 🏆	CAvo CBro EHyt EPar EPla EPot ERos LAma LBow MBal MDun NGar NHar NRog NSla WAbe WChr

ESCALLONIA † (Escalloniaceae)

'Alice'	CSte SLPl SPer
§ ***alpina***	CGre CPle MAll
'Apple Blossom' 🏆	CB&S CLan CTrw EBre ELan GRei IOrc LHop MBal MBri MGos MPla MWat NNor NPer NRoo SBod SHBN SLPl SPer WAbe WDin WHCG WWin
§ ***bifida***	CBot CGre CHan CPle LRHS WSHC WWat
'C.F. Ball'	CTri ELan GCHN GRei IOrc LBuc MAll MGos NFla NWea SEND SRms WAbe WDin WHer WRTC WStI
'Cardinalis'	MAll NCut
'Dart's Rosy Red'	CBlo MBri SLPl

'Donard Beauty'	CBlo CChe CDoC SRms
'Donard Brilliance'	MGos
'Donard Radiance' 🏆	CB&S CChe CDoC CShe ELan ENot ISea LHop MAll MGos MWat NHol SBod SPer SRms WAbe WBod WDin WGer WWeb
'Donard Rose'	WWeb
'Donard Seedling'	Widely available
'Donard Star'	CShe EBee ENot EPfP IOrc MGos SBid WWeb
'Donard Suprise'	NNor
'Edinensis' 🏆	CMHG ECtt EMil ENot MAll MBar NFla NNor SBid SEND SRms WDin WWat
'Erecta'	CBlo EPfP MAll SBid
x ***exoniensis***	SRms
fonkii	See ***E. alpina***
'Glory of Donard'	CDoC ENot
* ***gracilis alba***	CPle
'Gwendolyn Anley'	CLTr CMHG MAsh MGos NTow SBod SLPl SPer WWat WWeb
'Hopleys Gold'	See ***E. laevis* 'Gold Brian'**
illinita	CPle MAll
'Iveyi' 🏆	CB&S CChe CHan CLan CMHG CPle CTrw EBre ELan ENot ERav GWht IOrc ISea LHop MBal MBri MWat NSti SHBN SPer SPla SRms WAbe WHCG WRTC WSHC WWat
§ ***laevis***	CTrw SDry
§ – 'Gold Brian'	CMHG CSam CTrC EBee EBre EHic EHoe ELan IOrc MGos MSta MWat NEgg NPSI SAga SBid SPer WHar WStI WWeb
– 'Gold Ellen' (v)	CBlo EBre EFol EMil LHop LRHS NHol NTow SAga SCoo SEND SPla
'Langleyensis' 🏆	CB&S CDoC CTri MAll MWat NFla NNor NWea SBod WDin WFar WSHC
leucantha	CGre CPle MAll
littoralis	CPle
mexicana	CBot CHan WWat
montevidensis	See ***E. bifida***
'Newryensis'	SPer
organensis	See ***E. laevis***
'Peach Blossom' 🏆	CDoC CPle CWLN EBar EBee ELan EMil ENot MGos SAga SBid SHBN SLPl SPer WGwG WHCG WWeb
'Pink Elf'	ECtt IOrc MBri NCut WLRN
'Pink Pearl'	SRms
'Pride of Donard' 🏆	CB&S CDoC CLan IOrc LHop MAll SPla SRms WWeb
punctata	See ***E. rubra***
'Rebecca'	GOrc
'Red Dream'	CBlo CChe CFai CSte EBre IOrc LBuc LRHS MAsh MBri MGos NFla NPSI NPro SCoo WGer WLRN WStI
'Red Dwarf'	WAbe
'Red Elf'	CMHG EBre ECtt ELan EMil GOrc IOrc LHop MAll MBar MBri MGos MPla MTis MWat NHol SLPl SPer SRms WHen
'Red Hedger'	CBlo CDoC EHic EMil MTis SBid SCoo
resinosa	CPle SArc SMrm
revoluta	CPle CTri SDry
rosea	CPle
***rubra* 'Crimson Spire'** 🏆	CB&S CChe CLan CShe EBar EBre ENot GRei MAll MAsh MBri MGos MRav MWat NNor SAga SBod SHBN SPer SPla SRms WHen WRTC WStI WTyr WWeb
– 'Ingramii'	CChe CMHG MAll SBod SHBN
§ – var. ***macrantha***	CB&S CChe CHEx EMil GRei ISea MAll MAsh SPer SPla WAbe WDin WGer WGwG WRTC WStI
– 'Pubescens'	CPle
– 'Pygmaea'	See ***E. rubra* 'Woodside'**
– var. ***uniflora***	SDry
§ – 'Woodside'	CPle EHic MAll MGos NHol NPro SBid SIng SRms WHCG
'Silver Anniversary'	CGre CPMA CPle ELan LHop MAll MAsh MGos MPla SBid SPer WLRN WWeb
'Slieve Donard'	CBlo ENot MAll MGos MRav SHhN SLPl SRms WWeb
tucumanensis	CGre CPle
virgata	CPle WWat
viscosa	CPle MAll

EUCALYPTUS † (Myrtaceae)

aggregata	MAll SArc SPer WCel
¶ ***amygdalina***	CMHG
approximans subsp. ***approximans***	WCel
archeri	CTho GQui ISea MBal MCCP WCel
¶ ***brookeriana***	CMHG
caesia	GCHN
camphora	WCel
cinerea	CTrC GQui IOrc WCel
citriodora	EOHP GQui SIde WCel WNor
coccifera 🏆	CB&S CDoC CHEx CSte ELan GAri IOrc ISea LPan MAll MBal SEND SSpi WCel WNor
consideniana	LLew
cordata	CGre CMHG LHop MAll MBal WCel
crenulata	CTrC GQui WCel
dalrympleana 🏆	CB&S CDoC CMHG CSam CTho CTrC EBee EBre ELan ENot EWes IOrc MAll MBal MGos SBid SPer SPla WCel WPat
deanei	WCel
◆ ***debeuzevillei***	See ***E. pauciflora*** subsp. ***debeuzevillei***
delegatensis	CAgr CMHG CTrC GAri IOrc WCel
divaricata	See ***E. gunnii divaricata***
ficifolia	CDoC IDee
fraxinoides	LLew WCel
glaucescens	CGre CMHG GQui LPan LRHS SArc SBid SPer WCel
globulus 🏆	CHEx CMHG MAll MBal MSal SBid SSoC WCel WPLI
goniocalyx	WCel
§ ***gregsoniana***	ISea LLew WCel
§ ***gunnii*** 🏆	Widely available
§ ***gunnii divaricata***	GQui LPan WCel
haemastoma	MAll
johnstonii	CAgr MAll SPer
kitsoniana	MAll MBal WCel
¶ ***kruseana***	CTrC
kybeanensis	GQui LPan WCel
lehmannii	SOWG

leucoxylon WCel
– subsp. *megalocarpa* MAll
macarthurii WCel
macrocarpa CTrC
mannifera subsp. *elliptica* WCel
– subsp. *maculosa* MAll
mitchelliana WCel
* *moorei nana* CPle WNor
neglecta WCel
nicholii CSpe EWes GQui MAll WCel
niphophila See *E. pauciflora* subsp. *niphophila*
nitens CMCN GAri LLew MAll MBal WCel
§ *nitida* CGre CMHG WCel WNor
nova-anglica CMHG GAri
¶ *ovata* CMHG
parvifolia ♀ CAgr CB&S CDoC CLnd GAri ISea LPan SArc SDry SEND SSte WCel
pauciflora CBlo CDoC CTri EBee EBre ELan GAri MBal MUlv NBee SBid SEND SPer WCel WNor
§ – subsp. *debeuzevillei* CSte GQui LRHS MCCP SArc WCel
pauciflora nana See *E. gregsoniana*
§ *pauciflora* subsp. *niphophila* ♀ CB&S CHEx CLnd CMHG CSam CSte CTho EBar EBre ELan ENot GWht IOrc ISea MAll MBal MBri MGos MUlv MWat SDry SHFr SPer SReu SSta WCel WDin WNor WOrn WPat
– – 'Pendula' CMHG GAri WCel
perriniana CAgr CB&S CHEx CMHG CSte EBee ELan ENot IBlr LPan MBal SArc SDry SPer SPla WCel WNor WPat
phoenicea SOWG
polyanthemos WLRN
pulchella CGre
pulverulenta CAgr CBlo CGre MAll WCel
regnans CGre ISea MBal
remota CGre
risdonii GAri WNor
¶ *rodwayi* CMHG
rubida CGre CMHG CTho IOrc WCel
sideroxylon MAll
sieberi CGre
simmondsii See *E. nitida*
stellulata GAri MAll WCel
stuartiana See *E. bridgesiana*
sturgissiana GCHN
subcrenulata CMHG GAri GQui ISea WCel
tenuiramis CGre
urnigera CAgr CGre CTho GAri MAll WCel
vernicosa WCel
– subsp. *johnstonii* CMHG GAri WCel
viminalis CMHG GAri LLew WCel

EUCHARIDIUM See CLARKIA

EUCHARIS (Amaryllidaceae)

§ *amazonica* LAma NRog SDeJ
grandiflora hort. See *E. amazonica*
– Plan. & Lind. LBow WChr

EUCODONIA (Gesneriaceae)

'Adele' NMos WDib
andrieuxii NMos
– 'Naomi' CHal NMos WDib
'Cornell Gem' See x *Achicodonia* 'Cornell Gem'
'Tintacoma' NMos
verticillata 'Frances' NMos

EUCOMIS (Hyacinthaceae)

§ *autumnalis* CAvo CBro CPou CSWP CTrC GBin GSki LAma MCCP NRai WCot
bicolor CArc CAvo CBro CChu CFir CHEx CLon CTrC EBak EBee EGoo ETub LAma LBow LHil MHlr NGar NRog SAga SDix SMad SPer SSoC WCru WHil WPen
– 'Alba' CAvo CChu GSki
– hybrids EFou
§ *comosa* CAvo CB&S CBro CChu CFir CHEx CLon EMon GSki LAma LBow NGar NRog SMad WCru WLRN
pallidiflora EBee WChr
pole-evansii CChu CFir GBin GCal WChr WCot WLRN
punctata See *E. comosa*
undulata See *E. autumnalis*
zambesiaca CFee GBin LBow
'Zeal Bronze' CChu CFil CMHG NSti WCot WPGP

EUCOMMIA (Eucommiaceae)

ulmoides CFil CPle SMad WCoo WPGP

EUCROSIA (Amaryllidaceae)

See Plant Deletions

EUCRYPHIA † (Eucryphiaceae)

'Castlewellan' ISea
cordifolia CB&S CGre CTrw ISea MBal SCog
¶ – Crarae hardy form GGGa
– x *lucida* CB&S CGre CWLN IOrc ISea MBal SCog SPer WDin WWat
glutinosa ♀ CB&S CGre ELan GOrc ICrw ISea LHyd MAsh MBal MBri NBir SHBN SPer SSpi SSta WAbe WBod WDin WNor WPat WWat
– Plena Group ISea
x *hillieri* 'Winton' CMHG ISea MBal
x *intermedia* CGre CSam CWLN ELan GCHN GGGa NPal SCog SHBN SPer SRms SSpi WDin WPat WWat
– 'Rostrevor' ♀ CB&S CChu CLan CMHG CPMA ELan ICrw ISea MAsh MBal MBel SAga SCog SPer SReu SSta WBod WFar
lucida CGre CMHG ELan GGGa GSki ISea LHyd MBal WNor WWat
– 'Ballerina' ISea
– 'Gilt Edge' (v) ISea
– 'Leatherwood Cream' (v) ISea
– 'Pink Cloud' CFai CMHG CPMA ELan ISea LRHS SPer SSpi

milliganii	CB&S CDoC CFil CGre CMHG CWLN ELan GQui ISea LHop MBal MUlv NPal SCog SHBN SPer SSpi SSta WAbe WSHC WWat
moorei	CAbP CB&S CFil CKni ELan ISea MBal SSta
x ***nymansensis***	CB&S EBre EMil EPfP LHop MBal SAga SArc SCog SReu SRms SSpi WHCG WStI
– 'George Graham'	GGGa ISea MBal
– 'Mount Usher'	IOrc ISea
– 'Nymansay' ♀	CB&S CLan CMHG CPMA CTrC ELan GGGa ISea LHyd MAsh MBal MBar MBri MGos NPal SDix SHBN SPer SSta WAbe WDin WMou WPat WPyg WWat
N 'Penwith'	CPMA ISea MBal NCut SPer

EUGENIA (Myrtaceae)

myrtifolia	CPle CSev ERea STre
– 'Variegata'	ERea

EUMORPHIA (Asteraceae)

* ***canescens***	WHer
prostrata	CSpe
sericea	CHan CNic GAbr GOrc NNor WSHC

EUNOMIA See AETHIONEMA

EUODIA (Rutaceae)

daniellii	See ***Tetradium daniellii***
hupehensis	See ***Tetradium daniellii* Hupehense Group**

EUONYMUS † (Celastraceae)

alatus ♀	CB&S CChu CPMA EBre ELan ENot GRei IOrc LHop LNet MBal MBar MWat NBee SHBN SPer SReu SSpi SSta WBod WCoo WDin WGwG WHCG WMou WSHC WWat
– var. ***apterus***	SHBN
– 'Ciliodentatus'	See ***E. alatus* 'Compactus'**
§ – 'Compactus' ♀	CChu CDoC CEnd CPMA EBre EHic ESis IOrc LNet MAsh MBlu MBri MGos MPla MUlv SBid SPan SPla SReu SSpi WDin WWat
* ***atropurpureus cheatumii***	CPMA
bungeanus	CMCN
cornutus var. ***quinquecornutus***	CPMA EPla WMou WOMN WPat
europaeus	CArn CDoC CKin CLnd CPer CShe EBre ELan EPla EWFC LBuc LPan NWea SRms WDin WHar WMou
– f. ***albus***	CBot CWSG EMil EPla
¶ – 'Atropurpureus'	LPan
– 'Atrorubens'	CBrd CPMA
– 'Aucubifolius' (v)	CFil EPla WPGP
* – 'Aureus'	CNat
– var. ***intermedius***	ENot EPla
– 'Red Cascade' ♀	CB&S CChu CEnd CMCN CMHG CPMA EBre ELan ENot EPla IOrc LHop MBar MBel MBri MGos MWat NHol SHBN SPer SSpi WAbe WBod WDin WHCG WPat WWat WWin
farreri	See ***E. nanus***
fimbriatus	CB&S
fortunei Blondy	COtt CPMA EBee EBre ECle ELan EMil EPla MAsh MBri MGos MPla SBid SCoo SMad SPer SPla SSta WPyg WWeb WWes
– 'Canadale Gold' (v)	EBee EPla ESis MGos NBee NFai NHol SPer WWeb
– 'Coloratus'	CBlo CLan EBre ENot MBar NCut SBid SHBN SPer WDin WGwG
– 'Croftway'	SCro
– 'Dart's Blanket'	CBlo EBre ELan ENot EPla MRav SBid SLPl SSta SSto WDin
* – 'Emerald Carpet'	SHhN
– 'Emerald Cushion'	ENot ESis SPer SSto
– Emerald Gaiety (v) ♀	CB&S CBot CLan EBre ELan EPot ESis GRei LBuc LGro LHop LHyd MBal MBar MBri MGos MPla MWat NFai NRoo SMad SPer SReu SSta WDin WEas WHCG WPat WWin
– Emerald 'n' Gold (v) ♀	Widely available
– 'Emerald Surprise'	MBri NPro WRHF
– 'Gold Spot'	See ***E. fortunei* 'Sunspot'**
– 'Gold Tip'	See ***E. fortunei* Golden Prince**
– 'Golden Pillar' (v)	EBee EHic EHoe GWht MDHE
§ – Golden Prince (v)	CB&S CPle CWSG EFol ENot EPla IOrc MBar NFai NHol SPer WGor WStI
– 'Harlequin' (v)	COtt CPMA CSam CWSG EBre EHoe ELan EPla GOrc LBuc LHop MAll MAsh MBar MBlu MGos MPla SAga SHBN SIng SMad SPer SSta WGwG WWeb
– 'Highdown'	EHic WWat
– 'Hort's Blaze'	MGos
– 'Kewensis'	CMGP CMHG CNic CPle ENot MBar MPla MRav MWat NTow SArc SBod SHhN WCot WCru WWat
* – 'Minimus Variegatus'	ECho
– 'Minimus'	CBlo CTri EHal EHic EPla ESis GAri MGos NHol SIng SPla WFar WPer
§ ***fortunei*** var. ***radicans***	CPlN
fortunei 'Sheridan Gold'	EBee ECtt EHic EHoe EPla MPla MRav NHol SEas SHBN
– 'Silver Gem'	See ***E. fortunei* 'Variegatus'**
– 'Silver Pillar' (v)	EBar EBee EHic EHoe ENot ERav ESis GOrc LRHS
– 'Silver Queen' (v) ♀	CB&S CLan CPle ELan ENot EPla GOrc IOrc MBal MBar MGos MWat NBir NBrk NFla SHBN SMad SPer SReu SSta WDin WGwG WHCG WRTC WSHC WWat
– 'Sunshine' (v)	EHic ELan EPla MAll MAsh MGos NCut SBid

§ – 'Sunspot' (v) CMHG EBre ECtt ELan EPla ESis GOrc LHop MBar MGos MRav NFai NHed NHol NTow SAga SChu SEas SPla SSta WDin
– 'Tustin' EPla SLPl
§ – 'Variegatus' CMHG EFol ELan ENot MAll MBar NNor SPer SRms STre WBod WDin WPat WPyg WRHF
– var. ***vegetus*** EPla SPer
grandiflorus CPMA
hamiltonianus CMCN
– 'Fiesta' CPle
– subsp. ***hians*** See ***E. hamiltonianus*** subsp. ***sieboldianus***
§ – subsp. ***sieboldianus*** CMCN CPMA EBee LHop MBal MGos SLPl SMrm SPan WCoo WWat
– – 'Coral Charm' SMrm SMur WWes
– 'Winter Glory' CPMA LRHS MBri WWes
– var. ***yedoensis*** See ***E. hamiltonianus*** subsp. ***sieboldianus***
* ***hibarimisake*** SBla
japonicus EBee ENot EPfP LRHS SBid SHhN SPer WDin
– 'Albomarginatus' CB&S CBlo CTri EBee LFis MBar MPla NBrk SBid SEND SRms WSHC
– 'Aureopictus' See ***E. japonicus* 'Aureus'**
– 'Aureovariegatus' See ***E. japonicus* 'Ovatus Aureus'**
§ – 'Aureus' (v) CB&S CChe EGoo ELan ENot EPla GOrc LPan MBal MBri SBid SDix SEas SHBN SPla WDin WHar WWeb
– 'Bravo' CDoC EHic NHol
– 'Chollipo' ELan LRHS MAsh
* – 'Compactus' LPan
– 'Duc d'Anjou' Carrière (v) CB&S CLTr EBre EFol EHoe ELan EPla ESis EWes LPan MAsh SDry SMad SPla
– 'Duc d'Anjou' hort. See ***E. japonicus* 'Viridivarigatus'**
– 'Golden Maiden' ELan LRHS MAsh SPla
– 'Golden Pillar' (v) ESis
§ – 'Latifolius Albomarginatus' ♀ EBre EHic EHoe MNrw SBid SPer
– 'Luna' See ***E. japonicus* 'Aureus'**
– 'Macrophyllus Albus' See ***E. japonicus* 'Latifolius Albomarginatus'**
– 'Maiden's Gold' SBid
– 'Marieke' See ***E. japonicus* 'Ovatus Aureus'**
– 'Mediopictus' MBri
– 'Microphyllus' EMil MBal MUlv SSca
§ – 'Microphyllus Albovariegatus' CChe CLTr CMHG EAst ELan EMil EPla EPot ESiP MBal MBar MGos MHig MRav NHol SAga SHBN SPla SSca WHCG WPat WPyg WSHC WStI WWat
– 'Microphyllus Aureovariegatus' EMil WPat WPyg WWin
– 'Microphyllus Aureus' See ***E. japonicus* 'Microphyllus Pulchellus'**
§ – 'Microphyllus Pulchellus' (v) CB&S CMHG CNic EFol EPla EPot ESis LFis LHop MBar MNrw MRav NHed NHol SAga SBid WHCG WPyg WWeb
– 'Microphyllus Variegatus' See ***E. japonicus* 'Microphyllus Albovariegatus'**
§ – 'Ovatus Albus' (v) EAst SBid
§ – 'Ovatus Aureus' (v) ♀ CChe CTri EFol ENot LPan MBal MBar MGos MPla MRav SBid SEas SPer SPla SRms WDin WPat WRHF WStI
– 'Président Gauthier' (v) CDoC EBee EFol LPan MGos NCut
– 'Robustus' CDoC EPla
* – 'Silver Princess' SHBN
– 'Susan' CSte EHic NHol
kiautschovicus CBrd CPle EPla
latifolius CMCN CPMA
– × ***hamiltonianus*** CMCN
macropterus EPla
myrianthus CBrd EPfP SBid WWat
§ ***nanus*** CNic CPle EPla ESis MBal NHol WPat WPyg WSHC
– var. ***turkestanicus*** EHic EPla ESis NPal SRms WWat
obovatus CHan
oxyphyllus CBrd CMCN CPMA WMou WWat
§ ***pendulus*** CChu CGre
phellomanus EBar EHic GDra LHop LNet MBar MBlu MBri MUlv SMrm SPan WWat
§ ***planipes*** ♀ CGre CMHG CPle CTri EBar ELan ENot EPla MBlu MBri NHol NSti SPer SSpi WNor WWat
radicans See ***E. fortunei radicans***
'Rokojo' NHol WPat
rosmarinifolius See ***E. nanus***
sachalinensis hort. See ***E. planipes***
sanguineus CPMA
sp. B&L 12543 EHic EPla ESis EWes
tingens CChu CFil CPle SBid
velutinus CChu
verrucosus CPMA EPla
yedoensis See ***E. hamiltonianus*** subsp. ***sieboldianus***

EUPATORIUM (Asteraceae)

§ ***album*** CHad CSWP CVer EPPr WPer
– 'Braunlaub' CSte EFou EMon MCli MHlr MUlv SMad WCot WRus
altissimum CBot CGle EPar GCal MSal SChu WCHb WEas
– JLS 88029 EMon
aromaticum CArn CSev EBee ECro ELan GAul LFis MRav NBro SCro SMrm SWat WCHb WPer WWye
cannabinum CArc CArn CKin CSev CWGN EBar ECED ECWi ECoo EHon ELan EMFW EWFC GPoy LHol MHew MSal MSta NMir NSti SWat SWyc WApp WCer WOak WPer WWye
– 'Album' EMon GBar
– 'Flore Pleno' CSev ECha ECro EFou EGar EMon EOrc GCal LFis MBel MFir MHlr MRav MSte MUlv NBrk NHol NSti SHig SWat WCot WPbr WWat
* – 'Not Quite White' WAlt
– 'Spraypaint' CNat
capillifolium MHlr SMrm WCot
– 'Elegant Feather' EWes GCal LFis SMad
¶ ***chinense*** WCot
coelestinum LBuc WCot
* ***fistulosum*** WCot
* – 'Atropurpureum' WPer

* ***hyssopifolium*** 'Bubba'	WCot
§ ***ligustrinum***	CB&S CDec CDoC CElw CLan CPle CWit ECha ELan IOrc ISea LGre MAll SAga SDix SMrm SPer SUsu WCHb WSHC
¶ ***maculatum***	See ***E. purpureum* subsp. *maculatum***
madrense	CLTr
micranthum	See ***E. ligustrinum***
occidentale	EBee
perfoliatum	CArn ELau GBar GPoy LHol MNrw MSal SIde WPer
purpureum	CArc CArn CChu CWGN ECED ECha GBar GPoy LHol MGra MHew MSal MSte MWat NBro NDea NHol SChu SIde SMrm SPer SSvw SWat WEas WHer WOld WPer WRus WSHC WWye
– subsp. ***maculatum***	CSam EBee EBre EMon GCal LFis MUlv WHil WPer
– – 'Album'	EMon WCot
– – 'Atropurpureum' ♀	CChu CGle CHan CSev CVer EBre ECha EFol EFou ELan EOrc GCal LFis LHol MBel MBri MFir NBir NCat NPri NRoo NSti SAxl SUsu SWat WFar
– – 'Berggarten'	GCal
– – 'Riesinschirm'	CArc SMad
– 'Purple Bush'	ECha
* ***rotundifolium***	WCot
rugosum	CArc CGle CHan CSam ECro ELan GAul GBar GCra LHol MFir MHew SIde WCHb
rugosum album	See ***E. album***
* 'Snowball'	SMrm
§ ***sordidum***	ERea GCal LHil SLMG
triplinerve	EGar LHol MSte WLRN
weinmannianum	See ***E. ligustrinum***

EUPHORBIA † (Euphorbiaceae)

acanthothamnos	LFlo LGre
amygdaloides	CKin CRow ECWi EWFC SHel SSpi WCer WTyr WWye
– 'Brithembottom'	CSam
– 'Craigieburn'	GCal GCra
§ – 'Purpurea'	Widely available
§ – var. ***robbiae*** ♀	Widely available
– 'Rubra'	See ***E. amygdaloides* 'Purpurea'**
– 'Variegata'	CHad CRow ECha ELan EMon EOrc LGre MHar MTho SUsu WRus
¶ ***balsamifera***	GBin
biglandulosa	See ***E. rigida***
brittingeri	EGar
¶ ***broteroi***	WCot
capitata	WPat
capitulata	EFol EGar ELan EWes LHop MBro MTho NMen WWin
ceratocarpa	CB&S CEnd CLTr EBee EGar EMon EPla EWes GAbr GBuc GCal NHol SMad SPan SSea WCHb WFar WFox WOve WWeb
characias ♀	CB&S CBot CGle CRow CWGN ECha ECtt EMon GAul MBri NHol NNor NOak NPer NPri NSti SPan SPer SRms SSpi WByw WGwG WHoo WPer WTyr WWat
* – 'Amber Eye'	IBlr
¶ – Ballyrogan hybrids	IBlr
– subsp. ***characias*** ♀	WCru
– – 'Blue Hills'	EFou EGar EMon EPPr GBuc GCal IBlr LBlm NLak SMrm WRus
characias characias 'Burrow Silver' (v)	CAbb CBot CRDP CTrC EGar NLak SCoo SHam SSta SWat
characias* subsp. *characias 'H.E. Bates'	NBir
– – 'Humpty Dumpty'	COtt EBre LHop LRHS NPer NWes SMad WCra WGer WHil WRus
– – 'Percy Picton'	CHan
– dwarf	SMrm
– 'Forescate'	EBre EMil GCal LRHS SPan WGer WMer WRus
– 'Goldbrook'	CSev EBee EMan LBuc LFis NCat NHol SChu SHBN SHam SMrm SWat
* – 'Green Mantle'	IBlr
– JCA 475.500	GCal
– 'Jenetta'	NCat
– 'Portuguese Velvet'	CHan CMil EBre EGle EMan LGre MHar SMad SMrm SPan SWas WCot WKif
* – 'Sombre Melody'	IBlr
– 'Variegata'	CRow SMad
– subsp. ***wulfenii*** ♀	Widely available
– – 'Bosahan' (v)	EGar SMad SPan
– – 'Emmer Green' (v)	CElw ECha EGar SBla SWat WCot WRus
– – JCA 475.603	GCal SAga
§ – – 'John Tomlinson' ♀	CMil ECha EGar EMon EPPr EPla EWes LHop MSte MUlv WEas
– – Kew form	See ***E. characias* subsp. *wulfenii* 'John Tomlinson'**
– – 'Lambrook Gold' ♀	CMHG CRow CSam EBar EBre ECtt EGar EGol ELan EOrc EPar EWes LHop MBro MRav MWat NPer NRoo SChu SPer WHoo WPyg WRus WWat
– – 'Lambrook Yellow'	CMil EMon GBuc MWat SMur
– – Margery Fish Group	EFou EHic EMan EPla LRHS MFir NCat NWes SChu SMrm SWat WMer
– – 'Minuet'	CShe
– – 'Perry's Tangerine'	NPer SMad
– – 'Perry's Winter Blusher'	ECtt NPer
§ – – 'Purple and Gold'	EMon SBla SChu SPan WCot WCra WPen WRus
– – 'Purpurea'	See ***E. characias* subsp. *wulfenii* 'Purple and Gold'**
– – var. ***sibthorpii***	MUlv WCot WOld
¶ ***clava***	GBin
cognata CC&McK 607	EWes GCHN
– CC&McK 724	GBin
¶ ***confinalis***	GBin
conifera	CB&S
corallioides	CArc CArn CMea EBee EBre ECha EGar ELan EMan EPPr IBlr MCLN NFai NLak NPer SMac WHer WPen WWhi
§ ***cornigera***	CChu CFil CHad CLon CRDP EBre EGar EHic EHoe EMon GAbr GBin GCal GMac IBlr MMil SAxl SWat WSHC
¶ – CC 720	CPou
¶ ***cylindrica***	GBin
cyparissias	Widely available
– 'Betten'	See ***E. × gayeri* 'Betten'**

¶ – 'Bushman Boy'	EGar GBri IBlr NLak WCot
– 'Clarice Howard'	EBee ECha EDAr EGar ELan EMar GCal LGan NFla NOak NRar NSti SCoo SMrm SPan WHal WPbr
– 'Fens Ruby'	Widely available
– 'Orange Man'	CMil EBar EBee ECoo EFou EGar EMar EMon EWes GBin GBri GCal IBlr MBro NBrk NHol NLak SAxl SChu SMad SPan SWat WFox WPbr
–'Purpurea'	See ***E. cyparissias* 'Clarice Howard'**
– red	SPan
– 'Red Devil'	IBlr SChu SMrm SUsu WOve
– 'Tall Boy'	CArc EGar EMon EWes GBri IBlr NLak
dendroides	GBin
§ ***donii***	ELan GCra IBlr LHop NSti SDix SUsu
dulcis	CGle CRow CSte ECha ECtt EFol EFou ELan EOrc LGan NBrk NBro NHex NOak NSti SEas SMac SUsu WByw WCot WEas WFox WHen WOld WRus WWat
– 'Chameleon'	Widely available
I – 'Nana'	CBlo EHic EWll GBin NHol SPan
epithymoides	See ***E. polychroma***
erubescens	SChu WDav
esula	CGle EGar
Excalibur	See ***E.* Excalibur = 'Froeup'**
¶ ***fasciculata***	GBin
¶ ***fimbriata***	GBin
Excalibur = 'Froeup'	SSpi
fulgens	CHal
'Garblesham Enchanter'	EPPr
§ × ***gayeri*** 'Betten'	GCal
glauca	CFee ECou IBlr WCot
'Golden Foam'	See ***E. stricta***
griffithii	CRow CSte NBrk NBro NCat SSpi SWat WAbb WCru WGer
– 'Dixter' 🏆	Widely available
– 'Fern Cottage'	EWes GAbr SMrm SWas
– 'Fireglow'	Widely available
– 'King's Caple'	EGar
– 'Robert Poland'	CSWP
– 'Wickstead'	EGar EPla GCal LHop LRHS SMrm
* ***hiemale***	GCLN
horrida	SLMG
hyberna	GBri IBlr MTho MUlv NMen SWat WFox
¶ ***ingens***	GBin
jacquemontii	GCal MRav SPan
× ***keysii***	MBri
lathyris	CJew CRow EGoo ELan EMar ERav LHol MHew NCat NHex NPer SIng SRms WEas WFox WOak WWye
¶ ***leucocephala***	GBin
longifolia D Don	See ***E. donii***
– hort.	See ***E. cornigera***
– Lamarck	See ***E. mellifera***
mammillaris	GBin SLMG
× ***martinii*** 🏆	Widely available
– 'Red Dwarf'	EOrc
§ ***mellifera***	Widely available
¶ ***meloformis***	GBin
milii 🏆	CHal EBak SRms
– 'Koenigers Aalbäumle'	MBri
¶ ***monteiroi***	GBin
myrsinites 🏆	Widely available
nicaeensis	CB&S CChu CFil EMan EMon EOrc GCal LGre LHop MBro SBla SBod SChu SCro SDix SMrm SPer SSpi SUsu WCot WWat
oblongata	CB&S EBee ELan EMon EPla EWes GBuc IBlr LRHS NHol NLak NSti NWes SBod WCHb WFox WWeb
¶ ***obtusifolia***	GBin
palustris 🏆	CChu CHad CHan CMHG CRDP CRow CShe EFou EGol ELan ERav GAul GCal LBlm LHop LPBA MNrw MSta NDea NHol NSti SAxl SDix SHel SMad SPer SUsu WEas WWat WWin
– 'Walenburg's Glorie'	EBee EGar NBrk NLak NRoo SMad
¶ ***pekinensis***	MSal
pilosa	CNat NSti
– 'Major'	See ***E. polychroma* 'Major'**
pithyusa	CBot CGle CHan CMea EBre ECha EGar EMan EMon LFlo LHop NLak SAlw SAxl SChu SHBN SPan SUsu WCot WRus WWat WWhi
§ ***polychroma*** 🏆	Widely available
§ – 'Candy'	CBot CMea CRow EBre ECha EGol ELan EOrc ERav GCHN GCal LHop MUlv NHar NHol NOak NRoo NSti SChu SMad SPan WHoo
– 'Emerald Jade'	EGar GBri IBlr NLak
§ – 'Lacy' (v)	EBee ELan EWes MMil NBir NLak SMad SPan WPbr WPen
§ – 'Major'	CMHG ECha EGar ELan EPPr GCal MUlv NCat SPan WCot WEas
– 'Midas'	CFee EGle EMon SMrm
– 'Orange Flush'	WHoo
I – 'Purpurea'	See ***E. polychroma* 'Candy'**
– 'Sonnengold'	ECha EGar EWes GCal LBlm MBro WHoo WPyg WRHF WSHC
I – 'Variegata'	See ***E. polychroma* 'Lacy'**
portlandica	EBee EFol EHic ELan EMar GBin LFis MBri NPSI WCHb WHer
§ × ***pseudovirgata***	EHal EMon IBlr LHop SAxl SPan SUsu
pugniformis	MBri
pulcherrima	EWes MBri
'Purple Preference'	EPPr NPri
reflexa	See ***E. seguieriana*** subsp. ***niciciana***
resinifera	SLMG
§ ***rigida***	CBot CFil EFol EGoo GCal SBid SBla SIgm SWas WCot
robbiae	See ***E. amygdaloides*** var. ***robbiae***
schillingii 🏆	CAbb CB&S CChu CFee CHan CMHG CPle CSam EBre EGol EOrc GCal GCra ISea LFis LHop MBri NHol SBla SBod SDix SMad SPer WGle WWat
¶ ***schoenlandii***	GBin
seguieriana	EBee ECha EMan GBin

§ – subsp. ***niciciana*** CArc CBot CGle CHan CMGP CMea CSam EBre ECha ELan ERav IBlr MRav NBir SBla SDix SMrm SSpi WEas WHoo WRus WWat
serrulata See ***E. stricta***
sikkimensis CBot CBre CChu CElw CFee CGre CHan CMHG CRow EBre ECha ELan EMon EOrc NBrk SMrm WCHb WCru WEas WOld WWat WWin
¶ ***soongarica*** EJud
spinosa SIgm SMad
§ ***stricta*** CArc CRow EBee ECha EGar ELan EMan EWes GBri IBlr MCCP MFir NBro NCat NSti WLRN WRHF WWat CArc CRDP CVer
* ***submammillaris*** 'Variegata' MBri
¶ ***susannae*** SLMG
¶ ***transvaalensis*** GBin
uralensis See ***E.*** × ***pseudovirgata***
villosa GBin MBro SPan
§ ***virgata*** EMon EWes NSti SPan WCHb WCot
× ***waldsteinii*** See ***E. virgata***
wallichii Hook.f. CChu CSam ECha EGol EMan EOrc IBlr LFlo MBri MUlv NFla NHol NOrc NRoo NSti SMrm SPer SSoC WAbb WRus WWat
◆ – Kohli See ***E. cornigera***
◆ – misapplied See ***E. donii***
* 'Welsh Dragon' WCot
¶ ***zoutpansbergensis*** GBin

EUPTELEA (Eupteleaceae)
franchetii See ***E. pleiosperma***
§ ***pleiosperma*** CMCN
polyandra CBrd CGre

EURYA (Theaceae)
japonica CFil
– 'Variegata' See ***Cleyera japonica* 'Fortunei'**

EURYOPS (Asteraceae)
abrotanifolius CKni LHil SVen
§ ***acraeus*** ♀ CBot CPle CShe EHyt ELan EPot GCHN GDra GTou LBee LHop MBro MPla NGre NHol NNor NRoo NTow NWCA SBar SIgm SIng WAbe WWin
candollei WAbe
§ ***chrysanthemoides*** CB&S CBrk CMHG CPle CSam EBar ERav ERea IBlr LHil MMil MSte SVen WPer WRHF
aff. ***decumbens*** JJ&JH 9401309 NWCA
evansii See ***E. acraeus***
* ***grandiflorus*** CBot
pectinatus ♀ CB&S CBrk CMHG CPle CSam CSev ERea IBlr LHil MBlu MFir MNrw MRav NSty SDry SHBN SIgm SMrm SOWG SRms SVen WEas WPer WWye
sericeus See ***Ursinia sericea***
¶ ***speciosissimus*** CTrC
tysonii CPle GGar
virgineus CB&S CMHG IBlr

EUSTEPHIA (Amaryllidaceae)
jujuyensis WChr

EUSTOMA (Gentianaceae)
§ ***grandiflorum*** MBri
russellianum See ***E. grandiflorum***

EUSTREPHUS (Philesiaceae)
latifolius CPlN ECou

EVOLVULUS (Convolvulaceae)
convolvuloides ERea
glomeratus 'Blue Daze' See ***E. pilosus* 'Blue Daze'**
§ ***pilosus*** 'Blue Daze' ERea SSad

EWARTIA (Asteraceae)
nubigena NWCA

EXACUM (Gentianaceae)
affine MBri
– 'Rococo' MBri

EXOCHORDA (Rosaceae)
alberti See ***E. korolkowii***
giraldii CPle GOrc
– var. ***wilsonii*** CBlo CChu CPMA CSam EBar EBre EHic MBlu MPla MUlv SBid SSpi SSta WWat
§ ***korolkowii*** CGre WWat
¶ × ***macrantha*** GOrc
– 'The Bride' ♀ Widely available
racemosa CGre CPMA EHal ISea LHop MBal MGos NNor SHBN SPer WHCG WWat
serratifolia 'Snow White' CPMA

FABIANA (Solanaceae)
imbricata CBot CLan CPle EHic EMil GQui MBar SAga SBra SPer SSpi SSta WAbe
– 'Prostrata' CBlo CPle EHic EPfP GCal NNrd SBid SDry SSpi WWat WWin
– f. ***violacea*** ♀ CB&S CFee CGre CPle CTri EMil EPla EWes GQui MBar SAga SBid SIng SPan SPer SSta WKif

FAGOPYRUM (Polygonaceae)
cymosum See ***F. dibotrys***
§ ***dibotrys*** EBee ELan EPPr NSti

FAGUS † (Fagaceae)
crenata CMCN WNor
engleriana CMCN
grandifolia CMCN
japonica CMCN
lucida CMCN
orientalis CMCN GAri WCoo
sylvatica ♀ CB&S CDoC CDul CKin CLnd CPer ELan ENot GRei IOrc ISea LBuc LHyr LPan MAsh MBar MBri MGos NBee NWea SHBN SPer WDin WMou WNor WOrn WStI
§ – 'Albomarginata' CMCN IOrc MBlu
– 'Albovariegata' See ***F. sylvatica* 'Albomarginata'**
– 'Ansorgei' CDul CEnd CMCN CTho MBlu MBri

N– Atropurpurea Group	CB&S CDoC CDul CKin EBre ELan EMil ENot GAri GRei IOrc LBuc LHyr MAsh MBal MBar MBri MGos MWat NBee NHol NWea SHBN SPer WDin WFar WMou WOrn WStI
¶– – 'Swat Magret'	SMad
– 'Aurea Pendula'	CEnd CMCN MBlu SMad
– 'Birr Zebra'	CEnd
– 'Black Swan'	CBlo CDul CEnd CMCN MBlu MBri SMad WGer
– 'Bornyensis'	CMCN
– 'Cochleata'	CMCN
– 'Cockleshell'	CMCN CTho
– 'Cristata'	CMCN GAri MBlu
§ – 'Dawyck' ♕	CB&S CDoC CLnd CMCN COtt CTho EBre ELan EMil ENot IHos IOrc ISea LHyr MAsh MBal MBar MWat NWea SPer WDin WOrn
– 'Dawyck Gold' ♕	CAbP CDoC CDul CEnd CMCN COtt CSte CTho EBee IOrc LPan MAsh MBar MBlu MBri SMad SSpi WOrn
– 'Dawyck Purple' ♕	CAbP CDoC CDul CEnd CMCN COtt CTho CTri IOrc LPan MAsh MBar MBlu MBri MGos SMad SPer SSpi WOrn
– 'Fastigiata'	See ***F. sylvatica* 'Dawyck'**
¶– 'Felderbach'	MBlu
* – 'Franken'	MBlu SMad
– 'Frisio'	CEnd CMCN
¶– 'Grandidentata'	CMCN
¶– 'Greenwood'	MBlu
– var. ***heterophylla***	CBlo CLnd CTho GAri ISea NWea SHhN WOrn
– – 'Aspleniifolia' ♕	CBlo CDoC CDul CEnd CMCN COtt CPMA CSte EBee ELan EMil ENot EPfP IOrc LPan MAsh MBal MBar MBri SPer WDin WMou WNor
– – f. ***laciniata***	CMCN MBlu
– 'Horizontalis'	CMCN COtt
– 'Luteovariegata'	CDoC CEnd CMCN
– 'Mercedes'	CDul CMCN MBlu
– 'Miltonensis'	CMCN
N– 'Pendula' ♕	CB&S CDoC CDul CEnd CLnd CMCN CTho ELan ENot GRei IOrc ISea MAsh MBal MBar NWea SMad SPer WDin WGwG WMou WOrn WPyg WStI
– 'Prince George of Crete'	CEnd CMCN CTho
– 'Purple Fountain' ♕	CDoC CEnd CMCN COtt ELan EMil IOrc LPan MAsh MBar MBlu MBri MGos MUlv NBee SMad SPer WPyg WWeb
– Purple-leaved Group	See ***F. sylvatica* Atropurpurea Group**
– 'Purpurea Nana'	CMCN
– 'Purpurea Pendula'	CEnd CMCN CSte CTho ELan ENot GRei IOrc LPan MAsh MBal MBar MBlu MGos MWat NBee NWea SPer WDin WPyg WStI
§ – 'Purpurea Tricolor'	CDoC CEnd CMCN IOrc LPan MBar MGos NBee SHBN SMer SPer WDin WPyg
– 'Quercifolia'	CMCN
– 'Quercina'	CMCN
– 'Red Obelisk'	CDul CMCN CSte MBlu
– 'Remillyensis'	CMCN
– 'Riversii' ♕	CB&S CDoC CDul CEnd CLnd CMCN CTho ELan EMil ENot IOrc LPan MAsh MBal MBri MWat NWea SHBN SMer SPer SSta WDin WOrn WStI
– 'Rohan Gold'	CDul CEnd CMCN EBee EMil MBlu MBri
– 'Rohan Obelisk'	CEnd EBee MBlu
I – 'Rohan Pyramidalis'	CEnd CMCN
– 'Rohan Trompenburg'	CMCN MBlu
– 'Rohanii'	CAbP CB&S CDoC CDul CEnd CLnd CMCN COtt CTho ELan EMil IHos IOrc LPan MBal MBlu MWat NBee SHBN SPer SSpi WDin
– 'Roseomarginata'	See ***F. sylvatica* 'Purpurea Tricolor'**
– 'Rotundifolia'	CDoC CTho NWea SPer
– 'Silver Wood'	CMCN MBri
– 'Spaethiana'	CMCN MBri
– 'Striata'	CMCN
– 'Tortuosa Purpurea'	CMCN CTho MBlu
– 'Tricolor' (v)	CB&S CDul CLnd COtt EBee ELan MAsh MBal MUlv WDin
– 'Tricolor' hort.	See ***F. sylvatica* 'Purpurea Tricolor'**
– 'Viridivariegata'	CMCN
– 'Zlatia'	CB&S CDoC CLnd CMCN COtt CTho ELan ENot IOrc MAsh MBal MBar MBri MGos NBee SHBN SPer WDin WOrn WStI

FALLOPIA (Polygonaceae)

aubertii	See ***F. baldschuanica***
§ ***baldschuanica*** ♕	CChe CMac CRHN CShe EBre ELan ENot GRei IHos ISea LBuc MBar MGos MPla MRav MWat NBee NEgg NFla NRoo SBra SHBN SPer WFar WHar WWeb
§ ***japonica***	CRow ELan
§ – var. ***compacta***	CDoC CRow EPla MFir NPri SAxl SMrm
* – – 'Midas'	IBlr
– – 'Variegata'	CRow EPla IBlr SMad
– 'Spectabilis' (v)	CRow ELan WCot
§ ***multiflora***	EGol MSal
¶– var. ***hypoleuca*** B&SWJ 120	WCru
sachalinensis	CRow ELan EMon

FALLUGIA (Rosaceae)

See Plant Deletions

FARFUGIUM (Asteraceae)

§ ***japonicum***	CHEx MTho
– 'Argenteum' (v)	CFir CHEx CRDP WSan
* – 'Aureomaculatum' (v)	CAbb CBrP CB&S CFir CHEx CHan CSev EGar EHoe EOas LHil MTho SAxl SLod SMad SWat WCot WHal WHer WHil WSan
– 'Crispatum'	WCot
tussilagineum	See ***F. japonicum***

FARGESIA (Poaceae - Bambusoideae)

dracocephala	EPla SBam SDry WJun
fungosa	ISta WJun

§ ***murieliae*** 🏆	CHEx EBre EFul EHoe EJap ELan ENot EPla LNet LPan MBar MBri MGos NBee SBam SDry SMer SPer SRms WHow WJun
* ***murieliae dana***	WJun
§ ***murieliae*** 'Leda' (v)	EPla SDry
– 'Simba'	CDoC CEnd EBee EBre EPla ESiP MAsh MGos WCru WJun WLRN
§ ***nitida*** 🏆	CHEx CShe EBre EFol EFul EHoe EJap ENot EOas EPla ESiP ETPC IOrc LPan MBri MGos MUlv NBee SBam SDry SHig SPer SSoC WHow WJun
– 'Eisenach'	CDoC WCru
– 'Nymphenburg'	CPMA EPla ISta
robusta	EFul EPla ISta SBam SDry WJun
spathacea hort.	See ***F. murieliae***
utilis	EPla ISta SBam SDry WJun

FARSETIA (Commelinaceae)

clypeata	See ***Fibigia clypeata***

FASCICULARIA (Bromeliaceae)

andina	See ***F. bicolor***
§ ***bicolor***	CFil CGre CHEx CWGN EOas GCal IBlr ICrw LHil LHop MTho SArc SLMG SSpi SSta WAbe WCot WEas
kirchhoffiana	SLMG
pitcairniifolia	CFil CFir CGre CHEx EBak EWes GGar IBlr MFir SArc SLMG WCot

× FATSHEDERA (Araliaceae)

lizei 🏆	CB&S CBot CDoC CHEx CWLN EPla GOrc GQui IBlr MAll MBal MBri NRog SArc SBid SBra SDix SDry SMac SPer SPla SSoC WDin WGwG WStI WWat
§ – 'Annemieke' (v) 🏆	CBot CDec CSWP IBlr MBri SMac SMad
§ – 'Aurea' (v)	EPfP LRHS SBra SDry SEND
– 'Aureopicta'	See **× *F. lizei* 'Aurea'**
– 'Lemon and Lime'	See **× *F. lizei* 'Annemieke'**
– 'Maculata'	See **× *F. lizei* 'Annemieke'**
– 'Pia'	CSWP MBri
– 'Variegata' 🏆	CB&S CDoC CHEx CMHG CWLN IBlr LRHS MBal MBri SBid SBra SDry SEND SMer SPla WFar WWat

FATSIA (Araliaceae)

§ ***japonica*** 🏆	Widely available
– 'Variegata' 🏆	CB&S CBot MBri MGos MUlv NPal SArc SEND SHBN
papyrifera	See ***Tetrapanax papyrifer***

FAUCARIA (Aizoaceae)

tigrina	MBri

FAURIA See NEPHROPHYLLIDIUM

FEIJOA See ACCA

FELICIA (Asteraceae)

§ ***amelloides***	CCan CLTr EGar ERea ESis SChu SHel SRms
– 'Astrid Thomas'	CBrk CInt CSpe LHil MRav
– 'Read's Blue'	CCan CSev CSpe GMac LHil LHop LIck NPla
– 'Read's White'	CBrk CCan EOrc ERav ERea ESis GMac LHil LIck MSte
§ – 'Santa Anita' 🏆	CBrk CCan CSev CSpe CTri EBar ECtt EOrc ERea LHil LHop LIck NPer SCro SVen WEas
– 'Santa Anita' large flowered	LHil
§ – variegated	CBar CBot CBrk CCan CSev EBar ECtt ELan ERav ERea ESis IBlr LHil LHop LIck MBri MSte NPer SVen WEas WRus
amethystina	See ***F.* 'Snowmass'**
§ ***amoena***	CBrk CHad CTri ELan GBri LHil MHar SChu SRms WWin
– 'Variegata'	CTri EOrc SChu
bergeriana	WOMN
capensis	See ***F. amelloides***
– 'Variegata'	See ***F. amelloides* variegated**
coelestis	See ***F. amelloides***
drakensbergensis	NTow
¶ ***filifolia***	CTrC
natalensis	See ***F. rosulata***
pappei	See ***F. amoena***
§ ***petiolata***	CBrk CHan ECha EMan EMon ERea IBlr LHil LIck NSti WCot WHil WHow WOMN WWin
§ ***rosulata***	EHyt ELan EMan EMon GAri LGan LHop MRPP MTho NBro NGre NMen NNrd NRoo NTow SSmi WHil WWin
§ 'Snowmass'	CBot
uliginosa	CFee CHan EWes GGar GTou LBee MDHE MTho NTow SAlw WFar WHil

FERRARIA (Iridaceae)

§ ***crispa***	CMon LBow
uncinata	CMon
undulata	See ***F. crispa***

FERREYRANTHUS (Asteraceae)

excelsus	CB&S CPle

FERULA (Apiaceae)

assa-foetida	CArn MSal
* 'Cedric Morris'	ECha
chiliantha	See ***F. communis* subsp. *glauca***
§ ***communis***	CArc CArn CHad CRDP ECGP ECha EGoo EPla LGre LHol SDix SMad SMrm WCot WRHF
– 'Gigantea'	See ***F. communis***
§ – subsp. ***glauca***	SIgm
'Giant Bronze'	See ***Foeniculum vulgare* 'Giant Bronze'**
tingitana	SIgm

FESTUCA (Poaceae)

alpina	ETPC
amethystina	CCuc CDoC EBee EBre EFol EHoe EMon EPPr EPla EPot ESOG ETPC GBin GBri MBri MBro NHol NPla NSti WCra WPer
– 'Aprilgrün'	EHoe EPPr ETPC
– 'Bronzeglanz'	ETPC
ampla	ETPC
arundinacea	CKin

californica	ETPC
curvula subsp. ***crassifolia***	EBee EPPr EPla ESOG ETPC
dalmatica	ETPC
dumetorum	ETPC
elatior 'Demeter'	ETPC
elegans	EPPr ETPC
erecta	EHoe EPPr ESOG
eskia	CCuc CSWP EBee EBre EHoe EPGN EPPr EPla ESOG ETPC GAri GBin GFre NEgg NHol WCot WPbr WPer
extremiorientalis	ETPC
filiformis	EMon EPPr ETPC LRHS
§ ***gautieri***	CSte ECED ELan EPPr ESOG ESiP ETPC GBin LHil MBar NOrc WFoF
– 'Pic Carlit'	EMon ETPC
gigantea	CKin ETPC GBin
glacialis	EHoe ETPC MBal MDHE NHol
– 'Czakor'	ETPC
glauca	CFee CInt CKel CMea EBar EBre EGol ELan ENot EOrc ESOG ESiP ETPC GCHN LGro MBal MBar NBee NBro NEgg NSti SHFr SHel SPer SSmi WEas WHil WHoo WWat WWin
– 'Azurit'	EFou EMon EPPr EPla ESOG ETPC EWes LRHS
§ – 'Blaufuchs' 🏆	CDoC CLTr CM&M CSam CWLN CWSG EBee EBre ECot EHoe EPPr EPla EPot ESOG ETPC EWes GBin GFre IOrc LHop MBri MSte NHol SHBN WFox WWat
§ – 'Blauglut'	EBee EBre ECED EGar EHoe EPGN EPla ESOG GAri NFla NHar NHol NMir NRoo WGer WLRN
◆ – Blue Fox	See ***F. glauca* 'Blaufuchs'**
◆ – Blue Glow	See ***F. glauca* 'Blauglut'**
– 'Elijah Blue'	Widely available
– 'Golden Toupee'	Widely available
– 'Harz'	CCuc EBre EGar EHoe EMil EPla ESOG ETPC IBlr MBar
§ – 'Meerblau'	CCuc
* – ***minima***	CVer EFol ESOG ESis NGre NHol
–'Pallens'	See ***F. longifolia***
◆ – Sea Blue	See ***F. glauca* 'Meerblau'**
◆ – Sea Urchin	See ***F. glauca* 'Seeigel'**
§ – 'Seeigel'	CCuc EBee EBre EGar EGle EGoo EHoe EPPr EPla ESOG ETPC GFre LHil MAvo MBel MBri NPro WLeb WPbr
– 'Seven Seas'	See ***F. valesiaca* 'Silbersee'**
heterophylla	ETPC
juncifolia	ETPC
§ ***longifolia***	CKin ESOG ETPC
mairei	CCuc CLTr EHoe EMon EPPr ESOG ETPC IBlr
novae-zelandiae	ETPC GBin
ovina	CSWP EHoe SIng SPla WFox WPer
– subsp. ***coxii***	EHoe EPPr ETPC
– 'Söhrewald'	EBee EPPr ESOG
paniculata	EHoe EMon EPla ESOG ETPC GFre
pulchella	ETPC

punctoria	CCuc CMea EBee ECha EFol EHoe EPPr EPla ESOG ETPC EWes NFai NGre NHar SAlw SBla SSmi
rubra 'Jughandles'	SAsh
– var. ***viridis***	NHol SIng
sclerophylla	ETPC
scoparia	See ***F. gautieri***
sp. B&SWJ 1555	NGre
tenuifolia	CKin ETPC
valesiaca var. ***glaucantha***	EPPr ESOG ETPC NHol
§ – 'Silbersee'	CCuc CInt EBre ECha EFol EFou EHoe EPPr EPla ESOG ETPC IBlr MBar MBri MSte NCat NHol SIng SRms WFar
◆ – Silver Sea	See ***F. valesiaca* 'Silbersee'**
vivipara	CCuc CInt EGoo EHoe EMon EPPr ESOG NHol
* 'Willow Green'	CBlo

FIBIGIA (Brassicaceae)

§ ***clypeata***	NBro SMrm WEas WPer

FICUS † (Moraceae)

* ***alii***	CHal
australis hort.	See ***F. rubiginosa* 'Australis'**
benghalensis	MBri
benjamina 🏆	CHal EBre MBri SRms
– 'Exotica'	MBri
– 'Golden King'	MBri
– var. ***nuda***	MBri
– 'Starlight' (v)	MBri
carica (F)	GAri LPan MBri
– 'Adam' (F)	ERea
– 'Alma' (F)	ERea
– 'Angélique' (F)	ERea
– 'Beall' (F)	ERea
– 'Bellone' (F)	ERea
– 'Bifère' (F)	ERea
– 'Black Ischia' (F)	ERea
– 'Black Mission' (F)	ERea
– 'Boule d'Or' (F)	ERea
– 'Bourjassotte Grise' (F)	ERea
– 'Brown Turkey' (F) 🏆	Widely available
– 'Brunswick' (F)	CDoC CGre ERea ESim GBon GTwe WCot
– 'Castle Kennedy' (F)	ERea
– 'Col de Dame' (F)	ERea
– 'Conandria' (F)	ERea
– 'Figue d'Or' (F)	ERea
– 'Goutte d'Or' (F)	ERea
– 'Grise de Saint Jean' (F)	ERea
– 'Grise Ronde' (F)	ERea
– 'Grosse Grise' (F)	ERea
– 'Kaape Bruin' (F)	ERea
– 'Kadota' (F)	ERea
– 'Lisa' (F)	ERea
– 'Longue d'Août' (F)	ERea
– 'Malcolm's Giant' (F)	ERea
– 'Malta' (F)	ERea
– 'Marseillaise' (F)	ERea ESim GTwe SDea
– 'Negro Largo' (F)	ERea
◆ – 'Noir de Provence'	See ***F. carica* 'Reculver'**
– 'Osborn's Prolific' (F)	ERea
– 'Panachée' (F)	ERea
– 'Pastilière' (F)	ERea
– 'Petite Grise' (F)	ERea
– 'Pied de Boeuf' (F)	ERea
– 'Pittaluse' (F)	ERea
– 'Précoce Ronde de Bordeaux' (F)	ERea
§ – 'Reculver' (F)	ERea

- – 'Rouge de Bordeaux' (F) ERea
- – 'Saint Johns' (F) ERea
- – 'San Pedro Miro' (F) ERea
- – 'Sollies Pont' (F) ERea
- – 'Sugar 12' (F) ERea
- – 'Sultane' (F) ERea
- – 'Tena' (F) ERea
- – 'Verte d'Argenteuil' (F) ERea
- – 'Violette Dauphine' (F) ERea
- – 'Violette de Sollies' (F) ERea
- – 'Violette Sepor' (F) ERea
- – 'White Genoa' See ***F. carica* 'White Marseilles'**
- – 'White Ischia' (F) ERea
- § – 'White Marseilles' (F) ERea
- ***cyathistipula*** MBri
- ***deltoidea*** var. ***diversifolia*** MBri
- ¶ ***elastica*** SLMG
- – 'Robusta' MBri
- ***foveolata*** Wallich See ***F. sarmentosa***
- ***lyrata*** ♀ MBri
- ***microcarpa*** STre
- – 'Hawaii' (v) CHal MBri
- ***natalensis*** subsp. ***leprieurii*** 'Westland' MBri
- ***pumila*** ♀ CB&S CHEx CHal EBak MBri SArc
- – 'Minima' CFee MHig
- – 'Sonny' (v) CHal MBri
- – 'Variegata' CHEx CHal MBri
- ***radicans*** See ***F. sagittata***
- § ***rubiginosa*** 'Australis' MBri
- § ***sagittata*** 'Variegata' MBri
- § ***sarmentosa*** MBri
- ***triangularis*** See ***F. natalensis* subsp. *leprieurii***

FILIPENDULA (Rosaceae)

- ***alnifolia*** 'Variegata' See ***F. ulmaria* 'Variegata'**
- ***camtschatica*** CRow CWGN ECoo EFol ELan NDea NMir WCot
- ***camtschatica rosea*** IBlr LHop NBrk
- ***digitata*** 'Nana' See ***F. palmata* 'Nana'**
- ***hexapetala*** See ***F. vulgaris***
- – 'Flore Pleno' See ***F. vulgaris* 'Multiplex'**
- 'Kahome' CHan CRow EFol EGol EOrc GMaP LFis MBro NHol NMir NOrc NRoo NSti NTow SMrm SPer WCot WCra WFar WRus
- ***kamtschatica*** See ***F. camtschatica***
- ***kiraishiensis*** B&SWJ 1571 WCru
- ***palmata*** CWGN ECha EFou MCli NFla WByw
- – 'Alba' GCal
- – 'Digitata Nana' See ***F. palmata* 'Nana'**
- § – 'Elegantissima' CRow EBee ECha GCal GGar MTol SAsh
- § – 'Nana' CRow ECha ECro GCal MBal MBro MCli SAsh WChe WHoo WPyg
- ***palmata purpurea*** See ***F. purpurea***
- ***palmata*** 'Rosea' CGle IBlr NBir NCat WCHb
- – 'Rubra' CBlo
- ***palmata rufinervis*** B&SWJ 941 WCru
- § ***purpurea*** ♀ CDoC CRow CWGN ECha EFou EGar GGar LGan MBel MTis MUlv NFla SSoC WCru WEas
- – f. ***albiflora*** CBre EGol GAbr MUlv NCat WNdy
- – 'Elegans' NFai WHil
- * 'Queen of the Fairies' CBlo
- ***rubra*** CHan CRow CWGN EAst ECED LSyl NWoo WCra
- § – 'Venusta' ♀ CArc CBre CGle CRDP CRow CSev EBre ECha ECoo EFol EFou EGol ELan EOrc GAbr GCal LFis LGan MUlv MWat NSti NTay SChu SHig SMrm SPer WCot WHal WRus WWye
- – 'Venusta Magnifica' See ***F. rubra* 'Venusta'**
- § ***ulmaria*** CArn CKin CWGN ECWi ECoo EHon ELau EPla EWFC GMaP GPoy LHol MChe MGam MGra MHew MTho MTol NHol NLan NMir SIde SWat WCla WOak WPer WShi WWye
- – 'Aurea' Widely available
- – 'Flore Pleno' CArc CBre CRDP CRow CWGN EAst EBre EHon MCli NHol NSti SHig SPer SWat WCot WLRN WNdy
- – 'Rosea' IBlr SHig SPer
- § – 'Variegata' CBre CFee CRDP CRow CWGN ECha EFol EGol EHoe ELan EOrc EPla LHol LHop MTho MUlv NFla NHar NOak NRoo NSti SPer WAbe WByw WEas WHal WPbr WRus WWye
- § ***vulgaris*** CArn CFee CKin CWGN EAst ECWi ECtt EWFC LHol LPBA MChe MGra MHew MSal MTol NBro NLan NMir NOrc NPri SIde WByw WChe WCla WPer WWye
- – 'Grandiflora' EOrc NCat WCot
- § – 'Multiplex' CDoC CGle CRow ECha EGol ELan EOrc GAbr LGan LHop MBal MCLN MTho MUlv NDea NHol NSti SEas SPer WEas WHal WRus WWat
- – 'Plena' See ***F. vulgaris* 'Multiplex'**

FINGERHUTHIA (Poaceae)

- ***sesleriiformis*** S&SH 1 CHan ETPC

FIRMIANA (Sterculiaceae)

- ***simplex*** CFil CHEx LPan

FITTONIA (Acanthaceae)

See Plant Deletions

FITZROYA (Cupressaceae)

- ***cupressoides*** CMac GAri IOrc LCon MBal MBar SIng

FOENICULUM (Apiaceae)

- ***vulgare*** CArn CHad ECWi ECha EEls ELan GBar GPoy LHol MChe MGra MHew MSal NMir NRoo SIde WByw WCer WOak WPer WWye
- – 'Bronze' See ***F. vulgare* 'Purpureum'**
- – var. ***dulce*** CSev SIde
- § – 'Giant Bronze' CGle ELan SPer WHen
- § – 'Purpureum' Widely available
- – 'Smokey' CWit EFou MRav WOve

FOKIENIA (Cupressaceae)

- ***hodginsii*** LCon

FONTANESIA (Oleaceae)
phillyreoides WDin

FONTINALIS (Sphagnaceae; moss)
antipyretica SAWi

FORESTIERA (Oleaceae)
neomexicana CB&S

FORSYTHIA (Oleaceae)
'Arnold Dwarf' CBlo EHal NHol SEas SRms
N 'Beatrix Farrand' CTri EBee ECtt MGos MPla MWat NHol NNor SEas SPer SRms WLRN
§ Boucle d'Or = 'Courtacour' COtt ENot
'Courtasol' See *F.* **Marée d'Or = 'Courtasol'**
§ Marée d'Or = 'Courtasol' COtt EBee ENot MBri MGos SPer WLRN
'Fiesta' (v) CPMA CPle CSam EAst EBre EFol ELan IOrc LHop MBar MBel MBlu MBri MHlr MPla NHol NRoo SHBN SLod SPer SSta WCot WHer WPat
giraldiana CPle SRms WBod
'Gold Cluster' See *F.* **Melée d'Or**
'Gold Splash' EBee
'Gold Tide' See *F.* **Marée d'Or = 'Courtasol'**
'Golden Curls' See *F.* **Boucle d'Or = 'Courtacour'**
'Golden Nugget' CBlo EBre EHic ELan ESis IOrc MAsh MWat NRoo SHBN SPer WWeb
'Golden Times' (v) CDec CSte EFol EHic EHoe EPla EWes IOrc MBri MGos NPro SApp SCoo SEas SMad WCot WPat
x *intermedia* 'Arnold Giant' CBlo CShe MBlu WBod
– 'Densiflora' NWea
– 'Karl Sax' CChe NWea SBid WLRN
* – 'Liliane' EMil
– 'Lynwood' ♀ CB&S CChe CShe ELan ENot GRei ISea MBal MBar MBri MGos NBee NFla NHol NNor NRoo NWea SDix SPer SReu SSta WBod WDin WFar WRTC WWeb
– 'Lynwood' LA '79 CDec EHic MLan MUlv SPla
– 'Minigold' ECtt MAsh MGos MWat NHol SEas SHBN SRms WPat WPyg WRHF WRTC WStI WWeb
– 'Spectabilis' CWLN EBee ELan IOrc LBuc MBar NBee NWea SHBN SPer WBod WDin WGwG WRHF WRTC
– 'Spectabilis Variegated' CPle CWan EBar EFol EHic EPla MPla NPro WCot WPyg WWeb
– 'Spring Glory' EBee ECtt ENot MBri MRav
– 'Variegata' CBlo MUlv NHol NWea SPer SSta
– Week-End CBar CBlo ENot GAri MBri MGos
Marée d'Or See *F.* **Marée d'Or = 'Courtasol'**
§ Melée d'Or EBee ENot SHhN SPer
* 'Melissa' NWea WDin
'Northern Gold' CB&S EPfP
ovata EPla
– forms MUlv
– 'Tetragold' CB&S CBlo GOrc MBal MBar NWea SHBN
'Paulina' CBlo ESis GAri
* *pumila* EWes
* 'Spring Beauty' EHal MAsh
suspensa ♀ CB&S CShe CTri ENot EOHP IOrc MBel MWat NWea SEas SHBN SPer WStI
– f. *atrocaulis* CPle GAri NWea
– 'Cynthia Barber' (v) CNat
– 'Decipiens' WBod
– var. *fortunei* WGwG
– 'Nymans' MBri MUlv NSti SBid SBra
§ – 'Taff's Arnold' (v) CBlo CMil CPMA WBcn
– 'Variegata' See ***F. suspensa* 'Taff's Arnold'**
'Tremonia' EHal MBal MGos
viridissima CBlo NNor NWea
– 'Bronxensis' ELan EPar EPot ESis MHig MPla NBir NHol NNrd NWea SMad WOMN WPat WPyg WRTC
– var. *koreana* EPla
* – – 'Variegata' CPMA SBid
– 'Weber's Bronx' MBar

FORTUNEARIA (Hamamelidaceae)
See Plant Deletions

FORTUNELLA (Rutaceae)
x *crassifolia* (F) SCit
– 'Meiwa' (F) ERea
'Fukushu' ECon ERea SCit
hindsii (F) SCit
§ *japonica* (F) LPan SCit
§ *margarita* (F) CGOG LPan MBri SCit
– 'Nagami' (F) ECon ERea

FOTHERGILLA (Hamamelidaceae)
gardenii CPMA EBee EBre ELan IOrc MBlu MBri SPer SSpi WDin WWat
– 'Blue Mist' CAbP CDoC CPMA CSam CSte EBee ELan MAsh MBri NHed SMad SPer SPla SReu SSpi SSta WWat
'Huntsman' CAbP CKni COtt
major ♀ CB&S CPMA EBre ECtt EHoe ELan MAsh MBal MBri MGos MHlr MUlv NBee NFla NHol SChu SHBN SPer SReu SSpi WDin WHar WNor WPat WStI WWat
– Monticola Group CChu CPMA CSam ELan ENot IHos MBal MBar MBri MPla NHed SChu SHBN SPer SSpi SSta WBod WHar

FRAGARIA † (Rosaceae)
alpina See ***F. vesca* 'Semperflorens'**
– 'Alba' See ***F. vesca* 'Semperflorens Alba'**
x *ananassa* 'Aromel' (F) ♀ CWSG GTwe MBri SDea WWeb
– Bogota™ (F) GTwe LRHS NBee
* – 'Bolero' EMui GTwe
– 'Bounty' (F) GTwe
– 'Calypso' (F) CSut EMui GTwe WLRN
– 'Cambridge Favourite' (F) ♀ CMac CTri CWSG EMui GRei GTwe MBri MMor NDal NRog SDea WWeb

– 'Cambridge Late Pine' (F)	CWSG EMui GTwe
– 'Cambridge Vigour' (F)	GTwe MMor NBee NRog SDea
– Elsanta® (F)	CDoC CTri CWSG EMui GRei GTwe NDal SDea
– Elvira® (F)	CSut EMui
* – 'Emily'	EMui GTwe
– 'Evita' (F)	EMui
– 'Fraise des Bois'	See *F. vesca*
– 'Gorella' (F)	NDal SDea WWeb
– 'Hapil' (F)	EMui GTwe LRHS NDal WLRN
– 'Honeoye' (F) ♀	EMui GTwe LRHS WLRN
– Korona® (F)	CSut
– 'Kouril' (F)	LRHS
* – 'Laura'	EMui GTwe
– Marastil (F)	EMui
– 'Maxim' (F)	EMui
– 'Melody' (F)	GTwe
– 'Ostara' (F)	GTwe
– 'Pandora' (F)	GTwe WWeb
– 'Pegasus' (F)	EMui GTwe LRHS
– Rapella® (F)	GTwe NDal
– 'Redgauntlet' (F)	GTwe NRog SDea
– 'Rhapsody' (F)	CSut EMui GTwe
– 'Royal Sovereign' (F)	CMac EMui GTwe SDea
¶ – 'Serenata' (F)	MHlr
– 'Tamella' (F)	EMui GRei GTwe NDal
– 'Totem' (F)	GTwe
§ – 'Variegata' (F)	CGle CHid CLTr CMea CSev CShe ECro EFol ELan EOrc EPla MAsh MCCP MHar MRav NEgg NHol NNrd NRoo NSti NTay SIng SPer WBea WOak WRha WRus WWin
'Baron Solemacher' (F)	EJud WHer
'Bowles' Double'	See *F. vesca* **'Multiplex'**
chiloensis (F)	EMon
– 'Chaval'	CHid ECha EGoo EMon EPPr MRav NChi NWoo
N – 'Variegata'	GCal LBuc WByw WEas
– x ***virginiana***	CArn
daltoniana	NHol SIng
– CC&McK 390	LKoh
– CC&McK 559	GCHN
indica	See ***Duchesnea indica***
'Pink Panda' (F)	CM&M CTri EBee EBre ECtt MArl MAsh MBri MOne NEgg NHol NRoo SHFr SIng SPer WByw WEas WElm WMaN
'Red Ruby'	EBre NRoo SPer
* 'Ruby Surprise'	LRHS
'Variegata'	See *F.* x *ananassa* **'Variegata'**
§ ***vesca*** (F)	CArn CKin ECWi ECoo ELau EWFC GPoy LHol MGam MHew NMir SIde WBea WCla WJek WOak WPer WShi WWye
– 'Alexandra' (F)	CArn GAbr MChe NRog SIde WCHb
– 'Flore Pleno'	See *F. vesca* **'Multiplex'**
– 'Fructu Albo' (F)	CRow CWan WPer
– Mara des Bois (F)	EMui GTwe
– 'Monophylla' (F)	CRow EJud EMon NHol SIde WHer
§ – 'Multiplex'	CGle CJew CRow CSev EMon EMou EOrc ERav GAbr MInt NHex NHol NSti SSvw WByw WCHb WHer WOak
§ – 'Muricata'	CFee CHid CLTr CPou CRow EMon GAbr NBrk NChi NSti WAlt WCer WHer
* – 'Pineapple Crush'	WHer
– 'Plymouth Strawberry'	See *F. vesca* **'Muricata'**
– 'Rügen' (F)	CHal WGwy WHoo WPyg
§ – 'Semperflorens' (F)	CLTr CWan EBar ILis MGra NBrk WAlt WOak
§ – 'Semperflorens Alba' (F)	WOMN
N – 'Variegata'	CHid EAst EHoe EPar MCLN MSCN NMir WPer WSel

FRANCOA (Saxifragaceae)

appendiculata	CChr CGre ETen MEas WHer
¶ Ballyrogan strain	IBlr
'Confetti'	WCot
* dwarf purple	GCal
I 'Purple Spike'	See ***F. sonchifolia* Rogerson's form**
§ ***ramosa***	CGle CHan CSpe CTrC CTri GAbr GBuc IBlr LFis MHlr MNrw MTol NBro NRog NRoo NSti SHel WElm WFar
ramosa alba	See ***F. ramosa***
§ ***sonchifolia***	CElw CFee CGle CGre CMHG CNic CRDP CSam EBar GCal IBlr MBal MFir MUlv NBro NFai NHol NPer SCro SLMG SPer WEas WHow WMer WPer WWin
– 'Alba'	CRDP CSpe SUsu WCot
§ – Rogerson's form	CGle CNic CSpe ECha EGar GBuc IBlr MAvo SDix SOkh WSan

FRANKENIA (Frankeniaceae)

laevis	CShe CTri GGar NVic SRms WWin WWoo WWye
thymifolia	CHal CInt CMHG ELan EPar EPot ESis GCHN MBar MPla MRav MWat NMen NNrd NRoo SAga SAlw SBod SChu SIng SSmi WFar WHoo WPer WPyg WWin

FRANKLINIA (Theaceae)

alatamaha	SSpi

FRASERA (Gentianaceae)

See Plant Deletions

FRAXINUS † (Oleaceae)

americana	CDul CMCN CTho WLRN
– 'Autumn Purple'	CBlo CEnd CTho MAsh SSpi
¶ – 'Rose Hill'	CTho
§ ***angustifolia***	CMCN CTho
– 'Elegantissima'	CTho
– 'Flame'	See ***F. angustifolia* 'Raywood'**
– var. ***lentiscifolia***	CTho
§ – 'Monophylla'	CLnd CTho
§ – 'Raywood' ♀	CB&S CDoC CDul CEnd CLnd CSte CTho ELan ENot IOrc MAsh MBlu MGos NWea SMad SPer WDin WJas WMou WOrn
* – 'Variegata'	CBot CPMA
chinensis	CDul CLnd CMCN CTho
– subsp. ***rhyncophylla***	WMou
elonza	CTho
excelsior ♀	CB&S CDoC CDul CKin CLnd CPer ENot GRei LBuc LHyr LPan MBar MGos MWat NBee NWea SHBN SPer WDin WMou WOrn WStI
– 'Allgold'	CEnd

– 'Aurea Pendula'	CMCN LMer
– 'Crispa'	EMon WMou
– f. ***diversifolia***	CDul CLnd CTho EMon WMou
– 'Diversifolia Pendula'	See ***F. excelsior* 'Heterophylla Pendula'**
– 'Geesink'	ENot IHos SLPl
§ – 'Heterophylla Pendula'	GAri WMou
– 'Jaspidea' 🏆	CB&S CDoC CDul CEnd CLnd COtt CTho ENot GRei IOrc MBar MBlu MBri MGos MRav SHBN SPer SSpi SSta WDin WJas WMou WOrn WStI
¶ – 'Nana'	EMon
– 'Pendula' 🏆	CDoC CDul CEnd CLnd CTho EBre ELan ENot IOrc LPan MAsh MBlu MBri NBee NWea SHBN SPer WDin WJas WMou WOrn WStI
– 'Pendula Wentworthii'	WMou
– 'R.E. Davey'	CTho
– 'Stanway Gold'	EMon
– 'Stripey'	EMon
– 'Westhof's Glorie' 🏆	CDoC CLnd CSte ENot SHhN SLPl WJas WOrn
holotricha	CTho
mariesii	See ***F. sieboldiana***
nigra	CFil CMCN
– 'Fallgold'	CBlo
oregona	See ***F. latifolia***
ornus 🏆	CBot CLnd CTho ELan ENot EPfP IOrc MBri SPer WCoo WDin WFar WMou WWat
– 'Arie Peters'	WStI
oxycarpa	See ***F. angustifolia***
pennsylvanica	CMCN WWes
– 'Aucubifolia'	CTho WMou
– var. ***lanceolata***	See ***F. pennsylvanica*** var. ***subintegerrima***
¶ – 'Patmore'	CBlo
– 'Summit'	CTho
– 'Variegata'	CBlo CLnd CSte CTho MAsh WMou
¶ ***quadrangulata***	WDin
§ ***sieboldiana***	CFil CLnd CPMA CTho SSpi WCoo WMou
spaethiana	WMou
'Veltheimii'	See ***F. angustifolia* 'Monophylla'**
velutina	CBot CDul CMCN CSto CTho SLPl

FREESIA (Iridaceae)

alba Foster	See ***F. lactea***
'Diana'	LAma
¶ double mixed	ETub
elimensis	MSto
'Fantasy' (d)	LAma
hybrids	CSut NRog
§ ***lactea***	LAma NRog
'Romany' (d)	LAma
'White Swan'	LAma
xanthospila	LBow MSto

FREMONTODENDRON (Sterculiaceae)

'California Glory' 🏆	CB&S CBot CMHG CPMA CSam CTrC CTrw EBar EBre EHoe GQui LHop LHyd MBal MGos SAga SArc SBra SCog SDry SMad SPer SPla SReu SSoC SSta WHar WPat WSHC
californicum	CAbb CBar CChu CHEx ELan EMil IOrc MBlu MBri MGos NBee SHBN SOWG WAbe WBod WDin WNor WStI WWat WWin
¶ ***decumbens***	SSpi
mexicanum	CBot CChu CGre SAga
'Pacific Sunset'	CPMA ENot LHop LRHS MBri SBid SMad SMur SPer

FREYLINIA (Scrophulariaceae)

cestroides	See ***F. lanceolata***
§ ***lanceolata***	CB&S CPle CTre

FRITILLARIA † (Liliaceae)

acmopetala 🏆	CAvo CBro CMon CNic ECha ELan EPar EPot ERos ETub EWal ITim LAma MBal MHig MS&S MTho NMen NRog NWCA SWas WAbe WChr WDav
– subsp. ***wendelboi***	EPot LAma
§ ***affinis***	EHyt EPot EWal LAma MS&S MSto NHar SBid WDav
§ – var. ***gracilis***	LAma MSto SBid SPer WDav
– 'Limelight'	EPot ETub GCrs
– 'Sunray'	NHar
– 'Vancouver Island'	EPot
– 'Wayne Roderick'	EPot
alburyana	EPot
arabica	See ***F. persica***
armena	EHyt LAma MSto
◆ ***assyriaca***	See ***F. uva-vulpis***
atropurpurea	MSto
aurea	EPot LWoo NHar
biflora	EHyt LWoo MSto
– 'Martha Roderick'	CAvo CBro EBre EDAr EPot ETub EWal LAma SBid
§ ***bithynica***	EPot LAma MSto NMen WChr
brandegeei	EWal LAma WChr
bucharica	CAvo CGra EPot LWoo MFos WChr
camschatcensis	CAvo CBro CRDP ECha EFEx EHyt EPar EPot ETub LAma MS&S MSto MTho NHar NMen NRog WAbe WChr WDav
– black	MSto
¶ – f. ***flavescens***	EFEx
carduchorum	See ***F. minuta***
carica	CAvo EHyt EPot WChr
– subsp. ***serpenticola***	EPot
caucasica	LAma LWoo WChr
'Chatto'	ECha
citrina	See ***F. bithynica***
¶ ***conica***	GCrs NHar
crassifolia	EPot LAma
¶ – subsp. ***crassifolia***	CGra
§ – subsp. ***kurdica***	EPot GCrs WChr
davisii	CMea EHyt EPot LAma MRPP MSto NHar WChr
delphinensis	See ***F. tubiformis***
eastwoodiae	EPot ETub GCrs LAma
ehrhartii	EHyt MSto
elwesii	CAvo EHyt LRHS MSto WChr
¶ ***forbesii***	MSto
glauca	LAma WChr
– 'Goldilocks'	EPot ETub
graeca	EPot MSto MTho
– subsp. ***graeca***	MSto WChr
– subsp. ***ionica***	See ***F. graeca*** subsp. ***thessala***
§ – subsp. ***thessala***	EHyt LAma MSto MTho WChr
§ ***grayana***	EHyt MSto WChr

¶ – tall form	LWoo
¶ ***gussichiae***	MS&S MSto
hermonis subsp. ***amana***	CAvo EHyt EPot LAma NHar NMen SBid WChr
hispanica	See ***F. lusitanica***
imperialis	CAvo CB&S CHEx MBal MBri NRog
– 'Aureomarginata'	LAma LBow MBri NRog
– 'Aurora'	CAvo EBar EBre EMon EPar ETub LAma LBow LFis NCut NRog
– 'Crown upon Crown'	See ***F. imperialis*** **'Prolifera'**
¶ – 'Lutea'	EMon
– 'Lutea Maxima'	See ***F. imperialis*** **'Maxima Lutea'**
– 'Maxima'	See ***F. imperialis*** **'Rubra Maxima'**
§ – 'Maxima Lutea' 🏆	CBro CHEx EBee EBre ELan EPar ETub LAma LBow LFis NRog WHil
§ – 'Prolifera'	EPar LAma LBow NCat
– 'Rubra'	ELan EPar ETub LAma LBow NBir NCut NRog
§ – 'Rubra Maxima'	CBro EMon EPfP LAma MLLN SMad
– 'Sulpherino'	LRHS
– 'The Premier'	EPar LAma NCat
involucrata	CAvo CBro LAma MS&S MSto SWas WChr
ionica	See ***F. graeca*** subsp. ***thessala***
¶ ***japonica*** var. ***koidzumiana***	EFEx
karadaghensis	See ***F. crassifolia*** subsp. ***kurdica***
lanceolata	See ***F. affinis***
latakiensis	LAma
§ ***latifolia***	GCrs LAma WChr
– var. ***nobilis***	See ***F. latifolia***
liliacea	LAma
§ ***lusitanica***	GCrs LAma MS&S MSto WDav
– MS 440	CMon
lutea	See ***F. collina***
macrocarpa SB&L 258	CMon
meleagris 🏆	CArn CAvo CBro CMea ELan EPot ETub EWFC EWal LAma LBow MBal MBri MBro MHig MRPP MS&S NBir NGar NHar NMen NRog SChu WAbe WCla WHil WHoo WPat WShi
meleagris alba 🏆	CBro CMea ECtt ELan EPot ETub LAma LBow MBri MBro MHig MS&S NHar NRya SUsu WCru
meleagris 'Aphrodite'	CAvo EPot WChr WCot
– 'Jupiter'	LRHS WChr WOMN
– 'Mars'	LRHS WChr
§ ***messanensis***	CMon EHyt LAma MBal MS&S WChr
– subsp. ***gracilis***	EHyt MBal MS&S MSto
– subsp. ***messanensis***	CBro
michailovskyi 🏆	CAvo CBro ECtt ELan EPar EPot ETub EWal GBuc GCra LAma MBri MRPP MSto MTho NMen NNrd NRog SSoC WAbe WChr WCla WPat WPyg
micrantha	LAma
minima JCA 500.100	MSto
montana	LRHS MS&S
nigra hort.	See ***F. pyrenaica***
olivieri	GCrs MSto WChr
pallidiflora 🏆	CAvo CBro EMon EPar EPot ERos ETub EWal LAma LWoo MBal MFos MS&S MSto MTho NHar NNrd NSla SSpi WAbe WChr WCru WDav WOMN
§ ***persica***	CB&S CMea EBar EPar LAma MBri NPSI SBid SMad WCra WPen
– 'Adiyaman' 🏆	CAvo CBro CMil EBre ELan EMon ETub LBow NRog
– S&L 118	CMon
phaeanthera	See ***F. affinis*** var. ***gracilis***
pinardii	EPot
pluriflora	WChr
pontica	CAvo CBro CMea CMon EHyt EPar EPot ERos ETub EWal ITim LAma MBal MFos MS&S MTho NHar NSla SBid SBla SSpi SWas WChr WCru WDav WHil
pudica	EHyt LAma MS&S MSto MTho NHar WDav
* – 'Fragrant'	EPot
– 'Richard Britten'	EHyt
purdyi	CAvo EPot LWoo NMen SPer
§ ***pyrenaica*** 🏆	CAvo CBro CMon ECha EHyt LAma LWoo MBal MS&S NHar NMen NSla SChu
raddeana	LAma LWoo MSto WChr
¶ ***recurva***	LWoo
¶ ***rhodocanakis***	EHyt EPot
– JCA 502.600	MSto
roderickii	See ***F. grayana***
¶ ***roylei***	MS&S
rubra major	See ***F. imperialis*** **'Rubra Maxima'**
ruthenica	EHyt ERos MS&S NMen WChr
sewerzowii	LAma MSto WChr
sibthorpiana	CBro EPot LAma WChr
¶ ***spetsiotica***	EHyt
sphaciotica	See ***F. messanensis***
stenanthera	LAma MSto WChr
¶ ***striata***	EHyt
stribrnyi	WChr
tenella	See ***F. orientalis***
thunbergii	EHyt NMen SBid
§ ***tubiformis***	GCrs WChr
§ ***uva-vulpis***	CAvo CBro CMea EBee EHyt ELan EPar EPot ETub EWal ITim LAma MFos MTho NNrd NWCA SCro SSpi WAbe WCru WHil
verticillata	CAvo CBro ECha EPar EPot LAma MTho NHar SSpi WChr WCru
whittallii	EPot LAma MS&S MSto
zagrica	MSto

FUCHSIA † (Onagraceae)

'A.M. Larwick'	CSil EBak
'A.W. Taylor'	EBak SMer
'Aalt Groothuis'	EGou
'Abbé Farges'	CLit CLoc CSil EBak EBly ECtt EKMF LCla LFli MAsk MWhe NArc SKen SLBF
'Abigail'	EKMF
'Achievement' 🏆	CLoc CSil LCla MAsk MJac NArc SKen
'Ada Perry'	ECtt NArc
'Adagio'	CLoc
'Ada's Love'	MAld
'Adinda'	EGou

'Adrian Young'	MAsk
'Ailsa Garnett'	EBak
'Aintree'	CLit CSil NArc
'Airedale'	MAsk MJac NArc
'Ajax'	EGou
'Alabama Improved'	MAsk SKen
'Aladna'	CSil
'Aladna's Sanders'	EGou NArc
'Alan Ayckbourn'	CSil LCla MWar NArc
'Alan Stilwell'	SLBF
'Alaska'	CLoc EBak EKMF MAsk NArc
'Albertus Schwab'	EGou
'Alde'	CSil NArc
'Alf Thornley'	CSil EKMF LFli MAsk MWhe NArc
'Alfie'	CSil
'Alfred Rambaud'	CSil NArc
'Algerine'	SLBF
'Alice Ashton'	CLit EBak EKMF NArc
'Alice Doran'	SLBF
'Alice Hoffman'	CLit CLoc CSil EBak EBly EGou EKMF LCla LFli LVer MAld MAsk MBar MBri MGos MJac MWat MWhe NArc SKen SPer SSea
'Alice Mary'	CLit EBak EBly EKMF EMan
'Alice Rowell'	EKMF
'Alice Stringer'	ECtt
'Alice Travis'	CLit EBak
'Alipatti'	EKMF
'Alison Ewart'	CLit CLoc CSil EBak EKMF MAsk MJac MWhe NArc
'Alison June'	MBri
'Alison Patricia'	CLit CSil EBak EKMF EMan LCla MAld MWhe SLBF
'Alison Reynolds'	MBri NArc
'Alison Ryle'	CSil EBak
'Alison Sweetman'	EKMF MJac MWhe SKen
'Allure'	EGou
'Alma Hulscher'	EGou
'Alma Muir'	CLit
§ ***alpestris***	CLit EBak EGou EKMF LCla
'Alton Water'	EGou EKMF
'Alwin'	CLit CSil MWhe NArc
'Alyce Larson'	CLit CSil EBak MAsk MJac NArc
'Amanda Bridgland'	EKMF LCla
'Amanda Jones'	CLit EKMF MAsk MWhe NArc
'Ambassador'	CLit EBak MAsk SKen SMer
'Amelie Aubin'	CLoc EBak EKMF NArc
'America'	EBak NArc
'American Dream'	NArc
'American Flaming Glory'	CSil EGou NArc
'Amethyst Fire'	CSil
'Amigo'	CLit EBak NArc
§ ***ampliata***	EGou
ampliata hitchcockii	EKMF
'Amy Lye'	CLit CLoc CSil CWLN EBak EKMF MAsk NArc SKen
§ 'Andenken an Heinrich Henkel'	CLoc EBak EKMF LCla MAsk MWhe
'André Le Nostre'	EBak NArc
andrei	EGou EKMF LCla
'Andrew'	EBak EKMF MAsk NArc
'Andrew Carnegie'	CLoc
'Andrew George'	MJac
'Andrew Hadfield'	CSil EKMF MAsk MWar NArc SLBF
'Andrew Ryle'	NArc
'Angela Leslie'	CLoc CSil EBak EKMF NArc
'Angela Rippon'	CLit MJac MWhe NArc
'Angel's Dream'	CSil MAsk
'Angel's Flight'	EBak
'Anita'	CLit CSil EGou EKMF MAld MWhe NArc SLBF
'Anjo' (v)	EGou EKMF NArc SLBF SSea
'Ann Adams'	CSil MJac
'Ann Howard Tripp'	CLoc CSil MAsk MBri MJac MWhe NArc
'Ann Lee'	CLoc EBak
'Ann Roots'	EGou
'Anna Douling'	NArc
'Anna of Longleat'	CLit CLoc EBak EMan NArc SKen SLBF
'Annabel' 🏆	CGre CLit CLoc CSil EBak EBly EGou EKMF EMan LCla LFli LVer MAld MAsk MBri MJac MWar MWhe NArc NFai NHaw SLBF SSea
'Annabelle Stubbs'	NPri
'Annie Earle'	EKMF
'Anthea Day'	CLoc
¶ 'Anthonetta'	NArc
'Antigone'	SLBF
'Aphrodite'	CLoc EBak NArc
'Applause'	CLoc CSil EBak EBly EGou EKMF EMan LCla LVer MAld MAsk MJac MWhe NArc
¶ 'Apple Blossom'	EKMF
aprica hort.	See ***F. × bacillaris***
– Lundell	See ***F. microphylla*** subsp. ***aprica***
'Aquarius'	MWhe
¶ 'Arabella Improved'	EKMF
arborea	See ***F. arborescens***
§ ***arborescens***	CLit CLoc CSil EBak EGou EKMF ERea LCla MAsk NArc SLBF SMrm
'Arcadia'	MWar
'Arcadia Aubergine'	NArc
'Arcadia Gold'	ECtt LFli MWhe NArc
'Arcadia Lady'	CLit MAsk MJac NArc
'Arcady'	CLoc
'Archie Owen'	MAsk
'Arel's Avondzon'	NArc
'Ariel'	CLit CSil EGou NArc
'Army Nurse' 🏆	CLit CLoc CSil EKMF GCHN LFli LVer MAsk MWhe NArc SLBF
'Art Deco'	CSil NArc
'Ashley Jane'	MAld
'Ashmore'	CLit NArc
'Athela'	EBak
'Atlantic Crossing'	CLit
'Atlantic Star'	EBly EKMF MBri MJac NArc
'Atlantis'	CLit MAsk MJac NArc
'Atomic Glow'	EBak NArc
'Aubergine'	CLoc SLBF SSea
'Audray'	CLit LFli MAsk NArc
'Audrey Booth'	EGou
'Audrey Hepburn'	EKMF NArc
'Aunt Juliana'	CLit EBak
'Auntie Jinks'	CLit CSil EBak EKMF LCla MAsk MJac MWar MWhe NArc NHaw SLBF
* ***aureifolia***	EPfP
'Aurora Superba'	CLit CLoc CSil EBak EKMF SLBF
'Australia Fair'	CLoc CSil EBak MAsk NArc
§ ***austromontana***	EBak
'Autumnale'	CLit CLoc CSil EBak EKMF EMan LCla LFli LHil MAsk MBri MWhe NArc SKen SLBF SMrm SSea

'Avalanche'	CLit CLoc CSil EBak MAsk NArc
'Avocet'	CLoc EBak NArc
'Avon Celebration'	CLoc
'Avon Gem'	CLoc CSil
'Avon Gold'	CLoc
ayavacensis	EKMF
'Azure Sky'	EKMF
'Babette'	EKMF
'Babs'	MAsk
'Baby Blue Eyes'	CLit CSil SLBF
'Baby Bright'	CLit CSil LCla MWar SLBF
'Baby Chang'	CSil MWhe
'Baby Face'	NArc
'Baby Pink'	CLit CSil LFli NArc
'Baby Thumb'	CSil
§ × ***bacillaris***	CMHG CRDP CSam CWit EBak EGoo EHic GAri LCla MBlu SLBF SSoC
§ – 'Cottinghamii'	CSil EPla WPen WSHC
§ – 'Oosje'	CSil EGou EKMF LCla
§ – 'Reflexa'	GQui
'Bagworthy Water'	CLoc
'Baker's Tri'	EBak
'Balkonkönigin'	CLit CLoc CSil EBak MAsk SKen SMer
'Ballet Girl'	CLit CLoc CSil EBak ECtt EKMF LCla NPri SLBF
'Bambini'	CSil EBly
'Banks Peninsula'	GQui
'Banzai'	EKMF
'Barbara'	CLit CLoc CSil EBak EKMF LCla LFli MAsk MJac MWar MWhe NArc SKen
'Baron de Ketteler'	CSil EKMF NArc SMur
'Baroness van Dedem'	CSil
'Baroque Pearl'	EKMF NArc
'Barry M. Cox'	EGou
'Barry's Queen'	EBak
'Bashful'	CLit CSil EBly LCla LFli MAsk MBri NArc SKen
'Basketfull'	CLit CSil NArc
'Beacon'	CLoc CSil EBak EKMF EMan IHos LCla LFli LVer MAsk MBri MJac MWhe NArc NHaw SKen SSea WStI
'Beacon Rosa'	CLit CLoc CSil EGou EKMF EMan EOHP LCla LFli MAld MAsk MBri MJac MWar MWhe NArc SKen SLBF
'Bealings'	CLit CLoc CSil ECtt EGou EMan LCla LFli LVer MAsk MBri MJac MWar MWhe NArc
'Beatrice Burtoft'	EKMF
'Beau Nash'	CLoc
'Beauty of Bath'	CLoc EBak NArc
'Beauty of Clyffe Hall'	EBak
'Beauty of Exeter'	CLit CSil EBak EKMF MAsk NArc
'Beauty of Prussia'	CLoc CSil ECtt
'Beauty of Swanley'	EBak
'Beauty of Trowbridge'	LCla NArc SKen
'Becky'	EGou
'Becky Jane'	CSil
'Bella Forbes'	CLoc CSil EBak NArc
'Bella Rozella'	CSil EGou MAsk SCoo SLBF
'Belsay Beauty'	CLit MJac NArc
'Belvoir Beauty'	CLoc MJac
'Ben Jammin'	EGou SLBF
N 'Beranger'	CSil EBak
'Berba's Coronation'	EKMF NArc
'Berba's Happiness'	EGou
'Berba's Ingrid'	MAld
'Bergnimf'	EKMF LCla NArc
'Berliner Kind'	EBak
'Bermuda'	CSil EKMF
'Bernadette'	CLTr
'Bertha Gadsby'	EKMF MAsk
'Beryl Shaffery'	EGou
'Beryl's Choice'	CLit
'Beth Robley'	CLit CSil MAsk
'Betsy Ross'	EBak NArc
'Bette Sibley'	CSil LCla SLBF
'Beverley'	CSil EBak EBly LFli SLBF
'Bewitched'	EBak NArc
'Bianca'	CLit LFli SMur
'Bicentennial'	CLit CLoc CSil EBak EBly EGou EKMF LCla LVer MAsk MJac MWar MWhe NHaw SKen SSea
¶ 'Big Slim'	EGou
'Bill Gilbert'	LCla
'Bill Stevens'	EKMF
'Billy Green' ♀	CLTr CLit CLoc CSil EBak EBly ECtt EKMF LCla LFli MAld MAsk MJac MWar MWhe NArc SKen SLBF SSoC
'Bishop's Bells'	CSil MAsk MJac NArc
'Bits'	NArc
'Bittersweet'	CLit CSil LFli MAsk NArc
'Black Beauty'	CSil
'Black Prince'	CSil MAsk MBri MWar NArc
I 'Blanche Regina'	MJac MWhe
'Bland's New Striped'	EBak EKMF NArc SLBF
'Blazeaway'	CLit MBri MWar
'Blood Donor'	EKMF MJac SLBF
'Blowick'	CLit EMan LFli MAsk MBri NArc SMer
'Blue Beauty'	CSil EBak NArc
'Blue Bush'	CSil EKMF MAsk MJac NArc
'Blue Butterfly'	EBak NArc
'Blue Gown'	CLit CLoc CSil EBak EKMF LCla LFli LVer MAsk MWar MWhe NArc SBid SKen
'Blue Halo'	NArc
'Blue Ice'	CSil MWhe
'Blue Lace'	CSil LFli
N 'Blue Lagoon'	MAsk
'Blue Lake'	CLit CSil LVer MAsk
'Blue Mink'	EBak
'Blue Mirage'	CSil LCla MAsk NPri
'Blue Mist'	EBak
'Blue Pearl'	CLit EBak LFli MAsk NArc
'Blue Petticoat'	CLoc
'Blue Pinwheel'	CSil EBak
'Blue Sails'	LFli NArc
'Blue Satin'	CLit MAld MWhe NArc
'Blue Tit'	CSil LFli SKen
'Blue Veil'	CLit CLoc CSil EKMF LFli LVer MAsk MJac MWar SKen SLBF
'Blue Waves'	CLit CLoc CSil EBak EBly EGou EKMF EMan LFli MAsk MJac MWar MWhe NArc
'Blush of Dawn'	CLit CLoc CSil EBak EBly EGou EKMF LCla LFli LVer MAld MAsk MWar NArc SLBF
'Blythe'	EBly EGou SLBF
'Bob Pacey'	MJac
'Bob Paisley'	MBri
'Bobby Boy'	EBak
'Bobby Dazzler'	CSil ECtt EKMF MJac NArc
'Bobby Shaftoe'	EBak EKMF MAsk MWhe NArc

'Bobby Wingrove'	EBak NArc
'Bobolink'	EBak NArc
'Bob's Best'	CSil EBly LVer MJac
'Bob's Choice'	MAsk
'Boerhaave'	EBak MAsk
◆ ***boliviana*** 'Alba'	See ***F. boliviana* Carrière** var. ***alba***
§ ***boliviana*** Carrière	CAbb CBrk CLit CLoc CSil EBak EKMF GCra LCla MWhe NArc SBid SMrm
§ – var. ***alba*** ♀	CBrk CLit CLoc CSil EBak EGou EKMF LCla LFli MAsk MWhe NArc SBid SMrm
– var. ***boliviana***	EGou
– var. ***luxurians***	See ***F. boliviana* Carrière** var. ***alba***
◆ – f. ***puberulenta***	See ***F. boliviana* Carrière**
boliviana Britton	See ***F. sanctae-rosae***
'Bon Accorde'	CLoc CSil EBak EBly EKMF LCla MAsk SSea
'Bon Bon'	CLit CSil EBak LFli NArc
'Bonita'	CLit CSil MAsk MJac NArc
'Bonnie Doan'	NArc
'Bonnie Lass'	CLit CSil EBak NArc
'Bonny'	CLoc
'Bora Bora'	CSil EBak EKMF
'Border Princess'	EBak LCla
'Border Queen' ♀	CLit CLoc CSil EBak EKMF EMan LCla LFli MAld MAsk MJac MWar NArc SLBF
'Border Reiver'	CLit CSil EBak LCla NArc
'Börnemanns Beste'	CLoc CSil EBak EKMF LCla MAsk SKen
'Bouffant'	CLoc CSil EBak MAsk MJac SMer
'Bountiful'	CGre CLit CLoc CSil EKMF MAsk MWhe NArc SKen
'Bouquet'	CSil EKMF LCla SKen
'Bouvigne'	NArc
'Bow Bells'	CLoc CSil MAld MAsk MJac MWhe NArc
'Boy Marc'	CLit EGou
'Brandt's Five Hundred Club'	CLoc EBak
'Breckland'	EBak MJac NArc
'Breeders' Delight'	MBri
'Breeder's Dream'	EBak NArc
'Brenda'	CLit CLoc CSil EBak NArc
'Brenda Pritchard'	CSil ECtt LVer
'Brenda White'	CLit CLoc CSil EKMF MAsk MWar NArc
'Brentwood'	EBak
brevilobis	EGou EKMF LCla
'Brian A McDonald'	EGou
'Brian Breary'	EGou
'Brian C. Morrison'	EGou EKMF LCla MAsk
'Brian Ellis'	NArc
'Brian Soames'	EBak
'Brian Stannard'	EGou LCla
'Bridal Pink'	LFli
'Bridal Veil'	EBak NArc
'Bridesmaid'	CSil EBak EKMF LFli MAsk NArc
'Brigadoon'	CLit CLoc EBak
'Brightling'	CSil SLBF
'Brighton Belle'	CLit EGou NArc SSoC
N 'Brilliant'	CLit CLoc CSil EBak LHil MAsk MGos MPla MWat MWhe SKen
'Briony Caunt'	EKMF
'British Jubilee'	CSil EKMF MAsk NArc
'British Sterling'	NArc
'Brodsworth'	CSil MAsk
'Brookwood Belle' ♀	CLit EBly LCla MAld MJac SLBF
'Brookwood Dale'	MWhe
'Brookwood Joy'	CLit CSil EGou MAsk MJac NArc SLBF
'Brookwood Lady'	MAld MWhe
'Brutus' ♀	CChe CLit CLoc CSil EBak EBly EKMF EMan LCla LFli LVer MAsk MWat MWhe NArc NHaw SKen WStI
'Bryan Breary'	EKMF
'Bubble Hanger'	CSil NArc
'Buddha'	EBak
'Bunny'	CSil EBak LFli NArc
'Burton Brew'	MJac
'Buttercup'	CLoc CSil EBak LFli MAsk NArc
'Butterfly'	MAsk
'C.J. Howlett'	CSil EBak
'Caballero'	EBak NArc
'Cable Car'	NArc
'Caesar'	CSil EBak EGou EKMF MAsk NArc
'Caledonia'	CSil EBak
¶ 'Calumet'	EGou
'Cambridge Louie'	CLit CSil EBak LCla LFli MAld MAsk MBri MWar MWhe NArc
'Camel Estuary'	NArc
'Camelot'	EBak NArc
* ***campii***	EGou EKMF
* – var. ***rubra***	EGou
campos-portoi	EKMF LCla
'Cancun'	MJac
'Candlelight'	CGre CLoc CSil EBak NArc
'Candy Kisses'	CLit
'Candy Stripe'	CLoc
canescens Bentham	EBak
– Munz	See ***F. ampliata***
'Capri'	CSil EBak LFli NArc
'Cara Mia'	CLoc CSil SKen
'Caradela'	MAld
'Cardinal'	CLoc NArc
'Cardinal Farges'	CLit CLoc CSil EKMF LCla LFli NArc SKen SLBF
¶ 'Carillon van Amsterdam'	CLit EKMF MWhe
'Carioca'	EBak
'Carisbrooke Castle'	EKMF
'Carl Drude'	LCla
'Carl Wallace'	EKMF MJac
'Carla Johnston'	CLTr CLit CLoc CSil EBly EKMF LCla MAld MAsk MBri MJac MWar MWhe NArc SSea
'Carlisle Bells'	NArc
'Carmel Blue'	CLTr CLoc CSil LFli MAsk MWhe NArc
'Carmen'	CSil
'Carmen Maria'	CLit LCla MJac NArc
'Carmine Bell'	EKMF
'Carnea'	CSil
'Carnival'	LCla NArc
'Carnoustie'	EBak EGou NArc
'Carol Grace'	CLoc NArc
'Carol Nash'	CLoc
'Carol Roe'	EBly EKMF SLBF
'Caroline'	CGre CLoc CSil EBak EBly EKMF LFli MAsk MBlu NArc SLBF
'Cascade'	CLit CLoc CSil ECtt EKMF EMan LCla LFli MAsk MBri MJac MWar MWhe NArc NHaw SKen SRms SSea

'Casper Hauser'	CLit CSil EGou EKMF MAsk NArc
'Catherina'	EGou
'Catherine Bartlett'	EKMF NArc
'Catherine Claire'	CLit
'Cathie MacDougall'	EBak NArc
'Cecile'	CSil EBly ECtt EGou EKMF LCla LFli LVer MAld MAsk MJac MWhe NArc SLBF
'Celadore'	CLit CSil LCla MJac NArc SKen
'Celebration'	CSil EGou LCla LFli
'Celia Smedley' 🏆	CGre CLit CLoc CSil EBak EBly EGou EKMF LCla LFli LVer MAld MAsk MBri MJac MWar MWhe NArc SKen SLBF
'Centerpiece'	EBak SMer
'Central Scotland'	CLit SLBF
'Ceri'	CLoc NArc
'Cerrig'	NArc
'Chameleon'	CSil NArc
'Champagne Celebration'	CLoc
'Chandleri'	LCla NArc SLBF
'Chang'	CLit CLoc CSil EBak EKMF LBlm LCla LFli MAsk MWar MWhe NArc SLBF
'Chantry Park'	EGou LCla
'Charisma'	NArc SLBF
¶ 'Charles Edward'	EKMF
'Charlie Gardiner'	EBak EGou MWhe NArc
'Charlie Girl'	EBak
'Charlotte Clyne'	SLBF
'Charming'	CLoc CSil CWLN EBak GCHN MAsk MJac MWar MWhe NArc
'Chase Delight'	CLit CSil EKMF LFli MWar NHaw
'Checkerboard' 🏆	CLit CLoc EBak EGou EKMF LCla LFli LVer MAld MAsk MJac MWar MWhe NArc SKen SLBF SSea WEas
'Cheers'	CSil EGou EKMF LFli MAsk MWar MWhe
'Chessboard'	CLoc CSil
'Chillerton Beauty' 🏆	CLTr CLit CLoc CSil CTri ECtt EKMF LCla MAsk MJac MWhe NArc SLBF SPer
'China Doll'	CLit EBak LFli MWhe NArc SKen
'China Lantern'	CLit CLoc CSil EBak MAsk
'Chiquita Maria'	NArc
'Chris'	EGou
'Christ Driessen'	EGou
'Christina Becker'	NArc
'Christine Bamford'	EGou
'Christine Shaffery'	EGou
'Christmas Ribbons'	EGou LFli
cinerea	EGou EKMF LCla
'Cinnabarrina'	SLBF
'Circe'	CLit EBak EKMF MAsk NArc
'Circus'	EBak
'Circus Spangles'	CSil EGou NPri SCoo SMur
'Citation'	CLoc CSil EBak EKMF LFli MJac SSea
'City of Adelaide'	CLoc CSil MWhe SMur
'City of Leicester'	CSil LCla MAsk MBri
'Claire Belle'	SLBF
'Claire de Lune'	EBak LFli MAsk NArc SLBF
'Claire Evans'	CLoc SMer
'Claire Oram'	CLoc SSea
'Cliantha'	MWhe NArc
'Clifford Gadsby'	EBak NArc
'Cliff's Hardy'	EKMF LCla MAsk NArc
'Cliff's Own'	CSil NArc
'Cliff's Unique'	CSil EBly MAsk MWar
'Clifton Beauty'	MAsk MJac
'Clifton Charm'	CSil EBly MJac
'Clipper'	CSil
'Cloth of Gold'	CLit CLoc EBak MAsk MJac MWhe SKen SLBF SSea
'Cloverdale Jewel'	CSil EBak ECtt LCla MWhe NArc
'Cloverdale Joy'	EBak MAsk
'Cloverdale Pearl' 🏆	CLit CSil EBak EBee EKMF EMan ENot LCla LFli MAsk MJac MWhe NArc WPyg
'Coachman'	CLit CLoc CSil EBak EBly EKMF EMan LCla LFli MAld MAsk MWar MWhe NArc NHaw SLBF
coccinea	CGre CSil EKMF LCla
'Coconut Ice'	NArc
× ***colensoi***	ECou EKMF LCla MAsk SHFr
'Colin Chambers'	EGou
'Collingwood'	CLit CLoc CSil EBak MAsk NArc
¶ 'Colne Fantasy'	EKMF
'Colne Greybeard'	CSil NArc
'Come Dancing'	CLit CSil ECtt LCla LFli LVer MAsk NArc SKen
N 'Comet'	CLit CLoc CSil EBak NArc
'Conchilla'	EBak
'Confection'	NArc
'Congreve Road'	EGou MAsk
'Connie'	CSil EBak
'Conspicua'	CSil EBak EGou EKMF NArc
'Constable Country'	CLit NArc
'Constance'	CLit CLoc CSil EGou EKMF LCla MAsk MJac MWar MWhe NArc SKen SLBF
'Constance Comer'	MJac
N 'Constellation'	CLoc EBak MAsk MWhe NArc
'Continental'	EGou NArc
'Copycat'	CSil
'Coquet Bell'	EBak MAsk NArc
'Coquet Dale'	EBak MAsk MJac MWhe NArc
'Coquet Gold'	CSil ECtt NArc
¶ 'Coral Baby'	EGou
'Coral Seas'	EBak
§ 'Coralle' 🏆	CLit CLoc CSil EBak EBly EGou EKMF EMan LBlm LCla MAsk MJac MWar MWhe NArc SKen SLBF
'Corallina' 🏆	CLit CLoc CMHG CSil EBak EKMF IHos LFli MAsk MWhe NArc SKen SRms SSea WWat
cordifolia Bentham	CBrk CTre EBak MAsk NArc
– hort.	See ***F. splendens***
'Core'ngrato'	CLoc EBak
'Cornelia Smith'	EGou
'Cornwall Calls'	CLit
'Corsage'	NArc
'Corsair'	CLit CSil EBak EGou EKMF LFli NArc SLBF
§ ***corymbiflora***	EBak EKMF
corymbiflora alba	See ***F. boliviana*** var. ***alba*** **Carrière**
'Cosmopolitan'	CLit CSil EBak NArc
'Costa Brava'	CLoc EBak NArc
'Cotta Bella'	EKMF MJac NArc
'Cotta Bright Star'	CLit EKMF MAsk NArc SLBF
'Cotta Fairy'	EKMF
'Cotta Princess'	EKMF
'Cotta Vino'	EKMF MAsk NArc

'Cottinghamii'	See ***F.* × *bacillaris* 'Cottinghamii'**
'Cotton Candy'	CLit CLoc CSil EBly EGou LCla LFli MAsk MWhe SLBF
'Countdown Carol'	EBly
'Countess of Aberdeen'	CLoc CSil EBak EGou EKMF LVer MAld MAsk NArc SLBF
'Countess of Maritza'	CLoc
'County Park'	ECou EWes
'Court Jester'	CLoc EBak NArc
'Cover Girl'	CLit EBak MWhe NArc NHaw
'Coxeen'	EBak
'Crackerjack'	CLit CLoc EBak
crassistipula	EKMF LCla
'Creampuff'	NArc
'Crescendo'	CLoc SKen
'Crinkley Bottom'	EBly EKMF LCla LVer SLBF
'Crinoline'	EBak NArc
'Crosby Serendipidy'	CLoc
'Crosby Soroptimist'	CLit CSil EBly LCla MAsk MWar MWhe
'Cross Check'	CLit EMan MAsk MBri MJac NArc
'Crusader'	CSil
'Crystal Blue'	EBak MAsk NArc
'Crystal Stars'	CSil NArc SKen SMur
'Cupcake'	CLit NArc
'Cupid'	EBak NArc
'Curly Q'	CLit CSil EBak EKMF LFli MAsk NArc
'Curtain Call'	CLit CLoc EBak NArc SKen
cylindracea	EKMF
¶ – (f)	EGou
¶ – (m)	EGou
'Cymon'	CSil MAsk MWhe
'Cymru'	NArc
'Cyril Holmes'	NArc
¶ ***cyrtandroides***	EKMF
'Daffodil Dolly'	NArc
'Dainty'	EBak
'Dainty Lady'	EBak
'Daisy Bell'	CLit CLoc CSil EBak ECtt EGou EKMF LCla LFli MAsk MJac MWhe NArc NHaw
'Dalton'	EBak NArc
'Dancing Flame'	CLit CLoc CSil EBly EGou EKMF EMan LCla LFli LVer MAld MAsk MBri MJac MWar MWhe NArc NHaw SKen SLBF
'Danish Pastry'	LFli NArc
'Danny Boy'	CLoc EBak EGou EKMF EMan MAsk MWhe NArc
'Daphne Arlene'	CSil
'Dark Eyes' 🏆	CLit CLoc CSil EBak EGou EKMF EMan LCla LFli LVer MAld MAsk MBri MJac MWar MWhe NArc NFai NHaw NPri SLBF
'Dark Secret'	EBak NArc
'Dark Treasure'	CDoC CLit CSil LFli
'Darreen Dawn'	SLBF
'David'	CSil EGoo EGou EKMF EOHP LCla MAsk MPla SKen SLBF
'David Alston'	CLoc EBak
'David Lockyer'	CLoc EGou
'David Ward'	EGou EKMF LCla
'Dawn'	EBak LCla SKen SMer
'Dawn Carless'	EGou
'Dawn Sky'	EBak LAyl
'Dawn Star'	CSil MJac MWhe NArc NPri SMur
'Dawn Thunder'	NArc SMur
'Dawning'	EGou
'Day by Day'	MAsk
'Day Star'	EBak
'Daytime Live'	EBly EKMF
¶ 'De Groot's Pipes'	EGou
'Debby'	EBak NArc
'Deben Petite'	CSil
'Deben Rose'	CSil MAsk NArc
'Deborah Street'	CLoc
N ***decussata***	EBak EGou EKMF LCla
'Dee Copley'	EBak NArc
'Dee Star'	CLit NArc
'Deep Purple'	CSil EGou EKMF SCoo SLBF
'Delaval Lady'	CLit CSil
'Delicia'	CSil
'Delilah'	EKMF MJac
'Delta's Bride'	EGou SLBF
'Delta's Delight'	NArc
'Delta's Dream'	NArc
'Delta's Groom'	EGou
'Delta's K.O.'	NArc
'Delta's Night'	EGou
'Delta's Paljas'	NArc
'Delta's Parade'	EGou NArc
'Delta's Song'	NArc SLBF
'Delta's Sprinkler'	NArc
'Delta's Symphonie'	EGou
'Delta's Trick'	EGou
'Delta's Wonder'	CSil NArc
§ ***denticulata***	CKni CLit CLoc CMHG CSil EBak EGou EKMF ERea LCla MAsk NArc SLBF
dependens	See ***F. corymbiflora***
'Derby Imp'	CLit MAsk NArc
'Derby Star'	CSil
'Desperate Daniel'	LCla
'Destiny'	NArc
'Deutsche Perle'	CLit
'Devonshire Dumpling'	CGre CLTr CLit CLoc CSil EBak EBly ECtt EGou EKMF EMan LCla LFli LVer MAld MAsk MBri MJac MWar MWhe NArc NHaw SKen SLBF
'Diablo'	CSil EBak EGou
'Diamond Wedding'	NArc
'Diana'	EBak MAsk
'Diana Wills'	MWhe SKen
'Diana Wright'	CSil
'Diane Brown'	CLit EKMF MAsk MWhe SSea
'Dick Swinbank'	EKMF
'Die Fledermaus'	NArc
'Dilly-Dilly'	MAsk
'Dimples'	CSil MAsk MBri
'Diny Hetterscheid'	EGou
'Dipton Dainty'	CLoc CSil EBak LCla NArc
'Display' 🏆	CLit CLoc CSil EBak ECtt EKMF EMan IHos LCla MAld MAsk MBri MJac MWar MWhe NArc NHaw SLBF SSea WStI
'Doc'	CLit CSil LCla LFli MAsk
'Docteur Topinard'	CLoc EBak
'Doctor'	See ***F.* 'The Doctor'**
'Doctor Brendan Freeman'	MJac NArc
'Doctor Foster'	CLoc CSil CTri EBak ENot NArc SBid WEas
'Doctor Olson'	CLoc EBak
'Doctor Robert'	EBly EKMF MBri MJac MWhe NArc

§ 'Dollar Princess' 🏆	CLit CLoc CSil EBak EBly ECtt EGou EKMF EMan IHos LCla LVer MAld MAsk MBri MJac MWar MWhe NArc NFai NHaw SChu SKen SLBF WStI
'Dolly Daydream'	EKMF NArc
'Domacin'	CSil MWhe
'Dominyana'	EBak EKMF LCla SLBF
'Don Peralta'	EBak
'Dopey'	CSil LCla LFli MAsk
'Doreen Gladwyn'	SLBF
'Doreen Redfern'	CLoc CSil EKMF LFli MAsk MJac MWhe NArc
'Doris Coleman'	CLit EMan LFli
'Doris Hobbs'	EKMF
'Dorothea Flower'	CLoc CSil EBak
'Dorothy'	CSil SLBF
'Dorothy Day'	CLoc
'Dorothy Hanley'	EGou
'Dorothy Shields'	CLit MJac
'Dorrian Brogdale'	EGou LCla
'Dove House'	CSil EKMF
'Drake 400'	CLoc
'Drame'	CLit CSil EBak EKMF LCla LFli MAsk MWar NArc SKen SSea
'Drum Major'	EBak NArc
'Du Barry'	EBak NArc
'Duchess of Albany'	CLit CLoc CSil EBak MAsk NArc
'Duchess of Cornwall'	CSil
'Duet'	CLit CSil SMur
N 'Duke of Wellington'	CLoc
'Dulcie Elizabeth'	CLit CSil EBak LCla LFli MJac MWar MWhe NArc
'Dusky Beauty'	CLit CSil MJac NArc
'Dusky Rose'	CLoc CSil EBak EGou LFli MAsk MJac MWhe NArc SMer
'Dutch King Size'	EGou
'Dutch Mill'	CLoc EBak
'Duyfken'	CLit CSil NArc
'Earl of Beaconsfield'	See ***F.* 'Laing's Hybrid'**
'Earre Barré'	CLit EGou
'East Anglian'	CLoc CSil EBak NArc
'Easter Bonnet'	CLoc
'Easterling'	CSil LCla NArc
'Ebbtide'	CLoc EBak NArc
'Echo'	CLit CLoc
'Ed Largarde'	EBak EKMF MAsk
'Edale'	CSil
'Eden Beauty'	NArc
'Eden Lady'	CLoc CSil MBri MWar NArc
'Eden Princess'	MJac MWhe
'Edith'	CSil EKMF LCla SLBF
'Edith Emery'	LFli
'Edith Hall'	EGou EKMF
'Edna W. Smith'	CSil ECtt
'Edwin J. Goulding'	EGou LCla
'Eileen Raffill'	EBak
'Eileen Saunders'	CSil EBak
'Eira Goulding'	EGou
'El Camino'	CLit CSil LFli MAsk MWhe NArc NFai
'El Cid'	CLoc CSil EBak EKMF MAsk NArc
'Elaine Ann'	EBly MJac
'Eleanor Clark'	EKMF LCla NArc
'Eleanor Leytham'	CLit EBak EKMF LCla MAsk NArc
'Eleanor Rawlins'	EBak EKMF NArc SKen
'Elfin Glade'	CLoc CSil EBak
'Elfrida'	CSil EKMF
'Elfriede Ott'	CLit CLoc EBak EKMF MWhe SLBF
'Elisabeth Honorine'	NArc
N 'Elizabeth'	EBak NArc
¶ 'Elizabeth Broughton'	EKMF
'Elizabeth Tompkins'	EKMF LFli MJac
'Elizabeth Travis'	EBak
'Ellen Morgan'	EBak
'Elma'	EGou
'Elsa'	CLit ECtt
'Elsie Downey'	NArc
'Elsie Mitchell'	CLit CSil LCla MAsk MWar MWhe NArc
§ 'Emile de Wildeman'	EBak EKMF
'Emily Austen'	EKMF MAld NArc
'Emma Louise'	NArc
'Emma Massey'	MAld
'Emma Rowell'	EKMF
'Empress of Prussia' 🏆	CLit CLoc CSil EBak EBee EKMF EMan LFli MAsk NArc SKen SLBF SSea
'Enchanted'	CLit EBak MWar
encliandra subsp. ***encliandra***	EGou EKMF LCla
encliandra tetradactyla	EKMF LCla
§ 'Enfant Prodigue'	CLTr CLoc CSil EKMF
'English Rose'	CSil MAsk
'Enstone'	See ***F. magellanica*** var. ***molinae* 'Enstone'**
'Eppsii'	CSil
'Erica Julie'	NArc SLBF
'Eric's Hardy'	CSil
'Eric's Majesty'	EKMF
'Erika Frohmann'	SLBF
'Erika Köth'	CSil
'Ernest Rankin'	CSil EKMF NArc
'Ernestine'	EBly EGou MWhe
'Ernie Bromley'	EGou NArc SLBF
'Eroica'	NArc
'Errol'	CLoc
'Estelle Marie'	CLit CLoc CSil EBak EGou EKMF LCla MAsk MBri MJac MWar MWhe SLBF SSea
'Esther Divine'	CSil MAsk
'Eternal Flame'	CLit CSil EBak LFli MBri MWhe NArc SKen
'Eureka Red'	EGou SLBF
'Eurydice'	CLoc
'Eusebia'	EGou EKMF MAsk MJac NArc SLBF
'Eva Boerg'	CLit CLoc CSil EBak ECtt EKMF EMan IHos LCla LFli MAsk MBri MWar MWhe NArc NFai NHaw SKen WKif
'Eva Twaites'	EGou
'Evanson's Choice'	SKen
'Eve Hollands'	EGou LCla
'Evelyn Stanley'	EGou
'Evelyn Steele Little'	EBak
'Evening Sky'	EBak NArc
'Evensong'	CLit CLoc CSil EBak LFli MWhe NArc
'Excalibur'	CLit EGou NArc
excorticata	CB&S CGre CTre CTrw ECou EGou EKMF LHop WSHC
'Exton Beauty'	NArc
'Fabian Franck'	CLit EGou LCla
'Fairytales'	NArc
'Falklands'	CSil LFli MAsk
'Falling Stars'	CLit CLoc CSil EBak MWhe
'Fan Dancer'	EBak
'Fancy Flute'	CLit CSil NArc

'Fancy Free'	MBri WLRN
'Fancy Pants'	CLoc EBak EGou MAsk MBri
'Fanfare'	CDoC EBak EKMF NArc
'Fascination'	See ***F.* 'Emile de Wildeman'**
'Fashion'	EBak
'Fasna 1100'	NArc
'Favourite'	EBak
'Fenman'	EBly MJac NArc
'Fergie'	LCla LVer
'Festival'	MAsk
'Festoon'	EBak
'Fey'	CLit EGou EKMF MAsk SMur
'Fiery Spider'	EBak NArc
'Figaro'	EGou
§ 'Filigraan'	CSil NArc
◆ Filigree	See ***F.* 'Filigraan'**
'Fine Lady'	CLit
'Finn'	EBly EGou
'Fiona'	CLit CLoc CSil EBak EGou LFli MAsk NArc
'Fiona Jane'	EKMF
'Fiona Lynn'	EGou
'Fiona Pitt'	CLit EGou LCla
'Fire Mountain'	CLit CLoc CSil MWhe NArc SKen SSea
'Firefly'	NArc
'Firefox'	NArc
'Firelite'	EBak NArc
'Firenza'	MWar SLBF
'First Lady'	CLit MAsk NArc
'First Success'	EGou EKMF MAsk SLBF
'Flair'	CLoc
'Flame'	EBak
'Flamenco Dancer'	EGou SLBF
'Flash' ♀	CLit CLoc CSil CTri EBak EKMF EOHP LCla LVer MAld MAsk MJac MWhe NArc SLBF WFar WStI
'Flashlight'	EGou ELan
'Flat Jack o'Lancashire'	ECtt EKMF
'Flavia'	EBak LFli
'Flirtation Waltz'	CGre CLit CLoc CSil EBak EKMF EMan LCla LFli MAld MAsk MBri MJac MWhe NArc
'Flocon de Neige'	EBak NArc
'Floral City'	CLoc EBak NArc
'Florence Mary Abbott'	CSil EGou EMan LCla MWar
'Florence Turner'	CSil EBak EKMF MAsk MWhe SKen
'Florentina'	CLoc CSil EBak EGou EKMF NArc
'Floretta'	NArc
'Fluffy Frills'	CLit CSil
'Flyaway'	EBak NArc
'Fly-by-night'	NArc
'Flying Cloud' ♀	CLoc CSil EBak EKMF LFli MAsk MBri MWhe NArc
'Flying Scotsman'	CLoc CSil EBak EBly EGou EKMF LVer MAsk MJac NArc SLBF
'Folies Bergères'	EBak
'Foline'	NArc
'Foolke'	CSil EBak EBly
'Forest King'	CLit NArc
N 'Forget Me Not'	CLoc EBak EKMF MAsk NArc
'Formosissima'	NArc
'Fort Bragg'	EBak NArc SKen SMur
'Forward Look'	CSil MWhe
'Fountains Abbey'	EMan NArc
'Foxgrove Wood'	CLit EBak EBly LCla NArc SLBF
'Frank Sanford'	NArc
'Frank Saunders'	CSil LCla
'Frank Unsworth'	ECtt EKMF MAsk MWar MWhe NArc
'Frau Hilde Rademacher'	CLit CSil EBak EBee EKMF EMan LFli MAld MPla NArc NHaw NPri SLBF
'Frauke'	NArc
'Fred Swales'	CSil EKMF
'Freefall'	EBak
'Freeland Ballerina'	SLBF
'Friendly Fire'	CLit CLoc EKMF NArc
'Friendship'	MAsk
'Frosted Flame'	CLit CLoc CSil EKMF LCla LFli MAsk MJac MWar MWhe NArc SLBF SSea
'Frühling'	EBak
I 'Fuchsia Fan'	EBly LFli
'Fuchsiade '88'	CLoc CSil EBak LCla MAsk MWhe
¶ 'Fuchsiarama'	EKMF
'Fuchsiarama '91'	EBly EGou NArc
'Fuji San'	EGou LCla
'Fuksie Foetsie'	CSil EGou EKMF MAsk SLBF
fulgens ♀	CMHG EKMF LCla LHil MAsk MBal MWhe NArc
◆ – 'Gesneriana'	See ***F.* 'Gesneriana'**
– 'Rubra Grandiflora'	See ***F.* 'Rubra Grandiflora'**
* – 'Variegata'	CSil EGou LCla
¶ ***furfuracea***	EKMF LCla
'Für Elise'	CLit EBak NArc
'Gala'	CLit EBak NArc
'Galadriel'	CLit EGou
'Galahad'	EBak NArc
'Garden News' ♀	CLit CLoc CSil EBly ECtt EGou EKMF LCla LFli LVer MAld MAsk MJac MPla MWar MWhe NArc NHaw SKen SLBF
'Garden Week'	CLit CSil MAsk MWhe
'Gartenmeister Bonstedt' ♀	CLit CLoc CSil EBak EBly EKMF LBlm LCla MAsk MLan NArc SKen WEas
'Gay Anne'	EKMF LFli NArc
'Gay Fandango'	CLit CLoc CSil EBak LCla LFli MWar NArc SKen
¶ 'Gay Future'	EKMF
'Gay Parasol'	CLit CLoc EGou LFli MWhe
'Gay Paree'	CSil EBak MAsk
'Gay Senorita'	EBak
'Gay Spinner'	CLoc
'Geertien'	See ***F.* 'Dutch Geertien'**
gehrigeri	EBak EKMF LCla
'Geisha Girl'	CSil
¶ 'Gelre'	EGou
'Général Charles de Gaulle'	EGou
'Général Monk'	CLit CSil EBak ECtt EKMF EMan LVer MBri MPla NArc
'Général Voyron'	CSil MPla
'General Wavell'	CLit LFli NArc
'Genii' ♀	Widely available
'Geoffrey Smith'	CSil ECtt EKMF
'Georg Börnemann'	NArc
'Georgana'	MWhe NArc
'George Barr'	CSil EKMF NArc SKen
'George Johnson'	CLit CSil NArc
'George Travis'	EBak NArc
'Gerda Manthey'	EKMF
'Gerharda's Aubergine'	EGou EKMF
'Gerharda's Kiekeboe'	EKMF
'Gerharda's Sophie'	NArc
§ 'Gesneriana'	CLoc CSil EBak EGou
'Ghislaine'	EGou SLBF

'Giant Pink Enchanted'	CLit CLoc EBak NArc SMer
'Gilda'	CSil MAsk NArc
'Gillian Althea'	NArc
'Gilt Edge'	CLoc CSil
'Gina's Gold'	MAsk
'Gingham Girl'	MAld SLBF
'Gipping'	EGou
'Girls Brigade'	EKMF
'Gladiator'	CLit CSil EBak LCla LFli NArc
'Gladys Haddaway'	SLBF
'Gladys Miller'	CLoc
glaziouana	CLit CSil EKMF LCla SLBF
'Glenby'	CLit NArc
'Glitters'	EBak EKMF NArc
§ 'Globosa'	EBak EKMF SKen SRms
'Gloria Johnson'	EKMF NArc SLBF
'Glow'	CSil EBak
'Glowing Embers'	EBak MAsk NArc
Glowing Lilac	CSil EKMF EMan NArc
'Glyn Jones'	EKMF
'Gold Brocade'	CLit CSil NArc
'Gold Crest'	EBak NArc
'Gold Leaf'	NArc
'Golden Anniversary'	CLoc CSil EBak EGou EKMF EMan LCla LFli MAld MAsk MJac MWar SSea
'Golden Arrow'	EGou LHil NArc
'Golden Border Queen'	CLoc
'Golden Dawn'	CLoc EBak ECtt LVer NArc
'Golden Drame'	MAsk
'Golden Eden Lady'	MWhe
'Golden Herald'	SLBF
'Golden Jessimae'	MAsk NArc
'Golden La Campanella'	CLit CLoc CSil ECtt MBri NArc SSea
'Golden Lena'	CSil EKMF EMan MAsk NArc
'Golden Marinka' 🏆	CLit CLoc EBak ECtt EKMF LFli LHil MAsk MBri MWhe NArc
'Golden Melody'	CSil
'Golden Penny Askew'	MAsk
'Golden Runner'	MAsk
'Golden Swingtime'	CSil EGou LFli MAsk MBri MJac MWhe NArc NHaw SSea
'Golden Tolling Bell'	MAsk
'Golden Treasure'	CBrk CLit CLoc CSil ECtt EKMF LCla MBri
'Golden Vergeer'	EGou
'Golden Wedding'	CSil EKMF
'Goldsworth Beauty'	CSil LCla LFli
'Golondrina'	EBak MWhe
'Goody Goody'	EBak
'Gordon Thorley'	EKMF MWhe
'Gordon's China Rose'	LCla SKen
'Gottingen'	EBak
'Göttinger Ruhm'	NArc
'Governor 'Pat' Brown'	EBak MAsk
'Grace Darling'	EBak MWhe
'Grace Durham'	EGou
gracilis	See ***F. magellanica*** var. ***gracilis***
'Graf Spee'	EGou
'Graf Witte'	CLTr CLit CSil LFli NArc
'Grand Duchess'	EGou
¶ 'Grand Duke'	EGou
'Grand Prix'	CLit CSil MAsk NArc SKen
'Grand Slam'	LFli SKen
'Grandma Sinton'	CLoc CSil EBly EMan LCla MAld MBri MJac MWar MWhe NArc
'Grandpa George'	CLit CSil LCla
'Grasmere'	MAsk
'Grayrigg'	CSil EKMF EPPr
'Great Ouse'	EBly
'Great Scott'	CLoc CSil SKen
'Green 'n' Gold'	CSil EBak
'Greenpeace'	EKMF LCla MAsk SLBF
'Greg Walker'	CLit CSil
'Greta'	CSil EGou
'Gretna Chase'	MBri MWhe NArc
¶ 'Grey Lady'	CSil
'Grietje'	EGou
'Groene Kan's Glorie'	CGre CLit EKMF NArc
'Grumpy'	CLit CSil EBly LCla LFli MAsk MBri NArc
'Gruss aus dem Bodethal'	CLit CLoc EBak EBly EGou EKMF LCla
'Guinevere'	EBak
'Gustave Doré'	CSil EBak NArc
'Guy Dauphine'	EBak
'Gwen Dodge'	EGou
'Gwen Wakelin'	NArc
'Gwen Wallis'	EGou
'Gwendoline'	EGou
'Gypsy Girl'	CLit MAsk NArc SKen
'Gypsy Prince'	CLoc
'H.G. Brown'	CSil EBak MWhe
'Halsall Beauty'	MBri
'Halsall Belle'	MBri
'Halsall Pride'	MBri
'Hampshire Beauty'	MJac
'Hampshire Blue'	CSil NArc SLBF
'Hampshire Prince'	CSil
'Hampshire Treasure'	CSil
'Hanna'	CSil
'Hannah Louise'	EBly
'Hannah Williams'	CLTr MAsk NArc
'Hans van Beek'	NArc
'Happiness'	CSil
'Happy'	CLit CSil EBly LCla LFli MAsk MWhe NArc
'Happy Anniversary'	CLoc EKMF MAsk NArc
'Happy Fellow'	CLoc CSil EBak
'Happy Wedding Day'	CLit CLoc CSil EKMF LCla LFli MAsk MWhe NPri SLBF
'Hapsburgh'	EBak
'Harlow Car'	CLit EKMF LCla LFli MAsk MWar NArc
'Harlyn'	NArc
N 'Harmony'	EBak
'Harnser's Flight'	CSil EGou LCla
'Harriett'	MAsk
'Harrow Pride'	CSil
'Harry Dunnett'	EBak
'Harry Gray'	CLit CLoc CSil EBak EBly ECtt EMan LCla LFli MAsk MBri MJac MWar MWhe NArc NHaw SKen SLBF SSea
hartwegii	EGou EKMF LCla MAsk
'Hathersage'	EBak
¶ 'Hathor'	EGou
'Hatschbachii'	EGou EKMF LCla
'Haute Cuisine'	CLoc CSil EGou EKMF EMan LVer MAsk MWhe NArc SLBF
'Hawaiian Night'	NArc
'Hawaiian Princess'	ECtt
'Hawaiian Sunset'	SLBF
'Hawkshead'	CGle CLit CLoc CSil EBly ECha EGou EKMF ELan GCal GOrc GQui LCla LHil MAsk MJac MWhe NArc NRoo SAxl SBid SChu SLBF SMac SMrm SWas WCru
* 'Hazel'	CLit CSil EKMF LFli MAsk MWhe

'Heart Throb'	EBak
'Hebe'	EBak MWhe
'Heidi Ann' 🏆	CLit CLoc CSil EBak EBly EKMF EMan IHos LCla LFli LVer MAsk MBri MJac MWar MWhe NArc NHaw SKen SLBF
'Heidi Weiss'	NArc
'Heinrich Henkel'	See ***F.* 'Andenken an Heinrich Henkel'**
'Heirloom'	ECtt EKMF
'Helen Clare'	CLoc EBak NArc
'Helen Elizabeth'	EKMF MBri
'Helen Spence'	EKMF NArc
'Hellan Devine'	MJac
'Hello Dolly'	CLoc
'Hemsleyana'	See ***F. microphylla*** subsp. ***hemsleyana***
'Henri Poincaré'	EBak EKMF
'Henriette Prins'	EGou
'Herald' 🏆	CLit CSil EBak LFli MWhe NArc SLBF
'Herbe de Jacques'	EKMF SKen
'Heritage'	CLoc CSil EBak NArc
¶ 'Herman de Graaff'	EGou
'Hermiena'	CLit CLoc CSil EGou EKMF LCla LFli MAld MWar NArc SLBF
'Heron'	CSil EBak EKMF SKen
'Hessett Festival'	CLit CSil EBak EGou LFli LVer MWhe NArc
'Heston Blue'	EKMF NArc
'Hi Jinks'	EBak LFli MAsk
'Hiawatha'	NArc
hidalgensis	See ***F. microphylla*** subsp. ***hidalgensis***
'Hidcote Beauty'	CLit CLoc CSil EBak EKMF LFli MAsk MWhe NArc SKen SLBF
'Hidden Beauty'	NArc
'Highland Pipes'	CSil EKMF LCla NArc
'Hilda May Salmon'	NArc
'Hindu Belle'	EBak
'Hinnerike'	CSil EGou EKMF MAsk NArc SLBF
'Hiroshige'	EGou
'His Excellency'	CSil EBak
'Hobo'	EGou
'Hobson's Choice'	LCla LVer MWar SLBF
'Hokusai'	EGou EKMF
'Holly's Beauty'	NPri SMur
'Hollywood Park'	EBak
'Horatio'	CSil ECtt MJac
'Hot Coals'	CLit CSil EGou
'Howlett's Hardy'	CLit CLoc CSil EBak EBee ECtt EKMF GCHN LFli MAsk MBal MBri NArc
'Hula Girl'	CLit CSil EBak EKMF LCla LFli MAsk MJac MWar MWhe SLBF
'Humboldt Holiday'	CSil EKMF LCla LFli MAsk NArc
♦ 'Hummeltje'	See ***F. microphylla* 'Hummeltje'**
'Huntsman'	CLit EKMF LFli NPri WLRN
'Ian Brazewell'	CLoc
'Ian Leedham'	CSil EBak EKMF
'Ice Cream Soda'	EBak NArc
'Iceberg'	CSil EBak NArc
'Icecap'	CSil EKMF LFli MBri NArc
'Iced Champagne'	CLit CLoc EBak LCla LFli MAsk MJac MWar NArc NPri
'Ichiban'	CLoc
'Ida'	EBak

'Igloo Maid'	CLit CLoc CSil EBak EGou EKMF LFli MAsk MJac MWhe NArc SSea
'Impala'	EGou
'Imperial Crown'	CSil
'Imperial Fantasy'	EGou NArc
'Impudence'	CLoc CSil EBak MAsk
'Impulse'	CLoc EKMF NArc SKen SLBF
'Ina'	MAsk
'Independence'	CSil
'Indian Maid'	EBak EKMF LVer MAsk MBri MJac NArc SKen
'Inferno'	CLit CSil
'Ingleore'	NArc
'Ingram Maid'	MAsk
'Insa'	NArc
'Insulinde'	CLit EGou EKMF LCla MAld MWar NArc SLBF
'Intercity'	NArc
'Interlude'	EBak
'Iolanthe'	EGou
'Irene L. Peartree'	EGou LCla
'Irene van Zoeren'	EGou MAld NArc
'Iris Amer'	CLoc CSil EBak
'Isis'	CSil EKMF
'Isle of Mull'	CLit NArc SKen
'Isle of Purbeck'	MJac NArc
'Italiano'	MJac
'Ixion'	NArc
'Jack Acland'	ECtt EGou SKen
'Jack Shahan' 🏆	CLit CLoc CSil EBak EKMF EMan IHos LCla LFli MAsk MBri MJac MWar MWhe NFai SKen SLBF SSea
'Jack Stanway'	CLit CSil EGou MAsk WEas
'Jackie Bull'	EBak
'Jackpot'	EBak
'Jackqueline'	CSil EGou EKMF LCla MAsk NArc
'Jam Roll'	MAsk
'Jamboree'	EBak MAsk NArc
'James Lye'	EBak MAsk SKen
'James Travis'	EBak LCla
'Jan Bremer'	NArc
'Jane Humber'	EGou EKMF LCla NArc
'Jane Lye'	EBak
'Janet Goodwin'	NArc
¶ 'Janice Ann'	EKMF SLBF
'Janie'	CLit LFli
¶ 'Janneke Brinkman-Salentijn'	EGou
'Jap Van't Veer'	EGou
'Jasper's Likkepot'	NArc
'Jayess Wendy'	CLit
'Jayne Louise Mills'	NArc
'Jean Campbell'	EBak
'Jean Clark'	MWar SLBF
'Jean Pidcock'	NArc
'Jeane'	EKMF
'Jennie Rachael'	NArc
'Jennifer Hampson'	CSil
'Jennifer Haslam'	EGou LCla
'Jenny Sorensen'	CLit CSil EKMF LCla MAld MAsk MWar NArc SLBF
'Jess'	LCla NArc SLBF
'Jessimae'	CLit LFli MAsk NArc
N 'Jester'	CLoc CSil
'Jet Fire'	CSil EBak NArc
'Jiddles'	SLBF
'Jill Storey'	EKMF
'Jim Coleman'	CLit MWhe NArc SLBF
'Jim Missin'	MAld MAsk

'Jim Muncaster'	CLit EKMF MAsk NArc
jimenezii	EGou EKMF
'Jimmy Carr'	EKMF
'Joan Barnes'	CSil
'Joan Cooper'	CLoc CSil EBak EKMF
'Joan Gilbert'	CSil
'Joan Goy'	EBly EKMF LCla MAsk MJac MWar MWhe
'Joan Knight'	CLoc
'Joan Margaret'	MJac
¶ 'Joan Morris'	SLBF
'Joan Pacey'	CSil EBak LFli MAsk NArc SKen
'Joan Smith'	CLit CSil EBak
'Joan Young'	EGou LCla
'Jo-Anne Fisher'	EBly
'Joe Kusber'	CSil EBak EKMF MAsk MJac NArc SKen
'Joe Nicholls'	EKMF
'Joel'	SLBF
'John Boy'	EGou
'John E. Caunt'	EKMF
'John Grooms'	CLit EKMF MJac
'John Lockyer'	CLoc EBak NArc
'John Maynard Scales'	CLit EGou LCla MAsk MJac MWhe NArc
'John Oram'	CLit
'John Pitt'	EGou
'John Suckley'	EBak SMer
'Johnny'	CLoc
'Jomam'	CSil LCla MAld MAsk MWar MWhe NArc SLBF
'Jon Oram'	CLoc
'Jose's Joan'	CLit MAsk MWhe NArc
'Joy Bielby'	EGou EKMF LCla NArc
'Joy Patmore' 𝕐	CLit CLoc CSil EBak EBly EKMF LCla LFli MAsk MBri MWar MWhe NArc SKen SLBF
'Joyce Sinton'	EKMF EMan MBri NArc
¶ 'Jubie-Lin'	EGou
'Judith Alison Castle'	GCHN
'Julchen'	EGou
'Jules Daloges'	EBak
'Julia'	CSil EKMF
'Julie'	MAsk
'Julie Marie'	CSil LCla MJac NArc SLBF
'June Gardner'	EKMF
N 'Juno'	EBak SMer
¶ ***juntasensis***	EGou
'Jupiter Seventy'	EBak
'Justin's Pride'	CLit CSil EKMF MAsk
'Kaboutertje'	EKMF
'Kaleidoscope'	CSil EBak LFli NArc
'Karen Bielby'	EKMF
'Karen Louise'	CLoc
'Karin de Groot'	EKMF NArc
'Karin Siegers'	CSil
'Kate Harriet'	CLit LCla
'Kathleen Muncaster'	EKMF
'Kathleen Smith'	ECtt EKMF NArc
'Kathryn Maidment'	EKMF NArc
'Kathy Louise'	EMan LFli SLBF
'Kathy's Prince'	ECtt EKMF NArc
'Kathy's Sparkler'	CSil EGou EKMF NArc
'Katinka'	EGou LCla
'Katrina'	CLoc EBak NArc
'Katrina Thompsen'	CLoc EKMF LCla MAld MWar SLBF SSea
'Keele '92'	EKMF
'Keepsake'	CLoc CSil EBak
'Kegworth Beauty'	MAsk
'Kegworth Carnival'	CLit LCla MAsk NArc SKen

'Kegworth Delight'	NArc
'Kegworth Supreme'	MJac
'Kelly Rushton'	MWar
'Ken Goldsmith'	EBly EGou LCla MAsk
'Ken Jennings'	MJac
'Ken Sharp'	CLit MJac NArc
'Kenny Dalglish'	CSil EKMF
'Kernan Robson'	CLoc EBak EGou NArc
'Kerry Anne'	EBly
'Keystone'	EBak
'Khada'	EKMF MWhe
'Kim Wright'	MWhe
'Kimberly'	EBak
¶ 'King George V'	MBlu
'King of Bath'	EBak
'King of Hearts'	EBak
'King's Ransom'	CLit CLoc CSil EBak MAsk MWhe NArc
'Kiss 'n' Tell'	EBly MJac MWhe NArc
'Kit Oxtoby'	CLit CSil ECtt EGou EKMF EMan LCla MAld MAsk MJac NArc SKen
'Kiwi'	EBak MAsk SKen
'Klassic'	EGou
'Kleine Gärtnerin'	NArc
'Knight Errant'	CSil SLBF
'Knockout'	CLit CSil EKMF MAsk
'Kolding Perle'	CLit CSil
'Königin der Frühe'	NArc
'Kon-Tiki'	CLit CLoc CSil EKMF NArc
'Koralle'	See ***F.* 'Coralle'**
'Kwintet'	EBak LCla MJac SKen
'Kyoto'	CSil EKMF
'La Apache'	EBak
'La Bianca'	EBak
'La Campanella' 𝕐	CLoc CSil EBak EBly ECtt EKMF EMan LCla LFli LVer MAld MAsk MBri MJac MWar MWhe NArc NFai NHaw NPri SLBF
'La Fiesta'	CLit CSil EBak LFli NArc SMer
'La France'	EBak
N 'La Neige'	CLit CSil EBak MAsk
'La Porte'	CLit CLoc
'La Rosita'	CSil EBak MAsk SLBF
N 'La Traviata'	EBak
'Lace Petticoats'	EBak EKMF NArc
'Lady Beth'	CLit NArc
'Lady Boothby'	CHEx CLit CPle CSil EBak EKMF LCla MAsk NArc SBid SKen SLBF SMrm SRms
'Lady in Grey'	EKMF
'Lady Isobel Barnett'	CLit CLoc CSil EBak EKMF IHos LCla LFli MAld MAsk MBri MJac MWar MWhe NArc NHaw
'Lady Kathleen Spence'	CLit CSil EBak EKMF MAsk MWhe NArc
'Lady Love'	MBri
'Lady Patricia Mountbatten'	CSil EKMF EMan LCla MAsk MBri MWhe NArc
'Lady Ramsey'	CLit EBak MJac NArc
'Lady Rebecca'	CLoc
'Lady Thumb' 𝕐	CChe CLit CLoc CMHG CSil EBak EBly EKMF LCla LFli LVer MAsk MBal MBar MBri MJac MPla MWat MWhe NArc SKen SLBF SPer SSea
'Lady's Smock'	EKMF
'Lakeland Princess'	EBak NArc
'Lakeside'	CLoc EBak
'Lambada'	SLBF

	'Lamme Goedzak'	NArc
	'Lancashire Lass'	EMan MBri NArc WLRN
	'Lancelot'	CLit EBak EGou LCla
	'Land van Beveren'	MWar NArc SLBF
	'Lark'	EBly EGou
	'L'Arlésienne'	CLit CLoc
	'Lassie'	CLoc EBak LFli MJac NArc SMer
N	'Laura'	CLit CLoc CSil CWLN EBly EKMF MAsk MWhe SLBF
	'Laura Amanda'	EBly LFli
	'Lavender Kate'	CLoc EBak MJac
	'Lavender Lace'	MWhe
	'Lavender Lady'	CSil MAld
	'Lazy Lady'	EBak
	'Le Berger'	EKMF
	'Lechlade Apache'	EGou LCla
	'Lechlade Chinaman'	CSil MLan NArc
	'Lechlade Debutante'	EGou LCla
	'Lechlade Fire-eater'	EGou LCla
	'Lechlade Gorgon'	CSil EKMF LCla NArc
	'Lechlade Magician'	CLit CSil EKMF LCla MAsk NArc
	'Lechlade Maiden'	CSil
	'Lechlade Marchioness'	EGou EKMF
	'Lechlade Potentate'	EGou MAsk
	'Lechlade Rocket'	EGou EKMF
	'Lechlade Tinkerbell'	EGou LCla
	'Lechlade Violet'	CLit SSoC
	'Lee Anthony'	EGou
	'Leica'	EKMF SLBF
	'Leicestershire Silver'	MJac NArc
	'Len Bielby'	CLit EKMF LCla
	'Lena' 🏆	CLit CLoc CMHG CSil EBak EBly EGou EKMF LCla LVer MAld MAsk MBal MBri MJac MPla MWhe NArc NFai NHaw SKen SPer SRms WEas
	'Lena Dalton'	CLit CLoc EBak EKMF IHos MAsk MBri MJac MWhe NArc SKen
	'Leonora' 🏆	CLoc CSil EBak EKMF LCla MAsk MBri MWar MWhe NArc SLBF
	'Lesley'	EGou
	'Lett's Delight'	EBly EGou
	'Letty Lye'	EBak
	'Leverhulme'	See ***F.* 'Leverkusen'**
§	'Leverkusen'	CLit CLoc CSil EBak EGou EKMF LCla LHil MJac MWhe SKen SLBF SSoC
*	'Li Kai Lin'	CSil
N	'Liebesträume'	EBak
	'Liebriez'	CLit CSil EBak EBly EKMF LCla NArc
*	'Lilac'	EBak
	'Lilac Lady'	MJac
	'Lilac Lustre'	CGre CLoc CSil EBak EKMF MBri NArc
	'Lilac Princess'	MJac
	'Lilac Queen'	EBak
	'Lillibet'	CLoc CSil EBak LFli NArc SKen
	'Lillydale'	CLit CSil
	'Lilo Vogt'	EGou NArc
	'Linda Goulding'	CSil EBak EGou LCla MAld MAsk MWhe NArc
	'Linda Grace'	CLit EKMF SLBF
	'Lindisfarne'	CLit EBak EKMF LCla LFli MAsk MJac MWar NArc
	'Linet'	EBak
	'Lisa'	CSil EBly LFli
	'Lisa Ashton'	NArc
	'Lisi'	EKMF NArc
	'Little Beauty'	EKMF MWhe NArc SLBF
	'Little Gene'	EBak
	'Little Jewel'	SKen
	'Little Ouse'	EGou LCla MWhe
	'Little Ronnie'	MWhe
	'Little Witch'	EGou EKMF SLBF
	'Lively Lady'	CLit
	'Liver Bird'	NArc
	'Liz'	CLit EBak NArc
	'Lochinver'	CSil
	'Loeky'	CLoc CSil EBak LCla SLBF
	'Logan Garden'	See ***F. magellanica* 'Logan Woods'**
	'Lolita'	CLit EBak MAsk SMer
	'Lonely Ballerina'	CLoc
¶	'Long Distance'	SLBF
	'Long Preston'	EGou
	'Long Wings'	CSil EKMF LCla MAld MAsk NArc
	'Lord Byron'	CLoc EBak LCla NArc
	'Lord Derby'	NArc
	'Lord Lonsdale'	CLit CSil EBak EBly LCla MAsk MWhe NArc SKen WEas
	'Lord Roberts'	CLoc CSil NArc SKen
	'Lorelei'	CLit
	'Lorna Swinbank'	CLit CLoc NArc
	'Lorraine's Delight'	CLit CSil
	'Lottie Hobby'	CDec CInt CLoc CMGP CSil EBly ECtt EKMF LBlm LFli MAld MAsk MHar NArc SKen WFoF WPyg
	'Louise Emershaw'	CSil EBak LFli MAsk MJac
	'Lovable'	EBak MAsk SMer
	'Loveliness'	CLoc CSil EBak EKMF MWhe
	'Love's Reward'	CLit CLoc CSil EBly LCla MJac MWar MWhe SLBF
I	'Loxensis' 🏆	EBak EKMF LCla
N	***loxensis***	EGou LCla MAsk
	'Loxhore Angelus'	CSil
	'Loxhore Calypso'	EKMF
	'Loxhore Cancan'	CSil EKMF
	'Loxhore Cavalcade'	CSil
	'Loxhore Clarion'	CSil
	'Loxhore Cotillon'	CSil
	'Loxhore Mazurka'	CSil
	'Loxhore Minuet'	CSil
	'Loxhore Operetta'	CSil
	'Loxhore Posthorn'	CSil
	'Lucille'	CLit NArc
	'Lucky Strike'	CLit CLoc CSil EBak NArc SMer
	'Lucy Harris'	CSil
	'Lucy Locket'	MJac
	'Lula Bell'	LCla
	'Lunter's Trots'	NArc
	'Luscious'	CLit LFli
	'Lustre'	CLit EBak NArc SLBF
§	'Lycioides'	CSil LCla
§	***lycioides*** Andrews	CSil EBak EGou EKMF
	– hort.	See ***F.* 'Lycioides'**
	'Lye's Elegance'	CSil MAsk
	'Lye's Excelsior'	EBak LCla
	'Lye's Own'	EBak MAsk SLBF
	'Lye's Unique'	CLTr CLit CLoc CSil EBak EBly EGou EKMF LCla LFli MAld MAsk MJac MWar MWhe NArc SKen SLBF
	'Lylac Sunsa'	EKMF
	'Lynette'	CLoc
	'Lynn Ellen'	EBak NArc

'Mabel Greaves'	CSil LCla MAsk
'Machu Picchu'	CLoc CSil EBly EKMF LCla MWar NArc
macrophylla	EKMF
'Madame Butterfly'	CLoc
'Madame Cornélissen' 🏆	CLit CLoc CSil EBak EBly EKMF ENot LFli LVer MAsk MBar MBri MJac MWhe NArc SPer SRms
'Madame Eva Boye'	EBak
'Madelaine Sweeney'	MBri
'Maes-y-Groes'	EKMF
¶ ***magdalenae***	EKMF
magellanica	CMHG EKMF GOrc LHil NNor NPer SPer WOak WRha WWat
– 'Alba'	See ***F. magellanica*** var. ***molinae***
I – 'Alba Aureovariegata'	EPfP LHop MBri MRav SPer SSea WCru
– 'Alba Variegata'	CLit CMHG CSil EKMF NHaw WEas
¶ – var. ***conica***	EKMF
◆ – 'Globosa'	See ***F.* 'Globosa'**
§ – var. ***gracilis*** 🏆	CLit CLoc CSil EGoo EKMF LBlm MAsk NArc NFla SRms
– – 'Aurea'	CBot CLit CMHG CSil CTre EGou EHoe EKMF ELan ENot GCHN GQui LCla LFli MAld MAsk MWat MWhe SAxl SDix SKen SLBF SPer SPla WRus
§ – – 'Tricolor' (v)	CSil EBly EKMF EWes GOrc LCla LFli MAld MAsk SLBF SRms SSea
– – 'Variegata' 🏆	CGle CMHG CSil CTre EBak ECha EGou ENot LCla LVer MAsk MBal MGos NArc SChu SDix SKen SPer SUsu WAbe WEas WHil
§ – 'Logan Woods'	CSil EKMF GCal SAxl SLBF
– 'Longipedunculata'	EKMF
– var. ***macrostema***	EKMF
– – 'Variegata'	EGou
§ – var. ***molinae***	CGle CMHG CSil EBak EGou EKMF ELan ERav ISea LCla LFli MAld MBlu MWhe NFai NNor NPer NRoo SMac SPer WAbe WBod WEas WOak WRus
– – 'Golden Sharpitor'	WAbe WCot
§ – – 'Sharpitor' (v)	CB&S CDec CSil CTre EBak ECha EGou EHoe EKMF ELan LHop MAsk MBar MBri MPla MWat SAxl SMrm SPer SPla SRms SSea WCru WRus WSHC
– var. ***pumila***	CSil EAst EGoo GCal SIng
– 'Riccartonii'	See ***F.* 'Riccartonii'**
§ – 'Thompsonii' 🏆	ECGP EKMF EMon GCal SAxl SKen SRms
§ – 'Versicolor' (v) 🏆	Widely available
'Magic Flute'	CLoc CSil MJac
'Maharaja'	CLit EBak NArc
'Maike'	NArc
'Majebo'	NArc
'Major Heaphy'	CSil EBak EKMF MAsk MWar MWhe NArc
'Malibu Mist'	CSil EGou EKMF LCla MAsk NArc
'Mama Bleuss'	EBak NArc
'Mancunian'	CLit CSil EGou LCla LFli MAsk NArc
N 'Mandarin'	EBak LFli NArc
'Mandi'	EGou EKMF SLBF
¶ 'Mandy'	CLit
'Mantilla'	CLit CLoc CSil EBak EGou EKMF LFli MAsk MJac MWhe NArc SLBF
'Maori Pipes'	CSil EGou
'Marbled Sky'	MJac NArc
¶ 'Marco Jan'	EGou
'Marcus Graham'	CLit CLoc CSil EGou EKMF LCla LFli MAsk MWar MWhe NArc SLBF SMer
'Marcus Hanton'	CSil EKMF LCla MAsk NArc
'Mardi Gras'	EBak
'Margaret' 🏆	CLit CLoc CSil EBak EGou EKMF ENot GCHN ISea LCla LFli LVer MAsk MBal MWar MWhe NArc NHaw SKen SLBF SRms WStI
'Margaret Brown' 🏆	CLTr CLoc CSil CTri EBak EKMF LCla LFli MAsk MPla MWhe NArc SKen SLBF WStI
'Margaret Davidson'	CLoc
'Margaret Dawson'	MAsk
'Margaret Hazelwood'	EKMF
'Margaret Kendrick'	MBri
'Margaret Pilkington'	CGre EKMF LCla MAsk MBri MWar NArc SSea
'Margaret Roe'	CLit CSil EBak EKMF LCla MJac MWhe NArc SKen
'Margaret Rose'	MJac
'Margaret Susan'	EBak
'Margarite Dawson'	CLit CSil NArc
'Margery Blake'	CSil EBak
'Maria Landy'	CLit EKMF EMan LCla MAld MAsk MWar NArc SLBF
'Maria Merrills'	EKMF EMan LCla NArc
'Marietta'	CLit
'Marilyn Olsen'	CSil EBly EKMF LCla LFli MAld MWar NArc SLBF
'Marin Belle'	EBak LCla NArc
'Marin Glow' 🏆	CLit CLoc CSil EBak EKMF LCla LFli MAsk MWhe NArc SLBF
'Marinka' 🏆	CLit CLoc CSil EBak ECtt EKMF EMan IHos LCla LFli LVer MAld MAsk MBri MJac MWar MWhe NArc NFai NHaw SKen SLBF
'Marjory Almond'	EGou
'Mark Kirby'	EKMF
'Marlea's Vuurbol'	EGou
'Marlene Gilbee'	CLit MAsk MWar SMur
'Martin Hayward'	SKen
¶ 'Martin's Catherina'	EGou
'Martin's Midnight'	MAsk
¶ 'Martin's Yellow Suprise'	EGou EKMF SLBF
'Marton Smith'	MWhe
'Marty'	EBak
'Mary' 🏆	CLit CLoc CSil EBly EGou EKMF LCla LFli MAld MAsk MLan MWar MWhe NArc SKen SLBF
'Mary Caunt'	EKMF
¶ 'Mary Ellen Guffey'	EGou SLBF
'Mary Fairclo'	EGou
'Mary Joan'	EKMF MAsk
'Mary Lockyer'	CLoc EBak NArc
'Mary Neujean'	MBri
'Mary Poppins'	LCla NArc SLBF
'Mary Reynolds'	CLit
'Mary Thorne'	CSil EBak
'Mary Wright'	MWhe

'Masquerade'	EBak EKMF EMan MWhe NArc
'Matador'	CSil
mathewsii	EKMF
'Maureen'	NArc
'Maureen Ward'	EKMF
'Mauve Beauty'	CSil EGou EKMF
'Mauve Lace'	CSil
'Mauve Wisp'	NArc
'Max Jaffa'	CSil MAsk NArc
'May Rogers'	EGou
'Mayblossom'	ECtt LFli LVer SLBF
'Mayfayre'	CLoc
'Mayfield'	MWhe NArc SKen
'Meadowlark'	CLit EBak ECtt EKMF NArc
'Meditation'	CLoc CSil
'Melanie'	CSil EGou NArc SLBF
'Melody'	CSil EBak LFli MAsk MWhe NArc
'Melody Ann'	EBak
'Melting Moments'	EKMF NArc
'Mendocino Mini'	EGou EKMF
'Menna'	NArc
'Merlin'	CSil
'Merry England'	MAsk
'Merry Mary'	CSil EBak EKMF LCla NArc SMur
'Mexicali Rose'	CLoc
'Michael'	CSil EBly MAsk
'Michael Kurtz'	NArc
¶ ***michoacanensis***	EGou
'Micky Goult'	CLoc CSil EBly EKMF LCla LFli LVer MAld MAsk MJac MWhe NArc SLBF
'Microchip'	SLBF
microphylla	CB&S CGle CLit CLoc CMHG CSil CTre EBak EBar ERav ERea GRei LVer SMad SSea STre WCru WEas WRha
§ – subsp. ***aprica***	CGre EKMF LCla MAsk
§ – subsp. ***hemsleyana***	CSil EKMF LCla MWhe SKen
§ – subsp. ***hidalgensis***	CKni CLit CSil EGou EKMF GAri LBlm LCla SLBF SRms
§ – 'Hummeltje'	EGou
– subsp. ***microphylla***	CSil EGou LCla
¶ – subsp. ***quercetorum***	EGou LCla
'Midas'	MAsk MBri NArc
'Midnight Sun'	CSil EBak EBly LFli NArc SKen
'Midwinter'	NArc
'Mieke Meursing'	CLit CLoc CSil EBak ECtt EKMF LCla LFli MBri MJac MWar MWhe NArc SKen SLBF
'Miep Aalhuizen'	EGou EKMF LCla SLBF
N 'Mikado'	EGou
'Mike Oxtoby'	EKMF MAsk
'Millrace'	EGou LCla
'Mimi Kubischta'	NArc
'Mina Knudde'	NArc
'Ming'	CLoc CSil
'Miniature Jewels'	SLBF
minimiflora	See ***F. microphylla*** subsp. ***hidalgensis***
'Minirose'	CSil EBly EKMF LCla MAsk MWar MWhe SKen
'Minnesota'	EBak
'Mipam'	SLBF
'Mirjana'	NArc
'Mischief'	CSil NArc
'Miss Aubrey'	EGou
'Miss California'	CLit CLoc CSil EBak ECtt EKMF LFli MAsk MBri MWhe NArc
'Miss Debbie'	EGou
'Miss Great Britain'	CLit CSil MAsk
'Miss Marilyn'	CLit
'Miss Vallejo'	EBak NArc
'Mission Bells'	CLit CLoc CSil EBak EKMF LCla LVer MAsk MWhe NArc SKen
'Mistoque'	CSil NArc
'Misty Blue'	CSil NArc
'Misty Haze'	CSil MWar
'Misty Pink'	EKMF NArc
'Moira Ann'	ECtt
'Molesworth'	CLit CSil EBak LFli MJac MWhe NArc SKen SMer
'Mollie Beaulah'	CLit CSil ECtt EKMF NArc
'Molly Chatfield'	NArc
'Money Spinner'	CLoc EBak
'Monsieur Thibaut'	ENot LCla MAld SKen
'Monte Rosa'	CLoc SKen
'Monterey'	MWhe
'Montevideo'	EGou
'Montrose Village'	CSil MWhe
'Monument'	CSil
'Mood Indigo'	CLit CSil EGou LVer MWar NArc SLBF
'Moonbeam'	CLoc CSil MAsk MWhe
'Moonlight Sonata'	CLit CLoc CSil EBak MAsk MJac NArc SKen
'Moonraker'	CSil LFli LVer NArc
'Moonshot'	NArc
'Morcott'	NArc
'More Applause'	CLoc EGou EKMF LVer MWhe NArc
'Morning Cloud'	LFli NArc
'Morning Glow'	LFli NArc
'Morning Light'	CLit CLoc CSil EBak NArc SMer SMur
'Morning Mist'	EBak NArc
'Morning Star'	MBri
'Morrells'	EBak
'Moth Blue'	CLit CSil EBak NArc SMer
'Mountain Mist'	CSil EKMF LFli MJac
'Moyra'	EKMF
'Mr A. Huggett'	CLit CLoc CSil EBly LCla MAsk MWhe NArc SLBF
'Mr P.D. Lee'	MWhe
'Mr W. Rundle'	CLit EBak NArc
'Mrs Churchill'	CLoc
'Mrs Janice Morrison'	EGou
¶ 'Mrs John D. Fredericks'	CSil
'Mrs Lawrence Lyon'	EBak
'Mrs Lovell Swisher'	CLit CSil EBak EKMF LCla MBri MJac MWhe NArc SLBF
'Mrs Marshall'	CSil EBak MAsk NArc SLBF
'Mrs Popple' 🏆	CChe CLit CLoc CMHG CSil EBak EKMF ELan ENot ERav LCla LFli LVer MAld MAsk MBar MBri MGos MJac MPla MWar MWat MWhe NArc NHaw SKen SLBF SPer WBod
'Mrs Susan Brookfield'	LCla NArc
'Mrs Victor Reiter'	CSil
'Mrs W. Castle'	CSil NArc
'Mrs W. Rundle'	CLoc CSil EBak EKMF LFli MAld MWhe NArc SLBF
'Mrs W.P. Wood' 🏆	CLoc EKMF NArc
'Multa'	SLBF
'Muriel'	CLit CLoc EBak ECtt EKMF MWhe NArc SKen

'My Dear'	CLoc
'My Fair Lady'	CLoc CSil EBak NArc
'My Honey'	CSil MAsk NArc
'Mystique'	CLit MAsk
'Nancy Darnley'	EKMF
'Nancy Lou'	CGre CLit CLoc EBly EGou EKMF LCla LFli LVer MAld MAsk MJac MWar MWhe NArc SKen SLBF
'Nancy Scrivener'	NArc SLBF
'Nanny Ed'	MBri
'Natalie Jones'	EGou
'Natasha Sinton'	CLit CLoc CSil ECtt EKMF EMan LCla LFli MAld MAsk MBri MJac MWar MWhe NArc NHaw SLBF WLRN
'Native Dancer'	EBak
'Nautilus'	EBak
'Navy Blue'	CSil NArc
'Neapolitan'	EBly MAsk MWhe SKen SLBF
'Neil Clyne'	MWhe
'Nell Gwyn'	CLit CLoc CSil EBak NArc
'Nellie Nuttall' ♀	CLit CLoc CSil EBak EBly EGou EKMF LCla LFli LVer MAld MAsk MWar MWhe NArc NHaw SLBF SSea
'Neopolitan'	CSil EGou EKMF LCla NArc
'Nettala'	CLit EGou SLBF
'Neue Welt'	CSil EBak
'Neville Young'	MAsk
'New Fascination'	EBak NArc SKen
'Nice 'n' Easy'	CLit LVer MBri MJac MWhe NArc
'Nicholas Hughes'	NArc
¶ 'Nicky Veerman'	EGou
'Nicola'	CLoc EBak
N 'Nicola Claire'	EGou NArc
'Nicola Jane'	CSil EBak EBly EKMF LCla LFli MAld MAsk MBri MJac MWhe NArc SLBF
'Nicolette'	MJac
'Night and Day'	NArc
'Nightingale'	CLoc CSil EBak NArc
nigricans* × *gehrigeri	EKMF
'Nikkis Findling'	CSil EGou EKMF NArc SLBF
'Nimue'	EGou MAsk NArc
'Nina Wills'	EBak
'Niobe'	EBak
'Niula'	EKMF
'No Name'	EBak
'Norah Henderson'	NArc
'Norfolk Belle'	LFli
'Norfolk Ivor'	EGou
'Norma Nield'	LCla
'Norman Greenhill'	SLBF
'Norman Mitchinson'	EGou
'Normandy Bell'	CSil EBak
'North Cascades'	MAsk
'Northern Pride'	MAsk
'Northilda'	NArc
'Northumbrian Belle'	CSil EBak MJac NArc
'Northway'	CLit CLoc CSil LCla LFli MAsk MJac MWhe NArc
'Norvell Gillespie'	EBak
'Novato'	CLit EBak NArc
'Novella'	EBak NArc
'Noyo Star'	CSil LFli
'Nunthorpe Gem'	CSil NArc
¶ 'Nuwenspete'	EGou
obconica	EGou LCla
'Obergärtner Koch'	EKMF LCla NArc SMrm
'Ocean Beach'	EBly MAsk NArc
'Oddfellow'	CSil NArc
'Oetnang'	SCoo
'Old Somerset'	CLit CSil LCla LFli MAsk MWhe
'Ole 7 Up'	MAld
'Olive Moon'	EBly SLBF
'Olive Smith'	CSil EBly MAld MAsk MJac MWhe NArc
'Olympic Lass'	EBak NArc
'Olympic Sunset'	EKMF
'Oosje'	See ***F.* × *bacillaris* 'Oosje'**
'Opalescent'	CLit CLoc
'Orange Crush'	CLoc CSil EBak LFli MAsk MWar MWhe NArc
'Orange Crystal'	CLit CSil EBak EKMF IHos LFli MAsk MBri MJac MWhe NArc NFai NHaw SKen
'Orange Drops'	CLit CLoc CSil EBak EBly EKMF LFli MAsk MWhe NArc SKen
'Orange Flare'	CLit CLoc CSil EBak EKMF LCla MJac MWhe NArc SLBF
'Orange King'	CLoc CSil EGou EMan SSea
'Orange Mirage'	CLit CLoc CSil EBak LCla LFli LVer MAld MAsk MBri MWar MWhe NArc SKen
'Orangeblossom'	CSil LCla NArc SLBF
'Oranje van Os'	MJac MWhe
'Orient Express'	CLit CSil EGou LCla LFli MAsk MWar MWhe NArc
Oriental Flame	EKMF NArc
'Oriental Sunrise'	MAsk MWhe
'Ornamental Pearl'	CLoc EBak NArc SLBF
'Ortenburger Festival'	NArc
'Orwell'	CLit CSil
'Other Fellow'	CLit CSil EBak EBly EKMF LCla MAsk MJac NArc SLBF
'Our Darling'	CSil MWhe NArc
¶ 'Our Ted'	EGou
'Overbecks'	See ***F. magellanica* var. *molinae* 'Sharpitor'**
'Overbecks Ruby'	EMon GBuc WCot
'P.J.B.'	LCla NArc SLBF
'Pabbe's Teudebel'	EGou
'Pabbe's Tudebekje'	CSil EGou
¶ ***pachyrrhiza***	EKMF
'Pacific Grove'	EBak
'Pacific Queen'	CLoc EBak NArc
'Pacquesa' ♀	CLit CSil EBak EBly EKMF IHos LFli MAsk MJac MWar MWhe NArc SLBF
'Padre Pio'	MJac
'Pale Flame'	MWhe NArc
pallescens	EGou EKMF
'Pamela Hutchinson'	MAld NArc
'Pamela Knights'	EBak EGou
'Pan'	EGou NArc
'Pan America'	EBak
'Pangea'	EGou
paniculata	CBot CKni CLTr EAst EBak EGou EKMF LCla LHop MAsk NArc SHFr SLBF SLod SMrm WFoF
* – var. ***mixensis***	EGou
'Pantaloons'	EBak NArc
'Papa Bleuss'	CLoc EBak
'Papoose'	CLit CSil EBak EKMF LCla MAsk MPla NArc
'Paramour'	LFli NArc
'Party Frock'	CLit CLoc CSil EBak LCla LFli NArc SMer
parviflora hort.	See ***F.* × *bacillaris***

– Lindley	EBak
'Pastel'	EBak
'Pat Crofts'	NArc
'Pat Meara'	CLoc EBak
'Pathetique'	CLoc
'Patience'	CSil EBak EGou LCla MJac NArc SLBF
'Patio Party'	MBri
'Patio Princess'	CSil LCla LFli MBri MJac MWar MWhe NArc NPri
N 'Patricia'	CSil EBak
'Patricia Ann'	EKMF MWar
'Patty Evans'	EBak MBri NArc
'Patty Sue'	CLit LCla MBri WLRN
'Paul Berry'	EKMF
'Paul Cambon'	EBak EKMF NArc
'Paul Roe'	EKMF MBri MJac
'Paula Jane' ♀	CLit LCla MAsk MBri MJac MWar MWhe SLBF
'Paula Johnson'	MJac
'Pauline Rawlins'	CLoc EBak
¶ PC&H 247	CFee
'Peace'	EBak SMer
'Peachy'	EGou SLBF
'Peachy Keen'	EBak
'Peacock'	CLoc
'Pee Wee Rose'	CSil EBak EKMF NArc
'Peggy King'	CSil EBak LCla MWhe NArc SRms
'Peloria'	CLoc EBak MAsk NArc
'Pennine'	MBri MWar
'Peper Harow'	EBak
'Pepi'	CLoc EBak
'Peppermint Candy'	NPri SCoo
'Peppermint Stick'	CLit CLoc CSil EBak EKMF EMan LCla LFli LVer MAsk MBri MJac MWhe NArc NHaw SKen SSea
'Perestroika'	SLBF
'Perky Pink'	CLit EBak EBly LCla MAsk MWhe NArc SKen
'Perry Park'	CLit EBak MAsk MBri MJac NArc
'Perry's Jumbo'	NPer
perscandens	EGou EKMF ISea LCla SLBF
'Personality'	EBak NArc
'Peter Bielby'	EGou EKMF MWar SLBF
'Peter Crooks'	CSil EGou EKMF LCla MAsk MJac NArc
'Peter James'	EKMF
'Peter Pan'	CLit CSil SPer
'Peter Sanderson'	EKMF LCla NArc
petiolaris	EGou EKMF LCla MAsk
'Petit Fleur'	CSil
'Petit Four'	CSil
'Petite'	EBak NArc
'Petronella'	MAsk MWar
'Pharaoh'	CLoc
'Phénoménal'	CLit CSil EBak EBly EKMF LFli MAsk SKen
'Phyllis' ♀	CLit CLoc CSil EBak EBly EKMF LCla LFli LHil MAsk MBal MJac MWhe NArc NFai NHaw SKen SLBF SPla SSoC
'Phyrne'	CSil EBak NArc
'Piet G. Vergeer'	NArc
'Piet Heemskerke'	EGou
'Pinch Me'	CLTr CLit CSil EBak EKMF LCla LFli LVer MAsk SKen
'Pink Aurora'	CLoc CSil
'Pink Ballet Girl'	CLoc EBak ECtt NArc
'Pink Bon Accorde'	CLoc CSil NArc
'Pink Bouquet'	CSil
'Pink Chiffon'	NArc
'Pink Cloud'	CLoc EBak NArc
'Pink Crystal'	LVer
'Pink Darling'	CLit CLoc EBak MWhe SKen
'Pink Dessert'	CSil EBak NArc SKen
¶ 'Pink Domino'	EKMF
'Pink Fairy'	CLit CSil EBak NArc
'Pink Fandango'	CLoc
'Pink Fantasia'	CLit CLoc CSil EBak EBly EGou EKMF LCla LFli MAld MAsk MJac MWar MWhe
'Pink Flamingo'	CLit CLoc CSil EBak NArc SMer
'Pink Galore'	CLoc CSil EBak EKMF EMan IHos LCla LFli LVer MAld MAsk MBri MJac MWhe NFai NHaw
'Pink Goon'	CLit CSil LCla LFli MAsk SLBF
'Pink Jade'	EBak SMer
'Pink la Campanella'	CLit CSil EMan LCla MBri MJac MWhe NArc SMer WLRN
'Pink Lace'	CSil
N 'Pink Lady'	MWhe
'Pink Marshmallow'	CLit CLoc CSil EBak EGou EKMF EMan LCla LFli MAld MAsk MJac MWar MWhe NHaw SKen SLBF
'Pink Panther'	EKMF NArc
N 'Pink Pearl'	CSil EBak EKMF
'Pink Picotee'	LCla MJac
'Pink Profusion'	EBak
'Pink Quartet'	CLoc CSil EBak LCla LFli NArc
'Pink Rain'	CSil EGou EKMF MAsk MJac NArc
'Pink Slipper'	CLoc
'Pink Spangles'	CLit EMan IHos LFli MAsk MBri NHaw
'Pink Surprise'	MJac NArc
'Pink Temptation'	CLit CLoc CSil EBak NPri
'Pinkmost'	ECtt
'Pinto'	LFli NArc SMur
'Pinwheel'	CLoc CSil EBak
'Piper'	CSil LFli MWar
'Piper's Vale'	EGou EKMF SLBF
¶ 'Pirbright'	EKMF
'Pixie'	CLoc CSil EBak EKMF MAsk MJac MWhe NArc SKen SLBF
'Pixie Bells'	CMHG
'Playford'	EBak NArc
'Plenty'	EBak
'Ploughman'	EGou
'Plumb-bob'	EGou EKMF
¶ 'Poacher'	EGou
'Pop Whitlock' (v)	EKMF NArc
'Popely Pride'	EGou
'Popsie Girl'	EGou LCla SLBF
'Port Arthur'	EBak NArc
'Postiljon'	CLit CSil EBak EKMF MAsk NArc SLBF
N 'Powder Puff'	CLit CLoc CSil ECtt EKMF LVer MAsk MBri NArc NPri SKen
N 'Prelude'	CLoc CSil EBak NArc
'President'	CSil EBak LCla SKen
'President B.W. Rawlins'	EBak
§ 'President Elliot'	CSil MWhe
'President George Bartlett'	EKMF

'President Leo Boullemier'	CLit CSil EBak ECtt EKMF LCla LFli MAsk MJac NArc
'President Margaret Slater'	CLit CLoc CSil EBak EMan LFli MAsk MJac MWhe NArc SLBF
'President Moir'	CSil LFli
'President Norman Hobbs'	EKMF MWar NArc
'President Roosevelt'	CDoC CSil ECtt
'President Stanley Wilson'	EBak EBly ECtt LFli MAsk
'President Wilf Sharp'	NArc
'Preston Belle'	EGou
'Preston Field'	CSil SLBF
'Preston Guild'	CLit CLoc CSil EBak EGou EKMF LBlm LFli MAsk MWhe NArc NPer SLBF
'Pride of the West'	CSil EBak
'Prince of Orange'	CLoc CSil EBak LCla NArc
'Prince of Peace'	CSil
'Princess Dollar'	See ***F.* 'Dollar Princess'**
'Princess of Bath'	CLoc
'Princess Pamela'	SLBF
'Princess Pat'	EKMF
'Princessita'	CLit CSil EBak ECtt EKMF EMan LFli MAld MAsk MBri MJac MWar MWhe NArc NHaw SKen
procumbens ♀	CGre CLit CLoc CSil EBak ECou EGou EKMF ELan ERea ESis GCHN LCla MAsk MHar MWhe NArc NWCA SHFr SLBF SSea SSoC WAbe WOMN WPer
I – 'Argentea'	EKMF GCal
'Prodigy'	See ***F.* 'Enfant Prodigue'**
'Prosperity' ♀	CLit CLoc CSil EBak EBee EBly EGou EKMF LCla MAld MAsk MJac MWar MWhe NArc
N 'Pumila'	CTri EKMF ELan MAsk MBal NArc
'Purbeck Mist'	EKMF
'Purperklokje'	CSil EBak EGou EKMF MAld MAsk NArc
'Purple Emperor'	CLoc
'Purple Graseing'	MAsk
'Purple Heart'	CLoc CSil EBak NArc SKen
'Purple Patch'	CLit LCla MBri SLBF WLRN
'Purple Pride'	MBri
'Purple Rain'	CSil EKMF
'Purple Showers'	CSil NArc
'Purple Splendour'	CSil
'Pussy Cat'	CLoc CSil EBak EKMF LCla MAsk SKen SSoC
'Putney Pride'	EBly
'Put's Folly'	EBak MJac SKen SMer
putumayensis	CLit CSil EBak
'Quasar'	CLit CLoc CSil EBly EKMF LCla LFli MAsk MJac MWhe NHaw SLBF
'Queen Mabs'	EBak
'Queen Mary'	CLoc CSil EBak EKMF
'Queen of Bath'	EBak
'Queen of Derby'	CSil LCla MAld MAsk
'Queen's Park'	EBak
'Query'	CSil EBak NArc SKen
'R.A.F.'	CLit CLoc CSil EBak EBly ECtt EKMF LCla LFli MAsk MJac MWar NArc SKen SLBF
'Rachel Craig'	MWar
'Rachel Sinton'	EMan LFli MBri WLRN
'Radcliffe Beauty'	MWhe
'Radcliffe Bedder'	CSil MAsk SKen
¶ 'Radings Gerda'	EGou
'Radings Inge'	EGou EKMF
'Rading's Juma'	EGou
'Radings Karin'	CDoC EGou EKMF
'Radings Mapri'	EKMF
¶ 'Rading's Marjorie'	EGou
'Radings Michelle'	CSil EGou
'Raintree Legend'	NArc
'Ralph Oliver'	EGou
'Ralph's Delight'	EGou
'Rambling Rose'	CLit CLoc CSil EBak ECtt EGou LFli MAsk MJac NArc
'Rambo'	NArc
'Rams Royal'	LCla LVer MAsk MJac NArc
* 'Raspberry'	CLit CLoc CSil EBak LCla LFli MAsk MWar MWhe NArc
'Ratatouille'	CSil EKMF LFli MAsk NArc
ravenii	EGou EKMF LCla
'Ravensbarrow'	NArc
'Ravenslaw'	EKMF
'Ray Redfern'	MJac
'Raymond Scopes'	EGou
'Razzle Dazzle'	EBak
'Reading Show'	CSil EBly LCla LVer SLBF
'Rebecca Williamson'	EGou LCla MJac MWhe NArc
'Rebekah Sinton'	CLit EBak LCla LFli MBri MWar
'Red Ace'	CSil
'Red Imp'	CSil
'Red Jacket'	EBak LFli NArc
'Red Ribbons'	EBak
'Red Rum'	CSil
'Red Shadows'	CLit CLoc CSil EBak LFli MJac MWhe NArc
'Red Spider'	CLit CLoc CSil EBak EKMF EMan LFli LVer MAsk MWar MWhe NArc NHaw SKen SSea
'Red Sunlight'	EGou
'Red Wing'	CLoc
'Reflexa'	See ***F.* × *bacillaris* 'Reflexa'**
'Reg Dickenson'	MJac MWhe
'Reg Gubler'	SLBF
'Regal'	CLoc
'Regal Robe'	CLit CSil
regia	CSil
– var. ***alpestris***	See ***F. alpestris***
– var. ***regia***	EGou EKMF LCla
– subsp. ***reitzii***	EKMF
– subsp. ***serrae***	EKMF
'Remembrance'	EKMF
'Remus'	CSil EKMF LCla MAsk MBri NArc
'Requiem'	CLoc IHos
'Reverend Doctor Brown'	EBak NArc
'Reverend Elliott'	See ***F.* 'President Elliot'**
N 'Rhapsody'	CLoc
'Riant'	NArc
§ 'Riccartonii' ♀	CB&S CChe CLit CLoc EBak EKMF ELan ENot LCla LHil MBar MBri NBee NFla NPer NWea SMrm SPer WGwG WStI
'Riccartonii Variegated'	WEas
'Richard John'	NArc
'Richard John Carrington'	CSil
'Ridestar'	CLit CLoc CSil EBak EMan LCla MAsk MJac MWhe
'Rina Felix'	EGou
'Ringwood Market'	CLit EBly ECtt EKMF LCla LFli MJac MWhe NArc
'Robbie'	CLit EGou EKMF NArc
'Robert Lutters'	NArc
'Robin'	LFli
¶ 'Robin Hood'	CSil

'Rodeo'	EGou
'Rolla'	EBak EGou EKMF NArc
'Rolt's Ruby'	EBly NArc
'Roman City'	CLoc NArc
'Romance'	EKMF
'Romany Rose'	CLoc
'Ron Chambers Love'	EGou
'Ron Ewart'	EKMF MWhe
'Ron Venables'	MAld
'Ronald L. Lockerbie'	CLit CLoc EKMF MAsk SMur
'Roos Breytenbach'	EGou EKMF LCla
'Rosamunda'	CLoc
'Rose Aylett'	EBak NArc
'Rose Bradwardine'	EBak NArc SMer
'Rose Churchill'	CLit LCla LFli LVer MBri MJac
'Rose Fantasia'	CLit CLoc CSil EBly EGou EKMF LCla MAld MWar MWhe SLBF
'Rose Lace'	CLit
'Rose Marie'	CLit CLoc NArc
'Rose of Castile' 🏆	CLit CLoc CSil EBak EKMF LCla MAsk MJac MWhe NArc SRms
'Rose of Castile Improved'	CSil EBak EKMF LCla MAsk MJac MWar SKen
'Rose of Denmark'	CLoc CSil EBak LFli MAsk MBri MJac MWar MWhe NHaw WLRN
'Rose Reverie'	EBak NArc
'Rose Winston'	CLit EKMF MWhe
rosea hort.	See ***F.* 'Globosa'**
– Ruiz & Pav.	See ***F. lycioides* Andrews**
'Rosebud'	EBak NArc
'Rosecroft Beauty'	CSil EBak MAsk MWhe NArc SKen
'Rosemary Day'	CLoc
'Roslyn Lowe'	CLit CSil NArc
'Ross Lea'	CSil
'Rosy Frills'	CSil EGou LCla LFli MJac MWhe NArc
'Rosy Morn'	CLoc EBak
Rosy Ruffles	EKMF
'Rough Silk'	CLit CLoc CSil EBak LCla LFli SMer
'Roy Walker'	CLit CLoc CSil EGou EKMF LVer MAld MAsk MJac MWar MWhe NArc
'Royal and Ancient'	CLTr EGou
'Royal Orchid'	EBak
'Royal Purple'	CLit CSil EBak EKMF MAsk MBri NArc
'Royal Touch'	EBak
'Royal Velvet' 🏆	CLTr CLit CLoc CSil EBak EBly EGou EKMF EMan LCla LFli LVer MAld MAsk MJac MWar MWhe NArc NHaw SKen SLBF
'Royal Wedding'	CLit CSil LCla LFli NArc SLBF
'Rozientje'	NArc
'Rubicon'	NArc
§ 'Rubra Grandiflora'	EBak EKMF LCla SLBF
'Ruby'	CLit
'Ruby Wedding'	CLit CSil EGou LCla SLBF
'Ruddigore'	CSil MAsk NArc
'Ruffles'	CLit CSil EBak NArc
§ 'Rufus'	CLoc CSil CTri EBak EBly EKMF LCla LFli LVer MAsk MJac MWar MWhe NArc SKen SLBF
'Rufus the Red'	See ***F.* 'Rufus'**
'Ruth'	CLit CSil
'Ruth Brazewell'	CLoc

'Ruth King'	CLit EBak ECtt LFli
'Rutland Water'	LFli MAsk NArc
'Sailor'	MAld MJac
'Sally Ann'	CLit
'Salmon Cascade'	CLit CSil EBak EBly ECtt EKMF EMan LCla LFli MAld MAsk MJac MWar MWhe NArc SLBF
'Salmon Glow'	MAsk MJac MWhe NArc
'Sampson's Delight'	MAsk
'Sam's Song'	MJac
'Samson'	CLit EBak
'San Diego'	CLit CSil NArc SMur
'San Francisco'	EBak
'San Leandro'	EBak NArc
'San Mateo'	EBak NArc
§ ***sanctae-rosae***	EBak EGou EKMF LBlm LCla
'Sandboy'	CSil EBak
'Sanrina'	EKMF
'Santa Cruz'	CLit CSil EBak EGou EKMF LCla LVer MAsk MWhe NArc SMer SSea
'Santa Lucia'	CLoc EBak NArc
'Santa Monica'	EBak
'Sapphire'	CSil EBak NArc
'Sara Helen'	CLoc EBak
¶ 'Sarah Eliza'	MJac
'Sarah Greensmith'	EKMF NArc
'Sarah Jayne'	CSil EBak LCla NArc
'Sarong'	CSil EBak NArc
'Saskia'	EKMF NArc
'Satellite'	CLoc EBak EKMF LFli MAsk NArc
'Saturnus'	EBak
scabriuscula	EKMF LCla
scandens	See ***F. decussata***
'Scarborough Rock'	NArc
'Scarborough Rosette'	EGou
'Scarcity'	CLit CSil EBak NArc SKen
¶ 'Scarlett O'Hara'	EGou
¶ 'Schiller'	EKMF
'Schneeball'	CSil EBak EKMF NArc
¶ 'Schneewittchen' Hoech	EKMF
'Schneewittchen' Klein	CSil EBak EBly
'Schönbrunner Schuljubiläum'	EBak SLBF
'Schöne Wilhelmine'	NArc
'Scotch Heather'	NArc
'Sea Shell'	EBak MAsk NArc
'Seaforth'	EBak
'Sealand Prince'	CLit CSil ECtt EKMF MAsk NArc
'Sebastopol'	CLoc ECtt EKMF LFli NArc
serratifolia Hooker	See ***F. austromontana***
– Ruiz & Pavón	See ***F. denticulata***
sessilifolia	EKMF LCla
'Seventh Heaven'	CLit CLoc CSil EGou LFli MAsk MWar SLBF
'Severn Queen'	CSil
'Shady Lady'	NArc
'Shangri-La'	CSil EBak SMur
'Shanley'	NArc
'Sharon Allsop'	CSil MWhe
'Sharon Caunt'	EKMF
'Sharpitor'	See ***F. magellanica* var. *molinae* 'Sharpitor'**
'Shawn Rushton'	EKMF MWar
'Shawna Ree'	EKMF LCla
'Sheila Crooks'	EBak EMan LCla MAsk MJac MWhe
'Sheila Kirby'	MJac
'Sheila Mary'	EKMF MJac

'Shelford' 🏆	CLit CLoc CSil EBak EBly EKMF EMan LCla LFli MAld MAsk MJac MWar MWhe NArc SLBF
'Shell Pink'	CSil
'Shelley Lyn'	NArc SKen
'Shining Knight'	CSil
'Shirley Halladay'	EKMF
'Shooting Star'	EBak
'Showtime'	CSil
'Shugborough'	EKMF MWar
'Shy Lady'	MWhe
'Sierra Blue'	CLoc EBak EKMF NArc
'Silver Anniversary'	EKMF NArc
'Silver Dawn'	CSil EBly EKMF MAsk MWhe SLBF
'Silver Dollar'	CLit LFli MWhe NArc SKen
'Silverdale'	CSil EKMF LFli MAsk MWhe NLak SLBF
'Simon J. Rowell'	EKMF LCla
simplicicaulis	EBak EGou EKMF LCla MAsk
'Sincerity'	CLit CLoc CSil
'Sinton's Standard'	MBri
'Sir Alfred Ramsey'	EBak MJac MWhe
N 'Siren'	EBak NArc
'Sister Ann Haley'	CLit CSil EBly EKMF SLBF
'Sleepy'	CLit CSil LCla LFli LVer MAsk MBri NArc
'Sleigh Bells'	CLoc CSil EBak EKMF MAsk MWhe NArc
'Small Pipes'	EGou EKMF NArc
'Smokey Mountain'	EKMF MAsk NArc SMur
'Smoky'	CSil
'Sneezy'	CLit CSil LFli MAsk MWhe NArc
'Snow Burner'	NPri SLBF
'Snow Country'	LFli
'Snow Goose'	EGou
'Snow White'	CLit CSil EGou LFli LVer MAsk NArc SMur
§ 'Snowcap' 🏆	CLit CLoc CSil EBak EBly EKMF EMan IHos LCla LFli LVer MAld MAsk MBri MJac MWar MWhe NArc NFai NHaw NPer SKen SLBF WStI
'Snowdon'	MWar
N 'Snowdrift'	CLoc EBak
'Snowfire'	CLoc CSil ECtt EGou EKMF LFli MAld MAsk MJac MWhe NArc
'Snowstorm'	CSil ECtt
'Snowy Summit'	CLit CSil SMur
'So Big'	CLit EKMF NArc
Software	EGou MAsk NArc
'Son of Thumb' 🏆	CLit CLoc CSil EAst EBly EKMF ELan EMan LCla LFli MAsk MBri MJac MWhe NArc SLBF
'Sonota'	CLoc CSil EBak EKMF NArc
'Sophie Claire'	EGou EKMF LCla
'Sophie Cochrane'	NArc
'Sophie's Surprise'	EGou EKMF
'Sophisticated Lady'	CLoc CSil EBak EBly ECtt EKMF LVer MAsk MJac MWar NArc
'South Lakeland'	CLit
'South Seas'	EBak NArc
'Southgate'	CLit CLoc CSil EBak EGou EKMF EMan LFli LVer MAsk MBri MJac MWar MWhe NArc NHaw
'Southlanders'	EBak

'Southwell Minster'	EKMF NArc
'Space Shuttle'	CLoc CSil EKMF LCla LFli MAsk MWhe NArc
'Sparky'	CLit EGou LCla MAsk SLBF
'Speciosa'	EBak EKMF LCla MWhe
'Spellbinder'	EGou
'Spion Kop'	CLit CSil EBak EKMF LFli LVer MAsk MJac MWar MWhe NArc NFai NHaw
§ ***splendens*** 🏆	CFee CKni CLoc CSil EBak EGou EKMF LCla NPer SMrm
– 'Karl Hartweg'	LBlm
'Squadron Leader'	CLit EBak EBly EGou LCla
'Square Peg'	NArc
'Stanley Cash'	CLTr CLit CLoc CSil EKMF LFli LVer MAsk MWar MWhe NArc SCoo
'Stan's Choice'	CSil
'Star of Pink'	MWhe
'Star Rose'	EKMF
'Stardust'	CSil EBak LCla MJac MWhe NArc
'Steeley'	MWhe
'Steirerblut'	EGou
'Stella Ann'	CLit CSil EBak EBly EGou LCla MAld MWhe NArc
'Stella Marina'	CLoc EBak
'Sterretje'	EGou
'Stormy Sunset'	CLit NArc
'Strawberry Delight'	CLit CLoc CSil EBak ECtt EKMF LCla LFli LVer MAsk MJac MWhe NArc SKen
'Strawberry Mousse'	LVer
'Strawberry Sundae'	CLoc CSil EBak NArc
'Strawberry Supreme'	CSil EKMF MAsk
'String of Pearls'	CLit CLoc CSil EKMF LCla MAsk MBri MJac NArc SKen SLBF
'Stuart Joe'	EKMF
'Sugar Almond'	MJac
'Sugar Blues'	EBak NArc
◆ Sugarbush	See ***F.* 'Suikerbossie'**
§ 'Suikerbossie'	MJac NArc
'Sunkissed'	CLit EBak
'Sunlight Path'	LCla
'Sunningdale'	EGou LCla
'Sunny'	SKen
'Sunny Smiles'	EKMF NArc
'Sunray' (v)	CBrd CLTr CLit CLoc CSil EBak EGou EKMF LFli MAsh MAsk MWhe NArc NPri SKen SPla WWeb
'Sunset'	CLit CLoc CSil EBak MAsk MWhe NArc SKen SMer SPer
'Supernova'	NArc
'Superstar'	CLit CSil EBly LCla MBri
'Surrey Symphony'	LCla
'Susan'	LCla
'Susan Arnold'	MAsk
'Susan Ford'	CLit CSil LFli MAsk NArc
'Susan Green'	CLit CSil EBak EKMF EMan LCla LFli MJac MWar MWhe NArc
'Susan McMaster'	CLoc
'Susan Olcese'	EBak NArc
'Susan Travis'	CLTr CLit CLoc CSil EBak EKMF MAsk MWhe NArc SBid SKen
'Susan Young'	MAsk
'Swanley Gem' 🏆	CLit CLoc EBak EKMF LCla LFli LVer MAsk SLBF
'Swanley Pendula'	CLoc

'Swanley Yellow' EBak NArc SKen
'Sweet Leilani' CLit CLoc CSil EBak NArc SKen
'Sweet Sixteen' CLoc
N 'Sweetheart' EBak NArc
'Swingtime' ♀ CGre CLit CLoc CSil EBak EBly EKMF EMan IHos LCla LFli LVer MAld MAsk MJac MWar MWhe NArc NFai NHaw NPri SKen SLBF
'S'Wonderful' CLoc EBak SMer
¶ *sylvatica* Benth. EKMF
– Munz See ***F. nigricans***
'Sylvia Barker' EGou LCla MAld MAsk
'Sylvia Foster' NArc
'Sylvy' CLit CSil MWhe NArc
'Symphony' CLoc EBak MAsk
'Taddle' EMan MJac NArc SLBF
'Taffeta Bow' CLTr CLit CLoc CSil EKMF LFli LVer MAsk SMer
'Taffy' EBak
'Tam O'Shanter' CLit CSil LFli
'Tamworth' CLit CLoc EBak LCla LFli MAsk MJac NArc SSea
'Tangerine' CLit CLoc CSil EBak EKMF MWhe NArc
'Tania Leanne' CLit CSil NArc
'Tanya' CLoc EKMF
'Tanya Bridger' EBak NArc
'Tarra Valley' EGou LCla NArc SLBF
'Task Force' CLit CSil LFli MAsk NArc
'Tausendschön' CLit CLoc ECtt EKMF NArc NPri
'Tear Fund' EGou
'Ted Heath' MAsk NArc
'Ted Perry' CSil
'Television' LFli MAsk NArc
'Tempo Doelo' CLit
N 'Temptation' CGre CLit CLoc CSil EBak ECtt MBri
'Tennessee Waltz' ♀ CGre CLit CLoc CSil EBak EBly EKMF EMan LCla LFli LVer MAld MAsk MJac MWar MWhe NArc SChu SKen SLBF SPer SPla
'Terrysue' EKMF
tetradactyla SLBF
'Teupels Erfolg' NArc
'Texas Longhorn' CLit CLoc CSil EBak EKMF LFli NArc
'Thalia' ♀ CGre CLit CLoc CSil EBak EBly ECtt EGou EKMF EMan ERea IHos LBlm LCla LFli LHil LVer MAld MAsk MBri MJac MWar MWhe NArc NHaw NPri SKen SLBF SPla WEas
'Thamar' CLoc EGou EKMF LCla MWar MWhe
'That's It' EBak NArc
'The Aristocrat' CLoc CSil EBak
§ 'The Doctor' CLoc CSil EBak EKMF MAsk MWhe NArc
'The Jester' EBak
'The Madame' CSil EBak MAsk NArc
'The Patriot' NArc
'The Rival' EKMF
'The Tarns' CLit CSil EBak EKMF MAsk NArc NPla WCru
'Therese Dupois' CSil
'Théroigne de Méricourt' EBak NArc
'Thilco' EKMF
'This England' CSil NArc
¶ 'Thistle Hill' EKMF
◆ 'Thompsonii' See ***F. magellanica* 'Thompsonii'**
'Thornley's Hardy' CLit CSil EKMF EMan LFli MAsk MBri NArc
'Three Cheers' CLoc EBak
'Three Counties' EBak
'Thumbelina' EGou
'Thunderbird' CLoc EBak
thymifolia EBur ELan EMon ESis GCra GMac GQui LFli LHil LHop MAsk MBal MPla NArc SBid SHFr SMrm WKif
– subsp. ***minimiflora*** EKMF LCla
– subsp. ***thymifolia*** EGou EKMF LCla
'Tiara' EBak
N 'Tiffany' EBak
tillettiana EGou EKMF
'Tillingbourne' LCla
'Tillmouth Lass' EKMF MAsk
'Timlin Brened' CSil EBak MAsk MWhe NArc
'Ting-a-ling' CLit CLoc CSil EBak EBly EKMF LFli LHil LVer MAld MAsk MWhe NArc SLBF
N 'Tinker Bell' CLit EBak EKMF NArc WLRN
'Tintern Abbey' NArc
'Toby Bridger' CLoc EBak NArc
'Tolling Bell' CLit CSil EBak EKMF LCla LFli MAsk MJac MWhe NArc
'Tom H. Oliver' EBak
'Tom Knights' EBak EGou EKMF LCla MAsk MWhe NArc
'Tom Redfern' MJac
'Tom Thorne' EBak
'Tom Thumb' ♀ CLit CLoc CMHG CShe CSil EBak EBly EKMF ELan EMan ENot GRei LCla LFli LVer MAld MAsk MBar MBri MGos MJac MPla MWar MWat MWhe NArc SKen SLBF SPer
'Tom West' (v) CBrk CGre CInt CLit CLoc CMHG CSil EBak EGou EKMF ERav LBlm LCla LFli LHil LHop MAld MAsk MJac MWhe NArc NHaw SKen SLBF SMrm WEas
'Tom Woods' LCla MWhe
'Toos' EGou
'Topaz' CLoc EBak NArc
'Topper' EMan NArc
'Torch' CLit CLoc CSil EBak EKMF MJac NArc
'Torchlight' CSil EBly LCla MAsk
'Torvill and Dean' CLit CLoc CSil EBly EGou EKMF LFli LVer MAsk MJac MWar MWhe NArc SLBF
'Towi' NArc
'Tracid' CLoc CSil
'Tracie Ann' EKMF
'Trail Blazer' CLit CLoc CSil EBak LCla MJac NArc
'Trailing Queen' CLit CSil EBak EKMF MAsk MJac NArc
'Trase' CLit CSil EBak EBly EKMF LVer MAsk NArc
'Traudchen Bonstedt' CLoc CSil EBak EBly LCla MAsk MWhe NArc SLBF
'Traviata' LFli NArc
'Treasure' EBak
'Trés Long' EGou
'Trewince Twilight' MAsk NArc

'Tricolor'	See ***F. magellanica*** var. ***gracilis*** **'Tricolor'**
'Tricolorii'	See ***F. magellanica*** var. ***gracilis*** **'Tricolor'**
¶ 'Trientje'	EGou
'Trio'	CLoc
triphylla	EBak EGou EKMF LCla
'Tristesse'	CLoc CSil EBak MAsk MJac MWhe NArc
'Troika'	EBak EKMF
'Troon'	MAsk NArc
'Tropic Sunset'	CSil LFli MAsk MBri MWhe NArc
'Tropicana'	CLit CLoc EBak LFli NArc
'Troubadour'	CLoc
'Trudy'	CSil EBak EKMF LCla MAsk NArc
N 'Trumpeter'	CLit CLoc CSil EBak EBly EGou EKMF LCla LFli LHil MAsk MJac MWhe NArc
'Tsjiep'	MAsk
'Tuonela'	CLoc CSil EBak EKMF MAsk MWhe NArc
'Tutone'	MAsk MJac NArc
'Tutti-frutti'	CLoc MWhe SMer
'Tutu'	EKMF NArc
'T'Vosk'	NArc
'Twink'	EGou
'Twinkling Stars'	CSil EKMF LCla MJac NArc
'Twirling Square Dancer'	LFli
'Two Tiers'	EKMF NArc
'UFO'	CSil LFli NArc
'Uillean Pipes'	EGou
'Ullswater'	CLit CSil EBak LVer MAsk NArc
'Ultramar'	EBak NArc
'Uncle Charley'	CLoc EBak EKMF LFli WEas
'Uncle Steve'	CLit EBak LFli NArc
'Upward Look'	EBak EKMF MAsk SMer SSea
'Vale of Belvoir'	CLit
'Valentine'	EBak
'Valerie Ann'	CLit EBak LCla LFli SKen
'Valiant'	EBak
'Vanessa'	CLoc
'Vanessa Jackson'	CLoc CSil LCla LFli MAsk MJac MWar MWhe NArc SKen SLBF
'Vanity Fair'	CLoc CSil EBak NArc
vargarsiana	EKMF LCla
'Variegated Brenda White'	EKMF MAsk NArc SLBF
'Variegated La Campanella'	MWar MWhe
'Variegated Snowcap'	MWhe
'Variegated Superstar'	MBri
'Variegated Swingtime'	CSil EBak
'Variegated Vivienne Thompson'	MBri
'Variegated Waveney Sunrise'	MBri
'Variegated White Joy'	EKMF
'Veenlust'	EGou
'Velma'	NArc
'Venus Victrix'	EBak EGou EKMF MAsk SLBF
venusta	EBak EGou EKMF LCla MAsk
'Vera Wilding'	NArc
'Versicolor'	See ***F. magellanica*** **'Versicolor'**
'Vi Whitehouse'	CSil
'Victorian'	CSil SMur
'Victory'	EBak
¶ 'Vielliebchen'	CSil
'Vincent van Gogh'	EGou
'Violet Bassett-Burr'	CLoc CSil EBak NArc
'Violet Gem'	CLoc
'Violet Rosette'	EBak NArc
'Viva Ireland'	EBak ECtt MAsk NArc SMer
'Vivien Colville'	CLoc
'Vivienne Davis'	EGou
'Vivienne Thompson'	NArc
¶ 'Vobeglo'	EKMF
'Vogue'	EBak
'Voltaire'	CSil EBak
'Voodoo'	CGre CLit CLoc CSil EBak EKMF EMan LFli MAsk MWar NPri SCoo SLBF SSea
'Vulcan'	CSil
vulcanica André	See ***F. ampliata***
¶ – Berry	EKMF
'Vyvian Miller'	MJac
'W.F.C. Kampionen'	NArc
'W.P. Wood'	MAsk
'Waldfee'	CSil EGou EKMF LCla MAsk MWhe
'Walsingham'	CSil EBak EGou LCla MAld MAsk MJac MWhe SKen SLBF
'Waltraud'	NArc
'Waltzing Matilda'	CLit
'Walz Bella'	CLit LCla SLBF
'Walz Blauwkous'	EGou
'Walz Citer'	NArc
'Walz Doedelzak'	LCla
'Walz Freule'	EKMF MJac
'Walz Gamelan'	NArc
'Walz Gitaar'	NArc
'Walz Harp'	CLit EGou LCla NArc SLBF
'Walz Jubelteen'	CLoc CSil EGou EKMF EMan LCla MJac MWar SLBF SSea
'Walz Lucifer'	EGou EKMF SLBF
'Walz Luit'	EGou NArc
'Walz Mandoline'	EGou NArc
'Walz Parasol'	NArc
'Walz Tamtam'	CSil
'Walz Triangel'	CSil EKMF NArc
'Walz Trommel'	NArc
'Walz Waterval'	CSil
'Walz Wipneus'	NArc
'Wapenfeld's 150'	EGou
'Wapenfeld's Bloei'	CKni CLit CSil EGou LCla MAsk NArc SLBF
'War Dance'	MWhe
'War Paint'	CLoc CSil EBak NArc
'Warton Crag'	CSil NArc
'Wassernymph'	CSil
¶ 'Water Nymph'	CLit CLoc SLBF
'Waterways'	EGou
'Wave of Life'	CSil EKMF MAld MAsk MWhe SKen
'Waveney Gem'	CLit CSil EBak EGou EKMF EMan LCla MAld MAsk MJac MWar NArc SLBF
'Waveney Queen'	MJac NArc
'Waveney Sunrise'	CSil EGou EKMF LCla MAsk MJac MWar MWhe NArc
'Waveney Valley'	EBak MJac NArc
'Waveney Waltz'	CSil EBak LCla MAsk MJac MWar MWhe NArc
'Wedding Bells'	LCla
'Wee Lass'	CSil
'Welsh Dragon'	CLoc EBak MAsk NArc
'Wendy'	See ***F.*** **'Snowcap'**
'Wendy Atkinson'	EKMF
'Wendy Harris'	MJac
'Wendy Leedham'	ECtt EKMF

'Wendy's Beauty'	CLoc EBly
'Wessex Belle'	LCla
'Westgate'	ECtt EKMF
'Westminster Chimes' ♀	CLit CLoc CSil EKMF MAsk MJac MWhe NArc
'Wharfedale'	CSil MAld MJac NArc
'Whickham Beauty'	CSil
¶ 'Whickham Blue'	MWar
'Whirlaway'	CLoc CSil EBak EKMF MAsk NArc SMer
'Whirlybird'	NArc
'White Ann'	CLit CLoc LCla MBri
'White Clove'	CLit CSil EGou
'White Falls'	MAsk NArc
'White Galore'	CLit EBak EKMF EMan LVer MAsk NArc SMer
'White Gold'	EBak
'White Heidi Ann'	MAsk
'White Joy'	CLit CSil EBak EKMF MAsk MWhe NArc
'White King'	CLit CLoc CSil EBak EKMF EMan MAld MAsk MWhe SLBF
'White Lady Patricia Mountbatten'	EMan
'White Marshmallow'	LFli
'White Pixie'	CLit CSil EBly EKMF LCla LFli LVer MAld MAsk MJac MPla NArc SPer
'White Pixie' Wagtail'	EBak MWhe
N 'White Queen'	CLit CSil EBak MWhe NArc
'White Spider'	CLit CLoc CSil EBak EKMF LBlm LFli MAsk MWhe NArc SKen
'Whitehaven'	NArc
'Whiteknights Amethyst'	CSil SKen SLod
'Whiteknights Blush'	CSil GCal GQui SBid SKen SLod
'Whiteknights Cheeky'	CSil EBak EGou NArc
¶ 'Whiteknights Glister'	CSil
'Whiteknights Goblin'	See ***F. denticulata* 'Whiteknights Goblin'**
'Whiteknights Pearl'	CLit CSil ECtt EKMF LCla MAsk NArc SLBF
'Whiteknights Ruby'	CSil EKMF
'Whitton Pride'	MJac
'Wicked Queen'	CSil LCla LFli NArc
'Wickham Blue'	LCla MJac
'Wiebke Becker'	EKMF NArc
'Wild and Beautiful'	CLit EKMF LFli MAsk NArc
'Wildfire'	NArc
'Wilfred C. Dodson'	EGou
'William Caunt'	EKMF
'William Jay'	EGou
'Wilson's Colours'	EBly
'Wilson's Pearls'	CLit CSil NArc SLBF
'Wilson's Sugar Pink'	CLit EBly LCla MJac
'Win Oxtoby'	EKMF NArc
'Wine and Roses'	EBak NArc SMer
'Wingrove's Mammoth'	CSil LFli MAsk NArc
'Wings of Song'	CSil EBak NArc SMer
'Winifred'	NArc
'Winston Churchill' ♀	CLit CLoc CSil EBak EBly EKMF EMan IHos LCla LFli LVer MAsk MBri MJac MWar MWhe NArc NFai NHaw NPri SRms
'Woodnook'	CSil MAsk
¶ 'Woodside'	CSil
'Woodside Gem'	NArc
wurdackii	EKMF ERea MAsk SSea
'Xmas Tree'	MAsk
'Y Me'	CLit
¶ 'Ymke'	EGou SLBF
'Yolanda Franck'	CSil
'Yorkshire Rally'	MJac
'Yuletide'	CSil LFli
'Zara'	CSil MWhe
'Ziegfield Girl'	EBak NArc SMer
'Zulu King'	EGou NArc SLBF
¶ 'Zulu Queen'	EGou
'Zwarte Dit'	EGou
'Zwarte Snor'	EGou NArc

FUMANA (Cistaceae)

¶ ***procumbens***	WHil
thymifolia	NWCA

FUMARIA (Papaveraceae)

lutea	See ***Corydalis lutea***
officinalis	MSal

FURCRAEA (Agavaceae)

§ ***foetida*** var. ***mediopicta***	CB&S
– 'Variegata'	See ***F. foetida*** var. ***mediopicta***
gigantea	See ***F. foetida***
longaeva	CAbb CHEx CTrC LHil SArc
selloa	CHEx LHil
– var. ***marginata***	CHEx LHil

GAGEA (Liliaceae)

¶ ***fibrosa***	WDav
lutea	EPot
pratensis	EPot

GAHNIA (Cyperaceae)

See Plant Deletions

GAILLARDIA (Asteraceae)

aristata hort.	See ***G. × grandiflora***
'Bremen'	CBot CPou EPfP NPri NTow
'Burgunder'	CBot CDoC CMGP EBre ECtt EFou ELan LBlm MBri MNrw NBro NFai NFla NMir NOak SPer SRms WBea WGor WOve WRHF WRus
'Dazzler' ♀	CTri EBre ECtt ELan EMan ENot MBri NNor SPer WBea WCra WStI WTyr WWtk
§ 'Fackelschein'	CMdw NFai
◆ Goblin	See ***G.* 'Kobold'**
§ 'Goldkobold'	ELan EPar MLLN SIde
§ × ***grandiflora***	NOak
– 'Aurea Plena'	EBee
§ 'Kobold'	CB&S EBee EBre ECtt EMan GAbr MBri MLsm MTis NBus NPri NRoo SPer SPla SRms WFar WRHF WTyr WWin
'Mandarin'	COtt CSte EBre SRms
'Nana Nieske'	NTow
* New Giant hybrids	MRav
* 'Summer Fire'	MCLN
'Tokajer'	EBee EPfP NFla
◆ Torchlight	See ***G.* 'Fackelschein'**
'Wirral Flame'	EPar
◆ Yellow Goblin	See ***G.* 'Goldkobold'**

GALACTITES (Asteraceae)

tomentosa	CArc CInt CPle CRDP CSpe ECha ELan EMan EMar EMon GBri MAvo MHlr NChi SUsu WBea WEas WWye

GALANTHUS † (Amaryllidaceae)

allenii	CBro EMor EPot WChr
alpinus	LAma LWoo WChr
'Armine'	LFox
'Atkinsii' 🏆	CAvo CBro EMon EMor EOrc EPot ERav LAma LFox LWoo MBri MRav NGar NRar WChr WWat WWye
'Augustus'	CAvo EMor LFox WIvy
'Benhall Beauty'	LFox
'Bertram Anderson'	LFox
'Bitton'	CBro LFox NGar
'Blewbury Tart'	CMea
bortkewitschianus	CBro LFox
'Brenda Troyle'	CBro EPar EPot LFox LWoo NGar WChr WIvy
byzantinus	See ***G. plicatus*** subsp. ***byzantinus***
cabardensis	See ***G. transcaucasicus***
'Cassaba'	EPot
caucasicus 🏆	CAvo CBro ECha EMon EMor EPot ERav LAma LFox MTho NGar WChr
– var. ***hiemalis***	CBro ECha EMor LAma
'Clare Blakeway-Phillips'	SWas
corcyrensis Spring flowering	See ***G. reginae-olgae*** subsp. ***vernalis***
– Winter flowering	See ***G. reginae-olgae*** subsp. ***reginae-olgae* Winter-flowering Group**
'Cordelia' (d)	EMon LFox
* 'Curly'	EMor
* 'David Shackleton'	EMor
'Desdemona'	LFox LWoo
'Dionysus' (d)	CBro EMor EPot LFox LWoo NGar WChr
§ ***elwesii*** 🏆	CAvo CBro CMon EMon EMor EPot ERav ERos LAma LFox MBri NBir NGar NRar NRog WChr WCot WIvy WShi
– 'Flore Pleno'	LFox
* – 'Grumpy'	EMon
* – 'Magnus'	LWoo
¶ – var. ***whitallii***	LWoo
* – 'Zwanenburg'	EMon
fosteri	CAvo CBro EHyt EPot LAma LRHS WChr
– PD 256830	EMor
'Galatea'	EMon EMor LFox LWoo WIvy
§ ***gracilis***	CBro EMor EPar ERav LFox LWoo MTho NGar WIvy WOld
– Highdown form	EHyt
graecus Boissier	See ***G. elwesii***
– hort.	See ***G. gracilis***
Greatorex double	EMon LRHS LWoo
'Hill Poë' (d)	CBro EPot LFox
'Hippolyta' (d)	CBro ECha EMor EPot LFox LWoo
¶ ***ikariae*** 🏆	EHyt EOrc EPar EPot ERav LAma
§ – Latifolius Group	CAvo CBro EMor EOrc EPot LAma LFox NGar WChr WOld
– Woronowii Group	EMon LAma WChr
'Jacquenetta' (d)	CBro EMor EPot LWoo NGar
'John Gray'	CBro EMon EMor LFox
kemulariae	See ***G. transcaucasicus***
ketskovelii	See ***G. transcaucasicus***
'Ketton'	CAvo CBro EMon EOrc ERav LFox WIvy
'Kite'	CBro MPhe
'Lady Beatrix Stanley' (d)	CBro EMon EMor EPot ERav LAma LFox LWoo MTho NGar NHar WChr
lagodechianus	See ***G. transcaucasicus***
latifolius	See ***G. ikariae* Latifolius Group**
¶ 'Lavinia' (d)	CAvo ERav
'Lime Tree'	LFox
lutescens	See ***G. nivalis* 'Sandersii'**
'Magnet' 🏆	CAvo CBro CFee EMor EPot ERav LAma LFox LWoo NGar NHar SWas WChr
¶ 'Maidwell C'	EMor
'Maidwell L'	CAvo EMor LFox LRHS WChr
'Melvillei'	NHar
'Merlin'	EMor EOrc LFox NGar NHar
'Mighty Atom'	LFox
'Moccas'	WOld
¶ 'Modern Art'	EMor
¶ 'Mrs Backhouse's Spectacles'	EPot
'Neill Fraser'	LFox
'Nerissa' (d)	EPot NGar
nivalis 🏆	CBro CKin ECWi ELan EMor EPar EPot ERav ETub EWFC LAma LFox MBri MBro MRPP NGar NRar NRog WShi
– var. ***angustifolius***	CBro
– 'April Fool'	LFox
– dwarf form	LFox
– 'Flore Pleno' 🏆	CBro CMon EBre EPar EPla EPot ERav ETub LAma LFox MBro MFos NGar NMGW NRog NRya WHen WShi WWye
– 'Humberts Orchard'	EMor EOrc LFox
– subsp. ***imperati*** 'Ginns'	EMor LFox LWoo
– 'Lady Elphinstone' (d)	CAvo CBro CRow ECha EMor EPar EPot ERav LFox MTho NGar NHar WAbe WChr
– 'Lutescens'	See ***G. nivalis* 'Sandersii'**
– 'Pewsey Vale'	EMor
¶ – (Poculiformis Group) 'Sandhill Gate'	EMor
– 'Pusey Green Tip' (d)	CBro EMor EPar EPot ERav ITim LFox LWoo NGar WChr
§ – 'Sandersii'	CBro EMor NGar SSpi WChr
§ – Scharlockii Group	CAvo CBro EHyt EMor EOrc EPot LAma LFox NGar NHar SWas WChr
– 'Tiny'	CAvo EMor NGar NHar
§ – 'Virescens'	EMor LWoo SWas
– 'Viridapicis'	CAvo CBro ECha EHyt EMor EPar EPot ERav LAma LFox NGar
– 'Warei'	EMor LFox
¶ – WM 9615 from E. Slovenia	MPhe
¶ – WM 9630 from C. Hungary	MPhe
'Ophelia' (d)	CAvo CBro EPar EPot ERav LAma LFox NGar
* 'Paradise Double'	EPar
* 'Paradise Giant'	EPar
'Peg Sharples'	ERav
platyphyllus	See ***G. ikariae* Latifolius Group**
plicatus 🏆	CAvo CFee CMea EMon EPot LFox NGar WChr WOMN
§ – subsp. ***byzantinus*** 🏆	CAvo CBro EMor EOrc LFox NGar
– large form	EOrc
– 'Ron Ginns'	LFox
– 'Warham'	CBro EOrc EPot WOld
¶ – 'Washfield Warham'	EMon

reginae-olgae CBro CMea CMon EHyt EMor ERos LAma NGar SSpi WChr WCot
¶ – from Sicily ERav
§ – subsp. ***reginae-olgae*** Winter-flowering Group CBro ECha EMor ERav LAma LFox
§ – subsp. ***vernalis*** EMor NGar
– – AJM 75 EMor
– – CE&H 541 EMor
rizehensis CBro EPot
'Robin Hood' EMor LFox LRHS WChr
'S. Arnott' ♀ CAvo CBro CMea EMon EMor EPar EPot ERav LAma LFox LWoo NBir NGar NHar WChr WOld
'Sally Ann' LFox
'Scharlockii' See ***G. nivalis* Scharlockii Group**
'Straffan' CAvo CBro EHyt EMor EOrc EPot ERav LAma LFox NHar WOld
'Titania' (d) CBro NGar
§ ***transcaucasicus*** CBro EPot ERav NGar WChr
'Trotter's Merlin' EMor
'Tubby Merlin' LFox
'William Thomson' LFox
'Winifrede Mathias' LFox

GALAX (Diapensiaceae)

aphylla See ***G. urceolata***
§ ***urceolata*** CFil IBlr MBal SBar SSpi WCru WThi

GALEGA (Papilionaceae)

bicolor CMdw CWit EBre EGar IBlr MSte NBir NBrk SIde SMad SRms SWat WCot WFar WPri WWhi
'Duchess of Bedford' MAvo WCot
× ***hartlandii*** IBlr MRav
– 'Alba' ♀ EMon GBar GCal IBlr LGan MAvo MHlr NBrk NBro SWas WCot WPer
– 'Candida' CChu CGle NTow SPer
'Her Majesty' See ***G.* 'His Majesty'**
§ 'His Majesty' CChu EBee EMon MAvo NBrk WBea WCot
'Lady Wilson' CChu CGle MAvo NBrk NCat WBea WCot WFoF WRus
officinalis CArn CBot CHan CSev ECro EFou ELan ELau EOrc GPoy IBlr LHol LHop MChe MHew MNrw MTol NBir NBro NSti SIde WByw WCer WEas WHoo WMer WOak WPer WWin WWye
– 'Alba' CBot CHad CHan CHid CMdw EBee EBre ECED ECro ELan EMan EMar ERav ESiP IBlr LFis LHol WBea WByw WCHb WEas WHer WHoo WPyg WRus
orientalis CGle CHan ECha GCal MArl SWat WAbb WBea WCot WRus

GALEOBDOLON See LAMIUM

GALEOPSIS (Lamiaceae)

segetum EBee
speciosa ECWi
¶ ***tetrahit*** 'Contrast' WAlt
– 'Dirbach Variegated' MInt

GALIUM (Rubiaceae)

aristatum WCot
aureum See ***G. firmum***
cruciata See ***Cruciata laevipes***
mollugo CArn CKin CTiv ECWi MHew MSal NCGP NLan SIde WCHb
§ ***odoratum*** CArn CBre CGle CKin EEls EFou ELan ELau EOHP EOrc EWFC GPoy LHol MBar MBri MGam MNrw MSal NMir NSti SIde SPer WApp WBon WCer WHer WMer WOak
palustre CKin
perpusillum See ***Asperula perpusilla***
verum CArn CKin ECWi EJud EWFC MChe MGra MHew MSal NLan NMir SIde WCHb WGwy WHer WOak WPer

GALPHIMIA (Malpighiaceae)

See Plant Deletions

GALTONIA (Hyacinthaceae)

§ ***candicans*** CAvo CB&S CBro CGre CSev EBre ECha ECro ELan EMon GBuc GMac LAma LBow LHop MBri MCLN MHFP NFai SDeJ SPer SUsu WEas WGwG WHoo WPer WWat
princeps CAvo CBro EBre ECha ECro EPla GBuc GCra NRoo WEas
¶ ***regalis*** CHan GCal
viridiflora ♀ CArc CAvo CBot CBro CEnd CHar EAst ECha ECro ELan GCHN GCal MHFP MHlr NHol NPSI NRoo SAga SDix SIgm WHer WOMN WPer WWat

GAMOCHAETA (Asteraceae)

See Plant Deletions

GAMOLEPIS See STEIRODISCUS

GARDENIA (Rubiaceae)

§ ***augusta*** EBak MBri SLMG
– 'Prostrata Variegata' See ***G. augusta* 'Radicans Variegata'**
– 'Veitchiana' ERea
florida See ***G. augusta***
globosa See ***Rothmannia globosa***
grandiflora See ***G. augusta***
jasminoides See ***G. augusta***
thunbergia CTrC MSto

GARRYA † (Garryaceae)

elliptica CB&S CPle CShe EB&P EBre ELan ENot GOrc GRei LPan MBri MGos NFla NHol NNor SPer SReu SSoC WBod WPat WRTC WWat WWin
– (f) WPat
– 'James Roof' (m) ♀ CB&S CEnd CFee EB&P EBar EBre ELan GWht IOrc LHop LNet MBal MBri MGos MWat NBee NHed NHol SEas SHBN SPer SPla SReu SSoC SSta WAbe WDin WPat WStI WWat

fremontii	CKni ELan ISea SEas SSta
× ***issaquahensis*** 'Glasnevin Wine'	CFai CKni CPMA CSte CWSG EBre ELan LRHS MAsh MBlu SBra SReu SSta WWat
– 'Pat Ballard' (m)	CKni CSte ELan EPfP LRHS MAsh SReu SSta

GAULNETTYA See GAULTHERIA

GAULTHERIA † (Ericaceae)

adenothrix	EPot GDra MBal NGre SIng WAbe
antipoda	MBal SSta
– × ***macrostigma***	CMHG
crassa	MHig NHol
cuneata 🏆	ELan EPot GDra MAsh MBal MBar MGos MHig NGre SReu SSta WAbe
– 'Pinkie'	CRos CSte ELan EPfP MAsh
depressa	MBal
– × ***crassa***	MBal
§ ***fragrantissima***	NHol
furiens	See ***G. insana***
'Glenroy Maureen'	EHic MBal MCCP
griffithiana BM&W 69	MBal
§ ***hispida***	GDra MBal MDun MGos
hispidula	See ***G. hispida***
hookeri	IBlr NHol
– B 547	MBal
humifusa	MBal
§ ***insana***	MBal
itoana	GDra MBal MBar MGos MHig NGre WAbe
littoralis	MBal
macrostigma	MBal
miqueliana	EHic EHyt MBal MDHE MGos NHar SSta WFro WWat
mucronata 🏆	CMHG ELan ENot MBal MBar WGwG
– 'Alba' (f)	GRei MBar MGos MRav
– 'Atrococcinea' (f)	WPat WPyg WRTC
– 'Barry Lock' (f)	WPat WPyg WRTC
– 'Bell's Seedling' (f) 🏆	CChe CDoC CTri EPfP GRei MBri MGos SHBN SPer SReu SSta WPat WPyg WRTC
¶ – C 9510	GGGa
– 'Cherry Ripe' (f)	CDoC IOrc SEas SHBN
– 'Crimsonia' (f) 🏆	CChe CTri ELan MAsh MBar MGos SEas SHBN SPer SReu SRms WPat WPyg WRTC
– 'Indian Lake'	CDoC CEnd GAul NHol SEas SPan
– 'Lilacina' (f)	CBlo MBal MGos NCut
– 'Lilian' (f)	CBlo CTri GSki NHol SEas SHBN SPer
– (m)	CTri ELan GRei MBar MBri MGos MRav NHol SEas SPer SReu SRms WPat
♦ – Mother of Pearl	See ***G. mucronata* 'Parelmoer' (f)**
– 'Mulberry Wine' (f) 🏆	CBlo CChe CDoC EPfP GAul IOrc NHol
– 'October Red' (f)	NHol SEas SPan
§ – 'Parelmoer' (f)	CBlo ELan ENot GAul SEas SPer WPat WPyg WRTC
– 'Pink Pearl' (f) 🏆	MAsh NHol SRms WLRN WPat
– RB 94095	GTou
– 'Rosalind' (f)	CEnd GAul SEas SPer WWeb
– 'Rosea' (f)	GRei MBar
– 'Rosie' (f)	MBri
– 'Sea Shell' (f) 🏆	IOrc
§ – 'Signaal' (f)	CBlo ELan ENot MBri MGos MPla SPer SReu WLRN WPat
♦ – Signal	See ***G. mucronata* 'Signaal' (f)**
§ – 'Sneeuwwitje' (f)	CBlo CChe ENot GAul GSki MAsh MBri NHol SHBN SReu WPat
♦ – Snow White	See ***G. mucronata* 'Sneeuwwitje' (f)**
– 'Stag River' (f)	GDra MGos NCut NHar
– 'Thymifolia' (m)	CChe EPfP GAri SHBN SPan SPer SPla
– 'White Pearl' (f)	IOrc WLRN
– 'Wintertime' (f) 🏆	ELan MAsh SRms WWeb
§ ***myrsinoides***	GAri GDra MBal
nana Colenso	See ***G. parvula***
nummularioides	GAri MHig NHol NMen
– B 673	MBal
§ – var. ***elliptica***	SSta
nummularioides minor	MBal
nummularioides 'Minuta'	See ***G. nummularioides*** var. ***elliptica***
ovalifolia	See ***G. fragrantissima***
I ***paraguayensis***	MBal
§ ***parvula***	ECou
phillyreifolia	CMHG SSta
'Pink Champagne'	SSta
poeppigii	CMHG NHol WPyg
poeppigii racemosa	SSta
procumbens 🏆	CB&S CMHG EBre ELan ENot GDra GPoy IOrc LHol MBal MBar MBri MGos NHar NHol NWea SHBN SIng SPer SReu SRms SSta WAbe WDin WWat
prostrata	See ***G. myrsinoides***
– subsp. ***pentlandii***	MBal NHar SRms
* ***prostrata purpurea***	See ***G. myrsinoides***
pumila	ECou GAri MBal MBar NHar NHol NMen
§ – C&W 5226	MBal NHol
– 'E.K. Balls'	EPot NHar NHol
pyroloides	MBal
– BM&W 5	MBal
rupestris	GDra MBal
schultesii	SSta
shallon	CB&S CDoC ENot GAul GOrc GRei MBar MGos MHlr MPla NRoo SHBN SPer SRms SSta WDin WFar WFro
– dwarf form	MBal
sinensis	MBal MDun WThi
tasmanica	ECou GDra MBal MBar NHol
– × ***pumila***	MBal
– white-berried	GDra
– yellow-berried	MBal
thymifolia	MBal
trichophylla	GDra MBal MDun NMen WAbe
willisiana	See ***G. eriophylla***
× ***wisleyensis***	MAsh MBal SRms SSta WAbe WBod WPat WPyg WRTC
– 'Pink Pixie'	CMHG EHic ELan EPla MAsh MBar MGos SIng SPer SSta WAbe
– 'Wisley Pearl'	EHic GDra IBlr MBar MGos NHar SBid SIng SReu WPat
yunnanensis	EPla

GAURA (Onagraceae)

lindheimeri 🏆	Widely available

– 'Corrie's Gold' (v)	CArc CMil CSpe EBar EBee ECha ECtt EFou EHoe ELan EMan LGre LHop SAga SChu SUsu WRus WWye
– 'Jo Adela' (v)	CArc EBar EBee ECha ELan LHop SUsu SWat
– 'The Bride'	EFou MArl MLan MNrw NCGP NFai NRai WOve
– 'Whirling Butterflies'	CSte EBee EHic EMil EMon EPfP MCli MMil NCut SMrm WCot WMer

GAYLUSSACIA (Ericaceae)

brachycera	GGGa
ursinum	CKni

GAZANIA (Asteraceae)

'Aztec' 🏆	CBrk CHal CKni LHil NHaw
'Blackberry Ripple'	EAst NPri WLRN
'Brodick'	GCal
'Christopher'	CBrk CHal CKni CSpe LHil NHaw NPla NPri SVen WPer
'Circus'	WLRN
'Cookei' 🏆	CBrk CKni CSpe ELan MSte SMrm WCot WEas
'Cornish Pixie'	CHal
cream	CHal EAst LHop MRav NPla
cream and purple	LHop LLWP NPla SUsu WPer
'Cream Beauty'	EOrc LHil MSte NTow SAga SUsu
'Cream Dream'	CBrk WLRN
crimson and green	MSte
'Daybreak Bronze'	LIck MLan
'Dorothy' 🏆	CBrk LHil WPen
double yellow	See ***G.* 'Yellow Buttons'**
'Dwarf Orange'	LLWP
'Evening Sun'	CHal NHaw
'Flash'	WEas
'Freddie'	SMrm
'Garden Sun'	MLan
hybrids	ELan MRav SDix WPer
krebsiana	CSpe
'Lemon Beauty'	NPri WCot
'Magenta'	LHop
'Magic'	WLRN
'Mini Star Yellow'	SRms WHen
¶ 'Northbourne' 🏆	LHil
'Orange Beauty'	ELan
'Orange Magic'	WLRN
'Red Velvet'	CSpe LHop
§ ***rigens***	CB&S MBri
– var. ***uniflora*** 🏆	CBrk EOrc MSte WEas
– – 'Variegata'	CBot
– 'Variegata' 🏆	CB&S CBrk CHal ELan EOrc NPri WLRN WPer
'Silver Beauty'	CBot NTow
'Silverbrite'	CHal LLWP
splendens	See ***G. rigens***
'Sundance'	SVen
'Talent' 🏆	CHal SRms
§ 'The Serpent'	CSpe
'Tiger'	EOrc NPri
§ 'Yellow Buttons' (d)	CBrk CHal CSpe EHic EMon WLRN

GEISSORHIZA (Iridaceae)

aspera	CMon NRog
inflexa	NRog
monantha	NRog
radians	NRog
¶ ***splendidissima***	WCot
¶ ***tulbaghensis***	WCot

GELASINE (Iridaceae)

azurea	See ***G. coerulea***
§ ***coerulea***	WCot

GELIDOCALAMUS (Poaceae - Bambusoideae)

fangianus	See ***Chimonobambusa microphylla***

GELSEMIUM (Loganiaceae)

rankinii	CChu CMCN CPlN CPle
sempervirens 🏆	CArn CB&S CLTr CMCN CPlN EBee ERea LCns MSal SOWG
– 'Flore Pleno'	CB&S CPlN ERea
– 'Pride of Augusta'	CMCN

GENISTA (Papilionaceae)

aetnensis 🏆	CB&S CMCN CPle CSam EBre ELan ENot GAul IOrc LHop MBri MWat SArc SDix SHBN SIgm SMad SPer SSpi SSta WDin WOMN WWat
anglica 'Cloth of Gold'	WDav
§ ***canariensis***	CGre ERea LCns MAll WAbe
cinerea	CBlo CShe MAll
decumbens	See ***Cytisus decumbens***
delphinensis	See ***G. sagittalis*** subsp. ***delphinensis***
'Emerald Spreader'	See ***G. pilosa* 'Yellow Spreader'**
fragrans	See ***G. canariensis***
hispanica	CB&S EBre ELan ENot IOrc MBal MBar MGos MWat NFla NHol SHBN SHel SMer SPer WAbe WDin WGwG WPyg WRHF WRTC WStI
– 'Compacta'	EPla ESis SIng SPer
humifusa	See ***G. pulchella***
lydia 🏆	CB&S CPle EBre ELan ENot GOrc GRei GWht LBuc LGro LHop MBal MBar MGos MWat NBee NFla NNor SHBN SIng SPer SReu SSta WDin WFar WWat
monosperma	See ***Retama monosperma***
§ ***monspessulana***	MAll
pilosa	CTri ENot EPot ISea LNet MBar MBro MGos MHew MPla NHar NMen NRoo SPer SRms WAbe WBod WWin
– 'Goldilocks'	ECtt EHic MAll MBar MLan MPla NHar
– 'Lemon Spreader'	See ***G. pilosa* 'Yellow Spreader'**
* ***pilosa major***	MHig
pilosa var. ***minor***	GTou WAbe
– 'Procumbens'	CMea GDra MBal NHol WHoo WPat WPyg
– 'Vancouver Gold'	CB&S EBre EHal ELan GOrc IHos IOrc LBuc MGos MNrw MRav NHar WGor WHar WStI WWat WWeb
§ – 'Yellow Spreader'	CB&S CHan CLTr CMHG ECtt EHoe GOrc MBal WWat WWeb
'Porlock'	CDoC ELan
§ ***pulchella***	CTri MBro MHig NHol NMen
sagittalis	CHan CWGN LHop MAll MBal MBro NNor NWoo SPer
§ – subsp. ***delphinensis*** 🏆	ELan EPot MHig
sagittalis minor	See ***G. sagittalis*** subsp. ***delphinensis***
subcapitata	EPot
– dwarf form	NWCA

tenera 'Golden Shower' ♀	SLPl
tinctoria	CAgr CArn CJew CKin EWFC GBar GPoy ILis MBar MChe MHew MNrw MSal NNor SIde WDin WHer WOak WWye
– 'Flore Pleno' ♀	CLyd CMHG ELan MBal MBar MInt MPla NHar NMen SPer WHar WHil WRTC
– 'Humifusa'	EPot NHar NMen NWCA
– var. ***humilior***	MHig
– var. ***prostrata***	WOak
– 'Royal Gold' ♀	ECtt ENot MAll MGos MRav NNor SHBN SPer SRms WBod WWeb
tournefortii	MBal
umbellata	MAll
villarsii	See ***G. pulchella***

GENNARIA (Orchidaceae)

See Plant Deletions

GENTIANA † (Gentianaceae)

§ ***acaulis*** ♀	CGle CLyd CPBP CPla CShe EBre ELan EMNN EPot GDra GTou ITim LBee LHop MBri MFos MHig MWat NGre NHar NHol NRoo NWCA SAlw SBla SIng WAbe WEas WHoo WPat
– f. ***alba***	WDav
– Andorra form	GDra
– 'Belvedere'	GCLN MHig WAbe WDav
– 'Dinarica'	See ***G. dinarica***
– Excisa Group	WDav
– 'Holzmannii'	NNrd
– 'Krumrey'	EHyt EPot GDra NMGW WAbe
– 'Rannoch'	EPot NMen NNrd
– 'Undulatifolia'	NHar WDav
– 'Velkokvensis'	EHyt
algida	CPla MSto
– white	MSto
'Alpha'	See ***G. × hexafarreri* 'Alpha'**
¶ 'Amethyst'	NHar
'Amythyst'	WAbe
andrewsii	CPla EBee WHil
angustifolia	EHyt NSla NTow WAbe
– 'Montagne d'Aurouze'	WAbe
'Ann's Special'	ELan GMaP MDHE NHar NHol NRoo
asclepiadea ♀	CFil CGle CPla CVer CWGN EBre ELan EPar GCHN LSyl MBri MBro MTho NRoo SBla SDix SIng SOkh SPer SSpi WAbe WHoo WPyg WWat
– var. ***alba***	CBot CFil CLyd CPla LHop MBri MBro MTho NRoo SAlw SBla SPer SUsu WAbe WHoo WOMN WWat
– 'Knightshayes'	EGle LHop MBri MBro SWas WHoo
– 'Nymans'	ELan
– pale blue	CFil NRoo WOMN WPGP
– 'Phyllis'	CLyd MBro MTho WHoo
– 'Pink Cascade'	SBla
– 'Rosea'	GBuc
'Barbara Lyle'	NHol WAbe
¶ ***bavarica*** var. ***subacaulis***	WDav
bellidifolia	GTou
× ***bernardii***	See ***G. × stevenagensis* 'Bernardii'**
'Blauer Diamant'	MDHE
'Blue Flame'	GDra NHar WAbe
'Blue Heaven'	GCHN GCra GDra NHar WAbe
'Blue Silk'	NHar WAbe
N ***cachemirica***	GTou MTho NGre
¶ ***caelestis*** CLD 1087	EPot
'Cairngorm'	EWes GMaP MDHE NHar NHed NRoo WHil
Cambrian Hybrids	WAbe
× ***caroli***	GAri NHar SBla WAbe WPat
'Christine Jean'	GTou MBro MDHE NHar NHed NMen SIng
clusii	CNic
– ***clusii***	WDav
– subsp. ***costei***	WAbe
coelestis CLD 1087	GCrs
'Compact Gem'	EPot NHar WAbe
¶ ***corymbifera***	WAbe
crassicaulis	GCra
– SBEL 220	MSte
crinita	See ***Gentianopsis crinita***
§ ***cruciata***	CMGP EBee EMan GTou LHop MLan MTho WGwG WLRN
§ ***dahurica***	CPea EBee ELan GCal GDra LBee NHar SMrm
decumbens	GCal LHop MHar MSto NChi
depressa	MTho WAbe WThi
'Devonhall'	WAbe
§ ***dinarica***	CLyd CNic EHyt GDra MTho NRoo WAbe
I ***doeringiana***	ECho
Drake's strain	GDra LRHS WAbe
'Dumpy'	EPot NHar WAbe WPat
'Dusk'	GDra NHar
'Eleanor'	NHar
'Elizabeth'	EWes MDHE MOne NHar NHed NRoo
× ***farorna***	NRoo
farreri	EWes NWCA WAbe
– 'Duguid's Clone'	WAbe
freyniana	GCrs LHop
froelichii	WDav
gelida	NHol WOMN
Glamis Strain	GMaP NHar NHed NRoo
'Glen Isla'	EWes MDHE MOne NHar NHed NRoo
'Glen Moy'	EWes GMaP MDHE MOne NRoo
'Glendevon'	WAbe
§ ***gracilipes***	ECho ELan LBee MSte MWat NWCA SRms
– 'Yuatensis'	See ***G. wutaiensis***
grossheimii	SAlw
× ***hascombensis***	See ***G. septemfida*** var. ***lagodechiana* 'Hascombensis'**
'Henry'	WAbe
× ***hexafarreri***	NHar
§ – 'Alpha'	GCHN GMaP WAbe
hexaphylla	NHar
'Indigo'	WAbe
Inshriach Hybrids	GDra GMaP MOne NHar NHol NNrd
'Inverleith' ♀	ELan EWes MBri MBro MOne NHar NHol NRoo SSpi WGor WPat
ishizuchii	EDAr
kauffmanniana	NHol
kesselringii	See ***G. walujewii***
'Kirriemuir'	EWes NHed NRoo
kochiana	See ***G. acaulis***
kurroo	EHyt ELan MHar WPat
– var. ***brevidens***	See ***G. dahurica***

lagodechiana	See ***G. septemfida*** var. ***lagodechiana***
¶ 'Leslie Delaney'	NHar
lucerna	MDHE NHar NRoo
lutea	CArn CPla ECha EHoe EMan EMar GCra GDra GPoy LFis LHop MHar MSte NGar NHar NHol NSla NSti SDix SMad WDav WGle WSan WWye
x ***macaulayi*** ♀	CLyd CPla MBri MHig NHol NRoo NRya SIng WDav WHoo WTre
– 'Blue Bonnets'	MDHE NHar
– 'Edinburgh' ♀	MDHE
– 'Elata'	ELan MBri MDHE MOne NHar NHed NHol NRoo WHil
– 'Kidbrooke Seedling'	ELan EWes GTou MOne NGre NHar NRoo NRya WAbe WHil
– 'Kingfisher'	CMHG CPla ELan GCra GDra MHig MOne NHar NMen NNor NNrd NRoo SBla SBod SIng WAbe WDav
§ – 'Praecox'	ELan GCHN GTou MBri MDHE NHar NHed NRoo WHil
§ – 'Wells's Variety'	EPot MBri MDHE WAbe
macrophylla	See ***G. burseri*** var. ***villarsii***
makinoi	NWCA
– ***alba***	LRHS
'Margaret'	WAbe
melandriifolia	WAbe
– ACE 2515	NHar
¶ ***microdonta*** ACE 1161	EPot NHar
'Multiflora'	EWes MDHE NRoo
¶ aff. ***obconica*** ACE 2140	EPot
ochroleuca	See ***G. villosa***
x ***oliviana***	CSam NHol
olivieri	WAbe
oreodoxa	GMaP GTou MDHE NRoo WAbe
pannonica	GDra
– hybrids	GDra
paradoxa	CNic EDAr EHyt EPot GCHN GCra LBee MFos NHar NSla SBla WAbe WDav WOMN
¶ ***parryi***	EPot GCrs
phlogifolia	See ***G. cruciata***
pneumonanthe	LHop NSla
prolata	NHar WAbe
przewalskii	WWin
pumila	SIgm WAbe
purdomii	See ***G. gracilipes***
purpurea	EBee NHol
robusta	CRDP ELan EMon NWCA
'Royal Highlander'	MDHE NHar NHol
¶ ***rubicunda***	EFEx
saxosa	CRDP ECou EPot GTou ITim LHop MLan MSte MTho NBir NGre NHar NMen NWCA WAbe WOMN
scabra	MHar WWye
§ – var. ***buergeri***	GAri LRHS
– var. ***saxatilis***	See ***G. scabra*** var. ***buergeri***
¶ 'Sensation'	NHar
septemfida ♀	CPla ELan EMNN EMan EPot GDra LBee LHop MBri MBro MTho MWat SBla WAbe WCla WHoo WPat
§ – var. ***lagodechiana*** ♀	CSam GAbr NGre NRoo NWCA SRms WHil
§ – – 'Doeringiana'	GCHN NMen NRoo
§ – – 'Hascombensis'	CPla ECho ELan GCHN
'Serenity'	NHar NMen WAbe
'Shot Silk'	NHar NHol NMen WAbe WWin
sikkimensis	WAbe
sino-ornata ♀	CPla EHyt ELan EMan GCHN GDra LFis MBri NHar NHol NMen NNrd NRoo SBla SIng SRms WAbe
– 'Alba'	CPla GDra NHar NHol NRoo WWin
– 'Angel's Wings'	ELan GTou MBri MDHE NHar NHol NRoo WAbe
– 'Brin Form'	NNrd NRoo SBod SIng SRms WAbe WHil
– 'Downfield'	MOne NHar NHed NHol SBar
– 'Edith Sarah'	CMea ELan MBri MBro MHig MOne NHar NHol NNrd NRoo SBla WAbe WDav WPat WWin
– 'Lapis'	NHol
– 'Mary Lyle'	CHid GGar MBri MBro MOne MTho NHar NRoo WAbe
– 'Praecox'	See ***G.*** x ***macaulayi*** **'Praecox'**
– 'Trogg's Form'	EWes MDHE MOne NHar NHed NHol NRoo
– 'White Wings'	ELan EWes NHar NHed NHol NRoo
– 'Woolgreaves'	SAlw WAbe
x ***stevenagensis*** ♀	CLyd CPla MBri MBro NHar NRoo SIng WDav WHoo WPyg
§ – 'Bernardii'	MBri MDHE SIng WAbe
– dark form	NRoo WAbe WPat
– 'Frank Barker'	MBri MDHE WAbe
stragulata	WAbe
straminea	MHar WCot
'Strathmore'	EHyt ELan EWes MBri MDHE MOne NHar NHol NRoo SIng WAbe WFar
'Susan Jane'	GTou
ternifolia	ELan GDra MSte NRoo
– 'Cangshan' ex SBEC 1053	NHar NHol WAbe
– 'Dali' ex SBEC 1053	EWes MBri MOne NHar NHol WAbe WHil
– SBEC 1053	GGGa
thunbergii	WHil
tibetica	CBot CNic CPea CPla EFol EGar GCal GPoy MNrw NHol NRoo WEas WWye
trichotoma	CNic WAbe
– ACE 1768	EHyt EPot NHar
¶ – ACE 1812	EPot
– ACE 2241	NHar
triflora	GBuc
– 'Alba'	GBuc
– var. ***japonica***	GBuc NGre
– var. ***montana***	GDra
– 'Royal Blue'	GCal
Tweeddale Strain	NRoo
veitchiorum	MBri NRoo WAbe
verna	CGle CPBP ELan EWes LHop MBro MOne MTho NNrd NRoo NSla NTow SAlw SBla WAbe WOMN WPat
– 'Alba'	GCLN NHar SBla WAbe WPat WPyg
– subsp. ***angulosa***	See ***G. verna*** subsp. ***balcanica***
§ – subsp. ***balcanica*** ♀	CPla ELan GAbr GDra GTou MBro MHig MTho NGre NHar NHol SBla SIng WAbe WHoo WPat WPyg
– x ***pumila***	WAbe
¶ – slate blue form	WPat
'Violette'	MDHE

waltonii ECho ELan EWes
wellsii See ***G.* × *macaulayi* 'Wells's Variety'**
§ *wutaiensis* CMea CNic ECho ELan GDra SSca

GENTIANELLA (Gentianaceae)

cerastioides JCA 14003 WAbe
hirculus JCA 13880/93 WAbe
¶ sp. K&LG 94/63 EPot

GENTIANOPSIS (Gentianaceae)

See Plant Deletions

GEOGENANTHUS (Commelinaceae)

undatus See ***G. poepigii***

GERANIUM † (Geraniaceae)

aconitifolium L'Héritier See ***G. rivulare***
albanum CElw CHil CSev EMar EMou EOrc EPPr EPla GCHN MHFP MNFA MNrw NSti SCou SDix WBea WByw WCra WCru
albiflorum EBre EPPr GCHN LCom MHFP MNFA MWhe NCat NRoo SAxl
anemonifolium See ***G. palmatum***
'Ann Folkard' Widely available
'Anne Thomson' CElw CMil EMon EOrc GCHN GCal MHFP NRoo NTay SAxl SCro SHel WBea WCru
argenteum 'Purpureum' See ***G.* × *lindavicum* 'Alanah'**
'Aria' WCru
aristatum CPou EMar EOrc GAbr GCHN GFle MHFP SCou SDad SRGP WCra WCru WIvy WPer
¶ – NS 649 NWCA
armenum See ***G. psilostemon***
asphodeloides CElw CGle CHil CLyd EBar ECro EFol EMon EMou EOrc ERav GAbr GCHN LFis MNrw NCat NHex NSti SWat WBea WByw WCra WCru WEas WHCG WHal WHen WPbr WRus
§ – subsp. *asphodeloides* white CElw EBre ECGP EOrc EPPr SCou SRGP WHen WRus
– subsp. *crenophilum* SCou
– forms CBre LBlm MHFP NCat SCou WCru WHal WHen WHil
– 'Prince Regent' CHid EPPr GCHN MHFP NCat NRoo SCou SHel
– subsp. *sintenisii* EPPr
– 'Starlight' CElw GCHN LBlm MHFP NRoo SCou SHel WCra WCru
– white CVer WHil
atlanticum Hooker f. See ***G. malviflorum***
'Baby Blue' CElw GCHN GCal NBrk NBus NCat SAxl SHel SSoC WBea WCru WHen
'Bertie Crûg' CElw WCru
'Bethany' CMHG
¶ *biflorum* GCal
biuncinatum EMar LCom SCou WCot WWin
'Black Ice' GBuc WCru
'Blue Cloud' CHil MHFP NBrk NCat SAxl SCou SHel SMrm
bohemicum GCHN GFle LFis MHFP NRai NSti SCou SHel SRGP SWat WBea WByw WCra WCru WHen WHer
– DS&T 89077T EMon
'Brookside' CElw CHil EBre ECha EFou EGle EMar EOrc EPla GAbr GCHN MBel MHFP MNFA MSte MTol NBir NBrk NRoo SAga SAxl SCro SHel SWas WBea WCra WEas WHen
brutium EJud GCHN WCra WHen
brycei MNrw
'Buxton's Blue' See ***G. wallichianum* 'Buxton's Variety'**
caffrum CHan EOrc GBuc GCHN NBus SCou SRGP WBea WCru WEas
canariense CGre CHid CSpe EWes LCom SCou SDad SRGP WCru
candicans hort. See ***G. lambertii***
§ × *cantabrigiense* Widely available
– 'Biokovo' Widely available
– 'Cambridge' Widely available
– 'Karmina' CElw CHil EBre EGoo EMil EPPr EPla LBlm LCom MBro MCli NBus NRoo NTay SAxl SCou SHel WHoo
– 'Saint Ola' CElw CHil EBee EFou EPPr GBuc GCHN GCal LCom LLWP MHFP MNFA MNrw NBro NCat NHaw NRoo SAxl SCou SCro SHel SSpi SUsu SWas WCra WCru WFar WHen WRus
– 'Show Time' SCro
¶ *carolinianum* SCou
cataractarum GCHN SCou WCru
'Chantilly' CElw CMil CSam EPPr GAbr MHFP NBir NCat NRoo SAxl SCou SCro SUsu WBea WCra WCru WNdy WPbr
cinereum CGle CSev SIng
– 'Apple Blossom' See ***G.* × *lindavicum* 'Apple Blossom'**
– 'Ballerina' 🏆 Widely available
– var. *cinereum* GCHN SWat WCru
– – 'Album' GCHN MBal
– 'Lawrence Flatman' CHil CMea CSam EBre EFou ELan GCHN LGre MHFP MWhe NBrk NHar NRoo SAxl SBla SCou SHel WByw WCra WCru WHCG WHen WPat WRus WWin
¶ – subsp. *nanum* NCat
– var. *subcaulescens* 🏆 Widely available
– – 'Giuseppii' CTri CWGN EBre EFou GCHN LGro MBro MHFP MWhe NBro NCat NRoo SAxl SCou SHel SRGP WBea WCra WCru WHoo WPyg
¶ – subsp. *subcaulescens* var. *ponticum* NGre
– var. *subcaulescens* 'Splendens' 🏆 CSpe EBre ECha EFou ELan GCHN GFle GMac LFis MBal MBri MCLN MHFP MTis MWhe NRoo NSla SRGP SRms SWat WCru WHoo WIvy WRus
'Claridge Druce' See ***G.* × *oxonianum* 'Claridge Druce'**
clarkei 'Kashmir Blue' GCHN LCom NCat
– 'Kashmir Pink' CBos CElw CGle CHil CLon CMea ECha EWes GBur GCHN LCom MCLN MHFP NBir NBus NCat NRoo SBla SCro SHel SOkh SWat WBea WCra WHCG WHal WHen

§ – 'Kashmir Purple' Widely available
§ – 'Kashmir White' Widely available
– Raina 82.83 SCou
collinum GBuc GCHN GMac MNrw NBus NCat NRoo SCou SCro SUsu WByw WCru WHen WIvy
columbinum SCou
'Coombland White' CElw SHel WCru
'Crûg Dusk' MCLN
'Crûg's Darkest' WCru
dalmaticum ♀ Widely available
– 'Album' Widely available
– × ***macrorrhizum*** See ***G.*** × ***cantabrigiense***
delavayi Franchet CBot CChu
– hort. See ***G. sinense***
'Dilys' CElw CFis CMil CRDP CVer EPPr GCHN LCom MCLN MHFP NBus NCat NRoo SAxl SCou SHel SRGP SUsu SWas WBea WCru WHal WHen WRus
dissectum EWFC MSal SCou SIde
'Distant Hills' CHil GBuc GCHN NRoo
'Diva' CElw EPPr LCom MHFP NCat SAxl SCou WCot WCru
donianum CC 1074 CPou
'Dusky Crûg' WCru
'Elizabeth Ross' CElw LCom WCru
endressii ♀ Widely available
– ***album*** CElw SApp SCro SHel
– 'Castle Drogo' CElw CHil NCat NFai WBea
– dark form NBus WCru
– 'Prestbury White' See ***G. 'Prestbury Blush'***
– 'Priestling's Red' CElw EMar SMrm
– 'Rose' CHil GBur LBlm WPer
erianthum EBee GBuc GCHN MSCN MSte NBus NCat NGre NRoo NSti SAxl SCou SRGP WBea WCru WPbr
– 'Calm Sea' GBuc GCHN SHel SMrm WCru WPbr
– 'Neptune' WCra WCru WPbr
eriostemon Fischer See ***G. platyanthum***
§ ***farreri*** ♀ CBot CLyd EHyt GBri GBuc GCHN GMac MHFP MNrw NGre NRoo NWCA SBla SCou SWat WCru WEas WHal WOMN
flanaganii CElw GCHN WCru
fremontii CRDP GBuc GCHN SCou SDad
'Gillian Perrin' WWeb
gracile CChr CElw CHil CMea EMon EMou GBuc GCHN GMac LCom MCLN MHFP MNrw NBir NRoo SCou SCro SDad WCra WCru WHal
– 'Blanche' LCom NCat
– 'Blush' EPPr LCom MNFA NCat SAxl SHel WBea
– pale form CElw LBlm SCou
grandiflorum See ***G. himalayense***
– var. ***alpinum*** See ***G. himalayense* 'Gravetye'**
gymnocaulon GCHN WBea WCru
'Harmony' NCat
harveyi CElw CHan CHil CPBP CSpe CVer GCal LCom LHop SAxl SDad WCot WCru WKif WPnn
hayatanum B&SWJ 164 WCru
§ ***himalayense*** CElw CFee CHil CWGN EBar ECha ELan EMou GCHN LBlm MHFP MTho MWat MWhe NBir NBrk NBro NHol NNrd NSti SEas SMrm SRms SWat WCra WCru WHCG WHen WMer WPer
– ***alpinum*** See ***G. himalayense* 'Gravetye'**
– 'Birch Double' See ***G. himalayense* 'Plenum'**
¶ – 'Frances Perry' SMur
§ – 'Gravetye' ♀ Widely available
– 'Irish Blue' CElw CHad CHil EBee EBre EFou EGar EPPr GBuc GCHN GCal LCom MBel MBri MHFP MNFA MSte MTol NCat NRoo SAxl SCou SCro SHel SOkh WAbb WBea WCra WCru WHen
– ***meeboldii*** See ***G. himalayense***
§ – 'Plenum' Widely available
ibericum CChr CShe ECED EGoo EPad EPla MBal MMiN MTol MWat MWhe NRoo SCou SWat WByw WCra WCru WEas WHen WPLl WWat WWin
– subsp. ***jubatum*** CElw CHil EGle EPPr GCHN GCal LCom MHFP MNFA SAxl WBea
– var. ***platypetalum*** Boissier See ***G. platypetalum* Fischer & Meyer**
◆ – – hort. See ***G.*** × ***magnificum***
incanum CMHG CMea CSev CShe CSpe ECoo EEls EOrc EWes GCHN LHop MNrw NBir NTow SCou SDad SMrm SRGP
– var. ***incanum*** GCHN WCru
– var. ***multifidum*** GCHN SUsu SWat WCru
– white form SRGP
'Ivan' CElw LGre NCat SCou SHel SWas
* 'Janette' LRHS MAsh MBri MWhe NCat WCra WWeb
'Johnson's Blue' ♀ Widely available
'Joy' CElw CHad CHil CVer EGle EPPr GCHN MHFP NHaw SAxl SHel SMrm SUsu SWat WBea WCra WCru WRHF
§ 'Kate' GCHN NBus NRoo SWat WCru WPnn
'Kate Folkard' See ***G. 'Kate'***
kishtvariense ECGP GCHN GCal MBri MHFP NRoo SBla SCou WCru
– 'Blackthorn Garnet' SBla
¶ ***koraiense*** B&SWJ WCru
koreanum CChu CFil EBee GCHN WBea WCru WPGP
§ ***kotschyi*** var. ***charlesii*** WCru
krameri B&SWJ 1142 WCru
§ ***lambertii*** CVer EWes NBir SCou WEas WHoo
– CC 1077 CPou
– 'Coombland White' WBea
– 'Swansdown' EPPr GCHN GCal WCru
lanuginosum MCCP SCou SRGP
libani CElw CHan CHil EBre EMou GBuc GCHN GCal MBel MCLN MHFP MHlr MNFA MTho NBus NRoo NSti SAxl SCou SCro WByw WCot WCra WCru WEas WHal
'Libretto' WCru
§ × ***lindavicum*** 'Alanah' EMon

§ – 'Apple Blossom'	CFis LCom MHFP NRoo SAga SAsh SAxl WCra WCru WHCG WIvy
– 'Lissadell'	SBla
§ 'Little David'	SAxl
'Little Devil'	See ***G.* 'Little David'**
'Little Gem'	GCHN LCom SAxl SUsu WCru
lucidum	ECWi EJud EWFC GCHN GCra MGam MHew MSal MTol NCat NSti SCou SDad
¶ × ***luganense***	SCou
§ ***macrorrhizum***	Widely available
– 'Album' 🏆	Widely available
– 'Bevan's Variety'	Widely available
– 'Bulgaria'	EPPr SAxl
– 'Czakor'	Widely available
– 'Ingwersen's Variety' 🏆	Widely available
– 'Lohfelden'	CElw EGoo EPPr GCHN MHFP SAxl SHel WCra WCru WRHF
– ***macrorrhizum***	CElw SRms
– 'Mount Olympus'	WPbr
– 'Mount Olympus White'	CBos CElw WSan
– 'Pindus'	CElw CHid EGoo EPPr GCHN LCom MHFP MHar MNFA NCat SAxl SHel SUsu WCru
– 'Ridsko'	CElw CFee CFis CHil EBee EPPr GCHN GCal LCom MHFP NBro NCat NTow SAxl SCou SCro SHel WCru WHen
– ***roseum***	See ***G. macrorrhizum***
– 'Spessart'	CDoC CRos EBee EPPr ERav MBel MOne MUlv NBee NTay NTow SCou SHel SHig WCra WCru WPbr WPyg WRHF
– 'Variegatum'	CElw CHan CLon CRDP CShe ECha EFol EFou EGol ELan EPla GBur GCal MBri MHFP MTho MWhe NBir NRoo NSti NTay SPer WBea WByw WHCG WHen WHil WOld WWin
– 'Velebit'	CElw EPPr GCHN LCom NBus NCat SAxl WCru
– 'White-Ness'	GCHN WCru
macrostylum	GCHN MBro SSvw WCot WCru WPer
maculatum	CChu CElw CRDP CSev CVer ECha EFou ELan EMou GCHN GCal GMac GPoy MBro MHFP MHew MNFA MRav MSal NRoo SAxl SCou SCro SHel WCra WCru WHal WHen WHoo WPbr
– f. ***albiflorum***	CElw CGle CHil CRDP CVer EMon EMou GCHN GCal MBel MBro MHFP MNFA NSti SAxl SCou SHel SSpi SUsu WCra WCru WHal
– 'Chatto'	CMil CSpe CSte EFou EGol EMil LBuc MRav WCra WRus WWat
– 'Shameface'	LCom MHFP NBrk SAxl SHel
maderense 🏆	Widely available
§ × ***magnificum*** 🏆	Widely available
magniflorum	CHil GCHN SCou WBea WCru
§ ***malviflorum***	Widely available
– pink	CDoC LCom SBla WCru
'Mary Mottram'	MMil NBir WEas
microphyllum	MNrw
molle	EWFC MSal SCou SDad
molle album	WNdy
§ × ***monacense***	CBre CElw CHid CHil CSam EFou ELan EMar GGar MBel MHFP MWat MWhe NFai NRoo NSti SCou SCro SWat WBea WByw WCra WCru WHer WPbr
– var. ***anglicum***	CArc CHil ECtt EGle EOrc GAbr GCHN MBel MNFA NBus NSti SAxl SCou SCro SHel
– var. ***monacense***	CElw LCom WHen
§ – 'Muldoon'	CInt CMHG CSev EBre ECha ECoo EMon EPla GAbr MCLN MHFP MRav MTis MUlv NBrk NBro NOak NRoo NTay SAxl SRGP WCot WCra WCru WHCG WHen WOak WPbr WPer
§ – 'Variegatum'	CChr EBee EFol EFou EGol ELan EMar EPla LFis MCLN MSCN MWhe SCou SPer SRGP SWat WAbb WBea WCru WEas WGwG WRha WRus
'Mourning Widow'	See ***G. phaeum***
multisectum	WCru
napuligerum Franchet	NSla
– hort.	See ***G. farreri***
'Natalie'	NCat
nepalense	MHFP NBus SCou SRGP WHer
nervosum	LCom NBus SCou
'Nicola'	NCat SAxl
'Nimbus'	CElw CHil ECha EGle EMon EOrc EPPr GAbr GBuc GCHN LCom LFis MBro MCLN MHFP MNFA NCat SAxl SCou SCro SHel SMrm SOkh SUsu SWas WBea WCra WHCG WHoo WPyg
nodosum	Widely available
– dark form	See ***G. nodosum* 'Swish Purple'**
– pale form	See ***G. nodosum* 'Svelte Lilac'**
§ – 'Svelte Lilac'	CElw ECGP EMon EPPr EPla LCom LRHS MHFP MNFA NBrk NCat NWes SAxl SCou SMrm SWat WBea WCru WPbr
§ – 'Swish Purple'	CElw EMon EPPr LCom MNFA SWat WCru WHen WPbr
– 'Whiteleaf'	CElw EBee EMon NBrk NBus SBla SWat WBea WCru
ocellatum	SCou
oreganum	CElw GCHN LCom NBrk SCou SCro SHel
§ ***orientalitibeticum***	Widely available
'Orkney Pink'	CHil EPPr GCal NRoo SAxl WCot WCru WHoo WWin
× ***oxonianum***	SAga SCou SHel WCru WRHF
– 'A.T. Johnson' 🏆	Widely available
– 'Armitage'	EPPr LCom NCat SAxl SHel
– 'Breckland Sunset'	EPPr
– 'Bregover Pearl'	CBre CElw CHil LCom
– 'Bressingham Delight'	EBee EBre LCom MCLN MWhe NRoo SHel
– 'Buttercup'	EPPr
§ – 'Claridge Druce'	Widely available
– 'Coronet'	LCom NBrk SAxl WBea
– 'Crûg Star'	CElw CHil
– 'David McClintock'	CElw CHil EMon EPPr LCom SAxl
– 'Frank Lawley'	CElw CHil EPPr LCom MHFP NCat NChi NHex NRoo SAxl SCou SCro SHel SUsu WBea

– 'Hexham Pink'	NCat
– 'Hollywood'	CChr CElw CHil EBee ELan EMon EOrc EPPr GAbr GCHN LBlm LFis MHFP MSte MTho NBus NPer NRoo SAxl SCou SCro SHel SMrm SSpe WBea WCra
– 'Julie Brennan'	LCom NCat SAxl WBea
– 'Kate Moss'	CElw CHil EPPr GCHN LCom NCat NChi NHex NRoo NSti
– 'Lace Time'	CArc CElw CHil EBee EPPr LCom LFis MBro MWhe NOak SAxl SCro SHel WBea
– 'Lady Moore'	CElw CHil EBre EMar EPPr EPla GAbr GBuc GCHN LCom LGan MHFP MNFA MNrw MTol MWhe NBro NRoo SAxl SCou SCro SHFr SHel WBea WHen WPbr
– 'Lambrook Gillian'	CElw CHil EPPr LCom MHFP SAxl SCou SHel SMer WBea
– 'Lasting Impression'	EPPr
– 'Miriam Rundle'	CElw CHil EBre EOrc EPPr EPla LCom MHFP MNFA NBus NRoo SAxl SCou SHel WBea WCru
– 'Mrs Charles Perrin'	CElw
– 'Old Rose'	CElw CHil EMon EPPr GCHN LCom MBri MHFP MNFA NBus NCat NPla SAxl SCou WBea WCru
– pale form	EOrc
– 'Pat Smallacombe'	CElw CHil LCom NCat WBea WCru
– 'Phoebe Noble'	CElw CHil CMil EPPr LCom MNFA NCat NRoo SAxl SCro SHel SRGP SUsu SWas WBea WCra
– 'Phoebe's Blush'	CElw NCat NChi SAxl WBea
– 'Pink Lace'	WRus
– 'Prestbury White'	See **G. 'Prestbury Blush'**
– 'Rebecca Moss'	CChu CElw CHil CMil CSev EPPr GCHN GCal LCom MCLN MSte NCat NChi NHex NRoo SAxl SHel SSpe SUsu SWas WCra WCru WEas WHal
– 'Red Sputnik'	EPPr
– 'Rohina Moss'	SCou
– 'Rose Clair'	CElw CHid CHil CMil CShe EBre ECED EMou EOrc MCLN MNFA NFai NRoo SAxl SChu SCou SHel WBea WCru WEas WElm WHen WPer WWeb
– 'Rosenlicht'	CHil CSev EBee EFou EPPr LCom MHFP MNFA NCat NEgg NRoo NTow SAxl SChu SCou SHel SMrm SRGP SSpi WBea WCru WPbr
– x ***sessiliflorum*** subsp. ***novae-zelandiae*** 'Nigricans'	CHil
– 'Sherwood'	CElw CHan CHid CHil EBee EOrc EPPr GCHN GCal LCom MBro MCLN MHFP MSCN MTho NBro NCat NMGW NRoo NTay SAxl SCou SCro SHel SRGP WBea WCra
– 'Southcombe Double'	CElw CHil CM&M CMil CSev CWGN EBre EGle EMar EMou MCLN MFir MHFP MNFA MUlv MWhe NCat NRoo SAxl SChu SUsu WBea WByw WCru WHal WHen WWin
§ – 'Southcombe Star'	CElw EAst EBee EGar EHal EPPr GAbr GCal LCom MBel MHFP NBrk NBro NBus NRoo NSti SAxl SHel WBea WCru WHal WHen WPer
– 'Stillingfleet'	GCHN
§ – 'Thurstonianum'	Widely available
I – 'Thurstonianum Isherwood'	CSev
– 'Wageningen'	CBre CHil EBee EGar EPla GCal GMac LBlm LCom MMil NBus NCat NLak NPro NRoo SAxl SCou SHel WBea WCru WHen
– 'Walter's Gift'	Widely available
– 'Wargrave Pink' ♀	Widely available
– 'Waystradi'	EPPr
– 'Winscombe'	Widely available
'Pagoda'	EOrc
§ ***palmatum*** ♀	CAbb CBos CBot CDec CElw CPle CSpe EMar EPad LFis MHFP MHlr NBro NFai NPer SAxl SCou SDad SMad SMrm SUsu WCru WEas WHal WHer WKif WOMN WPer
palustre	CElw CHil EBee EMou GCHN MBel MBro MHFP MNFA MNrw NBro NSti SCou SDad SRGP WCra WCru WHen
papuanum	CElw GCHN SBla
'Patricia'	CElw CFis EFou GCHN LCom MAvo MCLN MHFP MMil MSte NBus NChi NHaw SAxl SCou SCro SWas WBea WCra WCru WHal WRus WSan
peloponnesiacum NS 660	CElw CPou
§ ***phaeum***	Widely available
– 'Album'	Widely available
– black	See ***G. phaeum*** **'Mourning Widow'**
– 'Calligrapher'	CElw EPPr MHFP NBrk SHel WBea
– 'Charles Perrin'	CElw
– forms	EMou EPPr SSvw
¶ – 'Golden Spring'	NCat
– 'Hannah Perry'	CElw CVer EPPr WBea
– var. ***hungaricum***	CHil EBee EGar GCal MFir NCat SCou SHel WBea WCru
– 'Joan Baker'	CBre CChr CElw CGle CHil CLTr CMil CRDP CSam CVer EBee EPPr LCom MHFP MNFA NCat NRoo SAxl SCou SCro SHel SSoC SWat WBea WCra WCru WSan
– 'Langthorn's Blue'	CElw CSev EFol ELan LCom MHFP NBus NCat NRoo SCro SHel WHal WHen WPbr
§ – 'Lily Lovell'	Widely available
* – 'Little Boy'	EMon
– var. ***lividum***	CBre CElw CFee CGle CHil CMea EBre EMar EMou GCHN LFis LGan SAxl SChu SCou SCro SHel SPer SWas WBea WByw WCra WCru WElm WHal WHen WHer WPer WWin

– – 'Majus'	CElw CHil EBre EGle EMil EMon EPPr GCal LGan MHFP MNFA NRoo NTay SAxl SCou SCro WBea
– 'Mierhausen'	CElw CGle
§ – 'Mourning Widow'	CElw CMil EPPr GBin GCal MWhe NCat NRoo NTay SAxl SCro SHel SRms WBea WCru WHen WPbr
– 'Night Time'	SCro SHel WBea
¶ – red form	MRav
– 'Rose Air'	EPPr LCom NBrk SAxl
– 'Rose Madder'	CArc CBos CFis CHad CHil GCal LCom MHFP SAxl SCou SHel WBea
– 'Samobor'	Widely available
– 'Saturn'	WHer
– 'Small Grey'	CHil
– 'Stillingfleet Ghost'	NHex NSti
– 'Taff's Jester' (v)	CElw CHad LCom LFis MTol NBus NSti SCro SHel WBea WCru WHer WHil
– 'Variegatum'	CElw CHan EBre ECED ECro EGol ELan EMon EMou ERav GBur MFir MHFP MNrw MRav NCat SCro WBea WCru WHer WPbr
'Phillippe Vapelle'	CChu CElw CHil CMil EMou EPPr GCHN GCal LCom MCLN MHFP NBir NBus NChi NRoo SCou SCro SHel SMrm SOkh SWat WBea WCot WCra WCru
§ *platyanthum*	CElw CGle CHil CVer EMou GCHN GCal LBlm MNrw MTol NRoo NSti SAxl SCou WBea WByw WCru WHCG WHal WHen WPer
§ *platypetalum* Fischer & Meyer	CElw CHan EBre ELan EMou ENot GAri GBur GCHN MHig MNFA MWhe NBir NCat NFla SCou SRms SWat WBea WCru WHil
– Franchet	See ***G. sinense***
– 'Georgia Blue' Fischer & Meyer	CFil LCom SSpi WCru
pogonanthum	GBuc GCHN GCal GMac NBir NBro SCou WCru
polyanthes	CElw CHil CRDP GAbr GAri GBuc GCra GDra GTou NGre SCou WCru
potentilloides	CHid GCHN MHFP NBir NBus NCat NHex SCou WBea WHil
pratense	Widely available
– f. *albiflorum*	CBot CElw CGle CHil ECED GCHN GCal LGan LHop MBri MHew MNrw NFai NOrc NRoo NSti SCou SDad SPer WBea WByw WCra WHCG WHal WHen WPbr WRus WWin
¶ – – 'Whimble White'	WWhi
– 'Bittersweet'	CHil EJud EMon NBrk SAxl SHel
¶ – 'Blue Chip'	EMon SHel
– 'Bodenfalle'	CHil
– 'Catforth Carnival'	NCat
– CC&McK 442	GTou
– 'Cluden Ruby'	GCHN
– 'Cluden Sapphire'	GCHN WCru
– 'Elizabeth Yeo'	SAxl SCou SCro SHel
– 'Flore Pleno'	See ***G. pratense* 'Plenum Violaceum'**
– forms	CHil GCHN MHFP SCou WCru
¶ – from Nepal	CHil
– 'Galactic'	CHan EMar EMon MBro NCat SDad SHel WBro WCru WHen WOMN
– 'Mrs Kendall Clark' 🏆	Widely available
– 'Numwood Purple'	CHil
– 'Plenum Album'	CHil SCou
§ – 'Plenum Caeruleum'	CChu CElw CGle CM&M CSam EOrc EPPr GCHN GCal MBri MHFP MWat NNor NRoo SCou WCru WEas WHCG
– 'Plenum Purpureum'	See ***G. pratense* 'Plenum Violaceum'**
§ – 'Plenum Violaceum' 🏆	CB&S CBos CBot CHad CM&M COtt EBre ECha ELan EOrc EPPr GCHN GFle MHFP MUlv NNor NRoo NTow NWes SChu SCou SCro SHel SOkh WCru WHCG WOld WWin
– 'Rectum Album'	See ***G. clarkei* 'Kashmir White'**
– 'Rose Queen'	NCat NRai SDad SHel WBea WCru WHen WPbr
– ***roseum***	CGle CHil ELan EOrc GBur MBro NBir NChi NHex NSti SSpi WHoo
– 'Silver Queen'	CBre CChr CGle CHil ELan EOrc EPPr GCHN MBro MHFP MNrw MWhe NBrk NRoo SCou SDad SOkh SRGP WBea WCru WHen WHoo WPyg
– subsp. ***stewartianum***	CElw LLew MRav WCru
– – ex CC 31	LKoh
– 'Striatum'	Widely available
¶ – 'Striatum' pale form	CBre
¶ – Tibetan Border form	LLew
– 'Wisley Blue'	LCom SCou SCro SHel SOkh
– 'Yorkshire Queen'	MTol NHex SHel
'Prelude'	CElw NCat WBea
§ 'Prestbury Blush'	CElw EMon GCHN SAxl SCou WBea WCot WCru
'Prima Donna'	NCat
procurrens	Widely available
pseudosibiricum	SCou
§ ***psilostemon*** 🏆	Widely available
– 'Bressingham Flair'	EBre ECha EFou EGol EMou GCal LHop MBel MHFP MWhe NHol NOrc NRoo SChu SCou SMrm WCra WCru WHal WWat
– 'Gold Leaf'	WCot
pulchrum	CElw CHan CSpe EMon EOrc GCHN MNrw SAxl SCou SHel SRGP SWas SWat WCot WCru
punctatum hort.	See ***G. × monacense* 'Muldoon'**
◆ – ***variegatum*** hort.	See ***G. × monacense* 'Variegatum'**
¶ ***purpureum***	SCou
pusillum	CKin MSal SCou
pylzowianum	CElw CNic CShe GBur GCHN LGan MNFA NGre NMen NNrd NRoo NRya NTay SAxl SChu SSmi WBea WByw WCru WHal WHen WHer
pyrenaicum	CElw CHil CKin CRDP CSev ECWi EOrc EPPr EWFC GAbr GCHN MHew NRoo NSti SCou SCro SIng WBea WHen

– f. ***albiflorum***	CElw EFol EMar EMou EOrc EPPr ESis GAbr GCHN LLWP MNrw MTho NBir NRai NRoo NSti SCou SCro SHel WBea WCla WCra WHen WWin
– 'Bill Wallis'	CHil CMea EEls EFol EMan EMar EOrc ESiP GBri LBlm LFis LLWP MCLN MHFP MHar MHlr MSCN MTho MUlv NPer SAxl SHel SRGP WBea WCot WCra WCru WEas WNdy
'Rambling Robin'	WCru
rectum	NBus SAxl WCru
– 'Album'	See ***G. clarkei* 'Kashmir White'**
'Red Dwarf'	GCHN
reflexum	CBre CChu CElw CHid CSev EGol EPPr GBur GCHN LFis MHFP MNFA NCat NRoo NVic SAxl SCou SCro SHel WCru WHCG WHal
– dark form	SAxl
regelii	CElw CMil CSam CVer EBee EPPr LCom MHFP NGre NSla SAxl SHel WCra WCru
¶ – CC 806	CPou
renardii 🏆	Widely available
– blue	See ***G. renardii* 'Whiteknights'**
– 'Tcschelda'	CFai CSte EFou SPla
§ – 'Whiteknights'	CElw CHil CSpe CSte CWGN EGol GCHN NBir NBus WBea WCru WEas WIvy
– 'Zetterland'	CElw CMil CSpe EBre EPPr LFis SHel SWat WBea WPbr
richardsonii	EPPr GCHN GCal LCom MHFP MNrw NBir NBus NCat NChi NRoo SAxl SChu SCou SCro SDad SRms WBea WCru
× ***riversleaianum***	GBur SCou WCru
– 'Jean Armour'	CHil GCHN WCru
– 'Mavis Simpson'	Widely available
– 'Russell Prichard' 🏆	Widely available
§ ***rivulare***	CElw GCHN LCom MNFA WBea WHCG
– 'Album'	CHil LCom MBro
robertianum	CKin ECWi EEls EFol EPPr EWFC MChe MGam SCou SIde SRms WHen WJek
§ – 'Album'	MGam MHar NSti SCou SIde SRms WElm
– f. ***bernettii***	See ***G. robertianum* 'Album'**
– 'Celtic White'	CBre EFol EJud EMon GBin GCal LCom MHFP NBus NCat NHex NRoo NSti SRGP WHal WHen
robustum	CElw CGle CHan CSpe EFol EFou EMar EMon EPri GAbr GCHN LBlm MNrw NBro NCat SAxl SCou SDad SIgm SRGP SUsu SVen WBea WByw WCra WCru WEas WHal WWin
¶ – Hannays' form	CSpe
– × ***incanum***	CElw WCru
– 'Norman Warrington'	WHer
– S&SH 14	CHan CMea WBea WCru
¶ ***rotundifolium***	SCou
rubescens	GBur GGar MFir MNFA MNrw NBir NBro NCat SCou SRGP WCra WCru WHal WWye
rubifolium	ECGP MHFP NBrk NBus SAxl SCou WCru
ruprechtii	CElw CHil CRDP EMar GCHN LCom MHFP MNrw NBus NCat NRai SCou SRGP WBea
'Salome'	CElw CGle CMHG CMil CSev EBre MCLN MTho SAga SAxl SBla SCou SWas WCot WCru
sanguineum	Widely available
– 'Alan Bloom'	EBre LRHS MCLN MWhe NRoo NWes
– 'Album' 🏆	Widely available
– 'Ankum's Pride'	CGle CRDP EBee EPPr LCom SAxl WCot
– 'Barnsley'	SCou
– 'Belle of Herterton'	GCHN SAxl WCru
– 'Bloody Graham'	MWhe NBrk SAxl
– 'Cedric Morris'	CBos CElw CFil CHil ECha EFou EPPr ERav LBlm LCom MHFP MNFA MTho SAxl SCou SHel SUsu SWas WCot WCru
– 'Elliott's Variety'	SIng
– 'Elsbeth'	CElw CHil CMil CRDP EPPr EWes GBuc GCHN LCom MCLN NBus NCat SAxl SCou SHel SWas WCru WSan
– 'Farrer's Form'	EPPr GBuc WCru
– 'Glenluce'	Widely available
– 'Holden'	CElw CMea NRoo WCru
– 'John Elsley'	CElw CHil CPou EBee EBre EGol EMou EPPr LCom MMil MSCN MWhe NBus NRoo SWat WCra WPer
– 'Jubilee Pink'	CHil EGar EPPr NRoo SBla SCou SHel WCru
– var. ***lancastrense***	See ***G. sanguineum* var. *striatum***
– 'Max Frei'	Widely available
– 'Minutum'	MHFP NSla SCou WCru
– 'Nanum'	CMea EPar NHol NMen NNrd WCru
– 'Nyewood'	CFis ECGP EMon EPPr GCHN LCom MHFP SAxl SEND SRGP WCru
– var. ***prostratum*** (Cav.) Pers.	See ***G. sanguineum* var. *striatum***
* – – hort.	WHil
– 'Sara'	SDad WHen
– 'Shepherd's Warning' 🏆	CHil CMea CSev CShe EBre ECED ECtt GAbr GCHN LHop MHFP MHig MRav NRoo SCou SPer SRGP SWat WBea WByw WCra WCru WHCG WHoo WIvy WRus
§ – var. ***striatum*** 🏆	Widely available
– – deep pink	SCro
I – – 'Splendens'	CElw ECha EGol ELan EPPr GDra LHop MWat NChi NNor NRoo NWes SAga SCou SSmi WCru WEas WOld WWhi
– × ***swatense***	EPPr
– 'Vision'	LGan NWes
'Sea Fire'	GCHN MTho WCru
'Sea Pink'	CElw GCHN MTho SHel WCru
'Sea Spray'	EWes GBuc GCHN MTho NRoo SWat WCra
sessiliflorum	CHid ECou EPar GBur NHar SAga SCou WElm
– subsp. ***novae-zelandiae*** green-leaved	GCHN NChi SWat
– – 'Nigricans'	Widely available
– – 'Nigricans' × ***traversii*** var. ***elegans***	CBos CHan CMea CRDP CWGN ESis GCHN NCat NSti SWat WCot WCru

– – 'Nigricans' × ***traversii*** var. ***elegans*** Crûg strain	CMil GCal MHFP NPSI SSpi WCru
§ – – 'Porter's Pass'	CBos CDec CHil CMea EFol EHoe EWes GBri GCHN MHFP MNrw NBir NHex NRoo SCou SDad SUsu SWat WCru
¶ – – 'Porter's Pass' hybrid	GCal
– – red-leaved	See ***G. sessiliflorum*** subsp. ***novae-zelandiae* 'Porter's Pass'**
shikokianum var. ***yoshiianum***	CElw GBuc GCHN
sibiricum	GBur GCHN SCou
§ ***sinense***	CChu CElw CHil EMon GCHN GCal GCra GMac LGre MHFP MNFA NRoo SCou SSoC WBea WCru WHCG WHal WHer WWhi
'Sirak'	GCal NCat NChi SAxl WBea
soboliferum	CFis GBuc GCal NBir NChi SCro WCru
'Sonata'	NRoo
'Southcombe Star'	See ***G.*** × ***oxonianum* 'Southcombe Star'**
¶ sp. from Pamirs, Tadzhikistan	EPPr
'Spinners'	CChu CElw CHil CMil CSam EBre EOrc GBuc GCHN GCal MBri MCLN MTol NCat NHex NRoo SAxl SCou SCro SHel SMrm SSpi WBea WByw WCra WHCG WHen WHoo
'Stanhoe'	EFol EMar EPPr MCLN SCou SCro SHel SOkh SUsu WBea
stapfianum var. ***roseum***	See ***G. orientalitibeticum***
'Stephanie'	NCat
'Strawberry Frost'	MMil WCot
'Sue Crûg'	GCHN NBus SAxl WBea WByw WCot WCru WHen
suzukii B&SWJ 016	WCru
swatense	EMou MBri MNrw NCat NGre SAxl SCou SWat WCru WHal
sylvaticum	CM&M CSev EMou EWFC GMac MBal MNFA MSCN MSal NHex SCou SRGP SSpi WCra WHal WHen WPer WShi
– f. ***albiflorum***	CBot CBre CElw CMil EGol ELan EMar EMou EPad GCHN MBro NRoo NSti SCou SSpi WCru WOld WWin
– 'Album' ♀	Widely available
– 'Amy Doncaster'	CElw CHad CHil CMea CMil ECha ELan EMou GCHN MBri MBro MCLN MHFP NCat NTay SAga SAxl SCou SHel SPer SWas WBea WCru WHal WNdy WRus
– 'Angulatum'	EPPr SAxl SCou
– 'Baker's Pink'	CElw CFil CHil CMea CMil EMou GCHN LCom MHFP MNFA NCat SAxl SBla SHel SMrm SSpi WBea WCru WHCG WRHF
– 'Birch Lilac'	CHil EGar EMou EPPr GBuc GCal MHFP MTol NBus NCat NRoo SAxl SCou WBea WCra WPbr
– 'Cyril's Fancy'	NCat
– 'Mayflower' ♀	Widely available
– f. ***roseum***	ECGP EGle EMou GCHN MHFP NCat NRoo SCro SIng SPer WCra
– 'Silva'	CGle CSte GCHN NBrk SAxl SCou WCru
– subsp. ***sylvaticum*** var. ***wanneri***	CGle CHil CMea EMou EPPr GCHN MBro NCat SCou SCro SHel WCra WCru
§ ***thunbergii***	CLTr CVer EAst EFol EMar EMou GAbr GCHN LCom LGro MHFP MHew MNrw MTol NBro NHol NOak SCou SHel WBea WByw WCra WHal WHen WPer
– purple	LBlm
– ***roseum***	SHel SRGP WCru
– white	CHil LBlm SRGP
thurstonianum	See ***G.*** × ***oxonianum* 'Thurstonianum'**
transbaicalicum	CPou EBre EMon EPPr GCHN MBri MHFP MNrw SCro SRGP WBea WCru
traversii	CBot CLyd MDHE WSan
– var. ***elegans***	CBos CChr CFee CSpe EFol ELan GCHN GMac LGre MHFP MNrw MTho NPSI NRoo SCou SHel SRGP SSca SWas WCra WCru WEas WHCG WOMN
– 'Seaspray'	CHil EBre GCal SCou
tuberosum	Widely available
– var. ***charlesii***	See ***G. kotschyi*** var. ***charlesii***
– 'Leonidas'	LRHS
– M&T 4032	CMon
– S&L 99	CMon
versicolor	Widely available
– ***album***	CElw CHan LCom MHFP NBus NRoo SHel WBea WHer
– 'Snow White'	EPPr NBrk NMGW SAxl SCou SHel
– 'White Lady'	WCru
violareum	See ***Pelargonium* 'Splendide'**
viscosissimum	EPPr GCal GMac LLWP MBri MFir MHFP NRoo NTay SCou SRGP WCot WOMN
wallichianum	CBod CFis CPou ECGP NBir NSti SBla WBea WCra WHal WHen WPyg WWat
§ – 'Buxton's Variety' ♀	Widely available
¶ – magenta form	GCHN
– pink	GBuc WCru
– purple	WCru
– 'Syabru'	CElw CMea MHFP SHel SWas WCru WFar
* 'Welsh Guiness'	WCru
wilfordii hort.	See ***G. thunbergii***
– Maximowicz	WThi
'Wisley Hybrid'	GCHN NBus SAxl WCru
wlassovianum	Widely available
yesoense	CMea EPPr GBin GCHN MHFP NBir NBus NRoo SCou SWat WCru WHal
yoshinoi	GBin GBuc SAsh SCou SHel SRGP SWat
yunnanense	EBee GGar SCou

GERANIUM hort. See PELARGONIUM

GERBERA (Asteraceae)

jamesonii	CB&S

GESNERIA (Gesneriaceae)

cardinalis	See ***Sinningia cardinalis***
× ***cardosa***	See ***Sinningia*** × ***cardosa***

GEUM † (Rosaceae)

aleppicum	CLyd MSto

– CLD 610	EPla
alpinum	See ***G. montanum***
'Beech House Apricot'	CElw CGle CRDP CSev GBri LGre MBel MHFP SMac SOkh SUsu WBro WPbr WRus
N 'Borisii'	Widely available
'Borisii' × ***montanum***	LCom LHop
bulgaricum	CMea LCom LRHS NBir NPro NRya NTow WByw WMer
canadense	ECro
capense JJ&JH 9401271	EBee
'Carlskaer'	CBre CElw CMil CRDP GCal
§ ***chiloense***	CLyd EBar NSla WBro
– P&W 6513	CHan MSte NWCA
¶ ***coccineum***	WRha
– hort.	See ***G. chiloense***
¶ – Sibth. & Sm. NS 653	MRPP
'Coppertone'	CChu CElw CGle CHad CLon CMil CRDP EBar ECha ECtt EHal ELan GCal GMac IBlr MCLN MMil NBir NBro NCat NRoo SAga SAxl SPer SUsu WElm WHal WHoo WSan
'Dingle Apricot'	EFol NBir
'Dolly North'	ECED EGar EPPr GAbr GGar MBri NBro NCat NFai WMer
I 'Farmer John Cross'	CBre
'Feuermeer'	LCom LHop MBel MSte NLak NPro
'Fire Opal' ♀	CSam NBir SPer WTyr
'Georgenburg'	CElw CHad CRDP EBre ECtt MCLN MNrw NBir NFai NHol NOak SAxl SChu SPer SRms WByw WHal WHil WMer WOld WSan WTyr
* ***hybridum luteum***	MBel NSti
× ***intermedium***	CBre CChu CRow EMan EMon MCLN NLak SChu SCro SUsu
– 'Muriel' (v)	MInt
'Lady Stratheden' ♀	Widely available
'Lemon Drops'	CBre CElw CGle CMil EBee ECha EGol EPPr GCra GMac MSte NCat SAxl SChu SOkh
'Lionel Cox'	Widely available
macrophyllum	GBar NBus
magellanicum	See ***G. parviflorum***
* 'Mandarin'	GCal
'Marika'	CElw CRow NBrk SChu
§ ***montanum*** ♀	CChr CHan CSam ECha EHyt ELan GDra GTou MBro MHig NBir NBro NHol NLak NRoo SRms WCla WHal WPer WWin
'Mrs J. Bradshaw' ♀	Widely available
¶ 'Mrs W. Moore'	NCat
§ ***parviflorum***	EGar MBro MSto NBro NBus NCut
pentapetalum	CGle CLyd MSto NSla WAbe
'Prince of Orange'	CElw EGar GAbr NLak SOkh
'Prinses Juliana'	CBos CHan EFou EGar GCal MUlv NCat NHol NLak WCot WMer
pyrenaicum	MSto NBus NLak
quellyon	See ***G. chiloense***
'Red Wings'	CM&M EGar GCal WCra WMer WRus
reptans	See ***Sieversia reptans***
× ***rhaeticum***	MHig NMen NTow
'Rijnstroom'	LBuc MBel MUlv NFai WCra
rivale	Widely available
– 'Album'	Widely available
– apricot	WWin
* – 'Leonard's Double'	ECtt
– 'Leonard's Variety'	Widely available
'Rubin'	EBar MBel
'Sigiswang'	GAbr MBel MFir NCat
'Tangerine'	GGar MRav NRoo
× ***tirolense***	EBee
triflorum	EHyt EMan GTou LGre MBri MSto WHil
– var. ***campanulatum***	EDAr EHyt NGar
urbanum	CArn CKin ECWi EWFC GPoy MChe MCli MGam MHew NLan NPri SIde SWat WCla WHer
– 'Checkmate' (v)	EMon EPla
'Werner Arends'	GCal MBri MRav WFar

GEVUINA (Proteaceae)

avellana	CB&S CGre CHEx CTrw GSki

GIBASIS (Commelinaceae)

See Plant Deletions

GIGASPERMUM (Gigaspermaceae)

See Plant Deletions

GILIA (Polemoniaceae)

aggregata	See ***Ipomopsis aggregata***
californica	See ***Leptodactylon californicum***
stenothyrsa	See ***Ipomopsis stenothyrsa***

GILLENIA (Rosaceae)

stipulata	CRDP EMon LGre LHol MSal
trifoliata ♀	Widely available

GINKGO (Ginkgoaceae)

biloba ♀	Widely available
– 'Autumn Gold' (m)	CDul CEnd ETen LNet LRHS MBlu SMad WMou
– 'Fairmount' (m)	MBlu
– 'Fastigiata' (m)	CMCN CSte MGos WMou
– 'Hekt Leiden'	CMCN
– 'Horizontalis'	CMCN MBlu
– 'Icho'	MBlu
– 'King of Dongting' (f)	MBlu WMou
– 'Ohazuki' (f)	WMou
– 'Pendula' (m)	CMCN LPan WMou
– 'Princeton Sentry' (m)	LRHS MBlu WMou
I – 'Prostrata'	CPMA WWes
– 'Saratoga' (m)	CEnd CMCN CPMA LNet LPan MBlu SMad
– 'Tit'	CMCN LNet
– 'Tremonia'	LNet LRHS MBlu WMou
– 'Tubifolia'	MBlu WMou
– 'Umbrella'	CMCN
– 'Variegata' (f)	CMCN CPMA LNet MBlu

GLADIOLUS † (Iridaceae)

alatus	NRog WCot
'Alice' (Min)	LAma
'Aloha' (L)	CSut
'Amanda Mahy' (N)	CBro GCra LAma MUlv NRog
'Applause' (L)	LAma NRog
'Atom' (P)	CBro LAma
'Avalanche' (B)	LAma
'Bell Boy' (B)	LAma
'Blackpool' (M)	LAma NRog
blandus var. ***carneus***	See ***G. carneus***
* 'Bread and Butter'	CSut
byzantinus	See ***G. communis*** subsp. ***byzantinus***
callianthus ♀	CArc CSWP WFar

§ – 'Murieliae' ♀	CAvo CBro CSut LAma LBow MDun NRog SDeJ
'Cambourne' (Min)	LAma NRog
cardinalis	CFil CHan CMea CRDP GCal IBlr WCot WPGP
carinatus	NRog
carmineus	CMon LBow
§ ***carneus***	CBro MSto NRog WCot
'Charm' (N)	CAvo CBro LAma
'Charming Beauty' (Tub)	NRog
'Chartres' (B)	LAma
'Chiquita' (M)	CSut
'Christabel' (L)	LBow
citrinus	LBow
'City Lights'	CSut
'Columbine' (P)	LAma NRog
x ***colvillei***	ECha
'Comet' (N)	NRog
communis	LAma
§ – subsp. ***byzantinus*** ♀	CAvo CB&S CBro CFee CGle CHEx CHad CLon EBre ECha ELan EPar ETub LAma LBow MBri MUlv NRog SHel WCra WEas WOMN WShi
'Côte d'Azur' (G)	WCot
'Don Juan'	CSut
'Dyanito' (B)	LAma
¶ ***ecklonii***	WCot
'Elvira' (N)	CBos LAma NRog
¶ 'Eurovision' (L)	CSut
'Fair Lady' (Tub)	NRog
'Fidelio' (L)	LAma
floribundus	LBow
'Flower Song' (L)	LAma
'Frosty Pink'	CSut
garnieri	CMon SSpi
'Georgette' (B)	LAma
'Giallo Antico'	CSut
'Good Luck' (N)	CAvo CBro
grandis	See ***G. liliaceus***
'Green Woodpecker' (M) ♀	LAma NRog
'Guernsey Glory' (N)	NRog
'Halley'	CBro
'Holland Pearl' (B)	LAma NRog
'Hunting Song' (L)	LAma NRog
illyricus	CFil CMon CNat CSam WPGP
'Impressive' (N)	NRog
§ ***italicus***	MSto
'Jacksonville Gold' (L)	LAma
§ kotschyanus	MSto
'Lady Godiva' (P/Min)	LAma NRog
'Leonore' (S)	LAma
§ ***liliaceus***	LBow WThi
'Lowland Queen' (L)	CSut
'Madonna' (L)	CSut
marlothii	MSto
'Mary Housley' (L)	LAma
'Mirella' (N)	NRog
'Murieliae'	See ***G. callianthus*** **'Murieliae'**
'My Love' (L)	LAma
§ ***natalensis***	GCal IBlr WCot
nerineoides	CMon
'Nova Lux' (L)	LAma NRog
'Nymph' (N)	CAvo ETub LAma MNrw NRog
'Obelisk' (P)	NRog
¶ ***orchidiflorus***	CSWP LBow
'Oscar' (G)	LAma NRog
papilio	Widely available
§ – Purpureoauratus Group	CBro CFis CGle CSam EBee EMan IBlr MFir MSto SOkh SRms
'Perky' (Min)	LAma
'Perseus' (P/Min)	LAma
'Peter Pears' (L)	LAma NRog
'Picturesque' (P)	NRog
'Plum Tart' (L)	CSut
'Praha' (L)	LAma NRog
primulinus	See ***G. natalensis***
Primulinus Hybrids	SDeJ
'Princess Margaret Rose' (Min)	LAma
'Prins Claus' (N)	CBro LAma NRog
priorii	NRog
'Priscilla' (L)	LAma
¶ ***punctulatus***	LBow
purpureoauratus	See ***G. papilio*** **Purpureoauratus Group**
quadrangularis	MSto
'Ramona'	CSut
'Richmond' (B)	NRog
'Robinetta'(*recurvus* hybrid) ♀	LAma NRog
'Rougex'	NRog
saundersii	CFil WPGP
scullyi	LBow NRog
segetum	See ***G. italicus***
'The Bride' (Colv.) ♀	CAvo CBos CBro CGle CMil CSpe EBre LAma MUlv NCat NRog WPen
'Tout à Toi'	CSut
'Trader Horn' (G)	LAma NRog
tristis	CBro CFee CPou CRow ECha ELan LBow NRog SAga SDix SSpi SWas WAbe WCot WHal WThi
– var. ***concolor***	WHer WOMN
undulatus	CSWP LBow
'Velvet Joy' (P)	LAma
'Vera Lynn'	CSut
'Victor Borge' (L)	NRog
violaceolineatus	MSto
'Violetta' (M)	CSut
¶ ***virescens***	LBow
¶ ***watsonioides***	ERos
'White City' (P/B)	LAma
'White Friendship' (L)	LAma NRog
'Wind Song' (L)	LAma

GLANDULARIA (Verbenaceae)

bipinnatifida	See ***Verbena bipinnatifida***
pulchella	See ***Verbena tenera***

GLAUCIDIUM (Glaucidiaceae)

palmatum ♀	EFEx EMan GDra MBal MDun NHar NSla WCru
– 'Album'	See ***G. palmatum*** var. ***leucanthum***

GLAUCIUM (Papaveraceae)

* ***caucasicum***	EEls
§ ***corniculatum***	CBot CGle CLon CSpe EBee EBre MHlr SEND SSoC SUsu WCot WCru WEas WPyg
flavum	CArc CArn CGle CLon CSpe ECWi ECha EWFC NBro SMrm WCru WHer WOld WPer WWin
– ***aurantiacum***	See ***G. flavum*** **f. *fulvum***
§ – f. ***fulvum***	ECha EPPr LHop MSCN
– orange	See ***G. flavum*** **f. *fulvum***

– red	See ***G. corniculatum***
grandiflorum	WWin
phoenicium	See ***G. corniculatum***

GLAUX (Primulaceae)

maritima	ELan WPer
– dwarf form	NWCA

GLECHOMA (Lamiaceae)

hederacea	CArn CKin ECWi EWFC GBar GPoy IHos MHew NBro NMir SIde SRms WCer WHer WWye
– 'Rosea'	EMon LRHS
– 'Spot Check'	EMon
§ – 'Variegata'	CHal CRow ECro EEls EJud ELan GBar ILis MBri MRav SIde
hirsuta AL&JS 90069YU	EMon

GLEDITSIA (Caesalpiniaceae)

caspica	CB&S
japonica	SMad
¶ ***koraiensis***	CMCN
triacanthos	CAgr CPle ENot GAri IOrc LPan SHhN WFox WNor
– 'Emerald Cascade'	CBlo CEnd CLnd LRHS
– f. ***inermis***	WNor
– 'Rubylace'	CDoC CEnd CLnd COtt ELan EMil EPfP LPan MAsh MBar MBlu MGos SHBN SMad SMer SSpi WDin WOrn
– 'Shademaster'	ENot
– 'Skyline'	LPan
– 'Sunburst' ♀	CB&S CEnd CLnd CSPN ELan EMil ENot GQui IOrc LBuc LHyr LNet LPan MAsh MBar MBlu MBri MGos MWat NBee SHBN SMad SPer SSpi SSta WDin WJas WOrn

GLOBBA (Zingiberaceae)

¶ ***marantina***	LLew
winitii	LChe

GLOBULARIA (Globulariaceae)

bellidifolia	See ***G. meridionalis***
bisnagarica NS 695	NWCA
cordifolia ♀	CMHG CMil CTri LBee MBro MTho NHar NHol NMen NTow SAga SBla SIng WHoo WOld WPer
– NS 696	NWCA
cordifolia purpurescens	CLyd
incanescens	CLyd LBee MLsm WCla WWin
§ ***meridionalis***	CPBP EWes ITim LBee MBro MHig MWat NHar NNrd NWCA SBla SSmi WFar WHal
– 'Hort's Variety'	CTri GMaP LBee MTho NNrd WAbe
nana	See ***G. repens***
nudicaulis	MBro NHar SBla WPer
– 'Alba'	CLyd WIvy
§ ***punctata***	LBee LFis MBro NTow NWCA SRms WHil WHoo WPer
pygmaea	See ***G. meridionalis***
§ ***repens***	CLyd CPBP MBro MTho
¶ ***spinosa***	WDav
¶ ***stygia***	NSla
trichosantha	GAbr LBee LCom MHig SMrm WDav
vulgaris	CInt ELan

GLORIOSA (Colchicaceae)

carsonii	See ***G. superba* 'Carsonii'**
lutea	See ***G. superba* 'Lutea'**
rothschildiana	See ***G. superba* 'Rothschildiana'**
§ ***superba*** ♀	IBlr LAma MBri NRog SDeJ SLMG
§ – 'Lutea'	LAma LBow NRog
§ – 'Rothschildiana'	CB&S CHal CPlN CRHN LAma LBow SLMG SRms SSoC

GLOXINIA (Gesneriaceae)

'Chic'	NMos
* ***latifolia***	ECon
¶ 'Medusa'	WDib
perennis	NMos
sylvatica	CHal WDib
– 'Bolivian Sunset'	WDib

GLUMICALYX (Scrophulariaceae)

¶ ***flanaganii*** HWEL 0325	NWCA

GLYCERIA (Poaceae)

aquatica variegata	See ***G. maxima*** var. ***variegata***
grandis	ETPC
maxima	ECWi WChe
§ – var. ***variegata***	Widely available
plicata	See ***G. notata***
spectabilis 'Variegata'	See ***G. maxima*** var. ***variegata***

GLYCYRRHIZA (Papilionaceae)

echinata	CAgr CArn MSal
§ ***glabra***	CAgr CArn EOHP LHol MHew MSal SIde WHer WJek WWye
– 'Poznan'	GPoy
glandulifera	See ***G. glabra***
uralensis	EOHP MSal

GLYPTOSTROBUS (Taxodiaceae)

lineatus	See ***G. pensilis***

GMELINA (Verbenaceae)

See Plant Deletions

GNAPHALIUM (Asteraceae)

'Fairy Gold'	See ***Helichrysum thianschanicum* 'Goldkind'**
keriense	See ***Anaphalis keriensis***
¶ ***norvegicum***	WHil
subrigidum	See ***Anaphalis subrigida***
trinerve	See ***Anaphalis trinervis***

GNIDIA (Thymelaeaceae)

See Plant Deletions

GODETIA See CLARKIA

GOMPHOCARPUS (Asclepiadaceae)

§ ***physocarpus***	CArn SHFr

GONIOLIMON (Plumbaginaceae)

§ ***tataricum*** var. ***angustifolium***	EBee LFis NMir SRms WByw WPer

GOODENIA (Goodeniaceae)

See Plant Deletions

GOODIA (Papilionaceae)

lotifolia	CHan

GOODYERA (Orchidaceae)

¶ *biflora*	EFEx
¶ *hachijoensis* var. *yakushimensis*	EFEx
¶ *oblongifolia*	SWes
pubescens	CSte EFEx WChr WCot WCru WThi
¶ *schlechtendaliana*	EFEx

GORDONIA (Theaceae)

axillaris	CB&S CHEx ICrw

GOSSYPIUM (Malvaceae)

¶ *herbaceum*	MSal

GRAPTOPETALUM (Crassulaceae)

bellum	MBri
– 'Super Star'	SLMG
§ *paraguayense*	CHal SLMG

GRATIOLA (Scrophulariaceae)

officinalis	CArn EHon EMan LHol MGra MHew MSal SIde WHer WSel WWye

GREENOVIA (Crassulaceae)

aizoon	NTow
§ *aurea*	MOne SIng

GREVILLEA † (Proteaceae)

alpina	CFee CKni CPle GQui MAll SBid SMur SOWG WAbe
– 'Olympic Flame'	CB&S CDoC CTrw MAll SOWG
* 'Apricot Queen'	CB&S
aspleniifolia 'Robyn Gordon'	SBid
¶ *banksii*	CTrC
'Canberra Gem' ♀	CAlt CGre CHan CPle CWSG ECou LCns LHop MAll MBal SAga SBar SDry SIgm SMrm SOWG SSpi WCru WPat
'Cranbrook Yellow'	SBid
crithmifolia	CTrC
¶ *juniperina*	CTrC
– 'Aurea'	MAll
– f. *sulphurea* ♀	CDoC CFil CHEx COtt CTrw CWLN EHic GQui MAll SBid SIgm WAbe WBod WPat WRTC
¶ *lanigera*	MAll
prostrata 'Aurea'	CB&S
robusta ♀	CHal MBri
rosmarinifolia ♀	CFil CHEx COtt CPle CTrw CWLN EHoe EMil EPfP GQui MAll MBal SAga SArc SBid SIgm SOWG WAbe WBod WCru WPat WRTC WSHC
– 'Jenkinsii'	CB&S
x *semperflorens*	CGre MAll
thelemanniana	CPle ECou MAll
thyrsoides	CB&S MAll SDry
* *tolminsis*	MAll
victoriae	MAll

GREWIA (Tiliaceae)

parviflora	See ***G. biloba***

GREYIA (Greyiaceae)

radlkoferi	CHEx
sutherlandii	CHEx CTrC

GRINDELIA (Asteraceae)

chiloensis	CAbb CPle ECha IBlr LLWP SAxl SDix SDry SMad WCot
robusta	EBee EMan GCal SIgm SMrm WCot WWye
sp. G&K 4423	CGre
squarrosa	WCot
stricta	CArn

GRISELINIA † (Cornaceae)

* 'Crinkles'	EPla SDry SMad
littoralis ♀	CB&S CBot CChe CGre CHEx CLan CTre CWSG EBre ENot GOrc GRei LPan MBal MBri MGos MTis NFla NNor SAga SArc SDix SPer WAbe WBod WDin WRTC WSHC WWin
– 'Bantry Bay' (v)	CAbP CDoC CLan CSte CTrC CWSG EHoe ELan EPla IOrc MAll MBal SAga SEND SPer WAbe
– 'Dixon's Cream' (v)	CAbb CB&S CDec GQui SBid SDry
– 'Green Jewel' (v)	CB&S CDoC EHic MAll SDry SPla
– 'Variegata'	CB&S CBot CChe CLan CTre CTrw CWSG EHoe ELan ENot GOrc GQui GRei IOrc LPan MBal MGos MTis NPer SAga SHBN SPer SPla SSta WAbe WDin WSHC
lucida	CHEx MUlv
scandens	CPle WSHC

GUICHENOTIA (Sterculiaceae)

See Plant Deletions

GUNNERA (Haloradigaceae)

arenaria	GAri GGar IBlr
chilensis	See ***G. tinctoria***
dentata	CFee IBlr
flavida	CFee CRow GAri GGar IBlr
fulvida	IBlr
hamiltonii	CHEx CRow ECha ECou EFol GGar IBlr WFar
magellanica	CArc CB&S CFee CHEx CRow CWGN EBre ECha ECoo EPot GAbr GWht IBlr MBal NBee NDea NHol NMen NNor NWCA SBid SMad SPer SWat SWyc WCru WWat
manicata ♀	CAbb CB&S CBot CHEx CHad CRow CTre CWGN EBre ECha EFol EHon ELan ENot ISea LNet LPBA MBal MBri NDea NOrc SArc SDix SHig SMad SPer SWyc WPat WWat WWin
monoica	CRow IBlr
prorepens	CFee CTre ECha IBlr SAlw SSpi SWat WWat WWye
scabra	See ***G. tinctoria***
§ *tinctoria*	CFil CHEx CRow CWSG ECha EHon ISea MSta SAWi SBid SDix SSoC SSpi WCru WPat WStI WTre WWat WWeb
– 'Nana'	IBlr

GUTIERREZIA (Asteraceae)

spathulata F&W 8005	CPBP

GUZMANIA (Bromeliaceae)
'Amaranth' MBri
'Cherry' MBri
'Claret' See *Neoregelia* **Claret Group**
dissitiflora MBri
'Exodus' MBri
Festival Group MBri
'Gran Prix' MBri
lindenii MBri
lingulata 🏆 MBri
– 'Empire' MBri
– var. *minor* 🏆 MBri
Marlebeca Group MBri
monostachya 🏆 MBri
'Orangeade' MBri
sanguinea 🏆 MBri
* 'Surprise' MBri
'Vulkan' MBri
* 'Witten Lila' MBri

GYMNADENIA (Orchidaceae)
conopsea EFEx

GYMNOCARPIUM (Thelypteridaceae)
dryopteris 🏆 CCuc CM&M EBee EFer EFol EMar EMon EPar EPot LSyl MBri NGar NMar NWCA SAxl SDix SRms WAbe WFib WNor WRic
– 'Plumosum' CBar CCuc CFil EMon GQui NHar NHed NHol NLak NMar SChu SHam WAbe WFib WHal WRic
robertianum EFer NHed NMar SRms WRic

GYMNOCLADUS (Caesalpiniaceae)
dioica CB&S CChu CFil CSam ELan EOas EPfP GBin MBlu MBri NPal SHhN SMad SPer SSpi WDin

GYMNOGRAMMA See GYMNOPTERIS

GYMNOPTERIS (Adiantaceae)
¶ *vestita* EMon

GYMNOSPERMIUM (Berberidaceae)
§ *albertii* LAma

GYNANDRIRIS (Iridaceae)
setifolia CMon WThi
sisyrinchium SSpi WThi
– MS 416 CMon
* – *purpurea* AB&S 4447 CMon

GYNERIUM (Poaceae)
argenteum See *Cortaderia selloana*

GYNURA (Asteraceae)
§ *aurantiaca* 'Purple Passion' 🏆 MBri
sarmentosa hort. See *G. aurantiaca* **'Purple Passion'**

GYPSOPHILA (Caryophyllaceae)
acutifolia ELan
altissima CArc CPou
aretioides LRHS NMen NNrd NSla
§ – 'Caucasica' CPBP EBur EHyt EPot MHig NHar NHed SIng
– 'Compacta' See *G. aretioides* **'Caucasica'**
briquetiana MHig MRPP NTow WPat
– Mac&W 5920 EPot NNrd WDav
cerastioides CMHG CTri ELan EMNN EMan ESis GTou LBee LHop MHig MRPP NBro NMen NNrd NTow NWCA WAbe WHoo WPbr WPer WRus WWin
* *cerastioides farreri* WEas
dubia See *G. repens* **'Dubia'**
fastigiata EGar WPer
'Festival' CB&S CDoC CHan EBre
◆ *gracilescens* See *G. tenuifolia*
nana EPot SIng
– 'Compacta' CLyd CPBP
oldhamiana CBlo CChu EMar LFis MLLN NLak WFar
pacifica EBee ECtt GBuc NBro NCut NOak NRoo WCot WHer
§ *paniculata* CTri EHic NMir NNor SRms SWat WEas WWin
– 'Bristol Fairy' (d) 🏆 CB&S CHad CSam CShe CTri EBre ECha EFou ELan EMan ENot ERav MBri NFai NFla NOrc NRoo SMad SPer SPla SRms WHoo
– 'Compacta Plena' CFis EBee EBre EFou ELan GCal LHop MMil NHol NRoo SMrm SPer SRms WLRN WPer
¶ – double pink WRHF
¶ – double white WRHF
– 'Flamingo' (d) CB&S CDoC EBre ECha ECot ECtt EFou MBri NFai SPer SRms WGwG WMaN
– 'Perfecta' EBee WWeb
§ – 'Schneeflocke' (d) CTri EBre ECtt LFis MWat NPri NRoo NTow NVic SEas SIde SRms WHoo
– 'Snow White' NOrc WLRN
◆ – Snowflake See *G. paniculata* **'Schneeflocke'**
§ *petraea* EPot SIng
repens 🏆 CSpe CWan GTou LBee MHig MOne MPla MWat WPer
repens alba CM&M CSpe CTri EFou ELan ESis GAul GLil MPla NNor SAlw SIde WAbe WPer WWtk
repens 'Dorothy Teacher' 🏆 CLyd CShe EMNN EPPr LHop MHig NHol SIng WAbe WEas WGor WPat WPyg
§ – 'Dubia' CLyd CMHG CShe ECha EFol ELan EMNN EPot ESis LBee MHig MPla NHol SBod SChu SIgm SRms WPer WWin
– 'Fratensis' ELan EMNN ESis MPla NMen NPro
– 'Letchworth Rose' EWes
◆ – Pink Beauty See *G. repens* **'Rosa Schönheit'**
§ – 'Rosa Schönheit' EBre ECha EGar EWes MMil NRoo SMrm SPer
– 'Rose Fountain' NHol WPat WPyg
– 'Rosea' CMHG EFou EMNN ESis GAul LBuc LFis MWat NHar NMen NNor NNrd NOak NRoo NWCA SAlw SBla SIde SRms WHal WMaN WPLl
§ 'Rosenschleier' (d) 🏆 CHad EBre ECha EFou ELan LFis LGan NFla NHol NMen NRoo SIgm SMer SMrm SOkh SPer SWat WEas WElm WGwG WHoo WMaN WOld
'Rosy Veil' See *G.* **'Rosenschleier'**

§ ***tenuifolia***	CLyd CMea EHyt EPot ITim LBee MBro MHig MPla MWat NGre NHed NHol NMen NTow WAbe
transylvanica	See ***G. petraea***
◆ Veil of Roses	See ***G.* 'Rosenschleier'**

HAASTIA (Asteraceae)

See Plant Deletions

HABENARIA (Orchidaceae)

radiata	See ***Pecteilis radiata***

HABERLEA (Gesneriaceae)

ferdinandi-coburgii	CGle LWoo MFos NWCA SIgm SIng WAbe
rhodopensis ♀	CChu EHyt EPar MBal MBro MHig MSte MWat NHar NRya NTow NWCA SBar SBla SIng SRms WAbe WOMN WOld WPat
– 'Virginalis'	CChu GDra LWoo NHar WOMN

HABLITZIA (Chenopodiaceae)

¶ ***tamnoides***	CPlN

HABRANTHUS (Amaryllidaceae)

andersonii	See ***H. tubispathus***
brachyandrus	CBro SRms WChr
gracilifolius	CBro CMon WChr
howardii	WChr
martinezii	CBro WChr
§ ***robustus***	CBro CMon GCra LAma MBri NRog
texanus	CBro CMon LBee SIng WChr
§ ***tubispathus***	CBro CFee CMon LBow MFos NWCA SAlw SUsu WChr WWin

HACQUETIA (Apiaceae)

§ ***epipactis*** ♀	Widely available
* – 'Thor'	EMon

HAEMANTHUS (Amaryllidaceae)

albiflos	CAvo CHal CMon LAma LHil SLMG SRms WChr
coccineus	CMon WChr
crispus	WChr
deformis	WChr
humilis subsp. ***hirsutus*** S&SH 72	CHan
kalbreyeri	See ***Scadoxus multiflorus*** subsp. ***multiflorus***
katherinae	See ***Scadoxus multiflorus*** subsp. ***katherinae***
natalensis	See ***Scadoxus puniceus***
sanguineus	NRog WChr

HAKEA (Proteaceae)

¶ ***bucculenta***	CTrC
¶ ***dactyloides***	MAll
¶ ***epiglottis***	CTrC
¶ ***laurina***	CTrC
§ ***lissosperma***	CChu ECou MAll SArc
microcarpa	CB&S
¶ ***salicifolia***	MAll
◆ ***sericea***	See ***H. lissosperma***
¶ ***teretifolia***	CTrC MAll

HAKONECHLOA (Poaceae)

macra	CFil EBre EHoe EPar NFai
§ – 'Alboaurea'	CB&S CFee CFil CHad CPMA CShe EBre ECha EGol ELan EOas EPla ETPC IOrc LGan LHil MBar MUlv NHed NOak NPSI SApp SAxl SMrm SPer SPla WRus WWye
– 'Aureola' ♀	CAbb CChu CCuc CElw CFil CHan CHid CInt CRDP ECha ECtt EHoe EPla LHop MBal MBri NGre SAga SAxl SBar WCot WEas WPat WWat
* – 'Mediovariegata'	CFil EPPr WPGP
– 'Variegata'	See ***H. macra* 'Alboaurea'**

HALENIA (Gentianaceae)

elliptica	GCra GTou

HALESIA (Styracaceae)

§ ***carolina***	CAgr CChu CDoC CLnd CMCN CPMA CTho EHoe ELan IOrc ISea LPan MBri MGos NSti SMer SPer SSta WWat
diptera	CMCN MBlu
monticola	CB&S CChu CMCN COtt EBre ELan EPfP MAsh MBal MBri NSti SPer SReu SSpi WFro WNor WWat
– var. ***vestita*** ♀	CAbP CChu CMHG CPMA CSam CTho CWSG CWit IOrc MBlu NPSI SHBN SPer SRms SSpi SSta WPat WWat
– – f. ***rosea***	CPMA ELan MAsh MBlu MSta SSpi SSta
tetraptera	See ***H. carolina***

× HALIMIOCISTUS (Cistaceae)

algarvensis	See ***Halimium ocymoides***
§ 'Ingwersenii'	CB&S CLTr CMHG CVer EGoo EWes NHol NTow SIng SPer SRms SVen WAbe WBod WCru WPer
revolii hort.	See **× *H. sahucii***
§ ***sahucii*** ♀	EBar EBre ECha ELan GCHN LFis LHop MBal MBel MGrG MPla MRav MWat NTow SEas SHBN SPan SPer WCru WElm WFar WKif WOMN WWin
* – 'Ice Dancer'	LRHS
'Susan'	See ***Halimium* 'Susan'**
§ ***wintonensis*** ♀	CB&S CChe CFee CHan CMHG EBre ECtt ELan EPla GOrc LHop MBri MPla MRav MWat NSti NTow SAxl SEas SHBN SPan SPer SRms SSpi WAbe WCru WGwG WHar WSHC WWat
§ – 'Merrist Wood Cream' ♀	CB&S CFee CSam CWLN EBre ELan EPla GCal GOrc IHos LHop MBri MGrG MPla MUlv NBir NSti SAxl SChu SPer SSpi SSta WAbe WOve WPat WRTC WSHC WWat

HALIMIONE (Chenopodiaceae)

§ ***portulacoides***	EEls

HALIMIUM † (Cistaceae)

N ***alyssoides***	CSam GCHN WAbe

§ *calycinum* — CHan ELan GCHN LRHS MBel MTis SAga SAxl SCoo SIgm SPan WAbe WPyg
commutatum — See ***H. calycinum***
formosum — See ***H. lasianthum***
N *halimifolium* — EBee SIgm WCru WSHC
§ *lasianthum* ♀ — CB&S CWit ECha ELan ENot GAbr GCHN LGre MBal MBel SChu SEas SPer WEas WPyg WWat WWin
– f. *concolor* — LHop NTow SAxl SDry WCru WDin WWin
– subsp. *formosum* — CKni CMil GBin GCal MBri MTis SDix WCru WSHC
– 'Sandling' — CKni EGoo ELan MAsh NTow WCru
libanotis — See ***H. calycinum***
§ *ocymoides* ♀ — CB&S EGoo ELan LGre MBal MPla MWat SIgm SPer WBod WCru WHar WRTC WSHC WWat
¶ × *pauanum* — MAsh
§ 'Susan' ♀ — CDoC CMHG EBre ELan LHop MBri MPla NFai NMen NNor SAxl SEas WAbe WPat WPyg WSHC WWat
§ *umbellatum* — LGre MBri SAga WAbe WCru WDin WKif WPat
wintonense — See **× *Halimiocistus wintonensis***

HALIMODENDRON (Papilionaceae)

halodendron — CB&S CPle ELan EMil EPfP MBlu SBid

HALLERIA (Scrophulariaceae)

lucida — CGre

HALOCARPUS (Podocarpaceae)

§ *bidwillii* — CDoC ECou

HALORAGIS (Haloradigaceae)

colensoi — ECou
erecta — CPle ECou
– 'Rubra' — CElw EBee WCot WFar
* – 'Wellington Bronze' — CVer MCCP MTis NChi NSti SMad

HAMAMELIS † (Hamamelidaceae)

§ 'Brevipetala' — CB&S IOrc MAsh MBri NHol SBid SSta
× *intermedia* 'Angelly' — SSta
– 'Arnold Promise' ♀ — CDoC CEnd COtt CPMA ELan IOrc LNet LPan MAsh MBal MBri NBee SBid SPer SPla SReu SSpi SSta
– 'Aurora' — SSta WDin
– 'Barmstedt Gold' — CSte LPan MAsh MBri MGos NHol SReu SSta
– 'Boskoop' — SSta
– 'Carmine Red' — SMur SSta WNor
– 'Copper Beauty' — See ***H.* × *intermedia* 'Jelena'**
– 'Diane' ♀ — CAlt CB&S CDoC CEnd CPMA EBre ELan IOrc ISea LNet LPan MBar MBri MGos NHol SAga SBid SMad SPer SReu SSoC SSpi SSta WDin WWat
§ – 'Feuerzauber' — IOrc LBuc SPer SSta WPyg
* – 'Fire Cracker' — SMur
– 'Hiltingbury' — LRHS SMur WWat
§ – 'Jelena' ♀ — CAlt CB&S CDoC CEnd CPMA EBre ELan ENot IHos IOrc LNet LPan MBal MBri MGos NFla SAga SBid SEas SHBN SPer SReu SSoC SSpi SSta WDin WWat
– 'Luna' — SSta
♦ – Magic Fire — See ***H.* × *intermedia* 'Feuerzauber'**
– 'Moonlight' — CAlt CBlo CPMA
– 'Orange Beauty' — CB&S CBlo CPMA MBal MGos SReu SSta
– 'Pallida' ♀ — Widely available
– 'Primavera' — CBlo CDoC IOrc MBal MBri SSta
– 'Ruby Glow' — CB&S CBlo ELan ISea MBal SPer SSta
– 'Sunburst' — CBlo MBri SSta WWeb
– 'Vezna' — CBlo MBlu MBri SSta
§ – 'Westerstede' — CBlo COtt EBee IOrc LBuc LPan MAsh MGos NHol SBid SSta WDin
japonica — MBal WWat
– 'Arborea' — SSta WNor
– var. *flavopurpurascens* — SSta
– 'Sulphurea' — SSta
– 'Zuccariniana' — CB&S CBlo
mollis ♀ — CArn CB&S CEnd ELan ENot GRei ISea LNet MBal MBar MBri MGos NFla NHol NWea SHBN SMad SPer SReu SSpi SSta WDin WWat
– 'Brevipetala' — See ***H.* 'Brevipetala'**
– 'Coombe Wood' — CAbP
– 'Goldcrest' — CBlo CPMA
– 'Nymans' — CAbP
– 'Select' — See ***H.* × *intermedia* 'Westerstede'**
– 'Superba' — SSta
– Wilson Clone — SSta
¶ *vernalis* — WDin
– 'Carnea' — SSta
– 'Christmas Cheer' — SSta
– Compact form — SSta
– 'Orange Glow' — SSta
– 'Pendula' — SSta
– 'Red Imp' — SSta
– 'Sandra' ♀ — LPan MBri SBid SReu SSpi SSta WWat
– f. *tomentella* — SSta
virginiana — CB&S CBlo EBee GPoy LHol WDin WGwG WWat

HANABUSAYA (Campanulaceae)

asiatica — EPad

HANNONIA (Amaryllidaceae)

hesperidum SF 21 — CMon

HAPLOCARPHA (Asteraceae)

rueppellii — NBro NNrd SIng SRms WHil WPer

HAPLOPAPPUS (Asteraceae)

acaulis — See ***Stenotus acaulis***
brandegeei — See ***Erigeron aureus***
coronopifolius — See ***H. glutinosus***
§ *glutinosus* — CHan CMHG CSev ECha ECtt EFol EMan EPot LBee LCom LHop MHig MMil MTho NNrd NTow NWCA SAga SRms SSmi

lyallii — See ***Tonestus lyallii***
microcephalus — WPer
– AJW 93/559 — NWCA
prunelloides — LBee MHig NNrd NTow
rehderi — GLil WFar

HARDENBERGIA (Papilionaceae)

comptoniana ♀ — CPlN CRHN CSpe MSto
* *comptoniana rosea* — ERea
violacea ♀ — CAbb CPlN CSpe CTrC ELan EMil ERea GQui IBlr LBlm LCns SBid SBra
– 'Alba' — See ***H. violacea* 'White Crystal'**
– 'Happy Wanderer' — CB&S EBee EMil ERea SOWG
– 'Rosea' — EBee
§ – 'White Crystal' — EBee ERea

HARRIMANELLA See CASSIOPE

HAWORTHIA † (Aloeaceae)

x *cuspidata* — SLMG
reinwardtii — CHal

HAYNALDIA See DASYPYRUM

HEBE † (Scrophulariaceae)

albicans ♀ — CChe CLan CShe ECou ELan ENot ESis GIsl MAll MBal MBar MBel MBri MGos MWat NMen NNor NSti SHBN SPer SSmi WBod WEas WHCG WWin
– 'Cobb' — ECou
– 'Cranleigh Gem' — ECou GIsl NFai NHed
– 'Pewter Dome' — See ***H.* 'Pewter Dome'**
– prostrate form — See ***H. albicans* 'Snow Cover'**
– 'Red Edge' — See ***H.* 'Red Edge'**
§ – 'Snow Cover' — ECou EWes GIsl
– 'Snow Drift' — NHed
– 'Snow Mound' — ECou
§ – 'Sussex Carpet' — ECou ESis
§ 'Alicia Amherst' ♀ — CBlo CLTr CSam ECou GCHN LHop SRms WLRN
allanii — See ***H. amplexicaulis* var. *hirta***
'Amanda Cook' (v) — EBee ECou EHoe ESis MPla NHed NPer SDry
amplexicaulis — CNic GIsl MAll NHed
§ – var. *hirta* — ECou GDra GIsl MAll MBro NHed NTow
§ 'Amy' — CSam ECou ELan ESis GIsl IOrc MAll MUlv NFai NPer NSti SHBN SPer WASP WAbe WRTC WRus WSHC
x *andersonii* 'Argenteovariegata' — See ***H.* x *andersonii* 'Variegata'**
§ – 'Aurea' — ECou GIsl SDry
– 'Aureovariegata' — See ***H.* x *andersonii* 'Aurea'**
* – 'Compacta' — GIsl MAll
§ – 'Variegata' — CB&S EBee ECou IOrc MAll MBri MSte NSti NTow SDry SRms WEas WLRN WPri
'Anne Pimm' (v) — WSHC
anomala hort. — See ***H.* 'Imposter'**
– (J B Armstr.) Ckn. — See ***H. odora***
'Aoira' — See ***H. recurva* 'Aoira'**
§ *armstrongii* — CBot CInt CMHG ECou EHic EHoe ELan GIsl MBar NHed NNor SPer WASP WDin WPer
– yellow — GIsl
astonii — MHig
'Autumn Blush' — MPla
'Autumn Glory' — CB&S CChe CMHG CShe EBre ECou ELan ERav ESis GCHN GIsl ISea LGro MAll MBar MGos NNor NSti SBod SHBN SPer SReu WASP WAbe WBod WDin WSHC WTyr
'Autumn Joy' — EBar MPla
'Autumn Queen' — NNor
'Azurea' — ELan ESis MBri MRav NMen SMrm WPer
'Baby Marie' — CAbP CLyd COtt ECot ECou ELan ESis GIsl MAll MAsh MGos NBee NHed NPer STre WASP WPer WStI
'Balfouriana' — GIsl MAll NHed
barkeri — ECou MAll
'Beatrice' — ECou NHed
§ x *bishopiana* — ECou ESis LRHS MAll
◆ – 'Champagne' — See ***H.* x *bishopiana***
'Blonde' — NNor
'Blue Clouds' ♀ — EBee ECou EHal EHoe ELan EPla ESis GIsl GMac MLan NHed SAga SIgm SPer SSmi WASP WRTC WRus
'Blue Diamond' — WEas
'Blue Wand' — MBal
'Bluebell' — ECou
'Blush Wand' — GIsl MAll NCut WAbe
bollonsoi — ECou GIsl MAll MSte
'Boscawenii' — GIsl MAll MGos
'Bowles' Variety' — CNic SHhN WASP
§ 'Bowles's Hybrid' — CShe ECou EHoe GIsl LHil MGos MPla MRav NBee NFai NGre NNor SChu SRms WASP WAbe WEas
brachysiphon — ECou ENot GOrc MGos SPer WDin WHCG WTyr
◆ – 'White Gem' — See ***H.* 'White Gem' (*brachysiphon* hybrid)**
'Bracken Hills' — GIsl
breviracemosa — ECou
'Brill Blue' — CLyd NMen WWin
'Brockiei' — ECou GIsl
buchananii — ECou ESis GAbr GDra GIsl GTou MAll MDHE MGos MTho NFai NHed NNor NPer WPer
– 'Christchurch' — ECou
– 'Minima' — CDoC
§ – 'Minor' — CLyd ECou EPot ESis GAbr GCHN GIsl LBee MBar MBri MHig NBir NHar NHed NHol NMen NNrd WASP
– 'Nana' — See ***H. buchananii* 'Minor'**
– 'Ohau' — ECou
– 'Otago' — ECou
§ – 'Sir George Fenwick' — ECou WHoo
– 'Wanaka' — ECou
buxifolia (Benth.) Ckn.& Allan — CMHG EBre ELan ENot GAbr GCHN GIsl IHos MAll MBal NFai NSti NWea SPer WDin WStI
– – 'Nana' — CLyd CSam EBre EPot ESis GIsl MAsh MBri MHig NCut NPer NPla SRms WASP WWin
◆ – 'Champagne' — See ***H.* x *bishopiana***
– hort. — See ***H. odora***
* – 'Nana' — EHoe NFla
N 'C.P. Raffill' — ECou GIsl MUlv

§ 'Caledonia'	CDec CNic CShe ECou ESis GAbr GIsl MAll MBri MGos MHig MSte NFai NHed NHol NPer NTow SPer WASP WEas WHoo WOMN WOld WPat WPer WPyg WSHC
'Candy'	ECou
§ *canterburiensis*	ECou EHal GIsl MAll WASP
N 'Carl Teschner'	See ***H.* 'Youngii'**
'Carnea'	GIsl
'Carnea Variegata'	EBee ECou EHoe ESis GIsl LHop MAll SBod SPer
carnosula	CMHG ECou EHoe ESiP ESis GIsl MAll MGos NNor SPer WASP WPer WTyr
'Cassinioides'	ESis MAll WASP
catarractae	See ***Parahebe catarractae***
I 'Chalk's Buchananii'	CNic
chathamica	ECou ESis MAll MBal MPla NMen NTow SDry SHhN WSHC
cheesemanii	ECou EHyt ESis GDra MHig
'Christabel'	ECou ESis GIsl MAll
§ 'Christensenii'	ECou GIsl MAll NFai NHed NMen
ciliolata	ECou
coarctata	CMHG ECou GIsl MAll
¶ *cockayniana*	ECou GIsl MAll
colensoi	ECou ESis
– 'Glauca'	See ***H.* 'Leonard Cockayne'**
'Colwall'	CBlo CLyd EBee ECho EHic ESis WAbe WHen
* 'Colwall Blue'	CInt
'Cookiana'	See ***H. stricta macroura* 'Cookiana'**
'Coral Blue'	LHop
'Coral Pink'	LHop WWeb
corrigana	ECou
corstorphinensis	GIsl
'County Park'	CLyd CNic ECou ECtt EMNN ESis EWes MAll MBal MGos MHig MMil MUlv NHed NHol NMen SBod SSmi WTyr
'Craig Park'	MAll
'Craigpark'	GIsl
'Cranleighensis'	ECou GIsl MAll SBod SMac SSto
'Cressit'	GIsl
'Cupins'	ESis GIsl WHoo
cupressoides	CMHG ECou GIsl GOrc MAll MAsh MBal MBar MGos NHed NNor SEND SUsu WDin WGwG
– 'Boughton Dome' 🏆	EAst ECha ECou EHoe EHyt EMNN ESis GCHN GIsl GTou MAsh MBar MBri MBro MGos MHig MPla MTho NCat NMen NNrd SAga SMac WAbe WEas WHoo WOld WPer WSHC
– 'Golden Dome'	CB&S EAst ESis MAll WAbe
– 'Nana'	ECou GIsl NNrd
darwiniana	See ***H. glaucophylla***
'David Hughes'	NFai
* 'Deans Fya'	ESis
'Debbie'	ECou
decumbens	CLyd CNic ECou EHic ESis EWes GDra GIsl MAll NHol
* 'Denise'	EBee ELan MAsh NFai WWeb
dieffenbachii	ECou GIsl
diosmifolia	CBot CChe CDoC CLan ECou ESis GIsl ISea SUsu WSHC
– 'Marie'	ECou ESis GIsl MAll

divaricata	ECou
* – 'Marlborough'	ECou
* – 'Nelson'	ECou
× *divergens*	CLan GIsl NHed
'Dorothy Peach'	See ***H.* 'Watson's Pink'**
'Douglasii'	GIsl NHed
'E.A. Bowles'	CBlo ECou EHoe
'E.B. Anderson'	See ***H.* 'Caledonia'**
'Early Blue'	CSpe GIsl NBir
'Edinensis'	CMHG CNic ECou GIsl NMen NNor WPer WSHC
'Edington'	CHal ECou GIsl SCoo
'Ellen'	WRus
elliptica	ECou GIsl IBlr LFis SPer
– 'Anatoki'	CLTr ECou
– 'Bleaker'	ECou
– 'Charleston'	ECou MAll
– 'Dwarf Blue'	GIsl
– 'Kapiti'	ECou
– 'Variegata'	See ***H.* ×*franciscana* 'Variegata'**
'Emerald Dome'	NGre NMen WPer
'Emerald Gem'	See ***H.* 'Emerald Green'**
§ 'Emerald Green' 🏆	CChe CSam ECou EPot ESis GIsl MAll MBar MBri MBro MGos MPla MTis MWat NBro NHed NHol NMen NWCA SEas SIng WASP WAbe WPat WPer WPyg
epacridea	CGra ECou EHyt ESis EWes GDra GIsl GTou MAll MHig NHed NHol NMen WAbe
§ 'Eveline'	CChe CTri EBee MBal NBir SPer WASP
'Evelyn'	GIsl
evenosa	ECou GIsl MAll NMen
'Eversley Seedling'	See ***H.* 'Bowles's Hybrid'**
'Fairfieldii'	ESis IBlr NMen NTow SDry WSHC
'Fairlane'	CNic ECou NHed
'Fragrant Jewel'	EBre ELan SEND SEas SMrm WASP
× *franciscana*	ECou WTyr
§ – 'Blue Gem' 🏆	CLan EHal EHoe ENot ESis GIsl MAll MGos NBir NFai NFla NPer SEND SPer SRms WASP WBod WHar
– 'Jura'	ECou
◆ – 'Purple Tips'	See ***H. speciosa* 'Variegata'**
– 'Red Gem'	GIsl
– 'Tresco Magenta'	ECou
§ – 'Variegata' 🏆	CB&S CChe EBre ECou ELan EMil ENot ESis GIsl GOrc GRei MAll MBal MBar MGos NFai NPer NSti SHBN SPer SSoC WASP WBod WHar WStI
– 'White Gem'	ESiP GIsl SRms
'Franjo'	ECou SSmi
fruticeti	GIsl
'Gauntlettii'	See ***H.* 'Eveline'**
gibbsii	ECou
'Gibby'	ECou
§ *glaucophylla*	ECou GIsl NMen SBod
– 'Clarence'	ECou NHed
'Glaucophylla Variegata'	CB&S CNic CTri EAst ECou ESis GIsl MAll MBel MHig NFai NHed NSti SBod SPer WASP WCru WHer WKif WRus WSHC
'Glengarriff'	CChu MAll NHol
§ 'Gloriosa'	CSam IOrc MAll NPla
'Gnome'	CBlo ECou GIsl
'Godefroyana'	CNic GIsl

gracillima	CBlo CMHG ECou GIsl SHhN
'Gran's Favourite'	ECou
'Great Orme' 🏆	CB&S CBot CSam CShe EBre ECou ECtt ELan ENot GIsl LFis MAll MBal MRav NFai NPer NRoo NTow SBod SEas SHBN SPer WASP WAbe WDin WHCG WHen WSHC WStI
'Green Globe'	See ***H.*** **'Emerald Green'**
'Greensleeves'	CBlo CMHG CSam EBee ECou ESis GIsl MGos NHed
'Gruninard's Seedling'	GIsl
haastii	CBlo ECou EPot ESis GDra GIsl MHig NHed NNor
'Hagley Park'	CSam ECou ESis LFlo LHil MMil MPla SAga SAlw SUsu WASP WEas WHCG WKif WSHC
§ 'Hartii'	GIsl MRav SPer
'Havering Green'	ECou MHig
'Headfortii'	GIsl
hectorii	CBlo ESis GIsl GTou LBuc MAll MBal MHig NFla NHed
– var. ***demissa***	ECou GIsl NHed
'Heidi'	ESis GIsl MBri
'Hidcote'	WTyr
'Hielan Lassie'	GIsl
'Highdownensis'	EBee ECou GIsl SEas SSto
'Hinderwell'	NPer
'Hinerua'	ECou GIsl
hookeriana	See ***Parahebe hookeriana***
hulkeana 🏆	CBot CSam ECou EHoe ELan GIsl LHil LLew MAsh MBel MHig MPla NBir NFai NPer NTow SAga SUsu WASP WAbe WEas WHCG WHoo WKif WOMN WPat WWat
– 'Averil'	ECou
– 'Lilac Hint'	ECou
– 'Sally Blunt'	ECou
§ 'Imposter'	EBee ECou NFai SRms
'Inspiration'	CDoC ECou
insularis	CBlo ECou LFis
'Jack's Surprise'	ECou
'James Platt'	ECou ESis MAll NHed
'James Stirling'	See ***H. ochracea*** **'James Stirling'**
'Jane Holden'	NLak SBla WSHC
'Jasper'	ECou ESis MAll
'Jewel'	EHoe SDix
'Joan Lewis'	ECou NHed
'Joyce Parker'	ECou NHed
'Judy'	ECou
'June Small'	CNic
'Killiney Variety'	CLan ECou MBal
'Kirkii'	CBlo ECou EMil LWak MUlv SPer WASP
'Knightshayes'	See ***H.*** **'Caledonia'**
§ 'La Séduisante' 🏆	CB&S CLTr EBar EBee ECou ENot IOrc MAll MLan SEND SHBN SPer WASP WSHC
'Lady Ardilaun'	See ***H.*** **'Amy'**
laevis	See ***H. venustula***
laingii	ECou GIsl
lapidosa	See ***H. rupicola***
latifolia	See ***H.*** × ***franciscana*** **'Blue Gem'**
lavaudiana	ECou ESis MRPP WAbe WWat
* 'Lavender Lady'	WRHF
'Lavender Queen'	CWan GIsl
'Lavender Spray'	See ***H.*** **'Hartii'**
leiophylla	GIsl

§ 'Leonard Cockayne'	CBlo EBee GIsl NFai NSti WSHC
ligustrifolia	ECou
'Lilac Haze'	MAll
'Lindleyana'	CLyd GIsl
'Lindsayi'	CNic CPle ECou GIsl MAll MUlv NHed
§ 'Loganioides'	CTri ECou EMNN ESis GAbr GIsl MAll MBal NMen NNor SBod SSmi WASP WPer
'Long Acre Variety'	ECou
'Lopen' (v)	ECou EWes GIsl
'Louise'	SHBN
lyallii	See ***Parahebe lyallii***
lycopodioides	ECou EHoe ESis EWes GIsl NHed
– 'Aurea'	See ***H. armstrongii***
– var. ***patula***	ECou
– 'Peter Pan'	ECou GIsl MBro SRms WAbe
§ 'Macewanii'	CMHG ECou EPla ESis GIsl MAll NFai NHed WHCG
mackenii	See ***H.*** **'Emerald Green'**
macrantha 🏆	CShe ECou EMon EPla ESis GAbr GCHN ITim LGre MAll MAsh MBal MHig MPla NHed NHol NMen NNor SIng SPer SRms WAbe WOMN WSHC WWin
– var. ***brachyphylla***	ECou
macrocarpa	ECou
– var. ***brevifolia***	ECou EWes
– var. ***latisepala***	ECou GIsl
'Maori Gem'	GIsl SEND SMrm WASP WLRN
'Margery Fish'	See ***H.*** **'Primley Gem'**
'Margret'	CHid COtt EBar EBre EMil GRei MAsh MGos NMen NRoo SHBN SMrm SPer WASP WStI WWhi
'Marjorie'	CChu ECou ENot GIsl GOrc MAll MBal MGos MRav NFai NHed NNor NPer NRoo NWea SBod SPer WASP WDin WTyr
matthewsii	ECou
'Mauve Queen'	GIsl
'McEwanii'	See ***H.*** **'Macewanii'**
'McKean'	ECou NHed SAlw
'Megan'	ECou
'Melanie'	WRus
'Menzies Bay'	GIsl MAll
'Mercury'	ECou
'Midsummer Beauty' 🏆	CB&S EBre ECou EHoe ELan ENot GIsl GOrc IOrc MAll MGos MLan MRav NFai NFla NNor NTow SBod SDix SHBN SPer WASP WAbe WDin WGwG WStI
'Milmont Emerald'	See ***H.*** **'Emerald Green'**
'Mini'	ECou
'Miss E. Fittall'	ECou
'Mist Maiden'	ESis NHed
'Monica'	ECou GCHN NHed NHol
¶ 'Monticola'	SHhN
* 'Moppets Hardy'	SPer
'Morning Clouds'	ECou
§ 'Mrs Winder' 🏆	CSam CShe EBar EBre ECou ECtt EHoe ELan EPla ESis GAbr GIsl GRei LHop MBar MRav MSte MWat NFai NNor NPer NRoo SHBN SPer WASP WDin WHCG WStI WWin
× ***myrtifolia***	MRav

'Mystery'	ECou
'Nantyderry'	CHal MSCN NMen WEas WLRN WWat
'Neil's Choice'	ECou EWes GIsl MSte WASP
'Netta Dick'	ECou
'Nicola's Blush'	CLTr CSam CSpe EBar EBre ECou ESis GIsl GMac LHop LLWP MAsh MBel MPla MRav MWat NBee NFai SHBN SMrm SPer SSta SUsu WASP WRus WWhi
'Northumbria Beauty'	NNor SRms
'Northumbria Gem'	NNor
obtusata	ECou
ochracea 🏆	ECou GIsl MAll MGos NFla NSti STre
§ – 'James Stirling' 🏆	Widely available
'Oddity'	ECou
§ ***odora***	CBlo CChe CDoC EBee ECou ESis GIsl SMac SPer WASP WGwG WIvy
– 'New Zealand Gold'	CNic CSam EBee ECou ESis GIsl MAll MAsh NFai NHed SAga SEND WASP WPyg WStI
* – *patens*	MGos WHCG
– prostrate form	ECou GIsl
– 'Stewart'	ECou
– 'Wintergreen'	EBee GIsl
'Oratia Beauty'	CDoC GIsl NCut NFai
'Orientale'	NHed
'Otari Delight'	CMHG
'Pageboy'	ECou NHed
§ ***parviflora*** var. ***angustifolia*** (Vahl) Ckn. & Allan 🏆	ECou EPla EWes GIsl LBlm MAll SArc SHFr
– hort.	See ***H.* 'Bowles's Hybrid'**
– 'Palmerston'	ECou
* 'Patti Dussett'	CLTr
pauciflora hort.	See ***H.* 'Christensenii'**
– Simpson & Thomson	ESis NMen
pauciramosa	ECou GIsl MAll NTow SRms SSto
'Penny Day'	ECou
perfoliata	See ***Parahebe perfoliata***
'Perryhill Lilac'	SPer
* 'Perry's Cerise'	NFai
'Perry's Rubyleaf'	NPer
* 'Peter Chapple'	EPot
'Petra's Pink'	ECou ESis MAll WEas
§ 'Pewter Dome' 🏆	CSam EBre ECou ECtt EHoe EPla ESis GIsl IOrc LHop MBal MBri MGos NBee NHed NNor SBod SDix SEas SIng SPer WASP WAbe WHen WWat
'Pimeba'	GIsl NHol
pimeleoides	ECou GIsl MAll MHig MNrw NHed NMen NTow
– 'Glauca'	GIsl NPer SHBN
– 'Glaucocaerulea'	CMHG EBee ECou ESis GIsl NHed SPer WKif
– var. ***minor***	ECou EHyt ESis GDra WPat
– – 'Elf'	ECou
– – 'Imp'	ECou
– 'Quicksilver' 🏆	CChu EBre ECou EHoe ELan ESis GIsl GOrc LHop MBar MBri MGos NFai NHar NPer NSti SHBN SPer SSmi WASP WAbe WEas WGwG WHCG WPat WSHC
– var. ***rupestris***	ECou ESis
pinguifolia	ECou GIsl NHed SPer
– 'Forma'	MAll

– 'Godefroyana'	ECou
– 'Hutt'	ECou
– 'Mount Dobson'	ECou GIsl NHol
– 'Pagei' 🏆	Widely available
– 'Sutherlandii'	CDoC CNic EBee ECou EHoe ESis GCHN GDra GIsl MBar NBee NFai NHed NSti SAlw SMac WASP
'Pink Payne'	See ***H.* 'Eveline'**
'Pink Pearl'	See ***H.* 'Gloriosa'**
'Pink Wand'	CB&S CLTr GIsl LHop
'Polly Moore'	MBal NTow
poppelwellii	ITim NHed
'Porlock Purple'	See ***Parahebe catarractae* 'Delight'**
§ 'Primley Gem'	EBar ESis WSHC
'Princess'	ECou
propinqua	ECou ESis GIsl NMen
§ – 'Aurea'	MBal
– 'Minor'	GIsl NHed
'Prostrata'	CChu ECou MAll NHed
* 'Pulchella'	CSam
* 'Purple Elf'	EHic SPer
'Purple Emperor'	MAsh MBri SPla
'Purple Picture'	ECou ECtt GIsl NCut NFai SDry WASP
* 'Purple Pixie'	COtt MAsh MGos WGor WLRN
'Purple Prince'	GIsl MAll
'Purple Queen'	See ***H.* 'Amy'**
'Purple Tips' hort.	See ***H. speciosa* 'Tricolor'**
rakaiensis 🏆	CMHG ECou EHoe ELan ENot GAbr GIsl ISea LHop MBar MBri MGos MWat NBir NNor SPer STre WASP WAbe WBod WDin WHCG WPer WTyr WWin
ramosissima	ESis GIsl GTou NHed
raoulii	CShe ECou GAbr WHCG WHoo WSHC
– var. ***maccaskillii***	ECou ESis
– 'Mount Hutt'	GTou
– var. ***pentasepala***	ESis
§ ***recurva***	CMHG CNic CPle CSam ECou EPla ESis LHop MAll MAsh MBri MFir NBee NFai NNor SHFr SRms WAbe WDin WPer WRus
§ – 'Aoira'	ECou NHed SPer WASP
– 'Boughton Silver' 🏆	EBar SDry SMac
– green-leaved	NHed
– 'White Torrent'	ECou
§ 'Red Edge' 🏆	CChe CMHG EBre ECou ELan EMil EPla ESis GAbr ISea LHop MBal MBar MBri MGos MRav MSCN MWat NBir NFai NSti SAga SPer SPla SSmi SSta WASP WAbe WHCG
'Red Ruth'	See ***H.* 'Eveline'**
rigidula	ECou ESis GIsl MAll NHed NMen
'Ronda'	ECou
'Rosie'	ELan GBur MAsh NBee SCoo WEas WGor WLRN
'Royal Purple'	See ***H.* 'Alicia Amherst'**
salicifolia	CChe CLTr ECou EHoe ELan ENot GCHN GIsl LGro MLan NFai NNor SHBN SPer SRms WASP WFar WHCG WRTC
– 'Snow Wreath' (v)	ECou IBlr
salicornioides	ECou GIsl
– 'Aurea'	See ***H. propinqua* 'Aurea'**

'Sapphire'	CDoC ECou ESis GIsl MAll MAsh MBar MGos NFai NPla NTow SPla WTyr
'Sarana'	ECou
selaginoides hort.	See ***H.* 'Loganioides'**
'Silver Gilt'	CBot
'Silver Wings'	NFai
'Simon Delaux' 🏆	CB&S CChu CSam ECou EHoe GAbr GIsl MAll MBal NPla NTow SHBN SPer WASP WEas WRus
speciosa	MLan
– 'Dial Rocks'	ECou
– 'Johny Day'	ECou
– 'Rangatira'	ECou EWes
– 'Ruddigore'	See ***H.* 'La Séduisante'**
§ – 'Variegata' (v)	CHal ECou EMil IBlr NPer NSti SDry WEas
'Spender's Seedling' 🏆	CLan ECou GIsl GOrc MAll NBee NSti SEND SMad SPer SRms STre WASP
'Spender's Seedling' hort.	See ***H. parviflora*** **var. *angustifolia* (Vahl) Ckn. & Allan**
stricta	ECou
– ***cookiana***	See ***H. stricta*** **var. *macroura* 'Cookiana'**
* – var. ***egmontiana***	ECou
– var. ***macroura***	ECou EPla GIsl SDry
subalpina	CLan CShe EBee EBre ECou ESis MOne MTis NCut NHed
subsimilis var. ***astonii***	ESis MHig NHed WThi
'Sussex Carpet'	See ***H. albicans*** **'Sussex Carpet'**
tetrasticha	GIsl
* – AGS 74	MRPP
'Tiny Tot'	CLyd ECou EHyt ESis MTho
'Tom Marshall'	See ***H. canterburiensis***
topiaria	CAbP EBre ECou EFol EMil EPla ESiP ESis GAbr GIsl LHop MAll MAsh MBri NBee NFai NHed NHol NNor SAlw SMrm SPer SPla SSmi SSta WASP WAbe WEas WTyr
'Torlesse'	ECou
townsonii	ECou MAll
traversii	CBlo ECou GIsl MSte SPla SRms
– 'Mason'	ECou
– 'Woodside'	ECou
'Trenchant Rose'	CBlo EHoe
'Tricolor'	See ***H. speciosa*** **'Tricolor'**
'Trixie'	CNic ECou MUlv
tumida	ECou
'Underway'	WWat
urvilleana	ECou GIsl
'Veitchii'	See ***H.* 'Alicia Amherst'**
§ ***venustula***	CMHG ECou GIsl MAll NHed
– 'Blue Skies'	ECou NFai WPer
– 'Patricia Davies'	CLTr ECou NHed
vernicosa	CMHG ECou EFol EPla ESis GDra GIsl GRei LFis LHop MAll MBar MBri MGos MHig NBee NHed NHol NNor NPer NTow SIgm SPer WASP WAbe WHCG
'Waikiki'	See ***H.* 'Mrs Winder'**
'Walter Buccleugh'	ECou GIsl WOMN
'Wardiensis'	CMHG ECou GIsl
'Warleyensis'	See ***H.* 'Mrs Winder'**
§ 'Watson's Pink'	CLTr EBee ECou GIsl MAll SPer SUsu WASP WAbe WKif
§ 'White Gem' (*brachysiphon* hybrid)	COtt ECou ECtt EHoe ESis GRei MAll MBal MGos NBee NFla NHed NNor NPer WASP WEas WStI
'White Heather'	ESis GIsl
'White Summer'	SHBN
'White Wand'	CB&S NFai
* 'White Wings'	WWhi
'Willcoxii'	See ***H. buchananii*** **'Sir George Fenwick'**
'Wingletye'	CAbP CLyd CMHG ECou EHoe ESis GIsl MBal MBri MGos NHed WAbe WPat WPer WPyg
'Winter Glow'	CLyd CMHG COtt ECou EHic ELan NFai
'Wiri Charm'	CDoC COtt EBee ECle EHoe ELan EMil ESis IOrc MAll MAsh MGos MLan MTis SPla SSto WASP WWeb
'Wiri Cloud'	ECle ELan ESis IOrc LRHS MAsh MGos MTis SSto WASP WWeb
'Wiri Dawn'	COtt CSte ECle EHoe ELan ESis EWes IOrc LRHS MAsh SPla WASP WWeb
'Wiri Gem'	EMil LRHS
'Wiri Image'	CDoC COtt EBee EMil IOrc LRHS MAll MGos WASP
'Wiri Joy'	LRHS
'Wiri Mist'	COtt EMil ESis IOrc LRHS MAsh WASP
'Wiri Splash'	CDoC COtt ECle ELan EMil WWeb
'Wiri Vision'	CDoC COtt LRHS
§ 'Youngii' 🏆	CChe CMea CSam CShe ECha ECou ELan EMNN ESis GDra GIsl GOrc GRei MBal MBar MBro MGos MPla NBee NMen NNrd NWCA SPer SSmi WASP WEas WSHC WTyr WWat WWin

HEBENSTRETIA (Scrophulariaceae)

See Plant Deletions

HECHTIA (Bromeliaceae)

¶ ***tillandsioides***	LHil

HECTORELLA (Hectorellaceae)

See Plant Deletions

HEDEOMA (Lamiaceae)

pulegioides	CArn

HEDERA † (Araliaceae)

algeriensis	See ***H. canariensis*** **hort.**
§ ***azorica***	CWhi WCot WFib WWat
– 'Aurea'	EMon
– 'Pico'	CWhi WFib
– typica	See ***H. azorica*** **'São Miguel'**
¶ – 'Variegata'	WCot
§ ***canariensis*** hort.	CHEx SArc WFib
– 'Algeriensis'	See ***H. canariensis*** **hort.**
– 'Argyle Street'	WFib
◆ – var. ***azorica***	See ***H. azorica***
– 'Cantabrian'	See ***H. maroccana*** **'Spanish Canary'**
* – 'Casablanca'	CWhi
* – 'Etna'	CWhi
§ – 'Gloire de Marengo' (v)	Widely available

– 'Marginomaculata' ♀	EPla SEND WFib WLeb WWeb
* – 'Mirandela'	CWhi
– 'Montgomery'	EBee WFib
* – 'Nevada'	CWhi
¶ – 'Ravensholst' ♀	CMac EHic NSti WFib WWat
– 'Stauss'	WFib
– 'Variegata'	See ***H. canariensis* hort. 'Gloire de Marengo'**
canariensis Willdenow	CDoC
◆ ***caucasigena***	See ***H. helix* f. *caucasigena***
◆ ***chinensis***	See ***H. nepalensis* var. *sinensis***
– typica	See ***H. nepalensis* var. *sinensis***
§ ***colchica*** ♀	CBlo CHEx ENot SPer WDin WFib
◆ – 'Arborescens'	See ***H. colchica* 'Dendroides' Arborescent**
* – 'Arborescens Variegata'	SPer
– 'Dentata' ♀	CBlo CHEx CWhi EPla LBuc LPri MBal MHlr SEas WFib
– 'Dentata Aurea'	See ***H. colchica* 'Dentata Variegata'**
§ – 'Dentata Variegata' ♀	CB&S CMac CWhi EHoe ELan ENot EPla GOrc GRei LPan MAsh MBal MBar MBri MWat NFai NHol SBra SDix SHBN SPer STre WFib WLeb WPat WRTC WWat
– 'My Heart'	See ***H. colchica***
– 'Paddy's Pride'	See ***H. colchica* 'Sulphur Heart'**
§ – 'Sulphur Heart' (v) ♀	CHEx CMHG CMac CWhi EHoe ELan ENot EPla IHos LPri MBal MBar MBri MGos MWat NBee NHol NWea SBra SHBN SMad SPer SSoC WDin WEas WFib WLeb WWat
– 'Variegata'	See ***H. colchica* 'Dentata Variegata'**
cristata	See ***H. helix* 'Parsley Crested'**
§ ***cypria***	EPla WFib
helix	CKin CTiv CTri CWhi EWFC MBar MGos NWea WFib WHer
◆ – 'Abundance'	See ***H. helix* 'California'**
– 'Adam' (v)	CBlo CWhi EPPr ESis MBri MGos MTho NPla SEND SHFr STre WByw WFib WLeb WWat WWeb
I – 'Ahorn'	CWhi WFib
◆ – 'Albany'	See ***H. hibernica* 'Albany'**
¶ – 'Alpha'	CWhi
– 'Alt Heidelberg'	CWhi WFib
– 'Alten Brücken'	CWhi WFib
– 'Amberwaves'	WFib
I – 'Ambrosia' (v)	CWhi WFib
¶ – 'Anchor'	CWhi
§ – 'Angularis'	CWhi ECot
– 'Angularis Aurea' ♀	CWhi EHoe EPla MPla NBir NPla SHBN SMad WFib
– 'Anne Borch'	See ***H. hibernica* 'Anne Marie'**
◆ – 'Anne Marie'	See ***H. hibernica* 'Anne Marie'**
– 'Annette'	See ***H. helix* 'California'**
¶ – 'Appaloosa'	WFib
– 'Aran'	See ***H. hibernica* 'Aran'**
◆ – 'Aran' misapplied	See ***H. helix* 'Rutherford's Arran'**
– 'Arapahoe'	WFib
– 'Arborescens'	CNat EPla
– 'Ardingly' (v)	CWhi EFol SPer WFib
◆ – 'Arran'	See ***H. helix* 'Rutherford's Arran'**
– 'Asterisk'	CWhi EPla NBrk WFib WLeb
– 'Astin'	CWhi WFib
– 'Atropurpurea' ♀	CBlo CNat CWhi EPPr EPla ETen MBar MHlr NHol SLPl WFib
◆ – 'Aurea Densa'	See ***H. helix* 'Aureovariegata'**
§ – 'Aureovariegata'	CMac CWhi WFib
– 'Avon' (v)	WFib
¶ – 'Baby Face'	CWhi
– 'Baccifera'	CWhi WFib
– 'Baden-Baden'	CWhi WFib
¶ – var. ***baltica***	CWhi WFib
¶ – 'Big Deal'	CWhi
– 'Bill Archer'	CWhi EPPr EPla WFib
– 'Bird's Foot'	See ***H. helix* 'Pedata'**
– 'Blodwen' (v)	WFib
– 'Bodil' (v)	CWhi SHFr WFib
– 'Boskoop'	CWhi WFib
– 'Bowles Ox Heart'	WFib
– 'Bredon'	WFib
– 'Brigette'	See ***H. helix* 'California'**
– 'Brightstone'	WFib
– 'Brokamp'	CWhi EPPr NFai SLPl WFib
– 'Bruder Ingobert' (v)	CWhi WFib
– 'Buttercup' ♀	Widely available
– 'Butterflies'	WFib
§ – 'Caecilia' (v)	CBlo ELan EPPr EPla ESiP LHop NFai NSti SMad WCot WCru WDin WFib WLRN WLeb WStI
I – 'Caenwoodiana'	See ***H. helix* 'Pedata'**
– 'Caenwoodiana Aurea'	CWhi WFib
– 'Calico' (v)	See ***H. helix* 'Schäfer Three'**
§ – 'California'	CWhi MBri NSti WFib
¶ – 'California Fan'	CWhi
– 'California Gold' (v)	CWhi EBre ESis NPro WFib
– 'Caristian'	WFib
– 'Carolina Crinkle'	CNat CWhi EPla WFib
– 'Cascade'	WFib
– 'Cathedral Wall'	WFib
§ – 'Cavendishii' (v) ♀	CWhi EFol MPla NBrk WCru WFib WLRN
§ – 'Ceridwen' (v)	CWhi EPPr MBri WFib
– 'Chester' (v)	CWhi MBri WFib WWat
– 'Chicago'	CBlo EBee WFib
◆ – 'Chicago Variegated'	See ***H. helix* 'Harald'**
– 'Christian'	See ***H. helix* 'Direktor Badke'**
– 'Chrysanna'	WFib
– 'Chrysophylla'	CWhi EPla
– 'Cleeve'	WFib
– 'Clotted Cream'	See ***H. helix* 'Caecilia'**
– 'Cockle Shell'	CWhi WFib
– 'Congesta' ♀	CWhi EPPr EPla EPot GDra MBal MTho SRms SSmi STre WEas WFib WLeb
– 'Conglomerata'	CWhi ELan EPPr EPla MAsh MBal MBar MBri MBro NBir NNor NRya SMad SPer SRms SSmi WAbe WDin WEas WFib WPat WPyg
– 'Conglomerata Erecta'	CSWP MAsh WFib
– 'Corrugata'	WFib
– 'Crenata'	CWhi WFib
– 'Crispa'	MRav NNor
◆ – 'Cristata'	See ***H. helix* 'Parsley Crested'**
– 'Cristata Melanie'	See ***H. helix* 'Melanie'**
– 'Curleylocks'	See ***H. helix* 'Manda's Crested'**
– 'Curley-Q'	See ***H. helix* 'Dragon Claw'**
– 'Curvaceous' (v)	WFib
◆ – 'Cuspidata Major'	See ***H. hibernica* 'Cuspidata Major'**
◆ – 'Cuspidata Minor'	See ***H. hibernica* 'Cuspidata Minor'**
– 'Cyprus'	See ***H. cypria***

* – 'Dead Again' WCot
– 'Dean' (v) WFib
◆– 'Deltoidea' See ***H. hibernica* 'Deltoidea'**
– 'Denmark' (v) WFib
– 'Denticulata' CWhi WFib
¶– 'Diana' CWhi
¶– 'Dicke von Stauss' CWhi
§ – 'Direktor Badke' CWhi WFib
– 'Discolor' See ***H. helix* 'Minor Marmorata'**
– 'Domino' (v) CWhi EFol EPla EWes WFib WLeb
§ – 'Donerailensis' CWhi GAri NFai WFib
– 'Dovers' WFib
§ – 'Dragon Claw' CNat CWhi EHic EPPr EPla ETen NPla SMad WCot WCru WFib WLeb
– 'Duckfoot' CLTr CWhi EPPr MTho NFai NPla NSti WFib WLeb WWat
– 'Dunloe Gap' EPla
¶– 'Edison' CWhi
– 'Elegance' CWhi WFib
– 'Elfenbein' (v) CWhi WFib
◆– 'Emerald Gem' See ***H. helix* 'Angularis'**
– 'Emerald Globe' CWhi EPla WFib
– 'Emerald Jewel' See ***H. helix* 'Pittsburgh'**
– 'Erecta' ♀ CMac CNat CTri CWhi EHic EPPr EPla GAri MBar MBri MTho NFla NRya SMac WFib WPat WRTC
– 'Erin' See ***H. helix* 'Pin Oak'**
◆– 'Ester' See ***H. helix* 'Harald'**
– 'Eugen Hahn' (v) CWhi EPPr EPla WCot WFib WHer
§ – 'Eva' (v) ♀ CMac CWhi WFib MBal MBri MGos NBir WFib WWeb
– 'Evesham' WFib
– 'Fallen Angel' CWhi EPPr WFib
¶– 'Fan' CWhi
– 'Fantasia' (v) CMac CWhi WFib
– 'Ferney' WFib
– 'Filigran' CNat CWhi SMad WFib WHer WLeb
– 'Flamenco' CWhi EPla WFib
¶– 'Flava' (v) CWhi
– 'Fleur de Lis' CNat CWhi WFib
– 'Florida' WFib
– 'Fluffy Ruffles' CWhi EPla WLeb
* – 'Francis' MBri
– 'Fringette' See ***H. helix* 'Manda Fringette'**
– 'Frosty' (v) EHic
– 'Gavotte' CWhi EPPr EPla MTho WFib
– 'Gertrud Stauss' (v) CWhi MBri WFib
– 'Glache' (v) SHFr WFib
– 'Glacier' (v) ♀ CMac CSam CWhi EBre EHoe ELan EPla ESis GOrc IHos LPri MAsh MBal MBar MBri MGos MHlr MLan NFla NNor NSti SEas SHBN SMac SPer SRms WFib WHen
§ – 'Glymii' CWhi EPPr EPla SLPl WFib
– 'Gold Harald' See ***H. helix* 'Goldchild'**
¶– 'Gold Nugget' CWhi
§ – 'Goldchild' (v) ♀ CB&S CSam CWhi EBre ELan EPla GOrc MAsh MBar MBri MGos MTho NBir NFla SEas SHFr SPer WByw WFib WLeb
– 'Goldcraft' (v) CWhi WFib
– 'Golden Ann' See ***H. helix* 'Ceridwen'**
¶– 'Golden Curl' (v) EPPr
– 'Golden Ester' See ***H. helix* 'Ceridwen'**
– 'Golden Gate' (v) MBri
– 'Golden Ingot' CWhi ELan EPPr MAsh MBar MGos NFai WFib WLeb
– 'Golden Kolibri' See ***H. helix* 'Midas Touch'**
– 'Golden Mathilde' CHal
– 'Golden Medal' EPPr WFib
◆– 'Golden Shamrock' See ***H. helix* 'Golden Envoy'**
– 'Golden Snow' (v) MBri
◆– 'Goldfinger' See ***H. helix* 'Goldstern'**
– 'Goldheart' See ***H. helix* 'Oro di Bogliasco'**
§ – 'Goldstern' (v) CNat CWhi WFib WLeb WWat
– 'Goldwolke' (v) SLPl
◆– 'Gracilis' See ***H. hibernica* 'Gracilis'**
§ – 'Green Feather' CWhi EGoo ESis SMac WFib WHer WOak
– 'Green Finger' See ***H. helix* 'Très Coupé'**
§ – 'Green Ripple' CB&S CMac CNat CSam CTri CWhi IOrc MAsh MBar MHlr NCat NNor NPla SEND SEas SPer WFib WHen WLeb WRHF WWeb
– 'Green Spear' See ***H. helix* 'Spear Point'**
– 'Hahn's Green Ripple' See ***H. helix* 'Green Ripple'**
– 'Hamilton' See ***H. hibernica* 'Hamilton'**
§ – 'Harald' (v) CBlo CDoC CWhi EBar MBal MBri NSti WFib WLeb WPat
– 'Harlequin' (v) WFib
¶– 'Harrison' CWhi
◆– 'Harry Wood' See ***H. helix* 'Modern Times'**
* – 'Hazel' (v) EPPr WFib
– 'Heise' (v) CWhi WFib
– 'Heise Denmark' (v) WFib
¶– 'Helvetica' CWhi
– 'Helvig' See ***H. helix* 'White Knight'**
– 'Heron' EMon SMad
◆– subsp. ***hibernica*** See ***H. hibernica***
– 'Hispanica' See ***H. maderensis*** subsp. ***iberica***
◆– 'Hite's Miniature' See ***H. helix* 'Merion Beauty'**
– 'Humpty Dumpty' CDoC MBar
– 'Ideal' See ***H. helix* 'California'**
– 'Ingelise' See ***H. helix* 'Sagittifolia Variegata'**
– 'Ingrid' See ***H. helix* 'Harald'**
– 'Innuendo' WFib
– 'Ivalace' ♀ CB&S CNat CWhi ECha EPla ESiP ESis GOrc MBal MGos MHlr MNrw MRav NFai NSti SEas SMac SRms WFib WLeb
– 'Jack Frost' (v) EHic ETen
– 'Jane's Findling' (v) CNat
– 'Jasper' WFib
– 'Jerusalem' See ***H. helix* 'Schäfer Three'**
– 'Jubilee' (v) CWhi ELan EPPr EPla NPla WFib WLeb
– 'Knülch' EHic EPla WFib
– 'Kolibri' (v) ♀ CBlo CChe CDoC CWan CWhi EAst EBre EMil MAsh MBar MBri NPla WFar WFib
– 'Königers Auslese' CWhi EPla ESiP SLPl WFib
– 'Kurios' CNat CWhi
¶– 'La Plata' CWhi
§ – 'Lady Kay' WFib
– 'Lalla Rookh' CWhi EPPr WFib
– 'Lemon Swirl' (v) CWhi WFib
– 'Leo Swicegood' CWhi EPla WFib
– 'Light Fingers' CNat SPer WFib
* – 'Lime Regis' CWhi
¶– 'Limey' CWhi
– 'Little Diamond' (v) ♀ CLTr CSam CTri CWhi EBee EHoe EMil EPPr EPla MAsh MBar MBri MGos MHar NPla SHBN SMac WAbe WFib WWat WWye

– 'Little Gem' CWhi WFib
– 'Little Luzii' (v) WFib
– 'Little Picture' WFib
– 'Little Witch' EPla
– 'Liz' (v) See ***H. helix* 'Eva'**
– 'Liziz' (v) WFib
– 'Lopsided' CNat
– 'Lucy Kay' See ***H. helix* 'Lady Kay'**
§ – 'Luzii' (v) EBee EHic EHoe MBar MGos NFai NNor NSti SHBN SPer SRms WByw WFib
– 'Maculata' See ***H. helix* 'Minor Marmorata'**
– 'Malvern' WFib
§ – 'Manda's Crested' 🏆 CBlo CDec CSWP CWhi ELan MBal NPla WFib
– 'Manda's Fan' WFib
§ – 'Manda Fringette' CWhi MTho NFai WFib WLeb
– 'Maple Leaf' CNat CWhi EPla WCot WFib
– 'Maple Queen' MBri
– 'Marginata' (v) CBlo SRms
– 'Marginata Elegantissima' See ***H. helix* 'Tricolor'**
– 'Marginata Major' (v) CWhi WFib WLeb
– 'Marginata Minor' See ***H. helix* 'Cavendishii'**
– 'Marie-Luise' WFib
– 'Marmorata' See ***H. helix* 'Luzii'**
– 'Masquerade' (v) CBlo WGor WLeb
– 'Mathilde' (v) CSpe CWhi WFib WWeb
– 'Meagheri' See ***H. helix* 'Green Feather'**
§ – 'Melanie' ECha ELan EPla NBrk NPla SAxl WCot WCru WFib WLeb WRHF
– 'Meon' WFib
§ – 'Merion Beauty' CWhi EHic EPla GAri NPro WFib
§ – 'Midas Touch' (v) 🏆 CBlo COtt CWhi EPla LHop MBri SHFr SPer WFib
– 'Midget' WEas WFib
– 'Mini Ester' (v) CWhi MBri
– 'Mini Heron' MBri
– 'Miniature Knight' CNat
– 'Minima' See ***H. helix* 'Donerailensis'**
§ – 'Minor Marmorata' (v) CWhi EHal EPla MBal MTho WEas WFib
– 'Mint Kolibri' EFol EHoe MBri
– 'Minty' (v) EPPr WLeb
* – 'Minutissima' CRow EPPr
– 'Miss Maroc' See ***H. helix* 'Manda Fringette'**
– 'Misty' (v) CWhi WFib
§ – 'Modern Times' CWhi
– 'Mrs Pollock' (v) CWhi WFib
¶ – 'Mrs Ulin' CWhi
– 'Needlepoint' CBlo IOrc
– 'Neilson' CLTr CWhi SPer STre WFib
¶ – 'Neptune' CWhi
– 'New Ripples' CWhi EHal NBrk WFib
¶ – 'Nigra' CWhi
– 'Nigra Aurea' (v) CWhi WFib
– 'Norfolk Lace' EWes
– 'Northington Gold' WFib
¶ – 'Obovata' CWhi
– 'Olive Rose' CWhi EPla MTho WCot WFib
§ – 'Oro di Bogliasco' (v) CChe CMac CSam CWhi EBee ELan ENot GOrc MBal MBar MBri NBee NFai NFla NSti NWea SBra SPer SRms WEas WPat WRTC WWat
– 'Pallida' See ***H. hibernica* 'Hibernica Variegata'**
¶ – 'Paper Doll' (v) CWhi
– 'Parasol' (v) EPla
§ – 'Parsley Crested' CNat EBee ECha EFol ELan GOrc MAsh MBal MBar MHlr NSti SPer SRms WCru WFib WLeb WOak WRHF WTyr WWat WWye
§ – 'Pedata' 🏆 CSWP CWhi ELan WFib WLeb
¶ – 'Pencil Point' CWhi
¶ – 'Pennsylvanian' CWhi
– 'Perkeo' CWhi EPPr EPla ESis NPla SPan WFib
– 'Perle' (v) CWhi EPPr NBir WFib
– 'Persian Carpet' CWhi LMer WFib
– 'Peter' (v) NBrk WFib
* – 'Pin Oak' CBlo NPla WCru
– 'Pink 'n' Curly' See ***H. helix* 'Melanie'**
* – 'Pink 'n' Very Curly' WCot
– 'Pirouette' WFib
§ – 'Pittsburgh' WFib WGwG
– 'Pixie' CWhi WFib
– 'Plume d'Or' CHal CSam MTho WFib
§ – subsp. ***poetarum*** EPla IOrc WFib
– – 'Poetica Arborea' ECha SDix
– 'Poetica' See ***H. helix* subsp. *poetarum***
– 'Preston Tiny' NBir
– 'Professor Friedrich Tobler' CBos CNat CWhi EPla NPro WFib WLeb
– 'Quatermas' WFib
– 'Ralf' CWhi EPla WFib
– 'Rambler' NBir
– 'Ramsgate' EMon
¶ – 'Rauschgold' (v) CWhi
– 'Ray's Supreme' See ***H. helix* 'Pittsburgh'**
– 'Reef Shell' (v) WFib
¶ – 'Regency' (v) CWhi
– subsp. ***rhizomatifera*** EPla WFib
– 'Ritterkreuz' CWhi WFib
– 'Romanze' (v) CWhi WFib
– 'Rüsche' CNat CWhi EPla WFib
– 'Russell's Gold' WFib
§ – 'Rutherford's Arran' CWhi WFib
– 'Sagittifolia' CLTr CMac CNic CTri CWhi ELan GOrc MAsh MBal NChi NNor SHFr SMac SRms SSta WCot WEas WFib WWat
§ – 'Sagittifolia Variegata' CMac CWhi EBee EHal EMil EPla ESis GOrc MBri SBra SPer SRms WAbe WFib WLeb WRHF
– 'Sally' (v) CWhi WFib
– 'Salt and Pepper' See ***H. helix* 'Minor Marmorata'**
§ – 'Schäfer Three' EPPr WFib
– 'Serenade' (v) WFib
– 'Shamrock' 🏆 CWhi EGoo EPPr EPla MBri SPer WCot WFib
¶ – 'Shannon' CWhi
– 'Silver Emblem' (v) WFib
– 'Silver King' (v) EPla NBir NPla SHFr WFib
– 'Silver Queen' See ***H. helix* 'Tricolor'**
– 'Sinclair Silverleaf' WFib
– 'Small Deal' CWhi WFib
§ – 'Spear Point' CWhi WFib
– 'Spectabilis Aurea' WLeb
– 'Spectre' (v) CNat CWhi ELan EPPr EPla MTho WFib WHer WLeb
– 'Spetchley' 🏆 CNic CSWP CWhi EFol EPPr EPla ESis EWes MAsh MBar MRav MTho NChi NHar NPer SMac SMad WBcn WFib WLeb WPat
– 'Spinosa' CWhi EPla
– 'Spiriusa' EPPr WFib
¶ – 'Staghorn' CWhi

– 'Stevenage' (v) WFib
– 'Stift Neuberg' (v) WFib
– 'Stuttgart' CWhi EPla WFib
– 'Succinata' EPPr WFib
– 'Sunrise' WFib
– 'Suzanne' See ***H. nepalensis*** var. ***nepalensis*** **'Suzanne'**
– 'Sylvanian' WFib
¶ – 'Symmetry' CWhi
– 'Tango' EPPr WFib
¶ – 'Teardrop' EPPr
– 'Telecurl' CWhi EPPr EPla WFib
– 'Tenerife' ELan WFib
– 'Thorndale' CWhi WFib
– 'Tiger Eyes' CWhi
* – 'Touch of Class' CWhi
§ – 'Très Coupé' CB&S CSWP EBee EPPr MBal MTho NPla SArc SPer WDin WFib WLeb
§ – 'Tricolor' (v) CB&S CMac CTri CWhi ELan EPla SBra SHBN SPer
– 'Trinity' (v) WByw WFib
– 'Tristram' (v) CWhi WFib
– 'Triton' CWhi MBal MBar MTho WFib WHer
– 'Troll' CWhi WLeb
¶ – 'Trustee' CWhi
– 'Tussie Mussie' (v) CWhi WFib
– 'Ursula' (v) CSWP EPPr WFib
¶ – 'Ustler' CWhi
* – 'Verity' CWhi
– 'Victoria' WWeb
– 'Walthamensis' CWhi WFib
– 'Wanda's Fan' WFib
§ – 'White Knight' (v) CWhi MBri WFib
– 'White Kolibri' MBri
– 'Whitehall' WFib
¶ – 'Wichtel' CWhi
– 'William Kennedy' (v) CWhi WFib
¶ – 'Williamsiana' (v) CWhi
– 'Woener' CWhi SLPl WFib
– 'Woodsii' See ***H. helix*** **'Modern Times'**
– 'Zebra' (v) CWhi WFib
§ ***hibernica*** 🏆 CB&S CWhi ELan LBuc MBar MBri MHlr MRav NNor SBra SMac SPer SRms WFib WLeb WStI WWat
§ – 'Albany' WFib
§ – 'Anna Marie' (v) CMac CWhi GOrc MBri WEas WFib WLeb
– 'Aracena' EMon EPla
§ – 'Cuspidata Major' CWhi WFib
§ – 'Cuspidata Minor' CWhi WFib
– 'Dealbata' (v) CMac CWhi GOrc WFib
§ – 'Deltoidea' CWhi EMon EPPr EPla MBal MBri WCot WFib
– 'Digitata' WFib
I – 'Digitata Crûg Gold' WCru
§ – 'Gracilis' CWhi WFib
§ – 'Hamilton' (v) WFib
– 'Helena' (v) WFib
* – 'Lactimaculata' CWhi
– 'Lobata Major' SRms
– 'Maculata' (v) EFol EPla WLeb
– 'Palmata' WFib
– 'Rona' CWhi WFib
– 'Sulphurea' (v) CWhi WFib
– 'Tess' CNat EPla WFib
– 'Variegata' CWhi MBar WWat
maderensis WFib
§ – subsp. ***iberica*** WFib
maroccana 'Morocco' WFib
§ – 'Spanish Canary' WFib
nepalensis MBal MBlu WFib
– CC&MR 460 LKoh
§ – var. ***nepalensis*** 'Suzanne' WFib
§ – var. ***sinensis*** CWhi WFib
pastuchovii CNat CWhi EFol WFib
– from Troödos, Cyprus See ***H. cypria***
* – 'Volga' CWhi
§ ***rhombea*** CWhi WCot WFib
– var. ***formosana*** WFib
– 'Japonica' See ***H. rhombea***
– var. ***rhombea*** 'Variegata' EFol WFib

HEDYCHIUM † (Zingiberaceae)

aurantiacum CMon NRog SLMG WCru
chrysoleucum CGle LAma LBow LHil NRog
coccineum 🏆 CB&S CMon LAma LBlm LBow LChe NRog SLMG WCru
– var. ***aurantiacum*** LAma LBow
– 'Tara' 🏆 CChu CFil CGle EOas MSte SArc SLMG
coronarium CAvo CBrk CGle EOrc LBlm LBow LChe LHil MSte NFai SLMG WHal WPer
– var. ***flavescens*** See ***H. flavescens***
densiflorum CBrk CFil CMon CTre LHil SDix SSpi
– 'Assam Orange' CB&S CBrk CChu CFil CGle CHEx CInt EOas GCal LChe MSte SArc
– 'Stephen' CFil SDix
ellipticum CFir LAma LBlm LBow NRog
§ ***flavescens*** LAma LHil NRog WCru
forrestii CChu CFil CGle CHEx CTre EOas MSte SArc
gardnerianum CFil CFir CGre CHEx CHan CLTr CTrC EOas ERea LAma LBlm LBow LChe MSte NRog SArc SDix SLMG SMad SSoC WCru WFar
greenei CFil CFir CGle CGre CHEx LBow MSte NRog SLMG
longicornutum LChe MSte
¶ × ***raffillii*** WCot
spicatum CFil CFir CGre CHEx CHan CMdw CMon LHil MSte NRog SLMG
villosum LAma LBow NRog
¶ ***yunnanense*** CFil

HEDYSARUM (Papilionaceae)

coronarium CArn CGle CHan CPle CSev CSpe ELan EMan GCra LFis LIck MHlr MNrw MSte NCGP NPSI SAga SHFr SMad SUsu WCot WCra WFar WOMN WOve WWin
hedysaroides EMan
multijugum CB&S CDoC MBlu NFla SMad SPer WSHC
– var. ***apiculatum*** ELan
occidentale SIgm

HEDYSCEPE (Arecaceae)

See Plant Deletions

HEIMERLIODENDRON See PISONIA

HEIMIA (Lythraceae)
salicifolia CArn CGre CPle ELan MAll MBlu MSal NSti SOWG SPan WWin WWye

HELENIUM † (Asteraceae)
autumnale CTri EBar EHal MBel MSal NBus NCGP NMir SEas SSvw WBea
– 'All Gold' WPer
– JLS 88007WI EMon
'Baudirektor Linne' CSam CWit ECED SCro
* 'Biedermeier' EFou
bigelovii WByw
'Blütentisch' SUsu
'Bruno' EBre ELan MArl MMil MRav SMrm SOkh
'Butterpat' CArc CB&S CWit ECED EFou EGar EHic EMan EPPr GMaP LFis MBel MCLN MMil NFai NPri NTow NVic SChu SPer WCra WHoo
'Chipperfield Orange' CArc CHad CMGP EBee EBre EFou EGar EMan EPPr LRHS MHlr MMil NCat NLak WLRN
'Coppelia' CSam CShe EBre ECED MUlv
◆ Copper Spray See *H.* **'Kupfersprudel'**
'Crimson Beauty' EBre ELan MBri MRav NCat NFai NRoo WMer
'Croftway Variety' SCro
◆ Dark Beauty See *H.* **'Dunkelpracht'**
§ 'Dunkelpracht' LRHS
'Feuersiegel' EFou
* 'Flammendes Kätchen' EFou
'Gold Fox' CKel CSam CWit WMer
◆ Golden Youth See *H.* **'Goldene Jugend'**
§ 'Goldene Jugend' ELan MRav NRoo SSpe WEas
'Goldrausch' EFou
hoopesii CKel CPea EBar EBre EFou GMaP MFir MRav NBro NFai NOak NPri NSti SCro SMrm SRms SSvw WBea WGwG WHil WPer WWye
¶ 'Indianersommer' CSte EFou
¶ 'July Sun' SSpe
'Kanaria' EFou EPPr SPla
§ 'Kupfersprudel' MRav
'Kupferzwerg' EFou LGre
'Mahogany' See *H.* **'Goldlackzwerg'**
'Moerheim Beauty' CBot CHad CRDP CSam CShe EFou ELan ERav LHop MFir MRav MWat NFai NRoo NSti SChu SCro SDix SEas SPer SSpe SUsu WEas WHil WHoo WMer WOld WRus WTyr
'Pumilum Magnificum' CArc CDoC CSam EPar EPfP MBri MWat NRoo SCro SPer WByw
◆ Red and Gold See *H.* **'Rotgold'**
'Riverton Beauty' CBre
'Riverton Gem' ECtt
§ 'Rotgold' CM&M CMGP ECtt GBur GLil MSCN NOak SIde SRms WHil WLRN WPer WRHF
'Septemberfuchs' EBee EFou EPPr
'Sonnenwunder' CWit ECha EFou EGar
¶ 'Sunshine' WSan
'The Bishop' CArc CSam EFou EGar LFis MBri MRav MTis NCut NFai NLak NSti SChu SSpe WCra WMer
'Waldtraut' CKel CM&M CMGP EBee ECot EFou EGar ELan EPfP MRav MUlv NCat NFai NOak SCro SPer WMer
¶ 'Wonadonga' EFou
'Wyndley' CB&S CSam EBre ECED EFou EGar MBel MRav NFai NRoo SChu SEas WCot WCra WMer
'Zimbelstern' ECha EFou EGar EGle SOkh WFar

HELIAMPHORA (Sarraceniaceae)
heterodoxa WMEx
¶ – × ***ionasii*** WMEx
¶ – × ***minor*** WMEx
¶ – × ***nutans*** WMEx
minor MHel WMEx
nutans WMEx
tatei WMEx

HELIANTHELLA (Asteraceae)
§ ***quinquenervis*** EBre EFou EMan GCal MSte NTow WFar

HELIANTHEMUM † (Cistaceae)
'Alice Howarth' CMea CShe ESis EWes MBro MDHE SHel SRms WHCG WHoo WPnn WPyg
◆ ***alpestre serpyllifolium*** See *H.* ***nummularium*** subsp. ***glabrum***
'Amabile Plenum' CPBP EBar EPfP GCal GDra NCut SIgm
* 'Amber' GAbr
'Amy Baring' 🏆 EBre EGle EGoo EMNN GAbr GDra LBee LHop NMen NRoo SAlw SBod SIng SMer WPer WRHF WSHC
'Annabel' EOrc GAbr GCHN LCom MPla NMGW NRoo NSla NSti SChu SIde SMer WHCG WPer
apenninum GTou MDHE WCla WPer
– var. ***roseum*** WCla
'Apricot' SBod
'Apricot Blush' WAbe
'Baby Buttercup' CLyd CMea CPBP GAbr MBro MPla NPro SIng WPat
'Barbara' MHig
'Beech Park Red' CMea CPBP CShe ESis GAbr LBee LBuc MBro MDHE MMil MWat SChu SHel SIgm WCer WHoo WKif WPyg
'Ben Afflick' EBar GAbr LBee MHig NHol NSty SAga SBod SIgm SRms WCer WPnn
'Ben Alder' GAbr LFis MDHE NHol NMen NSty
'Ben Dearg' CMea ECtt EGle EGoo EMNN ESis GAbr NSty SBod SIng SRms
'Ben Fhada' CMHG CMea CPBP EGle ELan EMNN GAbr GDra LBee MBal MHig NSti NSty SAga SAlw SBod WAbe WEas WPer WPnn WWin
'Ben Heckla' CMHG CSam GAbr GCHN MSte NMen NRoo WEas WPer
'Ben Hope' EMNN GAbr GDra MBal MOne NMen NRoo NSty SAga SAlw SRms WPer WWin
'Ben Lawers' NHol

'Ben Ledi'	CInt CMea EAst EFol ELan EMNN ESis GAbr GCHN GDra LBee LHop MBal MHig MTis NSla NSty NVic SBod WAbe WCer WHoo WPer WPnn WWin
'Ben Lomond'	GAbr MBal
'Ben Macdui'	GAbr LRHS
'Ben More'	CB&S EGle ELan EMNN ESis GAbr GDra GTou IHos LBuc MBal MWat NLak NMen SBod SHel SIng SSmi WPat WWin
'Ben Nevis'	CLon CShe CTri ECha ELan GAbr GDra MDHE SAlw SRms WHoo WPyg WWin
'Ben Vane'	EGle EMNN MDHE NHol SIng
'Birch White'	GAbr SIng
'Bishopsthorpe'	CShe
'Boughton Double Primrose' (d)	CGle EFol ELan EMan EWes GAbr GCal GMac GOrc LHop NSti SChu SHel SIgm SMer WEas WHoo WPen WSHC
'Broughty Beacon'	GAbr GDra MDHE WGor
'Broughty Sunset'	CLTr CSam GAbr MBro MDHE NBir SIgm WHoo WPyg
'Brown Gold' (d)	EOrc
'Bunbury'	CMea GAbr NRoo
* 'Butter and Eggs'	CInt SRms
'Butterball' (d)	MDHE
canum	NHol WPer
– subsp. ***balcanicum***	NTow
'Captivation'	EFol EGoo NHol
'Cerise Queen' (d)	EBre ECha GAbr GMac LHop MBro MPla NCut SDix SIgm SRms SSoC WCla WHoo WPer WPnn WPyg
chamaecistus	See ***H. nummularium***
'Cheviot'	CMea CWan MBro MDHE WEas WHoo WPer WPyg WWat
'Chocolate Blotch'	ECtt GAbr LBuc LFis MHar MSCN NPri NSty SAlw SChu SEND WPer WRHF
'Coppernob'	SRms
'Cornish Cream'	CLTr EWes GAbr
croceum	NTow
cupreum	EFou NHol
'David'	EGoo
'Doctor Phillips'	CShe WHCG
double apricot	CShe EGle EWes GAbr SAlw
double cream	CMea ECha ECtt EGar EOrc ESis MDHE NHol
'Double Orange'	EBar LHop MWat NCut SAlw
double pink	CMGP ECha GAbr MWat NWoo
'Double Primrose'	CElw SIng
double red	ECha NChi SAlw
double yellow	ECha MPla
¶ 'Elaine'	ELan
'Elisabeth'	EGoo
'Fairy'	EDAr EGle ESis MDHE
§ 'Fire Dragon' ♀	CPea CSam CTri EGle ELan GAbr GCHN GOrc LBee LBuc MHig MTis NRoo NWCA SChu SHel SIgm SRms WAbe WPyg WRHF
'Fireball'	See ***H. 'Mrs C.W. Earle'***
'Firegold'	WAbe
'Georgeham'	CMHG CSam CShe ELan EMan GAbr LBee LHop MDHE NCat SAlw SMer SRms WEas WGor WHCG WPer

¶ ***georgicum***	NSla
globulariifolium	See ***Tuberaria globulariifolia***
§ 'Golden Queen'	ECtt GAbr MOne NHol NMen NSty SChu WCla WHil WPer WPyg WRHF
'Henfield Brilliant' ♀	CInt CMHG CPBP CShe EAst EBre EGle EMar GAbr GDra GOrc LBee LHop MBro MHar NHol NRoo SMad SMer SRms SSmi SSoC WDav WEas WHoo WPer WSHC WWat
'Hidcote Apricot'	MTis NHol
'Highdown'	GAbr LCom SRms WAbe
¶ 'Highdown Apricot'	SAlw
'Honeymoon'	MDHE SIde WLRN
'John Lanyon'	LRHS MDHE
'Jubilee' (d) ♀	CMHG EGle ELan EMNN EOrc GAbr GOrc LBuc LFis LHop NNor NRoo NSti NSty SAlw SChu SDix SRms WAbe WCla WEas WHCG WHoo WWin
I 'Jubilee Variegatum'	GAbr NRoo SIgm
'Kathleen Druce' (d)	EWes GAbr GMac LHop MWat NHol WHoo
ledifolium	WPer
'Lucy Elizabeth'	GAbr MDHE
lunulatum	CInt CLyd EGoo EMon ESis LBee MBro MPla MSto NMen NTow SIgm WAbe WPat WWin
'Magnificum'	MDHE MWat
'Moonbeam'	WWin
§ 'Mrs C.W. Earle' (d) ♀	CInt CLTr CMHG CTri ELan EOrc ESis GAbr LFis LHop NHol NRoo NSti NSty SBod SDix SRms WAbe WPer WWin
'Mrs C.W. Earle Variegated' (d)	ELan WWin
'Mrs Clay'	See ***H. 'Fire Dragon'***
'Mrs Croft'	LCom WPer
'Mrs Hays'	GMac
'Mrs Jenkinson'	CMHG
'Mrs Lake'	EMNN GAbr NSty
'Mrs Moules'	SRms
'Mrs Mountstewart Jenkinson'	LHop MBro
mutabile	WPer
§ ***nummularium***	CKin EHic EOHP EWFC GOrc GPoy MHew NMir NWCA SIde WCla WHil WPat
§ – subsp. ***glabrum***	CMHG GAbr LCom MBro NHol NMGW NMen NTow SIng WHoo WPat WPer WPyg
– subsp. ***grandiflorum*** 'Variegatum'	MWat
* – 'Lemon Queen'	WBcn
§ – subsp. ***tomentosum***	MWat
oelandicum subsp. ***alpestre***	CLyd MBro NNrd NTow SRms SSmi WPer
– var. ***piloselloides***	MHig WAbe WWin
'Old Gold'	CLTr EBre GAbr LBee MHar MHig NRoo SIgm SRms WAbe WPer WPnn
ovatum	See ***H. nummularium*** subsp. ***obscurum***
pilosum	LRHS SIgm
¶ 'Pink Beauty'	WBcn
'Pink Glow'	WPer
'Pink Perfection'	CMHG CSam
'Praecox'	CMea CTri EHic LBee LCom MBal MPla NRoo NSty SMer WHoo WPer WPyg

'Prostrate Orange'	SRms
'Raspberry Ripple'	CInt CPBP CShe EAst EBre EFol EGle ELan EOrc GAbr GCHN LBuc LFis LHop MPla NEgg NHol NRoo SAxl SChu SRms WAbe WHoo WPat WPer WRus WWin
'Red Dragon'	WAbe
'Red Orient'	See ***H.* 'Supreme'**
§ 'Rhodanthe Carneum' ♀	CMHG CMea CShe EFou ELan EOrc GAbr GCHN GDra GTou LBee LGro LHop MBal NHol NMir NRoo NSty SSmi WAbe WDav WEas WHil WHoo WSHC WWin
§ 'Rosa Königin'	EMNN LBee LCom MDHE MOne NMen NSty SAlw SEND WAbe
'Rose of Leeswood' (d)	CInt CMea CShe ELan EOrc GAbr GMac LCom LFis LHop MBro MHar NEgg SAga SAlw SChu SIgm SIng SMrm SRms WEas WHCG WHoo WKif WPyg WSHC WWin
◆ Rose Queen	See ***H.* 'Rosa Königin'**
'Roxburgh Gold'	SRms
'Rushfield's White'	WHCG WRus
'Saint John's College Yellow'	CMHG CSam EBar EHal GAbr MOne SSmi WFar WHCG WPer
'Salmon Bee'	CShe MDHE
'Salmon Queen'	CMHG EMNN ESis GAbr LBee MHar MSCN NCat NPri NRoo SAga SHel SIng WPer WWin
serpyllifolium	See ***H. nummularium*** subsp. ***glabrum***
'Shot Silk'	EWes MDHE NRoo
'Silvery Salmon'	EGoo WAbe
'Snow Queen'	See ***H.* 'The Bride'**
'Snowball'	EGoo EMon
'Southmead'	GAbr
'Sterntaler'	GAbr GDra SRms WDav
'Sudbury Gem'	CTri EBre ECha GAbr LHop NRoo NSla SMer WPer WPnn
¶ 'Sulphureum Plenum'	EPfP
'Sunbeam'	CSam EMNN GAbr MDHE MOne NHol NMen NSty SRms
'Sunburst'	GAbr
§ 'Supreme'	CLTr CShe ELan EWes GAbr LBee LHop MWat SAlw SChu SDix SIgm WHCG WPer
'Tangerine'	GAbr
§ 'The Bride' ♀	CMea CTri EAst EBre ECha EFou EGle ELan EOrc ESis GCHN GOrc LBuc LHop MBro MSte MWat NHol NRoo NSty SChu SDix SRms SSoC WAbe WHoo WPer WPnn WSHC
'Tigrinum Plenum' (d)	CPBP ESis EWes LBee MDHE NPro NRoo WPer WWin
'Tomato Red'	ECha NSla SAlw SMrm
umbellatum	See ***Halimium umbellatum***
'Venustum Plenum' (d)	CInt MBro WEas
'Voltaire'	EMNN GAbr MDHE MOne NHol NPri WRHF WWin
'Watergate Rose'	MWat NBir
'Welsh Flame'	EGoo WAbe
'White Queen'	WPer
'Windermere'	SIgm
'Wisley Pink'	See ***H.* 'Rhodanthe Carneum'**
'Wisley Primrose' ♀	Widely available
'Wisley White'	CLon CSam CTri ECha GAbr LHop MBal MBro NRoo SChu SIgm WHCG WHoo WPyg
'Yellow Queen'	See ***H.* 'Golden Queen'**

HELIANTHUS † (Asteraceae)

¶ ***angustifolius***	WCot
atrorubens	CDoC LFis MBri MRav
'Capenoch Star' ♀	CArc CBre ECha EFou GBuc LFis MArl MHlr MUlv SDix SMad WByw WCot
¶ ***decapetalus***	WCot
* – 'Kastle Kobena'	CMGP
– 'Maximus'	SRms
– 'Morning Sun'	CTri WCot
– 'Soleil d'Or'	CTri ECtt EHic WCot
– 'Triomphe de Gand'	CArc EMon GBri LGre MWat WCot WFar WOld
doronicoides	CFee
'First Light'	WCot
giganteus 'Sheila's Sunshine'	WCot
'Golden Pyramid'	WCot
¶ ***grosseserratus***	WCot
'Gullick's Variety'	CBre EFou EPfP IBlr LLWP NBro WCot
× ***kellermanii***	EMon SMad WCot
§ × ***laetiflorus***	ELan EMon MTis NChi NOrc WCot
§ 'Lemon Queen'	CBre CElw CShe CVer ECha ECtt EFou EGar EHal EMon EPar ESiP GBuc LFis MHlr NFai NPer SDix SMad SPla WCot WEas WHal WOld WRHF WRus WWye
§ 'Loddon Gold' ♀	CSte EBre ECED ECtt EFou ELan EMan IBlr LFis MHlr MTis NVic WCot WWye
§ ***maximilianii***	MSte NPri
¶ ***mollis***	EMon
'Monarch' ♀	ECED EMon MFir WCot WOld WOve
nuttallii	EMon WCot
orgyalis	See ***H. salicifolius***
quinquenervis	See ***Helianthella quinquenervis***
rigidus	See ***H.* × *laetiflorus***
§ ***salicifolius***	EBre ECED ECha EGar EMon EPla LFis MBri MSte MUlv SDix SMad SSoC SSpe WCot WOld
scaberrimus	See ***H.* × *laetiflorus***
¶ ***strumosus***	WCot
'Summer Gold'	EFou
tuberosus	GPoy NRog

HELICHRYSUM † (Asteraceae)

acuminatum	See ***Bracteantha subundulata***
alveolatum	See ***H. splendidum***
ambiguum	CHan EFou LHop MPla NNor NOak
angustifolium	See ***H. italicum***
– Cretan form	See ***H. italicum*** subsp. ***microphyllum***
arenarium	SSmi
§ ***argyrophyllum***	WHil
§ ***arwae***	EHyt GTou NWCA SBla WAbe
asperum	See ***Ozothamnus purpurascens***
basalticum	LBee NWCA
bellidioides	CArc CShe ECha ECou ELan MBal MHig NGre NMen NSla SMer WCru WOMN WPer
bellum	LHop NHol

◆ ***bracteatum***	See ***Bracteantha bracteata***
¶ ***chionophilum***	EHyt
'Coco'	See ***Bracteantha* 'Coco'**
confertum	MHig
coralloides	See ***Ozothamnus coralloides***
'County Park Silver'	CMHG CSam ECou EHyt ESis EWes MSto NHar NSla NTow NWCA SBla SSmi
diosmifolium	See ***Ozothamnus diosmifolius***
doerfleri	MHig
'Elmstead'	See ***H. stoechas* 'White Barn'**
ericifolium	See ***Ozothamnus purpurascens***
ericoides	See ***Dolichothrix ericoides***
fontanesii	LHil SPer WHer
frigidum	CPBP ITim LBee MHig NNrd NTow NWCA SBla WOMN
glomeratum	See ***H. aggregatum***
gmelinii	CHan
heldreichii	CGra EHyt NHol SIng SMrm
– NS 127	NWCA
hookeri	See ***Ozothamnus hookeri***
§ ***italicum*** ♀	CArn CHan CShe ECha ELau GCHN GPoy LGro LHol MBar MBri MGra MPla NRoo SRms WCer WDin WEas WHCG WOak WOve WRHF WRTC WWat WWin WWye
– 'Dartington'	CBod WJek WSel
§ – subsp. ***microphyllum***	CSam CWan ECha ELan ESis GBar LHol NPri NWoo SIde SIgm WEas WOak WSel
– 'Nanum'	See ***H. italicum*** subsp. ***microphyllum***
§ – subsp. ***serotinum***	CChe CTri EPfP GPoy LHop NFla SPer SPla SRms SSoC STre SVen WAbe WPer WSel WWeb
lanatum	See ***H. thianschanicum***
ledifolium	See ***Ozothamnus ledifolius***
lingulatum JJ&JH 9401733	NWCA
lobbii	NGre
marginatum	See ***H. milfordiae***
microphyllum Bentham & Hooker	See ***Ozothamnus microphyllus***
– Cambessedes	See ***H. italicum***
– hort.	See ***Plecostachys serpyllifolia***
§ ***milfordiae*** ♀	CMHG EPot ITim MBal MWat NGre NHar NHol NNrd NSla NTow NWCA SBla SIng SRms WPat
'Mo's Gold'	See ***H. argyrophyllum***
orientale	CHan EPot NHol SIng SMer
pagophilum	CPBP MHig
¶ ***pagophyllum*** JJH from Lesotho	EHyt
§ ***petiolare*** ♀	CHad EBak EBar ECtt IHos LBlm MRav SRms SVen WEas
– 'Aureum'	See ***H. petiolare* 'Limelight'**
– 'Goring Silver'	CBrk CHal LHil NPri
§ – 'Limelight'	CBrk EBar ECtt IHos LBlm MRav SIng SLod
– 'Roundabout' (v)	CBrk LBlm LHil NPri WEas
– 'Variegatum' ♀	CHal EBar ECtt IHos LBlm MRav SIng WEas
petiolatum	See ***H. petiolare***
plicatum	CBrk EBar LHol WCra
plumeum	GCLN ITim MHig NWCA
populifolium	CBrk WHer
¶ aff. ***praecurrens***	CGra
praecurrens	CPBP EHyt ITim NHol NWCA
purpurascens	See ***Ozothamnus purpurascens***
rosmarinifolium	See ***Ozothamnus rosmarinifolius***
§ 'Schwefellicht'	CSam CShe ECED ECha EFou MBri MCLN MRav NFla NRoo SChu SMer SPer SPla SWat WBea WEas WGwG WSHC
scorpioides	ECou MAll
selaginoides	See ***Ozothamnus selaginoides***
selago	See ***Ozothamnus selago***
serotinum	See ***H. italicum*** subsp. ***serotinum***
serpyllifolium	See ***Plecostachys serpyllifolia***
sessile	See ***H. sessilioides***
§ ***sessilioides***	EPot ITim NHar NSla NTow NWCA SBla
§ ***sibthorpii***	CPBP CSev ITim LBee LHil MDHE NMen NTow WAbe
siculum	See ***H. stoechas*** subsp. ***barrelieri***
'Silver Bush'	LHil
* 'Skynet'	GCal
sp. from Drakensburg Mountains, South Africa	GAbr NHol NWCA
sp. H&W 336	EHyt
sp. JJ&JH 9401733	NWCA
§ ***splendidum*** ♀	CFee CHan CShe ECha EHoe EOrc GAbr GCHN LFis LHil LHol NBro NNor SBar SDix SPer SRms WDin WHer WPer WWat WWye
stoechas	CArn
§ – subsp. ***barrelieri***	CNic WHer
§ – 'White Barn'	EBee ECha
◆ Sulphur Light	See ***H.* 'Schwefellicht'**
'Sussex Silver'	EPla WKif
§ ***thianschanicum***	EBee EMan MRav NWCA SRms
◆ – Golden Baby	See ***H. thianschanicum* 'Goldkind'**
§ – 'Goldkind'	GAbr LFis NBir NMen NPri
thyrsoideum	See ***Ozothamnus thyrsoideus***
trilineatum	See ***H. splendidum***
aff. – JJ&JH 9401783	NWCA
tumidum	See ***Ozothamnus selago*** var. ***tumidus***
virgineum	See ***H. sibthorpii***
woodii	See ***H. arwae***

HELICHRYSUM × RAOULIA

'Rivulet'	ECou
'Silver Streams'	ECou

HELICODICEROS (Araceae)

¶ ***muscivorus***	CAvo

HELICONIA (Musaceae)

¶ ***bihai***	LChe
¶ ***psittacorum***	ECon LChe
rostrata	LChe
stricta 'Dwarf Jamaican'	LChe

HELICTOTRICHON (Poaceae)

filifolium	EPla ETPC
pratense	EHoe EMon EPPr ESOG ETPC
§ ***sempervirens*** ♀	Widely available
– var. ***pendulum***	CMil CSte EMon EPla GAul GBin MUlv SPer SPla
* ***splendens***	SSoC

HELIOPHILA (Brassicaceae)

longifolia	CSpe

HELIOPSIS † (Asteraceae)

◆ 'Golden Plume'	See ***H. helianthoides*** var. ***scabra*** **'Goldgefieder'**
helianthoides	EMon
¶ – 'Benzinggold'	SMrm
– 'Hohlspiegel'	ECha EMan WFar WLRN
– 'Limelight'	See ***Helianthus*** **'Lemon Queen'**
– var. ***scabra***	EPfP MSCN WCot
◆ – – Golden Plume	See ***H. helianthoides*** var. ***scabra*** **'Goldgefieder'**
§ – – 'Goldgefieder' ♀	EPfP WBea WCra
– – 'Goldgrünherz'	ECED MBri
– – 'Incomparabilis'	ECED
– – 'Light of Loddon'	MWat
§ – – 'Sommersonne'	CM&M EBre ECtt EFou GMaP LHop MRav NFai NMir NPer NTow SPer SRms WHoo WPer WRHF WWin WWtk
◆ – – Summer Sun	See ***H. helianthoides*** var. ***scabra*** **'Sommersonne'**
– – 'Sunburst'	WPyg
– 'Sonnenglut'	MBri
– 'Spitzentänzerin'	MBri

HELIOTROPIUM (Boraginaceae)

§ ***amplexicaule***	SIgm SSad
anchusifolium	See ***H. amplexicaule***
§ ***arborescens***	CArn CKni WSel
'Chatsworth'	CBrk CHad CPle CSev ERea LBlm LHil MSte SAxl SIde SMer SSad SSoC WEas WLRN WPen
'Dame Alicia de Hales'	CBrk ERea WEas
'Gatton Park'	CBrk ERea LHil MRav SMrm SSad
'Lord Roberts'	CBrk ERea EWoo LHil
* 'Midnight'	CSpe NPri
¶ 'Mrs J.W. Lowther'	LHil
'Netherhall White'	ERea
'P.K. Lowther'	CBrk ERea WEas
peruvianum	See ***H. arborescens***
'President Garfield'	CBrk LHil
'Princess Marina' ♀	CBrk CSev ERea LHil MSte SSad WEas
'The Speaker'	CBrk
'W.H. Lowther'	LChe
'White Lady'	CBrk CSev ERea LBlm LHil SSad WEas
'White Queen'	LHil

HELIPTERUM (Asteraceae)

albicans	See ***Leucochrysum albicans***
anthemoides	See ***Rhodanthe anthemoides***

HELLEBORUS † (Ranunculaceae)

§ ***argutifolius*** ♀	Widely available
– mottled-leaved	See ***H. argutifolius*** **'Pacific Mist'**
§ – 'Pacific Mist' (v)	ECha EMon
atrorubens hort.	See ***H. orientalis*** **hort Early Purple Group**
– Waldst. & Kit.	CLCN ECha MCli WStI
– – WM 9028 from Slovenia	MPhe
– – WM 9101 from Slovenia	MPhe
– – WM 9216 from Slovenia	MPhe WCru
– – WM 9317	MPhe
– – WM 9319 from Slovenia	MPhe
× ***ballardiae***	MBri
colchicus	See ***H. orientalis*** **Lamarck** subsp. ***abchasicus***
corsicus	See ***H. argutifolius***
croaticus WM 9313	MPhe
– WM 9416	MPhe
cyclophyllus	CFil CRos CSte EBee NRar SPer WFar WPGP
– JCA 560.625	CLCN
* – WM 9412	WDav
dumetorum	CAvo CFil WPGP
– WM 9209/9307 from Hungary	MPhe
–WM 9307 from Hungary	MPhe
– WM 9301 from Slovenia	MPhe
– WM 9025 from Croatia	MPhe
– WM 9413	WCru
§ × ***ericsmithii***	CRDP MBri SBla WAbe
foetidus	Widely available
– Bowles' form	CBro EWes
– 'Chedglow'	CNat LHop
* – 'Curio' (v)	CNat
– 'Green Giant'	MTho WCru
– Italian form	CEnd EBee GBin NHol NTow WElm WRus
– Kurt's Strain	WCot
– 'Ruth'	MPhe
– 'Sopron'	GBin WCru
– Wester Flisk Group	CBot CBro CNat ECha ELan EMar EPar ERav MBri MPhe NHol NPer NRar NTow SBla SPer WAbe WCru WGwG WHoo WOMN WRus WWat
lividus ♀	CAvo CBot CBro CChu CGle CHan CLCN CLon EBre EHyt ELan EWes GCra LBlm NHar NRar SBla SWas SWat WCru
– subsp. ***corsicus***	See ***H. argutifolius***
multifidus	CRos EBee NBir SPer
– subsp. ***bocconei***	WOMN
– subsp. ***hercegovinus*** WM 9105	MPhe
– subsp. ***istriacus***	CBro CChu WCot
– – WM 9222	MPhe
– – WM 9322	MPhe
– – WM 9324	MPhe
– subsp. ***multifidus***	SWas
– – WM 9104	MPhe
– – WM 9529	MPhe
– WM 9225	WCru
niger ♀	CAvo CB&S CBro CShe EBre ECha EFou EGol ELan ENot EOrc GPoy LHop MBri MBro MPhe MTho NHar NHol NNor NRoo SIng SMad SPer WEas WFib WWat
– Blackthorn Group	SBla
– 'Crûg Hybrid'	WCru
– Harvington hybrids	COtt LRHS
– 'Louis Cobbett'	CRDP EBre
§ – subsp. ***macranthus***	GCal
– – WM 9030	WCru
– 'Madame Fourcade'	MBri
niger major	See ***H. niger*** subsp. ***macranthus***
¶ ***niger*** pink strain	NRar
– 'Potter's Wheel'	CChu CDoC CHan CPMA CRDP EBre ECot LFis NRar SBla SSpi WCru WFar WPyg WWat
– 'Saint Brigid'	NRar
– Sunrise Group WM 9519	MPhe
– Sunset Group WM 9113	MPhe NRar SPla
– 'White Magic'	CBlo CPMA GDra
× ***nigercors*** ♀	CHan CRDP LHop MBri WCru
¶ – 'Alabaster'	NBir
× ***nigristern***	See ***H.*** × ***ericsmithii***

odorus	CFil CLCN CRos NRoo SBla SSpi
– WM 9103	MPhe
– WM 9202	MPhe WCru
– WM 9415	MPhe
N ***orientalis*** hort.	Widely available
– Aquarius	SApp
– 'Agnes Brook'	WFib
– 'Albin Otto'	EBre
– Anderson's Red Hybrids	CLCN
– 'Angela Tandy'	WFib
– 'Apricot'	LCTD
¶ – 'Ariel'	LCTD
– 'Baby Black'	ECot
– Ballard's Group	EBre ECha LBlm MBri NRar WCru WRus
– black seedlings	CGle CRDP GDra NRar NRoo WCru
– 'Carlton Hall'	WFib
– 'Chartreuse'	MUlv
– 'Cheerful'	LCTD NBir
– 'Citron'	LCTD
– 'Cygnus'	ECha
¶ – 'Dawn'	LCTD
– Draco strain	CLCN
– 'Dusk'	LCTD
§ – Early Purple Group	CLCN CTri NBee NFla WCru
– 'Elizabeth Coburn'	WFib
– 'Eric's Best'	ECha
– 'Fred Whitsey'	WFib
– Galaxy Group	SHig
– 'Gertrude Raithby'	WFib
– 'Gladys Burrow'	WFib
– 'Greencups'	LCTD
– green spotted	CRDP EBre
– Hadspen hybrids	CHad
– 'Helen Ballard'	LCTD
– ivory	CLCN
– 'Ian Raithby'	WFib
– 'Ingot'	LCTD
– 'Joan Bridges'	LCTD
– 'John Raithby'	WFib
– Kochii Group	CAvo ECha MUlv NBrk NRar WCru
– 'Lady Charlotte Bonham-Carter'	WFib
– 'Leo'	MUlv
– 'Limelight'	ECha
– 'Little Black'	ECho WFib
– 'Mary Petit'	WFib
– maroon	EBre ERav MLsm MTis NRar
– 'Maureen Key'	WFib
– Midnight Sky Group	WPyg WWat
¶ – 'Orion'	LCTD
– 'Pebworth White'	WFib
– 'Philip Ballard'	LCTD
– 'Philip Wilson'	LCTD
– 'Picotee'	CRDP
– pink	CLCN CPMA CRDP EBee LFis MBro NRar NRoo SApp WCru
– pink spotted	CRDP EBre NRar
– primrose	EBre NRar SPer
– purple	CLCN CPMA CRDP ECha MBro NRar NRoo SApp WCru
– 'Plum Stippled'	ECha
– 'Queen of the Night'	CRDP
– 'Red Mountain'	EBar
– 'Rubens'	LCTD
– slatey blue	EBre WCot
– 'Sunny'	LCTD
– 'Sylvia'	LCTD
– 'Trotter's Spotted'	GDra
– 'Ushba'	LCTD
– 'Ushba' seedlings	GCal
– 'Victoria Raithby'	WFib
– white	CGle EBre ECha MBal MBro NRar NRoo WCru
– white spotted	CRDP EBre
– Zodiac Group	CLCN EOrc SApp
orientalis Lamarck	MPhe
§ – subsp. ***abchasicus***	CDec EBre GCra WCru
¶ – subsp. ***guttatus***	CAvo CChu CLCN EBre LBlm MUlv SBla SHig SSpi Wcot Wcru
– – cream	ECha
– – light purple	ECha
– – pink	ECha WCru
– JCA 562.402	CLCN
– ***olympicus***	See ***H. orientalis* Lamarck®** subsp. ***orientalis***
§ – subsp. ***orientalis***	WPyg WWat
purpurascens	CAvo CRos CSte EBee NBir NRoo SBla SPer SWas WPyg
– Hungary WM 9208/9211	MPhe
– Hungary WM 9211	MPhe
– WM 9303	MPhe
– WM 9412	MPhe
x ***sternii***	CBos CBot CBro CChu CElw CLCN CRDP CSpe EBre ELan GCal LFis MBal MFir NHar NHol NPSI NRar NSti NTow SBod SEas SMad SPer SWas WAbe WEas WGwG WWat
– Blackthorn Group ♀	CChu CDec CFil CPMA CRos EBre ELan MBri MUlv NRoo SPla SSpi WByw WCru WHoo WWat
– 'Boughton Beauty'	CAvo CChu CMea ECha MTho WByw WCot
– Boughton Group	CBot LBlm
– Cally Strain	GCal
torquatus	CAvo CBro CFil CLCN CRos CSte MTho WMer
– hybrids	ECGP SBla WCru
– Party Dress Group	SBla
– WM 9003 from Bosnia	MPhe
– WM 9106 from Montenegro	MPhe
– WM 9111 from Bosnia	MPhe
– Wolverton Hybrids	SBla WFar
viridis	CSte EBee EBre ECha MSal SBla SRms WCru WUnd
– from Germany	MPhe
– subsp. ***occidentalis***	CAvo CBro SBla
– – WM 9401	MPhe

HELONIOPSIS (Melanthiaceae)

¶ ***acutifolia*** B&SWJ 218	WCru
japonica	See ***H. orientalis***
§ ***orientalis***	CBro CPou EPot WCot WCru
* – var. ***albiflora***	WCru
§ – var. ***breviscapa***	CFil LBee WCru WPGP WThi
§ – var. ***kawanoi***	WCru
– var. ***yakusimensis***	See ***H. orientalis*** var. ***kawanoi***

HELWINGIA (Helwingiaceae)

¶ ***chinensis***	CPle
japonica	CBot CPle EFEx WWat

HELXINE See SOLEIROLIA

HEMEROCALLIS † (Hemerocallidaceae)

'Addie Branch Smith'	EGol
'Adoration'	SPer
'Aglow'	NCut

'Alan'	EBre SCro SHig WNdy WTre
'Albany'	SApp
'Alec Allen'	SRos
altissima	EMon
'Amadeus'	SApp
'Amazon'	LRHS
'Ambassador'	CKel
'Amber Star'	LPBA
'Amen'	WGle
'American Revolution'	EGar EWll LBuc WCot WRus
'Amersham'	EBee ECGP GSki MNFA SMrm WLRN
'Angel Curls'	EGol
'Angel's Delight'	WGle
'Anne Welch'	EPla
'Anzac'	EBre ECha ECro ECtt EPla ERou GAri NHol NMir NWes WCot WFar WSan WTyr
'Apricot Beauty'	CBlo EBee LBuc
'Apricot Surprise'	WGle
'Apricotta'	CKel WCot
'Arctic Snow'	SRos
'Arriba'	NBro WCot WFox WLRN
'Artistic Gold'	EGol
'Artist's Brush'	LBuc
'Atalanta Bouquet'	SRos
'Aten'	EBre
¶ 'Atlanta Full House'	SDay
'Attention Please'	WGle
'Aurora Raspberry'	WGle
'Autumn Red'	CBlo ERou NBir NCat NFai NHaw NOak NWes
'Ava Michelle'	SDay
'Aztec Furnace'	SDay
'Baby Betsy'	SDay
'Baby Darling'	SDay
'Baby Julia'	WGle
* 'Bailey Hay'	LRHS
¶ 'Bald Eagle'	SDay
'Ballerina Girl'	SRos
'Ballet Dancer'	ERou
'Baroni'	ECha
'Beauty Bright'	MAus
'Beauty to Behold'	SApp SDay SRos
'Bed of Roses'	MNFA
'Bedarra Island'	SDay
¶ 'Beijing'	SDay
'Bejewelled'	CSte EBee EBre EGol SApp
'Beloved Country'	CSte EHal
'Berlin Red'	LRHS MNFA SApp
'Berliner Premiere'	MNFA
'Bernard Thompson'	SApp
'Bertie Ferris'	EBee LBuc SDay
'Bess Ross'	MAus
'Bess Vestale'	ERou MWat NHol
'Bette Davis Eyes'	SRos
'Betty Woods' (d)	CRDP EGar SRos
'Bibury'	SCro
'Big World'	LRHS MNFA
'Bitsy'	EBee EGol MSte SDay WTre
'Black Knight'	SRms WNdy
'Black Magic'	CBro CHad CSev CSpe ECED EGol ELan EMan EPla ERou GMaP GMac MAus MBri MBro MNFA MRav NHol NWes SChu SMad SPer SUsu WHal
'Blonde Is Beautiful'	SRos
¶ 'Blushing Angel'	SDay
'Blushing Belle'	CMil EBee LRHS MNFA WWin
'Bold Courtier'	CKel
'Bold One'	SRos
'Bonanza'	CBro CKel CM&M CMGP CTri EBre ECha ECtt EHon ELan EPla ERou MAus MBri MRav NBro NFai SHBN SHig SPer SUsu WFox WPer WWin
'Border Honey'	WGle
'Bourbon Kings'	EBee EGar EGol EPla ERou MBel SDay
'Bowl of Roses'	WGle
'Brand New Lover'	SDay
'Bright Spangles'	SApp SDay SRos
'Brocaded Gown'	SRos
'Brunette'	SApp
'Bruno Müller'	SApp
'Buffy's Doll'	SDay SRos
'Bugs Ears'	SDay
¶ 'Bumble Bee'	SDay
'Buried Treasure'	LRHS MNFA
'Burlesque'	SDay
'Burning Daylight'	CMGP EBee EBre EGar EPla ERou LHop MBel MHlr MNFA MNrw NHol NVic SMrm SPer SRms WOld
'Butterfly Charm'	SDay
'Buttons'	CShe
'Buzz Bomb'	CRDP EBee EBre SHig SPer SRos WGwG WLRN
'California Sunshine'	SRos
'Camden Gold Dollar'	SDay
'Canary Glow'	CTri EBre ECro ERav NCat NWes SRos SSpe WWat
'Caramea'	EAst EBee NFai WGwG
'Cartwheels' 🏆	EBee EBre ECha EPla MBel MCli MMil MNFA NFai SPer SUsu
'Casino Gold'	SRos
'Catherine Woodbery'	COtt CSev EAst EBre ECro ECtt EFou EGol ELan EMar EPla ERav MAus MNFA MRav NFla NRoo SAga SApp SPer SSpe WCot WCra WNdy WPyg
'Cedar Waxwing'	EGol
¶ 'Chantilly Lace'	CMHG
'Charles Johnston'	SRos
'Charlie Pierce Memorial'	MBel SRos
'Chartreuse Magic'	ECro EGol EPla NHol SPer
'Cherry Cheeks'	EBre ECro ECtt EGol ELan EPla ERav ERou MAus MBri MRav SRos WCot WTyr
'Cherry Kiss'	SRos
'Chic Bonnet'	SPer
'Chicago Apache'	MBel MBri MUlv SRos
'Chicago Arnie's Choice'	WGle
'Chicago Cattleya'	EGol MRav
'Chicago Coral'	WGle
'Chicago Fire'	EGol
¶ 'Chicago Heirloom'	COtt EGol
'Chicago Knobby'	WGle
'Chicago Petite Lace'	WGle
'Chicago Petticoats'	EGol SApp WGle
'Chicago Picotee Memories'	WGle
'Chicago Picotee Pride'	WGle
'Chicago Picotee Queen'	EBre LRHS MBri MTol MUlv WGle
'Chicago Plum Pudding'	WGle
'Chicago Princess'	WGle
'Chicago Royal Crown'	MBri
'Chicago Royal Robe'	EBar EBre EFou EGol MBel MRav MSte MUlv NCat SDay WCot WWin
¶ 'Chicago Silver'	COtt

'Chicago Sunrise'	CHad EBar EGol EPla GMaP IBlr MNFA MSta NHaw NHol NOrc NWes SApp SDay SRos WMer WPer
'Chief Sarcoxie'	MAus
'Children's Festival'	CHad CMGP CSev CSte EBar EBre ECtt EGol EMil GMaP MBel MRav NHol SCro SRos SSpe WCra WPer WRus
'Childscraft'	CLTr
'Chinese Autumn'	SRos
'Chinese Coral'	CKel WBcn
'Chinese Imp'	SDay
'Chloe's Child'	SCro
'Choral Angel'	WGle
'Chorus Line'	MBel SRos
'Christmas Candles'	EBre MUlv
'Christmas Is'	EFou SApp
'Cinnamon Glow'	WGle
citrina	CAvo CSte ECED ELan EMon MAus NPla SEas SPla
'Civil Rights'	SRos
'Classic Simplicity'	EBre LRHS MAus MUlv
'Classy Lassie'	MUlv WGle
'Colonial Dame'	CKel
'Coming up Roses'	SRos
'Conspicua'	CShe
'Contessa'	CBro ECro ELan SCro
'Cool Jazz'	SDay SRos
¶ 'Coral Mist'	EFou
'Coreana Yellow'	LRHS
'Corky' ♀	CHad EBre ECGP ECha ERav GCal GMaP MBel MNFA SAxl SChu SDay SDix SPer SRos SSpi WCra
'Cosmic Hummingbird'	SDay
¶ 'Countess Zora'	CMHG
'Court Magician'	SRos
'Cranberry Baby'	SDay SRos
'Cream Cloud'	WGle
'Cream Drop'	EBre ECtt EGol GMaP LBlm LGan MBel MRav NHol NOrc NPla NWes SSpe WCra WHow WMer WRus
'Crimson Icon'	MSte SDay
'Crimson Pirate'	EMil ERou
'Croesus'	NHol SCro SRms
'Croftway'	SCro
'Cupid's Bow'	EGol
'Cupid's Gold'	SDay SRos
'Cynthia Mary'	LRHS
'Dad's Best White'	EGol SCro
¶ 'Daily Bread'	SDay
'Daily Dollar'	MBri
'Dainty Pink'	EGol
'Dance Ballerina Dance'	SDay SRos
'Dawn Play'	CKel
'Decatur Imp'	EGol
'Decatur Piecrust'	MBel
'Demetrius'	MNFA
'Devon Cream'	SChu
'Devonshire'	SDay SRos
¶ 'Diamond Dust'	LRHS
'Dido'	CTri ERou GBuc MSte
'Display'	CKel
'Dominic'	SRos
'Dorethe Louise'	CRDP SDay
'Dorothy McDade'	EGol
'Double Cutie'	EFou
¶ 'Double Gardenia'	WGle
'Double Honey'	WGle
'Double Oh'	WGle

'Double Oh Seven'	SDay
'Double Pleasure'	MBel
'Double Pompom'	MAus WGle
'Double River Wye'	EGol LBuc SHBN
'Dresden Doll'	SPer
§ 'Dubloon'	CKel CMGP ERou GAbr GBuc NHol WHil
dumortieri	CBot CBro CDec EBre ECha ECro EFou EGol ELan EMon EOrc ERav MUlv MWat NBir NHaw NHol NSti NVic SHig SPer SSpe WWin
'Dutch Beauty'	EBre
'Dutch Gold'	NBro
'Ed Murray'	MAus SRos
'Edelweiss'	SDay
'Edna Spalding'	EBre SRos
'Eenie Allegro'	CBro EFou SPer SPla
'Eenie Fanfare'	WCra
'Eenie Weenie'	CBro CFee CKel EBre ECtt EGol EMil MBel MBri NHol SApp SDay WMer WPer WRus
'Eenie Weenie Non-stop'	ECha SAxl SWas
'Elaine Strutt'	SDay WCot
'Elegant Greeting'	EBee LBuc
¶ 'Elizabeth Ann Hudson'	SDay
'Erica Nichole Gonzales'	SDay
'Esther Walker'	CKel WBcn
'Evelyn Claar'	CKel SCro
'Evening Gown'	WGle
'Fairy Charm'	WGle
'Fairy Frosting'	SDay
'Fairy Tale Pink'	CRDP MBel SDay SRos
'Faith Nabor'	SRos
'Fan Dancer'	EGol
'Fandango'	SPer
'Fashion Model'	CKel WPer
¶ 'Feather Down'	SDay
'Felicity'	CKel
'Femme Osage'	SRos
'Fire Dance'	SCro
'First Formal'	SPer
'Flames of Fantasy'	CKel MUlv NCut SRos
'Flaming Sword'	GBuc
flava	See ***H. lilioasphodelus***
'Florissant Charm'	WGle
forrestii 'Perry's Variety'	EMon
'Fragrant Pastel Cheer'	WGle
'Frances Fay'	SRos
'Francis Russell'	CKel
'Frans Hals'	EBre EPla ERou LLWP MBri MBro MNFA MNrw MRav NFai SPer SPla SRos WHal WHoo WPer WPyg
fulva	CRow CWGN ECED ECro EPla IBlr MHar SChu SHBN SHig SRms WWin
N– 'Flore Pleno'	CAvo CFee CHan CKel CRow CWGN EFou EGol EHon ELan EMon EOrc EPla IBlr LFis LHop MAus MFir NBro NFai NSti SAxl SHBN SHig SPer SSvw SWat WEas WFox WWin
N– 'Green Kwanso'	CRow CSWP EMon IBlr NTow SPla WNdy WRha WTre
§ – 'Kwanzo Variegata'	CBot CGle CRow ELan EMon ERav IBlr LHop MTho SAxl WCot WSan
'Garnet Garland'	CKel
'Gay Nineties'	CKel
'Gay Rapture'	SPer
'Gay Troubadour'	CKel

'Gemini'	SDay SRos
'Gentle Country Breeze'	SRos
'Gentle Shepherd'	CKel CMil CSpe EAst EBar EBre EFou EGar EGol EMil LBuc LFis MAus MNFA MUlv NCut NHaw SApp SDay SHBN SRos WWat
'George Cunningham'	CMGP CSev EBre ECro ECtt EGol ELan EPla ERou MAus MBri MCli SChu SDay
'Georgette Belden'	WGle
'Giant Moon'	EBre ECro EGol ELan EPla EPri ERou MBri MUlv SChu WHal WRus
'Giddy Go Round'	SApp
'Gingerbread Man'	CRDP SDay
¶ 'Gold Crest'	LRHS MNFA
'Gold Imperial'	CShe NFla
'Golden Bell'	EGar LWak NHol
'Golden Chimes' 🏆	CAvo CBro CDec CFee CWGN EBre ECha EFou EGol ELan ERou MBel MBri MBro MRav MSta NBir NBro NFai NHol SApp SAxl SCro SDix SHig SPer SRos WCra WHoo WWat
'Golden Gate'	SHig
'Golden Ginko'	EBre LRHS MBri
'Golden Orchid'	See *H.* **'Dubloon'**
'Golden Peace'	SRos
'Golden Prize'	EBre EFou SRos
'Golden Scroll'	SDay SRos
'Grape Magic'	EGol
'Green Chartreuse'	ECha
'Green Drop'	WTyr
'Green Flutter' 🏆	CSev EWll NBir SApp SAsh SRos WCot
'Green Glitter'	LRHS
'Green Gold'	CMHG LRHS MNFA
'Grumbly'	EBee ELan
'Guardian Angel'	WGle
'Halo Light'	CKel
'Happy Returns'	ECha EGol SApp SRos
'Hawaian Punch'	EGol
'Hazel Monette'	EGol WGle
'Heather Green'	SApp
'Heavenly Treasure'	EBre SRos WGle
'Heaven's Trophy'	WGle
'Heirloom Lace'	EBre MAus MUlv SDay WFar
'Helios'	SHig
'Her Majesty'	CKel
¶ 'Hercules'	NFla
'Heron'	WGle
'Hey There'	SRos
'High Tor'	GCal GQui
'Holiday Mood'	ELan ERou NWes
'Honey Redhead'	CKel
'Hope Diamond'	CRDP SDay
'Hornby Castle'	CBro NHol NVic WPer
'Hot Ticket'	SRos
'Humdinger'	SRos
'Hyperion'	CSev CShe EBre ECED ECGP ECha ECtt EGol EMan GAri MAus MNFA MRav NHol SChu SHBN SPer SUsu WOld
'Ice Cap'	EBre MCli
¶ 'Ice Carnival'	LRHS
'Icy Lemon'	SRos
'Imperator'	CBen CWGN EPla LPBA NHol
'Imperial Blush'	CKel
'Inspired Word'	SRos
'Invictus'	SRos
'Irish Elf'	SApp
'Iron Gate Gnome'	WTre
'Jade Bowl'	WGle
'James Marsh'	SRos
'Jedi Dot Pearce'	SRos
'Jenny Wren'	MNFA
'Jo Jo'	WWin
'Joan Senior'	EGol LBlm MAus MBel SDay SRos
'John Bierman'	SRos
'Joylene Nichole'	SRos
'Judah'	SRos
'Kate Carpenter'	SRos
'Katie'	MAus WTre
'Katie Elizabeth Miller'	SRos
'Kelly's Girl'	SApp
'Kindly Light'	SRos
N 'Kwanso Flore Pleno'	See *H. fulva* **'Green Kwanso'**
N 'Kwanso Flore Pleno Variegata'	See *H. fulva* **'Kwanzo Variegata'**
¶ 'La Mer'	EFou
'Lady Cynthia'	CKel
'Lady of Leisure'	MBel
'Ladykin'	SDay
'Lark Song'	CKel EBre EGol WBcn
'Late Cream'	WGle
'Lavender Aristocrat'	WGle
'Lavender Bonanza'	MAus NWes
'Lemon Bells'	EMan EMar EPfP EWll GMaP GSki MAus MNFA MUlv NCat SChu SMrm WLRN
¶ 'Lemon Mint'	EGol
'Lenox'	SRos
'Lilac Wine'	ECha SMrm WMer
§ ***lilioasphodelus*** 🏆	CAvo CBre CGle CHad CHan EBre ECha ELan GCal IBlr LBlm LGan MBro MCli MFir NSti NTow SAxl SDix SHig SMad SPer SPla SSpi WHal WHoo WNdy WPyg WWat
'Lillian Frye'	EGol
'Linda'	CBlo CMGP ERou EWll MRav NHol
'Lion Cub'	WGle
¶ 'Little Bee'	EFou
'Little Beige Magic'	EGol
'Little Big Man'	SDay
'Little Bugger'	MBri
'Little Bumble Bee'	EGol
'Little Business'	SDay
'Little Cameo'	EGol
'Little Cranberry Cove'	EGol
'Little Dandy'	EGol
'Little Dart'	ECha
'Little Deeke'	SRos
'Little Fantastic'	EGol
'Little Fat Dazzler'	SDay
'Little Grapette'	CHad EGol MNFA SApp SRos
'Little Gypsy Vagabond'	SDay SRos
'Little Lavender Princess'	EGol
'Little Maggie'	MSte SDay
'Little Missy'	EFou SDay
'Little Prince'	SDay
'Little Pumpkin Face'	EGol
'Little Rainbow'	EGol MNFA
'Little Red Hen'	LRHS SDay
'Little Violet Lace'	GSki SDay
'Little Wart'	EGol

'Little Wine Cup'	CHad CLTr EAst EBre ECtt EGol GMaP LFis LHop MBel NHaw NHol NOrc NPla SApp SChu SDay SPla SRms SSvw WCra WGwG WPer WRus WTyr
'Little Woman'	SDay
'Little Zinger'	SDay
'Lochinvar'	ENot
longituba B&SWJ 625	GCra
'Look'	WTre
'Lotus Land'	CKel
'Lullaby Baby'	EGol SDay SRos
luna	GMac LWak NOak WFox
'Lupine'	WGle
x ***luteola***	SDay
'Luxury Lace'	CDec EAst EBre EFol EFou EGol ELan EOrc EPla MBel MNFA MOne MUlv NBir NHaw NMGW NWes SChu SPer WFox WWhi
'Lynn Hall'	EBre EGol
'Mabel Fuller'	SCro SPer
'Malaysian Monarch'	MBel
'Mallard'	EBre ECro ECtt EGol EPla MBri MRav MUlv SRos WCot WCra WGle WMer WPer
'Manchurian Apricot'	SRos
'Marion Moss'	CKel
'Marion Vaughn' 🏆	CMil CSev EBre ECGP ECot EGol ELan EMan GSki MAus MMil MNFA MUlv MWat NWes SDix SSpi WCot
'Mariska'	SDay
'Mary Todd'	CSte EGol MNFA
'Mary's Gold'	SRos
'Matador Orange'	SHam
'Matt'	SRos
'Mauna Loa'	SApp
'Mavoureen Nesmith'	SCro
'May Colven'	EBre EGol
'Meadow Gold'	CKel
'Meadow Mist'	EGol
'Meadow Sprite'	SDay
'Melody Lane'	EGol
'Meno'	EGol
¶ 'Metaphor'	SDay
'Michele Coe'	EMan LBuc LRHS MNFA SChu SMrm WLRN
middendorffii	EPPr GCal GDra GMaP MCli
– var. ***esculenta***	EMon WDav
'Mikado'	GAul SHam
'Millie Schlumpf'	SRos
'Ming Lo'	SDay
'Ming Porcelain'	SApp SRos
'Ming Snow'	WGle
'Mini Pearl'	EGol SDay SRos WPer
'Mini Stella'	CBro EMil EPla LRHS MBri SDay
Miniature Hybrids	SRms WPer WWtk
minor	CBro CMea EBre EGol GCal SPla SRms
'Missenden'	MNFA NHaw
¶ 'Mission Moonlight'	COtt
'Missouri Beauty'	CRos SHhN
'Monica Marie'	SRos
'Moonlight Mist'	SDay SRos
'Morocco Red'	CBro CTri CWGN ELan GSki SMrm WWat
'Mosel'	SDay
'Mountain Laurel'	LRHS MBri MUlv
'Mrs David Hall'	CKel SCro SMrm

'Mrs Hugh Johnson'	CHad CMGP CSev ECot EHon LGan LWak NHol SHBN
'Mrs John J. Tigert'	ERou
'Mrs Lester'	CKel SDay
multiflora	NHol SHig
'My Belle'	SDay
'My Hope'	WGle
'Naomi Ruth'	CSpe EGol
'Nashville'	CBro EBre ELan ERou IBlr
'Neal Berrey'	SRos
'Neyron Rose' 🏆	CSte EGar EGol ERou GSki MAus MNFA SAxl SChu SMrm
'Night Raider'	SRos
'Nigrette'	CBen LPBA MUlv MWat NHol
'Nob Hill'	CLTr ECGP EGol SRos
'North Star'	GCal
'Norton Beauté'	MBel
'Numinous Moments'	WGle
'Olive Bailey Langdon'	EGol SRos
'Oom-pa-pa'	ECha
'Optic Elegance'	SAsh
'Orangeman' hort.	CDoC GSki
'Orchid Beauty'	ECha
'Orford'	WWin
'Oriental Ruby'	SApp SDay
'Paige Parker'	EGol
'Painted Lady'	CKel
'Painted Trillium'	WGle
'Pandora's Box'	EGol SApp SDay
'Paper Butterfly'	SRos
'Paradise Prince'	EGol
'Pardon Me'	CMHG EGol SApp SDay
'Parian China'	WGle
'Pastel Ballerina'	SDay SRos
'Pastel Classic'	SRos
'Penelope Vestey'	LRHS MNFA SDay
'Penny's Worth'	EGol EMil MBri
'Persian Princess'	CKel WBcn
'Persian Shrine'	EGol
'Phoebe'	WGle
'Piccadilly Princess'	MBel SRos
'Pink Charm'	CM&M CMGP CWGN EMan LPBA MAus MBal MNFA MWat NHol NOrc SChu SEas SHBN WCra WTyr
'Pink Damask' 🏆	CKel CShe CTri CWGN EBre ECED ECha EFou EGol EHon ELan EPla GLil LBlm LGro LWak MAus MBel MBri MFir MNrw MWat NOak SAxl SChu SCro SDay SPer SRos WEas
'Pink Dream'	EGar MNFA NHol
'Pink Heaven'	EGol
'Pink Interlude'	CKel
'Pink Lady'	ERou MNrw MRav SHBN SRms
¶ 'Pink Lavender Appeal'	EGol
'Pink Opal'	CKel
'Pink Prelude'	CBlo LRHS SChu
'Pink Salute'	SRos
'Pink Sundae'	ECha
'Pink Super Spider'	SRos
'Piquante'	EBee
'Pixie Pipestone'	SApp
'Pojo'	SDay
'Pompeian Purple'	EGol WGle
'Poneytail Pink'	EGol
'Pony'	EGol WGle
'Pookie Bear'	SApp
'Potter's Clay'	WGle
'Prairie Bells'	CSWP CSte EHal MAus MBro NFai NPla WHoo WNdy

'Prairie Blue Eyes'	EGol SApp WTre
'Pretty Mist'	WGle
'Pretty Peggy'	MNFA
'Prima Donna'	CKel SCro
'Primrose Mascotte'	NBir WCot WWin
'Prize Picotee Deluxe'	WGle
'Prize Picotee Elite'	WGle
'Puddin'	See ***H.* 'Brass Buckles'**
'Pumpkin Kid'	SRos
'Puppet Show'	SDay
¶ 'Purple Rain'	EFou SDay
¶ 'Purple Waters'	EPfP NHaw
'Pursuit of Excellence'	SRos
'Pyewacket'	SDay
'Queen of May'	WCot
'Quick Results'	SRos
'Quietness'	SRos
'Radiant'	WRHF
'Raindrop'	EGol
'Rajah'	GAul LWak MBel NBro NBus WFox
'Raspberry Wine'	ECha
'Real Wind'	SDay
'Red Cup'	GLil
'Red Damask'	SHam
'Red Joy'	SApp
'Red Precious' ♀	EGol MBel MNFA SAsh
'Red Rum'	EWll MCli
'Red Torch'	CKel
'Romany'	LPBA
'Root Beer'	MAus WGle
'Rose Emily'	SRos
'Rose Festival'	WGle
'Royal Corduroy'	MBel
'Royal Heritage'	SDay
'Royal Palace Prince'	WGle
'Royal Prestige'	SApp
'Royal Robe'	EFou EGar
'Royalty'	CKel
'Ruffled Apricot'	LRHS SDay SRos
'Russell Prichard'	ERou
'Russian Rhapsody'	SDay
'Salmon Sheen'	CKel SPer
'Sammy Russell'	CMGP CWGN EAst EBre ECro EFou EGol EMar EOrc EPla GBuc GMac LHop MBal MBro MCli MNFA NBro NFai NHol SBod SEas SRms WCra WFox WPer WWhi
'Sandra Walker'	EGol
'Satin Clouds'	EGol WGle
'Satin Glow'	ECha
'Satin Silk'	EBre
'Scarlet Flame'	ECha
* 'Scarlet Oak'	MBri
'Scarlet Orbit'	SRos
'Scarlet Romance'	WGle
'Scarlet Royalty'	WGle
'Scarlet Tanager'	LRHS MUlv WMer
'Schoolgirl'	EBre
'Screech Owl'	LRHS WMer
'Searcy Marsh'	EGol
'Sebastian'	SRos
'Serena Sunburst'	MBel SRos
¶ 'Shaman'	SRos
'Shooting Star'	EGol SPla
'Silent Stars'	WGle
'Silken Fairy'	EGol SDay
'Siloam Angel Blush'	SDay
'Siloam Baby Doll'	SDay
'Siloam Baby Talk'	CRDP EGol NBir SRos WGle
'Siloam Bo Peep'	CRDP EGol SDay
'Siloam Brian Henke'	SRos
'Siloam Button Box'	EGol
'Siloam Byelo'	EGol SDay
'Siloam Cinderella'	EGol SRos
'Siloam David Kirchhoff'	SRos
'Siloam Doodlebug'	EGol WGle
'Siloam Double Classic'	MBel SRos
'Siloam Edith Scholar'	EGol WGle
'Siloam Ethel Smith'	EGol SDay
'Siloam Fairy Tale'	CRDP EGol SDay
'Siloam Grace Stamile'	SRos
¶ 'Siloam Gumdrop'	WGle
'Siloam Joan Senior'	EGol
'Siloam June Bug'	EGol WCot
'Siloam Kewpie Doll'	EGol WGle
'Siloam Little Girl'	EGol SDay WGle
'Siloam Merle Kent'	SRos
'Siloam Orchid Jewel'	EGol
'Siloam Pee Wee'	EGol
'Siloam Pink Glow'	EGol WGle
'Siloam Pink Petite'	EGol
'Siloam Plum Tree'	EGol
'Siloam Pocket Size'	EGol
'Siloam Prissy'	EGol
'Siloam Purple Plum'	EGol
'Siloam Red Ruby'	EGol
'Siloam Red Toy'	EGol
'Siloam Red Velvet'	EGol
'Siloam Ribbon Candy'	EGol
'Siloam Rose Dawn'	SDay SRos
'Siloam Shocker'	EGol
'Siloam Show Girl'	EGol
'Siloam Sugar Time'	EGol
'Siloam Tee Tiny'	EGol
'Siloam Tinker Toy'	EGol WGle
'Siloam Tiny Mite'	EGol SDay
'Siloam Toddler'	EGol WGle
'Siloam Tom Thumb'	EGol
'Siloam Ury Winniford'	CRDP EGol SDay
'Siloam Virginia Henson'	EGol SRos
'Silver Ice'	SRos
'Silver Veil'	SDay
'Sirius'	NHol
'Snowfall'	EGol
'Someone Special'	SRos
'Song Sparrow'	CBro WPer
'Sparkling Dawn'	MBel
'Sparkling Stars'	WGle
'Spiderman'	SRos
'Stafford'	CMGP EBre ECED ECtt EFou ELan EPla ERou LGro LHop MBel MBri MNFA MNrw MTis NBrk NHol NOrc NVic NWes SChu SDay SHig SPer SRos WCra WHoo WPer
'Starling'	EGol
'Stars and Stripes'	MNFA
'Stella de Oro' ♀	CBro EBar EBre ECha ECtt EFou EGol ELan EOrc EPla ERou LHop MAus MBel MBri MRav MTho MUlv NMir NRoo NSti SAxl SChu SDay SPer SPla WHoo WHow WMer WRus
'Stineette'	WCot
'Stoke Poges' ♀	CSev EBee ECGP EMar EPfP LRHS MMil MNFA SChu SMrm WLRN
'Strawberry Candy'	SRos
'Streaker' hort. (v)	WCot
'Sugar Cookie'	CRDP SApp
'Summer Air'	MBri

'Summer Wine'	CMGP CRos CSpe EBar EFou EGol EMar EPla LRHS MAus MBro MNFA MUlv NFai NPri SChu SDay SMrm SUsu WCot WCra WHoo WNdy WPyg WWat
'Sunday Gloves'	EGol
'Superlative'	SRos
'Suzie Wong'	MNFA
'Sweet Pea'	EGol
'Sweet Refrain'	CBot
'Swirling Water'	SDay
'Tasmania'	SPer
'Techny Peach Lace'	WGle
'Techny Spider'	SRos
'Teenager'	EGol
'Tejas'	CSte EMil
'Tender Sheperd'	EGol WGle
'Tetraploid Stella de Oro'	SDay
'Thousand Voices'	WGle
'Thumbelina'	ECha MNFA
§ ***thunbergii***	ECha EPla SMac SSpi
'Time Lord'	SDay
¶ 'Timeless Fire'	SRos
¶ 'Tinker Bell'	SRos
'Tiny Temptress'	SDay
¶ 'Todd Munroe'	WGle
'Tom Wise'	SRos
'Tonia Gay'	CRDP SRos
'Tootsie Rose'	SRos
'Torpoint'	LRHS MNFA
'Towhead'	EBre EGol LRHS MUlv SDay WCot WMer
'Toyland'	CMGP CSev EBee EBre EGar EGol GSki LRHS MNFA NRoo SAxl SSpe WLRN
'Triple Threat'	SDay
'Tropical Toy'	SDay
'Upper Class Peach'	WGle
'Varsity'	EBre EGol MAus NBir SRos
vespertina	See ***H. thunbergii***
'Vicountess Byng'	LFis
'Victoria Aden'	CBro
¶ 'Virgin's Blush'	SPer
'Walk Humbly'	WGle
'Wally Nance'	LRHS
'Water Witch'	EGol
'Waxwing'	CKel WPer
'Wayside Green Imp'	EGol WGle
'Wayside Princess'	WGle
'Wee Chalice'	EGol
'Whichford' ♀	CBro CMea EBre ECro ECtt EGol ELan MNFA NHol NRoo SChu SHig SUsu WGwG WWat WWin
'White Coral'	MNFA
'White Dish'	EGol
'White Temptation'	EGol MBel
'Whooperie'	MBel
'Wild Welcome'	EBre MAus
'Window Dressing'	EGol
'Windsor Tan'	MAus
'Wine Bubbles'	EGol
'Winsome Lady'	EBre ECha
'Wishing Well'	SChu
* 'Witch Hazel'	WGle
'Woodbury'	WRus
'Wren'	WGle
'Wynn'	MBel
'Yellow Lollipop'	SDay SRos
'Yellow Mantle'	MNFA
'Yellow Petticoats'	MUlv
'Yellow Rain'	SAsh WCot
'Yesterday Memories'	SDay SRos
'Zampa'	SDay
'Zara'	SPer

HEMIGRAPHIS (Acanthaceae)

§ ***alternata***	LChe
◆ ***colorata***	See ***H. alternata***

HEMIONITIS (Adiantaceae)

¶ ***arifolia***	NMar

HEMIPHRAGMA (Scrophulariaceae)

See Plant Deletions

HEMIZYGIA (Lamiaceae)

transvaalensis	CGre

HEPATICA † (Ranunculaceae)

acutiloba	CBro EPar GMaP LAma LWoo MAvo NGar NHol WChr WCot WCru WWat
americana	CArn NGar WChr WCot WCru WWat
angulosa	See ***H. transsilvanica***
× ***media*** 'Ballardii' ♀	IBlr
§ ***nobilis*** ♀	Widely available
– blue	GAbr MS&S NGar NHar NRar NSla SBla SWas
– double pink	See ***H. nobilis* 'Rubra Plena'**
– var. ***japonica***	CBro CRDP EPar LAma NGar NHol WChr WCru WWat
– lilac	MTho SWas
– mottled leaf	EHyt MTho
– pink	CRDP ELan EPot MS&S NGar SBla SWas WChr WIvy
* – 'Pyrenean Marbles'	LWoo
¶ – red	NNrd
– var. ***rubra***	CRDP LWoo NMen NSla
§ – 'Rubra Plena'	NGar NHar
– white	CNic ELan MHig MS&S NGar NSla SBla SIng WIvy
§ ***transsilvanica*** ♀	CBro EBre ECha EHyt ELan EPar EPot GDra LAma LHop LWoo MBro MHig MS&S MWat NGar NHar NRya SBla SMad SPer WChr WCru WWat
– ***alba***	NGar
– 'De Buis'	CAvo MDun
– 'Eisvogel'	EPot NGar WChr
– 'Elison Spence' (d)	IBlr WIvy
– 'Lilacina'	NGar
– 'Loddon Blue'	NGar
triloba	See ***H. nobilis***

× HEPPIMENES (Gesneriaceae)

I 'Purple Queen'	NMos

HEPTACODIUM (Caprifoliaceae)

jasminoides	CBot CChu CFil CPMA CPle ELan ERav GBin GQui MBlu MTis SAga SMac SMad WWat

HEPTAPLEURUM See SCHEFFLERA

HERACLEUM (Apiaceae)

antasiaticum	See ***H. stevenii***
lehmannianum	GAul WCot
mantegazzianum	CRow EOas MFir NSti WOak
minimum 'Roseum'	ELan MSte WFar WOMN WPat

¶ ***sphondylium***	CTiv
¶ – ***roseum***	CNat

HERBERTIA (Iridaceae)

§ ***lahue***	LRHS

HERMANNIA (Sterculiaceae)

candicans	See ***H. incana***
erodioides	See ***H. depressa***
§ ***incana***	CBrk CHal
* ***stricta***	MFos
verticillata	See ***H. pinnata***

HERMODACTYLUS (Iridaceae)

§ ***tuberosus***	CAvo CBro CChu CMea CMil CMon CTri EBre ECha ELan ERav LAma MNrw MRav MSto NFai NRog SCro WHil
– MS 976/762	CMon

HERNIARIA (Caryophyllaceae)

glabra	EOHP EWFC GBar GPoy LHol MHew MSal NHol WHer WWye

HERPOLIRION (Anthericaceae)
See Plant Deletions

HERTIA See OTHONNA

HESPERALOE (Agavaceae)

funifera	CTbh
parviflora	CTbh EOas SIgm
– 'Rubra'	SArc

HESPERANTHA (Iridaceae)

§ ***baurii***	GBuc MDun NMen SSpi WAbe WCot WHal
buhrii	See ***H. cucullata* 'Rubra'**
§ ***cucullata*** 'Rubra'	NWCA
huttonii	GBuc GCal MFir WCot
mossii	See ***H. baurii***

HESPERIS † (Brassicaceae)

lutea	See ***Sisymbrium luteum***
matronalis	Widely available
◆ – ***alba***	See ***H. matronalis*** var. ***albiflora***
§ – var. ***albiflora***	CBot EFou EMar MAvo SMrm SPer SSvw WCot WHil WOve WWat
– – 'Alba Plena'	CGle CMea CRDP LHol MTis SIde SWat WCot WRus
– double form	CHad CRow CSev ELan MBri SSpe WCru
– double pink	SWat
– 'Lilacina Flore Pleno'	CBot CBre CGle CHan CMil EBar EMon GMaP LFis MOne MRav NBrk NHaw NHol NPri SWat
steveniana	CHan EBar ECoo MEas MTis NSti SWat WEas
* ***sylviniana***	WCot

HESPEROCHIRON (Hydrophyllaceae)
See Plant Deletions

HETEROCENTRON (Melastomataceae)

§ ***elegans***	CLTr CTre

HETEROMELES See PHOTINIA

HETEROMORPHA (Apiaceae)

¶ ***arborescens***	CTrC

HETEROPAPPUS (Asteraceae)

altaicus	WPer

HETEROTHECA (Asteraceae)

mucronata	LKoh LLew
§ ***villosa***	CChr CChu CRDP EMon LBuc MAvo WCot

HEUCHERA † (Saxifragaceae)

§ ***americana***	CRDP CRow CShe ECha EFol EOrc EPar GBar GMaP MHar MUlv NBir NFai SCro SLod WCot WHal WWat
– 'Picta'	EBre EPPr
Bressingham Hybrids	EAst EBre EGoo GDra LSyl MBri MUlv NBir NFla NMir NOak NRoo SCro SPer SRms WHoo WPLl WPer WWin WWoo
x ***brizoides*** 'Gracillima'	CGle EPPr
'Canyon Delight'	WCot
'Cascade Dawn'	CDec CSte EHoe EMan EPPr LFis LHop MHlr NCut NHol NLak NPro SApp SBid SWat WFox
'Cathedral Windows'	WCot
§ Charles Bloom = 'Chablo'	EBre
◆ Charles Bloom	See ***H.* Charles Bloom = 'Chablo'**
'Cherry Red'	ECha
chlorantha	CPea WHil
'Chocolate Ruffles'	CRDP CSpe EBre EHal EHic LHop MCLN MHlr MLLN MMil NBir NCut NHol NWes SApp SMrm WCot WFox WGle WRus
Coral Bells	See ***H. sanguinea***
'Coral Cloud'	CB&S EBre ENot GCHN
cylindrica	CHid EBar GCHN GCra MBel MRav MSte NChi SHel WPer WWin
– var. ***alpina***	MFos NGre WDav
– 'Chartreuse'	CGle
– 'Greenfinch'	Widely available
– 'Hyperion'	EBre EPPr MBal MUlv
'David'	WCot
'Dennis Davidson'	See ***H.* 'Huntsman'**
I 'Eco Magnififolia'	CBos NWes WCot WGle
'Edge Hill'	SRms WRHF
'Firebird'	CBlo ELan EPPr MBal NVic
◆ Firefly	See ***H.* 'Leuchtkäfer'**
glabra	EMon
glauca	See ***H. americana***
'Green Ivory'	CGle CHar CWGN EBre EGol EHal ELan EMan EPPr GCHN GMaP LBlm MBal MBel MBri MRav MUlv NBus NCat SPer WRHF
grossulariifolia	MTho NHar NPri WCot WPer
'Helen Dillon' (v)	CElw CSte MCLN NWes SPla WCot WFox WSan
§ Rosemary Bloom = 'Heuros'	EBre SPer SWat
hispida	MSte Saga WPbr
§ 'Huntsman'	CGle CSte EBee ECha EGar ELan EPPr GBri GBuc WPbr
'Jack Frost'	NWes WGle
'Lady Romney'	GCal SHel

§ 'Leuchtkäfer'	CFee ESis LFis MCli MFir MRav NBrk NFai NMir NOrc NRoo SCro SMac SPer SWat WAbe WBro WHoo WPer
¶ ***mexicana***	WCot
* ***micans***	EHyt NHar NMen SIng WThi
micrantha	ELan GGar LBlm SRms WCot
– var. ***diversifolia***	GMaP LRHS MOne SPer
Bressingham Bronze = 'Absi'	
N– – 'Palace Purple' ♀	Widely available
– JLS 86275CLOR	EMon
– 'Martha Roderick'	WCot
'Mother of Pearl'	ECha
¶ 'Orphei'	NChi
'Painted Lady'	CDec GBuc SHam WPbr WWeb
'Pearl Drops'	EBre EPPr
'Persian Carpet'	CDec CMil CRDP EHal EHic GCal LHop MCLN MHlr MLLN NBir NCut NHaw NHol NLak NPSI SApp SBid SMad SMrm SSpi WCot WFox WGle WRus WWeb
'Pewter Moon'	Widely available
'Pewter Veil'	CBos WCot WEas WGle
pilosissima	GBuc WCot
Rain of Fire = 'Pluie de Feu'	CFir CTri EBre EPPr GBri GCal MCli SSte WGle WTyr
¶ 'Plum Puddin''	WCot
'Pretty Polly'	EBre MHFP
pringlei	NBro WHil WPer
pubescens	GBri GCHN MHlr
– 'Alba'	CWan GBur WCot WHoo WThi
pulchella	CPBP ESis NFla NGre NTow SSca
– JCA 9508	NMen
'Rachel'	CAbP CBro CGle CRDP CSev EBre EFol EFou EGol EPla GCal LGan LHop LRHS MArl MCLN MMil MUlv NBir NBrk NCat NHol SChu SMac SMrm SPer SPla WGle WHoo WWat
'Raspberry Regal'	NWes WCot WFox
'Red Spangles' ♀	CGle CKel EBre GCHN NBir
'Regal Robe'	WCot
richardsonii	ECED
◆ Rosemary Bloom	See ***H.*** **Rosemary Bloom = 'Heuros'**
rubescens	EDAr ELan EPPr MTho NHar WWin
rubra 'Redstart'	SHel SUsu
'Ruby Ruffles'	WGle
'Ruby Veil'	NWes WCot WGle
'Ruffles'	CRow
§ ***sanguinea***	CGle GCHN MBal NBro NCat NNor NRoo SHel WByw WHal WPer
– 'Alba'	EMon MArl WPbr
– 'Sioux Falls'	EPPr
– 'Splendens'	EPPr GLil
– 'White Cloud' (v)	WHil
'Santa Anna Cardinal'	WCot
'Schneewittchen' (v)	CSte ECha EPPr WMer
'Scintillation' ♀	CB&S CKel EBre ECED ECtt GCHN NCat SRms
'Silver Veil'	CRow
'Snow Storm' (v)	CB&S CDec EBre EFou ELan GCHN GMaP LHop MBar MBel MBri NHar NNrd SMad SPer SUsu WAbe WGle WPbr WWhi
¶ 'Souvenir de Wolley-Dod'	WCot
'Splish Splash'	WGle
'Stormy Seas'	CDec CSpe EGol EHic ELan EPPr LFis LHop MCLN MLLN MMil MSCN NBir NCut NHaw NHol NLak NPri NWes SBid SMad SWat WFox
'Strawberry Swirl'	CDec CSte EHal EHic LHop MLLN MMil NHol NWes SSpi WCot WFox
'Taff's Joy' (v)	CRow EFol EPPr EWes LHop MBel MCLN MNrw NPro SMac WCot
versicolor	GCal
villosa	EBre ECha EGar GCHN MRav WCot
– 'Royal Red'	ECha EGar
'Wendy Hardy'	WCot
¶ 'Widar'	EPPr
'Zabelliana'	GCal NRoo

× HEUCHERELLA (Saxifragaceae)

alba 'Bridget Bloom'	CB&S CDoC CGle CSam CShe ECha ELan GCHN GMaP LGro LHop MBri MRav MUlv NOrc NRoo SPer WHil WHoo WRus
– 'Rosalie'	CBos CDec CElw CFee CGle CMHG CMea EBre ECha EPri MBri MNrw MSte NChi NLak SAxl SLod SOkh SSpe SUsu SWas WAbe WFar WHal WHoo WRus WWhi
'Pink Frost'	WThi
tiarelloides ♀	CMGP CSev EBar EBee EMan EPfP NCat NFai NNor NRoo SOkh SPer WPer WRus
* 'White Blus'	WThi

HEXAGLOTTIS (Iridaceae)

See Plant Deletions

× HIBANOBAMBUSA (Poaceae - Bambusoideae)

tranquillans	EFul EPla SDry WJun
– 'Shiroshima' (v)	CPMA EBee EOas EPla ESOG SDry WCot WJun

HIBBERTIA (Dilleniaceae)

aspera	CGre CPle LHil SAga WWat
§ ***cuneiformis***	CAbb CPle ERea LHil
dentata	SLMG
procumbens	ESis ITim MHig WAbe
§ ***scandens*** ♀	CChu CGre CHEx CPlN CPle ECou ELan ERea GQui LBlm LCns LHil SAga
tetrandra	See ***H. cuneiformis***
volubilis	See ***H. scandens***

HIBISCUS † (Malvaceae)

biseptus	MSto
cardiophyllus	MSto
coccineus	MSte MSto SOWG
hamabo	MSto
huegelii	See ***Alyogyne huegelii***
leopoldii	IOrc SPer SRms
◆ ***manihot***	See ***Abelmoschus manihot***
* ***moesiana***	MBri
moscheutos	CArn CFir CHan MSte MSto WCot
mutabilis	SOWG

paramutabilis	SMad
rosa-sinensis	EBak MBri SLMG SOWG
– 'Casablanca'	MBri
– 'Cooperi'	CHal LChe SOWG
◆– 'Dainty Pink'	See ***H. rosa-sinensis* 'Fantasia'**
§ – 'Dainty White'	LChe
– 'El Capitolio'	SOWG
¶ – 'El Capitolio' sport	LChe
§ – 'Fantasia'	LChe
– 'Full Moon'	LChe
– 'Helene'	ELan MBri
– 'Herm Geller'	LChe
– 'Holiday'	MBri
– 'Kardinal'	MBri
– 'Koeniger'	MBri
– 'La France'	See ***H. rosa-sinensis* 'Fantasia'**
– 'Lemon Chiffon'	LChe
– 'Meteor'	LChe
◆– 'Pink La France'	See ***H. rosa-sinensis* 'Fantasia'**
– 'Rose of China'	MBri
– 'Swan Lake'	See ***H. rosa-sinensis* 'Dainty White'**
¶ – 'Thelma Bennell'	SOWG
– 'Tivoli'	Mbri
– 'Weekend'	LChe Mbri
– 'White La France'	See ***H. rosa-sinensis* 'Dainty White'**
rubis	ELan
sabdariffa	LLew MSal MSto
schizopetalus 🏆	LChe
sinosyriacus 'Lilac Queen'	WBcn
– 'Ruby Glow'	MGos
syriacus	CHEx LPan WNor WOMN
– 'Admiral Dewey'	IOrc SPla
– 'Ardens' (d)	CBlo CEnd ELan IOrc MGos MRav SPer WSel
◆– Blue Bird	See ***H. syriacus* 'Oiseau Bleu'**
– 'Coelestis'	IOrc MGos SPer WSel
– 'Diana' 🏆	EPfP EPla SBid WBcn
– 'Dorothy Crane'	CBlo CEnd EBee ENot WWes
– 'Duc de Brabant' (d)	IOrc NFla SCoo SEas SHBN SPer SRms
– 'Elegantissimus'	See ***H. syriacus* 'Lady Stanley'**
– 'Hamabo' 🏆	CDoC EBee ECle ELan EMil ENot IHos IOrc MBri MGos MRav MWat SBid SHBN SPer SPla WSel WStI
– 'Jeanne d'Arc' (d)	IOrc
§ – 'Lady Stanley' (d)	CHar CMil IOrc NFla SEas SPer SPla
§ – 'Meehanii' (v)	CBot CEnd EAst EBee ELan MAsh MBri MGos SBid SCoo SPla WWeb
– 'Monstrosus'	CBlo IOrc
§ – 'Oiseau Bleu' 🏆	CB&S CDoC CShe CTri ELan EMil ENot EPla IHos IOrc MBri MGos MWat NBee NFla SEas SHBN SPer SPla SReu SSpi WDin WSHC WStI
– Pink Giant™ 🏆	CB&S CEnd CWLN EBee EBre ELan IOrc MGos SBid SPer WDin
– 'Red Heart' 🏆	CDoC CEnd EBee ECle ELan EPfP IOrc MWat SBid SPer SRms WDin WFar WStI WWeb
¶ – 'Roseus Plenus' (d)	NFla
– Russian Violet	CDoC CEnd COtt CWLN ELan IOrc MRav
– 'Speciosus'	IOrc SPer
– 'Totus Albus'	EMil IOrc
– 'Variegatus'	See ***H. syriacus* 'Meehanii'**
– 'William R. Smith'	CBlo CHar EBee ECle ELan ENot IOrc SHBN SPer WWeb WWes
– 'Woodbridge' 🏆	CB&S CEnd CTri ELan EMil ENot EPfP IHos IOrc MBri MGos MRav NFla SEas SHBN SPer SPla SReu SSpi WDin WSel WStI
trionum	CArn CHad CInt CSpe ECou MSCN MSto SLMG SOWG WSan
– 'Spirits Bay'	ECou
– 'Sunny Day'	ELan

HIERACIUM (Asteraceae)

argenteum	WGwy
aurantiacum	See ***Pilosella aurantiaca***
bombycinum	See ***H. mixtum***
brunneocroceum	See ***Pilosella aurantiaca*** subsp. ***carpathicola***
§ ***glaucum***	MTol NHol WByw WEas WWin
§ ***lanatum***	CGle EBar GAul GBin NBir NBro NChi NNrd WEas WPer WWin
maculatum	CInt CRow ECoo EFol EHoe ELan EMar EPar EPla GGar MFir MUlv MWat NCat NPer NSti WOak WPer WWye
murorum	CPea
pilosella	See ***Pilosella officinarum***
praecox	See ***H. glaucum***
scotostictum	EMon LRHS
× ***stoloniflorum***	See ***Pilosella stoloniflora***
variegatum	See ***Hypochaeris variegata***
villosum	CBot CInt CNic CSam EHoe EMil GAul MAvo MDun MSte NBro NNor SIng WCru WHer WPer WWin
waldsteinii	MBro NNor SIng WCru
welwitschii	See ***H. lanatum***

HIEROCHLOE (Poaceae)

odorata	ETPC GPoy NCGP
redolens	ETPC GAbr GAri GFre NCGP

HIMALAYACALAMUS (Poaceae - Bambusoideae)

§ ***falconeri***	EFul EPla SBam
§ – 'Damarapa'	EPla SBam SDix WJun
§ ***hookerianus***	CWLN WJun

× HIPPEASPREKELIA (Amaryllidaceae)

See Plant Deletions

HIPPEASTRUM (Amaryllidaceae)

× ***acramannii***	CMon GCal
advenum BCW 4764	MSto
'Ambiance'	ETub
'Apple Blossom'	ETub LAma NRog
'Baby Star'	ETub
'Beautiful Lady'	LAma
'Bestseller' 🏆	LAma
bifidum	See ***Rhodophiala bifida***
'Byjou'	NRog
'Christmas Gift'	ETub
'Double Record'	ETub
'Dutch Belle'	LAma
elwesii	MSto
– BCW 4999	MSto
'Fantastica'	LAma
'Germa'	ETub

'Green Goddess' ETub
'Jewel' ETub
'Lady Jane' ETub
'Ludwig's Goliath' LAma
'Oskar' NRog
papilio LAma NRog WChr
– 'Butterfly' ETub
'Papillon' ETub LAma
'Pasadena' ETub
'Picotee' LAma
'President Johnson' ETub
'Red Lion' ETub
roseum See ***Rhodophiala rosea***
sp. BCW 5038 MSto
sp. BCW 5154 MSto
'Star of Holland' 🏆 ETub
¶ ***stylosum*** CMon
'United Nations' LAma
'White Dazzler' LAma
'Yellow Pioneer' LAma

HIPPOBROMA See LAURENTIA

HIPPOCREPIS (Papilionaceae)

§ ***comosa*** CKin ECWi EWFC WHil
– 'E.R. Janes' MPla
§ ***emerus*** CChu CMHG CPle CTri EHic ELan ERea GOrc LHop MBal SUsu WCot WHCG WSHC

HIPPOLYTIA (Asteraceae)

§ ***herderi*** CHan EHoe LHop LLWP NBro WCot

HIPPOPHAE (Elaeagnaceae)

rhamnoides 🏆 CB&S CHan CKin CLnd EBre ELan EMil ENot GPoy GRei IHos IOrc LBuc MBar MBlu MWat NWea SPer WDin WFar WGwG WHCG WMou WRTC WStI WWat
– 'Leikora' (f) MGos NFla SPer
– 'Pollmix' (m) MGos NFla SPer
salicifolia CLnd CPle

HIPPURIS (Hippuridaceae)

vulgaris CBen CRDP ECWi EHon EMFW MHew WMAq WWye

HIRPICIUM (Asteraceae)

See Plant Deletions

HISTIOPTERIS (Dennstaedtiaceae)

incisa CFil

HOHERIA † (Malvaceae)

§ ***angustifolia*** CBot CChu CHan ECou
'Borde Hill' CChu SBid SPer SSpi SSta WHCG
glabrata 🏆 CB&S CBot CChu CPle ECou MBal
'Glory of Amlwch' 🏆 CAbb CChu CFil CGre CMHG CSam GCal SBid SSpi SSta WCru WSHC
§ ***lyallii*** 🏆 CB&S CDoC CSam ECou ELan IOrc SHBN SSta WDin
microphylla See ***H. angustifolia***
populnea CBot
sexstylosa 🏆 CAbb CBot CDoC CFee CGre CHid CPle ELan EPfP EPla IOrc ISea MBlu SPer SSta WOMN
– 'Pendula' CB&S
– 'Stardust' 🏆 CFil CKni CPMA CSte LRHS SMad SPer SReu SSpi WWat

HOLBOELLIA (Lardizabalaceae)

coriacea CBot CChu CPlN CSam SArc SBra WCru
latifolia CGre COtt CPlN CSam CTri EHic SArc WCot WCru WSHC WWat
¶ – SF 95134 ISea

HOLCUS (Poaceae)

lanatus CKin
mollis 'Albovariegatus' Widely available

HOLODISCUS (Rosaceae)

discolor CFil CGre CPle ELan EPla EWes GCal GOrc MBlu MTis NFla SBid SHBN SSpi SSta WHCG WSHC
dumosus CPle

HOMALOCLADIUM (Polygonaceae)

§ ***platycladum*** CHal

HOMALOTHECA (Asteraceae)

See Plant Deletions

HOMERIA (Iridaceae)

breyniana See ***H. collina***
– var. ***aurantiaca*** See ***H. flaccida***
§ ***collina*** CFee ETub SLMG SMrm
§ ***flaccida*** LAma LBow NRog
marlothii CMon
ochroleuca LAma LBow NRog

HOMOGLOSSUM See GLADIOLUS

HOMOGYNE (Asteraceae)

alpina NGar SIng

HOOKERIA (Hookeriaceae)

See Plant Deletions

HORDEUM (Poaceae)

jubatum CArc CCuc CFee CInt EHoe ESOG ETPC EWes GAri GBin NChi NSti SLod WWhi

HORKELIA (Rosaceae)

See Plant Deletions

HORMINUM (Lamiaceae)

pyrenaicum CNic ELan GDra MBro MFir MHig NGre NMen SAlw SBar SBla SRms SSmi WCla WHil WPat WPer WPyg WWin
– pale blue MSte

HOSTA † (Hostaceae)

¶ 'Abba Dabba Do' (v) CBdn EGol
'Abby' CBdn EGol LHos
'Abiqua Ariel' SApp
'Abiqua Blue Krinkles' SApp

¶ 'Abiqua Drinking Gourd'	EGol GSki
¶ 'Abiqua Moonbeam' (v)	CBdn
¶ 'Abiqua Recluse'	EGol
¶ 'Abiqua Trumpet' (*tokudama*)	EGol
aequinoctiiantha	EGol LHos
'Aksarben'	EMic
'Alba' (*sieboldiana*)	See ***H.* 'Elegans Alba' (*sieboldiana*)**
albomarginata	See ***H.* 'Paxton's Original' (*sieboldii*)**
'Albomarginata' (*fortunei*)	CB&S CBdn CWGN EGol EMic EPGN LFis MBar MOne NBir NFai SPer WHoo
'Allan P. McConnell' (v)	EGol EMic EPGN LHos NHar SApp
'Alpine Aire'	EMic
'Amanuma'	EGol EMic NWes
'Amber Maiden' (v)	EGol LHos
'Antioch' (*fortunei*) (v)	CBdn EGol EMic MMiN MRav SApp
'Aoki' (*fortunei*)	EMic EPGN NHol NWes
'Aphrodite' (*plantaginea*) (d)	EGol EPGN LRHS
'Apple Green'	EMic
'Aqua Velva'	EGol
'Argentea Variegata' (*undulata*)	See ***H. undulata* var. *undulata***
'Aspen Gold' (*tokudama* hybrid)	EMic
'August Moon'	CBdn CBro CKel CMHG CSam CWGN EBre EFou EGol EJap ELan EMic EOrc EPGN LHos MBar MMiN MUlv NBee NFai NOrc SApp SPer SPla WCra WFox WHoo WWat
I 'Aurea' (*nakaiana*)	NWoo
'Aurea' (*sieboldii*)	See ***H. sieboldii* f. *subcrocea***
aureafolia	See ***H.* 'Starker Yellow Leaf'**
'Aureoalba' (*fortunei*)	See ***H.* 'Spinners'**
'Aureomaculata' (*fortunei*)	See ***H. fortunei* var. *albopicta***
§ 'Aureomarginata' (*montana*)	CBdn EBre EGol EHoe EMic EPGN GAri MMiN NHol NWes SApp SCro SPla SSpi WRus WWoo
§ 'Aureomarginata' (*ventricosa*) 🏆	CBdn CBro CHad EBre ECha EGol EMic EPGN MBro NRoo SAxl SPer SRms WHil Wrus
'Aureostriata' (*tardiva*)	See ***H.* 'Inaho'**
'Aurora Borealis' (*sieboldiana*) (v)	EGol EPGN LHos
'Azure Snow'	EGol
'Banyai's Dancing Girl'	EMic
'Barbara White'	EGol
bella	See ***H. fortunei* var. *obscura***
'Bennie McRae'	EGol
'Betcher's Blue'	EGol EMic
'Betsy King'	EMic EPGN LBuc LHos MRav WMer
¶ 'Bette Davis Eyes'	EGol
¶ 'Betty'	EGol
'Big Boy' (*montana*)	EGol
'Big Daddy' (*sieboldiana* hybrid)	Widely available
'Big Mama' (*sieboldiana* hybrid)	EGol EMic LHos LRHS
¶ 'Bill Brincka' (v)	EGol
§ 'Birchwood Parky's Gold'	CBdn CHan EGol EMic EPGN LHos MMiN NHar NHol SApp SAxl SRms SSpi SWas
'Birchwood Ruffled Queen'	EGol EMic
¶ 'Black Beauty'	EPGN
§ 'Blonde Elf'	EGol EMic EPGN LHos
'Blue Angel' (*sieboldiana*) 🏆	CB&S CBdn EBre ECha EGol EHoe ELan EMic EOrc EPGN LFis LHos MBal MBro MMiN MWat NOrc NTay SApp SMrm
'Blue Arrow'	CBdn EGol
'Blue Boy'	CBdn CHad CSte EGol EMic EPGN LHos MMiN NHol
'Blue Cadet'	CBdn CHad EAst ECha EGol EMic GSki MBar MMiN NCat NCut WCra
'Blue Edger'	CBdn Echa
'Blue Heart' (*sieboldiana* var. *elegans*)	ECha EMic
'Blue Jay'	EGol
'Blue Lake'	SMrm
'Blue Mammoth' (*sieboldiana*)	CBdn EGol EMic EPGN SApp
'Blue Seer' (*sieboldiana*)	CBdn EGol
'Blue Shadows' (*tokudama*) (v)	LHos
'Blue Umbrellas' (*sieboldiana* hybrid)	CBdn EBre EFou EGol EJap ELan EMic EOrc EPGN GSki LHos MMiN NHol NWes SApp
'Blue Velvet'	CBdn
'Blue Vision'	EMic EPGN LHos
'Bold Ribbons' (v)	CBdn EGol EMic LHos NWes
'Bold Ruffles' (*sieboldiana*)	EGol LRHS SApp
'Bonanza' (*fortunei*)	EMic
¶ 'Border Bandit' (v)	EGol
'Borsch 1'	CBdn
'Borwick Beauty' (*sieboldiana*) (v)	CBdn MMiN
'Bountiful'	EGol EMic
'Bouquet'	EGol
'Bressingham Blue'	CBdn EBre ECtt EGol EMic LHos NDea NMir SAxl SPer
'Bright Lights' (*tokudama*) (v)	CBdn EGol EMic EPGN LHos
'Brim Cup' (v)	CBdn EGol EMic EPGN LHos MMiN
'Brooke'	EGol EMic
'Bruce's Blue'	EGol GSki
'Buckshaw Blue'	CBdn EGol EMic EPGN GBin MBal MMiN NBir NTay SApp SAxl SSpi WCot
'Butter Rim' (*sieboldii*) (v)	EGol
'Camouflage'	ECha
'Candy Hearts'	CBdn CHan EGol EMic EPGN MMiN SApp WMer
capitata MSF 850	CFil WPGP
caput-avis	See ***H. kikutii* var. *caput-avis***
¶ 'Carnival' (v)	CBdn
'Carol' (*fortunei*) (v)	CBdn EGol EMic EPGN LHos MMiN SApp
'Carrie' (*sieboldii*) (v)	EGol EMic
'Celebration' (v)	EGol ELan EMic EPGN LBuc LHos MRPP
'Challenger'	EMic
'Change of Tradition' (v)	EMic
¶ 'Chantilly Lace' (v)	EGol
'Chartreuse Wiggles' (*sieboldii*)	CBdn EGol LHos SApp
'Cheatin Heart' (v)	EGol
'Chelsea Babe' (v)	EGol LHos
'Chinese Sunrise' (*cathayana*) (v)	CBdn EGol EMic EPGN MMiN NHol SCro WHil WMer
'Chiquita'	EGol LHos
'Chôkô Nishiki' (*montana*) (v)	CBdn EGol EPGN MMiN

'Christmas Tree' (v)	CBdn EGol EMic EPGN LHos LRHS NWes
¶ 'Citation' (v)	EGol
'Clarence'	CBdn
clausa	EMic
– var. ***normalis***	CBdn EBre EGol EMic GCal GQui LHos MCli*
'Color Glory' (*sieboldiana*) (v)	CBdn EGol EPGN LHos MMiN
'Colossal'	EGol EMic LRHS
'County Park'	EGol
'Cream Delight' (*undulata*)	See ***H. undulata*** var. ***undulata***
'Cream Edge'	See ***H. 'Fisher Cream Edge' (fortunei)***
'Crepe Suzette' (v)	EGol LHos LRHS
'Crested Reef'	EGol EMic
§ ***crispula*** 🏆	CB&S CBdn CHad CRow EGol EHon EMic EOrc EPGN EPar GGar LGro LHos MBal MBar NFai SChu SHig SRms SSpi WTyr
'Crown Jewel' (v)	EMic EPGN LHos SApp
'Crown Prince'	CBdn EGol EMic
§ 'Crowned Imperial' (*fortunei*) (v)	CBdn EMic EPGN NHol
'Crusader' (v)	CBdn EGol LHos
¶ 'Cupid's Dart' (v)	EGol
'Dawn'	EGol LHos
'Daybreak'	CBdn EGol EPGN LRHS
decorata	CBdn EBre EGol EMic LHos MBar MCli
'Delia'	EPGN
'Devon Gold'	CBdn
'Devon Green'	CBdn EPGN SApp WRus
'Devon Mist'	CBdn NWes
'Devon Tor'	CBdn EPGN NWes
¶ 'Dew Drop' (v)	CBdn EGol
'Diamond Tiara' (v)	CBdn EGol LHos LRHS SApp
'Dimple'	ECha
'Don Stevens' (v)	EGol
'Dorothy'	EMic
'Dorset Blue'	EGol EMic EPGN GSki
'Doubloons'	EGol LHos LRHS
'Drummer Boy'	EGol EMic MGan
'Duchess'	LHos
'DuPage Delight' (*sieboldiana*) (v)	CBdn EGol LHos
'El Capitan' (v)	CBdn EGol EPGN LRHS
§ ***elata***	EBre EGol EMic ISea MCli MMiN MUlv NWes WWat
'Elatior' (*nigrescens*)	EMic
'Eldorado'	See ***H. 'Frances Williams' (sieboldiana)***
'Elegans'	See ***H. sieboldiana*** var. ***elegans***
§ 'Elegans Alba' (*sieboldiana*)	EGol
'Elfin Power' (*sieboldii*) (v)	EGol
'Elisabeth'	CBdn EAst LBuc
'Elizabeth Campbell' (*fortunei*) (v)	EMic EPGN LHos MMiN MSte SSpi
'Ellen'	EMic
'Ellerbroek' (*fortunei*) (v)	EGol EMic GSki MMiN
¶ 'Elsley Runner'	EGol
'Emerald Carpet'	EMic
'Emerald Skies'	EGol
'Emerald Tiara' (v)	CBdn EGol EPGN LRHS
'Emily Dickinson' (v)	EGol LRHS
'Eric Smith Gold'	ECha
¶ 'Evelyn McCafferty' (*tokudama* hybrid)	EGol
'Evening Magic' (v)	EGol EMic EPGN LHos
'Excitation'	EGol EMic
'Fair Maiden' (v)	EGol

'Fall Bouquet' (*longipes hypoglauca*)	EGol
'Fall Emerald'	CBdn EMic
¶ 'Fantastic' (*sieboldiana* hybrid)	EGol
'Feather Boa'	EMic EPGN NHar SApp
* 'Fenman's Fascination'	EMic
§ 'Fisher Cream Edge' (*fortunei*)	CBdn WMer
'Floradora'	CBdn EGol EMic EPGN
'Flower Power'	EGol LHos LRHS
fluctuans	EMic
¶ 'Fond Hope' (*sieboldiana*)	MMiN
'Fool's Gold' (*fortunei*)	CBdn EMic SApp Wmer
'Formal Attire' (*sieboldiana* hybrid) (v)	EGol
'Forncett Frances' (v)	EGol LHos
'Fortis'	See ***H. undulata*** var. ***erromena***
fortunei	CBdn CHad CMHG CRow CWGN EGol EMic EOrc MBal NDea NHol SChu SPer WEas WGwG
§ – var. ***albopicta*** 🏆	CBdn CBro CGle CRow CShe EGol EHoe EHon ELan EMic ENot EOrc EPGN LBuc LGro LHos MBal MBri MMiN NDea NHar NHol NRoo SApp SHig SMad SPer WEas WRus
§ – – f. ***aurea*** 🏆	CHad CMGP CMHG CRow ECha EGol EHoe ELan EPGN EPla GMaP LHyd MBal SChu SCro SPer SPla WHil WRus
¶ – – – dwarf form	EMic
– f. ***aurea***	See ***H. fortunei*** var. ***albopicta*** f. ***aurea***
§ – var. ***aureomarginata*** 🏆	Widely available
– var. ***gigantea***	See ***H. montana***
§ – var. ***hyacinthina*** 🏆	CBdn CGle CHad EGol EMic EOrc EPGN GCal GGar MBal MBar MMiN NBus NCut NDea NOrc SSpi WFox WRHF Wwin body
§ – var. ***obscura***	CBdn ECho EGol EMic LHos LHyd
– var. ***rugosa***	EMic
'Fountain'	NHol
'Fragrant Blue'	CBdn EGol
'Fragrant Bouquet' (v)	CBdn EGol EMic EPGN LHos
'Fragrant Gold'	EGol EMic EPGN LHos SApp
'Francee' (*fortunei*) (v) 🏆	CB&S CBdn CBro EBar EBre EGol EJap ELan EMic EOrc EPGN LHos MBal MBri MUlv MWat NBro NFai NHar NHol NSti SApp SChu SPer SPla SUsu WCra WRus WWat
§ 'Frances Williams' (*sieboldiana*) (v) 🏆	Widely available
'Frances Williams Improved' (*sieboldiana*) (v)	EGol MMiN
'Fresh' (v)	EGol EPGN LHos
'Fringe Benefit' (v)	CBdn EBre EGol EMic EPGN LHos MMiN NHar NWes WMer
'Frosted Jade' (v)	CBdn EGol EMic EPGN LHos LRHS NWes SApp
'Gaiety' (v)	EGol EMic
¶ 'Gala' (v)	EMic EPGN
¶ 'Gay Blade' (v)	EGol
'Geisha' (v)	CBdn EGol EPGN LHos
'Gene's Joy'	EPGN LHos
◆ 'Gigantea' (*sieboldiana*)	See ***H. elata***

'Gilt Edge' (*sieboldiana*) (v)	EMic
'Ginko Craig' (v)	CAbb CBdn CBro CHad CRow EAst EBre ECha EFou EGol EHoe EJap ELan EOrc EPGN LHos MRPP MRav NBee NHar NHol NOak NSti NTay SApp SPer WAbe WHil WWat
glauca	See ***H. sieboldiana*** var. ***elegans***
* 'Glauca' (*fortunei*)	MMiN
'Gloriosa' (*fortunei*) (v)	EGol EMic EPGN MMiN
'Gold Drop'	CBdn ECho EGol EMic EPGN LHos MMiN NHol
'Gold Edger'	Widely available
'Gold Flush' (*ventricosa*)	EMic
§ 'Gold Haze' (*fortunei*)	CHad EGol EMic EOrc EPGN NHol NTay
'Gold Leaf' (*fortunei*)	EGol
'Gold Regal'	CBdn EGol EMic MMiN
'Gold Standard' (*fortunei*) (v)	CBdn CBos EBre ECha EGol ELan EMic EPGN EPla GMaP LGre LHos MMiN MWat NFai NRoo NTay SApp SChu SSpe SSpi WRus
'Goldbrook' (*fortunei*) (v)	EGol WBcn
'Goldbrook Genie'	EGol
'Goldbrook Glamour' (v)	EGol
'Goldbrook Gold'	EGol
'Goldbrook Grace'	EGol
'Goldbrook Gratis' (v)	EGol
'Goldbrook Grayling'	EGol
'Goldbrook Grebe'	EGol
'Golden Age'	See ***H.* 'Gold Haze' (*fortunei*)**
'Golden Anniversary'	CBdn EMic
'Golden Bullion' (*tokudama*)	CBdn EGol EMic
'Golden Circles'	See ***H.* 'Frances Williams' (*sieboldiana*)**
¶ 'Golden Decade'	EGol
'Golden Isle'	EGol EMic
'Golden Medallion' (*tokudama*)	CBdn CBro CTri EBar EBre EGol EJap ELan EMic EOrc EPGN LHos MBel MMiN NFai NHol NSti SApp WWat
'Golden' (*nakaiana*)	See ***H.* 'Birchwood Parky's Gold'**
'Golden Nakaiana'	See ***H.* 'Birchwood Parky's Gold'**
'Golden Prayers' (*tokudama*)	CAbb CBdn CBro CHad EGol ELan EMic EOrc EPGN ERos LGre LHos MMiN MRPP MRav NBro NFai NHol NOrc NSti NTay SApp SChu SPer SSpi WAbe WHow WRus
'Golden Scepter' (*nakaiana*)	CBdn EGol EMic EPGN SApp
'Golden Sculpture' (*sieboldiana*)	CBdn EGol
'Golden Spider'	EGol EMic
'Golden Sunburst' (*sieboldiana*)	CBdn CHad EGol EJap ELan EMic EPGN GGar LHos MBal MMiN MOne NEgg NHol
'Golden Tiara' (v) 🏆	Widely available
'Goldsmith'	EGol EMic
'Good as Gold'	EMic EPGN LHos
gracillima	CRow EPGN EPar LHyd NGre NHar
'Granary Gold' (*fortunei*)	EGol EPGN LHos LRHS
'Grand Master'	EGol EMic EPGN LHos
¶ 'Grand Tiara' (v)	EPGN
'Great Expectations' (*sieboldiana*) (v)	CBdn EBar EGol EPGN LHos LRHS SApp WRus
'Green Acres' (*montana*)	EMic
¶ 'Green Angel'	EGol
'Green Fountain' (*kikutii*)	CBdn EGol EMic EPGN LHos MMiN SApp
'Green Gold' (*fortunei*) (v)	CBdn EMic MMiN WMer
'Green Piecrust'	CBdn EGol EMic EPGN
'Green Sheen'	EGol EMic EPGN LHos SApp
'Green Velveteen'	EGol
'Green with Envy' (v)	EGol
'Greenwood'	EMic
'Ground Master' (v)	CBdn CBro COtt EBre ECha ECtt EGol EJap ELan EMic EOrc EPGN GMaP GSki LHos MBri MRav NBro NFai NHol NRoo NSti SApp SAxl SMad SPer SPla WAbe WRus
'Ground Sulphur'	EGol EMic
¶ 'Guacamole' (v)	CBdn EGol
'Gum Drop'	EMic
'Hadspen Samphire'	CHad CHan EGol EMic EPGN
'Hadspen Seersucker'	CHad SLod
'Hadspen White' (*fortunei*)	EMic LHos
'Haku-chu-han' (*sieboldii*) (v)	CBdn
'Hakujima' (*sieboldii*)	EGol LGre
'Happy Hearts'	EGol EMic MMiN
'Harrison'	EMic
'Harvest Glow'	EGol EMic
* 'Hazel'	EMic
'Heartleaf'	EBre EMic
'Heartsong' (v)	EGol LHos
¶ 'Heideturm'	EGol LHos
'Helen Doriot' (*sieboldiana*)	EGol EMic LRHS
'Helen Field Fischer' (*fortunei*)	CBdn EMic
helonioides f. ***albopicta*** hort.	See ***H. rohdeifolia***
'Herifu' (v)	CBdn EGol EMic
'Hirao Majesty'	EGol
'Hirao Supreme'	EGol
'Hoarfrost'	EMic
'Holstein'	See ***H.* 'Halcyon' (Tardiana Group)**
§ 'Honeybells' 🏆	CB&S CBdn CBro CHad CKel CMHG CRow EBre ECha EGol EJap ELan EMic EOrc EPGN LHos LHyd LPBA MBal MBar MMiN NHol NRoo NSti NTay SAxl SPer SSpi WFox WHoo
'Honeysong' (v)	CBdn EPGN
¶ 'Hoosier Harmony' (v)	EGol
¶ 'Hyacinthina Variegata' (*fortunei*)	CMHG
'Hydon Gleam'	EMic EPGN LHos
'Hydon Sunset' (*nakaiana*)	CBdn CHan CMHG EBre EGol EMic EOrc EPGN LHyd MBal MHig MMiN NFai NHol NOak NOrc NSti NTay SAxl WAbe WHoo WWat
hypoleuca	EGol NGre WDav
§ 'Inaho'	EGol EMic EPGN LHos MMiN NWes
'Inniswood' (*montana*) (v)	CBdn EGol EPGN LHos MMiN NWes
'Invincible'	CBdn EFou EGol EMic EPGN LHos MMiN NWes
'Iona' (*fortunei*)	CBdn EGol EMic EPGN LHos SSpi
'Irish Breeze'	EPGN
'Iron Gate Glamor'	EGol EPGN LHos
¶ 'Iron Gate Supreme' (v)	EMic
¶ 'Iwa Soules'	EGol
¶ 'Jade Beauty'	CBdn

'Jade Cascade'	CMil CSte EGol NWes SApp WCot
'Jade Scepter' (*nakaiana*)	EGol EMic LRHS
¶ 'Jadette' (v)	EGol
'Janet' (*fortunei*) (v)	CBdn EGol EMic EOrc WMer
'Japan Boy'	See ***H.* 'Montreal'**
'Japan Girl'	See ***H.* 'Mount Royal' (*sieboldii*)**
'Joker' (*fortunei*) (v)	CBdn
¶ 'Jolly Green Giant' (*sieboldiana* hybrid)	EMic
'Journeyman'	EBre EGol LHos
'Julie Morss'	CBdn EGol EMic EPGN LHos MMiN
'Jumbo' (*sieboldiana*)	EMic
¶ 'June Beauty' (*sieboldiana*)	MMiN
'Just So' (v)	CBdn EGol LHos
'Kabitan'	See ***H. sieboldii* f. *kabitan***
'Kelly'	SApp
'Kelsey'	EMic
'Kifukurin' (*kikutii*) (v)	CBdn
I 'Kifukurin' (*pulchella*) (v)	Egol
'Kifukurin Ubatake' (*pulchella*)	EPGN
kikutii	EGol EMic NGre
§ – var. ***caput-avis***	EBre EGol EMic
– var. ***polyneuron***	EGol
¶ – var. ***tosana***	EGol
§ – var. ***yakusimensis***	CRDP EGol EMic GDra SMad
§ 'Kirishima'	CBdn CSev EMic EPGN NHar SIng
kiyosumiensis	CRow NHol
'Klopping Variegated' (*fortunei*)	EGol EMic
'Knave's Green'	EPGN
'Knockout' (v)	CBdn EGol EPGN LHos
'Krinkled Joy'	EMic NWes
'Krossa Regal' ♀	Widely available*
'Lady Helen'	EMic MMiN
'Lady Isobel Barnett' (v)	SApp
'Lakeside Symphony' (v)	EGol LHos
§ ***lancifolia*** ♀	CBdn CBro CHad CHan CKel CMHG CRow CWGN EBre ECha EGol EJap ELan EMic EPGN GMaP LFis LGro LHos LHyd MBal NHol NSti SAxl SPer SSpi WDav WFox WGwG WWat
'Leather Sheen'	EGol EMic EPGN
¶ 'Lee Armiger' (*tokudama* hybrid)	EGol
'Lemon Delight'	CBdn EPGN LHos
'Lemon Lime'	CBdn CWGN EGol EMic EPGN EPPr LHos MMiN SApp SIng WMer
'Leola Fraim' (v)	CBdn EGol EPGN LHos
'Leviathan'	EMic
* ***lilacina***	SCro
'Little Aurora' (*tokudama* hybrid)	EGol EMic EPGN MBal SIng
'Little Blue' (*ventricosa*)	EGol EMic SLod
¶ 'Little Fatty'	MMiN
'Little Razor'	EGol
'Little White Lines' (v)	EGol EMic EPGN LHos LRHS
'Little Wonder' (v)	EGol
longipes	EGol
longissima	EGol EPGN LHyd WCru
– var. ***longissima***	LHyd
'Louisa' (*sieboldii*) (v)	ECha EGol EPGN LHos MSte NNrd
'Love Pat' (*tokudama*) ♀	CBdn EGol EMic EPGN GSki LHos NWes

'Lucky Charm'	EMic MMiN
'Lunar Eclipse' (v)	EGol EMic EPGN LGre MMiN
'Maculata Aurea'	SCro
'Maekawa'	EGol
N 'Marginata Alba' (*fortunei*)	CBot CHad ECha LPBA MMiN NDea WWin
'Marilyn'	EGol EMic EPGN LHos LRHS
¶ 'Marquis' (*nakaiana* hybrid)	EGol
'Mary Jo'	EMic
'Mary Marie Ann' (*fortunei*) (v)	EMic EPGN
¶ 'Maruba' (*longipes* var. *latifolia*)	EGol
§ 'Masquerade' (v)	CBdn EGol EPGN LHos NHar
'Mediovariegata' (*undulata*)	See ***H. undulata* var. *undulata***
'Mentor Gold'	EGol EMic
'Mesa Fringe' (*montana*)	CBdn
* 'Metallic Sheen'	LHos
'Midas Touch' (*tokudama* hybrid)	CBdn EGol EJap EMic EPGN NBus NHol WRus
'Middle Ridge'	EMic
¶ 'Midwest Magic' (v)	CBdn EGol LHos
'Mildred Seaver'	CBdn EGol EMic LHos LRHS NWes
'Minnie Klopping'	EMic
§ ***minor***	CBro EBre EGol ELan EMic EPot ERos GDra MTho NHol NTow SSpi WAbe WOMN
– f. ***alba*** hort.	See ***H. sieboldii* var. *alba***
– Goldbrook form	EGol
'Minor' (*ventricosa*)	See ***H. minor***
* 'Minuta' (*undulata*)	CBdn WMer
'Misty Waters' (*sieboldiana*)	EMic
'Moerheim' (*fortunei*) (v)	CBdn EGol EMic EPGN EPar LHos MBar MBri MMiN NHol SChu WMer
monatana 'Mount Fuji'	MMiN
N ***montana***	CBdn CBlo CHad ECha EGol EMic MMiN NHol
§ 'Montreal'	EMic
'Moon Glow' (v)	EGol EMic EPGN LHos LRHS
¶ 'Moon River' (v)	EGol EPGN
'Moonlight' (*fortunei*) (v)	CBdn EGol EMic LRHS MMiN
'Moscow Blue'	EGol
* 'Mount Hope' (v)	EGol
'Mount Kirishima' (*sieboldii*)	See ***H.* 'Kirishima'**
§ 'Mount Royal' (*sieboldii*)	EMic
'Mountain Snow' (*montana*) (v)	CBdn EGol EMic EPGN LHos
nakaiana	WWat
'Nakaimo'	EMic NHol
'Nameoki'	NHol
'Nana' (*ventricosa*)	See ***H. minor***
§ 'Nancy Lindsay' (*fortunei*) (v)	CBdn EBee EGol EMic EPGN LHos SApp SChu SHam SMrm
'Neat Splash' (v)	CBdn
'Neat Splash Rim' (v)	EMic
'New Wave'	EGol
¶ 'Night before Christmas' (v)	EGol
nigrescens	EGol EMic EPGN GCal LHos LRHS NGre SApp
'Nokogiryama'	EGol EMic
'North Hills' (*fortunei*) (v)	CBdn EBee EGol EMic EPGN LHos MMiN NBir NWes SChu SMrm WWat
'Northern Halo' (*sieboldiana*) (v)	EGol ELan EMic LHos LRHS MMiN
'Northern Lights' (*sieboldiana*)	EGol LHos LRHS

'Northern Sunray' (*sieboldiana*) (v)	EMic
'Obscura Marginata' (*fortunei*)	See ***H. fortunei*** var. ***aureomarginata***
'Okazuki Special'	CBdn EGol
'Olga's Shiny Leaf'	EGol EMic
'Oriana' (*fortunei*)	CBdn EGol EMic
'Oxheart'	EMic
pachyscapa	EMic
'Pacific Blue Edger'	EFou EGol EPGN SApp
'Pastures Green'	EGol
'Pastures New'	EFou EGol EMic EPGN LHos MOne NHol SApp
'Patriot' (v)	CBdn CSte EBar EGol EPGN LHos LRHS NWes SApp WFar
'Paul's Glory' (v)	EGol EMic LHos MMiN
§ 'Paxton's Original' (*sieboldii*) (v) 🏆	CMGP EBre ECha EGol EPGN LHyd MBal MBar MRav SApp SRms WPer
'Peace' (v)	EGol EPGN LHos
'Pearl Lake'	CBdn CSte EGol EMic EPGN LGre MMiN NHol NTay NWes
'Peedee Gold Flash'	CBdn EPGN LHos NHar
'Pelham Blue Tump'	EGol
'Perry's True Blue'	EMic
'Peter Pan'	EGol EMic
¶ 'Phoenix'	EGol
'Phyllis Campbell' (*fortunei*)	See ***H.* 'Sharmon' (*fortunei*)**
'Picta' (*fortunei*)	See ***H. fortunei*** var. ***albopicta***
'Piedmont Gold'	EBre EGol EMic EPGN LGre MMiN MSte NTay
'Pineapple Poll'	CBdn EMic EPGN LHos LRHS MMiN NWes SApp
'Pizzazz' (v)	CBdn EGol EPGN LHos
plantaginea	CBdn CWGN EBee EGol EMic EPar SSpi
– var. ***grandiflora***	See ***H. plantaginea*** var. ***japonica***
§ – var. ***japonica***	CBot CGle CHad CHan EBre ECha EPGN EPar MOne NBus SChu WWat
'Platinum Tiara' (*nakaiana*) (v)	CBdn LHos SApp
¶ 'Pooh Bear' (v)	EGol
'Popo'	EGol
'Potomac Pride'	EPGN
'Puck'	EGol
'Purple Dwarf'	EGol LBuc NHol WCra WFox
'Purple Profusion'	EGol EMic
pycnophylla	EGol SWas
¶ 'Queen Josephine' (v)	EGol
'Radiant Edger' (v)	CBdn EGol EPGN LHos LRHS
'Raleigh Remembrance'	EGol LHos LRHS
¶ 'Rascal' (v)	CBdn EGol
¶ 'Raspberry Sorbet'	EGol
rectifolia	CMHG EMic LHos
'Regal Splendor' (v)	CBdn EGol EMic EPGN GSki LHos
'Resonance' (v)	EBre EMic EPGN LHos LRHS MMiN NTay
'Reversed' (v)	CBdn EGol ELan EMic EPGN LHos WRus
¶ 'Rhapsody' (*fortunei*) (v)	EGol
'Richland Gold' (*fortunei*)	EGol EMic LRHS
* 'Rippling Waters'	EGol
'Rippling Waves'	EMic
'Robusta' (*fortunei*)	See ***H. sieboldiana*** var. ***elegans***
§ ***rohdeifolia*** (v)	EGol EMic LBuc
§ – f. ***albopicta***	CBdn EGol ELan EPGN EPar NHol SChu
'Rosemoor'	EGol SApp
'Rough Waters'	SApp
§ 'Royal Standard' 🏆	Widely available
'Royalt'	EGol LHos
rupifraga	EGol EMic SApp
'Russell's Form' (*ventricosa*)	EMic
'Ryan's Big One'	EMic
§ 'Sagae' 🏆	CBdn CSte EBre EGol EMic LRHS NWes SApp
§ 'Saishu Jima' (*sieboldii spathulata*)	EGol NHol WCru
'Samual Blue'	EMic
'Samurai' (*sieboldiana*) (v)	CBdn EGol EMic LHos MRav
'Sazanami' (*crispula*)	See ***H. crispula***
'Sea Bunny'	EGol
'Sea Dream' (v)	CBdn EGol EMic EPGN LHos SApp
'Sea Drift'	EGol EPGN
'Sea Fire'	EGol
'Sea Gold Star'	EGol EPGN LRHS
'Sea Lotus Leaf'	EGol EMic EPGN LRHS
'Sea Monster'	EGol LRHS
'Sea Octopus'	EGol EMic SApp
'Sea Sapphire'	EGol LHos LRHS
'Sea Sprite' (v)	EPGN LBuc LHos MRPP
¶ 'Sea Thunder' (v)	EGol
'Sea Yellow Sunrise'	EGol EMic SApp
'See Saw' (*undulata*)	CBdn EGol EMic
¶ 'Sentinels'	MMiN
'September Sun' (v)	CBdn EGol EMic EPGN LHos LRHS SApp
'Serendipity'	CBdn EGol EMic EPGN LHos
'Shade Fanfare' (v) 🏆	CBdn CBro CHid EBar EBre ECha EGol EJap ELan EMic EOrc EPGN EPar LHos MBal MBri MMiN MRav MWat NFai NSti NTay SCro SPer WHil WHoo
'Shade Master'	CBlo EBre EGol EMic GBin MMil MOne NHol
§ 'Sharmon' (*fortunei*) (v)	CBdn EGol EMic MMiN NHol NTay NWes SChu SPer
¶ 'Shelleys' (*kikutii*) (v)	EGol
'Sherborne Swift'	CBdn EGol EMic MMiN
'Shining Tot'	EGol EPGN LHos
'Shogun' (v)	EGol LHos
* 'Showboat'	CBdn EPGN
sieboldiana	CHad CHan CMHG CRow CShe EBar EGol ELan EMic EOrc EPar EPot LFis LHos LHyd MBal MMiN NHol NNor SPer WAbe WWat
§ – var. ***elegans*** 🏆	Widely available
¶ – var. ***mira***	MMiN
§ ***sieboldii*** var. ***alba***	CHad CHan CMGP CSte EGol ELan SSpi
§ – f. ***kabitan*** (v)	CBdn EGol EPGN LHos MHig NHar
– f. ***shiro-kabitan*** (v)	EGol EPGN
– var. ***thunbergiana***	See ***H. sieboldii* f. *spathulata***
* 'Silver Chimes'	WHil
'Silver Lance' (v)	EGol EMic EPGN
¶ 'Sitting Pretty' (v)	EGol
'Snow Cap' (v)	CBdn EGol EPGN LHos NWes
'Snow Crust' (*elata*) (v)	CBdn EGol EMic LRHS
¶ 'Snow Flakes' (*sieboldii*)	CBdn EGol EMic EMil EPGN GCal LHos MBar MBri MCli NFla NHol NPro SLod SPer WMer

'Snowden'	CBdn CHad EBre ECha EGol EMic EPGN GMaP LHos MBal MMiN NBir NHol NTay SApp SCro SSpi WHoo WRus WWat
'So Sweet'	CBdn CSte EGol EMic EPGN LHos SApp
¶ 'Something Blue'	LHos
¶ sp. from Japan	EPPr
¶ 'Sparkling Burgundy'	CBdn EGol
'Special Gift'	EGol EMic
§ 'Spinners' (*fortunei*) (v)	CBdn CHad ECha EGol EMic MMiN SChu SSpi
'Sprengeri'	MMiN
'Spritzer' (v)	CBdn EGol EMic EPGN LHos
'Squash Edge' (*sieboldiana*) (v)	EPGN
'Squiggles' (v)	EGol LHos
§ 'Starker Yellow Leaf'	EMic
'Stiletto' (v)	CBdn EGol EPGN LHos NHar SApp
'Sugar and Cream' (v)	CBdn EGol EMic EPGN LHos MMiN NWes SApp
'Sugar Plum Fairy' (*gracillima*)	EGol
'Sum and Substance' ♀	CB&S CBdn CHad CSte EAst EBre EGol ELan EMic EPGN GBin GMaP MMiN MOne MRav MUlv NBro NEgg NTay NWes SApp WCot
'Summer Fragrance'	CBdn EGol EMic EPGN LHos LRHS SApp
'Summer Music' (v)	CBdn EPGN LHos
¶ 'Summer Snow' (*sieboldiana*) (v)	EPGN
'Sun Glow'	EMic
'Sun Power'	CBdn CBro EBre EGol EJap EMic EPGN EPar MMiN MWat NTay SApp WRus
'Sundance' (*fortunei*) (v)	EGol EMic
* 'Sunflower'	NOak
'Super Bowl'	EGol LRHS
'Super Nova' (v)	EGol
'Suzuki Thumbnail'	EMic
'Sweet Standard'	SApp
'Sweet Susan'	CSte EGol EMic MMiN SApp SPer
'Sweet Tater Pie'	EPGN
'Sweetheart'	EMic
'Tall Boy'	CSev EBee EBre ECha EGol EMic EPGN GCal LHos NHol SApp SPer SSpi WWat
'Tall Twister'	EMic
¶ 'Tamborine' (v)	EGol
Tardiana Group	CBdn CBro CMGP CShe EGol ELan EMon MBal NHol SPer WKif
– 'Blue Belle'	CBdn ECha EGol EMic LHos MBro MMiN MSte WHoo
– 'Blue Blush'	CBdn EGol
– 'Blue Danube'	ECha EGol EMic MMiN
– 'Blue Diamond'	CHad EGol EMic MMiN
– 'Blue Dimples'	EGol EMic LRHS MMiN
– 'Blue Moon'	CBro CMHG EBar EBre EFou EGol ELan EMic EOrc EPGN ERos LGre LHop LHos MBri MRPP NHol SApp SMad WEas WWat
– 'Blue Skies'	CBlo EGol EMic EPGN LHos MBri
– 'Blue Wedgwood'	CBro CMHG CRow EGol ELan EMic EOrc EPGN LHos MWat NHol NTay SApp SChu SPer SPla WRus WWat
– 'Bright Glow'	EGol EMic
– 'Brother Ronald'	EGol LRHS
– 'Camelot'	EGol EMic LRHS
– 'Curlew'	CBdn ECha EGol EMic
– 'Devon Blue'	CWGN EGol EMic MMiN NWes
– 'Dorset Charm'	CBdn EGol EMic MBal MMiN
– 'Dorset Flair'	EGol EMic
– 'Eric Smith'	EGol EMic EPGN SChu WFar
– 'Goldbrook Glimmer' (v)	EGol
– 'Hadspen Blue'	CMHG EBar EBre ECha EGol EJap EMic EOrc EPGN MRav NBir NBro NHol NRoo SApp SChu SMrm SUsu WHow WRus WWat
– 'Hadspen Blue Jay'	CBro CHad
¶ – 'Hadspen Dolphin'	EMic
– 'Hadspen Hawk'	CBdn EGol LGre LRHS
– 'Hadspen Heron'	CBdn CHad CSte ECha EGol EMic EPGN LHos MBal SApp SChu
§ – 'Halcyon' ♀	Widely available
– 'Happiness'	ECha EGol EHoe EMic LHos MRav WCot
– 'Harmony'	EGol EMic LRHS
– 'Irische See'	SApp
– 'June' (v)	CBdn EBre EGol EPGN GSki LHos NHar SApp SPer WWeb
– 'Nicola'	EGol EMic EPGN WCot WRus
– 'Osprey'	EGol LRHS
¶ – pink-flowered	MMiN
– 'Serena'	SApp
– 'Sherborne Profusion'	EMic
– 'Sherborne Songbird'	EMic
– 'Sherborne Swan'	EMic
– 'Silvery Slugproof'	SApp
– 'Wagtail'	EMic
tardiflora	CFil EGol EMic ERos MBal MHig
tardiva	CMHG LHos NGre
'Tenryu'	EGol LHos
'The Twister'	EGol EMic
'Thomas Hogg'	See ***H. undulata*** var. ***albomarginata***
'Thumb Nail'	ECha EGol
tibae	EMic
'Tiny Tears' (*venusta*)	EGol
tokudama	CHad CHan EGol ELan EPGN IHos LWak MBri NBir NFai NHol NSti SApp SChu SPla WKif WWat
§ – f. ***aureonebulosa***	EGol EPGN LGre LHos
– f. ***flavocircinalis*** (v)	CBdn EBre ECha EGol EMic EPGN LHos MMiN SApp
'Tot Tot'	EMic
'Trail's End'	EMic
'True Blue'	CBdn EGol EMic EPGN LHos MMiN
¶ 'Tutu'	EGol
'Twinkle Toes'	EMic
undulata	EMic LFis NDea
§ – var. ***albomarginata***	Widely available
§ – var. ***erromena*** ♀	CBdn CHan CMGP CWGN EHon EMic LFis LHos LPBA MBro NFla NHol SChu SPer SSpi WCot

§ – var. ***undulata*** (v) 🏆 CBdn CBot CBro CRow CWGN EHoe EHon EJap ELan ENot EOrc EPGN LGro LHyd LPBA MBri MMiN SChu SHig SPer WEas WKif WRus WWin
– var. ***univittata*** (v) 🏆 CBro CRow ECha EGol EMic EPGN LHos LHyd MAvo MMiN NFai NTay SPla WKif
'Urajuro' (*hypoleuca*) EGol
'Valentine Lace' CBdn CSte EGol EMic
'Vanilla Cream' (*cathayana*) EGol EMic EPGN LHos SApp
'Variegata' (*gracillima*) See ***H. 'Vera Verde'***
'Variegata' (*tokudama*) See ***H. tokudama* f. *aureonebulosa***
'Variegata' (*undulata*) See ***H. undulata* var. *undulata***
'Variegata' (*ventricosa*) See ***H. 'Aureomarginata' (ventricosa)***
◆ 'Variegated' (*fluctuans*) See ***H. 'Sagae'***
body
– var. ***aureomaculata*** CHad EBee EGol EMic EPGN LHos MMiN NCut NTay SPer WCru
I 'Venucosa' EGol EMic
'Venus Star' EPGN GSki
venusta 🏆 CBdn CBro CMHG CRow CSWP EBre ECha EGol ELan EMic EPGN EPar ERos LGre LHil MBal MHig NHar NMen NNrd SHFr WEas WHil WOMN WWat
– dwarf form CSWP LGre
– × ***sieboldiana*** CHan
– ***yakusimensis*** See ***H. kikutii* var. *yakusimensis***
§ 'Vera Verde' (v) CBdn CHid GCra GQui MLan
'Verte' (*sieboldii*) See ***H. sieboldii* f. *spathulata***
'Viette's Yellow Edge' (*fortunei*) (v) MMiN
'Vilmoriniana' EGol EMic
'Viridis Marginata' See ***H. sieboldii* f. *kabitan***
'Vrajiro' EGol
'Vrajiro Hachijo' EGol
¶ 'Wahoo' (*tokudama*) (v) EGol
¶ 'Waving Winds' (v) EGol
'Wayside Blue' EMic
'Wayside Perfection' See ***H. 'Royal Standard'***
¶ 'Weihenstephan' (*sieboldii*) EGol
¶ 'Wheaton Blue' CBdn
¶ 'Whirlwind' (*fortunei*) (v) EGol
'White Fairy' (*plantaginea*) CBdn EPGN
'White Gold' EGol EPGN LHos
'White Tacchi' EMon
'Wide Brim' (v) 🏆 CBdn CBro EBre ECtt EFou EGol EHoe EJap ELan EMic EOrc EPGN LHos MBal MBri MMiN MWat NBir NBro NFai NHol NTay SApp SPer SPla WAbe WHil WHoo WRus WWat
'Wind River Gold' EGol SApp
'Windsor Gold' See ***H. 'Nancy Lindsay' (fortunei)***
* 'Winfield Gold' CBdn EGol
'Winning Edge' (*tokudama*) CBdn EGol
'Wogon Giboshi' See ***H. 'Wogon' (sieboldii)***
§ 'Wogon' (*sieboldii*) CBdn CM&M CRDP CRow EFou EGol EMic EPGN EPla GMaP NHar NHol
'Wogon's Boy' EGol EPGN
'Wrinkles and Crinkles' EMic LRHS
'Yakushima-mizu' (*gracillima*) CBdn EGol EMic
* ***yakushimana*** NHar
'Yellow Boa' EMic
'Yellow Edge' (*fortunei*) See ***H. fortunei* var. *aureomarginata***
'Yellow Edge' (*sieboldiana*) See ***H. 'Frances Williams' (sieboldiana)***
'Yellow River' (*montana*) (v) CBdn ECha EGol EMic LHos LRHS
'Yellow Splash' (v) CBdn ECha EPGN MMiN NTay
'Yellow Splash Rim' (v) EGol LHos
yingeri EGol
– B&SWJ 546 WCru
'Zager Blue' EMic
'Zager Green' EMic
'Zager White Edge' (*fortunei*) (v) EMic LHos
'Zounds' CBdn CBot CHad CKel CMHG EBre EFou EGol EHoe EJap ELan EMic EOrc EPGN GMaP IHos LHos MBri MMiN NFai NFla NHol NOrc NSti SApp SCro SPla WAbe WRus WWat

HOTTONIA (Primulaceae)

palustris CBen CWGN ECoo EHon ELan EMFW LPBA MSta NDea NVic SWat SWyc

HOUSTONIA (Rubiaceae)

caerulea Linnaeus var. ***alba*** CInt ELan EWes NGre WPer
– hort. See ***H. michauxii***
– Linnaeus CSam ECho ELan NGre NPri WWin
§ ***michauxii*** GAri
– 'Fred Mullard' EHyt EPot EWes NHol

HOUTTUYNIA (Saururaceae)

cordata CHan GBar IBlr MUlv NLak NSti SWat WBea WRHF
§ – 'Chameleon' (v) Widely available
– 'Flore Pleno' CBen CGle CRDP CRow CWGN ECha EFol EHon ELan EPla LGan LPBA MBal MRav MSta NBir NBro NWes SIde SIng SPer SWat SWyc WByw WChe WMAq WOld WRus WWin
– 'Tricolor' See ***H. cordata* 'Chameleon'**
– Variegata Group EPot GBar IBlr NDea WByw WChe
* 'Joseph's Coat' NBro

HOVEA (Papilionaceae)

celsii See ***H. elliptica***
§ ***elliptica*** LLew

HOVENIA (Rhamnaceae)

dulcis CB&S CGre CMCN CPle ELan EPfP

HOWEA (Arecaceae)

forsteriana 🏆 LPal MBri

HOYA † (Asclepiadaceae)

¶ ***acuta*** LChe
angustifolia LChe
arnottiana SLMG
§ ***australis*** ECon SLMG
bandaensis SLMG
bilobata LChe

carnosa 🏆	CB&S EBak ELan GQui LCns NRog SLMG SRms
– 'Compacta'	CHal SLMG
* – ***compacta*** 'Hindu Rope'	NPer
– 'Exotica' 🏆	SLMG
* – 'Jungle Garden'	SLMG
* – 'Krinkle'	NPer
– 'Krinkle Eight'	SLMG
– 'Red Princess'	MBri
– 'Rubra'	SLMG
– 'Variegata'	LCns MBri SLMG SRms
¶ ***cinnamomifolia***	LChe
cumingiana	LChe
darwinii hort.	See ***H. australis***
engleriana	SLMG
fusca 'Silver Knight'	SLMG
fuscomarginata	See ***H. pottsii***
¶ ***globulosa***	LChe
imperialis	SLMG
kerrii	LChe
lacunosa	LChe
lanceolata subsp. ***bella*** 🏆	CB&S CHal GQui MBri NRog SRms
linearis	LChe
longifolia	LChe
macgillivrayi	ECon
motoskei	LChe
multiflora	LChe MBri
neocaledonica	SLMG
nicholsoniae	LChe
pauciflora	LChe
polyneura	SLMG
pubicalyx 'Red Buttons'	LChe SLMG
* – 'Silver Pink'	LChe
¶ ***purpureofusca***	LChe
shepherdii	LChe
'Shibata'	LChe

HUGUENINIA (Brassicaceae)

alpina	See ***H. tanacetifolia***

HUMATA See DAVALLIA

HUMEA (Asteraceae)

elegans	See ***Calomeria amaranthoides***

HUMULUS (Cannabaceae)

japonicus	ECoo MSal
lupulus	CArn CB&S CJew CPlN ECoo GAri GBar GPoy ILis LHol MHew MSal NBee SIde WBea WHer WSel WStI WWye
– 'Aureus' 🏆	Widely available
¶ – 'Aureus' (f)	WWat
¶ – 'Aureus' (m)	WWat
– 'Fuggle'	GPoy
¶ – 'Hip-hop'	EMon
* – 'Taff's Variegated'	EMon EWes
– 'Wye Challenger'	GPoy

HUNNEMANNIA (Papaveraceae)

fumariifolia 'Sunlite'	CPle

HUTCHINSIA See THLASPI

HYACINTHELLA (Hyacinthaceae)

lineata M&T 5048	CMon
millingenii	EHyt

HYACINTHOIDES (Hyacinthaceae)

§ ***hispanica***	CAvo CBro CHid EPot EWFC IBlr MBri NHol WWye
– 'Alba'	CMea
– ***algeriensis*** AB&S 4337	CMon
♦ – Donau	See ***H. hispanica* 'Danube'**
¶ – 'Excelsior'	ETub
– 'La Grandesse'	CBro
– 'Rosabella'	CBro
– 'Rose'	CMea
§ ***italica***	CMon
§ – ***vicentina***	CMon
– – ***alba***	WChr
§ ***non-scripta***	CArn CAvo CBro CKin ECWi EPar EPot ETub EWFC GDra IBlr LAma LFox MBri NMir NRog WCla WShi
– pink bell	MSto

HYACINTHUS † (Hyacinthaceae)

amethystinus	See ***Brimeura amethystina***
azureus	See ***Muscari azureum***
comosus 'Plumosus'	See ***Muscari comosum* 'Plumosum'**
fastigiatus	See ***Brimeura fastigiata***
orientalis 'Amethyst'	EWal LAma NRog
– 'Amsterdam'	ETub EWal LAma NRog
– 'Anna Liza'	NRog
– 'Anna Marie' 🏆	CAvo CBro ETub EWal LAma MBri NRog
– 'Ben Nevis' (d)	LAma MBri NRog
– 'Bismarck'	LAma NRog
– 'Blue Giant'	LAma NRog
– 'Blue Jacket' 🏆	CBro ETub LAma NRog
– 'Blue Magic'	EWal LAma NRog
– 'Blue Orchid' (d)	LAma
– 'Blue Star'	LAma
– 'Borah' 🏆	EWal LAma NRog
– 'Carnegie'	CBro ETub EWal LAma NRog
– 'City of Haarlem' 🏆	CBro ETub EWal LAma NRog
– 'Colosseum'	LAma
– 'Concorde'	LAma
– 'Delft Blue' 🏆	CAvo CBro EWal LAma MBri NRog
– 'Distinction'	LAma
– 'Edelweiss'	LAma
– 'Fondant'	LAma
– 'Gipsy Queen' 🏆	CBro ETub EWal LAma MBri NRog
– 'Hollyhock' (d)	ETub EWal LAma MBri NRog
– 'Jan Bos'	CAvo EWal LAma NRog
– 'King Codro' (d)	LAma MBri NRog
– 'King of the Blues'	LAma NRog
– 'La Victoire'	LAma NRog
– 'Lady Derby'	EWal LAma
– 'L'Innocence' 🏆	CBro LAma NRog
– 'Lord Balfour'	LAma
– 'Madame Krüger'	LAma
– 'Marconi' (d)	LAma NRog
– 'Marie'	LAma NRog
– 'Mont Blanc'	EWal
– 'Mulberry Rose'	EWal LAma NRog
– 'Myosotis'	LAma
§ – 'Oranje Boven'	LAma
– 'Ostara' 🏆	CBro EWal LAma MBri NRog
– 'Peter Stuyvesant'	EWal NRog
– 'Pink Pearl' 🏆	CBro LAma NRog
– 'Pink Royal' (d)	LAma NRog
– 'Princess Margaret'	LAma
– 'Prins Hendrik'	LAma
– 'Queen of the Pinks'	LAma NRog
– 'Queen of the Violets'	NRog

– 'Rosalie'	EWal NRog
– 'Rosette' (d)	LAma NRog
– 'Salmonetta'	See ***H. orientalis* 'Oranje Boven'**
§ – 'Sneeuwwitje'	LAma NRog
◆ – Snow White	See ***H. orientalis* 'Sneeuwwitje'**
– 'Violet Pearl'	CBro LAma NRog
– 'Vuurbaak'	LAma
– 'White Pearl'	CAvo LAma NRog
* 'Woodstock'	ETub

HYBANTHUS (Violaceae)

See Plant Deletions

HYDRANGEA † (Hydrangeaceae)

anomala	CChu
§ – subsp. ***petiolaris*** 🏆	Widely available
§ – – ***cordifolia***	CFil CHan EBar EPla MTho SBra SReu SSta WWeb
– – dwarf form	See ***H. anomala* subsp. *petiolaris cordifolia***
– – ***tiliifolia***	EPfP MBlu SNut
– – 'Yakushima'	CFil WPGP
§ ***arborescens***	CArn CFil MRav NNor WPGP WWeb
– 'Annabelle' 🏆	CAbb CB&S CFil EBar ECtt ELan ENot IOrc ISea LHop MBri MGos MPla NHar NHol NPal SBod SEas SHBN SMad SNut SPer SPla SSpi SSta WBod WDin WHen WPat WWat
– subsp. ***discolor*** 'Sterilis'	CFil EHic EPla SPla SSpi WCru WPGP
– 'Grandiflora' 🏆	CB&S CBot ELan GOrc SBod SPer SReu WDin WHCG WSHC WWin
– subsp. ***radiata***	CFil CHan ELan MAsh NHlc SNut SSpi WCru WWat
aspera	CBlo CFil CGre GOrc IOrc SAga SChu SMac SSpi SSta WCru
– Kawakamii Group	CFil EPla WPGP
§ – 'Macrophylla' 🏆	CBlo CFil MBri MMor NPal WCru WPGP WWat
– 'Mauvette'	CFil MBlu NPal SSta WCru WPGP
¶ – 'Peter Chappell'	SSpi
§ – subsp. ***robusta***	CChu CMil GAri SMac SNut
– 'Rosthornii'	See ***H. aspera* subsp. *robusta***
§ – subsp. ***sargentiana*** 🏆	CAbP CB&S CBot CChu CFil CHEx CHad COtt ELan LNet MAsh MBal MBlu MBri NPal SArc SHBN SMad SPer SSpi SSta WAbe WCru WDin WWat
– subsp. ***strigosa***	CChu CFil ELan SBid WPGP
– 'Taiwan'	SSpi
§ – Villosa Group 🏆	Widely available
§ 'Blue Deckle' (L)	CFil CMHG EBar EPla NHlc SBid SNut SSpi
'Blue Tit'	See ***H. macrophylla* 'Blaumeise'**
cinerea	See ***H. arborescens* subsp. *discolor***
§ 'Grant's Choice' (L)	EHic NHlc NHol
heteromalla	CFai CFil CMHG WCru
– Bretschneideri Group 🏆	CChu CMCN EHal GAri GQui NHlc WCru WWat
¶ – 'Morrey's Form'	WCru
¶ – SF 338	ISea
– 'Snowcap'	EBee GQui NHlc WBcn WCru
– f. ***xanthoneura***	CFil GAri WPGP
– 'Yalung Ridge'	NHlc
integerrima	See ***H. serratifolia***
¶ ***integrifolia***	CPlN
– B&SWJ 022	WCru
involucrata	CFil MBal MPla NHlc SBid SMrm SSpi SSta WCru
– 'Hortensis' (d) 🏆	CFil IOrc SSpi WCru WKif WSHC
longipes	CFil WPGP
luteovenosa	WCru
◆ ***macrophylla*** Alpen Glow	See ***H. macrophylla* 'Alpenglühen'**
§ – 'Alpenglühen' (H)	CB&S CFil ELan ESis IOrc NHar NHlc NPro SBid SBod SHBN SPla SRms
– 'Altona' (H) 🏆	CB&S CFil EPla GAri IOrc ISea MAll MBal MGos MRav NHlc SAxl SBid SBod SPer WStI
– 'Amethyst' (H/d)	CFil WPGP
– 'Ami Pasquier' (H) 🏆	CB&S CBlo CDoC CFil EBee EPla IOrc MAsh NHlc SBid SSpi
– 'Aureovariegata'	CFil EFol ELan SNut
– 'Ayesha' (H) 🏆	Widely available
– 'Beauté Vendômoise' (L)	CFil SBid SSpi WPGP
– 'Belzonii' (L)	NHlc
– 'Benelux' (H)	CB&S CWSG EHic MAll SBid WLRN
§ – 'Blauer Prinz' (H)	CB&S GCHN IOrc MAll NHlc SAxl SHBN WLRN WTyr
§ – 'Blaumeise' (L)	CFil GAul MAsh NHlc SBid SSpi WPGP WRTC
– 'Blue Bird'	CWSG
– 'Blue Bonnet' (H)	COtt EPfP MAsh SPer WHen WLRN
◆ – Blue Prince	See ***H. macrophylla* 'Blauer Prinz'**
– 'Blue Sky'	See ***H. macrophylla* 'Blaumeise'**
– 'Blue Wave'	See ***H. macrophylla* 'Mariesii Perfecta'**
– 'Bodensee' (H)	COtt EBee NFla SBod SPla WLRN WStI
– 'Bouquet Rose' (H)	CBlo COtt ECtt EHal EHic MAll MGos NBee NFla
¶ – 'Brunette' (H)	CFil
– 'Buchfink'	CFil WPGP
– 'Cordata'	See ***H. arborescens***
– 'Covent Garden'	MAll
– 'Deutschland' (H)	CTri IOrc
– 'Domotoi' (H/d)	CFil WPGP
* – 'Dwaag Pink'	MRav
§ – 'Enziandom' (H)	CB&S CFil SMrm WAbe WPGP
– 'Europa' (H) 🏆	CB&S CTrw CWLN IOrc MAll MAsh MGos NCut NHlc SBod SEND WGwG WStI
– Twilight = 'Fasan'®	CFil GAul NHlc
– 'Fischers Silberblau' (H)	CFil
– 'Forever Pink'	EBre EPla MAsh
– 'Frillibet' (H)	CFil EPla LRHS SBid WCru WPGP
¶ – 'Gartenbaudirektor Kuhnert' (H)	SMer
§ – 'Générale Vicomtesse de Vibraye' (H) 🏆	CB&S CEnd CFil CMHG CTri EPfP GCHN ISea MBal MBar MBri NFla NHlc SAxl SBid SHBN SNut SPer SReu SSpi WBod WLRN WWin
◆ – Gentian Dome	See ***H. macrophylla* 'Enziandom'**

– 'Geoffrey Chadbund' (L) 🏆	CB&S CEnd CFil ECtt EPla IHos MBri NHlc SAxl SBod SChu SDix SMad SNut SPer SRms SSpi SSta WRTC WWeb
– 'Gerda Steiniger'	CB&S CBlo
– 'Gertrud Glahn' (H)	CB&S CBlo CWLN NCut
– 'Glowing Embers'	CFil SEND WPGP
– 'Goliath' (H)	CBlo CFil MBri SBid WPGP
– 'Hamburg' (H)	CB&S CEnd CFil CTri EBee ECtt ENot EPfP IOrc MGos NBee NCut NHlc SAxl SBid SDix WAbe WStI WWeb
– 'Harlequin'	CFil WPGP
– 'Harry's Pink Topper' (H)	MAsh
– 'Hatfield Rose' (H)	CB&S
– 'Heinrich Seidel' (H)	CB&S CFil MAll NHlc WPGP
– 'Holstein' (H)	CFil MAsh NBee SBid WPGP
§ – 'Hörnli'	CFil WPGP
– 'Intermezzo'	MAll WLRN
– 'James Grant'	See ***H.* 'Grant's Choice'**
§ – 'Joseph Banks' (H)	EHic
– 'Kardinal'	CFil WPGP
– 'King George' (H)	CB&S CFil CWSG EBee EBre EHic IOrc MBar MGos MRav NHlc SBid SPer WGwG WLRN WPGP WStI
– 'Kluis Superba' (H)	CB&S CBlo CFil CTri CWLN IOrc MRav NHlc
§ – 'Koningin Wilhelmina' (H)	CFil WPGP
– 'La France' (H)	CB&S CBlo COtt CTri CWSG EBee EHic MBar MRav SBid
– 'Lanarth White' (L) 🏆	CB&S CFil CTri CWLN EBee EHic ELan MPla NHlc SBid SDix SHBN SPer SReu SRms SSpi WBod WWat WWeb
§ – 'Libelle' (L)	CB&S CBlo CFil CWSG EBee EHic GAul MBri NHlc SLPl SMrm SNut SPer SSpi WKif WWat
– 'Lilacina' (L)	CFil CGre EHic EPla MAll NHlc SAxl SBid SLPl SPer WKif
§ – 'Maculata' (L)	EAst EFol ELan EPla GQui IOrc MAll SEas WWat
– 'Madame A. Riverain' (H)	COtt CWLN CWSG EHic MAll SBod WLRN
§ – 'Madame Emile Mouillère' (H) 🏆	CB&S CBot CEnd CFil ENot IOrc MAll MBri NFla NHlc SAga SAxl SBod SDix SHBN SMad SMer SNut SPer SPla SRms SSoC SSpi SSta
– 'Maréchal Foch' (H)	CFil CTri IOrc WPGP
– 'Mariesii' (L)	CMHG CTri EBee ELan ENot EPla ISea MAll MBal NBee NHlc SAxl SBid SDix SPer WKif WLRN WStI WWat
§ – 'Mariesii Perfecta' (L) 🏆	CChe CMHG CTri ELan ISea MBar MGos MRav NFla SAxl SDix SNut SPer WGwG WHen WStI WWat
– 'Mariesii Variegata' (L)	WCot
– 'Masja' (H)	CB&S COtt CWSG EHic IHos IOrc MBri MGos NBee NFla SHBN WAbe
– 'Mathilda Gutges' (H)	CFil CWSG EHic WPGP WStI
– 'Mini Hörnli'	See ***H. macrophylla* 'Hörnli'**
– 'Miss Belgium' (H)	CTri IOrc MBal MBri MTis MUlv NHlc SBod SEas
– 'Miss Hepburn'	COtt NHlc SPer
♦ – Morning Red	See ***H. macrophylla* 'Morgenrot'**

– 'Mousmée'	CFil WPGP
– 'Münster' (H)	NHlc
– 'Niedersachsen' (H)	CFil EPla MRav NHlc SBid SMer WPGP
– 'Nigra' (H) 🏆	CChe CChu CFil CGre CHan CTre ELan EPla IOrc MAll MBal MGos SBid SDix SHBN SNut SPer SSta WAbe WCru WGwG WStI
– 'Nikko Blue'	CB&S CBlo CFil CWLN SBid SEND WPGP
– var. ***normalis***	NHlc
– 'Otaksa' (H)	MAll NHlc
– 'Parzifal' (H) 🏆	CB&S CFil CTrw CWLN EHic MBri NHlc WGwG
* – 'Pax'	SNut
– 'Pia' (H)	CB&S CDec CFil EFol ELan ESis IOrc LHop MAsh MBal MGos MHig MPla MTho MUlv NHar NHol SApp SBod SIng SMad SMrm SPer SPla SRms WOMN WPat WWat
– 'Pink Wave' (L)	CB&S
– 'Prinses Beatrix'	CChe CFil WBcn WPGP
– 'Quadricolor' (L/v)	CAbb CDec CFil CMil EHoe EPla MBri MRav MUlv NRoo NSti SApp SDix SHBN SNut SPer SPla SRms WCru WHCG WSHC
♦ – Queen Wilhelmina	See ***H. macrophylla* 'Koningin Wilhelmina'**
– 'R.F. Felton'	CB&S
¶ – 'Red Emperor' (H)	EPfP
♦ – Redbreast	See ***H. macrophylla* 'Rotkehlchen'**
– 'Regula' (H)	CTrw
– 'Rex'	NHlc
– 'Rosita' (H)	LPan MAsh
§ – 'Rotkehlchen'	CFil SBid WCru WPGP
– Red Star = 'Rotschwanz' (L)	CFil NHlc WPGP
– Redstart = 'Rotschwanz' (L)	CFil
– 'Saint Claire'	CB&S
– 'Sea Foam' (L)	CKni EPla IOrc NHlc
– 'Seascape'	NHlc
* – 'Shower'	GAul
– 'Sibylla' (H)	CB&S CFil MAll NHlc WPGP WWeb
♦ – Sister Therese	See ***H. macrophylla* 'Soeur Thérèse'**
§ – 'Soeur Thérèse' (H)	CB&S CBlo CFil GAri IOrc MAll MAsh MGos WLRN WStI WWeb
– 'Souvenir du Président Paul Doumer' (H)	CB&S CBlo
– 'Taube'	CB&S CFil GQui WPGP
* – Teller Blau (L)	CBlo COtt MBri NHlc SCoo SSta WDin Wweb
– Teller Rosa (L)	EBre SCoo SSta
– Teller Rot (L)	CBlo EHic IHos MAsh MBri NHol SCoo WDin
– Teller Variegated	See ***H. macrophylla* 'Tricolor'**
– Teller Weiss	See ***H. macrophylla* 'Libelle'**
¶ – 'Thomas Hogg' (H)	EPfP
– 'Tokyo Delight'	CB&S CBlo CBrd CChe CEnd CFil CWLN EHic IOrc NHlc SBid SSpi
– 'Tovelit'	GAri MBri WWeb

§ – 'Tricolor' (L/v) 🏆	CB&S CBot CFil CGre EAst EPla ERav GOrc MAll MAsh MBri MGos NBee SAga SBod SPer SReu WCru WGwG WKif WPyg
– 'Universal' (H)	NHlc
– 'Ursula'	WLRN
– 'Val de Loire'	CBlo CWSG
– 'Variegata'	See ***H. macrophylla* 'Maculata'**
– 'Veitchii' (L) 🏆	CB&S CBot CFil CGre CMHG ENot EPfP MBri SAxl SBid SBod SDix SPer SSpi WWat
– 'Vicomte de Vibraye'	See ***H. macrophylla* 'Générale Vicomtesse de Vibraye'**
♦ – Vulcan	See ***H. macrophylla* 'Vulcain'**
– 'Westfalen' (H) 🏆	NCat NHlc SMrm SPla WGwG
– 'White Lace' (L)	ELan
– 'White Swan'	See ***H. macrophylla* 'Le Cygne'**
– 'White Wave' (L) 🏆	CBlo CFil EBee ENot MBar NFla SBid SBod SEND SHBN SNut SPer SRms SSpi WDin WLRN WStI
paniculata	CFil CMCN CTrw SHhN
– 'Brussels Lace'	CFil CKni CPMA CSte LRHS MAsh SNut SPla SSpi
– 'Burgundy Lace'	CPMA
– 'Everest'	SNut
– 'Floribunda' 🏆	CFil LRHS SNut SSpi WRHF
– 'Grandiflora' 🏆	Widely available
– 'Greenspire'	CPMA LRHS SPla WBcn
– 'Kyushu' 🏆	Widely available
– 'Pink Diamond'	CAbP CMCN CPMA CSte EBee EBre LHop LRHS MAsh NRoo SMad SPla SSpi SSta WCru WHCG
– 'Praecox' 🏆	SPer WPat WWin
– 'Tardiva'	CB&S CBot EMil EPla LPan MAsh MRav SDix SPer SPla SRms WFar WHCG WLRN WPat WPyg WRTC
– 'Unique' 🏆	CB&S CDoC CFil CPMA CSte EBar EHic LHop MAsh MBri SNut SPer SPla SSpi WCru WWat
– 'White Moth'	CFil CPMA MAsh MUlv SNut WPGP
§ 'Preziosa' 🏆	Widely available
quelpartensis	CB&S CHan CPlN CRHN CTre GQui SBid WCru
quercifolia 🏆	Widely available
– 'Flore Pleno'	See ***H. quercifolia* Snow Flake**
– 'Harmony'	CEnd CFil CHad SSta WPGP
– 'Sike's Dwarf'	CEnd CFil SSpi SSta WPGP
* – 'Snow'	CWSG
§ – Snow Flake™ (d)	CB&S CChu CEnd CFil COtt CPMA CSPN CTrC ELan EMil MAsh MBri SMad SPer SSpi SSta WHCG WPGP WWat
– 'Snow Queen'	CB&S CDoC CMil CPMA MAsh MBal MBri MGos SPer SPla SSta WHCG WWat
– 'Stardust'	CRos
– 'Tennessee Clone'	CFil WPGP
sargentiana	See ***H. aspera*** subsp. ***sargentiana***
scandens	CPle
¶ – subsp. ***liukiuensis***	WCru
seemannii	CB&S CBot CChu CFil CGre CHEx CMac CPlN CRHN CSam CTrw ELan GQui ISea LHop NHlc SArc SBra SSpi WCru WGwG WSHC WWat
serrata	CTrw NHlc WCru
– 'Acuminata'	See ***H. serrata* 'Bluebird'**
– 'Belle Deckle'	See ***H.* 'Blue Deckle'**
– 'Beni-gaku'	CB&S CFil NFla SBid WLRN WPGP
§ – 'Bluebird' 🏆	CFil CWLN EBre EHic ELan ISea LPan MBal MBar MBlu MBri MGos NBee NHlc SBid SBod SDix SHBN SMad SNut SPer SSpi SSta WGwG WLRN WStI WWat WWeb
* – ***chinensis***	NHlc
– 'Diadem'	CBrd CFai CFil CPle EPla NHlc NPro SBid SBod SDix SHBN SNut WCru WLRN
– 'Grayswood' 🏆	CEnd CHig CPle CWLN ENot GQui LHop MBal NHlc SBid SDix SPer WAbe WKif WLRN WWat
– 'Intermedia'	CFil ENot WPGP
– 'Macrosepala'	EHic
– 'Miranda' (L)	CBrd CEnd CFil COtt EHic MUlv NHlc SBid WLRN
– 'Preziosa'	See ***H.* 'Preziosa'**
* – 'Pulchella'	SPla
* – 'Pulchra'	SSpi SSta
– 'Rosalba' 🏆	CFil MRav SPer SPla WSHC
– var. ***thunbergii***	CB&S CFil CMHG CPle GQui WPGP
¶ – 'Tiara'	SSpi
– subsp. ***yezoensis*** 'Wryneck' (H)	CFil NHlc WPGP
§ ***serratifolia***	CBot CChu CFil CGre CPlN EPfP EPla SArc SBra SSpi WCru WSHC
sinensis	See ***H. scandens*** subsp. ***chinensis***
tiliifolia	See ***H. anomala*** subsp. ***petiolaris***
umbellata	See ***H. scandens*** subsp. ***chinensis***
villosa	See ***H. aspera* Villosa Group**

HYDRASTIS (Ranunculaceae)

canadensis	CArn GPoy MSal NGar WCru WThi

HYDROCHARIS (Hydrocharitaceae)

morsus-ranae	CBen CRDP CRow CWGN CWat EHon EMFW LPBA MSta NDea NVic SWat WChe

HYDROCLEYS (Limnocharitaceae)

See Plant Deletions

HYDROCOTYLE (Apiaceae)

§ ***americana***	NHol
asiatica	See ***Centella asiatica***
moschata	GAri WPer WWin
* ***palustris***	SBla
ranunculoides	See ***H. americana***
* ***sibthorpioides*** 'Variegata'	EMon EPPr
vulgaris	CRDP EMFW EWFC MSta WChe WKen

HYDROPHYLLUM (Hydrophyllaceae)

canadense	EMar EMon WCot WCru
virginianum	EBee MSal

HYLOMECON (Papaveraceae)

japonica — CRDP EPar EPot ERos MSte MTho MTol MUlv NBir NCat NGar NHol NMGW NRya NTow WCru WOMN WRHF

HYLOTELEPHIUM See SEDUM

HYMENANTHERA See MELICYTUS

HYMENOCALLIS (Amaryllidaceae)

'Advance' — LAma LBow
§ *caroliniana* — LAma
× *festalis* — CMon ERea LAma LBow MBri NRog SDeJ SLMG WChr
– 'Zwanenburg' — ETub SMad
harrisiana — LBow WChr
littoralis — NRog WChr
§ *longipetala* — LBow WChr
narcissiflora — WChr
occidentalis — See ***H. caroliniana***
'Sulphur Queen' — LBow NRog SDeJ SLMG SMad WChr

HYMENOSPORUM (Pittosporaceae)

See Plant Deletions

HYMENOXYS (Asteraceae)

◆ *grandiflora* — See ***Tetraneuris grandiflora***
subintegra — NNrd WDav

HYOPHORBE (Arecaceae)

§ *lagenicaulis* — LPal

HYOSCYAMUS (Solanaceae)

albus — GBar MChe MSal WWye
niger — CArn CJew EWFC GPoy MChe MSal NLak WHer WWye
* – 'Capel Ulo' — WHer

HYPERICUM † (Clusiaceae)

acmosepalum SBEC 93 — CChu
§ *addingtonii* — EPla
adenotrichum — CNic GCHN
aegypticum — CLyd CTri EDAr EHyt ELan EPot GCHN LBee MHig NMen NWCA NWoo SAlw WAbe WFar WPat WPer WPyg
amblycalyx — SIgm
androsaemum — CArn CKin CPle ECha EGoo ELan ENot GAul MHew MSal NMir NPer NRoo WDin
§ – 'Albury Purple' — CHan CPle EBee EPla GBuc MHlr NLak WCot
* – 'Autumn Blaze' — MBal SSte
§ – 'Dart's Golden Penny' — SLPl SPer WBcn
§ – 'Gladys Brabazon' (v) — CBlo EBee WCot WWeb
– 'Orange Flair' — See ***H. × inodorum* 'Orange Flair'**
– 'Variegatum' — See ***H. androsaemum* 'Gladys Brabazon'**
§ *annulatum* — ELan EMon
ascyron — EBee EWes
athoum — CLyd ESis GCHN LHop MBro MHig MPla NBir NTow WPat WPer
augustinii — CChu CPle
balearicum — CHan CLyd CPle EPot MAll MAsh MHar MPla MTho SAlw SChu SDry SIgm
§ *beanii* — CChu LRHS MBlu WAbe
bellum — CPle EPfP GCal SBid
– subsp. *latisepalum* — CChu
buckleyi — GCHN MDHE MHig NGre SIng WPat
calycinum — CB&S CLan ELan ENot LBuc LGro MBal MBar MGos MWat NNor NWea SHBN SPer SRms WDin WPLl
§ *cerastioides* — CMHG ECGP ESis GCHN LBee MBro MHar MHig MPla NGre NTow SIgm SIng SRms WAbe WPer WWin
choisyanum B&L 12469 — CChu
coris — CLyd CShe ECED ECha EHyt EPot EWes GTou LBee MBro MHar MTho MWat NMen NTow SAlw SRms SUsu WCla WHoo
cuneatum — See ***H. pallens***
× *cyathiflorum* 'Gold Cup' — MBal SBid
× *dummeri* 'Peter Dummer' — CBlo CChu EMil MBri SMac WWat
elatum — See ***H. × inodorum***
elodeoides — CLyd MSta SRms
elongatum — EMon ESis
empetrifolium — EWes MHig SIng
§ – subsp. *oliganthum* — ECha ESis GCHN NHar WPer
– 'Prostatum' — See ***H. empetrifolium*** subsp. ***tortuosum***
§ – subsp. *tortuosum* — CLyd MDHE
* 'Excellent Flare' — NPro
§ *forrestii* ♀ — CBot CLan CPle EBee ENot GAul MBal MGos SBid WWat
N *fragile* hort. — See ***H. olympicum* f. *minus***
frondosum — CLTr
– 'Buttercup' — CBlo SPan SPla
– Sunburst® — CBlo EPfP MBri MGos SBid SPan
'Gold Penny' — See ***H. androsaemum* 'Dart's Golden Penny'**
grandiflorum — See ***H. kouytchense***
henryi L 753 — CChu SRms
'Hidcote' ♀ — CArn CB&S CDec CLan CShe CTrw EBre ECha ELan ENot GCHN GRei ISea LGro LHop MBal MBar MBri MGos MWat NNor NRoo NWea SHBN SPer SReu WBod WDin WWin
* 'Hidcote Gold' — WRHF
'Hidcote Variegated' — COtt CWLN EBee ELan EMon GCHN GOrc MBal SHFr SPer SRms WWeb
hircinum — CPle SIde
¶ – subsp. *albimontanum* — SPan
– subsp. *cambessedesii* — EMon LRHS
– subsp. *majus* — EMon
hirsutum — CKin CTiv
hookerianum — CPle
humifusum — ECWi EHyt GAri WCla
hyssopifolium — CPle
× *inodorum* 'Albury Purple' — See ***H. androsaemum* 'Albury Purple'**
– 'Elstead' — CShe ECtt ELan MBal MBar MGos MWat NFla NRoo SHBN SRms WDin WHCG WWin
§ – 'Orange Flair' — CBlo CDoC MGos NFla
– 'Summergold' — CBlo
– 'Ysella' — ECha ECtt EFol ELan EPla EWes SDry
japonicum — ECou EWes
kalmianum — CBot CChe EWes SBid
kamtschaticum — CChu EDAr

kelleri	GCHN
§ ***kiusianum*** var. ***yakusimense***	GCHN MBar MTho NGre NWCA
§ ***kouytchense*** 🏆	CPle CSam EWes GQui MBri SDry SPan WKif WPat WPyg WRTC
lagarocladum	CChu ELan MBlu SPan
lancasteri	CBlo CKni CPle CSte ELan EMon EPfP LRHS SMac WWat
– L 750	CChu
leschenaultii hort.	See ***H. 'Rowallane'***
linarioides	GTou
maclarenii L 863	CChu CPle
montanum	MSal
× ***moserianum*** 🏆	CB&S CLan CShe EBre ENot MBal MBar MBri NNor NPer SHBN SPer SRms WStI
§ – 'Tricolor' (v)	CB&S CBot CSpe EBre EHoe ELan ENot GCHN GOrc IOrc LGro LHop MBal MBar MBri MGos MWat NNor SHBN SMad SPan SPer SReu WAbe WDin WEas WPyg WSHC WWin
– 'Variegatum'	See ***H.*** × ***moserianum*** **'Tricolor'**
'Mrs Brabazon'	See ***H. androsaemum*** **'Gladys Brabazon'**
nummularium	NBir
oblongifolium	CPle WLRN
olympicum 🏆	CArn CInt CMea CNic CShe ECha EFer ELan EPot GCHN GDra GLil LGro MFir MPla MWat NMen NNor SAlw SBla SEas SHel SIng SPer SPla SRms SSmi WHen
I – 'Calypso'	CBlo NPro
* – 'Eden Star'	NPro
– 'Edith'	NCat SAsh WPyg
– 'Grandiflorum'	See ***H. olympicum*** **f. *uniflorum***
§ – f. ***minus***	ECtt EGoo ELan EMNN GCHN GCal GDra LCom MOne MRav NRoo SMer SRms WPer WPnn WStI WWin
§ – – 'Sulphureum'	CBot EGoo ESis EWes MHar MRav NRoo SPer SPla SRms WSHC WWin
§ – – 'Variegatum'	EFol EGoo ELan EWes LBee LHop MHar MHig NRoo WPat WPyg
§ – f. ***uniflorum***	CM&M EBar GAri GAul LIck MBal MBar MBro NBro NPri NRoo NVic SEND WAbe WCla WHoo
– – 'Citrinum' 🏆	CLyd CMea ECha ECtt EFol EHyt EPot GCHN LBee LHop MBal MWat NBro NRoo SBid SBla SIgm WAbe WCla WEas WHoo WKif WOMN WPat WWat
orientale	CMHG EWes GCHN MBro MPla NMen NRoo WCla WPer
– JCA 3302	NHol
§ ***pallens***	ECho MDHE SIng
patulum var. ***forrestii***	See ***H. forrestii***
♦ – var. ***henryi*** Rehder et hort.	See ***H. pseudohenryi***
♦ – – Veitch ex Bean	See ***H. beanii***
* – 'Variegatum'	LHop SEas
perforatum	CArn CJew CKin ECWi EWFC GAul GPoy LHol MChe MHew NHex NMir SIde WCla WHer WJek WOak WSel WWye
polyphyllum	See ***H. olympicum*** **f. *minus***
– 'Citrinum'	See ***H. olympicum*** **f. *minus*** **'Sulphureum'**
– 'Grandiflorum'	See ***H. olympicum*** **f. *uniflorum***
– 'Sulphureum'	See ***H. olympicum*** **f. *minus*** **'Sulphureum'**
– 'Variegatum'	See ***H. olympicum*** **f. *minus*** **'Variegatum'**
prolificum	CChu CMHG ECtt ELan GCHN MAsh SChu SPan SSpi WRTC
pseudohenryi B&L 12009	CChu
– L 1029	CChu
pseudopetiolatum	GTou
– var. ***yakusimense***	See ***H. kiusianum*** var. ***yakusimense***
pulchrum	CKin ECWi
quadrangulum Linnaeus	See ***H. tetrapterum***
reptans Dyer	CMea ECha ESis EWes
– hort.	See ***H. olympicum*** **f. *minus***
rhodoppeum	See ***H. cerastioides*** subsp. ***meuselianum***
roeperianum	SBid
§ 'Rowallane' 🏆	CB&S CBot CLTr CLan CPle CTrw ISea MArl SDix SHBN
¶ ***scouleri*** subsp. ***nortoniae***	EWes
sp. ACE 2321	CPle
sp. ACE 2524	CPle
stellatum	CGre EGoo EPla WWat
subsessile B&L 12486	EMon
'Sungold'	See ***H. kouytchense***
tenuicaule KR 743	ISea
§ ***tetrapterum***	CArn CKin ECWi EWFC MHew MSal WHil
tomentosum	GCHN WPer
trichocaulon	CLyd ELan EWes GCHN MBro NMen NRoo WPat WPyg WWin
uralum	CPle
– CC 1225	WHCr
wilsonii	CChu
yakusimense	See ***H. kiusianum*** var. ***yakusimense***

HYPOCALYMMA (Myrtaceae)

robustum	MAll

HYPOCHAERIS (Asteraceae)

radicata	CKin ECWi NMir
uniflora	NGre
§ ***variegata***	CLTr EPfP

HYPOCYRTA See NEMATANTHUS

HYPOESTES (Acanthaceae)

aristata	ERea
§ ***phyllostachya*** (v) 🏆	MBri SRms
– 'Bettina' (v)	MBri
– 'Carmina' (v)	MBri SRms
– 'Purpuriana' (v)	MBri SRms
– 'Wit' (v)	MBri SRms
sanguinolenta	See ***H. phyllostachya***

HYPOLEPIS (Hypolepidaceae)

millefolium	CFil EBre GAri

HYPOXIS (Hypoxidaceae)

argentea	WChr
hirsuta	CSte SAlw WThi
hygrometrica	CRDP ECou EPot SAlw WAbe
parvula	SBla
¶ – var. ***albiflora***	EPot
¶ – pink-flowered	EPot

setosa	WChr
villosa	WChr

HYPOXIS × RHODOHYPOXIS

See also RHODOHYPOXIS × HYPOXIS	
¶ ***H. parvula* × *R. baurii***	CRDP NHar SBla SIng SWas

HYPSELA (Campanulaceae)

longiflora	See ***H. reniformis***
§ ***reniformis***	CNic EBre ELan EMNN ESis LBee MHig MRav NGre NHar NMen NNrd NOak NWCA SRms SSmi WAbe WFar WRHF WWin
– 'Greencourt White'	CLyd GBuc GGar
sp. RB 94066	ELan MNrw

HYSSOPUS (Lamiaceae)

officinalis	CArn CChr CHan CSev EBar ECha ELan ELau GPoy LBuc LHol MBar MBri MChe NFai NRoo SChu SIde WCHb WHer WHil WOak WOve WPer WWye
– f. ***albus***	ECED ECha EGoo ELau GPoy MChe SChu SIde WCHb WCer WHer WJek WPer WSel WWye
– subsp. ***angustifolius***	See ***H. officinalis officinalis***
– subsp. ***aristatus***	EBre ELau ESis GPoy LHol LLWP MChe NRoo SIde WCHb WEas WJek WSel WWin WWye
– ***roseus***	CHar EBar ECha ELau GPoy MChe NFai NNor SChu SEND SIde WCHb WCer WHer WJek WKif WPer WWye
§ – f. ***ruber***	LLWP
tianschanicus	MFos

HYSTRIX (Poaceae)

patula	CArc CCuc EBee EHoe EMon EPPr EPla ESOG ETPC GBin GCal MCCP NBro NFai NHol WHal WLRN WPer

IBERIS (Brassicaceae)

amara	EWFC MSal WUnd
candolleana	See ***I. pruitii* Candolleana Group**
commutata	See ***I. sempervirens***
'Correvoniana'	WEas
'Dick Self'	EBre EDAr
gibraltarica	CFir EMan GBur NNor NPri SRms WGor WWhi WWtk
jordanii	See ***I. pruitii***
§ ***pruitii***	CPBP EBur MBal SBla
§ – Candolleana Group	EHyt
saxatilis	NSla SIng
– ***candolleana***	See ***I. pruitii* Candolleana Group**
semperflorens	MHlr NFla SAlw WCot WOve
§ ***sempervirens*** 🏆	CB&S CMHG CTri EAst ELan EMan GBur LGro MBal MWat NBro NFai NGre NNor NOrc SRms WCot WGwG WPer WWtk
– 'Little Gem'	See ***I. sempervirens* 'Weisser Zwerg'**
– 'Pinky Perpetual'	NPer
– 'Pygmaea'	CLyd EWes MHig MWat NHar NMen NRai WHil
§ – 'Schneeflocke' 🏆	CShe CWan ENot GAri MBro MOne SIng SMrm SPer WBea WHoo WPyg
◆ – 'Snowdrift'	See ***I. sempervirens* 'Zwergschneeflocke'**
◆ – Snowflake	See ***I. sempervirens* 'Schneeflocke'**
– 'Starkers'	EMon
§ – 'Weisser Zwerg'	CMea CShe EBre ECha EFou ELan EMNN EPla GLil LBee MBro MHig MPla MTho NGre NHar NHol NMen NTow SBla SIng WHoo WWin
spathulata	MHig

IDESIA (Flacourtiaceae)

polycarpa	CB&S CFil CMCN CPle LRHS SSpi SSta WWat

ILEX † (Aquifoliaceae)

¶ × ***altaclerensis***	SHHo
– 'Atkinsonii' (m)	CRos
– 'Belgica' (f)	SHHo
N – 'Belgica Aurea' (f/v) 🏆	CB&S CMHG CRos ELan LNet MAsh MBal MBar MBri MWat SEND SHBN SHHo
– 'Camelliifolia' (f) 🏆	CMCN CMHG CRos EBee LPan MBlu MBri MMea MRav MWat NWea SBid SBod SHHo SPer WWat
– 'Golden King' (f/v) 🏆	CB&S CDec CLan CMHG CRos CShe EBre ELan ENot GRei ISea LNet MBal MBar MBri MGos MWat NHol NWea SBod SDix SHBN SHHo SPer SReu SSta WAbe WDin WPat WWat
– 'Hendersonii' (f)	CBlo SBod WBcn
– 'Hodginsii' (m) 🏆	CBlo CDoC CRos ECot IOrc MBar SBid SEND SHHo
¶ – 'Howick' (f)	SHHo
– 'Lady Valerie' (f/v)	SHHo
– 'Lawsoniana' (f/v) 🏆	CB&S CDec CMHG CPle CRos CSam EBre ELan LNet MBal MBar MBri MGos MMea MWat NHol NWea SBod SHBN SHHo SPer SSta WDin WPat WRTC
– 'Maderensis Variegata'	See ***I. aquifolium* 'Maderensis Variegata'**
– 'Marnockii' (f)	NHed SHHo
– 'Nigrescens' (m)	MWat
– 'Purple Shaft' (f)	SHHo
– 'Ripley Gold' (f/v)	CBlo CMHG EBre MAsh NHol SAga SBid SHHo
– 'Silver Sentinel'	See ***I.* × *altaclerensis* 'Belgica Aurea'**
¶ – 'W.J. Bean' (f)	SHHo
– 'Wilsonii' (f) 🏆	CMHG IOrc LPan MMea MWat SBid SBod SHHo
aquifolium 🏆	CB&S CChe CKin CPer CSam CTri ELau GRei IOrc LHyr LNet MBar MBri MGos MWat SHBN SHHo WDin WMou WOrn WStI
– 'Alaska' (f)	CBlo CDoC CEnd CMCN EBee EBre EMil IHos LBuc MAsh MBal MMea SHHo WMou
– 'Alcicornis' (m)	CMCN
– 'Amber' (f) 🏆	CTri MWat SHHo SMad WLRN

– 'Angustifolia' (m or f)	CB&S EBee EPla GAri IOrc MBar MWat SHHo WPat WRTC
– 'Angustimarginata Aurea' (m)	WPyg
§ – 'Argentea Marginata' (f) 🏆	CB&S CSam CShe CTri EBre ECtt ENot LHyr LPan MAsh MBri MGos MLan MMea MRav NBee NWea SHHo SPer SReu SRms WAbe WDin WGwG WPat WStI WWeb
§ – 'Argentea Marginata Pendula' (f)	CTri ELan LPan MAsh MBal MBri NHol NWea SBod SHHo SPer SRms WPat WPyg WWat
– 'Argentea Pendula'	See ***I. aquifolium*** **'Argentea Marginata Pendula'**
– 'Argentea Variegata'	See ***I. aquifolium*** **'Argentea Marginata'**
– 'Atlas' (m)	CB&S CDoC LBuc SHHo
– 'Aurea Marginata' (f)	CMHG EBee ECtt EHic EHoe ELan LPan MGos MMea SBod SHBN SHHo WAbe WPat WRHF
– 'Aurea Marginata Pendula' (f)	CDoC CRos EBee NHol WPat WPyg
¶ – 'Aurea Marginata Stricta' (f)	WCru
– 'Aurea Ovata'	See ***I. aquifolium*** **'Ovata Aurea'**
– 'Aurea Regina'	See ***I. aquifolium*** **'Golden Queen'**
– 'Aureovariegata Pendula'	See ***I. aquifolium*** **'Weeping Golden Milkmaid'**
– 'Aurifodina' (f)	EHic NHol WLRN
§ – 'Bacciflava' (f)	CEnd CPle CSam CTri ECtt ELan GCHN IOrc MAsh MBal MBlu MGos MMea MRav MWat NBee SHHo SPer SRms WDin WGwG WWat WWeb
– 'Crassifolia' (f)	EPla SHHo SMad
– 'Crispa' (m)	CPle EHic ISea MBal MBlu MWat NHol SHHo
– 'Crispa Aureomaculata'	See ***I. aquifolium*** **'Crispa Aureopicta'**
§ – 'Crispa Aureopicta' (m)	WPat
– 'Ferox' (m)	CBlo CLan EHal ELan LPan MBal SHHo
– 'Ferox Argentea' (m/v) 🏆	Widely available
* – 'Ferox Argentea Picta' (m)	LRHS SPla
– 'Ferox Aurea' (m/v)	CBlo CMHG CPle EBee ELan LRHS MWat NHol SHHo SPer WPat WPyg WRTC
§ – 'Flavescens' (f)	CBot EPla NHed NHol SHHo WLRN
* – 'Forest Weeping'	LRHS
– 'Foxii' (m)	SHHo
– 'Fructu Luteo'	See ***I. aquifolium*** **'Bacciflava' (f)**
– 'Gold Flash' (f/v)	ECtt ELan EMil MAsh MBri NBee NHol SHHo
– 'Golden Milkboy' (m/v) 🏆	CB&S CLan CRos EAst EBee ECtt ELan EMil ENot IHos LNet MBal MBlu NHol SBid SHHo SPla WPat WPyg WRTC
– 'Golden Milkmaid' (f/v)	CBlo CRos IOrc SBid
§ – 'Golden Queen' (m/v) 🏆	CB&S CRos EBre ELan ENot LHyr LNet MBal MGos MWat SPer SReu SRms
* – 'Golden Tears'	SHHo WBcn
– 'Golden van Tol' (f/v)	CB&S CRos CTri EBre ECtt ELan ENot IOrc LNet LPan MAsh MBal MBar MBlu MBri MGos NBee NHol SHBN SHHo SRms WGwG WStI
– 'Green Pillar' (f) 🏆	CMCN MMea SHHo
– 'Handsworth New Silver' (f/v) 🏆	CB&S CDec CPle CRos CSam EBre EHoe ELan IOrc LNet MAsh MBal MBar MBri MMea MWat NHol NTow NWea SBod SHHo SPer SPla WMou WPat WRTC WStI WWat
– 'Harpune' (f)	SHHo
§ – 'Hascombensis'	CRos EPot GAul GDra LGre LHop MBal MGos MPla NHar SAxl SMac WFar WPyg WWat
– 'Hastata' (m)	CMHG EPla MWat SHHo
– 'Ingramii' (m/v)	EHic SHHo WBcn
– 'J.C. van Tol' (f) 🏆	Widely available
– 'Latispina' (f)	SHHo
* – 'Laurifolia Aurea' (m)	WGwG
– 'Lichtenthalii' (f)	SHHo WBcn
– 'Madame Briot' (f/v) 🏆	CDoC CMHG CTri ELan ENot IOrc LHyr MAsh MBal MBar MBri MMea MWat NHol NWea SBod SHHo SPer SPla SReu SRms WDin WGwG WWeb
§ – 'Maderensis Variegata' (m)	SHHo
– 'Monstrosa' (m)	SHHo
– Moonlight holly	See ***I. aquifolium*** **'Flavescens'**
– 'Myrtifolia' (m)	CDoC ELan EPfP EPla LRHS MBar MBlu MBri MGos
§ – 'Myrtifolia Aurea Maculata' (m/v) 🏆	CDoC CMHG CPle CRos EBar EHoe ELan LNet LRHS MAsh MBal MBri MWat NHol NWea SMad SPer WPat WRTC
◆ – 'Myrtifolia Aureovariegata'	See ***I. aquifolium*** **'Myrtifolia Aurea Maculata'**
§ – 'Ovata Aurea' (m/v)	CRos SHHo SSta
– 'Pendula' (f)	CRos EPfP MAsh MBri MWat SBod SHHo
– 'Pendula Mediopicta'	See ***I. aquifolium*** **'Weeping Golden Milkmaid'**
§ – 'Pyramidalis' (f) 🏆	CEnd CTri EBre ELan ENot GCHN GRei IHos LHyr MAsh MBar MBri MGos MLan NBee NHol NWea SHHo SPer SPla SRms WDin WOrn
– 'Pyramidalis Aureomarginata' (f)	CDoC MGos SHHo WGwG
– 'Pyramidalis Fructu Luteo' (f) 🏆	CBlo MBar SHHo WBcn
– 'Recurva' (m)	MWat
– 'Rubricaulis Aurea' (f/v)	MBal WBcn
– 'Silver King'	See ***I. aquifolium*** **'Silver Queen'**
– 'Silver Milkboy' (f/v)	CB&S ELan EMil MBal MBlu SEas
– 'Silver Milkmaid' (f/v) 🏆	CMHG EAst EPfP GAul MBar MRav MWat NHol SHBN SHHo SPla SSta WGwG
§ – 'Silver Queen' (m/v) 🏆	CB&S CEnd CLan EBre ELan GRei MBal MBar MBri MGos MMea MWat NBee NWea SHHo SPer SPla WDin WHen WOrn WStI WWeb
– 'Silver Sentinel'	See ***I.*** × ***altaclerensis*** **'Belgica Aurea'**
– 'Silver van Tol' (f/v)	ELan IOrc MBri NHol SHHo WAbe WLRN WStI WWeb
§ – 'Watereriana' (m/v)	MAsh MBal SBod SMur
– 'Waterer's Gold'	See ***I. aquifolium*** **'Watereriana'**

§ – 'Weeping Golden Milkmaid' (f/v)	SHHo WPat
× ***aquipernyi***	SHHo
◆– Dragon Lady	See ***I.*** × ***aquipernyi*** **'Meschick'**
§ – Dragon Lady = 'Meschick' (f)	COtt CSte SHHo
¶ – 'San Jose' (f)	CMCN
× ***attenuata***	CMCN CRos
– 'Sunny Foster' (f) 🏆	CMCN EBee MAsh MBlu MGos
bioritsensis	CMCN MMea NWea
chinensis misapplied	See ***I. purpurea***
ciliospinosa	CMCN CPle GWht
¶ ***colchica***	CMCN
corallina	CMCN
cornuta	CLan CMCN CRos LPan SHHo
* – 'Aurea'	SHHo
– 'O'Spring' (f/v)	CMHG EPla SBid SHHo
crenata	CBlo CMCN EHic GAri MBar SReu SRms STre WNor WWat
– 'Aureovariegata'	See ***I. crenata*** **'Variegata'**
– 'Compacta'	See ***I. crenata*** **'Bennett's Compact'**
– 'Convexa' (f) 🏆	CB&S EBee EHic ENot GDra GWht MBal MBar MBri NHol NWea WPat WPyg WRTC WWat
– 'Fastigiata'	CBlo CRos EBar EBee EBre ECle LHol LHop MAsh MBri MGos MLan SCoo SHHo SPer WGwG WWes
– 'Fukarin'	See ***I. crenata*** **'Shiro-fukurin'**
– 'Golden Gem' (f) 🏆	CLan CRos EBre EHoe ELan ENot ISea ITim LPan MBar MBri MGos MLan MWat NBee NEgg NGre NHed NHol NWea SHHo SIng SPer SReu SSta WDin WHar WPat WRTC WWat
– 'Green Island' (m)	CRos LRHS SHHo
– 'Helleri' (f)	CMCN EPla MAsh MBar MBro NHol SSta WPat WPyg
– 'Luteovariegata'	See ***I. crenata*** **'Variegata'**
– 'Mariesii' (f)	CMCN GWht MBlu MBro MHig MPla NGre NHed NHol SBla SIng WPat WPyg
– 'Mount Halla' (f)	CMCN GWht
I – 'Pyramidalis' (f)	CMil EHic LPan MPla NHar NHol WPat
§ – 'Shiro-fukurin' (f/v)	CMCN CMHG EAst EFol EHic ELan NHar NHol SBid SHHo SPla SSta WCru WPat WPyg
– 'Snowflake'	See ***I. crenata*** **'Shiro-fukurin'**
– 'Stokes' (m)	GAri LRHS MBri WPat WPyg
– upright form	CMCN
§ – 'Variegata'	CMCN CMHG ELan EPla GAri MBar MBlu NHol SHHo SRms WPat
'Dazzler'	SHHo
decidua	CMCN
dimorphophylla	CChu CMCN EPla SHHo
– 'Somerset Pixie'	SHHo WRTC
'Doctor Kassab' (f)	CMCN
'Drace' (f)	ELan
'Elegance' (f)	CRos
fargesii	CMCN
ficoidea	CMCN
glabra 'Snow White' (f)	MBal
hascombensis	See ***I. aquifolium*** **'Hascombensis'**
'Indian Chief' (f)	CSam MBlu SMad WWat
insignis	See ***I. kingiana***

'John T. Morris' (m)	MBal
§ ***kingiana***	CB&S CMCN WWat
× ***koehneana***	CBot
– 'Chestnut Leaf' (f) 🏆	CMCN CMHG MMea MRav MWat SHHo SMad WCru
§ ***kusanoi***	CMCN
latifolia	CHEx CMCN SHHo SMad
longipes	CMCN
'Lydia Morris' (f)	CMHG CSam SBid SHHo WWat
¶ ***macropoda***	CMCN
× ***makinoi***	CMCN
'Mary Nell' (f)	SHHo
¶ × ***meserveae***	SHHo
§ – 'Blue Angel' (f) 🏆	Widely available
◆– Blue Maid	See ***I.*** × ***meserveae*** **Blue Maid = 'Mesid'**
– 'Blue Prince' (m)	CB&S CMHG COtt CRos EHoe IOrc LBuc LHol MAsh MBal MBar MBlu MMea NHed NHol SHBN SHHo SPer WDin WStI WWeb
– 'Blue Princess' (f) 🏆	CB&S CDec CMHG COtt CRos ENot LBuc LPan MAsh MBal MBar MBlu MMea NBee NHol SHBN SHHo SPer WDin WStI
* – 'Glenroy Purple'	MBal
– 'Golden Girl' (f)	EMil
§ – Blue Maid = 'Mesid' (f)	EMil
muchagara	CB&S CMCN
myrtifolia	CBlo CMCN ECot NHar SBid WLRN
'Nellie R. Stevens' (f)	CBlo EBee ENot IHos
nothofagifolia C&H 424	GAri GGGa
opaca	CMCN
pedunculosa	CMCN SHHo
perado latifolia	See ***I. perado*** subsp. ***platyphylla***
§ ***perado*** subsp. ***platyphylla***	CB&S CHEx CMCN CMHG MBlu SArc SHHo
pernyi	EHoe EPla IOrc LBuc MBal NHol SHHo WWat
– var. ***veitchii***	CMCN CRos CTri NWea
poneantha	See ***I. kusanoi***
pringlei	CMCN
'Pyramidalis'	See ***I. aquifolium*** **'Pyramidalis'**
rotunda	CMCN
rugosa	CMCN
'September Gem' (f)	CMCN
serrata	CMCN WWes
'Sparkleberry' (f)	LPan
¶ ***suaveolens***	CMCN
verticillata	CGre CMCN LPan NWea WRTC
– 'Afterglow' (f)	MBlu
– f. ***aurantiaca*** (f)	CBlo MBlu SMur
– f. ***chrysocarpa***	CMCN
◆– 'Compacta'	See ***I. verticillata*** **'Nana'**
N – early male (late-flowering) (m)	MBlu
– (f)	CPle CRos ELan GAri SBid SMur
* – 'Fructu Albo'	CMCN
* – 'Golden Male'	CMCN
* – 'Golden Rain'	CMCN
N – late male (late-flowering) (m)	MBlu
– (m)	CDoC ELan GAri SBid SMur WWat
§ – 'Nana' (f)	CMCN MBlu
– 'Red Sprite'	See ***I. verticillata*** **'Nana'**
– 'Stop Light' (f)	MBlu
– 'Sunset' (f)	MBlu

– 'Winter Red' (f) CDoC CMCN CWSG MBlu WWat
¶ ***vomitoria*** CMCN
x ***wandoensis*** CMCN SHHo
'Washington' (f) CPle EPla NHol WRTC
yunnanensis CMCN CMHG GAri GWht

ILIAMNA See SPHAERALCEA

ILLICIUM (Illiciaceae)
anisatum CArn CChu CFil CHan CPle SSpi WPat WPyg WRTC WSHC WWat WWye
floridanum CChu CPle GOrc MBal SBid SPer SSpi SSta WBod WSHC WWat
henryi CChu CMCN CPle WSHC

ILYSANTHES (Scrophulariaceae)
See Plant Deletions

IMPATIENS (Balsaminaceae)
auricoma EBak
balfourii MSto
¶ 'Ballerina' CInt
'Blackberry Ice' CHal CSpe
capensis CSpe MSto
'Cardinal Red' CHal CInt
'Dapper Dan' (v) CHal CSpe
'Diamond Rose' CHal
'Diamond Scarlet' CHal
double flowered EBak
¶ 'Evening Blush' CInt
glandulifera WHer
– 'Candida' CBre EMon
'Golden Surprise' SMrm WLRN
hawkeri EBak
'Madame Pompadour' CHal
New Guinea Group CHal EBak MBri WLRN
niamniamensis EBak ERea GCra LBlm LCns LHil
– 'Congo Cockatoo' CHal CInt ECon EOHP LIck SRms SVen
¶ ***omeiana*** WCot
'Orange Surprise' CHal
'Peach Ice' CHal CSpe
pseudoviola LHil SHFr
* – 'Alba' CSpe
¶ – 'Woodcote' CSpe LHil
¶ 'Purple Chico' CInt
'Raspberry Ripple' CHal
¶ 'Salmon Princess' CInt
sodenii LHil
¶ ***sulcata*** SHFr
sultani See ***I. walleriana***
tinctoria CChu CFil CFir CGre CTre GCal LHil SIgm SVen WCot WCru WPGP
– subsp. ***elegantissima*** CFee
– subsp. ***tinctoria*** GCra
¶ ***ugandensis*** GCal
§ ***walleriana*** EBak MBri
* – 'Variegata' CHal

IMPERATA (Poaceae)
cylindrica EPar MHlr MSal NSti WCot
– 'Red Baron' See ***I. cylindrica* 'Rubra'**
§ – 'Rubra' Widely available

INCARVILLEA (Bignoniaceae)
§ ***arguta*** CBot CChu CHan CSpe GCal GCra LGre MSto SAxl SSca WOld WPer WThi WWin
brevipes See ***I. mairei***
compacta EMon GBin MSto NHar SIng
– ACE 1455 EBee
delavayi CAvo CBot CHan EBre ECha EFou ELan EMon ENot EPot LBow LHop MBri MDun MFir NFla NRoo SBla SDeJ SPer SRms WCla WHil WHoo WOld WTyr WWin
delavayi alba CBot CRDP EAst EBee EBre EHic EMan GCal LHop LWoo MCCP MMil NPSI SCro SMrm SVen WFar WHil WPen WSan WWoo
delavayi 'Bees' Pink' EBee ELan GBuc GCra
forrestii KGB 43 GBin MSto
lutea L 1986 SBla
§ ***mairei*** CSpe EAst EBar GDra LHop MHar MSCN MTho MTis NPSI SAxl SLod SMrm WPen WPer
– B&L 12602 SWas
– 'Frank Ludlow' GBuc GDra NGre NHar NSla SBla SIgm
– var. ***grandiflora*** ELan EPot LWoo MSto MTho NWoo SBla
– var. ***mairei*** ACE 1600 WDav
¶ – – ACE 2233 Nhar
◆ – – f. ***multifoliata*** See ***I. zhongdianensis***
– 'Nyoto Sama' GBuc GDra SBla
§ ***olgae*** CSam EBee ELan EMan MHar MSto WCot
sinensis 'Alba' CLon CSpe MSte MSto SMac SMrm WCot WCru
– 'Cheron' SRms SSca WSan
* 'Snowcap' NNrd
'Snowtop' CBlo CMil COtt CSpe EHic ELan EPfP ETub MDun MTis NCut NPSI NPro NTow SMad SPla WHil WPyg
sp. ACE 2420 NHar
younghusbandii MSto
§ ***zhongdianensis*** ACE 2201 NHar
¶ – ACE 2278 NHar

INDIGOFERA (Papilionaceae)
amblyantha ♀ CChu CPle EHic EMil EPfP GCal MBlu NSti SBid SDry SSpi WCru WKif WOMN WSHC
¶ ***australis*** CTrC SOWG
dielsiana CB&S CChu CPle
gerardiana See ***I. heterantha***
hebepetala WBod WCru WDin WSHC
§ ***heterantha*** ♀ CArn CB&S CBot CMCN CPle EHoe ELan EMil ENot IOrc LHop MBlu MPla NFla SHBN SPer SReu SSpi SSta WAbe WFar WPer WSHC WWat WWye
kirilowii CGre SOWG WSHC
potaninii SHBN SMur WCru WHer
pseudotinctoria CChu CSte SRms
tinctoria CArn MSal

INDOCALAMUS (Poaceae - Bambusoideae)
hamadae EPla SDry
latifolius EOas EPla ISta SBam SDry WJun

longiauritus SBam SDry
solidus EPla ISta SBam SDry WJun
§ ***tessellatus*** CFil CSte EBee EFul EOas EPfP EPla WJun

INULA † (Asteraceae)

acaulis NNrd SSca WCot
conyzae CKin MHew MSal
crithmoides WHer
dysenterica See ***Pulicaria dysenterica***
ensifolia CHan CSam ECro ELan IBlr LFis MHar MRav MSte MTho NBro NDea NFai SSvw WBea WEas WHil WHoo WMer WPyg
– 'Gold Star' ECtt GAul NBir NNor NOak NRoo WLRN WPer WTyr
glandulosa See ***I. orientalis***
'Golden Beauty' See ***Buphthalmum salicifolium* 'Golden Wonder'**
helenium CArn CKin CSev ECWi ECro ELau EWFC GPoy ILis LHol MChe MFir MHew MSal MSto NMir SIde SRms WBea WByw WCer WHer WOak WPer WWye
helianthus-aquaticus EMon
CLD 658
hookeri CBre CMea CRDP CSam CSev ECED ECha ELan ELau EMar GMac IBlr LFis MBel MCLN MFir MSte NDea NHol NPer NWes SDix SUsu WBea WByw WEas WHal WOld WTyr
magnifica CHan CSam EBre ECha ECro ELan EMon GGar LFis MBro MFir MGam MNrw MRav MUlv NBro NDea NHol SDix SMad SMrm WBea WHer WHoo WMer WOld WPer WWin WWye
* 'Mediterranean Sun' MCLN SIde
oculus-christi ECro EWes LFis NHol
* 'Oriental Star' WHil
§ ***orientalis*** CKel CPea ECro EFou GCra MBri MBro MSCN NCat NFai NLak NMir NRoo NSti SMad WBea WByw WHoo WOld WPer WPyg
racemosa ECha ECro EMon EPPr GAul GBin GCal IBlr MNrw MSte NChi SMad SMrm SRms WFar
– CC&McK 620 GCHN
rhizocephala CSam
royleana CArc CHan ECED EGar GCal GCra MBro MNrw MSte SMad SSca WHil
verbascifolia EMan WHil

IOCHROMA (Solanaceae)

coccinea ECon
cyanea CGre CPle ECon ERea LCns LHil SLMG SOWG
– dark form LHil
grandiflora CHEx CSev LHil SLMG SOWG
violacea See ***Cestrum violaceum***
¶ ***warscewiczii*** ECon

IPHEION (Alliaceae)

'Alberto Castillo' CBro CMea CMon EHyt ELan EWes MTho WChr WCot
dialystemon CMon
§ 'Rolf Fiedler' 🏆 CAvo CBro CMea CMon EBre EBur ECho EHyt ELan EPar EPot EWes LAma LHil MHig MRPP MTho SBla WChr WCot WOMN
sellowianum EHyt
§ ***uniflorum*** CAvo CBro CHal EBre ECha EFol ETub LAma MBri MBro MNrw MRav MTol NGar NMen NRog NWCA NWoo SIng SRms WAbb WCla WHil WHoo WPer
– 'Album' CAvo CBro CMea ECha EHyt ELan EPar EPot ERos ETub EWes GDra MTho NGar NMGW SBla SIng WFar
– 'Froyle Mill' 🏆 CAvo CBro CHal CMea EBur EHyt ELan EPar EPot ERos EWes GDra LGan MHig MTho NMGW SAga SBla SIng WChr WHoo
– 'Wisley Blue' 🏆 CAvo CBro CMea ECha ELan EPar EPot ERos ETub LAma LHil MFos MHig MS&S MTho NNrd NRar SBla SIng SRms WHil WHoo WPyg

IPOMOEA (Convolvulaceae)

acuminata See ***I. indica***
alba CPlN
* ***andersonii*** CPlN MSto
* ***batatas*** 'Blackie' CPlN
¶ ***bonariensis*** SVen
carnea LChe
¶ – subsp. ***fistulosa*** NGno
coccinea MSto
horsfalliae 🏆 CPlN
§ ***indica*** 🏆 CB&S CHEx CHal CKni CLTr CPlN ERea LCns SLMG WCru
learii See ***I. indica***
§ ***lobata*** CSpe LIck MSto
palmata See ***I. cairica***
pennata 'Relli Valley' MSto
purpurea WHer
– 'Kniola's Purple-black' MSto
quamoclit CPlN
'Scarlett O'Hara' WGor
tuberosa See ***Merremia tuberosa***
◆ ***versicolor*** See ***I. lobata***
violacea hort. See ***I. tricolor***

IPOMOPSIS (Polemoniaceae)

§ ***aggregata*** CPBP
– subsp. ***aggregata*** NTow

IRESINE (Amaranthaceae)

herbstii CHal EBak ERea IBlr LHil SLMG
– 'Aureoreticulata' CHal LHil SLMG
– 'Brilliantissima' CBrk CHal LHil
lindenii 🏆 CBrk CLTr LHil SLMG

IRIS † (Iridaceae)

'A.W. Tait' (Spuria) GCal
'Abracadabra' (SDB) LBro MS&S
'Abridged Version' (MTB) NZep
'Acapulco Gold' (TB) SCro
'Ace of Clubs' (SDB) NZep
'Action Front' (TB) COtt EHic ERou NCat WLRN
'Actress' (TB) EFou

'Adobe Sunset' (Spuria)	LBro
'Adrienne Taylor' (MDB) 🏆	LBro MAus WWin
afghanica	MSto
'Ain't She Sweet' (IB)	SCro
'Alastor' (TB)	MS&S
'Albatross' (TB)	CKel
albicans 🏆	CMea CMon SCro
'Alcazar' (TB)	EPfP GLil
'Alenette' (TB)	MAus
'Alice Goodman' (TB)	LIri
'Alien' (IB)	LBro
'All Right' (IB)	NZep
'Allegiance' (TB)	WEas
'Alpine Lake' (MDB)	NZep
'Already' (MDB)	EHyt
'Altruist' (TB)	SCro
'Amadora' (TB)	LBro
'Amaranth Gem' (SDB)	LBro
'Ambassadeur' (TB)	CKel ERou GLil
'Amber Blaze' (SDB)	NZep
'Amber Queen' (DB)	CGle COtt ECtt ELan EMan ERos NMen SChu SCro SPer WGwG WLRN WWeb
'Amethyst Crystal' (CH)	EBre LBro
'Amethyst Flame' (TB)	EBre ERou MAus MS&S NMGW WFar
'Amethyst Sunset' (MTB)	LBro
'Amigo' (TB)	SCro
'Amphora' (SDB)	CBro NNrd
'Anastasia' (TB)	CKel
'Ancilla' (Aril)	LWoo
'Angel Unawares' (TB)	MAus
'Angelic' (SDB)	LBro
'Angel's Tears'	See ***I. histrioides* 'Angel's Eye'**
anglica	See ***I. latifolia***
'Anna Belle Babson' (TB)	MAus SCro
'Annabel Jane' (TB)	LBro MAus SCro
'Anne Elizabeth' (SDB)	CBro ERos
'Apache Warrior' (IB)	LBro
aphylla	NOrc
'Apollodorus' (TB)	LIri
* 'Apple Court'	SApp
'Appledore' (SDB)	CBro NNrd
'Apricot Skies' (BB)	NZep
'April Ballet' (MDB)	NZep
'Arab Chief' (TB)	CKel
'Arabi Pasha' (TB)	MAus SCro SPer WGor WLRN
'Arabi Treasure' (IB)	LBro
'Archie Owen' (Spuria)	LBro
'Arctic Fancy' (IB) 🏆	LBro MMil
'Arctic Star' (TB)	CKel CShe MFir
'Arctic Tern' (TB)	LBro
'Arden' (BB)	LBro
arenaria	See ***I. humilis***
¶ 'Argus Pheasant' (SDB)	LBro
'Arnold Sunrise' (CH) 🏆	EBre LBro
'Arnold Velvet' (SDB)	LBro
'Ask Alma' (IB)	NZep
atrofusca MS&CL 56	CMon
'Attention Please' (TB)	CKel
§ ***attica***	CBro CFai CHan CMea CMon CNic CPBP EHyt ERos LBee MSto NNrd WAbe WDav
– S&L 486	CMon
§ ***aucheri***	CBro EPot LAma WChr
'Audacious' (BB)	NZep
'Aunt Martha' (BB)	MAus MBri NMGW
'Austrian Sky' (SDB)	CMea CSam EBee EBre ELan MBro MMil SIng WCot
'Autumn Leaves' (TB)	MAus MMil
'Avanelle' (IB)	EFou ERou LBro WBcn
'Az Ap' (IB)	NZep SCro
'Aztec Star' (SDB)	LBro
¶ 'Azurea' (MDB)	NFla
¶ 'Babushka' (SDB)	LBro
'Baby Bibs' (MTB)	NZep
'Baby Blessed' (SDB)	CBro NSti NZep
'Baby Face' (TB)	MMil
'Baccarat' (TB)	CKel
'Baked Alaska' (TB)	MMil
bakeriana	LAma LRHS WChr
'Ballerina Blue' (TB)	ERou
'Ballyhoo' (TB)	LRHS MAus MBri
'Banbury Beauty' (CH)	LWoo NSti
'Banbury Fair' (CH)	Lbro
'Banbury Gem' 🏆	LBro
'Banbury Melody' (CH)	CFee WBcn
'Banbury Ruffles' (SDB)	CKel EBee MAus NMGW NMen NSti SCro
'Banbury Welcome' (CH)	IBlr
'Bang' (TB)	CKel
'Baria' (SDB)	LBro
barnumae	EHyt
barnumae polakii	See ***I. polakii***
'Baroque Prelude' (TB)	CKel MMil
'Basso' (IB)	SCro
'Batik' (BB)	SCro
'Batsford' (SDB)	CBro NNrd
'Battle Shout' (IB)	LBro
'Bayberry Candle' (TB)	LIri
'Be Dazzled' (SDB)	EFou
'Be Happy' (SDB)	NZep
'Beauty Mark' (SDB)	NZep
'Beckon' (TB)	CKel
'Bee Wings' (MDB)	NZep WEas
'Before the Storm' (TB)	LIri SCro
'Belise' (Spuria) 🏆	LBro
'Belissinado' (Spuria)	LBro
'Belvi Queen' (TB)	MNrw
* 'Ben Hasel'	ECha
N 'Benton Arundel' (TB)	SCro
'Benton Cordelia' (TB)	SCro
'Benton Dierdre' (TB)	SCro SRms
'Benton Evora' (TB)	ENot
N 'Benton Lorna' (TB)	SCro
'Benton Nigel' (TB)	MAus
'Benton Sheila' (TB)	SCro
'Berkeley Gold' (TB)	CMGP COtt EBre ECtt ERav EWes LBro LWak NMGW NOrc SPer SWat WLRN WWtk
'Best Bet'	LIri
'Betsey Boo' (SDB)	CKel NZep
'Betty Chatten' (TB)	MHig NMen NNrd WLRN
'Betty Cooper' (Spuria)	LBro
'Betty my Love' (Spuria)	LBro
'Betty Wood' (SDB)	LBro
'Beverly Sills' (TB)	CKel LBro LIri MAus SCro
¶ 'Bewdley' (IB)	LBro
'Beyond' (TB)	SCro
'Bibury' (SDB) 🏆	EGle LBro MAus MMil SCro
N 'Big Day' (TB)	CKel WBcn
◆ ***biglumis***	See ***I. lactea***
biliottii	CBro
'Black as Night' (TB)	LIri
'Black Dragon' (TB)	SCro
'Black Flag' (TB)	LIri
'Black Hills' (TB)	CKel MUlv
'Black Lady' (MTB)	LBro
'Black Swan' (TB)	CHad COtt EBre ECtt ELan EMan ERav MAus MMil MRav WCot WGwG
'Black Watch' (IB)	CKel
'Blazing Saddles' (TB)	NZep

'Blenheim Royal' (TB)	SCro
'Blitz' (SDB)	NZep
¶ ***bloudowii***	CPBP LWoo
'Blue Ballerina' (CH) 🏆	LBro
'Blue Denim' (SDB)	CBro CM&M EBar EBre ECtt EGle EHyt ENot GMaP LBro LCom MRav NNrd WHoo WMer WWeb
'Blue Doll' (MDB)	MS&S NZep
'Blue Duchess' (TB)	CKel
'Blue Eyed Blond' (IB)	SCro
'Blue Hendred' (SDB)	LBro MAus NBir
'Blue Horizon'	ERos NMen
¶ 'Blue Lassie' (Spuria)	LBro
'Blue Line' (SDB)	NZep
'Blue Luster' (TB) 🏆	LBro LIri SCro
'Blue Magic' (Dutch)	NRog
'Blue Moss' (SDB)	LBro
'Blue Pigmy' (SDB)	CGle CMil EBre LCom NCat NMen NNrd SCro SPer WGwG WLRN
'Blue Pools' (SDB)	EFou EGle LBro MBri MHFP NZep SCro
'Blue Reflection' (TB)	MMil
'Blue Rhythm' (TB)	CKel CM&M EMan ERou LBro NFai SCro SMrm WLRN
'Blue Shimmer' (TB)	COtt EBre ECro ELan EMan ENot MAus MRav NFai SChu SCro SPer SWat WGwG WLRN
'Blue Smoke' (TB)	CKel
'Blue Staccato' (TB)	LIri MAus SCro
'Blue Zephyr' (Spuria)	LBro
'Blushes' (IB)	SCro
'Blushing Pink' (TB)	SCro
'Bodderlecker' (SDB)	EFou
'Bold Lassie' (SDB)	WHer
'Bold Print' (IB)	MAus SCro
'Bonny' (MDB)	CBro
'Boo' (SDB)	CKel MAus NZep
'Bourne Graceful'	EBee GCal MRav NHol NSti SSpi WGwG WHow WLRN
bracteata	CFil CNic EWoo MHig SIng WPer
– JCA 13427	LWoo
'Braithwaite' (TB)	CKel CMGP COtt EBre EHic ELan ERou LBro MAus NLak SChu SCro SMrm SRms SSpe SWat WLRN
brandzae	See ***I. sintenisii*** subsp. ***brandzae***
'Brannigan' (SDB)	CBro EHyt LBro MMil NBir NNrd NSti
'Brass Tacks' (SDB)	LBro NZep
'Brassie' (SDB)	CBro CKel ERos LBro NNrd
'Breakers' (TB) 🏆	LIri
'Bridal Crown' (TB)	SCro
§ 'Bride' (DB)	CM&M NNrd
'Bride's Halo' (TB)	SCro
'Bright Button' (DB)	CKel
'Bright Moment' (SDB)	LBro
'Bright Vision' (SDB)	NZep
'Bright White' (MDB)	CBro CKel EHyt ERos LBro NMen NNrd
'Bright Yellow' (DB)	EBre MRav
'Brighteyes' (IB)	EBre ELan ESis LBro MBro MHig MTho NNrd SChu SCro SRms WPer
'Brilliant Excuse' (TB)	NZep
'Brindisi' (TB)	SCro SSte
'Bristo Magic' (TB)	SCro
'Bristol Gem' (TB)	SCro
'Broad Grin' (SDB)	LBro
'Broadleigh Ann' (CH)	CBro

'Broadleigh Carolyn' (CH) 🏆	CBro
¶ 'Broadleigh Charlotte'	CBro
'Broadleigh Clare' (CH)	CBro
'Broadleigh Dorothy' (CH)	CBro
'Broadleigh Elizabeth' (CH)	CBro
N 'Broadleigh Emily' (CH)	CBro
N 'Broadleigh Florence' (CH)	CBro EGle
¶ 'Broadleigh Jean'	CBro
'Broadleigh Joan' (CH)	CBro
'Broadleigh Joyce' (CH)	CBro
'Broadleigh Lavinia' (CH)	CBro
'Broadleigh Mitre' (CH)	CBro
'Broadleigh Nancy' (CH)	CBro
'Broadleigh Peacock' (CH)	CBro CHad IBlr MMil
N 'Broadleigh Rose' (CH)	CBro CElw CHad IBlr SMrm
'Broadleigh Sybil' (CH)	CBro
'Broadleigh Victoria' (CH)	CBro
'Broadway' (TB)	NZep SCro
'Bromyard' (SDB) 🏆	CBro
'Bronzaire' (IB) 🏆	MAus
'Bronze Beauty' (*hoogiana* hybrid)	CMon EPot
'Bronze Bird' (TB)	CKel MS&S
N 'Bronze Charm' (TB)	CKel
'Bronze Cloud' (TB)	CKel
'Broseley' (TB)	LBro
'Brown Lasso' (BB)	LBro SCro SSte
'Brown Trout' (TB)	CKel
'Brownstone' (Spuria)	LBro
'Brummit's Mauve'	MAus
'Bryngwyn' (TB)	LBro
'Bubbling Over' (TB)	LIri SCro
bucharica Foster	CBro CMon EBee EHyt EPar EPot GCra LAma MFos NRog SCro WChr
– hort.	See ***I. orchioides***
bulleyana	EWoo SIgm SRms SWas WCot
– ACE 1665	EBee
¶ – ACE 2296	EHyt
'Bumblebee Deelite' (MTB)	NZep
¶ 'Burford' (BB)	LBro
'Burgundy Brown' (TB)	NZep
'Burmese Dawn' (TB)	CKel
'Butter Pecan' (IB)	SCro
'Buttercup Bower' (TB)	MBri NMGW
'Buttercup Charm' (MDB)	NZep
'Buttermere' (TB)	SRms
'Butterpat' (IB)	NZep
'Butterscotch Kiss' (TB)	EBre ECGP ELan EMan ERou MMil MRav MS&S SCro SMrm WLRN
'Button Box' (SDB)	NZep
'Byword' (SDB)	LBro
caerulea	See ***I. albomarginata***
'Caliente' (TB)	EPfP MAus
'California Style' (IB)	NZep
§ Californian Hybrids	CChu CElw CGle CLTr CWGN ELan GCra MBal NSti SChu SSpi WBon WCru WWhi
'Calypso Mood' (TB)	SCro
'Cambridge Blue'	See ***I.* 'Monspur Cambridge Blue'**
'Campbellii'	See ***I. lutescens* 'Campbellii'**
'Can Can Red' (TB)	LIri

canadensis	See ***I. setosa*** subsp. ***canadensis***
'Canary Bird' (TB)	CKel
'Cannington Bluebird' (TB)	LBro
¶ 'Cannington Skies' (IB)	LBro
'Cannington Sweet Puff' (TB) 🏆	LBro
'Cantab' (Reticulata)	CAvo CBro EBre EHyt ELan EPar EPot ETub LAma NRog
'Capricious' (TB)	SCro
'Captain Gallant' (TB)	MAus
'Caramba' (TB)	SCro
'Caramel' (TB)	EWoo
'Cardew' (TB) 🏆	LBro
N 'Carey' (TB)	CKel
'Carilla' (SDB)	LBro LGre
'Carnaby' (TB)	LBro MAus
'Carnival Time' (TB)	EFou
'Carnton' (TB)	CKel WEas
'Carolina Gold' (TB)	SCro
'Carolyn Rose' (MTB)	LBro NZep
'Carved Pink' (TB)	SCro
'Casbah' (TB)	SCro
'Cascadian Skies' (TB)	ERou
'Catalyst' (TB)	SCro
'Cayenne Capers' (TB)	MMil MWat
'Celestial Glory' (TB)	MAus
'Centering Point' (Spuria)	LBro
'Centerpiece' (SDB)	LBro
'Centre Court' (TB)	SCro
'Chain White'	See ***I.* 'Chian Wine'**
chamaeiris	See ***I. lutescens***
'Champagne Elegance' (TB)	LBro LIri MAus
'Change of Pace' (TB)	SCro
'Chanteuse' (TB)	SCro
'Chantilly' (TB)	CM&M COtt EBre ELan EMan ERav MRav NOrc SCro
'Chapeau' (TB)	LIri
'Chapel Hill' (SDB)	LBro
'Charger' (TB)	MMil
'Charm Song' (IB)	LBro
'Charmaine' (TB)	CKel
I 'Charming' (TB)	CKel
'Chartreuse Ruffles' (TB)	SCro
'Cheers' (IB)	LBro NZep
'Cherry Falls' (TB)	LBro
'Cherry Garden' (SDB)	CBro CKel EBar EBee EBre ECro ECtt EFol ELan EWes GMaP LGre MMil MRav MS&S NBir NNrd NRoo SAlw SCro WWeb
'Cherry Orchard' (TB)	NNor
¶ 'Cherry Ripe' (TB)	EHyt
'Cherry Smoke' (TB)	SCro
'Cherub Tears' (SDB)	NZep
'Cherub's Smile' (TB)	SCro
§ 'Chian Wine' (MTB)	LBro
'Chicken Little' (MDB)	CBro
'Chief Chickasaw' (TB)	LBro
'Chief Moses' (TB)	MAus
'Chief Quinaby' (TB)	SCro
'Chief Waukesha' (TB)	SCro
I 'Chieftain' (SDB)	MRav NSti
'China Dragon' (TB)	SCro
¶ 'Chivalry' (TB)	LBro
'Chorus Girl' (TB)	CKel
'Christening Party' (TB)	CKel
'Christmas Angel' (TB)	EBre ERou MAus
'Christmas Time' (TB)	NMGW NZep
Chrysofor Group	WRHF

chrysographes	CGle CVer EBar EBre GCra LBro MBal MRav MSCN MTho NRya SHel SRms SUsu SWas WRHF WWin
chrysographes alba	NBir
chrysographes B&L 12617	EMon
– black	CBos CHad CHan CMil CRow CSam CWGN GAbr GCal GDra IBlr MBal MBro MFir NBrk NHar NMen SChu SWyc WCru WHal WHoo WPyg
I – 'Black Beauty'	CFir SPer
I – 'Black Knight'	CBot ECha EFol GCal NChi NNor NOrc SPer WPen WWin
I – 'Black Velvet'	ECha SMad
– crimson	IBlr NCat
– × ***forrestii***	GDra NBir
N – 'Inshriach'	CFai CHan EHyt GBuc GDra IBlr NHol
– 'Kew Black'	EFol
– 'Mandarin Purple'	CWGN EBee GCal NCat SPer SWyc WThi
– purple	MBro MS&S
– red	MBal
§ – var. ***rubella***	CBos CRow GDra GMac LGre MMil MSte NHol SCro SWyc
* – – 'Wine'	CHad
– 'Rubra'	See ***I. chrysographes*** var. ***rubella***
chrysophylla	MSto
– JCA 13233	LWoo SSpi
'Church Stoke' (SDB)	SCro
N 'Cider Haze' (TB)	CKel
'City of David' (TB)	SCro
'Clairette' (Reticulata)	CBro LAma
'Clap Hands' (SDB)	LBro
'Clarke Cosgrove' (Spuria)	LBro
clarkei	CHan ELan LGan NNrd NSti
'Clay's Caper' (SDB)	EFou LBro
'Cleeton Buff' (Sino-Sib)	MAus
N 'Cleo' (TB)	CKel NBir
'Cliffs of Dover' (TB)	CKel MS&S WBcn
N 'Climbing Gold'	NPri
N 'Clotted Cream'	ECha MRav
'Cloudcap' (TB)	SRms
'Cloudless Sunrise' (TB)	ERou
'Cold Cold Heart' (TB)	LIri
'Color Brite' (BB)	SCro
'Color Focus' (Spuria)	LBro
'Color Splash' (TB)	SCro
'Columbia Blue' (TB)	SCro
'Colwall' (TB)	LBro
'Combo' (SDB)	CKel
'Condottiere' (TB)	SCro
'Confetti' (TB)	MBri
confusa	CAvo CGle CHEx CHad CHan ECha EPla LHil MTho MUlv SArc SEND SSpi
§ – 'Martyn Rix'	CHad CPou LHil LWoo MHlr NPla WCot
'Conjuration' (TB)	LIri
'Connoisseur' (Spuria)	LBro
'Constant Wattez' (IB)	CKel LBuc
'Consummation' (MTB)	MS&S NZep
'Copper Classic' (TB)	NZep SCro
'Coral Chalice'	ERou LIri
'Coral Joy' (TB)	LBro
'Coral Strand' (TB)	MAus
'Coral Wings' (SDB)	NZep
'Corn Harvest' (TB)	MMil NZep
'Corrida' (TB)	LBuc
'Côte d'Or' (TB)	SCro

'Cotton Blossom' (SDB)	LBro
* 'Cotton Plantation' (La)	LBro
'Cozy Calico' (TB)	SCro
'Cracklin Burgundy' (TB)	LIri SCro
'Cranberry Ice' (TB)	CKel LIri SCro
'Cream Cake' (SDB)	NZep
'Creative Stitchery' (TB)	SCro
'Cregrina' (TB)	LBro
cretensis	See ***I. unguicularis*** subsp. ***cretensis***
'Cricket Lane' (SDB)	NZep
'Crimson Fire' (TB)	SCro
N 'Crispen Rouge' (TB)	CKel
cristata	CAvo CPBP EPot ITim LAma MDHE SRms
– 'Alba'	LBee MBal MDHE NHar NNrd SChu SIng SWas WAbe
– × ***gracilipes***	EPot
– × ***lacustris***	CHan EPot NMen NTow
croatica	See ***I. germanica***
crocea	GCra LKoh MSto WDav
'Croftway Lemon' (TB)	SCro
'Cross Stitch' (TB)	MMil NZep
'Crown Sterling' (TB)	SCro
'Cruzin' (TB)	LIri
'Cum Laude' (IB)	SCro
* ***cuniculifomis*** ACE 2224	EHyt
'Cup Race' (TB)	MAus NZep
'Cutie' (IB)	NZep
cycloglossa	SWas WChr
– HW&E 7727	LWoo
'Daisy Fresh' (MDB)	LBro
'Dale Dennis' (DB)	LBro
'Dame Judy' (TB)	CKel
'Dancer's Veil' (TB) 🏆	CKel EBre ECtt EFou EHic ELan ERou LBro MAus NVic SCoo SCro SMer
'Dancin'' (IB)	NZep
'Dancing Eyes' (SDB)	LBro
'Dancing Gold' (MTB)	NZep
danfordiae	CAvo CB&S CBro EBar EBre ELan EPar EPot ETub LAma MBri NRog
'Dante' (TB)	CKel
'Dappled Pony' (MTB)	NZep
'Dark Blizzard' (IB)	NZep
'Dark Bury' (TB)	LBro
'Dark Rosaleen' (TB)	LBro
'Dark Spark' (SDB)	NSti
'Dark Vader' (SDB)	NZep
'Darkover' (SDB)	LBro
'Darkside' (TB)	SCro
'David Chapman' (TB)	LBro
'Dawn Candle' (Spuria)	LBro
'Dawn Favour' (SDB)	LBro
'Dawn Glory' (TB)	SCro
'Dazzling Gold' (TB)	LIri SCro
§ ***decora***	CBro
'Deep Black' (TB)	CMGP COtt CRDP EMan ERav MAus NOrc SCro SPer SWat
'Deep Fire' (TB)	LIri SCro
'Deep Pacific' (TB)	LRHS MAus MBri
'Deft Touch' (TB)	MAus
delavayi	GMaP IBlr MRPP WCot
'Delicate Air' (SDB)	LBro
'Delphi' (TB)	SCro
'Demelza' (TB)	LBro
'Demon' (SDB)	CKel EFou LBro LRHS MBri MS&S
'Denys Humphries' (TB)	LBro
'Depth of Field' (TB)	LRHS
'Deputé Nomblot' (TB)	CKel CShe
'Derring Do' (SDB)	LBro MS&S
'Derwentwater' (TB)	CBlo CKel MAus MMil SRms
'Desert Dream' (AB)	GDra NHol SWyc
'Desert Echo' (TB)	EFou LIri
'Desert Quail' (MTB)	LBro
'Desert Song' (TB)	CKel
'Designer Gown' (TB)	ERou LIri
'Designer's Choice' (TB) 🏆	LBro
'Dew Point' (IB)	SCro
'Die Braut'	See ***I.*** **'Bride'**
'Discretion' (TB)	SCro
'Doctor Behenna' (TB)	LBro
'Doll Dear' (SDB)	LBro
'Doll House' (MDB)	CBlo CMea
'Doll Ribbons' (MTB)	NZep
'Doll Type' (IB)	LBro
'DoSiDo' (SDB)	SCro
'Dotted Doll' (MTB)	NZep
'Double Lament' (SDB) 🏆	CBro LBro MMil NNrd SCro SSte
douglasiana	CBre CHad CMil EPar EPla EPot GDra IBlr LGan MLsm NNrd NSti SMac SSpi WPer
¶ – 'Agnes James'	LBro
'Dovedale' (TB) 🏆	LBro
'Doxa' (IB)	SCro
'Dreamcastle' (TB)	CKel
'Dreamsicle' (TB)	SCro
'Dresden Candleglow' (IB)	CWGN MAus
¶ 'Driftwood' (Spuria)	LBro
'Drive You Wild' (CH)	LBro
'Dualtone' (TB)	CKel
'Dundee' (TB)	SCro
'Dunlin' (MDB)	CBro ERos NMen NNrd
'Dusky Challenger' (TB)	LBro LIri MAus SCro SSte
dykesii	CRow
'Eagle's Flight' (TB)	LBro LIri NMGW NZep
'Eardisland' (IB)	LBro
'Earl' (TB)	MMil
'Earl of Essex' (TB)	MMil SCro
'Early Edition' (IB)	LBro
'Early Light' (TB) 🏆	LBro
¶ 'East Indies' (TB)	MS&S
'Eastertime' (TB)	LIri
'Easy Strolling' (SDB)	LBro
'Edge of Winter' (TB)	CKel
'Edith Wolford' (TB)	LBro LIri MAus SCro
'Edward' (Reticulata)	EPot LAma
'Edward of Windsor' (TB)	CHad CMil EBre EHic ELan ERou GLil NOrc WLRN
'Eirian' (TB)	LBro
'Eleanor's Pride' (TB)	CKel LBro MAus MMil
elegantissima	See ***I. iberica*** subsp. ***elegantissima***
'Elixir' (Spuria)	LBro
'Elizabeth Arden' (TB)	CKel
'Elizabeth Poldark' (TB)	LBro
'Elvinhall'	CBro
'Ember Days' (TB)	MMil
'Enchanted Gold' (SDB)	NZep
'English Cottage' (TB)	EGar GCal MMil MWat SCro
'Ennerdale' (TB)	MAus SRms
§ ***ensata***	CBen CMHG CWGN ECGP ELan LBro LPBA MAus MSta NBro NRoo SAWi SHig SWat WDav WHil WPer WPyg WWin
– 'Activity'	CBlo LRHS
– 'Agrippine'	LBro
– 'Alba'	CGle CWGN ECha

– 'Apollo'	CBen CRow ETub
– 'Bellender Blue'	LBro
– 'Blue Embers'	LBro
I – 'Blue Peter'	CBen CRow
– 'Blue Skies'	SIng
– 'Butterflies in Flight'	LBro
– 'Calamari'	LBro
– 'Caprician Butterfly'	SWyc
– 'Center of Attention'	LBro
* – 'Chico Geisho'	SWyc
– 'Chitose-no-tomo'	CRow
– 'Chiyo-no-haru'	LBro
* – 'Cry of Rejoice'	MAus
– 'Crystal Halo'	LBro NBrk
– 'Dancing Waves'	CRow NBrk
– 'Darling' (I)	IBlr LBuc LRHS NBrk
– 'Dresden China' (TB)	CRow NBrk
– 'Emotion' (I)	LBuc
– 'Enchanting Melody'	CRow
– 'Fairy Carillon'	LBro
– 'Flashing Koi'	NBrk
– 'Freckled Geisha'	CRow LBro
– 'Frilled Enchantment'	LBro
* – 'Fringed Cloud'	SWyc
– 'Frosted Pyramid'	LBro NBrk
– 'Galatea Marx'	CRow CWGN
* – 'Geisha Parasol'	SWyc
– 'Gei-sho-mi'	CWGN
N – 'Ghost'	CGle
– 'Gipsy'	CSpe LRHS
– 'Glitter and Gayety'	CRow NBrk
– 'Hakug-yokuro'	CRow
– 'Hana-aoi'	CRow IBlr
– 'Happy Awakening'	SWyc
– 'Hatsu-shimo'	CRow IBlr
– 'Hercule'	CDoC CWGN NBrk
– Higo Hybrids	CRow IBlr MSta SCro
N – 'Hokkaido'	See ***I. ensata* 'Perry's Hokkaido'**
– 'Imperial Magic' ♀	SWyc
* – 'Innocence'	CBlo EHoe MBri
N – 'Iso-no-ob'	MBri WMer
– 'Kalamazo'	LBro
– 'Komo-no-ibo'	EBee LBuc SWat
– 'Kuma-funjin'	CWGN IBlr
* – 'Labby White'	SWyc
– 'Laced'	SPer
¶ – 'Landscape at Dawn'	CMHG CRow
* – 'Laughing Lion'	CDoC COtt LBro LRHS MBri
– 'Light at Dawn'	LBro
– 'Lilac Blotch'	SPer
– 'Magic Opal' ♀	CRow
– 'Manadzuru'	IBlr
I – 'Mandarin'	CGle CRow NBrk
¶ – 'Midnight Stars'	LBro
– 'Midsummer Reverie'	CRow
¶ – 'Miss Coquette'	LBro
§ – 'Moonlight Waves'	CDoC CMGP CRDP CRow CWGN ELan LHop MAus MFir MSte NBrk NRoo SChu SCro SSpi SWat WElm WGwG WHow WRus WWat
– 'Narihira'	CRow IBlr
– 'Oku-banri'	CDoC CWGN IBlr
– 'Oriental Eyes'	LBro
– pale mauve	SPer
– 'Peacock'	SChu SMrm SUsu
§ – 'Perry's Hokkaido'	CGle CRow IBlr NBrk
– 'Pink Frost'	CHad CRow EBre EGle GAri LRHS MBri
– 'Prairie Twilight'	LBro NBrk
– purple	SPer
I – 'Purple East'	CDoC CKni CRow CWGN NBrk
– 'Ranpo'	CRow
I – 'Red Dawn'	CRow
§ – 'Rose Queen'	CRDP CRow CWGN EBre ECha EGle ELan EMFW EPar ERou GCal LPBA MAus MSta NBrk NBro NHol NRoo SChu WChe WRus
– 'Rowden'	CRow
– 'Royal Crown'	CRow NBrk SWyc
– 'Royal Purple'	CGle CMHG
I – 'Ruby King'	CBlo LRHS MBri
N – 'Shihainami'	IBlr
– 'Silverband'	NBrk
– 'Summer Storm' ♀	SPer SWyc
– 'Taga-sode'	CRow NBrk SWyc
– 'The Great Mogul' ♀	SWyc
* – 'Time and Tide'	SWyc
– 'Umi-botaro'	CRow
– 'Valiant Prince'	CRow
– 'Variegata'	CBen CMil CRDP CRow CWGN EBee ECha EHoe EHon IBlr LPBA MBri MSta MUlv SCro SWat WCot WRus
* – 'Vintage Festival'	SWyc
– 'Waka-murasaki'	MBri WMer WRus
I – 'White Pearl'	CRow NBrk
– 'Worley Pink'	CRow
– 'Yako-no-tama'	CRow
– 'Yezo-nishiki'	EHoe LBro LRHS
– 'Yusho'	CRow
'Erleen Richeson' (TB)	LIri SCro
'Escalona' (CH)	LBro
'Essay' (Spuria)	LBro
¶ 'Etched Apricot' (TB)	MAus
¶ 'Evening Gown' (TB)	LBro
'Evening Magic' (TB)	SCro
'Everything Plus'	ERou LIri
ewbankiana	See ***I. acutiloba*** subsp. ***lineolata***
I 'Excelsior' (DB)	CShe
'Exotic Isle' (TB)	NZep
'Exotic Shadow' (SDB)	LBro
'Exotic Star' (TB)	LIri
'Extravagant' (TB)	SCro
'Eyebright' (SDB)	CBro LBro MAus SCro WThi
¶ 'Fairy Footsteps' (SDB)	LBro
'Fairy Time' (IB)	LBro
'Fancy Tales' (TB)	NZep
'Fanfaron' (TB)	SCro
'Fantaisie' (TB)	CKel
'Farolito' (Spuria)	LBro WBcn
'Fashion Jewel' (TB)	LIri
'Fashion Lady' (MDB)	CBro NNrd WThi
'Favorite Angel' (SDB)	NMGW NZep
'Feminine Charm' (TB)	CKel MAus
'Feminist' (TB)	SCro
'Femme Fatale' (TB)	LIri
fernaldii	MSto SSpi
– J&JA 12807	SSpi
'Festival Crown' (TB)	LBro
'Festive Skirt' (TB)	CKel
'Fierce Fire' ♀	MAus
'Fiery Song' (TB)	CKel
filifolia	CBro
– var. ***latifolia*** SF 332	CMon
– MS 437	CMon
N 'Fire and Flame' (TB)	NBir
'Fire One' (SDB)	LBro
'Fire Siren' (TB)	MMil
'Firecracker' (TB)	EBre ERou MAus MBri MRav
'First Interstate' (TB)	SCro

'First Violet' (TB)	LBro
'Five Star Admiral' (TB)	SCro
'Flaming Dragon'	CKel EBee
I 'Flamingo' (TB)	CKel
'Flapjack' (SDB)	NZep
'Flashing Beacon' (MTB)	NZep
flavescens	MAus NSti
'Flea Circus' (MDB)	NZep
'Flirty Mary' (SDB)	EGle
'Florentina' (IB)	CArn CBro CRow EBre ECha EFou ELau ERav GPoy IBlr LBro LHol MChe MHew MRav NFai SCro SIde WWye
'Focal Point'	LBuc
'Focus' (TB)	SCro
§ ***foetidissima***	Widely available
– 'Aurea'	CMon
foetidissima aurea MS 902	CMon
foetidissima chinensis	See ***I. foetidissima*** var. ***citrina***
§ ***foetidissima*** var. ***citrina***	CFil CKel CRow ECha EFou EGle EGol ELan EPla GAbr GCal IBlr LBro MBal MBro NSti SChu SPer SSpi SUsu WAbe WHoo WOMN WPyg WRus WWin
– 'Fructu Albo'	CRow EGol
– var. ***lutescens***	EMon
– 'Moonshy Seedling'	CSWP EGol
– 'Variegata'	CBro CFil CGle CRow CSam CSpe EFol EGle EGol ELan EOrc ESiP LHil MBri NDea NHol NPSI NPer NRoo SSpi WAbe WEas WHil WRus WWat WWhi
– yellow seeded	EFou
'Foggy Dew' (TB)	MBri
'Forest Hills' (TB)	CKel MS&S
'Forest Light' (SDB)	CBro LBro NNrd
formosana	CHEx
forrestii	CHad CHan CLon CNic CRow CWGN EOrc GCal GDra IBlr LGan LPBA MBri MNrw NBro NHed NHol NNrd NRya NSla NSti SPer SSea SSpi WAbe WCla WDav WHal WHer WWat
– hybrids	IBlr NHol WDav
'Fort Apache' (TB)	SCro
'Fort Regent' (TB)	LBro
N 'Foxtor' (TB)	CKel
'Frank Elder' (Reticulata)	CBro EHyt LAma MTho WIvy
'French Gown' (TB)	EFou
'Fresno Calypso' (TB)	LIri
'Fresno Flash' (TB)	NZep SCro
'Frontier Marshall' (TB)	CKel
'Frost and Flame' (TB)	EBre ECtt ELan ERav ERou MRav NOrc SCro SPer
'Full Tide' (TB)	SCro
fulva	ECha GCal IBlr LBro MUlv NBro NSti SWyc WChe WCot WEas
× ***fulvala***	CWGN EMon GCal IBlr MAus NSti SWyc WChe WCot WRus WWat
'Furnaceman' (SDB)	CBro MMil NNrd
'Fuzzy' (MDB)	LBro
'Fuzzy Face' (SDB)	NZep
* 'Galathea'	GCal
gatesii	EPot LAma
'Gay Parasol' (TB)	LBro
N 'Gay Prince' (TB)	CKel MS&S
N 'Gay Trip' (TB)	CKel WBcn
§ 'Gelbe Mantel' (Chrysographes)	CBot EHic GCra NBir NSti
'George' (Reticulata)	CAvo CBro EBar EBre EPar EPot ERos MHlr WCot
◆ 'Gerald Darby'	See ***I. × robusta* 'Gerald Darby'**
§ ***germanica***	LBro MAus NCut NNor WPyg WRHF
– 'Amas'	MAus
– 'Kharput'	EGol LBro
* – 'Mel Jope'	LBuc
'Gibson Girl' (TB)	MMil
'Gigglepot' (SDB)	LGre MMil
'Ginger Swirl' (TB)	SCro
'Gingerbread Man' (SDB)	CBro CLon CMea EFou EGle ERos LBro LGre MS&S NMen NNrd SIng WHoo
'Glad Rags' (TB)	NZep
N 'Glen' (TB)	CKel
'Godfrey Owen' (TB)	MAus
'Going My Way' (TB)	LIri LRHS MAus MBri SCro
'Gold Burst' (TB)	SCro
'Gold Canary' (MDB)	NZep
I 'Gold Flake' (TB)	CKel
'Gold Galore' (TB)	SCro
'Gold of Autumn' (TB)	CKel
'Golden Alps' (TB)	ENot LBro MAus
I 'Golden Bow' (TB)	CKel
'Golden Dewdrops' (SDB)	LBro
'Golden Encore' (TB)	CKel MAus MWat
'Golden Fair' (SDB)	NBir SIng
'Golden Harvest' (Dutch)	CB&S LAma
'Golden Lady' (Spuria)	LBro
'Golden Muffin' (IB)	LBro NZep
'Golden Oldie' (La)	LBro
'Golden Planet' (TB)	CKel MS&S WBcn
'Golden Ruby' (SDB)	LBro
'Golden Spice' (TB)	LBro
'Golden Starlet' (SDB)	LBro
N 'Golden Surprise' (TB)	CKel
'Golden Veil' (TB)	CKel
'Golden Waves' (Cal-Sib) 🏆	CMHG LBro
N 'Goldfinder' (TB)	CKel
I 'Goldilocks' (TB)	CKel
'Good and True' (IB)	SCro
'Good Nature' (Spuria)	LBro
'Good Show' (TB)	SCro
'Gordon' (Reticulata)	EPot LAma
gormanii	See ***I. tenax***
gracilipes	MBal
– 'Alba'	SSpi SWas
graeberiana	EPot LWoo
– white fall	LRHS
– yellow fall	LRHS
graminea	CAvo CBro CHad CHan CMon CRow ECha EFou ELan EPla IBlr LBee LBlm LBro MBro MRPP NHol NMen NNrd NSti SAxl SCro SMrm WOMN WPer WPyg WRus WWat
– 'Hort's Variety'	GCal
– var. ***pseudocyperus***	CMon CRow
graminifolia	See ***I. kerneriana***
'Grand Baroque' (TB)	MMil
'Grand Waltz' (TB)	SCro
'Grandpa's Girl' (MTB)	LBro
'Grapelet' (MDB)	NZep
'Grapesicle' (SDB)	NZep
'Graphic Arts' (TB)	NZep
'Grecian Skies' (TB)	SCro
'Green Halo' (DB)	EGle EGol LBro

'Green Ice' (TB) EFou MRav
'Green Jungle' (TB) LBro
N 'Green Little' (DB) CKel
'Green Spot' (IB) CBot CBro CHan CKel EBre ECtt ELan EPla ESis LGre MAus MHig MMil MRav MWat NMGW NMen NNrd NRoo SChu SPer WEas WHoo
'Greenstuff' (SDB) LBro MMil
'Gypsy Boy' (SDB) NMGW NZep
'Gypsy Caravan' (TB) CKel SCro
'H.C. van Vliet' (Dutch) LAma NRog
'Hagar's Helmet' (IB) LBro
'Hallowed Thought' (TB) MMil MWat
halophila See ***I. spuria*** subsp. ***halophila***
'Happening' (SDB) NZep
'Happy Choice' (Spuria) EFou LBro
'Happy Song' (BB) LBro
'Happy Thought' (IB) CKel
'Harbor Blue' (TB) CKel MAus MWat
'Harleqinade' (BB) LBro
'Harlow Gold' (IB) NZep
'Harmony' (Reticulata) CAvo CBro EBre EPot ETub LAma MBri MHlr NRog
'Harriette Halloway' (TB) CBlo ECGP SMrm
hartwegii subsp. ***pinetorum*** WCot
'Hazy Skies' (MTB) LBro
'Headlines' (TB) CKel GMaP MAus
'Helen Boehm' (TB) SCro
'Helen McGregor' (TB) CKel
'Helen Proctor' (IB) NZep SCro
'Helge' (IB) EPfP NFai
'Hellcat' (IB) NZep
'Hell's Fire' (TB) SCro
'Hercules' CKni GCal LAma SIng WRHF
'Hers' (IB) SCro
'High Command' (TB) CKel SCro
'High Life' (TB) SCro
'Highline Halo' (Spuria) EFou
'Hills of Lafayette' (IB) NZep
'Hindenburg' (TB) LIri
¶ 'Hindu Magic' (TB) LBro
'His' (IB) SCro
¶ ***histrio*** LAma
– subsp. ***aintabensis*** EHyt EPot LAma
– var. ***histrio*** EPot
histrioides 'Angel's Tears' See ***I. histrioides* 'Angel's Eye'**
¶ – 'Lady Beatrix Stanley' LWoo
N – 'Major' ♡ CBro LAma MBal MBri NRog
¶ – 'Reine Immaculée' GCLN
'Hocus Pocus' (SDB) EFou LBro
'Holden Clough' ♡ CBot CBre CGle CHad CHar CRDP CWGN EFou ELan EMFW EPri LBro MAus MFir MHFP MMil MRav MUlv NHol NSti SSvw SUsu SWat SWyc WChe WEas WOld WSan WWin
'Hollywood Blonde' LIri
'Holy Night' (TB) LIri
'Honey Crunch' (TB) LIri
'Honey Glazed' (IB) LBro MAus MS&S NZep SCro
'Honey Mocha' (TB) SCro
'Honey Pot' (MDB) CKel
'Honington' (SDB) LBro MAus MMil
'Honky Tonk Blues' (TB) LIri
'Honorabile' (MTB) CKel MAus
hoogiana EPot LAma MTho
– 'Alba' EPot
– 'Purpurea' EPot LRHS
hookeriana WRHF
'Hopscotch' (BB) SCro
'Hot Fudge' (IB) NZep
'Hot Spice' (IB) NZep
'Howard Weed' (TB) CKel
'Hubbub' (IB) SCro
'Hula Doll' (MDB) CBlo CMea EGle NMen
§ ***humilis*** NNrd
hyrcana CBro LAma WChr
'I Do' (TB) MMil NZep
§ ***iberica*** EPot
§ – subsp. ***elegantissima*** EPot
– subsp. ***iberica*** WThi
'Ice Chip' (SDB) LBro
'Ida' (Reticulata) EPot LAma
'Ideal' (Dutch) LAma
'Ila Remembered' (Spuria) LBro
illyrica See ***I. pallida***
'Immortality' (TB) MAus SCro
'Imperator' (Dutch) CB&S
'Imperial Bronze' (Spuria) EFou LBro MAus
'Impetuous' (BB) LBro
'Inaugural Ball' (TB) LIri
'Indeed' (IB) LBro MS&S
'Indian Chief' (TB) CKel CWan LBro LRHS MBri
'Indian Jewel' (SDB) EGle
'Indian Pow Wow' (SDB) LBro
N 'Indian Sunset' (TB) CKel
'Indigo Flight' (IB) EFou LBro
'Infinite Grace' (TB) SCro
'Ingenuity' (SDB) LBro
'Innocent Heart' (IB) LBro SCro
innominata CFil CGle CLon CRDP CRow CSam ECha EPot IBlr LBee MNrw MRPP MSto MTho NBro NGre NHar NHol NMen NSti NTow SUsu WCla WEas WGwG WOMN WWat
– 'Alba' NGre
– apricot IBlr
– Ballyrogan Hybrids IBlr
– copper IBlr
N – 'Doctor Riddle's Form' CGle CRDP GDra MBal
– J&JA 12897 SSpi
– JCA 13225 LWoo SSpi
¶ – JCA 13227 SSpi
– JCA 1460800 CPBP
– rose CNic ERos
N – 'Spinners' SSpi SWas WDav
– yellow NNrd
'Inscription' (SDB) EGle LBro NZep
'Irish Doll' (MDB) CMea EGle LBro
'Irish Tune' (TB) SCro
'Ishmael' (SDB) EGle LBro
'J.S. Dijt' (Reticulata) CAvo CBro EBar EBre EPar EPot LAma MBri NRog
'Jack o' Hearts' (SDB) CMea LBro
'Jade Mist' (SDB) EGle LBro LRHS MBri
'Jaime Lynn' (TB) LIri
'Jan Reagan' (SDB) NZep
'Jane Phillips' (TB) CHad CKel CMGP CRDP CShe EBre ECha ECtt EGle ELan ENot ERav ERou LBro MAus MCLN MHFP MMil MRav MS&S NCat NOrc SChu SCro SMrm SPer SWat
'Jane Taylor' (SDB) CBro EGle NNrd
'Janice Chesnik' (Spuria) LBro
japonica NPer WHil
– 'Aphrodite' (v) WCot
– L 638 SCro

N– 'Ledger's Variety'	CAvo CBro CHan CMon CRow ECha ELan EPar EPri LGan LHil MRav MTol MUlv SCro WAbe WEas WRus WWat
– 'Variegata'	CAvo CBot CHad CHan CKel CLon CMon CRow ECha EFol EPar EPla MBal MUlv NFai NOrc NPer SArc SCro SSpi WHal WHer WHil
'Jasper Gem' (MDB)	EGle LBro MMil MS&S
'Java Charm' (TB)	MMil
'Jay Kenneth' (IB)	LBro
* 'Jazzamatazz' (SDB)	LBro
'Jazzebel' (TB)	SCro
'Jean Guymer' (TB)	MMil NBir WBcn
'Jeannine' (Reticulata)	LAma
'Jeremy Brian' (SDB) ♀	LBro NZep SUsu
'Jersey Lilli' (SDB)	EFol LRHS NSti
'Jesse's Song' (TB)	LBro LIri MAus NZep SCro
'Jewel Baby' (SDB)	CBro NMGW NZep
'Jewel Bright' (SDB)	EFou
'Jo Jo' (TB)	CKel
'Joanna Taylor' (MDB)	CBro ERos NMen NNrd NZep
N 'Joe Elliott' (CH)	EGle EWes
'Joette' (MTB)	LBro
'John' (IB)	SCro
'Jolly Fellow' (SDB)	LBro SUsu WThi
jordana S&L 38	CMon
'Joyce' (Reticulata)	CAvo CBro ELan EPar EPot LAma MBri NRog
'Joyce Terry' (TB)	CKel LIri LRHS MBri
'Joyful' (SDB)	LBro SCro
'Joyous Isle' (SDB)	NZep
'Jubilee Gem' (TB)	CKel
'Juliet' (TB)	CKel
juncea	CArn CMon
'June Prom' (IB)	SCro
'Juneau' (TB)	WCot
'Jungle Fires' (TB)	MAus
'Jungle Shadows' (BB)	LGre MRav
'Just Jennifer' (BB)	LBro MAus
¶ 'Just Magic' (TB)	LBro
kaempferi	See ***I. ensata***
kamaonensis	GDra NHar WOMN
'Karen Christine' (TB)	SCro
'Karen Maddock' (TB)	LBro
kashmiriana	LKoh
'Katharine Hodgkin' (Reticulata)	CAvo CBro EBre EHyt EOrc EPot ERos GAbr LAma LWoo MRPP MTho NGar NHar NRog SMrm WAbe WIvy
'Katinka' (CH)	LBro
'Katy Petts' (SDB)	EFou NZep
'Kayo' (SDB)	EFou EGle LBro MS&S NZep
'Kent Pride' (TB)	EBee EBre EFou EHic ERou LBro MRav MS&S MWat NLak SCro SMrm SPer SWat
'Kentucky Bluegrass' (SDB)	EFou LBro MMil SUsu WWin
'Kentucky Derby' (TB)	SCro
'Kermit' (IB)	SCro
§ ***kerneriana***	CBro CMil ELan ERos GBuc MBro MNrw SIgm WEas
'Keyhaven' (SDB)	LBro
'Kilt Lilt' (TB)	SCro
'Kirkstone' (TB)	MBri
kirkwoodii MS&CL 555	CMon
'Kissing Circle' (TB)	LBro
'Kista' (SDB)	MS&S
'Kiwi Capers' (SDB)	NZep
klattii	See ***I. spuria*** subsp. ***musulmanica***
'Knick Knack' (MDB)	CBro CGle CM&M CPBP EGle EHyt ELan EMan ERos GMaP LGre MHig MRav NMen NNrd SChu SCro SIng WGwG WWin
¶ ***kochii***	LBro
¶ ***kopetdagensis***	EPot
korolkowii 'Violacea'	LRHS
kuschakewiczii	MSto
¶ 'La Nina Rosa' (BB)	MAus
'Lace Artistry' (TB)	SCro
'Laced Cotton' (TB)	SCro
'Laced Lemonade' (SDB)	EBre EFou LBro LRHS MBri
§ ***lactea***	GBin SCro WThi
– CC 220	MRPP
– SULE 1	LKoh
lacustris	ELan EPot ERos MBro MSto NBro NCat NGre NHar NMen NTow NWCA WAbe
– x ***gracilipes***	CRDP EPot GDra SIng SWas WAbe
'Lady Belle' (MTB)	LBro
'Lady Friend' (TB)	ERou SCro
'Lady Madonna' (TB)	SCro
'Lady Mohr' (AB)	CKel
'Lady of Nepal' (IB)	LBro
§ ***laevigata*** ♀	CBen CRow CWat EBre ECha EGle EGol EHon ELan LPBA MRav MSta NBrk NBro NDea SHig SPer SWat SWyc WAbe WChe WMAq WShi
– 'Alba'	CBen CRDP CRow CWGN ECha EGol EHon LPBA SAWi SWat SWyc WChe
¶ – 'Albopurpurea'	EMFW
– 'Atropurpurea'	CRDP CRow EGol IBlr LPBA MSta
¶ – 'Colchesterensis'	CBen CRDP CRow CWGN CWat EBre ECGP EGol EHon EMFW LPBA MSta SCro SWat SWyc WChe
I – 'Dorothy'	CWGN MSta SAWi SCro WChe
◆ – 'Elegant'	See ***I. laevigata* 'Weymouth Elegant'**
I – 'Elegante'	CRow CWGN SWat SWyc
– 'Goshobeni'	CRow
I – 'Midnight'	See ***I. laevigata* 'Weymouth Midnight'**
N– 'Monstrosa'	SWyc
– 'Mottled Beauty'	CBen CRow MSta SWyc
– 'Murasama'	CRow
– 'Odiham'	SWyc
– 'Plena'	SWyc
N– 'Plum Purple'	EGle
◆ – 'Purity'	See ***I. laevigata* 'Weymouth Purity'**
– 'Regal'	SWyc
I – 'Reveille'	EGle
– 'Richard Greany'	CRow
– 'Rose Queen'	See ***I. ensata* 'Rose Queen'**
– 'Shirasagi'	CRow
I – 'Snowdrift'	CBen CRow CWGN CWat EGol EHon EMFW LPBA MBri MSta NDea SAWi SCro SWat SWyc WChe WMAq
◆ – 'Surprise'	See ***I. laevigata* 'Weymouth Surprise'**
– 'Tamagawa'	CRow

– 'Variegata'	CBen CChu CRDP CRow CWGN CWat ECha EGol EHon EMFW LPBA MAus MHar MSta NDea NRoo SCro SPer SSpi SWat SWyc WChe WMAq WRus WWat
– 'Violet Garth'	CRow
I – 'Weymouth'	See ***I. laevigata* 'Weymouth Blue'**
§ – 'Weymouth Blue'	CRDP CRow CWGN EBre EGol SAWi SCro SWyc
§ – 'Weymouth Midnight'	CRow CWGN CWat ECGP EGol EHon SAWi SCro SWat SWyc
'Lake Placid' (TB)	SCro
'Land o' Lakes' (TB)	SCro
N 'Langport Chapter' (IB)	CKel
N 'Langport Chief' (IB)	CKel
N 'Langport Chimes' (IB)	CKel
N 'Langport Claret' (IB)	CKel
N 'Langport Curlew' (IB)	CKel
N 'Langport Duchess' (IB)	CKel
N 'Langport Duke' (IB)	CKel
N 'Langport Fairy' (IB)	CKel
N 'Langport Fashion' (IB)	CKel
N 'Langport Flame' (IB)	CKel MMil
N 'Langport Flush' (IB)	SCro SSte
N 'Langport Haze' (IB)	CKel
N 'Langport Hero' (IB)	CKel
N 'Langport Honey' (IB)	CKel
N 'Langport Hope' (IB)	CKel
N 'Langport Jane' (IB)	CKel
N 'Langport Lord' (IB)	CKel
N 'Langport Magic' (IB)	CKel MMil
N 'Langport Minstrel' (IB)	CKel
N 'Langport Myth' (IB)	CKel
N 'Langport Pagan' (IB)	CKel
N 'Langport Pearl' (IB)	CKel
N 'Langport Phoebe' (IB)	CKel
N 'Langport Pinnacle' (IB)	CKel
N 'Langport Pleasure' (IB)	CKel
N 'Langport Prince' (IB)	CKel MMil
N 'Langport Robe' (IB)	CKel
N 'Langport Robin' (IB)	CKel
N 'Langport Romance' (IB)	CKel
N 'Langport Song' (IB)	CKel MMil
N 'Langport Star' (IB)	CKel
N 'Langport Storm' (IB)	CKel EFou WBcn
N 'Langport Sultan' (IB)	CKel
N 'Langport Sun' (IB)	CKel
N 'Langport Sunbeam' (IB)	CKel
N 'Langport Swift' (IB)	CKel
N 'Langport Tempest' (IB)	CKel
N 'Langport Vale' (IB)	CKel
N 'Langport Violet' (IB)	CKel
N 'Langport Vista' (IB)	CKel
N 'Langport Warrior' (IB)	CKel MS&S
N 'Langport Wren' (IB)	CBro CKel CMil LBro LGre MMil
'Late Lilac' (TB)	LIri
§ ***latifolia*** 🏆	SAxl WCot
latifolia alba	ELan
'Latin Rock' (TB)	SCro
N 'Lavendula Plicatee'	NNrd
§ ***lazica***	CAvo CBro CMea CMon EPot IBlr MBel MUlv NChi NSti SAxl SChu SCro SIng SUsu WCot WEas WRus WWat
'Leda's Lover' (TB)	LIri SCro
'Lemon Brocade' (TB)	MAus MBri
I 'Lemon Drop' (TB)	CKel
'Lemon Flare' (SDB)	EBre ECtt LBro MAus MRav NRoo
'Lemon Flurry' (IB)	LBro
'Lemon Glitter' (TB)	EFou EPri
'Lemon Ice' (TB)	MMil
'Lemon Mist' (TB)	LIri MMil
'Lemon Puff' (MDB)	CBro LBro NNrd
'Lemon Reflection' (TB)	MMil
'Lemon Tree' (TB)	MAus
N 'Lena' (SDB)	CBro EBee
¶ 'Lent A Williamson' (TB)	CBlo
'Libation' (MDB)	LBro
'Light Cavalry' (IB)	NZep
'Lighted Signal' (Spuria)	LBro
'Lighted Within' (TB)	SCro
'Lilac and Lavender' (SDB)	MMil NZep
'Lilli-white' (SDB)	CKel EBre EGle LBro MRav NNrd NSti SPer
'Lime Grove' (SDB)	SIng
'Limpid Pools' (SDB)	SCro
'Listowel' (IB)	LBro
'Little Amigo' (SDB)	NZep
'Little Amoena'	ERos NMen
'Little Annie' (SDB)	NZep
'Little Bill' (SDB)	EFou EGle WThi
'Little Black Belt' (SDB)	EFou LBro NZep
'Little Blackfoot' (SDB)	CHad MAus MMil WWin
'Little Chestnut' (SDB)	LBro
'Little Cottage' (SDB)	SCro
'Little Dandy' (SDB)	EGle
'Little Dogie' (SDB)	EGle LBro
'Little Dream' (SDB)	NZep
'Little Episode' (SDB)	NZep
'Little Paul' (MTB)	LBro
'Little Pearl' (MDB)	NZep
'Little Rosy Wings' (SDB)	CBro ERos LBro LGre MMil
'Little Sapphire' (SDB)	CKel
'Little Shadow' (IB)	EBre ECtt EFol GMaP LBro MRav
'Little Sheba' (AB)	LBlm
'Little Snow Lemon' (IB)	NZep
'Live Jazz' (SDB)	NZep
'Lively Rose' (MTB)	LBro
¶ 'Llanthony' (SDB)	MAus
loczyi	MSto
'Lodestar' (TB)	LBro
'Lodore' (TB)	CKel MBri SRms
longipetala	NBir NSti
'Look Again' (Spuria)	LBro
'Lookin' Good' (IB)	NZep
'Loop the Loop' (TB)	CKel SMer
'Lord Baltimore' (TB)	SCro
'Lord Warden' (TB)	EFou
'Lord Wolseley' (Spuria)	LBro
'Lorilee' (TB)	LIri SCro
'Los Angeles'	MBri
'Lothario' (TB)	CKel MAus MS&S
'Loud Music' (TB)	MBri
'Loudmouth' (AB)	LBro
Louisiana hybrids	MSta
'Louisiana Lace' (TB)	SCro
'Louvois' (TB)	CKel MAus
'Loveday' (TB)	LBro
'Lovely Again' (TB)	MAus MWat
'Lovely Kay' (TB)	SCro
'Lovely Letty' (TB)	MBri
'Lovely Light' (TB)	MBri
'Love's Tune' (IB)	SCro
'Loveshine' (SDB)	NZep
'Low Snow' (SDB)	NZep
'Lucky Charm' (MTB)	LBro

'Lucky Devil' (Spuria)	LBro
'Lucky Duck' (SDB)	NZep
'Lugano' (TB)	MMil
'Lullaby of Spring' (TB)	LIri
'Luscious One' (SDB)	LBro
§ ***lutescens***	CPBP MAus
§ – 'Campbellii'	CBro LGre MBro MHig MSto NMen NNrd SIng
lutescens cyanea	NNrd
lutescens subsp. ***lutescens***	CMon
'Lydia Jane' (Spuria) 𝕻	LBro WBcn
'Madeira Belle' (TB)	MAus
I 'Maestro' (TB)	CKel
N 'Magenta and Peach' (TB)	MAus
'Magic Carpet' (TB)	CKel
'Magic Flute' (MDB)	EGle LBro
'Magic Hills' (TB)	CKel
'Magic Man' (TB)	LBro
magnifica	CBro EPot LWoo NWCA WChr WCot
– f. ***alba***	LRHS
'Mahogany Snow' (SDB)	NZep
I 'Mandarin' (TB)	CKel GDra
'Mandarin Purple'	IBlr NHol
maracandica	MSto
'Margot Holmes' (Cal-Sib)	EBee GCal GDra IBlr LBro NCat NHol SChu
'Marhaba' (MDB)	CBro ERos NNrd
'Maria Tormena' (TB)	SCro
'Mariachi' (TB)	CKel
'Marilyn Holloway' (Spuria)	ECha
'Marmalade Skies' (BB)	LBro MS&S NZep
'Marshlander' (TB)	EFou SCro
'Marty' (IB)	MS&S
'Martyn Rix'	See ***I. confusa* 'Martyn Rix'**
'Mary Frances' (TB)	LBro LIri SCro
'Mary McIlroy' (SDB)	CBro LBro
'Mary Randall' (TB)	MS&S
'Master Touch' (TB)	LIri SCro
'Matchpoint' (TB)	LBro
'Matinata' (TB)	CKel EBee
'Maui Moonlight' (IB) 𝕻	NZep
'May Melody' (TB)	CKel MAus MBri
'Meadow Court' (SDB)	CBro CKel MAus NNrd NZep WMer
'Media Luz' (Spuria)	LBro
'Meg's Mantle' (TB) 𝕻	LBro
'Melbreak' (TB)	CKel EBre
'Melissa Sue' (TB)	SCro
mellita	See ***I. suaveolens***
– var. ***rubromarginata***	See ***I. suaveolens***
'Melon Honey' (SDB)	CKel EGle LBro MAus MMil MS&S WWin
'Menton' (SDB)	LBro
I 'Merry Day' (IB)	CKel
'Merseyside' (SDB)	EGle LBro
'Metaphor' (TB)	MAus MMil
'Michael Paul' (SDB)	LBro
'Michele Taylor' (TB)	SCro
'Midnight Fire' (TB)	ERou
'Midnight Madness' (SDB)	NZep
milesii	CPou NBir SCro WPer
– CC&McK 741	GCHN
– CR 346	WPer
'Minnesota Glitters' (TB)	SCro
'Minnie Colquitt' (TB)	SCro
'Miss Carla' (IB) 𝕻	LBro MMil SCro
'Mission Ridge' (TB)	CKel
'Mission Sunset' (TB)	EBre MAus
'Missouri Gal' (Spuria)	LBro
missouriensis	CRow EWoo IBlr LBro MSto NMen SSpi
¶ – var. ***arizonica***	GCal
'Mister Roberts' (SDB)	LBro NZep
'Moment' (SDB)	NZep
¶ 'Monaco' (TB)	EFou
'Money' (TB)	SCro
monnieri	CMon EFou IBlr
§ 'Monspur Cambridge Blue' (Spuria)	MAus
Monspur Group	GCal SSpi WCot
'Moon Sparkle' (IB)	CKel
'Moonlight' (TB)	LBro MRav NNor NNrd
'Moonlight Waves'	See ***I. ensata* 'Moonlight Waves'**
'Moon's Delight' (TB)	LIri
'Morning Hymn' (TB)	SCro
'Morning Show' (IB)	SCro
'Morocco' (TB)	SCro
'Morwenna' (TB) 𝕻	LBro
* 'Mount Stewart Black'	EBee GCal
'Mrs Horace Darwin' (TB)	CFir
'Mrs Kate Rudolph' (SDB)	EBre EFou EGle LBro MBri WThi
munzii	EPot EWoo
'Muriel Neville' (TB)	MAus
¶ 'Murmuring Morn' (TB)	MAus
'Music Box' (SDB)	NZep
'My Honeycomb' (TB)	MAus MBri MS&S
'My Mary' (TB)	CKel
N 'My Seedling' (MDB)	CBro ERos NMen NNrd
'My Smoky' (TB)	CKel MS&S
'Mystique' (TB)	SCro
'Nambe' (MTB)	LBro
'Nampara' (TB)	LBro
'Nancy Hardy' (MDB)	CBro ERos NNrd
'Nancy Lindsay'	See ***I. lutescens* 'Nancy Lindsay'**
'Nashborough' (TB)	CKel
'Natascha' (Reticulata)	EHyt ELan EPot LAma
'Navajo Blanket' (TB)	SCro
'Nectar' (TB)	CKel MS&S
'Needlecraft' (TB)	CKel MMil
'Needlepoint' (TB)	SCro
'Neon Pixie' (SDB)	NZep
'Neophyte' (Spuria)	LBro
nepalensis	See ***I. decora***
nertschinskia	See ***I. sanguinea***
'New Idea' (MTB)	LBro MAus MS&S
'New Snow' (TB)	LBlm WCot
'Nibelungen' (TB)	CKel EPfP NFai
'Nice 'n' Nifty' (IB)	NZep
nicolai	WChr
'Night Owl' (TB)	MMil SCro
'Night Ruler' (TB)	LIri
nigricans S&L 148	CMon
¶ 'Nimble Toes' (SDB)	LBro
'No-name'	NSti
'Nylon Ruffles' (SDB)	EBre LBro SUsu
'Ochraurea'	EBee GCal
ochroleuca	See ***I. orientalis***
'Offenham' (TB)	LBro
'Oklahoma Bandit' (IB)	LBro
'Ola Kala' (TB)	CMGP EBre ECle ECro EHic ERou LBro MAus SCro WLRN
'Old Flame' (TB)	NZep
'Oliver' (SDB)	LBro
'Olympiad' (TB)	LIri
'Olympic Challenger' (TB)	LIri
'Olympic Torch' (TB)	CKel MAus
'One Accord' (SDB)	SCro
'One Desire' (TB)	NZep

'Open Sky' (SDB)	NZep
'Orange Blaze' (SDB)	CBro
'Orange Caper' (SDB)	EBre MRav NZep
'Orange Dawn' (TB)	LBro
¶ 'Orange Maid' (Spuria)	WBcn
N 'Orange Plaza'	NMen NPri
'Orange Tiger' (SDB)	NZep
'Orchardist' (TB)	CKel
'Orchidarium' (TB)	CKel
§ ***orchioides***	ELan EPot
– yellow	LRHS
'Oregold' (SDB)	NZep
'Oregon Skles' (TB)	SCro
'Oriental Blush' (SDB)	LBro
'Oriental Glory' (TB)	MAus
'Oriental Touch' (SpecHybrid)	CRow
§ ***orientalis***	CAvo CBot CHan CMil CRow ECGP ELan LBlm LBro LPBA MAus MBal SChu WWat WWin
– 'Alba'	See ***I. sanguinea* 'Alba'**
¶ 'Orinoco Flow' (BB) 🏆	CKel
'Oritam' (TB)	SCro
'Ornament' (SDB)	LBro
'Out Yonder' (TB)	MAus
'Ovation' (TB)	SCro
'Overnight Sensation' (TB)	SCro
'Pacer' (IB)	NZep
'Pacific Coast Hyb'	See ***I.* Californian Hybrids**
¶ 'Pacific Gambler' (TB)	EFou
'Pacific Mist' (TB)	SCro
'Palace Gossip' (TB)	LIri
'Pale Primrose' (TB)	MAus WEas
'Pale Shades' 🏆	LBro
'Pale Suede' (SDB)	LBro
§ ***pallida***	CSWP EFou LHol MAus MCCP
– 'Argentea Variegata'	CGle CHad EAst EBee ECro EFol EHoe ESiP LHop MBro MTis MUlv NCat NMir NPla NRoo NSti NTay SCro SSpi WHoo WHow WRus WWat WWeb
– 'Aurea'	See ***I. pallida* 'Variegata'**
– 'Aurea Variegata'	See ***I. pallida* 'Variegata'**
– subsp. ***cengialtii***	CMon WThi
– var. ***dalmatica***	See ***I. pallida*** subsp. ***pallida***
§ – subsp. ***pallida***	CBot CKel EBre ECha EGol ELan LBro LHil MBri MUlv NSti SCro SDix SMrm SPer WGwG
N – 'Variegata'	CAvo CB&S CBot CBro CChu CHan EBre ECha EFol EFou EGol ELan ENot EPla EPot IHos LBro LGre MBri MUlv MWat NRoo SCro SHig SPer WAbe WEas WHer WRus WWin
'Paltec'	CHad CPou LGre SCro
'Pandora's Purple' (TB)	LIri SCro
'Paradise' (TB)	EPfP LBro LIri SCro
'Paradise Bird' (TB)	LBro
paradoxa f. ***choschab***	EHyt EPot
'Paricutin' (SDB)	CBro EGle NNrd
'Paris Lights' (TB)	SCro
'Party Dress' (TB)	EBee EBre ECro ECtt EHic ELan ENot EPla ERav ERou LBro MRav MS&S NOrc SChu SCoo SCro SMrm SPer WGwG WLRN
'Pascoe' (TB)	LBro

'Pastel Charm' (SDB)	CKel
'Pastel Delight' (SDB)	NZep
'Path of Gold' (DB)	CBro CKel LBro NNrd SIng
'Patterdale' (TB)	NBir NMGW NVic
'Pauline' (Reticulata)	CAvo CBro EPot LAma NRog
'Peach Band' (TB)	ERou
'Peach Bisque' (TB)	LIri
'Peach Eyes' (SDB)	LBro NZep
'Peach Petals' (BB)	LBro NZep
'Peach Picotee' (TB)	SCro
'Peach Spot' (TB)	MAus
'Peaches 'n' Topping' (BB)	LBro
'Peachy Face' (IB)	LBro
'Pearly Dawn' (TB)	CHad EBre ECtt MTis MWat SCro SPer WLRN
'Pegasus' (TB)	SCro
'Peggy Chambers' (IB) 🏆	EFou LBro
'Peking Summer' (TB)	SCro
'Pennies' (MDB)	NZep
'Pennyworth' (IB)	SCro
'Penrhyn' (TB)	LBro
'People Pleaser' (SDB)	SCro
'Peppermint Twist' (SDB)	NZep
'Perfect Interlude' (TB)	LIri
'Persian Berry' (TB)	SCro
'Persian Doll' (MDB)	NZep
'Persian Romance' (TB)	MS&S
persica	LAma
'Pet' (SDB)	NSti NZep
'Pied Pretty' (SDB)	SCro
'Pigeon' (SDB)	NZep
'Pigmy Gold' (IB)	ECro ENot LBro
'Pinewood Amethyst' (CH)	LBro
'Pinewood Charmer' (CH)	LBro
'Pinewood Poppet' (CH)	LBro
'Pinewood Sunshine' (CH)	LBro
'Pink Angel' (TB)	SCro
'Pink Bubbles' (BB)	NZep
'Pink Clover' (TB)	LBro
'Pink Confetti' (TB)	LIri SCro
'Pink Divinity' (TB)	MMil
'Pink Horizon' (TB)	CKel
'Pink Kitten' (IB)	NZep
'Pink Lamb' (BB)	LBro
N 'Pink Lavender' (TB)	SCro
'Pink 'n' Mint' (TB)	SCro
'Pink Pussycat'	MBri
N 'Pink Randall' (TB)	SCro
'Pink Ruffles' (IB)	CKel WBcn
'Pink Taffeta' (TB)	CKel SCro
'Pinnacle' (TB)	MAus
'Pipes of Pan' (TB)	MAus MRav
'Piquant Lass' (MTB)	NZep
'Pixie Flirt' (MDB)	LBro
planifolia AB&S 4609	CMon
* – 'Alba'	CMea
– S&L 301	CMon
'Playgirl' (TB)	SCro
'Pledge Allegiance' (TB)	LIri MMil SCro
'Plickadee' (SDB)	EPot NNrd
'Plum Perfect' (SDB)	SCro
'Pogo' (SDB)	CMil EBre ECtt EGle EHyt ELan ENot GMaP MMil MRav NNrd NRoo SCro
'Pogo Doll' (AB)	LBro
'Pojaro Dunes' (CH) 🏆	LBro
§ ***polakii*** (Oncocyclus)	WThi
'Pony' (IB)	LBro MS&S
'Port of Call' (Spuria)	LBro
'Post Time' (TB)	SCro

'Pot Luck' (IB)	MS&S
'Powder Pink' (TB)	MS&S
'Praise the Lord' (TB)	LBro
'Prancing Pony' (TB)	CKel SCro
'Pretender' (TB)	LRHS MBri
'Prettie Print' (TB)	SCro
'Pride of Ireland' (TB)	SCro
'Prince' (SDB)	EFou EGle LBro
'Princess' (TB)	CKel
'Princess Beatrice'	See ***I. pallida*** subsp. ***pallida***
prismatica	CMon EFol NNrd
prismatica alba	GAbr LWoo
'Professor Blaauw' (Dutch)	ETub LAma
'Prosper Laugier' (IB)	SCro
'Protégé' (Spuria)	LBro
'Proud Tradition' (TB)	SCro
'Provencal' (TB)	CKel
pseudacorus	CArn CBen CKin CRow CWGN CWat EBre EHon ELan EWFC GCHN GPoy LPBA MChe MHew MSta MUlv NDea NLan NNor SWat SWyc WChe WHer WMAq WPyg WShi WWin
– 'Alba'	CRow GCal SSpi SWyc WChe
– var. ***bastardii***	CRDP CRow CWGN CWat ECGP ECha EGol EMFW MUlv SWyc WChe
– 'Beuron'	CRow
– cream	EGol MUlv NBir NBrk
– dwarf form	SWyc
N– 'Ecru'	CRow SWyc
N– 'Esk'	GCal
N– 'Flore Pleno'	CBot CRDP CRow EMFW GCra MAus MInt SWyc WCot
– 'Golden Daggers'	CRow
I – 'Golden Fleece'	SPer
– 'Golden Queen'	CRow MSta MUlv SWyc
– 'Ilgengold'	CRow
N– 'Ivory'	CRow
– 'Roy Davidson'	CKel
– 'Sun Cascade'	CRow
– Tangarewa Cream Group	SWyc
– 'Tiggah'	CRow NSti
– 'Turnipseed'	CRow WChe
– 'Variegata'	Widely available
– × ***versicolor***	SCro
– 'Wychwood Multifloral'	SWyc
¶ ***pseudocaucasica***	EPot
pseudopumila	EHyt
– MS 986/975	CMon
pumila	CMon CNic EHyt EPla EPot MBro MHig NCut NGre NMGW NMen NNor NWCA WCla
pumila atroviolacea	CDoC CKel MBro WPen
pumila subsp. ***attica***	See ***I. attica***
– 'Aurea'	CDoC MBro NTow WWeb
– 'Goldcrest' (I)	NNrd
– 'Violacea'	MBro SCro
– yellow	NFla
'Pumpkin Center' (SDB)	NZep
'Puppet' (SDB)	EGle LBro
'Puppet Baby' (MDB)	NZep
'Puppy Love' (MTB)	NMGW NZep
'Purgatory' (TB)	LIri
'Purple Gem' (Reticulata)	CBro EPot LAma
'Purple Landscape' (SDB) 🏆	LBro
'Purple Sensation' (Dutch)	CB&S LAma

'Purple Song' (TB)	MS&S
'Purple Streaker' (TB)	SCro
purpurea	See ***I. galatica***
purpureobractea	EPot
¶ 'Pushy' (SDB)	LBro
¶ 'Quark' (SDB)	LBro
'Quechee' (TB)	CBlo EHic ERou GMaP MRav NLak SCro WLRN
'Queen in Calico' (TB)	MAus SCro
'Queen of Hearts' (TB)	SCro
'Queen's Ivory' (SDB)	MAus
'Queen's Pawn' (SDB)	NMGW NZep
'Quiet Lagoon' (SDB)	NZep
'Quiet Thought' (TB)	LBro
'Quintana' (CH)	LBro
'Rabelais' (TB)	CKel
'Radiant Summer' (TB)	SCro
'Rain Dance' (SDB)	LBro NMGW NZep
'Rainbow Trout' (TB)	LBro
'Rajah' (TB)	EBee EBre EHic ERav ERou LBro MRav NLak NOrc WGwG
'Rancho Grande' (TB)	LIri
'Rancho Rose' (TB)	SCro
'Ranger' (TB)	CKel
'Rapture in Blue' (TB)	LIri
'Rare Edition' (IB)	CKel EBre EFou LBro MBri MS&S NZep SCro
'Rare Treat' (TB)	NZep
'Raspberry Acres' (IB)	MAus MBri
'Raspberry Blush' (IB) 🏆	CKel NZep SCro
'Raspberry Frills' (TB)	LIri
'Raspberry Jam' (SDB)	EGle LBro MMil MS&S NZep
'Raspberry Sundae' (BB)	NZep
'Rathe Primrose' (IB)	SCro
'Real Jazzy' (MTB)	CKel
I 'Red Flash' (TB)	CKel
'Red Hawk' (TB)	SCro
'Red Heart' (SDB)	CBlo MRav WPer
'Red Lion' (TB)	NZep
'Red Orchid' (IB)	CKel MAus
'Red Revival' (TB)	MAus MWat SCro
'Red Rufus' (TB)	EFou
N 'Red Rum' (TB)	CKel
'Red Tornado' (TB)	LIri
'Red Zinger' (IB)	NZep SCro
'Redwing' (TB)	MWat WPer
'Redwood Supreme' (Spuria)	LBro
'Regal Surprise' (SpecHybrid)	CRow WCot
'Regards' (SDB)	CBro CKel EGle LBro MS&S NNrd
'Reginae'	See ***I. variegata*** var. ***reginae***
§ ***reichenbachii***	ERos LBee LRHS
– Balkana Group	SIng
'Repartee' (TB)	SCro
§ ***reticulata*** 🏆	CB&S CBro CMon EBar EPar EPot ERav ETub NRog SIng
'Riches' (SDB)	NZep
'Ride the Wind' (TB)	SCro
'Rime Frost' (TB)	MAus MMil
'Ringo' (TB)	CKel LIri MAus SCro
'Ripple Chip' (SDB)	NZep
¶ 'Rippling Waters' (TB)	WBcn
'Rising Moon' (TB)	SCro
'Ritz' (SDB)	CKel
'River Hawk' (TB)	SCro
'River Patrol' (TB)	EFou
'Robert J. Graves' (TB)	MAus
§ × ***robusta*** 'Dark Aura'	CRDP

§ – 'Gerald Darby' CBro CFee CHad CMGP CRDP CRow CWGN ECha EFol EGol EMFW EPar IBlr LBlm MBro MUlv NSti SCro SWat SWyc WChe WEas WRus
– 'Mountain Brook' CRow
– 'Nutfield Blue' NSti
§ 'Rocket' (TB) CKel CMGP ECGP ERav GMaP MRav NBir SCro SMrm WLRN
'Role Model' (TB) LIri
'Roman Emperor' (TB) EFou
'Romance' (TB) ERou
'Romantic Mood' (TB) LIri
¶ 'Romp' (IB) LBro
'Ron' (TB) SCro
'Rose Queen' See ***I. ensata* 'Rose Queen'**
'Rose Violet' (TB) NMGW
'Roselene' (TB) SCro
'Rosemary's Dream' (MTB) CKel
rosenbachiana WChr
'Rosy Air' (SDB) NZep
'Rosy Wings' (TB) NNrd
'Roustabout' (SDB) EFou LBro
N 'Roy Elliott' CBos CHad NHol NMen WPer
'Royal Ascot' (TB) LBro
'Royal Contrast' (SDB) LBro NZep
¶ 'Royal Fairy' (SDB) LBro
'Royal Intrigue' (TB) SCro
¶ 'Royal Magician' (SDB) WHoo
'Royal Midget' (SDB) LBro
'Royal Regency' (TB) SCro
N 'Royal Toss' (TB) CKel
'Royal Touch' (TB) EFou
'Royal Viking' (TB) LIri
'Royal Yellow' (Dutch) NRog
'Royalist' (TB) LIri
'Ruby Chimes' (IB) LGre MAus MS&S SCro
'Ruby Contrast' (TB) CHad MS&S NSti
'Ruby Gem' (TB) CKel
'Ruby Locket' (SDB) LBro
'Ruby Mine' (TB) MAus
rudskyi See ***I. variegata***
'Ruffled Ballet' (TB) SCro
'Ruffled Surprise' (TB) SCro
'Ruffles and Lace' (TB) SCro
¶ 'Russian White' (Spuria) LBro
'Rustam' (TB) CKel
'Rustic Cedar' (TB) EPfP
N 'Rustic Jewel' (TB) CKel
'Rustler' (TB) SCro
'Rusty Dusty' (SDB) NZep
'Ruth Couffer' (BB) LBro MS&S
'Ruth Knowles' (SDB) LBro
'Ruth Margaret' (TB) CKel
ruthenica CMon ERos NMen NNrd SIng SSpi WOMN WPer
– var. ***nana*** L 1280 SBla
'Sable' (TB) CHad EBre EHic MAus MWat NCut NOrc SCro SMrm SPer WGor
'Sable Night' (TB) CKel ERou MAus
'Sager Cedric' MAus
'Sahara Sands' (Spuria) ECha
'Saint Crispin' (TB) CM&M EBre ERou LBro LBuc MRav MUlv MWat NLak SChu SCro SMrm SPer WGwG WLRN WTyr
'Sally Jane' MAus
'Salonique' (TB) CKel EBee NFai
'Saltwood' (SDB) 🏆 CBro LBro
'Sam' (SDB) NZep
'Samurai Warrior' (TB) SCro
'Sand and Sea' (TB) LBro
¶ 'Sand Princess' (MTB) EFou
'Sangreal' (IB) CKel GLil
§ ***sanguinea*** CAvo CWGN MSto WCot
– AGSJ 625 NGre
§ – 'Alba' CRow GCHN WThi
– × ***laevigata*** SCro
§ – 'Snow Queen' CHad CKel CRow CWGN ECED EGle EHon ELan EMan ERou LGan LPBA MBro NSti SCro SPer SSpe SSpi SUsu WPer
'Santana' (TB) SCro
'Sapphire Beauty' (Dutch) NRog
'Sapphire Gem' (SDB) CKel
'Sapphire Hills' (TB) SCro
'Sapphire Jewel' (SDB) NZep
'Sarah Taylor' (SDB) 🏆 CBro EFou LBro SCro
sari EPot LAma
'Satin Gown' (TB) EPri MBri
'Saturnalia' (TB) SCro
'Saucy Peach' (BB) LBro
'Saxon Princess' (TB) LBro
'Scarlet Ribbon' (TB) CKel
schachtii MS&CL 510 CMon
'Schortman's Garnet Ruffles' (TB) LIri SCro
'Scintilla' (IB) MMil SCro SSte
'Scintillation' (TB) SCro
'Scribe' (MDB) CBro EGle LRHS MBri
'Scrimmage' (SDB) NZep
'Sea Double' (TB) MMil
'Sea Fret' (SDB) CBro
'Sea of Joy' (TB) LIri SCro
'Second Opinion' (MTB) NZep
'Secret Melody' (TB) LIri
'Senlac' (TB) CKel GLil
serbica See ***I. reichenbachii***
'Serenity Prayer' (SDB) NZep
setosa CBro CRow ECha EGle EMNN ERos GAul GCra GMaP ITim LGan MHig MHlr MNrw MOne MSta NHed SCro
setosa alba CMea CRow EBee LGan MBro NRai WDav
setosa var. ***arctica*** CRDP CRow EMon EPot GCHN LBee MBro NHol NMen NWCA SBla SCro SIng SUsu SWas WHoo WPer WPyg
§ – subsp. ***canadensis*** CMea EDAr EHyt ELan GDra MBal MHar NTow SPer WAbe WHil WOMN
– dwarf form See ***I. setosa*** subsp. ***canadensis***
– 'Hondoensis' EMon
– 'Hookeri' See ***I. setosa*** subsp. ***canadensis***
– var. ***nana*** See ***I. setosa*** subsp. ***canadensis***
setosa tricuspis NNrd
'Shampoo' (IB) EFou
'Sheila Ann Germaney' (Reticulata) EHyt EPot
'Shelford Giant' (Spuria) 🏆 CRow LBro
'Shepherd's Delight' (TB) MBri
'Sherbet Lemon' (IB) MAus
'Short Order' (CH) 🏆 LBro
'Show Me Yellow' (SDB) NZep SCro
'Showcase' (TB) LIri NMGW
'Showman' (TB) ERou LIri
shrevei See ***I. virginica* var. *shrevei***
'Shrinking Violet' (MTB) LBro

'Shy Violet' (SDB)	NZep
sibirica	CChr CMHG CMea CNic CShe CVer CWGN EGle EHon LAma LLWP LSyl MBro MFir MWat NCut NDea NNor SEas SHel SMad WEas WHer WHoo WShi WWhi WWin
§ 'Sibirica Alba'	CRow ECGP ECha EHic GDra LLWP SBla
sibirica 'Alba'	See ***I.* 'Sibirica Alba'**
– 'Anglesey'	LBro
– 'Ann Dasch'	EFou EGar LBro WDav
– 'Annemarie Troeger' 🏆	EFou LBro NCat
– 'Anniversary'	LBro MBri SCro
§ 'Sibirica Baxteri'	CFee CRow WDav
sibirica 'Baxteri'	See ***I.* 'Sibirica Baxteri'**
– 'Beaumaris'	LBro
– 'Berliner Runde'	LBro
¶ – 'Blue Brilliant'	WDav
– 'Blue Burgee'	ECha SCro
– 'Blue King'	CKel COtt EPfP MBro MRav NFla
– 'Blue Mere'	LBro
– 'Bracknell'	CWGN
– 'Brynmawr'	LBro
– 'Butter and Sugar'	CRos CSWP EBee EBre EFou EGar LBlm LBro MAus MCLN MNrw MSte NFai NPri NSti SChu WCot WHoo WPen
– 'Caesar'	CKel LBro NCat
– 'Caesar's Brother'	CMGP IBlr MSta MUlv SPer WRHF WWin
¶ – 'Camberley'	WDav
– 'Cambridge' 🏆	EFou LBro MWat NHol
– 'Clee Hills'	WDav
– 'Clouded Moon'	See ***I. sibirica* 'Forncett Moon'**
– 'Cool Spring'	WDav WThi
– cream	See ***I. sibirica* 'Primrose Cream'**
– 'Crème Chantilly' 🏆	SCro
– 'Dance Ballerina Dance'	EBee EGar LBro NBrk
– 'Dark Desire'	MRav SCro
N – 'Dark Lavender'	GMac
– 'Dear Delight'	EBee SAxl
– 'Dragonfly'	WWhi
– 'Dreaming Green'	ECha
– 'Dreaming Spires'	LBro WCot
– 'Dreaming Yellow' 🏆	CBre CFee EBre ECha EFou EGar EGle EPri LBro MAus MUlv NBro NRoo SCro SPer SSpe WHal WRus
– 'Ego'	CDoC COtt CSte CWGN EBre ECha GMaP MUlv NHol WThi WWat
¶ – 'Elinor Hewitt'	LBro
– 'Ellesmere'	WDav
– 'Emperor'	CB&S CKel CRow ERou LPBA NHol WElm
– 'Eric the Red'	CB&S CMHG
– 'Ewen'	CBot CPou EFou LBro SCro WCot
– 'Flight of Butterflies'	CMil CRDP CRow EBre ECGP EFou EGle EGol ELan ERou MAus MCLN MRav NBrk NBro NCat NHol SOkh SPer SPla SSvw WRus
§ – 'Forncett Moon'	EFou LBro
– 'Fourfold Lavender'	LBro NBrk
– 'Fourfold White'	LBro
– 'Friendly Welcome'	LBro
– 'Gatineau'	GDra NHol WDav WThi
– 'Germantet One'	LBro
– 'Glaslyn'	LBro

– 'Harpswell Happiness' 🏆	LBro WGwG
– 'Harpswell Haze'	ECha
– 'Heavenly Blue'	EHon LPBA MWat SSpe
– 'Helen Astor'	CMea CRow CWGN ECED GAbr GAri GDra NCat NHol SWyc WCot
– 'Hoar Edge'	LBro
¶ – 'Isla Serle' 🏆	LBro
¶ – 'Kingfisher'	LBro
– 'Lady of Quality'	LBro SCro
– 'Lady Vanessa'	MRav SCro
– 'Langthorns Pink'	CRDP ELan MRav
– 'Laurenbuhl'	LBro SCro
¶ – 'Lavender Light'	WDav
– 'Limeheart'	CPou EGle ELan ERou LBro NHol NRoo NSti
N – 'Limelight'	SRms
– 'Little Blue' (TB)	SCro
– 'Llangors'	LBro
– 'Llyn Brianne'	LBro
N – 'Marcus Perry'	CRow ECED MSte
– 'Marilyn Holme'	MHlr WCot
– 'Mikiko' 🏆	LBro
– 'Mrs Rowe'	CPou CRow ECED EFou EGar LBro MAus MSte SWat WCot
– 'Mrs Saunders'	CRow WDav WNdy
– 'Navy Brass'	LBro
– 'Nottingham Lace'	LBro NBrk SWyc WBcn WDav
– 'Oban'	LBro
– 'Orville Fay' 🏆	EBee EFou EGar LBro SApp SAxl SCro WCot
– 'Ottawa'	CLTr CPou CRow CWGN ELan ERou NRoo SChu SCro SPer
– 'Papillon'	CLTr CMGP EBre EGle ELan ERou MBri MBro MCli MUlv MWat NBro NCat NHol NRoo NSti SChu SPer SSpi SUsu WKen WPer WRus WWat
– 'Perry's Blue'	CArn CB&S CHad CWGN EBre ECGP EFou ERou GAbr GDra LBlm LBro MAus NBrk NBro NHol NNrd NPer SChu SCro SEas SPer SRms SSvw WPer WRus WWat
I – 'Perry's Favourite'	CFee CRow
– 'Perry's Pigmy'	CRow EBre GBuc MSte
– 'Persimmon'	CFir CRos EBee EBre EGar EGle EMan EMou ERou MArl MCli MWat
– 'Pink Haze'	EGar SCro
– 'Pirate Prince'	LBro NPer
– 'Pontypool'	LBro
§ – 'Primrose Cream'	CMea WCot
– 'Purpeller'	LBro
– 'Purple Cloak'	LBro MSte WBcn
– 'Purple Mere'	LBro WDav
– 'Rebeboth Gem'	WRHF
N – 'Red Flag'	NHol
– 'Reddy Maid'	LBro NBrk
I – 'Redflare'	See ***I. sibirica* 'Towanda Redflare'**
– 'Rimouski'	LBro
N – 'Roger Perry'	CFee CRow
I – 'Royal Blue'	ECha GBuc SBla
– 'Ruffled Velvet'	CBlo EBee EFou LBro MSte NBrk SCro WKen
– 'Ruffles Plus'	LBro
– 'Sally Kerlin'	SCro
– 'Savoir Faire'	CRDP CWGN ECha EGle EPla LBro

– 'Sea Horse'	NCat
– 'Sea Shadows'	LBro NBir
– 'Shirley Pope'	EGar LBro
– 'Showdown'	CB&S EBre ECtt EGar LBro MBri MUlv NHol SAxl WHal WWat
– 'Silver Edge'	CRos EFou EGar LBlm LBro MAus MBri NFai SCro SWat WEas WHoo WPen
– 'Sky Wings'	CB&S CWGN EBee ECha EGle EMou MArl
– 'Snow Queen'	See ***I. sanguinea* 'Snow Queen'**
– 'Snowcrest'	CBre NBrk NPla
– 'Soft Blue'	LBro SCro
N – 'Southcombe White'	CRow CVer EGar GBuc GCal SWas WRHF
– 'Sparkling Rosé'	CBot CWGN EBre ECtt EFou EGol LBlm LBro MBri MBro MNrw NHar NHol NPla SChu SCro SMrm SSvw SUsu WGwG WHoo WPer WRus WWhi
– 'Summer Sky'	WCot
– 'Swank'	LBro WDav
– 'Teal Velvet'	LBro MAus
¶ – 'The Gower'	LWoo
– 'Thelma Perry'	WCot WDav
§ – 'Towanda Redflare'	EBee EGle EHon ELan LBro WHer
– 'Tropic Night'	CHad CWGN EBre ECGP EFou ERou GAbr LHop MAus MBri MRav MSta NBrk NHol NRoo NRya SCro SMad SPer SSoC WFar WHal WRus WWat
– 'Tycoon'	CWGN NChi NHol SPer WDav WLRN
– 'Vi Luihn'	CB&S ECha LBro
¶ – 'Violetmere'	LBro WDav
– 'Welcome Return'	LBro
– white	EGle
I – 'White Queen'	LBro SSvw
– 'White Swirl'	CB&S CBot COtt EBre ECtt EGol EPla ERou LBro MAus MBri MBro MCli MSCN MUlv MWat NBro NFla NHol NRoo SAxl SCro SHel SPer SSpi SWyc WHoo WWat WWin
– 'Wisley White'	EGle LBro NFai WKen
* ***sieboldii***	EMon
'Sierra Nevada' (Spuria)	EFou LBro WBcn
'Silent Strings' (IB)	LBro
'Silhouette' (TB)	LIri
¶ 'Silkirim' (TB)	LBro
'Silver Tide' (TB)	WEas
'Silverado' (TB)	LIri SCro
'Silvery Moon' (TB)	SCro
sindjarensis	See ***I. aucheri***
'Sing Again' (IB)	CBlo SCro
sintenisii	CBro CHan EHyt LBlm NGre SIng
'Sister Helen' (TB)	MMil
'Siva Siva' (TB)	EBre ERou WHer
'Skating Party' (TB)	LIri
'Skiers' Delight' (TB)	LIri SCro
'Skip Stitch' (SDB)	LBro
'Sky and Snow' (SDB)	NZep
'Sky Hooks' (TB)	LIri SCro
'Skyfire' (TB)	SCro
'Slap Bang' (SDB)	NZep
'Sleepy Time' (MDB)	NZep
'Slim Jim' (MTB)	LBro
'Small Sky' (SDB)	CBro LBro NNrd
'Small Wonder' (SDB)	LBro
N 'Smart Girl' (TB)	CKel
'Smarty Pants' (MTB)	LBro
'Smell the Roses' (SDB)	NZep
'Smoke Rings' (TB)	SCro
'Smokey Dream' (TB)	CKel
N 'Smooth Orange' (TB)	MAus
'Sneak Preview' (TB)	NZep
'Sno Jo' (TB)	SCro
'Snow Elf' (SDB)	LBro
'Snow Fiddler' (MTB)	NZep
'Snow Tracery' (TB)	ENot
'Snow Tree' (SDB)	NZep
'Snowbrook' (TB)	LIri SCro
'Snowdrift'	See ***I. laevigata* 'Snowdrift'**
'Snowmound' (TB)	SCro
'Snowshill' (TB)	LBro
'Snowy Owl' (TB)	LBro
'Snowy Wonderland' (TB)	NZep
'Soaring Kite' (TB)	LBro
'Soft Breeze' (SDB)	NZep
'Soft Caress' (TB)	LIri
'Solid Gold' (TB)	CKel
'Solid Mahogany' (TB)	MAus MMil MRav MUlv
N 'Somerset Vale' (TB)	CKel
'Song of Norway' (TB)	LIri MAus NZep SCro
'Sonoran Senorita' (Spuria)	LBro
'Sooner Seranade' (TB)	LIri
'Soul Power' (TB)	ERou
'Southern Clipper' (SDB)	LRHS MBri
sp. AGSJ 431	EWoo NGre
'Spanish Coins' (MTB)	LBro NZep
'Spanish Lime' (Spuria)	LBro
'Sparkling Cloud' (SDB)	EGle
N 'Specify' (TB)	CKel
'Spiced Custard' (TB)	SCro
'Spin-off' (TB)	SCro
'Spirit of Memphis' (TB)	MMil
'Splash of Red' (SDB)	LBro NZep
'Split Decision' (SDB)	NZep
'Spring Bells' (SDB)	EFou
'Spring Dancer' (IB)	SCro
'Spring Festival' (TB)	CKel MAus
'Spring Signal' (TB)	LBro
'Springtime' (Reticulata)	EPot LAma NRog
spuria	ECGP ELan GAul MSto SWyc WDav
N 'Spuria Alba'	SWyc
spuria subsp. ***carthaliniae***	EHic WPer
§ – subsp. ***halophila***	CMon EHic LBro MSto
– subsp. ***maritima***	NNrd
§ – subsp. ***musulmanica***	EHic LBro SRms WThi
– subsp. ***ochroleuca***	See ***I. orientalis***
¶ – subsp. ***sogdiana***	WDav
'Spyglass Hill' (TB)	LIri
x ***squalens***	LBro
'Squeaky Clean' (SDB)	NZep
'Stapleford' (SDB)	CBro EGle NNrd
'Star Sailor' (TB)	SCro
'Star Shine' (TB)	CKel
'Starcrest' (TB)	LIri SCro
'Starry Eyed' (SDB)	EGle LBro
'Startler' (TB)	SCro
'Staten Island' (TB)	CKel ELan ENot MMil MS&S SRms
'Stella Polaris' (TB)	SCro
'Stellar Lights' (TB)	LIri
'Step by Step' (BB)	MBri
'Stepping Out' (TB) 🏆	EBre EFou LIri MCLN SCro
'Sterling Prince' (TB)	LIri
'Stitch in Time' (TB)	SCro
'Stockholm' (SDB)	CKel LBro NSti NZep

stolonifera	CMon
'Stop the Music' (TB)	SCro
N 'Storrington' (TB)	SCro
'Strange Child' (SDB)	NZep
'Strawberry Love' (IB)	NZep
'Strawberry Sensation' (TB)	NZep
stylosa	See ***I. unguicularis***
'Suave' (TB)	SCro
§ ***suaveolens***	CBro EHyt ELan EPot MBro MSto NNrd NTow SIng WIvy
– 'Rubromarginata'	ERos NNrd
subbiflora	CMea
'Sudeley' (SDB)	SCro
'Sugar' (IB)	MAus NSti
'Sugar Candy' (CH)	LBro
'Sultan's Palace' (TB)	CKel SCro
'Sultry Mood' (TB)	LIri
'Summer Luxury' (TB)	NMGW NZep
'Sumptuous' (TB)	SCro
'Sun Dappled'	ERou LIri MMil
'Sun Doll' (SDB)	NZep
'Sunday Chimes' (TB)	SCro
'Sunlit Sea' (Spuria)	LBro
'Sunny Dawn' (IB)	LBro
'Sunny Day' (Spuria) 🏆	LBro
'Sunny Heart' (SDB)	CKel
'Sunny Honey' (IB)	SCro
'Sunset Sky' (TB)	CKel
'Sunshine Isle' (SDB)	NZep
'Superlation' (TB)	SCro
'Superstition' (TB)	EFou LIri MAus SCro
'Supreme Sultan' (TB)	SCro
'Surprise Orange' (MDB)	NZep
'Susan Bliss' (TB)	CKel EBre ELan EPfP GMaP MAus NFai SMer
susiana	LAma
'Swazi Princess' (TB)	SCro
'Sweertii'	WThi
'Sweet Kate' (SDB) 🏆	MAus
'Sweet Musette' (TB)	SCro
'Sweet 'n' Neat' (SDB)	SCro
'Sweeter than Wine' (TB)	SCro
'Swizzle' (IB)	LBro
'Sybil'	GCra
'Syllable' (SDB)	NZep
'Syncopation' (TB)	LBro
'Tall Chief' (TB)	EBre MAus MTis NBrk SCro
¶ 'Tan Tingo' (IB)	EFou
'Tangerine Sky' (TB)	SCro
'Tangerine Sunrise' (TB)	LBro
'Tantara' (SDB)	SCro
taochia	MSto
'Tarheel Elf' (SDB)	LBro
'Tarn Hows' (TB)	LBro MAus SRms
'Taupkin' (SDB)	LBro
tauri	See ***I. stenophylla***
'Tease' (SDB)	LBro
tectorum	CMon GCra LGre WHil WOMN
– 'Alba'	CMea CPou EHic WThi
– Burma form	WThi
– 'Variegata'	EBee EHic ESiP MRav NFai NPla
'Temple Meads' (IB)	MAus
¶ 'Templecloud' (IB)	CKel
'Ten' (SDB)	NZep SCro
§ ***tenax***	CBlo ECho EPot LBee LWoo MBal MFos
– 'Alba'	EPot
tenuis	NNrd
¶ ***tenuissima***	MRPP
'The Bride'	See ***I.* 'Bride'**
'The Citadel' (TB)	CKel SCro
N 'The Monarch' (TB)	CKel
'The Rocket'	See ***I.* 'Rocket'**
'Theatre' (TB)	LIri NZep SCro
'Theda Clark' (IB)	SCro
'Theseus' (Aril)	LWoo
'Third Charm' (SDB)	CBro
'Third World' (SDB)	CBro
¶ ***thompsonii***	EPot
'Thornbird' (TB)	LIri
'Thousand Lakes' (SDB)	NZep
'Three Cherries' (MDB)	CBro EGle
'Thriller' (TB)	LIri NZep
thunbergii	See ***I. sanguinea***
'Thundercloud' (TB)	MAus
'Tide's In' (TB)	ERou SCro
'Tiger Butter' (TB)	WCot
'Time for Love' (TB)	NZep
'Timeless Moment' (TB)	SCro
'Timmie Too' (BB)	LBro
tingitana var. ***fontanesii*** AB&S 4452	CMon
– SB&L 218	CMon
'Tinkerbell' (SDB)	CKel COtt CPBP EGle EMan LBro LGre NLak NRoo SChu SCro WGwG WLRN WWin
'Tinted Crystal' (TB)	LIri
'Tiny Freckles' (MDB)	NZep
'Tirra Lirra' (SDB)	LBro
'Titan's Glory' (TB)	CKel LBro LIri MAus MHlr SCro WCot
'Tomingo' (SDB)	MAus
'Tomorrow's Child' (TB)	SCro
'Toni Lynn' (MDB)	EHyt NNrd
'Toots' (SDB)	EGle LBro
'Top Flight' (TB)	ENot ERou WGor WLRN
N 'Topolino' (TB)	CKel WBcn
'Topsy Turvy' (MTB)	LBro
'Torchlight' (TB)	CKel MS&S
'Total Eclipse'	SRms
'Touch of Spring' (TB)	MMil
'Toy Boat' (SDB)	NMGW
'Trevaunance Cove' (TB)	LBro
'Triffid' (TB)	LIri
'Triplicate' (SDB)	LGre
trojana	CMon EWes LBro SIng
'Truly' (SDB)	CKel SCro
'Tu Tu Turquoise' (SDB)	NZep
tuberosa	See ***Hermodactylus tuberosus***
'Tumbleweeds' (SDB)	NZep
N 'Tuscan' (TB)	CKel WBcn
'Tut's Gold' (TB)	SCro
'Twist of Fate' (TB)	SCro
'Two Rubies' (SDB)	NZep
'Tyke' (MTB)	NZep
typhifolia	WThi
'Ultra Pretty' (TB)	SCoo
'Unfurled Flag'	LIri
§ ***unguicularis*** 🏆	CAvo CB&S CBro CKel CSev CShe EBre ECED EFou ELan EPot ERav GCHN IBlr IHos LBro MAus MBri MWat NFla NRoo NSti SDix SIng SPer SSvw WCra WEas WHoo
– 'Abington Purple'	CAvo CBro
– 'Alba'	CBos CBro ECha
– f. ***angustifolia***	IBlr SWas
N – 'Bob Thompson'	CAvo ECha
– broken form	MHlr
§ – subsp. ***cretensis***	EHyt EPot WHil
– – MS 720	CMon

– – S&L 478	CMon
– – S&L 550	CMon
N– 'Francis Wormsley'	ECha MRav
– L&R 65	CMon
– var. ***lazica***	See ***I. lazica***
– 'Mary Barnard'	CAvo CBro CFee CGle CMon CPou CRDP CSam CSev ECGP ECha GCHN LBro MRav NMen SApp SBla SIng SMad SOkh SPer SWas WRus
N– 'Oxford Dwarf'	CBro ECho ELan
– 'Palette'	ELan
– 'Unguicularis Marginata'	LBro
§ – 'Walter Butt'	CAvo CGle CMea ECGP ECha MRav NBir SBla SWas WCot WRus
uniflora caricina	WCot
urmiensis	See ***I. barnumae* f. *urmiensis***
uromovii	MBro WHoo WPyg
'Vanity' (TB)	LBro LIri NZep SCro
'Vanity's Child' (TB)	ERou
§ ***variegata***	CRDP EPar GCal NCut SIng SUsu
* ***variegata pontica***	SCro
'Vegas Showgirl' (SDB)	NZep
'Velvet Bouquet' (MTB)	LBro
'Vera' (Aril)	EPot ETub LWoo
verna	CGle CNic NHol WThi
versicolor	CArn CBen CRow CWGN EGol EHon EMFW EPar IBlr LBro LPBA MAus MHew MSal MSta NDea NRoo SRms SWyc
– 'Between the Lines'	CRow
– 'Blue Light'	CBlo WChe
– 'Dottie's Double'	CRow
– 'Goldbrook'	EGol
– 'Kermesina'	CRDP CRow CWGN ECha EGol EHon ELan EMFW EPar GCal GGar IBlr MSta NDea NRoo NSti SRms SWat WChe WRus
– 'Mysterious Monique'	CRDP CRow
– 'Party Line'	CRow
– purple	CRow
– 'Rosea'	CRow
* – 'Signagoniga Ridska'	NCat
– 'Silvington'	CRow
– 'Version'	CRow
vicaria	LRHS WChr
'Victor Herbert' (TB)	SCro
'Victoria Falls' (TB)	SCro
'Vigilante' (TB)	LIri MAus
'Viking Princess' (TB)	LIri
'Vintage Year' (Spuria)	EFou LBro
violacea	See ***I. spuria*** subsp. ***musulmanica***
'Violet Beauty' (Reticulata)	EPot LAma
'Violet Classic' (TB)	EFou MAus MMil
'Violet Icing' (TB)	LBro
'Violet Lass' (SDB)	NZep
'Violet Lulu' (SDB)	NZep
'Violet Miracle' (TB)	MMil
I ***virginica*** 'Crown Point'	CRow
– 'De Luxe'	See ***I.* × *robusta* 'Dark Aura'**
– 'Lilac Dream'	CRow
– 'Purple Fan'	CRow
§ – var. ***shrevei***	CRow MSto WThi
'Visual Arts' (TB)	SCro
'Vitality' (IB)	SCro
'Vivien' (TB)	SCro
'Voila' (IB)	EFou LBro NZep
¶ 'Volts' (SDB)	LBro
'Wabash' (TB)	CBlo EBre ERou LBro MAus MMil MS&S
'Walter Butt'	See ***I. unguicularis* 'Walter Butt'**
'War Sails' (TB)	LIri
'Warleggan' (TB)	LBro
'Warrior King' (TB)	LIri
'Watercolor' (SDB)	NZep
wattii	CHEx
'Webelos' (SDB)	CLon LBro LGre SAlw
'Wedding Candles' (TB)	SCro
'Wedgwood' (Dutch)	GLil
'Well Endowed' (TB)	SCro
'Wenlock' (IB)	MAus
¶ 'West Vale' (IB)	LBro
'Westar' (SDB)	LBro NZep
¶ 'Westwell' (SDB)	MAus
'What Again' (SDB)	SCro
'White Bridge' (Dutch)	NRog
'White Canary' (MTB)	LBro
'White City' (TB)	CHad CMGP EBee EGle EMan ERav LBro MAus MBro MMil MWat NPer SChu SRms SWat
'White Excelsior' (Dutch)	CB&S LAma
'White Gem' (SDB)	WWin
'White Heron' (Spuria)	LBro
'White Knight' (TB)	ELan EPfP SMer WCot WDav
'White van Vliet' (Dutch)	NRog
'Whiteladies' (IB)	LBro
'Whoop 'em Up' (BB)	LBro NZep
'Why Not' (IB)	NMGW NZep WBcn
'Widecombe Fair' (SDB)	WWin
'Widget' (MTB)	LBro
'Wild Dancer' (TB)	SCoo
N 'Wild Echo' (TB)	CKel
'Wild Thing' (TB)	SCro
'Wild West' (TB)	EBee
willmottiana	WChr
– 'Alba'	EPot WChr
'Willow Ware' (IB)	SCro
'Willowmist' (SDB)	NZep
wilsonii	CVer GBuc MMil WThi
– 'Gelbe Mantel'	See ***I.* 'Gelbe Mantel'**
'Windsor Rose' (TB)	CKel SCro
'Winged Melody' (TB)	MBri
winogradowii	ECha EPot ERos LAma MTho NHar SDix
'Winter Olympics' (TB)	EFou MRav
'Wisteria Sachet' (IB)	NSti
'Witch of Endor' (TB)	MMil
'Wizard of Id' (SDB)	EGle LBro NZep
'World News' (TB)	SCro
'Wow' (SDB)	LBro
N 'Wright's Pink' (SDB)	MAus
¶ 'Wyckhill' (SDB)	LBro
¶ 'Wyevale' (TB)	LBro
xanthospuria LT 10	CMon
xiphioides	See ***I. latifolia***
xiphium	SSpi WThi
'Yellow Girl' (SDB)	NMGW NZep
'Yo-yo' (SDB)	NZep
'Zantha' (TB)	CKel
'Zeeland' (BB)	LBro
'Zink Pink' (BB)	SCro
'Zowie' (SDB)	NZep
'Zua' (IB)	MUlv SCro
'Zulu Chief' (Spuria)	LBro
¶ 'Zwanenburg Beauty'	EPot

ISATIS (Brassicaceae)
tinctoria CArn CSev EOHP EWFC GPoy ILis LHol MChe MHew MSal SIde WCHb WHer WJek WOak WPer WSel WWye

ISCHYROLEPIS (Restionaceae)
§ *subverticillata* CHEx

ISMENE See HYMENOCALLIS

ISOLEPIS (Cyperaceae)
§ *cernua* CHal EMFW MBri

ISOLOMA See KOHLERIA

ISOMERIA See CLEOME

ISOPLEXIS (Scrophulariaceae)
canariensis CAbb CBot CFil CHEx CSpe EOas GCra SSoC WEas
sceptrum CBot CFil CFir CHan GSki LLew SArc SIgm SSoC

ISOPOGON (Proteaceae)
¶ *anethifolius* MSto
¶ *dubius* CTrC

ISOPYRUM (Ranunculaceae)
§ *nipponicum* var. *sarmentosum* NTow
ohwianum See ***I. nipponicum*** var. ***sarmentosum***
thalictroides CGle

ISOTOMA See SOLENOPSIS, LAURENTIA, LOBELIA

ITEA (Escalloniaceae)
ilicifolia ♀ CB&S CBot CMCN CPlN CShe EBre ELan ENot GOrc ISea LHop MBal MBri MGos NHol NPSl SArc SDix SHBN SPer SReu SSpi SSta WCru WHCG WPat WRTC WSHC WWat
japonica 'Beppu' MGos SLPl
virginica CB&S CDoC CLTr CMCN CPle CWit ECro ELan MBal MBlu MGos SBid SPer SSta WBod WDin WHCG WSHC WWat
§ – 'Henry's Garnet' CMCN CPMA CWSG LMer MBlu
– Swarthmore form See ***I. virginica* 'Henry's Garnet'**
yunnanensis IOrc

ITOA (Flacourtiaceae)
orientalis SF 92300 ISea

IVESIA (Rosaceae)
gordonii NWCA

IXIA (Iridaceae)
◆ Bird of Paradise See ***I.* 'Paradijsvogel'**
'Blue Bird' LAma
¶ 'Castor' ETub
flexuosa NRog
'Hogarth' LAma
hybrids SDeJ
'Mabel' NRog
maculata NRog
'Marquette' NRog
¶ *monadelpha* LBow
paniculata LBow NRog
§ 'Paradijsvogel' LAma
polystachya LBow NRog
'Rose Emperor' LAma NRog
'Venus' LAma
viridiflora NRog WCot

IXIOLIRION (Amaryllidaceae)
pallasii See ***I. tataricum***
§ *tataricum* LAma MBri NRog
– Ledebourii Group CAvo LAma

IXORA (Rubiaceae)
¶ *coccinea* MCCP

JABOROSA (Solanaceae)
integrifolia CFee CFir CLon EBee ELan GCal MTol WCot WCru
squarrosa F&W 7836 EBee EWes

JACARANDA (Bignoniaceae)
acutifolia HBK MBri
– hort. See ***J. mimosifolia***
§ *mimosifolia* CB&S ECon GQui LCns SOWG

JACOBINIA See DICLIPTERA, JUSTICIA

JAMESIA (Hydrangeaceae)
¶ *americana* CPle WWin

JASIONE (Campanulaceae)
¶ *amethystina* EPad
§ *crispa* ECro EPad
§ *heldreichii* EPad GAbr MBro MHig NNrd NRoo SBar SBla SChu SIng SRms WElm WHoo WPyg WWin
humilis See ***J. crispa*** subsp. ***amethystina***
jankae See ***J. heldreichii***
§ *laevis* ECot ELan EPad GMac NBro SAga SRms SSca WCot
§ – 'Blaulicht' EAst EBar ECha EMan ESis MBri NBrk SLod WGwG WPer WTyr
◆ – Blue Light See ***J. laevis* 'Blaulicht'**
montana CKin ECWi EPad EWFC LCom MChe SSca WCla WHer
perennis See ***J. laevis***

JASMINUM † (Oleaceae)
angulare CGre CPlN CRHN ERea SOWG
azoricum ♀ CB&S CGre CPlN ECon ELan ERea GQui LCns LRHS NPal
beesianum CArn CB&S CBot CChe CHal CPlN CPle EBre EPla GOrc LBlm LHol MBlu MPla MRav NEgg NFla SBra SEas SHBN SPan SPer SSvw WDin WHer WSHC
¶ *bignoniaceum* CPlN
¶ *floridum* CPlN
fruticans CDoC CMac CPle ECro ELan EPla MAll MWat WCru
grandiflorum 'De Grasse' CPlN ERea
humile CBlo CPle GOrc GSki IBlr MAsh SHFr WBod WKif

¶ – f. ***farreri***	WCru
§ – 'Revolutum' 🏆	CArn CB&S CBot CMHG CMac CPle EAst EBre ELan EPla IOrc ISea LHol LHop MBal MGos MMor NBrk NHol SHBN SPer SUsu WAbe WEas WHCG WRTC WSHC WWat
– f. ***wallichianum***	Cple
§ ***laurifolium*** f. ***nitidum***	CPlN ERea LChe
§ ***mesnyi*** 🏆	CAbb CBot CDoC CGre CHan CMac CPlN CPle EBak ECtt ELan EOvi ERea ERom IOrc ISea LBlm LPan SBra SLMG SOWG SSta WSHC
multipartitum	CSpe
◆ ***nitidum***	See ***J. laurifolium*** **f.** ***nitidum***
§ ***nobile*** subsp. ***rex***	CPlN LChe
nudiflorum 🏆	Widely available
– 'Argenteum'	See ***J. nudiflorum*** **'Mystique'**
– 'Aureum'	CDec CDoC EFol ELan EPla GQui MAsh MRav NHol NSti SPer SPla WHCG WPat WRTC WRus
§ – 'Mystique' (v)	CPMA CSte ELan LRHS MAsh SPla WCot WPat
– 'Nanum'	ELan MBro WPat
odoratissimum	ERea
officinale 🏆	CArn CBot CMac CSev CShe GOrc GQui LHol LPan MBri MGos MWat NFla NNor NPer SBra SHBN SHFr SPer SReu SSta WDin WEas WHCG WHil WOak WPat WRTC WWat WWin
§ – f. ***affine***	CB&S CRHN CTri EBre ELan ENot EOrc EPla ERea IOrc LPri MAsh NHol SDix SEas SMad SRms WCru WWeb
§ – 'Argenteovariegatum' 🏆	CArn CB&S CBot CDec ECha EFol EHoe ELan EPla GQui LHop MAsh MBri MGos MSta NHol SApp SBra SHBN SHFr SMad SPer SPla SSta WPat WSHC WWat
– 'Aureovariegatum'	See ***J. officinale*** **'Aureum'**
§ – 'Aureum'	CB&S CBot CMac EBre ECtt EFol EHal ELan EPla LHol LPri MAsh MBri MWat NBir NHol SApp SHBN SMad SPer SSta WFar WHCG WPat WSHC WWat
– 'Fiona Sunrise'	CAbb CChu CSte EBre ECle LHop LPan MAsh MBri MCCP MGos NCut NHol NPSI SCoo SHBN WCru WSHC WWat WWeb
– 'Grandiflorum'	See ***J. officinale*** **f.** ***affine***
– 'Inverleith'	CAbb CSte EBar EHic ELan GCal LHop SMad SPan SPla SSoC WGwG
– 'Variegatum'	See ***J. officinale*** **'Argenteovariegatum'**
parkeri	CB&S CBot CFee EBar EMil EPla EPot ESis LBee LHop MAsh MBlu MBro MPla NHar NHol SAlw SHBN SIgm SIng WAbe WCru WOMN WPat WPyg WWat
polyanthum 🏆	CArn CB&S CPlN CRHN CSpe CTri CTrw EBak ELan ERea ERom GQui ISea LBlm LHop MBri NRog SRms
primulinum	See ***J. mesnyi***
reevesii	See ***J. humile*** **'Revolutum'**
◆ ***rex***	See ***J. nobile*** subsp. ***rex***
sambac	CPlN ECon ELan LChe LCns LPri NPal SOWG
– 'Grand Duke of Tuscany'	ERea LChe SOWG
– 'Maid of Orleans'	ERea LChe SOWG
X ***stephanense*** 🏆	CB&S CBot CMac CRHN EBre EEls ELan ENot EPla LHol LHop LPan LPri MBlu MBri MGos MWat NHol SBra SHBN SPer WEas WHCG WHil WPat WRTC WSHC WTyr WWin
¶ ***tortuosum***	CPlN
¶ ***volubile***	CPlN

JATROPHA (Euphorbiaceae)

¶ ***multifida***	ECon
¶ ***podagrica***	LChe

JEFFERSONIA (Berberidaceae)

diphylla	CArn CBro CChu CElw CGle EBre EPar LAma MDun MSal MTho NBir NGar NHar NHol NRog SBla WAbe WChr WCru WFar WWat
dubia	CPBP NBir NRog NTow SAxl SBla SIgm SWas WCru

JOVELLANA (Scrophulariaceae)

punctata	CDec CGre CHan CPle LHil MBlu
repens	ECou LFis WCot
sinclairii	CGle CPle ECha ECou EHyt EMan SBar SBla WCru
violacea 🏆	CAbP CAbb CB&S CDec CGle CMHG CPle CWit EMil ERea GCal ITim LHil LHop MAll MBal MTho SArc SBar SBid SDry SMad WSHC

JOVIBARBA (Crassulaceae)

§ ***allionii***	CMea CTri CWil EPot LBee MBro MOne NNrd SIng SSmi WAbe WHil WPer
– X ***hirta***	CWil GAbr MBro NHol NNrd SSmi
– X ***hirta*** 'Oki'	CWil MOne NHed
– X ***sobolifera***	SSmi
§ ***arenaria***	CWil ESis GAbr GCHN MBro MDHE MOne MRPP NMen SIng SSmi
– from Murtal	CWil MDHE SSmi
'Emerald Spring'	CWil
§ ***heuffelii***	CWil NMen NPri WPer
– 'Aga'	SSmi
– 'Alemene'	SSmi
– 'Almkroon'	SSmi
– 'Angel Wings'	CWil SSmi
– 'Apache'	SSmi
– 'Aquarius'	CWil SSmi
– 'Artemis'	SSmi
– 'Beacon Hill'	CWil SSmi
– 'Belcore'	CWil SSmi
– 'Bermuda'	CWil SSmi
– 'Bermuda Sunset'	SSmi
– 'Brandaris'	SSmi
– 'Bronze Ingot'	CWil
– 'Bros'	SSmi
– 'Chocoleto'	CWil

– 'Cleopatra'	SSmi
– 'Copper King'	SSmi
– 'Cythera'	SSmi
– 'Fandango'	CWil SSmi
– 'Gento'	CWil SSmi
– 'Giuseppi Spiny'	CWil NHol SSmi
– var. ***glabra***	NGre
– – from Anabakanak	CWil
– – from Anthoborio	CWil SSmi
– – from Backovo	SSmi
– – from Bansko Vihren	SSmi
– – from Galicica	SSmi
– – from Haila	CWil
– – from Jakupica, Macedonia	CWil
– – from Kapaenianum	SSmi
– – from Koprovnik	CWil
– – from Kosovo, Yugoslavia	SSmi
– – from Ljuboten	CWil NGre SSmi
– – from Osljak	SSmi
– – from Pasina Glava	CWil
– – from Pelister	SSmi
– – from Rhodope	CWil NGre SSmi
– – from Stogovo	SSmi
– – from Treska Gorge, Macedonia	CWil
– – from Vitse	CWil
– 'Goya'	SSmi
– 'Grand Slam'	Ssmi
– 'Green Land'	CWil
– 'Greenstone'	CWil SSmi
– 'Harmony'	SSmi
– 'Helena'	SSmi
– 'Henry Correvon'	CWil SSmi
– 'Iason'	SSmi
– 'Ikaros'	SSmi
– 'Inferno'	CWil
– 'Iole'	SSmi
– 'Iuno'	CWil SSmi
– 'Jade'	CWil SSmi
– 'Kapo'	SSmi
– var. ***kopaonikensis***	CWil
– 'Mary Ann'	SSmi
– 'Miller's Violet'	CWil
– 'Minuta'	CWil SSmi
– 'Mont Rose'	SSmi
– 'Mystique'	CWil
– 'Nannette'	SSmi
– 'Nobel'	SSmi
– 'Orion'	CWil SSmi
– 'Pampero'	SSmi
– 'Passat'	SSmi
– 'Pink Skies'	SSmi
– 'Prisma'	CWil SSmi
– 'Purple Haze'	SSmi
– 'Pyrope'	SSmi
– 'Red Rose'	SSmi
– 'Springael's Choice'	SSmi
– 'Suntan'	CWil SSmi
¶ – 'Sylvan Memory'	CWil
– 'Tan'	CWil SSmi
– 'Tancredi'	SSmi
– 'Torrid Zone'	CWil SSmi
– 'Tuxedo'	CWil SSmi
– 'Vesta'	SSmi
– 'Violet'	CWil SSmi
– 'Vulcan'	SSmi
§ ***hirta***	CHal CWil GAbr MDHE NHol NMen STre WPer
– subsp. ***borealis***	CWil MBro NHed NHol
* – 'Dunbar Red'	NHol
– subsp. ***glabrescens***	ESis
– – from Belansky Tatra	CWil GCHN MDHE NGre NHed SSmi
– – from High Tatra	MDHE
– – from Smeryouka	CWil MBro SIng SSmi
– – var. ***neilreichii***	SIng
– 'Preissiana'	CWil MBro MOne NHed NHol NMen NNrd
x ***mitchellii*** 'Sandy'	SSmi
– 'Suzan'	SSmi
x ***nixonii*** 'Jowan'	SSmi
§ ***sobolifera***	CNic CWil ESis GCHN MBro NGre NHol SIng SSmi WPer
– 'Green Globe'	CWil MDHE NGre NNrd
– 'Miss Lorainne'	CWil

JUANIA (Arecaceae)

See Plant Deletions

JUANULLOA (Solanaceae)

aurantiaca	See ***J. mexicana***

JUBAEA (Arecaceae)

§ ***chilensis***	CHEx LPal NPal SArc
spectabilis	See ***J. chilensis***

JUGLANS † (Juglandaceae)

§ ***ailanthifolia***	CHEx CMCN ESim SSta
– var. ***cordiformis***	CAgr
§ x ***bixbyi***	ESim WGWT
¶ ***californica*** (F)	WGWT
¶ ***cathayensis*** (F)	WGWT
cinerea (F)	CMCN ESim WGWT
– x ***ailanthifolia***	See ***J.*** x ***bixbyi***
– 'Craxezy' (F)	CAgr
¶ x ***intermedia*** (F)	WGWT
mandschaurica	CMCN WGWT
¶ ***microcarpa***	WGWT
nigra (F) 🏆	CB&S CLnd CMCN ESim GTwe IOrc LHol LHyr LNet MGos NRog NWea SDea SHBN SKee SPer WDin WGwG WMou WStI
¶ – 'Emma Kay' (F)	CAgr
– 'Laciniata'	MBlu WGWT
regia (F) 🏆	Widely available
– 'Axel' (F)	WGWT
– 'Broadview' (F)	CBlo CTho ERea ESim GTwe MAsh MBlu MBri MGos SCoo SDea WGWT WMou
– 'Buccaneer' (F)	CTho ERea ESim GTwe SDea WGWT WMou
– 'China B' (F)	WGWT
– 'Coenen' (F)	WGWT WMou
– 'Franquette'	CTho EBee GTwe MAsh SKee WMou
¶ – 'Hansen' (F)	WGWT
¶ – 'Hartley' (F)	SKee
– 'Laciniata'	MBlu WGWT WMou
– 'Lara'	GTwe
– 'Mayette' (F)	SKee
– Number 139	ESim
– Number 16 (F)	WGWT
– Number 26	ESim
– 'Parisienne' (F)	SKee
– 'Plovdivski' (F)	WGWT
– 'Proslavsk' (F)	WGWT WMou
– 'Purpurea'	CDul MBlu WGWT
– 'Rita'	WGWT WMou
– 'Soleze' (F)	SKee WGWT
sieboldiana	See ***J. ailanthifolia***

JUNCUS (Juncaceae)

acutus	ETPC WWye
articulatus	CKin WKen
* ***balticus*** 'Spiralis'	WCot
bulbosus	Ckin
'Carmen's Grey'	WCot
compressus	CKin
concinnus	ETPC
conglomeratus	CKin EHoe ETPC
§ ***decipiens*** 'Curly-wurly'	CCuc CMea CRDP CSpe EBre EHoe EMon EPla ESOG EWes GCal MFir MUlv NWCA SAxl SWat WHal WHil
– 'Spiralis'	See ***J. decipiens* 'Curly-wurly'**
effusus	CKin ECWi EMFW ETPC SWat SWyc WMAq
– 'Cuckoo' (v)	CNat WAlt
§ – 'Spiralis'	CArc CCuc CFee CFil CRow CWGN CWat EHoe ELan EMFW EMon ESOG ETPC GCal GDra GMaP IBlr LPBA MBal MSta NCat NDea SAxl SUsu WChe WHal WPbr
ensifolius	CAgr CRow CWat ESOG MSta WChe
inflexus	CAgr CKin EHon ETPC SWat SWyc
– 'Afro'	CMea CRDP EMon EPGN EPla LRHS WAlt
pallidus	ETPC GCal
squarrosus	CKin
tenuis	ETPC
xiphioides	ESOG ETPC
¶ – JLS 86161LACA	EPPr

JUNELLIA (Verbenaceae)

¶ ***wilczekii***	WFar

JUNIPERUS † (Cupressaceae)

chinensis	SEND
– 'Aurea' 🏆	CKen CMac CTri EHul EPla LCon LNet MAsh MBal MBar MGos
§ – 'Blaauw' 🏆	CDoC CMac EHul ENHC ENot EPla GAri LCon LLin MBar MGos SHBN SLim STre WStI
– 'Blue Alps'	CDoC CMHG CSte EBre EHul EPla LCon LLin LNet LPan MAsh MBal MBar MBri MGos SEND SLim WStI
– 'Blue Point'	CBlo EHul MBar
– 'Densa Spartan'	See ***J. chinensis* 'Spartan'**
– 'Echiniformis'	CKen CMac
– 'Expansa Aureospicata'	CBlo CDoC CKen CMac EBre EHul ENHC EPfP LCon LLin MBar SBod SLim SRms SSmi
§ – 'Expansa Variegata'	CMac EBre EHul GAri LCon LLin MBal MBar MGos MPla NHol SBod SLim SRms SSmi WDin WGwG WStI
– 'Globosa Cinerea'	MBar
* – 'Golden Rod'	CBlo
– 'Japonica'	MBar SMer
– 'Japonica Variegata'	EBre
– 'Kaizuka' 🏆	CBlo CDoC EBre EHul ENHC GAri LCon MAsh MBal MBar SLim SMer WLRN
– 'Kaizuka Variegata'	See ***J. chinensis* 'Variegated Kaizuka'**
– 'Kuriwao Gold'	CBlo CMac CWLN EBre EHul ENHC GRei GWht LBee LCon LLin LNet MBar MGos NHol SBod SLim SPla WStI
– 'Kuriwao Mist'	CBlo
– 'Kuriwao Sunbeam'	NHol
– 'Obelisk' 🏆	CBlo CDoC CTri CWLN EHul LBee LCon MBar MGos SBod WLRN
– 'Oblonga'	EHul LLin MBar SMer STre
§ – 'Parsonsii'	CMac EHul MBar SHBN STre
– 'Plumosa'	MBar
– 'Plumosa Albovariegata'	LCon MBar
– 'Plumosa Aurea' 🏆	CBlo CDoC EHul ENHC ENot LCon MBar WDin
– 'Plumosa Aureovariegata'	CKen EPla LCon MBar
– 'Pyramidalis' 🏆	CDoC CMac EBre EHul ENHC ENot GAri LCon LLin MGos MWat NPSI NRoo SBod SRms WAbe WWeb
– 'Pyramidalis Variegata'	See ***J. chinensis* 'Variegata'**
I – 'Robusta Green'	CBlo ENHC LCon MBar SLim
– 'San José'	CDoC CWLN EHul LCon LLin MAsh MBar MPla SLim WLRN WWeb
– 'Shimpaku'	CKen EPla LCon LLin MBar
§ – 'Spartan'	EHul
– 'Stricta'	CKen EHul ENHC IHos LBee MAsh MBal MBar MGos MPla NBee NEgg SLim SPla STre WDin WStI
– 'Stricta Variegata'	See ***J. chinensis* 'Variegata'**
– 'Sulphur Spray'	See ***J. virginiana* 'Sulphur Spray'**
§ – 'Variegata'	EBee EHul MBar MPla
§ – 'Variegated Kaizuka'	EHul EPla LCon MBar NHol WWeb
communis	CArn CKin CSev EHul GAri GPoy GRei ITim LHol MSal NHex NWea SIde
– 'Arnold'	CBlo LCon MBar MGos
– 'Arnold Sentinel'	CKen
– 'Atholl'	CKen GAbr
I – 'Aureopicta'	MBar
– 'Barton'	CBlo LLin MBar NHol
– 'Berkshire'	CKen
– 'Brien'	CDoC CKen
– 'Compressa' 🏆	Widely available
§ – 'Constance Franklin' (v)	ECho EHul MBar
– 'Corrielagen'	CKen MBar MGos MPla MWat
– 'Cracovia'	EHul
– var. ***depressa***	GPoy MBal MBar
– 'Depressa Aurea'	CDoC CKen CMac EHul ENHC ENot LBee LLin LPan MBal MBar MBri MGos MPla MWat NHed NHol NRoo SBod SHBN WDin WStI
– 'Depressed Star'	MBar
– 'Derrydane'	EHul
– 'Gelb'	See ***J. communis* 'Schneverdingen Goldmachandel'**
§ – 'Gold Cone'	CDoC CKen EBre EHul EPla ESis LBee LCon LLin MAsh MBar MBri MOne MPla NHed NHol SLim SPla WAbe
– 'Golden Showers'	See ***J. communis* 'Schneverdingen Goldmachandel'**

– 'Green Carpet' ♀ CDoC CKen EBre EPla LCon LLin MAsh MBar MBri SLim SMer SSmi WFar WStI WWeb
– 'Greenmantle' SPla
– var. ***hemispherica*** ECho MBar NHed SRms
– 'Hibernica' ♀ CChe CDoC CKen CMac CSam EHul ENHC EPot GRei ISea LBee LCon LLin MBal MBar MGos MPla MWat NWea SBod SHBN SLim SPer SPla WDin WStI
– 'Hibernica Variegata' See ***J. communis* 'Constance Franklin'**
– 'Hornibrookii' ♀ CDoC CMac EHul ENot GDra LLin MBal MBar MGos MWat NWea SBod SHBN SLim SPla STre WDin WWin
– 'Horstmann' EPla GAri LPan MBar
I – 'Horstmann's Pendula' CBlo
§ – 'Minima' ENHC LCon SBod
§ – var. ***montana*** EHul
– 'Pyramidalis' WGor
– 'Repanda' ♀ CB&S CDoC CMac EHul ENHC ENot EPfP EPot GRei IHos LCon LLin MBar MGos NHed NRoo NWea SBod SLPl SLim SPer SSta
§ – 'Schneverdingen Goldmachandel' CBlo LCon SLim SMer WAbe WWeb
– 'Sentinel' CDoC EBre EHul ENHC EPfP IHos IOrc LBee LCon LPan MBar MBri MPla NBee SLim WWeb
– 'Sieben Steinhauser' CKen
– 'Silver Mist' CKen
– 'Spotty Spreader' (v) SCoo SLim
– f. ***suecica*** EHul ENot IHos MBar NWea SBod SRms
– 'Suecica Aurea' CBlo EHul
– 'Zeal' CKen
conferta CDoC EBee EHul LBee LCon LLin MBar MWat SAga SBod SLim SPer SRms WGwG
* – 'Blue Ice' LLin
– 'Blue Pacific' CBlo CMac COtt EHul GAri MBar MBri SLim
– 'Emerald Sea' EHul
– var. ***maritima*** See ***J. taxifolia* var. *lutchuensis***
davurica EHul
– 'Expansa' See ***J. chinensis* 'Parsonsii'**
– 'Expansa Albopicta' See ***J. chinensis* 'Expansa Variegata'**
deppeana* var. *pachyphlaea GAri
– 'Silver Spire' MBar MGos
× ***gracilis*** 'Blaauw' See ***J. chinensis* 'Blaauw'**
horizontalis NWea SIng
– 'Alpina' CKen
§ – 'Andorra Compact' CKen CMac ESis MBar
– 'Banff' CKen MBar
– 'Bar Harbor' CB&S CKen CMac CWLN EHul ENHC LLin LPan MBar MGos NWea SBod WGor
§ – 'Blue Chip' CKen CMac EBre EHul ENHC ENot EPfP LBee LCon LLin MAsh MBar MBri MGos NRoo SBod SLim SPer SPla SSmi
– 'Blue Moon' See ***J. horizontalis* 'Blue Chip'**
– 'Blue Pygmy' EPot
– 'Blue Rug' See ***J. horizontalis* 'Wiltonii'**
– 'Douglasii' CKen CMac EHul MBal MBar WGor
– 'Emerald Spreader' CKen EHul ENHC ENot MBar MGos SLim
– 'Glacier' CKen
– Glauca Group CMac EHul ENHC ENot GDra GOrc LLin MBal MBar MGos MOne WLRN WWin
– 'Glomerata' CKen MBar
– 'Golden Spreader' CDoC
– 'Grey Pearl' CKen EBre EHul EPla ESis GAul LCon MAsh MBri NHed NHol SBod SLim SMer SPer WWeb
– 'Hughes' CKen CMac EBre EHul ENot IHos LBee LCon LLin MAsh MBar MBri MGos MPla NHed SBod SLim WWeb
– 'Jade River' CKen LRHS MGos NEgg SLim WLRN
– 'Montana' See ***J. communis* var. *montana***
¶ – 'Mother Lode' CKen
– 'Neumänn' CKen
– 'Petraea' CBlo
– 'Plumosa' ♀ NHed
– 'Plumosa Compacta' See ***J. horizontalis* 'Andorra Compact'**
– 'Prince of Wales' CDoC CKen EBre EHul GRei LBee LCon LLin MAsh MGos NHol SLim WGor WLRN WStI
– var. ***saxatalis*** See ***J. communis* var. *montana***
– 'Turquoise Spreader' CBlo CKen EHul MBar MPla WWeb
– 'Variegata' MBar
– 'Venusta' CBlo CKen
– 'Villa Marie' CKen
– 'Webberi' LCon MAsh MBar SLim WWeb
– 'Wilms' CBlo EPla
§ – 'Wiltonii' ♀ CKen EHul ENot IHos LLin MBal MGos MWat NEgg
– 'Winter Blue' ENHC LBee LRHS SLim SPla
– 'Youngstown' CBlo CMac CSWP EBre LCon MBar NHol SBod SPla SSta WGor
– 'Yukon Belle' CKen
macropoda See ***J. excelsa* var. *polycarpos***
◆ × ***media*** See ***J.* × *pfitzeriana***
oxycedrus GAri
× ***pfitzeriana*** 'Armstrongii' EHul
◆ – 'Blaauw' See ***J. chinensis* 'Blaauw'**
– 'Blue and Gold' CKen EHul MBar SHBN SLim SPer
§ – 'Carbery Gold' CDoC CMac CSam EBar EBee EHul LBee LCon MAsh MBar MGos MOne NHol SAga SLim SSmi WLRN WWeb
– 'Gold Coast' CDoC CKen CMac EBee EBre EHul ENHC ENot IHos LBee LCon MBar MBri MGos MWat SLim
– 'Gold Sovereign' EBre MAsh MGos NHol SMer NEgg
¶ – 'Gold Star' NEgg
– 'Golden Saucer' MAsh MBar MBri SBod SCoo
– 'Goldkissen' MBri
§ – 'Mint Julep' CDoC CMac EBre EHul ENHC ENot GRei LBee LCon LLin LPan MBar MGos MPla SLim SPer WWeb
– 'Mordigan Gold' EHul LPan

– 'Old Gold' 🏆	CChe CDoC CKen CMac EHul ENHC ENot EPfP GOrc GRei LBee LBuc LCon LLin MAsh MBal MBar MGos MPla MWat NHed NHol NRoo NWea SBod SLim SPer WAbe WDin
♦– 'Old Gold Carbery'	See ***J.*** × ***pfitzeriana* 'Carbery Gold'**
§ – 'Pfitzeriana' 🏆	CMac EHul ENHC ENot EOHP GAul LLin MBal MBar MGos NWea SBod SLim SPer SRms WDin WStI WWin
– 'Pfitzeriana Aurea'	CB&S CDoC CMac EHul ENHC ENot EPfP EPot GAul GDra IHos LCon MBal MBar MBri MGos MPla MWat NFla NWea SBod SHBN SLim SPer SRms WDin WGwG
– 'Pfitzeriana Compacta' 🏆	CMac ECho EHul MBar SLim
– 'Pfitzeriana Glauca'	EHul LCon LPan MWat SLim WGor
– 'Richeson'	MBar
♦– 'Sea Green'	See ***J.*** × ***pfitzeriana* 'Mint Julep'**
– 'Silver Cascade'	EBee EHul
– 'Winter Surprise'	CBlo LCon MGos
§ ***pingii*** 'Glassell'	ECho LCon MBar
§ – 'Loderi'	CKen EHul LCon MBar
§ – 'Pygmaea'	CBlo CDoC LCon MBar MPla SLim
§ – 'Wilsonii'	CBlo CKen ECho MBar
procumbens	WBod
– 'Bonin Isles'	CSam LLin MBal MBar MGos SLim SPla SRms
– 'Nana' 🏆	CDoC CKen CMac EBre EHul LBee LCon LLin MAsh MBal MBri MGos MPla MWat NHar NHol SHBN SLim SPla SSmi SSta WGwG WPyg
recurva 'Castlewellan'	LCon MGos SMad
– var. ***coxii***	CMac EHul GGGa ISea LCon MBar MBri MGos SLim SRms
§ – 'Densa'	CKen EHul GAri LLin MBar NHol SHBN SPla
– 'Embley Park'	EHul MAsh MBar SLim
– 'Nana'	See ***J. recurva* 'Densa'**
rigida	GAri MBar SIng
sabina	LHol
– 'Arcadia'	CMac SRms
§ – 'Blaue Donau'	CBlo CMac EHul GAul MBar MGos SRms WGor
♦– Blue Danube	See ***J. sabina* 'Blaue Donau'**
– 'Broadmoor'	EHul
– 'Buffalo'	EHul
– 'Cupressifolia'	MBar
– 'Hicksii'	CMac MBar MGos NWea
– 'Knap Hill'	See ***J.*** × ***pfitzeriana* 'Pfitzeriana'**
– 'Mountaineer'	EHul
– 'Rockery Gem'	CBlo EHul EOrn MGos MOne SLim SPla WGor
– 'Skandia'	CKen
– 'Tamariscifolia'	CB&S CDoC CMac EBre EHul ENot EOrn GOrc LBee LCon LPan MAsh MBal MBar MBri MGos MPla MWat NRoo NWea SBod SHBN SLim SPer SSmi WAbe WPyg
– 'Tripartita'	MBar
– 'Variegata'	CMac EBee EHul GWht LBee MAsh MBar SLim WPyg
sargentii	CBlo GAri LCon MBal STre WWeb

– 'Glauca'	GAri
– 'Viridis'	GAri
scopulorum 'Blue Arrow'	CKen COtt LCon LLin MAsh MBri MGos MWat NEgg SCoo SLim
– 'Blue Banff'	CKen
– 'Blue Heaven' 🏆	EHul ENHC GAri LCon MBal MBar SLim SPla
– 'Blue Pyramid'	EHul
– 'Boothman'	EHul
– 'Gray Gleam'	EHul ENHC
– 'Moonglow'	EBre EHul MBar MBri
– 'Mrs Marriage'	CKen
– 'Repens'	MBar MGos
– 'Silver Star'	CBlo CKen EBre EHul MBar MGos
– 'Skyrocket'	CB&S CDoC CKen CMHG CMac EBre EHul ENot EPfP GAul GRei LBee LCon LLin LPan MAsh MBal MBar MGos MPla NWea SBod SLim SPer WDin
– 'Springbank'	EHul ENHC LBee LCon MBar SLim
– 'Table Top'	MBar WBcn
– 'Wichita Blue'	CBlo EBee EHul EOrn LCon SEND WGor
seravshanica	See ***J. excelsa* var. *polycarpos***
squamata	NWea
– 'Blue Carpet' 🏆	CChe CDoC CKen CMHG CMac EBre EHul ENot GDra GRei IHos LBee LBuc LCon LLin MBal MBar MBri MGos MPla MWat NHar NHol NRoo SBod SLim SPer WAbe WDin
– 'Blue Spider'	CKen LCon LLin LRHS MBar MBri WLRN
– 'Blue Star' 🏆	Widely available
– 'Blue Star Variegated'	See ***J. squamata* 'Golden Flame'**
– 'Blue Swede'	See ***J. squamata* 'Hunnetorp'**
– 'Chinese Silver'	CMHG EHul LCon MBar WLRN
– var. ***fargesii***	ISea
– 'Filborna'	CBlo CDoC CKen EOrn LBee MBar MWat NHol SLim SMer
– 'Forrestii'	See ***J. pingii* 'Forrestii'**
– 'Glassell'	See ***J. pingii* 'Glassell'**
§ – 'Golden Flame'	CKen EPla
– 'Holger' 🏆	CDoC CKen CMac EBre EHul EOrn EPla GAri LBee LCon LLin MAsh MBar MBri MGos MPla MWat SBod SLim WStI WWeb
§ – 'Hunnetorp'	CBlo EOrn LCon MBar MBri MGos
– 'Loderi'	See ***J. pingii* 'Loderi'**
– 'Meyeri'	EHul ENHC ENot EOrn GDra GOrc MBal MBar MWat NWea SBod SLim SPer SRms STre WStI WWin
– 'Pygmaea'	See ***J. pingii* 'Pygmaea'**
– 'Wilsonii'	See ***J. pingii* 'Wilsonii'**
§ ***taxifolia*** var. ***lutchuensis***	LBee MBal MPla MWat WWeb
virginiana	CAgr
– 'Blue Cloud'	CDoC EHul LCon MBar SLim
– 'Burkii'	EHul LCon MBal
– 'Frosty Morn'	CKen ECho EHul LCon MBar
– 'Glauca'	CSWP EHul NWea
– 'Golden Spring'	CKen

- 'Grey Owl' ♀ CMHG CMac EHul ENot GRei LCon LLin MBal MBar MGos MPla SLim SPla SRms STre WDin WGor WGwG WPyg WWeb
- 'Helle' See *J. chinensis* **'Spartan'**
- 'Hetz' CB&S CBlo CKen CMac ECho EHul ENHC LCon MBal MBar NWea SBod WWtk
- 'Hillii' MBar
- 'Hillspire' EHul
- 'Nana Compacta' MBar
- 'Pendula' EPla SMad
- 'Silver Spreader' CBlo EHul LCon MGos WLRN
- 'Staver Blue' EHul
§ - 'Sulphur Spray' ♀ CBlo CDoC CKen CMac EBre EHul ENHC EOrn EPla GAul GRei GWht LBee LCon MBar MBri MGos MPla NHol SLim SPer SPla SSmi

JURINEA (Asteraceae)
ceratocarpa See ***Saussurea ceratocarpa***
mollis EMan GBuc

JURINELLA See JURINEA

JUSSIAEA See LUDWIGIA

JUSTICIA (Acanthaceae)
§ ***brandegeeana*** ♀ CHal MBri SLMG
- 'Lutea' See ***J. brandegeeana* 'Yellow Queen'**
§ - 'Yellow Queen' CHal SLMG
§ ***carnea*** CHal CSev EBak ERea GCal LCns MBri SMad
floribunda See ***J. rizzinii***
guttata See ***J. brandegeeana***
* 'Norgard's Favourite' MBri
pauciflora See ***J. rizzinii***
¶ ***pectoralis*** NGno
Puerto Rican cultivar
* - var. ***stenophylla*** NGno
peruviana GCra
pohliana See ***J. carnea***
§ ***rizzinii*** ♀ CHal CInt CSev CSpe ERea IBlr LBlm LCns LHil
spicigera ERea LHil
suberecta See ***Dicliptera suberecta***

KADSURA (Schisandraceae)
japonica CGre CPlN CPle EMil EPfP SBid
- 'Shiromi' CPlN EMil SMur
- 'Variegata' CPle EAst EMil EPfP GOrc SAga SBid SBra SPer WSHC

KAEMPFERIA (Zingiberaceae)
ovalifolia See ***K. parishii***
rotunda LAma LChe

KALANCHOE (Crassulaceae)
beharensis CHal MBri SLMG
blossfeldiana EOHP
daigremontiana CHal GBur SRms
§ ***delagoensis*** CHal STre
fedtschenkoi CHal
manginii CHal EOHP
pumila ♀ CHal EWoo IBlr WEas
'Tessa' ♀ MBri MLan SLMG
tomentosa ♀ CHal WEas
tubiflora See ***K. delagoensis***
'Wendy' ♀ MBri

KALIMERIS (Asteraceae)
§ ***incisa*** EGar EMil EMon EWll SMrm SUsu
- 'Alba' EFou EMon SHel SUsu
- 'Blue Star' EFou
integrifolia CArc ECha SChu WCot
§ ***mongolica*** EBee LFis WPer
§ ***yomena*** 'Shogun' (v) CArc CBos CDec CElw CHal CRDP EBee EBre ECha EFol EFou EHal EHoe ELan EMan EMon GBri LFis LHop MAvo MTho NBir NRoo SHel SUsu WCot WFar WHil WOve
- 'Variegata' See ***K. yomena* 'Shogun'**

KALMIA † (Ericaceae)
angustifolia ♀ EBee GAul ISea MBar NHol SRms WDin
- f. ***candida*** GGGa
- var. ***pumila*** WAbe
- f. ***rubra*** CB&S CDoC CMHG EBre ELan ISea MBal MGos NHed NHol NRoo SHBN SPer SReu SSta WPat WPyg WRTC WWat
cuneata SSta
latifolia ♀ CB&S CLan ELan EMil ENot GGGa GRei ISea LNet MBal MBar MGos NBee NWea SPer SReu SSpi SSta WDin WNor WPyg WStI WWat
- 'Alpine Pink' CPMA CTrh ISea WAbe
- 'Brilliant' NHol
- 'Bullseye' GGGa
- 'Carol' SBid
- 'Carousel' CAbP CPMA CSte ELan GGGa SHBN
- 'Clementine Churchill' CBlo ECot MRav
- 'Elf' MGos
- 'Freckles' CPMA ELan GGGa MDun NHed
¶ - 'Fresca' CBlo
- 'Goodrich' CBlo
- 'Heart of Fire' CAbP CPMA CSte GGGa MBri NHed
- 'Heart's Desire' GGGa SBid
- 'Little Linda' CBlo CDoC CPMA CTrh GGGa GWht NHed SBid
- 'Minuet' CAbP CBlo CDoC CPMA CTrh GGGa NHed SSpi
- 'Nipmuck' CDoC
- 'Olympic Fire' CDoC ELan GGGa MBal MGos MLea NHed SPer SSpi
- 'Ostbo Red' ♀ CB&S CBlo CPMA CTrh EMil GGGa IOrc ISea LNet MBal MBri MDun MGos MLea NHed SHBN SPer SReu SSpi SSta WLRN
- 'Pink Charm' CSte EHic ELan GGGa LRHS MBal MGos MLea NHed SHBN WLRN
- 'Pink Frost' CB&S CTrh GGGa MGos MLea SBid SHBN SPer WWat
- 'Pink Star' MLea SHBN
- 'Sarah' SBid SSpi
- 'Silver Dollar' GGGa NHol WFar
- 'Snowdrift' LRHS SPer
§ ***microphylla*** GGGa MBal WPat
- 'Mount Shasta' GGGa
- var. ***occidentalis*** GGGa

polifolia — CB&S EHoe GGGa MBar MRav NHol WPat WPyg WRTC
polifolia compacta — WSHC
polifolia 'Glauca' — See ***K. microphylla***
– f. *leucantha* — GGGa

KALMIOPSIS (Ericaceae)
leachiana 🏆 — CNic EPot GTou MBal NHar SIng SSta WAbe
– Cedar Park form — WAbe
– 'Glendoick' — GGGa MAsh MDun NHar NHol WPat WPyg
– 'Marcel le Piniec' — GGGa MGos
* – 'Shooting Star' — WPat
– Umpqua Valley form — EPot

× KALMIOTHAMNUS (Ericaceae)
ornithomma — GGGa WAbe

KALOPANAX (Araliaceae)
pictus — See ***K. septemlobus***
§ *septemlobus* — CB&S CHEx ELan EOas NPal SMad
– var. *maximowiczii* — CHEx MBlu NBee SMad

KECKIELLA (Scrophulariaceae)
§ *antirrhinoides* — NWCA
§ *cordifolia* — CPle EMan LHop SIgm
corymbosa — CGra
– JCA 11618 — NWCA

KELSEYA (Rosaceae)
¶ *uniflora* — CGra

KENNEDIA (Papilionaceae)
beckxiana — LChe
coccinea — CB&S CPlN GQui LPan SOWG
¶ *macrophylla* — CPlN SHFr
nigricans — CPlN LChe
rubicunda — CPlN CRHN

KENTIA (Arecaceae)
belmoreana — See ***Howea belmoreana***
canterburyana — See ***Hedyscepe canterburyana***

KENTRANTHUS See CENTRANTHUS

KERNERA (Brassicaceae)
See Plant Deletions

KERRIA (Rosaceae)
japonica — CB&S CPle CTrw EBee IOrc NBee NFla WDin WFar
– 'Albescens' — CBot NPro WWat
– 'Golden Guinea' 🏆 — CChu CDoC EBre ECtt ELan EPfP GAul MAsh MGos MNrw NPro SBra SCoo SPer SPla WWat WWeb
§ – 'Picta' (v) — CB&S CPle CShe EAst EBre EHoe ELan GOrc IOrc LFis MBar MBri MGos MHar NFla SHel SPer WDin WGwG WRTC WSHC WWat
– 'Pleniflora' 🏆 — CB&S CChe CPle CShe EBre ELan ENot GOrc GRei IOrc MAsh MBar MBri MGos MPla MRav MWat NFla NNor NWea SHBN SHel SPer SRms WDin WGwG
– 'Simplex' — ELan NWea
– 'Variegata' — See ***K. japonica* 'Picta'**

KICKXIA (Scrophulariaceae)
elatine — EWFC
spuria — EWFC MHew

KIRENGESHOMA (Hydrangeaceae)
palmata 🏆 — CB&S CChu CHEx CSam EBre ECha ECro ELan LHop MBri MTho MUlv NBir NBro NFla NHol NSti SMac SPer SSpi WFar WWhi
§ – Koreana Group — CRDP EBee ECha ELan EPar LHop MBel MBri SCro SLod SPer WMer

KITAIBELA (Malvaceae)
vitifolia — CFee CGle CHan CPea CSam ECoo ECro ELan EMar EMon EOrc GAul GCal LFis LGan MHlr MNrw MTol NBro NSti SPla WBea WCer WCot WFar WHer WPer WWin WWye

KITCHINGIA See KALANCHOE

KLEINIA (Asteraceae)
articulata — See ***Senecio articulatus***
senecioides — WEas

KNAUTIA (Dipsacaceae)
arvensis — CArn CKin ECWi ECoo EMan EWFC LHol MChe NLan NMir WCla WGwy WHer WHil WJek WOak
dipsacifolia — WCot
* *jankiae* — WHer
§ *macedonica* — Widely available
– Melton Pastels — EBee MCLN NRai SWat
– pink — CBos CMil SWas WPbr
– 'Red Dress' — EMon

KNIGHTIA (Proteaceae)
excelsa — CHEx

KNIPHOFIA † (Asphodelaceae)
'Ada' — EBre ECGP EGar ERou GCHN MRav
'Alcazar' — CArc CMGP CSte EBee ECot EFou EGar EPar MHlr MNrw NPri WCot WMer
* 'Amber' — IBlr
¶ 'Apple Court' — NBir
'Apricot' — CHad CMdw
'Apricot Souffle' — CArc ECha EGar MHlr WCot
'Atlanta' — EBre EGar GCal IBlr SHel WCot
¶ 'Bees' Flame' — SMad
'Bees' Lemon' — EGar IBlr WCot
'Bees' Sunset' 🏆 — ECED EGar IBlr SHBN SMrm WCot WHil WLRN
* *bicolor* — MHlr WCot
'Border Ballet' — CMHG ECtt EGoo EMan MFir MOne NBir NBro NFai NMir SMrm SPla WByw
'Bressingham Comet' — CArc CGle CLon CPea EBee EBre EGar EGle NPri
'Bressingham Gleam' — WCot
Bressingham Hybrids — EBre IBlr NBir
'Bressingham Sunbeam' — EGar

'Brimstone' 🏆	EGar EPla IBlr WAbb WCot
'Buttercup' 🏆	CArc CChu CGle CMHG
'C.M. Prichard' hort.	See ***K. rooperi***
¶ 'C.M. Prichard' Prichard	WCot
'Candlelight'	EGar SApp SAxl WWin
'Candlemass'	EGar
'Catherine's Orange'	WCot
caulescens 🏆	CBot CHEx CHan CMil CPou CSam EBre EMan EMon GCra LLew MUlv SArc SBla SCro SHig SMad WCot
citrina	CB&S CBot CFir EBee EFou EGar EMan MBal NBus SIgm WWat
'Cobra'	CArc CPou CRDP EBee EFou EGar ERou GCHN WCot
'Corallina'	CMGP CSte EHal EWll MNrw NPri WCot
¶ 'Dawn Sunkiss'	WCot
'Dorset Sentry'	WCot
* 'Drummore Apricot'	WCot
'Earliest of All'	COtt SPer
'Early Buttercup'	CMGP CWGN EBee ECot EOrc GBri MMil MUlv NCat NHaw WCot
* 'Early Yellow'	EGar
elegans	See ***K. schimperi***
§ ***ensifolia***	CSte EGar LLew MBal WBcn
'Erecta'	IBlr
'Ernest Mitchell'	MRav WCot
Express hybrids	EBee WCot
'Fairyland'	EGar NBus WCot
'Fiery Fred'	CBlo CMHG EBee EFou EGar EGle ELan WCot
foliosa	EBee LLew
galpinii Baker 🏆	CBot CChu CGle CHan CMGP CMdw EBee EGar ENot LHil MBal NBir NFla SAga SPer SRms WCot WWat
– hort.	See ***K. triangularis*** subsp. ***triangularis***
'Goldelse'	CArc CChu CLon ECha EGar EGle EOrc IBlr NBir SBla
'Goldfinch'	SMrm
'Green Jade'	CChu COtt CRow ECha EFol EGar EPar GBri IBlr LGre NBir NCat SChu SEND SIgm WCot
'H.E. Beale'	EGar GCal WCot
hirsuta	EBre
– H&B 16444	EMon
'Hollard's Gold'	WCot
'Ice Queen'	EBre EGar EGle EGol EOrc MRav WCot
ichopensis	CHan GBuc IBlr LLew WCot
'Innocence'	CChu EGar EGle WCot
isoetifolia	IBlr
'Jenny Bloom'	CLon CSte EAst EBee EGar EHic MHFP MHlr SBla SWas WCot WFar WSan
'John Benary'	IBlr WCot
¶ 'Kingston Flame'	WCot
late orange	WCot
laxiflora	LLew
¶ 'Lemon Ice'	WCot
'Light of the World'	CSte MMil
'Limelight'	EOrc
linearifolia	EGar GBin IBlr LLew NRai SMrm
'Little Elf'	CLon EGar EMan SBla SWas WCot
'Little Maid' 🏆	Widely available

littoralis	EBee GCal
¶ 'Lord Roberts'	WCot
¶ 'Lye End'	WCot
macowanii	See ***K. triangularis*** subsp. ***triangularis***
'Maid of Orleans'	CChu EGar IBlr WCot
'Mellow Yellow'	IBlr
'Mermaiden'	CMHG EGar SApp WCot
'Modesta'	EGar EGle GBri IBlr MSte SUsu WCot
'Mount Etna'	CGle WCot
multiflora	EBee GCal
'Nancy's Red'	CArc CChu COtt ECha GBri MSte SSvw WCot
natalensis	EBee GBuc LLew WCot
nelsonii	See ***K. triangularis*** subsp. ***triangularis***
'Nobilis'	See ***K. uvaria* 'Nobilis'**
northiae	CBot CFil CPou EGar EOas IBlr SArc SBla SIgm SMad SSpi WCot
'Notung'	IBlr
* 'Old Court Seedling'	WCot
'Painted Lady'	CTri EGar GCal MHlr MRav WCot WHoo
pauciflora	WCot
'Percy's Pride'	CDec CMil COtt CRDP CSam EAst EBee EGar EHal EHic EOrc IBlr MCLN MHlr MMil MSCN NBir NCut NHaw NHol SApp SAsh SChu WCot WElm WSan
'Pfitzeri'	SRms
praecox	EBee LLew WCot
'Primrose Beauty'	WCot WMer
'Prince Igor'	EBre ECha EFou EGar MBal SIgm
pumila	EGar LLew MTis SAsh WCot
¶ ***ritualis***	GCal
§ ***rooperi***	CBlo CBot EGar GCal IBlr LGre LLew MBal WCot
'Royal Caste'	EBee MMil MRav NCut NOrc WWeb
'Royal Standard' 🏆	CB&S CChu CHEx CMHG COtt EBee EBre ELan EMan ENot EPfP IBlr LHil MNrw MRav SAga SMad SPla WCot
rufa	EBee WCot
'Safranvogel'	CSte EFou EGar IBlr SApp
'Samuel's Sensation' 🏆	EBre EGar IBlr SHBN WCot
sarmentosa	EBee LLew WCot WWoo
¶ 'September Sunshine'	MRav
'Shining Sceptre'	CChu CMHG CSam CSte EBee EBre ECha ECtt EFou EGar MUlv NCut SMad WCot WMer
'Sir C.K. Butler'	EGar IBlr
¶ ***splendida***	GCal
¶ 'Springtime'	WCot
'Star of Baden-Baden'	NBir WCot
'Strawberries and Cream'	MGrG MSte SAga SUsu WCot
stricta	EBee LLew WCot
'Sunbeam'	NBir
'Sunningdale Yellow' 🏆	CPou ECha EGar NRai SChu SLod SRms WCot WEas
'Tawny King'	WCot
§ ***thomsonii*** var. ***snowdenii***	CBot CChu CFir CMil CMon EBee ECha EFol EOrc GBri IBlr LHil MNrw MSte NTow SAxl WCot WHal
¶ – – triploid variety	WCot
'Timothy'	EFou EGle SAga WCot
'Toasted Corn'	EGar

'Toffee Nosed' ♀	EFou EGar ERou GBri GCal IBlr NBir WCot
'Torchbearer'	EGar IBlr WCot WTre
triangularis ♀	CBot CInt CMon CSte EBee EPfP SMrm
§ – subsp. ***triangularis***	CBot CGle EBee GBuc IBlr LLew NBro SIgm WCot
¶ 'Tubergeniana'	WCot
I 'Tuckii'	CDoC CHan EBee EWll LHil MBal MNrw SAsh SIgm
◆ ***tuckii*** Baker	See ***K. ensifolia***
'Underway'	SSvw
uvaria	CHEx CShe EAst EBee EOas LRHS MHFP NBir NVic SIgm SPer SRms SSpi WByw WHoo WPyg
* – Fairyland hybrids	LIck
§ – 'Nobilis' ♀	EGar IBlr MHlr SDix WCot
'Vanilla'	WCot
¶ 'Vesta'	EGar
'Wrexham Buttercup'	EGar IBlr WCot
'Yellow Hammer'	CBot EGar GBri IBlr NCat
'Zululandiae'	WCot

KNOWLTONIA (Ranunculaceae)

bracteata	CSpe
transvaalensis	SBla

KOBRESIA (Cyperaceae)

See Plant Deletions

KOCHIA See BASSIA

KOELERIA (Poaceae)

cristata	See ***K. macrantha***
glauca	CCuc CInt CPea EBar ECha ECoo EHoe EMon EOrc EPla ESOG ESiP ESis ETPC GCHN LHop MBri MSCN MSto NBro NFai NMir NSti SLod WCot WCra WHal WHoo WPer WWat
§ ***macrantha***	EPPr ETPC
§ ***pyramidata***	ETPC
vallesiana	CCuc EHoe EJud EMon EPPr EPla ESOG ETPC LRHS

KOELLIKERIA (Gesneriaceae)

'Red Satin'	NMos

KOELREUTERIA (Sapindaceae)

bipinnata	CGre WCoo
paniculata ♀	Widely available
– var. ***apiculata***	CMHG
– 'Fastigiata'	MBlu SSpi

KOHLERIA (Gesneriaceae)

'Clytie'	MBri
'Dark Velvet'	CHal WDib
digitaliflora	See ***K. warscewiezii***
eriantha ♀	CHal CPle MBri SLMG WDib
'Hanna Roberts'	WDib
hirsuta	CPle
* x ***hybrida***	NMos
'Jester'	WDib
'Strawberry Fields' ♀	MBri NMos
§ ***warscewiezii***	CHal WDib

KOLKWITZIA (Caprifoliaceae)

amabilis	CB&S CGre CTrw ELan EMil GOrc GRei LPan MGos MHar MPla MWat NBee NNor NWea SEas SRms WDin WFar WFro WHCG WHar WNor WStI WWin
– 'Pink Cloud' ♀	CB&S CShe CTrw EAst EBre ENot IOrc LHop MAsh MBal MBar MBri MGos NHol SHBN SPer SPla SReu SSpi SSta WBod WDin WGwG WSHC WWat WWeb

KUMMEROWIA (Papilionaceae)

See Plant Deletions

KUNZEA (Myrtaceae)

ambigua	CGre ECou MAll SOWG
baxteri	CTrC SOWG
capitata	CTrC MAll SOWG
§ ***ericoides***	ECou GAbr MAll SOWG SUsu
muelleri	MAll
parvifolia	CB&S MAll SOWG
pomifera	MAll
recurva	MAll

LABICHEA (Caesalpiniaceae)

See Plant Deletions

LABLAB (Caesalpiniaceae)

See Plant Deletions

+ LABURNOCYTISUS (Papilionaceae)

'Adamii'	CDoC COtt CPMA EBee ELan GAri IOrc LBuc MBlu MBri MNes SHBN SPer SSpi

LABURNUM † (Papilionaceae)

alpinum 'Pendulum'	CDoC CSte EBee EBre ELan EPfP IOrc LNet MAsh MBar MBri MGos MRav MWat NBee SHBN SPer WDin WStI
§ ***anagyroides***	GAri GRei NWea SEND SRms WDin WHut WLRN
– 'Aureum'	SPer
– 'Pendulum'	CLnd EBee
vulgare	See ***L. anagyroides***
x ***watereri*** 'Vossii' ♀	CB&S CLnd EBre ELan EMil ENot GOrc GRei IOrc LBuc LHyr LNet LPan MAsh MBar MBri MGos MHlr MRav MWat NBee NWea SFam SHBN SPer SSta WDin WFar WJas
* – 'Vossii Pendulum'	CBlo

LACCOSPADIX (Arecaceae)

See Plant Deletions

LACHENALIA (Hyacinthaceae)

§ ***aloides***	LBow LHil MBri WOMN
– var. ***aurea*** ♀	LBow MSte
– var. ***luteola***	LBow
– var. ***quadricolor*** ♀	LBow WCot
– var. ***vanzyliae***	LBow
§ ***bulbifera***	LBow MBri NRog
– 'George'	LBow
contaminata	LBow
hybrid Lac. 213	LBow
liliiflora	CMon

pallida	NRog
pendula	See *L. bulbifera*
purpureocoerulea	CMon
pustulata	NRog
rubida	NRog
tricolor	See *L. aloides*

LACHNANTHES (Haemodoraceae)

§ *caroliana*	MSal
♦ *tinctoria*	See *L. caroliana*

LACTUCA (Asteraceae)

alpina	See *Cicerbita alpina*
perennis	MAvo MTho NChi SChu
virosa	MSal

LAGAROSIPHON (Hydrocharitaceae)

§ *major*	CBen CRow EHon ELan EMFW NDea SRms SWyc WChe

LAGAROSTROBOS (Podocarpaceae)

§ *franklinii*	IOrc LLin

LAGENOPHORA (Asteraceae)
See Plant Deletions

LAGERSTROEMIA (Lythraceae)

indica ♈	ECon LPan SEND SLMG
– 'Rosea'	CB&S LPan SEND
subcostata	CB&S

LAGUNARIA (Malvaceae)

patersonii	LHil
– 'Royal Purple'	ERea

LALLEMANTIA (Lamiaceae)
See Plant Deletions

LAMARCKIA (Poaceae)
See Plant Deletions

LAMBERTIA (Proteaceae)

¶ *formosa*	CTrC

LAMIASTRUM See LAMIUM

LAMIUM † (Lamiaceae)

album	CKin CTiv CWan ECWi EWFC SMrm WWtk
– 'Aureovariegatum'	See *L. album* **'Goldflake'**
– 'Brightstone Gem'	EMon NBrk
– 'Friday' (v)	EFol EGar EHoe EMon EPPr LHop MBel MCLN MSCN MTho NPla NRar WCHb WCot WCru WHer WHil WPbr WPri
– 'Golden Halo'	EMon
§ – 'Goldflake' (v)	EMon MBel WCHb
– 'Pale Peril'	EMon NBrk
¶ *armenum*	EHyt
¶ *eriocephalum* subsp. *eriocephalum*	EHyt
flexuosum	EMon MBel
§ *galeobdolon*	CArn CTri EBre ECWi EMon EWFC LGro MHar MSal MWat NFai SRms WOak
§ – 'Florentinum'	CRow CShe ECha ECro EFol EHoe ELan EMar ENot EPPr EPar NVic SEas SHel SIng WFar WPer
– subsp. *galeobdolon*	EMon
– 'Hermann's Pride'	CElw CHan CMHG COtt CSam EAst EBre ECtt EFol EHoe EMon EPot GAbr GCal GCra LHop MBel MBri MCLN MUlv NFai NFla NMir NWes SPer SRms WByw WCru WHil WWye
– 'Kirkcudbright Dwarf'	EBee EMon EWes
– subsp. *montanum* 'Canford Wood'	EMon
– 'Purple Heart'	EMon
§ – 'Silberteppich'	CRow ECha EFou ELan EMar EMon EOrc EPla GGar MTho NNor NSti NVic SBla SMad WCru WPer WWat
– 'Silver Angel'	EMon MBel NSti
♦ – Silver Carpet	See *L. galeobdolon* **'Silberteppich'**
– 'Silver Spangled'	EGar EMon
– 'Variegatum'	See *L. galeobdolon* **'Florentinum'**
garganicum subsp. *garganicum*	CFis CGle CHan EBee EGar EMon EPPr EWes NChi WCot WCru WPer WWye
– – LM&S 94023B	EMon
– 'Laevigatum'	EMon MBel
– subsp. *pictum*	See *L. garganicum* subsp. *striatum*
– subsp. *reniforme*	See *L. garganicum* subsp. *striatum*
§ – subsp. *striatum*	CMil EFol ELan LFlo SBla SMrm
– – DS&T 89011T	EMon
luteum	See *L. galeobdolon*
maculatum	CArn CRow EGoo EMon SEND SRms WByw WWye
– AL&JS 90226JU	EMon
– 'Album'	CGle CRow EFou ELan EMon LGro MTol MWat NChi SHel SPer SRms WByw WCru WWat
– 'Annecy'	MInt
§ – 'Aureum'	CArn CB&S CGle CInt EBre EHoe ELan EMon EOrc EPla LGro LHop MBel MCLN MTho NFai SMad WEas WHil WOak WPer WWhi
– 'Beacon Silver'	CArn CGle CMHG CRow CShe EBre ECha EFol ELan EMar ENot EOrc GMac LGro LHop MBri MFir MWat NBee NFla NNor NNrd NSti SPer WEas WPer WWat WWhi WWin
– 'Beedham's White'	MRav NBir NSti SCro WCru WRus
– 'Brightstone Pearl'	EGoo EMon WCer
– 'Cannon's Gold'	EBee ECha ECtt EGar EHoe ELan EMon GBuc MCLN NPri WCru
N – 'Chequers'	CDoC CJew EBee EBre EMon ENot LCom SPer SPla
– 'Dingle Candy'	CElw EFol EMon MCLN
– 'Edinburgh Broadstripes'	EPla
– 'Elaine Franks'	NCat
– 'Elizabeth de Haas' (v)	CLTr EBee EFol EGar EGoo EMan EMon EPla EWes LHil LHop WCHb WCer WCru WHer WNdy WPer
– 'Gold Leaf'	See *L. maculatum* **'Aureum'**

– 'Golden Nuggets'	CWan EAst EBee LCom LFis LHop NCut NPla NPro NTay SMrm SPla WEas
– 'Hatfield'	EMon GAbr GBuc NCat
– 'Ickwell Beauty' (v)	EMon ESiP EWes GBri LFis NCat NLak WCot WRHF
– 'Immaculate'	CBre EMon EPla
– 'James Boyd Parselle'	CLTr EMon EPPr MHlr SCro WCHb WCot WRHF WWat
– 'Margery Fish'	SRms WEas
– 'Pink Nancy'	CBot CMea EGoo GAbr LCom MTho WCer
– 'Pink Pearls'	CWan EGar EMan EPPr NHaw NPla
– 'Pink Pewter'	CElw CGle CLTr EBre ECGP ECha ECtt EFou EMon EPla LGro MBel MTol NBrk NSti SCro SPer SUsu WBea WByw WCHb WCru WPer WRus WWhi
– 'Purple Winter'	EPla
– 'Red Nancy'	CBre EGar EMar EMon EPPr EPla GCal MCLN NChi WCer WPri
§ – 'Roseum'	CBre CGle CHan CRow CShe EFer EFol EFou ELan EMar EPla LGro LHop MRav MWat NFai NFla NMir NNor SPer WBon WHil WPer WTyr WWat WWhi
– 'Shell Pink'	See ***L. maculatum* 'Roseum'**
– 'Sterling Silver'	EWes WPer
– 'White Nancy' ♀	Widely available
– 'Wild White'	EPla
– 'Wootton Pink'	CBos CLTr CWan EGar GBuc GCal GMac LFis MBri NBir NChi NLak SSvw WCra WEas WHoo WPer
orvala	CArc CBot CGle CHan CLyd CPle EBre ECha EGar EMon EPla MFir NGar SIgm WBon WByw WCot WCru WHer WPer WWat WWye
– 'Album'	CBot CHan CPle ECro EGar ELan EMon EPPr EPla MFir NGar SEas SMrm WCot
¶ ***sandrasicum***	EHyt
sp. HH&K 315	CHan
sp. HH&K 332	CHan

LAMPRANTHUS (Aizoaceae)

aberdeenensis	See ***Delosperma aberdeenense***
aurantiacus	CB&S CHEx NBrk
aureus	CTrC
blandus	CB&S CHEx
§ ***brownii***	CB&S CHEx CHal ECho ELan EOas NBir WPat
'Carn Brea'	CB&S CHal
¶ ***coccineus***	SLMG
¶ ***coralliflorus***	CTrC
§ ***deltoides***	CHEx CTrC MRav SLMG
edulis	See ***Carpobrotus edulis***
falcatus	SLMG
glaucus	CB&S CHEx SEND
haworthii	CHal SLMG
lehmannii	See ***Delosperma lehmannii***
multiradiatus	SEND
oscularis	See ***L. deltoides***
pallidus	See ***Delosperma pallidum***
roseus	SSoC
spectabilis	CB&S EOas SArc SLMG
– 'Tresco Apricot'	CB&S
– 'Tresco Brilliant'	CB&S
– 'Tresco Fire'	CHal
– 'Tresco Peach'	WLRN
– 'Tresco Red'	CB&S

LANTANA (Verbenaceae)

'Aloha'	LHil NPri
camara	ELan ERea MBri SRms
– 'Brasier'	ERea
♦ – Cloth of Gold	See ***L. camara* 'Drap d'Or'**
– 'Cocktail'	NPri
– 'Feston Rose'	ERea
– 'Firebrand'	SLMG
– forms	ERea IBlr
– 'Mine d'Or'	ERea
– 'Mr Bessieres'	ERea LBlm
– 'Snow White'	ERea SLMG
* 'Cocktail'	CLTr LIck
'Gold Dust'	SLMG
'Gold Mound'	CBrk
§ ***montevidensis***	CBrk ELan ERea LHil NPri SLMG WEas
* ***montevidensis alba***	ERea LHil
§ ***montevidensis*** 'Boston Gold'	CBrk CHal
– 'Malans Gold'	ERea
– 'White Lightning'	LHop
– 'Whiteknights'	CBrk
'Radiation'	ERea
sellowiana	See ***L. montevidensis***
'Spreading Sunset'	SOWG

LAPAGERIA (Philesiaceae)

rosea ♀	CB&S CGre CHEx CMac CPlN CSam CWSG ERea GQui MBal MDun NPal SArc SHBN SPer SReu SSpi WNor WWat
– var. ***albiflora***	CPlN
– – 'White Cloud'	CGre
– 'Flesh Pink' ♀	CB&S CGre CPlN ISea NPal
– 'Nash Court' ♀	CB&S CGre CMac CPlN CSam ECot ELan EMil ERea ICrw ISea NPal SSpi WStI

LAPEIROUSIA (Iridaceae)

cruenta	See ***Anomatheca laxa***
laxa	See ***Anomatheca laxa***

LAPIEDRA (Amaryllidaceae)

martinezii MS 423	CMon

LAPSANA (Asteraceae)

communis 'Inky'	CNat
– 'Patchy' (v)	CNat

LARDIZABALA (Lardizabalaceae)

biternata	CGre CPlN

LARIX (Pinaceae)

decidua ♀	CB&S CDoC CPer ENHC ENot GRei IHos LCon LPan MBal MBar NWea SHBN SPer WDin WFar WGwG WMou WStI
– 'Corley'	CKen LCon LLin MBlu
– 'Little Bogle'	CKen NHol
– 'Oberförster Karsten'	CKen
– 'Pendula'	CB&S EBre
– 'Poulii'	CEnd COtt MBlu NHol
× ***eurolepis***	See ***L. × marschlinsii***
I ***europaeus***	SHhN
gmelinii	ETen GAri ISea

– var. ***olgensis***	CMCN GAri
– 'Tharandt'	CKen
§ ***kaempferi*** ♡	CDoC CLnd CPer ENHC ENot GRei LBuc LCon LNet MBar MGos NWea SLim SPer STre WFro WMou WNor WStI
– 'Bambino'	CKen
– 'Blue Ball'	CKen LLin
– 'Blue Dwarf'	CEnd CKen COtt EBee LCon LNet LPan MAsh MGos SLim
– 'Blue Rabbit Weeping'	CBlo COtt LLin LPan MGos NHol SLim WDin
– 'Cruwys Morchard'	CKen
– 'Diane'	CBlo CEnd CKen EBre GAri LLin MBlu NHol SLim
– 'Elizabeth Rehder'	CKen
– 'Grant Haddow'	CKen LLin
– 'Green Pearl'	CKen LLin
– 'Grey Pearl'	CKen
– 'Hobbit'	CKen
* – 'Jacobsen's Pyramid'	LLin NHol
– 'Little Blue Star'	CDoC
– 'Nana'	CKen GAri LLin
I – 'Nana Prostrata'	CKen
– 'Pendula'	CDoC CEnd IOrc MBar MBlu MBri MGos NHol SLim SPer
– 'Varley'	CKen
– 'Wehlen'	CKen
– 'Wolterdingen'	CKen LLin MBlu
– 'Yanus Olieslagers'	CKen
laricina	GAri
– 'Arethusa Bog'	CKen
* – 'Bear Swamp'	CKen
leptolepis	See ***L. kaempferi***
§ × ***marschlinsii***	ENot GRei NWea WMou
– 'Domino'	CKen LLin
– 'Gail'	CKen
– 'Julie'	CKen
occidentalis	GAri
× ***pendula*** 'Pendulina'	GAri
russica	See ***L. sibirica***
§ ***sibirica***	GAri ISea MBar
sukaczevii	See ***L. sibirica***

LARREA (Zygophyllaceae)

¶ ***tridentata***	MSal

LASER (Apiaceae)

See Plant Deletions

LASERPITIUM (Apiaceae)

¶ ***siler***	SIgm

LASIAGROSTIS See STIPA

LATHYRUS † (Papilionaceae)

¶ ***albus***	CEnd
amphicarpos	MSto
angulatus	MSto
angustifolius	MSto
annuus	MSto
aphaca	MSto
§ ***articulatus***	MSto
aurantius	MSto WLRN
§ ***aureus***	CBos CHan ECha EMon GCal GCra MAvo MBro MHar MSto MTho SUsu WCru WEas WHal WOMN
azureus hort.	See ***L. sativus***
chilensis	MSto
chloranthus	EWll MSto WWye
cicera	MSto
¶ ***cirrhosus***	EMon
clymenum articulatus	See ***L. articulatus***
* ***cyaneus*** 'Alboroseus'	CGle MTho
◆ – hort.	See ***L. vernus***
– (Steven)K.Koch	MSto
¶ ***davidii***	MSto
◆ ***fremontii*** hort.	See ***L. laxiflorus***
gmelinii 'Aureus'	See ***L. aureus***
gorgonii	MSto
grandiflorus	CGle CSev ECha EMon LGre MSto NChi SAxl SMad SMrm SWat WCot
heterophyllus	EMon MNrw MSto WHal WHil
hierosolymitanus	MSto
hirsutus	MSto
inermis	See ***L. laxiflorus***
japonicus	WGwy
japonicus maritimus	LFis MHlr MSto WCot
laetiflorus var. ***vestitus***	See ***L. vestitus***
laevigatus	EBee
lanzwertii	MSto
latifolius ♡	CGle CRHN EAst EBre ECGP ELan GCHN LHop MFir MGam NPer NSti SHFr SIng SUsu WCot WEas WHer WOak WPer WStI WWin WWye
– 'Albus'	CBot ELan EMan EMon GDra LGre MNrw MSte SRms SSpi SUsu WCot WEas WHoo
– 'Blushing Bride'	WCot
– deep pink	NSti
– pale pink	CSam NSti
◆ – Pink Pearl	See ***L. latifolius* 'Rosa Perle'**
– 'Red Pearl'	CPlN EBre ECtt EFou MBri NCut SMrm SPer SSvw WHil WPer WRus
§ – 'Rosa Perle'	CDoC CHid CTri ECtt EFou EMan GAbr MBri MSte NCut NPer SMrm SPer SSvw WPri WRus
– 'Rose Queen'	CB&S
I – 'Rubra'	EPfP
– 'Splendens'	CB&S
◆ – Weisse Perle	See ***L. latifolius* 'White Pearl'**
§ – 'White Pearl' ♡	CB&S CGle CHad CMea EBar EBre ECha EFou EOrc GAbr LFis MBri MSte NPer NSti SMad SPer SSoC SSvw WCra WHil WOve WPer WPri WRus WWat
§ ***laxiflorus***	CSpe EMon EOrc MNrw MSto MTho NTow SSca WCot WWin
¶ ***linifolius***	EMon MSto
– var. ***montanus***	CKin EBee WGwy
luteus 'Aureus'	See ***L. aureus***
§ ***nervosus***	CBot CPlN CPla CPou CSpe MSCN MTho SBla SIgm SMad SRms WOMN
neurolobus	CNic MOne MSto
niger	EMar EMon MSto SHFr SMrm
nissolia	ELan MSto
ochrus	MSto
odoratus	CGle CHan SAga WEas
– 'Bicolor'	ELan
– 'Matucana'	EJud WOMN
– 'Painted Lady'	CGle EJud
palustris	MSto
pannonicus	MFir MSto
¶ ***polyphyllus***	WCot
pratensis	CKin ECWi EWFC MSto
pubescens	GBuc GCra MSto SUsu

rotundifolius CPlN ECoo EPad GCal GDra LGre MBro MHlr MNrw MTho NSti SUsu SWas WCot WEas WHoo WPyg
– hybrids LGre MSto
– 'Tillyperone' EMon
§ ***sativus*** CHad CSpe LHop MSto SHFr SMrm SUsu WEas WWye
– var. ***azureus*** See ***L. sativus***
sphaericus MSto
sylvestris CKin CMGP ELan EMon GAul MSCN MSto WGwy
tingitanus CRHN SHFr WHer
– 'Flame' MSto
– salmon pink MSto
tuberosus EBee EMon MNrw MSto WCot WOMN
× ***tubro*** EMon
undulatus EBee
* ***uniflorus*** MSCN MSto
venetus EMon MNrw
§ ***vernus*** 🏆 CBot CGle CHan CRDP EAst ELan GAbr GCal LGre LHop MHlr MTho NRoo NSti SAlw SAxl SHFr SRms SUsu WCru WEas WFar WHal WHil WKif WRus WWhi WWye
– 'Alboroseus' CGle CHan EFol ELan EMon GCal LGre LHop MBri MBro MCCP MSto NBir NSla NTow NWCA SAga SBla SHFr SMrm SOkh SUsu WCot WHoo WKif WOMN WPyg WRus WWhi
– var. ***albus*** MNrw SIng SRms
vernus aurantiacus See ***L. aureus***
vernus 'Caeruleus' CRDP LGre SMrm SOkh
* ***vernus cyaneus*** NTow SWat WRus WSan
vernus 'Flaccidus' EMon WKif
– 'Rosenelfe' CBot EMan NSla WHil WSan
– f. ***roseus*** ECha EHyt SAlw
– 'Spring Melody' LFis SMrm WRHF
§ ***vestitus*** MSto
– var. ***alefeldii*** MSto

LAURELIA (Monimiaceae)

§ ***sempervirens*** CAbb CB&S CGre CTrw SArc
serrata See ***L. sempervirens***

LAURENTIA (Campanulaceae)

minuta EPad

LAURUS (Lauraceae)

§ ***azorica*** CB&S CGre WWat
canariensis See ***L. azorica***
nobilis 🏆 Widely available
– f. ***angustifolia*** CPle CSWP GQui LHol MBlu SArc SDry WCHb WSel
– 'Aurea' 🏆 CB&S CDec CGre CMHG CPle CSev ELan ELau EMil ERav ERea GQui IOrc LHol LNet MBlu MChe SMad SPer WCHb WDin WPat WPyg WRTC WWat
¶ – 'Crispa' MRav

LAVANDULA † (Lamiaceae)

N 'Alba' CArn CB&S CBot CJer CSev EFou ELan EOrc ERav GCHN LHol NLee NYoL SIde SPer SWat WEas WOak WPer WWye
× ***allardii*** CArn CJer CLon ELau ENor EOHP GBar MChe NHHG NLee SPan WJek WPen WSel
– 'African Pride' SDow SPan
– Clone B SDow
– forms WTus
§ ***angustifolia*** 🏆 CArn CLan CShe ELau ENot GOrc GPoy LBuc MBar MBri MChe MGos MPla MWat NFla NLee NNor NPer NYoL SEas SHBN SMac WAbe WPyg WTus WWye
– 'Alba' CChe EBar EFol EHic EHoe ELau GPoy LBuc LHop MChe NFai NLee NMen WAbe WPbr WSel WWat
– 'Alba Nana' See ***L. angustifolia* 'Nana Alba'**
– 'Ashdown Forest' CSev CWan ECle MChe SDow WLRN WTus
– 'Beechwood Blue' NYoL SDow WTus
§ – 'Bowles' Early' CJer CSam CWan GBar MChe SDow WJek WTus
– 'Bowles' Grey' See ***L. angustifolia* 'Bowles' Early'**
– 'Bowles' Variety' See ***L. angustifolia* 'Bowles' Early'**
– 'Cedar Blue' CSev ELau NYoL SDow SHDw SIde SPla WTus
¶ – 'Compacta' WTus
– 'Dwarf Blue' EFol EMil LHop SAxl
– 'Folgate' CArn CB&S CHad CJer EAst EFou LHol MChe MOne MPla MWat NHHG NLee NYoL SDow SIde WSel WTus
– 'Fring Favourite' NLee WTus
§ – 'Hidcote' 🏆 Widely available
– 'Hidcote Pink' CArn CGle CJer EBre EFou ELan EOrc ESis LHol MWat NBee NFai NFla NHHG NNor NRoo NSti SDow SMad SPer SSoC SSvw WPbr WPer WSel WStI WTus WWat
– 'Imperial Gem' CJer CRos EBee EHic ENor ESis GBar MAsh MBri MChe NHHG NLee NPer SDow SEas SIde WSel WTus WWeb
§ – 'Jean Davis' CJer EBee ELau GBar LHop NBee NHHG NLee SDow SIde WSel WTus
– 'Lady' EOHP GBar LFis LRHS MChe MWat NOrc NRoo SDow SHDw WLRN WTus
N – 'Lavender Lady' CJer EAst NYoL WHil
– 'Loddon Blue' CJer CWSG CWan EBee GBar LHol NFla NHHG NLee NYoL SDow SIde WJek WSel WTus
§ – 'Loddon Pink' CJer CWSG CWan ECle ELan ENor EOHP ERea GBar GCra MAsh MChe MPla NHHG NLee NYoL SDow WAbe WGwG WJek WSHC WSel WStI WTus WWeb
– 'Maillette' CJer
– Miss Katherine ENor
– 'Munstead' Widely available
§ – 'Nana Alba' CB&S CJer CSev CShe ECha EFou ELan ENor EOrc GPoy LHol LHop MBar MBri MPla NHHG NLee SBla SDow SHBN SMad SPer WEas WHow WKif WSel WWin
– 'Nana Atropurpurea' CJer SDow WTus

– 'Princess Blue'	CJer EBar EBee ELan ENor ESis GBar LFis MAsh NLee NYoL SDow SIde SSca WSel WTus WWeb WWoo
§ – 'Rosea'	CArn CB&S CJer CMea CShe EBre ECha EHoe ELau GPoy LHop MBar MBri NBee NHHG NLee SDow SIde SPer WHer WOMN WOak WTus WWat WWeb
– 'Royal Purple'	CArn CJer ENor EWes GBar LHol NHHG NLee NYoL SDow SIde WSel WTus WWye
N– 'Twickel Purple' 🏆	CJer EBar EBee LHop MChe MOne MPla NHHG NLee NYoL SAga SAxl SCoo SDow SIde SSoC WSel WTus
'Blue Cushion'	EBre MAsh
* 'Bowers Beauty'	WTus
¶ ***buchii*** var. ***buchii***	CJer NLee SDow
¶ – var. ***gracilis***	SDow WTus
canariensis	CJer CSev ENor ERea NHHG NLee SDow SHDw WCHb WJek WTus
'Cornard Blue'	See ***L.*** **'Sawyers'**
dentata	CArn CInt CJer CLon CSev ELan ELau ENor EPri ERea LBlm LFis LHol MChe NBrk NHHG NLee SDow SDry SUsu SVen WAbe WHer WOak WTus WWye
§ – var. ***candicans***	CGle CJer ELau ENor EOrc LHil LHol LHop MAll MChe NHHG NLee SAga SDow SIde SMrm SSad WCHb WPer WTus WWye
– 'Royal Crown'	SDow WTus
– silver	See ***L. dentata*** var. ***candicans***
'Dilly Dilly'	SAxl WTus
'Fragrant Memories'	EBee EBre ELau ERea GAbr MAsh NLee SDow SSoC WTus
* 'Goodwin Greek'	MChe
'Hidcote Blue'	See ***L. angustifolia*** **'Hidcote'**
¶ × ***intermedia*** 'Abrialii'	WTus
– 'Alba'	ECle ENor NHHG SDow SSca WLRN WTus
N– 'Arabian Night'	LRHS SDow WTus
§ – Dutch Group 🏆	CArn CJer EFou ELan ENot EPfP MBar MBri NLee NYoL SChu SCoo SDow SPer SWat WHen WHil WJek WPer WSel WTus
– 'Grappenhall'	CArn CEnd CJer CShe EBar ELau EMil ENor EOrc LHol LHop MAsh MChe MPla NFai NFla NHHG NLee NVic NYoL SChu SDow SPer WOak WPer WSel WTus WWat WWye
– 'Grey Hedge'	LHol NHHG NLee SDow WTus
– 'Grosso'	CJer COtt EBee ELau ENor LHol NHHG NLee NYoL SDow WAbe WJek WLRN WTus
– 'Hidcote Giant'	CJer CRos EHal MAsh NPer SAga SDow WSel WTus WWat
* – 'Hidcote White'	WTus
– 'Lullingstone Castle'	CBod NLee NYoL SDow SIde WSel WTus
– Old English Group	CArn CBod ELan MGra NBrk NLee NYoL SDow SPla WJek WOak WSel WTus WWat
– 'Seal'	CArn CEnd CJer ECle EFou ELau GBar LHol MChe NHHG NLee NSti NWoo NYoL SDow SIde SVen WGwG WPer WSel WTus WWat WWye
¶ – 'Super'	SDow
N– 'Twickel Purple'	CArn CMHG CSev ELau ENot EWes LFis LHol NFai NHHG NLee SChu SWat WJek WOak WPer WWat WWye
'Jean Davis'	See ***L. angustifolia*** **'Jean Davis'**
lanata 🏆	CAbb CArn CBot CChr CGle CHan CJer CLon ECha ELan ENor GPoy LHol MBro MChe MPla MWat NHHG NLee NSti SDow SDry SMad WEas WOMN WPer WRTC WSHC WTus WWye
– × ***angustifolia***	CJer NHHG SDow
§ ***latifolia***	CArn CJer EBee GBar NLee SDow SIde WSel WTus
* – 'Alba'	SVen
'Loddon Pink'	See ***L. angustifolia*** **'Loddon Pink'**
¶ ***mairei*** × ***intermedia***	WTus
¶ ***minutolii***	SDow
multifida	CAbb CArn CJer CSev ELau ENor ERea LFlo LHol MChe NHHG NLee NPla SDow SIde SSad WCHb WGwG WHer WTus WWye
officinalis	See ***L. angustifolia***
§ ***pinnata***	CArn CJer CWan ELau ENor ERea GBar LHol MChe NHHG NLee SDow SDry SSad WCHb WEas WTus
pterostoechas pinnata	See ***L. pinnata***
'Richard Gray'	EMon GBar LHop SAxl WAbe WTus
'Rosea'	See ***L. angustifolia*** **'Rosea'**
§ 'Sawyers'	Widely available
◆ ***spica*** 'Hidcote Purple'	See ***L. angustifolia*** **'Hidcote'**
N– nom. rejic.	See ***L. angustifolia***, ***L. latifolia***, ***L. × intermedia***
stoechas 🏆	Widely available
– var. ***albiflora***	See ***L. stoechas*** **f. *leucantha***
– dark form	NHol SDow WTus
¶ – 'Fathead'	SDow
– 'Helmsdale'	CJew CKni CRos CSam EBre ELan ENor IOrc LHop MAsh MBri MLan NYoL SAga SApp SCoo SDow SPer SPla WTus WWat WWeb
§ – f. ***leucantha***	CArn CBot CJer CMHG CMea CSev CTre EBar ECha ELan EOrc LHol MBri MChe MPla MRav NHHG NLee NSti NWoo SChu SDow SPer SUsu SVen WAbe WCHb WPer WTus
¶ – subsp. ***luisieri***	WAbe WHer
– 'Marshwood'	CKni CRos EBre ELan ENor EPfP IOrc LBuc MAsh MBri NYoL SAga SApp SCoo SDow SMad SPer SPla SVen WTus WWeb
* – 'Nana'	CArn
– 'Papillon'	See ***L. stoechas*** subsp. ***pedunculata***
§ – subsp. ***pedunculata*** 🏆	Widely available
¶ – – 'Avonview'	SDow

– subsp. ***pendunculata*** 'James Compton'	CHid EHic ELau EMon ERea LHop MPla NHHG NLee NPSI SDow SSoC SVen WKif WTus
– 'Snowman'	ENor IOrc LRHS MWat NLee SDow SSte WFar WGwG WTus
– 'Willow Vale'	CMHG LGre SDow SPan WTus
¶ ***subnuda***	WTus
vera De Candolle	See ***L. angustifolia***
– hort.	See ***L. × intermedia* Dutch Group**
viridis	CArn CChr CJer CSev EEls ELan ENor ERav LGre LHol MAsh MChe MRav NHHG NLee NPer SDow SPer SSad SUsu WCHb WEas WHer WPer WTus WWat WWye

LAVATERA (Malvaceae)

arborea	CArn GBar WHer
– 'Rosea'	See ***L.* 'Rosea'**
– 'Variegata'	CB&S CHan CInt ECro ELan EMon GBar LHop MHlr NChi NPer NRai SEND WCru WEas WGwG WHer WHil WPbr
assurgentiflora	EMon GBri LHil
'Barnsley' 🏆	CB&S CBot CChe CFee CMHG CShe EBre ECha GCHN GMac GRei IOrc LHop MBar MBri MGos NFai SChu SHBN SIng SPer SUsu WAbe WDin WHCG WHil WOld WPbr WWat
'Barnsley Perry's Dwarf'	NPer
bicolor	See ***L. maritima***
'Blushing Bride'	CBlo EBee EBre EHic LRHS MAsh MSCN SHBN SMad SMrm WHar
'Bredon Springs'	CB&S EBre ECha EMil EMon GBri GMac LFis LHop MAsh MBri MGos NBrk SBid SMad SMrm SPan SSoC WGwG WPyg WStI WWeb
* 'Bressingham Pink'	SMad
'Burgundy Wine'	CB&S CChe EBre ECtt ELan GRei MBar MBri MGos MRav NBee NPer NRoo SHBN SMad SPer WDin WHar WHen WHil WOld WStI WWeb
cachemiriana	ELan GBuc GCal MAvo MFir NPer NSti WRus WWat
'Candy Floss'	CB&S EBar ELan MAsh MBar MGos MRav NPer SHBN SIng SMrm SPer WAbe WDin WGwG WHil WOld WStI WWeb
'Chedglow' (v)	CNat MAvo
'Eye Catcher'	LRHS MAsh
'Kew Rose'	CB&S CBlo EBee EMil EOrc EPfP LHop MAll NPer SBid SMad SMrm SPla SSoC
* 'Laura Rose'	MGos
'Lavender Lady'	SMrm
'Lilac Lady'	LRHS MAsh SLod SMad SPer WPbr
'Lisanne'	EHic EOrc MCCP
§ ***maritima*** 🏆	CBot CDoC CGle CGre CHan CMHG CShe ELan GMac LHil LHop MAll SDry SHBN SMrm SPer SUsu WEas WHCG WKif WOMN WOld
maritima bicolor	See ***L. maritima***
'Mary Hope'	CHan LHop WWeb
'Moonstone'	SMrm
oblongifolia	CBlo CBot MAll SMad
N ***olbia***	CGle MPla MSCN MWat NFai SDix SIde
'Pavlova'	CSte EBee EBre MAll MTis
'Peppermint Ice'	See ***L. thuringiaca* 'Ice Cool'**
'Pink Frills'	CBot CFee EBre EMil EPla LHop MAll MBar MHlr MNrw NBrk NRoo SAxl SBid SDry SHBN SMad SSoC WHar WPyg WRus WStI WWeb
plebeia	MSto
§ 'Rosea' 🏆	CB&S CChe CMHG CShe EBre ECha ELan ENot GRei LHop MBar MBri MGos NNor SHBN SIng SMad SPer WAbe WBod WDin WHCG WOld WPbr WWin
'Shorty'	ELan NBrk WFar
'Snowcap'	CBlo CDoC
N ***thuringiaca***	LFis NBro NPri
– AL&JS 90100YU	EMon
§ – 'Ice Cool'	CBot CElw CMil ECha ECtt ELan EOrc ERav GCal LHop MAll MBar NBee NBrk NPer NRoo SBid SChu SHBN SMad SMrm SPer SSoC WHen WHil WTyr
'Variegata'	See ***L.* 'Wembdon Variegated'**
§ 'Wembdon Variegated'	EBar ELan EMon NPer SMad

LAWSONIA (Lythraceae)

¶ ***inermis***	MSal

LEDEBOURIA (Hyacinthaceae)

adlamii	See ***L. cooperi***
§ ***cooperi***	CHal CMon CRDP EHyt ELan ERos ESis GCal IBlr LHil NGar SIng WCot WHil
* ***pauciflora***	NGar
§ ***socialis***	CHEx CHal CMon CSWP EOHP ERav ERos IBlr LCns LHil MBro NChi NGar NRog
violacea	See ***L. socialis***

× LEDODENDRON (Ericaceae)

§ 'Arctic Tern' 🏆	CDoC CSam EHic EPot GGGa ITim LHyd LMil MAsh MBal MBar MGos NHar NHol SPer SReu WAbe

LEDUM (Ericaceae)

glandulosum var. ***columbianum***	MBal
groenlandicum	MBar WAbe WSHC
– 'Compactum'	LRHS MAsh MBal
hypoleucum	See ***L. palustre* f. *dilatatum***
palustre	EPot GPoy MBal MGos
'Teshio'	SSta

LEEA (Leeaceae)

coccinea	See ***L. guineensis***
guineensis	MBri

LEGOUSIA (Campanulaceae)

hybrida	EWFC

LEIBNITZIA (Asteraceae)

anandria	NWCA

LEIOPHYLLUM (Ericaceae)
buxifolium ♀ LRHS MBal MHig NHol SSpi SSta WPat WPyg
– var. *hugeri* NHar WAbe

LEMBOTROPIS See CYTISUS

LEMNA (Lemnaceae)
gibba CBen CWat LPBA MSta SAWi
minor CBen CWat EHon EMFW LPBA MSta SAWi SWat WKen
minuscula WKen
polyrhiza See *Spirodela polyrhiza*
trisulca CWat EHon EMFW LPBA MSta SAWi SWat WKen

LEONOTIS (Lamiaceae)
dysophylla CPle WCot
– 'Toastytoes' WCot
leonurus See *L. ocymifolia*
nepetifolia WCot
§ *ocymifolia* CAbb CFee CPle EGoo LBlm SAxl SLMG WHer WWye
¶ 'Staircase' WSan

LEONTICE (Berberidaceae)
albertii See *Gymnospermium albertii*

LEONTODON (Asteraceae)
autumnalis CKin
hispidus CKin CTiv NMir
¶ *rigens* WHil

LEONTOPODIUM (Asteraceae)
alpinum EBre GAbr GCHN GLil GTou MBal MBro NFla NHol NMen NNor NNrd SIng SRms WHoo WPer WWin
– 'Mignon' ELan EMNN EWes GDra GTou MBro NHol NMen NNrd NRoo NVic SIng SSmi WHoo
hayachinense miyabeanum CLyd
himalayanum EWes
kamtschaticum EWes
§ *ochroleucum* var. *campestre* WPer
palibinianum See *L. ochroleucum* var. *campestre*
sibiricum See *L. leontopodioides*
tataricum See *L. discolor*
wilsonii ECha

LEONURUS (Lamiaceae)
artemisia MSal
cardiaca CArn CPle CSev EBee ECoo EMan EMar EMon EPla EWFC GBar GPoy MChe MGam MHew MSal NCGP NHex SIde WHer WOak WSel WWye
sibiricus EMar GBar MSal SMad

LEOPOLDIA (Hyacinthaceae)
comosa See *Muscari comosum*
spreitzenhoferi See *Muscari spreitzenhoferi*
tenuiflora See *Muscari tenuiflorum*

LEPECHINIA (Lamiaceae)
floribunda CGre CPle

LEPIDIUM (Brassicaceae)
barnebyanum CGra NTow
– NNS 93-420 MFos
nanum CGra MFos MRPP

LEPIDOTHAMNUS (Podocarpaceae)
§ *laxifolius* CMHG SIng

LEPIDOZAMIA (Zamiaceae)
hopei LPal
peroffskyana LPal

LEPTARRHENA (Saxifragaceae)
See Plant Deletions

LEPTINELLA (Asteraceae)
§ *albida* LGro
§ *atrata* MDHE NMen
– subsp. *luteola* GAri GGar MDHE MHig NGre NMen NWCA SChu
§ *dendyi* EWes LBee MHig NMen
– 'Southley' WCru
filicula ECou
* *hispida* NGre
maniototo ECou
§ *minor* ECou MOne SSmi
§ *pectinata* ECou NGre WCru
– var. *sericea* See *L. albida*
§ *potentillina* CTri EBar ECha EFol EHoe ELan EMon ESis MRav NHol NNrd SChu SIng SRms WCru WPer WRHF WWin
§ *pusilla* SSmi
§ *pyrethrifolia* GAri GGar GTou SSmi
– var. *linearifolia* ELan SIng
reptans See *L. scariosa*
§ *rotundata* CArc ECou WCru WPer WRHF
§ *scariosa* ECou LHop
serrulata GCHN GCLN MBar NHol WCru
* aff. *socialis* JJ&JH 9401641 NGre
§ *squalida* CNic ECha ECou ESis IBlr MBar NNrd NRya NVic SIng SSmi WByw WPer

LEPTODACTYLON (Polemoniaceae)
§ *californicum* CPBP LGre
– subsp. *glandulosum* WDav

LEPTOPTERIS (Osmundaceae)
¶ *hymenophylloides* WRic
* *laxa* WRic
* *media* WRic
¶ *moorei* WRic
¶ *superba* WRic
¶ *wilkesiana* WRic

LEPTOSPERMUM † (Myrtaceae)
¶ *arachnoides* MAll
argenteum CB&S
citratum See *L. petersonii*
cunninghamii See *L. myrtifolium*
epacridoideum MAll
ericoides See *Kunzea ericoides*
N *flavescens* See *L. polygalifolium*
glaucescens MAll
§ *grandiflorum* CChu CFil CHan CPle ELan ISea MAll SOWG WSHC WWeb
¶ *grandifolium* ECou MAll SSpi

'Green Eyes' (*minutifolium* × *scoparium*)	ECou MAll
humifusum	See ***L. rupestre***
juniperinum	CB&S CPle MAll
laevigatum	ISea
– 'Yarrum'	ECou
§ ***lanigerum*** 🏆	CB&S CMHG CPle CTri ECou GCHN IOrc ISea MAll SBar SOWG WBod WWin
* – 'Citratum'	ECou
– 'Cunninghamii'	See ***L. myrtifolium***
– 'King William'	ECou
– 'Silver Sheen'	See ***L. myrtifolium* 'Silver Sheen'**
– 'Wellington'	ECou
liversidgei	CChe CPle ECou MAll
macrocarpum	ISea
minutifolium	ECou MAll
§ ***myrtifolium***	CDoC CPMA CTri ECou ELan EPla EWes MAll SDry SPer WPyg
– 'Newnes Forest'	ECou
¶ – × ***scoparium***	ECou
§ – 'Silver Sheen'	CSte EPfP MAll SOWG SSta WPat
nitidum	ECou
obovatum	CMHG MAll
§ ***petersonii***	CPle ECou
phylicoides	See ***Kunzea ericoides***
'Pink Surprise' (*minutifolium* × *scoparium*)	ECou MAll SOWG
polyanthum	MAll
§ ***polygalifolium***	CTrC MAll SRms
prostratum	See ***L. rupestre***
pubescens	See ***L. lanigerum***
rodwayanum	See ***L. grandiflorum***
¶ ***rotundifolium***	CTrC ECou EOHP
– from Jervis Bay	MAll
§ ***rupestre*** 🏆	CChu CPle CTri ECou EPot GTou ISea LHop MAll MBal MBar MGos NHar NHol SDry SIng SRms WDav WSHC WWat
– × ***scoparium***	ECou
scoparium	CArn CDoC ECou GAri IOrc WDin
– 'Autumn Glory'	EHoe MAll SMrm WStI
– 'Avocet'	ECou EWes
– 'Black Robin'	SOWG
– 'Blossom'	CB&S ECou MAll SOWG
– 'Bunting'	ECou
– 'Burgundy Queen'	CB&S ECou EHoe
– 'Chapmanii'	CB&S CMHG CTri
– 'Charmer'	CB&S
– 'Cherry Brandy'	CB&S MAll
– 'Chiff Chaff'	ECou
– 'Coral Candy'	CB&S CTrC
– 'Elizabeth Jane'	CB&S EWes GCHN GQui
– 'Fascination'	CB&S CGre
– 'Firecrest'	ECou
– 'Fred's Red'	EWes
– 'Grandiflorum'	CTrw GCHN
– var. ***incanum*** 'Keatleyi' 🏆	CGre CMHG ECou MAll SOWG WFar WPyg
– – 'Wairere'	ECou
– 'Jubilee' (d)	CB&S ISea
– 'Leonard Wilson' (d)	CTri ECou EWes LBlm MAll
– 'Lyndon'	ECou
– 'Martini'	CB&S CDoC CTrC IOrc SOWG WWeb
– 'McLean'	ECou
– (Nanum Group) 'Nanum'	LBee SBod SHBN SIng
– – 'Huia'	CB&S ECou EMil ENot IOrc
– – 'Kea'	ECou EHoe EPot ESis GQui MHig WPyg
¶ – – 'Kiwi' 🏆	CB&S CWLN ECou ELan ENot EPot EWes GQui IOrc ISea ITim MAll MAsh MDun NHol WLRN WPat WPyg
– – 'Kompakt'	EPot
– – 'Kotuku'	EPot
– – 'Pipit'	EPot EWes
– – 'Tui'	CTrC MAll
scoparium 'Nichollsii' 🏆	CB&S CGre CHan CMHG CTri CWLN ENot GQui ITim SOWG WHar WSHC
– 'Nichollsii Nanum' 🏆	EPot NHar NHol NSla SIng WAbe WPat WPyg
– 'Pink Cascade'	CB&S CBlo CTri IOrc ISea MAll MBal SAga
– 'Pink Champagne'	ECou
– var. ***prostratum*** hort.	See ***L. rupestre***
– 'Red Damask' (d) 🏆	CB&S CChe CGre CLan CTrC CTre CWLN ELan ENot GQui IOrc ISea LHop MAll MAsh SBod SHBN SOWG SRms WDin WSHC WStI WWeb
– 'Red Ensign'	MAll SBod
– 'Red Falls'	CDoC ECou MAll SOWG
– 'Redpoll'	ECou
– 'Redstart'	ECou
– 'Robin'	ECou
– 'Rosy Morn'	ISea
– 'Ruby Glow' (d)	WBod
– 'Ruby Wedding'	CSte
* – 'Silver Spire'	SOWG
– 'Snow Flurry'	CB&S CTrC ENot ISea MAll SSte WDin WWeb
– 'Sunraysia'	CDoC CTrw LBlm MAll
– 'Winter Cheer'	CB&S
¶ ***sphaerocarpum***	MAll
squarrosum	MAll
trinervium	MAll

LESCHENAULTIA (Goodeniaceae)

See Plant Deletions

LESPEDEZA (Papilionaceae)

bicolor	CAgr CB&S CWit EHal EOrc GOrc SLPl WDin
buergeri	CSte ELan LRHS SMur SSta
floribunda	CPle WSHC
hedysaroides	See ***L. juncea***
thunbergii 🏆	CB&S ELan EMil LHop LPan MBlu MGos NFla SBid SMad SOWG SPer SReu SSpi SSta WDin WFar WSHC
– 'Albiflora'	WThi
* – 'Variegata'	LRHS
tiliifolia	See ***Desmodium elegans***
yakushima	MPla

LESQUERELLA (Brassicaceae)

alpina	NWCA
arctica var. ***purshii***	WHil

LEUCADENDRON (Proteaceae)

argenteum	CBrP CHEx CTrC SIgm
¶ ***comosum***	CTrC
¶ ***discolor***	CTrC
¶ ***salicifolium***	CTrC
¶ ***tinctum***	CTrC

LEUCAENA (Mimosaceae)

leucocephala	See *L. latisiliqua*

LEUCANTHEMELLA (Asteraceae)

§ *serotina* ♀	CArc CBre CGle CHan CSev ECGP ECha EJud ELan EMan ESiP GAbr GMaP LBlm LCot LFis LGan MHlr MSte NSti SHel SPer WEas WHoo WOve WPri WWin

LEUCANTHEMOPSIS (Asteraceae)

§ *alpina*	LBee MDHE
hosmariensis	See ***Rhodanthemum hosmariense***
§ *pectinata*	NSla
– JCA 627.801	CPBP
radicans	See *L. pectinata*

LEUCANTHEMUM † (Asteraceae)

◆ *atlanticum*	See ***Pyrethropsis atlantica***
◆ *catananche*	See ***Pyrethropsis catananche***
'Fringe Benefit'	EMon NPer
hosmariense	See ***Rhodanthemum hosmariense***
mawii	See ***Rhodanthemum gayanum***
maximum hort.	See *L. × superbum*
§ *maximum* (Ramond) DC.	CWan GAbr GCHN NBro NPer NPla NVic WBea WByw WCer WOak WRha WWin
– *uliginosum*	See ***Leucanthemella serotina***
nipponicum	See ***Nipponanthemum nipponicum***
§ × *superbum*	LCom MNrw
– 'Aglaia' (d) ♀	CMil EMon LFis LRHS MAvo MCLN MHlr NPer WCot WRHF
– 'Alaska'	CDoC EMan EOrc NFai NOak SPer WGwG WPer
¶ – 'Anita Allen'	CMil MAvo
– 'Annie House'	CArc
– 'Antwerp Star'	MFir NCat
– 'Beauté Nivelloise'	CBre CMil CShe ECha LFis MAvo MBel WCot WPer WRha
– 'Bishopstone'	CBre CDec CMil ELan MAvo MRav NCat WEas
– 'Christine Hagemann'	LBuc MBri
– 'Cobham Gold' (d)	CBre CElw CMil ECha ERea GBuc NFla NOrc
– 'Coconut Ice'	EWll GAbr WPer
– 'Esther Read' (d)	CGle CM&M CMdw CShe EAst ECED ECle ELan EMan ERea EWes NFla NRoo SRms SWat WByw
– 'Everest'	EMan NOak SRms
– 'Fiona Coghill'	CArc CElw EBee GBri IBlr LFis MAvo WCot
– 'H. Seibert'	CMil CSam ECED MArl
– 'Horace Read' (d)	CMil CSev ECED ECha EFol ELan EMon ERea LFis NPer WEas WPer
– 'Jennifer Read'	ERea
– 'John Murray'	LRHS WAbb
– 'Little Miss Muffet'	LRHS NFai
– 'Little Princess'	See *L. × superbum* **'Silberprinzesschen'**
– 'Manhattan'	EMon GBuc LRHS
– 'Mayfield Giant'	WPer
– 'Mount Everest'	CBlo EGar SRms WCot
– 'Phyllis Smith'	CArc CGle CMdw CVer CWan ECha EGar EJud EMan GAbr LFis MAvo MBel MBri MTis NFai NPla SSvw WAbb WBea
– 'Polaris'	NFai NOak WHer
– 'Shaggy'	CBos CVer GMaP LFis NFla NRoo SWat WRHF
§ – 'Silberprinzesschen'	CDoC CMea CShe EJud GAbr MFir NHol NMir NOak NPri NRoo SRms SSea WBea WCot WHen WPer
– 'Snow Lady'	GCHN NMir NPer NRoo SHel WFar WHen WHil
– 'Snowcap'	EBre ECGP ECha EGar EHic EMan ENot GAri MBri MOne NFla SMrm SPer WTyr
§ – 'Sonnenschein'	CElw CPou CSam EBee ECha EFol EFou EGar EMan EMon GBuc LCom LRHS MArl MAvo MHlr NBrk NFai SMrm WBea WCot WHoo
– 'Starburst' (d)	EFou EMan MBri NRoo SHel SRms WHen
– 'Summer Snowball'	CElw EBre EWes MAvo MBri NCat
◆ – Sunshine	See *L. × superbum* **'Sonnenschein'**
– 'T.E. Killin' (d) ♀	CGle ECha EGar EJud EMon
– 'White Iceberg'	WPer
§ – 'Wirral Supreme' (d) ♀	CArc EAst EBre ECED EFou ELan ENot EOrc GAbr GMaP LFis MBro MCLN MFir MRav MWat NFai NFla SPer SRms SSvw WBea WByw WEas WHil
'Tizi-n-Test'	See ***Rhodanthemum gayanum* 'Tizi-n-Test'**
§ *vulgare*	CArn CKin ECWi ECoo EPar EWFC MGam MHew NLan NMir WCla WHen WHer WJek WOak WWye
– 'Avondale'	MAvo
– 'Hullavington' (v)	EMon
§ – 'Maikönigin'	GCal NSti WRHF
◆ – May Queen	See *L. vulgare* **'Maikönigin'**
* – 'Sunny'	CBre
– 'Woodpecker's'	WAlt WCot

LEUCOCHRYSUM (Asteraceae)

§ *albicans* subsp. *albicans* var. *incanum*	GDra

LEUCOCORYNE (Alliaceae)

'Andes'	WChr
'Caravelle'	WChr
coquimbensis	CMon
ixioides	LBow
ixioides alba	CMon
purpurea	WChr

LEUCOGENES (Asteraceae)

* *aclandii*	NHar NSla
grandiceps	GCLN GTou ITim NHar NSla SBla WAbe
leontopodium	GCLN GGar GTou ITim NHar NMen NRoo NSla WAbe

LEUCOJUM † (Amaryllidaceae)

aestivum	CB&S CFee ECWi LAma MBri NEgg NMGW NMen NRog SRms WAbe WCla WCra WCru WGwy WHil WHoo WShi

– 'Gravetye Giant' ♀	CAvo CBro CHad ECha ELan EMar EPar EPot ERav ETub LAma LFox LHop MBro MRav NRog SIng WAbb
autumnale ♀	CAvo CBro CFee CLyd CRDP EBre EHyt ELan ERos ESis EWes ITim LAma LBee LBow MFos MHig MTho NGar NMen SAlw SSpi SWas WHil WOMN
– 'Cobb's Variety'	GCal LHop
– var. ***oporanthum***	CMon EPot NRog
– var. ***pulchellum***	CBro CMon EPot
nicaeense ♀	CBro CGra CLyd CRDP EBur EHyt EPot LHop MFos MHig MTho NGar NHar NMen SSpi WAbe WChr WOMN
roseum	CLyd EBur EHyt EPot LAma SAlw SWas WChr
tingitanum	CMon EHyt
trichophyllum	CBro CMon ERos
trichophyllum purpurascens	EPot
valentinum	CAvo CBro CMon WChr
vernum ♀	CBro ELan EMon EPar ETub GDra LAma MBri MNrw MRav NGar NMGW NRar SRms WBod WHil WShi
– var. ***carpathicum***	ECha EMon EPot LAma MRav NRar WChr
– 'Podpolozje'	WChr
– var. ***vagneri***	CMea ECha LFox WChr

LEUCOPHYTA (Asteraceae)

§ ***brownii***	CBrk ECou LHil MRav SChu SVen

LEUCOPOGON (Epacridaceae)

ericoides	MBar
§ ***fasciculatus***	ECou
§ ***fraseri***	ECou EHyt MHig WAbe
parviflorus	See ***Cyathodes parviflora***

× LEUCORAOULIA (Asteraceae)

§ hybrid (***Raoulia hectorii* × *Leucogenes grandiceps***)	EPot GTou MHig NSla SIng
§ ***loganii***	EPot GDra ITim MHig NHar NWCA WAbe

LEUCOSCEPTRUM (Lamiaceae)

stellipilum formosanum B&SWJ 1804	WCru

LEUCOSPERMUM (Proteaceae)

¶ ***cordifolium***	CTrC

LEUCOTHOE (Ericaceae)

carinella	LRHS MBri MGos
catesbyi	GCHN
davisiae	GGGa MBal
fontanesiana	See ***L. walteri***
grayana	MBal
keiskei	MAsh WAbe
– 'Royal Ruby'	MAsh SEas WDin WWeb
populifolia	See ***Agarista populifolia***
Scarletta	CB&S CHig CKni CMHG COtt CSam EBre ELan EMil IOrc LBuc LHop MAsh MBal MBar MBri MGos MUlv NHol SPer SPla SReu SSta WDin WFar WHar WRTC WWeb
§ ***walteri*** ♀	EHic MBal MGos STre WStI WWat
– Lovita	GCal MBri MRav SBid SSta
– 'Nana'	CSte MAsh SSto
– 'Rainbow'	CB&S CLan CTrw ELan EMil ENot GRei IOrc LHop LNet MAsh MBal MBar MGos NBee NHol SHBN SPer SReu SSta WDin WGwG WRTC
* – 'Red Pimpernel'	EPfP
– 'Rollissonii' ♀	MBal MBar NHol SPla SReu SRms SSta WBod

LEUZEA (Asteraceae)

§ ***centauroides***	CGle EBre ECED ECha EGle ELan EMan GCal LGre MBro MFir NWoo WByw
conifera macrocephala	WAbe
§ ***rhapontica***	EMan

LEVISTICUM (Apiaceae)

officinale	CAgr CArn CSev ECha EJud ELan ELau GPoy LHol MBar MChe MGam MHew SDix SIde SWat WBea WHer WOak WPer WTyr WWye

LEWISIA † (Portulacaceae)

'Archangel'	NRya
'Ashwood Pearl'	MAsh
'Ben Chace'	MAsh
Birch strain	CB&S ECho ELan SIng
brachycalyx ♀	CGra EWes GDra GTou MAsh MBal MTho NGre NHar NNrd NWCA WLRN
cantelovii	CPBP MAsh NGre
columbiana	EHyt GTou MAsh MDHE NGre NHar NTow SIng
– 'Alba'	EHyt GCHN GDra LWoo MAsh
– 'Edithiae'	MFos
– 'Rosea'	CMea MAsh NGre SIng WAbe WGor
– subsp. ***rupicola***	CNic GCHN MAsh MFos NGre NWCA WGor
– subsp. ***wallowensis***	CGra EHyt EPot MAsh NMen WGor
congdonii	MAsh NGre WAbe
cotyledon ♀	CPla ESis MAsh MNrw MOne NNrd NWCA WHil WPat WWtk
– f. ***alba***	CLyd CPla EHyt EPot ESis GDra GTou LHop MAsh MBro NGre SBla WAbe WCla WHoo WPyg
– Ashwood Ruby Group	LWoo MAsh NHar
– Ashwood strain	CNic EBre EHyt ESis EWes LBee MAsh MBri MOne NRoo NRya NSla SRms WAbe WGor WHoo WPyg
– Crags Hybrids	NCLN
– var. ***heckneri*** ♀	GDra MAsh WGor
¶ – – JCA 11031	LWoo
– var. ***howellii***	CPla ELan SRms WGor
– hybrids	CFee CGra CMHG CNic EMNN EPot GDra GTou ITim LHop MBro MFos NGre NHar NMen WAbe WDav WGor WHil WWin
– J&JA 12959	NWCA
– 'John's Special'	GCHN GDra LWoo
– magenta strain	MAsh WGor WPyg

– 'Rose Splendour'	ELan EPar MAsh WGor
– 'Sundance'	GDra
– Sunset Group ♀	ELan GAbr GCHN GDra MBal MBri NGre NHar NHol NTow WCla WPer
– 'White Splendour'	MAsh SIng WGor
'George Henley'	EBre EHyt EWes LHop LWoo MAsh NHar NHed NMen NNrd NRya SIng SRms WAbe
leana	SIng
¶ ***leeana***	MAsh WGor
'Little Plum'	GCHN SIng
longifolia	See ***L. cotyledon*** var. ***cotyledon***
§ ***longipetala***	GCHN GDra GTou MAsh MHig MOne NGre NHol NTow NWCA WAbe
– x ***cotyledon***	GTou
* ***longiscapa***	MAsh NGre
'Margaret Williams'	EHyt
§ ***nevadensis***	CMea CNic CPla EHyt ELan EPot ESis GCHN GDra GTou ITim MAsh MBri MNrw MTho NGre NMen NNrd NWCA SIng WAbe WCla WFar WPer WPyg
nevadensis bernardina	See ***L. nevadensis***
nevadensis 'Rosea'	WAbe
oppositifolia	EHyt MAsh NNrd WGor
– J&JA 13450	NWCA
'Phyllellia'	MAsh
'Pinkie'	CPBP EHyt EPot LWoo MAsh MDHE NMen NNrd
pygmaea	CGra CNic EHyt EPot ESis EWes GCHN GTou ITim MAsh MBri NBir NGre NHar NNrd NWCA WAbe WPer
– subsp. ***longipetala***	See ***L. longipetala***
rediviva	CGra EWes GCHN GDra GTou ITim LWoo MAsh MBro MFos NGre NHar NSla NWCA WAbe WDav
– Jolon strain	MAsh WGor
– subsp. ***minor***	CGra EPot NMen WAbe
– white	MAsh NGre NWCA
'Regensbergen'	WPer
serrata	CGra MAsh NGre
sierrae	MAsh MOne NGre NMen NNrd SIng
'Trevosia'	EHyt MAsh MDHE MHig SIng
triphylla	MAsh NGre NNrd NWCA
tweedyi ♀	CPBP EBre EHyt EPad EWes GDra GTou LHop LWoo MAsh MOne NGre NHar NWCA SIng SRms WAbe WDav WGor
– 'Alba'	GDra LWoo MAsh NGre WGor
– 'Elliott's Variety'	MAsh WGor
– 'Rosea'	GDra MAsh NGre NTow WAbe WGor

LEYCESTERIA (Caprifoliaceae)

crocothyrsos	CAbb CGre CInt CPle GQui MCCP MSte NRai WRHF WWat
formosa	Widely available

LEYMUS (Poaceae)

§ ***arenarius***	CCuc CElw CHan CInt CWGN ECha EHoe ELan EOrc EPla ESOG ETPC GBur GCal MBar MUlv NBro NFai NSti SMad SSoC WRus WWat
hispidus	See ***Elymus hispidus***
mollis	EBee
§ ***racemosus***	ETPC

LHOTZKYA See CALYTRIX

LIATRIS (Asteraceae)

aspera	EMan SIgm
ligulistylis	EMan SIgm
pycnostachya	CMil ECro EMon NRai SRms WPer WRHF WWin
scariosa 'Magnifica'	CB&S
§ ***spicata***	CArn CB&S CDoC CKel CMea ECha EFou ELan ETub GCHN GPoy LAma LBow LHol LHop MChe MSal MWat NBir NFai NMir NNor SDeJ SIde SPer WChe WOld WPer WWye
– 'Alba'	ECha ECro EFou ELan GGar LAma LBow LHol MLsm NFai SDeJ SPer WFox WHoo WPer WWhi
spicata callilepis	See ***L. spicata***
spicata 'Floristan Violett'	CSam EAst EBee ECGP EPfP GAbr NPla NPri NRoo SCoo SHam SMer WFar WHil WLRN WPer
– 'Floristan Weiss'	CArn CMGP CSam EBre EMan GAbr GBuc GCHN GMaP MRav MTis NOak NRoo SCro SMrm WHil WLRN WPer WWin
◆ – Goblin	See ***L. spicata* 'Kobold'**
§ – 'Kobold'	CB&S CHan CSam EBre ECED ECtt EMan ENot EPfP MBri MRav NLak NRoo SPla SSea WHil WHoo WMer WPer

LIBERTIA † (Iridaceae)

'Amazing Grace'	CFir IBlr SAxl SLod SMrm
¶ 'Ballyrogan Blue'	IBlr
Ballyrogan Hybrid	IBlr
* ***breunioides***	IBlr
caerulescens	CAbb CHan CPou ECro EGoo GBin IBlr MHar NBir NChi WOMN WSan WWhi
chilensis	See ***L. formosa***
elegans	CChu CGre GBuc IBlr
§ ***formosa***	CDoC CElw CFee CGle CHan CHid CWGN EAst EBre ERav ERos GCHN LGan MBal MBri MUlv MWat NHol NSti SArc SChu SPer WCra WEas WHer WOld WPer WWin WWye
¶ – brown-stemmed form	IBlr
– form	IBlr LBlm
grandiflora	CAbb CB&S CDoC CElw CHEx CHan ECha ECro ELan EPla GAbr GCHN GCal GMac IBlr MBel MFir MNrw NCat NFai SLPl SMad SPer SUsu WAbe WBod WCru WPer
ixioides	CAvo CElw CGle CSam ECou EGoo GGar IBlr SDix WHoo WPyg WRHF
– 'Tricolor'	IBlr
'Nelson Dwarf'	ECou IBlr
paniculata	CHan IBlr
peregrinans	CAbb CChu CDoC CElw CFee CHan CNic EBre ECha EMan EPla ESis GCal IBlr MFir SAxl SChu SUsu WAbe WHal WThi
– East Cape form	IBlr
– 'Gold Leaf'	CB&S IBlr

* ***procera*** CChu CDoC CGre IBlr
pulchella CGle IBlr
¶ – Tasmanian form LLew
sessiliflora CFee IBlr NBir
– RB 94073 CNic MNrw SMad
Shackleton Hybrid IBlr
* ***umbellata*** IBlr

LIBOCEDRUS (Cupressaceae)
chilensis See ***Austrocedrus chilensis***
decurrens See ***Calocedrus decurrens***

LIBONIA See JUSTICIA

LICUALA (Arecaceae)
grandis MBri

LIGULARIA † (Asteraceae)
alatipes GBin
amplexicaulis GCra IBlr
calthifolia CRow EBre GCal
clivorum See ***L. dentata***
§ ***dentata*** CHEx CHan CRow EGar NBro SPla SRms SWat WCru WOld
– 'Dark Beauty' GSki
– 'Desdemona' ♀ Widely available
– 'Orange Princess' EBee NPer WPer
– 'Othello' CRow CWGN EAst EBee EGar EHoe EMan GAul IBlr MBal MBri NCut SCro SMad SWat WCot WCra WHil WMer
– 'Rubrifolia' GDra
– 'Sommergold' CKni ECha EGar IBlr
fischeri EGar GCal GCra WCot
– B&SWJ 2570 WCru
– B&SWJ 606a WCru
glabrescens CRow
§ 'Gregynog Gold' ♀ CDoC CHad CRow CWGN EAst EBre ECha EGol ENot GMaP IBlr LBlm MBri MRav NBro NDea NMir NOrc SCro SMrm SPer WCru WHoo WMer WPyg WTyr
× ***hessei*** CRow ECha EGar GAri SWat WCot WFar
hodgsonii EBre EGar IBlr MBri MNrw NMGW WCru WMer WPer
japonica CChu CRow ECha EGar WCot
macrophylla CHan CRow EBre EGar
oblongata See ***Cremanthodium oblongatum***
× ***palmatiloba*** CChu CFir CWGN EBre ECha EGar EGol EPar EPla GCal IBlr MCli MUlv NDea NOak NSti SCro SWat WCot WCra
§ ***przewalskii*** Widely available
reniformis See ***Cremanthodium reniforme***
sachalinensis GBin GCal WCot
sibirica WCot
smithii See ***Senecio smithii***
* ***speciosa*** ECha EGar
stenocephala CHEx EGar EGol EMil IBlr LFis MSCN NBro NDea
– B&SWJ 283 WCru
tangutica See ***Sinacalia tangutica***
'The Rocket' ♀ CBos CWGN EAst EBre ECha EFou EGol ELan EOas GMaP IBlr MBri MBro MCLN NBro NMir NNor SCro SMad SPer SSoC SWat WCot WHil WHoo WOld WWat WWhi WWin
tussilaginea See ***Farfugium japonicum***
veitchiana CChu CHan CRow EBee EGar EOas EOrc GCal GDra IBlr MSte NDea SWat WCot WCru
'Weihenstephan' IBlr LRHS MBri MUlv WGer WMer
wilsoniana CHan CRow EBee EBre ECtt EGar EOas MCli MRav NCut WCot
¶ 'Zepter' EGar

LIGUSTICUM (Apiaceae)
lucidum MSal SIgm
porteri MSal
scoticum GBar GPoy ILis LHol MHew MSal NLak

LIGUSTRUM † (Oleaceae)
chenaultii CDoC WWat
compactum CPle
delavayanum CB&S CPle GAri LPan SArc WWat
japonicum EBee ENot SMur WDin WWat
– 'Coriaceum' See ***L. japonicum* 'Rotundifolium'**
§ – 'Rotundifolium' CDec CDoC CPle EMil LNet MUlv SBid SMad SPer WCru
* – 'Silver Star' CPMA
§ – 'Texanum' CDec LPan
* – 'Texanum Argenteum' LPan
lucidum ♀ CChu CDoC CPle CShe ELan ENot IOrc MGos MUlv SArc SMad SPer SSpi WDin WRTC WWat
– 'Excelsum Superbum' (v) ♀ CAbP CDoC CEnd CPMA ELan LPan MAsh MBar MGos MMea SPer SPla SSpi WWat
¶ – 'Golden Wax' MRav WBcn
– 'Latifolium' MUlv
– 'Tricolor' (v) CPMA ELan IOrc MAsh MBal SHBN SPer SPla SSpi WWat
obtusifolium 'Dart's Elite' SLPl
ovalifolium CB&S CChe CDoC CLnd CTri EBre GRei ISea LBuc LPan MBar MBri MGos NBee NNor NWea SPer WDin WGwG WMou
§ – 'Argenteum' (v) CB&S CDoC CGle EFol EHoe ISea LBuc MBar MBri NBee NFla NHol SPer SPla WFar WPat WRTC WWin
– 'Aureomarginatum' See ***L. ovalifolium* 'Aureum'**
§ – 'Aureum' (v) ♀ CB&S CChe CLnd CMHG EBre EFol ELan ELau ENot GOrc GRei LBuc LNet LPan MBar MBri MGos MWat NFla NNor NWea SHBN SPer WDin WWin
* – 'Lemon and Lime' (v) SPla
– 'Taff's Indecision' (v) CNat CPMA
– 'Variegatum' See ***L. ovalifolium* 'Argenteum'**
quihoui ♀ CChu CHan CMHG ELan MGos SDix SPer SSpi WHCG WWat
sempervirens B&L 12033 EPla
sinense CHan CMCN MRav WWat
– 'Midsummer Lady' LRHS
– 'Multiflorum' WWat
– 'Pendulum' EPla NHol
– 'Variegatum' CMHG CPMA EBar EFol EHic SBid SPer SPla WRTC WWat
– 'Wimbei' CPMA EPla ESis NHol NPro SSpi WWat

♦ ***texanum***	See ***L. japonicum*** **'Texanum'**
tschonoskii	CBlo SLPl SMad
'Vicaryi'	CBlo CPMA EBre ELan EMon EPla MBar NHol NPro SPer WPyg WRTC WWat
vulgare	CCVT CKin CPer CTri EBre EWFC GRei LBuc NWea WDin WHer WMou
– 'Lodense'	SLPl
– variegated	WWat

LILAEOPSIS (Apiaceae)

See Plant Deletions

LILIUM (Liliaceae)

'Acapulco' (VIId)	CB&S LAma
African Queen Group (VIa)	CB&S EBre ECot LAma NRog SDeJ SMad SRms
albanicum	WChr
'Alliance' (VII)	CB&S
¶ ***amabile***	LWoo
'Angela North' (Ic)	MBri WFar
¶ 'Annabelle' (Ia)	CSut
'Anton Geesink'	CB&S
'Apeldoorn' (Ie)	LAma
'Apollo' (Ia)	CB&S ETub MBri NCat SDeJ WCra
'Aristo'	See ***L.*** **'Orange Aristo'**
Asiatic Hybrids (VI/VII)	LAma SDeJ
'Attila' (Ib)	SDeJ
auratum	CB&S EFEx LAma LGre SDeJ
– 'Crimson Beauty' (IX)	LAma
– 'Gold Band'	See ***L. auratum*** var. ***platyphyllum***
§ – var. ***platyphyllum*** (IX) 🏆	CB&S GCra
¶ – var. ***virginale***	ETub
'Avignon' (Ia)	LAma
'Barcelona' (Ia)	ETub MNrw
'Bel Ami'	CB&S
¶ Bellingham Group (IV) 🏆	SSpi
'Bellona' (Ia)	NRog
'Berlin' (VIId)	CB&S
'Black Beauty' (VIId)	CB&S
'Black Dragon' (VIa) 🏆	LAma
Black Magic Group (VIa)	SDeJ
bolanderi (IX)	MSto
'Bonfire' (VIIb)	SDeJ
'Brandywine' (Ib)	WRHF
'Bright Star' (VIb)	EBre ETub LAma SDeJ
¶ ***brownii***	EFEx
'Buff Pixie' (Ia)	CB&S ETub LAma
bulbiferum	ETub GCrs LWoo MSto NHar SIng
¶ 'Bums' (Ia)	EMon
'Butter Pixie' (Ia)	CB&S
§ ***canadense***	GGGa LAma MBal NRog SDeJ SSpi WChr
– var. ***editorum***	LAma LWoo
– var. ***flavum***	See ***L. canadense***
candidum 🏆	CArn CAvo CB&S CBro CGle CHEx CSWP EBre ECha ECtt ELan EMon ETub GAbr GCra LAma MBri NRog SDeJ SIgm
– 'Plenum'	EMon
'Capitol' (VII)	CB&S
'Carmen' (VIIc)	CB&S
carniolicum	WChr
'Casa Blanca' (VIIb) 🏆	CB&S CBro EBre ETub LAma NRog SDeJ SMad
'Casa Rosa'	CB&S CSWP SWat WCra
cernuum	SDeJ WChr
chalcedonicum 🏆	LWoo
'Charisma' (Ia)	MBri
'Chinook' (Ia)	NRog
Citronella Group (Ic)	CAvo CBro LAma NRog
columbianum (IX)	MSto
concolor var. ***partheneion*** (IX)	MSto
'Concorde' (Ia)	SDeJ
'Connecticut King' (Ia)	CB&S CBro EBre ETub LAma MHlr NBrk NRog SAga SDeJ
'Corina' (Ia)	CB&S MBri NCat SDeJ
'Corsage' (Ib)	NRog
'Côte d'Azur' (Ia)	CB&S CBro EBre ETub LAma NCat SDeJ WCra
'Crimson Pixie' (Ia)	CB&S
¶ × ***dalhansonii***	LWoo
§ – 'Marhan' (II) 🏆	LAma
'Darling' (VII)	CB&S
§ ***dauricum***	CPou
§ ***davidii*** var. ***willmottiae*** (IX)	EPot LAma SRms WAbe
'Delta'	See ***L. leichtlinii*** **'Delta'**
'Denia' (Ib)	CB&S
'Destiny' (Ia)	NRog
'Dominique' (VII)	NRog
duchartrei	CBro WAbe
'Electric' (Ia)	CB&S
'Elfin Sun'	CB&S LAma LRHS
'Elite'	See ***L.*** **'Gibraltar'**
'Elvin's Son'	CB&S WCra
'Elysee'	CB&S
'Enchantment' (Ia) 🏆	CB&S LAma LBow MBri MHlr NRog SDeJ
'Esperanto'	CB&S
¶ ***euxanthum*** ACE 1268	EHyt
¶ – KGB 492	EHyt
'Exception' (Ib)	LAma
'Festival' (Ia)	CB&S LAma
'Fire King' (Ib)	CB&S LAma NRog SDeJ
formosanum	CNic NBro NGre WCot
– B&SWJ 1589	WCru
– var. ***formosanum***	NBro
– var. ***pricei*** (IX) 🏆	CGle CGra CInt CLon CMea CSWP ELan EPot ITim LBee LGre LHop MBal MBri MFir MHlr MNrw MSto MTho NMen NNrd NWCA NWoo SAga SBla WAbe WPer WPyg
'Fresco' (VII)	CB&S
'Friendship' (VII)	CB&S
'Furore' (VIIc)	CB&S
'Geisha' (VII)	CB&S
'Golden Melody' (Ia)	CB&S
'Golden Pixie' (Ia)	CB&S
Golden Splendor Group (VIa)	ETub LAma NRog SWat
¶ 'Golden Sunrise' (Ia)	CSut
'Gran Cru' (Ia)	CB&S
'Gran Paradiso' (Ia)	CB&S LAma
'Grand Cru'	SDeJ
¶ Green Magic Group (VIa)	CHar
'Hannah North' (Ic)	LGre
hansonii 🏆	IBlr LAma NRog
Harlequin Group (Ic)	SDeJ
henryi 🏆	CAvo CB&S CSWP EFEx GAul LAma LBow NRog SDeJ SSoC WCot
humboldtii (IX)	SIgm
Imperial Gold Group (VIIc)	LAma
Imperial Silver Group (VIIc)	CB&S LAma

¶ ***japonicum***	EFEx
'Jetfire' (Ia)	CB&S SDeJ
¶ 'John Dix' (Ib)	ETub
'Journey's End' (VIId)	CB&S ETub LAma NRog SDeJ
§ 'Joy' (VIIb)	LAma
'Karen North' (Ic) 🏆	MBri
§ ***kelleyanum***	GGGa WChr
¶ ***kelloggii***	MSto
'King Pete' (Ib)	NOak SDeJ
'Kiss Proof' (VIIb)	CB&S
'Kiwi Fanfare'	WLRN
'Lady Ann' (VIb)	SDeJ
'Ladykiller' (Ia)	NRog
§ ***lancifolium***	CLTr LAma LBow MHar MHlr SDeJ WRHF
– 'Flore Pleno' (IX)	CAvo CSWP EBre EMar EMon GCal GSki IBlr MHar NSti WCot
– Forrest's form	IBlr
¶ – var. ***fortunei***	EMon
§ – var. ***splendens*** (IX)	CBro EMon LAma LBow SDeJ
¶ ***lankongense***	GCrs NHar NPro
¶ – ACE 2210	EPot
'Le Rêve'	See ***L.*** **'Joy'**
¶ 'Lemon Pixie' (Ia)	LAma LRHS
'Liberation' (I)	CB&S NBir
'Limelight' (VIa) 🏆	LAma
'Little Snow White' (V)	NOak WHer
longiflorum (IX) 🏆	CAvo CB&S LAma MHlr NRog WCot
– 'Gelria' (IX)	SDeJ
– 'White American' (IX)	CB&S CBro CSWP MBri
lophophorum	WChr
¶ – ACE 1767	EHyt GCLN
¶ 'Lovely Girl' (VIIb)	ETub
'Luxor' (Ib)	CSut NBir NCat
mackliniae 🏆	ECha EHyt GBuc GCra GGGa GTou IBlr MBal MSto NHar WAbe WChr
maculatum var. ***davuricum***	See ***L. dauricum***
maculatum monticola	EHyt
'Marhan'	See ***L.*** × ***dalhansonii*** **'Marhan'**
× ***marhan*** 'J.S. Dijt'	See ***L.*** **'Jacques S. Dijt'**
'Marie North' (Ic)	MBri
martagon	CArn CAvo CB&S CBro ECha EFou EMon ETub LAma LBow MBal NBir NPSI NRog SDeJ WAbe WShi WWat
– var. ***album*** (IX) 🏆	CAvo CB&S CBro CMea CPou ECGP EFou EPot ETub LAma MFir MHlr MTho NPSI SDeJ SHig WAbe
– var. ***cattaniae*** (IX) 🏆	EMon
– 'Netherhall Pink' (IX/d)	EMon
– 'Netherhall White' (IX/d)	EMon
– 'Plenum' (IX)	EMon
'Mecca'	CB&S
'Medaillon' (Ia)	LAma NRog
¶ ***medeoloides***	EFEx
michiganense	WChr
'Milano' (Ia)	CB&S CSut
¶ 'Miss America'	LRHS
'Mona Lisa' (VIIb/d)	CB&S ETub MBri
§ ***monadelphum*** 🏆	CAvo CBro LAma MHar NRog SIgm WChr
'Mont Blanc' (Ia)	CB&S CBro ETub LAma NBir NCat SDeJ
'Monte Rosa' (Ic)	SDeJ
'Montreux' (Ia)	CB&S LAma NCat
'Moonflower' (Ia)	CB&S

'Moulin Rouge' (Ib)	NRog
◆ 'Mr Ruud'	See ***L.*** **'Ruud'**
¶ 'Muscadet' (VII)	CSut
§ ***nanum***	EHyt GGGa MSto NRog NSla WAbe WChr
– CH&M	WChr
– var. ***flavidum*** (IX)	EHyt WChr
– 'Len's Lilac' (IX)	MSto WChr
nepalense	CBro CFir CLon CSWP LAma LWoo NGre NRog SDeJ SPla SSpi WCru WOMN
'New Yellow'	MBri
¶ ***nobilissimum***	EFEx
'Olivia' (Ia)	CSut ETub LAma SDeJ
Olympic Group (VIa)	LAma SDeJ
'Omega' (VII)	CB&S LAma SDeJ
§ 'Orange Aristo' (Ia)	MBri
'Orange Pixie' (Ia)	EBre LAma LRHS MBri
'Orange Triumph' (Ia)	LAma
'Orchid Beauty' (Ia)	MBri
oxypetalum	EHyt GGGa NGre WChr
– var. ***insigne*** (IX)	EHyt GCLN GDra GGGa LAma NHar NSla NTow SSpi WAbe WChr WCru
'Pandora' (Ia)	CB&S
pardalinum	CAvo CGle CMea ELan MSto
– var. ***giganteum*** (IX) 🏆	LWoo
¶ ***parryi***	WAbe
parvum	WChr
'Peachblush' (Ia)	CB&S
'Peggy North' (Ic)	MBri
¶ ***philadelphicum***	CGra MSto
philippinense	EGar NTow
Pink Perfection Group (VIa) 🏆	CAvo CB&S CBro EBre LAma NRog SWat
I 'Pink Regale'	CSut
'Pink Sunburst' (VId)	SDeJ
'Pink Tiger' (Ib)	CB&S CBro
'Pirate' (Ia)	LAma
pitkinense	EMon
pomponium	MSto
'Prominence'	See ***L.*** **'Firebrand'**
§ ***pumilum*** 🏆	CAvo CBro EBre EHyt ETub LAma LWoo MSto MTho NBir SDeJ WCru
pyrenaicum 🏆	CBro CMea ELan GDra MSto NTow WByw WCot WOMN WRha WShi
– var. ***aureum***	See ***L. pyrenaicum*** var. ***pyrenaicum***
– yellow	See ***L. pyrenaicum*** var. ***pyrenaicum***
'Red Carpet' (Ia)	CB&S CBro ETub MBri NBir NCat
Red Jewels Group (Ic)	LAma
◆ Red Knight	See ***L.*** **'Roter Cardinal'**
'Red Lion' (Ia)	SDeJ
'Red Night' (I)	NRog
regale 🏆	CArn CAvo CB&S CBro CSam CSut EBre EFEx EFou ETub GAul LAma LBow MBal MCLN NEgg NRog SDeJ WCru WEas WPyg WWat
– 'Album' (IX)	CAvo CHad CSWP EBre EFou LAma LBow NRog SDeJ SHel
§ – 'Royal Gold' (IX)	CB&S LAma NEgg SAga SDeJ SRms
'Roma' (Ia)	LAma NBir SHel
'Rosita' (Ia)	LAma MBri NRog
◆ 'Royal Gold'	See ***L. regale*** **'Royal Gold'**
¶ ***rubellum***	EFEx
§ 'Ruud' (VII)	CBro

'Sancerre' (Ia)	CB&S
'Sans Pareil' (Ia)	ETub SDeJ
'Sans Souci' (VIId)	MBri
sargentiae	CPou EPot NGre
'Sensation'	CB&S
shastense	See ***L. kelleyanum***
'Silly Girl' (Ia)	CB&S
'Simoen' (Ia)	SDeJ
'Snow Princess'	LAma
'Snow Trumpet' (V)	CSam WLRN
¶ ***souliei*** ACE 1192	EHyt
speciosum var. ***album*** (IX)	CB&S CBro EFEx LAma NBir SDeJ
– 'Grand Commander' (IX)	LAma SDeJ
– var. ***roseum*** (IX)	EFEx LAma SDeJ
– var. ***rubrum*** (IX)	CAvo CB&S CBro EFEx ETub LAma LBow LWoo NBir NRog SAga SDeJ
§ – 'Uchida' (IX)	LAma SDeJ
'Star Gazer' (VIIc)	CB&S CBro CSut EBre ECot LAma MHlr NRog SDeJ SSoC
* 'Sterling Silver'	LAma
'Sterling Star' (Ia)	CB&S ETub LAma NRog SDeJ
'Sun Ray' (Ia)	LAma NRog
superbum ♀	LAma NRog WChr
szovitsianum	See ***L. monadelphum***
'Tamara' (Ib)	CB&S MBri NRog
tenuifolium	See ***L. pumilum***
× ***testaceum*** (IX) ♀	EBre LAma NRog SDeJ
tigrinum	See ***L. lancifolium***
'Trance' (VIIb)	CB&S MBri
'Uchida Kanoka'	See ***L. speciosum* 'Uchida'**
¶ ***vollmeri***	GCLN
wallichianum	CPou LAma NRog SDeJ WChr WCru
'Walter Bentley' (Ic)	SRms
washingtonianum (IX)	MSto
¶ – var. ***purpurascens***	MSto
'White America'	CB&S CBro ETub
'White Happiness' (Ia)	LAma
'White Henryi' (VId)	EFEx
'White Journey's End' (VIId)	CB&S
'White Mountain' (VIIc)	SDeJ
¶ ***wigginsii***	GGGa
willmottiae	See ***L. davidii*** var. ***willmottiae***
Yellow Blaze Group (Ia)	LAma NRog
'Yellow Giant'	See ***L.* 'Joanna'**
'Zephyr' (Ia)	CSut

LIMNANTHES (Limnanthaceae)

douglasii ♀	CDoC CFee CKni CMGP CTri ELan IBlr NBus SIng WEas WElm WFox WHer

LIMONIUM (Plumbaginaceae)

bellidifolium	CShe ECha ELan ESis MBro MHig NTow SBla WCla WEas WHoo WPer
cosyrense	CInt CMea NMen SIng SRms WAbe WPer WWin
dumosum	See ***Goniolimon tataricum*** var. ***angustifolium***
globulariifolium	See ***L. ramosissimum***
gmelinii	LFis WPer
– 'Perestrojka'	CDoC NMir SIgm WTre
gougetianum	CLyd NTow
latifolium	See ***L. platyphyllum***
* ***maritimum***	CSpe
minutum	ELan MHig
otolepis	CLTr CM&M GAbr
paradoxum	ELan
peregrinum	CSpe
§ ***platyphyllum***	CGle EFou GLil LFis MLsm MTol MWat NFla NMir SDix SPer SRms SUsu WEas WGwG WHoo WOld WPer
– 'Robert Butler'	GCal MMil MRav
– 'True Blue'	LRHS
– 'Violetta'	CTri EBre ECED ECGP ECha ELan MBri MRav MUlv SPer WHoo
purpuratum	CSpe
rumicifolium	EEls
tataricum	See ***Goniolimon tataricum***
tetragonum	See ***L. dregeanum***
tomentellum	EBee
vulgare	EEls

LINANTHASTRUM See LINANTHUS

LINANTHUS (Polemoniaceae)

¶ ***nuttallii***	WHil

LINARIA (Scrophulariaceae)

aeruginea	MSto NMir
– subsp. ***nevadensis***	WCla WHil
alpina	CMea ELan EWes GTou LFis MSto MTho NWCA SRms WCla WPer WPri
– 'Purpurea'	NMGW WCru
– 'Rosea'	NMGW WCla WCru
'Anstey'	CElw EMan
anticaria	LCom MSto
¶ – 'Antique Silver'	CSpe ECha EMan EPPr GBuc WCot WHoo WPbr
cymbalaria	See ***Cymbalaria muralis***
dalmatica	CChr CGle CHan CSpe ECha ECro ELan MFir MInt MTol NBro NCat NSti SChu SIgm WGwy WKif WPer
× ***dominii*** 'Carnforth'	CGle CHan ECGP EJud EMar EPPr ERav ESiP LHop MArl NBro NLak NSti WWhi
– 'Yuppie Surprise'	EMon NBir NCat SMad WLRN
genistifolia	CArc CBlo LFis
'Globosa Alba'	See ***Cymbalaria muralis* 'Globosa Alba'**
glutinosa	See ***L. bipunctata***
hepaticifolia	See ***Cymbalaria hepaticifolia***
'Natalie'	CArc LGre SAga
nevadensis	MSto
origanifolia	See ***Chaenorhinum origanifolium***
pallida	See ***Cymbalaria pallida***
pilosa	See ***Cymbalaria pilosa***
purpurea	CGle CKin CTrC CWGN ECro EFou ELan EWFC LHil LHol MCLN MChe MFir NBro NCat NFai NNor NPer SRms WApp WCla WCra WHen WOve WPer WWin
– 'Alba'	See ***L. purpurea* 'Springside White'**
– 'Canon Went'	Widely available
– 'Radcliffe Innocence'	See ***L. purpurea* 'Springside White'**
§ – 'Springside White'	CArc CElw CGle ECha EFou EMan EMon EOHP GBuc LGre LHop MAvo MCLN MSte NChi SUsu SWat WCot WLRN WRha WRus
– 'Thurgarton Beauty'	WCot

– 'Winifrid's Delight'	CArc CBlo CMil EBee EBre EMan EWll GCal LBuc LHop MCLN NLak SChu SCoo SUsu SWat WCot WGle WHow WLRN WPbr
repens	CKin EWFC MHlr WCot WHer
'Sue'	LHop
supina	MSto WCla WHer
'Tony Aldis'	CArc CSpe LFis SBla SSvw WKif
triornithophora	CBrd CChr CFir CGle CHar CPea CSpe ECha ECro EMar GBuc GCra MBel MFir MHlr MSCN NLak SMad WBea WByw WCot WFar WRha WWin WWye
– pink	CBot CGle CHan CSpe WEas WPer
– purple	CHan ELan WBea
tristis* var. *lurida 'Toubkal'	SBla WOMN
vulgaris	CArn CKin ECWi EJud EOHP EWFC LHol MChe MGam MHew NMir SIde WApp WHer WJek WPer
– peloric form	CNat CPBP WAlt

LINDELOFIA (Boraginaceae)

anchusoides hort.	See ***L. longiflora***
§ – Lehmann	CHan
§ ***longiflora***	CFir CKni GAul GBin GBuc GCal LLew NVic SBar WPer
– 'Alba'	ECha

LINDERA (Lauraceae)

aggregata	CMCN
benzoin	CB&S CFil CMCN SBid WPGP
erythrocarpa	CFil CMCN WCoo WPGP
obtusiloba ♀	CFil CMCN WCoo WNor WPGP
praecox	CFil
triloba	CFil
umbellata	CFil

LINNAEA (Caprifoliaceae)

borealis	GAri GDra MBal MHig NGre WOMN
– var. ***americana***	MHig NHar NMen NWCA

LINUM † (Linaceae)

altaicum	MSto
arboreum ♀	CLon MBro MPla MSto NHol NMen SBla SIgm SMrm WOMN WPat WWat
¶ ***aretioides***	WDav
austriacum	EBee MSto
bienne	CKin
bulgaricum	See ***L. tauricum***
campanulatum	MSto SIng
capitatum	CPBP EBee WAbe WDav
* ***columbianum***	MSto
dolomiticum	WAbe
flavum	CGle CTri GTou NLak WBea WHoo
– 'Compactum'	ECha ELan LHop MHar NMen NRoo SBla SMer SMrm SRms WCot WMer WWin
'Gemmell's Hybrid' ♀	CLyd CMea CShe EPot LBee MBro MHig NBir NGre NHar NHol NMen NRya NWCA SBla WAbe WDav WPat
leonii	EMon WKif WRus
marginale	MSto
monogynum	CRDP ECha ECou MTho NTow NWCA SAlw SBla SChu
§ – var. ***diffusum***	ECou EWes
– dwarf form	CLyd EHyt GTou SOkh
– 'Nelson'	See ***L. monogynum* var. *diffusum***
narbonense	CLon CLyd CSam CShe ECha GMaP LGre LGro MBri MBro MUlv NFai NHol NOak SIgm SMrm SRms WCra WHoo WKif WMer WOMN WOld WPyg
– 'Heavenly Blue' ♀	WEas WElm WHen
§ ***perenne***	CArn CMea ECWi ECha EFer EFol ELan EWFC GCal GMaP LHol MBri MCLN MChe MHew NMir NNor NVic NWoo SIde SPer WHer WHil WPer WWin WWye
perenne album	CArc CGle CHan CLon ECha EFou ELan EMan LHol SPer WFar WHen WPer WRus
perenne* subsp. *alpinum	WPer
– – 'Alice Blue'	NHar NMen SBla SMrm WDav WWin
– subsp. ***anglicum***	NMir
§ – 'Blau Saphir'	CSam EGar EOrc ESis GAbr LFis NOrc NRoo SMrm WAbe WBea WHen WHil WLRN
♦ – Blue Sapphire	See ***L. perenne* 'Blau Saphir'**
– 'Diamant'	CBod EBar NPri NRoo WBea WLRN WPLl
¶ – subsp. ***extra-axillare***	CLyd
– subsp. ***lewisii***	EBee EHyt LHop MSto NBir NTow SMrm
I – 'Nanum Sapphire'	See ***L. perenne*** 'Blaue Saphir'
– 'White Diamond'	WHen
rubrum	MChe WBea
sibiricum	See ***L. perenne***
¶ ***suffruticosum***	CPBP
– subsp. ***salsoloides*** 'Nanum'	CLyd MBro NHar NWCA SBla SIng WPat
– var. ***salsoloides*** 'Prostratum'	GBuc SIgm
§ ***tauricum***	MSto
tenuifolium	MSto
* ***tweedyi***	NBir
¶ ***viscosum***	MSto

LIPARIS (Orchidaceae)

¶ ***cordifolia***	EFEx
¶ ***fujisanensis***	EFEx
¶ ***krameri* var. *krameri***	EFEx
kumokiri	EFEx
makinoana	EFEx
¶ ***nigra***	EFEx
¶ ***sootenzanensis***	EFEx

LIPPIA (Verbenaceae)

canescens	See ***Phyla canescens***
chamaedrifolia	See ***Verbena peruviana***
citriodora	See ***Aloysia triphylla***
dulcis	CArn EOHP MSal
nodiflora	See ***Phyla nodiflora***
repens	See ***Phyla nodiflora***

LIQUIDAMBAR (Hamamelidaceae)

acalycina	SSta WPat
formosana	CChu CGre CLnd CMCN CTho ELan GAri LPan MBlu SSta WCoo WNor

– Monticola Group SSta
orientalis CMCN CPMA LPan SSta
styraciflua CB&S CChu CLnd CMCN CMHG EBre ELan ENot GOrc IHos LHop LHyr LPan MBal MBar MBri MGos NFla SHBN SPer SSta STre WBod WCoo WDin WNor WPat WWat
– 'Andrew Hewson' CLnd CPMA SMad SSta
– 'Anja' SSta
– 'Anneke' SSta
– 'Aurea' CBlo CLnd COtt IOrc LNet WPat
– 'Aurea Variegata' CDoC CPMA
– 'Burgundy' CBlo CLnd CPMA WPat WWes
* ***styraciflua festeri*** CEnd SSta
styraciflua 'Golden Treasure' (v) CPMA ELan LNet WPat
– 'Gumball' CLnd CPMA SSta
– 'Kia' CEnd CPMA LPan SSta
– 'Lane Roberts' ♀ CDoC CLnd CMCN CTho IOrc LNet LPan SMad SReu SSta WDin WPat WPyg
– 'Manon' (v) CEnd CPMA SPla
– 'Moonbeam' (v) CBlo CEnd CPMA SSta WPat
– 'Palo Alto' SSta WPat
– 'Parasol' CPMA
– 'Pendula' CPMA SSta WWes
– 'Silver King' (v) CPMA EPfP SPer SSta
– 'Stared' CLnd CPMA
– 'Thea' SSta
– 'Variegata' CBot CPMA ELan LNet LPan LRHS SHhN SPer SSpi SSta WDin WPat
– 'Worplesdon' ♀ CB&S CChu CDoC CEnd CMCN COtt CTho EBre ELan ENot IHos IOrc LMer LNet LPan MAsh MBri MGos SMad SPer SReu SSpi SSta WAbe WDin WPat WWat

LIRIODENDRON † (Magnoliaceae)

chinense CAbP CChu CGre CMCN CPle ELan ISea MBlu SSpi SSta WWat
tulipifera ♀ Widely available
¶ – 'Ardis' CMCN
– 'Arnold' CMCN
– 'Aureomarginatum' ♀ CB&S CBot CEnd CLnd CMCN COtt CSte CTho CWSG EBre ELan ENot IOrc LNet LPan MAsh MBri MDun MGos MUlv NHol SHBN SMad SPer SReu SSpi SSta WPat WWat
– 'Aureum' CMCN
– 'Crispum' CMCN
– 'Fastigiatum' ♀ CB&S CMCN COtt CTho EBee ELan ENot LPan MBlu MBri SPer SSta WOrn
– 'Glen Gold' SMad
– 'Mediopictum' CMCN CTho ELan LNet MBlu

LIRIOPE † (Convallariaceae)

§ ***exiliflora*** CRDP EBre ECha EGol LHop
'Ariaka-janshige' (v) MCLN SHel SWat WCot WGle
♦ – Silvery Sunproof See ***L. exiliflora* 'Ariaka-janshige'**
gigantea SWat
graminifolia hort. non (L.) Bak. See ***L. muscari***
hyacinthifolia See ***Reineckea carnea***
koreana GCal
§ ***muscari*** ♀ CAbb CAvo CB&S CBot CBro CChu CHEx CHad CHan CRow CShe EBre ECha EGol ELan LHop MBal MBri MBro MHig MTho NRoo NSti SHel SPer WGle WGwG WOMN WRus WWat
– 'Alba' See ***L. muscari* 'Monroe White'**
– 'Aztec Gold' WGwG
– 'Big Blue' CSte EBee EMan EWll LRHS MRav NFla
– 'Christmas Tree' WGle WGwG
– 'Evergreen Giant' WGwG
– 'Gold-banded' EGol GCal IOrc LRHS MAvo NOrc SAxl SWat WCot WFar WGle WGwG
– 'Ingwersen' LRHS
– 'John Burch' (v) EGol NOrc WCot WPer
– 'Lilac Beauty' WGle
– 'Majestic' CAvo EBee EBre EMan EPPr EPar GCal SApp SMad WCot
– 'Mini Mondo' WGwG
§ – 'Monroe White' CBro CHad EBee EBre EMan EPar EPla GCal MBri MUlv NCat NFai NOrc SAlw SLMG SMad SPla SWat WCot WGle
– 'Royal Purple' EBre NOrc WCot WGwG WPer
– 'Silvery Midget' (v) MCLN WCot WGwG
– 'Superba' SApp WCot
– 'Variegata' CAbb CChu CFir CRow CSte CTrC CWSG CWan EBee ECot ELan EMan EPPr EPar EPla ERav EWes IOrc MCLN MTho NBir SBid SMad SPla WCot WRus
– variegated white bloom SAga WCot
– 'Webster Wideleaf' WCot WPer
'New Wonder' SApp
platyphylla ECro NRai SSpi
'Samantha' CAvo LRHS SPla
§ ***spicata*** EBre NFai NOrc SSpi SWat WEas WHoo
– 'Alba' CRow EBre EGol EPPr GCal MRav MTho MUlv SAxl WWin
– 'Silver Dragon' (v) CAvo CFir EBee EGol EPPr LHop MBel MCLN MSte WCot WGwG

LISTERA (Orchidaceae)

ovata WHer

LITHOCARPUS † (Fagaceae)

densiflorus CMCN
edulis CHEx SArc
§ ***glaber*** CHEx

LITHODORA (Boraginaceae)

§ ***diffusa*** NBro SBla
– 'Alba' CFee CMHG ELan EMil EPot GAri IOrc LBee LHop MAsh MBri MGos MPla NEgg NHar NMen NRoo SIng WAbe
– 'Cambridge Blue' EPfP MPla NCut NHol SAga SMer
– 'Compacta' EGle ELan EWes LHop
– 'Grace Farwell' EGle
– 'Grace Ward' ♀ CGle EWes MBro MGos MPla NHar NHol NRoo SBod SEas SIng WAbe WHen WPat
– 'Heavenly Blue' ♀ Widely available
– 'Inverleith' CMHG ELan EWes LHop LRHS WFar

– 'Picos'	CLyd EDAr EGle EHyt EPot GTou MHig NHol NMen SIgm WAbe WDav WOMN WPat
– 'Star'	MAsh MHig SCoo WWeb
graminifolia	See ***Moltkia suffruticosa***
hispidula	NMen SIng WCru
× ***intermedia***	See ***Moltkia*** × ***intermedia***
§ ***oleifolia*** ♀	CLyd CMea CShe EPot MBro MHig MWat NBir NMen NSla NTow WCot WCru WOMN WPat
rosmarinifolia	CSpe EBre
zahnii	CGra CMHG EHyt MHar NTow SIgm SIng WDav WHil

LITHOPHRAGMA (Saxifragaceae)

bulbiferum	See ***L. glabrum***
parviflorum	CMea EHyt EPot GDra MHig MNrw MSte MTho NBir NHol NMen NRya NWCA SIng WCru WDav WGle WOMN

LITHOSPERMUM (Boraginaceae)

diffusum	See ***Lithodora diffusa***
doerfleri	See ***Moltkia doerfleri***
¶ ***erythrorhizon***	MSal
officinale	EWFC GBar GPoy MSal WCla WCot WHer
oleifolium	See ***Lithodora oleifolia***
purpureocaeruleum	See ***Buglossoides purpurocaerulea***

LITSEA (Lauraceae)

japonica	CHEx

LITTONIA (Colchicaceae)

modesta	CGre CHal CMon CRHN

LITTORELLA (Plantaginaceae)

§ ***uniflora***	WCot

LIVISTONA (Arecaceae)

australis	CHEx CTrC LPal NPal
chinensis ♀	CTrC LPal NPal
decipiens	NPal
saribus	NPal

LLOYDIA (Liliaceae)

See Plant Deletions

LOASA (Loasaceae)

lateritia	See ***Caiophora lateritia***
triphylla var. ***volcanica***	GCal MSto

LOBELIA † (Campanulaceae)

'Alice'	WCot
anatina	CFai CFir CPBP EPad EWll LCom WLRN WRha
angulata	See ***Pratia angulata***
'Bees' Flame'	CFir CRos CRow EBre GBri LCom SWat WLRN
* 'Bees Ridge'	WCot
¶ ***bridgesii***	CSpe CTbh
'Brightness'	CRos CRow EBee EBre ELan SPer
'Butterfly Blue'	CB&S CSte EBre EGle GBuc MTis NCat WAbe WWat
'Butterfly Rose'	CSte EBre EGle EOrc GBuc LFis SAga WAbe WCHb
cardinalis ♀	CArn CRDP CRow CWGN CWat EFou EHon GCHN GCal GCra GMac LHol LPBA MHew MSal MSta MSte NDea SChu SPer SRms SUsu SWyc WChe WMAq WMer WOld WWin WWye
– 'Alba'	WCot WPyg
¶ – ***multiflora***	CFir WCot
–'Rose Beacon'	WCot
– 'Shrimp Salad'	WCot
'Cherry Ripe'	CElw CRos CSev CWGN ELan LHil MSte NHol SChu SCro SHFr SMrm WCHb WEas
♦ 'Cinnabar Deep Red'	See ***L.* 'Fan Tiefrot'**
Cinnabar Rose	See ***L.* 'Fan Zinnoberrosa'**
'Complexion'	CHad GCHN LHop SWat
Compliment Blue	See ***L.* 'Kompliment Blau'**
♦ Compliment Deep Red	See ***L.* 'Kompliment Tiefrot'**
Compliment Purple	See ***L.* 'Kompliment Purpur'**
Compliment Scarlet	See ***L.* 'Kompliment Scharlach'**
'Dark Crusader'	CBos CElw CHad CMHG CRos CRow CWGN ECtt EFou ELan LFis LHil LHop MBri MCLN NBro NDea NHol NSti SChu SMrm WCHb WEas WRus WSan
¶ ***dortmanna***	EMFW
erinus 'Kathleen Mallard' (d)	CSpe ELan EOrc LHop NPri WEas
♦ – 'Richardii'	See ***L. richardsonii***
'Eulalia Berridge'	CDoC CGle CRos EFou GBuc LBlm LHop MMil MSte SAga SHFr SMrm SWas
excelsa	CGre CHEx CPle CSpe CTbh EWes GCal
'Fan Zinnoberrosa'	CB&S CFir CGle EAst EMan EOrc LGan MHlr NCut NVic NWes SAga SRms WCHb WCot WHil WPer WRus WWin WWye
'Fan Deep Red'	GBuc GCHN GMac SMad SRms SSpi SWat WCHb WChe WLRN
* Fan Orchid Rose	EMan LIck WHil WLRN
¶ 'Fan Scharlach'	LIck WHil
§ 'Fan Tiefrot'	WPer
'Fan Zinnoberrosa'	SMad
'Flamingo'	See ***L.* 'Pink Flamingo'**
'Frances'	WCot
fulgens	CWGN IBlr MHlr WByw WCot WEas
¶ – 'Elmfeuer'	SMrm
– 'Illumination'	GBuc GMac
'Galen'	CRow
× ***gerardii***	EWll NHol NLak SSca
– 'Eastgrove Pink'	WEas
– 'Rosencavalier'	CFai LRHS SMrm WRus
§ – 'Vedrariensis'	Widely available
gibberoa	CHEx
inflata	CArn GPoy MSal SIde WCHb WWye
'Jack McMaster'	CBos
'Kimbridge Beet'	SHig
'Kompliment Blau'	CFir CSpe EMan LIck NCut WHil WPer
'Kompliment Purpur'	CSpe
'Kompliment Scharlach' ♀	CRos CRow CSWP CWan EBar EBre GCHN LGan NBro NCut NPer SSpi WCHb WHil WPer
§ 'Kompliment Tiefrot'	WPer
laxiflora	CBot CInt MTho SIgm WHer

- var. ***angustifolia*** — CGre CHEx CPle CRDP CSpe CTbh ELan ERea GCal IBlr LBlm LHil LHop MSte NWes SHFr SMac SMrm SUsu SVen WPer WWye
'Lena' — SWat
lindblomii — CLTr CPBP EHic EWes GAri
linnaeoides — EWes GCHN MTho NGre NMen WCru WEas
¶ ***lutea*** — WLRN
macrodon — NGre
pedunculata — See ***Pratia pedunculata***
perpusilla — See ***Pratia perpusilla***
physaloides — See ***Pratia physaloides***
'Pink Elephant' — CGle CMHG CRos CSWP CSev EFou SHFr SWas WCot
§ 'Pink Flamingo' — CRow EAst EBre ECha EFou EMFW EPar GCHN GMac NFai NHol NNor NSti SAga SChu SCro SMrm SPer SWat WCHb WPer WPyg WWye
¶ ***puberula*** — CFir
'Purple Towers' — WCot
pyramidalis B&SWJ 316 — CPou
'Queen Victoria' ♀ — CGle CMHG CRow EBre ECha EFol EFou EHoe ELan EMFW EOrc GCHN LHil LHop MBri NFai NHol NNor NSti SBla SChu SDix SHig SMad SPer SSoC WMer WWat
repens — See ***Pratia repens***
§ ***richardsonii*** — CBrk CInt LHil SDix SVen WEas WLRN
roughii — EPad
'Rowden Magenta' — CRow
'Royal Robe' — CRow
'Ruby Slippers' — WCot
N 'Russian Princess' — CBrk CGle CRDP CRos CRow CSam CWGN EMFW LHil MBri NBrk SChu SHFr SMad WCHb WFar WMer
'Sandy's Pink' — SWat
sessilifolia — EPad GBuc GCal NGre SMrm SRms SUsu WChe WCot WLRN WPer WTyr WWye
- B&SWJ 520 — GCra
siphilitica — Widely available
- 'Alba' — CB&S CNic CPea CPou CSam ECro EPfP EPri LBlm LGan LHil MCLN NSti SSca WByw WCHb WChe WCra WHoo WPer WPyg WWye
'Sonia' — CGle
'Spark' — WCot
'Sparkle Divine' — WCot
× ***speciosa*** — CRow MNrw WLRN
- dark form — CRos CRow EPPr NCat SHFr SMrm SUsu
'Tania' — CFir CGle CRDP CRow EBre EFou GBri IBlr LHil MHlr MUlv NHol SChu SCro SHig SMad SMrm WByw WRus WWeb
treadwellii — See ***Pratia angulata* 'Treadwellii'**
tupa — CBot CChu CDoC CGre CHEx CHan CInt CSam CSpe CTrC ECha ELan EOrc EPad GCal GGar IBlr LFis LHop WCHb WCru WHer WPer WSan WWat WWin WWye
- dark orange form — GCal SArc SMrm
- JCA 12527 — WCot
¶ ***urens*** — SSpi
valida — CFai CFir CInt EPad GBuc GQui WLRN
vedrariensis — See ***L.* × *gerardii* 'Vedrariensis'**
¶ 'Wildwood Splendour' — WCot
'Will Scarlet' — CRos EBre
'Zinnoberrosa' — See ***L.* 'Fan Zinnoberrosa'**

LOBELIA × PRATIA

Lobelia* × *Pratia — NGre

LOBOSTEMON (Boraginaceae)

montanus — CSpe

LOESELIA (Polemoniaceae)

mexicana — ERea LHop

LOISELEURIA (Ericaceae)

procumbens — NHar WAbe
- 'Saint Anton' — WPat

LOMANDRA (Xanthorrhoeaceae)

longifolia — ECou

LOMARIA See BLECHNUM

LOMATIA (Proteaceae)

dentata — CB&S
ferruginea — CAbb CFil CHEx CLan ISea MAll MBal SArc WCru WWat
longifolia — See ***L. myricoides***
§ ***myricoides*** — CAbb CDoC CFil CHEx CTrw ELan MAll SArc SPer SSpi WBod WWat
§ ***tinctoria*** — CB&S CHEx CTrw ELan EPfP ISea MAll SArc SPer SSpi

LOMATIUM (Apiaceae)

brandegeei — SIgm
columbianum — SIgm
grayi — MFos SIgm
utriculatum — MSal SIgm

LONICERA † (Caprifoliaceae)

§ ***acuminata*** — EHic ETen WCru WSHC
albertii — EBar EHic MRav SPan WHCG
¶ ***albiflora*** — CPlN CPle
- var. ***albiflora*** — SBra
alpigena — MSto
alseuosmoides — CChu CPlN ETen SBra WWeb
altmannii — CPle
N × ***americana*** hort. — See ***L.* × *italica***
§ - (Miller) K. Koch ♀ — CChu CHad CSPN EOrc EPfP LHop MAsh MBri MGos SAxl SBra SEas SReu SSta WCru WWeb
× ***brownii*** — CMac CRHN
§ - 'Dropmore Scarlet' — CB&S CBot CChe CChu CHad CMac CPlN EBre ELan ENot EPla GRei LPan LPri MAsh MBar MBri MGos NPer SBra SHBN SMad SPer SSoC WASP WDin
N - 'Fuchsioides' — MBro MUlv NBrk NSti SPer WPat WRTC WSHC WWat
¶ ***caerula*** var. ***altaica*** — CPle
caerulea — CPle EHal MRav STre WHCG
- var. ***edulis*** — ESim MSto
caerulea emphyllocalyx — CPle

§ ***caprifolium*** ♀	CChu CDoC CPlN CRHN CShe ELan EOrc EPla GAul LBuc LHol LPri MBar MBri NMGW NSti SBra SHBN SPan SPer WCru WWat
– 'Anna Fletcher'	EBar ELan MUlv NHol SBra SPan WCru WEas WWat WWeb
– f. ***pauciflora***	See ***L.*** x ***italica***
chaetocarpa	CMHG MBro NHol WPat
chrysantha	CMCN CPle
ciliosa	CPlN MSto SBra
'Clavey's Dwarf'	IOrc MPla NBrk NHol
cyanocarpa KGB 438	MSto
deflexicalyx KGB 165	MSto
dioica	SBra
'Early Cream'	See ***L. caprifolium***
etrusca	EHal EMon EPla LHol LPri WWeb
– 'Donald Waterer'	CBlo CChu CSam EHic LHop MUlv SBra WASP WFar WGor WWat
– 'Michael Rosse'	CSte EBar EBre ETen SBra SRms WASP
– 'Superba'	CPlN CRHN EBre ECtt ELan MUlv NSti SBra SEND WASP WCru WPen WSHC WWat
ferdinandii	MSto
flexuosa	See ***L. japonica*** var. ***repens***
fragrantissima	CB&S CBot CShe EBre EGol ELan ENot EPla GOrc LHol LPan LPri MAsh MBlu MGos MWat NBee NFla NHol NNor NPer SChu SHBN SPer SReu SSta STre WAbe WHCG WRTC
giraldii hort.	See ***L. acuminata***
– Rehder	CB&S CBot CChu CPlN EBee EOrc ETen GAul LPri NHol SBra
glabrata	EHic SBra WCru
glaucohirta	See ***L. periclymenum*** var. ***glaucohirta***
grata	See ***L.*** x ***americana* (Miller) K. Koch**
x ***heckrottii***	CDoC CMac CRHN CTri EBee ECtt GOrc LPan LPri MAsh MBar SPer WASP WCru WDin WLRN WStI WWeb
N– 'Gold Flame'	CB&S CChe EBre ELan EPla GAri LBuc MAsh MBal MBar MBri MGos MHlr MWat SBra SEas SHBN SRms SSoC WASP WGwG WSHC WStI WWat WWeb
§ ***henryi***	CB&S CChu CMac CPlN CRHN EBre ELan EOrc EPla GAul GOrc IOrc LHop LPri MAsh MBar MBri MWat NBrk NHol NSti SBra SHBN SPer WASP WAbe WBod WDin WRTC WSHC
– var. ***subcoriacea***	See ***L. henryi***
hildebrandiana	CGre CHEx CPlN
hirsuta	NBea SBra
implexa	CChu CHan CPlN EBar EFol EPla GCal LGre MBlu NPro SBra SEas WPat
insularis	CMCN CPle MBlu
involucrata	CB&S CChu CHan CMCN CMHG CPMA CPle EBar GBin GOrc LHil LHop MBar MBlu MRav SMac SPer SUsu WDin WHCG WPyg
– var. ***ledebourii***	CHan CPle ELan EPla GRei MBel MSto MWat NHol SBid WOve WPat WRTC WTyr WWin
§ x ***italica***	CMac CRHN CShe EBre ELan ENot LHol LPri MWat NSti SBra SPer SPla SSpi WASP WCru WPyg WSHC WWat
§ – 'Harlequin' (v)	CBot EBee EMil ENot MAsh MBel MGos MUlv NBea NEgg NRoo NSti SBra SMad SPer SPla WCot WCru WLRN WWat WWeb
§ ***japonica*** 'Aureoreticulata'	CB&S CMac CRHN CShe EBar EBre EHoe ELan ENot EPla GOrc LPri MBal MBar MBri MGos MHlr NFla NNor NPer SBra SEas SHBN SRms WASP WEas WGwG WWin
– 'Dart's Acumen'	SLPl
– 'Dart's World'	CSte SBra SLPl WLRN
– 'Halliana' ♀	Widely available
– 'Hall's Prolific'	CSam EBee EBre ECtt EHic ELan EOrc EWll GAul LBuc MAsh MBlu MBri MGos MUlv NBea NHol SBra SCoo SPla WASP WPyg WWat WWeb
– 'Horwood Gem' (v)	ECtt EHic NHol WWeb
– 'Peter Adams'	See ***L. japonica* 'Horwood Gem'**
§ – var. ***repens***	CDoC CMac CShe EBar EBre ECtt ELan ENot EOrc EPla GOrc IHos LPri MPla MRav NBea NEgg SBra SHBN SLPl SPer SRms WASP WCru WWat WWeb
– 'Variegata'	See ***L. japonica* 'Aureoreticulata'**
korolkowii	CBot CChu CPle CSam EBar EBee EHic LFis MUlv MWat NBir SBid SPan SPla WHCG WSHC WWat
– var. ***zabelii***	EFol ELan SEas
lanceolata KGB 488	MSto
maackii	CMCN CPMA MRav WHCG WWat
– f. ***podocarpa***	CPle
¶ ***microphylla***	CPle MSto
¶ ***morrowii***	MSto
x ***muscaviensis***	CPle
myrtillus KGB 298	MSto
nigra	CPle EPla
nitida	CB&S CKin EBee EBre ELan EOHP GOrc LHyr MRav NWea SHBN SPer STre WDin WHar WHen WRTC WStI
– 'Baggesen's Gold' ♀	CB&S CLan CShe EBre EFol EHoe ELan ENot GRei ISea LBuc LGro MBar MBel MBri MGos MPla MWat NHol NNor SDix SHBN SMad SPer STre WDin WWat WWin
– 'Elegant'	ELan IOrc LBuc WWtk
– 'Ernest Wilson'	MBar SRms
– 'Fertilis'	SPer SRms
– 'Hohenheimer Findling'	MUlv SLPl
§ – 'Maigrün'	CChe ECle EMil EPla MBri NFla NPro SPer

♦ – Maygreen	See *L. nitida* **'Maigrün'**
– 'Red Tips'	CWSG EHic LBuc MGos
– 'Silver Beauty'	Widely available
* – 'Silver Cloud'	CWSG EHic
– 'Silver Lining'	See *L. pileata* **'Silver Lining'**
¶ ***nummulariifolia***	CPle
periclymenum	CArn CKin CTri ECWi EPla EWFC GPoy MHew NBea NMir NNor NWea SHFr WDin WHCG WMou WOak
N – 'Belgica' 🏆	Widely available
– 'Cornish Cream'	NTay
– 'Florida'	See *L. periclymenum* **'Serotina'**
– 'Graham Thomas' 🏆	Widely available
– 'Harlequin'	See *L.* × *italica* **'Harlequin'**
– 'Heaven Scent'	EMil
– 'La Gasnaérie'	EPla GAri NHol SPan WASP
– 'Liden'	SBra
– 'Munster'	MBri SBra WASP WBcn
– 'Red Gables'	CBlo CWan EBar EHic MBri MHlr NHol SPan SPla WASP WGor WPat WRTC WWat
N – 'Serotina' 🏆	Widely available
– 'Serotina' EM '85	MBri MUlv
– 'Serpentine'	SBra
– ***sulphurea***	EPla EWll WASP
– 'Sweet Sue'	CSte ELan EPfP SBla SBra WBcn WWeb
– 'Winchester'	WASP
– yellow	SPer
pileata	CB&S CChe CHan CLan CShe EBre ELan EMar ENot GOrc GRei LBuc MBar MGos MRav NBee NHol NNor NPer SPer SRms WAbe WDin WGwG WHar WRTC WStI WWat WWin
– 'Moss Green'	CDoC MGos MUlv SBid SHhN SLPl WHCG WRHF WWat
§ – 'Silver Lining' (v)	EPla WCot
– 'Stockholm'	SLPl
pilosa Maxim.	See *L. strophiophora*
praeflorens	CChu
prolifera	SBra
¶ ***prostrata***	MSto SIgm
× ***purpusii***	CChe CPle CSam EBar EBre ECle EMil LHol MBar MBel MPla SRms WBea WBod WCru WEas WHCG WHar WPyg WSHC WWeb WWin
– 'Winter Beauty' 🏆	CChe CDoC CEnd CPMA CSam EBre ECtt ELan GAbr GAul LHop MAsh MBlu MBri MGos MRav NBrk NHol NSti SBra SEas SPer SPla SSpi SSta WAbe WPat WWat WWeb
pyrenaica	CPle LGre
quinquelocularis	CPle EHal EPla
– f. ***translucens***	MBlu
ramosissima	CMCN MSto
reflexa	NBrk
§ ***rupicola*** var. ***syringantha***	CChu CHan CMHG CPle CSam ELan LHol LHop MBlu MGos MHlr MWat SHBN SPan SPer SPla WFar WHCG WRTC WSHC WWat WWin
– – 'Grandiflora'	GQui WPyg
ruprechtiana	CPle
segreziensis	CPle
sempervirens 🏆	CBot CPlN CRHN EPar EPfP GAri LBlm LPri SBra WASP WLRN WWeb
– 'Dropmore Scarlet'	See *L.* × *brownii* **'Dropmore Scarlet'**
N – f. ***sulphurea***	CBlo CPlN EHic SBra WWat WWeb
serotina 'Honeybush'	CPle LRHS MAsh MBlu
setifera	CBot CPle
similis var. ***delavayi***	CBot CDoC CHan CLTr CPlN CSPN CSam EPla LBuc NBea SBra SDix SPan SWas WCru WEas WPen WSHC WWat
'Simonet'	SBra
sp. ACE 1413	CPle MSto
sp. CLD 315	CPle
sp. KBE 062	NHol
sp. LS&H 17465	WWat
splendida	CBot CRHN SBra WCru
standishii	CB&S ECle LHol MBel MGos MRav MUlv SPer WDin WHCG WRha WWat WWin WWye
'Stone Green'	NPro SPla
§ ***strophiophora***	WWat
– CD&R 1216	CHan
syringantha	See *L. rupicola* var. *syringantha*
tangutica KGB 535	MSto
tatarica	CFai CHan CMHG CPle GAul MHlr WHCG
– 'Alba'	CHan CPle
– 'Arnold's Red'	CB&S CBot CDoC CPle EBee EHal ELan MBal MBlu MPla NFla
– 'Hack's Red'	CB&S CFai EPfP MPla SPan SPer WHCG WPyg WRTC
¶ – 'Rosea'	NFla
– f. ***sibirica***	EHal
– 'Zabelii'	CChu MGos
× ***tellmanniana*** 🏆	CB&S CBot CHad CHan CPlN EBre ELan GOrc IOrc LHol LPri MAsh MBal MBar MBri MWat NHol NSti SBra SDix SEas SHBN SPer SReu WASP WBod WGwG WSHC WWat
¶ – 'Joan Sayers'	EBar EBre EHic GCal LHop MUlv SBra WWat
thibetica	CPle MBlu SPer
tragophylla 🏆	CB&S CChu CHad CMac CPlN EBar EBre ELan EPla GCal ICrw IOrc LHop LPri MAsh MBri NHol SBra SPer SSpi SSta WASP WCru WDin WSHC WWat
trichosantha KGB 404	MSto
¶ × ***xylosteoides***	MRav
– 'Clavey's Dwarf'	MBel MGos SLPl
– 'Miniglobe'	ESis NPro
* ***yunnanensis*** 'Variegata'	ESis

LOPHOMYRTUS (Myrtaceae)

§ ***bullata***	CGre CPle CTre ECou GQui MAll WCHb
'Gloriosa'	CB&S CPle WCHb
§ ***obcordata***	CGre CPle MAll WWat
§ × ***ralphii***	MAll WCHb WWat
– 'Andrea'	MAll
§ – 'Kathryn'	CB&S CHan CPle CTre ERea ISea MAll WCHb WFar WSHC WWat
– 'Pixie'	SBid
– 'Variegata'	EBre ERea MAll
'Sundae'	CPle MAll
'Tricolor'	CPle CTre MAll
'Versicolor'	CB&S

LOPHOSORIA (Lophosoriaceae)
quadripinnata CFil WRic

LOPHOSPERMUM (Scrophulariaceae)
§ ***erubescens*** ♀ CBot CHEx CHal CPlN CRHN CSam ERav LFis LHop MSte SLMG WOMN WOld
– 'Garnet' CSpe
§ ***scandens*** CPlN

LOPHOSTEMON (Myrtaceae)
§ ***confertus*** CPle

LOROPETALUM (Hamamelidaceae)
chinense CFil CMCN SBid

LOTUS (Papilionaceae)
berthelotii ♀ CBrk CFee CGle CHEx CHad CHal CSev CSpe ELan ERav ERea IHos LBlm LHil SChu SHFr SLMG SRms SSoC SVen WEas WKif WPer
¶ – deep red LIck
– Kew form LFlo
– × ***maculatus*** CBar CBrk CLTr CSpe ERav LFlo LHil SAxl WIvy WPer
corniculatus CArn CKin CLTr CTri EWFC MHew NLak NLan NRai SIde
– 'Plenus' CInt ELan EPot IBlr LFis MTho NHol WAlt WPer
'Gold Flash' IHos LIck
§ ***hirsutus*** Widely available
– dwarf form CHan
– 'Silver Mist' SCro
jacobaeus LHil
maculatus ♀ CBrk CGle CSpe LBlm SChu SHFr SOWG SSoC SVen WIvy
maritimus CMea SHFr WHal
mascaensis hort. See ***L. sessilifolius***
pedunculatus See ***L. uliginosus***
¶ ***pentaphyllus*** subsp. ***herbaceus*** GCal
§ – subsp. ***pentaphyllus*** MTol NBrk
§ ***sessilifolius*** CBrk CSpe ERea LHil
suffruticosus See ***L. pentaphyllus*** subsp. ***pentaphyllus***
§ ***uliginosus*** CTiv EWFC NMir NRai

LOXOSTYLIS (Anacardiaceae)
¶ ***alata*** CTrC

LUCULIA (Rubiaceae)
gratissima ♀ CB&S CHEx

LUDWIGIA (Onagraceae)
grandiflora CRow SWyc WChe
palustris WKen

LUETKEA (Rosaceae)
pectinata GCHN GDra MHig NHol NMen WAbe

LUMA (Myrtaceae)
§ ***apiculata*** ♀ CAbb CEnd CMHG CPle CTre CTri CTrw EBre ISea MBal MBlu SArc SDix SEND SPer STre WBod WCHb WRTC WSHC WWat WWye
§ – 'Glanleam Gold' (v) CChe CHan CPle CSam CTrC CTre CTrw EBre ELan GCHN GOrc IOrc LHol LHop MBal MBlu MGos MPla MUlv NFla NHol SChu SPer SRms SSta WAbe WDin WEas WPat WSHC
– 'Variegata' CMHG CTri ISea NHol WWat WWye
§ ***chequen*** CChu CGre CPle GAri LHol MAll NHex WCHb WJek WWat

LUNARIA (Brassicaceae)
§ ***annua*** ECWi EGoo GAbr LSyl NCat SIde SWat WByw WHer WOak WRha
I – 'Alba Variegata' CArc CChr CSWP CSpe EFol EJud EMan EMar EMon MAvo MFir WByw WCru WHil
– var. ***albiflora*** ♀ CSev NBir NCat SIde SWat WCer WHer WHil WOak
– 'Ken Aslet' NHol
* – 'Stella' GCal WHen
annua variegata CJew IBlr MTho NBir SWat WEas WHer WOMN WRha WSan
annua violet NBir
biennis See ***L. annua***
rediviva EBre ECGP ECha EJud EMon GAri GCHN GCra GGar GLil IBlr MTol NBro NSti SAxl SSpi SUsu WCot WEas WHen WHer

LUPINUS † (Papilionaceae)
'Alan Titchmarsh' MWoo
albifrons LFis LHil SIgm
* ***albifrons flumineus*** MSto
alopecuroides MSto
angustifolius MSto
'Ann Gregg' ♀ MWoo
arboreus ♀ Widely available
– 'Barton on Sea' CNat
– cream SMad
– 'Golden Spire' SMad
– 'Mauve Queen' CB&S SEND SMad
¶ – mixed NFla
– 'Snow Queen' CB&S MAsh
arcticus MSto
argenteus MSto
– var. ***depressus*** MSto
Band of Nobles Series ♀ ECtt GAbr NVic
'Barnsdale' MWoo
bicolor MSto
breweri MSto
caespitosus MSto SIgm
chamissonis CHan CRDP EBee EBre EWes LGre LHop MTho SDry SIgm SMad SMrm SSpi SUsu WRus
'Chandelier' CHad CTri EBre ECtt EFou ELan EMan GAbr GAri GCHN MBri MCLN NBrk NFai NMir NRoo SPer SPla WHen WPer WRHF
'Chelsea Pensioner' MWoo
'Deborah Woodfield' ♀ MWoo
densiflorus var. ***aureus*** MSto
Dwarf Gallery Hybrids LIck NOak
'Dwarf Lulu' See ***L. 'Lulu'***
'Esmerelder' ♀ MWoo
Gallery Series EBre EFou NCut NFai NPri NRoo SCoo WHil WLRN

'Garden Gnome'	WPer
'Helen Sharman' 🏆	MWoo
'Household Brigade'	MWoo
'Judith Chalmers'	MWoo
'Kayleigh Ann Savage' 🏆	MWoo
¶ ***latifolius***	WAbe
lepidus	MSto
– var. ***lobbii***	SIgm WAbe
– var. ***sellulus***	SIgm
– var. ***utahensis***	MSto
leucophyllus	SIgm
'Little Eugenie'	MWoo
littoralis	GDra MHar MSto SIgm WPer
§ 'Lulu'	COtt EBre ECtt ELan MRav NCat NMir SIde SPer WPer
luteus	MSto
micranthus	MSto
¶ ***microcarpus***	LCom
microphyllus	MSto
Minarette Group	CBlo ECtt MBri NCut SRms WGor
Mirakel Hybrids	CBlo
'Misty'	MWoo
montanus	MSto
'Mrs Perkins'	SMrm
mutabilis var. ***cruckshanksii***	MSto
'My Castle'	EBre ECtt EFou ELan GAbr GAri GCHN GLil MBri MCLN MRav NBrk NFai NMir NOak NRoo SPer SPla WFar WPer
nanus	MSto
'Noble Maiden'	CHad EBre ECtt EFou ELan EMan GAbr GAri GCHN GLil MBri NBrk NFai NMir NOak NRoo SPer SPla WHen WPLl WPer WRHF
nootkatensis	CFir EDAr MSto WPat
'Olive Tolley' 🏆	MWoo
oreophilus F&W 7353	SIgm
'Party Dress'	MWoo
perennis	CGle EBee
pilosus	See ***L. varius*** subsp. ***orientalis***
'Pink Fortune'	EBee
'Poached Salmon'	SMrm
'Polar Princess'	EBar EBee EWll LRHS MCLN MGrG SUsu SWat WLRN WRus WTyr
polyphyllus	MSto
'Pope John Paul' 🏆	MWoo
propinquus	MSto
'Royal Wedding'	MWoo
Russell Hybrids	CB&S CKel CWan ELan NFla SSea
sericatus	SIgm
sericeus	MSto
succulentus	MSto
'Sundown'	LCom
'Sunset'	MWoo
'Sunshine'	CGle
texensis	MSto
'The Chatelaine'	CHad EBre ECtt EFou ELan GAbr GAri GCHN GLil LWak MBri MRav NBrk NFai NMir NRoo SPer SPla WHen WPer
'The Governor'	CTri EBre ECtt EFou ELan EMan GAbr GAri GCHN GLil MBri MCLN MRav NBrk NFai NMir NRoo SPer SPla WPer
'The Page'	CDoC EBre EFou ELan EMan GAbr GAri LWak MBri MCLN MRav NBrk NFai NMir NRoo SPer SPla WPer
'Thundercloud'	CHad SMrm
variicolor	CHid CSpe NChi SIgm
– JJA 11167	MSto NChi
versicolor	CPea EDAr EMan LGro MCCP MSCN MSto WLRN
'Yellow Boy'	CB&S

LUZULA (Juncaceae)

× ***borreri*** 'Botany Bay' (v)	CCuc EMon EPPr EPla ESOG WCot
campestris	CKin
¶ ***canariensis***	CPle
forsteri	ETPC
lactea	EMon EPPr ETPC
¶ ***leptophylla***	NHar
¶ ***luzuloides***	WPer
– 'Schneehäschen'	CInt EFol EGar EMon EPla ESOG ETPC GBin GCal WCot
maxima	See ***L. sylvatica***
multiflora	EHoe
nivea	Widely available
pilosa	EGar EPla GCal IBlr
plumosa	ETPC
pumila	ECou
purpureosplendens	ETPC MTol
rufa	ECou
§ ***sylvatica***	CCuc CKin CRow CSWP ECWi EFou EPPr EPla ETPC GBur LWak MFir NBro NOrc WHer WShi
– 'A. Rutherford'	See ***L. sylvatica* 'Taggart's Cream'**
– 'Aurea'	CDoC CHan CLTr CRDP CSWP EBee ECha EFou EPPr EPla ESOG ETPC GAbr GCal MBri NSti SHel SMac SMad SPla WCot WRus WWat
– 'Aureomarginata'	See ***L. sylvatica* 'Marginata'**
I – 'Auslese'	ETPC GBin
– 'Hohe Tatra'	CArc CCuc CElw CMil EBar EBee EFol EHoe EMon EPPr EWes GAbr GBin LFis NBro NHar NHol NPla SPla WFox WLeb
§ – 'Marginata'	Widely available
– 'Select'	SLPl
§ – 'Taggart's Cream' (v)	CRow EHoe
– 'Tauernpass'	EHoe EMon EPPr EPla ETPC GCal NRar WRus
– 'Wäldler'	CCuc EHoe EMon EPPr
ulophylla	CInt EBee ECou EPPr GBin GBuc NHar

LUZURIAGA (Philesiaceae)

radicans	CFee WCot WCru WSHC

× LYCENE (Caryophyllaceae)

See Plant Deletions

LYCHNIS † (Caryophyllaceae)

alpina	CMHG CTri ECro ELan EWFC GAul GDra GTou NFla NMen NNor NPri NRoo WBea WCla WGwG WPer WWin
– 'Alba'	CLyd GTou NBir
– compact form	GTou
– 'Rosea'	SIng SRms WWtk

§ × ***arkwrightii***	CGle EBre ECha EFou ELan EPot LBee NMen SAga WBea WCla WOMN WWin
– 'Vesuvius'	CB&S CDoC CGle CRDP EAst EBre LFis MCLN MNrw MTis NBir NFai SRms WBro WCot WMer WOve WPbr WPer
chalcedonica 🏆	CArn CGle CKel CRow EBar EBee EBre ECha ECro ELan ENot ERav GCHN MBri MWat NBro NFai NMir NNor NOak SDix SPer SSvw WOMN WOak WOve WPer WTyr WWin
– var. ***albiflora***	CSam ECha ECro EFou ELan EMon ERav IBlr LFis LGan MBri MCLN NBro NFai NOak NSti SPer WCer WHen WPer WWhi
– – 'Snow White'	EWll WHil
– apricot	MBro WPyg
– Beverley seedling	CHan
– 'Carnea'	CVer ECro EMon GCal LCom MUlv NCat WCot
– 'Flore Pleno'	CArc CBos CMil ECha ECle ELan GBuc GCal MCLN MMil MOne MUlv NHaw NHol NPri NSti NWes SPer SSvw WCot WFar WOld WSan
– 'Rosea'	CGle CHad EAst ECro EFou EHal EJud EMan MCLN MUlv NFai NHol NMir WByw WCer WHen WPer
– 'Rosea Plena'	CBot
* – 'Salmonea'	EAst EBar ECle MBri MHlr MTis SHam SPer WCot WLRN
– salmon-pink	WWhi
– 'Valetta'	MEas
cognata	CGle EBee EGoo MSto SHel
§ ***coronaria***	CArn CChr CGle EBar EBre ECha EEls EHoe ELan EPar MBri MCLN MFir MGam MHew NFla NMir NOak NSti SPer SSvw WBea WByw WCla WHil WPyg WTyr
– 'Abbotswood Rose'	See *L.* × ***walkeri* 'Abbotswood Rose'**
– Alba Group 🏆	CGle EBar ECha EFou EHoe ELan GCHN MBri MCLN MHew NFai NOak NOrc NSti SPer SSvw WCla WEas WHer WHil WMer WOMN WPer WWhi WWin
– 'Angel's Blush'	CArc CSev EBar ECro EMan GCHN MTis NBus SPer WGwG WPer WPri WRHF WRha WRus WTyr
– Atrosanguinea Group	CBre EBee EBre ECro EFou EPPr GCHN IBlr MCLN MLsm NFai SPer WPer WRHF
– 'Cerise'	MArl NBus
– 'Dancing Ladies'	WRHF
– 'Eastgrove Pink'	WEas
– 'Hutchinson's Cream' (v)	WCot
– Oculata Group	CGle CHan CMHG ECro ELan EMar EMon GCHN IBlr LGan MCLN MFir MTho NFai NOak NSti SApp SSvw WCer WHen WHer WWhi
* – 'Purple Queen'	SPer
§ ***coronata*** var. ***sieboldii***	EBee
dioica	See ***Silene dioica***
flos-cuculi	CArn CKin CNic CWGN EBre EHon EMFW EWFC GAbr GCHN MGam MHew MHig MSal MSta MTol NDea NLan NMir NOrc SAlw WApp WBon WCla WHen WHer WWhi WWye
– var. ***albiflora***	CSam ECoo EJud EPar MEas NBro NBus NDea SIde WAlt WCla WHer WWhi
– 'Nana'	CBre CInt CNic ELan GAbr GGar LHop MBro MFir MTol NGre NHol NRya WCla WHil WPat WPer WPyg WWin
flos-jovis	CElw CGle CTri ECha EEls ELan EMan EPfP MCLN MFir NOak SRms WEas WPer
– 'Alba'	CMdw WCot
– 'Hort's Variety'	CDec CKel CLTr CSpe EFou EJud EPPr MAvo MHig MHlr NFla NSti NTow SBla SUsu WCla WCot WHil
– 'Minor'	See ***L. flos-jovis* 'Nana'**
§ – 'Nana'	CNic CRow EPPr GCHN MSCN NFai NPla NPro NWCA SSca WHoo WOMN WPyg
– 'Peggy'	GCal MCCP
× ***haageana***	EBee EOrc NWCA SIng SRms SSca WOve WTre
– 'Burning Desire'	WRHF
kubotae	See **× *Lycene kubotae***
lagascae	See ***Petrocoptis pyrenaica*** subsp. ***glaucifolia***
miqueliana	CMdw EBar EGar LFis MTis NBrk
'Molten Lava'	CBlo CInt CM&M EBre GMaP MCli MLan NLak NOrc SRms WBea WPer WTyr WWtk
nutans	MHew MSal
sp. Andes	WOMN
§ ***viscaria***	CGle CKin ECha EGar GAul MHew MSal NNor NPla SCro WBea WCla WGwy WHer WWhi
viscaria alba	ECha EEls EMan GCal NBro NPri
viscaria alpina	See ***L. viscaria***
viscaria subsp. ***atropurpurea***	GCal
– 'Firebird'	EFou
– 'Plena'	CDoC EFou EMFW LFis NSti WHil WOld
– 'Snowbird'	EFou
– 'Splendens'	CBlo EPfP NChi NFla WBro
* – 'Splendens Alba'	EPPr
– 'Splendens Plena' 🏆	CGle CHan CSpe ECha EGar ELan GMac MArl MBal MBri NBro NVic WEas WOve
§ × ***walkeri*** 'Abbotswood Rose' 🏆	EMan EMon GBuc
wilfordii	CMil CPou EBee EHic EJud WBea
§ ***yunnanensis***	CMdw CPea CSam EBee ECro EGar EMon GBuc GCHN GCra LLWP MFir MSte NHol NOak WPer WWhi
yunnanensis alba	See ***L. yunnanensis***

LYCIANTHES (Solanaceae)

◆ ***rantonnetii***	See ***Solanum rantonnetii***

LYCIUM (Solanaceae)

barbarum	CAgr ELan WApp WSHC WWye
chinense	CArn CPlN
europaeum	WTyr

LYCOPODIUM (Lycopodiaceae)

clavatum	GPoy

LYCOPSIS See ANCHUSA

LYCOPUS (Lamiaceae)

europaeus	CArn CJew ECWi ELau EWFC GBar GPoy MChe MHew MSal NCGP WChe WHer WJek WWye
exaltatus	WChe
sp. JLS 88040	EMon
virginicus	MSal

LYCORIS (Amaryllidaceae)

albiflora	SDeJ

LYGODIUM (Schizaeaceae)

¶ ***palmatum***	WCot

LYONIA (Ericaceae)

ligustrina	CChu EHic ELan SMur SSta
¶ ***ovalifolia*** var. ***elliptica***	SSta

LYONOTHAMNUS (Rosaceae)

floribundus subsp. ***aspleniifolius***	CAbb CChu EOas SArc SIgm WCru WWat

LYSICHITON (Araceae)

americanus ♈	CB&S CBen CHEx CHad CRDP CRow CTrw CWGN CWat ECha EHon ELan EMFW EPar GAbr GDra LPBA MRav MSta NDea NHol SPer SRms SSoC SSpi SWat WChe WNor WWat
camtschatcensis ♈	CB&S CBen CHEx CRow CWGN CWat ECha EHon ELan EMFW EPar LPBA MSta NDea SPer SSpi SWat WChe
¶ – x ***americanus***	SSpi

LYSIMACHIA † (Primulaceae)

atropurpurea	CHal CLTr CPle CSte EAst EBee EGar ELan EMar GBin MEas MNrw MTis NFai NPri WByw WCot WFar WPer
– 'Geronimo'	CBlo
barystachys	CKni CRow GCHN GMaP MRav WCot WOve
ciliata	CGle CMHG CRow ECha EFer EFol EGol EHoe ELan EMar EPar LFis LWak MBri MFir MNrw NDea SChu WDav WEas WHal WHoo WOld WOve WPbr WPer WRus WWin
§ – 'Firecracker'	Widely available
– 'Purpurea'	See ***L. ciliata* 'Firecracker'**
clethroides ♈	Widely available
¶ – from Guizhou, China	EWes
– 'Lady Jane'	CBlo
§ ***congestiflora***	CBrk CLTr LHil LHop NCut NPer WLRN
– 'Outback Sunset'	CHal CSpe LHop NPri WCot WLRN
– 'Silver Bird'	LIck WCot
– 'Sunbeam'	WCot
– 'Sunset Gold'	CInt
ephemerum	Widely available
fortunei	EMon SHel WCot
henryi	CHal CLTr EHic EWes GBuc LHil MHlr
japonica 'Minutissima'	CInt CRow EPPr GBuc GCHN MTho WAbe WCru WPer
lanceolata	WCot
lichiangensis	CFir CKel CSpe GBri GBur GSki MCCP MEas NRai SHFr SMac WPer
– B&L 12317	CGle NChi
– B&L 12464	CRow WCot WThi
lyssii	See ***L. congestiflora***
minoricensis	CBot CPle CRow EBre ECro EEls EFol ELan EPri GBri MLsm SMad SWat WByw WCot WLRN WOve WPer WWin
nemorum	ECWi EFer EWFC WCot WPer WRHF WTyr
nummularia	Widely available
– 'Aurea' ♈	Widely available
ovata	NHol WCot
pseudohenryi	WCot WRHF
punctata	CHal CKel CRow CShe CWGN EBre ECha EEls EHon ELan EWFC GAul LHol MWat NBro NHol NMir NNor NPer NSti SPer SWat SWyc WBea WByw WEas WOld WOve WPer WWin
– 'Alexander' (v)	CRDP EMon NCat WCot WSan
– dwarf form	EHic
punctata verticillata	See ***L. verticillaris***
* ***serpyllifolia***	SHFr
sertulata	WCot
thyrsiflora	CRow EBre MSta NDea SWat WChe WCot WHer WMAq
§ ***verticillaris***	MHlr WCot
vulgaris	CArn CWGN ECWi EHon EWFC MGam MHew SIde WChe WGwy WHil WPer WWye
– var. ***davurica***	WCot

LYSIONOTUS (Gesneriaceae)

pauciflora B&SWJ 1679	WCru
– B&SWJ 303	WCru
pauciflorus	NTow WCru
– B&SWJ 189	WCru
– B&SWJ 335	WCru

LYTHRUM (Lythraceae)

'Croftway'	CDoC
'Red Wings'	NBro
salicaria	Widely available
– 'Blush'	CHad CRDP EAst EBre ECha EFou EGar EHic ELan EMan GAri GMaP LFis MBel MBri MCLN NHol NPro NRoo SChu SMrm SOkh SUsu SWat WCot WPbr WWeb WWoo
– 'Brightness'	NCat NFla NHol WTyr
§ – 'Feuerkerze' ♈	CRDP CRow EBre EFou EHal ELan GCal LFis MBel MCLN MRav MUlv NCat NFai NHol NSti SChu SPer WFar WPer
◆ – Firecandle	See ***L. salicaria* 'Feuerkerze'**

– 'Florarose'	EFou
¶– 'Happy'	SMrm
– 'Lady Sackville'	EFou GBuc GCal GGar GMaP LFis NCat SAxl WAbe
– 'Morden Pink'	CDoC EFou LBuc MBri
– 'Robert'	CMGP CRow CShe CTri EBre ECha ELan EPar EPfP MCLN MHlr MTis MWat NCut NHol NOak SChu SPer WChe WEas
– 'Rose'	ELan
¶– 'Stichflamme'	EFou
– 'The Beacon'	CDoC CRow EMan GCal MAvo SRms WCot
– Ulverscroft form	MUlv
– 'Zigeunerblut'	LBuc LGre
virgatum 'Dropmore Purple'	CLTr MBri NCut
– 'Rose Queen'	ECha WPer
– 'Rosy Gem'	CM&M CRow EBar ECtt EGar EMar LSyl MFir MOne MWat NBro NCGP NOak NPri NRoo NTow SRms SSvw WHoo WPer
– 'The Rocket''	CRow CTri EBre LFis NCat NHol NLak NSti SPer WChe WWin

LYTOCARYUM (Arecaceae)

§ ***weddellianum*** ♀	MBri

MAACKIA (Papilionaceae)

amurensis	CAgr CB&S CChu ELan EPfP WFro WNor
chinensis	MBlu

MACFADYENA (Bignoniaceae)

§ ***unguis-cati***	CPlN CRHN EOas GCra

MACHAERANTHERA (Asteraceae)

¶ ***lagunensis***	EPPr WDav
pattersonii	See ***M. bigelovii***

MACHILUS See PERSEA

MACKAYA (Acanthaceae)

§ ***bella*** ♀	ERea

MACLEANIA (Ericaceae)

¶ ***insignis***	CPlN

MACLEAYA (Papaveraceae)

N ***cordata*** ♀	CArn CHEx CWGN EAst EBee ECoo ELan EMar EPar MRav MSCN MTis MTol MWat NOrc NTow SPer SRms WEas WFar WHal WHoo WKif WPLl WPer WWhi WWin
– 'Flamingo'	EAst EBee EBre ECha EOrc GCHN GCal GMaP MCLN MRav MUlv SMrm WWye
× ***kewensis***	CWan MBro WHoo WPyg
§ ***microcarpa***	EGar EHal EPPr LBlm SHhN SWat WHer WSel
– 'Kelway's Coral Plume' ♀	CB&S CGle CHEx CHad CShe CSte CWGN EBre ECha EFol ELan EOrc EPar GMaP MBri MCLN MRav NBro NFla SChu SPer SSoC WEas WGwG WOld WOve WWat

MACLURA (Moraceae)

pomifera	CB&S CLnd CMCN CPle SHhN WDin WPGP

MACRODIERVILLA See WEIGELA

MACROPIPER (Piperaceae)

crocatum	See ***Piper ornatum***
§ ***excelsum***	CHEx ECou
– 'Aureopictum'	CHEx

MACROZAMIA (Zamiaceae)

communis	CBrP LPal WNor
¶ ***diplomera***	CBrP
dyeri	See ***M. riedlei***
miquelii	LPal
moorei	CBrP LPal
mountperiensis	CBrP
riedlei	CBrP LPal

MAGNOLIA † (Magnoliaceae)

acuminata	CB&S CBlo CFil CMCN MBal SSpi
– var. ***subcordata*** 'Miss Honeybee'	CFil
'Ann' ♀	CDoC CTrh SSpi
'Apollo'	CB&S CFil CPMA WPGP
'Athene'	CB&S CMHG CPMA
'Atlas'	CB&S CDoC CEnd CFil CMHG CPMA WPGP
'Betty' ♀	CB&S CBlo CDoC CSte EMil IOrc LNet MGos SSta WDin WLRN WPyg
'Big Dude'	CFil WPGP
biondii	CFil
× ***brooklynensis*** 'Woodsman'	CB&S CPMA SSta
'Caerhays Belle'	CB&S CFil CPMA
campbellii	CAbb CB&S CFil CMCN CRos CSam CTho ELan ICrw IOrc ISea
– var. ***alba***	CB&S CTho
¶– 'Betty Jessel'	CTho
– subsp. ***mollicomata***	CB&S CEnd CPMA CTrw EPfP SPer
– – 'Lanarth'	CB&S CEnd SSta
– (Raffillii Group) 'Charles Raffill' ♀	CB&S CDoC CPMA EBee ELan GGGa MDun MLan SHBN SMad WDin
– – 'Kew's Surprise'	CB&S
– 'Strybing White'	CPMA
'Charles Coates'	CKni
'Columbus'	CFil
cordata	See ***M. acuminata*** var. ***subcordata***
'Cup Cake'	CKni
cylindrica ♀	CB&S CKni CMCN GGGa IOrc SSpi SSta
dawsoniana	CB&S CMCN
delavayi	CB&S CFil CHEx EOas GGGa SArc SSpi WPGP
I – SF 432	ISea
§ ***denudata*** ♀	CB&S CMCN CTho CTrw IOrc LPan MBal SPer SReu SSpi SSta WBod WNor WWat
– 'Forrest's Pink'	CFil CPMA
– var. ***purpurascens***	See ***M. sprengeri*** var. ***diva***
'Elizabeth' ♀	CFil CMCN ELan EPfP GGGa LHyd LRHS MAsh SSpi SSta
'Frank Gladney'	CKni
'Full Eclipse'	CFil

'Galaxy' ♀	CB&S CEnd CFil CKni CPMA MBar MBlu SSpi WPGP
'George Henry Kern'	CBlo CDoC COtt CPMA EB&P IOrc LPan MAsh MGos SSta WDin
globosa	CB&S CFil GGGa WPGP
'Goldstar'	CFil SSpi WPGP
grandiflora	CHEx CMCN EBre EMil ISea MRav MWat SArc SSta WDin WNor WWat
– 'Edith Bogue'	SBid
– 'Exmouth' ♀	CB&S CBot CChu CGre CLan CMCN EBre ELan ENot IOrc ISea LHyd LNet MAsh MBal MBri SBid SFam SHBN SMad SPer SReu SSpi SSta WBod WStI WWat
– 'Ferruginea'	CLan ISea
– 'Galissonière'	CBlo CDoC COtt CSte IOrc ISea LPan SBid SSpi
I – 'Galissonière Nana'	LPan
– 'Goliath' ♀	CB&S CEnd CFil CHEx CTrC CWLN ELan IOrc ISea LHyd LNet MBal SBid SPer SSpi SSta
– 'Little Gem'	CDoC CPMA CTrC MAsh SPla SSpi
– 'Russet'	CPMA LNet
– 'Saint Mary'	CPMA
– 'Samuel Sommer'	CMCN CPMA EHoe SArc SSpi
– 'Undulata'	IOrc ISea
– 'Victoria'	CFil ELan ISea MAsh MBlu MBri SReu SSta WWeb
'Heaven Scent' ♀	CAbP CB&S CMCN COtt CSam CTho CTrw IOrc LHyd LPan MAsh MBal MBar MBlu MGos SPer SSpi SSta WPyg
heptapeta	See ***M. denudata***
hypoleuca ♀	CDoC CFil CHEx CTho GGGa ISea MBlu MLan SHBN SSpi WWat
'Iolanthe' ♀	CB&S CDoC CEnd CFil CMCN CMHG CPMA CTho EBee MAsh NHol SPer SSpi SSta
'Jane' ♀	CDoC COtt ELan IOrc MAsh MBri MGos NHol SSta
'Joe McDaniel'	CDoC
'Jon Jon'	CFil
x ***kewensis*** 'Kewensis'	CB&S
– 'Wada's Memory' ♀	CB&S CFil CMCN CMHG CTho EBee EHoe GGGa MAsh MBri NFla SPer SSpi SSta WBod
kobus	CB&S CBot CGre CMCN CTho IOrc LHyd LPan SHBN SPer SSpi SSta WNor WWat
¶ – var. ***borealis***	CTho
§ – 'Norman Gould'	CKni CMCN CWLN EPfP
'Lilenny'	CKni
§ ***liliiflora***	CTrw MAsh MBar SHhN
§ – 'Nigra' ♀	CB&S CGre EBre ELan EMil ENot IOrc LPan MGos NFla SDix SHBN SPer SPla SReu SSpi SSta WDin WFar WStI
x ***loebneri***	CB&S WNor
– 'Ballerina'	CDoC CMCN SSta
– 'Leonard Messel' ♀	CB&S CEnd CLan CMCN CMHG CShe CTho CTrh CTrw EBre ELan IOrc LNet LPan MAsh MBal MBri MGos NHed NHol SHBN SPer SReu SSpi SSta WBod WDin WWat
– 'Merrill' ♀	CB&S CFil CKni CMCN CMHG CPMA CSam CTho CTrh EBre ELan IOrc ISea LPan MAsh MBal MBri NHol SPer SReu SSpi SSta WDin WPyg WWat
– 'Neil McEacharn'	CDoC IOrc
– 'Snowdrift'	CMCN SSta
– 'Star Bright'	CMCN
macrophylla	CBrP CFil CMCN EOas SArc SSpi WCoo WPGP
– 'Sara Gladney'	CHEx
'Manchu Fan'	CPMA GWht IOrc
'Mark Jury'	CB&S CPMA
¶ 'Marwood Spring'	CTho
'Maryland' ♀	CFil CPMA SSpi WPGP
'Milky Way'	CB&S CFil CMHG COtt CPMA CTho SSpi WPGP
'Nimbus'	CFil
officinalis	LPan
'Peppermint Stick' ♀	CPMA MGos SSta
'Peter Smithers'	CFil IOrc
'Pickard's Coral'	MBal
'Pickard's Crystal'	CKni
'Pickard's Opal'	CDoC LHyd
'Pickard's Pink Diamond'	CKni
'Pickard's Ruby'	CDoC COtt CPMA
'Pickard's Schmetterling'	See ***M. 'Schmetterling'***
'Pickard's Sundew'	See ***M. x soulangeana 'Pickard's Sundew'***
'Pinkie' ♀	CKni IOrc MAsh MBri SSta
x ***proctoriana*** ♀	CFil CKni ELan EPfP IOrc ISea MAsh SSta
– 'Proctoriana'	EBre LHyd
'Purple Prince'	CFil WPGP
quinquepeta	See ***M. liliiflora***
'Raspberry Ice'	CDoC CKni COtt CRos CTho CTrw MBal SSta
'Ricki' ♀	COtt CPMA EB&P IOrc MBri MGos SSta
'Royal Crown'	CKni SSta
salicifolia ♀	CFil CKni ISea MAsh SBid SPer SSpi SSta
– 'W.B. Clarke'	CMCN
sargentiana	CFil IOrc WPGP
– var. ***robusta***	CB&S CEnd CKni CTrw ELan EPfP GWht IOrc MAsh SSpi SSta
– – ***alba***	CDoC CTrw
'Sayonara' ♀	CB&S CKni COtt CPMA EPfP IOrc MBlu SSpi SSta
§ 'Schmetterling'	CDoC SSta
'Serene'	CB&S CFil CPMA SSpi
* 'Seyu'	SSpi
sieboldii ♀	CAbb CB&S CGre CMCN CPMA EHoe ELan EMil IOrc LPan MAsh MBal MBar MBri MDun MGos SHBN SSpi SSta WBod WCoo WNor
– subsp. ***sinensis*** ♀	CB&S CMCN CSam ELan GGGa MDun SPer SSpi WDin WWat
x ***soulangeana***	CB&S CLan CShe CTrh CTrw EBre ELan EMil ENot IOrc ISea MAsh MBal MBar MBri MGos MWat NBee SHBN SPer WDin WNor
– 'Alba'	See ***M. x soulangeana 'Alba Superba'***
§ – 'Alba Superba'	CB&S CEnd CGre EHoe ENot IOrc LPan MAsh MGos SPer SSpi WWat

– 'Alexandrina' 🏆	CDoC COtt CWLN ELan IOrc MAsh MBri SPer
¶ – 'Alexandrina Alba'	CTho
– 'Amabilis'	CDoC COtt IOrc
– 'Brozzoni' 🏆	CB&S CGre CMCN CMHG CSam CTrh CWLN IOrc ISea LPan SSpi
N – 'Burgundy'	CB&S CBot CDoC SSta
– 'Lennei' 🏆	CB&S CEnd CMCN CMHG CTrh CWLN ENot GWht IOrc LPan MAsh MGos NHol SHBN SPer SRms WNor WPyg WStI WWat
– 'Lennei Alba' 🏆	CMCN ELan IOrc SPer
– 'Nigra'	See ***M. liliiflora* 'Nigra'**
– 'Pickard's Sundew'	CB&S CDoC CMCN CPMA EB&P EPfP IOrc MBri MGos SHBN
– 'Picture'	CBlo CDoC CMCN IOrc WBod
– 'Rubra'	See ***M.* × *soulangeana* 'Rustica Rubra'**
§ – 'Rustica Rubra' 🏆	CB&S CEnd CMCN CPMA CSam CTrh CWLN EBre ELan ENot IOrc LNet LPan MAsh MBri SHBN SPer SReu SSpi SSta WWat
– 'San José'	CMCN CRos EB&P IOrc MAsh SPer SSta
– 'Verbanica'	LRHS MAsh
– 'White Giant'	CDoC SHhN
'Spectrum'	CFil CPMA GWht SSpi
sprengeri	CTrw
§ – var. ***diva***	CB&S CFil CMCN SSpi
– – 'Burncoose'	CB&S
– var. ***elongata***	COtt IOrc ISea
¶ – 'Lanhydrock'	SSpi
'Star Wars'	CB&S CDoC CFil CPMA CTho SHhN SSpi SSta
§ ***stellata*** 🏆	CB&S CMHG CTrh CTrw EBre ELan ENot GRei ISea LHyd LNet MAsh MBal MBar MBri MGos MWat NFla NHol SHBN SMad SPer SReu SSta WCoo WDin WNor WWat
– 'Centennial'	CDoC SSta
– 'Chrysanthemiflora'	CMCN LHyd LRHS SPer SSpi SSta
– f. ***keiskei***	CEnd COtt NFla
– 'King Rose'	CB&S CDoC COtt CWLN ISea MAsh MBlu MBri NHed SPer SPla
– 'Massey'	ISea WBod
– 'Norman Gould'	See ***M. kobus* 'Norman Gould'**
– 'Rosea'	COtt ELan IOrc ISea MGos SHBN WPyg
– 'Royal Star'	CB&S CBot CEnd CLan CMCN CWLN ECtt EMil ENot IOrc ISea LPan MAsh MBri MGos NHol SPer SSpi SSta WHCG WStI
– 'Waterlily' 🏆	CB&S CBot CEnd CMCN CRos CSam CWLN EBre ELan IOrc ISea MAsh SPer SPla SSpi SSta WPyg
'Sundance'	CFil WPGP
'Susan' 🏆	CAbP CB&S CEnd CMCN COtt CSam ELan EMil IOrc LPan MAsh MBal MBar MBri MGos MWat NBee NHed NHol SHBN SMad SPer SReu SSpi SSta WDin WStI WWeb
× ***thompsoniana***	CMCN WBod
tripetala	CB&S CHEx CMCN LPan MDun MLan SHBN SSta WCoo WDin WWat
× ***veitchii***	CDoC CGre
– 'Peter Veitch'	CFil CGre CTho
virginiana	CGre CMCN SSpi
'Vulcan'	CB&S CFil CMHG COtt CPMA CTho
× ***watsonii***	See ***M.* × *wiesneri***
§ × ***wiesneri***	CFil CKni CPMA ELan MBlu SSta
wilsonii 🏆	CB&S CFil CMCN CTho CTrw EHoe ELan GGGa ICrw IOrc MAsh MBal SHBN SMad SPer SReu SSpi SSta WDin WNor WWat
'Yellow Bird'	CFil SSpi WPGP
'Yellow Fever'	CFil WPGP

× MAHOBERBERIS (Berberidaceae)

aquisargentii	CAbP CPle ENot EPla GBin LHop MAll MGos MPla MRav NHol SBid SPer WPat WPyg WRTC WWat
'Dart's Treasure'	EPla WFar
'Magic'	MRav WWeb
miethkeana	CMHG MAll MBar

MAHONIA † (Berberidaceae)

acanthifolia	See ***M. napaulensis***
§ ***aquifolium***	CB&S CPer EAst ELan ENot GCHN GOrc GRei ISea MAsh MBal MBar MBri MGos MHew MWat NFla NNor NRoo NWea SHBN SPer SReu SSoC WDin WHCG WStI
– 'Apollo' 🏆	CShe ECtt ELan EMil ENot EPla IOrc MAsh MBar MBri MGos NBee NHol SHBN SPer SReu SSta WPat WPyg WWat
– 'Atropurpurea'	CDoC ELan ENot EPla MHlr NBee NFla SHBN SPer SPla WWat
* – 'Cosmo Crawl'	MGos
– 'Fascicularis'	See ***M.* × *wagneri* 'Pinnacle'**
– 'Green Ripple'	COtt EPfP EPla MBri SPla WFar
¶ – 'Mirena'	MGos
– 'Orange Flame'	MBlu
– 'Smaragd'	CDoC ELan EPla IOrc MBlu MUlv NHol WHCG WPyg
– 'Versicolor'	MBlu
bealei	See ***M. japonica* Bealei Group**
confusa	CChu CFil WPGP
eutriphylla	EPla
fortunei	EPla MBal WSHC
fremontii	GCal LGre WSHC
– × ***haematocarpa***	GCal
gracilipes	NHol
'Gulf Tide'	CEnd
haematocarpa	GCal
japonica 🏆	CBot CChe CEnd CHEx CShe CTre CTrw ELan ENot ISea MAsh MBal MBar MBri MWat NHol SHBN SPer SReu SSpi SSta WDin WGwG WHCG WPat WSHC WWat
§ – Bealei Group	CB&S CLan EBee EBre ELan GRei IOrc MAsh MBar MGos SEas SSoC WDin WWeb
– 'Hiemalis'	See ***M. japonica* 'Hivernant'**
§ – 'Hivernant'	NFla WPyg WWat

lomariifolia 🏆 CB&S CBot CHEx CPle ENot IHos IOrc ISea MBal MUlv NSti SArc SDry SPer SPla SSpi WSHC
× *media* 'Buckland' 🏆 CAbP CAlt CB&S CEnd CSam CTrw ECtt ISea MAsh MBal MBri NHol SBid SPer SRms WPat WPyg WRHF WWat WWeb
– 'Charity' 🏆 CAlt CB&S CLan CShe EBre ELan ENot GOrc GRei LHop MBal MBar MBri MGos NFla NHol NRoo SHBN SMad SPer SReu SSoC SSta WBod WDin WHCG WPat WWat
– 'Charity's Sister' EPla MBri
– 'Faith' EPla
– 'Lionel Fortescue' 🏆 CB&S CEnd CSam CTre CTrw EBre ELan EPla GCHN LHop MAsh MBal MBri MPla SBid SEas SMad SPer SReu SSpi SSta WHCG WWat
– 'Underway' 🏆 CSam EPla MAsh MBri SMur SPla WWat WWes
– 'Winter Sun' 🏆 CB&S CBot CEnd COtt CSte EBre ELan EMil EPla IOrc MAsh MBal MBlu MBri MGos MWat SBid SHBN SPla SSta WDin WPyg WWat WWin
nervosa COtt EPla EPot LPan MBlu NBee NHol SBid SHBN SPer SReu SSta WRTC
pallida CFil EPla WPGP WWat
– T&K 553 CChu
N***pinnata*** EBee ELan ENot EPla IOrc MAsh MBal MBar MBro SPer WDin WPat WRTC
piperiana MUlv
pumila EPla
repens CPle EPla ERav SRms
– 'Rotundifolia' EPla
* × ***savillii*** EPla
siamensis CGre
trifoliolata var. ***glauca*** CEnd
× ***wagneri*** 'Fireflame' MUlv
– 'Moseri' SPer SPla SSpi WBcn
§ – 'Pinnacle' 🏆 EPla MGos SMur SPer
– 'Undulata' 🏆 ECtt ENot EPla IHos MUlv SDix SRms WHCG

MAIANTHEMUM (Convallariaceae)

bifolium CAvo CRDP CRow CVer ELan EMon EPot EWFC GBuc MBal MDun MTho NBro NMen SRms WAbe WCru WWat WWye
§ – var. ***kamtschaticum*** CAvo CRDP ECro EMon EPar LSyl WCot
canadense GCal MSal
dilatatum See ***M. bifolium*** var. ***kamtschaticum***

MAIHUENIA (Cactaceae)

poeppigii JCA 1253 GCHN

MALEPHORA (Aizoaceae)

lutea CNic MHig

MALLOTUS (Euphorbiaceae)

japonicus CGre

MALPIGHIA (Malpighiaceae)

See Plant Deletions

MALUS † (Rosaceae)

× ***adstringens*** 'Hopa' CLnd
– 'Simcoe' CDoC CLnd EBee MGos
'Aldenhamensis' See ***M.*** × ***purpurea*** **'Aldenhamensis'**
× ***atrosanguinea*** NWea
§ – 'Gorgeous' CBlo COtt GTwe MAsh MBri SIgm WDin WJas
baccata CLnd CMCN CTho GTwe WNor
– 'Lady Northcliffe' CLnd SFam
'Butterball' CMCN MBri WJas
* 'Cheal's Weeping' SPer WStI
coronaria var. ***dasycalyx*** 'Charlottae' (d) CBlo CDoC CEnd CLnd COtt CSam CTho ENot MAsh SPer
'Crittenden' EBee
* 'Directeur Moerlands' EPfP MAsh MGos WJas
domestica (F) MGos
¶ – 'Acklam Russet' (D) SKee
– 'Acme' (D) SDea SKee
– 'Adam's Pearmain' (D) CTho GTwe SDea SFam SIgm SKee WHow WJas
¶ – 'Admiral' (D) SKee
– 'Advance' (D) SKee
– 'Akane' (D) SDea
§ – 'Alexander' (C) GTwe SKee
– 'Alfriston' (C) SKee
– 'Alkmene' (D) GTwe SKee
– 'Allen's Everlasting' (D) GTwe SDea SKee
– 'Allington Pippin' (D) CCVT CSam CTho CTri NRog SDea SKee WHow WJas
– 'American Mother' See ***M. domestica*** **'Mother'**
– 'Anna Boelens' (D) SDea
– 'Annie Elizabeth' (C) CCVT CTho GTwe MMor SDea SFam SKee WJas
– 'Api Noir' (D) SKee
– 'Api Rose' (D) CCVT SKee WJas
– 'Ard Cairn Russet' (D) GTwe SDea SKee
– 'Aromatic Russet' (D) SKee
– 'Arthur Turner' (C) 🏆 CCVT CDoC EMui GTwe LBuc MGos NRog SDea SFam SKee WJas
– 'Ashmead's Kernel' (D) 🏆 CCVT CSam CTho EBre EMui ERea GTwe LBuc MWat NRog SDea SFam SIgm SKee WHow WJas
– 'Ashton Bitter' (F) CCSL CCVT CEnd CSam CTho GTwe
– 'Ashton Brown Jersey' (Cider) CTho
– 'Autumn Pearmain' (D) CTho SDea WJas
– 'Baker's Delicious' (D) SDea SIgm SKee
¶ – 'Ballarat Seedling' (D) SKee
– 'Balsam' See ***M. domestica*** **'Green Balsam'**
¶ – 'Banns' (D) SKee
– 'Barnack Beauty' (D) CTho SKee
– 'Barnack Orange' (D) SKee
¶ – 'Bascombe Mystery' (D) SKee
– 'Baumann's Reinette' (D) SKee
– 'Baxter's Pearmain' (C/D) SKee
¶ – 'Beachamwell' (D) SKee
– 'Beauty of Bath' (D) CCVT CDoC CTri GTwe IOrc NRog SFam SKee WJas
– 'Beauty of Hants' (D) SKee
– 'Beauty of Kent' (C) SDea SKee
– 'Beauty of Moray' (C) SKee

– 'Bedwyn Beauty' (C)	CTho
– 'Beeley Pippin' (D)	GTwe SDea SKee
– 'Bell Apple' (Cider/C)	CTho
– 'Belle de Boskoop' (C/D) 🏆	CSam GTwe SKee
– 'Bembridge Beauty' (F)	SDea
– 'Ben's Red' (D)	CEnd CTho SKee
– 'Bess Pool' (D)	SFam SKee
– 'Billy Down Pippin' (F)	CTho
– 'Bismarck' (C)	CTho SKee
– 'Black Dabinett' (Cider)	CTho
– 'Black Tom Putt' (C/D)	CTho
– 'Blaze' (D)	GTwe
– 'Blenheim Orange' (C/D) 🏆	CCVT CDoC CTho EMui EWar GBon GTwe LBuc MBri MMor MWat NRog SDea SFam SIgm SKee SPer WHow WJas WStI WWeb
– 'Blenheim Red'	See *M. domestica* **'Red Blenheim'**
– 'Bloody Ploughman' (F)	SKee
– 'Blue Pearmain' (D)	SKee
– 'Blue Sweet' (Cider)	Ctho
◆– Bolero	See *M. domestica* **Bolero = 'Tuscan'**
– 'Boston Russet'	See *M. domestica* **'Roxbury Russet'**
– 'Bountiful' (C)	COtt EMui GTwe MGos SIgm WStI
– 'Bow Hill Pippin' (D)	SKee
– 'Box Apple' (D)	SKee
– 'Braddick Nonpareil' (D)	SKee
– 'Braeburn' (D)	SDea SKee
– 'Bramley's Seedling' (C) 🏆	CB&S CCVT CMac CSam EBre EMui ERea EWar GBon GChr GRei GTwe IOrc LBuc MBri MMor MWat NBee NDal NRog SDea SFam SIgm SKee SPer WJas WWeb
– 'Bread Fruit' (C/D)	CEnd
– 'Breakwell Seedling' (Cider)	CTho
– 'Bridgwater Pippin' (C)	CTho WJas
¶– 'Bringewood Pippin' (D)	WJas
– 'Broad-eyed Pippin' (C)	SKee
– 'Brown Snout' (Cider)	CCSL CTho
– 'Brown Thorn' (Cider)	CCSL
– 'Brownlees Russet' (D)	CTho EMui GTwe NRog SDea SFam SKee
– 'Brown's Apple' (Cider)	CCSL GTwe
– 'Broxwood Foxwhelp' (Cider)	CTho
– 'Burn's Seedling' (D)	CTho
– 'Burr Knot' (C)	SKee
– 'Burrow Hill Early' (Cider)	CTho
– 'Bushey Grove' (C)	SDea SKee
– 'Calville Blanc d'Hiver' (D)	SKee
– 'Calville des Femmes' (C)	SKee
– 'Cambusnethan Pippin' (D)	SKee
– 'Camelot' (Cider/C)	CCSL CTho
– 'Cap of Liberty' (Cider)	CCSL
– 'Captain Broad' (Cider)	CEnd CTho
¶– 'Captain Kidd' (D)	SKee
– 'Captain Smith' (F)	CEnd
– 'Carlisle Codlin' (C)	GTwe SKee
¶– 'Caroline' (D)	SKee
– 'Carswell's Orange' (D)	SKee

– 'Catherine' (C)	EPfP SKee
– 'Catshead' (C)	CCVT GQui SDea SKee WJas
– 'Cellini' (C/D)	SDea
– 'Charles Ross' (C/D) 🏆	CCVT CMac CSam CTho EBre EMui EWar GBon GRei GTwe MWat NDal NRog SDea SFam SIgm SKee WHow WJas
– Charlotte™ (C/Ball)	LBuc MGos
– 'Chaxhill Red' (Cider/D)	CTho
– 'Cheddar Cross' (D)	CTri SKee
– 'Chelmsford Wonder' (C)	SKee
– 'Chisel Jersey' (F)	CCSL CTho
– 'Chiver's Delight' (D)	EMui GTwe MMor SDea SIgm SKee WJas
– 'Chorister Boy' (D)	CTho
– 'Christmas Pearmain' (D)	CTho GTwe SDea SFam SKee WHow
– 'Cider Lady's Finger' (Cider)	CCSL
– 'Claygate Pearmain' (D) 🏆	CTho GTwe SDea SFam SIgm SKee WJas
¶– 'Close' (D)	SKee
– 'Cockle Pippin' (D)	CTho GTwe SDea SKee
¶– 'Cockpit' (C)	SKee
– 'Coeur de Boeuf' (C/D)	SKee
– 'Coleman's Seedling' (Cider)	CTho
– 'Colloget Pippin' (C/Cider)	CCSL CEnd CTho
– 'Colonel Vaughan' (C/D)	CTho SKee
– 'Cornish Aromatic' (D)	CDoC CSam CTho EMui GTwe SDea SFam SIgm SKee WJas
– 'Cornish Crimson Queen' (F)	GTwe
– 'Cornish Gilliflower' (D)	CCSL CDoC SDea SFam SIgm SKee WJas
– 'Cornish Honeypin' (D)	CTho
– 'Cornish Longstem' (D)	CEnd CTho
– 'Cornish Mother' (D)	CEnd
– 'Cornish Pine' (D)	CEnd CTho SDea SKee
– 'Coronation' (D)	SDea SKee
– 'Costard' (C)	GTwe SKee
– 'Cottenham Seedling' (C)	SKee
– 'Coul Blush' (D)	SKee
– 'Court of Wick' (D)	CTho SKee
– 'Court Pendu Plat' (D)	CCVT CTho LBuc MWat NRog SDea SFam SIgm SKee WJas
– 'Court Royal' (Cider)	CCSL CTho
– 'Cox's Orange Pippin' (D)	CB&S CCVT CMac EBre EWar GTwe LBuc MBri MMor MWat NRog SDea SFam SKee SPer WJas WWeb
– 'Cox's Pomona' (C/D)	CTho SDea SKee WJas
– 'Cox's Rouge de Flandres' (D)	SKee
– 'Cox's Selfing' (D)	CBlo CWSG ERea GTwe LBuc MGos SKee WJas WWeb
– 'Crawley Beauty' (C)	GTwe SDea SFam SKee WHow WJas
– 'Crimson Cox' (D)	SDea
– 'Crimson King' (F)	CCSL CTho
– 'Crimson Queening' (D)	SKee WJas
– 'Crimson Victoria' (Cider)	CTho
– 'Crispin'	See *M. domestica* **'Mutsu'**
– 'Crown Gold' (F)	CEnd EMui GBon
– 'Cummy Norman' (Cider)	CCSL

– 'Curl Tail' (D)	SKee
– 'Dabinett' (Cider)	CCSL CCVT CEnd CTho CTri EMui GTwe LBuc SDea SKee
– 'D'Arcy Spice' (D)	SDea SFam SIgm SKee
– 'Dawn' (D)	SKee
– 'Deacon's Blushing Beauty' (C/D)	SDea
– 'Decio' (D)	SKee
◆ – 'Delbards'	See *M. domestica* **Jubilee (Delbards)**
– 'Delkid' (F)	GTwe
– 'Devon Crimson Queen' (D)	CTho
– 'Devonshire Buckland' (C)	CEnd CTho WJas
– 'Devonshire Quarrenden' (D)	CEnd CSam CTho EMui SDea SFam SKee WJas
– 'Dewdney's Seedling' (C)	GTwe
– 'Diamond Jubilee' (D)	SKee WJas
– 'Discovery' (D) 🏆	CB&S CSam EBre EMui EWar GBon GChr GRei GTwe IOrc LBuc MBri MMor MWat NBee NDal NRog SDea SFam SIgm SKee SPer WJas WWeb
– 'Doctor Hare's' (C)	WJas
– 'Doctor Harvey' (C)	SFam
– 'Doctor Kidd's Orange Red' (D)	SDea
– 'Domino' (C)	SKee
– 'Don's Delight' (C)	CTho
– 'Doux Normandie' (Cider)	CCSL
– 'Dove' (F)	CTho
– 'Downton Pippin' (D)	SKee WJas
– 'Dredge's Fame' (D)	CTho
– 'Duchess of Oldenburg' (C/D)	SKee
– 'Duchess's Favourite' (D)	SKee
¶ – 'Duck's Bill' (D)	SKee
– 'Dufflin' (Cider)	CTho
– 'Duke of Devonshire' (D)	CSam CTho SDea SFam SKee WJas
– 'Duke of Gloucester' (C)	WJas
N – 'Dumeller's Seedling' (C)	CTho GTwe SDea SKee
– 'Dunkerton Late Sweet' (Cider)	CCSL CTho
– 'Dunn's Seedling' (D)	SDea
– 'Dutch Codlin' (C)	CTho
§ – 'Dutch Mignonne' (D)	SKee
– 'Early Blenheim' (D/C)	CEnd CTho
– 'Early Bower' (F)	CEnd
– 'Early Julyan' (C)	SKee WJas
– 'Early Victoria'	See *M. domestica* **'Emneth Early'**
– 'Early Worcester'	See *M. domestica* **'Tydeman's Early Worcester'**
– 'Easter Orange' (D)	GTwe SFam SKee WJas
– 'Ecklinville' (C)	SDea SKee WJas
– 'Edward VII' (C) 🏆	CDoC GTwe SDea SFam SKee WJas
– 'Egremont Russet' (D) 🏆	CCVT CSam CTho EBre EMui EWar GBon GChr GTwe IOrc LBuc MBri MMor MWat NBee NRog SDea SFam SIgm SKee SPer WJas WWeb
– 'Ellis' Bitter' (Cider)	CCSL CEnd CTho GTwe
– 'Ellison's Orange' (D) 🏆	CSam CTri EWar GBon GTwe MBri MMor NRog SDea SFam SIgm SKee WJas WStI
– 'Elstar' (D) 🏆	EMui GTwe IOrc SDea SIgm SKee
– 'Elton Beauty' (D)	SDea SKee
§ – 'Emneth Early' (C) 🏆	CSam CTho GTwe MMor NRog SDea SFam SKee WHow WJas
◆ – 'Emperor Alexander'	See *M. domestica* **'Alexander'**
– 'Empire' (D)	SKee
– 'Encore' (C)	SDea SKee
– 'English Codling' (C)	CTho
§ – 'Epicure' (D) 🏆	CDoC CSam CTho GBon GTwe IOrc NRog SFam SIgm SKee WJas
– 'Ernie's Russet' (D)	SDea
– 'Evening Gold' (C)	SDea
– 'Eve's Delight' (D)	SDea
– 'Exeter Cross' (D)	SDea SFam SKee
¶ – 'Eynsham Dumpling' (C)	SKee
– 'Fair Maid of Taunton' (D)	CCSL WJas
– 'Fairfield' (D)	CTho
¶ – 'Fall Pippin' (D)	SKee
– 'Fall Russet' (D)	GTwe
– 'Falstaff' (D) 🏆	CCSL CDoC EMui GTwe MGos SIgm SKee WJas
– 'Fameuse' (D)	SKee
– 'Fearn's Pippin' (D)	SKee
– 'Feuillemorte' (D)	SKee
– 'Fiesta' (D) 🏆	CDoC CSam EBre EMui GBon GTwe LBuc MBri MGos NDal SDea SFam SIgm SKee WJas WWeb
– 'Fillbarrel' (Cider)	CCSL CTho
– 'Fillingham Pippin' (C)	SKee
– 'Fireside' (F)	SIgm
– 'Firmgold' (D)	SDea
– 'Five Crowns' (F)	SKee
– Flamenco™ (D/Ball)	MGos
§ – 'Flower of Kent' (C)	SDea SIgm SKee
– 'Flower of the Town' (D)	SKee WJas
– 'Folkestone' (D)	SKee
◆ – 'Forfar'	See *M. domestica* **'Dutch Mignonne'**
– 'Forge' (D)	SDea SKee
– 'Formosa Nonpareil' (C)	WJas
§ – 'Fortune' (D) 🏆	CDoC CMac CSam CTri EMui GChr GRei GTwe MGos NRog SDea SFam SIgm SKee WHow WJas
– 'Foster's Seedling' (D)	SKee
¶ – 'Foulden Pearmain' (D)	SKee
– 'French Crab' (C)	CTho SDea
– 'Freyberg' (D)	SKee
– 'Fuji' (D)	SDea SKee
– 'Gala' (D)	CSam GBon GTwe MBri SDea SFam SIgm SKee
– 'Gala Mondial' (F)	SKee
– 'Gala Royal' (F)	SKee
– 'Galloway Pippin' (C)	GTwe SKee
– 'Gascoyne's Scarlet' (D)	SDea SFam SKee
– 'Gavin' (D)	SDea SKee
– 'Genesis II' (D/C)	SDea
– 'Genet Moyle' (C)	CTho WJas
– 'George Carpenter' (D)	SKee
– 'George Cave' (D)	CCVT GTwe NBee NRog SDea SFam SIgm SKee WJas
– 'George Neal' (C) 🏆	SDea SFam SIgm SKee

– 'Gilliflower of Gloucester' (D)	CTho
– 'Gin' (Cider)	CCSL
– 'Gladstone' (D)	CTho SIgm SKee WJas
§ – 'Glass Apple' (C/D)	CEnd
– 'Gloria Mundi' (C)	SDea
– 'Glory of England' (C)	WJas
– 'Gloster '69' (D)	GTwe SDea SIgm SKee
– 'Gloucester Cross' (D)	SKee
– 'Golden Bittersweet' (D)	CTho
– 'Golden Delicious' (D) 🏆	CB&S CMac EBre EWar GBon MBri MMor NRog SDea SKee SPer WStI WWeb
– 'Golden Harvey' (D)	CTho SKee
– 'Golden Knob' (D)	CTho SKee
– 'Golden Noble' (C) 🏆	CDoC CSam CTho EMui GTwe LBuc SDea SFam SIgm SKee
– 'Golden Nugget' (D)	SIgm SKee
– 'Golden Pearmain' (D)	SIgm
– 'Golden Pippin' (C)	CTho SKee
– 'Golden Reinette' (D)	GTwe SKee
– 'Golden Russet' (D)	GTwe SDea SKee WJas
– 'Golden Spire' (C)	CTho NRog SDea SKee
– 'Golden Wonder' (C)	CEnd
– 'Goldilocks' (F)	GTwe WLRN
– 'Gooseberry' (C)	SKee
– 'Goring' (Cider)	CTho
– 'Grand Sultan' (D)	CTho
– 'Granny Smith' (D)	GTwe SDea SIgm SKee SPer
– 'Gravenstein' (D)	SDea SFam SKee
§ – 'Green Balsam' (C)	NRog
– 'Green Roland'	See *M. domestica* **'Greenup's Pippin'**
– 'Greensleeves' (D) 🏆	CDoC CSam EBre EMui GTwe MBri MGos NBee NDal NRog SDea SIgm SKee WJas WWeb
§ – 'Greenup's Pippin' (D)	SKee
– 'Grenadier' (C) 🏆	CDoC EWar GRei GTwe IOrc MBri MGos MMor NBee NDal NRog SDea SIgm SKee SPer WJas WStI
– 'Halstow Natural' (Cider)	CTho
– 'Hambledon Deux Ans' (C)	SDea SKee WJas
– 'Hambling's Seedling' (C)	SKee
– 'Hangy Down' (Cider)	CTho
– 'Haralson' (D)	SIgm
– 'Harry Master's Jersey' (Cider)	CCSL CTho CTri SDea
– 'Harvey' (C)	SDea SKee
– 'Hawthornden' (C)	CTho SKee
– 'Hereford Cross' (D)	SKee
– 'Herefordshire Beefing' (C)	CEnd SKee WJas
– 'Herring's Pippin' (D)	CTri GTwe SDea SKee
– 'Heusgen's Golden Reinette' (D)	SKee
– 'High View Pippin' (D)	SKee
– 'Hills Seedling' (F)	SKee
– 'Histon Favourite' (D)	SKee
– 'Hoary Morning' (C)	CTho SDea SKee
– 'Hocking's Green' (C/D)	CEnd CTho
– 'Holland Pippin' (C)	SKee
– 'Hollow Core' (C)	CTho
– 'Holstein' (D)	COtt CSam CTho GTwe SDea SIgm SKee
– 'Horneburger Pfannkuchen' (C)	SKee
– 'Houblon' (D)	SKee
– 'Howgate Wonder' (C)	CDoC CSam EMui GBon GChr GTwe IOrc LBuc MBri MGos MMor NBee NRog SDea SFam SIgm SKee SPer WJas
– 'Hubbard's Pearmain' (D)	SKee
– 'Idared' (D) 🏆	GBon GTwe MGos SDea SKee
– 'Improved Cockpit' (D)	NRog
– 'Improved Keswick' (C/D)	CEnd
– 'Improved Lambrook Pippin' (Cider)	CCSL CTho
– 'Improved Redstreak' (Cider)	CTho
– 'Improved Woodbine' (Cider)	CCSL
– 'Ingrid Marie' (D)	SDea SKee WJas
– 'Irish Peach' (D)	GTwe SDea SFam SIgm SKee WHow WJas
– 'Isaac Newton's Tree'	See *M. domestica* **'Flower of Kent'**
– 'Isle of Wight Pippin' (D)	SDea
– 'Isle of Wight Russet' (D)	SDea
– 'James Grieve' (D) 🏆	CB&S CCVT CMac EMui EWar GBon GChr GRei GTwe IOrc LBuc MBri MMor MWat NBee NDal NRog SDea SFam SIgm SKee SPer WJas WWeb
– 'Jerseymac' (D)	SDea
– 'Jester' (D)	GTwe SDea SIgm SKee
– 'John Apple' (C)	SKee
– 'John Standish' (D)	GTwe SDea SKee
– 'Johnny Andrews' (Cider)	CTho
– 'Johnny Voun' (D)	CEnd CTho
– 'Jonagold' (D) 🏆	GTwe MBri SDea SFam SHhN SIgm SKee WJas
– 'Jonagold Crowngold' (D)	GTwe
– 'Jonagored' (D) 🏆	EBee
– 'Jonared' (D)	GTwe
– 'Jonathan' (D)	SDea SKee
– 'Jordan's Weeping' (F)	GTwe SDea WJas
– 'Josephine' (D)	SDea
– 'Joybells' (D)	SKee
– 'Jubilee'	See *M. domestica* **'Royal Jubilee'**
– 'Jupiter' (D) 🏆	CDoC CSam CTri GBon GTwe IOrc MGos MWat NDal NRog SDea SFam SIgm SKee WJas
¶ – 'Kandil Sinap' (D)	SKee
– 'Kapai Red Jonathan' (D)	SDea
– 'Karmijn de Sonnaville' (D)	SDea SKee
§ – 'Katja' (D)	CDoC CSam EMui GBon GChr GTwe IOrc LBuc MBri NBee SDea SIgm SKee SPer WJas
– 'Katy'	See *M. domestica* **'Katja'**
¶ – 'Kendall' (D)	SKee
– 'Kent' (D)	GTwe SDea SKee
– 'Kentish Fillbasket' (C)	SKee
– 'Kentish Pippin' (C/Cider/D)	SKee
– 'Kentish Quarrenden' (D)	SKee
– 'Kerry Pippin' (D)	SKee
– 'Keswick Codling' (C)	CSam GTwe NRog SDea SKee WJas

– 'Kidd's Orange Red' (D) 🏆	COtt EBre EMui GTwe LBuc MMor SFam SIgm SKee WJas
– 'Kilkenny Pippin' (F)	GTwe
– 'Killerton Sharp' (Cider)	CTho
– 'Killerton Sweet' (Cider)	CTho
– 'King Byerd' (C/D)	CEnd CTho
– 'King Charles' Pearmain' (D)	CTho SKee
¶ – 'King Coffee' (D)	SKee
– 'King George V' (D)	SKee
– 'King Luscious' (D)	SDea
§ – 'King of the Pippins' (D) 🏆	CCSL CSam CTho CTri GTwe SDea SFam SKee WJas
– 'King of Tompkins County' (D)	SKee
– 'King Russet' (D) 🏆	SDea
– 'King's Acre Bountiful' (C)	SKee WJas
– 'King's Acre Pippin' (D)	CTho SDea SFam SKee WHow WJas
– 'Kingston Bitter' (Cider)	CTho
– 'Kingston Black' (Cider)	CSam CTho SDea SKee
– 'Knobby Russet' (D)	SKee
– 'Lady Henniker' (D)	CTho GTwe SDea SKee WJas
– 'Lady Lambourne' (C/D)	SKee
– 'Lady of the Wemyss' (C)	SKee
– 'Lady Stanley' (D)	SDea
– 'Lady Sudeley' (D)	CTho SDea SKee WJas
– 'Lady's Finger' (C/D)	CEnd
– 'Lady's Finger of Hereford' (D)	CTho WJas
– 'Lady's Finger of Lancashire' (C/D)	CSam SKee
– 'Lady's Finger of Offaly' (D)	SDea
– 'Lamb Abbey Pearmain' (D)	SKee
– 'Landsberger Reinette' (D)	SKee
– 'Lane's Prince Albert' (C) 🏆	CCVT CSam EMui EWar GBon GTwe MGos MWat NRog SDea SIgm SKee WJas
– 'Langley Pippin' (D)	SDea SKee
– 'Langworthy' (Cider)	CCSL CTho
– 'Lass o' Gowrie' (C)	SKee
◆ – 'Laxton's Epicure'	See ***M. domestica* 'Epicure'**
– 'Laxton's Fortune'	See ***M. domestica* 'Fortune'**
– 'Laxton's Rearguard' (D)	SKee WJas
– 'Laxton's Royalty' (D)	SDea SFam
§ – 'Laxton's Superb' (D)	CB&S CCVT CSam CTri EWar GBon GTwe IOrc LBuc MBri MMor NRog SDea SIgm SKee SPer WJas
– 'Leathercoat Russet' (D)	CTho SKee
– 'Lemon Pippin' (C)	CTho SDea SKee WJas
– 'Lewis's Incomparable' (C)	SKee
– 'Liberty' (D)	SDea
– 'Limberland' (C)	CTho
– 'Linda' (D)	SKee
– 'Listener' (Cider/D)	CTho
¶ – 'Lobo' (D)	SKee
§ – 'Loddington' (C)	SKee
– 'Lodi' (C)	SDea
¶ – 'London Pearmain' (D)	SKee WJas
– 'London Pippin' (C)	CTho
– 'Longkeeper' (F)	CEnd CTho
– 'Longstem' (Cider)	CTho
– 'Lord Burghley' (D)	GTwe SDea SKee
– 'Lord Derby' (C)	CMac CSam CTho EMui GTwe MBri MWat NRog SDea SKee WJas
– 'Lord Grosvenor' (C)	GTwe SKee
– 'Lord Hindlip' (D)	GTwe LBuc SDea SFam SKee WJas
– 'Lord Lambourne' (D) 🏆	CCVT CDoC CSam EBre EMui EWar GChr GTwe IOrc MMor MWat NDal NRog SFam SIgm SKee WJas
– 'Lord Stradbroke' (C)	SKee
– 'Lord Suffield' (C)	SKee
– 'Lucombe's Pine' (D)	CEnd CTho
– 'Lucombe's Seedling' (D)	CTho SKee
– 'Madresfield Court' (D)	SDea SKee WJas
– 'Major' (Cider)	CCSL CTho
– 'Malling Kent' (D)	CSam EMui SDea SFam
– 'Maltster' (D)	GTwe SKee WJas
– 'Manaccan Primrose' (C/D)	CEnd
– 'Manks Codlin' (C)	CTho SKee
– 'Margil' (D)	CTho GTwe SDea SFam SIgm SKee
– 'May Queen' (D)	SDea SFam SKee WJas
– 'Maypole' (D/Ball)	MGos SDea
– 'McCutcheon' (F)	SIgm
– 'McIntosh Red' (D)	SKee WJas
– 'Medina' (D)	GTwe
– 'Melba' (D)	CSam SKee
– 'Melcombe Russet' (D)	CTho
– 'Melon' (D)	SDea
– 'Melrose' (D)	GTwe SKee
– 'Merchant Apple of Illminster' (D)	CTho
– 'Merton Knave' (D)	GTwe MGos SDea
– 'Merton Russet' (D)	SDea
– 'Merton Worcester' (D)	SDea SKee
– 'Michaelmas Red' (D)	GTwe SKee WJas
– 'Michelin' (Cider)	CCSL CCVT CEnd CTho EMui GTwe LBuc SDea
– 'Miel d'Or' (F)	CEnd SKee
– 'Miller's Seedling' (D)	GTwe SIgm SKee WHow WJas
– 'Millicent Barnes' (D)	SDea
– 'Mollie's Delicious' (D)	GTwe SKee
– 'Monarch' (C)	CTri GTwe MMor NRog SDea SFam SKee WHow WJas
– 'Mondial Gala' (F)	WJas
– 'Morgan's Sweet' (C/Cider)	CCSL CTho CTri SDea SKee
– 'Moss's Seedling' (D)	GTwe SDea
§ – 'Mother' (D) 🏆	GTwe SDea SFam SKee WJas
– 'Mrs Phillimore' (D)	SKee
– 'Muscadet de Dieppe' (F)	CSam
§ – 'Mutsu' (D)	GTwe MMor NRog SDea SIgm SKee
– 'Neasdale Favorite' (F)	SKee
– 'Nettlestone Pippin' (D)	SDea
– 'Newton Wonder' (D/C) 🏆	CDoC CMac CSam CTri EWar GTwe MMor NDal NRog SDea SFam SIgm SKee WJas
– 'Newtown Pippin' (D)	SDea
– 'Nittany Red' (D)	SDea
– 'Nobby Russet' (F)	GTwe
– 'Nonpareil' (D)	CTho SKee
– 'Norfolk Beauty' (C)	SKee
– 'Norfolk Beefing' (C)	SFam SKee
– 'Norfolk Royal' (D)	CDoC GTwe MGos SDea SFam SIgm SKee

– 'Norfolk Summer Broadend' (F)	SKee
– 'Norfolk Winter Coleman' (F)	SKee
– 'Northcott Superb' (D)	CTho
– 'Northern Greening' (C)	GTwe SKee
– 'Northwood' (Cider)	CCSL CTho
– 'Oaken Pin' (C)	CTho
– 'Old Pearmain' (D)	CTho SDea SKee
– 'Old Somerset Russet' (D)	CTho
– 'Opalescent' (D)	SKee
– 'Orange Goff' (D)	SKee
¶ – 'Orin' (D)	SKee
– 'Orkney Apple' (F)	SKee
– 'Orleans Reinette' (D)	CCVT CTho EMui GTwe LBuc MWat SDea SFam SIgm SKee WHow WJas
– 'Oslin' (D)	SKee
– 'Owen Thomas' (D)	CTri SKee
– 'Paignton Marigold' (Cider)	CTho
– 'Paulared' (D)	SDea SKee
– 'Payhembury' (C/Cider)	CTho
– 'Peacemaker' (D)	SKee
– 'Pear Apple' (D)	CEnd
– 'Pearl' (D)	CTho SDea
– 'Peasgood's Nonsuch' (C) 🏆	GTwe LBuc SDea SFam SKee WJas
– 'Peck's Pleasant' (D)	SKee
– 'Pendragon' (F)	CTho
– 'Penhallow Pippin' (D)	CTho
– 'Peter Lock' (C/D)	CEnd CTho
– 'Pickering's Seedling' (D)	SKee
– 'Pig Snout' (Cider)	CCSL CEnd CTho
– 'Pig's Nose Pippin' (D)	CEnd CTho SKee
– 'Pig's Nose Pippin'Type III (D)	CTho
– 'Pine Golden Pippin' (D)	SKee
– 'Pitmaston Pine Apple' (D)	CSam CTho SDea SFam SKee WJas
– 'Pitmaston Pippin Nonpareil' (F)	SKee
– 'Pixie' (D) 🏆	CCVT CSam GTwe SFam SIgm SKee WJas
– 'Plum Vite' (D)	CTho CTri
– 'Plympton Pippin' (C)	CEnd CTho
– 'Polly' (F)	CEnd
– 'Polly Prosser' (D)	SKee
– 'Polly Whitehair' (F)	CTho SDea Skee
◆ – Polka	See *M. domestica* **Polka = 'Trajan'**
– 'Pomeroy of Somerset' (D)	CTho
– 'Ponsford' (C)	CTho
– 'Porter's Pefection' (Cider)	CCSL CTho
– 'Pott's Seedling' (C)	SKee
– 'Priscilla' (D)	GTwe
– 'Queen' (C)	CEnd CTho SKee
– 'Queen Cox' (D)	EMui GBon MRav SDea SIgm SKee
* – 'Queens' (D)	CTho
– 'Racky Down' (F)	SKee
– 'Red Astrachan' (D)	SKee
§ – 'Red Blenheim' (C/D)	SKee
– 'Red Charles Ross' (C/D)	SDea
– 'Red Devil' (D)	COtt CWSG EMui GTwe LBuc MBri NDal SIgm SKee WJas

– 'Red Ellison' (D)	CTho CTri GTwe NRog SDea
– 'Red Fuji' (F)	SDea
– 'Red James Grieve' (D)	SDea
– 'Red Jersey' (Cider)	CCSL
– 'Red Joaneting' (D)	SKee
– 'Red Miller's Seedling' (D)	COtt SDea
– 'Red Robin' (F)	CEnd
– 'Red Ruby' (F)	CTho
– 'Red Victoria' (C)	GTwe WJas
– 'Redfree' (F)	GTwe
– 'Redsleeves' (C)	GTwe SDea SIgm
– 'Redstrake' (Cider)	CCSL
– 'Reine de Pommes' (Cider)	CCSL
◆ – 'Reine des Reinettes'	See *M. domestica* **'King of the Pippins'**
– 'Reinette Doreé de Boediker' (D)	GTwe
– 'Reinette du Canada' (D)	CTho SKee
– 'Reinette Rouge Etoilée' (D)	SDea
– 'Reverend Greeves' (F)	SDea
– 'Reverend W. Wilks' (C)	CCVT CDoC COtt EMui LBuc MWat NDal NRog SFam SIgm SKee WJas
– 'Ribston Pippin' (D) 🏆	CTho CTri EMui GTwe LBuc MWat SDea SFam SIgm SKee WJas WWeb
– 'Rival' (D)	SDea SKee WJas
¶ – 'Rivers' Nonsuch' (D)	WJas
– 'Robin Pippin' (D)	GTwe
– 'Rome Beauty' (D)	SDea
– 'Rosemary Russet' (D) 🏆	COtt CSam CTho GTwe LBuc SDea SFam SIgm SKee WHow WJas
– 'Ross Nonpareil' (D)	GTwe SDea SKee
– 'Rough Pippin' (D)	CEnd CTho
– 'Roundway Magnum Bonum' (D)	CTho SDea SFam SKee
§ – 'Roxbury Russet' (D)	SKee
– 'Royal Gala' (F) 🏆	EMui SDea
§ – 'Royal Jubilee' (C)	SKee
– 'Royal Russet' (C)	SDea
– 'Royal Snow' (D)	SKee
– 'Royal Somerset' (C/Cider)	CCSL CTho
– 'Rubens' (D)	SKee
– 'Rubinette' (F)	CDoC COtt GTwe MBri MGos NDal WHow WJas
– 'S.T. Wright' (C)	SKee
– 'Saint Albans Pippin' (D)	SKee
– 'Saint Augustine's Orange' (F)	SKee
– 'Saint Cecilia' (D)	SDea SKee WJas
§ – 'Saint Edmund's Pippin' (D) 🏆	CSam CTho ERea GTwe SDea SFam SIgm SKee
– 'Saint Edmund's Russet'	See *M. domestica* **'Saint Edmund's Pippin'**
– 'Saint Everard' (D)	SKee
– 'Saint Magdalen' (F)	SKee
– 'Saltcote Pippin' (D)	SKee
– 'Sam Young' (D)	SKee
– 'Sandringham' (C)	SKee
– 'Sanspareil' (D)	CTho SKee
– 'Saw Pits' (F)	CEnd SKee
– 'Scarlet Nonpareil' (D)	SKee
¶ – 'Scilly Pearl' (C)	WJas
– 'Scotch Bridget' (C)	SKee WHow WJas
– 'Scotch Dumpling' (C)	EBee GTwe

– 'Seaton House' (C)	SKee
– 'Sercombe's Natural' (Cider)	CTho
– 'Shakespeare' (D)	WJas
– 'Sheep's Nose' (C)	CCSL SDea SKee
– 'Shenandoah' (C)	SKee
– 'Shoesmith' (C)	SIgm
– 'Sidney Strake' (C)	CEnd
– 'Sir Isaac Newton's'	See *M. domestica* **'Flower of Kent'**
– 'Sir John Thornycroft' (D)	SDea
¶ – 'Sisson's Worksop Newtown' (D)	SKee
– 'Slack Ma Girdle' (Cider)	CCSL CTho
– 'Smart's Prince Arthur' (C)	SDea
– 'Snell's Glass Apple'	See *M. domestica* **'Glass Apple'**
¶ – 'Somerset Lasting' (C)	CTho
– 'Somerset Red Streak' (Cider)	CCSL CTho
– 'Sops in Wine' (C/Cider)	CCSL CTho SKee
¶ – 'Sour Bay' (Cider)	CTho
– 'Spartan' (D)	CDoC CSam EBre EMui GBon GTwe MBri MGos MMor NRog SDea SFam SIgm SKee WJas WStI
– 'Spencer' (D)	CTri SKee
¶ – 'Spotted Dick' (Cider)	CTho
– 'Spur Mac' (D)	SDea
– 'Star of Devon' (D)	CTho SDea
– 'Stark' (D)	SDea
– 'Starking' (D)	SKee
– 'Starkrimson' (D)	SKee
– 'Starkspur Golden Delicious' (D)	SKee
– 'Stembridge Clusters' (Cider)	CCSL
– 'Stembridge Jersey' (Cider)	CCSL
– 'Steyne Seedling' (D)	SDea
– 'Stirling Castle' (C)	GTwe SKee
– 'Stobo Castle' (F)	SKee
¶ – 'Stockbearer' (C)	CTho
– 'Stoke Edith Pippin' (D)	WJas
– 'Stoke Red' (Cider)	CCSL CTho
– 'Stone's'	See *M. domestica* **'Loddington'**
– 'Stoup Leadington' (C)	SKee
– 'Strawberry Pippin' (F)	WJas
– 'Striped Beefing' (C)	SKee
– 'Stub Nose' (F)	SKee
– 'Sturmer Pippin' (D)	GTwe MWat SDea SFam SIgm SKee WJas
¶ – 'Sugar Bush' (C/D)	CTho
– 'Summer Golden Pippin' (D)	SKee
– 'Summer Granny' (F)	SDea
¶ – 'Summer Stubbard' (D)	CTho
– 'Summerred' (D)	CWSG SKee WStI
– 'Sunburn' (D)	SIgm
– 'Sunset' (D) 🏆	CDoC CMac CSam EMui GTwe LBuc MBri NBee NRog SDea SFam SIgm SKee SPer WJas
– 'Suntan' (D) 🏆	CSam CTho GBon GTwe MWat NBee SDea SKee
– 'Superb'	See *M. domestica* **'Laxton's Superb'**
– 'Surprise' (D)	GTwe
– 'Sweet Alford' (Cider)	CCSL CTho
– 'Sweet Bay' (Cider)	CTho
– 'Sweet Blenheim' (Cider)	CCSL
– 'Sweet Cleave' (Cider)	CTho
– 'Sweet Coppin' (Cider)	CCSL CTho
◆ – Swiss Orange	See *M. domestica* **'Schweizer Orange'**
– 'Tale Sweet' (Cider)	CTho
– 'Tamar Beauty' (F)	CEnd
– 'Tan Harvey' (F)	CEnd
– 'Taunton Fair Maid' (Cider)	CCSL CTho
– 'Taylor's' (Cider)	SDea
– 'Taylor's Sweet' (Cider)	CCSL
– 'Telamon'	See *M. domestica* **Waltz = 'Telamon'**
§ – Waltz = 'Telamon' (D/Ball)	MGos SDea
– 'Ten Commandments' (D)	SDea SKee WJas
– 'The Rattler' (F)	CEnd
– 'Thomas Rivers' (C)	CTho SDea SKee
– 'Thorle Pippin' (D)	SKee
– 'Tillington Court' (C)	WJas
– 'Tom Putt' (C)	CCSL CCVT COtt CSam CTho CTri GTwe SDea SKee WHow WJas
– 'Tommy Knight' (D)	CEnd
– 'Tower of Glamis' (C)	GTwe SKee
– Town Farm Number 59 (Cider)	CTho
– 'Trajan'	See *M. domestica* **Polka = 'Trajan'**
§ – Polka = 'Trajan' (D/Ball)	MGos SDea
¶ – 'Transparente de Croncels' (C)	CTho
– 'Tregoana King' (C/D)	CEnd CTho
– 'Tremlett's Bitter' (Cider)	CCSL CTho SDea
– 'Tuscan'	See *M. domestica* **Bolero = 'Tuscan'**
§ – Bolero = 'Tuscan' (D/Ball)	MGos SDea
– 'Twenty Ounce' (C)	GTwe SKee WJas
– 'Twinings Pippin' (D)	SKee
§ – 'Tydeman's Early Worcester' (D)	GTwe NBee NRog SDea SKee WHow WJas
– 'Tydeman's Late Orange' (D)	GTwe MMor NRog SDea SFam SKee
¶ – 'Underleaf' (D)	SKee
– 'Upton Pyne' (D)	CSam CTho SDea SKee
– 'Veitch's Perfection' (F)	CTho SKee
– 'Venus Pippin' (C/D)	CEnd
– 'Vickey's Delight' (D)	SDea
– 'Vista-bella' (D)	GTwe NBee SDea SKee WJas
– 'Wagener' (D)	SDea SFam Skee
◆ – Waltz	See *M. domestica* **Waltz = 'Telamon'**
– 'Wanstall Pippin' (D)	SKee
– 'Warner's King' (C) 🏆	SDea SKee WJas
– 'Wealthy' (D)	SDea SKee
– 'Wellington'	See *M. domestica* **'Dumeller's Seedling'**
– 'Wellspur Red Delicious' (F)	GTwe
– 'Welsh Russet' (D)	SDea
¶ – 'Wheeler's Russet' (D)	SKee
¶ – 'White Alphington' (Cider)	CTho
– 'White Close Pippin' (Cider)	CTho

– 'White Joaneting' (D) (F)	CTho
– 'White Melrose' (C)	GTwe SDea SKee
– 'White Paradise' (C)	SKee
– 'White Transparent' (C/D)	GTwe SDea SKee
– 'William Crump' (D)	SDea SFam SKee WHow WJas WWeb
– 'Winston' (D) 🏆	CCVT CTri GTwe NRog SDea SFam SIgm SKee WJas
– 'Winter Banana' (D)	SDea SKee
* – 'Winter Gem'	COtt EBee EMui LBuc MGos
¶ – 'Winter Majetin' (C)	SKee
– 'Winter Peach' (D/C)	CEnd CTho
– 'Winter Pearmain' (D)	SKee
– 'Winter Quarrenden' (D)	SDea SKee
– 'Winter Queening' (D/C)	CTho SDea
¶ – 'Winter Stubbard' (C)	CTho
– 'Woodbine' (Cider)	CCSL
– 'Woolbrook Pippin' (D)	CTho
– 'Woolbrook Russet' (C)	CTho SKee
– 'Worcester Pearmain' (D) 🏆	CB&S CCVT CTho EMui EWar GBon GChr GRei GTwe LBuc MBri MMor MWat NRog SDea SFam SIgm SKee SPer WJas WStI WWeb
– 'Wormsley Pippin' (D)	SKee WJas
– 'Wyken Pippin' (D)	GTwe SDea SFam SKee WJas
– 'Yarlington Mill' (Cider)	CCSL CTho CTri SDea SKee
– 'Yellow Ingestrie' (D)	SFam SKee WJas
¶ – 'Yorkshire Greening' (C)	SKee
– 'Young America' (F)	SIgm
– 'Zabergäu Renette' (D)	SKee
'Echtermeyer'	See ***M.* × *gloriosa* 'Oekonomierat Echtermeyer'**
§ 'Evereste' 🏆	CBar CDoC CLnd EMui GChr GTwe LPan MAsh MBlu MBri SIgm WDin WJas
florentina	CTho WMou
floribunda 🏆	CDoC CLnd CSam CTho ELan ENot GTwe IHos IOrc LBuc LHyr LPan MAsh MBri MGos MHlr MRav NBee SChu SHBN SIgm SPer SSta WDin WJas WNor WOrn
§ × ***gloriosa*** 'Oekonomierat Echtermeyer'	CBlo GQui SSta WDin WJas
'Golden Gem'	CEnd GTwe SIgm WJas
'Golden Hornet'	See ***M.* × *zumi* 'Golden Hornet'**
'Goldsworth Purple'	CTho
× ***heterophylla*** 'Redflesh'	CTho WHut
'Hillieri'	See ***M.* × *schiedeckeri* 'Hillieri'**
hupehensis 🏆	CB&S CLnd CMCN CTho ENot GTwe IHos MBri SFam SHBN SIgm SLPl SPer WMou WWat
'John Downie' (F) 🏆	CB&S CLnd CMac CTho CWSG EBre ELan EMui ENot GChr GRei GTwe LBuc LHyr MBal MBar MBri MGos NRog NWea SDea SFam SHBN SIgm SKee SPer WDin WJas WMou WOrn
'Kaido'	See ***M.* × *micromalus***
kansuensis	CLnd WMou
× ***magdeburgensis***	CLnd EBee MRav SIgm
* 'Mamouth'	EPfP
§ × ***micromalus***	CLnd GAri
× ***moerlandsii***	CLnd
– 'Liset'	CLnd COtt EBee EBre ECtt ENot GChr MAsh SFam SIgm SPer WFar WJas WStI
§ – 'Profusion'	CLnd EBre ELan ENot IOrc LHyr LPan MAsh MBar MBri MGos NBee NWea SHBN SIgm SPer SSta WDin WJas WStI
orthocarpa	CLnd
◆ Perpetu	See ***M.* 'Evereste'**
'Pink Perfection'	CLnd ENot SHBN SPer
¶ ***prattii***	CTho
◆ 'Profusion'	See ***M.* × *moerlandsii* 'Profusion'**
prunifolia 'Cheal's Crimson'	NRog
– 'Pendula'	GAri
pumila 'Cowichan'	CBlo LRHS MBri
– 'Dartmouth'	CLnd CTho CTri NRog SFam SPer
– 'Montreal Beauty'	MAsh MBri WJas
– 'Niedzwetzkyana'	CLnd MAsh
§ × ***purpurea*** 'Aldenhamensis'	CBlo CLnd SDea WDin
– 'Eleyi'	CBlo CLnd ENot EPfP MAsh MGos NWea WDin
– 'Lemoinei'	CTho EBee IOrc SDea
– 'Neville Copeman' 🏆	CDoC CLnd EPfP MAsh WJas
– 'Pendula'	See ***M.* × *gloriosa* 'Oekonomierat Echtermeyer'**
'Red Glow'	CDoC CLnd COtt EBee GQui LHyr WHut WJas WLRN
× ***robusta***	CDoC CLnd CTri EBee GTwe MAsh MBal NWea WHut
– 'Red Sentinel' 🏆	CDoC CLnd COtt CSam CTho EBre ELan EMui ENot MAsh MBar MBri NBee SFam SIgm SPer WJas
– 'Red Siberian' 🏆	SDea SHBN SPer
– 'Yellow Siberian' 🏆	CLnd
'Royal Beauty' 🏆	CLnd COtt EBee EBre GTwe LBuc MAsh MBri
'Royalty'	CB&S CLnd CTho EBre ELan ENot GRei GTwe IHos LBuc LPan MAsh MBar MBri MGos MHlr MRav SFam SHBN SIgm SPer SSta WJas WStI
'Rudolph'	EBee ENot LPan
sargentii	See ***M. toringo*** subsp. ***sargentii***
× ***schiedeckeri*** 'Exzellenz Thiel'	SIgm
§ – 'Hillieri'	CLnd CTho LPan SFam
– 'Red Jade'	CLnd EBre ECtt ELan ENot GTwe IOrc LBuc MAsh MBar MBri MGos MRav MWat NBee SHBN SIgm SPer WDin WJas WOrn WStI
sieboldii	See ***M. toringo***
– 'Professor Sprenger'	CLnd
sikkimensis	CMCN
'Snowcloud'	CLnd ENot MBri SHBN SPer
sp. CLD 417	EMon
spectabilis	CLnd
'Sun Rival'	CBlo CEnd GTwe MAsh MGos SCoo SFam
sylvestris	CKin CLnd CPer GAri GChr LBuc LHyr NBee NRog NRoo NWea WDin WLRN
§ ***toringo***	CBlo CSto
§ – subsp. ***sargentii***	ECtt ENot MBri MGos NWea SFam SIgm SPer WNor WWat
toringoides	CLnd CTho MBri SFam SHBN SIgm SPer WNor

transitoria ♀	CEnd CLnd CTho EPfP MBri SSpi WWat
– 'R.J. Fulcher'	CTho
– 'Thornhayes Tansy'	CTho
trilobata	CLnd WMou
tschonoskii ♀	CDoC CLnd CSam CTho EBre ELan ENot GRei GTwe IOrc LBuc LHyr LPan MAsh MBal MBri MGos MRav MWat NBee NWea SHBN SIgm SPer SSta WDin WJas WStI WWat
'Van Eseltine'	CLnd CSam EBee EBre GTwe MAsh MBri SIgm SPer WJas
'White Star'	CBlo CEnd LPan MAsh WDin
'Winter Gold'	CDoC CLnd CSam EBee ECtt MAsh SIgm WStI
'Wisley'	CLnd GTwe SDea SFam SKee
'Veitch's Scarlet'	CLnd CTho GQui GTwe NRog SFam SIgm
¶ × ***zumi*** var. ***calocarpa***	CLnd
§ – 'Golden Hornet' ♀	CB&S CLnd CMac CSam CTho EBre ELan EMui ENot GChr GRei GTwe IOrc LBuc LHyr MBar MBri MGos MRav NRog NWea SDea SFam SHBN SIgm SPer WDin WJas

MALVA (Malvaceae)

alcea	CShe
– var. ***fastigiata***	CArn CGle CMGP EBre ECED ELan EMan LGan NBro NCat NRoo NVic SAga SPer SRms WEas WHil
'Bibor Fehlo'	WRha
bicolor	See ***Lavatera maritima***
crispa	See ***M. verticillata***
'Gibbortello'	CHar NBro
hispida	CNat
moschata	CArn CB&S CElw CGle CKin CSev CShe ECWi ELan EOrc EWFC GCHN LHol MChe MHew NBrk NBro NMir NRoo SIde SMad SPer SWat WCla WHer WOak WPer WWye
– f. ***alba*** ♀	Widely available
– 'Pirouette'	CM&M WHen WOve WRHF
moschata 'Romney Marsh'	See ***Althaea officinalis* 'Romney Marsh'**
moschata rosea	ECha LFis MHFP NCut NNor NPer WByw WPbr
neglecta	EWFC WPer
sylvestris	CGle CKin ECWi EWFC GCHN MChe MGam NBro SMad SSoC SWat WHer WJek WPer WWin WWye
– 'Brave Heart'	ECoo EOrc GBri MLsm NPer SLod SWat WHer WRha
– 'Highnam'	WAlt
– 'Inky Stripe'	WHil
– 'Marina'	LRHS MArl MAvo MBri
sylvestris mauritiana	CHan CNic ECoo ECro ELan EMar EPfP GBri LHop MGam NFai NNor NPer WHil WRus
sylvestris 'Perry's Blue'	NPer
– 'Primley Blue'	CB&S CBot CElw CGle CHad CHan ECha EFol ELan ERav GBri GMac LFis LGre LHop MTho NBrk NPer NRoo SAxl SMad WBea WHal WOld WWin
– 'Zebrina'	CM&M ECro GBri NBrk NFai NPer SLod SMad SSoC WBea WOve WRha
§ ***verticillata***	ELan
– 'Crispa'	MChe WRha

MALVASTRUM (Malvaceae)

× ***hypomadarum***	See ***Anisodontea* × *hypomadara* (Sprague) Bates**
lateritium	Widely available
– 'Eastgrove Silver' (v)	GBri
* – 'Variegatum'	ELan SMrm
peruvianum	See ***Modiolastrum peruvianum***

MALVAVISCUS (Malvaceae)

arboreus var. ***mexicanus***	ERea LHil

MANDEVILLA (Apocynaceae)

¶ × ***amabilis***	LRHS
× ***amoena*** 'Alice du Pont' ♀	CB&S CHEx CPlN CSpe ECon ELan EMil ERea GQui IHos LCns SLMG SOWG
boliviensis	CPlN CSpe ECon ELan LChe SOWG
§ ***laxa***	CAbb CBot CChu CHEx CHan CPlN CPle CSPN ELan ERea IHos LBlm LHil LLew NPal SOWG WCot WCru WOMN WSHC
sanderi	CSpe MBri
– 'Rosea'	ERea
splendens	EBak SLMG SOWG
suaveolens	See ***M. laxa***
¶ yellow form	SOWG

MANDRAGORA (Solanaceae)

autumnalis	EEls GCal MSal WThi
§ ***officinarum***	EEls GCal GPoy MSal SMad WWye

MANETTIA (Rubiaceae)

inflata	See ***M. luteorubra***
§ ***luteorubra***	CPlN ELan LHop SLMG

MANGIFERA (Anacardiaceae)

See Plant Deletions

MANGLIETIA (Magnoliaceae)

See Plant Deletions

MANIHOT (Euphorbiaceae)

See Plant Deletions

MANSOA (Bignoniaceae)

hymenaea	CPlN

MARANTA (Marantaceae)

leuconeura var. ***erythroneura***	MBri
– var. ***kerchoveana*** ♀	CHal LBlo MBri

MARCHANTIA (Marchantiaceae)

See Plant Deletions

MARGYRICARPUS (Rosaceae)

§ ***pinnatus***	CFee ESis NMen NWCA WPer
setosus	See ***M. pinnatus***

MARISCUS See CYPERUS

MARKHAMIA (Bignoniaceae)
platycalyx See ***M. lutea***

MARRUBIUM (Lamiaceae)
candidissimum See ***M. incanum***
¶ *catariifolium* EMon
cylleneum ECha EGar EGoo EMar ERav WPer WWin
* – 'Velvetissimum' CArc CMGP EGle EGoo EOrc GMaP LHop SBla SChu SCro SHel WCHb
'Gold Leaf' EBar ECha NSti
§ *incanum* CGle CMHG EBee EBre EHal MBri NTow WEas
libanoticum ECha EGar EMon MSte WPer
supinum ECGP EMon GLil NWoo WDav
velutinum CGle EGar EMon
vulgare CArn CSev EEls EJud ELau EMar GBar GPoy MChe MHew NOrc SIde WCHb WCer WHer WOak WPer WSel WWye

MARSDENIA (Asclepiadaceae)
erecta See ***Cionura erecta***

MARSHALLIA (Asteraceae)
¶ *caespitosa* WCot
grandiflora EBee
¶ *trinerva* WCot

MARSILEA (Marsileaceae)
mutica MSta SWyc
quadrifolia SWyc
* *schelpiana* SWyc

MASCAGNIA (Malpighiaceae)
¶ *macroptera* CPlN

MASCARENA See HYOPHORBE

MASSONIA (Hyacinthaceae)
echinata WChr

MATRICARIA (Asteraceae)
chamomilla See ***M. recutita***
maritima See ***Tripleurospermum maritimum***
parthenium See ***Tanacetum parthenium***
§ *recutita* EJud GPoy MChe MGra MHew SIde

MATTEUCCIA (Aspidiaceae)
orientalis NHar NMar NOrc WRic
pensylvanica CCuc NHar
struthiopteris ♀ Widely available

MATTHIOLA (Brassicaceae)
arborescens WPer
§ *fruticulosa* CArn NMen
– subsp. *perennis* MAvo NSti NWCA WHal
incana MArl MHlr WCot WRHF WRha WRus
incana alba NBir SUsu
pink perennial CHan
scapifera CPBP MFos NTow
sinuata CNat EWFC
thessala See ***M. fruticulosa***
white perennial CArn CGle CHad CHan CMil CRDP CSpe LCot MCLN NBrk NFai NPer NTow SEND WEas WHoo WPyg

MAURANDELLA (Scrophulariaceae)
See Plant Deletions

MAURANDYA (Scrophulariaceae)
§ *barclayana* CBot CFee CPlN CRHN GCra MBri MNrw SAxl SLMG
barclayana alba CBot
erubescens See ***Lophospermum erubescens***
lophantha See ***Lophospermum scandens***
lophospermum See ***Lophospermum scandens***
* 'Pink Ice' CLTr SLMG SOWG
purpusii CPlN
'Red Dragon' CPla
§ *scandens* CPlN CRHN ELan EWes
* 'Victoria Falls' SLMG SOWG

MAYTENUS (Celastraceae)
boaria CGre CMCN CPle SArc WWat

MAZUS (Scrophulariaceae)
alpinus B&SWJ 119 WCru
pumilio ECou WCru
radicans ECou WCru WThi
reptans CNic ELan EPar NNrd NPri NRoo NWCA SBla WPer WPyg
– 'Albus' ECha ELan LHop NNrd SBla WCru WPer

MECONOPSIS † (Papaveraceae)
aculeata EHyt GCra GGGa GPoy GTou
baileyi See ***M. betonicifolia***
x *beamishii* GBuc GCal GGar WAbe WCru
§ *betonicifolia* ♀ CB&S CBot CGle CHar EBre ELan EMil GGGa GTou IBlr ITim LHop MBal MBri MDun MFir MNes NChi NHar NHol NNor NPal NRoo SPer WCru WOMN WWin
– var. ***alba*** CB&S EBre GAbr GBuc GCan GCra GGGa IBlr LSyl MBal MBri NChi NHar NHol NLak NRoo SPer SRms WAbe WCru
– Harlow Carr strain GMac
* – 'Hensol Lilac' GCal
¶ – var. ***pratensis*** GGGa
– purple IBlr
¶ – violet GCra
cambrica CGle CKin CMea CNic EBre ECWi EJud ELan EMar EWFC GTou LSyl MCLN NCat NFla NHol NMir NVic SChu SIng WAbe WBon WCru WHen WHer WOve WPer WTyr WWye
– var. ***aurantiaca*** CTri EBee EGoo ELan NBir NLak WAbe WBon WHen
cambrica flore-pleno CArc CGle CPBP CSpe EPar GBuc MTho NBro NCat WAbe WFar
– orange CHar WCru
– yellow WCru
§ *cambrica* 'Frances Perry' EGoo GBuc GCal IBlr NBro NTow WAbe WCru WOMN
– 'Muriel Brown' (d) MAvo NBro WAbe WCot
– 'Rubra' See ***M. cambrica* 'Frances Perry'**

chelidoniifolia	CFil EBre GCal GCra IBlr SSpi WCru WPGP WPbr
delavayi	GGGa
dhwojii	GCan GCra MNes WAbe WOMN
grandis ♀	CElw CGle CNic CSam GAbr GCan GCra GGGa NHar NLak NRoo NSla SBla SRms WAbe WEas
– Balruddry form	GGGa
– GS 600	GAbr GCra IBlr NBir SRms
– PS&W 5423	GDra
horridula	CNic CSam EBee EHyt GCan GCra GGGa MTho SMrm
– Rudis Group	GCra WCru
integrifolia	GCra GDra GGGa LSyl
– ACE 1798	EPot GTou
lancifolia	GGGa
§ ***napaulensis***	CB&S CSam ELan GCan GCra GDra GGGa IBlr LHop MBal MBri MNes NHar NRoo WEas WHil WWin
– ex CMC 127	GCra
– forms	GAbr NHar WDav
– red	GBuc NBir
¶ – scarlet	GCra
nudicaulis	See ***Papaver nudicaule***
paniculata	EBee GCra GGGa IBlr NBir WAbe
– BC 9314	GCra
– CC&McK 296	GTou
– compact form	GCra
– ginger foliage	WAbe
¶ ***pseudointegrifolia*** var. ***robusta***	GCra
punicea	GCan GCra GGGa NHar
* ***quintuplinerva*** 'Kay's Compact'	IBlr
quintuplinervia ♀	GCan GCra GDra GGGa GTou IBlr LWoo NBir NHar NRoo NRya NSla SBla
regia	CBot CSam EBee GCra NHar NLak NRoo SMrm WFar
– x ***grandis***	GCra
– hybrids	CAbP GTou
¶ ***robusta***	GCra
x ***sarsonsii***	GCan GCra
x ***sheldonii*** ♀	CBrd CSam GAbr GBuc GGGa MBri MFir NBir NHar NRoo SSpi
– Ballyrogan form	IBlr
– 'Blue Ice'	GTou
– 'Branklyn'	IBlr
– Crewdson Hybrids	GBuc GCra GDra MNes MOne WAbe
– 'Jimmy Bayne'	GCra
– 'Lingholm'	GCal GCra GCrs GGar WCru
* – 'Miss Jebb'	IBlr
* – 'Mrs McMurtrie'	IBlr
– 'Ormswell'	IBlr NRoo SRms
– 'Silver'	GCra
– 'Slieve Donard' ♀	EBre GCra GDra GGar IBlr MNes NHar NRoo
– 'Springhill'	IBlr
simplicifolia	GCra
sp. CH&M 1013	GCra
superba	EBee GBuc GCan GCra GGGa MBal MNes NRoo
villosa	CArc GBuc GCra GGGa GTou IBlr MOne NBir WAbe
wallichii	See ***M. napaulensis***
wallichii alba BC 9370	GCra
wallichii BC 9361	GCra

MEDEMIA (Arecaceae)

argun	LPal

MEDEOLA (Convallariaceae)

virginica	LAma WCru

MEDICAGO (Papilionaceae)

arborea	CPle ELan IBlr WHer
echinus	See ***M. intertexta***
sativa	CKin EWFC MAvo WHer
– subsp. ***sativa***	IBlr

MEDINILLA (Melastomataceae)

magnifica	LCns LRHS MBri

MEEHANIA (Lamiaceae)

¶ ***cordata***	CSte
urticifolia	EMon MHar SMrm WOMN

MEGACARPAEA (Brassicaceae)

polyandra	GDra

MELALEUCA (Myrtaceae)

acerosa	SOWG
alternifolia	ECou MAll MSal SOWG
armillaris	CPle MAll SOWG
¶ ***bracteata***	CTrC MAll
coccinea	SOWG
cuticularis	MAll
decora	SOWG
decussata	ECou MAll SOWG
§ ***diosmatifolia***	ECou MAll
ericifolia	CTri MAll SOWG
erubescens	See ***M. diosmatifolia***
filifolia	SOWG
¶ ***fulgens***	CTrC
gibbosa	CPle MAll SBid
halmaturorum	MAll
holosericea	SOWG
huegelii	SOWG
hypericifolia	CPle ECou LPan MAll SBid SOWG
incana	MAll SOWG
lateritia	MAll
¶ ***leucadendra***	MSal
linariifolia	ECou
nesophila	ECou MAll SOWG
pauciflora	See ***M. biconvexa***
platycalyx	SOWG
pulchella	MAll WThi
pustulata	ECou MAll SOWG
◆ ***quinquenervia***	See ***M. viridiflora*** var. ***rubriflora***
* ***rosmarinifolia***	SOWG
spathulata	SOWG
squamea	ECou MAll
squarrosa	CGre CLTr CTrC ECou MAll SOWG
styphelioides	MAll
thymifolia	ECou MAll
viridiflora	CB&S GQui MAll
§ – var. ***rubriflora***	MAll
wilsonii	MAll SOWG

MELANDRIUM See SILENE

MELANOSELINUM (Apiaceae)

§ ***decipiens***	CHEx EOHP LHil SIgm WCot

MELANTHIUM (Melanthiaceae)
See Plant Deletions

MELASPHAERULA (Iridaceae)

graminea	See ***M. ramosa***
§ ***ramosa***	CAvo CBre CMon CSpe EHic NRog WThi

MELASTOMA (Melastomataceae)

¶ ***malabathricum***	ECon

MELIA (Meliaceae)

§ ***azedarach***	CB&S CPle LPan
– var. ***japonica***	See ***M. azedarach***

MELIANTHUS (Melianthaceae)

comosus	CPle CTrC GCal LFlo LLew
major ♀	Widely available
minor	CFir CHEx LLew
pectinatus	LBlo
villosus	GCal LFlo LLew

MELICA (Poaceae)

altissima	EMon ETPC
– 'Alba'	CArc
– 'Atropurpurea'	CArc CCuc CDec CHan CWSG ECha EGar EHoe EMon EPPr EPla ESOG ETPC LBlm LGan LGre LLWP MNrw MSte NHol NSti WBro WCot WFoF WOve WPer WWye
ciliata	CCuc CPea CSam EBee EHoe EMon EPPr EPla ETPC GBin GCHN WPer
– bronze	ETPC
– subsp. ***magnolii***	ETPC
* – 'Pearl Eyelash'	CInt
– subsp. ***taurica***	ETPC
macra	EHoe EPla ESOG
* ***minima***	ESOG ETPC
nutans	CCuc EHoe ETPC GBin NHol WHal
penicillaris	WPer
picta	ETPC
subulata	ETPC
transsilvanica	EBee ETPC GBin
– 'Atropurpurea'	EBee NHol
uniflora	CKin
– f. ***albida***	CCuc CFil EHoe EMon EPPr ETPC WCot
– 'Variegata'	CArc CCuc CFil CVer EHoe EMon EPPr EPla ETPC GCal MAvo MBri MHlr WCot WCru

MELICOPE (Rutaceae)

ternata	ECou

MELICYTUS (Violaceae)

alpinus	ECou
angustifolius	CPle ECou MAll MHig
crassifolius	CBot CChu CPle ECou EMon MAll WHCG WSHC
obovatus	CPle ECou MAll
ramiflorus	CPle ECou MAll

MELILOTUS (Papilionaceae)

officinalis	CArn CJew CKin ECWi EJud GBar GPoy MChe SIde WHer WSel
– subsp. ***albus***	SIde WHer

MELINIS (Poaceae)
See Plant Deletions

MELIOSMA (Meliosmaceae)

myriantha	WCoo
pendens	See ***M. dilleniifolia*** subsp. ***flexuosa***
simplicifolia subsp. ***pungens***	CB&S
veitchiorum	CHEx

MELISSA (Lamiaceae)

officinalis	CArn CChe CHal EBar EFer EJud ELau GAul GPoy LHol MBal MBar MBri MChe MHew SIde SSoC WBea WEas WOak WPer WTyr WWye
– 'All Gold'	CHal CSev ECha EFol EGoo EHoe EJud ELan ELau LHol MBri MCLN MChe NFai NSti NVic SPer SSpi WWye
§ – 'Aurea' (v)	CArn CFee CHal CMHG CSev ECha EFol EHoe ELan GPoy LGro LHol MBar MBri MCLN MFir MHew NBro NFai NRoo NSti SIde SPer WBea WHil WOak WWin
* – 'Compacta'	GPoy
– 'Small-Ness'	MNes
N– 'Variegata' hort.	See ***M. officinalis* 'Aurea'**

MELITTIS (Lamiaceae)

melissophyllum	CFir CHan CRDP ECha EMan MRav SIgm SIng SRms SSpi WAbb WWye
– subsp. ***albida***	CChu SSpi
– pink	EMon MInt SOkh

MENISPERMUM (Menispermaceae)

canadense	CPlN GPoy MSal SHBN
¶ ***davuricum***	CPlN

MENTHA † (Lamiaceae)

aquatica	CArn CBen CKin CRow CWGN CWat EBre ECWi ECoo EHon EJud ELau EWFC GAbr GPoy LPBA MChe MHew MSta SWat SWyc WApp WChe WHer WMAq WOak
arvensis	CArn ELau MHew MSal SIde WHer
asiatica	ELau EOHP SIde
cervina	CBen CWat EMFW MSta SWat WChe
cervina alba	WChe
citrata	See ***M. × piperita* f. *citrata***
cordifolia	See ***M. × villosa***
corsica	See ***M. requienii***
crispa Tashkent	ELau
¶ ***diemenica***	EOHP
* – var. ***koiscikoko***	EOHP
'Eau de Cologne'	See ***M. × piperita* f. *citrata***
gattefossei	CArn
× ***gentilis***	See ***M. × gracilis***
§ × ***gracilis***	CArn EOHP EOrc GBar LHol MChe NDea NPri SIde WApp WBea WJek WOak WRHF WWye
– 'Aurea'	See ***M. × gracilis* 'Variegata'**

§ – 'Variegata'	CDec CSev CWGN ECha ECoo EFol EHoe EMar GPoy ILis MBal MBar NRoo NSti WHer WOak WOve WPer
* 'Hillary's Sweet Lemon'	EOHP
Lavender Mint	CBod GBar GPoy NPri WRha
§ ***longifolia***	CAgr CRDP ECha ECoo ELau EMar EOrc GBar LHop NSti WEas WHer WJek WOak WPer WSel WWye
– Buddleia Mint Group	ELau EWes GAbr NBus WBea WRha WSel
* – 'Variegata'	NCat NSti
× ***piperita***	CAgr CArn CSev EBar ECha EHoe EJud ELau GAul GBar GPoy ILis LHop MBri MChe MHew NNor NRoo WBea WOak WPLl WPer WWye
§ – f. ***citrata***	CArn ECha ECoo ELau GAbr GBar GPoy LHol MBar MBri MChe MHew NFai NSti NVic SIde WApp WBea WCer WOak WOve WPLl WPer WSel WWye
* – – 'Basil'	CBod EJud ELau EOHP WJek
– – 'Chocolate'	EOHP SIde WBea WJek
– – 'Lemon'	CWan ELau EOHP GAbr MBri SIde WBea WJek WPer WRha WSel
– – 'Lime'	EOHP SIde WBea
– f. ***officinalis***	SIde
* – 'Variegata'	CNat EOHP EWes WCHb
pulegium	CArn CSev CWGN EBar ECha ELau EPar EWFC GPoy LHol MChe MHew SIde WHer WJek WOak WPer WWye
– 'Upright'	CArn CBod EOHP GPoy MGra SHDw SIde WJek WPer WSel
§ ***requienii***	CArn CRow ELan EPot ESis GBar GPoy ILis LHol MBal MBar MBri MChe NRoo SDix SIng SRms WCla WEas WOMN WOak WPat WPer WWhi WWye
rotundifolia 'Bowles'	See ***M. × villosa* f. *alopecuroides* Bowles' Mint**
– hort.	See ***M. suaveolens***
rubra var. ***raripila***	See ***M. × smithiana***
§ × ***smithiana***	CArn EJud ELau EOHP GAbr GBar GPoy ILis MChe NPri SIde WBea WChe WHer WPer WRha WSel WWye
– 'Capel Ulo'	WHer
sp. Nile Valley Mint	CArn ELau
§ ***spicata***	CAgr CArn CSev EBar GPoy ILis LHol MBal MBar MBri MChe MHew NFai NNor NRoo WApp WBea WHer WJek WOak WPer WWye
– 'Crispa'	CArn CBre CWan EJud ELau EMon EOHP GAbr GAri GAul GBar MGra NFai NPri NRoo WApp WCer WCot WPer WRha WSel WWye
– 'Moroccan'	CArn CInt CJew CSev CWan EJud ELau EOHP GAbr GPoy NPri SIde WBea WCer WHer WJek WOak WPer WSel WWye
– 'Newbourne'	ELau
¶ – 'Tashkent'	WJek
§ ***suaveolens***	CAgr CArn CWGN EJud ELau GAul GBar GPoy ILis LHol MBal MBri MHew NRoo WBea WHer WOak WPer
¶ – subsp. ***timija***	WJek
§ – 'Variegata'	CArn CDec CRow CShe CWGN EBar ECha EFol EHoe ELau EOrc GAbr GAul GPoy MBal MBar MBri MChe NFai NHol NNor NSti SRms WBea WHer WOak WOve WPer WTyr
sylvestris	See ***M. longifolia***
§ × ***villosa*** f. ***alopecuroides*** Bowles' Mint	CBre EGoo GBar GPoy ILis LHol MChe NFai SIde SWat WHer WJek WOak WWye
viridis	See ***M. spicata***

MENYANTHES (Menyanthaceae)

trifoliata	CBen CNic CRow CWGN CWat EBre ECWi ECha ECoo EHon EMFW EWFC GPoy LPBA MHew MSta NDea NVic SRms SWyc WChe WMAq WShi WWye

MENZIESIA (Ericaceae)

alba	See ***Daboecia cantabrica* f. *alba***
ciliicalyx dwarf form	CNic SSta
ciliicalyx lasiophylla	See ***M. ciliicalyx* var. *purpurea***
ciliicalyx var. ***multiflora***	GDra GGGa MBal MDun NHar
§ – var. ***purpurea***	EPfP GGGa SSta
– 'Spring Morning'	SSta
ferruginea	MBal
polifolia	See ***Daboecia cantabrica***

MERCURIALIS (Euphorbiaceae)

perennis	GPoy WHer WShi
– 'Cae Rhos Llingwy'	WHer

MERENDERA (Colchicaceae)

attica	EPot
eichleri	See ***M. trigyna***
filifolia AB&S 4665	CMon
kurdica	EPot LAma
§ ***montana***	EHyt ERos WIvy
– MS 900/913	CMon
– SF 221	CMon
pyrenaica	See ***M. montana***
raddeana	See ***M. trigyna***
sobolifera	EHyt EPot
§ ***trigyna***	EPot LAma

MERREMIA (Convolvulaceae)

§ ***tuberosa***	CPlN

MERTENSIA (Boraginaceae)

ciliata	CHan EBee EBre ELan MArl MBri MRav MTol SPer SWat WPbr WRus
echioides	NTow
franciscana	GCal WCru
maritima	GPoy MHlr MSal NWCA SMer WCru WFar WOMN WWin
– subsp. ***asiatica***	See ***M. simplicissima***
primuloides	GCal
pterocarpa	See ***M. sibirica***

§ ***pulmonarioides*** 🏆	CArc CBot CBro CGle CRDP EAst EBre EHoe ELan EPot GDra GGar LAma LHop LWoo MHlr MLsm NSti SMac SPer SRms WCru WHal WHoo WWat
§ ***sibirica***	CHan CMea CSpe CSte EAst EHyt LGre LWoo MDun NTow NVic
§ ***simplicissima***	CBot CHad CLon CSpe EBre ECho EHyt ELan EMan LHop MHar MHig MNrw MTho NBir NGre NWCA SBla SMad SWas WCru WHoo
virginica	See ***M. pulmonarioides***
¶ ***viridis***	NGre

MERYTA (Araliaceae)

sinclairii	CHEx
– 'Variegata'	See ***M. sinclairii* 'Moonlight'**

MESEMBRYANTHEMUM (Aizoaceae)

'Basutoland'	See ***Delosperma nubigenum***
brownii	See ***Lampranthus brownii***
ornatulum	See ***Delosperma ornatulum***
putterillii	See ***Ruschia putterillii***

MESPILUS (Rosaceae)

germanica (F)	CB&S CBlo CLnd ELan IOrc LHol LPan MWat NDal SHBN WDin WMou
– 'Breda Giant' (F)	GTwe
– 'Dutch' (F)	SDea SFam SKee
– 'Large Russian' (F)	ERea ESim GTwe SKee
– 'Monstrous' (F)	CBar GTwe SDea
– 'Nottingham' (F)	CDoC CSam CTho EMui ERea EWar GTwe LBuc MBlu MMor NBee SDea SFam SIgm SKee SPer WJas WMou
– 'Royal' (F)	ESim

METAPANAX See PSEUDOPANAX

METASEQUOIA (Taxodiaceae)

glyptostroboides 🏆	CB&S CGre CMCN CMac EHul ELan ENot GRei ISea LCon LHyr LNet MBal MBar MBri MGos NWea SHBN SMad SPer SReu SSta STre WBod WDin WGwG WMou WNor WWat
– 'Fastigiata'	See ***M. glyptostroboides* 'National'**
* – 'Green Mantle'	EHul
§ – 'National'	CSam
– 'Sheridan Spire'	CEnd LNet

METROSIDEROS (Myrtaceae)

carmineus	CHEx
– 'Carousel'	ERea
– 'Ferris Wheel'	ERea
¶ ***diffusus***	CPlN
§ ***excelsus***	CAbb CHEx ECou SPer
– 'Aureus'	ECou
– 'Parnell'	CTrC
– 'Scarlet Pimpernel'	ERea NPal SOWG
– 'Spring Fire'	CAbb CB&S GQui
fulgens	ECou
'Goldfinger'	ERea NPal
kermadecensis	ECou LHil
– 'Radiant' (v)	NPal
– 'Variegatus'	CAbb CB&S ECou ERea GQui LHil SBid
lucidus	See ***M. umbellatus***
'Moon Maiden'	ERea
'Pink Lady'	ERea
robustus	CB&S CHEx GQui
'Thomasii'	ECon SOWG
tomentosus	See ***M. excelsus***
§ ***umbellatus***	CChu CGre CHEx ECou SOWG
villosus	
– 'Tahiti'	CB&S CTrC GQui

MEUM (Apiaceae)

athamanticum	CBos CGle CRDP CSev EFou EGol EMan EPla GCal GPoy LHop MHew MRav MSal MTho MUlv NBrk NHol NRoo SIgm SMad SMrm WFar WPbr WPer

MIBORA (Poaceae)

See Plant Deletions

MICHAUXIA (Campanulaceae)

campanuloides	CBrd CSpe EPad NChi SMrm
laevigata	EPad
tchihatchewii	CBot CSpe EPad EWll MNrw SMac

MICHELIA (Magnoliaceae)

compressa	CGre
doltsopa	CChu CFil CGre CHEx CPle GQui SBid SSpi
figo	CAbb CFil CGre EMil ERea GQui SBid
wilsonii	See ***M. sinensis***

MICRANTHUS (Iridaceae)

alopecuroides	NRog

MICROBIOTA (Cupressaceae)

decussata 🏆	CDoC CKen CMHG CMac EBre EHul ENHC EOrn EPla EPot ESis GRei LBee LCon LLin MAsh MBar MBri MGos MWat NHol SRms SSmi WPyg WWat
– 'Jakobsen'	CKen
– 'Trompenburg'	CKen

MICROCACHRYS (Podocarpaceae)

tetragona	ECho ECou EPla ESis LCon SIng

MICROCOELUM See LYTOCARYUM

MICROGLOSSA (Asteraceae)

albescens	See ***Aster albescens***

MICROLEPIA (Dennstaedtiaceae)

speluncae	MBri

MICROLOMA (Asclepiadaceae)

hereroense	MSto
sagittatum	MSto

MICROMERIA (Lamiaceae)

¶ ***chamissonis***	EOHP
corsica	See ***Acinos corsicus***
croatica	EHyt NTow WThi
rupestris	See ***M. thymifolia***

§ *thymifolia*	EMan MPla NMen

MICROSERIS (Asteraceae)

ringens	CArc EBre ECha EMan GAri GBri GBuc NTow SMrm WCot
– 'Girandole'	EBee LBuc NHol SUsu WGwG WPer

MICROSORUM (Polypodiaceae)

diversifolium	CFil CHEx

MICROSTROBOS (Podocarpaceae)

fitzgeraldii	CKen

MIKANIA (Asteraceae)

§ *dentata*	CPlN MBri
scandens	CPlN
ternata	See ***M. dentata***

MILIUM (Poaceae)

effusum	CKin
– 'Aureum'	Widely available
– var. *esthonicum*	EBee EMon EPPr ESOG

MILLIGANIA (Asteliaceae)

See Plant Deletions

MIMOSA (Mimosaceae)

¶ *hostilis*	NGno
pudica	MLan
¶ *scabrella*	NGno

MIMULUS (Scrophulariaceae)

'A.T. Johnson'	GCHN MSCN NVic
§ 'Andean Nymph' Mac&W 5257 🏆	CLTr CMea EBre ELan ESis GCHN MBal MSCN NHol NMGW NNrd SWat WBea WCla WOMN
* 'Andean Nymph' F & W 8384	CPBP
'Andean Nymph' forms	CGle
§ *aurantiacus* 🏆	CBot CFee CInt CPle CSpe EBak EBre EFol ELan EOrc ERea IBlr LHil LHop MPla NPer SDry SHFr SMrm SUsu WEas WHal WHil WPer
– orange	See ***M. aurantiacus*** var. ***puniceus***
§ – var. *puniceus*	CBot CBrk CLTr CSpe EBee EDAr ELan LHil LHop SDry SLMG SMrm SUsu
× *bartonianus*	CWGN EBee LFis WCot WFar
bifidus	CSpe EOrc LHop
– 'Verity Buff'	CSpe LHil LIck
– 'Verity Purple'	CSpe
– 'Verity Rose'	CLTr CSpe LHil
– 'Wine'	LIck
× *burnetii*	LPBA MRav NVic SRms
californicus	CHan
Calypso Hybrids 🏆	SRms SWat
cardinalis 🏆	CArc CWGN EHon ELan LGan LHop MFir MHar MNrw MTho NDea NMGW NNor SHFr SPer WBea WHer WOve WPer WWhi WWin
– 'Dark Throat'	WPer
cupreus	MBal
¶ – 'Minor'	ECho
– 'Whitecroft Scarlet' 🏆	CWGN EBre ECha ELan GDra LFis LPBA MOne NGre NHar NMen NNrd SBod WBea WPer WWin
'Eleanor'	SMrm
glutinosus	See ***M. aurantiacus***
– *atrosanguineus*	See ***M. aurantiacus*** var. ***puniceus***
– *luteus*	See ***M. aurantiacus***
§ *guttatus*	CBen CKin CRow EBre ECWi EMan EWFC GAbr GAri GBar MGam NDea SRms WBea WChe WPer
– variegated	See ***M. guttatus* 'Richard Bush'**
– 'Richard Bush'	CMea CRDP CSpe EPot LHop MAvo NCat SAga WBea WByw WCot WHal
'Highland Orange'	GAri GCHN MOne NHar NMen WGor WPer WRHF
'Highland Pink'	ECtt EMan MOne NHar NRoo SBod WGor WPer
'Highland Red' 🏆	ECtt GCHN GDra MOne NMen NNrd WBea WHal WHen WPer WWin
'Highland Yellow'	ECtt GAri GCHN NLak NMen NRoo SBod WBea WHal WHen WPer
hose-in-hose	CDec CLTr CRow EBee ECha NDea WCot WHer
¶ hose-in-hose yellow	GCal
'Inca Sunset'	EFol EWes WOMN
'Inshriach Crimson'	GAri GCHN GDra
langsdorffii	See ***M. guttatus***
lewisii 🏆	CMea ELan EMan GCra GDra GTou LGan MFir MTho NTow NWCA SRms WOMN WPer
longiflorus	CBot CBrk CLTr CSpe LHil LHop WCot
– 'Santa Barbara'	CBrk CLTr LHil SMrm SUsu
luteus	CBen CKel CRow CWGN CWat ECha EHon LPBA MBal MSta NDea NFai SHFr WByw WChe WHal WMAq WWin
* – 'Variegatus'	CRow EAst GBar GMac NGar NNrd NPer
* 'Major Bees'	CDoC EPfP GCal
Malibu Series	NNor
'Mandarin'	EBre
moschatus	CRow CSam NCat NMen WCla WEas WHal
nanus	MSto
'Old Rose'	EBee ECha
'Orange Glow'	EPfP WHal
'Orkney Gold'	NCat
'Popacatapetl'	CBrk CHal CLTr CSpe LHil LHop LIck SChu SMrm
primuloides	ELan EPot GCHN NGre NHar NMen NNrd NWCA SBod WPnn
'Puck'	ECtt GAri NCat NPro
'Queen's Prize'	WBea WKen
'Quetzalcoatl'	CBrk SMrm
◆ Red Emperor	See **M. 'Roter Kaiser'**
ringens	CBen CDoC CRow CWGN CWat EBre EHon EMFW GBri LPBA MSCN MSta NDea SPer SRms WBon WChe WHal WMAq WOMN WPer
§ 'Roter Kaiser'	SRms
'Royal Velvet'	WKen
sp. Mac&W 5257	See **M. 'Andean Nymph'**
Threave variegated	EBee GBri GBuc GCal NRoo

tilingii	CFee CHal ECho ELan GTou NLak NNrd WOMN
Verity Hybrids	CBrk ERea SMrm
* 'Wine Red'	CSpe
'Wisley Red'	ECha ECot ELan SIng
'Yellow Velvet'	WKen

MINA See IPOMOEA

MINUARTIA (Caryophyllaceae)

¶ ***capillacea***	MSto
§ ***circassica***	CLyd ESis MDHE MHig NTow NWCA WAbe WPer
juniperina NS 270	NWCA
laricifolia	LBee
parnassica	See ***M. stellata***
§ ***recurva***	GCLN
§ ***stellata***	EPot LBee NHed NMen NNrd NTow SIng
– NS 758	NWCA
§ ***verna***	CLyd NHar NHed NMen
– subsp. ***caespitosa*** 'Aurea'	See ***Sagina subulata* 'Aurea'**
– subsp. ***gerardii***	See ***M. verna*** subsp. ***verna***

MIRABILIS (Nyctaginaceae)

jalapa	CArn CSWP ELan LAma MBri MHlr NRog SEND SLMG SRms WCot

MISCANTHUS (Poaceae)

§ ***floridulus*** ♀	CSev CSte EFou EHoe GCal MUlv SApp SDix SMad SSoC WCot
nepalensis	EHoe EPla
– CLD 1314	EPla
oligostachyus	EBee EPPr GCal
– 'Nanus Variegatus'	CRow EHoe EPPr EPla
sacchariflorus	CB&S CHEx CRow CSte CWGN EBre ECED ECha EJap ELan EOas EPPr EPla ESOG ESiP GAul GFre LPBA MUlv NHol NVic SHig SPer SPla WWat WWye
§ 'Silberfeder'	Widely available
sinensis ♀	CArn CHEx CHan EPla
¶ – 'Adagio'	CSte
¶ – 'Augustfeder'	CSte
¶ – 'Autumn Light'	CSte
– C&L 143a	EPla
* – 'China'	EHoe EPPr
– var. ***condensatus***	EFou
¶ – – 'Cabaret'	SMad SRos WCot
¶ – – 'Cosmopolitan' (v)	WCot
– dwarf form	MUlv
– 'Ferne Osten'	CCuc CSte EBre ECha EFou EGar EPPr EPla ETPC MBri MUlv SApp WFar
– 'Flamingo'	CSte EBre EHoe EPPr EPla MAvo MBri
◆ – 'Giganteus'	See ***M. floridulus***
– 'Goldfeder' (v)	EBre EPla WBcn
– 'Goliath'	CSte EFou
– 'Gracillimus'	CB&S CDoC CFil CHEx CHid CRow CSte CWGN EBre ECha EFou ELan ENot EPla ESOG ESiP ETPC EWes GFre LHil MBal NBro SAxl SDix SPer
– 'Graziella'	CSte EBee EBre EPPr EPla MBri NHol SAxl WLRN
– 'Grosse Fontäne'	CSte ECha EFou EPla SMad WCot
– 'Hercules'	EFou
– 'Kaskade'	CSte EBre EPla MBri SApp SWas
– 'Kleine Fontäne'	CFee CSte EBee EBre EGar EHoe EMan EPPr EPla GBri MBri NHol SAxl SBla SChu SMad SWas WCra
– 'Kleine Silberspinne'	CCuc CLon CMil CSte EBre EFou EGle EHoe EPPr EPla ESOG ETPC GCal NHol WRus
– 'Malepartus'	CHad CLon CMil CRow CSte EBre ECha EGar EHoe EPPr EPla GCal NHol SAxl SChu SWas WCot
– 'Morning Light' (v)	CCuc CSte CVer EBre ECha EFou EMan EMon EPPr EPla ETPC MUlv SAxl WCot
– 'Nippon'	EBar EHoe EPPr EPla ESOG MBri NHol SAxl SChu SMad SMrm WRus
– 'Poseidon'	EBee EPPr SAxl
– var. ***purpurascens***	CInt CSte CWan EBee EBre ECha EGar EGol EHoe EMan EOas EPPr EPla ESOG ESiP ETPC GAri MBro MUlv SApp SMad SSoC WWat
– 'Pünktchen' (v)	ECha EFou EPPr EPla SMad SWas
– 'Roterpfeil'	EPla
– 'Rotfuchs'	CLon
– 'Rotsilber' (v)	EBre ECha EFou EGle EHoe EPPr EPla MUlv SApp SHBN
¶ – 'Sarabande'	CSte EHoe
¶ – SF 92302	ISea
– 'Silberpfeil' (v)	EPla ETPC SMad
– 'Silberspinne'	EFou EPla ESOG ETPC LHil SApp
◆ – Silver Feather	See ***M.* 'Silberfeder'**
– 'Sioux'	EBre EPla WBcn
– 'Sirene'	CSte EBre EPla SMad
– 'Slavopour'	EPla
– 'Spatgrun'	EPPr EPla ETPC
– 'Strictus' (v)	ECha EGar EHoe EPPr EPla ESOG MBri MHlr NBee SDix WCot
– 'Undine'	CCuc EBee EBre ECha EGle EHoe EMan EPPr EPla ETPC LHil MAvo MBri MUlv NHol SAxl SChu SMad SPla SUsu WLRN
– 'Variegatus'	Widely available
– 'Vorläufer'	EHoe EPla
– 'Yakushima Dwarf'	CSte CVer EBee EBre EGle EHoe EMil EPPr EPla ETPC GBin GCal LHil NHol NPSI SSoC SWas WCot
– 'Zebrinus' (v)	Widely available
sp. from Yakushima	EPla
tinctorius 'Nanus Variegatus'	See ***M. oligostachyus* 'Nanus Variegatus'**
transmorrisonensis	EBee EHoe EPPr EPla ESOG GBin SLPl
yakushimensis	EBee ECha EGle EPPr EPla ETPC

MISOPATES (Scrophulariaceae)

orontium	EWFC WCla

MITCHELLA (Rubiaceae)

repens	MHig WCru WWat

MITELLA (Saxifragaceae)
breweri CGle CHal CHan CLyd CNic ECha ECro EEls ELan MFir MSte NHol NRoo NSti SHFr SRms SSpi WBea WByw WEas WFar WOMN WPbr WPer WWat
caulescens ECha ECro GAbr LFis NBro NHol WPer
formosana B&SWJ 125 WCru
stauropetala CArc NCat NWoo

MITRARIA (Gesneriaceae)
coccinea CAbb CB&S CMac CPlN CPle CRHN CTrC CTrw ELan ERea GGGa IOrc MBal MHig MPla NSti SArc SBar SPer SSoC SSpi WAbe WBod WSHC WWat
– 'Lake Caburgua' GCal
– Lake Puye form CFee CGre ERea GQui LHop SAga SBra WAbe WCru WGwG

MITRASACME (Loganiaceae)
See Plant Deletions

MITRIOSTIGMA (Rubiaceae)
See Plant Deletions

MNIUM See PLAGIOMNIUM

MODIOLA (Malvaceae)
See Plant Deletions

MODIOLASTRUM (Malvaceae)
See Plant Deletions

MOEHRINGIA (Caryophyllaceae)
See Plant Deletions

MOLINIA (Poaceae)
altissima See ***M. caerulea*** subsp. ***arundinacea***
caerulea CInt COtt ECWi
§ – subsp. *arundinacea* CCuc ECha EFou EPla ETPC GBin LHil WPer
– – 'Bergfreund' EHoe EMon EPPr EPla ETPC GBin GCal SAxl
– – 'Fontäne' EFou EPla ETPC MSte
– – 'Karl Foerster' EFou EHoe EPPr EPla GBin GCal SApp WCot
¶ – – 'Skyracer' WCot
– – 'Transparent' CLon EBre EFou EGle EHoe EPla ETPC GCal SAxl WChe WCot
– – 'Windspiel' CLTr CRow EBee ECha EHoe EMil EPPr EPla ESOG ETPC GCal NHol NSti WChe WCot
caerulea arundinacea 'Zuneigung' EHoe ETPC SApp
caerulea subsp. *caerulea* 'Edith Dudszus' CCuc ECha EHoe EMon EPPr EPla ESiP ETPC
– – 'Heidebraut' (v) CCuc ECha EGle EHoe EMon EPPr EPla ETPC NHol
¶ – – 'Moorflamme' EPPr
– – 'Moorhexe' CArc EBee EBre ECha EHoe EMan EMon EPPr EPla ESOG ETPC GBri GCal NSti SSoC WChe WCra
– – 'Variegata' ♀ Widely available
– 'Carmarthen' (v) CNat EMon EPPr WCot
– 'Claerwen' EPPr EPla GBuc GCal
– 'Strahlenquelle' EMon EPPr EPla ETPC GCal WChe
litoralis See ***M. caerulea*** subsp. ***arundinacea***

MOLOPOSPERMUM (Apiaceae)
peloponnesiacum ECoo LGre SIgm WPer

MOLTKIA (Boraginaceae)
§ *doerfleri* CPle MBro MHar NChi SIng WWat
graminifolia See ***M. suffruticosa***
§ x *intermedia* ♀ CMea ELan LHil MHig SMrm WOMN WWin
petraea ECha EMan MWat SIgm SIng WHil
§ *suffruticosa* LBee

MOMORDICA (Cucurbitaceae)
balsamina CPlN MSal
charantia CPlN MSal MSto

MONADENIUM (Euphorbiaceae)
lugardae MBri
'Variegatum' MBri

MONARDA † (Lamiaceae)
'Adam' ECED GAbr GCal LBlm MBri MSte NTow SMad
'Aquarius' CGle CLTr ECha EFou EGle EMon MBel MSte NHol NLak NRoo SChu SCro SHel SMrm SOkh WCHb WMer WRha WRus WWat WWeb WWhi
austromontana CArc CArn CBlo CElw ECoo EWes EWll MEas MGra SIde WHer WMaN
§ 'Balance' CArc CGle CSev CWan EGar EGle EMon GCal LHol MSte NHol NRoo NSti SChu SCro SMrm SOkh WCHb WHoo WOve WPyg WRha WRus WWat
'Beauty of Cobham' ♀ CGle CHad CHan ECha EFou EHal EOrc GAbr GMaP LFis MBri MCLN MRav MSte MUlv NHol NRoo NSti SChu SLod SMad SMrm SPer WHal WMer WOve WRus WSan WWye
'Blaukranz' EFou
§ 'Blaustrumpf' CElw EBre EFou EHic LFis MArl MCli MSte NOrc NPla SPer WMer WRus
◆ Blue Stocking See ***M. 'Blaustrumpf'***
◆ Bowman See ***M. 'Sagittarius'***
bradburyana CBot CWan EMon SMrm WHil
'Cambridge Scarlet' ♀ Widely available
'Capricorn' CGle CLTr CMGP CSev EBee EFou EGar EGle EMon GBuc GMaP LHol LRHS MCLN MSte NCat NSti SChu SCro SHel SOkh WCHb WGwG WHoo WPyg WRus
'Cherokee' EGar MAvo MRav WCHb
citriodora CArn EBre GPoy MChe MSal SIde SRms SWat WJek WPer WSel WWye
– PC&H 215 CPle
'Comanche' EFou LGre SMrm WCHb

'Croftway Pink' 🏆	CB&S CGle CHid EBre ECha EFol EFou EGar ELan GCHN LSyl MCLN MGrG NOrc NRoo NSti NTay SHel SPer WCHb WHil WMer WOld WOve WRus
'Dark Ponticum'	EFol EGar EMon LRHS MCLN MGrG
didyma	CArn CJew CTri CWan EAst LHol MChe MFir MHew MSal NBro SWat WHoo WJek WOak WOld
– 'Alba'	CBot EOrc GAbr MGra MSCN WSel
– 'Duddiscombe'	CSam
¶ – 'Red Explode'	NFla
'Donnerwolke'	SChu
'Elsie's Lavender'	CHal CLTr EFou EGar EGle EMon GBuc GCal NBro NChi WCHb
§ 'Feuerschopf'	EBre EFou MSte SAga SBla WRHF
◆ Firecrown	See ***M.* 'Feuerschopf'**
§ 'Fishes'	CHid CRDP ECha EFou EGle EHal EMon EWes GCal MSte NCat NHol NLak SChu SHel SIde SMrm SOkh WCHb WHoo WRus WTyr
fistulosa	CArc CArn EBee EMon GPoy LHol MChe MHew MSal NLak NTay SIde WHer WJek WPer WWye
'Forncett Bishop'	EFou
'Gardenview'	GCal WRHF
¶ 'Gardenview Scarlet'	EFou NChi
'Hartswood Wine'	LBlm MRav SMad
'Kardinal'	CGle EFou MSte NTay SIde
'Kruisbekje'	SMrm
'Lambada'	MGra
◆ 'Libra'	See ***M.* 'Balance'**
'Loddon Crown'	CBos CLTr EFou EMon
* 'Mahogany'	CDoC CSam EFou EGle EHic EMon GAbr LHop MCLN MHlr MMil NHaw NHol NPla NRoo NSti SHel SPer WCHb WSan WTyr WWye
'Marshall's Delight'	WMer WRus
* 'Melissa'	CGle EFou EGle EHal
menthifolia	CArn EBee EGar EOHP EWll LBlm LGre MGra NLak SAga WCot
'Mohawk'	EFou EGle LFis MAvo NCat NHol SIde SMrm WCHb WLRN WRus WTyr
'Mrs Perry'	EFou LBuc WMer WRHF
'Osage'	EFou
'Ou Charm'	EFou EMon SCro SMad SMrm WCHb
'Pale Ponticum'	EMon MBel
'Panorama'	CBot ECtt GCra MBal MLsm MSal NRoo WFar WPer
'Pawnee'	EFou MUlv SMrm WCHb
'Pink Tourmaline'	LGre LRHS MBri MCli SMad
◆ 'Pisces'	See ***M.* 'Fishes'**
'Poyntzfield Pink'	GPoy
◆ Prairie Night	See ***M.* 'Prärienacht'**
'Präriebrand'	MBri SUsu
Prairie Glow = 'Prärieglut'	MBri

§ 'Prärienacht'	CGle CKel CSam CSev EBre ECha ELan GAbr LBlm MCLN MRav NBro NRoo NVic NWes SPer SSea WCHb WEas WHil WMer WOld WPer WSan WWin WWye
punctata	CArn CBot CGle CInt ELan EMan GCal MAvo MSal SIde SMad SMrm SWat WCHb WCot WHer WHil WWye
¶ purple	MGra
'Ruby Glow'	MArl MBri MTis NCat NHol NPla SMrm WLRN
§ 'Sagittarius'	CArc CGle CSev EGar EGle EMon LBlm LRHS MBel MCLN NCat NHol NRoo SChu SMrm SOkh WCHb WGwG WHoo WLRN WRus WWat
§ 'Schneewittchen'	CArc CKel EAst EBre ECED ECha ECtt EGar ELan EMon EOrc GAbr MSCN MTis NBro NOrc NRoo NSti SChu SIde SPer WHil WMer WRus WWin WWye
◆ 'Scorpio'	See ***M.* 'Scorpion'**
§ 'Scorpion'	CGle CM&M CWan EFou EMon LBlm MBel MSte NCat SAga SChu SHel SMad SMrm SOkh WCHb WHil WHoo WOve WPyg WRHF WRus
'Sioux'	EFou EWes GBuc MAvo SMrm WCHb WCot
'Snow Maiden'	See ***M.* 'Schneewittchen'**
'Snow Queen'	CMGP EFou EGle EPfP LBuc NHol SCoo SMrm SPla WSan WWat
◆ Snow White	See ***M.* 'Schneewittchen'**
'Squaw'	Widely available
stipitatoglandulosa	EBee
'Talud'	EGar EMon SMrm
'Twins'	CBod EFou SWat WHil WMer WRus
'Vintage Wine'	CLTr ECtt EGar EGle ELan EMon NFla WCHb WHal WRus WWye

MONARDELLA (Lamiaceae)

¶ ***cinerea***	CPBP
* ***nana arida***	CPBP WDav
odoratissima	CGle EMan LHol
¶ ***villosa*** subsp. ***neglecta***	SBla
viridis	EBee

MONOPSIS (Campanulaceae)

◆ ***lutea***	See ***Lobelia lutea***
¶ ***unidentata***	CSpe

MONOTOCA (Epacridaceae)

See Plant Deletions

MONSONIA † (Geraniaceae)

emarginata	GCHN
speciosa	CSpe MHul

MONSTERA (Araceae)

deliciosa 🏆	MBri SRms
– 'Variegata' 🏆	MBri SRms

MONTBRETIA See CROCOSMIA, TRITONIA

MONTIA (Portulacaceae)

australasica	See *Neopaxia australasica*
californica	See *Claytonia nevadensis*
parvifolia	See *Naiocrene parvifolia*
perfoliata	See *Claytonia perfoliata*
sibirica	See *Claytonia sibirica*

MORAEA (Iridaceae)

alpina	SBla
alticola	SBla
– CBR 180	CHan
§ *aristata*	LBow NRog
§ *bellendenii*	LBow MSto
§ *fugax*	CMon IBlr
gawleri	CMon
glaucopsis	See *M. aristata*
huttonii	CGre CHan
iridioides	See *Dietes iridioides*
longifolia	See *Hexaglottis longifolia*
– Sweet	See *M. fugax*
loubseri	CMon NRog
pavonia var. *lutea*	See *M. bellendenii*
polystachya	NRog
sp. S&SH 4	CHan
sp. S&SH 47	CHan
sp. S&SH 78	CHan
spathacea	See *M. spathulata*
§ *spathulata*	CBro CHan CMon EBee GCal MAvo MFir MHig MSto SBla WCot WSHC
villosa	LBow NRog

MORINA (Morinaceae)

longifolia	CBot CChu CGle CHan CSpe ECha ELan EMon EOrc GMac LFis MBri MFir MNrw MTis NBrk NTow SHig SMrm WEas WHal WHoo WPer WRus WWye
persica	EGar SIgm

MORISIA (Brassicaceae)

hypogaea	See *M. monanthos*
§ *monanthos*	CInt CMea LBee MBar MHig NTow WAbe WLRN WPat
– 'Fred Hemingway'	EBre EHyt EPot LBee NHar NMen SBla WAbe

MORUS (Moraceae)

§ *alba*	CB&S CHEx CLnd CMCN CPle CTho ELan ERea GTwe IOrc LBuc SHBN SPer WDin WGwG WMou WWat
– 'Globosa'	See *M. alba* **'Nana'**
– var. *multicaulis*	ERea
– 'Pendula'	CDoC CEnd ELan ERea GTwe LHol LNet LPan MAsh MBlu MBri MWat NFla SHBN SPer WDin
bombycis	See *M. alba*
'Illinois Everbearing' (F)	ESim
nigra (F) ♀	Widely available
– 'Chelsea' (F)	ERea
– 'King James' (F)	GTwe SPer
– 'Wellington' (F)	MAsh WDin
¶ *platanifolia*	MBlu

MUCUNA (Papilionaceae)

¶ *bennettii*	CPlN
¶ *macrocarpa*	CPlN
¶ *pruriens* var. *utilis*	CPlN

MUEHLENBECKIA (Polygonaceae)

astonii	ECou ELan
australis	MAll
axillaris hort.	See *M. complexa*
§ – Walpers	CPle CTri ECou EPla ESis GAri MAll MHar MUlv NCat NTow SDry
§ *complexa*	CB&S CChu CDoC CHEx CHal CPlN CPle ECou EPla ESis GQui IBlr ISea LBlm MAll MUlv NFai NRar SArc SBra SDry WCru WSHC WWat WWye
– 'Nana'	See *M. axillaris* **Walpers**
– var. *trilobata*	CPlN CPle EGar EPla IBlr SMad WCru
ephedroides	ECou MAll
– 'Clarence Pass'	ECou
– var. *muriculata*	ECou
gunnii	CPlN ECou MAll WCru
platyclados	See *Homalocladium platycladum*

MUHLENBERGIA (Poaceae)

japonica 'Cream Delight' (v)	CCuc EBee EHoe EMon EPPr EPla ESOG WCot
¶ *lindheimeri*	WCot
¶ *mexicana*	ETPC
rigens	ETPC WCot

MUKDENIA (Saxifragaceae)

§ *rossii*	CChu CLTr CRDP ECro EPla GCal NCat WCot WOld

MUNDULEA (Papilionaceae)

See Plant Deletions

MURBECKIELLA (Brassicaceae)

See Plant Deletions

MURRAYA (Rutaceae)

* *elliptica*	SOWG
exotica	See *M. paniculata*
¶ *koenigii*	LChe
§ *paniculata*	ERea LChe

MUSA (Musaceae)

§ *acuminata* (F)	LPal MBri
basjoo	CAbb CB&S CBrP CFil CHEx CTrC EHoe EOas LPal SArc SSoC WJun
cavendishii	See *M. acuminata* **'Dwarf Cavendish'**
◆ *coccinea*	See *M. uranoscopus*
ensete	See *Ensete ventricosum*
§ *lasiocarpa*	LPal
nana	See *M. acuminata*
¶ × *paradisiaca*	LBlo
§ *uranoscopus* ♀	LBlo
¶ *velutina*	LBlo WCot

MUSCARI (Hyacinthaceae)

ambrosiacum	See *M. muscarimi*
armeniacum ♀	CBro EHyt EPar ETub MBri NMGW NRog WPer WShi
– 'Argaei Album'	LAma NEgg
– 'Blue Spike'	CBro EHyt EPar ETub LAma MBri MHlr NEgg NRog WPer
– 'Cantab'	EPot
– 'Early Giant'	LAma
– 'Fantasy Creation'	ETub LRHS WCot

- 'Heavenly Blue' LAma
- 'Saffier' LAma LRHS

§ *aucheri* ♀ CNic EHyt EPar EPot LAma MFos NRog
§ *azureum* ♀ CAvo CBro CNic CSWP ELan ERos LAma MHlr NMen NRog SAlw
- 'Album' CAvo CBro EPar ETub LAma MHlr NRog WCot

botryoides LAma NRog
- 'Album' CAvo CBro CMea ELan EMon EPot LAma MBri NRog WShi

chalusicum See ***M. pseudomuscari***
§ *comosum* CBro EHyt EPar SAlw WPer
* - 'Album' EHyt
- 'Monstrosum' See ***M. comosum* 'Plumosum'**
§ - 'Plumosum' CAvo CBro CHad CRDP ELan EMan EMon EPar ETub LAma MBri MHlr

grandifolium JCA 689.450 CMil
- var. *populeum* AB&S 5357 CMon

inconstrictum S&L 19/20 CMon
latifolium CAvo CBro CMea CMon EHyt EPar ETub LAma NMGW NRog WHil WPen WPer
§ *macrocarpum* CAvo CBro EHyt EPot LAma MHig WChr
mirum EHyt
moschatum See ***M. muscarimi***
§ *muscarimi* CAvo CBro EPar LAma WChr
- var. *flavum* See ***M. macrocarpum***

§ *neglectum* CSWP EHyt ELan LAma SEND WShi
- B&S 349 CMon

pallens CMon
paradoxum See ***Bellevalia paradoxa***
§ *pseudomuscari* ♀ CMon
¶ - BSBE 842 EHyt
racemosum See ***M. neglectum***
'Sky Blue' WChr
§ *spreitzenhoferi* LIck
- MS 712 CMon

§ *tenuiflorum* EHyt
- S&L 91 CMon

tubergenianum See ***M. aucheri***
'White Beauty' WChr

MUSCARIMIA (Hyacinthaceae)
ambrosiacum See ***Muscari muscarimi***
macrocarpum See ***Muscari macrocarpum***

MUSSCHIA (Campanulaceae)
wollastonii CHEx CTrC

MUTISIA (Asteraceae)
brachyantha × *oligodon* MSto
¶ *clematis* CRHN
coccinea CPlN EOvi
decurrens CB&S CPlN IBlr MSto
ilicifolia CPlN EOvi IBlr ISea MSto SBra SIgm SMur WSHC
latifolia MSto
oligodon CGre CPlN EOvi IBlr SBra
retrorsa CPlN
- JCA 14345 MSto

retusa See ***M. spinosa* var. *pulchella***
sinuata JCA 14351 MSto
spinosa CGre CPlN MSto
§ - var. *pulchella* EOvi MSto SHFr SSpi
subulata CPlN MSto

MYOPORUM (Myoporaceae)
acuminatum See ***M. tenuifolium***
debile CPle ECou MAll SIgm
insulare CPle
laetum CAbb CHEx CPle ECou LHil MAll SMad
§ *tenuifolium* CPle

MYOSOTIDIUM (Boraginaceae)
§ *hortensia* CFil CHEx CPla CTrC EWes GBin GBuc GCal IBlr LHop SBid SSpi WCot WCru
- white LHop WCot

nobile See ***M. hortensia***

MYOSOTIS (Boraginaceae)
alpestris 'Ruth Fischer' NBir NMen NNrd NTow
arvensis EWFC
australis CArc EBur GCal GGar NChi NMen NNrd NWCA
'Bill Baker' CHan
colensoi ECou EHic ELan EPot MHig MRPP MTho NHol NNrd NWCA
explanata CFir MAvo NMen NNrd WEas
palustris See ***M. scorpioides***
'Popsy' ECou
rakiura GTou WCla
rehsteineri LBee LRHS
rupicola See ***M. alpestris***
§ *scorpioides* CBen CRow CWGN ECWi ECoo EHon ELan EWFC LPBA MHew MSta NDea SHig SRms SWat SWyc WChe WEas WFar WMAq
- Maytime = 'Blaqua' (v) EBre NSti WWeb
- 'John Beaty' LBlm
- 'Mermaid' CBen CLyd CMGP CNic CRow CWat EBre ECha EPPr GMac LHop MFir MSta NBrk NCat NNrd SDix SWat WChe WPer
- 'Pinkie' CRDP CRow CWat LHop MAvo SWat WChe WMAq

secunda CKin
sylvatica EWFC
◆ *sylvatica alba* See ***M. sylvatica* f. *lactea***
§ *sylvatica* f. *lactea* CRow
¶ *traversii* AGS 90 MRPP
uniflora CGra

MYOSURUS (Ranunculaceae)
See Plant Deletions

MYRCEUGENIA (Myrtaceae)
chrysocarpa CGre

MYRICA (Myricaceae)
californica CAgr CFil CPle GAri MAll SSta WPGP
cerifera CAgr CArn GAri MAll
gale GAri GPoy LHol MGos MGra MUlv SWat WDin WGwy WSel WWye
pensylvanica CBlo LHol MAll MBal

MYRICARIA (Tamaricaceae)
See Plant Deletions

MYRIOPHYLLUM (Haloradigaceae)

§ ***aquaticum***	CBen CHEx CRow CWGN CWat EBre EHon ELan EMFW LPBA MSta NDea SHig SWat SWyc WChe WFar WMAq
brasiliense	See ***M. aquaticum***
proserpinacoides	See ***M. aquaticum***
spicatum	CBen EHon EMFW SAWi SWyc WChe
verticillatum	CBen EHon

MYRRHIS (Apiaceae)

odorata	CArn CKin CSev ECha EEls EFer EJud ELan ELau EWFC GMaP GPoy ILis LHol MCLN MChe MHew MSal SIde SPer WApp WByw WCer WEas WHer WOak WPer WWye
– 'Forncett Chevron'	EFou

MYRSINE (Myrsinaceae)

africana	CPle EPfP SArc SBid WWat
¶ ***australis***	MAll
nummularia	ECou

MYRTEOLA (Myrtaceae)

§ – ***nummularia***	CMHG CNic EPot GAri GDra MAll MBal MHig NHar SIng

MYRTUS (Myrtaceae)

apiculata	See ***Luma apiculata***
bullata	See ***Lophomyrtus bullata***
chequen	See ***Luma chequen***
communis 🏆	Widely available
– 'Flore Pleno'	CChu GQui LHol MPla
– 'Jenny Reitenbach'	See ***M. communis*** subsp. ***tarentina***
– 'Microphylla'	See ***M. communis*** subsp. ***tarentina***
– 'Nana'	See ***M. communis*** subsp. ***tarentina***
§ – subsp. ***tarentina*** 🏆	CB&S CChe CHan CInt CLan CMHG CPle CShe EEls ELan ELau ENot ERav ESis ISea LBlm LHol LHop MBal MBlu SLMG SPer STre WAbe WDin WEas WOak WRTC WWat
– – 'Compacta'	WWye
§ – – 'Microphylla Variegata'	CInt CMHG CPle EJud ELan EPla ERav LHol MBal MPla SAga SArc SLMG SPer WHal WJek WOak WSHC WWat
– 'Tricolor'	See ***M. communis* 'Variegata'**
§ – 'Variegata'	CArn CBot CEnd CMCN COtt CPle ECtt EMil ERav LHop SDry SHBN SLMG SPer SPla STre WCru WFar WHar WSel WStI WWat WWye
'Glanleam Gold'	See ***Luma apiculata* 'Glanleam Gold'**
lechleriana	See ***Amomyrtus luma***
luma	See ***Luma apiculata***
nummularia	See ***Myrteola nummularia***
obcordata	See ***Lophomyrtus obcordata***
× ***ralphii***	See ***Lophomyrtus* × *ralphii***
'Traversii'	See ***Lophomyrtus* × *ralphii* 'Traversii'**
ugni	See ***Ugni molinae***

NAIOCRENE (Portulacaceae)

§ ***parvifolia***	CNic

NANDINA (Berberidaceae)

domestica 🏆	CB&S CBot CDoC CSam ELan GOrc IOrc ISea LHop LPan MUlv NFla NPal NRog SPla SReu SRms SSpi SSta WCru WDin WSHC WStI WWat
– 'Fire Power'	CB&S CDoC CSte EBre ECtt ELan EMil ENot EPla GAri IOrc LHop LNet LPan MAsh MGos MUlv NHol NPal SHBN SPer SSta WAbe WPat WWat
– 'Harbor Dwarf'	WWat
– 'Nana'	See ***N. domestica* 'Pygmaea'**
– 'Nana Purpurea'	EPla
§ – 'Pygmaea'	GAri WDin
– 'Richmond'	CB&S EBee ELan EMil EPla MAsh MBlu MGos MMea MUlv SHBN SPer SPla WFar

NANNORRHOPS (Arecaceae)

ritchieana	LPal NPal

NARCISSUS † (Amaryllidaceae)

'Abalone' (2)	EWal
'Accent' (2)	CQua ICar
'Accord' (2)	ICar
'Achduart' (3)	CQua EHof ICar
'Achentoul' (4)	ICar
'Achnasheen' (3)	CQua ICar
'Acropolis' (4)	CQua ETub EWal ICar LAma
'Actaea' (9) 🏆	ETub MBri NRog
'Admiration' (8)	CQua
'Advocat' (3)	CQua
'Affable' (4)	ICar
'Aflame' (3)	LAma MBri
'Ahwahnee' (2)	IDun
'Aintree' (3)	CQua
'Aircastle' (3)	CQua EHof ICar
'Akepa' (5)	ICar
* ***albidus occidentalis***	ERos
'Albus Plenus Odoratus'	See ***N. poeticus* 'Plenus'**
'Alley Inn' (4)	IDun
'Alliance' (1)	EWal
alpestris	See ***N. pseudonarcissus*** subsp. ***moschatus***
'Alpine Glow' (1)	CQua
'Altruist' (3)	CQua EWal
'Altun Ha' (2)	CQua EHof
'Ambercastle' (2)	CQua EHof ICar
'Ambergate' (2)	EWal LAma
'Amberglow' (2)	EWal
'Amboseli' (3)	IDun
'Amor' (3)	EWal
'Amstel' (4)	CQua
'Andalusia' (6)	CQua ICar
'Androcles' (4)	ICar IDun
'Angel' (3)	ICar
Angel's Tears	See ***N. triandrus*** var. ***triandrus***
'Angkor' (4)	ICar
'Ann Abbott' (2)	EWal
'Annalong' (3)	IBal
'Anniversary' (2)	EWal
'Anthea' (2)	EWal
'Apostle' (1)	ICar
'Apotheose' (4)	EWal
'Apricot' (1)	CBro
'Apricot Sundae' (4)	ICar
'April Charm' (2)	ICar
'April Love' (1)	CQua IBal ICar
'April Snow' (2)	CBro CQua
'April Tears' (5) 🏆	EWal LAma NRog
'Apropos' (2)	CQua

'Aranjuez' (2)	LAma
'Arbar' (2)	EWal
'Arcady' (2)	EWal
'Arctic Char' (2)	ICar
'Arctic Gold' (1) 🏆	CQua EHof ICar
'Ardglass' (3)	IBal ICar
'Ardour' (3)	ICar
'Ardress' (2)	CQua IDun
'Argosy' (1)	CQua
'Arish Mell' (5)	CQua EWal ICar IDun
'Arizona Sunset' (3)	IDun
'Arkle' (1)	ICar
'Armley Wood' (2)	ICar
'Arpege' (2)	CQua
'Arran Isle' (2)	IDun
'Arthurian' (1)	IDun
'Artillery' (3)	EWal
'Asante' (1)	IDun
'Ashmore' (2)	CQua EHof IDun
'Asila' (2)	IDun
'Aslan' (4)	ICar
'Aspasia' (8)	CBro
§ ***assoanus***	CBro EBre EPar LAma LWoo
assoanus juncifolius	EPot
assoanus MS 582/581/511	CMon
§ – var. ***praelongus*** MS 656	CMon
§ ***asturiensis*** 🏆	CBro CSam ELan EPar IBlr LAma WChr
'Atholl Palace' (4)	IDun
atlanticus	EHyt
– SB&L 78	CMon
'Attrus' (2)	EWal
'Audubon' (3)	CQua ETub EWal
'Auntie Eileen' (2)	CQua
§ ***aureus***	CQua
'Avalanche' (8)	CQua EWal
'Avalon' (2)	CQua
'Ave' (2)	ICar
'Avenger' (2)	ICar
'Baby Doll' (6)	EWal ICar
'Baby Moon' (7)	CMea CQua EBar ELan EPar EPot ETub LAma MBri NRog WBro
'Baccarat' (11)	ICar LAma MBri
'Badbury Rings' (3)	IDun
baeticus	See ***N. assoanus*** var. ***praelongus* MS 656**
'Bailey' (2)	ICar
'Balalaika' (2)	CQua EHof
'Baldock' (4)	IDun
'Ballyarnett' (1)	ICar
'Ballycastle' (3)	ICar
'Ballyfrema' (1)	ICar
'Ballygarvey' (1)	CQua EWal
'Ballygowan' (4)	IBal
'Ballykinler' (3)	IBal
'Ballylig' (1)	ICar
'Ballylough' (1)	ICar
'Ballymorran' (1)	IBal
'Ballynahinch' (3)	IBal
'Ballynichol' (3)	IBal
'Ballyrobert' (1)	EHof
'Ballyvoy' (1)	ICar
'Baltic Shore' (3)	IBal
'Balvenie' (2)	CQua
'Bambi' (1)	CBro ERos NRog
'Banbridge' (1)	IBal ICar
'Bandesara' (3)	IDun
'Bandleader' (2)	EWal
'Bantam' (2) 🏆	CBro CQua ERos EWal
'Barley Sugar' (3)	ICar
'Barleygold' (2)	IBal
'Barleythorpe' (1)	EWal
'Barleywine' (4)	IBal
'Barlow' (6)	CQua
'Barnesgold' (1)	IDun
'Barnum' (1)	IDun
'Baronscourt' (1)	ICar
'Barrett Browning' (3)	MBri NRog
'Bartley' (6)	EWal
'Bastion' (1)	EWal
¶ 'Beach Party' (2)	IDun
'Beauvallon' (4)	IDun
'Bebop' (7)	CBro
'Bedgebury' (3)	ICar
'Beefeater' (2)	EWal
'Beige Beauty' (3)	EHof EWal ICar
'Belcanto' (11)	CQua
'Belisana' (2)	LAma
'Bell Song' (7)	CAvo CBro CQua ERos EWal WShi
'Beltrim' (2)	ICar
'Ben Aligin' (1)	CQua
'Ben Hee' (2)	CQua
'Ben Vorlich' (2)	ICar
'Bere Ferrers' (4)	CQua
'Bergerac' (11)	CQua
'Berkeley Court' (4)	IDun
¶ 'Berlin' (2)	EWal
bertolonii	CMon
'Beryl' (6)	CBro CQua ERos EWal ICar LAma
'Best of Luck' (3)	IBal
'Bethany' (2)	EWal
'Betsy Macdonald' (6)	CQua
'Bilbo' (6)	CQua IDun
'Binkie' (2)	CBro EWal LAma MBri
'Birdsong' (3)	CQua
'Birma' (3)	ETub EWal LAma
'Birthright' (1)	EWal
'Biscayne' (1) 🏆	EWal
'Bishopstone' (1)	ICar
'Bittern' (2)	ICar
'Blarney' (3)	EWal
'Blessing' (2)	EWal
'Blue Bird' (2)	EWal
'Blushing Maiden' (4)	CQua
'Bob Minor' (1)	CQua
'Bobbysoxer' (7)	CBro CQua EWal ICar LAma MTho
'Bobolink' (2)	CQua
'Bodilly' (2)	EWal
'Bodwannick' (2)	CQua
¶ 'Bolton' (7)	CBro
'Bonamargy' (2)	ICar
'Border Beauty' (2)	IDun
'Border Chief' (2)	ICar
'Borrobol' (2)	EHof
'Bosbigal' (11)	CQua
'Boslowick' (11)	CQua
'Bosmeor' (2)	CQua
'Bossa Nova' (3)	CQua IDun
'Boudoir' (1)	ICar
'Bouzouki' (2)	IDun
'Bowles' Early Sulphur' (1)	CRow
'Bracken Hill' (2)	ICar
'Brandaris' (11)	CQua
'Brave Journey' (2)	ICar
'Bravoure' (1) 🏆	CQua EWal
'Breakthrough' (2)	EWal
'Brentswood' (8)	CQua
'Bridal Crown' (4)	ETub EWal LAma
'Bridesmaid' (2)	IBal

'Bright Flame' (2)	CQua
'Brighton' (1)	LAma
¶ 'Brindle Pink' (2)	IDun
'Broadland' (2)	CQua
'Broadway Star' (11)	EWal LAma
'Brodick' (2)	IDun
'Brookdale' (1)	IDun
'Broomhill' (2)	CQua
broussonetii	CFil
– SF 269	CMon
'Brunswick' (2)	EWal LAma
'Bryanston' (2)	IDun
'Bryher' (3)	ICar
'Buffawn' (7)	EWal
'Bulbarrow' (2)	IDun
bulbocodium 🏆	CBro CFil CMea ESis ETub LBee LBow MFos MHig NMGW NWCA WCla
– subsp. ***bulbocodium***	CBro WChr
– – var. ***citrinus***	EHyt MS&S SSpi
– – var. ***conspicuus***	CAvo CBro CQua CSam CVer EHyt EPar EPot ERos LAma MBal MBri MS&S NMen NRog NRya WChr WHil WPyg WShi
§ – – var. ***graellsii***	EHyt
– – – MS 567/ 408	CMon
§ – – var. ***tenuifolius***	CAvo CMon CQua EHyt EPot WChr
– – – × ***triandrus***	EHyt
– – – S&B 189	CMon
* – ***filifolius***	CBro CQua EHyt
– subsp. ***genuinus*** S&F 177/180	CMon
– subsp. ***mairei*** S&F 181	CMon
– var. ***mesatlanticus***	See *N.* ***romieuxii*** subsp. ***romieuxii*** var. ***mesatlanticus***
* – 'Monserrat'	EHyt
– subsp. ***praecox*** var. ***paucinervis***	EHyt
– ***tananicus***	See *N.* ***tananicus***
– subsp. ***viriditubus*** MS 453	CMon EHyt
'Bullseye' (3)	EWal
'Bunclody' (2)	CQua ICar
'Bunting' (7)	CQua ICar IDun
'Burma Star' (2)	ICar
'Burning Bush' (3)	IDun
'Burntollet' (1)	CQua IDun
'Bushmills' (3)	ICar
'Buster' (2)	EWal
'Buttercup' (7)	CBro
'Butterscotch' (2)	CQua ICar
'By Jove' (1)	EWal
'Cabra' (1)	ICar
'Cadence' (3)	ICar
'Caedmon' (9)	CQua
'Cairn Toul' (3)	CQua EHof
'Cairndhu' (2)	CQua ICar
'Cairngorm' (2)	ICar
'Calabar' (2)	EWal
calcicola B&S 413	CMon
– MS 450	CMon
'California Rose' (4)	IDun
'Callaway' (3)	ICar
'Camelford' (2)	CQua
'Camelot' (2)	EHof EWal
♦ 'Campernelli Plenus'	See *N.* × ***odorus* 'Double Campernelle'**
'Campion' (9)	CQua IDun
'Canaliculatus' (8)	CBro CMon CQua EHyt EPar LAma LBow MBri
canaliculatus Gussone	See *N.* ***tazetta*** subsp. ***lacticolor***

'Canarybird' (8)	CBro
'Canasta' (11)	CQua
'Candida' (4)	EWal
'Canisp' (2)	CQua ICar
'Cantabile' (9)	CBro CQua IBal
cantabricus	CFil CQua
– subsp. ***cantabricus*** 🏆	EHyt ERos SWas WChr
– – var. ***foliosus*** 🏆	CAvo CQua EPot LRHS WChr
– – – S&F 284/2	CMon
– – var. ***petunioides***	LAma
– – – S&F 365/2	CMon
– – S&F 396	CMon
– ***eualbidus*** S&F 362	CMon
– S&F 385	CMon
– subsp. ***monophyllus*** var. ***laciniatus***	CMon EHyt
– × ***romieuxii***	NHar
'Cantatrice' (1)	CQua
'Canticle' (9)	IBal
'Capax Plenus'	See *N.* **'Eystettensis'**
'Cape Cool' (2)	ICar
'Capisco' (3)	CQua IBal
'Caracas' (2)	CQua
'Caramba' (2)	CQua
'Carbineer' (2)	LAma
'Carclew' (6)	CQua
'Cardinham' (3)	CQua
'Cargreen' (9)	CQua
'Cariad' (5)	CQua
'Carlingford' (2)	IBal
'Carlton' (2)	ETub LAma MBri NRog
'Carnearny' (3)	ICar
'Carnkief' (2)	CQua
'Caro Nome' (2)	EWal
'Carrickbeg' (1)	CQua
'Carson Pass' (2)	IDun
'Cassata' (11)	CQua EWal LAma NBir NRog
'Casterbridge' (2)	IDun
'Castle Dobbs' (4)	ICar
'Castlehill' (3)	IBal
'Catistock' (2)	CQua
'Cauldron' (2)	CQua IDun
'Cavendish' (4)	IDun
'Cavoda' (1) or (2)	ICar
'Cazique' (6)	CQua
× ***cazorlanus***	WChr
'Ceasefire' (2)	IDun
'Cedric Morris' (10)	CBro ECha IBlr SWas
'Ceylon' (2)	EWal LAma
'Changing Colors' (11)	ETub
'Chania' (1)	ICar
'Chanterelle' (11)	EWal ICar LAma NRog
'Charity May' (6) 🏆	CBro CQua EWal IBal ICar LAma MBri NRog
'Charleston' (2)	IDun
'Charter' (2) 🏆	EWal
'Chat' (7)	CQua ICar
'Cheer Leader' (3)	CQua
'Cheerfulness' (4)	EWal LAma MBri NRog
¶ 'Cheetah' (1)	IDun
'Chemeketa' (2)	IDun
'Chenoweth' (2)	CQua
'Chérie' (7)	CBro CQua
'Cherrygardens' (2)	CQua EHof
'Chesterton' (9)	CQua IDun
'Chickadee' (6)	CBro CQua
'Chickerell' (3)	IDun
'Chief Inspector' (1)	CQua IDun
'Chig' (2)	EWal
'Chilmark' (3)	IDun
'Chiloquin' (1)	CQua
'Chinchilla' (2)	IDun

'Chinese White' (3)	ICar
'Chinita' (8)	CBro CQua EWal
'Chit Chat' 🏆	CBro
'Chivalry' (1)	EWal
¶ 'Chobe River' (1)	IDun
'Churchfield' (2)	ICar
'Churchman' (2)	IBal ICar
'Churston Ferrers' (4)	CQua
'Citronita' (3)	CQua
'Clady Cottage' (2)	ICar
'Clare' (7)	CBro CQua
'Claridges' (4)	IDun
'Clockface' (3)	EWal
'Cloneytrace' (1)	ICar
'Close Encounter' (2)	ICar
'Cloud Nine' (2)	CBro EWal
¶ 'Clouds Rest' (2)	IDun
'Colblanc' (11)	ICar
'Collector's Choice' (3)	ICar
'Colorama' (11)	CQua
'Colour Sergeant' (2)	IBal
'Columbus' (2)	ICar
'Colville' (9)	CQua
compressus	See ***N.*** × ***intermedius***
§ ***concolor***	CBro MS&S
'Conestoga' (2)	IBal
'Congress' (11)	CQua EWal
* 'Connie Number 1'	EHyt
* 'Connie Number 2'	EHyt
'Connor' (2)	ICar
'Conval' (2)	CQua
'Cool Autumn' (2)	CQua
'Cool Crystal' (3)	CQua EHof ICar IDun
'Coolattin' (2)	ICar
'Cophetua' (1)	ICar
'Copper Nob' (2)	IBal
'Coppins' (4)	CQua
'Cora Ann' (7)	CBro
'Coral Light' (2)	ICar
'Corbiere' (1)	CQua
'Corbridge' (2)	EWal
cordubensis	EHyt WChr
– MS 434	CMon
– MS 91-71	EHyt
'Cornerstone' (2)	EWal
'Cornet' (6)	CQua
'Corofin' (3)	CQua
'Coromandel' (2)	IDun
'Cosmic Dance' (3)	IDun
'Cotehele' (1)	CQua
'Country Morning' (3)	ICar
'Crackington' (4)	CQua IDun
'Cragford' (8)	EWal LAma
'Craig Stiel' (2)	CQua EHof
'Craigarusky' (2)	IBal
'Craigdun' (2)	ICar
'Craigywarren' (2)	EWal
'Creag Dubh' (2)	CQua ICar IDun
'Crenelet' (2)	IDun
'Crimson Chalice' (3)	IDun
'Crinoline' (2)	EWal
'Cristobal' (1)	CQua
'Crock of Gold' (2)	EWal
'Croila' (2)	CQua
'Crown Royalist' (2)	IBal
'Cryptic' (2)	IDun
'Crystal River' (3)	EWal
'Cuan Gold' (4)	IBal
cuatrecasasii	CMon WChr
– MS 429	CMon
– var. ***segimonensis*** MS 559	CMon
'Cuesta' (2)	IDun

'Cul Beag' (3)	CQua
'Cupid's Eye' (2)	IDun
cyclamineus 🏆	CBro CFil EPot LAma NRog SBla SRms SSpi SWas WCru
'Cyclataz' (8)	CQua
cypri (8)	CBro CQua
'Cyros' (1)	CQua
'Dailmanach' (2)	CQua EHof IDun
'Daiquiri' (3)	ICar
'Dallas' (3)	CQua
'Dalliance' (2)	ICar
'Dancer' (2)	EWal
'Dancing Partner' (2)	EWal
'Danes Balk' (2)	ICar
'Dateline' (3)	CQua IDun
'Daviot' (2)	ICar
'Dawn' (5)	CBro
'Dawn Chorus' (1)	CQua
'Dawn Mist' (2)	EWal
'Dawn Run' (2)	IDun
'Daydream' (2)	CQua EHof ETub EWal ICar LAma
'Debutante' (2)	CQua
'Decoy' (2)	ICar
'Del Rey' (1)	CQua
'Delabole' (2)	CQua
'Delia' (6)	IDun
'Delibes' (2)	LAma
'Dell Chapel' (3)	EHof ICar
'Delnashaugh' (4)	CQua ICar
'Delos' (3)	CQua
'Delphin Hill' (4)	IBal
'Delta Flight' (6)	IDun
'Delta Wings' (6)	IDun
'Demand' (2)	ICar
'Derryboy' (3)	IBal
'Desdemona' (2)	EWal NRog
'Desert Bells' (7)	CQua
'Desert Rose' (2)	ICar
¶ 'Diane' (6)	EWal
'Diatone' (4)	IDun
'Dick Wilden' (4)	EWal LAma
'Dickcissel' (7)	CBro CQua ICar
'Dimity' (3)	CQua
'Dimple' (9)	IDun
'Dinkie' (3)	CBro
'Discovery' (4)	ICar
'Dispatch Box' (1)	IDun
'Diversion' (3)	ICar
'Divertimento' (7)	ICar
'Doctor Alexander Fleming' (2)	EWal
'Doctor Hugh' (3)	CQua EHof EWal IDun
'Dolly Mollinger' (11)	EWal ICar LAma
'Don Carlos' (2)	ICar
'Dorchester' (4)	IDun
'Double Blush' (4)	ICar
◆ 'Double Campernella'	See ***N.*** × ***odorus*** **'Double Campernelle'**
'Double Diamond' (4)	CQua
'Double Fashion' (4)	EWal
Double Roman (4)	CQua
¶ 'Doubleday' (4)	IDun
'Doubtful' (3)	CQua ICar
'Dove of Peace' (6)	IBal
'Dove Wings' (6) 🏆	CBro CQua EWal IBal ICar LAma
'Dovekie' (12)	ICar
'Dover Cliffs' (2)	CQua
'Downpatrick' (1)	CQua ICar
'Dream Castle' (3)	EWal
'Drenagh' (2)	ICar

'Drumadarragh' (1)	ICar
'Drumawillan' (2)	ICar
'Drumbeg' (2)	IBal
'Drumboe' (2)	CQua
'Drumlin' (3)	IBal
'Drumnabreeze' (2)	ICar
'Drumrunie' (2)	ICar
dubius var. ***dubius*** MS 512	CMon
'Duet' (4)	EWal
'Dulcimer' (9)	CQua
¶ 'Dunadry Inn' (4)	IDun
'Dunkery' (4)	IDun
'Dunmurry' (1)	CQua
'Dunskey' (3)	CQua
'Dutch Master' (1)	ETub EWal LAma MBri NRog
'Dynamite' (2)	EWal
'Earendil' (2)	IDun
'Early Blossom' (1)	ICar
'Early Splendour' (8)	CQua LAma
'Earthlight' (3)	EHof
'East Wind' (1)	ICar
'Easter Bonnet' (2)	ETub LAma
'Easter Moon' (2)	EHof ICar
¶ 'Eastern Dawn' (2)	EWal
'Eastertide' (4)	CQua
'Eaton Park' (3)	IDun
'Eaton Song' (12)	CBro CQua
'Eclat' (2)	ICar
'Edge Grove' (2)	ICar
'Edward Buxton' (3)	LAma MBri
'Egard' (11)	CQua EWal
'Egg Nog' (4)	ICar
'Eland' (7)	CQua IDun
'Elburton' (2)	CQua
elegans var. ***elegans*** S&F 316	CMon
'Elf' (2)	CBro CQua
'Elfin Gold' (6)	IDun
'Elizabeth Ann' (6)	CQua IDun
'Elka' (1)	CQua IBal ICar
'Elmley Castle' (1)	EHof
'Elphin' (4)	CQua ICar
'Elrond' (6)	CQua IDun
'Elven Lady' (2)	IDun
'Elvira' (8)	CBro CQua
'Elwing' (6)	IDun
'Elysian Fields' (2)	EWal
'Emily' (2)	CQua IBal ICar
'Eminent' (3)	CQua EWal
'Emperor's Waltz' (6)	CQua
'Empress of Ireland' (1) 🏆	CQua EHof EWal IBal IDun
'Englander' (6)	EPot
'Ensemble' (4)	CQua
'Entrancement' (1)	CQua EWal
'Erlicheer' (4)	CQua
'Eskylane' (2)	ICar
'Estrella' (3)	CQua
'Estremadura' (2)	ICar
'Ethereal Beauty' (2)	IDun
'Ethos' (1)	IDun
'Euphony' (2)	EHof
'Euryalus' (1)	CQua
'Evendine' (2)	EWal
'Everglades' (4)	IDun
'Everpink' (2)	CQua
'Exalted' (2)	ICar
'Exemplar' (1)	EWal
'Eye Level' (9)	IBal
'Eyecatcher' (3)	ICar
§ 'Eystettensis' (4)	CBro CQua ECha IBlr
'Fair Prospect' (2)	CQua EHof ICar
'Fairgreen' (3)	ICar
'Fairhead' (9)	CQua IBal
'Fairsel' (3)	IBal
'Fairy Chimes' (5)	CBro CQua
'Fairy Footsteps' (3)	IBal ICar
'Fairy Island' (3)	ICar
'Fairy Spell' (3)	IBal
'Falconet' (8)	CBro CQua EWal
'Falstaff' (2)	CQua EHof EWal ICar
'Fanad Head' (9)	IBal
'Far Country' (2)	CQua ICar
'Faro' (1)	IBal
'Farranfad' (2)	IBal
'Fastidious' (2)	CQua
'Favor Royal' (3)	IBal
'Favourite' (2)	EWal
'February Gold' (6) 🏆	CAvo CBro CNic EBar EPar ETub EWal IBal LAma LBow MBri NBir NMGW NRog SRms WShi
'February Silver' (6)	CBro EPar ETub EWal LAma NMGW NRog WShi
'Feeling Lucky' (2) 🏆	EWal
'Felindre' (9)	CQua EWal IBal
'Feock' (3)	CQua
fernandesii	CBro CMon EHic EHyt WChr
'Ferndown' (3)	CQua EHof IDun
'Festivity' (2)	CQua EWal
'ffitch's Ffolly' (2)	CQua
'Fieldfare' (3)	ICar
'Fiji' (4)	ICar
'Filly' (2)	EWal
'Fine Gold' (1)	CQua
'Fionn' (2)	ICar
'Fire Raiser' (2)	ICar
'Firestorm' (2)	IBal
'First Hope' (6)	CQua
'Flaming Meteor' (2)	ICar
'Flirt' (6)	CQua ICar
'Flomay' (7)	CBro
'Florida Manor' (3)	IBal
'Flower Carpet' (1)	LAma
'Flower Drift' (4)	LAma
'Flower Record' (2)	LAma
'Fly Half' (2)	CQua
'Flycatcher' (7)	CQua
'Flying Saucer' (2)	EWal
'Focal Point' (2)	ICar
'Fool's Gold' (4)	ICar
'Foray' (2)	EWal
'Foresight' (1)	ICar LAma
'Forge Mill' (2)	CQua ICar
'Fort Knox' (1)	EWal
'Fortissimo' (2)	ETub
'Fortune' (2)	EWal LAma NRog
'Foundling' (6)	CBro CQua EHof EWal IBal ICar IDun
'Foxfire' (2)	ICar
'Fragrant Breeze'	EWal
'Fragrant Rose' (2)	CQua EWal ICar IDun
¶ 'Francolin' (1)	IDun
'Frank's Fancy' (9)	IBal
'Fresh Season' (12)	CQua
'Fresno' (3)	IDun
'Frigid' (3)	EHof IBal ICar
'Frolic' (2)	EWal
'Front Royal' (2)	CQua ICar
'Frostbite' (4)	IBal
'Frostkist' (6)	CBro CQua
'Frou-frou' (4)	ICar
'Fruit Cup' (7)	CQua
'Fuego' (2)	ICar
'Fulwell' (4)	IDun

'Furnace Creek' (2)	IDun
¶ 'Fynbos' (3)	IDun
'Gabriël Kleiberg' (11)	ICar
gaditanus (10)	CBro CMon
– MS 526/633	CMon
'Galway' (2)	EWal
'Garden News' (3)	IDun
'Garden Princess' (6)	CBro LAma
'Gay Cavalier' (4)	CQua
'Gay Kybo' (4)	CQua IDun
'Gay Mood' (2)	EWal
'Gay Song' (4)	CQua ICar
'Gay Time' (4)	EWal
gayi	CQua
'Geevor' (4)	CQua
genuinus × 'Jessamy'	EHyt
'George's Pink' (2)	ICar
'Georgie Girl' (6)	CQua IDun
'Geranium' (8)	CBro CQua ETub EWal LAma MBri NRog
'Gettysburg' (2)	CQua EHof
'Gigantic Star' (2)	EWal LAma MBri
'Gilda' (2)	IBal
'Gin and Lime' (1)	CQua EHof ICar IDun
'Gipsy Queen' (1)	CQua
'Gironde' (11)	CQua
'Glasnevin' (2)	ICar
'Glaston' (2)	ICar
'Glen Clova' (2)	CQua EHof
'Glenamoy' (1)	ICar
'Glendermott' (2)	ICar
'Glendun' (3)	ICar
'Glenfarclas' (1/2)	EHof ICar
'Glenganagh' (4)	ICar
'Glenside' (2)	CQua EHof
'Gloriosus' (8)	CQua
'Glowing Red' (4)	CQua
'Gold Bond' (2)	IDun
'Gold Bullion' (1)	ICar
'Gold Convention' (2)	CQua IDun
'Gold Medal' (1)	EWal LAma
'Gold Mine' (2)	IBal
'Gold Phantom' (1)	ICar
'Gold Strike' (1)	ICar
'Golden Amber' (2)	CQua IBal ICar
'Golden Aura' (2)	CQua EHof EWal IBal ICar IDun
'Golden Bear' (4)	IDun
¶ 'Golden Bells' (12)	EWal WHil
'Golden Cycle' (6)	CQua
'Golden Dawn' (8) 🏆	CQua EWal
'Golden Ducat' (4)	EWal ICar LAma MBri NRog
'Golden Girl' (1)	ICar
'Golden Halo' (2)	IBal ICar
'Golden Harvest' (1)	LAma MBri NRog
'Golden Jewel' (2)	EHof ICar IDun
'Golden Joy' (2)	CQua ICar IDun
'Golden Orchid' (11)	LAma
'Golden Perfection' (7)	LAma
'Golden Radiance' (1)	IBal
'Golden Rapture' (1) 🏆	CQua
'Golden Riot' (1)	EWal
¶ 'Golden Sceptre' (7)	CBro
'Golden Sheen' (2)	IDun
'Golden Sovereign' (1)	IBal
'Golden Strand' (2)	IBal
'Golden Topaz' (2)	IBal
'Golden Vale' (1)	CQua
'Golden Wings' (6)	IBal
'Goldfinger' (1)	IDun
'Goldsithney' (2)	CBro
'Golly' (4)	EWal
'Good Measure' (2)	EWal
'Goose Green' (3)	IBal
'Gossamer' (3)	EWal
'Gouache'	EWal
'Gourmet' (1)	LAma
'Grace Note' (3)	CQua ICar
gracilis	See ***N.*** × ***tenuior***
'Gracious Lady' (2)	IDun
graellsii	See ***N. bulbocodium*** subsp. ***bulbocodium*** var. ***graellsii***
'Grand Monarque' (8)	CQua
'Grand Primo Citronière' (8)	CQua
'Grand Prospect' (2)	CQua
'Grand Soleil d'Or' (8)	CQua LAma NRog
'Gransha' (3)	IBal
'Green Bridge' (3)	ICar
'Green Glens' (2)	ICar
'Green Gold' (2)	EWal
'Green Lodge' (9)	IBal
'Greenfinch' (3)	ICar
'Greenlet' (6)	CQua
'Greenodd' (3)	CQua
'Greenpark' (9)	IBal
'Greenstar' (4)	EWal
'Gresham' (4)	CQua IDun
'Grey Lady' (3)	ICar
'Gribben Head' (4)	CQua
'Grosvenor' (4)	IDun
'Gwennap' (1)	CQua
'Gwinear' (2)	CQua
'Halley's Comet' (3)	CQua IDun
'Hallworthy' (2)	CQua
'Halolight' (2)	EWal
'Halstock' (2)	IDun
'Halvose' (8)	CBro
'Hambledon' (2)	CQua EHof IDun
'Hammoon' (3)	EWal
'Happy Face' (2)	ICar
'Harmony Bells' (5)	CQua ICar
'Hartington' (2)	CQua
'Hartlebury' (3)	CQua
* 'Hat' (10)	SWas
'Hawaii' (4)	IBal
¶ 'Hawangi' (3)	IDun
'Hawera' (5) 🏆	CAvo CBro CMea CQua EPar EPot ETub EWal LAma MBri MBro MRPP NMGW NRog WHil
'Haye'	CQua
'Heart's Desire' (4)	EWal
'Heat Haze' (2)	ICar
hedraeanthus	EPot
– MS 543/419	CMon
'Helen's Tower' (2)	IBal
hellenicus	CQua
henriquesii	See ***N. jonquilla*** var. ***henriquesii***
'Hero' (1)	CQua EWal IDun
'Hesla' (7)	CBro ICar
'Hessenford' (2)	CQua
'Hexameter' (9)	CQua
'Hexworthy' (3)	CQua
'High Note' (7)	EWal
'High Society' (2)	CQua EWal IDun
'Highfield Beauty' (8)	CQua EWal IDun
'Highland Wedding' (2)	ICar
'Highlite' (2)	ICar
'Highway Song' (2)	ICar
'Hilford' (2)	IBal
'Hill Head' (9)	IBal
'Hillstar' (7)	CQua
'Hilltown' (2)	IBal

'Holiday Fashion' (2)	EWal
'Holland Sensation' (1)	LAma
'Hollypark' (3)	IBal
'Homage' (2)	EWal
'Honey Guide' (5)	CQua
'Honeybird' (1)	CQua EWal ICar
¶ 'Honolulu' (4)	EWal
'Hoopoe' (8)	CBro CQua ICar
'Hope' (4)	EWal
'Horace' (9)	ICar
'Horn of Plenty' (5)	CQua
'Hors d'Oeuvre' (8)	CBro
'Hot Gossip' (2)	CQua EHof
'Hot Toddy' (4)	ICar
'Hotspur' (2)	CQua
* ***humilis humilis*** AB&S 4301	CMon
* – ***mauretanicus*** S&F 260	CMon
¶ 'Ice Dancer' (2)	IDun
'Ice Follies' (2) 🏆	ETub EWal LAma MBri NRog
'Ice King' (4)	EWal
'Ice Wings' (5)	CAvo CBro CQua EWal IDun
'Idless' (1)	CQua
'Immaculate' (2)	CQua ICar
'Inara' (4)	CQua
'Inca' (6)	CQua
'Indian Maid' (7)	CQua
'Indora' (4)	CQua
'Inglescombe' (4)	LAma
'Ingrid Evensen' (2)	CQua
'Initiation' (1)	ICar
'Innis Beg' (2)	ICar
'Inniswood' (1)	ICar
'Interloper' (6)	IDun
§ x ***intermedius***	CBro
'Interval' (2)	IBal
'Intrigue' (7)	ICar IDun
'Inverpolly' (2)	EHof ICar
'Ireland's Eye' (9)	IBal
'Irene Copeland' (4)	EWal
'Irish Light' (2)	CQua ICar
'Irish Linen' (3)	EHof ICar
'Irish Luck' (1)	EWal LAma
'Irish Minstrel' (2) 🏆	CQua
'Irish Mist' (2)	CQua ICar
'Irish Nymph' (3)	ICar
'Irish Ranger' (3)	ICar
'Irish Rover' (2)	EHof
'Irish Splendour' (3)	ICar
'Islander' (4)	ICar
'Islandhill' (3)	IBal
'It's True' (1)	EWal
'Itzim' (6)	CAvo CBro CQua
jacetanus MS 580	CMon
'Jack Snipe' (6)	CAvo CBro CNic CQua EBar EPot ERos ETub EWal LAma LBow MBri NRog WShi
¶ 'Jackadee' (2)	IDun
¶ 'Jacobin' (1)	IDun
'Jamage' (8)	CQua
'Jamaica Inn' (4)	CQua
'Jambo' (2)	IDun
'Jamboree' (2)	CQua
'Jamestown' (3)	IBal
'Jana' (6)	CQua ICar
'Janis Babson' (2)	ICar
'Jennie Tait' (2)	ICar
'Jenny' (6) 🏆	CAvo CBro CQua EPar EPot ETub EWal IBal ICar LAma NBir NRog SUsu WBro
'Jessamy' (12)	EHyt
'Jetfire' (6)	CBro CQua EWal ICar IDun LAma
'Jewel Song' (2)	ICar
'Jezebel' (3)	CBro
'Johanna' (5)	CBro
'John Ballance' (1)	IBal
'John Daniel' (4)	CQua
'John of Salisbury' (2)	EWal
§ 'Jolity' (2)	EWal
jonquilla 🏆	CAvo CBro CQua EPar EPot LAma LBow MHig MSto NRog WHil WShi
§ – var. ***henriquesii***	CBro CFil
– – MS 455	CMon
– var. ***jonquilla*** B&S 420	CMon
– var. ***stellaris*** MS 466	CMon
'Joppa' (7)	CQua
'Joseph Macleod' (1)	EWal
'Joy'	See ***N.* 'Jolity'**
'Joy Bishop'	See ***N. romieuxii* 'Joy Bishop'**
'Joybell' (6)	CQua
'Jubilation' (2)	EWal
'Jules Verne'	LAma
'Julia Jane'	See ***N. romieuxii* 'Julia Jane'**
'Jumblie' (12)	CBro CMea CQua EHyt EPot EWal LAma MBri NRog WShi
'Jumbo Gold' (1)	IDun
juncifolius	See ***N. assoanus***
'June Lake' (2)	IDun
'Kamau' (9)	IDun
'Karachi' (2)	CQua
'Karamudli' (1)	CQua
'Kaydee'	CQua IDun
'Kea' (6)	CQua
'Keats' (9)	CBro CQua ICar
'Kebaya' (2)	IDun
'Kehelland' (4)	CBro
'Kelanne' (2)	IDun
'Kenbane Head' (9)	IBal
'Kenellis' (12)	CBro
'Ken's Favourite' (2)	CQua
'Kernow' (2)	CQua
'Kidling' (7)	CQua
'Kildrum' (3)	EWal ICar
'Kilkenny' (1)	EWal
'Killara' (8)	CQua
'Killearnan' (9)	CQua
'Killeen' (2)	IBal
'Killyleagh' (3)	IBal
'Kilmood' (2)	IBal
'Kiltonga' (2)	IBal
'Kilworth' (2)	EWal LAma
'Kimmeridge' (3)	CQua
'Kindled' (2)	ICar
'King Alfred' (1)	LAma
'King Size' (11)	CQua
'Kinglet' (7)	ICar
'King's Bridge' (1)	IDun
'King's Grove' (1)	CQua IDun
'King's Pipe' (2)	CQua
'King's Stag' (1)	ICar IDun
'Kingscourt' (1) 🏆	CQua ICar
'Kirkcubbin' (3)	IBal
'Kirkinriola' (3)	ICar
'Kirklington' (2)	CQua
'Kissproof' (2)	EWal LAma
'Kitty' (6)	CBro
'Klamath' (2)	EWal
'Knockanure' (2)	ICar
'Knocklayde' (3)	ICar
'Krakatoa' (2)	EWal
'La Vella' (2)	IDun

'Ladies' Choice' (7)	IDun
'Lady Ann' (2)	IDun
'Lady Emily' (2)	IBal
'Lady Serena' (9)	CQua
'Lake Tahoe' (2)	IDun
'Lamanva' (2)	CQua
'Lamerton' (2)	CQua
'L'Amour'	See *N.* **'Madelaine'**
'Lanarth' (7)	CBro
'Lancaster' (3)	CQua IBal
'Landmark' (2)	EWal
'Lapwing' (5)	CBro CQua EWal
'Larkelly' (6)	CBro CQua
'Larkfield' (2)	ICar
'Larkhill' (2)	CQua
'Larkwhistle' (6) 🏆	CBro
'Last Promise' (1)	ICar
'Last Word' (3)	EWal
'Latchley' (2)	CQua
'Late Call' (3)	IBal
'Lavender Lass' (6)	CQua
'Lee Moor' (1)	CQua
'Lemon Beauty' (11)	EWal
'Lemon Cloud' (1)	EWal
'Lemon Heart' (5)	CBro
'Lemon Silk' (6)	CQua
'Lemonade' (3)	CQua
'Lennymore' (2)	IDun
'Leonaine' (2)	EWal
'Leslie Hill' (1)	ICar
'Lewannick' (2)	CQua
'Liberty Bells' (5)	CBro CQua EWal LAma MBri NRog
'Lichfield' (3)	EWal
'Lighthouse' (3)	IDun
'Lilac Charm' (6)	CQua IDun
'Lilac Hue' (6)	CBro IDun
'Lillande' (4)	ICar
'Limbo' (2)	CQua EWal IDun
'Limegrove' (3)	EHof
'Limehurst' (2)	CQua
'Limelight' (1)	EWal
'Limerick' (3)	EWal
'Lintie' (7)	CBro CQua EWal LAma MBri NRog
'Lionheart' (4)	EWal
'Lisanore' (2)	ICar
'Lisbarnett' (3)	IBal
'Lisnamulligan' (3)	IBal
¶ 'Lisnamurrican' (2)	ICar
'Lisrenny' (1)	ICar
'Little Beauty' (1)	CAvo CBro CQua EPot LAma
'Little Dancer' (1)	CBro
'Little Gem' (1)	CAvo CBro CQua EPot LAma NRog
'Little Princess' (6)	ICar
'Little Rusky' (7)	CQua
'Little Sentry' (7)	CBro CQua
'Little Soldier' (12)	CQua
'Little Spell' (1)	CBro CQua
'Little Witch' (6)	CAvo CBro CQua EPot ERos ETub EWal LAma MBri NRog
'Lizard Light' (2)	EWal
lobularis	See ***N. pseudonarcissus* 'Lobularis'**
'Loch Assynt' (3)	CQua ICar
'Loch Brora' (2)	CQua ICar
'Loch Carron' (2)	ICar
'Loch Fada' (2)	CQua
'Loch Hope' (2)	CQua EHof ICar
'Loch Lundie' (2)	CQua EHof ICar IDun
'Loch Maberry' (2)	CQua
'Loch Naver' (2)	CQua IDun
'Loch Stac' (2)	CQua ICar
'Logan Rock' (7)	CQua
longispathus MS 546	CMon SSpi
'Lorikeet' (1)	CQua NZep
'Lostwithiel' (2)	CQua
'Lothario' (2)	LAma NRog
'Lough Bawn' (2)	ICar
'Lough Cuan' (1)	IBal
'Lough Ryan' (1)	IBal
'Loughanisland' (1)	IBal
'Loughanmore' (1)	ICar
'Lovable' (3)	EWal
'Loveny' (2)	CQua
'Ludgvan' (4)	CQua
'Lunar Sea' (1)	EWal
'Lurgain' (1)	EWal
'Lurig' (2)	ICar
'Lyrebird' (3)	CQua
'Lyric' (9)	CQua
'Lysander' (2)	CQua
§ 'Madelaine' (2)	EWal
* 'Madison'	EWal
'Magic Flute' (2)	ICar
'Magna Carta' (2)	IDun
'Magnet' (1)	LAma MBri
'Magnificence' (1)	LAma
'Majestic Star' (1)	CQua
¶ 'Makasa Sun' (2)	IDun
'Malin Head' (5)	IBal
'Manchu' (2)	EWal
'Manly' (4)	CQua EWal
'Manon Lescaut' (2)	EWal
'Marabou' (4)	CQua IDun
'Maraval' (1)	EWal
'March Sunshine' (6)	CBro EWal LAma
'Marie-José' (11)	LAma
'Marjorie Treveal' (4)	CQua
'Marlborough' (2)	CQua
'Martha Washington' (8)	CBro CQua
'Martinette' (7)	CQua
marvieri	See ***N. rupicola*** **subsp. *marvieri***
'Mary Bohannon' (2)	EWal
'Mary Copeland' (4)	EWal LAma
'Mary Kate' (6)	CQua IDun
'Mary Lou' (6)	IDun
'Mary Sumner' (1)	ICar
'Mary's Pink' (2)	ICar
¶ 'Marzo' (7)	IDun
'Masai Mara' (2)	IDun
'Matador' (8)	CQua
'Max' (11)	CQua
'Mayan Gold' (1)	IBal
× ***medioluteus***	CBro CMon
¶ 'Medusa' (8)	CBro
'Megalith' (2)	IDun
'Melbury' (2)	CQua EHof
'Meldrum' (1)	EHof
'Mellon Park' (3)	IDun
'Melodious' (6)	CQua
'Menabilly' (4)	CQua
'Men-an-Tol' (2)	CQua
'Menehay' (11)	CQua
'Mentor' (2)	IDun
'Menucha' (2)	ICar
'Mercato' (2)	LAma
'Meredith' (3)	ICar
'Merida' (2)	IBal
'Merlin' (3) 🏆	CQua EHof IBal
'Merlin's Castle'	ICar
'Merry Bells' (5)	CQua ICar
'Merrymeet' (4)	CQua

'Mexico City' (2)	IBal
'Midas Touch' (1)	CQua IDun
'Midget'	CAvo CBro EPot
'Milan' (9)	CQua
'Millennium' (1)	CBro
'Millgreen' (1)	EWal
'Minicycla' (6)	CBro LRHS
minimus	See ***N. asturiensis***
'Minnow' (8)	CAvo CBro CMea CQua EPot ERos ETub EWal LAma MBri NRog WShi
§ ***minor*** 🏆	CBro CQua LAma
§ – var. ***pumilus***	ERos
– – 'Plenus'	See ***N.* 'Rip van Winkle'**
– Ulster form	IBlr
'Mint Cup' (3)	ICar
minutiflorus B&S 412	CMon
'Miss Kitty' (2)	ICar
'Mission Bells' (5)	CQua ICar
'Missouri' (2)	EWal
'Mistral' (11)	ICar
'Misty Dawn' (3)	IBal
'Misty Glen' (2)	CQua ICar
'Misty Moon' (3)	ICar
¶ 'Mite' (6)	CBro
'Mockingbird' (7)	IDun
'Modern Art' (2)	ETub EWal
'Mol's Hobby' (11)	EWal LAma
¶ 'Mona Lisa' (2)	EWal
'Mondragon' (11)	CQua EWal
'Mongleath' (2)	CQua
'Montego' (3)	CQua
'Monza' (4)	IDun
'Moon Jade' (3)	IBal
'Moon Ranger' (3)	IBal
'Moon Rhythm' (4)	IBal
'Moon Tide' (3)	IBal
'Moon Valley' (2)	IDun
'Moonshine' (5)	CBro
'Moonshot' (1)	EWal
'Moonspell' (2)	IBal ICar
'Moralee' (4)	IDun
'Mother Catherine Grullemans'	LAma
'Mount Angel' (3)	IDun
'Mount Fuji' (2)	CQua IDun
'Mount Hood' (1)	ETub EWal LAma MBri NBir
'Mount Oriel' (2)	IBal
'Mountjoy' (7)	EWal
'Mourneview' (1)	IBal
'Movie Star' (2)	IDun
¶ 'Mowana' (2)	IDun
'Moyarget' (3)	ICar
'Moyle' (9)	IBal
'Moyola' (2)	ICar
'Mrs R.O. Backhouse' (2)	LAma MBri WShi
'Mrs William Copeland' (4)	EWal
'Mulatto' (1)	EWal
'Mulroy Bay' (1)	IDun
'Murlough' (9)	CQua IBal
'Murrayfield' (3)	IDun
'Muscadet' (2)	CQua
'My Lady' (2)	EWal
'My My' (2)	EWal
'My Word' (2)	ICar
'Naivasha' (2)	IDun
'Nampa' (1)	CQua EWal
'Namraj' (2)	CQua EHof
'Nancegollan' (7)	CBro CQua
'Nansidwell' (2)	CQua
nanus	See ***N. minor***
'Narok' (4)	IDun
'Neahkahnie' (1)	IDun
'Nether Barr' (2)	IDun
¶ ***nevadensis***	SSpi
'New Penny' (3)	ICar
'New Song' (2)	EWal
'New Star' (2)	EWal
'New World' (2)	EWal
¶ 'New-baby' (7)	EWal
'Newcastle' (1)	CQua EHof ICar IDun
'Newton Ferrers' (4)	CQua
'Night Music' (4)	CQua
'Nightcap' (1)	CQua
'Nirvana' (7)	CBro
'Niveth' (5)	CQua ICar
nobilis var. ***nobilis*** MS 486	CMon
– var. ***primigenius*** MS 593	CMon
'Nor-nor' (2)	CBro
'North Rim' (2)	IDun
'Northern Sceptre' (2)	IBal ICar
'Noss Mayo' (6)	CBro CQua
'Notable' (3)	IBal
'Notre Dame' (2)	IDun
'Nouvelle' (3)	IBal
'Nuage' (2)	EWal
'Numen Rose' (2)	IDun
'Nylon' (12)	CBro CQua EHyt EPot LWoo SSpi WChr
'Oadby' (1)	CQua
'Oakwood' (3)	EWal
¶ 'Obdam' (4)	EWal
'Obelisk' (11)	CQua
obesus	EHyt EPot ERos ESis LWoo MMil
– MS 451	CMon
'Obsession' (2)	IDun
obvallaris	See ***N. pseudonarcissus*** subsp. ***obvallaris***
'Ocarino' (4)	CQua
§ x ***odorus*** 'Double Campernelle' (4)	CQua ETub LAma
– 'Rugulosus' (10) 🏆	CAvo CBro EPar ERos LAma NRog
'Odyssey' (4)	ICar
'Oecumene' (11)	CQua
'Ohio' (2)	EHof
Old Pheasant's Eye	See ***N. poeticus*** var. ***recurvus***
'Olympic Gold' (1)	IDun
'Omaha' (3)	IBal
'Orange Beacon' (2)	ICar
'Orangery' (11)	LAma MBri NRog
'Oratorio' (2)	EWal
'Ormeau' (2) 🏆	CQua
'Oryx' (7)	CQua IDun
'Osmington' (3)	CQua EHof IDun
'Ottoman Gold' (2)	IBal
'Ouma' (1)	CQua
'Ouzel' (6)	CQua
'Owen Roe' (1)	IBal
'Owston Wood' (1)	EHof
'Oykel' (3)	CQua ICar
'Oz' (6)	CQua
'Painted Desert' (3)	CQua ICar
'Pale Sunlight' (2)	CQua ICar
'Palmares' (11)	EWal
'Palmyra' (3)	ICar
'Panache' (1)	CQua EHof EWal ICar
panizzianus	CMon
'Pankot' (2)	ICar
'Paolo Veronese' (2)	EWal
'Paper White'	See ***N. papyraceus***
'Papillon Blanc' (11)	EWal LAma

'Papua' (4) ♀	CQua
§ ***papyraceus*** (8)	CQua ETub EWal LAma LBow MBri NRog
– subsp. ***papyraceus*** AB&S 4399	CMon
'Parcpat' (7)	CBro
'Parfait' (4)	ICar
'Paricutin' (2)	EWal
'Parisienne' (11)	EWal LAma NRog
'Park Avenue' (4)	IDun
¶ 'Park Gate' (2)	ICar
'Park Springs' (3)	CQua EHof IBal ICar
'Parterre' (2)	IDun
'Parthenon' (4)	ICar
'Passionale' (2) ♀	CQua EWal IBal LAma NBir WShi
'Pastiche' (2)	CQua
'Pastorale' (2)	EWal
'Patabundy' (2)	CQua IDun
'Patois' (9)	IDun
patulus	CMon
'Paula Cottell' (3)	CBro
'Pawley's Island' (2)	IDun
'Pay Day' (1)	EHof ICar
'Peach Prince' (4)	CQua
'Peacock' (2)	ICar
'Pearl Shell' (11)	CQua
'Pearlax' (11)	EWal
'Peeping Tom' (6)	CBro EPar ETub EWal LAma MBri NRog SRms
'Pelynt' (3)	CQua
'Pencrebar' (7)	CAvo CBro CQua LAma MBri WShi
'Pengarth' (2)	CQua
'Penkivel' (2)	CQua
'Pennine Way' (1)	CQua
'Penpol' (7)	CBro CQua
'Penril' (6)	CQua
'Pentille' (1)	CQua
'Penvose' (2)	EWal
'Pepper' (2)	CBro
'Pequenita' (7)	CBro
'Percuil' (6)	CQua
perez-chiscanoi MS 560	CMon SSpi
'Perimeter' (3)	CQua IBal ICar
'Peripheral Pink' (2)	CQua
'Perseus' (1)	ICar
'Pet Finch' (7)	EWal
'Petit Four' (4)	ETub EWal LAma NRog
'Petrel' (5)	CAvo CBro CQua ETub ICar NMGW
'Phantom' (11)	CQua
'Picasso' (3)	ICar
'Pick Up' (11)	ICar
¶ 'Picoblanco' (2)	CBro
'Pinafore' (2)	EWal
'Pink Angel' (7)	CQua ICar
'Pink Champagne' (4)	CQua
'Pink Charm' (2)	EWal
'Pink Gin' (4)	EWal
'Pink Monarch' (2)	EWal
'Pink Pageant' (4)	CQua EWal IDun
'Pink Panther' (2)	EHof
'Pink Paradise' (4)	CQua ICar IDun
'Pink Silk' (1)	CQua EHof NZep
'Pink Wing' (2)	CQua
'Pinza' (2) ♀	CQua
'Pipe Major' (2)	CQua EWal
'Piper's Barn' (7)	CBro CQua
'Pipit' (7)	CAvo CBro CMea CQua EWal ICar IDun LAma NBir WShi
'Piraeus' (4)	IDun

'Pismo Beach' (2)	CQua EHof ICar
'Pitchroy' (2)	CQua
'Playschool' (3)	ICar
poeticus	CAvo LAma
– var. ***hellenicus***	EWal
– Old Pheasant's Eye	See ***N. poeticus*** var. ***recurvus***
* ***poeticus physaloides***	ICar WChr
§ ***poeticus*** 'Plenus'	CAvo CBro CQua ETub
– 'Praecox' (9)	CBro CQua MFos
§ – var. ***recurvus*** ♀	CBro CGle CQua ETub EWal LAma LBow NBir WShi
'Poet's Way' (9)	CQua
'Polar Circle' (2)	ICar
'Polar Imp' (3)	ICar
'Polbathic' (2)	CQua
¶ 'Polglase' (8)	CBro
'Polindra' (2)	EWal
'Polly's Pearl' (8)	CQua
'Polnesk' (7)	CBro
'Pomona' (3)	LAma
'Pops Legacy' (1)	IBal
'Port Patrick' (3)	IBal
'Port William' (3)	IBal
'Porthchapel' (7)	CQua
'Portnagolan' (2)	ICar
'Portrait' (2)	CQua
'Portrush' (3)	EWal
'Portstewart' (3)	IBal
'Post House' (4)	IDun
'Powder Room' (2)	ICar
'Prairie Fire'	CQua IDun
'Preamble' (1)	CQua IBal ICar
'Premiere' (2)	CQua
'President Carter' (1)	LAma
'Pride of Cornwall' (8)	CBro
'Primrose Path' (2)	ICar
'Prince of Brunswick' (2)	IBal
'Princess Zaide' (3)	CQua
'Professor Einstein' (2)	LAma NRog
'Prologue' (1)	EWal
'Prophet' (1)	EWal
'Prosperity' (1)	ICar
'Prototype' (6)	IDun
'Pryda' (2)	ICar
pseudonarcissus ♀	CBro CGle CQua CRow EMon ETub EWFC LAma LBow SSpi WChr WJek WShi
– subsp. ***gayi***	CBro
§ – 'Lobularis'	CAvo CBro NRog
§ – subsp. ***moschatus***	CBro
– – 'Cernuus Plenus' (4)	ICar
– subsp. ***nevadensis***	MFos WOMN
§ – subsp. ***obvallaris*** ♀	CAvo CBro EPot LBow NRog WCla WShi
– subsp. ***pallidiflorus***	See ***N. pallidiflorus***
'Pueblo' (7)	ICar
'Pukawa' (7)	ICar
pumilus	See ***N. minor*** var. ***pumilus***
'Puppet' (5)	CQua ICar
'Puppy' (6)	EWal
'Purbeck' (3)	CQua EHof EWal ICar IDun
'Quail' (7)	CBro CQua EWal ICar LAma NRog
'Quasar' (2)	ICar IDun NZep
'Queen Anne's Double'	See ***N.*** **'Eystettensis'**
'Queenscourt' (1)	ICar
'Quetzal' (9)	CQua
'Quick Step' (7)	CQua
'Quiet Day' (2)	CQua ICar
'Quince' (12)	CAvo CBro CQua EWal
'Quirinus' (2)	LAma
¶ 'Raceview' (2)	ICar

'Radiation' (2)	EWal
'Radjel' (4)	CQua
'Rainbow' (2)	CQua EWal ICar
'Ramada' (2)	ICar
'Rame Head' (1)	CQua
'Rameses' (2)	CQua EHof
'Rapture' (6)	CQua
'Rarkmoyle' (2)	ICar
'Rashee' (1)	EHof ICar
'Raspberry Ring' (2)	CQua EHof
'Ravenhill' (3)	CQua EHof IDun
readinganorum B&S 434	CMon
'Recital' (2)	CQua
'Reckless' (3)	ICar
'Red Arrow' (1)	IBal
'Red Cameo' (2)	IDun
'Red Cottage' (2)	ICar
'Red Devil' (2)	ICar
'Red Ember' (3/2)	IDun
'Red Goblet' (2)	LAma
'Red Haze' (2)	IDun
'Red Hot' (2)	CQua
'Red Hugh' (9)	IBal
'Red Mission' (2)	IDun
'Red Spartan' (2)	IDun
'Redhill' (2)	EWal
'Redman' (2)	IBal
'Redstart' (3)	EWal
'Regal Bliss' (2)	CQua IDun
'Reggae' (6)	ICar IDun
'Rembrandt' (1)	LAma MBri
'Replete' (4)	CQua ICar
'Reprieve' (3)	EHof
requienii	See ***N. assoanus***
'Resplendent' (2)	ICar
'Revival' (4)	EWal
'Ridgecrest' (3)	IDun
'Riding Mill' (3)	EWal
'Riesling' (11)	CQua
rifanus	See ***N. romieuxii*** subsp. ***romieuxii*** var. ***rifanus***
'Rijnveld's Early Sensation' (1) 🏆	CBro CQua EWal MBri
'Rikki' (7)	CBro CQua ERos
'Rim Ride' (3)	ICar
'Rima' (1)	CQua
'Rimmon' (3)	CQua EHof IDun
'Rimski' (2)	IDun
'Ringhaddy' (3)	IBal
'Ringleader' (2)	CQua EHof EWal IDun
'Ringmaster' (2)	CQua ICar
'Ringwood' (3)	IDun
'Rio Bravo' (2)	IBal
'Rio Gusto' (2)	IBal
'Rio Lobo' (2)	IBal
'Rio Rondo' (2)	IBal
'Rio Rouge' (2)	IBal ICar
§ 'Rip van Winkle' (4)	CAvo CBro EFol EPar EPot ERos ETub LAma LBow MBri NMGW NRog WShi
'Rippling Waters' (5)	CBro CQua ICar LAma
'Riptide' (1)	ICar
'Ristin' (1)	CQua
'Rivendell' (3)	ICar IDun
'River Dance' (2)	IDun
'Rob Roy' (3)	EWal
'Rock Creek' (3)	IDun
'Rockall' (3)	CQua ICar
'Rockport' (2)	ICar
'Rococo' (2)	EWal
'Roger' (6)	CBro
'Romance' (2)	CQua EHof EWal LAma

'Romany Red' (3)	IDun
romieuxii 🏆	CAvo CBro CFil CGra CNic CQua EHyt EPot ERos MFos MHig NMen SSpi
– AB&S 4384	EPot NHar
– subsp. ***albidus***	CQua
– – S&F 256	EHyt
– – S&F 110	CMon
– – var. ***zaianicus***	CQua MMil
§ – – – f. ***albus*** MS168	CMon
§ – – – f. ***lutescens***	EHyt
§ – – – f. ***lutescens*** SF374	CMon NHar
– 'Atlas Gold'	EPot
– JCA 805	EHyt EPot NHar WChr
§ – 'Joy Bishop' (10)	EHyt EPot WChr
§ – 'Julia Jane' (10)	EHyt ERos NHar
§ – subsp. ***romieuxii*** var. ***mesatlanticus***	CMon EHyt EPot SWas
§ – – var. ***rifanus*** SB&L 207	CMon
¶ – – var. ***romieuxii*** JCA 805Y	NHar
– S&F 370	CMon
– 'Treble Chance'	EPot
'Roscarrick' (6)	CQua
'Rose Gold' (1)	IDun
'Rose of May' (4)	ICar
'Rose Royale' (2)	CQua IBal ICar
'Roseate Tern' (2)	CQua IDun
'Rosedown' (5)	CBro
'Roseworthy' (2)	LAma
'Rossferry' (2)	IBal
'Rosy Sunrise' (2)	LAma
'Rosy Trumpet' (1)	CBro
'Rosy Wonder' (2)	EWal
'Round Robin' (2)	ICar
'Royal Coachman'	ICar
'Royal Command'	See ***N.*** **'Royal Decree'**
§ 'Royal Decree' (2)	EWal
'Royal Orange' (2)	EWal
'Royal Princess' (3)	CQua EHof IDun
'Royal Regiment' (2)	CQua ICar
'Royal Wedding' (2)	ICar
'Rubh Mor' (2)	CQua
'Ruby Rose' (4)	IDun
'Ruby Tail' (2)	EWal
'Rubyat' (6)	IBal
rupicola 🏆	CMon CQua EPot ERos LAma LWoo MRPP MS&S
§ – subsp. ***marvieri*** 🏆	WChr
– – AB&S 4414	CMon NHar
– – S&F 126	CMon
– MS 567/455	CMon
'Rushmore' (2)	IDun
'Ruth Haller' (5)	ICar
'Rutland Water' (2)	EHof
'Rytha' (2)	CQua
'Saberwing' (5)	CQua ICar
'Sabine Hay' (3)	CQua ETub EWal ICar IDun
'Sacajawea' (2)	EWal
'Saint Dilpe' (2)	CQua
'Saint Keverne' (2) 🏆	CQua EWal IBal LAma NRog
'Saint Keyne' (8)	CQua
'Saint Mawes' (2)	CQua
'Saint Patrick's Day' (2)	ETub EWal LAma
'Saint Piran' (7)	CQua
'Salmon Trout' (2)	CQua EWal LAma
'Salomé' (2)	EWal LAma MBri NBir NRog
'Samantha' (4)	CQua
'Samaria' (3)	CBro
¶ 'Samba' (5)	ERos
'Samite' (1)	EWal
'Sancerre' (11)	CQua

'Sandy Cove' (2)	IDun
'Sandymount' (2)	IBal
'Sarah' (2)	EWal
'Sarah Dear' (2)	CQua
'Sateen' (2)	EWal
'Satellite' (6)	EWal ICar
'Satin Pink' (2)	EWal MBri
'Saturn' (3)	CQua ICar
'Savoir Faire' (2)	IDun
scaberulus	CBro LAma WChr
'Scarlet Elegance' (2)	LAma
'Scarlet Gem' (8)	ETub EWal LAma
'Scarlett O'Hara' (2)	LAma
'Sea Dream' (3)	CQua EWal
'Sea Gift' (7)	CBro CQua
'Sea Green' (9)	CQua
'Sealing Wax' (2)	CQua EWal
'Segovia' (3) 🏆	CBro CQua ERos
'Sempre Avanti' (2)	LAma MBri NRog
'Sennocke' (5)	CBro
'Serena Beach' (4)	IDun
'Serena Lodge' (4)	IDun
serotinus	CMon EHyt EPot WChr WThi
– S&F 298/285	CMon
'Sextant' (6)	CQua EWal
'Shanes Castle' (1)	ICar
'She' (2)	EWal
'Sheer Joy' (6)	IDun
'Sheerline' (2)	IDun
'Sherborne' (4)	IDun
'Sherpa' (1)	IDun
'Sheviock' (2)	CQua
'Shimna' (1)	IBal
'Shining Light' (2)	CQua ICar
'Shorecliffe' (2)	IDun
'Shot Silk' (5)	LAma
'Show Band' (2)	IDun
'Sidley' (3)	CQua IDun
'Sidney' (9)	CQua
'Signorina' (2)	IDun
'Silent Valley' (1)	CQua EHof IDun
'Silk Cut' (2)	CQua IDun
'Silken Sails' (3)	ICar
'Silver Bells' (5)	IDun
'Silver Blaze' (2)	IDun
'Silver Chimes' (8)	CBro CQua ETub EWal LAma NRog
'Silver Crystal' (3)	IDun
'Silver Plate' (11)	CQua
'Silver Princess' (3)	EWal
'Silver Standard' (2)	EWal
'Silver Surf' (2)	CQua IDun
'Silverwood' (3)	IDun
'Simply Bloomfield' (2)	ICar
'Sir Winston Churchill' (4)	CQua EWal LAma NRog
'Skerry' (2)	ICar
'Slaney' (3)	ICar
'Small Fry' (1)	EWal
'Small Talk' (1)	CQua
'Smokey Bear' (4)	CQua IDun
'Snoopie' (6)	CQua
'Snow Bunting' (7)	CBro
'Snowcrest' (3)	CQua IDun
'Snowfire' (4)	ICar
'Snowshill' (2)	CQua
'Society Belle' (2)	IDun
'Solar Tan' (3)	IDun
'Soldier Brave' (2)	EWal
'Soledad' (2)	ICar
'Soleil d'Or' (8)	EWal MBri
'Sonata' (9)	CQua
'Songket' (2)	IDun
'Sophia' (2)	CQua
'Soprano' (2)	IDun
¶ 'Sorbet' (11)	EWal
'Sorcerer' (3)	CQua
'South Street' (2)	CQua
¶ 'Sovereign' (11)	ETub
sp. C M Stocken (10)	CBro
'Spaniards Inn' (4)	CQua
'Spanish Moon' (1)	EWal
'Sparkling Eye' (8)	IBal
'Spellbinder' (1) 🏆	EWal LAma MBri
'Sperrin Gold' (1)	IDun
'Spirit of Rame' (3)	CQua
¶ 'Split Image' (2)	IDun
'Sportsman' (2)	CQua EHof IDun
'Spring Dawn' (2)	EWal
'Stadium' (2)	EWal
'Standard Value' (1)	LAma
'Stanway' (3)	CQua
'Star Glow' (2)	IDun
'Star War' (2)	CQua
'Starfire' (7)	CQua ICar
'State Express' (2)	CQua IDun
'Statue' (2)	EWal
¶ 'Steenbok' (3)	IDun
'Stilton' (9)	CQua
'Stint' (6)	CBro CQua IDun
* 'Stockens Gib'	EHyt
'Stoke Charity' (2)	EHof ICar
'Stormy Weather' (1)	ICar
'Stourbridge' (2)	ICar
'Strathkanaird' (1)	ICar
'Stratosphere' (7)	CQua ICar IDun
'Stray' (6)	ICar
'Strines' (2)	CQua EHof EWal
'Stromboli' (2)	EWal
'Suave' (3)	EHof
'Suda Bay' (2)	ICar
'Sugar Loaf' (4)	CQua
'Sugarbush' (7)	CBro LAma MBri NRog
'Sumo Jewel' (6)	CQua
'Sun Disc' (7) 🏆	CAvo CBro CQua ERos EWal IDun LAma MBri WShi
'Sunapee' (3)	EHof
'Sundial' (7)	CAvo CBro CQua EPot ERos EWal ICar LAma
'Suntory' (3)	CQua IDun
'Surfside' (6)	CQua
'Surrey' (2)	IDun
'Susan Pearson' (7)	ICar
¶ 'Suzie Dee' (6)	IDun
'Suzy' (7) 🏆	CBro EWal ICar LAma MBri NRog WShi
'Swaledale' (2)	CQua
'Swansdown' (4)	EWal ICar
'Sweet Charity' (2)	EWal
'Sweet Pepper' (7)	CBro
'Sweetness' (7) 🏆	CAvo CBro CQua EWal IBal LAma NRog WShi
'Swing Wing' (6)	CQua IDun
'Sydling' (5)	CQua
'Sylvan Hill' (1)	IBal
'Taffeta' (12)	CAvo CBro CQua EHyt LRHS WChr
'Tahiti' (4)	CQua EWal LAma MBri NRog
'Tain' (1)	ICar
'Takoradi' (4)	ICar
'Talwyn' (1)	CQua
'Tamar Fire' (4)	CQua
'Tamar Snow' (2)	CQua
'Tamara' (2)	CQua
§ ***tananicus***	WChr

– SF 44	CMon
'Tangent' (2)	CQua EWal ICar
'Tara Rose' (2)	EHof
'Tardree' (1)	ICar
'Tarlatan' (12)	CBro
'Taslass' (4)	CQua
'Tater-Du' (5)	CQua
tazetta aureus	See ***N. aureus***
tazetta compressus	CQua
tazetta subsp. ***lacticolor***	CMon
MS 517	
– – MS 519	CMon
tazetta orientalis	CQua
tazetta papyraceus	See ***N. papyraceus***
'Tedstone' (1)	EWal
§ 'Telamonius Plenus' (4)	CBro LAma WShi
◆ ***tenuifolius***	See ***N. bulbocodium*** subsp. ***bulbocodium*** var. ***tenuifolius***
§ x ***tenuior***	CAvo CQua
'Terracotta' (2)	IDun
'Testament' (2)	EWal
'Tête-à-tête' (12) 🏆	CAvo CBro CQua EBar EPar EPot ERos ETub EWal IBal LAma LBow MBri WHil
'Texas' (4)	CQua LAma MBri
'Thalia' (5)	CAvo CBro CRDP EFol ETub EWal ICar LAma LBow MBri NRog WShi
'The Alliance' (6)	CQua
'The Knave' (6)	CQua
'The Little Gentleman' (6)	CBro
'Thoughtful' (5)	CBro CQua EWal
'Three Trees' (1)	ICar
'Thunderbolt' (1)	EWal
'Tibet' (2)	EWal
'Tiercel'	CQua
'Tiffany' (12)	EHyt
'Tiger Moth' (6)	IDun
'Timolin' (3)	CQua ICar
'Tinnell' (1)	CQua
'Tiri Tomba' (11)	CQua EWal
'Titania' (6)	CQua
'Tittle Tattle' (7)	CBro CQua EWal IBal LAma
'Toby' (2)	EWal
'Toby the First' (6)	CQua
'Tonga' (4)	ICar
'Top Hit' (11)	CQua
'Top of the Hill' (3)	IBal ICar
'Topkapi' (2)	IBal
'Topolino' (1)	CAvo CBro CQua EPot LAma NRog
'Torcross' (3)	IDun
'Torr Head' (9)	IBal
'Torridon' (2)	CQua EHof ICar IDun
'Tracey' (6)	CQua
'Tranquil Morn' (3)	EWal
'Trebah' (2)	CQua
'Trefusis' (1)	CQua
'Tregarrick' (2)	CQua
'Trehane' (6)	CQua
'Trena' (6)	CQua EWal IDun
'Tresamble' (5)	CBro CQua EWal LAma
'Trevelmond' (2)	CQua
'Treverva' (6)	CQua
'Treviddo' (2)	CQua
'Trevithian' (7)	CBro CQua EWal IBal LAma NRog
'Trewidland' (2)	CQua
'Trewirgie' (6)	CBro CQua
triandrus 🏆	CQua WChr
– var. ***albus***	See ***N. triandrus*** var. ***triandrus***
– var. ***concolor***	See ***N. concolor***
– var. ***pulchellus***	LAma
§ – var. ***triandrus***	EPot MSto
¶ 'Tricollet' (11)	EWal
'Triller' (7)	ICar
'Tripartite' (11)	CQua EWal ICar NZep
'Triple Crown' (3)	IDun
'Tristram' (2)	CQua EHof
'Tropic Isle' (4)	ICar
'Trousseau' (1)	CQua EWal LAma
'Troutbeck' (3)	CQua
'Tudor Grove' (2)	IDun
'Tudor Minstrel' (2)	CQua EWal
'Tuesday's Child' (5)	CQua EBar EWal ICar IDun
'Tullygirvan' (2)	ICar
'Tullynog' (4)	ICar
'Tullyroyal' (2)	IBal
'Turncoat' (6)	CQua
'Tutankhamun' (2)	CQua
'Tweeny' (2)	CQua
'Twicer' (2)	IDun
'Tyee' (2)	CQua
'Tynan' (2)	ICar
'Tyneham' (3)	IDun
'Tyrian Rose' (2)	IDun
'Tyrone Gold' (2)	IDun
'Ufo' (3)	EWal
'Ulster Bank' (3)	IDun
'Ulster Bullion' (2)	IBal
'Ultimus' (2)	EWal
'Uncle Duncan' (1)	CQua EHof
'Uncle Remus' (1)	EWal
'Unique' (4)	CQua EWal ICar IDun LAma
'Unsurpassable' (1)	LAma
'Urchin'	See ***N.*** **'Pzaz'**
'Vahu' (2)	IDun
'Val d'Incles' (3)	IDun
'Valdrome' (11)	CQua ICar MBri
'Valediction' (3)	IDun
'Valinor' (2)	EHof IDun
'Value' (2)	IDun
'Van Dyke' (2)	IDun
'Van Sion'	See ***N.*** **'Telamonius Plenus'**
'Verdin' (7)	CQua ICar
'Verger' (3)	LAma MBri
'Vernal Prince' (3)	CQua IDun
'Verona' (3) 🏆	CQua IDun
'Vers Libre' (9)	CQua IDun
'Verwood' (3)	IDun
'Victory' (2)	EWal
'Vigil' (1) 🏆	CQua EWal
'Vigilante' (1)	IDun
'Viking' (1)	CQua EHof
'Vilna' (2)	EWal
'Violetta' (2)	CQua EWal ICar
'Vireo' (7)	ICar
viridiflorus	WThi
– MS 500	CMon
– S&F 323	CMon
'Vivarino' (11)	EWal
'Volare' (2)	CQua
'Voltage' (2)	IDun
'Vulcan' (2) 🏆	CQua EHof EWal
'W.P. Milner' (1)	CAvo CBro CMea LAma MBri NRog WOMN
'Waldorf Astoria' (4)	CQua IDun
'Walesby' (2)	CQua
'Warleigh' (2)	CQua
¶ 'Warm Day' (2)	ICar
'Waterperry' (7)	CBro ETub LAma NRog
watieri	CBro CGra CMon MTho WChr
– AB&S 4518	CMon
'Waxwing' (5)	CQua

'Wee Bee' (1) CQua
'Wendy Walsh' (2) ICar
'Westbury' (4) IDun
'Westward' (4) CQua EWal
'Wetherby' (3) IDun
'Whang-hi' (6) CQua
'Wheal Kitty' (7) CQua
'Whetstone' (1) CQua
¶ 'Whipcord' (7) IDun
'Whisper' (5) EWal
'Whitbourne' (3) EWal
'White Butterfly' (2) EWal
'White Cross' (2) IBal
'White Hill' (2) IBal
'White Lady' (3) CQua
'White Lion' (4) ♀ EWal LAma NRog
'White Marvel' (4) CQua EWal LAma NRog
'White Mist' (2) ICar
'White Phantom' (1) ICar
'White Plume' (2) EWal
'White Star' (1) CQua ICar IDun
'Whiteabbey' (2) IBal
'Widgeon' (2) EWal
willkommii CBro
'Winchester' (2) EWal
'Windjammer' (1) EWal
'Winfrith' (2) EWal
'Winged Victory' (6) CQua
'Witch Doctor' (3) IBal
'Witch Hunt' (4) IBal
'Woodcock' (6) CBro CQua
'Woodgreen' (2) EWal
'Woodland Prince' (3) CQua
'Woodland Star' (3) CQua
'Woodvale' (2) CQua
'Worcester' (2) EWal
'Xit' (3) CAvo CBro CQua SWas
'Yeats' (9) ICar
'Yellow Cheerfulness' (4) ETub EWal LAma MBri NRog
'Yellow Standard' (2) LAma
'Yellow Sun' (3) LAma
'Yes Please' (2) EWal
'Yoshiko' (2) IDun
'Young Blood' (2) IDun
'Young Idea' (7) EWal
* ***zaianicus*** var. ***albus*** MS 168 See ***N. romieuxii* subsp. *albidus* var. *zaianicus* f. *albus* MS168**
– ***lutescens*** SF 374 See ***N. romieuxii* subsp. *albidus* var. *zaianicus* f. *lutescens* SF374**
'Zelah' (1) CQua
'Zion Canyon' (2) IDun

NARDOPHYLLUM (Asteraceae)
bryoides GTou ITim NTow

NARDOSTACHYS (Valerianaceae)
grandiflora GPoy

NARTHECIUM (Melanthiaceae)
ossifragum WShi

NASSAUVIA (Asteraceae)
gaudichaudii EHyt

NASSELLA (Poaceae)
trichotoma EGar EGoo EHoe EPPr EPla ESOG ETPC LHil

NASTURTIUM (Brassicaceae)
officinale CBen SWat WHer

NECTARBERRY See RUBUS

NECTAROSCORDUM (Alliaceae)
§ ***siculum*** CArn CAvo CBro CGle CMea CMil CNic EBre ELan EMan EOrc EPar ERav LGan MBal NBir NEgg NSti SSoC SSvw SUsu WFar WHil WRHF
§ – subsp. ***bulgaricum*** CBro CHad CRDP ECha EFou EPar EPot ERos ETub IBlr LBow LFis MNrw SChu SIng SSpi WAbb WBro WElm

NEILLIA (Rosaceae)
affinis CDec CPle ECro EHal EHic MBal MUlv NPro WHCG
longiracemosa See ***N. thibetica***
rubiflora CC&McK 18 LKoh
sinensis CMCN CPle MRav
§ ***thibetica*** CB&S CChu CGre CHan CPle EAst ELan EMil ENot IOrc ISea MBri MBro MTis MUlv SMac SPer SPla SSpi SSta WAbe WHar WWat WWin

NELUMBO (Nymphaeaceae)
'Kermesina' MSta
lutea 'Flavescens' MSta
nucifera LLew MSta
– 'Alba Grandiflora' MSta
– 'Alba Striata' MSta
– 'Pekinensis Rubra' MSta
– 'Rosea' MSta
– 'Rosea Plena' MSta
'Osiris' MSta
'Pulchra' MSta

NEMASTYLIS (Iridaceae)
tenuis subsp. ***pringlei*** CTbh

NEMATANTHUS (Gesneriaceae)
'Black Magic' CHal MBri WDib
'Christmas Holly' WDib
'Freckles' WDib
§ ***glaber*** MBri
§ ***gregarius*** CHal EBak MBri WDib
§ – 'Golden West' (v) CHal MBri WDib
– 'Variegatus' See ***N. gregarius*** **'Golden West'**
radicans See ***N. gregarius***
strigillosus MBri
'Tropicana' ♀ CHal MBri WDib

NEMESIA (Scrophulariaceae)
'Blue Bird' LIck
§ ***caerulea*** CBar CBot CBrk CDoC ECtt EPot LHil MArl MTho NFai NPri NTow SLMG SUsu WPer WWin
– 'Elliott's Variety' CBar EBee LHil
– 'Joan Wilder' (clonal) EMan NPri WOMN
N– 'Joan Wilder' (seed raised) See ***N. caerulea*** **lilac/blue**
§ – lilac/blue CBrk CSam CSpe EBar EOrc LHil LHop NPri SUsu WPer WPyg WWin
– 'Woodcote' CBrk CSpe EBee LHil MArl NPri

§ ***denticulata***	CBar CBrk CDec CHad CSpe EBar ECtt EMar EOrc LHil LHop MArl MAsh NPri SAxl SCoo SUsu WFar WFoF WRus WWeb WWhi
– 'Confetti'	See ***N. denticulata***
foetens	See ***N. caerulea***
'Fragrant Cloud'	EOrc MAsh SPer
'Innocence'	CBrk CSpe EBee EHic EMan LFis LHil LHop LIck MArl WLRN WRus
umbonata hort.	See ***N. caerulea* lilac/blue**

NEMOPANTHUS (Aquifoliaceae)

See Plant Deletions

NEMOPHILA (Hydrophyllaceae)

menziesii	NRai

NEODYPSIS (Arecaceae)

decaryi	LPal

NEOLITSEA (Lauraceae)

glauca	See ***N. sericea***
§ ***sericea***	CHEx

NEOMARICA (Iridaceae)

northiana	SLMG WThi

NEOPANAX See PSEUDOPANAX

NEOPAXIA (Portulacaceae)

§ ***australasica***	CMHG ECou ESis NGre WWin
– blue-leaved	See ***N. australasica* 'Kosciusko'**
– bronze-leaved	See ***N. australasica* 'Ohau'**
§ – 'Great Lake'	ECou
– green-leaved	See ***N. australasica* 'Great Lake'**
– grey	See ***N. australasica* 'Kosciusko'**
§ – 'Kosciusko'	GAri GDra NBir
– 'Lakeside'	ECou
– 'Lyndon'	ECou
§ – 'Ohau'	ECou GAri GGar

NEOREGELIA (Bromeliaceae)

carolinae	MBri SRms
§ – (Meyendorffii Group) 'Flandria'	MBri
– – 'Meyendorffii'	MBri
– f. ***tricolor*** (v) ♀	CHal MBri
§ Claret Group	MBri

NEOTTIANTHE (Orchidaceae)

¶ ***cucullata***	EFEx

NEPENTHES (Nepenthaceae)

alata	WMEx
¶ ***bongso* × *hamata***	WMEx
× ***coccinea***	MBri
gracilis	WMEx
¶ ***gymnamphora***	WMEx
hybrids	MHel
khasiana	WMEx
¶ ***lowii***	WMEx
madagascariensis	WMEx
maxima	WMEx
mirabilis	WMEx
¶ ***muluensis***	WMEx
rafflesiana	WMEx
– × ***ampullaria***	See ***N.* × *hookeriana***
rajah	WMEx
¶ ***reinwardtiana***	WMEx
sanguinea	WMEx
¶ ***tentaculata***	WMEx
¶ ***tobaica***	WMEx
¶ ***tomoriana***	WMEx
¶ ***truncata***	WMEx
ventricosa	WMEx
¶ – slim × ***spectabilis***	WMEx
¶ ***vieillardii***	WMEx

NEPETA † (Lamiaceae)

argolica	See ***N. sibthorpii***
'Blue Beauty'	See ***N. sibirica* 'Souvenir d'André Chaudron'**
bucharica	GBuc
camphorata	CArc CSam GAbr GTou LHol MSCN MSte SIde WElm WOve WPer WWye
cataria	CArn CSev EJud ELau GBar GPoy LHol MChe MHew MSal NBro SIde WHer WOak WPer WSel WWye
– 'Citriodora'	CArn CBot CLTr EFol EFou EHal ELau EMon GBar GPoy LHol MSal NFai SChu SSca SSpe WCHb WHer WHil WRha WSel WWye
clarkei	CArc CHan CLon CMea CSam EBee EFou MSte NCat NLak SBla SCro SHel SWat WPer
× ***faassenii***	CGle CHad EBre EMon GLil MRav MTol MWat NPer NVic SAga SChu SCro SEas SIng SPla SRms
◆ ***glechoma*** 'Variegata'	See ***Glechoma hederacea* 'Variegata'**
govaniana	CChu CHad CHan CPle CSam ECha EFou ELan EOrc GCal LGre LHol MMil NBro NSti NTow SIgm SPer SUsu WCHb WHoo WHow WOld WPer WWin WWye
grandiflora	CLTr CPle EFol EFou LFis LHol MGrG MRav NFai SIde SMrm WHer WWhi
¶ – 'Bramdean'	CArc CSam
– 'Dawn to Dusk'	CArc CLon CMil CRDP CSev EBee ECha EFou EMon GAbr GBri MCLN MMil NFai NRoo SChu SHel SMrm SWat WHow WLRN WPbr WRus WWoo
◆ ***hederacea*** 'Variegata'	See ***Glechoma hederacea* 'Variegata'**
lanceolata	See ***N. nepetella***
latifolia	EEls EMon WCot
* ***longipes***	CHan CSam EMon MSte SAga SBla SChu SCro SHel SMrm SWas WCot WHal WPbr WRus
macrantha	See ***N. sibirica***
mariae JJH 948425	EBee
melissifolia	CWan EBee WCHb WPer WWye
mussinii	See ***N. racemosa***
§ ***nepetella***	CSam GBar GBri LHol NChi SIde WPer
nervosa	CArn CDec CLon CPle CSam ECED ECha ELan EMar LGre LHol MCLN MFir MRav MSte NBro NFai NOak NSti SChu SCro SDix SEas SPer WHoo WPer WPyg
¶ – 'Forncett'	CSam

– 'Forncett Select' CArc EFou SWas
§ ***nuda*** CPle CSam EBee ECha EHal EMan EMon LHol NWoo WCot WPbr WPer WRus
– subsp. ***albiflora*** CArc CHan EGar EMon
* – 'Anne's Choice' WCot
– 'Nacre' EMon
– subsp. ***nuda*** CHan EGar
pannonica See ***N. nuda***
¶ ***parnassica*** CPea LCom LLew LRHS SWat WBea
– CDB 13073 SCro
§ ***phyllochlamys*** CBot CLTr CPBP MSte NTow SAga SBla WHil
'Pool Bank' ECoo EFou EGoo EMon MBel NCat NFai SChu WTre
'Porzellan' CLTr EFou EMon MSte WTre
§ ***prattii*** EBee EHal EPPr
§ ***racemosa*** CArn CBot CPle CSev EBre ELan ELau GBar LHol MChe MFir NFai NRoo NWes SIde SPla WTyr WWin WWye
– 'Blue Ice' GBuc SMer WHoo
– 'Grog' EFou
– 'Little Titch' CArc EFou GCal MSte SChu SMrm SSpe
– 'Snowflake' CBot CGle CMea EAst EBee EFou EGoo EHal ELan EMil ERav GCal GCra LHop MSte MWat NBir NBrk NCat NSti SChu SCro SEas SHel SPer SSpe WHow WPbr
§ – 'Superba' CBlo CLTr CWan EFou EGoo ELan EMon GBuc SEas WHoo WPbr
– 'Walker's Low' CArc CEnd CSev EBee ECGP EFou EGar GBar GCal NCat NChi NRoo SChu SHel SMrm SSpe SWat WLRN WPen WRha WRus WWoo
reichenbachiana See ***N. racemosa***
§ ***sibirica*** CGle CHan CLTr CPle ECha EFou EJud LGan LGre LHol MBri MNrw MRav MSal NBro NPri NSti NWes SChu SCro SIgm SSvw SUsu WCot WHal WHil WMer WOve WPer WWye
§ – 'Souvenir d'André Chaudron' CDoC CGle CMHG CRDP CSam EFou EMon GCal GMaP LFis LGan LHop MBri MNrw NFai SBla SCro SEas SPer SUsu WEas WHil WHoo WOld WPer WPyg WRus WWhi
§ ***sibthorpii*** CWan NChi WPer
sintenisii EGar EMar EMon LBlm
'Six Hills Giant' Widely available
sp. DS&T 89048T EMon
sp. DS&T 89054T EMon
stewartiana GBuc LCom WSan
– ACE 1611 SMrm
– CLD 551 EBee
subsessilis CBot CGle CHad CLon CRDP EBee EBre EMan GAbr GBuc LGan LGre LHol MHlr MSte NSti SAga SBla SChu SMrm SOkh SWas WHer WHil WOld WPer WWhi WWye
– forms MNrw WBon WCot
¶ ***subsessilis*** pink form WPbr
* ***subsessilis sensibilis*** CBot SWat
subsessilis var. ***yesoensis*** CHan
¶ ***tenuifolia*** MSal
teydea MNrw
'Thornbury' CShe
transcaucasica EWll
tuberosa CFir CHan CPle EBee ECha EMan GBar LGan NSti SChu SCro WPen WWhi WWye
ucranica NHex

NEPHROLEPIS (Oleandraceae)

cordifolia GQui MBri NMar
exaltata ERea
– 'Bostoniensis' MBri SRms
– 'Rooseveltii' MBri
– 'Smithii' MBri
– 'Smithii Linda' MBri
– 'Teddy Junior' MBri
– 'Todeoides' NMar

NEPHROPHYLLIDIUM (Menyanthaceae)

cristagalli CRDP IBlr

NERINE † (Amaryllidaceae)

¶ ***angustifolia*** LLew
'Baghdad' CMon
'Betty Hudson' CRDP
¶ 'Blanchefleur' SSpr
* 'Borde Hill White' SSpr
bowdenii ♀ Widely available
¶ – 'Manina' WCot
– 'Mark Fenwick' CAvo CB&S EBre ECha ECro EPot ERav LHop SAxl WCot
* – 'Mollie Cowie' IBlr
– 'Pink Triumph' CB&S CLyd EBee GBuc IBlr LAma LWak NRog SDeJ SPer
– 'Wellsii' CMon CRDP WCot
'Brocade' CMon
'Camellia' LHop
'Canasta' LHop SSpr
'Catherine' LHop SSpr
'Catkin' LHop
'Christmas' LHop
¶ 'Clent Charm' SSpr
corusca 'Major' See ***N. sarniensis*** var. ***corusca***
crispa See ***N. undulata***
'Dover' LHop
'Druid' LHop
¶ 'Dunkirk' SSpr
'Enchantress' LHop
¶ 'Eve' SSpr
'Evening' LHop
¶ 'Ffiske' SSpr
filamentosa CMon SWas
filifolia CAvo CLyd CRDP EHyt EPot GCal MNrw WChr WCot
flexuosa CMon MRav SLMG SSpr
– 'Alba' CAvo CBro EBre LAma LGre LHop SDeJ SLMG SSpr WChr
– pink CMon WChr
'Gaby Deslys' CMon
'Gaiety' LHop
'Gloaming' LHop
'Grilse' CMon LHop
¶ 'Hamlet' SSpr
'Harlequin' SSpr
'Harry Dalton' SSpr
'Helen Smith' LHop SSpr
* ***hirsuta*** WChr
humilis CMon WCot
– Breachiae Group CMon
– Tulbaghensis Group CMon
¶ 'Inchmery Kate' SSpr

¶ ***innominata***	SSpr
¶ 'Janet'	SSpr
¶ 'Jill'	SSpr
* 'Killi'	CRDP
'King of the Belgians'	LAma
krigei	WChr
¶ 'Lady Cynthia Colville'	SSpr
¶ ***laticoma***	LLew
'Lindhurst'	LHop
'Lord Grenfell'	IBlr
'Mansellii'	CMon LHop WChr
'Marnie Rogerson'	CBro CGle LGre
masoniorum	CBro CLyd EBee EHyt LGre MTho WCot WOMN
pudica	CMon WChr
* 'Red Pimpernel'	LAma
'Rose Camellia'	CMon
'Rushmere Star'	LHop
sarniensis	CBro ECha NRog SLMG WChr WThi
* – 'Alba'	LHop
§ – var. ***corusca***	LAma
– – 'Major'	LBow LHop SSpr
– var. ***curvifolia*** f. ***fothergillii***	LHop SSpr WCot
– – –'Queen Mary'	CMon
Smee No. 11	CMon
'Smokey Special'	SSpr
¶ 'Snowflake'	SSpr
'Solent Swan'	LHop
'Stephanie'	LAma LHop
'Stephanie' x 'Moscow'	SSpr
§ ***undulata***	CAvo CBro CMon ECha LAma LBow MBri NRog SPer WChr WCot
* – 'Alba'	WCot
¶ 'Vestal'	SSpr
'Vicky'	CRDP
* 'White Swan'	EBar LAma LHop
¶ 'Wolsey'	SSpr
'Zeal Giant'	CAvo

NERIUM † (Apocynaceae)

oleander	CBrP CHEx CMdw CPle EBak LHil LPan SRms WHil WOMN
– 'Album'	EEls
– 'Album Plenu'	EEls
– 'Alsace'	EEls ERea
¶ – 'Altini'	EEls
– 'Angiolo Pucci'	LHil
* – 'Avalanche'	CB&S
– 'Belle Hélène'	EFlo
* – 'Clare'	EEls ERea SOWG
– 'Emilie'	EEls ERea
– forms	EEls SLMG
– 'Géant des Batailles'	EEls ERea SOWG
– 'Hardy Pink'	ERea
– 'Hardy Red'	EEls ERea
¶ – 'Hawaii'	EEls
* – 'Isabelle'	EEls
– 'Isle of Capri'	ERea SOWG
– 'Italia'	ERea
– 'Jannoch'	EEls EFlo ERea
– 'Luteum Plenum'	CFee EEls EFlo ERea
– 'Madame Allen'	EEls EFlo LHil
¶ – 'Madame Léon Blum'	EFlo
– 'Madame Planchon' (d)	ERea
– 'Magaly'	ERea
– 'Maresciallo Graziani'	EEls
– 'Margaritha'	EEls ERea
¶ – 'Papa Gambetta'	EFlo
* – 'Peach Blossom'	ERea
¶ – 'Petite Salmon'	EEls
– 'Professeur Granel'	EEls ERea LHil
– 'Provence'	EEls ERea SOWG
– 'Rosario'	ERea
– 'Rosée du Ventoux'	EEls ERea SOWG
– 'Roseum'	EEls SLMG
– 'Roseum Plenum'	CB&S EEls
– 'Rosita'	EEls ERea
– 'Sealy Pink'	CB&S
* – 'Snowflake'	EEls ERea SOWG
– 'Soeur Agnès'	ERea
– 'Soleil Levant'	EEls ERea LHil
¶ – 'Souvenir d'Emma Schneider'	EEls
¶ – 'Souvenir des Iles Canaries'	EFlo
– 'Splendens'	ERea SOWG
¶ – 'Splendens Giganteum' (d)	EEls
– 'Tito Poggi'	ERea LHil
– 'Variegatum'	CBot CGre EEls ERea LHil LHop LPan SLMG
¶ – 'Variegatum Plenum' (d)	WCot
– 'Ville de Carpentras'	EEls EFlo ERea
* – 'Yellow Queen'	CB&S

NERTERA (Rubiaceae)

balfouriana	ECou
depressa	ECou
granadensis	MBri WOMN

NEVIUSIA (Rosaceae)

alabamensis	CHan

NICANDRA (Solanaceae)

physalodes	CArn EJud EMan GBur NBir NHex SIde SSoC WWye
– ***alba***	LCot NBir WHer WRha
– 'Violacea'	SLod SRms
– 'Blacky'	WCot

NICOTIANA (Solanaceae)

acuminata	MSto
alata	MSto
glauca	CGle CMdw EEls ERea LFlo LLew MAll MSte SLMG
knightiana	MEas MSto
langsdorffii ♀	CB&S CBrk CHad CHan ECro EMon GBri NBro NRai SLMG SMrm SUsu WEas WHal WHer WOve WPer WRus WWye
– 'Cream Splash' (v)	CPla
noctiflora	EBar
rustica	ECro MSto
suaveolens	WRus
sylvestris ♀	CBrk CHEx CHad CHan CJew EBar EMan GBri SEND SMrm WEas WRus WWye
tabacum	CArn CHEx EJud WWye

NIDULARIUM (Bromeliaceae)

flandria	See ***Neoregelia carolinae* (Meyendorffii Group) 'Flandria'**

NIEREMBERGIA (Solanaceae)

§ ***caerulea*** ♀	ECha EMan WRus WThi
frutescens	See ***N. scoparia***
hippomanica	See ***N. caerulea***

§ ***repens***	CMHG CTri ELan EPot NBus NMen NNrd NRoo SBla WHil WOMN WPer WWin
rivularis	See ***N. repens***
§ ***scoparia***	CGle CHan EWes GOrc LHop MTho WRus
– 'Mont Blanc'	WRus
¶ – 'Purple Robe'	WRus

NIPHAEA (Gesneriaceae)

oblonga	NMos

× NIPHIMENES (Gesneriaceae)

'Lemonade'	NMos

NIPPONANTHEMUM (Asteraceae)

§ ***nipponicum***	CHan CMGP CNic CSam ECha GCal NFai NRoo NSti WCot WEas
– ***roseum***	CSam

NIVENIA (Iridaceae)
See Plant Deletions

NOCCAEA See THLASPI

NOLANA (Nolanaceae)
See Plant Deletions

NOLINA (Agavaceae)

beldingii	SIgm
brevifolia	SIgm
durangensis	CTbh
greenii	SIgm
longifolia	CTbh
palmeri	SIgm
§ ***recurvata*** 🏆	LCns LPal MBri
texana	SIgm

NOMOCHARIS (Liliaceae)

aperta	CPea EHyt EPot GBuc GDra LAma MDun WChr WCru
farreri	WChr
mairei	See ***N. pardanthina***
nana	See ***Lilium nanum***
§ ***pardanthina***	GBuc NHar WAbe WChr
– f. ***punctulata***	GDra GGGa MDun WAbe
saluenensis	GTou

NONEA (Boraginaceae)

lutea	CMea MFir NChi NOrc NRoo WAbb WByw WHal WPen

NOTELAEA (Oleaceae)

ligustrina	GWht

NOTHOFAGUS † (Fagaceae)

alessandrii	CMCN ISea
§ ***alpina***	CDoC CLnd CMHG CPer GAri GRei IOrc MBal NWea SMad WMou WNor
antarctica	CB&S CDoC CLnd CMHG ELan EMil IOrc ISea LPan MBal MBar MBri MGos NBee NHol NPal SPer WDin WNor WSHC
– 'Prostrata'	See ***N. antarctica* 'Benmore'**
cunninghamii	GAri GGGa ISea STre WNor
dombeyi	GAri IOrc ISea SArc WBod WNor
menziesii	CLnd CMHG GAri
moorei	CFil
obliqua	CDoC CGre CLnd CMCN CPer CSam GAri IOrc ISea MBal WDin WFro WMou WNor
procera	See ***N. alpina***
pumilio	GAri
solandri	CMHG
– var. ***cliffortioides***	CChu CFai CLnd MBal STre

NOTHOLAENA See CHEILANTHES

NOTHOLIRION (Liliaceae)

bulbuliferum	CRDP GCra SAlw WChr
¶ – C 5074	GGGa
¶ ***campanulatum***	SWat
macrophyllum	WChr WCru
¶ ***thomsonianum***	GCrs

NOTHOPANAX See PSEUDOPANAX, POLYSCIAS

NOTHOSCORDUM (Alliaceae)

¶ ***inodorum***	GBuc
inodorum macrostemon CL 7/76	CMon
neriniflorum	See ***Caloscordum neriniflorum***

NOTOBUXUS (Buxaceae)

¶ ***natalensis***	SLan

NOTOSPARTIUM (Papilionaceae)

carmichaeliae	ECou MAll
glabrescens	ECou MAll
torulosum	ECou MAll
– × ***glabrescens***	ECou MAll

NOTOTRICHE (Malvaceae)

compacta	MTho

NUPHAR (Nymphaeaceae)

advena	MSta WKen
japonica var. ***variegata***	CRow
lutea	CBen CRow EHon EMFW LPBA MSta NDea SWat WChe
– subsp. ***variegata***	See ***N. variegata***
pumila	MSta
– ***variegata***	MSta
'Shirley Bryne'	MSta

NYMPHAEA † (Nymphaeaceae)

'Afterglow' (T/D)	MSta
alba	CBen CRow CWGN EHon EMFW LPBA MSta NVic SAWi SWat SWyc WChe WKen WMAq WStI
§ – subsp. ***occidentalis*** (H)	MSta SWyc WKen
– 'Plenissima' (H)	MSta SWyc
– var. ***rubra*** (H)	MSta
'Albatros' (H)	EHon LPBA MSta SWat SWyc WBcn WKen
'Albatros' hort.	See ***N.* 'Hermine'**
'Albert Greenberg' (T/D)	MSta
'Amabilis' (H)	CBen CRow EMFW LPBA MSta SWat SWyc WKen WMAq
'American Star'	CWat MSta SWat SWyc WKen WMAq
'Andreana' (H)	CWat EMFW LPBA MSta SWat SWyc WKen

'Anna Epple'	SWyc WKen
'Apple Blossom Pink'	See *N.* **'Marliacea Carnea'**
'Apricot Pink' (T)	MSta
'Arc-en-ciel' (H)	MSta SWat SWyc WKen
'Arethusa' (H)	MSta SWyc
'Atropurpurea' (H)	CBen EMFW LPBA MSta SWat SWyc WKen WMAq
'Attraction' (H)	CBen CRow CWGN EHon EMFW LPBA MSta NVic SHig SWat SWyc WChe WKen WMAq WStI
'Aurora' (H)	CWat EMFW LPBA MSta SWat SWyc WKen WMAq
'Ballerina'	SWyc
'Barbara Davies'	MSta
'Barbara Dobbins'	MSta SWyc
'Baroness Orczy' (H)	MSta SWyc
'Bateau' (H)	MSta
'Berit Strawn'	SWyc
'Berthold'	MSta SWyc
'Betsy Sakata'	SWyc
¶ 'Bleeding Heart'	SWyc
'Blue Beauty' (T/D)	CBen
'Bory de Saint-Vincent' (H)	MSta
'Brakeleyi Rosea' (H)	EMFW LPBA MSta SWyc WKen
'Burgundy Princess'	SWyc WKen
caerulea (T/D)	MSta
candida	CBen EHon EMFW LPBA MSta SWyc WKen
– var. ***biradiata*** (H)	SWyc
– var. ***neglecta*** (H)	SWyc
– var. ***rubra*** (H)	MSta
'Candidissima' (H)	MSta SWyc WKen
'Candidissima Rosea' (H)	MSta SWyc
'Cardinal' (H)	SWyc
'Carolina Sunset'	SWyc
'Caroliniana' (H)	CWat MSta SWyc
'Caroliniana Nivea' (H)	CBen CWat EMFW MSta SWyc WKen
'Caroliniana Perfecta' (H)	CBen LPBA MSta SWat SWyc WKen
'Caroliniana Rosea' (H)	MSta SWyc
'Celebration'	MSta SWyc WKen
§ 'Charlene Strawn'	EMFW MSta SWat SWyc WKen
'Charles de Meurville' (H)	CBen CRow CWat EMFW LPBA MSta SWyc WKen WMAq
'Charles's Choice'	SWyc
'Château la Rouge'	MSta
'Cherokee'	SWyc
'Chromelia'	SWyc
'Chrysantha' (H)	EMFW MSta SWyc WKen
'Chubby'	MSta SWyc
'Citrus Star'	SWyc
'Colonel A.J. Welch' (H)	CBen CRow CWGN EHon EMFW LPBA MSta SAWi SWat SWyc WChe WKen WMAq
'Colonel Lindbergh' (T/D)	MSta
'Colorado'	SWyc
colorata	CBen MSta WKen
'Colossea' (H)	CBen EHon EMFW LPBA MSta SWyc WKen WMAq
'Comanche' (H)	CBen EMFW MSta SWat SWyc WKen WMAq
'Comte de Bouchaud'	MSta
'Conqueror' (H)	CWat EMFW LPBA MSta SAWi SWat SWyc WKen WMAq
cordata 'Pink Pons'	SWyc

'Dallas'	SWyc WKen
'Danieda'	SWat
§ 'Darwin' (H)	CBen MSta SWat SWyc WKen WMAq
× ***daubenyana*** (T/D)	MSta
'David'	MSta
'Denver'	SWyc
'Deva'	MSta
'Director George T. Moore' (T/D)	MSta
'Doll House'	SWyc
'Ellisiana' (H)	CBen CWGN EMFW LPBA MSta SWat SWyc WKen
'Elysée' (H)	MSta
'Ernst Epple Senior'	SWyc
'Escarboucle' (H) 🏆	CBen CRow CWGN CWat EHon EMFW LPBA MSta SAWi SWat SWyc WBcn WKen WMAq
'Esmeralda' (H)	MSta SWat SWyc
'Eucharis' (H)	MSta
'Evelyn Randig' (T/D)	CBen MSta
'Evelyn Stetston'	SWyc
♦ 'Exquisita'	See *N.* **'Odorata Exquisita'**
§ 'Fabiola' (H)	CBen CRow EHon EMFW LPBA MSta SAWi SWat SWyc WBcn WKen WMAq
'Fantastic Pink'	SWyc
'Fiesta'	SWyc
'Firecrest' (H)	CBen CWat EHon EMFW LPBA MSta SWat SWyc WBcn WKen WMAq
'Florida Sunset'	SWyc
'Formosa' (H)	MSta SWyc WKen
'France'	MSta
'Fritz Junge' (H)	MSta SWyc
'Froebelii' (H)	CBen CRow CWGN CWat EHon EMFW LPBA MSta SHig SWat SWyc WBcn WChe WKen WMAq
'Fulva' (H)	MSta SWyc
'Galatée' (H)	MSta SWyc
'General Pershing' (T/D)	MSta
gigantea	MSta
'Gladstoneana' (H) 🏆	CBen CRow CWGN EHon EMFW LPBA MSta SAWi SHig SWat SWyc WKen WMAq
'Gloire du Temple-sur-Lot' (H)	CBen EMFW MSta SWat SWyc WKen WMAq
'Gloriosa' (H)	CBen EMFW LPBA MSta SWat SWyc WKen
'Gold Medal' (H)	SWyc WKen
'Golden West' (T/D)	MSta
'Goliath' (H)	MSta SWyc
'Gonnère' (H) 🏆	CBen CRow CWGN CWat EHon EMFW LPBA MSta SHig SWat SWyc WKen WMAq
'Gracillima Alba' (H)	SWyc
'Granat'	SWyc
'Graziella' (H)	CWGN EMFW LPBA MSta SWat SWyc WBcn WKen WMAq
'Green Smoke' (T/D)	MSta
'Grésilias' (h)	MSta
'H.C. Haarstick' (T/D)	MSta
'Hal Miller' (H)	EMFW MSta SWyc WKen
'Helen Fowler' (H)	EMFW MSta SWat SWyc WMAq
♦ × ***helvola***	See *N.* **'Pygmaea Helvola'**
§ 'Hermine' (H)	CBen EMFW MSta SWat SWyc WKen WMAq
'Hever White' (H)	MSta SWyc WKen

◆ 'Hollandia' hort.	See ***N.* 'Darwin'**
¶ 'Hollandia' Koster (H)	SWyc
'Improved Firecrest'	SWyc
'Indiana' (H)	CBen CWGN CWat EMFW LPBA MSta SWat SWyc WKen WMAq
'Irene' (H)	SWyc
'Irene Heritage'	SWyc
'J.C.N. Forestier' (H)	MSta WKen
'Jack Wood' (T)	MSta
'James Brydon' (H) 🏆	CBen CRow CWGN CWat EHon EMFW LPBA MSta SAWi SHig SRms SWat SWyc WBcn WKen WMAq
'James Hudson' (H)	MSta SWyc
'Jean de la Marsalle' (H)	MSta
'Jean Laydeker'	MSta
'Jean Marie'	SWyc
'Jim Saunders'	SWyc
'Joanne Pring'	MSta SWat SWyc
'Joey Tomocick'	SWyc WKen
'Julian Decelle'	MSta
'Juliana' (h)	CWat EMFW MSta
'Kiss of Fire' (H)	SWyc
'Lactea' (H)	MSta
'Laydekeri Fulgens' (H)	CBen EMFW LPBA MSta SWat SWyc WKen WMAq
'Laydekeri Lilacea' (H)	CBen CRow EMFW LPBA MSta SWat SWyc WKen WMAq
'Laydekeri Purpurata' (H)	EMFW LPBA MSta SWat SWyc WBcn WKen WMAq
◆ 'Laydekeri Rosea' hort.	See ***N.* 'Laydekeri Rosea Prolifera'**
§ 'Laydekeri Rosea Prolifera' (H)	CBen EMFW LPBA MSta SWyc WKen
'Lemon Chiffon'	SWyc WKen
'Leviathan' (H)	MSta
'Lily Pons'	SWyc
'Limelight'	SWat
'Liou'	SWyc
'Little Sue'	SWyc WKen
'Livingstone' (H)	MSta SWyc
'Louise' (H)	SWyc
'Louise Villemarette'	SWyc
◆ 'Luciana'	See ***N.* 'Odorata Luciana'**
'Lucida' (H)	CBen CWat EMFW LPBA MSta SWat SWyc WKen
'Lusitania' (H)	MSta SWyc
¶ 'Lustrous' (H)	SWyc
'Madame Bory Latour-Marliac' (H)	MSta
'Madame de Bonseigneur' (H)	MSta
'Madame Julien Chifflot' (H)	MSta
'Madame Maurice Laydeker' (H)	MSta SWyc
'Madame Wilfon Gonnère' (H)	CBen CWGN CWat EHon EMFW LPBA MSta SWat SWyc WBcn WKen WMAq
'Margaret Randig' (T/D)	MSta
'Marguerite Laplace' (H)	MSta SWyc
'Marliacea Albida'	CBen CWGN CWat EHon LPBA MSta SWat SWyc WChe WKen
§ 'Marliacea Carnea' (H)	CBen CRow CWGN EHon EMFW LPBA MSta NVic SWat SWyc WBcn WKen WMAq
'Marliacea Chromatella' (H) 🏆	CBen CRow CWGN EHon EMFW LPBA MSta NVic SAWi SHig SWat SWyc WBcn WChe WKen WMAq
'Marliacea Flammea' (H)	MSta SWyc
'Marliacea Ignea' (H)	MSta SWyc
'Marliacea Rosea' (H)	EMFW MSta SHig SWyc WKen WMAq
'Marliacea Rubra Punctata' (H)	MSta SWyc WKen
'Maroon Beauty' (T/N)	MSta
'Martha'	SWyc WKen
'Mary'	SWyc
'Mary Exquisita' (H)	MSta
'Mary Patricia' (H)	MSta SWyc
'Masaniello' (H)	CBen CRow CWGN EHon EMFW LPBA MSta SWat SWyc WBcn WKen WMAq
'Maurice Laydeker' (H)	EMFW MSta SWyc
'Mayla'	SWyc
§ 'Météor' (H)	CWat EMFW MSta SWyc WKen
mexicana	MSta WKen
'Moorei' (H)	CBen CWGN EHon EMFW LPBA MSta SHig SWat SWyc WKen WMAq
'Mount Shasta'	SWyc
'Mrs C.W. Thomas' (H)	MSta SWyc
'Mrs C.W. Ward' (T/D)	MSta
◆ 'Mrs Richmond'	See ***N.* 'Fabiola'**
'Murillo' (H)	MSta SWyc
'Neptune' (H)	MSta
'Newton' (H)	CWat EMFW MSta SWat SWyc WMAq
'Nigel' (H)	MSta SWat SWyc WKen
'Nobilissima' (H)	MSta
'Norma Gedye' (H)	CBen CWat MSta SWat SWyc WKen WMAq
'Occidentalis'	See ***N. alba*** subsp. ***occidentalis***
'Odalisque' (H)	CWat EMFW MSta SWyc WBcn
§ ***odorata*** (H)	CBen CRow CWGN EHon LPBA MSta SHig SWyc WBcn WKen WMAq
'Odorata Alba'	See ***N. odorata***
'Odorata Eugène de Land' (H)	MSta
§ 'Odorata Exquisita' (H)	MSta SWyc
¶ ***odorata*** var. ***gigantea*** (H)	MSta
* – 'Jasmine'	SWyc WKen
'Odorata Juliana' (H)	SWyc
§ 'Odorata Luciana'	EMFW MSta SWyc WKen
odorata 'Maxima' (H)	SWyc
§ – var. ***minor*** (H)	CBen CRow CWGN EMFW LPBA MSta SWat SWyc WKen WMAq
◆ – 'Pumila'	See ***N. odorata*** var. ***minor***
– var. ***rosea*** (H)	EMFW MSta SAWi SWyc
– 'Roswitha' (H)	SWyc
– f. ***rubra*** (H)	MSta
'Odorata Sulphurea' (H)	MSta SWat SWyc WBcn WKen
§ 'Odorata Sulphurea Grandiflora' (H)	CRow CWGN EHon EMFW LPBA MSta SWat SWyc WKen WMAq
'Odorata Turicensis' (H)	CWGN EMFW LPBA MSta SWyc WKen
◆ 'Odorata William B. Shaw'	See ***N.* 'W.B. Shaw'**
'Pam Bennett' (H)	MSta WKen
'Pamela' (T/D)	CBen MSta WKen

'Paul Hariot'	CWGN CWat EHon EMFW LPBA MSta SWat SWyc WBcn WMAq
'Peach Blossom'	SWyc
'Peaches and Cream'	SWyc
Pearl of the Pool (H)	MSta SWat SWyc WKen
'Pennsylvania' (T/D)	MSta
'Perry's Almost Black'	SWyc
'Perry's Baby Red'	SWyc WKen
'Perry's Black Opal'	SWyc WKen
'Perry's Cactus Pink'	SWyc WKen
'Perry's Crinkled Pink'	SWyc WKen
'Perry's Darkest Red'	SWyc
'Perry's Double White'	SWyc WKen
'Perry's Dwarf Red'	SWyc WKen
'Perry's Fire Opal'	SWyc WKen
'Perry's Magnificent'	SWyc WKen
'Perry's Pink'	MSta SWat SWyc WKen WMAq
'Perry's Pink Beauty'	SWyc WKen
'Perry's Pink Bicolor'	SWyc WKen
'Perry's Pink Delight'	SWyc WKen
'Perry's Pink Heaven'	SWyc
'Perry's Red Beauty'	SWyc WKen
'Perry's Red Bicolor'	SWyc WKen
'Perry's Red Blaze'	SWyc
'Perry's Red Glow'	SWyc WKen
'Perry's Red Sensation'	WKen
'Perry's Red Star'	SWyc WKen
'Perry's Red Wonder'	SWyc WKen
'Perry's Rich Rose'	SWyc WKen
'Perry's Stellar Red'	SWyc WKen
'Perry's Strawberry Pink'	SWyc WKen
'Perry's Super Red'	SWyc WKen
'Perry's Super Rose'	SWyc
'Perry's Vivid Rose'	SWyc
'Perry's Viviparous Pink'	SWyc WKen
'Perry's White Star'	SWyc WKen
'Perry's White Wonder'	SWyc WKen
'Perry's Wildfire'	SWyc WKen
'Peter Slocum'	MSta SWat SWyc WKen
'Philippe Laydeker'	MSta
'Phoebus' (H)	MSta SWat SWyc WBcn
'Phoenix' (H)	MSta
'Picciola' (H)	MSta SWyc
'Pink Beauty'	SWyc
'Pink Cameo'	SWyc
'Pink Glory' (H)	SWyc
'Pink Opal' (H)	CBen CWat EMFW LPBA MSta SWyc WKen
'Pink Peony'	SWyc WKen
'Pink Platter' (T/D)	CBen WKen
'Pink Pumpkin'	SWyc WKen
'Pink Sensation' (H)	CBen CWat EMFW MSta SWat SWyc WKen WMAq
'Pink Shadow'	SWyc
'Pink Starlet'	SWyc
'Pink Sunrise'	MSta SWyc WKen
'Pöstlingberg' (H)	MSta SWyc WKen WMAq
'Président Viger'	MSta
'Princess Elizabeth' (H)	EMFW LPBA MSta SWyc
'Pygmaea Alba'	See ***N. tetragona***
§ 'Pygmaea Helvola' (H) ♀	CBen CRow CWGN EHon EMFW LPBA MSta NVic SWat SWyc WKen WMAq
'Pygmaea Rubis' (H)	CRow EHon LPBA MSta NVic SWat SWyc
'Pygmaea Rubra' (H)	CBen CWat EMFW MSta SWyc WKen WMAq
'Queen of the Whites' (H)	SWyc WKen
¶ 'Radiant Red' (T/D)	SWyc
'Ray Davies'	MSta SWyc WKen
'Red Beauty'	MSta
'Red Cup' (T)	MSta
'Red Flare' (T/N)	MSta
'Red Sensation'	SWyc WKen
'Red Spider'	SWyc WKen
'Regann'	SWyc
'Rembrandt' hort.	See ***N.* 'Météor'**
¶ 'Rembrandt' Koster (H)	SWyc
'René Gérard' (H)	CBen CWat EHon EMFW LPBA MSta SAWi SHig SWat SWyc WBcn WKen WMAq
'Rio'	SWyc
'Robinsoniana' (H)	EMFW MSta SWyc
'Rosa Mundi'	SWyc
'Rosanna'	SWyc
'Rosanna Supreme' (H)	MSta SWat SWyc WKen
'Rose Arey' (H)	CBen CRow CWGN EHon EMFW LPBA MSta SWat SWyc WBcn WKen WMAq
'Rose Magnolia' (H)	EMFW MSta SWat SWyc WKen
§ 'Rosea' (H)	CBen CWGN EMFW LPBA MSta SWyc WKen
'Rosennymphe' (H)	CBen LPBA MSta SWat SWyc WKen WMAq
'Rosette'	SWyc
'Rosita' (H)	MSta
'Rosy Morn' (H)	EMFW MSta SWyc WKen
'Saint Louis' (T/D)	MSta
'Saint Louis Gold' (T/D)	MSta
'Sanguinea' (H)	EMFW MSta SWyc
'Seignouretti' (H)	EMFW MSta SWyc WBcn
'Senegal' (H)	MSta SWyc
'Sioux' (H)	CBen CWGN CWat EHon EMFW LPBA MSta SHig SWat SWyc WKen WMAq
'Sir Galahad' (T/N)	MSta
'Sirius' (H)	CWat EMFW MSta SWat SWyc WKen
'Solfatare' (H)	EMFW MSta SWyc WKen
'Somptuosa' (H)	CWat EMFW MSta SWyc WKen
'Souvenir de Jules Jacquier' (H)	MSta
'Speciosa' (H)	MSta
'Spectabilis'	MSta
'Splendida' (H)	MSta SWyc WKen WMAq
'Stardust'	SWyc
'Steven Strawn'	SWyc
'Sturtevantii' (T/N)	MSta
'Suavissima' (H)	MSta
'Sultan' (H)	EMFW MSta SWyc WKen
'Sunburst'	SWyc
'Sunrise'	See ***N.* 'Odorata Sulphurea Grandiflora'**
'Superba' (H)	MSta
'Sylphida' (H)	MSta
'Temple Fire' (H)	MSta
§ ***tetragona*** (H)	CBen CRow EHon EMFW LPBA MSta SWyc WKen
– 'Alba'	See ***N. tetragona***
– 'Johann Pring' (H)	EMFW
§ – var. ***rubra*** (H)	MSta
'Texas Dawn'	EMFW MSta SWyc WKen
tuberosa (H)	CBen LPBA MSta SWyc
– 'Maxima' (H)	MSta SWyc
– 'Richardsonii' (H)	CWGN EHon EMFW MSta SWyc WKen
◆ – 'Rosea'	See ***N.* 'Rosea'**
'Tulipiformis' (H)	MSta
'Venus'	SWyc WKen
'Venusta' (H)	MSta SWyc
'Vera Louise' (H)	MSta SWyc

'Vésuve' (H) CWat EMFW MSta SWat SWyc WKen
'Victoria Longwood' (T) MSta
'Virginalis' (H) EMFW MSta SWat SWyc WKen
'Virginia' (H) EMFW MSta SWyc WKen
§ 'W.B. Shaw' (H) CBen CWGN EHon EMFW LPBA MSta SWat SWyc WKen WMAq
'Walter Pagels' MSta SWyc
'White Cup' SWyc
'White Sultan' SWyc
'William Doogue' (H) EMFW MSta SWyc WBcn WKen WMAq
'William Falconer' (H) CBen CWGN CWat EMFW LPBA MSta SAWi SWat SWyc WKen
'Wood's White Knight' (T/N) MSta
'Wow' SWyc
'Wucai' SWyc
'Yellow Dazzler' (T/D) MSta
'Yellow Princess' SWyc WKen
'Yellow Queen' SWyc WKen
'Yellow Sensation' SWyc WKen
'Yogi-gi' SWyc
'Yul Ling' EMFW SWat SWyc
'Ziyu' SWyc

NYMPHOIDES (Menyanthaceae)

peltata CRDP CWat ECoo EMFW MHew NDea SWat SWyc WChe
§ – 'Bennettii' CBen CWGN EHon IBlr LPBA MSta

NYSSA (Nyssaceae)

aquatica CFil CMCN SSpi SSta
sinensis ♀ CAbP CB&S CChu CDoC CEnd CGre CHan CMCN CPMA CSam CTho ELan MBri MUlv SPer SReu SSpi SSta WPat WWat
sylvatica ♀ CB&S CChu CLnd CMCN CPMA CPle CTho ELan EMil ISea LPan MBal MBar MBri MMea MUlv SHBN SPer SReu SSpi SSta WBod WCoo WDin WFro WNor WWat
¶ – 'Sheffield Park' LRHS
– 'Windsor' LRHS SSpi
– 'Wisley Bonfire' LRHS SSpi

OAKESIELLA See UVULARIA

OCHAGAVIA (Bromeliaceae)

rosea CFil CHEx

OCHNA (Ochnaceae)

serrulata CSpe

OCIMUM (Lamiaceae)

¶ 'African Blue' EOHP
§ ***americanum*** WHer WPer
– 'Meng Luk' See ***O. americanum***
basilicum CArn CSev EEls GPoy LHol MBri MChe SIde SWat WHer WPer WSel WWye
– 'Anise' See ***O. basilicum* 'Horapha'**
– 'Cinnamon' CSev MChe MGra MSal SHDw SWat WHer WJek WPer WSel WWye
– var. ***citriodorum*** CArn MChe MSal SHDw SIde SWat WJek WPer WSel
– 'Dark Opal' CBod MGra NRai SHDw SWat WJek WSel
– 'Genovese' ELau EOHP
– 'Glycyrrhiza' See ***O. basilicum* 'Horapha'**
– 'Green Globe' MChe
– 'Green Ruffles' MChe MGra SWat WJek WSel
– 'Holy' See ***O. tenuiflorum***
§ – 'Horapha' CArn CSev EOHP GPoy MChe MLan MSal SIde WJek WPer
– 'Horapha Nanum' WJek
– var. ***minimum*** CArn CBod CJew CSev ELau EOHP GPoy LHol MBri MChe SIde WHer WJek WPer WSel WWye
– 'Napolitano' MChe MGra SIde SWat WJek WPer
– 'Purple Ruffles' EOHP MChe MGra NRai SIde SWat WJek WPer WSel
– var. ***purpurascens*** CArn CSev ELau GPoy LHol MBri MChe SIde WHer WPer
– 'Red Rubin' MChe
* – 'Rubin' EOHP
◆ – 'Thai' See ***O. basilicum* 'Horapha'**
canum See ***O. americanum***
kilimandscharicum GPoy
× ***basilicum*** var. ***purpurascens***
sanctum See ***O. tenuiflorum***
'Spice' MChe WPer
§ ***tenuiflorum*** CArn CSev GPoy MChe MSal NOak SHDw SIde SWat WHer WJek WPer

ODONTONEMA (Acanthaceae)

strictum LHil

OEMLERIA (Rosaceae)

§ ***cerasiformis*** CB&S CFil CHan ELan SSpi WCot WEas WHCG WWat WWin

OENANTHE (Apiaceae)

aquatica 'Variegata' EMFW
crocata ECWi WChe
fluviatilis WKen
japonica See ***O. javanica***
* ***javanica*** 'Atropurpurea' EHoe
– 'Flamingo' CBen CBre CHid CRow CSpe EBar EFol EHal ELan EMar EMon EPla EPri LFis LHop MBel MNrw MRav MSCN NBro NRoo NWes SLod WBea WCru WFar WHer WOve WPbr WPer
pimpinelloides ECWi

OENOTHERA † (Onagraceae)

§ ***acaulis*** CBot CHan CSpe GCal GMac LHop MNrw SAlw SAxl SChu SOkh SSpi
acaulis alba MAvo WCot
§ ***acaulis*** 'Aurea' LHop NTow NWCA WCla WPer
– BC&W 4110 MFos
– 'Lutea' hort. See ***O. acaulis* 'Aurea'**
* ***alpina*** CPle
'Apricot Delight' MCCP
argillicola MSto WPer
'Beach' SUsu

berlandieri	See ***O. speciosa* 'Rosea'**
§ ***biennis***	CKin CRow CSev EBre ECWi ECha EHoe EWFC GPoy LHol MChe MHew NBro SIde SIng WHer WJek WOak WPer WSel
brachycarpa	MSto
brevipes	MSto
caespitosa	CPBP EMan MFos MTho WHer
* ***campylocalyx***	LHop WCot
cheiranthifolia	SAlw WPer
childsii	See ***O. speciosa* 'Rosea'**
cinaeus	See ***O. fruticosa*** subsp. ***glauca***
'Colin Porter'	CInt EBur EFou EOHP MNrw NWCA SAlw SOkh SUsu
¶ ***coryi***	WCot
deltoides	MSto
– var. ***howellii***	CPou CSpe
§ ***elata*** subsp. ***hookeri***	WPer
erythrosepala	See ***O. glaziouana***
flava	CNic MTho
fremontii	MSto
§ ***fruticosa***	EBre MSto NBro
* – 'Camel' (v)	CBos CRDP CVer SUsu
◆ – Fireworks	See ***O. fruticosa* 'Fyrverkeri'**
– subsp. ***fruticosa***	CHan
§ – 'Fyrverkeri' 🏆	CDoC CSam CShe EBre ECED ECro EFou ELan ENot EPla GMaP LHop MCLN MRav MTis NVic SOkh SPer SUsu WGwG WHil WHoo WPyg WRus WTyr WWin
§ – subsp. ***glauca*** 🏆	CElw CHan EBee EBre MNrw MTho NBro NTow WEas WPer
– – 'Erica Robin' (v)	CMil EBee EFou EMan EMon GBuc LHop SOkh WCot WSan
– – 'Frühlingsgold' (v)	EMon WCot
◆ – – Solstice	See ***O. fruticosa*** subsp. ***glauca* 'Sonnenwende'**
§ – – 'Sonnenwende'	EBee EBre EMon NPro SOkh WCot
◆ – Highlight	See ***O. fruticosa* 'Hoheslicht'**
– 'Lady Brookborough'	LHop MRav
– 'Michelle Ploeger'	EBee
– var. ***riparia***	ELan SAga WRus
¶ – 'Silberblatt'	LBuc
– 'Yellow River'	CB&S CSte ECED EOrc WWeb
– 'Youngii'	CM&M EJud LFis SSte WPer
glabra hort.	CLyd LHop NSti SIng SUsu
– Miller	See ***O. biennis***
§ ***glaziouana***	ECoo IBlr NBir WPer WWye
heterantha	EBee MSto
* 'Hollow Meadows'	MTho NMen
hookeri	See ***O. elata*** subsp. ***hookeri***
kunthiana	CElw EDAr EGoo EMan MSto NLak NWCA WCru WHil WPen WPer
§ ***laciniata***	SIde
lamarckiana	See ***O. glaziouana***
lavandulifolia	MSto
'Lemon Sunset'	EBee MCCP SWat
linearis	See ***O. fruticosa***
'Longest Day'	EPfP NFai WHil
§ ***macrocarpa*** 🏆	CSev EBre ECha ELan ENot EOrc LHop MCLN MTho MTol MWat NFai NRoo SDix SMad SPer WBea WFar WHoo WOld WWin
– 'Greencourt Lemon'	LRHS NSti
mexicana	See ***O. laciniata***
missouriensis	See ***O. macrocarpa***
* 'Moonlight'	SAsh SIng
muricata	EBee
odorata Hook. & Arn.	See ***O. biennis***
– hort.	See ***O. glaziouana***
– Jacquin	CArn CSam CSev CSpe EFol GBar GCal IBlr LGan LHil NOrc SSvw WCru
– 'Sulphurea'	See ***O. stricta* 'Sulphurea'**
organensis	EBee
pallida	IBlr NFai NLak SWat
– 'Innocence'	CBot CM&M LRHS WHer WPer
– subsp. ***trichocalyx***	LHol
– 'Wedding Bells'	EBee NPer
'Penelope Hobhouse'	SUsu
§ ***perennis***	CNic EBre EMan LFis MTho NFai NNrd NPri SAlw SMac SOkh SRms SWat WCla WEas WHil WPer WWin
primiveris	MSto
pumila	See ***O. perennis***
rosea	CHan CMea MSto NPer SIde SUsu WOMN WWye
serrulata	MSto
sp. South America	CLyd MTho
speciosa	CMea CSev CSte EFou MBel MTol SEND SPer SWat WCot WPer WSan
– 'Ballerina'	CSpe EMan LHop
– var. ***childsii***	See ***O. speciosa* 'Rosea'**
– 'Pink Petticoats'	CChr CM&M CPou CSpe EBee EBre ECoo EHal MCCP NCGP NFai NPer SIde SOkh SWat WBea WBro WElm WHil WSan
§ – 'Rosea'	CBot CFir CGle CMea CNic CRDP ECGP ELan EMon MCCP MNrw WCot WHer WPer WWin
– 'Siskiyou'	COtt CSpe EMan LRHS MTis NLak SCoo SIng SMrm WCru WMaN WWeb
– 'Siskiyou' variegated	LRHS
§ ***stricta***	CHad CHan CKin CSpe ECGP EWFC MSto WPer WWye
§ – 'Sulphurea'	CHad CHan CM&M CMil CSam ECoo ELan EMan GCal IBlr LBlm LGre MBel NPer SAga SAxl SChu SMrm SUsu WAbb WBea WBro WCot WHoo WPer
taraxacifolia	See ***O. acaulis***
tetragona	See ***O. fruticosa*** subsp. ***glauca***
– var. ***fraseri***	See ***O. fruticosa*** subsp. ***glauca***
◆ – 'Sonnenwende'	See ***O. fruticosa*** subsp. ***glauca* 'Sonnenwende'**
tetraptera	NWCA
texensis	SWat
– 'Early Rise'	CSev ELan EMan LHop SAga
triloba	MSto
versicolor 'Sunset Boulevard'	CHad CMil CPou CRDP EBee ECoo EFou EOHP MCCP NBus WBea WSan
'Woodside White'	LRHS

OLEA (Oleaceae)

europaea 🏆	CArn CFil CSWP ERea GAri LBlm LCns LHol LPan SArc STre WNor
§ – var. ***europaea*** 'Cipressino'	ERea LPan
– – 'El Greco'	CB&S ERea GAri
– – 'Picholine'	ERea

– – 'Pyramidalis'	See ***O. europaea*** var. ***europaea*** **'Cipressino'**

OLEARIA † (Asteraceae)

albida var. ***angulata***	CPle MAll
– Hooker f.	CB&S
– – × ***paniculata***	CPle
– hort.	See ***O.*** **'Talbot de Malahide'**
algida	CPle ECou
arborescens	GSki MAll
argophylla	ECou MAll
avicenniifolia	CPle ECou EPla MAll WLRN WSHC
– 'White Confusion'	MAll WPen WWat
canescens	SBid
capillaris	CChe CPle ECou EPla GGar IDee ISea MAll SDry SIgm WPen WWat
chathamica	ICrw IDee
§ ***cheesemanii***	CMHG CPle MAll WSHC
coriacea	MAll
erubescens	CPle MAll
floribunda	CPle MAll
fragrantissima	MAll
frostii	CPle MSto SBar WFar WKif
furfuracea	CB&S CDoC CHEx CPle
glandulosa	CPle ECou MAll
gunniana	See ***O. phlogopappa***
× ***haastii***	Widely available
– 'McKenzie'	ECou
§ 'Henry Travers' 🏆	CDoC CPle GQui IBlr MAll MBal
§ ***ilicifolia***	CFil CPle EBee GSki IDee MAll SDry SPla SSpi WCru
insignis	WCru
– var. ***minor***	WCru
lacunosa	ICrw
lepidophylla	ECou WThi
– green	ECou
– silver	ECou MAll
lineata 'Dartonii'	ECou MAll
lirata	CPle ECou MAll
macrodonta 🏆	Widely available
– 'Intermedia'	MAll
– 'Major'	EBee EPfP SHBN SSoC WTyr
– 'Minor'	CChu CWLN ELan GQui
microphylla	CPle
× ***mollis*** hort.	See ***O. ilicifolia***
– (Kirk) Ckn.	CB&S CPle GQui MAll NNor SBid SPer SSpi WCru WSHC
– – 'Zennorensis' 🏆	CAbb CGre CLan CMHG CPle ISea MAll SDry SOWG SSpi WCru
moschata	CPle ECou GSki MAll SBid SSpi
myrsinoides	CMHG CPle MAll
§ ***nummulariifolia***	CMHG COtt CPle CTri ECou EPla GAul MAll MBal NBee NNor SArc SDry SEND SIng WBod WGwG WSHC
– var. ***cymbifolia***	ECou MAll
– hybrids	ECou MAll
obcordata	MAll
odorata	CPle ECou MAll WHCG
oleifolia	See ***O.*** **'Waikariensis'**
paniculata	CAbb CChu CGre CMHG CPle CTri GIsl GSki ISea MAll SDry WCru
§ ***phlogopappa***	CMHG CPle ECou GIsl ISea MAll MTis SVen WCot
– 'Comber's Blue'	CB&S CDoC CPle IBlr ISea SAga SPer SSta
§ – 'Comber's Pink'	CB&S CDoC CGre CPle ELan EMil IBlr SAga SPan SPer SPla
– pink	MAll SReu SSta
– 'Rosea'	See ***O. phlogopappa*** **'Comber's Pink'**
– Splendens Group	CAbb
– var. ***subrepanda***	CGre CPle MAll SEND WBod
§ ***ramulosa***	CInt CPle LHil SBid WCot WGwG WWat
– 'Blue Stars'	ECou
ramulosa ramulosa	ECou
rani hort.	See ***O. cheesemanii***
× ***scilloniensis*** hort.	See ***O. stellulata*** **De Candolle**
– 'Master Michael' Dorrien-Smith	CBlo CBot CTrw EMil MRav NFai SEND SOWG SPer SPla WSHC
semidentata	See ***O.*** **'Henry Travers'**
solandri	CMHG COtt CPle CSam CWSG ECou EMil EPla GBin GIsl GOrc ISea MAll NFai SDix SDry SHFr SPer
– 'Aurea'	CB&S GQui
§ ***stellulata*** De Candolle 🏆	CBot CGre CMHG CTrw CWit EAst EBar ECou EEls ELan ENot IHos ISea MWat SDix SOWG SPer SPla SSta WAbe WBea WHCG WRTC WStI WWeb
– hort.	See ***O. phlogopappa***
traversii	CAbb CDoC CMHG CPle CTre EHic GIsl IOrc MAll SEND WCru WDin WLRN
§ – 'Tweedledum' (v)	CPle ECou EHoe MAll
– 'Variegata'	See ***O. traversii*** **'Tweedledum'**
virgata	CMHG COtt CPle ECou ELan GSki ISea
– 'Laxifolia'	CTre
– var. ***lineata***	CChu CPle MAll SArc SEND WCru WDin WSHC
– – 'Dartonii'	GIsl SHhN SLPl
– var. ***ramuliflora***	MAll
viscosa	CPle MAll
§ 'Waikariensis'	CBlo CBot CPle CSam ECou EHic LHop MAll SChu SEND WBod WDin WWat

OLSYNIUM (Iridaceae)

§ ***douglasii*** 🏆	CBro EBur EHyt ELan EPar EPot GDra NHar NHol NMen NNrd NRya NTow WOMN
douglasii album	EBur EHyt EPot GAbr GDra NHar NHol NNrd NRya
douglasii var. ***inflatum***	EWes
– JCA 11132	SBla
§ ***filifolium***	CLyd EMar MHar MNrw WWhi
junceum JCA 12289	MTho

OMPHALODES (Boraginaceae)

cappadocica 🏆	CBos CElw CGle CRow EBre ECha ELan EOrc EPot LFis MBro NBrk NBro NNor NPer SDix SMac SSpi WEas WHal WHoo WOMN WPbr WWat
– 'Alba'	EBre LLWP SRms WEas
– 'Anthea Bloom'	EBre IBlr NTow SPer
– 'Cherry Ingram'	CArc CFil CLyd CRow ECha EHyt GBuc MAvo MBel MBri MCLN NBir NCat SAxl SBid SBla SDix SLod SMrm SSpe SSpi SUsu SWas WCer WCot WCru WFar WWhi
– 'Starry Eyes'	Widely available

§ *linifolia* 🏆	CLyd CRDP CSpe ECoo MHlr NTow NWes SUsu WEas
linifolia alba	See ***O. linifolia***
luciliae	NTow WHoo
nitida	MAvo
verna	Widely available
– 'Alba'	CBot CBre CGle CRow CShe EAst EBre ECha EFol EFou ELan GAbr GCal LFis LHop MTho NHol SIng SPer SSvw WBea WDav WHal WHoo WMer WOve WPbr WRus WWat
verna grandiflora	SWas

OMPHALOGRAMMA (Primulaceae)

delavayi	NHar

ONCOBA (Flacourtiaceae)

See Plant Deletions

ONIXOTIS (Colchicaceae)

See Plant Deletions

ONOBRYCHIS (Papilionaceae)

viciifolia	CKin ELan ESis EWFC MHew MSal SOkh WGwy WWye

ONOCLEA (Aspidiaceae)

sensibilis 🏆	Widely available
– copper	CFil CVer SRms WPGP

ONONIS (Papilionaceae)

cenisia	See ***O. cristata***
repens	CArn CInt CKin ECWi EWFC GAul MHew MSal NMir WGwy
rotundifolia	CHan CLyd CPle MBro MSal WOMN WPat
spinosa	CKin CLyd ECWi EWFC GAul LFis MHew MSal WFar WGwy WPer
– 'Alba'	EMon

ONOPORDUM (Asteraceae)

acanthium	CArc CArn CHad CKin CLTr ECGP ECha ECoo ELan EMan EMil GAbr GBar GCra LHol MGam MHar MWat NPSI SIde SSoC WCHb WCot WCru WHer WHil WWye
arabicum	See ***O. nervosum***
bracteatum	WPer
§ *nervosum* 🏆	CArn EBee ERav LFis LHil NBro NVic SMad WFar WWhi

ONOSMA (Boraginaceae)

alborosea	CLyd CMea CSev ECha EFol EGoo ELan EOrc GBri GCal GCra MFir NGar SBla SChu WEas WOMN WPer WWye
echioides	EPad
helvetica	MSto WPat
nana	EPot LFlo MSto NChi
– Mac&W 5785	WOMN
rutila	SIgm
stellulata	CLyd NChi
taurica 🏆	NBir NChi WDav WWin

ONYCHIUM (Polypodiaceae)

contiguum	CFil WAbe
japonicum	CFil CRDP ECha GQui NMar SAxl SBar SBla SChu SWas WAbe
– 'Dali' L 1649	SBla

OPHIOPOGON † (Convallariaceae)

'Black Dragon'	See ***O. planiscapus* 'Nigrescens'**
bodinieri	EWes SApp SIng SMac
– B&L 12505	CHid CRDP EBee EMon EPPr EPla SAxl
¶ *chingii*	EMon
graminifolius	See ***Liriope muscari***
intermedius	CHid EMon EPPr EPla MSte WCot
§ – 'Argenteomarginatus'	EWes LHop WChr
intermedius parviflorus	NSti
intermedius 'Variegatus'	See ***O. intermedius* 'Argenteomarginatus'**
§ *jaburan*	CArc CHan CHid CMGP CTrC LAma LHil MHFP MSte MUlv SBar WPri WWat
– 'Variegatus'	See ***O. jaburan* 'Vittatus'**
§ – 'Vittatus' (v)	EBee EFol EHoe EPPr LRHS SMad SPla WCot WFar WRus
japonicus	CBro CRow EPPr EPla NSti WBea
– 'Albus'	NHol
– B&SWJ 561	WCru
– 'Compactus'	CArc CFil CHid SMac SPla WCot WPGP
¶ – 'Kigimafukiduma'	CDec CElw CSte CWSG EPPr WCot
– 'Minor'	CInt EFol EGar EPla
– 'Nippon'	EGol EPPr
* – Tamaryu Number Two	ECho EHic EHyt ESis EWes NHar WChr
planiscapus	CFee CPea CSWP CSev EPar EPla GCal GFre LHil MBel MSte MTho MWat NBro NGar NHar NHol WGwG WHil
– *leucanthus*	WCot
¶ – 'Little Tabby'	SBla WCot
* – *minimus*	ERos
§ – 'Nigrescens' 🏆	Widely available
– 'Silver Ribbon'	SWat
* *tamaryu*	EPPr WThi
wallichianus	WCot WOMN WWat

OPHRYS (Orchidaceae)

¶ *apifera*	WHer

OPITHANDRA (Gesneriaceae)

See Plant Deletions

OPLISMENUS (Poaceae)

§ *africanus* 'Variegatus' 🏆	CHal
hitellus	See ***O. africanus***

OPUNTIA † (Cactaceae)

humifusa	EOas SMad
§ *lindheimeri*	CHEx SArc
linguiformis	See ***O. lindheimeri***
phaeacantha	CHEx SArc

ORCHIS (Orchidaceae)

elata	See ***Dactylorhiza elata***
foliosa	See ***Dactylorhiza foliosa***
fuchsii	See ***Dactylorhiza fuchsii***
¶ *laxiflora*	SWes
maculata	See ***Dactylorhiza maculata***
maderensis	See ***Dactylorhiza foliosa***

majalis	See ***Dactylorhiza majalis***
§ ***mascula***	SWes WChe WHer
¶ ***morio***	LAma SWes
¶ ***spectabilis***	EFEx

OREOBOLUS (Cyperaceae)
See Plant Deletions

OREOPANAX (Araliaceae)

epremesnilianus	CHEx

OREOPTERIS (Thelypteridaceae)

§ ***limbosperma***	CCuc CFil NHar SRms

ORIGANUM † (Lamiaceae)

acutidens	WCHb
amanum 🏆	CLon CLyd CPBP ECha EDAr EHyt ELan EWes LBee LHop MBro MFos MHig MTho NBir NTow SAga SBla SChu WFar WOMN WPat WRus WWye
amanum album	CPBP ECho WOMN WPat
'Barbara Tingey'	CElw CLon CLyd CRDP CSpe ECha ECou EHyt ELan EPot EWes LBee LHop MBro MHig MTho NTow SBla SChu SUsu WAbe WCru WHil WHoo WPat
I 'Bristol Cross'	CElw ECha GBri NHex WPat
'Buckland'	CGle CLon CLyd ESis LBee LGre MSte NWCA SBla SWas SWat WPat WPyg WRus
caespitosum	See ***O. vulgare* 'Nanum'**
§ ***calcaratum***	CLyd CShe ELan LBee MTho SBla SSad WAbe WByw WPat WPyg
dictamnus	CMea EEls EHyt ELan EPot GPoy LBee SSad SWas WAbe WOMN WRus
'Dingle Fairy'	EBee EFol EWes NHex WWye
'Erntedank'	EFou EMon WTre
'Frank Tingey'	CElw ECho EHyt ELan
'Gold Splash'	GBar
'Gouldgeel'	WCot
heracleoticum hort.	See ***O.*** × ***applei***
– Linnaeus	See ***O. vulgare*** subsp. ***hirtum***
§ × ***hybridinum***	CLyd EBee LBee LHop MBro SBla SChu WDav WPat WPyg WWat WWin
'Kent Beauty'	CDec CLTr CLon CMHG CMea CSpe ECha ELan EPot LGre LLWP MSte NLak SAga SBla SChu SUsu SWas WHoo WOMN WPat WRus
kopatdaghense	See ***O. vulgare*** subsp. ***gracile***
laevigatum 🏆	CArn CElw CGle CLyd CMHG CMea CShe ELan EPot MBro MHig NBro NHol NMir NPer SAga SBla SMer SUsu SWas WAbe WByw WDav WEas WHil WHoo WPer WWat WWin WWye
* – ***aureum***	WJek
– 'Herrenhausen' 🏆	Widely available
– 'Hopleys'	Widely available
– hybrids	SIng
– 'Springwood'	WCot
* – ***album***	EOHP
libanoticum	EBee NTow
– hybrids	WDav
majorana	CArn CJew CSev ELan ELau GPoy LHol MChe MSal NHex SIde SWat WJek WOak WPer WSel WTyr WWye
microphyllum	CArn CBot CFee CGle CLon CLyd CMHG CShe EDAr EHyt ESis GBar ITim LBee LGre MBro MHig MTho SBla SChu SIng SUsu SWas WCru WHoo WPat WPyg WWye
minutiflorum	ECho ELan EPot
'Norton Gold'	CArc CElw CJew CLTr EBee ECha EFol ELau EPot GBar GBuc LHop LRHS MBro NHex NPer SIde WCHb WHoo WPyg
'Nymphenburg'	CFee ECha EHic MBro MSte SUsu SWas WCru WDav
onites	CArn EEls ELau GBar GPoy ILis LHol MChe MSal MWat NRoo SBla SIde WHer WJek WOak WPer WSel WWye
pulchellum	See ***O.*** × ***hybridinum***
'Rosenkuppel'	CGle CLon EBee ECha ELan ELau EMan EPot GBar GCal MRav MSte NCat NFai NHex NHol NTow SChu SHel SIde SMrm SOkh SPla SSpe SUsu SWas WOve WRus WWeb
* 'Rotkugel'	CElw LGre
rotundifolium 🏆	CArn CElw CGle CLon CLyd CRDP CSev ECha ELan LGre LHop NBir NHex SAlw SBla SChu SMer SUsu SWas WMer WOve WRus WSan
scabrum	CArn NHex WWye
– subsp. ***pulchrum***	CElw
¶ ***sipyleum***	EHyt
sp. from Santa Cruz	CArn
¶ sp. from Yunnan, China	NWoo
sp. Mac&W 5882	See ***Nepeta phyllochlamys***
tournefortii	See ***O. calcaratum***
villosum	See ***Thymus villosus***
vulgare	CArn CKin CSev ECWi ECoo EWFC GBar GPoy LHol MBar MChe MHew NBro NFai NHex NMir NRoo SIde WByw WHer WOak WPer WWye
– var. ***album***	CElw CWan LGre WHer WJek
– 'Aureum' 🏆	Widely available
– 'Aureum Album'	CWan EMar MCLN WDav WHer WHil WWhi
– 'Aureum Crispum'	CWan ELau EOrc GAbr GBar ILis NFai NHex NLak NSti SIde SWat WCer WJek WRha WSel WWye
– 'Compactum'	CArn CJew CLyd CRDP CSev CWan ECha EGoo ELau EOHP GAbr GCal GPoy ILis LHol MHig NHex NLak SAga SBla SIde SWat WCHb WPer WWye
– 'Compactum Album'	MHig SIde
– 'Corinne Tremaine' (v)	WHer
– 'Country Cream' (v)	CArc CArn CBar CHid EBar EHic EHoe EMan EWes GAbr MCLN MMil NFai NLak NPri NRoo SChu SHDw SPer SWat
§ – 'Gold Tip' (v)	CArc CLTr CMea CSev EBre EHoe EJud ELau EOrc GAbr ILis NFai NHex NHol NRoo NSti SWat WCHb WHer WPat WWye

– 'Golden Shine' CBod EWes MWat NRoo SIde WRha
§ – subsp. ***hirtum*** GPoy MSal NWoo WJek WPer
¶ – – 'Greek' CBod MGra
– x ***majorana*** ELau
§ – 'Nanum' EOHP EPla GBar LHop NCat WCla WCot WJek
– 'Polyphant' (v) CBre CElw CFis CInt CLTr CMil CRDP CSev CWan EMan EOHP LHop NHex NPro NWoo WCHb WCot WHil WJek WNdy WOve WSel WWye
– 'Thumble's Variety' CTri EBre ECGP ECha ECoo EGoo EHic EHoe ELau GBar MRav NHex SIde SWat WCot
– 'Variegatum' See ***O. vulgare* 'Gold Tip'**
'Webb's White' SIde

ORIXA (Rutaceae)
japonica CBot CMCN SSpi WDin

ORLAYA (Apiaceae)
grandiflora CRDP WCot WHal

ORNITHOGALUM (Hyacinthaceae)
arabicum CBro CGle CMil LAma LBow MBri NRog WCot
arcuatum CMon
balansae See ***O. oligophyllum***
caudatum See ***O. longibracteatum***
chionophyllum CMon
comosum CNic
concinnum MS 452 CMon
¶ ***dubium*** ETub WCot
exscapum CMon
¶ ***fimbriatum*** EPot
lanceolatum CAvo EHyt LRHS
§ ***longibracteatum*** CGre CHEx ELan EOHP LHil SLMG WCot WHer
¶ ***magnum*** CAvo ETub
montanum BSBE 2360 CMon
nanum See ***O. sigmoideum***
narbonense CBro GBuc
nutans ♀ CAvo CBro CMea CMon CRDP EPar EPot ETub EWFC LAma LBow MNrw MTho NMen NRog WCot WPer WShi
§ ***oligophyllum*** CBro EPot WCot
¶ ***ponticum*** ERos
pyramidale CLyd
pyrenaicum CArn CAvo ECha ERos WShi
– AB&S 4600 CMon
– Flavescens Group CMon
reverchonii CAvo CMea CMon
saundersiae LBow
sessiliflorum AB&S 4619 CMon
sibthorpii See ***O. sigmoideum***
§ ***sigmoideum*** EPot
spicatum MS 585 CMon
tenuifolium CMon EPot WOMN
thyrsoides LAma MBri SRms
umbellatum CAvo CBro CMea ELan EPar ETub EWFC GPoy LAma MBri MNrw NHol NRog WCot WPer WShi WWye
unifolium MS 435 CMon

ORONTIUM (Araceae)
aquaticum CBen CHEx CWGN CWat EBre EHon EMFW LPBA MSta NDea SBar SHig SWat WChe

OROSTACHYS (Crassulaceae)
§ ***aggregata*** NGre
chanetii NMen
iwarenge ESis
malacophylla See ***O. aggregata***
§ ***spinosa*** MOne NGre NMen NTow SIng

ORPHIUM (Gentianaceae)
frutescens CSpe

ORTHOSIPHON (Lamiaceae)
See Plant Deletions

ORTHROSANTHUS (Iridaceae)
chimboracensis CFir EBee WAbe WPer
– JCA 13743 CPou
laxus CInt CPBP ERos GBuc SMad WCot WWin
multiflorus CHan NTow
polystachyus CHan

ORYZOPSIS (Poaceae)
lessoniana EBee SVen WCot
miliacea CLTr ETPC

OSBECKIA (Melastomataceae)
See Plant Deletions

OSCULARIA (Aizoaceae)
deltoides See ***Lampranthus deltoides***

OSMANTHUS (Oleaceae)
armatus CFil CTri EPfP NHol WWat
§ x ***burkwoodii*** ♀ CB&S CBot CLan CPle EBre ELan ENot GRei ISea LHop LNet MBal MBar MBlu MBri MGos MPla MWat NBee NHol NNor NWea SPer SReu SRms SSta WDin WWat WWin
§ ***decorus*** CB&S CDoC CTri ELan ENot GOrc GWht MGos MRav MUlv NWea SPer SSta WPat WRTC WWat
delavayi ♀ CB&S CBot CChu CLan CShe CTrw EBre ELan ENot GWht ISea LHop LNet MBar MBri MGos MWat NHed NHol NWea SDix SHBN SPer SSpi SSta WPat WWat WWin
– 'Latifolius' WWat
forrestii See ***O. yunnanensis***
x ***fortunei*** CDoC CGre CPle
– 'Variegatus' See ***O. heterophyllus* 'Latifolius Variegatus'**
fragrans SArc
§ ***heterophyllus*** CB&S CGre CLan EMil ENot ERav GCHN GOrc LPan MBar MUlv NFla NHol NNor SPer SReu SRms SSpi SSta WDin WStI WWat
§ – all gold CPMA MBlu
– 'Argenteomarginatus' See ***O. heterophyllus* 'Variegatus'**

§ – 'Aureomarginatus'	CB&S CDoC CFil CMHG CPMA CPle EBee EHoe ELan EMil IOrc ISea LHop MBal MPla SAga SHBN SPer
◆ – 'Aureus' misapplied	See ***O. heterophyllus* all gold**
◆ – 'Aureus' Rehder	See ***O. heterophyllus* 'Aureomarginatus'**
§ – 'Goshiki' (v)	Widely available
N – 'Gulftide' ♀	CBlo CChu EHic ELan EMil EPfP MGos MUlv NHol WFar WWat
– 'Purple Shaft'	CAbP ELan EPfP LRHS WWat
– 'Purpureus'	CAbP CB&S CBot CMHG CPle EAst EHoe ELan MAll MBal MBri MGos MRav NHed SDry SSpi SSta WHCG WRTC WStI
– 'Rotundifolius'	CB&S CFil MBri
◆ – Tricolor	See ***O. heterophyllus* 'Goshiki'**
§ – 'Variegatus' ♀	CB&S CBot CGre EBre ELan EMil ENot ERav GWht IOrc MAll MAsh MBal MBar MPla MRav MWat NBee NFla NHol SHBN SPer SPla SReu SSta WDin WHar WPat WRTC
ilicifolius	See ***O. heterophyllus***
serrulatus	CBot EPla
§ ***yunnanensis***	CMHG EPfP MBlu SArc WWat

× OSMAREA (Oleaceae)

burkwoodii	See ***Osmanthus* × *burkwoodii***

OSMARONIA See OEMLERIA

OSMORHIZA (Apiaceae)

See Plant Deletions

OSMUNDA † (Osmundaceae)

cinnamomea	CFil GBin NHar NMar WFib WPGP WRic
claytoniana	CFil NMar WRic
regalis ♀	Widely available
– 'Crispa'	NMar
§ – Cristata Group	CFil CRDP ELan EMon MBri NHol SAxl WFib WRic
– 'Purpurascens'	CCuc CFil CRDP CRow EBre EFer ELan EMan EMon GBuc GMaP GQui IOrc MBri NBro NHar NHol NOrc SApp SAxl SBid SSpi SWat WCru WFib WRic WWat
§ – 'Undulata'	ELan EMon GBin NHol SAxl WFib WRic WWoo
– Undulata Group	See ***O. regalis* Cristata Group**

OSTEOMELES (Rosaceae)

¶ ***schweriniae*** B&L 12360	SAga
subrotunda	CPle

OSTEOSPERMUM † (Asteraceae)

'African Queen'	See ***O.* 'Nairobi Purple'**
'Anglia Yellow'	CBrk EOrc
'Ballyrogan Pink'	See ***O. jucundum* 'Ballyrogan Pink'**
barberae hort.	See ***O. jucundum***
'Blackthorn Seedling'	See ***O. jucundum* 'Blackthorn Seedling'**
'Bloemhoff Belle'	See ***O.* 'Nairobi Purple'**
'Blue Streak'	CBrk CCan CMHG EBar EBee ECtt ELan ERav SMrm WRus
'Bodegas Pink'	CBrk ELan ERav SChu
'Brickell's Hybrid'	See ***O.* 'Chris Brickell'**
'Buttermilk' ♀	Widely available
'Cannington John'	CCan CMHG ELan EOrc LBlm LHop MArl NPla SUsu
'Cannington Joyce'	CCan
'Cannington Katrina'	CCan NPla
'Cannington Roy'	CBar CCan CGle CLTr CMHG CSam CSpe CTrw EBar EBre ECtt ELan LFis LHop LLWP MBri NBrk NFai NHaw NPer SMrm SRms WAbe WHer
'Catriona'	GAbr
◆ ***caulescens*** hort.	See ***O.* 'Prostratum'**
'Chris Brickell'	CBrk CCan CLTr CMHG CSam CSev EBar GCal MSte NHaw WHen WPer
'Coconut Ice'	See ***O.* 'Croftway Coconut-ice'**
'Croftway Coconut-ice'	NBrk NPla
'Croftway Silver Spoons'	EBee
'Dennis Weston'	ECtt
'Durban'	WRus
ecklonis	CGle CHEx CMHG CSam CShe CTbh GMaP ISea LHil MCLN MTho NBro NFla SCro SMrm SVen WFar WPer WWin
* – deep pink	MBri
◆ – var. ***prostratum***	See ***O.* 'Prostratum'**
§ – 'Starshine'	EBar EOrc
'Edna Bond'	WEas
'Giant'	CCan CSpe
'Giles Gilbey' (v)	CLTr CTbh EBar EBee EOrc LHil LHop NHaw NPri SVen WEas WLRN
'Glistener'	CB&S
'Gold Sparkler' (v)	LHop NHaw SAga SMrm
'Gweek Variegated'	CBrk CLTr EBar EBee EOrc ERav NPer WWin
'Hopleys'	EBar EOrc LHop
'James Elliman'	CBrk CCan EBar ECtt EOrc LHop LLWP MSte NHaw SAga SRms
'Jewel'	COtt
§ ***jucundum*** ♀	CBrk CCan CChr CMHG CMea CShe ECha ELan ENot EOrc MCLN MNrw MRav MTis MWat NBrk NFai NHol NPer NSti SDix SIng SRms WHen WHil WPat
– 'Ballyrogan Pink'	IBlr
§ – 'Blackthorn Seedling'	CSWP EBee ECha MBri NPla SAga SBla
– var. ***compactum***	CB&S CLyd CMea CPBP ECha ELan LBlm LHop MHig MSte NMGW WAbe
¶ – 'Jackarandum' ♀	EBee
– 'Killerton Pink'	CCan CMHG EOrc WPer
– 'Langtrees'	CCan ECtt GAbr LHop NBrk NPla SMrm
¶ – 'Merriments Joy'	SMrm
'Kerdalo'	CKni
'Killerton Pink'	See ***O. jucundum* 'Killerton Pink'**
'Kriti'	EOrc
'La Mortola'	CHad CLTr
§ 'Lady Leitrim'	CCan CHEx CLTr CSam EBar ECha EFol EOrc GBri LHop LLWP MArl NBrk NBus SAxl SChu SSvw SUsu SVen WAbe WRus
'Langtrees'	See ***O. jucundum* 'Langtrees'**
'Merriments Joy'	See ***O. jucundum* 'Merriments Joy'**
'Molly's Choice'	EOrc SMrm

§ 'Nairobi Purple' CBrk CCan CFee CHEx CShe EBar EBee EBre ELan EOrc GBuc GMac MLan NBrk NPla SVen WLRN WOMN WPer
'Pale Face' See *O.* **'Lady Leitrim'**
'Peggyi' See *O.* **'Nairobi Purple'**
'Penny Pink' CCan CSpe EBee ECtt EOrc NFai WHer
'Pink Whirls' 🏆 CB&S CBot CBrk CCan CHEx CMHG CTrw ELan EOrc ERav GMac LFis LHop MBri NFai NHaw NSti SRms SSoC SUsu SVen WOMN WPer WRus
'Port Wine' See *O.* **'Nairobi Purple'**
N 'Prostratum' 🏆 CBrk CHan CLTr CLyd ELan IBlr NPer SAxl SChu SCro SDix SLMG SMad SPla SUsu SWas
'Royal Purple' WCot
'Seaspray' COtt
'Silver Sparkler' (v) 🏆 CBar CBrk CCan CMHG CSpe CTbh EBar EBre ECha EFol ELan EOrc ERav IHos LHop MLan NFai NHaw SAxl SChu WEas WRus
'Silver Spoons' See *O.* **'Croftway Silver Spoons'**
'Snow White' SMrm
* 'Sophie' CSpe
'Sparkler' CHEx EBre EOrc LHil MSte SVen
'Stardust' COtt EBee NPer SCoo WWeb
'Starshine' See *O.* ***ecklonis*** **'Starshine'**
'Sunny Boy' EBar LIck
'Sunny Girl' EBee ECtt GBuc LHil LIck SSte
'Sunny Gustav' LIck
'Sunny Lady' CTbh LIck
'Tauranga' See *O.* **'Whirligig'**
'Tiberias' EBar EBee
'Tresco Peggy' See *O.* **'Nairobi Purple'**
'Tresco Pink' IBlr
'Tresco Purple' See *O.* **'Nairobi Purple'**
'Tresco Sally' SMrm
'Weetwood' CBrk EBar ECtt GAbr GCal GMaP LHop MBri MHar MSte NBrk SAga SChu SIng SMrm SVen SWas WAbe
§ 'Whirligig' 🏆 CB&S CBrk CCan CMHG CShe CTrw EBre ECha ELan EOrc ERav GMac LHop MBri MLan NHaw SHFr SRms SUsu SVen WEas WOMN WPer WRus
* 'White Pim' LHil
'Wine Purple' See *O.* **'Nairobi Purple'**
Wisley Hybrids WEas WElm WRus
'Zambesi' CSpe
'Zimbar' ELan
'Zulu' CSpe EBar LHop MLan SSoC

OSTROWSKIA (Campanulaceae)
See Plant Deletions

OSTRYA (Corylaceae)
carpinifolia CB&S CDoC CGre CLnd CMCN ELan IOrc MBar MBlu SPan WMou WNor
virginiana CDoC WFro WNor

OTACANTHUS (Scrophulariaceae)
caeruleus CSpe

OTANTHUS (Asteraceae)
See Plant Deletions

OTHONNA (Asteraceae)
capensis CHal
§ ***cheirifolia*** CBot CHan CPle CSam CSev EBar ECha ELan EOrc MAll NBir NNor NTow SDry SIgm SMac SPer SRms WEas WPer WRus

OTHONNOPSIS See OTHONNA

OURISIA † (Scrophulariaceae)
caespitosa ELan EPot GGar NMen NWCA
– var. ***gracilis*** GGar GTou IBlr NGre
§ ***coccinea*** CGle GBuc GCra GDra GGar NBir NTow SMac SRms SSpi WAbe WCru WGle WWat
crosbyi IBlr
elegans See *O.* ***coccinea***
¶ ***fragrans*** NGre
'Loch Ewe' GAbr GCal GDra GGar IBlr MDun NBro NHar NHol NRoo WAbe WCru
macrophylla CPea GAbr GAri GBuc GDra GGar IBlr NGre NHar NHol NRoo WAbe WCru WDav
modesta NBro
¶ ***polyantha*** F & W 8487 CPBP
'Snowflake' 🏆 CFir CNic EHyt EMan EPot GAbr GDra GGar IBlr MDun MOne NBir NBro NHar NMen NSla NWCA SBla WAbe WGle WWin

OXALIS † (Oxalidaceae)
acetosella CKin CTiv EWFC LWak MSal NGre NMir WBon WGwy WHer WShi
¶ – deep pink WCot
adenophylla 🏆 CBro CElw CMea ELan EPot ESis ETub GAbr GDra LAma LHop MBal MBar MHig NEgg NGre NHar NMen NNrd NRog SIng WAbe WDav WEas WHil WPat
– dark form GDra MHig MTho
§ ***articulata*** EMan LGro MTho MTol NPer NRai WCot WHil WWin
– 'Aureoreticulata' MTho
'Beatrice Anderson' CPBP EHyt GDra MDHE MTho NHar NHol NNrd SBla WAbe
bowiei EPot NGre WOMN
'Bowles' White' MTho SUsu WHil
brasiliensis EPot GCrs MTho NNrd
chrysantha CRow WAbe
compacta F&W 8011 CPBP
corniculata var. ***atropurpurea*** MTho
¶ ***corymbosa*** 'Aureoreticulata' WCot
deppei See *O.* ***tetraphylla***
§ ***depressa*** ELan EPPr EPot EWes MTho NBir NGre NHol NMen NNrd NRya NSla SRms
§ ***drummondii*** GCal
enneaphylla 🏆 ECou EPot MTho NMen NRya SIng
– x ***adenophylla*** See *O.* **'Matthew Forrest'**

– 'Alba'	CGra EHyt EPot MDHE MFos MHig NHol NNrd NTow WAbe WIvy
– 'Minutifolia'	EHyt EPot MHig MTho NGre NHol NMen NNrd NRya SSmi WAbe WIvy
* – 'Minutifolia Rosea'	CGra
– 'Rosea'	CBro EPot GDra MBal MTho NGre NHar NHol NMGW NNrd NRya SBla
– 'Rubra'	GDra NHar NHol WAbe
flava	LAma NNrd
floribunda	See ***O. articulata***
glabra	CMon
hedysaroides	GCra
'Hemswell Knight'	EHyt
hirta	CBro CMon LBow LHil MTho NGre NNrd
– 'Gothenburg'	LBow MHig MTho WHil
incarnata	NChi
inops	See ***O. depressa***
'Ione Hecker' 🏆	CAvo CGra CLyd EHyt EPot ERos GTou LBee LHop MHig MRPP MTho NHar NHol NMen NNrd NRya NSla NTow WAbe WIvy
§ ***laciniata***	EHyt EPot MFos MTho NHar NHol NMen NSla SBla WChr
¶ – dark form	EHyt
– x ***enneaphylla***	NGre
¶ – hybrid seedlings	NHar
lactea double form	See ***O. magellanica* 'Nelson'**
lasiandra	CAvo
lobata	CBro EHyt ELan EPPr EPot LBow LHop MTho NTow SWas WOMN
magellanica	CFee CHal CHid CMHG CNic CSam CSpe CVer ELan ESis GCHN LRHS MTho NHol SAlw SIng WCru WDav WPer
– 'Flore Pleno'	See ***O. magellanica* 'Nelson'**
§ – 'Nelson' (d)	CElw CFee CHal CHan CHid CLyd CRDP CRow CSpe CVer EPot ESis EWes GCHN GCal LBee MTho NBir NBro NHar NHol NPer NRya NWoo WCru WPer
– 'Old Man Range'	ECou
§ 'Matthew Forrest'	NHol WAbe
melanosticta	LBow
obtusa	CLyd CMon ECha ELan EPot ESis MTho NCat NTow SSad SWas WFar WHil WOMN
oregana	CAvo CChu CNic CPBP CRDP CRow ECha EPla GBuc NChi WCru WPbr
– f. ***smalliana***	WCru
palmifrons	CMon MTho
patagonica	MDHE MHig NHar NHol
§ ***purpurea***	LBee LHop NGre NHol WHil
– 'Ken Aslet'	CBro CFee CLyd CMon CNic CRow EDAr EHyt EPot MFos MTho NGre NHol NNrd NTow WAbe WOMN
regnellii	See ***O. triangularis*** subsp. ***papilionacea***
rosea hort.	See ***O. rubra***
– Jacquin	See ***O. articulata***
'Sheffield Swan'	EHyt NNrd
speciosa	See ***O. purpurea***
¶ ***squamata***	CPBP
squamosoradicosa	See ***O. laciniata***

stipularis	CMea CMon WChr
succulenta Barnèoud	CFee LHil
§ ***tetraphylla***	CM&M CRow CSam EPot LAma MBri MTho NCat NOrc NPer NRog SLMG SSoC WByw
tetraphylla alba	NNrd
tetraphylla 'Iron Cross'	CAvo CMea CRow EBee ELan EMan LAma MSCN NBir NHol SAga SAxl SBid WCot WHal WHil
triangularis	CSWP EMan ETub GAri LAma NHol NPer NRai NTay SBid WChr WPat WPyg
– 'Cupido'	CB&S CRDP EBee EOrc WPer WWin
§ – subsp. ***papilionacea***	CMon LAma LHop NRog WChr WHal WWin
– – 'Atropurpurea'	WCot
– subsp. ***papilionacea rosea***	CMon
– subsp. ***triangularis***	MDun
tuberosa	CFir GPoy WHer
versicolor	EPot EWes MTho SBla
vespertilionis Torrey & A Gray	See ***O. drummondii***
– Zuccarini	See ***O. latifolia***
vulcanicola	CFee SBid SDix WLRN

OXERA (Verbenaceae)

¶ ***pulchella*** — CPlN

OXYCOCCUS See VACCINIUM

OXYDENDRUM (Ericaceae)

arboreum	CAbP CB&S EHic EMil MBal MBri MGos SSpi SSta WCru WDin WNor WWat
– 'Chameleon'	CKni CSte EPfP LRHS MBlu SPer SSta

OXYLOBIUM (Papilionaceae)

¶ ***ellipticum*** — CTrC

OXYPETALUM (Asclepiadaceae)

caeruleum — See ***Tweedia caerulea***

OXYRIA (Polygonaceae)

digyna — CAgr GCHN GGar NBro WGwy WHer

OXYTROPIS (Papilionaceae)

oreophila JCA 13585	CPBP
– var. ***jonesii*** NNS 93-517	MFos
podocarpa	NWCA

OZOTHAMNUS (Asteraceae)

antennaria	MAll WSHC
§ ***coralloides*** 🏆	EPot MHig NWCA SIng
§ ***hookeri***	CAbb CPle ECou MHig SChu SPer
§ ***ledifolius*** 🏆	CMHG CPle CSam ECha ELan EMil GTou LHop MAll MBri MPla NNor SChu SIgm SPer SSpi WHCG WHar WPat WRTC WSHC WWat
¶ ***lycopodioides***	ECou
§ ***microphyllus***	ITim
'Rose Dazzler'	MAll

§ ***rosmarinifolius*** CB&S CDoC CMHG CPle CWit ELan EPla ERea IOrc MAll MBlu MNrw NNor SChu SPer WAbe WBod WHCG WRTC WSHC WWat
– 'Purpureus' CMHG
– 'Silver Jubilee' ♀ CB&S CDoC CEnd CHan CMHG CSam CTrC EBar ELan EPla GOrc LHop MAll NNor NSti SAga SHBN SPer SSpi WHCG WSHC WStI
scutellifolius ECou
§ ***selago*** ESis EWes ITim LBee MHig SBla
– 'Minor' EWes GCrs MHig NWCA
'Sussex Silver' CPle MAll SBid SVen WPyg
'Threave Seedling' SMrm SPer
§ ***thyrsoideus*** CB&S CPle MAll WWat

PACHYLAENA (Asteraceae)

See Plant Deletions

PACHYPHRAGMA (Brassicaceae)

§ ***macrophyllum*** CSev EBre ECha ELan EMon ERav IBlr MRav NChi NPla NSti SSpi WCru WEas WWin

PACHYPODIUM (Apocynaceae)

lamerei MBri

PACHYSANDRA (Buxaceae)

procumbens CSte EPla WCot WCru WThi
stylosa EPla MRav SMad
terminalis ♀ CB&S CChe CHal CHan CRow CWGN EBre ECED ECha ELan ENot GRei IHos LBuc MBar MGos NHol NNor NWea SHBN SPer SReu WDin WGwG WHar WOve WStI WWat WWin
– 'Green Carpet' CDoC EBre ECot EFou EGol EPfP EPla GAri MAsh MBar MBri MGos NPro SCoo SPla WRHF WRus WWat
– 'Variegata' ♀ CB&S CBot CHal CHan CRDP CRow CSam EAst EBre ECha EGol EHoe ELan ENot MBal MBar MBri MGos NFla NHol SHBN SHel SPer SPla WDin WGwG WHar WRus WWat WWin

PACHYSTACHYS (Acanthaceae)

lutea ♀ CHal MBri

PACHYSTEGIA (Asteraceae)

¶ ***insignis*** MAll

PACHYSTEGIA See OLEARIA

PACHYSTEMA See PAXISTIMA

PACKERA (Asteraceae)

§ ***aurea*** MSal

PAEDERIA (Rubiaceae)

scandens CPlN WCru WSHC
– var. ***velutina*** WCru

PAEDEROTA (Scrophulariaceae)

§ ***bonarota*** CLyd
¶ ***lutea*** WDav

PAEONIA † (Paeoniaceae)

albiflora See ***P. lactiflora***
¶ 'Angel Cobb Freeborn' MAus
anomala CFil EPot WPGP
arietina See ***P. mascula*** subsp. ***arietina***
'Avant Garde' WKif
'Ballerina' CKel
banatica See ***P. officinalis*** subsp. ***banatica***
beresovskii CFil WPGP
broteroi CMon LGre LWoo SBla WPGP
¶ ***brownii*** MFos
'Buckeye Belle' MAus MBri WGle
'Burma Ruby' MAus
* 'Byzantine' CKel
californica LWoo MFos
cambessedesii ♀ CBrd CBro CFil CKel CLyd CMon EPot LGre LWoo MTho NBir SBla SIgm SSpi WAbe WOMN
* 'Carl G.Klehm' WGle
¶ 'Carol' MAus
caucasica See ***P. mascula*** subsp. ***mascula***
¶ ***chamaeleon*** WPGP
'Chocolate Soldier' MUlv
¶ 'Claire de Lune' MAus WGle
clusii CBro CMon WPGP
'Coral Fay' MAus WGle
corallina See ***P. mascula*** subsp. ***mascula***
* ***coriacea*** var. ***maroccana*** SSpi
daurica See ***P. mascula*** subsp. ***triternata***
'Daystar' CKel
decora See ***P. peregrina***
'Defender' ♀ MAus
delavayi ♀ CAbb CB&S CGre CHad CKel CSam EBre EOrc GAbr GCal IBlr MBal MBri MDun MTis NBir NBro NRoo NSti SLPl SMad SMrm SPer SRms SSpi WBod WEas WGle WSHC WWat
¶ – dark red GGGa
§ – var. ***ludlowii*** (S) ♀ CB&S CGle CGre CKel CSam ELan GGGa ISea MBal NBrk NPer NRoo SBla SMad SPer SSpi WEas WHoo WSHC WWat
§ – var. ***lutea*** (S) CKel ELan MBro SAxl SHBN SRms STre WEas WHar WPyg WWat
– 'Mrs Sarson' CBlo EBee SLPl SWat
* 'Eastgrove Ruby Lace' WEas
emodi CKel
¶ 'Heritage' WGle
'High Noon' CKel MAus
¶ 'Horizon' WGle
humilis See ***P. officinalis*** subsp. ***microcarpa***
¶ 'Illini Belle' MAus
'Illini Warrior' MAus
japonica hort. See ***P. lactiflora***
¶ ***kavachensis*** WPGP
kevachensis See ***P. mascula*** subsp. ***mascula***
'Kinkaku' See ***P. × lemoinei* 'Souvenir de Maxime Cornu'**
'Kinko' See ***P. × lemoinei* 'Alice Harding'**
'Kinshi' See ***P. × lemoinei* 'Chromatella'**

'Kintei'	See ***P.* × *lemoinei* 'L'Espérance'**
¶ Kohlein's hybrid	LWoo
§ ***lactiflora***	ECha SSpi
– 'A.F.W. Hayward'	CKel
– 'Adolphe Rousseau'	CB&S CKel LRHS MBri
* – 'Afterglow'	CKel
– 'Agida'	EBre GCHN MRav
– 'Albâtre'	CKel
– 'Albert Crousse'	CB&S CKel MAus
– 'Alexander Fleming'	CKel EBre ECot MAus MUlv SMrm
– 'Alice Harding'	MAus WCot
– 'Anna Pavlova'	CKel
– 'Antwerpen'	CKel
– 'Arabian Prince'	CKel
– 'Argentine'	CB&S CKel
– 'Armance Dessert'	CKel
– 'Artist'	CKel
– 'Asa Gray'	CKel
– 'Auguste Dessert'	CB&S CBlo CKel MAus
– 'Aureole'	CKel
– 'Avant Garde'	MAus
– 'Bahram'	CKel
– 'Ballerina'	CKel
– 'Banner of Purity'	CKel
– 'Baroness Schröder'	ELan MAus
– 'Barrington Belle'	MBri
– 'Barrymore'	CKel
– 'Beacon'	CKel
– 'Beatrice Kelway'	CKel
– 'Beau Geste'	CKel
– 'Beauty Spot'	CKel
– 'Beersheba'	CKel
– 'Belle Center'	MAus
– 'Belle of Somerset'	CKel
– 'Bertha Gorst'	CKel
– 'Bethcar'	CKel
– 'Blaze of Beauty'	CKel
– 'Blaze of Glory'	CKel
– 'Blenheim'	CKel
– 'Blithe Spirit'	CKel
– 'Bloodshot'	CKel
– 'Bloodstone'	CKel
– 'Blush Queen'	CKel EBre ELan MAus
– 'Blush White'	CKel
– 'Border Gem'	EBre GCHN MRav
– 'Bouchela'	CKel
– 'Boulanger'	CKel
– 'Bower of Roses'	CKel
– 'Bowl of Beauty' 🏆	CB&S CKel EBre ELan EOrc MAus MBri MUlv NRoo NVic SMad SMrm SPer SSpe SSpi WEas WKif WPyg
– 'Bowl of Cream'	EBre MAus MBri
– 'Boy Kelway'	CKel
– 'Break o' Day'	MAus
– 'Bridal Veil'	CKel
– 'Bridesmaid'	CKel
– 'British Beauty'	CKel
– 'British Empire'	CKel
– 'Bunker Hill'	CB&S CBlo CDoC CKel CShe MAus SMur
– 'Butch'	MAus
– 'Calypso'	CKel
– 'Candeur'	CKel
– 'Captain Alcock'	CKel
– 'Captivation'	CKel
– 'Carmen'	CKel
– 'Carnival'	CKel
– 'Cascade'	CKel
– 'Catherine Fontijn'	CKel
– 'Charles' White'	MAus SPer
– 'Charm'	MAus
– 'Cheddar Cheese'	WGle
– 'Cheddar Gold'	MBri
– 'Cherry Hill'	CKel
– 'Chestine Gowdy'	CKel
– 'Chocolate Soldier'	SPer
– 'Christine Kelway'	CKel
– 'Cincinnati'	WGle
– 'Claire Dubois'	EBre MAus
– 'Colonel Heneage'	SPer
– 'Cornelia Shaylor'	CKel EBre ELan MAus
– 'Coronation'	CKel
– 'Countess of Altamont'	CKel
– 'Country Girl'	CKel
– 'Couronne d'Or'	MAus
– 'Crimson Banner'	CKel
– 'Crimson Glory'	CKel
– 'Crimson Velvet'	CKel
– 'Dark Lantern'	CKel
– 'Dark Song'	CKel
– 'Dark Vintage'	CKel
– 'David Kelway'	CKel
– 'Dawn Crest'	CKel
– 'Dayspring'	CKel
– 'Daystar'	CKel
– 'Denise'	CKel
– 'Desire'	CKel
– Diana Drinkwater	CKel
– 'Dinner Plate'	MAus MBri
– 'Display'	CKel
– 'Docteur H. Barnsby'	CKel
– 'Dominion'	CKel
– 'Doreen'	MAus MRav
– 'Dorothy Welsh'	CKel
– 'Dragon'	CKel
– 'Dresden'	CKel
– 'Duchess of Bedford'	CKel
– 'Duchess of Somerset'	CKel
– 'Duchesse de Nemours' 🏆	CKel CMGP COtt EBar EBre EFou EPfP GMaP MAus MBri MTis MUlv NBro NRoo SPer SSpe WWeb
– 'Duke of Devonshire'	CKel
– 'Edith Cavell'	CKel
– 'Edmund Spencer'	CKel
– 'Edouard Doriat'	CKel
– 'Edulis Superba'	CKel CKni EBar EBre ELan MAus SPer WWeb
– 'Ella Christine Kelway'	CKel
– 'Elsa Sass'	MAus
– 'Emperor of India'	CKel
– 'Empire State'	EBee
– 'Enchantment'	CKel
– 'English Princess'	CKel
– 'Ethelreda'	CKel
– 'Eugénie Verdier'	MUlv
– 'Evening Glow'	CKel
– 'Evening World'	CKel MUlv
– 'Fantin-Latour'	CKel
– 'Félix Crousse' 🏆	CKel CTri EBre ELan GMaP MAus MBri NRoo SMrm SPer SWat WWeb
– 'Festiva Maxima' 🏆	CKel CTri EBee EBre ECot ELan LFis MBri SMrm SPer SRms WGwG WHoo WPyg WWeb
– 'Flag of War'	CKel
– 'Flamboyant'	CKel
– 'Flamingo'	CKel
– 'France'	CKel
– 'Gainsborough'	CKel
– 'Garden Beauty'	CKel

– 'Gay Ladye'	CKel
– 'Gay Paree'	MAus
– 'Gay Sister'	CKel
– 'Gayborder June'	CKel EBre MAus
– 'Gazelle'	CKel
– 'Général Joffre'	CKel
– 'Général MacMahon'	See ***P. lactiflora*** **'Augustin d'Hour'**
– 'General Wolfe'	CKel
– 'Germaine Bigot'	CKel
– 'Gertrude'	CKel
– 'Gilbert Barthelot'	MAus
– 'Gleam of Light'	CKel
– 'Glory of June'	CKel
– 'Glory of Somerset'	CKel
– 'Gold Mine'	CKel
¶ – 'Golly'	WGle
– 'Grace Loomis'	CKel MAus
– 'Great Lady'	CKel
– 'Great Sport'	CKel
– 'Grover Cleveland'	CKel
– 'Gypsy Girl'	CKel
– 'Heartbeat'	CKel
– 'Heirloom'	CKel
¶ – 'Helen Hayes'	MAus
– 'Henri Potin'	CKel
– 'Her Grace'	CKel
– 'Her Majesty'	CKel
– 'Herbert Oliver'	CKel
¶ – 'Honey Gold'	WGle
– 'Huge Delight'	CKel
– 'Hyperion'	CKel
– 'Immaculée'	CKel
– 'Indian Pink'	CKel
– 'Ingenieur Doriat'	CKel
– 'Inspecteur Lavergne'	CDoC CKel EFou MAus MRav MUlv NBee SPer WWeb
– 'Instituteur Doriat'	CKel
– 'Jacques Doriat'	CKel
– 'James Kelway'	CKel
– 'James Pillow'	MAus
– 'James R. Mann'	CKel
– 'Jan van Leeuwen'	CKel
– 'Jeanne d'Arc'	CKel
– 'Joan Kelway'	CKel
– 'Joseph Plagne'	CKel
– 'Joy of Life'	CKel
– 'June Morning'	CKel
– 'June Rose'	MAus
– 'Kansas'	CKel ELan MAus
– 'Karl Rosenfield'	CKel EBre ECot MBri NBee SMrm SPla SSpe WHoo WWeb
– 'Katherine Havermeyer'	CKel
– 'Kathleen Mavoureen'	CKel
– 'Kelway's Brilliant'	CKel
– 'Kelway's Fairy Queen'	CKel
– 'Kelway's Glorious'	CBlo CKel EBar MAus
– 'Kelway's Lovely'	CKel
– 'Kelway's Majestic'	CKel
– 'Kelway's Malmaison'	CKel
– 'Kelway's Queen'	CKel
– 'Kelway's Scented Rose'	CKel
– 'Kelway's Supreme'	CKel MUlv SWat
– 'Kelway's Unique'	CKel
– 'Kestrel'	CKel
– 'King Arthur'	CKel
– 'King George VI'	CKel
– 'King of England'	CKel
– 'Knight of the Thistle'	CKel
– 'Knighthood'	CKel
– 'Krinkled White'	MAus MBri MRav WGle
– 'La France'	CKel
– 'Lady Alexandra Duff' 🏆	CB&S CDoC CKel COtt EBee EBre EPfP MAus MRav
– 'Lady Ley'	CKel
– 'Lady Mayoress'	CKel
¶ – 'Lady Orchid'	MAus
– 'Langport Triumph'	CKel
– 'Laura Dessert' 🏆	CKel EBre LRHS MBri
– 'Le Jour'	MBri
– 'L'Eclatante'	CKel WGwG
– 'Legion of Honor'	CKel
– 'Lemon Ice'	CKel
– 'Letitia'	CKel
– 'Lois Kelsey'	MAus
¶ – 'Lora Dexheimer'	MAus
– 'Lord Avebury'	CKel
– 'Lord Cavan'	CKel MAus WGle
– 'Lord Kitchener'	CKel
– 'Lord Rosebery'	CKel
– 'Lorna Doone'	CKel
– 'Lottie Dawson Rea'	CKel
¶ – 'Lotus Queen'	MAus
– 'Louis Barthelot'	CKel MAus
– 'Louis van Houtte'	CKel
– 'Lyric'	CKel
– 'Madame Calot'	CKel EBre MAus SRms
– 'Madame Claude Tain'	LRHS MBri MHlr WCot
– 'Madame Ducel'	CKel MAus
– 'Madame Emile Debatène'	CKel EBar
– 'Madame Jules Dessert'	CKel MAus
– 'Madelon'	CKel
– 'Magic Melody'	CKel
– 'Magic Orb'	CKel
– 'Major Loder'	CKel
– 'Margaret Truman'	CKel
– 'Marguérite Gerard'	CKel
– 'Marie Lemoine'	CKel MAus SMur
– 'Marquisite'	CKel
– 'Mary Brand'	CKel
– 'Meteor Flight'	CKel
– 'Mischief'	MAus
– 'Miss America'	MAus
– 'Miss Eckhart'	CKel MAus
– 'Mister Ed'	MAus
– 'Monsieur Jules Elie' 🏆	CBot CKel EBee EBre EFou MAus MBri SPer SPla
– 'Monsieur Martin Cahuzac'	MAus
¶ – 'Mother's Choice'	WGle
– 'Mr G.F. Hemerik'	CKel LRHS MAus MBri
– 'Mrs F.J. Hemerik'	MAus
– 'Mrs Franklin D. Roosevelt'	ELan
– 'Mrs J.V. Edlund'	MAus
– 'My Pal Rudy'	MAus
– 'Myrtle Gentry'	CKel
¶ – 'Nancy Nicholls'	MAus
– 'Nectar'	CKel
– 'Newfoundland'	CKel
– 'Nice Gal'	MAus
– 'Nick Shaylor'	MAus WGle
– 'Nobility'	CKel
– 'Noonday'	CKel
– 'Ornament'	CKel
– 'Orpen'	CKel
– 'Othello'	CKel
– 'Pageant'	CKel
– 'Paper White'	CKel
– 'Paul M. Wild'	MAus
– 'Pauline Maunder'	CKel
– 'Peregrine'	CKel
– 'Peter Brand'	LRHS MBri

– 'Peter Pan'	CKel
¶ – 'Petticoat Flounce'	WGle
– 'Phedar White'	MPhe
– 'Philomèle'	MAus
– 'Pillow Talk'	MAus
– 'Pink Dawn'	CKel
– 'Pink Delight'	CKel
¶ – 'Pink Lemonade'	WGle
¶ – 'Pink Parfait'	MAus
– 'Pink Princess'	MAus
– 'President Franklin D. Roosevelt'	CKni EBre ELan GCHN SPer SWat
– 'Président Poincaré'	CBlo CKel EBre MRav SMur SPer SWat
– 'President Taft'	See ***P. lactiflora* 'Reine Hortense'**
– 'President Wilson'	CKel
– 'Pride of Huish'	CKel
– 'Pride of Somerset'	CKel
– 'Primevere'	LBuc LRHS MAus MBri
– 'Princess Beatrice'	CKel
– 'Pure Delight'	CKel
– 'Queen Elizabeth'	CKel
– 'Queen of the Belgians'	CKel
– 'Queen's Grace'	CKel
– 'Raspberry Sundae'	MAus MRav
– 'Red Dwarf'	CKel
– 'Red King'	CKel
– 'Red Warrior'	CKel
§ – 'Reine Hortense'	CKel MAus MRav WGle
– 'Rembrandt'	CKel
– 'Rose of Delight'	CKel MUlv
– 'Ruby Light'	CKel
– 'Sainfoin'	CKel
– 'Sarah Bernhardt' ♀	CB&S CKel CMGP CShe EBre ELan GCHN IHos MAus MBri MRav MUlv NBee NBro NRoo NVic SChu SPer SPla SSpe WEas WGwG WHoo WWeb
– 'Shimmering Velvet'	CKel
– 'Shirley Temple'	CKel EBar EFou ELan MAus MBri WCot WFar WPyg
– 'Silver Flare'	CKel
– 'Sir Edward Elgar'	CKel
– 'Smiling Morn'	CKel
– 'Solange'	CKel MAus
– 'Souvenir de Louis Bigot'	CKel
– 'Spearmint'	CKel
– 'Strephon'	CKel
– 'Surugu'	ELan
– 'Sweet Sixteen'	MAus
– 'Thérèse'	CKel MAus
– 'Top Brass'	CBot MAus MRav
– 'Toro-no-maki'	MAus
– 'Torpilleur'	CKel
– 'Tourangelle'	CKel
– 'Translucient'	CKel
¶ – var. ***trichocarpa***	WPGP
– 'Utopia'	CKel
– 'Victoire de la Marne'	CKel SMur
– 'Vogue'	CBlo CKel LRHS MAus SMur
¶ – 'Westerner'	MAus
– 'White Wings'	CB&S CKel COtt EBre EFou ELan MAus MBri SSpe WGle
– 'Whitleyi Major' ♀	CKel LRHS
– 'Wiesbaden'	CKel MAus
– 'Wilbur Wright'	CKel
– 'Windsor Lad'	CKel
– 'Wings of Love'	CKel
– 'Winston Churchill'	CKel
– 'Wladyslawa'	SPla
– 'Zus Braun'	CKel
– 'Zuzu'	MAus
'Late Windflower'	ECha
§ x ***lemoinei*** 'Chromatella' (S)	CKel LAma
§ – 'L'Espérance'	LAma
§ – 'Souvenir de Maxime Cornu' (S)	CKel LAma MAus
lobata 'Fire King'	See ***P. peregrina***
lutea	See ***P. delavayi*** var. ***lutea***
– var. ***ludlowii***	See ***P. delavayi*** var. ***ludlowii***
'Mai Fleuri'	LRHS SHig
§ ***mascula***	CBro CKel WPGP
§ – subsp. ***arietina***	LFlo WKif
– – 'Northern Glory'	MBri SHig WCot
§ – subsp. ***mascula***	EPot NTow
§ – subsp. ***triternata***	LWoo WHoo
mlokosewitschii ♀	CAvo CBro CFil CKel EBre ECha EOrc EPot LGre LHop LWoo NPSI NTow SAxl WAbe WEas WHoo WPyg
mollis	See ***P. officinalis*** subsp. ***villosa***
'Montezuma'	MAus MBri
'Nymphe'	CKel MAus MRav
obovata ♀	LWoo WPGP
– var. ***alba*** ♀	WAbe WEas
– 'Grandiflora'	EBre MRav
officinalis	CFil NBrk WPGP
– 'Alba Plena'	CKel CPou MAus MBri MRav SPer WCot
– 'Anemoniflora Rosea' ♀	LRHS MAus MBri
§ – subsp. ***banatica***	WPGP
– 'China Rose'	ELan LRHS MAus MBri
– subsp. ***humilis***	See ***P. officinalis*** subsp. ***microcarpa***
– 'James Crawford Weguelin'	CKel
– 'Lize van Veen'	EBre ELan SPer
§ – subsp. ***microcarpa***	WPGP
– 'Mutabilis Plena'	IBlr
– 'Rosea Plena' ♀	CDoC CKel EBee GAbr LRHS MAus MRav NMGW SPer SWat
– 'Rosea Superba Plena'	CKel NRoo
– 'Rubra Plena' ♀	CDoC CKel CPou EBee EBre EGoo MAus MBri NRoo SPer SWat WHoo WWeb
§ – subsp. ***villosa***	EBee ELan
paradoxa	See ***P. officinalis*** subsp. ***microcarpa***
'Paula Fay'	MAus MRav
* 'Peppermint Stick'	WGle
§ ***peregrina***	CFil ECho LWoo MAus MPhe NHar SSpi
§ – 'Otto Froebel' ♀	EBre ELan MBri SHig SMad SPer
– 'Sunshine'	See ***P. peregrina* 'Otto Froebel'**
potaninii	See ***P. delavayi* Potaninii Group**
* 'Raspberry Ice'	MAus WGle
* 'Reine Supreme'	WGle
¶ 'Requiem'	WGle
♦ ***rockii***	See ***P. suffruticosa*** subsp. ***rockii***
romanica	See ***P. peregrina***
'Roselette'	MAus
russoi	See ***P. mascula*** subsp. ***russoi***
'Scarlett O'Hara'	EBre MAus
sinensis	See ***P. lactiflora***
'Smouthii'	EBre
* 'Sorbet'	COtt
¶ ***steveniana***	LWoo
suffruticosa	CBlo CHad CPMA ELan GOrc MGos WStI

* – 'Alice Palmer'	CKel
– White Jade = 'Bai-yu' (S)	MPhe
– 'Bang-ning-zi' (S)	MPhe
♦ – Bird of Rimpo	See *P. suffruticosa* **'Rimpo'**
♦ – Black Dragon Brocade	See *P. suffruticosa* **'Kokuryu-nishiki'**
♦ – Brocade of the Naniwa	See *P. suffruticosa* **'Naniwa-nishiki'**
– 'Cai-die' (S)	MPhe
* – 'Cai-jing-qui' (S)	MPhe
– 'Cardinal Vaughan' (S)	CKel
♦ – Charming Age	See *P. suffruticosa* **'Howki'**
♦ – Cherries of Imperial Palace	See *P. suffruticosa* **'Gosho-zakura'**
– Great Brown-Purple = 'Da-zong-zi' (S)	MPhe
♦ – Double Cherry	See *P. suffruticosa* **'Yae-zakura'**
– Pea Green = 'Dou-lu' (S)	MPhe
– 'Duchess of Kent' (S)	CKel
♦ – Eternal Camellias	See *P. suffruticosa* **'Yachiyo-tsubaki'**
– Powder Blue Pearl = 'Fen-lan-zhu' (S)	MPhe
– 'Fen-qiao' (S)	MPhe
♦ – Flight of Cranes	See *P. suffruticosa* **'Renkaku'**
♦ – Floral Rivalry	See *P. suffruticosa* **'Hana-kisoi'**
– Kudzu Purple = 'Ge-jin-zi' (S)	MPhe
* – 'Glory of Huish'	CKel
– 'Godaishu' (S)	LAma SPer
§ – 'Hakuojisi' (S)	EBee MAus
§ – 'Hana-daijin' (S)	LAma MAus
§ – 'Hana-kisoi' (S)	LAma MAus SPer
– Lotus Green = 'He-hua-lu' (S)	MPhe
* – 'Hei-hue-kui' (S)	MPhe
§ – 'Higurashi' (S)	EBee LAma
– 'Hou-lian-jin-dan' (S)	MPhe
§ – 'Howki' (S)	MAus
– Cloud of Butterflies = 'Hu-die-qun-wu' (S)	MPhe
♦ – Jewel in the Lotus	See *P. suffruticosa* **'Tama-fuyo'**
♦ – Jewelled Screen	See *P. suffruticosa* **'Tama-sudare'**
– 'Jiao-rong-san-bian' (S)	MPhe
– Red Brocade Gown = 'Jin-pao-hong' (S)	MPhe
♦ – Kamada Brocade	See *P. suffruticosa* **'Kamada-nishiki'**
§ – 'Kamada-fuji' (S)	LAma
§ – 'Kamada-nishiki' (S)	MAus
§ – 'Kaow' (S)	MAus
♦ – King of Flowers	See *P. suffruticosa* **'Kaow'**
♦ – King of White Lions	See *P. suffruticosa* **'Hakuojisi'**
* – 'Kingdom of the Moon'	MAus
– 'Kinkaku'	See *P.* × *lemoinei* **'Souvenir de Maxime Cornu'**
– 'Kinshi'	See *P.* × *lemoinei* **'Alice Harding'**
♦ – Knight's Dance	See *P. suffruticosa* **'No-kagura'**
§ – 'Kokuryu-nishiki' (S)	LAma
– 'Lan-tian-yu'' (S)	MPhe
* – 'Large Globe'	MAus
– Pearblossom Snow = 'Li-hua-xue' (S)	MPhe
– 'Liu-li-guan-zhu' (S)	MPhe
– 'Lord Selbourne' (S)	CKel LRHS
♦ – Magnificent Flower	See *P. suffruticosa* **'Hana-daijin'**
¶ – 'Montrose' (S)	CKel
♦ – Moon World	See *P. suffruticosa* **'Gessekai'**
* – 'Mrs Shirley Fry'	CKel
– 'Mrs William Kelway' (S)	CKel LRHS
§ – 'Naniwa-nishiki' (S)	MAus
♦ – Palace of Gems	See *P. suffruticosa* **'Shugyo-kuden'**
♦ – Pride of Taisho	See *P. suffruticosa* **'Taisho-no-hokori'**
– 'Qing-long-wo-mo-chi' (S)	MAus MPhe
– 'Raphael' (S)	CKel LRHS
§ – 'Renkaku' (S)	MAus
§ – 'Rimpo' (S)	EBee LAma
♦ – Seven Gods of Fortune	See *P. suffruticosa* **'Sitifukujin'**
§ – 'Shugyo-kuden' (S)	MAus
– Lotus-like = 'Si-he-lian' (S)	MPhe
§ – 'Sitifukujin' (S)	MAus
– 'Superb' (S)	CKel
§ – 'Taisho-no-hokori' (S)	MAus
§ – 'Taiyo' (S)	LAma SPer
§ – 'Tama-fuyo' (S)	LAma
§ – 'Tama-sudare' (S)	MAus
– Elegant Charming Red = 'Tao-hong-xian-mei' (S)	MPhe
♦ – The Sun	See *P. suffruticosa* **'Taiyo'**
♦ – Twilight	See *P. suffruticosa* **'Higurashi'**
♦ – Wisteria at Kamada	See *P. suffruticosa* **'Kamada-fuji'**
– Snow Osmanthus = 'Xue-gui' (S)	MPhe
§ – 'Yachiyo-tsubaki' (S)	CKel LAma MAus
§ – 'Yae-zakura' (S)	LAma
¶ – 'Yin-fen-jin-lin' (S)	MAus
– 'Yoshinogawa' (S)	EBee
– Jade Butterfly = 'Yu-hu-die' (S)	MPhe
– 'Yu-pan-zheng-yan' (S)	MPhe
– Purple-spotted White = 'Zi-ban-bai' (S)	MPhe
'Sunshine'	See *P. peregrina* **'Otto Froebel'**
tenuifolia	CBot EPot GCal LWoo MAus
¶ – subsp. ***biebersteiniana***	GCal
* – subsp. ***lithophila***	GCal
– 'Plena'	EMon LRHS LWoo MBri
– 'Rosea'	MAus
veitchii	CKel LGre LWoo MBal MTho SIgm SSpi WAbe
– var. ***woodwardii***	CLyd EBee GCal GDra LGre MTho NHar NSla SSpi WCot WHoo
¶ 'Windchimes'	WGle
wittmanniana	CBot EBre LWoo MAus NTow
Elegant Yellow = 'Yao-huang' (S)	MAus MPhe

PAESIA (Hypolepidaceae)

scaberula	CBos CFil GCal SSpi WAbe WRic

PALISOTA (Commelinaceae)

See Plant Deletions

PALIURUS (Rhamnaceae)

spina-christi	CPle SMad

PALLENIS (Asteraceae)

spinosus	See ***Asteriscus spinosus***

PANAX (Araliaceae)	
ginseng	GPoy
japonicus	GPoy
quinquefolius	GPoy
PANCRATIUM (Amaryllidaceae)	
canariense	WChr
foetidum S&L 354	CMon
maritimum	CAvo CMon CSpe WChr
PANDANUS (Pandanaceae)	
See Plant Deletions	
PANDOREA (Bignoniaceae)	
jasminoides	CAbb CPlN CSpe EBak ECon ECot ELan IBlr SBid SLMG SOWG
– 'Alba'	See ***P. jasminoides* 'Lady Di'**
§ – 'Charisma' (v)	CAbb CPlN CSpe EBee ELan EMil LCns SHFr
§ – 'Lady Di'	CB&S CPlN CSpe EMil ERea LCns
– 'Rosea Superba' ♀	CB&S CRHN EBee ECon EHic ELan EMil ERea SPer
♦ – 'Variegata'	See ***P. jasminoides* 'Charisma'**
lindleyana	See ***Clytostoma callistegioides***
pandorana	CB&S CPlN CRHN CSpe ERea WCot
* – 'Alba'	CPlN
* – 'Golden Rain'	LCns
– 'Golden Showers'	CPlN ERea SOWG
* – 'Ruby Heart'	CPlN
PANICUM (Poaceae)	
bulbosum	CHan EHoe EPPr EPla ESOG ETPC
clandestinum	EHoe EPPr EPla ESOG ETPC EWes MCCP NPro WCot
coloratum 'Bambatsi'	ETPC
miliaceum	EFou EGle ETPC
virgatum	CTri ECha MSte NHol WBro WHil WPer WWat
– 'Hänse Herms'	CInt EHoe EPla ETPC MBri
– 'Heavy Metal'	CSte SApp SMad WCot
– 'Pathfinder'	ETPC
– 'Rehbraun'	CDec EFou EHoe ETPC LBuc MHlr WCot WRus
– 'Rotstrahlbusch'	EFou EPPr ETPC LBuc SPla
– 'Rubrum'	Widely available
¶ – 'Squaw'	CSte WCot
– 'Strictum'	EHoe EMil ETPC EWes
'Warrior'	CSte EFou ETPC SApp
PAPAVER † (Papaveraceae)	
aculeatum	MSto
alboroseum	EDAr GCHN GTou
¶ ***alpinum***	MPla
¶ – cut petal form	CInt
– subsp. ***ernesti-mayeri***	MSto
– 'Flore Pleno' Linnaeus	NBir
§ – Linnaeus	CSpe EMNN ESis GCHN GDra GTou LHol MBal MOne MRPP MWat NGre NNrd SIng SPla SRms WByw WPer WWin
anomalum	EMan MSto
anomalum album	ECGP EMon EWll GAbr NFai NLak WElm WSan
argemone	EWFC
§ ***atlanticum***	CNic ECoo EMan EMar GBuc GCHN NBro WPer WRha
– 'Flore Pleno'	CM&M LFis NBro NFai WCot WOld
bracteatum	See ***P. orientale*** var. ***bracteatum***
burseri	MSto SIng
§ ***commutatum*** ♀	ELan LHol MAvo SMrm WEas
– 'Ladybird'	See ***P. commutatum***
¶ ***corona-sancti-stephani***	MSto
degenii	CGra GCHN
dubium	ECWi
§ 'Fireball'	CBre CMHG CRow ECha ELan EWes GCal LHop MTis MWat NCat NGar WCot WMaN WRHF
heldreichii	See ***P. spicatum***
x ***hybridum*** 'Flore Pleno'	EMon MCLN NBrk SWat WGwG
¶ ***julicum***	CGra
kluanense	MSto NLak NWCA
lapponicum	MSto
lapponicum occidentale	MSto
lateritium	CPou MSto SRms
– 'Flore Pleno'	CSpe WSan
§ ***miyabeanum***	CGle CGra CMea CSpe ELan EPot GCHN GCra GDra GTou LHop MPla NWCA WOMN WPer WWin
miyabeanum album	ECho ELan
* ***miyabeanum*** 'Pacino'	ESis
miyabeanum tatewakii	See ***P. miyabeanum***
nanum 'Flore Pleno'	See ***P.* 'Fireball'**
§ ***nudicaule***	ELan GBur MHlr NChi WOMN WPer
– Champagne Bubbles Group	EBre SRms WLRN
– Constance Finnis Group	EMon EPot GBuc LHop
– var. ***croceum***	MSto NWCA WDav
♦ – Garden Gnome Group	See ***P. nudicaule* Gartenzwerg Group**
§ – Gartenzwerg Group	CSpe EMil GAbr MBri MPla NPri NTay WPbr
– 'Pacino'	SRms WFar WLRN WPer WWeb
– Wonderland Hybrids	NRoo
oreophilum	MSto
orientale	CB&S MBro NBee NCut SWat WBod WHil WPer
¶ – 'Aglaja'	WCot
– 'Allegro'	CSam CShe EBar EBre ECtt EFou GAbr MBri MCLN MRav NBrk NFai NRoo NVic SPer SSvw SWat WByw WGwG
– 'Avebury Crimson'	MWat
– 'Beauty Queen'	EBre ECot EOrc MBri MRav NBrk NCat NRoo SCoo WLRN WPbr
– 'Black and White' ♀	CElw CGle CHad CLon CRDP CShe EBre ECha EFou ELan EMan GCHN MRav MUlv NBrk NRoo SChu SPer SSoC SWat WCot WPbr WWin
– 'Blue Moon'	CArc CHad CMil EBre EFou GGar MRav NBir SMrm SWat WLRN
– 'Bonfire Red'	ELan
§ – var. ***bracteatum*** ♀	ECha EMon GCHN GDra NBir WBro WRHF
– 'Brilliant'	CM&M NFai
orientale carneum	CM&M SMrm
orientale 'Cedar Hill'	EFou WMer
– 'Cedric Morris' ♀	CHad CMil EGle GCra MSto NFai WCot WEas

– 'Cedric's Pink' CGle CMil EBee ECha EFou EMan EPri GCal MRav NRoo SChu SMrm SWat WLRN
– 'Charming' CLon LGre MHlr SWat WCot
¶ – 'China Boy' EFou
* – 'Choir Boy' NBrk SPla
– 'Curlilocks' CMGP CSte EBre ELan GAbr MCLN MRav MUlv NBrk NRoo SMrm SPer SRms SWat WCot WPbr WWeb WWin
* – 'Diana' CHad
– 'Doubloon' CDoC EBre GMac MBri NBrk NRoo
– 'Dwarf Allegro' GBuc MFir MOne NNor NOak
– 'Elam Pink' CLon ECha LGre MTis WCot
* – 'Erste Zuneigung' ECha
– 'Fatima' CHad EBee EFou LBuc LFis NPri SMrm
N – 'Flore Pleno' EFou GLil SSvw
¶ – 'Garden Glory' EFou SMrm
– 'Glowing Embers' EBre
* – 'Goldie' ELan WPbr
– Goliath Group CGle CHan CMil CSev EBee EFou MUlv NBrk NBro NOak NVic SDix SWat WCot WEas WHoo WPyg
– – 'Beauty of Livermere' 🏆 CDoC CHad CM&M CMea EMan MBro MTis NCat SAga SChu SLod SRms SWat WCot WElm WLRN WPyg WWhi
– 'Graue Witwe' CLon EFou GBuc NBrk SWat WRha
– 'Harvest Moon' CFir CShe EBre GLil MBri MRav NCut WCot WWeb
– 'Helen Elisabeth' EBre ECtt EFou EHal GCra GMac MHlr MRav MUlv NBrk NFai NRoo SChu SWat WCot WCra WMer
¶ – 'Hewitt's Old Rose' WCot
– 'Indian Chief' CSte EGle WCot WCra WMer
¶ – 'John Metcalf' EFou
– 'Juliane' ECha EGle EPri LGre WCot WPbr
– 'Karine' ECha LGre MBri NBrk NCat NRoo SChu SMrm SWas SWat WBro WCot WLRN WPen WWoo
– 'King George' GBuc MWat
– 'Kleine Tänzerin' CLon CMil CPou EBee EFou LGre MTis SWat WCot WLRN
– 'Lady Frederick Moore' LBuc SWat WMer WPbr
– 'Ladybird' CKel EBre ELan MRav NBrk NRoo SPla WCot
– 'Lilac Girl' CLon ECha EGle NSti WCot WPbr
– 'Marcus Perry' CDoC EBee GGar GMaP NFla NPri SPer SWat WCot WMer WRHF WTyr
– 'May Queen' (d) GBuc IBlr WCot WPen
– 'May Sadler' ENot LBuc SCoo
– 'Midnight' EBre
– 'Mrs Marrow's Plum' See ***P. orientale* 'Patty's Plum'**
– 'Mrs Perry' 🏆 CM&M CMGP CSam CSev CShe EBre EFou ELan EOrc GAbr GMac LHop MBri MFir MNrw MUlv MWat NBrk NFai NPer NRoo NSti SChu SMrm SPer WHoo WTyr
– 'Nanum Flore Pleno' See ***P.* 'Fireball'**
– 'Orange Glow' WMer
– 'Oriana' MBri MMil NCat SMrm WLRN
¶ – pale pink form WWhi
§ – 'Patty's Plum' CArc CBos CGle CHad CLon CMea CMil CPou CRDP CSWP CShe CSpe LGre MAvo SAga SChu SMrm SPla SWas WBro WCot WGle WHoo WRha WSan WWeb
– 'Perry's White' CGle CMea CRDP CSam CSpe EBre ECtt EFou ELan GMaP MBri MCLN MRav MWat NBro NFai NRoo NSti NVic SChu SPer SSoC SSvw WBro WByw WEas WHal WHoo WMer WWhi
– 'Picotée' CMGP CShe EBre EFou ELan EMan EOrc GMac MCLN MGrG MRav MUlv MWat NBro NRoo SChu SPer WBro WByw WCot WGwG WPbr WTyr
– 'Pinnacle' CSWP EBee GLil NFai NPri WCot
– 'Pizzicato' CM&M LGre NPer NRoo SMrm SWat WLRN WOve
♦ – Princess Victoria Louise See ***P. orientale* 'Prinzessin Victoria Louise'**
§ – 'Prinzessin Victoria Louise' CSWP EFou EHal EMan GLil GMaP LCom MMil SSoC SSvw SWat WCer WCot WMer WPer
– 'Raspberry Queen' CSte EFou ELan MAvo MHlr MTis NCut SWat WBro WCot WMer WPbr
– 'Redizelle' EBre
– 'Rembrandt' ECot MMil NCut NFla NPri WMer WPer
¶ – 'Rose Queen' WCot
* – 'Royal Wedding' CMil CSev MMil SChu SMrm WRha
– 'Salmon Glow' EBee GLil SCoo WMer WPbr WPer
– 'Scarlet King' EWll MMil NPri WLRN WTyr
– 'Showgirl' CRDP
– 'Sindbad' EFou NCat SMrm WCot
– 'Snow Queen' MBro NCut
* – 'Springtime' MRav
♦ – Stormtorch See ***P. orientale* 'Sturmfackel'**
§ – 'Sturmfackel' SCoo
¶ – 'Suleika' EFou
– 'Sultana' ECha GMac LGre SSoC WPbr
* – 'Turkish Delight' 🏆 EFou ELan EOrc GCHN GMaP GMac MMil MRav MTis NBir NBro NCat SChu SLod SPer SSoC SWat WPbr WTyr
– 'Türkenlouis' EFou WCot
– 'Watermelon' COtt EBee EHal LBuc MRav WBro WMer WPbr

paucifoliatum CHan
pilosum EMan EMar GBuc MSto NCat SRms SWat
radicatum MSto
rhaeticum ELan EMan
rhoeas CArn CJew ECWi EWFC GPoy MHew WElm WJek WSel
¶ – angels choir SWat WHer
– 'Mother of Pearl' SWat
– Shirley WSel
– 'Valerie Finnis' ELan
rupifragum CArc CFir CGle ECha ESis GAbr GCHN GCra LGan LHil MFir MRPP MSto NHex SUsu WEas WOve WPer WRha WWin

– 'Flore Pleno'	CSWP MRPP SMrm WCot WCru WHer WWhi
sendtneri	GCLN MSto WDav
§ ***spicatum***	CSWP CSam CSpe ECGP ECha GAbr GCal LHop MHar MHlr NBir NFai SMrm WBro WCot WEas WPbr
triniifolium	CInt CSpe SMrm

PARABENZOIN See LINDERA

PARADISEA (Asphodelaceae)

liliastrum ♀	EMan ERos LGan NCat NWoo SSpi WWhi
– 'Major'	CAvo
lusitanica	CAvo CGle CLon CMHG CMil CRDP CSpe NRai NSti SSpi WDav

PARAHEBE † (Scrophulariaceae)

x ***bidwillii***	CMHG ECou EMNN GAri GGar LFis MHig NHed NMen SBod SRms WWat
– 'Kea'	CFee ECou ECtt ELan EMNN ESis GCHN MAll MHig NHar NMen SBla SHel SUsu WASP WPer WRHF
canescens	ECou
§ ***catarractae*** ♀	CLyd CMHG CShe ECou ELan EMNN EMar MFir MNrw MPla MWat NBee NBro NMen NNor NTow SBod SMer SOkh SUsu WASP WHen WOve WPer WWhi
– blue	EHic GIsl GMac NBee SAlw SPan SPer SPla WWat
§ – 'Delight' ♀	CChe CGre CLTr ECou ELan ESis EWes GCHN GCal GGar LFis LHop MAsh MBro NBrk NPer SDix WASP WEas WHen WHoo WPyg
– subsp. ***diffusa***	CMHG ECou EMNN IOrc MAsh MMil NHar NMen NPer NVic WASP
– – 'Annie'	ECou
– – 'Pinkie'	CLTr ECou
– garden form	ECha LLWP SBla WAbe
– subsp. ***martinii***	ECou EWes MAll NCut
– 'Miss Willmott'	CShe GIsl LGan MAll MSCN NMen NVic SPer WASP WBod WPer
– 'Porlock Purple'	See ***P. catarractae* 'Delight'**
– 'Rosea'	ESis LGan MAll NVic SAlw SBla SIng WWat
– 'Tinycat'	MAll
– white	CBot ECha ELan EMNN ESis GCHN GIsl GMac IBlr LHop MBro MFir NCat NFla NMen SHel SOkh SUsu WASP WEas WPer WWat WWhi
decora	CLyd ECou GAri GCHN NSla WASP
derwentiana	ECou EMon
§ ***formosa***	CPle ECou MAll
– erect form	ECou
– lax form	ECou
– white	ECou
'Gillian'	CLTr CNic ECou ECtt EHyt GAri GGar GIsl LFis MMil NMen WFar WPer
'Greencourt'	See ***P. catarractae* 'Delight'**
§ ***hookeriana***	CNic CShe GGar MAll NMen SAga SMrm WHoo WPyg WRHF WStI WWat
'Joy'	ECou
linifolia	CTri EMNN NMen NNrd
– 'Blue Skies'	ECou EDAr EHyt GIsl LHop MHig
§ ***lyallii***	CBot EAst ECou ELan ESis GIsl LHop MAll MBar MPla MRav MWat NBee NHed NHol NMen NNor NWCA SAga SIng SRms WASP WAbe WWin
– 'Clarence'	CLyd ECou GIsl MAll
– 'Engel's Blue'	LGan
– 'Glacier'	CLTr ECou
– 'Julie-Anne'	CMHG ECou ELan ESis GCal GIsl LRHS MAsh
– 'Rosea'	CTri GGar LFis MBal WASP WHoo WPer WPyg
'Mervyn'	CLyd CPBP ECou ECtt GCHN GGar GIsl LFis LHop MAll NHed NHol NMen SPan WASP WHen WPer
olsenii	ECou GGar MAll NTow
§ ***perfoliata*** ♀	Widely available
– dark blue	GBuc GCal MBro SMad
'Snowcap'	ELan LRHS MAsh WCot

PARAJUBAEA (Arecaceae)

cocoides	LPal

PARAQUILEGIA (Ranunculaceae)

adoxoides	See ***Semiaquilegia adoxoides***
§ ***anemonoides***	GGGa GTou NHar WAbe WDav
grandiflora	See ***P. anemonoides***

PARASERIANTHES (Mimosaceae)

distachya	See ***P. lophantha***
§ ***lophantha*** ♀	CAbb CGre CHEx CHan CPle CTrC ISea LHil SArc SOWG

PARASYRINGA See LIGUSTRUM

× PARDANCANDA (Iridaceae)

norrisii	CArn CFir EAst EBee EMan EWes GSki NPri WLRN WPer

PARDANTHOPSIS (Iridaceae)

dichotoma	WThi

PARIETARIA (Urticaceae)

§ ***judaica***	ELau EWFC GPoy MHew MSal WHer
– 'Corinne Tremaine'	WHer
officinalis	See ***P. judaica***

PARIS (Trilliaceae)

incompleta	EPot
japonica	WCru
§ ***polyphylla***	CFir WChr WCot WCru
polyphylla yunnanensis alba	WChr
quadrifolia	CAvo CFil CFir CRDP GPoy LGre SSpi WChr WCot WCru WHer
– JMH 79	MDun

PARKINSONIA (Caesalpiniaceae)

See Plant Deletions

PARNASSIA (Parnassiaceae)
cabulica GDra
nubicola GDra MBal NHar
palustris WHer
palustris palustris NTow

PAROCHETUS (Papilionaceae)
africana CHan CHid GBuc
communis ♀ CB&S CFee CGle CNic GCra GDra GMac LBlm NBro NPer SIng SVen WAbe WOMN WWhi
* – 'Blue Gem' CArc
– dark form GCal
– Himalayan form IBlr

PARONYCHIA (Illecebraceae)
argentea EPot MBro WPer
§ *capitata* CHal CLyd CMHG CNic CTri ELan NMen NNrd SRms WPat WPer WRHF WWin
§ *kapela* MHig NPri NTow SAlw SSmi WPer
– 'Binsted Gold' (v) CElw CHid EMon SSmi
¶ – subsp. *serpyllifolia* CPea
nivea See *P. capitata*
serpyllifolia See *P. kapela*

PARROTIA (Hamamelidaceae)
persica ♀ CB&S CGre CPMA CSte CTho CWSG ELan EMil ENot ISea LHyr LPan MAsh MBal MBri MGos NBee NPal SHBN SPer SReu SSpi SSta WAbe WBod WDin WHCG WHar WWat
– 'Pendula' CPMA ELan IOrc MBal
– 'Vanessa' CMCN CPMA LPan LRHS MBri SSpi SSta
– 'Variegata' CPMA

PARROTIOPSIS (Hamamelidaceae)
jacquemontiana CEnd CPMA SMur SSpi

PARRYA (Brassicaceae)
menziesii See *Phoenicaulis cheiranthoides*

PARSONSIA (Apocynaceae)
capsularis CPlN ECou MAll
heterophylla ERea

PARTHENIUM (Asteraceae)
integrifolium CArn GPoy MSal

PARTHENOCISSUS † (Vitaceae)
§ *henryana* ♀ Widely available
himalayana ECtt
♦ – 'Purpurea' See *P. himalayana* var. *rubrifolia*
§ – var. *rubrifolia* CBlo CSte EHic EPfP ETen LHol MAsh WCru WWat
¶ *inserta* GOrc
§ *quinquefolia* ♀ Widely available
– var. *engelmannii* LBuc MGos NFla SPer WAbe
striata See *Cissus striata*
thomsonii See *Cayratia thomsonii*
§ *tricuspidata* ♀ CChe CHEx CShe EBee ECtt GOrc MBal MGos NNor SBid SPer SReu SSoC WDin
– B&SWJ 1162 WCru
– 'Beverley Brook' CMac CShe EBre ETen MBri SBid SBra SPla SRms WAbe
– 'Green Spring' CDoC IHos MBlu MBri MGos NBrk
– 'Lowii' CDoC CMac EBre ECot EPla MBlu MGos SMad
– 'Robusta' CSam LPan
§ – 'Veitchii' Widely available

PASITHEA (Asphodelaceae)
See Plant Deletions

PASPALUM (Poaceae)
quadrifarium ETPC

PASSIFLORA † (Passifloraceae)
actinia CPas CPlN LChe
¶ *acuminata* CPas
adenopoda CPas
¶ 'Adularia' CPas LChe LPri
alata (F) ♀ CAbb CPas CPlN ECon ELan ERea LChe LCns
– 'Shannon' (F) CPas
x *alatocaerulea* See *P.* x *belotii*
allantophylla CPas
'Allardii' CPas SMad
ambigua CPas
'Amethyst' CAbb CPas CPlN CSPN ELan EMil EOrc LBlm LHop LPri SAga SBid SBra
§ *amethystina* ♀ CAbb CB&S CDoC CPas CPlN CRHN ECon ERea LCns NPal SLMG
ampullacea (F) CPas
anfracta CPas
N *antioquiensis* Karst ♀ CB&S CBot CGre CHEx CPlN CSPN CTbh ELan EOrc ERea GQui IBlr ISea LChe LPri MBlu MTis SLMG
apetala CPas
§ *aurantia* CPas ERea
auriculata CPas
banksii See *P. aurantia*
§ x *belotii* CPas ELan ERea LChe LCns LPri WDin WWeb
– 'Impératrice Eugénie' See *P.* x *belotii*
* *biflora* CPas
– Lamarck CPas
boenderi CPas
brevipes CPas
¶ 'Byron Beauty' LPri
§ *caerulea* (F) ♀ Widely available
– 'Constance Elliot' (F) ♀ CB&S CBot CChe CMac CPas CPlN CRHN CSPN ELan EMil EOrc LBlm LChe LHop LPri SBra SLMG SOWG SPer SPla SReu SSta WBod WCru WHen WWeb
I x *caerulea racemosa* See *P.* x *violacea*
caerulea rubra CChu ECtt SBid SEND
* *caerulea* 'Star of Kingston Seymour' CPlN
I x *caeruleoracemosa* See *P.* x *violacea*
x *caponii* ERea
capsularis CPas MSto SLMG WCot
chinensis See *P. caerulea*
cincinnata CPas
cinnabarina CPas
citrina CPas CPlN ECon ELan ERea LChe LPri
coccinea (F) CB&S CPas CPlN LRHS
¶ *colinvauxii* CPas

× ***colvillii***	CPas CPlN
¶ ***conzattiana***	CPas
§ ***coriacea***	CPas CPlN LChe LRHS
costaricensis	CPas
cumbalensis	CPas
– var. ***cumbalensis*** JCA 13988	MSto
¶ ***cuneata***	CPas SLMG
¶ ***cuprea***	CPas
¶ ***cuspidifolia***	CPas
§ ***cyanea***	CPas
¶ × ***decaisneana*** (F)	CPas
§ – 'Innesii'	CPas
¶ ***dioscoreifolia***	CPas
discophora	CPas
edulis (F)	CPas CPlN EBak LCns LPri SLMG
– 'Crackerjack' (F)	CB&S COtt ERea
– f. ***flavicarpa*** (F)	CPas ECon ELan LChe
* – 'Golden Nuggett' (F)	CPas
¶ – 'Norfolk' (F)	CPas
– 'Supreme'	CB&S
'Elizabeth' (F)	CPas LChe
'Empress Eugenie'	See ***P.*** × ***belotii***
* ***escorbariana***	CPas
* 'Evatoria'	CPas
× ***exoniensis*** ♀	CBot CGre CPas CPlN LPri
* ***exura***	CPas
¶ ***filipes***	CPas
foetida	CPas MSto
– var. ***hirsuta*** (F)	CPas
– var. ***hirsutissima***	CPas
– var. ***orinocensis***	CPas
* ***garayaglia***	CPas
¶ ***garckei***	CPas
gibertii	CPas
gigantifolia	CPas
gilbertiana	CPas
glandulosa	CPas
gracilis	CPas MSto
gracillima	CPas
guatemalensis	CPas SLMG
hahnii	CPas
helleri	CPas CPlN
herbertiana (F)	CPas CPlN
holosericea	CPas
incana	See ***P. seemannii***
incarnata (F)	CArn CBlo CPas CPlN ELan LChe LPri MSal NBrk
'Incense' (F) ♀	CBlo CPas CPlN ELan LChe LPri LRHS
× ***innesii***	See ***P.*** × ***decaisneana*** **'Innesii'**
¶ ***jilekii***	CPas
jorullensis	CPas
¶ ***juliana***	CPas
kalbreyeri	CPas
¶ ***karwinskii***	CPas
× ***kewensis***	CPas LChe LPri
* ***kirkii***	CPlN
¶ ***lancearia***	CPas
laurifolia (F)	CPas
§ ***ligularis*** (F)	CPas LBlo LRHS
◆ 'Lilac Lady'	See ***P.*** × ***violacea*** **'Tresederi'**
lindeniana	CPas
* ***lourdesae***	CPas
lowei	See ***P. ligularis***
lutea	CPas
maliformis (F)	CPas CPlN
manicata (F)	CPas CPlN NBrk WHer
¶ ***matthewsii***	CPas
'Mavis Mastics'	See ***P.*** × ***violacea*** **'Tresederi'**
mayana	See ***P. caerulea***

menispermifolia	See ***P. pilosa***
* ***microstipula***	CPas
misera	CPas
mixta (F)	CPlN ERea
– × ***antioquiensis***	CPas SAga
mollissima (F) ♀	CAbb CB&S CBot CGre CPas CPlN CRHN CSPN EBak ELan EOrc ERea LBlm LChe LPri SLMG SVen WHer
morifolia	CPas CPlN CTrC LPri MSto WHer
¶ ***mucronata***	CPas
¶ ***multiflora***	CPas
¶ ***murucuja***	CPas
naviculata	CPas
nelsonii	CPas
nitida (F)	CPas
¶ ***oblongata***	CPas
◆ ***obtusifolia***	See ***P. coriacea***
oerstedii	CPas
– var. ***choconhiana***	CPas
onychina	See ***P. amethystina***
organensis	CPas
pallens	CPas
perfoliata	CPas
* 'Perfume'	CPas
¶ ***phoenicea***	CPas
¶ – 'Ruby Glow' (F)	CPas
pinnatistipula (F)	CGre CPas
¶ × ***piresii***	CPas
platyloba	CPas CPlN
punctata	CPas
¶ 'Pura Vida'	CPas
¶ 'Purple Haze'	CPas LPri
'Purple Passion'	See ***P. edulis*** **f. *edulis* (F)**
quadrangularis L. (F) ♀	CB&S CPas CPlN CTbh ERea LChe LPan LPri WHer
* ***quadrangularis macrocarpa*** (F)	CPas
¶ ***quadrifaria***	CPas
¶ ***quadriflora***	CPas
¶ ***quinquangularis***	CPas
racemosa ♀	CPas CPlN CSPN ELan ERea ERom IBlr LChe SOWG WGor
¶ 'Red Inca'	CPas
◆ ***retipetala***	See ***P. cyanea***
rovirosae	CPas LRHS
rubra	CBlo CPas ELan EWes LPri WStI
* ***rufa***	CPas
'Saint Rule'	CPas
sanguinolenta	CAbb CPas CRHN ELan ERea LChe LPri
¶ 'Sapphire'	CPas
§ ***seemannii***	CPas
◆ ***serrata***	See ***P. serratodigitata***
serratifolia	CPas
§ ***serratodigitata***	CPas
serrulata	CPas
sexflora	CPas
¶ 'Smythiana'	CPas
standleyi	CPas
'Star of Bristol' ♀	CPas
'Star of Clevedon'	CPas CPlN
'Star of Kingston'	CPas
¶ ***stipulata***	CPas
suberosa	CPas LPri
subpeltata	CPas LPri
'Sunburst'	CPas CPlN
¶ ***talamancensis***	CPas
¶ ***tatei***	CPas
¶ ***tenuifila***	CPas

§ ***tetrandra*** CGre CPas ECou
tica CPas
◆ × ***tresederi*** See ***P.* × *violacea* 'Tresederi'**
tricuspis CPas
¶ ***tridactylites*** CPas
trifasciata CPas CPlN
¶ ***tripartita*** CPas
– JCA 13982 MSto
* ***triphostemmatoides*** CPas
¶ ***trisecta*** CPas
tuberosa CPas
¶ ***tulae*** CPas
umbilicata CBot CPas CPlN WCru
urbaniana CPas
vespertilio CPas
§ × ***violacea*** ♀ CAbb CB&S CBlo CPas CPlN CRHN ECon ERea ISea MBri
¶ – 'Dedorina' CPas
– 'Eynsford Gem' CPas
◆ – 'Lilac Lady' See ***P.* × *violacea* 'Tresederi'**
§ – 'Tresederi' CPas
– 'Victoria' CPas LPri
viridiflora CPas
vitifolia (F) CAbb CPas CPlN ECon ELan ERea LChe LPri
¶ – 'Scarlet Flame' (F) CPas
xiikzodz CPas
yucatanensis CPas
zamorana CPas

PASTINACA (Apiaceae)

sativa CKin

PATRINIA (Valerianaceae)

gibbosa CLyd CRDP ECha ECro GCHN LGan MHig SIde SMrm WCru
scabiosifolia CMil ECha EMan GBuc SMrm WWin
triloba CLyd CRDP ECha NGre NMen NRya NWoo SSpi
* – 'Minor' ECho
– var. ***palmata*** CShe NBro NBus WFar
– var. ***triloba*** CGle GCal MHig NTow WWin
¶ ***villosa*** WCot

PAULOWNIA (Scrophulariaceae)

coreana CGre
fargesii Franchet CEnd CHEx CLnd ICrw SLPl SMad
– Osborn See ***P. tomentosa* 'Lilacina'**
fortunei CChu CMCN CWSG GAri WLRN WNor
tomentosa ♀ CB&S CBot CHEx CLnd CPle ELan EMil ENot EWes ICrw IOrc LPan MUlv NPal SBid SHBN SMad SPer SRms SSta WHCG WMou WNor

PAVONIA (Malvaceae)

§ × ***gledhillii*** LHil
× ***intermedia*** See ***P.* × *gledhillii***
multiflora hort. See ***P.* × *gledhillii***
– Jussieu ERea
praemorsa CBot LHil

PAXISTIMA (Celastraceae)

canbyi MAll NPro WPat WWin
myrsinites See ***P. myrtifolia***
§ ***myrtifolia*** CPle

PECTEILIS (Orchidaceae)

* ***dentata*** EFEx
§ ***radiata*** EFEx
* – 'Albomarginata' EFEx
* – 'Aureomarginata' EFEx

PEDICULARIS (Scrophulariaceae)

See Plant Deletions

PEDILANTHUS (Euphorbiaceae)

¶ ***tithymaloides*** 'Variegatus' LChe

PEGANUM (Zygophyllaceae)

harmala MSal NGno

PELARGONIUM † (Geraniaceae)

'A Happy Thought' See ***P.* 'Happy Thought'**
'A.M. Mayne' (Z/d) CWDa SDen
¶ 'Abba' (Z/d) CWDa
'Abel Carrière' (I/d) SDen SKen WFib
abrotanifolium (Sc) CNat CSev ERav MHul SKen WEas WFib
– broad-leaved SDen
'Acapulco' NPri WLRN
acerifolium hort. See ***P. vitifolium***
– L'Héritier See ***P. cucullatum*** subsp. ***strigifolium***
acetosum CSpe GCal LHil MHul MSte SAga SHFr SMrm SUsu
* – 'Variegatum' CSpe
acraeum MHul WFib
Action (Z/d) WFib
'Ada Sutterby' (Dw/d) SKen WFib
'Adagio' (Dw) ESul
'Adam's Quilt' (Z/C) SKen WEas
'Adele' (Min/d) ESul WFib
'Aerosol' (Min) ESul WFib
'Afterglow' (Z) WFib
'Ailsa' (Min/d) ESul MBri
'Ainsdale Angel' (A) ESul LDea
'Ainsdale Claret' (Z) LVer
'Ainsdale Eyeful' (Z) LVer
'Akela' (Min) ESul
'Alan West' (Z/St) LHil SDen
'Alberta' (Z) SKen WFib
'Albert's Choice' (R) WFib
album CWDa MHul
alchemilloides CNat MHul SIng WFib
'Alcyone' (Dw/d) ESul IHos SKen WFib
'Alde' (Min) ESul LHil LVer MWhe SKen SSea WEas
'Aldenham' (Z) WFib
'Aldham' (Min) ESul LVer WFib
'Aldwyck' (R) EBSP LDea WFib
'Alex' (Z) CWDa SKen
'Alex Mary' (R) SDen SSea WFib
'Alfred Wolfe' SDen
'Algenon' (Min/d) ESul WFib
'Alice Crousse' (I/d) ♀ SDen SKen WFib
'Alison' (Dw) ESul SDen
¶ 'Alison Jill' (Z/d) CWDa
'Alison Wheeler' (Min/d) MWhe
'All My Love' (R) LDea WFib
'Alma' (Min/C) ESul
'Almost Heaven' (Dw/Z/v) MWhe
'Alpine Glow' (Z/d) EBSP MWhe
'Alpine Orange' (Z/d) CWDa SDen
'Alta Bell' (R) WFib
'Altair' (Min/d) ESul WFib
alternans CSev MHul WEas

	'Always' (Z/d)	SDen WFib
*	'Alys Collins' (Z/d)	WFib
	'Amarantha' (Z)	WFib
	'Amari' (R)	LDea
	'Ambrose' (Dw/d)	ESul LVer WFib
§	'Amethyst' (I/d) 🏆	ECtt GDTE IHos LDea LVer MWhe NPri WFib WLRN
	'Amethyst' (R)	EBSP LDea MBri SDen SKen WFib
	'Ami' (R)	WFib
	'Anabell Stephenson' (Dw/d)	WFib
	'Andersonii' (Sc)	EWoo WFib
	'Andrew Salvidge' (R)	LDea WFib
I	'Andromeda' (Min)	SDen WFib
	'Ange Davey' (Z/d)	WFib
*	'Angela Brook'	CWDa
	'Angela Read' (Dw)	ESul
*	'Angela Woodberry' (I/d)	CWDa
	'Angelique' (Dw/d)	ESul LVer WFib
	'Anglia' (Dw)	ESul SDen
	'Ann Hoysted' (R) 🏆	WFib
	'Ann Redington' (R)	LDea WFib
	'Ann Sothern' (Z)	WFib
	'Anna' (Dw)	ESul SDen WFib
	'Anne Wilkie-Millar' (Z/d)	WFib
	antidysentericum	MHul
	'Antigua' (R)	LDea WFib
¶	'Antoine Crozy' (ZxI/d)	WFib
	'Antoinette' (Min)	ESul
	'Apache' (Z/d) 🏆	CHal CWDa WFib
	'Aphrodite' (Z)	CWDa ECtt WFib
	'Apollo' (R)	CWDa
	'Apple Betty' (Sc)	LDea WFib
	'Apple Blossom Rosebud' (Z/d) 🏆	CLit EBSP ECtt LVer MBri MWhe SDen SKen SMrm SUsu WEas WFib
	'Apricot' (Z/St/d)	ESul SDen SKen
	'Apricot Queen' (I/d)	LDea SDen
	'Apricot Star'	CSpe MWhe
*	'April Hamilton' (I)	WFib
	'Apuldram' (R)	EBSP LDea WFib
	'Aquarell' (R)	CKni SDen
	'Arctic Frost'	SDen
	'Arctic Queen' (R)	SDen
§	'Arctic Star' (Z/St/d)	CSpe ESul LHil LVer WEas
	'Arcturus' (Min)	WFib
x	***ardens***	CSpe LHil MHul
	'Ardwick Cinnamon'	ESul GDTE LDea
	aridum	MHul
	'Aries' (Min/C)	ESul MBri MWhe
	'Arizona' (Min/d)	ESul SDen SKen WFib
	'Arnside Fringed Aztec' (R)	LDea
	'Aroma' (Sc)	WFib
	'Arthington Slam' (R)	LDea
	'Arthur Biggin' (Z)	MWhe SKen
	articulatum	MHul
*	'Ashey'	SDen
	'Ashfield Blaze' (Z/d)	SDen WFib
	'Ashfield Jubilee' (Z/C)	SKen
	'Ashfield Monarch' (Z/d) 🏆	LVer MWhe WFib
	'Ashfield Serenade' (Z) 🏆	SDen SKen WFib
	'Ashley Stephenson' (R)	WFib
	'Askham Fringed Aztec' (R) 🏆	EBSP LDea LVer SDen
	'Askham Slam' (R)	LDea
	asperum Ehr. ex Willd.	See ***P.* 'Graveolens'**
	'Astrakan' (Z/d)	SDen
	'Athabasca' (Min)	ESul

	'Atomic Snowflake' (Sc/v)	CArn CHal CInt ERav ESul GBar GDTE LDea LHil LVer MSte MWhe SDen SIde WCHb WEas WFib WJek WWye
	'Attar of Roses' (Sc) 🏆	CArn CHal CInt CLTr CLit CNat ERav ESul GBar IHos LBlm LDea LHil LVer MWhe NHHG NSty SDen SIde SKen WApp WCHb WEas WFib WWye
	'Attraction' (Z/St/d)	WFib
	'Aubusson' (R)	WFib
	'Audrey' (Z/d)	SDen WFib
*	'Audrey Baghurst' (I)	CWDa
	'Audrey Clifton' (I/d)	ECtt SDen WEas WFib
	'Augusta'	LHil LHop SMrm
	Auralia (Z/d)	WFib
	auritum	CMon
	'Aurora' (Z/d)	MWhe SKen
	'Aurore'	See ***P.* 'Unique Aurore'**
	australe	CFir CNat EWes MHul MSte SMrm SSpi WFib
	'Australian Mystery'	LHil
	'Autumn' (Z/d)	IHos LVer MWhe WFib
	'Autumn Colours' (Min)	ESul
	'Autumn Festival' (R)	WFib
	'Autumn Haze' (R)	EBSP WFib
	'Autumn Mist' (R)	WFib
	'Avril'	ESul
	'Aztec' (R) 🏆	EBSP LDea LVer MSte WEas WFib
	'Aztec Fimbriant'	SMrm
	'Baby Birds Egg' (Min)	CSpe ESul SDen WFib
	'Baby Brocade' (Min/d)	ESul LVer WFib
	'Baby Helen' (Min)	ESul
	'Baby James' (Min)	ESul
	'Baby Snooks' (A)	WEas
	'Babylon' (R)	WFib
	'Badley' (Dw)	ESul
	Balcon Imperial	See ***P.* 'Roi des Balcons Impérial'**
	'Balcon Lilas'	See ***P.* 'Roi des Balcons Lilas'**
	'Balcon Rose'	See ***P.* 'Hederinum'**
	'Balcon Rouge'	See ***P.* 'Roi des Balcons Impérial'**
	'Balcon Royale'	See ***P.* 'Roi des Balcons Impérial'**
	'Bali Surprise' (Z/St)	ESul
	'Ballerina' (Dw/d)	MWhe
	'Bandit' (Min)	ESul
	'Bantam' (Min/d)	ESul WFib
§	'Barbe Bleu' (I/d)	EBSP ECtt LDea MWhe SDen SKen SSea WFib
	'Barking' (Min)	ESul
	barklyi	MHul
	'Barnston Dale' (Dw)	ESul
	'Baron de Layres' (Z/d)	SDen WFib
	'Baronne A. de Rothschild' (Z/d)	WFib
	'Bashful' (Min)	ESul
	'Bath Beauty' (Dw)	SDen SKen WEas
	'Baylham' (Min)	ESul
	'Beacon Hill' (Min)	ESul LVer
	'Beatrice Cottington' (I/d)	SKen WFib
	'Beatrix' (Z/d)	ESul LVer SDen SKen WFib
	'Beau Geste' (R)	EBSP
	'Beauty' (Z)	WFib
	'Beauty of Bath' (R)	WFib
	'Beauty of Calderdale' (Z/C)	WFib
N	'Beauty of Eastbourne'	See ***P.* 'Lachskönigin'**

'Beauty of El Segundo' (Z/d)	SKen WFib
'Beauty of Jersey' (I/d)	EBSP WFib
'Beckwith's Pink' (Z)	SDen SKen
'Belinda Adams' (Min/d) ♀	ESul MWhe WFib
§ 'Belladonna' (I/d)	ECtt IHos
'Bembridge'	SDen
'Ben Franklin' (Z/v) ♀	CLit EBSP IHos LVer MWhe SDen WFib
'Ben Matt' (R)	WFib
'Ben Nevis' (Dw/d)	ESul LVer SDen
'Bentley' (Dw)	ESul
Bergpalais (Z/d)	WFib
'Berliner Balkon' (I)	SDen SKen
* 'Bern'	CLit
'Bernado'	WLRN
'Beromünster' (Dec)	ERav ESul EWoo LDea LHil LIck MSte SKen WEas WFib
'Bert Pearce' (R)	EBSP LDea WFib
'Beryl Bodey'	See ***P.* 'Mrs L.R. Bodey'**
'Beryl Gibbons' (Z/d)	LVer MWhe
'Beryl Read' (Dw)	ERea ESul
'Beryl Reid' (R)	LDea WFib
'Berylette' (Min/d)	ESul WFib
'Bess' (Z/d)	ESul SDen SKen
'Beta' (Min/C)	ESul
'Bette Shellard' (Z/d)	LVer MWhe
'Betty Dollery' (Z/d)	SDen
'Betty Hulsman' (A)	ESul LDea
'Betty Read' (Dw)	ESul
'Betty West' (Min/d)	SDen
betulinum	MHul WFib
'Betwixt' (Z/v)	SDen SKen WFib
'Bewerley Park' (Z/C/d)	LVer WFib
'Bianca' (Min/d)	ESul
'Bicester Gem'	SDen
'Bi-coloured Startel' (Z/St/d)	LVer MWhe
'Biedermeier' (R)	LVer
'Bildeston' (Z/C)	ESul SDen
'Bill West' (I)	SDen
'Billie Read' (Dw/d)	ERea ESul
'Bingo' (Min)	ESul
'Bird Dancer' (Dw/St) ♀	CInt CSpe ERav ESul GBur LHil LVer MSte MWhe SDen SKen SSea WEas WFib
'Birthday Girl' (R)	WFib
'Bitter Lemon' (Sc)	ESul
'Black Butterfly'	See ***P.* 'Brown's Butterfly'**
¶ 'Black Country Bugle' (Z/d)	CWDa SDen
'Black Knight' (R)	CMdw CSpe ESul LVer MSte WFib
'Black Magic' (R)	WFib
'Black Night' (A)	ESul
'Black Pearl' (Z/d)	LVer SDen WFib
'Black Prince' (R)	WEas WPen
'Black Velvet' (R)	LDea LVer
'Black Vesuvius'	See ***P.* 'Red Black Vesuvius'**
'Blackcurrant Sundae'	LVer
'Blakesdorf' (Dw)	ESul MWhe
'Blanche Roche'	NPri SCoo WLRN
§ 'Blandfordianum' (Sc)	EWoo LVer SSad
§ 'Blauer Frühling' (I/d)	IHos LVer SKen
'Blaze Away'	SDen SSea
'Blazonry' (Z/v)	CBrk MWhe WFib
'Bloomfield Abundance'	LBlm
'Blooming Gem' (Min/I/d)	LDea
'Blue Beard'	See ***P.* 'Barbe Bleu'**
'Blue Blizzard'	NPri WLRN
'Blue Fox' (Z)	CWDa SDen
'Blue Orchid' (R)	LDea WFib
'Blue Peter' (I/d)	SKen
'Blue Spring'	See ***P.* 'Blauer Frühling'**
'Bluebeard'	ERav
§ 'Blues' (Z/d)	CWDa IHos
'Blush Kleine Liebling' (Min)	WFib
'Blush Mariquita' (R)	WEas WFib
'Blush Petit Pierre' (Min)	ESul
'Blushing Bride' (I/d)	IHos LDea SKen
'Blushing Emma' (Z)	ESul WFib
'Bob Legge' (Z/d)	WFib
* 'Bode's Trina' (I)	CWDa
'Bodey's Picotee' (R) ♀	WFib
'Bold Flame' (Z/d)	WFib
'Bold Sunrise' (Z)	LVer
'Bold Sunset' (Z/d)	LVer WFib
'Bolero' (U) ♀	EWoo IHos LVer WFib
'Boogy'	WLRN
'Bosham' (R)	EBSP LDea WFib
'Botley Beauty' (R)	EBSP LDea WFib
'Boudoir' (Z/C/d)	ESul
'Bouldner'	SDen
bowkeri	MHul
'Brackenwood' (Min/d) ♀	ESul LVer WFib
'Bramford' (Dw)	ESul
'Braque' (R)	LDea WFib
'Brasil'	WLRN
'Bravo' (Z/d)	MWhe WFib
'Break o' Day' (R)	LDea LVer SDen WEas
'Bredon' (R) ♀	WFib
'Brenda' (Min/d)	ESul LVer
'Brenda Hyatt' (Dw/d)	ESul WFib
'Brenda Kitson' (Z/d)	LVer MWhe WFib
'Brialyn Beauty' (A)	LDea
'Brialyn Moonlight' (A)	ESul LDea SSea
'Bridesmaid' (Dw/C/d)	ESul LVer WFib
'Brightstone'	SDen
'Brightwell' (Min/d)	ESul WFib
'Brilliant' (Dec)	CNat EWoo LVer WFib
'Bristol' (Z/v)	SDen SKen WFib
'Britannia' (R)	LDea
'Brixworth Boquet' (Min/C/d)	MWhe
'Brixworth Charmer' (Z/v)	MWhe
'Brixworth Melody' (Z/v)	MWhe
'Brixworth Pearl' (Z)	MWhe
'Brixworth Rhapsody' (Z/v)	MWhe
'Brixworth Starlight' (I/v)	MWhe
'Broadway' (Min)	WFib
'Brocade' (Z/d)	IHos LVer WFib
'Brockbury Scarlet' (Ca)	WFib
'Bronze Corinne' (Z/C/d)	SDen SKen
¶ 'Bronze Nuhulumby' (R)	EBSP WFib
'Bronze Queen' (Z/C)	LIck MWhe
'Bronze Velvet' (R)	WFib
'Brook'	SDen
'Brook's Purple'	See ***P.* 'Royal Purple'**
'Brookside Astra'	LVer
'Brookside Betty' (Dw/C/d)	ESul SDen
'Brookside Bolero' (Z)	ESul
'Brookside Candy' (Dw/d)	ESul WFib
'Brookside Champagne' (Min/d)	ESul
'Brookside Cinderella' (Z/C/d)	ESul
'Brookside Flamenco' (Min/d)	ESul LVer MWhe WFib
'Brookside Primrose' (Min/C/d)	ESul MWhe WFib

'Brookside Rosita' (Min)	ESul
'Brookside Serenade' (Z)	ESul WFib
'Brookside Spitfire' (Dw/d)	ESul
§ 'Brown's Butterfly' (R)	EBSP ERav LDea LHop SAga SUsu WFib
§ 'Bruni' (Z/d)	CHal MWhe WFib
'Brunswick' (Sc)	ESul EWoo LVer MSte SDen WFib
'Brutus' (Z)	CWDa
'Bucklesham' (Dw)	ESul
'Bumblebee' (Dw)	ESul
'Burgenlandmädel' (Z/d)	LVer SKen WFib
'Burgundy' (R)	LDea LVer WFib
'Burnaby' (Min)	WFib
'Burstall' (Min/d)	SDen
'Bushfire' 🏆	EBSP LDea WFib
'Butley' (Min)	ESul
'Buttercup Don' (Z/d)	EBSP
§ Butterfly (I)	IHos WFib
'Butterfly' (Min/v)	ECtt NPri
§ Cabaret (Z/d)	MBri
caffrum	MHul
'Cal'	See ***P.* 'Salmon Irene'**
'Caledonia' (Z)	LVer SKen
'Caledonian Maiden' (Z)	WFib
'Caligula' (Min/d)	WFib
'Calypso' (Z)	WFib
'Cameo' (Dw/d)	LVer MWhe WFib
'Camilla' (Dw)	SDen
'Camphor Rose' (Sc)	CLTr ESul GBar SSea
* 'Canadian Centennial'	CBar
'Can-can' (I/d)	WFib
candicans	MHul WFib
'Candy' (Min/d)	ESul
'Candy Dancer' (Sc) 🏆	EOHP ESul LDea
'Candy Kisses' (D)	ESul
canescens	See ***P.* 'Blandfordianum'**
'Capel' (Dw/d)	ESul
'Capella' (Min)	WFib
Capen (Z/d)	WFib
capitatum	CInt CNat MHul SDen SVen WCHb WEas WFib
'Capri' (Sc)	WFib
'Caprice' (R)	EWoo SDen WFib
'Capricorn' (Min/d)	ESul
'Captain Starlight' (A)	CLit ESul EWoo LDea LHil LVer SSea WEas WFib
'Cardinal'	See ***P.* 'Kardinal'**
¶ 'Cardinal Pink' (Z/d)	CWDa
'Carefree' (U)	EWoo WFib
'Cariboo Gold' (Min/C) 🏆	ESul
'Carisbrooke' (R) 🏆	LDea SDen SKen SSea WEas WFib
'Carmel' (Z)	WFib
'Carnival' (R)	See ***P.* 'Marie Vogel'**
'Carnival' (Z)	WFib
carnosum	MHul
'Carol Ann' (Z)	SDen
'Carol Gibbons' (Z/d)	LVer MWhe
'Carol Munroe' (Z/d)	LVer SDen
'Carole' (R)	EBSP
'Caroline Plumridge' (Dw)	ESul WFib
'Caroline Schmidt' (Z/d/v) 🏆	CBrk CHal CLit EBSP LDea LVer MBri MWhe SDen SKen SSea WFib
'Carousel' (Z/d)	CWDa LVer
¶ 'Casanova' (Z/d)	WLRN
* 'Cascade Lilac'	WFib
* 'Cascade Pink'	WFib
* 'Cascade Red'	WFib
§ Casino (Z/d)	IHos
'Cassata' (R)	WFib
'Catford Belle' (A) 🏆	CLit CSpe EBre ESul GDTE LDea LHil LVer MWhe SDen SKen SSea WEas WFib
'Cathay' (Z/St)	ESul
caucalifolium subsp. ***caucalifolium***	MHul
– subsp. ***convolvulifolium***	MHul WFib
caylae	MHul
'Cayucas' (I/d)	SKen
'Celebration' (Z/d)	ESul LVer
'Celia' (Min)	SDen WFib
ceratophyllum	MHul
'Cerise Carnation'	See ***P.* 'Mrs H.J. Jones'**
'Cézanne' (R)	LDea LVer SAga SMrm WFib
§ Champagne (Z)	CWDa
'Chantilly Claret' (R)	EBSP LDea
'Chantilly Lace' (R)	EBSP LDea
'Charity' (Sc) 🏆	ERav LDea WFib
§ Charleston (Z)	IHos
'Charlie Boy' (R)	LDea SDen WFib
'Charlotte Bidwell'	ESul
'Charlotte Read' (Dw)	ERea ESul
'Charm' (Min)	ESul
* 'Charmant'	CWDa
'Charmer' (R)	LDea
'Charmy Snowflake'	WFib WHer
'Chelmondiston' (Min/d)	ESul MWhe
§ 'Chelsea Gem' (Z/d/v) 🏆	CBrk EBSP LVer SDen SKen WFib
* 'Chelsea Morning' (Z/d)	WFib
'Chelsworth' (Min/d)	ESul LVer SDen WFib
'Chelvey' (R)	WFib
'Cherie' (Min)	WFib
'Cherie' (R)	LDea WFib
'Cherie Bidwell'	ESul SDen
'Cherie Maid' (Z/v)	LHil WFib
'Cherry' (Min)	LVer WFib
'Cherry' (Z/d)	WFib
'Cherry Cocktail' (Z/v)	MWhe SDen
'Cherry Hazel Ruffled' (R)	LDea
'Cherry Orchard' (R)	LDea LVer SDen SKen SSea WFib
'Cherry Sundae' (Z/d/v)	ESul LVer SDen WFib
'Cherryade' (Dw)	SDen
'Chew Magna' (R)	WFib
'Chi-Chi' (Min)	ESul LVer
'Chieko' (Min/d)	ESul MWhe SDen WFib
'Chime' (Min/d)	ESul
'China Doll' (Dw/d)	WFib
'Chintz' (R)	LDea
'Chiquita' (R)	LDea WFib
'Chocolate Blotch' (Z/C)	CNat
§ 'Chocolate Peppermint' (Sc) 🏆	CHal CInt CLTr CSev ERav ESul IHos LDea LHil MWhe NHHG SDen SKen WCHb WEas WFib WHer WJek WPer
'Chocolate Tomentosum'	See ***P.* 'Chocolate Peppermint'**
'Choice Cerise' (R)	LDea SDen
'Chorus Girl' (R)	LVer SDen
'Chrissie' (R)	EBSP
'Christie' (Z/d)	WFib
'Christopher Ley' (Z)	LVer SDen SKen
'Cindy' (Dw/d)	ESul
'Circus Day' (R)	LDea WFib
'Citriodorum' (Sc) 🏆	CArn CInt LDea NHHG SIde WCHb WEas WFib WPer
'Citronella' (Sc)	LDea MSte NHHG WCHb WFib
citronellum (Sc)	CInt MHul NSty SDen SKen WFib WHer WPer

'Clair' (Min)	WFib
'Clara Read' (Dw)	ESul LVer
* 'Claret Cruz' (I)	CWDa
'Claret Rock Unique' (U)	CLTr EWoo SDen SKen SMrm WFib
'Clarissa' (Min)	ESul
'Clatterbridge' (Dw)	ESul LVer WFib
'Claude Read' (Dw)	ERea ESul
'Claudette' (Min)	ESul
'Claudius' (Min)	ESul SDen
'Claydon' (Dw/d)	ESul LVer
'Claydon Firebird' (R)	EBSP
'Cleopatra' (Z)	WFib
'Clorinda' (U/Sc)	CHal CSev EOHP ERea ESul EWoo GBar LHil LVer MEas MSte SDen WCHb WFib WHer WJek
'Clorinda Variegated'	See ***P.* 'Variegated Clorinda'**
'Clown' (R)	WFib
'Coddenham' (Dw/d)	ESul LVer WFib
'Colette' (Min)	WFib
§ 'Colonel Baden-Powell' (I/d)	LDea
'Colonel Drabbe' (Z/d)	SDen WFib
§ Columbia (Z/Sc)	IHos
columbinum	MHul
¶ 'Comedy'	WLRN
'Concolor Lace' (Sc)	CLTr CLit ESul LVer MEas
'Conspicuous' (R)	WFib
'Contrast' (Z/d/C/v)	EBSP MBri MWhe SDen SKen SSea WFib
'Cook's Red Spider' (Ca)	WFib
'Copdock' (Min/d)	ESul
'Copthorne' (Sc) 🏆	CLTr CMdw CNat CSpe ESul LVer WFib
'Coral Frills' (Dw)	ESul
* 'Coral Sunset' (d)	CWDa
'Coralglow' (Z/d)	IHos
cordifolium	EWoo LHil MHul WFib WHer
'Coriand' (Z/d)	WFib
coriandrifolium	See ***P. myrrhifolium***
'Cornell' (I/d)	ECtt IHos MBri WFib
¶ 'Coronia' (Z/Ca)	CWDa
coronopifolium	MHul
'Corsair' (Z/d) 🏆	MWhe WFib
cortusifolium	MHul
'Cotswold Queen' (Z/d)	WFib
'Cottenham Surprise' (A)	LDea
'Cotton Candy' (Dw/d)	ESul
'Cottontail' (Min/d)	ESul LVer
cotyledonis	MHul WFib
'Countess Mariza'	See ***P.* 'Gräfin Mariza'**
'Countess of Birkenhead' (Z)	WFib
'Countess of Scarborough'	See ***P.* 'Lady Scarborough'**
'Country Girl' (R)	IHos WFib
* 'Courbet'	SDen
'Cover Girl' (Z/d)	WFib
'Cramdon Red' (Dw)	SKen WFib
'Crampel's Master' (Z)	LVer SKen
'Cranbrook Black'	EWoo
'Cransley Blends' (R)	EBSP LDea WFib
'Cransley Star' (A)	ESul LDea WEas WFib
crassicaule	MHul
'Cream and Green'	CSpe
'Creamery' (Z/d)	WFib
§ 'Creamy Nutmeg' (Sc/v)	CArn CHal CKni CLTr ESul GBar LDea LVer MWhe NSty SSea
'Creed's Seedling' (Z/C)	ERav
'Creeting St Mary' (Min)	ESul
'Creeting St Peter' (Min)	ESul

'Crescendo' (I/d)	ECtt
* 'Crimson Crampel' (Z)	CWDa
'Crimson Fire' (Z/d)	MBri MWhe SKen WFib
'Crimson Unique' (U) 🏆	EWoo LHil SKen WFib
crispum (Sc)	CJew CNat GBar GPoy LDea NHHG SDen WApp WCHb WEas WFib WJek WRha
– 'Major' (Sc)	ESul NSty SDen SKen WFib WHer WPer
– 'Minor'	MGra
– 'Peach Cream' (Sc/v)	CHal CInt CSev MGra MWhe SDen WFib WJek
– 'Variegatum' (Sc/v) 🏆	CBrk CHal CSev GBar GDTE GPoy IHos LDea LHil LVer MWhe NSty SDen SKen SSea WCHb WEas WFib WHer WWye
'Crocketta' (I/d)	EBSP LVer SSea
'Crocodile'	See ***P.* 'The Crocodile'**
'Crowfield' (Min/d)	ESul
'Crystal Palace Gem' (Z/v)	LVer MWhe SDen SKen SMrm WFib
cucullatum	EWoo MHul WFib
§ 'Culm' (A)	LDea
'Culpho' (Min/C/d)	ESul
'Cupid' (Min/Dw/d)	ESul WFib
'Cynthia' (Min)	ESul
'Cyril Read' (Dw)	ERea ESul
§ 'Czar' (Z/C)	WFib
'Dainty Lassie' (Dw/v)	ESul
'Dainty Maid'	ESul
'Dale Queen' (Z)	WFib
'Dame Anna Neagle' (Dw/d) 🏆	ESul LVer WFib
'Dancer' (Dw)	ESul
'Dandee' (Z/d)	WFib
'Danny West'	SDen
'Dark Lady' (Sc)	WFib
'Dark Presidio'	See ***P.* 'Dark Mabel'**
'Dark Red Irene' (Z/d)	LVer MWhe WFib
'Dark Secret' (R)	CSpe EBSP LDea SDen SKen WFib
'Dark Venus' (R)	LDea SDen WFib
'Darmsden' (A) 🏆	ESul LDea
§ 'Dart' (A)	LDea
dasyphyllum	MHul
'David John' (Dw/d)	ESul LVer SDen
'Davina' (Min/d)	ESul WFib
'Dawn' (Z/d)	WFib
'Dawn Star' (Z/St)	CSpe ESul WFib
'Deacon Arlon' (Dw/d)	ESul LVer MWhe SKen
'Deacon Avalon' (Dw/d)	WFib
'Deacon Barbecue' (Z/d)	ESul MWhe SDen
'Deacon Birthday' (Z/d)	ESul LVer MWhe SDen WFib
'Deacon Bonanza' (Z/d)	CLit ESul LVer MWhe SDen SKen WFib
'Deacon Clarion' (Z/d)	ESul LVer SKen
'Deacon Constancy' (Z/d)	CLit ESul LVer MWhe SDen
'Deacon Coral Reef' (Z/d)	CLit ESul LVer MWhe SKen WFib
'Deacon Finale' (Z/d)	ESul LVer SDen
♦ 'Deacon Finito'	See ***P.* 'Finito'**
'Deacon Fireball' (Z/d)	ESul LVer MWhe SDen SKen WFib
'Deacon Flamingo' (Z/d)	ESul MWhe SDen
'Deacon Gala' (Z/d)	ESul LVer MWhe SDen
'Deacon Golden Bonanza' (Z/C/d)	ESul SDen WFib
'Deacon Golden Gala' (Z/C/d)	ESul
I 'Deacon Golden Lilac Mist' (Z/C/d)	ESul SDen WFib

◆ 'Deacon Golden Mist'	See ***P.* 'Golden Mist'**
'Deacon Jubilant' (Z/d)	ESul MWhe SDen SKen
'Deacon Lilac Mist' (Z/d)	CLit ESul LVer MWhe SDen SKen WFib
'Deacon Mandarin' (Z/d)	ESul MWhe SKen
'Deacon Minuet' (Z/C/d)	CLit ESul LVer MWhe SDen SKen
'Deacon Moonlight' (Z/d)	ESul LVer MWhe
'Deacon Peacock' (Z/C/d)	ESul MWhe SDen SKen
'Deacon Picotee' (Z/d)	ESul IHos LVer MBri MWhe SDen
'Deacon Regalia' (Z/d)	CLit ESul MWhe SDen SKen WFib
'Deacon Romance' (Z/d)	ESul LVer MWhe SDen SKen WFib
'Deacon Summertime' (Z/d)	CLit ESul LVer MWhe
'Deacon Sunburst' (Z/d)	ESul LVer MWhe SDen SKen
'Deacon Suntan' (Z/d)	ESul LVer MWhe SDen SKen WFib
'Deacon Trousseau' (Z/d)	ESul LVer MWhe SDen WFib
'Decora Impérial' (I)	LDea LVer SKen
* 'Decora Lavender' (I)	LVer
§ 'Decora Lilas' (I)	ECtt LDea SKen
'Decora Mauve'	See ***P.* 'Decora Lilas'**
§ 'Decora Rose' (I)	ECtt IHos LDea SKen
'Decora Rouge' (I)	ECtt LDea NPri SKen
'Deerwood Lavender Lad' (Sc)	ESul WFib
'Degas' (R)	WFib
'Delhi' (R)	WFib
'Delightful' (R)	WFib
'Delilah' (R)	LDea SDen
'Delta' (Min/d)	ESul
'Denebola' (Min/d)	ESul LVer WFib
Denticulatum Group (Sc)	NHHG SDen SKen WApp WCHb WFib WJek
§ – 'Filicifolium' (Sc)	CHal CInt CLTr CLit EWoo GBar IHos NHHG SDen SKen WFib WHer WJek WWye
desertorum	MHul
'Destiny' (R)	WFib
¶ 'Diabolo'	WLRN
'Diadem' (R)	WFib
'Diana Palmer' (Z/d)	LVer SKen WFib
'Diane' (Min/d)	ESul SDen WFib
'Dibbinsdale' (Z)	ESul
dichondrifolium	EWoo MHul NSty WFib
'Diddi-Di' (Min/d)	ESul
'Didi' (Min)	ESul WFib
'Dinky' (Min/d)	ESul
§ Disco (Z/d)	CWDa
'Distinction' (Z)	CBrk CSpe EBSP IHos LHil MWhe SDen SKen WFib WPer
'Doctor A. Chipault' (I/d)	LDea WFib
* 'Doctor A. Vialetts'	CWDa
'Doctor Margaret Sturgis' (Z/d)	WFib
'Dodd's Super Double' (Z/d)	CHal LVer WFib
'Dolce Vita'	WLRN
'Dollar Bute' (R)	LDea
'Dollar Princess' (Z/C)	SDen SKen
'Dolly Daydream' (C)	SDen
'Dolly Moon' (C)	SDen
'Dolly Read' (Dw)	ERea ESul WFib
'Dolly Varden' (Z/v) 🏆	CLit IHos LDea LHil LVer MBri MWhe SDen SKen SLMG SSea WFib
dolomiticum	MHul WFib
'Dolphin' (Min)	WFib
'Don Quixote' (A)	EWoo LDea
¶ 'Don's Carosel' (Z/v)	SDen
¶ 'Don's Mona Noble' (Z/C/v)	SDen
¶ 'Don's Silva Perle' (Dw/v)	SDen
'Dopey' (Min)	ESul
'Doreen Featherby' (R)	WFib
* 'Doreen Maddison'	LDea
'Doris Brook' (Z/d)	WFib
'Doris Frith' (R)	LDea SDen WFib
'Doris Hancock' (R)	WFib
'Doris Moore' (Z)	LVer
'Doris Shaw' (R)	WFib
'Double Bird's Egg' (Z/d)	CWDa
'Double Grace Wells' (Min/d)	ESul
'Double Henry Jacoby'	See ***P.* 'Double Jacoby'**
§ 'Double Jacoby' (Z/d)	SDen WFib
'Double Lilac White' (I/d)	IHos
'Double New Life' (Z/d)	CHal CWDa
'Double Orange' (Z/d)	SKen
'Double Pink Bird's Egg' (Z/d)	SKen
'Double White Lilac Eye' (I)	SDen
'Dove' (Z)	WFib
'Dovedale' (Dw/C)	ESul LVer
'Downlands' (Z/d)	LVer SDen
'Dream' (Z)	CWDa WFib
'Dresden China' (R)	LDea SDen
'Dresden Pink' (Dw)	CLit LVer WFib
'Dresden White' (Dw)	CSpe LHil LVer
'Drummer Boy' (Z)	CWDa SKen
'Dryden' (Z)	LVer SDen SKen WFib
'Dubonnet' (R)	LDea WFib
'Duchess of Devonshire' (Z)	SDen SKen
'Duke of Buckingham' (Z/d)	LVer SDen
'Duke of Devonshire' (Z/d)	LVer
'Duke of Edinburgh'	See ***P.* 'Hederinum Variegatum'**
'Dulcie' (Min)	ESul
'Dunkery Beacon' (R)	LDea WFib
'Dusty Rose' (Min)	ESul WFib
§ 'Dwarf Miriam Baisey' (Min)	SDen WFib
'Dwarf Miriam Read'	See ***P.* 'Dwarf Miriam Baisey'**
'E. Dabner' (Z/d)	CWDa SDen SKen WFib
'Earl of Chester' (Min/d) 🏆	WFib
'Earliana' (Dec)	ESul LDea SKen
'Earls Four' (R)	LDea
'Eastbourne Beauty' (I/d)	SLMG WFib
'Easter Greeting'	See ***P.* 'Ostergruss'**
'Easter Morn' (Z/St)	WFib
echinatum	LVer MHul
– 'Album'	SDen
– 'Miss Stapleton'	See ***P.* 'Miss Stapleton'**
'Eclipse' (I)	ESul MWhe SDen SKen WFib
'Eden Gem' (Min/d)	ESul LVer SDen WFib
* 'Eden Rose' (Sc)	MEas
'Edith Steane' (Dw/d)	ESul LVer
'Edmond Lachenal' (Z/d)	WFib
'Edna' (Z/d)	WFib
'Edward Hockey' (Z)	WFib
'Edward Humphris' (Z)	SDen SKen
'Edwin Clarke' (Dw/Min)	ESul
'Eileen' (I)	SDen WFib
'Eileen Postle' (R) 🏆	WFib
'Eileen Stanley' (R)	LDea
'Elaine' (R)	LDea
'Eldorado'	WLRN

'Eleanor' (Z/d)	SDen
'Electra' (Z/d)	CWDa LVer SDen WFib
elegans	MHul
'Elfin Rapture' (R)	WFib
'Elgar' (R)	WFib
'Elizabeth Angus' (Z)	SDen SKen WFib
'Elizabeth Cartwright' (Z)	WFib
'Elizabeth Read' (Dw)	ERea ESul WFib
'Elmsett' (Z/C/d)	ESul LVer
'Elna' (Min)	ESul
elongatum	MHul
'Els' (Min/St)	ERav ESul LHil LVer SKen
* 'Els Variegated'	SMrm
'Elsi' (I/d/v)	LVer WFib
'Elsie Hickman' (R)	LDea SDen WFib
'Elsie Portas' (Z/C/d)	ESul
'Embassy' (Dw)	ESul WFib
'Emerald' (I)	SDen SKen
'Emma Hössle'	See ***P.* 'Frau Emma Hössle'**
'Emma Jane Read'	CLit ERea ESul MWhe WFib
(Dw/d)	
'Emma Louise' (Z)	LVer SKen
'Emperor Nicholas' (Z/d)	MWhe SDen SKen
'Empress' (Z)	SKen
'Ena' (Min)	ESul
'Enchantress' (I)	MBri SDen
'Encore'	LVer MWhe
endlicherianum	CMon EPot MHul NGre SIgm
'Endora' (Min)	ESul SDen
'Endsleigh' (Sc)	MEas SDen
englerianum	MHul
'Enid Blackaby' (R)	WFib
'Enid Read' (Dw)	ERea WFib
'Eric Ellis' (Dw/d)	WFib
'Eric Hoskins' (Z/d)	WFib
* 'Eric Lee'	CWDa
'Erwarton' (Min/d)	ESul LVer SDen
'Escapade' (Dw/d)	ESul WFib
'Esteem' (Z/d)	WFib
'Etna' (Min)	WFib
'Evelyn'	ESul
'Evesham Wonder' (Z/d)	SDen WFib
¶ 'Evka (I)' (I/v)	NPri
exhibens	MHul
'Explosive'	WLRN
exstipulatum	CSpe MHul WFib
'Fair Dinkum' (Z/v)	MWhe SDen
§ 'Fair Ellen' (Sc)	CLTr ERav EWoo SKen WFib
	WPer
'Fairlee' (DwI)	SDen
'Fairy Orchid' (A)	CLit ESul LDea LVer SDen
'Fairy Princess' (R)	LDea
'Fairy Queen'	CLit EWoo LDea WEas
'Fairy Tales' (Dw)	ESul WFib
¶ 'Falkland Brother' (Z/C/v)	WFib
¶ 'Falkland Hero' (Z/v)	LVer MWhe SDen SKen SSea
	WFib
'Fandango' (Z/St/d)	ESul LHil WFib
* 'Fanfare'	CWDa
'Fanny Eden' (R)	WFib
¶ 'Fantasia' white (Dw/d) 🏆	ESul MWhe WFib
'Fareham' (R) 🏆	EBSP LDea WFib
'Fascination' (Z/Ca)	SDen WFib
'Feneela' (Dw/d)	ESul
'Fenton Farm' (Z/C)	ESul SDen
'Festal' (Min/d)	ESul
'Feuerriese' (Z)	LVer
'Fiat' (Z/d)	CWDa SKen
'Fiat Queen' (Z/d)	SKen WFib
'Fiat Supreme' (Z/d)	SKen WFib
§ 'Fidelio' (Z/d)	IHos
'Fiery Sunrise' (R)	EBSP LDea LVer

¶ 'Fiesta' (I/d)	LDea
'Fiesta' (R)	WFib
'Fifth Avenue' (R)	CSpe MSte SDen WFib
'Filicifolium'	See ***P.* (Denticulatum Group)**
	'Filicifolium'
§ 'Finito' (Dw/d)	CLit ERea
'Fire Cascade' (I)	NPri
'Fire Dragon' (Z/St/d)	SDen SKen
'Fire Light' (Min/d)	WFib
'Firebrand' (Z/d)	LVer
'Firefly' (Min/d)	ESul WFib
'Fireglow' (Z/d)	ESul
'Firestone' (Dw)	ESul
'First Blush' (R)	SSea WFib
¶ 'First Love' (Z)	LVer
fissifolium	MHul
'Flair' (R)	WFib
'Flakey' (I/d/v) 🏆	CSpe ERav ESul LDea MWhe
	SDen WFib
'Flame' (Z)	WFib
¶ 'Flesh Pink' (Z/d)	CWDa
'Fleur d'Amour' (R)	WFib
'Fleurette' (Dw/d)	CHal ESul MWhe SDen SKen
	WFib
§ Flirt (Min)	ESul MBri WFib
'Floral Cascade' (Fr/d)	WFib
'Florence Storey' (Z/C/d)	WFib
¶ 'Flower Basket' (R)	LDea
'Flower of Spring' (Z/v) 🏆	CHal EWoo LVer MWhe SDen
	SKen SSea WFib
'Flowerfield' (Z)	SDen WFib
'Flowton' (Dw/d)	ESul
* 'Forever' (d)	CWDa
'Fox' (Z/d)	CHal WFib
'Foxhall' (Dw)	ESul
Fragrans Group (Sc)	CHal CLTr CLit CMil CSev
	ERav ESul EWoo GCra GDTE
	GPoy LVer MGra MWhe
	NHHG NSty SDen SKen WApp
	WFib WHer WPer WWye
– 'Creamy Nutmeg'	See ***P.* 'Creamy Nutmeg'**
§ – 'Fragrans Variegatum'	CInt CMil CSev CSpe ERav
(Sc/v)	MWhe NSty SDen SKen WCHb
	WFib WJek WPer
– 'Snowy Nutmeg'	See ***P.* (Fragrans Group)**
	'Fragrans Variegatum'
'Fraiche Beauté' (Z/d)	CWDa WFib
'Francis James' (Z)	SDen WFib
'Francis Parrett' (Min/d)	ESul LVer MWhe WFib
🏆	
'Francis Read' (Dw/d)	ERea ESul
'Frank Headley' (Z/v) 🏆	CBrk CHal CLit CSpe ERav
	ESul IHos LDea LHil LVer
	MMil MSte MWhe SDen SKen
	SMrm SSea WEas WFib
'Frank Parrett' (Min/d)	ESul
§ 'Frau Emma Hössle'	WFib
(Dw/d)	
'Frau Käthe Neubronner'	CWDa SDen
(Z/d)	
'Freak of Nature' (Z/v)	EBSP IHos LHil MWhe SDen
	SKen SSea WEas WFib
'Freckles' (Z/d)	WFib
'Frensham' (Sc)	ESul IHos MEas WFib
'Freston' (Dw)	ESul
'Freya' (Min)	ESul
'Friary Wood' (Z/C/d)	ESul WFib
'Friesdorf' (Dw)	ERav ESul LHil LVer MWhe
	SDen SKen WEas WFib
'Frills' (Min/d)	ESul LHil SKen WFib
§ 'Fringed Aztec' (R) 🏆	EBSP LDea LVer SAga SDen
	SKen WFib

'Fringed Rouletta' (I)	LDea
'Frosty'	See *P.* **'Variegated Kleine Liebling'**
'Frosty Petit Pierre'	See *P.* **'Variegated Kleine Liebling'**
frutetorum	MHul
fruticosum	MHul WFib
'Frühlingszauber Lilac' (R)	EBSP
fulgidum	MHul WFib
'Funny Girl' (R)	WFib
'Fynn' (Dw)	ESul
'Galilee' (I/d) 🏆	IHos LDea LVer SDen SKen WFib
'Galway Star' (Sc/v) 🏆	CNat CSpe LVer SDen WFib
'Garda' (I/d)	ECtt
'Garibaldi' (Z/d)	CWDa WFib
'Garland' (R)	ESul
'Garnet' (Z/d)	ESul LVer WFib
'Garnet Rosebud' (Min/d)	ESul LVer
'Garnet Wings' (R)	WFib
¶ 'Gartendirektor Herman' (Dec)	ERav EWoo SMrm WFib
'Gary Salvidge' (R)	LDea
'Gay Baby' (DwI)	ESul LDea MWhe SDen
'Gay Baby Supreme' (DwI)	ESul SDen SKen
'Gazelle' (Z)	SDen SKen
§ 'Gemini' (Z/St/d)	ESul SKen WFib
'Gemma' (Min/C)	LVer SKen WFib
'Gemma' (R)	LDea LVer
'Gemma Jewel' (R) 🏆	EBSP
'Gemstone' (Sc) 🏆	ESul LDea WFib
'Genetrix' (Z/d)	WFib
'Genie' (Z/d)	LVer MWhe SDen WFib
'Gentle Georgia' (R)	WFib
'Geoff May' (Dw)	ESul SDen WFib
'Geoffrey Harvey' (Z/d)	WFib
'Geoffrey Horsman' (R)	WFib
'Georgia' (R)	WFib
'Georgia Peach' (R)	EBSP SDen WFib
'Georgina Blythe' 🏆	WFib
'Geo's Pink' (Z/v)	MWhe
'Gerald Portas' (Dw/C)	ESul LIck
'Gerald Wells' (Min)	ESul
'Geraldine' (Min)	ESul LVer
'Geronimo' (R)	WFib
'Gess Portas' (Z/v)	ESul SKen
'Giant Butterfly' (R)	LDea SDen
'Giant Oak' (Sc)	MSte WFib
gibbosum	CNat LBlm MHul SDen WFib
'Gilbert West' (Z)	SDen SKen
'Gilda' (R)	EBSP LDea
'Gill' (Min/Ca)	ESul
'Gillian Clifford' (Z/d)	SDen
'Glacier Claret' (Z)	IHos
Glacis (Z/d)	WFib
'Gladys Evelyn' (Z/d)	WFib
'Gladys Stevens' (Min/d)	ESul
× ***glaucifolium***	MHul
glaucum	See ***P. lanceolatum***
'Gleam' (Z/d)	LVer
'Glenn Barker' (Z/d)	WFib
'Glenshree' (R)	LDea LVer WFib
'Gloria Pearce' (R)	LDea SDen WFib
'Glory' (Z/d)	WFib
'Glowing Embers' (R)	LDea WFib
§ ***glutinosum***	CSev
'Goblin' (Min/d)	ESul IHos SDen SKen WFib
* 'Godshill'	LDea
* 'Gold Medallion'	CLit
'Gold Star' (Z/St/C)	ESul
'Golden Baby' (DwI/C)	ERav LDea MWhe
'Golden Brilliantissimum' (Z/C)	LVer MWhe SKen WFib
'Golden Butterfly' (Z/C)	ESul
'Golden Chalice' (Min/v)	LVer MWhe
'Golden Clorinda' (U/Sc/C)	EWoo SDen WEas
'Golden Crest' (Z/C)	SDen SKen SMrm
'Golden Ears' (Dw/St/C)	ESul LVer MBri MWhe SDen SKen WFib
'Golden Everaarts' (Dw/C)	ESul
'Golden Fleece' (Min/C/d)	ESul SDen
'Golden Gates' (Z/C)	ESul SDen SKen
'Golden Harry Hieover' (Z/C)	CBrk ESul LVer MBri SDen SKen SSea WEas
'Golden Mirage' (Z/v)	WFib
§ 'Golden Mist' (Dw/C/d)	CLit LVer
'Golden Orange' (Dw/C)	ESul
'Golden Orfe' (Dw/C)	WFib
'Golden Petit Pierre' (Min/C)	ESul SSea
'Golden Princess' (Min/C)	ESul WFib
'Golden Princess' (R)	LDea
'Golden Roc' (Min/C)	ESul
'Golden Ruth' (Z)	WFib
'Golden Staphs' (St/C)	ESul LIck LVer SDen WFib
'Golden Tears' (MinI/C/d)	ESul
'Golden Wedding' (Z/d/v)	LVer MWhe
'Golden Well Sweet' (Sc)	ERav WFib
'Goldie' (R)	WFib
'Goldilocks' (A)	ESul LDea WFib
'Gooseberry Leaf'	See ***P. grossularioides***
'Gordano Midnight' (R)	WFib
'Gordino Pixie' (R)	LDea
'Gosbeck' (A)	ESul LDea SDen SSea
'Gosport Girl' (R)	EBSP LDea
'Grace Read' (Min)	ESul
'Grace Thomas' (Sc) 🏆	WFib
'Grace Wells' (Min)	ESul SDen WFib
'Gracious Lady' (Z/d)	WFib
§ 'Gräfin Mariza' (Z/d)	IHos SDen SKen WFib
'Grand Slam' (R)	CKni EBSP LDea LVer SDen SKen WFib
grandiflorum	MHul WFib
'Grandma Fischer'	See *P.* **'Grossmutter Fischer'**
'Grandma Ross' (R)	EBSP LDea
'Granny Hewitt' (Min/d)	ESul
§ 'Graveolens' (Sc)	CHal CLTr CNat CSev ESul GDTE GPoy LVer MWhe NSty SDen SKen SSea WApp WFib WJek
'Great Blakenham' (Min)	ESul LVer
'Great Bricett' (Min/d)	ESul LVer
'Green Ears' (Z/St)	ESul WFib
'Green Eyes' (I/d)	LDea SDen
'Green Goddess' (I/d)	LDea SKen
'Green Gold Petit Pierre' (MiN)	ESul SDen
'Green Lady' (Sc)	WFib
'Green Woodpecker' (R)	LDea LVer SDen SSea
§ 'Greengold Kleine Liebling' (Min/C/v)	ESul SDen SKen
'Greengold Petit Pierre'	See *P.* **'Greengold Kleine Liebling'**
'Greetings' (Min/v)	ESul MBri SDen WFib
§ 'Grenadier' (Z)	CWDa
§ 'Grenadier' (Z/St/d) 🏆	SDen
'Grey Lady Plymouth' (Sc/v)	ESul EWoo GBar LBlm LDea SIde WFib
'Grey Monk' (Z)	EBSP
'Grey Sprite' (Min/v)	ESul WFib

greytonense	MHul
griseum	MHul WFib
* 'Groombridge Success' (d)	CWDa
§ 'Grossmutter Fischer' (R)	LDea WEas WFib
§ ***grossularioides***	CInt CNat ESul MHul
'Grozser Garten' (Dw)	ESul
'Grozser Garten Weiss' (Dw)	ESul
Wico = 'Guimongol'	NPri WLRN
Vinco = 'Guivin'	CWDa
'Gurnard'	SDen
'Gustav Emich' (Z/d)	SDen SKen WFib
'H. Guinier'	See ***P.* 'Charles Gounod'**
'H. Rigler' (Z)	SDen
'Hadleigh' (Dw)	CSpe ESul
'Hamble Lass' (R)	EBSP LDea
'Hanchen Anders' (Z)	WFib
§ 'Hannaford Star' (Z/St/d)	ESul SDen WFib
'Hannah' (A)	ESul
'Hans Rigler' (Z/d)	WFib
§ 'Happy Thought' (Z/v) 🏆	CHal CLTr CLit EBSP IHos LDea MBri MWhe SDen SKen
'Happy Valley' (R)	LVer WFib
'Harbour Lights' (R)	EBSP LDea WFib
'Harewood Slam' (R)	LDea LVer MSte SDen SMrm WEas WFib
'Harkstead' (Min)	ESul
'Harlequin Alpine Glow' (I)	LDea LVer MWhe SDen WFib
* 'Harlequin Candy Floss' (I/d)	CWDa
'Harlequin Liverbird' (I)	WFib
'Harlequin Mahogany' (I/d)	LDea LVer MBri MWhe SDen SKen WFib
§ 'Harlequin Miss Liver Bird' (I)	LDea SDen SKen
'Harlequin My Love' (I)	SKen
'Harlequin Picotee' (I/d)	LDea LVer SDen
'Harlequin Pretty Girl' (I)	LVer MWhe SDen SKen WFib
'Harlequin Rosie O'Day' (I)	LDea LVer MWhe SDen SKen WFib
'Harlequin Ted Day' (I)	LDea LVer
'Harold Bowie' (Z/d)	WFib
'Harold Headley' (Z/v)	WFib
'Harriet Le Hair' (Z)	SKen
'Harvard' (I)	LVer SDen WFib
'Harvey' (Z)	MWhe
'Hayley Charlotte' (Z/v)	MWhe
'Hay's Radiant' (Z/d)	WFib
* 'Hazel' (R)	LVer SDen WFib
* 'Hazel Adair'	LDea
'Hazel Anson' (R)	LDea
'Hazel Barolo' (R)	LDea
'Hazel Beauty' (R)	LVer
'Hazel Birkby' (R)	EBSP LDea SDen WFib
'Hazel Blake' (R)	EBSP WFib
'Hazel Burgundy' (R)	EBSP
'Hazel Burtoff' (R)	EBSP LDea WFib
'Hazel Carey' (R)	LDea
'Hazel Cherry' (R)	LDea WFib
'Hazel Chick' (R)	LDea
'Hazel Choice' (R)	EBSP LDea SDen WFib
'Hazel Gipsy' (R)	LDea SDen WFib
'Hazel Glory' (R)	LDea WFib
'Hazel Gowland' (R)	LDea
'Hazel Harmony' (R)	LDea
'Hazel Heather' (R)	LDea
'Hazel Henderson' (R)	LDea LHil
'Hazel Herald' (R)	EBSP LDea SDen
'Hazel Mistique' (R)	LDea
'Hazel Peach' (R)	LDea
'Hazel Perfection' (R)	LDea

'Hazel Rose' (R)	LDea
'Hazel Saga' (R)	EBSP WFib
'Hazel Satin' (R)	LDea
'Hazel Shiraz' (R)	LDea
'Hazel Star' (R)	EBSP LDea
'Hazel Stardust' (R)	EBSP LDea
* 'Hazel Whitaker'	LDea
'Hazel Wright' (R)	LDea
§ 'Hederinum' (I)	EAst IHos LDea NPri SKen WEas
§ 'Hederinum Variegatum' (I/v)	CHal CSpe GBur LDea SKen WFib
'Heidi' (Min/d)	ESul SKen
* 'Helen Bowie'	CWDa
'Helen Christine' (Z/St)	WFib
'Helena' (I/d)	EBSP LDea MWhe SDen SKen WFib
'Helter Skelter' (Z/v)	SDen
'Hemingstone' (A)	ESul LDea
'Henhurst Gleam' (Dw/C/d)	ESul WFib
'Hermione' (Z/d)	CHal MWhe WFib
'High Tor' (Dw/C/d)	ESul LVer SKen WFib
'Highfields Always' (Z/d)	IHos LVer
'Highfields Appleblossom' (Z/d)	IHos LVer SKen
'Highfields Attracta' (Z/d)	LVer SDen SKen
'Highfields Ballerina' (Z/d)	LVer WFib
'Highfields Candy Floss' (Z/d)	LVer SDen
'Highfields Charisma' (Z/d)	LVer
'Highfields Choice' (Z)	LVer SDen SKen
'Highfields Comet' (Z)	SKen
'Highfields Contessa' (Z/d)	LVer SDen SKen WFib
'Highfields Dazzler' (Z)	LVer
'Highfields Delight' (Z)	LVer
'Highfields Fancy' (Z/d)	IHos LVer SDen SKen
'Highfields Fantasy' (Z)	SKen
'Highfields Festival' (Z/d)	LVer MWhe SDen
'Highfields Joy' (Z/d)	SDen SKen
'Highfields Melody' (Z/d)	SDen
'Highfields Orange' (Z)	LVer MWhe
'Highfields Paramount' (Z)	SDen SKen
'Highfields Pearl' (Z)	LVer
¶ 'Highfields Perfecta' (Z)	CWDa
'Highfields Pink' (Z)	LVer
'Highfields Prestige' (Z)	SKen
'Highfields Pride' (Z)	LVer SDen SKen
'Highfields Prima Donna' (Z/d)	LVer MWhe SDen SKen WFib
'Highfields Promise' (Z)	SDen SKen
'Highfields Serenade' (Z)	LVer
'Highfields Snowdrift' (Z)	LVer SKen
'Highfields Sonata' (Z/d)	LVer
'Highfields Sugar Candy' (Z/d)	ECtt IHos LVer SDen SKen WFib
'Highfields Supreme' (Z)	LVer
'Highfields Symphony' (Z)	LVer WFib
'Highfields Vogue' (Z)	LVer
'Highscore' (Z/d)	WFib
¶ 'Hi-jinks' (Z/v)	MWhe
'Hildegard' (Z/d)	CHal SKen WFib
'Hills of Snow' (Z/v)	CHal LVer MBri SDen SKen WFib
'Hillscheider Amethyst'	See ***P.* 'Amethyst'**
'Hindoo' (R)	CNat WFib
'Hintlesham' (Min)	ERav ESul
hirtum	MHul

hispidum	MHul
'Hitcham' (Min/d)	ESul WFib
'Holbrook' (Min/C/d)	ESul SDen
'Holly West'	SDen
'Holmes Miller' (Z/d)	ESul
'Honeywood Hannah' (R)	EBSP WFib
'Honeywood Jonathan' (R)	EBSP WFib
'Honeywood Lindy' (R)	EBSP LDea LVer SDen
'Honeywood Matthew' (Dw)	ESul
'Honeywood Suzanne' (Min/Fr)	ESul LVer WFib
'Honne Früling' (Z)	SKen WFib
'Honneas' (Min)	ESul
'Honnestolz' (Min)	ESul SKen
'Hope' (Z)	WFib
'Hope Valley' (Dw/C/d) 🏆	ESul MWhe SKen
'Horace Parsons' (R)	LDea WFib
'Horace Read' (Dw)	ERea ESul
'Horning Ferry' (Dw)	ESul
'House and Garden' (R)	SDen WFib
'Howard Stanton' (R)	SDen WFib
'Howard's Orange' (R)	LDea SKen
'Hugo de Vries' (Dw/d)	CWDa WFib
'Hula' (U)	EWoo LVer WFib
'Hulda Conn' (Ca/d)	WFib
'Hunter's Moon' (Z/C)	ESul SDen
'Hurdy-gurdy' (Z/d/v)	ESul MWhe SDen WFib
HWD Corelli	IHos
HWD Gabrieli	IHos
HWD Monteverdi	IHos
HWD Onyx	IHos
HWD Romanze	IHos
HWD Vivaldi	IHos
hypoleucum	MHul
'Ian Read' (Min/d)	ERea ESul WFib
* 'Ice Crystal'	CWDa WLRN
'Icing Sugar' (I/d)	ESul LDea SDen SSea WFib
* 'Ilse Fisher'	CWDa
'Immaculatum' (Z)	WFib
'Imperial Butterfly' (Sc)	CLit CSpe ERav ESul LDea LVer WFib
'Improved Petit Pierre' (Min)	ESul
'Improved Ricard' (Z/d)	WFib
Ina (Z/d)	WFib
'Inca' (R)	EBSP LDea SDen WFib
incrassatum	MHul
'Ingres' (I/d) 🏆	ECtt IHos
inquinans	MHul WFib
iocastum	MHul
ionidiflorum	CSpe MHul
'Ipswich Town' (Dw/d)	ESul
'Irene' (Z/d) 🏆	LVer SLMG WFib
'Irene Cal' (Z/d) 🏆	SKen
'Irene Corsair' (Z/d)	SKen
'Irene La Jolle' (Z/d)	SKen
* 'Iris Monroe'	CWDa
'Isaac Middleton' (Z)	LVer
§ 'Isabell' (Z/d)	WFib
'Isidel' (I/d) 🏆	SKen WFib
'Isobel Gamble' (Z/d)	LVer SKen
'Italian Gem' (I)	SKen
'Ivalo' (Z/d)	IHos MWhe SDen SKen WFib
'Ivory Snow' (Z/d/v)	LVer MWhe SDen SKen
'Jacey' (Z/d)	LVer SDen SKen
'Jack Read' (Dw)	ERea
'Jack Wood' (Z/d)	ESul
'Jackie' (I)	WFib
'Jackie's Gem' (I/d)	MWhe
'Jacky Gall' (I/d)	IHos MBri SKen
'Jacqueline' (Z/d)	SDen SKen
'Jana' (Z/d)	WFib
'Jane Biggin' (Dw/C/d)	ESul MWhe SKen
'Janet Hofman' (Z/d)	WFib
'Janet Kerrigan' (Min/d)	ESul MWhe WEas WFib
¶ 'Janet Scott' (Z)	CWDa
'Janna Whelan' (Dw/d)	SDen
'Jasmin' (R)	EBSP LDea
'Jaunty' (Min/d)	ESul SDen WFib
'Jayne Eyre' (Min/d)	CHal CLit ESul MWhe SDen WFib
§ 'Jazz'	CWDa IHos
¶ 'Jean Bart' (I)	CWDa SDen
'Jean Beatty' (Dw/d)	LVer
'Jean Oberle' (Z/d)	SDen SKen WFib
§ 'Jeanne d'Arc' (I/d)	SKen WFib
'Jenifer Read' (Dw)	ERea ESul
'Jennifer' (Min)	ESul
'Jessel's Unique' (U)	LBlm LHil SDen
'Jessika' (Z/d)	WFib
* 'Jetfire' (d)	CWDa
'Jewel' (R)	EBSP
'Jeweltone' (Z/d)	WFib
'Jill Portas' (Z/C)	ESul SKen
'Jim Field' (R)	WFib
'Jimmy Read' (Min)	ERea
'Jinny Reeves' (R)	EBSP LDea WFib
'Joan Cashmore' (Z/d)	SDen WFib
'Joan Fairman' (R)	WFib
'Joan Fontaine' (Z)	WFib
'Joan Hayward' (Min)	ESul
'Joan Morf' (R)	EBSP LDea SDen SSea WFib
'Joan of Arc'	See ***P.* 'Jeanne d'Arc'**
'Joanna Pearce' (R)	EBSP LDea SKen
'John Thorp' (R)	LDea
'John West'	SDen
'John's Angela'	LVer
¶ 'John's Chameleon'	LVer
'John's Pride'	MBri
'Joseph Haydn' (R)	CKni EBSP
'Joseph Haydon' (R)	LDea
'Joseph Paul' (R)	SDen SSea
'Joseph Warren' (I/d)	LDea
'Joseph Wheeler' (A)	MWhe
'Joy' (R) 🏆	EBSP LDea LVer SSea WFib
'Joy' (I)	SDen
'Joy Lucille' (Sc)	CNat CSev ESul LDea SDen WCHb WFib
'Joyce Delamere' (Z/C/d)	WFib
¶ 'Joyden'	CWDa
'Jubel Parr' (Z/d)	CWDa SDen
'Judith Thorp' (R)	EBSP
'Judy Read' (Dw)	ESul
'Julia' (R) 🏆	EBSP LDea
'Julie' (A)	CLit ESul
'Julie Smith' (R)	LDea WFib
'Jungle Night' (R)	EBSP WFib
'Juniper' (Sc)	WFib
'Jupiter' (Min/d)	WFib
'Jupiter' (R)	EBSP LDea
'Just William' (Min/C/d)	ESul
'Kamahl' (R)	WFib
§ 'Kardinal' (Z/d)	IHos
'Kardino'	WLRN
'Karl Hagele' (Z/d)	LVer SKen SLMG WFib
'Karmin Ball'	CWDa WFib
karooicum	MHul
karrooense 'Graham Rice'	See ***P.* 'Grollie's Cream'**
'Kath Peat' (Z/d)	WFib
'Kathleen Gamble' (Z)	SKen
'Kathryn' (Min)	ESul
'Kathryn Portas' (Z/v)	ESul SKen

'Kayleigh West' (Min)	ESul SDen SSea
'Keepsake' (Dw/d)	ESul LVer WFib
'Keith Vernon' (Fr/d)	LVer SDen
'Kelvedon Beauty' (Min)	WEas
'Ken Salmon' (Dw/d)	ESul
¶ 'Kennard Castle' (Z)	CWDa
'Kenny's Double' (Z/d)	SDen WFib
'Kerensa' (Min/d)	ESul SKen
'Kershy' (Min)	ESul
'Kesgrave' (Min/d)	ESul LVer
'Kettle Baston' (A) 🏆	ESul LDea LHil LVer MWhe WFib
'Kimono' (R)	EBSP LDea LVer
'Kinder Charm' (R)	SDen
'King Edmund' (R)	LDea SDen WFib
'King of Balcon'	See ***P.* 'Hederinum'**
'King of Denmark' (Z/d)	LVer SKen WFib
'Kingsmill' (R)	LDea SDen
'Kingswood' (Z)	SDen
'Kirton' (Min/d)	ESul
'Kiwi'	MBri
§ 'Kleine Liebling' (Min)	EWoo LHop MWhe SKen WFib
'Krista' (Min/d)	ESul SDen WFib
* 'Kristy'	CLit
'Kyra' (Min/d)	ESul WFib
'L.E. Wharton' (Z)	SDen SKen
'La France' (I/d) 🏆	EBSP LDea LVer MBri MWhe SDen SKen WEas WFib
'La Jolla' (Z/d)	SDen
'La Paloma' (R)	LDea WEas WFib
'Laced Mini Cascade'	ESul
'Laced Red Mini Cascade' (I)	LVer SDen
Lachsball (Z/d)	EBSP SKen WFib
§ 'Lachskönigin' (I/d)	IHos LDea LVer SDen SKen WEas WFib
◆ 'Lady Alice of Valencia'	See ***P.* 'Grenadier' (Z)**
'Lady Churchill' (Z/v)	WFib
'Lady Cullum' (Z/C/v)	MWhe
'Lady Ilchester' (Z/d)	SDen SKen WFib
'Lady Love Song' (R)	EBSP
'Lady Mary' (Sc)	ESul EWoo GBar LVer SDen WFib
'Lady Plymouth' (Sc/v) 🏆	CHal CInt CLTr CMil CSpe ESul IHos LBlm LDea LHil LVer MSte MWhe NHHG NSty SDen SKen SVen WApp WEas WFib WHer WWye
§ 'Lady Scarborough' (Sc)	CArn LDea SKen WFib WWye
laevigatum	MHul
'Lakis' (R)	LDea
'Lamorna' (R)	LDea SDen SKen WFib
'Lancastrian' (Z/d)	WFib
§ ***lanceolatum***	MHul
'Langley' (R)	LDea SDen
'Lanham Lane' (I)	LDea MWhe
'Lanham Royal' (Min/d)	ESul
'Lara Aladin' (A)	WFib
'Lara Candy Dancer' (Sc)	WFib
'Lara Jester' (Sc)	EWoo WFib
'Lara Maid' (A) 🏆	ESul WEas WFib
'Lara Nomad' (Sc)	EWoo
'Lara Starshine' (Sc) 🏆	ESul EWoo SSea WFib
'Lark' (Min/d)	ESul
N 'Lass o'Gowrie' (Z/v)	CBrk LVer MWhe SDen SKen WFib
'Lass o'Gowrie' (American) (Z/v)	WFib
'Laura' (Z/d)	WFib
'Laura Wheeler' (A)	MWhe
* 'Laurel Heywood' (R)	WFib
'Lauripen' (Z/d)	WFib

'Lavender Feathers' (R)	WFib
'Lavender Frills' (R)	LDea
'Lavender Grand Slam' (R) 🏆	EBSP IHos LDea LVer SDen WFib
'Lavender Harewood Slam' (R)	LDea
'Lavender Mini Cascade'	See ***P.* 'Lila Mini Cascade'**
'Lavender Sensation' (R)	WFib
'Lavender Wings' (I)	LDea
laxum	MHul
'Layham' (Dw/d)	ESul
'Layton's White' (Z/d)	CWDa SDen SKen
'Le Lutin' (Z/d)	CWDa WFib
'L'Elégante' (I/v) 🏆	CHal CLit CSpe EAst EBSP ERav IHos LDea LVer MBri MWhe SDen SKen SSea WEas WFib WLRN
'Lemon Air' (Sc)	ESul
'Lemon Fancy' (Sc)	CInt ESul IHos LVer MWhe SDen WFib WJek
'Lemonii'	EWoo
'Len Chandler' (Min)	ESul
'L'Enfer'	See ***P.* 'Mephistopheles'**
'Lenore' (Min)	ESul
'Leo' (Min)	ESul
'Leonie Holbrow' (Min)	ESul
¶ 'Leopard' (I/d)	CWDa SDen
'Leslie Judd' (R)	WFib
'Leslie Salmon' (Min/C)	ESul MWhe
'Lethas' (R)	LDea
'Letitia' (A)	ESul LHil
§ Leucht-Cascade	WFib
'Levington' (Min/d)	WFib
Lila Compakt-Cascade	See ***P.* 'Decora Lilas'**
§ 'Lila Mini Cascade' (I)	ESul MWhe
'Lilac Cascade'	See ***P.* 'Roi des Balcons Lilas'**
'Lilac Domino'	See ***P.* 'Telston's Prima'**
'Lilac Elaine' (R)	LDea
'Lilac Gem' (Min/I/d)	IHos LDea LVer MWhe SDen SKen WFib
'Lilac Jewel' (R)	EBSP
'Lilac Mini Cascade' (I)	LDea LVer SDen
'Lili Marlene' (I)	LVer SKen
'Lilian' (Dw)	ESul
'Lilian Pottinger' (Sc)	CArn CHal CInt ESul GDTE LDea LVer NSty SDen SIde SKen WEas WFib WHer
'Limoneum' (Sc)	CSev SDen SKen WEas WFib
'Lin Davis' (Z/C)	WFib
'Linda' (R)	EBSP LDea WFib
'Linda' (Z/d)	WFib
'Lindsey' (Min)	ESul
'Lindy Portas' (I/d)	SKen
'Lisa' (Min/C)	ESul WFib
'Little Alice' (Dw/d) 🏆	ESul LVer MWhe SDen WFib
'Little Blakenham' (A)	ESul LDea SDen
¶ 'Little Fi-fine' (Dw)	ESul SDen WFib
'Little Gem' (Sc)	EWoo LDea LVer NSty SDen WFib
'Little John' (Min/d)	WFib
'Little Margaret' (Min/v)	ESul SDen
'Little Primular' (Min)	ESul
'Little Trot' (Z/v)	WFib
'Little Vectis' (D)	SDen
'Lively Lady' (Dw/C)	ESul SDen
'Liverbird'	See ***P.* 'Harlequin Miss Liver Bird'**
lobatum	MHul
'Lolette' (Min)	ESul
'Lollipop' (Z/d)	SDen WFib
'Longshot' (R)	WFib
* 'Loraine Howarth'	ERav

'Lord Baden-Powell'	See ***P.* 'Colonel Baden-Powell'**
'Lord Bute' (R) 🏆	CLit CNat CSpe EBSP ERav EWoo LCot LDea LHil LHop LIck LVer MSCN MSte NPla SBid SIde SKen SMer SMrm SUsu WEas WFib
* 'Lord Constantine'	LDea
'Lord de Ramsey'	See ***P.* 'Tip Top Duet'**
'Lord Roberts' (Z)	WFib
'Lorelei' (Z/d)	CWDa WFib
'Loretta' (Dw)	ESul
'Loripen' (Z/d)	WFib
'Lorna' (Dw/d)	ESul
* 'Lotus'	WLRN
'Louise' (Min)	ESul
'Love Song' (R)	EBSP EWoo LDea LVer
'Love Story' (Z/v)	ESul
* 'Loverly' (Min/d)	ESul
Lovesong (Z/d)	WFib
'Lowood' (R)	WFib
'Lucilla' (Min)	ESul SDen
'Lucinda' (Min)	ESul
'Lucy' (Min)	ESul
'Lucy Gunnett' (Z/d/v)	EBSP ERav MWhe SDen WFib
'Lucy Jane' (R)	LDea
¶ 'Luna'	NPri
luridum	MHul
'Lustre' (R)	WFib
'Luz del Dio' (R)	WFib
'Lyewood Bonanza' (R)	EBSP LDea
'Lyn West'	SDen
'Lynne Valerie' (A)	LDea
'Lyric' (Min/d)	ESul LVer WFib
'M.J. Cole' (I/d)	LDea
'Mabel Grey' (Sc) 🏆	CSev CSpe ERav ESul EWoo IHos LBlm LVer MWhe NHHG SDen SKen WEas WFib WHer WJek WWye
§ 'Madame Auguste Nonin' (Sc)	CHal LHil LVer MEas SAga SDen WFib
'Madame Butterfly' (Z/C/d)	ESul MWhe SKen
'Madame Crousse' (I/d) 🏆	SDen WEas WFib
'Madame Dubarry' (Z)	WFib
'Madame Fournier' (Min/C)	ESul
'Madame Guinier'	See ***P.* 'Charles Gounod'**
'Madame Hibbault' (Z)	SDen SKen
'Madame Kingsbury' (U)	SDen
'Madame Layal' (A)	CSpe ESul EWoo LDea LIck SDen SKen WFib
'Madame Margot'	See ***P.* 'Hederinum Variegatum'**
'Madame Recamier' (Z/d)	WFib
'Madame Salleron' (Min/v) 🏆	CBrk CLit LDea LHil LVer MSte SDen SKen
'Madame Thibaut' (R)	LDea WFib
'Madge Hill' (Min)	ESul SDen WFib
'Magaluf' (I/C/d)	ERav SDen SSea WFib
'Magda' (Z/d)	ESul LVer WFib
magenteum	MHul
'Magic'	WLRN
'Magic Lantern' (Z/C)	IHos SKen
'Magic Moments' (R)	WFib
'Magnum' (R)	WFib
* 'Mahogany' (I/d)	EBSP ECtt
'Maid of Honour' (Min)	ESul SDen
'Mairi' (A)	ESul LDea WEas WFib
'Maja' (R)	WFib
'Maloja' (Z)	SDen SKen WFib
'Mamie' (Z/d)	SDen SKen
'Mandarin' (Z)	SDen
'Mangles' Variegated' (Z/v)	SDen SKen
'Manx Maid' (A)	ESul LDea SDen SKen WFib
'Marble Sunset'	See ***P.* 'Wood's Surprise'**
'Marchioness of Bute' (R)	LDea MSte WFib
'Maréchal MacMahon' (Z/C)	CBrk SDen SKen WFib
'Margaret Pearce' (R)	LDea
'Margaret Salvidge' (R)	LDea WFib
'Margaret Soley' (R) 🏆	LDea
'Margaret Stimpson' (R)	LDea
'Margaret Thorp'	LVer
'Margaret Waite' (R)	WFib
'Margery Stimpson' (Min/d)	ESul LVer SDen WFib
'Maria Wilkes' (Z/d)	WFib
'Marie Rober' (R)	SKen WFib
§ 'Marie Vogel' (R)	WFib
'Marion' (Min)	ESul
'Mariquita' (R)	WFib
* 'Marja'	LDea
'Marktbeherrscher' (Z/d)	WFib
'Marmalade' (Dw/d)	ESul LVer MWhe SDen WFib
§ 'Mars' (Z/d)	WLRN
'Martin Parrett' (Min/d)	ESul WFib
'Martin's Splendour' (Min)	ESul
'Martlesham'	ESul
'Mary Ellen Tanner' (Min/d)	ESul
'Mary Read' (Min)	ERea ESul
'Mary Webster' (Min)	ESul
'Masquerade' (R)	ESul
'Masterpiece' (Z/C/d)	ESul SDen SKen
'Mataranka' (Min/d/C/v)	MWhe SDen
'Matisse' (I)	SDen
'Matthew Salvidge' (R)	EBSP LDea WFib
¶ 'Maureen' (Min)	SDen
'Maureen Mew'	SDen
'Mauve Beauty' (I/d)	IHos SKen WFib
'Mauve Duet' (A)	ESul
'Maxime Kovalevski' (Z)	WFib
'May Day' (R)	LDea SDen
'May Magic' (R)	WFib
'May Rushbrook' (Z)	LVer
* 'Maya'	SCoo
'Mayor of Seville' (Z/d)	WFib
'Maytime' (Z/d)	WFib
¶ 'Meadowside Midnight'	LHil
'Meadowside Orange'	LVer
'Medallion' (Z/C)	SKen WFib
'Meditation' (Dw)	ESul
'Medley' (Min/d)	ESul LVer MWhe WFib
'Melanie' (R)	ESul LDea WFib
* 'Melissa' (Min)	ESul
* 'Meloblue'	WLRN
Melody (Z/d)	WFib
¶ 'Melva Bird' (Z/d)	WFib
'Memento' (Min/d)	ESul LVer SKen WFib
'Memories' (Z/d)	LVer SDen WFib
'Mendip' (R)	SDen WFib
'Meon Maid' (R)	EBSP ERav LDea WFib
§ 'Mephistopheles' (Min/C)	ESul
Mercutio (Z/d)	WFib
'Mere Casino' (Z)	LVer
* 'Mere Champagne'	LDea
'Mere Cocktail' (R)	WFib
'Mere Flamenco' (R)	WFib
'Mere Greeting' (Z/d)	MWhe
'Mere Iced Cocktail' (R)	WFib
'Mere Meteor' (R)	WFib
'Mere Sunglow' (R)	LDea WFib

'Merry-go-round' (Z/C/v)	ESul MWhe SDen WFib
'Meshed Pink Gay Baby'	See ***P.* 'Laced Sugar Baby'**
'Mexically Rose' (R)	WFib
'Mexican Beauty' (I)	CHal MWhe SDen SKen WEas WFib
'Mexicanerin'	See ***P.* 'Rouletta'**
'Michelle' (Min/C)	LDea WFib
'Michelle West' (Min)	ESul SDen
'Milden' (Z/C)	ESul LHil SDen
'Milkmaid' (Min)	SDen WFib
'Millbern Choice' (Z)	MWhe
'Millbern Clover' (Min/d)	MWhe
'Millbern Engagement' (Min/d)	MWhe
'Millbern Peach' (Z)	MWhe
'Millbern Sharna' (Min/d)	MWhe
'Miller's Valentine'	ESul WFib
'Millfield Gem' (I/d)	LBlm LDea LVer SDen SKen WFib
'Millfield Rival' (Z)	SDen WFib
'Millfield Rose' (I/d)	CLit IHos LVer MWhe SDen SKen
'Millie' (Z/d)	CWDa WFib
'Mimi' (Min/C/d)	ESul
'Mini-Czech' (Min/St)	ESul LVer
minimum	MHul
'Minnie Clifton'	SDen
'Minstrel'	ESul SDen
'Minstrel Boy' (R)	EBSP LDea SDen WFib
'Minuet' (Z/d)	WFib
'Minx' (Min/d)	ESul WFib
* 'Mirage'	CWDa
'Miranda' (Dw)	ESul
'Miriam Basey'	See ***P.* 'Dwarf Miriam Baisey'**
'Miss Australia' (R/v)	EWoo LDea SKen WFib
'Miss Burdett Coutts' (Z/v)	ESul IHos LVer MWhe SDen SKen WFib
'Miss Farren' (Z/v)	SDen SSea
'Miss Flora' (I)	CWDa MWhe
'Miss Liverbird' (I/d)	ECtt
'Miss Muffett' (Min/d)	ESul
§ 'Miss Stapleton'	SDen
'Miss Wackles' (Min/d)	ESul SDen WFib
'Misty' (Z)	ESul
'Modesty' (Z/d)	SDen WFib
'Modigliani' (R)	SDen SMrm
'Mohawk' (R)	WFib
§ 'Mole' (A)	LDea LVer
¶ 'Molina'	SCoo
mollicomum	MHul
'Mollie' (R)	LDea WFib
* 'Molly'	LDea
'Monarch' (Dw/v)	ESul
'Monica Bennett' (Dw)	ESul SDen SKen WEas
'Monks Eleigh'	ESul
'Monkwood Charm' (R)	LDea
'Monkwood Delight' (R)	SDen
'Monkwood Dream' (R)	LDea
'Monkwood Rhapsody' (R)	SDen
'Monkwood Sprite' (R)	LDea SMrm
'Monsal Dale' (Dw/C/d)	ESul
'Monsieur Ninon' (U)	CLTr EWoo WFib
'Monsieur Ninon' hort.	See ***P.* 'Madame Auguste Nonin'**
'Mont Blanc' (Z/v)	EWoo MWhe SDen SKen WFib
'Moon Maiden' (A)	CLit ESul LDea LVer WFib
'Moonflight' (R)	WFib
'Moonlight'	SDen
'Moor' (Min/d)	ESul
'Moppet' (Min/d)	ESul
'Morello' (R)	SDen WFib
'Morning Cloud' (Min/d)	ESul SDen
'Morning Star' (Z/St/d)	WFib
'Morning Sunrise' (Min/v)	ESul
* 'Morph Red' (R)	WFib
'Morval' (Dw/C) 🏆	ESul LVer MWhe SKen WFib
'Morwenna' (R)	CKni CMdw LDea LVer SDen SKen WFib
'Mountie' (Dw)	ESul
'Mr Everaarts' (Dw/d)	ESul MWhe WFib
'Mr Henry Apps' (Dw/C/d)	MWhe
'Mr Henry Cox' (Z/v) 🏆	CBrk CLit IHos LDea LVer MWhe SKen SLMG WFib
'Mr Pickwick' (Dw)	ESul
'Mr Ritson' (Min)	ESul
'Mr Wren' (Z)	CHal LVer MWhe SDen SKen WFib
'Mrs Cannell' (Z)	SKen
'Mrs Dumbrill' (A)	ESul LDea LIck SDen SKen
¶ 'Mrs E G Hill' (Z)	CWDa
'Mrs Farren' (Z/v)	SKen WFib
'Mrs G. More' (R)	SSea WFib
'Mrs G.H. Smith' (A)	CLit ESul EWoo LDea LHil LVer MSte MWhe SDen SSea WFib
'Mrs J.C. Mappin' (Z/v) 🏆	EBSP EWoo SDen SKen
'Mrs Kingsbury' (U)	EWoo SKen WEas WFib
'Mrs Kingsley' (Z/v)	WPer
'Mrs Langtry' (R)	LDea
'Mrs Lawrence' (Z/d)	SDen SKen WFib
'Mrs Margaret Thorp' (R)	EBSP WFib
'Mrs Martin' (I)	WFib
'Mrs Mary Bard' (R)	WFib
'Mrs McKenzie' (Z/St)	WFib
'Mrs Morf' (R)	EBSP LDea
'Mrs Parker' (Z/v)	CLit IHos LVer MWhe SDen WFib
'Mrs Pat' (Min/St/C)	ESul LVer MWhe SDen
'Mrs Pollock' (Z/v)	CBrk LDea LVer MWhe SDen SKen SSea WFib
'Mrs Quilter' (Z/C)	LDea LIck LVer MBri MWhe SDen SKen SMrm SSea WFib
'Mrs Reid's Pink'	EWoo
'Mrs Salter Bevis' (Z/Ca/d)	ESul LVer SDen WFib
'Mrs Strang' (Z/d/v)	LVer SKen SSea WEas
'Mrs Tarrant' (Z/d)	SDen WFib
'Mrs W.A.R. Clifton' (I/d)	ERav LDea SKen WFib
multibracteatum	MHul
multicaule	MHul
'Muriel'	SDen
'Music Man' (R)	WFib
mutans	MHul
'Mutzel' (I/v)	LDea
'My Choice' (R)	LDea
'My Love' (I/d)	LDea SDen
§ ***myrrhifolium***	CNat SDen
– var. ***coriandrifolium***	CSpe MHul
'Mystery' (U) 🏆	WFib
'Müttertag' (R)	EBSP
'Nacton' (Min)	ESul
'Nadine' (Dw/C/d)	ESul WFib
Nadja (Z/d)	WFib
namaquense	CMon MHul
'Nan Greeves' (Z/v)	SDen
'Nancy Grey' (Min)	ESul
'Nancy Hiden' (R)	WFib
nanum	MHul
'Naomi' (R)	LDea
'Natalie' (Dw)	ESul
'Naughton' (Min)	ESul
'Naunton Velvet' (R)	WFib
'Naunton Windmill' (R)	WFib

'Navajo' (R)	WFib
'Nedging Tye' (A)	ESul
'Needham Market' (A)	CLit CSpe ESul EWoo LDea LHil
'Neene' (Dw)	ESul
'Neil Clemenson' (Sc)	ESul WFib
'Neil Jameson' (Z/v)	LVer SKen
'Nell Smith' (Z/d)	WFib
'Nellie' (R)	LDea
'Nellie Nuttall' (Z)	WFib
'Nels Pierson' (I)	WFib
'Neon Fiat' (Z/d)	WFib
'Nervosum' (Sc)	ESul
'Nervous Mabel' ♀	ESul LDea SDen WFib
'Nettlestead' (I)	ESul
'Nettlestead' (Dw)	LVer WFib
'Neville West' (Z)	SDen SSea
'New Life' (Z)	ESul LHil MWhe SDen SKen
'New Phlox' (Z)	SDen WFib
'Nicholas Purple' (R)	LDea
* 'Nicky'	LDea
'Nicola Gainford'	SDen
'Nicor Star' (Min)	ESul SDen WFib
'Nimrod' (R)	LDea
'Noche' (R)	LDea SAga SDen SKen SMrm WFib
nodosum	WEas
'Noel' (Z/Ca/d)	LVer SDen WFib
'Noele Gordon' (Z/d)	LVer WFib
'Noir' (R)	LDea
'Nono' (I)	LDea WFib
'North Star' (Dw)	ESul
'Northern Lights' (R)	LDea
* 'Norvic' (d)	CWDa
'Notting Hill Beauty' (Z)	SKen
'Nouvelle Aurore' (Z)	WFib
¶ 'Nuhulumby' (R)	EBSP WFib
'Oakfield'	SDen SSea
'Obergarten' (Z/d)	WFib
'Occold Embers' (Dw/C/d)	ESul LVer SDen WFib
'Occold Lagoon' (Dw/d)	ESul SDen SKen WFib
'Occold Orange Tip' (Min/d)	ESul
'Occold Profusion' (Min/d)	ESul SDen
¶ 'Occold Ruby' (Dw/C)	CWDa
'Occold Shield' (Dw/C/d)	ESul LVer SDen SSea WFib
'Occold Surprise' (Min/d)	ESul
'Occold Volcano' (Dw/d)	ESul
* 'Odessy' (Min)	WFib
odoratissimum (Sc)	CHal ESul GPoy IHos LDea LVer MHul NHHG NSty SDen SIde SKen WApp WCHb WEas WFib WJek WWye
– 'Variegatum' (Sc)	WEas
oenothera	MHul
'Offton' (Dw)	ESul
'Old Rose' (Z/d)	WFib
'Old Spice' (Sc/v)	ESul GBar LVer WFib
'Olga' (R)	IHos LDea
'Olive West'	SDen
'Olivia' (R)	EBSP
'Olympia' (Z/d)	CWDa WFib
'Onnalee' (Dw)	ESul
'Opera House' (R)	WFib
'Orange Fizz' (Z/d)	LVer
'Orange Imp' (Dw/d)	ESul
'Orange Parfait' (R)	WFib
'Orange Puff' (Min)	WFib
'Orange Ricard' (Z/d)	SDen SKen WFib
'Orange River' (Dw/d)	ESul SKen WFib
'Orange Sal' (R)	LDea
'Orange Splash' (Z)	SKen
'Orangeade' (Dw/d)	ESul LVer WFib
'Orangesonne' (Z/d)	LVer WFib
'Orchid Paloma' (Dw/d)	ESul LVer SDen SKen
'Oregon Hostess' (Dw)	ESul
oreophilum	MHul
'Orion' (Min/d)	CLit ESul LVer MWhe SDen SKen WFib
'Orsett' (Sc) ♀	LVer
* 'Oscar'	CWDa
'Osna' (Z)	SKen
otaviense	MHul
ovale subsp. ***hyalinum***	MHul
– subsp. ***ovale***	MHul WFib
– subsp. ***veronicifolium***	MHul
'Oyster' (Dw)	ESul
PAC cultivars	See under cultivar name
'Paddie' (Min)	ESul
'Pagoda' (Z/St/d)	CSpe ESul LVer SDen SKen WFib
'Paisley Red' (Z/d)	LVer WFib
'Palais' (Z/d)	SKen WFib
'Pamela Underwood' (R)	WFib
panduriforme	MHul WFib
papilionaceum	CHEx EWoo LHil MHul WEas WHer
'Parasol' (R)	WFib
'Parisienne' (R)	EBSP LDea SDen
'Parmenter Pink' (Min)	ESul
'Partisan' (R)	SDen
'Party Dress' (Z/d)	MWhe SDen WFib
'Pascal' (Z)	SKen
'Pat Thorpe' (R)	WFib
'Patience' (Z/d)	IHos SDen WFib
'Paton's Unique' (U/Sc) ♀	CHal ERav EWoo IHos LBlm LHil LVer SDen SKen WEas WFib
* 'Patricia' (I)	CWDa
'Patricia Andrea' (T)	LVer SDen
'Patricia Read' (Min)	ERea ESul
'Patsy 'Q'' (Z/C)	SKen
patulum	MHul
'Paul Crampel' (Z)	CBrk CHal LVer WFib
'Paul Gotz' (Z)	SKen
'Paul Gunnett' (Min)	MWhe
'Paul Humphries' (Z/d)	WFib
'Paul Sloan' (Z)	WFib
'Paul West' (Min/d)	SDen
'Paula Scott' (R)	LDea
'Pauline' (Min/d)	ESul MWhe WFib
'Pavilion' (Min) ♀	ESul
'Pax' (R)	LDea WFib
'Peace' (Min/C)	WFib
'Peace Palace' (Dw)	ESul
¶ 'Peach' (Z)	LDea
'Peach Princess' (R)	EBSP
'Pearl Brocade' (R)	WFib
'Pearl Eclipse' (I)	SDen SKen
◆ Pearl Necklace	See ***P.*** **'Perlenkette'**
'Pearly Queen' (Min/d)	ESul
'Pegasus' (Min)	CLit
'Peggy Sue' (R)	EBSP LDea LVer SDen
'Peggy West' (Min/C/d)	SDen
PELFI cultivars	See under cultivar name
peltatum	MHul SDen WFib
– 'Lateripes'	MHul
'Penny' (Z/d)	MWhe SDen WFib
'Penny Lane' (Z)	LVer SDen
'Penny Serenade' (Dw/C)	ESul SKen
'Pensby' (Dw)	ESul
'Penve' (Z/d)	WFib

'Percival' (Dw/d)	SDen
'Perfect' (Z)	SDen SKen
* 'Perle Blanche' (I)	CWDa
§ 'Perlenkette' (Z/d)	SDen
§ Perlenkette Orange (Z/d)	WFib
§ Perlenkette Weiss = 'Perlpenei'	WFib
'Persian King' (R)	LDea
'Persimmon' (Z/St)	WFib
'Petals' (Z/v)	SKen SSea
'Peter Godwin' (R)	EBSP LDea WFib
'Peter Grieve' (Z/v)	WFib
'Peter Read' (Dw/d)	ERea ESul
'Peter's Choice' (R)	EBSP LDea LVer
'Petit Pierre'	See ***P.* 'Kleine Liebling'**
'Petite Blanche' (Dw/d)	LVer SDen WFib
'Petronella' (Z/d)	ESul
'Phil Rose' (I)	CWDa MWhe
'Philomel' (I/d)	SDen SKen WFib
'Philomel Rose' (I/d)	LDea
'Phlox New Life' (Z)	ESul
'Phyllis' (U/v)	LHil
'Phyllis Mary' (R)	SDen WFib
'Phyllis Read' (Min)	ERea ESul WFib
'Phyllis Richardson' (R/d)	LDea LVer SDen WFib
'Phyllis Variegated'	LHop
'Pickaninny' (Min)	ESul
'Pin Mill' (Min/d)	ESul
'Pink Aura'	ESul
'Pink Aurore' (U)	LVer
'Pink Black Vesuvius' (Min/C)	WFib
'Pink Blizzard'	ERav NPri WLRN
'Pink Bonanza' (R)	EBSP LDea WFib
'Pink Bouquet' (Z/d)	IHos
'Pink Bouquet' (R)	EBSP WFib
'Pink Capitatum'	See ***P.* 'Pink Capricorn'**
§ 'Pink Capricorn' (Sc)	WFib
'Pink Carnation' (I/d)	IHos LDea SDen SKen
'Pink Cascade'	See ***P.* 'Hederinum'**
'Pink Champagne' (Sc)	ESul SDen WFib
¶ 'Pink Charm' (I)	SDen
'Pink Cloud' (Z/d)	WFib
'Pink Countess Mariza' (Z)	SKen
¶ 'Pink Crampel' (Z)	CWDa
'Pink Eggshell' (Dw)	LVer
'Pink Flamingo' (R)	LDea
'Pink Fondant' (Min/d)	ESul
'Pink Gay Baby' (DwI)	See ***P.* 'Sugar Baby'**
'Pink Golden Harry Hieover' (Z/C)	ESul
'Pink Grace Wells' (Min)	ESul
'Pink Grozser Garten' (Dw)	SDen
'Pink Happy Thought' (Z/v)	LVer WFib
'Pink Ice' (Min/d)	ESul LVer
'Pink Kewense' (Min)	ESul
'Pink Lively Lady' (Dw/C)	ESul
'Pink Margaret Pearce' (R)	SDen WFib
'Pink Mini Cascade'	See ***P.* 'Rose Mini Cascade'**
'Pink Parfait' (Z)	EWoo
'Pink Pearl' (Z/d)	WFib
'Pink Rambler' (Z/d)	MWhe SKen WFib
'Pink Raspail' (Z/d)	WFib
'Pink Rosebud' (Z/d)	IHos SDen WFib
'Pink Ruffles' (R)	EBSP
'Pink Satisfaction' (Z)	IHos
'Pink Snow' (Min/d)	ESul
'Pink Splash' (Min/d)	ESul SDen
'Pink Star' (Z/St)	WFib
'Pink Tiny Tim' (Min)	ESul WFib
'Pinnochio' (R)	WFib
'Pixie' (Dw)	ESul
'Pixie Rose' (Z/St)	WFib
'Platinum' (Z/v)	EWoo SDen
'Playmate' (Min/St)	ESul LVer SKen WFib
'Plenty' (Z/d)	CWDa WFib
'Plum Rambler' (Z/d)	EWoo SKen WFib
'Poetesse' (A)	EWoo LDea
'Polka' (U)	EWoo WFib
'Pom Pom' (Z/d)	WFib
'Pompeii' (R)	LDea SAga WFib
'Portsmouth' (R)	SDen
'Potpourri' (Min)	SKen
'Potter Heigham' (Dw)	ESul
'Powder Puff' (Dw/d)	ESul
praemorsum	MHul
'Prairie Dawn' (Z/d)	WFib
'Presto' (Min)	ESul MWhe
'Preston Park' (Z/C)	CBrk LBlm SDen SKen SMrm WFib
'Pretty Girl' (I)	EBSP LDea
'Pretty Polly' (Sc)	WFib
'Pride of the West' (Z)	SDen SKen
'Prim' (Min/d)	ESul LVer
'Primavera' (R)	EBSP LDea
'Prince Consort' (R)	LVer
'Prince of Orange' (Sc)	CArn CInt CLTr CNat CSev ESul EWoo GBar GPoy IHos LDea LVer MSte MWhe NHHG NSty SDen SKen SSea WCHb WFib WHer WPer WWye
'Prince of Wales' (Z)	WFib
'Prince Regent' (R)	LVer
'Princeanum' (Sc) ♀	CSpe EWoo WFib
'Princess Alexandra' (R)	LVer SSea
'Princess Alexandra' (Z/d/v)	MWhe SDen WFib
'Princess Anne' (Z)	CSpe LHil SDen
'Princess Josephine' (R)	WFib
'Princess of Balcon'	See ***P.* 'Roi des Balcons Lilas'**
'Princess of Wales' (R)	EBSP LDea WFib
'Princess Virginia' (R/v)	EBSP LDea WFib
'Professor Eckman' (R)	WFib
'Promenade' (Z/d)	WFib
'Prospect' (Z/d)	MWhe
pseudofumarioides	MHul
pseudoglutinosum	WFib
pulchellum	MHul
pulverulentum	MHul
'Purple Ball'	See ***P.* Purpurball**
'Purple Emperor' (R)	LDea WFib
'Purple Heart' (Dw/St)	ESul LHil
'Purple Light'	See ***P.* 'Purple Gem'**
'Purple Orchard' (R)	LDea
* 'Purple Pride' (I/d)	CWDa
'Purple Rambler' (Z/d)	EBSP MWhe SDen
'Purple Unique' (U/Sc)	EWoo IHos SDen SKen WCHb WFib
Purple Wonder (Z/d)	WFib
§ Purpurball (Z/d)	EBSP SDen SKen WFib
'Pygmalion' (Z/d/v)	SDen WFib
'Quakeress' (R)	LDea WFib
'Quakermaid' (Min)	ESul
'Quantock' (R)	WFib
'Queen Ingrid' (Z)	IHos
'Queen of Denmark' (Z/d)	LVer SDen SKen WFib
'Queen of Hearts' (I/d)	LVer WFib
I 'Queen of the Lemons'	EWoo

N ***quercifolium*** (Sc)	CNat CSev EWoo GDTE GPoy MHul NHHG NSty SKen SSea WCHb WEas WFib WJek WWye
– 'Fair Ellen'	See ***P.* 'Fair Ellen'**
quinquelobatum	CSpe MHul
'R.A. Turner' (Z/d)	WFib
'Rachel' (Min)	ESul
'Rachel Fisher' (Z)	WFib
radens (Sc)	CTrC MHul NHHG SIde WFib
'Radiance' (Z/d)	WFib
'Radiant' (Z/d)	WFib
'Radio' (Z/d)	WFib
'Radior' (Min)	WFib
'Rads Star' (Z/St)	ESul WFib
Radula Group (Sc)	CLTr CSev ERav ESul GBar LVer MWhe SDen SKen WApp WCHb WFib WPer
'Radula Roseum'	LHil SSea
radulifolium	MHul
'Ragamuffin' (Min/d)	ESul MWhe WFib
'Rager's Pink' (Dw/d)	ESul
'Rager's Star' (Min)	ESul
'Rakastani' (Z)	SKen
ranunculophyllum	MHul
rapaceum	MHul
'Rapture' (R)	LDea WFib
'Raspberry Parfait' (R)	LDea SDen
'Raspberry Ripple' (A)	CLit ERav ESul LDea WEas WPen
'Raspberry Sundae' (R)	CLTr LDea
'Raspberry Sweet' (Z/St)	LHil WFib
'Raviro' (I)	WFib
'Ray Bidwell'	ESul SDen
'Ray Coughlin' (Z/C/d)	WFib
'Raydon' (Min)	ESul
'Rebecca' (Min/d)	ESul WFib
'Red Admiral' (Min/d/v)	ESul
§ 'Red Black Vesuvius' (Min/C)	CHal CLit CSpe ESul LHil LVer MWhe SDen SKen WEas WFib
'Red Cascade' (I) 🏆	MWhe SKen
'Red Fox' (Min)	SDen
'Red Galilee' (I/d)	MWhe SKen
'Red Gem' (Min)	ESul
'Red Glow' (Min)	ESul
'Red Ice' (Min/d)	ESul LVer
* 'Red Irene' (Z/d)	CWDa
* 'Red Kewense'	ESul
'Red Light' (Z/d)	WFib
'Red Magic Lantern' (Z/C)	SKen
'Red Mini Cascade'	See ***P.* 'Rote Mini-cascade'**
'Red Pandora' (T)	LVer SDen
'Red Rambler' (Z/d)	CHal CKni CLit EBSP LVer MWhe SDen SKen WFib
'Red Satisfaction' (Z)	IHos
'Red Silver Cascade'	LVer
'Red Spangles' (R)	WFib
'Red Spider' (Min/Ca/d)	ESul WFib
'Red Startel' (Z/d)	LVer MWhe
'Red Susan Pearce' (R)	EBSP LDea
'Red Tiny Tim' (Min)	WFib
'Red Velvet' (R)	WFib
'Red Witch' (Dw/St)	ESul LVer SDen WFib
'Redondo' (Min/d)	ESul LHil LVer MWhe SDen WEas WFib
'Reflections' (Z/d)	WFib
'Regal Perchance'	SDen
'Regina' (Z/d)	LVer SKen WEas WFib
'Reifi Vanderlea'	EWoo
'Rembrandt' (R)	LDea LVer SDen SSea WEas WFib
'Remo' (Z/d)	WFib
'Rene Roué' (Dw)	ESul
'Renee Ross' (I/d) 🏆	CWDa WFib
reniforme	CNat CSpe GBar LVer MHul WEas WFib
'Retah's Crystal' (Z/v)	MWhe SDen
'Rhineland' (I)	SKen
'Rhodamant' (I/d) 🏆	MWhe WFib
'Rhodamine' (R)	EBSP LDea
'Rhodo' (R)	WFib
ribifolium	MHul
Rica (Z/d)	WFib
'Richard Gibbs'	ERav EWoo
'Richard Key' (Z/d/v)	WFib
'Richard West' (I/d)	CWDa SDen
'Rietje van der Lee' (A)	ESul WFib
'Rigel' (Min/d)	ESul LVer MWhe SKen WFib
'Rigi' (I)	ECtt IHos LDea LVer MBri SDen SKen WFib
'Rigoletto' (I)	EBSP LDea MWhe
'Rimfire' (R)	EBSP LDea WFib
'Rio' (Z)	WLRN
'Rio Grande' (I/d)	EBSP LDea LVer MWhe SDen SKen WEas WFib
'Rising Sun'	LDea
'Rita Brook' (Z/d)	WFib
'Rita Coughlin' (R)	WFib
'Rita Scheen' (A)	ESul LDea LVer MWhe SSea WFib
'Rita Thomas' (Z)	WFib
'Robbie Hare' (R)	WFib
'Robe' (Z/d)	WFib
'Rober's Lavender' (Dw)	ERav ESul
'Rober's Lemon Rose' (Sc)	CInt CNat ERav ESul EWoo GBar LBlm LHil LVer NHHG SDen SIde WCHb WEas WFib WHer WJek WWye
'Rober's Salmon Coral' (Dw/d)	ESul
'Robert Fish' (Z/C)	CLit ESul SDen SSea
'Robert McElwain'	WFib
'Robin' (R)	EWoo LDea WEas
rodneyanum	MHul
'Roger's Delight' (R)	WFib
rogersianum	See ***P. worcesterae***
'Rogue' (R)	EBSP LDea SDen WFib
'Roi des Balcons'	See ***P.* 'Hederinum'**
§ 'Roi des Balcons Impérial' (I)	IHos LDea MWhe
§ 'Roi des Balcons Lilas' (I)	IHos LDea MWhe SKen
'Roi des Balcons Rose'	See ***P.* 'Hederinum'**
§ Rokoko (Z)	CWDa IHos
'Roller's David' (I)	CWDa LVer SDen
'Roller's Echo' (A)	ESul LDea LIck
'Roller's Pathfinder' (I/v)	LDea LVer
'Roller's Pioneer' (I/v)	CLit LDea LVer SKen
'Roller's Satinique' (U) 🏆	WFib
'Rollisson's Unique' (U)	ERav LVer MGra SDen SKen WFib
§ Romy (I)	LDea
'Rosaleen' (Min)	ESul
'Rosalie' (Min)	ESul
'Rosamunda' (Z/d)	WFib
'Roscobie' (Z/d)	SDen SKen
'Rose Bengal' (A)	CLit CMil ESul LDea LVer NSty SDen SKen WEas WFib
'Rose Irene' (Z/d)	MWhe SDen WFib
§ 'Rose Mini Cascade' (I)	ESul LVer MWhe SDen WLRN
'Rose of Amsterdam' (Min/d)	ESul

'Rose Silver Cascade' (I)	LDea LVer
'Rose Slam' (R)	LDea WFib
'Rose Startel' (Z/St)	LVer
¶ 'Rose Unique' (Z)	CLit
'Rosebud Supreme' (Z/d)	EBSP
'Rosee Normande' (Z/d)	WFib
* 'Roselo'	CWDa
'Rosemarie' (Z/d)	MWhe
'Rosemie' (Z/d)	WFib
'Rose's Orange'	EWoo
'Rosette' (Dw)	SKen WFib
'Rosina Read' (Dw)	ERea ESul LVer WFib
'Rosita' (Dw/d) 🏆	SDen
'Rosmaroy' (R)	EBSP LDea LVer SDen
§ 'Rospen' (Z/d)	WFib
* 'Rosseau' (Min)	WFib
'Rosy Dawn' (Min/d)	WFib
Rote Mini-Cascade	See ***P.* 'Rote Mini-cascade'**
§ 'Rote Mini-cascade' (I)	IHos LDea LVer MWhe SDen SKen WFib
'Rotherfield' (I/d)	LDea
'Rotlieb' (Z/d)	WFib
§ 'Rouletta' (I)	ECtt GDTE IHos LDea LVer MWhe NPri SDen SKen WFib WLRN
'Rousillon' (R)	LDea WFib
'Roussseau' (Dw/C)	ESul
'Royal Ascot' (R)	CBrk ERav EWoo LDea LHil MSte SMrm
'Royal Blaze' (Z/v)	SDen SKen
'Royal Carpet' (Min/d)	ESul
'Royal Fiat' (Z/d)	WFib
'Royal Norfolk' (Min/d)	ESul LVer MWhe SDen SKen
'Royal Oak' (Sc) 🏆	CInt CJew CSev CSpe GBar LDea LHil LVer MWhe WFib WHer WPer WRha
* 'Royal Princess' 🏆	LVer
§ 'Royal Purple' (Z/d)	CHal WFib
* 'Royal Salmon'	CWDa
'Royal Sovereign' (Z/d/v)	LHil LVer
'Royal Star' (R)	LVer
'Royal Surprise' (R)	LDea
'Royal Wedding' (R)	LDea SDen
'Rubella' (Z/d)	WFib
* 'Rubican'	CWDa
'Rubin Improved' (Z/d)	WFib
'Ruby' (Min/d)	ESul WFib
'Ruby Orchid' (A)	LDea
'Ruffled Velvet' (R)	EWoo SDen SSea
'Rushmere' (Dw/d)	ESul WFib
* 'Russet Wings' (R)	WFib
'Rustler' (Min)	WFib
'Rusty' (Dw/C/d)	ESul SDen
'Ruth Bessley'	LVer
'Ruth Karmen' (I/d)	LDea
'Ryan Dollery' (Z)	SDen
'Ryecroft Pride' (Z/d)	WFib
'Ryecroft White' (Z/d)	WFib
'Sally Anne' (R)	LDea WEas
'Sally Munro' (R)	LDea
'Sally Read' (Dw/d)	ERea ESul
'Salmon Beauty' (Min/d)	WFib
'Salmon Black Vesuvius' (Min/C)	ESul
'Salmon Comet' (Min)	ESul
§ 'Salmon Irene' (Z/d)	WFib
'Salmon Queen'	See ***P.* 'Lachskönigin'**
'Salmon Slam' (R)	LVer SDen WFib
'Salmon Startel' (Z/St/d)	MWhe
salmoneum	SDen
'Saltford' (R)	WFib
'Samantha' (R)	EBSP LDea WFib

'Samantha Stamp' (Dw)	WFib
'Samba' (R)	WFib
'Sancho Panza' (Dec) 🏆	CLit CSpe ESul LDea LVer MSte SDen SKen SSea WEas WFib
'Sandra Haynes' (R)	WFib
§ × ***sanguineum***	MHul
'Santa Maria' (Z/d)	LVer SDen SKen WFib
'Santa Marie' (R)	LDea
'Santa Paula' (I/d)	ECtt LDea LVer MWhe SDen SKen
'Sante Fe' (Z/C)	SDen SSea
'Sasha' (Min)	WFib
Sassa (Z/d)	CWDa WFib
§ Satellite (Z/St)	IHos WFib
'Satsuki' (R)	EBSP LDea
'Saxifragoides'	SDen SSea
§ ***scabrum***	MHul WFib
scandens	MHul
* 'Scarlet Kewense'	ESul
'Scarlet Nosegay'	CHal
'Scarlet Pet' (U)	CLTr ESul
'Scarlet Pimpernel' (Z/C/d)	ESul WFib
¶ 'Scarlet Queen' (Z)	LHil
'Scarlet Rambler' (Z/d)	LVer SKen SMrm WEas WFib
'Scarlet Unique' (U)	CLit EWoo LHil LVer SDen SKen WCHb WFib
¶ 'Scatterbrain' (Z)	CWDa
schizopetalum	MHul
§ 'Schneekönigen' (I/d)	ECtt IHos LDea LVer MSte WEas
§ Schöne Helena (Z/d)	CWDa
* 'Schone von Grenchen (I)'	NPri
× ***schottii***	See ***P.* × *sanguineum***
'Seaview Star' (Z/St)	SDen
'Secret Love' (Sc)	WFib
'Seeley's Pansy' (A)	CLit CSpe ESul LDea WFib
'Sefton' (R) 🏆	EBSP LDea WFib
'Selby' (Z/C/d)	WFib
'Selina'	ESul
'Semer' (Min)	ESul LVer SDen SKen
senecioides	MHul
'Senorita' (R)	LDea
¶ 'Sensation' (Z)	SDen
'Serena' (Min)	ESul
sericifolium	MHul
'Shalimar' (St)	CSpe LHil SDen WFib
'Shanks' (Z)	SDen
'Sharon' (Min/d)	ESul WFib
'Sharon Louise' (Min)	SDen
'Sharon West' (Dw)	CNat SDen SSea
'Shaun Jacobs' (Min/d)	SDen
'Shaunough' (Min)	ESul
'Sheila' (Dw)	ESul SDen
'Shelley' (Dw)	ESul
'Shenandoah' (Min)	WFib
'Sheraton' (Min/d)	ESul
'Shimmer' (Z/d)	IHos LVer MWhe SKen WFib
'Shirley Anne' (Dw/d)	SDen
'Shirley Ash' (A)	ESul LDea SKen WEas WFib
'Shirley Maureen' (R)	LDea WFib
'Shiva'	NPri WLRN
'Shocking' (Z/d)	SDen
'Shotley' (Min)	ESul
'Shottesham Pet' (Sc)	EWoo
'Shrubland Pet' (U/Sc)	LHil SDen SKen
'Shrubland Rose' (Sc)	WFib
sidoides	MHul
'Sienna' (R)	LDea
'Silberlachs' (Z/d)	SDen WFib
'Silky'	ESul

'Silpen' (Z/d)	EBSP WFib
* 'Sils'	CWDa
'Silver Anne' (R)	WFib
* 'Silver Cascade'	ERav NPri
'Silver Kewense' (Dw/v)	ERav ESul SDen SKen WFib
* 'Silver Lights'	CWDa
'Silver Monarch'	ESul
'Silver Wings' (Z/v)	CSpe EBSP ESul MWhe SDen SSea WFib
'Simon Portas' (I/d)	SKen
'Simon Read' (Dw)	ERea ESul
'Simplicity' (Z)	LVer
'Single New Life' (Z)	LVer
'Sir Arthur Hort' (I)	SDen WFib
'Sister Henry' (Z/d)	SDen WFib
'Sister Teresa' (Z/d)	IHos SDen SKen
'Skelly's Pride' (Z)	LVer SDen SKen WEas
'Skies of Italy' (Z/C/d)	MBri SKen SSea WFib
'Sleuring's Robin' (Min/d)	SDen WFib
'Small Fortune' (Dw)	ESul SKen
'Smuggler' (R)	LDea
'Snape'	ESul
'Sneezy' (Min)	ESul
♦ Snow Queen	See ***P.* 'Schneekönigen'**
'Snow White' (Min)	ESul
'Snowbaby' (Min/d)	ESul
'Snowball' (Z/d)	SDen
'Snowberry' (R)	EBSP
'Snowdon' (Min)	WFib
'Snowdrift' (I/d)	LVer SDen WFib
'Snowflake' (Min)	ESul LDea SDen WFib WPer
'Snowmass' (Z/d)	CHal MWhe SDen SKen
'Snowstorm' (Z)	SKen WFib
'Snowy Baby' (Min/d)	SDen WFib
'Sofie'	See ***P.* 'Decora Rose'**
'Solano' (R)	WFib
'Solent Star'	SDen
'Solent Waves' (R)	EBSP LDea WFib
'Solferino' (A)	ESul LDea
§ Solidor (I/d) 🏆	LDea WFib
'Sombrero' (R)	WFib
'Somersham' (Min)	ESul
'Something Special' (Z/d)	LVer MWhe SDen WFib
'Sonata' (Dw/d)	ESul
'Sonnesport' (Z)	WFib
'Sophie Cascade'	CWDa
'Sophie Dumaresque' (Z/v)	LVer MBri MWhe SDen SKen SSea WFib
'Sophie Koniger' (Z/d)	WFib
'Sorcery' (Dw/C)	ESul IHos MWhe
'South American Bronze' (R) 🏆	LDea SDen SKen SMrm WFib
* 'Southern Belle' (A)	LDea
'Southern Belle' (Z/d)	WFib
'Southern Charm'	SDen
'Souvenir' (R)	CHal LDea LVer SDen SSea
'Spanish Angel' (A) 🏆	ESul LDea SSea
'Special Moment' (R)	WFib
'Speckles' (Z)	MWhe
'Spellbound' (R)	WFib
'Spital Dam'	ESul
'Spitfire' (Z/Ca/v)	ESul WFib
'Spithead Cherry' (R)	EBSP LDea WFib
'Splash Down'	SDen
§ 'Splendide'	CMdw CRDP CSpe LHil LHop LVer MHul SAga SIgm WEas
* 'Spotlight Winner'	LDea
'Spot-on-Bonanza' (R)	LDea WFib
'Spring Bride' (R)	LDea SDen
'Spring Park' (A)	CLit ESul LVer SDen WFib
'Springfield Ann' (R)	EBSP
'Springfield Betty' (R)	EBSP
'Springfield Black' (R)	EBSP LDea LVer
'Springfield Charm' (R)	EBSP
'Springfield Kate' (R)	EBSP
'Springfield Mary Parfitt' (R)	EBSP
'Springfield Pearl' (R)	LDea
'Springfield Purple' (R)	EBSP
'Springfield Stripey' (R)	EBSP
'Springfield Unique' (R)	EBSP LDea
'Springtime' (Z/d)	EBSP LVer MWhe SDen WFib
¶ 'Sprite' (Min/v)	SDen
'Sproughton' (Dw)	ESul
'St Helen's Favourite' (Min)	ESul SDen
'Stacey' (R)	LDea
'Stadt Bern' (Z/C)	LVer MBri MWhe SDen SKen WEas WFib
'Stanton Drew' (Z/d)	WFib
'Staplegrove Fancy' (Z)	SDen SKen
x ***stapletoniae***	See ***P.* 'Miss Stapleton'**
'Star Flecks'	SDen
'Star Glitter'	SDen
'Star of Persia' (Z/Ca)	LVer WFib
'Starlet' (Ca)	WFib
'Starlight' (R)	WFib
* 'Starlight Magic' (A)	LDea
'Starlight Magic' (R) 🏆	ESul WEas
'Starry Eyed' (Dw)	ESul
'Startel Red' (Z/St)	WFib
'Startel Salmon' (Z/St)	WFib
'Stella Ballerina'	ERav
'Stella Read' (Dw/d)	ERea ESul WFib
'Stellar Apricot' (Z/St)	ERav LHil LVer
'Stellar Arctic Star'	See ***P.* 'Arctic Star'**
'Stellar Cathay' (Z/St/d)	CSpe ERav LVer WFib
'Stellar Dawn Star' (Z/St)	LVer WEas WFib
'Stellar Grenadier'	See ***P.* 'Grenadier'**
'Stellar Hannaford Star'	See ***P.* 'Hannaford Star'**
'Stellar Orange' (Z/St)	SDen
* 'Stellar Orange Pixie' (d)	CWDa
'Stellar Ragtime' (Z/St/d)	LHil LVer SDen
'Stellar Telstar' (Z/St/d)	LVer
stenopetalum	MHul
'Stephen Read' (Min)	ERea ESul
'Stewart Read' (Dw)	ERea ESul
stipulaceum	MHul
'Stirling Stent' (Z)	CWDa LVer SDen
* 'Strasbourg'	LHil
'Strawberry Fayre'	LVer
'Strawberry Sundae' (R)	EBSP LDea LVer SDen WFib
'Stringer's Delight'	ESul LVer
'Stringer's Souvenir'	ESul LVer
'Stutton' (Min)	ESul
sublignosum	MHul
suburbanum subsp. ***bipinnatifidum***	MHul
'Suffolk Gold' (Min/C)	SDen
§ 'Sugar Baby' (DwI)	ECtt ESul GDTE IHos LDea MBri MWhe SDen SKen WEas WFib
'Summer Cloud' (Z/d)	SKen WFib
'Summertime' (R)	SDen
'Sun Kissed' (Min)	ESul
'Sun Rocket' (Dw)	ESul LIck LVer MWhe SDen WFib
'Sundridge Moonlight' (Z/C)	SDen WFib
'Sunraysia' (Z/St)	WFib
'Sunrise' (R)	EBSP LDea SDen SKen WEas WFib
'Sunset' (Z)	WFib
'Sunset Snow' (R)	LDea LVer WFib

'Sunspot Petit Pierre' (Min/v)	ESul SDen
'Sunstar' (Min/d)	ESul LVer WFib
'Super Rose' (I)	MBri MWhe SDen SKen
'Supernova' (Z/St/d)	CWDa ESul SKen WFib
'Supernova' (Min/d)	LVer
'Surcouf' (I)	WFib
'Susan Baldwin'	See ***P.* 'Salmon Kovalevski'**
'Susan Payne' (Dw/d)	ESul LVer
'Susan Pearce' (R)	LDea LVer SKen WFib
'Susan Read' (Dw)	ERea ESul
* 'Susan Screen'	CWDa
'Susie 'Q'' (Z/C)	ESul LHil LVer MWhe SDen SKen
'Sussex Beauty' (Dw/C/d)	CWDa ESul SDen
'Sussex Delight' (Min)	CWDa ESul SDen
'Sussex Gem' (Min)	LVer SKen
'Sussex Jewel' (Min)	SKen
'Sussex Lace'	See ***P.* 'White Mesh'**
'Swanland Lace' (I)	LVer WFib
'Swedish Angel' (A)	ESul LDea LVer SDen SSea
'Sweet Charlotte' (R)	EBSP
* 'Sweet Lady Mary' (Sc)	WFib
'Sweet Mimosa' (Sc) 🏆	CInt CLTr CLit CSpe EWoo LDea LHil LVer MEas SDen SKen SSea WEas WFib
'Sweet Sue' (Min)	ESul SDen WFib
'Swilland' (A)	ESul LDea LVer MWhe SDen
'Sybil Bradshaw' (R)	LDea WFib
'Sybil Holmes' (I/d)	EBSP ECtt IHos LVer MBri MWhe SDen SKen WFib
'Sylvia Gale' (R)	SDen WFib
'Sylvia Marie' (Dw/d)	LVer MWhe SDen SKen
'Sylvia Mariza'	IHos
* 'Tamara'	CWDa
'Tami' (Min)	ESul
'Tamie' (Dw/d)	ESul LVer MWhe
'Tamie D' (Min)	SKen
'Tammy' (Dw/d)	ESul LVer MWhe WFib
'Tangerine' (Min/Ca/d)	ESul SDen WFib
§ 'Tango' (Z/d)	IHos
'Tanzy' (Min)	ESul
* 'Tapestry' (R)	LDea
'Tapestry' (Min/v)	SDen WEas
'Tashmal' (R)	EBSP
'Tattingstone' (Min)	ESul
'Tavira' (I/d)	LDea LVer SDen SKen WFib
'Ted Brooke' (Z/d)	WFib
'Ted Dutton' (R)	SDen WFib
'Teddy Roosevelt' (Z/d)	WFib
'Telstar' (Min/d)	ESul WFib
§ 'Telston's Prima' (R)	LDea
'Tenderly' (Dw/d)	ESul
'Tenerife Magic' (MinI/d)	ESul
tenuicaule	MHul WFib
'Terence Read' (Min)	ERea ESul
ternatum	MHul
tetragonum	MHul SSea WFib
'The Barle' (A) 🏆	LDea
'The Boar' (Fr)	CBrk CSpe EWoo LVer MSte SRms WEas WPer
'The Creedy' (A)	LDea
§ 'The Crocodile' (I/C/d)	CSpe ECtt GBur IHos LDea MWhe SDen SKen WEas WFib
I 'The Culm'	See ***P.* 'Culm'**
'The Czar'	See ***P.* 'Czar'**
I 'The Dart'	See ***P.* 'Dart'**
'The Duchess' (I/d)	WFib
'The Joker' (I)	WFib
'The Lowman' (A)	LDea
'The Lynn' (A)	LDea
I 'The Mole'	See ***P.* 'Mole'**
'The Prince' (Min)	ESul
'The Speaker' (Z/d)	SDen SKen WFib
'The Tamar' (A)	LDea
'The Tone' (A) 🏆	LDea
'Thomas Earle' (Z)	WFib
'Thomas Gerald' (Min/C)	ESul SKen
'Thorley'	SDen
'Tiberias' (I/d)	WFib
'Tiffany' (Min/d)	WLRN
'Tilly' (Min)	CHal
'Tim' (Min)	ESul
'Timothy Clifford' (Min/d)	ESul MWhe SDen WFib
§ 'Tip Top Duet' (A) 🏆	CLit ESul EWoo LDea LHil LIck LVer MWhe SAga SDen SLod SSea WEas WFib WPer
'Token' (Z)	IHos
'Tom Portas' (Dw/d)	ESul
'Tomcat' (Z/d)	WFib
tomentosum (Sc) 🏆	CArn CHEx CHal CSev CSpe EWoo GPoy LDea LHop LVer MHul MSCN MWhe NHHG NSty SAga SDen SKen SVen WEas WFib WWye
– 'Chocolate'	See ***P.* 'Chocolate Peppermint'**
'Tommay's Delight' (R)	EBSP LDea WFib
tongaense	CSpe MHul WEas WFib
'Tony' (Min)	ESul
'Topscore' (Z/d)	WFib
'Toreador' (Z/d)	WFib
'Torento' (Sc)	CNat ESul SDen WFib
'Tornado' (R)	EBSP LDea WFib
'Tortoise Shell' (R)	WFib
'Toyon' (Z/d)	SDen WFib
'Tracy' (Min/d)	ESul LVer
tragacanthoides	MHul
transvaalense	MHul WFib
'Trautlieb' (Z/d)	CWDa WFib
¶ 'Treasure' (Z/d)	LVer
'Treasure Chest' (Z)	LVer SDen
¶ 'Trésor' (Dw/d)	CWDa
tricolor Curt.	CSpe MHul SDen SSad
– hort.	See ***P.* 'Splendide'**
trifidum	MHul SSad SSea WEas WFib
'Trimley' (Dw/d)	ESul
'Trinket' (Min/d)	IHos SKen
'Triomphe de Nancy' (Z/d)	SDen WFib
triste	CSpe CTrC MHul SDen WFib
'Trudie' (Dw)	ESul LVer SKen WFib
'Trulls Hatch' (Z/d)	LVer MWhe SDen SKen
'Tu Tone' (Dw/d)	ESul
'Tuddenham' (Min/d)	WFib
'Tuesday's Child' (Dw/C)	SKen
'Tunias Perfecta' (R)	WFib
'Turkish Coffee' (R)	EBSP WFib
'Turkish Delight' (Dw/v)	ESul LVer MWhe SDen WFib
'Turtle's Surprise' (Z/d/v)	SDen SKen
'Turtle's White' (R)	LDea SKen
'Tuyo' (R)	WFib
'Tweedle-Dum' (Dw)	MWhe
'Twinkle' (Min/d)	ESul WFib
'Tyabb Princess' (R)	WFib
'Ullswater' (Dw/C)	ESul
§ 'Unique Aurore' (U)	LVer MSte SKen WEas WFib
'Unique Mons Ninon'	EWoo
'Unity'	LVer
'Urchin' (Min)	CSpe ESul MWhe SDen WFib
'Ursula Key' (Z/v)	SKen WFib
'Valanza' (A)	ESul LDea
'Valcandia' (Dw)	ESul
'Valencia' (R)	EBSP LDea
'Valenciana' (R)	WFib

'Valentin' (R)	LDea
'Valentina' (Min/d)	ESul WFib
'Vancouver Centennial' (Dw/St/C) ♀	CInt CLit CSpe ERav ESul LDea LVer MBri MWhe SDen WFib
§ 'Variegated Clorinda' (Sc/v)	EWoo WCHb WFib WHer
'Variegated Fragrans'	See *P.* **(Fragrans Group) 'Fragrans Variegatum'**
§ 'Variegated Kleine Liebling' (Min/v)	ESul SDen SKen WFib
'Variegated La France' (I)	WFib
'Variegated Lorelei' (Z/d/v)	SDen
'Variegated Madame Layal' (A/v) ♀	ESul LDea WFib
* 'Variegated Peppermint'	MGra
'Variegated Petit Pierre'	See *P.* **'Variegated Kleine Liebling'**
'Vasco da Gama' (Dw/d)	ESul WFib
'Vectis Cascade'	SDen
'Vectis Glitter'	LVer SDen
'Vectis Gold' (Z/St/C)	SDen
'Vectis Star'	SDen
'Velvet' (Z)	CWDa IHos LVer
'Velvet Duet' (A) ♀	ESul EWoo LDea LIck LVer SDen SKen SSea
'Venus' (Dw/d)	ESul LVer
'Vera Dillon' (Z)	SKen WFib
'Verdale' (A)	WFib
'Verity Palace' (R)	WFib
'Verona' (Z/C)	CHal MBri SDen
'Verona Contreras' (A)	CLit LDea WFib
* 'Veronica' (Z)	MWhe SKen
'Vibrant'	SDen
'Vicki Town' (R)	LDea WFib
'Vicky Claire' (R)	EBSP LDea SBid SDen SKen SMrm WFib
'Victoria' (Z/d)	SKen
'Victoria Regina' (R)	LDea SDen WFib
¶ 'Video Blush' (Min)	CLit
'Viking' (Min/d)	SKen
'Viking Red' (Z)	MWhe
'Village Hill Oak' (Sc)	ESul LVer
* 'Ville de Dresden' (I)	CSpe SDen
'Ville de Paris'	See *P.* **'Hederinum'**
'Vina' (Dw/C/d)	ESul LVer MWhe SDen SKen WFib
'Vincent Gerris' (A)	ESul LDea MWhe SDen
violareum hort.	See *P.* **'Splendide'**
'Violet Lambton' (Z/v)	SDen WFib
'Violetta' (R)	LDea WFib
'Virginia' (R)	IHos LDea WEas WFib
'Virginia Ley' (Z)	LVer SKen
'Viscossisimum'	WCHb
viscosum	See ***P. glutinosum***
'Vivat Regina' (Z/d)	WFib
'Voodoo' (U) ♀	CMdw CSpe EWoo LHil MSte NPla WFib
§ Vulcan (Z/d)	IHos WLRN
'W.H. Heytman' (R)	WFib
'Wallace Fairman' (R)	LDea
'Wallis Friesdorf' (Dw/C/d)	ESul LHil MWhe
'Wantirna' (Z/v)	ECtt LVer SDen
'Warrior' (Z/d)	WFib
'Washbrook' (Min/d)	ESul
'Watersmeet' (R)	LDea
'Wattisham' (Dec)	ESul LDea WEas
'Waveney' (Min)	ESul
'Wayward Angel' (A) ♀	CLit ESul EWoo LDea LVer SKen WFib

'Wedding Gown' (R)	LDea
'Wedding Royale' (Dw/d)	ESul LVer SDen
Weisse Perle (Z/d)	WFib
'Welcome' (Z/d)	WFib
'Welling' (Sc)	LVer
'Wellington' (R)	LDea WFib
'Wendy' (Min)	SDen
'Wendy Anne'	SDen SKen
'Wendy Hawley' (R)	LDea
'Wendy Read' (Dw/d)	ERea ESul LVer MWhe WFib
'Wensum' (Min/d)	ESul LVer SDen WFib
'West Priory'	SDen
* 'Westdale Beauty' (d)	CWDa
'Western Zoyland' (R)	WFib
'Whisper' (R)	CSpe WFib
'White Birds Egg' (Z)	WFib
¶ 'White Blizzard'	NPri WLRN
'White Boar' (Fr)	CBrk EWoo LBlm SDen
'White Bonanza' (R)	EBSP LDea WFib
'White Charm' (R)	EBSP LDea
'White Chiffon' (R)	CSpe EBSP LDea LVer
'White Eggshell' (Min)	ESul LVer
'White Feather' (Z/St)	WFib
'White Frills' (Z/d)	WFib
'White Gem' (Min)	ESul
'White Glory' (R) ♀	LDea SDen WFib
'White Lively Lady' (Dw/C)	ESul
§ 'White Mesh' (I/v)	ECtt MBri MWhe SDen SKen WEas WFib
◆ White Pearl Necklace	See *P.* **Perlenkette Weiss = 'Perlpenei'**
¶ 'White Queen' (Z/d)	CWDa
'White Unique' (U)	EWoo NSty SDen SKen WFib
whytei	MHul
* 'Wickham Lad'	LDea
* 'Wild Spice'	LDea
'Wilhelm Kolle' (Z)	WFib
'William Sutton' (R)	WFib
'Winnie Read' (Dw/d)	ERea ESul
'Winston Churchill' (R)	LDea
'Wirral Moonglow'	SDen
'Wirral Target' (Z/d)	EBSP ESul MWhe
'Wishing Star'	ESul
'Witnesham' (Min/d)	ESul
§ 'Wood's Surprise' (MinI/d)	ESul LDea LVer MWhe SDen WFib
'Wookey' (R)	WFib
§ ***worcesterae***	MHul
'Wrington' (R)	WFib
'Wroxham' (Dw)	ESul
* 'Wychwood'	LDea
'Wyck Beacon' (I/d)	SKen
'Wycombe Maid' (Min/d)	SDen WFib
'Xenia Field' (Z)	SDen SKen
xerophyton	MHul
'Yale' (I/d) ♀	CHal EBSP GDTE IHos LBlm LDea LVer MBri MSte MWhe SDen SKen SLMG WFib
'Yarrabee Jane' (R)	WFib
'Yhu' (R)	EBSP LDea LVer WFib
'Yolanda' (Min/C)	ESul
'York Florist'	LVer
'York Minster' (Dw/v)	SDen SKen
'Yours Truly' (Z)	SKen
'Yvonne' (Z)	SDen SKen WFib
'Zinc' (Z/d)	WFib
'Zoe' (D)	SDen
zonale	MHul SVen WFib
'Zulu King' (R)	WFib
'Zulu Warrior' (R)	WFib

PELLAEA (Sinopteridaceae)

boivinii var. *viridis* NMar
§ *calomelanos* NMar SBla
falcata MBri
hastata See *P. calomelanos*
paradoxa WRic
rotundifolia ♀ CHal MBri NMar
sagittata NMar

PELLIONIA See ELATOSTEMA

PELTANDRA (Araceae)

alba See *P. saggitifolia*
§ *saggitifolia* SWyc
§ *undulata* CRow CWGN EHon LPBA MSta NDea SRms SWat SWyc
virginica Rafinesque SWyc
– Schott See *P. undulata*

PELTARIA (Brassicaceae)

alliacea ECha

PELTIPHYLLUM See DARMERA

PELTOBOYKINIA (Saxifragaceae)

§ *tellimoides* EBre NHol SMac
watanabei CHan GTou LFis WFar WTre

PENNANTIA (Icacinaceae)

corymbosa ECou MAll

PENNISETUM (Poaceae)

§ *alopecuroides* CLTr EBre EGar EGol ETPC GBin GCal MHar MHlr NHol NVic SApp SOkh SPer WHil WWat
– 'Hameln' CDoC CInt CMea EBee EBre ECha EFou EHoe EMan EMon EPPr EPla ESOG ETPC LHop MBri MSte NFai SApp SLod SMad SPla WPer WRus
– f. *viridescens* CCuc EBee ECha EFou EHoe ELan EMan ESOG ETPC NPSI NSti SLPl SSoC WWat
– 'Woodside' CCuc EBre EGol EHoe EPPr EPla
* 'Burgundy Blaze' CSte EFou EPPr NPSI
'Cassian's Choice' EFou
compressum See *P. alopecuroides*
flaccidum EMon EPPr
imcomptum purple EPPr ETPC
incomptum EBee EBre
longistylum See *P. villosum*
macrourum CHan CInt EHoe EPPr EPla ESOG ETPC
orientale ♀ CInt CPea EBee EBre ECha EGar EMan ETPC LFis LHop MHlr MMil MNrw NBir SAxl SMrm SUsu SWas WBro WCot WHoo WOMN WPyg
rueppellii See *P. setaceum*
§ *setaceum* ♀ EOrc ETPC MNrw WLRN
§ *villosum* CArc CCuc CInt CKel CRDP EBar EBre ECha EHoe ETPC LHop NBro NPSI NSti SApp SAxl SLPl SLod SMad SPla SUsu SVen WCot

PENSTEMON † (Scrophulariaceae)

* 'Abberley' WPer
§ 'Alice Hindley' ♀ CBot CGle CGre CSam EBee EBre ECha EFou EOrc GMac LHil LHop LLWP MMil MNes MWat NHaw NHol NSti SAga SChu SPer WEas WHCG WHoo WMaN WMer WRus WSPU WWat
alpinus CLyd EWes GAbr GTou MSto NOak WPLl WRHF WThi
– subsp. *brandegeei* See *P. brandegeei*
§ 'Andenken an Friedrich Hahn' ♀ Widely available
§ *angustifolius* MHew MNrw SRms WPer
antirrhinoides See *Keckiella antirrhinoides*
'Apple Blossom' ♀ Widely available
'Apple Blossom' hort. See *P.* **'Thorn'**
aridus EPot
arizonicus See *P. whippleanus*
arkansanus MNrw
'Astley' WPer
attenuatus MSto WPer
azureus EPot WPer
'Barbara Barker' See *P.* **'Beech Park'**
§ *barbatus* CBot CGle CKel CLon EBre ECha ELan EMar ERav GCHN LBlm LGre LPen MBel MWat NMir SChu SMac SPer SSea SUsu WEas WHCG
– 'Jingle Bells' EHic
– K 92.319 CMdw NHar
– Limoges form GCal
– var. *praecox* WPer
– – f. *nanus* CBot EMil GCHN GSki MSte SRms
barrettiae CMea GCHN NRoo
§ 'Beech Park' ♀ CInt ELan LHil LHop MBel SAga SMrm SPer SUsu WHCG WHil WRus WSPU
'Bisham Seedling' See *P.* **'White Bedder'**
'Blackbird' Widely available
'Blue Spring' CBot CLon EBre LFis MAsh MBri NBrk
'Bodnant' EBee SSte WPer
§ *brandegeei* EBee
'Breitenbush Blue' LCom LHop SAga
bridgesii See *P. rostriflorus*
'Bridget's White' CSam
'Burford Purple' See *P.* **'Burgundy'**
'Burford Seedling' See *P.* **'Burgundy'**
'Burford White' See *P.* **'White Bedder'**
§ 'Burgundy' CDec CDoC CElw CLTr CMHG CSam ECha EFol EOrc GCHN GMac IHos LHil LLWP LPen NBrk NFai NPer NSti SChu SPer WHCG WPer WRus
caeruleus See *P. angustifolius*
caespitosus EBre
caespitosus albus CPBP
caespitosus 'Cloud Barr' CPBP
§ – subsp. *suffruticosus* MFos WDav
¶ *calcyosus* NLak
§ *campanulatus* CMHG CSam EHyt EPot EWes GCal LFis LHop MBro MTho NBrk NHar NHol NMen NNrd NTow SAga WAbe WGwG WHCG WPat WPer WRus WSPU
– var. *chihuahuensis* SAga
campanulatus pulchellus See *P. campanulatus*
campanulatus roseus WEas WSPU
'Candy Pink' WEas

cardwellii	CMea ECha EPot EWes GTou LGan LGre NHar SAga SRms
– K 92.321	WDav
'Castle Forbes'	GMac WEas WHCG WPer WWoo
'Catherine de la Mare' 🏆	CGle CLTr CLyd EBar EBre ECtt EFou ELan ERav GCHN LBlm LFis LGre LHil LHop MHFP MRav MSCN MWat NBir NBro SAga SChu SCro SMrm SOkh WHil WHoo WPer WSPU
centranthifolius JJA 13106	SIgm
'Charles Rudd'	CBod CGle LPen NFai NLak SAga SChu WHCG WMaN WOMN WPri
'Cherry Ripe'	EBar EBee LHil LRHS SCro SMrm SPla SSte WHCG WHal WPer WPyg WRus WSPU WWoo
§ 'Chester Scarlet' 🏆	EBre EOrc GBri GCHN GGar GMac LHop LPen MBel MBri MNrw MRav NBrk NFai SAga SSte SVen WEas WHCG WPbr WPer WRus WSPU WWhi WWye
clevelandii var. ***connatus***	SIgm
confertus	CMHG CTri EBar ECtt EHyt ELan EMNN EPot GAbr LPen MHig MSto NGre NLak NMen NRoo NTow NWCA SAlw SHFr SRms WAbe WHCG WHil WPat WPer WSPU
'Connie's Pink' 🏆	MSte WHCG WSPU
* 'Coral Pink'	GMac
cordifolius	See ***Keckiella cordifolia***
'Cottage Garden Red'	See ***P.* 'Windsor Red'**
§ 'Countess of Dalkeith'	CLTr CLon CRos EBee EOrc EWes GBri LHil LHop LLWP MNes NHaw NLak SOkh SSte SVen WHCG WRHF WSPU WWhi
'Craigieburn Chenille'	GCra
'Craigieburn Taffeta'	GCra
¶ ***crandallii***	CPBP
– subsp. ***glabrescens***	CPBP LGre NHar SAga SUsu WHCG
cristatus	See ***P. eriantherus***
cyaneus	SRms WRHF
davidsonii	CLyd EWes LGre MHig WAbe
¶ – subsp. ***davidsonii***	GCLN NHar
§ – var. ***menziesii*** 🏆	CPBP EPot GTou MFir NBus NHar NLak NWCA SBla WAbe WEas WIvy WSPU
– – 'Microphyllus'	CLyd CMea EPot GCLN MAsh MBro MSto NBus NHar NMen NSla WDav WPat
– var. ***praeteritus***	CGra CHan GCLN LGre NHar WDav
'Dazzler'	CBlo CBod CKni CM&M CMdw CWan NRoo WPer WSPU
deustus	MBel SRms
'Devonshire Cream'	WHCG WPer
'Diane'	WMer
diffusus	See ***P. serrulatus***
digitalis	CHan CLyd CMdw CNic CSpe ECha EGar GCra LGan LGre LPen MBel WAbb WEas WHCG WPer WTyr
§ – 'Husker's Red'	Widely available
– pink	SUsu

– 'Purpureus'	See ***P. digitalis* 'Husker's Red'**
discolor	CMea LGre SAga SMrm
§ 'Drinkstone'	CGle CMGP EGoo LGre LHop LPen NChi SAga SDix SMrm WHCG WPer WSPU
'Drinkwater Red'	See ***P.* 'Drinkstone'**
duchesnensis	CGra
eatonii	SRms WOMN
'Edithiae'	CPBP EOrc LFis LFlo MBal NLak NRoo SChu WDav WEas WHCG WHoo WIvy WKif
§ ***eriantherus***	CElw CPBP WCot WHCG
¶ ***euglaucus***	WDav
§ 'Evelyn' 🏆	Widely available
'Fanny's Blush'	CSpe
'Firebird'	See ***P.* 'Schoenholzeri'**
'Flame'	CGle EBee EMan LHop LPen NPla WHCG WPer WSPU
'Flamingo'	CSpe EBar EWes LPen MCLN NHaw SAga SMrm SSte SUsu SVen WHoo WLRN WMaN WSPU WWoo
frutescens	GTou WSPU
fruticosus	EBee MBro MNrw NHar NWCA SRms WDav
§ – var. ***scouleri*** 🏆	EHic MAsh MBro MHar MOne SRms WIvy WSPU
– – f. ***albus*** 🏆	CBot CMea ELan GDra LFlo LGre LHop LPen SAga SBla SChu WAbe WEas WIvy WKif WSPU WSan
– – 'Amethyst'	EGoo WAbe
– – 'Hopleys'	LHop
¶ – var. ***serratus***	WDav
* – – 'Holly'	LGre
* 'Gaff's Pink'	EOrc SChu
'Garden Red'	See ***P.* 'Windsor Red'**
'Garnet'	See ***P.* 'Andenken an Friedrich Hahn'**
'Garnet Variegated'	CLyd NLak WThi
gentianoides	CMdw NBro NLak WRus WSPU
'George Elrick'	EBar
§ 'George Home' 🏆	CGle CLTr EBee ECGP ECtt EHic EWes GAbr LHil WByw WHCG WRus WWoo
glaber	CElw CMHG CSev EBee GMac LGre LHop LLWP LPen MRav NBro SAga SHFr SMrm WEas WHCG WHoo WKif WPer WRus WSPU WWhi
gormanii	CNic SIng
gracilis	CNic GCHN SRms WPer WSPU
grandiflorus	NLak
hallii	CLyd EWes GTou LPen NSla SIng WSPU
hartwegii 🏆	CGre CShe EOrc GMac LHil LHop NCat SAga SChu SSea WAbe WHCG WPer WRus WSPU
hartwegii albus	EBee EOrc LGan LGre LHop LRHS MMil MSte NNor SPer WHCG WRus WSPU WWhi
harvardii	WAbe
heterodoxus	WDav
§ ***heterophyllus***	CLyd CVer EBre IHos LBlm LGre LGro LHop LPen MCLN MNrw NBir NRoo SAga SChu SHFr SRms SUsu WAbe WEas WHCG WHil WPer WRus WSPU WWin

– subsp. ***australis***	See ***P. australis***
– 'Blue Eye'	WMaN WSPU
– 'Blue Fountain'	LPen WSPU
– 'Blue Gem'	CBod CElw CTri CVer EBre EOrc NRoo SIng SMrm SPla SSte WHoo WSPU
– 'Blue Springs'	CGle CM&M CShe EOrc MSte NBir NFla SAga SBla SMrm SPla WAbe WRus
– 'Heavenly Blue'	EBre ECtt LFis LHop MCLN MTis NHaw NPla SWat WGwG WLRN WOve WRus WWhi
* – 'John D.'	EAst
– subsp. ***purdyi***	NLak SMrm WHCG
– 'True Blue'	See ***P. heterophyllus***
– 'Züriblau'	SMrm WWat
'Hewell Pink Bedder' ♀	CGle CLTr CWan EAst EBar EBee EBre EFou GBri GMaP LHil LPen MCLN NRoo SChu SSte SUsu WHCG WPer WSPU
'Hewitt's Pink'	LHil
§ 'Hidcote Pink' ♀	Widely available
'Hidcote Purple'	CElw LHil NBrk NPla SChu
* 'Hidcote White'	CBot CM&M EOrc MBel SUsu WAbe WRus
¶ 'Hillview Red'	WHil
§ ***hirsutus***	CGle CLon EBee EPPr NHol SOkh WOMN WPer WRHF WSan WThi
– bronze-leaved	WThi
– var. ***minimus***	WHil WThi
– var. ***pygmaeus***	CChr CHan CLyd CNic CRDP CWGN ELan GCLN GTou LFis MBro MHar MHig MPla NHar NMen NWCA SAlw SBla SRms WByw WHoo WOMN WPer WRus WThi WWin
– – f. ***albus***	EHyt WPer
'Hopleys Variegated'	EFol EGar EMon EOrc EWes LFis LHop MBel MNrw MSCN NBir NLak SLod SSte WCot WHil WSPU WSan WWeb WWye
'Hower Park'	WPer
humilis	EAst NWCA WHil
¶ – Mckay's form	WDav
– 'Pulchellus'	LGre NWCA
* 'Hyacinth'	ELan
isophyllus ♀	CBrk CLyd EBee MMil MNes SChu WCot WEas WFar WHCG WPer WSPU
jamesii	CHan EBee EOrc NChi
janishiae	CBlo
'John Booth'	WEas
'John Nash'	CMil CSWP CSam EBar LHil NLak SHFr SIgm SMrm SSte
'John Nash' hort.	See ***P. 'Alice Hindley'***
'Joy'	CBlo EBre MBro MSte SSte WOve WPer WPri WPyg WWoo
'June'	See ***P. 'Hidcote Pink'***
'King George V'	CBrk CGre CKel EBar EBee EBre ECtt EFou ELan GMac IHos LFis LHil LHop MBri MNrw NBrk NBro NHaw NPer NRoo SChu SPer WHCG WPer WRus WSPU
* 'Knight's Purple'	WHCG
'Knightwick'	WPer WSPU
'Kummel'	ELan
kunthii	See ***P. campanulatus***
¶ ***laetus*** var. ***laetus***	GCLN
§ – var. ***roezlii***	EDAr GDra MLan MPla MSto NHar NLak NMen SIng SRms WAbe WEas WWin
laricifolius	CPBP
leiophyllus	CGra
linarioides	CPBP EWes WAbe WPat
– subsp. ***coloradensis***	WDav
– JCA 9694	WDav
'Little Witley'	SUsu WHCG WPer
* 'Logan Pink'	GMac
'Lord Home'	See ***P. 'George Home'***
lyallii	CKel EBee ELan EMar EMon ESis LFis MNrw MSCN NLak SMac WSPU WSan
* 'Lynette'	CElw CLyd CWan EHic LFis WHCG WHil WPer
'Macpenny's Pink'	EBar EBee WWoo
'Madame Golding'	CGle CSWP EBee LGre LHil MMil SAga SMrm SSte SUsu WHCG WPer WSPU
'Margery Fish' ♀	CElw CLyd CM&M CPou EHic ESis LFlo LGan MMil MNrw MSte NFai SMac SSte WPer WRha WSPU WSel
'Maurice Gibbs' ♀	SIgm WHCG WSPU
menziesii	See ***P. davidsonii*** var. ***menziesii***
'Merlin'	CLTr EBee EHic
'Midnight'	CBrk CElw CGle CLTr EOrc GBri LHil MMil NBrk NCat SAga SChu SIgm SMrm WCot WHCG WMer WPer WRus WSPU WWin
'Modesty'	EBar LPen LRHS NPla SMac WHCG WSPU
montanus	GCHN
'Mother of Pearl'	CElw EBar ECtt EFou EOrc GMac LHil LHop MBel MNrw NFai NHaw NRoo SAga SChu SIgm SPer SUsu WHCG WHal WMaN WOve WPer WSPU
* 'Mountain Wine'	WThi
'Mrs Miller'	EBar LPen
'Mrs Morse'	See ***P. 'Chester Scarlet'***
'Myddelton Gem'	CGle CLTr ECGP EMon LPen MWat NPla WFoF WHCG WSPU
'Myddelton Red'	CRos
newberryi ♀	CMHG CMea CPBP ELan LGre MAsh MFos NBir NMen NRoo NTow WAbe WKif WSPU WWin
– subsp. ***berryi***	See ***P. berryi***
– f. ***humilior***	MSto
§ – var. ***sonomensis***	GCLN NHar NWCA WAbe WDav
§ ***nitidus***	CGra
'Oaklea Red'	ECtt EMar LHil SSoC SWat
* old candy pink	EOrc LLWP LPen MBel MBri WPer WRus WSPU WWhi
'Osprey' ♀	CGle CLyd CMil EBar EBre EOrc EWes GMac LFis LHil LLWP MHlr MNrw NBrk NHaw NHol SUsu WCot WEas WHCG WHal WMaN WPer WRha WRus WSPU WSel WWin
ovatus	CChr CLyd CSpe ELan GCHN GCal GCra LFis LGan LPen MBro MTol NLak SAga SIgm WHCG WKif WSan
palmeri	EWll GCra LGre NLak

'Papal Purple'	CKel CLyd CM&M CMHG EBar GMac LLWP LPen MMil MSte NBrk NLak SAga SChu SMac SMrm SRms WHCG WHil WHoo WPer WRus WSPU WWhi WWye
parvulus	CGra CPBP NWCA
'Patio Coral'	MBri
'Patio Pink'	MBri
'Patio Shell'	MBri
'Patio Swirl'	MBri
'Patio Wine'	MBri
'Peace'	CLTr CRos EBar EBee LHop LPen LRHS NLak NPla SSca SSte WHCG WRus WSPU WWhi
peckii	MSto WHil
'Pennington Gem' 🏆	CGle EBre ECtt ELan EOrc GAbr GBri GMac LHil LHop LLWP LPen MNrw MSte NBrk NFla SAga SIng SMac SMrm SPer WEas WHCG WMaN WMer WPer WRus WSPU
'Pershore Pink Necklace'	EBre LPen MCLN WEas WHCG WSPU WSan
'Phare'	CBod CWan WHCG WPer WSPU
'Phyllis'	See ***P.* 'Evelyn'**
pinifolius 🏆	Widely available
– 'Mersea Yellow'	CLyd CMea EBre EPot ESis GDra LHop LPen MBro MHig MPla NHar NHed NHol NMen NWCA SAga SAlw SBla SIng SMac WDav WEas WHal WPat WPer WSPU WWat WWin
– 'Wisley Flame'	ESis SIgm SWas
'Pink Dragon'	CLyd CMea CPBP EOrc GCHN GDra LGre MPla NHar SAga SChu SMrm WHCG WRus WSPU
§ 'Pink Endurance'	CMea EBre ELan EOrc LGan LLWP LPen MBro MCLN MMil NHaw NRoo SAga WEas WHCG WHal WHoo WMaN WPer WSPU
'Pink Ice'	NPla WHil
'Pink Profusion'	SIgm SMrm
'Port Wine' 🏆	CGle CLTr CRDP CSam GCHN LHil LPen NPla SPer SSte WHCG WOve WPer WSPU WSel
'Powis Castle'	WPer WWye
¶ 'Prairie Dusk'	LPen
'Prairie Fire'	LPen WSPU
* 'Prairie Pride'	LPen
'Primrose Thomas'	MBel
'Priory Purple'	NLak WHCG WPer
procerus	CM&M GBri GCra LPen MDHE SRms SSte WPer
– subsp. ***brachyanthus***	WDav
– subsp. ***tolmiei***	EPot GCHN GCal LGre LPen NChi NHol NRoo NTow NWCA WCla
pruinosus	CGra EPot GCLN WDav
pubescens	See ***P. hirsutus***
pulchellus Lindley	See ***P. campanulatus***
pulcherrimus	NBro
pumilus	MSto
'Purple and White'	See ***P.* 'Countess of Dalkeith'**

'Purple Bedder'	CGle CGre EBee EHic EMar GAbr LPen MCLN MWat NHol NPla SSoC SWat WGor WGwG WHCG WSPU WSel
'Purple Dragon'	MPla SBla
'Purple Gem'	GDra
'Purple Passion'	EBre EWes NRoo WLRN
'Purpureus Albus'	See ***P.* 'Countess of Dalkeith'**
purpusii	EPot LGre SIgm WAbe WDav
'Rajah'	CVer EBee LHop SUsu
'Raspberry Ripple'	WLRN
rattanii	EBee
'Raven'	CLon EOrc GBri LBlm LHil MArl MBel MBro MCLN MSte NBrk NBro NHaw SChu SUsu WCot WEas WHCG WHal WHoo WMaN WMer WPer WPyg WRus WSPU WWin
'Razzle Dazzle'	WPer
'Red Ace'	MNrw
'Red Emperor'	CMHG ECtt NFai WEas WHCG WMer WPer WSPU WWhi
'Red Knight'	EBar
'Rich Purple'	SPer
'Rich Ruby'	CBrk CGle CMGP EBre ELan EWes LGre LHil LHop LLWP MGrG MNrw SAga SChu SMrm SOkh SUsu SVen WCot WEas WHCG WPer WRus WSPU WWhi
richardsonii	CGra CPBP ECro MSCN NChi NLak SIgm SRms WOMN
'Ridgeway Red'	WSPU
roezlii	See ***P. laetus* var. *roezlii***
* 'Rose Blush'	NLak WHCG
* ***roseocampanulatus***	SPan WSPU
§ ***rostriflorus***	SAga
– JJA 9548	SBla
'Rosy Blush'	LPen
'Roundhay'	CFee
* 'Roy Davidson'	LBee SBla WDav
'Royal White'	See ***P.* 'White Bedder'**
'Rubicundus' 🏆	CBot CGle CLyd EBar EBee ECtt ELan GMac LHil LHop LPen MCLN NSti SAga SMrm WAbe WCot WGwG WHCG WHoo WMer WRus WSPU WWeb
'Ruby'	See ***P.* 'Schoenholzeri'**
'Ruby Field'	EBee GAbr NPla WHCG WWoo
rupicola 🏆	CInt CMea GDra GTou LHop MBro MPla NSla NWCA SBla SIgm WAbe WOMN WWin
– 'Albus'	LGre WAbe
– 'Diamond Lake'	CPBP NHar WDav WIvy WPat
– mauve hybrid	GDra LGre
'Russian River'	CLTr CSWP CSpe EAst EBee EFou EHic LHil LLWP MBro SMrm SOkh SSte WHCG WHoo WPer WPyg WSPU
rydbergii	EPot WDav
Saskatoon hybrids	NChi
'Scarlet Queen'	CSWP
§ 'Schoenholzeri' 🏆	CElw CLTr EBee EOrc LGre LHop LLWP LPen MBri MNes MNrw NFai NRoo NSti SAga SChu SIgm SPer SUsu WAbe WEas WHCG WHil WHoo WPer WRus WSPU WWat
scouleri	See ***P. fruticosus* var. *scouleri***

secundiflorus	CNic
serratus 'Holly'	CHan CPBP SAga SBla SMrm
§ ***serrulatus***	CSWP EBee ECha EWes GTou LRHS MBel MSte SMad SRms WEas WSPU
– 'Albus'	EBee MSte SIgm WSPU WWin
'Shell Pink'	CWan WPer
* 'Sherbourne Blue'	WPer
* 'Shrawley'	WPer
'Sissinghurst Pink'	See ***P.* 'Evelyn'**
'Six Hills'	CPBP MHig MPla NHar NHol NRoo SAga WDav WHCG WPer WSPU
* 'Skyline'	ECtt EPfP WHil
smallii	LPen NLak SIgm WPer
¶ 'Snow Storm'	See ***P.* 'White Bedder'**
'Snowflake'	See ***P.* 'White Bedder'**
'Snowstorm'	WEas WHCG
sonomensis	See ***P. newberryi*** var. ***sonomensis***
'Sour Grapes' hort.	See ***P.* 'Stapleford Gem'**
§ 'Sour Grapes' M. Fish	Widely available
'Southcombe Pink'	WHCG WPen
'Southgate Gem'	MNrw MWat SCro WHCG
'Souvenir d'Adrian Regnier'	EHic GCHN
'Souvenir d'André Torres'	CBod LLWP
'Souvenir d'André Torres' misapplied	See ***P.* 'Chester Scarlet'**
sp. CD&R 1355	CHan
¶ sp. P&C 150	CFee
¶ ***speciosus*** subsp. ***kennedyi***	EPot NTow
§ 'Stapleford Gem' 🏆	CElw CGle CKel CMHG CMil CSam CShe CWGN EBre ELan GCHN LHil LPen NBro SAga SIgm SMad SRms WEas WGwG WHCG WSPU WSel WWat WWhi
strictus	EBar EBee ECro GCHN LGre NBro NChi NLak SIde SIgm WDav WPer WRHF WSPU
– 'Bandera'	MHlr WCot
'Sutton's Pink Bedder'	WSPU
N 'Taoensis'	CLTr EOrc EWes LHil SChu SMac SSea WAbe WCot WRus
♦ ***taosensis***	See ***P. crandallii*** subsp. ***taosensis***
ternatus	See ***Keckiella ternata***
teucrioides	EPot NMen NWCA SMrm WThi
§ 'Thorn'	CBod CGle CLTr CLon CSWP CSam CSpe EAst EFou ELan LHop LRHS MBel MNrw NBrk NFai NRoo SAga SCro SMrm SOkh WGwG WHCG WHoo WRus WSPU
'Threave Pink'	See ***P.* 'Pink Endurance'**
* 'Threave White'	CMil WPen
'Torquay Gem'	CElw CKni CVer GBuc LHop LPen NLak WHCG WPer WRus
¶ ***traceyi***	NLak
♦ 'True Sour Grapes'	See ***P.* 'Sour Grapes' M. Fish**
tusharensis	See ***P. caespitosus*** subsp. ***suffruticosus***
uintahensis	CGra
unilateralis	MSto
utahensis	CBot EBre EPla EWes GBri MHlr WCot WPer WTyr
venustus	CFir CSam EBar GBuc GBur MHar MNrw NChi SRms WHCG WHil WPer WWye
virens	MHig NRoo NTow NWCA SIng WPat WWhi
virens albus	GCHN LFis NPri WWin
virens R/Mr 7890	WPer
virgatus subsp. ***arizonicus***	CPBP EBee SIng WSPU
watsonii	EHic EMan LHop SAga SWat WCot WHCG WPer WTyr
§ ***whippleanus***	CBot CGle CHan CLon CLyd CRDP ECro EWes GCra LFlo LGre MBel MSte NLak SAga WAbb WPer
– dark form	MBro
§ 'White Bedder' 🏆	CGle CMea EBre EFou EOrc GMac LHil LHop LLWP LPen MBel MNes MSte NCat NFai SAga SChu SIgm SOkh SPer WHCG WHil WMaN WPbr WPer WRus WSPU WWat WWin
'Whitethroat'	CGre LPen MHlr SOkh WCot WHCG WMer WPer WSPU WWin
wilcoxii	MFos
§ 'Windsor Red'	CBod EBar EFou EHic LHil MHFP MSte NPla SUsu WCot WGor WHCG WSPU WSel WWoo
§ ***wislizenii***	EAst EBre EHic LGre MLan MTis NBro NOak SBid SPla SRms WFar WGwG WMaN

PENTAGLOTTIS (Boraginaceae)

§ ***sempervirens***	CArn CKin ECWi EGoo EJud MHew MSal WBea WHen WOak WWye

PENTALINON (Apocynaceae)

See Plant Deletions

PENTAPTERYGIUM See AGAPETES

PENTAS (Rubiaceae)

lanceolata	CHal ELan MBri

PENTASCHISTIS (Poaceae)

See Plant Deletions

PEPEROMIA (Piperaceae)

§ ***argyreia*** 🏆	CHal MBri
arifolia	CHal
caperata	MBri
– 'Little Fantasy' 🏆	CHal
clusiifolia	CHal
– 'Variegata' 🏆	CHal
glabella	CHal
griseoargentea	CHal
magnoliifolia	See ***P. obtusifolia* Magnoliifolia Group**
obtusifolia 'Jamaica'	MBri
§ – Magnoliifolia Group	SRms
– – 'Golden Gate'	MBri
– – 'Greengold'	CHal MBri
– – 'USA'	MBri
– 'Tricolor'	MBri
orba 'Pixie'	MBri
I – 'Pixie Variegata'	MBri
pulchella	See ***P. verticillata***
resediflora	See ***P. fraseri***
sandersii	See ***P. argyreia***
scandens 🏆	MBri
– 'Variegata'	CHal MBri

§ *verticillata*	CHal

PERESKIA (Cactaceae)

aculeata f. *rubescens*	WCot
corrugata	ECon

PERESKIOPSIS (Cactaceae)

§ *diguetii*	CHal
spathulata	See ***P. diguetii***

PEREZIA (Asteraceae)

linearis	GBuc
recurvata	EPot GTou NNrd NWCA WFar

PERICALLIS (Asteraceae)

§ *lanata*	CBrk CSev ELan LHil LHop MBlu MTol SMrm SRms WEas WNdy
– Kew form	CSpe SMrm

PERILLA (Lamiaceae)

§ *frutescens* var. *crispa* ♀	CArn MChe NRai WJek
– var. *nankinensis*	See ***P. frutescens*** var. ***crispa***
frutescens rubra	CArn MChe WJek

PERIPLOCA (Asclepiadaceae)

graeca	CArn CB&S CMac CPlN CPle CRHN EGar GQui NFla SBra SPer WCru WSHC
sepium	CPlN CPle

PERISTROPHE (Acanthaceae)

speciosa	ERea SLMG

PERNETTYA See GAULTHERIA

PEROVSKIA (Lamiaceae)

atriplicifolia ♀	CArn CBot CChe CPle CShe GPoy LGre LHol MBri SIde SLod WHCG WOld WSel
'Blue Haze'	GCal
'Blue Spire' ♀	Widely available
'Filigran'	GCal
¶ *scrophulariifolia*	CPle
'Superba'	WWeb

PERROTTETIA (Celastraceae)

See Plant Deletions

PERSEA (Lauraceae)

thunbergii	CGre

PERSICARIA (Polygonaceae)

§ *affinis*	CB&S CBen CHan CTri CWGN ECha EFol MBar MTho NBro NVic SWat WEas WHil WOld WOve WWat WWin
– 'Darjeeling Red' ♀	CB&S CRow CSev ECED ELan ENot EPla GCal LGro LHil MBal MBri NBir NFla NHol SMrm WAbe WBea WHen
– 'Dimity'	See ***P. affinis* 'Superba'**
– 'Donald Lowndes' ♀	CRow CShe ECha EGol ELan EMar ENot EOrc EPla LHop MBal MSta MWat NDea NFla NGre NHol NRoo SPer SRms WAbe WOld WPer
– 'Ron McBeath'	ECha
§ – 'Superba' ♀	CRow EBre EFou EGol EPla ERav LFis MBri MFir MHlr MRav NBro NFai NHol NRoo SIng SMrm SSpi WHoo WPer WPyg WRus
alata	CRow NHol SMad
alpina	CRow
amphibia	CRow
§ *amplexicaulis*	CBre CRow CShe EBre ELan EMar ERav GMaP LGro MBal MSCN MWat NChi NDea NNor NOrc SChu SEND SUsu WHoo WPyg WRHF
– 'Alba'	CArc CRow ECha EGar EPla LGre
– 'Arun Gem'	See ***P. amplexicaulis*** var. ***pendula***
– 'Atrosanguinea'	CKel CNic CRow EBre ECED ECha EMan EPla LFis MFir NBir NDea NFai NFla NHol NTow NVic SPer SRms WOld WWin
– 'Cottesbrooke Gold'	CRow
– 'Firetail' ♀	CDec CHan CRow EBre ECED ECha ECtt EFou EGar EPla LHop LLWP NHol NRoo NSti WBea WHil WOld WRus WWhi
– 'Gold Leaf'	WCot
– 'Inverleith'	CBre CRow EBre ECha ECtt EGar EPla NCat NLak NRoo WRHF WWye
§ – var. *pendula*	CRow CShe ECha GAri NBir NRoo NSti
– 'Rosea'	CRow CWGN ECha ELan EMon EPla
– 'Rowden Gem'	CRow
– 'Taurus'	CWGN EGar WFar
§ *bistorta*	CArn CJew CKin CRow CShe ELau GPoy LHol MChe MHew MSal SWat WSel WWye
– subsp. *carnea*	CRow ECha EGar ELan EMon EPPr ERav NBir
¶ – 'Hohe Tatra'	CRow SMrm
– 'Superba' ♀	Widely available
bistortoides	MSal
campanulata	CElw CHan COtt CRow CWGN ECED ECha ECro EFol ELan EMar EOrc EPar LBlm LHop MHar MSCN MWat NBro NFai NNor NRoo SPer WBea WOve WPer WWat WWin WWye
– Alba Group	CRow ELan EMar EOrc GCal NBro NSti SChu WElm WHer WWat
– pale pink	GBuc GCal WBcn
– 'Rosenrot'	CBre CJew CRow EGol ELan EOrc GBuc GCal IBlr LFis NHol SSpi SWat WBea WOld
– 'Southcombe White'	CRow EBar EPla LBlm WBea
capitata	CLTr CNic CRow CWGN EFol ELan MMil SCro SIng SMac SRms WBea WEas WPer
– from Afghanistan	WBea
coriacea	CRow
elata	CArc EGoo GAri GBuc GGar SLod
emodi	CRow WWat
filiformis	See ***P. virginiana***
§ *macrophylla*	CRow EBre NFla WCot
microcephala	CRow EWes SAga SCro SMac WCot

milletii	CRDP CRow EPPr GAri GBuc GDra MTho NLak NOak NSti WCot WCru WMer
§ ***mollis***	CHan CRow EHal
¶ ***odorata***	CArn WJek
¶ ***orientalis***	MSal SMrm
polymorpha	EFou EMon LGre SMrm WPbr
polystachya	ECha
runcinata	CLTr CRow ECED EHal LHop MTol NBro NFai SAxl SChu SEas WCot WCru WDav WFox WHer WOld WPer WWin
scoparia	See ***Polygonum scoparium***
sphaerostachya Meissner	See ***P. macrophylla***
tenuicaulis	CArc CBre CLyd CRow EBre EMon EPar EPla GGar MBal NDea NHol WCru WOMN
vacciniifolia 🏆	Widely available
– 'Ron McBeath'	CRow
§ ***virginiana***	CMHG EPla MFir
¶ – Compton's form	WCot
§ – 'Painter's Palette' (v)	CArn CB&S CBot CGle CHad CRow EBre ECha ECtt EFou ELan EPla ERav GCal LHop NVic SAga SMad SMrm SPer WCru WEas WMer WOld WPer
§ – Variegata Group	CBot CHan CRow EBee ECha EGar EMar EPla GCal LHop SAxl WCot WOld
vivipara	CRow
§ ***wallichii***	CRow IBlr NSti
weyrichii	GCal MTol NBir NBro WCot

PETALOSTEMON See DALEA

PETAMENES See GLADIOLUS

PETASITES (Asteraceae)

albus	CRow EMon GPoy LRHS MCli MSal NSti
fragrans	CHEx CNat ELan EMon EPar MSta MUlv SWat WOak
hybridus	CKin EMFW MCli WHer
* – 'Variegatus'	WNdy
japonicus var. ***giganteus***	CHEx CRow CWGN ECha EGol ELan EMan EMon EPar EPfP MSCN MTol MUlv NDea NVic SBid WCra WCru
– ***giganteus*** 'Variegatus'	CArc CRow ECoo EEls EFol EGar EMon EPla IBlr MSCN MUlv NTow SBid WCHb WCru WHer WHil
palmatus	CRDP GCal MHlr WCru
– JLS 86317CLOR	EMon WCot
paradoxus	CRDP EMon WCot

PETREA (Verbenaceae)

volubilis	CPlN ECon LChe

PETROCALLIS (Brassicaceae)

lagascae	See ***P. pyrenaica***
§ ***pyrenaica***	NHol NWCA WPer

PETROCOPTIS (Caryophyllaceae)

–	EBur MDHE NMen SRms SSca
§ – subsp. ***glaucifolia***	ESis GTou MPla NBir WHil WPer WWin
– – 'Alba'	SSca

PETROCOSMEA (Gesneriaceae)

kerrii	WCru

PETROMARULA (Campanulaceae)

See Plant Deletions

PETROPHYTUM (Rosaceae)

caespitosum	CGra GTou NHar NHol NWCA
cinerascens	NWCA
§ ***hendersonii***	GCLN NHol WAbe

PETRORHAGIA (Caryophyllaceae)

nanteuilii	CNat EWFC
§ ***saxifraga*** 🏆	CSpe EBur GAul MNrw NMen NPri SAxl SRms WPer WWhi
§ – 'Rosette'	ECha MTho WAbe WWin

PETROSELINUM (Apiaceae)

§ ***crispum***	CArn CJew CSev CWan EJud ELau GPoy ILis LHol MBar MChe NPri SIde WPer WSel WWye
– var. ***crispum***	CWan
¶ – 'Darki'	CSev
– French	CArn CBod ELau WJek
– 'Greek'	ELau
– 'Italian'	See ***P. crispum*** var. ***neapolitanum***
§ – var. ***neapolitanum***	CBod EBar ELau EOHP MGra
– var. ***tuberosum***	CBod SIde WHer
hortense	See ***P. crispum***
tuberosum	See ***P. cripsum var. tubersum***

PETTERIA (Papilionaceae)

ramentacea	CB&S CFil CPle SLPl SMad

PEUCEDANUM (Apiaceae)

officinale	ECWi
ostruthium	GPoy LHol
palustre	ECWi
verticillare	EBre SMrm

PEUMUS (Monimiaceae)

boldus	CGre

PHACELIA (Hydrophyllaceae)

bolanderi	CHan CPBP EBee
sericea subsp. ***ciliosa***	MFos SIgm
¶ – subsp. ***sericea***	MFos
tanacetifolia	WWye

PHAEDRANASSA (Amaryllidaceae)

dubia	CMon
tunguraguae	WChr
viridiflora	CMon WChr

PHAEDRANTHUS See DISTICTIS

PHAENOCOMA (Asteraceae)

¶ ***prolifera***	CTrC

PHAENOSPERMA (Poaceae)

globosa	EBee EGar EHoe EPPr EPla ESOG ETPC LHil

PHAGNALON (Asteraceae)

See Plant Deletions

PHAIOPHLEPS (Iridaceae)

biflora	See ***Olsynium biflorum***
nigricans	See ***Sisyrinchium striatum***

PHAIUS (Orchidaceae)

minor	EFEx

PHALARIS (Poaceae)

§ *aquatica*	ETPC
arundinacea	CKin CWGN EBar ETPC MLan SWat
– 'Elegantissima'	See *P. arundinacea* var. *picta* **'Picta'**
– 'Luteovariegata'	EMon
¶ – 'Picta'	NFla WFar
– var. *picta* 'Aureovariegata'	CB&S CRow CSWP CWGN MRav NPer SAga SWat
– – 'Feesey' (v)	Widely available
– – 'Luteopicta'	EBee EHoe EPPr EPla ESOG WChe WCot
§ – – 'Picta' (v) 🏆	CRow CWGN EBre ECED EHoe EHon ELan EMar EPPr EPla EPot ESOG ETPC GCHN IBlr LGro MBal MBar NFai NHol NNor NSti SPer SWat SWyc WChe WEas WRha WWin WWye
– – 'Tricolor' (v)	EBee EHoe EMon EPPr EPla ETPC GAri GFre LRHS SMad SSoC WBea
– 'Streamlined' (v)	EMon EPla WCot WLeb
tuberosa stenoptera	See *P. aquatica*

PHANEROPHLEBIA (Dryopteridaceae)

caryotidea	See *Cyrtomium caryotideum*
falcata	See *Cyrtomium falcatum*
fortunei	See *Cyrtomium fortunei*

PHARBITIS See IPOMOEA

PHASEOLUS (Papilionaceae)

caracalla	See *Vigna caracalla*

PHEGOPTERIS (Thelypteridaceae)

§ *connectilis*	CCuc CFil EFer MBal NHed NMar SRms
decursive-pinnata	CCuc EMon NMar WRic

PHELLODENDRON (Rutaceae)

amurense	CB&S CGre CMCN ELan EPfP SSpi WDin WNor
¶ *lavalleei*	WPGP

PHILADELPHUS † (Hydrangeaceae)

'Avalanche'	CMHG EBre MAsh NFla NPro SEas SPer SRms WDin WHCG WWat
'Beauclerk' 🏆	CB&S CDoC CMHG CShe EBre ENot MBri MGos MRav NBee NHol SEas SPer SPla SReu SRms SSpi WHCG WWat WWin
'Belle Etoile' 🏆	CB&S CBot CPle CShe CTrw EBre ELan ENot ESis GRei LHop MBal MBar MBri MGos MWat NHol NRoo SHBN SPer SReu SSpi SSta WDin WEas WHCG WWat WWin
'Boule d'Argent'	CMHG
'Bouquet Blanc'	GQui SEas SPer SRms WKif
brachybotrys	CFil NHol WPGP
¶ 'Buckley's Quill'	WBcn
'Burfordensis'	MAsh SBid SPer WLRN WWat WWeb
'Burkwoodii'	SBid
coronarius	CTri EBee LBuc MWat NNor SHBN SPer
– 'Aureus' 🏆	Widely available
– 'Bowles' Variety'	See *P. coronarius* **'Variegatus'**
– 'Gold Mound'	MGos
§ – 'Variegatus' (v) 🏆	Widely available
'Coupe d'Argent'	MRav
'Dame Blanche' (d)	EBee NPro
delavayi	CFil WCru WPGP
– var. *calvescens*	See *P. purpurascens*
'Enchantment'	MRav MTis SBid SDix WLRN
'Erectus'	EBee ENot GAul MBal MRav NWea WHCG WWat
'Frosty Morn'	CB&S CDoC EHal EHic MGos NHol NTow SPer SPla
§ 'Innocence' (v)	CBot CDec CEnd CPMA CPle ECtt EFol EHoe ELan EMil EPla LHop MBri MGos MPla MRav MUlv SApp SEas SHBN SMac SPer SReu SSta WHCG WRus
'Innocence Variegatus'	See *P.* **'Innocence'**
§ *insignis*	MRav
x *lemoinei*	CTri EBee EMil MGos NNor SEas SHBN WFar WGwG WStI
madrensis	LHop
– CD&R 1226	CHan
'Manteau d'Hermine' 🏆	Widely available
'Marjorie'	CHan CHar
¶ *mexicanus*	WPGP
microphyllus	CBot CHan CMHG EBre ESis LGre MBro MPla NHol SPer SReu SSpi WCot WHCG WPat WRTC WSHC WWat
'Minnesota Snowflake'	EBee ECtt EHic IOrc NCut NPro SBid
x *monstrosus* 'Monster'	SSte
'Mrs E.L. Robinson'	CBlo ECtt EPla SBid WWoo
'Natchez'	EBar ECtt MPla SPan
'Perryhill'	SPer
§ *purpurascens*	MRav SSta
§ 'Silberregen'	CPle ECtt IOrc MBal MBar MGos MUlv NBee SBid SEas SHBN SRms WAbe WDin WPat WWat
◆ Silver Showers	See *P.* **'Silberregen'**
'Snowflake'	EBre EMil MBal NHol SEas WAbe WLRN
'Souvenir de Billiard'	See *P. insignis*
subcanus	GOrc MRav
'Sybille' 🏆	CMHG ENot GOrc MBri MRav SBid SPer SPla SRms SSpi SSta WHCG WKif WSHC WWat
tomentosus	CFil WHCG WPGP
'Virginal' 🏆	Widely available
'Virginal' LA '82	MBal MUlv
¶ 'Voie Lactée'	MRav
White Rock	COtt EBee LRHS MBal MBri SPer WLRN

PHILESIA (Philesiaceae)

buxifolia	See *P. magellanica*
§ *magellanica*	EMil GGGa GSki MBal SArc SBid SPer SSpi WBod WCru

PHILLYREA (Oleaceae)

angustifolia	CFil CHan COtt CPle SHFr WPGP WWat
– f. *rosmarinifolia*	CFil WPGP
decora	See *Osmanthus decorus*
§ *latifolia*	CFil CPle SArc SHBN SSpi WWat

media	See ***P. latifolia***

PHILODENDRON (Araceae)

§ ***angustisectum*** 🏆	MBri
elegans	See ***P. angustisectum***
'Emerald Queen'	MBri
epipremnum	See ***Epipremnum pinnatum***
erubescens 🏆	MBri
– 'Burgundy' 🏆	MBri
– 'Imperial Red'	MBri
– 'Red Emerald'	CHal EBak MBri
melanochrysum	MBri
'New Red'	MBri
panduriforme	See ***P. bipennifolium***
pedatum	MBri
'Purple Queen'	MBri
radiatum	MBri
scandens 🏆	CHal
sodiroi	See ***P. ornatum***
tuxtlanum 'Royal Queen'	MBri
– 'Tuxtla'	MBri

PHLEBODIUM See POLYPODIUM

PHLEUM (Poaceae)

hirsutum	ETPC
pratense	EHoe EPla
– subsp. ***bertolonii***	CKin

PHLOMIS † (Lamiaceae)

alpina	WCru
* ***anatolica***	CHan CKni EFou ELan LRHS
* – 'Lloyd's Variety'	CAbP CChu CKni EHic ELan EPla GCal LHop MSte SBid SMad SPan WPen WWat
angustifolia	SBid
¶ aff. ***anisodonta***	WPhl
armeniaca	SIgm
atropurpurea	EMon WPhl
betonicoides	WPhl
– B&L 12600	EMon
bourgaei JMT 260	WPhl
– 'Whirling Dervish' JMT 271	WPhl
bovei subsp. ***maroccana***	CBot CChu CHan CPle CRDP EPPr EPla GCal LFis NLak NTow SAxl WCot WPbr WPhl WWat
breviflora	WPhl
cancellata	CHan
cashmeriana	CAbb CBot CGle CHan CPle ECha SPan WPhl
– CC&MR 31	LKoh
chrysophylla 🏆	CAbP CBot CChu CHan CMil CPle CSam ELan MBlu MDun NTow SBid SDix SDry SPan SPer SRms WPhl WWat
crinita	SWas WPhl
cypria	WPhl
§ 'Edward Bowles'	SDry SPan WCot WCru WPhl
fruticosa 🏆	CArn CB&S CBot CChr CPle EBre ELan EMil ENot GOrc GPoy LHol LHop MBal MBri MWat NFla SDix SHBN SIde SMad SPer SUsu WDin WPLl WPhl WSHC WWat WWin
¶ – SCH 3149	WHCr
grandiflora	CBot CChu ELan SEND
– JMT 256	WPhl
italica	CB&S CBot CHad CHan ELan EMil IDee LFis LHil LHol LHop NBir NSti SBid SChu SPer SSpi SUsu WCot WCru WEas WFar WHer WPbr WPhl WSHC WWat WWin WWye
lanata	CAbP CAbb CChu CHan CMil ELan EPPr IDee LHop SBid SBla SDry SPan SPer WEas WPhl WRHF WWat WWye
leucophracta	CKni EFou LRHS
– 'Golden Janissary' JMT 255	WPhl
longifolia	CBot CHad CHan SPer WCru
– var. ***bailanica***	CKni CPle EMon LRHS WWat
– var. ***longifolia***	WPhl
lunariifolia JMT 258	WPhl
lychnitis	WPhl
lycia	CHad CHan CKni EFou LRHS SEND SIgm WPhl
monocephala	WPhl
nissolii JMT 268	WPhl
platystegia	WPhl
purpurea	CHan CPle CSam EFou ELan NBir SBid WCot WPhl WSHC
purpurea alba	CBot CHan LHop SBid WPhl WSHC
purpurea subsp. ***almeriensis***	CHan NLak WPhl
rigida	WCru
§ ***russeliana*** 🏆	CArn CChu CHan CSev ECha EFou ELan EPla EPri GMac LHol LLWP MBri MCLN MFir MNrw NBro NFai SHBN SPer WAbb WBea WCru WEas WOak WPer WPhl WSHC WWat WWye
samia Boissier	See ***P. russeliana***
– Linnaeus JMT 285	WPhl
sp. B&SWJ 2210	WCru
tuberosa	CBot CFir CHan CMil CPou EGar EPPr GCal SIgm SOkh WCot WCru WPhl
– 'Amazone'	EAst EBee ECha EFou NPSI WHil
viscosa hort.	See ***P. russeliana***
– Poiret	WPhl

PHLOX † (Polemoniaceae)

adsurgens 🏆	ITim SBla WAbe
– 'Alba'	CMea NHar SBla
– 'Red Buttes'	CGle CLyd ELan EPot LHop NTow SAga SBla SCro
– 'Wagon Wheel'	CLyd EBre ELan EPot EWes LBee LGan LHop MHig NGre NHar NMen SMrm SUsu WFar WHal WPat WRus WWin
albomarginata	CGra
amoena hort.	See ***P.*** × ***procumbens***
× ***arendsii*** 'Anja'	WCot
– 'Hilda'	EMon WCot
– 'Lisbeth'	WCot
– 'Luc's Lilac'	EFou MHlr WCot
¶ – 'Suzanne'	WCot
austromontana	EPot NWCA
bifida	CMea CPBP ITim LFlo MBro NHol WThi WWin
– 'Alba'	CGra EHyt
– blue	CMea ELan LBee LRHS SUsu
– 'Colvin's White'	CLyd CPBP EPot LBee SBla WPer
– 'Minima Colvin'	ECtt EPot

– 'Petticoat'	CLyd CPBP LBee MDHE NCat NGre SBla SWas
– 'Ralph Haywood'	CLyd MHig NGre
– 'Starbrite'	CLyd CMea CPBP ITim LBee MBro MDHE MHig MOne NGre NMen SBla WThi
– 'Sunset'	SBla
* – 'The Fi'	EWes NCat WIvy
'Black Buttes'	CLyd CPBP EPot NNrd NTow WIvy
'Bleeklila'	WCot
borealis	CShe ELan GDra ITim WThi
* ***borealis arctica***	EPot
caespitosa	CLyd CMea CPBP EPot EWes GCHN ITim NHed NMen
– subsp. ***condensata***	NWCA
canadensis	See ***P. divaricata***
carolina 'Bill Baker'	Widely available
– 'Magnificence'	EBee EMon GBuc MSte SOkh
– 'Miss Lingard' ♀	CGle CSam EBee EFou EMan EMon GBuc GCal LRHS MBel MGrG MMil MSte NTow SDix SMrm SOkh WCot WMaN
'Casablanca'	EFou
* 'Chanel'	MLan
'Charles Ricardo'	CMil ERav GBuc LFlo MBro NCat NTow SMrm SSca SUsu SWas SWat WHoo WPbr WPyg WRus
'Chattahoochee'	See ***P. divaricata*** subsp. ***laphamii***
covillei	CPBP GCrs
'Daniel's Cushion'	See ***P. subulata*** **'McDaniel's Cushion'**
◆ ***depressa***	See ***P. multiflora*** subsp. ***depressa***
diffusa	LHop
§ ***divaricata*** ♀	EMou MSte WPer WRus WWin
– f. ***albiflora***	ELan
– 'Blue Dreams'	CFir CRDP EBee ECha GBuc LCom MAvo MSte SAga SAxl SCro SLod SMrm SUsu SWas SWat WPbr WRHF
– 'Blue Perfume'	EFou
– 'Clouds of Perfume'	EFou GBri MRav NCat SBla SMrm SWat WRus
– 'Dirigo Ice'	CLyd CMil EMan ERav LFis LFlo LGre SBla WIvy WRHF WRus
– 'Eco Texas Purple'	CGra CRDP
– 'Fuller's White'	CLyd MAvo WPbr
§ – subsp. ***laphamii***	CGra CLyd EBre EWes LCom LFlo NVic SBla WCru WFoF WHer WKif WRus WThi
– – 'Chattahoochee' ♀	CBot CMea CSpe EBre ELan EMNN EPot EWes GMac LBee LHop MBro NGre NSti NWes SBla SIng SLod SMrm SUsu WAbe WMaN WPat WSHC WWin
– – 'Chattahoochee Variegated'	EHyt EWes LHop LRHS SUsu WCot
– 'May Breeze'	CLyd CRDP EBee EBre ECha EMan GMaP LCom LHop MHar MHlr MNrw MSte NGar SAga SAxl SBla SMrm SWas WCot WHil WIvy WPbr WRHF WRus
– 'White Perfume'	MRav
douglasii	EBar NHol NWCA SOkh SRms
– 'Apollo'	CLyd ELan EMNN EPot GDra MHig NGre NHol NMen WAbe WWin
– 'Boothman's Variety' ♀	CGle CLyd CShe ECha ELan EPar EPot MHig MPla MWat NMen SAlw SBod SRms WEas WWin
– 'Concorde'	GDra NHar
– 'Crackerjack' ♀	CLyd CShe ELan EMNN EPot ESis GAbr GDra ITim LBee MHig MPla MWat NGre NHar NMen NRoo SBod SIng STre WAbe WDav
– 'Eva'	CLyd CNic EBre ELan EMNN EPot GTou LBee MHig MOne MRav NBir NGre NHar NHol NRoo SBod SMrm WPer WThi WWin
– 'Galaxy'	CLyd ESis EWes GDra NHar
– 'Holden Variety'	NHol
– 'Ice Mountain'	ECho ELan IHos NPri SMrm WLRN
– 'Iceberg' ♀	CLyd EPot GDra ITim NHar NHol NMen SIng WAbe WWin
– 'J.A. Hibberson'	CLyd EPot ESis MHig SIng WThi
◆ – Lilac Queen	See ***P. douglasii*** **'Lilakönigin'**
§ – 'Lilakönigin'	CLyd
¶ – x ***multiflora*** subsp. ***depressa***	MBro WDav
– 'Red Admiral' ♀	CMHG CShe EBre EMNN EPot EWes GCHN GDra IHos MHig MOne NHar NHol NMen NNrd NRoo SAlw SBod SMrm
– 'Rose Cushion'	CNic EWes GDra LRHS MDHE MPla NHol SIng
– 'Rose Queen'	CLyd CMHG ESis GDra
– 'Rosea'	EBre ELan EMNN EPar LBee MBal MRav NGre NRoo SBod SMer SMrm SSmi
– 'Silver Rose'	GTou SAlw
– 'Sprite'	SRms
– 'Tycoon'	See ***P. subulata*** **'Tamaongalei'**
– 'Violet Queen'	ELan EMNN EWes GDra NHar NHol NNrd
– 'Waterloo'	CLyd CPBP CTri EBre EPot GAri LHop MOne MRav NHar NHol NMen SChu WWin
'Herfstsering'	EFou
'Hesperis'	EFou
¶ ***hirsuta***	NWCA WDav
hoodii	CLyd CPBP ECho EPot SIde
'Hortensia'	EFou
'Kelly's Eye' ♀	CLyd CMHG CSam ECha ECtt ELan EMNN EPot GAbr LBee LHop MHig MMil NMen NRoo SBod SIng SWas WPer
kelseyi	NWCA WDav
– 'Rosette'	CLyd EPot ESis LBee MHig NGre NMen WOMN WPer
¶ ***longifolia***	WDav
maculata	NOrc WPer
– 'Alba'	WCot
– 'Alpha' ♀	CArc CGle EBre ECha EFou GCHN GMaP GMac MBri MRav MUlv NHol NOrc NRoo NVic SBla SChu SCro SMrm SPer WMaN WRus
◆ – Avalanche	See ***P. maculata*** **'Schneelawine'**
– 'Delta'	CArc EBee EBre EFou NCut NSti SPla WHil WMaN WRus
– 'Good White'	SMrm

* – 'Natascha'	CArc EBee EBre EFou EWes GBuc MBri SPer SPla WCot WHil WPbr
– 'Omega' 🏆	CArc CDec CHad CHan EFou EOrc GCHN GMaP GMac MBri MBro MRav MUlv NRoo NSti SChu SMrm SPer SSpi WByw WMaN WPer WRus WSHC
– 'Rosalinde'	EFou MBel MRav NRoo SChu WMaN
§ – 'Schneelawine'	EBee EBre EFou MRav NCat WRus
mesoleuca	See ***P. nana*** subsp. ***ensifolia***
Mexican Hybrids	See ***P. nana***
'Millstream'	See ***P. × procumbens* 'Millstream'**
'Millstream Jupiter'	NHol
missoulensis	SIng
'Mrs Campbell'	See ***P. paniculata* 'Elizabeth Campbell'**
§ ***nana*** subsp. ***ensifolia***	EPot
nivalis	MHig NMen
– 'Camla'	CLyd ECha ELan EPot ITim LHop WPat WThi
– 'Jill Alexander'	NHol
– 'Nivea'	LBee NGre NTow WLRN
paniculata	CHad CShe NNor SChu SDix WCot WOld WRHF
– 'A.E. Amos'	CTri EFou ERou
– 'Aida'	CB&S EFou EGar ERou MWat
– var. ***alba***	CBos GCal SDix WCot WCra
– 'Alba Grandiflora' 🏆	MUlv WEas
– 'Albert Leo Schlageter' 🏆	CShe ERou SRms WMer
– 'Amethyst'	CDoC CFir CSam EBar EBee EBre EFou EGar EPfP ERou GDTE LFis MBel NBir WCra WHil WHoo WPer WWoo
– 'Annie Laurie'	SRms
– 'Anthony Six'	WPer
– 'Balmoral'	CDoC CGle CM&M ECtt MRav MSte NCat NFla NMir SChu SMrm SWat WGwG WHil WLRN WWoo
– 'Barnwell'	EFou ELan WMer
– 'Betty Symons-Jeune'	ERou
– 'Bill Green'	EBee EBre ECGP LBuc LRHS SMrm
– 'Blue Boy'	CM&M EFou ERou NCut WCra WMer
– 'Blue Ice' 🏆	CMGP CSev EBee EBre EFou ELan EMan MWat NRoo SMrm SUsu WCot WLRN WWoo
– 'Blue Moon'	GDTE
– 'Blue Paradise'	EFou LGre SMrm
– 'Blushing Bride'	SRms
– 'Bonny Maid'	CBla
– 'Border Gem'	CB&S CDoC EBre ECED EFou EMan EMon ENot MHlr MSte NCut NRoo SMrm SWat WCot
– 'Branklyn'	EBre MArl MGrG MRav
– 'Brigadier' 🏆	CBla CDoC CSam CTri ELan EMan ENot GDTE GMaP MFir MWat NRoo SMrm SPer SSoC
– 'Bright Eyes' 🏆	CBla CBlo COtt EBre EFou EPfP LRHS MArl NRoo SUsu
– 'Caroline van den Berg'	CTri EGar ERou SMer SRms WCot
– 'Cecil Hanbury'	CBlo CDoC ERou SRms WHoo WWoo
– 'Charmaine'	CBla
– 'Chintz'	SRms
– 'Cinderella'	CDoC ERou NPri WMer
– 'Cool of the Evening'	CBla CDec WCot
– 'Count Zeppelin'	See ***P. paniculata* 'Graf Zeppelin'**
– 'Darwin's Joyce'	EFou
– 'Dodo Hanbury Forbes' 🏆	CBla CKel EGar
– 'Dresden China'	ERou GCra
¶ – 'Düsterlohe'	CArc GBuc SMrm
– 'Eclaireur'	EBee
– 'Elie'	LBuc LFis
– 'Elizabeth Arden'	EFou ERou MSte WMaN WMer
– 'Endurance'	ERou
– 'Etoile de Paris'	SWas
– 'Europe'	CB&S CGle CMGP EBee EFou ELan EMan ERou MFir MWat NFai SMrm SPer WGwG WHil WHoo WMer
– 'Eva Cullum'	CM&M CTri EBre EFou LHop MArl MRav NFai NRoo SHel WCot
– 'Eventide' 🏆	CDoC EBre ECED ECtt EFou EGar EHal ENot ERou MArl NFla NMir SMrm SOkh SPer WCot WCra
– 'Excelsior'	CBlo CDoC EBre MRav
– 'Fairy's Petticoat'	MWat WCot
– 'Firefly'	EFou
– 'Flamingo'	EBar EBre EFou
– 'Franz Schubert'	CTri EBee EBre EFou EGar EMan MHlr MTis NRoo SHFr WCot WSan WWoo
§ – 'Frau A. von Mauthner'	LBuc
§ – 'Fujiyama' 🏆	CArc CKel CSam EBee EBre ECha EFou EMon EOrc GCra LHop LLWP MSte MWat NBir NRoo NSti NWes SApp SHel SMad SMrm WAbb WCot WEas WHil WMaN WThi WWoo
– 'Glamis'	CBla MWat
§ – 'Graf Zeppelin'	CBla ELan MWat NCat SRms WMer
– 'Hampton Court'	NBrk WCot
– 'Harewood'	ERou
– 'Harlequin' (v)	EBre ECha GBuc MRav SPla WCot
– 'Iceberg'	MFir
– 'Iris'	CArc GBuc SMrm SRms SWas
– 'Jules Sandeau'	WWeb
§ – 'Juliglut'	ELan MWat NCat WCot
◆ – July Glow	See ***P. paniculata* 'Juliglut'**
– 'Kirmesländler'	CB&S EBee ERou
– 'Lady Clare'	SRms
– 'Latest Red'	See ***P. paniculata* 'Spätrot'**
* – 'Laura'	COtt LFis
§ – 'Lavendelwolke'	ELan
◆ – Lavender Cloud	See ***P. paniculata* 'Lavendelwolke'**
– 'Le Mahdi' 🏆	ELan MWat SRms WCot WCra
– 'Lilac Time'	CBla CPou CWan EBee GLil MWat NCat
– 'Look Again'	ERou
– 'Mary Fox'	CSam ERou MRav NRoo
– 'Mia Ruys'	EFou EHal ERou MArl WMer
– 'Mies Copijn'	CDoC CShe GMaP WMer
– 'Miss Kelly'	EBee
* – 'Miss Pepper'	CM&M EBee EFou LFis SSte WHil

* – 'Monica Lynden-Bell'	WCot
– 'Mother of Pearl' ♀	CBla CGle CHad CMGP CMil EBre EFou ELan MHlr MWat NCat NVic SChu SPer WCot WLRN
– 'Mount Fujiyama'	See ***P. paniculata* 'Fujiyama'**
– 'Mrs A.E. Jeans'	SRms
– 'Mrs Fincham'	LFis
– 'Newbird'	ERou SRms
* – 'Nicky'	EBee EFou LFis MRav NPri SSte WHil
– 'Norah Leigh' (v)	CArc CBot CRow EBee EBre ECha EFou EHoe ELan EMon EOrc GCal LGre LHop MTho MWat NPer NRoo SBla SChu SCro WCot WHil WPbr WWin
– 'Orange Perfection'	CB&S CBlo CM&M EBar EPfP NCut NPri
– 'Othello'	CBla
– 'Otley Choice'	CMil EMan LFis MSte MWat NRoo NSti SCoo SMrm WLRN
– 'Pastorale'	MWat WCot
– 'Pax'	EMon
– 'Pike'	MHlr WCot
– 'Pink Posy' (v)	SCoo SPer
– 'Prince of Orange' ♀	CBla CGle CMGP CSam EBre EFou ELan EMan ERou MRav MUlv MWat NCat NRoo SAga SMrm SPer SSoC WCot WGwG
– 'Prospero' ♀	CBla CMil EBee EBre EMan EOrc LFis MBel MRav NRoo SChu SMrm SPer SUsu WCot WOld
– 'Rapture'	MWat
– 'Red Indian'	EBre ERou MWat
– 'Rembrandt'	CShe ERou WCot
– 'Rheinländer'	WPer
– 'Rijnstroom'	CB&S ECot EFou ERou GLil LFis MBel NCat NFai SMrm WCot WGwG WHoo WTyr WWoo
– 'Rosa Spier'	WMer
– 'Rougham Supreme'	ERou
– 'Russian Violet'	MRav MWat
– 'San Antonio'	MRav NCat SMrm WCot WLRN
– 'Sandringham'	CDec CSam CTri EBee EBre ELan EMan ENot MArl MNrw MRav MSte MUlv NBir NCat NFla NLak NMir NRoo NVic SChu SMrm SPer
– 'Schneerausch'	WCot
– 'Septemberglut'	EBee SSte WHil
– 'Silver Salmon'	WCot
– 'Sir John Falstaff'	WMer
– 'Sir Malcolm Campbell'	ERou
– 'Skylight'	CShe MGrG MWat NCat SMrm SPer SSte SUsu WCot WGwG WLRN WWoo
¶ – 'Snowball'	NFla
– 'Snowdrift'	ERou
§ – 'Spätrot'	EFou WMer
– 'Spitfire'	See ***P. paniculata* 'Frau A. von Mauthner'**
– 'Starfire'	CB&S CBla CGle CSam EBar EBre EFou ELan ENot ERou GMaP LFis MArl MFir MHlr MRav NRoo NSti SChu SPer WCot WHil WHoo WMer WRus
– 'Steeple Bumpstead'	WCot
– 'Sternhimmel'	CGra ERou LGre

– 'Tenor'	CFir CM&M EBee ECGP EFou MSte NCut NFla NMir NPri SMrm SSea WFar WHil WTyr WWoo
– 'The King'	WCra
– 'Toits de Paris'	EFou MLLN MWat
– 'Úspech'	EFou
– 'Vintage Wine'	CTri LBuc WMer
¶ – 'Violetta Gloriosa'	EFou
– 'White Admiral' ♀	CB&S CBla CGle CHad CM&M EBar EBre ELan ENot EOrc GMaP GMac MBel MRav MUlv MWat NFai NFla NRoo SChu SMrm SPer WGwG WHil WHoo WMer WTyr
– 'William Ramsay'	CTri ELan
– 'Windsor' ♀	CBla CMGP EFou ERou LFis MBel MGrG MTis NFla NMir SCoo SMrm
pilosa	CMGP EBre ECha EFou NSti SMrm SUsu WRus
§ × ***procumbens*** 'Millstream' ♀	CGra ELan LCom LHop NTow SAga SBla WOMN WThi WWin
– 'Variegata'	CBot CGra CPBP ECha EHyt ELan EMNN ESis MHig MPla MTho NGre NHol NNor NRoo NWCA SBla SMrm WAbe WDav WPat WThi WWin
× ***rugellii***	NHol SRms WWin
stolonifera	EPar MHar MNrw MTho SAga WCot WMer WPbr
– 'Ariane'	ECha ELan EPar LCom LHop MAvo SAga SBla SMrm SWas SWat WAbe WHal WHer WPbr WWin
– 'Blue Ridge' ♀	CFir CHan CPea CSpe ECha EGle ELan EMan EPar GBuc LCom LFis LHop NGre NHar NPSI NRoo SAga SBla SMrm SRms SSca SWat WSan WWin
– 'Bob's Motley' (v)	WCot
¶ – 'Bruce's White'	CGra
– 'Compact Pink'	LHop NCat SAga SWas
– 'Fran's Purple'	CGra CLyd CRDP LCom NCat NHar SCro SWas WAbe WDav
– 'Mary Belle Frey'	CDec CNic CPBP ECha EMan LCom LHop MSte SAga SBla SCro SMrm SWas WWin
– 'Pink Ridge'	CGra GBuc NCut SIng WDav
– variegated	MHlr MRav NCat WCot WPen
– 'Violet Vere'	CLyd CMil CPBP EGle GBuc LCom LHop MBro MHlr MNrw SAga SBla SIng SLod SMrm SUsu WHal WHoo WKif WPyg WRus
subulata	EPar NWCA
– 'Alexander's Surprise'	CGle CMea CShe EBre ECtt EPot GAbr GCHN LHop MBal NBir NCat NGre NHol NMen SChu
– 'Amazing Grace'	CTri ELan EPot EWes LHop MOne MPla NMen NPri NRoo NSla SAlw SChu WAbe WPbr WPer WThi WWin
– 'Apple Blossom'	GAbr GDra NPri SChu WLRN
– 'Atropurpurea'	EBre GCHN NNor WWin
– 'Beauty of Ronsdorf'	See ***P. subulata* 'Ronsdorfer Schöne'**
– 'Betty'	CTri ECtt EMNN MDHE NMen NRoo WPer
– 'Blue Eyes'	See ***P. subulata* 'Oakington Blue Eyes'**

– 'Blue Saucer' EPot MDHE NHol NNrd
– 'Bonita' EMNN GAri LBee MRav NMen NPri NRoo SAlw SMer SMrm SWas WWin
– 'Bressingham Blue Eyes' See ***P. subulata* 'Oakington Blue Eyes'**
– 'Brightness' CTri GCHN GTou LRHS SIng
– subsp. ***brittonii*** 'Rosea' EPot NHol WPer
– 'Candy Stripe' EPfP
– 'Coral Eye' EPfP
– 'Daisy Hill' NHol
– 'Drumm' See ***P. subulata* 'Tamaongalei'**
– 'Emerald Cushion' EMan
– 'Emerald Cushion Blue' CLyd EBre ELan GTou LBee LGan MBal NHol NNrd NRoo SBod SMrm SSmi WAbe WPer WThi
– 'Fairy' WPer
– 'G.F. Wilson' CLyd CMea CShe ECha ECtt ELan GTou LBee LGro MBal MHig MWat NGre NMen NNor NNrd NRoo NVic SChu SSca SSmi WAbe WDav WPer WWin
– 'Greencourt Purple' NCat
* – 'Holly' EPot MDHE
– 'Jupiter' SChu
– 'Kimono' See ***P. subulata* 'Tamaongalei'**
§ – 'Maischnee' CLyd EBre ECtt ELan EMNN EPot GAbr LBee LGro LHop MBal MHig MOne MPla MWat NGre NNor NNrd NRoo SMrm WEas WWin
◆ – May Snow = 'Maischnee' See ***P. subulata* 'Maischnee'**
– 'Marjorie' CLyd ECtt ELan EMNN MBal MHar MOne NMen NPri SChu SSca WEas WLRN
§ – 'McDaniel's Cushion' ♀ CLyd CMHG CShe EBre ECha ELan EMNN EPot ESis GTou ITim LBee MHig MMil NGre NMen NNor NRoo WHil WPer WWin
– 'Mikado' See ***P. subulata* 'Tamaongalei'**
– 'Model' LGro MWat NSla
– 'Moonlight' CLyd ECtt NNrd SAga SLod SWas WPer WRHF
– 'Nelsonii' CShe
* – 'Nettleton Variation' CGra CMea CPBP EDAr EPot LHop WAbe
§ – 'Oakington Blue Eyes' CMHG EBre EPar GCHN GDra LBee NGre NNrd NRoo SMrm SRms WPer
– 'Pink Pearl' EWes
– 'Red Wings' ♀ CPBP EBre ECtt GCHN MBal MRav NMen NNor NPri NRoo SAga SAlw SRms
§ – 'Ronsdorfer Schöne' EPot LBee NNrd
– 'Samson' CNic ELan GAbr GTou LBee MHar SBod SMer WPer WThi WWin
– 'Scarlet Flame' EBre ECha ECtt ELan EMNN GDra LGro MBal MOne MRav MWat NHol SBod SMrm WPer WWin
– 'Schneewittchen' CLyd NHol
– 'Sensation' GTou SRms
– 'Snow Queen' See ***P. subulata* 'Maischnee'**
– 'Southcroft' CGra
– 'Starglow' GTou LRHS MOne SIde SIng WPer
§ – 'Tamaongalei' CGra CLyd CMea CMil EDAr EHyt EMan EWes GDra LHop MDHE MNrw NCat NHar NHol NRoo SAga SBla SChu SCoo SIde SLod SMrm SRms SUsu SWas WDav WMaN WRHF WWin
– 'Temiskaming' CGra CMHG EBre ECha ELan EMNN EWes GCHN GDra LGro MHar NGre NMen NRoo SChu SRms WAbe WEas
– violet seedling CLyd NHol
– 'White Delight' CLyd EBre ECha ECtt ELan EMNN GCHN GTou MHig MOne NHol NMen NRoo SBod SChu SRms WPer
– 'White Swan' WThi
'Sweet William' EFou
'Vivid' EDAr LRHS MDHE SAlw

PHOEBE (Lauraceae)

See Plant Deletions

PHOENICAULIS (Brassicaceae)

§ ***cheiranthoides*** MFos NHol NTow WOMN

PHOENIX (Arecaceae)

canariensis ♀ CBrP CGre CHEx CTbh CTrC EOas LPal MBri NPal SEND
dactylifera (F) LPal
paludosa LPal
reclinata NPal
roebelenii ♀ CBrP CTrC LPal MBri
rupicola LPal
sylvestris LPal
theophrasti CFil LPal NPal

PHORMIUM † (Agavaceae)

'Apricot Queen' (v) CAbb CB&S CDoC CTrC EFou GQui IBlr IOrc MBal
¶ Ballyrogan variegated IBlr
'Black Edge' MRav
'Bronze Baby' CAbb CB&S CEnd CLTr CSam CTrC EB&P ECtt EHoe ELan EMil GQui IBlr IOrc ISea LPan MBal MNrw MSte MWat SHBN SPer SPla WPat WRTC WStI WWat
colensoi See ***P. cookianum***
§ ***cookianum*** ♀ CAgr CB&S CHEx CHan CTrC CTrw EMil GIsl IBlr LPal MAll MBal MGos SArc WWat
– 'Alpinum Purpureum' See ***P. tenax* 'Nanum Purpureum'**
* – 'Flamingo' SApp
– subsp. ***hookeri*** 'Cream Delight' (v) ♀ CAbb CB&S CEnd EBee EBre EHoe ELan ENot IOrc LHil MBal MBlu NFla SAga SHBN SPer
– – 'Tricolor' ♀ CB&S CFil CHEx CMGP CTrC EBre ELan ENot EPPr EPla IBlr IOrc ISea MBal SApp SArc SHBN SRms SSpi WDin WWye
* 'Copper Beauty' CBlo CDoC COtt WLRN
'Dark Delight' CB&S CDoC IBlr
'Dazzler' (v) EBee IBlr IOrc MBal SHhN
'Duet' (v) ♀ CB&S CDoC COtt CTrC EHoe IBlr IOrc
'Dusky Chief' CTrC
* 'Emerald Pink' COtt CTrC EBee
'Evening Glow' IBlr SApp

'Gold Sword' (v)	CDoC COtt EFou IBlr
'Guardsman' (v)	IBlr
'Jack Spratt' (v)	COtt ECou EHoe IBlr IOrc SApp
'Jester'	CB&S COtt EFou EHoe EWll GQui IBlr SApp SPla
§ 'Maori Chief' (v)	CB&S CFil EBee GQui IBlr IOrc SHBN WLRN
'Maori Eclipse'	CBlo
§ 'Maori Maiden' (v)	CB&S CDoC CSam EHoe GQui IOrc MBal NBrk SMad
§ 'Maori Queen' (v)	CB&S CDoC EFou EHic GQui IBlr IOrc WLRN
§ 'Maori Sunrise' (v)	CAbb CB&S CBlo CDoC EBee IBlr IOrc MSte SAga SSoC WLRN WWye
'Pink Panther' (v)	CAbb CB&S CDoC CKni CTrC EFou ELan EWll GQui IBlr IOrc SPla
* 'Pink Stripe'	CTrC EBee IBlr
¶ 'Platt's Black'	CAbb SMad
'Rainbow Chief'	See ***P.* 'Maori Chief'**
Rainbow Hybrids	CSpe MBal SEas
'Rainbow Maiden'	See ***P.* 'Maori Maiden'**
'Rainbow Queen'	See ***P.* 'Maori Queen'**
'Rainbow Sunrise'	See ***P.* 'Maori Sunrise'**
'Sea Jade'	IBlr
'Sundowner' (v) 🏆	CB&S CSpe CTrC EBre ELan EMil ENot GQui IBlr IOrc MBal MGos SHBN SMad SPla SSoC WFar WStI
'Sunset' (v)	IBlr IOrc
'Surfer' (v)	COtt EHoe IBlr IOrc LRHS WLeb
tenax 🏆	CAgr CB&S CHEx EAst ELan EMil ENot EOas ISea LPan MBal MNrw MWat NNor SArc SMad SPer SReu SSoC SVen WBod WCot WDin WOld WWat
– 'Co-ordination'	CAbb IBlr SApp SMad WBcn
* – 'Dwarf'	EMil IBlr
* ***tenax lineatum***	CTrC EBee SEND
§ ***tenax*** 'Nanum Purpureum' 🏆	CHad CRDP IBlr MAsh SAxl SEND SWas
– Purpureum Group 🏆	CAbb CB&S CBot CElw CGre CHEx CHad CSpe EBre EHoe ELan EMil ENot EOas IOrc ISea MBal MSte SEND SEas SMad SPer SSoC WDin
– 'Radiance' (v)	IBlr MBal
– 'Rainbow Queen'	See ***P.* 'Maori Queen'**
– 'Rainbow Sunrise'	See ***P.* 'Maori Sunrise'**
– 'Variegatum' 🏆	CFil CHEx IBlr LPal LPan MBal SArc SEND SRms WPat
– 'Veitchianum' (v)	IBlr SHig
– 'Yellow Queen'	ESiP
'Thumbelina'	CB&S EHoe MSte SApp
'Tom Thumb'	CB&S IOrc WDin
'Yellow Wave' (v) 🏆	CAbb CB&S CDoC CEnd CHEx CSte CTrC EBre EHoe ELan EMil IBlr IOrc MBal SMad SPer SPla SReu SRms WAbe WDin

PHOTINIA † (Rosaceae)

§ ***arbutifolia***	CPle MAll
beauverdiana 🏆	CB&S CChu CPle CTho SRms WWat
§ ***davidiana***	CPle CTrw ELan EMil GRei GWht IOrc LHop MBal MBar MBri MGos MRav MWat SEas SPer SRms WNor WTyr WWat
– 'Palette' (v)	Widely available
– var. ***undulata***	CMHG MRav
– – 'Fructu Luteo'	CMHG CPle CTrw EHic EPla MBri MRav WWat
– – 'Prostrata'	EBee ELan MBar NHol SPer WWat
× ***fraseri***	CMCN ISea
– 'Birmingham'	CChu CLan CWLN EHoe LPan MBal SHBN SRms WDin WPyg WSHC WWeb
– 'Red Robin' 🏆	Widely available
– 'Robusta' 🏆	CBlo CWLN MBal WWat
§ – 'Rubens'	ELan MBri SDry SPer SPla SSta WPat WPyg WRTC WWat
§ ***glabra*** 'Parfait' (v)	CPle ELan EWll LHop MBal MUlv SDry SHBN SPer WFar WPat WPyg WWeb
– 'Pink Lady'	See ***P. glabra* 'Parfait'**
– 'Rubens'	See ***P.* × *fraseri* 'Rubens'**
– 'Variegata'	See ***P. glabra* 'Parfait'**
glomerata	CHEx CMHG
lasiogyna	CMCN
microphylla SF 92307	ISea
§ 'Redstart' 🏆	CEnd CPle EPfP MGos MUlv SPer SSta SSto WWat
§ ***serratifolia***	CBot CHEx CPle MBal SArc SDry SPer SSta WPat WPyg WRTC WWat
serrulata	See ***P. serratifolia***
villosa 🏆	CAbP CChu CPle CTho GAri IOrc MBal MBar SPer
– var. ***laevis***	CB&S

PHRAGMITES (Poaceae)

§ ***australis***	CBen GBin LPBA NDea SWat
australis giganteus	See ***P. australis*** subsp. ***altissimus***
australis 'Variegatus'	CBen CCuc CInt CRDP EHoe EMFW EPPr EPla ESOG ETPC IBlr MAvo MUlv SMad SWyc WChe WRus
communis	See ***P. australis***
karka 'Variegatus'	WChe

PHUOPSIS (Rubiaceae)

§ ***stylosa***	CElw CLTr CMea CSev EAst ECha ELan EMar EMil LGan MFir NBro NRoo NSti SChu SHFr SMac SRms SSpe WBea WFar WHal WOve WPer WWhi WWin WWye
– 'Purpurea'	CElw CMea ECha ELan LCot MNrw MRav NBrk NCat NChi SChu WByw WGwy WHal

PHYGELIUS † (Scrophulariaceae)

aequalis	CBot CFee CGle CKno CMHG CSev ELan EMil EOrc EPla LFis MFir MNrw SChu SDix SMac SSpi SUsu WPer WPri WSHC WSan WWat WWhi
aequalis albus	See ***P. aequalis* 'Yellow Trumpet'**
aequalis 'Aureus'	See ***P. aequalis* 'Yellow Trumpet'**
– 'Cream Trumpet'	See ***P. aequalis* 'Yellow Trumpet'**
– 'Indian Chief'	See ***P.* × *rectus* 'African Queen'**

* – 'Pink Trumpet'	CLTr EFou NNor SCoo SMrm
§ – 'Yellow Trumpet' 🏆	Widely available
capensis 🏆	CBot CGle CKno CLTr CMea CShe EBar ELan ENot EOrc EPla GOrc MAsh MBel NNor NRoo SHFr SMac SPer SRms WAbe WEas WHil WPer WWye
– × ***aequalis***	See ***P.*** × ***rectus***
capensis coccineus	CAbb CChe CKno CTrw EMil EOrc ISea MBal NFai SMad SSoC WBod
capensis orange	CKno EGar LHop
capensis roseus	CTrw
capensis S&SH 50	CHan
'Golden Gate'	See ***P. aequalis* 'Yellow Trumpet'**
* 'Janet's Jewel'	CKno SBid
§ × ***rectus***	EPla
§ – 'African Queen' 🏆	CFee CGle CKno EBar EBre ECtt EFou ELan EOrc EPla ESis LBlm LHop MBri MBro MPla MRav NBir NHol NTow SMac WBea WHil WMer WPer WRus WWin WWye
– 'Devil's Tears'	CAbb CFee CKno CMHG EBar EMil EOrc GGar LHop MBro NFai SAga SCro SMac WHil WHoo WMer WPer WWat WWeb WWye
– 'Moonraker'	CAbb CKno CLTr CMHG EBar ECtt EFol ELan EMil EOrc EPla ERav ESis GGar GMac LFis MAsh MBro NFai NRoo SMac SMad WBea WHoo WMer WWat
– 'Pink Elf'	CKno ELan EOrc ESis SMac
– 'Salmon Leap'	CAbb CKno CMHG EBar EBre EOrc GGar LHop MAsh MGrG NTow SHFr SMac WHal WHil WOve WPer WWeb
§ – 'Winchester Fanfare'	CAbb CKno CMHG EBre ELan EMil EOrc EPla ESis LFis LHil MBro MSCN SChu SCro SMac SOkh SPer WBea WEas WFar WHal WHoo WMer WPer WPyg WSHC WWat WWye
– 'Winton Fanfare'	See ***P.*** × ***rectus* 'Winchester Fanfare'**
'Trewidden Pink'	CKni CKno EHic LHop MAvo MBel MMil SMac WHoo WPbr WRus

PHYLA (Verbenaceae)

§ ***canescens***	WCru WHal
§ ***nodiflora***	CHal CNic ECha EEls SEND WPer WPri
– 'Alba'	CNic

PHYLICA (Rhamnaceae)

¶ ***ericoides***	MAll

× PHYLLIOPSIS (Ericaceae)

'Coppelia'	CMHG CNic EPot GGGa MAsh MBal MDun NHar NHol SSta WAbe WPat WPyg
hillieri 'Askival'	GGGa
– 'Pinocchio'	EPot GDra GGGa GTou MAsh MBal MDun NHar NHol WAbe WPat WPyg
'Hobgoblin'	EPot MBal WPat
¶ 'Mermaid'	GGGa WAbe
'Puck'	WAbe
'Sprite'	GCrs NHol WAbe WPat

PHYLLITIS See ASPLENIUM

PHYLLOCLADUS (Phyllocladaceae)

aspleniifolius var. ***alpinus***	CDoC

PHYLLODOCE † (Ericaceae)

aleutica	EPot GGGa MBal MBar MHig NHar SSta WAbe
§ – subsp. ***glanduliflora***	GDra MBal NHol
§ – – 'Flora Slack'	CMHG GGGa MBal MHig
– – white	See ***P. aleutica*** subsp. ***glanduliflora* 'Flora Slack'**
× ***alpina***	GDra
breweri	GDra GGGa
caerulea 🏆	GDra GGGa MBal MHig NHar NHol WAbe
caerulea japonica	See ***P. nipponica***
empetriformis	GDra GGGa MBal MBar MBri MGos MHig NHar NHed NHol SRms SSta WAbe
glanduliflora	See ***P. aleutica*** subsp. ***glanduliflora***
× ***intermedia***	GDra MBal
– 'Drummondii'	CMHG GGGa
– 'Fred Stoker'	CMHG GGGa MHig NHol
§ ***nipponica*** 🏆	GDra MBal NHar WAbe
– var. ***oblongo-ovata***	WAbe

PHYLLOSTACHYS † (Poaceae - Bambusoideae)

angusta	SBam SDry WJun
arcana	EPla ISta SBam SDry WJun
– 'Luteosulcata'	EPla SDry
§ ***atrovaginata***	EPla SBam SDry
aurea 🏆	CB&S CHEx CTrC CWLN EBee EFul EOas EPfP EPla GAri LNet LPan SArc SBam SDry SPla WJun WNor
– 'Flavescens Inversa'	EPla SBam SDry WJun
– 'Holochrysa'	CB&S EFul EPla SBam SDry WJun
– 'Koi'	EPla SBam SDry
– 'Variegata'	EFul EPla SBam SDry
aureosulcata	EBee EFul EJap EOas EPfP EPla SBam SDry WJun
– f. ***alata***	EPla SDry
– 'Aureocaulis'	CFil EFul EPla SBam SDry WJun
– 'Harbin'	SDry
– 'Spectabilis'	EFul EOas EPla LNet SBam SDry WJun
bambusoides	CB&S EJap EPla SBam SDix SDry WJun
§ – 'Allgold'	EPla SBam SDry
– 'Castilloni' 🏆	CB&S EFul EPla LNet SBam SDix SDry WJun
– 'Castilloni Inversa'	EPla SBam SDry WJun
◆ – Holochrysa	See ***P. bambusoides* 'Allgold'**
– 'Katashibo'	EPla
– 'Kawadana'	EPla SDry
– f. ***subvariegata***	SBam SDry
– 'Sulphurea'	See ***P. bambusoides* 'Allgold'**
– 'Tanakae'	SDry
bissetii	EFou EFul EOas EPla SBam SDry WJun
congesta hort.	See ***P. atrovaginata***
decora	SBam SDry WJun
dulcis	EOas EPla SBam WJun

§ ***edulis***	CGre EFul EHoe EJap GAri ISta MBal SBam SDry WJun
– 'Bicolor'	SBam SDry WJun
§ – var. ***heterocycla***	EBee SBam SDry SMad
– f. ***pubescens***	See ***P. edulis***
edulis subconvexa	See ***P. viridiglaucescens***
flexuosa	CWLN EBee EFul EPfP EPla LNet SBam SDry WJun
fulva	EPla
glauca	EPla
– 'Yunzhu'	EPla SDry WJun
§ ***heteroclada***	SBam SDry
♦ – 'Solid Stem' misapplied	See ***P. heteroclada* 'Straight Stem'**
§ – 'Straight Stem'	EPla SBam SDry
heterocycla	See ***P. edulis*** var. ***heterocycla***
♦ – f. ***pubescens***	See ***P. edulis***
humilis	CWLN EBee EPla MUlv SBam SDry WJun
iridescens	EPla SDry WJun
lithophila	WJun
makinoi	WJun
mannii	SBam SDry WJun
meyeri	EFou EPla SBam SDry WJun
nidularia	EBee EPla MUlv SBam SDry WJun
nigra 🏆	CB&S CHEx CSWP CWLN EBee EFul EOas EPla LNet LPal LPan NPal SArc SBam SDry SPla SSoC WJun
– 'Boryana'	CFil CWLN EFul EPla MUlv SBam SDix SDry WJun
– var. ***henonis*** 🏆	EBee EFul EPfP EPla SBam SDry WJun
– 'Megurochiku'	EPla SBam SDry WJun
– f. ***punctata***	CFil EPla SBam SDry WJun
nuda	EPla SBam SDry WJun
– f. ***localis***	SBam SDry
parvifolia	EPla WJun
praecox	EPla WJun
propinqua	CDoC EPla ISta SBam WJun
purpurata	See ***P. heteroclada***
rubicunda	WJun
rubromarginata	EPla SBam SDry
stimulosa	EPla WJun
sulphurea 'Houzeau'	EPla SBam SDry
– 'Robert Young'	CB&S EPla SBam SDry WJun
– 'Sulphurea'	See ***P. bambusoides* 'Allgold'**
§ – var. ***viridis***	EFul SBam SDry WJun
– – 'Mitis'	See ***P. sulphurea*** var. ***viridis***
violascens	CB&S EFul EPla SBam SDry WJun
§ ***viridiglaucescens*** 🏆	CB&S CHEx CWLN EFul EPla SArc SBam SDry SEND WCot WJun
vivax	EFul EPla ISta SBam SDry WJun
– 'Aureocaulis'	EFul EOas EPla ISta SDry WJun

× PHYLLOTHAMNUS (Ericaceae)

erectus	GDra GGGa MHig NHar NHol WAbe WPat WPyg

PHYMOSIA (Malvaceae)

§ ***umbellata***	CBot CGre LCns SOWG

PHYODINA See CALLISIA

PHYSALIS (Solanaceae)

alkekengi 🏆	WOak
– var. ***franchetii***	CArn CB&S ECED ELan ENot EPla GAbr GLil MBri MCLN NBir NBro NFai NFla NMir NRoo SEas SHel SPer SRms WBea WOve WPer WWhi WWin
– – 'Gigantea'	ECGP GBuc NNor SMrm
– – 'Variegata'	CDec CRDP EBee EPla EWes IBlr MUlv
pubescens (F)	CArn

PHYSARIA (Brassicaceae)

See Plant Deletions

PHYSOCARPUS (Rosaceae)

opulifolius	MSal
– 'Dart's Gold' 🏆	EBre EHoe ELan EMil ENot IOrc LBuc LHop MAsh MBar MHar MMor MTis MWat NNor NSti SLPl SMac SPer SRms SSpi SSta WDin WGwG WRTC WWin
– 'Diabolo'	EBee ECle MAsh MBri MGos NBir SCoo SPer WWes
§ – 'Luteus'	CBot CPle CSam ENot ESis ISea MBar MGos MRav NNor SPer SRms WBod WDin WFar
ribesifolius 'Aureus'	See ***P. opulifolius* 'Luteus'**

PHYSOCHLAINA (Solanaceae)

orientalis	CRDP EMon MSal NChi

PHYSOPLEXIS (Campanulaceae)

§ ***comosa*** 🏆	CLyd EPad MBro NTow WAbe WHoo WPyg

PHYSOSTEGIA (Lamiaceae)

angustifolia	CHan EBee NLak
§ ***virginiana***	CTri EBar EBee ECoo EOrc GBar GCHN GMaP LGan MHew NRoo SWat WByw WRHF
– 'Alba'	CBot CGle EBre ECro GBri GMaP LHop LWak MSte NOrc NRoo SHel SUsu WEas WPLl WRHF
§ – 'Crown of Snow'	CBot CFir CMdw CMil EBar ECoo ECtt GBur MCLN MSCN NMir NPla NRai SPla WCot WHil WPer WRHF WWhi
– dwarf form	ECha
– 'Galadriel'	EMon LRHS
– 'Grandiflora'	CFir SIde WLRN
– pale pink	EFou LGan SUsu SWat
– 'Red Beauty'	CFir EBee EGar EHal LRHS MTis SMrm WPyg WWin
– 'Rosea'	CB&S CBot GBur LWak MBel MLsm WOve WPer
♦ – Schneekrone	See ***P. virginiana* 'Crown of Snow'**
– 'Snow Queen'	See ***P. virginiana* 'Summer Snow'**
– subsp. ***speciosa***	EMon
§ – – 'Bouquet Rose'	CDec CHan EBre ECED ECha EMar LFis LLWP MBri MFir MRav MSte NCat NFla NMir NPri SChu SPer SSea WHal WHoo WPyg WRus WTyr
♦ – – Rose Bouquet	See ***P. virginiana*** subsp. ***speciosa* 'Bouquet Rose'**

§ – – 'Variegata'	CB&S CGle CMHG CRDP EBre ECha ECro EFol EFou EHoe ELan EMon LFis LHop MBel MBri MCLN MRav MUlv NOak SCro SHFr SOkh SPer WCot WEas WOld WPer WWhi WWin
§ – 'Summer Snow' ♡	CB&S CKel EAst ECha EFol EFou ELan ENot EOrc LHop MBel MBri MFir MWat NFla NHol SHFr SPer SRms WBea WHal WHoo WOld WOve WRus WWin
– 'Summer Spire'	ECha ECro ELan EMan MSte NHol SPer WBea WFar
– 'Vivid' ♡	CGle CMGP CRDP EBre ECED ECha ECro EFou ELan EMon LGan MBro MCLN MRav MWat NFla NHol NOak SDix SMac SPer SRms WEas WGwG WHoo WPyg WWin

PHYTEUMA (Campanulaceae)

balbisii	See ***P. cordatum***
betonicifolium	WHil
charmelii	NBro WThi
comosum	See ***Physoplexis comosa***
§ ***cordatum***	MFos
¶ ***globulariifolium***	NSla
halleri	See ***P. ovatum***
hemisphaericum	EPad NGre SWas
humile	CNic
japonicum	EPad
nigrum	ELan EPad GCal LBee MNrw NBro SSca WHoo WPyg WThi
orbiculare	WHoo WPyg
§ ***ovatum***	NPri
scheuchzeri	CNic CPea CRDP ECha ECro ELan EMan GTou LFis LGan MBro NBro NMGW NOrc NPri NRoo SAlw SBla SRms SSca WThi
sieberi	ELan GDra NBir WRHF
spicatum	NBro WWye
– subsp. ***coeruleum***	GBin
tenerum	CKin

PHYTOLACCA (Phytolaccaceae)

acinosa	ELan IBlr LHol MHew MSal SWat WHer
§ ***americana***	CArn CAvo CHEx CSev EBar ECha ELan ELau EMar GPoy IBlr LHol MChe MSal SIde SRms SWat WByw WEas WHer WPer WWye
clavigera	See ***P. polyandra***
decandra	See ***P. americana***
¶ ***dioica***	GBin
esculenta	EBee NPSI
– B&SWJ 1000	WCru
§ ***polyandra***	CArc ECGP ECha GBin GBuc GCHN LHol NBro NHex SAxl SRms WWye

PICEA † (Pinaceae)

§ ***abies***	CPer CTri EHul ENot GRei LBuc LCon MBar MBri MGos NBee NRoo NWea WDin WGwG WMou
– 'Acrocona'	CDoC EHul EOrn LCon MBar MBri MGos MPla
– 'Argenteospica' (v)	LCon NHol
– 'Aurea'	LLin LPan
– 'Aurea Magnifica'	LCon MAsh
– 'Capitata'	CBlo CKen GAri LCon MBar
* – 'Cinderella'	MAsh
– 'Clanbrassiliana'	CBlo CKen LCon MBar
– 'Columnaris'	GAri
– 'Compacta'	LBee
I – 'Congesta'	CKen
– 'Crippsii'	CKen
I – 'Cruenta'	CKen
– 'Cupressina'	CKen
– 'Diffusa'	CBlo CKen LCon MBar
– 'Elegans'	LCon MBar
– 'Ellwangeriana'	CBlo LCon
– 'Excelsa'	See ***P. abies***
– 'Finedonensis'	LCon
– 'Formanek'	CKen LCon LLin
– 'Four Winds'	CAbP
– 'Frohburg'	CDoC COtt ENHC GAri LCon MBar MBri MGos NHol
– 'Globosa'	CBlo CWLN MBar WStI
– 'Globosa Nana'	MGos
– 'Gregoryana'	CDoC CKen LCon MBar NHar NHed WAbe
– 'Humilis'	LCon SIng
– 'Inversa'	CDoC EHul ENHC EOrn GAri IOrc LCon LLin LPan MBar
– 'Little Gem' ♡	CDoC CKen CMac EBre EHul ENHC EOrn LBee LCon LLin MAsh MBar MBri MGos MPla MWat NBee NHar NRoo SAga SLim WAbe
– 'Maxwellii'	EHul MBar MGos NHar
– 'Merkii'	GAri
– 'Nana'	MBar
– 'Nana Compacta'	CKen CWLN EHul ESis LCon LLin MBar MOne SLim
– 'Nidiformis' ♡	CDoC CKen CMac EBre EHul ENHC ENot EOrn GRei IOrc LCon LLin LPan MBal MBar MBri MGos MPla MWat NBee NHar NRoo NWea SAga SHBN SLim SRms WDin WStI
– 'Norrkoping'	CKen
– 'Ohlendorffii'	CKen CSte EHul ENHC EOrn LCon LPan MBar MBri MPla MWat NHar NHol NRoo SHBN SLim WDin WStI
– 'Pachyphylla'	CKen
– 'Pendula Major'	SHBN
– 'Procumbens'	LCon MBar
– 'Pseudomaxwellii'	CBlo LCon NHol
– 'Pumila'	EOrn NHed
– 'Pumila Nigra'	CMac EHul LCon LLin MAsh MBar MGos MPla NHar SLim
¶ – 'Pusch'	CKen
– 'Pygmaea'	CKen GDra LCon MBar MGos MPla
– 'Reflexa'	CWLN EHul LCon LLin
– 'Repens'	MBar MBlu MGos NBee
– 'Rydal'	EBre LCon MAsh MBri
– 'Saint James'	CKen
– 'Tabuliformis'	MBar
– 'Tufty'	EOrn
– 'Veitchii'	See ***P. abies* 'Gregoryana Veitchii'**
– 'Waugh'	CBlo MBar
◆ – Will's Dwarf	See ***P. abies* 'Wills Zwerg'**
§ – 'Wills Zwerg'	LCon MAsh
alcockiana 'Prostrata'	LCon MBal MBar NHol
asperata	ETen LCon
§ ***balfouriana***	LCon NHol

bicolor	See ***P. alcockiana***
brachytyla	LCon SIng
breweriana 𝕐	CB&S CChu CDoC CMac EBre EHul ENot GRei IHos IOrc ISea LCon LLin LNet LPan MBar MBri MWat NBee NHol NWea SHBN SLim SPer SSta WNor
engelmannii	CBlo GAul LCon MBar
– f. ***glauca***	EHul LCon LPan MBar SSta
glauca	GAul NRoo NWea
– 'Alberta Blue'	LLin LPan SCoo SLim WWeb
– var. ***albertiana*** 'Alberta Globe'	CDoC CFee EBre EHul ENHC EOrn EPot GRei LBee LCon LLin MAsh MBar MBri MGos MPla NBee NHar NHed NRoo SAga SLim SSmi WDin WFar
– – 'Conica' 𝕐	CB&S CDoC CMac EBre EHul ENHC ENot EPot GDra ISea LBee LCon LLin LNet MBal MBar MBri MGos MPla MWat NBee NHar NHed NRoo NWea SBod SHBN SLim SPer WDin
– – 'Gnome'	CKen
– – 'Laurin'	CDoC CKen EBre EOrn LBee LCon LLin MAsh MBar MBri NHar SSmi SSta WAbe
– var. ***albertiana*** 'Tiny'	CKen EHul EOrn EPot LCon LLin MBar MOne WAbe
– 'Arneson's Blue'	LCon SLim
– 'Coerulea'	LCon MBar
– 'Densata'	CBlo
– 'Echiniformis' 𝕐	CKen EHul EPot GAri LBee LCon LLin LPan MBal MBar MBri NHar
* – 'J.W. Daisy's White'	LLin
– 'Lilliput'	EHul EPot LCon MBar MBri MGos
– 'Nana'	CBlo CKen
– 'Piccolo'	CDoC CKen CSte LLin MBri SLim
– 'Rainbow's End'	CKen
– 'Sander's Blue'	CKen
– 'Zucherhut'	LCon LRHS MBri
glehnii 'Sasanosei'	CKen
– 'Shimezusei'	CKen
jezoensis	ETen GAri MGos NWea
– subsp. ***hondoensis***	LCon WNor
kosteri 'Glauca'	See ***P. pungens* 'Koster'**
§ ***koyamae***	CBlo CLnd ETen LCon
likiangensis	CBlo LCon MBal WWat
– var. ***balfouriana***	See ***P. balfouriana***
– var. ***purpurea***	See ***P. purpurea***
mariana 'Aureovariegata'	LCon
– 'Doumetii'	EOrn LCon
– 'Ericoides'	GAri
– 'Fastigiata'	CKen EOrn
– 'Nana' 𝕐	CKen CMac EBre EHul ELan ENHC ESis GDra LCon LLin LNet MBar MBri MGos MNrw MPla MWat NBee NHed NHol SLim SSmi SSta WDin
× ***mariorika***	MBar
omorika 𝕐	CB&S CDoC CMCN CPer EHoe ENHC ENot GRei LBuc LCon LNet MBal MBar MGos NBee NWea SIng SPer SReu WCoo WDin WGwG WMou
– 'Gnom'	See ***P.* × *mariorika* 'Gnom'**
– 'Nana'	CMac EBre ENHC GAri LCon LNet LPan MBar NBee SLim

– 'Pendula' 𝕐	CBlo IOrc LCon MAsh MBar SHBN SSta
– 'Pimoko'	CKen LCon MBri
– 'Schneverdingen'	CKen
– 'Treblitsch'	CKen
orientalis 𝕐	CLnd ETen LCon MBal STre WMou
§ – 'Aurea' 𝕐	CDoC CMac EBre EHul ELan ENHC IOrc LCon LLin LPan MBar MBri SHBN SLim
– 'Bergman's Gem'	CKen
– 'Gowdy'	MBar
– 'Kenwith'	CKen
– 'Pendula'	MGos
– 'Reynolds'	CKen
– 'Skylands'	CBlo CKen LCon MAsh MGos SLim
pungens	EBee LCon MBar NWea SPer WDin WNor
¶ – 'Blaukissen'	CKen
– 'Drayer'	EBee
– 'Erich Frahm'	CDoC CSte EBre ENHC GAri LCon LPan MBri MGos SCoo SLim SMad WWeb
– 'Fat Albert'	EBre LPan
– f. ***glauca***	EHul GAul GRei LBee MBal MBar NBee NWea WDin WMou WStI
– 'Glauca Globosa'	See ***P. pungens* 'Globosa'**
– 'Glauca Procumbens'	LNet
§ – 'Glauca Prostrata'	CKen EBre EHul LCon MBal SLim SSta
– 'Globe'	CKen LCon NHol
§ – 'Globosa' 𝕐	CDoC CKen EBre EHul ELan ENHC EOrn IOrc LBee LCon LLin LPan MBar MBri MGos MWat NBee NHol SHBN SLim SPer SRms WPyg WStI
I – 'Globosa Viridis'	EHul
– 'Gloria'	CKen LCon
– 'Hoopsii' 𝕐	CDoC CMac EBre EHul ELan ENHC ENot EOrn IHos IOrc LCon LNet LPan MBal MBar MGos MWat NBee SHBN SLim SPla WDin
– 'Hoto'	EBee EHul ENHC IOrc LCon MBar WPyg WWeb
– 'Hunnewelliana'	EOrn
– 'Iseli Fastigiate'	EBre LCon MAsh MBri
§ – 'Koster' 𝕐	CDoC CMac EHul ENHC EOrn GRei IOrc LCon LLin LNet LPan MAsh MBar MGos NBee NWea SLim SMad SPer SRms SSta WDin WStI
– 'Koster Prostrate'	MBal
– 'Lucky Strike'	CKen LCon MAsh MGos
– 'Maigold'	CKen
– 'Moerheimii'	EHul LCon LNet LPan MBar MGos
– 'Montgomery'	CBlo CKen LCon LLin MBar NHol
– 'Procumbens' 𝕐	CKen LCon
– 'Prostrata'	See ***P. pungens* 'Glauca Prostrata'**
– 'Saint Mary's Broom'	CKen
– 'Schovenhorst'	EHul
– 'Thomsen'	CKen EHul LCon MAsh MBal MBri
– 'Thuem'	EBee EHul LCon MGos
– 'Wendy'	CKen
rubens	GAri LCon NWea
schrenkiana	ETen LCon

sitchensis	CPer GRei LBuc LCon MGos NWea WMou
– 'Nana'	CDoC NHol
– 'Papoose'	See ***P. sitchensis* 'Tenas'**
– 'Silberzwerg'	CKen
– 'Strypemonde'	CKen
§ – 'Tenas'	LCon MBri NHol
smithiana 🏆	GAri ISea LCon MBal SLim WFro

PICRASMA (Simaroubaceae)

ailanthoides	See ***P. quassioides***

PICRIS (Asteraceae)

echioides	CKin EWFC WHer

PIERIS † (Ericaceae)

'Bert Chandler'	ELan SPer SSpi
'Flaming Silver' (v) 🏆	CB&S CEnd CHig CKni CLan COtt CSam EBre EHoe ELan IHos IOrc MAsh MBar MBri MGos NFla NHed NHol SHBN SReu SRms SSta WAbe WGwG WHar WPat WWat WWeb
'Flamingo'	CB&S CHig CTrh CTrw EHoe MAsh MBal MBar MGos NHed NHol SExb SPer WAbe WPat WPyg
floribunda	IOrc MBal SEas SPer
'Forest Flame' 🏆	CB&S CHig CMHG CTrh CTrw EBre ELan ENot GWht IOrc LHyd MBal MBar MBri MGos NBee NHed NHol NRoo SExb SHBN SPer SReu SSta WAbe WBod WDin WPat WRTC WWat
formosa	CHig
– var. ***forrestii***	CDoC CTre CTrw GRei ISea NWea SExb
– – 'Fota Pink'	WHar WSHC
– – 'Jermyns' 🏆	CB&S CEnd CHig GWht IOrc MBal SHBN
– – 'Wakehurst' 🏆	CB&S CHig CLan EHoe GWht IOrc LHyd MAsh MBal MRav NWea SArc SPer SReu SSta WBod WGwG WPat WRTC
Havila	CDoC CHig EHic IOrc MAsh MBal MBri MGos NHed NHol WLRN
japonica	CB&S CHig CLan CTrw MBal MBar MGos NWea SArc SReu WDin
– 'Balls of Fire'	CTrh
– 'Bisbee Dwarf'	CTrh MBar MBro NHar NHol WAbe WPat WPyg
– 'Blush' 🏆	CHig NHol SBod SEas SHBN SPer WSHC
– 'Cavatine'	CMHG LRHS SBod
§ – 'Christmas Cheer'	CDoC CLan CWLN IOrc MBal MGos NHed SPer WDin WLRN
– 'Coleman'	CMHG
– 'Compact Crimson'	MBal
– 'Compacta'	NHol WAbe
– 'Crispa'	CHig
– 'Cupido'	CBlo CWLN EMil MAsh MBar MGos NHol WLRN
– 'Daisen'	CLan CTrw
§ – 'Debutante' 🏆	CDoC CHig CWLN ELan EPfP MAsh MPla NHol SSpi WStI WWat
– 'Don'	See ***P. japonica* 'Pygmaea'**
– 'Dorothy Wyckoff'	CB&S CDoC CLan CMHG CWLN MAsh NHed NHol SHBN SPer SSta
– 'Firecrest' 🏆	CB&S CChe CHig CMHG CTrh CWLN IOrc MBal MBri NHed NRoo SSpi WPat
– 'Flaming Star'	ECot
– 'Geisha'	WPat
– 'Glenroy Pink Plenty'	MBal
– 'Grayswood' 🏆	CChe CHig CMHG CSam EPfP IOrc MBri
– 'Little Heath' (v) 🏆	CDoC CEnd CFee CHig CMHG CTrh CWLN EBar EBre EHoe GCHN IOrc MAsh MBar MBri MGos MHig NHed NHol SPer SReu SRms SSta WAbe WBod WPat WPyg WWeb
– 'Little Heath Green' 🏆	CChe CDoC CHig CMHG CTrh EBre EPla GAri LHyd MAsh MBar MBri MGos NHar NHed NHol SPer SSta WFar WWeb
– 'Minor'	MBar NHar NHol WPat WPyg
– 'Mountain Fire' 🏆	CB&S CChe CDoC CMHG CTrh ECle GCHN GOrc IOrc MAsh MBal MBar MBri MGos NHol SBod SCoo SEas SHBN SPer SReu WGwG WHar WPat WWeb
– 'Pink Delight' 🏆	CAbP CB&S CHig MAsh MBal MBar MGos MPla MRav NHol SBid SHBN SPer SRms WPat WRTC
– 'Prelude' 🏆	GCHN MBri MRav NHol WPat
– 'Purity' 🏆	CB&S CDoC CHig CMHG CTrh CWLN IOrc MBal MBar MGos NHol SEas SPer SReu SSta WDin WPat WStI
§ – 'Pygmaea'	GDra MBal MBro MHig NHar NHol WPat WPyg
– 'Red Mill'	CAbP CBlo CDoC CEnd CHig CMHG CWLN EBee GOrc MAsh NHol SBod SPer SSpi WPat
– 'Robinswood'	SBid WBcn
– 'Rosalinda'	MAsh
– 'Rosea'	LHyd
– 'Rowallane'	IBlr
– 'Sarabande' 🏆	COtt MBri MGos SPer WPat WPyg
– 'Scarlett O'Hara'	CB&S MGos WBcn
– 'Select'	CWLN MGos
– 'Snowdrift'	GCHN MAsh MSta SPer SSta
– 'Spring Candy'	CB&S MGos SBid body
– Taiwanensis Group	CGre CHig CMHG CTre CTrh GCHN GRei IOrc LHyd MBal MBar MRav NHol NWea SPer SRms SSta WAbe WPat WRTC WWat
– 'Tickled Pink'	CB&S CWLN EHic
– 'Tilford'	CHig MBal MBri MPla NHar SSta WFox WPat
¶ – 'Valley Fire'	CTrh
– 'Valley Rose'	CChe COtt CSam CTrh CWLN EHoe ENot GCHN MAsh MBal MGos NBee NHol SBid SPer SSpi WStI
– 'Valley Valentine' 🏆	CLan COtt EHic EPfP MAsh MBal MBri MGos NFla NHed NHol SBid SPer SReu SSta WWeb

§ – 'Variegata' (Carrière) Bean	CChe CHig CMHG CWLN ELan EPot GRei IOrc LHyd MBal MBar MGos NBee NHed NHol SArc SExb SHBN SIng SPer SReu SSta WAbe WDin WHar WPat WSHC WWat
– 'Variegata' hort.	See ***P. japonica* 'White Rim'**
– 'Wada's Pink'	See ***P. japonica* 'Christmas Cheer'**
– 'White Caps'	CTrh MBal
– 'White Cascade'	CTrh
– 'White Pearl'	CAbP CLan MAsh MBal MBri MGos SPer
§ – 'White Rim' (v) 𝕍	CB&S EHoe MAsh MGos MPla
– 'William Buchanan'	MBar MBro MHig NHar NHol WPat WPyg WRTC
nana	GAri MBal MBar NHar
– 'Redshank'	MBal
ryukuensis 'Temple Bells'	EHic SBid WFox
yakushimensis	CBlo WSHC
– 'Brookside Miniature'	WPat

PILEA (Urticaceae)

* 'Anette'	MBri
cadierei 𝕍	CHal MBri SLMG
nummulariifolia	CHal MBri
peperomioides	CSev EPad SRms WCot
repens	MBri

PILEOSTEGIA (Hydrangeaceae)

viburnoides 𝕍	CB&S CChu CGre CHEx CLan CMac CPlN CSPN CTrw EMil EPla GQui LHop MGos SArc SBid SBra SDix SHBN SPer SSpi SSta WBod WCru WPat WPyg WSHC WWat

PILOSELLA (Asteraceae)

§ ***aurantiaca***	CLTr CNic CRow CWGN EBar ECWi EFol ELan EWFC MFir MGam MHew MRav NOrc NSti SIng SSmi WBea WCer WCla WElm WHer
§ ***officinarum***	CKin CRow ECWi EWFC WGwy
§ ***stoloniflora***	CRow

PILULARIA (Marsileaceae)

globulifera	CNat NVic

PIMELEA (Thymelaeaceae)

arenaria	ECou
coarctata	See ***P. prostrata***
drupacea	ECou
filiformis	ECou MAll
§ ***prostrata***	CLyd CTri ECou EPot MAll MBar MHig NHar NMen NWoo SAlw SIng WAbe WCru WPer
– f. ***parvifolia***	ECou WCru
– Tennyson's form	SBla
sericeovillosa	ECou
suteri	ECou

PIMENTA (Myrtaceae)

See Plant Deletions

PIMPINELLA (Apiaceae)

anisum	CArn LHol MSal SIde WHer WSel
¶ ***bicknellii***	WCot
major 'Rosea'	CHan CRDP ECha GBri LHop MHlr SMrm WBro WCot WFar WHal
saxifraga	EWFC LHol

PINELLIA (Araceae)

cordata	CMon CRDP EPot WCru
pedatisecta	CRDP MRav SAxl SSoC WCru
pinnatisecta	See ***P. tripartita***
ternata	CMon CRDP EPar EPot MSal SIng WCru WOld WWye
§ ***tripartita***	CMon EPot SAxl
– B&SWJ 1102	WCru

PINGUICULA † (Lentibulariaceae)

acuminata	WMEx
agnata	MHel WMEx
ehlersiae	EFEx MHel WMEx
emarginata	WMEx
esseriana	EFEx MHel WMEx
gracilis	WMEx
grandiflora	CRDP EFEx EPot MHel NGre NHar NMen NRya NSla WAbe WHer WMEx
– subsp. ***coenocantabrica*** NS 307	NWCA
gypsicola	WMEx
¶ ***hemiepiphytica***	WMEx
'Kewensis'	MHel WMEx
laueana	MHel WMEx
longifolia subsp. ***longifolia***	EFEx
macrophylla	WMEx
moranensis alba	MHel WMEx
moranensis var. ***caudata***	EFEx MHel WMEx
moranensis flos-mulionis	MHel WMEx
moranensis 'Kirkbright'	MHel
– var. ***mexicana***	CRDP WMEx
moranensis moreana	EFEx
moranensis morelia	WMEx
moranensis superba	EFEx
potosiensis	WMEx
¶ ***primuliflora***	MHel WMEx
reticulata	WMEx
rotundifolia	WMEx
'Sethos'	MHel WMEx
vulgaris	EFEx MHel WMEx
'Weser'	MHel WMEx
zecheri	MHel WMEx

PINUS † (Pinaceae)

¶ ***albicaulis***	WNor
– 'Flinck'	CKen
– 'Nana'	See ***P. albicaulis* 'Noble's Dwarf'**
§ – 'Noble's Dwarf'	CKen
N ***aristata***	CAbP CDoC CKen CMCN EBre EHul EOrn LCon LLin MAsh MBal MBar MGos NHol SMad SReu SSta STre WCoo WFro
– 'Cecilia'	CKen
– 'Sherwood Compact'	CKen
armandii	CDul CFil CGre CMCN CSWP ETen LCon SMad
– SF 313	ISea
– TW 415	GWht
attenuata	CBlo
austriaca	See ***P. nigra* subsp. *nigra***
N ***ayacahuite***	LCon SLim SMur
banksiana	CSam EHul ETen LCon MBal
– 'Chippewa'	CKen NHol

I – 'Compacta'	CKen
– 'H.J. Welch'	CKen
– 'Manomet'	CKen
– 'Neponset'	CKen LCon
– 'Wisconsin'	CKen
brutia	See ***P. halepensis*** **subsp.** ***brutia***
bungeana	CGre CKen CLnd CMCN EHul LCon LLin MBal MBlu SLPl STre WFro WNor
canariensis	EHul ISea
cembra ♀	CDoC CDul EHul ENHC LBee LCon MBal MBar NWea STre WAbe
– 'Aurea'	See ***P. cembra*** **'Aureovariegata'**
§ – 'Aureovariegata'	CKen
– 'Barnhourie'	CKen
– 'Blue Mound'	CKen
– 'Chalet'	CKen
– 'Compacta Glauca'	LRHS
* – 'Griffithii'	WDin
– 'Inverleith'	CKen MBri
– 'Jermyns'	CKen
– 'King's Dwarf'	CKen
– 'Nana'	See ***P. pumila*** **'Nana'**
– 'Roughills'	CKen
– 'Stricta'	CKen
– Witches' broom	CKen
¶ ***cembroides*** var. ***edulis***	ETen
contorta	CB&S CBlo CDoC CDul CPer GRei LCon MBal MBar MGos NWea STre WDin WMou
– 'Asher'	CKen
– 'Frisian Gold'	CKen
– var. ***latifolia***	CLnd ETen LPan MBal
– 'Spaan's Dwarf'	CBlo CKen LCon LLin MBar MGos NHol SLim
coulteri ♀	CAgr CMCN ETen LCon MBal SMad WNor
densiflora	CDul CMCN EHul ENHC ETen LCon MBal STre WFro WNor
– 'Alice Verkade'	CBlo LCon LLin LRHS SLim
– 'Aurea'	EBre LCon MBar MGos NHol SLim
– 'Jane Kluis'	CKen COtt LRHS MBri
– 'Oculus Draconis'	CDoC LCon MBar MGos SLim SMur
– 'Pendula'	CKen LLin MBal SLim
– 'Pygmy'	CKen
– 'Umbraculifera'	CDoC IOrc LCon LLin LPan MBar MBri MGos MOne NHar SLim SSta
edulis	LCon
flexilis	CBlo CDul ETen LCon MBal
– 'Firmament'	CDoC LCon LLin
– 'Glenmore Dwarf'	CKen
– 'Nana'	CKen
– 'Pendula'	EBre LLin MAsh
– WB No. 1	CKen
– WB No. 2	CKen
gerardiana	LCon MBal
greggii	CFil ISea
griffithii	See ***P. wallichiana***
halepensis	CLnd ETen
¶ ***hartwegii***	ETen
§ ***heldreichii*** var. ***leucodermis*** ♀	CMac ETen LCon LNet MBal MBar SCoo WDin WNor
– – 'Aureospicata'	LCon LLin MBar SIng
– – 'Compact Gem'	CDoC CKen EBre IOrc LCon LLin MBar MBri MGos NHar SCoo SLim SSta WPyg
– – 'Groen'	CKen

– – 'Malink'	CKen
– – 'Pygmy'	CKen
– – 'Satellit'	CDoC ENHC EOrn IOrc LBee LLin LPan MBri SLim
– 'Schmidtii' ♀	CDoC CKen EBre LCon LLin MAsh MBar MBri SLim
jeffreyi ♀	CBot CDul CLnd CMCN ETen ISea LCon MBal MBar WFro
– 'Joppi'	CKen
koraiensis	ETen LCon MBal STre WNor
– 'Bergman'	CKen
– 'Dragon Eye'	CKen
– 'Jack Corbit'	CKen
– 'Shibamichi'	CKen
– 'Silver Lining'	MAsh MBri
– 'Silvergrey'	CKen
– 'Winton'	CDoC CKen
¶ ***lambertiana***	ETen
leucodermis	See ***P. heldreichii*** **var.** ***leucodermis***
magnifica	See ***P. montezumae***
¶ ***massoniana***	WNor
monophylla	ETen MBal
N ***montezumae***	CB&S CGre CLnd CMCN IOrc ISea LCon LLin SArc SMad WDin WNor
monticola	CLnd LCon
– 'Pendula'	MBar
– 'Pygmy'	See ***P. monticola*** **'Raraflora'**
§ – 'Raraflora'	CKen
– 'Skyline'	LCon MBar
– 'Windsor Dwarf'	CKen
mugo	CB&S CDul CTri EHul ENot GRei MAsh MBal MBar MGos SRms WDin WStI
* – 'Benjamin'	CKen
– 'Bisley Green'	LLin
– 'Brownie'	CKen
– 'Carsten'	CKen
– 'Carsten's Wintergold'	See ***P. mugo*** **'Winter Gold'**
I – 'Columnaris'	LPan
– 'Corley's Mat'	CKen EBre LCon LLin MAsh SCoo SLim
– 'Gnom'	CKen CMac EHul LCon LLin MBar MBri MOne NBee WDin WFar
– 'Hoersholm'	CKen
– 'Humpy'	CKen CWLN EBre ENHC EOrn GAri LBee LCon LLin MAsh MBar MBri MGos MOne NHar NHol SLim WAbe
– 'Jacobsen'	CKen
– 'Kissen'	CBlo CKen LCon MGos
– 'Klosterkotter'	MGos
– 'Knapenburg'	LCon NHol
– 'Kobold'	CBlo NHol
– 'Krauskopf'	CKen
– 'Laarheide'	MBri
– 'Laurin'	CKen
– 'March'	CKen LCon NHol
– 'Mini Mops'	CKen
– 'Minikin'	CKen
– 'Mops' ♀	CDoC CMac CWLN EBre EHul ENHC IHos LBee LCon LLin LPan MAsh MBar MBri MGos NBee NHar NHol SLim SPer SSta WPyg
– 'Mops Midget'	LLin MBri
– var. ***mughus***	See ***P. mugo*** **var.** ***mugo***
§ – var. ***mugo***	CMCN EHic GRei LPan MBar WGwG
– 'Mumpitz'	CKen

– 'Ophir'	CKen EBre EHul ENHC IOrc LBee LCon LLin LNet MAsh MBar MBri MGos NHar NHol SLim SPer SPla SSta WDin
– 'Pal Maleter'	CDoC LCon LLin MBri
– var. ***pumilio*** 🏆	CDoC CDul CMac EHul ENot GRei IOrc LCon LLin LPan MBar MBro MGos NFla NWea SHBN SLPl STre WNor
– var. ***rostrata***	See ***P. mugo*** subsp. ***uncinata***
– 'Spaan'	CKen
§ – subsp. ***uncinata***	CLnd ETen GRei LCon NWea
– 'White Tip'	CKen
§ – 'Winter Gold'	CKen EBre EHul IOrc LBuc LCon LLin MAsh NHar SSta
– 'Winzig'	CKen
– 'Zundert'	CBlo CKen LCon LLin MBar MBri MGos NHar
muricata 🏆	CAbP CDoC CDul CLnd ETen LCon MBal MGos NWea
nigra 🏆	CB&S CDoC CDul ENHC GRei LCon LNet MBar MGos NWea SHBN WDin WMou
– var. ***austriaca***	See ***P. nigra*** subsp. ***nigra***
– 'Black Prince'	CBlo CKen LBee LCon LLin NHol SCoo SLim
N – 'Cebennensis Nana'	CKen
– var. ***corsicana***	See ***P. nigra*** subsp. ***laricio***
– 'Géant de Suisse'	LCon
– 'Hornibrookiana'	CKen LCon LPan
§ – subsp. ***laricio*** 🏆	CDoC CKen ENot GRei IHos LBuc LCon MBar NWea WMou
– – 'Bobby McGregor'	CKen LLin
– – 'Globosa Viridis'	GAri LLin NHol
– – 'Goldfingers'	CKen LLin
* – – 'Moseri' 🏆	CKen GAri LCon LLin SLim SSta
– – 'Pygmaea'	CKen
– – 'Spingarn'	CKen
– – 'Talland Bay'	CKen
– – 'Wurstle'	CKen
– subsp. ***maritima***	See ***P. nigra*** subsp. ***laricio***
– 'Molette'	CMCN LCon
– 'Nana'	LPan MBri
§ – subsp. ***nigra***	EBee LBuc LPan NWea WStI
– – 'Bright Eyes'	CFee CKen EHul EOrn LBee LCon LLin
– – 'Helga'	CKen
– – 'Schovenhorst'	CKen
– – 'Strypemonde'	CKen
– – 'Yaffle Hill'	CKen
– 'Obelisk'	CKen
* ***nigra serotina***	CMCN
nigra 'Uelzen'	CKen
palustris	LCon LLin
parviflora 🏆	GAri LCon LPan NWea STre WCoo WDin WNor
– 'Adcock's Dwarf' 🏆	CDoC CKen GAri LCon LLin MBar MGos NHol SCoo SLim WAbe
– 'Aizu'	CKen
– 'Al Fordham'	CKen
– 'Aoi'	CKen
– 'Azuma-goyo'	CKen NHol
I – 'Baasch's Form'	CKen
– 'Bergman'	CBlo CDoC LCon MAsh MBar NHol
– 'Bonnie Bergman'	CKen
– 'Brevifolia'	GAri
– 'Dai-ho'	CKen
– 'Daisetsusan'	CKen
– 'Fukai Seedling'	CKen

– 'Fukiju'	CKen
– 'Fukushima-goyo'	CKen
¶ – 'Fukuzumi'	LLin
– f. ***glauca***	CDoC CMac EHul ENHC GAri IHos IOrc LCon LLin MBar MBri MGos NFla NHol NPal WDin
I – 'Glauca Nana'	CKen
– 'Gyok-kan'	CKen
– 'Gyok-ke-sen'	CKen
– 'Gyo-ko-haku'	CKen
– 'Gyokuei'	CKen
– 'Gyokusen Seedling'	CKen WAbe
– 'Gyo-ku-sui'	CKen
– 'Hagaromo Seedling'	CKen
– 'Hakko'	CKen NHol
– 'Hatsumi'	NHol
– 'Ibo-can'	CKen
– 'Ichi-no-se'	CKen
– 'Iri-fune'	CKen
¶ – 'Ishizuchi-goyo'	CKen
¶ – 'Jyu-roko-ra-kan'	CKen
– 'Ka-ho'	CKen
– 'Kanzan'	CKen
– 'Kiyomatsu'	CKen
– 'Kobe'	CKen
– 'Kokonde'	CKen
– 'Kokonoe'	CBlo CKen LCon NHol
– 'Kokuho'	CKen NHol
– 'Koraku'	CKen
– 'Kusu-dama'	CKen
– 'Meiko'	CKen EBre
– 'Michi-noku'	CKen
– 'Nasu-goyo'	CKen
– 'Negishi'	CKen EBre GAri LCon LPan MBal MBlu MBri
– 'Ogonjanome'	CKen
– 'Ryokuho'	CKen
– 'Ryuju'	CKen
– 'Sanbo'	CDoC CKen LCon MBar
§ – 'Saphir'	CKen EBre LCon MBri
– 'Setsugekka'	CKen
– 'Shikashima'	CKen
– 'Shiobara'	CKen
– 'Shizukagoten'	CKen
– 'Shure'	CKen
– 'Tempelhof'	COtt ENHC GAri LNet MBar SLim
I – 'Zelkova'	LLin
– 'Zui-sho'	CKen
patula 🏆	CAbb CDul CGre CSam GAri ISea LCon MBal MBlu SArc SCoo SIgm WWat
peuce	CDul LCon MBar NWea SIng STre WFro
– 'Arnold Dwarf'	CKen
pinaster 🏆	CB&S CBlo CDoC CDul CLnd EHul GWht ISea LCon MBal
pinea 🏆	CAgr CHEx CKen CMac IOrc LCon LLin LPan MGos SArc SEND WNor
– 'Queensway'	CKen
ponderosa 🏆	CDul CFil CLnd ETen ISea LCon LLin LPan SIgm
pseudostrobus	MBal
¶ ***pumila***	CAgr
– 'Buchanan'	CKen
– 'Draijer's Dwarf'	CDoC LLin SLim
– 'Dwarf Blue'	See ***P. pumila*** **'Glauca'**
§ – 'Glauca' 🏆	CBlo CKen LCon LLin LNet MBar MBri NHar NHol
– 'Globe'	LCon LLin MBri

– 'Jeddeloh'	CKen
– 'Knightshayes'	CKen
§ – 'Nana'	SRms
– 'Säntis'	CDoC CKen EBre MAsh
– 'Saphir'	See ***P. parviflora* 'Saphir'**
radiata ♀	CB&S CDoC CDul CHEx CPer CTrw EBre ENot IHos IOrc LCon MBal SArc SHBN SLim STre WDin
– 'Aurea'	CKen EBre LCon LLin MAsh SLim SMur
– 'Bodnant'	CKen
– 'Isca'	CKen
– 'Marshwood'	CKen
resinosa 'Don Smith'	CKen
– 'Joel's Broom'	CKen
– 'Nobska'	CKen
– 'Quinobequin'	CKen
– 'Watnong'	CKen
rigida	EHul LCon STre
sabineana	LCon
x ***schwerinii***	CDoC LCon LRHS
sibirica	See ***P. cembra*** subsp. ***sibirica***
strobiformis	LCon
strobus	CDoC CDul EHul GAri GAul IOrc ISea LCon MBar NWea SEND STre WNor
§ – 'Alba'	LCon MGos NHol
– 'Amelia's Dwarf'	CBlo CKen
– 'Anna Fiele'	CKen
– 'Bergman's Mini'	CKen
– 'Bergman's Pendula Broom'	CKen
I – 'Bergman's Sport of Prostrata'	CKen
– 'Blue Shag'	CBlo CKen COtt LLin LPan MBri MGos SLim WPyg
– 'Densa'	CKen LCon MBri
– 'Dove's Dwarf'	CKen
– 'Fastigiata'	CKen EBee LLin
– 'Hillside Gem'	CKen
– 'Horsford'	CKen
– 'Jericho'	CKen
– 'Krügers Lilliput'	CKen LCon LLin MBri SLim
– 'Macopin'	MGos
– 'Merrimack'	CBlo CKen
– 'Minima'	CDoC CKen LCon LLin MBar MBlu MBri NHar SLim
– 'Minuta'	CKen LCon
– 'Nana'	See ***P. strobus* 'Radiata'**
– 'Nivea'	See ***P. strobus* 'Alba'**
– 'Northway Broom'	CKen LLin
– 'Pendula'	SMad
§ – 'Radiata' ♀	EBee EHul ENHC IHos IOrc LBee LNet MBar NBee NHar SLim WAbe
– 'Reinshaus'	CKen LCon LLin
– 'Sayville'	CKen
– 'Sea Urchin'	CKen
– 'Uncatena'	CKen
– 'Verkade's Broom'	CKen
sylvestris ♀	CB&S CDoC CDul CGre CKin CPer CSam EHul ENot EOrn GRei IHos LBuc LCon LHyr LLin MAsh MBal MBar MGos NBee NWea SHBN SPer SReu STre WDin WMou WNor WStI
– 'Abergeldie'	CKen
– 'Andorra'	CKen
§ – 'Argentea'	LNet
– 'Aurea' ♀	CKen CMac CWLN EBre EHul IOrc LBee LCon LLin LNet MAsh MBal MBar SHBN SLim SPer SSta
– 'Avondene'	CKen
– 'Beuvronensis' ♀	CKen CMac CWLN EOrn GAri LBee LCon LLin LNet MAsh MBlu MGos NHol SLim SSta
– 'Brevifolia'	CBlo LCon MBar NHol
– 'Buchanan's Gold'	CKen
– 'Burghfield'	CBlo CKen LCon LLin NHol
– 'Chantry Blue'	CBlo CFee CWLN EOrn LBee LCon LLin MAsh MBar MGos NHol SLim
– 'Clumber Blue'	CKen
– 'Compressa'	GAri
– 'Dereham'	CKen LLin
– 'Doone Valley'	CKen LLin
– 'Edwin Hillier'	See ***P. sylvestris* 'Argentea'**
– 'Fastigiata'	CDoC CEnd CKen EOrn LCon LLin MAsh MBar MGos NHar SLim SSta
– 'Frensham'	CBlo CKen LCon LLin MGos MOne
– 'Globosa'	GAri
– 'Gold Coin'	CDoC CKen LCon LLin MBri MGos NHol SLim WPyg
– 'Gold Medal'	CKen LLin
– 'Grand Rapids'	CKen
– 'Green Flare'	CKen
– 'Hibernia'	ENHC
– 'Hillside Creeper'	CBlo CKen LLin SLim
– 'Inverleith' (v)	GAri LCon LLin MAsh MBar MGos NHol SLim
– 'Jade'	See ***P. sylvestris* 'Iceni'**
– 'Jeremy'	CKen LCon LLin WAbe
– 'Kelpie'	CKen
– 'Kenwith'	CKen NHol
¶ – 'Lakeside Dwarf'	LLin
– 'Little Brolly'	CKen
– 'Lodge Hill'	CBlo CKen CWLN EBre EOrn LCon LLin MAsh MOne SLim WAbe
– 'Longmoor'	CDoC CKen
– 'Martham'	CKen
– 'Nana'	See ***P. sylvestris* 'Watereri'**
– 'Nana Compacta'	LLin
– 'Nisbet'	CKen
§ – 'Nisbet's Gem'	LLin
– 'Padworth'	CKen
– 'Pixie'	CKen LCon
– 'Pyramidalis Compacta'	NHol
– 'Reedham'	LLin
– 'Repens'	CKen
– 'Sandringham'	CBlo LCon LLin NHol
– 'Saxatilis'	CBlo LCon LLin
– 'Scott's Dwarf'	See ***P. sylvestris* 'Nisbet's Gem'**
– 'Scrubby'	LCon
– 'Sentinel'	CKen
I – 'Skjak I'	CKen
I – 'Skjak II'	CKen
– 'Spaan's Slow Column'	CKen
– 'Tage'	CKen LLin
– 'Tanya'	CKen
– 'Tilshead'	CKen
– 'Treasure'	CKen
– 'Variegata'	CBlo
§ – 'Watereri'	CDoC CMac EHul ENHC ENot IHos IOrc LBee LCon LLin LNet LPan MAsh MBar MBri MGos NHar NHol SLim SPer SSta WDin

– 'Westonbirt' CKen NHol
– 'Wishmoor' LLin
* – 'Yaff Hill' LLin
tabuliformis CLnd CMCN LCon
taeda SIng
taiwanensis ISea
thunbergii CDoC CDul EHul LCon LLin MBal MGos SEND SPla STre WFro WNor
– 'Akame' CKen
¶ – 'Aocha-matsu' CKen
– 'Banshosho' CKen
– 'Compacta' CKen
– 'Dainagon' CKen
– 'Iwai' CKen
– 'Kotobuki' CKen
– 'Ko-yo-sho' CKen
– 'Kujaku' CKen
– 'Miyajuna' CKen
– 'Nishiki-ne' CKen
– var. ***oculus draconis*** LLin
– 'Ogon' CKen
§ – 'Sayonara' CBlo CKen GAri LCon NHol
– 'Senryu' CKen
– 'Shio-guro' CKen
– 'Sunsho' CKen
– 'Taihei' CKen
I – 'Thunderhead' CKen
– 'Yatsubusa' See ***P. thunbergii* 'Sayonara'**
uncinata See ***P. mugo*** subsp. ***uncinata***
– 'Paradekissen' CKen
virginiana MBal
– 'Wate's Golden' CKen
§ ***wallichiana*** CAbP CDoC CDul CKen CMCN EHoe EHul ENHC IOrc LCon LLin LPan MBal MBar MGos NBee SLim STre WCoo WNor
– 'Densa' MBri
– 'Nana' CKen EHul MBar
– 'Umbraculifera' LRHS MBal
– 'Zebrina' (v) EBre LCon MBar MGos SMad
yunnanensis ETen WNor

PIPER (Piperaceae)

¶ ***betle*** CPlN
♦ ***excelsum*** See ***Macropiper excelsum***
¶ ***nigrum*** MSal

PIPTANTHUS (Papilionaceae)

forrestii See ***P. nepalensis***
laburnifolius See ***P. nepalensis***
§ ***nepalensis*** CB&S CBot CHEx CHan CMac CPle ECha ELan EMil EPla LHop MGos MNrw MWat NSti SDix SHBN SOWG SPer SRms SSpi WCru WDin WOMN WPat
tomentosus SDry

PISONIA (Nyctaginaceae)

brunoniana See ***P. umbellifera***
§ ***umbellifera*** CHEx
– 'Variegata' CHEx

PISTACIA (Anacardiaceae)

chinensis CB&S CMCN ELan
terabinthus CFil

PISTIA (Araceae)

stratiotes MSta

PITTOSPORUM † (Pittosporaceae)

anomalum ECou MAll SDry
¶ – (f) ECou
¶ – (m) ECou
* ***argyrophyllum*** IOrc
'Arundel Green' CBlo CDoC ECou LRHS SDry
bicolor CFil ECou GQui MAll SArc WPGP
buchananii CHid CPle
colensoi ECou
– 'Wanaka' ECou
crassifolium CB&S CFil ECou IOrc NRai WPGP
– 'Havering Dwarf' ECou
– 'Napier' ECou
– x ***tenuifolium*** ECou MAll
– 'Variegatum' CGre
dallii CHEx
daphniphylloides var. ***adaphniphylloides*** CFil CGre
divaricatum ECou
'Essex' (v) ECou
eugenioides CB&S CMHG IDee MAll
– 'Platinum' CB&S
– 'Variegatum' 🏆 CB&S CGre GQui IOrc SBid WSHC
'Garnettii' (v) 🏆 CB&S CBot CChe CDec CEnd CLan CMHG CPle CShe CTrw EBre EHoe ELan EMil ENot IOrc LHop MAll MBal SMad SPer WAbe WDin WSHC
heterophyllum CPle ECou
¶ – variegated ECou
'Limelight' (v) CB&S CBlo CGre EMil WWes
lineare ECou
§ 'Margaret Turnbull' (v) CB&S CDoC ECou EMil LHop MGos
michiei ECou
¶ – (f) ECou
¶ – (m) ECou
'Nanum Variegatum' See ***P. tobira* 'Variegatum'**
obcordatum var. ***kaitaiaense*** ECou
¶ ***phillyreoides*** MAll
pimeleoides var. ***reflexum*** ECou
ralphii ECou
– 'Green Globe' ECou
revolutum MAll
'Saundersii' (v) CBlo CGre CMHG EMil MBal
tenuifolium 🏆 CB&S CShe EBre ECou EHoe ELan EMil ENot GOrc ISea LHop MAll MBal MBri MHlr MUlv SPer SReu SRms STre WAbe WDin WOMN WSHC WStI WTyr WWat
– 'Abbotsbury Gold' (v) CAbb CBot CChe CDoC CSam CTri CWSG ECou ELan EMil EWes MAll SDry SHBN SPer WSHC WStI
– 'Atropurpureum' CB&S
– 'County Park Dwarf' ECou WCru
– 'Deborah' (v) CB&S ECou LHop SBid
– 'Dixie' CMHG ECou
§ – 'Eila Keightley' (v) CBlo CDoC CMHG CSam EHic EHoe IOrc MBal
– 'French Lace' ECou
– 'Gold Star' CB&S CDoC ECou EMil
– 'Golden King' CB&S CDoC CMHG CWLN EBee MBal MRav MUlv SPla SRms
– 'Green Elf' ECou
* – 'Green Thumb' CMHG

– 'Irene Paterson' (v) 🏆 CAbb CB&S CGre CMHG CPle CSam ECou ELan IOrc LHop MBal MGos MUlv SAga SDry SPer SPla SRms SSpi SSta WAbe WFar WSHC
– 'James Stirling' CDoC ECou IOrc MAll WSHC
– 'John Flanagan' See ***P.* 'Margaret Turnbull'**
– 'Katie' CB&S
– 'Marjory Channon' (v) CB&S CDoC MUlv
– 'Nigricans' CB&S CLan
– 'Purpureum' CBot CPle CSam CTri CTrw ELan EPfP IOrc MBal SDry SHBN SPer SPla SRms WSHC
* – 'Silver Dollar' MBri
– 'Silver Magic' CB&S EMil
– 'Silver Queen' (f/v) 🏆 CB&S CEnd CLan CMHG CSam EBre ECou EHoe GOrc IOrc MAll MBal MNrw SHBN SPer SPla WAbe WSHC WStI WWat
– 'Stirling Gold' (v) CB&S ECou EWes EWll
– 'Sunburst' See ***P. tenuifolium* 'Eila Keightley'**
– 'Tiki' CB&S ECou
– 'Tom Thumb' 🏆 CB&S CEnd CFee CMHG CTrw CWLN ECou EHoe EMil IOrc LHop MAll MBal MLan MPla MUlv NRoo SAga SDry SHBN SPer SPla SSpi SSta WAbe WSHC WStI WWat
– 'Tresederi' (f/m) CTrw CWLN ECou MBal
– 'Variegata' CB&S ECou EMil
– 'Warnham Gold' 🏆 CB&S CDoC CHan CMHG COtt CTrw EBee ECou ELan IOrc MUlv SDry SPla SSpi WAbe WDin WWat
– 'Wendle Channon' (v) CB&S CDoC CEnd CMHG CPle CSam CWSG ECot ECou LHop MAll MBal MUlv SPer SPla WSHC WStI WWat
– 'Winter Sunshine' EFou SSta
tobira 🏆 CB&S CBot CFil CHEx CHan CLTr CPMA CPle CTrC ECou ELan IOrc MAll MGos NPal SApp SArc SBid SHBN SPer SSpi SSta WAbe WCru WEas WOMN WPat WPyg WSHC
– 'Nanum' CB&S EBee ECou ERea IOrc SBid
§ – 'Variegatum' 🏆 CB&S CBot CDoC CGre CHEx CPle CWLN ECou ERea GQui LHop MBri NPal SBid SPer SPla SSta WCru
undulatum CB&S CHEx IDee MAll
– 'Variegatum' CGre

PITYROGRAMMA (Hemionitidaceae)
triangularis CFil

PLAGIANTHUS (Malvaceae)
betulinus See ***P. regius***
lyallii See ***Hoheria lyallii***
§ ***regius*** ECou GQui ISea LRHS SBid

PLAGIOMNIUM (Sphagnaceae)
See Plant Deletions

PLAGIORHEGMA See JEFFERSONIA

PLANERA (Ulmaceae)
See Plant Deletions

PLANTAGO (Plantaginaceae)
¶ ***alpina*** EPPr
argentea EGoo GAul
asiatica MSal
– 'Variegata' CRow EBar EGoo EHoe ELan EMar EMon EPPr GBuc LFlo NBro NEgg NSti WBea WHer WSan
coronopus CKin EWFC
cynops EMon EPPr LRHS MTho WCot
gaudichaudii EOHP
lanceolata CNat CTiv ECWi EWFC MHew
– 'Burren Rose' CNat CRow
– 'Streaker' (v) CRow WCot WHer
major CTiv EWFC
– 'Atropurpurea' See ***P. major* 'Rubrifolia'**
– 'Frills' CNat CRow WAlt WCot WHer
§ – 'Rosularis' CArn CInt CRow CSpe CWGN ECha ECro ELan EMon ILis LHol MFir MTho NBro NEgg NGar NMir NRoo NSti WBea WBon WHal WHer WHil WPer WWye
§ – 'Rubrifolia' CArn CBos CRow CWGN EBar ECha ECoo EHoe ELan EMar EMon EPla LFis LHol LWak MFir MNrw MRav NBro NEgg NGar NHar NMir NSti WCer WHer WPer WWye
– 'Variegata' CJew LHol WPer
maritima CKin GBin WHer
media CKin ECWi EWFC MHew
nivalis EGoo EHyt GBin GCLN NNrd NTow SMad WWin
psyllium MSal WHer
raoulii NBro NHol
rosea See ***P. major* 'Rosularis'**
sempervirens ECro WHer
uniflora See ***Littorella uniflora***

PLATANTHERA (Orchidaceae)
hologlottis EFEx
metabifolia EFEx

PLATANUS † (Platanaceae)
× ***acerifolia*** See ***P.* × *hispanica***
§ × ***hispanica*** 🏆 CB&S CDoC CGre CKin CLnd CMCN CTho EMil ENot IOrc LBuc LPan MGos NWea SEND SHBN SPer WDin WFar WMou
¶ – 'Pyramidalis' CTho
– 'Suttneri' (v) CBlo CDoC CEnd CLnd CMCN LBuc LMer LNet SMad
occidentalis CSto
orientalis 🏆 CLnd CMCN EBee EPfP IOrc WMou
– 'Cuneata' CDoC LRHS MBri
§ – f. ***digitata*** CLnd CTho SLPl WMou
– 'Laciniata' See ***P. orientalis* f. *digitata***
– 'Mirkovec' CDoC MBri SMad SPer WMou

PLATYCARYA (Juglandaceae)
strobilacea CMCN WCoo

PLATYCERIUM (Polypodiaceae)
alcicorne hort. See ***P. bifurcatum***
§ ***bifurcatum*** 🏆 LCns MBri
grande hort. See ***P. superbum***
§ ***superbum*** 🏆 LCns

PLATYCLADUS (Cupressaceae)

orientalis	See ***Thuja orientalis***

PLATYCODON † (Campanulaceae)

grandiflorus ♀	CGle CNic CWGN ECha EPad GLil LFis LHop MFir MHFP MSal NBro NCut NFai NGre NOrc NVic SIng WCla WHoo WOld WWye
grandiflorus albus	CArc CBro CRDP EAst ECro EFou ELan EPad LHop MBri MBro NBro NFai NGre NOak SIng SPer WHoo WOve WPer WWin
grandiflorus apoyama ♀	CLyd CPBP EPad GMac LBee MBro MHig SAlw SIng SWas WAbe WHil WHoo WPer WWin
– *albus*	ECro LGre SIde SWas WCru WEas WHoo WPyg
grandiflorus 'Baby Blue'	EOHP EPad SRms
– 'Blue Pearl'	WHoo
– 'Blue Pygmy'	SSca
– 'Blue Surf'	SPla WPer
– 'Florist Blue'	CMdw
– 'Florist Rose'	ECro EPad NOak
– 'Florist Snow'	CMdw ECro NOak
– 'Fuji Blue'	CBlo EBre MCCP
– 'Fuji Pink'	CArc CBlo CBro CRDP CSpe EAst EBee EBre MCCP NHol NSti SMrm SPer SPla SSte SUsu WAbe WTre
– 'Fuji White'	CBlo CMil MCCP NHol SMrm SPla WHil WTre
– 'Hakone'	CArc CBlo CRDP EMan LHop MBro NCat SMrm WGwG WHil WHoo WPyg
– 'Hakone Double Blue'	CBro
¶ – 'Hakone White'	WHil
– Purple Princess = 'Hime-murasaki'	EBee
– 'Mammoth Blue'	ECro NMir
– 'Mammoth White'	ECro NMir
grandiflorus mariesii ♀	CBro CGle CLyd CNic EBre ECtt EFou ELan ENot EPad GMaP LFis MBal MHig NBir SPer SRms WEas WHoo WPer WWin
grandiflorus mariesii albus	MBro WHoo WPyg
grandiflorus 'Misato Purple'	NHol NSla SMrm
♦ – Mother of Pearl	See ***P. grandiflorus* 'Perlmutterschale'**
– 'Park's Double Blue'	MBro MHFP MTis NOak WHoo WPen WPyg WWhi
§ – 'Perlmutterschale'	CArc CGle CMil EBre ELan EPad MBri WHoo WPyg WWeb
grandiflorus pumilus	EBee NWCA WDav WHoo WPyg
grandiflorus 'Purple Dwarf'	EPad
grandiflorus roseus	ECro EFou NCut NGre WHoo
grandiflorus 'Sentimental Blue'	EPad WLRN
– 'Shell Pink'	See ***P. grandiflorus* 'Perlmutterschale'**
– 'Zwerg'	LGre NSla WHil

PLECOSTACHYS (Asteraceae)

§ ***serpyllifolia***	CHal CLTr IHos LBlm SDix WPer

PLECTOCOLEA (Jungermanniaceae)

See Plant Deletions

PLECTRANTHUS (Lamiaceae)

¶ ***amboinicus***	LHil
argentatus	CHad CSev CSpe LHil SMrm
australis	CHal EOHP SLMG
behrii	See ***P. fruticosus***
ciliatus	LHil
coleoides 'Marginatus'	See ***P. forsteri* 'Marginatus'**
– 'Variegatus'	See ***P. madagascariensis* 'Variegated Mintleaf'**
excisus	EMon
§ ***forsteri***	LHil
§ – 'Marginatus'	CHal CLTr ERea LHil MRav NFai SIde SVen
§ ***fruticosus***	CHal LHil SLMG
§ ***madagascariensis*** 'Variegated Mintleaf'	CHal LHil MRav SRms
oertendahlii ♀	CBrk CHal EBak LHil SLMG
podena	CArn
purpuratus	EOHP
Swedish Ivy	See ***P. australis***
§ ***thyrsoideus***	CHal
¶ ***zatarhendii***	LHil
zuluensis	CPle

PLEIOBLASTUS † (Poaceae - Bambusoideae)

akebono	SBam SDry
§ ***auricomus*** ♀	CChu CCuc CHEx CRDP CRow EBee ECha EFul EGol EHoe EJap ELan ETPC MBal MBar MBri MGos MRav NHol SAxl SBam SBla SDix SDry SMad SPer WJun WPat WRus
– 'Bracken Hill'	EPla SBam SDry WJun
– f. ***chrysophyllus***	EPla SBam SDry SMad WJun
§ ***chino***	CWLN EFou SBam SDry
§ – f. ***angustifolius***	EPla LHil SBam SDry
– 'Aureostriatus' (v)	EFou EPla SBam SDry
chino chrysanthus	See ***Sasa chrysantha***
chino f. ***elegantissimus***	COtt EPla ISta SBam SDry WJun
– 'Kimmei'	SDry
– 'Murakamianus'	EPla SBam SDry
fortunei	See ***P. variegatus***
'Gauntlettii'	See ***P. humilis*** var. ***pumilus***
glaber 'Albostriatus'	See ***Sasaella masamuneana* f. *albostriata***
gramineus	EPla SBam SDry WJun
§ ***hindsii*** hort.	EPla SArc SBam SDry
§ ***humilis***	CBlo ELan SBam
§ – var. ***pumilus***	CArc CCuc CPMA CRow CWLN EHoe EPar EPla ETPC ISea ISta MBlu MBri SBam SDry WBea WJun WNor WPat WPer
kongosanensis 'Aureostriatus' (v)	EPla SBam SDry
linearis	CB&S CWLN EFul EPla SBam SDry WJun
longifimbriatus	WJun
oleosus	EPla SDry WJun
§ ***pygmaeus***	CArc CCuc CEnd CPMA CRow CWit EBre ECro EFul EHoe ELan EOas EPla ESiP ESis IOrc ISea MBar MBri NBro NFai SBam SDry SIng SPer SRms SSoC WJun WNor WPer
§ – var. ***distichus***	CWLN EFul EPPr EPla GBin LHil SArc SBam SDry WJun
– – 'Mini'	WCot

§ – 'Mirrezuzume'	EPla GBin SBam WWat
shibuyanus 'Tsuboi'	CArc COtt EFou EPla ISta SDry WJun
§ ***simonii***	CHEx CWLN EBee EBre EFul GBin SBam SDry
– var. ***heterophyllus***	See ***P. simonii* f. *variegatus***
§ – f. ***variegatus***	EOas EPla ISta MBlu SBam SDry SPer WJun
§ ***variegatus*** ♀	CCuc CEnd CPMA EBre ECha EFul EGol EHoe EJap ELan ENot EPla ESiP ETPC LHop MBal MBri MGos NHol SArc SBam SChu SDix SDry WCot WJun WNor WPat WPer WRus
– var. ***viridis***	SDry
viridistriatus	See ***P. auricomus***

PLEIONE † (Orchidaceae)

§ ***albiflora*** 'Pinchbeck Diamond'	LBut SWes
g. **Alishan**	CNic LBut MRPP NSpr SWes
– 'Mount Fuji'	LBut
– 'Soldier Blue'	LBut
'Asama'	LBut SWes
§ ***aurita***	EFEx LAma NSpr WChr
g. **Bandai-san**	LBut
g. **Barcena**	LBut
g. **Beerenberg**	LBut
'Berapi'	LBut SWes
g. **Brigadoon**	LBut MRPP
g. **Britannia**	LBut
– 'Doreen'	LBut
§ ***bulbocodioides***	EPot ERos IBlr LBut MRPP NSpr WFar
– 'Lapwing'	LBut
§ – Limprichtii Group ♀	EFEx EPot MRPP NTow SWes WChr
– – 'Primrose Peach'	EPot
◆ – Pricei Group	See ***P. formosana* Pricei Group**
§ – 'Yunnan'	EPot LBut NSpr SWes WChr
g. **Captain Hook**	LBut
chunii	See ***P. aurita***
× ***confusa***	EFEx SWes WChr
g. **Cotopaxi**	LBut
g. **Danan**	LBut SWes
g. **Deriba**	LBut
g. **Eiger**	EPot LBut NSpr SWes WChr
– cream form	EPot LBut
g. **El Pico**	LBut SWes
– 'Goldcrest'	LBut
– 'Kestrel'	LBut
– 'Pheasant'	LBut
– 'Starling'	LBut
g. **Erebus**	LBut SWes
– 'Quail'	LBut
'Erh Hai'	NSpr
g. **Etna**	CNic LBut SWes
– 'Bullfinch'	LBut
formosana ♀	CBos CNic EFEx EPot ETub IBlr LAma NHar NSpr NTow SDeJ SIng SWes WChr
– 'Achievement'	LBut
I – 'Alba'	CNic EPot IBlr MRPP SWes
– ***alba*** g. **Kate**	SWes
– g. **Polar Sun**	SWes
– g. **Snow Cap**	SWes
– 'Avalanche'	EPot LBut NSpr
– 'Ben Nevis'	LBut
– 'Blush of Dawn'	EPot LBut NSpr
– 'Cairngorm'	NSpr SWes WChr
– 'Christine Anne'	NSpr
– 'Clare'	EPot LBut NSpr

– g. **Eugene**	SWes
– 'Greenhill'	LBut
I – 'Iris'	LBut NSpr
– 'Lilac Beauty'	SWes
– 'Little Winnie'	SWes
– 'Lucy Diamond'	LBut
– g. **Lulu**	SWes
– 'Oriental Grace'	EFEx EPot LAma LBut SWes
– 'Oriental Jewel'	SWes
– 'Oriental Splendour'	EPot LBut MRPP NNrd NSpr SIng SWes WChr
– 'Polar Sun'	EPot NSpr WChr
§ – Pricei Group	EPot NTow
– 'Serenity'	LBut
– 'Snow Cap'	EFEx SWes
– 'Snow White'	LBut MRPP
forrestii	EFEx EPot LAma NSpr SWes WChr
g. **Fuego**	LBut NSpr SWes
– 'Wren'	LBut
g. **Fujiyama**	LBut
g. **Gerry Mundey**	LBut
g. **Hekla**	EPot LBut SWes
– 'Partridge'	LBut SWes
hookeriana	LAma MRPP SWes WChr
humilis	LAma MRPP SDeJ WChr
g. **Irazu**	LBut
g. **Jorullo**	LBut SWes
– 'Long-tailed Tit'	LBut
g. **Katla**	LBut SWes
g. **Katmai**	LBut
g. **Keith Rattray**	LBut
g. **Kilauea**	LBut SWes
g. **Krakatoa**	LBut
g. **Lascar**	LBut
limprichtii	LBut NSpr
g. **Lipari**	LBut
maculata	EFEx LAma SWes
g. **Marco Polo**	LBut NSpr
g. **Matupi**	LBut NSpr
g. **Mayon**	LBut
g. **Mazama**	LBut
g. **Myojin**	LBut SWes
g. **Novarupta**	LBut
g. **Orinoco**	LBut SWes
– 'Gemini'	LBut
g. **Paricutin**	LBut
g. **Pavlof**	LBut
'Phoenix'	NSpr
pinkepankii	See ***P. albiflora***
g. **Piton**	EPot LBut SWes WChr
pogonioides hort.	See ***P. speciosa***
– Rolfe	See ***P. bulbocodioides***
praecox	SWes WChr
g. **Rakata**	LBut
– 'Shot Silk'	LBut
g. **Ranier**	LBut
scopulorum	LBut
g. **Shantung**	EPot LAma LBut MRPP NSpr SWes WChr
– 'Candyfloss'	NSpr
– 'Ducat'	LBut
– 'Gerry Mundey'	LBut
– 'Golden Jubilee'	NSpr
– 'Golden Plover'	LBut
– 'Muriel Harberd' ♀	CRDP NSpr
– 'Piton'	LAma
– 'R6.7'	NSpr
– 'Ridgeway'	EPot NSpr SWes WChr
g. **Sorea**	LBut
g. **Soufrière**	LBut NSpr SWes
§ ***speciosa***	EPot LBut MRPP SWes WChr

– 'Blakeway Phillips'	LBut NSpr SWes
g. **Stromboli**	LBut NSpr SWes
– 'Fireball'	LBut NSpr
– 'Robin'	LBut
g. **Surtsey**	LBut
g. **Tacana**	LBut
g. **Tambora**	LBut
g. **Tarawera**	LBut SWes
g. **Tolima**	CNic EPot LAma LBut NSpr SWes WChr
g. **Tongariro**	EPot LBut NSpr SWes WChr
– 'Jackdaw'	LBut SWes
g. **Versailles**	EFEx EPot LAma LBut NSpr SWes WChr
– 'Bucklebury' ♀	CNic EPot LBut NSpr SWes WChr
– 'Heron'	LBut
– 'Muriel Turner'	EPot LAma LBut NSpr SWes WChr
g. **Vesuvius**	EPot LBut NSpr
– 'Aphrodite'	EPot WChr
– 'Leopard'	LBut
g. **Volcanello**	LBut NSpr SWes
'Wunzen'	LBut
yunnanensis hort.	See ***P. bulbocodioides* 'Yunnan'**
– Rolfe	LAma LBut SWes
g. **Zeus Weinstein**	LBut

PLEOMELE See DRACAENA

PLEUROCHAETE (Sphagnaceae)
See Plant Deletions

PLEUROSPERMUM (Apiaceae)

brunonis	EDAr NGre WHal

PLEXIPUS (Verbenaceae)
See Plant Deletions

PLUMBAGO (Plumbaginaceae)

§ ***auriculata*** ♀	CB&S CEnd CLTr CPlN CPle CRHN EBak ELan ERav ERea ERom ISea LBlm LHol LHop MBri MRav NEgg NPal NRog SIde SLMG SOWG SPer SRms SVen WBod
– var. ***alba***	CB&S CBot CBrk CPlN CRHN CSev EBak ELan EMil ERav ERea ERom IBlr ISea LBlm LHol SLMG SOWG SPer SVen
– Royal Cape = 'Monott'	ERav
capensis	See ***P. auriculata***
§ ***indica***	CPle SLMG
indica rosea	See ***P. indica***
larpentiae	See ***Ceratostigma plumbaginoides***
zeylanica	ERea

PLUMERIA (Apocynaceae)

§ ***obtusa***	LChe
rubra	ECon LChe
¶ – f. ***lutea***	LChe
'Singapore'	See ***P. obtusa***

PNEUMATOPTERIS See CYCLOSORUS

POA (Poaceae)

¶ ***abyssinica***	ETPC
acicularifolia	ESOG NHol
alpina nodosa	ETPC GBin
araratica	ETPC
badensis 'Ingelkissen'	ETPC
bulbosa	EPPr ETPC
chaixii	CCuc EHoe EMan EMon EPPr EPla ESOG ETPC GBin WFoF
cita	EBee EWes
colensoi	CCuc EBee EFou EHoe ETPC GBin MHlr NHar NHol NPSI WCot
eminens	EBee
¶ – from Magadan, Siberia	EPPr
fawcettiae	ETPC
glauca	ETPC
hothamensis	ETPC
imbecilla	ESOG ETPC
× ***jemtlandica***	EBee ESOG NHol
labillardierei	ECha EPPr ESOG ETPC
nemoralis	ETPC

PODALYRIA (Papilionaceae)

¶ ***biflora***	CSpe
¶ ***calyptrata***	CSpe CTrC
sericea	CSpe CTrC SIgm

PODANTHUS (Asteraceae)

ovatifolius G&K 4386	CGre

PODOCARPUS (Podocarpaceae)

acutifolius	CDoC ECou MBar STre
andinus	See ***Prumnopitys andina***
'Autumn Shades' (m)	ECou
'Blaze' (f)	ECou
chilinus	See ***P. salignus***
'Chocolate Box' (*lawrencei* × *nivalis*) (f)	ECou
'County Park Fire' (*lawrencei* × *nivalis*) (f)	ECou MGos
cunninghamii	See ***P. hallii***
dacrydioides	See ***Dacrycarpus dacrydioides***
¶ ***elongatus***	CTrC
ferrugineus	See ***Prumnopitys ferruginea***
'Golden Dwarf'	See ***Prumnopitys ferruginea* 'Golden Dwarf'**
§ ***hallii***	ECou
* – 'Kiwi' (f)	ECou
– × ***nivalis*** (f)	ECou
– 'Roro' (m)	ECou
'Havering' (f)	ECou
¶ ***henkelii***	CTrC
¶ ***latifolius***	CTrC
lawrencei	CBlo ECho EHul GAri IOrc
– 'Alpine Lass' (f)	ECou
– 'Blue Gem' (f)	ECou EOrn LCon MAsh MGos WBcn
– 'Bluey'	CBlo CDoC LBee LLin MBar MOne SLim WLRN WWat
– (f)	ECou MBar MGos MPla SSmi WWat
– 'Kiandra'	ECou
macrophyllus	CGre CMCN EOrn SArc SMad STre WWat
¶ – (m)	ECou
– 'Angustifolius'	CHEx
nivalis	CMHG CMac EBre ECou EOrn EPla LLin MBar MHig MPla SIng SPla SRms SSmi WWat
– 'Arthur' (m)	ECou
– 'Bronze'	EPla
– 'Clarence' (m)	ECou
– 'Green Queen' (f)	ECou
– 'Jack's Pass' (m)	ECou
– 'Kaweka' (m)	ECou
– 'Little Lady' (f)	ECou

– 'Livingstone' (f)	ECou
– 'Lodestone' (m)	ECou
– 'Moffatt' (f)	ECou
– 'Otari' (m)	ECou
– 'Park Cover'	ECou
– 'Princess' (f)	ECou
– 'Ruapehu'	ECou
§ ***salignus*** ♡	CB&S CChu CDoC CGre CHEx EPla IOrc ISea SArc WWat
¶ – (m)	ECou
spicatus	See ***Prumnopitys taxifolia***
'Spring Sunshine'	ECou
totara	CHEx CHan ECou STre
– 'Aureus'	CB&S CDoC ECou EPla LLin MBal MBar MUlv SHBN WLRN WSHC
– 'Pendulus'	ECou
'Young Rusty'	ECou

PODOLEPIS (Asteraceae)
See Plant Deletions

PODOPHYLLUM (Berberidaceae)

difforme	WCru
emodi	See ***P. hexandrum***
◆ – var. ***chinense***	See ***P. hexandrum*** var. ***chinense***
* ***hendersonii***	WCot
§ ***hexandrum***	CChu CHEx CRDP CRow EBre GAbr GCal GCra GDra GPoy MBal MBri MHig MSal MTol NHar SBid SSpi WCot WWye
§ – var. ***chinense***	CPou CRow EGar EHyt IBlr SMad WCru WWat
– 'Majus'	EBee NHol WCot WCru
peltatum	CArn CBro CChu EBee EBre GPoy IBlr LAma MBri MSal NHar NSti SSpi WChr WCot WCru WThi WWat
pleianthum	WCru
versipelle	WCru

PODRANEA (Bignoniaceae)

§ ***ricasoliana***	CPlN ERea LChe SLMG SOWG

POGONATHERUM (Poaceae)

paniceum	See ***P. saccharoideum***
§ ***saccharoideum***	MBri

POGONIA (Orchidaceae)

¶ ***ophioglossoides***	SSpi

POGOSTEMON (Lamiaceae)

§ ***cablin***	GPoy
patchouly	See ***P. cablin***

POINSETTIA hort. See EUPHORBIA
pulcherrima cvs

POLEMONIUM † (Polemoniaceae)

acutifolium var. ***nipponicum***	See ***P. caeruleum*** subsp. ***nipponicum***
'Apricot Beauty'	See ***P. carneum* 'Apricot Delight'**
N ***archibaldiae***	CPea LBlm NCGP
boreale	GGar MNrw MSto NChi
brandegeei Greene	ECro MHig NBro NCGP NGre WByw WPer WSan
– subsp. ***mellitum***	CArn GCHN LCot MSto NTow WBea
§ ***caeruleum***	CArn CGle CKin CSev CShe EBre ECED ECha EFou ELan EWFC GPoy LHol LHop MBal MChe MGam NBro NGre NMir NNor NNrd NOak SIde SPer WCla WEas WHil WWin WWye
– var. ***album***	See ***P. caeruleum*** subsp. ***caeruleum* f. *album***
– 'Blue Bell'	MAvo WPbr
– Brise d'Anjou = 'Blanjou' (v)	COtt EBre EOrc EWes LRHS MCLN MGra NLak NRoo SCoo SPer SWat WWeb
§ – subsp. ***caeruleum*** f. ***album***	CBre CGle CHan CShe EBar ECED ECha EFou ELan EOrc GAbr LHop NBro NFai NOak SPer SSte WBea WCla WEas WHen WHil WPer WWin
– subsp. ***dissectum*** f. ***album***	CBre
– var. ***grandiflorum***	See ***P. caeruleum*** subsp. ***himalayanum***
◆ – Himalayan - misapplied	See ***P. cashmerianum***
§ – subsp. ***himalayanum***	GCra WCot WPer
– 'Humile'	See ***P.* 'Northern Lights'**
– 'Newark Park'	EPPr
§ – subsp. ***nipponicum***	WPer
carneum	CGle EBre ECha EMan EMon EOrc MFir MTho NHar NMir WBea WOMN WPer WSan WWin
§ – 'Apricot Delight'	CBot CBre CMil EAst ECoo ELan EMar GAbr GBri GMac MHFP MNrw NBir NFai NGar NLak SAga SIde SOkh WCot WElm WHil WOve WThi WWhi WWin
§ ***cashmerianum***	CBre CLTr CMdw EBee ECGP ECro EMon GAbr GBuc GCHN LFis MBro NOak SMrm WBea WEas WHen WHoo WPyg
cashmerianum album	NRai
¶ ***chartaceum***	NGre
'Churchills'	CBos CBre CChu NFai
confertum	See ***P. viscosum***
'Dawn Flight'	EBre NCat
'Daydawn'	MAvo
delicatum	MHar MHig MTho NHar NWCA
elegans	MSto
¶ ***eximium***	WFox
flavum	See ***P. foliosissimum*** var. ***flavum***
foliosissimum A Gray	CBot CGle EBre ECha EPPr MNrw SRms WPer
◆ – var. ***albiflorum***	See ***P. foliosissimum*** var. ***alpinum***
§ – var. ***alpinum***	ECro LGan NBir WGwG
§ – var. ***flavum***	CBre MHig WHil
– hort.	See ***P. archibaldiae***
'Glebe Cottage Lilac'	CBre CElw CGle CHar CMil WBea
'Golden Showers' (v)	CPla MCCP
'Hannah Billcliffe'	LCot
¶ 'Hopleys'	CHan GBar GCal LBlm LFis LHop MAvo NBrk SAxl WByw WCot WFar WPbr
× ***jacobaea***	WBea WCot WPbr
§ 'Lambrook Mauve' ♡	Widely available
liniflorum	LCot MSto

¶ 'Mary Mottram'	CBre
mellitum	ECoo MSto
§ 'Northern Lights'	CHid ELan EMon EPPr LRHS MBri MCCP
occidentale	See ***P. caeruleum*** subsp. ***amygdalinum***
pauciflorum	CBre CChr CGle CLon CMea CVer ECro ELan EOrc ESis GTou LHop MCLN MNrw MTho MTis NBir NMir NOak SHel WBea WCla WHer WOMN WPer WWhi WWin WWye
– form	LBlm
– subsp. ***hinckleyi***	NChi NGre
– silver-leaved	EBee MHFP MSto NRai WElm WOve WSan
'Pink Beauty'	CBre CMGP ECro EFou ELan LCom LRHS NCat SCro WBea WCer WGwG
'Pink Pearl'	WWhi
pulchellum Salisbury	See ***P. reptans***
– Turczaninow	See ***P. caeruleum***
– Willdenow	WCot
pulcherrimum album	CGra
– Hooker	CArc CHan EBre EHyt ELan EPla GAbr GBar GCal GTou LHop MSCN NBro NHar NLak NTow SAlw SPer WBea WHen WPer WWye
– 'Tricolor'	NBus NLak
pulcherrimum hort.	See ***P. boreale***
– 'Tricolor' hort.	See ***P. boreale***
§ ***reptans***	CArn CLTr ECha ECoo ELau GBar GBri GCra GPoy LHol MHew MSal NBro NHar NRoo WBea WHil WPer WRHF WWye
– 'Album'	See ***P. reptans* 'Virginia White'**
– 'Blue Pearl'	CBre CGle CMGP CMea EMan EPPr GAri LFis MNrw NBro NCat NRoo SCro SHel SOkh SPer SUsu WByw WHen WOve WRHF
– 'Lambrook Manor'	See ***P.* 'Lambrook Mauve'**
* – 'Sky Blue'	NBro
– 'Virginia White'	CBre NChi
richardsonii Graham	See ***P. boreale***
richardsonii hort.	See ***P.* 'Northern Lights'**
'Sapphire'	CBre CDoC EMon MBel NFai NNor WBea
scopulinum	MSto NChi WPer
'Sonia's Bluebell'	CGle CMil EBee MSte NLak WPbr
¶ 'Theddingworth'	MAvo
§ ***viscosum***	CFir CPea GBuc GCHN MSto NGre WByw WHen
¶ – NNS 93-658	MRPP
yezoense	CM&M GBri MHFP MNrw WCot
yezoense hidakanum	CPla MAvo
¶ ***yezoense*** 'Purple Rain'	CBre CPea MCCP NRai WDav WSan

POLIANTHES (Agavaceae)

§ ***geminiflora***	LAma
tuberosa 🏆	CAvo CB&S NRog
* – 'Marginata' (v)	WCot
– 'The Pearl' (d)	CSpe LAma

POLIOMINTHA (Lamiaceae)

* ***bustamanta***	CLon LGre NBir WCot

POLIOTHYRSIS (Flacourtiaceae)

sinensis	CAbP CB&S CChu CFil CGre SSpi WWat WWes

POLYGALA (Polygalaceae)

calcarea	MBro MDun NHar NTow NWCA WPat
– Bulley's form	LBee LRHS SIng WAbe
– 'Lillet' 🏆	CLyd ELan EPot MHig MTho NHar NHol NMen SBla SWas WAbe WPat WWin
chamaebuxus 🏆	EBre GDra GGGa MAsh MBal MDun MHig MPla NHar NHol NWoo SRms WAbe WHil WWin
chamaebuxus alba	LBee LRHS WAbe
§ ***chamaebuxus*** var. ***grandiflora*** 🏆	CB&S CNic ELan EPot GDra GGGa LBee LHop MAsh MBal MBar MBro MDun MGos MHig MPla NHar NHol NMen NWCA SBla SChu SIng WAbe WBod WPat WSHC WWin
– 'Kamniski'	CMHG EPot GGGa NHar NMen
– 'Loibl'	EPot GGGa MAsh SBla
– 'Purpurea'	See ***P. chamaebuxus*** var. ***grandiflora***
– 'Rhodoptera'	See ***P. chamaebuxus*** var. ***grandiflora***
§ × ***dalmaisiana*** 🏆	CAbb CLTr CSpe EMil ERea GQui LBlm LHop MAsh SAga SBla
'Dolomite'	GGGa NHar
myrtifolia	CBrk CPle CSpe IBlr LCns SAxl SChu SEND SMrm SUsu WWye
– 'Grandiflora'	See ***P.* × *dalmaisiana***
¶ ***vayredae***	WPat
virgata	CArn CSpe ECon ERea LHil
vulgaris	EWFC IOrc

POLYGONATUM (Convallariaceae)

§ ***biflorum***	CArn CBro CPou EBre EGar EGol ELan EMan EPot GCHN MSal NCat NRoo SSpi WCot WCru WHer
– dwarf form	EPla WChr WCot
canaliculatum	See ***P. biflorum***
cirrhifolium	MDun SWas WCru
commutatum	See ***P. biflorum***
¶ ***cryptanthum***	WCru
curvistylum	CMea CRDP ECha LGre WFar
cyrtonema B&SWJ 271	WCru
– hort.	See ***Disporopsis pernyi***
§ ***falcatum***	CBro CHan CLyd CMea EBre EPla ERav MBal MDun MHig NOak SIng WChr WHer WWat WWin
– 'Variegatum'	CChu CDoC CHad CLyd CRow CSpe ECha EFou ELan EPar LGre MBri MBro MDun NDea NFla NHol NSti SBla SCro SMac WHoo WNdy WPyg WWat WWhi
'Falcon'	See ***P. humile***
geminiflorum	SWas
giganteum	See ***P. biflorum***
§ ***graminifolium***	EPot ERos LGre WCru
– GW 803	MDun SWas
§ ***hirtum***	EMon EPla EPot LWoo SAxl WCot WCru

hookeri	CBro CChu CLyd CMea ECha EDAr EPla EPot ERos LBee LGre LHop MBal MHig MTho NGar NGre NHar NHol NNrd NRya NSla NWCA SIng SMac WAbe WChr WDav WHal WHil
§ ***humile***	CGle CRDP CSpe ELan EPla EPot ERos LWoo MBel NGar NHar SAxl SBar SWas WChr WCot WCru WHal WRus
§ × ***hybridum*** ♀	Widely available
– 'Flore Pleno'	WHer
§ – 'Striatum' (v)	Widely available
– 'Variegatum'	See ***P. × hybridum* 'Striatum'**
latifolium	See ***P. hirtum***
multiflorum giganteum hort.	See ***P. biflorum***
multiflorum hort.	See ***P. × hybridum***
– Linnaeus	CMHG CRow EAst EGar MDun MGra SRms WSel
§ ***odoratum***	CBro CRow CSWP EOHP EPar EPla EPot EWFC MSal NRya SSpi
– 'Flore Pleno' ♀	CRow ECha LWoo NRar SBla SWas WChr
– 'Grace Barker'	See ***P. × hybridum* 'Striatum'**
– Kew form	EPot
¶ – var. ***pluriflorum***	SSpi
N– – 'Variegatum'	CBro CChu EFol EGol EOrc EPla LGan LGre MBal MBro MCli MRav NRoo SPer WCru WRus WWat WWin
– 'Silver Wings'	ECha
officinale	See ***P. odoratum***
pluriflorum	See ***P. graminifolium***
¶ ***pubescens***	MSto
pumilum	See ***P. falcatum***
punctatum	WCru
racemosum	SIng
roseum	WHer
sibiricum	WCru
sp. Himalaya	WCru
stewartianum	EBee LWoo
verticillatum	CBro CHid CLyd CRow ECha EPla EPot LBuc MBal MDun MTho NHol SAxl SMad WCot WCru WWat
verticillatum rubrum	CArn CHid CRow EGar MSte MTho MUlv SAxl WCot

POLYGONUM † (Polygonaceae)

affine	See ***Persicaria affinis***
amplexicaule	See ***Persicaria amplexicaulis***
aubertii	See ***Fallopia baldschuanica***
baldschuanicum	See ***Fallopia baldschuanica***
bistorta	See ***Persicaria bistorta***
cuspidatum	See ***Fallopia japonica***
equisetiforme hort.	See ***P. scoparium***
molle	See ***Persicaria mollis***
♦ ***multiflorum***	See ***Fallopia multiflora***
polystachyum	See ***Persicaria wallichii***
reynoutria	See ***Fallopia japonica*** var. ***compacta***
§ ***scoparium***	CRow EGoo EPla LHil MFir NFai NSti SDry SVen WCot

POLYLEPIS (Rosaceae)

¶ ***australis***	SMad

POLYMNIA (Asteraceae)

See Plant Deletions

POLYPODIUM † (Polypodiaceae)

aureum ruffled form	NMar
australe	See ***P. cambricum***
§ ***cambricum***	NHar NMar WCot WRic
§ – 'Barrowii'	CCuc NMar WRic
– 'Cambricum'	WRic
– 'Cristatum'	WRic
– 'Diadem'	WRic
– 'Grandiceps Forster'	WRic
– 'Grandiceps Fox'	WRic
– 'Hornet'	WRic
– 'Oakley'	EGoo SWas WAbe
¶ – Omnilacerum Group	EMon
– 'Omnilacerum Oxford'	WRic
– Plumosum Group	EMon
– 'Prestonii'	WRic
– Pulcherrimum Group	EGol NHar SWas
– – 'Pulcherrimum Addison'	WRic
– Semilacerum Group	NMar WRic
– – 'Falcatum O'Kelly'	WRic
– – 'Jubilee'	NMar WRic
– – 'Robustum'	NMar WRic
– 'Wilharris'	CCuc CFil WPGP WRic
glycyrrhiza	EFer WRic
– Grandiceps Group	WRic
– 'Longicaudatum'	EMon NMar WFib WRic
– 'Malahatense' (sterile)	WRic
– 'Malahatense' (fertile)	WRic
interjectum	EFer EFou NMar NOrc NVic SPer WAbe WFib WRic
– 'Bifidograndiceps'	WRic
– 'Cornubiense'	CBos CFil CRDP CWGN ECha EFer EMon GCal NBir NBro NHar NHol NMar NVic SDix SSpi SWas WAbe WPGP WRic
– 'Ramosum Hillman'	WRic
× ***mantoniae***	SWas
scouleri	NBro
vulgare	CBar CKin CWGN EBre ECWi EGoo EPfP GPoy LSyl MBal MBro NBro NEgg NHol NMar NOrc NPSI SApp SChu SRms WFib WHil WRic
– 'Acutum'	NMar
– 'Bifidocristatum'	EGoo EMon GBin NHar NHol WFib WWat
– 'Bifidograndiceps'	NMar SChu
¶ – 'Bifidomultifidum'	ETen
§ – 'Congestum Cristatum'	WRic
– 'Cornubiense'	CCuc EGoo NGar SRms WFib
– 'Cornubiense Grandiceps'	WRic
– 'Cornubiense Multifidum'	MBri NHar
– 'Crispum Cristatum'	See ***P. vulgare* 'Congestum Cristatum'**
– (Cristatum Group) 'Forster'	CCuc
– 'Jean Taylor'	See ***P. vulgare* 'Congestum Cristatum'**
– 'Longicaudatum'	WFib
– Ramosum Group	NMar

POLYPOGON (Poaceae)

See Plant Deletions

POLYSCIAS (Araliaceae)

'Elegans'	MBri
fruticosa	MBri
sambucifolia	SBid
scutellaria 'Pennockii' (v)	MBri

POLYSTICHUM † (Aspidiaceae)

acrostichoides	CCuc EFer GQui IOrc NHar NMar WFib WRic
aculeatum ♀	CCuc EBee EBre ECha EFer EFou EHon ELan EMon GQui IOrc MBri NFla NHar NHol NMar NOrc SAxl SMer SRms WFib WHil WRic WWoo
– Grandiceps Group	NMar
andersonii	NHar NHol WRic
braunii	CB&S EGol MLan NMar WRic
californicum	CFil
caryotideum	See ***Cyrtomium caryotideum***
setiferum Percristatum Group	See ***P. setiferum*** **'Cristatogracile'**
falcatum	See ***Cyrtomium falcatum***
falcinellum	CFil
fortunei	See ***Cyrtomium fortunei***
imbricans	NHar
makinoi	NHol WCot WFib WRic
mohrioides	CFil
munitum	CBar CCuc CFil CMil IOrc NFla NHar NHol NOrc SArc SDix SRms SSpi SWas WFib WRic WWoo
neolobatum	SWas WRic
polyblepharum	CCuc CFil CHid EBre EFer ELan EMon IOrc MBri NHar NHol SPla SRms SWas WAbe WCot WFib WRic
proliferum hort.	See ***P. setiferum*** **Acutilobum Group**
– (R.Br.) C. Presl.	SWas
¶ ***retrorsopaleaceum***	WRic
rigens	EHic NHar NHol NLak NMar SHam WFib WRic
§ ***setiferum*** ♀	CBar CCuc CFil CHan CKin CSam CWGN EBre EFer EFou EGol ELan EMon IOrc MBri NEgg NFla NHol NOrc SApp SArc SBla SPer WFib WStI
§ – Acutilobum Group	CB&S CFil CRDP ECha EHic EPot GAri MBal NCat NHar NVic SAxl SDix SMad SSpi WAbe WCot WCru
◆ ***setiferum angulare***	See ***P. setiferum***
¶ ***setiferum*** 'Congestum'	EMon WGor
– Congestum Group	CMil CRDP EHic IOrc MBri NHar NHol NMar SAxl SChu SPla SRms WFib WRic
§ – 'Cristatogracile'	NHar NMar
– 'Cristatopinnulum'	CFil EMon NHar NMar WRic
– Cristatum Group	EMon SRms
– Dahlem Group	CCuc CDoC ECha EFer ELan MBri WAbe WRic
– Divisilobum Group	CCuc CDec CFee CFil CM&M CRow CWGN EBre EFer ELan EMon EPar LSyl MBri MBro NHol NMar SApp SMad SPla SRms WBon WEas WHoo WPGP WRic
– – 'Divisilobum Densum'	MBal NMar NOrc SPla SSoC SSpi
– – 'Divisilobum Iveryanum'	EPot NHol SRms
– – 'Herrenhausen'	CDoC CSte EBee EBre ECha EFer ELan EPfP LHop MBri NFla NMar NOrc SPer SPla WAbe WFar WHil WRic
– – 'Mrs Goffy'	NMar
¶ – – 'Madame Patti'	EMon
¶ – – 'Ray Smith'	EMon
– 'Divisilobum Laxum'	CBlo EPar MHlr SChu
¶ – Foliosum Group	EMon
– 'Gracile'	MBri
– Lineare Group	CFil WFib WPGP
– Multilobum Group	WRic
◆ – 'Plumosodensum'	See ***P. setiferum*** **'Plumosomultilobum'**
– Plumosodivisilobum Group	CCuc CMil CRow EBre ECha EGol EHyt NHar SPla SWas WAbe WCru WFib
§ – 'Plumosomultilobum'	EMon NFla SRms WRic
– ***plumosum grande*** 'Moly'	WFib
– Plumosum Group	CBar CSam CSpe CWGN MBri NOrc SApp SAxl SChu SPer SSoC WFib WStI
– Proliferum Group	See ***P. setiferum*** **Acutilobum Group**
– 'Pulcherrimum Bevis'	EMon SDix WFib WRic
* – ***ramopinnatum***	NMar
* – ***ramulosum***	NMar
– Rotundatum Group	CRDP EMon NMar WFib
¶ – – 'Cristatum'	EMon
¶ – 'Wakeleyanum'	SRms
N – 'Wollaston'	MBri WAbe WWoo
¶ ***silvaticum***	EMon
stenophyllum	CFil WPGP
triangulum	NMar
tsussimense	CCuc CRDP EBre EFou GQui MBri NFla NHol NMar SApp SBla SMad SPer SRms WAbe WFib WRic

POLYXENA (Hyacinthaceae)

§ ***ensifolia***	LBow
odorata	CLyd MHig WAbe
pygmaea	See ***P. ensifolia***

POMADERRIS (Rhamnaceae)

¶ ***apetala***	MAll
elliptica	MAll

PONCIRUS (Rutaceae)

§ ***trifoliata***	CAgr CB&S CChu CDoC CGre CMCN CPle ELan EMil ENot ERea GOrc MBel MBlu SArc SBid SMad SPer STre WDin WFar WPat WRTC WSHC WWat
– 'Flying Dragon'	CAgr

PONERORCHIS (Orchidaceae)

¶ ***taiwanensis***	SWes

PONTEDERIA (Pontederiaceae)

cordata ♀	CBen CRow CWGN CWat EBre ECha ECtt EHon ELan EMFW LPBA MSta NDea SCoo SHig SWat SWyc WChe WMAq
cordata alba	CBen CRow EMFW NDea SWyc WChe
§ ***cordata*** var. ***lancifolia***	CRow CWGN EMFW MSta SRms SWat SWyc
– 'Pink Pons'	CRow
dilatata	CWat SRms SWyc
lanceolata	See ***P. cordata*** var. ***lancifolia***

POPULUS † (Salicaceae)

× ***acuminata***	WMou

alba	CDoC CKin CLnd CPer CTri EBre ENot GRei IOrc LBuc MAsh MBar MRav NBee NWea SHBN SPer WDin WMou WStI
– 'Bolleana'	See ***P. alba* f. *pyramidalis***
§ – f. ***pyramidalis***	CB&S NBee SRms WMou
§ – 'Raket'	CLnd CTho ELan ENot EPfP IOrc MGos NWea SPer
– 'Richardii'	CBot CGre CLnd CTho EBre ECtt EPla ESis IOrc MAsh MBar MUlv SPer WFar WMou
♦ – Rocket	See ***P. alba* 'Raket'**
§ 'Balsam Spire' (f) 🏆	CDoC CLnd CTho ENot GRei IOrc LBuc NWea WMou
§ ***balsamifera***	CDoC CTho CTri ELan EMil ENot MGos NWea SHBN SPer SRms WDin
× ***berolinensis***	CDoC
× ***canadensis*** 'Aurea' 🏆	CDoC CLnd CTho EMil ENot MDun MRav NWea SPer WDin WMou
– 'Eugenei' (m)	CTho WMou
– 'Robusta' (m)	CDoC CKin CLnd CTri EMil ENot IOrc LBuc NWea WDin WMou
– 'Serotina' (m)	CDoC CTho GRei MAsh NWea WDin WMou
× ***candicans***	WDin
– 'Aurora' (v)	CB&S CKin CTrw EBre ELan ENot GOrc GRei IOrc ISea LBuc MAsh MBar MBri MGos MWat NBee NWea SHBN SPer SRms SSta WDin
× ***canescens***	CDoC CPer ELan GAul WDin WMou
– 'De Moffart' (m)	ENot
– 'Tower'	WMou
× ***euroamericana***	See ***P.* × *canadensis***
× ***interamericana*** 'Beaupré'	CTho WMou
lasiocarpa 🏆	CBot CLnd CTho ENot EPfP MBlu MRav SHhN SLPl SMad WMou
§ – var. ***tibetica***	CBot WMou
maximowiczii	WMou
nigra	CPer ELan ENot SPer WDin WHut
– subsp. ***betulifolia*** 🏆	CBlo CCVT CKin CTho CWan LBuc MGos NWea WMou
– – (f)	WMou
– – (m)	WMou
¶ – (f)	SLPl
N – var. ***italica*** 🏆	CB&S CDoC CLnd CMHG CTho CTri EBre ELan ENot EPfP IOrc LBuc MBri MGos NBee NWea SHBN SPer SRms WDin
– 'Italica Aurea'	See ***P. nigra* 'Lombardy Gold'**
§ – 'Lombardy Gold' (m)	CEnd CTho GRei LMer SSpi WMou
¶ – (m)	SLPl
– 'Pyramidalis'	See ***P. nigra*** var. ***italica***
simonii	CTho
– 'Fastigiata'	NSti WMou
– 'Obtusata'	WMou
szechuanica	WMou
tacamahaca	See ***P. balsamifera***
'Tacatricho 32'	See ***P.* 'Balsam Spire'**
¶ ***tomentosa***	WMou
tremula 🏆	CKin CLnd CPer CTho EBre ELan ENot GRei IOrc LBuc LHyr MBar NBee NWea SFam SHBN SPer WDin WMou
§ – 'Erecta'	CLnd CTho EBee LPan SMad WMou
– 'Fastigiata'	See ***P. tremula* 'Erecta'**
– 'Pendula' (m)	CLnd CTho EBee WDin WMou
trichocarpa	CBlo CTho GRei SPer
– 'Fritzi Pauley' (f)	CTho WMou
violascens	See ***P. lasiocarpa*** var. ***tibetica***
wilsonii	WMou
yunnanensis	WMou

PORTULACA (Portulacaceae)

grandiflora	MBri
oleracea	CArn ELau MChe MGra SIde WHer WJek WWye
– var. ***aurea***	MChe MGra WJek

POTAMOGETON (Potamogetonaceae)

crispus	CBen EHon EMFW SAWi SRms SWyc
pectinatus	EHon

POTATO See SEED Supplier's Index

POTENTILLA † (Rosaceae)

alba	CGle CLyd CSev CShe CSpe EBar ECha EFou ELan EMar GCHN ISea LBlm LGro MHar MHig MRav MTho NFai NRoo SCro SPer SUsu WByw WCra WPer
alchemilloides	MHig MNrw SMer SOkh WHil WPer
alpicola	WBro WPer
ambigua	See ***P. cuneata***
anserina	CArn CKin CTiv ECWi EEls EFol EGoo EWFC GBar MHew WHer
– 'Golden Treasure'	WHer
anserinoides	GCal MBel NTay WCot WPer
arbuscula D Don	See ***P. fruticosa*** var. ***arbuscula* (D. Don) Maxim.**
– hort.	See ***P. fruticosa* 'Elizabeth'**
argentea	CSWP CSev CWan EBar ELan GAul LIck MTis NChi NFai WBea WCla WCru WPer
arguta	EBee
argyrophylla	See ***P. atrosanguinea*** var. ***argyrophylla***
atrosanguinea	CGle CHan CInt CMea CRDP CShe EBre ECha EOrc GCal GTou LBlm LHop MBal MBri MRav NFai NNor NRoo NSti SUsu WCru WGwG WHoo WPLl WPyg WTyr
§ – var. ***argyrophylla***	CGle CHan CMHG ECha EFer ELan EPla GCHN GCal GTou LGan MBel MRav NBir NBro NFai NGre NMir NNrd NOak SCro SRms SUsu WByw WCot WHil WPer WTyr WWhi WWin
– – SS&W 7768	GDra MPla MSte NGre NMGW
¶ – CC 1384	CPou
– var. ***leucochroa***	See ***P. atrosanguinea*** var. ***argyrophylla***
aurea	CPea ECtt ELan EMNN MBri MHig MTho NFla NGre NMen NMir NOrc NWCA SAlw SIng SRms SSmi WRHF

– 'Aurantiaca'	CElw GCHN MRav NNrd NRoo SBod SUsu
§ – subsp. ***chrysocraspeda***	EGle NHol NMen NNrd SIng
§ – 'Goldklumpen'	EGar GAbr MRav NPro SCro
– 'Plena'	GCHN GDra GTou LCom MHar MRav NGre NHar NNrd NSla SBod WWin
'Blazeaway'	EBee EBre EPPr MBel MBri NCat NHol SCoo SHam WLRN WTyr WWeb
brevifolia NNS 94-25	MFos
calabra	ECha EDAr EMan SIgm SMer WByw WHer WHil WPer WWin
§ ***cinerea***	CLyd CShe CTri LBee NHar NMen NNrd SIgm SSmi
clusiana	NWCA
'Craigieburn Cochineal'	GCra WCru
§ ***crantzii***	CMea CTri EWFC GCHN GTou LBee MBar MHar MHig MSte NMen NNrd NTow NWCA SIng SRms WCla WHil
– 'Nana'	See ***P. crantzii* 'Pygmaea'**
§ – 'Pygmaea'	ECtt ESis MOne
§ ***cuneata*** 🏆	CLyd CNic ELan ESis GDra GTou MHig MPla MTho NHar NMen NRya NWCA SIng SSmi WPer WWin
aff. – CC 1461	MRPP NGre
delavayi	MBro NBus
detommasii	WPer
dickinsii	NTow
dombeyi	EBee GCHN
* 'Emilie'	GCal MAvo MBri WCra WFar
§ ***erecta***	CArn CKin ECWi EOHP GBar GPoy LFis MChe MHew MSal
eriocarpa	CLyd EMNN GCHN GDra MBro MHar MHig MPla MWat NGre NHar NMen NNrd NRoo SBod SSmi WAbe WCla
'Etna'	CElw CLon ECtt EJud ELan EMon GAbr GCal GCra GTou LFis LGre MNrw NBrk NCat NFai NNor NRoo SAga SMad WByw WCru WHen WMer WPer WWhi
'Everest'	See ***P. fruticosa* 'Mount Everest'**
'Fireflame'	ECha LBlm
fissa	LBlm MSte
'Flambeau'	CHad MRav
'Flamenco'	CB&S CSam CTri EBre EFou ELan MBri MNrw MRav NCat NRoo WAbb WByw WHoo WOld WPbr WTyr
fragiformis	See ***P. megalantha***
fruticosa	LBuc NMen NWea
– 'Abbotswood' 🏆	CB&S CMHG CWLN EAst ELan ENot GOrc LHop MAsh MBal MBar MBri MGos MRav NFla NHol NNor NRoo SPer WDin WGwG WHCG WHar WSHC WWat WWeb
– 'Abbotswood Silver'	CB&S CLTr CLyd EBar ECtt ELan MAsh MRav SPla WFar WGwG WHCG WHar WWat WWeb
– 'Annette'	CBlo NPro WHCG WWeb
– var. ***arbuscula*** (D. Don) Maxim. KW 5774	WWeb
– – hort.	See ***P. fruticosa* 'Elizabeth'**
– 'Argentea Nana'	See ***P. fruticosa* 'Beesii'**
– 'Beanii'	NHol SPer WWeb
§ – 'Beesii' 🏆	CDoC CShe ELan ESis MAsh MBar MBlu MPla NHol NRoo SIng SPer WAbe WDin WHCG WSHC WWat WWeb WWin
– 'Beverley Surprise'	NPro SPer WHCG WWeb
◆ – Blink	See ***P. fruticosa* 'Princess'**
– 'Buttercup'	WHCG WWeb
– 'Cascade'	WBcn WHCG
* – 'Chelsea Star'	WHCG
* – 'Chilo'	MGos
– 'Clotted Cream'	MBar
– var. ***dahurica***	WHCG
– – 'Hersii'	See ***P. fruticosa* 'Snowflake'**
– – 'Rhodocalyx'	CPle WHCG WWat
– 'Dart's Cream'	MBri MRav
– 'Dart's Golddigger'	CB&S CTri EBee ECtt MBal NRoo SLPl WHCG WRHF WWeb
§ – 'Dart's Nugget'	WHCG WWeb
– 'Daydawn' 🏆	CB&S CLan CMHG CShe CWLN ELan GOrc GRei LHop MBal MBar MBri MPla MWat NBir NRoo SPer WAbe WDin WHCG WRTC WWat WWeb WWin
– 'Donard Orange'	See ***P. fruticosa* 'Donard Gold'**
– 'Eastleigh Cream'	SPer
– 'Eden Lemonlight'	NPro
§ – 'Elizabeth' 🏆	CB&S CLan CShe CWLN ELan ENot GDra ISea LGro LHop MBar MBri MGos MWat NFla NHol NNor NRoo NWea SHBN SPer SSoC WDin WHCG WWat WWeb
– 'Farreri'	See ***P. fruticosa* 'Gold Drop'**
– 'Farreri Prostrata'	See ***P. fruticosa*** var. ***pyrenaica***
– 'Floppy Disc'	CDoC CFai ECtt EFou ELan MGos NCut NWoo SEas SHBN SPer SPla SSta
– 'Frances Lady Daresbury'	ISea MPla WWeb
– 'Friedrichsenii'	NHol WWeb
– 'Glenroy Pinkie'	CFai CSam EBee MBal NPro SAga SEas WAbe WHCG WWeb
– 'Glenroy Seashell'	MBal
§ – 'Gold Drop'	NHol WHCG WWeb
– 'Golden Dwarf'	MBri MGos
* – 'Golden Nugget'	WLRN
– 'Golden Spreader'	EBre NPro
– 'Goldfinger' 🏆	CChe CDoC ELan ENot GOrc GRei IOrc MAsh MBri MGos MRav SEas WAbe WDin WHCG WHar WStI WWeb
◆ – Goldkugel	See ***P. fruticosa* 'Gold Drop'**
– 'Goldstar'	CMHG EBee EBre EPla GAri GCHN IOrc MBri MGos WHCG WWeb
– 'Goldteppich'	LBuc MBar SHBN
– 'Goscote'	MGos
– 'Hachmann's Gigant'	WWeb
– 'Hopleys Little Joker'	NHol WPat WPyg
– 'Hopleys Orange'	CB&S CChe CDoC CMHG EBee EWes GAri GCHN LHop MBri SAga WGor WHCG WWin
– 'Hurstbourne'	WWeb
– 'Jackman's Variety'	CSam ECtt ENot MAsh SPan SPer SRms WBod WDin WWeb
– 'Judith'	WWeb

– 'Katherine Dykes' ♀	CChe CDoC CWLN ELan ENot GDra MAsh MBal MBar MHlr SPer SRms WBod WDin WHCG WHar WRTC WStI WWeb
* – 'King Cup'	CWLN WLRN WWeb
– 'Klondike' ♀	CB&S CLan CWLN EBee ELan MAsh NNor NRoo NWea SBid WDin WWeb
§ – 'Knap Hill'	ENot EPar GDra NNor WWeb
– 'Knap Hill Buttercup'	See ***P. fruticosa* 'Knap Hill'**
– 'Kobold'	CBlo EBee MBar SHhN WWeb
* – 'Lemon and Lime'	MBlu
– 'Logan'	WWeb
– 'London Town'	CMHG
– 'Longacre Variety' ♀	CTri GDra MBar NHol NWea SLPl WWat WWeb
§ – 'Maanelys' ♀	CTrw ECtt ELan MBal MWat NFla NWea SPer SPla SRms WDin WHCG WWeb
– 'Macpenny's Cream'	WHCG
§ – 'Manchu'	ENot EPar EPla GDra MBar MBri MHlr MPla MRav NFla NHol NNor NRoo SChu SHBN SMac SPer SRms SSta WWat WWeb WWin
* – 'Medicine Wheel Mountain'	CKni EFou EHal ELan EWes MAsh NPro NTow SPer WHCG WWeb
– 'Milkmaid'	WWeb
◆ – Moonlight	See ***P. fruticosa* 'Maanelys'**
§ – 'Mount Everest'	CChe CDoC ELan MBar MWat NCut NHol NWea SRms WHCG WWeb
– 'Nana Argentea'	See ***P. fruticosa* 'Beesii'**
– 'Northman'	WWeb
– 'Nugget'	See ***P. fruticosa* 'Dart's Nugget'**
– 'Ochroleuca'	WWeb
– 'Orange Star'	CBlo WHCG WWeb
– 'Orange Stripe'	WWeb
– 'Orangeade'	CKni EFou MAsh SMur SPla SReu SSta WWeb
– 'Peaches and Cream'	EBee WHCG WWeb
– 'Peachy Proud'	NPro
– 'Pierce Ogon'	CBlo
– 'Pink Glow'	GDra
– 'Pink Pearl'	EBre WWin
– 'Pink Queen'	WWeb
– 'Pretty Polly'	CDoC CWLN EAst EBre ELan IOrc MBar MBlu MBri MGos NHol SHBN SPer SSta WDin WGwG WHCG WHar WStI WWeb
– 'Primrose Beauty' ♀	CLan CShe CWLN EAst ELan ENot ISea MBal MBar MGos MPla MRav NFla NNor NRoo WAbe WDin WHCG WHar WRTC WStI WWat WWeb
§ – 'Princess'	CWLN EBre ELan GRei MBal MBar MBri MGos MHlr MWat NHol NRoo SPer SReu SRms WDin WHCG WHar WStI WWat WWeb
¶ – 'Prostrate Copper'	NPro
– var. ***pumila***	WPat
– Red Ace	CWLN EBre ELan ENot GOrc GRei LHop MBar MBri MGos MWat NHol NRoo NWea SPer WDin WGwG WHCG WHar WWeb
– 'Red Robin'	CDoC CWLN EBee EBre ELan EPfP GCHN GRei MAsh MBri MGos MWat NFla NRoo SCoo SPer WDin WStI WWeb
– 'Royal Flush'	GAri LHop MAsh MBar MBri SAga WHCG WStI WWeb
– 'Ruth'	LRHS WWeb
– 'Sandved'	WWeb
– 'Silver Schilling'	LHop
– 'Snowbird'	EBre EPfP MAsh MBlu MGos NLak NPro WWeb
§ – 'Snowflake'	CB&S WHCG WWeb
– 'Sommerflor'	ENot WWeb
– 'Sophie's Blush'	CLTr EAst MBal MRav NHol NRoo NWea SBid WRus WSHC WWeb
– 'Sunset'	CB&S CChe CDoC CSam CWLN ELan ENot GDra MAsh MBal MBar MBri MGos MHlr MPla MTis NNor NWea SPer SReu SRms SSta WGwG WStI WWeb
– 'Tangerine' ♀	CB&S CLan CTrw CWLN ELan GOrc GRei ISea MAsh MBal MBar MRav MWat NFla NHol NWea SPer SRms WAbe WBod WDin WHCG WHar WRTC WWat WWeb WWin
– 'Tilford Cream' ♀	CChe CWLN EBre ELan ENot GDra MAsh MBar MBri MPla MRav MWat NFla NHol NMen NRoo SAga SHBN SPer SReu SRms WAbe WDin WHCG WStI WWat WWeb
– 'Tom Conway'	LBuc MUlv WHCG WWeb
§ – var. ***veitchii***	CDoC SHBN SPer WHCG WStI WWeb
– 'Vilmoriniana'	CBot CHad EFol ELan MAsh NNor SBid SMac SSpi WAbe WHCG WSHC WWat WWeb
– 'Walton Park'	MBal WWeb
– 'Wessex Silver'	WHCG
– 'Whirligig'	CWan WHCG
– 'White Rain'	CLTr GDra NNor WWeb
– 'William Purdom'	GAul NHol WHCG WWeb
– 'Yellow Bird'	MGos
– 'Yellow Carpet'	WHCG
– 'Yellow Giant'	WWeb
fulgens	See ***P. lineata***
'Gibson's Scarlet' ♀	CHad CKel CSam ECha ECtt EFou ELan GCal MBri MCLN MFir NFai NFla NHol NRoo SCro SPer WHil WMer WPer WSHC WTyr WWat
glandulosa	EBee WPer
'Gloire de Nancy'	EBre ELan GAri GCal MRav NBir SPer
'Gold Clogs'	See ***P. aurea* 'Goldklumpen'**
'Grace Darling'	CWit MTis NEgg WGor WWeb
¶ ***gracilis***	EBee NNrd
§ – var. ***glabrata***	EPPr
– subsp. ***nuttallii***	See ***P. gracilis* var. *glabrata***
'Helen Jane'	CGle EBre EFou LHop MBel MBri NBir NBro NRoo SAga SHam SLod WAbb WHoo WMer WPer
'Herzblut'	EBee EPfP GBuc
× ***hopwoodiana***	CBos CGle CHad EPPr LBlm MBri MUlv NBir SAga SUsu SWas WAbb WByw WHal
× ***hybrida*** 'Jean Jabber'	EWll NRai

hyparctica nana	CLyd LBee MBro NHol WAbe WPat WPyg
* 'Limelight'	CKni ECle EFou ELan EPla MAsh MRav SSta WHCG
'Mandshurica'	See ***P. fruticosa* 'Manchu'**
§ ***megalantha*** ♀	CBot CSam EBar ECha EFou GCal GTou LFis LHop MBal MRav NBro NFai NGre NMen NMir NNrd NSti NWCA SBla SChu SPer WPer WSHC WWhi WWin
'Melton'	EBee ECoo EFou EMon MNrw NBir NBrk NOak SAga WElm WHen
'Monarch's Velvet'	See ***P. thurberi* 'Monarch's Velvet'**
'Monsieur Rouillard'	CGle CLon EBar EPPr LFis MBel MNrw MSCN MUlv MWat NBrk NNor NRoo SUsu WByw WCru WHoo WSan
'Mont d'Or'	MBri
montana	GCHN MBel NHol WHer WPer
nepalensis	CNic CSam ECha EDAr GAbr LHop LLWP MFir NBro NNor NPro NRai SMac SWas
– 'Craigieburn'	GCra
– forms	EAst
– 'Kirsten'	WHil
§ – 'Miss Willmott' ♀	CB&S CBot CGle CShe ECtt EFou ELan EOrc MBri MBro MRav NFai NFla NMir NRoo SBla SPer SSoC SUsu WBea WEas WHen WHil WOMN WPer WWat WWhi WWin
– 'Roxana'	CGle CShe EBar EBee ECGP ELan EOrc MBel MFir MRav NBro NFai WAbb WByw WCra WHil WPer
§ ***neumanniana***	EWFC WAbe
– 'Goldrausch'	ECha MBri MRav SRms
§ – 'Nana'	CInt CSam CSev EMNN EPot ESis LBee LHop MBro MHig MPla MRPP MWat NHar NMen NNrd NRoo SBla SRms WEas WWin
nevadensis	CLyd CTri ECho MHig WPer
* 'New Dawn'	LRHS MAsh MBri
nitida	NGre NHar NMen WDav
– 'Alba'	EPot
– 'Lissadell'	CPBP
– 'Rubra'	CLyd CMea CShe EHyt GTou MWat NBir NHol NMGW NNrd NTow NWCA SBla SRms SSmi WAbe WPat WWin
nivea	GTou NHol SIng
'Nunk'	CBlo MBar WWeb
* 'Olympic Mountains'	WPer
ovina	WPer
palustris	ECWi MSta WCla WGwy
pamirica	EBee
pedata	LLWP
peduncularis	SUsu WCot
– CC&McK 532	GCHN
'Pink Panther'	See ***P. fruticosa* 'Princess'**
'Pyrenaica'	See ***P. fruticosa* var. *pyrenaica***
recta	CArc ELan EMan EWFC GTou MHew SIgm WHil
– 'Alba'	CBlo EAst ECoo GMaP LGan LIck NFai NPri NRoo SMac WPer
– 'Citrina'	See ***P. recta pallida***
– 'Macrantha'	See ***P. recta* 'Warrenii'**

§ ***recta pallida*** ♀	Widely available
recta* var. *sulphurea	See ***P. recta pallida***
§ – 'Warrenii'	CPea CSam EBar EBre ECro EFou GMaP LGan MCLN MFir MRav MTis MWat NFai NMir NOrc NRoo SAlw SCro SPer WHal WHoo WPLl WPer WPyg WTyr WWhi
reptans	CArn CKin ECWi EWFC
– 'Pleniflora'	EMon MInt WAlt
rupestris	CGle CHan CInt CLTr CM&M CTri EBre ECha EMan EWFC GCra GLil MCLN MFir MNrw NRoo NSti SUsu WByw WCla WHal WPer WSHC WWin
schillingii	CBot
speciosa	EHyt EMan WOMN
– var. ***discolor***	SAlw
– var. ***speciosa***	NTow NWCA
– – NS 765	MRPP
sterilis	CHid ECWi ELan EWFC WHer
¶ – 'Turncoat' (v)	WAlt
'Sungold'	CBlo ECho ESis WThi
tabernaemontani	See ***P. neumanniana***
ternata	See ***P. aurea* subsp. *chrysocraspeda***
thurberi	CGle CLon EWes GCal LGre MRav NChi WMaN
§ – 'Monarch's Velvet'	CBot CLTr CMdw EBee MOne NFla NRai WBro WGor WHil
tommasiniana	See ***P. cinerea***
× ***tonguei*** ♀	CFee CLyd CShe ECha ECtt EFou ELan ESis GCHN GDra LHop MBal MBri MCLN MRav NFai NHar NHol NNrd NRoo SAlw SBla SSmi WMer WPer WWat
tormentilla	See ***P. erecta***
tridentata	See ***Sibbaldiopsis tridentata***
verna	See ***P. neumanniana***
– 'Pygmaea'	See ***P. neumanniana* 'Nana'**
'Versicolor Plena'	GCal WCru
villosa	See ***P. crantzii***
'Volcan'	CBos GCal MBri
***wallichiana* 'Cream Cracker'**	EMon
* 'White Beauty'	CKni
'White Queen'	CMea EWll MLsm MNrw WBea WGor
'Wickwar Trailer'	CLyd CShe EPot ESis MPla WHCG WHoo
'William Rollison' ♀	CB&S CBre CHad CSam EBar EBre ECro EFou ELan GLil LFis LHop MBel MBri MRav NHol NOrc NVic SCro SPer SRms SUsu WPer WSHC WTyr
willmottiae	See ***P. nepalensis* 'Miss Willmott'**
'Yellow Queen'	CB&S CTri EBre ELan MRav NFai NHol NRoo SCro SPer SWat WMer WTyr WWeb

POTERIUM See SANGUISORBA

PRATIA (Campanulaceae)

§ ***angulata***	CMea NGre NHar NHol NMen SSmi WWeb
– 'Jack's Pass'	GAri NHar
– 'Messenger'	ECou
– 'Ohau'	ECou
– 'Tim Rees'	ELan SBla

§ – 'Treadwellii'	ECha ELan LBee MHar NPro NRoo SUsu WHal WHen WLRN WPri WWin
– 'Woodside'	ECou EWes
macrodon	WCru
§ ***pedunculata***	CHan CMHG CMea CRow ECha ECou ELan ESis GCHN GTou LBee MBar NBro NFla NGre NNrd NRoo NRya NVic SHFr SIng SSmi WAbe WHen WHil WHoo WPer WWhi WWin
– 'Blue Stars'	ECou WCru WThi
– 'Clear Skies'	ECou
– 'County Park'	CInt CMea CSpe CVer ECha ECou ELan EPot ESis LRHS MBar NGre NHar NHol NMen NRoo NWCA SIng SRms SSmi WHal WHen WHoo WOMN WPat WPer WPyg WRus WThi WWin
– 'Kiandra'	ECou
– 'Kinsey'	ECou
– 'Tom Stone'	CLTr EBar ECou EPot NHar NNrd
§ ***perpusilla***	ECou
– 'Fragrant Carpet'	ECou
– 'Summer Meadows'	ECou WPer
§ ***repens***	ECou

PRESLIA See MENTHA

PRIMULA † (Primulaceae)

acaulis	See ***P. vulgaris***
'Aire Mist' (2)	CLyd EHyt EMNN GCLN NGar NGre NHar NHol
§ 'Aire Waves' (2)	EHyt EMNN
'Alan Robb' (D.Prim)	EBar ECtt EHic MBri MCLN NNrd SIng SPer WHal WHil
algida (11)	CPla ECho GCra NGre
allionii (2)	CTri EHyt EMNN EPot GTou ITim LBee MBro MHig MRPP NCra NHar NHol NNrd NWCA WAbe WDav WWin
– 'A.K. Wells' (2)	EHyt EPot NGre WAbe
– 'Adrian Jones' (2)	EHyt NNrd WAbe
◆ – 'Aire Waves'	See ***P. 'Aire Waves'***
– var. ***alba*** (2)	EHyt EMNN MHig NHol NTow
– 'Alexina' (2)	EHyt NHar NHol WDav
– 'Anna Griffith' (2)	CGra EHyt EPot GCHN ITim MHig MRPP NGre NHol NNrd NTow WAbe WHil
– 'Anne' (2)	EHyt
§ – 'Apple Blossom' (2)	CGra CLyd EHyt EMNN EPot GAbr MDHE MFie NNrd NTow SIng WDav
– 'Archer' (2)	EMNN NGre NMen
– × ***auricula*** 'Blairside Yellow' (2)	CLyd CPBP EMNN NGre
– × ***auricula*** 'Old Red Dusty Miller' (2)	MDHE NHar NNrd
¶ – × ***auricula*** 'Old Red Dusty Miller' hort. (2)	MFie
– 'Austen' (2)	EHyt EPot MHig NHol NMen NNrd WAbe
– 'Avalanche' (2)	CLyd EHyt ITim MHig NGre NHar NMen NTow SWas WAbe
– 'Bill Martin' (2)	EPot
¶ – 'Brilliant' KRW 448/69 (2)	EHyt
– Burnley form (2)	EPot
§ – 'Clarence Elliott' (2)	CGra CLyd EHyt NGre NHar SIng WDav
– 'Claude Flight' (2)	NHar
– × ***clusiana*** (2)	NGre WDav
– 'Crowsley Variety' (2)	CLyd CNic CPBP EHyt EPot MHig NGre NMen NSla NTow NWCA SBla WAbe
– 'Crusader' (2)	EHyt NGar NNrd WDav
* – 'E.G. Watson'	EHyt
§ – 'Edinburgh' (2)	CNic EHyt EMNN EPot ITim MHig NNrd
– 'Edrom' (2)	ITim MHig
– 'Elizabeth Baker' (2)	EHyt EMNN GCLN WAbe
– 'Elizabeth Earle' (2)	EPot NHol NMen SIng WAbe
◆ – 'Elliott's Large'	See ***P. allionii* 'Edinburgh'**
– 'Elliott's Variety'	See ***P. allionii* 'Edinburgh'**
– 'Fairy Rose' KRW 180/48 (2)	WAbe
– 'Fanfare' (2)	CGra EHyt WDav
– 'Frank Barker' (2)	EPot NGre NHol
– 'Gavin Brown' (2)	EHyt EPot
– GFS 1984 (2)	CGra
§ – 'Gilderdale Glow' (2)	MFie NGre NHar
◆ – 'Giuseppi's Form'	See ***P. allionii* 'Mrs Dyas'**
– 'Grandiflora' (2)	EHyt NGre
◆ – Hartside 383/12	See ***P. allionii* 'Gilderdale Glow'**
– Hartside 383/3 (2)	EPot NHol NMen NNrd
¶ – Hartside 383/6	NGre
– 'Hemswell' (2)	EMNN
◆ – 'Hemswell Blush'	See ***P.* 'Hemswell Blush'**
◆ – 'Hemswell Ember'	See ***P.* 'Hemswell Ember'**
– × ***hirsuta*** (2)	See ***P.* × *pubescens***
– 'Hocker Edge' (2)	NNrd
¶ – 'Horwood' KD/KRW 397/60 (2)	EHyt
– Ingwersen's form (2)	EPot GTou NHol
– JCA 4161/16 (2)	EPot
◆ – JCA 4161/21	See ***P. allionii* 'Travellers' JCA 4161/21**
◆ – JCA 4161/22	See ***P. allionii* 'Jenny' JCA 4161/22**
¶ – JCA 4161/23	CGra EPot
§ – 'Jenny' JCA 4161/22 (2)	CGra EHyt EPot
– 'Joan Hughes' (2)	CLyd NGar NHar SIng WAbe
– K R W	See ***P. allionii* 'Ken's Seedling'**
§ – 'Kath Dryden' (2)	WHil
§ – 'Ken's Seedling' (2)	CLyd EHyt EMNN EPot NGre NHar NHol NNrd WAbe
– KRW 1971 (2)	WDav
– KRW 455/70 (2)	EHyt
– KRW 525/76 (thrum, white) (2)	EHyt
– KRW 56/392 (2)	EHyt
– 'Lea Gardens' (2)	NHar
– 'Lee Myers' (2)	CLyd CNic EHyt EMNN MBro NHar NHed NMen NNrd
¶ – 'Lindisfarne' (2)	WDav
– × 'Lismore Treasure' (2)	CGra EHyt NWCA WDav
– 'Margaret Earle' (2)	NHol WAbe
– × ***marginata*** (2)	EBre EHyt EPot NHar WHil
– 'Maria Talbot' (2)	NNrd
– 'Marion' (2)	EHyt EMNN EPot ITim NHed NMen
– 'Marjorie Wooster' KRW 331/52 (2)	MRPP NGre NWCA
– 'Mars' (2)	EMNN NGre NHar NNrd WDav
– 'Martin' (2)	EPot MHig NGre NNrd
– 'Mary Berry' (2)	EHyt EMNN EPot MHig NGre NHar WAbe WHil
§ – 'Mrs Dyas' (2)	EHyt EMNN NHar NHol NNrd WAbe WOMN
– Nettleton 8824 (2)	EPot

¶ – × ***pedemontana*** (2)	MFie
– 'Peggy Wilson' (2)	EPot EWes NHol
– 'Pennine Pink' Hartside 383/7 (2)	EMNN EPot MRPP NGre NHol SIng
– 'Perkie' JCA 4161/12 (2)	EHyt NNrd WDav
– 'Phobos' (2)	EMNN MFie
– 'Picton's Variety' (2)	EPot NHed
◆ – 'Pink Aire'	See ***P.* 'Pink Aire'**
– 'Pink Beauty' (2)	EPot
◆ – 'Pink Ice'	See ***P.* × *pubescens* 'Pink Ice'**
– 'Pinkie' KRW 271/51 (2)	CGra WDav
– 'Praecox' (2)	EPot NHol NNrd NSla
– × ***pubescens*** 'Harlow Car' (2)	CLyd NHar
– 'Raymond Wooster' KRW 321/52 (2)	EPot
– 'Roger Bevan' (2)	EHyt
– × ***rubra*** (2)	MBro NHol
– 'Saint Dalmas' (2)	EPot
– 'Scimitar' (2)	EMNN NHar
– 'Serendipity' (2)	EHyt
– 'Snowflake' KRW 367/56 (2)	CGra CLyd CPBP EHyt EMNN EPot NHar NTow NWCA WAbe
¶ – 'Stanton House' (2)	NHed NHol WAbe
– 'Stephen' JCA 4161/6 (2)	EMNN
– 'Tranquillity' Hartside 383/1 (2)	EHyt MFie NGre NHar NHol NMen NNrd
§ – 'Travellers' JCA 4161/21 (2)	CGra EPot
– 'Viscountess Byng' (2)	EMNN
– 'William Earle' (2)	CNic EHyt EMNN EPot NGre NHar NHed NHol NMen NTow WAbe
alpicola (26)	CBot CRow CSWP CWGN EBre GAbr GDra GFle GPot LPBA MBal MFie NBro NCra NGre NHol SPer WAbe WHil WRus WWat
– var. ***alba*** (26)	CMil CNic CPla CRow CSWP GBin GCra LSyl MBal MNrw NGre NRoo SWat
– hybrids (26)	NHol
– var. ***luna*** (26)	CNic GBuc LSyl
– var. ***violacea*** (26)	CPla CRow GAbr GDra LSyl MBal MBri MFie MNrw NHar SWat WWhi
'Altaica'	See ***P. elatior*** subsp. ***meyeri***
altaica grandiflora	See ***P. elatior*** subsp. ***meyeri***
amoena	See ***P. elatior*** subsp. ***meyeri***
anisodora (4)	CNic CPla EPot GCan GCra GMaP MBal MNrw
'April Rose' (D.Prim)	CMea EBar ECtt NHar SPer
× ***arctotis***	See ***P.* × *pubescens***
¶ ***atrodentata*** (9)	WAbe
aurantiaca (4)	CPla GAbr GAri GFle LSyl MSta NGar NGre SRms WChe WLRN
aureata (21)	EPot GCra GGGa NCra
auricula hort. 'A.H. Spring' (A)	MFie
– 'Adrian' (A)	EJap MFie NCra NNrd SHya
– 'Aga Khan'	SHya
– 'Agamemnon'	NCra
– 'Alamo'	NCra
– 'Alan Ravenscroft' (A)	MFie
– 'Albury' (d)	MFie
– 'Alfred Niblett' (S)	EMNN MFie NNrd
– 'Alice Haysom' (S)	ELan MFie NNrd SHya WDav WHil
– 'Alicia' (A)	SHya
– 'Alien' (S)	MFie
– 'Alison Jane' (A)	CLyd MFie NCra SHya
– 'Allansford'	EMNN
– 'Almondbury' (S)	SHya
– Alpine mixed (A)	CNic GCra GDra NCra SRms
– 'Amicable' (A)	SHya
– 'Andrea Julie' (A)	EJap EMNN MFie MOne NCra NHar NHol NMen NNrd SHya WHil
– 'Ann Taylor' (A)	NCra SHya
– 'Antoc' (S)	EMNN MFie
– 'Anwar Sadat' (A)	EMNN MFie
– 'Applecross' (A)	EJap EMNN MFie NCra NHar NNrd SHya
– 'Arctic Fox'	NCra
– 'Argus' (A)	CLyd EJap MFie NBir NCra NHar NMen NNrd SHya SUsu WHil
¶ – 'Arundell' (S/St)	EMNN NMen SHya WHil
– 'Astolat' (S)	EMNN MFie NCra NNrd SHya
– 'Athur Delbridge' (A)	MFie
– 'Aurora' (A)	MFie SHya
– 'Austin'	NCra
– 'Aviemore' (A)	MFie
– 'Avril Hunter' (A)	MFie SHya
– 'Aye Aye'	NCra
– 'Bacchus' (A)	MFie
– 'Ballet' (S)	MFie
– 'Barbara Mason'	NCra
– 'Barbarella' (S)	EMNN MFie
– 'Basuto' (A)	EMNN MFie SHya
– 'Beatrice' (A)	CLyd EMNN GAbr MFie NCra NNrd SHya
– 'Bedford Lad' (A)	SHya
– 'Beechen Green' (S)	EMNN SHya
– 'Ben Lawers' (S)	SHya WHil
– 'Ben Wyves' (S)	SHya
– 'Bendigo' (S)	SHya
– 'Bilton' (S)	CLyd MFie NCra
– 'Blackfield' (S)	MFie
– 'Blackhill' (S)	EMNN MFie
– 'Blairside Yellow' (B)	CLyd EWes MRPP NHar NHol NMen WAbe WWin
– 'Blossom' (A)	EJap EMNN MFie NCra NNrd SHya
– 'Blue Heaven'	NCra
– 'Blue Jean' (S)	EJap EMNN MFie NCra
– 'Blue Nile' (S)	EMNN MFie NCra NMen
– 'Blue Steel' (S)	SHya
– 'Blue Velvet' (B)	EMNN MFie NBro NSti SHya WHil
– 'Blue Wave' (d)	NNrd
– 'Bob Lancashire' (S)	EMNN MFie NHar NMen NNrd SHya WHil
– 'Bolero' (A)	SHya
– 'Bookham Firefly' (A)	EJap EMNN GAbr MFie NCra NHar NHol NNrd SHya
– 'Bravura'	NCra
– 'Brazil' (S)	EBee EMNN MFie NCra NHol NNrd WHil
– 'Bredon Hill' (S)	SHya
– 'Brenda's Choice' (A)	MFie SHya
– 'Bright Eyes' (A)	MFie SHya
– 'Broad Gold' (A)	SHya
– 'Broadwell Gold' (B)	CLyd EPot MFie SHya
– 'Brookfield' (S)	EMNN MFie NMen NNrd SHya WDav
– 'Broughton' (S)	MFie SHya
– 'Brown Bess' (A)	EMNN GCLN MFie NCra NNrd SHya WDav
– 'Buccaneer'	NCra
– 'Bunty' (A)	MFie
– 'Butterwick' (A)	MFie NHar SHya WDav

– 'C.F. Hill' (A) EMNN SHya
– 'C.G. Haysom' (S) EJap EMNN MFie NCra NHar NNrd SHya
– 'C.W. Needham' (A) EJap EMNN MFie NCra NHol NNrd SHya WHil
* – 'Cambodumun' NCra
– 'Camelot' (d) CLyd EJap ELan EMNN MFie MOne NCra NHar NHol NMen NNrd NPri SHya WHil
– 'Camilla' (A) MFie
– 'Candida' (d) SHya
– 'Carole' (A) MFie NNrd SHya
– 'Carreras' NCra
– 'Catherine' (d) EJap MFie NCra NNrd
– 'Chaffinch' (S) MFie SHya
– 'Chamois' (B) NMen
– 'Chelsea Bridge' EMNN
– 'Cherry' (S) EMNN GAbr MFie NCra SHya
– 'Cherrypicker' (A) SHya
– 'Cheyenne' (S) EMNN MFie
– 'Chloë' (S) EJap SHya
– 'Chloris' (S) NBir
– 'Chorister' (S) CLyd ELan EMNN EPot GAbr MBro MFie MOne NCra NHed NHol NMen NNrd NPri SHya SUsu WDav
– 'Cicero' (A) SHya
– 'Cindy' (A) MFie
* – 'Cinnamon' (S) SHya
– 'Clare' (S) NMen SHya
– 'Claudia Taylor' NHar SHya WDav
¶ – 'Clunie' (S) GCLN WHil
– 'Clunie II' (S) SHya
– 'Coffee' (S) MFie SHya
– 'Colbury' (S) MFie NCra NHar SHya WDav
– 'Colonel Champney' (S) MFie NNrd SHya
– 'Comet' (S) MFie NNrd
– 'Connie' (S) MFie
– 'Conservative' (S) MFie SHya
– 'Consett' (S) EMNN MFie NCra NNrd SHya
– 'Coppernob' (S) SHya
– 'Coral' (S) MFie NCra NHed
– 'Corona' (S) SHya
– 'Corrie Files' (d) SHya
– 'Cortina' (S) EJap EMNN MOne NCra NHar NHol NMen NNrd
– 'County Park Red' (B) ECou
– 'Craig Vaughan' (A) MFie NCra NNrd SHya
– 'Creenagh Stripe' (A) MFie
– 'D.S.J.' (S) SHya
– 'Daftie Green' (S) EMNN NNrd SHya
– 'Dakota' (S) EMNN MFie NCra
– 'Daphnis' (S) SHya
– 'Deep Wilson' EWes
– 'Delilah' (d) MFie NHar WDav
– 'Denna Snufer' EMNN
– 'Devon Cream' (d) EJap MFie NCra NHol
– 'Diane' EMNN MFie SHya
– 'Divint Dunch' (A) SHya
– 'Doctor B. Sharma' (S) SHya
– 'Doctor Duthie' (S) SHya
– 'Doctor Lennon's White' (B) MFie
– 'Donhead' (A) MFie SHya WHil
– 'Donna Clancy' (S) MFie SHya
– 'Doris Jean' (A) SHya
– 'Dorothy' (S) SHya
– double maroon (d) WHil
– double yellow (d) WHil
– 'Doublet' (d) CLyd EMNN GAbr MFie NCra NNrd NSla SHya WDav WHil
– 'Doubloon' (d) SHya
– 'Doublure' (d) SHya
– 'Douglas Black' (S) SHya
– 'Douglas Green' (S) MFie SHya
– 'Douglas White' (S) EMNN MFie SHya
– 'Dovedale' (S) SHya
– 'Dowager' (A) MFie
¶ – 'Dubarii' (A) NCra
– 'Dusky Maiden' (A) EMNN NCra SHya WDav
– 'Dusky Yellow' (B) MBro
– 'Dusty Lemon' (d) SHya
¶ – 'Dusty Miller' (B) GPot
– 'E' NNrd
– E82 (S) MFie
– 'Ed Spivey' (A) SHya
– 'Edith Allen' (A) SHya
– 'Eglinton' NCra
– 'Eileen K' (S) SHya
– 'Elegance' (S) MFie SHya
– 'Elizabeth Ann' (A) EMNN MFie NCra SHya
– 'Ellen Thompson' (A) MFie NNrd SHya WDav
– 'Elmor Vete' (S) SHya
– 'Elsie' (A) EMNN MFie
– 'Elsie May' (A) EMNN MFie NCra NNrd SHya WHil
– 'Embley' (S) CLyd NCra
– 'Emery Down' (S) MFie NNrd SHya
– 'Enlightened' (A) NCra SHya
I – 'Erica' (A) EMNN MFie NHar NMen SHya WDav
– 'Ethel' NNrd
– 'Ettrick' (S) SHya
– 'Eve Guest' (A) SHya
– 'Everest Blue' (S) SHya
– 'Fairy' (A) SHya
– 'Falcon' (S) SHya
– 'Fanciful' (S) CLyd MFie SHya
– 'Fanny Meerbeck' (S) EJap EMNN LRHS MFie NCra NHol NNrd WHil
– 'Favorite' EMNN NNrd SHya
– 'Figaro' (S) SHya
– 'Finchfield' (A) EMNN MFie SHya
– 'Firenze' NCra
– 'Flamingo' (S) MFie
– 'Fleminghouse' (S) EJap NNrd SHya
– 'Forsinard' (S) SHya
– 'Fradley' (A) SHya
– 'Frank Crosland' (A) MFie NCra SHya WHil
– 'Frank Faulkner' (A) SHya
– 'Frank Taylor' (S) SHya
– 'Frosty' (S) SHya
– 'Fuller's Red' (S) CLyd MFie
– 'Gaia' hort. (d) NHol SHya
– 'Galen' (A) MFie NCra NNrd SHya
– 'Gay Crusader' (A) EMNN MFie SHya
– 'Gee Cross' (A) EMNN MFie
§ – 'Geldersome Green' (S) EMNN MFie NHar SHya
– 'Generosity' (A) SHya
– 'George Rudd' (S) SHya
¶ – 'George Swinford's Leathercoat' (B) SHya
– 'Geronimo' (S) EMNN MFie SHya
– 'Gizabroon' (S) CLyd EMNN MFie NCra NHar NNrd WDav
– 'Gleam' (S) EMNN MFie NHar NNrd SHya
– 'Glencoe' (S) SHya
– 'Gleneagles' (S) SHya
– 'Glenelg' (S) MFie SHya
– 'Glenluce' (S) SHya
– 'Gnome' (B) NHol
– 'Goldcrest' (S) SHya
– 'Golden Chartreuse' (d) WHil
– 'Golden Eagle' NCra

– 'Golden Splendour' (d)	SHya WDav
– 'Goldthorn' (A)	SHya
– 'Good Report'	NCra
– 'Gordon Douglas' (A)	EMNN MFie NCra SHya SUsu
– 'Gorey'	NCra
– 'Grace Ellen' (S)	SHya
– 'Green Isle' (S)	EMNN MFie NBir NNrd SHya WHil
– 'Green Jacket' (S)	SHya WHil
– 'Green Mouse' (S)	MFie SHya
– 'Green Parrot' (S)	CLyd EMNN NHar SHya WHil
– 'Green Shank' (S)	MFie NNrd SHya WDav WHil
– 'Greenfinger' (S)	SHya
– 'Greenheart' (S)	EMNN SHya
– 'Greenpeace' (S)	LRHS NHar SHya
– 'Greensleeves' (S)	SHya
– 'Greta' (S)	ELan EMNN NHar NMen NNrd SHya WDav WHil
– 'Gretna Green' (S)	MFie NMen SHya
– 'Grey Bonnet' (S)	SHya
– 'Grey Friar' (S)	SHya
– 'Grey Hawk' (S)	SHya
– 'Grey Lag'	EMNN MFie NNrd SHya
– 'Grey Monarch' (S)	GCLN MFie SHya
– 'Grey Shrike' (S)	SHya
– 'Grey Tarquin' (S)	SHya
– 'Grizedale' (S)	MFie
– 'Guildersome Green'	See ***P. auricula* 'Geldersome Green'**
– 'Guinea' (S)	EMNN MFie NCra NNrd SHya
– 'Gwen' (A)	SHya
– 'Habanera'	NCra
– 'Haffner' (S)	SHya
– 'Harmony' (B)	MFie
– 'Harrison Weir' (S)	SHya
– 'Harry 'O'' (S)	SHya
– 'Harvest Moon' (S)	MFie
– 'Haughmond' (A)	EMNN MFie
– 'Hawkwood' (S)	EMNN NCra NHar NNrd WHil
– 'Hawkwood Fancy' (S)	MFie SHya WDav
* – 'Hazel' (A)	MFie NCra SHya
– 'Hazel's Fancy' (S)	SHya
– 'Headdress' (S)	MFie
– 'Heady'	NCra
– 'Hebers'	NCra
– 'Helen' (S)	NMen SHya
– 'Helen Barter' (S)	SHya
– 'Helena' (S)	EMNN MFie NHar NMen NNrd SHya WHil
– 'Helena Brown' (S)	SHya
– 'Hetty Woolf'	EMNN NMen NNrd SHya
– 'Hew Dalrymple' (S)	SHya
– 'Hinton Admiral' (S)	SHya
– 'Hinton Fields' (S)	MFie SHya
– 'Hoghton Gem' (d)	SHya
– 'Holyrood' (S)	MFie SHya
– 'Hopley's Double Mauve' (d)	MFie
– 'Humphrey' (S)	SHya
– 'Hurstwood Midnight'	NNrd WDav
* – 'Hyacinth' (S)	EJap NMen NWCA
– 'Ibis' (S)	MFie SHya
– 'Ice Maiden'	NCra
– 'Idmiston' (S)	SHya
– 'Imber' (S)	SHya
¶ – 'Impassioned' (A)	NCra
– 'Impeccable'	NCra
– 'Indian Love Call'	NCra
– 'Jack Dean' (A)	MFie SHya WHil
– 'Jack Stant' (S)	SHya
– 'James Arnot' (S)	MFie NCra NHar NMen SHya
– 'Jane Myers' (d)	MFie SHya

– 'Janet'	SHya
– 'Janie Hill' (A)	SHya
– 'Jeanne' (A)	SHya
– 'Jeannie Telford' (A)	NCra
– 'Jenny' (A)	EMNN GAbr MFie MYat NHar NNrd SHya
– 'Jessie' (d)	SHya
– 'Jezebel' (B)	SHya
– 'Joan Elliott' (A)	CLyd GAbr MFie MYat
– 'Joanne' (A)	SHya
– 'Joe Perks'	NCra
– 'Johann Bach' (B)	MFie
– 'John Stewart' (A)	EMNN MFie
– 'John Wayne' (A)	EMNN MFie SHya
– 'John Woolf' (S)	SHya
– 'Joy' (A)	CLyd EMNN MFie NCra NNrd SHya
– 'Joyce'	GAbr MFie NBir SHya WDav
– 'Julia' (S)	SHya
– 'July Sky' (A)	SHya
– 'Jupiter' (S)	SHya
– 'K.H.B.' (S)	NNrd
– 'Karen Cordrey' (S)	SHya WDav
◆ – 'Kath Dryden'	See ***P. allionii* 'Kath Dryden'**
– 'Kathy' (A)	SHya
– 'Kelso' (A)	MFie
– 'Kercup' (A)	MFie NCra NNrd
– 'Khachaturian'	NCra
– 'Kim' (A)	EMNN MFie NNrd SHya
– 'Kincraig' (S)	SHya
– 'Kingcup' (A)	MFie NCra SHya
– 'Kiowa' (S)	MFie
– 'Kirklands' (d)	MFie SHya
– 'Lady Croft' (S)	SHya
– 'Lady Daresbury' (A)	EMNN MFie NCra SHya
– 'Lady Emma Monson' (S)	SHya
– 'Lady Joyful' (S)	SHya
– 'Lady Zoë' (S)	MFie NCra
– 'Lamplugh'	MFie NNrd
– 'Landy' (A)	SHya
– 'Langley Park' (A)	MFie SHya WHil
– 'Larkhill' (A)	SHya
– 'Laverock' (S)	NBro SHya
– 'Laverock Fancy' (S)	EMNN MFie WDav
– 'Leather Jacket'	GAbr NHol
– 'Lechistan' (S)	EJap EMNN MFie NHar NHol NNrd
– 'Lee Paul' (A)	EMNN MFie NCra SHya WDav
– 'Lee Sharpe' (A)	SHya
– 'Lemon Drop' (S)	NMen SHya
– 'Lemon Sherbet' (B)	MFie
– 'Lewis Telford' (A)	SHya
– 'Lich'	EMNN
– 'Lichfield' (A)	SHya
¶ – 'Light Hearted'	NCra
– 'Lilac Domino' (S)	MFie NCra NGar SHya WDav
– 'Lillian Hill' (A)	SHya
– 'Lindley' (S)	EMNN NHar
– 'Lindsey Moreno' (S)	SHya
– 'Ling' (A)	CLyd EMNN MFie NCra SHya
– 'Lisa' (A)	CLyd MBal MFie NCra NHar NNrd SHya
– 'Lisa Clara' (S)	EMNN SHya
– 'Lisa's Smile' (S)	MFie NCra NMen SHya
– 'Lismore Yellow'	NNrd
– 'Little Rosetta' (d)	WHil
– 'Louisa' (d)	MFie
– 'Lovebird' (S)	EJap EMNN GAbr MFie NCra NHar NHol NNrd SHya SUsu WHil
– 'Madame Gina' (S)	MFie

- 'Maggie' (S) EMNN SHya
- 'Magnolia' (B) MFie
- 'Maid Marion' (d) SHya
- 'Manka' (S) MFie NCra SHya
- 'Mansell's Green' MFie NNrd SHya
- 'Margaret' (S) SHya
- 'Margaret Faulkner' (A) EMNN GCLN MFie NCra NMen SHya WHil
- 'Margaret Martin' (S) SHya WHil
- 'Margot Fonteyn' NCra
- 'Marigold' (d) CLyd EJap MFie NCra NNrd WDav
- 'Mark' (A) EJap EMNN MFie NCra NHol SHya WHil
- 'Marmion' (S) SHya
- 'Martin Luther King' (S) MFie
- 'Mary' (d) MFie SHya
- 'Mary of Dunoon' (S) SHya
- 'Mary Taylor' (S) SHya
- 'Mary Zac' NNrd
- 'Matthew Yates' (d) CHad GAbr MFie MOne NCra NHol SHya
- 'Maureen Millward' EMNN MFie NNrd
- 'May Tiger' (S) SHya
- 'Meadow Lark' NCra
- 'Mellifluous' NCra
- 'Merlin' (A) SHya
- 'Mermaid' GAbr MFie NCra SHya WHil
- 'Merridale' (A) EMNN MFie NCra SHya
- 'Metha' NCra

¶ – 'Mick' (A) NCra
- 'Midnight' (S) CBot CLyd EMNN MOne NCra NHar
- 'Mikado' (S) MFie SHya
- 'Millicent' (A) MFie SHya
- 'Mink' (A) MFie SHya WHil
- 'Minley' (S) EMNN MFie NHar NMen NNrd SHya
- 'Minstrel' (S) SHya
- 'Mipsie Miranda' (d) MFie SHya
- 'Mirabella Bay' NCra
- 'Miriam' (A) SHya
- 'Mish Mish' (d) SHya WHil
- 'Mojave' (S) EMNN MBro MFie NCra NHar NHol NMen WDav
- 'Moneymoon' (S) MFie NMen
- 'Monica' (A) MFie
- 'Monk' (A) CLyd MFie NNrd SHya
- 'Moonglow' (S) EBee EJap EMNN MFie NCra
- 'Moonrise' (S) EMNN MFie
- 'Moonstone' (d) MFie
- 'Moscow' (S) MFie
- 'Moselle' (S) SHya
- 'Mr 'A'' (S) CLyd WHil

¶ – 'Mrs L. Hearn' EMNN MFie NCra NNrd SHya WHil
- 'Mrs R. Bolton' (A) SHya WRha
- 'Murray Lakes' NCra
- 'Nankenan' WHil
- 'Neat and Tidy' (S) CLyd EJap EMNN MFie MHig NCra NHar NMen NNrd SHya WHil
- 'Nefertiti' NCra
- 'Neville Telford' (S) EMNN MFie NMen
- 'Nickity' (A) SHya

¶ – 'Nigel' (d) NHar WDav
- 'Night and Day' (S) EMNN MFie NCra
- 'Nocturne' (S) EMNN GAbr MFie NCra SHya
- 'Norma' (A) EMNN MFie NNrd
- 'Notability' (A) NCra SHya
- 'Oake's Blue' (S) MFie NCra
- 'Oban' (S) SHya
- 'Old Double Green' (d) MFie
- 'Old England' (S) SHya
- 'Old Gold' (S) SHya
- 'Old Gold Dusty Miller' (B) MFie NNrd
- 'Old Irish Blue' (B) CLyd MBro MFie SHya
- 'Old Irish Scented' (B) WHil
- 'Old Lilac' (B) MFie
- 'Old Mustard' SWas
- 'Old Red Dusty Miller' (B) ECha MFie MHig NBir SHya WHil
- 'Old Red Velvet' GCLN
- 'Old Suffolk Bronze' (B) MFie NBro SHya
- 'Old Tawny' (B) MFie
- 'Old Wine' (A) CLyd MFie
- 'Old Yellow Dusty Miller' (B) CLTr CLyd EMNN EWes GAbr MBro MFie MHig NBro NHol NNrd SHya WAbe WDav WHil WWin
- 'Olton' (A) MFie NNrd SHya
- 'Orb' (S) CLyd EJap EMNN MFie NMen NNrd SHya WHil
- 'Osbourne Green' (B) MFie WDav WHil
- 'Overdale' (A) SHya
- 'Paradise Yellow' (B) EMNN MFie NMen SHya
- 'Paris' (S) SHya
- 'Party Dress' (S) SHya
- 'Pastiche' (A) MFie NCra
- 'Pat' (S) EMNN MFie MOne NCra NMen SHya
- 'Pat Barnard' NNrd
- 'Patience' (S) NNrd
- 'Patricia Barras' (S) SHya
- 'Pauline' (A) MFie SHya
- 'Peggy' (A) EPot MFie NNrd NWCA
- 'Petite Hybrid' MFos
- 'Pharaoh' NCra
- 'Phyllis Douglas' (A) EMNN MFie NCra SHya
- 'Pierot' (A) MFie

¶ – 'Piers Telford' NCra
- 'Pink Lady' (A) MFie
- 'Pinstripe' NNrd
- 'Pippin' (A) MFie SHya
- 'Pixie' (A) SHya
- 'Plush Royal' (S) MFie
- 'Portree' (S) EMNN SHya
- 'Pot o' Gold' (S) MFie NCra NHar SHya
- 'Prague' (S) MFie NBir NMen SHya
- 'Prince Charming' (S) MFie SHya
- 'Prince John' (A) EJap MFie NBro NCra NNrd SHya WHil
- 'Purple Mermaid' (d) MFie
- 'Purple Sage' (S) EMNN GCLN NHar

¶ – 'Purple Velvet' (S) EHyt
- 'Queen Bee' (S) SHya
- 'Queen's Bower' (S) EMNN NNrd SHya
- 'Quintessence' NCra
- 'Quiquern' (S) SHya
- 'Rabley Heath' (A) CLyd EMNN MFie SHya
- 'Radiant' (A) MFie SHya
- 'Rajah' (S) EJap ELan MFie NCra NHar NMen SHya WHil
- 'Ray's Grey' (S) SHya
- 'Red Beret' (S) EJap MFie NCra
- 'Red Gauntlet' (S) EJap EMNN MFie NCra NHar NMen NNrd SHya
- 'Red Mark' (A) MFie
- 'Red Rum' (S) MFie NCra
- 'Remus' (S) ELan MFie NCra NHar NHol NNrd NWCA SHya WHil
- 'Renata' (S) MFie
- 'Rene' EMNN

- 'Riatty' (d) MFie
- 'Richard Shaw' (A) MFie NNrd
- 'Rishworth' (S) SHya
- 'Roberto' (S) SHya
- 'Rock Sand' (S) EMNN GCLN MFie NHar NNrd
- 'Rodeo' (A) MFie NCra SHya
- 'Rolts' (S) CLyd ELan EMNN MFie NBir NCra NHar NHol NMen NNrd SHya WFar WHil
- 'Rondy' (S) SHya
- 'Ronny Simpson' NCra
- 'Rosalie Edwards' (S) EMNN MFie NCra NNrd SHya
- 'Rosamund' (d) SHya
- 'Rosanna' (S) MFie
- 'Rosebud' (S) MFie
- 'Rosemary' (S) EMNN MFie NNrd
- 'Rossiter's Grey' (S) SHya
- 'Rowena' (A) CLyd EJap EMNN MFie MOne NCra NHar NHol NNrd NPri SHya
- 'Roxburgh' (A) EMNN SHya
- 'Royal Purple' (S) NNrd
- 'Royal Velvet' (S) NNrd
- 'Royalty' (S) MFie
- 'Ruby Hyde' (B) MFie
- 'Rusty Dusty' GAbr
- 'Sailor Boy' (S) MFie SHya
- 'Saint Boswells' (S) MFie SHya
- 'Saint Elmo' (d) MFie
- 'Saint Gerrans' White' (B) MFie
- 'Saint Quentin' (S) SHya
- 'Salad' (S) MFie SHya
- 'Sale Green' (A) SHya
- 'Salome' (A) SHya
- 'Sam Hunter' NCra
- 'Sandhills' (A) SHya
- 'Sandmartin' (S) MFie SHya
- 'Sandra' (A) ELan EMNN GAbr MFie SHya WHil
- 'Sandwood Bay' (A) CLyd EBee EMNN GAbr MFie NCra NHar NMen NNrd SHya WHil WPen
- 'Sarah Lodge' (d) EMNN MFie
- 'Satchmo' EMNN
- 'Scipio' (S) SHya
- 'Seaton Burn' (S) SHya
- 'Serenity' (S) EMNN MFie NNrd SHya
- 'Shalford' (d) MFie WDav
- 'Sharman's Cross' (S) SHya
- 'Sheila' (S) GAbr MFie NHar NNrd SBla SHya
- 'Shere' (S) EMNN MFie NCra NNrd SHya
- 'Sherwood' EMNN MFie NHar NNrd SHya
- 'Shirley Hibberd' (S) SHya
- 'Shotley' (A) EMNN MFie
- 'Shrewton' (S) SHya
- 'Silverway' (S) SHya
- 'Sir Hardy Amies' (A) SHya
- 'Sir John Hall' NCra
- 'Sirius' (A) CLyd EBee MFie MOne NCra NHar NHol SHya WHil
- 'Slioch' (S) EMNN MFie NHar NNrd SHya WHil
- 'Snooty Fox' (A) EMNN MFie NNrd WDav
- 'Snooty Fox II' (A) SHya
- 'Snowy Owl' GCLN MFie SHya
- 'Soncy Face' NCra
- 'Sonya' (A) NNrd
- 'South Barrow' (d) EMNN MFie WHil
- 'Space Age' (S) SHya
- 'Splendour' (S) SHya
- 'Spring Meadows' (S) MFie MOne NCra SHya
- 'Springtime' NCra
- SS TY 72 (S) MFie
- 'Standish' (d) EJap GAbr MFie NCra NHol SHya
- 'Stant's Blue' (S) EJap EMNN MFie NHol SHya
- 'Star Wars' (S) SHya

¶ – 'Starry' (S) NHar WDav

- 'Stella' (S) MFie
- 'Stoke Poges' (A) SHya
- 'Stonnal' (A) MFie NHar SHya
- 'Streamlet' (S) SHya
- 'Stripey' (d) SHya
- 'Stubb's Tartan' (S) NHar SHya
- 'Sue' (A) MFie
- 'Sue Douglas' (A) SHya
- 'Sugar Plum Fairy' EMNN
- 'Summer Sky' (A) SHya
- 'Sumo' NCra
- 'Sunflower' (S) MFie NHar WDav
- 'Sunsal' (S) MFie
- 'Sunstar' (S) EMNN MFie NMen
- 'Super Para' (S) EMNN MFie NNrd SHya
- 'Superb' (S) SHya
- 'Susan' (A) MFie SHya
- 'Susannah' (d) EBee EFol MFie MOne NHol SHya
- 'Sweet Pastures' (S) EJap EMNN MFie NCra NHol SHya
- 'Swift' (S) MFie
- 'Swinley' (S) SHya
- 'Sword' NNrd SHya
- 'Symphony' (A) SHya WHil
- 'Tall Purple Dusty Miller' (B) MFie
- 'Tally-ho' (A) SHya
- 'Tarantella' (A) EJap EMNN MFie NCra NNrd SHya
- 'Tawny Owl' NBro
- 'Ted Roberts' (A) EMNN MFie NCra SHya
- 'Teem' (S) EJap EMNN MFie NCra NMen SHya WHil
- 'Tenby Grey' (S) MFie
- 'The Baron' (S) EJap MFie MOne NHar WHil
- 'The Bishop' (S) MFie NCra
- 'The Bride' (S) EJap EMNN NCra SHya
- 'The Cardinal' (d) SAsh
- 'The Czar' (A) SHya
- 'The Maverick' (S) SHya
- 'The Raven' (S) EMNN MFie NMen
- 'The Sneeps' NCra SHya WHil
- 'The Snods' (S) EMNN MFie NCra
- 'Thebes' NCra
- 'Thetis' (A) MFie NCra SHya WDav
- 'Thirlmere' (d) MFie SHya
- 'Three Way Stripe' WHil
- 'Tinkerbell' (S) EJap MFie SHya
- 'Tomboy' (S) MFie
- 'Tomma' NCra
- 'Tosca' (S) EMNN NMen NNrd SHya WDav WHil
- 'Trojan' (S) SHya
- 'Trouble' (d) CSpe EMNN MFie MHlr MOne NCra NHar NMen SHya SMrm
- 'Trudy' (S) EMNN MFie NCra NHar NMen NNrd
- 'True Briton' (S) MFie SHya
- 'Trumpet Blue' (S) MFie
- 'Tumbledown' (A) MFie SHya
- 'Tummel' NCra
- 'Tuthmoses' NCra

– 'Tye Lea' (S)	MFie SHya
– 'Typhoon' (A)	MFie SHya
– 'Unforgetable'	NCra
– 'Upton Belle' (S)	NMen
– 'Valerie' (A)	MFie NCra NMen NNrd SHya WHil
– 'Valerie Clare'	NCra
– 'Vee Too' (A)	MFie SHya
– 'Velvet Moon'	NCra
– 'Venetian'	NCra
– 'Vera' (A)	MFie
– 'Verdi' (A)	EJap EMNN MFie NCra SHya
– 'Victoria' (S)	SHya
– 'Victoria de Wemyss' (A)	MFie
– 'Vulcan' (A)	MFie NCra NMen SHya
– 'Waincliffe Fancy' (S)	SHya
– 'Waincliffe Red' (S)	MFie
– 'Walhampton' (S)	EMNN MFie NMen SHya
– 'Walton' (A)	MFie SHya
– 'Walton Heath' (d)	EMNN MFie SHya WDav WHil
– 'Warwick' (S)	NMen SHya
– 'Watt's Purple' (d)	MFie
– 'Wedding Day' (S)	MFie
– 'White Ensign' (S)	EMNN MFie NNrd SHya WHil
– 'White Water'	NCra
– 'White Wings' (S)	EMNN MFie NCra NHar SHya
– 'Wide Awake' (A)	MFie
– 'Wincha' (S)	MFie SHya
– 'Windways Mystery' (B)	MFie
– 'Winifrid' (A)	CLyd EMNN MFie MOne NCra NHar NHol SHya WHil
– 'Woodmill' (A)	SHya
– 'Woodstock' (S)	SHya
– 'Wor Jackie' (S)	EMNN MFie NHar
– 'Y.I. Hinney' (A)	EMNN MFie
– 'Yelverton' (S)	SHya
– 'Yorkshire Grey' (S)	MFie SHya
– 'Zambia' (d)	CLyd MFie SHya WHil
§ – L. 🏆	CArn ELan GDra GTou MBal MTho NBro NCra NHar NRoo NSla NWCA SPer SSmi WCla
– subsp. ***auricula*** (2)	GTou
– ***balbisii*** (2)	NNrd
– subsp. ***bauhinii*** (2)	MBro
'Barbara Midwinter' (30x6)	CMea
Barnhaven Blues Group (Prim)	GAbr NRya
Barnhaven doubles (d.Poly)	CSWP EGol
Barnhaven Gold-laced Group (Poly)	GAbr MFie
Barnhaven Reds	See ***P.* Tartan Reds Group**
Barnhaven Traditional Group	CSWP
'Beamish Foam' (Poly)	CVer MDHE
'Beatrice Wooster' (2)	CLyd CNic EMNN EPot EWes LRHS MBro MFie NGre NHar NHed NHol NMen NNrd NTow NWCA SIng WAbe WDav WHil
'Beeches' Pink'	GAbr
beesiana (4)	CInt CRow CSam EAst EBar EHon ELan GAbr GCHN GFle LPBA LSyl MBri MFie MSta MSte NHar NOak NSti SHel SMrm SPer WChe WCra WGwG WHil WPer WPyg WWat
'Bellamy's Pride'	CLyd
bellidifolia (17)	CPla NGre
beluensis	See ***P.* × *pubescens* 'Freedom'**
Bergfrühling Julianas Group (Prim)	MFie
§ × ***berninae*** 'Windrush' (2)	CLyd EHyt NHar NNrd SIng WAbe
'Betty Green' (Prim)	MBri
'Bewerley White'	See ***P.* × *pubescens* 'Bewerley White'**
bhutanica	See ***P. whitei* 'Sherriff's Variety'**
× ***biflora*** (2)	CBlo
'Big Red Giant' (d.Prim)	CBlo LFis MOne NHar
bileckii	See ***P.* × *forsteri* 'Bileckii'**
'Blue Riband' (Prim)	CCot CGle EPot GGar LSur MBri MHig WAbe WHil
'Blue Sapphire' (d.Prim)	CBlo CMil GAbr LHop MOne NRoo SLod WHil
Blue Striped Victorians Group (Poly)	GAbr
'Blutenkissen' (Prim)	EPot GAbr GMaP LSur NNrd
'Bon Accord Purple' (d.Poly)	CGle EJud WFar
'Bonfire' (4)	GDra NHol
'Bootheosa' (21)	NHol
boothii alba (21)	GGGa
◆ 'Boothman's Ruby'	See ***P.* × *pubescens* 'Boothman's Variety'**
boveana (12)	MFie SBla
§ ***bracteosa*** (21)	ITim NHar NHol WAbe
brevicula ACE 1689 (18)	EPot
'Brimstone' (Poly)	CGle
¶ 'Broadwell Pink' (2)	CGra EHyt
'Bronwyn' (30)	LSur NHol SSvw
'Broxbourne'	CLyd NHar
'Buckland Wine' (Prim)	CCot CVer LSur
× ***bulleesiana*** (4)	EAst LFis NBro NPri NRoo SMrm SRms SWat WHil WPer WRha
bulleyana (4) 🏆	CGle CPla CRow CWGN EAst ECha EHon ELan EPot GAbr GDra GFle GTou LHop LPBA LSyl MBal MBri MSta NCra NDea NHar SBla SPer SSpi WAbe WChe WHil WPer WWat
– ACE 2484 (4)	GGGa
burmanica (4)	CInt CPla CSam CWGN EBee GAbr GDra GFle GGar LSyl MBal MSta NCra NDea NGar NHar NPri SRms WCru
'Butterscotch' (Prim)	CGle CSWP GPot
'Caerulea Plena' (d.Prim)	GAbr GCal
calderiana (21)	GDra NHar
– subsp. ***strumosa*** BC 9347 (21)	GCra
Candelabra Hybrids (4)	CBre CBro EMNN NCra
Candy Pinks Group (Prim)	GAbr
capitata (5)	CBot CGle CInt CPla GDra GFle GTou LSyl MBal MBri MSte NCra NGre NHar WChe WCla WPer
– subsp. ***crispata*** AGS/ES 407 (5)	GCra
– dark forms (5)	MFie
– KEKE 274 (5)	MFie
– subsp. ***mooreana*** (5)	CFir CHan CPea CWGN GCan GFle LPBA NLak WCla WHil WHoo
– subsp. ***sphaerocephala*** (5)	GCra NWCA
'Captain Blood' (d.Prim)	ECtt GAbr NHar SPer SUsu WRha
'Carmen' (Prim)	CLyd

Carnation Victorians Group (Poly)	EJap EWoo GAbr MFie
'Casquet'	CSWP
cernua (17)	GCan GDra GFle MFie NGre NHar WCru
'Charlen' (d.Prim)	NHar SRms
Chartreuse Group (Poly)	CGle CSWP EJap GAbr MFie
'Cherry' (Prim)	CCot CVer GAbr
chionantha (18) 🏆	CBot CGle CPla CWGN EJap ELan GDra GFle GPot GTou LBee LSyl MBal MBri MFie MNrw NCra NDea NGre NHar NHed NMen NNor NRoo SPer WHil
§ – Sinopurpurea Group (18)	CGle CPla EBee EMNN EWes GAbr GCra GDra GFle GGGa GTou LSyl MBal NCra SPer WPer WWhi
'Chocolate Soldier' (d.Prim)	ECtt EJap GGar MBal MOne
chungensis (4)	CGle GCra GTou MBri NHar SRms WAbe
§ – x *pulverulenta* (4)	EBre NPri SMrm WAbe
x *chunglenta*	See ***P. chungensis* x *pulverulenta***
'Clarence Elliott' (2)	See ***P. allionii* 'Clarence Elliott'**
clarkei (11)	CLyd EHyt GFle GGGa GTou MHig NWCA
clusiana (2)	GDra MBal NGre NHol NSla
cockburniana (4)	CInt CMil CRow GAbr GDra GFle GGGa GGar GTou MBal MBri MFie NCra NGre NHar SMrm SRms
concholoba (17)	CPla GAbr GCan GCra GGGa GGar GTou MFie NGre NHar WAbe
'Corporal Baxter' (d.Prim)	EBar LHop MBri MOne SLod SMrm
cortusoides (7)	CPla GCra MNrw NCra NWCA SRms
Cowichan (Poly)	CCot CInt EGar EJap GAbr MBri NCra NSti
Cowichan Amethyst Group (Poly)	CSWP GAbr
Cowichan Blue Group (Poly)	CSWP EWoo GAbr LHop WPen
Cowichan Garnet Group (Poly)	CSWP EWoo GAbr GCan MFie
Cowichan Venetian Group (Poly)	CSWP GAbr GCan WFar
Cowichan Yellow Group (Poly)	GAbr NWoo WCot WPen
'Craven Gem' (Poly)	GAbr LSur NRoo
Crescendo Series (Poly)	GAbr NRoo
'Crimson Cushion'	NNrd
'Crimson Queen' (Prim)	GAbr LSur
'Crimson Velvet' (2)	EMNN EPot GAbr MBro MFie MHig NNrd SRms
crispa	See ***P. glomerata***
x *crucis* (2)	NGar
* *cuneata*	GTou
cuneifolia (8)	GCLN
cuneifolia alba (8)	GCLN
daonensis (2)	NMen SIng
darialica (11)	CGle CNic CPla ELan GDra MYat NChi NCra NMen
'David Green' (Prim)	CVer
'David Valentine'	GAbr LSur
'Dawn Ansell' (D.Prim)	CBre CElw CGle CRow CSpe EBar EBre ECtt EFol ELan EPri GGar LFis LHop LSur MBal MBri MCLN MOne MRav NEgg NHar NHol NRoo SLod SPer SSvw WHer WHil WPnn
Daybreak Group (Poly)	CSWP EWoo MFie
deflexa ACE 2283 (17)	EPot
denticulata (9) 🏆	CGle CPla CRow CShe CWGN EBre ECha EHon ELan LPBA MBal MBri MCLN MFir MSta MWat NCra NGre NHed NNor NRoo SIng WAbe WCla WPer WWin
– var. *alba* (9)	CGle EBre ECha EGol EJap ELan EMNN EPot ERav GAbr GMac GPot GTou LHop MBal MBri MFie MWat NCra NHar NHed NHol NOrc NRoo WHen WHil WPer
– 'Bressingham Beauty' (9)	EBre MUlv
– var. *cachemiriana* hort. (9)	ELan EPfP WCla
– 'Glenroy Crimson' (9)	CRDP MBal SRms
– 'Inshriach Carmine' (9)	GDra
– lilac (9)	EHon EJap GTou MFie NPri
– purple (9)	GAbr IBlr
– red (9)	CRow EMNN EPar NOrc NPri
– 'Robinson's Red' (9)	EPot GBuc
– 'Ronsdorf' (9)	LHop
– rose (9)	NCut NHar
– 'Rubinball' (9)	EBre EPfP GAri NHol NRoo
– ruby (9)	CInt EHon EJap GAbr GTou LWak MBri MCLN MFie NBro NOak SMrm SRms WHen WHil WPer WPyg
– 'Snowball' (9)	MCLN MFir NOak WHen WPyg
¶ *deorum* (2)	CGra WDav
x *deschmannii*	See ***P.* x *vochinensis***
'Desert Sunset' (Poly)	EWoo GAbr MFie
deuteronana alba (21)	NHar
'Devon Cream' (Prim)	ECha
'Dianne'	See ***P.* x *forsteri* 'Dianne'**
'Doctor Mary' (Prim)	GAbr
'Dora'	MDHE
'Dorothy' (Poly)	GAbr LSur MRav NNrd
'Double Lilac'	See ***P. vulgaris* 'Lilacina Plena'**
¶ *drummondiana*	GFle
'Duchess of York'	CBos SApp
'Duckyls Red' (Prim)	GBuc LSur SRms
'Dusky Lady'	MTis
'Early Irish Yellow' (Prim)	LSur
'Easter Bonnet'	CBlo MOne
edelbergii (12)	GTou MFie
edgeworthii	See ***P. nana***
elatior (30) 🏆	CBro CGle CKin CNic CPla CRow CSev EJap GDra GFle GLil LFox LSyl MHar MHew MNrw MSal NCra NMen NMir NOrc NRoo NSla NSti SIng SPer SRms SSpi WCla WUnd
¶ – hose in hose (30)	GAbr
– subsp. *intricata* (30)	CNic
¶ – subsp. *leucophylla* (30)	ECho
§ – subsp. *meyeri* (30)	NSla
– subsp. *pallasii* (30)	NSla
elliptica (11)	GTou
ellisiae (21)	MFie NMen NSla

'Erin's Gem' (Poly)	CGle
§ ***erythra*** (26)	NGre
'Ethel Barker' (2)	CLyd EHyt EMNN EPot ITim LFox MHig NGre NHar NHed NHol NMen NNrd NTow SIng SSmi WAbe WHil
'Ethel M. Dell' (D.Prim)	MOne NHar SRms
'Eugénie' (D.Prim)	CGle CSpe ELan MOne NChi NHar WWeb
farinosa	CLyd CNic CPla GFle MBal MBri MSal NCra NGre NHar NMen NRya SSpi WCla WPer WUnd
– JCA 786.500 (11)	MFie
fasciculata (11)	EDAr
– CLD 345 (11)	NHar
¶ 'Fife Yellow' (D.Poly)	GBuc
'Fire Dance' (Poly)	EWoo MFie
Firefly Group (Poly)	GAbr LFox
firmipes (26)	NTow WLRN
§ ***flaccida*** (28) 🏆	GCra GDra GFle GGGa MBal NCra NGre NHar WAbe
× ***flagellicaulis***	See ***P.*** × ***polyantha***
Flamingo Group (Poly)	CSWP EJap GAbr MFie
§ × ***floerkeana*** (2)	NGre NHol WAbe
¶ – f. ***biflora alba*** (2)	NGre
florida (29)	GGGa
florindae (26) 🏆	Widely available
– hybrids (26)	CVer GAbr LFox MFie MSCN NHol WHil
– orange (26)	CSam IBlr LSyl MNrw NChi WChe WCru
– 'Ray's Ruby' (26)	GBuc MCLN MNrw NBro WWhi
– red (26)	GAbr GGGa LSyl MSta SMrm WChe
Footlight Parade Group (Prim)	CSWP EWoo
forrestii (3)	LSyl MFie NGre NHar WAbe WHil
– C&Cu 9431 (3)	GGGa
§ × ***forsteri*** (2)	EMNN ITim MHig NHar NHed NHol NMen WAbe
§ – 'Bileckii' (2)	ELan EPot LBee MBal MBro MHig NBro NHar NHed NNrd NWCA SRms SSmi WAbe WDav WHil
§ – 'Dianne' (2)	EHyt EPot GAbr MBro MHig MYat NBro NHar NHol NNrd WAbe
'Freckles' (D.Prim)	ELan GGar MCLN MOne NHar SIng SPer
'Freedom'	See ***P.*** × ***pubescens* 'Freedom'**
frondosa 🏆	CGle CGra CInt CLyd CPla EJap GCra GPot LFox LHop MBal MBri MBro MFie NCra NHar NMen NWCA SMrm WAbe WHoo
'Frühlingszauber' (Prim)	NHol
Fuchsia Victorians Group (Poly)	CSWP EJap EWoo MFie
Galligaskins Group (Poly)	NGar
'Garryard Guinevere'	See ***P.* 'Guinevere'**
'Gartenmeister Bartens' (Prim)	LSur
gaubana (12)	MFie NMen
gemmifera (11)	GGGa NHar
– ACE 1427 (11)	NHar
– var. ***zambalensis*** (11)	WAbe
geraniifolia (7)	NRoo
§ 'Gigha' (Prim)	CSpe EWoo GPot MBro

glaucescens (2)	CLyd CNic MBro MFie NHar NSla
– subsp. ***calycina***	See ***P. glaucescens*** subsp. ***glaucescens***
§ – subsp. ***glaucescens*** (2)	NHol
– JCA 786.900 (2)	MFie
'Glebe Grey' (Prim)	CGle
§ ***glomerata*** (5)	GBuc GGGa
'Gloriosa' (Prim)	CCot LSur
'Glowing Embers' (4)	CGle EJap ELan MBri MFie NBir
glutinosa (2)	ITim
Gold Laced Group (Poly)	CBre CCot CDec CGle CPla CRDP ELan EWoo GAbr GMac LFox LSur MBri NCra NGar NGre NHar NHol NNrd NWCA SUsu WHal WHer WHil WHoo
'Gordon'	NGar
gracilipes (21)	CGle GGGa MOne NHar SRms WAbe
– early form (21)	NHar NHol
– L&S 1 (21)	NHar NHol
– L&S 1166 (21)	NHar NHol
– late form (21)	NHar NHol
– 'Major'	See ***P. bracteosa***
– 'Masterton' (21)	NHar NHol
– 'Minor'	See ***P. petiolaris***
– 'Winter Jewel' (21)	NHar NHol
'Graham'	NGar
Grand Canyon Group (Poly)	EJap EWoo GPot MFie
'Granny Graham' (Prim)	SRms
griffithii (21)	GFle GGGa NGre
'Groeneken's Glory' (Prim)	CGle CInt CNic CVer ELan EPot GAbr LSur MBri MRav NBro NCra NFla SIng WPbr
§ 'Guinevere' (Poly) 🏆	Widely available
'Hall Barn Blue'	LSur NHol
§ ***halleri*** (11)	CPea CPla GCHN GCan GCra GFle GTou MBal MBro MFie NCra NHar NMen NWCA SAlw WAbe WCla
– 'Longiflora'	See ***P. halleri***
Harbinger Group (Prim)	CGle GPot NNrd
'Harbour Lights'	CSWP EWoo MFie
Harlow Carr hybrids (4)	EHyt NCat NDea NGar NRoo SPer WPen
Harvest Yellows Group (Poly)	EWoo GPot MFie
× ***heeri*** (2)	EPot NHol
'Helge' (Prim)	LSur
helodoxa	See ***P. prolifera***
§ 'Hemswell Blush' (2)	EMNN NGre NHol WDav
§ 'Hemswell Ember' (2)	EMNN MFie NHar NHed NMen
heucherifolia (7)	CBot CPla GCan LFox MSCN SAlw
hirsuta (2)	CNic GTou MFie
¶ – 'Lismore Snow' (2)	NHar NNrd
Hose in Hose (Poly)	CCot CGle CSWP MNrw MOne NCra NGar NNrd NPri NRoo SAlw SSvw WRus
'Hurstwood Midnight'	MFie
'Husky' 🏆	NRoo
§ 'Hyacinthia' (2)	CLyd EMNN EPot NGre NNrd WAbe
hyacinthina (17)	NMen WHil
ianthina (4)	GGar NLak
Indian Reds Group (Poly)	EJap EWoo MFie
¶ 'Ingram's Blue' (Prim)	LSur

Inshriach Hybrids (4)	CMHG GAbr GCan GDra GGar LHop MBri MFie MSCN MSte NHol SBar SPer WGwG
integrifolia (2)	NGre WAbe WHil
× ***intermedia*** (2)	MHig WHil
§ 'Inverewe' (4) 🏆	GAbr GAri GCal GDra GGar NHar NHol NRoo
§ ***involucrata*** (11)	CBot GCLN GCan GFle GGGa NHar NMen SWat WHil
§ – subsp. ***yargongensis*** (11)	CGle CPla GGar GTou MBal MBri MFie NGre NNrd NWCA SWat
ioessa (26)	CPla EBre EJap EWes GCra GGGa MBal MBri NWCA
– hybrids (26)	MFie SAlw
'Iris Mainwaring' (Prim)	CVer EPot GAbr GMaP LSur MDHE NCra NHol NNrd
irregularis	GGGa
Jack in the Green Group (Poly)	CCot CDec CGle CMGP CNic CSWP LSur MNrw NCra NGar SAlw WHer WRus
Jackanapes Group (Poly)	LSur NGar
Jackanapes on Horseback Group (Poly)	NGar
'Jackaroo' (4)	GFle
japonica (4) 🏆	CBre CGle CMHG CRow CWGN ECha GFle GMac GTou LPBA MFir NBro NCra NHar NMen NNor NRoo SUsu SWat WChe WCla WCru WPer
– 'Alba' (4)	EBee GBin NPri WHil
– 'Apple Blossom' (4)	EHon LSyl NHed
– 'Fromfield Pink' (4)	WWoo
– 'Fuji' (4)	CSam EJap GCan GCra GDra MBal MBri MSta
– 'Miller's Crimson' (4)	CGle CPla CRow CTrw CWGN EAst EBre ECha EHon ELan GAbr GDra LHop LSyl MBal MBri MCLN MFie NBro NDea NFla NHar NSti SMrm SPer WHil WOve WPer WWat WWhi
– 'Oriental Sunrise' (4)	CMil EJap
– 'Postford White' (4)	CBot CBro CGle CPla CRow CTrw CWGN EBre ECha EHon EJap ELan EPot LSyl MBri MCLN NCra NDea NGar NSti SPer SUsu WCla WPer WRus WWat WWhi
– red shades (4)	EJap NSti WAbe
– 'Valley Red' (4)	GBin GBuc GCra GGar LSyl
jesoana (7)	NSla NTow
– B&SWJ 618 (7)	WCru
Jewel Group	LSur
'Jill'	CVer GAbr LSur
'Johanna' (11)	CGle EBre GFle GGar LSyl NBro NGar NGre NHar NWCA
'Jo-Jo' (2)	CLyd
juliae (30)	CGle CPla CRDP GFle LSur MHlr NGre NMen NNrd WCot WEas
– white (30)	CGle
× ***juliana***	See ***P.*** × ***pruhonicensis***
× ***juribella*** (2)	EHyt NHar
'Kate Haywood'	CLyd
'Ken Dearman' (D.Prim)	CSpe EBar ECtt EFol ELan GGar MBal MCLN MHlr MOne MRav NEgg NHol NSti SIng SMrm WHil WPnn
kewensis (12) 🏆	MFie NWCA
'Kinlough Beauty' (Poly)	CCot CDec CVer EPPr EPar GAbr LFox LSur NCra NRoo NSti NWes WEas
kisoana (7)	CPla MTho WCru
kisoana alba (7)	CPla LWoo MTho
'Lady Greer' (Poly) 🏆	CCot CGle CInt CPla ELan GAbr LFox LGan LSur MRav NBir NCra NGre NHar NMen NNrd NRoo NRya NSti NWCA SAlw SIng SLod SMac SSmi WEas WHal WPbr WWat
'Lambrook Lilac' (Poly)	CVer
§ ***latifolia*** (2)	NCra NHar WLRN
– cream (2)	NGre NHed
latisecta (7)	GGGa
laurentiana	See ***P. mistassinica*** var. ***macropoda***
'Lilac Fairy'	NHar NNrd
'Lilian Harvey' (D.Prim)	CElw CGle ECtt ELan MOne MRav NBir SIng SPer
Limelight Group (Poly)	EWoo GAbr MFie
'Lingwood Beauty' (Prim)	CVer GMaP LSur
'Linnet' (21)	ITim
¶ 'Lismore' (2)	EHyt
'Lismore Pink Ice'	NGre
'Lismore Yellow' (2)	GTou NGre NHar NHol WAbe WHil
Lissadel Hybrids (4)	NHol
'Little Egypt' (Poly)	EWoo
'Little Poppet'	GAbr
littoniana	See ***P. vialii***
§ × ***loiseleurii*** (2)	EBre MBro
◆ ***longiflora***	See ***P. halleri***
luteola (11)	GFle MFie MNrw NPri WHil WWoo
macrophylla (18)	GFle GLil GTou MBal
– H 78 (18)	GDra MSte
magellanica (11)	WAbe
malacoides (3)	MBri
marginata (2) 🏆	EMNN EPot GAbr GDra GFle LFox LHop MBro MRPP MYat NCra NGre NHar NHed NNrd SSmi WAbe
marginata alba (2)	EPot EWes GCLN MBro MHig MYat NCra NGar NGre NHar NHed NNrd SSmi WAbe WDav WHil
marginata 'Amethyst' (2)	EPot
– 'Arthur Branch' (2)	EPot WAbe
– 'Baldock's Mauve' (2)	NGar
– 'Barbara Clough' (2)	CLyd MFie NGar WAbe
– 'Beamish' (2)	CLyd EPot NGar NRya
– 'Beatrice Lascaris' (2)	EPot ITim MBro MFie MHig MYat NGar NHar NHol NMen NNrd SIng WAbe WDav WHil
– 'Beverley Reid' (2)	EHyt
– 'Caerulea' (2)	CLyd EPot MFos MHig MYat NGar WAbe
– 'Clear's Variety' (2)	EHyt EMNN EPot MHig MYat NHar NMen NNrd WHil
– 'Correvon's Variety' (2)	CLyd NCra NGar WAbe
– 'Doctor Jenkins' (2)	NHar NHol WDav
– 'Drake's Form' (2)	EPot ITim MHig NHol NNrd
– 'Earl L. Bolton' (2)	EPot NGar NHol NNrd WAbe
– 'Elizabeth Fry' (2)	CLyd LFox MBro NNrd
– 'F.W. Millard' (2)	MBro NHar
– 'Grandiflora' (2)	MBro NHar NNrd SIng WDav
– 'Highland Twilight' (2)	CPBP NNrd SAlw
– 'Holden Variety' (2)	EHyt EMNN MBal MBro MHig NGar NGre NHar NHed NHol NMen NNrd WAbe WDav
– 'Hyacinthia' (2)	See ***P.*** **'Hyacinthia'**

¶ – 'Ivy Agee'	CLyd EPot NGar WAbe
– 'Janet' (2)	CLyd EHyt EMNN EPot MHig WAbe WDav WHil
– 'Jenkins Variety' (2)	CLyd EPot
– 'Kesselring's Variety' (2)	CLyd EHyt ELan EPot MBro MHig MRPP MYat NGar NHar NHed NNrd SSmi WAbe WDav WHil WWin
– 'Laciniata'	NGar
* – 'Lilac' (2)	EHyt GDra LFox NGar NHar NNrd
– 'Lilac Domino'	WAbe
– 'Linda Pope' (2) 🏆	CLyd EHyt EMNN EPot ITim NCra NGar NHar NHed NHol NMen NNrd NSla WAbe WHil
¶ – maritime form (2)	NNrd
– 'Messingham' (2)	EPot
– 'Millard's Variety' (2)	CLyd NGar NMen
– 'Mrs Carter Walmsley' (2)	NGar
– 'Nancy Lucy' (2)	WAbe
– 'Napoleon' (2)	NHar NHol NNrd
– 'Prichard's Variety' (2)	CLyd ELan EMNN EPot GDra ITim LBee LFox MBro MFie MYat NCra NGar NGre NHar NHed NMen NRya SSmi WAbe WCla WDav WEas WHil WOMN
– 'Rheniana' (2)	EPot NGar
– 'Rosea' (2)	EPot SIng
– 'Sheila Denby' (2)	EMNN NGar NNrd
– small flowered form (2)	NGar
– 'Snowhite' (2)	WAbe
– 'Violet Form' (2)	EMNN MBro NHar WHil
– 'Waithman's Variety' (2)	EPot GTou
'Marianne Davey' (D.Prim)	CGle EPri MBri MCLN MRav NHar NMGW NSti SPer
'Marie Crousse' (D.Prim)	CGle EBar EHic GAbr LHop MBal MBro MFie MOne NHar NHol NNrd SHya SMrm SSvw WHil WRha
Marine Blues Group (Poly)	CSWP EWoo GAbr MFie
'Marven' (2)	CLyd EPot MBro NCra NGar NHol NNrd NWoo
'Mary Anne'	LSur
'Mauve Queen' (Prim)	LSur
Mauve Victorians Group	CSWP EWoo MFie
'Mauvekissen'	WHil
'McWatt's Claret' (Poly)	CSWP CVer GAbr LSur NCra
'McWatt's Cream' (Poly)	CPBP CSWP GAbr GGar LHop LSur NBro NChi NCra NHol NMen SIng
megaseifolia (6)	NHar
melanops (18)	CGle CPla ELan GCan GFle GMaP NGre NHar
'Mexico'	EWoo MFie
Midnight Group	CSWP EWoo GAbr MFie
'Miniera' (2)	CLyd CPBP EPot SBla SIng
minima (2)	CGra CLyd GTou NBro NGre NHar NWCA WAbe
– var. ***alba*** (2)	EPot GGGa NSla
– x ***glutinosa*** (2)	See ***P.*** x ***floerkeana***
– x ***hirsuta*** (2)	See ***P.*** x ***forsteri***
– x ***villosa*** (2)	See ***P.*** x ***truncata***
– x ***wulfeniana*** (2)	See ***P.*** x ***vochinensis***
'Miss Indigo' (D.Prim)	CGle CWGN EBar EBre ECtt ELan LFis MBri MCLN MOne MRav NEgg NHar NHol NRoo SIng SLod SMrm SPer WHil WPnn
'Miss Luck'	CVer
mistassinica alba (11)	MFie
§ ***mistassinica*** var. ***macropoda*** (11)	GFle NWCA
modesta (11)	CNic
modesta alba (11)	GCLN GFle
modesta var. ***faurieae*** (11)	GCLN MFie NGre
– 'Flore Pleno' (11)	CPBP
– var. ***samanimontana*** (11)	NGre
mollis (7)	CMGP
'Morton'	NGre
'Mrs Eagland'	NGre
'Mrs McGillivray' (Prim)	GAbr LSur NNrd
Munstead Strain (Poly)	LSur
x ***murettiana*** (2)	WAbe
muscarioides (17)	CGle CPla GCan GCra GFle GTou LGan MFie NGre NHar WAbe WHil
Muted Victorians Group (Poly)	EWoo MFie
nepalensis	See ***P. tanneri*** subsp. ***nepalensis***
New Pinks Group (Poly)	CSWP EWoo GAbr MFie
'Nightingale'	WAbe
nivalis (18)	CPla GGGa
nutans Delavay	See ***P. flaccida***
§ – Georgi (25)	GCra GDra NHar
obconica (19)	MBri
'Old Port' (Poly)	CSWP GBin NNrd WPat
Old Rose Victorians Group (Poly)	EWoo MFie
'Olive Wyatt' (D.Prim)	EPri MOne
'Oriental Sunrise' (4)	GPot MBri MFie
Osiered Amber Group (Prim)	CMil CSWP GAbr GPot
'Our Pat' (D.Poly)	IBlr
Pagoda Hybrids (4)	EJap ELan MBri
palinuri (2)	MFie
palmata (7)	GGGa NHar WAbe
Pantaloons Group (Poly)	NGar
'Paris '90' (Poly)	CSWP EWoo GAbr MFie NNrd
parryi (20)	CGra CNic NCra NGre NHar NWCA WHil
¶ 'Peardrop' (2)	CGra WDav
pedemontana (2)	MSte NGre NHar NHol NSla
– 'Alba' (2)	EHyt
'Perle von Bottrop' (Prim)	GAbr LSur MHig
'Peter Klein' (11)	EPot GDra GFle ITim MBal MBro NGar NHar SBar WHoo WOMN WPyg
§ ***petiolaris*** (21)	EHyt GCHN GGGa ITim MOne NCra NHar NHol WAbe
– LS&H 19856	See ***P.*** **'Redpoll'**
'Petticoat'	MOne NHar NHol WWoo
§ 'Pink Aire' (2)	EHyt MFie
'Pink Gem' (D.Prim)	NWes
¶ 'Pink Profusion' (Prim)	NGre
pinnatifida (17)	GGGa
poissonii (4)	CBot CGle CHar CPla CWGN EJap GAbr GCan GCra GFle GGar IBlr LPBA MBal NGre
– ACE 1946 (4)	MFie
– CLD 193 (4)	LSyl
Polyanthus (30)	GDra NCra
polyneura (7)	CBot CInt CNic CPla ECha GCra GFle GMaP LSyl MBal MFie MHig MNes MNrw NDea NHol NWCA SRms
– ACE 1429 (7)	SBla
praenitens	See ***P. sinensis***
¶ ***prenantha*** (4)	WAbe
'Prince Silverwings' (D.Poly)	WEas

§ ***prolifera*** (4) 🏆	CMHG CTrw ECha GCra GFle GGGa GGar LGan LPBA LSyl MFir MNrw NSti NVic SBla SPer SPla SRms SSpi SWat WAbe WHil WPer WWat
pseudosikkimensis	See ***P. sikkimensis***
§ × ***pubescens*** (2) 🏆	CInt EMan EPot GAbr GDra LFox MBro MYat NVic SMrm SRms SSmi WLRN WPer
– 'Alba' (2)	NHar WAbe
– 'Alison Gibbs' (2)	MHig
– × ***allionii*** (2)	NNrd
– 'Apple Blossom' (2)	See ***P. allionii* 'Apple Blossom'**
– 'Balfouriana' (2)	CNic LFox MBro WDav
§ – 'Bewerley White' (2)	EHyt ELan EPot MBal MBro MRPP NCra NHed NMen NNrd SBla WWin
– 'Blue Wave' (2)	MFie
§ – 'Boothman's Variety' (2)	CInt CLyd EMNN EPot ITim MBro MFie MHig MRPP MYat NCra NGar NGre NHar NHed NHol NMen NNrd NWCA SBla SSmi WCla WWin
– 'Carmen'	See ***P.* × *pubescens* 'Boothman's Variety'**
– 'Chamois' (2)	MFie
– 'Christine' (2)	CLyd CNic EMNN EPot LBee MBro MFie MHig MYat NCra NHar NHed NHol NMen NNrd SBod WDav
– 'Cream Viscosa' (2)	EMNN MFie NHed NMGW NMen NNrd
– 'Deep Mrs Wilson' (2)	EHyt MFie SWas
– 'Ellen Page' (2)	MFie
¶ – 'Elphenor' (2)	NNrd
– 'Faldonside' (2)	CInt CLTr CLyd EMNN EPot GCHN MBro MHig NCra NHed NHol NMGW NMen NNrd WWin
§ – 'Freedom' (2)	CLyd ELan EMNN EPot GTou ITim MBro MFie MHig MYat NCra NGre NHar NHed NHol NMen NNrd SBla SBod SRms SSmi WDav WWin
– 'George Harrison' (2)	MFie
– 'Greenslacks Yellow'	NGre
– 'Harlow Car' (2)	CLyd EMNN EPot ITim LFox MBro MFie MHig MYat NGre NHar NHed NMen NNrd SBla WAbe WDav
– 'Henry Hall' (2)	CLyd EWes MFie
¶ – 'Herbert Beresford' (2)	NMen
– 'Hurstwood Red Admiral' (2)	EMNN
– 'Joan Danger' (2)	CLyd EMNN MFie NHol NNrd WLRN
– 'Joan Gibbs' (2)	CLyd ELan EPot MBro MFie MHig NCra NHar NHed NMen NNrd
– 'Kath Dryden' (2)	MFie
– 'Lilac Fairy' (2)	EMNN NHed
¶ – mixed (2)	WWtk
– 'Mrs J.H. Wilson' (2)	CGra CLyd EHyt ITim MBal MBro MFie MHig NCra NGre NHed NHol NMen NNrd SBla WAbe
– 'Pat Barwick' (2)	EMNN EPot LFox MBro MFie NHed NMen WDav
– 'Peggy Fell' (2)	MDHE MFie
– 'Pink Freedom' (2)	NHed
§ – 'Pink Ice' (2)	CGra CLyd CPBP EHyt EMNN EPot MDHE NMen NNrd
– 'Roseille' (2)	EHyt
– 'Rufus' (2)	CGra CLyd EHyt ITim MBal MHig NCra NHol NNrd SBla
– 'S.E. Matthews' (2)	EHyt NNrd
– 'Sid Skelton' (2)	EMNN
¶ – 'Snowcap'	CGra WDav
– 'Sonya' (2)	MFie
– 'The General' (2)	CLyd EPot MBro MHig NCra NNrd WWin
– 'Victoria' (2)	EMNN
§ – 'Wedgwood' (2)	EMNN GCLN
– white (2)	WCru
– 'Winifred'	NHed
pulverulenta (4) 🏆	CInt CRow CTrw CWGN EAst ECha EHon ENot GDra GFle GPot GTou LGan LPBA LSyl MBal MBri MFie MNes NDea NWCA SPer SSpi WAbe WChe WGwG WPLI WPer WWat
– Bartley Hybrids (4) 🏆	CBot CGle CMil GBuc MFie SMur WChe
– 'Bartley Pink' (4)	CPla LSyl
'Purple Splendour'	LSur
'Purpurkissen' (Prim)	NHol
'Quaker's Bonnet'	See ***P. vulgaris* 'Lilacina Plena'**
¶ 'Rachel Kinnen' (2)	EHyt MFie
'Ramona' (Poly)	EWoo MFie
'Raven'	NMen
'Ravenglass Vermilion'	See ***P.* 'Inverewe'**
'Red Sunset' (4)	GDra
'Red Velvet' (D.Prim)	LHop MOne SMrm WWeb
§ 'Redpoll' (21)	NHar WAbe
reidii (28)	MBri NCra NHar
– var. ***williamsii*** (28)	CPla EBre GDra GFle GGGa GTou MBal MBri NGre NHar NSla
– var. ***williamsii alba*** (28)	GDra MBal MBri NGre NHar
'Reverie' (Poly)	EWoo MFie
'Rhubarb and Custard' (Poly)	CGle
'Romeo' (Prim)	CVer NCra
'Rose O'Day' (D.Prim)	ELan MBal MCLN MOne NHol NRoo WWoo
rosea 🏆	CBot CPla CRow EJap EPar GDra GGGa GTou LHop MBal MFie NCra NDea NFla NGre NHar NSti NVic NWes SIng SSpi WChe WEas WRus
– CC&McK 367 (11)	GCHN
– 'Delight'	See ***P. rosea* 'Micia Visser-de Geer'**
– 'Gigas' (11)	MSta
– 'Grandiflora' (11)	CGle CNic CPea CWGN EHon ELan EMNN EPar LPBA LSyl MBri MRav NHed NMen NRoo SAlw SRms WOMN WPer
* ***rosea splendens*** (11)	SChu
rotundifolia	See ***P. roxburghii***
'Rowallane Rose' (4)	CBro SSpi
§ ***roxburghii*** (25)	WCru
'Roy Cope' (D.Prim)	CHad CLTr EBar EHic GGar MBal MCLN MOne MRav NBir NEgg NNrd SIng WHil WPnn
rubra	See ***P. erythra***
rusbyi (20)	MFie NHar
Rustic Reds Group (Poly)	EJap EWoo MFie
'Sandy's Form' (21)	NHol
saxatilis (7)	GGar MFie
scandinavica (11)	GCan MFie
× ***scapeosa*** (21)	MBal NHar
§ 'Schneekissen' (Prim)	CCot CElw CHid GAbr MBri MOne NBro WHil WPbr WRus

scotica (11)	CNic GTou LFox MBal MFie MRPP NCra NSla NWCA WAbe WCla WUnd
secundiflora (26)	CBre CGle CInt CLTr CPla CWGN ELan GAbr GCra GDra GFle GGGa GTou LSyl MBal MBro MNrw NCra NMen NRoo SBla SPer SRms WAbe WHil WHoo
× ***serrata***	See ***P.*** × ***vochinensis***
serratifolia (4)	GGGa GMaP SBla
sibirica	See ***P. nutans* Georgi**
sibthorpii	See ***P. vulgaris*** subsp. ***sibthorpii***
sieboldii (7) 🏆	CBre CGle CRow CShe EGol EMNN LFox MBal MBri MNrw NCra NHar NMen NRya NWCA SIng SRms SSpi WEas WHil
sieboldii alba (7)	MBro SWas WCru
sieboldii 'Carefree' (7)	GMac NNrd
– 'Cherubim' (7)	EBre ECtt GCHN NNrd
– 'Dancing Ladies' (7)	CGle CMil CNic EJap
– 'Galaxy' (7)	WAbe
– 'Geisha Girl' (7)	EBre ECtt GCHN MRav
– 'Lilac Sunbonnet' (7)	CGle NHol NNrd
– 'Manakoora' (7)	CDec CGle EJap MFie SUsu
– 'Mikado' (7)	EBre ECtt GCHN MFie MRav NNrd
– 'Pago-Pago' (7)	CGle CInt CNic EJap MFie
– 'Seraphim' (7)	EBre
– 'Snowflake' (7)	CGle CMea EBre GCHN NHol NSla WAbe
– 'Tah-ni' (7)	CNic EJap GPot
– 'Winter Dreams' (7)	CGle CInt CNic EJap MFie
§ ***sikkimensis*** (26)	CBot CBro CGle CMea CWGN EBre EHon EMNN ENot GCHN GGGa LPBA LSyl MBal MBri MBro MNrw MSta NCra NDea NGre NHar SIng SPer WAbe WChe WHil WOMN
– ACE 1822 (26)	EPot NRya
– B&SWJ 2471 (26)	WCru
– CC&McK 1022 (26)	GTou
– crimson and gold (26)	MBro MFie
– 'Tilman Number 2' (26)	EWes GAbr GDra GFle WDav
Silver-laced Group (Poly)	CGle CRDP EPar
§ ***sinensis*** (27)	MBri
sinoplantaginea (18)	CPla GAbr
sinopurpurea	See ***P. chionantha* Sinopurpurea Group**
'Sir Bedivere' (Prim)	CElw
smithiana	See ***P. prolifera***
'Snow Carpet'	See ***P.* 'Schneekissen'**
'Snow Cushion'	See ***P.* 'Schneekissen'**
'Snow Queen'	LSur
'Snow White' (Poly)	LSur
'Snowruffles'	EHyt
sonchifolia (21)	GDra GGGa
sorachiana (11)	EHyt
sp. B&SWJ 2165	WCru
sp. BC 9331	GCra
spectabilis (2)	NHar NMen
– JCA 789.400 (2)	MFie
– JCA 789.401 (2)	MFie
Spice Shades Group (Poly)	CMil CSWP EWoo GAbr MFie
× ***steinii***	See ***P.*** × ***forsteri***
¶ 'Stradbrook Charmer' (2)	EPot WDav
¶ 'Stradbrook Dainty' (2)	EHyt WDav
'Stradbrook Gem' (2)	EHyt NGar WAbe WDav
¶ 'Stradbrook Lilac Lustre' (2)	EHyt
¶ 'Stradbrook Lucy' (2)	EHyt WDav
Striped Victorians Group	CMil CSWP EWoo GAbr MFie NChi
'Sue Jervis' (D.Prim)	CSpe CVer EBre EHic GAbr LFis MBri NEgg NHar NNrd WHer WRus
suffrutescens	WAbe
'Sunshine Susie' (D.Prim)	CGle EBar EBre ECtt ELan EPri GAbr MBri MOne MRav MYat NCat NEgg NHol SIng SMrm WHil WPnn
'Sylvia' (Prim)	LSur
tanneri (21)	NHol WAbe
§ – subsp. ***nepalensis*** (21)	ITim
– subsp. ***tsariensis*** var. ***alba*** (21)	GGGa
'Tawny Port' (Poly)	CBrd CCot CGle CLTr CMea CVer LSur NBro NCra NNrd SIng SRms
¶ ***tibetica*** (11)	GFle
'Tinney's Moonlight'	EHyt
'Tipperary Purple' (Prim)	GAbr
'Tomato Red' (Prim)	CFee CVer GAbr LBee LSur NCra
'Tony'	NHar WDav
'Torchlight' (D.Prim)	LHop
tosaensis (24)	NMen
'Tournaig Pink' (4)	GGar
¶ ***tschuktschorum*** (18)	GCLN
uralensis	See ***P. veris*** subsp. ***macrocalyx***
'Val Horncastle' (D.Prim)	CHad CSpe EBar ECtt EFol MCLN MOne MRav MYat NEgg NHar NRoo NSti SMrm SPer SPla WCla WHil WPnn
Valentine Victorians (Poly)	CSWP EWoo MFie
× ***variabilis***	See ***P.*** × ***polyantha***
veris (30) 🏆	Widely available
– subsp. ***canescens*** JCA 789.600 (30)	MFie
– hybrids (30)	WDav WGwG
– red (30)	CRDP EBee
– 'Rhandirmwyn Red'	WRha
vernalis	See ***P. vulgaris***
verticillata (12)	MFie
§ ***vialii*** (17) 🏆	Widely available
§ ***villosa*** (2)	GFle GTou NHol
– var. ***cottica***	See ***P. villosa***
Violet Victorians Group (Poly)	CSWP MFie
viscosa Allioni	See ***P. latifolia***
§ × ***vochinensis*** (2)	CFee CLyd EPot MBro NHar NHol NNrd NWCA WAbe
§ ***vulgaris*** (30)	Widely available
vulgaris alba (30)	CGle CRow ECha MHig NSla WAbe
vulgaris 'Alba Plena' (30)	CGle CHad CRow GAbr GGar IBlr NChi SRms
– Ballyrogan cream edge (30)	IBlr
– 'Double Sulphur' (30)	ELan
– green-flowered	See ***P. vulgaris* 'Viridis'**
¶ § – 'Lilacina Plena' (D.Prim)	CBot CDec CGle EBar EFol GAbr IBlr LFis MCLN NNrd NSti SIng SMrm WCla WEas WHil
§ – subsp. ***sibthorpii*** (30) 🏆	CElw CGle CShe EJud EPot GAbr GTou LFox LSur MBro MFos MRav NBro NCra NHol NWCA SBla SChu SRms SSvw WDav WHoo WPyg
– – HH&K 265 (30)	CHan

– – HH&K 337 (30) CHan
– – JCA 790.401 (30) MFie
– 'Viridis' semi-double (30) CRDP
§ – 'Viridis' (30) IBlr
¶ – white hose-in-hose (Prim) LSur
waltonii (26) CBot CPla CWGN GCra GFle MBal MNrw WCru
– hybrids (26) GGar
'Wanda' (Prim) ♀ CCot CGle CRow CShe CVer CWGN ELan GAbr GAul LSur NGre NHol NSti SBla SIng SPer SRms WHoo WTyr
'Wanda Hose in Hose' (Prim) CGle CVer EMon GAbr LSur NChi NMir SRms WHer WHil
'Wanda Jack in the Green' (Prim) CRow MBro WFar
wardii See ***P. involucrata***
warshenewskiana (11) CInt CLyd CNic CPla EWes GAbr GCHN GTou MBal MBro MRPP NCra NGar NGre NHar NMen NNrd NWCA SBod SRms WAbe WFar WPat
watsonii (17) EWes GCan GGGa GTou NHar
'Wedgwood' See ***P. × pubescens* 'Wedgwood'**
'Wharfedale Bluebell' (2) CLyd NGar NHar
'Wharfedale Butterfly' (2) NGar NHar
¶ 'Wharfedale Crusader' (2) MRPP
'Wharfedale Gem' (2) EHyt EMNN MDHE NGar NGre NHar NHol NNrd WAbe
'Wharfedale Ling' (2) CGra CPBP EPot MRPP NGar NHar NHol WAbe
'Wharfedale Superb' (2) EMNN NGar NHar NHol NNrd WAbe WHil
'Wharfedale Village' (2) CLyd MDHE NGar NHar NHol
¶ 'White Linda Pope' (2) CLyd MFie NHar
'White Wanda' (Prim) CGle CRow CVer GAbr LSur WCru
whitei (21) CBrd MBal MDun NHar
§ – 'Sherriff's Variety' (21) IBlr
'William Genders' (Poly) GAbr LSur
wilsonii (4) CPla GBuc GCra GGGa LSyl MNes MNrw SWat WHer WHoo WPyg
'Windrush' See ***P. × berninae* 'Windrush'**
¶ 'Windward Blue' SBla
'Winter White' See ***P.* 'Gigha'**
◆ 'Wisley Crimson' See ***P.* 'Wisley Red'**
wollastonii (28) GFle GGGa
wulfeniana (2) CGra GFle MFie NHol NMen WAbe
yargongensis See ***P. involucrata*** subsp. ***yargongensis***
yuparensis (11) CInt NMen
'Zenobia' NGar

PRINSEPIA (Rosaceae)

sinensis CPle MBlu

PRITCHARDIA (Arecaceae)

See Plant Deletions

PROBOSCIDEA (Pedaliaceae)

louisianica EFEx
parviflora EFEx

PROSOPIS (Mimosaceae)

chilensis See ***P. glandulosa***

PROSTANTHERA (Lamiaceae)

aspalathoides CPle ECon ECou LGre
cuneata ♀ Widely available
– 'Alpine Gold' CMHG CPle CTrC CWSG EHic LHop SEND
– 'Fastigiata' CPle SPan
incisa 'Rosea' CPle SChu WSHC
lasianthos CB&S CPle CSev ECou LGre MAll SOWG WWye
lasianthos coriacea CPle
melissifolia ECon LBlm LCns LHil
– var. ***parvifolia*** CTrw GCHN MAll NChi WAbe WSHC
nivea CPle LGre MAll
ovalifolia EBee ECou EFou LHop MAll MMil SMrm
'Poorinda Ballerina' CPle CSev CSpe ECon LGre LHop SAga
rotundifolia ♀ CAbb CB&S CGre CInt CPle CSam CSev CSpe CTri ERea ISea MAll SAga SEND SLMG SMad SOWG WBod WOld WWye
– 'Chelsea Girl' See ***P. rotundifolia rosea***
§ ***rotundifolia rosea*** CGre CPle CSpe ERea LHop MAll MLan SAga WWye
saxicola var. ***montana*** CPle LGre SBla
sieberi CChu CTrw LBlm WRTC
walteri CAbb CChu CPle CSpe ECou LBlm LGre MAll

PROTEA (Proteaceae)

cynaroides CHEx CTrC SIgm
¶ ***eximia*** CTrC
¶ ***grandiceps*** CTrC
¶ ***laurifolia*** CTrC
¶ ***subvestita*** CTrC
¶ ***venusta*** CTrC

PRUMNOPITYS (Podocarpaceae)

§ ***andina*** CGre WWat
elegans See ***P. andina***
§ ***ferruginea*** ECou
§ – 'Golden Dwarf' CLTr
§ ***taxifolia*** ECou

PRUNELLA (Lamiaceae)

§ ***grandiflora*** CArn EFer GBar MNrw MWat NGre SRms SWat WBea WCHb WHoo WOve WWhi WWye
– 'Alba' CDoC EPfP NChi NCut NOrc NTay NWoo SPla WCHb WOve WPbr WWhi
– 'Blue Loveliness' CLyd ELan EMan GAbr GDra GTou SPla WCHb
– 'Little Red Riding Hood' See ***P. grandiflora* 'Rotkäppchen'**
– 'Loveliness' ♀ CDoC CLyd EBre ECha ECtt ELan EOrc EPar LGro MBel MRav NBro NMir NNrd NVic SBod SPer SPla WTyr WWeb WWin
– 'Pagoda' EAst LIck NBrk NOak NTay SIng WCHb WElm
– 'Pink Loveliness' CInt CLyd CNic EBre ECha EOrc EPar GCHN GDra GMac GTou LGro MBal NMir SRms WByw WPer WWin WWye
¶ – purplish blue WWhi
grandiflora rosea EPfP LBuc WByw WWhi
§ ***grandiflora*** 'Rotkäppchen' EBre ECtt GCHN SPer WPbr

– 'White Loveliness'	CLyd EBre ECha EOrc EPar GCHN GDra GGar GMac NBrk NCat NMir SPer SPla WByw WEas WPer WRus WTyr WWin WWye
hyssopifolia	WHil
incisa	See ***P. vulgaris***
* 'Inshriach Ruby'	NBir SPla WCHb
laciniata	CLyd LFis WCHb WHil WPbr
¶ – white form	GBin
§ ***vulgaris***	CAgr CArn CKin ECWi EJud ELan EWFC GAbr GBar GPoy MChe MHew MSal NLan NMir NSti SIde WCHb WCla WHer WOak WWye
vulgaris alba	WAlt WHer
x ***webbiana***	See ***P. grandiflora***

PRUNUS † (Rosaceae)

'Accolade' ♀	CAbP CDoC CLnd COtt CSam CTho ECtt ENot IOrc LPan MAsh MBri NWea SEND SHBN SIgm SPer SSta WDin WJas WStI
§ 'Amanogawa' ♀	CB&S CLnd CSam EBre ELan ENot GRei LBuc LHyr LNet LPan MAsh MBal MBar MBri MGos NWea SHBN SIgm SPer WJas
x ***amygdalopersica*** 'Pollardii'	CBlo ENot WJas
– 'Spring Glow'	CDoC MAsh MBri WJas
amygdalus	See ***P. dulcis***
armeniaca 'Alfred' (F)	EMui ERea GTwe MBri SDea SIgm
– 'Bredase' (F)	SDea
– 'De Nancy'	See ***P. armeniaca* 'Gros Pêche'**
– 'Early Moor Park' (F)	CDoC ERea EWar GBon GRei GTwe SDea SFam SIgm WWeb
– 'Farmingdale' (F)	ERea SDea SKee
– 'Goldcot' (F)	ERea SDea
§ – 'Gros Pêche' (F)	CMac
– 'Hongaarse' (F)	SDea
– 'Moor Park' (F)	CEnd EMui ERea GTwe MGos NDal NRog SDea SKee WStI
– 'New Large Early' (F)	ERea GTwe SDea SEND SIgm SKee
– 'Royal' (F)	CMac
– 'Tross Orange' (F)	SDea
'Asano'	See ***P.* 'Geraldinae'**
avium	CB&S CKin CLnd CPer ENot GRei LBuc LHyr LPan MBar MBri MGos MRav NBee NRoo NWea SFam SHBN SKee SPer WDin WMou WOrn
– 'Amber Heart' (F)	SDea SKee
– 'August Heart' (F)	SKee
– 'Bigarreau Gaucher' (F)	SDea SKee
§ – 'Bigarreau Napoléon' (F)	GTwe MGos SDea SKee
– 'Birchenhayes' (F)	CTho
– 'Black Eagle' (F)	CTho SKee
– 'Black Elton' (F)	SKee
– 'Black Glory' (F)	SKee
– 'Black Tartarian' (F)	SKee
– 'Bottlers' (F)	CTho
– 'Bradbourne Black' (F)	SKee
– 'Bullion' (F)	CTho
– 'Burcombe' (F)	CTho
– 'Cherokee'	See ***P. avium* 'Lapins'**
– 'Circassian Black' (F)	SKee
– 'Colney' (F)	GTwe WJas

– 'Dun' (F)	CTho
– 'Early Rivers' (F)	EWar GTwe SDea SKee
– 'Elton Heart' (F)	CTho SKee
¶ – 'Fastigiata'	CTho
– 'Florence' (F)	SKee
– 'Governor Wood' (F)	GTwe SKee
– 'Grandiflora'	See ***P. avium* 'Plena'**
– 'Greenstem Black' (F)	CTho
¶ – 'Hertford' (F)	SKee
– 'Inga' (F)	SKee
– 'Ironsides' (F)	SKee
– 'Kassins Frühe Herz' (F)	SKee
– 'Kentish Red' (F)	CTho
§ – 'Lapins' (F)	CSam EMui GTwe SDea SFam SKee WJas
– 'May Duke'	See ***P.* x *gondouinii* 'May Duke'**
– 'Merchant' (F)	CDoC GTwe SKee
– 'Mermat' (F)	GTwe
– 'Merpet' (F)	GTwe
– 'Merton Bigarreau' (F)	SDea
– 'Merton Crane' (F)	SKee
– 'Merton Favourite' (F)	SKee
– 'Merton Glory' (F)	CDoC EWar GChr GTwe MGos SDea SKee
– 'Merton Heart' (F)	SDea SKee
– 'Merton Late' (F)	SKee
– 'Merton Marvel' (F)	SKee
– 'Merton Premier' (F)	SKee
– 'Merton Reward' (F)	SKee
– 'Napoléon'	See ***P. avium* 'Bigarreau Napoléon'**
¶ – 'Newstar' (F)	EMui
– 'Noble' (F)	SKee
– 'Noir de Guben' (F)	GChr GTwe SKee
– 'Nutberry Black' (F)	SKee
– 'Old Black Heart' (F)	SKee
§ – 'Plena' ♀	CB&S CLnd CSam CTho ELan ENot EPfP IOrc LBuc LHyr LPan MBal MGos NBee NWea SFam SPer WDin WJas WOrn
– 'Ronald's Heart' (F)	SKee
– 'Roundel' (F)	SDea SKee
– 'Sasha' (F)	GTwe
– 'Small Black' (F)	CTho
– 'Smoky Dun' (F)	SKee
– 'Stark Hardy Giant' (F)	SKee
– 'Starkrimson' (F)	GTwe
– 'Stella' (F) ♀	CMac CSam EMui ERea EWar GBon GChr GRei GTwe LBuc MBri MGos NBee NDal NRog SDea SFam SIgm SKee SPer WJas WWeb
– 'Stella Compact' (F)	COtt GTwe MBri SKee
– 'Sunburst' (F)	EMui GTwe LBuc MBri NDal SDea SFam SKee WJas WWeb
– 'Turkish Black' (F)	SKee
– 'Upright'	CTho
– 'Van' (F)	CDoC GTwe SKee
– 'Vega' (F)	GTwe
– 'Waterloo' (F)	CTho SKee
– 'White Heart' (F)	CTho SKee
¶ 'Benden'	CTho
* 'Beni-no-dora'	SMur
* 'Beni-yutaka'	MBri
* 'Birch Bark'	GRei
x ***blireana*** ♀	CDoC CLnd EBee MAsh MBri MRav MWat NBee SPer SSta
'Blushing Bride'	See ***P.* 'Shôgetsu'**
bucharica JJH 98807	NWCA
capuli	See ***P. salicifolia***
cerasifera	CAgr GAri LBuc NWea SKee WDin WMou

– 'Cherry Plum' (F)	SKee
– 'Crimson Dwarf'	CBlo CDoC
– 'Green Glow'	CBlo
– 'Hessei' (v)	CBlo MBri SPer WRTC
– 'Kentish Red' (F)	SKee
§ – Myrobalan Group (F)	CBlo CKin SDea SKee
N – 'Nigra' 🏆	CDoC CLnd ELan IOrc LBuc LNet LPan MAsh MBri MGos NBee SDea SHBN SPer SRms WDin WOrn WStI
– 'Pendula'	WMou
§ – 'Pissardii'	CTho CTri EBre GRei MAsh MBar NNor NWea SFam SIgm SPer WJas
– 'Rosea'	MBri SLPl
– 'Spring Glow'	CEnd
cerasus 'Montmorency' (F)	SDea SKee
– 'Morello' (F) 🏆	CMac CSam EBre EMui EWar GBon GChr GRei GTwe LBuc MBri MGos NBee NDal NRog SDea SFam SIgm SKee SPer WJas WWeb
– 'Nabella' (F)	EWar
– 'Rhexii' (d)	CBlo MAsh MGos SPer
– 'Wye Morello' (F)	SKee
'Cheal's Weeping'	See ***P.* 'Kiku-shidare-zakura'**
§ 'Chôshû-hizakura' 🏆	CBlo CLnd GRei IOrc LNet SDea SPer
§ × ***cistena*** 🏆	CB&S CBot CShe EBre EFol ELan ENot IOrc MBar MBri MGos MWat NBee NRoo SEas SHBN SPer SPla WDin WPat WRTC WStI
– 'Crimson Dwarf'	See ***P.* × *cistena***
conradinae	See ***P. hirtipes***
¶ ***davidiana***	CTho
domestica 'Angelina Burdett' (D)	GTwe NRog SKee
– 'Anna Späth' (C/D)	SKee
– 'Ariel' (C/D)	SDea SKee
– 'Autumn Compote' (C)	SKee
– 'Avalon' (F)	GTwe SIgm SKee
– 'Belgian Purple' (C)	SKee
– 'Belle de Louvain' (C)	CTho ERea GTwe NRog SDea SKee
– 'Birchenhayes' (F)	CEnd
– 'Blue Imperatrice' (C/D)	SKee
– 'Blue Tit' (C/D)	EMui GTwe SKee
– 'Bonne de Bry' (D)	SKee
– 'Brandy Gage' (C/D)	SKee
– 'Bryanston Gage' (D)	CTho SFam SKee
– 'Burbank' (C/D)	SDea
– 'Burcombe'	CEnd
– 'Bush' (C)	SKee
– 'Cambridge Gage' (D)	CDoC CSam CTho EBre EMui ERea GBon GTwe LBuc MBri MGos MWat NDal NRog SDea SFam SIgm SKee SPer WJas WStI WWeb
– 'Chrislin' (F)	CTho
– 'Coe's Golden Drop' (D)	CTho CTri EMui ERea GTwe MBri MGos SCoo SDea SFam SIgm SKee
– 'Count Althann's Gage' (D)	GTwe NRog SDea SFam SIgm SKee
– 'Cox's Emperor' (C)	SKee
– 'Crimson Drop' (D)	SKee
– 'Cropper'	See ***P. domestica* 'Laxton's Cropper'**
– 'Curlew' (C)	SDea

– 'Czar' (C) 🏆	CDoC CSam CTri EBre EMui EWar GChr GTwe IOrc LBuc MGos NRog SDea SFam SIgm SKee SPer WWeb
– 'Delicious'	See ***P. domestica* 'Laxton's Delicious'**
– 'Denniston's Superb'	See ***P. domestica* 'Imperial Gage'**
– 'Diamond' (C)	SKee
– 'Dittisham Black' (C)	CTho
– 'Dittisham Ploughman' (C)	CSam CTho SKee
– 'Dunster Plum' (F)	CTho
– 'Early Laxton' (C/D) 🏆	GTwe SDea SFam SKee
– 'Early Orleans'	See ***P. domestica* 'Monsieur Hâtif'**
– 'Early Prolific'	See ***P. domestica* 'Rivers's Early Prolific'**
– 'Early Rivers'	See ***P. domestica* 'Rivers's Early Prolific'**
– 'Early Transparent Gage' (C/D)	CTho CTri EMui ERea GTwe LBuc SDea SFam SIgm
– 'Edwards' (C/D)	EWar GTwe LBuc NBee NDal SDea SFam SIgm SKee
– 'Excalibur' (F)	GTwe NDal SIgm
– 'Fice' (F)	CEnd CTho
– 'Giant Prune' (C)	GTwe NRog SKee
– 'Godshill Blue' (C)	SDea
– 'Golden Transparent' (D)	CTho ERea GTwe NRog SFam
– 'Goldfinch' (D)	GTwe NRog SKee
§ – Green Gage Group (C/D)	EMui GTwe NRog SDea SFam SKee SPer
– – 'Old Green Gage' (D/C)	ERea SIgm WJas
– 'Grey Plum' (F)	CTho
– 'Grove's Late Victoria' (C/D)	SKee
– 'Guthrie's Late Green' (D)	SKee
– 'Herman' (C/D)	CSam GTwe SIgm
– 'Heron' (F)	GTwe
– 'Imperial Epineuse' (D)	SKee
§ – 'Imperial Gage' (C/D) 🏆	CTho GRei GTwe LBuc SDea SFam SIgm SKee
– subsp. ***insititia***	See ***P. insititia* (F)**
– 'Jan James' (F)	CEnd
– 'Jefferson' (D)	EMui ERea GTwe NRog SDea SFam SIgm SKee
– 'Kea' (C)	CTho SKee
– 'Kirke's' (D)	CTho CWSG GTwe MBri SDea SFam SIgm SKee
– 'Landkey Yellow' (F)	CTho
– 'Late Muscatelle' (D)	SKee
– 'Laxton's Bountiful'	See ***P. domestica* 'Bountiful'**
§ – 'Laxton's Cropper' (C)	GTwe NRog SKee
§ – 'Laxton's Delicious' (D)	GTwe
– 'Laxton's Delight' (D)	GTwe
– 'Laxton's Gage' (D)	SDea SKee
¶ – 'Manaccan' (C)	CTho
– 'Marjorie's Seedling' (C) 🏆	CDoC CTho EBre EMui ERea GBon GTwe LBuc MGos MWat SDea SEND SFam SIgm SKee WJas
– 'McLaughlin' (D)	SKee
– 'Merton Gem' (C/D)	GTwe SFam SKee
– 'Monarch' (C)	GTwe SKee
– 'Ontario' (C/D)	GTwe SKee
– 'Opal' (D)	CDoC EMui EWar GTwe IOrc MGos MWat SDea SEND SFam SIgm SKee WWeb
– 'Orleans' (C)	SKee

– 'Oullins Gage' (C/D) 🏆	CMac EMui ERea EWar GBon GTwe LBuc MBri MWat NRog SDea SFam SIgm SKee SPer WJas WWeb
– 'Pershore' (C) 🏆	CTho ERea
– 'Pond's Seedling' (C)	SDea SKee
– 'President' (C/D)	GTwe SDea
– 'Prince Englebert' (C)	SKee
– 'Priory Plum' (D)	SDea
– 'Purple Pershore' (C)	CTri CWSG GTwe NRog SDea SFam SKee
– 'Quetsche d'Alsace'	See ***P. domestica* German Prune Group**
– 'Reeves' (C)	GTwe SFam SIgm SKee
– 'Reine Claude de Bavais' (D)	CTho GTwe NRog SFam SKee
– 'Reine Claude Dorée'	See ***P. domestica* Green Gage Group**
– 'Reine Claude Violette' (D)	CTho SKee
§ – 'Rivers's Early Prolific' (C)	CTho ERea GTwe MWat NRog SCoo SDea SIgm SKee
– 'Royale de Vilvoorde' (D)	SKee
– 'Sanctus Hubertus' (D) 🏆	EWar GTwe SDea SFam SIgm SKee
– 'Severn Cross' (D)	GTwe SKee
– 'Stint' (C/D)	SKee
– 'Swan' (C)	GTwe SIgm
– 'Transparent Gage' (D)	SKee
– 'Upright' (F)	CEnd
– 'Utility' (D)	SKee
– 'Victoria' (C/D) 🏆	CMac CSam CTho EBre EMui ERea EWar GBon GChr GRei GTwe IOrc LBuc MBri MGos MWat NBee NDal NRog SDea SFam SIgm SKee SPer WJas WWeb
– 'Warwickshire Drooper' (C)	CSam CTho ERea EWar GBon GTwe SDea SFam SKee SPer
– 'Washington' (D)	CTho SKee
– 'White Magnum Bonum' (C)	CTho SDea
– 'Willingham Gage' (F)	GTwe
– 'Wyedale' (C)	GTwe
– 'Yellow Egg' (C)	GTwe SDea SFam
– 'Yellow Pershore' (C)	NRog SFam SKee
§ ***dulcis***	CLnd CTri LHyr MAsh MWat NWea SDea SFam SKee WDin
– 'Balatoni' (F)	MBri
– 'Macrocarpa' (F)	ESim
– 'Roseoplena'	CBlo MBri
fruticosa 'Globosa'	CBlo CWSG
'Fugenzô'	CBlo
§ 'Geraldinae'	CLnd WPyg
glandulosa 'Alba Plena' 🏆	CB&S CBot CPMA CPle ECtt ELan ESis GOrc MBal MBar MGos MPla MWat NBee NHol SHBN SPan SPer SPla SReu SRms SSpi SSta WDin WHCG WRTC WSHC
– 'Rosea Plena'	See ***P. glandulosa* 'Sinensis'**
§ – 'Sinensis' (d) 🏆	CBot CPMA CPle ELan ESis GOrc MBal MGos MHlr MPla SHBN SPan SPer SPla SReu SRms SSpi SSta WHCG WRTC WSHC
§ × ***gondouinii*** 'May Duke' (F)	SKee
¶ 'Gyoikô'	CTho
'Hally Jolivette'	CEnd COtt ELan MAsh MBri SCoo
'Hillieri'	MBar MGos
'Hillieri Spire'	See ***P.* 'Spire'**
§ ***hirtipes***	CTho
'Hisakura'	See ***P.* 'Chôshû-hizakura'**
Hollywood	See ***P.* 'Trailblazer'**
'Ichiyo'	See ***P.* 'Chôshû-hizakura'**
incisa	GAri IOrc SLPl SPer SSpi
– 'Beniomi'	GAri MRav
– 'February Pink'	CPMA LBuc MPla MRav NPro
– 'Fujima'	NHol SMur WPat WPyg WRTC WWat
– 'Kojo-no-mai'	CEnd CHar CMil EBre ECtt EPla ESis GAri GBin MAsh MBlu MBri NPro SPan WPat WWeb
– 'Mikinori'	MBri
– 'Oshidori'	MGos MRav NHol WPat WPyg WRTC
* – 'Otome'	MBri
– 'Praecox' 🏆	LRHS MBri
– 'The Bride'	CEnd MBri
insititia 'Blue Violet Damson' (F)	SKee
§ – 'Bradley's King Damson' (F)	SKee
¶ – 'Dittisham Damson' (C)	CTho
– 'Farleigh Damson' (C)	GTwe NBee SDea SFam SKee WJas
– 'Godshill Damson' (C)	SDea
– 'Golden Bullace'	See ***P. insititia* 'White Bullace'**
– 'King of Damsons'	See ***P. insititia* 'Bradley's King Damson' (F)**
– 'Langley Bullace' (C)	CTho ERea SKee
– 'Merryweather Damson' (C)	CDoC CMac CTho EBre EMui ERea GBon GChr GRei GTwe LBuc MBri NBee NDal NRog SDea SFam SKee SPer WJas WStI WWeb
– 'Mirabelle de Nancy' (C)	CTho GTwe SDea SKee
– 'Mirabelle de Nancy (Red)' (C)	SDea
– 'Mirabelle Petite'	See ***P. insititia* 'Mirabelle de Metz'**
§ – 'Prune Damson' (C)	CSam CTho EMui ERea EWar GBon GTwe LBuc MBri MGos MWat NRog SDea SFam SIgm SKee WJas
– 'Shepherd's Bullace' (C)	CTho SKee
– 'Shropshire Damson'	See ***P. insititia* 'Prune Damson'**
– 'Small Bullace' (F)	SKee
§ – 'White Bullace' (F)	SKee
– 'Yellow Apricot' (F)	SKee
§ ***jamasakura***	CTho GAri
'Jô-nioi'	CEnd CLnd CTho
§ 'Kanzan' 🏆	CB&S CLnd EBre ELan GRei LBuc LHyr LPan MAsh MBal MBar MBri MGos NWea SDea SHBN SPer SSta WFar WJas
§ 'Kiku-shidare-zakura' 🏆	CB&S CLnd EBre ELan GRei LBuc LHyr LNet MBal MBar MBri MGos MRav NBee NWea SFam SHBN SIgm SPer WDin WJas WStI
Korean Hill Cherry	See ***P.* × *verecunda***
kurilensis	See ***P. nipponica* var. *kurilensis***
'Kursar' 🏆	COtt EBee EPfP GRei IOrc LNet MAsh MBri SFam WHut
laurocerasus 🏆	CB&S CChe CKin ELan GRei LHyr LNet LPan MRav MWat NNor NWea SPer SReu WMou WStI

– 'Aureovariegata'	See ***P. laurocerasus* 'Taff's Golden Gleam'**
– 'Camelliifolia'	CChu CTri EPla ISea MBlu WHCG WPyg
N– 'Castlewellan' (v)	CBot CChu CHan CLTr CPle CTrw EFol ELan EPla IOrc ISea MBar MGos NHol SEND SPer SPla SSta WPat
– 'Cherry Brandy'	ENot SPer WLRN
– 'Dart's Low Green'	ENot
– 'Golden Splash'	EFol
♦– Green Carpet	See ***P. laurocerasus* 'Grünerteppich'**
– 'Green Marble' (v)	CPMA CTri MUlv WSHC
§ – 'Latifolia'	CHEx EPla SArc SLPl SMad
– 'Magnoliifolia'	See ***P. laurocerasus* 'Latifolia'**
– 'Marbled White'	See ***P. laurocerasus* 'Castlewellan'**
– 'Mischeana'	ENot MBri SLPl
– 'Mount Vernon'	MBar MBri MGos NBee WDin
– 'Otto Luyken' 🏆	CB&S CMHG EBre ELan ENot GRei ISea LBuc MBal MBar MBri MGos MWat NBee NBir NFla NHol NNor NWea SHBN SPer SPla WDin WFar WGwG WWin
– 'Reynvaanii'	EPla MBri MGos WBcn
– 'Rotundifolia'	CDoC CTri EBar ELan ENot LBuc MBar MBri MGos NFla SRms WDin
– 'Rudolf Billeter'	EPla
– 'Schipkaensis'	GAul NNor SLPl SPer WCot
§ – 'Taff's Golden Gleam' (v)	CPMA MGos SMad
– 'Van Nes'	EMil IOrc MUlv
N– 'Variegata'	EHic MGos
– 'Zabeliana'	CDoC CLan CMHG ENot MBar SHBN SPer SRms WDin WPyg WRHF WWin
lusitanica 🏆	CB&S CChe CHan CKin CLan CMHG EBre ELan ENot GAul GRei ISea LBuc LNet MBal MBar MBri MGos MHlr NFla NNor NWea SLPl SPer SSta WDin WHCG WRTC WWat
– subsp. ***azorica*** 🏆	EPfP EPla SPer WWat
– 'Myrtifolia'	EBee EPla MRav MUlv SMad WWat
– 'Variegata'	CB&S CBot CMHG EBre EFol EHoe ELan ENot EPla IOrc ISea MBal MBri MGos MHlr MWat SDix SHBN SPer SSta WDin WSHC WWat
maackii	CTho EPfP LPan SEND SSpi WWat
– 'Amber Beauty'	CPMA MAsh MBri MRav WPyg
mahaleb	CTho
* 'Mahogany Lustre'	MBlu
'Mount Fuji'	See ***P.* 'Shirotae'**
mume	WNor
– 'Alboplena'	CChe
§ – 'Beni-chidori'	CB&S CBlo CEnd CPMA LBuc MBlu MBri SIgm SPan SSpi SSta
– 'Beni-shidori'	See ***P. mume* 'Beni-chidori'**
– 'Ken Kyo'	SSta
– 'Kyo Koh'	SSta
§ – 'Omoi-no-mama' (d)	CEnd CPMA LRHS MAsh MBri SPan
– 'Omoi-no-wac'	See ***P. mume* 'Omoi-no-mama'**
– 'Pendula'	CLnd MBri

myrobalana	See ***P. cerasifera* Myrobalan Group**
§ ***nipponica*** var. ***kurilensis***	CB&S MAsh
– – 'Ruby'	CEnd COtt LRHS MGos SMur
'Okame' 🏆	CLnd CSam CTho EBee EBre MAsh MBri MGos NBee NWea SPer
§ 'Okumiyako'	CB&S CBlo CEnd SFam
'Opal'	LBuc
padus	CKin CLnd CPer IOrc LBuc LHyr LNet MGos NBee NRoo NWea SSpi WDin WMou
– 'Albertii'	CTho LPan SLPl WJas
– 'Colorata' 🏆	CDoC CEnd CMHG CSam CTho ELan IOrc LBuc LNet LPan NBee SHBN SPer SSpi WDin WJas
– 'Dropmore'	SPer
– 'Grandiflora'	See ***P. padus* 'Watereri'**
¶ – 'Plena' (d)	CTho
– 'Purple Queen'	CBlo CEnd CTho ENot MGos
§ – 'Watereri' 🏆	CB&S CDoC CLnd CTho ELan ENot IOrc LPan SHBN SPer SSta WDin WJas
'Pandora' 🏆	CDoC CLnd EBee ENot LHyr LPan MAsh MBal MWat NBee NWea SEND SHBN SPer
§ ***pendula*** var. ***ascendens*** 'Rosea'	CBlo CLnd
§ – 'Pendula Rosea' 🏆	CB&S CDoC ENot LPan MAsh MBar SPer WJas
§ – 'Pendula Rubra' 🏆	CDoC COtt CTri ENot LNet MAsh MBri MGos SFam SHBN SPer
persica 'Amsden June' (F)	ERea GTwe SDea SFam
– 'Bellegarde' (F)	ERea GTwe SDea SFam SKee
– 'Bonanza' (F)	EMui ERea
– 'Doctor Hogg' (F)	SDea
– 'Duke of York' (F)	ERea EWar GTwe SDea SFam SKee WWeb
– 'Dymond' (F)	ERea GTwe
– 'Early Rivers' (F)	CMac EMui ERea GTwe NRog SDea SFam
– 'Flat China'	ERea
– 'Francis' (F)	SKee
– 'Garden Anny' (F)	ERea
– 'Garden Lady' (F)	ERea GTwe WWeb
– 'Garden Silver'	CLon
– 'Hale's Early' (F)	ERea GTwe SDea SEND SFam SKee SPer
– 'Kestrel' (F)	GTwe
– 'Klara Mayer' (d/F)	EBee NFla WJas
– 'Melred'	MGos
– var. ***nectarina*** Crimson Gold (F)	SDea
– – 'Early Gem' (F)	ERea SDea
– – 'Elruge' (F)	ERea GTwe SEND SFam
– – 'Fantasia' (F)	ERea SDea
– – 'Fire Gold' (F)	SDea
– – 'Humboldt' (F)	ERea GTwe
– – 'John Rivers' (F)	ERea GTwe SFam
– – 'Lord Napier' (F)	CDoC CWSG EMui ERea LBuc MGos SDea SEND SFam SIgm SKee SPer WStI WWeb
– – 'Nectared' (F)	GTwe
– – 'Nectarella' (F)	ERea GTwe
– – 'Pineapple' (F)	CDoC CTri ERea GTwe SDea SFam SIgm WWeb
– – 'Red Haven' (F)	CDoC GTwe SIgm SKee
– – 'Rivers Prolific' (F)	SDea
– – 'Ruby Gold' (F)	SDea

Name	Suppliers
– 'Peregrine' (F)	CMac CTri CWSG EMui ERea EWar GBon GRei GTwe LBuc MBri MGos NBee NDal NRog SDea SFam SIgm SKee SPer WJas WWeb
– 'Reliance' (F)	SDea
– 'Robin Redbreast' (F)	SDea
– 'Rochester' (F)	CWSG EMui ERea EWar GBon GTwe MBri SDea SEND SFam SIgm WStI
– 'Royal George' (F)	GTwe NRog SFam
– 'Rubira' (F)	EPla
¶ – 'Saturne' (F)	EMui
– 'Springtime' (F)	ERea SDea
'Pink Perfection' 🏆	CB&S CLnd EBee EBre LBuc LHyr LPan MAsh MBri NBee SFam SHBN SPer SSta WHut WOrn
'Pink Shell' 🏆	CLnd CTho MAsh MBri SFam WHut WStI
pissardii	See ***P. cerasifera* 'Pissardii'**
'Pissardii Nigra'	See ***P. cerasifera* 'Nigra'**
* *pissardii* 'Princess'	CBlo MAsh
prostrata	NHol WPat WWat
– 'Anita Kistler'	ECho
– var. *discolor*	WNor
– 'Pygmaea'	EHyt
pumila	SEas
– var. *depressa*	CPMA CPle GAri MBar MBlu MPla MRav NPro SPla
'Red Cascade'	SDea
rufa	CTho
– FK 40	EBee
sargentii 🏆	CDoC CLnd CSam CTho ELan ENot IHos IOrc LBuc LHyr LPan MAsh MBri MGos NWea SFam SHBN SPer SSta STre WDin WMou
– Rancho™	CLnd ENot SHhN SLPl SPer SSta WOrn
× *schmittii*	CLnd CTho SPer WJas
'Sekiyama'	See ***P.* 'Kanzan'**
serotina	NWea
§ *serrula* 🏆	CBar CDoC CEnd CLnd CTho ELan ENot IOrc LPan MBal MBar MBlu MBri MGos NBee NBir NWea SChu SHBN SPer SSta WDin WMou WNor WWat
– var. *tibetica*	See ***P. serrula***
serrulata 'Erecta'	See ***P.* 'Amanogawa'**
– 'Grandiflora'	See ***P.* 'Ukon'**
¶ – var. *hupehensis*	SLPl
– 'Longipes'	See ***P.* 'Okumiyako'**
– 'Miyak'	See ***P.* 'Okumiyako'**
N – var. *pubescens*	See ***P.* × *verecunda***
– 'Rosea'	See ***P.* 'Kiku-shidare-zakura'**
– var. *spontanea*	See ***P. jamasakura***
'Shidare-zakura'	See ***P.* 'Kiku-shidare-zakura'**
'Shimizu-zakura'	See ***P.* 'Okumiyako'**
'Shirofugen' 🏆	CB&S CDoC CLnd EBee IOrc LBuc LPan MAsh MBri MWat SDea SFam SPer SSta WDin WOrn
§ 'Shirotae' 🏆	CDoC CLnd CSam CTho EBee ELan ENot IOrc LBuc LHyr MAsh MBal MGos MRav NBee NWea SPer SSta
§ 'Shôgetsu' 🏆	CLnd CTho EBee ELan IOrc MBal MBri SFam SHBN SPer
'Shosar'	CLnd EBee MBri SPer
'Snow Goose'	LPan MBri
spinosa	CDoC CKin CPer CSam CTri LBuc LHol MBri MHlr NBee NWea SPer STre WDin WHer WMou WNor
– 'Purpurea'	MBlu WHCG WMou WPat
§ 'Spire' 🏆	CDoC CLnd CTho EBee ENot GRei IOrc LBuc LHyr LPan SPer WHut WJas
× *subhirtella*	WNor
– var. *ascendens*	See ***P. pendula* var. *ascendens***
– 'Autumnalis' 🏆	CB&S CEnd CLnd CTho EBre ELan ENot IHos LPan MAsh MBal MBar MBri MGos NWea SDea SFam SHBN SIgm SPer SSpi SSta WDin WWat
– 'Autumnalis Rosea' 🏆	CB&S CEnd CPMA CSam CTho ENot GRei LBuc LNet LPan MAsh MBar MBri MGos NBee NWea SChu SHBN SIgm SPer WDin WHCG WHen WWat
– 'Fukubana' 🏆	CBlo CLnd CTho ELan LPan MAsh MBri SEND
– 'Pendula' (hort.)	See ***P. pendula* 'Pendula Rosea'**
– 'Pendula Rubra'	See ***P. pendula* 'Pendula Rubra'**
N – 'Rosea'	CLnd
– 'Stellata'	See ***P. pendula* 'Stellata'**
'Taihaku' 🏆	CB&S CDoC CEnd CLnd CSam CTho CTri EBre ELan ENot IOrc LBuc LNet LPan MAsh MBri MGos NBee NWea SFam SHBN SPer WDin WJas WOrn WStI
'Takasago'	See ***P.* × *sieboldii* 'Caespitosa'**
* *takesimensis*	CMCN
'Taoyame'	CLnd WPyg
tenella	CB&S CEnd EBee ECtt ELan NBee WCot WHCG WWat
– 'Fire Hill' 🏆	CDoC CEnd CPMA CShe ELan LNet MBar MGos MPla NFla SHBN SPer SSpi SWas WCot WJas WOrn WPat WPyg
tibetica	See ***P. serrula***
tomentosa	EPla
§ 'Trailblazer' (C/D)	CEnd CLnd CTho IOrc LPan MGos NWea SKee SSta
triloba	CB&S CLnd ECtt LBuc LPan MBar MPla NBee NFla NWea SHBN SIgm WDin
– 'Multiplex' 🏆	EBre ENot MGos MRav SPer SRms WJas
– Rosemund	MBri
§ 'Ukon' 🏆	CB&S CDoC CLnd CTho CTri ENot IOrc LBuc LNet MBal MBar MBri NBee NWea SChu SFam SPer SSta WDin WPyg WStI
'Umineko'	CDoC CLnd EBee ENot IOrc MGos SPer
§ × *verecunda*	CDoC CLnd EBee NWea WJas
– 'Autumn Glory'	CTho SLPl SPer
virginiana 'Schubert'	CDoC CLnd CTho EBee ELan ENot EPla IOrc LPan SSta WJas
'Wood's Variety'	See ***P. cerasifera* 'Woodii'**
§ × *yedoensis* 🏆	CLnd CSam CTho EBee ENot NWea SFam SPer WDin WJas WOrn WWat
– 'Ivensii'	CB&S CDoC MAsh MBri SFam SHBN SPer WStI
– 'Pendula'	See ***P.* × *yedoensis* 'Shidare-yoshino'**

- 'Perpendens' See *P.* × *yedoensis* **'Shidare-yoshino'**
§ - 'Shidare-yoshino' CDoC CEnd CLnd EBee LNet MBar MBri MRav MWat NWea SPer WOrn WPyg WWat
- 'Tsubame' MBri
'Yoshino' See *P.* × *yedoensis*
'Yoshino Pendula' See *P.* × *yedoensis* **'Shidare-yoshino'**

PSEUDERANTHEMUM (Acanthaceae)
¶ *reticulatum* 'Eldorado' LChe

PSEUDOCYDONIA (Rosaceae)
§ *sinensis* LNet

PSEUDOFUMARIA (Papaveraceae)
♦ *alba* See *Corydalis ochroleuca*
♦ *lutea* See *Corydalis lutea*

PSEUDOFUMARIA See CORYDALIS

PSEUDOLARIX (Pinaceae)
§ *amabilis* ♀ CAbP CDoC CFil CGre CMCN EHul ISea LCon LNet MBal MBar MBlu MBri SMad STre WCoo WNor WWat
kaempferi See *P. amabilis*

PSEUDOMERTENSIA (Boraginaceae)
See Plant Deletions

PSEUDOMUSCARI See MUSCARI

PSEUDOPANAX † (Araliaceae)
(Adiantifolius Group) 'Adiantifolius' CB&S CHEx GQui
- 'Cyril Watson' ♀ CB&S CTrC
arboreus CAbb CHEx SMad
chathamicus CHEx MAll SArc SMad
crassifolius CAbb CBot CHEx ECou SArc SMad
davidii SBla
delavayi SBla
discolor ECou
ferox CAbb CHEx ERea SArc SMad
laetus CAbb CHEx
lessonii CB&S CHEx ECou
- 'Gold Splash' (v) ♀ CB&S
- hybrids CHEx
* - 'Purpureus' ♀ EOas
¶ 'Linearifolius' CTrC
'Sabre' CTrC SMad
¶ 'Trident' CTrC

PSEUDOPHEGOPTERIS (Thelypteridaceae)
levingei CCuc EMon

PSEUDOPHOENIX (Arecaceae)
* *nativo* MBri

PSEUDOSASA (Poaceae - Bambusoideae)
§ *amabilis* SBam SDry
- hort. See *Arundinaria tecta*
§ *japonica* ♀ CB&S CHEx EBee EBre EFul EJap EOas EPfP EPla ESiP MBal SBam SDry SMad SPer WDin WJun
§ - 'Akebonosuji' (v) EFul EPla SBam SDry
- 'Tsutsumiana' EPla SBam SDry WJun
- 'Variegata' See *P. japonica* **'Akebonosuji'**
owatarii SDry
pleioblastoides EPla SBam SDry
usawai WJun

PSEUDOTSUGA (Pinaceae)
§ *menziesii* ♀ CB&S CDoC CPer IOrc LBuc LCon MBar NRoo NWea WMou
- 'Bhiela Lhota' CKen
- 'Blue Wonder' CKen MAsh
- 'Densa' CKen
- 'Fastigiata' CKen
- 'Fletcheri' CBlo CKen MBar SLim
- var. *glauca* CBlo CMCN LCon MBar STre
- 'Glauca Pendula' ♀ CDoC LCon MBar MGos
I - 'Gotelli's Pendula' CKen
- 'Graceful Grace' CKen
- 'Julie' CKen
- 'Little Jamie' CKen
- 'Little Jon' NHol
- 'Lohbrunner' CKen
- 'McKenzie' CKen
- 'Nana' CKen
- 'Stairii' CKen
- 'Tempelhof Compact' SLim
- f. *viridis* GRei
taxifolia See *P. menziesii*

PSEUDOWINTERA (Winteraceae)
§ *colorata* CB&S CDec CDoC CMCN CPle CTrw IOrc ISea MAll MBlu WCru WPat WPyg WRTC WWat

PSIDIUM (Myrtaceae)
cattleyanum See *P. littorale* var. *longipes*
littorale (F) ERea
§ - var. *longipes* LBlo WHer

PSILOSTROPHE (Asteraceae)
See Plant Deletions

PSORALEA (Papilionaceae)
affinis CHEx
glandulosa CGre
pinnata CTrC LHil

PSYCHOTRIA (Rubiaceae)
capensis SLMG
¶ *viridis* NGno

PTELEA (Rutaceae)
trifoliata ♀ CB&S CChu CFil CLnd CMCN CPMA ELan LHol SPer SRms SSpi WCoo WFar WHCG WNor WOMN
- 'Aurea' ♀ CAbP CBot CChu CEnd CLnd CPMA CPle ELan ICrw LHol MBlu MBri MGos SHBN SPer SSpi SSta WHCG WPat WPyg WRTC

PTERACANTHUS See STROBILANTHES

PTERIDIUM (Hypolepidaceae)
aquilinum Percristatum Group IOrc

PTERIDOPHYLLUM (Papaveraceae)
¶ ***racemosum*** EFEx WCru

PTERIS (Pteridaceae)
argyraea MBri NMar
bulbifera SLMG
cretica ♀ MBri SArc
cretica albolineata ♀ GQui MBri SRms
cretica cristata MBri
cretica 'Gautheri' MBri
– 'Parkeri' MBri
– 'Rivertoniana' MBri
– 'Rowei' MBri
– 'Wimsettii' MBri
ensiformis MBri NMar
– 'Arguta' MBri
– 'Victoriae' MBri
longifolia NMar
tremula GQui MBri NMar SRms
umbrosa MBri
vittata SRms

PTEROCARYA (Juglandaceae)
fraxinifolia ♀ CAbb CAgr CB&S CDoC CLnd CMCN CTho ENot IOrc MBlu SHhN SPer WDin WMou
– var. ***dumosa*** WMou
× ***rehderiana*** CTho WMou
rhoifolia CMCN WCoo WMou
stenoptera CB&S CLnd CMCN CTho SLPl WMou
– 'Fern Leaf' WMou

PTEROCELTIS (Ulmaceae)
tatarinowii CMCN WHCr

PTEROCEPHALUS (Dipsacaceae)
parnassi See ***P. perennis***
§ ***perennis*** CLyd CShe ELan ESis GCHN LBee MBro NBir NHar NMen NTow NWCA SAlw SBla SIng SMer SRms WAbe WEas WHoo WOMN WOld WPat WPyg WWin
pinardii NTow WDav

PTEROSTYLIS (Orchidaceae)
¶ ***alata*** SWes
g. **Bantam** SWes
¶ ***coccinea*** SSpi SWes
¶ ***concinna*** SWes
curta CFil CRDP WCot
g. **Cutie** 'Harold's Pride' AM-OCSA SWes
g. **Dunkle** SWes
¶ ***fischii*** SWes
g. **Hookwink** SWes
¶ × ***ingens*** SWes
g. **Joseph Arthur** SWes
g. **Marelba** SWes
g. **Mary Eleanor** SWes
g. **Nodding Grace** SWes
¶ ***obtusa*** SWes
¶ ***ophioglossa*** SWes
¶ ***procera*** SWes
¶ ***robusta*** SWes
¶ ***russellii*** SWes
g. **Sentinel** SWes
¶ ***stricta*** SWes
g. **Talhood** SWes
¶ ***taurus*** SWes
¶ × ***toveyana*** SWes
¶ ***truncata*** SSpi SWes

PTEROSTYRAX (Styracaceae)
corymbosa CChu CMCN WWat
hispida ♀ CB&S CBrd CChu CFil CLnd CMCN CPMA CPle CTho EPfP MBlu SSpi SSta WCoo WWat
psilophylla CMCN

PTILOSTEMON (Asteraceae)
¶ ***afer*** WCot

PTILOTRICHUM (Brassicaceae)
◆ ***spinosum*** 'Roseum' See ***Alyssum spinosum* 'Roseum'**

PTILOTRICHUM See ALYSSUM

PTYCHOSPERMA (Arecaceae)
See Plant Deletions

PUERARIA (Papilionaceae)
montana var. ***lobata*** CAgr CPlN
thunbergiana SBra

PULICARIA (Asteraceae)
§ ***dysenterica*** CArn CKin ECWi EWFC MChe MSal NMir SIde WBea WCHb WGwy WOak WWye

PULMONARIA † (Boraginaceae)
'Abbey Dore Pink' CMea WAbb
affinis EMon LRHS WPbr
angustifolia ♀ CArc CHad CRow CSam GDra MCLN MSal NBrk NFla NHol NOrc SChu WEas WHil WWin
– subsp. ***azurea*** CBro CElw CMil CRow CSpe CVer CWGN EAst EBar EBre EFou EGol ELan EPla ERav LWak MBri MCLN MRav NBro NGar NRoo NSti NTow SPer SPla SRms SSvw WTyr WWye
– 'Blaues Meer' CSte EBar GBuc NSti SAxl WCru WThi
– 'Blue Pearl' MBel NSti
– 'Munstead Blue' CArc CElw CGle CShe CWit ECha EFou EGol EPar LFis MBel MTho NBrk NRya NSti SAga SRms WCru WRus
– 'Rubra' See ***P. rubra***
'Barfield Regalia' CGle EMon MBro NCat NChi NSti WCer
'Beth's Blue' ECha EOrc MBri MGrG WByw WCru
'Beth's Pink' ECha MBel NCat WCHb WCru
'Blauhügel' EMon
'Blue Crown' CBos CElw CGle CSev EMon EPPr NSti NTow SWas WDav WHal
'Blue Ensign' CGle CMea CRDP CVer EBee ECha EFou EMon LHop LRHS LWoo MArl MBel MBri MGrG NSti SAxl SMad SMrm WCHb WCot WCru WHal WPbr
* 'Blue Moon' WHoo
'Botanic Hybrid' NCat
'British Sterling' WGle
'Buckland' NCat
Cally hybrid GCal NSti
'Cedric Morris' CElw NSti

'Chintz'	CElw MAvo SUsu WCru WHal WPbr
'Cleeton Red'	NSti WCru
'Corsage'	CElw EBee
'Crawshay Chance'	SWas WPbr
'Esther'	NSti WCot WRus
¶ 'Excalibur'	ECha
'Fiona'	EFou NHaw
'Glacier'	CElw CGle CMea CMil ECha EMon EPPr LRHS MArl MBel NCat SAxl WCer WCru WHal
'Hazel Kaye's Red'	NSti
'Highdown'	See ***P.* 'Lewis Palmer'**
'Joan's Red'	CElw
§ 'Lewis Palmer' 🏆	Widely available
'Little Star'	EMon GBuc WGle
longifolia	Widely available
– 'Ankum'	CGle CSpe EMan EPla GBuc LWoo MBel NSti SBid SWas WCot WPbr
– 'Bertram Anderson'	CGle CHad CWGN EAst EBre EGol GAbr GMaP LWoo MBel MBri MUlv NTow NVic SAga SBla SMrm SUsu WCHb WCot WCru WHil
¶ – subsp. ***cevennensis***	NSti SSpi
¶ – 'Coen Jansen'	NCat
– 'Dordogne'	CGle ECha EGle EPPr EPla MGrG MRav SBla SPla SUsu WCot WCru
– forms	ECha GAbr
¶ – from France	EPPr
¶ – wild-collected	WCot
'Lovell Blue'	CElw WRus
'Macuson's Blue'	EWes
'Majestic'	ECha
'Mary Mottram'	CCot MBel MHFP MMil MUlv NBir WCer WCru WGle WHal
'Mawson's Blue'	CGle CMea EBre ECha EMon LWoo MAvo MBel MBri MWat NRoo NSti WCHb WCot WCru WEas WElm WMaN WPbr WWat
'Merlin'	EMon LRHS LWoo WCHb
mollis	CBot CMHG EMon EOrc EPla GCal MBel MBri NBrk NCat NSti SAxl WByw WCot WPbr
– 'Royal Blue'	CMea EGol GCHN MRav NRoo SLod WCHb
– 'Samobor'	WCot
¶ ***mollissima***	WHil
'Mournful Purple'	CElw CGle CRow EBre ECha EMon EPla ERav MBel MHFP MUlv NBrk SWat WCot WCru
'Mrs Kittle'	CMil NSti SAxl SSpi SWas WByw WCHb WCot WHal WMer WPbr WRus
'Nürnberg'	EFou EHoe EMon EPPr LFis LRHS MBel NSti WCHb WCru WHal WPbr
obscura	EGar EMon LRHS MBel
officinalis	CArn CBro CGle CRow ECED ECWi EMon EOrc EPar EWFC GPoy LHol LLWP MChe MFir MHew NBrk SIde WCru WEas WHal WOak WWye
– 'Alba'	NCat WByw
– 'Blue Mist'	CElw CMil ECha EGar EMon NCat NSti SAxl SMrm WByw WCru WHal WPbr
– 'Bowles' Blue'	CFis CGle CVer EBre LWoo SHel WAbb WFox WPbr WRus WThi
– Cambridge Blue Group	CElw CHan ECha EFou EGar EGol EMon EOrc EPla ERav MCLN MRav MWat NHol NSti WByw WCru WEas WHal WRus
– 'Plas Merdyn'	IBlr
– ***rubra***	See ***P. rubra***
–'Sissinghurst White' 🏆	Widely available
– 'White Wings'	CElw CHan CMil EFou EPPr EPla EPri MAvo NHol SSpi WCHb WCot WCra WEas WFar WMaN WPbr
'Oliver Wyatt's White'	EMon
Opal = 'Ocupol'	EFou GBuc LWoo WCot WRha WWeb
'Patrick Bates'	MBel
'Paul Aden'	WGle
* 'Rowlatt Choules'	SSpi
'Roy Davidson'	CElw CGle CMHG CMil CSte CVer CWGN EBre EPPr GAbr LFis MBel MBri NRoo NSti SAga SAxl SBla SMrm WCru WGle WHal WRus WWat
§ ***rubra*** 🏆	CElw CGle CHan CSWP ECha ELan EMar EOrc LFis MFir MSCN NHol NOrc NSti SChu SEas SRms SUsu WBon WByw WCHb WCru WElm WRha
– var. ***alba***	See ***P. rubra*** var. ***albocorollata***
§ – var. ***albocorollata***	CBre CElw CGle ECha EMon LRHS MBel MCLN MFir MSte NCat NSti SApp SAxl SOkh WByw WCru WRus
– 'Ann'	CElw EBee EFou EMon LRHS NSti SOkh
* ***rubra argentea***	WCot
rubra 'Barfield Pink'	Widely available
– 'Barfield Ruby'	EMon GBuc LRHS LWoo MAvo SOkh
– 'Bowles' Red'	CArc CBot CBre CMea CWit EBre ECtt EFol ENot ERav GAbr LGan LHop NHol NRoo NSti SCro SMrm SPer WCra WHal WTyr
– 'David Ward' (v)	CRDP CRow CSpe EBre ECha ECtt EFol EHal ELan EMon LFis MBel MGrG MUlv MWat NBir NCut NWes SApp SBid SMrm SSpi WBcn WCHb WCot WCru WHoo WPbr WRus WSan
– 'Prestbury Pink'	EMon
– 'Redstart'	Widely available
– 'Warburg's Red'	EMon
§ ***saccharata***	CHEx CRow CShe ECha ELan LGro MFir NHol SChu SCro SSvw WCHb WCru WEas WHoo WPbr WPyg WWat WWin
– 'Alba'	CBro CRow ECha EGar MBel NOak SIng SRms WCru
– Argentea Group 🏆	CBro CGle CRow CSev CWGN EAst ECha ECoo EFou EGol ELan EMar EOrc EPla GAbr MTho NBro NFla NSti SPer SSpi WCru WSan
– 'Blauhimmel'	CCot EMon NSti WHoo
– 'Bofar Red'	EFou
– 'Brentor'	CElw CRow

– 'Cotton Cool' SApp SBid
– 'Diana Chappell' MBel SSpi
– 'Dora Bielefeld' Widely available
– 'Frühlingshimmel' CBro CElw CGle CMil ECha EFou EOrc EPla LGre MBel MHFP MRav MUlv NTow SAxl SBla SMrm SUsu SWas WCHb WHal WRus
– 'Jill Richardson' EGar ELan WPbr
– 'Lady Lou's Pink' LFis WCru
– 'Leopard' CElw CGle CMea CSam CSte EBre ECtt EFou GMaP LFis MBel MCli MHFP MUlv NSti SBid SBla SMrm WCru WMer WRus
– 'Mrs Moon' CDoC CSpe CWGN CWit EBar EBee EBre ECtt EFou ENot GMaP LHop MCli MHFP NBrk NBro NFla NHol NMir NOrc SChu SPer SSvw WCHb WCru WFox WGwG WHen WHil WPyg
– 'Old Rectory Silver' LWoo
– 'Picta' See ***P. saccharata***
– 'Pink Dawn' CDoC EAst EBee EMan EOrc LFis MBri MCli MUlv NBus NPri NSti SEas SPer WCru
– 'Reginald Kaye' CRow ECha EGar EHic NBrk NSti
– 'Snow Queen' NHol
– 'White Leaf' WRus
'Saint Ann's' CElw NSti
'Skylight' CElw
'Smoky Blue' CBlo EAst EBee EFou EGol EPPr EPfP GBri MCLN NCat NPri NSti SMer SWat WByw WCot WMer WWeb
'Snowy Owl' WGle
'Tim's Silver' ECha NBrk WBcn
vallarsae 'Margery Fish' ♀ CBro CGle COtt EGol EOrc LFis MBri MUlv NBro NRoo NSti NWes SHFr SMad SMer SPer WByw WCHb WCru WEas WMer WWye
'Weetwood Blue' CBre CChu CElw MSte
'Wisley White' CElw

PULSATILLA (Ranunculaceae)

alba CBro GCLN MSto
albana CAvo CBro MSto NTow SBla
– 'Lutea' MSto SBla
– white MSto
alpina CBot NRoo SRms WAbe WRHF
§ – subsp. ***apiifolia*** ♀ CBot CLyd ELan GAbr GDra GTou NGre NHar NRoo WCot WDav WOMN WSan
– subsp. ***sulphurea*** See ***P. alpina*** subsp. ***apiifolia***
ambigua ESis MSto
¶ ***aurea*** MSto
bungeana MSto
campanella MSto
caucasica CBro
cernua MSto SIgm
chinensis MSto
dahurica MFos
georgica MSto
halleri ♀ ECGP EDAr MMil MSto NRoo NSla SIgm
halleri alba EDAr
halleri subsp. ***slavica*** ♀ CBro MFos NNrd NSla SWas WWin
koreana CBro LRHS MSto
* ***lutea*** WDav
montana EWes MSto WDav
¶ – var. ***australis*** MSto
occidentalis MSto WOMN
§ ***patens*** EBee GCLN MSto NTow WDav
– subsp. ***trisecta*** CGra
pratensis GTou MSto MTho NRoo
– subsp. ***nigricans*** CBro EDAr LRHS
turczaninovii MFos MSto SIgm
§ ***vernalis*** ♀ EDAr GDra GTou MSto NGre NHar NSla NTow NWCA SRms WAbe
¶ – Czech Fringed hybrids GCLN
§ ***vulgaris*** ♀ Widely available
vulgaris alba ♀ Widely available
vulgaris 'Barton's Pink' EFou EHyt SBla WRus
– 'Eva Constance' CAvo CBro CLyd CRDP EBre EHyt LHop LRHS SIng SWas WAbe
– 'Flore Pleno' CNic
– 'Gotlandica' CLyd GDra NHol SIgm
– subsp. ***grandis*** LWoo
¶ – Heiler Hybrids EMan
– 'Miss Beveridge' NOak
– pale pink NRoo
– 'Papageno' CBot CGle EMan LGre NRoo NSla SIgm SMrm WFar WHil
I – 'Red Clock' See ***P. vulgaris* 'Röde Klokke'**
§ – 'Röde Klokke' CBot LGre MBro WHil
♦ – Rote Glocke See ***P. vulgaris* 'Röde Klokke'**
– var. ***rubra*** CB&S CGle CShe CSpe EFou EHyt ELan EOrc GAbr GLil LHop MBal MBri MBro MHig MSto NFla NHar NNrd NRoo SBla SUsu WHoo WPer WRus
§ – 'Weisse Schwan' CBlo LFis MBro NFla NMen
♦ – White Swan See ***P. vulgaris* 'Weisse Schwan'**

PULTENAEA (Papilionaceae)

¶ ***daphnoides*** MAll

PUNICA (Punicaceae)

granatum EMil ERea GAri LPan SOWG STre WSHC
– 'Flore Pleno Luteo' GAri
– 'Flore Pleno Rubro' GAri LPan
– var. ***nana*** CArn CHal CPle ERea GAri LHop LPan MPla SMrm SRms WPat WWat
– f. ***plena*** CB&S
– 'Striata' SOWG

PURSHIA (Rosaceae)

See Plant Deletions

PUSCHKINIA (Hyacinthaceae)

§ ***scilloides*** var. ***libanotica*** CAvo CBro ELan EPar EPot ETub LAma MBal NEgg NRog WPer WShi
– – 'Alba' CAvo EPar EPot LAma NRog WCot
– Polunin 5238 CMon

PUTORIA (Rubiaceae)

calabrica CLyd

PUYA (Bromeliaceae)

alpestris CFil CHEx CTbh CTrC EOas SArc SMad WPGP

berteroniana	CHEx CTrC LHil LLew
chilensis	CAbb CB&S CHEx CPle CTrC EOas MAll SArc
coerulea	CFir CHEx GBin MAll SIgm
¶ – var. *coerulea*	SAxl
¶ – RB 94100	LLew
– var. *violacea*	CGre
conquimbensis	MAll
laxa	CHEx
mirabilis	CHEx GCra LLew
raimondii	CHEx
venusta	CHEx GBin
weberbaueri	CHEx

PYCNANTHEMUM (Lamiaceae)

¶ *montanum*	WCot
muticum	MRav
pilosum	CArn CHal CPou CSev ELau EMan GBar GPoy LHol MSal NPri SIde WPer WWye
tenuifolium	EBee
virginiana	ECha

PYCNOSTACHYS (Lamiaceae)

¶ *urticifolia*	GCra

PYGMAEA See CHIONOHEBE

PYRACANTHA † (Rosaceae)

Alexander Pendula	CWLN EBee ENot GAri LHop MGos MRav SEas SRms WHar WWat
angustifolia	CB&S CBlo EHic WWat
§ *atalantioides*	CB&S CMac CSam CShe SPla SRms WRTC WWat
§ – 'Aurea'	CBlo CChe SRms WWin
'Brilliant'	CB&S EPfP SLPl
'Buttercup'	EPla GAri WBcn
Saphyr® Orange = 'Cadange'	COtt IOrc MBri SBid SHhN SPer WLRN WWeb
§ Saphyr® Jaune = 'Cadaune'	CBlo CDoC IOrc SPer WLRN WWeb
Saphyr® Rouge = 'Cadrou'	COtt IOrc MBri SBid SPer WLRN WWeb
coccinea	CTrw
§ – 'Lalandei'	CMac CSam EBee MGos NNor SPer WGwG
– 'Red Column'	CChe CMac EBar ECtt ELan GOrc GRei LBuc MBar MGos MRav MWat NBee NFla SAga SCoo SEas WDin WGwG WHar WRHF WWeb
– 'Red Cushion'	ENot IHos MGos MRav SRms
– 'Rutgers'	SLPl
– 'Telstar'	CB&S CBlo
Dart's Red	CBlo EBee MBri WLRN WWeb
gibbsii	See ***P. atalantioides***
– 'Flava'	See ***P. atalantioides* 'Aurea'**
'Golden Charmer'	EBee EBre ECtt ELan EPfP MBal MGos SHBN SPer SRms WBod WDin WHar
'Golden Dome'	SEas
'Golden Glow'	CBlo
'Golden Sun'	See ***P.* 'Soleil d'Or'**
'Harlequin' (v)	CB&S CBot ECtt EPla MBal MBar NSti SBid SHBN SReu WLeb WWeb
'John Stedman'	See ***P.* 'Stedman's'**
'Knap Hill Lemon'	CChe MBlu WLRN
'Mohave'	CB&S CChe CMac CWLN EBre ELan ENot MBal MBar MGos MRav MWat NHed NNor SHBN SPer SReu SRms WDin WGwG WStI
'Mohave Silver' (v)	CWLN EAst EBar ELan MBar MWat NNor SEas SPla WGwG
'Monrovia'	See ***P. coccinea* 'Lalandei'**
'Mozart'	WWeb
'Navaho'	CBlo CWLN EBee MPla MRav SEas SReu WAbe WBod
'Orange Charmer'	CChe CShe CTri CWLN ELan ENot MAsh MBal MBar MGos MWat NBee SHBN SPer WLRN WRHF WRTC WStI WWeb
'Orange Giant'	See ***P. coccinea* 'Kasan'**
'Orange Glow' ♀	CChe CMac CShe CWLN EBre ECtt ENot GOrc GRei IHos LBuc MAsh MBar MGos NFla NNor NWea SPer SRms WDin WHar WRTC WStI
* 'Red Pillar'	CBlo CDoC
'Renault d'Or'	SLPl
rogersiana ♀	EBee ENot EPfP MRav NNor WGwG
– 'Flava' ♀	CLTr CTri EBee ENot EPfP MAsh MBal MBar MGos NNor NWea WGwG
Saphyr® Jaune	See ***P.* Saphyr® Jaune = 'Cadaune'**
'Shawnee'	CB&S CMac ECot EHic MAsh MRav MWat NHed SPla WWeb
§ 'Soleil d'Or'	CMac CSam CShe CWLN EBre ECtt ELan ENot EPla IHos LBuc MBar MBri MPla MRav NBee NCut NNor SPer SReu WDin WHar WStI
'Sparkler' (v)	CMac CPMA EAst EBar EHoe ELan LHop MAsh NHol NNor SAga SBid SEas SPer SPla WHar
§ 'Stedman's'	MBri WLeb
'Teton'	CDec CMHG CMac ELan ENot EPla LHop MAsh MBar MBri MGos MRav NHed NHol SEas SPla SRms WAbe WBod WDin WFar WLRN WRTC WStI
'Watereri' ♀	CBlo SBid SLPl SPer
'Yellow Sun'	See ***P.* 'Soleil d'Or'**

× PYRACOMELES (Rosaceae)

See Plant Deletions

PYRETHROPSIS (Asteraceae)

§ *atlantica*	ECho
§ *catananche*	ECho

PYRETHROPSIS See RHODANTHEMUM

PYRETHRUM (Asteraceae)

◆ *roseum*	See *Tanacetum coccineum*

PYRETHRUM See TANACETUM

PYROLA (Ericaceae)

rotundifolia	WHer

PYROSTEGIA (Bignoniaceae)

venusta	CPlN LChe

PYRROCOMA (Asteraceae)
clementis EBee

PYRROSIA (Polypodiaceae)
heterophylla NMar

PYRUS † (Rosaceae)
amygdaliformis CTho
– var. *cuneifolia* CTho
betulifolia CMCN WJas
calleryana CAgr
– 'Bradford' CLnd
– 'Chanticleer' 🏆 CDoC CEnd CLnd CTho ENot IOrc LHyr LPan MAsh NBee SHBN SLPl SPer SSta WDin WHut WJas WOrn WWat
× *canescens* CTho
communis (F) CAgr CCVT CKin MBlu SKee SPer STre WMou
– 'Autumn Bergamot' (D) CTho SKee
– 'Barland' (Perry) WMou
– 'Barnet' (Perry) CTho
– 'Baronne de Mello' (D) CTho SFam SKee
– 'Beech Hill' (F) CLnd CTho ENot SHhN
– 'Belle Guérandaise' (D) SKee
– 'Belle Julie' (D) SKee
– 'Bergamotte d'Automne' (D) SKee
– 'Bergamotte Esperen' (D) SKee
– 'Beth' (D) 🏆 CDoC CWSG EMui EWar GBon GChr GTwe LBuc MBri MGos NBee NDal NRog SDea SFam SIgm SKee SPer
– 'Beurré Alexandre Lucas' (D) SKee
– 'Beurré Bedford' (D) NRog SIgm
– 'Beurré Bosc' (D) SKee
– 'Beurré Clairgeau' (C/D) SKee
– 'Beurré d'Amanlis' (D) SKee
– 'Beurré d'Avalon' (D) CTho
– 'Beurré de Naghin' (C/D) SKee
– 'Beurré Dumont' (D) SFam
¶ – 'Beurré Gris d'Hiver' (D) SKee
– 'Beurré Hardy' (D) 🏆 CDoC CTho EMui ERea GTwe MBri MWat NRog SDea SFam SIgm SKee
– 'Beurré Mortillet' (D) SKee
– 'Beurré Six' (D) SKee
– 'Beurré Superfin' (D) ERea GTwe SFam SIgm SKee
– 'Bianchettone' (D) SKee
¶ – 'Bishop's Thumb' (D) SKee
– 'Black Worcester' (C) GTwe SFam SKee WJas WMou
– 'Blakeney Red' (Perry) CTho SDea WMou
– 'Blickling' (D) SKee
– 'Bonne de Beugny' (F) SKee
– 'Brandy' (Perry) CTho SDea WMou
– 'Bristol Cross' (D) GTwe SKee
– 'Brown Bess' (Perry) WMou
– 'Catillac' (C) 🏆 CTho GTwe NRog SFam SKee
– 'Chalk' See ***P. communis* 'Crawford'**
– 'Chaumontel' (D) SKee
– 'Clapp's Favourite' (D) CTho GTwe IOrc SIgm SKee
– 'Colmar d'Eté' (D) CTho
– 'Comte de Lamy' (D) SKee
– 'Concorde' (D) 🏆 CDoC CWSG EMui ERea EWar GTwe LBuc MBri MGos NBee NDal SDea SFam SIgm SKee WJas WWeb
– 'Conference' (D) 🏆 CMac CSam CTho CWSG EBre EMui ERea EWar GBon GChr GRei GTwe IOrc LBuc MBri MGos MWat NBee NDal NRog SDea SFam SIgm SKee SPer WJas WWeb
– 'Craig's Favourite' (D) GTwe
– 'Crassane' CTho
§ – 'Crawford' (D) SKee
– 'Deacon's Pear' (D) SDea
– 'Docteur Jules Guyot' (D) SKee
– 'Double de Guerre' (C/D) SKee
¶ – 'Doyenné Boussoch' (D) SKee
– 'Doyenné d'Eté' (D) ERea SFam SKee
– 'Doyenné du Comice' (D) 🏆 CDoC CMac CSam CTho CWSG EBre EMui ERea EWar GBon IOrc MBri MWat NRog SDea SFam SIgm SKee SPer WJas WWeb
– 'Doyenné Georges Boucher' (D) SKee
– 'Duchesse d'Angoulême' (D) SKee
– 'Durondeau' (D) CTho GTwe NRog SFam SIgm SKee
– 'Easter Beurré' (D) SKee
– 'Emile d'Heyst' (D) CTho GTwe SIgm
¶ – 'English Caillot Rosat' (D) SKee
– 'Eva Baltet' (D) SKee
¶ – 'Fair Maid' (D) SKee
– 'Fertility Improved' See ***P. communis* 'Improved Fertility'**
– 'Fondante d'Automne' (D) CTho SKee
– 'Forelle' (D) ERea SKee
– 'Gansel's Bergamot' (D) CTho SKee
– 'Gin' (Perry) CTho WMou
– 'Glou Morceau' (D) CTho EMui GBon GTwe MWat NRog SDea SFam SIgm SKee
– 'Glow Red Williams' (D) SFam
– 'Gorham' (D) CTho GTwe NBee SFam SKee
– 'Gratiole de Jersey' (D) CTho
– 'Green Horse' (Perry) CTho WMou
– 'Green Pear of Yair' (D) SKee
– 'Hacon's Imcomparable' (D) SKee
– 'Hendre Huffcap' (Perry) WMou
– 'Hessle' (D) GTwe NRog SDea SFam SKee
– 'Highland' (D) SKee
§ – 'Improved Fertility' (D) CDoC GBon GTwe SDea SKee
– 'Jargonelle' (D) GTwe NRog SDea SFam SKee
– 'Joséphine de Malines' (D) 🏆 CTho GTwe SDea SFam SIgm SKee
– 'Judge Amphlett' (Perry) WMou
– 'Laxton's Foremost' (D) SKee
– 'Laxton's Satisfaction' (D) SFam
¶ – 'Le Lectier' (D) SKee
– 'Louise Bonne of Jersey' (D) CDoC CTho CTri EMui EWar GTwe MBri NRog SDea SFam SIgm SKee
¶ – 'Madame Treyve' (D) SKee
– 'Maggie Duncan' (F) GTwe
– 'Marguérite Marillat' (D) GTwe

– 'Marie-Louise' (D)	SKee
– 'Martin Sec' (C/D)	SKee
– 'Merton Pride' (D)	CTho GTwe MWat SDea SFam SKee
– 'Merton Star' (D)	SKee
– 'Moorcroft' (Perry)	WMou
– 'Nouveau Poiteau' (C/D)	CTho GTwe SKee
– 'Oldfield' (Perry)	WMou
– 'Olivier de Serres' (D)	SFam SKee
– 'Onward' (D) 🏆	EMui GChr GTwe LBuc MGos NBee NDal NRog SDea SFam SIgm SKee
§ – 'Packham's Triumph' (D)	CDoC GBon GTwe NRog SKee
– 'Passe Colmar' (D)	CTho
– 'Passe Crassane' (D)	SKee
– 'Pear Apple' (D)	SDea
– 'Pitmaston Duchess' (C/D) 🏆	CTho CWSG GTwe SDea SKee
– 'Red Comice' (D/C)	GTwe SKee
– 'Robin' (C/D)	ERea SDea SKee
– 'Roosevelt' (D)	SKee
– 'Santa Claus' (D)	SDea SFam SKee
– 'Seckle' (D)	GTwe SFam SIgm SKee
– 'Soleil d'Automne' (F)	SKee
– 'Souvenir du Congrès' (D)	NRog
¶ – 'Sucrée de Montluçon' (D)	SKee
– 'Swan's Egg' (D)	CTho SKee
– 'Sweet Huffcap'	See ***P. communis* 'Hellen's Early'**
– 'Thompson's' (D)	GTwe SFam SIgm
– 'Thorn' (Perry)	CTho WMou
– 'Triomphe de Vienne' (D)	SFam SKee
– 'Triumph'	See ***P. communis* 'Packham's Triumph'**
– 'Uvedale's St Germain' (C)	CTho SKee
– 'Vicar of Winkfield' (C/D)	GTwe SDea SKee
– 'Williams' Bon Chrétien' (D/C) 🏆	CMac CWSG EBre EMui ERea EWar GBon GChr GRei IOrc LBuc MBri MGos MWat NDal NRog SDea SFam SIgm SKee SPer WJas WWeb
– 'Williams Red' (D/C)	GTwe SKee
– 'Winnal's Longdon' (Perry)	CTho WMou
– 'Winter Christie' (F)	GTwe
– 'Winter Nelis' (D)	CTho GTwe SDea SFam SKee
– 'Yellow Huffcap' (Perry)	WMou
¶ – 'Zéphirin Grégoire' (D)	SKee
cordata	CTho
cossonii	CTho
elaeagnifolia	CTho WWat
– var. ***kotschyana***	CDoC CEnd
nivalis	CLnd CTho EHoe ENot SHBN SLPl SPer
pyraster	CPer
pyrifolia '20th Century'	See ***P. pyrifolia* 'Nijisseiki'**
– 'Chojura' (F)	IOrc
– 'Kumoi' (F)	ESim LBuc MGos SDea
* – 'Nashi Kumoi'	LPan
– 'Shinseiki' (F)	EMui SDea
– 'Shinsui' (F)	SDea SKee
salicifolia 'Pendula' 🏆	CB&S CEnd CGre CLnd CTho EBre ELan ENot GRei LHyr LNet LPan MBal MBar MBri MGos NBee NWea SChu SHBN SIgm SMad SPer SReu SSta WDin WFar WJas WWat
ussuriensis	CMCN

QUAMOCLIT See IPOMOEA

QUERCUS † (Fagaceae)

acuta	CB&S CHEx CMCN
§ ***acutissima***	CLnd CMCN WDin WNor
– subsp. ***chenii***	CMCN
aegilops	See ***Q. macrolepis***
¶ ***affinis***	CMCN SBir
agrifolia	CB&S CMCN
alba	CMCN
aliena	WCoo
– var. ***acuteserrata***	CMCN
alnifolia	CDul CMCN
arkansana	CMCN
austrina	CMCN
¶ ***baloot***	CMCN
¶ × ***beadlei***	SBir
bicolor	CDul CMCN IOrc WDin WNor
borealis	See ***Q. rubra***
¶ ***brantii***	CMCN
breweri	CMCN
× ***bushii***	CMCN MBlu
canariensis 🏆	CFil CLnd CMCN CTho WMou WPGP
¶ ***canbyi***	CMCN
castaneifolia	CDul CLnd CMCN WMou
– 'Greenspire' 🏆	CDoC CDul CLnd CMCN EBee MBlu MBri SMad SPer
cerris 🏆	CB&S CDoC CDul CKin CLnd CMCN EMil ENot IOrc NWea SEND SPer SSta STre WDin WFro WMou
§ – 'Argenteovariegata'	CDul CMCN CTho MBlu MBri SMad WMou
– 'Variegata'	See ***Q. cerris* 'Argenteovariegata'**
– 'Wodan'	CMCN MBlu
chapmanii	CMCN
chrysolepis	CMCN MBlu
coccifera	CDul CFil CMCN WPGP
coccinea	CAbP CB&S CChu CDul CLnd CMCN CWSG EHic EPfP IOrc NBee NWea SPer SSta WCoo WNor
– 'Splendens' 🏆	CDoC CDul CEnd CFil CMCN COtt CTho ELan IOrc LPan MBlu SHBN SMad SPer SSpi WDin
¶ ***comptoniae***	CMCN
¶ ***crassipes***	CMCN
dentata	CMCN
– 'Carl Ferris Miller'	CFil SMad WPGP
– 'Pinnatifida'	CMCN MBlu SMad
douglasii	CMCN WCoo
dumosa	CMCN
durata	CMCN
ellipsoidalis	CAbP CDoC CDul CGre CMCN WWat WWes
¶ – 'Hemelrijk'	CFil MBlu
engelmannii	CMCN
faginea	CMCN MNes
falcata	CDul CLnd CMCN
– var. ***pagodifolia***	CMCN MBlu
× ***fernaldii***	CMCN

frainetto	CDoC CDul CLnd CMCN CTho EBee IOrc LPan MBlu MBri SEND SMad SPer SSpi WDin WMou WWat
¶ – 'Trump'	MBlu
fruticosa	See ***Q. lusitanica*** **Lamarck**
gambelii	CMCN
garryana	CMCN MBlu
¶ – × ***turbinella***	SBir
¶ ***geminata***	CMCN
georgiana	CMCN
gilva	CMCN
glabra	See ***Lithocarpus glaber***
glabrescens	CB&S
glandulifera	CMCN
glauca	CMCN
hartwissiana	CMCN
× ***hastingsii***	CMCN
hemisphaerica	CMCN
× ***heterophylla***	CDul CMCN
× ***hickelii***	CMCN
× ***hispanica***	See ***Q.*** × ***lucombeana***
◆ – 'Lucombeana'	See ***Q.*** × ***lucombeana*** **'William Lucombe'**
ilex 🏆	CAgr CB&S CDoC CDul CKin CLnd CMCN CSam CTrw ELan EMil IOrc ISea LHyr LPan MAsh MBlu MBri MGos NWea SArc SHBN SPer SSta STre WDin WMou WNor WOrn
ilicifolia	CDul CMCN MBlu WNor WWat
imbricaria	CDul CMCN MBlu WWes
incana Bartram	CMCN
– Roxburgh	See ***Q. leucotrichophora***
infectoria	CDul
¶ – subsp. ***veneris***	CMCN
ithaburensis	CMCN
kelloggii	CMCN WWes
× ***kewensis***	CMCN WMou
laevis	CMCN MBlu
laurifolia	CDul CMCN
§ ***leucotrichophora***	CMCN
liaotungensis	CMCN
× ***libanerris*** 'Rotterdam'	CMCN
libani	CDul CMCN WCoo
lobata	CMCN
§ × ***lucombeana***	CLnd
– 'Diversifolia'	CMCN MBlu WMou
– 'Suberosa'	CTho
– 'Wageningen'	CMCN WMou
§ – 'William Lucombe' 🏆	CDul CMCN CTho MBlu WMou
× ***ludoviciana***	CMCN SArc
§ – Lamarck	CDul CMCN
lyrata	CMCN
macranthera	CMCN EMil
macrocarpa	CMCN WDin WNor
¶ – × ***gambelii***	SBir
¶ – × ***robur***	SBir
§ ***macrolepis***	CMCN MBlu
marilandica	CDul CEnd CMCN WWes
mexicana	CMCN
michauxii	CMCN
mongolica var. ***grosseserrata***	CMCN
§ ***montana***	CMCN MBlu
muehlenbergii	CDul CMCN CTho
myrsinifolia	CB&S CMCN SArc WNor
nigra	CMCN CMHG MBlu
nuttallii	CMCN
obtusa	CDul CMCN
palustris 🏆	CChu CDoC CDul CLnd CMCN CTho IOrc LPan MBal MBri SPer SSpi WDin WNor WOrn
– 'Pendula'	CEnd CMCN
– 'Swamp Pygmy'	CMCN MBlu
pedunculata	See ***Q. robur***
pedunculiflora	CMCN
§ ***petraea*** 🏆	CDoC CDul CKin CLnd CPer EMil GRei IOrc LBuc MBal NWea SPer WDin WFro WMou
– 'Columna'	EBee
§ – 'Insecata'	CDoC CEnd CMCN
– 'Laciniata'	See ***Q. petraea*** **'Insecata'**
– 'Mespilifolia'	CTho
– 'Purpurea'	CMCN
§ ***phellos*** 🏆	CDul CLnd CMCN CTho MBlu SLPl SSpi WCoo WDin WNor WWat WWes
* ***phellos latifolia***	IOrc MBlu
phillyreoides	CB&S CDul CMCN SSpi WCoo WNor WWat
¶ ***planipocula***	CMCN
'Pondaim'	CMCN
pontica	CMCN MBlu
¶ ***prinoides***	SBir
◆ ***prinus*** Engelm.	See ***Q. montana***
§ – Linnaeus	CMCN MBlu
pubescens	CDul CMCN
pumila Michaux	See ***Q. prinus*** **Linnaeus**
– Walt.	See ***Q. phellos***
pyrenaica	CMCN CTho
– 'Pendula'	CMCN MBlu
§ ***robur*** 🏆	CB&S CDoC CDul CKin CLnd CMCN CPer EBre ENot GRei IOrc LBuc LHyr LPan MBar MBri MGos MWat NBee NWea SHBN SPer WCoo WDin WMou WOrn WStI
– 'Argenteomarginata'	CDul CMCN MBlu SMad
– 'Atropurpurea'	EMil SPer
– 'Compacta'	MBlu
– 'Concordia'	CB&S CEnd CFil CMCN COtt MBlu SMad
– 'Cristata'	CDul CMCN
– 'Cucullata'	CMCN
* ***robur dissecta***	CMCN
robur 'Facrist'	CBlo CDul CEnd
– f. ***fastigiata***	CDoC CDul CLnd CTho EMil ENot IOrc LBuc LPan MAsh MBar MWat NBee NWea SCoo SPer WOrn
– 'Fastigiata Koster' 🏆	CDul CMCN COtt EMil EPfP
– 'Fastigiata Purpurea'	IOrc
– 'Fennessii'	CMCN MBlu SMad
– 'Fürst Schwarzenburg'	CMCN MBlu
– 'Hentzei'	CMCN
– 'Hungaria'	MBlu
¶ – × ***lobata***	SBir
¶ – ***robur*** × ***macrocarpa*** × ***muehlenbergii***	SBir
¶ – ***robur*** × ***macrocarpa*** × ***virginiana***	SBir
– 'Pectinata'	MBlu
– f. ***pendula***	CDul CEnd CMCN CTho
– 'Purpurascens'	CEnd CMCN MBlu
– 'Raba'	CMCN
– 'Salicifolia Fastigiata'	CMCN
– 'Strypemonde'	CMCN
¶ – × ***turbinella***	SBir
× ***rosacea*** 'Filicifolia'	CEnd WMou

§ ***rubra*** ♀	CB&S CDoC CDul CKin CLnd CMCN CPer CTho EBre ELan EMil ENot GRei IOrc LBuc LHyr LPan MBal MBar MBri MGos NBee NWea SHBN SPer SSta WDin WMou WNor
– 'Aurea'	CDul CEnd CFil CMCN MBlu SMad SSpi
* – 'Sunshine'	CMCN MBlu MBri SMad
rugosa	CMCN
sadleriana	CMCN
¶ ***sartorii***	CMCN
× ***saulii***	CMCN
¶ × ***schuettei***	SBir
serrata	See ***Q. acutissima***
sessiliflora	See ***Q. petraea***
shumardii	CDul CMCN WDin WNor WWes
stellata	CMCN
suber	CB&S CDoC CDul CLnd CMCN CTho GAri ISea SArc SEND SSpi WDin
texana	CMCN WWes
trojana	CMCN
turbinella	CMCN
× ***turneri***	CDoC CDul CLnd CMCN CTho LBuc MBri WMou
– 'Pseudoturneri'	CB&S ELan EMil
vacciniifolia	CMCN MBal
variabilis	CDul CMCN MBlu WCoo WWes
velutina	CDul CGre CLnd CMCN WCoo WWat
– 'Rubrifolia'	CMCN
virginiana	CMCN
'Warburgii'	CMCN
wislizenii	CMCN IOrc

QUESNELIA (Bromeliaceae)
See Plant Deletions

QUILLAJA (Rosaceae)

saponaria	CGre CPle

QUIONGZHUEA (Poaceae - Bambusoideae)

tumidinoda	See ***Chimonobambusa tumidissinoda***

RACOPILUM (Sphagnaceae)
See Plant Deletions

RACOSPERMA See ACACIA

RAMONDA (Gesneriaceae)

§ ***myconi*** ♀	CMea CPBP CShe EHyt GDra LWoo MBro MHig NHar NRai NSla NTow NWCA SAlw SBla SIgm SIng SRms SWas
– var. ***alba***	SIng
¶ – 'Rosea'	LWoo
nathaliae ♀	GCLN LWoo NHar SIgm
– 'Alba'	SBla SWas WFar
pyrenaica	See ***R. myconi***
serbica	GDra SIgm SIng

RANUNCULUS † (Ranunculaceae)

abnormis	SWas
aconitifolius	CGle EBre ECha EPar NSti
– 'Flore Pleno' ♀	CRDP CRow EBre EPri IBlr LGre NBir NRya NTow SBla WByw
acris	CTiv ECWi EWFC
* ***acris citrinus***	ECoo EPri EWoo WRha WSan
acris 'Farrer's Yellow'	CRow
– 'Flore Pleno'	CArc CAvo CElw CFee CFir CGle CMea CRow ECha ELan EMan EPar GAbr MInt NBro NFai NHex NHol NRya SMac WByw WGwG WHal WHil WHow WSan
– 'Hedgehog'	EMon
– 'Stevenii'	CArc CBos CFee CRow
– 'Sulphureus'	CBre CGle CMea EMon MSte NCat SMrm WEas WHal
alpestris	NMen
amplexicaulis	CMon EPot ERos GDra GTou NHar SBla
aquatilis	CBen EHon EMFW NDea SWat SWyc WChe
asiaticus	CAvo CMon ETub WOMN
– Accolade	NNrd SCoo WStI
– red	EEls WChr
* – Tecolote Hybrids	LAma
– white	SBla
– yellow	SBla
auricomus	CKin
bulbosus	CKin EWFC
§ – 'F.M. Burton'	CRDP EGar EMon GCal MHlr NCat NTow WCot WHal
bulbosus farreri	See ***R. bulbosus* 'F.M. Burton'**
bulbosus 'Speciosus Plenus'	See ***R. constantinopolitanus* 'Plenus'**
calandrinioides ♀	CMon SBla WAbe WCot
– dwarf form	SIgm
– SF 37	CMon
§ ***constantinopolitanus*** 'Plenus'	CArc CBos CDec CElw CGle CRDP CRow ECha GCal GGar MBri MBro MInt NBro NChi NRya NTow SUsu WCot WEas
cortusifolius	CRDP WCot
crenatus	CLyd EHyt ELan GTou ITim LBee MBal MHig NGre NHar NMen NNrd NRya NSla NTow SBla WAbe WHal WHil
¶ ***creticus***	EMon
eschscholtzii	NGre
ficaria	CArn CHid CJew CKin CNat CRow ECWi EWFC GBar GCal MChe MHew MSal SIde WHer WOak WShi WWye
I – 'Aglow in the Dark'	CNat
– var. ***albus***	CBre CElw CGle CMil CMon CRow CVer EMon NGar NGre NRya SIng WByw
– anemone centred	See ***R. ficaria* 'Collarette'**
– 'Ashen Primrose'	CRow
§ – var. ***aurantiacus***	CBre CMil CNic CRow CVer ECha EMon EPar EPot GDra MBro NGar NGre NHol NMen NNrd NRya SAlw SAxl SBla SIng SRms SSvw WAbe
– 'Blackadder'	CRow
– 'Bowles' Double'	See ***R. ficaria* 'Double Bronze'**, ***R. ficaria* 'Picton's Double'**
– 'Brambling'	CHid CRow EMon LWoo WCot
– 'Brazen Daughter'	CRow
– 'Brazen Hussy'	Widely available
– 'Bregover White'	CRow
– 'Bunch' (d)	CBre CRow
– 'Button Eye'	CMon
– 'Champernowne Giant'	CRow
– 'Chedglow'	WAlt
– 'Chocolate Cream'	CRow

– subsp. ***chrysocephalus***	CBre CHid CRow ECha EMon EPot NGre NRya SIng SSvw WCot WHer
– 'Coffee Cream'	CRow
§ – 'Collarette' (d)	CArc CBre CGle CHid CInt CMil CRDP CRow ECha EHyt EMon EPar EPot ERos GAbr GBar GCal GGar MTho NGar NGre NMGW NNrd NRya NSla SAlw SAxl SBla SIng WAbe WCla WCot WHil WCot
– 'Coppernob'	CAvo CBos CRDP CRow CVer SSvw SWas WCot
– 'Coy Hussy' (v)	CNat
– 'Crawshay Cream'	SWas
– 'Cupreus'	See ***R. ficaria*** var. ***aurantiacus***
– 'Damerham'	CHid CRow EMon
– 'Double Bronze' (d)	CHid CMil EMon EPar MTho NGre NRya
– double cream	See ***R. ficaria* 'Double Mud'**
– double green eye (d)	CHid CRow NGre
§ – 'Double Mud' (d)	CBos CBre CMil CRDP CVer EMon LWoo MTho NGar NNrd NRya SBla SIng SUsu SWas WCot WHal
– double yellow	See ***R. ficaria flore-pleno***
– 'Dusky Maiden'	CRow EMon
– 'E.A. Bowles' (d)	See ***R. ficaria* 'Collarette'**
– 'Elan' (d)	CRow
– subsp. ***ficariiformis***	EMon
§ – ***flore-pleno*** (d)	CFee CGle CInt CMil CMon CRow ECha ELan EMar EMon EPar ERos GAbr GDra MHig NDea NGre NHol NNrd NRya NSla SAxl SIng SRms WCot WHil WWin
– 'Fried Egg'	CRow
– 'Green Petal'	CArc CHid CMil CRDP CRow EMon EPar MS&S MTho NGar NGre NNrd NRya NSla SIng SSvw SUsu WCot
– 'Holly Green'	CRow
– 'Hoskin's Miniature'	NGre
– 'Ken Aslet' (d)	CHid CRow EMon SWas
– 'Lemon Queen'	MBro NHol SIng WCot
– 'Limelight'	CRow
– 'Little Southey'	CHid CRow
– subsp. ***major***	See ***R. ficaria* subsp. *chrysocephalus***
– 'Mimsey' (d)	CRow
– 'Mobled Jade'	CNat
– 'Newton Abbot'	CRow
– 'Picton's Double' (d)	CGle CHid CRDP CRow CVer EHyt EMou GBar GCal LGan MTho NNrd NRya
– 'Primrose'	CArc CBre CRow EMon GGar MTho NCat NGre NHol NRya SUsu WCot
– 'Quillet' (d)	CBre CRow
– 'Randall's White'	CGle CHid CRDP CRow ECha MTho NTow SSvw WCot
– 'Rowden Magna'	CRow NGre
– 'Salmon's White'	CAvo CFee CRow CVer ELan EMar EPPr EPar EPot NGre NNrd NRya SBla SSvw WHal WHil
– 'Sheldon'	CNat
– 'Sheldon Silver'	CNat
– single cream	EMon GAbr
– 'Suffusion'	CNat WAlt
– 'Sutherland's Double'	CRow
– 'Sweet Chocolate'	CRow
– 'Tortoiseshell'	CBos CRow CVer WCot
– 'Trenwheal' (d)	CRow
– 'Wisley Double Yellow'	CBos CVer NSti SUsu
– 'Yaffle'	CBre CHid CRow EMon WAlt WCot
flammula	CArn CBen CKin CRow ECWi EHon EMFW GBar LPBA MSta NDea SWat SWyc WChe
* – ***minor***	CRow
gouanii	EPot NBro NGre NTow
gramineus ♀	CDec CLyd CMea CRDP EBre EHyt ELan EPot LBee LGan LHop MBro MNrw MTho MWat NGre NMen NNrd NRya SIgm SRms SSmi WByw WCot WHil WPer
¶ – 'Pardal'	WFar
hederaceus	EMFW SWyc
illyricus	EMon
insignis	CRDP GCal
kochii	EPot
lanuginosus	WCot
– AL&JS 89066YU	EMon
lingua	CKin ECWi ECoo EMFW MHew WChe
– 'Grandiflorus'	CBen CRow CWGN EHon LPBA MSta NDea SWat SWyc WMAq WSan WWye
lyallii	CPla GCal SBla SIgm
macrophyllus	WCru
millefoliatus	EHyt ERos MTho NMen NNrd NRya WHil
montanus	MBal
– 'Molten Gold' ♀	ELan EPot MHig MRav MTho NBro NHar NHol NMen NNrd NRya NTow SBla SIng
muelleri var. ***brevicaulis***	CMHG
nivicola	NTow
ophioglossifolius	CNat
parnassiifolius	CPBP GTou NGre NHar NTow SBla WAbe
platanifolius	CBre LGre
repens	CKin CTiv ECWi EWFC
– 'Joe's Golden'	EFol EHoe EMon NSti WAlt WCer
– var. ***pleniflorus***	CBre CDec CInt CNic CRow ECha ELan EMon GCal NSti WAlt WEas
– 'Timothy Clark' (d)	MInt WHil
rupestris	See ***R. spicatus***
sceleratus	WHer
from Morocco	WHil
speciosus 'Flore Pleno'	See ***R. constantinopolitanus* 'Plenus'**
§ ***spicatus***	CRDP NRya WCot WOMN

RANZANIA (Berberidaceae)

See Plant Deletions

RAOULIA (Asteraceae)

australis Hooker	CLTr CLyd ECou EHoe ELan EMNN EPot GAbr GCHN GDra ITim MBal MBar MHig MRPP MWat NBro NGre NHol NNrd NRoo NWCA SIng WAbe WHoo WPyg
– 'Calf'	ITim NHol
§ – Lutescens Group	ECha EPot GAri ITim LBee MHig NTow
– 'Saxon Pass'	GCHN NHol
– hort.	See ***R. hookeri***
glabra	ECou GAbr NTow

haastii CLyd ECou EPot GDra NHol
§ *hookeri* CLyd EBre ECha ECou ELan EPot GCHN ITim LBee NHol NMen NNrd NTow NWCA SBla SIng WDav WFar
– var. *laxa* EPot EWes
× *loganii* See × *Leucoraoulia loganii*
lutescens See *R. australis* Lutescens Group
monroi ECou ELan GCHN ITim NHol NTow
* *nova* GDra
petriensis EPot NSla
× *petrimia* 'Margaret Pringle' NHar WAbe
subsericea CLyd CMHG ECou MHig NGre NMen
tenuicaulis ECha ECou GAbr GAri NHol WDav

RAOULIA See × LEUCORAOULIA

RATIBIDA (Asteraceae)
columnifera EBee MCCP
– f. *pulcherrima* MCCP WCot WHil
pinnata EBee WHil

RAUVOLFIA (Apocynaceae)
¶ *serpentina* MSal

RAVENALA (Musaceae)
madagascariensis LBlo LPal

RAVENEA (Arecaceae)
rivularis LPal

RECHSTEINERIA See SINNINGIA

REEVESIA (Sterculiaceae)
See Plant Deletions

REGELIA (Myrtaceae)
ciliata MAll
velutina SOWG

REHDERODENDRON (Styracaceae)
macrocarpum CB&S

REHMANNIA (Scrophulariaceae)
angulata See *R. elata*
§ *elata* CBot CChr CGle CMGP CSev CSpe EBre ECro ELan GMac LBlm LFis MCLN MNrw NPer SMrm WCru WFar WGwG WHer WHil WPer WRus WWhi WWin WWye
glutinosa 🏆 CSpe LGre MSal MSto SMrm WOMN WWye

REINECKEA (Convallariaceae)
§ *carnea* CHan CHid CNic CRDP ECha EGar ELan EMan EMar EPar EPla ERos GCal LFis LGan LWak MFir MRav MTho MUlv NNrd NRoo NSti SBar SOkh WBon WCru WGwG
– 'Variegata' WCot

REINWARDTIA (Linaceae)
§ *indica* CGre CPle LHil
– S&SH 106 CHan
trigyna See *R. indica*

RELHANIA (Asteraceae)
See Plant Deletions

RESEDA (Resedaceae)
alba EMon
lutea CKin CTiv ECWi EWFC MGam MSal SIde
luteola CJew CKin ECWi EJud EWFC GBar GPoy LHol MChe MHew MSal SIde WCHb WHer WWye

RESTIO (Restionaceae)
subverticillatus See *Ischyrolepis subverticillata*

RETAMA (Papilionaceae)
§ *monosperma* CPle

REYNOUTRIA See FALLOPIA

RHABDOTHAMNUS (Gesneriaceae)
solandri WCru

RHAGODIA (Chenopodiaceae)
triandra ECou

RHAMNUS (Rhamnaceae)
alaternus CFil SBid WPGP
– var. *angustifolia* CFil WPGP WWat
§ – 'Argenteovariegata' 🏆 CB&S CHan CMHG CPle CSam CShe CWSG EBar EBre ELan ENot GOrc LHol LHop NSti SArc SChu SHBN SHFr SPer SPla SReu SSpi SSta WDin WHCG WPat WRTC WSHC WWat
– 'Variegata' See *R. alaternus* **'Argenteovariegata'**
cathartica CCVT CKin LBuc WDin WMou
frangula CArn CCVT CDoC CKin CPer CSam ENot LBuc SLPl STre WDin WMou WRTC
– 'Aspleniifolia' EBee EPfP MBri SMad SMur
– 'Columnaris' EMil SLPl
× *hybrida* 'Billardii' ESis
japonica SPer
¶ *prinoides* CPle

RHAPHIOLEPIS (Rosaceae)
× *delacourii* CChu CMHG EPfP GQui SBid WBod
– 'Coates' Crimson' CChu CSPN EHic EMil GOrc GQui LPan MBlu SBid SHBN SOWG SPer WSHC
– 'Enchantress' EBre SMur
– 'Spring Song' EBee LPan
indica CGre CPle CTrC NPSI SEND WAbe WWat
ovata See *R. umbellata*
§ *umbellata* 🏆 CAbb CB&S CBot CChu CDoC CHEx CPle CSam CTri GQui LHop MAll MBlu MUlv SAga SAxl SMac WHCG WSHC WWat

RHAPHITHAMNUS (Verbenaceae)
cyanocarpus See *R. spinosus*

§ *spinosus* CGre CHan CPle EPla ERea SBid SMad WBod

RHAPIDOPHYLLUM (Arecaceae)

hystrix LPal NPal

RHAPIS (Arecaceae)

§ *excelsa* ♀ LPal
multifida LPal

RHAZYA (Apocynaceae)

orientalis See ***Amsonia orientalis***

RHEKTOPHYLLUM See CERCESTIS

RHEUM † (Polygonaceae)

§ 'Ace of Hearts' CBot CChu CRow CWGN CWit EBre ECha EGol EHoe ELan EMFW EOrc EPar EPla GTwe MBri MUlv NDea NHol NSti SChu SMrm SSpi SWat WCot WRus
'Ace of Spades' See ***R. 'Ace of Hearts'***
acuminatum CRow GBin WCot
– HWJCM 252 WCru
alexandrae CArc GAri GCal GLil IBlr WWhi
§ *australe* CArn CRow GAul MSal NBro SMrm WCot WHoo WPyg
× *cultorum* See ***R.* × *hybridum***
emodi See ***R. australe***
forrestii ACE 2286 SWas
§ × *hybridum* NVic SEND
– 'Baker's All Season' GTwe
– 'Canada Red' GTwe
N – 'Cawood Delight' GTwe SEND
– 'Champagne' GTwe SEND
– 'Daw's Champion' GTwe
– 'Early Champagne' GTwe
– 'Early Cherry' GTwe
– 'Fenton's Special' GTwe
– 'German Wine' GTwe
– 'Goliath' GTwe
– 'Grandad's Favorite' EBre
– 'Greengage' GTwe
– 'Hammond's Early' GTwe SEND
– 'Harbinger' GTwe
– 'Hawke's Champagne' GTwe
– 'Mac Red' GTwe
– 'Prince Albert' GTwe
– 'Red Prolific' GTwe
– 'Reed's Early Superb' GTwe
– 'Stein's Champagne' GTwe
– 'Stockbridge Arrow' GTwe SEND
– 'Stockbridge Bingo' GTwe
¶ – 'Stockbridge Emerald' GTwe
– 'Stockbridge Guardsman' GTwe
* – 'Strawberry' EMui GTwe
¶ – 'Sutton's Cherry Red' GTwe
– 'The Sutton' GTwe LBuc
– 'Timperley Early' CDoC CMac CSam CTri ECtt EMui GChr GTwe LBuc MMor NDal NFai SDea
– 'Tingley Cherry' GTwe
– 'Valentine' GTwe
– 'Victoria' GTwe SEND
¶ – 'Zwolle Seedling' GTwe
kialense EBee GCal WChe WCot
* *maximum* WCot
nobile HWJCM 307 WCru
¶ – SF 95170 ISea
officinale CHEx GCal MBri SWat
palmatum ♀ CArn CB&S CHEx EBee ECha EHal ELan GAul LHil MRav MSal NCut NDea NFla NNor SHig SPer SSpi SWat WBea WGwG WHoo WHow WPyg WStI
– 'Atropurpureum' See ***R. palmatum* 'Atrosanguineum'**
§ – 'Atrosanguineum' CBot CHEx CRow EBre ECha ECtt EGar EGol ELan EPar GBuc LBlm NBro NNor SPer SSoC SWat WCru WWin
– 'Bowles' Crimson' CHad LRHS MBri SAga SSoC
– 'Hadspen Crimson' CHad
– 'Red Herald' MBri WCot
palmatum rubrum CDoC COtt CWGN EBre EHic EHoe GCHN MEas MHlr WCot
palmatum 'Saville' EHoe MBri
– var. *tanguticum* CRow EBee ECha EGar EOrc MBri MSCN MSal MSta MUlv NCat NPri NSti SMrm SPer SRms SSoC SWat WCot WCru WWat
I – – 'Rosa Auslese' SMrm
* *robertianum* GPoy
spiciforme GPoy
¶ *tataricum* GCal
tibeticum WWoo
undulatum CRow

RHEXIA (Melastomataceae)

¶ *mariana* WCot
¶ – var. *purpurea* WCot

RHINANTHUS (Scrophulariaceae)

See Plant Deletions

RHINEPHYLLUM (Aizoaceae)

broomii NGre

RHIPSALIS (Cactaceae)

cassytha See ***R. baccifera***

RHODANTHE (Asteraceae)

§ *anthemoides* ECou

RHODANTHEMUM (Asteraceae)

atlanticum ELan EWes
catananche CPBP ELan EOrc EPot EWes LHop NTow SMrm WAbe
§ *gayanum* CSpe EBar ELan EWes IHos LBee LFlo LHil NSty NTow SCro SUsu WKif WOMN
– 'Flamingo' See ***R. gayanum***
§ – 'Tizi-n-Test' SBla SWas
– 'Tizi-n-Tichka' CInt CPBP ELan EWes LBee LHop LRHS NBir NTow SBla SLod WAbe WDav
§ *hosmariense* ♀ CElw CMHG CSam CSev ECha ELan EPot LBee LFis LHop MBal MTho NHol SBla SIng SPer SRms SSmi SUsu WAbe WEas WOMN WRus WWin

RHODIOLA (Crassulaceae)

alsia NGre
arctica NGre
bupleuroides CLD 1196 EMon

crassipes	See ***R. wallichiana***
§ ***fastigiata***	EMon GCal NGre NRoo
– × ***kirilovii***	NGre
¶ ***gelida***	NGre
§ ***heterodonta***	ECha EGle ELan WCot
◆ ***himalensis***	See ***R.* 'Keston'**
§ 'Keston'	NGre SSmi
§ ***kirilovii***	GTou
– var. ***rubra***	EBre NGre SSmi WFar
I ***kirilowii***	EMon
pachyclados	See ***Sedum pachyclados***
pamiroalaica	NGre
§ ***primuloides***	CLyd NGre NMen WHil
§ ***quadrifida***	NGre
rhodantha	NGre
§ ***rosea***	ECha ECro EHoe ELan EMan GGar LBlm MBal MFir NGre NNor NRoo SCro SIng SRms SSmi STre WAbb WEas WWhi
§ – subsp. ***integrifolia***	NGre
semenowii	EBee MHar WCot
sp. CC&McK 158	GCHN
sp. EMAK 0516	NHol
§ ***trollii***	MHig NGre
§ ***wallichiana***	GAri NGre WCot
§ ***yunnanensis***	EMon

RHODOCHITON (Scrophulariaceae)

§ ***atrosanguineus*** ♀	CArn CEnd CGle CHEx CMac CPlN CRHN EDAr ELan ERea LHop MNes NEgg NFai SOWG SSoC WEas WWhi
volubilis	See ***R. atrosanguineus***

RHODODENDRON † (Ericaceae)

'A.J. Ivens'	See ***R.* 'Arthur J. Ivens'**
'Abegail'	NMun SLeo
'Abendrot'	MBri
aberconwayi	IOrc LMil MBal NMun SLeo SReu
– 'His Lordship'	GGGa LHyd
– pink	NMun
'Accomplishment'	CWri
'Achilles'	SLeo
* ***acpunctum*** SF 313	ISea
'Actress'	IOrc LHyd NMun SLeo
'Addy Wery' (EA) ♀	CMac CWLN GDTE GWht IOrc LKna MBal MBar MGos NMun SBod SCog SExb SLeo SPer SReu WBod WStI
adenogynum	GGGa MDun NMun SLeo
§ – Adenophorum Group	SLeo
– – F 20444	SLeo
– – 'Kirsty'	NMun
– – R 11471	NMun
¶ – Cox 6502	GGGa
– CLD 795	LMil
– white	NMun
adenophorum	See ***R. adenogynum*** **Adenophorum Group**
adenopodum	GGGa NMun SLeo SReu
adenosum	LMil NHol NMun
– Kuluense Group	NMun SLeo
– R 18228	GGGa
'Admiral Piet Hein'	SReu
'Adonis' (EA/d)	CMac IOrc MBar SCog SPer
§ 'Adorable' (EA)	IOrc
'Adriaan Koster'	IOrc
adroserum R/USDA 59201	See ***R. lukiangense*** **R 11275***
'Advance' (O)	NMun SExb SLeo
aeruginosum	See ***R. campanulatum*** subsp. ***aeruginosum***
aganniphum	GGGa NMun SLeo
§ – var. ***aganniphum*** Doshongense Group	GGGa NMun SLeo
¶ – – – C&V 9541	GGGa
– – – KW 5863	NMun
– – F 16472	NMun
– – Glaucopeplum Group	GGGa
– – Schizopeplum Group	GGGa
– var. ***flavorufum***	GGGa NMun SLeo
– – P Cox 5070	GGGa
– – SSNY 143	GGGa
– P Cox 6003	GGGa
– 'Rusty'	NMun
– SSNY 138	GGGa
– SSNY 320	GGGa
agapetum	See ***R. kyawii*** **Agapetum Group**
agastum	NMun SLeo
– PW 98	GGGa
'Aida' (R/d)	GGGa SReu
'Aksel Olsen'	CDoC ECho MBal MBar MDun NHol WBod
'Aladdin' (EA)	ECho IOrc WFar
Aladdin Group & cl.	CWri SReu
Albatross Group & cl.	LHyd LKna LMil SLeo SPer SReu SSta
'Albatross Townhill Pink'	LMil
'Albert Schweitzer'	CWri LMil MBal MBar MBri SLeo SReu SSta
albertsenianum	SLeo
albiflorum (A)	GGGa SReu
albrechtii (A) ♀	GGGa GWht LHyd NGre SReu WAbe
'Alena'	GGGa
'Alex Hill'	WLRN
'Alexander' (EA)	CB&S CTrh CWLN GQui IOrc LMil MBri MGos SBod SCog SHBN
'Alfred'	LRHS
'Alice' (EA)	CMac IHos LHyd LKna
'Alice' ♀	IOrc LHyd LKna NMun SCog SLeo SPer SReu
'Alice Street'	SLeo
¶ 'Alisa Nicole' (V)	CEqu
Alison Johnstone Group & cl.	CB&S GGGa GWht ISea MBal MDun MLea NMun SCog SExb SLeo SPer SReu WAbe WBod
'Aloha'	CAbP LMil MAsh MBar MLea MMor NHed SCog SHBN SReu
'Alpine Dew'	GGGa
Alpine Gem Group	GGGa GQui NHol
'Alpine Glow' ♀	NMun SLeo
alutaceum	NMun
– var. ***alutaceum***	GGGa
§ – – Globigerum Group	LMil
– – – R 11100	GGGa NMun SLeo
§ – var. ***iodes***	GGGa LMil NMun
§ – var. ***russotinctum***	GGGa NMun SLeo
§ – – Triplonaevium Group	NMun
– – – R/USDA 59442/ R10923	GGGa
§ – – Tritifolium Group	GGGa NMun
– – – R 158*	NMun
amagianum (A)	LMil
Amaura Group	WBod
ambiguum	CDoC CHig LMil NMun SLeo SReu
– 'Jane Banks'	LMil
– KR 185 select	GGGa
'America'	CB&S CWLN IOrc MAsh MBal MBar MGos SLeo WWeb
amesiae	NMun SLeo
'Amethyst'	LHyd
§ 'Amethystinum' (EA)	LKna

'Amoenum' (EA/d)	CBlo CChe CMHG CMac CTrw GWht IOrc LHyd LKna MBar MGos NMun SCog SExb SLeo WBod WFar
'Amoenum Coccineum' (EA/d)	GWht SCog
Amor Group & cl.	LHyd NMun SLeo
'Analin'	See *R.* **'Anuschka'**
'Anatta Gold' (V)	GGGa
'Anchorite' (EA)	GQui LMil
'Andre'	NMun SLeo SReu
'Andrea'	NMun
Angelo Group & cl.	CWri LHyd LMil SCog SReu
Anita Group	NMun SLeo
'Anita Dunstan'	LMil LRHS MLea
'Ann Lindsay'	SReu
'Anna Baldsiefen' 🏆	CSam GGGa LMil MAsh MBri NHol SPer SReu SSta
'Anna H. Hall'	IOrc MDun SCog
'Anna Rose Whitney' 🏆	CB&S CWri GGGa GRei IOrc LHyd LKna LMil MBar MBri MGos MLea NMun SHBN SLeo SPer SReu SSta
'Annabella' (K) 🏆	LHyd MBri MMor SReu
annae	GGGa LMil NMun SLeo
§ – Hardingii Group	NMun
'Anne Frank' (EA)	EBee MGos SReu WBod
'Anne George'	LHyd
'Anne Rothwell'	LHyd
'Anneke' (K)	MBar MBri MMor SReu SSta
'Anniversary Gold'	GGGa
'Anny' (EA)	CMac IOrc LKna
anthopogon	LMil NMun SLeo
– 'Betty Graham'	LMil NMun
– BL&M 322	GGGa
– CH&M 2052	GGGa
§ – subsp. *hypenanthum*	LMil
– – 'Annapurna'	CSam GGGa SReu
– Sch 2259	GGGa
anthosphaerum	GGGa NMun SReu
– F 17943	NMun
– F 26432	NMun SLeo
– Gymnogynum Group	NMun
§ – Heptamerum Group	NMun
– KW 5684	NMun
§ 'Antilope' (Vs)	MMor SPer SReu SSta
'Antje'	LRHS MAsh SCog
Antonio Group & cl.	SCog
§ 'Anuschka'	CDoC LRHS MBri
anwheiense	See *R. maculiferum* subsp. *anwheiense*
aperantum	GGGa
– F 227022*	GGGa
– F 26933	SLeo
'Aphrodite' (EA)	GQui
apodectum	See *R. dichroanthum* subsp. *apodectum*
'Apotheose' (EA)	EBee
N 'Appleblossom'	See *R.* **'Ho-o'**
'Apricot Fantasy'	LMil SMur
'Apricot Surprise'	MLea
'April Dawn'	GGGa
'April Gem'	GGGa
§ 'April Glow'	LHyd SLeo
'April Showers'	GWht
'April Snow' (d)	GGGa
'April White'	GGGa
'Arabesque'	EBee MBri MMor
araiophyllum	GGGa NMun SLeo
Arbcalo Group	SLeo
§ *arborescens* (A)	GGGa LKna LMil NMun SLeo SReu
arboreum	CB&S CWri GGGa GWht IOrc ISea LMil MDun NMun SLeo SReu
– f. *album*	SReu
– B 708	MBal
– 'Blood Red'	NMun
– BM&W 172	MBal
– C&S 1651	NMun
– C&S 1695	NMun
– subsp. *cinnamomeum*	GGGa NMun SLeo SReu
– – Campbelliae Group	NMun SLeo
– – var. *roseum*	NMun
– – – BB 151	NMun
* – – var. *roseum crispum*	NMun
– subsp. *delavayi*	GGGa ISea NMun SLeo
¶ – – C&H 7178	GGGa
– – C&S 1515	NMun
– – KW 21796	NMun
– 'Heligan'	SReu
– KR 966	NMun
* *arboreum nigrescens*	SLeo
§ *arboreum* subsp. *nilagiricum*	GGGa NMun
§ – 'Sir Charles Lemon' 🏆	NMun SLeo SPer SReu SSta
– 'Tony Schilling' 🏆	LHyd LMil NMun SLeo
– TSS 26	NMun
§ – subsp. *zeylanicum*	NMun SLeo
'Arborfield'	SLeo
Arbsutch Group	SLeo
× *arbutifolium*	See *R.* **Arbutifolium Group**
'Arcadia' (EA)	LKna
¶ 'Arctic Regent' (K)	GQui
'Arctic Tern'	See × *Ledodendron* **'Arctic Tern'**
§ *argipeplum*	NMun SLeo
– KR 1231	NMun
'Argosy' 🏆	LMil NMun SBid SReu
argyrophyllum	CDoC NMun SLeo
– 'Chinese Silver' 🏆	LHyd LMil NMun SLeo SReu
§ – subsp. *hypoglaucum*	NMun SLeo
§ – – 'Heane Wood'	GGGa
– KR 184	GGGa
– subsp. *nankingense*	GGGa IOrc LMil NMun
– W 1210	NMun
Ariel Group	SLeo
arizelum	See *R. rex* subsp. *arizelum*
'Arkle'	LHyd
'Armantine'	LKna
¶ *armitii* Woods 2518	GGGa
'Arneson Gem' (M)	GGGa LMil
§ 'Arpege' (Vs)	MBal SReu WWat
'Arthur Bedford'	CWri GGGa LHyd LKna LRHS SLeo SReu
'Arthur Osborn'	CHig GGGa NMun SLeo
'Arthur Stevens' 🏆	SLeo
'Arthur Warren'	LKna
'Asa-gasumi' (EA)	LHyd
'Ascot Brilliant'	NMun SLeo
¶ *asterochnoum* C&H 7051	GGGa
Asteroid Group	NMun
atlanticum (A)	GAri GGGa NMun SLeo SSpi
– 'Seaboard' (A)	LMil
'Atlantis'	CWri
'Audrey Wynniatt' (EA)	MAsh SExb
Augfast Group	CB&S CTrw EPot IOrc MBal SBod WBod
'August Lamken'	SBid
augustinii	CB&S CSam CTrw CWri GGGa IOrc ISea LHyd LMil MBal MLea NMun SCog SExb SLeo SPer SSpi SSta WBod
¶ – subsp. *augustinii* C 7008	GGGa
¶ – – Cox 7048	GGGa

¶ – – 'Smoke'	CGre
§ – subsp. ***chasmanthum***	GGGa LMil
¶ – – C&Cu 9407 white	GGGa
¶ – – C&Cu 9418 pale pink	GGGa
§ – Electra Group & cl. 🏆	GGGa LHyd LMil MDun NMun SCog SLeo
– EN 3527	GGGa
– Exbury best form	SReu
§ – subsp. ***hardyi***	GGGa LHyd SLeo
§ – subsp. ***rubrum***	GGGa
– – 'Papillon'	NMun
– W A 1207	NMun
I – 'Werrington'	MUlv SReu
§ ***aureum***	GGGa LMil NMun SLeo
auriculatum	GGGa LHyd LMil MBal NHol SLeo SReu SSta
¶ – x ***degronianum***	SReu
– PW 50	GGGa
– Reuthe's form	SReu
auritum	CBlo GGGa NMun
'Aurora' (K)	NMun SLeo
'Autumn Gold'	CDoC COtt LMil MBal NHol SMur SReu
Avalanche Group & cl. 🏆	SReu
'Award'	GGGa LMil
'Aya Kammuri' (EA)	LHyd
¶ 'Ayah'	SReu
Azor Group & cl.	CHig LHyd NMun SLeo SReu SSta
'Azorazie'	NMun SLeo
'Azuma-kagami' (EA) 🏆	CB&S LHyd LKna LMil SCog WBod
¶ 'Azuray'	GGGa
'Azurika'	GGGa NHol
'Azurro'	GGGa LMil MDun SBar SMur
'Azurwolke'	GGGa
'Baby Scarlet'	SSta
'Baden-Baden'	EPot GCHN GRei GWht LHyd LKna MAsh MBal MBar MDun MGos MMor NHol NMun NWea SBod SCog SExb SHBN SPer SSta WBod
'Bagshot Ruby' 🏆	LKna NWea SBod
baileyi	GGGa LHyd LMil NMun
– LS&H 17359	NMun
bainbridgeanum	NMun SLeo
R/USDA 59184/ R11190	
bakeri	See ***R. cumberlandense***
balangense EN 3530	GGGa
balfourianum	GGGa MDun NMun
– Aganniphoides Group	LMil NMun
– F 16811	NMun
– F 29256*	NMun
– SSNY 224	GGGa
'Ballerina' (K)	MBal
'Balsaminiflorum'	See ***R. indicum*** **'Balsaminiflorum'**
'Balzac' (K)	CSam IOrc MBri MGos
'Bambi'	LHyd NMun SCog SLeo SReu
'Bambino'	CAbP COtt LNet MAsh MLea SBar SLeo
'Bandoola'	SReu
'Banzai' (EA)	NMun SLeo
'Barbara Coates'	LHyd
'Barbara Reuthe'	SReu
barbatum	CWri GGGa LHyd LMil NMun SLeo SReu
– B 235*	NMun
– BB 152	MBal
– BL&M 325	NMun
aff. – Cave 6714	NMun
– DF 525	MBal
– KW 5659*	NMun
– LS&H 17512	NMun
– TSS 30	NMun
Barclayi Group	LHyd
'Barclayi Helen Fox'	NMun
'Barclayi Robert Fox'	NMun SLeo
'Barmstedt'	SBar
'Barnaby Sunset'	CSam GAri GGGa NHol
'Bashful' 🏆	CWLN EPfP GRei IOrc LHyd MAsh MBal MGos MMor NMun SCog SExb SLeo SReu
§ ***basilicum***	CWri GGGa IDee LHyd LMil NMun SLeo
– SF 381	ISea
– TW 368	GWht
bathyphyllum	NMun SLeo
¶ – Cox 6542	GGGa
bauhiniiflorum	See ***R. triflorum*** var. ***bauhiniiflorum***
beanianum	GGGa LMil NMun SLeo
– compact form	See ***R. piercei***
– KW 6805	NMun
'Beatrice Keir' 🏆	LHyd NMun SLeo SReu
Beau Brummel Group & cl.	LMil
'Beaulieu Manor'	GQui
'Beauty of Littleworth' 🏆	LHyd LKna LMil NMun SLeo SReu
'Beaver' (EA)	MBri
beesianum	GGGa LMil NMun SLeo
– F 10195	NMun
– R 176	NMun
– SSNY 250	GGGa
– SSNY 303	GGGa
'Beethoven' (EA) 🏆	CBlo LHyd LKna MBal NMun SBod SExb SLeo SReu WBod WGor
'Belle Heller'	CSam CWri MBal MBri SExb WLRN
'Belle of Tremeer'	LHyd
¶ Bellerophon Group	NMun
'Bengal'	CDoC ISea MAsh MBal MBar MBri NHol SCog SReu
'Bengal Beauty' (EA)	GQui LMil
'Bengal Fire' (EA)	CMac SExb
§ 'Benifude' (EA)	WBod
'Beni-giri' (EA)	CMac
I 'Benjamen'	GGGa
¶ 'Bergie Larson'	LMil
bergii	See ***R. augustinii*** subsp. ***rubrum***
¶ 'Berg's Yellow'	CWri
'Bernard Shaw'	SReu
'Berryrose' (K) 🏆	CB&S CTri GWht IOrc LHyd LKna LMil MAsh MBal MBar MBri MLea MMor NMun SExb SPer
¶ 'Better Half'	GGGa
'Betty' (EA) 🏆	LHyd SRms
'Betty Anne Voss' (EA)	LHyd LRHS MAsh SCoo SExb
'Betty Stewart'	NMun SLeo
'Betty Wormald' 🏆	CHig CWri IHos LHyd LKna LMil MGos MLea NMun SBid SCog SHBN SLeo SPer SReu SSta WGer
¶ ***beyerinckianum*** (V)	CEqu
bhutanense	MDun
– AC 119	NMun
– AC 124	NMun
– EGM 077	GGGa LMil
– KR 1753	LMil
'Big Punkin'	LMil
'Bijou de Ledeberg' (EA)	SSta

'Billy Budd'	SCog
'Binfield'	SLeo
'Birthday Girl'	COtt LMil SExb
'Birthday Greeting'	NMun
'Biscuit Box'	NMun SLeo
Biskra Group & cl.	GGGa
'Blaauw's Pink' (EA) 🏆	CHig CMac CWLN GQui GWht IOrc ISea LHyd LKna LMil MAsh MBar MBri MGos NMun SBod SCog SExb SLeo SPer SReu WFar
'Black Hawk' (EA)	CB&S
'Black Magic'	COtt CWri LMil SExb
'Black Satin'	COtt GGGa LMil
◆ Blaue Donau	See ***R.* 'Blue Danube'**
'Blazecheck'	LRHS MGos SCoo
'Blewbury' 🏆	LHyd LMil SCog SPer SReu SSta
'Blitz'	MBri SLeo
'Blizzard' (EA)	CTrh
'Blue Bell'	LKna
'Blue Boy'	LMil LRHS SMur
'Blue Carpet'	MAsh
'Blue Chip'	LHyd NMun SLeo
§ 'Blue Danube' (EA) 🏆	CMac CWLN EBee GRei GWht IOrc LHyd LKna LMil LRHS MBal MBar MBri MMor MRav NMun SBod SCog SExb SLeo SPer SReu SSta WBod WStI
Blue Diamond Group & cl.	CB&S CChe CMHG CWLN CWri GRei GWht LHyd LKna MAsh MBal MBar MDun MGos NHol NMun SBod SCog SHBN SLeo SReu SRms WBod
'Blue Gown'	LKna
'Blue Haze'	LHyd
'Blue Monday'	MBri WBod
'Blue Moon'	MBar
'Blue Mountain'	GDra MBal
'Blue Pacific'	SBod
'Blue Peter' 🏆	CB&S CHig CWri GGGa IHos IOrc LHyd LKna MAsh MBar MBri MDun MGos MMor NMun SCog SHBN SLeo SPer SReu SSta WStI
'Blue Pool'	LMil LRHS MBal MBar WBod
Blue Ribbon Group	CMHG CTrw CWLN ISea
'Blue River'	CWri
'Blue Silver'	GGGa NHol
'Blue Star'	CMHG LHyd MBri MLea NHed SExb SReu WAbe
'Blue Steel'	See ***R. impeditum* 'Blue Steel'**
Blue Tit Group	CB&S CSam CTre CWLN CWri EPot GDra ITim LHyd LKna MAsh MBal MBar MMor NHol NMun SHBN SLeo SReu SSta STre WBod
Bluebird Group & cl.	ECho ENot IOrc LKna MBal MBar MGos MMor SPer SRms WBod
Bluestone Group	MMor WBod
'Bluette'	GWht ISea MBal MLea NHed SLeo
¶ 'Blumiria'	GGGa
'Blushing Belle' (V)	CEqu
'Bob's Blue'	ISea SBar
'Bob's Choice' (V)	CEqu
'Boddaertianum' 🏆	LHyd SReu
bodinieri	NMun
R/USDA 59585/ R11281	
'Bodnant Yellow'	CSam
'Bonfire'	SReu

Bonito Group & cl.	SCog
'Bonnie Babe'	LMil
Bo-peep Group & cl. 🏆	CB&S CHig CSam LHyd LMil MBal MLea NMun SLeo
'Borderer'	SCog SLeo
'Boskoop Ostara'	MBri
'Boule de Neige'	MDun SBod SLeo
'Boulodes'	CWri
'Bounty'	GGGa
'Bouquet de Flore' (G) 🏆	LMil MBar MBri SPer SReu
Bow Bells Group & cl. 🏆	CSam CWLN CWri EBre GWht IOrc ISea LHyd LKna LMil MAsh MBal MBar MBri MDun MGos MLea MMor SBod SCog SExb SHBN SPer SReu SRms WStI
'Bow Street'	LHyd
brachyanthum	GGGa NMun SLeo
– subsp. ***hypolepidotum***	GGGa LMil MBal NMun SLeo
§ – L&S 2764	LMil
brachycarpum	GGGa MBal NMun SLeo
– subsp. ***brachycarpum*** Tigerstedtii Group	SReu
§ – subsp. ***fauriei***	NMun SLeo
– pink	NMun SLeo
– 'Roseum Dwarf'	GGGa NMun
brachysiphon	See ***R. maddenii*** subsp. ***maddenii***
bracteatum CH&M 2586	GGGa
'Brazier' (EA)	LHyd NMun SLeo
'Brazil' (K)	LKna SBid SExb SReu
Break of Day Group & cl.	SLeo
'Brentor'	SLeo
'Breslau' (EA)	SSta
'Brets Own'	NMun SLeo
Bric-a-brac Group & cl. 🏆	CB&S CSam CTrw LHyd MAsh MBal NMun SLeo SReu SRms
'Bride's Bouquet' (EA/d)	LRHS
'Bridesmaid' (O)	GWht SExb
'Brigadoon'	GGGa
'Bright Forecast' (K)	MBri SExb WGor
'Brigitte'	CDoC GGGa
'Brilliant' (EA)	EBee MGos
'Brilliant'	GGGa NHol
'Brilliant Blue'	MAsh
'Brilliant Crimson'	WLRN WWeb
'Brilliant Pink'	MAsh WLRN WWeb
'Britannia' 🏆	CB&S CSam CWLN CWri IOrc ISea LHyd LKna LNet MAsh MBal MBar MBri MGos MMor NMun NWea SBod SCog SExb SHBN SLeo SPer SReu SSta WWeb
'Brocade' 🏆	CSam LHyd LKna LMil MBri NMun SCog SLeo SPer
'Bronze Fire' (A)	MMor SReu
'Broughtonii'	CWri NMun SLeo
¶ 'Brown Eyes'	CWri
'Bruce Brechtbill'	CWri EHoe GGGa GWht LMil LRHS MAsh MBal MLea NHol SExb SReu SSta
'Bruce Hancock' (Ad)	LMil
'Buccaneer' (EA)	CWLN IOrc LHyd MBal SBod SCog SExb SPer
'Bud Flanagan'	LMil NMun
'Buketta'	GGGa MBri
bullatum	See ***R. edgeworthii***
¶ ***bulu*** C&V 9503	GGGa
'Bungo-nishiki' (EA/d)	CMac SRms WPat
bureaui 🏆	CAbP GGGa IOrc LHyd MBal MDun NMun SLeo SReu SSta
– 'Ardrishaig'	GGGa

¶ – C&H 7158	GGGa
¶ – CNW 1039	GGGa
¶ – CNW 957	GGGa
¶ – CNW 965	GGGa
¶ – CNW 969	GGGa
– EGM 141	LMil
– F 15609	NMun
I – 'Lem's Variety'	LMil SBar
– R 25439	NMun
¶ – SF 517	ISea
bureauoides	NMun
– P Cox 5039, 5066, 5076	GGGa
burmanicum ♀	GGGa LMil NMun SLeo
Bustard Group	SLeo
'Butter Brickle'	GGGa
'Butter Yellow'	SLeo
¶ 'Buttercup' (K)	MBar
'Buttered Popcorn'	LMil
'Butterfly'	LKna LRHS NMun SExb SLeo
'Buttermint'	CSam CWri GAri GGGa ISea LMil MAsh MBal MBri MLea NMun SBar SCog SHBN SLeo SReu SSta
'Buttersteep'	NMun SLeo
'Buttons and Bows' (K)	GGGa LMil
'Buzzard' (K)	LKna LMil
'C.I.S.'	NMun SExb SLeo
'Caerhays Lavender'	CB&S IOrc
caesium	GGGa
calendulaceum (A)	LHyd LMil MBal SLeo SReu
– yellow	LMil
Calfort Group & cl.	NMun
¶ ***caliginis*** (V)	CEqu
callimorphum	GGGa LMil NMun
– var. ***myiagrum*** F 21821A	NMun SLeo
– – KW 6962	NMun
calophytum ♀	CHEx CWri GGGa GWht LHyd LMil MDun NMun SLeo
– W A 4279	NMun
– W V 1523	NMun
calostrotum	LMil SIng SRms WAbe
– 'Gigha' ♀	CSam CWri GGGa LHyd LMil MOne NHar WAbe
§ – subsp. ***keleticum*** ♀	GAri GDra GWht LHyd MBal MBar MGos NHol SBod SRms WAbe WBod
– – Cox 6157	GGGa
– – F 19915	NHol
– – F 21756	NMun SLeo
– – R 58	LMil NHol
§ – – Radicans Group	GWht LHyd LMil MBar MBro MLea NHol SRms WAbe WBod WPat WPyg
– – – mound form	NHol
– – – R 59182	MLea
– R/USDA 03954/ R18453	GGGa
– subsp. ***riparium***	MBal
– – Calciphilum Group	GGGa GWht WAbe WBod
– – – Yu 19754	GGGa
§ – – Nitens Group	CBlo CMHG GGGa LMil NHed WAbe
– – Rock's form R 178	GGGa NHol
– SF 357	ISea
caloxanthum	See ***R. campylocarpum*** subsp. ***caloxanthum***
'Calsap'	GGGa
Calstocker Group	SLeo
Calsutch Group	SLeo
calvescens var. ***duseimatum***	NMun
camelliiflorum	GGGa LMil
– Rump 5696A	NMun

'Cameronian' (Ad)	LKna
campanulatum	COtt IOrc LHyd LKna LMil MDun NMun SLeo SReu
§ – subsp. ***aeruginosum***	GGGa LMil MDun NMun SReu
– – EGM 068	LMil
campanulatum album	NMun SLeo
– SS&W	NMun
campanulatum B 643	MBal
– BL&M 283	NMun
– Bu 249	GGGa
– Bu 258	GGGa
– DF 563	MBal
– 'Graham Thomas'	SReu
– 'Knap Hill' ♀	LHyd NMun SReu
– 'Roland Cooper'	NMun
– SS&W 9107	GGGa SLeo
– TSS 11	NMun SLeo
– TSS 7	SLeo
– 'Waxen Bell'	LHyd NMun SLeo
¶ ***camplyogynum***	SSpi
campylocarpum	CHig GGGa LHyd LMil NMun SCog SLeo SReu
– BM&W 150	MBal
§ – subsp. ***caloxanthum***	GGGa IOrc
– – forms	NMun SLeo
§ – – Telopeum Group	NMun
§ – – – KW 5718B	NMun SLeo
– subsp. ***campylocarpum*** Elatum Group	NMun
– DF 558	MBal
– LS&H 16495	NMun
– TSS 12	NMun
– TW 31	GWht
campylogynum 'Album'	See ***R. campylogynum*** var. ***leucanthum***
– apricot	LMil
– 'Beryl Taylor'	GGGa NMun
– 'Bodnant Red'	CHig GGGa LHyd LMil MDun NMun SLeo
– Castle Hill form	LMil SReu
– Charopoeum Group	GGGa GWht LMil MBal MBar MGos NHar NHol WAbe
– – 'Patricia'	GGGa MBal MBri WBod
– claret	ECho GGGa LMil MBal WAbe
§ – Cremastum Group	GGGa LHyd LMil NHol NMun SLeo
– – 'Cerise'	GGGa
– KW 21481	NHol
§ – var. ***leucanthum***	CHig GGGa LMil
– Myrtilloides Group	CB&S CHig CMHG CTrh CTrw EPot GAri GGGa GQui GWht IOrc LHyd LMil MBal MBri MDun NHar NMun SLeo SReu WAbe WBod
– – Farrer 1046	EPot GGGa NHar NHol
– pink	CTrh MBar WAbe
– plum	GGGa WAbe
– salmon pink	ECho EPot GGGa MBal NHar NHol WAbe WBod
camtschaticum	GAri GDra GGGa MBal MLea WAbe
– var. ***albiflorum***	GGGa
– red	GGGa
canadense (A)	GGGa MBal NHol NMun SLeo SReu
– f. ***albiflorum*** (A)	GGGa
– 'Deer Lake' (A)	SReu
'Canary'	LKna MBal NMun SLeo SReu
'Canby' (K)	LMil
§ × ***candelabrum***	NMun SLeo
'Cannon's Double' (K)	GGGa LMil
'Canzonetta' (EA)	MGos

capitatum	GGGa
'Captain Jack'	GGGa
'Caractacus'	IOrc MBar SLeo WFar
'Carat'	MBri SReu
cardiobasis	See ***R. orbiculare*** subsp. ***cardiobasis***
Carex Group & cl.	SCog
¶ 'Carillon Bells'	CEqu
Carita Group	LKna SReu
'Carita Golden Dream' 🏆	LKna LMil NMun SLeo
'Carita Inchmery' 🏆	LHyd LKna NMun SCog SLeo
'Carmen' 🏆	CSam EPot GDra GGGa GRei GWht ISea LHyd LKna LMil MBal MBar MBri MDun MLea MMor NHar NHol NMun NWea SBod SHBN SLeo SReu SRms WBod
carneum	GGGa
'Caroline Allbrook' 🏆	CHig CSam CWri GGGa ISea LHyd LMil MAsh MBri MGos MOne NHed NHol NMun SCog SExb SLeo SReu
'Caroline de Zoete'	LHyd
carolinianum	See ***R. minus*** var. ***minus* Carolinianum Group**
'Cary Ann'	CDoC CSam CWri GCHN GRei ISea LMil MAsh MBal MLea NMun SBid SLeo SReu
'Cassley' (Vs)	LMil
catacosmum	GGGa SLeo
– R 11185	SLeo
catawbiense	CHig GGGa LHyd NMun SLeo
'Catawbiense Album'	ECho IOrc
'Catawbiense Boursault'	IOrc
'Catawbiense Grandiflorum'	IOrc LRHS
'Catherine Hopwood'	NMun SLeo
caucasicum	LHyd MBal
– ex AC&H	GGGa NMun SLeo
'Caucasicum Pictum'	GGGa LHyd LMil MBri
'Cayenne' (EA)	SExb
'Cecile' (K) 🏆	CB&S GWht LHyd LKna LMil MAsh MBal MBar MBri MGos MLea NMun SExb SPer SReu SSpi
'Celestial' (EA)	CMac
'Centennial'	See ***R.* 'Washington State Centennial'**
'Centennial Celebration'	GGGa IOrc MLea
cephalanthum	GGGa LMil
– subsp. ***cephalanthum***	MBal
– – Crebreflorum Group	GAri GGGa LMil
– – – Week's form	GDra
– subsp. ***platyphyllum***	GGGa
– SBEC 0751	GGGa
cerasinum	CDoC GGGa LMil NMun SLeo
¶ – C&V 9504	GGGa
– 'Cherry Brandy'	LHyd NMun
– 'Coals of Fire'	NMun SLeo
– deep pink	NMun SLeo
– × ***forrestii*** subsp. ***forrestii***	MBal
– KW 11011	NMun
– KW 5830	NMun SLeo
– KW 6923	NMun
– KW 8258	NMun
'Cetewayo'	SLeo SReu
chaetomallum	See ***R. haematodes*** subsp. ***chaetomallum***
'Chaffinch' (K)	LKna
chamaethomsonii	GGGa GWht LMil MBal NHar NMun SLeo
– var. ***chamaethauma*** F 21768	LMil
– – KW 5847	LMil
– var. ***chamaethomsonii*** Exbury form L&S	GGGa
– – pink forms L&S	GGGa
– – Rock form	GGGa
'Chameleon' (EA)	IOrc
chameunum	See ***R. saluenense*** subsp. ***chameunum***
§ 'Champagne' 🏆	CWri IOrc LHyd LMil MGos NMun SCog SLeo SReu
championiae	GGGa
'Chanel' (Vs)	MMor SReu SSta
'Chanticleer' (EA)	LRHS SCog SExb
charitopes	GGGa LMil MBal MBri NMun SLeo
¶ – F 25570	SReu
§ – subsp. ***tsangpoense***	GGGa GQui LMil NHol
'Charlotte Currie'	SLeo
'Charlotte de Rothschild' 🏆	LMil
* 'Charlotte de Rothschild' (A)	SExb
Charmaine Group & cl.	CSam EPot GGGa MBal MDun NHol WBod
¶ 'Charme La'	GGGa
'Charming Valentino' (V)	CEqu
chasmanthum	See ***R. augustinii*** subsp. ***chasmanthum***
'Cheer'	COtt CWri EHoe IOrc LMil MAsh MBal MBar MBri SExb SSta WGor
'Cheerful Giant' (K)	GGGa LMil MLea
'Chelsea Reach' (K/d)	LKna SExb
'Chelsea Seventy'	COtt IHos MAsh MBal NHol NMun SCog SLeo SReu
'Chenille' (K/d)	LKna
'Chetco' (K)	GGGa LMil
'Chevalier Felix de Sauvage' 🏆	CWri LMil MGos NMun SBod SLeo SReu SSta
'Cheyenne'	SLeo
'Chicago' (M)	LKna
'Chiffchaff'	EPot LHyd MLea SLeo SPer WAbe
'Chikor'	CSam CWLN EPot GDra GGGa GWht LKna MAsh MBal MBar MBri MDun MGos MLea MMor NFla NHar NHol NMun NRoo SExb SLeo SReu SRms WBod WSHC
China Group & cl.	LKna SReu
'China A'	LKna
'Chinchilla' (EA)	GQui GWht MBri
'Chink'	CB&S CSam LHyd MAsh MBal MBar NMun SCog SExb SLeo SPer WBod
'Chionoides'	GGGa IOrc LKna SBid
'Chipmunk' (E/d)	GWht
'Chippewa' (EA)	GGGa GWht LMil MBri
chlorops	NMun SLeo
'Chocolate Ice' (K/d)	LKna
'Chopin' (EA)	WBod
'Choremia' 🏆	CTrw SCog SReu
'Chorister' (K)	LKna
christii (V)	CEqu
¶ – Sandham 61/86 (V)	GGGa
'Christina' (EA/d)	CMac GDTE GWht MBri MMor SPer WBod WGwG
'Christmas Cheer' (EA)	See ***R.* 'Ima-shojo'**

'Christmas Cheer'	CDoC CHig CWLN GGGa GWht IOrc ISea LHyd LKna LMil MBri MGos MLea NMun SCog SExb SHBN SLeo SPer SReu
'Christobel Maude'	LHyd
§ 'Christopher Wren' (K)	ELan MBal
chrysanthum	See ***R. aureum***
chryseum	See ***R. rupicola*** var. ***chryseum***
chrysodoron	GGGa LMil NMun
chrysomanicum	See **R. Chrysomanicum Group & cl.**
§ Chrysomanicum Group & cl. 🏆	NMun SLeo
ciliatum 🏆	CB&S CHig CSam EPot GGGa GWht IOrc LHyd MBal NMun
– 'Multiflorum'	See **R. 'Multiflorum'**
♦ ***ciliicalyx*** subsp. ***lyi***	See ***R. lyi***
¶ – SF 535	ISea
Cilpinense Group 🏆	CB&S CHig CSam CWri EHoe GGGa GWht IOrc ISea LHyd LKna LMil MAsh MBal MBar MDun NFla NHol NMun SCog SExb SLeo SPer SReu WAbe WBod
cinnabarinum	LMil MBal NMun SLeo
– B 652	MBal
– BL&M 234	LMil
– Bu 268	GGGa
– 'Caerhays Lawrence'	MBal NMun SLeo
– 'Caerhays Philip'	MBal
– subsp. ***cinnabarinum*** 'Aestivale'	LMil MDun
– – Blandfordiiflorum Group	GGGa MBal MDun NMun SLeo
I – – 'Mount Everest'	SLeo
– – 'Nepal'	LHyd LMil SLeo
– – Roylei Group	GGGa LHyd LMil MBal MDun MLea NMun SExb SLeo SReu
– – – KW 8239	NMun
– – 'Vin Rosé'	LMil
§ – 'Conroy' 🏆	GGGa LHyd LMil MBal MDun SPer SReu
– LS&H 21283	NMun
– SHE 638	NMun
§ – subsp. ***tamaense***	GGGa NMun SLeo
– – KW 21003	NMun
– – KW 21021	GGGa NMun
§ – subsp. ***xanthocodon*** 🏆	ISea LMil MBal NMun SCog SExb SLeo SReu
§ – – Concatenans Group	CB&S CSam GGGa NMun SCog SLeo WBod
¶ – – – 'Amber'	LMil
¶ – – – C&V 9523	GGGa
– – – KW 5874	LMil LRHS
– – – LS&T 6560	NMun SLeo
– – – mustard form	NMun SLeo
– – 'Daffodilly'	NMun SLeo
– – EGM 088	LMil
– – forms	NMun SLeo
– – Purpurellum Group	GGGa LMil MDun NMun SLeo
Cinnkeys Group & cl.	GGGa LMil
Cinzan Group	SReu
citriniflorum	NMun
– var. ***citriniflorum***	LMil
– var. ***horaeum***	NMun
– – F 21850	GGGa LMil
– – F 25901	GGGa LMil NMun
– R 108	GGGa
'Clarissa' (EA/d)	IOrc
'Claydian Variegated'	GGGa
clementinae	GGGa LHyd NMun SLeo SReu

– F 25705	LMil NMun SLeo
– F 25917	LMil
'Cliff Garland'	CDoC GQui LMil
Clio Group	NMun SLeo
'Coccineum Speciosum' (G) 🏆	GGGa IOrc LHyd LMil MBar SReu SSta
'Cockade' (EA)	LKna
'Cockatoo' (K)	LKna
coelicum F 21830	SLeo
¶ – F 25625	GGGa
coeloneuron	GGGa MDun
– EGM 108	LMil
'Colin Kenrick' (K/d)	LKna
collettianum H&W 8975	GGGa
'Colonel Coen'	CWri LMil MBal SHBN
Colonel Rogers Group	LHyd NMun SLeo SReu
Comely Group	LHyd NMun SLeo
complexum F 15392	GGGa
– SSNY 296	GGGa
'Comte de Gomer'	CB&S
concatenans	See ***R. cinnabarinum*** subsp. ***xanthocodon*** **Concatenans Group**
concinnum	CHig CTrw LHyd LMil MBal NMun SLeo WAbe
– Benthamianum Group	NMun
– C 5011, 5085	GGGa
– Pseudoyanthinum Group 🏆	GGGa LMil NMun SLeo
'Concorde'	CHig LHyd MBri MMor SCog
'Congo'	See **R. 'Robin Hill Congo'**
'Conroy'	See ***R. cinnabarinum*** **'Conroy'**
'Consolini's Windmill'	LMil
'Constable'	LHyd NMun SLeo
'Constant Nymph'	LKna
'Contina'	GGGa
Conyan Group	LHyd
cookeanum	See ***R. sikangense*** **Cookeanum Group**
'Cora Grant' (EA)	SExb
'Coral Beauty'	CWLN
'Coral Reef'	NMun SLeo SReu
'Coral Sea' (EA)	SReu
'Coral Velvet'	COtt
coriaceum	GGGa LMil NMun SLeo
– F 16364	NMun
– F 21843	NMun
– P Cox 6531	GGGa
– R 120	NMun
– SF 348	ISea
'Corneille' (G/d) 🏆	LKna LMil SBar SBid SPer SReu
'Cornish Cracker'	NMun SLeo
Cornish Cross Group	LHyd NMun SLeo SReu
Cornish Early Red Group	See **R. Smithii Group**
'Cornish Red'	See **R. Smithii Group**
Cornubia Group	NMun SLeo
'Corona' 🏆	LKna SCog
'Coronation Day'	SReu
'Coronation Lady' (K)	EBee LKna MBri MMor
'Corringe' (K) 🏆	SExb
'Corry Koster'	LKna
coryanum	GGGa NMun SLeo
– 'Chelsea Chimes' ex KW 6311	GGGa LMil
'Cosmopolitan'	CDoC CWri GGGa IOrc LMil MGos WLRN
'Costa del Sol'	NMun SLeo
'Countess of Athlone'	IOrc LKna
'Countess of Derby'	IOrc SReu
'Countess of Haddington' 🏆	CB&S ERea ISea LMil NMun SLeo

'County of York'	See ***R.*** **'Catalode'**
cowanianum	GGGa
Cowslip Group	CSam LHyd LKna LMil MBal MBar MBri MDun MGos NHol NMun SCog SHBN SLeo SReu
coxianum C&H 475B	GGGa
¶ 'Craig Faragher' (V)	CEqu
'Cranbourne'	SReu
'Crane'	GGGa GQui
crassum	See ***R. maddenii*** subsp. ***crassum***
'Cream Crest'	GQui ISea MDun SHBN SLeo
'Cream Glory'	SCog SReu
'Creamy Chiffon'	CSam CWri GCHN GGGa LHyd MBal MGos MLea MOne SLeo SReu SSta
§ 'Creeping Jenny' 🏆	GGGa LHyd MAsh MBal MBar MLea NHol SCog WBod
cremastum	See ***R. campylogynum*** **Cremastum Group**
§ 'Crest' 🏆	CSam CWri GGGa IOrc ISea LHyd LKna LMil MAsh MBal MGos MLea SCog SHBN SLeo SPer SReu SSta
'Crete'	COtt LMil MAsh MDun MGos SReu
'Crimson Glory'	See ***R.*** **'Natalie Coe Vitetti'**
'Crimson Pippin'	GGGa LMil
crinigerum	GGGa LMil NMun SLeo
– var. ***crinigerum*** R 100	NMun
– – R 38	NMun
– var. ***euadenium***	NMun
– KW 7123	NMun
– KW 8164	NMun
'Crinoline' (K)	SCog SPer WWeb
Crossbill Group	CB&S MBal SLeo
* ***crossium***	SReu
'Crosswater Red'	LMil
'Crowthorne'	SCog
cruttwellii (V)	GGGa
cubittii	See ***R. veitchianum*** **Cubittii Group**
cucullatum	See ***R. roxieanum*** var. ***cucullatum***
§ ***cumberlandense*** (A)	GGGa LMil
¶ – 'Sunlight' (A)	LMil
cuneatum	GGGa LMil NMun
– F 27119*	NMun SLeo
– R 11392	NMun
§ – Ravum Group	CHig
'Cunningham's Blush'	GAri GGGa SHBN
'Cunningham's Sulphur'	See ***R. caucasicum*** **'Cunningham's Sulphur'**
'Cunningham's White'	CB&S CHig CPMA CSam CWri EHoe GGGa GRei IOrc LKna LMil MAsh MBar MBri MGos MMor NMun SExb SLeo SPer SReu WStI WWeb
'Cupcake'	GGGa
'Curlew' 🏆	Widely available
'Cutie'	SLeo
cyanocarpum	GGGa LMil MDun NMun SLeo
– Bu 294	GGGa
– EN 2458	GGGa
'Cynthia' 🏆	CB&S CHig CWri GGGa IOrc ISea LHyd LKna LMil MAsh MBal MBar MBri MGos MMor NMun NWea SBod SHBN SLeo SPer SReu SSta
'Dagmar'	GGGa
'Daimio' (EA)	SPer
¶ 'Dainty Drops' (V)	CEqu
'Dairymaid'	LHyd LKna NMun SLeo SReu
dalhousieae	GGGa SLeo
§ – var. ***rhabdotum*** 🏆	GGGa SLeo
Damaris Group	NMun SLeo
'Damaris Logan'	See ***R.*** **'Logan Damaris'**
Damozel Group & cl.	SCog SExb WStI
'Dandy'	LKna
Dante Group	SLeo
'Daphne'	SLeo
'Daphne Jewiss'	SReu
'Daphne Magor'	SLeo
'Daphnoides'	MLea SBar
'Dartmoor Dawn'	MBal
'Dartmoor Rose'	GGGa
dasycladum	See ***R. selense*** subsp. ***dasycladum***
dasypetalum	ECho MBal MBar
dauricum	EPot LMil MBal SLeo WBod
– 'Album'	See ***R. dauricum*** **'Hokkaido'**
– 'Arctic Pearl'	GGGa
– 'Dark St Andrews'	GGGa
§ – 'Hokkaido'	GAri LHyd
¶ – 'Hokkaido' x ***leucaspis***	GGGa
– 'Midwinter' 🏆	GGGa LHyd LMil MBri SLeo
– 'Nanum'	MBal
– 'Suzuki'	SLeo
'David' 🏆	GGGa LHyd LKna NMun SLeo SReu
'David Grant'	GDra
davidsonianum 🏆	CB&S CTrw GGGa IOrc ISea LHyd LMil MBal MMor NMun SCog SLeo SPer SSta WBod
– Bodnant Form	LMil
– C 5007, 5091	GGGa
¶ – C 7023	GGGa
– 'Caerhays Pink'	GGGa
– 'Ruth Lyons'	LMil
'Daviesii' (G) 🏆	CB&S CWLN GGGa LHyd LKna LMil MAsh MBal MBri MLea MMor SExb SPer SReu SSpi WWat WWeb
'Dawn's Delight'	NMun
* 'Day Dawn'	SReu
Day Dream Group & cl. 🏆	IOrc LHyd LKna SCog SReu
¶ 'Daybreak' (K)	GQui
N 'Daybreak' (EA/d)	See ***R.*** **'Kirin'**
'Dayspring' (EA)	LMil
N 'Debutante'	GRei GWht IHos MMor
decorum	COtt IOrc LHyd LMil NMun SLeo SReu
¶ – CNW 582	ISea
– 'Cox's Uranium Green'	SReu
§ – subsp. ***diaprepes***	CWri IOrc NMun
– – 'Gargantua'	NMun SLeo SReu
– forms	GGGa NMun
¶ – x hybrid	CTrC
– R 54021*	NMun
– SBEC 1060	NMun
– SBEC 181	NMun
– SBEC 439	NMun
– SF 252	ISea
– TW 384	GWht
– TW 388	GWht
degronianum	GGGa NMun SReu
§ – subsp. ***degronianum***	NMun SLeo
– – 'Gerald Loder'	GGGa LHyd
§ – subsp. ***heptamerum***	GGGa NMun SLeo
– – 'Ho Emma'	LMil
– – var. ***macranthum***	LMil
– 'Metternianum'	See ***R. degronianum*** subsp. ***heptamerum*** var. ***kyomaruense***
delavayi var. ***peramoenum***	See ***R. arboreum*** subsp. ***delavayi*** var. ***peramoenum***

'Delicatissimum' (O) ♀	GGGa GQui LHyd LRHS MBri SExb WWeb
dendricola KW 20981	GGGa
dendrocharis	GGGa
¶ – C 5016	GGGa
¶ – CC&H 4012	GGGa
'Denny's Rose' (A)	MMor
¶ 'Denny's Scarlet'	SReu
'Denny's White'	SReu
¶ ***denudatum*** C 7012	GGGa
¶ – C 7118	GGGa
'Desert Orchid'	LHyd
'Desert Pink' (K)	LKna
desquamatum	See ***R. rubiginosum*** **Desquamatum Group**
x ***detonsum***	NMun SLeo
'Dexter's Spice'	LMil
'Diabolo' (K)	LKna
Diamant Group (EA)	CDoC GAri GGGa
– lilac (EA)	GGGa MBri
– pink (EA)	ECho GGGa MGos
§ – purple (EA)	ECho MGos
§ – red (EA)	WAbe
– rosy red (EA)	COtt ECho GAri GGGa GWht MBri
– white (EA)	ECho WAbe
◆ 'Diamant Purpur'	See ***R.*** **Diamant Group purple**
◆ 'Diamant Rot'	See ***R.*** **Diamant Group red**
'Diana Pearson'	LHyd NMun SLeo
'Diane'	LKna NMun SLeo
◆ ***diaprepes***	See ***R. decorum*** subsp. ***diaprepes***
– Farrer 979	NMun SLeo
dichroanthum	CHig GGGa IOrc MBal NMun SCog SLeo SReu
§ – subsp. ***apodectum***	GGGa GWht LMil MDun NMun SLeo
– F 27137	NMun
– F 6781	NMun
– forms	NMun
– SBEC 0545	GGGa
– SBEC 0601	GGGa
§ – subsp. ***scyphocalyx***	GGGa LMil MBal NMun SLeo
¶ – – F 24546	GGGa
¶ – – F 27115	GGGa
¶ – – Farrer 1024	GGGa
dictyotum	See ***R. traillianum*** var. ***dictyotum***
didymum	See ***R. sanguineum*** subsp. ***didymum***
'Dietrich'	SReu SSta
¶ ***dignabile*** C&V 9569	GGGa
dimitrum	CWri LMil
'Diny Dee'	MBal MGos SSta
'Diorama' (Vs)	CBlo MBri MMor SReu SSta
diphrocalyx	NMun
discolor	See ***R. fortunei*** subsp. ***discolor***
'Doc' ♀	CB&S GRei IOrc ISea LMil MAsh MBal MBar MGos MMor NHed NMun SCog SLeo SReu WStI
'Doctor Arnold W. Endtz'	CWri IOrc MAsh MBri MMor NMun SLeo
'Doctor Ernst Schäle'	GGGa MAsh
'Doctor H.C. Dresselhuys'	CWLN IOrc SHBN
'Doctor M. Oosthoek' (M) ♀	ECho MMor SReu
'Doctor Stocker'	NMun SLeo
'Doctor Tjebbes'	ISea
'Doctor V.H. Rutgers'	IOrc MGos
'Doncaster'	GRei IOrc LKna MAsh MGos NHol NMun NWea SBod SCog SHBN SLeo
'Dopey' ♀	CDoC CSam CWri GGGa GRei GWht IHos IOrc ISea LHyd LMil MAsh MBal MBar MBri MDun MLea MMor NHed NHol NMun SCog SExb SHBN SLeo SPer SReu WAbe WWeb
'Dora Amateis' ♀	COtt CSam CWLN GGGa ISea LHyd LMil MAsh MBal MBar MBri MGos MLea MMor NHar NHol NMun SBid SCog SLeo SPer SReu
Dormouse Group	CDoC LMil
'Dorothea'	SLeo
'Dorothy Amateis'	SSta
'Dorothy Corston' (K)	LKna
'Dorothy Hayden' (EA)	LHyd
doshongense	See ***R. aganniphum*** var. ***aganniphum*** **Doshongense Group**
'Double Beauty' (EA/d)	CTrh IOrc LKna MMor SBod SCog SPer SReu SSta WGwG
'Double Damask' (K/d) ♀	LHyd LKna
'Double Date'	GGGa
'Double Delight' (K/d)	GGGa MLea
¶ 'Doubloons'	NMun
Dragonfly Group	SLeo SReu
'Drake's Mountain'	ECho MBar
'Dreamland'	COtt CWri LHyd LMil MAsh MBri MMor SBid SExb SReu
'Driven Snow' (EA)	SBod
drumonium	See ***R. telmateium***
¶ 'Drury Lane'	GQui
dryophyllum Balfour & Forrest	See ***R. phaeochrysum*** var. ***phaeochrysum***
– hort.	See ***R. phaeochrysum*** var. ***levistratum***
¶ 'Duchess of Rothesay'	NMun
'Duchess of Teck'	SReu
'Dusky Dawn'	NMun
'Dusky Orange'	SReu
'Dusty Miller'	CAbP CDoC COtt IHos ISea LHyd MBal MBar MGos MLea NHed SCog SExb SHBN SLeo WAbe
'Earl of Athlone'	LHyd SReu
'Earl of Donoughmore' ♀	LHyd LKna MMor SReu SSta
'Early Beni' (EA)	CWLN LHyd
Early Brilliant Group	LKna
'Eastern Fire'	See ***R. kaempferi*** **'Eastern Fire'**
'Ebony Pearl'	GGGa
eclecteum	LHyd LMil NMun SLeo
– var. ***bellatulum***	NMun
– – R 110*	NMun
– 'Kingdon Come'	NMun
– P Cox 6054	GGGa
– R 23512	NMun
– 'Rowallane Yellow'	NMun
'Eddy' (EA)	LKna NMun SExb SLeo
edgarianum	LMil
§ ***edgeworthii*** ♀	GGGa LHyd MBal NMun SLeo WBod
– forms	GGGa WBod
– x ***leucaspis***	CB&S
– x ***moupinense***	CB&S GGGa
– SF 607	ISea
– Yu 17431*	LMil
Edmondii Group	LHyd
'Edna Bee' (EA)	GQui LMil

'Egret' ♀	CDoC CHig CSam CTrh EPot GAri GGGa GWht ITim MAsh MBal MBar MBri MGos MLea NHar NHol SBid SExb SLeo SPer SSta WAbe WGer
'Ehrengold'	MBri
'Eider'	COtt GCHN GGGa ISea MAsh MBal NMun SCog SLeo SReu WAbe
'Eileen'	LMil SReu
'El Alamein'	SLeo
'El Camino'	COtt CWri MAsh MBal MLea NMun SHBN SLeo WWeb
'El Greco'	NMun SLeo
¶ Eldorado Group	GQui
Eleanore Group & cl.	IOrc
Electra Group & cl.	See ***R. augustinii* Electra Group & cl.**
elegantulum	GGGa LHyd LMil MDun NMun SLeo
'Elfenbein'	SCog
¶ 'Elfin Gold'	GGGa SReu
'Elisabeth Hobbie' ♀	GDra GGGa LKna LMil MBal MBar MGos SCog
N 'Elizabeth' (EA)	IOrc MGos SCog
'Elizabeth de Rothschild'	LMil NMun
'Elizabeth Gable' (EA)	GWht
Elizabeth Group	CB&S CMHG CSam CTrw CWLN CWri EBee GDra GGGa GWht IOrc LHyd LKna LMil MAsh MBal MBar MGos MMor NHol NMun NWea SBod SCog SHBN SLeo SPer SReu WBod
'Elizabeth Jenny'	See ***R.* 'Creeping Jenny'**
'Elizabeth Lockhart'	GGGa GQui MBal MBar MGos MLea
'Elizabeth of Glamis'	GGGa
'Elizabeth Red Foliage'	GGGa MAsh MDun NHol
elliottii	GGGa NMun SLeo SReu
– KW 7725	NMun
Elsae Group & cl.	NMun SLeo SReu
'Else Frye'	GGGa
'Elsie Lee' (EA)	CGre GGGa LMil MAsh SBod SCog SReu SSta
'Elsie Pratt' (K)	MBar MBri MMor SReu SSta
'Elsie Straver'	CWri MBal NHol SExb SHBN SReu
¶ 'Elsie Watson'	LMil
'Elspeth'	LHyd LKna
§ 'Emasculum' ♀	CGre COtt CSam LKna SPer SReu
¶ 'Ember Glow'	NMun
¶ Emerald Isle Group	SReu
'Empire Day'	LKna
'Ems'	EPot
'Enborne'	NMun SLeo
'Endre Ostbo'	SLeo
'English Roseum'	IOrc
Erato	GGGa LMil
eriogynum	See ***R. facetum***
eritimum subsp. ***heptamerum***	See ***R. anthosphaerum* Heptamerum Group**
'Ernest Inman'	LHyd NMun SLeo
erosum	NMun SLeo
erubescens	See ***R. oreodoxa*** var. ***fargesii* Erubescens Group**
§ × ***erythrocalyx*** Panteumorphum Group	NMun SLeo
N 'Esmeralda'	CMac SBod
Ethel Group & cl.	CHig WBod
'Etta Burrows'	CWri GGGa MBal MLea
'Euan Cox'	GGGa MBal NHar SCog
euchaites	See ***R. neriiflorum*** subsp. ***neriiflorum* Euchaites Group**
euchroum	NMun
eudoxum	GGGa NMun
¶ – C 6036	GGGa
– var. ***eudoxum*** R 10950	NMun
– – R 6C	NMun
– KW 5879	NMun
'Eunice Updike' (EA)	LHyd
'Europa'	SReu
eurysiphon	NMun
– KW 21557*	NMun
'Eva Goude' (K)	LKna
'Evening Fragrance' (A)	SReu
'Evening Glow'	NHol
'Evensong' (EA)	LKna
'Everbloom' (EA)	NMun SCog
'Everest' (EA)	EBee GWht LHyd MBri WBod
'Everestianum'	IOrc LKna MBar SLeo SSta
exasperatum	NMun SLeo
– KW 8250	GGGa
'Exbury Albatross'	LKna
'Exbury Fabia'	SReu
'Exbury May Day'	SReu
'Exbury White' (K)	EPfP GQui GWht MAsh SExb WWeb
excellens AC 146	GGGa
– SF 92074	ISea
– SF 92079	ISea
– SF 92303	ISea
eximium	See ***R. falconeri*** subsp. ***eximium***
¶ ***exquisitum***	ISea
'Exquisitum' (O) ♀	EPfP GGGa LMil MBri SReu SSpi WWeb
F H 8	LMil
F.C. Puddle Group & cl.	SLeo
§ ***faberi***	GGGa MDun NMun SLeo
– EGM 111	LMil
§ – subsp. ***prattii***	CWri LMil NMun SLeo
– – EGM 147	LMil
Fabia Group & cl. ♀	EHoe GCHN GGGa IOrc LHyd LKna LMil MDun NMun SCog SLeo SSpi
§ 'Fabia Tangerine'	COtt MBal MLea SReu SRms WBod
§ ***facetum***	GGGa LMil NMun SLeo
– CLD 1522	MDun
– F 1022	NMun
– SF 315	ISea
– TW 360	GWht
'Faggetter's Favourite' ♀	LKna LMil MMor NMun SLeo SReu SSta
Fairy Light Group	ISea LMil SRms
* 'Fairy Mary'	GGGa
falconeri ♀	CHEx COtt GGGa GWht IOrc ISea LHyd LMil MDun NMun SArc SLeo SPer SReu
– BM&W 66	MBal
– Cox's species	SReu
– DF 526	MBal
– EGM 055	LMil
§ – subsp. ***eximium***	GGGa LMil
'Faltho'	SLeo
'Fanny'	See ***R.* 'Pucella'**
'Fantastica'	CWri EHoe GGGa LHyd LMil MAsh SReu
fargesii	See ***R. oreodoxa*** var. ***fargesii***
'Fashion'	CChe
fastigiatum ♀	GDra LMil MBal MBar NMen NMun SLeo
– 'Blue Steel'	See ***R. impeditum* 'Blue Steel'**

I – 'Harry White'	LMil
– pink	GGGa LMil
– SBEC 0804/4869	GGGa NHol
'Fastuosum Flore Pleno' (d) ♀	CHig CWri EHoe GGGa IOrc ISea LHyd LKna LMil MBal MBar MBri MGos MMor NMun NWea SCog SLeo SPer SReu SSta
faucium	GGGa NMun SLeo
¶ – C&V 9508	GGGa
– KW 5732	NMun
§ – KW 6401	NMun
¶ 'Faulk Lemon'	CHig
fauriei	See ***R. brachycarpum*** subsp. ***fauriei***
'Favorite' (EA)	CMac CTrw GWht IOrc LHyd LKna MBri MMor NMun SLeo SSta
'Fedora' (EA) ♀	CB&S GWht LHyd LKna MRav SPer
'Fernanda Sarmento'	SReu
ferrugineum	CHig GGGa LKna LMil MBal MBar MGos NMun SLeo SReu
– Ascreavie form	NHol
* ***ferrugineum compactum***	ECho
ferrugineum Glenarn form	NHol
* – 'Hill of Tarvit'	NHol
'Festive'	LHyd
fictolacteum	See ***R. rex*** subsp. ***fictolacteum***
'Fidelio' (EA)	SCog
fimbriatum	See ***R. hippophaeoides*** var. ***hippophaeoides* Fimbriatum Group**
Fire Bird Group	LHyd SCog SLeo
'Fireball' (K)	CB&S CTri GGGa GRei LHyd LMil MLea SExb SPer WWeb
'Fireball'	WGwG
Firedrake Group	CWri SReu
'Firefly' (K)	LMil SExb
'Firefly' (EA)	See ***R.* 'Hexe'**
'Fireglow'	WFar
'Fireman Jeff'	MBal SExb SPer
'Flamenco Dancer' (V)	ERea
¶ 'Flaming Bronze'	SReu
'Flaming June' (K)	LKna
Flashlight Group	SLeo
§ Flava Group & cl.	GGGa LMil MAsh MBar MGos NHed SSta
'Flava Glendoick'	GGGa
flavidum	GGGa MBal SSta
– 'Album'	LMil SBod SExb
– C 5064	MDun
– P Cox 6143	GGGa
fletcherianum	MBal NMun WAbe
– R 22302	NMun SLeo
– 'Yellow Bunting'	GGGa NMun
¶ ***fleuryi*** KR 3286	GGGa
§ ***flinckii***	GGGa GWht LMil MDun NMun
– CH&M 3080	GGGa
floccigerum	GGGa LHyd LMil NMun SLeo
– bicolored	NMun
– F 20305	NMun SLeo
– R 10	NMun
– R/USDA 03966/ R18465	NMun
'Floradora' (M)	SReu
'Flora's Garden'	CWLN
'Flora's Green'	CWLN
'Florence Archer'	SSta
'Floriade'	LHyd LKna
floribundum	LMil NMun SLeo
– P. Cox 5090	GGGa
'Florida' (EA/d) ♀	CMac GWht LKna LMil MAsh SBod SCog SPer SSta WBod WFar WGwG
formosanum	GGGa
formosum ♀	CB&S CGre ERea GGGa GQui NMun
§ – var. ***formosum*** Iteaphyllum Group	GGGa SLeo
– var. ***inaequale*** C&H 301	GGGa GWht
– 'Khasia'	GGGa
forrestii	GGGa NMun
– subsp. ***forrestii*** F 21723	NMun
– – LS&T 5582	NMun
– – Repens Group	GGGa GWht LMil MBal NHar NMun SLeo WBod
– Tumescens Group	GGGa NHar NHol NMun SLeo
¶ – – C&V 9517	GGGa
Fortorb Group	NMun SLeo
Fortune Group & cl.	NMun SLeo
Fortune Seedling Group	LKna
fortunei	COtt GGGa IOrc LHyd LMil MDun NMun SLeo SReu SSpi
§ – subsp. ***discolor*** ♀	GGGa LMil NMun SLeo
§ – – Houlstonii Group	LMil NMun SLeo
– 'Foxy'	NMun SLeo
– 'Mrs Butler'	See ***R. fortunei* 'Sir Charles Butler'**
§ – 'Sir Charles Butler'	LMil
'Fox Hunter'	LKna
¶ ***fragariiflorum*** LS&E 15828	GGGa
'Fragrantissimum' ♀	CB&S CGre CTre CTrw ELan ERea GGGa IOrc ISea LHyd LMil MBal MDun MRav SReu
'Francis B. Hayes'	IOrc
Francis Hanger (Reuthe's) Group	NMun SLeo SReu
'Frank Baum'	CBlo CWri MBal NMun SLeo SReu SSta
'Frank Galsworthy' ♀	LKna LMil SExb SLeo SReu SSta
'Fred Peste'	CAbP GGGa IOrc LMil MDun MLea MMor SCog SReu SSpi
'Fred Rose'	SLeo
'Fred Wynniatt' ♀	CWri ISea LMil NMun
◆ 'Fred Wynniatt Stanway'	See ***R.* 'Stanway'**
'Freya' (R/d)	LMil
'Frigate'	WLRN
'Frilled Petticoats'	MLea NMun SLeo SReu
'Frills' (K/d)	LHyd
'Frilly Lemon' (K/d)	LMil
'Frome' (K)	LKna
'Frontier'	LMil
'Frosthexe'	GGGa
'Fudetsukasi'	SLeo
'Fuju-kaku-no-matsu'	MGos
'Fuko-hiko' (EA)	NMun SLeo
'Fulbrook'	LHyd
'Fulgarb'	SLeo
fulgens	GGGa LHyd LMil NMun SLeo SReu
– DF 543	MBal
fulvum ♀	GGGa GWht IOrc LHyd LMil MDun NMun SExb SLeo SReu SSta
– F 24110	SLeo
– Fulvoides Group	GGGa NMun
¶ – – C 6026	GGGa
¶ – – C 6532	GGGa
– R 143	NMun
– R 180	NMun
– TW 379	GWht

'Furnivall's Daughter' 🏆	CSam CWri GGGa IOrc LHyd LKna LMil MBal MBri MGos MMor NMun SExb SLeo SPer SReu SSta
Fusilier Group & cl. 🏆	LHyd SReu
'Gabriele' (EA)	GQui SSpi
'Gabrielle Hill' (EA)	COtt CWLN SCog
'Gaiety' (EA)	GGGa GWht IOrc LMil SCog
'Galactic'	NMun SLeo
galactinum	GGGa LMil NMun SLeo
– CC&H 4023	GGGa
– EN 3537	GGGa
– W A 4254	NMun
'Galathea' (EA)	GGGa GWht LMil
'Gallipoli' (K)	CBlo
'Garden State Glow' (EA/d)	SBod SCog
'Gartendirektor Glocker'	CSam CWri EHic GGGa LMil SSta WWeb
'Gartendirektor Rieger'	GGGa LMil MBri NHol SReu
¶ 'Gauche'	GQui
¶ 'Gaugin'	GQui
'Geisha' (EA)	MBar
'Geisha Lilac' (EA)	COtt ECho MBar MBri WLRN WWeb
'Geisha Orange' (EA)	COtt GGGa GWht MBar MBri MGos NHed WLRN WWeb
'Geisha Purple' (EA)	COtt MBar WFar
'Geisha Red' (EA)	COtt EBee EPfP MBar MBri MOne STre WAbe WFar
'Gekkeikan' (EA)	CB&S
'Gena Mae'	GGGa LMil
'General Eisenhower'	SReu
'General Eric Harrison'	LHyd NMun SCog SLeo
'General Practitioner'	NMun
'General Wavell' (EA)	CMac COtt GAri LKna
'Gene's Favourite'	SReu
'Genghis Khan'	MBri MLea
'Geoffroy Millais'	LMil
'George Hardy'	CWri SExb
'George Johnstone' 🏆	MBal
'George Reynolds' (K)	MLea
'George's Delight'	CWri GGGa
'Georgette'	LHyd NMun SCog SLeo
§ × ***geraldii***	CWri SLeo
Gertrud Schäle Group	CDoC CTri MBal MBar MLea NHol SReu
'Getsutoku' (EA)	GAri
'Gibraltar' (K) 🏆	CB&S CSam CWLN EBre GGGa GRei GWht IOrc LHyd LKna LMil MAsh MBal MBar MBri MGos MLea MMor MRav SPer SReu SSta WGwG
giganteum	See ***R. protistum*** var. ***giganteum***
'Gigi'	GGGa
'Gilbert Mullier'	MBri
'Ginger' (K)	EPfP LMil MAsh MBal NMun SExb WWeb
'Ginny Gee' 🏆	CDoC COtt CSam CWri EHoe EPot GGGa GWht ISea LHyd LMil MAsh MBal MBar MBri MDun MGos MLea NHar NHol NRoo SExb SReu SSta WAbe WBod WFar
§ 'Girard's Hot Shot' (EA)	ECho GGGa GQui LMil SBod SSta
'Glad Tidings'	SLeo
Gladys Group & cl.	SCog
¶ 'Glamora' (EA)	LHyd
¶ ***glanduliferum*** C&H 7131	GGGa
glaucophyllum	GGGa LHyd LMil NMun SLeo
– BH form	LMil

* – 'Branklyn'	GGGa
– 'Glenarn'	GGGa
– L&S 2764	See ***R. brachyanthum* L&S 2764**
§ – var. ***tubiforme***	NMun SCog SLeo
– white	GGGa
'Glencora' (EA)	LHyd
'Glenn Dale Adorable'	See ***R.* 'Adorable'**
glischrum	GGGa NMun SLeo
– C&Cu 9316	GGGa
– subsp. ***glischroides***	LMil NMun SLeo
– subsp. ***glischrum***	GGGa
§ – subsp. ***rude***	GGGa NMun SLeo
¶ – – C&V 9524	GGGa
globigerum	See ***R. alutaceum*** var. ***alutaceum*** **Globigerum Group**
'Glockenspiel' (K/d)	LKna
glomerulatum	See ***R. yungningense*** **Glomerulatum Group**
'Gloria'	EHoe LMil
'Glory of Leonardslee'	SLeo
'Glory of Penjerrick'	NMun SLeo
'Glowing Embers' (K)	CSam CWLN EBee GAri GRei MAsh MBal MBri MLea MMor SBid SExb SPer SReu SSpi WFar WWeb
'Gloxineum'	CWri
'Gog' (K)	LHyd LKna MAsh MBal SPer WLRN
'Gold Crest' (K)	LKna
'Gold Dust' (K)	SExb
'Gold Mohur'	SLeo SReu
'Goldball'	See ***R.* 'Christopher Wren'**
'Goldbukett'	LHyd LMil MBri
'Golden Bee'	GGGa NHol
'Golden Belle'	CWri LMil MBal MLea SLeo SMur
'Golden Coach'	COtt ISea LMil LRHS MAsh MBri MLea NMun
'Golden Eagle' (K)	CB&S CBlo CDoC COtt MBri MGos SCoo
'Golden Eye' (K)	LKna
'Golden Flare' (K)	CB&S CBlo ISea LHyd MBri WWeb
'Golden Fleece'	LKna SCog SLeo SReu
'Golden Gate'	CDoC CWri NMun SLeo WGor WWeb
'Golden Horn' (K)	GQui MAsh WGor WWeb
Golden Horn Group & cl.	IOrc MBal NMun SCog SLeo
'Golden Horn Persimmon'	See ***R.* 'Persimmon'**
'Golden Lights'	LMil
'Golden Orfe' 🏆	LHyd SCog
'Golden Oriole' (K)	LKna SReu
Golden Oriole Group	CB&S NHol NMun SLeo
§ – 'Talavera' 🏆	CB&S MBal SCog
'Golden Princess'	COtt LMil NHol
¶ 'Golden Splendour'	LMil
'Golden Star'	GGGa LMil LRHS
'Golden Sunlight'	See ***R.* 'Directeur Moerlands'**
'Golden Sunset' (K)	COtt LMil MAsh MBri MGos MMor SExb
'Golden Torch' 🏆	CAbP CMHG COtt CWri GGGa GWht IOrc ISea LHyd LMil LNet MBal MBri MDun MGos MLea MMor NHed NMun SCog SExb SHBN SLeo SPer SReu SSta WWeb
'Golden Wedding'	CWri GGGa LMil MAsh MBal MLea
'Golden Wit'	ECho MBal SBod SCog
'Goldfee'	LHyd LMil
'Goldfinch' (K)	LKna
'Goldfinger'	MBal

'Goldflimmer' (v)	CDoC GGGa LMil MGos NHol SReu WWeb
'Goldfort'	LKna SLeo SReu
'Goldika'	LMil
'Goldilocks'	GGGa
'Goldkrone'	CWri EHoe GGGa LHyd LMil MGos NMun SCog SExb SReu
'Goldsworth Crimson'	LHyd
'Goldsworth Orange'	GGGa LHyd LKna MBal MGos MMor NMun SLeo SPer SReu SSpi SSta
'Goldsworth Pink'	LKna SReu
'Goldsworth Yellow'	CBlo CSam LKna MGos SLeo SReu
'Gomer Waterer' 🏆	CHig CWLN CWri GGGa IOrc LHyd LKna LMil MAsh MBal MBar MBri MDun MGos MLea MMor NMun NWea SBod SCog SLeo SPer SReu SSta
'Gordon Jones'	GGGa
'Govenianum' (Ad)	LKna
'Grace Seabrook'	COtt CSam CWLN CWri EHoe GGGa GWht ISea LHyd LMil MAsh MBri MDun MLea SExb SLeo SPer SReu
¶ ***gracilentum*** (V)	CEqu
'Graciosum' (O)	LKna SReu
'Graf Zeppelin'	GGGa
grande	GGGa IOrc NMun
– DF 524	MBal
– EGM 058	LMil
– pink	NMun
– TSS 37	NMun
gratum	See ***R. basilicum***
'Grayswood Pink'	CSam
'Graziella'	GGGa
'Greensleeves'	CDoC LKna LMil
'Greenway' (EA)	CB&S CGre CTre IOrc SPer
'Greta' (EA)	LHyd
'Gretzel'	MLea NMun SLeo
'Grierdal'	GGGa
Grierocaster Group	SCog
griersonianum	GGGa IOrc ISea MBal NMun SCog SLeo
– F 24116	NMun
griffithianum	GGGa NMun SLeo
– EGM 101	LMil
'Grisette'	SLeo
'Gristede'	COtt GGGa LMil MAsh MOne NHol SReu SSta
Grosclaude Group & cl. 🏆	NMun SCog SLeo
'Grouse'	MBal MLea NHar
¶ 'Grouse' x ***keiskei*** 'Yaku Fairy'	ECho
'Grumpy'	CDoC EBre GGGa GRei IHos IOrc LHyd LMil LNet MBal MBar MBri MGos MLea MMor NHed NHol NMun SCog SHBN SLeo SReu WAbe
Guardsman Group	SLeo
§ 'Gumpo' (EA)	CMac EPot SCog
'Gumpo Pink' (EA)	WAbe
'Gumpo White' (EA)	EPot SBod SSta WBod
'Gwenda' (EA)	LHyd SCog
'Gwillt-king'	NMun SLeo
gymnocarpum	See ***R. microgynum*** **Gymnocarpum Group**
'Gyokushin' (EA)	MBal
'H. Whitner'	NMun SLeo
'H.H. Hume' (EA)	MBal
habrotrichum	GGGa LMil NMun SLeo
– F 15778	NMun
¶ 'Hachmann's Brasilia'	CWri
'Hachmann's Charmant'	GGGa LMil
'Hachmann's Feuerschein'	LMil
'Hachmann's Marlis'	LHyd LMil SReu
¶ 'Hachmann's Polaris'	LMil
'Hachmann's Porzellan'	LHyd
'Hachmann's Rokoko' (EA)	GGGa
'Hachmann's Rosita'	LHyd MAsh WLRN
haematodes	GGGa MBal MBri MDun NMun SLeo SRms
– Bu 290	GGGa
¶ – C&Cu 9445	GGGa
§ – subsp. ***chaetomallum***	GGGa LMil NMun
– – F 25601	NMun
– – KW 21077	NMun SLeo
– – R 18359	NMun SLeo
– – R 41	NMun
– CLD 1282	LMil
– ex Hobbie	GGGa
– F 6773	NMun SLeo
– McLaren S124A	NMun SLeo
– SBEC 0585	GGGa
'Haida Gold'	GWht ISea MBal MBri MGos MLea NMun SReu SSta WWeb
¶ 'Hakurakuten' (EA)	CMHG
Halcyone Group	SLeo
'Halfdan Lem'	CAbP CSam EHoe GGGa ISea LHyd LMil MBal MGos MLea MMor NMun SCog SExb SHBN SLeo SPer SReu SSta
'Hallelujah'	CWri MBal SExb SMur WWeb
¶ 'Halton'	NMun
'Hamlet' (M)	LMil
'Hammondii' (Ad)	LKna
'Hana-asobi' (EA)	CB&S LHyd
hanceanum	CHig NMun SLeo
– 'Canton Consul'	EHoe EPot GGGa LHyd
– EN 2104	GGGa
– Nanum Group	CB&S EPot GGGa LMil MBal NMun SBar WBod
'Handsworth Scarlet'	SLeo
¶ ***haofui*** Guiz 75	GGGa
Happy Group	IOrc SHBN
'Harbinger' (EA)	NMun SBod SCog SLeo
§ 'Hardijzer Beauty' (Ad) 🏆	IOrc LKna MBal MBri
'Hardijzer's Beauty'	See ***R.* 'Hardijzer Beauty'**
hardingii	See ***R. annae*** **Hardingii Group**
'Hardy Gardenia' (EA/d)	SCog SSta
hardyi	See ***R. augustinii*** **subsp. *hardyi***
¶ 'Harkwood Friendship'	LPan
'Harkwood Moonlight'	LPan LRHS MBri WWeb
'Harkwood Premiere'	LMil LRHS MBri MGos
'Harkwood Red'	GQui LMil LRHS
'Harry Tagg'	GGGa LHyd
'Harumiji' (EA)	NMun SLeo
'Harvest Moon'	LHyd MBal MBri MGos NMun SExb SLeo SReu SSta
'Harvest Moon' (K)	CSam IHos MBri MLea SCoo SReu
'Hatsugiri' (EA) 🏆	CHig CMac EBee IOrc LHyd LKna LMil MBar MMor SBid SBod SCog SReu SSta
(Hawk Group) 'Crest'	See ***R.* 'Crest'**
– 'Jervis Bay'	See ***R.* 'Jervis Bay'**
'Haze'	NMun SLeo
'Hazel Fisher'	LMil
headfortianum	See ***R. taggianum*** **Headfortianum Group**
'Heather Macleod' (EA)	LHyd
heftii	NMun
'Heidelberg' (K/d)	WAbe

'Heiwa' (EA)	CWLN
'Heiwa-no-kagami' (EA)	GAri
'Helen Close' (EA)	LHyd LRHS SExb
'Helen Curtis' (EA)	SCog SReu
'Helene Schiffner' 🏆	GGGa NMun SLeo SReu
§ ***heliolepis***	GGGa IOrc LMil MBal SLeo
§ – var. ***brevistylum***	NMun SLeo
Pholidotum Group	
F 6762	
¶ – Bu 292	GGGa
– C&Cu 9313	GGGa
◆ – var. ***fumidum***	See ***R. heliolepis***
¶ – SF 489	ISea
¶ – SF 516	ISea
– SSNY 314	GGGa
– SSNY 66	GGGa
– Yu 7933*	NMun
hemidartum	See ***R. pocophorum*** var. ***hemidartum***
× ***hemigynum***	NMun SLeo
hemitrichotum	NMun SExb
– KW 4050	NMun
hemsleyanum	GGGa IOrc NMun SLeo
¶ aff. – C&H 7189	GGGa
¶ – EN 2097	GGGa
'Henry Street'	SLeo
heptamerum	See ***R. degronianum*** subsp. ***heptamerum***
'Herbert' (EA)	CMac
§ 'Hexe' (EA)	WBod
¶ ***hidakanum***	SReu
'Higasa' (EA)	CHig GAri
'High Gold'	LMil
'High Summer'	LMil
'Hilda Margaret'	SReu
himantodes (V)	CEqu
'Hino-crimson' (EA) 🏆	CGre CMac CWLN IOrc LKna LMil MAsh MBar MBri MGos MMor SPer SReu SSta WFar WLRN WStI WWeb
'Hinode-giri' (EA)	CB&S CHig CMac CTrw CWLN LHyd LKna NMun SBod SCog SExb SLeo SReu WBod
'Hinode-no-kumo' (EA)	NMun SLeo
'Hino-mayo' (EA) 🏆	CB&S CMHG CMac CTre GQui GRei IOrc LHyd LKna LMil MBar MBri NMun SCog SExb SLeo SPer SReu SSta WAbe WBod WStI
'Hino-scarlet'	See ***R.* 'Campfire'**
'Hino-tsukasa' (EA)	NMun SLeo
hippophaeoides 🏆	CHig EHic EPfP LKna LMil MBri MDun NMun SExb SLeo SSta WAbe
– 'Bei-ma-shan'	See ***R. hippophaeoides* 'Haba Shan'**
– F 22197A	NMun SLeo
§ – 'Haba Shan'	GGGa LMil MBri
– var. ***occidentale*** C&Cu 9314	GGGa
– Yu 13845	GGGa
hirsutum	GGGa GWht LMil MBal SReu WPyg
– f. ***albiflorum***	GGGa
– 'Flore Pleno' (d)	EPot GGGa MBal MBar WAbe
hirtipes	GGGa
¶ – C&V 9546	GGGa
– KW 10616	GGGa
– KW 5659	GGGa SLeo
– KW 6223	NMun SLeo
– LS&E 15765	GGGa

– LS&T 3624	NMun
× ***hodconeri***	NMun
– LS&H 21296	NMun
– 'pink'	NMun
– TSS 9	NMun
hodgsonii	CWri GGGa IOrc LMil MDun NMun SLeo SReu
– B 653	MBal
– BL&M 232	NMun
– DF 532	MBal
– EGM 081	LMil
– 'Poet's Lawn'	NMun
– SU 323	GGGa
– TSS 42A	NMun
'Hojo-no-odorikarako' (EA)	NMun SLeo
'Holden'	CWri
'Hollandia'	IOrc MMor SHBN
'Homebush' (R/d) 🏆	CB&S CMHG GGGa GWht IOrc ISea LHyd LKna LMil MAsh MBal MBar MBri SExb SPer SReu SSpi SSta
'Honey'	LKna NMun SLeo
'Honey Bee'	MAsh
'Honeymoon'	NMun WLRN WWeb
'Honeysuckle' (K)	IOrc MBar MMor SReu
'Hong Kong'	MDun
hongkongense	GGGa NMun SLeo
§ 'Ho-o' (EA)	CB&S CGre SCog
hookeri	NMun SLeo
– KW 13859	NMun
– Tigh-na-Rudha form	GGGa
'Hope Findlay'	LHyd
'Hoppy'	CWri GWht LMil MAsh MBal MDun MLea MMor MOne NMun SCog SExb SLeo SReu WWeb
'Horizon Dawn'	CWri
'Horizon Lakeside'	GGGa
'Horizon Monarch'	GGGa LMil
'Horizon Snowbird'	LMil
horlickianum	GGGa NMun SLeo
– KW 9403	NMun
'Hortulanus H. Witte' (M)	MMor SReu
'Hot Shot'	See ***R.* 'Girard's Hot Shot'**
'Hotei' 🏆	CWri GCHN GGGa ISea LHyd LMil MAsh MBal MBar MBri MGos MLea MMor NMun SCog SHBN SLeo SPer SReu SSta WGer WWeb
Hotspur Group (K) 🏆	CWLN ELan GGGa ISea SCoo SExb SPer WLRN WWeb
'Hotspur Red' (K) 🏆	CSam EBee EPfP LKna LMil MBri SCog SReu
'Hotspur Yellow' (K)	SReu
houlstonii	See ***R. fortunei*** subsp. ***discolor*** **Houlstonii Group**
¶ ***huanum*** C&H 7073	GGGa
¶ – EN 4028	GGGa
'Hugh Koster'	CB&S CWLN IOrc LKna MBri MGos NMun SLeo SPer
Humming Bird Group	CB&S CMHG CSam CTrh CWLN CWri EPot GGGa GWht ISea LHyd LKna MBal MBar MBri MGos MMor NHol NMun SCog SHBN SLeo SPer SReu SRms WBod
hunnewellianum	GGGa
'Hurricane'	COtt EHoe MBri
'Huzzar'	MDun
¶ 'Hyde and Seek'	GQui
'Hydon Ball'	LHyd

'Hydon Ben'	LHyd
¶ 'Hydon Comet'	LHyd
'Hydon Dawn' 🏆	COtt GGGa ISea LHyd LMil MAsh MGos MLea NHed NMun SCog SExb SLeo SReu SSta WAbe
'Hydon Glow'	LHyd NMun SLeo
'Hydon Gold'	LHyd
¶ 'Hydon Haley'	LHyd
'Hydon Hunter' 🏆	COtt GGGa IOrc ISea LHyd LMil LNet NHed NMun SCog SLeo SReu SSta
¶ 'Hydon Juliet'	LHyd
'Hydon Mist'	LHyd
'Hydon Pearl'	LHyd
'Hydon Pink'	LHyd
¶ 'Hydon Primrose'	LHyd
'Hydon Rodney'	LHyd
'Hydon Salmon'	LHyd NMun SLeo
'Hydon Velvet'	LHyd
hylaeum	NMun
– KW 6401	See ***R. faucium* KW 6401**
– KW 6833	NMun SLeo
hypenanthum	See ***R. anthopogon*** subsp. ***hypenanthum***
Hyperion Group	LKna SReu SSta
hyperythrum	CWri GGGa LHyd LMil NHol NMun SLeo
* ***hyperythrum album***	NMun
hyperythrum ETOT 183	GWht ISea
– pink	NMun
hypoglaucum	See ***R. argyrophyllum*** subsp. ***hypoglaucum***
– 'Heane Wood'	See ***R. argyrophyllum*** subsp. ***hypoglaucum* 'Heane Wood'**
Ibex Group & cl.	NMun
'Ice Cream'	LHyd SCog
¶ 'Ice Cube'	CWri
'Ice Maiden'	SReu
'Iceberg'	See ***R.* 'Lodauric Iceberg'**
'Icecream Flavour'	See ***R.* 'Flavour'**
'Icecream Vanilla'	See ***R.* 'Vanilla'**
Idealist Group & cl. 🏆	CWri EHoe LHyd NMun SLeo SReu
'Ightham Gold'	SReu
'Ightham Peach'	SReu
'Ightham Yellow'	MMor NMun SLeo SReu
'Il Tasso' (R/d)	LKna SRms
§ 'Ilam Melford Lemon'	LMil
§ 'Ilam Ming'	LMil
'Ilam Violet'	LKna LMil
'Imago' (K/d)	LKna
§ 'Ima-shojo' (EA/d) 🏆	GAri IHos LHyd LMil SPer WBod
'Impala' (K)	LKna
impeditum 🏆	CB&S CHig CSam ELan GGGa GRei GWht ISea LHyd LKna MBal MBar MDun MGos MLea MPla NBir NHar NHol NMun NWea SCog SPer SReu SSta WPat
§ – 'Blue Steel'	CB&S COtt CPMA CTri CWSG CWri GGGa LMil MAsh MBal MBri MBro NHar NHol NMun SLeo SReu WAbe WPat WPyg
* – 'Compactum'	EPfP
– dark compact form	LKna
– F 20454	LMil
– 'Indigo'	CMHG EHoe GWht MAsh MBri NHar SCog
– 'Johnston's Impeditum'	LKna
– 'Moerheim'	See ***R.* 'Moerheim'**
– 'Pygmaeum'	NHol WPat
– Reuthe's form	SReu
– 'Russell's Blue'	SReu
imperator	See ***R. uniflorum*** var. ***imperator***
Impi Group & cl.	LKna NMun SLeo
'Ina Hair'	CB&S
inconspicuum (V)	CEqu
§ ***indicum*** (EA)	MBal
§ – 'Balsaminiflorum' (EA/d)	CMac
– 'Crispiflorum' (EA)	GWht
– var. ***eriocarpum*** 'Gumpo'	See ***R.* 'Gumpo'**
◆ 'Indigo Diamant'	See ***R.* Diamant Group indigo**
inopinum	GGGa NMun
insigne 🏆	CWri GGGa IOrc LMil MDun MGos NMun SLeo
– Reuthe's form	SReu
Intermedium Group	MBal
X ***intermedium*** white	GGGa
intricatum	GGGa
¶ – C 5060	GGGa
– KW 4184	NMun SLeo
Intrifast Group	GAri GGGa GWht LHyd MAsh MBal NHar NHol
iodes	See ***R. alutaceum*** var. ***iodes***
'Irene Koster' (O) 🏆	CMHG CWLN ELan GGGa GWht ISea LHyd LKna LMil MBri SPer SReu WWeb
'Irohayama' (EA) 🏆	CHig CMac CTrw GQui LHyd LKna LMil SCog SExb SPer SReu SSta
irroratum	CWri LMil NMun SLeo
¶ – C&H 7185	GGGa
¶ – subsp. ***irroratum*** C&H 7100	GGGa
– pale pink	NMun
§ – subsp. ***pogonostylum***	NMun SLeo
– – KR 3121	GGGa
– 'Polka Dot'	GGGa NMun SLeo
– R 72	NMun
– SF 384	ISea
– SF 92304	ISea
– white	GGGa
'Isabel Pierce' 🏆	CSam CWLN LMil MBal SLeo
'Isabella Mangles'	LHyd
'Ishiyama' (EA)	SCog
Italia Group	SLeo
iteaphyllum	See ***R. formosum*** var. ***formosum* Iteaphyllum Group**
Ivanhoe Group & cl.	ISea
'Ivery's Scarlet'	IOrc
'Ivette' (EA)	CMac LHyd LKna
Iviza Group	SReu
'Iwato-kagami' (EA)	NMun SLeo
'Izayoi' (EA)	WBod
'J.C. Williams'	CB&S
'J.G. Millais'	LHyd
'J.M. de Montague'	See ***R.* 'The Hon Jean Marie de Montague'**
'Jabberwocky'	LHyd
'Jack A Sand' (K)	MLea
'Jack Skelton'	LHyd
'Jacksonii'	IOrc ISea LKna MBal MBar NMun SLeo SReu
Jacques Group	NMun SCog SLeo
'Jade'	SLeo
Jalisco Group & cl.	NMun SLeo
'Jalisco Eclipse'	LKna
'Jalisco Elect' 🏆	CWri LKna LMil NMun
'Jalisco Goshawk'	NMun SLeo
'James Barto'	IOrc LHyd NMun SLeo SSta

'James Burchett' 🏆	GGGa LKna LMil SLeo SReu
'James Gable' (EA)	MAsh
'Jan Bee'	MBal
'Jan Dekens'	SReu
¶ Jan Steen Group & cl.	NMun
'Jan Wellen' (EA)	EBee IOrc
¶ 'Jane Abbott' (A)	GGGa
¶ 'Janelle Marie' (V)	CEqu
¶ 'Janet Blair'	CWri
'Janet Ward'	CBlo LHyd LKna SReu
'Janine Alexandre Debray'	NMun SCog SLeo
japonicum Schneider var. ***japonicum***	See ***R. degronianum*** subsp. ***heptamerum***
– var. ***pentamerum***	See ***R. degronianum*** subsp. ***degronianum***
japonicum Suringar	See ***R. molle*** subsp. ***japonicum***
jasminiflorum (V)	ERea
'Jasorbit' (V)	CEqu
'Java Light' (V)	CDoC ERea
javanicum Sands 74 (V)	GGGa
¶ – var. ***teysmannii*** (V)	CEqu
'Jazz Band' (V)	CEqu GGGa
Jean Group	SCog
'Jean Mary Montague'	See **R. 'The Hon Jean Marie de Montague'**
'Jean Read'	LHyd
'Jeanette' (EA)	LKna
'Jeff Hill' (EA)	ECho LMil MOne
'Jennie Dosser'	LMil
'Jenny'	See **R. 'Creeping Jenny'**
§ 'Jervis Bay' 🏆	SReu
'Jingle Bells'	CWri GGGa MAsh
'Jo Madden'	LHyd
'Joan Scobie'	SLeo
Jock Group	CB&S CMHG CTrw
'Jock Brydon' (O)	GGGa LMil
'Jock Coutts'	LKna
'Jock's White'	MBal SPer
'Joe Paterno'	CWri
'Johann Sebastian Bach' (EA)	WBod WWeb
'Johann Strauss' (EA)	WBod
'Johanna' (EA)	CDoC CMac EBee GDTE GGGa LMil MAsh MBar MBri MMor SExb SPer WBod
'John Barr Stevenson'	LHyd SLeo
'John Cairns' (EA) 🏆	CMac CWLN LHyd LKna LMil MBal MBar SCog SPer SReu WBod
'John Eichelser'	LMil
'John Tremayne'	SLeo
'John Walter'	GRei MBri MGos SBid
'John Waterer'	CBlo CWri IOrc LKna SPer
Johnnie Johnston Group & cl.	SLeo
'Johnny Bender'	MAsh MLea
johnstoneanum 🏆	CB&S CGre CSam GGGa ISea LMil MBal NMun SLeo WBod
– 'Double Diamond' (d)	CGre LHyd
– 'Rubrotinctum' KW 7723	NMun SLeo
'Jolie Madame' (Vs)	CBlo MBri SReu
'Jonathan Shaw'	GGGa
'Joseph Hill' (EA)	CWLN ECho LMil SSpi WPat
'Joy's Delight' (Ad)	LKna
'Jubilee'	LKna
Jubilee Queen Group & cl.	SLeo
'Julischka'	MGos
¶ 'June Bee'	GGGa
'Juwel'	MGos
kaempferi (EA) 🏆	CGre CHig GGGa LHyd LMil
– 'Damio'	See ***R. kaempferi*** **'Mikado'**
– dark form (EA)	SCog
– 'Firefly'	See **R. 'Hexe'**
– light form (EA)	SCog
§ – 'Mikado' (EA)	SBod SCog SPer SReu SSta
– orange (EA)	IOrc
– pink (EA)	IOrc
'Kaho-no-hikari' (EA)	GAri
'Kakiemon' (EA)	LHyd SPer
'Kalinka'	GGGa LHyd MGos NHol
¶ 'Kantilene'	LMil
'Kaponga'	CDoC MGos
'Karen Triplett'	LMil
'Karin'	COtt MBal MDun SBod SHBN
'Kasane-kagaribi' (EA)	LHyd
'Kate Waterer' 🏆	IOrc LKna MBar MGos NMun SLeo SReu
N 'Kathleen' (A)	IOrc LHyd LKna MMor SCog
'Katinka' (EA)	MBal MGos
'Katisha' (EA)	LHyd
'Katy Watson'	SReu
¶ ***kawakamii*** (V)	GGGa
'Keija'	SCog
'Keinohana' (EA)	NMun SLeo
keiskei	CHig LHyd MBal NMun
– 'Cordifolium'	NHol SLeo
– 'Ebino'	GGGa NHol WAbe
– 'Yaku Fairy' 🏆	GAri GGGa LMil LRHS MBal NHar SIng SReu
– 'Yaku Fairy' × ***campylogynum***	GGGa
– 'Yaku Fairy' × ***spinuliferum***	GGGa
keleticum	See ***R. calostrotum*** subsp. ***keleticum***
§ 'Ken Janeck'	GGGa LMil SMur WWeb
§ ***kendrickii***	GGGa NMun SLeo
¶ – MH 62	GGGa
'Kermesinum' (EA)	CHig COtt EBee GGGa GWht MBar SReu WPat
'Kermesinum Album' (EA)	GGGa MBar MGos
I 'Kermesinum Rose' (EA)	MBri SCog
* 'Kermesinum Wit'	SReu
kesangiae CH&M 3058, 3099	GGGa
– EGM 061	LMil
– KR 1136	NMun
– KR 1640	GGGa MDun NMun
N Kewense Group	See **R. Loderi Group**
keysii	GGGa LMil MBal NMun SLeo
– KR 974	NMun
– KW 8101*	NMun
– 'Unicolor'	NMun SLeo
'Kijei'	CB&S
Kilimanjaro Group & cl. 🏆	NMun SLeo SReu SSta
'Kimberly'	GGGa
'Kimbeth'	GGGa
'Kimigayo' (EA)	LHyd
¶ 'King Fisher'	NMun
kingianum	See ***R. arboreum*** subsp. ***zeylanicum***
'Kingston'	LRHS MAsh MLea SSpi
§ 'Kirin' (EA/d) 🏆	CGre CMac CTrw CWLN GDTE IOrc LHyd LKna LMil MOne SBod SCog WBod
'Kirishima' (EA)	LKna SRms
'Kiritsubo' (EA)	GAri IOrc LHyd
kiusianum (EA) 🏆	GGGa LHyd SReu SRms WAbe
– 'Album' (EA)	GAri LHyd LMil SReu WAbe
– 'Hillier's Pink' (EA)	LMil
* – 'Mount Fuji' (EA)	WAbe

– 'Mountain Gem' (EA)	SSta
¶ – var. ***sataense*** (EA)	SReu
'Kiwi Majic'	GGGa LMil
'Klondyke' (K) 🏆	CB&S CSam CTri EBee EBre ELan GGGa GWht IOrc LMil MAsh MBri MGos MLea SPer SReu
'Kluis Sensation' 🏆	CB&S CWLN CWri IOrc LHyd LKna LMil MGos MMor NMun SHBN SLeo SReu
'Kluis Triumph'	LKna SReu
'Knap Hill Apricot' (K)	CBlo LKna LMil SMur
'Knap Hill Red' (K)	LKna LMil SMur
'Kobold' (EA)	NMun SLeo
'Koichiro Wada'	See ***R. yakushimanum* 'Koichiro Wada'**
'Kokardia'	GGGa LMil LRHS
'Komurasaki' (EA)	NMun SLeo
kongboense	GGGa
§ 'Koningin Emma' (M)	LMil MBri
§ 'Koningin Wilhelmina' (M)	IOrc SCog SMer WBod
konorii M Black (V)	GGGa
¶ – var. ***phaeopeplum*** (V)	GGGa
'Koster's Brilliant Red' (M)	MBal MBar SReu
kotschyi	See ***R. myrtifolium***
'Kozan' (EA)	MBal
§ 'Kure-no-yuki' (EA/d) 🏆	CMac LHyd LKna LMil MAsh SBod SCog SExb SReu WBod
'Kusudama' (EA)	GAri
kyawii	NMun SLeo
§ – Agapetum Group	NMun SLeo
'Lacs'	SLeo
lacteum	LMil MDun NMun SLeo
– bright yellow	NMun
¶ – C 7164	GGGa
¶ – CNW 930	GGGa
¶ – CNW 936	GGGa
¶ – CNW 966	GGGa
– forms	NMun SLeo
– KR 2760	GGGa
– SBEC 0345	GGGa
– SF 374	ISea
'Ladt Decis'	SReu
'Lady Adam Gordon'	NMun SLeo
'Lady Alice Fitzwilliam' 🏆	CB&S CGre CMHG ERea GGGa GWht ISea LHyd LMil MBal NMun SLeo
'Lady Annette de Trafford'	LKna
'Lady Armstrong'	CWri
Lady Bessborough Group & cl.	SLeo
'Lady Bessborough Roberte'	See ***R.* 'Roberte'**
'Lady Bowes Lyon'	LHyd NMun SCog SLeo
Lady Chamberlain Group & cl.	GGGa LMil MBal MGos NMun SLeo
'Lady Chamberlain Exbury'	See ***R.* 'Exbury Lady Chamberlain'**
'Lady Chamberlain Golden Queen'	See ***R.* 'Golden Queen'**
'Lady Chamberlain Salmon Trout'	See ***R.* 'Salmon Trout'**
'Lady Clementine Mitford' 🏆	CWri GGGa IHos LHyd LKna LMil MAsh MDun MGos NMun SBid SExb SHBN SLeo SPer SReu SSta
¶ 'Lady Decies'	SReu
'Lady Eleanor Cathcart' 🏆	CHig CWri GGGa IOrc LKna NMun SLeo

'Lady Elphinstone' (EA)	LHyd
'Lady Grey Egerton'	LKna MMor
Lady Linlithgow Group	SCog SLeo
'Lady Longman'	LHyd SSta
¶ 'Lady Louise' (EA)	LHyd
'Lady Primrose'	SReu
'Lady Romsey'	LMil
'Lady Rosebery' (K)	LKna MBri
Lady Rosebery Group & cl.	MLea NMun SLeo
'Lady Rosebery Pink Delight'	See ***R.* 'Pink Lady Rosebery'**
Ladybird Group & cl.	SReu
laetum (V)	CEqu GGGa
Lamellen Group	LHyd SLeo
'Lampion'	GGGa LMil
'Lamplighter' 🏆	LMil SLeo SReu
lanatoides	NMun
– KW 5971	NMun
lanatum	LHyd LMil NMun SLeo
– 716652	NMun
– BB 185B	NMun
– Cooper 2148	NMun SLeo
– DF 538	MBal
– dwarf cream	GGGa
– Flinckii Group	See ***R. flinckii***
– KR 873	GGGa
'Langmans'	LKna
'Langworth'	CWri ECho LKna LMil SReu
lanigerum	NMun SLeo SReu
¶ – C&V 9530	GGGa
– 'Chapel Wood'	NMun
– KW 6258	NMun
– KW 8251	GGGa
– pink	NMun SLeo
– red	NMun
– 'Round Wood'	LHyd
lapponicum	LMil
– Japanese	GGGa
'Lapwing' (K)	GAri LKna MBri
'Lascaux'	SReu
lasiostylum ETOT 136	GWht ISea
'Late Love' (EA)	CWLN MGos SSpi
late pink Inverewe	WBod
§ ***latoucheae*** (EA)	MBal SLeo
– PW 86 (EA)	GGGa
laudandum var. ***temoense***	GGGa LMil
Laura Aberconway Group & cl.	SLeo
'Laura Morland' (EA)	LHyd
'Lava Flow'	LHyd NHol SCog
'Lavender Girl' 🏆	GGGa GRei LHyd LKna LMil MBal MGos NMun SLeo SReu SSta
'Lavender Princess'	LMil
'Lavender Queen'	CWri NMun SExb WWeb
'Lavendula'	CSam GGGa LMil
'Le Progrès'	SReu
'Lea Rainbow'	MLea
'Ledifolium'	See ***R. mucronatum*** var. ***mucronatum***
'Ledifolium Album'	See ***R. mucronatum*** var. ***mucronatum***
ledifolium 'Bulstrode'	See ***R.* 'Bulstrode'**
– 'Magnificum'	See ***R.* 'Magnificum'**
– 'Ripense'	See ***R. mucronatum*** var. ***ripense***
'Lee's Dark Purple'	CWri LMil NMun SPer
'Lee's Scarlet'	LKna LMil
¶ 'Lemon Cloud'	GGGa
* 'Lemon Drop' (A)	GGGa
¶ 'Lemon Grove'	SReu
'Lemon Ice'	SCog

'Lemon Lodge'	CB&S CDoC
'Lemon Minuet' (V)	CEqu
'Lemonora' (M)	ELan MBri
'Lem's Cameo' ♀	GGGa LHyd LMil NMun SReu SSta
'Lem's Monarch' ♀	GGGa LMil MGos MLea SReu SSta
'Lem's Stormcloud'	MLea SSta
¶ 'Lem's Tangerine'	LMil
'Lemur' (EA)	EPot GGGa MAsh MBri MGos NHar WAbe WPat
'Leny'	NHol
'Leo' (EA)	GQui LHyd LKna LMil NMun SBod SCog SExb SLeo SReu WWeb
'Leo'	NMun SLeo
'Leonardslee Brilliant'	SLeo
'Leonardslee Giles'	SLeo
'Leonardslee Pink Bride'	SLeo
'Leonardslee Primrose'	SLeo
Leonore Group & cl.	NMun SReu
lepidostylum ♀	CB&S CHig CWri EHoe EPot GGGa GWht LHyd LMil MBar MBri MDun NHar NMun SBar SCog SIng SLeo SReu SSta WAbe WBod WSHC
lepidotum	GGGa LHyd LMil NMun SLeo WAbe
¶ – Elaeagnoides Group	GGGa
– FMB 279	MBal
– × ***lowndesii***	WAbe
¶ – M. Black 602	GGGa
◆ – 'Reuthe's Purple'	See ***R.*** **'Reuthe's Purple'**
– TW 40	GWht
– white	GGGa
¶ ***leptocarpum***	GGGa
§ – C&H 420	NMun SLeo
leptothrium	GGGa NMun SLeo
Letty Edwards Group & cl.	LKna NMun SCog SLeo SReu
leucaspis ♀	CGre CHig EPot ERea GGGa IOrc ISea LHyd MBal NMun SCog SReu
– KW 7171	NMun SLeo
'Leverett Richards'	LHyd SReu
levinei	GGGa
'Lila Pedigo'	COtt CWri GGGa GWht ISea MBal MLea
'Lilac Time' (EA)	MBar
'Lilacinum'	SCog
liliiflorum Guiz 163	CWri GGGa
'Lillie Maude' (EA)	CTrh
'Lilliput'	MAsh SBod SPer
'Lily Marleen' (EA)	CBlo CDoC CTri CWLN MMor SCoo SReu
'Linda'	CSam CTri GGGa MBal MBar MBri MDun MGos MLea SBod SCog SReu WWeb
'Linda R' (EA)	LMil
lindleyi ♀	GQui LMil NMun SLeo
– 'Dame Edith Sitwell'	GGGa
– L&S	GGGa MBal
'Linearifolium'	See ***R. macrosepalum*** **'Linearifolium'**
'Linnet' (K/d)	LKna
'Linwood Salmon' (EA/d)	SCog
Lionel's Triumph Group & cl.	LHyd LMil NMun SLeo
'Lissabon Rosa'	SExb
litiense	See ***R. wardii*** **var. *wardii* Litiense Group**
'Little Beauty' (EA)	SExb

'Little Ben'	ECho GWht MBal MBar SCog WAbe
'Little Bert'	SLeo
¶ 'Little Grace' (V)	CEqu
'Little Jessica'	SReu
'Little Jock'	MBal
¶ 'Little One' (V)	CEqu
'Loch o'the Lowes'	GGGa LMil
'Loch Rannoch'	GGGa
'Loch Tummel'	GGGa
lochiae (V)	CEqu GGGa
¶ 'Lochinch Spinbur'	GQui
Lodauric Group	SReu
§ 'Lodauric Iceberg' ♀	LKna LMil SReu
'Lodbrit'	SReu
'Loderi Fairy Queen'	NMun SLeo
'Loderi Fairyland'	LHyd NMun SLeo
§ 'Loderi Game Chick'	LHyd LMil MBal NMun SLeo SPer SReu SSta
'Loderi Georgette'	NMun SLeo
'Loderi Helen'	NMun SLeo
§ 'Loderi Julie'	NMun SLeo SReu
'Loderi King George' ♀	CB&S CSam CWLN CWri EHoe GGGa ISea LHyd LKna LMil MBlu MDun MLea NMun SCog SHBN SLeo SPer SReu SSta
'Loderi Patience'	LHyd NMun SLeo
'Loderi Pink Diamond' ♀	LMil
'Loderi Pink Topaz'	CWri LHyd LMil NMun SLeo
'Loderi Pretty Polly'	NMun SLeo
'Loderi Princess Marina'	NMun SLeo
'Loderi Sir Edmund'	LHyd NMun SLeo
'Loderi Sir Joseph Hooker'	LHyd NMun SLeo
'Loderi Titan'	SReu
§ 'Loderi Venus' ♀	GGGa IOrc LHyd LKna LMil MBal MLea NMun SCog SHBN SLeo SPer SReu SSta
'Loderi White Diamond'	LHyd NMun SLeo
'Loder's White' ♀	CWri GGGa IHos LHyd LKna LMil MBal MLea NMun SCog SLeo SPer SReu SSta
'Lodestar'	CWri
§ 'Logan Damaris'	LHyd NMun SLeo SReu
'Loki'	SLeo
longesquamatum	GGGa LMil NMun SLeo
¶ ***longipes*** var. ***chienianum*** EN 4074	GGGa
¶ – var. ***longipes*** C&H 7072	GGGa
¶ – – C&H 7113	GGGa
longistylum	GGGa NMun
'Longworth'	NMun
'Looking Glass'	SHBN
lopsangianum	See ***R. thomsonii*** subsp. ***lopsangianum***
loranthiflorum (V)	CEqu
'Lord Roberts'	CB&S CHig CSam CWLN CWri EHoe GGGa GRei GWht IOrc LKna LMil MAsh MBal MBar MBri MGos MMor NMun SHBN SLeo SPer SReu SRms WWeb
'Lord Swaythling'	LHyd SLeo
'Lori Eichelser'	CSam LMil MAsh MBal MLea NHar NHed
'Lorna' (EA)	GQui LMil
'Louis Pasteur'	SReu
'Louisa' (EA)	SExb SSpi WLRN
'Louise Dowdle' (EA)	CDoC CTrh LMil MMor SExb SPer
'Lovely William'	CSam MBal

lowndesii	WAbe
¶ – × ***keiskei*** 'Yaku Fairy'	EPot
'Lucy Lou'	CSam GGGa NHol SExb
ludlowii	GGGa LMil MBal
– × ***viridescens***	NHol
ludwigianum	GGGa
lukiangense	GGGa NMun SLeo
§ – R 11275*	NMun SLeo
'Lullaby' (EA)	LKna
'Lunar Queen'	LHyd
Luscombei Group	LHyd
luteiflorum	LMil
– KW 21040	GGGa NMun
¶ – KW 21556	GGGa
– TW 390	GWht
lutescens	CB&S CGre CHig CTre CWri GWht IBlr IOrc LMil MAsh MBal MBri MDun NMun SCog SReu SSta WAbe WBod WWat
– 'Bagshot Sands' 🏆	GGGa LHyd LMil NMun SPer SReu
– C 5092, 5100	GGGa NHol
¶ – C&H 7124	GGGa
§ ***luteum*** (A) 🏆	CB&S CPMA CTre CTri CWri GDra GGGa GWht ISea LKna LMil LPan MBal MBar MBri MGos MLea MUlv NMun SLeo SReu SRms SSta WBod WWat
§ ***lyi***	NMun SLeo
– KR 2861	GGGa
– KR 2962	GGGa
lysolepis KW 4456	GGGa
* 'Mac Ovata'	CMac
macabeanum 🏆	CB&S CHEx GGGa GWht LMil MBal MDun NMun SLeo SPer SReu SSta
– DT 10	GGGa
– KW 7724	NMun SLeo
– Reuthe's form	SReu
¶ – × ***sinogrande***	SReu
macgregoriae (V)	CEqu ERea
– P Woods 2646 (V)	GGGa
macranthum	See ***R. indicum***
'Macranthum Roseum' (EA)	SBod SExb
macrophyllum	GGGa LMil
§ ***macrosepalum*** 'Linearifolium' (A)	CMac ISea LMil NMun SLeo SReu WAbe
§ ***macrosmithii***	NMun SLeo
'Macrostemon'	See ***R.* (Obtusum Group) 'Macrostemon'**
maculiferum	NMun
§ – subsp. ***anwheiense*** 🏆	CWri GGGa LHyd LMil NMun SLeo
– Guiz 120	GGGa
¶ – Guiz 121	GGGa
¶ – Guiz 148	GGGa
'Madame Albert Moser'	LKna
'Madame de Bruin'	LKna MBal NWea SLeo
¶ 'Madame F. J. Chauvin'	ISea
'Madame Knutz'	SCog
'Madame Masson'	CDoC CHig CSam CWri GGGa GWht LMil MAsh MGos NHol NMun SCog SExb SHBN SLeo SReu SSta WWeb
'Madame van Hecke' (EA)	COtt EPfP GWht MAsh MBri SReu WFar
maddenii 🏆	CGre LHyd LMil NMun SLeo
§ – subsp. ***crassum*** 🏆	CTrw GGGa LMil MBal SReu
§ – – Obtusifolium Group	NMun SLeo
§ – subsp. ***maddenii***	NMun SLeo
§ – – Polyandrum Group	GQui ISea MBal NMun SLeo
magnificum	GWht LMil NMun SLeo SReu
N 'Magnificum' (A)	MBri SCog
'Maharani'	GGGa
§ ***makinoi*** 🏆	CHig GGGa LHyd LMil NMun SLeo SReu SSta
mallotum	GGGa LHyd LMil MDun NMun SLeo SReu
– F 17853	NMun
– Farrer 815	NMun
'Malvaticum' (EA)	WBod
'Manda Sue'	GGGa LMil MAsh MBal MLea SBar
Mandalay Group	LHyd MBri NMun SLeo
manipurense	See ***R. maddenii*** subsp. ***crassum*** **Obtusifolium Group**
'Marchioness of Lansdowne'	MGos
'Marcia'	LHyd SLeo
'Mardi Gras'	GGGa
Margaret Dunn Group & cl.	SLeo
'Margaret Falmouth'	SReu
'Margaret George' (EA)	LHyd
'Maria Elena' (EA/d)	LMil
'Marianne' (EA/d)	LMil MOne
'Marie' (EA)	CMac SCog
'Marie Curie'	SReu
'Marilee' (EA)	MGos
Mariloo Group	NMun SLeo
'Marinus Koster' 🏆	LKna MMor
'Marion'	LMil
'Marion Merriman' (K)	LKna
'Marion Street'	LHyd LMil NMun SCog SLeo SReu
'Markeeta's Prize' 🏆	CBlo CHig CSam CWri EHoe GAri GGGa GWht LMil MBri MLea
'Marlene Peste'	CAbP
'Mars'	SReu
'Martha Hitchcock' (EA)	LKna SCog SRms
'Martha Isaacson' (Ad)	GGGa MBal MBri MGos MLea SReu
'Martine' (Ad)	LHyd LKna MBri MGos SLeo
martinianum	NMun SLeo
– KW 21557	GGGa
'Mary Drennen'	LMil
'Mary Fleming'	SBod SCog SExb SSta WLRN
'Mary Forte'	SLeo
'Mary Helen' (EA)	CDoC LHyd LRHS SCoo SExb WBod
'Mary Meredith' (EA)	LHyd
'Mary Poppins'	EBee GRei GWht SCoo
'Master Mariner'	LHyd
'Master of Elphinstone' (EA)	SCog
Matador Group & cl. 🏆	GWht LHyd NMun SCog SReu WBod
'Mauna Loa' (K)	LKna
'Maurice Skipworth'	CB&S CDoC
maximum	GGGa NMun SLeo
– 'Weeldon's Red'	GGGa
'Maxine Childers'	LMil
'Maxwellii' (EA)	CMac SCog
May Day Group & cl. 🏆	CB&S CSam CTrw CWri ISea LHyd LKna MBal MBri MDun MGos NMun SCog SHBN SLeo SReu SSta WBod
'May Glow'	MGos
May Morn Group & cl.	SReu
'Mayor Johnstone'	CDoC
'Mazurka' (K)	LKna
meddianum	GGGa NMun SLeo

– var. ***atrokermesinum***	NMun SLeo
– – F 26476	NMun SLeo
– – KW 21006A	GGGa
– F 24219	NMun
Medusa Group	GGGa SReu
megacalyx	GGGa NMun SLeo
‘Megan’ (EA)	GGGa GWht IOrc MAsh
megaphyllum	See ***R. basilicum***
megeratum	GGGa NMun SLeo SReu
– ‘Bodnant’	WAbe WBod
‘Meicho’ (EA)	GAri
mekongense	GGGa NMun
¶ – var. ***mekongense***	SReu
– – Rubroluteum Group	See ***R. viridescens*** **Rubroluteum Group**
– – Viridescens Group	See ***R. viridescens***
◆ – – – ‘Doshong La’	See ***R. viridescens*** **‘Doshong La’**
– – – KW 5829	See ***R. viridescens*** **KW 5829**
§ – var. ***melinanthum***	NMun SLeo
– var. ***rubrolineatum***	NMun SLeo
‘Melford Lemon’	See ***R.*** **‘Ilam Melford Lemon’**
melinanthum	See ***R. mekongense*** var. ***melinanthum***
‘Merganser’ 🏆	GGGa LMil MAsh MBal MDun MLea MOne NHol SReu WAbe WBod
N ‘Merlin’ (EA)	COtt LMil MBal SExb
metternichii	See ***R. degronianum*** subsp. ***heptamerum***
‘Michael Hill’ (EA)	CB&S COtt CTrh CWLN EHic LHyd MAsh SCog SExb SSpi
‘Michael Waterer’ 🏆	NMun SBod SLeo
‘Michael’s Pride’ 🏆	CB&S CGre GQui MBal NMun
micranthum	CGre GGGa NMun
microgynum	NMun SLeo
– F 14242	GGGa NMun SLeo
microleucum	See ***R. orthocladum*** var. ***microleucum***
micromeres	See ***R. leptocarpum*** **C&H 420**
microphyton	NMun
‘Midori’ (EA)	SExb
‘Midsummer’	SLeo
‘Mikado’ (EA)	See ***R. kaempferi*** **‘Mikado’**
mimetes	LMil NMun SLeo
‘Mimi’ (EA)	CMac LHyd
‘Ming’	See ***R.*** **‘Ilam Ming’**
‘Minterne Cinnkeys’	MBal
minus	GQui
§ – var. ***minus*** Carolinianum Group	GGGa LHyd LMil
§ – – Punctatum Group	GRei MBar
‘Misomogiri’	CHig
‘Miss Muffet’ (EA)	SExb
‘Mizu-no-yamabuki’ (EA)	SLeo
§ ‘Moerheim’ 🏆	CSam MAsh MBal MBar MMor MOne MRav NHol SReu SSta WStI
§ ‘Moerheim’s Pink’	GGGa LHyd LKna LMil NHol SPer
‘Moerheim’s Scarlet’	LKna
‘Moidart’ (Vs)	LMil
‘Moira Salmon’ (EA)	LHyd
‘Molalla Red’	LMil MAsh
§ ***molle*** subsp. ***japonicum*** (A)	GGGa LHyd
– – JR 871 (A)	GGGa
mollicomum	NMun
– F 10347	NMun
– F 30940	NMun SLeo
Mollis orange	MBar SRms
Mollis pink	GGGa GWht MBar SRms
Mollis red	MBar SRms
Mollis salmon (M)	GGGa GQui
Mollis yellow	GQui GWht MBar SRms
‘Molly Ann’	GGGa MAsh MDun MLea SReu
‘Monaco’	CWri ISea
‘Monica’	SCog
◆ ***monosematum*** CNW 956	See ***R. pachytrichum*** **Monosematum Group CNW 956**
montroseanum	LHyd LMil NMun SLeo WCru
* – ‘Baravalla’	CWri GGGa
– ‘Benmore’	GGGa NMun
‘Moon Maiden’ (EA)	CWLN GQui LMil MMor
Moonbeam Group	LKna
Moonshine Group & cl.	SReu
‘Moonshine Bright’	LHyd SReu
‘Moonshine Crescent’	SReu
‘Moonshine Supreme’	LKna SReu
Moonstone Group	CHig EPot GAri GWht MBal MBar MLea NMun SCog SLeo WAbe
– pink-tipped	NHol
‘Moonstone Yellow’	GGGa
‘Moonwax’	CSam LMil MBal SMur
§ ‘Morgenrot’ 🏆	GGGa LMil MBri MGos SReu
morii 🏆	CWri GGGa LHyd LMil MDun NMun SLeo
– ETOT 90	GWht ISea
– W A 10955	NMun SLeo
‘Morning Cloud’ 🏆	CAbP IOrc LHyd LMil MAsh MBar NHed NMun SCog SLeo SReu
‘Morning Magic’	LHyd NMun SCog SExb SLeo
◆ Morning Red	See ***R.*** **‘Morgenrot’**
‘Morvah’	SLeo
‘Moser’s Maroon’	LHyd LKna MGos NMun SLeo
‘Moser’s Strawberry’	LKna
‘Motet’ (K/d)	LKna
‘Moth’	GGGa NHol
‘Mother Greer’	GGGa MAsh
‘Mother of Pearl’	LKna SCog SPer SReu
‘Mother Theresa’	LKna
‘Mother’s Day’ (EA) 🏆	CB&S CGre CMac CWLN EBre GDTE GQui GRei GWht IOrc LHyd LKna LMil MBal MBar MBri MGos MMor NMun SBod SCog SExb SLeo SPer SReu SSta WFar WLRN WPLl
§ ***moulmainense***	NMun SLeo
¶ ‘Mount Everest’ 🏆	LHyd SReu SSta
‘Mount Rainier’ (K)	LMil
‘Mount Saint Helens’	GGGa
‘Mountain Star’	SLeo
moupinense 🏆	CB&S CHig CWri ERea GGGa IDee LHyd LMil NMun SCog SLeo SPer SReu WBod
– C&K 140	GGGa
– pink	GGGa NMun WBod
‘Mozart’ (EA)	SBod WBod
‘Mrs A.T. de la Mare’ 🏆	GGGa IOrc LHyd LKna LMil MBri MMor NMun SLeo SPer SReu SSta
‘Mrs Anthony Waterer’ (O)	LKna
‘Mrs Anthony Waterer’	CBlo LKna SSta
‘Mrs Ashley Slocock’	SReu
‘Mrs Betty Robertson’	CHig CWri GWht MBri MLea SReu
Mrs C. Whitner Group	NMun SLeo
‘Mrs C.B. van Nes’	SReu
‘Mrs Charles E. Pearson’ 🏆	CB&S CWLN CWri LHyd LKna LMil MLea NMun SCog SExb SHBN SLeo SPer SReu

'Mrs Davies Evans' 🏆	LHyd LKna MBar MMor SReu SSta
'Mrs Dick Thompson'	SReu
'Mrs Donald Graham'	SReu
'Mrs Doorenbos'	CMac
'Mrs E.C. Stirling'	LHyd LKna SRms
'Mrs Emil Hager' (EA)	LHyd
'Mrs Furnivall' 🏆	CB&S CHig CWri LHyd LKna LMil MAsh MBri MGos SExb SReu WGer
'Mrs G.W. Leak'	CSam CWri EHoe EPfP GGGa ISea LHyd LKna LMil MBri MLea MMor NMun SCog SExb SHBN SLeo SPer SReu SSta
'Mrs Helen Koster'	LKna
'Mrs Henry Agnew'	NMun SLeo
'Mrs J.C. Williams'	LKna LMil NMun SLeo
'Mrs J.G. Millais'	LKna LMil NMun SLeo
'Mrs James Horlick'	LHyd NMun SLeo
'Mrs Kingsmill'	SLeo
'Mrs Lindsay Smith'	LKna
Mrs Lionel de Rothschild Group & cl. 🏆	LKna LMil SReu
'Mrs P.D. Williams' 🏆	LKna SReu
'Mrs Philip Martineau'	LKna
'Mrs R.S. Holford' 🏆	LKna NMun SLeo
'Mrs T.H. Lowinsky'	EHoe MBri
'Mrs Tom H. Lowinsky' 🏆	CHig CWri GCHN GGGa LKna LMil MAsh MGos NMun SLeo SReu SSta
'Mrs W.C. Slocock'	LHyd LKna NMun SLeo SPer SReu SSta
'Mrs William Agnew'	LKna SLeo
'Mucronatum'	See ***R. mucronatum*** var. ***mucronatum***
'Mucronatum Amethystinum'	See **R. 'Amethystinum'**
§ ***mucronatum*** var. ***mucronatum*** (EA)	CHig GGGa NMun SLeo SPer SRms WBod
§ – var. ***ripense*** (EA)	GWht
mucronulatum	GGGa LHyd LMil NMun SLeo
– var. ***chejuense***	GGGa
– 'Cornell Pink'	GGGa LMil
– 'Mahogany Red'	GGGa
§ 'Multiflorum'	SReu
¶ 'Muncaster Bells'	NMun
'Muncaster Hybrid'	NMun
'Muncaster Mist'	LHyd NMun
'Muriel'	SLeo
'My Lady'	GGGa
myiagrum	See ***R. callimorphum*** var. ***myiagrum***
§ ***myrtifolium***	LHyd NMun SLeo
nakaharae (EA)	MBal NMun SCog SLeo SReu WAbe
§ – 'Mariko' (EA)	EPot GGGa LHyd LMil MBal MBar MBro MGos MOne NHol SCog WAbe WPat WPyg
– 'Mount Seven Stars' (EA)	CHig ECho GGGa LHyd LMil MBro MOne NHol SCog WPat
§ – orange (EA)	LMil MAsh SCog SHBN SPer SReu SSta
– pink (EA)	CHig LHyd LMil MAsh SCog SPer SSta
'Nakahari Orange'	See ***R. nakaharae*** **orange**
'Nakahari-mariko'	See ***R. nakaharae*** **'Mariko'**
'Nancy Evans'	COtt CSam GGGa ISea LMil MAsh MBal MDun MLea MMor SBid SCog SReu SSpi
'Nancy of Robinhill' (EA)	LHyd
'Nancy Waterer' (G) 🏆	SReu
'Nanki Poo' (EA)	LHyd SPer

'Naomi' (EA)	GQui GWht IOrc LKna LMil SCog SHBN
Naomi Group & cl.	CSam CWri ISea LKna MLea SReu
– 'Paris'	See ***R.*** **'Paris'**
'Naomi Astarte'	LKna SLeo
¶ 'Naomi Early Dawn'	NMun
'Naomi Exbury'	GGGa LHyd LKna LMil NMun SExb SLeo SReu
'Naomi Glow'	LMil
'Narcissiflorum' (G/d) 🏆	CDoC IOrc LHyd LKna LMil SPer SReu
'Naselle'	GGGa LMil
'Nassau' (EA/d)	LMil
neriiflorum	GGGa GWht ISea LMil NMun SCog SLeo SSpi
– Bu 287	GGGa
– L&S 1352	GGGa
§ – subsp. ***neriiflorum*** Euchaites Group	NMun SLeo
§ – – Phoenicodum Group	NMun
– – – Farrer 877	GGGa NMun
§ – subsp. ***phaedropum***	NMun
– – C&H 422	NMun SLeo
– – KR 1778	LMil
– – KW 6845*	NMun SLeo
– – KW 8521	NMun SLeo
– SF 366	ISea
– SF 375	ISea
Neriihaem Group	NMun SLeo
¶ ***nervulosum*** Argent (V)	GGGa
'Nettie' (EA)	SCog
'New Comet'	LHyd LMil NMun SReu
'New Moon'	SLeo SReu
'Newcomb's Sweetheart'	GGGa LMil SMur
'Niagara' (EA) 🏆	CTrh CWLN EPfP GQui LHyd LMil MBal SCog SExb WBod
'Nichola' (EA)	MAsh SBod SCog
'Nico'	CDoC CMac MAsh MBri SPer WBod WPat
'Night Sky'	GGGa LMil MOne SLeo
'Nightingale'	LMil SReu
nigroglandulosum	GGGa
nigropunctatum	See ***R. nivale*** subsp. ***boreale*** **Nigropunctatum Group**
nilagiricum	See ***R. arboreum*** subsp. ***nilagiricum***
'Nimbus'	LKna LMil SLeo
Nimrod Group	CWri NMun SLeo
'Nishiki' (EA)	CMac
nitens	See ***R. calostrotum*** subsp. ***riparium*** **Nitens Group**
nitidulum	NMun
¶ – var. ***nitidulum*** C 5059	GGGa
¶ – – C 5107	GGGa
– var. ***omeiense*** KR 185	GGGa LMil NHol
¶ ***nivale*** subsp. ***boreale*** Ramosissimum Group	GGGa
§ – – Stictophyllum Group	GGGa LMil
– subsp. ***nivale*** Sch 2269	NMun
niveum 🏆	GGGa LMil MBal NMun SLeo SReu SSta
– 'Nepal'	LHyd
'Noble Mountain'	LMil SMur
nobleanum	See ***R.*** **Nobleanum Group**
§ Nobleanum Group	GGGa ISea LHyd LKna LMil NMun SCog SLeo SSta
'Nobleanum Album'	LHyd LKna LMil MBal NMun SLeo SReu SSta
'Nobleanum Coccineum'	ISea NMun SLeo SReu
'Nobleanum Lamellen'	SLeo

'Nobleanum Venustum'	ISea LHyd LKna LMil SReu SSpi SSta WBod
'Nofretete'	GGGa
N 'Norma' (G) ♀	LMil SReu
Norman Shaw Group & cl.	LHyd
'Northern Star'	SLeo
'Northlight'	MBri
¶ ***notiale*** (V)	CEqu
'Nova Zembla'	CWLN GGGa MAsh MBar MGos SHBN SLeo SReu SSta WLRN WStI
nudiflorum	See ***R. periclymenoides***
nuttallii ♀	GGGa LMil MBal
'Oban'	GGGa WAbe
Obtusum Group (EA)	CHig LHyd
§ – 'Macrostemon'	WBod
occidentale (A) ♀	CGre GGGa LMil MBal SReu
– forms (A)	GGGa
¶ ***ochraceum*** C&H 7052	GGGa
'Odee Wright' ♀	CWri GGGa GWht LMil MAsh MDun MLea NMun SLeo SPer SReu SSpi SSta
'Oi-no-mezame' (EA)	LHyd
'Old Copper'	LNet MBri MLea NHol WGer
'Old Gold' (K)	SReu
'Old Port'	CWri LHyd MLea SHBN SReu SSta
Oldenburgh Group	NMun SLeo
oldhamii (EA)	CTre NMun SLeo
– ETOT 60 (EA)	GWht ISea
¶ – ETOT 601 (A)	GGGa
oleifolium 'Penheale Pink'	See ***R. virgatum*** subsp. ***oleifolium* 'Penheale Pink'**
'Olga'	LHyd LKna LMil NMun SPer SReu SSta
'Olga Mezitt'	GGGa LHyd LMil NHol
¶ 'Olin O. Dobbs'	WGer
'Olive'	LHyd LKna LMil SLeo
'Olive Judson'	SLeo
'Oliver Cromwell'	SReu
Olympic Lady Group	LHyd MLea NMun SLeo
'Olympic Sunrise'	LMil
Omar Group	MBar
§ 'One Thousand Butterflies'	COtt CWri GGGa LRHS MAsh MLea
'Optima' (EA)	SCog
'Orange Beauty' (EA) ♀	CMac CWLN GGGa GWht LHyd LKna MBal MBar MGos MMor NMun SBod SCog SExb SLeo SPer SReu SSta WBod WFar
'Orange Scout'	WGor WGwG
'Orangengold'	GGGa
orbiculare	GGGa IDee LHyd LMil NMun SCog SLeo SSta
– C&K 230	GGGa
§ – subsp. ***cardiobasis***	NMun
– Sandling Park form	SReu
– W V 1519	NMun SLeo
'Oregon Trail'	LMil
Oreocinn Group	MBal
oreodoxa	LMil NMun SLeo
§ – var. ***fargesii*** ♀	GGGa IOrc LHyd LMil NMun SLeo
§ – – Erubescens Group	NMun SLeo
– var. ***oreodoxa*** EN 4212	GGGa
– var. ***shensiense***	GGGa
– W A 4245	NMun
oreotrephes	IOrc LHyd LMil MBal MBri MDun NMun SLeo SReu
¶ – C&Cu 9449	GGGa
¶ – C&V 9557	GGGa
– 'Davidian's Favourite'	GGGa
– Exquisitum Group	SReu
– F 20489	NMun
– F 20629	NMun
– KW 9509	NMun
– R 96	NMun
¶ – SF 640	ISea
– Timeteum Group	SReu
orthocladum	LHyd LMil
– F 20488	GGGa NHol SLeo
§ – var. ***microleucum*** ♀	GGGa ISea LMil MBal NHar NMun SLeo
'Oryx' (O)	LKna
'Osmar'	GGGa MDun MGos
'Ostara'	CB&S COtt MGos
'Ostfriesland'	SRms
'Ouchiyama'	LKna
'Oudijk's Favorite'	MBal MGos
'Oudijk's Sensation'	GCHN LKna MGos MMor MOne SExb
'Ovation'	GGGa NHol
ovatum (A)	CB&S NMun SLeo WBod
– W A 1391 (A)	GGGa NMun SLeo
Oxlip Group	SLeo
'Oxydol' (K) ♀	GWht LHyd MAsh MLea
P J M Group	CSam CWri MAsh MBal MBri MLea SExb SSta
'P.J. Mezitt'	See ***R.* 'Peter John Mezitt'**
§ ***pachypodum***	GGGa
pachysanthum ♀	CWri LHyd MDun NHol NMun SMur SPer SReu SSpi
– 'Crosswater'	LMil
¶ – × ***proteoides***	GGGa
– RV 72/001	GGGa LMil NMun SLeo
pachytrichum	GGGa NMun SLeo
§ – Monosematum Group CNW 956	GGGa
– – W V 1522	NMun SLeo
– 'Sesame'	LMil
– W A 1203	NMun
'Palestrina' (EA) ♀	CB&S CChe CMac CWLN EPot GDTE GWht IOrc LHyd LKna MBal MMor NMun SBod SCog SExb SLeo SPer SReu SSta WFar
'Pallas' (G)	MBri SReu
'Palma'	See ***R. parmulatum* 'Palma'**
'Pamela Miles'	LHyd
'Pamela-Louise'	LHyd
'Pancake'	CMac
'Panda' (EA)	CDoC CMac EBee GGGa LHyd LMil MBar MBri NHar NHed SCog SCoo SReu WAbe
panteumorphum	See ***R.* × *erythrocalyx* Panteumorphum Group**
'Papaya Punch'	LMil
papillatum	NMun
'Paprika Spiced'	COtt CWri GWht LMil LRHS MAsh MBal MLea
'Parade' (A)	LMil
paradoxum	NMun
– C&K 228	GGGa
– CC&H 3906	GGGa
'Paramount' (K/d)	LKna
§ 'Paris'	LHyd
'Parisienne'	SCog
parmulatum	LMil NMun SLeo
– KW 5875	NMun
– mauve	NMun
– 'Ocelot'	GGGa LHyd
– pink	GGGa NMun
'Party Pink'	CWri LMil

'Patty Bee' 🏆	CSam CWri EPot GGGa LHyd LMil LRHS MAsh MBar MBri MGos MLea NHar NHol SBod SExb SReu SSpi SSta WAbe
patulum	See ***R. pemakoense*** **Patulum Group**
'Pavane' (K)	LKna
'Peace'	GGGa MBal NMun SLeo
'Peach Blossom'	See ***R.*** **'Saotome'**
'Pearl Diver'	LHyd
'Peep-bo' (EA)	LHyd SPer
'Peeping Tom'	LMil MAsh MDun MLea SBid SExb SHBN SLeo SReu
pemakoense	CMHG EPot GGGa GWht LHyd LMil MBal MBar MGos NHol NMun SIng SLeo SReu SRms WAbe WBod
§ – Patulum Group	GGGa MBar MDun NHol NMun SLeo WPat WPyg
'Pematit Cambridge'	SBod
pendulum	GGGa LMil
¶ – CH&M 3094	GGGa
– LS&T 6660	GGGa NMun
Penelope Group	SReu
'Penheale Blue' 🏆	CDoC CTre CWLN GGGa LMil NHed NHol SLeo WGer
Penjerrick Group & cl.	GGGa
'Penjerrick Cream'	NMun SLeo
'Penjerrick Pink'	NMun SLeo
pennivenium	See ***R. tanastylum*** var. ***pennivenium***
'Penrose'	CB&S
peramoenum	See ***R. arboreum*** subsp. ***delavayi*** var. ***peramoenum***
'Percy Wiseman'	CB&S CHig CSam CWri GGGa GWht IHos IOrc LHyd LMil LNet MBal MBar MBlu MBri MDun MLea MMor NHed NHol NMun SBar SCog SExb SLeo SPer SReu SSta WAbe
peregrinum	NMun SLeo
'Perfect'	MBal SPer
'Perfect Lady'	LMil LRHS
§ ***periclymenoides*** (A)	GGGa LMil
I 'Periwinkle' (V)	CEqu
'Persil' (K) 🏆	CB&S CSam ELan GGGa GRei LHyd LKna MBar MBri MGos MLea MMor SCoo SExb SPer SReu
§ 'Persimmon'	LKna NMun SLeo
'Peter Alan'	CWri MLea
'Peter Berg'	MGos
§ 'Peter John Mezitt' 🏆	GGGa LHyd LMil NMun SLeo SReu WGer
'Peter Koster' 🏆	CWri NMun SExb SHBN SLeo SMur WStI WWeb
'Petrouchka' (K)	LKna MAsh MBri
phaedropum	See ***R. neriiflorum*** subsp. ***phaedropum***
phaeochrysum	GGGa MDun NMun SLeo
– var. ***agglutinatum***	GGGa NMun
– – EGM 134	LMil
§ – var. ***levistratum***	NMun SReu
– – EGM 143	LMil
– McLaren cup winner	NMun SLeo
– var. ***phaeochrysum*** EGM 129	LMil
– – 'Greenmantle'	NMun
– R/USDA 59929/ R11325	NMun
'Phalarope'	CSam CWLN CWri GGGa LHyd MAsh MBal MBar MBri MDun MGos SReu WBod
'Pheasant Tail'	NMun SCog SLeo
'Phoebe'	SReu
phoenicodum	See ***R. neriiflorum*** subsp. ***neriiflorum*** **Phoenicodum Group**
pholidotum	See ***R. heliolepis*** var. ***brevistylum*** **Pholidotum Group F 6762**
'Phyllis Korn'	CAbP CHig CWri ISea LHyd LMil MLea SExb SPer
'Piccolo' (K/d)	LKna
§ ***piercei***	GGGa LMil NMun SLeo
– KW 11040	GGGa NMun SLeo
Pilgrim Group & cl.	LKna NMun
pingianum	CWri NMun
– KR 150	NMun
'Pink and Sweet' (A)	LMil MLea
'Pink Bountiful'	LKna
'Pink Cherub' 🏆	CWLN GWht IHos LHyd MBal MBar MBri MMor MOne NMun SCog SLeo SReu
N 'Pink Delight'	ERea LHyd LKna SExb WBod
'Pink Drift'	EPot GDra GWht ISea LKna MAsh MBal MBar MDun MGos MLea MMor NHar NHol NMun NRoo SBod SExb SHBN SLeo SReu STre WAbe WBod
'Pink Frills'	CB&S
'Pink Ghost'	NMun SLeo
'Pink Gin'	LMil
'Pink Glory'	NMun SLeo
'Pink Leopard'	ISea LMil MAsh NMun SBid WWeb
'Pink Pancake' (EA)	CB&S CTrh GQui LMil MGos MOne SCog SSpi WLRN WWeb
'Pink Pearl'	CB&S CHig CWLN GGGa ISea LHyd LKna LMil MAsh MBal MBar MGos MMor NHol NMun NWea SBod SCog SLeo SPer SReu SSta
'Pink Pebble' 🏆	CTrw LHyd NMun SLeo SReu
'Pink Perfection'	MGos NMun SLeo SReu
¶ 'Pink Poppet' (V)	CEqu
'Pink Rosette'	LKna
N 'Pink Ruffles'	EBee WBod
'Pink Sensation'	MBri
'Pinkerton'	LKna
'Pintail'	GGGa
'Pipaluk'	LHyd
'Pipit'	GGGa LMil MBal WAbe
'Pippa' (EA) 🏆	CMac SRms
'PJM Elite'	GGGa
¶ (PJM Group) 'Rim Checkmate'	GGGa
¶ × ***planecostatum*** (V)	CEqu
planetum	SLeo
pleistanthum	NMun
– F 15002	GGGa
– R 11288*	NMun
pocophorum	GGGa LHyd NMun SLeo
– forms	NMun SLeo
§ – var. ***hemidartum***	GGGa NMun SLeo
– – R/USDA 59190/ R11201	NMun
– KW 21075	NMun
– R/USDA 59190/ R11201	NMun
pogonostylum	See ***R. irroratum*** subsp. ***pogonostylum***
'Point Defiance'	GGGa MLea
'Polar Bear' (EA)	MBal MBar MGos
Polar Bear Group & cl. 🏆	COtt CSam CWri GAri GGGa ISea LHyd LMil NMun SLeo SReu WGer

'Polar Haven' (EA)	LKna
'Polar Sea'	CTrh SBod
'Polaris'	LHyd LMil MBri MGos SReu
'Polgrain'	CB&S
§ ***poluninii***	GGGa
polyandrum	See ***R. maddenii*** subsp. ***maddenii* Polyandrum Group**
'Polycinn'	SCog
§ ***polycladum***	CSam GGGa LHyd LMil MBal MLea
– Scintillans Group 🏆	GDra MBar MBri MLea NHol NMun SLeo
polylepis	GGGa NMun SLeo
– C&K 284	GGGa
¶ – EN 3619	GGGa
'Ponticum'	See ***R. ponticum***
§ ***ponticum***	CWri GGGa ISea LHyd MBar MGos MLea MMor NWea SPer
– (A)	See ***R. luteum***
– AC&H 205	GGGa
– 'Cheiranthifolium'	NMun SLeo
– 'Foliis Purpureis'	SReu
– 'Silver Edge'	LMil SMur
– 'Variegatum' (v)	CB&S CHig EBre GGGa IOrc ISea MBal MBar MBri MGos MMor MUlv NMun SPer SReu SRms SSta WGer WWeb
'Pooh-Bah' (EA)	LHyd
'Pook'	LHyd
'Popacatapetl'	SReu
'Port Knap' (EA)	LKna
'Port Wine' (EA)	LKna
'Potlatch'	GGGa
poukhanense	See ***R. yedoense*** var. ***poukhanense***
'Powder Puff'	LMil
§ 'Praecox' 🏆	CB&S CHig CSam CTrw ENot GGGa GRei ISea LHyd LKna LMil MAsh MBal MBar MBri MGos MMor NHol NMun NWea SBar SBod SCog SHBN SPer SReu SSta WBod
praecox	See ***R.* 'Praecox'**
◆ – 'Emasculum'	See ***R.* 'Emasculum'**
praestans	GGGa LMil MDun NMun SLeo
– KW 13369	NMun
– P Cox 6025A	GGGa
praeteritium	SLeo
praevernum	GGGa LMil NMun SReu
prattii	See ***R. faberi*** subsp. ***prattii***
'Prawn'	LKna SReu
preptum	GGGa NMun SLeo
'President Roosevelt' (v)	CHig IHos IOrc LKna LNet MBal MGos MMor NMun SHBN SLeo SPer SReu SSta WWeb
'Pretty Girl'	LKna
'Pridenjoy'	LMil
'Prima Donna'	LMil SReu
primuliflorum	GGGa LMil SReu
– Cephalanthoides Group	GGGa
– 'Doker-La'	LMil
– KW 4160	NMun
'Prince Camille de Rohan'	LMil SMur
'Princess Alice' 🏆	CB&S CGre CHig COtt ERea GGGa ISea LHyd MBal SCog
'Princess Anne' 🏆	CHig CMHG CSam CWLN EPot GDra GGGa GRei LHyd LMil MAsh MBal MBar MDun MGos MLea NHol NMun SBod SCog SHBN SLeo SPer SReu SSta

'Princess Ida' (EA)	LHyd
'Princess Juliana'	WGor
¶ 'Princess Margaret of Windsor' (K)	GQui
principis	GGGa LMil MDun NMun
¶ – C&V 9547	GGGa
– LS&E 15831	NMun
§ – Vellereum Group	NMun SLeo
'Prins Bernhard' (EA)	IOrc LKna MAsh
'Prinses Juliana' (EA)	MMor MOne SExb SReu WFar
'Professor Hugo de Vries' 🏆	LKna MGos SReu
'Professor J.H. Zaayer'	MGos SLeo
pronum	GGGa
– R 151*	NMun
¶ – R.B. Cooke form	GGGa
¶ – Towercourt form	GGGa
§ 'Prostigiatum'	GDra GGGa MGos
prostigiatum	See ***R.* 'Prostigiatum'**
prostratum	See ***R. saluenense*** subsp. ***chameunum* Prostratum Group**
proteoides	GGGa
* – 'Ascreavie'	GGGa
¶ – C 6542	GGGa
¶ – KGB 700	GGGa
– R 151	NMun
protistum	LMil NMun SLeo
§ – var. ***giganteum***	CWri LMil NMun SLeo SReu
– KR 1986	GGGa
– KW 8069	NMun
pruniflorum	GGGa NMun SLeo
– KW 7038	NMun
prunifolium (A)	LMil
– 'Summer Sunset' (A)	NMun
przewalskii	GGGa NMun SLeo
¶ – C 5073	GGGa
¶ – C&K 370	GGGa
– CH&M 2545	NHol
– var. ***dabanshanense***	GGGa
pseudochrysanthum 🏆	CWri GGGa LHyd LMil MBal NHol NMun SCog SLeo SReu SSta
– ETE 442	GGGa
– ETE 443	GGGa
– ETOT 162	GWht
– ETOT 164	GWht
– ETOT 167	ISea
Psyche Group	See ***R.* Wega Group**
'Ptarmigan' 🏆	CB&S CMHG CSam EPot GGGa GWht LHyd LMil MBal MBar MDun MGos MMor NHar NHol NMun SBod SCog SLeo SReu SSta WBod WPat
pubescens	LMil NMun SLeo
– KW 3953	GGGa
pudorosum	NMun
– L&S 2752	GGGa
'Puget Sound'	SLeo
pumilum	GDra GGGa MBal MDun WAbe
'Puncta'	GGGa NHol
punctatum	See ***R. minus*** var. ***minus* Punctatum Group**
purdomii	GGGa SLeo
◆ 'Purple Diamond'	See ***R.* Diamant Group purple**
'Purple Emperor'	LKna
'Purple Gem'	NHar NHol SBar
'Purple Heart'	ENot
'Purple Peterli'	GGGa
'Purple Queen' (EA/d)	MAsh
'Purple Splendor' (EA)	CChe CMac CWLN IOrc LKna MGos

'Purple Splendour' 🏆	CB&S CHig CWLN CWri GGGa GWht LKna LMil MBal MBar MBri MDun MGos MMor NMun NWea SCog SHBN SLeo SPer SReu SSta WWeb
'Purple Triumph' (EA)	CB&S IOrc LKna LMil NMun SLeo SReu SSta WBod
'Purpur Geisha'	GGGa
¶ 'Purpurtraum' (A)	GGGa
Quaver Group	SRms
'Queen Alice'	MDun
'Queen Anne's'	LMil MBal SSta
'Queen Elizabeth II' 🏆	LHyd LMil SPer SReu SSta
◆ Queen Emma	See ***R.* 'Koningin Emma'**
'Queen Mary'	MBar MMor
'Queen Mother'	See ***R.* 'The Queen Mother'**
Queen of Hearts Group & cl. 🏆	LHyd NMun SLeo
'Queen Souriya'	SReu
Queen Wilhelmina	See ***R.* 'Koningin Wilhelmina'**
quinquefolium (A) 🏆	NMun SLeo
racemosum	CB&S CGre CSam GWht LMil MBar NMun SLeo SPer SReu SSpi SSta
– 'Glendoick'	GGGa
– 'Rock Rose' 🏆	EPfP GGGa LHyd LMil NMun
– SF 365	ISea
– SSNY 47	GGGa
– x ***tephropeplum***	MBal MBar
– x ***trichocladum*** SBEC	NHol
– TW 385	GWht
– 'White Lace'	LHyd
'Racil'	LHyd LKna MBal MBar MGos MLea MMor
'Racoon' (EA)	GGGa
radicans	See ***R. calostrotum* subsp. *keleticum* Radicans Group**
'Rainbow'	LKna
'Ramapo' 🏆	CHig GGGa LMil MAsh MBal MBar MGos MLea MOne NHar NHol SPer SReu SSta WAbe WBod
ramsdenianum	GGGa NMun SLeo
¶ 'Rangoon'	GGGa
'Raphael de Smet' (G/d)	SReu
rarum (V)	CEqu
'Rashomon' (EA)	LHyd NMun SLeo WBod
¶ 'Raspberry Delight' (K/d)	SMur
'Raspberry Ripple'	LKna SReu
ravum	See ***R. cuneatum* Ravum Group**
'Razorbill' 🏆	EPot GGGa LHyd LMil MBri MGos NHar SReu WAbe
recurvoides	GGGa LHyd LMil NMun SReu SSta
– Keillour form	GGGa
– KW 7184	NMun SLeo
recurvum	See ***R. roxieanum* var. *roxieanum***
Red Admiral Group	NMun SLeo
Red Argenteum Group	NMun SLeo
'Red Bird' (EA)	CMac
'Red Carpet' 🏆	LMil LRHS
'Red Delicious'	LMil
◆ 'Red Diamond'	See ***R.* Diamant Group red**
'Red Dragon'	SLeo
'Red Fountain' (EA)	CWLN LMil SCog WLRN WWeb
'Red Glow'	LHyd SLeo
'Red Jack'	CDoC
'Red Poll'	LHyd
'Red Red'	GGGa
'Red Riding Hood'	CWri LKna
'Red Rum'	LHyd
'Red Sunset' (EA/d)	LMil
'Red Velour'	CAbP
'Red Wood'	GGGa
¶ 'Redmond' (EA)	LHyd
'Redshank' (K)	MBri
'Redwing' (EA)	LRHS SPer
'Reich's Schneewittchen'	GGGa
Remo Group	MBal SCog SLeo
'Rendezvous'	LMil SReu
'Renoir' 🏆	LHyd LMil SCog SLeo SReu
Repose Group & cl.	LKna
reticulatum (A) 🏆	GWht LMil NMun SLeo SReu SSta
* ***reticulatum leucanthum***	GGGa
reticulatum 'Sea King' (A)	LHyd
¶ ***retusum*** (V)	GGGa
§ 'Reuthe's Purple' 🏆	GGGa MBal NHol NMun SLeo SReu SSta
'Rêve d'Amour' (Vs)	MMor SReu SSta
Rêve Rose Group & cl.	SCog
'Revlon'	LHyd
'Rex' (EA)	CWLN EBee
rex	COtt GGGa IDee IOrc LHyd LMil MBal MDun NMun SLeo
§ – subsp. ***arizelum***	GGGa LMil MDun NMun SLeo
– – R 25	GGGa
– – Rubicosum Group	NMun SLeo
§ – subsp. ***fictolacteum***	GGGa LHyd LMil MBal NMun SLeo SReu
– – 'Cherry Tip' R 11395	NMun SLeo
– – var. ***miniforme*** F 25512	GGGa
– – R/USDA 59104/ R11043	NMun SLeo
– – SF 649	ISea
– – TW 407	GWht
– Sich 1037	GGGa
– Sich 1134	GGGa
– Sich 1154	GGGa
– Sich 1159	GGGa
– Sich 1236	GGGa
– x Sincerity Group	NMun SLeo
rhabdotum	See ***R. dalhousieae* var. *rhabdotum***
'Ria Hardijzer'	LKna MBri
Rickshaw Group	SLeo
rigidum	LHyd LMil NMun SCog SLeo
* ***rigidum album***	CHig NMun
'Ring of Fire'	CDoC CWri LMil SReu
'Ripe Corn'	CBlo LKna NMun SLeo SReu
ripense	See ***R. mucronatum* var. *ripense***
Riplet Group 🏆	EPot GAri GGGa MLea NHar SLeo WAbe
ririei	GGGa LHyd NMun
– Guiz 75	GGGa
– W 5139	NMun
– W V 1808	NMun
'Robert Keir' 🏆	LHyd NMun SLeo
'Robert Korn'	LMil MDun
'Robert Seleger'	GGGa LMil MAsh MBri NHar
'Robert Whelan' (A)	MMor SReu
§ 'Roberte'	SCog
'Robin Hill Frosty' (EA)	LHyd
'Robin Hill Gillie' (EA)	LHyd
Robin Hood Group	NMun
'Robin Redbreast'	LHyd NMun SLeo
'Robinette'	GGGa
'Rocket'	CAbP LMil MAsh MDun MLea NMun WWeb
Romany Chai Group	LHyd LMil MBal SCog SPer
'Romy'	NMun SLeo
'Rosa Mundi'	EBee ENot

'Rosabelle'	CEqu
'Rosata' (Vs)	GGGa MBri MMor SReu SSta
'Rose Elf'	MBal MOne NHar NHol
'Rose Glow'	MMor SReu
'Rose Greeley' (EA)	CDoC CHig GQui IOrc SBod SCog SExb SReu WFar WLRN WWeb
'Rose Haze'	MMor SReu
'Rose Ruffles' (K)	GGGa LMil SMur
'Rose Torch'	MMor SReu
roseatum F 17227	GGGa
'Rosebud' (EA/d) 🏆	CB&S CGre CHig CMac CTrw CWLN ECho GDTE GGGa GWht IOrc LHyd LKna MBar MGos MMor NMun SBod SCog SExb SLeo SPer SReu WBod WLRN
roseotinctum	See ***R. sanguineum*** subsp. ***sanguineum*** var. ***didymoides*** **Roseotinctum Group**
roseum	See ***R. austrinum***
'Roseum Elegans'	ECho LMil MBar NMun SLeo
'Rosie Posie' (V)	CEqu
'Rosiflorum'	See ***R. indicum*** **'Balsaminiflorum'**
'Rosy Bell'	LKna
'Rosy Cream'	SPer
'Rosy Dream'	CAbP LMil MLea MOne SMur
'Rosy Fire' (A)	SReu
'Rosy Lea'	MLea
'Rosy Lights'	CTri LMil
'Rothenburg'	LHyd LMil SReu
rothschildii	GGGa LHyd LMil MDun NMun SLeo SMur
– C&Cu 9312	GGGa
roxieanum	LMil NMun SLeo SReu
§ – var. ***cucullatum***	NMun
¶ – – CNW 680	GGGa
¶ – – dwarf Dawyck	GGGa
– – R 10920	NMun
– – SBEC 0345	NMun SLeo
– var. ***oreonastes*** 🏆	GGGa LHyd LMil MDun NMun SLeo SSta
¶ – – CNW 307	GGGa
¶ – – CNW 723	GGGa
¶ – – CNW 740	GGGa
¶ – – CNW 743	GGGa
– – Nymans form	SReu
– – R/USDA 59222/ R11312	GGGa NMun
– R 25422	NMun SLeo
– R/USDA 59159/ R11141	NMun SLeo
§ – var. ***roxieanum***	NMun
¶ – – CNW 727	GGGa
– – F 16508	NMun
'Royal Blood'	LHyd
'Royal Command' (K)	COtt GAri GRei MAsh MBar MMor SExb
Royal Flush Group	CB&S ISea
'Royal Lodge' (K) 🏆	SBid
'Royal Pink'	SBod
'Royal Ruby' (K)	MBri MMor
'Roza Stevenson' 🏆	LHyd NMun SLeo SPer
'Rozanne Waterer' (K)/d	LKna
'Rubicon'	CB&S CWri
rubiginosum	CSam GGGa GWht IOrc ISea LHyd LMil MBal NMun SCog SLeo SReu
§ – Desquamatum Group	LHyd NMun SLeo
– SF 368	ISea
– SF 404	ISea
– white	LMil
Rubina Group	SLeo
'Rubinetta' (EA)	WFar
rubroluteum	See ***R. viridescens*** **Rubroluteum Group**
'Ruby F. Bowman'	CWri MGos MLea NMun SLeo SReu
'Ruby Hart'	GGGa NHol SReu
rude	See ***R. glischrum*** subsp. ***rude***
rufum	GGGa NMun SLeo
– Hummel 31	NMun
– Sich 155	GGGa
– W V 1808*	NMun SLeo
¶ ***rugosum*** Sinclair 240 (V)	GGGa
'Rumba' (K)	LKna
'Rumplestilzchen'	GGGa
rupicola	CHig GDra LMil MBal NMun
§ – var. ***chryseum***	GGGa LHyd LMil NMun SLeo
– var. ***muliense***	LMil NMun
¶ – – Yu 14042	GGGa
russatum 🏆	CSam EBee EPot GDra GGGa GWht LHyd LMil MBri NGre NMun SLeo
– blue-black	LMil
¶ – C&Cu 9315	GGGa
– 'Purple Pillow'	NHar
* – 'Tower Court'	NMun
– Waterer form	LMil
russotinctum	See ***R. alutaceum*** var. ***russotinctum***
'Sacko'	CHig ECho GGGa LMil MOne
'Saffron Queen'	CB&S CGre CTrw ISea MBal
'Sahara' (K)	LKna
'Saint Breward'	GGGa LHyd MBal MLea NHol SBod SCog SPer WAbe WBod
'Saint Merryn' 🏆	CTrh GAri GGGa LHyd MAsh MBri NHol NMun SLeo WGer WWeb
'Saint Michael'	SReu
'Saint Minver' 🏆	LHyd
'Saint Tudy' 🏆	CB&S LHyd LKna MBal MMor NMun SBid SLeo SPer WAbe WBod
'Sakata Red' (EA)	CGre CMac IOrc SExb WBod
'Sakon' (EA)	NMun SLeo
'Salmon's Leap' (EA/v)	CB&S COtt GQui LMil MAsh MGos SCog SCoo SHBN SPer WFar WWeb
saluenense	GGGa LHyd LMil MBal NMun
§ – subsp. ***chameunum*** 🏆	GGGa LMil MBal NMun SLeo WAbe WGer
¶ – – C 6112	GGGa
– – Exbury form R 11005	LMil
§ – – Prostratum Group	GGGa MBal WAbe
– F 19479	NMun
¶ 'Sammetglut'	CWri
'Samuel Taylor Coleridge' (M)	MMor
sanctum	LMil NMun SLeo
'Sandling'	LHyd
'Sang de Gentbrugge' (G)	SReu
sanguineum	GGGa GWht LMil NMun SLeo
§ – subsp. ***didymum***	GGGa NMun SLeo
– P Cox 6056	GGGa
– subsp. ***sanguineum*** var. ***cloiophorum*** F 25521	LMil
– – – R 10899	NMun SLeo
– – – R/USDA 59096/ R11029	NMun SLeo
– – – R/USDA 59553/ R11212	NMun SLeo
– – var. ***didymoides*** Consanguineum Group	NMun SLeo
– – – – KW 6831	LMil
– – – R 10903	GGGa LMil NMun SLeo
§ – – – Roseotinctum Group	LMil

– – – – R/USDA 59038/ R10903	NMun
– – var. ***haemaleum***	GGGa LMil NMun SLeo
– – – F 21732	NMun SLeo
– – – F 21735	GGGa NMun SLeo
– – – R 10893	NMun SLeo
¶ – – – R 31	GGGa
– – – R/USDA 59303/ R10895	NMun SLeo
– – – R/USDA 59453/ R10938	NMun SLeo
'Santa Maria'	COtt SReu SSta
santapaui (V)	CEqu
§ 'Saotome' (EA)	CMac LHyd
'Sapphire' ♀	EBee EHic EPot GWht LKna MBal MBar SBod SLeo SPer SRms
'Sappho' ♀	CB&S CWLN CWri GGGa IHos IOrc ISea LHyd LKna LMil MBal MBar MGos MMor NMun SBid SCog SHBN SLeo SPer SReu SSta WGer WWeb
'Sapporo'	GGGa
sargentianum ♀	LMil MLea NMun SLeo
– 'Maricee'	GGGa MAsh MBri WGer
– 'Whitebait'	GGGa NMun WPat
Sarita Loder Group & cl.	SLeo
Sarled Group ♀	EPot GDra GGGa LHyd LMil MAsh MBal NHar NMun SBid SLeo SPer SReu SRms WAbe WWat
'Saroi' (EA)	NMun SLeo
'Saskia' (K)	LKna
'Satan' (K) ♀	COtt ELan GAri GGGa LKna MBri MMor SReu
'Satsuki' (EA)	CGre ECho LNet MAsh MOne WWeb
'Saturnus' (M)	ELan
scabrifolium	NMun SLeo
§ – var. ***spiciferum***	GGGa MBal NMun SLeo WAbe
'Scarlet Wonder' ♀	CWLN CWri EBre GGGa GRei GWht LKna LMil MBal MBar MBri MGos MLea MMor NHol NMun SBod SCog SExb SLeo SReu SSta WBod
Scarlett O'Hara Group	LHyd
schlippenbachii (A) ♀	CGre GGGa GWht LHyd LMil MBal NMun SLeo SPer SReu SSta WWat
– 'Sid's Royal Pink' (A)	LMil SReu
'Schneekrone'	GGGa LMil NHol
'Schubert' (EA)	MBar MGos WBod
scintillans	See ***R. polycladum***
'Scintillation'	CDoC CSam CWri EBee GGGa ISea LMil MBal MLea NMun SBid SHBN SLeo
scopulorum	LHyd NMun SLeo
– KW 6354	GGGa NMun
scottianum	See ***R. pachypodum***
scyphocalyx	See ***R. dichroanthum*** subsp. ***scyphocalyx***
Seagull Group & cl.	NMun SLeo
searsiae	LMil NMun SLeo
– W A 1343	NMun
'Sea-Tac'	MLea
¶ 'Second Honeymoon'	CWri GWht ISea LRHS MAsh MLea SHBN SReu SSta WWeb
'Seikai' (EA)	CBlo
seinghkuense KW 9254	GGGa
selense	GGGa NMun
§ – subsp. ***dasycladum***	LMil NMun SLeo
– – F 11312	NMun
– – KW 7189	NMun
– – R 11269	NMun
– subsp. ***jucundum***	GGGa LMil NMun
– P Cox 6024	GGGa
– P Cox 6041	GGGa
§ – subsp. ***setiferum***	NMun
– – F 14458	NMun SLeo
semnoides	GGGa NMun SLeo
– F 21870	NMun
– F 25639	NMun
– R 25388	NMun
'Senator Henry Jackson'	GGGa LMil
'Sennocke' ♀	GGGa LHyd
'September Song'	CDoC CHig COtt CWri GGGa LHyd LMil MAsh MBal MLea
'Serendipity'	GGGa
serotinum	CWri NMun SLeo SReu
serpyllifolium (A)	CB&S GGGa NMun SLeo
– var. ***albiflorum*** (A)	GAri
'Sesterianum'	CMHG
Seta Group & cl. ♀	CB&S CHig EPot LHyd MBal MLea NMun SLeo SReu
setiferum	See ***R. selense*** subsp. ***setiferum***
setosum	GGGa LMil MBal NMun SLeo
– TW 30	GWht
'Seven Stars' ♀	LHyd NMun SCog SLeo SReu WPyg
'Shamrock'	CDoC CSam GWht ISea MAsh MBal MBar MLea NHar NHol SBar WBod
'Sham's Candy'	ERea
'Shanty' (K/d)	LKna
¶ × ***sheilae*** (V)	CEqu
shepherdii	See ***R. kendrickii***
sherriffii	GGGa LHyd NMun SLeo
– L&S 2751	NMun
Shilsonii Group	LHyd NMun SLeo SReu
'Shin Seikai' (EA/d)	CB&S
¶ 'Shinimiagagino' (EA)	NMun SLeo
'Shinnyo-no-hikari'	GAri
'Shi-no-noe' (EA)	NMun SBod SLeo
'Shinsei' (EA)	GAri
'Shintoki-no-hagasane' (EA)	LHyd
'Shintsune' (EA)	NMun SLeo
¶ Shot Silk Group	NMun
'Shrimp Girl'	CDoC CWLN EBee IHos ISea LHyd MBal MGos MLea MMor NMun SCog SLeo SReu
'Shukishima' (EA)	NMun SLeo
'Shuku-fuku' (EA)	GAri
shweliense	GGGa LMil SReu
sidereum	GGGa LMil NMun SLeo
¶ – KR 2710	GGGa
– KW 13649	NMun SLeo
– KW 6792	NMun
– SF 314	ISea
– SF 318	ISea
– TW 345	GWht
– TW 350	GWht
siderophyllum	NMun
sikangense	MDun NMun
– C&K 246	GGGa
§ – Cookeanum Group	NMun
– EGM 108	LMil
– P Cox 5012	GGGa
– P Cox 5105	GGGa NHol
– R 18142	NMun
* ***sikkimense*** SD 1108	GGGa
§ 'Silberwolke'	EBee MBri SReu
'Silkcap'	WWeb
'Silky'	MBal
◆ Silver Cloud	See ***R.* 'Silberwolke'**

'Silver Glow' (EA)	CMac
'Silver Jubilee'	LHyd LMil
'Silver Moon' (EA)	CBlo IOrc NMun SBod SCog SExb SLeo SPer
'Silver Sixpence' 🏆	CDoC CMHG GWht IHos IOrc MAsh MBal MBar MDun MLea NMun SCog SExb SHBN SLeo SMad SReu WWeb
'Silver Skies'	LMil
'Silver Slipper' (K) 🏆	CGre CWLN GAri GWht LHyd LKna LMil MBal MBar MBri MLea MMor SExb SReu SSta WGor
'Silverwood' (K)	LMil
'Silvester' (EA)	COtt EBee MBri MMor WPat
simiarum	GGGa
'Simona'	CWri SReu
simsii (EA)	CMac
– SF 431 (EA)	ISea
simulans	NMun
– F 20428	GGGa NMun
'Sinbad'	SLeo
¶ ***sinofalconeri*** C&H 7183	GGGa
– SF 92142	ISea
sinogrande 🏆	CB&S CHEx GGGa IOrc LMil MBal NMun SArc SLeo SPer
– KW 21111	NMun SLeo
– SF 327	ISea
– SF 329	ISea
– SF 350	ISea
– TW 341	GWht
– TW 383	GWht
'Sir Charles Lemon'	See ***R. arboreum* 'Sir Charles Lemon'**
Sir Frederick Moore Group & cl.	SCog
* 'Sir G.E. Simpson'	NMun SLeo
'Sir William Lawrence' (EA)	LKna SReu
Siren Group & cl.	MBal
'Skookum'	LMil MGos MOne SMur
'Sleepy'	ELan IHos IOrc NHed NMun SCog SExb SLeo SPer SReu WLRN
smirnowii	GGGa LHyd LMil MBal NMun SLeo SReu SSta
smithii	See ***R. macrosmithii***
– Argipeplum Group	See ***R. argipeplum***
'Sneezy'	CB&S CDoC GGGa GRei IHos LHyd LMil MAsh MBal MBar MGos MLea NHol NMun SCog SLeo SReu SSta
'Snipe' 🏆	CSam EBre EPot GGGa LHyd LMil MAsh MBal MBar MBri MGos MLea MOne NHar NHol SReu
'Snow' (EA)	CMac LMil MBar
'Snow Crown'	MAsh MOne
'Snow Hill' (EA)	GQui LHyd LMil
'Snow Lady' 🏆	EBee GWht LMil MAsh MBal MBar MGos MLea NHar NHol SBid SCog SIng WAbe
Snow Queen Group & cl. 🏆	GGGa LKna LMil SExb SReu WWeb
'Snowbird'	GGGa
'Snowflake'	See ***R.* 'Kure-no-yuki'**
'Soho' (EA)	GAri GQui LNet
'Soir de Paris' (Vs)	MBar MBri MMor SReu SSta
'Soldier Sam'	SReu SSta
'Solidarity'	MBal MBri WLRN
'Solway' (Vs)	LMil
'Sonata'	GAri GGGa MBal MBri MDun SReu
'Songbird'	CSam EPot GCHN GDra LHyd LKna LMil MAsh MBal MBar MBri SBid SReu WBod
'Songster'	SLeo
'Sophie Hedges' (K/d)	LKna
sororium KR 3080	GGGa
Souldis Group	LMil SMur
souliei	GGGa IOrc LHyd LMil NMun SLeo
– C&K 371	GGGa
– P Cox 5056	GGGa
– white	GGGa
'Southern Cross'	CSam CWri GGGa LHyd LMil NMun
'Souvenir de Doctor S. Endtz' 🏆	CBlo LKna MBal MBar MMor
'Souvenir du Président Carnot' (G/d)	LKna
'Souvenir of Anthony Waterer' 🏆	LHyd LKna MMor SReu SSta
'Souvenir of W.C. Slocock'	CSam LKna NMun SHBN SLeo SReu SSta
¶ 'Sparkler' (Vs)	GGGa
'Sparkler'	MGos MLea WWeb
'Spek's Orange' (M) 🏆	LHyd MAsh MGos SReu
sperabile	NMun
– F 26446	SLeo
– F 26453	SLeo
– var. ***weihsiense***	GGGa NMun SLeo
sperabiloides	GGGa NMun
– R 125	NMun
sphaeranthum	See ***R. trichostomum***
sphaeroblastum	GGGa LMil NMun SLeo
– F 20416	SLeo
¶ – KR 1481	NMun
¶ – var. ***wumengense*** CNW 510	ISea
¶ – – CNW 942	GGGa
¶ – – CNW 963	GGGa
¶ – – CNW 968	GGGa
¶ – – SF 515	ISea
spiciferum	See ***R. scabrifolium*** var. ***spiciferum***
'Spicy Lights'	LMil
spilotum	GGGa NMun SLeo
spinuliferum	GGGa LHyd NMun SLeo
– SF 247	ISea
'Spinulosum'	LHyd
'Spitfire'	MGos MMor SLeo SReu
'Spoonbill' (K)	LKna
'Spring Beauty' (EA)	CMac SExb
'Spring Dream'	See ***R.* 'Frühlingstraum'**
'Spring Magic'	LMil MAsh
'Spring Pearl'	See ***R.* 'Moerheim's Pink'**
'Spring Rose'	SBid
'Spring Sunshine'	LMil
'Springbok'	LHyd
'Squirrel' (EA)	CDoC CMac COtt EBre GGGa GRei LHyd LMil MAsh MBal MBri MGos NHar NHed NHol SCog SReu WAbe WPat
¶ 'Staccato'	GGGa
Stadt Essen Group & cl.	GGGa LMil
stamineum	NMun
– W V 887	NMun SLeo
'Stanley Rivlin'	LHyd SCog SLeo
§ 'Stanway'	LMil NMun
'Starcross'	LHyd
'Starfish'	SReu
'Stella'	NMun SLeo

stenaulum	See ***R. moulmainense***
stewartianum	GGGa MDun NMun SLeo
– CLD 1300	LMil
– F 26921	NMun
– SF 370	ISea
'Stewartstonian' (EA) ♀	CMac CTrh GWht IOrc LHyd LMil MBal MBar MMor SBod SReu SSta WFar
stictophyllum	See ***R. nivale*** subsp. ***boreale*** **Stictophyllum Group**
'Stoat' (EA)	GQui MBri
'Stranraer'	MAsh MBri
'Strawberry Cream'	GGGa NHol
'Strawberry Ice' (K) ♀	CMHG CWLN EPfP GGGa GWht IOrc LHyd LKna LMil MAsh MBar MBri MGos MLea SExb SPer SReu
'Streatley' ♀	SCog SLeo
strigillosum	GGGa NMun SLeo
¶ – C&H 7035	GGGa
¶ – C&H 7047	GGGa
– Reuthe's form	SReu
'Striped Beauty'	MBal
'Suave'	SCog
subansiriense C&H 418	GGGa NMun SLeo
suberosum	See ***R. yunnanense*** **Suberosum Group**
succothii	GGGa LHyd NMun SLeo
– BB 185A	NMun
– CH&M 3079	GGGa
– CH&M 3105	GGGa
– CH&M 3109	GGGa NHol
– CH&M 3125	GGGa NHol
– EGM 086	LMil
– LS&H 19850	NMun
– LS&H 21295	NMun SLeo
'Suede'	SReu
'Sugar Pink'	CDoC LMil
'Sugared Almond' (K) ♀	MBal
'Sugi-no-ito'	See ***R.*** **'Kumo-no-ito'**
sulfureum	GGGa NMun
¶ – SBEC 0249	GGGa
'Sumatra'	GGGa
'Summer Blaze'	SReu
'Summer Flame'	SReu
'Summer Fragrance' (O) ♀	MMor SReu SSta
'Sun Chariot' (K) ♀	CB&S CWLN GRei LHyd LKna LMil MBri MLea SReu SSpi
'Sunbeam' (EA)	See ***R.*** **'Benifude'**
'Sunbeam'	CBlo LKna SReu
I 'Sundance'	LMil
¶ 'Sunny' (V)	GGGa
'Sunny Splendour' (V)	ERea
'Sunset over Harkwood'	LRHS
'Sunset Pink' (K)	CBlo CWLN ISea LHyd LMil MAsh WWeb
'Sunte Nectarine' (K) ♀	GQui LHyd LMil MBri SCoo
¶ 'Superbum' (O)	SReu
superbum (V)	GGGa NMun
'Surprise' (EA)	CTrh CTri EBee MAsh NMun SCog SCoo SExb SLeo
'Surrey Heath' ♀	CB&S COtt CWri GGGa GRei GWht LHyd LMil LNet MAsh MBal MBar MBri MDun MGos MLea MMor NHed NHol NMun SCog SExb SLeo SReu SSpi SSta WAbe
'Susan' ♀	CHig CWri GGGa LHyd LKna LMil MLea MMor NMun SCog SLeo SReu

'Susannah Hill' (EA)	CB&S CTrh CWLN LMil SBod SPer WPat
'Sussex Bonfire'	NMun SLeo
sutchuenense	CB&S CHig GGGa IDee LMil MDun NMun SLeo
– var. ***geraldii***	See ***R.*** × ***geraldii***
'Swamp Beauty'	CWri GGGa LMil
'Swansdown'	CWri MDun SPer
'Swansong' (EA)	CMac SCog
¶ 'Sweet Mac' (V)	CEqu
'Sweet Seraphim' (V)	CEqu
'Sweet Simplicity' ♀	LKna MBal
'Sweet Sixteen'	CWri NMun SLeo
'Sweet Sue'	EBee MAsh MBal NMun SCog SLeo SReu WLRN
'Swift'	GGGa GQui
'Sylphides' (K)	GAri LKna MBri
'Sylvester'	CDoC MGos SReu
¶ 'Sylvia' (EA/d)	EPfP
taggianum 'Cliff Hanger'	LMil
'Takasago' (EA/d)	LHyd LMil SCog
◆ 'Talavera'	See ***R.*** **(Golden Oriole Group) 'Talavera'**
taliense	GGGa LHyd LMil NMun SLeo
– F 6772	NMun SLeo
– KR 2765	GGGa
– SBEC 0350	GGGa
– SF 92069	ISea
– SSNY 352	GGGa
Tally Ho Group & cl.	ISea NMun SLeo SReu
tamaense	See ***R. cinnabarinum*** subsp. ***tamaense***
'Tama-no-utena' (EA)	LHyd
'Tan Crossing'	SReu
'Tanager' (EA)	CTrh LKna
¶ ***tanastylum*** var. ***pennivenium*** SF 593	ISea
'Tangerine'	See ***R.*** **'Fabia Tangerine'**
'Tangiers' (K)	SExb
tapetiforme	GGGa NMun
'Tara'	SLeo
tashiroi (EA)	NMun
¶ 'Tatjana'	LMil
tatsienense	GGGa
'Taurus' ♀	COtt CWri GGGa LMil MBri MLea MMor WWeb
'Tay' (K)	LMil
'Teal'	CSam CTrh CTri GGGa GWht MBal MBar MLea NHol NMun SCog SLeo SPer SReu
'Teddy Bear'	GGGa LMil LRHS MDun SMur
§ ***telmateium***	NMun
telopeum	See ***R. campylocarpum*** subsp. ***caloxanthum*** **Telopeum Group**
temenium var. ***dealbatum***	LMil
– – Glaphyrum Group F 21902	NMun SLeo
– F 21809	NMun
– var. ***gilvum*** 'Cruachan' R 22272	GGGa LMil NMun SLeo
– – R 22271	NMun
– P Cox 6037B	GGGa
– R 101	NMun
– R 10909	NMun SLeo
– var. ***temenium*** F 21734	NMun SLeo
Temple Belle Group ♀	CSam LHyd LKna LRHS MBal MLea NHed NMun SCog SLeo
§ ***tephropeplum*** ♀	CB&S GGGa NMun SLeo
◆ – Deleiense Group	See ***R. tephropeplum***
– KW 6303	NMun SLeo
– R/USDA 03914	GGGa
'Tequila Sunrise'	LMil MBal MLea NMun SLeo

'Terra-cotta'	LKna LMil SMur
'Terra-cotta Beauty' (EA)	WPat
Tessa Group & cl.	LKna LMil MGos MOne SBod
¶ 'Tessa Bianca'	GGGa
'Tessa Roza' 🏆	EPot GGGa GQui LHyd MAsh
thayerianum	GGGa NMun
§ 'The Hon. Jean Marie de Montague' 🏆	CAbP CWri EHoe EPfP IOrc LKna LMil MBal MBri MLea MMor NMun SLeo WWeb
'The Master' 🏆	LHyd LKna NMun SLeo SReu
§ 'The Queen Mother'	LHyd
'Theme Song'	SExb
thomsonii	CWri GGGa LHyd LMil NHol NMun SLeo
– BL&M 153	MBal
– Bu 270	GGGa
– var. ***candelabrum***	See ***R.*** × ***candelabrum***
– DF 540	MBal
– L&S 2847	GGGa NMun
§ – subsp. ***lopsangianum***	GGGa
§ – – LS&T 6561	NMun SLeo
– LS&H 1949*	NMun
– MH 70	GGGa
– subsp. ***thomsonii*** BL&M 228	NMun
Thomwilliams Group	MBal
Thor Group & cl.	GGGa SLeo SReu
'Thousand Butterflies'	See ***R.* 'One Thousand Butterflies'**
'Thunderstorm' 🏆	LHyd LKna SReu
thymifolium	GGGa
'Tiana'	GGGa
'Tibet'	GQui MBal MBar NHar SExb SHBN WWeb
'Tidbit'	GGGa LHyd LKna LMil MAsh MBal MBri MGos MLea NMun SLeo WGer
'Tilford Seedling'	LKna
'Timothy James'	CDoC SReu
'Tiny' (EA/d)	LMil
'Tit Willow' (EA)	GRei LHyd SCoo SPer
'Titian Beauty' 🏆	CB&S COtt CWri GGGa IHos IOrc LHyd LMil LNet MBal MBri MDun MGos MLea MMor NHed NMun SCog SExb SLeo SMad SPer SReu WAbe WWeb
'Titipu' (EA)	LHyd
'Toff' (V)	CEqu
'Tolkien'	SReu SSta
¶ 'Tomba'	GGGa
¶ ***tomentosum*** var. ***subarcticum***	GGGa
¶ – var. ***tomentosum***	GGGa
'Tonkonatsu' (EA)	SLeo
'Too Bee'	GGGa MAsh MBri NHol
'Top Banana'	LMil MBal MLea SMur SPer
'Top Hat'	MLea
'Topsvoort Pearl'	SReu
'Torch'	LKna
'Toreador' (EA)	CMac SExb
'Torridon' (Vs)	LMil
'Tortoiseshell Champagne'	See ***R.* 'Champagne'**
'Tortoiseshell Orange' 🏆	LHyd LKna LMil MBri SCog SHBN SReu SSta WGer
'Tortoiseshell Pale Orange'	LKna
'Tortoiseshell Salome'	LKna SReu SSta
'Tortoiseshell Scarlet'	LKna SReu
'Tortoiseshell Wonder' 🏆	LHyd LKna LMil MBal MGos NMun SLeo SPer SReu SSta
tosaense	LHyd
– 'Ralph Clarke' (EA)	SLeo
'Totally Awesome' (K)	GGGa MLea
'Tottenham'	MBal
'Tower Beauty'	LHyd
'Tower Dainty'	LHyd
'Tower Daring'	LHyd
'Tower Dexter'	LHyd
'Tower Dragon'	LHyd
'Trail Blazer'	GGGa
traillianum	GGGa LMil NMun SLeo
§ – var. ***dictyotum***	NMun
– – from Katmandu	NMun
– F 5881*	NMun SLeo
'Travis L'	SPer
Treasure Group	GDra IOrc LHyd MBal
'Trebah Gem'	NMun SLeo
'Tregedna'	NMun SLeo
'Tretawn'	SLeo
'Trewithen Orange'	CSam CTrw MBal MBar NMun SCog SHBN SLeo SPer
'Trewithen Purple'	CTrw
'Trianon'	LMil
trichanthum	CHig GGGa IOrc LMil NMun SLeo
– 'Honey Wood'	LHyd
trichocladum	LMil NMun SLeo
§ ***trichostomum*** 🏆	GGGa NMun SSpi WAbe
– KW 4465	NMun
– Ledoides Group	LMil NMun SLeo SReu
– – 'Collingwood Ingram'	LMil SReu
– Radinum Group	SSta
triflorum	GGGa IOrc ISea LMil MBal NMun SLeo
§ – var. ***bauhiniiflorum***	LMil NMun SLeo
¶ – C&V 9573	GGGa
– var. ***triflorum*** Mahogani Group	NMun SLeo
'Trilby'	CWri SLeo SReu
triplonaevium	See ***R. alutaceum*** var. ***russotinctum* Triplonaevium Group**
tritifolium	See ***R. alutaceum*** var. ***russotinctum* Tritifolium Group**
'Troll' (EA)	SReu
'Troupial' (K)	LKna
'Trude Webster'	CHig CSam CWri GGGa MLea SExb SReu SSta
¶ aff. ***tsaii*** C&H 7022	GGGa
¶ aff. ***tsaii*** H&M 1490	GGGa
tsangpoense	See ***R. charitopes*** subsp. ***tsangpoense***
tsariense	GGGa LMil NHol NMun
– forms	NMun SLeo
– L&S 2766	NMun
– var. ***magnum***	NMun
♦ – Poluninii Group	See ***R. poluninii***
¶ – × ***proteoides***	GGGa
– var. ***trimoense***	GGGa NMun
– 'Yum Yum'	NMun SLeo
§ ***tsusiophyllum***	GAri GGGa WAbe
'Tsuta-momiji' (EA)	LHyd
tubiforme	See ***R. glaucophyllum*** var. ***tubiforme***
'Tulyar'	LKna
'Tunis' (K)	ECho MBri MLea
'Turkish Delight'	MLea
N 'Twilight'	MBri
'Twilight Pink'	MLea NMun SExb
'Twilight Sky'	MAsh WWeb
'Tyermannii' 🏆	SLeo
'Ukamuse' (EA/d)	LHyd
'Uki Funei' (EA/v)	LMil

'Umpqua Queen' (K)	MAsh MLea
Ungerio Group	NMun SLeo
ungernii	CWri GGGa GWht NMun
uniflorum	GGGa LMil NHol NMun
§ – var. ***imperator***	LMil
– – KW 6884	GGGa
– KW 5876	NMun SLeo
'Unique' 🏆	CB&S CHig CSam CWLN CWri GGGa GWht ISea LHyd LKna LMil LNet MAsh MBal MBri MDun MLea MMor NMun SExb SHBN SLeo SPer SReu SSta WWeb
'Unique' (G)	LKna
'Unknown Warrior'	MMor SReu
uvariifolium	GGGa NMun SLeo
– Griseum Group LS&E 15817	GGGa
– P Cox 6519	GGGa
– R/USDA 59623/ R11391	NMun
– 'Reginald Childs'	LMil
– 'Yangtze Bend'	GGGa
¶ 'Valentine' (EA)	GGGa
valentinianum	CB&S CGre CSam GGGa MBal NMun SLeo
– F 24347	NMun SLeo SReu
Valpinense Group & cl.	WBod
'Van Nes Sensation'	LMil
Vanessa Group & cl.	LHyd LMil SCog SReu WBod
'Vanessa Pastel' 🏆	CHig GGGa LHyd LMil MBal MDun NMun SCog SLeo SReu WBod
§ 'Vanilla'	LKna
vaseyi (A) 🏆	GGGa GWht LHyd LMil MBal
veitchianum 🏆	GGGa
§ – Cubittii Group 🏆	GGGa NMun SLeo
– – 'Ashcombe'	LHyd
– K Cox 9001	GGGa
'Veldtstar'	LHyd
vellereum	See ***R. principis*** **Vellereum Group**
'Velvet Gown' (EA)	GWht IOrc LMil LRHS MBri SBid
venator	GGGa LHyd NMun SLeo
'Venetia' (K)	MBri MMor
'Venetian Chimes'	IHos IOrc ISea MBal MLea NMun SCog SExb SLeo SPer SReu WWeb
vernicosum	GGGa GWht LMil MDun NMun SLeo
¶ – C&H 7009	GGGa
¶ – C&H 7150	GGGa
– Euanthum Group F 5880	NMun
– F 5881	NMun SLeo
– McLaren T 71	NMun
– SF 416	ISea
– Yu 13961	NMun
– Yu 14694	NMun
verruculosum	SLeo
'Veryan Bay' 🏆	CB&S LMil
vesiculiferum	NMun SLeo
'Vespers' (EA)	CTrh
'Victoria Hallett'	SReu
'Vida Brown' (EA/d)	CMac GWht LKna LMil MAsh MBri SBid SBod SCog SReu SSta WPat
'Viking' (EA)	LHyd
'Vincent van Gogh'	GGGa LMil
¶ 'Vineland Fragrance'	CWri
'Vinestar'	LHyd
'Vintage Rose' 🏆	LMil MBal MBri MLea NMun SCog SLeo SReu WAbe

'Violet Longhurst'	LHyd
'Violetta' (EA)	GGGa ISea
virgatum	NMun
– subsp. ***oleifolium*** KW 6279	NMun SLeo
Virginia Richards Group & cl.	CDoC CHig CWLN GAri GGGa LHyd MBal MBri MDun MGos MLea NMun SCog SExb SLeo SReu SSta WBod WGer
§ ***viridescens***	LMil MBal
§ – 'Doshong La'	LMil
§ – KW 5829	NMun SLeo
§ – Rubroluteum Group	GGGa LMil
viscidifolium	GGGa NMun
viscosum (A) 🏆	GGGa GQui LHyd LKna LMil SReu
* ***viscosum aemulans*** (A)	SReu
viscosum 'Antilope'	See ***R.* 'Antilope'**
– 'Arpege'	See ***R.* 'Arpege'**
– var. ***montanum*** (A)	IBlr
– f. ***rhodanthum*** (A)	LMil
'Viscount Powerscourt'	ENot
'Viscy'	CWri ECho GGGa GQui GWht LHyd LMil WGer
'Vital Spark'	MBri
Volker Group	See ***R.* Flava Group & cl.**
'Vulcan' 🏆	CB&S CWLN CWri GGGa LMil MBal MLea SHBN
¶ 'Vulcan's Flame'	CDoC
'Vuyk's Rosyred' (EA) 🏆	CB&S CHig CMac CWLN GQui GRei GWht IOrc LHyd LKna LMil MBar MBri MGos MMor SBod SCog SExb SPer SReu WBod WFar WStI WWeb
'Vuyk's Scarlet' (EA) 🏆	CB&S CChe CMac EBee EPot GGGa GQui GWht IOrc ISea LHyd LKna LMil MBar MBri MGos MMor NMun SCog SExb SLeo SPer SReu SSta WFar WWeb
'W.E. Gumbleton' (M)	SReu
W.F.H. Group 🏆	CWri LMil NMun SCog SLeo
wadanum var. ***leucanthum***	LMil
'Wagtail'	GGGa LRHS NHar NHol WAbe
wallichii	GGGa LHyd
¶ – Bu 249	GGGa
¶ – Bu 262	GGGa
¶ – Bu 290	GGGa
– KR 813	NMun
– KR 882	NMun
– LS&H 17527	NMun SLeo
– TW 32	GWht
Walloper Group	NMun SLeo SReu
'Wallowa Red' (K)	LMil
'Wally Miller'	SReu SSta
walongense	NMun
– C&H 373	GGGa
wardii	IDee IOrc ISea LHyd LMil MBal MDun NMun SLeo
¶ – C&V 9548	GGGa
¶ – C&V 9558	GGGa
¶ – C&V 9606	GGGa
– L&S form*	GGGa NMun SLeo SReu
– LS&T 6591	NMun
– P Cox 6119	GGGa
– var. ***puralbum***	GGGa NMun
– – F 10616	NMun
– – Yu 14757	NMun
– SHEG 5672	NMun
– SSNY 99	GGGa
– var. ***wardii*** F 21551	NMun

– – KW 4170	GGGa
– – KW 5736	NMun
§ – – Litiense Group	NMun SLeo
– – LS&E 15764	NMun
– – LS&T 5679	NMun
– – LS&T 5686	NMun
– – R 18333	NMun
– – R 25391	NMun
– yellow	GGGa
'Ward's Ruby' (EA)	CTrh CTrw CWLN
§ 'Washington State Centennial'	GGGa
wasonii	GGGa LHyd LMil NMun
– McLaren AD 106	NMun
– f. ***rhododactylum***	NMun SLeo SReu
¶ – – KW 1876	GGGa
– white	NMun SLeo SReu
'Waterfall'	MBal
watsonii	GGGa MDun NMun SLeo SReu
– CC&H 3939	GGGa
– EGM 109	LMil
– P Cox 5075	GGGa
'Waxwing'	LKna
websterianum C 5123A	MDun
– EGM 146	LMil
– P Cox 5123	GGGa
'Wee Annie' (V)	CEqu
'Wee Bee'	EPot GGGa LMil MAsh MBri MLea NHar NHed NHol SSpi WAbe
§ Wega Group	LHyd
'Wellesleyanum'	NMun SLeo
'Werei'	NMun SLeo
'Werrington'	CGre
'Westminster' (O)	LKna LMil
'Weston's Innocence'	MLea
'Weston's Pink Diamond'	GGGa LMil
'Weybridge'	NMun SLeo
weyrichii (A)	GGGa
¶ 'Whidbey Island'	LMil
'Whisperingrose'	CSam LMil MAsh MBal MBri MDun NHol
'White Frills' (EA)	LMil MBal SExb SMur
White Glory Group & cl.	NMun SLeo
'White Jade' (EA)	SExb
'White Lady' (EA)	CWLN LKna MBar SRms
'White Lights'	GGGa LMil LRHS MLea
'White Olympic Lady'	LKna
'White Swan' 🏆	LKna LMil MBal SReu
'White Wings'	GQui SLeo
'Whitethroat' (K/d) 🏆	GQui IOrc LKna LMil MAsh MBri SExb
'Whitney's Dwarf Red'	SLeo
'Wigeon'	GGGa LMil LRHS NHol SBar SPer
wightii	GGGa MDun NMun SLeo
– BM&W 153	MBal
– DF 542	MBal
– KR 877	LMil
'Wilbrit Rose'	SBod
'Wild Affair'	LRHS
'Wilgen's Ruby' 🏆	CSam CWLN LKna MBri MGos MMor SBod SHBN SPer WLRN WStI
'Willbrit'	CDoC CHig CWri ECho GWht LHyd MAsh MBri MDun MOne SCog SExb WGor
williamsianum 🏆	CB&S CHig CSam EPot GGGa GWht ISea LHyd LMil MBal MBar MGos MLea NMun NWea SCog SLeo SPer SReu SRms SSpi WAbe WBod WGer
– Caerhays form	MPla
– pink	WWat
– 'Special'	GGGa
– white	CDoC CPMA GWht ISea MBal NHol NMun SLeo WWat
'Willy' (EA)	GGGa GWht LHyd LKna
wilsoniae	See ***R. latoucheae***
'Wilsonii' (Ad)	LKna
wiltonii	GGGa LHyd LMil MDun NMun
– CC&H 3906	GGGa
'Windbeam'	SBod
'Windlesham Scarlet' 🏆	EBee LHyd LMil
'Windsor Lad'	LKna SReu
Winsome Group & cl. 🏆	CB&S CHig CSam CTrw CWri GCHN GGGa IOrc ISea LHyd LKna MBal MBar MDun MLea MMor NHol NMun SBid SCog SLeo SSta WBod
'Winston Churchill' (M)	MBar MMor
I 'Winter Green' (EA)	CWLN
'Wintergreen' (EA)	CB&S COtt CTrh EBee
'Wishmoor' 🏆	LMil NMun SCog SLeo SReu
'Witch Doctor'	CDoC ECho LMil SBod
'Witchery'	GGGa
'Wojnar's Purple'	LMil
'Wombat' (EA)	CDoC COtt EPot GGGa GRei GWht LHyd LMil MBal MBar MBri MGos NHar NHed NHol SCog SReu WPat
'Wonderland'	LKna
wongii	CSam GQui LMil NMun
'Woodcock'	LHyd
'Woodside'	SLeo
'Wren'	CSam GGGa ISea MAsh MBal MBar MBri MDun MOne NHar NHol SExb SReu WAbe
'Wryneck' (K) 🏆	LHyd LMil MBri SReu
xanthocodon	See ***R. cinnabarinum*** subsp. ***xanthocodon***
xanthostephanum	NMun
'Yachiyo Red'	LMil
'Yaku Angel'	MDun SPer
'Yaku Prince'	CAbP IOrc SPer
'Yaku Princess'	CAbP IOrc MAsh MLea SLeo SPer
'Yaku Queen'	SBar SLeo
yakushimanum	CB&S CMHG CNic CSam CWri GGGa GWht IOrc LKna LMil MBar MBri MDun MGos NHol NMun SCog SPer SReu SSta WAbe WGer
I – 'Angel'	MLea SCog WWeb
I – 'Beefeater'	SCog
– x ***bureaui***	MBal MLea SBar SCog
¶ – x ***campanulatum*** 'Roland Cooper'	GGGa
– x ***decorum***	GGGa MMor SReu
– 'Edelweiss'	GGGa
¶ – x 'Elizabeth'	GGGa
– Exbury form	SReu
– FCC form	CPMA EBee MUlv SReu
§ – 'Koichiro Wada' 🏆	GGGa LHyd MBal MBri MGos NMun SLeo
– x ***lanatum***	GGGa
– subsp. ***makinoi***	See ***R. makinoi***
– 'Mist Maiden'	MLea SBar

– x ***pachysanthum***	GGGa SReu
¶ – x ***ponticum***	GGGa
¶ – x ***proteoides***	GGGa
– x ***rex***	GGGa SReu
¶ – x 'Sappho'	GGGa
I – 'Torch'	SCog
– x ***tsariense***	GGGa
– subsp. ***yakushimanum*** 'Ken Janeck'	See ***R.* 'Ken Janeck'**
* 'Yaya'	CWLN
'Yellow Dane'	GGGa
Yellow Hammer Group ♀	CB&S CHig CMHG CSam CWri GGGa ISea LKna LMil MBal MBar MGos MMor NMun SBid SBod SExb SHBN SLeo SPer SReu SRms SSta WAbe WBod
'Yellow Petticoats'	LMil MBri MLea SBar SLeo SSpi
¶ 'Yellow Pippin'	CWri LMil
'Yellow Rolls Royce'	LMil
'Yoga' (K)	LKna
'Youthful Sin'	MBal
'Yo-zakura' (EA)	NMun SLeo
yungningense	LMil NMun WAbe
– F 29268	GGGa NMun
yunnanense	GGGa IOrc ISea LHyd LMil NMun SCog SLeo WGer
¶ – C&H 7145	GGGa
– KGB 551	SReu
– KGB 559	SReu
– 'Openwood' ♀	GGGa LMil
– pink	GGGa
– SF 379	ISea
– SF 400	ISea
§ – Suberosum Group	NMun
– TW 400	GWht
– white	GGGa SCog
'Yvonne Dawn'	CWri NMun SLeo
zaleucum F 15688	GGGa
– F 27603	NMun SLeo
– Flaviflorum Group KW 20837	NMun SLeo
– TW 373	GWht
Zelia Plumecocq Group & cl.	CWri NMun SExb
zeylanicum	See ***R. arboreum*** subsp. ***zeylanicum***
zoelleri (V)	CEqu
Zuiderzee Group	SLeo

RHODOHYPOXIS (Hypoxidaceae)

'Albrighton'	CAvo CBro CRDP ELan EPot EWes LAma NHar SBla WAbe WChr WPat
'Appleblossom'	CAvo EWes NHar NMen SIng WAbe WChr
baurii ♀	CAvo CElw CMHG CNic CRDP ELan EPot MFos MHig MTho NHar NNrd NRoo NTow SAlw WPyg WWin WWye
– 'Alba'	CBro CMea CRDP CTri EDAr NNrd WWye
– var. ***baurii***	EHyt EPot EWes NHar WChr
– var. ***confecta***	EPot EWes SIng
– 'Dulcie'	EDAr EPot NHar NTow SWas WAbe
* – x ***parousia***	EWes
– 'Pinkeen'	EPot WAbe
– var. ***platypetala***	CRDP EHyt EPot EWes NHar NHol NMen WAbe WChr
– – x ***milloides*** , Burtt 6981	NHar
– 'Susan Garnett-Botfield'	EPot EWes NHar NMen WAbe
'Betsy Carmine'	NHar WChr
'Confusion'	EHyt WAbe WChr
'Dawn'	CAvo EHyt EPot EWes LAma NHar NHol SBla WAbe WChr
deflexa	CGra EHyt GCrs WChr
'Donald Mann'	EHyt
'Douglas'	CRDP EHyt EPot LAma NHar NHol NNrd SBla WAbe WLRN WPat WPyg
'Dusky'	EPot
'E.A. Bowles'	EWes GCrs WAbe WChr
'Emily Peel'	EPot WAbe WChr
'Eva-Kate'	EPot EWes LAma NHar NHol SBla WAbe WChr WPat
'Fred Broome'	CBro ELan EPot EWes LAma NHar NHol NTow SBla WAbe WChr WFar WPat WPyg
'Garnett'	EDAr EPot EWes NHol NMen SBla WChr
'Great Scott'	ECho EPot EWes NHar WAbe WChr
'Harlequin'	CBro ELan EPot EWes LAma NHar NHol SBla SIng WAbe WChr
'Hebron Farm Biscuit'	EWes WAbe WChr
'Hebron Farm Cerise'	EWes
'Hebron Farm Pink'	EWes WAbe WChr
'Hebron Farm Red-eye'	EWes WAbe WChr
§ 'Helen'	EPot EWes NHar NHol SBla WAbe WChr
hybrids	ELan
'Knockdolian Red'	NHol
'Margaret Rose'	EPot EWes NHar WAbe WChr
milloides	CRDP EHyt EPot EWes LBee NHar NHol NMen NWCA SBla SSpi WAbe WChr
– 'Claret'	CRDP
– 'Damask'	CRDP WChr
– giant form	WChr
'Monty'	EPot EWes WAbe WChr
'New Look'	EWes NHar WAbe WChr
'Perle'	EPot EWes NHar NMen NNrd WAbe WChr
'Picta'	CAvo CRDP EHyt EPot EWes LAma NHar NHol NNrd SBla SSpi WAbe WChr
'Pink Pearl'	EPot EWes NHol
'Pinkeen'	EWes GCrs NHar WChr
'Ruth'	EHyt EPot EWes LAma NHar NHol SBla WAbe WChr
'Shell Pink'	SBla
'Stella'	CAvo EPot EWes NHol SBla WAbe
'Tetra Pink'	SIng WChr
'Tetra Red'	EPot EWes NHar NHol NMen SIng WAbe WChr
'Tetra White'	See ***R.* 'Helen'**
thodiana	CAvo CGra CRDP EPot SIng SSpi

RHODOHYPOXIS × HYPOXIS

¶ ***R. baurii*** x ***H. parvula***	EWes NHar WAbe
– x ***H. parvula***, JJ's pink	NHar

RHODOMYRTUS (Myrtaceae)

¶ ***tomentosa***	ECon

RHODOPHIALA (Amaryllidaceae)

advena	WChr WCot
¶ – yellow form	LWoo
bakeri F&W 7196	SIgm

§ *bifida*	CMon LBow WChr
bifida spathacea	CMon WChr
chilensis	WChr
elwesii	EHyt

RHODORA See RHODODENDRON

RHODOTHAMNUS (Ericaceae)
See Plant Deletions

RHODOTYPOS (Rosaceae)

kerrioides	See ***R. scandens***
§ *scandens*	CB&S CBot CChu CPle GBin MPla MTis NTow SBid SSpi WCru WWin

RHOEO See TRADESCANTIA

RHOICISSUS (Vitaceae)
See Plant Deletions

RHOPALOBLASTE (Arecaceae)
See Plant Deletions

RHOPALOSTYLIS (Arecaceae)

baueri	LPal
sapida	CHEx ECou LPal NPal

RHUS † (Anacardiaceae)

copallina	SMur
cotinus	See ***Cotinus coggygria***
glabra	CAgr CArn CB&S CDoC MBlu NFla SPer
– 'Laciniata' hort.	See ***R.* × *pulvinata* Autumn Lace Group**
N *hirta*	See ***R. typhina***
¶ *incisa*	CTrC
integrifolia	CArn
¶ *leptodictya*	CTrC
pendulina	CGre
potaninii	EPfP WRTC WWat
§ × *pulvinata* Autumn Lace Group	EBee MBlu MGos SDix SHBN WFar
– (Autumn Lace Group) 'Red Autumn Lace' ♀	CDoC MBlu SPer
punjabensis	SSpi
§ *radicans*	CArn GPoy
toxicodendron	See ***R. radicans***
trichocarpa	SMur
trilobata	CArn CFil WPGP
§ *typhina* ♀	CAgr CB&S CLnd EBre ECtt ELan ENot IOrc ISea MBar MBri MGos MWat NFla NNor NWea SHBN SPer SSta WDin WGwG WStI WWin
§ – 'Dissecta' ♀	CB&S CLnd CSpe ELan ENot GRei IOrc MBar MBri MWat NBee NFla SEND SEas SMad SPer WDin
¶ – f. *laciniata*	MAsh
– 'Laciniata' hort.	See ***R. typhina* 'Dissecta'**
verniciflua	CFil

RHYNCHELYTRUM See MELINIS

RIBES † (Grossulariaceae)

alpinum	CAgr CWLN ELan ENot GAul GRei IOrc LBuc NSti NWea SBid SPer SRms WDin
– 'Aureum'	CMHG CTri EFol EHoe ELan MHig NNor WCot WDin WSHC
americanum	EPla
– 'Variegatum'	EBee EFol EHoe ELan EPla NHol SPan WBea WPat WPyg WRha
atrosanguineum	See ***R. sanguineum* 'Atrorubens'**
aureum hort.	See ***R. odoratum***
'Black Velvet'	LBuc
bracteosum	CPle
californicum	CPle
× *culverwellii* Jostaberry (F)	EMui GTwe LBuc
¶ *divaricatum*	CAgr
– 'Worcesterberry' (F)	CMac CPle CWSG EMui MBri MGos MMor NDal NRog SDea SPer
gayanum	CGre CPle LHop SLPl WHCG
glutinosum	See ***R. sanguineum* var. *glutinosum***
× *gordonianum*	CChu CGre CMHG CPMA CPle CWSG LHop MBal MRav SBid SEND SMrm WCot WHCG WPyg WWat
laurifolium	CB&S CBot CPle CSam EFol IOrc MBal SBid SChu SPer SSpi WCot WCru WDin WGwG WHCG WPyg WSHC WWat WWin
– 'Mrs Amy Doncaster'	EPla
¶ *lobbii*	SIgm
nigrum 'Amos Black' (F)	GTwe
– 'Baldwin' (F)	CMac EWar GBon NDal SDea SPer WStI WWeb
– 'Barchatnaja'	CAgr
– 'Ben Alder' (F)	SDea
– 'Ben Connan' (F)	COtt EMui GTwe MGos SCoo
– 'Ben Lomond' (F) ♀	CTri EMui EWar GBon GRei GTwe LBuc MBri MGos NBee NDal NRog SDea SPer WStI
– 'Ben Loyal' (F)	GTwe
– 'Ben More' (F)	GRei GTwe MBri NBee NDal SDea SPer WStI
– 'Ben Nevis' (F)	GTwe NDal NRog SDea
– 'Ben Sarek' (F) ♀	CSam CSut EBre EMui ERea GChr GRei GTwe LBuc MBri MGos NDal SDea SPer WWeb
– 'Ben Tirran' (F)	CDoC LBuc MGos
– 'Blackdown' (F)	SDea
– 'Blacksmith' (F)	WLRN
– 'Boskoop Giant' (F)	CMac EWar GTwe NRog SPer
– 'Byelorussian Sweet' (F)	CAgr
– 'Cascade' (F)	CAgr
– 'Cherry' (F)	CAgr
– 'Consort' (F)	CAgr
– 'Daniel's September' (F)	GTwe
– 'Hystawneznaya' (F)	CAgr
– 'Jet' (F)	GTwe LRHS SDea SPer
– 'Kosmicheskaya' (F)	CAgr
– 'Laxton's Giant' (F)	GTwe SDea
– 'Malling Jet' (F)	NRog WLRN
– 'Mendip Cross' (F)	GTwe NRog
– 'Pilot Alek Mamkin' (F)	CAgr
– 'Seabrook's' (F)	EWar
– 'Wellington XXX' (F)	CTri ERea EWar GTwe LBuc MBri NBee NRog SDea WStI WTyr WWeb
– 'Westwick Choice' (F)	GTwe

§ ***odoratum***	CB&S CMHG CPle CSam ECoo ELan ENot ERav GOrc GRei LHol MBar MGos MHar MPla NBee NWea SEas SHBN SPer SRms SSpi WBea WHCG WStI WWat WWin
– 'Crandall'	CAgr
praecox	CB&S CBlo CPle MBlu SEND
¶ ***propinquum***	CPlN
rubrum 'Hollande Rose' (P)	GTwe
– 'October Currant' (P)	GTwe
– 'Fay's New Prolific' (R)	GTwe
– 'Jonkheer van Tets' (R) 🏆	EMui LRHS MGos SDea
– 'Junifer' (R)	CSut EMui
– 'Laxton Number One' (R)	CMac CSam CTri EBre EMui GBon GChr GRei MBri NRog SDea SPer WWeb
– 'Raby Castle' (R)	GTwe
– 'Red Lake' (R) 🏆	CB&S CMac CSam EBre ERea GBon GRei LBuc MBri MGos NBee NDal NRog SDea SPer WStI
– 'Redstart' (R)	COtt LBuc LRHS MBri SDea WWeb
– 'Rondom' (R)	SDea
– 'Rovada' (R)	CSut EMui
– 'Stanza' (R) 🏆	SDea
– 'Wilson's Long Bunch' (R)	GTwe
– 'Blanka' (W)	CSut
– 'White Grape' (W) 🏆	CTri GTwe NRog
– 'White Pearl' (W)	CB&S GRei
– 'White Transparent' (W)	GTwe
◆–White Versailles	See ***R. rubrum* (White Currant Group) 'Versailles Blanche'**
§ – 'Versailles Blanche' (W)	CDoC CMac CSam CTri GTwe LBuc MBri MGos SDea SPer WWeb
sanguineum	CLTr CPle CSam MBal MBar NCut NNor WStI
– 'Albescens'	SPer WBcn
– 'Brocklebankii' 🏆	CAbP CBrd EPar EPla LFis LHop MGos MPla SAga SBid SHBN SPer SPla WFar WPat WSHC WWat
– double	See ***R. sanguineum* 'Plenum'**
– 'Flore Pleno'	See ***R. sanguineum* 'Plenum'**
– var. ***glutinosum*** 'Albidum'	SChu WWat
– 'King Edward VII'	CDoC ECtt LBuc MBar MBri MGos MWat NBee NHol NNor NRoo NWea SHBN SPer SPla SReu SRms WDin WStI WWeb
– 'Koja'	LRHS MBri NPro
– 'Lombartsii'	CBlo CShe EPla MRav
§ – 'Plenum' (d)	CBot MBlu MUlv
– 'Porky Pink'	EBre GSki LRHS MAsh MGos MRav
– 'Pulborough Scarlet' 🏆	CB&S CChe CDoC CLTr CShe ELan ENot GOrc MAsh MBri MGos MPla MRav MWat NBee NBir NFla SPer SPla SRms WWeb
– 'Pulborough Scarlet Variegated'	CBlo CPMA EPla LHop MPla SBid
– 'Red Pimpernel'	EBar MBri WBcn
– 'Roseum'	See ***R. sanguineum* 'Carneum'**
– 'Splendens'	GRei
– 'Taff's Kim' (v)	CPMA
– 'Tydeman's White' 🏆	CBlo CChe CPMA CPle ECtt EPfP MBar MBlu SBid SSpi
– 'White Icicle'	CBlo CBot CMil EBre ELan GSki MAsh MGos MUlv NBir SPla WBea
speciosum 🏆	Widely available
tenue	CPle EPla NHol
uva-crispa var. ***reclinatum*** 'Achilles' (C/D)	GTwe
– – 'Admiral Beattie' (F)	GTwe NRog
– – 'Alma' (D)	NRog
– – 'Annelii' (F)	SDea
– – 'Aston Red'	See ***R. uva-crispa* var. *reclinatum* 'Warrington'**
– – 'Australia' (F)	NRog
– – 'Bedford Red' (D)	GTwe NRog
– – 'Bedford Yellow' (D)	GTwe
– – 'Beech Tree Nestling' (F)	GTwe
– – 'Bellona' (C)	NRog
– – 'Black Velvet' (F)	CMac COtt MBri SPer
– – 'Blucher' (F)	NRog
– – 'Bright Venus' (D)	GTwe
– – 'Broom Girl' (D)	GTwe NDal NRog
– – 'Captivator' (F)	CSam GTwe SDea
– – 'Careless' (C) 🏆	CMac CSam CTri EMui ERea EWar GBon GRei GTwe IOrc MBri MGos NBee NRog SDea SPer WTyr WWeb
– – 'Catherina' (C/D)	SDea
– – 'Champagne Red' (F)	GTwe
– – 'Clayton' (F)	NRog
– – 'Cook's Eagle' (C)	GTwe
– – 'Cousen's Seedling' (F)	GTwe
– – 'Criterion' (C)	GTwe NRog
– – 'Crown Bob' (C/D)	GTwe NRog
– – 'Dan's Mistake' (D)	GTwe NRog
– – 'Drill' (F)	GTwe
– – 'Early Sulphur' (D/C)	GTwe NRog SDea WStI
– – 'Edith Cavell' (F)	GTwe
– – 'Firbob' (D)	GTwe NRog
– – 'Forester' (D)	GTwe
– – 'Freedom' (C)	GTwe NRog
– – 'Gipsey Queen' (F)	GTwe
– – 'Glenton Green' (F)	GTwe
– – 'Golden Ball' (D)	SDea
– – 'Golden Drop' (D)	GTwe
– – 'Green Gascoigne'	See ***R. uva-crispa* var. *reclinatum* 'Early Green Hairy'**
– – 'Green Gem' (C/D)	GTwe NRog
– – 'Green Ocean' (F)	GTwe NRog
– – 'Greenfinch' (F)	EMui GTwe MGos
– – 'Greengage' (D)	NRog
– – 'Gretna Green' (F)	GTwe
– – 'Guido' (F)	GTwe NRog
– – 'Gunner' (D)	CTri GTwe NRog
– – 'Heart of Oak' (F)	GTwe NRog
– – 'Hebburn Prolific' (D)	GTwe
– – 'Hedgehog' (D)	GTwe
– – 'Hero of the Nile' (C)	GTwe NRog
– – 'High Sheriff' (D)	GTwe
– – 'Hinnonmäki Röd' (F)	SDea
– – 'Howard's Lancer' (C/D)	GTwe NRog SDea
– – 'Invicta' (C) 🏆	CDoC CMac CSut CTri CWSG EBre EMui EWar GBon GChr GRei LBuc MBri MGos NDal SDea SPer WStI WWeb
– – 'Ironmonger' (F)	GTwe
– – 'Jubilee' (C/D)	COtt CTri LBuc MBri MGos NRog

– – 'Keen's Seedling' (D)	GTwe
– – 'Keepsake' (C/D)	GTwe NRog
– – 'King of Trumps' (F)	GTwe NRog
– – 'Lancashire Lad' (C/D)	GTwe NRog
– – 'Langley Gage' (D)	GTwe NRog
– – 'Laxton's Amber' (D)	GTwe
– – 'Leveller' (C/D) ♀	CMac CTri EBre EMui EWar GBon GTwe LBuc MBri MGos NRog SDea SPer WStI WWeb
– – 'London' (C/D)	GTwe NRog
– – 'Lord Derby' (C/D)	GTwe MBri NRog
– – 'Lord Kitchener' (F)	NRog
– – 'Macherauch's Seedling' (F)	NRog
– – 'Marigold' (F)	NRog
– – 'Matchless' (D)	NRog
– – 'May Duke' (C/D)	LBuc NRog SDea
– – 'Mitre' (C)	GTwe
– – 'Pax'	CDoC EMui GTwe
– – 'Peru'	GTwe
– – 'Pitmaston Green Gage' (D)	GTwe
– – 'Plunder' (F)	NRog
– – 'Prince Charles' (F)	GTwe
– – 'Queen of Hearts' (F)	NRog
– – 'Queen of Trumps' (C)	GTwe NRog
– – 'Red Rough' (D)	GTwe
– – 'Rifleman' (D)	GTwe
– – 'Rokula'	CDoC GTwe
– – 'Roseberry' (D)	GTwe
– – 'Scottish Chieftan' (D)	GTwe
– – 'Sir George Brown' (D)	NRog
– – 'Snowdrop' (C)	GTwe
– – 'Speedwell' (F)	NRog
– – 'Spinefree' (F)	GTwe
– – 'Sultan Juror' (F)	NRog
– – 'Surprise' (C)	GTwe NRog
– – 'Suter Johnny' (F)	NRog
– – 'Telegraph' (F)	GTwe
– – 'The Leader' (F)	NRog
– – 'Tom Joiner' (F)	GTwe
– – 'Trumpeter' (C)	NRog
– – 'Victoria' (F)	GTwe NRog
§ – – 'Warrington' (D)	GTwe NRog
– – 'Whinham's Industry' (C/D) ♀	CMac CSam CSut EMui ERea EWar GBon GRei GTwe IOrc LBuc MBri MGos NBee NDal NRog SDea SPer WStI
– – 'White Eagle' (C)	NRog
– – 'White Lion' (C/D)	GTwe NRog
– – 'White Transparent' (C)	GTwe
– – 'Whitesmith' (C/D)	CTri GTwe NRog SDea
– – 'Woodpecker' (F)	GTwe NRog
– – 'Yellow Champagne' (F)	GTwe NRog
viburnifolium	CPle WWat

RICHEA (Epacridaceae)

dracophylla	CFil LLew SArc
milliganii	CFil
scoparia	CFil MAll SArc

RICINUS (Euphorbiaceae)

¶ ***communis*** 'Carmencita' ♀	LBlo
¶ – 'Gibsonii'	EOas LBlo
– 'Impala'	EOas LBlo MLan NRai SSoC
¶ – 'Zanzibarensis'	EOas LBlo

RIVINA (Phytolaccaceae)

humilis	LHil

ROBINIA (Papilionaceae)

boyntonii	CTho
fertilis	SIgm
hispida ♀	CEnd CLnd CTho EBee ELan ICrw LNet MBlu MHlr SHBN SSpi WPyg WSHC
– 'Macrophylla'	CBlo CEnd SSpi
N – 'Rosea'	CB&S CBlo CBot EBee LRHS MGos NFla SPer
kelseyi	CBlo IOrc MUlv SPer WPyg
◆ × ***margaretta*** Casque Rouge	See ***R.*** × ***margaretta* 'Pink Cascade'**
§ – 'Pink Cascade'	CDoC CEnd CSPN CSte CTho EBee LNet LPan MBri MGos MMea SBid SHBN SLPl SPer WDin WPyg
neomexicana	CLnd
pseudoacacia ♀	CAgr CB&S CHEx CLnd CPer ELan ENot GAri LPan NWea WDin WFar WFox WHut WNor
– 'Bessoniana'	CBlo CLnd CTho ENot
– 'Fastigiata'	See ***R. pseudoacacia* 'Pyramidalis'**
– 'Frisia' ♀	CB&S CEnd CHEx CLnd CSam CTho EBre ELan EMil ENot IOrc LHyr LNet LPan MAsh MBal MBri MGos NWea SFam SHBN SPer SReu SSta WDin WJas WMou WOrn WWat
– 'Inermis' hort.	See ***R. pseudoacacia* 'Umbraculifera'**
– 'Lace Lady'	EBee ELan ENot LPan MAsh MBri MRav SCoo SMad WWes
§ – 'Pyramidalis'	CTho ENot
– 'Rozynskiana'	CTho
– 'Sandraudiga'	SMad
– 'Tortuosa'	CEnd CLnd CTho EBee ELan EMil LPan MAsh MBri MMea SPer
§ – 'Umbraculifera'	CLnd CSte EMil LPan MGos
– 'Unifoliola'	CLnd CTho
× ***slavinii*** 'Hillieri' ♀	CEnd CLnd CTho ELan IOrc LPan MAsh MWat SBid SPer SSpi WWat
* 'Twisty Baby'	EPfP

ROCHEA See CRASSULA

RODGERSIA † (Saxifragaceae)

aesculifolia ♀	Widely available
– 'Irish Bronze'	IBlr
¶ – pink form	IBlr
henrici	CRow EBre IBlr LBuc MCli SPer WRus
– hybrid	GAri MUlv NHol WCru
¶ ***nepalensis***	IBlr
'Parasol'	CFil CHad ELan IBlr NHol SSpi
pinnata	CDoC CGle CHEx CHad CRow CWGN EBre EFol EGol EHon ERav IBlr LHil MBal MBri MCli MSta NDea NFla NHol NVic SAxl SChu SHig SPer WHil WHoo WPyg WWat WWhi
– 'Alba'	IBlr NHol

– 'Elegans'	CChu CHad EBre EFou ELan EMan EPar GCal GGar GMaP IBlr NFla NHol NOrc SChu SMrm SSoC WGer WWat WWin
¶ – 'Rosea'	IBlr
– 'Superba' ♀	CArc CBos CHEx CHad CShe CTrC EBar ECha ECtt GAbr GCal IBlr LBlm LFis LGro MBal MBri MBro MCLN MUlv NBee NFla NHar NPer NSti SApp SSpi WAbe WCru WKif
podophylla ♀	CB&S CChu CHEx CHad CHan CRow CWGN CWit EBre ECha EFol EGol EOas GMaP NBir NDea NHol SAxl SBla SHig SMac SMad SPer SSoC SSpi WCru WEas WGer WWat
– Donard form	CFil IBlr WCot
– 'Rotlaub'	EBre GCal IBlr MBri MUlv WCot WTre
– 'Smaragd'	CRow EBre GCal IBlr MUlv
purdomii	CRow EBre EGar IBlr SSpi
sambucifolia	CB&S CDoC CHEx CRow CShe EBee EBre EMan LFis MBri MCli MFir MUlv NDea NFla NHar SMac SPer SSoC SSpi WCru WFar WGer WMer WWat
¶ – dwarf pink-flowered	IBlr
¶ – dwarf white-flowered	IBlr
¶ – large green-stemmed	IBlr
¶ – large red-stemmed	IBlr
¶ – x ***pinnata***	IBlr
– – x 'Panache'	IBlr
sp. ACE 2303	SWas
sp. CLD 1329	NHol
sp. CLD 1432	NHol
¶ sp. from Castlewellan	IBlr
tabularis	See ***Astilboides tabularis***

ROELLA (Campanulaceae)

ciliata	CSpe
¶ ***maculata***	CSpe

ROHDEA † (Convallariaceae)

japonica	CFil WCru
¶ – long-leaved form	WCru
– 'Talbot Manor' (v)	CRDP SApp WCot
– 'Tuneshige Rokujo'	WCot
– variegated	WCot
watanabei B&SWJ 1911	WCru

ROMANZOFFIA (Hydrophyllaceae)

§ ***sitchensis***	CLyd CTri EBar
suksdorfii Green	See ***R. sitchensis***
– hort.	See ***R. californica***
tracyi	CArc WThi
unalaschcensis	CNic ELan GTou MHig NBro NTow NWCA SRms SSca WOMN WPer WWin

ROMNEYA (Papaveraceae)

coulteri ♀	CAbb CB&S CBot CChu COtt CPle CShe EBre ELan GCal IBlr LHop MBlu MBri MGos MLan SBid SBla SPer SReu SSta WDin WSHC WWat
– var. ***trichocalyx***	CDoC GMac IBlr SCro WAbe
§ – 'White Cloud'	ERea IBlr MRav SMad SPer SSoC
– 'White Sails'	IBlr
x ***hybrida***	See ***R. coulteri* 'White Cloud'**

ROMULEA (Iridaceae)

battandieri AB&S 4659	CMon
bifrons AB&S 4359/4360	CMon
bulbocodium	CBro CMon EHic MFos MHig
– var. ***clusiana***	LAma
¶ – – MS 239	EHyt
– – Serotina Group	EPot
– – SF 237	CMon
– 'Knightshayes'	EHyt
* – var. ***leichtliniana*** MS 784	EHyt
campanuloides	CMon
columnae AB&S 4659	CMon
engleri SF 3	CMon
hirta	CMon
ligustica var. ***rouyana*** SF 360	CMon
linaresii	EPot LAma
– var. ***graeca***	CNic
– – CE&H 620	CMon
longituba	See ***R. macowanii***
§ ***macowanii***	MHig WAbe
– var. ***alticola***	EHyt WAbe WOMN
minutiflora	NRog
monticola	CMon
nivalis	CAvo LAma WChr WThi
pratensis	CNic WThi
ramiflora	CMon WChr
– SF 63	CMon
requienii	WOMN
¶ – L65	EHyt
rosea	NRog
sabulosa	CBro
saldanhensis	EHyt
sp. SF 367	CMon
tabularis	WCot
tempskyana	CMon EPot WChr
'Zahni'	CMon EHic LAma

RORIPPA (Brassicaceae)

nasturtium-aquaticum	MHew

ROSA † (Rosaceae)

◆ A Shropshire Lad	See ***R.* A Shropshire Lad = 'Ausled'**
Aalsmeer Gold (HT)	MJon
'Abbandonata'	See ***R.* 'Laure Davoust'**
Abbeyfield Rose (HT) ♀	GCoc GGre SApu SJus SPer
§ 'Abbotswood' (*canina* hybrid)	EBls
Aberdeen Celebration (F)	GCoc
Abigaile (F)	MJon NBat
'Abington Park' (HT)	MHay
Abraham Darby (S)	CDoC CGro CSam EBre EWar GGre IHar LGod LStr MAus MFry MGan MHlr MJon MTis NPri SPer SWCr WAct WHCG WHow WStI
'Acapulco' (HT)	IDic MFry NBat
Ace of Hearts (HT)	MBur
acicularis	EPla WWat
– var. ***nipponensis***	EBls EWar
'Adam' (ClT)	EBls MAus
'Adam Messerich' (Bb)	EBls MAus WHCG
'Adélaïde d'Orléans' (Ra) ♀	EBls MAus NPri SPer SRum WAct WHCG WPen
Admirable (Min)	MBur

'Admiral Rodney' (HT)	EWar MGan MHay MJon NBat NRog
Adolf Horstmann (HT)	MGan
'Adrienne Burnham' (HT)	MHay
'Agatha' (G)	EBls
Agatha Christie (ClF)	CGre EWar MBri MJon MMat SApu SJus
'Agathe Incarnata' (GxD)	EWar
¶ 'Aglaia' (Ra)	WHCG
'Agnes' (Ru)	EBls ENot GCoc IHar IHos MAus MGan MMat NSty SJus SPer SWCr WAct WHCG WOVN
'Aimée Vibert' (Ra)	EBls MAus MHlr NPri SMer SPer WAct WHCG WSHC
Air France (Min)	EWar
'Alain Blanchard' (G)	EBls MAus WHCG
× ***alba*** (A)	EBls MSto NRog
§ – 'Alba Maxima' (A) ♀	CHad EBls ENot EWar GCoc MAus MHlr MMat NFla NPri NSty SFam SPer WAct WHCG
§ – 'Alba Semiplena' (A) ♀	EBls EWar MAus NSty SJus SPer WAct WGer WHCG
◆ – Celestial	See ***R.* 'Céleste'**
◆ – 'Maxima'	See ***R.* × *alba* 'Alba Maxima'**
N Alba Meidiland (GC)	EWar WOVN
'Albéric Barbier' (Ra) ♀	CHad CSam EBls EOrc EWar IHos LHol LStr MAus MBri MBur MGan MHlr MJon MMat MMor NRog NSty SApu SJus SPer SRum SWCr WAct WHCG WHow WOVN WSHC WWeb
'Albert Weedall' (HT)	MHay
'Albertine' (Ra) ♀	Widely available
'Alchymist' (S/Cl)	CHad CNat EBee EBls MAus MBri MGan MJon MMat SPer SWCr WAct WHCG WHow
◆ Alec C. Collie	See ***R.* Alec C. Collie = 'Cococrust'**
Alec's Red (HT)	CB&S CGro EBls ESha EWar GCoc IHar IHos LPlm LStr MBri MECR MGan MHay MJon MMat MMor NRog SPer WWeb
Alexander (HT) ♀	CGro EBls ESha EWar GCoc IHos LGod LPlm LStr MFry MGan MHay MJon MMat MMor NRog SApu SPer
'Alexander Hill Gray' (T)	EBls
'Alexander von Humbolt' (Cl)	MGan
Alexandra Rose (S)	WHow
'Alexandre Girault' (Ra)	EBls EMFP MAus MHlr NPri SPer SWCr WAct WHCG WHow
§ 'Alfred Colomb' (HP)	EBls NSty
'Alfred de Dalmas' hort.	See ***R.* 'Mousseline'**
'Alida Lovett' (Ra)	EBls MAus
Alison (F)	GCoc SApu
§ 'Alister Stella Gray' (N)	EBls EMFP LHol MAus MGan MHlr NPri SPer WAct WHCG WHow
All in One	See ***R.* Exploit**
'Allen Chandler' (ClHT)	EBls MAus NSty
Allgold (F)	CB&S CGro EBls EWar GCoc LStr MAus MGan MJon MMor NPri SRum WStI
'Aloha' (ClHT)	CB&S CDoC CGro CHad EBls EBre IHar IHos IOrc MAus MBur MECR MFry MGan MJon MMat NBat NRog NSty SApu SJus SPer SRum SSoC WAct WHCG WHow WSHC
alpina	See ***R. pendulina***
Alpine Sunset (HT)	CTri EBee EBls ESha EWar GGre MGan SPer SRum
altaica hort.	See ***R. pimpinellifolia* 'Grandiflora'**
Altissimo® (Cl) ♀	CHad EBee EBls EMFP LPlm MAus MGan MHlr MJon MMat SPer SWCr WGer
'Amadis' (Bs)	EBls MAus SWCr WHCG
Amanda (F)	LStr MBri MJon SApu
'Amatsu-otome' (HT)	MHay
'Amazing Grace' (HT)	GGre
'Amber Nectar' (F)	LStr
Amber Queen (F) ♀	CDoC CGro EBls ELan ESha EWar GCoc GGre IHos LGod LPlm LStr MAus MBri MBur MECR MFry MGan MHay MJon MMat MMor NRog SApu SJus SPer SRum SWCr
Ambridge Rose (S)	MAus MBri MTis WWeb
'Amélia'	See ***R.* 'Celsiana'**
'Amelia Louise' (Min)	MHay
'American Pillar' (Ra)	CB&S CDoC CGro CSam EBls EBre EOrc ESha EWar ISea LGod LStr MAus MGan MHlr MMat NBat NRog NSty SApu SPer SRum WFar WHCG
'Améthyste' (Ra)	NSty
'Amy Robsart' (RH)	EBls MAus SJus
'Anais Ségalas' (G)	MAus
§ 'Andersonii' (*canina* hybrid)	EBls MAus WAct
§ 'Anemone' (Cl)	EBls MAus
anemoniflora	See ***R.* × *beanii***
anemonoides	See ***R.* 'Anemone'**
– 'Ramona'	See ***R.* 'Ramona'**
Angela Rippon (Min)	EWar IHos MFry MGan MJon MMat SPer WGer WStI
'Angela's Choice' (F)	MGan
'Angèle Pernet' (HT)	EBls
'Angelina' (S)	EBls EWar
Anisley Dickson (F) ♀	EBee GCoc IDic LGod MGan MHay MJon NBat SApu SPer
'Ann Aberconway' (F)	MJon MMat
'Anna de Diesbach' (HP)	EBls
Anna Ford (Min/Patio) ♀	EWar GGre IHar IHos LGod LPlm LStr MAus MGan MJon SApu SRum SWCr
Anna Livia (F)	EBee IHos MGan MJon MMat MMor SApu SJus
'Anna Olivier' (T)	EBls
'Anna Pavlova' (HT)	EBls
Anna Zinkeisen (S)	WAct WOVN
Anne Cocker (F)	EBls GCoc MGan
'Anne Dakin'	MAus
Anne Harkness (F)	EWar LStr MAus MGan MHay MJon NRog SPer
Anne Moore (Min)	MHay
'Anne of Geierstein' (RH)	EBls MAus MGan
'Anne Watkins' (HT)	EBls
◆ Antique	See ***R.* Antique = 'Kordalen'**
Antique '89 (ClF)	EBls MBri MJon MMat SJus
'Antoine Rivoire' (HT)	EBls
'Antonia d'Ormois' (G)	EBls
Anusheh (F)	MHay
Anvil Sparks (HT)	MGan
Apothecary's Rose	See ***R. gallica* var. *officinalis***

'Apple Blossom' (Ra)	EBls EWar NSty WHCG
'Applejack' (S)	EBls
'Apricot Garnet'	See ***R.* 'Garnette Apricot'**
'Apricot Nectar' (F)	LStr MAus MGan SPer SWCr
'Apricot Silk' (HT)	CB&S CGro CTri EBls EWar IHar IHos MAus MGan NPri NRog SPer WWeb
Apricot Summer (Patio)	GCoc MJon MMat WGer
Apricot Sunblaze (Min)	EBls EWar IHos MJon SJus WWeb
¶ 'Apricot Wine' (F)	IHar
◆ Arc Angel	See ***R.* Arc Angel = 'Fryyorston'**
Arcadian (F)	MJon
'Archiduc Joseph'	See ***R.* 'Général Schablikine'**
'Archiduchesse Elisabeth d'Autriche' (HP)	EBls
'Ardoisée de Lyon' (HP)	EBls
Ards Beauty (F)	IDic MGan MJon SApu SPer
'Ards Rover' (ClHP)	EBls
'Arethusa' (Ch)	EBls
'Arizona Sunset' (Min)	MHay
§ ***arkansana*** var. ***suffulta***	EBls WHCG
Armada (S)	GCoc SApu
'Artful Dodger' (Patio)	MBur
'Arthur Bell' (F) 🏆	EBls EBre ESha EWar GCoc GGre IHar IHos LPlm LStr MAus MBur MECR MGan MHay MMat NBat NRog SApu SPer SRum WWeb
'Arthur de Sansal' (DPo)	EBls MAus MRav
'Arthur Scargill' (Min)	MHay
arvensis	CCVT CKin EBls MAus SLPl
'Ash Wednesday' (Cl)	EBls
'Assemblage des Beautés' (G)	EBls MAus
'Astrid Späth Striped' (F)	EBls
Atco Royale (F)	MFry
Atlantic Star (F)	MFry MJon
Audrey Gardner (Min/Patio)	SRum
Audrey Wilcox (HT)	MFry
'August Seebauer' (F)	EBls MAus
'Auguste Gervais' (Ra)	EBls IHar MAus SPer SRum WHCG
'Augustine Guinoisseau' (HT)	EBls MAus
'Augustine Halem' (HT)	EBls
'Aunty Dora' (F)	EWar
§ Dapple Dawn = 'Ausapple' (S)	MAus SPer SWCr
§ Moonbeam = 'Ausbeam' (S)	MAus
§ Jayne Austin = 'Ausbreak' (S)	CGro EBre MAus MJon MTis NPri SApu SPer
§ Mayor of Casterbridge = 'Ausbrid' (S)	IHar MAus MJon NPri
§ Canterbury = 'Ausbury' (S)	MAus
§ John Clare = 'Auscent'	EBre MAus
§ Heather Austin = 'Auscook'	MAus NPri
§ Cressida = 'Auscress' (S)	MAus
§ Windflower = 'Auscross' (S)	EBre MAus
§ Bibi Maizoon = 'Ausdimindo'	EWar IHar IHos MAus SPer
§ Jude the Obscure = 'Ausjo' (S)	IHar MAus MJon
§ Mistress Quickly = 'Ausky' (S)	IHar MAus MJon NPri
§ A Shropshire Lad = 'Ausled' (S)	MAus MJon

§ Eglantyne = 'Ausmark' (S)	EBre IHar MAus MHlr MJon SPer SWCr
§ Heavenly Rosalind = 'Ausmash'	MAus
§ Molineux = 'Ausmol' (S)	EBre IHar MAus MHlr MJon NPri WHCG
§ Trevor Griffiths = 'Ausold' (S)	EBre MAus
§ Radio Times = 'Aussal' (S)	EBre IHar MAus MJon NPri
Austrian Copper	See ***R. foetida* 'Bicolor'**
Austrian Yellow	See ***R. foetida***
§ Noble Anthony = 'Ausway' (S)	MAus MJon NPri SWCr
'Autumn' (HT)	NRog
'Autumn Bouquet' (S)	EBls
'Autumn Delight' (HM)	EBls MAus WHCG
'Autumn Fire'	See ***R.* 'Herbstfeuer'**
'Autumn Sunlight' (ClHT)	EWar MBur MGan SPer
'Autumn Sunset' (S)	EBls
'Autumnalis'	See ***R.* 'Princesse de Nassau'**
'Aviateur Blériot' (Ra)	EBls MAus
Avocet (F)	GGre MBri
◆ Avon	See ***R.* Avon = 'Poulmulti'**
'Awakening' (Cl)	EBls WHCG
'Awareness' (HT)	MFry
'Ayrshire Splendens'	See ***R.* 'Splendens'**
Babie Kate (Min)	MHay NBat
'Baby Bio' (F)	CB&S MBri MGan NPri NRog SRum
'Baby Darling' (Min)	MAus MGan
'Baby Faurax' (Poly)	MAus
'Baby Gold' (Min)	LPlm
'Baby Gold Star' (Min)	MAus MGan SPer
◆ Baby Love	See ***R.* Baby Love = 'Scrivluv'**
Baby Masquerade (Min)	ELan EWar GCoc IHos LGod LPlm MBur MGan MJon MMat MMor NRog SWCr WStI
Baby Sunrise (Min)	MJon SJus
'Bad Neuenahr' (Cl)	MGan
'Ballerina' (HM) 🏆	Widely available
◆ Ballindalloch Castle	See ***R.* Ballindalloch Castle = 'Cocneel'**
'Baltimore Belle' (Ra)	EBls EWar MAus WHCG
banksiae (Ra)	CGre GQui LPan SPer SRms
banksiae alba	See ***R. banksiae*** var. ***banksiae***
§ ***banksiae*** var. ***banksiae*** (Ra/d)	CBot CPMA EPfP ERea MAus NSty SBid SBra WWat
– 'Lutea' (Ra/d) 🏆	CB&S CFee CGre CPMA CPlN CSPN CSam CTrw EBls ELan ERea GQui ISea MAus MHlr MMat NSty SBra SMad SPer SSoC SUsu WAct WBod WHCG WSHC WWat WWeb
– var. ***normalis*** (Ra)	CBot CGre MAus NSti NSty
– 'Purezza'	See ***R.* 'Purezza'**
Bantry Bay (ClHT)	EBls EWar LStr MGan MMat SJus SPla SRum SWCr
'Barbara Carrera' (F)	EBls
Barkarole (HT)	EWar LStr MJon SApu SJus
'Baron de Bonstetten' (HP)	EBls
'Baron de Wassenaer' (CeMo)	EBls MGan
'Baron Girod de l'Ain' (HP)	CPou EBee EBls EMFP MAus MHlr NSty SPer SPla SWCr WAct WHCG WHow
Baron Sunblaze	See ***R.* Baron Meillandina**
◆ 'Baroness Rothschild' (HT)	See ***R.* Baronne Edmond de Rothschild**
§ 'Baronne Adolph de Rothschild' (HP)	CPou EBee EMFP IHos IOrc MGan WHCG

'Baronne de Rothschild' (HP)	See *R.* **'Baronne Adolph de Rothschild'**
§ Baronne Edmond de Rothschild (HT)	EWar WAct
'Baronne Henriette de Snoy' (T)	EBls
'Baronne Prévost' (HP) 🏆	EBls MAus SFam WAct WHCG
◆ Barry Fearn	See ***R.* Barry Fearn = 'Korschwana'**
'Bashful' (Poly)	MGan
Basildon Bond (HT)	IHar MJon
'Battersby Beauty' (HT)	NBat
§ x ***beanii*** (Ra)	EPla SMad
'Beauté' (HT)	EBls MAus MGan NPri
Beautiful Britain (F)	EBls GGre IDic IHos LStr MAus MBri MGan MJon NRog SJus SRum WFar
'Beauty of Rosemawr' (ClT)	EBls
Beauty Star	See ***R.* Liverpool Remembers**
Belfast Belle (HT)	IDic
'Belle Amour' (DxA)	EBls MAus NSty WHCG
'Belle Blonde' (HT)	MGan SPer
'Belle de Crécy' (G) 🏆	EBls EWar GCoc IOrc MAus MHlr MMat NSty SFam SJus SMer SPer SWCr WAct WHCG
'Belle des Jardins'	See *R.* **'Centifolia Variegata'**
Belle Epoque (HT)	GCoc MBur MFry MJon SApu
'Belle Isis' (G)	EBls MAus SPer
'Belle Lyonnaise' (ClT)	EBls
'Belle Poitevine' (Ru) 🏆	EBls MAus NSty
'Belle Portugaise' (Cl)	EBls MAus
Belle Story (S)	MAus
¶ Belle Sunblaze (Min)	IHar
Bellevue (HT)	MJon
'Belvedere' (Ra)	MAus SWCr WHCG
* 'Bengal Beauty'	WWat
◆ Benita	See ***R.* Benita = 'Dicquarrel'**
'Bennett's Seedling' (Ra)	MAus
Benson and Hedges Gold (HT)	EWar
Benson and Hedges Special (Min)	ELan GGre MJon MMor
Berkshire (GC)	ENot LStr MHlr MJon MMat NPri SWCr WOVN WWeb
◆ Best Wishes	See ***R.* Best Wishes = 'Chessnut'**
Bettina (HT)	MAus MGan NRog
Betty Driver (F)	MBri MGan SPer
'Betty Prior' (F)	GCoc MGan
'Betty Uprichard' (HT)	EBls NSty
'Beyreuth' (S)	MGan
Bianco (Patio/Min)	GCoc MAus SJus
◆ Bibi Maizoon	See ***R.* Bibi Maizoon = 'Ausdimindo'**
Biddulph Grange (S)	MFry
Biddy (Min)	MHay
§ ***biebersteinii***	EBls
'Big Chief' (HT)	MHay MJon NRog
Big Purple (HT)	MJon SApu SRum
Birthday Girl (F)	GCoc MJon SApu
'Bishop Darlington' (HM)	EBls
Bishop Elphinstone (F)	GCoc
'Bit o'Sunshine' (Min)	MGan MMor
'Black Beauty' (HT)	MAus MJon
'Black Ice' (F)	MGan
'Black Jack' (Ce)	See *R.* **'Tour de Malakoff'**
Black Jack (Min/Patio)	MBur MHay NBat
Black Jade (Patio)	MHay
'Black Prince' (HP)	EBls
'Blairii Number One' (Bb)	EBls NSty
'Blairii Number Two' (ClBb) 🏆	CHad EBee EBls EMFP MAus MHlr NPri NSty SFam SPer SWCr WAct WHCG WHow WSHC
'Blanche de Vibert' (DPo)	EBls MAus
'Blanche Double de Coubert' (Ru) 🏆	CHad CSam EBls ELan ENot EWar GCoc IHos IOrc LHol LStr MAus MFry MGan MHlr MJon MMat NFla NRog NSty SApu SJus SPer SRum WAct WHCG WHow WOVN WSHC
'Blanche Moreau' (CeMo)	EBls IHar IHos MAus MGan MHlr NSty SPer WAct
'Blanchefleur' (Ce)	EBls IHos MAus NSty
blanda	EBls
'Blaydon Races'	NBat
◆ Blenheim	See ***R.* Blenheim = 'Tanmurse'**
Blessings (HT) 🏆	CB&S CDoC CGro EBls EBre ESha EWar GCoc GGre IHos LGod LPlm LStr MAus MBri MBur MECR MFry MGan MHay MJon NBat NRog SApu SPer SWCr WWeb
'Bleu Magenta' (Ra)	EBls EWar MAus WHCG
'Bloomfield Abundance' (Poly)	CPou EBls MAus MMat NSty SPer SRum SWCr WHCG WHer
'Bloomfield Dainty' (HM)	EBls
'Blossomtime' (Cl)	NRog SMad SPer
'Blue Diamond' (HT)	MGan
Blue Moon (HT)	CGro EBls EBre ELan ESha EWar GCoc GGre IHos LGod LPlm MAus MBur MGan MHay MJon MMor NRog SApu SPer SRum WWeb
Blue Parfum®	MAus MJon
Blue Peter (Min)	IHos MFry MJon SApu WWeb
'Blush Boursault' (Bs)	EBls MAus
'Blush Damask' (D)	EBls WHCG
'Blush Noisette'	See *R.* **'Noisette Carnée'**
'Blush Rambler' (Ra)	EBee EBls EWar MAus MHlr SPla WHCG WHow
'Blushing Lucy' (Cl)	MAus WAct WSHC
'Bob Collard' (F)	SRum
'Bob Woolley' (HT)	MHay
'Bobbie James' (Ra) 🏆	CHad EBls EBre EWar IHos LStr MAus MGan MHlr MMat NBat NSty SJus SPer SRum WAct WHCG WHow
'Bobby Charlton' (HT)	MFry MGan MHay NRog
'Bobolink' (Min)	MGan
'Bon Silène' (T)	EBls
Bonfire Night (F)	CGro MBur MGan MMat
Bonica (GC) 🏆	CSam EBls EBre ELan ENot GCoc IHar IHos LGod LStr MAus MBur MECR MFry MGan MHlr MJon SApu SJus SPer SRum SWCr WAct WHCG WOVN
'Bonn' (HM)	CB&S MAus MGan NRog
'Bonnie Scotland' (HT)	MGan
Bonsoir (HT)	MGan MHay
'Border Coral' (F)	NRog
'Botzaris' (D)	EBls SFam
'Boule de Nanteuil' (G)	EBls
'Boule de Neige' (Bb)	CHad EBls EMFP ENot GCoc IHar LHol LStr MAus MHlr MMat NFla NSty SFam SJus SPer SPla WAct WHCG WOVN WWeb
'Bouquet d'Or' (N)	EBls MAus WHCG

◆ 'Bouquet Tout Fait' misapplied	See ***R.* 'Nastarana'**
'Bourbon Queen' (Bb)	EBee EBls MAus MHlr NSty WHCG
Bow Bells (S)	MAus MHlr
◆ Boy O Boy	See ***R.* Boy O Boy = 'Dicuniform'**
Boys' Brigade (Patio)	CGro EWar GCoc MGan NBat SApu
§ ***bracteata***	GQui MAus WWat
'Brave Heart' (F)	NBat
Breath of Life (ClHT)	CGro CSam EBls ELan ESha EWar GGre IHar LGod LStr MAus MBri MFry MGan MJon NBat SApu SJus SPer SRum SWCr
Bredon (S)	IHar MAus MBri
'Breeze Hill' (Ra)	EBls MAus
§ 'Brenda Colvin' (Ra)	MAus
'Brennus' (China hybrid)	EBls
'Briarcliff' (HT)	EBls
Bridal Pink (F)	EWar MJon
◆ Bride	See ***R.* Bride = 'Fryyearn'**
Bright Smile (F/Patio)	CDoC GCoc IDic IHar LStr MAus MECR MFry MGan SPer SWCr
Bright Spark (Min)	MFry
'Brindis' (ClF)	MGan
◆ Broadlands	See ***R.* Broadlands = 'Tanmirson'**
Brother Cadfael (S)	EWar IHar MAus MHlr MJon NPri SPer SSoC
Brown Velvet (F)	MJon SApu
'Browsholme Rose'	NSty
§ ***brunonii*** (Ra)	CHan EBls EWes MAus SBra WLRN
– CC 1235 (Ra)	WHCr
– CC&McK 362 (Ra)	LKoh
§ – 'La Mortola' (Ra)	MAus SPer
Buck's Fizz (F)	EWar GGre MBur MGan SApu SJus
'Buff Beauty' (HM) ♀	Widely available
'Bullata'	See ***R.* × *centifolia* 'Bullata'**
§ Katie Crocker = 'Burbringley' (F)	MBur
§ 'Burgundiaca' (G)	EBls MAus WAct WHCG
Burgundian Rose	See ***R.* 'Burgundiaca'**
'Burma Star' (F)	EWar GCoc
Burnet, Double Pink	See ***R. pimpinellifolia* double pink**
Burnet, Double White	See ***R. pimpinellifolia* double white**
§ Good Luck = 'Burspec' (Patio)	MJon
Bush Baby (Min)	LGod LStr MJon SApu SWCr
Buttons (Min/Patio)	IDic IHos MFry WWeb
By Appointment (F)	GGre MJon SJus SRum
'C.F. Meyer'	See ***R.* 'Conrad Ferdinand Meyer'**
¶ 'Café' (F)	WBcn
'Cairngorm' (F)	GCoc
¶ 'Caledonian' (HT)	NBat
californica (S)	MAus
– 'Plena'	See ***R. nutkana* 'Plena'**
'Callisto' (HM)	EBee EWar MAus WHCG
'Camaïeux' (G)	EBls MAus MHlr MMat SPer SWCr WAct WHCG
Cambridgeshire (GC)	ENot LGod LStr MMat NBat NPri SPer SWCr WWeb
'Camélia Rose' (Cl)	EBls WHCG
'Cameo' (Poly)	EBls IHar MAus MGan SMer
Can-can	See ***R.* Can-can = 'Legglow'**
'Canary Bird'	See ***R. xanthina* 'Canary Bird'**
Candy Rose (S)	EWar
canina (S)	CB&S CCVT CKin CPer CTri ECWi LBuc MAus MHew NWea WMou
– 'Abbotswood'	See ***R.* 'Abbotswood' (*canina* hybrid)**
– 'Andersonii'	See ***R.* 'Andersonii' (*canina* hybrid)**
– 'Inermis' (S)	MSto
'Cantabrigiensis' (S)	EBee EBls ENot MAus MHlr NBus NFla NRog SPer WAct WHCG WOVN WWat
◆ Canterbury	See ***R.* Canterbury = 'Ausbury'**
'Capitaine Basroger' (CeMo)	EBls MAus
'Capitaine John Ingram' (CeMo) ♀	EBee EBls EWar MAus NSty SFam SPer WHow
Captain Cook (F)	NBat
'Captain Hayward' (HP)	EBls
'Cardiff Bay' (HT)	MHay
'Cardinal de Richelieu' (G) ♀	CHad EBls EMFP EWar GCoc IOrc MAus MFry MHlr MMat NSty SApu SFam SPer WAct WHCG
Cardinal Hume (S)	EBls EWar LStr MGan SApu SPer
Carefree Beauty (S)	EWar
'Carmen' (Ra)	EBls MAus
§ 'Carmenetta' (S)	EBls EWar MAus
'Carol'	See ***R.* 'Carol Amling'**
carolina	CGre LHop SIng SLPl WHCG
Caroline de Monaco (HT)	MJon
'Caroline Testout'	See ***R.* 'Madame Caroline Testout'**
§ Casino (ClHT)	CGro EBls ESha EWar IHar LPlm MBur MFry MGan MJon MMor SPer SRum WStI WWeb
Castle of Mey (F)	GCoc MJon
Catherine Cookson (HT)	NBat
'Catherine Mermet' (T)	EBls MAus NSty
'Catherine Seyton' (RH)	EBls
§ 'Cécile Brünner' (Poly)	CBos CHad EBls ELan EMFP ENot EWar GCoc LHol LStr MAus MGan MHlr MMat NRog NSty SJus SPer SPla SRum SWCr WHCG WHow WWat
§ 'Cécile Brünner, White' (Poly)	EBls MAus WHCG
Cecily Gibson (F)	MJon
§ 'Céleste' (A) ♀	EBls EMFP ENot GCoc IHar IHos MAus MFry MHlr MMat NSty SApu SFam SJus SPer SRum SWCr WAct WGer WHCG WOVN
'Celestial'	See ***R.* 'Céleste'**
'Célina' (CeMo)	EBls MGan
'Céline Forestier' (N)	EBee EBls MAus SFam SPer SPla WAct WHCG
§ 'Celsiana' (D)	EBls EWar IHar MAus MHlr NPri SFam SPer WAct WHCG
Centenaire de Lourdes (F)	EBls
§ × ***centifolia*** (Ce)	CTri EBls IOrc MHlr NRog SJus SMad WAct WHCG
§ – 'Bullata' (Ce)	EBls MAus
§ – 'Cristata' (Ce) ♀	EBls EMFP ENot EWar IHos MMat NBus NPri NRog SFam SJus SPer WAct WHCG
§ – 'Muscosa' (Ce) ♀	CPou CTri EBls EMFP ENot EWar GCoc IHos IOrc MGan MMat NRog NSty SFam SJus

– 'Parvifolia'	See ***R.* 'Burgundiaca'**
§ 'Centifolia Variegata' (Ce)	EBls MGan
'Cerise Bouquet' (S) ♀	EBls EMFP IHar MAus MMat NSty SJus SPer WAct WHCG WKif WWeb
Cha Cha (Patio/Min)	SApu
Champagne (F)	MJon
Champagne Cocktail (F)	EWar GGre MJon NBat SApu
'Champion' (HT)	MAus MHay
'Champneys' Pink Cluster' (China hybrid)	EBls
Champs Elysées (HT)	MGan
'Chanelle' (F)	EBls EWar GCoc MAus MGan NRog SPer
Chapeau de Napoléon	See ***R.* × *centifolia* 'Cristata'**
'Chaplin's Pink Climber' (Cl)	EBls MGan
Chardonnay (HT)	MBri MJon
Charisma (F)	EBee
Charles Austin (S)	IHar MAus MBri NSty SJus WAct WHCG
Charles Aznavour (F)	EWar
'Charles de Mills' (G) ♀	CHad EBls EMFP ENot GCoc IHar MAus MFry MHlr MJon MMat NSty SFam SJus SPer SRum WAct WHCG WHow WWeb
'Charles Gater' (HP)	EBls
'Charles Lefèbvre' (HP)	EBls
'Charles Mallerin' (HT)	EBls
Charles Rennie Mackintosh (S)	EWar MAus MJon NPri WGer
Charleston (F)	MGan
Charleston '88 (HT)	EWar
Charlotte (S)	EWar IHar MAus MHlr MJon NPri SApu SWCr WAct
Charmian (S)	MAus
'Charter 700' (F)	MFry
'Château de Clos-Vougeot' (HT)	MGan
◆ Chatsworth	See ***R.* Chatsworth = 'Tanotax'**
Chaucer (S)	MAus MBri
Chelsea Belle (Min)	MHay
Chelsea Pensioner (Min)	LPlm SApu
Cherry Brandy (HT)	MBur MFry MGan MJon SRum
'Cherryade' (S)	MGan
§ Thank You = 'Chesdeep' (Patio)	EWar GGre MJon
'Cheshire Life' (HT)	ESha MAus MBur MFry MGan MJon MMor NPri SRum WStI
§ Best Wishes = 'Chessnut' (Cl/v)	GGre LStr MJon SWCr
§ Golden Hands = 'Chessupremo' (Min/Patio)	CDoC GGre SPer
Chester Cathedral (HT)	MJon
§ Open Arms = 'Chewpixcel' (ClMin)	LGod MFry MJon WGer
§ Pathfinder = 'Chewpobey' (GC)	MJon
§ Little Rambler = 'Chewramb' (MinRa)	MJon MMat SApu
§ Good as Gold = 'Chewsunbeam' (ClMin)	EBre EWar LStr MBur MFry MJon SApu WGer WOVN
'Chianti' (S)	EBls MAus MBri NSty WHCG
Chicago Peace (HT)	EBls ESha EWar GGre IHos LGod LPlm MAus MGan MJon MMor NRog SRum SWCr WStI
Child's Play (Min)	MHay
Chilterns (GC)	ENot EWar SWCr
Chinatown (F/S) ♀	CB&S CGro EBls EBre ELan ESha EWar GCoc GGre IHos LPlm LStr MAus MECR MGan MHay MJon MMor NRog NSty SApu SJus SRum
***chinensis* 'Mutabilis'**	See ***R.* × *odorata* 'Mutabilis'**
– 'Old Blush'	See ***R.* × *odorata* 'Pallida'**
'Chloris' (A)	EBls EMFP
'Chorus Girl' (F)	MGan
Christian Dior (HT)	EBls
'Christine Gandy' (F)	MGan
◆ Christopher	See ***R.* Christopher = 'Cocopher'**
Christopher Columbus (HT)	MBri MJon MMat SApu
'Chrysler Imperial' (HT)	EBls MAus MGan
Cider Cup (Min/Patio)	CDoC ESha EWar GCoc GGre IDic MBur MFry MJon NBat SApu SJus
'Cinderella' (Min)	GAri MGan
cinnamomea	See ***R. majalis***
'Circus' (F)	MAus MGan
◆ City Lights	See ***R.* City Lights = 'Poulgan'**
City of Belfast (F)	EBls IHos MAus
City of Birmingham (S/HT)	MMat
'City of Cardiff' (HT)	MHay
'City of Leeds' (F)	EBls ESha GGre MAus MGan MHay MMat NRog SPer WStI
City of London (F) ♀	EBls EWar LStr MBur MJon SApu SPer
'City of Portsmouth' (F)	CB&S MGan
'City of Worcester' (HT)	MHay
'City of York' (Ra)	EBls
Clair Matin (ClS)	CHad EBls MAus SPer SPla WAct
'Claire Jacquier' (N)	EBls MAus SPer WAct WHCG
Claire Rayner (F/Patio)	LPlm MJon WGer
Claire Rose (S)	CGro CSam EBar EWar IHar IHos MAus MJon NPri SChu SPer SWCr
Claire Scotland (Patio)	GCoc
Clarissa (Min)	IHos MAus
'Clementina Carbonieri' (T)	EBls
Cleopatra (HT)	ENot MBur MMat
'Cliff Richard' (F)	EWar WWeb
Climbing Alec's Red (ClHT)	SPer
'Climbing Allgold' (ClF)	EBls EWar GGre IHos MGan SRum
'Climbing Arthur Bell' (ClF)	CTri NRog SApu SPer SRum
Climbing Bettina (ClHT)	EBls MAus SRum
Climbing Blessings (ClHT)	EBls
'Climbing Blue Moon' (ClHT)	MBur MGan
'Climbing Captain Christy' (ClHT)	EBls MAus
'Climbing Cécile Brünner' (ClPoly) ♀	CHad CHan EBls EFol LGod LStr MAus NFla NPri NSty SApu SFam SJus SPer SWCr WAct WHCG WHow WSHC WWat
'Climbing Château de Clos-Vougeot' (ClHT)	EBls MAus
'Climbing Cherryade' (ClHT)	MGan
'Climbing Christine' (ClHT)	MAus

'Climbing Columbia' (ClHT)	NSty
'Climbing Comtesse Vandal' (ClHT)	EBls MAus
'Climbing Crimson Glory' (ClHT)	EBls EMFP GCoc MAus MGan NRog SRum WStI
'Climbing Devoniensis' (ClT)	EBls MAus NSty
'Climbing Ena Harkness' (ClHT)	CB&S CGro CTri EBls GCoc GGre IHos MAus MBri MBur MGan NRog SPer SPla SRum WStI WWeb
'Climbing Ernest H. Morse' (ClHT)	MGan
'Climbing Etoile de Hollande' (ClHT) ♀	CSam EBls EBre GCoc LHol LStr MAus MGan MHlr MJon MRav NFla NRog NSty SApu SJus SPer SRum WHCG WHow WOVN
'Climbing Fashion' (ClF)	EBls
Climbing Fragrant Cloud (ClHT)	CB&S ELan MGan SRum
§ 'Climbing Frau Karl Druschki' (ClHP)	EBls MGan NRog
'Climbing General MacArthur' (ClHT)	EBls MAus
Climbing Gold Bunny (ClF)	EWar MJon WGer
'Climbing Grand-mère Jenny' (ClHT)	EBls
'Climbing Home Sweet Home' (ClHT)	MAus
'Climbing Iceberg' (ClF) ♀	CGro EBls EBre ELan EWar GGre LPlm LStr MAus MBri MGan MJon MMor NRog SPer SRum WHCG WOVN WSHC WWeb
'Climbing Irish Fireflame' (ClHT)	MAus
'Climbing Josephine Bruce' (ClHT)	MAus MGan
'Climbing la France' (ClHT)	MAus
'Climbing Lady Hillingdon' (ClT) ♀	EBls EBre EMFP EWar MAus MGan MHlr NSty SApu SPer WAct WHCG WSHC
'Climbing Lady Sylvia' (ClHT)	EBls EMFP MAus MGan NRog SApu SPer WStI
◆ 'Climbing Little White Pet'	See ***R.* 'Félicité Perpétue'**
'Climbing Madame Abel Chatenay' (ClHT)	EBls MAus SPer
'Climbing Madame Butterfly' (ClHT)	EBls EBre MAus MGan NPri SJus SPer
'Climbing Madame Caroline Testout' (ClHT)	EBls LHol MAus NRog NSty SPer WBcn WSHC
§ 'Climbing Madame Edouard Herriot' (ClHT)	EBls MAus MGan SPer
'Climbing Madame Henri Guillot' (ClHT)	EBls MAus
'Climbing Maman Cochet' (ClT)	EBls MAus
'Climbing Masquerade' (ClF)	EBls EBre GGre LPlm MAus MGan MJon NRog SRum WStI WWeb
'Climbing McGredy's Yellow' (ClHT)	MGan
§ 'Climbing Mevrouw G.A. van Rossem' (ClHT)	EBls MAus
'Climbing Mrs Aaron Ward' (ClHT)	EBls MAus
◆ 'Climbing Mrs G.A. van Rossem'	See ***R.* 'Climbing Mevrouw G.A. van Rossem'**
'Climbing Mrs Herbert Stevens' (ClHT)	CPou EBee EBls EMFP MAus MHlr NRog NSty SPer WHCG WHow
'Climbing Mrs Sam McGredy' (ClHT) ♀	CGro CTri EBls LPlm MAus MBri MGan MJon NRog SPla SRum
'Climbing My Love' (ClHT)	MGan
'Climbing Ophelia' (ClHT)	CPou EBee EBls MAus MHlr
Climbing Orange Sunblaze (ClMin)	EWar LStr MBri MJon NPri SApu SPer
'Climbing Pascali' (ClHT)	CB&S MGan
'Climbing Paul Lédé' (ClT)	EBee EBls EBre EMFP IHar MAus MHlr WHCG WHow
'Climbing Picture' (ClHT)	EBls MAus MGan
'Climbing Pompon de Paris' (ClCh)	CBot CDec CHan EBls LHop MAus MRav NSty SIng SMer SPer WHCG WSHC
'Climbing Richmond' (ClHT)	EBls MAus
'Climbing Roundelay' (Cl)	EBls
'Climbing Shot Silk' (ClHT) ♀	EBee EBls MAus MGan SJus SPer SRum
§ 'Climbing Sombreuil' (ClT)	CHad EBee EBls EBre MAus MHlr MRav SBid SFam SJus SPer SPla WAct WHCG WHow
'Climbing Souvenir de la Malmaison' (ClBb)	EBls MAus SPer WAct WHCG
'Climbing Spartan' (ClF)	EWar
'Climbing Spek's Yellow' (ClHT)	MAus
'Climbing Summer Sunshine' (ClHT)	MBri
Climbing Super Star (ClHT)	MAus MMor WWeb
'Climbing Sutter's Gold' (ClHT)	MAus MGan
'Climbing Talisman' (ClHT)	EBls
'Climbing the Doctor' (ClHT)	MGan
'Climbing the Queen Elizabeth' (ClF)	EBls MGan SRum
'Clio' (HP)	MJon
'Cloth of Gold' (N)	EBls MAus
§ Rosabell = 'Cocceleste' (F/Patio)	GCoc GGre LPlm MFry SApu
§ Gingernut = 'Coccrazy' (Patio)	EBre ESha GCoc GGre NBat SApu
§ Honey Bunch = 'Cocglen'®	GCoc LGod LStr MBri MJon NBat SApu
§ Toprose = 'Cocgold' (F)	EBre GCoc GGre SJus
§ Gordon's College = 'Cocjabby' (F)	GCoc SApu
§ Marguerite Anne = 'Cockredward' (F)	GCoc NBat SApu
Cocktail (S)	EBls MGan
§ Ballindalloch Castle = 'Cocneel' (F)	GCoc
§ Constance Fettes = 'Cocnest' (F)	GCoc
§ Ray of Hope = 'Cocnilly' (F)	GCoc
§ Alec C. Collie = 'Cococrust' (F)	GCoc
§ Greer Garson = 'Cocoddy' (HT)	GCoc

§ Christopher = 'Cocopher' (HT) — GCoc
Colchester Beauty (F) — EBee
Colibre (Min) — LGod MGan SPer
§ Colibre '79 (Min) — ELan EWar LStr SWCr WStI
Colibre '80 — See ***R.* Colibre '79**
§ 'Colonel Fabvier' — EBls
◆ Colonial White — See ***R.* 'Climbing Sombreuil'**
Colorama (HT) — MBri
'Columbian' (Cl) — ERea WHCG
'Commandant Beaurepaire' (Bb) — EBls MAus NSty SPer SWCr
Common Moss — See ***R.* × *centifolia* 'Muscosa'**
'Compassion' (ClHT) 🏆 — Widely available
§ 'Complicata' (G) 🏆 — EBls EWar IHar MAus MBri MGan MHlr MMat MRav NRog NSty SApu SJus SPer SSpi WAct WHCG WOVN WSHC
N Comte de Chambord — See ***R.* 'Madame Knorr'**
'Comtesse Cécile de Chabrillant' (HP) — EBls MAus
'Comtesse de Lacépède' — See ***R.* 'Du Maître d'Ecole'**
'Comtesse de Murinais' (DMo) — EBls IHar MAus SFam SWCr
§ 'Comtesse du Cayla' (Ch) — MAus
'Comtesse Vandal' (HT) — MAus
'Condesa de Sástago' (HT) — EBls
§ 'Conditorum' (G) — EBls SFam
Congratulations® (HT) — EBee EWar GCoc GGre IHos LGod LPlm LStr MFry MGan MJon MMat MMor NPri SApu SJus SPer SWCr
§ 'Conrad Ferdinand Meyer' (Ru) — EBls IHos MAus MGan NSty SPer SRum WAct
Conservation (Min/Patio) — ESha GCoc GGre LStr MJon NBat SApu WWeb
◆ Constance Fettes — See ***R.* Constance Fettes = 'Cocnest'**
Constance Spry (ClS) 🏆 — CHad EBls EBre ENot EWar GCoc IHar IOrc LStr MAus MBri MGan MHlr MJon MMat MMor NFla NSty SApu SJus SPer SRum SSoC SWCr WAct WGer WHCG WHow WOVN WWeb
Cooper's Burmese — See ***R.* *laevigata* 'Cooperi'**
'Copenhagen' (S) — EBls MAus MBri
'Copper Delight' (F) — NRog
Copper Pot® — MGan SPer
'Coral Cluster' (Poly) — EBls MAus MGan SMer
'Coral Creeper' (ClHT) — EBls
Coral Dawn (ClHT) — EBls IHar MFry MJon
Coral Reef® (Min/Patio) — GCoc GGre LStr SWCr
'Coral Satin' (Cl) — EBls MGan
'Coralie' (D) — EBls
'Coralin' (Min) — LGod MGan
Cordon Bleu (HT) — MBur
'Cornelia' (HM) 🏆 — CB&S CHad CSam EBls ENot EWar GCoc IHos LHol LStr MAus MBri MFry MHlr MJon MMat MMor NRog NSty SApu SJus SPer SRum WAct WHCG WOVN WWeb
'Coronation Gold' (F) — ESha GCoc
'Coryana' — EBls
I 'Corylus' (Ru) — See ***R.* 'Hazel Le Rougetel'**
corymbifera — EBls
corymbulosa — EBls
'Cosimo Ridolfi' (G) — EBls
◆ Cottage Garden — See ***R.* Cottage Garden = 'Haryamber'**
Cottage Maid — See ***R.* 'Centifolia Variegata'**
Cottage Rose (S) — MAus MJon NPri SChu SJus WHow
Country Lady (HT) — MBur SApu SJus SRum
Country Living (S) — EBls EMFP EWar IHos MAus
'Country Maid' (F) — EWar
'Coupe d'Hébé' (Bb) — EBls MAus
'Cramoisi Picotée' (G) — EBls MAus
'Cramoisi Supérieur' (Ch) — EBee EBls MAus WHCG
'Cramoisi Supérieur Grimpant' (ClCh) — EBls
Crathes Castle® — GCoc
'Crépuscule' (N) — EBls NSty WHCG
◆ Cressida — See ***R.* Cressida = 'Auscress'**
Crested Moss — See ***R.* × *centifolia* 'Cristata'**
Cricri (Min) — MAus MGan
Crimson Cascade (Cl) — EWar MBri MFry NBat SApu SJus SWCr
'Crimson Conquest' (ClHT) — EBls
Crimson Damask — See ***R.* *gallica* var. *officinalis***
Crimson Gem (Min) — MGan
'Crimson Globe' (Mo) — MGan
'Crimson Glory' (HT) — CTri EBls MBur MGan WAct
'Crimson Rambler' (Ra) — MAus MRav WBcn
'Crimson Shower' (Ra) 🏆 — EBre EMFP EWar IHos LPlm MAus MGan MHlr MJon MMat NRog SPer WGer WHCG WHer WStI
'Cristata' — See ***R.* × *centifolia* 'Cristata'**
◆ Crystal Palace — See ***R.* Crystal Palace = 'Poulrek'**
'Cuisse de Nymphe' — See ***R.* 'Great Maiden's Blush'**
'Cupid' (ClHT) — EBee EBls EWar MAus SPer
Curiosity (HT/v) — GGre MJon
Cymbeline (S) — MAus SPer SRum
'Cynthia Brooke' (HT) — EBls
'D'Aguesseau' (G) — EBls MAus SPer
Daily Express (HT) — MFry
'Daily Mail' — See ***R.* 'Climbing Madame Edouard Herriot'**
Daily Post (F) — MFry
Daily Sketch (F) — MGan
'Dainty Bess' (HT) — CHad EBls MAus MRav NSty
Dainty Dinah (Min/Patio) — GCoc LStr SApu
'Dainty Maid' (F) — EBls MAus
'Dairy Maid' (F) — MAus
'Daisy Hill' (*macrantha* hybrid) — EBls
Dalli Dalli (F) — MJon
× ***damascena*** var. ***bifera*** — See ***R.* × *damascena* var. *semperflorens***
§ – var. ***semperflorens*** (D) — EBls EMFP IHos WHCG WHow
N – 'Trigintipetala' hort. — See ***R.* 'Professeur Emile Perrot'**
§ – var. ***versicolor*** (D) — CGro EBee EBls ENot IHos MGan NSty SFam WAct
'Dame Edith Helen' (HT) — EBls
Dame of Sark (F) — ESha
Dame Wendy (F) — EBee EWar GCoc LGod MAus MBri MGan MJon SApu
'Danaë' (HM) — CHad EBls EMFP MAus MHlr WHCG
¶ Dancing Pink (F) — NBat
'Danny Boy' (ClHT) — SRum
Danse des Sylphes (Cl) — EBls
'Danse du Feu' (Cl) — CB&S CGro EBls ELan ESha EWar GCoc GGre GOrc IHos LGod LPlm LStr MAus MBri MECR MFry MGan MJon MMat MMor NRog SApu SPer SRum WWeb

'Daphne Gandy' (F)	MGan
◆ Dapple Dawn	See ***R.* Dapple Dawn = 'Ausapple'**
Darling Flame (Min)	ELan EWar GGre MGan SApu SPer
'Dart's Defender'	SLPl
'Dave Hessayon' (HT)	MECR
David Whitfield (R)	MGan MJon
davidii	EBls MAus
◆ Dawn Chorus	See ***R.* Dawn Chorus = 'Dicquaser'**
'Daybreak' (HM)	EBls MAus NRog WAct WHCG
Daylight (F)	IDic MBur
Dazzler (Patio)	MJon
§ 'De Meaux' (Ce)	EBls EMFP ENot MAus MMat NFla NSty SPer SPla WHCG WHow
§ 'De Meaux, White' (Ce)	EBls MAus
§ 'De Rescht' (DPo) 🏆	EBls IHar LHol MAus MGan MJon MMat NSty SPer WAct WGer WHCG WHow
'Dearest' (F)	CB&S CDoC EWar GGre MBri MGan MHay MJon MMor NRog SPer SRum WStI
'Debbie Thomas' (HT)	MHay
Deb's Delight (F)	ELan EWar GCoc MFry MJon
'Debutante' (Ra)	EBls MAus MHlr SFam
'Deep Secret' (HT)	CDoC CGro EBre ESha EWar GCoc GGre LPlm MBur MECR MFry MGan MJon MMor NRog SApu SJus SPer SRum WWeb
'Delambre' (DPo)	EBls MAus MRav
'Dembrowski' (HP)	EBls
Denman™	MJon SApu
'Dentelle de Malines' (S)	EBls MAus MHlr WAct
'Deschamps' (N)	EBls
'Desprez à Fleurs Jaunes' (N)	EBee EBls EMFP IHar MAus NPri NSty SFam SPer SPla WHCG WHow WSHC
'Deuil de Paul Fontaine' (Mo)	EBls
'Devoniensis' (ClT)	See ***R.* 'Climbing Devoniensis'**
Diadem (F)	MFry MJon
'Diamond Jubilee' (HT)	EBls EWar MHay
§ Memento = 'Dicbar' (F)	EWar IDic MBri MGan MMat
§ Elina = 'Dicjana'® (HT) 🏆	ESha EWar GCoc GGre IDic LGod LStr MBur MFry MGan MHay MJon MMat NBat NRog SApu SJus SPer
'Dickson's Flame'	MGan
§ Benita = 'Dicquarrel' (HT)	GCoc IDic MJon
§ Dawn Chorus = 'Dicquaser' (HT)	CGro EBre EWar GCoc GGre IHar LGod LPlm LStr MBri MFry MGan MHay MJon MMat NPri SApu SJus SPer SRum WWeb
§ Our Molly = 'Dicreason' (GC/S)	IDic SApu
§ Pure Bliss = 'Dictator' (HT)	EBee GCoc IDic MFry MJon NBat
§ Pretty in Pink = 'Dicumpteen' (GC)	IDic MJon
§ Boy O Boy = 'Dicuniform' (GC)	IDic
§ Roche Centenary = 'Dicvantage' (Patio)	IDic
Die Welt (HT)	MHay NBat
'Diorama' (HT)	MAus MGan NRog
'Directeur Alphand' (HP)	EBls WHCG
Disco Dancer (F)	GGre IDic IHos

¶ 'Dixieland Linda' (ClHT)	EBls
'Doc' (Poly)	MGan
'Docteur Andry' (HP)	EBls
'Docteur Grill' (T)	EBls MAus
'Doctor A.J. Verhage' (HT)	MGan
'Doctor Abrahams' (HT)	MJon
Doctor Dick™	GCoc MHay NBat
'Doctor Eckener' (Ru)	EBls IHar MGan
'Doctor Edward Deacon' (HT)	EBls
Doctor Goldberg (HT)	MGan
Doctor Jackson (S)	MAus
'Doctor John Snow' (HT)	MGan
Doctor McAlpine (F/Patio)	MBri MJon SPer
'Doctor W. Van Fleet' (Ra/Cl)	EBls MAus WAct WSHC
'Don Charlton' (HT)	MHay NBat
'Don Juan' (Cl)	MGan
Donald Davis (F)	MJon
§ 'Doncasteri'	EBls MAus MSto
'Dopey' (Poly)	MGan
'Doreen'	NRog
Doris Tysterman (HT)	CGro EBls EBre ESha EWar GGre LPlm LStr MAus MBur MGan MMor NRog SRum WWeb
'Dorothy Perkins' (Ra)	CB&S CGro EBls EWar GGre GOrc LPlm LStr MAus MGan MJon MMat MMor NPer NRog NSty SApu SPer SRum WHCG
'Dorothy Wheatcroft' (F)	MGan MHay SRum
'Dorothy Whitney Wood' (HT)	MFry
'Dorothy Wilson' (F)	EBls
Dortmund (ClHScB)	EBls LPlm MAus MGan MMat MMor SPer WAct WHCG
Double Delight (HT)	CGro EBee ELan ESha GCoc GGre LPlm LStr MBri MECR MGan MJon NRog SApu SPer SRum
Dove (S)	EBee
Dream Girl (Cl) 🏆	MAus MBri NSty
'Dream Time' (HT)	MHay
'Dream Waltz' (F)	MHay
'Dreamglo' (Min)	MHay NBat
'Dreaming Spires' (Cl)	IHos MBri MJon MMat SApu SJus SPer
Dreamland (F)	MFry MGan
'Dresden Doll' (MinMo)	EBls MAus SApu SPer
Drummer Boy (F/Patio)	GGre SPer
§ 'Du Maître d'Ecole' (G) 🏆	EBls MAus WHCG
Dublin Bay (Cl) 🏆	CDoC CTri EBls EBre ELan ESha EWar IHar IHos LGod LPlm LStr MBri MBur MFry MGan MJon MMat MMor NRog SApu SPer WGer WHow
'Duc de Fitzjames' (G)	EBls
'Duc de Guiche' (G) 🏆	CPou EBee EBls MAus SFam SPer WAct WHCG
'Duchess of Portland'	See ***R.* 'Portlandica'**
Duchess of York	See ***R.* Sunseeker**
'Duchesse d'Albe' (T)	EBls
'Duchesse d'Angoulême' (G)	EBee EBls MAus NSty SFam
'Duchesse d'Auerstädt' (N)	EBls
'Duchesse de Buccleugh' (G)	EBls MAus
§ 'Duchesse de Montebello' (G) 🏆	EBee EBls MAus MHlr SFam SPer SRms WHCG WHow

'Duchesse de Rohan' (CexHP)	EBls
'Duchesse de Verneuil' (CeMo)	EBls MAus SFam
§ Duke Meillandina (Min)	SApu
'Duke of Edinburgh' (HP)	EBls MAus
'Duke of Wellington' (HP)	EBls WHCG
'Duke of Windsor' (HT)	IHar MGan NRog SPer
'Duke of York' (Ch)	EBls
Duke Sunblaze	See ***R.* Duke Meillandina**
'Dundee Rambler' (Ra)	EBls MAus
'Dupontii' (S)	EBee EBls MAus SFam SPer WAct WHow WOVN
'Dupuy Jamain' (HP)	EBls WHCG
'Durham Prince Bishop' (HT)	NBat
'Dusky Maiden' (F)	EBls MAus WHCG
'Dusterlohe' (R)	EBls
Dutch Gold (HT)	CGro CTri EWar LStr MAus MECR MGan MJon NRog SPer
'Dwarf King'	See ***R.* 'Zwergkönig'**
'E.H. Morse'	See ***R.* 'Ernest H. Morse'**
'Easlea's Golden Rambler' (Ra)	EBee EBls EBre EWar MAus NPri NSty WAct WHCG
'Easter Morning' (Min)	ELan MAus MGan MJon SApu SPer
'Eblouissant' (Poly)	MGan
ecae	EBls MAus
– 'Helen Knight'	See ***R.* 'Helen Knight' (*ecae* hybrid)**
'Eclair' (HP)	EBls
'Eddie's Jewel' (*moyesii* hybrid)	EBls IHar MAus MGan NSty
Eden Rose (HT)	EBls MGan SRum
Eden Rose '88 (ClHT)	EWar MJon SApu SJus SPer
'Edith Bellenden' (RH)	EBls
Edith Holden (F)	LGod MAus MBri MJon SApu SJus
◆ ***eglanteria***	See ***R. rubiginosa***
◆ Eglantyne	See ***R.* Eglantyne = 'Ausmark'**
'Elegance' (ClHT)	EBls MAus MGan
§ ***elegantula*** **'Persetosa'** (S)	EBls ENot MAus SPer WAct WHCG
◆ Elina	See ***R.* Elina = 'Dicjana'**
¶ 'Eliza Boëlle' (HP)	WHCG
Elizabeth Harkness (HT)	EBls MAus MBur MGan SPer
Elizabeth Heather Grierson (ClHT)	MMat
Elizabeth of Glamis (F)	CDoC CGro CTri EBls ELan EWar GCoc IHar IHos MBri MGan MMor NRog SPer SRum
'Elizabeth Philp' (F)	LPlm
Ellen (S)	MAus MBri
'Ellen Poulsen' (Poly)	MGan
'Ellen Willmott' (HT)	EBee EBls MAus
'Elmshorn' (S)	CB&S MGan WHCG
Elsie Warren (F)	NBat
Emanuel (S)	MAus SPer
Emily (S)	MAus SApu
'Emily Gray' (Ra)	CGro EBls EBre EWar IHos LStr MAus MBur MGan MHlr MJon MMor NRog NSty SPer SRum WHCG
Emily Louise (Patio)	NBat
Emma Kate (F)	MHay
'Emma May' (HT)	MHay
Emma Mitchell (Patio)	NBat
'Emma Wright' (HT)	MAus
'Emmerdale' (F)	WStI
'Empereur du Maroc' (HP)	EBls MAus MMat NSty WAct WHCG
'Empress Josephine'	See ***R.* × *francofurtana***
'Empress Michiko' (HT)	EWar GCoc IDic SApu
Ena Baxter (HT)	GCoc
'Ena Harkness' (HT)	CGro EBls ELan EWar GGre LStr MBur MGan NRog SRum WStI
§ 'Enfant de France' (HP)	EBls
English Elegance (S)	MAus
English Garden (S)	CAbP CGro EBar EBre EMFP ENot EWar GCoc GGre IHar LStr MAus MBri MMat SApu SPer WAct WHow WWeb
'English Miss' (F)	CDoC EBls EWar IHos LPlm LStr MAus MFry MGan MJon SApu SJus SPer SRum WStI WWeb
'Eos' (*moyesii* hybrid)	EBls MAus
'Erfurt' (HM)	EBls MAus MGan NSty SPla SRms WHCG
'Erinnerung an Brod'	WHCG
§ 'Ernest H. Morse' (HT)	CTri EBls ESha EWar GCoc GGre IHar IHos MAus MBur MGan MHay MJon NPri NRog SApu SPer SRum
Eroica (HT)	NRog
Escapade (F)	EBls MAus MGan NBat
◆ 'Especially for You'	See ***R.* Especially for You = 'Fryworthy'**
Essex (GC)	EBee EBre ENot EWar IHos MGan MMat NPri SApu SPer WHCG WOVN
Esther Ofarim (F)	EWar
'Eternally Yours' (HT)	MJon
Ethel Austin (F)	MFry
¶ 'Etoile de Hollande' (HT)	CHad GOrc
'Etoile de Lyon' (T)	EBls
'Eugène Fürst' (HP)	EBls WHCG
'Eugénie Guinoisseau' (Mo)	EBls EWar WHCG
Euphrates (*persica* hybrid)	MGan WAct
Europeana (F)	CGro MAus MGan SRum
◆ Eurostar	See ***R.* Eurostar = 'Poulreb'**
'Eva' (HM)	EBls
'Evangeline' (Ra)	EBls MAus NSty SPer
Evelyn (S)	CAbP CGro EBee EBre EMFP EWar GCoc IHar LGod MAus MHlr MJon MMat NFla SApu SPer SSoC WHow
◆ Evelyn Fison	See ***R.* Evelyn Fison = 'Macev'**
◆ Evelyn Grace	See ***R.* Evelyn Grace = 'Horavme'**
'Evening Star' (HT)	MAus
'Evening Telegraph' (HT)	MHay
'Everest Double Fragrance' (F)	EBls
'Excelsa' (Ra)	CTri EBls EMFP EWar GCoc GGre LGod LStr MAus MGan MJon MMor NBus NRog NSty SRum WAct WStI
Exception (Ru)	WLRN
§ Exploit (Cl)	EWar GGre SCoo WWeb
Eye Paint (F)	EWar MAus MGan MJon NRog SMrm
'Eyecatcher' (F)	EBee
Eyeopener (S/GC)	CGro EBls EWar IDic MGan MJon SRum
'F.E. Lester'	See ***R.* 'Francis E. Lester'**
§ 'F.J. Grootendorst' (Ru)	EBls EWar IHos IOrc LGod LStr MAus MGan MJon MMor NRog NSty WAct
'Fabvier'	See ***R.* 'Colonel Fabvier'**
Fair Bianca (S)	IOrc MAus MBri MHlr

Fairhope (Min)	MHay
Fairy Changeling (Poly)	MAus
Fairy Damsel (Poly/GC)	EBls MAus MBur
Fairygold (Patio)	MFry SRum
Fairyland (Poly)	EBls ESha EWar MAus MBur SApu
Fairysnow (S)	MFry
Fancy Pants (Min)	MHay
'Fantin-Latour' (*centifolia* hybrid) 🏆	CHad EBls ELan ENot EWar GCoc IHar IHos LStr MAus MBri MGan MHlr MMat NRog NSty SApu SJus SMad SPer WAct WGer WHCG WHow WSHC
fargesii hort.	See ***R. moyesii*** **var.** ***fargesii***
farreri	See ***R. elegantula***
– var. ***persetosa***	See ***R. elegantula*** **'Persetosa'**
'Fashion Flame' (Min)	MGan
Father's Day (Min)	EWar MJon
Favorite Rosamini (Min)	MFry
fedtschenkoana	EBls MAus MGan NSty SPer WAct WHCG
◆ Fée des Neiges	See ***R.*** **Iceberg = 'Korbin'**
'Felicia' (HM) 🏆	CHad CSam EBls ENot EWar GCoc IHar IHos LHol LStr MAus MBri MFry MHlr MJon MMat MMor NRog NSty SApu SJus SPer SRum WAct WHCG WHow WOVN
'Félicité Parmentier' (AxD) 🏆	EBls EBre MAus NPri NSty SFam SJus SPer WAct WHCG
§ 'Félicité Perpétue' (Ra) 🏆	EBls ELan EWar GCoc IHar IHos LHol LStr MAus MBri MGan MHlr MMat NFla NSty SApu SFam SJus SPer SRum WAct WHCG WSHC
Felicity Kendal (HT)	EWar MBri MJon
'Fellenberg' (Ch)	EBls MAus WHCG
Fellowship (F)	EWar GCoc LGod LPlm LStr MAus MBri MBur MFry MGan MJon MMat SRum WGer WWeb
'Femina' (HT)	MGan
§ 'Ferdinand de Lesseps' (HP)	EBls
'Ferdinand Pichard' (Bb) 🏆	EBls EMFP ENot EWar IHar MAus MHlr MJon MMat NSty SJus SPer WAct WGer WHCG WHow WOVN
Ferdy (GC)	EBls ELan ENot MAus MGan SApu SPer WOVN
Fergie (F/Patio)	MGan
Festival (Patio)	CDoC CGro EBee EBre ENot ESha GCoc GGre IHar LPlm LStr MBri MFry MMat NBat NPri SApu SPer WGer WOVN WWeb
◆ Fiesta	See ***R.*** **Fiesta = 'Macfirinlin'**
Figurine (Min)	MHay
filipes 'Brenda Colvin'	See ***R.*** **'Brenda Colvin'**
§ – 'Kiftsgate' (Ra) 🏆	Widely available
§ 'Fimbriata' (Ru)	EBls MAus MBri SPer WAct WHCG WHow
Financial Times Centenary (S)	EWar IHos MAus
Fine Gold (HT)	EWar
Fiona (S/GC)	EBls GGre IHos SApu SHhN WHCG WOVN
'Fire Princess' (Min)	MHay
'Firecracker' (F)	EBls
Firefly (Min)	MJon
'First Love' (HT)	EBls MGan
'Fisher and Holmes' (HP)	EBls MAus WAct WHCG
Fisherman's Friend (S)	CDoC EWar IHos MAus SPer SRum
Flair (F)	IDic LStr MJon
'Fleur Cowles' (F)	MBur MECR
'Flora' (Ra)	EBls MAus
'Flora McIvor' (RH)	EBls MAus MGan
Florence Nightingale (F)	MBri MBur MGan SApu SPer
Flower Carpet (GC) 🏆	CTri EBee EBre ELan EWar GGre IHar MAus MFry MGan MJon MMat NPri SCoo SJus SPer SPla SRum WWeb
§ ***foetida*** (S)	EBls MAus NSty
§ – 'Bicolor' (S)	EBee EBls ENot IHar MAus MGan MMat NRog NSty SPer WAct
§ – 'Persiana' (S)	EBls MAus MGan SPer
foliolosa	EBls SLPl WHCG
'Forgotten Dreams' (HT)	MJon
forrestiana	EBls MAus MMat
× ***fortuneana***	EBls
Fortune's Double Yellow	See ***R.*** **×** ***odorata*** **'Pseudindica'**
'Fountain' (S)	CSam EBls EWar LStr MAus MGan SApu SPer SRum
Fragrant Cloud (HT)	CDoC CGro EBls EBre ESha EWar GCoc GGre IHar IHos LStr MAus MBri MBur MECR MFry MHay MJon MMat MMor NBat NRog SApu SPer WWeb
Fragrant Delight (F)	ESha EWar GCoc IHos LPlm LStr MECR MFry MGan MJon NBat SApu SPer WWeb
Fragrant Dream (HT)	EWar GGre IDic LStr MBri SApu
Fragrant Gold (HT)	GCoc LStr SRum
'Fragrant Hour' (HT)	MGan MMat
'Francesca' (HM)	EBls MAus MGan NSty SPer WAct WHCG
Francine Austin (S/GC)	IHos MAus NPri SPer WAct
'Francis Dubreuil' (T)	EBls
§ 'Francis E. Lester' (HM/Ra)	CHad CSam EBee EBls EBre EWar MAus MBri NSty SPer WAct WHCG WHow
§ × ***francofurtana*** 🏆	EBls IHos MRav SFam WAct WHCG
'François Juranville' (Ra) 🏆	EBls EWar LStr MAus MBri MGan MHlr MMat NBus NPri NRog SApu SMad SPer SSoC WAct
'Frank MacMillan' (HT)	MHay
'Frank Naylor' (S)	EWar
'Frau Astrid Späth' (F)	NRog
§ 'Frau Karl Druschki' (HP)	EBls MAus MGan NSty WAct
'Fraulein Octavia Hesse' (Ra)	EBls
'Fred Gibson' (HT)	MHay
'Fred Loads' (S) 🏆	CSam EBls EWar MAus MFry MGan SApu
Freddie Mercury (HT)	NBat
Freedom (HT) 🏆	EWar GCoc GGre IDic IHar LGod LPlm LStr MBur MECR MFry MGan MMat NBat NRog SApu SJus WWeb
'Freiherr von Marschall' (T)	EBls
'Frensham' (F)	CB&S CGro EBls LStr MGan MMat
Fresh Pink (Min)	MGan
Friday's Child (HT)	NBat
Friend for Life (F)	EWar GCoc MJon
'Fringette' (Min)	MGan

'Fritz Nobis' (S) 🏆	CHad EBls ENot EWar GCoc IHar IHos LStr MAus MGan MHlr MRav NSty SJus SPer WAct WHCG WHow
Frothy (Min)	MJon
'Fru Dagmar Hastrup' (Ru) 🏆	CDoC CSam EBls EBre ELan ENot EWar GCoc IHos IOrc LStr MAus MFry MGan MHlr MJon MMat MMor NRog NSty SApu SJus SPer SRum WAct WHCG WOVN
§ Langdale Chase = 'Fryrhapsody' (F)	MFry
§ Especially for You = 'Fryworthy' (HT)	LGod LStr MBur SApu
§ Bride = 'Fryyearn' (HT)	LPlm LStr MFry MJon SApu SWCr
§ Rosie Larkin = 'Fryyippee' (S)	MFry
§ Arc Angel = 'Fryyorston' (HT)	MFry
§ The Cheshire Regiment = 'Fryzebedee' (HT)	MFry
'Frühlingsanfang' (PiH)	EBls MAus MBri WAct
'Frühlingsduft' (PiH)	EBee EBls NRog NSty SPer
Frühlingsgold (PiH) 🏆	CB&S CGro EBls EBre ELan ENot EWar GCoc IOrc LGod LStr MAus MBri MFry MGan MMat MMor NBat NFla NRog NSty SApu SJus SPer SRum WAct WHCG WOVN WWeb
'Frühlingsmorgen' (PiH)	EBls EBre ENot EWar GCoc IHos LStr MAus MBri MGan MHlr MMat MMor NFla NRog NSty SApu SJus SPer WAct WHCG WOVN
'Frühlingsschnee' (PiH)	EBls EWar
'Frühlingszauber' (PiH)	EBls
'Fulgens'	See ***R.* 'Malton' (China hybrid)**
Fulton Mackay (HT)	GCoc MFry MGan SApu
Fyvie Castle (HT)	GCoc MGan
'Gail Borden' (HT)	MAus MGan
§ ***gallica*** (G)	EBls
– 'Complicata'	See ***R.* 'Complicata'**
– 'Conditorum'	See ***R.* 'Conditorum'**
§ – var. ***officinalis*** (G) 🏆	EBls GCoc GPoy LHol MAus MBri MMat NRog NSty SApu SFam SJus SPer WAct WHCG WHow
– 'Velutiniflora' (G)	EBls
§ – 'Versicolor' (G) 🏆	CHad CSam EBls ELan ENot EWar GCoc LStr MBri MFry MGan MJon MMor NRog NSty SApu SJus SPer SPla WHCG WHow WWeb
Galway Bay (ClHT)	EBee EBre MFry MGan MMat SPer
'Gardenia' (Ra)	MHlr SPer WHCG
§ 'Garnette' (Gn)	SRum
§ 'Garnette Apricot' (Gn)	SPla
'Garnette Carol'	See ***R.* 'Carol Amling'**
◆ 'Garnette Golden'	See ***R.* 'Golden Garnette'**
'Garnette Pink'	See ***R.* 'Carol Amling'**
'Garnette Red'	See ***R.* 'Garnette'**
Gary Lineker (F)	MBri
'Gary Player' (HT)	MHay
'Gateshead Festival' (HT)	NBat
'Gaujard'	See ***R.* Rose Gaujard**
'Gavotte' (HT)	MHay
Gee Gee (Min)	MHay
'Général Galliéni' (T)	EBls

'Général Jacqueminot' (HP)	EBls MAus WAct
'Général Kléber' (CeMo)	EBls MAus NSty SFam SPer WAct WHCG
§ 'Général Schablikine' (T)	EBls MAus WBcn WSHC
N ***gentiliana*** (Ra)	EBls WHCG
Gentle Touch (Min/Patio) 🏆	CDoC CGro EBls EBre ESha EWar GGre IDic IHar MBri MECR MFry MGan MJon MMat NBat SApu SJus SPer SRum
'Geoff Boycott' (F)	ESha
Geordie Lad (HT)	NBat
'Georg Arends' (HP)	EBls MAus
'George Dickson' (HT)	EBls MAus SRms
'George R. Hill' (HT)	NBat
'Georges Vibert' (G)	EBls MAus WHCG
Geraldine (F)	ESha MBri MGan MJon
§ 'Geranium' (*moyesii* hybrid) 🏆	CB&S CGro EBre ELan ENot EWar GCoc IHar IOrc LStr MAus MBri MGan MHlr NSty SApu SPer SRum WAct WHCG WOVN WSHC WWeb
Gerbe d'Or	See ***R.* Casino**
'Gerbe Rose' (Ra)	EBls MAus NSty
Gertrude Jekyll (S)	CDoC CGro CHad CSam EBar EBre EMFP ENot EWar GCoc IOrc LGod LPlm LStr MAus MFry MHlr MJon MMat MTis SApu SChu SJus SPer WAct WHCG WHow WOVN WStI
'Ghislaine de Féligonde' (S/Ra)	EBls WHCG
gigantea	EBls
– 'Cooperi'	See ***R. laevigata* 'Cooperi'**
◆ Gingernut	See ***R.* Gingernut = 'Coccrazy'**
Ginny-Lou (Min)	SJus
'Gipsy Boy'	See ***R.* 'Zigeunerknabe'**
Glad Tidings (F)	CGro ESha EWar GGre LPlm LStr MBri MBur MECR MGan MJon NBat SApu SJus SPer SRum WWeb
Glamis Castle (S)	CBlo EBls EBre EWar IHar MAus MBri MJon NPri SJus SPer WAct WHow
§ ***glauca*** (S) 🏆	CHad CHar EBls EFol ELan ENot ESha IOrc LBuc LHop MAus MBri MFry MGan MJon MMat NRog NRoo NSty NWea SApu SJus SPer SPla SRum WAct WEas WOVN WWat
'Glenfiddich' (F)	CGro ESha EWar GCoc GGre IHar IHos LPlm LStr MAus MBri MFry MGan MJon NRog SPer SRum WStI WWeb
'Glenn Dale' (Cl)	EBee
'Glenshane' (S)	IDic
'Gloire de Bruxelles' (HP)	EBls
'Gloire de Dijon' (ClT) 🏆	CHad CSam EBls EBre EWar GCoc IOrc LGod LStr MAus MBri MGan MHlr MJon MMat NFla NRog NSty SApu SFam SJus SMad SPer SPla SRum SSoC WAct WHCG WHow
'Gloire de Ducher' (HP)	CPou MAus MGan WAct WHCG
'Gloire de France' (G)	EBee EBls MAus
'Gloire de Guilan' (D)	EBls MAus NSty WAct
'Gloire des Mousseuses' (CeMo)	EBee EBls MAus SFam WAct WHCG
'Gloire du Midi' (Poly)	MAus
'Gloire Lyonnaise' (HP)	EBee EBls

'Gloria Mundi' (Poly)	EBee EBls MGan
glutinosa	See ***R. pulverulenta***
'Goethe' (CeMo)	EBls
Gold Bunny (F)	EWar MBri MGan MJon
◆ Gold Crown	See ***R.* 'Goldkrone'**
'Goldbusch' (S)	EBls MAus MGan SRms
¶ 'Golden Anniversary' (Patio)	GGre
Golden Celebration (S)	EBee EBre GGre IHar LStr MAus MBri MGan MHlr MJon NPri SApu SJus SPer WGer WWeb
Golden Chersonese (S)	EBls MAus NRog NSty
'Golden Dawn' (ClHT)	MAus
Golden Days (HT)	EWar MBri MFry
§ 'Golden Garnette' (Gn)	SRum
'Golden Glow' (Cl)	EBls MGan
Golden Halo (Min)	MHay
◆ Golden Hands	See ***R.* Golden Hands = 'Chessupremo'**
◆ Golden Jewel™	See ***R.* 'Goldjuwel'**
Golden Jubilee (HT)	ELan EWar GCoc GGre LPlm LStr MAus MBur NBat
'Golden Melody' (HT)	EBls
Golden Moments (HT)	EWar MBur MFry MJon
'Golden Moss' (Mo)	EBls
'Golden Ophelia' (HT)	EBls
◆ Golden Quill	See ***R.* Golden Quill = 'Tanellog'**
'Golden Rambler'	See ***R.* 'Alister Stella Gray'**
Golden Rosamini (Min)	MFry
'Golden Salmon' (Poly)	MGan
'Golden Salmon Supérieur' (Poly)	EBls
'Golden Shot' (F)	ESha MGan
Golden Showers (Cl) 🏆	Widely available
'Golden Slippers' (F)	CB&S MGan
'Golden Sunblaze'	See ***R.* 'Rise 'n' Shine'**
◆ Golden Symphonie	See ***R.* Golden Symphonie = 'Meilolcil'**
Golden Wedding (F/HT)	EBre ELan EWar GCoc GGre IHar LGod LPlm LStr MBri MBur MFry MGan MHay MJon MMat MMor NBat SApu SJus SPer WStI WWeb
'Golden Wings' (S) 🏆	CHad EBls EMFP ENot EWar GCoc IHar IHos LStr MAus MBri MFry MGan MJon MMat NSty SApu SJus SPer SRum WHCG WHow WOVN WWeb
Golden Years (F)	EWar GCoc MAus MFry MJon
'Goldfinch' (Ra)	CHad EBls EBre EMFP EWar GGre IHar MAus MBri MHlr NSty SApu SPer WAct WHCG WHow
◆ Goldfinger	See ***R.* Goldfinger = 'Pearoyal'**
'Goldilocks' (F)	NRog
§ 'Goldjuwel' (F/Patio)	NBat
§ 'Goldkrone' (HT)	MGan
Goldstar (HT)	EBee EWar MFry MGan SApu
◆ Good as Gold	See ***R.* Good as Gold = 'Chewsunbeam'**
◆ Good Luck	See ***R.* Good Luck = 'Burspec'**
'Good Morning' (F)	MFry
'Good News' (F)	EWar
◆ Gordon's College	See ***R.* Gordon's College = 'Cocjabby'**
'Grace Abounding' (F)	EWar NBat
'Grace Darling' (T)	EBls
Grace de Monaco (HT)	EBls MAus MGan
Graceland (Patio)	MJon
Graham Thomas (S) 🏆	Widely available
Granada (HT)	EBls
Grand Hotel (ClHT)	IHos MBri MJon MMat SPer SWCr
'Grand-mère Jenny' (HT)	EBls MGan
'Grandpa Dickson' (HT)	EBls EBre ESha EWar GGre IHar IHos LGod LPlm MAus MBur MFry MGan MHay MJon MMor NBat NRog SApu SPer SRum WWeb
§ 'Great Maiden's Blush' (A)	EBls GCoc MFry MMat NSty SFam WAct
'Great News' (HT)	MAus
'Great Ormond Street' (F)	EBls
'Great Western' (Bb)	EBls
'Green Diamond' (Min)	MAus MFry MJon
Greenall's Glory (F/Patio)	CDoC EBee LStr MAus MJon WHow
'Greenmantle' (RH)	EBls MAus MGan WAct
Greensleeves (F)	EBls LStr MAus SPer SWCr
◆ Greer Garson	See ***R.* Greer Garson = 'Cocoddy'**
'Grootendorst Supreme' (Ru)	MAus SPer
N 'Gros Choux de Hollande' (Bb)	EBls WHCG
Grouse (S/GC)	EBls ENot GCoc IHar IHos MAus MHlr MJon MMat SApu SPer WAct WOVN
'Grumpy' (Poly)	MGan
'Gruss an Aachen' (Poly)	CHad EBls LStr MAus MBri MGan NSty SPer WAct WHCG WHow
'Gruss an Teplitz' (China hybrid)	EBls MAus SPer SWCr WHCG
Guernsey Love (Min)	MJon SJus
'Guinée' (ClHT)	CHad EBls EBre ELan IHar IHos LStr MAus MBur MGan MMat NPri NSty SChu SPer SPla WHCG WHow
'Guletta'	See ***R.* Rugul**
'Gustav Grünerwald' (HT)	EBls MAus
Gwent (GC)	EBre ELan EWar LGod LPlm LStr MBur MFry MGan MHlr MMor NPri SApu SPer WAct WOVN WRHF
'Gypsy Boy'	See ***R.* 'Zigeunerknabe'**
§ Smooth Romance = 'Hadromance' (HT)	LStr MHay
'Hakuun' (F/Patio)	EBee MAus MGan
'Hamburger Phönix' (Ra)	CGro EBls MGan SPer WAct
Hampshire (GC)	ENot EWar IHos MAus MGan MMat MMor SApu
Hand in Hand (Patio)	MFry MJon NBat
Handel (Cl) 🏆	CGro EBls EBre ELan ESha EWar GGre IHos LGod LPlm LStr MBri MBur MECR MFry MGan MJon MMat MMor NBat NRog SApu SPer SRum WWeb
Hannah Gordon (F)	EBee EWar LStr MBur MGan MJon MMat NBat
'Hannah Hauwxell' (Patio)	NBat SRum
'Hanne' (HT)	IHar NRog
'Hansa' (Ru)	CHad EBls ENot IHar IHos LBuc MAus MGan MMat WHCG WHow WOVN
'Happy' (Poly)	MGan
Happy Anniversary (F)	CTri EWar GGre MJon WWeb
'Happy Birthday' (Min/Patio)	GGre

Happy Child (S)	EBre IHar MAus MHlr MJon NPri SPer WGer
'Happy Ever After' (F)	IDic MFry
'Happy Thought' (Min)	MJon
Happy Wanderer (F)	EWar
§ Sunset Boulevard = 'Harbabble' (F)	LGod LPlm LStr MAus MBur MFry MHay NBat SApu
§ Ruby Anniversary = 'Harbonny' (Patio)	EWar MFry
◆ Harewood	See ***R.* Harewood = 'Taninaso'**
§ x ***harisonii*** 'Harison's Yellow' (PiH)	EBls MAus SPer WAct
§ – 'Lutea Maxima' (PiH)	EBls MAus
§ – 'Williams' Double Yellow' (PiH)	EBls GCoc MAus
'Harry Maasz' (GC/Cl)	EBls
Harry Wheatcroft (HT)	CB&S CGro EBls GGre IHos MAus MBri MBur MGan MJon NRog
Harvest Fayre (F)	CGro EWar IDic LGod LStr MAus MBri MBur MGan MMat NBat SApu SPer SRum
§ Jacqueline du Pré = 'Harwanna' (S)	EWar GCoc IHar MAus MHlr MJon SApu SJus SPer WAct WGer WHCG WHow
§ Cottage Garden = 'Haryamber' (Patio)	GGre
'Hazel Rose' (HT)	MHay
'Headleyensis'	EBee EBls MAus
'Heart of England' (F)	MBur
Heartbreaker (Min)	MHay
◆ Heather Austin	See ***R.* Heather Austin = 'Auscook'**
¶ Heather Honey (HT)	EWar
§ 'Heather Muir' (*sericea* hybrid) (S)	EBls MAus NSty
'Heaven Scent' (F)	MJon NBat
◆ Heavenly Rosalind	See ***R.* Heavenly Rosalind = 'Ausmash'**
§ 'Hebe's Lip' (DxSwB)	EBls MAus WAct
'Hector Deane' (HT)	EBls MBur MGan NSty
'Heidi Jayne' (HT)	MBur SRum
'Heinrich Schultheis' (HP)	EBls
§ 'Helen Knight' (*ecae* hybrid)	EBls MAus MBri MMat NSty WHCG
'Helen Traubel' (HT)	EBls MGan
helenae	EBls GCal MAus SPer WHCG
Hello (Min/Patio)	GCoc
hemisphaerica (S)	EBls MAus WAct
'Henri Fouquier' (G)	EBls
§ 'Henri Martin' (CeMo) 🏆	CTri EBls IOrc MAus NBus NRog SPer WAct WHCG
'Henry Nevard' (HP)	EBls MAus
'Her Majesty' (HP)	EBls
§ 'Herbstfeuer' (RH)	EBls NSty
Heritage (S)	Widely available
'Hermosa' (Ch)	EBls EMFP MAus MHlr NBus NPri NSty WAct WHCG WHow
Hero (S)	MAus
Hertfordshire (GC)	EBre ENot EWar LPlm MMat NPri SPer WOVN WRHF
'Hiawatha'	EBls MAus WHCG
'Hibernica' (*canina* hybrid)	MAus
'Hidcote Gold'	EBls MAus
High Hopes (Cl)	EBee EWar GGre LStr MBri MBur MFry MGan MJon SApu SJus SRum WHCG WWeb
§ 'Highdownensis' (*moyesii* hybrid)	EBls ELan MAus MMat SPer
Highfield (Cl)	ESha EWar IHar LGod MAus MBri MJon SApu SJus SPer
Highland Laddie™	GCoc

Hilda Murrell (S)	MAus
§ 'Hillieri' (S)	EBls MAus SRms
'Hippolyte' (G)	EBls MAus WSHC
¶ 'Hole-in-one' (F)	GGre
holodonta	See ***R. moyesii* f. *rosea***
Holy Rose	See ***R.* x *richardii***
'Home Sweet Home' (HT)	EBls MAus
'Homère'	EBls MAus
◆ Honey Bunch	See ***R.* Honey Bunch = 'Cocglen'**
'Honey Favorite' (HT)	MAus
'Honeymoon' (F)	CB&S GCoc GGre MMor NPri SRum
'Honorine de Brabant' (Bb)	EBee EBls EWar IHar MAus MHlr MMat SFam SPer SPla WAct WHCG
'Horace Vernet' (HP)	EBls
§ Evelyn Grace = 'Horavme' (F)	NBat
horrida	See ***R. biebersteinii***
'Horstmanns Rosenresli' (F)	EBls
'Hugh Dickson' (HP)	EBls MAus NSty SJus
hugonis	See ***R. xanthina* f. *hugonis***
'Hula Girl' (Min)	LGod MBur MJon
Hume's Blush	See ***R.* x *odorata* 'Odorata'**
'Hunslet Moss' (Mo)	EBls
'Hunter' (Ru)	WAct
'Hutton Village' (HT)	EWar
Ice Cream (HT)	CTri ENot EWar GGre LStr MJon MMat NBat SApu SCoo SJus
◆ Iceberg	See ***R.* Iceberg = 'Korbin'**
'Iced Ginger' (F)	EWar MFry MGan SApu SPer
'Illusion' (Cl)	MGan
Ilse Krohn Superior (Cl)	EBls
¶ In the Pink (F)	GGre
Indian Summer™	EBee EWar GCoc LGod MBri MFry MJon
'Indian Sunblaze' (Min/Patio)	IHos
'Indigo' (S)	EBls MAus WHCG
Ingrid Bergman (HT) 🏆	EWar GCoc GGre LGod LStr MAus MBri MBur MECR MFry MGan MJon MMat MMor SApu
Inner Wheel (F)	MFry
'Intermezzo' (HT)	MBur MGan
International Herald Tribune (F/Patio)	ESha
Intrigue (F)	MMat
Invincible (F)	EWar MFry MGan
'Invitation' (HT)	MBur MGan
'Ipsilanté' (G)	EBls MAus SMer SWCr WAct WHCG
'Irene of Denmark' (F)	EBls
'Irène Watts' (Ch) 🏆	CHad EBls EMFP MAus MHlr SPla WAct WHCG WHow
Irene's Delight (HT)	NBat
'Irish Elegance' (HT)	EBls
'Irish Fireflame' (HT)	EBls
◆ Irish Wonder	See ***R.* Evelyn Fison = 'Macev'**
Irresistible (Min/Patio)	MBur MHay NBat
'Isis' (F)	MBri
Isobel Derby (HT)	EWar MJon
'Ispahan' (D) 🏆	EBls EMFP EWar MAus MHlr NSty SApu SFam SJus SPer WAct WHCG WSHC
'Ivory Fashion' (F)	EBls
Jack Collier (HT)	NBat

§ × ***jacksonii*** 'Max Graf' (GC/Ru)	EBls ELan ENot IHos MAus MGan MJon MMor NRog NSty SRum WAct
– Red Max Graf® (GC/Ru)	See ***R.* Rote Max Graf**
– 'White Max Graf' (GC/Ru)	ENot IHos
Jacobite rose	See ***R.* × *alba* 'Alba Maxima'**
◆ Jacqueline du Pré	See ***R.* Jacqueline du Pré = 'Harwanna'**
'Jacquenetta' (S)	MAus SRms
N Jacques Cartier	See ***R.* 'Marchesa Boccella'**
'James Bourgault' (HP)	EBls
'James Mason' (G)	EBls MAus SWCr
'James Mitchell' (CeMo)	EBls MAus WHCG
'James Veitch' (DPoMo)	EBls MAus WHCG
'Jan Guest' (HT)	MHay
Jane Asher (Min/Patio)	MBri MJon SApu
'Janet's Pride' (RH)	EBls MAus
Janina (HT)	MJon
'Japonica' (CeMo)	MAus
'Jason' (HT)	MHay
◆ Jayne Austin	See ***R.* Jayne Austin = 'Ausbreak'**
Jean Kenneally (Min)	MHay NBat
'Jean Mermoz' (Poly)	MAus NRog NSty SPer SRum WHCG
'Jean Rosenkrantz' (HP)	EBls
'Jean Sisley' (HT)	EBls
'Jeanne de Montfort' (CeMo)	EBls MAus
'Jeannie Deans' (RH)	MAus
'Jemma' (Patio)	NBat
Jennie Robinson (Min/Patio)	SApu
Jennifer (Min)	MHay
◆ Jenny Charlton	See ***R.* Jenny Charlton = 'Simway'**
'Jenny Duval'	See ***R.* 'Président de Sèze'**
'Jenny Wren' (F)	EBls MAus
¶ 'Jenny's Dream' (HT)	MHay
'Jens Munk' (Ru)	WAct
'Jersey Beauty' (Ra)	EBls MAus
'Jiminy Cricket' (F)	EBls
'Jimmy Greaves' (HT)	MGan
'Joan Bell' (HT)	MHay
'Joanna Hill' (HT)	EBls
'Joanna Lumley' (HT)	MHay
'Joanne' (HT)	EWar MHay MJon
'Jocelyn' (F)	EBls
'Joe Longthorne' (HT)	NBat
◆ John Clare	See ***R.* John Clare = 'Auscent'**
'John Hopper' (HP)	EBls MAus NSty
◆ John Keats	See ***R.* John Keats = 'Meiroupis'**
Johnnie Walker (HT)	MFry SApu
'Josephine Bruce' (HT)	CB&S CGro EBls EWar LGod MAus MBur MGan MHay NRog SRum WStI
'Josephine Wheatcroft'	See ***R.* 'Rosina'**
Joseph's Coat (S/Cl)	EBls IHos LGod LStr MFry MGan MMor SRum
'Journey's End' (HT)	MGan
'Jubilee Celebration' (F)	MJon
◆ Jude the Obscure	See ***R.* Jude the Obscure = 'Ausjo'**
'Judy Fischer' (Min)	EWar LGod NPri
Judy Garland (F)	SJus
'Julia Mannering' (RH)	MAus
Julia's Rose (HT)	CGro CHad EWar LStr MAus MBur MFry MGan MJon SApu SPer

Julie Andrews (F)	MFry
Julie Cussons (F)	MFry
'Juliet' (HP)	EBls
June Laver (Min)	MBur
'Juno' (Ce)	EBls EWar MAus WHCG
'Just Jenny' (Min)	MHay
Just Joey (HT) 🏆	CGro EBls ELan ESha EWar GCoc GGre IHos LGod LPlm LStr MAus MBri MBur MECR MFry MGan MHay MJon MMat MMor NRog SApu SJus SPer SRum SSoC WWeb
Just Magic (Min)	MJon
'Karl Foerster' (PiH)	EBls MAus
'Kassel' (S/Cl)	EBls MAus SPer WAct
'Katharina Zeimet' (Poly)	EBls MAus MGan NRog NSty WAct WHCG
'Kathleen' (HM)	EBls
'Kathleen Ferrier' (F)	EBls MGan
'Kathleen Harrop' (Bb)	EBls EBre ENot IHar LStr MAus MBur MHlr MMat NSty SPer WAct WHCG WSHC WWat
'Kathleen O'Rourke' (HT)	EWar
Kathleen's Rose (F)	MJon
'Kathryn McGrech' (HT)	MJon
Kathryn Morley (F)	EBre EWar IHar MAus MHlr MJon MTis NPri
'Katie' (ClF)	MGan
◆ Katie Crocker	See ***R.* Katie Crocker = 'Burbringley'**
'Kazanlik' hort.	See ***R.* 'Professeur Emile Perrot'**
Keepsake (HT)	EWar LPlm MGan MHay MMat NRog
Kent (S/GC)	EBee ELan EWar GGre IHos LPlm LStr MHlr MJon MMat NBat NPri SPer SPla SRum WAct WHCG WOVN WRHF
'Kerryman' (F)	EWar
'Kew Rambler' (Ra)	EBee EBls EWar MAus MRav WHCG
'Kiese' (*canina* hybrid)	MJon
'Kiftsgate'	See ***R. filipes* 'Kiftsgate'**
'Kilworth Gold' (HT)	MGan
'Kim' (Patio)	NRog
Kind Regards (F)	SRum
'Kingig' (Min)	MHay
King's Ransom (HT)	CB&S CGro EBls ESha EWar GGre IHos MBur MECR MGan MHay MJon MMor SPer SRum WWeb
§ Woman o'th North = 'Kirlon' (F/Patio)	WGer
'Kirsten Poulsen' (Poly)	EBls
Kiss 'n' Tell (Min)	MBur
'Kitchener of Khartoum'	See ***R.* 'K of K'**
'Kitty Hawk' (Min)	MHay
× ***kochiana***	EBls
'Köln am Rhein' (Cl)	MGan
§ 'Königin von Dänemark' (A) 🏆	CHad EBls EMFP EOrc EWar GCoc IHar MBri MMat NFla NSty SApu SJus SPer WAct WHCG WHow WSHC
'Korbell' (F)	MGan
§ Tradition = 'Korbeltin' (Cl)	EWar MMat

§ Iceberg = 'Korbin' (F) 🏆	CB&S CDoC CGro EBls EBre ESha EWar GCoc GGre IHos LFis LGod LStr MAus MFry MGan MJon MMat MMor NRog NSty SApu SJus SPer SRum WWeb
§ Antique = 'Kordalen' (Cl)	EWar WGer
§ Malverns = 'Kordehei' (GC)	MMat
◆ Kordes' Golden Times	See ***R.* Kordes' Golden Times = 'Kortimes'**
'Kordes' Robusta'	See ***R.* Robusta**
'Kordialo' (F/Patio)	MGan
§ Oxfordshire = 'Korfullwind' (GC)	CDoC LStr MMat NPri SWCr
§ Mary Pope = 'Korlasche' (HT)	MMat
§ Pink Pearl = 'Kormasyl' (HT)	LPlm MBri MJon MMat SApu
Korona (F)	MGan NRog
'Korresia' (F)	EBls ESha EWar GCoc GGre IHar IHos LGod LStr MAus MBri MECR MFry MGan MJon MMat MMor NRog SJus SPer SRum
§ Barry Fearn = 'Korschwana' (HT)	MMat
§ White Cloud = 'Korstacha' (S/ClHT)	ECho EWar LGod
§ Kordes' Golden Times = 'Kortimes' (F)	MECR MJon
§ Scarlet Patio = 'Kortingle' (Patio)	MMat
Kristin (Min)	MHay
Kronenbourg (HT)	EBls LPlm MAus
'Kronprinzessin Viktoria' (Bb)	EBls MAus MHlr WHCG
L.D. Braithwaite (S)	CDoC CHad CSam EBre IHar LGod LPlm LStr MAus MBri MFry MGan MHlr MJon MMat NBat NFla NPri SJus SPer SSoC WAct WHCG WHow WWeb
'La Belle Distinguée' (RH)	EBls MAus WHCG
'La Belle Sultane'	See ***R.* 'Violacea'**
'La Follette' (Cl)	EBls
'La France' (HT)	EBls MAus
'La Mortola'	See ***R. brunonii* 'La Mortola'**
'La Noblesse' (Ce)	EBls
'La Perle' (Ra)	MAus
'La Reine' (HP)	EBls NSty
'La Reine Victoria'	See ***R.* 'Reine Victoria'**
'La Rubanée'	See ***R.* 'Centifolia Variegata'**
La Sevillana (F/GC)	EBls EWar SApu SPer SRum WOVN
'La Ville de Bruxelles' (D) 🏆	EBls IHos MAus MRav NSty SFam SPer WAct WHCG WHow
'Lady Alice Stanley' (HT)	EBls
'Lady Barnby' (HT)	EBls
'Lady Belper' (HT)	EBls MBur
'Lady Curzon' (Ru)	EBls IHos MAus NSty
'Lady Elgin'	See ***R.* Thais**
'Lady Forteviot' (HT)	EBls
'Lady Gay' (Ra)	MAus WHCG
'Lady Godiva' (Ra)	MAus
'Lady Hillingdon' (T)	MAus NSty WHow
'Lady Hillingdon' (ClT)	See ***R.* 'Climbing Lady Hillingdon'**
'Lady Iliffe' (HT)	MGan
Lady in Red (Min)	MBur
'Lady Jane' (HT)	MHay

¶ 'Lady Love' (Patio)	GGre
'Lady MacRobert' (F)	GCoc
'Lady Mary Fitzwilliam' (HT)	EBls
Lady Mavis Pilkington (HT)	MFry MMat
'Lady of Stifford' (F)	EWar
§ 'Lady Penzance' (RH)	CB&S EBls EWar MAus MFry MGan NSty SApu SPer WAct
Lady Rachel (F)	EBee
'Lady Romsey' (F)	EBls
Lady Rose (HT)	MJon
'Lady Seton' (HT)	SPer
'Lady Stuart' (Ch)	NSty
'Lady Sylvia' (HT)	EBls MAus MGan NRog NSty SPer WHow WStI
Lady Taylor (F/Patio)	IHar MBur MECR
'Lady Waterlow' (ClHT)	EBee EBls MAus SPer WHCG
laevigata (Ra)	CBot EBls MAus
– 'Anemonoides'	See ***R.* 'Anemone'**
§ – 'Cooperi' (Ra)	CAbP EBls MAus SPer WAct WHow WSHC
'Lafter' (S)	EBls
'Lagoon' (F)	EBls
L'Aimant (F)	ECle GCoc LStr MFry MJon NBat SApu
'Lakeland' (HT)	MAus NRog
'Lamarque' (N)	MAus
Laminuette (F)	MJon
Lancashire Life (F)	MBri
'Lanei' (CeMo)	EBls
◆ Langdale Chase	See ***R.* Langdale Chase = 'Fryrhapsody'**
Langford Light (Min/GC)	MBur
Laughter Lines (F)	IDic MGan
Laura (HT)	EWar
Laura Anne (HT)	GCoc
Laura Ashley (ClMin)	EWar MAus MBur NBat
Laura Ford (ClMin) 🏆	CDoC EBre EWar GGre IHar LGod LStr MAus MBri MBur MGan MJon MMat NBat NPri SApu SJus SRum SWCr WWeb
'Laura Jane' (HT)	MGan
'Laura Louise' (Cl)	EBls
Laurence Olivier (F)	SApu
'Lavender Jewel' (Min)	IHar MAus MBur NPri
'Lavender Lassie' (HM) 🏆	EMFP IOrc MAus MFry MGan MHay MHlr MMat SPer SRum WHCG WHow
'Lavender Pinocchio' (F)	MAus
Lavinia (Cl)	EBee EWar LGod LStr MBri MGan SApu SJus SPer
'Lawrence Johnston' (Cl)	EBls MAus NPri NSty SPer WAct
'Le Havre' (HP)	EBls
'Le Rêve' (Cl)	EBls MAus
'Le Vésuve' (Ch)	EBls MAus
Leander (S)	MAus MBri SWCr
Leaping Salmon (ClHT)	CGro ELan EWar GCoc IHar IHos IOrc LGod LStr MBri MGan MJon SApu SPer SPla SRum WOVN WStI
'Leda' (D)	EBls EWar MAus SFam SPer WAct
Can-can = 'Legglow' (HT)	EWar MJon
'Lemon Pillar'	See ***R.* 'Paul's Lemon Pillar'**
Len Turner (F)	IDic SApu
'Léonie Lamesch' (Poly)	EBls
'Léontine Gervais' (Ra)	CAbP MAus MHlr NPri WAct WHCG
Leslie's Dream (HT)	IDic MBri

'Leuchtstern' (Ra)	EBls
'Leverkusen' (Cl)	CHad EBls EBre MAus MGan NSty SPer SPla SRum WAct WHCG WHow WSHC
'Leveson-Gower' (Bb)	EBls
'Ley's Perpetual' (ClT)	EBls WBcn
'Lilac Charm' (F)	EBls MAus
Lilac Rose (S)	MAus
Lilian Austin (S)	EWar IHos MAus MBri
Lilli Marlene (F)	CB&S CTri EBls ESha GCoc IHos LStr MAus MGan MMor NPri NRog SPer SRum
'Lilly the Pink' (HT)	MHay
'Lime Kiln' (S)	NSty
Lincoln Cathedral (HT)	MGan MJon SApu SPer
Lincolnshire Poacher (HT)	NBat
Little Artist (Min)	MJon
Little Bo-peep (Min/Patio)	EBre EWar MFry MJon MMat
'Little Buckaroo' (Min)	ELan EWar LGod MGan NPri SPer WStI
'Little Dorrit' (Poly)	NRog
'Little Flirt' (Min)	EWar MAus MGan
'Little Gem' (DPMo)	EBls MAus MGan
Little Jackie (Min)	MHay NBat
Little Jewel (Patio)	GCoc
'Little Len' (Min/Patio)	MJon
Little Marvel (Min)	MBri
Little Prince (F/Patio)	GCoc
◆ Little Rambler	See ***R.* Little Rambler = 'Chewramb'**
Little Russell (Min)	MJon
'Little White Pet'	See ***R.* 'White Pet'**
Little Woman (Patio)	IDic IHos LStr SApu SWCr
'Liverpool Echo' (F)	LPlm MJon
§ Liverpool Remembers (HT)	EWar LGod MBri MBur MFry MMor
'Living Fire' (F)	EBls MBur MGan
'Lollipop' (Min)	MGan
'Long John Silver' (Cl)	EBls
longicuspis Bertoloni (Ra)	EBls
– hort.	See ***R. mulliganii***
§ ***longicuspis sinowilsonii*** (Ra)	EBls GCal MAus
Longleat (Min)	MMat
Lord Byron (ClHT)	EKMF EWar LStr MBri MJon SApu SWCr
'Lord Penzance' (RH)	EBee EBls MAus MGan NSty SPer WAct WHow
L'Oréal Trophy (HT)	MAus MJon
'Lorraine Lee' (T)	EBls
'Los Angeles' (HT)	EBls
'L'Ouche'	See ***R.* 'Louise Odier'**
'Louis Gimard' (CeMo)	EBls IHos MAus SPer WAct WHCG
'Louis Philippe' (Ch)	EBls
'Louis XIV' (Ch)	CHad EBls LGre WHCG
§ 'Louise Odier' (Bb)	EBls EBre EMFP IHar LStr MAus MBri MHlr MMat NSty SApu SFam SJus SPer SPla SRum WAct WHCG WHow WOVN
'Love Token' (F)	MBur
◆ Lovely Fairy	See ***R.* Lovely Fairy = 'Spevu'**
Lovely Lady™ (HT) 🏆	CTri EBee IDic LStr MGan MJon SApu SJus
'Lovers' Meeting' (HT)	EBre GGre LPlm MBri MBur MECR MGan MJon MMor NBat SApu SPer SRum WStI
Loving Memory (HT)	EWar GCoc GGre LPlm LStr MFry MGan MMat MMor NPri SPer SRum

Loving Touch (Min)	MHay
Lucetta (S)	MAus SPer WAct
luciae	CMHG EBls
– var. ***onoei***	EPot NMen
'Lucilla' (Patio)	NBat
'Lucy Ashton' (RH)	MAus
Luis Desamero (Min)	MHay NBat
'Lutea Maxima'	See ***R.* × *harisonii* 'Lutea Maxima'**
'Lykkefund' (Ra)	EBls MAus
'Lyon Rose' (HT)	EBls
'Lübeck'	See ***R.* 'Hansestadt Lübeck'**
'Ma Perkins' (F)	EBls
'Ma Ponctuée' (DPMo)	EBls
'Mabel Morrison' (HP)	EBls MAus SWCr
Macartney Rose	See ***R. bracteata***
§ Evelyn Fison = 'Macev' (F)	ELan EWar GCoc GGre IHos MAus MGan MJon MMor NRog SApu SPer SRum
§ Fiesta = 'Macfirinlin'	LStr NBat SWCr WGer
§ Oranges and Lemons = 'Macoranlem'™ (F)	GCoc GGre LGod LPlm LStr MBri MBur MFry MGan MJon MMat SApu SJus WGer WWeb
'Macrantha' (Gallica hybrid)	EBls MAus SLPl SPer WAct
◆ ***macrantha*** 'Raubritter'	See ***R.* 'Raubritter' ('Macrantha' hybrid)**
§ Sexy Rexy = 'MacRexy' (F) 🏆	CGro EBre ELan EWar GGre IHar IHos LStr MBri MFry MGan MJon NBat SJus SPer SRum WWeb
macrophylla	MAus MMat
– 'Doncasteri'	See ***R.* 'Doncasteri'**
§ – 'Master Hugh' 🏆	EBls MAus NSty
'Madame Abel Chatenay' (HT)	EBls MAus
'Madame Alfred Carrière' (N) 🏆	Widely available
'Madame Alice Garnier' (Ra)	EBls SPer
'Madame Antoine Mari' (T)	EBls
'Madame Berkeley' (T)	EBls
'Madame Bravy' (T)	EBls MAus
'Madame Butterfly' (HT)	EBls MAus MBur MGan NSty SApu
§ 'Madame Caroline Testout' (HT)	MHlr
'Madame Charles' (T)	EBls SFam
'Madame d'Arblay' (Ra)	EBls
'Madame de Sancy de Parabère' (Bs)	EBee EBls MAus WHCG
'Madame de Watteville' (T)	EBls
'Madame Delaroche-Lambert' (DPMo) 🏆	EBls MAus WAct WHCG
'Madame Driout' (ClT)	EBls
'Madame Eliza de Vilmorin' (HT)	EBls
'Madame Ernest Calvat' (Bb)	EBls MAus NSty SPer
'Madame Eugène Résal' hort.	See ***R.* 'Comtesse du Cayla'**
'Madame Gabriel Luizet' (HP)	EBls
'Madame Georges Bruant' (Ru)	EBls MAus

§ 'Madame Grégoire Staechelin' (ClHT) 🏆	CHad CSam EBls EBre EWar IHar LStr MAus MBri MGan MHlr MJon MMat NBat NFla NRog NSty SApu SChu SJus SPer SRum WAct WHCG WOVN WWeb
'Madame Hardy' (ClD) 🏆	CPou EBls ENot EWar GCoc IHar LStr MAus MBri MGan MHlr MJon MMat NSty SApu SFam SJus SPer SRum WAct WHCG WHow WOVN
'Madame Isaac Pereire' (ClBb)	CHad EBls EBre ENot EWar GCoc IHos IOrc LHol LStr MAus MBri MFry MGan MHlr MJon MMat NFla NRog NSty SApu SFam SJus SMad SPer SSoC WAct WHCG
'Madame Jules Gravereaux' (ClT)	EBls MAus
'Madame Jules Thibaud' (Poly)	MAus
§ 'Madame Knorr' (DPo)	EBee EBls EBre EMFP IHos MAus NSty SJus SPer SWCr WAct WHow
'Madame Laurette Messimy' (Ch)	EBls MAus WHCG WSHC
'Madame Lauriol de Barny' (Bb)	CPou EBls MAus MGan NSty WHCG
'Madame Legras de Saint Germain' (AxN)	EBls EMFP IHar MAus NSty SFam SJus SPer WAct WHCG WHow
'Madame Lombard' (T)	EBls
'Madame Louis Laperrière' (HT)	EBls MAus MGan NSty SPer
'Madame Louis Lévêque' (DPMo)	EBls WHCG
'Madame Pierre Oger' (Bb)	EBls ENot EWar GCoc IHos LHol LStr MAus MHlr MMat NSty SApu SPer SRum WAct WHCG WWeb
'Madame Plantier' (AxN)	EBls IHar LHol MAus MHlr MMat NPri SPer WHCG WOVN
'Madame Scipion Cochet' (T)	EBls WHCG
'Madame Victor Verdier' (HP)	EBls
'Madame Wagram, Comtesse de Turenne' (T)	EBls
'Madame William Paul' (PoMo)	EBls
'Madame Zöetmans' (D)	EBls MAus NSty
'Madeleine Selzer' (Ra)	EBls MAus MGan
Maestro (HT)	MAus
'Magenta' (S/HT)	CHad EBls MAus SPer WAct WHCG
Magic Carpet (S/GC)	EPfP EWar GCoc GGre IDic LGod LPlm LStr MBri MFry MGan MJon MMat NBat SApu SPla
Magic Carrousel (Min)	LPlm MAus MHay NPri WStI
'Magna Charta' (HP)	EBls
'Magnifica' (RH)	EBls MAus MGan
N 'Maiden's Blush' (A)	CHad CSam EBls EBre ELan EMFP ENot IHar LHol MAus MGan MHlr SApu SFam SJus SPer SRum WHCG WWeb
'Maiden's Blush, Great'	See ***R.* 'Great Maiden's Blush'**
'Maigold' (ClHScB) 🏆	CB&S CGro EBls EBre ELan EWar GCoc GGre IHos LGod LPlm LStr MAus MBri MGan MJon MMat MMor NBat NFla NSty SApu SJus SPer SRum WAct WHCG WSHC WWeb
§ ***majalis***	MSto
◆ Make a Wish	See ***R.* Make a Wish = 'Mehpat'**
'Malaga' (ClHT)	EWar MMat
Malcolm Sargent (HT)	SPer
'Maltese Rose'	See ***R.* 'Cécile Brünner'**
§ 'Malton' (China hybrid)	EBls
◆ Malverns	See ***R.* Malverns = 'Kordehei'**
Mandarin (Min)	LStr MJon MMat NPri SWCr
'Manettii' (N)	EBls
'Manning's Blush' (RH)	EBls MAus NSty WAct WHCG
Manou Meilland (HT)	EWar MGan
Manuela (HT)	MGan
'Manx Queen' (F)	MGan MJon
Many Happy Returns (F) 🏆	EBre ESha EWar GCoc LGod LPlm LStr MAus MBri MBur MFry MGan MJon MMat NBat SApu SJus SPer SRum WOVN WWeb
'Marbrée' (DPo)	EBls MAus
'Marcel Bourgouin' (G)	EBls
'Märchenland' (S)	EBls MAus
§ 'Marchesa Boccella' (DPo) 🏆	EBee EBls IHar MAus MGan NPri SJus SMer SPer SPla WAct
'Marcie Gandy' (HT)	MGan
'Maréchal Davoust' (CeMo)	EBls MAus NSty SFam SPer
'Maréchal Niel' (N)	EBls ERea MAus MGan NSty SPer WHCG
'Margaret' (HT)	MBur MGan
'Margaret Merril' (HT/F) 🏆	CDoC EBls EBre ESha EWar GCoc GGre IHos LGod LPlm LStr MAus MBri MBur MFry MGan MJon MMat MMor NBat NRog SApu SJus SPer SRum WHCG WOVN WWeb
Margaret Thatcher (HT)	MJon
'Margo Koster' (Poly)	EBls MAus NRog SPer SRum
◆ Marguerite Anne	See ***R.* Marguerite Anne = 'Cockredward'**
'Marguerite Guillard' (HP)	EBls
'Marguerite Hilling' (S) 🏆	EBls ENot EWar GCoc MBri MGan MHlr MJon MMat MMor NRog NSty SApu SPer SRum WAct WHCG WOVN WWeb
Maria Therese (HT/S)	MHay
x ***mariae-graebnerae***	SLPl WHCG
Marianne Tudor (HT)	MFry
'Marie de Blois' (CeMo)	EBls
'Marie Louise' (D)	EBls IHar IHos MAus SFam WAct WHCG
'Marie Pavié' (Poly)	EBls MAus WHCG
'Marie van Houtte' (T)	EBls MAus
'Marie-Jeanne' (Poly)	EBls MAus
'Marijke Koopman' (HT)	MFry
Marjorie Fair (S/GC)	EBls EWar LPlm MAus MGan MMat NPri SApu SRum WAct WOVN WWeb
'Marlena' (F/Patio)	GCoc MAus MBri MFry MGan
'Martha' (Bb)	EBls MAus
'Martian Glow' (F/S)	MGan
'Martin Frobisher' (Ru)	EBls MAus
'Mary' (Poly)	LStr
Mary Donaldson (HT)	EWar MGan
Mary Gamon (Patio)	MFry
'Mary Manners' (Ru)	EBls SPer

◆ Mary Pope	See ***R.*** **Mary Pope = 'Korlasche'**
Mary Rose (S)	CGro CHad CSam EBls EBre ELan ENot EOrc EWar GCoc GGre IHos LGod LStr MAus MBri MECR MFry MGan MHlr MJon MMat NBat SApu SJus SPer SRum WOVN
'Mary Wallace' (Cl)	EBls MAus
Mary Webb (S)	MAus MBri
'Masquerade' (F)	CB&S CGro EBls ESha LGod LStr MAus MGan MJon NRog SRum WStI WWeb
'Master Hugh'	See ***R. macrophylla*** **'Master Hugh'**
Matangi (F)	EWar LGod MGan MMat
Matthias Meilland (F)	EWar
'Maurice Bernardin'	See ***R.*** **'Ferdinand de Lesseps'**
'Max Graf'	See ***R.*** ×***jacksonii*** **'Max Graf'**
'Maxima'	See ***R.*** × ***alba*** **'Alba Maxima'**
maximowicziana CC 541	WHCr
'May Queen' (Ra)	EBls EMFP MAus MHlr SFam SPer WHCG WHow
◆ Mayor of Casterbridge	See ***R.*** **Mayor of Casterbridge = 'Ausbrid'**
'McGredy's Sunset' (HT)	NRog
'McGredy's Yellow' (HT)	EBls MBur MGan
'Meg' (ClHT)	CHad EBee EBls MAus MBur MGan MHlr NSty SPer SRum WAct WHCG
'Meg Merilees' (RH)	EBls MAus MGan
'Megiddo' (F)	MGan
§ Make a Wish = 'Mehpat' (Min/Patio)	LStr SWCr
§ Golden Symphonie = 'Meilolcil' (Min/Patio)	MJon
§ John Keats = 'Meiroupis' (S)	SApu
Meirov (Min)	MGan
Flamingo Meidiland = 'Meisolroz'	EWar WOVN
melina	EBls
Melina (HT)	See ***R.*** **Sir Harry Pilkington**
'Melinda' (HT)	MBri
Melody Maker (F)	CDoC EWar IDic MBri MBur MGan MJon NBat SJus
◆ Memento	See ***R.*** **Memento = 'Dicbar'**
'Memoriam' (HT)	MGan
◆ Memory Lane	See ***R.*** **Memory Lane = 'Peavoodoo'**
Mercedes (F)	MJon
'Mermaid' (Cl) ♀	CB&S CDoC CGro EBls EBre EWar GCoc IHar IHos LHop LStr MAus MGan MJon MMat MMor NRog SApu SBra SJus SLPl SMad SPer SRum SSoC WAbe WAct WHCG WWat
'Merveille de Lyon' (HP)	EBls
Message (HT)	MGan
Meteor (F/Patio)	MGan
§ 'Mevrouw Nathalie Nypels' (Poly) ♀	CHad EBee EBls IHar LStr MAus SPer WAct WKif WOVN
'Mexico' (Min)	LPlm
Michael Crawford (HT)	GCoc LGod
'Michèle Meilland' (HT)	EBls MAus MGan NSty
¶ ***micrantha***	WUnd
× ***micrugosa***	EBls MAus
– 'Alba'	EBls MAus
Middlesex County (F)	NBat
Mimi (Min)	MGan
Mini Metro (Min)	MFry
Minijet (Min)	EWar
Minilights (Patio)	EWar IDic SApu SPer

'Minnehaha' (Ra)	EBls EMFP LGod MAus
Minnie Pearl (Min)	MHay
mirifica stellata	See ***R. stellata*** var. ***mirifica***
Mischief (HT)	EBls EWar GCoc GGre MAus MGan NPri NRog SPer SRum
'Miss Edith Cavell' (Poly)	EBls
Miss Harp (HT)	MGan NRog
Miss Ireland (HT)	NRog
'Miss Lowe' (Ch)	EBls
§ Miss Pam Ayres (S)	MMat
§ Mister Lincoln (HT)	EBls LGod MAus MBri MBur MGan SPer
◆ Mistress Quickly	See ***R.*** **Mistress Quickly = 'Ausky'**
'Mojave' (HT)	MAus MGan
Moje Hammarberg (Ru)	ENot IHos MJon WAct
◆ Molineux	See ***R.*** **Molineux = 'Ausmol'**
¶ ***mollis***	MSto
'Mona Ruth' (Min)	MGan
'Monique' (HT)	EBls MGan NSty
'Monsieur Tillier' (T)	EBls
'Moon Maiden' (F)	MMat
◆ Moonbeam	See ***R.*** **Moonbeam = 'Ausbeam'**
'Moonlight' (HM)	CTri EBls EWar IHar IHos MAus MGan MMat NBus NRog NSty SJus SPer SRum WAct WHCG
'Morgengruss' (Cl)	MGan
Moriah (HT)	MGan
'Morlettii' (Bs)	EBls MRav
Morning Jewel (ClF) ♀	CB&S EWar GCoc LPlm MFry MJon NBat NRog
moschata (Ra)	EBls MAus MHlr MRav
– 'Autumnalis'	See ***R.*** **'Princesse de Nassau'**
– var. ***nastarana***	See ***R.*** **'Nastarana'**
– var. ***nepalensis***	See ***R. brunonii***
'Mothers Day' (F)	ELan EWar MJon
Mother's Love (Min)	MHay
Mountain Snow (Ra)	MAus MBri
Mountbatten (F) ♀	CB&S CGro EBls EBre ELan ESha EWar GCoc GGre IHos LGod LPlm LStr MAus MBri MFry MGan MJon MMat NBat NRog SApu SJus SPer SRum WWeb
§ 'Mousseline' (DPoMo)	EBls EMFP MAus NSty WAct WHCG WHow
moyesii (S)	CSam EBls ELan ENot GCoc GOrc IHar IHos IOrc ISea MAus MFry MGan MJon MMat MMor NRog NSty NWea SPer WAct WOVN WRTC
– 'Evesbatch' (S)	WAct
§ – var. ***fargesii*** (S)	EBls
– 'Geranium'	See ***R.*** **'Geranium' (*moyesii* hybrid)**
– 'Highdownensis'	See ***R.*** **'Highdownensis' (*moyesii* hybrid)**
– 'Hillieri'	See ***R.*** **'Hillieri'**
moyesii holodonta	See ***R. moyesii*** **f.** ***rosea***
§ ***moyesii*** f. ***rosea*** (S)	EBls ENot GCal
– 'Sealing Wax'	See ***R.*** **'Sealing Wax' (*moyesii* hybrid)**
'Mozart' (HM)	MJon WHCG
'Mr Bluebird' (MinCh)	EWar MAus MGan WStI
'Mr Chips' (HT)	MBur
Mr J.C.B (S)	IDic
'Mr Lincoln'	See ***R.*** **Mister Lincoln**
'Mrs Anthony Waterer' (Ru)	EBls ENot IHos MAus NSty SPer WAct WHCG
'Mrs Arthur Curtiss James' (ClHT)	EBee

'Mrs B.R. Cant' (T)	EBls
Mrs Doreen Pike (S)	MAus WAct
'Mrs Eveline Gandy' (HT)	MGan
'Mrs Foley Hobbs' (T)	EBls
¶ 'Mrs Honey Dyson' (Ra)	CHad
'Mrs John Laing' (HP)	EBls EWar MAus MHlr NSty SJus SPer WHCG
'Mrs Oakley Fisher' (HT) 🏆	CHad EBls MAus NSty WAct WCot
'Mrs Paul' (Bb)	EBls MAus
'Mrs Pierre S. du Pont' (HT)	EBls
'Mrs Sam McGredy' (HT)	MAus MGan
'Mrs Walter Burns' (F/Patio)	MGan
'Mullard Jubilee' (HT)	EWar IHar MGan
§ ***mulliganii*** (Ra) 🏆	EBls ELan IHar MAus SBid SJus SPer SPla WHCG
multibracteata	EBls MAus WHCG
multiflora	EBls MAus
– 'Carnea'	EBls
– var. ***cathayensis***	EBls
§ – 'Grevillei'	EBee EBls NSty SPer WHow
– 'Platyphylla'	See ***R. multiflora* 'Grevillei'**
– var. ***watsoniana***	See ***R. watsoniana***
mundi	See ***R. gallica* 'Versicolor'**
mundi versicolor	See ***R. gallica* 'Versicolor'**
'Mutabilis'	See ***R.* × *odorata* 'Mutabilis'**
'My Choice' (HT)	MGan SWCr
'My Joy' (HT)	EWar MHay
'My Little Boy' (Min)	MBur
'My Love' (HT)	MBur MECR MGan MJon
My Valentine (Min)	MRav
Myra (HT)	NBat
Myriam (HT)	GCoc MJon SApu
'München' (HM)	MAus
¶ 'Nancy's Keepsake' (HT)	NBat
nanothamnus	LKoh
'Narrow Water' (Ra)	EBls WAct WHCG
§ 'Nastarana' (N)	EBls WHCG
'Nathalie Nypels'	See ***R.* 'Mevrouw Nathalie Nypels'**
'National Trust' (HT)	EBls EWar GGre IHar IHos MGan MJon MMor NBat NRog SPer WStI WWeb
'Nestor' (G)	EBls MAus
'Nevada' (S) 🏆	CB&S EBre ELan ENot EWar GCoc IOrc LGod LStr MAus MBri MFry MGan MHlr MJon MMat MMor NRog NSty SApu SJus SPer SRum WAct WHCG WOVN WWeb
New Daily Mail (F)	MECR
§ 'New Dawn' (Cl) 🏆	Widely available
New Fashion (Patio)	ENot MMat
New Horizon (F)	IDic
'New Look' (F)	MGan
'New Penny' (Min)	EWar IHar MGan
New Zealand (HT)	MHay MJon NBat SApu
News (F)	CHad MAus MGan
Nice Day (ClMin)	EBre EWar GGre LStr MBri MBur MFry MJon MMat NBat SApu WOVN
'Nicola' (F)	EWar MGan
Nigel Hawthorne (S)	WAct
Night Light (Cl)	EWar LPlm MBri MBur MFry MGan MJon SApu SJus
Nina Weibull (F)	MGan
'Niphetos' (ClT)	EBls MAus
nitida	EBee EBls ELan ENot MAus NSty NWea SLPl SPer WHCG WOVN WRTC
– 'Defender'	CWan
◆ Noble Anthony	See ***R.* Noble Anthony = 'Ausway'**
§ 'Noisette Carnée' (N)	CHad EBls NPri NSty SPer WAct WHCG WHow WSHC
Norfolk (GC)	EBls EBre ENot EWar GCoc LGod LStr MFry MGan MHlr MMat SApu SPer SPla WHCG WOVN
'Norma Major' (HT)	MHay
Northamptonshire (GC)	ENot EWar LGod MGan MMat NPri
Northern Lights (HT)	GCoc
'Norwich Castle' (F)	EBls
¶ 'Norwich Cathedral' (HT)	EBls
'Norwich Pink' (Cl)	MAus
'Norwich Union' (F)	EBls
'Nova Zembla' (Ru)	EBls MAus NSty
'Nozomi' (GC) 🏆	CGro EBls ELan ENot ESha EWar GCoc GGre IHos LPlm LStr MAus MBur MECR MFry MGan MHlr MJon MMat MMor NMen SApu SJus SPer SRum WAct WHCG WOVN
'Nuits de Young' (CeMo)	CHad CPou EBls GCoc IHar MAus MMat NSty SFam WHCG
'Nur Mahal' (HM)	EBls MAus WHCG
nutkana (S)	EBls MAus
§ – var. ***hispida*** (S)	EBls
§ – 'Plena' (S) 🏆	CHan EBls ENot NSty SPer WGer WHCG WRHF
'Nymphenburg' (HM)	EBls EMFP MAus SPer
'Nypels' Perfection' (Poly)	MAus
'Nyveldt's White' (Ru)	EBls IHos MAus
'Oakington Ruby' (MinCh)	GAri
Octavia Hill (F/S)	LStr MFry MJon SApu SPer SWCr WHCG WHow
× ***odorata*** 'Fortune's Double Yellow'	See ***R.* × *odorata* 'Pseudindica'**
§ – 'Mutabilis' (Ch) 🏆	CGre EBls EMFP ENot MAus MMat NSty SJus SMad SMrm SPer WHCG WKif WWat
§ – 'Ochroleuca' (Ch)	EBls
§ – 'Odorata' (Ch)	EBls
– Old Crimson China (Ch)	EBls
§ – 'Pallida' (Ch)	CHad EBls EMFP GCoc IHos MMat NPri NSty SPla WHCG WHow
§ – 'Pseudindica' (ClCh)	EBls WSHC
§ – Sanguinea Group (Ch)	EBls WHCG
§ – 'Viridiflora' (Ch)	CPou EBls MAus MBur MMat SMad SPer SRum SSoC WHCG
'Oeillet Flamand'	See ***R.* 'Oeillet Parfait'**
'Oeillet Panaché' (Mo)	WAct
§ 'Oeillet Parfait' (G)	EBls MAus
officinalis	See ***R. gallica*** var. ***officinalis***
'Ohl' (G)	EBls
Ohshima Rose (HT)	GCoc
'Oklahoma' (HT)	MGan
Old Blush China	See ***R.* × *odorata* 'Pallida'**
Old Cabbage	See ***R.* × *centifolia***
Old Master (F)	MAus MGan
Old pink Moss rose	See ***R.* × *centifolia* 'Muscosa'**
Old Port (F)	GGre MBri MJon SApu
Old Velvet Moss	See ***R.* 'William Lobb'**
Old Yellow Scotch	See ***R.* × *harisonii* 'Williams' Double Yellow'**
'Olde Romeo' (HT)	MHay
'Oliver Twist' (Patio)	MBur
'Omar Khayyám' (D)	EBls ENot MAus

§ 'Ombrée Parfaite' (G)	EBls
omeiensis f. ***pteracantha***	See ***R. sericea*** subsp. ***omeiensis*** **f. *pteracantha***
◆ Open Arms	See ***R.*** **Open Arms = 'Chewpixcel'**
'Ophelia' (HT)	EBls MAus MBur MGan NSty SApu
'Orange Honey' (Min)	MBur WWeb
§ Orange Sensation (F)	EBls ESha EWar MAus MGan MJon MMor NRog SRum
§ Orange Sunblaze (Min)	EBls EWar GGre IHos LStr MGan MJon SJus SPer WWeb
Orange Triumph (Poly)	EBls
'Orangeade' (F)	MGan
◆ Oranges and Lemons	See ***R.*** **Oranges and Lemons = 'Macoranlem'**
'Oriana' (HT)	CGro
'Orient Express' (HT)	MJon
'Orpheline de Juillet'	See ***R.*** **'Ombrée Parfaite'**
Othello (S)	CGro EWar MAus SApu WAct
¶ Our Love (HT)	GGre
◆ Our Molly	See ***R.*** **Our Molly = 'Dicreason'**
Owen's Pride (F)	MJon
◆ Oxfordshire	See ***R.*** **Oxfordshire = 'Korfullwind'**
Paddy McGredy (F)	CGro EWar GGre MAus MGan MJon NRog SRum
Painted Moon (HT)	GCoc IDic MFry
◆ Paint-pot	See ***R.*** **Paint-pot = 'Trobglow'**
'Pam Ayers'	See ***R.*** **Miss Pam Ayres**
◆ Panache	See ***R.*** **Panache = 'Poultop'**
'Panorama Holiday' (F/HT)	MBur
'Papa Gontier' (T)	EBls MAus
'Papa Hémeray' (Ch)	EBls
Papa Meilland (HT)	CB&S CGro EBls MAus MGan MHay MJon NRog SApu SPer SRum
'Papillon' (T)	EBls
Paprika (F)	MAus
'Pâquerette' (Poly)	EBls
'Para Ti'	See ***R.*** **'Pour Toi'**
'Parade' (Cl) 🏆	MAus MFry MGan MMat SJus WHCG
Paradise (HT)	MGan
Parkdirektor Riggers (Cl)	CHad CSam EBls EBre EWar LStr MAus MBri MGan MMat MMor SPer SRum WHCG WSHC
Park's Yellow China	See ***R.*** × ***odorata*** **'Ochroleuca'**
'Parkzierde' (Bb)	EBls
Parson's Pink China	See ***R.*** × ***odorata*** **'Pallida'**
Partridge (GC)	EBls ENot IHos MAus MGan MJon MMat SApu SJus SPer WAct WOVN
'Party Girl' (Min)	MHay NBat
Party Trick (F)	IDic MBri
parvifolia	See ***R.*** **'Burgundiaca'**
Pascali (HT)	CGro EBls EBre ELan ESha EWar GCoc GGre IHos LStr MAus MBur MECR MGan MJon MMor NRog SApu SPer SRum WWeb
Passion (Ru)	WLRN
Pat Austin (S)	MAus MJon NBus NPri SWCr WGer
◆ Pathfinder	See ***R.*** **Pathfinder = 'Chewpobey'**
Patricia (F)	SRum
'Paul Crampel' (Poly)	EBls MAus MGan NRog NSty SPer
'Paul Lédé' (ClT)	See ***R.*** **'Climbing Paul Lédé'**
Paul McCartney	See ***R.*** **The McCartney Rose**
'Paul Neyron' (HP)	EBls MAus MMat NSty SPer WAct WHCG
'Paul Ricault' (CexHP)	EBls MAus
Paul Shirville (HT) 🏆	CDoC EWar GCoc GGre IHar IHos LPlm LStr MAus MFry MGan MMat NRog SApu SJus SPer
'Paul Transon' (Ra) 🏆	EBee EBls EMFP IHar MAus MBri MHlr SJus SPer WHCG WHow
'Paul Verdier' (Bb)	EBls
§ 'Paulii' (Ru)	EBls ELan ENot IHos MAus MBur MHlr MMor SPer WAct WHCG WOVN
'Paulii Alba'	See ***R.*** **'Paulii'**
'Paulii Rosea' (Ru/Cl)	EBls MAus MBri WAct WHCG
'Paul's Early Blush' (HP)	EBls
'Paul's Himalayan Musk' (Ra) 🏆	CHad CRHN CSam EBls EBre EMFP EOrc EWar IHar ISea LHol LStr MAus MBri MHlr MJon NBat NSty SApu SFam SJus SPer WAct WHCG WHow WKif
§ 'Paul's Lemon Pillar' (ClHT)	CHad EBee EBls EBre MAus NPri NRog NSty SPer
'Paul's Perpetual White' (Ra)	EBls WHCG
'Paul's Scarlet Climber' (Cl/Ra)	CGro EBls ELan EOrc EWar GGre IHos LGod LStr MAus MGan MJon MMat MMor NBat NSty SApu SPer SRum WWeb
'Pax' (HM)	EBls MAus NSty SPer WHCG WKif
Peace (HT) 🏆	CB&S CGro EBls ELan ESha EWar GCoc GGre IHos LGod LPlm LStr MAus MBri MBur MECR MFry MGan MHay MJon MMat MMor NBat NRog SApu SPer SRum WWeb
Peace Sunblaze (Min)	EWar SApu
Peach Blossom (S)	EWar MAus MHlr SWCr
Peach Sunblaze (Min)	EWar MJon SApu SJus WWeb
'Peachy White' (Min)	MAus
'Pearl Anniversary' (Min/Patio)	EKMF EWar GGre LStr SWCr
Pearl Drift™	EBls EWar LStr MAus MJon SPer WHCG
§ Goldfinger = 'Pearoyal' (F)	ESha EWar MBri
Peaudouce	See ***R.*** **Elina = 'Dicjana'**
§ Stardust = 'Peavandyke' (Patio/F)	GGre MJon
§ Memory Lane = 'Peavoodoo' (F)	GGre
§ Ruby Celebration = 'Peawinner' (F)	GGre
Peek A Boo (Min/Patio)	EBre ELan EWar IDic IHar IHos LGod MECR MFry MGan SApu SPer WStI
Peer Gynt (HT)	EBre ESha EWar IHos LPlm MGan NPri
Pegasus (S)	IHar MAus MJon SSoC SWCr
'Peggy Netherthorpe' (HT)	MHay
'Pélisson' (CeMo)	EBls
§ ***pendulina***	EBls MAus WHCG

'Penelope' (HM) 🏆	CHad CSam EBls EBre ELan ENot EWar GCoc IHos LStr MAus MBri MFry MGan MHlr MJon MMat MMor NRog NSty SApu SJus SPer SRum WAct WHCG WKif WOVN
Penelope Keith (Min/Patio)	MJon MMat SApu
Penelope Plummer (F)	EBls
Pensioner's Voice (F)	MFry
Penthouse (HT)	EWar MJon
× *penzanceana*	See ***R.* 'Lady Penzance'**
Peppermint Ice (F)	MJon MRav SApu SRum
Perdita (S)	EWar IHos IOrc MAus MBri MHlr MTis SPer WAct WHCG
Perestroika (F/Min)	GCoc LStr MBur MJon MMat SApu SJus WGer
Perfecta (HT)	EBls MGan
'Perla d'Alcañada' (Min)	EWar
'Perla de Montserrat' (Min)	EWar
'Perle des Jardins' (T)	EBls MAus
'Perle des Panachées' (G)	EBls
'Perle d'Or' (Poly)	CHad EMFP ENot GCoc MAus MHlr MMat NRog NSty SMer SPer SPla WAct WHCG WWat
'Perle von Hohenstein' (Poly)	EBls
Pernille Poulsen (F)	EBls
Persian Yellow	See ***R. foetida* 'Persiana'**
Petit Four (Min/Patio)	IDic SApu
'Petite de Hollande' (Ce)	EBls EMFP MAus NSty SPer WAct WHCG WHow
'Petite Lisette' (CexD)	EBls MAus SPer
'Petite Orléannaise' (Ce)	EBls
Phantom (S/GC)	MBur MJon WGer
'Pharisäer' (HT)	EBls
Pheasant (GC)	ENot GCoc IHos MAus MHlr MJon MMat SJus SPer WAct WOVN
phoenicia	EBls
'Phyllis Bide' (Ra) 🏆	EBls EMFP EWar MAus MGan MHlr NSty SJus SPer WHCG WHow
Picasso (F)	EBls EWar MAus MGan
Piccadilly (HT)	CB&S CGro EBls ESha EWar GGre IHar LPlm MAus MGan MHay MJon MMor NRog SApu SPer SRum WWeb
Piccolo (F/Patio)	EWar GGre LStr MBri MECR MFry MJon MMor NPri SApu SJus SRum WGer WWeb
'Picture' (HT)	EBls MAus MGan NRog NSty SPer
'Pierre Notting' (HP)	EBls
Pierrine (Min)	MHay
Pigalle '84 (F)	SRum
Pillar Box (F)	MGan
§ ***pimpinellifolia***	CKin EBls ENot LBuc MAus MGan MMat NRoo NWea SPer WHCG WOVN WRTC
– 'Altaica' hort.	See ***R. pimpinellifolia* 'Grandiflora'**
§ – 'Andrewsii'	MAus WAct
– 'Bakewell Scots Briar'	NSty
§ – double pink	EBls
§ – double white	CNat EBls GCoc MAus WAct
– double yellow	See ***R.* × *harisonii* 'Williams' Double Yellow'**
§ – 'Dunwich Rose'	EBee EBls EBre ENot MAus MBri MGan MMat SPer WAct WHCG
– 'Falkland'	EBls MAus
§ – 'Glory of Edzell'	EBls MAus
§ – 'Grandiflora'	EBls MAus SJus
– 'Harisonii'	See ***R.* × *harisonii* 'Harison's Yellow'**
– 'Irish Marbled'	EBls
– 'Lutea'	See ***R.* × *harisonii* 'Lutea Maxima'**
– 'Marbled Pink'	EBls MAus
– 'Mary Queen of Scots'	EBls MAus NSty SRms WAct
– 'Mrs Colville'	EBls MAus
– 'Ormiston Roy'	MAus NSty
– × *pendulina*	See ***R.* × *reversa***
§ – 'Robbie'	MAus WAct
– 'Single Cherry'	EBls MAus
◆ – 'Stanwell Perpetual'	See ***R.* 'Stanwell Perpetual'**
– 'Variegata'	CArn
– 'William III'	EBls LHop MAus NSty SChu SLPl
Pink Bells (GC)	CGro EBls ENot EWar GCoc IHos LStr MAus MECR MGan MHlr MMat NFla SApu SPer WAct WHCG WOVN
'Pink Bouquet' (Ra)	MAus
Pink Chimo (S/GC)	IDic MJon
Pink Drift (Min/GC)	ENot MMat
'Pink Elizabeth Arden' (F)	EWar
'Pink Favorite' (HT)	IHos MAus MGan MHay NRog SPer SRum
'Pink Garnette'	See ***R.* 'Carol Amling'**
'Pink Grootendorst' (Ru) 🏆	CB&S EBls ENot EWar IHos IOrc LStr MAus MGan MHlr MJon MMat MMor NRog NSty SPer SRum WAct WHCG
'Pink Hedgrose'	See ***R.* Romantic Hedgrose**
◆ Pink Hit	See ***R.* Pink Hit = 'Poulink'**
Pink La Sevillana (F/GC)	EWar SRum
Pink Meidiland (GC)	MGan WOVN
Pink Moss	See ***R.* × *centifolia* 'Muscosa'**
Pink Panther (HT)	EWar
'Pink Parfait' (F)	EBls GCoc GGre MAus MGan NRog SPer SRum
Pink Peace (HT)	CB&S ESha EWar GGre MMor NPri WWeb
◆ Pink Pearl	See ***R.* Pink Pearl = 'Kormasyl'**
'Pink Perpétué' (Cl)	CDoC CGro EBls EBre ELan ESha EWar GCoc GGre IHos LGod LPlm MAus MBri MBur MECR MFry MGan MJon MMat MMor NBat NFla NRog NSty SApu SPer SRum WWeb
Pink Posy (Min/Patio)	MAus
'Pink Prosperity' (HM)	EBls MAus
Pink Sunblaze (Min/Patio)	GCoc SApu
Pink Surprise (Ru)	MAus
Pink Wave (GC)	IHos MMat
'Pinocchio' (F)	EBls
'Pinta' (HT)	EBls
Piroschka (HT)	MJon
'Pixie Rose' (Min)	IHos
Playgroup Rose (F)	IHar NBat
Pleine de Grâce (S)	EBls MAus SPer WAct
'Plentiful' (F)	EBls
'Poetry in Motion' (HT)	NBat SApu
Polar Star (HT)	EBls ESha EWar GCoc GGre IHos LGod LPlm LStr MFry MGan MHay MJon NBat NRog SApu SJus SPer SRum WWeb
× ***polliniana***	SLPl
'Polly' (HT)	EBls MGan NRog
polyantha grandiflora	See ***R. gentiliana***

pomifera	See ***R. villosa***
– 'Duplex'	See ***R.* 'Wolley-Dod'**
Pomona (F)	MFry
'Pompon Blanc Parfait' (A)	EBls MAus SFam
'Pompon de Bourgogne'	See ***R.* 'Burgundiaca'**
'Pompon de Paris' (ClCh)	see ***R.* 'Climbing Pompon de Paris'**
'Pompon Panaché' (G)	EBls MAus
Portland Dawn (Min)	MBur
Portland Rose	See ***R.* 'Portlandica'**
§ 'Portlandica'	EBls SPer WAct WHCG
Pot o' Gold (HT)	EBee ESha IDic IHos LStr MAus MFry MGan MJon SApu SPer SRum
§ Tiger Cub = 'Poulcub' (Patio)	MMat
§ Tivoli = 'Poulduce' (HT)	GGre MAus MJon MMat
§ City Lights = 'Poulgan' (Patio)	LGod MMat
§ Pink Hit = 'Poulink' (Min/Patio)	MMat
§ Avon = 'Poulmulti' (GC)	ELan EWar GCoc LGod LStr MGan MJon NPri SApu SRum WHCG WOVN
§ Salmo = 'Poulnoeu' (Patio)	MJon MMat
§ Eurostar = 'Poulreb' (F)	MMat
§ Crystal Palace = 'Poulrek' (Patio)	EWar MMat WHow
§ Panache = 'Poultop' (Patio)	GGre WGer
§ Pzazz = 'Poulzazz' (Min/Patio)	MJon WGer
§ 'Pour Toi' (Min)	EWar MGan MJon NPri SPer
Prairie Rose	See ***R. setigera***
'Precious Platinum' (HT)	IHar IHos LGod LStr MBri MJon SJus SPer
§ 'Président de Sèze' (G) 🏆	EBee EBls MAus NSty SFam SPer WAct WHCG WHow
'President Herbert Hoover' (HT)	EBls
'Prestige' (S)	NRog
♦ Pretty in Pink	See ***R.* Pretty in Pink = 'Dicumpteen'**
Pretty Jessica (S)	IHos MAus MHlr MJon SPer
'Pretty Lady' (F)	MJon
Pretty Polly (Min)	CGro CTri EBre EWar GGre LStr MBri MECR MFry MGan MJon MMat NPri SApu SJus WWeb
Prima Ballerina® (HT)	CB&S CGro EBls GCoc GGre IHos LPlm LStr MAus MBur MGan MJon MMor NBat NRog SPer SRum
primula (S) 🏆	CHad EBls EMFP ENot LHol MAus MJon MMat NSty SPer WAct WHCG WHow
'Prince Camille de Rohan' (HP)	EBls MAus WHCG
'Prince Charles' (Bb)	EBls MAus MHlr NSty WHCG
Princess Alice (F)	EWar LGod MGan SApu
¶ 'Princess Chichibu' (F)	SWCr
Princess Margaret of England (HT)	EWar
Princess Michael of Kent (F)	MGan
Princess Royal (HT)	COtt GCoc GGre IDic MBri
'Princesse Adélaïde' (Mo)	EBls
§ 'Princesse de Nassau' (Ra)	EBls MAus WAct WHCG
'Princesse Louise' (Ra)	MAus SFam
'Princesse Marie' (Ra)	EBls MBri
Priscilla Burton (F)	MAus
Pristine (HT)	EWar IDic IHos LPlm LStr MAus MGan MJon SPer SRum
N 'Professeur Emile Perrot' (D)	EBee EBls IHos NSty
'Prolifera de Redouté' hort.	See ***R.* 'Duchesse de Montebello'**
'Prosperity' (HM)	EBls EMFP ENot EWar GCoc IOrc MAus MFry MGan MHlr MJon MMat NRog SJus SPer WAct WHCG WOVN WWeb
Prospero (S)	MAus MBri WAct
'Prudhoe Peach' (F)	NBat
× *pruhoniciana* 'Hillieri'	See ***R. moyesii* 'Hillieri'**
'Pudsey Bear' (HT)	CDoC COtt GGre SPer
§ ***pulverulenta***	EBls SIng
♦ Pure Bliss	See ***R.* Pure Bliss = 'Dictator'**
'Purple Beauty' (HT)	MGan
'Purple Splendour' (F)	MAus
Purple Tiger (F)	EBee IDic LPlm MBri MBur MFry MJon SApu WGer
'Purpurtraum' (Ru)	WHCG
♦ Pzazz	See ***R.* Pzazz = 'Poulzazz'**
Quaker Star (F)	IDic
Quatre Saisons	See ***R.* × *damascena*** var. ***semperflorens***
'Quatre Saisons Blanche Mousseuse' (DMo)	EBls IHar
Queen Charlotte (HT)	MBri MBur
Queen Elizabeth	See ***R.* 'The Queen Elizabeth'**
Queen Mother (Patio)	EBls ELan EWar GCoc GGre IHos LGod LStr MAus MBur MFry MGan MJon MMat NPri SPer WWeb
Queen Nefertiti (S)	MAus
'Queen of Bedders' (Bb)	EBls
♦ Queen of Denmark	See ***R.* 'Königin von Dänemark'**
'Queen of Hearts'	See ***R.* 'Dame de Coeur'**
'Queen of the Belgians' (Cl)	EBls
Radiant (Min)	MHay
♦ Radio Times	See ***R.* Radio Times = 'Aussal'**
Radox Bouquet (F)	EWar GCoc MBur
'Radway Sunrise' (S)	EBls
'Rainbow' (S)	MMat
'Rambling Rector' (Ra) 🏆	CHad CSam EBls EBre ELan EMFP EWar GCoc GGre LGod LStr MAus MBri MBur MGan MHlr MMat MMor NBrk NSty SApu SJus SPer SPla SRum WAct WHCG WSHC
§ 'Ramona'	CHad EBls WHCG WSHC
§ 'Raubritter' ('Macrantha' hybrid)	EBee EBls IHos MAus MHlr NSty SApu SPer WAct WHCG
'Ravenswood Village' (HT)	MHay
♦ Ray of Hope	See ***R.* Ray of Hope = 'Cocnilly'**
Ray of Sunshine (Patio)	CGro ESha GCoc LPlm LStr MBri MFry
'Raymond Chenault' (Cl)	MGan
'Rebecca Claire' (HT)	GCoc MJon SApu
Red Ace (Min)	MFry MJon
Red Bells (Min/GC)	CGro EBls ENot EWar IHos LStr MAus MGan MMat SPer WHCG WOVN
Red Blanket (S/GC) 🏆	CGro EBls ENot EWar GCoc IDic IHos MAus MGan NFla SPer SRum WAct WOVN
'Red Coat' (F)	IHos MAus SWCr
'Red Dandy' (F)	MGan

Red Devil (HT)	ESha EWar GGre LPlm MAus MGan MHay MJon NBat NRog SRum
Red Dot (S/GC)	IDic MMat WOVN
'Red Elf' (Min)	GAri
'Red Garnette'	See ***R.* 'Garnette'**
'Red Grootendorst'	See ***R.* 'F.J. Grootendorst'**
'Red Max Graf'	See ***R.* Rote Max Graf**
Red Meidiland (GC)	WOVN
Red Moss	See ***R.* 'Henri Martin'**
Red New Dawn	MRav WAct
Red Rascal (Patio)	EWar IDic MBri MFry MJon SApu
Red Rose of Lancaster	See ***R. gallica* var. *officinalis***
Red Sunblaze (Min)	GCoc IHos MJon WWeb
Red Trail (S/GC)	EWar IDic MJon WOVN
§ 'Red Wing' (*hugonis* hybrid)	EBls MAus
Redgold (F)	EWar GGre MGan
Redouté (S)	EBre EWar MAus NPri SJus SPer
Regal Red (S)	GCoc
Regensberg (F/Patio)	CTri ESha EWar GCoc GGre IHos LPlm LStr MBri MFry MGan MJon MMat NRog SApu WFar
'Reine des Centifeuilles' (Ce)	EBls SFam
'Reine des Violettes' (HP)	CHad EBls EWar IHar LStr MAus MHlr NPri NSty SApu SJus SPer WAct WHCG WHow
'Reine Marie Henriette' (ClHT)	EBls
§ 'Reine Victoria' (Bb)	EBls EBre EMFP IHar IHos LStr MAus MGan NPri NSty SJus SPer SPla WAct
Remember Me (HT) 🏆	EBre ESha EWar GCoc GGre LGod LPlm LStr MBri MECR MFry MGan MHay MJon MMat NBat NRog SApu SJus SPer
Remembrance (F)	GCoc LStr MBri SApu SPer SRum SWCr
Rémy Martin (HT)	EWar MBri
Renaissance (HT)	ECle GCoc GGre LStr MBur MFry MJon SRum
'René André' (Ra)	EBee EBls MAus
'René d'Anjou' (CeMo)	EBls MAus
Repens Meidiland (S)	EWar WOVN
'Rescht'	See ***R.* 'De Rescht'**
¶ 'Rest in Peace' (Patio/F)	GGre
'Rêve d'Or' (N)	EBls EMFP MAus SPer WHow WSHC
'Réveil Dijonnais' (ClHT)	EBls MAus
'Reverend F. Page-Roberts' (HT)	EBls
'Rhodes Rose' (S)	NSty
◆ Richard Buckley	See ***R.* Richard Buckley = 'Smitshort'**
§ x ***richardii***	EBls MAus WHCG
§ 'Rise 'n' Shine' (Min)	EWar LGod MGan
'Ritter von Barmstede' (Cl)	MGan
'Rival de Paestum' (T)	EBls MAus
'River Gardens'	NPer
Rob Roy (F)	GCoc MBur MGan SPer
'Robert le Diable' (Ce)	EBls MAus NSty SPer WAct WHCG
'Robert Léopold' (DPMo)	EBls
'Robin Hood' (HM)	EBls
Robin Redbreast (Min/GC)	EBls IDic IHar MJon SApu WWeb
§ Robusta (Ru)	EBls MAus MJon

◆ Roche Centenary	See ***R.* Roche Centenary = 'Dicvantage'**
'Roger Lambelin' (HP)	EBls ENot MAus MMat NSty SPer
Romance (S)	MJon MRav WWeb
§ Romantic Hedgrose (F/S)	ENot MMat
◆ Rosabell	See ***R.* Rosabell = 'Cocceleste'**
'Rosalie Coral' (Cl)	EBre EWar MBri MJon NBat NPer SApu SJus
Rosarium Uetersen (Cl)	MJon
'Rose à Parfum de l'Hay' (Ru)	EBls
§ 'Rose d'Amour' 🏆	EBls EWar ISea MAus SJus WHCG
'Rose de Meaux'	See ***R.* 'De Meaux'**
'Rose de Meaux White'	See ***R.* 'De Meaux, White'**
'Rose de Rescht'	See ***R.* 'De Rescht'**
'Rose des Maures'	See ***R.* 'Sissinghurst Castle'**
'Rose d'Hivers' (D)	EBls
'Rose d'Orsay' (S)	EBls
'Rose du Maître d'Ecole'	See ***R.* 'Du Maître d'Ecole'**
'Rose du Roi' (HP/DPo)	EBls MAus NSty WAct WHCG
'Rose du Roi à Fleurs Pourpres' (HP)	EBls MAus
'Rose Edouard' (Bb)	EBls
§ Rose Gaujard (HT)	EBls ESha EWar GGre LGod LPlm MAus MBur MGan MHay NPri SRum
'Rosecarpe' (HT)	NBat
§ 'Rose-Marie Viaud' (Ra)	CFee MAus WHCG
'Rosemary Gandy' (F)	MGan
Rosemary Harkness (HT)	EWar IHos LStr MJon MMat SApu SPer WWeb
'Rosemary Rose' (F)	EBls MBri NRog SPer
'Rosenelfe' (F)	EBls
'Roseraie de l'Haÿ' (Ru) 🏆	Widely available
'Rosette Delizy' (T)	EBls
◆ Rosie Larkin	See ***R.* Rosie Larkin = 'Fryyippee'**
§ 'Rosina' (Min)	EWar GCoc MGan
'Rosy Cheeks' (HT)	EWar LPlm MBur MFry MGan MMor
Rosy Cushion (S/GC) 🏆	CSam ENot EWar GCoc IDic IHar IHos MAus MGan MHlr SApu SPer SRum WAct WHCG WOVN WWeb
Rosy Future (F/Patio)	EWar SApu
'Rosy Mantle' (Cl)	CB&S EWar GCoc LPlm MGan SPer
§ Rote Max Graf (GC)	EBls ENot EWar MJon WAct
'Rouletii' (MinCh)	EBls
'Roundelay' (S)	EBls MAus
Roxburghe Rose (HT)	GCoc
roxburghii (S)	CB&S MMat NSty WAct WHCG
– f. ***normalis*** (S)	CFee EBls MAus
– 'Plena' (S)	See ***R. roxburghii* f. *roxburghii***
§ – f. ***roxburghii*** (d/S)	MAus
'Royal Albert Hall' (HT)	EBls GCoc
Royal Baby (F/Min)	MBur
§ Royal Brompton Rose (HT)	EWar
'Royal Gold' (Cl)	EBls EWar IHos LPlm LStr MBri MFry MGan MMor NPri NRog SRum WStI
'Royal Highness' (HT)	CGro EBls MGan MHay SRum
'Royal Occasion' (F)	SPer
Royal Romance (HT)	EWar SJus
Royal Salute (Min)	EWar MJon MMat NRog SPer
'Royal Smile' (HT)	EBls
Royal Volunteer (HT)	GCoc

Royal William (HT) 🏆	CDoC CGro ELan ESha EWar GGre LGod LPlm LStr MAus MBur MGan MJon MMat MMor NPri SApu SJus SPer SRum
Royal Worcester (S)	MJon WGer WHow WWeb
'Rubens' (HP)	EBls
§ ***rubiginosa*** 🏆	CAgr CB&S CKin EBls ENot GPoy ILis LBuc LHol MAus MMat SPer WAct WMou WRTC
rubra	See ***R. gallica***
rubrifolia	See ***R. glauca***
– 'Carmenetta'	See **R. 'Carmenetta'**
'Rubrotincta'	See **R. 'Hebe's Lip'**
rubus (Ra)	MAus
¶ – SF 579 (Ra)	ISea
♦ Ruby Anniversary	See **R. Ruby Anniversary = 'Harbonny'**
♦ Ruby Celebration	See **R. Ruby Celebration = 'Peawinner'**
'Ruby Pendant' (Min)	MHay
'Ruby Wedding' (HT)	CB&S EBre ELan EWar GCoc GGre IHar LGod LPlm LStr MAus MBri MECR MFry MGan MHay MJon MMat MMor NBat NRog SApu SJus SPer SRum WOVN WWeb
'Ruga' (Ra)	EBls MAus
rugosa (Ru)	CAgr CPer EPla IHos ISea LBuc LHol MAus MBri NWea WRTC WStI
– 'Alba' (Ru) 🏆	CB&S CDoC CHad EBls ECGP ELan EWar IHos LBuc LStr MAus MBri MMat NRoo NSty NWea SJus SPer SRum WAct WOVN WRTC
'Rugosa Atropurpurea' (Ru)	NRog
rugosa var. ***kamtschatica***	See ***R. rugosa*** var. ***ventenatiana***
rugosa rubra (Ru) 🏆	CB&S CDoC CTri EWar LBuc MFry MMat NRoo NSty SPer SRum WAct
rugosa 'Scabrosa'	See **R. 'Scabrosa'**
'Rugspin' (Ru)	WAct
§ Rugul (Min)	MFry MGan MJon NPri WGer
'Ruhm von Steinfurth' (HP)	EBls
Running Maid (S/GC)	MAus WAct
'Ruskin' (RuxHP)	EBls MAus
'Russelliana' (Ra)	EBls EMFP MAus WAct WHCG WRha
Rutland (Min/GC)	ENot EWar MMat NPri WOVN
'Sadler's Wells' (S)	EBls
'Safrano' (T)	EBls
Saint Boniface (F/Patio)	ESha MMat
¶ 'Saint Catherine' (Ra)	CFee
Saint Cecilia (S)	EBar ELan EWar IHos MAus MHlr MJon SJus SRum
Saint Dunstan's Rose (S)	MBri MJon NBat SApu SPer
Saint Helena (F)	EBee
Saint John's Rose	See ***R.*** × ***richardii***
Saint Mark's Rose	See **R. 'Rose d'Amour'**
'Saint Nicholas' (D)	EBls MAus WHCG
'Saint Prist de Breuze' (Ch)	EBls
Saint Swithun (S)	EMFP GQui MAus MJon SWCr
'Salet' (DPMo)	EBls MAus WHCG
Sally Holmes (S) 🏆	CHad EBls GCoc IHar MAus MBri MFry MGan MJon MMat SApu WAct WHCG
Sally's Rose (HT)	EBee GCoc SApu WWeb
♦ Salmo	See **R. Salmo = 'Poulnoeu'**
¶ 'Salmon' (Cl)	EWar
Samaritan (HT)	CDoC SApu SJus
sancta	See ***R.*** × ***richardii***
'Sanders' White Rambler' (Ra) 🏆	CHad CRHN EBls EBre EMFP LGre LHol MAus MGan MJon MMor NBat NRog NSty SMad SPer SRum WAct WHCG WHow WWeb
'Sandringham Centenary' (HT)	EBls
'Sanguinea'	See ***R.*** × ***odorata*** **Sanguinea Group**
Sarabande (F)	MGan
§ Sarah (HT)	COtt EWar MBur MJon SApu
¶ Sarah Jo (HT)	COtt
Sarah Robinson (Min)	MJon
'Sarah van Fleet'	CGro EBls EBre ENot GCoc LStr MAus MFry MGan MHlr MMat MMor NRog NSty SApu SPer SRum WAct WOVN WWeb
Sarah, Duchess of York	See **R. Sunseeker**
Satchmo (F)	ESha EWar IHos
§ White Cloud = 'Savacloud' (Min)	ENot MBri MFry MMat SApu
Savoy Hotel (HT) 🏆	EWar GCoc GGre LGod LStr MAus MBri MBur MFry MGan MJon MMat SApu SJus SPer
§ 'Scabrosa' (Ru) 🏆	EBls EMFP GCoc IHos MAus MGan MJon MMat WAct WHCG WOVN
'Scarlet Fire'	See **R. 'Scharlachglut'**
§ Scarlet Gem (Min)	ELan EWar MGan MMor
'Scarlet Glow'	See **R. 'Scharlachglut'**
Scarlet Meidiland (S/GC)	EWar MGan WOVN
♦ Scarlet Patio	See **R. Scarlet Patio = 'Kortingle'**
'Scarlet Pimpernel'	See **R. Scarlet Gem**
Scarlet Queen Elizabeth (F)	CB&S CGro EBls GGre MBur MJon MMor NPri SRum WStI
'Scarlet Showers' (Cl)	MGan
Scarletta (Min)	IHos
'Scented Air' (F)	MGan SPer
§ 'Scharlachglut' (ClS) 🏆	EBls ELan ENot MGan MMat NSty SApu SPer WAct WHCG WSHC
* ***schmidtiana***	CFee
'Schneelicht' (Ru)	EBls MAus
Schneewittchen	See **R. Iceberg = 'Korbin'**
§ 'Schneezwerg' (Ru) 🏆	EBls EBre ELan ENot GCoc IHar IHos IOrc MAus MGan MJon MMat NSty SApu SPer SPla WAct WHCG WOVN WWeb
'Schoolgirl' (Cl)	CB&S CGro EBls EBre ELan EWar GGre IHos LGod LPlm LStr MBri MECR MFry MGan MJon MMat MMor NRog SApu SPer SRum WFar WWeb
'Scintillation' (S/GC)	EBls MAus
Scotch Rose	See ***R. pimpinellifolia***
♦ Scotch Yellow	See ***R.*** × ***harisonii*** **'Williams' Double Yellow'**
'Scotch Yellow' (HT)	MJon
Scotland's Trust (HT)	GCoc
Scottish Special (Min/Patio)	GCoc MJon
§ Baby Love = 'Scrivluv' (Patio)	MAus MFry MHay MJon MMat
'Sea Pearl' (F)	MGan

'Seagull' (Ra) 🏆	CWan EBls EBre ELan EMFP EWar GGre LGod LStr MAus MECR MGan MHlr MJon NBus NRog NSty SPer WAct WGer WHCG
§ 'Sealing Wax' (*moyesii* hybrid)	EBls MAus WAct
Selfridges (HT)	MMat NBat
'Semiplena'	See ***R.*** **×** ***alba*** **'Alba Semiplena'**
'Sénateur Amic' (Cl)	EBls
§ ***serafinoi***	GCal
sericea (S)	CFee MAus MBal NGre WHCG
– BC 9355 (S)	GCra
– 'Heather Muir'	See ***R.*** **'Heather Muir' (*sericea* hybrid)**
– var. ***morrisonensis*** B&SWJ 1549	NGre
§ – subsp. ***omeiensis*** f. ***pteracantha*** (S)	EBls ELan EMFP ENot EWar MAus MGan MMat NRog NSty SApu SMad SPer WAct
– 'Red Wing'	See ***R.*** **'Red Wing' (*hugonis* hybrid)**
– SF 95049	ISea
§ ***setigera***	EBls MAus
setipoda	EBls MAus WAct WHCG WWat
'Seven Seas' (F)	MBur
Seven Sisters Rose	See ***R. multiflora*** **'Grevillei'**
◆ Sexy Rexy	See ***R.*** **Sexy Rexy = 'MacRexy'**
§ 'Shailer's White Moss' (CeMo) 🏆	CDoC EBls EWar MAus MGan MMat NRog NSty SFam SJus WHCG
Sharifa Asma (S)	CAbP EBre EWar IHar LStr MAus MHlr MJon MMat NFla NPri SPer WAct WWeb
Sheer Delight (Patio)	EWar
Sheila's Perfume (HT/F)	EBee EWar GCoc GGre LPlm LStr MGan MJon NRog SApu SJus SPer
'Shepherd's Delight' (F)	MGan
¶ ***sherardii***	WUnd
Sheri Anne (Min)	MAus
Shine On (Patio)	COtt GCoc IDic MBri MFry MJon WWeb
Shirley Spain (F)	GCoc
Shocking Blue (F)	EBee LPlm MGan MJon MMat SPer
Shona (F)	EWar IDic SApu
'Shot Silk' (HT)	EBls GCoc MAus MBur MGan
Shrewsbury Show (HT)	MFry
'Shropshire Lass' (S)	MAus SPer SWCr
'Sightsaver' (HT)	MFry
Silver Anniversary (HT)	COtt EBee ELan EWar GGre LGod LStr MFry MGan MJon MMat SApu SCoo
Silver Jubilee (HT) 🏆	CB&S CDoC CGro EBls EBre ELan ESha EWar GCoc GGre IHos LGod LPlm LStr MAus MBri MBur MFry MGan MHay MJon MMat MMor NBat NRog SApu SJus SPer SRum WWeb
'Silver Lining' (HT)	EBls MAus MBur SWCr
'Silver Moon' (Cl)	EBls MAus
'Silver Tips' (Min)	MAus
'Silver Wedding' (HT)	EBls EBre EWar GCoc GGre IHar LPlm MBur MECR MFry MGan MHay MJon MMor NRog SApu SPer SRum WOVN WWeb
Simba (HT)	MBri MGan MMat SApu SJus

Simon Robinson (Min/GC)	EBls MJon
§ Jenny Charlton = 'Simway' (HT)	NBat
Singin' in the Rain (F)	MFry MJon SApu
sinowilsonii	See ***R. longicuspis sinowilsonii***
'Sir Cedric Morris' (Ra)	EBls ELan
'Sir Clough' (S)	MAus
'Sir Edward Elgar' (Cl)	EBls EBre MAus MJon NPri
'Sir Frederick Ashton' (HT)	EBls
'Sir Lancelot' (F)	MGan
'Sir Neville Marriner' (F)	NBat
Sir Walter Raleigh (S)	EWar MAus MBri
Sir William Leech (HT)	NBat
§ 'Sissinghurst Castle' (G)	EBls SBid
'Sleepy' (Poly)	MGan
Smarty (S/GC)	EBls ENot IDic IHar MAus MGan MJon SApu SPer WAct WOVN
§ Richard Buckley = 'Smitshort' (F)	MBur
Smooth Angel (HT)	CGro ELan EWar LGod LStr MGan MHay SApu
Smooth Lady (HT)	ELan EWar LGod LStr MGan MHay
Smooth Melody (F)	EWar LStr MHay
Smooth Prince (HT)	ELan EWar LGod LStr MGan MHay
◆ Smooth Romance	See ***R.*** **Smooth Romance = 'Hadromance'**
Smooth Satin (HT)	EWar LStr MHay
Smooth Velvet (HT)	CGro EWar LGod LStr MGan MHay
'Sneezy' (Poly)	MGan
Snow Carpet (Min/GC) 🏆	EBls ENot GCoc IHos MAus MFry MJon MMat WAct
'Snow Dwarf'	See ***R.*** **'Schneezwerg'**
Snowgoose (F)	MAus MJon
'Snow Queen'	See ***R.*** **'Frau Karl Druschki'**
Snow Sunblaze (Min)	SPer WWeb
Snow White (HT)	MBri MJon
Snowball (Min/GC)	MJon
'Snowdon' (Ru)	EBls MAus
'Snowdrift'	WHCG
Snowdrop (Min/Patio)	MFry
'Snowflake' (Ra)	WHCG
'Snowline' (F)	EWar MGan SPer
'Soldier Boy' (Cl)	WHCG
Solitaire (HT)	EWar MBri MJon SApu WFar WWeb
'Sombreuil' (ClT)	See ***R.*** **'Climbing Sombreuil'**
'Sophie's Perpetual' (ClCh)	EBls ENot MAus MGan MHlr MMat NFla SJus SPer WAct
soulieana 🏆	EBls MAus MMat WCot WKif
'Soupert et Notting' (PoMo)	EBls MAus MHlr SBid SPer
'Southampton' (F) 🏆	EBee EBls EWar GGre IHar LStr MAus MGan MMor NPri NRog SApu SPer
'Souvenir d'Alphonse Lavallée' (ClHP)	EBls WHCG
§ 'Souvenir de Brod'	See ***R.*** **'Erinnerung an Brod'**
'Souvenir de Claudius Denoyel' (ClHT) 🏆	CHad EBls MAus MMat NRog SPer SSoC
'Souvenir de François Gaulain' (T)	EBls
'Souvenir de Jeanne Balandreau' (HP)	EBls

'Souvenir de la Malmaison' (Bb) EBls EBre ENot EOrc GCoc IHar IHos IOrc MAus MGan MHlr MMat NFla NSty SJus SPer WAct WWeb
'Souvenir de la Malmaison' (ClBb) See ***R.* 'Climbing Souvenir de la Malmaison'**
'Souvenir de Madame Léonie Viennot' (ClT) COtt EBls MAus NSty
'Souvenir de Philémon Cochet' (Ru) EBls MAus
'Souvenir de Pierre Vibert' (DPMo) EBls
'Souvenir de Saint Anne's' (Bb) ♀ CHad EBls IHar MAus WAct WHCG WHow
'Souvenir d'Elise Vardon' (T) EBls
¶ 'Souvenir di Castagneto' MRav
'Souvenir du Docteur Jamain' (ClHP) CHad EBls EMFP LStr MAus MHlr MMat NSty SFam SJus SPer SWCr WAct WHCG
'Souvenir du Président Carnot' (HT) EBls MAus
'Souvenir d'un Ami' (T) EBls
spaldingii See ***R. nutkana*** var. ***hispida***
Spangles (F) MBur MGan
'Spanish Beauty' See ***R.* 'Madame Grégoire Staechelin'**
Sparkling Scarlet (Ra) EBre ELan EWar LPlm MGan WWeb
'Sparrieshoop' (ClS) EWar
Special Occasion (HT) EWar MFry
'Spectabilis' (Ra) EBls MAus WHCG
'Spek's Yellow' (HT) CB&S EBls
'Spencer' See ***R.* 'Enfant de France'**
§ Lovely Fairy = 'Spevu' IDic MBri MJon WAct
spinosissima See ***R. pimpinellifolia***
§ Spirit of Youth (HT) SApu
§ 'Splendens' (Ra) CHad EBls ELan MAus SLPl
'Spong' (G) EBls MAus WAct
'Stacey's Star' (Patio) NBat
§ 'Stanwell Perpetual' (PiH) EBls EMFP ENot EOrc EWar GCoc IHos LStr MAus MHlr MMat NSty SApu SPer WAct WHCG WOVN WWeb
Star Child (F) EWar
¶ 'Star of Waltham' (HP) WHCG
◆ Stardust See ***R.* Stardust = 'Peavandyke'**
Starina (Min) EWar MGan
'Stars 'n' Stripes' (Min) LGod LPlm MAus MFry
Stella (HT) EBls MGan
§ ***stellata*** var. ***mirifica*** EBls MAus MGan MMat
'Stephanie Diane' (HT) LPlm MHay
'Sterling Silver' (HT) EBls LStr MAus MGan
Strawberry Fayre (Min/Patio) COtt EBre GCoc MFry MJon NBat WWeb
'Strawberry Ice' (F) MJon
subcanina MSto
subcollina MSto
Sue Lawley (F) MBri MGan MJon NRog
Sue Ryder (F) EWar
Suffolk (S/GC) EBre ENot EWar GCoc IHos LGod LPlm LStr MAus MGan MHlr MMat NPri SApu SJus SPer SRum WAct WHow WOVN WRHF
suffulta See ***R. arkansana*** var. ***suffulta***
Suma (GC) ♀ EWar GCoc GGre LGod LPlm MFry MJon SApu SJus WAct WOVN
Summer Dream (HT) LStr MAus MFry SApu SJus SWCr
Summer Fragrance (HT) GCoc GGre MGan MJon
Summer Holiday (HT) MBur MMor SPer
Summer Lady (HT) MBri MBur MJon SApu
Summer Love (F) IHar MJon MMor
Summer Sérénade (F) MJon
'Summer Sunrise' (GC) EBls
'Summer Sunset' (GC) EBls
◆ Summer Sunset (Min) See ***R.* Summer Sunset = 'Brisun'**
Summer Wine (Cl) ♀ EBee EWar IHos MBri MGan MJon MMat NBat SApu SJus SMrm SPer
Sun Hit (Patio) ENot GGre MMat MRav
'Sunblaze' See ***R.* Orange Sunblaze**
Sunblest (HT) CTri ESha EWar GGre IHos LPlm MBri MBur MFry MMor NPri NRog SRum WWeb
Sunderland Supreme (HT) NBat
Sunmaid (Min) MJon
Sunny Sunblaze (Min) SJus
'Sunrise' (Cl) EWar GCoc MBur MFry MJon MMat SApu WGer
§ Sunseeker (F/Patio) EPfP GGre IDic LGod MJon
◆ Sunset Boulevard (F) See ***R.* Sunset Boulevard = 'Harbabble'**
Sunset Song (HT) ESha GCoc
'Sunshine' (Poly) MGan
'Sunsilk' (F) MBri MFry
Super Star (HT) CB&S CGro EBls EBre ESha EWar GCoc IHar LPlm LStr MAus MGan MJon MMat MMor NPri NRog SRum WWeb
'Super Sun' (HT) ESha SWCr
'Surf Rider' (S) MMor
'Surpasse Tout' (G) EBls MAus MRav WHCG
§ 'Surpassing Beauty of Woolverstone' (ClHP) EBls WHCG
Surrey (GC) ♀ EBre ELan ENot EWar GCoc IHos LFis LGod LPlm LStr MAus MECR MFry MGan MHlr MJon MMat SApu SJus SPer SPla SRum WAct WOVN WStI
Susan Hampshire (HT) EBls EWar MGan SRum
Sussex (GC) EBre ENot EWar GCoc LPlm LStr MBur MFry MGan MHlr MJon MMat MMor SApu SJus SPer SPla SRum WAct WHow WOVN WRHF
'Sutter's Gold' (HT) EBls MAus MBur MGan NRog
Swan (S) EBee EWar MAus MJon
'Swan Lake' (Cl) EBls EBre ELan ESha EWar GGre IHos LGod LStr MBri MBur MFry MGan MHlr MMat MMor NBat SPer SRum WWeb
'Swanland Gem' (F) NBat
Swany (Min/GC) EBls ELan EWar GGre IHos MAus MGan MMat SApu SPer SRum WAct WHCG WOVN
'Sweet Bouquet' (HT) MBur
Sweet Dream (Patio) ♀ CDoC CGro EBre ELan ESha EWar GCoc GGre LGod LPlm LStr MAus MBri MBur MECR MFry MGan MJon MMor NBat SApu SJus SPer SRum WOVN WWeb
'Sweet Fairy' (Min) EFol LPlm
Sweet Juliet (S) CAbP EBls EBre EWar IHar LGod LPlm MAus MBri MHlr MJon NBat NPri SApu SPer WAct WHow WOVN WWeb

Sweet Magic (Min/Patio) 🏆	CDoC CGro EBre ESha EWar GCoc GGre IDic IHar IHos LGod LPlm LStr MBri MBur MECR MFry MGan MJon MMat NBat SApu SJus SPer SRum WWeb
'Sweet Memories' (Patio)	COtt CTri EBre EPfP EWar GCoc LStr MJon SCoo SPla SWCr WGer
Sweet Nell (F)	LGod
Sweet Promise (GC)	MGan
'Sweet Repose' (F)	MAus MGan
Sweet Symphony (Min)	EBre MBri MFry MJon
'Sweet Velvet' (F)	MGan
¶ 'Sweet Wonder' (Patio)	COtt
N Sweetheart (HT)	GCoc MGan SJus SWCr
sweginzowii	GCal MAus MMat
– 'Macrocarpa'	EBls
'Sydonie' (HP)	EBls
Sympathie (ClHT)	IHar IHos LPlm MFry MGan MMat MMor SJus SPer SRum
Symphony (S)	CGro EWar MJon WAct
taiwanensis	CFil
'Talisman' (HT)	EBls
Tall Story (S/GC) 🏆	EBls EWar IDic MJon SApu SRms SRum WHCG WOVN
'Tallyho' (HT)	EBls
'Tamora' (S)	MAus
§ Golden Quill = 'Tanellog' (F)	MJon
Tango (F) 🏆	EWar LPlm MBri MJon
§ Harewood = 'Taninaso' (Patio/F)	ECle MJon SApu
§ Broadlands = 'Tanmirson' (GC)	CSam ECle MBur MGan MJon SApu WGer WHCG WHow
§ Blenheim = 'Tanmurse' (GC)	ECle MBur MGan MJon SApu WOVN
§ Chatsworth = 'Tanotax' (Patio/F)	CGro EBee ECle EWar GCoc LGod LPlm LStr MBri MBur MFry MGan MJon NBat SApu SCoo SPer WWeb
§ 'Tausendschön' (Ra)	EBls
'Tea Rambler' (Ra)	EBls NSty
Tear Drop (Min/Patio)	IDic LStr MFry MGan MJon NBat SApu SPer SRum
Ted Gore (F)	NBat
Teeny Weeny (Min)	MJon
'Telstar' (F)	MGan
'Temple Bells' (Min/GC)	EBls MAus NRog
Tender Loving Care (F)	EWar MHay NBat
'Tenerife' (HT)	ESha WStI
Tequila Sunrise (HT) 🏆	CTri ESha EWar GCoc GGre IDic IHar LPlm LStr MBri MBur MFry MGan MJon MMat NBat SApu SJus SPer
'Texas Centennial' (HT)	EBls
§ Thais (HT)	EBls
'Thalia'	MAus
♦ Thank You	See ***R.* Thank You = 'Chesdeep'**
The Alexandra Rose (S)	EWar MAus SWCr
'The Bishop' (CexG)	EBls MAus
'The Bride' (T)	EBls NSty
♦ The Cheshire Regiment	See ***R.* The Cheshire Regiment = 'Fryzebedee'**
The Children's Rose (F)	SApu SRum
'The Colwyn Rose'	See ***R.* Colwyn Bay**
The Countryman (S)	CAbP EBre EWar IHar MAus MFry MHlr NPri SJus
The Coxswain (HT)	GCoc
The Dark Lady (S)	EBre GGre IHar IHos MAus MBri MJon MTis NBus NPri SChu SJus
'The Doctor' (HT)	EBls MAus MGan
The Dove (F)	MGan
'The Ednaston Rose' (Cl)	WHCG
'The Fairy' (Poly) 🏆	CHad EBls EBre ELan ENot EWar GGre IHos IOrc LGod LPlm LStr MAus MBur MECR MFry MGan MHlr MJon MMat MMor NRog NSty SApu SPer SRum WAct WHCG WOVN WSHC
The Flower Arranger (F)	MFry MJon
'The Garland' (Ra) 🏆	EBls EBre MAus MHlr MMat NPri NSty SFam SPer SPla WAct WHCG
The Herbalist (S)	MAus
'The Holt' (F)	EKMF LStr
'The Honorable Lady Lindsay' (S)	NSty
'The Knight' (S)	NSty
The Lady (S) 🏆	EBee GCoc MAus MBur MFry MJon
§ The McCartney Rose (HT)	EWar GCoc GGre LPlm LStr MJon MMat SApu SJus SPer
'The New Dawn'	See ***R.* 'New Dawn'**
The Nun (S)	MAus
The Observer (HT)	MFry
The Painter (F)	EWar LStr MBur MFry MJon SApu
The Pilgrim (S)	CAbP CHad EBre EWar IHar MAus MBri MHlr MJon MTis SJus SPer WHow
The Prince (S)	CAbP EBar EBre EWar MAus MJon MTis NPri WHow
'The Prioress' (S)	MAus
§ 'The Queen Elizabeth' (F) 🏆	CB&S CDoC CGro EBls EBre ESha EWar GCoc GGre IHos LGod LPlm LStr MAus MBri MBur MECR MFry MGan MHay MJon MMat MMor NRog SApu SPer SRum WWeb
The Reeve (S)	MAus
'The Royal Brompton Rose'	See ***R.* Royal Brompton Rose**
The Seckford Rose (S)	ENot MJon MMat
The Squire (S)	MAus WAct
The Times Rose (F) 🏆	EWar IHos LGod LStr MGan MJon MMat SJus SPer
The Valois Rose (R)	MMat
'The Wife of Bath' (S)	IHar MAus MBri
'Thelma' (Ra)	EBls MAus
'Thérèse Bugnet' (Ru)	EBls
'Thisbe' (HM)	EBls MAus SPer WAct WHCG
Thomas Barton (HT)	LStr SApu
Thora Hird (F)	MAus
'Thousand Beauties'	See ***R.* 'Tausendschön'**
Threepenny Bit Rose	See ***R. elegantula* 'Persetosa'**
'Tiara' (RH)	SRum
♦ Tiger Cub	See ***R.* Tiger Cub = 'Poulcub'**
Tigris® (*persica* hybrid) (S)	WAct
'Till Uhlenspiegel' (RH)	EBls
'Tina Turner' (HT)	EWar MBur MJon NBat
'Tintinara' (HT)	GCoc IDic MFry
Tip Top (F/Patio)	CB&S CGro CTri EBls ELan EWar GCoc IHos LFis MBri MFry MGan MMor NRog SPer SRum WStI
'Tipo Ideale'	See ***R.* × *odorata* 'Mutabilis'**
'Tipsy Imperial Concubine' (T)	EBls
♦ Tivoli	See ***R.* Tivoli = 'Poulduce'**
'Toby Tristam' (Ra)	WWat
'Tom Foster' (HT)	NBat

tomentosa	MSto
Too Hot to Handle (S)	MJon SApu WGer
Top Marks (Min/Patio)	CDoC EBre EWar GCoc LGod LPlm LStr MAus MBri MBur MFry MGan MJon MMat MMor NBat SApu SCoo SJus SRum WStI WWeb
'Topeka' (F)	SRum
◆ Toprose	See ***R.* Toprose = 'Cocgold'**
Topsi (F/Patio)	EWar IHos MJon MMor NPri SPer SRum
Torvill and Dean (HT)	MJon NRog
Toulouse-Lautrec (S)	SApu
§ 'Tour de Malakoff' (Ce)	EBls IHar MAus MHlr SFam SPer WAct WHCG
Tournament of Roses (HT)	IDic MAus MJon
Toynbee Hall (F)	MMat
'Trade Winds' (HT)	MGan
Tradescant (S)	EBre IHar MAus MHlr NPri
◆ Tradition	See ***R.* Tradition = 'Korbeltin'**
Tranquility (HT)	MBur
'Treasure Trove' (Ra)	EBls EMFP IHar MAus MBur NPri SWCr WAct
◆ Trevor Griffiths	See ***R.* Trevor Griffiths = 'Ausold'**
'Tricolore de Flandre' (G)	EBls MAus
Trier (Ra)	EBls MAus MHlr MMat WHCG
'Trigintipetala' hort.	See ***R.* 'Professeur Emile Perrot'**
'Triomphe de l'Exposition' (HP)	MAus
'Triomphe du Luxembourg' (T)	EBls MAus
triphylla	See ***R.* × *beanii***
Troika (HT) 🏆	ESha IHar LStr MAus MBur MECR MFry MGan MHay MJon MMat SPer SRum
Troilus (S)	MAus
'Tropical Sunblaze' (Min/v)	MBri
Trumpeter (F) 🏆	ESha EWar GCoc IHar IHos LGod LPlm LStr MAus MBri MFry MGan MJon MMat NBat SApu SPer
'Tuscany' (G)	GCoc MAus SJus SPer WAct WHCG
'Tuscany Superb' (G) 🏆	CHad CPou EBls EMFP ENot EWar IHar IHos LHol MAus MHlr MMat NSty SPer WAct WHCG WHow WKif WSHC
¶ ***tuschetica***	MSto
Twenty One Again (HT)	GGre MBur MJon MRav SApu
'Twenty-fifth' (F)	EBls
Tynwald (HT)	EWar LStr MJon MMat SPer SWCr
'Typhoon' (HT)	IHar MBur MJon
'Ulrich Brunner Fils' (HP)	EBls MAus
'Uncle Bill' (HT)	EBls
Uncle Walter (HT)	EBls ESha NPri NRog SRum WStI
'UNICEF' (F)	GCoc
§ 'Unique Blanche' (Ce)	CPou EBee EBls MAus WHow
Valencia (HT)	EWar MBur MJon MMat NBat
Valentine Heart (F)	CDoC EBee IDic MFry MJon SApu SJus
'Vanguard' (Ru)	EBls
'Vanity' (HM)	EBls MAus SPer
'Variegata di Bologna' (Bb)	CHad EBee EBls EWar MAus MMat NSty WAct

'Veilchenblau' (Ra) 🏆	CHad EBls EBre ELan EWar LGod MAus MBri MBur MGan MHlr NSty SApu SJus SPer SRum WAct WHCG WHow WKif WSHC
Velvet Fragrance (HT)	EBee EWar GCoc LStr MAus MBur MFry MJon NBat SApu
'Venusta Pendula' (Ra)	EBls MAus
'Verschuren' (v)	ELan
versicolor	See ***R. gallica* 'Versicolor'**
'Vick's Caprice' (HP)	EBls MAus NSty
'Vicomtesse Pierre du Fou' (ClHT)	EBls MAus NSty
Victor Hugo	See ***R.* Spirit of Youth**
'Victoriana' (F)	MAus
Vidal Sassoon (HT)	EBee GCoc MBur MGan MJon MMat SApu
'Village Maid'	See ***R.* 'Centifolia Variegata'**
§ ***villosa***	EBls MAus MMat MSto NSty WUnd
– 'Duplex'	See ***R.* 'Wolley-Dod'**
§ 'Violacea' (G)	EBls
Violet Carson (F)	MAus MGan
'Violette' (Ra)	CHad EBls MAus NSty SPer WAct WHCG WHer
'Violinista Costa' (HT)	EBls
virginiana 🏆	CTri EBls GCal IHar MAus MGan MSte NWea SPer WHCG WHen WOVN
– 'Plena'	See ***R.* 'Rose d'Amour'**
'Virgo' (HT)	EBls
'Viridiflora'	See ***R.* × *odorata* 'Viridiflora'**
Vital Spark (F)	MGan
'Vivid' (Bourbon hybrid)	EBls
Voice of Thousands (F)	NBat
vosagiaca	MSto
'W.E. Lippiat' (HT)	EBls
Wandering Minstrel (F)	SApu
wardii* var. *culta	MAus
'Warley Jubilee' (F)	EWar
Warm Welcome (ClMin) 🏆	CDoC EBre EFol EWar GCoc GGre LGod LStr MAus MBri MBur MFry MJon MMat NBat SJus SMad SPer SSoC WWeb
Warm Wishes (HT)	CTri EBee EWar GCoc GGre LGod LPlm LStr MBur MFry MGan MJon NPri SApu WWeb
'Warrior' (F)	EWar MGan SPer
Warwick Castle (S)	EBar EBre MAus NBus NPri SPer
Warwickshire (GC)	ENot EWar MHlr MMat NPri WOVN
§ ***watsoniana***	EBls
webbiana	CPle EBls MAus WHCG
'Wedding Day' (Ra)	CDoC CHad EBls EBre ELan EWar IHar LHol LPlm LStr MAus MBri MBur MGan MJon MMat NBat NSty SApu SJus SPer SRum WAct WHCG WHow WWeb
'Wee Barbie' (Min)	SApu
'Wee Cracker' (Patio)	GCoc
Wee Jock (F/Patio)	GCoc GGre LStr SWCr
'Weetwood' (Ra)	MAus SPer
'Weisse aus Sparrieshoop' (S)	MGan
◆ Weisse Wolcke®	See ***R.* White Cloud = 'Korstacha'**
'Wembley Stadium' (HT)	MGan

'Wendy Cussons' (HT)	CB&S CGro EBls EWar GCoc IHos LPlm MAus MBur MECR MGan MJon MMor NRog SApu SPer SRum WWeb
Wenlock (S)	CSam EBar EBre EWar GGre IHar MAus NPri SPer
Westerland™ (F/S) ♀	MGan MJon MMat WGer
'Westfield Star' (HT)	MAus
'Whisky Gill' (HT)	MGan
Whisky Mac (HT)	CB&S CGro EBls EBre ELan ESha EWar GCoc GGre IHos LGod LPlm LStr MAus MBri MBur MFry MGan MJon MMat MMor NRog SApu SPer SRum WWeb
'White Bath'	See ***R.* 'Shailer's White Moss'**
White Bells (Min/GC)	EBls ENot EWar IHos LStr MAus MGan MMat SPer WAct WHCG WOVN
'White Cécile Brunner'	See ***R.* 'Cécile Brünner, White'**
'White Christmas' (HT)	ELan MBur MGan SRum
◆White Cloud (S/ClHT)	See ***R.* White Cloud = 'Korstacha'**
White Cloud™ (Min)	See ***R.* White Cloud = 'Savacloud'**
'White Cockade' (Cl) ♀	CB&S EBls GCoc LPlm MFry MGan SApu SJus SPer WHCG
¶ 'White Diamond' (S)	IDic MAus
White Flower Carpet (GC)	IHar MFry MMat SCoo SPer WGer WWeb
'White Grootendorst' (Ru)	EBls MAus WAct
White Max Graf (GC)	MAus
White Meidiland (S/GC)	EWar MGan WOVN
White Moss	See ***R.* 'Shailer's White Moss'**
§ 'White Pet' (Poly) ♀	CHad EMFP GCoc IHos LStr MBri MBur MGan MHlr MJon SApu SJus SPer SPla WAct WHow WSHC
White Provence	See ***R.* 'Unique Blanche'**
'White Queen Elizabeth' (F)	EBls SRum
White Rose of York	See ***R.* × *alba* 'Alba Semiplena'**
'White Spray' (F)	EBls
'White Wings' (HT)	CHad EBls MAus MGan NSty SPer WAct WHCG WKif
Whitley Bay (F)	NBat
N ***wichurana*** (Ra)	EBls MAus WHCG
* – 'Nana'	MRav
– 'Variegata' (Ra)	CB&S CSWP EBar EBee EFol EHoe ELan EPot MAus MPla NHol SCoo SDry WPat WPyg WRTC WWeb
* – 'Variegata Nana' (Ra)	LHop
'Wickwar' (Ra)	CSWP EBls ELan GCal MHlr WAct WCot WHCG
'Wilhelm' (HM) ♀	EBls IHar MAus MRav NSty WHCG
'Will Scarlet' (HM)	MAus
'Willhire Country' (F)	EBls
'William Allen Richardson' (N)	EBls MAus WHCG
'William and Mary' (S)	EBls
§ 'William Lobb' (CeMo) ♀	CHad EBls EBre ENot EOrc EWar GCoc GOrc IHar IHos IOrc MAus MGan MHlr MMat NFla NSty SApu SJus SPer SRum SSoC WAct WHCG WKif WWeb
'William Quarrier' (F)	GCoc
'William R. Smith' (T)	EBls
William Shakespeare (S)	CGro CTri ELan EWar GCoc GGre IHar IHos LStr MBri NBus SMad SPer SRum WStI
'William Tyndale' (Ra)	WHCG
'Williams' Double Yellow'	See ***R.* × *harisonii* 'Williams' Double Yellow'**
willmottiae	EBls MAus MGan MMat NSty SPer WAct WBod WHCG
Wiltshire (S/GC)	LStr MFry MJon MMat NPri SJus WHow WOVN
Wimi (HT)	EWar MGan MHay SApu
Winchester Cathedral (S)	CDoC CGro CHad EBls EBre EMFP EWar GGre IHar LGod LStr MAus MBri MHlr MJon SApu SChu SPer SPla SRum SSoC WOVN WWeb
◆Windflower	See ***R.* Windflower = 'Auscross'**
Windrush (S)	IHar MAus MBri SPer SWCr WAct WHCG
Wine and Dine (GC)	IDic
Winter Magic (Min)	MHay
× ***wintoniensis***	EHic WAct WHCG
Wise Portia (S)	MAus
Wishing (F/Patio)	GCoc IDic IHar MECR MFry MJon SApu WWeb
With Love (HT)	MJon SApu
'Woburn Abbey' (F)	CGro EBls GGre IHar MJon NPri NRog
§ 'Wolley-Dod' (S)	EBls MAus MRav WAct
'Woman and Home' (HT)	CBlo
◆Woman o'th North	See ***R.* Woman o'th North = 'Kirlon'**
'Woman's Hour' (F)	EBls
Woodland Sunbeam (Min/Patio)	MJon
'Woodrow's Seedling' (Cl)	MMor
Woods of Windsor (HT)	MMat
§ ***woodsii***	EBls MAus MMat SPer WHCG
– var. ***fendleri***	See ***R. woodsii***
'Woolverstone Church Rose'	See ***R.* 'Surpassing Beauty of Woolverstone'**
Wor Jackie (HT)	NBat
xanthina	EBls MGan MMat
§ – 'Canary Bird' (S) ♀	CGro EBls EBre ELan ENot EWar GCoc IOrc LGod LPlm LStr MAus MBri MMat NFla SApu SBod SJus SMad SPer SRum SWCr WAct WGer WHCG WHow WWeb
§ – f. ***hugonis*** ♀	EBls EFol ELan MAus MGan MMat NRog SPer WAct WHCG
¶ – var. ***spontanea***	IHar
'Xavier Olibo' (HP)	EBls
'Yellow Button' (S)	MAus MBri WAct
Yellow Charles Austin (S)	MAus MBri
'Yellow Cushion' (F)	EWar MAus
Yellow Dagmar Hastrup (Ru)	CTri EBee EBre MAus MBri MGan MHlr MJon SApu SJus SPer WAct WHCG WOVN
'Yellow Doll' (Min)	ELan EWar MAus MGan
'Yellow Pages' (HT)	MAus
'Yellow Patio' (Min/Patio)	LStr SWCr
'Yellow Ribbon' (F)	ESha
Yellow Scotch	See ***R.* × *harisonii* 'Williams' Double Yellow'**
Yellow Sunblaze (Min)	EWar IHos WWeb
Yesterday (Poly/F/S) ♀	EBls ESha EWar MAus MGan MMat SRum WHCG
'Yolande d'Aragon' (HP)	EBls
York and Lancaster	See ***R.* × *damascena* var. *versicolor***

Yorkshire Bank (HT)	MFry
'Yorkshire Lady' (HT)	MHay NBat
Yorkshire Sunblaze (Min)	EWar
Young Quinn (HT)	MBur
Young Venturer (F)	EWar
Yves Piaget	See ***R.*** **Royal Brompton Rose**
'Yvonne Rabier' (Poly) 🏆	EBls LStr MAus MHlr MMat NSty SPer WAct WHCG WHow
Zambra (F)	CB&S
'Zénobia' (Mo)	EBls
'Zéphirine Drouhin' (Bb) 🏆	Widely available
§ 'Zigeunerknabe' (S) 🏆	EBee EBls EMFP ENot EWar MAus NSty SPer WAct WHCG
Zitronenfalter (S)	MGan
'Zweibrücken' (Cl)	MGan
◆ Zwergkönigin	See ***R.*** **Dwarf Queen '82**

ROSCOEA (Zingiberaceae)

alpina	CBro CGra CPBP EBre GDra IBlr MTho NHol NWCA SBar SBla SWas WChr WCru WOMN WSan
auriculata	CAvo CBro CDoC CFir EBee IBlr LWoo MTho NHar NHol SBla SCro WChr WCot WCru WPyg WThi
'Beesiana'	CFir CRDP EBee EBre ECha ERos IBlr LAma LBow MDun MTho NHar NHol NPri SHig WChr WCot WCru WPyg
'Beesiana' white	EBar LWoo NHol
capitata	See ***R. scillifolia***
cautleyoides 🏆	CAvo CBro CChu CGle CRDP EBre EDAr EHyt EOrc EPot GDra LAma LBow MDun MNrw MTho NHar NHol NRog SAlw SAxl SHig SMad SMrm SPer WChr WCru WPyg WSan WThi
– 'Grandiflora'	EPot
– x ***humeana***	IBlr
¶ – hybrid	NGre
– 'Kew Beauty'	EBre MTho SAxl SBla
humeana 🏆	CBro CDec CFir CPea EHyt LAma LWoo NHar SAxl WChr WCru
§ ***purpurea***	CBro CChu CGle CRDP EBre ELan ERos GCal LAma LBow MDun MFir MUlv NBir NHar NHol SPer WChr WCot WCru WOMN WPyg WThi WWin
– var. ***procera***	See ***R. purpurea***
§ ***scillifolia***	CBro CFir CRDP EBee GCal LAma LBow MTho NBir NGre NHar NHol NMen NRog NTow SWas WChr WCru WThi
¶ – pink form	IBlr WChr
tibetica	SAxl

ROSMARINUS † (Lamiaceae)

* ***calabriensis***	WCHb
corsicus 'Prostratus'	See ***R. officinalis*** **Prostratus Group**
x ***lavandulaceus*** hort.	See ***R. officinalis*** **Prostratus Group**
– Noë	See ***R. eriocalyx***
officinalis	CArn CB&S CGle CLan CSev CShe ELan ENot ERav ESis GPoy GRei ISea LBuc LHol MBar MChe MPla MWat NFla NNor NSti SArc SIng SReu WOak WPLl WWin
– var. ***albiflorus***	CArn CSev EFou ELau ESis GAbr GPoy MBar MChe MPla NHHG NSti SChu SMac WCHb WEas WHer WOMN WPer WRTC WSHC WWye
§ – ***angustissimus*** 'Corsican Blue'	CArn GBar SCro SPer WPer
– 'Aureovariegatus'	See ***R. officinalis*** **'Aureus'**
§ – 'Aureus' (v)	CDec CLan CMil EFol ELau IBlr MHar NHHG SDry SEas SMad SUsu WByw WCHb WEas WHer WSel
§ – 'Benenden Blue'	CGle CSev EBar ECha GPoy LHop MChe MGos MWat NHHG NHar SAxl SBid SChu SDix SPan SPer STre WEas WSel WWat WWye
– 'Collingwood Ingram'	See ***R. officinalis*** **'Benenden Blue'**
– 'Corsicus Prostratus'	CB&S ELau SMac WSel
– dwarf blue	ELau MGra
– 'Fastigiatus'	See ***R. officinalis*** **'Miss Jessopp's Upright'**
– 'Fota Blue'	CArn CBod CMGP CSWP ELau GBar NHHG NHex NSti SAga SCro SIde WJek WWye
– 'Frimley Blue'	See ***R. officinalis*** **'Primley Blue'**
– 'Ginger-scented'	WRus
– 'Guilded'	See ***R. officinalis*** **'Aureus'**
– 'Gunnel's Upright'	GBar WRha
– 'Jackman's Prostrate'	CB&S EBee ECtt NHar WSel
– 'Lady in White'	CKni EFou ELan EPfP SPer WWat
– ***lavandulaceus***	See ***R. officinalis*** **Prostratus Group**
–'Lilies Blue'	GPoy
– 'Lockwood Variety'	WPer
– 'Majorca Pink'	CB&S CDec CSam EFol ELau GBar LHol MPla NSti SIde SPer SSoC WCHb WOMN WPer WRTC WWat WWye
– 'McConnell's Blue'	CArn CDoC CLTr CLan EBre ELan ELau GAbr MAsh MGos MWat SDry SPan WCHb WGer WPer WWat WWye
* – 'Miss Jessopp's Prostrate'	MGra
§ – 'Miss Jessopp's Upright' 🏆	CArn CB&S CShe EBre ELan ENot GAbr GPoy LHol MBal MGos MWat NHHG NHar NMir NNor NSti SMad SPer SPla SSta WAbe WBod WGwG WSel WWat
§ – 'Primley Blue'	CArn CChe CFee CSam CSev CWSG ELau EMil GBar LBlm LHol MChe MRav NHHG NHar NSti SBid SChu SMac SMer WCHb WHer WOak WPer WWye
§ – Prostratus Group 🏆	CArn CB&S CLan CSev CShe CTrw EFol ELau EMil MChe NHHG NSti NWCA SArc SPer SRms SSoC SUsu SWas WHar WOMN WOak WPer WRus WWat

– f. *pyramidalis*	See ***R. officinalis* 'Miss Jessopp's Upright'**
– *repens*	See ***R. officinalis* Prostratus Group**
– 'Roseus'	CArn CHan CWit EFol ELan ELau EMil GPoy LHop MChe NHHG NHar NSti SChu SEas SMad SSoC WEas WHer WPer WRTC WWat WWye
– 'Russell's Blue'	WHer
– 'Severn Sea' 🏆	CArn CB&S CBot CGle CHan CSev CShe EBar ECtt ELan GPoy LHol LHop NHHG NNor NSti SPer WAbe WEas WHil WPer WWat
– 'Sissinghurst Blue' 🏆	CArn CMGP CSev CShe ECha ELan ELau EMil ERav LHol MAsh MSta SBid SPer WCHb WRHF WSel WWat WWye
– 'Sudbury Blue'	ELau GBar MChe MGra NHHG NRoo NSti WEas WJek
– 'Trusty'	EBee ECtt EFou ELan ELau ERav LHop LRHS WPer
– 'Tuscan Blue'	CDoC CSWP ECGP ECot ELau EMil EPri GBar MWat NFla NHex SDry SIde SMer WCHb WHer WJek WPer WRha WWat WWye
– 'Variegatus'	See ***R. officinalis* 'Aureus'**
– 'Vicomte de Noailles'	ERea
repens	See ***R. officinalis* Prostratus Group**

ROSTRINUCULA (Lamiaceae)

dependens Guiz 18	CBot SMac

ROSULARIA (Crassulaceae)

acuminata	See ***R. alpestris*** subsp. ***alpestris***
§ *aizoon*	ESis MFos
alba	See ***R. sedoides***
alpestris	MSte
§ *chrysantha*	EBur ESis MBro NGre NMen NNrd SIng SSmi WFar WPer
– Number 1	CWil
crassipes	See ***Rhodiola wallichiana***
hissarica K 92.380	MBro
§ *muratdaghensis*	EBur MBro NGre NMen
pallida A. Berger	See ***R. chrysantha***
– Stapf	See ***R. aizoon***
platyphylla hort.	See ***R. muratdaghensis***
rechingeri	CWil
§ *sedoides*	CMHG CWil EGoo ELan GCHN MBar NNrd SChu SSmi WElm WPer WWin
§ – var. *alba*	CMHG CWil ELan EPot GCHN MBar MHig NGre SChu SRms WHoo WOMN WPyg WWin
sempervivum	CWil EWes NGre NMen
§ – subsp. *glaucophylla*	CWil NTow WPer
serpentinica	CWil
spatulata hort.	See ***R. sempervivum*** subsp. ***glaucophylla***
¶ *turkestanica*	CWil

ROTHMANNIA (Rubiaceae)

capensis	CTrC SOWG
§ *globosa*	CTrC

RUBIA (Rubiaceae)

peregrina	CArn CKin EHic EWFC GBar GPoy MHew MSal
tinctorum	CArn ELau GBar GPoy LHol MHew MSal NCGP NHex SIde SWat WHer WWye

RUBUS † (Rosaceae)

¶ *alceifolius*	CPMA
– Poiret	CGle
arcticus	CGle CInt ESim MBal MBro MCCP MHig NCat NHar SAlw SReu SRms SSta WCru WPat
– subsp. *stellarcticus* (F)	ESim
– – 'Anna' (F)	ESim
– – 'Beata' (F)	ESim
– – 'Linda' (F)	ESim
– – 'Sofia' (F)	ESim
¶ *australis*	CPlN
× *barkeri*	ECou
§ 'Benenden' 🏆	CB&S CBot CChu CGle CMHG CSam EBar ELan ENot ISea LHop MBal MBri MGos MHlr MRav MWat NFla NNor NSti SHBN SPer WDin WGwG WHCG WWat WWin
'Betty Ashburner'	CAgr CDoC CHan CWit EBre EPla GCal LBuc MGos NFla WHCG WWat
biflorus	ELan EMon EPla
'Boysenberry, Thornless' (F)	EMui GTwe LBuc NDal SDea SPer
buergeri 'Variegatus'	NPSI
caesius 'Sidings'	CNat
calophyllus	WCot
calycinoides Hayata	See ***R. pentalobus***
chamaemorus	GPoy WUnd
cockburnianus (F) 🏆	CB&S CGle CPle EBre ELan ENot EPla IOrc MBal MRav MWat NHol NWea SAga SEas SPer SRms WDin WWat
– Golden Vale™	CB&S CDoC CPle EBee EBre EMil EPla MBlu MPla NHol SEas SMrm SPer SSpi WRus WWye
coreanus	CFil CPle
crataegifolius	SMac WPat WWat
'Emerald Spreader'	LRHS MBri SBod
flagelliflorus	MBar WHCG
fockeanus hort.	See ***R. pentalobus***
× *fraseri*	EPla
fruticosus	CKin CTiv
– 'Ashton Cross' (F)	EMui GRei GTwe LBuc SDea
– 'Bedford Giant' (F)	GTwe MGos SDea SPer WWeb
– 'Black Satin' (F)	CSam GRei MBri SDea SPer WWeb
– 'Dart's Ambassador'	ENot
– 'Dart's Robertville'	SLPl
– 'Denver Thornless' (F)	EWar
– 'Fantasia' (F) 🏆	EMui GTwe LBuc
– 'Godshill Goliath' (F)	SDea
– 'Himalayan Giant' (F)	CSam EWar GTwe NRog SDea SPer
– 'John Innes' (F)	NRog
– 'Loch Ness' (F) 🏆	COtt CSam EMui GChr GTwe LBuc MBri MGos SDea SPer
– 'Merton Thornless' (F)	GTwe MGos NBee NRog SDea
– 'No Thorn' (F)	SDea
– 'Oregon Thornless' (F)	EMui EWar GTwe MBri NDal SDea SPer SRms
– 'Parsley Leaved' (F)	SDea
– 'Sylvan' (F)	MGos

– 'Thornfree' (F) NDal SDea WWeb
– 'Variegatus' CBot CPMA CRDP EFol EPla MBlu SAxl SMad WCot
– 'Waldo' COtt CSut EMui LBuc MBri MGos
henryi CBot CPlN CSWP EPla MRav WCot WHCG WWat
– var. ***bambusarum*** CDec CFil CHan CMCN CPlN CPle EBar EHic ELan EPar EPla SBid SMad WCru
hupehensis SLPl
ichangensis CBot CHan CMCN CPlN EPPr EPla MBal
idaeus CKin
– 'Augusta' (F) EMui
– 'Aureus' (F) ECha EFol EHal ELan EPla LHop NRoo NSti SDry SEas WCot WRus
– Autumn Bliss™ (F) ♀ CSam CSut CWSG EMui GRei GTwe LBuc MBri MGos MMor NBee NEgg SDea SPer WWeb
– 'Fallgold' (F) GTwe SDea
– 'Glen Ample' (F) EMui GTwe
– 'Glen Clova' (F) EWar GTwe NBee NRog SDea SPer WWeb
– 'Glen Coe' (F) GTwe
– 'Glen Lyon' (F) GRei GTwe LBuc MBri SCoo
¶ – 'Glen Magna' (F) EMui GTwe
– 'Glen Moy' (F) ♀ CSut CWSG EMui GChr GTwe LBuc MGos MMor NBee NRog SPer
– 'Glen Prosen' (F) ♀ CSam CWSG EMui GChr GTwe LBuc MBri MMor NRog SPer
¶ – 'Glen Rosa' (F) GTwe
¶ – 'Glen Shee' (F) GTwe
– 'Golden Everest' (F) EWar GTwe SDea
– 'Heritage' (F) EBee SDea SPer
¶ – 'Julia' (F) GTwe
– 'Leo' (F) ♀ CSut EMui GTwe MGos SCoo SDea
– 'Malling Admiral' (F) ♀ COtt GTwe MBri MMor NRog SPer
– 'Malling Delight' (F) GTwe MMor NRog SCoo SPer
– 'Malling Jewel' (F) ♀ COtt EMui EWar GRei GTwe LBuc NBee SDea SPer
– 'Malling Joy' (F) GTwe
– 'Malling Orion' (F) MGos MMor
– 'Malling Promise' (F) EWar SDea
– 'Redsetter' (F) EMui
– 'Ruby' (F) EMui
– 'September' (F) EWar
– 'Summer Gold' (F) GTwe
– 'Zefa Herbsternte' (F) EWar GTwe SDea WWeb
illecebrosus (F) MBro SMac WBea WCot WRTC
¶ ***intercurrens*** GCal
irenaeus CFil CHan CPlN CPle WPGP WWat
'Kenneth Ashburner' CDoC EPla MBri SLPl WWat
'King's Acre Berry' (F) EMui
laciniatus EPla
lineatus CAbb CBot CBrd CGre CHan CPle LHop MBal MBlu MBro SDix SDry SMad SSta WBea WCru WPat WRTC WWat
(Loganberry Group) 'LY 59' (F) ♀ CDoC EMui GTwe MMor NRog SDea SPer SRms
– 'LY 654' (F) ♀ CSam CSut GRei GTwe LBuc MBri MGos MMor SDea SPer WWeb
– 'New Zealand Black' (F) SDea
– Thornless (F) CTri ECot GTwe NDal NRog SDea
'Margaret Gordon' CBlo CPMA MRav NPro WHCG
microphyllus 'Variegatus' MRav SBid WPat WWeb
§ ***nepalensis*** CAgr CDoC CGle CLTr EGoo NPro NWoo WRHF
nutans See ***R. nepalensis***
odoratus CDoC CHEx CWit ELan LBlm MHlr NPal SBid SPer WCot WHCG WRTC WWat
palmatus var. ***coptophyllus*** SLPl
parviflorus CArn GAul
– 'Sunshine Spreader' GAri LHop NPro
parvus ECou
pectinellus var. ***trilobus*** B&SWJ 1669B EGoo SAxl WCru
§ ***pentalobus*** CGle CTri CWit EGoo ELan ENot EPla ESis LHop MAll MBal MBar SIng SMac SPer WAbe WCru WFar WWin
– 'Emerald Carpet' ESim SBod
– 'Green Jade' WWat
phoenicolasius CB&S ELan EMui EPla ESim
Japanese Wineberry (F) GTwe MBlu MBri NRog SDea SPer WAbb WBea WCru WHCG WPat WRTC WWat WWye
rosifolius 'Coronarius' (d) CHan CMil EHal ELan EPla LHop MAvo MHlr MMil MSCN NHaw NHol NPro SBid SMad WCot WRus WSan
setchuenensis CMCN CSWP
'Silvanberry' (F) CDoC EMui GTwe
sp. B&SWJ 1735 WCru
spectabilis CChu CMHG CPle CWit EBee ELan GAul LFis LHop MBal MRav SEas SPan SRms WNdy WRha
– 'Flore Pleno' See ***R. spectabilis* 'Olympic Double'**
– 'Gun Hildi' WCru
§ – 'Olympic Double' Widely available
* – 'Olympic Flame' CEnd
splendidissimus B&SWJ 2361 WCru
squarrosus CPle ECou EGoo EPla SMad
'Sunberry' (F) GTwe NDal
¶ ***taiwanicola*** WCot
– B&SWJ 317 CFee EGoo EPPr WCru
Tayberry (F) CSam CTri EMui EWar GChr GRei GTwe MBri MGos MMor NDal NRog SPer SRms WWeb
(Tayberry Group) 'Medana Tayberry' (F) CSut LBuc SDea
§ ***thibetanus*** ♀ CB&S CBot CDoC CHan CPle ELan EMil ENot EOrc GCal MBri MRav NBir NPal NSti SBod SDix SDry SEas SMac SPer SUsu WBea WDin WHCG WWat
– 'Silver Fern' See ***R. thibetanus***
treutleri WCot
tricolor CAgr CB&S CChe CDec CGle CHEx CHan CPlN ECha ELan ENot EPla GAul IHos LGro MBal MBar NHol NNor SDix SHBN SLPl SPer WBea WDin WEas WHCG WWat WWin WWye
– 'Dart's Evergreen' SLPl

– 'Ness'	SLPl
Tridel 'Benenden'	See ***R.* 'Benenden'**
'Tummelberry' (F)	GTwe LRHS
ulmifolius 'Bellidiflorus' (d)	CBot CSev ELan ENot EPla MAvo MBal MBlu NNor SBid SChu SMac SPer WAbb WBea WCot
'Veitchberry' (F)	EMui GTwe NDal NRog
'Walberton'	SPer
'Youngberry' (F)	SDea

RUDBECKIA † (Asteraceae)

◆ Autumn Sun	See ***R.* 'Herbstsonne'**
californica	CWan MNrw SHhN SSca WPer
echinacea purpurea	See ***Echinacea purpurea***
fulgida var. ***deamii*** ♀	CBre CVer EBre ECED ECha ECtt ELan GCal GMac LFis MCLN MRav MTis MWat NBrk NOak NRoo NSti NTow SAga SChu SCro SPer WByw WEas WFar WHoo WPyg
§ – var. ***speciosa***	CM&M CSam CShe ECha EHic ELan EPfP MBel NCGP NRoo SHel SPer SRms WCot WOld WPer WRus
– var. ***sullivantii*** 'Goldsturm' ♀	Widely available
gloriosa	See ***R. hirta***
'Goldquelle' ♀	ECED EFou EGar ELan EMan EPfP GMaP LHop MBel NOrc NPri SCro SMad SMrm SPer SRms WHil WWin
§ 'Herbstsonne'	CArc CChu CSte CTri ECGP ECha ECle LFis MBel MWat NFla NOrc NPer NPri NVic SAga SMad SPer SPla SSoC SSvw WBro WEas WTyr
§ ***hirta***	WRha
§ 'Juligold'	EFou EGar MUlv NCat SCro SMrm SSpe
◆ July Gold	See ***R.* 'Juligold'**
laciniata	CSam EBee ECGP ELan EMan EMon EPPr GCal LFis MArl NOrc SMrm WByw
– 'Golden Glow'	See ***R. laciniata* 'Hortensia'**
§ – 'Hortensia'	EBee EMon MFir MUlv
maxima	CGle CSte ECha EGar EMan EMon MBri MCCP SAga SIgm SMrm SSoC WCot
newmannii	See ***R. fulgida*** var. ***speciosa***
occidentalis	CHan CPou LFis WPer
– 'Green Wizard'	CHid CM&M CMdw CMil CPou EGar GCal GCra MCLN NBro NRai SMad WBea WBro WCot WWhi
purpurea	See ***Echinacea purpurea***
subtomentosa	CArc CPou EFou EGar EMon GCal MNrw NSti WOld
triloba	EBee EMan

RUELLIA (Acanthaceae)

amoena	See ***R. graecizans***
¶ ***caroliniensis***	WCot
'Chi Chi'	WCot
devosiana	SLMG
§ ***graecizans***	ERea
humilis	SHFr SIgm WCot WLRN
'Katie'	WCot
makoyana ♀	CHal IBlr MBri SLMG SRms
¶ ***strepens***	WCot

RUMEX (Polygonaceae)

§ ***acetosa***	CArn CKin CSev ECWi ECha EJud ELau GAbr GBar GPoy LHol MChe MHew NBir SIde WApp WHer WSel WWye
– 'Redleaf'	See ***R. acetosa*** subsp. ***vineatus***
§ – subsp. ***vineatus***	WCot
acetosella	ECWi MSal WSel
alpinus	WCot
flexuosus	CElw CRow EFol EHoe EMon EPPr GCal IBlr WCot
hydrolapathum	CArn ECWi EMFW EWFC MSta NDea
maritimus	EWFC
montanus 'Ruber'	See ***R. alpestris* 'Ruber'**
rubrifolius	SIde
rugosus	CWan
sanguineus	CHan EMFW EMan GGar MSCN WCer WChe WGwG WHil
– var. ***sanguineus***	CArn CElw CRow CSev EFol EHoe ELan EMon EPar EPla LHol MNrw MRav MTho NBro NHol NLak NSti WFox WHer WHow WOak WPer WSel WWye
scutatus	CArn CJew CSev EJud ELau GAbr GBar GPoy LHol MChe MHew MTho SIde WApp WCer WHer WJek WSel WWye
– 'Silver Shield'	CJew CMil CRDP EFol EMar EMon EPPr IBlr LBlm NSti SUsu WCHb WHer WJek WOak WWye
¶ ***venosus***	MSal

RUMOHRA (Davalliaceae)

See Plant Deletions

RUPICAPNOS (Papaveraceae)

africana	EPot NMen NWCA SBla WAbe WOMN

RUSCHIA (Aizoaceae)

putterillii S&SH 64	CHan
¶ ***uncinata***	CTrC

RUSCUS † (Ruscaceae)

aculeatus	CLTr CSte CTri ECED ENot EPfP GPoy MFir MRav MUlv SArc SSta WDin WHer WOMN WRHF WStI WWye
– var. ***angustifolius*** (f)	EPla
– (f)	WMou
– hermaphrodite	EPla GCal
– (m)	EGoo WMou WWat
* – 'Wheeler's Variety' (f/m)	CPMA EBee LRHS MPla MRav
hypoglossum	MUlv SArc
ponticus	EPla
racemosus	See ***Danae racemosa***

RUSPOLIA (Acanthaceae)

¶ ***pseuderanthemoides***	ECon

RUSSELIA (Scrophulariaceae)

§ ***equisetiformis*** ♀	CB&S ERea LLew SIgm
juncea	See ***R. equisetiformis***

RUTA (Rutaceae)

chalepensis	CArn EGoo WCHb WHil

§ – 'Dimension Two'	EMon LHol WCot WHer
– prostrate form	See ***R. chalepensis* 'Dimension Two'**
corsica	CArn
graveolens	CArn CChr CGle CJew CWSG EFer EJud LHol MChe MHew NOak SIde WHer WJek WOak WPLl WPer
– 'Jackman's Blue' 🏆	CGle CMHG CSev CShe EBre ECha EEls EFol EHoe ELan ENot EOrc LGro LHol MBal MBar MCLN MPla MWat NNor NSti SPer WEas WOak WOve WRTC WWin
– 'Variegata'	CArn CBot ECha EFol ELan EOrc GPoy MCLN MChe NNor NPer WHer WHil WJek WPbr WWye
montana	CBot WHer
prostrata	See ***R. chalepensis* 'Dimension Two'**

RUTTYA (Acanthaceae)

See Plant Deletions

SABAL (Arecaceae)

¶ ***mauritiiformis***	NPal
§ ***mexicana***	NPal
minor	CTrC LPal NPal
palmetto	CArn CTrC LPal NPal WNor
texana	See ***S. mexicana***

SACCHARUM (Poaceae)

ravennae	EHoe EMon EPla ETPC GBin MSte NSti SAxl SMad WChe

SAGERETIA (Rhamnaceae)

§ ***thea***	STre
theezans	See ***S. thea***

SAGINA (Caryophyllaceae)

boydii	EMNN GCLN ITim
glabra 'Aurea'	See ***S. subulata* 'Aurea'**
§ ***subulata*** 'Aurea'	CMea EBar ECha EFer EFol EGoo ELan EPPr LGro LHop MOne SIng SRms WEas WHal WPer WWin

SAGITTARIA (Alismataceae)

japonica	See ***S. sagittifolia***
latifolia	CHEx EMFW NDea WChe
§ ***sagittifolia***	CBen CRow CWGN ECWi EHon EMFW LPBA MHew MSta SHig SRms SWat WChe WMAq WShi
– 'Bloomin Baby'	CRow
– 'Flore Pleno'	CRow CWGN CWat EHon EMFW LPBA MBal MSta NDea SWat WChe
– var. ***leucopetala***	WMAq
subulata	CRow

SAINTPAULIA (Gesneriaceae)

See Plant Deletions

SALIX † (Salicaceae)

acutifolia	ELan EPla IOrc
– 'Blue Streak' (m) 🏆	CEnd EPla IOrc MAsh MBal MBlu NBir SWat
– 'Pendulifolia' (m)	IOrc
adenophylla Hooker	See ***S. cordata***
aegyptiaca	CDoC CLnd MBlu NWea WMou
alba	CCVT CKin CLnd EOHP LBuc SHhN SPer WDin WMou
– f. ***argentea***	See ***S. alba*** var. ***sericea***
– 'Aurea'	CLnd CTho EFol WMou
– subsp. ***caerulea***	CLnd EBee ENot NWea SPer WMou
– 'Chermesina' hort.	See ***S. alba*** subsp. ***vitellina* 'Britzensis'**
– 'Dart's Snake'	CBlo EBee ELan ENot MRav SCoo SPer
– 'Hutchinson's Yellow'	EPfP MBri MGos
– 'Liempde' (m)	ENot
– 'Orange Spire'	LMer
§ – var. ***sericea*** 🏆	CB&S CLnd CTho ENot IOrc MBal MBlu MBri MRav NNor NWea SHBN SPer WDin WGer WMou WWat
– 'Splendens'	See ***S. alba*** var. ***sericea***
N – 'Tristis'	CLnd CTri EBee ELan MAsh MBri MRav NWea SRms WDin WFar
– subsp. ***vitellina*** 🏆	CKin CPer EBar ELan LBuc NHol NWea WDin WOrn
§ – – 'Britzensis' 🏆	CDoC CKin CLnd CTho CTri ELan ENot GRei IOrc LBuc LHop MBal MBar MGos MRav NNor NWea SHBN SPer SPla SRms SSta WDin WMou WWat
– 'Vitellina Pendula'	See ***S. alba* 'Tristis'**
– 'Vitellina Tristis'	See ***S. alba* 'Tristis'**
§ ***alpina***	CLyd CShe EHyt EWes GAri MBal MBro MPla NHol NRoo NWoo
apoda (m)	CLyd ESis EWes MBal NHar NHol WPat WPer
§ ***arbuscula***	CBlo CDoC CShe EBar EPad ESis GBin MBal MPla NHar NWCA
arctica var. ***petraea***	WPat
babylonica	CBlo NBee SHBN WDin WMou
– 'Annularis'	See ***S. babylonica* 'Crispa'**
§ – 'Crispa'	EHic ELan EPla LHop SHBN SMad SPla WLRN
– var. ***pekinensis*** 'Pendula'	MUlv
§ – – 'Tortuosa' 🏆	CArn CDec CLnd CTho ELan ENot IOrc LHop LPan MAsh MBal MBar MGos MTis MWat NHol NNor NPer NWea SPer SRms WHar WWat
bockii	CBlo CDoC CSte MBar WPer
§ 'Bowles' Hybrid'	CDoC LBuc MRav WMou
'Boydii' (f) 🏆	CFee CSam EHyt ELan EPot ESis GDra GTou MAsh MBal MBri MBro MDun MGos MPla NHar NHol NMen NNor NRoo SIng SRms STre WAbe WPat
§ 'Boyd's Pendulous' (m)	CFee CLyd GAri MBal MBar
breviserrata	CLyd GDra NWCA
¶ ***calyculata***	EHyt
caprea	CB&S CCVT CKin CLnd CPer CTri ENot GRei LBuc LHyr NRoo NWea WDin WMou
– 'Curlilocks'	CBlo COtt EBee MBlu MGos WBcn
§ – 'Kilmarnock' (m) 🏆	CLnd ELan GRei LBuc LHyr LPan MAsh MBar MGos MWat NBee NHol NWea SHBN SMad SPer WDin WMou WTyr
– var. ***pendula*** (f)	See ***S. caprea* 'Weeping Sally'**

◆ – – (m)	See ***S. caprea*** **'Kilmarnock' (m)**
– var. ***variegata***	SPer
capusii	LMer
cashmiriana	CLyd MBro NHol WPat
× ***cernua***	NWCA
'Chrysocoma'	See ***S.*** × ***sepulcralis*** var. ***chrysocoma***
cinerea	CB&S CDoC CKin CPer GRei NWea WDin
– 'Tricolor'	CArn CDoC EFol
× ***cottetii***	CBlo CDoC
daphnoides	CDoC CLnd CSam ELan ENot GRei IHos IOrc NWea SHBN SPer SRms STre WDin WMou WWat
– 'Aglaia' (m) ♀	CB&S CTri MBal
– 'Meikle'	CAgr
'E.A. Bowles'	See ***S.*** **'Bowles' Hybrid'**
× ***ehrhartiana***	CNat
§ ***elaeagnos*** ♀	CBrd CCVT CDoC CPle CTho EBar EBee MBlu SPer SWat WDin WMou WRTC
§ – subsp. ***angustifolia***	CLnd ELan IOrc LBuc LHop MBal MTis MUlv NWea SMad SMrm SRms STre WWat WWin
'Elegantissima'	See ***S. pendulina*** var. ***elegantissima***
§ 'Erythroflexuosa'	CDoC CShe CTho EBee EBre ELan EPla MAsh MGos NHol NWea SMrm SWat WDin WHer WOak
exigua	CB&S CDoC CTho EBre ELan ENot EWes IOrc MBar MBlu MBri MGos NWea SDry SMad SPer WMou WWat
fargesii	CAbb CBot CChu CEnd CFee CFil CHan CMHG EBre LHop MBal MBlu MDun MGos MHlr MUlv NHar NHol SAxl SDix SMad SWas WCru WPat WRTC WWat
formosa	See ***S. arbuscula***
fragilis	CCVT CKin CLnd CPer NWea WDin WMou
§ ***fruticulosa***	CGle EPot GAri GDra GGar GTou LFlo MBal NWCA
'Fuiri-koriyanagi'	See ***S. integra*** **'Hakuro-nishiki'**
furcata	See ***S. fruticulosa***
glauca	CNat
glaucosericea	EBee EHic WLRN WWat
'Golden Curls'	See ***S.*** **'Erythroflexuosa'**
gracilistyla	WMou WWat
§ – 'Melanostachys' (m) ♀	CAbb CB&S CBot CHan CMHG EBar ECtt ELan EPla ERav GDra LHop MBal MBar MBlu MRav NEgg SRms STre WMou WPat WWat WWin
× ***grahamii*** (f)	MBal NHol
– 'Moorei' (f)	ESis MBal NWCA
× ***greyi***	CSam NPro
'Hagensis'	See ***S.*** **'The Hague'**
hastata 'Wehrhahnii' (m) ♀	Widely available
helvetica ♀	CB&S EBre ELan ENot GDra GRei IOrc LHop MBal MBar MBlu MBri MGos MPla NBee NHar NHol NNor NRoo SHBN SPer SSmi WDin WHar WPat WWat WWin
herbacea	ESis GAri GTou MBal MOne NMen WPer
hibernica	See ***S. phylicifolia***
× ***hirtei*** 'Reifenweide' (f)	CDoC
hookeriana	CMHG CTho ELan MBlu MRav SLPl SSpi WMou WPat WWat
humilis var. ***microphylla***	CBlo
hylematica	See ***S. fruticulosa***
incana	See ***S. elaeagnos***
integra 'Albomaculata'	See ***S. integra*** **'Hakuro-nishiki'**
§ – 'Hakuro-nishiki' (v)	CB&S CEnd CSpe EBre ELan LHop LPan MBar MBri MGos MPla MWat NHol NWea SHBN SMad SPer SPla SReu SSpi SSta WDin WPat
irrorata	CBot EBee GBin IOrc MRav WMou
'Jacquinii'	See ***S. alpina***
japonica hort.	See ***S. babylonica*** **'Lavalleei' (m)**
kinuyanagi (m)	ELan LHop SMrm
'Kuro-me'	See ***S. gracilistyla*** **'Melanostachys' (m)**
lanata ♀	CB&S CBot CChu CSam CShe EBre ELan ESis GDra GRei MBal MBro MGos MPla MWat NHol NMen NNor NRoo NWea SHBN SPer SSpi SSta WAbe WDin WPat WWat WWin
– hybrid	MBro WPat
¶ – Kew form	SMrm
– 'Stuartii'	See ***S.*** **'Stuartii'**
lapponum	GAri SRms WPat
§ ***lindleyana***	CHan CNic EHyt GAri MPla NMen NOak NRoo WWat
magnifica ♀	CBot CChu CEnd CFil CLnd CPle EFol EPar MBal MSte SBid SDry SMad SSpi SWat WCru WMou
'Mark Postill' (f)	CDoC EBar EHic
matsudana	See ***S. babylonica*** var. ***pekinensis***
– 'Tortuosa'	See ***S. babylonica*** var. ***pekinensis*** **'Tortuosa'**
– 'Tortuosa Aureopendula'	See ***S.*** **'Erythroflexuosa'**
'Melanostachys'	See ***S. gracilistyla*** **'Melanostachys' (m)**
moupinensis	CBrd IOrc WMou
× ***myricoides***	See ***S.*** × ***bebbii***
§ ***myrsinifolia***	EPla MBlu SPer
myrsinites var. ***jacquiniana***	See ***S. alpina***
myrtilloides	CLyd
– 'Pink Tassels' (m)	EHyt ESis GAri MBal MBlu SIng WPat
– × ***repens***	See ***S.*** × ***finnmarchica***
nakamurana var. ***yezoalpina***	CChu CFai CFee EFol GAri LHop MAsh MBal MBro NHol NPro SRms WPat WPyg WRTC WWat
nepalensis	See ***S. lindleyana***
nigricans	See ***S. myrsinifolia***
nivalis	EPot NHol
occidentalis	See ***S. humilis***
* 'Onoga'	CB&S
'Onusta' (m)	CDoC
× ***ovata***	CLyd NMen NRoo
pentandra	CBot CKin IOrc NWea WDin WMou WWat
§ ***phylicifolia***	CNat SPer WMou
polaris	CLyd ESis GAri MBal WWtk
procumbens	See ***S. myrsinites***
prunifolia	See ***S. arbuscula***

§ ***purpurea***	CB&S EBee EHic IOrc SRms WDin WMou
– 'Dicky Meadows'	CAgr
– 'Goldstones'	CAgr
– f. ***gracilis***	See ***S. purpurea* 'Nana'**
– 'Green Dicks'	CAgr
– 'Helix'	See ***S. purpurea***
– 'Howki'	WMou
§ – 'Nana'	CLTr CLyd CPle ELan EPla LBlm MBal NBee SChu SLPl SPla STre WStI WWat
– 'Nancy Saunders' (f)	CTho EBar EPPr EPla GBuc MBlu MSte NPro NSti SMrm SWas WSHC
– 'Pendula' 🏆	CTho ENot LHyr MAsh MBal MBar MBri NBee NHol NWCA NWea SMac SPer WDin WStI
– 'Richartii' (f)	WLRN
pyrenaica	CLyd EWes
repens	CNic GAri MBar SRms STre SWat WDin
– var. ***argentea*** 🏆	CGle CShe ENot GDra IOrc MBal MBar MRav NHol NWea SPer WDin WWin
– 'Iona' (m)	CBlo CLyd
– ***pendula***	See ***S.* 'Boyd's Pendulous' (m)**
– Saint Kilda form	WPat
– 'Voorthuizen' (f)	EBee EHyt ELan ESis MBar WGer WPyg
reticulata 🏆	EPot GDra GTou MAsh MBal MHig NHar NMen NWoo WPat
retusa	CTri GAri GDra GTou MBro MHig MPla NHar NHol NMen WPat WPyg
¶ – × ***pyrenaica***	ECho
rosmarinifolia hort.	See ***S. elaeagnos*** subsp. ***angustifolia***
× ***rubens*** 'Basfordiana' (m) 🏆	CDoC CLnd CTho EBar EPla LWak WLRN WMou WOrn
× ***rubra*** 'Eugenei' (m)	GQui SWat WBcn WMou WWat WWin
sachalinensis	See ***S. udensis***
schraderiana Willdenow	See ***S. bicolor* Willdenow**
× ***sepulcralis***	NWea
§ – var. ***chrysocoma*** 🏆	CDoC EBee ELan ENot GAri LBuc LHyr LPan MAsh MBal MGos MWat SCoo SHBN SPer WLRN
serpyllifolia	CLyd CTri ESis LFlo MBal MBro MHig NMen WPat WPyg
– × ***retusa***	NWCA
serpyllum	See ***S. fruticulosa***
'Setsuka'	See ***S. udensis* 'Sekka' (m)**
× ***simulatrix***	CLyd GAri NWCA WWat
× ***smithiana***	See ***S.* × *stipularis* (f)**
§ × ***stipularis*** (f)	CLnd WDin
§ 'Stuartii'	CSam ESis MBar NHol NMen SRms
subopposita	CDoC EBar EHic ELan MBar MBlu MPla NPro SMrm
syrticola	See ***S. cordata***
× ***tetrapla*** 'Hutchinson's Nigricans'	CNat
triandra	WMou
– 'Black Hollander'	CAgr
– 'Black Maul'	CAgr
– 'Semperflorens'	CNat
– 'Whissander'	CAgr
tristis	See ***S. humilis***
× ***tsugaluensis*** 'Ginme' (f)	CMHG SLPl WWat
§ ***udensis*** 'Sekka' (m)	CDec CLnd CTho ECtt ELan EPar EPla IOrc MBal NHol NWea SMrm STre SWat WMou WPyg
uva-ursi	CLyd GAri MBal SIng
viminalis	CAgr CCVT CKin CPer ENot GRei LBuc NWea WDin WMou
– 'Bowles' Hybrid'	See ***S.* 'Bowles' Hybrid'**
¶ – 'Brown Merrin'	CAgr
¶ – 'Reader's Red' (m)	CAgr
¶ – 'Yellow Osier'	CAgr
vitellina 'Pendula'	See ***S. alba* 'Tristis'**
× ***wimmeriana***	SRms
'Yelverton'	MBri MRav

SALVIA † (Lamiaceae)

acetabulosa	See ***S. multicaulis***
aethiopis	CLon CPle CSev ECoo ELan EMar LGre MSte NChi NSti WPer
afghanica	CPle WEas
§ ***africana-caerulea***	CPle WWye
§ ***africana-lutea***	CBrk CHal CPle CSev CWan EGar ELan LHil MMil SBid SMrm WPer WWye
– 'Kirstenbosch'	CPle CWan MRav WCot WPer
agnes	CPle
albimaculata	SBla
algeriensis	CPle
amarissima	CPle
ambigens	See ***S. guaranitica* 'Blue Enigma'**
§ ***amplexicaulis***	CPle WPer WWye
angustifolia Cavanilles	See ***S. reptans***
– Michaux	See ***S. azurea***
apiana	CPle SIgm WCot
argentea 🏆	CArn CB&S CGle CHad CMea CPle CRDP CSam EAst EBre ECha ELan GCal GMaP LGre LHop MBri MNrw SHFr SVen WCHb WCru WEas WHal WOMN WOve WPer WWin
arizonica	CPle GCal WPer
atrocyanea	CPle LHil SLod
aucheri	CPle EGar GBuc GCal
aurea	See ***S. africana-lutea***
austriaca	CArc CPle MBel SHFr WPer WWye
§ ***azurea***	CArn CChr CLyd CPle LHol LHop MNrw MSte SMrm WPer
bacheriana	See ***S. buchananii***
§ ***barrelieri***	CHan CPle MSto SLod WLRN
'Belhaven'	GCal
bertolonii	See ***S. pratensis* Bertolonii Group**
bicolor Desfontaines	See ***S. barrelieri***
blancoana	CArn CBot CBrk CHan CPle ECha EFol ELau EMan LHop MSte WRus WSel
blepharophylla	CCan CPle CSev CSpe GBri LHil LHop MWat SHel WPen WWye
'Blue Bird'	CPle
brachyantha	CPle EBee EGar
broussonetii	CPle LHil
§ ***buchananii*** 🏆	CAbb CCan CHal CHan CLon CPle CSWP CSam ELan EMil ERea GBri GQui LHop SAga SBid SCro SMrm SSoC WOld WPnn WWye

bulleyana	CChu CGle CLyd CPle CSev EBre ELan GBin GCal LHol MNrw SHFr SHel SIde SSoC SWas WOve WPer WWin WWye
cacaliifolia 🏆	CCan CChu CHan CLTr CLon CPle CSpe EEls ERav LBlm LHil LHol MSte MWat SBid SHFr SMrm SPer WCHb WEas WHer WWin WWye
caerulea hort.	See ***S. guaranitica* 'Black and Blue'**
– Linnaeus	See ***S. africana-caerulea***
caespitosa	CPle EHyt MSto NTow NWCA SBla
campanulata	CPle
aff. – ACE 2379	CPle
canariensis	CPle LHil MSte WSan WWye
– f. ***alba***	CPle
¶ – f. ***candidissima***	CPle
candelabrum 🏆	CHad CHan CPle CSev LGre NLak SAxl SVen WCHb WHer WKif WPen WSHC
candidissima	CPle
canescens	CPle
cardinalis	See ***S. fulgens***
carduacea	CPle
castanea	CPle
chamaedryoides	CCan CPle CSpe SHel WWye
– silver	CSpe LGre LHil
chapalensis	CPle
¶ ***chiapensis***	CPle
chinensis	See ***S. japonica***
cinnabarina	CPle
clevelandii	CPle GCal
coccinea	CBot CGle CMdw CPle EBar GBri MSte NBus SHFr WCHb WOMN WPen WPer WWye
– 'Cherry Blossom'	SWat
– 'Coral Nymph'	CKni CPle CSpe LIck SLod SSoC WPen
– 'Indigo'	EGar ELan EPfP GBri
– 'Lactea'	CBot CPle
– 'Lady in Red' 🏆	GBri LIck SMrm SWat
– pink	CPle
– 'Snow Nymph'	LIck
columbariae	CPle
compacta	CPle
concolor hort.	See ***S. guaranitica***
– Lamb.	CPle LHil
confertiflora	CAbb CCan CHal CPle CSev CWit ELan GBri GCal LHil LHop MSte SBid SLod SMrm WCHb WWhi WWye
¶ ***corrugata***	CPle LHil
cyanescens	CPle EPot WDav
darcyi	CHan CPle LGre LHop SIgm
davidsonii	CPle
'Dear Anja'	EFou
deserta	See ***S.* × *sylvestris***
digitaloides	CPle GBin
discolor 🏆	CBot CBrk CDec CHan CPle CSam CSev CSpe ELan ERav ERea GQui LBlm LHil LHop MTho MWat SAxl SSoC WCHb WHal WWye
* ***discolor nigra***	CMdw
¶ ***disermas***	CPle
¶ ***divinorum***	NGno
dolichantha	CPle
¶ ***dolomitica***	CPle
dombeyi	CPle
dominica	CPle
dorisiana	CArn CPle CSev ELan LBlm MSte WJek
eigii	CPle
§ ***elegans***	CCan CGre CPle CSev ELau EPri EWes LBlm LHol MSCN MSte SBid SCro SHel SIde WCer WOld
§ – 'Scarlet Pineapple'	CArn CBot CCan CFee CHal CInt CPle CSev ELan ELau ERea GPoy LHol LHop MChe SAga SIde SLMG SMac SMer SOWG SVen WEas WOak WPer WWye
fallax	CPle
farinacea 'Alba'	LBlm LGre
¶ – 'Rhea'	LIck
– 'Silver'	CPle
– 'Strata'	CPle EHic
– 'Victoria' 🏆	CPle LBlm
forreri CD&R 1269	CPle
forsskaolii	Widely available
frigida	CPle
§ ***fruticosa***	CArn CHan CPle EEls LHol SHFr SIde
§ ***fulgens*** 🏆	CGle CPle CSam CSev CWit LBlm LHil NBro SBid SHFr SHel SIde SUsu WCHb WEas WKif WWhi WWye
gesneriiflora	CAbb CCan CPle CSev LHop MSCN MSte SBid SIde SMrm WPer WWye
glutinosa	CChu CHad CHan CPle CSam EBre ECha ELan GCal LHol MNrw NBro NCat NHex NSti SAga WHil WPer WWye
– HH&K 294	CHan
grahamii	See ***S. microphylla* var. *microphylla***
greggii	CBrk CHan CPle EWes LHil MSCN MSte SAga SPer SWat WHil WOve WPer WWin WWye
– 'Alba'	CHal CPle LHop SBid WHil WWye
– 'Blush Pink'	See ***S. microphylla* 'Pink Blush'**
– CD&R 1148	LHop
– 'Keter's Red'	CPle
§ – × ***lycioides***	CMdw CPle CSev LCom LHil LHop SAga SBid SHel WSHC
– 'Peach' 🏆	CBrk CPle CSpe EOrc MSCN SAga SAxl WAbe WFoF WWye
– 'Peach' misapplied	See ***S.* × *jamensis* 'Pat Vlasto'**
– 'Raspberry Royal'	See ***S.* 'Raspberry Royale'**
– yellow	CKni
§ ***guaranitica*** 🏆	CAbb CArc CBot CCan CGle CPle CSpe EBre ELan GCal LHil LHol MRav SAga SUsu WCHb WEas WSan
– 'Argentine Skies'	CLon CPle LHil LHop
§ – 'Black and Blue'	CCan CGle CLTr CPle CSWP CSev CWit EPPr GCal LBlm MSte MWat SSoC SVen WPer WWye
§ – 'Blue Enigma' 🏆	CArc CArn CBot CCan CLon CSev ECha EFou EGar EPPr LHil LHop WEas
haematodes	See ***S. pratensis* Haematodes Group**
heldreichiana	CPle

hians	CFir CGle CHal CHan CPle EBre ECoo EMan EMar EPad GBar GBri GCra MBro MNrw NLak NSti NWoo SBla SRms SUsu WCer WHoo WOve WPer WPyg WWye
hierosolymitana	CChr CPle
hirtella	CPle
hispanica	CPle
– hort.	See ***S. lavandulifolia***
horminoides	CKin NMir WCla WWye
horminum	See ***S. viridis***
hypargeia	CPle
indica	SRms
'Indigo Spires' ♀	CBrd CLon CMdw CPle ECha EFou EPPr LBlm LHil SAga SBid SMrm SUsu WKif WPen
interrupta	CPle ECha EHal EOrc GBar LFis LHil SAga SChu SDix WCHb WEas
involucrata ♀	CFir CHan CPle CSev GCal GQui LHil LHol NBro SBid SCro SMrm SUsu WEas
– 'Bethellii'	Widely available
– 'Boutin' ♀	CCan CPle LBlm WEas
– dark form	GCal MSte
§ – 'Hadspen'	CArc CBot CCan CHad CSam
– 'Mrs Pope'	See ***S. involucrata* 'Hadspen'**
iodantha	CPle WWye
× ***jamensis*** 'Devantville'	CPle LHil SBid SLod SMrm WHil
– 'El Duranzo'	CPle LGre SMrm
– 'Fuego'	CPle
– 'James Compton'	LHil MSte SAxl SBid SHFr SIgm SMrm
– 'La Luna'	CBrk CHan CLon CPle CSev EPPr GCal LGre LHil LHop MSCN MSte SCro SHel SLod SSoC SUsu WHil
– 'La Siesta'	CLon CPle CSev SHel WHil
– 'La Tarde'	CBrk CLon CPle MSte WHil
– 'Los Lirios' ♀	CHan CPle EPPr SHel SLod SMrm SSoC SUsu
§ – 'Pat Vlasto'	CLon CPle LGre MSte SAga SBid SMrm SUsu WEas WHil
¶ – pink seedling	GCal
§ ***japonica***	CPle WWye
judaica	CPle EBee
jurisicii	CFir CPle EBee EMan EWll MBro SBid SHFr SIgm SMrm SSca WHoo WPyg WWye
karwinskyi	CPle
keerlii	CPle
koyamae	CPle
lanceolata	See ***S. reflexa***
§ ***lavandulifolia***	CArn CMHG CPle ECha EFou ELan ELau EMon EPri EWes NSti SAxl SPan SPla SUsu WAbe WApp WCHb WHer WOak WPer WWat WWye
– pink	CWan
lemmonii	See ***S. microphylla*** var. ***wislizenii***
leptophylla	See ***S. reptans***
leucantha ♀	CB&S CBrk CCan CHal CPle CSam CSev CSpe EBar ELan EOrc EPri ERea GCal LFlo LHil LHop MSte SAxl SBid SCro SHFr SIde SLMG SOWG SPer WHer WOMN WPer WWye
¶ – 'Purple Velvet'	CPle
leucophylla	CPle SIgm
longispicata	CPle WWye
lycioides hort.	See ***S. greggii* × *lycioides***
lyrata	CPle EBee EOHP MHew MSal SSca SUsu WWye
madrensis	CPle
mellifera	CArn CPle LHop
mexicana	CPle GBri LBlm LHil WEas
– var. ***minor***	CCan CPle LHop WPer
– T&K 550	CBot
microphylla	CArn CCan CGle CLTr CMHG CPle CWit ELau EWes GBar MAll MChe MSCN NFai SChu SHFr SLMG SOkh SVen WCru WHCG WPer
– 'Cerro Potosi'	CHan CLon CSev SHFr
– 'Huntingdon Red'	EOHP
– 'La Foux'	LGre NLak SMrm
¶ – 'Maraschino'	WHil
§ – var. ***microphylla***	Widely available
– var. ***neurepia***	See ***S. microphylla*** var. ***microphylla***
– – 'Newby Hall' ♀	CBrk CLon CPle LHil MBel SUsu WPer
– 'Oxford'	CPle
§ – 'Pink Blush' ♀	CBot CCan CPle ELan EMan EPri LHil LHop MMil MSte SHel SSpi WHil WOve
¶ – purple form	GCal
– 'Raspberry Ice'	LRHS
§ – 'Ruth Stungo' (v)	CPle
– 'Variegata' splashed	See ***S. microphylla* 'Ruth Stungo'**
§ – var. ***wislizenii***	CLyd CPle SCro WPer
microstegia	CPle
miniata	CPle
moelleri	MSCN
moorcroftiana	CPle NChi NLak WOve WPer
§ ***multicaulis*** ♀	CHan CPle ECha EMan GCal MSCN NLak NTow SChu SOkh SUsu WCHb WHer WOld WPer WSHC
munzii	CPle
nemorosa	CHan
– 'Amethyst' ♀	CHal CPle EFou LGre SMrm SWas WCot
♦ – East Friesland	See ***S. nemorosa* 'Ostfriesland'**
– HH&K 246	CHan
– 'Lubecca' ♀	CPle CSev CShe EBee EBre EFou NCat SMrm SOkh SPer WLRN WRus
§ – 'Ostfriesland' ♀	CLon CPle CSam EBre ECha ECtt EFou ELan EPla GCHN LHop MCLN MRav MSte MWat NCat NFai NFla SChu SCro SDix SMad SPer SPla WBea WCHb WHoo WRus WWin
– 'Plumosa' ♀	CHad ECha LGre WCot
– 'Rosenwein'	GBuc LGre
§ – subsp. ***tesquicola***	CHan CMdw CPle ECha
– 'Wesuwe'	CPle ECha LBuc
♦ ***neurepia***	See ***S. microphylla*** var. ***microphylla***
nilotica	CPle EBee MSto SHFr WHer WPen
nipponica	CPle WPer
– 'Fuji Snow' (v)	WCot
nubicola	CPle EHic SLod
nutans	CPle WKen

officinalis	CArn CChe CHal CShe ELau GBar GPoy MBal MBar MBri MChe MGos MWat NNor NPri SHBN SHFr WByw WDin WOak WPLl WPer WTyr WWat WWye
– 'Alba'	See ***S. officinalis* 'Albiflora'**
§ – 'Albiflora'	CBot CPle ECha EFou ELan GBar LHol LLWP SIde WJek WPer
N – 'Aurea'	CPle EPar GPoy MBar MFir NFla NPri SMad SUsu WLRN
– 'Berggarten'	EBre EFou EGar EMon EPPr EPri GBar GCal LGre LHol WHer
§ – broad-leaved	CBot CJew CSWP CWan EJud ELau MGra NSti SIde SWat WJek WWye
* ***officinalis extrakta***	EOHP
officinalis 'Giant'	MGra
– 'Grandiflora'	CPle
¶ – 'Grete Stolze'	EFou
– 'Herrenhausen'	CPle MSte WPen
§ – 'Icterina' (v) ♀	Widely available
– 'Kew Gold' ♀	EGar EGoo EMon GBar LHop SMad WJek
officinalis latifolia	See ***S. officinalis* broad-leaved**
officinalis narrow-leaved	See ***S. lavandulifolia***
officinalis prostrata	EOHP MGra
officinalis Purpurascens Group ♀	Widely available
– 'Purpurascens Variegata'	CPle EFol GBar NSti WEas WJek WRha
– 'Robin Hill'	GBar SHam WLRN
– 'Rosea'	CPle EGoo GBar SUsu
– 'Selsley Splash'	WSel
– tangerine	NPri
– Tomentosa Group	CArn
– 'Tricolor' (v) ♀	CArn CB&S CPle EBre ECha EFol EFou ELan EOrc ESis GCHN GPoy LFlo LGro LHol LHop MBri MChe MPla NHol NNor NPri NSti SAga SHBN SPer WEas WHCG WWat WWin
– 'Variegata'	See ***S. officinalis* 'Icterina'**
oppositiflora ♀	CPle EOrc SAga WWin
¶ ***oresbia***	CSev
pachyphylla	SIgm WDav
patens ♀	CB&S CCan CHad CPle CSam CSev EFou ELan EOrc EPot EPri LHil LHol LHop NFai NOrc NSti NWes SAga SBla SHel SOWG WCHb WEas WOMN WOld WPer WRus WWin
– 'Alba' misapplied	See ***S. patens* 'White Trophy'**
– 'Cambridge Blue' ♀	CBot CHad CPle CRDP CSam CSev CSpe ECha EFou ELan LBlm LHil LHol LHop MRav MWat NPer SAga SBla SCro SHel WEas WOMN WOld WPer WPnn WWye
– 'Chilcombe'	CArc CHan CPle CSpe EBar EMan EOrc LBlm LHil LHop MBel SAga SChu SCro SMrm WPer WWye
– 'Guanajuato'	CPle CSam LGre LHil LHol LHop SBid SCro SMad SMrm
– 'Lavender Lady'	CSam EBee MSCN WWhi
– 'Oxford Blue'	EOrc
– 'Royal Blue'	ECha EGle

§ – 'White Trophy'	CBot CLon CPle CSpe ELan EOrc EPri LBlm LHil LHol LHop SBid SCro SHel SLod SMad WRus WWhi WWye
'Peaches and Cream'	SMrm
penstemonoides	CPle
polystachya	CPle WWye
¶ ***populifolia***	LFis
pratensis	CArn CKin CLon CPle ECWi EJud ELan GBar MHew MSal SHFr SIde WHil WOve WPer WWye
§ – Bertolonii Group	CHan CPle EBee GCal
§ – Haematodes Group ♀	CHad CPle EBre ECha ELan EMon LFis MBel MBro MNrw NBro NBus NVic SCro SHFr SRms WBea WHoo WOld WPer WPyg WRus WWye
– 'Lapis Lazuli'	CPle
– 'Rosea'	CPle
– 'Tenorei'	WPer
prostrata	WRHF
przewalskii	CChu CPle CWan EBee ECro EGar MNrw MSal NChi SWas WPer WWye
– ACE 1157	CPle
– CLD 247	CPle
puberula	CHan CPle
– 'El Butano'	CPle
pulchella	CPle
'Purple Majesty'	CPle EFou EOrc SUsu SWas
purpurea	CPle EFou
§ 'Raspberry Royale' ♀	CHan CLon CPle ELan EOrc EPri EWoo LHil LHop MBel SAga SAxl SMrm SSpi SWat WPen WRus WWhi
recognita	CBot CPle GCal LGre MSto NChi
§ ***reflexa***	CPle
regeliana	CPle LFis NBir NChi NTow WPer
regla	CPle
repens	CPle
§ ***reptans***	CCan CPle CSam CSpe LHop SAga SLod WPer
ringens	CPle EBee GCHN
§ ***riparia***	CPle
roborowskii	CPle EBee
roemeriana ♀	CPle EBre EHic NWCA SSca WCru WHer WOMN
rutilans	See ***S. elegans* 'Scarlet Pineapple'**
'San Antonio'	CSpe
scabiosifolia	EBee MSto
scabra	CPle MSto
sclarea	CArn CGle CPle EJud ELau GPoy LFis LHol MChe MHew MWat NFai SIde WBea WCHb WHer WHoo WOak WPer WWye
* – 'Alba'	CPle
N – var. ***turkestanica*** hort.	Widely available
scutellarioides	CPle
semiatrata	CPle LHil MWat
sinaloensis	CPle MSte SAga SIgm
somalensis	CPle
sonomensis	CPle WWye
souliei	See ***S. brevilabra***
sp. ACE 2172	CPle
sp. CC&McK 77	GTou
sp. Iran	WOMN
spathacea ♀	CPle GBar SIgm

spinosa	CPle
splendens	MSto
sprucei	CPle
squalens	CPle
§ ***staminea***	CPle SIde SSca
stenophylla	CPle WPer
stepposa	CPle
× ***superba*** ♀	CBot CGle CHad CKel CPle CShe EBre ELan LHil MBri MBro MWat NRoo SAxl SCro SDix SMrm SRms SSvw WHoo WWhi WWye
– 'Adrian'	EFou
– 'Forncett Dawn'	EFou
– 'Rubin' ♀	EFou
– 'Superba'	CSev ECha EFou LGre MRav
× ***sylvestris*** 'Blauhügel' ♀	CLon CMGP CPle CSev EBre ECha EFou ELan EPPr EPar GCal LGre MArl MBri MSte MTis MWat NRoo SChu SHam SMrm WPer WWeb
§ – 'Blaukönigin'	CGle EBre ECro EPPr GBri GCHN LFis LWak MBro MTis MWat NCat NMir NOak NRoo SIgm WBea WHoo WPer WPyg
♦ – Blue Queen	See ***S.*** × ***sylvestris*** **'Blaukönigin'**
– 'Indigo'	EBre EFou EWll MRav
– 'Lye End'	EBre ECtt GCal LHop MRav NPla
§ – 'Mainacht' ♀	EBre ECro EFou EPar LHop MBri MCLN MRav MSte MWat NCat NFla NRoo NSti SAxl SChu SMrm SPer SPla SUsu SWas WEas WRus WWeb
♦ – May Night	See ***S.*** × ***sylvestris*** **'Mainacht'**
– 'Rose Queen'	CLTr CPle EBre ECha ECoo ECtt EFou ELan EPfP GBur GCHN LFis LHop MCLN MSte NCat NFla NOak NOrc NRoo SIgm WBea WFar WHoo WPer WPyg WRus WWin
– 'Rügen'	LCom WRus
– 'Tänzerin' ♀	EBar EFou LGre NCat SMrm WLRN
– 'Viola Klose'	EFou EMon MBri SUsu
– 'Wissalink'	SMad
tachiei	MRav SMrm
taraxacifolia	CPle LFlo NWoo SChu WWye
tarayensis	CPle
tesquicola	See ***S. nemorosa*** subsp. ***tesquicola***
tiliifolia	CPle SRms
tingitana	CPle
tomentosa	CPle
transcaucasica	See ***S. staminea***
transsylvanica	CArc CArn CChr CMdw CPle CSam EBee EMan EWll MEas NChi NLak SHam SWat WHil WOld WPer
trijuga	CPle
triloba	See ***S. fruticosa***
uliginosa ♀	Widely available
urica	CPle
'Van-Houttei'	CPle
verbenaca	CPle EGar EWFC GCHN MHew MNrw MSal WPer
– pink	CPle
verticillata	CArn CLTr CPle EBar ECha ELan GLil LHol MHew NNor NSti SHFr SVen WHoo WOve WPer WWhi WWye
– 'Alba'	CLTr CPle CSev ECha EMon LHol MBel SAxl SBid SIde WHer WPer
– subsp. ***amasiaca***	CPle
– HH&K 253	CHan
– HH&K 267	CHan
– HH&K 342	CHan
– 'Purple Rain'	CChr CLon CPle CSev EBee EBre ECha EFou EMil EMon EPPr EPar GCal MArl MBel MBri MCLN MMil MRav NSti SAxl SBid SMad SMrm SOkh SUsu WCot WRus
villicaulis	See ***S. amplexicaulis***
virgata	CPle LCot MNrw WHoo WPer
§ ***viridis***	CArn CPle LHol LHop MChe MGra SIde SIng
– var. ***alba***	CPle
viscosa Jacquin	CPle
– Sesse & Moc.	See ***S. riparia***
wagneriana	CPle
xalapensis	CPle

SALVINIA (Salviniaceae)

braziliensis	MSta

SAMBUCUS † (Caprifoliaceae)

adnata L 864	CPle
caerulea	EPla
canadensis	ESim
– 'Adams' (F)	ESim
– 'Aurea'	CWLN IOrc MBar NWea WHar
– 'Maxima'	CHEx ERav GCal SBid SMad SMrm
– 'York' (F)	ESim
coraensis	See ***S. sieboldiana*** var. ***coreana***
ebulus	CKin CRow
formosana B&SWJ 1543	WCru
nigra	CKin CPer ENot GAul GPoy GRei LBuc MBri NHol NNor NWea SIde WBea WMou WSel
– 'Albomarginata'	See ***S. nigra*** **'Marginata'**
– 'Albovariegata'	CWLN CWan MGra WWeb
– 'Ardwall'	GCal
N – 'Aurea' ♀	CB&S CInt CLnd CMHG CRow ELan EMon ENot EPla ERav GRei LHol MBar NFla NWea SPer WDin WSel
– 'Aureomarginata'	CInt CSam EBee ELan EPla ERav GAri MBal MRav NNor NSti SHBN WFar
– 'Cae Rhos Lligwy'	WHer
– 'Castledean'	EHal SMad WCot
– 'Din Dryfol' (v)	CNat
– 'Flex' (v)	CNat
– 'Frances'	CNat WCot
– 'Greener Later' (v)	CNat
§ – 'Guincho Purple' ♀	CHad CHan CMHG CNat CPMA CRow EFol EHoe ELan ERav GCal IOrc LFis LHol LHop MBal MBar MBlu MBri NBee NNor NSti SDix SMad SPer SSpi SSta WSHC WWat
– 'Heterophylla'	See ***S. nigra*** **'Linearis'**
– f. ***laciniata*** ♀	CB&S CMHG CNat CRow CSam EFol ELan EMon EPla ERav LHol MBal NNor NRoo NSti SChu SDix SEas SMad SPer SSpi SSta WCot WSHC WWat
§ – 'Linearis'	CPMA CPle EHal EHic ELan EPla SMad SPer WAbe WWat

– 'Luteovariegata'	EFol
– 'Madonna' (v)	CPMA CWLN EFol EPla MGos MPla NHol SEas SMad SMrm SPer WCot
§ – 'Marginata'	CMHG CRow EFol EHoe ELan GRei IOrc MBar MBri MGos MRav NRoo SAxl SDix SMad SPer WAbe WDin WHar WSHC WWat WWin
– 'Pendula'	EPla
– 'Plena' (d)	EPla MInt WCot
– 'Pulverulenta' (v)	CBrd CDoC CHan CRow EBre EFol ELan EPar EPla ERav GCal LHop NSti SAxl SEas SPer WCot WSHC
– 'Purpurea'	See ***S. nigra* 'Guincho Purple'**
– 'Pygmy'	EPla MBlu MPla NHol
– 'Pyramidalis'	CPMA EMon EPla MHlr SMad WCot
* – 'Tenuifolia'	CKni
– 'Thundercloud'	NPro
– 'Variegata'	See ***S. nigra* 'Marginata'**
– 'Witches Broom'	EMon
racemosa	GRei NWea WRTC WRha
– 'Aurea'	EHoe GRei
– 'Goldenlocks'	EFol EHal LHop MGos NPro SPer WPat WPyg
– 'Moerheimii'	EPla
– 'Plumosa Aurea'	CB&S CBot CMHG CRow CSpe CTrw EBre ELan ENot LHop MBal MBri NBee NNor NWea SDix SEas SHBN SMad SPer SReu SSpi SSta WDin WHCG WWin
– 'Sutherland Gold' ♀	CB&S CBot CHad CSam CSte CWLN EBre ELan ENot EOrc EPla ERav IOrc LNet MBar MBlu MGos MWat NBee NHol SHBN SReu SSpi SSta WAbe WDin WHCG WPat WSHC WWat
– 'Tenuifolia' ♀	CPMA CSWP CSte CWSG EHal ELan GSki MBro MGos MPla MUlv NHol NSti SMad SPer SSpi WCru WHCG WPat WPyg WWat
sieboldiana	CHan CPle EMon
tigrina	WWat
wightiana	See ***S. javanica***

SAMOLUS (Primulaceae)

repens	ECou

SANCHEZIA (Acanthaceae)

nobilis hort.	See ***S. speciosa***
§ ***speciosa***	CHal

SANDERSONIA (Colchicaceae)

aurantiaca	CMon LAma LBow NRog

SANGUINARIA (Papaveraceae)

canadensis	CArn CAvo CBro CChu CGle CSpe ECha ELan EPot GCal GPoy IBlr LAma LHop LSyl NGar NRog NRya SHig SMad SPer WAbe WChr WCru WWat WWin
– f. ***multiplex***	CRDP EPot LWoo NEgg WChr
– pink	WThi
– 'Plena' ♀	Widely available

SANGUISORBA (Rosaceae)

§ ***albiflora***	CArc CBlo CRow EBee EBre ECro EFol EFou ELan EPla GAri LCom MCLN MRav NRoo WCot WFar WWin
armena	SSvw
benthamiana	CHEx
canadensis	CHan CRow ECha EGar EHic GAbr GCal GPoy MFir NHex SPer WCot WOld WWye
hakusanensis	MNrw NBir NBro WWhi
magnifica alba	See ***S. albiflora***
menziesii	EFou WCot
§ ***minor***	CArn CKin EEls EWFC GPoy LHol MBar MChe MGam MHew NBro NMir SIde WCHb WCla WHer WOak WPer WWye
obtusa	CHan CInt CRow CShe CSte EBee ECha ECro EFol EFou ELan EPar GCal LFis LHil LHol MRav MTis MUlv NBro NFla NHex NHol NRoo NSti SMrm SPer SSoC WEas
– var. ***albiflora***	See ***S. albiflora***
officinalis	CArn CChr CInt ECWi EWFC GBar NMir SSca SWat WApp WCla WWin WWye
– 'Tanna'	EMon EPPr GCal SLod SMrm SWas WCot WPbr
pimpinella	See ***S. minor***
sitchensis	See ***S. stipulata***
§ ***stipulata***	GCal IBlr
tenuifolia	WWhi
– 'Alba'	CBlo ECha WCot
– 'Purpurea'	WCot

SANICULA (Apiaceae)

elata B&SWJ 2250	WCru
europaea	CKin EWFC GBar GPoy MSal WHer

SANIELLA (Hypoxidaceae)

verna	ERos MHig NMen

SANSEVIERIA † (Agavaceae)

trifasciata 'Golden Hahnii' (v) ♀	MBri
– 'Laurentii' (v) ♀	MBri

SANTOLINA † (Asteraceae)

§ ***chamaecyparissus*** ♀	CArn CB&S CGle CMHG CSev EBre ECha ENot ESis GCHN GPoy LBuc LGro LHol MBal MBri MGos NNor NSti NYor SHBN SIde SPer WEas WWin
– var. ***corsica***	See ***S. chamaecyparissus* var. *nana***
– 'Lambrook Silver'	EBee ECtt EOHP EPPr ESis GAbr LFis NHol NYor SAga SCoo SEas SPan SPla SSvw
– 'Lemon Queen'	CArn CDoC EAst ELau ESis GBar MBal MBel MGos NBir NSti NYor SAga SEas SIde SPla SWat WCHb WOak WPer
§ – var. ***nana*** ♀	CB&S CLyd EBre ECha ENot LHop MBar NFai NNor NYor SHFr SPer SRms SVen SWat WAbe WPer WWye
– – 'Weston'	CLyd CShe EWes GBar NYor

– 'Pretty Carol'	CAbP CKni EBre ELan EMil ESis LHop MAsh NFai NYor SAga SEas SIde SMad SPan WWeb
– 'Small-Ness'	CSWP EBre EDAr EGoo EMon EPPr ESis EWes LHop MAsh MBlu MBri MBro MSte NHol SIng SMad WAbe WCru WFar WPat WPyg
– subsp. ***squarrosa***	NYor
¶ ***dentata***	MGra
¶ ***elegans***	WAbe WDav
incana	See ***S. chamaecyparissus***
'Oldfield Hybrid'	MBel MLan NYor WCot
pectinata	See ***S. rosmarinifolia*** subsp. ***canescens***
§ ***pinnata***	CSev CTri LHol NYor WPer
§ – subsp. ***neapolitana*** ♀	CArn CMHG CSev CShe ECha ELan ENot LHol LHop MAll MBri MCLN NNor NSti NYor SDix SVen WEas WHCG WOak WTyr WWye
– – cream	See ***S. pinnata*** subsp. ***neapolitana* 'Edward Bowles'**
§ – – 'Edward Bowles'	CGle CLyd CMil EBar EFou EJud ELan EMil EOrc ESis GCal GOrc LHop MCLN MRav NBir NHol NPer NSti NYor SAga SAxl SChu SSvw SVen WAbe WBea WHen WHer WSHC
– – 'Sulphurea'	EBee EGoo EPfP LGre MBel MBlu NYor SPer WKif WPer WWhi
rosmarinifolia	CMil CWan EBee ELau ESis MBel SPan SRms WNdy WRha WSel WWye
§ – subsp. ***canescens***	NYor WWye
§ – subsp. ***rosmarinifolia***	CChe CMHG CSev ECha ELan ENot EOHP GCHN LHol MAll MBri MCLN NFai NSti NYor SDix SSvw WEas WHoo WSHC WWin WWye
– – 'Primrose Gem' ♀	CB&S CSam ECha EFol ELau EMil ESis LHop MBal MCLN MPla NSti NYor SAxl SBod SEas SPer SPla WGwG WPer WWye
* ***serratifolia***	EBee LHol NCut NYor WPer
tomentosa	See ***S. pinnata*** subsp. ***neapolitana***
virens	See ***S. rosmarinifolia*** subsp. ***rosmarinifolia***
viridis	See ***S. rosmarinifolia*** subsp. ***rosmarinifolia***

SAPINDUS (Sapindaceae)

See Plant Deletions

SAPIUM (Euphorbiaceae)

¶ ***japonicum***	WCoo

SAPONARIA (Caryophyllaceae)

'Bressingham' ♀	CPBP EBre ECha EPot LBee MHig MTho NHar NHol SBla WPat WPer WPyg WWin
caespitosa	EPot EWes GTou MHig NMen WAbe WOMN
x ***lempergii*** 'Max Frei'	ECro GAbr SBla SDix WCot
* 'Lilac Double'	MRav
lutea	NWCA WGor
ocymoides ♀	CB&S CLTr EAst ECha ECtt EHon ELan EMNN ESis GAbr GAul GCHN GTou LGro MPla NFla NRoo NVic SAlw SIng SRms WBea WOve WPbr WPer WStI WWin
– 'Alba'	ECha SAlw WFar
– 'Rubra Compacta' ♀	LBee MHig MTho WPyg
officinalis	CAgr CArn CBre CKin CRow ECWi EJud ELau EWFC GAbr GPoy LHol MChe MHew MSal NFai SIde SSea WGwG WHer WOak WPer WWye
– 'Alba Plena'	CGle CJew CMil CRDP CSam EBre ECha ECoo ECro EJud EMon GBar MAvo NBrk NSti SChu SUsu WCHb WElm WHer WPer WRha WWin
§ – 'Dazzler' (v)	EBar EFol EHoe ELau EMon GBri LBlm LHol MTho NBir NBrk NFai NRoo SIde WBea WCHb WCot WHer WPbr
– 'Rosea Plena'	CBre CFee CHan CMHG CMil CRDP CRow CSam ECoo ECro EEls EJud ELan EMon LLWP MBel MBri MCLN NCat NFla NOrc SMrm SPer SUsu WCHb WCot WOve WPbr WPer
– 'Rubra Plena'	CGle CHad CMHG CMil CRDP ECha ELan EMon LBlm LFis MCLN NSti SChu WCHb WCot WPbr WRha WThi
– 'Variegata'	See ***S. officinalis* 'Dazzler'**
x ***olivana*** ♀	CLyd ECha EPot ESis LFis MHig MPla MTho NMen SBla SBod WOMN WPat WPyg WWin
pamphylica	EBee
pulvinaris	See ***S. pumilio***
§ ***pumilio***	CLyd GCHN GTou NWCA
'Rosenteppich'	ESis NTow SWas WDav WPat WPyg
sicula	WPer WTyr
zawadskii	See ***Silene zawadskii***

SARCOCAPNOS (Papaveraceae)

baetica	NWCA
enneaphylla	EPot

SARCOCOCCA † (Buxaceae)

confusa ♀	CB&S CHan CMCN CPMA CPle CShe EBee EBre ELan EPla IHos ISea MBar MBri NHol SPan SPer SPla SReu SSpi SSta WAbe WBod WPat WRTC WSHC WWat
hookeriana ♀	CBlo ECot GSki GWht IOrc SHhN SReu
– B&SWJ 2585	WCru
– var. ***digyna*** ♀	CB&S CGre CHan CMCN CPMA CPle ELan ENot EPla IHos ISea LNet MBri MGos MWat NHed NHol SHBN SMac SPer SPla SReu SRms SSpi SSta WBod WPat WRTC WWat
– – 'Purple Stem'	EPla MGos MRav WDin
– var. ***humilis***	CDoC CHan CPMA CPle EBre ELan ENot EPla GOrc LHop MBal MBar MBri MGos MPla MWat NFla NHol NNor SEas SHBN SPer SPla SSpi WBod WCru WDin WSHC WWat

– Sch 2396	EPla
orientalis	CFil CMCN CPMA EFou EPla LRHS MAsh SMac SSpi WWat WWeb
'Roy Lancaster'	See ***S. ruscifolia* 'Dragon Gate'**
ruscifolia	CB&S CDoC CMCN CPMA CPle CWSG ELan ENot EPla IHos IOrc LFis LHop MGos MPla MTis SPer SSpi WWat
– var. ***chinensis*** 🏆	CBot CFil CSam EPla NHol SBid SSta WCru
– – L 713	EPla
§ – 'Dragon Gate'	CFil EFou EPla MAsh
saligna	CB&S CFil CPMA EPla WBod WCru

SARCOPOTERIUM (Rosaceae)

See Plant Deletions

SARMIENTA (Gesneriaceae)

repens 🏆	WAbe WCru

SARRACENIA † (Sarraceniaceae)

¶ x ***ahlesii*** (***rubra*** x ***alata*** 'Red Lid')	WMEx
alata	GTro WMEx
– copper lid	GTro
¶ – x ***flava*** 'Maxima'	WMEx
– purple lid	GTro
– 'Red Lid'	MHel
¶ – 'Red Lid' x ***flava*** red pitcher	WMEx
¶ – red x ***purpurea*** subsp. ***venosa***	WMEx
¶ – x ***willisii***	WMEx
x ***areolata***	GTro WMEx
– (x ***areolata*** x ***alata*** red throat)	WMEx
x ***catesbyi*** 🏆	CFil GTro MHel WMEx
– x ***excellens***	WMEx
x ***chelsonii*** 🏆	WMEx
x ***courtii***	MHel
x ***excellens*** 🏆	GTro MHel
x ***exornata***	WMEx
x ***farnhamii***	See ***S.* x *readii* 'Farnhamii'**
flava 🏆	CFil CRDP GTro MHel WMEx
¶ – 'Burgundy'	GTro WMEx
– copper lid	GTro
– 'Maxima'	WMEx WNor
– 'Maxima' x ***purpurea*** subsp. ***venosa***	MHel
– 'Maxima' x ***rubra*** subsp. ***jonesii***	MHel
x ***formosa***	MHel
x ***harperi***	WMEx
'Judy'	GTro MHel
leucophylla 🏆	GTro MHel WMEx
– x ***excellens***	MHel
x ***melanorhoda***	GTro MHel WMEx
x ***miniata***	WMEx
minor	GTro MHel WMEx
– 'Okefenokee Giant'	WMEx
x ***mitchelliana*** 🏆	GTro MHel WMEx
x ***moorei***	GTro MHel WMEx
– 'Brook's Hybrid'	GTro
¶ – (***leucophylla*** x ***moorei***)	WMEx
oreophila	EFEx GTro WMEx
– x ***leucophylla***	MHel
– x ***purpurea***	MHel
¶ x ***popei***	WMEx
– (x ***popei*** x ***flava*** giant)	WMEx
psittacina	GTro WMEx
purpurea	CFil
– subsp. ***purpurea***	GTro MHel WMEx
¶ – – f. ***heterophylla***	WMEx
– subsp. ***venosa***	GTro MHel WMEx
– – f. ***heterophylla***	MHel
¶ – – x ***oreophila***	WMEx
§ x ***readii***	GTro WMEx
¶ – (***leucophylla*** x ***readii***)	WMEx
x ***rehderi***	MHel WMEx
rubra	GTro WMEx
¶ – subsp. ***alabamensis***	MHel WMEx
– subsp. ***jonesii***	MHel WMEx
x ***swaniana***	GTro MHel WMEx
¶ – x ***popei***	WMEx
x ***wrigleyana*** 🏆	GTro

SASA † (Poaceae - Bambusoideae)

borealis	See ***Sasamorpha borealis***
chrysantha hort.	See ***Pleioblastus chino***
disticha 'Mirrezuzume'	See ***Pleioblastus pygmaeus* 'Mirrezuzume'**
glabra f. ***albostriata***	See ***Sasaella masamuneana* f. *albostriata***
kurilensis	EPla ISta SBam SDry WJun
– 'Shimofuri'	EPla ISta SBam SDry WJun
– short form	EPla
megalophylla 'Nobilis'	SBam SDry
nana	See ***S. veitchii* f. *minor***
nipponica	EPla SBam SDry WJun
– 'Aureostriata'	SBam SDry
oshidensis	EPla
§ ***palmata*** 🏆	CB&S CHad CHan CWLN ENot GAri NRar SBam
– f. ***nebulosa***	CHEx EFul EOas EPfP EPla MUlv SArc SBam SDry WJun
– 'Warley Place' (v)	SBam SDry
quelpaertensis	EPla GAri SBam SDry
senanensis	EPla SBam SDry
tessellata	See ***Indocalamus tessellatus***
tsuboiana	CB&S EBee EFou EPla MUlv SBam SDry
§ ***veitchii***	CB&S CCuc CGre CHEx CWLN CWit EBre ECha EJap EPar EPla IOrc LNet MBri MUlv SBam SDry SPer WFar WHil WJun WWye
§ – f. ***minor***	EPla SBam

SASAELLA (Poaceae - Bambusoideae)

bitchuensis hort.	SBam SDry
glabra	See ***S. masamuneana***
§ ***masamuneana***	EPla
§ – f. ***albostriata*** (v)	COtt CPMA CWLN EBee EFou EPPr EPla SBam SDry WCot WJun
– f. ***aureostriata*** (v)	COtt EPla SBam SDry
§ ***ramosa***	EBee EPla GAri GBin MBal NRya SBam SDry

SASAMORPHA (Poaceae - Bambusoideae)

§ ***borealis***	SBam

SASSAFRAS (Lauraceae)

albidum	CArn CHEx

SATUREJA (Lamiaceae)

§ ***coerulea*** 🏆	EWes LFis NBir NVic SIde WFar
hortensis	CBod CWan GPoy ILis LHol MChe MHew MLan WHer WJek WSel

montana	CArn EEls ELau EWFC GPoy ILis LHol MBri MChe MHew MPla NMen SDix SIde SRms WCHb WCer WHer WOak WPer WWye
montana citriodora	GPoy
montana 'Coerulea'	See ***S. coerulea***
§ – subsp. ***illyrica***	SIgm WThi
– prostrate white	CRDP MHar
– 'Purple Mountain'	GPoy
montana subspicata	See ***S. montana*** subsp. ***illyrica***
parnassica	WPer WWye
repanda	See ***S. spicigera***
seleriana	CInt CLTr
spicata	CLyd
§ ***spicigera***	CArn CLyd CPBP EDAr ELau EPot LFis LHol MHig NBir NMen NTow SIde SWas WCHb WHil WSel WWin WWye
thymbra	CArn EOHP GBar SHDw SIde

SATYRIUM (Orchidaceae)

See Plant Deletions

SAURAUIA (Actinidiaceae)

subspinosa	CHEx

SAUROMATUM (Araceae)

guttatum	See ***S. venosum***
§ ***venosum***	LAma MBri WCot WCru

SAURURUS (Sauruaceae)

cernuus	CBen CRow CWGN CWat EBre EHon ELan EMFW LPBA MSta NDea SRms SWat WChe WKen
chinensis	CRDP CRow

SAUSSUREA (Asteraceae)

¶ ***auriculata*** HWJCM 490	WCru

SAXEGOTHAEA (Podocarpaceae)

conspicua	CMCN ECou EPla LCon LLin SMad

SAXIFRAGA † (Saxifragaceae)

'Aemula' (X *borisii*) (8)	CLyd WAbe
aizoides var. ***atrorubens*** (6)	MBal MBro NGre
aizoon	See ***S. paniculata***
'Aladdin' (X *borisii*) (8)	NHol
'Alba' (X *apiculata*) (8)	CLyd CShe ELan EMNN EPot ESis GTou LFox MBal MBro MHig NHol NMen NRya SBla SChu SIng SSmi WAbe WCla WHoo WPat WWin
'Alba' (X *arco-valleyi*)	See ***S. 'Ophelia' (X arco-valleyi)***
'Alba' (*oppositifolia*) (9)	CLyd ELan EMNN EPot EWes GTou MYat NGre NHar NMen WAbe WWin
'Alba' (*sempervivum*)	See ***S. 'Zita'***
'Albert Einstein' (X *apiculata*) (8)	NMen WAbe
'Albertii' (*callosa*) (7)	CLyd CShe GTou MHig NNrd SIng SSmi WWin
¶ 'Albida' (*callosa*) (7)	NFla
'Aldebaran' (X *borisii*) (8)	EMNN MDHE NHar NMen
'Alfons Mucha' (8)	EPot MWat NGre NSla WAbe
'Alpenglow' (8)	MWat NMen
alpigena (8)	GCrs NGre NSla
'Amitie' (X *gloriana*) (8)	MYat
andersonii (8)	CLyd EHyt EMNN ITim MBal MWat NGre NMen NNrd NTow WAbe
X ***andrewsii*** (3X7)	MDHE MHig MTho SSmi
angustifolia	NHar
'Anne Beddall' (X *goringiana*) (8)	CLyd MWat NGre WAbe
'Aphrodite' (*sempervivum*) (8)	EPot
X ***apiculata***	See ***S. 'Gregor Mendel' (X apiculata)***
'Apple Blossom' (12)	GTou LBuc MOne NFla WGor
'Archfield White' (*callosa*) (7)	CNic NNrd
§ 'Arco' (X *arco-valleyi*) (8)	CLyd EPot MWat NNrd WAbe
X ***arco-valleyi***	See ***S. 'Arco' (X arco-valleyi)***
X ***arendsii*** (12)	WEas
§ 'Aretiastrum' (X *boydii*) (8)	EMNN EPot LFox MYat NGre NHed NMen
aretioides (8)	GCHN NMen
'Ariel' (X *hornibrookii*) (8)	LFox NNrd
'Assimilis' (X *petraschii*) (8)	CLyd MYat WAbe
'August Hayek' (X *leyboldii*) (8)	MWat NMen NNrd
I 'Aureopunctata' (X *urbium*) (3/v)	CMil CShe ECha EFol ELan EMar EPla GBuc GCal GCra LHop MBal MBro NHol NRoo SMrm SRms WFox WHen WHil
'Backhousei' (12)	NHol
'Balcana'	See ***S. paniculata*** var. ***orientalis***
'Baldensis'	See ***S. paniculata*** var. ***baldensis***
'Ballawley Guardsman' (12)	ECho EPar LFox MBal NRoo SIng
§ 'Beatrix Stanley' (X *anglica*) (8)	EMNN GCLN LFox MBal MBro MYat NGre NHar NMen WAbe
'Becky Foster' (X *borisii*) (8)	MWat NNrd
'Beechcroft White'	LBee LRHS
X 'Bettina' (X *paulinae*) (8)	GCHN
X ***biasolettoi***	See ***S. 'Phoenix' (X biasolettoi)***
biflora (9)	NHol
'Birch Baby' (12)	SIng
'Birch Yellow'	See ***S. 'Pseudoborisii' (X borisii)***
'Black Beauty' (12)	CMHG ECho LBee MBro NRoo
'Blackhouse White' (7)	NGre
¶ 'Blütenteppich' (11)	WPer
'Bob Hawkins' (12/v)	CLyd CMHG ELan GCHN GDra LBee LFox NHar NNrd SMer WRHF WWin
§ 'Bodensee' (X *hofmannii*) (8)	WAbe WPat
'Bohemia' (9)	CLyd NMen WGle
'Boston Spa' (X *elisabethae*) (8)	CLyd EMNN GCHN MBro MHig MYat NGre NHed NHol NMen NNrd NRoo NTow SChu WAbe WPat
'Bridget' (X *edithiae*) (8)	CLyd CMea CShe ELan ESis ITim LFox MBal NGre NHed NMen NRoo SSmi WAbe
'Brookside' (*burseriana*) (8)	EPot NMen SIng
brunoniana	See ***S. brunonis***
§ ***brunonis*** (2)	EPot LFox SAlw WCru
– CC&McK 108 (2)	NWCA
bryoides (5)	GTou MHig
X ***burnatii*** (7)	CLyd EPot LFox MBro MHig NHed NNrd NPro SIng WGor
burseriana (8)	GCHN MBro WAbe WPyg

'Buttercup' (× *kayei*) (8)	CPBP EPot GTou MBro MWat MYat NGre NHed NHol NNrd NWCA WAbe WHoo WPat WPyg
caesia (7)	SRms
§ ***callosa*** (7) 🏆	GCHN GTou MBro MWat NGre NHar NHol SBla WPat
§ – var. ***australis*** (7)	CNic EPot ESis MBro MDHE MHig NHol NMen NNrd
– var. ***bellardii***	See ***S. callosa***
§ – subsp. ***catalaunica*** (7)	MBro
– var. ***lantoscana***	See ***S. callosa*** var. ***australis***
– ***lingulata***	See ***S. callosa***
'Cambria Jewel' (12)	NMen NNrd
'Cambridge Seedling' (8)	MWat MYat NMen
§ ***camposii*** (12)	GAbr SIng
'Camyra' (8)	CGra MWat MYat NGre NHed NNrd WAbe
canaliculata (12)	NNrd
× ***canis-dalmatica*** (7)	CLyd CMHG ECtt EGoo EMNN ESis GGar GTou LBee MBro MHig NHar NHed NHol NMen NNrd SIng WGor WRHF
§ 'Carmen' (× *elisabethae*) (8)	CShe ELan EMNN ITim MBro MHig MOne MYat NHed NMen NNrd NRya WAbe
'Carniolica' (*paniculata*) (7)	CInt CLyd LBee LFox MDHE MHig NMen NWCA SBla WHil
'Carnival' (12)	LRHS WRHF
'Castor' (× *bilekii*) (8)	MWat NHed NHol SIng WAbe
catalaunica	See ***S. callosa*** subsp. ***catalaunica***
'Caterhamensis' (*cotyledon*) (7)	WEas
cebennensis 🏆	CLyd EPot EWes LFox NHed NMen NRya NTow SIgm SIng
– dwarf form (12)	NMen
cespitosa	NWCA
'Chambers' Pink Pride'	See ***S. 'Miss Chambers' (× urbium)***
§ ***cherlerioides*** (5)	EBar ELan NRya WCla WWin
'Cherrytrees' (× *boydii*) (8)	CLyd NMen NNrd
'Chetwynd' (*marginata*) (8)	MWat WAbe
'Chez Nous' (× *gloriana*) (8/v)	NGre NMen
'Christine' (× *anglica*) (8)	LFox MWat NMen NNrd SIng
chrysospleniifolia	See ***S. rotundifolia*** subsp. ***chrysospleniifolia***
¶ 'Clare' (× *anglica*) (8)	MDHE
'Clare Island' (12)	SIng
§ 'Clarence Elliott' (*umbrosa* var. *primuloides*) (3) 🏆	CNic CShe ELan EPPr EWes GCal GDra MBro MHig NHol NRya NVic WCla WCot WPat WWin
§ 'Cloth of Gold' (*exarata* subsp. *moschata*) (12)	CLyd CMea CShe EAst ECha ELan EPot GDra GTou LBee MBal MBar MPla NMen NRoo NRya NWCA SBla SBod SSmi WAbe WFar WWin
cochlearis (7)	CMea CShe ESis LBee MBal MOne MWat NBro NHed NMen NNor SSmi WPer WPyg WWin
'Cockscomb' (*paniculata*) (7)	MDHE
'Compacta' (*exarata* subsp. *moschata*) (12)	MBro
corbariensis	See ***S. fragilis***
'Corona' (× *boydii*) (8)	LFox MDHE MWat NGre NHol NMen
* 'Corrennie Claret'	GTou
'Correvoniana' (*paniculata*) (7)	EBre ECtt EPad ESis GCHN MBro MOne NBus NHed NNrd NRya SAlw WGor WRHF WWin
'Corrie Fee' (*oppositifolia*) (9)	GCrs GTou NHar NHol
corsica subsp. ***cossoniana*** (11)	WOMN
§ ***cortusifolia*** (4)	CChu CHEx MBal NHar SSpi
– dwarf form (4)	EPot
– var. ***fortunei***	See ***S. fortunei***
§ ***corymbosa*** (8)	NGre
cotyledon (7)	CLyd GDra LBee NHol NNor SIng WCla WEas WPer
§ 'Cranbourne' (× *anglica*) (8) 🏆	CLyd CShe EBre EMNN EPot LFox MBro MWat MYat NGre NHar NHol NMen SBla SSmi WAbe WPat
¶ 'Cream' (*paniculata*) (7)	NNrd SSmi
'Cream Seedling' (× *elisabethae*) (8)	EBre ESis MDHE MWat NGre NHed NMen
'Crenata' (*burseriana*) (8)	CLyd EPot GCHN LFox MBro MFos MWat MYat NGre NHar NHed NMen NNrd SAlw WAbe WHoo
'Crimson Rose' (*paniculata*) (7)	NNrd
§ ***crustata*** (7)	EHyt GCHN MDHE NWCA SIng
– var. ***vochinensis***	See ***S. crustata***
'Crystalie' (× *biasolettoi*) (8)	EPot MBro MDHE NGre NMen WAbe WPat
'Cultrata' (*paniculata*) (7)	NBro
'Cumulus' (*iranica* hybrid) (8)	EHyt WAbe
cuneata (12)	NHol
cuneifolia (3)	CHEx CLyd EAst GDra GGar LBee MBal MWat NFla NGre NHed NRoo NSti NWCA SSmi
– var. ***capillipes***	See ***S. cuneifolia*** subsp. ***cuneifolia***
¶ – var. ***subintegra*** (3)	ECho
cuscutiformis (4)	CInt EBee GCal LRHS MHlr NTow WCot WCru WOve
cymbalaria (13)	EBur WCla
– var. ***huetiana*** (13)	CNic
'Dainty Dame' (× *arco-valleyi*) (8)	CLyd LFox MWat NGre NHed NMen SIng WAbe
'Dana' (× *megaseiflora*) (8)	CLyd EMNN EPPr MWat NHol NMen
'Dartington Double' (12)	EBre EWes GCHN GDra GTou LBee MBal MOne NHar NNrd NVic
'Dawn' (8)	NNrd
¶ 'Dawn Frost' (9)	EHyt
'Delia' (× *hornibrookii*) (8)	CPBP NMen
§ 'Denisa' (× *pseudokotschyi*) (8)	MBal WAbe
densa	See ***S. cherlerioides***
§ 'Dentata' (× *polita*) (3)	CHan ECha EPPr EPla GAbr GGar NVic
'Dentata' (× *urbium*)	See ***S. 'Dentata' (× polita)***
desoulavyi (8)	GTou MHig NGre
diapensioides (8)	CLyd NGre NMen
'Doctor Clay' (7)	MDHE WAbe
'Doctor Ramsey' (7)	ELan EPPr ESis EWes GTou ITim LBee MBro MHig MRPP NBro NHed NNrd SIng SSmi WGor
¶ aff. ***doyalana*** SEP 45	CGra EHyt
'Drakula' (*ferdinandi-coburgi*) (8)	CLyd LRHS MDHE MWat NHed NMen WAbe

'Dubarry' (12)	ECho EWes SIde SIng SMrm
'Duncan Lowe' (*andersonii*) (8)	NGre
'Dwight Ripley' (8)	LFox
'Edgar Irmscher' (8)	LFox MWat WAbe
'Edie Campbell' (12)	NGre
'Edith' (× *edithiae*) (8)	LRHS NNrd
'Edward Elgar' (× *megaseiflora*) (8)	MWat NHol NMen
'Elf' (12)	ELan EMNN LBee MOne NBro NMen NNrd NRoo SIng SRms SSmi WCla WFar WGor
'Eliot Hodgkin' (× *millstreamiana*) (8)	LFox NNrd WAbe
× ***elisabethae*** hort.	See ***S.* 'Carmen' (× *elisabethae*)**
'Elizabeth Sinclair' (× *elisabethae*) (8)	EPot NMen NNrd
'Ellie Brinckerhoff' (× *hornibrookii*) (8)	CLyd NGre
¶ 'Ernst Heinrich' (× *heinrichii*) (8)	NMen
'Esther' (× *burnatii*) (7)	CLyd CMea EBre EHyt ELan ESis LBee MHig NNrd SBla SMer SSmi WAbe
§ 'Eulenspiegel' (× *geuderi*) (8)	CLyd EPot LBuc NNrd
exarata (12)	ITim LBee LFox NMen
§ – subsp. ***moschata*** (12)	NGre NWCA
exarata pyrenaica	See ***S. androsacea***
Fair Maids of France	See ***S.* 'Flore Pleno' (*granulata*)**
'Fairy' (*exarata* subsp. *moschata*) (12)	ELan NFla
'Faldonside' (× *boydii*) (8) 🏆	CLyd EPot LFox MBro MWat NGre NHed NHol NMen SBla WAbe WHoo WPat WPyg
'Falstaff' (*burseriana*) (8)	EPot LFox MDHE MWat MYat SBla SIng
× ***farreri*** (7)	NGre NHed NNrd
§ 'Faust' (× *borisii*) (8)	EMNN NGre NMen SBla SIng
federici-augusti	See ***S. frederici-augusti***
'Ferdinand' (× *hofmannii*) (8)	NMen NNrd WAbe
ferdinandi-coburgi 🏆	CLyd EPot LFox NGre NHed NNrd NTow NWCA WAbe WRHF
– var. ***pravislavii***	See ***S. ferdinandi-coburgi*** var. ***rhodopea***
– var. ***radoslavoffii***	See ***S. ferdinandi-coburgi*** var. ***rhodopea***
§ – var. ***rhodopea*** (8)	EPot LRHS NHed SIng
ferruginea	NTow
'Findling' (12)	CMHG EGoo EPot GCHN LGro MOne NGre NMen NNrd NRoo SBod SIng SSmi WAbe WWin
¶ 'Flavescens' (*paniculata*) (7)	NBro
× ***fleischeri*** (8)	NMen
§ 'Flore Pleno' (*granulata*) (11)	CFir CMil CRDP CVer ELan EWes GAbr GBri LFox MHlr NBir NHar NRya NSla NWoo SIng WAbe WCot WHil
'Florissa' (*oppositifolia*) (9)	EBre GCHN LRHS WAbe
'Flowers of Sulphur'	See ***S.* 'Schwefelblüte'**
§ ***fortunei*** 🏆	CLTr NBir SPer SSpi WCru
'Foster's Gold' (× *elisabethae*) (8)	NMen
'Four Winds' (12)	CWan EGle EWes GAbr LBee NMen NNrd SBla SIde SIng SSmi
'Francis Cade' (7)	ELan ITim NGre
× 'Franzii' (× *paulinae*) (8)	MDHE MYat NHed
§ ***frederici-augusti*** (8)	SBla
§ – subsp. ***grisebachii*** (8) 🏆	GTou MFos MYat NGre NSla WCla
– – 'Wisley' (*frederici-augusti* subsp. *grisebachii*) (8) 🏆	GCHN MBal NHar NHol NMen WHoo WPat WPyg
'Friar Tuck' (× *boydii*) (8)	MWat NMen
'Friesei' (× *salmonica*) (8)	CLyd CShe EMNN EPot MBro MYat NHar NHed NMen
§ × ***fritschiana*** (7)	EPPr MDHE NHol NNrd SIng
'Funkii' (× *petraschii*) (8)	MWat NMen
'Gaiety' (12)	ECho ELan GDra LBee NFla NRoo SIng
'Galaxie' (× *megaseiflora*) (8)	CLyd LFox MDHE NGre NHol NMen WAbe
¶ 'Ganymede' (*burseriana*) (8)	NNrd
'Gelber Findling' (8)	EPot LRHS MDHE WAbe
'Gem' (× *irvingii*) (8)	EMNN NHar NMen NNrd
'Geoides'	See ***S. hirsuta*** subsp. ***paucicrenata***
georgei (8)	EPot NGre
geranioides (11)	GCHN
'Gertie Pritchard' (× *megaseiflora*)	See ***S.* 'Mrs Gertie Prichard' (× *megaseiflora*)**
× ***geuderi***	See ***S.* 'Eulenspiegel' (× *geuderi*)**
§ × ***geum*** (3)	CHid ECha ELan EPar MRav NWoo
– Dixter form (3)	ECha EPPr EPla
* 'Gladys'	ELan
'Glauca' (*paniculata* var. *brevifolia*)	MDHE NGre
* 'Gleborg'	EWes
'Gloria' (*burseriana*) (8) 🏆	CLyd CNic CShe LFox MBal MBro MRPP MYat NGre NMen NNrd NSla SBla SRms WPat
× ***gloriana*** (8)	EMNN NMen
◆ 'Gloriosa' (× *gloriana*)	See ***S.* 'Godiva' (× *gloriana*)**
§ 'Godiva' (× *gloriana*) (8)	MWat WAbe
'Goeblii' (8)	MDHE NGre WAbe
'Gold Dust' (× *eudoxiana*) (8)	CLyd EMNN EPPr GTou LFox MHig MOne MWat MYat NHar NMen SBod SIng WAbe WWin
'Gold Leaf'	EPot
'Golden Falls' (12/v)	EPot EWes GTou LBee LHop MOne NGre NMen SIng WPat WRHF
◆ 'Golden Prague' (× *pragensis*)	See ***S.* 'Zlatá Praha' (× *pragensis*)**
'Grace Farwell' (× *anglica*) (8)	CLyd EMNN EPot GCHN ITim MBar MBro MYat NGre NHed NHol NMen NRya NWCA WAbe WHoo WPyg
◆ 'Gracilis' (× *geum*)	See ***S.* 'Gracilis' (× *polita*)**
§ 'Gracilis' (× *polita*) (3)	CNic
granulata	CNic ECWi EWFC MHew NMen NRya SAlw WCla WHil WOMN
'Gratoides' (× *grata*) (8)	MYat NGre WAbe
¶ 'Greenslacks Claire' (*oppositifolia*) (9)	NGre
¶ 'Greenslacks Heather' (*oppositifolia*) (9)	NGre
¶ 'Greenslacks Valerie' (*oppositifolia*) (9)	NGre
§ 'Gregor Mendel' (× *apiculata*) (8) 🏆	CMea ELan EMNN ESis GDra GTou MBal MBro MHig MNrw MPla MYat NGre NHed NHol NMen SAlw SBla SBod SIng SSmi WAbe WHoo WPyg
grisebachii	See ***S. frederici-augusti*** subsp. ***grisebachii***
– ***montenegrina***	See ***S. frederici-augusti***

'Gustav Hegi' (*x anormalis*) (8)	WAbe
'Haagii' (*x eudoxiana*) (8)	CInt CLyd ELan EMNN GCHN GTou MBal MBro MOne NGre NHed NMen NNrd NTow SAlw SIng SSmi WAbe WRHF WWin
hallii	GCHN WWin
'Harlow Car' (8)	CLyd LFox NMen
'Hartside Pink' (*umbrosa*) (3)	NWoo
'Hartswood White' (12)	SIng
'Hedwig' (*x malbyana*) (8)	MWat NMen
'Herbert Cuerden' (*x elisabethae*) (8)	NGre NHed NNrd
'Hi-Ace' (12/v)	ELan EMNN GTou LBee LFox MBro NGre NRoo NWCA SBla SBod SSmi WRHF WWin
¶ 'Highdownensis' (7)	MDHE
'Hindhead Seedling' (*x boydii*) (8)	CLyd EMNN LRHS MDHE MWat NHar NHed NMen NNrd WAbe
hirsuta (3)	CLyd MDHE NRya WCru
'Hirsuta' (*x geum*)	See ***S. x geum***
'Hirtella' (*paniculata*) (7)	MDHE SIng
'His Majesty' (*x irvingii*) (8)	EMNN LFox MDHE NHar NMen NNrd WAbe
'Hocker Edge' (*x arco-valleyi*) (8)	ITim LFox MHig MWat MYat NHed WAbe
'Holden Seedling' (12)	EMNN EPot EWes
hostii (7)	CLyd ESis GTou ITim LBee MHig SIng
§ – subsp. ***hostii*** (7)	MDHE
– – var. ***altissima*** (7)	STre
– subsp. ***rhaetica*** (7)	MDHE NMen
hypnoides (12)	GAbr MOne SSmi
§ – var. ***egemmulosa*** (12)	MBal
hypostoma (8)	NGre
'Icelandica' (*cotyledon*) (7)	NHol
'Icicle' (*x elisabethae*) (8)	MWat
'Ingeborg' (12)	ECha LBee SChu SIng
iranica (8)	EMNN GCHN MWat MYat NGre NHar NMen NNrd
'Irene Bacci' (*x baccii*) (8)	MWat NMen
'Iris Prichard' (*x hardingii*) (8)	CLyd EMNN MBro MYat NGre NNrd WAbe WHoo WPyg
irrigua (11)	EWes NChi SSca
x ***irvingii***	See ***S. 'Walter Irving' (x irvingii)***
'Ivana' (*x caroliquarti*)	MWat
'James Bremner' (12)	GGar LBee MOne NFla SBod SIng
'Jason' (*x elisabethae*) (8)	MWat
'Jenkinsiae' (*x irvingii*) (8) 🏆	Widely available
§ 'Johann Kellerer' (*x kellereri*) (8)	LFox MHig MYat NGre NHed WAbe
'John Tomlinson' (*burseriana*) (8)	NSla WAbe
'Josef Capek' (*x megaseiflora*) (8)	EPot NMen
'Josef Mánes' (*x borisii*) (8)	MDHE NMen
'Joy'	See ***S. 'Kaspar Maria Sternberg' (x petraschii)***
'Judith Shackleton' (*x abingdonensis*) (8)	CLyd EHyt MWat NGre NMen NNrd WAbe
'Juliet'	See ***S. 'Riverslea' (x hornibrookii)***
§ ***juniperifolia*** (8)	ELan EMNN EPPr GCHN GTou ITim MOne MWat NGre NHar NHed NMen NNrd NRoo NWCA SChu SMer SRms SSmi
– var. ***macedonica***	See ***S. juniperifolia***
'Jupiter' (*x megaseiflora*) (8)	CLyd EMNN MWat NGre NHar NMen NNrd WAbe
¶ 'Karasin' (9)	NNrd
'Karel Capek' (*x megaseiflora*) (8)	CGra CLyd CMea EPot MWat NGre NHed NHol NMen NNrd WAbe
'Karel Stivín' (*x edithiae*) (8)	EMNN MWat NGre NMen
'Karlstejn' (*x borisii*) (8)	WAbe
§ 'Kaspar Maria Sternberg' (*x petraschii*) (8)	EMNN EPPr GCHN ITim LFox MBro NGre NHar NHol NMen NNrd WPat
'Kath Dryden' (*x anglica*) (8)	CGra CLyd MDHE SIng WAbe
'Kathleen Pinsent' (7) 🏆	CShe EPot MBro NGre NHar NNrd NVic NWCA SIng SSmi WAbe
'Kathleen' (*x polulacina*) (8)	CLyd EHyt NGre NHol
x ***kellereri***	See ***S. 'Johann Kellerer' (x kellereri)***
'Kestoniensis' (*x salmonica*) (8)	MWat NNrd
'Kewensis' (*x kellereri*) (8)	MWat NMen NNrd SIng WAbe
'King Lear' (*x bursiculata*) (8)	EPot LFox LRHS MWat NRya SIng
'Kingii'	See ***S. hypnoides*** var. ***egemmulosa***
'Kingscote White'	SIng
'Klondike' (*x boydii*) (8)	MDHE
'Knapton Pink' (12)	CMHG LBee NRya SIng SSmi
'Knapton White' (12)	LBuc SIng WCla
§ x 'Kolbiana' (*x paulinae*) (8)	CLyd MDHE MWat MYat
'Koprvnik' (*paniculata*) (7)	EPPr MDHE SIng
'Krasava' (*x megaseiflora*) (8)	CLyd CPBP EHyt EMNN GCLN NGre NHar NHol NMen NNrd
'Kyrillii' (*x borisii*) (8)	EMNN NMen NNrd
'Labe' (*x arco-valleyi*) (8)	CLyd EPot LRHS NMen WAbe
'Labradorica' (*paniculata*)	See ***S. paniculata neogaea***
'Lady Beatrix Stanley'	See ***S. 'Beatrix Stanley' (x anglica)***
'Lagraveana' (*paniculata*) (7)	ELan NGre NHed WRHF WWin
x ***landaueri***	See ***S. 'Leonore' (x landaueri)***
'Lenka' (*x byam-groundsii*) (8)	EHyt EMNN ITim NGre NHar NMen NNrd NSla WAbe
'Leo Gordon Godseff' (*x elisabethae*) (8)	CLyd MHig MOne MYat NMen SBla SIng
§ 'Leonore' (*x landaueri*) (8)	MDHE MWat SIng WAbe
'Letchworth Gem' (*x urbium*) (3)	GCal
x ***leyboldii*** (8)	GTou NMen
'Lidice' (8)	EMNN NGre NHar NMen NNrd WAbe
lilacina (8)	CLyd EHyt EMNN NGre NHar NMen NNrd SIng WPat
'Lindau' (8)	MWat
lingulata	See ***S. callosa***
'Lismore Carmine' (*x lismorensis*) (8)	CGra CLyd EHyt MWat NGre NMen
'Lismore Pink' (*x lismorensis*) (8)	CLyd EHyt MWat NGre
'Lohengrin' (*x hoerhammeri*) (8)	MWat NNrd
'Lohmuelleri' (*x biasolettoi*) (8)	MWat
longifolia (7)	CGra ELan NSla WGor
– JJA 861600 (7)	SBla
◆ Love Me	See ***S. 'Miluj Mne' (x poluanglica)***
'Lowndes' (*andersonii*) (8)	WAbe

'Ludmila Šubrová' (X *bertolonii*) (8)	NGre
'Luna' (X *millstreamiana*) (8)	WAbe
'Lusanna' (X *irvingii*) (8)	MDHE NGre
'Lutea' (*marginata*)	See ***S.* 'Faust' (X *borisii*)**
'Lutea' (*paniculata*) (7) 🏆	CNic EPPr ESis GDra GTou LBee MBal MBro MRPP NBro NGre NHed NMen NNrd NRoo SBla SChu SIng SSmi
¶ 'Lutea' (X *stuartii*) (8)	MDHE
§ 'Luteola' (X *boydii*) (8) 🏆	MDHE WAbe
luteoviridis	See ***S. corymbosa***
'Luzníce' (X *poluluteopurpurea*) (8)	MWat NGre NHed
'Major' (*cochlearis*) (7) 🏆	LRHS NMen NNrd WAbe WGor
◆ 'Major Lutea'	See ***S.* 'Luteola' (X *boydii*)**
manshuriensis (1)	GDra
'Margarete' (X *borisii*) (8)	MWat NHed NNrd WAbe
marginata (8)	CLyd LFox MYat NGre
– var. ***balcanica***	See ***S. marginata*** var. ***rocheliana***
– var. ***boryi*** (8)	EHyt EPot MDHE MWat MYat NGre NMen SIng WAbe
– var. ***coriophylla*** (8)	EPot MDHE MYat NNrd NWCA
– var. ***karadzicensis*** (8)	EMNN LRHS NMen NNrd
§ – var. ***rocheliana*** (8)	CGra CLyd CMHG CPBP ELan EPot NGre NMen NNrd SIng
'Maria Luisa' (X *salmonica*) (8)	CLyd CPBP EMNN EPot LFox MBro MWat NGre NHed NNrd WAbe WPat
'Marianna' (X *borisii*) (8)	CLyd MYat NGre NHed NMen NNrd NRya
'Marie Stivínová' (X *borisii*) (8)	MWat
'Mars' (X *elisabethae*) (8)	MWat
'Marshal Joffre' (12)	LBuc
§ 'Martha' (X *semmleri*) (8)	CLyd EMNN NGre NMen NNrd
matta-florida	MWat
'May Queen' (9)	MWat NHol
media (8)	CLyd EHyt MWat NGre
X ***megaseiflora***	See ***S.* 'Robin Hood' (X *megaseiflora*)**
mertensiana (1)	CInt CLyd CPBP GTou NBir SAlw
– var. ***bulbifera*** (1)	CNic
'Meteor' (8)	NNrd NRya
micranthidifolia (1)	WThi
'Millstream Cream' (X *elisabethae*) (8)	CLyd EPot MDHE MWat NNrd
§ 'Miluj Mne' (X *poluanglica*) (8)	EHyt LFox NGre NHar NNrd
'Minehaha' (X *elisabethae*) (8)	MDHE WAbe
'Minor' (*cochlearis*) (7) 🏆	CInt EMNN EPad GDra GTou LBee LFox LRHS MBal MBro MHig MRPP NHol NMen NVic NWCA SChu SIng SSmi WCla WHoo WPat
'Minor Glauca' (*paniculata*)	See ***S. paniculata*** var. ***brevifolia* 'Glauca'**
'Minor' (*paniculata*)	See ***S. paniculata*** var. ***brevifolia***
'Minutifolia' (*paniculata*) (7)	CNic EPad EPot ESis LBee LFox MBal MBro MDHE NHed NWCA SIng
§ 'Miss Chambers' (X *urbium*) (3)	EGoo WCot
'Mona Lisa' (X *borisii*) (8)	MDHE MWat MYat SIng WAbe WPat
'Moonlight'	See ***S.* 'Sulphurea' (X *boydii*)**

'Moonlight Sonata' (X *boydii*)	See ***S.* 'Mondscheinsonate' (X *boydii*)**
moschata	See ***S. exarata*** subsp. ***moschata***
* 'Mossy Irish'	EPot
'Mother of Pearl' (X *irvingii*) (8)	EMNN NHar NMen WAbe
'Mother Queen' (X *irvingii*) (8)	MBro MDHE NHol WHoo WPat WPyg
'Mount Nachi' (*fortunei*) (4)	CFil ECha EHyt EWes NHar SBla SSpi SWas WCot WPer
'Mrs E. Piper' (12)	LBuc
§ 'Mrs Gertie Prichard' (X *megaseiflora*) (8)	LFox MWat NHol NMen WAbe
'Mrs Helen Terry' (X *salmonica*) (8)	CLyd EPot LRHS MDHE MYat NHed NMen
'Mrs Leng' (X *elisabethae*) (8)	EMNN NMen
'Myra' (X *anglica*) (8)	EMNN LFox MBro MWat MYat NHol NWCA WAbe WHoo WPat WPyg
'Myra Cambria' (X *anglica*) (8)	GCHN MWat MYat NGre NHol NMen NNrd WAbe
'Nancye' (X *goringiana*) (8)	CGra CLyd MDHE NGre NMen NNrd WAbe
§ ***nelsoniana*** (1)	NHol NNrd
nivalis (1)	NHol
'Norvegica' (*cotyledon*) (7)	CLyd GTou MDHE NGre WWin
'Notata' (*paniculata*) (7)	NNrd
'Nottingham Gold' (X *boydii*) (8)	CLyd MDHE MWat NGre NMen WAbe
'Nugget' (8)	SIng
'Obristii' (X *salmonica*) (8)	EMNN ITim NHol NMen WAbe
'Obtusocuneata' (*fortunei*) (4)	ECho EHyt ELan NHar SBla SWas WAbe
'Ochroleuca' (X *elisabethae*) (8)	CLyd EMNN ITim NMen WAbe
'Opalescent' (8)	CLyd LFox MWat NNrd WAbe
§ 'Ophelia' (X *arco-valleyi*) (8)	MWat NGre NHol
oppositifolia (9)	CMea EBre GTou ITim MOne MYat NHol NSla SIde SRms WAbe WWin
– X ***biflora*** (9)	NHar NTow
– subsp. ***latina*** (9)	CLyd ELan EMNN EPot GDra GGar GTou NHar WRHF
'Oriole' (X *boydii*) (8)	NMen
'Orjen' (*paniculata* var. *orientalis*) (7)	NNrd
¶ 'Pandora' (*burseriana*) (8)	SAlw
§ ***paniculata*** (7)	CShe ELan ESis GTou LBee MBal MBro MWat NHed NMen NRoo NSla WCla WHil WHoo WPyg
§ – var. ***baldensis*** (7)	CLyd ELan GDra GTou ITim MBar MBro MWat NBro NGre NHed NHol NMen NNrd SBla SIgm SSmi WAbe WCla WRHF WWin
§ – var. ***brevifolia*** (7)	CNic NNrd SIng SSmi
§ – subsp. ***cartilaginea*** (7)	NHol SBla
– subsp. ***kolenatiana***	See ***S. paniculata*** subsp. ***cartilaginea***
§ – ***neogaea*** (7)	MDHE
§ – var. ***orientalis*** (7)	MBro MDHE SSmi WCla
paradoxa (14)	CLyd EPot SBla SIng WGor
'Parcevalis' (X *finnisiae*) (8X6)	CLyd WAbe
X 'Parsee' (X *margoxiana*) (8)	EPot NRya WAbe
X 'Paula' (X *paulinae*) (8)	NGre
'Peach Blossom' (8)	CLyd EPot MWat MYat NGre NMen NRya SBla SIng WAbe

'Pearl Rose' (X *anglica*) (8)	LFox NGre
'Pearly Gates' (X *irvingii*) (8)	CLyd MWat NGre NMen NNrd WAbe
'Pearly Gold' (12)	CMea NRoo NRya SIde
'Pearly King' (12)	CLyd ECho ELan LBee MBal NMen NVic WAbe
X ***pectinata***	See ***S.*** X ***fritschiana***
'Penelope' (X *boydilacina*) (8)	CLyd CPBP EHyt EMNN EPot ITim LBee MBro MFos MYat NGre NHed NHol NNrd SAlw SBla WAbe WHoo WPat WPyg
'Peter Burrow' (X *poluanglica*) (8)	CGra CLyd CPBP MDHE NHar NMen NNrd WAbe
'Peter Pan' (12)	ELan EMNN EPot GDra GTou LBee LFox LGro MBro NFla NGre NHol NMen NNrd NRoo SBod SSmi WPat
'Petra' (8)	CLyd EPot NHol NNrd WAbe
X ***petraschii*** (8)	ITim
§ 'Phoenix' (X *biasolettoi*) (8)	LRHS NMen SIng
'Pilatus' (X *boydii*) (8)	MWat NMen SIng
'Pixie' (12)	EBre EMNN LBee MBal MPla MWat NFla NGre NHol NMen NNrd NRoo NRya SIng SRms SSmi
'Pixie Alba'	See ***S.* 'White Pixie'**
◆ 'Plena' (*granulata*)	See ***S.* 'Flore Pleno' (*granulata*)**
¶ 'Pluto' (X *megaseiflora*) (8)	MDHE
'Pollux' (X *boydii*) (8)	EPot
poluniniana (8)	CLyd EHyt EMNN EPPr ITim LFox NGre NHar NHol NMen NWCA WAbe
'Pompadour'	LBee
porophylla (8)	EHyt GDra NGre WAbe
aff. – (8)	NWCA
– var. ***thessalica***	See ***S. sempervivum* f. *stenophylla***
'Portae' (*paniculata*) (7)	NNrd SIng
'Primrose Bee' (X *apiculata*) (8)	EPot WAbe
'Primrose Dame' (X *elisabethae*) (8)	CShe EMNN ESis ITim MBal MWat MYat NHol NMen SIng WAbe WFar
X ***primulaize*** (6X3)	CLyd MBro MHlr NMen SRms WOMN
'Primulina' (X *malbyana*) (8)	LFox NHed WAbe
primuloides	See ***S. umbrosa* var. *primuloides***
'Prince Hal' (*burseriana*) (8)	EHyt EMNN EPot ESis ITim MDHE NHar NHed NMen NNrd
'Princess' (*burseriana*) (8)	EHyt NMen NNrd
'Probynii' (*cochlearis*) (7)	EPot MDHE MWat NNrd
'Prometheus' (X *prossenii*) (8)	NGre
'Prospero' (X *petraschii*) (8)	MWat NGre NNrd WAbe
X ***prossenii***	See ***S.* 'Regina' (X *prossenii*)**
§ 'Pseudoborisii' (X *borisii*) (8)	EPot ITim
X ***pseudokotschyi***	See ***S.* 'Denisa' (X *pseudokotschyi*)**
'Pseudosalomonii' (X *salmonica*) (8)	EPot
'Pseudoscardica' (X *wehrhahnii*) (8)	MWat
¶ 'Pseudovaldensis' (*cochlearis*) (7)	MDHE
pubescens subsp. ***iratiana*** (12)	EPot NMen
punctata	See ***S. nelsoniana***
'Pungens' (X *apiculata*) (8)	NHed NHol NMen WAbe
'Purpurea' (*fortunei*)	See ***S.* 'Rubrifolia' (*fortunei*)**
¶ 'Purpurteppich' (11)	WPer
§ X 'Pygmalion' (X *webrii*) (8)	CLyd CPBP ESis MYat NGre NHol NMen WAbe WPat
'Pyramidalis' (*cotyledon*) (7)	EPfP LBuc SRms
'Pyrenaica' (*oppositifolia*) (9)	EMNN GÇLN NHar NMen
'Quarry Wood' (X *anglica*) (8)	NMen
'Rainsley Seedling' (*paniculata*) (7)	MDHE NBro NMen
ramulosa	NMen
'Red Poll' (X *poluanglica*) (8)	CGra CLyd MDHE MWat NGre NMen WAbe
§ 'Regina' (X *prossenii*) (8)	GCHN ITim NNrd SIng WAbe
retusa (9)	CLyd EHyt EMNN EPot NGre NSla NWCA SSca
'Rex' (*paniculata*) (7)	LBuc NHol NMen NNrd SIng
§ 'Riverslea' (X *hornibrookii*) (8) 🏆	CGle CLyd CPBP EMNN LFox MBro MWat NGre NHar NHol NMen WAbe WPat
§ 'Robin Hood' (X *megaseiflora*) (8)	CLyd EMNN EPot ITim LFox LRHS MWat MYat NGre NHar NMen NNrd SBla SIng WAbe WPat
'Rokujô' (*fortunei*) (4)	EFou
rosacea subsp. ***hartii*** (12)	SIng
'Rosea' (*cortusifolia*) (4)	NHar
'Rosea' (*paniculata*) (7)	GDra GTou LBee MBal MBro NBro NGre NHed NHol NRoo NSla SAlw SBla SIng SSmi STre WCla WHoo WPyg WWin
'Rosea' (X *stuartii*) (8)	NHed WAbe
'Rosemarie' (X *anglica*) (8)	CLyd ITim MHig MYat WAbe
'Rosenzwerg' (12)	LBee
'Rosina Sündermann' (X *rosinae*) (8)	EPot LRHS NHed NNrd NSla WAbe
rotundifolia	CLyd GBin NHol SSpi WCot
§ – subsp. ***chrysospleniifolia*** (10)	WCot WCru WPer
'Rubella' (X *irvingii*) (8)	MDHE MWat
§ 'Rubrifolia' (*fortunei*) (4)	CFil CMil EBre ECha EFou MBri NHar NRoo SSpi SWas WCot WCru WFox WGer WSan
'Ruth Draper' (*oppositifolia*) (9)	CShe EMNN EPot GCHN NGre NHar SBla WAbe
'Ruth McConnell' (12)	CMea LBee LBuc
'Sabrina' (X *fallsvillagensis*) (8)	CLyd MWat NHol
'Saint John's' (*caesia*) (7)	EBur MDHE NNrd SAlw WWin
'Saint Kilda' (*oppositifolia*) (9)	CLyd GCrs GTou
'Salmon' (X *primulaize*) (6X3)	EPot ESis LBee LBuc MHig NHed NWoo WPer
'Salomonii' (X *salmonica*) (8)	CLyd EPPr EPot ITim MHig MOne NHed NMen NNrd SIng SRms WAbe
sancta (8)	CLyd EPot GCHN LFox MBal MHig SRms SSmi WAbe
– subsp. ***pseudosancta*** var. ***macedonica***	See ***S. juniperifolia***
'Sanguinea Superba' (X *arendsii*) (12) 🏆	GDra NNrd SIng
'Sara Sinclair' (X *arco-valleyi*) (8)	LRHS MYat NHol
sarmentosa	See ***S. stolonifera***
'Sartorii'	See ***S.* X 'Pygmalion' (X *webrii*)**
'Saturn' (X *megaseiflora*) (8)	EPot MWat NGre NHol NMen NNrd
'Sázava' (X *poluluteopurpurea*) (8)	MDHE MWat NGre NHed
scardica	CPBP EHyt EMNN MDHE MWat NMen WAbe

– var. ***dalmatica***	See ***S. obtusa***
– f. ***erythrantha*** (8)	NNrd
– var. ***obtusa***	See ***S. obtusa***
◆ 'Schelleri' (× *petraschii*)	See **S. 'White Star' (× *petraschii*)**
◆ 'Schleicheri' (× *kellereri*)	See **S. 'Schleicheri' (× *landaueri*)**
§ 'Schleicheri' (× *landaueri*) (8)	EMNN
¶ 'Schneeteppich' (11)	WPer
§ 'Schwefelblüte' (12)	GTou LBee MBal NRoo SIng SSmi WPat WRHF
¶ ***scleropoda***	NGre
'Seaspray' (× *arendsii*) (12/v)	EWes NVic
'Seissera' (*burseriana*) (8)	EPot NHol
× ***semmleri***	See **S. 'Martha' (× *semmleri*)**
sempervivum	EPot LFox MBro NWCA
– JCA 864.003 (8)	CPBP MBro
§ – f. ***stenophylla***	GCHN GTou MDHE NHed
sibirica (11)	GTou
'Silver Cushion' (12/v)	CMea EAst EBre ELan EPot GTou LBee MBro NPri NRoo SIng SMer SSmi WAbe
'Silver Edge' (× *arco-valleyi*) (8)	NMen WAbe
'Sir Douglas Haig' (12)	NNrd SIng
'Snowcap' (*pubescens*) (12)	EPot LBee NHed NMen NNrd NWCA
'Snowdon' (*burseriana*) (8)	MWat
'Snowflake' (7)	GCLN MHig NHed NNrd WHil
§ 'Sofia' (× *borisii*) (8)	EPot LFox NGre NNrd WAbe
§ 'Southside Seedling' 🏆	CLyd CShe ELan EPot ESis GTou LHop MBar MBro MFos MTho NBro NGre NHar NHol NMen NNrd NRoo SIng SSmi WAbe WCla WHoo WPat WPyg WWin
sp. BM&W 118	GDra
sp. SEP 22	MWat NGre NHol
'Spartakus' (× *apiculata*) (8)	NRya WAbe
spathularis	MHlr WCot WEas WWin
'Speciosa' (*burseriana*) (8)	MDHE NHed
'Splendens' (*oppositifolia*) (9) 🏆	ELan EMNN EPot ITim LFox MBal NHed NMen SMer SRms SSmi WAbe WGor WPat
'Sprite' (12)	GCHN LBee
spruneri	MYat NWCA
– var. ***deorum*** (8)	NGre
'Stansfieldii' (12)	EBre EMNN NGre NMen NNrd SBod SSmi WWin
§ 'Stella' (× *stormonthii*) (8)	SBla
stellaris (1)	GTou
stolitzkae	CLyd EMNN EPot NGre NMen
§ ***stolonifera*** (4) 🏆	CArn CHal CHan ECho ELan EPla GAri SDix WEas
'Stormonth's Variety'	See **S. 'Stella' (× *stormonthii*)**
stribrnyi (8)	EPot MWat NMen
– JCA 861-400	NWCA
'Sturmiana' (*paniculata*) (7)	MBro NMen SRms
'Suendermannii' (× *kellereri*) (8)	MWat NHed NWCA SIng WAbe
'Suendermannii Major' (× *kellereri*) (8)	CLyd SIng
'Suendermannii Purpurea' (× *kellereri*) (8)	GCHN
§ 'Sulphurea' (× *boydii*) (8)	CShe EMNN EPot LFox MBro MYat NGre NHar NHed NHol NMen NNrd NWCA SChu WAbe WHoo WPat WPyg
¶ 'Sun Dance' (× *boydii*) (8)	MDHE
'Superba' (*callosa australis*) (7)	GCra GDra GTou MBro MDHE NNrd SSmi
'Sylva' (× *elisabethae*) (8)	MWat NGre

taygetea (10)	NTow
× ***tazetta*** (10x3)	MBro
'Theoden' (*oppositifolia*) (9) 🏆	CPBP EHyt EMNN EPot EWes GTou MBro NGre NHar NHol NPro NWCA SBla WAbe WSan
'Thorpei' (8)	ITim NMen SIng
'Timballii' (× *gaudinii*) (7)	EPPr SIng
'Timmy Foster' (× *irvingii*) (8)	NGre
× ***tiroliensis*** (7)	NHed
'Tom Thumb' (12)	NMen NNrd
tombeanensis	NGre
'Tricolor' (*stolonifera*) (4) 🏆	EBak ELan SLMG
'Triumph' (× *arendsii*) (12)	CShe ECtt EMNN GCHN GDra GTou LBee NMen NRoo NVic SBod
'Tully' (× *elisabethae*) (8)	MBro NHol WPat
'Tumbling Waters' (7) 🏆	CInt GAbr LHop MBro MTho SIng SRms WAbe WGor WPat WWin
§ 'Tvůj Den' (8) (× *poluanglica*)	CGra EHyt NHed NMen NNrd WAbe
§ 'Tvuj Píseň' (8) (× *poluanglica*)	EHyt EPot MDHE NGre NHar NHed WAbe
§ 'Tvuj Polibek' (8) (× *poluanglica*)	EHyt MDHE NHar NHed
§ 'Tvuj Přítel' (8) (× *poluanglica*)	EHyt MDHE NGre NHar NHed WAbe
§ 'Tvuj Úsměv' (8) (× *poluanglica*)	CGra EHyt MDHE MWat NGre NHar NHed NMen NNrd WAbe
§ 'Tvuj Úspěch' (8) (× *poluanglica*)	EHyt MDHE NGre NHed WAbe
'Tycho Brahe' (× *doerfleri*) (8)	CLyd NMen WAbe
umbrosa	CLyd EAst EBre ECle EPar NNor SPer SRms WHen WWin
§ – var. ***primuloides*** (3) 🏆	CGle CShe EPot GCHN LFox MBro MYat NMen NPri SAlw SRms WBon WEas WFox
'Unique'	See **S. 'Bodensee' (× *hofmannii*)**
× ***urbium*** (3) 🏆	EGoo EJud ELan GDra LGro MBal NSti SIng WBon WFar WPer
urbium primuloides 'Elliott's Variety'	See ***S. umbrosa*** var. ***primuloides*** **'Clarence Elliott'**
'Vaccarina' (*oppositifolia*) (9)	EBre ECho MRPP NVic WAbe
'Václav Hollar' (× *gusmusii*) (8)	MWat NGre NMen
'Vahlii' (× *smithii*) (8)	WAbe
'Valborg'	See **S. 'Cranbourne' (× *anglica*)**
'Valentine'	See **S. 'Cranbourne' (× *anglica*)**
'Valerie Finnis'	See **S. 'Aretiastrum' (× *boydii*)**
'Variegata' (*cuneifolia*) (3)	CNic ECho ECtt ELan EPPr ESis GCHN MBar NMen NNrd NPri NRoo NTow NVic SHFr SIde SSmi WHil WPer
'Variegata' (*umbrosa*)	See **S. 'Aureopunctata' (× *urbium*)**
'Variegata' (× *urbium*) (3)	CDec ELan EPar GDra GGar LBee LGro MBal NCat NNor NSti SRms SSmi WCla WEas WGwG WWin
vayredana (12)	CLyd
veitchiana	EPla MHig NCat NNrd WCot WCru
'Venetia' (*paniculata*) (7)	MDHE NNrd SSmi
'Vesna' (× *borisii*) (8)	CLyd EMNN GCHN MHig MOne MWat NGre NMen NNrd WAbe WWin

'Vincent van Gogh' (× *borisii*) (8) ITim LBuc NHol NNrd
'Vladana' (× *megaseiflora*) (8) CLyd EHyt EMNN EPot GCLN MDHE NGre NHar NHol NMen NNrd NRya WAbe
'Vlasta' (8) MWat WAbe
'Vltava' (8) LRHS NGre
'W.A. Clark' (*oppositifolia*) (9) MBal WAbe
'Wada' (*fortunei*) (4) CChu CFil CGle CWit EPar GAbr GCHN MBal NBir NHar NRoo SCro SSpi SWas WCot WWin
'Waithman's Variety' (7) NNrd
§ 'Wallacei' (12) ECho
'Walpole's Variety' (*longifolia*) (7) NHar NNrd WPer
'Walter Ingwersen' (*umbrosa* var. *primuloides*) (3) SIng
§ 'Walter Irving' (× *irvingii*) (8) EHyt EMNN EPot MDHE MYat NHar NMen WAbe
'Welsh Dragon' (12) WAbe
'Welsh Red' (12) EGoo WAbe
'Welsh Rose' (12) WAbe
wendelboi CLyd EHyt EMNN LFox MWat MYat NGre NMen NNrd WAbe
'Wendrush' (× *wendelacina*) (8) MDHE NMen WAbe
'Wendy' (× *wendelacina*) (8) CLyd NGre NMen WAbe
'Wetterhorn' (*oppositifolia*) (9) EPot MBal NMen NNrd WAbe
¶ 'Wheatley Lion' (× *borisii*) MDHE NMen
'Wheatley Rose' (8) CLyd LRHS
§ 'White Pixie' (12) EMNN LBee LFox LGro NGre NNrd NPri SBla SIng SRms SSmi WCla
'White Spire' (12) NNrd
§ 'White Star' (× *petraschii*) (8) WAbe
'Whitehill' (7) CLyd CShe EBre ELan ESis GCHN GTou LBee LFox MBal MBro MHig NBro NEgg NGre NMen NNrd SAlw SIng SSmi WHoo WPat WPer WPyg WWin
'Whitlavei Compacta' (*hypnoides*) (12) NMen NWoo
'Wilhelm Tell' (× *malbyana*) (8) NMen
'William Boyd' (× *boydii*) (8) MDHE MWat WAbe
'Winifred' (× *anglica*) (8) CLyd EHyt EPot LFox MWat NGre NMen NNrd WAbe WFar
'Winifred Bevington' (7×3) CInt CLyd EBre ELan EMNN ESis GDra GTou LBee LHop MBro NBro NHar NHed NMen NNrd NRoo NRya SIng WCla WHoo WPat WPer WPyg WRHF
'Winston Churchill' (12) LBuc NHol NNrd SIng
'Winter Fire' See ***S.* 'Winterfeuer' (*callosa*)**
§ 'Winterfeuer' (*callosa*) (7) CShe
* 'Winton' MDHE
'Wisley Primrose' See ***S.* × 'Kolbiana' (× *paulinae*)**
I 'Wisley Variety' (*grisebachii*) GCLN
'Yellow Rock' (8) WAbe
◆ Your Day See ***S.* 'Tvûj Den'**
◆ Your Friend See ***S.* 'Tvuj Přítel'**
Your Good Fortune See ***S.* 'Tvuj Úspěch'**
◆ Your Kiss See ***S.* 'Tvuj Polibek'**
◆ Your Smile See ***S.* 'Tvuj Úsměv'**
◆ Your Song See ***S.* 'Tvuj Píseň'**
◆ Your Success See ***S.* 'Tvuj Úspěch'**
× ***zimmeteri*** (7×3) EWes NNrd NTow SSmi
§ 'Zlatá Praha' (× *pragensis*) (8) CGra NGre NMen NRya SIng WAbe
* ***zohlenschaferi*** NMen

SCABIOSA † (Dipsacaceae)

¶ ***africana*** WCot
alpina L. See ***Cephalaria alpina***
anthemifolia CHan
atropurpurea MSto SMrm SUsu
banatica See ***S. columbaria***
'Black Prince' NBir
'Butterfly Blue' EBar GMac MBri SCoo SPer WWeb
caucasica CSam ECha GBur LGan MBro MLsm NCat NLak SBla WHoo WOld WPyg WWin
– var. ***alba*** CBot CM&M MBri MEas MLsm NCut NNor NRoo WHoo
– Blue Seal = 'Blausiegel' EBre EFou
– 'Blue Lace' MBri
– 'Bressingham White' EBre EWes SAsh
– 'Challenger' MBri
– 'Clive Greaves' 🏆 CB&S CDoC CRDP CShe EAst ECED ECha EFou ELan LHop MBri MBro MWat NFla NMir NNor SPer WEas WRus
– 'Fama' EBar EBee NBir NRoo SMrm SRms WGor WHoo WPyg
– 'Floral Queen' ECha
– 'Goldingensis' EBar LFis NPri WFar
– House's Hybrids CBot CPou SRms
– 'Isaac House' SIde SWat
– 'Kompliment' ECGP EFou
– 'Miss Willmott' 🏆 CDoC CGle CMGP CRDP CSev EAst ECha EFou ELan LHop MBel MBri MUlv MWat NCut NFla NRoo SPer SRms SUsu WRus WTyr
– 'Moerheim Blue' ECha MBri MUlv NFla SPer
– 'Mount Cook' LHop SAsh
– 'Nachtfalter' MBri
– 'Penelope Harrison' CShe
– 'Perfecta' EAst GMaP MTis NPri SWat WHil WWhi
– 'Perfecta Alba' GMaP LFis MBro NOrc NPri NTay SWat WPyg
– 'Stäfa' CDoC EBee EFou LHop MBel MBri MUlv SChu SMrm WTyr
'Chile Black' CElw CHad CHan CHar CMea GBri GCal LGre WCot WRus
'Chile Red' GCal
cinerea WWin
§ ***columbaria*** CKin ECWi EWFC GMac MChe MHew NLan NMir NTow NWCA SSca WCla WGor WHoo WJek WPyg
– ***alba*** SSpi
– 'Nana' NBir NMen NPri SSmi WHoo WPyg
§ – var. ***ochroleuca*** CBot CChr CGle CHan CLon CMea CRDP CSam EBar ECha ERav LLWP MBro MCLN NBir NPla NPri NSti SMrm SRms SSpi SWas WBro WHil WHoo WOld WWin
farinosa CBot CElw CHan WAbe WPer
– 'Schofield's Variegated' WAbe
gigantea See ***Cephalaria gigantea***

graminifolia EDAr ELan EMan GBuc NBir NMen NTow SAlw WOld
– 'Pinkushion' EBre
graminifolia rosea EWes SCro
holosericea MSto
japonica MSto SAlw WPer
– var. *alpina* CInt CLTr EFou GDra GTou MBel MSCN NRai NTow NWoo WHoo
lucida CGle CNic CSev ELan EPar GDra GMac GTou LGan LHop MBro MHig NPri NRoo SBla SMrm WAbe WEas WPat WPer WTyr
¶ *maritima* NRai
minoana MSto
ochroleuca See ***S. columbaria*** var. ***ochroleuca***
parnassi See ***Pterocephalus perennis***
'Perfecta Lilac Blue' CSev
'Perpetual Flowering' EFou
'Pink Mist' CGle MBri NBir SCoo SPer SRms WWeb
pterocephala See ***Pterocephalus perennis***
rhodopensis MSto
rumelica See ***Knautia macedonica***
* 'Satchmo' NRai
succisa See ***Succisa pratensis***
tatarica See ***Cephalaria gigantea***
¶ *triandra* CHan MEas

SCADOXUS (Amaryllidaceae)

'König Albert' See ***Haemanthus* 'König Albert'**
membranaceus WChr
multiflorus LAma MBri NRog WChr
natalensis See ***S. puniceus***
§ *puniceus* NRog SLMG WChr

SCAEVOLA (Goodeniaceae)

aemula 'Alba' CSpe LHop
– 'Blue Fan' CBrk CHal CSpe EAst MMil SBid SHFr SMrm SRms
– 'Blue Wonder' CLTr LHil LHop NPri SVen
– 'New Wonder' WLRN
– 'Petite' CHal CLTr LHil
hookeri ECou
suaveolens See ***S. calendulacea***

SCANDIX (Apiaceae)

pecten-veneris EWFC

SCHEFFLERA (Araliaceae)

actinophylla 🏆 EBak MBri SRms
arboricola 🏆 MBri
– 'Compacta' MBri
– 'Gold Capella' 🏆 MBri
– 'Jacqueline' MBri
– 'Trinetta' MBri
digitata CHEx
elegantissima 🏆 CSpe

SCHIMA (Theaceae)

argentea See ***S. wallichii*** subsp. ***noronhae*** var. ***superba***
§ *wallichii* subsp. *noronhae* var. *superba* CHEx
– subsp. *wallichii* var. *khasiana* ISea

SCHINUS (Anacardiaceae)

molle IDee
¶ *patagonicus* MAll
polygamus CGre CPle

SCHISANDRA (Schisandraceae)

chinensis CChu CHan CPlN ETen WSHC
grandiflora CSte EBee EBre ECot ELan EOvi EPfP SSta
– B&SWJ 2245 WCru
– var. *cathayensis* See ***S. sphaerandra***
propinqua var. *sinensis* CBot
rubriflora CBar CRHN CSte CWSG EHic EPfP SHBN SSpi
– (f) CB&S CPlN ELan EOvi MBlu MGos SBid SBra WSHC WWat
– (m) CPlN EMil NHol
§ *sphaerandra* CPlN
sphenanthera EFou EHic ELan EMil EOvi ETen MDun NPal WSHC

SCHISTOSTEGA (Sphagnaceae)

See Plant Deletions

SCHIVERECKIA (Brassicaceae)

doerfleri CNic

SCHIZACHYRIUM (Poaceae)

§ *scoparium* CRow EBee EBre EHoe EPPr ESOG GBin GCal

SCHIZANTHUS (Solanaceae)

candidus WSan
– RB 94104 MSto
gilliesii MSto
grahamii JCA 12365 CPBP MSto
hookeri EWes MSto

SCHIZOCENTRON See HETEROCENTRON

SCHIZOCODON See SHORTIA

SCHIZOLOBIUM (Papilionaceae)

See Plant Deletions

SCHIZOPETALON (Brassicaceae)

See Plant Deletions

SCHIZOPHRAGMA (Hydrangeaceae)

hydrangeoides CChu CFil CHEx CPlN CPle EBre EMil MBal MBri MGos NHlc SBra SRms SSpi SSta WCru WDin WSHC
– 'Brookside Littleleaf' WCru
– 'Moonlight' (v) WCru
– 'Roseum' CBot CChu CFil MBlu SBla SSpi WCru
integrifolium 🏆 CB&S CChu CFil CHEx CMac CPlN EMil MBal SDix SHBN WSHC WWat
– *fauriei* B&SWJ 1701 WCru
* – var. *molle* CPlN

SCHIZOSTACHYUM (Poaceae - Bambusoideae)

§ *funghomii* SDry WJun

SCHIZOSTYLIS (Iridaceae)

coccinea CArn CAvo CB&S CBro CNic CPea CRDP CWGN EAst EFol ELan ERos ETub LAma MBal MFir MNrw NBro NHol NNor NRoo NSti SOkh WHal WHoo WOld WWhi WWye
– *alba* CAbb CB&S CElw CMHG CMea CMil CRDP CWGN ECha ELan EOrc GMac LHop LWak MNrw MRav NBro SApp SAxl SDix SMad SPer SUsu WHal WHil WPbr WRus WSHC WWat
– 'Ballyrogan Giant' IBlr
– 'Cardinal' CDec CPea NPla
– 'Elburton Glow' CChu
– 'Fenland Daybreak' EBee EBre ECro EFou EGar EMan IBlr LIck SSpe
– 'Gigantea' See ***S. coccinea* 'Major'**
– 'Grandiflora' See ***S. coccinea* 'Major'**
– 'Hilary Gould' CRDP GBuc IBlr MAvo MUlv SUsu SWas WCot WFar WHal
– 'Jennifer' ♀ CAvo CBro CElw CGle CHid CMHG COtt CRDP CTri EBre ECha EFou IBlr LGan MBri MUlv SApp SCro SRms SUsu WRus WWat
– 'Maiden's Blush' ECGP EFou EWll LCom LIck MUlv SPer WCot
§ – 'Major' ♀ CB&S CBro CDec CGle CSam CShe EBre ECha EFou EGol GCal GMac LHop LWak MBri NHol NMir SApp SAxl SDeJ SDix SMad SPer WAbe WBod WEas WOld WPer WWat WWin
– 'Mrs Hegarty' CB&S CHid CMHG EAst EFou EGol ELan EPot LAma LHop LPBA NFla NHol NRog SDeJ SMad SPer SSea SSoC WBod WEas WHil WHoo WOld WPer WWat
– 'November Cheer' CDec CMHG ECot EPPr IBlr LIck MSte NRoo SSpe WOld WPer
– 'Pallida' CMil CSam ECha EGar ELan GBuc GMac IBlr LHop NPla
– 'Professor Barnard' CFee CGle EPot GCal IBlr MBri MSte SApp WHoo WOld WPnn WPyg WWat
– 'Salmon Charm' EFou IBlr
– 'Snow Maiden' CFai LIck WCot
§ – 'Sunrise' ♀ CAvo CB&S CChu CFee CMHG CRDP CSam ECha EGol ELan GCal LHop LIck NHol NNor NRoo SAxl SIng SPer SSpi SWas WAbe WBod WHil WOMN WOld WPer WRus
– 'Sunset' See ***S. coccinea* 'Sunrise'**
– 'Tambara' CDec CMHG CPou EGar IBlr LGre MBro MHFP NCat SApp SAxl WElm WOld WWat WWeb
– 'Viscountess Byng' CB&S CBro CGle CMil CShe EGar EPot GCal MBri NRog SAga SPer WHal WPer WWat
– 'Zeal Blush' IBlr
– 'Zeal Salmon' CBro CPou ECha EGar IBlr SApp SCro SSpi WCot WHil
'Marietta' ETub

SCHOENOPLECTUS (Cyperaceae)

§ *lacustris* ECWi EMFW WChe
– subsp. ***tabernaemontani*** 'Albescens' (v) CBen CWGN EBre EHon EMFW LPBA MSta SRms SWat SWyc WChe WCot WKen
– – 'Zebrinus' (v) CBen CInt CWGN EBre EHon ELan EMFW LPBA MSta NDea SHig SWat SWyc WChe WCot

SCHOENUS (Cyperaceae)

pauciflorus CCuc CFil EBee ECou EHoe EPot ESOG ETPC GFre

SCHOTIA (Caesalpiniaceae)

¶ *brachypetala* SOWG

SCIADOPITYS (Sciadopityaceae)

verticillata ♀ CB&S CChu CDoC CKen EHul IOrc LCon LLin LNet LPan MBar MBlu MBri NBee SLim WCoo WDin WNor
– 'Gold Star' CKen
– 'Picola' CKen

SCILLA † (Hyacinthaceae)

adlamii See ***Ledebouria cooperi***
x *allenii* See ***x Chionoscilla allenii***
amethystina See ***S. litardierei***
amoena CMon LAma LRHS
autumnalis CAvo CMon EPot EWFC LAma WChr WOMN WShi
autumnalis fallax AB&S 4345 CMon
baurii WChr
bifolia ♀ CAvo CBro CMea EPar EPot LAma NRog WShi
– 'Rosea' CMea EPar EPot LAma NRog WPer
bithynica SSpi WWat
campanulata See ***Hyacinthoides hispanica***
chinensis See ***S. scilloides***
cilicica CBro CMon LAma
hanburyi S&L 78 CMon
hohenackeri BSBE 811 CMon
hyacinthoides CMon EHyt
italica See ***Hyacinthoides italica***
japonica See ***S. scilloides***
libanotica S&L 113 CMon
liliohyacinthus CAvo CBro CRDP CRow EHyt IBlr SSpi
– 'Alba' WChr
lingulata ciliolata CBro
lingulata MS 320 CMon
– S&L 253 CMon
– SF 288/281 CMon
§ *litardierei* CAvo CMon EPot ERos LAma MFos NEgg
litardierei hoogiana SWas
mauretanica alba CMon
mauretanica SF 65 CMon
messeniaca MBro SWas
§ *mischtschenkoana* CAvo CBro CMon EBre EHyt EPot ETub LAma LBow MBri NRog
monophyllos CFil LAma

– SB 184 — CMon
morrisii M 4015 — CMon
non-scripta — See ***Hyacinthoides non-scripta***
numidica MS&CL 288 — CMon
nutans — See ***Hyacinthoides non-scripta***
obtusifolia AB&S 4410 — CMon
ovalifolia — See ***Ledebouria ovalifolia***
paucifolia — SLMG
persica BSBE 1054 — CMon
peruviana — CAvo CB&S CBrd CBro CFee CHEx CHad CMil CSpe EBre EPar EPot ERos LAma MTho NRog SApp SMrm SSpi SUsu WAbe WWhi
– 'Alba' — CAvo CMon EBre LAma MTho NRog WCot
peruviana elegans — CMon
peruviana var. ***venusta*** — CMon
pratensis — See ***S. litardierei***
puschkinioides — LAma
ramburei — LAma
– B&S 406 — CMon
– MS 417 — CMon
¶ ***reverchonii*** — ERos
– MS 418 — CMon
rosenii — WChr
§ ***scilloides*** — CBro EPot ERos MHig WCot
¶ – MSF 782 — SSpi
siberica 🏆 — CAvo CMea ETub LAma NEgg NRog WPer WShi
– 'Alba' — CBro EPar EPot LAma NEgg NRog WPer
– 'Spring Beauty' — CAvo CBro EPar EPot LAma MBri MHlr NRog
– var. ***taurica*** M&T 4148 — CMon
tubergeniana — See ***S. mischtschenkoana***
verna — CMon ERos WShi
– JCA 878.000 — CNic
– MS 483 — CMon
vicentina — See ***Hyacinthoides italica vicentina***
violacea — See ***Ledebouria socialis***

SCINDAPSUS (Araceae)

aureus — See ***Epipremnum aureum***
pictus (v) — MBri

SCIRPOIDES (Poaceae)

§ ***holoschoenus*** — ETPC

SCIRPUS (Cyperaceae)

cernuus — See ***Isolepis cernua***
cespitosus — MBal
§ ***fauriei*** var. ***vaginatus*** 'Golden Spear' — CRow EHoe SWyc SRms
holoschoenus — See ***Scirpoides holoschoenus***
lacustris — See ***Schoenoplectus lacustris***
– 'Spiralis' — See ***Juncus effusus* 'Spiralis'**
mucronatus — MSta
sylvaticus — CKin SWyc
tabernaemontani — See ***Schoenoplectus lacustris*** subsp. ***tabernaemontani***
variegatus — CBot

SCLERANTHUS (Caryophyllaceae)

biflorus — CPea ECou EGle ELan EPPr ESis EWes MBro NTow SSca WPer
perennis — CNat
singuliflorus — ECou WPat WPyg
uniflorus — CLyd GAbr GAri GBin GCLN NHed NWCA
– CC 466 — NWCA

SCLEROCHITON (Acanthaceae)

See Plant Deletions

SCOLIOPUS (Trilliaceae)

bigelowii — SWas WFar

SCOLOPENDRIUM See ASPLENIUM

SCOLYMUS See CYNARA

SCOPOLIA (Solanaceae)

carniolica — CAvo CFir EGle GCal GDra GPoy MBel MBlu MHar MSal NSti WCru
– forms — ECha IBlr
– subsp. ***hladnikiana*** — CBlo EBre ECro EPPr WBcn
carniolica podolica — CMea
lurida — MSal
physaloides — MSal
sinensis — See ***Atropanthe sinensis***

SCORZONERA (Asteraceae)

humilis — GPoy
suberosa subsp. ***cariensis*** — NTow

SCROPHULARIA (Scrophulariaceae)

aquatica — See ***S. auriculata***
§ ***auriculata*** — ECWi ELau EWFC MSal NDea NOrc WHer WWye
– 'Burdung' (v) — EMon
§ – 'Variegata' — CAbb CGle CRow EBre EHoe ELan LHop MBri MSta MWat NRoo NSti SPer SRms WBea WEas WFar WHal WOve WRus WWin
buergueriana 'Lemon and Lime' (v) — EMon WCot
canina subsp. ***bicolor*** — WHer
nodosa — CArn CJew CKin ELau MChe MSal NMir SIde WApp WCla WHer
nodosa tracheliodes — CNat
nodosa variegata — See ***S. auriculata* 'Variegata'**
sambucifolia — EJud GBin MNrw MSto NChi
scorodonia — SRms
umbrosa — MSal
vernalis — EWFC

SCUTELLARIA (Lamiaceae)

§ ***alpina*** — CLyd CPBP EBre GCHN LBee MAvo MHig NWCA SBla SRms WGor WPer
altissima — CArc CGle EBee EGar EMan EMar EPPr GAul GBuc LFis MAvo MSal NBro NPla SSca WPbr WPer WWin WWye
baicalensis — CHan GAul IBlr LHop MSal SBla WOve WPer WWye
barbata — MNrw MSal
brevibracteata — SHFr
brittonii — EBee
canescens — See ***S. incana***
diffusa — CPBP ESis WPer WWye
¶ ***formosana*** — WCot

galericulata	CKin EWFC GPoy MHew MSal WApp WHer WJek
¶ – 'Corinne Tremaine' (v)	WHer
* ***glandulosissima***	EHyt
hastata	See ***S. hastifolia***
§ ***hastifolia***	CNic CPBP CTri ECot ECtt EMNN EPot SSea WCot WOMN WPer
§ ***incana***	CGle EBee EFou ELan EMan EPPr LFis LGre MNrw NSti SMrm SUsu SWas WCot WEas WWoo
indica var. ***japonica***	See ***S. indica*** var. ***parvifolia***
§ – var. ***parvifolia***	CPBP EBur ELan EWes LBee LFis MTho NMen NTow NWCA WCru WPbr
– – 'Alba'	CMHG LBee LRHS
integrifolia	MSal
lateriflora	CArn CBod CJew EFou ESis GBar GPoy LHol MChe MHew MSal SIde WCer WJek WPer WSel WWye
minor	CKin EWFC MSal
nana var. ***sapphirina***	CPBP MRPP
– – JJA 1840650	NWCA
novae-zelandiae	ECou LBee MTho SUsu WWye
orientalis	LBee NWCA SBla WCot WCru WPat WWin
– subsp. ***carica***	CMHG WOMN WWye
¶ – subsp. ***pinnatifida***	EHyt NWCA WDav
pontica	WDav WThi
prostrata	ESis SSca WDav WOMN WThi WWye
scordiifolia	CLyd CMea CMil CSam ECha EFou ELan EPot LFis MNrw NMen NRya SBla SUsu WCla WCot WHoo WPer WPyg WRus WWin WWye
serrata	CArn
supina	See ***S. alpina***
¶ ***tournefortii***	WPbr

SECURIGERA See CORONILLA

SECURINEGA (Euphorbiaceae)

¶ ***ramiflora***	CPle

SEDASTRUM See SEDUM

SEDUM † (Crassulaceae)

acre	CTri ECWi ECot EFer ELan GPoy LHol MBar NGre NNrd SIde
– 'Aureum'	CInt CNic ELan EPot MBar MHlr MOne MWat SChu WCot WHoo WPat WPyg
– 'Elegans'	ECtt GDra GTou MBal NGre NMen
§ – var. ***majus***	CChe NGre SIde SSmi
– 'Minus'	MOne NGre SIde SSmi
aggregatum	See ***Orostachys aggregata***
§ ***aizoon***	NGre NVic SChu SIde WEas WGwG WOve
– 'Aurantiacum'	See ***S. aizoon* 'Euphorbioides'**
§ – 'Euphorbioides'	EBre ECED ECha ECro ECtt EGoo ELan EMon EOrc MBel MRav NChi NFai NPro SPer WCot
albescens	See ***S. rupestre* f. *purpureum***
§ ***alboroseum***	EBre MTho
§ – 'Mediovariegatum'	CBot EBee ECro EGar ELan EMon LHop MBri MCLN MRav MSCN NFai NRoo WEas WGwG WPer
§ ***album***	CHal EBar EGoo NBro SIde WPer WRHF
§ – 'Chloroticum'	NGre SIde SSmi
– subsp. ***clusianum***	See ***S. gypsicola glanduliferum***
– 'Coral Carpet'	CNic EGoo ELan EPot GDra MBar MWat NGre NMen NNrd SChu SSmi
– var. ***micranthum***	See ***S. album* 'Chloroticum'**
§ – subsp. ***teretifolium*** 'Murale'	CTri MBar NGre
algidum	See ***S. alsium***
alpestre	NGre
§ ***alsium***	NGre
altissimum	See ***S. sediforme***
altum	EBee EMon WPer
amplexicaule	See ***S. tenuifolium***
§ ***anacampseros***	CHEx CNic EGoo GCHN MHar NGre NHol SIde SSmi WCla WCot WEas WPer
anglicum	ECWi NGre WCla
anopetalum	See ***S. ochroleucum***
– alpine form	See ***S. ochroleucum*** subsp. ***montanum***
athoum	See ***S. album***
atlanticum	See ***S. dasyphyllum*** subsp. ***dasyphyllum*** var. ***mesatlanticum***
atuntsuense	CBlo NGre
◆ Autumn Joy	See ***S.* 'Herbstfreude'**
batesii	See ***S. hemsleyanum***
§ 'Bertram Anderson'	CElw CLyd CMGP CRDP EBre ECha EGoo EMan EPot GAri GCal LHop MBel MBri MBro MCLN MNrw MRav MSte NFai NGre NRoo NSti SMrm SUsu SWas WMer WWin WWtk
beyrichianum hort.	See ***S. glaucophyllum***
bithynicum 'Aureum'	See ***S. hispanicum*** var. ***minus* 'Aureum'**
brevifolium	MDHE SChu
* ***brevifolium potsii***	NGre
§ ***brevifolium*** var. ***quinquefarium***	NGre
'Carl'	EMon
§ ***caucasicum***	NGre WAbb
– DS&T 89001T	EMon
cauticola ♀	CLyd CMHG CShe EGoo GCal ITim LHop MBro MFos MHar MHig MRav NGre NNor NRoo SBod SRms SSca SSmi WHil WWin
¶ – Lida	ECho NNrd
§ – 'Lidakense'	CMea CSam EBar EBre ELan EMon MBar MBri MBro MCLN MTis NFai NGre NHar NVic SBla SChu SHel SIng SSmi
¶ – 'Robustum'	EMon
¶ – × ***tatarinowii***	NGre
clusianum	See ***S. gypsicola glanduliferum***
crassipes	See ***Rhodiola wallichiana***
crassularia	See ***Crassula milfordiae***
cyaneum hort.	See ***S. ewersii*** var. ***homophyllum***
– Rudolph	GCHN LCom MDHE NGre NWCA

dasyphyllum	CNic ELan EPot ESis GTou MBal MBar MOne MRPP MWat NGre NRoo NVic SSmi WCla WRHF
– subsp. ***dasyphyllum*** var. ***glanduliferum***	CHEx CHal
– – var. ***macrophyllum***	MDHE NGre SSmi
§ – – var. ***mesatlanticum***	CNic MDHE NBir NGre SSmi
dasyphyllum mucronatis	See ***S. dasyphyllum*** subsp. ***dasyphyllum*** var. ***mesatlanticum***
dasyphyllum subsp. ***oblongifolium***	NGre
debile	NGre
divergens	NGre
– large form	NGre
douglasii	See ***S. stenopetalum* 'Douglasii'**
'Dudley Field'	CLyd GCHN LCom NGre NMen
'Eleanor Fisher'	See ***S. telephium*** subsp. ***ruprechtii***
ellacombeanum	See ***S. kamtschaticum*** var. ***ellacombeanum***
erythrostichum	See ***S. alboroseum***
§ ***ewersii***	CMHG CNic EBee EBre EGoo ELan EMNN ESis GCHN GTou MHar NBro NGre NMen SSmi WEas WOMN
§ – var. ***homophyllum***	MHig NGre SSmi
§ ***fabaria***	MCLN NGre WEas
farinosum	MHig
fastigiatum	See ***Rhodiola fastigiata***
floriferum	See ***S. kamtschaticum***
forsterianum	See ***S. rupestre***
'Frosty Morn'	WCot
'Gooseberry Fool'	LGre SUsu
gracile	NGre SSmi
'Green Expectations'	EFou
gypsicola	CHEx MDHE NGre WPer
'Harvest Moon'	EBur
§ 'Herbstfreude' 🏆	CShe EBre ECha EFou EGoo ELan GLil LBlm LGro LHop MBal MRav MWat NBee NFai NFla NGre NHol NRoo NSti SDix SIng SMad SPer SRms SSoC WBod WEas WOld WPer
heterodontum	See ***Rhodiola heterodonta***
hidakanum	CLyd ECha GTou MBro NBro NMen NTay WHoo WPat
hillebrandtii	See ***S. urvillei* Hillebrandtii Group**
himalense	See ***Rhodiola* 'Keston'**
§ ***hispanicum***	CTri ECho
– 'Albescens'	CNic NGre
– var. ***bithynicum***	NGre
hispanicum glaucum	See ***S. hispanicum*** var. ***minus***
§ ***hispanicum*** var. ***minus***	ECtt EGoo GAri GTou MBar NGre NNrd NPri SChu SIde SSmi STre
§ – – 'Aureum'	ECha MBar MHig MRPP NGre NMen NNrd SBod SSmi
humifusum	EBur EHyt MFos MHig NMen NTow SSmi WOMN
hybridum	CShe NGre
hyperaizoon	NGre
integrifolium	See ***Rhodiola rosea*** subsp. ***integrifolia***
ishidae	See ***Rhodiola ishidae***
jaeschkei	See ***S. oreades***
japonicum	NGre

'Joyce Henderson'	CArc EFou ERav MGrG MSCN SUsu WEas WOld
§ ***kamtschaticum*** 🏆	CLyd ESis MBar NGre
§ – var. ***ellacombeanum*** 🏆	CNic EGoo ELan EMon ESis NGre NMen WRHF
§ – var. ***floriferum*** 'Weihenstephaner Gold' 🏆	CMea CNic CTri EBre EGoo EMNN ESis MBal MBar MCLN MHar MHig MWat NBro NGre NMen NNor NNrd NRoo SChu SHFr SSmi WAbe WCla WDav WEas WHil WPat
– var. ***kamtschaticum*** 'Variegatum' 🏆	CHEx CTri ECro ELan ESis GCHN LBee LHop MHig MWat NFla NGre NPri NRoo SBla SBod SRms SSmi WEas WPyg
¶ – var. ***middendorffianum***	See ***S. middendorffianum***
– 'Takahira Dake'	NGre
kirilovii	See ***Rhodiola kirilovii***
kostovii	See ***S. grisebachii*** subsp. ***kostovii***
lanceolatum	NGre
laxum	NGre
– subsp. ***heckneri***	NGre
lineare	EAst ELan SLMG
– 'Variegatum'	ESis MBri SIde
litorale	NGre
§ ***lydium***	CLyd CTri EMNN GTou MBal MBar MHig MOne MRPP MWat NGre NMen NNrd NRoo SSmi
– 'Aureum'	See ***S. hispanicum*** var. ***minus* 'Aureum'**
– 'Bronze Queen'	See ***S. lydium***
'Lynda et Rodney'	CRDP SUsu
makinoi 'Variegatum'	EBre
'Matrona'	See ***S. telephium* 'Matrona'**
maweanum	See ***S. acre*** var. ***majus***
maximowiczii	See ***S. aizoon***
mexicanum	MBri
middendorffianum	CLyd ECho EGoo ELan EMon GTou LHop MDHE MHig MWat NGre NMen NNrd SAlw SBod SRms SSmi WHoo WWin
¶ – var. ***diffusum***	NGre SSmi
'Mohrchen'	EFou
monregalense	NGre
'Moonglow'	NGre NMen
moranense	CHal CNic NGre NTow SIde SSmi
¶ 'Morchen'	CArc SMrm SUsu SWas WCot WFar
morganianum 🏆	CHal EBak LCns MBri
morrisonense	NGre
multiceps	NGre SSmi
murale	See ***S. album*** subsp. ***teretifolium* 'Murale'**
N ***nevii***	CLyd CShe EGle
nicaeënse	See ***S. sediforme***
obcordatum	NGre
§ ***obtusatum***	EGle MBro MHig NBro NFla NGre NNrd NSla NTay SSmi
§ – subsp. ***retusum***	NGre
obtusifolium	NGre
* – 'Variegatum'	WWtk
ochroleucum 'Green Spreader'	SSmi
§ – subsp. ***ochroleucum glaucum***	NGre
oppositifolium	See ***S. spurium*** var. ***album***

§ ***oreganum***	CInt CMHG ECha EMNN ESis GTou MBar MHig MWat NGre NMen NRoo SBod SChu SHel SRms SSmi WPer WPyg WWin
– 'Procumbens'	See ***S. oreganum*** subsp. ***tenue***
§ – subsp. ***tenue***	CNic WPat
§ ***oregonense***	EBur GTou NGre NMen NNrd
oryzifolium	NGre
– 'Minor'	EBur
§ ***pachyclados***	CInt CLyd EBur EGoo ELan ESis GAbr GTou LBee MBar MDHE MOne NBir NGre NNrd SAlw SChu SIde SIng SSmi WCla WDav WPat WPer
pallidum	NGre
palmeri	NBir NTow SIng SSmi
pilosum	EBur NGre NWCA SBla WOMN
§ ***pluricaule***	EHoe EHyt GCHN GDra MBar MBro NGre NMen NNrd SBod SChu SRms WCla WRHF
◆ – Rose Carpet	See ***S. pluricaule* 'Rosenteppich'**
polytrichoides	See ***Rhodiola komarovii***
populifolium	CLyd CMHG ECha EGoo GCHN GCal MBel MHar NGre SDry SMad SSmi STre WEas WPer
¶ ***praealtum***	EOas SEND
primuloides	See ***Rhodiola primuloides***
pruinatum	NGre
pruinosum	See ***S. spathulifolium*** subsp. ***pruinosum***
pulchellum	CShe NGre
purdyi	NGre NMen
'Purple Emperor'	CArc EPPr
quadrifidum	See ***Rhodiola quadrifida***
quinquefarium	See ***S. brevifolium*** var. ***quinquefarium***
ramosissimum	See ***Villadia ramosissima***
'Red Bead'	NGre
◆ ***reflexum*** L.	See ***S. rupestre* L.**
reptans var. ***carinatifolium***	NGre
retusum	See ***S. obtusatum*** subsp. ***retusum***
rhodiola	See ***Rhodiola rosea***
rosea	See ***Rhodiola rosea***
rubroglaucum hort.	See ***S. oregonense***
– Praeger	See ***S. obtusatum***
x ***rubrotinctum***	CHal SLMG
§ 'Ruby Glow' ♀	CLon CMea EBre ECha EFou ELan EMar LGro MBal MBri MCLN MWat NFai NGre NHol NNrd NSti SAga SDix SPer SPla SUsu WEas WOve WPer WWhi
§ ***rupestre*** L.	CNic EBar EGoo ELan MBar NGre NPri SChu SIde SSmi WCla WEas WHer
¶ – subsp. ***elegans***	LGro
§ – f. ***purpureum***	SIde
– 'Minus'	CNic NGre
– 'Monstrosum Cristatum'	MBal NBir SIde SMad
ruprechtii	See ***S. telephium*** subsp. ***ruprechtii***
sarcocaule	See ***Crassula sarcocaulis***
sarmentosum	NGre SSmi
§ ***sediforme***	LHop MBro NGre SIde WRHF
sediforme nicaeense	See ***S. sediforme***
selskianum	GAul GDra GTou MOne NPri WWtk
sempervivoides	EBur NGre WThi
sexangulare	EMNN ESis GDra MBar MOne NGre NMen NNrd SSmi WPLl WWtk
¶ ***sibiricum***	WEas
sichotense	NGre
§ ***sieboldii***	CSam LCns LGro MBri MDHE NGre NNrd SSmi
– 'Mediovariegatum' ♀	EGoo ELan EMan LHop NGre NNrd SCro SSmi WEas WPer
'Silver Moon'	EBur EGoo ESis MDHE NGre SIng SSmi
sp. B&SWJ 054	WCru
spathulifolium	ECha ELan ESis GTou MOne MRPP NBus SChu WEas
– 'Aureum'	EBur ECtt EMNN GTou MBar MHig MWat NGre NNrd SBod WRHF
– 'Cape Blanco' ♀	Widely available
§ – subsp. ***pruinosum***	MDHE NGre
– 'Purpureum' ♀	CLyd CShe EBre EMNN GDra GTou LBee LHop MBal MBar MBri MHig MWat NFla NGre NNrd NRoo NVic SBla SBod SIng SMer SSmi STre WAbe WHil WHoo WPer WWhi WWin
– 'Roseum'	CBlo CLyd SSmi
§ ***spectabile*** ♀	CArn CDoC EJud ELan NBee NPla NSti SHFr SRms WBea WHil WTyr WWin
– 'Abendrot'	EMon
– 'Album'	EOrc
– 'Brilliant' ♀	CDoC CM&M CShe EBre ECED ECha EFou EGoo ELan EMon LBlm MBri NGre NOrc SDix SMad SPer SPla SSoC WEas
– 'Iceberg'	CArc CRDP CSev EBee ECha EFou EGoo EMan EMon EPPr ERav LBlm LGre LHop MCLN NHaw SMad SSoC WCot WHil
¶ – 'Indian Chief'	CBlo WCot WFar
– 'Meteor'	CArc EBar ECha EGoo MWat NCat NFai NGre SCro WAbe WCot
* – 'Mini'	ELan
– 'Rosenteller'	EFou EMon NGre SMrm
◆ – September Glow	See ***S. spectabile* 'Septemberglut'**
§ – 'Septemberglut'	EMan EMon
– 'Stardust'	CBlo EBar EFou EGar EMil GMaP MBri MTis NCut NGre SIde SPla WAbe WGor WWeb
– 'Variegatum'	See ***S. alboroseum* 'Mediovariegatum'**
spinosum	See ***Orostachys spinosa***
spurium	EJud ELan GBur LGro NGre NNor SBod SRms STre WRHF
§ – var. ***album***	ELan EMon ESis MHar NGre SIde
* – 'Atropurpureum'	CLyd ECha NNor NRoo SPla
– 'Coccineum'	GAul MBar NPri WWtk
◆ – Dragon's Blood	See ***S. spurium* 'Schorbuser Blut'**
– 'Erdblut'	CTri EBre MHig NFla NGre NMen NNrd NRoo
– 'Fuldaglut'	CHal EBre EHoe NGre NHar SChu SMac WPer WWin
– 'Glow'	CTri STre
– 'Green Mantle'	CBlo ECha SMer WPLl
◆ – Purple Carpet	See ***S. spurium* 'Purpurteppich'**

– 'Purpureum'	CHan CInt ELan GDra
§ – 'Purpurteppich'	CShe EBre EPot ESis LGro MHig MRav NBro NGre NHol SRms
– 'Roseum'	CLyd SRms
– 'Ruby Mantle'	CBlo NPro WCot
§ – 'Schorbuser Blut' ♀	CMea CNic EBar ELan EPot LHop MBal MBro MWat NBro NGre NVic SRms WEas WHoo WPat WPyg WRHF
– 'Splendens Roseum'	LGro
– 'Tricolor'	See ***S. spurium* 'Variegatum'**
§ – 'Variegatum'	CHan CLyd CMHG CNic CSam CShe ECha EHoe ELan ESis LHop MBar MHig NGre NRoo SBod SIng SPla SSmi STre WAbe WCla WEas WHil WOve WPat WPyg WWin
stenopetalum	NGre
§ – 'Douglasii'	CNic MOne NNrd SRms SSmi
stephanii	See ***Rhodiola crassipes*** var. ***stephanii***
'Stewed Rhubarb Mountain'	CArc CMil EBee GAri MRav WBea WCot
stoloniferum	NGre SSmi
'Strawberries and Cream'	MRav
stribrnyi	See ***S. urvillei* Stribrnyi Group**
'Sunset Cloud'	CArc CLyd CMHG CSam EMon GCal MRav NGre WOld
takesimense	NGre
§ ***tatarinowii***	CLyd EDAr NGre
– K 92.405	WDav
§ ***telephioides***	WCot
§ ***telephium***	CAgr CArn EBar EMon EWFC MHlr NSti SRms WCla WCot
– 'Abbeydore'	EMon NSti WAbb
– 'Arthur Branch'	CArc CElw CMil EGoo EHal EMon GBuc MTho SUsu WCot WDav
– subsp. ***fabaria***	See ***S. fabaria***
– 'Hester'	EFou
– 'Leonore Zuutz'	WCot
– 'Matrona'	ECha EFou EJud EMon SMrm WCot
§ – subsp. ***maximum***	ECha EMon MBel SChu
– – 'Atropurpureum' ♀	CBot CGle CHad CSev CWGN ECha ECoo ELan EMar EMon MBri MFir MRav NFai NRoo SChu SPer WEas WPer WWhi WWin
¶ – 'Munstead Red'	CArc CLyd CMil EBee EFou EGoo EJud EMan EMar EMon LFis LHop MRav MUlv NGre SPla SSpe SUsu WCot
– 'Roseovariegatum'	EMon
– 'Roseum'	EFol LHop
§ – subsp. ***ruprechtii***	CArc CLyd CMHG CMea EBee ECha EGoo EMan EMon MBri NGre SUsu SWas WCot WDav WEas WPer
– 'Variegatum'	CMHG COtt ECoo LFis MBel NRoo WHal WWin
– Washfield purple selection	EWes
§ ***tenuifolium***	EBur SSmi
§ – subsp. ***ibericum***	NGre
– subsp. ***tenuifolium***	EBur
ternatum	NGre
trollii	See ***Rhodiola trollii***
§ 'Vera Jameson' ♀	CLon CLyd CSam CShe ECha ECro EHoe MBri MFir MHlr MRav MTis NGre NHol SBla SChu SPer SUsu WEas WHil WOve WWat WWhi
verticillatum	NGre
'Weihenstephaner Gold'	See ***S. kamtschaticum*** var. ***floriferum* 'Weihenstephaner Gold'**
weinbergii	See ***Graptopetalum paraguayense***
yezoense	See ***S. pluricaule***
yunnanense	See ***Rhodiola yunnanensis***

SEEMANNIA See GLOXINIA

SELAGINELLA (Selaginellaceae)

apoda	MBri
braunii	NMar
douglasii	NMar
emmeliana	See ***S. pallescens***
helvetica	NHol
¶ ***involens***	WCot
kraussiana ♀	CHal MBal MBri NMar WRic
– 'Aurea'	CHal GGar MBri NMar SMad
– 'Brownii' ♀	MBri NMar NVic
– 'Variegata' ♀	MBri
martensii 'Watsoniana'	NMar
§ ***pallescens***	NMar
– 'Aurea'	NMar
sanguinolenta	SIng
vogelii	NMar

SELAGO (Selaginellaceae)

See Plant Deletions

SELINUM (Apiaceae)

¶ ***carvifolia***	EMon
tenuifolium	See ***S. wallichianum***
§ ***wallichianum***	CChu CGle CMil CPou CRDP EPla MBri NSti SDix SIgm SMrm WEas WHer

SELLIERA (Goodeniaceae)

radicans	NHol
– forms	ECou
– 'Lake Ellerman'	NHol

SEMELE (Ruscaceae)

androgyna	CHEx CPlN

SEMIAQUILEGIA † (Ranunculaceae)

§ ***adoxoides***	CLyd GBin NRya WPer
§ ***ecalcarata***	CBot CGle CHar CMil EBre ECro GBin LGan MNrw NHar NOak NWoo SAlw SIng SMrm SRms WCru WDav WPer WWhi WWin
– 'Flore Pleno'	CNic LGan NPSI NRoo WWhi
simulatrix	See ***S. ecalcarata***

SEMIARUNDINARIA (Poaceae - Bambusoideae)

§ ***fastuosa*** ♀	CHEx EBee EFul EJap EOas EPfP EPla SArc SBam SDry WJun
– var. ***viridis***	EPfP EPla SBam SDry WJun
kagamiana	CDoC EPla ISta SDry WJun
¶ ***lubrica***	ISta
makinoi	WJun

nitida	See ***Fargesia nitida***
§ ***okuboi***	EPla WJun
villosa	See ***S. okuboi***
yamadorii	EPla SBam SDry WJun
– 'Brimscombe'	SDry
yashadake	EPla ISta SBam SDry WJun
yashadake kimmei	EPla ISta SDry WJun

SEMPERVIVELLA See ROSULARIA

SEMPERVIVUM † (Crassulaceae)

'Abba'	MOne WPer
acuminatum	See ***S. tectorum*** var. ***glaucum***
'Aglow'	CWil SSmi
'Alcithoë'	CWil
'Aldo Moro'	CWil MOne NMen NNrd SSmi
allionii	See ***Jovibarba allionii***
'Alluring'	GAbr MOne
'Alpha'	CWil ESis LBee NGre NHol SIng SSmi STre
altum	CWil MOne NMen SSmi
'Amanda'	CWil MBro MOne NMen SSmi WHoo WPer
'Ambergreen'	CWil MOne NMen SSmi
andreanum	CWil MOne NGre NHol SIng SSmi
'Apache'	CWil MOne NNrd SSmi
'Apple Blossom'	CWil MOne NBus SSmi
arachnoideum ♀	CMea CShe CWil EGoo ELan EPot ESis GAbr LBee MBar MNrw MOne MTis MWat NHed NHol NNrd NRoo NWCA SBla SIng SLMG SSmi WAbe WEas WHoo WPyg WWin
– var. ***bryoides***	CWil GCHN MBro NMen
– × ***calcareum***	CWil NGre NMen SSmi
– 'Clairchen'	MBro
– subsp. ***doellianum***	See ***S. arachnoideum*** var. ***glabrescens***
– 'Form No. 1'	LRHS SSmi
§ – var. ***glabrescens***	NMen SSmi
– 'Laggeri'	See ***S. arachnoideum*** subsp. ***tomentosum***
– × ***nevadense***	CWil SIng SSmi
– × ***pittonii***	CWil MBro NGre NHol NMen SSmi
– 'Rubrum'	MOne
¶ – 'Sultan'	MOne
N – subsp. ***tomentosum*** ♀	EBre EMNN EPad GCHN MBro MOne MRPP NGre NHol NMen NPer NWCA SChu SIng SMer SSmi WPer WWin
– – 'Minor'	NHol SIng
§ – – 'Stansfieldii'	GAbr MOne NGre NMen STre
arenarium	See ***Jovibarba arenaria***
'Aross'	CLyd CWil MOne NMen SSmi
'Arrowheads Red'	MOne SSmi
arvernense	See ***S. tectorum***
'Ashes of Roses'	CWil EGoo MBro MOne NMen NTow SSmi WAbe
'Asteroid'	CWil NMen SSmi
atlanticum	CWil MOne NMen NNrd SSmi
– 'Edward Balls'	MOne SIng
– from Oukaimaden	CWil MOne NHol
'Atlantis'	MOne NHol
'Atropurpureum'	CWil GAbr MBro MOne
'Aureum'	See ***Greenovia aurea***
ballsii	CWil GCHN MOne NHed NMen
– from Smólikas	MOne NMen SSmi
– from Tschumba Petzi	MOne SSmi
'Banderi'	CWil MOne
§ × ***barbulatum***	GCHN MOne NMen SIng SSmi WHoo WPer WPyg
§ – 'Hookeri'	CWil EPad ESis EWes MOne NHol NRoo SSmi WAbe WPer
'Bascour Zilver'	CWil GAbr MOne SIng
'Beaute'	CWil
'Bedazzled'	CWil
'Bedivere'	CWil LCom NGre NMen SSmi
'Bedivere Cristate'	CWil
'Bella Meade'	CWil MOne NGre SSmi
I 'Belladonna'	CWil MDHE NHol NMen NTow SSmi WPer
¶ 'Bellotts Pourpre'	CWil
'Bennerbroek'	MDHE MOne
'Bernstein'	CWil MBro NHed NMen SIng
'Beta'	MOne NHol NMen NRoo SSmi WAbe
¶ 'Bethany'	MOne NMen
'Bicolor'	EPfP
'Big Slipper'	NHol
'Birchmaier'	CWil NMen
'Black Mini'	CWil MOne NHed NMen
'Black Mountain'	CWil
'Black Prince'	CLyd SWas
'Black Velvet'	CWil MBro MOne
'Bladon'	WPer
'Blari'	SSmi
'Blood Tip'	CLyd EBar ESis GAbr GCHN LBee MBro NHar SChu WGor WHal
'Blue Boy'	CWil ESis NHol SIng
'Blue Moon'	MOne
'Blush'	SSmi
'Boissieri'	See ***S. tectorum*** subsp. ***tectorum*** **'Boissieri'**
'Booth's Red'	MOne SIng SSmi
borisii	See ***S. ciliosum*** var. ***borisii***
borissovae	CWil NMen SSmi
'Boromir'	CWil MOne SSmi
'Bowles' Variety'	WPer
'Brock'	CWil MOne MRPP NHol
'Bronco'	CWil ELan EPad MOne NMen SSmi
'Bronze Pastel'	CWil MOne NGre NMen SSmi
'Brown Owl'	CWil MOne
'Brownii'	GAbr NMen WPer
'Brunette'	GAbr
'Burnatii'	CWil
'Butterbur'	CWil
'Café'	CWil MBro MOne NMen NNrd SIng SSmi WPer
× ***calcaratum***	SIng
calcareum	CWil MBro MOne NBro NGre SSmi WPer
* – 'Atropurpureum'	MBro
– from Colle St Michael	CWil
– from Gleize	CWil NMen
– from Gorges du Cains	CWil SSmi
– from Guillaumes, Mont Ventoux, France	GAbr NMen
– from Mont Ventoux, France	SSmi
– from Queyras	CWil MOne SSmi
– from Route d'Annôt	CWil SSmi
– from Triora	CWil NMen
– 'Greenii'	CWil MRPP NGre NHed NMen SSmi
§ – 'Grigg's Surprise'	CInt CWil NMen

– 'Limelight'	CWil ESis EWes MOne NMen SIng SSmi
– 'Monstrosum'	See ***S. calcareum* 'Grigg's Surprise'**
– 'Mrs Giuseppi'	ESis GAbr GCHN LBee MBro MOne NOak NRoo SChu SSmi STre WPer
– 'Pink Pearl'	CWil MOne NMen
– 'Sir William Lawrence'	CWil EPPr ESis MOne NRoo SChu WHal
'Caldera'	CWil MOne
californicum	NHed
¶ 'Caliph's Hat'	CWil
'Canada Kate'	CWil SSmi WPer
'Cancer'	CLyd MOne SSmi
'Candy Floss'	CWil SSmi
cantabricum	CWil MDHE SSmi
– subsp. ***cantabricum*** from Leitariegos	CWil NMen
– from Navafria	CWil SIng
– from Peña Prieta	MOne NMen SSmi
– from Piedrafita, Spain	SSmi
– from Riaño, Spain	CWil
– from San Glorio	CWil NMen
– from Santander, Spain	SSmi
– from Ticeros	CWil MOne NMen
– from Valvernera	CWil MOne
– subsp. ***guadarramense*** from Lobo No 1	CWil SSmi
– – from Lobo No 2	SSmi
¶ – – from Navafria No 1	SSmi
– – from Valvanera No 1	NMen SSmi
– × ***montanum*** subsp. ***stiriacum***	CWil NGre SSmi WEas
'Canth'	CWil MOne
'Caramel'	CWil MOne
'Carmen'	CHal CWil GAbr MBro MOne SSmi
'Carneus'	MOne
'Carnival'	CHal MBro MOne SSmi WPer
caucasicum	CWil MOne NMen SSmi
'Cavo Doro'	CWil MDHE NGre
¶ ***charadzeae***	CWil
'Cherry Frost'	MOne NGre NNrd SSmi
¶ 'Cherry Tart'	CWil MOne
'Chocolate'	SSmi
× ***christii***	NHol SSmi
chrysanthum	NMen
§ ***ciliosum*** var. ***borisii***	CNic ESis GCal GTou MBro MRPP NGre NHed NMen NNrd NRoo NTow SSmi
– × ***ciliosum*** var. ***borisii***	CHal CWil EPot
– from Ochrid	CWil NMen
– var. ***galicicum*** 'Mali Hat'	CWil NHol NMen
– × ***marmoreum***	CWil MBro SSmi
¶ 'Cindy'	CWil
'Circlet'	CWil NMen SSmi
* ***cistaceum***	WEas
'Clara Noyes'	MOne SSmi WPer
'Clare'	MOne NGre NNrd SSmi
'Cleveland Morgan'	CWil GAbr MOne NHar SSmi
¶ 'Climax'	MOne
¶ 'Cobweb Capers'	MOne
'Collage'	CWil
'Collecteur Anchisi'	NGre SSmi
'Commander Hay' 🏆	CLyd ESis EWes LHop MRPP NGre NHol NPer NTow SAxl WEas WFar WHal
¶ 'Compte de Congae'	MOne
'Congo'	CWil MOne SSmi
'Cornstone'	CWil MOne
'Corona'	WPer
'Coronet'	SSmi
'Correvons'	See ***S.* 'Aymon Correvon'**
'Corsair'	CWil MBro MOne NMen NNrd SIng WPer
'Crimson Velvet'	CWil MDHE NGre SSmi WPer
§ 'Crispyn'	CLyd CWil MBro MOne MRPP NHol NMen SSmi WEas
'Croton'	SIng WPer
'Cupream'	CWil MDHE MOne NGre NHed
'Dakota'	CWil
'Dallas'	CWil MOne
'Damask'	CWil GAbr MDHE MOne NGre SSmi
'Dark Beauty'	CWil MOne NMen SIng SSmi WHal
'Dark Cloud'	CWil MOne
'Dark Point'	CWil MOne NMen SSmi
'Darkie'	CWil
'Deep Fire'	CWil MOne SSmi
× ***degenianum***	MBro MOne
densum	See ***S. tectorum***
'Director Jacobs'	CWil GAbr GCHN MOne NGre NMen SSmi WEas
¶ 'Disco Dancer'	CWil
¶ ***dolomiticum***	MOne
– from Rif Sennes	CWil
– × ***montanum***	CWil NBro NHed NMen SSmi
'Downland Queen'	CWil
'Duke of Windsor'	CWil MOne MRPP NGre NMen SSmi
'Dusky'	CWil MOne SSmi
'Dyke'	CWil GAbr MBro MOne
¶ ***dzhavachischvilii***	CWil
'Edge of Night'	CWil
'El Greco'	CWil MOne
¶ 'El Toro'	MOne
'Elgar'	CWil
'Elizabeth'	WPer
'Elvis'	CWil MBro MOne NMen SSmi
'Emerald Giant'	CWil MOne
'Emerson's Giant'	CWil MOne
'Engle's 13-2'	CLyd CWil NHar NHol SChu
'Engle's Rubrum'	ESis GAbr GTou NHol NMen
erythraeum	CWil NGre WAbe
– from Pirin, Bulgaria	NGre
'Excalibur'	CWil MBro MOne SSmi
'Exhibita'	CWil MOne SSmi
'Exorna'	CWil NMen SIng SSmi WEas
'Fair Lady'	CWil MOne NMen
'Fame'	CWil MDHE
× ***fauconnettii***	CWil MOne NHol SSmi
× ***fauconnettii thompsonii***	NGre NHol SSmi
'Festival'	CWil NMen
'Fiesta'	CWil
fimbriatum	See ***S.* × *barbulatum***
'Finerpointe'	MBro SSmi
'Fire Glint'	CWil MOne
'Firebird'	CWil MOne
¶ 'First Try'	CWil MOne
'Flaming Heart'	CWil MOne NMen SSmi WPer
'Flander's Passion'	LBee LRHS WPer
'Flasher'	CWil MBro MOne WEas WPer
'Fluweel'	CWil MOne
'Forden'	MOne WGor
'Ford's Amability'	CWil ESis NGre SSmi
'Ford's Giant'	CWil

¶ 'Ford's Shadows'	SSmi
'Ford's Spring'	CWil MOne NHol SSmi WPer
'Freeland'	WPer
'Frigidum'	MOne NHed
'Frosty'	CWil MOne
'Fuego'	CWil SIng
× ***funckii***	CWil MBro NGre NHol NMen SIng WPer
'Fuzzy Wuzzy'	CWil MOne SSmi
¶ 'Galahad'	CWil MOne
'Gamma'	LBee MOne NHol NMen SChu
'Garnet'	MOne
'Gay Jester'	CWil MBro MOne NGre SSmi WHoo
¶ 'Gazelle'	MOne SSmi
'Georgette'	CWil MBro
'Ginnie's Delight'	CWil MOne SSmi
'Gipsy'	CWil MBro
giuseppii	CShe CWil EBar MBro MOne MRPP NGre NHol NMen SIng SRms SSmi
– from Peña Espigüete, Spain	CWil MOne NHol NMen SSmi
– from Peña Prieta, Spain	CWil
'Gizmo'	CWil
¶ 'Gleam'	MOne
'Gloriosum'	GAbr MBro MOne NBus NGre NRoo SIng SSmi
'Glowing Embers'	CWil MBro MOne SSmi
'Gollum'	MOne SSmi
'Granada'	MOne NGre
'Granat'	CWil GCal MOne WPer
'Granby'	MOne NMen
grandiflorum	CWil GCHN MRPP NGre NHed NMen SSmi WPer
¶ – × ***ciliosum***	CWil NMen
– 'Fasciatum'	CWil NMen SSmi
– 'Keston'	EWes NGre SSmi
'Grape Idol'	CWil
'Grapetone'	CWil NGre SSmi
¶ 'Graupurpur'	CWil
¶ 'Gray Dawn'	CWil MOne SSmi
'Green Apple'	CWil NGre SSmi
'Green Gables'	CWil MBro SSmi
'Greenwich Time'	CWil MOne NMen SSmi
* ***greigii***	NNrd
'Grey Ghost'	CWil
'Grey Green'	CWil MOne
'Grey Lady'	CWil SSmi
'Greyfriars'	CWil NMen WPer
'Greyolla'	CWil MOne SSmi WPer
'Hades'	CWil MOne
'Hall's Hybrid'	GAbr MOne NHar NNrd SIng
'Happy'	CWil MBro MOne
* 'Hart'	CWil MOne
¶ 'Haullauer's Seedling'	MOne
'Havana'	CWil MOne NMen
'Hayling'	CWil MOne NHol NMen SSmi
'Heigham Red'	CWil ESis MOne NGre SIng SSmi
helveticum	See ***S. montanum***
'Hester'	CWil ESis GAbr MBro MDHE NHar SIng SSmi
'Hey-Hey'	LBee MOne NMen WAbe WPer
'Hidde'	CWil MOne SSmi
'Hiddes Roosje'	SSmi
hirtum	See ***Jovibarba hirta***
'Hookeri'	See ***S.*** × ***barbulatum* 'Hookeri'**
'Hopi'	CWil NHol
'Hortulanus Smit'	SSmi
'Hot Peppermint'	CWil MOne
'Hot Shot'	CLyd
¶ 'Hurricane'	MOne
'Icicle'	CWil NGre NHol NMen SIng SSmi WGor
imbricatum	See ***S.*** × ***barbulatum***
'Imperial'	CWil SSmi
ingwersenii	MOne NGre SIng SSmi
'Interlace'	CWil SSmi
'Iophon'	SSmi
'Irazu'	CWil GAbr MBro
¶ ***ispartae***	CWil
italicum	CWil
'Itchen'	NMen SSmi
'IWO'	CWil GAbr MOne NMen
'Jack Frost'	CWil MOne NBro NGre NMen SChu SIng SSmi
¶ 'Jane'	MOne
¶ 'Jasper'	MOne
'Jaspis'	CWil MOne
'Jelly Bean'	CWil MOne NMen
'Jet Stream'	CWil MOne NMen SSmi
'Jewel Case'	CWil SSmi
'Jolly Green Giant'	CWil MOne
'Jo's Spark'	CWil
'Jubilee'	CLyd CNic EBar ELan GAbr MOne NHol NMen NRoo SSmi WEas WGor WPer WRHF WWin
'Jubilee Tricolor'	MBro MOne SSmi
¶ 'Jungle Fires'	CWil MOne
¶ 'Jupiter'	ESis
'Justine's Choice'	CWil MOne
'Kalinda'	NGre
'Kappa'	CWil MBro MOne NHol SIng SSmi
'Katmai'	CWil
'Kelly Jo'	CWil MOne NGre NHar NMen SIng SSmi
'Kermit'	MOne SSmi
¶ 'Kibo'	CWil
¶ 'Kilt'	CWil
'Kimble'	CWil WPer
kindingeri	CWil GTou NMen NWCA SSmi
'King George'	CWil ESis GAbr LBee MBro NGre NMen NPer SChu SSmi WGor WHoo WPer WPyg
'Kip'	CWil NMen SSmi
'Kismet'	CWil MOne NGre SSmi
'Kolibri'	GAbr MDHE
kosaninii	CWil MBro MOne NGre NMen SIng SSmi WPer
– from Koprivnik	CWil MOne NMen SSmi WAbe
¶ – from Visitor	CWil
¶ 'Krakeling'	CWil MOne
¶ 'Kramers Purpur'	CWil
'Kramers Spinrad'	CWil ESis GAbr MBro MOne NGre NMen SIng SSmi WEas WHoo
'Lady Kelly'	CLyd CWil ESis WCot
'Launcelot'	MOne WPer
'Lavender and Old Lace'	CWil GAbr MOne MRPP NGre NMen SChu SMer
'Laysan'	CWil MOne
'Leneca'	NGre SSmi
'Lennik's Glory'	See ***S.* 'Crispyn'**
* 'Lennik's Glory No. 1'	CWil
'Lennik's Time'	MBro MOne SSmi
¶ 'Lentevur'	CWil
'Lentezon'	CWil MOne SSmi

'Leocadia's Nephew' CWil MOne
'Lilac Time' CWil GAbr MOne NGre NNrd SChu SIng SSmi
'Lipari' CWil
'Lipstick' CWil NGre
'Lively Bug' CWil MBro MOne NNrd SIng SSmi WPer
'Lloyd Praeger' See ***S. montanum*** subsp. ***stiriacum***
'Lonzo' CWil
'Lou Bastidou' MOne SSmi
'Lowe's Rubicundum' MOne
'Lynne's Choice' CWil SIng
macedonicum CWil NGre SSmi
– from Ljuboten NMen SSmi
'Magic Spell' CWil MOne SSmi
'Magical' CWil MOne SSmi
'Magnificum' CWil MOne NMen
* 'Mahogany' GBin LBee MBro NHol NMen NRoo WGor WHal
'Maigret' CWil MOne SIng
'Majestic' CWil MOne NGre NMen SSmi
'Malabron' CWil MOne SSmi
'Malby's Hybrid' See ***S.* 'Reginald Malby'**
'Marella' CWil WPer
'Marijntje' MOne SSmi
'Marjorie Newton' CWil
'Marmalade' MOne SSmi
§ ***marmoreum*** CMea CWil EBar LBee NMen STre WEas WPer
– 'Brunneifolium' CWil EGoo ESis MBro NGre NHol SChu SSmi WPer
– from Kanzas Gorge NGre NHol SSmi
– from Monte Tirone CWil SSmi
– from Okol CWil NMen SSmi
– from Sveta Peta NGre
¶ – subsp. ***marmoreum*** var. ***dinaricum*** NMen
§ – – 'Rubrifolium' CShe GCal MRPP
§ – 'Ornatum' NGre NHed SRms SSmi
'Marshall' MBro
¶ 'Mary Ente' CWil
'Mate' MOne NMen SSmi
¶ 'Maubi' CWil
'Mauna Kea' MOne SSmi
'Mavbi' NNrd
'Medallion' CWil MOne
'Meisse' MOne SSmi
'Melanie' CWil MOne
'Mercury' CWil MDHE NHol SSmi
'Merlin' CWil MOne SSmi
'Midas' CWil
¶ 'Mila' CWil MOne
'Mini Frost' CLyd CWil MOne NMen SIng
'Minuet' CWil
'Moerkerk's Merit' CWil SSmi
'Mondstein' CWil MOne
'Montague' CWil
§ ***montanum*** CWil ESis NNrd SMer WPer
– subsp. ***burnatii*** NGre SIng SSmi
montanum carpaticum 'Cmiral's Yellow' MBro MOne
montanum from Anchisis CWil MOne
– from Arbizion CWil
– from Windachtal CWil MOne NMen
– subsp. ***montanum*** var. ***braunii*** MRPP
– 'Rubrum' See ***S.* 'Red Mountain'**
§ – subsp. ***stiriacum*** CWil MOne NMen SIng
– – from Mauterndorf, Austria SSmi
– – 'Lloyd Praeger' CWil MOne NGre SSmi
'More Honey' CWil MOne
'Mount Hood' CWil MOne
'Mulberry Wine' CLyd CWil MOne
'Myrrhine' CWil MOne
'Mystic' CWil MOne NMen NNrd WPer
¶ 'Neptune' CWil
nevadense CWil MBro MOne MRPP NGre NMen SRms SSmi
– var. ***hirtellum*** CWil MOne NMen SSmi
'Nico' CWil MOne
'Night Raven' CLyd CWil MOne NMen SSmi
'Nigrum' See ***S. tectorum* 'Nigrum'**
'Niobe' CWil
'Nixes 27' MOne
'Noir' CWil GAbr MOne NGre NMen SSmi
'Norbert' CWil MOne
'Nouveau Pastel' CWil
'Octet' MOne NMen
octopodes CLyd ESis MDHE NBir NHed
– var. ***apetalum*** CWil NMen SIng SSmi
'Oddity' CPBP CWil MOne WPer
'Ohio Burgundy' CWil MDHE MOne NMen SSmi WAbe WPer
'Olivette' SSmi WPer
'Omega' EBar MBro MOne SSmi WPer
'Opitz' CLyd CWil MOne WPer
'Ornatum' EPot NGre SSmi WAbe WEas
ossetiense CWil MOne NMen SSmi
'Othello' CHal EBre GAbr MRPP NBir NVic
'Packardian' CWil MOne NMen SSmi
'Painted Lady' CWil SSmi
'Palissander' CWil MOne NGre NNrd SSmi
'Pam Wain' MOne
¶ 'Paricutin' CWil
'Pastel' CWil NMen SSmi
patens See ***Jovibarba heuffelii***
'Patrician' CWil EBar EBre ESis
'Peach Blossom' CWil
'Pekinese' CWil EWes MBro MOne NBro NMen NNrd SIng SSmi WEas WPer WWin
'Peterson's Ornatum' MOne NGre SSmi
'Pilatus' CWil
'Pilosella' MOne
'Pink Cloud' CWil MBro
'Pink Dawn' CWil MOne
¶ 'Pink Delight' CWil
'Pink Mist' WPer
'Pink Puff' CWil SSmi
'Pippin' CWil MOne WPer
'Piran' CWil MOne
pittonii CMea CWil ESis GAbr MOne NMen SIng SSmi
'Pixie' CWil MOne NHed
'Plumb Rose' CWil MOne SChu
'Pluto' CWil MOne SSmi
'Poke Eat' MOne SSmi
'Polaris' CWil MOne SSmi
¶ 'Poldark' MOne
'Pottsii' CWil GAbr MOne NHed
'Prairie Sunset' CWil MOne
'Precious' CWil MOne SSmi
'President Arsac' SSmi
'Proud Zelda' CWil MOne SSmi
¶ 'Pruhonice' CWil
'Pseudo-ornatum' LBee SChu
'Pumaros' CWil NMen SSmi

pumilum	CWil MBar NGre NMen
– from Adyl Su No 1	CWil SSmi
– from Adyl Su No 2	SSmi
– from Armchi	CWil MRPP SSmi
– from Armchi × *ingwersenii*	NMen
– from El'brus No 1	CWil MOne MRPP NMen SSmi
– from El'brus No 2	SSmi
¶ – from Techensis	CWil NMen
¶ – × ***ingwersenii***	CWil
'Purdy'	WAbe
'Purdy's 50-6'	CWil MOne
'Purdy's 90-1'	MOne
'Purple Beauty'	CWil MOne
'Purple King'	CWil
'Purple Passion'	MBro
'Purpurriese'	CWil GAbr
'Queen Amalia'	See ***S. reginae-amaliae***
¶ 'Query'	MOne
'Quintessence'	CWil MOne
'Racy'	CWil
'Radiant'	CWil MOne
'Ramses'	MOne
'Raspberry Ice'	CLyd CWil MBro NHol NMen WAbe
'Red Ace'	CWil NBro NMen SSmi
'Red Beam'	CWil MDHE NGre SSmi
'Red Delta'	CWil SSmi
'Red Devil'	CWil MBro MOne NMen SSmi
¶ 'Red Indian'	CWil
§ 'Red Mountain'	CHal CWil MBro MOne MWat SSmi
'Red Prince'	CWil
'Red Rum'	WPer
'Red Shadows'	CWil ESis WPer
'Red Skin'	CWil MOne
'Red Spider'	NNrd
'Red Wings'	NGre SRms
'Regal'	MOne
¶ 'Regina'	MOne
reginae	See ***S. reginae-amaliae***
§ ***reginae-amaliae***	NHol SSmi STre
– from Kambeecho No 1	SSmi
– from Kambeecho No 2	MDHE NMen
– from Mavri Petri	CWil MOne SSmi
– from Peristéri, Greece	SSmi
– from Sarpun	CWil NMen SSmi
§ 'Reginald Malby'	CShe CWil MDHE NGre SSmi
'Reinhard'	CWil GAbr MOne NMen NNrd SIng SSmi WPer
'Remus'	CWil NMen SIng
'Rex'	NMen
'Rhone'	CWil MOne
* ***richardii***	MBar NBus
'Risque'	CWil MOne WPer
'Rita Jane'	CLyd CWil NMen SSmi
'Robin'	CLyd CWil MOne NHol NNrd
'Ronny'	CWil MOne
'Roosemaryn'	MBro
'Rose Splendour'	CWil
× ***roseum*** 'Fimbriatum'	MBro NHed NHol SSmi WEas
'Rosie'	CMea CWil GAbr MBro MOne NBus NGre NMen NRoo SIng SSmi WHoo WPer WPyg
'Rotkopf'	CWil MOne
'Rotmantel'	MOne NNrd SSmi
¶ 'Rotund'	CWil
'Rouge'	CWil MOne NMen SRms
'Royal Flush'	CWil SSmi
'Royal Mail'	MOne
'Royal Opera'	CWil NGre SSmi
'Royal Ruby'	CWil GCHN LBee MOne MRPP NRoo SChu SSmi
'Rubikon Improved'	MOne
'Rubin'	EGoo EPad ESis MBro MOne MRPP NGre NMen NNrd WAbe WEas WHoo WPer WPyg
'Rubrifolium'	See ***S. marmoreum*** subsp. ***marmoreum* 'Rubrifolium'**
'Rubrum Ash'	CWil NMen
'Rubrum Ornatum'	SIng
'Rubrum Ray'	CWil SSmi
'Ruby Glow'	ESis
'Ruby Heart'	NGre SSmi
'Rusty'	CWil MOne WFar
ruthenicum	NGre
'Safara'	CWil
'Saffron'	CLyd CWil MOne
'Saga'	CWil MOne
¶ 'Sanford's Hybrid'	MOne
'Santis'	MBro
'Saturn'	CWil GAbr NMen SSmi
schlehanii	See ***S. marmoreum***
'Seminole'	CWil MOne
¶ 'Sharon's Pencil'	CWil MOne
'Shawnee'	CWil MOne
'Sheila'	GAbr
'Shirley's Joy'	CHal CWil GAbr MOne NMen SSmi WEas
'Sideshow'	CWil MOne
¶ 'Sigma'	MOne
'Silberkarneol'	See ***S.* 'Silver Jubilee'**
'Silberspitz'	CWil MOne NMen WPer
§ 'Silver Jubilee'	CWil MDHE NGre NHed SSmi
¶ 'Silver Spring'	MOne
'Silver Thaw'	CWil NMen NNrd
'Simonkaianum'	See ***Jovibarba hirta***
'Sioux'	CWil MOne NGre NMen SIng SSmi WPer
'Skrocki's Bronze'	MOne NMen WPer
¶ 'Skrocki's Purple Rose'	CWil
'Slabber's Seedling'	CWil
'Smokey Jet'	CWil
'Snowberger'	CWil EBar ESis GAbr MOne NHar SIng WPer
soboliferum	See ***Jovibarba sobolifera***
¶ 'Soothsayer'	CWil MOne
'Sopa'	CWil MOne
sosnowskyi	CWil MOne NMen
sp. from Figaua Dhag	NGre
sp. Sierra del Cadi	MOne NHol
sp. Sierra Nova	NHed
'Spanish Dancer'	CWil MOne SSmi
'Spherette'	CWil MBro MOne NMen SSmi WPer
¶ 'Spice'	CWil
'Spinnelli'	NHed
'Spode'	SSmi
'Spring Mist'	CWil GCHN MBro NHar WPer
'Sprite'	CLyd CWil GAbr MOne NMen SSmi
stansfieldii	See ***S. arachnoideum*** subsp. ***tomentosum* 'Stansfieldii'**
¶ 'Starion'	CWil
'Starshine'	CWil MBro MOne NMen SIng SSmi
'State Fair'	CWil MOne NGre SSmi WPer
'Strawberry Fields'	CWil MOne
'Strider'	MBro
'Stuffed Olive'	CWil SSmi

'Sun Waves'	CWil MOne SSmi
¶ 'Super Dome'	CWil MOne
'Superama'	CWil
'Supernova'	CWil
¶ 'Syston Flame'	MOne
'Tamberlane'	CWil MOne
¶ 'Tambimuttu'	CWil
'Tambora'	CWil
'Tarn Hows'	CWil
¶ 'Teck'	CWil
§ ***tectorum*** ♀	CArn CNic CWil EJud ELan EWFC GAbr GPoy GTou MBar MDHE SIde SIng STre WAbe WJek WOak WWye
* – 'Alp Gasson'	SIng
– subsp. ***alpinum***	CWil SIng SSmi
– 'Atropurpureum'	GCal
– 'Atroviolaceum'	CWil ESis GCal SIng WFar
– from Sierra del Cadi	SSmi
§ – var. ***glaucum***	CWil ESis MOne SSmi
§ – 'Nigrum'	CWil ESis MBro NGre NHol NMen SSmi
– 'Red Flush'	CWil NHar NMen SIng SSmi
– 'Royanum'	ESis GAbr WEas
– 'Sunset'	CWil ESis MOne NMen SIng SSmi WEas
– subsp. ***tectorum***	MOne NGre
§ – – 'Atropurpureum'	CWil SIng SSmi
§ – – 'Boissieri'	CWil MBro NGre SSmi
– – 'Triste'	CWil EBar ESis LBee SSmi
– 'Violaceum'	MOne SIng WAbe
'Telfan'	SSmi
'Thayne'	NMen
thompsonianum	CWil ESis MRPP NGre NHed NHol NMen SIng SSmi
'Tiffany'	MOne NHol WPer
¶ 'Tina'	WPer
'Titania'	CWil NHar SSmi
¶ 'Tombago'	CWil
'Topaz'	CWil EBar GAbr LBee LRHS MOne SChu
'Tordeur's Memory'	CWil MOne NGre NMen SSmi
'Traci Sue'	CWil MOne SSmi
'Trail Walker'	CWil
transcaucasicum	CWil SIng SSmi
'Tree Beard'	CWil
'Tristesse'	CWil GCal MOne NMen WGor
'Tristram'	SSmi
'Truva'	CWil MOne SIng SSmi
'Twilight Blues'	CWil MOne
'Unicorn'	CWil
x ***vaccarii***	MOne NGre NMen SSmi
'Vanbaelen'	CWil MOne SSmi
'Vaughelen'	CWil MOne
'Velvet Prince'	CWil MOne
x ***versicolor***	NHol
vicentei	CWil NHed
¶ 'Victorian'	MOne
'Video'	CWil MOne NMen SSmi
'Violet Queen'	CWil
'Virgil'	CWil MBro SSmi WPer
'Virginus'	CWil MBro
'Vulcano'	CWil
webbianum	See ***S. arachnoideum*** subsp. ***tomentosum***
'Webby Flame'	CWil MOne
'Webby Ola'	MOne SSmi
'Weirdo'	CWil MOne
'Wendy'	CLyd CWil MOne NMen
'Westerlin'	CWil GAbr MOne NGre SIng SSmi
'Whitening'	CWil MOne NGre NMen SSmi
x ***widderi***	SSmi
'Wollcott's Variety'	GAbr MOne MRPP NBir NHar WPer
wulfenii	CWil NMen
¶ 'Zaza'	CWil MOne
¶ 'Zenith'	CWil MOne
'Zenocrate'	CWil
'Zeppelin'	CWil MBro
'Zinaler Rothorn'	LRHS
'Zircon'	NMen
'Zone'	CWil MOne NMen SSmi
'Zulu'	CWil MOne NHed SSmi

SENECIO (Asteraceae)

§ ***abrotanifolius***	MHar NNrd NTow
– var. ***tiroliensis***	See ***S. abrotanifolius***
aquaticus	CKin
§ ***articulatus***	CHal GBur
¶ ***aschenbornianus***	GCal
aureus	See ***Packera aurea***
bicolor subsp. ***cineraria***	See ***S. cineraria***
bidwillii	See ***Brachyglottis bidwillii***
buchananii	See ***Brachyglottis buchananii***
candicans	See ***S. cineraria***
cannabifolius	EBee
chrysanthemoides	See ***Euryops chrysanthemoides***
§ ***cineraria***	CHEx IBlr MBri
– 'Alice'	EFou
– 'Ramparts'	LHop WEas
– Sch 3129	WHCr
– 'White Diamond' ♀	CLTr ECha LGro WBod WWin
compactus	See ***Brachyglottis compacta***
confusus	CPlN ECon LCns LHil
doria	EBee EPPr SAxl SCro WCot WFar WLRN
¶ ***doronicum***	EMan
elaeagnifolius	See ***Brachyglottis elaeagnifolia***
eminens	WCot
fuchsii HH&K 293	CHan
– HH&K 318	CHan
glastifolius	CTrC ERea GBri LHil
'Gregynog Gold'	See ***Ligularia* 'Gregynog Gold'**
greyi Hooker	See ***Brachyglottis greyi***
– hort.	See ***Brachyglottis* (Dunedin Group) 'Sunshine'**
◆ ***hectoris***	See ***Brachyglottis hectoris***
heritieri	See ***Pericallis lanata***
herreanus	MBri SLMG
kirkii	See ***Brachyglottis kirkii***
laciniatus	CHEx
laxifolius Buchanan	See ***Brachyglottis laxifolia***
– hort.	See ***Brachyglottis* (Dunedin Group) 'Sunshine'**
'Leonard Cockayne'	See ***Brachyglottis* 'Leonard Cockayne'**
¶ ***leucophyllus***	LHil WDav
leucostachys	See ***S. viravira***
macroglossus	CPlN
– 'Variegatus' ♀	CB&S CHal CPlN ERea
maritimus	See ***S. cineraria***
mikanioides	See ***Delairea odorata***
monroi	See ***Brachyglottis monroi***
petasitis	CHEx LHil
polyodon	CInt GBri MAvo MNrw MTol SUsu
– S&SH 29	CFir CHan CRDP EBee SAga WCot WCru WHoo WWhi

populifolius	See ***Pericallis appendiculata***
przewalskii	See ***Ligularia przewalskii***
pulcher	CChu CFil CGle CHan CRDP CSam GBri MAvo MMil MNrw MTho NTow SMrm SUsu WCot WCru
reinholdii	See ***Brachyglottis rotundifolia***
rodriguezii	WOMN
rowleyanus	EBak
scandens	CB&S CFil CMac CPlN CPle ELan ERav ERea ISea MAvo MCCP MNrw MTho NRai SBra WCru
¶ *seminiveus*	WCot
serpens	MBri
§ *smithii*	CChu CHan CRDP CRow CWGN ECha ELan MSta NChi WCot WCru
spedenii	See ***Brachyglottis spedenii***
¶ *squalidus*	CTiv
'Sunshine'	See ***Brachyglottis* (Dunedin Group) 'Sunshine'**
takedanus	See ***Tephroseris takedanus***
tamoides 'Variegatus'	ERea WPyg
tanguticus	See ***Sinacalia tangutica***
§ *viravira* 🏆	CDec CGle CPle ELan ERea MBel MRav SMad SPer SUsu WByw WHal WPri WSHC WWat
werneriifolius	See ***Packera werneriifolius***

SENNA (Caesalpiniaceae)

acutifolia	CB&S
angustifolia	MSal
artemisioides 🏆	CTrC SOWG
N *corymbosa* Lam.	CAbb CB&S CBot CHEx CPlN CPle ERea LChe LCns LHil SLMG SOWG
didymobotrya	SOWG
hebecarpa	MSal
marilandica	CB&S EBee MSal WCru WSHC
obtusa Clos	See ***S. candolleana***
– (Roxb.) Wight	CGre SBid
§ *obtusifolia*	CPlN MSal
tomentosa	See ***S. multiglandulosa***
tora	See ***S. obtusifolia***

SEQUOIA (Taxodiaceae)

sempervirens	CB&S CDoC CGre CMCN EHul IOrc ISea LCon LPan MBlu WDin WMou WNor
– 'Adpressa'	CDoC CMac EBre EHul EOrn EPla LCon LLin MAsh MBal MBar MBri MGos MPla NHol NWea SAga SLim WPyg
– 'Prostrata'	EBre EOrn EPla GAri LBee LCon LLin MAsh MBar MBri MOne SIng

SEQUOIADENDRON (Taxodiaceae)

giganteum 🏆	CB&S CDoC CMCN CMac EBre EHul ELan ENot GRei IOrc ISea LCon LNet LPan MBar MBlu MBri NBee NPal NWea SMad SPer WFro WMou WNor
– 'Barabits' Requiem'	LRHS MBlu WMou
– 'Glaucum'	CBlo EBre LCon LPan MBlu MBri SMad WMou
– 'Hazel Smith'	MBlu WMou
– 'Pendulum'	CBlo CDoC EBre LCon LPan MBlu SMad WMou
– 'Variegatum'	WMou

SERAPIAS (Orchidaceae)

lingua	LAma SBla SSpi

SERENOA (Arecaceae)

See Plant Deletions

SERIPHIDIUM (Asteraceae)

caerulescens subsp. *gallicum*	EEls MAvo
§ *canum*	EEls
§ *ferganense*	EEls
§ *maritimum* 🏆	GBar GGar GPoy ILis
– var. *maritimum*	EEls
§ *nutans*	EBre EEls MWat NSti WWhi
§ *tridentatum*	CArn
– subsp. *tridentatum*	EEls
– subsp. *wyomingense*	EEls
tripartitum rupicola	EEls NWCA
§ *vallesiacum* 🏆	CJew EEls GBar SAga WEas
vaseyanaum	EEls

SERISSA (Rubiaceae)

foetida	See ***S. japonica***
§ *japonica*	GAri STre
japonica rosea	STre
japonica 'Variegata'	CPle ECon STre

SERRATULA (Asteraceae)

§ *seoanei*	CBos CMea CNic CRDP CSev CTri ECha EDAr EMan EMon LHop MHig MWat NNrd SDix SIng SMad SRms WByw WCot WHil WPat WRus WWin
shawii	See ***S. seoanei***
tinctoria	CArn CKin ECWi ELau EMan GBar MHew MSal
¶ – subsp. *macrocephala*	WFar

SESAMUM (Pedaliaceae)

indicum	CArn MSto

SESBANIA (Papilionaceae)

punicea	SOWG

SESELI (Apiaceae)

dichotomum	SIgm
elatum subsp. *osseum*	SIgm
globiferum	SIgm
gummiferum	CBot CGle CSpe LGre SMrm
hippomarathrum	CGle
libanotis	SIgm
pallasii	SIgm
varium	SIgm

SESLERIA (Poaceae)

§ *albicans*	EPPr
§ *argentea*	ETPC
autumnalis	ETPC
caerulea	CCuc CElw EGar EHoe ELan EMon EPla ETPC GBin MUlv
– subsp. *calcarea*	See ***S. albicans***
cylindrica	See ***S. argentea***
glauca	EHoe MAvo MSCN WPer
heufleriana	EHoe EMon EPPr EPla ESOG ETPC LRHS

insularis	CSWP EMon EPPr EPla ESOG ETPC LRHS
nitida	CCuc CElw EGar EHoe EMon ETPC LRHS
sadleriana	EBee EPPr EPla ESOG ETPC EWes

SETARIA (Poaceae)

palmifolia	LHil

SETCREASEA See TRADESCANTIA

SEVERINIA (Rutaceae)

buxifolia	SCit

SHEPHERDIA (Elaeagnaceae)

argentea	CAgr CB&S CPle MAll

SHERARDIA (Rubiaceae)

arvensis	EWFC MHew MSal

SHIBATAEA (Poaceae - Bambusoideae)

kumasasa	CB&S CBar CCuc CPMA EBee EJap EPla ESiP GCal IOrc ISta LNet MBal MCCP MGos MUlv SBam SDry WJun WNor
kumasasa aureastriata	CWLN EPla SDry
lancifolia	EPla SDry WJun

SHORTIA (Diapensiaceae)

galacifolia	CGra
soldanelloides	IBlr WCru
– f. ***alpina***	IBlr
– var. ***ilicifolia***	IBlr
– var. ***magna***	IBlr
uniflora 'Grandiflora'	IBlr

SIBBALDIA (Rosaceae)

parviflora NS 668	NWCA

SIBBALDIOPSIS (Rosaceae)

tridentata 'Nuuk'	CSpe GAri MGos

SIBIRAEA (Rosaceae)

altaiensis	See ***S. laevigata***

SIDA (Malvaceae)

hermaphrodita	EMon

SIDALCEA (Malvaceae)

'Brilliant'	CM&M EBar EBee EPfP MBel MTis NFai WHil WMer WTyr
candida	CChu CGle CHad CHan CMGP CRDP CSpe EFou ELan GAbr GCal GGar GLil LHop MFir MRav MSte MTis NFai NRoo NSti SApp SCro SHel SPer SUsu WGwG WHal WRus WTyr
– 'Bianca'	CBot CPea EAst EBar EBee LFis WHil WPer
'Crimson King'	LFis
'Croftway Red'	CB&S EBre ELan LFis MFir NRoo SAga SChu SCro SHel SOkh SPer WMaN WTyr
Crown Hybrids	CTri
'Elsie Heugh'	CBot CChu CDoC CHad CHan CSpe EAst EBre EFol EFou ELan GAbr GBri GCal MArl MBri MCLN MUlv NBro NFai NPla NSti SAga SChu SHel SOkh SRms WRus WWhi
hendersonii	EBee
'Interlaken'	NFla NHol NOrc WTyr
'Loveliness'	CGle CRDP ECED ELan EMan MTis NCat
malviflora	CBre MFir NSti SChu SRms
– dark form	GMac WTyr
¶ 'Monarch'	NCat NCut
'Mr Lindbergh'	EBre MCli NCat SPer WCot WRus
'Mrs Borrodaile'	EBre GBuc MCLN MTis MUlv WCot WRus WTyr
'Mrs Galloway'	LFis WTyr
'Mrs T. Alderson'	EBre EMan LCom WTyr
neomexicana	EBee GCal WTyr
'Oberon'	CHan GBuc NHol SAxl SPer WEas WFar WTyr
'Party Girl'	CM&M CSam EAst EBre ECot ECtt EFou EHal EMar GGar LGan MCLN MTis NCat NLak NOrc NPri NRoo NVic SHel WHil WHoo WOve WPer WRus
* ***purpetta***	CPea NPSI SMac
'Reverend Page Roberts'	CShe LFis MRav SMrm WTyr
'Rosaly'	WHoo
'Rosanna'	LBuc NRai WTyr
'Rose Bouquet'	MHlr WCot
'Rose Queen'	CGle EBre ECha EMan EMar LGan LHop MCLN MRav NFla NRoo SAga SChu SOkh SPer SRms WTyr
'Rosy Gem'	CBlo GLil NCat NCut WTyr
Stark's Hybrids	SRms
'Sussex Beauty'	CBos CRDP EBre ECha EFou LFis MCli NCat SChu WCot WTyr
'The Duchess'	CShe LFis WTyr
'Twixt'	LFis WTyr
'William Smith' ♀	CChu COtt CRDP CSam EAst EBre ECED ECha EMan EPfP EWes GMaP LFis LGan LHop MCLN NCat NFla NHol NOrc NPla NRoo SAga SPer SUsu WCot WTyr

SIDERITIS (Lamiaceae)

candicans	NSty
hyssopifolia	EBee SUsu
¶ ***macrostachys***	LHil
scordioides	CFis SHFr
syriaca	CBot ECha EMan SHFr SIgm
– subsp. ***syriaca***	NRai

SIEVERSIA (Rosaceae)

§ ***reptans***	WDav

SILAUM (Apiaceae)

silaus	CKin EWFC

SILENE (Caryophyllaceae)

acaulis	ESis GCHN GTou ITim LBee LFis MBro MPla MTho NMen NRoo NWCA SBla SRms SSmi WAbe WPat

§ – subsp. ***acaulis***	CMHG EPot GDra NCat SRms WPer
– 'Alba'	EHyt EPot EWes GDra LBee NHar NMen NNrd WAbe
§ – subsp. ***bryoides***	WPer
– subsp. ***elongata***	See ***S. acaulis*** subsp. ***acaulis***
– subsp. ***exscapa***	See ***S. acaulis*** subsp. ***bryoides***
– 'Frances'	EHyt EPot GAbr GCHN GDra GTou ITim MHig NHar NRya NSla NWCA WAbe WPat
– 'Francis Copeland'	ECho ELan
– 'Helen's Double'	EHyt EPot NNrd WAbe
* ***acaulis minima***	CLyd EPot
acaulis 'Mount Snowdon'	CInt EBre ELan EWes LBee MTho NBus NHar NHol NMen NPri NWCA WAbe WPat
– 'Pedunculata'	See ***S. acaulis*** subsp. ***acaulis***
– 'Plena'	NBrk
alba	See ***S. latifolia***
alpestris	ELan ESis LFis MBar MHig MNrw MPla MTho NGre NNrd NWCA WCla WFar WPer
– 'Flore Pleno' 🏆	CMil CShe EOrc ESis EWes LBee LBlm MHig WOMN WWin
* ***andina***	NWCA
¶ ***argaea***	EHyt
x ***arkwrightii***	See ***Lychnis*** x ***arkwrightii***
armeria	EMar WHer
asterias	CBre CSam EBar EJud MBel MNrw NBrk NBro NSti SMrm WCot WPer WPri WWin
– NS 657	NWCA
caroliniana	NWCA SSca
caryophylloides subsp. ***echinus***	WDav
¶ ***ciliata***	EPot
§ ***compacta***	CM&M WCot WEas WKif
conica	EWFC
delavayi	SIgm WCot
dinarica	SIng
§ ***dioica***	CArn CKin CNat ECWi ELan EWFC MChe MGam MHew MRav NFai NLan SWat WCla WHen WHer WJek WShi
dioica alba	WNdy
dioica 'Clifford Moor' (v)	SCoo
– 'Compacta'	See ***S. dioica*** **'Minikin'**
§ – 'Flore Pleno'	CBot CJew ECha GMac LFis LLWP MNrw MTho NBro SMrm WByw WCot WEas WHoo WNdy WPer WWin
§ – 'Graham's Delight' (v)	EMon GBri NCat WBea WCHb WCot WHer
– 'Inane'	CNat MAvo WAlt
§ – 'Minikin'	CLyd ECha ELan EMon GBri LRHS NCGP WCot
– 'Pat Clissold' (v)	EMon
– 'Richmond' (d)	ECha EMon GBuc MNrw
§ – 'Rosea Plena'	CBre CGle CSam ELan EMan EMon EOrc LFis MTho SChu SMrm SUsu WByw WHer WPer
– 'Rubra Plena'	See ***S. dioica*** **'Flore Pleno'**
– 'Thelma Kay' (v)	CMil GBuc WCHb WCot WPbr
– 'Variegata'	See ***S. dioica*** **'Graham's Delight'**
elisabethae	LRHS MRPP NWCA
– 'Alba'	WCla
§ ***fimbriata***	CHad CHan CMea EEls ELan GCal LFis MFir SAxl SMrm SUsu SWas WAbb WCot WRHF
– 'Marianne'	MNrw
fortunei B&SWJ 296	WCru
gallica	EWFC
hifacensis	EMon
hookeri	EMar MTho NWCA SIng WDav
– Ingramii Group	CGra WAbe
ingramii	MHew
italica	CKin
keiskei	ECha ELan NTow SBla SChu WPer
– var. ***minor***	EWes MTho NWCA SSca WAbe WOMN WWin
§ ***latifolia***	CArn ECWi EWFC NMir WCla WHen WHer WJek
lerchenfeldiana	CNic
maritima	See ***S. uniflora***
moorcroftiana	WPer
morrisonmontana	NBro
multifida	See ***S. fimbriata***
noctiflora	CKin EBee WCla
nutans	CArn CKin EJud EWFC MNrw NMir WGwy WHer WHil WUnd
– var. ***salmoniana***	WUnd
¶ – var. ***smithiana***	WUnd
orientalis	See ***S. compacta***
parishii var. ***viscida*** NNS 95-474	MRPP
parnassica	NGar
¶ ***pendula***	LLWP
¶ – 'Compacta'	CInt
petersonii	NWCA WDav
pusilla	CHal CLyd NMen NWCA
rubra 'Flore Pleno'	See ***S. dioica*** **'Flore Pleno'**
saxatilis	NHol
schafta 🏆	CHal CMea ECha ELan EMNN GCHN MBro MFir MPla MWat NFla NGre NNrd NRoo NWCA SRms WCla WHoo WPer WWin
– 'Abbotswood'	See ***Lychnis*** x ***walkeri*** **'Abbotswood Rose'**
§ – 'Shell Pink'	CInt CNic EPot EWes LHop MHig WAbe WHoo WOMN WThi
sieboldii	See ***Lychnis coronata*** var. ***sieboldii***
suksdorfii	CPea EPot MBro MHig NHol WHoo WPyg
* ***surortii***	WPer
§ ***uniflora***	ELan EMNN EMar EWFC MFir MHew MWat NBro NOak NWCA SBod WCla WHen WHer WHil WWin
– 'Alba Plena'	See ***S. uniflora*** **'Robin Whitebreast'**
§ – 'Druett's Variegated'	CElw CInt CLyd CMHG CPBP EBre ECha EFol EMan EPot EWes LBee LFis LHop MBar NHol NMen NNrd NPri NRoo SBla SIde SIng WAbe WBea WCot WHil WPat WPyg WWin
– 'Flore Pleno'	See ***S. uniflora*** **'Robin Whitebreast'**

§ – 'Robin Whitebreast' (d) CMHG CMil CPBP CVer EBar ECha ECtt ELan EOrc GCal MBar MRav MTho MTol MWat NBro NHol NOak SRms WEas WHoo WOve WPer WPyg WWin
– 'Rosea' CGle CMil ECtt EMNN EMar MRav NWCA SAxl SIng SMrm SSca SUsu WCot WPer
– 'Silver Lining' (v) ELan EMon GBuc
– 'Variegata' See *S. uniflora* **'Druett's Variegated'**
♦ – Weisskehlchen See *S. uniflora* **'Robin Whitebreast'**
– 'White Bells' CMea CTri EBee NNrd WBea WHoo WPyg WSHC
vallesia WPat WPer WRHF
§ ***vulgaris*** CKin CTiv ECWi EWFC MChe MGam NLan NMir
– subsp. ***alpina*** See *S. uniflora* subsp. ***prostrata***
– subsp. ***maritima*** See *S. uniflora*
wallichiana See *S. vulgaris*
'Wisley Pink' CHal NMen
§ ***zawadskii*** EBar EMar GBuc MNrw NGre SSca WHil WPer

SILPHIUM (Asteraceae)

laciniatum CArn ECro
perfoliatum CArn ECro GPoy NSti WCot

SILYBUM (Asteraceae)

marianum CArc CArn CGle CInt ECoo EFer ELan EMan EMar EPar GPoy LGan LHol MFir MSal NFai SIde SSoC SVen WCer WEas WFar WHer WHil WOak WWye

SIMMONDSIA (Simmondsiaceae)

chinensis MSal

SINACALIA (Asteraceae)

§ ***tangutica*** CGle CHEx CHan CRow CWGN EBar ELan GGar MBal MHlr MNrw NBro NDea NSti SDix SMrm WAbb WCot WCru WFar

SINARUNDINARIA (Poaceae - Bambusoideae)

anceps See ***Yushania anceps***
jaunsarensis See ***Yushania anceps***
maling See ***Yushania maling***
murieliae See ***Fargesia murieliae***
nitida See ***Fargesia nitida***

SINNINGIA (Gesneriaceae)

'Arion' NMos
'Blanche de Méru' NMos SDeJ
'Blue Wonder' MBri
'Boonwood Yellow Bird' NMos
canescens 🏆 CHal
§ ***cardinalis*** CHal EBak WDib
§ x ***cardosa*** MBri
'Cherry Belle' NMos
'Diego Rose' MBri
'Duchess of York' CSut
'Duke of York' CSut
'Etoile de Feu' LAma MBri NMos
'Hollywood' LAma NMos SDeJ
'Island Sunset' NMos
'Kaiser Friedrich' LAma MBri NMos NRog
'Kaiser Wilhelm' LAma MBri NMos NRog
'Medusa' NMos
'Mont Blanc' CSut LAma MBri NMos SDeJ
'Pegasus' NMos
'Princess Elizabeth' SDeJ
'Red Tiger' CSut
'Reine Wilhelmine' SDeJ
'Royal Crimson' CSut
Royal Pink Group CSut
'Royal Tiger' CSut
Tigrina Group NMos SDeJ
tubiflora CMon
'Violacea' MBri NMos NRog
'Waterloo' NMos NRog

SINOBAMBUSA (Poaceae - Bambusoideae)

tootsik SBam SDry WJun
§ – f. ***albostriata*** SDry
– 'Variegata' See ***S. tootsik* f. *albostriata***

SINOCALYCANTHUS (Calycanthaceae)

chinensis CMCN CPMA LNet LRHS SMad SSpi

SINOFRANCHETIA (Lardizabalaceae)

chinensis CPlN WCru WWat

SINOJACKIA (Styracaceae)

See Plant Deletions

SINOWILSONIA (Hamamelidaceae)

henryi CMCN

SISYMBRIUM (Brassicaceae)

§ ***luteum*** WHer WHil

SISYRINCHIUM † (Iridaceae)

x ***anceps*** See ***S. angustifolium* Miller**
angustifolium album CInt MSCN WDav
§ ***angustifolium*** Miller CHan CShe CWGN EBar EBur ECha ELan GCHN MBal MBar MSal MWat NDea NFla NHol NNrd SRms SSmi WCla WEas WPer WWin
§ ***arenarium*** EBur EHyt MDHE SBla
atlanticum CMea CPea EBur EHyt ESis MDHE NBro WAbe WPer
bellum hort. See ***S. idahoense* var. *bellum***
bermudianum 'Album' See ***S. graminoides* 'Album'**
– Linnaeus See ***S. angustifolium* Miller**
birameun See ***S. graminoides***
'Biscutella' CHad CHan CInt CLyd CMea EAst EBur ECtt ELan ESis LHop NDea NMen NNrd SAxl SChu SLod SOkh SSea SSmi SSvw SUsu WCla WHal WLRN WOMN
* 'Blue Ice' CInt CMea CPBP CSpe CVer EBur EGar LWak MBro MDHE MHig NBro NCat NHol WAbb WAbe WFar WHal WHoo WPat WPer WPyg
boreale See ***S. californicum***
brachypus See ***S. californicum* Brachypus Group**

'Californian Skies'	CBro CElw CGle CHan CLon CMil CRDP EBur ECha EHyt LBee LBlm LGre LWak MDHE MHig NBro NFla NHol SAsh SMrm SSmi SSvw SUsu SWas WKif WPat WWhi WWye
§ ***californicum***	CBen CBro CInt CLon CShe CWGN EBur EFol EHon ESis LPBA MBar MFir MSta MWat NBro NHol NMen NNrd SSmi SVen SWyc WCla WPer WRus WWin WWye
§ – Brachypus Group	CBro CMea EAst EBar ECtt EPot GCHN GCra GTou MNrw NDea NMen NWes SWat WBea WCer WEas WOak
§ ***chilense***	MSto SIng
coeleste	EBur EPPr MDHE
coeruleum	See ***Gelasine coerulea***
commutatum	CInt EBar EFol SIng WSan
¶ ***convolutum***	CInt
cuspidatum	See ***S. arenarium***
demissum	CLyd CNic EBur
depauperatum	CLyd EBur EMar ESis MSte NWCA WHer WNdy WPer
'Devon Skies'	CHid CInt CMHG EBur MNrw WSan WWin
douglasii	See ***Olsynium douglasii***
'E.K. Balls'	CInt CVer EAst EBur ELan EPla EPot LBee LWak MBro MHew MTho NBro NCat NFai NHol NMen NRya SBla SSmi SSvw SUsu WAbe WCla WHen WPat WWin
elmeri	EBur MSto WPer
filifolium	See ***Olsynium filifolium***
§ ***graminoides***	EBur NBro WPer
§ – 'Album'	EBur GAri MTol NBro WCla WPer
grandiflorum	See ***Olsynium douglasii***
'Hemswell Sky'	CInt CLyd EBur MDHE MMil WWye
§ ***idahoense***	CBro CInt CMHG EBar EBre EBur ECha EFol ELan GCHN GTou LBee MBal MNrw NMen NRya NWCA WBea WCla WHen WOMN WPat WPer
§ – 'Album'	CGle CHan CVer EBur ECha EHyt ELan EPot GTou LBee MHig MNrw MTho MWat NDea NEgg NHol NMen NNrd SIng SSmi SWas WAbe WCla WOMN WPat WPer WWin WWye
¶ – var. ***bellum*** 'Rocky Point'	EBur
– blue	ELan
iridifolium	See ***S. micranthum***
junceum	See ***Olsynium junceum***
littorale	EBur MSto WCla WPer
macrocarpon ♀	CBro CGra CInt CPBP EBur EHyt EPot ERos ESis GTou LBee MHig NMen NNrd NWCA SSpi WAbe WCla WCot WDav WHal WHoo WOMN WPer WWye
'Marie'	EBur ECha MDHE
'Marion'	NHar SAsh
'May Snow'	See ***S. idahoense* 'Album'**
§ ***micranthum***	CBro EBur ECGP EWes
montanum	EBur ERos MSto NHol WHer WThi
– var. ***crebrum***	CInt MSto
– var. ***montanum***	NHol
'Mrs Spivey'	CInt EBar EBur ECtt EMNN ESis MBal MBar NBro NHol NMen NOak WCla WRHF
mucronatum	EBur MSto
'North Star'	See ***S. 'Pole Star'***
nudicaule	EBur
– x ***montanum***	CFee EBur EMNN ESis GCal ITim LWak MDHE MNrw NHar NHol NNrd NRya WAbe WPer
patagonicum	EBur ERos MSto NCat NNrd WCla WLRN WPer
pearcei	EBur MSto
§ 'Pole Star'	CFee CInt CLyd CNic CSpe EBur GTou IBlr MFir NBro NHar NHol NMen NNrd SSmi SSvw WHal WPer
'Quaint and Queer'	CInt CMil CWGN EBur ECha EMar ERav ESiP GCra GMac LBlm LGan LWak MCLN MTho MTol NBro SSmi WAbe WBea WCra WPer WPri WRus WWhi WWin
* 'Raspberry'	EBur NHol WAbe
scabrum	See ***S. chilense***
'Sisland Blue'	EBur EHic EWes MDHE
sp. ex Tierra del Fuego	CRow
§ ***striatum***	CAvo CBro CFee CGle CHan CKel CM&M CRow CWGN EBur ECha ELan ERav GCHN NBro NDea NGar NHol NMir NNor NSti NWCA SPer WAbb WCla WEas WPer WTyr WWin
§ – 'Aunt May' (v)	Widely available
– 'Variegatum'	See ***S. striatum* 'Aunt May'**

SIUM (Apiaceae)

sisarum	ELau GBar GPoy LHol MHew MSal SIde WGwy WHer WOak WWye

SKIMMIA † (Rutaceae)

anquetilia	EPla MBar WBod WWat
x ***confusa***	EGol
– 'Kew Green' (m) ♀	CB&S CHan EBre ELan EPfP EPla IOrc LHop MAsh MBal MBar MBri MGos NHol SAga SPer SPla SReu SSta WPyg WWat
japonica (f)	CTri EBee ELan SRms
§ –	CHEx CLan CMHG CShe CTrw EBre EMil ENot GQui MBri MGos SDix SReu SSta STre WHCG WStI
– 'Alba'	See ***S. japonica* 'Wakehurst White' (f)**
– 'Bowles' Dwarf Female' (f)	CChu EMon EPla MBar MBri MGos MPla MRav NHol SMad SPer WWat
– 'Bowles' Dwarf Male' (m)	CChu EPla MBar MBri MPla SBid SMad SPer WWat
* – 'Bronze Beauty'	SBid SReu
– 'Bronze Knight' (m)	CDoC EBee EHic EMil GBin IHos MAsh MBar NHol SEas SPan SSta
– 'Cecilia Brown' (f)	WWat

– 'Emerald King'	MAsh MBar MBri
N– 'Foremanii'	See ***S. japonica* 'Veitchii' (f)**
– 'Fragrans' (m) ♀	CDoC CHig CSam CTrw EMil IOrc MAll MAsh MBal MBar MBri MGos MUlv SEas SHBN SPer SPla SReu SSta WBod WFar WRTC
– 'Fragrantissima' (m)	LRHS MBri
– 'Fructu Albo'	See ***S. japonica* 'Wakehurst White' (f)**
– 'Highgrove Redbud' (f)	MBar MBri MGos SSta
– 'Kew White' (f)	CBlo CDoC CSam EBre MAll MBal NHol WLRN
– 'Nymans' (f) ♀	CDoC CEnd EBre ELan EMil GWht IOrc MAll MAsh MBal MBar MBri MRav MUlv NHed NHol SHBN SPer SPla SReu SSpi SSta WGwG WStI WWat
– 'Oblata'	MBar
– 'Obovata' (f)	EPla
– 'Red Princess' (f)	LRHS MAsh MBri
– 'Redruth' (f)	CB&S CDoC CLan IOrc MAll MBal MBar MGos MUlv NHol SMad SSta
§ – subsp. ***reevesiana***	CDec CPMA EBre EPla GQui GWht IOrc ISea MAsh MBal MBar MBri MGos MPla NHol NRoo SHBN SPer SReu SSpi SSta WBod WDin WGwG WStI
– – 'Chilan Choice'	SAga SSta
– – 'Robert Fortune' ♀	MBar SCoo WWat
§ – Rogersii Group	CTri GRei IHos IOrc MBal MBar MGos MWat SChu SPla
– – 'Dunwood'	MBar
– – 'George Gardner'	MBar
– – 'Helen Goodall' (f)	MBar
§ – – 'Nana Femina' (f)	CSam IHos
§ – – 'Nana Mascula' (m)	CTri MGos MUlv
– – 'Rockyfield Green'	MBar
– – 'Snow Dwarf' (m)	EPla LRHS MBar MBri
– 'Rubella' (m) ♀	CB&S CLan CShe EBre EGol EMil ENot GRei IHos IOrc LNet MBal MBar MBri MGos MWat NHed NHol SHBN SPer SReu SSpi SSta WBod WDin WHCG WWat
– 'Rubinetta' (m)	EBee MAll MAsh MBar MGos WWeb
– 'Ruby Dome' (m)	MBar MBri WWat
– 'Ruby King'	CDoC CSam EBee EHic EPla MAll MBal MBar MBri MGos NHol SSta WStI
– 'Scarlet Dwarf' (f)	MBar MBri
– 'Tansley Gem' (f)	CDoC EFou ELan EPfP MAsh MBar
– 'Thelma King'	LRHS MBri
§ – 'Veitchii' (f)	CChe CTri EBee EBre GWht MAll MAsh MBar MGos NBee NHol SHBN SPer WBod WDin WGwG WStI WWeb
§ – 'Wakehurst White' (f)	CDec CDoC CPle CTrw EGol GWht LRHS MBar MBri MPla SAga SMad SPer SReu WWat
– 'Winifred Crook' (f)	MBar WWat
– 'Winnie's Dwarf'	CHig MGos
– 'Wisley Female' (f)	CDoC CTri ECtt EGol EHic EPla NHol SEas SPan WWat
laureola	CDoC CSam EBee ECot EHic ENot MAll MAsh MBal MGos NGar NHol SReu SRms WSHC
– T 132	WWat
reevesiana	See ***S. japonica* subsp. *reevesiana***
rogersii	See ***S. japonica* Rogersii Group**

SMELOWSKIA (Brassicaceae)

calycina	NTow WDav
¶ – NNS 94-137	MRPP

SMILACINA (Convallariaceae)

¶ ***formosana*** B&SWJ 349	WCru
¶ ***japonica***	WCru
racemosa ♀	CBos CBre CBro CChu CHEx CHan CLon CRDP CRow ECha EFol EGol ELan EMon EOrc EPla LAma LGan LGre LHop MBri MDun NDea SBla WAbb WChr WEas WPbr WTyr WWat
– dwarf form	IBlr
¶ – 'Emily Moody'	SSpi
stellata	CAvo CBre CMea CRDP CRow CVer EMou EPar EPla NGar WCot WCru WDav
– BH 319	MDun

SMILAX (Smilacaceae)

asparagoides 'Nanus'	See ***Asparagus asparagoides* 'Myrtifolius'**
aspera	CFil CPlN WPGP
discotis	CB&S CPlN CPle
¶ ***excelsa***	CPlN
¶ ***glaucophylla*** B&SWJ 2971	WCru
¶ ***rotundifolia***	CPlN
sagittifolia	CPlN
sieboldii	CPlN MRav
– B&SWJ 744	WCru

SMITHIANTHA (Gesneriaceae)

'Calder Girl'	NMos
'Carmel'	NMos
'Carmello'	NMos
'Castle Croft'	NMos
'Cinna Barino'	NMos
'Corney Fell'	NMos
'Dent View'	NMos
'Ehenside Lady'	NMos
'Harecroft'	NMos
'Little One'	NMos
'Matins'	NMos
'Meadowcroft'	NMos
'Multiflora'	NMos
'New Yellow Hybrid'	NMos
'Orange King'	NMos
'Orangeade'	NMos
'Pink Lady'	NMos
'Sandybank'	NMos
'Santa Clara'	NMos
'Starling Castle'	NMos
'Summer Sunshine'	NMos
'Vespers'	NMos
'Zebrina Hybrid'	NMos

× SMITHICODONIA (Gesneriaceae)

§ 'Cerulean Mink'	NMos

SMYRNIUM (Apiaceae)

olusatrum	CArn CGle CKin CSev ECWi EJud GBar LHol MChe MHew MSal SIde SWat WCer WCot WHer WOak WWye
perfoliatum	CGle EFou ELan EMar EPar GBuc MFir NRar

SOLANDRA (Solanaceae)

grandiflora	CPlN LChe
hartwegii	See ***S. maxima***
§ ***maxima***	ERea LChe LHil

SOLANUM (Solanaceae)

aviculare	CMdw CSWP ERea SLMG SMrm
* ***conchifolium***	LHil
crispum	CHan ELan ISea NEgg WDin WFar WStI
– 'Autumnale'	See ***S. crispum* 'Glasnevin'**
§ – 'Glasnevin' ♀	CB&S CBot CMHG CMac CPle CRHN CTrw ECha ELan ENot GMac GOrc GQui LHol LHop MAsh MBal MBri MGos MRav NSti SBra SHBN SLMG SPer SReu SSoC SSta WBod WSHC
– 'Variegatum'	MPla
dulcamara	CArn EWFC GPoy
– 'Hullavington' (v)	CNat
– 'Variegatum'	CB&S CChe CHan CMac CTrw EBar EHoe ELan IBlr IOrc ISea MAsh MBal MBri MRav NEgg NNor NSti SBra SRms WEas WStI WWeb
jasminoides	CB&S CChu CDoC CPlN EBee EOrc EPfP LPan NSti WDin WSHC
– 'Album' ♀	CB&S CBot CChu CGle CMac CPlN CPle ECha ELan GQui IHos LBlm LHol LHop MBri MRav SBra SDix SHBN SPer SReu SSta SUsu WBod WSHC
– 'Album Variegatum'	CChu ELan EPPr EPfP GQui LHop LRHS SBra WCot WHil WKif WSHC
* – 'Aureovariegatum'	CSte
laciniatum	CGle CInt CSev CSpe ERea EWes IBlr LHil LHop MBlu SArc SSoC SVen WHer
¶ ***linearifolium***	ISea
mauritianum	SLMG
muricatum 'Lima' (F)	ESim
– 'Otavalo' (F)	ESim
– 'Quito' (F)	ESim
pseudocapsicum	MBri
– 'Ballon'	MBri
¶ ***quitoense***	LBlo WHer
§ ***rantonnetii***	CBrk CPle ELan ERea LBlm LHil LHop LIck SDix SMrm SOWG
'Royal Robe'	CB&S GQui
seaforthianum	CPlN LCns LPan SOWG
sisymbriifolium	WKif
wendlandii	CB&S CPlN EOrc ERea LBlm LHil SLMG SOWG

SOLDANELLA (Primulaceae)

alpina	CShe ELan EPot GDra GTou MBal MTho NHar NHol NMen NNrd NRoo NWCA SBla SRms WAbe
carpatica ♀	GCal GTou MBal MHig NCat NHol NNrd NRya NTow WAbe
– 'Alba'	EDAr NHar NNrd SBla WAbe
cyanaster	EPot MBal NBir NNrd NRya WAbe
dimoniei	CFee EPot ITim MHig WAbe
hungarica	CLyd CNic EDAr MBal MHig MNrw MTho NGre NNrd NWCA WAbe
minima	CLyd NHar NSla WAbe
– 'Alba'	ITim
montana	CVer GTou MHig MTho NHol NMen NNrd WAbe WBea WRha
pindicola	ELan EWes MBal MBro MOne NHar NHol NMen NNrd NWCA SIng SSmi WAbe
pusilla	EHyt GDra ITim NHol WAbe
villosa	CRDP CTri MBal MHig MTho NHar NNrd NRya NSla NTow WAbe WFar WOMN WRHF WRus

SOLEIROLIA (Urticaceae)

soleirolii	CHEx CHal EPot LPBA MBri SHFr SIng STre WHer WOak
– 'Argentea'	See ***S. soleirolii* 'Variegata'**
§ – 'Aurea'	CHal EPot STre WOak
– 'Golden Queen'	See ***S. soleirolii* 'Aurea'**
– 'Silver Queen'	See ***S. soleirolii* 'Variegata'**
§ – 'Variegata'	CHal WOak

SOLENOMELUS (Iridaceae)

chilensis	See ***S. pedunculatus***
§ ***pedunculatus***	CFee EHic WThi
sisyrinchium	EHyt LLew WThi
sp. RB 94117	NHol

SOLENOPSIS (Campanulaceae)

§ ***axillaris***	CBar CLTr CSpe ECou EPad GBur LHil LHop LIck NPri SChu SCoo SHFr SUsu WWin
axillaris alba	CLTr CSpe EPad LHop LIck NPri SUsu
axillaris pink	CSpe EPad LHop LIck NPri SUsu
* 'Fairy Carpet'	CSpe
fluviatilis	CLTr ECou WCru

SOLENOSTEMON (Lamiaceae)

aromaticus	CHal SIde
'Autumn'	CBrk CHal
'Beauty' (v)	CBrk CHal
'Beauty of Lyons'	CBrk
'Beckwith's Gem'	CHal
'Bizarre Croton'	CBrk
'Black Prince'	CBrk CHal WDib
'Blackheart'	CBrk
'Brilliant' (v)	CBrk WDib
'Bronze Gloriosus'	CBrk
'Buttercup'	WDib
'Buttermilk' (v)	CBrk CHal
'Carnival' (v)	CBrk CHal
'Chamaeleon' (v)	CBrk WDib
'Cream Pennant' (v)	CBrk

'Crimson Ruffles' (v)	CBrk WDib
'Crimson Velvet'	CHal
'Dairy Maid' (v)	CBrk
'Dazzler' (v)	CBrk CHal
'Display'	CBrk CHal
'Etna'	CHal
'Firebrand' (v)	CBrk CHal
'Firedance'	CBrk
'Freckles' (v)	CBrk
'Funfair' (v)	CBrk
'Gloriosa'	CBrk CHal
'Glory of Luxembourg' (v)	CBrk CHal
'Goldie'	CBrk
* 'Holly' (v)	CBrk
'Inky Fingers' (v)	CBrk
'Jean' (v)	CBrk
'Joseph's Coat' (v)	CBrk
'Juliet Quartermain'	CBrk WDib
'Jupiter'	CHal
'Kentish Fire'	CBrk
'Kiwi Fern' (v)	CBrk CHal CInt WDib
'Klondike'	CBrk CHal
'Laing's Croton' (v)	CBrk
'Lemon Dash'	CBrk
'Lemondrop'	CHal
'Leopard' (v)	CBrk
'Lord Falmouth'	CBrk CHal WDib
'Luminous'	CBrk
'Melody'	CBrk
'Mission Gem'	CBrk
'Mrs Pilkington' (v)	CBrk
'Nettie' (v)	CBrk
'Ottoman'	CHal
'Paisley Shawl' (v)	CBrk CHal WDib
pentheri	CHal
'Percy Roots'	CBrk
'Petunia Gem'	CHal
'Picturatum' (v) 🏆	CBrk CHal WDib
'Pineapple Beauty' (v)	CBrk CHal WDib
'Pineapplette'	CBrk CHal
'Pink Showers'	CBrk
'Primrose Cloud'	CBrk
'Primrose Spray' (v)	CBrk
'Raspberry Ripple'	CHal
'Red Croton'	CBrk
'Red Heart'	CBrk
'Red Mars'	CBrk WDib
'Red Nettie' (v)	CBrk
'Red Paisley Shawl' (v)	CBrk
'Red Velvet'	CBrk
'Roseblush'	WDib
'Rosie'	CBrk
'Royal Scot' (v)	CBrk CHal WDib
'Salmon Plumes' (v)	CBrk CHal
'Scarlet Ribbons'	CBrk
scutellarioides	MBri
'Spire'	CBrk
'Stawberry Blush'	CHal
'Surprise'	CBrk
thyrsoideus	See ***Plectranthus thyrsoideus***
'Treales' (v)	CBrk CHal
'Vesuvius'	CBrk CHal
'Walter Turner' (v)	CBrk CHal WDib
'White Gem' (v)	CBrk CHal
'White Pheasant' (v)	CBrk
'Winsome' (v)	CBrk CHal WDib
'Winter Sun' (v)	CBrk CHal
'Wisley Flame'	CBrk
'Wisley Tapestry' (v) 🏆	CBrk WDib
'Yellow Croton'	CBrk

SOLIDAGO (Asteraceae)

altissima	See ***S. canadensis*** var. ***scabra***
brachystachys	See ***S. cutleri***
caesia	CArc ECha EGar EMan EWes LRHS WCot
canadensis	CTri ELan WByw WFar WPLl
'Cloth of Gold'	CB&S COtt EBre ECro MBri NPro WCot WLRN WOld WOve
§ 'Crown of Rays'	CLyd EBre ECtt EFou MArl MRav NFla WWin
§ ***cutleri***	CLyd CNic EFol ELan EMon MBar MTho MWat NGre NMen NMir NNrd SIng WHoo WPat WPer WPyg WWin
cutleri nana	EPPr EWes
§ ***flexicaulis***	GMaP
§ – 'Variegata'	CM&M CRDP EBee EBre ECoo EGar EJud ELan EMan EMar EMon ERav GBin LFis LGan LHop MAvo MHar NSti SEas SMad WCot WPbr
gigantea	EMon
glomerata	CHan EMon WPer
§ 'Golden Baby'	CLTr CM&M CTri ECtt EGar EMan GAbr GLil MBri MFir MLsm NFai NOak NOrc SPla WByw WPer WRHF
§ 'Golden Dwarf'	CDoC EBre EFou MCLN
'Golden Rays'	See ***S.* 'Goldstrahl'**
'Golden Shower'	MWat
'Golden Thumb'	See ***S.* 'Queenie'**
'Golden Wings'	CBre MWat
'Goldenmosa' 🏆	CDec CShe EBre EHal EMan EMon EPfP GMaP MBel MWat NFla SChu SPer WCot WRHF
'Goldilocks' (Prim)	NMir NPri
◆ Goldkind	See ***S.* 'Golden Baby'**
◆ Goldzwerg	See ***S.* 'Golden Dwarf'**
graminifolia	EMon
hybrida	See **x *Solidaster luteus***
latifolia	See ***S. flexicaulis***
'Laurin'	CWan EPfP NFai NHol WHoo WPyg
'Ledsham'	MMil WLRN
'Lemore'	See **x *Solidaster luteus* 'Lemore'**
microcephala	EMon
multiradiata	ESis WPer
odora	MSal
* 'Peter Pan'	NFla
§ 'Queenie'	CHan CPea ECha ECro ELan ESis GCHN MBri MCLN MWat NPro NVic SEas SPer SRms WHal WPer
randii	EMon
rigida	MRav WCot
– JLS 88002WI	EMon LFis
rugosa	EFol
– 'Fireworks'	EFou WCot WOve
sempervirens	CBlo EBre EMon WCot
shortii	NSti
'Spätgold'	EFou
spathulata f. ***nana***	CMHG WPer
sphacelata 'Golden Fleece'	LBuc WLRN WPbr WThi WWoo
◆ Strahlenkrone	See ***S.* 'Crown of Rays'**
'Tom Thumb'	EGle MRav SRms WEas WRHF

virgaurea	CArn CBod CKin ECWi GPoy LHol SIde WHer WJek WPer WSel WWye
– subsp. ***alpestris*** var. ***minutissima***	ITim LCom MHig WAbe WPat
– var. ***cambrica***	See ***S. virgaurea*** var. ***minuta***
§ – var. ***minuta***	WCla
– 'Praecox'	WLRN
§ – 'Variegata'	EFol EHoe EPla WDav WOld
vulgaris 'Variegata'	See ***S. virgaurea* 'Variegata'**

× SOLIDASTER (Asteraceae)

hybridus	See **× *S. luteus***
§ ***luteus***	CB&S CHan CMil CSte CTri EFou GBri MBri SPla SRms WEas WHal WHil WOld
§ – 'Lemore' 🏆	CDec CShe EBre ECha EFol EFou ELan EMon EPPr LFis MCli MRav MUlv MWat NBus NFla NSti NVic SEas SPer WCot WFar
'Super'	EFou WCot

SOLLYA (Pittosporaceae)

fusiformis	See ***S. heterophylla***
§ ***heterophylla*** 🏆	Widely available
– 'Alba'	CB&S CPle LGre
– mauve	ECou
¶ – pink	CPlN
– 'Pink Charmer'	ERea LRHS SBra
parviflora	CPlN ECou EWes

SONCHUS (Asteraceae)

palustris	EMon
platylepsis	CHEx

SOPHORA (Papilionaceae)

§ ***davidii***	CChu CPle SOWG WPGP
¶ ***flavescens***	ISea
japonica 🏆	CAbP CB&S CLnd ELan EMil ENot GAri IOrc ISea MBlu SHBN SPer WDin WNor
– 'Pendula'	LPan SMad
– 'Regent'	LPan
'Little Baby'	EMil EPfP ERea MBlu SHFr SMur WWeb
macrocarpa	CHan GQui ISea SBid WBod
microphylla	CPle CTrC ECou LHop MAll MBlu SArc SIgm SMad SVen
– 'Dragon's Gold'	CTrC ECou ELan EMil LRHS
– 'Early Gold'	CB&S CTrC ERea GQui SBid
– var. ***fulvida***	ECou
– var. ***longicarinata***	ECou
N ***prostrata***	CBot CChu ECou
– Pukaki form	ECou
tetraptera 🏆	CAbP CB&S CBot CHEx CHan CLnd CMac CPle CWit ECou EMil GQui IOrc ISea LHil LHop MBlu MLan NPSI SEND SIgm SRms
– 'Gnome'	CB&S
¶ – 'Goughensis'	WCru
viciifolia	See ***S. davidii***

SORBARIA † (Rosaceae)

aitchisonii	See ***S. tomentosa*** var. ***angustifolia***
arborea	See ***S. kirilowii***
§ ***kirilowii***	CChu IOrc SPer
lindleyana	See ***S. tomentosa***
sorbifolia	CAbP CChu CDoC EHic EMil EPla MBar NPro SEND SLPl SMac SPer STre WCot WDin WWat
– var. ***stellipila***	SLPl
sorbifolia stellipila B&SWJ 776	WCru
§ ***tomentosa*** 🏆	CAbP CPle EBre SBid SHBN WCru WHCG
§ – var. ***angustifolia*** 🏆	CChu CTri EBee ELan ENot EPfP MBal MBar MGos MRav SPer SPla WHer WWat

SORBUS † (Rosaceae)

§ ***alnifolia***	CLnd CMCN LSyl SLPl WWat
americana	CLnd CMCN NWea
– 'Belmonte'	LSyl MBri
americana erecta	See ***S. decora***
anglica	WMou
'Apricot Lady'	CLnd MBri WJas
¶ ***arachnoidea***	LSyl
aria	CKin CLnd CPer CTri EBre GRei LBuc LHyr MBar NRoo NWea WDin WMou WOrn
– 'Chrysophylla'	CDul CLnd CTho CWSG MAsh MBri NWea SPer
– 'Decaisneana'	See ***S. aria* 'Majestica'**
– 'Gigantea'	CDul
– 'Lutescens' 🏆	CB&S CDul CLnd CSam CTho EBre ELan ENot GRei LBuc LHyr LPan LSyl MAsh MBar MBri MGos NBee NWea SHBN SPer SReu SSta WDin WJas
– 'Magnifica'	CDoC CDul CTho ENot LPan SHhN WDin WJas
§ – 'Majestica' 🏆	CDoC CDul CLnd CTho EBee ELan LPan MAsh MGos NWea SPer WJas WOrn
– 'Mitchellii'	See ***S. thibetica* 'John Mitchell'**
♦ – var. ***salicifolia***	See ***S. rupicola***
× ***arnoldiana*** 'Apricot Queen'	CDul EPfP MAsh SHhN
– 'Brilliant Yellow'	MBlu
¶ – 'Chamois Glow'	WJas
¶ ***aronioides***	LSyl
aucuparia	CB&S CDul CKin CLnd CPer ELan ENot GRei ISea LBuc LHyr LPan MAsh MBal MBar MBri MGos NBee NRoo NWea SHBN SReu WDin WMou
¶ – 'Apricot Lady'	LSyl SSta
– 'Aspleniifolia'	CB&S CDul CLnd CTho EBre ENot LHyr LPan MGos NBee NWea SPer WDin WJas WOrn
§ – 'Beissneri'	CLnd CTho MGos WWat
– 'Cardinal Royal'	LSyl
– 'Dirkenii'	CBlo CDul CLnd COtt MAsh WJas
– 'Edulis' (F)	CDul CLnd CTho ESim IOrc LBuc MGos WDin
§ – 'Fastigiata'	CDoC CDul CEnd CSam CTho CTri IOrc MAsh MBri MGos SHBN WDin WStI
§ – 'Fructu Luteo' 🏆	CBlo ENot LPan LSyl MGos
– 'Hilling's Spire'	CBlo CTho SLPl
– 'Pendula'	CDul
aucuparia pluripinnata	See ***S. scalaris***
aucuparia 'Red Copper Glow'	MBlu
¶ – 'Rossica'	LSyl

– 'Rossica Major'	CDoC CDul CTho GQui
– 'Rowancroft Coral Pink'	CTho
– 'Scarlet King'	MBlu
– 'Sheerwater Seedling' 🏆	CB&S CDoC CDul CLnd CTho EBee EBre ELan ENot IOrc LHyr MGos NBee SCoo SPer SSta WDin WOrn
– 'Winterdown'	CNat
– 'Xanthocarpa'	See ***S. aucuparia* 'Fructu Luteo'**
bristoliensis	CTho LSyl WMou
caloneura	CFil LSyl SBid WAbe WPGP
'Cardinal Royal'	CBlo CEnd GQui MBri WJas
'Carpet of Gold'	CBlo CLnd CTho WHut
cashmiriana 🏆	CB&S CDul CEnd CLnd COtt CSam CTho ELan ISea LBuc LNet LPan LSyl MBal MBar MBri MGos NBee NWea SFam SPer SReu SSpi SSta WAbe WDin WJas WNor WOrn WWat
– 'Rosiness'	LRHS MBri
chamaemespilus	GDra LSyl
'Chinese Lace'	CEnd CLnd CTho EBee ECot LSyl MAsh MBlu MBri MGos MUlv SFam SHBN SMad WGor WJas WOrn WPyg WWat
§ ***commixta***	CB&S CDul CEnd CLnd CMCN CTho IOrc LSyl MBar MGos MUlv SPer WDin WJas WOrn
– 'Creamlace'	CBlo
– 'Embley' 🏆	CB&S CDul CLnd CSam CTho EBee ELan ENot LSyl MBar MBri MGos NBee SLPl SSpi SSta WOrn
– var. ***rufoferruginea***	GQui LSyl MBlu WAbe
– 'Serotina'	LSyl
conradinae hort.	See ***S. pohuashanensis* (Hance) Hedlund**
– Koehne	See ***S. esserteauana***
'Coral Beauty'	CLnd
cuspidata	See ***S. vestita***
¶ × ***decipiens***	WMou
§ ***decora***	CDul CLnd CTho LSyl SPer
* – 'Grootendorst'	CDul
– var. ***nana***	See ***S. aucuparia* 'Fastigiata'**
devoniensis	CDul CTho LSyl WMou
discolor Hedlund	CLnd ELan GRei MBar MGos MUlv NWea SReu WHut WJas
– hort.	See ***S. commixta***
domestica	CAgr CDul LBuc SLPl WMou
– 'Maliformis'	See ***S. domestica* var. *pomifera***
§ – var. ***pomifera***	WMou
§ – var. ***pyrifera***	WMou
– 'Pyriformis'	See ***S. domestica* var. *pyrifera***
'Eastern Promise'	CBlo CDul LRHS LSyl MAsh MBri SHhN SSta WJas
eminens	WMou
§ ***esserteauana***	CDoC CDul CSam CTho ENot LSyl
– 'Flava'	CTho EBee LSyl WWat
¶ – × ***scalaris***	LSyl
folgneri	CDoC CEnd CPMA LSyl
– 'Lemon Drop'	CBlo CDoC CEnd CLnd CPMA LRHS LSyl SSpi
foliolosa KR 3518	LSyl
forrestii	CDul CTho EHic LSyl MBlu NSti SLPl SSpi WAbe
§ ***fruticosa***	CChu CEnd CLnd COtt LSyl MBri MMea NHol NWea SLPl SSpi WAbe WJas

– 'Koehneana'	NTow SHFr
'Ghose'	CLnd CTho MBri SLPl SPer SSpi
glabrescens 'Roseoalba'	LSyl
'Golden Wonder'	LSyl
gonggashanica	LSyl
¶ ***gracilis***	LSyl
§ ***graeca***	LSyl MNes SEND
¶ 'Harvest Moon'	GQui
hedlundii	IBlr LSyl WWes
hemsleyi	CChu CFil CLnd SSpi WPGP
× ***hostii***	CLnd ENot SPer
§ ***hupehensis*** 🏆	CB&S CDul CEnd CLnd CMCN CSam CTho EFol GRei ISea LHyr LPan LSyl MAsh MBal MBar NBee NWea SHBN SLPl SPer SSpi SSta WAbe WDin WJas WNor WOrn WWat WWin
* – 'Apricot'	CBlo CEnd
§ – var. ***obtusa*** 🏆	CDoC CSam GAri MBlu NTow SFam SSpi SSta WWat
– 'Pink Pagoda'	CDoC CLnd GRei LSyl MAsh MBri MGos MSta MWat NWea SCoo SPer WGer WJas WPyg
– 'Rosea'	See ***S. hupehensis* var. *obtusa***
× ***hybrida*** 'Gibbsii' Linnaeus 🏆	CBlo CDoC CLnd CTho ELan SHhN
– hort.	See ***S. × thuringiaca***
– Linnaeus	NWea
insignis	CDoC CTho SSpi
intermedia	CAgr CB&S CDul CKin CLnd CPer ENot GRei LSyl MBal MGos NBee NWea SPer WDin WMou WStI
– 'Brouwers' 🏆	ELan
'Joseph Rock' 🏆	CB&S CDul CLnd COtt CSam CTho EBre ELan GRei ISea LBuc LSyl MBal MBar MBri MGos NBee NWea SHBN SPer SReu SSta WDin WHCr WJas WOrn WWat
§ × ***kewensis*** 🏆	CDul CLnd CTho LSyl SHhN SPer SSpi SSta
'Kirsten Pink'	CBlo CDoC CLnd LSyl MBlu MGos NEgg
koehneana hort.	See ***S. fruticosa***
¶ aff. – Schneider Harry Smith 12799	LSyl
¶ ***kurzii*** EGM	LSyl
lanata hort.	See ***S. vestita***
lancastriensis	CNat CTho WMou
latifolia	CAgr CLnd CTho ENot NWea SHhN WDin WMou
* ***laxiflora***	WAbe
'Leonard Messel'	CTho
'Leonard Springer'	ENot GQui SSta
leyana	WMou
¶ ***lingshiensis***	LSyl
'Lombart's Golden Wonder'	CB&S CBlo CDoC CTho EBee LBuc LPan MGos NWea WJas
¶ ***longii***	LSyl
'Lowndes'	CLnd CTho
matsumurana hort.	See ***S. commixta***
– (Makino) Koehne	ENot IHos
megalocarpa	CBlo CFil CGre CPMA CSam CTho LSyl SSpi WCru WNor WWes
meliosmifolia	LSyl WPGP
¶ ***microphylla*** Yu 13815	LSyl

minima CNat LSyl WMou
'Molly Sanderson' IBlr
¶ ***monbeigii*** CLD 311 LSyl
– McLaren D 84 LSyl
moravica 'Laciniata' See ***S. aucuparia* 'Beissneri'**
¶ ***mougeotii*** LSyl
'November Pink' CBlo CEnd IOrc MAsh WJas
parva L 937 LSyl
'Peachiness' LSyl
'Pearly King' CB&S CSam CTho LSyl WJas
pekinensis LSyl
'Pink-Ness' MBri
¶ ***pogonopetala*** Yu 14299 LSyl
§ ***pohuashanensis*** (Hance) Hedlund CSam CTho
– hort. See ***S.* × *kewensis***
porrigentiformis CNat CTho WMou
poteriifolia GCLN MFir NHar
§ ***prattii*** GAri LSyl WWat
¶ – var. ***subarachnoidea*** GBin
– var. ***tatsienensis*** See ***S. prattii***
¶ ***pseudofennica*** LSyl
* ***pseudovilmorinii*** LSyl
randaiensis LSyl WAbe
'Red Tip' CDoC CDul CLnd CTho LSyl MBlu NEgg
reducta 🏆 CB&S CBot CEnd CLyd CMCN CSWP GAbr GDra ISea ITim MBal MBri MBro MFir MPla NGre NHar SMac SPer SReu SSta WAbe WNor WPat WWat
reflexipetala See ***S. commixta***
rehderiana MBal MBri WNor
¶ – 'Pink Pearl' LSyl
§ ***rupicola*** CNat CTho LSyl
'Salmon Queen' CLnd
sargentiana 🏆 CBot CDul CEnd CLnd CSam CTho CTri EBre ELan ENot IHos LBuc LPan LSyl MAsh MBlu MBri NHol NWea SPer SSpi WJas WOrn WWat
* 'Savill Orange' LSyl
§ ***scalaris*** 🏆 CDul CEnd CTho CTri EBee IOrc LSyl MAsh MBri SPer WJas WOrn WWat
'Schouten' ENot MBlu MBri
scopulina hort. See ***S. aucuparia* 'Fastigiata'**
¶ ***semi-incisa*** LSyl
setschwanensis GAri
'Signalman' MBri SPer
¶ sp. CLD 237 LSyl
¶ sp. Ghose LSyl
sp. Harry Smith CChu MBri
¶ sp. Harry Smith 12732 LSyl
¶ sp. KR 3595 LSyl
¶ sp. KR 3733 LSyl
¶ sp. nova LSyl
'Sunshine' CDoC LSyl MAsh MBri WJas
thibetica LSyl
§ – 'John Mitchell' 🏆 CDul CLnd CMCN CSam CTho EBar EBee ENot LPan LSyl MAsh MBlu MBri MGos NWea SPer WJas WOrn WWat
§ × ***thuringiaca*** WMou
§ – 'Fastigiata' CB&S CDoC CDul CLnd EBee ENot MGos WDin WJas
torminalis CCVT CDul CKin CLnd CPer CSWP CSam CTho CTri LBuc NWea SPer SSta STre WCoo WDin WHut WMou
umbellata var. ***cretica*** See ***S. graeca***
ursina CAbP CLnd CTho
× ***vagensis*** CLnd WMou
§ ***vestita*** CLnd CTho LSyl WWat
vilmorinii 🏆 CBar CEnd CLnd CSam CTho EBre ELan GRei IOrc LBuc LPan MBal MBar NBee NWea SFam SHBN SPer SReu SSpi SSta WAbe WDin WJas WNor WOrn WWat
wardii CLnd CTho
'White Wax' CBlo MGos NEgg WFar
'Wilfrid Fox' CLnd EBee SHBN SLPl
willmottiana CNat WMou
¶ ***wilsoniana*** LSyl
¶ 'Winter Cheer' LSyl
zahlbruckneri hort. See ***S. alnifolia***

SORGHASTRUM (Poaceae)
§ ***avenaceum*** EBee ECha EHoe EMan EPPr ETPC
¶ – 'Indian Steel' ETPC MAvo MCCP
nutans See ***S. avenaceum***

SORGHUM (Poaceae)
halepense MSte
nigrum MLan

SPARAXIS (Iridaceae)
bulbifera NRog
elegans NRog
– 'Coccinea' LBow
fragrans subsp. ***acutiloba*** NRog
¶ – subsp. ***fimbriata*** LBow
– subsp. ***grandiflora*** WCot
hybrids LAma
tricolor EPar MBri NRog
§ ***variegata*** NRog

SPARGANIUM (Sparganiaceae)
§ ***erectum*** CRow CWGN ECoo EHon EMFW LPBA MHew MSta NDea SWat SWyc WHer WWye
ramosum See ***S. erectum***

SPARRMANNIA (Tiliaceae)
africana 🏆 CAbb CB&S CHEx CPle ERea GQui LBlm LCns LHil MBri SArc SVen WOak
– 'Variegata' ERea LCns

SPARTINA (Poaceae)
pectinata CHan GBin
– 'Aureomarginata' CCuc CInt CRow ECha ECoo EGol EHoe ELan EMon EPGN EPar EPla ESOG ETPC GCHN GCal GFre LHil MBar MSta MSte NDea NHol NSti SPer WRus WWye

SPARTIUM (Papilionaceae)
junceum 🏆 CB&S CPle ELan EMil ENot ISea MBal MBri MGos MWat SArc SDix SHBN SPer SPla SRms WBod WOMN WRTC

SPARTOCYTISUS See CYTISUS

SPATHANTHEUM (Araceae)
¶ *orbignyanum* — WCot

SPATHICARPA (Araceae)
See Plant Deletions

SPATHIPAPPUS See TANACETUM

SPATHIPHYLLUM (Araceae)
'Viscount' — MBri
wallisii — CHal EOHP MBri

SPEIRANTHA (Convallariaceae)
§ *convallarioides* — CFil CRDP LWoo SAxl WCot WCru
gardenii — See *S. convallarioides*

SPERGULARIA (Caryophyllaceae)
purpurea — WPer
rupicola — CKin EWFC

SPHACELE See LEPECHINIA

SPHAERALCEA (Malvaceae)
ambigua — ELan
¶ *coccinea* — EMan MFos
fendleri — CB&S CBot CBrk CLTr CMHG CSam EBar EOrc LFlo MSCN SMrm WKif WOMN WWye
fendleri venusta — CFir EBee
grossulariifolia — NGar
'Hopley's Lavender' — CSpe EBar LHil LHop
'Hyde Hall' — EOrc GBri MCCP SMad SMrm WRus WWeb
incana — CSev MAvo MCCP NRai SMad SMrm
malviflora — WPer
miniata — CAbb CMHG ELan GBri LGre LHil LHop SAga SMrm
munroana — CAbb CBot CMHG CSev CSpe ELan EOrc LBlm LHil LHop MCCP MSCN SMad SMrm SSpi SVen WEas WOMN WSHC WSan
– 'Dixieland Pink' — WEas
– pale pink — CSpe ECtt EMan LGre LHop SMrm
– 'Shell Pink' — ECGP
umbellata — See *Phymosia umbellata*

SPHAEROMERIA (Asteraceae)
argentea — See *Tanacetum nuttallii*
§ *capitata* — EPot NWCA
compacta — CPBP

SPHAGNUM (Sphagnaceae)
See Plant Deletions

SPHENOTOMA (Epacridaceae)
See Plant Deletions

SPIGELIA (Loganiaceae)
marilandica — CRDP EBee WPbr

SPILANTHES (Asteraceae)
See Plant Deletions

SPIRAEA † (Rosaceae)
albiflora — See *S. japonica* var. *albiflora*
arborea — See *Sorbaria kirilowii*
arcuata — CTri MBri
§ 'Arguta' — CShe EBre ELan ENot GRei ISea LBuc MBar MBri MGos MPla MWat NBee NNor NWea SHBN SPer SReu SRms SSta WAbe WBod WDin WHCG WRTC WWin
× *arguta* 'Bridal Wreath' — See *S.* **'Arguta'**
– 'Compacta' — See *S.* × *cinerea*
– 'Nana' — See *S.* × *cinerea*
bella — CPle MBar WHCG
betulifolia — CDoC EBee MRav WHCG WPyg
– var. *aemiliana* — CBot CMHG CPle EBre ECtt EHal EPla ESis LHop MGos MPla NHol SLPl SPan SSta WWat
× *billiardii* 'Macrothyrsa' — CB&S EBee
– 'Triumphans' — CBlo ENot NCut NFla NNor SHFr WWin
× *bumalda* — See *S. japonica* **'Bumalda'**
– 'Wulfenii' — See *S. japonica* **'Walluf'**
callosa 'Alba' — See *S. japonica* var. *albiflora*
canescens — GAul
cantoniensis — CPle
§ – 'Flore Pleno' — CPle EMon MBlu
– 'Lanceata' — See *S. cantoniensis* **'Flore Pleno'**
¶ *chamaedryfolia* — CPle
§ × *cinerea* — SSta
– 'Grefsheim' 🏆 — CB&S CBlo CDoC COtt CShe ECtt GOrc MBri MGos SPer SSta WStI
– 'Variegata' — MPla
crispifolia — See *S. japonica* **'Bullata'**
decumbens — CPle WDin
¶ *densiflora* — EPot
douglasii — GOrc MBar NRoo
– subsp. *menziesii* — CBlo CPle
× *fontenaysii* 'Rosea' — CBlo CPle
formosana — CPle
– CC 1597 — WHCr
fritschiana — CMCN CPle SLPl WHCG
hendersonii — See *Petrophytum hendersonii*
henryi — CPle
§ *japonica* — CPle SBod
– 'Alba' — See *S. japonica* var. *albiflora*
§ – var. *albiflora* — CB&S CPle CTri ESis MBal MBar MWat NRoo SChu SPer SRms WHCG
– 'Allgold' — NBee
– 'Alpina' — See *S. japonica* **'Nana'**
– 'Anthony Waterer' (v) 🏆 — CB&S CChe CPle CShe EBre ELan ENot GRei MBal MBar MBri MGos MRav NBee NFla NNor NRoo NWea SHBN SPer SRms WBod WDin WFox WSHC WWin
– 'Blenheim' — SRms
§ – 'Bullata' — CFee CMHG ELan ESis MBal MBar MBri MHig MPla NFla NHol NRoo NWCA SRms WBod WHCG WPat
– 'Candle Light' — CAbP CWLN CWSG EBre ECle EMil MAsh MGos NHol SCoo SPla WRHF
– 'Country Red' — CBlo WRHF
§ – 'Crispa' — EPfP MBar MBlu MBri NPro

– 'Dart's Red' CBlo IOrc MAsh MBlu MBri NFla SCoo SEas SSta WWeb
– 'Fire Light' CAbP CBlo CEnd CWLN EBre ELan MAsh MGos NHol SCoo SPer SPla SSta WRHF WWeb
– var. ***fortunei*** 'Atrosanguinea' WHCG
– 'Froebelii' ISea LBuc WFox
– 'Glenroy Gold' MBal WHen
– 'Gold Mound' ♀ CMHG CShe EBre ELan ESis GOrc MBal MBar MBel MBlu MBri MGos MRav MWat NBee NNor NRoo SChu SEas SHBN SHFr SPer SPla SRms WSHC WWat
– 'Gold Rush' CMHG EBar EFol MPla WHCG WRus
– 'Golden Dome' EHic WHCG
– 'Goldflame' ♀ Widely available
¶ – Golden Princess = 'Lisp' EAst EBre ECle ELan GRei IOrc MAsh MBal MBar MBlu MGos MPla MUlv NHol NRoo SEas SPer SReu SSta WWeb
– 'Little Maid' CBot
– 'Little Princess' CB&S CPle CShe ELan EMil ENot EPot ISea LHop MAsh MBal MBar MBri MRav MWat NBee NHol NRoo NWCA SPer SSta WDin WGwG WHCG WHar WWat
– 'Magic Carpet' LRHS MAsh SCoo
– 'Magnifica' WHCG
§ – 'Nana' ♀ CMHG ELan ENot ESis MBal MBar MBri MPla MRav MTho NHar SReu SRms WEas WHCG WPat WPer WPyg
– 'Nyewoods' See ***S. japonica* 'Nana'**
– 'Pamela Harper' EHic
N – 'Shirobana' ♀ CB&S CBot CPle EBre ELan ENot ESis GOrc GRei IOrc LHop MAsh MBal MBar MBri MGos MPla MWat NFla NHol NRoo SHBN SMac SPer SPla SRms SSta
§ – 'Walluf' COtt CPle EHic NNor SPan WHCG
latifolia CPle
'Margaritae' CPle NPro SHBN SLPl SPer
mollifolia CPle
myrtilloides CPle
nipponica CB&S MBar
– 'Halward's Silver' CBlo MGos MRav NPro SLPl WBcn
– 'June Bride' CBlo WHCG WRHF
§ – 'Snowmound' ♀ CB&S CPle EBre ELan ENot GOrc GRei IOrc MBal MBar MBri MGos MRav NBee NFla NHol NRoo SHBN SHFr SLPl SMac SPer SPla SSta WAbe WDin WStI WWat WWin
– var. ***tosaensis*** hort. See ***S. nipponica* 'Snowmound'**
– – (Yatabe) Makino LHop MWat SReu
palmata elegans See ***Filipendula palmata* 'Elegantissima'**
prunifolia (d) CFai CPle EBre ELan EPla LHop MPla SEas SPer SPla WHCG WWin
– 'Plena' EBee MBlu
salicifolia CPle SHBN
sp. CLD 1389 CPle
stevenii GAri SPla
'Summersnow' SLPl
tarokoensis CPle
thunbergii ♀ CChe CPle CTri EBee ELan ENot IOrc LHop MPla MRav NFla NNor NWea SCoo SMer SPer SRms WDin WGwG WHCG WRTC
– 'Mount Fuji' CFai EBre EFol EHoe ELan EPla GSki MAsh MGos NLak NPro SCoo SMac WFar
* – 'Variegata' EBee
trichocarpa CMCN
trilobata CPle WLRN
ulmaria See ***Filipendula ulmaria***
x ***vanhouttei*** ♀ CB&S CTri ELan ENot IOrc MBal MBar MRav MWat NFla NNor SHBN SHFr SMac SPer SRms WDin WGwG WRTC WWat WWin
– Pink Ice (v) CAbP CDoC COtt CPMA CWit EAst EBre ECle EFol EHoe ELan EMil LHop MAsh MBal MGos MPla MTis SHBN SPer SPla WDin WHar
veitchii MBal MRav
venusta 'Magnifica' See ***Filipendula rubra* 'Venusta'**
'Wyndbrook Gold' NHol

SPIRANTHES (Orchidaceae)

¶ ***aestivalis*** SWes WChr
¶ ***cernua*** EFEx
¶ – f. ***odorata*** 'Chadd's Ford' CSte WCot
¶ ***spiralis*** SSpi WHer

SPIRODELA (Lemnaceae)

§ ***polyrhiza*** MSta

SPODIOPOGON (Poaceae)

sibiricus ECha EPla ESOG ETPC MCCP WCot WHil

SPOROBOLUS (Poaceae)

fertilis ETPC
heterolepis EBee ETPC
wrightii ETPC

SPRAGUEA (Portulacaceae)

§ ***umbellata*** MFos WAbe WDav
§ ***umbellata glandulifera*** NGre

SPREKELIA (Amaryllidaceae)

formosissima ♀ CMon ETub GCra LAma LBow NRog WChr

STACHYS (Lamiaceae)

§ ***affinis*** CFir ELau GPoy
alopecuros WWin
¶ ***alpina*** CNat
x ***ambigua*** EWFC
betonica See ***S. officinalis***
§ ***byzantina*** CGle CHad CLyd CShe EAst EBre ELan EOrc EPar EPla GCal LHop MBri MFir MWat NBro NFla NOrc NPer SCro SHel SRms WBea WEas WGwG WPer WTyr WWin WWye

§ – 'Big Ears'	ECha EMon MCLN SAga SAxl SMrm WCot
§ – 'Cotton Boll'	CMGP CMil ECha EFou GCal MCLN MHar MTho MWat NSti SAxl SPer WCot WGwG WWat
– 'Countess Helen von Stein'	See ***S. byzantina* 'Big Ears'**
– gold-leaved	See ***S. byzantina* 'Primrose Heron'**
– large-leaved	See ***S. byzantina* 'Big Ears'**
– 'Limelight'	EPPr WCot
§ – 'Primrose Heron'	CMGP COtt ECha ECot EMan EPla GMaP MFir MHar NOrc NSti SMer SMrm SPer
– 'Sheila McQueen'	See ***S. byzantina* 'Cotton Boll'**
– 'Silver Carpet'	CB&S CGle CShe ECha EFou EGoo EHoe EOrc GCra GMaP LGro MBel MBri MCLN MFir NBro NFla NRoo SPer SPla SRms WPyg WWat
§ – 'Striped Phantom' (v)	CHan EGoo EPPr LFis MBel WBea WCot WPbr
– 'Variegata'	See ***S. byzantina* 'Striped Phantom'**
candida	CLyd EHyt MSto NMen SIng WThi
chrysantha	CPBP LGre
citrina	CLyd ECha GCal WCot WHal WPbr
coccinea	CElw CGle CHan CInt CLTr CPle EBar EBre GCra LBlm LGre LHop LLWP MFir NBir NFai SHFr WEas WHil WOve WSan WWye
¶ – apricot	WEas
– 'Axminster Lemon'	SAga
– 'Axminster Variegated'	SAga
– 'El Salto'	LHop SAga
cretica	CWan MTis SIgm WCot WHer
densiflora	See ***S. monieri***
§ ***discolor***	GBri MBri MLLN WCru WHil WPbr WPer
germanica	CNat EMan
grandiflora	See ***S. macrantha***
* 'Hidalgo'	LHop
iva	ESis LGre NTow
lanata	See ***S. byzantina***
lavandulifolia	WDav
§ ***macrantha***	CArn CShe EBre ECha ECoo LGan MBel MBro MHew MRav NOak NOrc NSti SMrm SOkh SRms WBea WEas WHal WHoo WOld WOve WPyg WTyr WWin
– 'Hummelo'	EFou
– 'Nivea'	EBee EBre ELan EMan GCal MCLN WGwG WPat WPbr
§ – 'Robusta' ♀	CGle ELan EPPr MBri NBro SCro SHel SUsu WCot WRHF WWye
– 'Rosea'	CNic EBee EFou ELan MCLN NWes SCro SHel WCra WEas WOld WPer WRha WWye
– 'Superba'	CDoC CGle CHan CRDP EBar EGar MBel MBri NFai NMGW SMrm SPla WByw WCot WHil
§ ***monieri***	CMGP CRDP EBre EMan ESis MCLN MRav SIgm SMrm WBea WDav WPer WSan
nivea	See ***S. discolor***
§ ***officinalis***	CArn CKin CSev ECWi EWFC GPoy MChe MGam MHew MHig MSal NLan NMir SIde SIng WApp WBea WCla WHal WHer WWye
– 'Alba'	CGle CJew MCLN MHig NBro NHol WPbr WRha
– 'Rosea Superba'	CGle CMil EBee ECha MCLN WCot WFar WPbr
olympica	See ***S. byzantina***
palustris	CKin ECWi ECoo MSta WChe
saxicola subsp. ***villosissima***	CPBP
spicata	See ***S. macrantha***
sylvatica	CArn CKin ECWi EMan EWFC GPoy MGam MHew WCla WHer
thirkei	EBee
tuberifera	See ***S. affinis***

STACHYTARPHETA (Verbenaceae)

¶ ***mutabilis***	LCns SOWG

STACHYURUS (Stachyuraceae)

chinensis	CB&S CMCN CPMA CRos MBri WFar
– 'Magpie' (v)	CChu CFil CPMA SBid SSpi SSta WCru WWat
himalaicus	CFil WPGP
leucotrichus	CPMA
praecox ♀	CB&S CBot CDoC CEnd CFil CPMA CPle CRos ELan EMil ENot GOrc IOrc MBar MBlu MBri MRav NPal SHBN SPer SReu SSpi SSta WCoo WDin WSHC WWat
– var. ***matsuzakii***	CFil WPGP
* – 'Rubriflora'	CPMA CSte ELan LRHS SPer

STAEHELINA (Asteraceae)
See Plant Deletions

STANLEYA (Brassicaceae)
See Plant Deletions

STAPHYLEA (Staphyleaceae)

bumalda	CMCN
colchica ♀	CB&S CHan CMHG IOrc SPer WSHC WWat
emodi	CPle
holocarpa	CPMA CPle WWat
N – var. ***rosea***	CPMA EBee ENot EPfP LHop SMad SPer
N – 'Rosea'	CBot MBlu MGos SMur SSpi WSHC
pinnata	ELan EPfP WCoo WNor WRTC
¶ ***trifolia***	CAgr

STARFRUIT See AVERRHOA *carambola*

STATICE See LIMONIUM

STAUNTONIA (Lardizabalaceae)

hexaphylla	CChu CDoC CHEx CPlN CSam CSte EMil GQui SBid SBra SPer SReu SSpi SSta WSHC

STEGNOGRAMMA (Thelypteridaceae)
See Plant Deletions

STEIRODISCUS (Asteraceae)

* ***euryopoides***	CKni NSty

STELLARIA (Caryophyllaceae)

graminea	CKin
holostea	CKin CTiv ECWi EWFC MChe NMir WHer

STEMODIA (Scrophulariaceae)

¶ ***tomentosa***	WCot

STENANTHIUM (Melanthiaceae)
See Plant Deletions

STENOCARPUS (Proteaceae)

¶ ***sinuatus***	CTrC

STENOCHLAENA (Blechnaceae)

palustris	MBri

STENOGLOTTIS (Orchidaceae)
See Plant Deletions

STENOMESSON (Amaryllidaceae)

§ ***miniatum***	EPot WChr
variegatum	CMon

STENOTAPHRUM (Poaceae)

secundatum 'Variegatum' 🏆	CHal CInt IBlr

STENOTUS (Asteraceae)

§ ***acaulis***	CGra NWCA

STEPHANANDRA (Rosaceae)

incisa	CB&S CBlo CGle CPle CShe EMil IOrc SChu SPla WGwG WHCG WRTC
§ – 'Crispa'	CGle CMHG CPle ELan EMil ENot GOrc GRei LHop MBar MBlu MWat NHol NNor SHBN SPer SRms WDin WFar WHCG WWat
– 'Prostrata'	See ***S. incisa* 'Crispa'**
tanakae	CDoC CGle CPle CShe ELan GOrc IOrc MBar MBlu MRav MUlv MWat NFla NNor SChu SHBN SLPl SPer SPla STre WDin WHCG

STEPHANIA (Menispermaceae)

glandulifera	CPlN

STEPHANOTIS (Asclepiadaceae)

floribunda 🏆	CB&S EBak GQui MBri SOWG

STERNBERGIA (Amaryllidaceae)

candida	CBro CMon LAma WChr
§ ***clusiana***	CMon LAma WChr
colchiciflora	EHyt EPot WChr
fischeriana	CBro CMon EHyt LAma
greuteriana	WChr
lutea	CAvo CBro CHan CTri EBre ECha EHyt ELan EPot EWes LAma LHil MBri NRog SDix SSpi WEas
– Angustifolia Group	CBro CMea CMon EMon WChr
– var. ***lutea*** MS 971	CMon
macrantha	See ***S. clusiana***
sicula	CBro EHyt EPot ETub
– Dodona form	WChr
– var. ***graeca***	CMon EHyt
– MS 796	CMon

STEVIA (Asteraceae)

rebaudiana	GPoy

STEWARTIA † (Theaceae)

'Korean Splendor'	See ***S. pseudocamellia* Koreana Group**
koreana	See ***S. pseudocamellia* Koreana Group**
malacodendron	CSte ELan LRHS MBri SSpi
monadelpha	CB&S CPMA WCoo WNor
ovata	CGre SSpi WWat
N– var. ***grandiflora***	LRHS SPer
pseudocamellia 🏆	CB&S CDoC CGre COtt CPMA ELan ICrw IOrc ISea LPan MBlu MBri MDun SHBN SPer SReu SSpi SSta WCru WNor WWat
♦ – var. ***koreana***	See ***S. pseudocamellia* Koreana Group**
§ – Koreana Group 🏆	CBlo CDoC CGre CMCN ISea MBri SReu SSpi SSta WDin WNor WWat
¶ ***pteropetiolata***	CWSG
¶ – var. ***koreana***	LRHS
serrata	CGre EPfP LRHS SPer SSpi
sinensis 🏆	CPMA SPer WNor

STICTOCARDIA (Convolvulaceae)

beraviensis	CPlN

STIGMAPHYLLON (Malpighiaceae)

cilliatum	CPlN

STIPA (Poaceae)

arundinacea	Widely available
– 'Autumn Tints'	ECou
– 'Gold Hue'	ECou ESOG
barbata	EBre EGar EGle EPPr ETPC LGre SAxl SUsu WCot
– 'Silver Feather'	GBin
* ***brachytricha***	CArc EBee ECha EGle EPPr EPla ESOG ETPC WCot
§ ***calamagrostis***	CCuc CElw CHan CVer CWGN EBre ECha EHoe EMon EPPr EPla ESOG ESiP ETPC GAbr GFre GMaP MBri NBro NCat NSti SMrm WHal
capillata	EBre EGle EPla ETPC GBin LBuc SAxl SMrm WCot
¶ ***comata***	ETPC
elegantissima	CInt ETPC LHil
extremiorientalis	EGle EPPr ETPC LGre
gigantea 🏆	Widely available
lasiagrostis	See ***S. calamagrostis***
mollis	ETPC
¶ ***offneri***	SBla
papposa	ETPC
patens	CCuc EBee EHoe EPPr ESOG

pennata	CB&S CSpe EMan EPPr ETPC GBin MFir SAxl SMad WCot WLRN
pulcherrima	EPPr EPla GCal SIgm
– 'Windfeder'	CFir ECha MCCP SMrm
¶ *pulchra*	MCCP
robusta	ETPC NGno
§ *splendens*	EFou EHoe EPPr EPla ESiP ETPC SDix
tenacissima	EFou EHoe EPPr EPla MHlr
tenuifolia	CCuc CInt CKni CMea CMil CSam EBee ECED EGar EMan EPGN MBri MCLN MRav NBir NBro NCat NChi NHar NHol NPla SPla WHal WWoo
tenuissima	Widely available

STOEBE (Asteraceae)

¶ *plumosa*	CTrC

STOKESIA (Asteraceae)

laevis	CChu CDoC CMea ECGP ECha EHic LFis NBro NNor SAga SAxl WCot WFar WHil WPer WWeb
– 'Alba'	CHan CM&M CMGP CRDP EAst EBre ECGP ECha EMar EOrc EPar LGre MBri MCLN NBrk NHol SAga SChu SMrm SUsu WHil WRus WTyr
– 'Blue Star'	CB&S CElw CGle CRDP CSam CShe EFou EGol ELan EMar LGre LHop MBri MFir MTho MUlv NHol NOak NRoo SChu SEas SMrm SPer WHow WRus WTyr WWin
– 'Mary Gregory'	WCot
– mixed	CPou
– 'Omega Skyrocket'	WCot
– 'Träumerei'	CChu CRDP EAst EBee EFou EHic EMan EMar LFis MGrG MTis NHol SOkh WCot WGwG WHow WLRN WTyr
– 'Wyoming'	EBre

STRANSVAESIA See PHOTINIA

STRATIOTES (Hydrocharitaceae)

aloides	CBen CHEx CWGN CWat EBre ECoo EHon EMFW LPBA MSta NDea SAWi SWat SWyc WChe

STRAVINIA See PHOTINIA

STRELITZIA (Musaceae)

nicolai	CTrC LBlo LPal LPan
reginae ♀	CB&S CBrP CHEx CTrC ECon ELan ERea GQui IBlr LCns LHil LPal LPan NPal SArc SRms SVen
¶ – 'Kirstenbosch Gold'	LBlo

STREPTOCARPELLA See STREPTOCARPUS

STREPTOCARPUS † (Gesneriaceae)

'Albatross' ♀	CKni WDib
'Amanda'	WDib
'Anne'	CKni WDib
'Athena'	CKni WDib
'Beryl'	WDib
'Bethan'	CKni WDib
'Black Panther'	WDib
'Blue Gem'	WDib
'Blue Heaven'	WDib
'Blue Moon'	WDib
¶ 'Blue Nymph'	WDib
'Blue Pencil'	CSpe
'Blue Trumpets'	CSpe
'Blushing Bride'	WDib
'Boysenberry Delight'	CSpe LHil WDib
'Branwen'	WDib
candidus	WDib
'Carol'	MBri WDib
'Catrin'	WDib
caulescens	LHil WDib
– var. *pallescens*	WDib
'Chorus Line'	CKni WDib
'Clouds'	CSpe
'Cobalt Nymph'	MBri
'Concord Blue' ♀	MBri WDib
¶ 'Constant Nymph'	WDib
cyaneus	MSto WDib
'Cynthia' ♀	MBri WDib
* 'Diana' ♀	WDib
¶ *dunnii*	WDib
'Elsi'	CKni WDib
'Falling Stars' ♀	CKni CSpe MBri WDib
'Festival Wales'	WDib
'Fiona'	WDib
gardenii	WDib
glandulosissimus	CHal LCns LHil WDib
'Gloria' ♀	CKni CSpe WDib
'Good Hope'	ERea
'Happy Snappy'	CKni WDib
'Heidi' ♀	CKni MBri WDib
'Helen' ♀	WDib
holstii	CHal CSpe LHil
'Huge White'	CSpe
'Jennifer'	WDib
'Joanna'	CKni MBri WDib
'Julie'	WDib
'Karen'	WDib
'Kim' ♀	CKni CSpe WDib
'Laura'	WDib
'Lisa' ♀	CSpe MBri WDib
'Louise'	WDib
'Lynette'	WDib
'Lynne'	WDib
'Maassen's White'	ERea WDib
'Mandy'	WDib
¶ 'Marie'	WDib
'Maureen'	CSpe
'Megan'	CKni WDib
'Mini Nymph'	WDib
'Myba'	MBri
'Neptune'	MBri
'Nicola'	MBri WDib
¶ 'Olga'	WDib
'Paula' ♀	CKni MBri WDib
pentherianus	CSpe SBla
'Pink Fondant'	CSpe
'Pink Upstart'	CSpe
'Plum Crazy'	CSpe
primulifolius subsp. *formosus*	WDib
'Purple Passion'	CSpe
rexii	MSto WDib
'Rhiannon'	WDib

'Rosebud'	CKni WDib
'Ruby' ♀	MBri WDib
'Sally'	WDib
'Sandra'	MBri WDib
'Sarah' ♀	WDib
saxorum ♀	CBrk CHal CInt CSWP LCns LHil LIck MBri NTow SRms WDib
– compact form	LCns WDib
'Snow White' ♀	CSpe WDib
'Something Special'	WDib
'Stella' ♀	WDib
¶ ***stomandrus***	WDib
'Sugar Almond'	CSpe
'Susan' ♀	CKni WDib
'Sweet Violet'	CSpe
'Tina' ♀	MBri WDib
'Tracey'	WDib
'Upstart'	CSpe
'Violet Lace'	CSpe
'Wiesmoor Red'	MBri WDib
'Winifred'	WDib

STREPTOLIRION (Commelinaceae)

¶ ***volubile***	CPlN

STREPTOPUS (Convallariaceae)

¶ ***amplexifolius***	EMan
roseus	LAma

STREPTOSOLEN (Solanaceae)

jamesonii ♀	CHal CPlN CPle CSev CSpe EBak ELan ERea IBlr LCns LHil NRog SLMG WBod
– yellow	CBrk ERea

STROBILANTHES (Acanthaceae)

anisophyllus	CSpe
atropurpureus	CBot CGle CGre CHan CPle EBre ECha EFou EHal ELan GCal LHil MHar NBrk NSti SAxl SMrm SUsu SVen WCot WCru WHer WOMN WOld WPer WWin WWye
attenuatus	SWas WCru WFar
¶ –subsp. ***nepalensis***	WWye
¶ – – TSS	CGle CHan CSpe EBee EMar WPbr WRHF
dyerianus ♀	CHal
violaceus	CArc ERav ERea LFis SAga SBar SMac WPer WWye

STROMANTHE (Marantaceae)

amabilis	See ***Ctenanthe amabilis***
'Freddy'	MBri
sanguinea	CHal MBri
'Stripestar'	MBri

STROPHANTHUS (Apocynaceae)

kombe	CPlN MSal SLMG
¶ ***preussii***	CPlN
¶ ***speciosus***	CPlN MSal

STRUTHIOPTERIS (Blechnaceae)

♦ ***niponica***	See ***Blechnum niponicum***

STUARTIA See STEWARTIA

STYLIDIUM (Stylidiaceae)

See Plant Deletions

STYLOMECON (Papaveraceae)

See Plant Deletions

STYLOPHORUM (Papaveraceae)

diphyllum	CHan CPou EBee EBre ECha EMar EMon LAma MSal SWas WCot WCru
lasiocarpum	CArc EBre EMon MBel MHlr NCat SMad SSca SWas WCot WCru WFar

STYPHELIA (Epacridaceae)

colensoi	See ***Cyathodes colensoi***

STYRAX (Styracaceae)

americanus	CB&S
hemsleyanus ♀	CAbP CChu CFil EPfP MBlu SMad SPer SSpi SSta WWat
japonicus ♀	CB&S CBlo CChu CEnd CMCN CPMA ELan GOrc ICrw IOrc LHop LPan MBal MBlu MBri MGos NPal SHBN SPer SReu SSpi SSta WBod WCoo WDin WNor WPat WWat
§ – Benibana Group	CDoC MAsh SPer SReu SSta
– – 'Pink Chimes'	CAbP CKni CPMA CSte ELan EPfP LRHS MAsh MBlu SPer SSta WWat WWes
– 'Carillon'	ELan LRHS MAsh SPer
– 'Fargesii'	CKni CSte LRHS SSpi SSta WFar
– 'Pendulus'	SSta
– 'Roseus'	See ***S. japonicus* Benibana Group**
obassia ♀	CB&S CChu CGre CMCN CPMA CTho CWSG SReu SSpi SSta WNor WWat
odoratissimus	CArn

SUCCISA (Dipsacaceae)

§ ***pratensis***	CArn CKin ECWi ECoo EMan EWFC MChe MFir MGam MHew MHig NLan SSpi WGwy WHer WJek WOak
pratensis alba	SSpi WNdy
pratensis dwarf form	CLyd GDra LBlm MBro NGre NTow
¶ ***pratensis rosea***	SSpi

SUTERA (Scrophulariaceae)

cordata	EBar LHop
– 'Knysna Hills'	CSpe LIck
– 'Lilac Pearls'	LHop
– mauve	CSpe
¶ – pale pink	NPri
– 'Pink Domino'	CSpe WLRN
§ – 'Snowflake'	CBar CBrk CHal CSpe EAst LHil MLan NPri SCoo SMac SMer SUsu WLRN
¶ ***grandiflora***	CSpe
jurassica	EHyt NMen
* ***rosea*** 'Plena'	WCot

SUTHERLANDIA (Papilionaceae)

frutescens	CAbb CSam CSpe CTrC LHop LLew NCGP SUsu SWat
– Edinburgh strain	LLew
– 'Prostrata'	SIgm SMrm
microphylla	LLew
– S&SH 56/61	CHan
montana	CFir LLew SIgm

SWAINSONA (Papilionaceae)

formosa	MSto
galegifolia 'Albiflora'	CSpe EWes LGre LHil SMrm
tephrotricha	MSto

SWERTIA (Gentianaceae)

kingii	WThi

SYAGRUS (Arecaceae)

§ ***romanzoffiana***	CBrP LPal

× SYCOPARROTIA (Hamamelidaceae)

semidecidua	CFil CKni CPMA CPle LRHS SBid SSta WWat

SYCOPSIS (Hamamelidaceae)

sinensis	EPfP ICrw SBid SSpi SSta WSHC WWat
tutcheri	See ***Distylium racemosum tutcheri***

SYMPHORICARPOS (Caprifoliaceae)

albus	CChe CKin CPer ENot NWea WDin
– 'Constance Spry'	MUlv SRms
§ – var. ***laevigatus***	CB&S ENot GRei LBuc MBar WDin
§ – 'Taff's White' (v)	EMon
– 'Variegatus'	See ***S. albus* 'Taff's White'**
× ***chenaultii*** 'Hancock'	EGoo ELan ENot GOrc GRei MBar MGos MRav MWat NPro SHBN SLPl SPer WDin WFar
× ***doorenbosii*** 'Magic Berry'	CBlo EBee ENot LBuc MBar NWea
– 'Mother of Pearl'	ECha ELan ENot LBuc MBar MGos NWea SPer WDin
– 'White Hedge'	EBee ELan ENot LBuc NWea SPer WDin
orbiculatus	GAul WThi
– 'Albovariegatus'	See ***S. orbiculatus* 'Taff's Silver Edge'**
– 'Argenteovariegatus'	See ***S. orbiculatus* 'Taff's Silver Edge'**
– 'Bowles' Golden Variegated'	See ***S. orbiculatus* 'Foliis Variegatis'**
§ – 'Foliis Variegatis'	CTri EFol EHal EHoe ELan EPla LHop MBal MGos MRav MTis SHBN SPer WAbe WDin WEas WGwG WHCG WSHC WWat WWin
§ – 'Taff's Silver Edge' (v)	EHoe ELan EPla IOrc ISea MBar MPla NSti WWat
– 'Variegatus'	See ***S. orbiculatus* 'Foliis Variegatis'**
rivularis	See ***S. albus*** var. ***laevigatus***

SYMPHYANDRA † (Campanulaceae)

armena	CLTr CPea EBur ECro ELan GBuc GDra LGan MSto NHol NPer SWat WBea
asiatica	CHan WWat
cretica	EBee EPad EWll NRai NTow SWat
hofmannii	CGle CSpe CWGN EBur ELan EPad ITim LGan MTho NBrk NFai NHol NWCA SRms SSca SWat WBea WCru WHer WHil WOve WPer WPri WSan WWin
§ ***ossetica***	CGle EPad NBro NWoo SSvw SUsu WCot WThi
§ ***pendula***	CFir EBar ECro EMan EPad EWes GBri GBuc GCra LCot LGan SBar SSca WCru WFar WPer WThi
pendula alba	See ***S. pendula***
* ***tianschanica***	LCot
wanneri	CMea CNic EBee EBur ECro EPad GCra LGan MAvo NBro NMen NRai WOMN WWin
zanzegura	CNic EBur ECro EEls EMan EPad MHar NBro SUsu SWat

SYMPHYTUM † (Boraginaceae)

asperum	ECha EGar ELan EMon MHew MSal WCHb WCer
* ***azureum***	CSte EAst LRHS MBri MSte WCHb WGwy
'Boking'	GAbr
caucasicum	CElw CHan CSam ECED ECha ELau EPad EPar GPoy LHol MBri MHar NFai NRar NSti SAxl SSvw WCHb WCru WHer WHil WRha WWye
– 'Eminence'	CGle CRDP EGoo EMon MGra MHlr WCHb WCot
– 'Norwich Sky'	CDoC CInt EJud NMir WCHb WNdy
'Denford Variegated'	MInt WCot
§ 'Goldsmith' (v)	CMil CRDP CWGN EAst ECha ELan EMon ENot EOrc EPla LHop MBri MRav MTho MUlv NOrc NPer NRoo SAxl SSpi WCru WDav WHer WPbr WPer WRus
grandiflorum	See ***S. ibericum***
'Hidcote Blue'	CBre CHan CMGP CTri ECha ELan ELau EPla ILis LHop MBri MSte NHol NSti SLPl SPer WCru WElm WWeb WWin
§ 'Hidcote Pink'	CGle EAst EBre ECha ELau ENot EPla LHol LHop MSte NFla NRoo NSti SLPl WCer
'Hidcote Variegated'	CGle SIng WCHb WRha
§ ***ibericum***	CArn CGle CHan CNic ECha ELau GPoy LGan LGro LHol MDun MFir MNrw NSti SAWi SIde SSvw WCHb WCru WWat
– 'All Gold'	EBee ECha EFol ELau LGan MBri WCru
– 'Blaueglocken'	CSev EBee ECha NCat NRoo WHow WSan
– 'Gold in Spring'	EGoo EMon WCHb WCer WRha
– 'Jubilee'	See ***S.* 'Goldsmith'**
– 'Langthornes Pink'	WPbr
– 'Lilacinum'	SAga WCer WHer WWat
– 'Pink Robins'	EMon WCHb
– 'Variegatum'	See ***S.* 'Goldsmith'**

– 'Wisley Blue'	ELan EPfP MCli NCat WCer WWoo
'Lambrook Sunrise'	CFis EBre NBus NRoo WCot WSan
¶ 'Langthorns Pink'	ELan EMar EMon GBar GBuc GCal MTol NRoo WCHb WCer
'Mereworth' (v)	EMon WCHb WPbr
officinale	CArn CKin CSev CShe ECWi EJud EPla GPoy LHol MChe MGam MHew MNrw MSal NFai NHex NMir NPer SIde SRms WHer WWye
* – blue	MGra WWat
officinale ochroleucum	WCHb WHer
orientale	CElw CGle EBre SSvw WCHb WRha
peregrinum	See ***S.*** × ***uplandicum***
'Roseum'	See ***S.* 'Hidcote Pink'**
'Rubrum'	CArc CMGP EAst ECot ELan ELau EOrc EPfP EPla EWes MCli MSte NOrc NPla NRoo SMrm SPer WCru
tuberosum	CBre CJew CRDP EGar ELau EOHP GPoy LGan MFir NCat NHol NSti SSvw WCHb WHer WRha WWat
– JMH 8106	MDun
§ × ***uplandicum***	CSev EJud ELan ELau EMar MHew MSal WCHb WCer WJek WOak WWin WWye
– 'Axminster Gold' (v)	CRDP IBlr SAga
– 'Bocking 14'	CAgr CBod CJew MGra
– 'Jenny Swales'	EMon
– 'Variegatum' ♀	CBot CChu CGle CWGN EBre ECha ELan ELau EOrc EWes GCal GPoy LHop MTho MUlv NRoo SSpi WBea WCHb WEas WFar WWat WWin

SYMPLOCARPUS (Araceae)

foetidus	WCot

SYMPLOCOS (Symplocaceae)

paniculata	WWat WWes

SYNADENIUM (Euphorbiaceae)

See Plant Deletions

SYNEILESIS (Asteraceae)

aconitifolia B&SWJ 879	WCru
intermedia B&SWJ 298	WCru
palmata B&SWJ 1003	WCru

SYNGONIUM (Araceae)

'Maya Red'	MBri
* ***podophyllum*** ♀	LBlo
– 'Emerald Gem'	CHal
– 'Silver Knight'	MBri
– 'Variegatum'	MBri
'White Butterfly'	CHal MBri

SYNNOTIA See SPARAXIS

SYNTHYRIS (Scrophulariaceae)

pinnatifida	NWCA
¶ – var. ***canescens***	MFos
¶ – var. ***lanuginosa***	CGra GCLN MFos
– var. ***pinnatifida***	WDav
reniformis	IBlr WCot WHil
stellata	EBre GCal GGar LFis WOMN WPbr

SYRINGA † (Oleaceae)

afghanica	See ***S. protolaciniata***
amurensis	See ***S. reticulata*** var. ***amurensis***
¶ × ***chinensis***	WWat
– 'Saugeana'	CDoC WPyg
'Correlata' (graft hybrid)	IOrc
¶ ***debelderorum***	SSta
emodi	CBot CChu WHCG
– 'Aureovariegata'	CEnd CPMA MMor
× ***hyacinthiflora***	WStI
– 'Esther Staley' ♀	CDoC EBee ENot MAsh MRav SFam WAbe
¶ – 'Pocohontas'	SSta
¶ – 'Sunset' (d)	SSta
¶ – 'The Bride'	SSta
¶ × ***hyacinthifolia*** 'Laurentian'	SSta
× ***josiflexa*** 'Bellicent' ♀	CChu CEnd CHan CPle ELan ENot ISea MAsh MBal MBar MGos MHlr MRav MTis MUlv NSti SChu SHBN SPer SPla SRms SSta WHCG WPat
– 'Lynette'	EPla
– 'Royalt'	CDoC
josikaea	CBlo CChu CPMA CPle LPan MBar SPer SSpi WHCG
komarovii subsp. ***reflexa*** ♀	CChu CDoC EBee EFol LPan MBar MGos WWat
§ × ***laciniata*** Miller	CBot CPMA CPle CWan MBri MRav SChu SMad SPer WGor WSHC WWat
§ ***meyeri*** var. ***spontanea*** 'Palibin' ♀	Widely available
microphylla	See ***S. pubescens* var. *microphylla***
¶ ***oblata*** var. ***donaldii***	SSta
palibiniana	See ***S. meyeri* 'Palibin'**
patula hort.	See ***S. meyeri* 'Palibin'**
patula (Palibin) Nakai	See ***S. pubescens* var. *patula***
pekinensis	CBot
× ***persica*** ♀	EHal ISea MGos MWat SPer SPla WPyg
– 'Alba' ♀	CBot CEnd GQui WSHC WWat
– var. ***laciniata***	See ***S.*** × ***laciniata* Miller**
pinnatifolia	CBot CPle
× ***prestoniae*** 'Agnes Smith'	MGos
– 'Audrey'	MGos
– 'Desdemona'	CB&S
– 'Elinor' ♀	CBlo CDoC CMHG CPMA CPle EBee ENot ISea NSti SPer
– 'Isabella'	MGos NFla
– 'Redwine'	MGos
§ ***protolaciniata***	CChu CMHG EPla MBlu MPla NPro SSta WFar
pubescens subsp. ***microphylla***	MHlr
– – 'Superba' ♀	CPle CShe ELan ENot IOrc MAsh MBel MBri MBro MGos NBee NFla NHol NRoo SHBN SPer SPla SSpi SSta WGwG WHCG WPat WPyg WRTC WSHC WWat
§ – subsp. ***patula***	CWLN EBee ELan IHos IOrc LNet MBal MWat NBee NRoo SPla WStI

– – 'Miss Kim' 🏆	CBlo EBee EBre ECle LRHS MAsh MBri MGos NPro SHBN SSta WPyg
reflexa	See ***S. komarovii* subsp. *reflexa***
reticulata	CPle
§ – subsp. ***amurensis***	MBal
– var. ***mandschurica***	See ***S. reticulata*** subsp. ***amurensis***
sweginzowii	CChu MBal SPer WRus WWat
tomentella	CEnd CPle CWSG
velutina	See ***S. patula* (Palibin) Nakai**
vulgaris	CBlo GOrc GRei LBuc MBar NWea
– 'Adelaide Dunbar' (d)	GCHN
– var. ***alba***	MBar
¶ – 'Albert F. Holden'	SSta
§ – 'Andenken an Ludwig Späth' 🏆	CB&S CBot CTho CTri EB&P ECtt ENot IOrc MBar MBri MGos NWea SHBN SPer WGwG WPyg
¶ – 'Arthur William Paul' (d)	MRav
– 'Aurea'	EFol EPla MRav WBcn
¶ – 'Avalanche'	SSta
– 'Belle de Nancy' (d)	ECtt EHic ELan MAsh MBri MWat SHBN WDin WLRN WPyg
– 'Charles Joly' (d) 🏆	CB&S CTho EB&P ELan ENot GCHN GRei IHos IOrc LNet MAsh MBal MBar MBri MGos MRav MTis NBee NWea SHBN SPer WDin WStI
– 'Charm'	GCHN
– 'Condorcet' (d)	LNet
– 'Congo'	ENot GCHN MAsh SCoo SPer
– 'Edward J. Gardner' (d)	SPer
¶ – 'Ellen Willmott' (d)	MRav
– 'Firmament' 🏆	EBee ELan ENot SCoo SHBN SPer SRms
– 'Glory of Horstenstein'	See ***S. vulgaris* 'Ruhm von Horstenstein'**
– 'Katherine Havemeyer' (d) 🏆	CB&S CBot CDoC CSam CTri CWLN EB&P ELan ENot GRei LBuc MAsh MBri MGos MHlr MRav SHBN SPer SReu WDin WStI
¶ – 'Krasavitsa Moskvy'	SSta
¶ – 'Lucie Baltet'	SSta
– 'Madame Antoine Buchner' (d) 🏆	ENot MRav SPer
– 'Madame Florent Stepman'	CBlo CDoC
– 'Madame Lemoine' (d) 🏆	CB&S CBot CTho ELan ENot GCHN GRei LBuc LNet MAsh MBal MBar MBri MGos MHlr MRav NBee NWea SFam SHBN SPer SReu WDin WStI
– 'Masséna'	ENot MRav SCoo SPer
– 'Maud Notcutt'	ENot SCoo SPer
– 'Michel Buchner' (d)	CB&S ECtt ENot GRei IHos IOrc MAsh MBar MBri MRav MWat
– 'Mrs Edward Harding' (d) 🏆	ECtt ENot LBuc LNet MBal MBri MGos SPer WLRN
¶ – 'Olivier de Serres'	SSta
¶ – 'Paul Thirion' (d)	SSta
– 'Président Grévy' (d)	CDoC CWLN ECle SPer
– 'Primrose'	CBot CTho EHic ELan ENot MBal SPer SSta WDin WLRN
¶ – 'Romance'	SSta
– 'Sensation'	CPle EBee EHic ENot MAsh MRav SCoo SHBN SPer SSta
¶ – 'Silver King'	SSta
– 'Souvenir de Louis Spaeth'	See ***S. vulgaris* 'Andenken an Ludwig Späth'**
– variegated double	EFol MBal
– 'Vestale' 🏆	CBlo ENot SCoo SRms
yunnanensis	ELan

SYZYGIUM (Myrtaceae)

See Plant Deletions

TABERNAEMONTANA (Apocynaceae)

coronaria	See ***T. divaricata***

TACITUS See GRAPTOPETALUM

TAGETES (Asteraceae)

lemmonii	SMac
lucida	MSal

TAIWANIA (Taxodiaceae)

See Plant Deletions

TALBOTIA (Velloziaceae)

¶ ***elegans***	WCot

TALINUM (Portulacaceae)

calycinum	NGre
okanoganense	MFos NGre NTow NWCA WAbe
¶ ***rugospermum***	WAbe
teretifolium	WThi
'Zoe'	SIng WAbe WFar WThi

TAMARILLO See CYPHOMANDRA *crassicaulis*

TAMARIX (Tamaricaceae)

africana	SEND WWin
gallica	CBlo ENot GCHN NWea SArc SEND WSHC
germanica	See ***Myricaria germanica***
§ ***parviflora***	CB&S CBlo EBee EMil IOrc MGos SSoC WGwG
pentandra	See ***T. ramosissima***
§ ***ramosissima***	CDoC CShe CSpe EBre ELan MUlv SEND SMrm SRms SSoC SSta WDin WWeb
– 'Pink Cascade'	CTri EBee EMil ENot MBri MRav SEas SPer WDin WGwG WStI
§ – 'Rubra' 🏆	CChe CDoC EMil ENot EPfP IOrc MBlu MGos WPyg
– 'Summer Glow'	See ***T. ramosissima* 'Rubra'**
tetrandra 🏆	CMHG EAst EBre ELan ENot GOrc LNet LPan MWat NBee NNor NPer SHBN SPer SReu SRms SSta WBod WFar WHCG WRHF WStI WWeb
– var. ***purpurea***	See ***T. parviflora***

TAMUS (Dioscoreaceae)

communis	CArn

TANACETUM † (Asteraceae)

§ ***argenteum***	LCom LRHS MRav MTho NTow SIng
– subsp. ***canum***	CKni ELan EWes LRHS MAsh

§ ***balsamita***	CArn CSev EEls EJud ELan ELau EOHP ERav GPoy MBri MHew MSal WJek WOak WPer WSel WWye
§ – subsp. ***balsametoides***	EJud ELau LHol MChe MGra NPri SIde WGwy WJek WWye
§ – subsp. ***balsamita***	EOHP GPoy LHol MSal SIde
– var. ***tanacetoides***	See ***T. balsamita*** subsp. ***balsamita***
– ***tomentosum***	See ***T. balsamita*** subsp. ***balsametoides***
capitatum	See ***Sphaeromeria capitata***
§ ***cinerariifolium***	CArn CBod CInt GPoy SIde WPer
§ ***coccineum***	CChr EEls GBar GPoy MHew MSal NVic SHam SRms WWin
I – 'Andromeda'	EBre
¶ – 'Aphrodite'	EFou SMrm
– 'Bees' Pink Delight'	EFou
– 'Brenda' 🏆	EBre EFou MRav SMrm
– 'Duplex'	EPfP
– 'Duro'	CMdw GBuc
– 'Eileen May Robinson' 🏆	EBee EBre ECED ECot EPfP NCut NFla SMrm
– 'Evenglow'	EFou SMrm
– 'James Kelway' 🏆	ECot MBri MRav NFai SMrm SRms
– 'Kelway's Glorious'	NCut
– 'King Size'	CSam MTis NFla NMir WFar
– 'Laurin'	EBre
– 'Phillipa'	EBre
– 'Pink Petite'	EBre
¶ – 'Queen Mary'	EFou
¶ – Robinson's giant flowered	WRHF
– 'Robinson's Pink'	EMan GMaP MGrG NFla NOrc NPla NPri NRoo SMrm SRms
– 'Robinson's Red'	GBur GMaP LIck MGrG NOrc NPla NPri NRoo SMrm
– 'Salmon Beauty'	EFou EMan LRHS
– 'Scarlet Glow'	MWat
– 'Snow Cloud'	EBee EFou EMan MGrG MWat SMrm
– 'Vanessa'	EBee EBre EFou SMrm
§ ***corymbosum***	CGle EMon GCal LFis NCat WCot
§ – subsp. ***clusii***	EEls
– 'Festafel'	ECha
densum	ECho EPot WWeb
– subsp. ***amani***	ECha ELan GTou LBee LGro MPla MRPP MWat NRoo NWCA SEND SRms SSmi WRus WWin
§ ***haradjanii***	CGle ELan EMNN GCHN MBro MHar MRPP NNor SBla SChu WByw WEas WHer WHoo WOld WSHC WWye
herderi	See ***Hippolytia herderi***
§ ***macrophyllum***	EMon GCal WCot WPer
niveum	CArn CHad EGar EOHP MSal WBea WCot
pallidum	See ***Leucanthemopsis pallida***
§ ***parthenium***	CArn CKin ECWi EEls EJud ELau EWFC GBar GPoy LHol MChe MHew NFai NHex NMir NPer NRoo SIde WHer WOak WWye
– 'Aureum'	CM&M CRow ECha EEls ELan ELau GPoy LGro MBri MChe NFai NHex SIng SMad SPer SRms WBea WEas WHer WOak WOve WPer WWin
– 'Ball's Double White'	SRms
– double white	CM&M CSWP GBar GPoy NPer SEND
– 'Golden Ball'	NTow WCot
– 'Plenum'	LBlm MBri SIng
§ – 'Rowallane' (d)	ELan EMon GBuc MBri WCot WSan
– 'Sissinghurst White'	See ***T. parthenium* 'Rowallane'**
– 'White Bonnet' (d)	CGle ECGP EGar ELan NBrk WEas
§ ***praeteritum***	LGre
pseudachillea	EEls
§ ***ptarmiciflorum***	SMer
sp. CC&McK 460	GTou
vulgare	CAgr CArn CKin CSev ECWi ECtt EEls EJud ELau EWFC GPoy LHol MChe MHew MSal NLan NMir SIde SPer WByw WCla WOak WWye
– var. ***crispum***	CJew CWan ELan EOHP GBar GCal GPoy LFis MBri NCGP NHex SIde WBea WCot WGwy WHer WJek WRha WSel
– 'Isla Gold'	CBod EFol EFou EMon EWes GCal LFis MMil SMad WCHb WCot WNdy WPbr WRha WWye
– 'Silver Lace' (v)	CRDP ECha EFol EMar EMon LFis MAvo NBrk NHex NSti WBea WCHb WCot

TANAKAEA (Saxifragaceae)

radicans	NHol WCru

TAPEINOCHILOS (Zingiberaceae)

See Plant Deletions

TARAXACUM (Asteraceae)

albidum B&SWJ 509	WCru
¶ ***carneocoloratum***	EPPr
I ***officinale***	CTiv MHew SIde
pamiricum JJH 395	EHyt EPPr

TASMANNIA See DRIMYS

TAXODIUM (Taxodiaceae)

ascendens	See ***T. distichum*** var. ***imbricatum***
§ ***distichum*** 🏆	CB&S CDoC CLnd CMCN CMac CWSG EHul ELan ENHC ENot ISea LCon LNet MBal MBar MBlu MBri NHol NPal NWea SHBN SPer SReu WDin WFro WGer WNor WWat
– var. ***imbricatum*** 'Nutans' 🏆	CEnd IOrc MBlu MBri SMur
mucronatum	WFro

TAXUS † (Taxaceae)

baccata 🏆	CB&S CDoC CKin CPer ELan ENot ERea GAul GRei ISea LBee LBuc LCon LHyr LLin LNet LPan MAsh MBar MBri MChe MGos NWea SMad SPer SReu WDin WHar WHen WMou
– 'Adpressa Aurea'	CKen EPla ESis GAri MPla
– 'Adpressa Variegata' 🏆	EBre EHul LCon MAsh SLim
– 'Aldenham Gold'	CKen
– 'Amersfoort'	EOrn EPla LCon SSpi
– 'Argentea Minor'	See ***T. baccata* 'Dwarf White'**
§ – Aurea Group	CBlo EBee EPot SRms
I – 'Aurea Pendula'	EBre ENHC
I – 'Aureomarginata'	CB&S ENHC EOrn WStI
¶ – 'Cavendishii'	ECho
– 'Compacta'	EPla
– 'Corley's Coppertip'	CBlo CKen CSam EBee EHul EPot LCon LLin MBar MOne NHol WGwG WLRN
– 'Cristata'	LCon
– 'Dovastoniana' 🏆	CDoC CMac LCon LPan MBar NWea
– 'Dovastonii Aurea' (v) 🏆	CDoC CMac EBee EHul EOrn EPla LCon LHol MBar MBri SLim WDin
– 'Drinkstone Gold'	EHul EPla WBcn
§ – 'Dwarf White'	EOrn LCon NHol
– 'Elegantissima' (f/v) 🏆	EHul LBuc MPla NWea
– 'Erecta' (m)	EHul SHBN
§ – 'Fastigiata' (f) 🏆	CB&S CDoC CMac EBre EHul ENHC ENot ERea GRei IOrc ISea LCon LLin LNet MAsh MBar MBri MGos NBee SLim SPer WDin WMou WStI WWin
– 'Fastigiata Aurea'	CKen CLnd EBee EHul ELan IHos LBuc LLin NBee NEgg NHol NPer NRoo SBla SRms WLRN
– 'Fastigiata Aureomarginata' 🏆	CDoC CKen CMac EBre EHul EOrn EPot GRei IOrc ISea LCon LPan MBal MBar MBri MGos MWat NHol NWea SLim WGwG WMou
– 'Fastigiata Robusta'	EBre EPla MBar WGer WPyg
– 'Glenroy New Penny'	MBal
– 'Green Diamond'	CKen
– 'Hibernica'	See ***T. baccata* 'Fastigiata' (f)**
– 'Ivory Tower'	MGos
– 'Melfard'	EHul
– 'Nutans'	CKen EHul ESis LCon LLin MBar MOne WLRN
– 'Overeynderi'	EHul
– 'Pendula'	MBal MRav
– 'Pumila Aurea'	ELan MAsh
– 'Pygmaea'	CKen IOrc
– 'Repandens' (f) 🏆	CDoC EHul ENHC LCon LPan MBar SHBN WFar WGer
– 'Repens Aurea' (v) 🏆	CDoC CHig CKen EHul ELan ENHC GCHN LCon LLin MAsh MBar MBri MGos MPla NRoo SAga
– 'Rushmore'	SCoo
– 'Semperaurea' (m) 🏆	CB&S CMac EBre EHul ELan ENHC EOrn EPla GCHN LBee LCon LHol LPan MBal MBar MBri MGos NBee NWea SAga SLim SPla WDin WWin
– 'Silver Spire' (v)	CB&S CKen
– 'Standishii' 🏆	CDoC CFee CKen EHul ELan ENHC EPla GCHN IOrc LBee LCon LLin LNet MAsh MBal MBar MBri MGos MPla MRav MWat NHol SAga SBla SHBN SLim WDin
– 'Summergold' (v)	CDoC EBre EHul ELan ENHC ENot EPla GCHN GRei IOrc LCon LPan MBar MGos NHol NRoo SLim WPyg WStI
– 'Variegata'	See ***T. baccata* Aurea Group**
– 'Washingtonii'	SHBN
brevifolia	EPla LCon
cuspidata	CMCN ETen LCon
– 'Aurescens'	CKen EPla LCon MAsh SRms
– f. *nana*	EHul EOrn GAri LCon MBar NBee NHol SIng WGwG WLRN
– 'Robusta'	EHul LLin
– 'Straight Hedge'	EHul WLRN
× *media* 'Brownii'	EHul LBuc
– 'Hicksii' 🏆	CEnd CLnd EHul ENHC LBuc LNet LPan MBar NRoo NWea SLim WLRN
– 'Hillii'	CBlo LCon MBar NHol

TECOMA (Bignoniaceae)

capensis 🏆	CB&S CHEx CPlN CPle CSev CTrC EBak ELan EMil ERea SLMG SSoC
– 'Aurea'	CPle CSev ERea SLMG
– subsp. *nyassae*	ERea
¶ *garrocha*	CPlN
ricasoliana	See ***Podranea ricasoliana***
× *smithii*	CPlN
stans	CPlN

TECOMANTHE (Bignoniaceae)

¶ *dendrophila*	CPlN
speciosa	CPlN ECou

TECOMARIA See TECOMA

TECOPHILAEA (Tecophilaeaceae)

cyanocrocus 🏆	CAvo EHyt EPot LAma WChr
– 'Leichtlinii' 🏆	CAvo EHyt EPot LAma SSpi WChr
– 'Purpurea'	See ***T. cyanocrocus* 'Violacea'**
§ – 'Violacea'	CAvo EHyt EPot WChr
violiflora	LAma

TECTARIA (Dryopteridaceae)

gemmifera	GQui NMar

TELANTHOPHORA (Asteraceae)

grandifolia	SArc

TELEKIA (Asteraceae)

§ *speciosa*	CHan CSam CWGN ECro ELan GAul LFis MFir NBro NBus NPSI SDix WBea WByw WHer WOld WPer WRHF

TELESONIX See BOYKINIA

TELINE See GENISTA

TELLIMA (Saxifragaceae)
grandiflora CGle CHan CMHG CSam EBre EEls EHon EJud ELan EMon GCHN MFir NBrk NFla NOrc NWCA SHel SIng SSpi WCot WHen WOak WPer WTyr WWhi WWye
– 'Delphine' CElw
– 'Forest Frost' WCot
– Odorata Group CBre CHid ECha EGoo EPPr EPla GAul NBrk NCat NLak SPer WGwG WWat WWye
– 'Purpurea' See *T. grandiflora* **Rubra Group**
– 'Purpurteppich' CDec CGle ECha MRav NCat
§ – Rubra Group CBre CDec CGle CHid CKel CRow CShe CWGN EBre ECha EHoe ELan EOrc LFis LGro LSyl MBri MCLN MWat NPer NRoo NSti SHel SMad SPer SRms WEas WHoo WWat WWin

TELOPEA (Proteaceae)
mongaensis SArc
speciosissima CHEx CTrC
truncata CFil CHEx ISea MAll SSpi

TEPHROSERIS (Asteraceae)
¶ *integrifolia* WHer

TERNSTROEMIA (Theaceae)
gymnanthera See *T. japonica*
§ *japonica* EPfP SBid

TETRACENTRON (Tetracentraceae)
sinense CB&S CChu CDoC CFil CGre CPle CWSG GQui SBid SSpi WWat

TETRACLINIS (Cupressaceae)
See Plant Deletions

TETRADIUM (Rutaceae)
§ *daniellii* CDoC CFil CMCN SSpi WCoo WWat
§ – Hupehense Group CMCN GCal GGGa SSpi WWat
¶ *velutinum* CMCN

TETRAGONOLOBUS See LOTUS

TETRANEURIS (Asteraceae)
§ *grandiflora* CPBP GCal SMrm WHil
– JCA 11422 SBla
§ *scaposa* EPot

TETRAPANAX (Araliaceae)
§ *papyrifer* ♀ CHEx SArc

TETRAPATHAEA See PASSIFLORA

TETRASTIGMA (Vitaceae)
voinierianum ♀ CHEx CPlN ECon LCns MBri SArc

TETRATHECA (Tremandraceae)
See Plant Deletions

TEUCRIUM (Lamiaceae)
* *ackermannii* CLyd CShe EGoo EHyt ESis LBee LHop MBro NVic SBla SChu SCro SMac WAbe WHoo WPat
* *arabii* NChi
arduinoi CPle
aroanium CLyd CMea CPBP EGle EPot LBee MBro MHig MPla MWat NGre NMen NTow SBla SHFr SMrm SWas WAbe
asiaticum SSca
bicolor CGre CPle SSta WWye
botrys MHew MSal
canadense LHop
chamaedrys hort. See *T.* × *lucidrys*
chamaedrys Linnaeus CHal CSam CWan EGoo ESis GBar LFis MHew NHol NRoo NWCA SRms SSea SVen WCer WHoo WSel
– 'Nanum' CLyd CNic CWan MBro SRms WPat WPyg WWye
– 'Rose Carpet' CMGP EGoo MHar
– 'Variegatum' CDec CNic EFol EGoo GBar LLWP MAll MHar NCGP NHol WBea WCHb WCot WHer WOve WPer WRha WSel
* *discolor* CPle
flavum LFlo LGan SIde WHer
fruticans CB&S CBot CChe CHan CLyd CPle CShe CTrw EBre EEls EHoe ENot ERea LHop NFai NSti SAxl SBla SHBN SPer SSta WDin WEas WHCG WHar WRTC WSHC WWin WWye
– 'Album' CPle
– 'Azureum' ♀ CB&S CBot CPle CSpe EBee ERav LGre MBro SAga SBra SPer WAbe WBod WPat WPyg
– 'Compactum' CChu CMil EHic ESis LHop SMad SMrm SPer SPla WSHC
¶ – dark form SMrm
hircanicum CArc CPle CSam ECoo EGoo EHic EJud ELan EMan GBin LHop LLWP MBro MFir MNrw MSte WCot WWye
§ × *lucidrys* CArn CChe CMea CSev EAst EHyt ELan ELau EPla EPot ERea GAbr GPoy IOrc LHol MBal MCLN MChe MPla SIde SMad SPer SRms WCla WDin WEas WWin
lucidum GBin WCla WOak
majoricum See *T. polium* **f.** ***pii-fontii***
marum CArn LHol MSal NMen SIgm
massiliense hort. See *T.* × *lucidrys*
– Linnaeus EGoo WHer
montanum CMea EGoo MHig NRoo
musimonum CLyd EPot MHig NNrd
polium CLyd CShe EGoo ESis MBro MWat SIgm WPat
– *aureum* SBla SIng
pulverulentum See *T. cossonii*
pyrenaicum CHal CMea EGoo EPot MBro MHig NNrd NSla NWCA SIng WOld WPat WPyg WWin
rosmarinifolium See *T. creticum*
scordium CNat ECWi MGam WWhi

scorodonia	CArn CKin CSev EGoo EJud ELau EWFC GPoy LHol MChe MHew MSal NMir SIde WCla WHer WJek WSel WWye
– 'Crispum'	CB&S CHan CInt ELan ELau EOrc GOrc LHol MBri MFir MHar MSCN MWat NBro NFai SMrm WBod WCHb WKif WPer WSel
§ – 'Crispum Marginatum' (v)	CBot CWGN ECha ECoo EFol EFou EGoo EHoe ELan EMar EMon EPla ESis GAbr IBlr ILis LFis MNrw NFai NOak NRoo NSti WBea WBon WEas WHoo WPyg
– 'Winterdown' (v)	CMea CNat WAlt WCHb WCot WDav WPbr
subspinosum	CMea CPle EHyt ITim LBee NMen NTow SBla WPat WPyg
¶ ***webbianum***	ECho

THALIA (Marantaceae)

dealbata	CHEx MSta

THALICTRUM † (Ranunculaceae)

actaeifolium	EBee
adiantifolium	See ***T. minus adiantifolium***
angustifolium	See ***T. lucidum***
aquilegiifolium	Widely available
– var. ***album***	CBot CBre CMil EAst EBre ECha EFou ELan EPla LFis LGan MBri MCli MHlr MNrw NSti NTow SChu SCro SSpi WCot WEas WHil WHoo WPer
– dwarf form	ECha
* – 'Hybridum'	EHic WHil WPer
♦ – Purple Cloud	See ***T. aquilegiifolium*** **'Thundercloud'**
– 'Purpureum'	CSev CSte EAst GCal LFis SPla WCru WHoo
§ – 'Thundercloud' ♀	CDoC CFir EBre ECro ECtt EFou GCal MBel MBri MUlv NHol WAbe WCot WMer
¶ ***calabricum***	EMon
chelidonii dwarf form	GDra
clavatum	EBee
coreanum	See ***T. ichangense***
§ ***delavayi*** ♀	Widely available
– 'Album'	CGle CHad ECha EFou ELan GCra LGan LGre MBro NDea NOak WBro WHoo WMaN
– 'Hewitt's Double' ♀	Widely available
– 'Sternhimmel'	NHol
diffusiflorum	NHar SBla WCot
dipterocarpum hort.	See ***T. delavayi***
fendleri	GBuc
finetii	EMon
flavum	CGle CHan EBee EBre ECWi EFou ELan GGar NBro NDea NPri SSpi WHil WRha
– 'Chollerton'	See ***T. sp. from Afghanistan***
§ – subsp. ***glaucum*** ♀	CBot CBre CChu CElw CLon CShe CSpe ECha ECro EFol EHoe ELan EOrc EPla EPot MBri MBro MCLN MFir MNrw NOak SHFr SMad SSoC SUsu WEas WPer WRha WWhi WWin
– 'Illuminator'	CSte MBel MOne NHol SBid WCot
foetidum	EMon
§ ***ichangense***	CBos CRDP GLil SMrm
isopyroides	CLTr CLon CPBP CRDP CSev CVer EAst EBee ECro EHic EMan EMon GBin MHar SMrm WAbe WCru WLRN
javanicum B&L 12327	EMon
kiusianum	CChu CLyd CMGP CMea EBee ECha EFol EGar EHyt EPot ESis EWes GAri LFis LGre MBel MTho NHar NMGW NTow SAga WAbe WFar WHil
– Kew form	CBos CRDP SWas WPbr
koreanum	See ***T. ichangense***
§ ***lucidum***	CPou EFol ELan EMan SSca WCot
minus	CHan ELan EMan EMon GAbr GBuc MBel MBri NOak NRoo NSti SPla WHil WWye
§ – ***adiantifolium***	CHan CMGP EAst EBee ECro EHic EJud EPla GAul LRHS MFir MUlv NHol NOak SMrm SRms WMer WPer WWat
§ – subsp. ***olympicum***	WPer
– subsp. ***saxatile***	See ***T. minus*** subsp. ***olympicum***
occidentale JLS 86255	EMon MNrw
orientale	SBla
pauciflorum	WCot WRus
polygamum	CBos EBee EBre LFis MHew MSal WCot
punctatum B&SWJ 1272	WCru
ramosum	EMon
¶ ***rhynchocarpum***	LLew
rochebruneanum	CChu CGle CHan EBee ECha EMan EWes MBri MNrw MUlv SMrm SSca WCru WPen WSHC
* ***rugosum***	GBuc
§ sp. from Afghanistan	CHan ELan EPot GBuc GTou WCot WHil WSan
sp. B&SWJ 2520	WCru
sp. B&SWJ 2622	WCru
sp. CLD 564	EMon
speciosissimum	See ***T. flavum*** subsp. ***glaucum***
¶ ***sphaerostachyum***	WGer
tuberosum	CChu CHan CRDP EMon EPot LGre SAga SBla SWas WCot
¶ ***uchiyamae***	WCot

THAMNOCALAMUS (Poaceae - Bambusoideae)

¶ ***aristatus***	ISta
crassinodus	EPla SDry
– dwarf from	EPla
– 'Kew Beauty'	EFul EPla ISta SDry WJun
– 'Lang Tang'	EPla WJun
– 'Merlyn'	EPla SDry WJun
falcatus	See ***Drepanostachyum falcatum***
falconeri	See ***Himalayacalamus falconeri***
funghomii	See ***Schizostachyum funghomii***
khasianus	See ***Drepanostachyum khasianum***
maling	See ***Yushania maling***
spathaceus hort.	See ***Fargesia murieliae***
§ ***spathiflorus***	EFul EPla SBam SDry WJun
§ ***tessellatus***	EFul EPla SBam SDry WJun

THAPSIA (Apiaceae)

decipiens	See ***Melanoselinum decipiens***
garganica	SIgm WCot

THEA See CAMELLIA

THELYMITRA (Orchidaceae)
See Plant Deletions

THELYPTERIS † (Thelypteridaceae)
limbosperma See ***Oreopteris limbosperma***
palustris EBee EMon MLan SRms WFib WRic
phegopteris See ***Phegopteris connectilis***

THEMEDA (Poaceae)
triandra subsp. ***australis*** from Adaminaby ETPC
– – from Cooma ETPC

THERMOPSIS (Papilionaceae)
¶ ***barbata*** NWoo
caroliniana See ***T. villosa***
fabacea See ***T. lupinoides***
lanceolata CHad CTri ECGP EMan GBin MBel MBri MMil MTis MTol SAga SMrm SOkh WFar WPer
§ ***lupinoides*** CArc ECha ECro EFol NOrc SLod WCot WCru WPer
mollis EBre EPla
montana CMGP CRDP EBre EFou ELan ERav GAbr MNrw NOrc NSti SChu WAbb WByw WGwG WPer WRus WWat
§ ***villosa*** CGle CHan CMdw EBee MSte NFai SBla SPer WCot

THEVETIA (Apocynaceae)
peruviana MSal SOWG

THLADIANTHA (Cucurbitaceae)
¶ ***dubia*** CPlN
oliveri (f) MSCN WCot

THLASPI (Brassicaceae)
alpinum CMHG CShe EPot MPla MWat NMen NNrd NWCA SAlw
arvense ECWi
bellidifolium GDra NBir
biebersteinii See ***Pachyphragma macrophyllum***
bulbosum GTou WThi
cepaeifolium subsp. ***rotundifolium*** GTou NGre
– – var. ***limosellifolium*** CMea
fendleri MNrw
stylosum NWCA

THRINAX (Arecaceae)
See Plant Deletions

THUJA † (Cupressaceae)
§ ***koraiensis*** ISea LCon MBar WHCr
occidentalis NWea WDin
– 'Aurea' MBar
– 'Aureospicata' EHul
– 'Beau Fleur' LLin
– 'Beaufort' (v) CKen EHul MBar MPla WGwG
– 'Caespitosa' CBlo CKen CNic ESis GAul LLin MOne NHol WLRN
– 'Cristata Aurea' CKen
– 'Danica' 🏆 CMac EBre EHul ENHC ENot EOrn GRei IOrc LCon LLin LPan MAsh MBar MGos MPla MWat SBod SLim SRms WGwG WStI
– 'Dicksonii' EHul
– 'Douglasii Aurea' CKen
– 'Ellwangeriana Aurea' ENHC LBee MGos
– 'Emerald' See ***T. occidentalis* 'Smaragd'**
– 'Ericoides' CDoC CTri EBee EHul ENHC LCon MAsh MBal MBar SRms SSmi WStI
– 'Europa Gold' CDoC EBee EHul IOrc LBee MBar MGos SLim WLRN
– 'Fastigiata' MBar
– 'Filiformis' CKen EPla
– 'Froebelii' WLRN
– 'Globosa' CBlo CMac MBar MGos SBod WGor WGwG
– 'Globosa Variegata' CBlo CKen MBar
– 'Golden Gem' LPan
– 'Golden Globe' CBlo EHul ENHC ENot LCon LNet LPan MBar MGos NHol SBod SLim SPla WDin WLRN
* – 'Golden Minaret' EHul
– 'Hetz Midget' CBlo CKen EHul EOrn ESis LCon LLin MBar MGos MOne NHol SLim SMer WLRN
– 'Holmstrup' 🏆 CDoC CMac CNic EBre EHul ENHC ENot EOrn GAul IOrc LCon LLin MAsh MBal MBar MBri MWat NBee NHol SLim SRms SSmi SSta WStI WWeb
– 'Holmstrup's Yellow' CBlo CDoC CKen EHul LCon MAsh MOne MPla WWeb
– 'Hoveyi' CTri EBee EHul ENHC LCon WLRN
– 'Little Champion' EHul GRei NHol
– 'Little Gem' CNic EBee EHul ENHC MGos NHol NPro SRms WDin WGor
– 'Lutea Nana' 🏆 CMac EHul ENHC EOrn MBal MBar
– 'Marrisen's Sulphur' CBlo EHul GAul LCon SLim WLRN
– 'Meineckes Zwerg' CKen EPla SSmi
– 'Miky' CKen WBcn
– 'Milleri' EPot
– 'Ohlendorffii' CBlo CKen EHul EOrn GWht LCon LLin MBar MWat NHol SSmi
– 'Orientalis Semperaurescens' See ***T. orientalis* 'Semperaurea'**
– 'Pygmaea' CKen MBar
– 'Pyramidalis Compacta' EHul LNet WGor
– 'Recurva Nana' EHul LLin MBal MBar NHol
– 'Rheingold' 🏆 Widely available
– 'Silver Beauty' (v) CMHG
§ – 'Smaragd' 🏆 CChe EBre EHul ENHC ENot GAul IOrc LBuc LCon LLin LNet LPan MAsh MBar MGos MPla SBod SPer WStI WWtk
– 'Southport' CBlo CKen MBri
– 'Sphaerica' MPla
– 'Spiralis' CBlo CMHG EBee ECho MBar
§ – 'Stolwijk' CBlo EHul MBar MGos SLim

– 'Sunkist'	CKen CMHG CMac EBre EHul ENHC ENot EOrn GRei IHos IOrc LCon LLin LNet LPan MAsh MBar MBri MGos MPla MWat NHol SBod SLim SPla WFar WWeb
– 'Suzie'	LLin
– 'Tiny Tim'	CBlo CMac EHul EPot ESis LCon LLin MBar MGos MOne SIng WGor WGwG WLRN WWeb
– 'Trompenburg'	CBlo EBee ECho EHul MAsh WBcn
– 'Wansdyke Silver' (v)	CBlo CMac EHul EOrn EPla LCon MBar MPla SIng SLim SPla
– 'Wareana'	CMac
– 'Wareana Aurea'	See ***T. occidentalis* 'Wareana Lutescens'**
§ – 'Wareana Lutescens'	CMHG CMac EBee EHul ENHC EOrn GRei LCon MBal MBar MGos MPla WGor
– 'Woodwardii'	EBee EHul MBar MOne SMer WDin WGor
– 'Yellow Ribbon'	CBlo EBre EHul LCon NHol SLim SMer SPla
§ ***orientalis***	NWea
§ – 'Aurea Nana' 🏆	CDoC CKen CMac CWLN EBre EHul ENHC ENot EPot ISea LBee LCon LLin LNet LPan MBal MBar MBri MGos MPla MWat NBee NWea SBod SLim SSmi WAbe WDin WStI
– 'Autumn Glow'	CBlo
– 'Bergmanii'	CBlo WWeb
– 'Beverleyensis'	LLin
– 'Blue Cone'	MBar
– 'Carribean Holiday'	EBre MAsh
– 'Collen's Gold'	CTri EHul MBar SPla
– 'Conspicua'	CKen EBee EHul ENHC LBee LCon MBar MWat
– 'Copper Kettle'	CBlo
– 'Elegantissima' 🏆	CMac EHul EOrn LBee LCon MBar MGos SBod
– 'Flame'	CBlo MGos
– 'Golden Minaret'	WBcn
– 'Golden Pygmy'	CKen EOrn MAsh WBcn
– 'Golden Wonder'	ENHC
– 'Juniperoides'	CBlo EHul EPla LCon LLin MBar WLRN
¶ – 'Madurodam'	LLin
– 'Magnifica'	EHul
– 'Meldensis'	CTri EBre EHul ENHC EPla LCon LLin MBal MBar WDin
– 'Miller's Gold'	See ***T. orientalis* 'Aurea Nana'**
– 'Minima'	CDoC EPot ESis MWat
– 'Minima Glauca'	CKen MBar SRms
– 'Purple King'	EPla LCon SLim
I – 'Pyramidalis Aurea'	LPan
– 'Rosedalis'	CKen CMac CNic EBre EHul ENHC EOrn EPla ESis LBee LCon LLin MAsh MBal MBar MBri MPla MWat SBod SLim SRms
– 'Sanderi'	CKen EBre EOrn MBar MBri
§ – 'Semperaurea'	CMac WGor
– 'Shirley Chilcott'	EBre MBri
– 'Sieboldii'	EHul
– 'Southport'	EBre LLin MAsh
¶ – 'Spaethii'	EOrn

– 'Summer Cream'	CBlo EHul MBar MGos
– 'Westmont'	EOrn
plicata	CChe CPer EHul GRei GWht IOrc LHyr MBal MBar MGos NEgg NWea SBod SPer WFro WMou WStI
– 'Atrovirens' 🏆	CChe CTri EBre ENot GAul LBee LBuc LCon LPan MAsh MBri SMer SRms WGwG WMou WWeb
– 'Aurea' 🏆	CBlo EHul SRms
– 'Can-can'	EPla MBri
I – 'Cole's Variety'	CBlo MBar MBlu
– 'Collyer's Gold'	EHul LCon SRms
– 'Copper Kettle'	CBlo CKen EBee EHul LCon MBar MPla SLim WLRN
– 'Cuprea'	CKen CNic CWLN EHul ESis LLin MBar
– 'Doone Valley'	CKen CMHG EHul EOrn MBar NHol WAbe
– 'Dura'	CDoC
– 'Fastigiata' 🏆	CMac
– 'Gelderland'	EHul
– 'Gracilis Aurea'	CBlo ECho EHul MPla WBcn
– 'Hillieri'	EHul EPla MBar
– 'Irish Gold' (v) 🏆	CAbP CBlo CMac EPla LCon LLin SAga
– 'Rogersii'	CDoC CKen CMHG CMac CWLN EBar EBre EHul EOrn EPot ESis IOrc LCon LLin MAsh MBar MGos MPla NHol SBod SIng SLim SPer SRms SSmi WAbe
– 'Semperaurescens'	CBlo
– 'Stolwijk's Gold'	See ***T. occidentalis* 'Stolwijk'**
– 'Stoneham Gold' 🏆	CDoC CKen CMHG CMac EBre EHul ENHC EOrn IOrc LBee LCon LLin MAsh MBar MPla SBod SLim SMer SPer SRms SSmi
– 'Winter Pink' (v)	CBlo CKen
– 'Zebrina' (v)	CB&S CDoC CMHG CMac EHul EOrn LBee LCon LLin MAsh MBal MBar MGos MWat NBee NEgg NFla NWea SBod SLim SPer WGwG WWin

THUJOPSIS (Cupressaceae)

dolabrata 🏆	CB&S CGre EHul IOrc MBar NHed NWea SHBN SPer WFar WWat
– 'Aurea' (v)	CDoC CKen EHul EOrn LCon MBar MGos SAga SHBN SLim
– 'Laetevirens'	See ***T. dolabrata* 'Nana'**
§ – 'Nana'	CDoC CKen CMac EHul EOrn ESis LCon LLin MBar MPla SLim SRms STre
– 'Variegata'	CDoC CMac EHul EOrn ESis LCon LLin MBal MBar NHed NHol SHFr SLim WDin WLRN
koraiensis	See ***Thuja koraiensis***

THUNBERGIA (Acanthaceae)

alata	CPlN MBri
¶ ***coccinea***	CPlN
erecta	CB&S CPlN ECon ELan LChe
– 'Alba'	LChe
fragrans	CPlN
grandiflora 🏆	CPlN ECon ELan LChe LCns SLMG SOWG

– 'Alba' CPlN LChe SLMG
gregorii CPlN LChe
¶ *laurifolia* CPlN
mysorensis ♀ CPlN ECon ERea
natalensis CHan LChe
¶ *petersiana* CPlN

THYMUS † (Lamiaceae)

'Anderson's Gold' See ***T.* × *citriodorus* 'Bertram Anderson'**
azoricus See ***T. caespititius***
'Belle Orchard' WRHF
'Bidwells' MRav
§ *caespititius* CArn CInt CLyd CShe ELau EPar EPot GAbr GDra GGar GPoy ILis LHol LLWP MBro MHig MRPP MSte NHex NMen NNrd NRya SSmi WCHb WHil WPer
– 'Aureus' ECha EGar GBar LHol SIde
camphoratus CBod CMea EHyt ELau EOHP EWes LHop MWat NHex SIde WApp WJek
carnosus LFis NHol SAxl SIng SSmi
'Carol Ann' (v) EWes LLWP NLak
¶ *cephalotos* EHyt
ciliatus LLWP WPer
cilicicus CLyd CPBP EHyt ESis EWes GCHN MChe MHig NRoo SBla WCHb WJek WPer WWye
× *citriodorus* CArn CDoC ELau ESiP GAbr GCHN GPoy MChe NHex NMen NOak WApp WHen WJek WOMN WOak WPer WWye
– 'Archer's Gold' EBre EHoe ELau EPot ESis GAbr LBee LGro LHop LLWP MBri MHig MRPP NHex NSti SChu SMer SRms SSmi WCHb WHil WJek WPat WPer
– 'Argenteus' LLWP MBro
– 'Aureus' ♀ CShe EBre EMNN ESis GBar GDra GTou LLWP MBal MBar MBri MBro MFos NFla NMen NNrd NRoo NWCA SBla SIng SRms WHen WHoo WPyg
♦ – 'Aureus' misapplied See ***T.* × *citriodorus* 'Golden Lemon'**
§ – 'Bertram Anderson' ♀ CArn CShe CTri EBre ECha EMNN GCHN LBee LHol LLWP MBro MHig NGre NHex NHol NMen NNrd NRoo NRya SBla SMac SSmi WAbe WDav WHoo WPLl WWin WWye
– 'Fragrantissimus' CArn CChr CJew EOHP ESis GAbr GPoy LHol LLWP MChe MWat NHex NPri NRoo SIde WJek WPer WWye
§ – 'Golden King' (v) EBre ECha ELan EPar LBee LHop LLWP MBar MBri MBro MChe NGre NHex NSti SAga WApp WCHb WHil WHoo WPer WSel WStI
§ – 'Golden Lemon' (v) CArn EOHP GPoy LLWP WJek WWye
– 'Golden Queen' (v) CLTr CMea ELau EOHP EPot GBar NLak NPri NRoo NSla SMrm WRHF WWin
– 'Nyewoods' GAbr MGra SIde
× *citriodorus repandus* SIde
× *citriodorus* 'Silver Posie' See ***T. vulgaris* 'Silver Posie'**
– 'Silver Queen' (v) ♀ CB&S CLyd CShe ECha ELan EOHP EPar GAul GDra GPoy MBal MBar MChe MHig NGre NHex NRoo SSmi WHoo WPyg WStI WWye
§ – 'Variegatus' CJew ESis LGro LHol LHop MBri MBro MChe MPla NGre NMen WEas WWin
♦ – 'Variegatus' misapplied See ***T.* × *citriodorus* 'Golden King'**
comosus CNic CPBP ESis LHol LLWP MChe MGra NTow SIde WHoo WPer
'Desboro' GAbr LLWP NHex NHol NNrd
doerfleri CLyd CShe ECha EGoo ELau EOHP GBar LHol LLWP NMen WPat WPer WSel WWye
– 'Bressingham' CArn CMea EBre ECtt ELau EMNN GAbr LBee LGro LHol LHop LLWP MBro MChe MHig MPla NGre NHex NHol NMen NNrd NRoo SBla SRms SSmi WHoo WPat WPer WPyg WWye
'Doone Valley' (v) CArn CSev EBre EFou ELan EPot ESis GCHN GTou LGro LHol LHop LLWP MBal MBar MBri MChe MPla MRPP NGre NHol NNor NNrd NRoo SBla SIng WAbe WHoo WOak
drucei See ***T. polytrichus*** subsp. ***britannicus***
'E.B. Anderson' See ***T.* × *citriodorus* 'Bertram Anderson'**
'Emma's Pink' NHex
erectus See ***T. vulgaris* 'Erectus'**
* *ericoides* MGra
* – 'Aureus' CArn EHal EPot SBla
'Golden Icing' MGra
§ 'Hartington Silver' (v) Widely available
herba-barona CArn CHad CTri ECha ELau ESis GAbr GBar GDra GPoy LHol LLWP MBal NHex NHol NNor NRoo NVic SIde SIng SRms SSmi WApp WOak WPer WWye
– *citrata* See ***T. herba-barona* 'Lemon-scented'**
§ – 'Lemon-scented' CArn ELau GPoy LLWP NHex NHol
'Highland Cream' See ***T.* 'Hartington Silver'**
* *hirsutus minus* CNic
hyemalis SIde
integer SBla
lanuginosus hort. See ***T. pseudolanuginosus***
¶ 'Lavender Sea' EWes LLWP
'Lemon Caraway' See ***T. herba-barona* 'Lemon-scented'**
leucotrichus CLyd GAbr ILis MHig SSmi WPat
'Lilac Time' EWes LLWP
longicaulis CArn EBar ECha EGoo LHol NHex SIde WJek WWye
marschallianus See ***T. pannonicus***
mastichina CArn CDoC ESis GBar LHol LHop MChe SBla SChu SMac SSca WPer WWye
– 'Didi' LLWP NHex
membranaceus CLyd EHyt EWes

micans	See ***T. caespititius***
I ***minus***	See ***Calamintha nepeta***
montanus	See ***T. pulegioides***
Waldstein & Kitaibel	
neiceffii	CArn CLyd ECha EGoo GAbr GBar LHol LLWP MHig NHex NTow SIde WPer
nummularius	ELau LGro SSca
odoratissimus	See ***T. pallasianus*** subsp. ***pallasianus***
'Onyx'	CLyd NHex NMen
pallasianus	ELau LLWP
§ – subsp. ***pallasianus***	CBod GBar GCal SIde WOak
§ ***pannonicus***	LLWP MGra NHex WPer
¶ 'Pink Ripple'	EWes LLWP MChe
'Pinkushion'	LLWP NHol SIng
§ ***polytrichus***	ECWi NHol NMir
§ – subsp. ***britannicus***	CKin EEls EPot EWFC GPoy LLWP MFos MHew NMen NSti WJek WPer WWye
§ – – 'Albus' 🏆	CHid ELan LBee LLWP
– – 'Minus'	EPot LLWP WPer
'Porlock'	CDoC CMea CSev EBar ELau ESis GPoy LHol LLWP MChe NHex NHol SRms WHoo WJek WPer WPyg
praecox	See ***T. polytrichus***
– subsp. ***arcticus***	See ***T. polytrichus*** subsp. ***britannicus***
§ ***pseudolanuginosus***	CArn CMea EBar ECha ELau GTou LBee LGro LHol LLWP MBar MBri MBro MRPP NFla NGre NHex NHol NNrd NRya NSti SHFr SRms SSmi WAbe WHoo WOak WPer WPyg
– 'Hall's Variety'	CHal
§ ***pulegioides***	CArn CBod CJew ELau GBar GPoy LHol LLWP MBri NHex NPri NRoo WJek WOak WPer WRHF WWye
'Redstart'	LBee LLWP WHil
richardii subsp. ***nitidus***	CShe LHol MGra WWye
– subsp. ***nitidus albus***	LLWP SSmi WPer
♦– subsp. ***nitidus***	See ***T. richardii*** subsp. ***nitidus***
'Compactus Albus'	**'Snow White'**
– – 'Peter Davis'	CArn CBod CMea CShe EBar EOHP ESis LHop MChe MGra MPla NHex NMen NTow SBla SChu WJek
§ – – 'Snow White'	EGoo EWes GBar LLWP MPla NBus NMen SIde WJek
rotundifolius	ELau LLWP SIde
¶ 'Ruby Glow'	EBre EWes LLWP MChe MGra NHex NRoo
serpyllum	CArn ELan ELau GAbr GCHN LLWP MBri MChe MPla MWat NOak SRms WJek WPer WRHF WWtk WWye
– var. ***albus***	CHal CShe ECha ELau EMNN ESis GDra GPoy GTou LLWP MBal MBro MHar NNrd NRoo NVic SBla SChu SMac SRms WHoo WOak WWye
– 'Albus Variegatus'	See ***T.* 'Hartington Silver'**
– 'Annie Hall'	CDoC CHal EBre EMNN EPot ESis GAbr LBee LGro LHol LLWP MBro MChe NHex NHol NMen NNor NNrd NRoo SBod SIng SSmi WHil WPer WWye
¶ – 'Carol Ann' (v)	CBod

– ***coccineus*** 🏆	CArn CShe ECha ELan EMNN EPot ESis GDra GTou LGro LHol LLWP MBal MBar MBri MBro MChe MHig MRPP MWat NHol NNrd NRoo SBla SIng WCla WHoo WOak WPat WWin
– 'Major'	EPPr GDra SIde WJek
– 'Minor'	EBre GAri GTou MChe NRoo
* – × ***zygis sylvestris***	ECho
–'Dartmoor'	GCal LLWP
– 'East Lodge'	LLWP
– 'Elfin'	CArn CLyd EPot ESis EWes GBar GTou LBee LHol MBri MBro MHar NGre NMen NNrd NWCA WAbe WCla WDav WHoo WPat
– 'Flossy'	LLWP NNrd
– 'Fulney Red'	EWes LLWP
– 'Goldstream'	CDoC CHal CLyd CMea ELau EMNN GAbr LBee LBuc LHop LLWP MBar MBri MChe MOne NHol NNrd NRoo NSti SRms WCHb WPer WWye
– subsp. ***lanuginosus***	See ***T. pseudolanuginosus***
– 'Lavender Sea'	See ***T.* 'Lavender Sea'**
– 'Lemon Curd'	CBod CDoC EOHP GAbr GBar LLWP MChe NSti SIde SMer WCHb WJek WRha WSel WWye
– 'Minimus'	CArn CDoC CHal CLyd ECha ELau EPPr ESis GAbr LHol MBri MChe NSti NTow SIde WOMN WPat WPer WRHF WSel WWye
§ – 'Minor'	CArn ELan EMNN EPot ESis GDra LBee LHol MBro MChe MHig NHol NMen NNrd NRya NSla SIng SSmi WAbe WCla WDav WHoo WPyg WWin
* – 'Minor Albus'	GBar
– 'Minus'	See ***T. serpyllum* 'Minor'**
– 'Petite'	EWes
– 'Pink Chintz' 🏆	Widely available
– 'Pink Ripple'	See ***T.* 'Pink Ripple'**
– subsp. ***pulchellus***	LLWP
– 'Rainbow Falls' (v)	CBod EWes GAbr GBar LLWP MChe NCat NHex NRoo SIde WPLI
– 'Roseus'	EOHP GBar
– 'Ruby Glow'	See ***T.* 'Ruby Glow'**
– 'Russetings'	CDoC CHal CLyd EMNN EPot LHol LLWP MBar MChe NHex NHol NMen NNrd NRoo SRms WOak WWin WWye
– 'September'	LLWP NHol WAbe
– 'Snowdrift'	CHal CMea EGar EOHP GBar LHol MBar MBro MChe NHex NHol NSti SIde SSmi WAbe WJek WPat WPer WRHF
– 'Splendens'	GMaP LLWP
– 'Variegatus'	See ***T.* 'Hartington Silver'**
– 'Vey'	CWan EGle EPPr ESis EWes GBar LLWP MChe NHex NHol SIng WMaN
¶ ***sibthorpii***	CArn
N 'Silver Posie'	See ***T. vulgaris* 'Silver Posie'**
sp. from Turkey	EPPr EWes LLWP
* ***taeniensis***	CArn
§ ***villosus***	CBot ESis

vulgaris	CArn CChe CSev ECha ELau GPoy LLWP MBar MBri MChe MHew NHex NRoo NVic SDix WJek WPer
– ***albus***	EOHP GBar LLWP NHex SIde
– ***aureus***	GBar LGro LLWP MChe NRoo WJek WSel
§ – 'Erectus'	CArn CLyd ELan ELau GBar LHol LLWP NTow SIde SRms WHer WPer WWye
– French	LLWP
– 'Lucy'	GBar LLWP SIde WJek
– 'Pinewood'	GPoy
– pink	LLWP
– 'Silver Pearl' (v)	EWes LLWP
§ – 'Silver Posie'	Widely available
– Turkish	ELau EOHP
zygis	CArn LHol

THYSANOTUS (Anthericaceae)

See Plant Deletions

TIARELLA (Saxifragaceae)

collina	See ***T. wherryi***
cordifolia ♀	Widely available
– 'Oakleaf'	CSte GCal SAxl SMrm WPbr
'Darkeyes'	WCot
'Eco Red Heart'	WPbr
'Elizabeth Oliver'	WThi
'Filigree Lace'	WThi
'Glossy'	GBuc SAxl WCot WPbr
lanciniate runner	WPbr
'Martha Oliver'	WPbr WThi
'Pinwheel'	NCat WCot
polyphylla	CLyd ELan EPar GAbr GBin LGro MRav NBro NNor NOrc NSti WCla WCra WCru WFar WWhi WWye
– 'Moorgrün'	GCal WWat
– pink	CGle CLTr EPar SAxl SWas
'Slick Rock'	WThi
'Tiger Stripe'	EBee MMil WCot WThi
trifoliata	CArc ELan LGan MRav SBla WPbr
– 'Incarnadine'	ECha EMon
unifoliata	NCat
§ ***wherryi*** ♀	CGle CHad CLyd CRow ECha ELan GAbr GCHN LGre MBri MTho NBrk NBro NFla NNor NOrc SBla SMac SPer WAbe WEas WHil WHoo WPer WWat WWin WWye
– 'Bronze Beauty'	CMea CMil CRDP EBee ECha EPar GBuc MCLN MRav NLak NPro SAga SAxl SUsu SWas WAbe WCot WPbr
– fig-leaved	WPbr WThi
– 'George Schenk'	WThi
– 'Pink Foam'	ECha

TIBOUCHINA (Melastomataceae)

* 'Edwardsii'	CBar CLTr CSev LChe LHil MLan NPSI SMrm
¶ ***grandifolia***	LHil
¶ ***granulosa***	EOHP
graveolens	ERea
holosericea 'Elsa'	ECon
'Jules'	ECon ERea
laxa 'Noelene'	ECon
– 'Skylab'	ECon
organensis	CB&S ERea GQui LBlm LChe
paratropica	CLTr CPle CSev LChe LHil
semidecandra	See ***T. urvilleana***
§ ***urvilleana*** ♀	CAbb CB&S CDoC CGre CHEx CPlN CPle CSPN CSpe CWit EBak ELan ERea IOrc ISea LBlm LCns LHop LPan SArc SBid SLMG SOWG SPer SRms SVen
– 'Grandiflora'	IBlr LHil

TIGRIDIA (Iridaceae)

hybrids	SDeJ
lutea	SDeJ
pavonia	CGre LAma LBow MBri NCut NRog

TILIA † (Tiliaceae)

americana	CLnd CMCN ENot WMou
– 'Dentata'	WMou
– 'Fastigiata'	WMou
– 'Nova'	CDoC CTho WMou
– 'Redmond'	CTho WMou
amurensis	CMCN WMou
argentea	See ***T. tomentosa***
begoniifolia	See ***T. dasystyla***
caucasica	WMou
– 'Select'	WMou
– 'Winter Red'	WMou
¶ 'Chelsea Sentinel'	WMou
¶ ***chenmoui***	WMou
chinensis	WMou
chingiana	CMCN WHCr WMou
cordata ♀	CDul CKin CLnd CPer ELan ENot GRei IOrc LBuc LHyr MBal NBee NWea SHBN SPer WDin WMou WStI WWye
– 'Erecta'	WMou
– 'Greenspire' ♀	CDoC CDul CLnd CTho ENot IOrc LPan SLPl WMou WOrn
– 'Len Parvin'	WMou
– 'Lico'	WMou
– 'Morden'	WMou
– 'Plymtree Gold'	CTho WMou
– 'Rancho'	WMou
– 'Roelvo'	WMou
– 'Swedish Upright'	CTho WMou
– 'Umbrella'	WMou
– 'Westonbirt Dainty Leaf'	WMou
– 'Winter Orange'	MBlu WMou
§ ***dasystyla***	WMou
× ***euchlora*** ♀	CDoC CDul CLnd EBee ENot EPfP LPan MBri MGos MWat NWea SPer WDin WFar WMou WOrn WStI
× ***europaea***	CDul CLnd ELan WMou
– 'Pallida'	CDul CTho WMou
– 'Pendula'	WMou
– 'Wratislaviensis' ♀	CBlo CDoC CDul CTho LBuc MBlu SMad WMou
– 'Zwarte Linde'	WMou
× ***flavescens*** 'Glenleven'	WMou
¶ 'Harold Hillier'	WMou
henryana	CEnd CLnd CMCN MBlu SMad WMou
– var. ***subglabra***	WMou
§ ***heterophylla***	CTho WMou
– var. ***michauxii***	WMou
'Hillieri'	See ***T. 'Harold Hillier'***

insularis	MBlu WMou
intonsa	WMou
japonica	CMCN WHCr WMou
kiusiana	CMCN WMou
ledebourii	WMou
mandshurica	WMou
maximowicziana	SSta WMou
¶ ***mexicana***	WMou
miqueliana	WMou
'Moltkei'	WMou
mongolica ♀	CDul CLnd CMCN ENot GAri WMou
monticola	See ***T. heterophylla***
neglecta	WMou
oliveri	CMCN CTho WMou
'Orbicularis'	WMou
paucicostata	WMou
'Petiolaris' ♀	CDoC CDul CEnd CLnd CTho EBee ELan ENot EPfP IOrc LHyr NBee NWea SHBN SMad SPer SSta WDin WMou
platyphyllos	CDoC CDul CKin CMCN ENot GRei LBuc NWea SPer WDin WHut WMou
– 'Aurea'	CTho WMou
– 'Corallina'	See ***T. platyphyllos* 'Rubra'**
– 'Delft'	WMou
– 'Erecta'	See ***T. platyphyllos* 'Fastigiata'**
§ – 'Fastigiata'	CDul CTho ENot MAsh SLPl WMou
– 'Grandiflora'	WMou
– 'Laciniata'	CEnd CMCN CTho SMad WMou
– 'Orebro'	SLPl WMou
– 'Pannonia'	WMou
* – 'Pendula'	CTho
– 'Prince's Street'	WMou
§ – 'Rubra' ♀	CDoC CLnd CTho EBee ENot IOrc LHyr MBri MGos NBee NWea SHhN WDin WMou
– 'Tortuosa'	SMad WMou
– 'Vitifolia'	WMou
tarquetii	WMou
§ ***tomentosa***	CDul CLnd CMCN CTho NWea SEND SHhN WDin WMou
– 'Brabant' ♀	CDoC ENot IOrc SPer WMou
– 'Erecta'	WMou
– 'Silver Globe'	WMou
– 'Szeleste'	WMou
– 'Van Koolwijk'	MBlu WMou
tuan	WMou

TILLAEA See CRASSULA

TILLANDSIA (Bromeliaceae)

abdita	MBri
acostae	MBri
argentea	MBri
baileyi	MBri
balbisiana	MBri
benthamiana	See ***T. erubescens***
brachycaulos	MBri
– var. ***multiflora***	MBri
bulbosa	MBri
butzii	MBri
caput-medusae	MBri
circinnatoides	MBri
cyanea	MBri
x ***erographica***	MBri
* ***fasciculata*** 'Tricolor' (v)	MBri
filifolia	MBri
flabellata	MBri
ionantha	MBri
– var. ***scaposa***	See ***T. kolbii***
juncea	MBri
§ ***kolbii***	MBri
magnusiana	MBri
§ ***matudae***	MBri
oaxacana	MBri
polystachia	MBri
punctulata	MBri
seleriana	MBri
sphaerocephala	MBri
tenuifolia var. ***surinamensis***	See ***T. tenuifolia* var. *tenuifolia***
tricolor var. ***melanocrater***	MBri
valenzuelana	See ***T. variabllis***
velickiana	See ***T. matudae***
vicentina	MBri
wagneriana	MBri
xerographica	MBri

TINANTIA (Commelinaceae)

See Plant Deletions

TIPUANA (Papilionaceae)

See Plant Deletions

TITHONIA (Asteraceae)

rotundifolia 'Torch'	SMrm

TOFIELDIA (Melanthiaceae)

calyculata	NHol

TOLMIEA (Saxifragaceae)

'Goldsplash'	See ***T. menziesii* 'Taff's Gold'**
menziesii ♀	CGle CHEx CWGN EBar ECha GAri LGro MBri NHol NOrc NRai WByw WFox
– JLS 86284CLOR	EMon
– 'Maculata'	See ***T. menziesii* 'Taff's Gold'**
§ – 'Taff's Gold' (v) ♀	CGle CMHG CRow CWGN ECha EFol EHoe ELan EOHP EPar GAul MBri MCLN MRav NHol NMir NNor NRoo NSti NVic SHel WBea WByw WEas WHil WHoo WOve WPyg WWye
– 'Variegata'	See ***T. menziesii* 'Taff's Gold'**

TOLPIS (Asteraceae)

barbata	MSal

TONESTUS (Asteraceae)

§ ***lyallii***	CWan MHar NWCA WPer WWin

TOONA (Meliaceae)

§ ***sinensis***	CChu CMCN CPle EMil ISea MBri
– 'Flamingo' (v)	CB&S CPMA EBee EMil

TORENIA (Scrophulariaceae)

concolor formosana B&SWJ 124	WCru
'Summerwave'	SCoo

TORREYA (Taxaceae)

See Plant Deletions

TORTULA (Sphagnaceae)

See Plant Deletions

TOVARA See PERSICARIA

TOWNSENDIA (Asteraceae)

condensata	MFos
exscapa	MFos
¶ – NNS 93-74	MRPP
florifera	CLyd MFos
formosa	CInt CLyd NBir NMen NNrd WOMN WWin
hookeri	CGra MFos WHil
incana	CGra MFos
leptotes	NWCA
mensana	NMen NTow
montana	CGra NTow WDav
parryi	CGra MFos NTow
§ ***rothrockii***	CPBP NMen NWCA
¶ sp. from California	CGra
spathulata	CGra EHyt MFos NTow
wilcoxiana hort.	See ***T. rothrockii***

TRACHELIUM (Campanulaceae)

§ ***asperuloides***	EPot
caeruleum ♀	CLTr EPad ERea LFis SBid WCot
– 'Purple Umbrella'	CSam WLRN
– 'White Umbrella'	CLTr WLRN
¶ ***jacquinii***	CPBP
– subsp. ***rumelianum***	CArc CPBP EPad MBro NTow NWCA WPat WPyg
¶ ***rumelianum***	WHoo

TRACHELOSPERMUM (Apocynaceae)

§ ***asiaticum*** ♀	CB&S CBot CChu CHan CMac CPlN CRHN CTrw EBre ELan EMil EPla GQui ISea LPri MBal MGos NHed NPal SArc SBra SHBN SPer SSpi SSta WPat WSHC WWat
– 'Aureum'	LRHS
– 'Goshiki'	CB&S GQui MGos SPer SSpi
– var. ***intermedium***	CFil WPGP
* ***bodinieri*** 'Cathayensis'	GCal
jasminoides ♀	CB&S CHEx CMCN CMac CPlN CPle CSam CSpe CTbh EMil ERea GOrc GQui IHos IOrc LHop LPan MBri MRav NPal SArc SBra SDry SLMG SPer SReu SSpi SSta WBod WWat
§ – 'Japonicum'	GCal NSti SBra
– 'Major'	CSPN SSpi
– 'Oblanceolatum'	GCal
– 'Tricolor' (v)	CRHN SMur SSta
– 'Variegatum' ♀	CB&S CBot CChu CMac COtt CTrw EBar ELan ERav ERea GCal GQui LHop MRav MSta NPal SApp SArc SHBN SLMG SPer SReu SSpi SSta WPat WSHC WWat
– 'Wilsonii' W 776	CBot CMac CPlN CSPN EBre EHic ELan EMil ETen GCal IOrc MSta MUlv SArc SLMG SPer SReu SSpi SSta WCru WWat
majus hort.	See ***T. jasminoides* 'Japonicum'**
– Nakai	See ***T. asiaticum***
sp. from Nanking, China	CHan

TRACHYCARPUS (Arecaceae)

§ ***fortunei*** ♀	Widely available
martianus	LPal
nanus	LPal
* ***oreophilus***	LPal
* ***sikkimensis***	LPal
wagnerianus	LPal NPal SDry

TRACHYMENE (Apiaceae)

See Plant Deletions

TRACHYSTEMON (Boraginaceae)

orientalis	CGle CHEx CRDP CSev EBre ECha EFou EGol ELan EPar EPla ERav MFir MRav MUlv NPSI SAxl SIng WCru WGwG WHer WWat WWin

TRADESCANTIA (Commelinaceae)

albiflora	See ***T. fluminensis***
x ***andersoniana***	MBro MFir MSal NNor WEas WFox WHil WPer WRHF WWin
– 'Bilberry Ice'	CSte EFou LFis MUlv NTow WSan
– 'Blaby Blue'	MUlv
– 'Blue Stone'	CMea CSpe ECha EMou EPla GLil NFai NPri NRya SRms WFar WThi
– 'Caerulea Plena'	See ***T. virginiana* 'Caerulea Plena'**
◆ – Carmine Glow	See ***T.* x *andersoniana* 'Karminglut'**
– 'Charlotte'	CSte MGrG NCut
– 'Croftway Blue'	SCro
– 'Domaine de Courson'	CHan
– 'Innocence'	CSpe EBre ECha ECtt EFou ELan EOrc EPla GMaP LHop MBel MBri MHFP MTho MUlv NCat NFai NOrc NRoo SPer WHoo WMer WRus
– 'Iris Prichard'	CHan CM&M CMGP CMil EBee EBre ELan EPar EPla GMaP LHop MHFP SChu SCro SEas WGwG
– 'Isis' ♀	CB&S CKel CMil CSpe EBre ECED ECtt EFou ELan EPar EPla GCHN LFis LHop MRav MUlv NFai NOrc NRoo SChu SLMG SPer SSoC WAbe WCer WTyr WWin
– 'J.C. Weguelin' ♀	CBlo EMil EPfP MBri NFai SRms WHoo WPnn WPyg
§ – 'Karminglut'	CB&S ELan EOrc EPar EPla GCHN GMaP MHFP NOrc NRoo NVic SHam WCer WHoo WPbr WPnn WRHF WRus
– 'Leonora'	CDoC CSte EAst ENot NCut NFai SHam WRHF WThi
– 'Little Doll'	WCot
– 'Maiden's Blush'	CHal CSpe NCut WFoF
– 'Osprey' ♀	CRDP CSpe EBre ECha EFou ELan ENot EOrc EPla LWak MNrw MTho NBro NDea NOak NOrc NPri NSti NWes SPer WEas WMer WPbr WPnn WTyr WWin

– 'Pauline' EBre ECro ECtt EFou EMan EPla GCHN MBel MRav MUlv NBir NFai NRoo SChu SUsu WCer WGwG WHoo WPyg WSan WWin
– 'Purewell Giant' CKel CTri ECot EPla NBro NCat SChu SPer WGor WHoo WKif WPyg
– 'Purple Dome' CHan CKel CMGP CNic CRDP EBre ECED ECtt EFou EPla GCHN GMaP MRav NBir NCat NFai NMir NWes WCer WHoo WPbr WPyg WTyr
– 'Rubra' CDoC CMea CSte EBee LFis MBel NDea NFai NOrc NPri SChu SCro SLod SRms
– 'Valour' CBlo GLil NCut WHil WTyr
– 'Zwanenburg Blue' CKni CMGP CSte EBre ECha ECro EFou EOrc EPla GCHN LFis MUlv NFai SEas WMer WPnn WRus

¶ ***blossfeldiana*** SLMG
bracteata NTow
bracteata alba SEas WThi
brevicaulis CMon ECha ECro EFou EPar EPla GBuc GDra MBel MTho NOrc SLMG
canaliculata See ***T. ohiensis***
'Chedglow' LHop
fluminensis 'Albovittata' CHal SLMG
– 'Aurea' 🏆 CHal MBri
– 'Laekenensis' (v) MBri
– 'Quicksilver' (v) 🏆 CHal MBri
multiflora See ***Tripogandra multiflora***
navicularis See ***Callisia navicularis***
§ ***ohiensis*** EBee EMan LPBA MHFP
§ ***pallida*** CHal IBlr
pendula See ***T. zebrina***
sillamontana 🏆 CHal LChe MBri
♦ ***tricolor*** See ***T. zebrina***
¶ ***virginiana*** SMrm
– 'Alba' GCal WPer WThi
§ – 'Caerulea Plena' CArc CHan CM&M CMGP CSpe ECED EFou ELan EMan EPla LHop SChu SLod WGwG WThi
– 'Rubra' CHan CM&M EAst NCut WThi
'White Domino' CSte
§ ***zebrina*** 🏆 CHal SLMG SVen
– ***pendula*** See ***T. zebrina***

TRAGOPOGON (Asteraceae)

porrifolius CJew ILis NLak WWye
pratensis CArn CKin CPou ECWi EWFC NMir
roseus See ***T. ruber***

TRAPA (Trapaceae)

natans CWGN MSta

TREVESIA (Araliaceae)

See Plant Deletions

TRICHOCOLEA (Trichocoleaceae)

See Plant Deletions

TRICHOPETALUM (Anthericaceae)

§ ***plumosum*** CBro

TRICHOPHORUM (Cyperaceae)

See Plant Deletions

TRICHOSANTHES (Cucurbitaceae)

cucumerina CPlN

TRICHOSTEMA (Lamiaceae)

¶ ***lanatum*** SHFr

TRICUSPIDARIA See CRINODENDRON

TRICYRTIS (Convallariaceae)

'Adbane' CBro ELan MBri MUlv WCru WPbr
affinis GBuc
– 'Variegata' SAxl WCru
bakeri See ***T. latifolia***
'Citronella' CM&M
'Emily' CM&M
formosana 🏆 CAvo CDoC CGle CInt CKel CWGN EAst EBre ECha ECro ECtt EGol ELan GCra MBri MTho MUlv SAxl SBla SCro SEas SMac WCru WEas WGwG WHil WMer WPbr WPer WThi WWye
– B&SWJ 306 WCru
– 'Dark Beauty' MCLN
– forms SEas WCru WPer
– 'Shelley's' EBee GCal NBro
§ – Stolonifera Group CAvo CB&S CBro CHan CM&M ECha EFou EGol ELan LHop MBal MRav MUlv NDea NFai SAxl SCro SPer WFar WHil WPbr WRus WThi WWat WWin
'Golden Gleam' WCot
§ ***hirta*** CB&S CBro CHan CSam EBre ECtt EFou GMaP MBri MBro MRav MTho MUlv NBro NFai NHol SCro SIng WAbe WBea WCru WHoo WOMN WRus WWat
§ – ***alba*** CBro CHan CWGN ELan MBal MBel MBro WCru WHoo WPbr WThi WWat WWin
– hybrids CM&M WCru WPbr
– 'Makinoi Gold' EBee MRav
– 'Miyazaki' CArc CChu CFir CHan EAst EFou EGar EGle ELan EMan EPar GBuc GCra GMaP MBel MUlv NLak SCro WCru WHoo WPbr WThi WWat
* – 'Nana' ELan
– 'Variegata' CLon ECha EFol EGol GBuc SMad WCot WCru WHil WPbr
– 'White Flame' (v) WCot WPbr
N Hototogisu CMea EBee EGle EMon EPar MTho WCot WPbr
* ***iishiana*** WPbr
japonica See ***T. hirta***
'Kohaku' EBee WCru WPbr
§ ***latifolia*** CBro CChu CGle CHad CHan EFou ELan GCra GMaP MBro MNrw NFai SAxl SWas WCot WCru WHil WHoo WPbr WPer WThi WWat WWye
'Lilac Towers' EPar WCru WKif WPbr
macrantha MBal SIng
– subsp. ***macranthopsis*** SWas WCru

* ***macrocarpa***	NFai
N ***macropoda***	CChu CGle CLon CMGP CPea CSam EGar ELan EMan EPar GGar GMaP NBus NHol NWCA SAga WThi
– B&SWJ 1271	WCru
¶ ***maculata*** HWJCM 470	WCru
¶ ***nana***	WCru
ohsumiensis	CChu CGle CHan CLon ECha ELan EPar EPot LGre MTho WCot WCru WPbr WThi
perfoliata	SWas WCru WThi
'Shimone'	CBro ELan LRHS MBri MUlv SOkh WCru WKif WPbr
stolonifera	See ***T. formosana* Stolonifera Group**
'Tojen'	CAvo CBro ECha EGar ELan LRHS MBri MMil NBro NTay SOkh WCru WPbr
'White Towers'	CFee CHid ECha EPar GCra MBel NBus NCut NSti SAga SAxl SOkh SWas WBea WCru WPbr WSan WThi

TRIDENS (Poaceae)

See Plant Deletions

TRIENTALIS (Primulaceae)

europaea rosea	CNat

TRIFOLIUM (Papilionaceae)

alpinum	GDra SIng
arvense	ECWi
campestre	CKin
incarnatum	SIde WHer
medium	ECWi
ochroleucum	EWFC
pannonicum	EPla GCal MBel MHlr MSte MTol SMrm SUsu WCot WRus
pratense	CTiv ECWi EWFC
– 'Chocolate'	See ***T. pratense* 'Purple Velvet'**
– 'Dolly North'	See ***T. pratense* 'Susan Smith'**
– 'Ice Cool'	See ***T. repens* 'Green Ice'**
– 'Speech House'	WAlt
§ – 'Susan Smith' (v)	CArc CElw CLyd CRow ECha EFol EHal EMar EMon EWes IBlr LHop MHar MSCN MTho WBea WByw WHer WHil WPri WRHF
repens	CHEx EWFC LWak NCat NGre
– 'Aureum'	MBal
– 'Gold Net'	See ***T. pratense* 'Susan Smith'**
– 'Good Luck'	CRow MTho WAlt
§ – 'Green Ice'	CBre CInt CSev EMan EWes LHop MTho WAlt WCot WRus
– 'Harlequin'	CBre
– 'Pale Centre'	WAlt
– 'Pentaphyllum'	See ***T. repens* 'Quinquefolium'**
– 'Purpurascens'	CArn CBre CHEx CInt CLyd CRow EBar GCal GDra GMac ILis MBal NRoo SSea WHen WOak WWhi
§ – 'Purpurascens Quadrifolium'	CDec CNic CSev EAst ECha EFol ELan EWes MBel NMir NNrd SIde SIng SPer WOve WPbr WRHF WRus WWin
– 'Quadrifolium'	EHoe EPar
§ – 'Quinquefolium'	WPer
– 'Tetraphyllum Purpureum'	See ***T. repens* 'Purpurascens Quadrifolium'**
– 'Velvet and Baize' (v)	CNat
– 'Wheatfen' (v)	CNat CRow ECha EMan EWes LFlo LHop MTho NCat WAlt WCot WGwy WRus
rubens	CArc EBee EGoo EMan MSte SMrm SSca SUsu WCot WNdy WRus

TRIGONELLA (Papilionaceae)

foenum-graecum	CArn EJud MSal SIde

TRIGONOTIS (Boraginaceae)

rotundifolia	EBee

TRILLIUM † (Trilliaceae)

albidum	CBro SSpi WChr
apetalon	WChr WCru
§ ***catesbyi***	CBro EBee LAma MGrG MSal NRog SSpi WChr WCot WCru
cernuum	CWGN EBre EPot LAma MGrG NRog SBid WChr WCot WCru
chloropetalum ♀	CBro CChu EBre GCra GDra NHol SAxl SSpi WAbb WChr WCru
– subsp. ***giganteum***	MSto
chloropetalum rubrum	CFil SSpi SWas WPGP
cuneatum	CB&S CBro CChu CWGN EBre EHyt ELan EOrc EPar EPot GAbr LAma MDun MTho NRog NRoo SBid SDeJ SPer WAbe WChr WCot WCru
– red	CRDP
erectum ♀	CAvo CB&S CBro CChu CRDP CWGN EBre EHyt ELan EOrc EPot GAbr GDra GPoy LAma LBow LWoo MBal MDun MSal MTho NRog SBid SDeJ SPer SSpi WAbe WChr WCot WHil
§ – f. ***albiflorum***	CBro CRDP EPot LAma MSal SSpi WChr WCot WCru
– 'Beige'	WChr
– f. ***luteum***	GCrs LAma SSpi WChr
flexipes	GCrs WChr
grandiflorum ♀	Widely available
– ***flore-pleno*** ♀	CChu EBre NHar SWas
– 'Snowbunting' (d)	WChr
kamtschaticum	CAvo GCrs LAma WChr WCru
kurabayashii	WChr
§ ***luteum*** ♀	CB&S CBro CWGN EHyt ELan EOrc EPar EPot GAbr LAma LBow MDun NFai NHar NRog NRoo SBid SPer WAbe WChr WCot WCru WFar WHil WRus
nivale	WChr
ovatum	GDra LAma MSto NHol WChr
– var. ***hibbersonii***	CBro GDra MBal NHar NMen NTow WAbe WChr
– 'Wayne Roberts'	WChr
parviflorum	GCrs MSto WChr
pusillum var. ***pusillum***	NHar WChr
– var. ***virginianum***	CBro LAma WCru
recurvatum	CB&S CWGN EBee EOrc EPar EPot LAma NFai NRog NRoo WAbe WChr WCru
rivale ♀	CBro LAma SBla SWas WAbe WChr

– 'Purple Heart' WChr
rugelii LAma WChr WCru
sessile CHEx CMea EBre ELan EPot LAma LBow NBir NHar NHol SPer WChr WCot WCru WRus WSHC WShi
– var. ***luteum*** See ***T. luteum***
smallii LAma WCru
stylosum See ***T. catesbyi***
sulcatum CAvo CBro EPot GDra MDun SSpi WChr WCru
tschonoskii LAma WChr
undulatum CHEx CWGN LAma WCru
vaseyi CBro LAma SSpi WChr
viride ELan EPot LAma WChr WCru

TRINIA (Apiaceae)
* ***grandiflora*** EPla

TRIOSTEUM (Caprifoliaceae)
See Plant Deletions

TRIPETALEIA (Ericaceae)
§ ***bracteata*** MDun

TRIPLEUROSPERMUM (Asteraceae)
See Plant Deletions

TRIPOGANDRA (Commelinaceae)
§ ***multiflora*** CHal

TRIPTEROSPERMUM (Gentianaceae)
japonicum B&SWJ 1168 WCru
lanceolatum B&SWJ 085 WCru
taiwanense B&SWJ 1205 WCru

TRIPTERYGIUM (Celastraceae)
¶ ***regelii*** CPlN

TRISETUM (Poaceae)
flavescens CKin

TRISTAGMA (Alliaceae)
'Rolf Fiedler' See ***Ipheion* 'Rolf Fiedler'**
uniflorum See ***Ipheion uniflorum***

TRISTANIA (Myrtaceae)
conferta See ***Lophostemon confertus***

TRISTANIOPSIS (Myrtaceae)
laurina CPle CTrC

TRISTELLATEIA (Malpighiaceae)
¶ ***australasiae*** CPlN

TRITELEIA (Alliaceae)
californica See ***Brodiaea californica***
grandiflora WCot
hyacintha ETub LAma MFos WChr WCot
¶ ***ixioides*** ERos
– subsp. ***ixioides*** WChr
– var. ***scabra*** WChr
– 'Splendens' ETub
§ ***laxa*** CAvo CMea EHic ELan LAma NRog WCot
§ – 'Koningin Fabiola' CTri ETub LAma MBri NRog
– PJC 951 WChr
♦ – Queen Fabiola See ***T. laxa* 'Koningin Fabiola'**
§ ***peduncularis*** LAma MFos WChr
× ***tubergenii*** LAma WCot WThi
uniflora See ***Ipheion uniflorum***

TRITHRINAX (Arecaceae)
acanthocoma LPal

TRITICUM (Poaceae)
See Plant Deletions

TRITOMA See KNIPHOFIA

TRITONIA (Iridaceae)
crocata LBow NRog SPer
– ***hyalina*** LBow SPer
§ ***disticha*** subsp. ***rubrolucens*** CAvo CBos CBro CChu CElw CFil CHan CMil CPou CSev EBre ECha EMan MBel MBri NRoo SAga SAxl WFar WGer WRHF
lineata LBow SPer
'Orange Delight' LBlm MHlr WCot
rosea See ***T. disticha*** subsp. ***rubrolucens***
securigera CMon
squalida LBow SPer WCot

TROCHETIOPSIS (Sterculiaceae)
melanoxylon EPad LHil

TROCHOCARPA (Epacridaceae)
See Plant Deletions

TROCHODENDRON (Trochodendraceae)
aralioides CB&S CFil CGre CMCN EGol ENot EPfP MBlu MGos SArc SMad SPer SReu SSpi SSta WCoo WCot WCru WSHC WWat

TROLLIUS (Ranunculaceae)
acaulis EGle EWes GDra LHop MTho NGre SMrm WPat WPyg
asiaticus GBuc
§ ***chinensis*** CGle ECha EPot LSyl NCut SWat
– 'Golden Queen' ♀ EBre ECtt EFou ELan EMar LFis MCLN MNrw MRav MUlv MWat NMir NNor NRoo SChu SEas SHel SMac SPer WCru WGor WHen WHil WHoo WPLl WPer
– 'Imperial Orange' CGle WGwG WWin
× ***cultorum*** 'Alabaster' CLon CRDP CRow ECha EGar SMad WSan
– 'Baudirektor Linne' EBre ECtt EGar GCHN LCom MRav NRoo
– Bressingham Hybrids EBre NRoo
– 'Bunce' NCut
– 'Canary Bird' EGol ELan NFla SMur SRms WCot WRus WTre
¶ – 'Cheddar' COtt EFou MRav
– 'Commander-in-chief' COtt EBee EBre
– 'Earliest of All' CDoC CGle EGol MBri NRoo SChu SHig SPla SRms WGor
– 'Etna' MBri
§ – 'Feuertroll' CDoC CWGN ECha LBuc MBri NPro SMur WRus
♦ – Fireglobe See ***T. × cultorum* 'Feuertroll'**

– 'Golden Cup' ECot NRoo
– 'Golden Monarch' CBlo CWGN EPar
– 'Goldquelle' 🏆 EHon NVic SHig SMur
– 'Goliath' CGle CMGP NRoo WFar
– 'Helios' CGle CSam ECha
– 'Lemon Queen' CWGN EBee EPar GCal MBri NCut NNor NRoo SWat WCot WRus
– 'Maigold' MBri
– 'Orange Crest' GCal
– 'Orange Princess' 🏆 CBos CWGN EBee EBre EGar LSyl MBal MBel NBro NDea SHig SPer SRms WCra
– 'Prichard's Giant' WCot WCra
¶ – 'Salamander' SMur
– 'Superbus' 🏆 COtt CRDP ELan EPar MBri NRoo SHig SSpi WCot WRus
europaeus CBot CRow CSam ECha EPot LHil LHop LSyl MBal MBro MNrw NDea NMir NRya SRms SWat WCla WHoo WPer WPnn WPyg WUnd
hondoensis WSan
ledebourii hort. See ***T. chinensis***
pumilus CBos CGle ECha ELan EPar LBee MHig NMGW NNrd NWCA WHil
* – ***albidus*** CRDP
– 'Wargrave' EPot NMen NNrd WPer
stenopetalus ECha
yunnanensis CGle GBuc MBal NGre NWoo

TROPAEOLUM † (Tropaeolaceae)

azureum CPla MSto
brachyceras MSto
ciliatum 🏆 CAvo CChu CFir CHan CMon CPlN CPla CSWP CSam EBre ELan EOrc GCal LBow LWoo MSto MTho SLMG WCru WHer WNor
incisum MSto
majus CHEx EMFW LHol SBid WSel
– 'Alaska' (v) CBod SBid SIde WJek
* – 'Clive Innes' ERea GCra
– 'Crimson Beauty' MHlr MMil WCot WCru
– 'Darjeeling Double' WCru
– 'Empress of India' SBid WEas WJek
– 'Hermine Grashoff' (d) 🏆 CRow CSWP CSpe CTbh ECtt ERea GCal LBlm LHil LHop NHaw SAxl SBid SDix SLod SMad SUsu WEas WHil WLRN
– 'Margaret Long' (d) CSpe LHil WCot WEas WHil WLRN
– 'Peaches and Cream' WJek
– 'Red Wonder' CSWP CSpe GCal LHil SBid SMad SUsu
¶ – Tom Thumb mixed WJek
– 'Variegatum' ERea
peltophorum MSto
pentaphyllum CAvo CRow ECha GCal IBlr LWoo MSto MTho WChr WCot
polyphyllum CPlN GBuc MSto SWas WOMN
sessilifolium EHyt MSto
speciosum 🏆 Widely available
sylvestre WCru
tricolorum 🏆 CAvo CChu CMon CPlN ECha EPot LWoo MTho SDix WChr WCot
tuberosum CB&S CGle CMHG ETub GPoy MBal NSti WAbe WWye
– var. ***lineamaculatum*** 'Ken Aslet' 🏆 CAvo CBro CGle CPlN CRDP CRHN CRow CSam CWit ECha ELan EOrc EPot ERea GCHN IBlr LAma LBow LFis LHop MBal MTho NPSI NRog SSpi WCru WHer WHil WNor WWat
– P.J. Christian's form NRog
– var. ***piliferum*** 'Sidney' CFil CGle IBlr WCru

TSUGA (Pinaceae)

canadensis EHul ENHC GAri GAul LCon MBar NWea SHBN SPer WDin
– 'Abbot's Dwarf' CKen MGos
§ – 'Abbott's Pygmy' CKen
– 'Albospica' ESis LBee LCon
– 'Aurea' (v) LCon MBar SMur
– 'Baldwin Dwarf Pyramid' MBar
– 'Bennett' EHul LCon MBar
– 'Brandley' CKen
§ – 'Branklyn' CKen
– 'Cinnamonea' CKen
– 'Coffin' CKen
– 'Cole's Prostrate' CKen EBre LCon MBar NHol SHBN
– 'Curley' CKen
– 'Curtis Ideal' CKen
– 'Dwarf Whitetip' EPla LCon
– 'Everitt Golden' CKen
– 'Fantana' EHul LBee LCon LLin MBar MOne NHol SBod SLim WLRN
– 'Gentsch Snowflake' CKen EPla MGos
– 'Golden Splendor' EPla
– 'Horsford' CKen
– 'Hussii' CKen
– 'Jacqueline Verkade' CKen
– 'Jeddeloh' 🏆 CChe CDoC EBar EBre EHul ENHC ENot EOrn EPot ESis LCon LLin MBal MBar MBri MGos MPla NBee NHar SLim SPer WPyg WStI
– 'Jervis' CKen LCon
– 'Kingsville Spreader' CKen
I – 'Lutea' CKen
– 'Minuta' CKen EHul EOrn ESis LBee LCon MBar MGos NHar
– 'Nana' CMac EHul IOrc WLRN
– 'Nana Gracilis' See ***T. canadensis* 'Gracilis'**
– 'Palomino' CKen MBar
– 'Pendula' 🏆 CDoC CKen EHul ENot EOrn LBee LCon MBar MBri MOne NHar SLim SPla
– 'Prostrata' See ***T. canadensis* 'Branklyn'**
– 'Pygmaea' See ***T. canadensis* 'Abbott's Pygmy'**
– 'Rugg's Washington' CKen
– 'Verkade Petite' CKen
– 'Verkade Recurved' CKen MBar WBcn
– 'Von Helms' CKen
– 'Warnham' CKen ECho LBee LCon MBri
caroliniana 'La Bar Weeping' CKen
diversifolia EPot
– 'Gotelli' CKen
heterophylla 🏆 CDoC CPer ENot GAri GAul GRei IOrc LBuc LCon MBar NWea SHBN SMad SPer STre WDin
– 'Iron Springs' CKen EOrn
menziesii See ***Pseudotsuga menziesii***

mertensiana 'Elizabeth' CKen
I – 'Glauca Nana' CKen
– 'Quartz Mountain' CKen
¶ *sieboldii* 'Nana' CKen

TSUSIOPHYLLUM (Ericaceae)
tanakae See ***Rhododendron tsusiophyllum***

TUBERARIA (Cistaceae)
guttata SSpi WCru
lignosa CInt CMHG EPot MSto SSpi WAbe WCla WCru

TULBAGHIA † (Alliaceae)
acutiloba CAvo
alliacea CFee LHil WCot
capensis CFee LGre
cepacea CChu LHil NBir WCot
– var. *maritima* CMon LLew WThi
coddii CFee CHan CRow LGre WCot
cominsii CAvo CHan CMon CRow LGre WCot
'Fairy Star' WCot
fragrans See ***T. simmleri***
galpinii CMon WCot
'John May's Special' WCot
'John Rider' WPer
¶ *leucantha* ERos LHil
ludwigiana WCot
natalensis CAvo CHan CMon CPou LGre
– pink WCot
§ *simmleri* CAvo CMon LAma LBlm LLew SSpi WCot
violacea CB&S CBro CChu CHan CMon CPea CPou CRow CSev ECha ERav ETub IBlr LAma LPan MBel MTho SMrm SSpi SUsu SWat
– 'Alba' CPea
– *pallida* CAvo CChu CRDP CRow EBee LGre LHil SAxl SLod SMrm SUsu WCot
§ – 'Silver Lace' (v) CAvo CBrk CChu CFee CGle CHad CHan CRDP CRow CSWP CSpe ELan ERav ERea EWes LGre LHop MTho SIgm SSpi SWas WCot WThi
– *tricolor* CMon
– 'Variegata' See ***T. violacea* 'Silver Lace'**

TULIPA † (Liliaceae)
'Abu Hassan' (3) ETub LAma
acuminata (15) CBro ETub LAma LBow
'Ad Rem' (4) LAma
'Addis' (14) LAma
'African Queen' (3) LAma
aitchisonii See ***T. clusiana***
'Aladdin' (6) LAma NRog
'Alaska' (6) LAma
albertii (15) LAma
'Albino' (3) LAma
aleppensis (15) LAma
'Aleppo' (7) LAma
'Alfred Cortot' (12) 🏆 LAma
'Ali Baba' (14) MBri
'Alice Leclercq' (2) LAma
'All Bright' (5) LAma
'Allegretto' (11) LAma NRog
altaica (15) EPot LAma
amabilis PF 8955 See ***T. hoogiana* PF 8955**
'Ancilla' (12) 🏆 CBro LAma
'Angélique' (11) CAvo ETub EWal LAma MBri NBir
¶ *anisophylla* (15) MSto
'Anne Claire' (3) LAma
'Antwerp' (3) LAma
'Apeldoorn' (4) ETub EWal LAma MBri NRog
'Apeldoorn's Elite' (4) 🏆 LAma NRog
'Apricot Beauty' (1) CAvo ETub LAma MBri NBir NRog WBro
'Apricot Jewel' See ***T. linifolia* (Batalinii Group) 'Apricot Jewel'**
'Apricot Parrot' (10) 🏆 LAma NRog
'Arabian Mystery' (3) CAvo LAma NBir
'Aristocrat' (5) 🏆 CAvo LAma
'Arma' (7) LAma
'Artist' (8) CAvo LAma NBir
'Athleet' (3) LAma
'Attila' (3) LAma NRog
aucheriana (15) 🏆 CBro CMea CMon EHyt EPot ERos ETub LAma LBow WChr
'Aurea' See ***T. greigii* 'Aurea'**
'Aureola' (5) LAma
australis (15) CMon
bakeri See ***T. saxatilis* Bakeri Group**
'Balalaika' (5) LAma
'Ballade' (6) 🏆 ETub LAma
'Ballerina' (6) CAvo LAma
batalinii See ***T. linifolia* Batalinii Group**
'Beauty of Apeldoorn' (4) LAma NRog
'Belcanto' (3) LAma
'Bellflower' (7) LAma
'Bellona' (3) ETub LAma
'Berlioz' (12) LAma
biebersteiniana (15) LAma
§ *biflora* (15) CAvo CBro EPot ETub LAma NRog
bifloriformis (15) MSto
'Big Chief' (4) 🏆 LAma MBri
'Bing Crosby' (3) ETub LAma
◆ 'Bird of Paradise' See ***T.* 'Mrs Keightley'**
'Black Parrot' (10) CAvo LAma
¶ 'Blenda' (3) ETub
'Bleu Aimable' (5) CAvo ETub LAma
'Blue Heron' (7) LAma
'Blue Parrot' (10) LAma NRog
'Blushing Lady' (5) LAma
'Bonanza' (11) LAma
'Boule de Neige' (2) LAma
'Bravissimo' (2) MBri
'Brilliant Star' (1) LAma MBri
'Burgundy' (6) ETub LAma
'Burgundy Lace' (7) LAma
'Burns' (7) LAma
butkovii (15) LAma
I 'Calypso' (14) ETub
'Candela' (13) LAma
'Cantata' (13) CBro LAma
'Cantor' (5) LAma
'Cape Cod' (14) LAma NRog
'Caprice' (10) LAma
'Captain Fryatt' (6) LAma
carinata (15) LAma
'Carlton' (2) ETub LAma NRog
'Carnaval de Nice' (11/v) CRDP ETub LAma MBri
'Cassini' (3) LAma
§ *celsiana* (15) CMon EPot LAma
'César Franck' (12) LAma
'Charles' (3) LAma

'China Pink' (6) CAvo ETub LAma NRog
'Chopin' (12) LAma NRog
'Christmas Marvel' (1) ETub LAma
◆ ***chrysantha*** Boiss. See ***T. montana***
– Boiss. ex Baker See ***T. clusiana*** var. ***chrysantha***
'Clara Butt' (5) LAma NRog
§ ***clusiana*** (15) CBro LAma
§ – var. ***chrysantha*** (15) ♀ CAvo EBar LAma LBow MSto NRog
– – 'Tubergen's Gem' (15) CSWP LAma MBri
– 'Cynthia' (15) CAvo CSWP EHyt EPot LAma SMad
§ – var. ***stellata*** (15) LAma
'Concerto' (13) CBro ETub LAma
'Cordell Hull' (5) NRog
'Corona' (12) ETub LAma
'Corsage' (14) ♀ LAma
'Couleur Cardinal' (3) ETub EWal LAma NRog
cretica (15) CMon MSto
'Crystal Beauty' (7) NRog
'Dancing Show' (8) CAvo LAma
dasystemon (15) EBar EPot LAma MRPP
'Diana' (1) LAma NRog
'Diantha' (14) LAma
'Dillenburg' (5) LAma
'Dix' Favourite' (3) LAma
'Doctor Plesman' (3) LAma
'Doll's Minuet' (8) LAma
'Don Quichotte' (3) LAma
'Donna Bella' (14) ♀ CRDP LAma
'Douglas Bader' (5) CAvo LAma NRog
'Dreaming Maid' (3) LAma
'Dutch Gold' (3) LAma
'Dyanito' (6) EWal LAma
'Early Harvest' (12) ♀ LAma
'Easter Parade' (13) EWal LAma
'Easter Surprise' (14) LAma
§ ***edulis*** (15) CMon LAma LRHS
eichleri See ***T. undulatifolia***
'Electra' (5) LAma MBri
'Elegant Lady' (6) ETub
'Elizabeth Arden' (4) LAma
'Elmus' (5) LAma
'Esperanto' (8/v) LAma NRog
'Estella Rijnveld' (10) ETub LAma NBir NRog
'Fair Lady' (12) LAma
'Fancy Frills' (7) LAma
'Fantasy' (10) ♀ LAma
'Fashion' (12) LAma
ferganica (15) CMon LAma
'Feu Superbe' (13) LAma
'Fireside' See ***T. 'Vlammenspel'***
'First Lady' (3) ♀ LAma
'Flair' (1) LAma
'Flaming Parrot' (10) LAma
'Flying Dutchman' (5) LAma
fosteriana (13) MBri
'Franz Léhar' (12) LAma
'Frasquita' (5) LAma
'Fresco' (14) LAma
¶ Fringed Group (7) ETub
'Fringed Apeldoorn' (7) NRog
'Fringed Beauty' (7) ETub MBri
'Fringed Elegance' (7) LAma
'Fritz Kreisler' (12) LAma
'Fulgens' (6) LAma
'Gaiety' (12) LAma
'Galata' (13) LAma
galatica (15) LAma
'Garden Party' (3) ETub LAma
'Generaal de Wet' (1) ETub LAma MBri
'General Eisenhower' (4) LAma
'Georgette' (5) EWal LAma MBri NRog
'Giuseppe Verdi' (12) EWal LAma LBow MBri NRog
'Glück' (12) EWal LAma
'Gold Medal' (11) LAma MBri
'Golden Age' (5) LAma
'Golden Apeldoorn' (4) EWal LAma MBri NRog
'Golden Artist' (8) LAma MBri NRog
'Golden Emperor' (13) LAma
'Golden Harvest' (5) LAma
'Golden Melody' (3) ETub LAma NRog
'Golden Oxford' (4) LAma
'Golden Parade' (4) LAma
'Golden Springtime' (4) LAma
'Gordon Cooper' (4) LAma
'Goudstuk' (12) LAma
'Grand Prix' (13) LAma
'Green Eyes' (8) LAma
'Green Spot' (8) LAma
greigii (14) CBro CMon
§ – 'Aurea' (14) CMon
grengiolensis (15) CAvo EPot LAma
'Greuze' (5) LAma
'Grével' (3) CAvo LAma
'Groenland' (8) LAma
'Gudoshnik' (4) LAma
hageri (15) CMon LAma
– 'Splendens' (15) ETub LAma
'Halcro' (5) ♀ ETub LAma
'Hamilton' (7) LAma
'Happy Family' (3) LAma
'Heart's Delight' (12) CBro ETub EWal LAma LBow NRog
'Hibernia' (3) LAma
'Hit Parade' (13) LAma
'Hoangho' (2) LAma
'Hollands Glorie' (4) ♀ LAma
'Hollywood' (8) LAma
hoogiana (15) LAma WChr
§ – PF 8955 (15) CMon
§ ***humilis*** (15) CAvo CBro EPar EPot LAma LBow MBri
– 'Eastern Star' (15) LAma MBri
§ – 'Lilliput' (15) CBro EPot GCrs
– 'Odalisque' (15) EPot LAma
– 'Persian Pearl' (15) EPot LAma MBri NRog
§ – var. ***pulchella*** Albocaerulea Oculata Group (15) EPot LAma MRPP WChr
§ – Violacea Group (15) CAvo CMea EPar EWal LAma MBri
§ – – black base (15) CBro LRHS
– – yellow base (15) CBro LAma LBow LRHS
'Humming Bird' (8) LAma
'Hytuna' (11) LAma NRog
'Ibis' (1) LAma
'Ile de France' (5) LAma
ingens (15) LAma
'Inzell' (3) ETub LAma
'Jacqueline' (6) LAma
'Jeantine' (12) ♀ LAma
'Jewel of Spring' (4) ♀ LAma
'Jimmy' (3) NRog
'Jockey Cap' (14) LAma
'Joffre' (1) LAma MBri
'Johann Strauss' (12) CBro LAma MBri
'Johanna' (3) LAma
'Juan' (13) LAma MBri
'Kansas' (3) LAma

'Karel Doorman' (10)	LAma
'Kareol' (2)	LAma
kaufmanniana (12)	CAvo CBro EPot LBow NRog SRms WRHF
§ 'Kees Nelis' (3)	LAma MBri NRog
'Keizerskroon' (1) ♀	EWal LAma NRog
'Kingsblood' (5) ♀	LAma
kolpakowskiana (15) ♀	LAma MBri NRog
kurdica (15)	LAma LRHS
'La Tulipe Noire' (5)	LAma
* 'Lady Diana' (14)	LAma MBri
lanata (15)	LAma
'Landseadel's Supreme' (5) ♀	LAma
'Large Copper' (14)	LAma
'Leen van der Mark' (3)	LAma
'Lefeber's Favourite' (4)	LAma
'Lilac Time' (6)	LAma
'Lilac Wonder'	See ***T. saxatilis*** **(Bakeri Group) 'Lilac Wonder'**
'Lilliput'	See ***T. humilis*** **'Lilliput'**
linifolia (15) ♀	CAvo CMea EHyt EPar EPot ETub LAma LBow NRog WAbe
§ – Batalinii Group ♀	CBro LAma LBow NRog WOMN
§ – – 'Apricot Jewel'	CAvo CBro
– – 'Bright Gem' (15)	CAvo CBro EPot LAma LBow MBro NRog WHoo WPyg
– – 'Bronze Charm' (15)	CAvo CBro CMea CSWP EPot ETub LAma
– – 'Red Gem'	CBro LAma
– – 'Yellow Gem'	CBro
– – 'Yellow Jewel'	LAma
§ – Maximowiczii Group	CBro LAma LBow
'London' (4)	LAma
'Love Song' (12)	LAma
'Lucifer' (5)	EWal LAma
'Lucky Strike' (3)	LAma
§ 'Lustige Witwe' (3)	ETub LAma
§ 'Madame Lefeber' (13)	CBro EWal LAma LBow MBri
'Madame Spoor' (3)	LAma
'Magier' (5)	LAma
'Maja' (7)	LAma
'Mamasa' (5)	LAma
'March of Time' (14)	MBri
'Maréchal Niel' (2)	LAma
'Mariette' (6)	LAma
'Marilyn' (6)	ETub LAma
marjolletii (15)	CBro LAma LBow NRog
'Mary Ann' (14)	LAma
'Maureen' (5) ♀	ETub LAma
mauritiana (15)	LAma
maximowiczii	See ***T. linifolia*** **Maximowiczii Group**
'Maytime' (6)	LAma
'Maywonder' (11)	LAma
¶ 'Melody d'Amour' (5)	ETub
'Menton' (5)	ETub
◆ Merry Widow	See ***T.*** **'Lustige Witwe'**
'Mickey Mouse' (1)	NRog
'Minerva' (3)	NRog
'Miss Holland' (3)	MBri
'Mona Lisa' (6)	LAma
§ ***montana*** (15)	CBro EPot ETub LAma
'Monte Carlo' (2) ♀	ETub LAma
'Mount Tacoma' (11)	ETub LAma MBri NRog
'Mr Van der Hoef' (2)	LAma MBri
'Murillo' (2)	LAma
'My Lady' (4) ♀	LAma
'Negrita' (3)	LAma
neustreuvae	CBro GCrs
'New Design' (3/v)	ETub EWal LAma MBri NRog
¶ 'New Look' (7)	ETub
'Orange Bouquet' (3) ♀	LAma NRog
'Orange Elite' (14)	LAma MBri
'Orange Emperor' (13)	LAma MBri NRog
'Orange Favourite' (10)	LAma
'Orange Sun'	See ***T.*** **'Oranjezon'**
'Orange Triumph' (11)	MBri
'Oranje Nassau' (2) ♀	LAma MBri NRog
§ 'Oranjezon' (4)	LAma
'Oratorio' (14)	LAma MBri
'Oriental Beauty' (14)	LAma NRog
'Oriental Splendour' (14) ♀	EWal LAma
orphanidea (15)	EPot LAma LBow WCot
– 'Flava' (15)	CBro CMon ETub LAma
§ – Whittallii Group (15)	CAvo CBro CMon LAma NRog SMad
ostrowskiana (15)	LAma
'Oxford' (4) ♀	LAma
'Oxford's Elite' (4)	LAma
'Page Polka' (3)	LAma
'Palestrina' (3)	LAma
'Pandour' (14)	LAma MBri
'Parade' (4) ♀	LAma MBri
'Paris' (3)	LAma
¶ ***passeriniana*** (15)	LAma
'Paul Richter' (3)	LAma
'Pax' (3)	LAma
'Peach Blossom' (2)	ETub LAma MBri NRog
'Peerless Pink' (3)	LAma
'Perlina' (14)	LAma
persica	See ***T. celsiana***
'Philippe de Comines' (5)	LAma
'Picture' (5)	LAma
'Pimpernel' (8/v)	CAvo LAma
'Pink Beauty' (1)	LAma
'Pink Impression' (4)	LAma
'Pink Trophy' (1)	LAma
'Pinkeen' (13)	LAma
'Pinocchio' (14)	EWal NRog
'Plaisir' (14) ♀	LAma MBri
platystigma (15)	LAma
polychroma	See ***T. biflora***
praestans (15)	LAma
– 'Fusilier' (15) ♀	CBro EPot ETub EWal LAma LBow MBri NRog
– 'Unicum' (15/v)	CRDP EBar EWal LAma MBri NRog
– 'Van Tubergen's Variety' (15)	LAma NRog
'Preludium' (3)	LAma
'President Kennedy' (4) ♀	LAma
primulina (15)	CMon
'Prince Karl Philip' (3)	NRog
'Prince of Austria' (1)	LAma
'Princeps' (13)	CBro EWal LAma MBri
'Princess Margaret Rose' (5)	LAma
'Prins Carnaval' (1)	LAma
'Prinses Irene' (3) ♀	ETub LAma MBri NBir
'Professor Röntgen' (10)	LAma
'Prominence' (3)	LAma
pulchella	See ***T. humilis*** var. ***pulchella*** **Albocaerulea Oculata Group**
pulchella humilis	See ***T. humilis***
§ 'Purissima' (13)	CAvo CBro ETub LAma LBow
'Queen' (4)	LAma

'Queen Ingrid' (14)	LAma
'Queen of Bartigons' (5)	LAma NRog
'Queen of Night' (5)	CAvo ETub EWal LAma MBri
'Queen of Sheba' (6)	CAvo LAma
'Queen Wilhelmina'	See ***T.* 'Koningin Wilhelmina'**
'Recreado' (5)	ETub
'Red Champion' (10)	LAma
'Red Emperor'	See ***T.* 'Madame Lefeber'**
'Red Georgette' (5) 🏆	MBri
'Red Matador' (4)	LAma
'Red Parrot' (10)	LAma
'Red Riding Hood' (14) 🏆	CBro ETub EWal LAma LBow MBri NBir NRog
'Red Sensation' (10)	LAma
'Red Shine' (6)	LAma
'Red Wing' (7)	LAma
'Reforma' (3)	LAma
Rembrandt Mix	ETub MBri
'Renown' (5)	LAma
rhodopea	See ***T. urumoffii***
'Rijnland' (3)	LAma
'Ringo'	See ***T.* 'Kees Nelis'**
'Rockery Beauty' (13)	LAma
'Rockery Wonder' (14)	LAma
'Rosario' (3)	ETub
* 'Rose Emperor' (13)	LAma
'Rosy Wings' (3)	LAma
'Safari' (14)	ETub
saxatilis (15)	CAvo CBro LAma MBri NRog
§ – Bakeri Group (15)	EPot LAma MRPP WChr
§ – – 'Lilac Wonder'	CAvo CBro EPot ETub LAma MBri NRog
– MS 769 (15)	CMon
'Scarlet Cardinal' (2)	LAma
'Scarlett O'Hara' (5)	LAma
'Schoonoord' (2)	ETub LAma MBri
schrenkii (15)	LAma LRHS
'Scotch Lassie' (5)	LAma
'Shakespeare' (12)	CBro LAma LBow NRog
'Shirley' (3)	CAvo ETub LAma MBri NRog
'Showwinner' (12) 🏆	CBro ETub LAma MBri
'Sigrid Undset' (5)	LAma
'Silentia' (3)	LAma
'Smiling Queen' (5)	LAma
'Snowflake' (3)	LAma
'Snowpeak' (5)	LAma
sogdiana (15)	LAma
'Sorbet' (5) 🏆	LAma
'Sparkling Fire' (14)	LAma
'Spectacular Gold'	See ***T.* 'Goldenes Deutschland'**
sprengeri (15) 🏆	CAvo CBro CFil CMon CNic EPar LAma LWoo SSpi WChr
– Trotter's form (15)	WCot
'Spring Green' (8) 🏆	CAvo ETub EWal LAma MBri NRog
'Spring Pearl' (13)	LAma
'Spring Song' (4)	LAma
stellata	See ***T. clusiana*** var. ***stellata***
'Stockholm' (2) 🏆	LAma
'Stresa' (12) 🏆	CBro LAma
'Striped Apeldoorn' (4)	LAma NRog
subpraestans (15)	EPot LAma
'Success' (3)	LAma
'Summit' (13)	LAma
'Sundew' (7)	LAma NRog
'Sunray' (3)	LAma
'Susan Oliver' (8)	LAma
'Swan Wings' (7)	LAma
'Sweet Harmony' (5) 🏆	LAma MBri NRog
'Sweet Lady' (14)	LAma NRog
◆ 'Sweetheart' (5)	See ***T.* 'Princess Juliana'**
'Sweetheart' (13)	CBro LAma NRog
sylvestris (15)	CAvo CBro EPar EWFC LAma LBow NRog WCot WRHF WShi
'Tamara' (3)	LAma
'Tango' (14)	LAma
tarda (15) 🏆	CAvo CBro CMea CNic EPar EPot ETub EWal LAma LBow MBri MBro MSto NMGW NRog WPat WPyg
'Teenager' (14)	LAma
'Temple of Beauty' (5) 🏆	LAma
'Tender Beauty' (4)	LAma
tetraphylla (15)	LAma
'Texas Flame' (10)	LAma
'Texas Gold' (10)	LAma
'The First' (12)	CBro LAma
'Toronto' (14) 🏆	ETub LAma MBri
'Toulon' (13)	MBri
'Towa' (14)	LAma
'Trance' (3)	LAma
'Trinket' (14)	LAma
'Triumphator' (2)	LAma
tschimganica (15)	LAma
tubergeniana (15)	LAma
– 'Keukenhof' (15)	LAma
turkestanica (15) 🏆	CAvo CBro EPar EPot ETub LAma LBow MBri NRog WHoo WRHF
'Uncle Tom' (11)	LAma MBri
§ ***undulatifolia*** (15)	CBro LAma LBow
'Union Jack' (5)	EWal LAma
urumiensis (15) 🏆	CAvo CBro CMea EHyt EPot LAma MBri MBro NMen NRog WAbe WHoo WPat WPyg
§ ***urumoffii*** (15)	LAma
'Valentine' (3)	LAma
'Van der Neer' (1)	LAma
'Varinas' (3)	LAma
violacea	See ***T. humilis* Violacea Group**
'Viridiflora' (8)	ETub
'Vivaldi' (12)	LAma
'Vivex' (4)	LAma
§ 'Vlammenspel' (1)	LAma
'Vuurbaak' (2)	LAma
vvedenskyi (15)	CBro LAma NRog
– 'Blanka' (15)	EPot
– 'Hanka' (15)	EPot
– 'Lenka' (15)	EPot
– 'Tangerine Beauty' (15)	MBri
'West Point' (6)	CAvo ETub LAma
* 'White Bouquet' (5)	NRog
'White Dream' (3)	LAma
'White Emperor'	See ***T.* 'Purissima'**
'White Parrot' (10)	CAvo LAma NRog
'White Swallow' (3)	NRog
'White Triumphator' (6)	CAvo ETub LAma NBir NRog
'White Virgin' (3)	LAma
whittallii	See ***T. orphanidea* Whittallii Group**
'Willem van Oranje' (2)	LAma
'Willemsoord' (2)	LAma MBri
wilsoniana	See ***T. montana***
'Yellow Dawn' (14)	LAma
'Yellow Dover' (4)	LAma
'Yellow Emperor' (5)	MBri
'Yellow Empress' (13)	LAma
'Yellow Present' (3)	LAma
'Yellow Purissima' (13)	NRog

- 'Yokohama' (3) — LAma
- 'Zampa' (14) ♀ — LAma
- *zenaidae* (15) — MSto
- 'Zombie' (13) — LAma
- 'Zomerschoon' (5) — ETub
- 'Zwanenburg' (5) — LAma

TUNICA See PETRORHAGIA, DIANTHUS

TURBINA (Convolvulaceae)

- ¶ *corymbosa* — NGno

TURRAEA (Meliaceae)

- *obtusifolia* — CSpe

TUSSILAGO (Asteraceae)

- *farfara* — CArn CJew CKin ECWi ELau EWFC GPoy MHew MSal SIde WHer

TUTCHERIA (Theaceae)

See Plant Deletions

TWEEDIA (Asclepiadaceae)

- § *caerulea* ♀ — CChr CGle CInt CRHN CSev CSpe ELan EMil EOrc ERea GCal IBlr LGre LHop LLWP SAxl SHFr SPer SUsu WEas WPer

TYLOPHORA (Asclepiadaceae)

- ¶ *ovata* — CPlN

TYPHA (Typhaceae)

- *angustifolia* — CBen CKin CRow CWGN CWat EBre ECWi EHon EMFW LPBA MSta SHig SWat SWyc WChe WWye
- *latifolia* — CBen CHEx CRow CWGN CWat ECWi EHon EMFW LPBA MSta SWat SWyc WChe WHer WMAq WWye
- – 'Variegata' — CBen CFai CRow CWat EGar ELan EMFW MSta SWyc WChe WCot
- § *laxmannii* — CBen EHon EMFW LPBA MSta SRms
- *minima* — CBen CRDP CRow CWGN EBre ECWi EHoe EHon EMFW ESOG LPBA MSta NDea SCoo SHig SMad SWat SWyc WChe WFar WMAq
- *shuttleworthii* — CRow
- *stenophylla* — See *T. laxmannii*

UGNI (Myrtaceae)

- § *molinae* — CDec CGre CMHG CPle CSam ESim GAri ISea MBal SHFr SOWG WCHb WGwG WJek WSHC WWat WWye

ULEX (Papilionaceae)

- *europaeus* — CCVT CDoC ECWi EMil ENot EWFC GRei LBuc NWea SEND WDin WMou
- – 'Aureus' — CB&S
- § – 'Flore Pleno' ♀ — CB&S CDoC CInt CTri ENot MBal SHBN SMad SPer WCot WWeb
- – 'Plenus' — See *U. europaeus* **'Flore Pleno'**
- – 'Prostratus' — MBar
- *gallii* 'Mizen' — EHic ESis GCal GGGa GSki LRHS MPla SMad
- *nanus* — See *U. minor*

ULMUS (Ulmaceae)

- 'Dodoens' — LBuc MGos NBee
- § *glabra* — CPer GRei NWea WDin WMou
- – 'Camperdownii' — CDoC ELan SPer WMou
- – 'Exoniensis' — CTho
- – 'Gittisham' — CTho
- – 'Horizontalis' — See *U. glabra* **'Pendula'**
- – 'Nana' — WPat
- ¶ – 'Pendula' — LPan
- × *hollandica* 'Commelin' — CDoC EMil
- – 'Groeneveld' — CDoC EMil
- – 'Jacqueline Hillier' — CInt CShe CTre EBre ELan ESis GDra GWht LHop MAsh MBal MBar MPla NHar NHol NNrd SHFr SIng SRms SSpi STre WAbe WHCG WPat WPyg
- – 'Lobel' — CDoC MGos
- – 'Wredei' — See *U. minor* **'Dampieri Aurea'**
- *minor* 'Cornubiensis' — CBlo CDoC CTho
- § – 'Dampieri Aurea' — CBot CEnd CLnd ELan LBuc LNet LPan MAsh MBar MBlu MBro NBee SHBN SMad SPer SSta WDin WPat
- – 'Variegata' — EPot
- *montana* — See *U. glabra*
- *parvifolia* — EHal EHic GAri NWea STre WFro WHCr WNor
- – 'Frosty' (v) — ECho ELan EPot
- – 'Geisha' (v) — CWSG ELan MGos SBla SMad STre WPat WPyg
- § – 'Hokkaido' — EHyt MBro SBla WAbe WPat WPyg
- – 'Pygmaea' — See *U. parvifolia* **'Hokkaido'**
- – 'Yatsubusa' — CLyd EPot ESis EWes MBro MHig SIng STre WAbe WGle WPat WPyg
- 'Plantijn' — CDoC
- *pumila* — CAgr GAri WNor
- 'Sapporo Autumn Gold' — CDoC

UMBELLULARIA (Lauraceae)

- *californica* — CArn SArc WSHC

UMBILICUS (Crassulaceae)

- *erectus* — CChu CRDP EWFC
- *rupestris* — CArc CNat EGoo ELan GAri GBar NGre NMen NWCA SIde WCla WCot WHer WPer WWye

UNCINIA (Cyperaceae)

- *clavata* — ETPC
- N *rubra* — Widely available
- – 'Dunn Valley' — WCot
- sp. ex Chile — GCal
- *uncinata* — CFil CSpe EBee ECha EHoe EMan EOas ESOG ETPC GFre MBal NHar NHol SUsu WByw
- – *rubra* — CFir ECot

UNGNADIA (Sapindaceae)

See Plant Deletions

UNIOLA (Poaceae)
latifolia See ***Chasmanthium latifolium***

URCEOLINA (Amaryllidaceae)
miniata See ***Stenomesson miniatum***
peruviana See ***Stenomesson miniatum***
urceolata WChr

URECHITES See PENTALINON

URGINEA (Hyacinthaceae)
fugax SF 62 CMon
maritima GPoy LAma MNrw MSal
– SF 275 CMon
ollivieri MS&CL 281 CMon
undulata SF 2/279/323 CMon

UROSPERMUM (Asteraceae)
delachampii CChu CGle CHan COtt CSam EBar EBre ECha EMan SAga SUsu

URSINIA (Asteraceae)
See Plant Deletions

URTICA (Urticaceae)
¶ ***dioica*** CTiv
– 'Chedglow' CNat
galeopsifolia CNat

UTRICULARIA (Lentibulariaceae)
alpina WMEx
australis EFEx
biloba GTro
bisquamata GTro WMEx
calcyfida GTro WMEx
capensis WMEx
dichotoma EFEx GTro MHel WMEx
exoleta See ***U. gibba***
§ ***gibba*** EFEx
intermedia EFEx
laterifolia EFEx GTro MHel WMEx
livida EFEx GTro MHel WMEx
longifolia GTro WMEx
menziesii EFEx GTro
monanthos EFEx
nephrophylla GTro
novae-zelandiae GTro
ochroleuca EFEx
praelonga GTro
prehensilis GTro WMEx
¶ ***pubescens*** WMEx
reniformis EFEx GTro MHel WMEx
reniformis nana EFEx
sandersonii GTro MHel WMEx
– blue GTro
subulata EFEx WMEx
tricolor GTro WMEx
vulgaris EFEx SAWi WMEx

UVULARIA (Convallariaceae)
disporum LAma
grandiflora ♀ Widely available
– var. ***pallida*** CChu CRDP ECha EMon EPar IBlr LGre SAxl SWas WCru
perfoliata CChu ECha EHyt EPar EPot LAma MBro SBla WAbe WCru WWat
pudica See ***U. caroliniana***

§ ***sessilifolia*** EBee EPar EPot LAma WCru

VACCARIA (Caryophyllaceae)
segetalis See ***V. hispanica***

VACCINIUM † (Ericaceae)
* ***alpinum*** CMHG
arctostaphylos SSta
caespitosum GDra
corymbosum ♀ CB&S CBlo ELan EPfP MBal MBar MGos MHlr NBee SReu SSta WDin
– 'Berkeley' (F) CTrh GTwe LBuc LRHS
– 'Bluecrop' (F) CDoC CMac CTrh ELan EMui GTwe LBuc MBri MGos WStI WWeb
– 'Bluejay' (F) CTrh LRHS
– 'Bluetta' (F) CTrh GTwe LRHS
– 'Concord' (F) EBee ENot
– 'Coville' (F) CTrh EMui
– 'Duke' (F) CTrh ELan LRHS
– 'Earliblue' (F) EMui MGos
– 'Elliott' (F) CTrh
– 'Goldtraube' (F) CDoC MBlu MBri MGos NDal
– 'Herbert' (F) EMui GTwe MGos
¶ – 'Jersey' (F) LRHS
– 'Nelson' CTrh
– 'Northland' (F) GAri GTwe
– 'Patriot' (F) CTrh GAri GTwe LRHS
– 'Pioneer' (F) MBar
– 'Spartan' (F) GAri GTwe LRHS
– 'Sunrise' (F) GTwe
– 'Toro' (F) GTwe
– 'Trovor' (F) ELan
crassifolium 'Well's Delight' (F) CKni CNic CSte LRHS MAsh
cylindraceum ♀ WAbe WBod WPat WPyg
– 'Tom Thumb' WAbe
delavayi CKni CSte EPot GCHN MAsh MBal MBar MBlu MHig SReu SSta WAbe
donianum See ***V. sprengelii***
duclouxii CB&S
dunalianum CB&S
emarginatum SSta
floribundum CFil CMHG GDra GSki GTou MAsh MBal SPer SSta WAbe WPGP
glaucoalbum ♀ CAbP CKni CSte GWht MBar MBlu MRav SPer SReu SSta WAbe WDin
– B 173 MBal
§ ***macrocarpon*** CMac CSte ELan ESim GTwe LRHS MBal MBar MBri SRms SSta
– 'CN' (F) CTrh ESim MGos
– 'Early Black' (F) CB&S CTrh
– 'Franklin' (F) CTrh EPot ESim
– 'Hamilton' (F) CGra EPot GDra NHol WAbe WPat WPyg
– 'Pilgrim' (F) ESim
* 'McMinn' GAri MBal
moupinense CNic ITim MAsh MBal MBlu MGos SPer SSta
– small-leaved MBal
– 'Variegatum' WPyg
myrtillus GPoy MBal WDin
'Nimo Pink' MBar
nummularia EPot GDra LRHS MBal MHig NHar SSpi WAbe

– LS&H 17294	NHar
ovatum	CMHG CSte GSki LRHS MBal MBar SPer SSta
§ ***oxycoccos***	CArn
* – ***rubrum***	LRHS
padifolium	CFil CGre MBal
¶ ***pallidum***	IBlr
palustre	See ***V. oxycoccos***
praestans	GAri NHol
retusum	CGre CTrw LRHS MBal WAbe
sikkimense	EHyt
virgatum	MBal
vitis-idaea	CAgr CNic ESim GPoy GWht MBal MBar MGos MHig SReu WPyg
– 'Compactum'	EWes MBal NHar
– Koralle Group 🏆	MAsh MBal MBar MBri MGos MRav NHol SPer SReu SSta WAbe WPat WPyg
– subsp. ***minus***	ECou EHyt GAri MAsh MBal MHig SSta
– 'Red Pearl'	CSte MAsh MGos
* – 'Variegatum'	EWes WPat

VAGARIA (Amaryllidaceae)

ollivieri SF 266	CMon

VALERIANA (Valerianaceae)

'Alba'	See ***Centranthus ruber albus***
alliariifolia	EMon GCal NBro NSti WCot
arizonica	CLyd LFis MSte MTho NCat WPat
'Coccinea'	See ***Centranthus ruber***
dioica	CRDP WNdy
montana	EHyt GTou MBro NBro NRya SRms SWat WHil
officinalis	CArn CKin CRDP CSev ECWi ECoo ELau EWFC GPoy ILis LHol MChe MGam MHew NBro NRoo SIde SWat WApp WHer WOak WPer WShi WWye
– subsp. ***sambucifolia***	CHan WCot WHil WPbr
* – 'Variegata'	WCHb WNdy
phu 'Aurea'	CBot CFil CGle CHan ECha EFol EHoe ELan EMon IBlr LHol LHop MBal MBel MBri MFir MUlv NBro NNor NRoo NSti SMad SPer SUsu WEas WHen WHil WPer WRus WWin
* – 'Purpurea'	ECoo
pyrenaica	ECha EFol EMon WCot
saxatilis	EFol LCom NRoo NRya
supina	NWCA
tatamana	WEas

VALERIANELLA (Valerianaceae)

eriocarpa	EJud
§ ***locusta***	GPoy
olitoria	See ***V. locusta***

VALLEA (Elaeocarpaceae)

stipularis pyrifolia	CGre CPle

VALLOTA See CYRTANTHUS

VANCOUVERIA (Berberidaceae)

chrysantha	CElw CFil CVer ECha EMon EPla SBar SLod SSpi SUsu WCru WPbr WSHC
hexandra	CFil CHEx CNic CVer EBre ECha EMan EMon ERos GCal LHop MBal NCat NRya NSti SSpi WBea WCru WPbr WRus WWin
planipetala	WHal

VANIA (Brassicaceae)

¶ ***campylophylla***	CGra

VEITCHIA (Arecaceae)

See Plant Deletions

VELLA (Brassicaceae)

See Plant Deletions

VELTHEIMIA (Hyacinthaceae)

§ ***bracteata*** 🏆	CHal CMon EBak ETub IBlr LBow NRog
§ ***capensis*** 🏆	CSev SLMG
viridifolia hort.	See ***V. capensis***
– Jacquin	See ***V. bracteata***

VENIDIOARCTOTIS See ARCTOTIS

VENIDIUM See ARCTOTIS

VERATRUM (Melanthiaceae)

album	CBot CFil CFir ECha GCal SBla WCru
¶ – var. ***oxysepalum***	WCru
californicum	ECha
caudatum	EBre
formosanum B&SWJ 1575	WCru
nigrum 🏆	CBot CBro CFir CHEx EBre GCal GDra LGre MBri MNrw SChu SMad WByw WCot WFar
¶ ***stamineum***	WCru
viride	CBot ECha GCal IBlr

VERBASCUM † (Scrophulariaceae)

acaule	GCLN
* – 'Album'	WCru
adzharicum	EWll SWat WSan
Allstree Hybrids	CFee
'Arctic Summer'	See ***V. bombyciferum 'Polarsommer'***
arcturus	ESis MSto NSti WPer
* ***bakerianum***	EBar WEas
blattaria	CGle CPou EBee ECWi ELan EPPr EWFC MCLN NBir NWCA SWat WEas WHer WPer
– f. ***albiflorum***	CLon CNic CSpe EMar LGan LGre MBro MGam NSti WBon WHer WHil WHoo WKif WPer WPyg WRus
– pink	CChr CLTr EGoo EWll GAbr NLak WOve
– yellow	EWll SWat
§ ***bombyciferum*** 🏆	CSWP CSam CSev EFol ERav NSti NVic SRms WByw WEas WHer
§ – 'Polarsommer'	CSam EBre EMan GAbr MBri MHlr NBir SRms WCot WFar WSan
– 'Silver Lining'	CWan NNor NPer
'Broussa'	See ***V. bombyciferum***

chaixii	CArc ECha GBuc MBro MRav NBir SHam WHoo WPer WPyg
– 'Album'	CArc CGle CSpe ECED ECoo EFou EOrc LFlo LGre LHop MBri MBro MFir MUlv NBir NBrk NBro SMrm SSvw SUsu WHen WHoo WPer WRus WWin
– x ***phoeniceum*** 'Clent Sunrise'	CHan
(Cotswold Group) 'Boadicea'	CShe
– 'Cotswold Beauty' ♀	CChu COtt CSam EAst EMan EMon NCat NSti SChu
– 'Cotswold Gem'	CRDP
– 'Cotswold King'	CGle WCot WGle WSan
– 'Cotswold Queen'	CChu CDoC CGle EBre ECED EFou ELan MWat NCut NFla SChu SMrm SPer WEas WRHF WRus WSan WWin
– 'Gainsborough' ♀	CDoC CGle CHad CRDP EAst EBre ECha ECtt EFou ELan MBri MCLN MUlv MWat SBla SChu SMrm SPer SUsu SWat WCra WRus WWeb
– 'Mont Blanc'	CBot CGle EBee EBre ECot EFou WRus WWeb
– 'Pink Domino' ♀	CBot CDoC CGle CHad EBre EFou ELan GBri GLil MBri MTis MWat NCat NCut NLak NSti SChu SMrm SPer SUsu SWat WRus
– 'Royal Highland'	CChu CGle CHad EAst EBee ECot EFou EHal ELan GBri NCut NLak SMrm SUsu SWat WCot WRus
– 'White Domino'	EFou WRus
creticum	EBar ECoo EPri GCra NLak WApp WCla WPer
§ ***densiflorum***	CArn CSte ECoo EMan LHol NCut SIde SPer WCla WPer
dumulosum ♀	EBre EDAr EHyt EPot GCal NWCA SBla SHFr WAbe WOMN WPer WSan
'Frosted Gold'	LGre
'Golden Wings' ♀	CPBP EPot ITim NTow WAbe WPat
'Helen Johnson' ♀	CGle CHad CLon CRDP EBre ECha ECot EFou EGol EOrc LHop LRHS MCLN MUlv NRoo NSti SCoo SMrm SSoC SUsu SWat WCra WRus WWeb
'Jackie'	CLon LGre SBla WKif
'Letitia' ♀	CShe EBre ELan EPot EWes GCal LBee MTho NNrd NTow SBla SIng SSmi SWas WAbe WEas WHoo WKif WPer WPyg WWin
longifolium var. ***pannosum***	See ***V. olympicum***
lychnitis	CArn CLTr ECWi WHer
nigrum	CArn CGle CJew EBar EOrc EPfP EWFC MChe MGam MHew MSto NChi SEND WHer WOak WPer
¶ – var. ***album***	WWhi
§ ***olympicum***	CGle CLTr CSam EBar ECha EGoo ELan MOne NOak SEND WCot WPer WRHF
phlomoides	MSto WHil WKif
phoeniceum	CArn CGle ECoo ELan MSCN NBro NCut NMir NOak NWCA SRms SVen WBro WCla WCra WEas WHen WHil WPer WWin
* – 'Album'	SSvw
– 'Flush of White'	CBot CM&M ECoo EMan EWll MLLN SMrm WWhi
– hybrids	CBot CSpe EBre EGoo EMan NChi SSea WGor WPer
pulverulentum	CKin EWFC
rorippifolium	EMan
¶ ***sinuatum***	CArn WCot
* 'Spica'	CGle EMan
spicatum	CBot
spinosum	CGle SHFr
Sunset shades	WGor
thapsiforme	See ***V. densiflorum***
thapsus	CJew CKin CSam CSev ECWi EGoo EJud EWFC GPoy MChe MHew NLak NMir NNor WApp WOak WSel WWye
'Vernale'	CBot
wiedemannianum	CSpe EWll GAbr WDav WPen

VERBENA (Verbenaceae)

'Aphrodite'	WLRN
¶ 'Apple Blossom'	WCot
'Artemis'	WLRN
'Aveyron'	EOrc SChu SMrm
* 'Batesville Rose'	WCot
'Blue Cascade'	NPri
'Blue Prince'	CSpe
§ ***bonariensis***	Widely available
'Boughton House'	CSpe MSte
'Bramley'	SChu SUsu
'Calcutta Cream'	WCot
canadensis 'Perfecta'	EBar MTis
'Candy Carousel'	CElw CSev EBar SCro SUsu
'Carousel'	NPri
chamaedrifolia	See ***V. peruviana***
corymbosa	CGre CM&M ECGP ECha EGar LLWP SMrm SUsu WCot WPer WRHF
– 'Gravetye'	EHal EMar GBuc GCal GMac LGan NChi WAbe
'Crimson Star'	NPri
'Edith Eddleman'	WCot
'Fiesta'	WCot
* 'Foxhunter'	EMan LIck
hastata	CHan CJew CSev ECot EFol EMan EMon EOrc GBar GCal LHol MChe MHew MNrw NChi NSti WCot WPer
– 'Alba'	CBre CSWP EHal EMan EMon GBuc MBel WCot WPer
– JLS 88010WI	EMon
– 'Rosea'	CSte EFou EMon GBuc LBuc
'Hecktor'	EMan
'Hidcote Purple'	CBrk GCal MSte
'Homestead Purple'	CBrk CSev EAst EBre ECGP EGar EHic EMan GBur GCal LFis LHop LLWP MCLN MFir MMil NFla SBid SCoo WCot WOve WWeb WWoo
'Huntsman'	GBuc GCal MSte WEas
N 'Kemerton'	CBrk CSev EMan MTis
'Kurpfalz'	IHos
* 'La France'	CElw CSam ECha EMan MRav SChu SDix SMrm SUsu

'Lawrence Johnston' ♀	CBrk EOrc GCal SLMG WEas WHen
'Loveliness'	EMan EOrc GCal IBlr MUlv SMer SMrm WEas
× ***maonettii***	CSpe EOrc WCot
'Nero'	NPri SMrm
officinalis	CArn ECWi EJud EWFC GPoy LHol MChe MGam MHew SIde WApp WHer WJek WOak WPer WSel WWye
patagonica	See ***V. bonariensis***
'Peach Blossom'	WCot
§ ***peruviana***	CBrk EBre EOrc LHop MRav SChu SCro SIng SRms WAbe WOMN
– 'Alba'	CBrk CSpe EOrc GCal NTow SCro SIde
phlogiflora	CBrk
'Pink Bouquet'	See ***V. 'Silver Anne'***
'Pink Parfait'	CBrk CHal EBar ELan EMan LHop MRav SMer SUsu WLRN
'Pink Pearl'	ECtt EOrc
'Pink Perfection'	SMrm
pulchella	See ***V. tenera***
'Purple Kleopat'	IHos
'Red Sissinghurst'	NPri SBid
§ ***rigida*** ♀	CAbb CFir CMea ECGP ECha LHil MHlr NCat SIde SMrm SRms SUsu WCot WEas WOve
* 'Royal Purple'	EMan NPri
§ 'Silver Anne' ♀	CB&S CBrk CHad CSam ECha ECtt EOrc GCal LFis LHop MRav MUlv NFai NPri NTow SChu SCro SDix SMer SMrm SRms SUsu WCot WEas WHen WHoo WOve
§ 'Sissinghurst' ♀	CArn CB&S CBrk CGle CHad CSam CSpe ECtt EOrc GCal LFis LHop NFai NPri SBid SCro SLMG SUsu WEas WHen WHoo WPyg WWin
'Snow Flurry'	WCot
* ***spicata*** 'Pam' (v)	WCot
stricta	EMan GBar
§ Tapien® Pearl = 'Sunvat'	NPri
§ Tapien® Pink = 'Sunver'	LIck NPri
§ Tapien® Violet = 'Sunvop'	LIck NPri
◆ Tapien® Pearl	See ***V. Tapien® Pearl = 'Sunvat'***
◆ Tapien® Pink	See ***V. Tapien® Pink = 'Sunver'***
◆ Tapien® Violet	See ***V. Tapien® Violet = 'Sunvop'***
'Tenerife'	See ***V. 'Sissinghurst'***
tenuisecta	CBrk CM&M SDix
¶ – f. ***alba***	WCot
– 'Edith'	LHop WCot WPen
'Texas Appleblossom'	WCot
venosa	See ***V. rigida***
'White Cascade'	ECtt EOrc NPri
* 'White Knight'	CBrk LIck
'White Sissinghurst'	SBid

VERNONIA (Asteraceae)

crinita	CHan ECha ECro GCal LFis SIgm
fasciculata	EMan GCal
¶ ***noveboracensis***	SMrm WCot WPer
– 'Albiflora'	GCal WCot WPer

VERONICA † (Scrophulariaceae)

amethystina	See ***V. spuria***
armena	CLyd CShe EWes MBro MSte MWat SBla SIgm WThi
§ ***austriaca***	SMac SMrm
– Corfu form	CLyd CMil EMan EWes LGre LHop MSCN SLod WPer
– var. ***dubia***	See ***V. prostrata***
– 'Ionian Skies'	CLon CLyd CPBP CRDP CSpe EBre ESis GBuc LCom MBel SAga SBla SChu SHel SIgm SPer SWas WCru WFar WKif
§ – subsp. ***teucrium***	CArn CHan CPle EBee EHal GAul LFis LHol NNor NRoo NWCA SChu SRms WPer
– – 'Blue Blazer'	SCro
– – 'Crater Lake Blue' ♀	CKel CLon CRDP ECha ECtt EFou ELan ESis LGre MFir MRav NFai NNor SMac SMrm SRms WByw WCot WEas WPat WPer WWin
– – 'Kapitän'	ECha EGar ELan LHop MFir SMrm WPer
– – 'Knallblau'	EBee EFou EMil MBri WLRN
– – 'Royal Blue' ♀	CLTr CMil EBee ECot EFou EPfP GBuc MArl NSti SIng WBea WBro WHoo WPyg WWtk
– – 'Shirley Blue'	See ***V. 'Shirley Blue'***
beccabunga	CArn CBen CKin CWGN CWat EBre ECWi EHon ELan EMFW EWFC GPoy LPBA MHew MSta NDea NMir SHig SRms SWat WChe WHer WMAq
– 'Don's Dyke' (v)	CRow
bellidioides	CLyd GTou NGre
'Blue Spire'	SWat WPer
bombycina	CLyd EHyt EPot NMen NTow NWCA SIgm
– subsp. ***bolkardaghensis***	CPBP SIgm
– Mac&W 5840	EHyt
bonarota	See ***Paederota bonarota***
caespitosa	WDav
– subsp. ***caespitosa***	CLyd EHyt SIgm
– Mac&W 5849	EHyt NTow
candida	See ***V. spicata*** subsp. ***incana***
× ***cantiana*** 'Kentish Pink'	EGoo GBuc MBel SHel SPla SUsu WHil
'Catforth Border Guard'	NCat
caucasica	EHal ELan EMon LCom LGre MSCN
chamaedrys	CKin ECWi NMir
§ – 'Miffy Brute' (v)	CHan CSpe ELan LFis LHop MRav WAlt WLRN WPbr WRus
– 'Variegata'	See ***V. chamaedrys 'Miffy Brute'***
– 'Waterrow'	EMon
cinerea ♀	CLyd CMHG CShe ECha LCom MBro MHar NHol NTow SIgm WAbe WEas WPat
¶ ***coreana***	CLon
dichrus	ELan
exaltata	CBrd EBee EHal EMan EMon GBuc GMac LGre LRHS MNrw MSte MTol SAxl WCot WPer
¶ – white	CBrd
filifolia	MHar
filiformis	ECWi MGam
formosa	See ***Hebe formosa***

§ ***fruticans***	CLyd GTou NCat NMen NSla WCla
fruticulosa	NWCA SIde SSmi
* ***galactites***	LLew
gentianoides ♀	Widely available
– 'Alba'	CMea CRDP EOrc GCal NSti
– 'Barbara Sherwood'	EBee EBre MFir
– 'Nana'	EBre EOrc MMil
– 'Pallida'	EBee NPri SHhN
– 'Robusta'	CArc ECha EFol GCra LCom WPbr
– 'Tissington White'	CArc CBre CLon CVer LCom MCLN MTis NCut NWes SAga SBla SHel SOkh SWat WAbb WPbr WPen
– 'Variegata'	Widely available
x ***guthrieana***	CNic MAll WCru WPer WRHF
hendersonii	See ***V. subsessilis hendersonii***
incana	See ***V. spicata*** subsp. ***incana***
* – 'Candidissima'	GCal
kellereri	See ***V. spicata***
kiusiana	CBot EBre MBel MTis
kotschyana	NGre
* 'Lila Karina'	WPer
liwanensis	ELan ESis EWes GCHN MBro NTow WThi
– Mac&W 5936	EPot MHig WHil
longifolia	CBre CHan CKel ECro EGar ELan GMac MBel MCLN MFir NCat WEas WRHF
– 'Alba'	EGar ELan EPfP MBel SIde SSca
– 'Blaubündel'	EFou WHil
– 'Blauer Sommer'	CMGP EBee EFou EGar SPer WLRN
§ – 'Blauriesin'	CM&M CTri ECtt EOrc GMaP MBri MUlv NCut NHol NVic
– Blue Bouquet	See ***V. longifolia* 'Blaubündel'**
◆ – Blue Giantess	See ***V. longifolia* 'Blauriesin'**
– 'Fascination'	SMrm
– 'Foerster's Blue'	See ***V. longifolia* 'Blauriesin'**
– 'Joseph's Coat' (v)	EBee EMon LFis WBro WCot WPbr
– 'Oxford Blue'	WRHF
– pink shades	WRHF
– 'Rose Tone'	ECha MTis SMrm WWhi
– 'Rosea'	CTri LCom MBel NCGP NTow WCru WPer
– 'Schneeriesin'	CMGP EBee EBre ECha ECtt EOrc GMaP MBri MCLN NHol NWoo SCro
lyallii	See ***Parahebe lyallii***
montana	CKin
– 'Corinne Tremaine' (v)	CArc CElw CNat EMon WCot WHer WPbr
morrisonicola B&SWJ 086	NBro
nipponica	NLak WPer
* ***nivalis nivea***	EGar
'Noah Williams' (v)	WCot
nummularia	ESis NGre NTow WOMN WPer
officinalis	CArn CKin ECWi EWFC
oltensis	CLyd CMHG CPBP EHyt EPot ESis EWes MHig WAbe WPat WWin
– JCA 984.150	MBro NTow
orientalis subsp. ***carduchorum***	SIgm
– subsp. ***orientalis***	EPot NMen
ornata	ECha SVen WPer
pectinata	EHic ESis GDra MBel NCat NMen SHel
– 'Rosea'	CMHG CMea CNic ESis EWes GDra NBus NMen SHel WPer WThi WWin
peduncularis	CNic EOrc LBee LRHS SBla WEas
§ – 'Georgia Blue'	Widely available
– 'Oxford Blue'	See ***V. peduncularis* 'Georgia Blue'**
perfoliata	See ***Parahebe perfoliata***
petraea 'Madame Mercier'	MMil SMrm
'Pink Damask'	CHad CLon EBee EFou EMon LBuc LGre SCro SOkh WRus
pinnata 'Blue Eyes'	ESis LHop WPbr
prenja	See ***V. austriaca***
§ ***prostrata*** ♀	CLyd CSam CShe CSpe ELan EMNN EPot ESis GDra MBar MBro MHig MPla MWat NGre NHol NNrd NRoo SHel SIng SRms SSmi SSoC WEas WHil WHoo WWin
– 'Alba'	CSpe MBro WHoo WPyg
§ – 'Blauspiegel'	CLon SBla SIgm SWas WCru
– 'Blue Ice'	SSmi
◆ – Blue Mirror	See ***V. prostrata* 'Blauspiegel'**
– 'Blue Sheen'	ECtt EGoo EHic ESis LBlm LGre NBus NPri SChu SMer WAbe WPer WRHF WWin
– 'Loddon Blue'	NRoo NVic SBla SMer WPer
– 'Miss Willmott'	See ***V. prostrata* 'Warley Blue'**
– 'Mrs Holt'	CLyd CMea CSam CShe EBre EMNN ESis LGan LGre NCat NMen NNor NNrd NRoo SBla SIng SRms SSmi SWas WPer WThi WWin
– 'Nana'	EMNN EPot ESis EWes LBee MHig MPla NHol NMen NNrd
– 'Rosea'	CLyd ELan ESis MPla SIgm WDav WKif WPer
– 'Silver Queen'	SRms
– 'Spode Blue'	CLTr CMea CShe ELan ESis LCom LGre LHop MHar MHig MMil NCat NWCA SBla SRms WDav
– 'Trehane'	CArc CLyd CShe EBre ECha ELan ESis LFis LGan LGro LHop MBro NGre NHar NNrd NOak NRoo NRya SHel SRms SSmi SWat WAbe WDav WThi WWhi
§ – 'Warley Blue'	CMGP
'Red Georgia'	LFis
repens	See ***V. reptans***
§ ***reptans***	EHal GBur LCom LWak MOne NCat WPer WRHF
'Rosalinde'	CBot EBre GBuc LFis NCat SPla WPer
rupestris	See ***V. prostrata***
saturejoides	CNic CPBP MBro SRms WPer
saxatilis	See ***V. fruticans***
schmidtiana	GTou LLew WPer
– 'Nana'	CLyd MBro NHol WOMN WPat
– 'Nana Rosea'	WThi
selleri	See ***V. wormskjoldii***
serpyllifolia	ECWi

§ 'Shirley Blue' ♀ EBar EBre ECro EFou GCHN LFis LWak MBel MCLN MFir MWat NFla NHol NMir NRoo SHel SPer SRms SWat WHen WHil WPer WWhi
§ ***spicata*** EBar ECWi ELan EWFC GDra LWak MBro MHew NNor NPri SRms SSea WCla WCot WOve WPer WWeb
– 'Alba' EBar EMan EMil LCom MRav NCut NPri WHil WPer
– 'Barcarolle' EBee ELan WPbr
§ – 'Blaufuchs' CBlo CMHG CSam EBre NRoo
♦ – Blue Fox See ***V. spicata* 'Blaufuchs'**
* – 'Corali' LFis
§ – 'Erika' EBee ECha ECtt EOrc GBuc MBro MTol NOak NPri NRoo SHel SIde WCla
– 'Heidekind' CGle CLon CMea CShe EBre ECha EFou ELan EOrc ESis GDra LHop MCLN MRav NHar NHol NNor NVic SBla SHel SIng SWat WEas WOve WWin
– hybrids CNat
§ – 'Icicle' EFou SAsh SLod WRus
§ – subsp. ***incana*** ♀ CBot CGle CLon CShe CSpe EAst EFol EHoe ELan ENot ESis GMaP GMac LFis LGan MBri MBro MWat NMir NNor NRoo SBla SPer WAbe WBea WPer WPyg WRus
– – 'Mrs Underwood' ECha
– – 'Nana' ECha ESis SAxl SRms
– subsp. ***incana*** 'Saraband' EBre WCot WPer
– –'Silver Carpet' CMGP CMil EBee EBre EFou EOrc MTis NHol NSti SCoo
– – 'Wendy' ♀ GCal
– 'Minuet' LFis WByw
¶ – 'Nana Blauteppich' EMan
– 'Pavane' LFis
– 'Pink Damask' LFis
¶ – red WHil
♦ – Red Fox See ***V. spicata* 'Rotfuchs'**
– 'Romiley Purple' ECGP EFou EMon ESiP LGre MBro MSte NFla NSti SAxl SChu SHel SLod WCot WHoo WPyg WWeb
– ***rosea*** See ***V. spicata* 'Erika'**
§ –'Rotfuchs' CGle CMHG CSam EBre ECha ECtt EFou ELan EPar MRav MWat NFla NRoo NSti SCro SMrm SPer SUsu WByw WEas WHoo WOve WPer WWeb WWin
* – 'Sightseeing' NBus NCut NRoo SWat WBea WHil
– subsp. ***spicata*** 'Nana' SSmi
– ***variegata*** NBir WPbr
§ ***spuria*** EFol EMon NWes WPer
stelleri See ***V. wormskjoldii***
§ ***subsessilis hendersonii*** EHal
'Sunny Border Blue' EPfP LBuc WCot
surculosa MFos SBla
tauricola NTow
– JH 92101536 LGre
– Mac&W 5835 EPot SIgm
telephiifolia CLyd EHyt EMNN ESis EWes LFis MPla NMen NTow NWCA WAbe WPat WPyg WWin
teucrium See ***V. austriaca*** subsp. ***teucrium***
thessalica NTow SBla
thymoides subsp. ***pseudocinerea*** NWCA
– subsp. ***thymoides*** ESis SIgm
virginica See ***Veronicastrum virginicum***
'Waterperry Blue' EGoo ELan MBel MHig MRav NWoo SBod SMer WPer
wherryi WPer
'White Icicle' See ***V. spicata* 'Icicle'**
'White Spire' CBot
whitleyi CLyd CTri LCom MHar NNrd WWin
§ ***wormskjoldii*** CHan ELan ESiP ESis LHop MBro MCLN MHar MHig NMen NNrd SBla SRms WCla WFar WHil WOMN WPer WWin
– 'Alba' WPer

VERONICASTRUM (Scrophulariaceae)

§ ***virginicum*** CArn CPou CRow ECha EFol EFou EMon MFir MUlv NSti WPer WWhi WWin
– 'Alboroseum' WCot
– ***album*** CBot CChu CDoC CHan CShe EBre EFol ELan GCal LBlm LFis LGan MBri MBro MRav MUlv MWat NFai NFla NRoo NSti SAxl SCro SHel SPer SRms WEas WHoo WRus
–'Fascination' CLon EFou GCal WCot
§ – var. ***incarnatum*** CSte LRHS MBri MUlv NFla SCro SHel SPer WCot
– 'Lavendelturm' LGre WCot
– 'Lila Karina' EPfP
– 'Pink Glow' EBre ELan EMil EPfP SMrm SOkh WCot
– ***roseum*** See ***V. virginicum*** var. ***incarnatum***
– var. ***sibiricum*** EMon WCot

VESTIA (Solanaceae)

§ ***foetida*** ♀ CB&S CGre CPle ELan ERea IBlr LHil MHar NRar SIgm SLod SOWG WPer WSHC
lycioides See ***V. foetida***

VETIVERIA (Poaceae)

¶ ***zizanioides*** MSal

VIBURNUM † (Caprifoliaceae)

acerifolium CFil WHCG WPGP WWat
'Allegheny' WWat
alnifolium See ***V. lantanoides***
atrocyaneum CFil CPle WGwG WHCG WWat
awabuki CFil EPfP
betulifolium CB&S CChu CFil CPle CTrw MBal WAbe WHCG WWat
bitchiuense CPle ELan
× ***bodnantense*** CBot CChu CTri CTrw ELan ENot GRei MRav MWat NHed NNor WStI WWat WWin
– 'Charles Lamont' ♀ CBot CEnd CSam ECtt EMil IBlr LPan MAsh MBri MGos MPla NHol SEND SHBN SPer SSpi WPat WPyg WWat WWeb
– 'Dawn' ♀ Widely available

– 'Deben' 🏆	EBee ENot LRHS MBri SPer WDin
bracteatum	CFil CPle WPGP
buddlejifolium	CChu CEnd CHan CPle WHCG WWat
burejaeticum	CPle
x ***burkwoodii***	CB&S CBot CLan CMHG CShe ELan ENot GAul GRei ISea LHop LPan MBal MBel MBri MGos MRav MWat NWea SHBN SPer SReu SSpi SSta WAbe WDin WHCG WPat WRTC
– 'Anne Russell' 🏆	CB&S CPMA CShe EBre EWes IOrc MAsh MGos MMor NSti SHBN SPer SPla WFar WRus
– 'Chenaultii'	EHal ELan SPer WCru
– 'Fulbrook' 🏆	CMHG CRos MBri NHol SSpi WWat
– 'Park Farm Hybrid' 🏆	CChu CPMA CSam CTri EBre ELan ENot IOrc MAsh MBal MRav SLPl SPan SPer SRms WCru WRHF WWat
x ***carlcephalum*** 🏆	CB&S CChu CEnd EBre ELan EMil ENot IOrc LPan MAsh MBri MGos MHlr MMor MRav MTis MWat NHol NNor SPer SReu SSpi WBod WDin WHCG WPat WSHC WWat
* – 'Variegatum'	CPMA
carlesii	CB&S ECtt ENot GRei GWht IOrc LHol MBlu NBee SCoo SPer SReu WStI
* – 'Aurea'	LPan MAsh SHBN
– 'Aurora' 🏆	CB&S CEnd CPMA EBre ELan ENot IOrc MBar MBri MGos MMor MWat NHol SPan SPer SReu SSpi SSta WBod WDin WHCG WPat WWat
– 'Charis'	CMHG MMor WBod WLRN
– 'Diana'	CBlo CEnd CMHG CPMA CRos SBid SSpi SSta WPat WWat
* ***carlesii sieboldii*** (v)	CPMA
cassinoides	CPle WPat WWat
'Chesapeake'	CChu CPMA CPle EWes MTis NHol NTow SBid SEND SSpi WWat
chingii	CFil CPle ELan GGGa WPGP WWat
cinnamomifolium 🏆	CFil CLan CPle ELan ISea LNet MAsh MHlr SArc SBid WHCG WLRN WWat
congestum	CPle ELan EMon
cotinifolium	CChu CPle
cylindricum	CBot CBrd CChu CFil CGre CPle ELan EPfP SBid WCru WWat
dasyanthum	EPfP EPla
davidii 🏆	CChe CDec CHEx CShe EBre ELan EMil ENot GRei ISea LHop MBal MBar MBri MGos MHlr MRav MWat NHol NNor NWea SHBN SSpi WDin WGwG WHCG WWin
– (f)	CB&S CBot CDoC ELan EPfP MAsh MBal MGos MUlv SHBN SPer SPla SReu SRms SSta WBod WHar WPat WWat WWeb
– (m)	CB&S CBot CDoC ELan EPfP MBal MGos MUlv SPer SPla SReu SRms SSta WBod WHar WPat WWat WWeb
dentatum	CFil CPle WPGP
§ – var. ***pubescens***	CPle
dilatatum	CBlo ELan WWat WWes
erosum	CFil
erubescens	CPle WWat
– var. ***gracilipes***	CHan CPle WWat
'Eskimo'	CBlo CPMA EBre LHop MBlu MBro SSpi WHCG WPat WPyg
§ ***farreri*** 🏆	CB&S CChu CPle CShe EBar ECtt ELan ENot GRei ISea LBuc LHol MBal MBar MGos MPla MRav NHol NWea SHBN SPer WDin WHCG WTyr WWat
– 'Album'	See ***V. farreri* 'Candidissimum'**
§ – 'Candidissimum'	CBot CFil ELan LHop NHol SBid SSpi WPat WPyg WWat
– 'Farrer's Pink'	CPMA WWat
– 'Nanum'	CFil CPMA CPle LHop MAsh MBar MPla NHol SChu SSta WHCG WPat WPyg WWat
¶ ***foetens***	SPer
foetidum	CPle
¶ – var. ***ceanothoides***	CPle
fragrans Bunge	See ***V. farreri***
furcatum 🏆	CChu SSpi WHCG WWat
x ***globosum*** 'Jermyns Globe'	CB&S CDoC CMHG CPle EBee MBar MGos SEas WAbe WHCG WWat
harryanum	CFil CPle ECou EPla IOrc MBal MUlv WCru WWat
henryi	CChu CFil CPle MBri NHol SPer WHCG WRTC WWat
x ***hillieri***	CAbP CFil CHan CPle WHCG WKif WWat
– 'Winton' 🏆	CAbP CDoC CGre EBee ISea MAsh MBri SBid SHBN WCot WCru WWat
japonicum	CChu CFil CHEx CPle CSam SBid SHBN WWat
x ***juddii*** 🏆	CB&S CBot CEnd CPMA CPle CShe EBre ECtt ELan EMil ENot IOrc MAsh MBal MBar MBlu MBri MGos MRav NBee SPan SPer SReu SSta WAbe WDin WHCG WPat WWat
lantana	CKin CPer CTri EHic ENot GAul IOrc LBuc NRoo NWea SPer WDin WMou
– 'Aureum'	EFol EHoe EPla MBlu WBcn
¶ – 'Mohican'	NPro
§ ***lantanoides***	SSpi
lentago	CPle
lobophyllum	CPle EPfP
macrocephalum	CPMA
– f. ***keteleeri***	CPMA
mariesii	See ***V. plicatum* 'Mariesii'**
'Mohawk'	CAbP CKni CRos ELan LRHS MAsh SCoo SPla SSpi WWat
mullaha CC 1241	WHCr
nudum 'Pink Beauty'	CChu CPMA CPle WWat
odoratissimum	CB&S CChu CFil CGre CHEx CPle SBid SHBN SMad WSHC

opulus	CAgr CB&S CKin CPer CSam ECtt ELan ENot GAul GPoy IOrc LBuc MBar MBlu MBri MRav MWat NBee NNor NRoo NWea SHBN SHFr SMac SPer WDin WMou
– 'Aureum'	CMHG CSam EBre EHoe ELan EMil GAul IOrc MAsh MBal MGos MPla MUlv NFla NHol SEas SHBN SPer SPla SSta WHCG WPat WRTC WWeb
– 'Compactum' 🏆	CB&S CChu CHan EBre ELan ENot IOrc LHop MAsh MBar MBri MGos MPla MWat NHol SDix SLPl SPer SReu WDin WHCG WPat WWat
N– 'Fructu Luteo'	ELan SPan
– 'Nanum'	CAbP CPle ELan EPla ESis GAul MBal MBar MBri MPla NHol NMen WDin WHCG WPat WWat
– 'Notcutt's Variety' 🏆	EBee ENot NTow SHBN SHFr SHhN SMur SRms
– 'Park Harvest'	CPle CRos CSWP EBee EPla MBri NSti SAga SLPl
§ – 'Roseum' 🏆	CB&S CBot CPle ELan ENot IOrc LPan MBar MBlu MBri MGos MPla MWat NBee NFla NWea SHBN SPer SPla WDin WGwG WStI
– 'Sterile'	See ***V. opulus* 'Roseum'**
N– 'Xanthocarpum' 🏆	CChu CMHG CSam EBre ELan EMon IOrc LHop MBar MGos MHlr MRav MUlv MWat NHol SEas SLPl SMac SPer SRms WDin WSHC WWat WWin
N***plicatum***	CB&S CShe EBee ENot MBar WDin
– 'Cascade'	SHBN
– 'Dart's Red Robin'	CEnd ECtt EHic MBri MGos MPla NHol SMad SSta
– 'Grandiflorum' 🏆	CBlo CPle EBee MBar SSta WAbe WHCG
– 'Lanarth'	CB&S CPle CSam CShe CTre ECtt EMil ENot IOrc LHop MBri MHlr MMor NFla SEas SPer SPla SSta WBod WDin WHCG WWat
§ – 'Mariesii' 🏆	CB&S CLan CMHG CPle CTrw EBre ELan GRei LGro LPan MBal MBar MBel MGos MMor MPla MWat NHed NNor SHBN SMad SPer SPla SSta WAbe WBod WDin WHCG WSHC WWat
– 'Nanum'	See ***V. plicatum* 'Nanum Semperflorens'**
§ – 'Nanum Semperflorens'	CBar EAst ECtt ELan EPla ESis IOrc LHop MAsh MBal MBlu MGos MPla SHBN SPer WFar WGwG WHCG WPat WSHC WWat
– 'Pink Beauty' 🏆	Widely available
* – 'Prostratum'	ESis
– 'Rotundifolium'	MBri SHBN
– 'Rowallane' 🏆	WWat
– 'Saint Keverne'	SHBN
N– 'Sterile'	GOrc

– 'Summer Snowflake'	CWLN EBee ELan EPfP IOrc MAsh MBal MBri MPla MWat NHol SHBN SPer SPla WDin WHCG WPat WWeb
– f. ***tomentosum***	CLan ELan EPla MRav SEas WDin WHCG WStI
– 'Watanabe'	See ***V. plicatum* 'Nanum Semperflorens'**
'Pragense' 🏆	CChu CMCN CPle EBee EPla MBar MGos NHol SPer WHCG WLRN WPat WPyg WWat
pubescens	See ***V. dentatum*** var. ***pubescens***
recognitum	CPle MUlv
x ***rhytidophylloides***	CPle NNor WWat
– 'Dart's Duke'	MBri SLPl
rhytidophyllum	CChu CHEx CLan CPle EBre ELan ENot GRei ISea LPan MBal MBar MGos SHBN SMad SPer SReu SRms SSpi WBod WDin WRTC WTyr WWat WWin
– 'Roseum'	CBot CShe MRav
– 'Variegatum'	CBot CPMA ELan EPla SPer
– 'Willowwood'	CKni ELan MAsh SSpi SSta WWat
rigidum	CFil
sargentii	CBlo GBin IOrc WWoo
– 'Onondaga' 🏆	Widely available
semperflorens	See ***V. plicatum* 'Nanum Semperflorens'**
§ ***setigerum***	CChu CPle EPla MUlv SLPl SSpi
'Shasta'	CDoC CMCN COtt CRos EHic MBri NHol SPla SSpi SSta
sieboldii	CPle
¶ ***suspensum***	CPle
theiferum	See ***V. setigerum***
tinus	CB&S CBot CLan CShe CTrw ELan EMil ENot GWht LBuc LNet MBal MBar MGos MWat NBee NFla NNor SArc SHFr SReu SRms SSta WDin WHCG WPat WWin
– 'Bewley's Variegated'	CB&S EBee EMil MGos SCoo WWeb
– 'Compactum'	EHic
– 'Eve Price' 🏆	CB&S CBot CTre EBre ELan ENot IOrc LHop LNet MBal MBar MBri MGos MRav MWat NHed NWea SHBN SLPl SPer SPla SReu SSpi SSta WAbe WDin WHCG WPat WSHC WWat
– 'French White'	CBlo CEnd EHic ELan EPla LRHS SBid SCoo SEas SRms WGwG WRHF WWat
– 'Gwenllian' 🏆	CDoC CEnd CHan EAst EBre ECtt ELan EMil ENot EPla MAsh MBal MGos MPla MRav MUlv NTow SEas SLPl SPer SPla SRms SSpi WAbe WPat WRTC WWat WWeb
– ***hirtellum***	CTre
–'Israel'	CEnd EBee EHic EMil SPer SPla
– 'Lucidum'	CB&S CBlo CPle CSam CShe EHic MGos SBid SHBN SPla
– 'Lucidum Variegatum'	CFil CLan CPMA SDry WPGP
* – 'Macrophyllum'	EHic LPan
– 'Pink Prelude'	CDoC EBee SEas SHhN

- 'Purpureum' CB&S CPle CWLN EBee EFol EHal EHoe ELan EPla MAsh SBid SEas SHBN SLPl SMac SPer SPla WGwG
- 'Pyramidale' See ***V. tinus* 'Strictum'**
* – ***rigidum*** CPle
–'Sappho' EHic
– var. ***subcordatum*** C 2002 GGGa
– 'Variegatum' CB&S CBot CPle CTre EBre ELan GOrc IOrc LHop MBal MBar MBel MBri MHlr MWat SHBN SPer SPla SReu SSta WAbe WDin WHCG WPat WRTC WSHC WWat WWin
tomentosum See ***V. plicatum***
utile CPle EHal WHCG WWat
wrightii NHol WHCG WPat WPyg
– var. ***hessei*** MUlv

VICIA (Papilionaceae)

angustifolia See ***V. sativa*** subsp. ***nigra***
cracca CKin ECWi EWFC NLan
orobus MSCN WGwy
§ ***sativa*** subsp. ***nigra*** CKin
sepium CKin EWFC
sylvatica WGwy

VICTORIA (Nymphaeaceae)

regia See ***V. amazonica***

VIGNA (Papilionaceae)

§ ***caracalla*** CPlN

VILLADIA (Crassulaceae)

hemsleyana See ***Sedum hemsleyanum***

VILLARESIA See CITRONELLA

VILLARSIA (Menyanthaceae)

bennettii See ***Nymphoides peltata* 'Bennettii'**

VINCA † (Apocynaceae)

difformis CGle CHar CLTr CTri EBre ECha ELan EPla LBlm LHop LLWP NCat SDix SDry WCru WFox WHer WWat
– subsp. ***bicolor*** 'Alba' EBar
– var. ***bicolor*** 'Jenny Pym' EMon LHop SMad
– subsp. ***difformis*** EMon
– Greystone form EBar EPla LHop SEND WRus
– 'Oxford' SLPl
– 'Snowmound' MRav WFox WWat
herbacea EGoo
'Hidcote Purple' See ***V. major*** var. ***oxyloba***
major CB&S CChe CDoC CShe ELan ENot EOrc GPoy GRei LBuc MBri MFir MGos MWat SBod SHBN SPer WDin WOak WPLl WStI WTyr WWin
– var. ***alba*** CWan EPla GBuc IBlr
– 'Caucasian Blue' LMer
– 'Elegantissima' See ***V. major* 'Variegata'**
§ – subsp. ***hirsuta*** (Boiss.) Stearn CShe EMon EOrc WCot WFox WWye
– ***hirsuta*** hort. See ***V. major*** var. ***oxyloba***
– 'Jason Hill' EMon MBel WCot
§ – 'Maculata' (v) EFol ELan EMar EMon ENot EPla LHop MBar MBri MSCN NRoo NSti SDry SPer WCru WHer WStI WWeb
§ – var. ***oxyloba*** CHid CLyd CNic ECtt ELan EMon EPla GSki LHop MRav SLPl SPla SRms WHen
– var. ***pubescens*** See ***V. major*** subsp. ***hirsuta* (Boiss.) Stearn**
– 'Reticulata' ELan EMon MBel MSCN NSti
– 'Surrey Marble' See ***V. major* 'Maculata'**
§ – 'Variegata' ♀ CB&S CGle CKel CShe ECha EFou EHoe ELan ENot ERav GCHN GPoy GRei LBuc LGro LHop LLWP MBal MBar MBel MBri MGos NNor NRoo SHBN SPer WDin WEas WOak WWin
minor CDoC CKin CLyd EGoo ELan ENot EPar ERav GCHN GPoy GRei MBar MBro MFir MSCN MWat WDin WOak WPLl WTyr WWin WWye
– f. ***alba*** CB&S CBot CDoC EBre ECha EGoo ELan EOrc EPla LHol LHop MBar MBri MGos NNor NOak SEas SHBN SPer STre WCot WOak WStI WWat WWye
– 'Alba Aureavariegata' See ***V. minor* 'Alba Variegata'**
§ – 'Alba Variegata' CGle EBre EGoo EHoe EJud EOrc EPPr EPla MBar MFir NHol NPro NRoo SPer SRms STre WEas WHer WWat
§ – 'Argenteovariegata' ♀ CB&S CChe CGle CShe EAst ECha EFou ELan ENot GDra GRei LBuc LGro MBar MBri MGos NFla NHol NRoo SBod SMac SPer STre WDin WEas WWat WWin WWye
§ – 'Atropurpurea' ♀ CB&S CSam CShe EAst EBre ECha ELan EPla LBuc LHol MBar MBri MGos MRav MSCN NFla NHol NRoo NSti SBod SChu SHBN SPer WEas WOak WWeb WWhi
– 'Aurea' EPla WRHF
§ – 'Aureovariegata' CB&S CBot EFol ELan EOrc EPla GPoy LHol MBal MBar MFir MRav NHol NNor NRoo WHen WWye
§ – 'Azurea Flore Pleno' ♀ CArn CB&S CElw CEnd CGle CWan EOrc EPla ERav GGar LHop LLWP MBal MBar MFir MPla NBrk NHol NRoo NSti SHBN SMac SPer WEas WFox WHen WHoo WTyr WWat WWhi
* – 'Blue and Gold' EGoo
– 'Blue Cloud' EBee NHol SBod
– 'Blue Drift' CBlo EBar EFou NHol SBod
– 'Blue Moon' EBee ECtt NHol
– 'Bowles' Blue' See ***V. minor* 'La Grave'**
– 'Bowles' Variety' See ***V. minor* 'La Grave'**
– 'Burgundy' CShe EPar GGar LLWP MBal SRms WWat WWye
– 'Caerulea Plena' See ***V. minor* 'Azurea Flore Pleno'**
– 'Dartington Star' See ***V. major*** var. ***oxyloba***
– 'Dart's Blue' MBri
– 'Double Burgundy' See ***V. minor* 'Multiplex'**

– 'Gertrude Jekyll' 🏆	CArc CLTr EBee ELan EMon EPla ILis MAsh MBri NHol NRoo SBod SChu SEND SPer WHer
◆ – Green Carpet	See *V. minor* **'Grüner Teppich'**
§ – 'Grüner Teppich'	EMon SPla
§ – 'La Grave' 🏆	CChe CDoC CEnd CSev CShe ECGP ECha EGoo ELan ENot EPla GAbr MBri MBro NHol SBod SPer SRms SSvw STre WBod WPyg WWat
– 'Maculata' (v)	EGoo ELan EPPr SCoo WAlt WBcn
– 'Marion Cran'	CEnd GSki
§ – 'Multiplex' (d)	CHid CNic ECtt EGoo ELan EPar EPla ERav MBri MInt NHol NNor NRoo SRms WCru WRHF WWat
* – 'Persian Carpet'	EGoo
– 'Purpurea'	See *V. minor* **'Atropurpurea'**
– 'Rubra'	See *V. minor* **'Atropurpurea'**
– 'Sabinka'	CHid EGoo EMon EPla
– 'Silver Service' (v)	CElw CHid EGoo EMon EPPr EPla GBuc LBlm MAvo MBel MInt NHol WCot WPbr
– 'Variegata'	See *V. minor* **'Argenteovariegata'**
– 'Variegata Aurea'	See *V. minor* **'Aureovariegata'**
– 'White Gold'	CChe EBee MPla NHol WFox

VINCETOXICUM (Asclepiadaceae)

§ ***hirundinaria***	EEls GPoy
nigrum	CPlN EMon NChi WThi
officinale	See ***V. hirundinaria***

VIOLA † (Violaceae)

'Abigail' (Vtta)	LPVe
'Achilles' (Va)	LPVe
'Adelina' (Va)	LPVe
'Admiral Avellan'	See *V.* **'Amiral Avellan'**
'Admiration' (Va)	CFul GDTE GMac LPVe NPla WBou
¶ ***adunca***	WHil
– 'Alba'	WLRN
– var. ***minor***	See ***V. labradorica***
aetolica	CInt
'Agnes Cochrane' (Ex Va)	GDTE
'Agneta' (Va)	LPVe
'Alanta' (Va)	LGre LPVe
§ ***alba***	CPla EFou ELan EWes NSti NWes SCro WEas WWin
albanica	See ***V. magellensis***
I 'Alcea' (Va)	LPVe
'Alethia' (Va)	LPVe
'Alexander Rayfield' (Va)	GDTE LPVe
'Alexia' (Va)	LPVe
¶ 'Alice Witter' (Vt)	CDev
'Alice Wood' (Ex Va)	GDTE
'Alice Woodall' (Va)	LPVe
'Alison'	GMaP WBou
¶ 'Alma' (Va)	GDTE
altaica	LPVe
'Alwyn' (Va)	LPVe
'Amelia' (Va)	GMac LPVe WWhi
'Amethyst' (C)	CDoC LHop
§ 'Amiral Avellan' (Vt)	CCot CDev NBro WRus
'Andrena' (Va)	LPVe
'Angela' (Va)	LPVe
'Anita' (Va)	LPVe
'Ann' (SP)	GDTE
'Ann Kean' (Vtta)	LPVe NRoo
'Anna' (Va)	LPVe
'Anna Leyns' (Va)	LPVe
'Annabelle' (Va)	LPVe
'Annaliese' (C)	LPVe
'Anne Mott' (Va)	LPVe
'Annette Ross' (Va)	LPVe
I 'Annona' (Va)	LPVe
'Anthea' (Va)	LPVe
'Antique Lace' (Va)	GMac NPla
'Aphrodite' (Va)	LPVe
'Apollo' (Va)	LPVe
'Arabella' (Va)	GDTE LBee LIck LPVe SIng SLod SMrm WBou WFar WHer WLRN
arborescens	MSCN
'Ardross Gem' (Va)	CFul CGle CMHG CPla CSam CShe GCHN GDTE GMac LBee LHop LPVe MCLN NHol NRoo SHel WBou WEas WIvy WKif WPer WWhi WWin
arenaria	See ***V. rupestris***
'Arkwright's Ruby' (Va)	CArn CLTr LPVe SSca
'Artemis' (Va)	LPVe
arvensis	ECWi
'Aspasia' (Va) 🏆	CFul GMac LBee LPVe NHol WBou
'Astrid' (Va)	LPVe
'Atalanta' (Vtta)	LPVe
'Athena' (Va)	LPVe
athois	LPVe
'Aurelia' (Va)	LPVe
'Aurora' (Va)	LPVe
'Avril' (Va)	LPVe
'Avril Lawson' (Va)	GDTE GMac NNrd
'Baby Lucia' (Va)	CElw
'Barbara' (Va)	CFul GDTE LPVe NRoo WBou
'Barbara Cawthorne' (C)	LPVe
'Baronne Alice de Rothschild' (Vt)	CDev LHop WLRN
'Becka' (Va)	LPVe
§ 'Belmont Blue' (C)	CFul CLon CLyd CShe EOrc EWes GMac LBee LPVe MBel MCLN MRav NHol NRoo SChu SHel SMrm WBou
§ ***bertolonii***	EBar LPVe WBou
'Beshlie' (Va) 🏆	GMaP GMac LPVe MArl MGrG WBou WEas WHil WKif
'Bessie Cawthorne' (C)	LPVe SChu
'Bessie Knight' (Va)	LPVe
betonicifolia	MSCN WPer
* – ***albescens***	NHar
'Bettina' (Va)	LPVe
'Betty' (Va)	GDTE LPVe
'Bianca' (Vtta)	LPVe
biflora	CMHG CPla EPar GDra MTho NChi NGre NRya
'Bishop's Belle' (FP)	GDTE
'Bishop's Gold' (FP)	GDTE
'Black Ace' (Va)	LPVe
'Black Beauty'	WCot
'Blue Carpet' (Va)	GMac
'Blue Cloud' (Va)	LPVe NChi
'Blue Moon' (C)	SChu SMrm WBou
'Blue Moonlight' (C)	CBos GBuc GMac NChi SMrm
'Blue Tit' (Va)	WBou
'Bonna Cawthorne' (Va)	LPVe
bosniaca	See ***V. elegantula bosniaca***
'Boughton Blue'	See *V.* **'Belmont Blue'**
'Bournemouth Gem' (Vt)	CDev

§ 'Bowles' Black' (T)	CArn CDev CHan CSWP ECha ELan GAbr NBro NLak NRai NRoo SBla SHBN SRms WBea WBou WEas WOve WRHF
'Boy Blue' (Vtta)	EHal LPVe
'Brenda Hall' (Va)	LPVe
'Bronwen' (Va)	LPVe
¶ 'Bruneau' (dVt)	WRus
* 'Bryony' (Vtta)	LPVe WBou
'Bullion' (Va)	LPVe WMer
'Burnock Yellow' (Va)	GDTE
'Buttercup' (Vtta)	CFul CInt GDTE GMac LBee LPVe NHar NRoo SChu SIng WBou WLRN WWin
'Buxton Blue' (Va)	CFul LPVe SHBN WBou
calaminaria	LPVe
'Calantha' (Vtta)	LPVe
calcarata	ELan LPVe SIng
§ – subsp. ***zoysii***	EWes GCHN GCrs GDra ITim NGre
'California' (Vt)	CDev
¶ 'Callia' (Va)	LPVe
I 'Calliandra' (Vtta)	LPVe
I 'Calypso' (Va)	LPVe
§ ***canadensis*** var. ***rugulosa***	CRDP
'Candida' (Vtta)	LPVe
canina	CKin NBro WUnd
– ***alba***	CBre
'Carberry Seedling' (Va)	LPVe
'Carina' (Vtta)	LPVe
'Carnival' (Va)	GMac NBrk
'Carola' (Va)	LPVe
'Caroline' (Va)	SMrm
I 'Cassandra' (Vtta)	LPVe
'Catforth Gold'	NCat
'Catforth Suzanne'	NCat
'Catherine Williams' (Ex Va)	GDTE
'Cat's Whiskers'	GBri GMac NBrk
chaerophylloides	See ***V. dissecta*** var. ***chaerophylloides***
'Chandler's Glory' (Va)	LPVe
'Chantal' (Vtta)	LPVe NRoo
'Chantreyland' (Va)	CMdw NBir SRms WCot WWhi
'Charity' (Va)	LPVe
'Charlotte'	EFol
'Charlotte Mott' (Va)	LPVe
'Chelsea Girl' (Va)	SMrm
'Chloe' (Vtta)	LPVe
'Christina'	LBee WLRN
¶ 'Christmas' (Vt)	CBre CDev
'Christobel' (Va)	LPVe
'Cinderella' (Va)	CFul GDTE
'Citrina' (Va)	LPVe
'Clare Harrison' (Va)	LPVe
'Clementina' (Va) ♈	CSWP EBre GCHN LPVe MRav NRoo SCro
'Cleo' (Va)	GMac
'Clive Groves' (Vt)	CDev CGro
'Clodagh' (Va)	LPVe
'Clover' (Va)	LPVe
'Coeur d'Alsace' (Vt)	CCot CDev CGro CHan CMea CNic CPla EFou ELan EPar GMac NBro SSvw WEas WPer WRus
'Colette' (Va)	LPVe
'Colleen' (Vtta)	LPVe

'Columbine' (Va)	CBos CElw CInt CLTr CLon CMHG CRDP CSam GDTE GMac LBee LIck LPVe MCLN SAga SChu SHBN SLod SMrm WBou WEas WLRN WMaN WWhi
§ 'Comte de Brazza' (dPVt)	CDev CTri GBar GMac
'Connie' (Va)	LPVe
'Coralie' (Vtta)	LPVe
'Cordelia' (Va)	CElw LPVe NBro SSvw
'Cornish White'	CDev
cornuta ♈	CElw CFul CGle CHad CMea CPla EOrc EPot LHop LPVe MBro MFir MHig MWat NBro NRoo SDix SMrm SPer SRms WAbe WBou WHen WHil WHoo WPyg
– Alba Group ♈	Widely available
§ – 'Alba Minor'	CFul CLyd CMHG EFol ELan EWes GMac LIck LPVe MBro MCLN MFir NBro NRoo SChu WAbe WCot WHoo WPyg
– blue	LPVe WWat
* – 'Bluestone Gold'	WCot
– Lilacina Group (C)	CFul CGle ECha EWes GMac LPVe NCat NChi NFla SChu SMrm SWat WHoo WPer
– 'Minor' ♈	CFul CInt CPla CSam ECGP EPot GMac LPVe MFir NBro NHol SBla WAbe WBou WBro WRus
– 'Minor Alba'	See ***V. cornuta*** **'Alba Minor'**
– 'Paris White'	EPfP
– Purpurea Group	CMea ECha GBuc WRus
– 'Rosea'	CBos CFul CLyd LPVe
– 'Seymour Pink'	CFul
– 'Variegata'	NHol
– 'Victoria's Blush'	NHar SMrm WRHF
corsica	EMan LPVe
'Cottage Garden' (Va)	GDTE NFai
¶ 'Countess of Shaftsbury' (dVt)	CDev
'Cox's Moseley' (ExV)	GDTE
'Cressida' (Va)	LPVe
§ ***cucullata***	CGro SChu
§ – 'Alba'	ECGP
– ***rosea***	CJew EFol EWes
cunninghamii	GDra
¶ – CC 463	MRPP
curtisii	See ***V. tricolor*** subsp. ***curtisii***
'Cyril Bell' (Va)	LPVe
§ 'Czar' (Vt)	CBre CPla ILis NRya
§ 'Czar Bleu' (Vt)	CDev
'Daena' (Vtta)	LPVe SMrm
'Daisy Smith' (Va)	CFul GDTE GMac NChi SChu WBou
'Dartington Hybrid' (Va)	LPVe
'Daveron' (C)	LPVe NRoo
'David Rhodes' (FP)	GDTE
'David Wheldon' (Va)	GDTE LPVe
'Davina' (Va)	LPVe SChu
'Dawn' (Vtta)	CCot CFul GDTE GMac LPVe MMil WBou
'Deanna' (Va)	LPVe
'Decima' (Va)	LPVe
'Delia' (Va)	GMac LPVe WBou
'Delicia' (Vtta)	LPVe NChi NRoo
'Delmonden' (Va)	CRDP SAsh
'Delphine' (Va)	CBos LPVe NPla NRoo SChu SMrm

'Demeter' (Va) LPVe
'Desdemona' (Va) CMHG GMac LBee LGre WBou
'Desmonda' (Va) LPVe SChu
'Devon Cream' (Va) GMac WBou
'Dimity' (Va) LPVe
¶ 'Dione' (Vtta) LPVe
I 'Diosma' (Va) LPVe
§ ***dissecta*** WCot WPer
§ – var. ***chaerophylloides*** f. ***eizanensis*** CRDP EBre ECro MTho NWCA WOMN
– var. ***sieboldiana*** CRDP EFol
'Dobbie's Bronze' (Va) LPVe
'Dobbie's Buff' (Va) LPVe
'Dobbie's Red' (Va) GDTE LPVe WLRN
'Doctor Smart' (C) LPVe
doerfleri LPVe
'Dominique' (Va) LPVe
'Dominy' (Vtta) LPVe
¶ 'Donau' (Vt) CDev
'Double White' (dVt) CGle
dubyana GBuc WOMN
'Duchesse de Parme' (dVt) CDev CGle CGro GBar GMac WHer
'D'Udine' (dVt) CDev CGro GBar GMac WRus
'Dusk' WBou
'E.A. Bowles' See ***V.* 'Bowles' Black'**
'Eastgrove Blue Scented' (Va) CLTr GMac MCLN WAbe WBou WCot WEas WIvy WRHF
eizanensis See ***V. dissecta*** var. ***chaerophylloides* f. *eizanensis***
'Elaine Cawthorne' (C) LPVe
'Elaine Quin' WBou
§ ***elatior*** CElw CMea CMil CPla CSWP EBar ECha EMon GBri LGan MBel MHar NHol NSti SChu SSca WFar WPer WWye
§ ***elegantula*** LPVe
§ – ***bosniaca*** LPVe
'Elisha' (Va) LPVe NRoo
'Elizabeth' (Va) GDTE GMac LPVe NPri SChu SMrm SRms WBou WLRN
¶ 'Elizabeth Cawthorne' (C) LPVe
'Elizabeth Lee' CGro
'Elizabeth McCallum' (FP) GDTE
¶ 'Elliot Adam' (Va) GDTE
'Elsie Coombs' (Vt) CDev WPer
'Emily Mott' (Va) LPVe
'Emma' (Va) CMea LPVe NHar
'Emma Cawthorne' (C) CLTr GDTE LPVe
'Enterea' (Va) LPVe
erecta See ***V. elatior***
'Eris' (Va) LPVe NRoo
'Eros' (Va) LPVe NRoo
'Etain' (Va) CSWP EBee ECha ELan GDTE GMaP LGre LIck LPVe MMil NRoo WBou WLRN
'Ethena' (Va) LPVe
'Etienne' (Va) LPVe
'Evelyn' (Ex Va) GDTE
'Evelyn Cawthorne' (C) LPVe NRoo
'Fabiola' (Vtta) GMac LBee LPVe NBir WBou
'Felicity' (Va) LPVe
'Finola Galway' (Va) LPVe
'Fiona' (Va) CLon CMHG GDTE GMac LPVe MCLN NBrk NCat NRoo SChu SHel SUsu WBou
'Fiona Lawrenson' (Va) LPVe
'Florence' (Va) LPVe NRoo
'Foxbrook Cream' (C) CFul CLTr CMea CRDP GBuc GDTE GMac LPVe MBel MOne NBrk NPla SHel WAbe WBou WCot WRus
'Frances' (Va) LPVe
'Francesca' (Va) LPVe
'Freckles' See ***V. sororia* 'Freckles'**
'Gatina' (Va) LPVe
I 'Gazania' (Va) CMea LPVe WBou
'Gazelle' (Vtta) ECha LPVe MCLN WPen
'Genesta Gambier' (Va) CFul CSam
'Georgina' (Va) LPVe
'Geraldine' (Vtta) LPVe
'Geraldine Cawthorne' (C) GDTE LPVe
'Gina' (Vtta) LPVe
'Giselle' (Va) LPVe
glabella CLTr SWas WOMN
'Gladys Findlay' (Va) GDTE GMac LPVe WBou
'Glenroyd Fancy' (Ex Va) GDTE
'Governor Herrick' (Vt) CDev EFou NSti WPer
'Grace' (Va) NRoo
§ ***gracilis*** CElw ECha ELan LPVe SBla
– × ***cornuta*** LPVe
– 'Lutea' CLon CSam NRoo SBla SMrm
* – 'Magic' CElw SMrm SUsu SWat WCot
'Grey Owl' (Va) CLon CMea LBee LGre LPVe NCat SChu SLod WBou WKif
grisebachiana GCLN NGre
– ***alba*** GCLN
'Griselda' (Vtta) LPVe
'Grovemount Blue' (C) CMea NCat WPen
§ ***grypoceras*** var. ***exilis*** CDec CInt CRDP EHyt EWes GBri NBus NChi SMad WHoo WWye
– 'Variegata' EHoe NBir
'Gustav Wermig' (C) GAbr LPVe MBel WBou
'Gwen Cawthorne' (C) LPVe
'H.H. Hodge' (Ex Va) GDTE
'Hadria Cawthorne' (C) GDTE LPVe
'Hansa' (C) CHid WMer
'Haslemere' See ***V.* 'Nellie Britton'**
'Heaselands' SMrm
I 'Hebe' (Vtta) LPVe
§ ***hederacea*** CArn CCot CDev CGro CHan CMHG CPla CShe CSpe ECou ELan ESis GCHN GMac GQui MNrw NBro NHar NOak SUsu WBea WHer WOMN WPri WWhi WWye
– blue CFee CLTr CPla SIng WPer
– 'Putty' ECou EWes
– var. ***sieberi*** See ***V. sieberiana***
'Helen Dillon' EWes NHaw
'Helen W. Cochrane' (Ex Va) GDTE
'Helena' (Va) LPVe SChu
¶ 'Hera' (Va) LPVe
¶ 'Hespera' (Va) LPVe
I 'Hesperis' (Va) LPVe
heterophylla subsp. ***epirota*** See ***V. bertolonii***
'Hextable' (C) LPVe
hirta CKin ECWi WCla
hispida LPVe
'Hopley's White' CGro
¶ 'Hudsons Blue' WWhi
'Hugh Campbell' (Ex Va) GDTE

'Huntercombe Purple' (Va) 🏆	CBos CFul CGle GDTE GMac LBee LPVe NPla SBla SChu SUsu WBou WKif
'Hunter's Pride'	SMrm
'Hyperion' (Va)	LPVe
'Iantha' (Vtta)	LPVe
'Iden Gem' (Va)	CFul GDTE LPVe
'Inkie' (Va)	CFul
'Inverurie Beauty' (Va) 🏆	EJud GMaP LPVe MFir NBrk NCat SChu WBou WKif
'Inverurie Mauve' (Va)	LPVe
'Iona' (Va)	LPVe
'Irina' (Va)	LPVe
'Irish Elegance' (Vt)	CDev CGro CRDP NBro WHal
'Irish Mary' (Va)	LPVe
'Irish Molly' (Va)	CBot CElw CFul CLon CMHG CSam CShe CSpe ECha ELan GCal GDTE GMac LBee LBlm LPVe MCLN NRoo SBla SMrm WBou WEas WHer WPer WSHC WWhi WWin
'Isata' (Vtta)	LPVe
'Isla' (Vtta)	LGre LPVe
'Isobel'	EWes
'Ita' (Va)	LPVe
'Iver Grove' (Va)	LPVe
'Ivory Queen' (Va)	CFul GDTE GMac LPVe NBrk WBou
'Ivory White' (Va)	CDev LPVe WOMN
'Jack Sampson'	CDev
'Jackanapes' (Va) 🏆	CBot CFul CMHG CShe ECha ECtt ELan GDTE GMac LPVe MHig NBrk NRoo SMrm SRms WBou WWin
'James'	EWes
'James Pilling' (Va)	CFul GDTE GMac NPla
'Jane Askew' (Va)	LPVe
'Jane Mott' (Va)	LPVe
'Janet' (Va)	GDTE LPVe SIng SMrm WLRN
'Janine' (Vtta)	LPVe
'Janna' (Va)	LPVe
japonica	EGar WThi
'Jean Arnot'	CGro
'Jeannie Bellew' (Va)	GDTE GMac LIck LPVe NCat NHar NPri SChu SMrm WBou WLRN
'Jemma' (Va)	LPVe
'Jenelle' (Vtta)	LPVe
'Jenny' (Vtta)	LPVe
'Jersey Gem' (Va)	GMac LPVe
'Jessica' (Va)	LPVe
'Jessie East'	WEas
'Jessie Taylor' (FP)	GDTE
'Jimmie's Dark' (Ex Va)	GDTE
'Joanna' (Va)	GDTE
I 'Jocunda' (Va)	LPVe
'Joella' (Va)	LPVe
'John Wallmark' (c)	WMer
'John Yelmark' (Va)	LPVe
'John Zanini' (Vtta)	LPVe
'Johnny Jump Up' (T)	EWll
jooi	CLyd CNic GTou NBir NBro NHol NMen SBla SIng SSca WOMN WRha
'Jordieland Gem' (c)	GMac WAbe
'Josie' (Va)	LPVe
'Joyce Gray' (Va)	GDTE NRoo WBou
'Judy Goring' (Va)	LPVe
'Julia' (Va)	LPVe WBou

'Julian' (Va)	CFul CLTr GDTE GDra GMac MOne NRoo SBla SRms WBou WIvy
'Juno' (Va)	GMac LPVe
'Jupiter' (Va)	CBos LPVe SMrm
'Kate' (Va)	CElw CFul GMac
'Katerina' (Va)	LPVe
'Kathy' (Vtta)	LPVe
'Katie Grayson' (C)	LPVe
'Katinka' (Va)	LPVe
keiskei	GCHN NCat WThi
'Kerrie' (Va)	LPVe
'Kerry Girl'	CDev
'Kiki McDonough' (C)	CBos LPVe SChu
¶ 'Kilruna' (Va)	LPVe
'King of the Blacks' (T&M)	ECoo
'King of the Blues' (Va)	LPVe
'Kinvarna' (Va)	LPVe
'Kirsty' (Va)	LPVe
'Kitten'	SChu WAbe WBou
'Kitty White' (Va)	LPVe
koraiensis	NWCA
koreana	See ***V. grypoceras*** var. ***exilis***
kusanoana	WThi
§ ***labradorica***	EPot GLil SMer
N – hort.	See ***V. riviniana*** **Purpurea Group**
N ***labradorica purpurea*** misapplied	See ***V. riviniana*** **Purpurea Group**
lactea	ECWi
'Lady Tennyson' (Va)	GMac LPVe SBla WBou
'Lamorna' (Vtta)	LPVe
lanceolata	CPla GCra
'Larissa' (Va)	LPVe
'Latona' (Va)	LPVe
'Laura' (C)	CFul GBuc GMac
'Laverna' (Va)	LPVe
'Lavinia' (Va)	GCrs GDTE GMac LBee LIck LPVe MOne NBrk WBou
'Lawrence' (c)	WMer
'Leander' (Va)	LPVe
'Leda' (Va)	LPVe
'Leora' (Vtta)	CFul GMac LPVe NRoo
'Leora Hamilton' (C)	CMHG LPVe NPla
'Lerosa' (Vtta)	LPVe
'Leta' (Vtta)	LPVe
'Letitia' (Va)	CFul EOrc GDTE GMaP GMac LPVe MMil NPri SMrm WBou
'Leto' (Va)	LPVe
'Lewisa' (Va)	LPVe
'Lianne' (Vt)	CDev WPer
'Lilac Rose' (Va)	CFul GMac NPla WBou
'Liliana' (Va)	LPVe
'Liriopa' (Va)	LPVe
'Lisa Cawthorne' (C)	LPVe
'Little David' (Vtta) 🏆	CFul CInt CSam CShe EHal GDTE GMac LBee LPVe MCLN NHol NPla NRoo WBou WEas
'Little Johnny' (Va)	GMac
'Little Liz' (Va)	GMac
'Livia' (Vtta)	LPVe
'Lola' (Va)	LPVe
'Lord Nelson' (Va)	EMou EWll LPVe WMer
'Lord Plunket' (Va)	CFul LPVe WBou
'Lorna' (Va) 🏆	LPVe SUsu
'Lorna Cawthorne' (C)	GDTE LPVe NCat
'Lorna Moakes' (Va)	LPVe SMrm
'Louisa' (Va)	LPVe

'Louise Gemmell' (Va)	LPVe SChu
'Luca' (Va)	LPVe
'Lucinda' (Va)	LPVe
'Lucy' (Va)	LPVe
'Ludy May' (Va)	LPVe
'Luna' (Vtta)	LPVe
§ ***lutea***	CShe LPVe WBou WGwy WUnd
– subsp. ***elegans***	See ***V. lutea***
'Luxonne' (Vt)	WLRN
lyallii	ECou
'Lydia' (Va)	CShe LPVe SChu WBou
'Lydia Groves'	CDev
'Lynn' (Va)	GDTE LPVe
'Lysander' (Va)	LPVe
macedonica	See ***V. tricolor*** subsp. ***macedonica***
'Madame Armandine Pagès' (Vt)	CBre CDev
'Madelaine' (Va)	LPVe
'Madge' (Va)	LPVe
'Maera' (Vtta)	LPVe
§ ***magellensis***	NChi
'Magenta Maid' (Va)	CFul GMac LBee MArl NCat
'Maggie' (Va)	LPVe
'Maggie Mott' (Va) 🏆	CCot CFul CGle CSam CShe ECha ECtt EOrc GDTE GMac LBee LBlm LHop LPVe MBri MCLN MHig NBrk NGar NRoo SBla WBou WEas WKif WRus WWhi WWin
'Magic'	GMac LBee MArl NPla SChu WBou WCru
'Maid Marion'	SRms
'Majella' (Vtta)	LPVe
'Malise' (Va)	LPVe
'Malvena' (Vtta)	LPVe
'Margaret Cawthorne' (C)	LPVe
'Marian' (Va)	LPVe
'Marie-Louise' (dPVt)	CCot CDev CGro CPla CTri EPar
'Marika' (Va)	LPVe
¶ 'Mark Talbot' (Va)	GDTE
'Maroon Picotee'	ELan GDTE NPla
'Mars' (Va)	CLon LPVe
'Marsland's Yellow' (Vtta)	LPVe
'Martin' (Va) 🏆	CFul CInt CMHG CSam CShe ECha EWes GCHN GDTE GMac LBee LHop LPVe NBrk NBro SChu WBou WIvy WKif WWin
'Mary Cawthorne' (C)	LPVe
'Mary Ellen' (Va)	CFul GDTE
'Mauve Beauty' (Va)	LPVe
'Mauve Haze' (Va)	GMac WBou WEas WPat
'Mauve Radiance' (Va)	CFul CShe GMac LPVe NVic WBou
'May Mott' (Va)	GMac NBrk WBou
'Mayfly' (Va)	GDTE GMac NBrk WBou
'Meena' (Vtta)	LPVe
'Megumi' (Va)	LPVe
'Melinda' (Vtta)	LPVe WBou
* 'Melissa' (Va)	CFul GMac LPVe SChu WBou
'Mercury' (Va)	GDTE LPVe WPen
'Merry Cheer' (C)	SMrm WBou
¶ 'Midnight Turk' (Va)	GBuc
'Milkmaid' (Va)	CGle ECha GCrs GDTE LBee NBir SIng WFar WKif
'Mina Walker' (Ex Va)	GDTE
'Minerva' (Va)	LPVe

minor subsp. ***calcarea***	WUnd
'Miranda' (Vtta)	LPVe
'Miss Brookes' (Va)	CFul GDTE GMac LPVe NPla SChu WBou
'Miss Helen Mount'	CM&M
'Mistral' (Va)	LPVe
'Misty Guy' (Vtta)	NChi
'Mitzel' (Vtta)	LPVe NRoo
'Molly Sanderson' (Va) 🏆	CB&S CBot CGle CMea CSam CSpe ECha ECtt EFol ELan EPot GDTE GMac LBee LHop LPVe MCLN MHig MRav NRoo SChu SIng SMrm SSoC SUsu WBou WEas WPer WWhi WWin
I 'Mona' (Va)	LPVe
'Monica' (Va)	LPVe SChu
'Moonlight' (Va) 🏆	CFul CMea ECha ELan GCHN GMac LBee LHop LPVe MOne NRoo SAga SBla SChu WBou WMaN
'Moonraker'	CBos CCot LIck NCat
'Morvana' (Va)	LPVe
'Morwenna' (Va)	LPVe NRoo
'Moscaria' (Va)	LPVe
'Moseley Ideal' (Ex Va)	GDTE
'Moseley Perfection' (Va)	LPVe
'Mrs Chichester' (Va)	GDTE GMac LPVe NBrk WBou
'Mrs David Lloyd George' (dVt)	CDev CGro
'Mrs Lancaster' (Va)	CFul CMea CSam EOrc EWes GDTE GMac LPVe MCLN NBir NRoo SChu SMrm SRms WBou WLRN
'Mrs M.B. Wallace' (Ex Va)	GDTE
'Mrs Pickett' (C)	CBos CRDP
'Mrs R. Barton' (Vt)	CCot CDev CGro CPla NBro WHil WLRN WRus
'Myfawnny' (Va)	ELan EWes GDTE LBee LPVe MOne NPla NPri NRoo SChu SHBN SMrm SRms WBou WHil WKif WLRN WPen
'Mylene' (Va)	LPVe
'Myntha' (Vtta)	LPVe
'Mysie' (Va)	CFul
'Nadia' (Va)	LPVe
'Naomi' (Va)	LPVe
'Natasha' (Va)	LPVe
'Neapolitan'	See ***V.* 'Pallida Plena'**
'Nell' (Va)	CFul
§ 'Nellie Britton' (Va) 🏆	CElw CFul CGle EOrc GDTE GMac LHop LPVe NRoo NSti SBla SChu WBou WEas WRus WWin
'Nemesis' (Va)	LPVe
'Neptune' (Va)	LPVe
'Nerena' (Vtta)	LPVe
'Nesta' (Vtta)	LPVe
'Netta Statham'	See ***V.* 'Belmont Blue'**
¶ 'Nicole' (Va)	LPVe
'Nigra' (Va)	LPVe
'Nina' (Va)	LPVe
'Nona' (Va)	LPVe
'Norah Church' (Vt)	CBre CCot CDev CGro
'Norah Leigh' (Va)	EBre WBou
obliqua	See ***V. cucullata***
occulta striata albe	EMar NBro
'Octavia' (Va)	LPVe

'Odile' (Va)	LPVe
odorata	CArn CB&S CDev CGle CGro CJew CKin CSWP ECWi ERav EWFC GBar GMac GPoy LHol MRav MWat NFla NLak NRoo NSti SIde SIng SSea WApp WCla WOak WWye
– 'Alba'	CBre CDev CGle CKin CSWP CTri CVer CWan EAst EFou ELan EMan ERav GMac ILis MCLN MFir NCat NNrd NOak NRai NRoo NSti SIde WBon WCla WRus WWat WWye
– 'Alba Plena'	CVer EFol ELan EPar
– apricot	See ***V.* 'Sulphurea'**
– ***dumetorum***	See ***V. alba***
– ***flore-pleno***	EPar
– pink	EPar WCla
– ***rosea***	GBar GMac MRav SIng WOMN
– subsp. ***subcarnea***	WUnd
– 'Sulphurea'	See ***V.* 'Sulphurea'**
'Olive Edmonds' (Va)	LPVe
'Olwyn' (Va)	LPVe
'Opéra' (Vt)	CCot
oreades	LPVe NTow
'Oriana' (Va)	LPVe
orphanidis	LPVe
ossea	LPVe
§ 'Pallida Plena' (dPVt)	CDev
'Palmer's White' (Va)	CFul LPVe
palustris	CKin CShe EWFC WChe WHer
'Pamela Zambra' (Vt)	CDev
'Pandora' (Va)	LPVe
papilionacea	See ***V. sororia***
'Parme de Toulouse' (dPVt)	CDev
'Pat Creasy' (Va)	GDTE GMac WBou
'Pat Kavanagh' (C)	GDTE GMac LPVe WBou
'Patricia Brookes' (Va)	LPVe
pedata	CBro CFai CRDP EMan MBri NHar SMad WAbe WWat
¶ – 'Bicolor'	SBla
pedatifida	EBar ECro EFol ELan EPla MBel MTho NMGW NNrd SChu WAbe WWye
'Penelope' (SP)	GDTE
pensylvanica	See ***V. pubescens*** var. ***eriocarpa***
'Perle Rose' (Vt)	CCot CDev CGro
'Pete'	SChu SUsu
'Petra' (Vtta)	LPVe
'Philippa Cawthorne' (C)	LPVe
'Phoebe' (Va)	LPVe
'Phyllida' (Va)	LPVe
'Pickering Blue' (Va)	CFul GDTE GMac LPVe WBou
'Pilar' (Va)	LPVe SChu
'Pippa' (Vtta)	LPVe SChu
'Poppy' (Va)	CLTr LPVe
'Priam' (Va)	LPVe
'Primrose Cream' (Va)	LPVe
'Primrose Dame' (Va)	CDoC GDTE GMac LPVe NCat WBou WMer
'Primrose Pixie' (Va)	WBou
'Prince John' (T)	EGar
'Princess Blue'	WWhi
'Princess Mab' (Vtta)	CFul GDTE LPVe NBrk NRoo WBou
'Princess of Prussia' (Vt)	CBre CDev
'Princess of Wales'	See ***V.* 'Princesse de Galles'**
'Princess Yellow'	EPfP
§ 'Princesse de Galles' (Vt)	CB&S CDev EPar NSti WRus WWtk
§ ***pubescens*** var. ***eriocarpa***	CBro
'Purity' (Vtta)	GDTE LPVe NRoo
'Purple Dove' (Va)	SMrm
'Purple Wings' (Va)	GMac WBou
'Putty'	WCru
'Queen Charlotte' (Vt)	CDev CFai CM&M GCHN ILis NBro NFai NHar NHol NMen WCot
'Queen Disa' (Vtta)	CMHG LPVe
'Queen Victoria'	See ***V.* 'Victoria Regina'**
'Quink' (Va)	CFul
'R.N. Denby' (Ex Va)	GDTE
'Ramona' (Va)	LPVe
'Rave' (Vtta)	GMac SChu WBou
'Raven'	NHar WBou
'Ravenna' (Va)	LPVe
'Rebecca' (Vtta)	Widely available
'Rebecca Cawthorne' (C)	LPVe NRoo
'Red Charm' (Vt)	EWll NBro NCat WHow WLRN
'Red Lion'	CDev
'Red Queen' (Vt)	CBre CCot
reichenbachiana	ELan EPar EWFC
'Reine des Blanches' (dVt)	EFou WRus
'Reliance' (Va)	CFul GDTE
'Remora' (Vtta)	LPVe
reniforme	See ***V. hederacea***
'Rhoda' (Va)	LPVe
'Richard Vivian' (Va)	LPVe
'Richard's Yellow' (Va)	GDTE LPVe
riviniana	CArn CKin EJud NChi SIde WApp WHer WJek WOak
§ – Purpurea Group	Widely available
– white	EWes NWoo
'Rodney Davey' (Vt/v)	CArc CDec CPla EBee EFol EGar GBri MCLN NBro NCut NFai NRai NWes SSca WLRN WRha WWhi WWye
'Romilly' (Va)	LPVe
'Rosalie' (Va)	LPVe
'Rosanna'	CDev
'Roscastle Black'	CLTr NPla NRai WBou WCot
'Rosemary Cawthorne' (C)	LPVe
'Rosine' (Vt)	CBre
'Rowan Hood' (ExV)	GDTE
'Rowena' (Va)	LPVe
'Royal Delft'	GCHN
'Royal Robe' (VT)	CDev
'Rubra' (Vt)	SMrm WPer
rugulosa	See ***V. canadensis*** var. ***rugulosa***
§ ***rupestris rosea***	CDev CLTr CNic CPla MNrw NCat NGre NSti NWCA STre WCla WEas WOMN
'Russian Superb' (Vt)	WLRN
'Ruth Blackall' (Va)	LPVe
'Ruth Elkans' (Va)	GDTE GMac LPVe NBrk
'Saint Helena' (Vt)	CDev
'Saint Maur' (Va)	CFul
'Sally' (Vtta)	LPVe
'Samantha' (Vtta)	LPVe
'Sammy Jo' (Va)	WBou
'Sandra Louise' (Va)	LPVe
'Sandra Louise' (C)	LPVe
'Sarah' (Va)	CFul
'Saughton Blue' (Va)	LPVe
saxatilis	See ***V. tricolor*** subsp. ***subalpina***

selkirkii	CNic CPla NBro NBus NWCA WCot WHal
– 'Variegata'	GBri GBuc NBir NWes WDav
septentrionalis	CCot CRDP ECha EGol ELan MNrw MOne NBro NGre NRya SSmi WHal WRus
– ***alba***	CHid CMHG CSWP CVer EFou NPla WHow WLRN WPer
'Septima' (Va)	LPVe
'Serena' (Va)	LPVe WBou
'Sheila' (Va)	WBou
'Sidborough Poppet'	CInt CNic CPBP EWes NHar SSca WOMN WPat WPer
§ ***sieberiana***	ECou
'Sigrid' (Va)	LPVe
'Sir Fred Warner' (Va)	LPVe
'Sissinghurst' (Va)	GMac LPVe MOne NBir
'Sky Blue' (Va)	LPVe
'Sophie' (Vtta)	LPVe SChu
§ ***sororia***	EMan GCHN GSki MSCN WBro WGwG WLRN WOMN
– 'Albiflora'	EMil EPPr EPfP GMaP GSki NHar NPro WCot WPer WRus
§ – 'Freckles'	Widely available
– 'Priceana'	CNic EBee EMan NCat SLod SMrm WCot WGwG WHow WLRN WPer WPri WWat
¶ 'Soula' (Vtta)	LPVe
'Stacey Proud' (v)	NPro
'Steyning' (Va)	LPVe
stojanovii	CMea ELan MOne SBla SChu WEas WOMN WPer
striata	CInt WWat
§ 'Sulphurea' (Vt)	CDev CHid CPla CSWP EFol ELan ERav GMac MHar NBrk WHil WOMN WPer
'Susanah' (Vtta)	GDTE GMac LPVe NPla
¶ 'Susie' (Va)	GDTE
'Swanley White'	See *V.* **'Comte de Brazza'**
'Sybil' (SP)	GDTE
'Sylvia Hart'	EWes MTho WBon
* ***takedana*** 'Variegata'	WThi
'Talitha' (Va)	GMac LPVe
'Tamsin' (Va)	LPVe
'Tanith' (Vt)	CBre CDev
'Tara' (Va)	LPVe
'Thalia' (Vtta)	CFul LPVe MCLN WBou
'The Czar'	See *V.* **'Czar'**
'Thea' (Va)	LPVe
'Thelma' (Va)	LPVe
'Thetis' (Va)	GDTE LPVe
'Thierry' (Va)	LPVe
'Tiffany' (Va)	LPVe
'Tina' (Va)	GDTE LPVe WBou
'Titania' (Va)	LPVe
'Tom' (SP)	GDTE
'Tom Tit' (Va)	LIck LPVe WBou
'Tomose' (Va)	CFul
'Tony Venison' (C/v)	CCot CElw EHal EHoe LHop MBel MTho NBus NSti WBou WByw WCot
tricolor	CKin CNic CSWP ECWi EFer EWFC GBar GPoy LHol MHew NWCA SIde WHer WJek WSel WWye
§ – subsp. ***curtisii***	LPVe
– 'Sawyer's Blue'	WPer
'Tullia' (Vtta)	LPVe
'Una' (Va)	LPVe
'Unity' (Vtta)	LPVe
'Velleda' (Vtta)	LPVe
velutina	See ***V. gracilis***
'Venetia' (Va)	LPVe
'Venus' (Va)	LPVe
§ ***verecunda*** var. ***yakusimana***	CNic CRDP ESis EWes NGre NHol
'Victoria'	See *V.* **'Czar Bleu'**
'Victoria Cawthorne' (C)	CElw CPBP GBuc GDTE GMac LIck LPVe MBel MBro MOne NChi NRoo SBla SChu WBou WHoo WPyg
§ 'Victoria Regina' (Vt)	CArc CDev CRow EMon
'Violacea' (C)	GDTE LPVe
'Virginia' (Va)	CFul GMac LPVe NChi SChu WBou
'Virgo' (Va)	LPVe
'Vita' (Va)	CFul CLTr CMea CSpe EBar GBuc GMac LBee LGre LPVe NRoo SBid SBla SChu SRms SUsu WBou WIvy WWhi
vourinensis	LPVe
'Wanda' (Va)	LPVe
'White Gem' (Va)	LBee
'White Ladies' (Vt)	See ***V. cucullata* 'Alba'**
'White Pearl' (Va)	GBuc GMac LGre NBrk WBou
'White Superior'	CB&S
'White Swan' (Va)	CBos GMac LPVe MOne
'William Fife' (Ex Va)	GDTE
'William Wallace' (Va)	LPVe
'Windward' (Vt)	CCot NBrk NCat
¶ 'Winifred Jones' (Va)	GDTE
'Winifred Warden' (Va)	GDTE
'Winifred Wargent' (Va)	LPVe NPri SIng SMrm WLRN
'Winona' (Vtta)	LPVe
'Winona Cawthorne' (C)	GDTE GMac LPVe NChi SChu WAbe WBou
'Woodlands Cream' (Va)	GDTE GMac NPla WBou
'Woodlands Lilac' (Va)	GDTE LPVe NRoo SChu WBou
'Woodlands White' (Va)	LPVe
'Xantha' (Va)	LPVe
yakusimana	See ***V. verecunda*** var. ***yakusimana***
yezoensis	CPla LFlo SBla
'Zalea' (Va)	LPVe
'Zara' (Va)	GMaP WBou
'Zenobia' (Vtta)	LPVe
'Zepherine' (Va)	LPVe
'Zeta' (Va)	LPVe
'Ziglana' (Va)	LPVe
'Zoe' (Vtta)	GDTE GMac LPVe MMil MOne NPla NPri NRoo SChu SMrm WBou WLRN
'Zona' (Va)	LPVe
zoysii	See ***V. calcarata*** subsp. ***zoysii***

VISCARIA (Caryophyllaceae)

vulgaris	See ***Lychnis viscaria***

VITALIANA (Primulaceae)

§ ***primuliflora***	CLyd GCrs GTou MBro NSla SIng WHoo WPyg
– subsp. ***canescens***	NHol
– subsp. ***praetutiana***	EHyt EPot GDra MBro MHig MRPP NHar NHol NNrd NTow NWCA WDav WPat WPyg
– subsp. ***praetutiana chionantha***	EPot
– subsp. ***tridentata***	EPot NMen NNrd

VITEX (Verbenaceae)

agnus-castus	CAgr CArn CB&S EEls ELan ELau EOas GPoy LHol LLew SBid SIgm SMad SPer WFar WHil WWye
– var. ***latifolia***	MBri
– 'Silver Spire'	CChu SBid
lucens	CHEx
negundo	CArn LLew NCGP
negundo cannabifolia	See ***V. incisa***

VITIS † (Vitaceae)

'Abundante' (F)	WSuF
amurensis	CPlN EHic EPla ETen WCru WWat
'Baco Noir' (O/B)	GTwe WSuF
Black Hamburgh	See ***V. vinifera* 'Schiava Grossa'**
§ 'Boskoop Glory' (F)	CMac GTwe SCoo SDea WSuF
'Brant' (O/B) ♀	CAgr CB&S CMac CPlN EBre ELan ENot ERea EWar GTwe LPri MAsh MBri MGos MWat NRog SDea SHBN SPer SRms WStI WSuF WWeb
californica (F)	ERea
§ 'Cascade' (O/B)	ERea LBuc SDea WSuF
'Chambourcin' (B)	WSuF
◆ Claret Cloak	See ***V. coignetiae* Claret Cloak = 'Frovit'**
coignetiae ♀	Widely available
§ – Claret Cloak = 'Frovit'	ELan LRHS MAsh
– 'Rubescens'	CPlN
'Dalkauer' (W)	WSuF
ficifolia	See ***V. thunbergii***
'Fiesta'	WSuF
§ 'Fragola' (O/R)	CAgr CMac CPlN EBre ECha EHic EPla ERav ERea GTwe SDea SEND SRms WSuF WWat
henryana	See ***Parthenocissus henryana***
'Himrod' (O/W)	ERea GTwe SDea WSuF
inconstans	See ***Parthenocissus tricuspidata***
'Kuibishevski' (O/R)	WSuF
labrusca 'Concord' (O/B)	ERea
Landot 244 (O/B)	WSuF
'Léon Millot' (O/G/B)	CAgr EMui ERea NDal SDea WSuF
'Maréchal Foch' (O/B)	WSuF
'Maréchal Joffre' (O/B)	GTwe WSuF
Oberlin 595 (O/B)	WSuF
'Orion'	WSuF
parsley leaved	See ***V. vinifera* 'Ciotat'**
¶ ***parvifolia***	CPlN
¶ 'Phönix' (O/W)	WSuF
'Pink Strawberry' (O)	WSuF
'Pirovano 14' (O/B)	CDoC ERea GTwe WSuF
§ 'Plantet' (O/B)	WSuF
* 'Polaske Muscat' (W)	WSuF
pseudoreticulata	CFil CPlN WPGP
'Pulchra'	WCru
quinquefolia	See ***Parthenocissus quinquefolia***
Ravat 51 (O/W)	WSuF
riparia	CPlN GAri WCru
'Schuyler' (O/B)	WSuF
Seibel (F)	EMui GTwe
Seibel 13053	See ***V.* 'Cascade'**
Seibel 5455	See ***V.* 'Plantet'**
Seibel 7053	WSuF
Seibel 9549	WSuF
'Seneca' (W)	WSuF
§ 'Seyval Blanc' (O/W)	ERea GTwe SDea WSuF
Seyve Villard 12.375	See ***V.* 'Villard Blanc'**
◆ Seyve Villard 5276	See ***V.* 'Seyval Blanc'**
'Tereshkova' (O/B)	ERea WSuF
'Thornton'	WSuF
§ ***thunbergii***	WCru
'Triomphe d'Alsace' (O/B)	SDea WSuF
'Trollinger'	See ***V. vinifera* 'Schiava Grossa'**
§ 'Villard Blanc' (O/W)	WSuF
vinifera 'Abouriou' (O/B)	WSuF
§ – 'Alicante' (G/B)	ERea GTwe WSuF
– 'Apiifolia'	See ***V. vinifera* 'Ciotat'**
– 'Appley Towers' (G/B)	ERea
– 'Auxerrois' (O/W)	WSuF
– 'Bacchus' (O/W)	WSuF
– 'Black Alicante'	See ***V. vinifera* 'Alicante'**
– 'Black Corinth' (G/B)	ERea
– 'Black Frontignan' (G/O/B)	ERea WSuF
◆ – Black Hamburgh	See ***V. vinifera* 'Schiava Grossa'**
– 'Black Monukka' (G/B)	ERea WSuF
– 'Blauburger' (O/B)	WCru
– 'Blue Portuguese'	See ***V. vinifera* 'Portugieser'**
– 'Buckland Sweetwater' (G/W)	ERea GTwe MBri WSuF
– 'Cabernet Sauvignon' (O/B)	WSuF
– 'Canon Hall Muscat' (G/W)	ERea
– 'Cardinal' (F)	ERea
– 'Chaouch' (G/W)	ERea
– 'Chardonnay' (O/W)	SDea WSuF
§ – 'Chasselas' (G/O/W)	CDoC CMac ERea EWar WSuF WWeb
– 'Chasselas d'Or'	See ***V. vinifera* 'Chasselas'**
– 'Chasselas Rosé' (G/R)	ERea WSuF
– 'Chasselas Vibert' (G/W)	ERea WSuF
– 'Chenin Blanc' (O/W)	WSuF
§ – 'Ciotat' (F)	EHic EPla ERea SDea WCru WSuF WWat
§ – 'Cot' (O/B)	WSuF
– 'Csabyongye' (W)	WSuF
– 'Dornfelder' (O/R)	WSuF
– 'Dunkelfelder' (O/R)	WSuF
– 'Early Van der Laan' (F)	LHol
– 'Ehrenfelser' (O/W)	WSuF
– 'Elbling' (O/W)	WSuF
– 'Excelsior' (W)	SDea WSuF
– 'Faber' (O/W)	WSuF
– 'Findling' (W)	WSuF
– 'Forta' (O/W)	WSuF
– 'Foster's Seedling' (G/W)	ERea GTwe SDea WSuF
– 'Gagarin Blue' (O/B)	ERea SDea WSuF
– 'Gamay Hatif' (O/B)	ERea
– 'Gamay Hatif des Vosges'	WSuF
– 'Gamay Noir' (O/B)	WSuF
– Gamay Teinturier Group (O/B)	WSuF
– 'Gewürztraminer' (O/R)	WSuF
– 'Glory of Boskoop'	See ***V.* 'Boskoop Glory'**
– 'Golden Chasselas'	See ***V. vinifera* 'Chasselas'**
– 'Golden Queen' (G/W)	ERea
– 'Goldriesling' (O/W)	WSuF
– 'Gros Colmar' (G/B)	ERea
– 'Gros Maroc' (G/B)	ERea

- – 'Grüner Veltliner' (O/W) WSuF
- – 'Gutenborner' (O/W) WSuF
- – 'Helfensteiner' (O/R) WSuF
- – 'Huxelrebe' (O/W) WSuF
- – 'Incana' (O/B) CPlN EPla ERav WCru WPen WSHC
- – 'Interlaken' (F) ERea
- ¶ – 'Jubiläumsrebe' (O/W) WSuF
- – 'Kanzler' (O/W) WSuF
- – 'Kerner' (O/W) WSuF
- – 'Kernling' (F) WSuF
- – 'King's Ruby' (F) ERea
- – 'Lady Downe's Seedling' (G/B) ERea
- – 'Lady Hastings' (G/B) ERea
- – 'Lady Hutt' (G/W) ERea
- – 'Lucombe' (F) SDea
- – 'Madeleine Angevine' (O/W) CDoC ERea GTwe NDal SDea WSuF WWeb
- – 'Madeleine Royale' (G/W) ERea WSuF
- – 'Madeleine Silvaner' (O/W) EMui ERea GTwe LBuc MGos SDea SPer WSuF
- – 'Madresfield Court' (G/B) ERea GTwe WSuF
- – 'Malbec' See *V. vinifera* **'Cot'**
- – 'Mireille' (F) GTwe WSuF
- – 'Morio Muscat' (O/W) WSuF
- – 'Mrs Pearson' (G/W) ERea
- – 'Mrs Pince's Black Muscat' (G/B) ERea
- – 'Muscadet' See *V. vinifera* **'Melon de Bourgogne'**
- – 'Muscat Blanc à Petits Grains' (O/W) WSuF
- – 'Muscat Bleu' (O/B) ERea
- – 'Muscat Champion' (G/R) ERea
- – 'Muscat de Saumur' (W) WSuF
- – 'Muscat Hamburg' (G/B) EMui ERea MGos WSuF
- – 'Muscat of Alexandria' (G/W) CB&S CMac CSam EMui ERea EWar MWat NDal SPer
- – 'Muscat of Hungary' (G/W) ERea
- – 'Muscat Ottonel' (O/W) WSuF
- § – 'Müller-Thurgau' (O/W) ECtt ERea GTwe MBri MGos SDea WSuF WWeb
- – 'New York Muscat' (O/B) ERea
- – 'No. 69' (W) WSuF
- – 'Noir Hatif de Marseilles' (O/B) ERea
- – 'Oliver Irsay' (O/W) ERea WSuF
- – 'Optima' (O/W) WSuF
- – 'Ortega' (O/W) WSuF
- – 'Perle' (O/W) WSuF
- – 'Perle de Czaba' (G/O/W) ERea
- – 'Perlette' (O/W) WSuF
- – 'Pinot Blanc' (O/W) WSuF
- – 'Pinot Gris' (O/B) WSuF
- – 'Pinot Noir' (F) WSuF
- § – 'Portugieser' (O/B) WSuF
- – 'Précoce de Bousquet' (O/W) WSuF
- – 'Précoce de Malingre' (O/W) ERea
- – 'Primavis Frontignan' (G/W) WSuF
- – 'Prince of Wales' (G/B) ERea
- – 'Purpurea' (O/B) ♀ Widely available
- – 'Reichensteiner' (O/G/W) WSuF
- – 'Reine Olga' (O/R) ERea
- – 'Rembrant' (R) WSuF
- – 'Riesling' (O/W) WSuF
- ◆ – Riesling-Silvaner See *V. vinifera* **'Müller-Thurgau'**
- – 'Royal Muscadine' (F) See *V. vinifera* **'Chasselas'**
- – 'Saint Laurent' (G/O/W) ERea WSuF
- – 'Sauvignon Blanc' (O/W) WSuF
- – 'Scheurebe' (O/W) WSuF
- § – 'Schiava Grossa' (G/B) CMac CRHN CSam ECtt ELan ERea EWar GRei GTwe LBuc LHol MBlu MBri MGos MWat NDal NRog SDea SPer WSuF
- – 'Schönburger' (O/W) WSuF
- – Seibel 138315 (R) WSuF
- – Seibel 5409 (W) WSuF
- – 'Septimer' (O/W) WSuF
- – Seyve Villard 20.473 (F) WSuF
- – 'Siegerrebe' (O/W) CDoC EMui ERea GTwe LBuc SDea WSuF WWeb
- – 'Silvaner' (O/W) WSuF
- – 'Spetchley Red' WCru
- – Strawberry Grape See *V.* **'Fragola'**
- § – 'Sultana' ERea GTwe WSuF
- – 'Syrian' (G/W) ERea
- – Teinturier Group (F) ERea
- – 'Thompson Seedless' See *V. vinifera* **'Sultana'**
- – 'Trebbiano' (G/W) ERea
- – 'Wrotham Pinot' (O/B) WSuF
- – 'Würzer' (O/W) WSuF
- – 'Zweigeltrebe' (O/B) WSuF
- 'White Strawberry' (O/W) WSuF

VITTADINIA (Asteraceae)

- ***cuneata*** See *V.* ***australis***

VRIESEA (Bromeliaceae)

- ***carinata*** MBri
- ***hieroglyphica*** MBri
- ×***poelmanii*** MBri
- ×***polonia*** MBri
- ***saundersii*** ♀ MBri
- ***splendens*** ♀ MBri
- 'Vulkana' MBri

WACHENDORFIA (Haemodoraceae)

- ***paniculata*** NRog
- ***thyrsiflora*** CGre CHEx CRDP CTrC IBlr NRog WCot
- – Trengwainton Form GCal

WAHLENBERGIA (Campanulaceae)

- ***albomarginata*** ECou EMan EPad GCHN GTou NHar NWCA WRHF
- – 'Blue Mist' ECou EPad
- ¶ – white form MHar
- * ***albosericea*** EPad
- ***cartilaginea*** EPad
- ***ceracea*** NNrd
- ***congesta*** EPad LBee LRHS WThi
- ***gloriosa*** CPBP CSpe EHyt EPPr EPad LBee MBro NHol NSla WAbe WFar WPat WPyg WWin
- ¶ ***matthewsii*** EPot

pumilio	See ***Edraianthus pumilio***
§ *saxicola*	CLyd CRow EHyt EPad GTou NSla NWCA SRms SSca WPer
serpyllifolia	See ***Edraianthus serpyllifolius***
simpsonii	GTou
species	ECou
stricta	LBlm
tasmanica	See ***W. saxicola***
trichogyna	EPad LRHS
undulata	CSpe EPad

WALDHEIMIA See ALLARDIA

WALDSTEINIA (Rosaceae)

fragarioides	ECro WPer
geoides	EBee EMan EPPr EPfP NPro SPer WLRN
ternata	CB&S CBro CGle CShe EBre ECha ELan EMil ESis GDra GTou LFis LGro LHop MBri MBro NBro NGar NHol NRoo NSti NTow SIng SPer WCla WEas WHil WRus WWat WWin
* – 'Variegata'	IBlr

WASABIA (Brassicaceae)

japonica	GPoy

WASHINGTONIA (Arecaceae)

filifera ♀	CAbb CBrP CHEx CTbh LPal MBri SArc
robusta	CTrC

WATSONIA (Iridaceae)

aletroides	LLew NRog SIgm
angusta	GCal IBlr LLew
ardernei	See ***W. borbonica*** subsp. ***ardernei***
beatricis	See ***W. pillansii***
§ *borbonica*	CChu IBlr LLew NRog
§ – subsp. *ardernei*	CHan GCal IBlr LLew NRog
¶ – pink form	CPou
brevifolia	See ***W. laccata***
bulbillifera	See ***W. meriana***
¶ *coccinea*	LLew
– Baker	See ***W. spectabilis***
– Herbert ex Baker dwarf form	NRog
¶ *densiflora*	LLew
¶ *distans*	LLew
¶ *fourcadei*	LLew
fulgens	CHan GCal LLew
§ *humilis*	CFil CHan
hysterantha	IBlr NRog
§ *laccata*	LLew
marginata	CHan CPou GCal LLew NRog SIgm
§ *meriniae*	CHan GCal IBlr LLew NRog WCot
'Mount Congreve'	SVen
§ *pillansii*	CChu CHan CPou EBre GCal IBlr SAxl SMrm
pyramidata	See ***W. borbonica***
roseoalba	See ***W. humilis***
§ *spectabilis*	NRog
'Stanford Scarlet'	CChu IBlr SCro WEas WSHC
tabularis	CHan GCal IBlr LLew
'Tresco Dwarf Pink'	GCal
vanderspuyae	IBlr LLew NRog
versfeldii	CHan
'White Dazzler'	SApp
wilmaniae	IBlr
wordsworthiana	GCal

WATTAKAKA See DREGEA

WEIGELA † (Caprifoliaceae)

'Abel Carrière' ♀	CShe CTri CWan ECtt EHic ENot GAul MRav NFla SEND SPla
'Avalanche' hort.	See ***W. 'Candida'***
'Avalanche' Lemoine	See ***W. praecox 'Avalanche'***
'Boskoop Glory'	CDoC GQui MBri SPer
§ Briant Rubidor	EBar ECtt EHoe GRei IOrc MAsh MBal MBar MBel MBri MGos MRav NFla NNor SEas SPer WBod WHCG WStI WWeb
'Bristol Ruby'	CChe CShe ELan ENot GRei LHop MBar MGos MPla NBee NNor NRoo NWea SHBN SPer SRms WDin WGwG WWin
§ 'Candida'	CTri EAst EBee ELan EPla EWes GSki MBri NHol SEas SMac SPan SPer SPla WGor
Carnaval	CBlo CDoC COtt EBee EHic GAri LPan MBri WLRN
'Centennial'	MGos
coraeensis	EHic MBlu
– 'Alba'	CChu GWht WSHC
decora	CPle GQui
'Eva Rathke'	CB&S CBlo CTri EPla ISea NWea SCoo
'Eva Supreme'	EHic
'Evita'	CMHG EHic IOrc MBar MGos MPla SEas SPer SPla
Feline	COtt SPer
florida	CTrw MWat SMer
– f. *alba*	CB&S MBar
§ – 'Aureovariegata'	CDec CMHG CTri GQui ISea MBal SPla SRms WHCG
– 'Bicolor'	CB&S
– 'Bristol Snowflake'	CSWP CWan EHic LHop MAsh WLRN
– 'Foliis Purpureis' ♀	CBot CChe CMHG CPle EHoe ELan ENot GRei LHop MBal MBar MBel MBri MPla MWat NHol NNor NRoo SHBN SMad SPer SReu SSta WAbe WBod WDin WHCG WSHC WWat WWin
– Rubigold	See ***W.* Briant Rubidor**
– 'Suzanne' (v)	EFol NPro WWeb
– 'Tango'	ECtt MAsh MBri NPro WBcn
'Florida Variegata'	CB&S CChe CPle CShe CTrw CWLN EBar EBre ELan ENot GRei LHop LPan MAsh MBar MGos MPla MWat NRoo NWea SDix SSta WAbe WBod WHen WSHC WTyr WWat WWin
* *florida* 'Variegata Aurea'	See ***W. florida 'Aureovariegata'***
– 'Versicolor'	CChu CMHG GQui LHop MBel
¶ 'Gustave Malet'	GQui
hortensis 'Nivea'	CPle
japonica	CPle
– Dart's Colourdream	EBee EBre ECtt EHal EHic EPla GAul IOrc MGos MRav SCoo SEas SLPl

'Kosteriana Variegata' CWLN EBee EHic NRoo WFar WLRN
'Looymansii Aurea' CChu CMHG CPle CTri EAst EFol ELan LHop MPla MRav NHol SEas SMac SPer SPla WAbe WDin WGwG WHCG WHar WWat WWin
Lucifer CBlo CDoC MHlr WDin WLRN
maximowiczii CPle GOrc GQui GSki NHol WHCG WLRN
§ ***middendorffiana*** CB&S CBot CChu CGre CMHG CPle CWit ELan EMil ENot ISea LHop MBal MBar MDun MNrw MPla MWat NSti SMac SPer SSpi WDin WHCG WSHC WTyr WWin
'Minuet' CBlo CMHG EHic GSki NPro SBid SEas WPat WRTC
'Mont Blanc' ♀ CBot SEND
Nain Rouge CBlo COtt NHol WLRN
'Nana Variegata' EAst EHal MBar MBri NBee NHol
'Newport Red' CBlo EBar EBee EHic ENot MRav MWat NBee NWea SMer SPla WGwG WLRN WStI
§ ***praecox*** 'Avalanche' ECtt MRav WStI
– 'Espérance' EPla
'Praecox Variegata' ♀ CChu CMHG CTri ELan MBri SPer SPla SReu SRms SSta WCru WHCG WSHC
'Red Prince' CBlo CWLN ELan MAsh MBri MGos SEas
'Rosabella' EHic
◆ Rubidor See ***W.* Briant Rubidor**
◆ Rubidor Variegata See ***W.* Briant Rubidor**
Rubigold See ***W.* Briant Rubidor**
'Rumba' EHic EMil GSki NPro NRoo
'Snowflake' CPle EBee ECtt EPla MPla SEas SRms WDin
sp. CC 1279 WHCr
subsessilis CC 1289 WHCr
'Victoria' CBlo CLTr CMHG CSWP CWLN EBre ECtt ELan MAsh MBel MBri NBee NRoo SCoo WDin WGor WHar WLRN WWeb
'Wessex Gold' CFai

WEINMANNIA (Cunoniaceae)

trichosperma CGre CHEx IBlr ISea MAll SArc

WELDENIA (Commelinaceae)

candida EHyt NHar WChr

WESTRINGIA (Lamiaceae)

angustifolia ECou
brevifolia ECou
– Raleighii Group ECou
§ ***fruticosa*** ♀ CPle LHil MAll SBid WJek
– 'Variegata' CPle GQui MAll SBid WJek WLRN WSHC
– 'Wynyabbie Gem' LHop
¶ ***longifolia*** ECon
rosmariniformis See ***W. fruticosa***

WIDDRINGTONIA (Cupressaceae)

cedarbergensis IBlr
cupressoides See ***W. nodiflora***
§ ***nodiflora*** IBlr MBri
¶ ***schwarzii*** CTrC
whytei See ***W. nodiflora***

WIGANDIA (Hydrophyllaceae)

urens CHEx

WISTERIA † (Papilionaceae)

* 'Captain Fuji' CMCN SPla
'Caroline' CB&S CDoC CEnd CMCN CPMA CSam ERea LNet MGos MMea SPer SPla SReu SSpi SSta
floribunda CB&S CRHN ELan MAsh SHBN WDin WNor
§ – 'Alba' ♀ CAlt CB&S CBot CDoC CEnd CPMA EBre ELan GAri LNet LPan MAsh NEgg NHol SBra SHBN SPer SSpi SSta WDin WStI
– 'Burford' CDoC CEnd CTri EBee MAsh MBri MMea MWat NHol WWeb
– 'Fragrantissima' CBlo
– 'Harlequin' LRHS MGos
– 'Hichirimen' EBee LNet MMea
◆ – 'Honko' See ***W. floribunda* 'Rosea'**
◆ – Jakohn-fuji See ***W. floribunda* 'Reindeer'**
§ – 'Kuchi-beni' CB&S CPMA EBee ELan LNet MGos MMea SPer SPla WWeb
* – 'Lavender Lace' CPMA
– 'Lipstick' See ***W. floribunda* 'Kuchi-beni'**
– 'Longissima Alba' CDoC EBee LPan MBar MGos
– 'Macrobotrys' See ***W. floribunda* 'Multijuga'**
§ – 'Multijuga' ♀ CAlt CDoC CEnd CHad CPMA ELan IOrc LNet LPan MBri MGos MMea MWat NHol SBra SMad SPer SPla SSoC SSpi SSta WSHC WWat WWeb
◆ – Murasaki-naga See ***W. floribunda* 'Purple Patches'**
– 'Murasaki-noda' MGos
– 'Nana Richin's Purple' LNet
– 'Peaches and Cream' See ***W. floribunda* 'Kuchi-beni'**
– 'Pink Ice' See ***W. floribunda* 'Rosea'**
§ – 'Purple Patches' CPMA ELan LNet MGos MMea MWat SPer WWeb
* – 'Purple Tassle' LNet
§ – 'Reindeer' NHol WWeb
§ – 'Rosea' ♀ CB&S CEnd CMac CPMA EBre ELan ENot EPfP IOrc LNet MAsh MBar MBri MGos MMea MWat NHol SBra SHBN SPer WStI WWat WWeb
– 'Royal Purple' CBlo EBee ERea MMea WGor
◆ – Shiro-nagi See ***W. floribunda* 'Snow Showers'**
§ – 'Snow Showers' CHad CPMA ELan IHos LNet MBri MGos MMea SPer SPla WGor WWeb
* – 'Variegata' CPMA
– 'Violacea Plena' CBlo EBee MBri MGos MMea SHBN SPer
floridunda 'Honbeni' See ***W. floribunda* 'Rosea'**
× ***formosa*** CPMA ETen WFro WWat
◆ – Black Dragon See ***W.* × *formosa* 'Kokuryû'**
– Domino See ***W.* × *formosa* 'Issai'**

§ – 'Issai' CB&S CBlo CEnd CPMA CSam EBee LNet MBar MGos MMea NEgg NHol NSti SBra SPla WWat WWeb
§ – 'Kokuryû' CAlt CB&S CDoC CEnd CPMA ELan EPfP IOrc LNet LPan MAsh MGos MMea NHol SBra SHBN SMad SPer SPla SReu SSpi SSta WGor WPyg WWat WWeb
frutescens WNor
¶ – 'Nivea' CMCN
* 'Kofuji' LNet
multijuga 'Alba' See ***W. floribunda* 'Alba'**
'Showa-beni' LNet
sinensis 🏆 CB&S CHEx CMac EBre ELan ENot GRei IHos ISea LNet LPan MBal MBar MGos MMea MPla MWat NFla SBra SHBN SPer SRms SSta WBod WDin WNor
§ – 'Alba' 🏆 CB&S CBlo ELan EPfP IOrc ISea LNet LPan MBar MMea MWat WDin
– 'Amethyst' CPMA ERea SPla
¶ – 'Blue Sapphire' CPMA
– 'Imp' ISea
– 'Plena' CPMA
– 'Prematura' MAsh NHol WSHC
– 'Prolific' CDoC CPMA CPlN EBee ELan LBuc LPan MBri MGos MMea SBra SPer SPla SSpi
* – 'Rosea' LPan
♦ – Shiro-capital See ***W. sinensis* 'Alba'**
venusta CEnd CPMA CTri ELan ENot LNet MAsh MBri MMea NHol SBra SHBN SMad SPer WWat
– ***purpurea*** See ***W. venusta*** var. ***violacea***
§ – var. ***violacea*** CEnd
* – 'Violacea Plena' LRHS
* – 'White Silk' CPMA

WITHANIA (Solanaceae)
somnifera CArn GPoy

WITTSTEINIA (Alseuosmiaceae)
vacciniacea WCru

WOODSIA (Aspidiaceae)
¶***fragilis*** EMon
intermedia NBro
obtusa EBee GMaP NHar WAbe WFib WRic
polystichoides EMon GQui NHar WRic

WOODWARDIA † (Blechnaceae)
fimbriata SArc SChu SPer WRic
martinezii CFil
orientalis var. ***formosana*** NMar
radicans 🏆 CAbb CFil CGre CHEx GQui ISea NMar SArc SMad WAbe
unigemmata NWoo WAbe

WULFENIA (Scrophulariaceae)
carinthiaca CNic GAbr MBro MHig NBir NMen

WYETHIA (Asteraceae)
helianthoides EMan

XANTHOCERAS (Sapindaceae)
sorbifolium 🏆 CAbb CAgr CB&S CBlo CBot CFil CLnd CMCN ELan SBid SIgm SMad SSpi WCoo WDin WNor WWat

XANTHORHIZA (Ranunculaceae)
simplicissima CChu CFil CRow GCal SPer SSpi WIvy WThi WWat

XANTHORRHOEA (Xanthorrhoeaceae)
australis CTrC SMad
preisii LPan

XANTHOSOMA (Araceae)
lindenii See ***Caladium lindenii***
sagittifolium CHEx SLMG

XERONEMA (Phormiaceae)
callistemon ECou

XEROPHYLLUM (Melanthiaceae)
tenax GBin WDav

XYLORHIZA See MACHAERANTHERA

XYLOSMA (Flacourtiaceae)
quichensis CPle

YUCCA † (Agavaceae)
aloifolia CHEx CTrC SArc SIgm
– 'Variegata' CHEx LPal LPan SArc
angustifolia See ***Y. glauca***
angustissima CTbh
arizonica CTbh
baccata CTbh
brevifolia CFil EOas
carnerosana CTbh
elata CTbh
§ ***elephantipes*** 🏆 CHEx MBri
filamentosa 🏆 CAbb CB&S CHEx CMHG CTrC EFou ELan ELau ENot GMaP ISea LPan MBal MBlu MGos MWat NCut NPSI SHBN SPer SRms SSoC SSpi WBod WDin WGwG WTyr WWat WWin
– 'Bright Edge' (v) 🏆 CAbb CB&S CDoC CMHG CPMA CTrC EBre ECtt EGol ELan EPla IHos IOrc LPan MAsh MBri MGos MTis MUlv MWat SArc SHBN SPer WAbe WStI WTyr WWin
– 'Variegata' 🏆 CB&S CBot EBre EGol ELan ENot IOrc LHop MBal MGos SAga SDix SPer SRms WDin WFar WStI
flaccida MAsh NBee NFla SDix
– 'Golden Sword' (v) 🏆 CAbb CDoC CMHG CPMA CTrC EBre EGol ELan IHos IOrc ISea LHop MAsh MBal MBri MHlr MSCN MUlv NCut NPSI SCoo SPer SPla WAbe WTyr
– 'Ivory' 🏆 Widely available
× ***floribunda*** SArc
'Garland's Gold' (v) CDoC CHEx COtt CTrC ELan GQui MAsh MBri MGos SMad SPla

§ *glauca* CB&S CBrP CHEx CMHG EHic GCal NCut SArc SIgm
gloriosa ♀ CB&S CDoC CHEx CShe CTrC ENot EPla LNet LPan NFla SArc SHBN SMad SPer SSpi WStI
– 'Aureovariegata' See ***Y. gloriosa* 'Variegata'**
– 'Nobilis' SDix
– 'Tricolor' CB&S
§ – 'Variegata' ♀ CBot CDoC CHEx EBre ELan ENot MRav MUlv SArc SCro SDry SEas SHBN SPer SRms WWeb
guatemalensis See ***Y. elephantipes***
harrimaniae CTbh SIgm
kanabensis CTbh
navajoa CTbh
neomexicana CTbh
recurvifolia ♀ CB&S CHEx MBal SArc
rigida CBrP CTbh
¶ *rostrata* CBrP
schidigera CTbh
schottii CBrP CTbh
thompsoniana CTbh
* *torcelli* CTbh
torreyi CTbh EOas SLMG
valida CTbh
'Vittorio Emanuele II' MUlv SArc SMad
whipplei CBot CBrP CDoC CFil CHEx CTbh CTrC EOas GCra LHil SArc SLMG SMad SSpi
– var. *parishii* SIgm

YUSHANIA (Poaceae - Bambusoideae)

§ *anceps* ♀ CDoC CFil CHEx CHad EFul EPla ESiP GAri IOrc MBri MGos MUlv NBee SArc SBam SDry SMad SPer SPla WCru
§ – 'Pitt White' EOas EPla SBam SDry WJun
maculata EPla ISta SBam SDry WJun
§ *maling* EPla ISta SBam SDry WJun

ZALUZIANSKYA (Scrophulariaceae)

'Katherine' GCal SIng WCot
ovata CPBP EHyt EPot EWes GCal LHop MTho NBir NWCA SAga SBla WAbe WLRN WPat

ZAMIA (Zamiaceae)

floridana LPal
furfuracea CBrP LPal

ZAMIOCULCAS (Araceae)

See Plant Deletions

ZANTEDESCHIA (Araceae)

§ *aethiopica* ♀ CBen CHEx CMHG CTrC CWGN CWat EHon EOas EWes ISea LAma LCns LPBA MBro MNrw MSta NDea NRog SDix SSoC SSpi SWat WChe WEas WFar WGwG WPri
– 'Apple Court Babe' CRow SApp
– 'Crowborough' CAvo CB&S CBro CHEx CHad CHan CRow EBre ECha EFou EGol EHon ELan EMFW LBlm MBal MBri MRav MSCN MUlv SArc SAxl SDeJ SMad SPer SRms SUsu SWat WCru WFib
– 'Gigantea' SLMG
– 'Green Goddess' ♀ CB&S CBro CDec CFir CHan CMon COtt CRow CTrC CWGN EBee EBre ECha EGar ELan EMFW GCra GQui MHlr NPSI SDeJ SRms SSoC SUsu WCot WFib WWat
– 'Little Gem' ECha
– 'Pershore Fantasia' WCot
¶ – pink CTrC
– 'Snow White' CDec
– 'White Sail' CRow GCal MUlv WFib
albomaculata CMon LAma NPSI NRog
– S&SH 35 CHan
'Best Gold' LAma
'Black Eyed Beauty' CBro LAma NRog WWeb
'Black Magic' LAma WWeb
'Bridal Blush' LAma
'Cameo' LAma
elliottiana ♀ CB&S CFir CHal CSut GQui LAma NRog SLMG
'Harvest Moon' CWit LAma
'Helen O'Connor' SLMG
'Lavender Petite' LAma NRog
'Majestic Red' WWeb
'Mango' EBre
'Maroon Dainty' LAma NRog
'Pacific Pink' LAma
pentlandii See ***Z. angustiloba***
'Pink Persuasion' WWeb
rehmannii ♀ CB&S CMon GQui LAma SRms
– *alba* SLMG
* – *superba* SLMG
'Romeo' SLMG
'Ruby' WWeb
'Shell Pink' LAma NRog
'Solfatare' LAma
* 'Sweet Suzie' EBre
'Treasure' WWeb

ZANTHORHIZA See XANTHORHIZA

ZANTHOXYLUM (Rutaceae)

americanum CFil CLnd WPGP
coreanum CFil
¶ *oxyphyllum* CFil WPGP
piperitum CAgr CFil WPGP
¶ *planispinum* MRav
simulans CB&S WCoo

ZAUSCHNERIA (Onagraceae)

arizonica See ***Z. californica* subsp. *latifolia***
§ *californica* GQui
– 'Albiflora' EPot LHop SUsu WOMN
§ – subsp. *cana* CLTr CSam ECGP ECha ELan IOrc MHar MPla NWCA SAga SChu SIgm SUsu WCru WEas
– – 'Sir Cedric Morris' CKni ELan
– 'Clover Dale' CMHG LGre
§ – 'Dublin' ♀ CBot CShe ECha EFou ELan EPot ERea LHop MBel MBro MFos MHar MPla SBla SChu SIng WAbe WEas WHer WHil WHoo WOld WPat WSHC WWat WWin
§ – subsp. *garrettii* LHop
– 'Glasnevin' See ***Z. californica* 'Dublin'**
§ – subsp. *latifolia* CPle LHop NMen SAga SIgm WHoo

§ – subsp. ***mexicana*** CLyd EPot SRms WOMN
– 'Olbrich Silver' LGre LHop MAvo MSCN NWCA SBla WAbe WCot WCru
– 'Sierra Sunshine' LGre MAvo
– 'Solidarity Pink' CLTr ELan MTho SAga SIng SUsu
– 'Western Hills' CBrk CFir EBee LGre LHop MAvo NWCA SAga SBla SIgm SIng SMrm WAbe
¶ ***cana*** subsp. ***garrettii*** SIgm
– ***villosa*** See ***Z. californica*** subsp. ***mexicana***
septentrionalis SIgm

ZEBRINA See TRADESCANTIA

ZELKOVA † (Ulmaceae)
carpinifolia CLnd CMCN CTho LRHS WNor
¶ ***hyrcana*** SBir
schneideriana CMCN
serrata ♀ CB&S CDoC CLnd CMCN CTho CWSG ELan EMil IOrc ISea MBal MBar NPal NWea SPer SSpi STre WCoo WDin WFro WMou WNor WWat
– 'Goblin' MBro NHol SSta WPat
– 'Nira' CPMA WWes
– 'Variegata' CPMA MBlu MGos SSta
– 'Yatsubusa' STre
– 'Yrban Ruby' MGos SSta
sinica CDoC CLnd CMCN GAri SSpi STre WNor
× ***verschaffeltii*** GAri

ZENOBIA (Ericaceae)
pulverulenta CAbb CB&S CChu CGre ELan GCal GOrc GQui IOrc MBal MBar MBlu MBri MBro MUlv NHol SHBN SPer SReu SSpi SSta WDin WNor WPat WPyg WRTC WSHC WWat
– f. ***nitida*** SSta

ZEPHYRANTHES (Amaryllidaceae)
atamasca WChr
candida CAvo CBro EMan ERea ERos LAma LHop NMen NRog SDeJ SDix WChr WCot WFox WRHF
'Capricorn' WChr
chlorosolen WChr
citrina LAma NMen NRog WChr
drummondii WChr
flavissima CBro WChr WCot
grandiflora WChr
'Grandjax' WChr
'La Buffa Rose' WChr
× ***lancasterae*** CMon WChr
macrosiphon WChr
morrisclintii WChr
'Prairie Sunset' WChr
primulina WChr
puertoricensis WChr
pulchella WChr
reginae WChr
robusta See ***Habranthus robustus***
rosea LAma WChr
smallii WChr
sulphurea LAma

ZIERIA (Rutaceae)
See Plant Deletions

ZIGADENUS (Melanthiaceae)
elegans ECha EHyt EMan LGre LWoo MBro NHol NWCA SMad SSpi WHoo WPyg
nuttallii CLyd EMan LBee LGre MSte NHol WCot
venenosus CHan WDav

ZINGIBER (Zingiberaceae)
officinale EOHP MSal NHex

ZINNIA (Asteraceae)
See Plant Deletions

ZIZANIA (Poaceae)
aquatica EMFW
caducifolia See ***Z. latifolia***
§ ***latifolia*** MSta

ZIZIA (Apiaceae)
aurea EBee

ZIZIPHORA (Lamiaceae)
See Plant Deletions

ZIZIPHUS (Rhamnaceae)
§ ***jujuba*** (F) CAgr LPan
sativa See ***Z. jujuba***

Nursery-Code Index

Nurseries that are included in **THE RHS PLANT FINDER** for the first time this year (or have been reintroduced) are marked in **Bold Type.**

Full details of the nurseries with a four letter Code will be found in the **Code-Nursery** Index on page 711.

Nurseries with a number are detailed in the **Additional Nursery** Index on page 808.

Nurseries marked **SEED, SUCC** or **ORCH** are listed in the **Seed Suppliers, Cactus & Succulent** or **Orchid Specialist Index**

Note: the first letter of each nursery Code indicates the main area of the country in which the nursery is situated, as follows: **C** = South West England, **E** = Eastern England, **G** = Scotland, **I** = Northern Ireland & Republic of Ireland, **L** = London area, **M** = Midlands, **N** = Northern England, **S** = Southern England, **W** = Wales & Western England. For further details refer to page 8.

39 Steps	**WThi**
A La Carte Daylilies	**SDay**
Abbey Dore Court Gardens	**WAbb**
Abbey Plants	**CAbP**
Abbotsbury Sub-Tropical Gardens	**CAbb**
Aberconwy Nursery	**WAbe**
Abriachan Nurseries	**GAbr**
Acton Beauchamp Roses	**WAct**
Agar's Nursery	**SAga**
Agroforestry Research Trust	**CAgr**
Agroforestry Research Trust	**SEED**
Alderton Plant Nursery	**MAld**
All Seasons Plants	**WASP**
Paul Allanson	**MAll**
Allwood Bros	**SAll**
Allwood Bros	**SEED**
Alternatives	**WAlt**
Altoona Nurseries	**CAlt**
Always Alpines	**SAlw**
Jacques Amand Ltd	**LAma**
Apple Court	**SApp**
Applegarth Nursery	**WApp**
Apuldram Roses	**SApu**
Arcadia Nurseries Ltd	**NArc**
Archangel Plants	**CArc**
Anthony Archer-Wills Ltd	**SAWi**
Architectural Plants	**SArc**
Arivegaig Nursery	**GAri**
Arley Hall Nursery	**MArl**
Arne Herbs	**CArn**
Ashenden Nursery	**SAsh**
Ashwood Nurseries Ltd	**MAsh**
Ashwood Nurseries	**SEED**
Askew's Nursery	**MAsk**
Asterby Nurseries	**EAst**
Aultan Nursery	**GAul**
David Austin Roses Ltd	**MAus**
Avon Bulbs	**CAvo**
Avondale Nursery	**MAvo**
Axletree Nursery	**SAxl**
Aylett Nurseries Ltd	**LAyl**
B & T World Seeds	**SEED**
Steven Bailey Ltd	**SBai**
B & H M Baker	**EBak**
Ballagan Nursery	**3**
Ballalheannagh Gardens	**MBal**
Ballydorn Bulb Farm	**IBal**
Ballyrogan Nurseries	**IBlr**
Bamboo Nursery Ltd	**SBam**
Banff & Buchan Nurseries Ltd	**12**
T H Barker & Sons	**NBrk**
Barncroft Nurseries	**MBar**
Barnhawk Nursery	**SBar**
Barnsdale Plants & Gardens	**EBar**
Barters Farm Nurseries Ltd	**CBar**
Barwinnock Herbs	**GBar**
Battersby Roses	**NBat**
Battle & Pears Ltd	**EB&P**
Beacon's Botanicals	**WBea**
Beacon's Nurseries	**WBcn**
Peter Beales Roses	**EBls**
Beamish Clematis Nursery	**NBea**
Beechcroft Nurseries	**NBee**
Beechcroft Nursery	**LBee**
Beeches Nursery	**EBee**
R F Beeston	**86**
Beetham Nurseries	**5**
Bellhouse Nursery	**MBel**
Bennett's Water Lily Farm	**CBen**
Biddenden Nursery at Garden Crafts	**SBid**
Binny Plants	**GBin**
Birchfleet Nursery	**SBir**
Birchwood Farm Nursery	**33**
Birkheads Cottage Garden Nursery	**NBir**
Blackmore & Langdon Ltd	**CBla**
Blackmore & Langdon Ltd	**SEED**
Blackthorn Nursery	**SBla**
Terence Bloch - Plantsman	**LBlo**
Bloomers Nurseries	**78**
Bloomsbury	**LBlm**
Blounts Court Nurseries	**CBlo**
Bluebell Nursery	**MBlu**
R J Blythe	**EBly**
Bodiam Nursery	**SBod**
Bodmin Plant and Herb Nursery	**CBod**
Bodnant Garden Nursery Ltd	**WBod**
S & E Bond	**WBon**
Bonhard Nursery	**GBon**
Bosvigo Plants	**CBos**
The Botanic Nursery	**CBot**
Bouts Cottage Nurseries	**WBou**
Ann & Roger Bowden	**CBdn**
Rupert Bowlby	**LBow**
S & N Brackley	**SEED**

Nursery-Code Index

Code-Nursery Index

Please note that all these nurseries are listed in alphabetical order of their Codes. All nurseries are listed in alphabetical order of their name in the **Nursery-Code Index** on page 703.
Addresses printed in **bold type** provide a Mail Order Service to the EU.

CAbb **Abbotsbury Sub-Tropical Gardens, Abbotsbury, Nr Weymouth, Dorset, DT3 4LA**
TEL: (01305) 871344/412 *FAX:* (01305) 871344 *CONTACT:* David Sutton
OPENING TIMES: 1000-1800 daily mid Mar-1st Nov. 1000-1500 Nov-mid Mar.
MIN. MAIL ORDER UK: £10.00 + p&p *MIN. VALUE EC:* £20.00 + p&p
CAT. COST: £2 + A4 Sae + 42p stamp *W/SALE or RETAIL:* Both *CREDIT CARDS:* not for telephone orders
SPECIALITIES: Less common & tender Shrubs. *MAP PAGE:* **2**

CAbP **Abbey Plants,** Chaffeymoor, Bourton, Gillingham, Dorset, SP8 5BY
TEL: (01747) 840841 *CONTACT:* K Potts
OPENING TIMES: 1000-1300 & 1400-1700 Tue-Sat Mar-Nov. Dec-Feb by appt.
No mail order
CAT. COST: Sae *W/SALE or RETAIL:* Retail *CREDIT CARDS:* None
SPECIALITIES: Flowering Trees & Shrubs. Shrub Roses incl. many unusual varieties.
MAP PAGE: **2**

CAgr **Agroforestry Research Trust,** 46 Hunters Moon, Dartington, Totnes, Devon, TQ9 6JT
TEL: *CONTACT:* Martin Crawford
OPENING TIMES: Not open - Mail Order only.
MIN. MAIL ORDER UK: No minimum charge *MIN. VALUE EC:*
CAT. COST: 3 x 1st class *W/SALE or RETAIL:* Retail *CREDIT CARDS:* None
SPECIALITIES: Mostly Trees, some Perennials, Alnus, Berberis, Citrus, Eucalyptus, Juglans & Salix. See also SEED Index.

CAlt **Altoona Nurseries,** The Windmill, Tigley, Dartington, Totnes, Devon, TQ9 6DW
TEL: (01803) 868147 *FAX:* (01803) 868147 *CONTACT:* Paul A Harber
OPENING TIMES: Any time by appt.
No mail order
CAT. COST: Sae *W/SALE or RETAIL:* Both *CREDIT CARDS:* None
SPECIALITIES: Japanese Maples. *MAP PAGE:* **1**

CArc **Archangel Plants,** 186 Ringwood Road, Longham, Ferndown, Dorset, BH22 9AP
TEL: 01202 872414 *CONTACT:* Carol Strafford
OPENING TIMES: 0900-1700 Mon-Thur & 1000-1600 Sat, 31st Mar-30th Sept. Please phone first.
MIN. MAIL ORDER UK: £10.00 + p&p *MIN. VALUE EC:*
CAT. COST: 4 x 1st class *W/SALE or RETAIL:* Retail *CREDIT CARDS:* None
SPECIALITIES: Traditional and unusual Hardy Perennials incl. Grasses, Erysimum, Eryngium, Nepeta, Phlox & Sedum *MAP PAGE:* **2**

CArn **Arne Herbs, Limeburn Nurseries, Limeburn Hill, Chew Magna, Avon, BS18 8QW**
TEL: (01275) 333399 *FAX:* (01275) 333399 *CONTACT:* A Lyman-Dixon & Jenny Thomas
OPENING TIMES: Most times - please check first.
MIN. MAIL ORDER UK: No minimum charge *MIN. VALUE EC:* Nmc *EXPORT:* Yes
CAT. COST: £1.50 UK, 6 x IRC *W/SALE or RETAIL:* Both *CREDIT CARDS:* None
SPECIALITIES: Herbs, Wild Flowers & Cottage Flowers. *MAP PAGE:* **2**

CAvo **Avon Bulbs, Burnt House Farm, Mid-Lambrook, South Petherton, Somerset, TA13 5HE**
TEL: (01460) 242177 *CONTACT:* C Ireland-Jones
OPENING TIMES: Thu, Fri, Sat mid Sep-end Oct & mid Feb-end Mar or by appt.
MIN. MAIL ORDER UK: £10.00 + p&p *MIN. VALUE EC:* £20.00 + p&p *EXPORT:* Yes
CAT. COST: 4 x 2nd class *W/SALE or RETAIL:* Retail *CREDIT CARDS:* Visa, Access
SPECIALITIES: Smaller & unusual Bulbs. *MAP PAGE:* **1/2**

◆ **See also Display Advertisements**

CB&S **Burncoose & South Down Nurseries, Gwennap, Redruth, Cornwall, TR16 6BJ**
TEL: (01209) 861112 *FAX:* (01209) 860011 *CONTACT:* C H Williams & D Knuckey NDH
OPENING TIMES: 0800-1700 Mon-Sat & 1100-1700 Sun.
MIN. MAIL ORDER UK: No minimum charge *MIN. VALUE EC:* Nmc* *EXPORT:* Yes
CAT. COST: £1.00 inc p&p *W/SALE or RETAIL:* Both *CREDIT CARDS:* Visa, Access, AmEx, Switch
SPECIALITIES: Extensive range of over 2500 Ornamental Trees & Shrubs and Herbaceous. 30 acre garden. *NOTE: Individual quotations for EC sales. Internet Web site: http://www.eclipse.co.uk/burncoose. *MAP PAGE:* **1**

CBar **Barters Farm Nurseries Ltd,** Chapmanslade, Westbury, Wiltshire, BA13 4AL
TEL: (01373) 832694 *FAX:* (01373) 832677 *CONTACT:* D Travers
OPENING TIMES: 0900-1700 Mon-Sat & 1000-1700 Sun & Bank Hols.
No mail order
CAT. COST: A4 Sae *W/SALE or RETAIL:* Both *CREDIT CARDS:* Visa, Switch
SPECIALITIES: Wide range of Shrubs. Ground Cover, Patio plants, container & open-ground Trees. Ferns, half-hardy Perennials, Grasses & Herbaceous. *MAP PAGE:* **2**

CBdn **Ann & Roger Bowden, Cleave House, Sticklepath, Okehampton, Devon, EX20 2NN**
TEL: (01837) 840481 *FAX:* (01837) 840482 *CONTACT:* Ann & Roger Bowden
◆ *OPENING TIMES:* Appt. only.
MIN. MAIL ORDER UK: No minimum charge *MIN. VALUE EC:* Nmc *EXPORT:* Yes
CAT. COST: 3 x 1st class *W/SALE or RETAIL:* Both *CREDIT CARDS:* Visa, Access, EuroCard
SPECIALITIES: Hosta only. *MAP PAGE:* **1**

CBen **Bennett's Water Lily Farm, Putton Lane, Chickerell, Weymouth, Dorset, DT3 4AF**
TEL: (01305) 785150 *FAX:* (01305) 781619 *CONTACT:* J Bennett
OPENING TIMES: Tue-Sun Apr-Aug, Tue-Sat Sep, Oct & Mar.
MIN. MAIL ORDER UK: No minimum charge *MIN. VALUE EC:* £25.00 + p&p
CAT. COST: 3 x 1st class *W/SALE or RETAIL:* Both *CREDIT CARDS:* Visa, Access
SPECIALITIES: Aquatic plants. NCCPG Collection of Water Lilies. *MAP PAGE:* **2**

CBla **Blackmore & Langdon Ltd, Pensford, Bristol, Avon, BS18 4JL**
TEL: (01275) 332300 *FAX:* (01275) 332300 *CONTACT:* J S Langdon
◆ *OPENING TIMES:* 0900-1700 Mon-Sat, 1000-1600 Sun.
MIN. MAIL ORDER UK: No minimum charge *MIN. VALUE EC:* Nmc *EXPORT:* Yes
CAT. COST: Sae *W/SALE or RETAIL:* Retail *CREDIT CARDS:* None
SPECIALITIES: Phlox, Delphinium & Begonias. See also SEED Index. *MAP PAGE:* **2**

CBlo **Blounts Court Nurseries,** Studley, Calne, Wiltshire, SN11 9NH
TEL: (01249) 812103 *FAX:* (01249) 812103 *CONTACT:* Mrs P E Rendell & Mr S N Fox
OPENING TIMES: 1030-1630 Sun, 0900-1700 Nov-Feb, 0900-1800 Apr-Jul, 0900-1730 Mon, Tue, Fri & Sat Aug-Oct.
No mail order
CAT. COST: 2 x 1st or 2nd class *W/SALE or RETAIL:* Retail *CREDIT CARDS:* Visa, Access, Switch
SPECIALITIES: Wide range of Shrubs, Fruit & Ornamental Trees, Conifers, Roses, container & open ground. Clematis, Climbers, Herbaceous, incl. unusual varieties. *MAP PAGE:* **2**

CBod **Bodmin Plant and Herb Nursery,** Laveddon Mill, Laninval Hill, Bodmin, Cornwall, PL30 5JU
TEL: (01208) 72837 *FAX:* (01208) 76491 *CONTACT:* Sarah Wilks
OPENING TIMES: 0900-1800 (or dusk if earlier) daily.
No mail order
CAT. COST: 2 x 1st class for herb list. *W/SALE or RETAIL:* Both *CREDIT CARDS:* MasterCard, Visa
SPECIALITIES: Herbs, & good range of Shrubs & Herbaceous Plants. *MAP PAGE:* **1**

CBos **Bosvigo Plants,** Bosvigo House, Bosvigo Lane, Truro, Cornwall, TR1 3NH
TEL: (01872) 275774 *FAX:* (01872) 275774 *CONTACT:* Wendy Perry
OPENING TIMES: 1100-1800 Wed-Sat Mar-end Sep.
No mail order
CAT. COST: 4 x 2nd class *W/SALE or RETAIL:* Retail *CREDIT CARDS:* None
SPECIALITIES: Rare & unusual Herbaceous. *MAP PAGE:* **1**

CBot **The Botanic Nursery,** Bath Road, Atworth, Nr Melksham, Wiltshire, SN12 8NU
TEL: (01225) 706597* *FAX:* (01225) 700953 *CONTACT:* T & M Baker
OPENING TIMES: 1000-1700 Wed-Mon, Closed Jan.
No mail order
CAT. COST: 4 x 1st class *W/SALE or RETAIL:* Both *CREDIT CARDS:* Visa, Access
SPECIALITIES: Rare hardy Shrubs & Perennials for lime soils. *Mobile Phone (0850) 328756. *MAP PAGE:* **2**

CBrd **Broadleas Gardens Ltd,** Broadleas, Devizes, Wiltshire, SN10 5JQ
TEL: (01380) 722035 *CONTACT:* Lady Anne Cowdray
OPENING TIMES: 1400-1800 Wed, Thu & Sun Apr-Oct.
No mail order
CAT. COST: 1 x 1st class *W/SALE or RETAIL:* Both *CREDIT CARDS:* None
SPECIALITIES: General range. *MAP PAGE:* **2**

CBre **Bregover Plants, Hillbrooke, Middlewood, North Hill, Nr Launceston, Cornwall, PL15 7NN**
TEL: (01566) 782661 *CONTACT:* Jennifer Bousfield
OPENING TIMES: 1100-1700 Wed-Fri Mar-mid Oct and by appt.
MIN. MAIL ORDER UK: No minimum charge *MIN. VALUE EC:* Nmc
CAT. COST: 2 x 1st class *W/SALE or RETAIL:* Retail *CREDIT CARDS:* None
SPECIALITIES: Unusual Hardy Perennials. *MAP PAGE:* **1**

CBrk **Brockings Exotics,** Petherwin Gate, North Petherwin, Cornwall, PL15 8LW
TEL: (01566) 785533 *CONTACT:* Ian K S Cooke
OPENING TIMES: Strictly by appt. ONLY. Apr-Sep.
MIN. MAIL ORDER UK: £15.00 + p&p* *MIN. VALUE EC:*
CAT. COST: 3 x 1st class *W/SALE or RETAIL:* Both *CREDIT CARDS:* None
SPECIALITIES: Tender Perennials, Canna, Coleus & Conservatory plants. *Note: mail order within UK only. *MAP PAGE:* **1**

CBro **Broadleigh Gardens, Bishops Hull, Taunton, Somerset, TA4 1AE**
TEL: (01823) 286231 *FAX:* (01823) 323646 *CONTACT:* Lady Skelmersdale
OPENING TIMES: 0900-1600 Mon-Fri for viewing ONLY. Orders collected if prior notice given.
MIN. MAIL ORDER UK: No minimum charge *MIN. VALUE EC:* Nmc
CAT. COST: 2 x 1st class *W/SALE or RETAIL:* Retail *CREDIT CARDS:* Visa, Access
SPECIALITIES: Two Catalogues. (Jan) - Bulbs in growth, (Galanthus, Cyclamen etc.) & Herbaceous. (June) - Dwarf & unusual Bulbs. *MAP PAGE:* **1/2**

CBrP **Brooklands Plants, 25 Treves Road, Dorchester, Dorset, DT1 2HE**
TEL: (01305) 265846 *CONTACT:* Mr I R Watt
OPENING TIMES: Weekends, please phone first.
MIN. MAIL ORDER UK: £25.00 + p&p *MIN. VALUE EC:* £25.00 + p&p
CAT. COST: 2 x 2nd class *W/SALE or RETAIL:* Both *CREDIT CARDS:* None
SPECIALITIES: Palms, Cycads & other distinctive Foliage Plants for the conservatory & outside. *MAP PAGE:* **2**

CCan **Cannington College Plant Centre, Cannington, Bridgwater, Somerset, TA5 2LS**
TEL: (01278) 652226 *FAX:* (01278) 652479 *CONTACT:* Nick Rigden
OPENING TIMES: 1400-1700 daily Easter-Oct.
MIN. MAIL ORDER UK: £15.00 + p&p *MIN. VALUE EC:* £15.00 + p&p *EXPORT:* Yes
CAT. COST: Free *W/SALE or RETAIL:* Retail *CREDIT CARDS:* None
SPECIALITIES: Abutilon, Argyranthemum, Osteospermum, Salvia, Felicia & Euryops. *MAP PAGE:* **1/2**

◆ **See also Display Advertisements**

CChe **Cherry Tree Nursery,** (Sheltered Work Opportunities), off New Road Roundabout, Northbourne, Bournemouth, Dorset, BH10 7DA
TEL: (01202) 593537 *FAX:* (01202) 590626 *CONTACT:* Chris Veale
OPENING TIMES: 0830-1600 Mon-Fri, 0900-1200 most Sats.
No mail order
CAT. COST: A4 Sae + 2 x 2nd class *W/SALE or RETAIL:* Both *CREDIT CARDS:* None
SPECIALITIES: Hardy Shrubs. *MAP PAGE:* **2**

CChr **Christina's Cottage Plants,** Friars Way, Church Street, Upwey, Weymouth, Dorset, DT3 5QE
TEL: (01305) 813243 *CONTACT:* Christina Scott
OPENING TIMES: 1100-1700 Wed, Sat, Sun Mar-Oct.
No mail order
CAT. COST: 2 x 1st class *W/SALE or RETAIL:* Retail *CREDIT CARDS:* None
SPECIALITIES: Hardy Perennials. *MAP PAGE:* **2**

CChu **Churchills Garden Nursery,** Exeter Road, Chudleigh, South Devon, TQ13 0DD
TEL: (01626) 852585 *FAX:* (01626) 852585 *CONTACT:* Mr M J S Henry
OPENING TIMES: 1400-1700 Mon-Fri, 1000-1700 Sat & Sun, mid Mar-mid Oct. Also by appt.
No mail order
CAT. COST: 3 x 2nd class *W/SALE or RETAIL:* Retail *CREDIT CARDS:* Visa, Access, MasterCard, EuroCard, Switch, Delta
SPECIALITIES: Extensive & interesting range of garden-worthy Trees, Shrubs, Climbers & Herbaceous - many unusual. *MAP PAGE:* **1**

CCot **Cottage Garden Plants Old & New, Cox Cottage, Lower Street, East Morden, Wareham, Dorset, BH20 7DL**
OPENING TIMES: Mainly Mail Order. Visitors by appt. only.
MIN. MAIL ORDER UK: £5.00 + p&p *MIN. VALUE EC:* £10.00 + p&p
CAT. COST: 2 x 1st class *W/SALE or RETAIL:* Retail *CREDIT CARDS:* None
SPECIALITIES: Pinks, Primroses, Cheiranthus, Viola & Violets. *MAP PAGE:* **2**

CCSL **Corkscrew Lane Nursery,** (Off.) 12 Tallowood, Shepton Mallet, Somerset, BA4 5QN
TEL: (01749) 343368 *CONTACT:* Mr J Dennis
OPENING TIMES: By appt. only.
No mail order
CAT. COST: Free *W/SALE or RETAIL:* Retail *CREDIT CARDS:* None
SPECIALITIES: Malus. NB Nursery at Corkscrew Lane, Woolston. Visits BY APPT. ONLY. *MAP PAGE:* **2**

CCuc **Cuckoo Mill Nursery,** Rose Ash, South Molton, Devon, EX36 4RQ
TEL: (01769) 550530 *CONTACT:* P A Woollard
OPENING TIMES: By appt. only. Please phone before 1000 or after 1800.
No mail order
CAT. COST: 3 x 1st class *W/SALE or RETAIL:* Retail *CREDIT CARDS:* None
SPECIALITIES: Hardy Ferns, Grasses & Astilbe. Shade & moisture loving plants. *MAP PAGE:* **1**

CCVT **Chew Valley Trees,** Winford Road, Chew Magna, Bristol, Avon, BS18 8QE
TEL: (01275) 333752 *FAX:* (01275) 333746 *CONTACT:* J Scarth
OPENING TIMES: 0800-1700 Mon-Fri all year. 0900-1600 Sat 1st Oct-30th Jun. Other times by appt.
No mail order
CAT. COST: 1 x 1st class *W/SALE or RETAIL:* Both *CREDIT CARDS:* None
SPECIALITIES: Native British Trees and Shrubs, Apple Trees & Hedging. *MAP PAGE:* **2**

CDec **Decorative Foliage,** Higher Badworthy, South Brent, Devon, TQ10 9EG
TEL: (01548) 821493 evening, (01364) 72768 daytime only. *FAX:* (01364) 72768
CONTACT: Amanda Hansford
OPENING TIMES: By appt. only.
MIN. MAIL ORDER UK: No minimum charge* *MIN. VALUE EC:*
CAT. COST: 2 x 1st class *W/SALE or RETAIL:* Retail *CREDIT CARDS:* None
SPECIALITIES: Flower arrangers plants & rarities. *Note: mail order to UK only.
MAP PAGE: **1**

CDev **Devon Violet Nursery, Rattery, South Brent, Devon, TQ10 9LG**
TEL: (01364) 643033 *FAX:* (01364) 643033 *CONTACT:* Joan & Michael Yardley
◆ *OPENING TIMES:* All year except Xmas. Please ring first.
MIN. MAIL ORDER UK: 6 plants *MIN. VALUE EC:* 6 plants *EXPORT:* Yes
CAT. COST: 2 x 2nd class *W/SALE or RETAIL:* Both *CREDIT CARDS:* None
SPECIALITIES: Violets & Parma Violets. Also Penstemon & Cottage Garden plants (but no list).
MAP PAGE: **1**

CDoC **Duchy of Cornwall,** Penlyne Nursery, Cott Road, Lostwithiel, Cornwall, PL22 08W
TEL: (01208) 872668 *FAX:* (01208) 872835 *CONTACT:* Andrew Carthew
OPENING TIMES: 0900-1700 Mon-Sat, 1000-1700 Sun. Closed Bank Hols.
MIN. MAIL ORDER UK: Ask for details *MIN. VALUE EC:*
CAT. COST: £1.50 *W/SALE or RETAIL:* Retail *CREDIT CARDS:* Visa, AmEx, Access, Switch, Delta
SPECIALITIES: Very wide range of all garden plants incl. Trees, Shrubs, Conifers, Roses, Perennials, Fruit & half-hardy Exotics. *MAP PAGE:* **1**

CDul **Dulford Nurseries,** Cullompton, Devon, EX15 2DG
TEL: (01884) 266361 *FAX:* (01884) 266663 *CONTACT:* David & Jean Brent
◆ *OPENING TIMES:* 0730-1630 Mon-Fri
MIN. MAIL ORDER UK: £10.00 + p&p *MIN. VALUE EC:*
CAT. COST: Free *W/SALE or RETAIL:* Both *CREDIT CARDS:* None
SPECIALITIES: Native, Ornamental & unusual Trees & Shrubs, incl. Oaks, Maples, Beech, Birch, Chestnut, Ash, Lime, Sorbus & Pines. *MAP PAGE:* **1**

CElm **Elm Tree Nursery,** Cadbury, Exeter, Devon, EX5 5LA
TEL: (01392) 861330 *FAX:* (01392) 861330 *CONTACT:* M Saunders
OPENING TIMES: Not open to the public.
MIN. MAIL ORDER UK: £10.00 + p&p *MIN. VALUE EC:*
CAT. COST: Free *W/SALE or RETAIL:* Retail *CREDIT CARDS:* None
SPECIALITIES: Cyclamen species.

CElw **Elworthy Cottage Plants,** Elworthy Cottage, Elworthy, Lydeard St Lawrence, Taunton, Somerset, TA4 3PX
TEL: (01984) 656427 *CONTACT:* Mrs J M Spiller
OPENING TIMES: 1130-1700 Tue, Thu & Fri mid Mar-mid Oct & by appt.
No mail order
CAT. COST: 3 x 2nd class *W/SALE or RETAIL:* Retail *CREDIT CARDS:* None
SPECIALITIES: Unusual Herbaceous plants esp. Hardy Geranium, Geum, Grasses, Campanula, Erysimum, Pulmonaria, Origanum & Viola. *MAP PAGE:* **1/2**

CEnd **Endsleigh Gardens,** Milton Abbot, Tavistock, Devon, PL19 0PG
TEL: (01822) 870235 *FAX:* (01822) 870513 *CONTACT:* Michael Taylor
◆ *OPENING TIMES:* 0800-1700 Mon-Sat, 1400-1700 Sun. Closed Sun Dec & Jan.
MIN. MAIL ORDER UK: £12.00 + p&p *MIN. VALUE EC:*
CAT. COST: 2 x 1st class *W/SALE or RETAIL:* Both *CREDIT CARDS:* Visa, Access
SPECIALITIES: Choice & unusual Trees & Shrubs incl. Acer & Cornus cvs. Old Apples & Cherries. Grafting service. *MAP PAGE:* **1**

CEqu **Equatorial Plant Co. (Vireyas), The White Cottage, Three Gates, Leigh, Nr Sherborne, Dorset, DT9 6JQ**
TEL: (01963) 210309 *FAX:* (01833) 690519 *CONTACT:* Blair & Jackie Sibun
OPENING TIMES: By appt.
MIN. MAIL ORDER UK: No minimum charge *MIN. VALUE EC:* Nmc
CAT. COST: Free *W/SALE or RETAIL:* Retail *CREDIT CARDS:* Visa, Access
SPECIALITIES: Vireya Rhododendrons

CFai **Fairhaven Nursery,** Clapworthy Cross, Chittlehampton, Umberleigh, Devon, EX37 9QT
TEL: (01769) 540528 *CONTACT:* Derek Burdett
OPENING TIMES: 1000-1600 all year, but please check first.
MIN. MAIL ORDER UK: £10.00 + p&p* *MIN. VALUE EC:*
CAT. COST: 2 x 1st class *W/SALE or RETAIL:* Retail *CREDIT CARDS:* None
SPECIALITIES: Wide selection of more unusual Hardy Trees, Shrubs & Perennials. *Note: mail order to UK only. *MAP PAGE:* **1**

CFee **Feebers Hardy Plants,** 1 Feeber Cottage, Westwood, Broadclyst, Nr Exeter, Devon, EX5 3DQ
TEL: (01404) 822118 *FAX:* (01404) 822118 *CONTACT:* Mrs E Squires
◆ *OPENING TIMES:* 1000-1700 Thur & 1400-1800 Sat Mar-Jul & Sep-Oct
No mail order
CAT. COST: Sae + 36p stamp *W/SALE or RETAIL:* Retail *CREDIT CARDS:* None
SPECIALITIES: Plants for wet clay soils, Alpines & Hardy Perennials. *MAP PAGE:* **1**

CFil **Fillan's Plants, Pound House Nursery, Buckland Monachorum, Yelverton, Devon, PL20 7LJ**
TEL: (01822) 855050 *FAX:* (01822) 614351 *CONTACT:* Mark Fillan
OPENING TIMES: By appt. only.
MIN. MAIL ORDER UK: £20.00 + p&p *MIN. VALUE EC:* £50.00 + p&p *EXPORT:* Yes
CAT. COST: 3 x 1st class *W/SALE or RETAIL:* Both *CREDIT CARDS:* None
SPECIALITIES: Ferns, Hydrangea & less usual plants. *MAP PAGE:* **1**

CFir **Fir Tree Farm Nursery,** Tresahor, Constantine, Falmouth, Cornwall, TR11 5PL
TEL: (01326) 340593 *CONTACT:* Jim Cave
OPENING TIMES: 1000-1700 Thu-Sun 1st Mar-30th Sep.
MIN. MAIL ORDER UK: £25.00 + p&p *MIN. VALUE EC:*
CAT. COST: 6 x 1st class *W/SALE or RETAIL:* Retail *CREDIT CARDS:* None
SPECIALITIES: Over 1000 varieties of Cottage Garden & rare Perennials & 90 types of Clematis. *MAP PAGE:* **1**

CFis **The Margery Fish Plant Nursery, East Lambrook Manor, East Lambrook, South Petherton, Somerset, TA13 5HL**
TEL: (01460) 240328 *FAX:* (01460) 242344 *CONTACT:* Mr M Stainer
OPENING TIMES: 1000-1700 Mon-Sat Mar-Oct, 1000-1700 Mon-Fri Nov-Feb.
MIN. MAIL ORDER UK: £10.00 + p&p *MIN. VALUE EC:* £25.00 + p&p *EXPORT:* Yes
CAT. COST: 4 x 1st class *W/SALE or RETAIL:* Retail *CREDIT CARDS:* None
SPECIALITIES: Hardy Geranium, Euphorbia, Helleborus, Primula vulgaris, Penstemon, Salvia & Herbaceous. *MAP PAGE:* **1/2**

CFul **Rodney Fuller,** Coachman's Cottage, Higher Bratton Seymour, Wincanton, Somerset, BA9 8DA
TEL: *CONTACT:* Rodney Fuller
OPENING TIMES: Not open.
MIN. MAIL ORDER UK: £25.00 *MIN. VALUE EC:*
CAT. COST: Sae *W/SALE or RETAIL:* Retail *CREDIT CARDS:* None
SPECIALITIES: Violas & Violettas. Buxus 'Suffruticosa'.

CGle **Glebe Cottage Plants,** Pixie Lane, Warkleigh, Umberleigh, Devon, EX37 9DH
TEL: FAX: (01769) 540554 *CONTACT:* Carol Klein
OPENING TIMES: 1000-1300 & 1400-1700 Tue, Wed, Thur & Fri.
No mail order
CAT. COST: £1.50 *W/SALE or RETAIL:* Retail *CREDIT CARDS:* None
SPECIALITIES: Extensive range of hard-to-find Perennials. *MAP PAGE:* **1**

CGOG **Global Orange Groves UK, PO Box 644, Poole, Dorset, BH17 9YB**
TEL: (01202) 691699 *CONTACT:* P K Oliver
◆ *OPENING TIMES:* Most weekends.
MIN. MAIL ORDER UK: No minimum charge *MIN. VALUE EC:* Nmc
CAT. COST: Sae *W/SALE or RETAIL:* Both *CREDIT CARDS:* None
SPECIALITIES: Citrus trees, Citrus fertiliser & book 'Success with Citrus'.

CGra **Graham's Hardy Plants, Southcroft, North Road, Timsbury, Bath, Avon, BA3 1JN**
TEL: (01761) 472187 *CONTACT:* Graham Nicholls
OPENING TIMES: 1000-1600 1st Apr-30th Sep but please phone on Wed, Thur & Fri first.
MIN. MAIL ORDER UK: £1.50 + p&p *MIN. VALUE EC:* £1.50 + p&p
CAT. COST: 2 x 1st class or 2 x IRC *W/SALE or RETAIL:* Retail *CREDIT CARDS:* None
SPECIALITIES: North American Alpines esp. Lewisia, Eriogonum, Penstemon, Campanula. *MAP PAGE:* **5**

CGre **Greenway Gardens,** Churston Ferrers, Brixham, Devon, TQ5 0ES
TEL: (01803) 842382 *CONTACT:* Roger Clark (Manager)
OPENING TIMES: 1400-1700 (Nov-Feb 1630) Mon-Fri, 1000-1200 Sat, ex Bank Hols. Also by appt.
MIN. MAIL ORDER UK: No minimum charge* *MIN. VALUE EC:*
CAT. COST: 3 x 1st class *W/SALE or RETAIL:* Retail *CREDIT CARDS:* None
SPECIALITIES: Unusual Trees & Shrubs particularly from temperate Southern hemisphere. *Note: mail order by Carrier only. *MAP PAGE:* **1**

CGro **C W Groves & Son, West Bay Road, Bridport, Dorset, DT6 4BA**
TEL: (01308) 422654 *FAX:* (01308) 420888 *CONTACT:* C W Groves
OPENING TIMES: 0830-1700 Mon-Sat, 1030-1630 Sun.
MIN. MAIL ORDER UK: No minimum charge* *MIN. VALUE EC:* £50.00 + p&p *EXPORT:* Yes
CAT. COST: Free *W/SALE or RETAIL:* Retail *CREDIT CARDS:* Access, Visa, Switch
SPECIALITIES: Nursery & Garden Centre specialising in Parma & Hardy Viola. *Note: Violets Mail Order ONLY. *MAP PAGE:* **1/2**

CHad **Hadspen Garden & Nursery,** Hadspen House, Castle Cary, Somerset, BA7 7NG
TEL: (01749) 813707 *FAX:* (01749) 813707 *CONTACT:* N & S Pope
OPENING TIMES: 0900-1800 Thu-Sun & Bank Hols. 1st Mar-1st Oct. Garden open at the same time.
No mail order
CAT. COST: 3 x 1st class *W/SALE or RETAIL:* Retail *CREDIT CARDS:* None
SPECIALITIES: Large leaved Herbaceous. Old fashioned and shrub Roses. *MAP PAGE:* **2**

CHal **Halsway Nursery,** Halsway, Nr Crowcombe, Taunton, Somerset, TA4 4BB
TEL: (01984) 618243 *CONTACT:* T A & D J Bushen
OPENING TIMES: Most days - please telephone first.
MIN. MAIL ORDER UK: £2.00 + p&p *MIN. VALUE EC:*
CAT. COST: 2 x 1st class* *W/SALE or RETAIL:* Retail *CREDIT CARDS:* None
SPECIALITIES: Coleus & Begonias (excl. tuberous & winter flowering). Also good range of Greenhouse & garden plants. *Note: List for Coleus & Begonias only, no nursery list. *MAP PAGE:* **1/2**

CHan **The Hannays of Bath,** Sydney Wharf Nursery, Bathwick, Bath, Avon, BA2 4ES
TEL: (01225) 462230 *CONTACT:* Mr V H S & Mrs S H Hannay
OPENING TIMES: 1000-1700 Wed-Sun (but open Bank Hols.) 1st Mar-12th Oct or by appt. esp in Winter.
No mail order
CAT. COST: £1.00 + 40p p&p *W/SALE or RETAIL:* Retail *CREDIT CARDS:* None
SPECIALITIES: Uncommon Perennials & Shrubs, many grown from seed collected abroad by ourselves. *NOTE: For Export items, Certificates arranged but collection only. *MAP PAGE:* **2**

CHar **West Harptree Nursery, Bristol Road, West Harptree, Bath & North East Somerset, BS18 6HG**
TEL: (01761) 221370 *FAX:* (01761) 221989 *CONTACT:* Bryn & Helene Bowles
OPENING TIMES: Daily from 10.00 except Mondays, 1st Mar-30th Nov.
MIN. MAIL ORDER UK: No minimum charge *MIN. VALUE EC:* Nmc *EXPORT:* Yes
CAT. COST: 2 x 1st class *W/SALE or RETAIL:* Both *CREDIT CARDS:* None
SPECIALITIES: Unusual Lilies and Herbaceous Perennials *MAP PAGE:* **2**

CHEx **Hardy Exotics, Gilly Lane, Whitecross, Penzance, Cornwall, TR20 8BZ**
TEL: (01736) 740660 *FAX:* (01736) 741101 *CONTACT:* C Shilton/J Smith
OPENING TIMES: 1000-1700 1st Apr-31st Oct. 1000-1600 Mon-Sat 1st Nov-31st Mar. Please phone first Nov-Mar.
MIN. MAIL ORDER UK: £13.50 carriage *MIN. VALUE EC:* P.O.A.
CAT. COST: 4 x 1st class *W/SALE or RETAIL:* Retail *CREDIT CARDS:* Visa, Access
SPECIALITIES: Trees, Shrubs & Herbaceous plants to create tropical & desert effects. Hardy & half-Hardy for gardens patios & conservatories. *MAP PAGE:* **1**

CHid **Hidden Valley Nursery, Umberleigh, Devon, EX37 9YY**
TEL: (01769) 560567 *CONTACT:* Linda & Peter Lindley
OPENING TIMES: By appt. only.
MIN. MAIL ORDER UK: No minimum charge *MIN. VALUE EC:* Nmc *EXPORT:* Yes
CAT. COST: 2 x 1st class *W/SALE or RETAIL:* Retail *CREDIT CARDS:* None
SPECIALITIES: Hardy Perennials, esp. shade lovers.

CHig **The High Garden, Courtwood, Newton Ferrers, South Devon, PL8 1BW**
TEL: (01752) 872528 *CONTACT:* F Bennett
OPENING TIMES: By appt.
MIN. MAIL ORDER UK: No minimum charge *MIN. VALUE EC:* £20.00 + p&p
CAT. COST: 60p *W/SALE or RETAIL:* Both *CREDIT CARDS:* None
SPECIALITIES: Pieris & Rhododendron. *MAP PAGE:* **1**

CHil **Hillside Cottage Plants,** Hillside, Gibbet Lane, Whitchurch, North East Somerset, BS14 0BX
TEL: (01275) 837505 *CONTACT:* Josephine Pike
◆ *OPENING TIMES:* Normally here but please phone first in case at show.
No mail order
CAT. COST: 4 x 1st class *W/SALE or RETAIL:* Retail *CREDIT CARDS:* None
SPECIALITIES: Hardy Geraniums & wide range of Hardy Perennials. *MAP PAGE:* **2**

CHor **Horton Vale Nursery,** Horton Heath, Wimborne, Dorset, BH21 7JN
TEL: (01202) 813473 *CONTACT:* David Wright
OPENING TIMES: 0900-1700 daily exc. Wed, Feb-Nov.
No mail order
CAT. COST: None issued *W/SALE or RETAIL:* Retail *CREDIT CARDS:* None
SPECIALITIES: Perennials *MAP PAGE:* **2**

CInt **International Animal Rescue Nursery,** Animal Tracks, Ash Mill, South Molton, Devon, EX36 4QW
TEL: (01769) 550277 *FAX:* (01769) 550917 *CONTACT:* Jo Hicks
OPENING TIMES: 1000-1800 or dusk 365 days a year.
No mail order
CAT. COST: 3 x 1st class *W/SALE or RETAIL:* Retail *CREDIT CARDS:* None
SPECIALITIES: Alpines, Grasses *MAP PAGE:* **1**

CJer **Jersey Lavender Ltd,** Rue du Pont Marquet, St Brelade, Jersey, Channel Islands
TEL: (01534) 42933 *FAX:* (01534) 45613 *CONTACT:* David Christie
OPENING TIMES: 1000-1700 Mon-Sat Jun-Sep. Also by appt.
No mail order
CAT. COST: Free *W/SALE or RETAIL:* Retail *CREDIT CARDS:* Access, AmEx, Diners, MasterCard, Switch, Visa
SPECIALITIES: National Collection of Lavandula *MAP PAGE:* **1**

CJew **Jean Jewels,** Millmoor Cottage, Burrington, Umberleigh, Devon, EX37 9EF
TEL: (01769) 520285 *CONTACT:* Jean Jewels & Peter Charnley
OPENING TIMES: Phone call first appreciated.
MIN. MAIL ORDER UK: No minimum charge *MIN. VALUE EC:*
CAT. COST: 3 x 1st class *W/SALE or RETAIL:* Retail *CREDIT CARDS:* None
SPECIALITIES: Herbs, culinary, medicinal & dye plants. Scented foliage plants & plants for the wild garden. *MAP PAGE:* **1**

CKel **Kelways Ltd, Langport, Somerset, TA10 9EZ**
TEL: (01458) 250521 *FAX:* (01458) 253351 *CONTACT:* Mr David Root
OPENING TIMES: 0900-1700 Mon-Fri, 1000-1600 Sat & Sun.
MIN. MAIL ORDER UK: £4.00 + p&p* *MIN. VALUE EC:* £8.00 + p&p *EXPORT:* Yes
CAT. COST: Free *W/SALE or RETAIL:* Both *CREDIT CARDS:* Visa, Access
SPECIALITIES: Paeonia, Iris, Hemerocallis & Herbaceous perennials. *Note: mail order for Paeonia, Iris & Hemerocallis only. *MAP PAGE:* **1/2**

CKen **Kenwith Nursery (Gordon Haddow), Blinsham, Nr Torrington, Beaford, Winkleigh, Devon, EX19 8NT**
TEL: (01805) 603274 *FAX:* (01805) 603663 *CONTACT:* Gordon Haddow
◆ *OPENING TIMES:* 1000-1200 & 1400-1630 Wed-Sat Nov-Feb & by appt. 1000-1630 daily Mar-Oct.
MIN. MAIL ORDER UK: £10.00 + p&p *MIN. VALUE EC:* £50.00 + p&p *EXPORT:* Yes
CAT. COST: 3 x 1st class *W/SALE or RETAIL:* Retail *CREDIT CARDS:* None
SPECIALITIES: All Conifer genera. Grafting a speciality. Many new introductions to UK. Also provisional National Collection of Dwarf Conifers. *MAP PAGE:* **1**

CKin **Kingsfield Conservation Nursery, Broadenham Lane, Winsham, Chard, Somerset, TA20 4JF**
TEL: (01460) 30070 *FAX:* (01460) 30070 *CONTACT:* Mrs M White
OPENING TIMES: Please phone for details.
MIN. MAIL ORDER UK: No minimum charge *MIN. VALUE EC:* Nmc
CAT. COST: 31p stamps *W/SALE or RETAIL:* Both *CREDIT CARDS:* None
SPECIALITIES: Native Trees, Shrubs, Wild flowers & Wild flower Seeds. See also SEED Index under Y.S.J. Seeds. *MAP PAGE:* **1/2**

CKni **Knightshayes Garden Trust,** The Garden Office, Knightshayes, Tiverton, Devon, EX16 7RG
TEL: (01884) 259010 (Shop) *FAX:* (01884) 253264 (Off) *CONTACT:* M Hickson
OPENING TIMES: 1030-1730 daily 1st Apr-31st Oct.
No mail order
CAT. COST: None issued *W/SALE or RETAIL:* Retail *CREDIT CARDS:* Access, AmEx, MasterCard, Switch, Visa, Diners
SPECIALITIES: Bulbs, Shrubs & Herbaceous. *MAP PAGE:* **1**

CKno **Knoll Gardens,** Hampreston, Stapehill, Nr Wimborne, Dorset, BH21 7ND
TEL: (01202) 873931 *FAX:* (01202) 870842 *CONTACT:* N R Lucas
OPENING TIMES: 1000-1730 every day Easter-October only.
No mail order
CAT. COST: None issued *W/SALE or RETAIL:* Retail *CREDIT CARDS:* Visa, Access
SPECIALITIES: Ceanothus & Phygelius National Collections (list available). Herbaceous & Grasses. Half-hardy Perennials. *MAP PAGE:* **2**

CLan **The Lanhydrock Gardens (NT),** Lanhydrock, Bodmin, Cornwall, PL30 5AD
TEL: (01208) 72220 *FAX:* (01208) 72220 *CONTACT:* The National Trust
OPENING TIMES: Daily - Easter (or Apr 1st)-31st Oct.
No mail order
CAT. COST: Free *W/SALE or RETAIL:* Both *CREDIT CARDS:* None
SPECIALITIES: Shrubs, especially Camellia, Azalea, Rhododendron, Magnolia & Ceanothus.
MAP PAGE: **1**

CLCN **Little Creek Nursery, 39 Moor Road, Banwell, Weston-super-Mare, Avon, BS24 6EF**
TEL: (01934) 823739 *CONTACT:* Rhys & Julie Adams
OPENING TIMES: 1000-1630 Thu & Fri March & April. Other times by appt. Please ring first.
MIN. MAIL ORDER UK: No minimum charge *MIN. VALUE EC:* Nmc *EXPORT:* Yes
CAT. COST: 3 x 1st class *W/SALE or RETAIL:* Retail *CREDIT CARDS:* None
SPECIALITIES: Species Cyclamen (from seed) & Helleborus. *MAP PAGE:* **2**

CLit **Littleton Nursery,** Littleton, Somerton, Somerset, TA11 6NT
TEL: (01458) 272356 *CONTACT:* G & R Seymour
◆ *OPENING TIMES:* 0900-1700 Mon-Sat.
No mail order
CAT. COST: £1.00 + A5 Sae *W/SALE or RETAIL:* Both *CREDIT CARDS:* None
SPECIALITIES: Fuchsia, Pelargoniums & half-hardy Perennials *MAP PAGE:* **1/2**

CLnd **Landford Trees,** Landford Lodge, Landford, Salisbury, Wiltshire, SP5 2EH
TEL: (01794) 390808 *FAX:* (01794) 390037 *CONTACT:* C D Pilkington
OPENING TIMES: 0800-1700 Mon-Fri.
No mail order
CAT. COST: Free *W/SALE or RETAIL:* Both *CREDIT CARDS:* None
SPECIALITIES: Deciduous ornamental Trees. *MAP PAGE:* **2**

CLoc **C S Lockyer,** Lansbury, 70 Henfield Road, Coalpit Heath, Bristol, BS17 2UZ
◆ *OPENING TIMES:* Appt. only. (Many open days & coach parties).
MIN. MAIL ORDER UK: 6 plants + p&p *MIN. VALUE EC:*
CAT. COST: 4 x 1st class *W/SALE or RETAIL:* Both *CREDIT CARDS:* None
SPECIALITIES: Fuchsia. *MAP PAGE:* **5**

CLon **Longhall Nursery, Stockton, Nr Warminster, Wiltshire, BA12 0SE**
TEL: (01985) 850914 *FAX:* (01985) 850914 *E-MAIL:* www.designbywire.com
CONTACT: H V & J E Dooley
OPENING TIMES: 0930-1730 19th Mar-27th Sep 1997, 18th Mar-26th Sep 1998.
MIN. MAIL ORDER UK: £5.00 + p&p *MIN. VALUE EC:* £5.00 + p&p
CAT. COST: 3 x 1st class *W/SALE or RETAIL:* Both *CREDIT CARDS:* None
SPECIALITIES: Many chalk tolerant plants, esp. Digitalis, Eryngium, Euphorbia & Salvia.
MAP PAGE: **2**

CLTr **Little Treasures, Wheal Treasure, Horsedowns, Cornwall, TR14 0NL**
TEL: (01209) 831978 *FAX:* (01209) 831978 *CONTACT:* Bernadette Jackson
OPENING TIMES: 1000-1600 Wed-Sat Mar-end Oct. Other times by appt. only
MIN. MAIL ORDER UK: £15.00 + p&p *MIN. VALUE EC:* £25.00 + p&p
CAT. COST: 4 x 1st class *W/SALE or RETAIL:* Retail *CREDIT CARDS:* None
SPECIALITIES: Cottage garden plants, Shrubs & tender Perennials. *MAP PAGE:* **1**

CLyd **Lydford Alpine Nursery,** 2 Southern Cottages, Lydford, Okehampton, Devon, EX20 4BL
TEL: (01822) 820398 *CONTACT:* Julie & David Hatchett
OPENING TIMES: 1000-1700 Tue & Thu Apr-Oct & by appt. Nov-Mar by appt. only.
No mail order
CAT. COST: 3 x 1st class *W/SALE or RETAIL:* Retail *CREDIT CARDS:* None
SPECIALITIES: Dianthus, Primula & Saxifraga. Very wide range of choice & unusual Alpines in small quanities. *MAP PAGE:* **1**

CM&M M & M Plants, Lloret, Chittlehamholt, Umbesleigh, Devon, EX37 9PD
TEL: (01769) 540448 *CONTACT:* Mr M Thorne
OPENING TIMES: 0930-1730 Tue-Sat Apr-Oct & 1000-1600 Tue-Sat Nov-Mar.
No mail order
CAT. COST: £1.00 (incl. p&p) *W/SALE or RETAIL:* Retail *CREDIT CARDS:* None
SPECIALITIES: Perennials. We also carry a reasonable range of Alpines, Shrubs, Trees & Roses.
MAP PAGE: **1**

CMac Macpennys Nurseries, 154 Burley Road, Bransgore, Christchurch, Dorset, BH23 8DB
TEL: (01425) 672348 *CONTACT:* T & V Lowndes
OPENING TIMES: 0800-1700 Mon-Fri, 0900-1700 Sat 1400-1700 Sun.
MIN. MAIL ORDER UK: No minimum charge *MIN. VALUE EC:* Nmc
CAT. COST: 50p & A4 Sae with 2x1st class *W/SALE or RETAIL:* Retail *CREDIT CARDS:* None
SPECIALITIES: General. *MAP PAGE:* **2**

CMCN Mallet Court Nursery, Curry Mallet, Taunton, Somerset, TA3 6SY
TEL: (01823) 480748 *FAX:* (01823) 481009 *CONTACT:* J G S & P M E Harris F.L.S.
OPENING TIMES: 0900-1300 & 1400-1700 Mon-Fri. Sat & Sun by appt.
MIN. MAIL ORDER UK: No minimum charge *MIN. VALUE EC:* Nmc *EXPORT:* Yes
CAT. COST: 29p Sae *W/SALE or RETAIL:* Both *CREDIT CARDS:* None
SPECIALITIES: Maples, Oaks, Magnolia, Hollies & other rare and unusual plants including those from China & South Korea. *MAP PAGE:* **1/2**

CMdw Meadows Nursery, 5 Rectory Cottages, Mells, Frome, Somerset, BA11 3PA
TEL: (01373) 813025 *CONTACT:* Sue Lees
OPENING TIMES: 1000-1800 Tue-Sun 1st Mar-31st Oct & Bank Hols.
No mail order
CAT. COST: 2 x 1st class *W/SALE or RETAIL:* Retail *CREDIT CARDS:* None
SPECIALITIES: Hardy Cottage garden plants. *MAP PAGE:* **2**

CMea The Mead Nursery, Brokerswood, Nr Westbury, Wiltshire, BA13 4EG
TEL: (01373) 859990 *CONTACT:* Steve Lewis-Dale
OPENING TIMES: 0900-1700 Wed-Sat, 1200-1700 Sun, 0900-1700 Bank Hols. 1st Feb-31st Oct. Closed Easter Sunday.
No mail order
CAT. COST: 5 x 1st class *W/SALE or RETAIL:* Retail *CREDIT CARDS:* None
SPECIALITIES: Perennials & Alpines incl. Bulbs. *MAP PAGE:* **2**

CMGP Milton Garden Plants, Milton-on-Stour, Gillingham, Dorset, SP8 5PX
TEL: (01747) 822484 *FAX:* (01747) 822484 *CONTACT:* Sue Hardy & Richard Cumming
OPENING TIMES: 0830-1700 Tue-Sat & Bank Hol Mons, 1000-1630 Sun.
MIN. MAIL ORDER UK: No minimum charge* *MIN. VALUE EC:*
CAT. COST: 5 x 1st class *W/SALE or RETAIL:* Retail *CREDIT CARDS:* Visa, Access
SPECIALITIES: Very wide range of Perennials. Ever changing selection of Trees, Shrubs, Conifers, Alpines & Herbs. *Note: mail order to UK only. *MAP PAGE:* **2**

CMHG Marwood Hill Gardens, Barnstaple, Devon, EX31 4EB
TEL: (01271) 42528 *CONTACT:* Dr Smart
OPENING TIMES: 1100-1700 daily.
No mail order
CAT. COST: 70p *W/SALE or RETAIL:* Retail *CREDIT CARDS:* None
SPECIALITIES: Large range of unusual Trees & Shrubs. Eucalyptus, Alpines, Camellia, Astilbe & Bog plants. *MAP PAGE:* **1**

CMil Mill Cottage Plants, The Mill, Henley Lane, Wookey, Somerset, BA5 1AP
TEL: (01749) 676966 *CONTACT:* Sally Gregson
OPENING TIMES: 1000-1800 Wed Mar-Sep or by appt. Ring for directions.
MIN. MAIL ORDER UK: £5.00 + p&p *MIN. VALUE EC:* £10.00 + p&p
CAT. COST: 3 x 1st class *W/SALE or RETAIL:* Retail *CREDIT CARDS:* None
SPECIALITIES: Unusual & period Cottage plants especially 'old' Pinks, Campanula, Hardy Geranium, Euphorbia, Ferns, Pulmonaria & Grasses. *MAP PAGE:* **1/2**

◆ **See also Display Advertisements**

CMon **Monocot Nursery, Jacklands, Jacklands Bridge, Tickenham, Clevedon, Avon, BS21 6SG**
TEL: (01275) 810394 *CONTACT:* M R Salmon
OPENING TIMES: 1000-1800 Mon-Fri, Sat & Sun by appt.
MIN. MAIL ORDER UK: No minimum charge *MIN. VALUE EC:* Nmc *EXPORT:* Yes
CAT. COST: Sae *W/SALE or RETAIL:* Retail *CREDIT CARDS:* None
SPECIALITIES: Rare & unusual Bulbous plants. Narcissus, Colchicum, Scilla, Crocus, Aroids, S. African & S. American species. See also SEED Index. *MAP PAGE:* **2**

CNat **Natural Selection,** 1 Station Cottages, Hullavington, Chippenham, Wiltshire, SN14 6ET
TEL: (01666) 837369 *E-MAIL:* @worldmutation.demon.co.uk *CONTACT:* Martin Cragg-Barber
OPENING TIMES: Wed afternoon Easter-end August. Other times please telephone first.
MIN. MAIL ORDER UK: £8.00 + p&p *MIN. VALUE EC:*
CAT. COST: 2 x 1st class *W/SALE or RETAIL:* Retail *CREDIT CARDS:* None
SPECIALITIES: Unusual British natives, Pelargoniums & others. See also SEED Index. *MAP PAGE:* **2/5**

CNCN **Naked Cross Nurseries,** Waterloo Road, Corfe Mullen, Wimborne, Dorset, BH21 3SR
TEL: (01202) 693256 *CONTACT:* Mr P J French & Mrs J E Paddon
OPENING TIMES: 0900-1700 daily.
MIN. MAIL ORDER UK: No minimum charge *MIN. VALUE EC:*
CAT. COST: 2 x 1st class *W/SALE or RETAIL:* Both *CREDIT CARDS:* Visa, Access, AmEx, Switch
SPECIALITIES: Heathers. *MAP PAGE:* **2**

CNic **Nicky's Rock Garden Nursery,** Broadhayes, Stockland, Honiton, Devon, EX14 9EH
TEL: (01404) 881213 *CONTACT:* Diana & Bob Dark
OPENING TIMES: 0900-dusk daily. Please telephone first to check & for directions.
No mail order
CAT. COST: 3 x 1st class *W/SALE or RETAIL:* Retail *CREDIT CARDS:* None
SPECIALITIES: Plants for Rock gardens, Alpine house, Scree, Troughs, Banks, Walls & front of border & Dwarf Shrubs. Many unusual. *MAP PAGE:* **1/2**

COCH **Otters' Court Heathers, Otters' Court, West Camel, Yeovil, Somerset, BA22 7QF**
TEL: (01935) 850285 *CONTACT:* Mrs D H Jones
OPENING TIMES: 0900-1700 Wed-Sun and by appt.
MIN. MAIL ORDER UK: £3.00 + p&p *MIN. VALUE EC:* No minimum charge
CAT. COST: 3 x 1st class *W/SALE or RETAIL:* Both *CREDIT CARDS:* None
SPECIALITIES: Lime-tolerant Heathers - Erica, & Daboecia. *MAP PAGE:* **2**

COtt **Otter Nurseries Ltd,** Gosford Road, Ottery St. Mary, Devon, EX11 1LZ
TEL: (01404) 815815 *FAX:* (01404) 815816 *CONTACT:* Mr K Owen
OPENING TIMES: 0800-1730 Mon-Sat, 1030-1630 Sun. Closed Xmas & Boxing day & Easter Sun.
No mail order
CAT. COST: Free *W/SALE or RETAIL:* Retail *CREDIT CARDS:* Visa, Access, AmEx, Diners, Switch
SPECIALITIES: Large Garden Centre & Nursery with extensive range of Trees, Shrubs, Conifers, Climbers, Roses, Fruit & hardy Perennials. *MAP PAGE:* **1/2**

CPas **Passiflora (National Collection), Lampley Road, Kingston Seymour, Clevedon, North Somerset, BS21 6XS**
TEL: (01934) 833350 *FAX:* (01934) 877255 *E-MAIL:* passion@3wa.co.uk
CONTACT: John Vanderplank
OPENING TIMES: 0900-1300 & 1400-1700 Mon-Sat
MIN. MAIL ORDER UK: No minimum charge *MIN. VALUE EC:* £20.00 + p&p *EXPORT:* Yes
CAT. COST: 3 x 1st class *W/SALE or RETAIL:* Both *CREDIT CARDS:* Visa, Access, EuroCard
SPECIALITIES: Passiflora. National Collection of over 200 species & varieties. See also SEED Index. Note: Retail nursery now at Kingston Seymour. *MAP PAGE:* **2**

CPBP **Parham Bungalow Plants, Parham Lane, Market Lavington, Devizes, Wiltshire, SN10 4QA**
TEL: (01380) 812605 *CONTACT:* Mrs D E Sample
OPENING TIMES: Please ring first.
MIN. MAIL ORDER UK: No minimum charge *MIN. VALUE EC:* Nmc
CAT. COST: Sae *W/SALE or RETAIL:* Retail *CREDIT CARDS:* None
SPECIALITIES: Alpines & dwarf Shrubs. *MAP PAGE:* **2**

CPea **Pear Tree Cottage Plants, Pear Tree Cottage, Prestleigh, Shepton Mallet, Somerset, BA4 4NL**
TEL: (01749) 831487 *CONTACT:* PJ & PM Starr
OPENING TIMES: 0900-1900 1st Mar-31st Oct.
MIN. MAIL ORDER UK: £12.50 + p&p *MIN. VALUE EC:* £20.00 + p&p
CAT. COST: 3 x 1st class *W/SALE or RETAIL:* Both *CREDIT CARDS:* None
SPECIALITIES: Wide General Range with many unusual plants. *MAP PAGE:* **2**

CPer **Perrie Hale Forest Nursery,** Northcote Hill, Honiton, Devon, EX14 8TH
TEL: (01404) 43344 *FAX:* (01404) 47163 *CONTACT:* N C Davey & Mrs J F Davey
OPENING TIMES: 0800-1630 Mon-Fri, 0900-1230 Sat, Mar-Nov. Retail sales by appt. please. Telephone first.
No mail order
CAT. COST: Sae *W/SALE or RETAIL:* Both *CREDIT CARDS:* None
SPECIALITIES: Forest Trees, native Hedging plants & Shrubs. *Note: no mail order but will send trees (TNT) if customers cannot collect. *MAP PAGE:* **1/2**

CPev **Peveril Clematis Nursery,** Christow, Exeter, Devon, EX6 7NG
TEL: (01647) 252937 *FAX:* (01647) 252937 *CONTACT:* Barry Fretwell
OPENING TIMES: 1000-1300 & 1400-1730 Fri-Wed, 1000-1300 Sun. Dec-Mar by appt.
No mail order
CAT. COST: 2 x 1st class *W/SALE or RETAIL:* Retail *CREDIT CARDS:* None
SPECIALITIES: Clematis. *MAP PAGE:* **1**

CPla **Plant World Botanic Gardens,** St Marychurch Road, Newton Abbot, South Devon, TQ12 4SE
TEL: (01803) 872939 *FAX:* (01803) 872939 *CONTACT:* Ray Brown
◆ *OPENING TIMES:* 0930-1700 open 6 days (incl. Sun), closed Weds. Easter-end Sept.
No mail order
CAT. COST: 3 x 1st class or $2 *W/SALE or RETAIL:* Both *CREDIT CARDS:* Visa, Access, EuroCard, MasterCard
SPECIALITIES: Alpines & unusual Herbaceous plants. 4 acre world botanic map. NCCPG Primula collections. See also SEED Index for choice seed list (Aquilegia, Geranium, Gentian, Viola). *MAP PAGE:* **1**

CPle **Pleasant View Nursery, Two Mile Oak, Nr Denbury, Newton Abbot, Devon, TQ12 6DG**
TEL: Please write with Sae *CONTACT:* Mrs B D Yeo
OPENING TIMES: 1000-1700 Wed-Sat mid Mar-mid Oct. (Closed for lunch 1245-1330)
MIN. MAIL ORDER UK: £20.00 + p&p *MIN. VALUE EC:* £20.00 + p&p
CAT. COST: 5 x 2nd class *W/SALE or RETAIL:* Retail *CREDIT CARDS:* None
SPECIALITIES: Salvias & unusual shrubs for garden & conservatory incl. Buddleja, Viburnum, Ceanothus, Berberis, Lonicera, Spiraea. Nat. Collections Salvia & Abelia. Off A381 at T.M. Oak Cross towards Denbury. *MAP PAGE:* **1**

CPlN **The Plantsman Nursery, North Wonson Farm, Throwleigh, Okehampton, Devon, EX20 2JA**
TEL: (01647) 231618 *FAX:* (01647) 231618 *CONTACT:* Guy & Emma Sisson
◆ *OPENING TIMES:* 0900-1700 Tues Apr-Sept, and by appt.
MIN. MAIL ORDER UK: 2 plants + p&p *MIN. VALUE EC:* £45.00 + p&p *EXPORT:* Yes
CAT. COST: £1.50 *W/SALE or RETAIL:* Both *CREDIT CARDS:* None
SPECIALITIES: Unusual hardy & tender Climbers & Conservatory plants. *MAP PAGE:* **1**

◆ **See also Display Advertisements**

CPMA P M A Plant Specialities, Lower Mead, West Hatch, Taunton, Somerset, TA3 5RN
TEL: (01823) 480774 *FAX:* (01823) 481046 *CONTACT:* Karan or Nick Junker
OPENING TIMES: STRICTLY by appt. only.
MIN. MAIL ORDER UK: No minimum charge *MIN. VALUE EC:* Nmc *EXPORT:* Yes
CAT. COST: 5 x 2nd class *W/SALE or RETAIL:* Both *CREDIT CARDS:* None
SPECIALITIES: Choice & unusual Shrubs incl. grafted Acer palmatum cvs, Cornus cvs, Magnolia cvs. and a wide range of Daphne. *MAP PAGE:* **1/2**

CPou Pounsley Plants, Poundsley Combe, Spriddlestone, Brixton, Plymouth, Devon, PL9 0DW
TEL: (01752) 402873 *FAX:* (01752) 402873 *CONTACT:* Mrs Jane Hollow
◆ *OPENING TIMES:* Normally 1000-1700 Mon-Sat but please phone first.
MIN. MAIL ORDER UK: £10.00 + p&p** *MIN. VALUE EC:*
CAT. COST: 2 x 1st class *W/SALE or RETAIL:* Both *CREDIT CARDS:* None
SPECIALITIES: Unusual Herbaceous Perennials & 'Cottage plants'. Selection of Clematis & Old Roses. *Note: mail order Nov-Feb only. *MAP PAGE:* **1**

CQua Quality Daffodils, 14 Roscarrack Close, Falmouth, Cornwall, TR11 4PJ
TEL: (01326) 317959 *CONTACT:* R A Scamp
OPENING TIMES: Mail Order only.
MIN. MAIL ORDER UK: No minimum charge *MIN. VALUE EC:* Nmc *EXPORT:* Yes
CAT. COST: 2 x 1st class *W/SALE or RETAIL:* Both *CREDIT CARDS:* None
SPECIALITIES: Narcissus Hybrids & Species.

CRDP R D Plants, Homelea Farm, Tytherleigh, Axminster, East Devon, EX13 7BG
TEL: (01460) 220206* *CONTACT:* Rodney Davey & Lynda Windsor
OPENING TIMES: 0900-1300 & 1400-1730 Mon-Fri & most weekends, Mar-end Sep. Please check first.
MIN. MAIL ORDER UK: £30 mainland only *MIN. VALUE EC:*
CAT. COST: 4 x loose 2nd class *W/SALE or RETAIL:* Retail *CREDIT CARDS:* None
SPECIALITIES: Choice & unusual Herbaceous, retentive shade & woodland plants, Helleborus, plus rarities. *NOTE Please 'phone between 0830 & 0930 only. *MAP PAGE:* **1/2**

CRHN Roseland House Nursery, Chacewater, Truro, Cornwall, TR4 8QB
TEL: (01872) 560451 *CONTACT:* C R Pridham
OPENING TIMES: 1200-1800 Tue Mar-Jul.
MIN. MAIL ORDER UK: £1.00 + p&p *MIN. VALUE EC:*
CAT. COST: 2 x 1st class *W/SALE or RETAIL:* Retail *CREDIT CARDS:* Visa, Access
SPECIALITIES: Climbing Plants. *MAP PAGE:* **1**

CRos Royal Horticultural Society's Garden, Rosemoor, Great Torrington, Devon, EX38 8PH
TEL: (01805) 624067 *FAX:* (01805) 622422 *CONTACT:* Plant Sales Manager
OPENING TIMES: 1000-1800 Apr-Sep, 1000-1700 Oct-Mar.
No mail order
CAT. COST: None issued *W/SALE or RETAIL:* Retail *CREDIT CARDS:* Visa, Access, AmEx
SPECIALITIES: National Cornus and part Ilex Collections. Many rare & unusual plants.
MAP PAGE: **1**

CRow Rowden Gardens, Brentor, Nr Tavistock, Devon, PL19 0NG
TEL: (01822) 810275 *CONTACT:* John R L Carter
OPENING TIMES: 1000-1700 Sat-Sun & Bank Hols 26th Mar-end Sep. Other times by appt.
MIN. MAIL ORDER UK: No minimum charge *MIN. VALUE EC:* Nmc *EXPORT:* Yes
CAT. COST: £1.50 *W/SALE or RETAIL:* Both *CREDIT CARDS:* None
SPECIALITIES: Aquatics, Bog, unusual & rare specialist plants. NCCPG Polygonum & Ranunculus ficaria Collection. *MAP PAGE:* **1**

CSam **Sampford Shrubs, Sampford Peverell, Tiverton, Devon, EX16 7EW**
TEL: (01884) 821164 *CONTACT:* M Hughes-Jones & S Proud
OPENING TIMES: 0900-1700 (dusk if earlier) Thu, Fri, Sat. 1000-1600 Sun. Closed 1st Dec-4th Feb.
MIN. MAIL ORDER UK: £15.00 + p&p *MIN. VALUE EC:* £30.00 + p&p
CAT. COST: Sae *W/SALE or RETAIL:* Retail *CREDIT CARDS:* None
SPECIALITIES: Extensive range of good common & uncommon plants including Herbaceous, Shrubs, Trees & Fruit. Internet Web site: http://members.aol.com/sampford/stock.htm.
MAP PAGE: **1**

CSCl **Scott's Clematis,** Lee, Nr Ilfracombe, Devon, EX34 8LW
TEL: (01271) 863366 *FAX:* (01271) 863003 *CONTACT:* John & Marianne McLellan-Scott
◆ *OPENING TIMES:* 1000-1700 Tue-Fri, Sun & Bank Hols Mon. Closed 31st Oct-31st Mar.
MIN. MAIL ORDER UK: * *MIN. VALUE EC:* *EXPORT:* Yes
CAT. COST: A5 Sae *W/SALE or RETAIL:* Retail *CREDIT CARDS:* Visa, Access
SPECIALITIES: Clematis only. *Note: mail order to UK by special arrangement only.
MAP PAGE: **1**

CSev **Lower Severalls Nursery,** Crewkerne, Somerset, TA18 7NX
TEL: (01460) 73234 *FAX:* (01460) 76105 *CONTACT:* Mary R Cooper
OPENING TIMES: 1000-1700 Fri-Wed, 1400-1700 Sun 1st Mar-20th Oct.
MIN. MAIL ORDER UK: £10.00 + p&p *MIN. VALUE EC:*
CAT. COST: 4 x 1st class *W/SALE or RETAIL:* Retail *CREDIT CARDS:* None
SPECIALITIES: Herbs, Herbaceous & Conservatory plants. *MAP PAGE:* **1/2**

CShe **Shepton Nursery Garden,** Old Wells Road, Shepton Mallet, Somerset, BA4 5XN
TEL: (01749) 343630 *CONTACT:* Mr & Mrs P W Boughton
OPENING TIMES: 0930-1730 Tue-Sat and by appt.
No mail order
CAT. COST: 4 x 2nd class *W/SALE or RETAIL:* Retail *CREDIT CARDS:* None
SPECIALITIES: Herbaceous, Alpines & Chaenomeles. *MAP PAGE:* **2**

CSil **Silver Dale Nurseries, Shute Lane, Combe Martin, Illfracombe, Devon, EX34 0HT**
TEL: (01271) 882539 *CONTACT:* Roger Gilbert
◆ *OPENING TIMES:* 1000-1800 daily
MIN. MAIL ORDER UK: No minimum charge *MIN. VALUE EC:* Nmc
CAT. COST: 3 x 1st class *W/SALE or RETAIL:* Retail *CREDIT CARDS:* None
SPECIALITIES: Fuchsia. *MAP PAGE:* **1**

CSpe **Special Plants, Hill Farm Barn, Greenways Lane, Cold Ashton, Chippenham, Wiltshire, SN14 8LA**
TEL: (01225) 891686 *E-MAIL:* derry@sclegg.demon.co.uk *CONTACT:* Derry Watkins
OPENING TIMES: 1100-1600 daily Mar-Sep. Other times please ring first to check.
MIN. MAIL ORDER UK: £10.00 + p&p* *MIN. VALUE EC:* £10.00 + p&p
CAT. COST: 4 x 2nd class *W/SALE or RETAIL:* Retail *CREDIT CARDS:* None
SPECIALITIES: Tender Perennials, Felicia, Diascia, Lotus, Pelargonium, Salvia, Streptocarpus, Osteospermum etc. New introductions of South African plants. *Note: mail order Sep-Mar only.
MAP PAGE: **2/5**

CSPN **Sherston Parva Nursery Ltd, Malmesbury Road, Sherston, Wiltshire, SN16 0NX**
TEL: (01666) 841066 *FAX:* (01635) 32104 *CONTACT:* Martin Rea
OPENING TIMES: 1000-1700 every day 1st Mar-31st Dec.
MIN. MAIL ORDER UK: £10.00 + p&p *MIN. VALUE EC:* £20.00 + p&p
CAT. COST: 4 x 1st class *W/SALE or RETAIL:* Retail *CREDIT CARDS:* None
SPECIALITIES: Clematis, wall Shrubs & Climbers. *MAP PAGE:* **5**

◆ See also Display Advertisements

CSte **Stewarts Country Garden Centre,** God's Blessing Lane, Broomhill, Holt, Wimborne, Dorset, BH21 7DF
TEL: (01202) 882462 *FAX:* (01202) 842127 *E-MAIL:* nsy@stewarts.co.uk
CONTACT: Vincent Blood
◆ *OPENING TIMES:* 0900-1730 Mon-Sat & 1000-1630 Sun.
No mail order
CAT. COST: None issued *W/SALE or RETAIL:* Both *CREDIT CARDS:* Visa, Access, MasterCard, Switch
SPECIALITIES: Wide range of Shrubs, Trees, Climbers, Perennials, Grasses & Conifers. Some unusual. *MAP PAGE:* **2**

CSto **Stone Lane Gardens, Stone Farm, Chagford, Devon, TQ13 8JU**
TEL: (01647) 231311 *FAX:* (01647) 231311 *CONTACT:* Kenneth Ashburner
OPENING TIMES: By appt. only.
MIN. MAIL ORDER UK: No minimum charge *MIN. VALUE EC:* Nmc
CAT. COST: See below* *W/SALE or RETAIL:* Both *CREDIT CARDS:* None
SPECIALITIES: Wide range of wild provenance Betula and Alnus. Also interesting varieties of Rubus, Sorbus etc. *£3.00 for descriptive Catalogue. *MAP PAGE:* **1**

CSut **Suttons Seeds Ltd,** Hele Road, Torquay, South Devon, TQ2 7QJ
TEL: (01803) 614455 *FAX:* (01803) 615747 *CONTACT:* Customer Services
OPENING TIMES: (Office) 0830-1700 Mon-Fri Oct-Apr. 0830-1615 Mon-Thu 0830-1200 Fri May-Sep. Answerphone also.
MIN. MAIL ORDER UK: No minimum charge *MIN. VALUE EC:*
CAT. COST: Free *W/SALE or RETAIL:* Retail *CREDIT CARDS:* Visa, MasterCard
SPECIALITIES: Over 1,000 varieties of flower & vegetable seed, bulbs, plants & sundries. See also SEED Index.

CSWP **Sonia Wright Plants,** (Off.) Westfield Farmhouse, West Street, Aldbourne, Wiltshire, SN8 2BS
TEL: (01672) 540995 Off.* *FAX:* (01672) 541047 *CONTACT:* Sonia Wright
OPENING TIMES: 1000-dusk all year. Closed Wed & Sun.
MIN. MAIL ORDER UK: £10 Primulas only *MIN. VALUE EC:*
CAT. COST: 4 x 1st class *W/SALE or RETAIL:* Retail *CREDIT CARDS:* None
SPECIALITIES: Barnhaven Polyanthus & Primula. Grasses, grey-leaved plants, Iris, Euphorbia, Penstemon. *NURSERY at: Grove Farm, Stitchcombe, Marlborough (01672) 514003.
MAP PAGE: **2**

CTbh **Trebah Enterprises Ltd,** Trebah, Mawnan Smith, Falmouth, Cornwall, TR11 5JZ
OPENING TIMES: 1030-1700 every day.
No mail order
CAT. COST: *W/SALE or RETAIL:* Retail *CREDIT CARDS:* Visa, Access, EuroCard
SPECIALITIES: Agave, Tree Ferns, Palms, Camellias, Gunnera & Conservatory Climbers.
MAP PAGE: **1**

CTho **Thornhayes Nursery, St Andrews Wood, Dulford, Cullompton, Devon, EX15 2DF**
TEL: (01884) 266746 *FAX:* (01884) 266739 *CONTACT:* K D Croucher
OPENING TIMES: By appt. only.
MIN. MAIL ORDER UK: No minimum charge *MIN. VALUE EC:* Nmc *EXPORT:* Yes
CAT. COST: 5 x 1st class *W/SALE or RETAIL:* Both *CREDIT CARDS:* None
SPECIALITIES: A broad range of forms of Broadleaved, Ornamental, Amenity & Fruit Trees, including West Country Apple varieties. *MAP PAGE:* **1**

CThr **Three Counties Nurseries, Marshwood, Bridport, Dorset, DT6 5QJ**
TEL: (01297) 678257 *FAX:* (01297) 678257 *CONTACT:* A & D Hitchcock
OPENING TIMES: Not open.
MIN. MAIL ORDER UK: No minimum charge *MIN. VALUE EC:* £15.00 + p&p
CAT. COST: 2 x 2nd class *W/SALE or RETAIL:* Both *CREDIT CARDS:* None
SPECIALITIES: Pinks & Dianthus.

CTiv **Tivoli Garden Ltd, Tivoli House, 15 Pine View, Woodfalls, Salisbury, Wiltshire, SP5 2LR**
TEL: (01725) 511287 *FAX:* (01725) 511287 *CONTACT:* Martin Allen
OPENING TIMES: Mail order only.
MIN. MAIL ORDER UK: £12.00 + p&p *MIN. VALUE EC:* £12.00 + p&p
CAT. COST: 2 x 1st class *W/SALE or RETAIL:* Both *CREDIT CARDS:* None
SPECIALITIES: English Wild Flowers from self-collected seed. *MAP PAGE:* **2**

CTor **The Torbay Palm Farm, St Marychurch Road, Coffinswell, Nr Newton Abbot, South Devon, TQ12 4SE**
TEL: (01803) 872800 *FAX:* (01803) 213843 *CONTACT:* T A Eley
OPENING TIMES: 0900-1730 Mon-Fri, 1030-1700 Sat & Sun.
MIN. MAIL ORDER UK: £3.50 + p&p *MIN. VALUE EC:* n/a *EXPORT:* Yes
CAT. COST: Free *W/SALE or RETAIL:* Both *CREDIT CARDS:* None
SPECIALITIES: Cordyline australis, Trachycarpus fortuneii & new varieties of Cordyline. *MAP PAGE:* **1**

CTrC **Trevena Cross Nurseries, Breage, Helston, Cornwall, TR13 9PY**
TEL: (01736) 763880 *FAX:* (01736) 762828 *CONTACT:* Graham Jeffery
◆ *OPENING TIMES:* 0900-1700 Mon-Sat, 1030-1630 Sun.
MIN. MAIL ORDER UK: No minimum charge *MIN. VALUE EC:* Nmc *EXPORT:* Yes
CAT. COST: A4 Sae *W/SALE or RETAIL:* Both *CREDIT CARDS:* Access, Visa
SPECIALITIES: South African & Australasian Plants, Aloe, Protea, Tree Ferns, Palms, wide range of Hardy Exotics. *MAP PAGE:* **1**

CTre **Trewidden Estate Nursery, Trewidden Gardens, Penzance, Cornwall, TR20 8TT**
TEL: (01736) 362087 *FAX:* (01736) 3331470 *CONTACT:* Mr M G Snellgrove.
OPENING TIMES:
MIN. MAIL ORDER UK: No minimum charge *MIN. VALUE EC:* Nmc
CAT. COST: 2 x 1st class *W/SALE or RETAIL:* Both *CREDIT CARDS:* None
SPECIALITIES: Camellia & unusual Shrubs. *MAP PAGE:* **1**

CTrh **Trehane Camellia Nursery, J Trehane & Sons Ltd, Stapehill Road, Hampreston, Wimborne, Dorset, BH21 7NE**
TEL: (01202) 873490 *FAX:* (01202) 873490 *CONTACT:* Chris, Lorraine or Jeanette
OPENING TIMES: 0900-1630 Mon-Fri all year (ex. Xmas & New Year) 1000-1630 Sat-Sun late Feb-May & Sep-Oct & by appt.
MIN. MAIL ORDER UK: No minimum charge *MIN. VALUE EC:* Nmc *EXPORT:* Yes
CAT. COST: Cat/Book £1.50 *W/SALE or RETAIL:* Both *CREDIT CARDS:* Visa, Access, MasterCard
SPECIALITIES: Extensive range of Camellia species, cultivars & hybrids. Many new introductions. Evergreen Azalea, Pieris, Magnolia, Blueberries & Cranberries. *MAP PAGE:* **2**

CTri **Triscombe Nurseries,** West Bagborough, Nr Taunton, Somerset, TA4 3HG
TEL: (01984) 618267 *CONTACT:* S Parkman
◆ *OPENING TIMES:* 0900-1300 & 1400-1730 Mon-Sat. 1400-1730 Sun & Bank Hols.
No mail order
CAT. COST: None issued *W/SALE or RETAIL:* Retail *CREDIT CARDS:* None
SPECIALITIES: Rock plants & Alpines, Herbaceous, Conifers and unusual Shrubs. *MAP PAGE:* **1/2**

CTrw **Trewithen Nurseries,** Grampound Road, Truro, Cornwall, TR2
TEL: (01726) 882764 *FAX:* (01726) 882764 *CONTACT:* M Taylor
OPENING TIMES: 0800-1630 Mon-Fri.
No mail order
CAT. COST: £1.25 *W/SALE or RETAIL:* Both *CREDIT CARDS:* None
SPECIALITIES: Shrubs, especially Camellia & Rhododendron. *MAP PAGE:* **1**

◆ **See also Display Advertisements**

CVer **Veryans Plants,** Glebe, Coryton, Okehampton, Devon, EX20 4PB
TEL: (01822) 860302 day* *CONTACT:* Miss R V Millar
OPENING TIMES: Essential to telephone first for appt. *Note: (01566) 783433 evenings.
MIN. MAIL ORDER UK: No minimum charge *MIN. VALUE EC:*
CAT. COST: 3 x 1st class *W/SALE or RETAIL:* Retail *CREDIT CARDS:* None
SPECIALITIES: Range of hardy Perennials inc. Aster, Geranium & large selection of Primroses, many rare. *MAP PAGE:* **1**

CWan **Wanborough Herb Nursery,** Callas Hill, Wanborough, Swindon, Wiltshire, SN4 0AG
TEL: (01793) 790327 *CONTACT:* Peter Biggs
OPENING TIMES: 0900-1830 1st May-30th Sep, 0900-1630 1st Oct-30th Apr. Closed Xmas Day & New Year's Day.
No mail order
CAT. COST: 2 x 1st or A4 Sae *W/SALE or RETAIL:* Retail *CREDIT CARDS:* None
SPECIALITIES: Herbs, Herbaceous, esp. Culinary, Diascia, Lavandula, Monarda & Origanum. *MAP PAGE:* **2/5**

CWat **The Water Garden,** Hinton Parva, Swindon, SN4 0DH
TEL: (01793) 790558 *FAX:* (01793) 791298 *CONTACT:* Mike & Anne Newman
OPENING TIMES: 1000-1700 Wed-Sun.
MIN. MAIL ORDER UK: £10.00 + p&p *MIN. VALUE EC:*
CAT. COST: 4 x 1st class *W/SALE or RETAIL:* Retail *CREDIT CARDS:* Visa, Access, Switch
SPECIALITIES: Water Lilies, Marginal & Moisture plants, Oxygenators & Alpines. *MAP PAGE:* **2/5**

CWDa **Westdale Nurseries, Holt Road, Bradford-on-Avon, Wiltshire, BA15 1TS**
TEL: (01225) 863258 *FAX:* (01225) 863258 *CONTACT:* Mr Clarke
OPENING TIMES: 0900-1800 7 days a week.
MIN. MAIL ORDER UK: £10.00 + p&p *MIN. VALUE EC:* £10.00 + p&p *EXPORT:* Yes
CAT. COST: 4 x 1st class *W/SALE or RETAIL:* Both *CREDIT CARDS:* None
SPECIALITIES: Bougainvillea, Geranium, Conservatory Plants. *MAP PAGE:* **2**

CWGN **The Water Garden Nursery, Highcroft, Moorend, Wembworthy, Chulmleigh, Devon, EX18 7SG**
TEL: (01837) 83566 *CONTACT:* J M Smith
OPENING TIMES: 0930-1230 & 1330-1700 Wed-Sun Apr-Sep & Bank Hol Mons. Also by appt.
MIN. MAIL ORDER UK: No minimum charge *MIN. VALUE EC:* Nmc
CAT. COST: 3 x 1st class *W/SALE or RETAIL:* Retail *CREDIT CARDS:* None
SPECIALITIES: Plants for shade, wetlands, bog & water. *MAP PAGE:* **1**

CWhi **Whitehouse Ivies, Eggesford Gardens, Chulmleigh, Devon, EX18 7QU**
TEL: (01769) 580250 *FAX:* (01769) 581041 *CONTACT:* Joan Burks
OPENING TIMES: 0900-1700 daily exc. Xmas & Boxing Day
MIN. MAIL ORDER UK: £17.70 + p&p *MIN. VALUE EC:* £17.70 + p&p *EXPORT:* Yes
CAT. COST: 6 x 1st class *W/SALE or RETAIL:* Retail *CREDIT CARDS:* Visa, MasterCard, Switch, Delta
SPECIALITIES: Hedera - over 350 varieties. *MAP PAGE:* **1**

CWil **H & S Wills, 2 St Brannocks Park Road, Ilfracombe, Devon, EX34 8HU**
TEL: (01271) 863949 *FAX:* (01271) 863949 *CONTACT:* H Wills
OPENING TIMES: By appt. only.
MIN. MAIL ORDER UK: £3.00 + p&p *MIN. VALUE EC:* £5.00 + p&p
CAT. COST: 3 x 1st class *W/SALE or RETAIL:* Retail *CREDIT CARDS:* None
SPECIALITIES: Sempervivum, Jovibarba & Rosularia.

CWit **Withleigh Nurseries,** Quirkhill, Withleigh, Tiverton, Devon, EX16 8JG
TEL: (01884) 253351 *CONTACT:* Chris Britton
OPENING TIMES: 0900-1730 Mon-Sat Mar-Jun, 0900-1730 Tue-Sat Jul-Feb.
No mail order
CAT. COST: None issued *W/SALE or RETAIL:* Retail *CREDIT CARDS:* None
SPECIALITIES: Shrubs & Herbaceous. *MAP PAGE:* **1**

CWLN **Watering Lane Nursery,** St Austell, Devon, PL26 6BE
TEL: (01726) 69695 *FAX:* (01726) 69335 *CONTACT:* Roger Noyce
OPENING TIMES: 0900-1700 daily
No mail order
CAT. COST: None issued *W/SALE or RETAIL:* Both *CREDIT CARDS:* Visa, Access
SPECIALITIES: Wide range of Cornish Garden plants. Camellias, Japanese Azaleas, Phormium, garden Palms & an increasing range of Bamboos. *MAP PAGE:* **1**

CWri **Nigel Wright Rhododendrons,** The Old Glebe, Eggesford, Chumleigh, Devon, EX18 7QU
TEL: (01769) 580632 *CONTACT:* Nigel Wright
OPENING TIMES: By appt. only.
No mail order
CAT. COST: 2 x 1st class *W/SALE or RETAIL:* Both *CREDIT CARDS:* None
SPECIALITIES: Rhododendron only. 200 varieties field grown. Root-balled, not potted - for collection only. Specialist grower. *MAP PAGE:* **1**

CWSG **West Somerset Garden Centre, Mart Road, Minehead, Somerset, TA24 5BJ**
TEL: (01643) 703812 *FAX:* (01643) 706470 *CONTACT:* Mrs J K Shoulders
OPENING TIMES: 0800-1700 Mon-Sat, 1100-1700 Sun (Winter times vary, please phone).
MIN. MAIL ORDER UK: No minimum charge *MIN. VALUE EC:* Nmc
CAT. COST: Free *W/SALE or RETAIL:* Retail *CREDIT CARDS:* Access, Visa
SPECIALITIES: Wide general range. *MAP PAGE:* **1**

EAst **Asterby Nurseries,** Dairy Farm, Church Lane, Asterby, Louth, Lincolnshire, LN11 9UF
TEL: (01507) 343549 *CONTACT:* Edwin & Elizabeth Aldridge
OPENING TIMES: Generally open but please phone first.
MIN. MAIL ORDER UK: See Cat for details *MIN. VALUE EC:*
CAT. COST: 2 x 1st class *W/SALE or RETAIL:* Retail *CREDIT CARDS:* None
SPECIALITIES: Hardy Shrubs, herbaceous & tender Perennials. *MAP PAGE:* **8**

EB&P **Battle & Pears Ltd, Glebe Farm, Bracebridge Heath, Lincolnshire, LN4 2HZ**
TEL: (01522) 722857 *FAX:* (01522) 723252 *CONTACT:* D J Carmichael or D J Harby
OPENING TIMES: By appt. For collection only.
MIN. MAIL ORDER UK: £15.00 + p&p *MIN. VALUE EC:* £15.00 + p&p
CAT. COST: 2 x 1st class *W/SALE or RETAIL:* Both *CREDIT CARDS:* None
SPECIALITIES: Daphne & other choice hardy ornamental Shrubs. *MAP PAGE:* **8**

EBak **B & H M Baker,** Bourne Brook Nurseries, Greenstead Green, Halstead, Essex, CO9 1RJ
TEL: (01787) 472900/476369 *CONTACT:* B, HM and C Baker
OPENING TIMES: 0800-1630 Mon-Fri, 0900-1200 & 1400-1630 Sat & Sun.
No mail order
CAT. COST: 20p + stamp *W/SALE or RETAIL:* Both *CREDIT CARDS:* None
SPECIALITIES: Fuchsia & Conservatory Plants. *MAP PAGE:* **6**

EBar **Barnsdale Plants & Gardens, Exton Avenue, Exton, Oakham, Rutland, LE15 8AH**
TEL: (01572) 813200 *FAX:* (01572) 813346 *E-MAIL:* hampho@dial.pipex.com
CONTACT: Nick Hamilton
OPENING TIMES: 1000-1700 1st Mar-31st Oct, 1000-1600 1st Nov-28/29th Feb. Closed Xmas & New Year.
MIN. MAIL ORDER UK: No minimum charge *MIN. VALUE EC:* Nmc
CAT. COST: A5 + 5 x 2nd class *W/SALE or RETAIL:* Retail *CREDIT CARDS:* Visa, Access
SPECIALITIES: Choice & unusual Garden Plants & Trees. *MAP PAGE:* **8**

◆ **See also Display Advertisements**

Code-Nursery Index

EBee **Beeches Nursery,** Village Centre, Ashdon, Saffron Walden, Essex, CB10 2HB
TEL: (01799) 584362 *FAX:* (01799) 584362 *CONTACT:* Alan Bidwell
◆ *OPENING TIMES:* 0830-1700 Mon-Sat, 1000-1700 Sun incl. Bank Hols.
MIN. MAIL ORDER UK: See catal.* *MIN. VALUE EC:*
CAT. COST: 2 x 1st class (specify tree, shrub or herbac.) *W/SALE or RETAIL:* Retail *CREDIT CARDS:* Visa, Access, AmEx
SPECIALITIES: Herbaceous specialists & extensive range of other garden plants. *Note: see catalogue for mail order details. *MAP PAGE:* **6**

EBls **Peter Beales Roses, London Road, Attleborough, Norfolk, NR17 1AY**
TEL: (01953) 454707 *FAX:* (01953) 456845 *E-MAIL:* sales@classicroses.co.uk
CONTACT: Mr Peter Beales
OPENING TIMES: 0900-1700 Mon-Fri, 0900-1630 Sat, 1000-1600 Sun. Jan closed Sun.
MIN. MAIL ORDER UK: No minimum charge *MIN. VALUE EC:* Nmc *EXPORT:* Yes
CAT. COST: Free *W/SALE or RETAIL:* Retail *CREDIT CARDS:* Visa, EuroCard, MasterCard
SPECIALITIES: Old fashioned Roses & Classic Roses. *MAP PAGE:* **8**

EBly **R J Blythe,** Potash Nursery, Cow Green, Bacton, Stowmarket, Suffolk, IP14 4HJ
TEL: (01449) 781671 *CONTACT:* R J Blythe
OPENING TIMES: 1000-1700 Sat, Sun & Mon mid Feb-end June.
No mail order
CAT. COST: 3 x 1st class *W/SALE or RETAIL:* Retail *CREDIT CARDS:* Visa, Access
SPECIALITIES: Fuchsia. *MAP PAGE:* **6**

EBre **Bressingham Plant Centre,** Bressingham, Diss, Norfolk, IP22 2AB
TEL: (01379) 687464/688133 *FAX:* (01379) 688061 *CONTACT:* Tony Fry
◆ *OPENING TIMES:* 0900-1730 daily. (Direct retail Plant Centre).
No mail order
CAT. COST: None issued *W/SALE or RETAIL:* Retail *CREDIT CARDS:* Visa, Delta, Switch, MasterCard
SPECIALITIES: Very wide general range. Many own varieties. Focus on Hardy Ornamental plants & grasses. *MAP PAGE:* **6/8**

EBSP **Brian Sulman, 54 Kingsway, Mildenhall, Bury St Edmunds, Suffolk, IP28 7HR**
TEL: (01638) 712297 *CONTACT:* Brian Sulman
OPENING TIMES: Mail Order only. Special open weekend June 7/8th 1997, June 6/7th 1998.
MIN. MAIL ORDER UK: £9.00 + p&p *MIN. VALUE EC:* £9.00 + p&p
CAT. COST: 2 x 1st class *W/SALE or RETAIL:* Retail *CREDIT CARDS:* None
SPECIALITIES: Regal Pelargoniums.

EBur **Jenny Burgess, Alpine Nursery, Sisland, Norwich, Norfolk, NR14 6EF**
TEL: (01508) 520724 *CONTACT:* Jenny Burgess
OPENING TIMES: Any time by appt.
MIN. MAIL ORDER UK: £5.00 + p&p* *MIN. VALUE EC:* £10.00 + p&p *EXPORT:* Yes
CAT. COST: 3 x 1st class *W/SALE or RETAIL:* Retail *CREDIT CARDS:* None
SPECIALITIES: Alpines, Sisyrinchium & Campanula. National Collection of Sisyrinchium. *Note: only Sisyrinchium by mail order. *MAP PAGE:* **8**

ECED **C E & D M Nurseries, The Walnuts, 36 Main Street, Baston, Peterborough, Lincolnshire, PE6 9PB**
TEL: (01778) 560483 *CONTACT:* Mr C E Fletcher
OPENING TIMES: 0900-1700 Fri-Tue all year & by appt.
MIN. MAIL ORDER UK: See Cat. for details *MIN. VALUE EC:* See Cat. *EXPORT:* Yes
CAT. COST: 2 x 1st class *W/SALE or RETAIL:* Retail *CREDIT CARDS:* None
SPECIALITIES: Hardy Herbaceous Perennials. *MAP PAGE:* **8**

ECGP **Cambridge Garden Plants,** The Lodge, Clayhithe Road, Homingsea, Cambridgeshire, CB5 9JD
TEL: (01223) 861370 *CONTACT:* Mrs Nancy Buchdahl
OPENING TIMES: 1100-1730 Thu-Sun mid Mar-31st Oct. Other times by appt.
No mail order
CAT. COST: 4 x 1st class *W/SALE or RETAIL:* Retail *CREDIT CARDS:* None
SPECIALITIES: Hardy Perennials incl. wide range of Geraniums, Alliums, Euphorbia, Penstemons, Digitalis. Some Shrubs, Roses & Clematis. *MAP PAGE:* **6**

ECha **The Beth Chatto Gardens Ltd, Elmstead Market, Colchester, Essex, CO7 7DB**
TEL: (01206) 822007 *FAX:* (01206) 825933 *CONTACT:* Beth Chatto
OPENING TIMES: 0900-1700 Mon-Sat 1st Mar-31st Oct. 0900-1600 Mon-Fri 1st Nov-1st Mar. Closed Sun & Bank Hols.
MIN. MAIL ORDER UK: See Cat. for details *MIN. VALUE EC:* Ask for details
CAT. COST: £2.50 incl p&p *W/SALE or RETAIL:* Retail *CREDIT CARDS:* Visa, Access, Switch
SPECIALITIES: Predominantly Herbaceous. Many unusual for special situations. *MAP PAGE:* **6**

ECho **Choice Landscapes, Priory Farm, 101 Salts Road, West Walton, Wisbech, Cambs, PE14 7EF**
TEL: (01945) 585051 *FAX:* (01945) 585051 *CONTACT:* Michael Agg
OPENING TIMES: 1000-1700 Thur-Sat, Bank Hols between 1st Apr & 31st Oct. Other times by appt.
MIN. MAIL ORDER UK: No minimum charge *MIN. VALUE EC:* £10.00 + p&p *EXPORT:* Yes
CAT. COST: 4 x 1st class *W/SALE or RETAIL:* Retail *CREDIT CARDS:* None
SPECIALITIES: Dwarf Conifers, Heathers, Alpines & Rhododendrons. *MAP PAGE:* **8**

ECle **Cley Nurseries Ltd,** Holt Road, Cley-Next-the-Sea, Holt, Norfolk, NR25 7TX
TEL: (01263) 740892 *FAX:* (01263) 741138 *CONTACT:* Alec or Gill Mellor
OPENING TIMES: 1000-1600 daily.
MIN. MAIL ORDER UK: £10.00 + p&p *MIN. VALUE EC:*
CAT. COST: List 2 x 1st class *W/SALE or RETAIL:* Retail *CREDIT CARDS:* Visa, Access
SPECIALITIES: Roses. *MAP PAGE:* **8**

ECon **Conservatory PlantLine, Nayland Road, West Bergholt, Colchester, Essex, CO6 3DH**
TEL: (01206) 242533 *FAX:* (01206) 242530 *E-MAIL:* 100724.3432@compuserve.com
CONTACT: Carol Golder
OPENING TIMES: By appt. only.
MIN. MAIL ORDER UK: No minimum charge *MIN. VALUE EC:* Nmc *EXPORT:* Yes
CAT. COST: £2.00 + p&p *W/SALE or RETAIL:* Both *CREDIT CARDS:* Access, MasterCard, EuroCard, Visa
SPECIALITIES: Conservatory Plants. *MAP PAGE:* **6**

ECoo **Patricia Cooper,** Magpies, Green Lane, Mundford, Norfolk, IP26 5HS
TEL: (01842) 878496 *CONTACT:* Patricia Cooper
OPENING TIMES: 0900-1700 Mon, Tue, Thu & Fri 1200-1700 Sat & Sun.
No mail order
CAT. COST: Free *W/SALE or RETAIL:* Retail *CREDIT CARDS:* None
SPECIALITIES: Unusual hardy Perennials, Grasses, Wild Flowers, Bog, Aquatic & Foliage plants. *MAP PAGE:* **8**

ECot **Cottage Gardens,** Langham Road, Boxted, Colchester, Essex, CO4 5HU
TEL: (01206) 272269 *CONTACT:* Alison Smith
OPENING TIMES: 0800-1730 daily Spring & Summer. 0800-1730 Thu-Mon Jul-Feb.
No mail order
CAT. COST: Free *W/SALE or RETAIL:* Retail *CREDIT CARDS:* Visa, Access
SPECIALITIES: 400 varieties of Shrubs, 390 varieties of Herbaceous. Huge range of Trees, Alpines, Herbs, Hedging - all home grown. Garden antiques. *MAP PAGE:* **6**

◆ **See also Display Advertisements**

ECou **County Park Nursery,** Essex Gardens, Hornchurch, Essex, RM11 3BU
TEL: (01708) 445205 *CONTACT:* G Hutchins
OPENING TIMES: 0900-dusk Mon-Sat ex Wed, 1000-1700 Sun Mar-Oct. Nov-Feb by appt. only.
No mail order
CAT. COST: 3 x 1st class *W/SALE or RETAIL:* Retail *CREDIT CARDS:* None
SPECIALITIES: Alpines & rare and unusual plants from New Zealand, Tasmania & Falklands. *MAP PAGE:* **6**

ECro **Croftacre Hardy Plants,** Croftacre, Ellingham Road, Scoulton, Norfolk, NR9 4NT
TEL: (01953) 850599 *FAX:* (01953) 851399 *CONTACT:* Mrs V J Allen
OPENING TIMES: By appt. Please phone first.
No mail order
CAT. COST: 2 x 1st class *W/SALE or RETAIL:* Retail *CREDIT CARDS:* None
SPECIALITIES: Rare & uncommon Perennials. *MAP PAGE:* **8**

ECtt **Cottage Nurseries,** Thoresthorpe, Alford, Lincolnshire, LN13 0HX
TEL: (01507) 466968 *FAX:* (01507) 466968 *CONTACT:* W H Denbigh
OPENING TIMES: 0900-1700 daily 1st Mar-31st Oct, 1000-1600 Thu-Sun Nov-Feb.
MIN. MAIL ORDER UK: £5.00 + p&p* *MIN. VALUE EC:*
CAT. COST: 3 x 1st class *W/SALE or RETAIL:* Both *CREDIT CARDS:* None
SPECIALITIES: Wide general range. *Note: mail order to UK only. *MAP PAGE:* **8**

ECWi **Countryside Wildflowers, Somersham, Cambridgeshire, PE17 3DN**
TEL: (01487) 841322 *FAX:* (01487) 740206 *E-MAIL:* nickmeakin@msn.com
CONTACT: Nick Meakin
OPENING TIMES: 0900-1700 Mon-Fri.
MIN. MAIL ORDER UK: £4.00 + p&p *MIN. VALUE EC:* £4.00 + p&p *EXPORT:* Yes
CAT. COST: £1.50 *W/SALE or RETAIL:* Both *CREDIT CARDS:* None
SPECIALITIES: Native British Wildflowers. *MAP PAGE:* **6/8**

EDAr **D'Arcy & Everest, (Off.) St Ives Road, Somersham, Huntingdon, Cambridgeshire, PE17 3ET**
TEL: (01487) 843650 *FAX:* (01487) 840096 *E-MAIL:* angalps@martex.com.uk
CONTACT: Barry Johnson
OPENING TIMES: By appt. ONLY.
MIN. MAIL ORDER UK: £10.00 + p&p *MIN. VALUE EC:* £50.00 + p&p
CAT. COST: 5 x 1st class *W/SALE or RETAIL:* Both *CREDIT CARDS:* None
SPECIALITIES: Alpines & Herbs *MAP PAGE:* **6**

EDen **Denbeigh Heather Nurseries, All Saints Road, Creeting St. Mary, Ipswich, Suffolk, IP6 8PJ**
OPENING TIMES: By appt. only.
MIN. MAIL ORDER UK: No minimum charge *MIN. VALUE EC:* Nmc *EXPORT:* Yes
CAT. COST: Free *W/SALE or RETAIL:* Retail *CREDIT CARDS:* None
SPECIALITIES: Rooted Heather cuttings. *MAP PAGE:* **6**

EEls **Elsworth Herbs, Avenue Farm Cottage, 31 Smith Street, Elsworth, Cambridgeshire, CB3 8HY**
TEL: (01954) 267414 *FAX:* (01954) 267414 *CONTACT:* Drs J D & J M Twibell
OPENING TIMES: Advertised weekends & by appt. only.
MIN. MAIL ORDER UK: £10.00 + p&p *MIN. VALUE EC:* £10.00 + p&p
CAT. COST: 2 x 1st class *W/SALE or RETAIL:* Retail *CREDIT CARDS:* None
SPECIALITIES: Herbs, Artemisia (NCCPG Collection), Cottage garden plants & Nerium oleanders. *MAP PAGE:* **6**

EEve **R G & A Evenden, 25 Penway Drive, Pinchbeck, Spalding, Lincolnshire, PE11 3PJ**
TEL: (01775) 767857 *FAX:* (01775) 713878 *CONTACT:* Richard Evenden
OPENING TIMES: By appt. only, weekends May-Jul.
MIN. MAIL ORDER UK: No minimum charge *MIN. VALUE EC:* Nmc *EXPORT:* Yes
CAT. COST: Sae *W/SALE or RETAIL:* Both *CREDIT CARDS:* None
SPECIALITIES: Bletilla species & hybrids. Pleiones. *MAP PAGE:* **8**

EFer **The Fern Nursery, Grimsby Road, Binbrook, Lincolnshire, LN3 6DH**
TEL: (01472) 398092 *CONTACT:* R N Timm
OPENING TIMES: 0900-1700 Sat & Sun Apr-Oct or by appt.
MIN. MAIL ORDER UK: No minimum charge *MIN. VALUE EC:* Nmc
CAT. COST: 2 x 1st class *W/SALE or RETAIL:* Both *CREDIT CARDS:* None
SPECIALITIES: Ferns & Hardy Perennials. *MAP PAGE:* **9**

EFEx **Flora Exotica, Pasadena, South-Green, Fingringhoe, Colchester, Essex, CO5 7DR**
TEL: (01206) 729414 *CONTACT:* J Beddoes
OPENING TIMES: Not open to the public.
MIN. MAIL ORDER UK: No minimum charge *MIN. VALUE EC:* Nmc *EXPORT:* Yes
CAT. COST: 6 x 1st class *W/SALE or RETAIL:* Both *CREDIT CARDS:* None
SPECIALITIES: Insectivorous plants, esp. Pinguicula, Drosera & rare & exotica Flora incl. Orchids.

EFlo **Flor do Sol,** Copenore Lodge, South Hanningfield Road, Wickford, Essex, SS11 7PF
TEL: (01268) 710499 *CONTACT:* Mrs M Heaton
OPENING TIMES: By appt. only from 1st Apr- 31st Oct
No mail order
CAT. COST: Sae + 1 x 1st class *W/SALE or RETAIL:* Retail *CREDIT CARDS:* None
SPECIALITIES: Conservatory plants esp. Nerium oleanders. *MAP PAGE:* **6**

EFol **Foliage & Unusual Plants,** Dingle Plants & Gardens, Stamford Road, Pilsgate, Stamford, Cambs, PE9 3HW
TEL: (01780) 740775 *CONTACT:* Margaret Handley
OPENING TIMES: 1000-1700 (dusk if earlier) daily Mar-14th Nov & Bank Hols.
No mail order
CAT. COST: 3 x 1st class *W/SALE or RETAIL:* Retail *CREDIT CARDS:* Visa, Access, EuroCard, MasterCard, Delta
SPECIALITIES: Variegated, coloured foliage & unusual plants. *MAP PAGE:* **8**

EFou **Four Seasons, Forncett St Mary, Norwich, Norfolk, NR16 1JT**
TEL: (01508) 488344 *FAX:* (01508) 488478 *CONTACT:* J P Metcalf & R W Ball
OPENING TIMES: No callers.
MIN. MAIL ORDER UK: £15.00 + p&p *MIN. VALUE EC:* £15.00 + p&p
CAT. COST: £1.00 *W/SALE or RETAIL:* Retail *CREDIT CARDS:* None
SPECIALITIES: Herbaceous Perennials. Aquilegia, Aconitum, Anemone, Aster, Campanula, Dendranthema, Digitalis, Erigeron, Geranium, Helenium, Iris, Salvia & Grasses.

EFul **Fulbrooke Nursery, Home Farm, Westley Waterless, Newmarket, Suffolk, CB8 0RG**
TEL: (01638) 507124 *FAX:* (01638) 507124 *CONTACT:* Paul Lazard
OPENING TIMES: By appt. most times incl. weekends.
MIN. MAIL ORDER UK: £6.00 + p&p *MIN. VALUE EC:* £6.00 + p&p
CAT. COST: 2 x 1st class *W/SALE or RETAIL:* Both *CREDIT CARDS:* None
SPECIALITIES: Bamboos *MAP PAGE:* **6**

EGar **Gardiner's Hall Plants, Braiseworth, Eye, Suffolk, IP23 7DZ**
TEL: (01379) 678285 *FAX:* (01379) 678285 *CONTACT:* Raymond Mayes or Joe Stuart
OPENING TIMES: 1000-1800 Wed-Sat 1st Apr-31st Oct.
MIN. MAIL ORDER UK: £15.00 + p&p *MIN. VALUE EC:* £15.00 + p&p *EXPORT:* Yes
CAT. COST: £1.00 or stamps *W/SALE or RETAIL:* Retail *CREDIT CARDS:* None
SPECIALITIES: Herbaceous Perennials, incl. Crocosmia, Euphorbia, Kniphofia, Monarda & Grasses. *MAP PAGE:* **6**

EGle **Glen Chantry,** Ishams Chase, Wickham Bishop, Essex, CM8 3LG
TEL: (01621) 891342 *CONTACT:* Sue Staines
OPENING TIMES: 1000-1600 Fri & Sat Apr-mid Oct. Also Sun & Mon on NGS open days.
No mail order
CAT. COST: 4 x 1st class *W/SALE or RETAIL:* Retail *CREDIT CARDS:* None
SPECIALITIES: A wide & increasing range of Perennials & Alpines, many unusual.
MAP PAGE: **6**

EGol Goldbrook Plants, Hoxne, Eye, Suffolk, IP21 5AN
TEL: (01379) 668770 *FAX:* (01379) 668770 *CONTACT:* Sandra Bond
OPENING TIMES: 1030-1800 or dusk if earlier, Thu-Sun Apr-Sep; Sat & Sun Oct-Mar, or by appt. Closed during Jan, & Chelsea & Hampton Court shows.
MIN. MAIL ORDER UK: £15.00 + p&p* *MIN. VALUE EC:* £100.00 + p&p *EXPORT:* Yes
CAT. COST: 4 x 1st class *W/SALE or RETAIL:* Retail *CREDIT CARDS:* None
SPECIALITIES: Very large range of Hosta (over 600), Hemerocallis & Bog Iris. Interesting Hardy plants esp. for shade & bog. *Note: mail order for Perennials & Grasses only. *MAP PAGE:* **6**

EGoo Elisabeth Goodwin Nurseries, The White Gate, 86 Cambridge Road, Girton, Cambridgeshire, CB3 0PJ
TEL: (01223) 276013 *CONTACT:* Elisabeth Goodwin
OPENING TIMES: The Nursery is moving to a new site in 1997 & will not be open at this address. Please phone or write for details.
MIN. MAIL ORDER UK: No minimum charge *MIN. VALUE EC:*
CAT. COST: 3 x 1st class *W/SALE or RETAIL:* Retail *CREDIT CARDS:* None
SPECIALITIES: Drought tolerant plants esp. Cistus, Helianthemum, Sedum, Teucrium & Vinca. See also SEED Index. *MAP PAGE:* **6**

EGou Gouldings Fuchsias, West View, Link Lane, Bentley, Nr Ipswich, Suffolk, IP9 2DP
TEL: (01473) 310058 *CONTACT:* Mr E J Goulding
OPENING TIMES: 1000-1700 everyday 11th Jan-25th August 1997.
MIN. MAIL ORDER UK: See Cat. for details *MIN. VALUE EC:* See Cat.
CAT. COST: 4 x 1st class *W/SALE or RETAIL:* Both *CREDIT CARDS:* None
SPECIALITIES: Fuchsia - new introductions, Basket, Hardy, Upright, Terminal flowering (Triphylla), Species, Encliandras & Paniculates. *MAP PAGE:* **6**

EHal Hall Farm Nursery, Harpswell, Nr Gainsborough, Lincolnshire, DN21 5UU
TEL: (01427) 668412 *FAX:* (01427) 668412 *CONTACT:* Pam & Mark Tatam
OPENING TIMES: 0930-1730 daily. Please telephone in winter to check.
No mail order
CAT. COST: Sae *W/SALE or RETAIL:* Retail *CREDIT CARDS:* Visa, MasterCard, Access
SPECIALITIES: Wide range of Shrubs, Perennials & old Roses. *MAP PAGE:* **8/9**

EHGC Harlow Garden Centre, Cane's Lane, Nr M11 Junction, Harlow, Essex, CM17 9LD
TEL: (01279) 419039 *FAX:* (01279) 428319 *CONTACT:* David Albone
♦ *OPENING TIMES:* 0830-1745 Mon-Sat, 1030-1630 Sun (closed Easter Sun).
No mail order
CAT. COST: None issued *W/SALE or RETAIL:* Retail *CREDIT CARDS:* Access, Visa
SPECIALITIES: 170 varieties of Clematis and wide general range of plants. *MAP PAGE:* **6**

EHic Hickling Heath Nursery, Sutton Road, Hickling, Norwich, Norfolk, NR12 0AS
TEL: (01692) 598513 *CONTACT:* Brian & Cindy Cogan
OPENING TIMES: 0930-1700 Tue-Sun & Bank Hol Mons. Please ring before visiting.
No mail order
CAT. COST: 4 x 1st class *W/SALE or RETAIL:* Retail *CREDIT CARDS:* None
SPECIALITIES: Shrubs & Herbaceous, many unusual inc. wide variety of Diascia, Euphorbia, Hydrangea, Lonicera, Penstemon & Viburnum. *MAP PAGE:* **8**

EHMN Home Meadows Nursery Ltd, Martlesham, Woodbridge, Suffolk, IP12 4RD
TEL: (01394) 382419 *CONTACT:* S D & M I O'Brien Baker & I D Baker
OPENING TIMES: 0800-1700 Mon-Fri, 0800-1300 Sat.
MIN. MAIL ORDER UK: No minimum charge *MIN. VALUE EC:* Nmc
CAT. COST: Sae *W/SALE or RETAIL:* Retail *CREDIT CARDS:* None
SPECIALITIES: Small general range plus Chrysanthemum esp. Korean. See also SEED Index. *MAP PAGE:* **6**

EHoe **Hoecroft Plants, Severals Grange, Holt Road, Wood Norton, Dereham, Norfolk, NR20 5BL**
TEL: (01362) 684206 *FAX:* (01362) 684206 *CONTACT:* M Lister
◆ *OPENING TIMES:* 1000-1600 Thur-Sun 1st Apr-1st Oct.
MIN. MAIL ORDER UK: No minimum charge *MIN. VALUE EC:* Nmc
CAT. COST: 5 x 2nd class/£1coin *W/SALE or RETAIL:* Retail *CREDIT CARDS:* None
SPECIALITIES: 240 varieties of Variegated and 300 varieties of Coloured-leaved plants in all species. 220 Grasses. *MAP PAGE:* **8**

EHof **Hofflands Daffodils, Bakers Green, Little Totham, Maldon, Essex, CM9 8LT**
TEL: (01621) 788678 *CONTACT:* John Pearson
OPENING TIMES: By appt. only. Normally Mail Order only.
MIN. MAIL ORDER UK: No minimum charge *MIN. VALUE EC:* Nmc *EXPORT:* Yes
CAT. COST: Free *W/SALE or RETAIL:* Retail *CREDIT CARDS:* None
SPECIALITIES: Narcissus.

EHon **Honeysome Aquatic Nursery,** The Row, Sutton, Nr Ely, Cambridgeshire, CB6 2PF
TEL: (01353) 778889 *CONTACT:* D B Barker & D B Littlefield
OPENING TIMES: At all times by appt. ONLY.
MIN. MAIL ORDER UK: No minimum charge *MIN. VALUE EC:*
CAT. COST: 2 x 1st class *W/SALE or RETAIL:* Both *CREDIT CARDS:* None
SPECIALITIES: Hardy Aquatic, Bog & Marginal. *MAP PAGE:* **6/8**

EHul **Hull Farm,** Spring Valley Lane, Ardleigh, Colchester, Essex, CO7 7SA
TEL: (01206) 230045 *FAX:* (01206) 230820 *CONTACT:* J Fryer & Sons
OPENING TIMES: 1000-1630 daily ex Xmas.
No mail order
CAT. COST: None issued *W/SALE or RETAIL:* Both *CREDIT CARDS:* None
SPECIALITIES: Conifers. *MAP PAGE:* **6**

EHyt **Hythe Alpines, Methwold Hythe, Thetford, Norfolk, IP26 4QH**
TEL: (01366) 728543 *CONTACT:* Mike Smith
OPENING TIMES: 1000-1800 Tue & Wed, Mar-Oct.
MIN. MAIL ORDER UK: No minimum charge *MIN. VALUE EC:* Nmc *EXPORT:* BO
CAT. COST: 4 x 1st class *W/SALE or RETAIL:* Retail *CREDIT CARDS:* None
SPECIALITIES: Rare & unusual Alpines, Rock garden plants & Bulbs for enthusiasts & exhibitors. *Export of dry Bulbs ONLY. *MAP PAGE:* **8**

EJap **The Japanese Garden Co., Wood Cottage, Ford Lane, Alresford, Colchester, Essex, CO7 8AY**
TEL: (01206) 793399 *FAX:* (01206) 793399 *CONTACT:* Susan Gott
OPENING TIMES: Mail Order only.
MIN. MAIL ORDER UK: No minimum charge *MIN. VALUE EC:* Nmc
CAT. COST: Sae for list *W/SALE or RETAIL:* Retail *CREDIT CARDS:* None
SPECIALITIES: Primula, Acer, Bamboo, Herbaceous. Japanese garden design service. Booklet on design £3.75 (cheques to K. Gott).

EJud **Judy's Country Garden,** The Villa, Louth Road, South Somercotes, Louth, Lincolnshire, LN11 7BW
TEL: (01507) 358487 *FAX:* (01507) 358487 *CONTACT:* M J S & J M Harry
OPENING TIMES: 0900-1800 most days mid Mar-end Sep.
No mail order
CAT. COST: 3 x 1st class *W/SALE or RETAIL:* Retail *CREDIT CARDS:* None
SPECIALITIES: Herbs, old-fashioned & unusual plants, including scarce & old varieties. *MAP PAGE:* **9**

EJWh **Jill White,** 6 Edward Avenue, Brightlingsea, Essex, CO7 OLZ
TEL: (01206) 303547 *CONTACT:* Jill White
OPENING TIMES: By appt. only
MIN. MAIL ORDER UK: No minimum charge *MIN. VALUE EC:*
CAT. COST: Sae *W/SALE or RETAIL:* Both *CREDIT CARDS:* None
SPECIALITIES: Cyclamen species especially Cyclamen parviflorum. See also SEED index.
MAP PAGE: **6**

EKMF **Kathleen Muncaster Fuchsias, 18 Field Lane, Morton, Gainsborough, Lincolnshire, DN21 3BY**
TEL: (01427) 612329 *E-MAIL:* 101713.730@compuserve.com *CONTACT:* Kathleen Muncaster
OPENING TIMES: 1000-dusk daily. After mid-July please phone for opening times.
MIN. MAIL ORDER UK: See Cat. for details *MIN. VALUE EC:* See Cat. *EXPORT:* Yes
CAT. COST: 2 x 1st class *W/SALE or RETAIL:* Retail *CREDIT CARDS:* None
SPECIALITIES: Fuchsia. *Note: mail orders to be received before April 1st. *MAP PAGE:* **9**

ELan **Langthorns Plantery,** High Cross Lane West, Little Canfield, Dunmow, Essex, CM6 1TD
TEL: (01371) 872611 *FAX:* (01371) 872611 *CONTACT:* P & D Cannon
OPENING TIMES: 1000-1700 or dusk (if earlier) daily ex Xmas fortnight.
No mail order
CAT. COST: £1.00 *W/SALE or RETAIL:* Retail *CREDIT CARDS:* Visa, Access, Switch, MasterCard
SPECIALITIES: Wide general range with many unusual plants. *MAP PAGE:* **6**

ELau **Laurel Farm Herbs,** Main Road, Kelsale, Saxmundham, Suffolk, IP13 2RG
TEL: (01728) 668223 *CONTACT:* Chris Seagon
OPENING TIMES: 1000-1700 Wed-Mon 1st Mar-31st Oct. 1000-1500 Wed-Fri only 1st Nov-28th Feb.
MIN. MAIL ORDER UK: * *MIN. VALUE EC:*
CAT. COST: 4 x 25p *W/SALE or RETAIL:* Retail *CREDIT CARDS:* None
SPECIALITIES: Herbs, esp. Rosemary, Thyme, Lavender, Mint, Comfrey & Sage. *Note: mail order to UK avail. from May; please phone for details. *MAP PAGE:* **6**

EMan **Manor Nursery,** Thaxted Road, Wimbish, Saffron Walden, Essex, CB10 2UT
TEL: (01799) 513481 *FAX:* (01799) 513481 *CONTACT:* William Lyall
◆ *OPENING TIMES:* 0900-1700 Summer. 0900-1600 Winter. Closed Xmas.
No mail order
CAT. COST: 2 x 1st class *W/SALE or RETAIL:* Both *CREDIT CARDS:* Visa, Access
SPECIALITIES: Uncommon Perennials, Grasses & Fuchsia. *MAP PAGE:* **6**

EMar **Lesley Marshall, Islington Lodge Cottage, Tilney All Saints, King's Lynn, Norfolk, PE34 4SF**
TEL: (01553) 765103 *CONTACT:* Lesley & Peter Marshall
OPENING TIMES: Weekends Mar-Oct & by appt.
MIN. MAIL ORDER UK: £5.00 + p&p *MIN. VALUE EC:* £20.00 + p&p
CAT. COST: £1 refundable *W/SALE or RETAIL:* Retail *CREDIT CARDS:* None
SPECIALITIES: Uncommon garden plants, hardy Perennials & plants for Foliage effect.
MAP PAGE: **8**

EMFP **Mills' Farm Plants & Gardens, Norwich Road, Mendlesham, Suffolk, IP14 5NQ**
TEL: (01449) 766425 *CONTACT:* Peter & Susan Russell
OPENING TIMES: 0900-1730 daily except Tue. (Closed Jan).
MIN. MAIL ORDER UK: No minimum charge* *MIN. VALUE EC:* Nmc *EXPORT:* Yes
CAT. COST: 5 x 2nd class *W/SALE or RETAIL:* Retail *CREDIT CARDS:* None
SPECIALITIES: Pinks, Old Roses, Wide general range. *Note: mail order for Pinks & Roses only.
MAP PAGE: **6**

EMFW Mickfield Fish & Watergarden Centre, Debenham Road, Mickfield, Stowmarket, Suffolk, IP14 5LP
TEL: 01449 711336 *FAX:* 01449 711018 *CONTACT:* Mike & Yvonne Burch
◆ *OPENING TIMES:* 0930-1700 daily
MIN. MAIL ORDER UK: No minimum charge *MIN. VALUE EC:* £25.00 + p&p *EXPORT:* Yes
CAT. COST: £1.00 *W/SALE or RETAIL:* Both *CREDIT CARDS:* Visa, Access
SPECIALITIES: Hardy Aquatics, Nymphaea & moisture lovers. *MAP PAGE:* **6**

EMic Mickfield Hostas, The Poplars, Mickfield, Stowmarket, Suffolk, IP14 5LH
TEL: (01449) 711576 *FAX:* (01449) 711576 *CONTACT:* Mr & Mrs R L C Milton
OPENING TIMES: By appt. only.
MIN. MAIL ORDER UK: See Cat. for details *MIN. VALUE EC:* See Cat.
CAT. COST: 4 x 1st class* *W/SALE or RETAIL:* Retail *CREDIT CARDS:* None
SPECIALITIES: Hosta, over 425 varieties (subject to availability) mostly from USA. *Catalogue cost refundable with order. *MAP PAGE:* **6**

EMil Mill Race Nursery, New Road Aldham, Colchester, Essex, CO6 3QT
TEL: (01206) 242521 *FAX:* (01206) 241616 *CONTACT:* Bill Mathews
OPENING TIMES: 0900-1730 daily.
No mail order
CAT. COST: Sae + 2 x 1st class *W/SALE or RETAIL:* Both *CREDIT CARDS:* Access, Visa, Diners, Switch
SPECIALITIES: Over 400 varieties of Herbaceous & many unusual Trees, Shrubs & Climbers. *MAP PAGE:* **6**

EMNN Martin Nest Nurseries, Grange Cottage, Harpswell Lane, Hemswell, Gainsborough, Lincolnshire, DN21 5UP
TEL: (01427) 668369 *FAX:* (01427) 668080 *CONTACT:* M & M A Robinson
OPENING TIMES: 1000-1600 daily
MIN. MAIL ORDER UK: No minimum charge *MIN. VALUE EC:* £30.00 + p&p
CAT. COST: 3 x 2nd class *W/SALE or RETAIL:* Both *CREDIT CARDS:* Visa, Access, Switch
SPECIALITIES: Alpines especially Primula, Auricula & Saxifraga. *MAP PAGE:* **9**

EMon Monksilver Nursery, Oakington Road, Cottenham, Cambridgeshire, CB4 4TW
TEL: (01954) 251555 *FAX:* (01954) 202666 *E-MAIL:* monksilver@dial.pipex.com
CONTACT: Joe Sharman & Alan Leslie
OPENING TIMES: 1000-1600 Fri & Sat 1st Mar-30th Jun, 14th Sep & Fri & Sat Oct.
MIN. MAIL ORDER UK: £10.00 + p&p *MIN. VALUE EC:* £30.00 + p&p
CAT. COST: 6 x 1st class *W/SALE or RETAIL:* Retail *CREDIT CARDS:* None
SPECIALITIES: Herbaceous plants, Grasses, Anthemis, Arum, Helianthus, Lamium, Nepeta, Monarda, Salvia, Vinca, Sedges & Variegated plants. Many NCCPG 'Pink Sheet' plants. See also SEED index. *MAP PAGE:* **6**

EMor John Morley, North Green Only, Stoven, Beccles, Suffolk, NR34 8DG
TEL: *CONTACT:* John Morley
OPENING TIMES: By appt. ONLY.
MIN. MAIL ORDER UK: Details in Catalogue *MIN. VALUE EC:* Details in Cat.
CAT. COST: 6 x 1st class *W/SALE or RETAIL:* Retail *CREDIT CARDS:* None
SPECIALITIES: Galanthus, species & hybrids. See also SEED Index.

EMou Frances Mount Perennial Plants, 1 Steps Farm, Polstead, Colchester, Essex, CO6 5AE
TEL: (01206) 262811 *FAX:* (01206) 262811 *CONTACT:* Frances Mount
OPENING TIMES: 1000-1700 Tue Wed Sat & Bank Hols. 1400-1800 Fri. Check weekends & Hols.
MIN. MAIL ORDER UK: £5.00 + p&p *MIN. VALUE EC:* £5.00 + p&p
CAT. COST: 3 x 1st class *W/SALE or RETAIL:* Retail *CREDIT CARDS:* None
SPECIALITIES: Hardy Geraniums. *MAP PAGE:* **6**

EMui **Ken Muir,** Honeypot Farm, Rectory Road, Weeley Heath, Essex, CO16 9BJ
TEL: (01255) 830181 *FAX:* (01255) 831534 *CONTACT:* Ken Muir
OPENING TIMES: 1000-1600.
MIN. MAIL ORDER UK: No minimum charge *MIN. VALUE EC:*
CAT. COST: 3 x 1st class *W/SALE or RETAIL:* Both *CREDIT CARDS:* Visa, Access
SPECIALITIES: Fruit. *MAP PAGE:* **6**

ENHC **Norwich Heather & Conifer Centre,** 54a Yarmouth Road, Thorpe, Norwich, Norfolk, NR7 0HE
TEL: (01603) 439434 *CONTACT:* B Hipperson
OPENING TIMES: 0900-1700 Mon Tue Wed Fri Sat, 1400-1700 Sun Mar-Dec. Closed Sun in Jan & Feb.
MIN. MAIL ORDER UK: No minimum charge *MIN. VALUE EC:*
CAT. COST: 2 x 1st class *W/SALE or RETAIL:* Retail *CREDIT CARDS:* None
SPECIALITIES: Conifers and Heathers. *MAP PAGE:* **8**

ENor **Norfolk Lavender, Caley Mill, Heacham, King's Lynn, Norfolk, PE31 7JE**
TEL: (01485) 570384 *FAX:* (01485) 571176 *CONTACT:* Henry Head
OPENING TIMES: 0930-1700 daily. Closed two weeks after Xmas.
MIN. MAIL ORDER UK: £15.00 + p&p *MIN. VALUE EC:* n/a *EXPORT:* Yes
CAT. COST: 2 x 1st class *W/SALE or RETAIL:* Retail *CREDIT CARDS:* Visa, Access, Switch
SPECIALITIES: National collection of Lavandula. *MAP PAGE:* **8**

ENot **Notcutts Nurseries, Woodbridge, Suffolk, IP12 4AF**
TEL: (01394) 383344 *FAX:* (01394) 445440 *E-MAIL:* sales@notcutts.demon.co.uk
CONTACT: Plant Adviser
OPENING TIMES: Garden Centre varies between 0830-1800 Mon-Sat & 1030-1630 Sun.
MIN. MAIL ORDER UK: £150.00 + p&p *MIN. VALUE EC:* £300.00 + p&p *EXPORT:* Yes
CAT. COST: £4.00 + £1.00 postage *W/SALE or RETAIL:* Both *CREDIT CARDS:* Visa, Access, Switch, Connect
SPECIALITIES: Wide general range. Specialist list of Syringa. National Collection of Hibiscus. *MAP PAGE:* **6**

EOas **Oasis,** 42 Greenwood Avenue, South Benfleet, Essex, SS7 1LD
TEL: (01268) 757666 *CONTACT:* Paul Spracklin
OPENING TIMES: Strictly by appt. ONLY.
MIN. MAIL ORDER UK: No minimum charge *MIN. VALUE EC:*
CAT. COST: Sae *W/SALE or RETAIL:* Retail *CREDIT CARDS:* None
SPECIALITIES: Small nursery offering a range of Hardy & Half-hardy Exotic plants esp. Bamboos, Palms, Tree Ferns, Bananas & unusual Xerophytes. *MAP PAGE:* **6**

EOHP **Old Hall Plants,** 1 The Old Hall, Barsham, Beccles, Suffolk, NR34 8HB
OPENING TIMES: By appt. most days - please phone first.
No mail order
CAT. COST: 3 x 1st class *W/SALE or RETAIL:* Retail *CREDIT CARDS:* None
SPECIALITIES: Herbs, over 450 varieties grown. *MAP PAGE:* **8**

EOrc **Orchard Nurseries,** Tow Lane, Foston, Grantham, Lincolnshire, NG32 2LE
TEL: (01400) 281354 *FAX:* (01400) 281354 *CONTACT:* R & J Blenkinship
OPENING TIMES: 1000-1800 daily 1st Feb-30th Sep.
No mail order
CAT. COST: Sae *W/SALE or RETAIL:* Retail *CREDIT CARDS:* Visa, Access
SPECIALITIES: Unusual herbaceous & small flowered Clematis both hardy & for the Conservatory. See also SEED Index. *MAP PAGE:* **7/8**

EOrn **Ornamental Conifers,** 22 Chapel Road, Terrington St Clement, Kings Lynn, Norfolk, PE34 4ND
TEL: (01553) 828874 *CONTACT:* Peter Rotchell
OPENING TIMES: 0930-1700 7 days a week, 1st Feb-20th Dec.
No mail order
CAT. COST: None issued *W/SALE or RETAIL:* Retail *CREDIT CARDS:* None
SPECIALITIES: Conifers & Heathers *MAP PAGE:* **8**

EOvi **M Oviatt-Ham, (Off.) Ely House, 15 Green Street, Willingham, Cambridgeshire, CB4 5JA**
TEL: (01954) 261654 *FAX:* (01954) 260481 *CONTACT:* M Oviatt-Ham
OPENING TIMES: Fri-Tue 1st Apr-31st Oct. Other times by appt. only.
MIN. MAIL ORDER UK: No minimum charge *MIN. VALUE EC:* Nmc *EXPORT:* Yes
CAT. COST: 50p + 2 x 1st class *W/SALE or RETAIL:* Both *CREDIT CARDS:* None
SPECIALITIES: Clematis & climbing plants. Nursery address: Black Pit Drove, Rampton Rd., Willingham. *MAP PAGE:* **6**

EPad **Padlock Croft,** 19 Padlock Road, West Wratting, Cambridgeshire, CB1 5LS
TEL: (01223) 290383 *CONTACT:* Susan & Peter Lewis
OPENING TIMES: 1000-1800 Wed-Sat 1st Apr-15th Oct & Bank Hol Mons. Winter by appt.
No mail order
CAT. COST: 4 x 2nd class *W/SALE or RETAIL:* Retail *CREDIT CARDS:* None
SPECIALITIES: National Collection of Campanula, Adenophora, Symphyandra & Platycodon & other Campanulaceae. *MAP PAGE:* **6**

EPar **Paradise Centre, Twinstead Road, Lamarsh, Bures, Suffolk, CO8 5EX**
TEL: (01787) 269449 *FAX:* (01787) 269449 *CONTACT:* Cees & Hedy Stapel-Valk
OPENING TIMES: 1000-1700 Sat-Sun & Bank Hols or by appt. Easter-1st Nov.
MIN. MAIL ORDER UK: £7.50 + p&p *MIN. VALUE EC:* £25.00 + p&p *EXPORT:* Yes
CAT. COST: 5 x 1st class *W/SALE or RETAIL:* Retail *CREDIT CARDS:* Visa, Access, Diners
SPECIALITIES: Unusual bulbous & tuberous plants including shade & bog varieties. See also SEED Index. *MAP PAGE:* **6**

EPfP **The Place for Plants,** East Bergholt Place, East Bergholt, Suffolk, CO7 6UP
TEL: (01206) 299224 *FAX:* (01206) 299224 *CONTACT:* Rupert & Sara Eley
OPENING TIMES: 1000-1700 (dusk if earlier) daily. Closed Xmas fortnight. Garden open Mar-Oct.
No mail order
CAT. COST: Free list *W/SALE or RETAIL:* Retail *CREDIT CARDS:* Visa, Access, MasterCard, EuroCard, Delta, Switch
SPECIALITIES: Wide range of specialist & popular plants. 15 acre mature garden.
MAP PAGE: **6**

EPGN **Park Green Nurseries, Wetheringsett, Stowmarket, Suffolk, IP14 5QH**
TEL: (01728) 860139 *FAX:* (01728) 861277 *CONTACT:* Richard & Mary Ford
OPENING TIMES: 1000-1700 daily Mar-Sep.
MIN. MAIL ORDER UK: No minimum charge *MIN. VALUE EC:* Nmc *EXPORT:* Yes
CAT. COST: 4 x 1st class *W/SALE or RETAIL:* Retail *CREDIT CARDS:* Visa, Access
SPECIALITIES: Hosta, Astilbe, ornamental Grasses & Herbaceous. *MAP PAGE:* **6**

EPla **P W Plants, Sunnyside, Heath Road, Kenninghall, Norfolk, NR16 2DS**
TEL: (01953) 888212 *FAX:* (01953) 888212 *CONTACT:* Paul Whittaker
OPENING TIMES: Every Friday & last Saturday in every month.
MIN. MAIL ORDER UK: No minimum charge *MIN. VALUE EC:* Nmc
CAT. COST: 5 x 1st class *W/SALE or RETAIL:* Retail *CREDIT CARDS:* None
SPECIALITIES: Choice Shrubs, Perennials, Grasses, Climbers, Bamboos, Hedera. Wide range of unusual hardy ornamental Shrubs. *MAP PAGE:* **8**

EPot **Potterton & Martin, The Cottage Nursery, Moortown Road, Nettleton, Caistor, Lincolnshire, LN7 6HX**
TEL: (01472) 851792 *FAX:* (01472) 851792 *CONTACT:*
◆ *OPENING TIMES:* 0900-1700 daily.
MIN. MAIL ORDER UK: No minimum charge *MIN. VALUE EC:* Nmc *EXPORT:* Yes
CAT. COST: £1 in stamps only *W/SALE or RETAIL:* Both *CREDIT CARDS:* Visa, Access, MasterCard, EuroCard
SPECIALITIES: Alpines, Dwarf Bulbs, Conifers & Shrubs. See also SEED Index.
MAP PAGE: **9**

EPPr **The Plantsman's Preference, Lynwood, Hopton Road, Garboldisham, Diss, Norfolk, IP22 2QN**

TEL: (01953) 681439 *CONTACT:* Jenny & Tim Fuller
OPENING TIMES: 0900-1700 Fri & Sun Mar-Oct. Other times by appt.
MIN. MAIL ORDER UK: No minimum charge *MIN. VALUE EC:* Nmc
CAT. COST: 4 x 1st class *W/SALE or RETAIL:* Retail *CREDIT CARDS:* None
SPECIALITIES: Hardy Geraniums, Grasses and unusual & interesting Perennials.
MAP PAGE: **6/8**

EPri **Priory Plants,** 1 Covey Cottage, Hintlesham, Nr Ipswich, Suffolk, IP8 3NY

TEL: (01473) 652656 *CONTACT:* Sue Mann
OPENING TIMES: 0930-1700 Fri-Mon 1st Mar-31st Oct
MIN. MAIL ORDER UK: £10.00 + p&p *MIN. VALUE EC:*
CAT. COST: 2 x 1st class *W/SALE or RETAIL:* Retail *CREDIT CARDS:* None
SPECIALITIES: Penstemon, hardy Geranium, Euphorbia, Campanula. Small range of Shrubs & hardy Herbaceous. *MAP PAGE:* **6**

ER&R **Rhodes & Rockliffe, 2 Nursery Road, Nazeing, Essex, EN9 2JE**

TEL: (01992) 463693 *FAX:* (01992) 440673 *CONTACT:* David Rhodes or John Rockliffe
OPENING TIMES: By appt.
MIN. MAIL ORDER UK: £2.50 + p&p *MIN. VALUE EC:* £2.50 + p&p *EXPORT:* Yes
CAT. COST: 2 x 1st class *W/SALE or RETAIL:* Retail *CREDIT CARDS:* None
SPECIALITIES: Begonias *MAP PAGE:* **6**

ERav **Raveningham Gardens, Norwich, Norfolk, NR14 6NS**

TEL: (01508) 548222 *FAX:* (01508) 548958 *CONTACT:* Ian Greenfield
OPENING TIMES: Mail Order only. Gardens open - please phone for details.
MIN. MAIL ORDER UK: No minimum charge *MIN. VALUE EC:* Nmc *EXPORT:* Yes
CAT. COST: 4 x 1st class *W/SALE or RETAIL:* Both *CREDIT CARDS:* None
SPECIALITIES: Plants noted for Foliage. Variegated & coloured leaf plants, Herbaceous, Galanthus & Hardy Agapanthus. *MAP PAGE:* **8**

ERea **Reads Nursery, Hales Hall, Loddon, Norfolk, NR14 6QW**

TEL: (01508) 548395 *FAX:* (01508) 548040 *CONTACT:* Terence & Judy Read
◆ *OPENING TIMES:* 1000-1700 (or dusk if earlier) Tue-Sat, 1200-1700 Sun & Bank Hols Easter-Oct & by appt.
MIN. MAIL ORDER UK: £10.00 + p&p *MIN. VALUE EC:* £10.00 + p&p *EXPORT:* Yes
CAT. COST: 4 x 1st class *W/SALE or RETAIL:* Both *CREDIT CARDS:* Visa, Access, Diners, Switch
SPECIALITIES: Conservatory plants, Vines, Citrus, Figs & unusual Fruits & Nuts. Wall Shrubs & Climbers. Scented & aromatic Hardy plants. Box & Yew hedging & topiary. UK grown.
MAP PAGE: **8**

ERob **Robin Savill Clematis Specialist, (Off.) 2 Bury Cottages, Bury Road, Pleshey, Chelmsford, Essex, CM3 1HB**

TEL: (01245 237380) *CONTACT:* Robin Savill
OPENING TIMES: Mail order only.
MIN. MAIL ORDER UK: 1 plant + p&p *MIN. VALUE EC:* 1 plant + p&p *EXPORT:* Yes
CAT. COST: £1.00 or 4 x 1st class *W/SALE or RETAIL:* Both *CREDIT CARDS:* None
SPECIALITIES: Clematis incl. many rare & unusual species & cultivars.

ERom **The Romantic Garden, Swannington, Norwich, Norfolk, NR9 5NW**

TEL: (01603) 261488 *FAX:* (01603) 871668 *CONTACT:* John Powles
◆ *OPENING TIMES:* 1000-1700 Wed, Fri & Sat all year.
MIN. MAIL ORDER UK: £5.00 + p&p *MIN. VALUE EC:* £30.00 + p&p *EXPORT:* Yes
CAT. COST: 4 x 1st class *W/SALE or RETAIL:* Both *CREDIT CARDS:* Visa, Access, AmEx
SPECIALITIES: Half-hardy & Conservatory. Buxus topiary, Ornamental standards, large specimen. *MAP PAGE:* **8**

ERos **Roseholme Nursery, Roseholme Farm, Howsham, Lincoln, Lincolnshire, LN7 6JZ**
TEL: (01652) 678661 *CONTACT:* P B Clayton
OPENING TIMES: By appt. for collection of orders.
MIN. MAIL ORDER UK: No minimum charge *MIN. VALUE EC:* Nmc *EXPORT:* Yes
CAT. COST: 2 x 2nd class *W/SALE or RETAIL:* Both *CREDIT CARDS:* None
SPECIALITIES: Underground Lines - Bulbs, Corms, Rhizomes & Tubers (esp. Crocus, Iris).
MAP PAGE: **9**

ERou **Rougham Hall Nurseries, Ipswich Road, Rougham, Bury St. Edmunds, Suffolk, IP30 9LZ**
TEL: (01359) 270577 *FAX:* (01359) 271149 *CONTACT:* A A & K G Harbutt
OPENING TIMES: 1000-1600 Thu-Mon.
MIN. MAIL ORDER UK: No minimum charge *MIN. VALUE EC:* Nmc
CAT. COST: 4 x 1st class *W/SALE or RETAIL:* Both *CREDIT CARDS:* None
SPECIALITIES: Hardy Perennials, esp. Aster (n-a, n-b & species), Delphinium, Hemerocallis, Iris, Kniphofia, Papaver & Phlox, *MAP PAGE:* **6**

ESCh **Sheila Chapman Clematis,** Writtle By-pass (A414), Ongar Road West, Writtle, Essex, CM1 3NT
TEL: (01245) 422245 (Clematis), (01245) 421020 (Roses, shrubs) *FAX:* (01245) 422293
CONTACT: Sheila Chapman
OPENING TIMES: 0900-1800 daily Summer, 0900-dusk daily Winter, excl. Xmas week.
No mail order
CAT. COST: 4 x 1st class *W/SALE or RETAIL:* Both *CREDIT CARDS:* Visa, Access, AmEx, Diners, Switch
SPECIALITIES: Over 400 varieties of Clematis, David Austin Roses, unusual shrubs & herbaceous plants. *MAP PAGE:* **6**

ESha **Shaw Rose Trees,** 2 Hollowgate Hill, Willoughton, Gainsborough, Lincolnshire, DN21 5SF
TEL: (01427) 668230 *CONTACT:* Mr K Shaw
OPENING TIMES: Vary, please check.
MIN. MAIL ORDER UK: £3.00 + p&p *MIN. VALUE EC:*
CAT. COST: Sae *W/SALE or RETAIL:* Both *CREDIT CARDS:* None
SPECIALITIES: Roses. *MAP PAGE:* **9**

ESim **Clive Simms,** Woodhurst, Essendine, Stamford, Lincolnshire, PE9 4LQ
TEL: (01780) 755615 *CONTACT:* Clive & Kathryn Simms
OPENING TIMES: By appt. for collection only.
MIN. MAIL ORDER UK: No minimum charge *MIN. VALUE EC:*
CAT. COST: 2 x 1st class *W/SALE or RETAIL:* Retail *CREDIT CARDS:* None
SPECIALITIES: Uncommon nut Trees & unusual fruiting plants.

ESiP **Simply Plants,** (Off.) 17 Duloe Brook, Eaton Socon, Cambridgeshire, PE19 3DW
TEL: (01480) 475312 *CONTACT:* Christine Dakin
OPENING TIMES: Please phone for opening dates or for an appointment.
MIN. MAIL ORDER UK: £10.00 + p&p *MIN. VALUE EC:*
CAT. COST: 2 x 1st class *W/SALE or RETAIL:* Both *CREDIT CARDS:* None
SPECIALITIES: Ornamental Grasses, Sedges & Bamboos. Also range of Shrubs & Perennials. Nursery at: 44 Rookery Road, Wyboston, Bedfordshire MK44 3AX. *MAP PAGE:* **6**

ESis **Siskin Plants, April House, Davey Lane, Charsfield, Woodbridge, Suffolk, IP13 7QG**
TEL: (01473) 737567 *FAX:* (01473) 737567 *CONTACT:* Chris & Valerie Wheeler
OPENING TIMES: 1000-1700 Tue-Sat Feb-Oct.
MIN. MAIL ORDER UK: No minimum charge *MIN. VALUE EC:* Nmc
CAT. COST: £1.00 *W/SALE or RETAIL:* Retail *CREDIT CARDS:* Access, Visa
SPECIALITIES: Alpines, miniature Conifers & dwarf Shrubs, esp. plants for Troughs. National Collection of Dwarf Hebe. *MAP PAGE:* **6**

◆ **See also Display Advertisements**

ESOG **Smallworth Ornamental Grasses,** Fourwynds, Smallworth, Garboldisham, Diss, Norfolk, IP22 2QW
TEL: (01953) 681536 *CONTACT:* Wally Thrower
OPENING TIMES: 0930-1530 Thu & Fri, 1330-1730 Sat & Sun 1st Mar-31st Oct. Other days by appt.
MIN. MAIL ORDER UK: No minimum charge* *MIN. VALUE EC:*
CAT. COST: 3 x 2nd class *W/SALE or RETAIL:* Retail *CREDIT CARDS:* None
SPECIALITIES: An increasing range of Grasses, Sedges & Rushes. *Note: mail order to UK only.
MAP PAGE: **6/8**

ESul **Pearl Sulman, 54 Kingsway, Mildenhall, Bury St Edmunds, Suffolk, IP28 7HR**
TEL: (01638) 712297 *CONTACT:* Pearl Sulman
OPENING TIMES: Not open. Mail Order only. Open weekend June 7/8th 1997 & 6/7th 1998.
MIN. MAIL ORDER UK: £9.00 + p&p *MIN. VALUE EC:* £9.00 + p&p
CAT. COST: 3 x 1st class *W/SALE or RETAIL:* Retail *CREDIT CARDS:* None
SPECIALITIES: Miniature, Dwarf & Scented-leaf Pelargoniums.

ETen **Tennyson Nurseries, Chantry Farm, Campsea Ashe, Wickham Market, Suffolk, IP13 0PZ**
TEL: (01728) 747113 *FAX:* (01728) 747725 *CONTACT:* Henry Rose
OPENING TIMES: 1000-1700 daily.
MIN. MAIL ORDER UK: £20.00 + p&p *MIN. VALUE EC:* £20.00 + p&p
CAT. COST: 5 x 1st class *W/SALE or RETAIL:* Both *CREDIT CARDS:* None
SPECIALITIES: Range of rare & unusual Hardy Plants. *MAP PAGE:* **6**

ETho **Thorncroft Clematis Nursery, The Lings, Reymerston, Norwich, Norfolk, NR9 4QG**
TEL: (01953) 850407 *CONTACT:* Ruth P Gooch
OPENING TIMES: 1000-1630 Thu-Tue 1st March-31st Oct.
MIN. MAIL ORDER UK: No minimum charge* *MIN. VALUE EC:* Nmc *EXPORT:* Yes
CAT. COST: 2 x 1st class *W/SALE or RETAIL:* Retail *CREDIT CARDS:* None
SPECIALITIES: Clematis. *Note: please enquire for mail order details. *MAP PAGE:* **8**

ETPC **Trevor Scott,** Thorpe Park Cottage, Thorpe-le-Soken, Essex, CO16 0HN
TEL: (01255) 861308 *FAX:* (01255) 861308 *CONTACT:* Trevor Scott
◆ *OPENING TIMES:* By appt. only.
No mail order
CAT. COST: 5 x 1st class *W/SALE or RETAIL:* Retail *CREDIT CARDS:* None
SPECIALITIES: Ornamental Grasses. *MAP PAGE:* **6**

ETub **Van Tubergen UK Ltd, Bressingham, Diss, Norfolk, IP22 2AB**
TEL: (01379) 688282 *FAX:* (01379) 687227 *E-MAIL:* sales@vantub.flexnet.co.uk
CONTACT: General Manager
OPENING TIMES: Not open to the public.
MIN. MAIL ORDER UK: No minimum charge *MIN. VALUE EC:* Nmc
CAT. COST: Free *W/SALE or RETAIL:* Both *CREDIT CARDS:* Visa, Access
SPECIALITIES: Bulbs. *Note: Retail & Wholesale sales by Mail Order only (wholesale bulbs not listed in Plant Finder).

EWal **J Walkers Bulbs, Washway House Farm, Holbeach, Spalding, Lincolnshire, PE12 7PP**
TEL: (01406) 426216 *FAX:* (01406) 425468 *CONTACT:* J W Walkers
OPENING TIMES: Not open to the public.
MIN. MAIL ORDER UK: See Cat. for details *MIN. VALUE EC:* See Catalogue
CAT. COST: 2 x 1st class *W/SALE or RETAIL:* Both *CREDIT CARDS:* Visa, Access
SPECIALITIES: Daffodils & Fritillaria.

EWar **Warley Rose Garden Ltd, Warley Street, Great Warley, Brentwood, Essex, CM13 3JH**
TEL: (01277) 221966/219344 *FAX:* (01277) 262239 *CONTACT:* J H G Deamer
OPENING TIMES: 0900-1730 Mon-Sat.
MIN. MAIL ORDER UK: No minimum charge *MIN. VALUE EC:* Nmc
CAT. COST: Free-30p at shop *W/SALE or RETAIL:* Both *CREDIT CARDS:* Visa, Access, AmEx, Delta, Switch
SPECIALITIES: Roses & container grown Nursery Stock. *MAP PAGE:* **6**

EWes **West Acre Gardens,** West Acre, Kings Lynn, Norfolk, PE32 1UJ
TEL: (01760) 755562/755989 *FAX:* (01760) 755989 *CONTACT:* J J Tuite
◆ *OPENING TIMES:* 1000-1700 daily 1st Mar-15th Nov. Other times by appt.
No mail order
CAT. COST: 4 x 1st class *W/SALE or RETAIL:* Retail *CREDIT CARDS:* None
SPECIALITIES: Unusual Shrubs, Herbaceous & Alpines. Large selection of Rhodohypoxis.
MAP PAGE: **8**

EWFC **The Wild Flower Centre,** Church Farm, Sisland, Loddon, Norwich, Norfolk, NR14 6EF
TEL: (01508) 520235 *FAX:* (01508) 528294 *CONTACT:* D G Corne
OPENING TIMES: 0900-1700 Fri, Sat, Sun & Tue
MIN. MAIL ORDER UK: £3.80 + p&p *MIN. VALUE EC:*
CAT. COST: 40p or A4 Sae *W/SALE or RETAIL:* Retail *CREDIT CARDS:* None
SPECIALITIES: British native and naturalised Wild Flower plants. 283+ varieties.
MAP PAGE: **8**

EWll **The Walled Garden,** Park Road, Benhall, Saxmundham, Suffolk, IP17 1JB
TEL: (01728) 602510 *FAX:* (01728) 602510 *CONTACT:* J R Mountain
◆ *OPENING TIMES:* 0930-1700 Tue-Sun Feb-Oct, Tue-Sat Nov-Jan.
No mail order
CAT. COST: 2 x 1st class *W/SALE or RETAIL:* Retail *CREDIT CARDS:* Visa, Access
SPECIALITIES: Tender & hardy Perennials & wall Shrubs. *MAP PAGE:* **6**

EWoo **Wootten's Plants,** Wenhaston, Blackheath, Halesworth, Suffolk, IP19 9HD
TEL: (01502) 478258 *CONTACT:* M Loftus
OPENING TIMES: 0930-1700 daily.
No mail order
CAT. COST: £2.50 illus. *W/SALE or RETAIL:* Retail *CREDIT CARDS:* Access, Visa, AmEx, Switch
SPECIALITIES: Pelargonium, Salvia, Penstemon, Viola, Aquilegia, Digitalis, Campanula & Polemonium. *MAP PAGE:* **6**

GAbr **Abriachan Nurseries, Loch Ness Side, Inverness, Invernesshire, Scotland, IV3 6LA**
TEL: (01463) 861232 *FAX:* (01463) 861232 *CONTACT:* Mr & Mrs D Davidson
OPENING TIMES: 0900-1900 daily (dusk if earlier) Feb-Nov.
MIN. MAIL ORDER UK: No minimum charge *MIN. VALUE EC:* Nmc
CAT. COST: 3 x 1st class *W/SALE or RETAIL:* Retail *CREDIT CARDS:* None
SPECIALITIES: Herbaceous, Primula, Helianthemum, Hebe & Hardy Geraniums.
MAP PAGE: **10**

GAri **Arivegaig Nursery,** Aultbea, Acharacle, Argyll, Scotland, PH36 4LE
TEL: (01967) 431331 *CONTACT:* E Stewart
◆ *OPENING TIMES:* 0900-1700 daily Easter-end Oct.
No mail order
CAT. COST: 4 x 1st class *W/SALE or RETAIL:* Both *CREDIT CARDS:* None
SPECIALITIES: A wide range of unusual plants, including those suited for the milder parts of the country. *MAP PAGE:* **10**

GAul **Aultan Nursery,** Newton of Cairnhill, Cuminestown, Turriff, Aberdeenshire, Scotland, AB53 5TN
TEL: (01888) 544702 *FAX:* (01888) 544702 *E-MAIL:* rlking@globalnet.co.uk
CONTACT: Richard King
OPENING TIMES: 1100-1600 Mon, 1330-1800 Sat, 1000-1800 Sun, Apr-Oct. Other times please phone first.
No mail order
CAT. COST: 2 x 1st class *W/SALE or RETAIL:* Retail *CREDIT CARDS:* None
SPECIALITIES: Herbaceous Perennials & Shrubs, mostly grown in peat-free composts. A very wide range including many unusual items. *MAP PAGE:* **10**

GBar **Barwinnock Herbs, Barrhill, by Girvan, Ayrshire, Scotland, KA26 0RB**
TEL: (01465) 821338 *FAX:* (01465) 821338 *E-MAIL:* 101344.3413@compuserve.com
CONTACT: Dave & Mon Holtom
◆ *OPENING TIMES:* 1000-1800 daily 1st April-31st Oct.
MIN. MAIL ORDER UK: No minimum charge *MIN. VALUE EC:* Nmc *EXPORT:* Yes
CAT. COST: 3 x 1st class *W/SALE or RETAIL:* Retail *CREDIT CARDS:* None
SPECIALITIES: Culinary, Medicinal & fragrant leaved plants organically grown.
MAP PAGE: **10**

GBin **Binny Plants,** West Lodge, Binny Estate, Ecclesmachen Road, Nr Broxbourn, West Lothian, Scotland, EH52 6NL
TEL: (01506) 858931 *FAX:* (01506) 858931 *E-MAIL:* binnycrag@aol.com
CONTACT: Billy Carruthers
◆ *OPENING TIMES:* 1000-1700 Fri, Sat & Sun only Easter Fri-Halloween.
MIN. MAIL ORDER UK: £25.00 + p&p *MIN. VALUE EC:*
CAT. COST: 2 x 31p *W/SALE or RETAIL:* Retail *CREDIT CARDS:* None
SPECIALITIES: Euphorbia, Grasses, hardy Geranium & many lesser known Shrubs. Herbaceous, Ferns, Alpines & Aquilegias. *MAP PAGE:* **10**

GBon **Bonhard Nursery,** Murrayshall Road, Scone, Perth, Tayside, Scotland, PH2 7PQ
TEL: (01738) 552791 *FAX:* (01738) 552791 *CONTACT:* Mr & Mrs Hickman
OPENING TIMES: 1000-1800, or dusk if earlier, daily.
No mail order
CAT. COST: Free (fruit trees & roses) *W/SALE or RETAIL:* Retail *CREDIT CARDS:* None
SPECIALITIES: Herbaceous, Conifers & Alpines. Fruit & ornamental Trees. Shrub & species Roses. *MAP PAGE:* **10**

GBri **Bridge End Nurseries,** Gretna Green, Dumfries & Galloway, Scotland, DG16 5HN
TEL: (01461) 800612 *FAX:* (01461) 800612 *CONTACT:* R Bird
OPENING TIMES: 0930-1700 all year. Evenings by appt.
No mail order
CAT. COST: None issued *W/SALE or RETAIL:* Retail *CREDIT CARDS:* None
SPECIALITIES: Hardy cottage garden Perennials. Many unusual & interesting varieties.
MAP PAGE: **10**

GBuc **Buckland Plants, Whinnieliggate, Kirkcudbright, Scotland, DG6 4XP**
TEL: (01557) 331323 *FAX:* (01557) 331323 *CONTACT:* Rob or Dina Asbridge
OPENING TIMES: 1000-1700 Thu-Sun Feb-Nov
MIN. MAIL ORDER UK: £15.00 + p&p *MIN. VALUE EC:* £50.00 + p&p *EXPORT:* Yes
CAT. COST: 3 x 1st class *W/SALE or RETAIL:* Retail *CREDIT CARDS:* None
SPECIALITIES: Very wide range of unusual perennials esp. for woodland gardens & flower arrangers. Meconopsis, Cardamine, Euphorbia, etc. *MAP PAGE:* **10**

GBur **Burnside Nursery, by Girvan, Ayrshire, Scotland, KA26 9JH**
OPENING TIMES: 1000-1900 daily except Weds, 1st Apr-31st Oct.
MIN. MAIL ORDER UK: No minimum charge *MIN. VALUE EC:* Nmc
CAT. COST: Sae *W/SALE or RETAIL:* Both *CREDIT CARDS:* None
SPECIALITIES: Dicentra & Hardy Geraniums. *MAP PAGE:* **10**

GCal **Cally Gardens, Gatehouse of Fleet, Castle Douglas, Scotland, DG7 2DJ**
TEL: Not on phone. *FAX:* Only (01557) 815029 *CONTACT:* Michael Wickenden
◆ *OPENING TIMES:* 1000-1730 Sat & Sun only from 29th March-5th Oct
MIN. MAIL ORDER UK: £15.00 + p&p *MIN. VALUE EC:* £50.00 + p&p *EXPORT:* Yes
CAT. COST: 3 x 1st class *W/SALE or RETAIL:* Both *CREDIT CARDS:* None
SPECIALITIES: Unusual perennials. Agapanthus, Crocosmia, Erodium, Eryngium, Euphorbia, Hardy Geraniums & Grasses. Some rare Shrubs, Climbers & Conservatory plants.
MAP PAGE: **10**

GCan **Candacraig Gardens,** Strathdon, Aberdeenshire, Scotland, AB3 8XT
TEL: (01975) 651226 *FAX:* (01975) 651391 *CONTACT:* Mrs E M Young
OPENING TIMES: 1000-1700 Mon-Fri & 1400-1800 Sat & Sun May-Sep or by appt.
MIN. MAIL ORDER UK: No minimum charge *MIN. VALUE EC:*
CAT. COST: 2 x 1st class *W/SALE or RETAIL:* Retail *CREDIT CARDS:* None
SPECIALITIES: A wide variety of Hardy Perennials, Meconopsis & Primula. *MAP PAGE:* **10**

GCHN **Charter House Nursery, 2 Nunwood, Dumfries, Dumfries & Galloway, Scotland, DG2 0HX**
TEL: (01387) 720363 *CONTACT:* John Ross
OPENING TIMES: 0900-1700 Mar-Oct. Other times by appt.
MIN. MAIL ORDER UK: No minimum charge *MIN. VALUE EC:* Nmc
CAT. COST: 3 x 1st class *W/SALE or RETAIL:* Retail *CREDIT CARDS:* None
SPECIALITIES: Aquilegia, Hypericum, Geranium, Erodium, Saxifraga and Campanula. Erodium National Collection. *MAP PAGE:* **10**

GChr **Christie Elite Nurseries,** The Nurseries, Forres, Moray, Grampian, Scotland, IV36 0TW
TEL: (01309) 672633 *FAX:* (01309) 676846 *CONTACT:* Dr S Thompson
◆ *OPENING TIMES:* 0800-1700 daily.
MIN. MAIL ORDER UK: No minimum charge *MIN. VALUE EC:*
CAT. COST: Free *W/SALE or RETAIL:* Both *CREDIT CARDS:* Visa, Access
SPECIALITIES: Hedging & screening plants. Woodland & less common Trees, Shrubs & Fruit. *MAP PAGE:* **10**

GCLN **Craig Lodge Nurseries,** Balmaclellan, Castle Douglas, Kirkcudbrightshire, Scotland, DG7 3QR
TEL: (01644) 420661 *CONTACT:* Sheila & Michael Northway
◆ *OPENING TIMES:* 1000-1700 Wed-Mon late Mar-mid Oct.
MIN. MAIL ORDER UK: £10.00 + p&p* *MIN. VALUE EC:*
CAT. COST: A5 Sae + 4 x 2nd class *W/SALE or RETAIL:* Retail *CREDIT CARDS:* None
SPECIALITIES: Alpines, Auriculas, dwarf Rhododendron, Bulbs & Conifers. Bulbs & Alpines are largely grown from wild seed. *Note: mail order to UK only. *MAP PAGE:* **10**

GCoc **James Cocker & Sons,** Whitemyres, Lang Stracht, Aberdeen, Scotland, AB9 2XH
TEL: (01224) 313261 *FAX:* (01224) 312531 *CONTACT:* Alec Cocker
OPENING TIMES: 0900-1730 daily.
MIN. MAIL ORDER UK: No minimum charge *MIN. VALUE EC:*
CAT. COST: Free *W/SALE or RETAIL:* Both *CREDIT CARDS:* Visa, Access
SPECIALITIES: Roses. *MAP PAGE:* **10**

GCra **Craigieburn Classic Plants, Craigieburn House, by Moffat, Dumfries, Scotland, DG10 9LF**
TEL: (01683) 221250 *FAX:* (01683) 221250 *CONTACT:* Janet Wheatcroft & Bill Chudziak
OPENING TIMES: 1230-1800 Tue-Sun Easter-end Oct. Nov-Apr by appt.
MIN. MAIL ORDER UK: £10.00 + p&p *MIN. VALUE EC:* £25.00 + p&p
CAT. COST: £1.00 *W/SALE or RETAIL:* Retail *CREDIT CARDS:* None
SPECIALITIES: Codonopsis, Digitalis, Meconopsis & Primula. National Meconopsis Collection. *MAP PAGE:* **10**

GCrs **Christie's Nursery, Downfield, Westmuir, Kirriemuir, Angus, Scotland, DD8 5LP**
TEL: (01575) 572977 *FAX:* (01575) 572977 *CONTACT:* Ian & Ann Christie & Ian Martin
◆ *OPENING TIMES:* 1000-1700 daily except Tue (closed) & 1300-1700 Sun, 1st Mar-31st Oct.
MIN. MAIL ORDER UK: 5 plants + p&p *MIN. VALUE EC:* On request *EXPORT:* Yes
CAT. COST: 2 x 1st class *W/SALE or RETAIL:* Both *CREDIT CARDS:* None
SPECIALITIES: Alpines, esp. Gentians, Cassiope, Primula, Lewisia, Orchids, Trillium & Ericaceous. *MAP PAGE:* **10**

◆ **See also Display Advertisements**

GDra **Jack Drake, Inshriach Alpine Nusery, Aviemore, Invernesshire, Scotland, PH22 1QS**
TEL: (01540) 651287 *FAX:* (01540) 651656 *CONTACT:* J C Lawson
OPENING TIMES: 0900-1700 Mon-Fri, 0900-1600 Sat & Bank Hol Suns.
MIN. MAIL ORDER UK: No minimum charge *MIN. VALUE EC:* £50.00 + p&p *EXPORT:* Yes
CAT. COST: £1.00 *W/SALE or RETAIL:* Both *CREDIT CARDS:* None
SPECIALITIES: Rare and unusual Alpines & Rock plants. Especially Primula, Meconopsis, Gentian, Heathers etc. See also SEED Index. *MAP PAGE:* **10**

GDTE **Down to Earth,** 55 Beresford, Ayr, Ayrshire, Scotland, KA7 2HD
TEL: (01292) 283639 *CONTACT:* Rose & Malcolm Macgregor
OPENING TIMES: Appt. only. Shop open 0900-1730 Mon-Sat & 1200-1700 Sun Apr-Aug.
MIN. MAIL ORDER UK: No minimum charge *MIN. VALUE EC:*
CAT. COST: 2 x 1st class *W/SALE or RETAIL:* Both *CREDIT CARDS:* None
SPECIALITIES: Pansies & Violas, plus range of quality Shrubs. *MAP PAGE:* **10**

GFle **Fleurs Plants,** 2 Castlehill Lane, Abington Road, Symington, Biggar, Scotland, ML12 6SJ
TEL: (01889) 308528 *CONTACT:* Jim Elliott
OPENING TIMES: Please phone to arrange a visit.
MIN. MAIL ORDER UK: £8.00 + p&p *MIN. VALUE EC:*
CAT. COST: Sae *W/SALE or RETAIL:* Retail *CREDIT CARDS:* None
SPECIALITIES: Primula, Hardy Geranium. *MAP PAGE:* **10**

GFre **John Frew, 14 Meadowside of Craigmyle, Kemnay, Inverurie, Aberdeenshire, Scotland, AB51 5LZ**
TEL: (01467) 643544 *CONTACT:* John & Lois Frew
OPENING TIMES: By appt.
MIN. MAIL ORDER UK: No minimum charge *MIN. VALUE EC:* Nmc
CAT. COST: 3 x 1st class *W/SALE or RETAIL:* Retail *CREDIT CARDS:* None
SPECIALITIES: Ornamental Grasses. *MAP PAGE:* **10**

GGar **Garden Cottage Nursery,** Tournaig, Poolewe, Achnasheen, Highland, Scotland, IV22 2LH
TEL: (01445) 781339 *CONTACT:* R & L Rushbrooke
OPENING TIMES: 1200-1900 Mon-Sat (Mar-Oct) or by appt.
MIN. MAIL ORDER UK: £10.00 + p&p *MIN. VALUE EC:*
CAT. COST: 4 x 2nd class *W/SALE or RETAIL:* Retail *CREDIT CARDS:* None
SPECIALITIES: Large range of Herbacous & Alpines esp. Primula, Hardy Geraniums & moisture lovers. Range of West Coast Shrubs. *MAP PAGE:* **10**

GGGa **Glendoick Gardens Ltd, Glencarse, Perth, Scotland, PH2 7NS**
TEL: (01738) 860205 *FAX:* (01738) 860630 *CONTACT:* P A, E P & K N E Cox
OPENING TIMES: By appt. only. Garden Centre open 7 days.
MIN. MAIL ORDER UK: £30.00 + p&p *MIN. VALUE EC:* £100.00 + p&p *EXPORT:* Yes
CAT. COST: £1.50 or £1 stamps *W/SALE or RETAIL:* Retail *CREDIT CARDS:* not for mail orders
SPECIALITIES: Rhododendron, Azalea and Ericaceous, Primula & Meconopsis. National collection of Kalmia & Enkianthus. Many Catalogue plants available at Garden Centre. *MAP PAGE:* **10**

GGre **Greenhead Roses, Greenhead Nursery, Old Greenock Road, Inchinnan, Renfrew, Strathclyde, PA4 9PH**
TEL: (0141) 812 0121 *FAX:* (0141) 812 0121 *CONTACT:* C N Urquhart
OPENING TIMES: 1000-1700 daily.
MIN. MAIL ORDER UK: No minimum charge* *MIN. VALUE EC:* Nmc
CAT. COST: Sae *W/SALE or RETAIL:* Both *CREDIT CARDS:* Visa
SPECIALITIES: Roses. Wide general range, dwarf Conifers, Heather, Azalea, Rhododendron, Shrubs, Alpines, Fruit, hardy Herbaceous & Spring & Summer bedding. *Note: mail order for bush roses only. *MAP PAGE:* **10**

GIsl **Island Plants, The Old Manse, Knock, Point, Isle of Lewis, HS2 0BW**
TEL: (01851) 870281 *CONTACT:* Mr D Ferris
◆ *OPENING TIMES:* Every afternoon ex. Sun.
MIN. MAIL ORDER UK: No minimum charge *MIN. VALUE EC:* Nmc
CAT. COST: 1 x 1st class *W/SALE or RETAIL:* Retail *CREDIT CARDS:* None
SPECIALITIES: Hebe & New Zealand plants esp. for coastal regions. *MAP PAGE:* **10**

GLil **Lilliesleaf Nursery,** Garden Cottage, Linthill, Melrose, Roxburghshire, Scotland, TD6 9HU
TEL: (01835) 870415 *FAX:* (01835) 870415 *CONTACT:* Teyl de Bordes
OPENING TIMES: 0900-1700 Mon-Sat, 1000-1600 Sun. In Dec-Feb please phone first.
No mail order
CAT. COST: None issued *W/SALE or RETAIL:* Both *CREDIT CARDS:* None
SPECIALITIES: Epimedium & wide range of common & uncommon plants. *MAP PAGE:* **10**

GMac **Elizabeth MacGregor, Ellenbank, Tongland Road, Kirkcudbright, Dumfries & Galloway, Scotland, DG6 4UU**
TEL: (01557) 330620 *CONTACT:* Elizabeth MacGregor
OPENING TIMES: Please phone.
MIN. MAIL ORDER UK: 6 plants £10.50+p&p *MIN. VALUE EC:* £30.00 + p&p *EXPORT:* Yes
CAT. COST: £1.00 *W/SALE or RETAIL:* Retail *CREDIT CARDS:* None
SPECIALITIES: Violets, Violas & Violettas, old and new varieties. Campanula, Geranium, Penstemon & other unusual Herbaceous *MAP PAGE:* **10**

GMaP **Macplants,** Berrybank Nursery, 5 Boggs Holdings, Pencaitland, E Lothian, Scotland, EH34 5BA
TEL: (01875) 340797 *FAX:* (01875) 340797 *CONTACT:* Claire McNaughton
OPENING TIMES: 1030-1700 daily mid-March-Oct
No mail order
CAT. COST: 4 x 2nd class *W/SALE or RETAIL:* Both *CREDIT CARDS:* None
SPECIALITIES: Herbaceous Perennials, Alpines, Hardy Ferns, Violas & Grasses.
MAP PAGE: **10**

GOrc **Orchardton Nurseries,** Gardeners Cottage, Orchardton House, Auchencairn, Castle Douglas, Kircudbrightshire, DG7 1QL
TEL: (01556) 640366 *CONTACT:* Fred Coleman
OPENING TIMES: 1200-1800 Sun, Mon & Tues Apr-end Oct.
No mail order
CAT. COST: None issued *W/SALE or RETAIL:* Retail *CREDIT CARDS:* None
SPECIALITIES: Unusual Shrubs & Climbers. *MAP PAGE:* **10**

GPot **The Potting Shed, Upper Scotstown, Strontian, Acharacle, Argyll, Scotland, PH36 4JB**
TEL: (01967) 402204 *CONTACT:* Mrs Jo Wells
OPENING TIMES: By appt. only.
MIN. MAIL ORDER UK: £1.80 + p&p *MIN. VALUE EC:* £1.80 + p&p
CAT. COST: 4 x 1st class *W/SALE or RETAIL:* Retail *CREDIT CARDS:* None
SPECIALITIES: Primula. *MAP PAGE:* **10**

GPoy **Poyntzfield Herb Nursery, Nr Balblair, Black Isle, Dingwall, Ross & Cromarty, Highland, Scotland, IV7 8LX**
TEL: (01381) 610352* *FAX:* (01381) 610352 *CONTACT:* Duncan Ross
OPENING TIMES: 1300-1700 Mon-Sat 1st Mar-30th Sep, 1300-1700 Sun June-Aug.
MIN. MAIL ORDER UK: £5.00 + p&p *MIN. VALUE EC:* £10.00 + p&p *EXPORT:* Yes
CAT. COST: Sae + 3 x 1st class *W/SALE or RETAIL:* Retail *CREDIT CARDS:* None
SPECIALITIES: Over 350 popular, unusual & rare Herbs, esp. Medicinal. See also SEED Index.
*Note: Phone only 1200-1300 & 1800-1900. *MAP PAGE:* **10**

◆ **See also Display Advertisements**

Code-Nursery Index

GQui **Quinish Garden Nursery, Dervaig, Isle of Mull, Argyll, Scotland, PA75 6QL**
TEL: (01688) 400344 *FAX:* (01688) 400344 *CONTACT:* Nicholas Reed
OPENING TIMES: By appt. only.
MIN. MAIL ORDER UK: No minimum charge *MIN. VALUE EC:* Nmc
CAT. COST: 2 x 1st class *W/SALE or RETAIL:* Both *CREDIT CARDS:* None
SPECIALITIES: Specialist garden Shrubs & Conservatory plants. *MAP PAGE:* **10**

GRei **Ben Reid and Co,** Pinewood Park, Countesswells Road, Aberdeen, Grampian, Scotland, AB9 2QL
TEL: (01224) 318744 *FAX:* (01224) 310104 *CONTACT:* John Fraser
OPENING TIMES: 0900-1700 Mon-Sat, 1000-1700 Sun.
MIN. MAIL ORDER UK: £10.00 + p&p *MIN. VALUE EC:*
CAT. COST: Free *W/SALE or RETAIL:* Both *CREDIT CARDS:* Visa, Access, Switch
SPECIALITIES: Trees & Shrubs. *MAP PAGE:* **10**

GSki **Skipness Plants, The Gardens, Skipness, Nr Tarbert, Argyll, Scotland, PA29 6XU**
TEL: (01880) 760201 *FAX:* (01880) 760201 *CONTACT:* Bill & Joan Mchugh
OPENING TIMES: 0900-1800 Mon-Fri, 0900-1600 Sat-Sun, Feb-Nov.
MIN. MAIL ORDER UK: No minimum charge *MIN. VALUE EC:* Nmc
CAT. COST: £1.00* *W/SALE or RETAIL:* Both *CREDIT CARDS:* None
SPECIALITIES: Unusual Herbaceous Perennials, Shrubs, Climbers & Grasses. *Catalogue cost refundable on first order. *MAP PAGE:* **10**

GSpe **Speyside Heather Garden Centre, Dulnain Bridge, Highland, Scotland, PH26 3PA**
TEL: (01479) 851359 *FAX:* (01479) 851396 *CONTACT:* D & B Lambie
OPENING TIMES: 0900-1730 7 days a week Feb-Dec with extended summer hours. Closed Jan.
MIN. MAIL ORDER UK: No minimum charge *MIN. VALUE EC:* Nmc
CAT. COST: £2.25 inc. p&p *W/SALE or RETAIL:* Retail *CREDIT CARDS:* Visa, AmEx, Access, Switch
SPECIALITIES: Heathers. *MAP PAGE:* **10**

GTou **Tough Alpine Nursery, Westhaybogs, Tough, Alford, Aberdeenshire, Scotland, AB33 8DU**
TEL: (01975) 562783 *FAX:* (01975) 563561 *CONTACT:* Fred & Monika Carrie
OPENING TIMES: 1st Mar-31st Oct. Please check first.
MIN. MAIL ORDER UK: £10.00 + p&p *MIN. VALUE EC:* £10.00 + p&p *EXPORT:* Yes
CAT. COST: 3 x 2nd class *W/SALE or RETAIL:* Both *CREDIT CARDS:* None
SPECIALITIES: Alpines *MAP PAGE:* **10**

GTro **Tropic House, Langford Nursery, Carty Port, Newton Stewart, Wigtownshire, Scotland, DG8 6AY**
TEL: (01671) 402485, (01671) 404050 *CONTACT:* Mrs A F Langford
OPENING TIMES: 1000-1700 daily Easter-end Oct. Other times by appt.
MIN. MAIL ORDER UK: No minimum charge *MIN. VALUE EC:* £20.00 + p&p *EXPORT:* Yes
CAT. COST: Sae *W/SALE or RETAIL:* Retail *CREDIT CARDS:* None
SPECIALITIES: Carnivorous. *MAP PAGE:* **10**

GTwe **J Tweedie Fruit Trees,** Maryfield Road Nursery, Maryfield, Nr Terregles, Dumfries, Dumfrieshire, Scotland, DG2 9TH
TEL: (01387) 720880 *FAX:* (01387) 720880 *CONTACT:* John Tweedie
◆ *OPENING TIMES:* Saturdays, 0930-1400 from 21st Oct-Mar. Other times by appt.
MIN. MAIL ORDER UK: No minimum charge *MIN. VALUE EC:*
CAT. COST: Sae *W/SALE or RETAIL:* Retail *CREDIT CARDS:* None
SPECIALITIES: Fruit trees & bushes. A wide range of old & new varieties. *MAP PAGE:* **10**

GWht **Whitehills Nurseries, Newton Stewart, Wigtownshire, Scotland, DG8 6SL**
TEL: (01671) 402049 *FAX:* (01671) 403106 *CONTACT:* Tony Weston
OPENING TIMES: 0830-1630 Mon-Fri or by appt.
MIN. MAIL ORDER UK: £30.00 + p&p *MIN. VALUE EC:* £50.00 + p&p
CAT. COST: 50p *W/SALE or RETAIL:* Both *CREDIT CARDS:* None
SPECIALITIES: Rhododendron, Azalea & Shrubs. *MAP PAGE:* **10**

IBal **Ballydorn Bulb Farm, Killinchy, Newtownards, Co. Down, N Ireland, BT23 6QB**
TEL: (01238) 541250 *CONTACT:* Sir Frank & Lady Harrison
OPENING TIMES: Not open.
MIN. MAIL ORDER UK: £15.00 + p&p *MIN. VALUE EC:* £25.00 + p&p *EXPORT:* Yes
CAT. COST: 4 x 1st class *W/SALE or RETAIL:* Retail *CREDIT CARDS:* None
SPECIALITIES: New Daffodil varieties for Exhibitors and Hybridisers.

IBlr **Ballyrogan Nurseries, The Grange, Ballyrogan, Newtownards, Co. Down, N Ireland, BT23 4SD**
TEL: (01247) 810451 eves *CONTACT:* Gary Dunlop
OPENING TIMES: Only open, by appt., for viewing of national collections of Crocosmia and Euphorbia.
MIN. MAIL ORDER UK: £10.00 + p&p *MIN. VALUE EC:* £20.00 + p&p
CAT. COST: 2 x 1st class *W/SALE or RETAIL:* Both *CREDIT CARDS:* None
SPECIALITIES: Choice Herbaceous & Shrubs. Agapanthus, Celmisia, Crocosmia, Euphorbia, Hardy Geraniums, Meconopsis, Grasses & Iris. *MAP PAGE:* **11**

IBro **Brookwood Nurseries, 18 Tonlegee Road, Coolock, Dublin 5, Rep. of Ireland**
TEL: (00) 353-1-847 3298 *CONTACT:* Jim Maher
OPENING TIMES: For Collection ONLY. 1st Feb-30th Apr.
MIN. MAIL ORDER UK: £5.00 + p&p *MIN. VALUE EC:* £5.00 + p&p
CAT. COST: 2 x 1st class *W/SALE or RETAIL:* Retail *CREDIT CARDS:* None
SPECIALITIES: Hybrid Crocosmia rarities & hardy Cyclamen.

ICar **Carncairn Daffodils, Broughshane, Ballymena, Co. Antrim, N Ireland, BT43 7HF**
TEL: (01266) 861216 *CONTACT:* Mr & Mrs R H Reade
OPENING TIMES: 1000-1700 Mon-Fri. Please phone in advance.
MIN. MAIL ORDER UK: No minimum charge *MIN. VALUE EC:* Nmc *EXPORT:* Yes
CAT. COST: Free *W/SALE or RETAIL:* Both *CREDIT CARDS:* None
SPECIALITIES: Old and new Narcissus cultivars, mainly for show. *MAP PAGE:* **11**

ICrw **Carewswood Garden Centre, Carewswood House, Castlemartyr, Co. Cork, Rep. of Ireland**
TEL: 00 353 (0)21 667283 *FAX:* 00 353 (0)21 667673 *CONTACT:* Gillian Hornibrook
OPENING TIMES: 0900-1800 Mon-Sat & 1200-1800 Sun.
MIN. MAIL ORDER UK: £20.00 + p&p *MIN. VALUE EC:* £20.00 + p&p *EXPORT:* Yes
CAT. COST: £1.00 *W/SALE or RETAIL:* Retail *CREDIT CARDS:* Visa, Access, AmEx
SPECIALITIES: Rare & unusual Shrubs, Alpines & Herbaceous plants. *MAP PAGE:* **11**

IDee **Deelish Garden Centre, Skibbereen, Co. Cork, Rep. of Ireland**
TEL: 00 353 (0)28 21374 *FAX:* 00 353 (0)28 21374 *CONTACT:* Bill & Rain Chase
OPENING TIMES: 1000-1300 & 1400-1800 Mon-Sat, 1400-1800 Sun.
MIN. MAIL ORDER UK: IR£50.00 + p&p *MIN. VALUE EC:* IR£100.00 + p&p
CAT. COST: Sae *W/SALE or RETAIL:* Retail *CREDIT CARDS:* Visa, Access
SPECIALITIES: Unusual plants for the mild coastal climate of Ireland. Conservatory plants. Sole Irish agents for Chase Organic Seeds. *MAP PAGE:* **11**

IDic **Dickson Nurseries Ltd, Milecross Road, Newtownards, Co. Down, N Ireland, BT23 4SS**
TEL: (01247) 812206 *FAX:* (01247) 813366 *CONTACT:* A P C Dickson OBE.
OPENING TIMES: 0800-1230 & 1300-1700 Mon-Thur. 0800-1245 Fri.
MIN. MAIL ORDER UK: One plant *MIN. VALUE EC:* £25.00 + p&p *EXPORT:* Yes
CAT. COST: Free *W/SALE or RETAIL:* Both *CREDIT CARDS:* None
SPECIALITIES: Roses, especially modern Dickson varieties. *MAP PAGE:* **11**

IDun **Brian Duncan, Novelty & Exhibition Daffodils, 15 Ballynahatty Road, Omagh, Co. Tyrone, N Ireland, BT78 1PN**
TEL: (01662) 242931 *FAX:* (01662) 242931 *CONTACT:* Brian Duncan
OPENING TIMES: By appt. only.
MIN. MAIL ORDER UK: £20.00 + p&p *MIN. VALUE EC:* £20.00 + p&p *EXPORT:* Yes
CAT. COST: £1.00 inc p&p *W/SALE or RETAIL:* Both *CREDIT CARDS:* None
SPECIALITIES: New hybrid & Exhibition Daffodils & Narcissus. *MAP PAGE:* **11**

IHar **Harry Byrne's Garden Centre,** Castlepark Road, Sandycove, Dublin, Eire
TEL: 01 2803887 *FAX:* 01 2801077 *E-MAIL:* dburn@indigo.ie *CONTACT:* H Byrne
OPENING TIMES: 0900-1730 Mon-Sat 1200-1730 Sun & Public Hols.
MIN. MAIL ORDER UK: £20.00 + p&p* *MIN. VALUE EC:*
CAT. COST: £1.00 Roses & Clematis only. *W/SALE or RETAIL:* Retail *CREDIT CARDS:* Visa, MasterCard
SPECIALITIES: Roses, Clematis, Patio & Basket Plants. Wide variety of Trees, Shrubs, Herbaceous, Alpines. *Note: mail order to UK & Eire only. *MAP PAGE:* **11**

IHos **Hosford's Geraniums & Garden Centre, Cappa, Enniskeane, Co. Cork, Rep. of Ireland**
TEL: 00 353 (0)2339159 *FAX:* 00 353 (0)2339300 *CONTACT:* John Hosford
OPENING TIMES: 0900-1800 Mon-Sat (except Mon Jul-Sep). 1430-1730 Sun March-Xmas.
MIN. MAIL ORDER UK: £10.00 + p&p *MIN. VALUE EC:* £10.00 + p&p *EXPORT:* Yes
CAT. COST: IR£1.50 *W/SALE or RETAIL:* Retail *CREDIT CARDS:* Visa, Access, AmEx, Diners
SPECIALITIES: Hardy Geraniums, Pelargoniums, Basket & Window box plants, Bedding & Roses. NOTE: Express Courier service available within Ireland. *MAP PAGE:* **11**

ILis **Lisdoonan Herbs,** 98 Belfast Road, Saintfield, Co. Down, N Ireland, BT24 7HF
TEL: (01232) 813624 *CONTACT:* Barbara Pilcher
OPENING TIMES: Most days - please phone to check.
No mail order
CAT. COST: 2 x 1st class *W/SALE or RETAIL:* Both *CREDIT CARDS:* None
SPECIALITIES: Aromatics, Herbs, kitchen garden plants, some native species. Freshly cut herbs & salads. *MAP PAGE:* **11**

IOrc **Orchardstown Nurseries, 4 Miles Out, Cork Road, Waterford, Rep. of Ireland**
TEL: 00 353 51384273 *FAX:* 00 353 51384422 *CONTACT:* Ron Dool
OPENING TIMES: 0900-1800 Mon-Sat, 1400-1800 Sun.
MIN. MAIL ORDER UK: No minimum charge* *MIN. VALUE EC:* Nmc *EXPORT:* Yes
CAT. COST: List £1.50 *W/SALE or RETAIL:* Retail *CREDIT CARDS:* None
SPECIALITIES: Unusual hardy plants incl. Shrubs, Shrub Roses, Trees, Climbers, Rhododendron species & Water plants. *Note: Only SOME plants Mail Order. *MAP PAGE:* **11**

ISea **Seaforde Gardens, Seaforde, Co. Down, N Ireland, BT30 8PG**
TEL: (01396) 811225 *FAX:* (01396) 811370 *CONTACT:* P Forde
OPENING TIMES: 1000-1700 Mon-Fri all year. 1000-1700 Sat & 1300-1800 Sun mid Feb-end Oct.
MIN. MAIL ORDER UK: No minimum charge *MIN. VALUE EC:* Nmc *EXPORT:* Yes
CAT. COST: Free *W/SALE or RETAIL:* Both *CREDIT CARDS:* None
SPECIALITIES: Over 700 varieties of self-propagated Trees & Shrubs. National Collection of Eucryphia. *MAP PAGE:* **11**

ISta **Stam's Nurseries,** The Garden House, Cappoquin, Co. Waterford, Rep. of Ireland
OPENING TIMES: By appt. only.
No mail order
CAT. COST: Sae *W/SALE or RETAIL:* Both *CREDIT CARDS:* None
SPECIALITIES: Bamboos *MAP PAGE:* **11**

ITim **Timpany Nurseries, 77 Magheratimpany Road, Ballynahinch, Co. Down, N Ireland, BT24 8PA**
TEL: (01238) 562812 *FAX:* (01238) 562812 *CONTACT:* Susan Tindall
OPENING TIMES: 1100-1800 Tue-Fri, 1000-1800 Sat & Bank Hols.
MIN. MAIL ORDER UK: No minimum charge *MIN. VALUE EC:* £30.00 + p&p *EXPORT:* Yes
CAT. COST: 75p in stamps *W/SALE or RETAIL:* Retail *CREDIT CARDS:* Visa, Access, MasterCard
SPECIALITIES: Celmisia, Androsace, Primula, Saxifraga, Helichrysum & Dianthus.
MAP PAGE: **11**

LAma **Jacques Amand Ltd, The Nurseries, 145 Clamp Hill, Stanmore, Middlesex, HA7 3JS**
TEL: (0181) 954 8138 *FAX:* (0181) 954 6784 *CONTACT:* Sales Office
OPENING TIMES: 0900-1700 Mon-Fri, 0900-1400 Sat-Sun. Limited Sun opening in Dec & Jan.
MIN. MAIL ORDER UK: No minimum charge *MIN. VALUE EC:* Nmc *EXPORT:* Yes
CAT. COST: Free *W/SALE or RETAIL:* Both *CREDIT CARDS:* Visa, AmEx, Access
SPECIALITIES: Rare and unusual species Bulbs. *MAP PAGE:* **6**

LAyl **Aylett Nurseries Ltd,** North Orbital Road, London Colney, St Albans, Hertfordshire, AL2 1DH
TEL: (01727) 822255 *FAX:* (01727) 823024 *CONTACT:* Roger S Aylett
OPENING TIMES: 0830-1730 Mon-Fri, 0830-1700 Sat, 1030-1600 Sun.
No mail order
CAT. COST: Free *W/SALE or RETAIL:* Both *CREDIT CARDS:* MasterCard, Switch, Visa
SPECIALITIES: Dahlias. *MAP PAGE:* **6**

LBee **Beechcroft Nursery,** 127 Reigate Road, Ewell, Surrey, KT17 3DE
TEL: 0181 393 4265 *FAX:* 0181 393 4265 *CONTACT:* C Kimber
OPENING TIMES: 1000-1700 May-Sept. 1000-1600 Oct-Apr, Bank Hols & Suns. Closed Xmas-New Year & August.
No mail order
CAT. COST: 2 x 1st class *W/SALE or RETAIL:* Both *CREDIT CARDS:* Visa, Access, Switch
SPECIALITIES: Conifers & Alpines *MAP PAGE:* **3**

LBlm **Bloomsbury,** Upper Lodge Farm, Padworth Common, Reading, Berkshire, RG7 4JD
TEL: (0118) 970 0239 *CONTACT:* Susan Oakley
OPENING TIMES: By appt. and NGS afternoons.
MIN. MAIL ORDER UK: £15.00 + p&p* *MIN. VALUE EC:*
CAT. COST: 5 x 1st class *W/SALE or RETAIL:* Retail *CREDIT CARDS:* None
SPECIALITIES: Selected range of good Conservatory and Garden perennials, esp. Geranium, Iris, Salvia, White flowers & borderline-hardy Exotics. *Note: mail order to UK only. *MAP PAGE:* **2**

LBlo **Terence Bloch - Plantsman,** 9 Colberg Place, Stamford Hill, London, N16 5RA
TEL: (0181) 802 2535 *CONTACT:* Mr T Bloch
OPENING TIMES: Mail order only.
MIN. MAIL ORDER UK: £15.00 + p&p* *MIN. VALUE EC:*
CAT. COST: 4 x 1st class *W/SALE or RETAIL:* Retail *CREDIT CARDS:* None
SPECIALITIES: Tropical Plants for the conservatory/home; plants for sub-tropical summer bedding; some rare fruiting species. *Note: mail order to UK only. *MAP PAGE:* **6**

LBow **Rupert Bowlby,** Gatton, Reigate, Surrey, RH2 0TA
TEL: (01737) 642221 *FAX:* (01737) 642221 *CONTACT:* Rupert Bowlby
OPENING TIMES: Sat & Sun pm in Mar & Sep-Oct.
MIN. MAIL ORDER UK: No minimum charge *MIN. VALUE EC:*
CAT. COST: 3 x 2nd class *W/SALE or RETAIL:* Retail *CREDIT CARDS:* None
SPECIALITIES: Unusual Bulbs & Corms. *MAP PAGE:* **3**

LBro **Mrs P J Brown, V H Humphrey-The Iris Specialist, Westlees Farm, Logmore Lane, Westcott, Dorking, Surrey, RH4 3JN**
TEL: (01306) 889827 *FAX:* (01306) 889371 *CONTACT:* Mrs P J Brown
◆ *OPENING TIMES:* Open days 1100-1500 Sat 17th & Sun 18th May 1997. Otherwise by appt. (16th & 17th May 1998.)
MIN. MAIL ORDER UK: No minimum charge *MIN. VALUE EC:* Nmc *EXPORT:* Yes
CAT. COST: Sae or 3 x 1st class *W/SALE or RETAIL:* Both *CREDIT CARDS:* None
SPECIALITIES: Bearded, Spuria, Siberian, Pacific Coast, species & Japanese Iris.
MAP PAGE: **3**

◆ See also Display Advertisements

LBuc **Buckingham Nurseries, 14 Tingewick Road, Buckingham, Buckinghamshire, MK18 4AE**
TEL: (01280) 813556 *FAX:* (01280) 815491 *CONTACT:* R J & P L Brown
◆ *OPENING TIMES:* 0830-1730 (1800 in summer) Mon-Fri, 0930-1730 (1800 in summer) Sun.
MIN. MAIL ORDER UK: No minimum charge *MIN. VALUE EC:* Nmc
CAT. COST: Free *W/SALE or RETAIL:* Retail *CREDIT CARDS:* Visa, Access
SPECIALITIES: Bare rooted and container grown hedging. Trees, Shrubs, Herbaceous Perennials, Alpines, Grasses & Ferns.. *MAP PAGE:* **5**

LBut **Butterfields Nursery, Harvest Hill, Bourne End, Buckinghamshire, SL8 5JJ**
TEL: (01628) 525455 *CONTACT:* I Butterfield
OPENING TIMES: 0900-1300 & 1400-1700. Please telephone beforehand in case we are attending shows.
MIN. MAIL ORDER UK: No minimum charge *MIN. VALUE EC:* £30.00 + p&p *EXPORT:* Yes
CAT. COST: 2 x 2nd class *W/SALE or RETAIL:* Both *CREDIT CARDS:* None
SPECIALITIES: Only Pleione by Mail Order. Dahlia for collection. *MAP PAGE:* **6**

LChe **Chessington Nurseries Ltd, Leatherhead Road, Chessington, Surrey, KT19 2NG**
TEL: (01372) 744490 *FAX:* (01372) 740859 *CONTACT:* Jim Knight
OPENING TIMES: 0900-1800 Mon-Sat, 1000-1600 Sun.
MIN. MAIL ORDER UK: No minimum charge *MIN. VALUE EC:* Nmc *EXPORT:* Yes
CAT. COST: 6 x 1st class *W/SALE or RETAIL:* Retail *CREDIT CARDS:* MasterCard, Visa
SPECIALITIES: Conservatory plants esp. Citrus & Passiflora. *MAP PAGE:* **3**

LCla **Clay Lane Nursery,** 3 Clay Lane, South Nutfield, Nr Redhill, Surrey, RH1 4EG
TEL: (01737) 823307 *CONTACT:* K W Belton
OPENING TIMES: 0900-1700 Tue-Sun 1st Feb-30th Jun & Bank Hols. From 1st Jul-31st Aug please telephone.
No mail order
CAT. COST: 2 x 1st class *W/SALE or RETAIL:* Retail *CREDIT CARDS:* None
SPECIALITIES: Fuchsia. *MAP PAGE:* **3**

LCns **The Conservatory, Gomshall Gallery, Gomshall, Surrey, GU5 9LB**
TEL: (01483) 203019 *FAX:* (01483) 203282 *CONTACT:* Marceline Siddons
OPENING TIMES: 1000-1730 Mon-Sat all year; 1400-1700 Sun Apr-Oct.
MIN. MAIL ORDER UK: No minimum charge *MIN. VALUE EC:* Nmc
CAT. COST: 3 x 2nd class *W/SALE or RETAIL:* Retail *CREDIT CARDS:* Visa
SPECIALITIES: Wide range of Conservatory & House plants. *MAP PAGE:* **3**

LCom **Combe Cottage Plants,** 20 High Street, Lambourn, Berkshire, RG17 8XN
TEL: (01488) 72121 *FAX:* (01488) 72121 *CONTACT:* Jenny Winch
OPENING TIMES: 1230-1530 Tue-Fri, 1200-1800 Sat, 1000-1800 Sun, 1st Apr-30th Sep. Also 1200-1800 Bank Hols.
No mail order
CAT. COST: 3 x 1st class *W/SALE or RETAIL:* Retail *CREDIT CARDS:* None
SPECIALITIES: Herbaceous Perennials & Alpines, esp. Hardy Geranium & Campanula. *MAP PAGE:* **2/5**

LCon **The Conifer Garden,** Hare Lane Nursery, Little Kingshill, Great Missenden, Buckinghamshire, HP16 0EF
TEL: (01494) 890624 (11-4), (01494) 862086 (9-6) *FAX:* (01494) 862086
CONTACT: Mr & Mrs M P S Powell
OPENING TIMES: Usually 1100-1600 Tue-Sat & Bank Hol Mons. Please phone first.
MIN. MAIL ORDER UK: No minimum charge *MIN. VALUE EC:*
CAT. COST: 2 x 1st class *W/SALE or RETAIL:* Retail *CREDIT CARDS:* None
SPECIALITIES: Conifers only - over 500 varieties always in stock. *MAP PAGE:* **5/6**

LCot **Cottage Garden Plants,** 9 Buckingham Road, Newbury, Berkshire, RG14 6DH
TEL: (01635) 31941 *CONTACT:* Mrs Hannah Billcliffe
OPENING TIMES: 1000-1700 Tue-Sat Mar-Oct, 1400-1700 Sun & Bank Hols Jun-Jul.
No mail order
CAT. COST: Sae + 1 x 1st class *W/SALE or RETAIL:* Retail *CREDIT CARDS:* None
SPECIALITIES: Wide range of unusual Perennials. *MAP PAGE:* **2**

LCTD **CTDA, 174 Cambridge Street, London, SW1V 4QE**
TEL: (0171) 976 5115 *FAX:* (01432) 820337 *CONTACT:* Basil Smith
OPENING TIMES: Not open.
MIN. MAIL ORDER UK: £10.00 + p&p *MIN. VALUE EC:* £10+p&p *EXPORT:* SO
CAT. COST: Free *W/SALE or RETAIL:* Both *CREDIT CARDS:* None
SPECIALITIES: Hardy cyclamen for the garden & named hellebores. See also SEED Index.

LDea **Derek Lloyd Dean, 8 Lynwood Close, South Harrow, Middlesex, HA2 9PR**
TEL: (0181) 864 0899 *CONTACT:* Derek Lloyd Dean
OPENING TIMES: Mail Order only.
MIN. MAIL ORDER UK: £2.50 + p&p *MIN. VALUE EC:* £2.50+p&p *EXPORT:* Yes
CAT. COST: 2 x 1st class *W/SALE or RETAIL:* Retail *CREDIT CARDS:* None
SPECIALITIES: Regal, Angel, Ivy & Scented Leaf Pelargoniums.

LFis **Kaytie Fisher,** The Nursery, South End Cottage, Long Reach, Ockham, Surrey, GU23 6PF
TEL: (01483) 282304 *FAX:* (01483) 282304 *CONTACT:* Kaytie Fisher
OPENING TIMES: 1000-1700 daily May-Jul, Wed-Fri Mar & Oct, Wed-Sun Apr, Aug & Sep. Oct-Feb by appt. only.
MIN. MAIL ORDER UK: £8.00 min. postage *MIN. VALUE EC:*
CAT. COST: 3 x 1st class *W/SALE or RETAIL:* Retail *CREDIT CARDS:* None
SPECIALITIES: Mainly hardy Herbaceous, Alpines some Shrubs. Old Shrub Roses & Climbing Roses. Nursery 1 mile South East of RHS Wisley. *MAP PAGE:* **3**

LFli **Flittvale Garden Centre & Nursery,** Flitwick Road, Westoning, Bedfordshire, MK45 5AA
TEL: (01525) 712484 *FAX:* (01525) 718412 *CONTACT:* Bernie Berry
OPENING TIMES: 0830-1800 Mon-Sat, 1030-1630 Sun.
MIN. MAIL ORDER UK: £10.00 + p&p *MIN. VALUE EC:*
CAT. COST: 4 x 1st class *W/SALE or RETAIL:* Retail *CREDIT CARDS:* Visa, Access
SPECIALITIES: Fuchsia. *MAP PAGE:* **6**

LFlo **Flora Arcana,** 8 Flitwick Road, Maulden, Bedfordshire, MK45 2BJ
TEL: (01525) 403226 *CONTACT:* Mark Todhunter
OPENING TIMES: 0900-1600 Fri & 1300-1700 Sat Mar-Nov. Please phone first.
No mail order
CAT. COST: 2 x 1st class *W/SALE or RETAIL:* Both *CREDIT CARDS:* None
SPECIALITIES: Digitalis. Also plants for dry gardens & scented plants.

LFox **Foxgrove Plants, Foxgrove, Enborne, Nr Newbury, Berkshire, RG14 6RE**
TEL: 01635 40554 *CONTACT:* Miss Louise Vockins
OPENING TIMES: 1000-1700 Wed-Sun & Bank Hols.
MIN. MAIL ORDER UK: No minimum charge* *MIN. VALUE EC:* Nmc
CAT. COST: £1.00 *W/SALE or RETAIL:* Retail *CREDIT CARDS:* None
SPECIALITIES: Hardy & unusual plants. Alpines & good selection of Saxifraga. Also Galanthus & Auriculas. *Note: mail order for Galanthus only. *MAP PAGE:* **2**

LGan **Gannock Growers, Gannock Green, Sandon, Buntingford, Hertfordshire, SG9 0RH**
TEL: (01763) 287386 *CONTACT:* Penny Pyle
OPENING TIMES: Usually 1000-1600 Thur-Sat Apr-Sept but please ring first.
MIN. MAIL ORDER UK: No minimum charge *MIN. VALUE EC:* £25.00 + p&p
CAT. COST: 3 x 1st class *W/SALE or RETAIL:* Retail *CREDIT CARDS:* None
SPECIALITIES: Unusual & some rare herbaceous plants. *MAP PAGE:* **6**

LGod **Godly's Roses, Redbourn, St Albans, Hertfordshire, AL3 7PS**
TEL: (01582) 792255 *FAX:* (01582) 794267 *CONTACT:* Colin Godly
OPENING TIMES: 0900-1900 Summer, 0900-dusk Winter Mon-Fri. 0900-1800 Sat & Sun.
MIN. MAIL ORDER UK: £2.50 + p&p *MIN. VALUE EC:* £50.00 + p&p
CAT. COST: Free *W/SALE or RETAIL:* Both *CREDIT CARDS:* Visa, Access, AmEx, not for mail orders
SPECIALITIES: Roses. *MAP PAGE:* **6**

LGre **Green Farm Plants,** Bury Court, Bentley, Farnham, Surrey, GU10 5LZ
TEL: (01420) 23202 *FAX:* (01420) 22382 *CONTACT:* J Coke & M Christopher
OPENING TIMES: 1000-1800 Wed-Sat, end Mar-end Oct.
No mail order
CAT. COST: 3 x 1st class *W/SALE or RETAIL:* Retail *CREDIT CARDS:* None
SPECIALITIES: Small Shrubs, Alpines, Sub-shrubs and Perennials. Many uncommon.
MAP PAGE: **2/3**

LGro **Growing Carpets,** Christmas Tree House, High Street, Guilden Morden, Nr Royston, Hertfordshire, SG8 0JP
TEL: (01763) 852705 *CONTACT:* Mrs E E Moore
◆ *OPENING TIMES:* 1100-1700 Mon-Sat 17th Mar-31st Oct. Other times by appt.
MIN. MAIL ORDER UK: £5.00 + p&p *MIN. VALUE EC:*
CAT. COST: 4 x 1st class *W/SALE or RETAIL:* Retail *CREDIT CARDS:* None
SPECIALITIES: Wide range of Ground-covering plants. *MAP PAGE:* **6**

LHil **Brian Hiley, 25 Little Woodcote Estate, Wallington, Surrey, SM5 4AU**
TEL: (0181) 647 9679 *CONTACT:* Brian & Heather Hiley
OPENING TIMES: 0900-1700 Wed-Sat (ex Bank Hols). Please check beforehand.
MIN. MAIL ORDER UK: No minimum charge *MIN. VALUE EC:* Nmc
CAT. COST: 3 x 1st class *W/SALE or RETAIL:* Retail *CREDIT CARDS:* None
SPECIALITIES: Penstemon, Salvia, Canna, Pelargoniums, tender & unusual plants.
MAP PAGE: **3**

LHol **Hollington Nurseries, Woolton Hill, Newbury, Berkshire, RG20 9XT**
TEL: (01635) 253908 *FAX:* (01635) 254990 *E-MAIL:* hnherbs@netcomuk.co.uk
CONTACT: S & J Hopkinson
OPENING TIMES: 1000-1700 Mon-Sat, 1100-1700 Sun & Bank Hols Mar-Sep. Please enquire for winter hours.
MIN. MAIL ORDER UK: No minimum charge* *MIN. VALUE EC:* Nmc
CAT. COST: 3 x 2nd class *W/SALE or RETAIL:* Both *CREDIT CARDS:* Visa, Access, AmEx, Switch
SPECIALITIES: Herbs, Thymes, Old fashioned Roses, Salvia & Lavandula. *Note: Ltd mail order service. *MAP PAGE:* **2**

LHop **Hopleys Plants Ltd,** High Street, Much Hadham, Hertfordshire, SG10 6BU
TEL: (01279) 842509 *FAX:* (01279) 843784 *CONTACT:* Aubrey Barker
OPENING TIMES: 0900-1700 Mon & Wed-Sat, 1400-1700 Sun. Closed Jan & Feb.
MIN. MAIL ORDER UK: No minimum charge* *MIN. VALUE EC:*
CAT. COST: 5 x 1st class *W/SALE or RETAIL:* Both *CREDIT CARDS:* Visa, Access, Switch
SPECIALITIES: Wide range of Hardy & Half-hardy Shrubs & Perennials. *Note: mail order in Autumn only. See also SEED Index. *MAP PAGE:* **6**

LHos **The Hosta Garden, 47 Birch Grove, London, W3 9SP**
TEL: (0181) 248 1300 *FAX:* (0181) 248 1300 *E-MAIL:* 101534.3273@compuserve.com
CONTACT: Ian Toop
OPENING TIMES: Mail order only.
MIN. MAIL ORDER UK: No minimum charge *MIN. VALUE EC:* £20.00 + p&p *EXPORT:* Yes
CAT. COST: 4 x 1st class *W/SALE or RETAIL:* Retail *CREDIT CARDS:* None
SPECIALITIES: Hosta. *MAP PAGE:* **3/6**

LHyd **Hydon Nurseries, Clock Barn Lane, Hydon Heath, Godalming, Surrey, GU8 4AZ**
TEL: (01483) 860252 *FAX:* (01483) 419937 *CONTACT:* A F George & Rodney Longhurst
◆ *OPENING TIMES:* 0800-1245 & 1400-1700 Mon-Sat. Sun during May and by appt. Open Bank Hols.
MIN. MAIL ORDER UK: No minimum charge *MIN. VALUE EC:* £25.00 + p&p *EXPORT:* Yes
CAT. COST: £1.50 *W/SALE or RETAIL:* Both *CREDIT CARDS:* None
SPECIALITIES: Large and dwarf Rhododendron, Yakushimanum hybrids & evergreen Azalea, & Camellias. *MAP PAGE:* **3**

LHyr **Hyrons Trees,** The Green, Sarratt, Rickmansworth, Hertfordshire, WD3 6BL
TEL: (01923) 263000 *FAX:* (01923) 270625 *CONTACT:* Graham Peiser
OPENING TIMES: 0900-1300 Mon-Fri, but please check first. Other times by appt.
No mail order
CAT. COST: 3 x 1st class *W/SALE or RETAIL:* Both *CREDIT CARDS:* Visa, Delta, MasterCard, EuroCard, Switch
SPECIALITIES: Full standard Broadleaved Trees, plus specimen Conifers, Hedging & Topiary - all in containers. *MAP PAGE:* **6**

LIck **Lower Icknield Farm Nurseries,** Meadle, Princes Risborough, Aylesbury, Buckinghamshire, HP17 9TX
TEL: (01844) 343436 *CONTACT:* S Baldwin
◆ *OPENING TIMES:* 0900-1730 daily ex. Xmas-New Year
No mail order
CAT. COST: Sae for Argy. list *W/SALE or RETAIL:* Retail *CREDIT CARDS:* None
SPECIALITIES: Argyranthemum. Patio & Basket plants. Tender & hardy Perennials
MAP PAGE: **6**

LIri **The Iris Garden,** 47 Station Road, New Barnet, Hertfordshire, EN5 1PR
TEL: (0181) 441 1300 *FAX:* (0181) 441 1300 *CONTACT:* Clive Russell
◆ *OPENING TIMES:* Show Garden by appt. only at: Roan Cottage, Dukes Kiln Drive, Gerrards Cross, Bucks SL9 7HD.*
MIN. MAIL ORDER UK: £15.00 + p&p *MIN. VALUE EC:*
CAT. COST: £1 full colour *W/SALE or RETAIL:* Retail *CREDIT CARDS:* None
SPECIALITIES: Modern Tall Bearded Iris from breeders in UK, USA, France & Australia. *Tel. for Garden appt. (01753) 884308 after 1700.

LKna **Knap Hill & Slocock Nurseries, Barrs Lane, Knaphill, Woking, Surrey, GU21 2JW**
TEL: (01483) 481214/5 *FAX:* (01483) 797261 *CONTACT:* Mrs Joy West
OPENING TIMES: 0900-1700 Mon-Fri by appt. only
MIN. MAIL ORDER UK: No minimum charge *MIN. VALUE EC:* Nmc *EXPORT:* Yes
CAT. COST: 3 x 1st class *W/SALE or RETAIL:* Both *CREDIT CARDS:* Visa, Access
SPECIALITIES: Wide variety of Rhododendron & Azalea. *MAP PAGE:* **3**

LKoh **Kohli Memorial Botanic Garden Nursery,** 81 Parlaunt Road, Slough, Berkshire, SL3 8BE
TEL: (01753) 542823 *CONTACT:* Chris Chadwell
OPENING TIMES: Most days May-Sep by appt. only. Occasional openings 1998.
No mail order
CAT. COST: None issued *W/SALE or RETAIL:* Retail *CREDIT CARDS:* None
SPECIALITIES: Himalayan species wild collected & Tibetan Medicinal plants. *MAP PAGE:* **6**

LLew **Michael Lewington Gardener - Plantsman,** 12a Tredown Road, Sydenham, London, SE26 5QH
TEL: 0181-778 4201 *CONTACT:* Michael Lewington
OPENING TIMES: May-Oct by appt. only.
No mail order
CAT. COST: 3 x 1st class *W/SALE or RETAIL:* Both *CREDIT CARDS:* None
SPECIALITIES: Datura & Brugmansia. Rare Perennials, Shrubs & Conservatory plants.
MAP PAGE: **3**

LLin **Lincluden Nursery, Bisley Green, Bisley, Woking, Surrey, GU24 9EN**
TEL: (01483) 797005 *FAX:* (01483) 474015 *CONTACT:* Mr & Mrs J A Tilbury
◆ *OPENING TIMES:* 0930-1630 Mon-Sat all year. 1000-1500 Sun & Bank Hols Easter-end Sept.
MIN. MAIL ORDER UK: No minimum charge *MIN. VALUE EC:* Nmc *EXPORT:* Yes
CAT. COST: 3 x 1st class *W/SALE or RETAIL:* Both *CREDIT CARDS:* Visa, MasterCard
SPECIALITIES: Dwarf, slow-growing & unusual Conifers. *MAP PAGE:* **3**

LLWP **L W Plants,** 23 Wroxham Way, Harpenden, Hertfordshire, AL5 4PP
TEL: (01582) 768467 *CONTACT:* Mrs M Easter
OPENING TIMES: 1000-1700 most days, but please phone first.
MIN. MAIL ORDER UK: £15 + p&p* *MIN. VALUE EC:*
CAT. COST: A5 Sae + 4 x 2nd class* *W/SALE or RETAIL:* Retail *CREDIT CARDS:* None
SPECIALITIES: Unusual Hardy Perennials & Herbs. Especially Diascia, Penstemon & Thymus. National Collection of Thymus. *Note:mail order to UK only, late Sept-April. *Sae for list.
MAP PAGE: **6**

LMer **Merrist Wood Plant Shop,** Merrist Wood College, Worplesdon, Guildford, Surrey, GU3 3PE
TEL: (01483) 232424 *FAX:* (01483) 236518 *CONTACT:* Danny O'Shaughnessy
OPENING TIMES: 0900-1700 Mon-Fri.
No mail order
CAT. COST: *W/SALE or RETAIL:* Both *CREDIT CARDS:* Visa, Access
SPECIALITIES: *MAP PAGE:* **3**

LMil **Millais Nurseries, Crosswater Lane, Churt, Farnham, Surrey, GU10 2JN**
TEL: (01252) 792698 *FAX:* (01252) 792526 *CONTACT:* David Millais
◆ *OPENING TIMES:* 1000-1300 & 1400-1700 Tue-Fri. Sats Mar, Apr, Oct & Nov. Also daily in May.
MIN. MAIL ORDER UK: £25.00 + p&p *MIN. VALUE EC:* £60.00 + p&p *EXPORT:* Yes
CAT. COST: 4 x 1st class *W/SALE or RETAIL:* Both *CREDIT CARDS:* Visa, Access
SPECIALITIES: Rhododendron & Azalea. *MAP PAGE:* **2/3**

LMor **Morehavens,** 28 Denham Lane, Gerrards Cross, Buckinghamshire, SL9 0EX
TEL: (01494) 871563 *CONTACT:* B Farmer
OPENING TIMES: Only for collection.
MIN. MAIL ORDER UK: £10.00 incl. p&p *MIN. VALUE EC:*
CAT. COST: Free *W/SALE or RETAIL:* Both *CREDIT CARDS:* None
SPECIALITIES: Camomile 'Treneague'. *MAP PAGE:* **6**

LNet **Nettletons Nursery,** Ivy Mill Lane, Godstone, Surrey, RH9 8NF
TEL: (01883) 742426 *FAX:* (01883) 742426 *CONTACT:* Jonathan Nettleton
◆ *OPENING TIMES:* 0900-1300 & 1400-1700 Mon Tue Thu-Sat.
No mail order
CAT. COST: 2 x 1st class *W/SALE or RETAIL:* Both *CREDIT CARDS:* Visa, Access
SPECIALITIES: Trees & Shrubs. Especially Conifers, Azalea, Camellia, Rhododendron, Climbers. 100 Japanese Acer. 27 Wisteria. *MAP PAGE:* **3**

LPal **The Palm Centre, 563 Upper Richmond Road West, London, SW14 7ED**
OPENING TIMES: 1000-1800 daily.
MIN. MAIL ORDER UK: £10.00 + p&p *MIN. VALUE EC:* £10.00 + p&p *EXPORT:* Yes
CAT. COST: £1.95 *W/SALE or RETAIL:* Both *CREDIT CARDS:* Visa, MasterCard
SPECIALITIES: Palms & Cycads, exotic & sub-tropical, hardy, half-hardy & tropical. Seedlings to mature trees. Colour Catalogue for Palms & Cycads £1.95. *MAP PAGE:* **3/6**

LPan **Pantiles Nurseries Ltd, Almners Road, Lyne, Chertsey, Surrey, KT16 0BJ**
TEL: (01932) 872195 *FAX:* (01932) 874030 *CONTACT:* Brendan Gallagher
◆ *OPENING TIMES:* 0900-1730 Mon-Sat, 0900-1700 Sun.
MIN. MAIL ORDER UK: £100.00 + p&p *MIN. VALUE EC:* £100.00 + p&p *EXPORT:* Yes
CAT. COST: Free *W/SALE or RETAIL:* Both *CREDIT CARDS:* Visa, Switch, MasterCard
SPECIALITIES: Large Trees, Shrubs & Climbers in containers. Australasian & other unusual plants. *MAP PAGE:* **3**

LPBA **Paul Bromfield - Aquatics, Maydencroft Lane, Gosmore, Hitchin, Hertfordshire, SG4 7QD**
TEL: (01462) 457399 *FAX:* (01462) 422652 *CONTACT:* P Bromfield
OPENING TIMES: 0900-1300 & 1400-1730 daily Feb-Oct. 1000-1300 Sat-Sun Nov-Jan.
MIN. MAIL ORDER UK: £5.00 + p&p *MIN. VALUE EC:* £50.00 + p&p *EXPORT:* Yes
CAT. COST: 50p *W/SALE or RETAIL:* Both *CREDIT CARDS:* None
SPECIALITIES: Water Lilies, Marginals & Bog. *MAP PAGE:* **6**

LPen **Penstemons by Colour, 76 Grove Avenue, Hanwell, London, W7 3ES**
TEL: (0181) 840 3199 *FAX:* (0181) 840 6415 *CONTACT:* Debra Hughes
OPENING TIMES: Any time by appt.
MIN. MAIL ORDER UK: £5.00 + p&p *MIN. VALUE EC:* £10.00 + p&p *EXPORT:* Yes
CAT. COST: Free *W/SALE or RETAIL:* Retail *CREDIT CARDS:* None
SPECIALITIES: Penstemons. *MAP PAGE:* **3/6**

LPlm **A J Palmer & Son, Denham Court Nursery, Denham Court Drive, Denham, Uxbridge, Middlesex, UB9 5PG**
TEL: (01895) 832035 *FAX:* (01895) 832035 *CONTACT:* Sheila Palmer
OPENING TIMES: 0900-dusk daily Jul-Oct, Rose field viewing. 0900-1700 Mon-Sat, 1000-1300 Sun Nov. Dec-Jun phone.
MIN. MAIL ORDER UK: No minimum charge *MIN. VALUE EC:* Nmc
CAT. COST: Free *W/SALE or RETAIL:* Both *CREDIT CARDS:* None
SPECIALITIES: Roses. *MAP PAGE:* **6**

LPri **Priorswood Clematis, Priorswood, Widbury Hill, Ware, Hertfordshire, SG12 7QH**
TEL: (01920) 461543 *FAX:* (01920) 461543 *CONTACT:* G S Greenway
OPENING TIMES: 0800-1700 Tue-Sun & Bank Hol Mondays.
MIN. MAIL ORDER UK: £8.75 + p&p *MIN. VALUE EC:* £10.00 + p&p *EXPORT:* Yes
CAT. COST: 4 x 1st class *W/SALE or RETAIL:* Both *CREDIT CARDS:* Visa, Access
SPECIALITIES: Clematis & other climbing plants. Lonicera, Parthenocissus, Solanum, Passiflora, Vitis etc. *MAP PAGE:* **6**

LPVe **Planta Vera, Lyne Hill Nursery, Farm Close, Lyne Crossing Road, Chertsey, Surrey, KT16 0AT**
TEL: (01932) 563011 *FAX:* (01932) 563011 *CONTACT:* Morris May
OPENING TIMES: Bank Hols & last weekend every month Apr-Sept incl. Otherwise by appt.
MIN. MAIL ORDER UK: £24.00 (12 plants) *MIN. VALUE EC:* £24 (12 plants) *EXPORT:* Yes
CAT. COST: 5 x 2nd class *W/SALE or RETAIL:* Both *CREDIT CARDS:* None
SPECIALITIES: Largest Viola collection in the world (415 named Violas & Violettas). NCCPG status (provisional). *MAP PAGE:* **3**

LRHS **Wisley Plant Centre,** RHS Garden, Wisley, Woking, Surrey, GU23 6QB
TEL: (01483) 211113 *FAX:* (01483) 212372 *CONTACT:*
◆ *OPENING TIMES:* 1000-1800 Mon-Sat 1100-1700 Sun Summer, 1000-1730 Mon-Sat 1000-1600 Sun Winter. Closed Easter Sun.
No mail order
CAT. COST: None issued *W/SALE or RETAIL:* Retail *CREDIT CARDS:* MasterCard, Access, AmEx, Switch, Visa
SPECIALITIES: Very wide range, many rare & unusual. *MAP PAGE:* **3**

LStr **Henry Street Nursery, Swallowfield Road, Arborfield, Reading, Berkshire, RG2 9JY**
TEL: 0118 9761223 *FAX:* 0118 9761417 *CONTACT:* Mr M C Goold
OPENING TIMES: 0900-1730 Mon-Sat, 1000-1600 Sun.
MIN. MAIL ORDER UK: No minimum charge *MIN. VALUE EC:* Nmc
CAT. COST: Free *W/SALE or RETAIL:* Both *CREDIT CARDS:* Visa, Access
SPECIALITIES: Roses. *MAP PAGE:* **2/3**

◆ **See also Display Advertisements**

LSur **Surrey Primroses, Merriewood, Sandy Lane, Milford, Godalming, Surrey, GU8 5BJ**
TEL: (01483) 416747 *CONTACT:* Val & Geoff Yates
OPENING TIMES: Not open to the public.
MIN. MAIL ORDER UK: No minimum charge *MIN. VALUE EC:* Nmc
CAT. COST: Sae *W/SALE or RETAIL:* Retail *CREDIT CARDS:* None
SPECIALITIES: Primroses, old named varieties.

LSyl **Sylvatica Nursery,** Crosswater Farm, Crosswater Lane, Churt, Farnham, Surrey, GU10 2JN
TEL: (01252) 792775 *FAX:* (01252) 792526 *CONTACT:* John Millais
◆ *OPENING TIMES:* By appt.
MIN. MAIL ORDER UK: No minimum charge* *MIN. VALUE EC:*
CAT. COST: 4 x 1st class *W/SALE or RETAIL:* Retail *CREDIT CARDS:* None
SPECIALITIES: Sorbus & Woodland Perennials. *Note: mail order to UK only. *MAP PAGE:* **3**

LVer **The Vernon Geranium Nursery, Cuddington Way, Cheam, Sutton, Surrey, SM2 7JB**
TEL: (0181) 393 7616 *FAX:* (0181) 786 7437 *E-MAIL:* mrgeranium@aol.com
CONTACT: Janet, Derek & Philip James
OPENING TIMES: 0930-1730 Mon-Sat, 1000-1600 Sun, 1st Feb-27th July 1997, 1st Feb-26th July 1998.
MIN. MAIL ORDER UK: No minimum charge *MIN. VALUE EC:* Nmc
CAT. COST: £2.00 UK* *W/SALE or RETAIL:* Retail *CREDIT CARDS:* Visa, Access, Switch
SPECIALITIES: Pelargoniums. *NOTE: Illustrated colour Catalogue. £2.50 for overseas. *MAP PAGE:* **3**

LWak **N & J Wake, 27 Clifton Road, Henlow, Bedfordshire, SG16 6BL**
TEL: (01462) 815223 *FAX:* (01462) 815223 *CONTACT:* N K Wake
OPENING TIMES: By appt. only.
MIN. MAIL ORDER UK: No minimum charge *MIN. VALUE EC:* Nmc
CAT. COST: 4 x 1st class *W/SALE or RETAIL:* Both *CREDIT CARDS:* None
SPECIALITIES: Herbaceous Perennials. *MAP PAGE:* **6**

LWoo **Woodland Plants, Creek Cottage, Heath Lane, Thatcham, Berkshire, RG18 3FB**
TEL: CONTACT: Nigel Rowland
OPENING TIMES:
MIN. MAIL ORDER UK: £10.00 + p&p *MIN. VALUE EC:* £20.00 + p£p
CAT. COST: 3 x 1st class stamps *W/SALE or RETAIL:* Retail *CREDIT CARDS:* None
SPECIALITIES: Paeonia, Lilium, shade tolerant Perennials & Rare Bulbs. *MAP PAGE:* **2**

MAld **Alderton Plant Nursery,** Spring Lane, Alderton, Towcester, Northamptonshire, NN12 7LW
TEL: (01327) 811253 *CONTACT:* Tom Hutchinson
OPENING TIMES: 1000-1630 Tue-Sun & Bank Hol Mons. Closed Jan 1997.
No mail order
CAT. COST: 2 x 1st class *W/SALE or RETAIL:* Retail *CREDIT CARDS:* None
SPECIALITIES: Fuchsia. *MAP PAGE:* **5**

MAll **Paul Allanson,** Rhendhoo, Jurby, Isle of Man, IM7 3HB
TEL: (01624) 880766 *FAX:* (01624) 880649 *CONTACT:* Paul Allanson
OPENING TIMES: By appt. only. Closed Dec & Jan.
MIN. MAIL ORDER UK: £10.00 + p&p *MIN. VALUE EC:*
CAT. COST: £1.50 cheque/PO* *W/SALE or RETAIL:* Retail *CREDIT CARDS:* None
SPECIALITIES: Shrubs for seaside locations, west coast & southern England. Particularly Australian, Tasmanian & New Zealand. *Note: English stamps not accepted in IoM. *MAP PAGE:* **4**

MArl **Arley Hall Nursery,** Northwich, Cheshire, CW9 6NA
TEL: (01565) 777479/777231 *FAX:* (01565) 777465 *CONTACT:* Jane Foster
OPENING TIMES: 1200-1730 Tue-Sun 28th Mar-28th Sep. Also Bank Hol Mons.
No mail order
CAT. COST: 4 x 1st class *W/SALE or RETAIL:* Retail *CREDIT CARDS:* None
SPECIALITIES: Wide range of Herbaceous. *MAP PAGE:* **7**

MAsh **Ashwood Nurseries Ltd,** Greensforge, Kingswinford, West Midlands, DY6 0AE
TEL: (01384) 401996 *FAX:* (01384) 401108 *CONTACT:* John Massey & Philip Baulk
OPENING TIMES: 0900-1800 Mon-Sat & 1100-1700 Sun. ex Xmas & Boxing day.
No mail order
CAT. COST: 4 x 1st class *W/SALE or RETAIL:* Both *CREDIT CARDS:* Visa, Access, AmEx
SPECIALITIES: Large range of hardy plants & dwarf Conifers; Lewisia, Cyclamen species (NCCPG Collection Holder for both). See also SEED Index. Note-Mail Order for SEEDS only. *MAP PAGE:* **7**

MAsk **Askew's Nursery,** South Croxton Road, Queniborough, Leicestershire, LE7 3RX
TEL: (01664) 840557 *FAX:* (01664) 840557 *CONTACT:* Mrs Longland
OPENING TIMES: 0900-1800 Mon-Fri Feb-end Sep. 10000-1800 Sat & Sun. Oct-Jan please telephone first.
MIN. MAIL ORDER UK: No minimum charge *MIN. VALUE EC:*
CAT. COST: 3 x 1st class *W/SALE or RETAIL:* Retail *CREDIT CARDS:* None
SPECIALITIES: Fuchsia. *MAP PAGE:* **7**

MAus **David Austin Roses Ltd, Bowling Green Lane, Albrighton, Wolverhampton, West Midlands, WV7 3HB**
TEL: (01902) 373931 *FAX:* (01902) 372142 *CONTACT:*
OPENING TIMES: 0900-1700 Mon-Fri, 1000-1800 Sat, Sun & Bank Hols. Until dusk Nov-Mar.
MIN. MAIL ORDER UK: No minimum charge *MIN. VALUE EC:* £25.00 + p&p *EXPORT:* Yes
CAT. COST: Free *W/SALE or RETAIL:* Both *CREDIT CARDS:* Access, Diners, Switch, Visa
SPECIALITIES: Roses, Paeonia, Iris & Hemerocallis & hardy plants. Also Roses & Herbaceous perennials at Nursery. *MAP PAGE:* **7**

MAvo **Avondale Nursery,** (Off.) 3 Avondale Road, Earlsdon, Coventry, Warwickshire, CV5 6DZ
TEL: (01203) 673662 *CONTACT:* Brian Ellis
OPENING TIMES: 1000-1700 daily Mar-Oct. Other times by appt.
No mail order
CAT. COST: 4 x 1st class *W/SALE or RETAIL:* Retail *CREDIT CARDS:* None
SPECIALITIES: Rare & unusual Perennials, esp. Adenophora, Campanula, Centaurea, Diascia, Leucanthemum & Grasses. NOTE: Nursery at Smith's Nursery, 3 Stoneleigh Road, Baginton, Nr Coventry CV8 3BA. *MAP PAGE:* **5**

MBal **Ballalheannagh Gardens, Glen Roy, Lonan, Isle of Man, IM4 7QB**
TEL: (01624) 861875 *FAX:* (01624) 861875 *CONTACT:* Clif & Maureen Dadd
OPENING TIMES: 1000-1300 & 1400-1700 or dusk if earlier in Winter. Closed w/ends Nov-Mar. Please telephone first.
MIN. MAIL ORDER UK: £10.00 + p&p* *MIN. VALUE EC:* £20.00 + p&p
CAT. COST: £1.50 *W/SALE or RETAIL:* Retail *CREDIT CARDS:* None
SPECIALITIES: Rhododendron & Ericaceous Shrubs. Small number of rare trees and shrubs for callers not in catalogue. *Note: mail order on some items only. *MAP PAGE:* **4**

MBar **Barncroft Nurseries,** Dunwood Lane, Longsdon, Nr Leek, Stoke-on-Trent, Staffordshire, ST9 9QW
TEL: (01538) 384310 *FAX:* (01538) 384310 *CONTACT:* S Warner
OPENING TIMES: 0900-1900 or dusk if earlier Fri-Sun.
No mail order
CAT. COST: None issued *W/SALE or RETAIL:* Both *CREDIT CARDS:* None
SPECIALITIES: Very large range of Heathers, Conifers & Shrubs. *MAP PAGE:* **7**

MBel **Bellhouse Nursery,** Bellhouse Lane, Moore, Nr Warrington, Cheshire, WA4 6TR
TEL: (01925) 740874* *FAX:* (01925) 740672 *CONTACT:* Elaine Soens & Doreen Scott
OPENING TIMES: 1000-1700 Wed-Mon Mar-Oct. 1000-1600 Wed-Mon Feb. Closed Nov-Jan & every Tue.
No mail order
CAT. COST: t£1.00 *W/SALE or RETAIL:* Retail *CREDIT CARDS:* None
SPECIALITIES: Wide range of Herbaceous plants & Shrubs. Good selection of unusual varieties. *NOTE: New telephone no. *MAP PAGE:* **7**

◆ **See also Display Advertisements**

MBlu **Bluebell Nursery, Annwell Lane, Smisby, Nr Ashby de la Zouch, LE65 2TA**
TEL: (01530) 413700 *FAX:* (01530) 417600 *E-MAIL:* castell@bigfoot.com
CONTACT: Robert & Suzette Vernon
OPENING TIMES: 0900-1700 Mon-Sat & 1030-1630 Sun 1st Mar-31st Oct, 0900-1600 Mon-Sat 1st Nov-28th Feb. Closed Xmas/New Year. Mon-Sat, 1030-1630 Sun. Closed 25th Dec-2nd Jan.
MIN. MAIL ORDER UK: No minimum charge *MIN. VALUE EC:* Nmc *EXPORT:* Yes
CAT. COST: £1.00 + 2 x 1st class *W/SALE or RETAIL:* Retail *CREDIT CARDS:* Visa, Access
SPECIALITIES: Uncommon Trees & Shrubs. Display Garden & Arboretum. *MAP PAGE:* **7**

MBri **Bridgemere Nurseries,** Bridgemere, Nr Nantwich, Cheshire, CW5 7QB
TEL: (01270) 521100 *FAX:* (01270) 520215 *CONTACT:* Keith Atkey
◆ *OPENING TIMES:* 0900-2000 Mon-Sat, 1000-2000 Sun summer, until 1700 in winter.
No mail order
CAT. COST: None issued *W/SALE or RETAIL:* Both *CREDIT CARDS:* Visa, Access, MasterCard, Switch
SPECIALITIES: Perennials, Shrubs, Trees, Roses, Rhododendrons & Azaleas, Alpines, Heathers & Houseplants. *MAP PAGE:* **7**

MBro **Broadstone Nurseries,** 13 The Nursery, High Street, Sutton Courtenay, Abingdon, Oxfordshire, OX14 4UA
TEL: (01235) 847557 (day/eve) *CONTACT:* J Shackleton
OPENING TIMES: 1400-1700 Tue, 1400-1800 Sat (except Show days). By appt on other days/times.
No mail order
CAT. COST: 3 x 1st class *W/SALE or RETAIL:* Retail *CREDIT CARDS:* None
SPECIALITIES: Plants for rock garden, scree, troughs & borders. Lime tolerant hardy Alpines, Perennials & unusual plants. *MAP PAGE:* **5**

MBur **Burrows Roses, Meadow Croft, Spondon Road, Dale Abbey, Derby, Derbyshire, DE7 4PQ**
TEL: (01332) 668289 *CONTACT:* Stuart & Diane Burrows
OPENING TIMES: Mail Order only.
MIN. MAIL ORDER UK: £3.00 + p&p *MIN. VALUE EC:* 1 plant + p&p
CAT. COST: 2 x 1st class *W/SALE or RETAIL:* Retail *CREDIT CARDS:* None
SPECIALITIES: Roses

MCad **Caddick's Clematis Nurseries, Lymm Road, Thelwall, Warrington, Cheshire, WA13 0UF**
TEL: (01925) 757196 *CONTACT:* H Caddick
◆ *OPENING TIMES:* 1000-1700 Tue-Sun 1st Feb-31st Oct. 1000-1600 Tue-Sat in Nov. 1000-1700 Bank Hols. Closed Dec & Jan.
MIN. MAIL ORDER UK: £11.00 + p&p *MIN. VALUE EC:* £11.00 + p&p
CAT. COST: £1.00 cheque/PO *W/SALE or RETAIL:* Both *CREDIT CARDS:* Visa, Access, MasterCard
SPECIALITIES: Clematis. *MAP PAGE:* **7**

MCCP **Collectors Corner Plants,** 33 Rugby Road, Clifton-under-Dunsmore, Rugby, Warwickshire, CV23 0DE
TEL: (01788) 571881 *CONTACT:* Pat Neesam
◆ *OPENING TIMES:* By appt. only.
MIN. MAIL ORDER UK: No minimum charge *MIN. VALUE EC:*
CAT. COST: 4 x 1st class *W/SALE or RETAIL:* Retail *CREDIT CARDS:* None
SPECIALITIES: General range of choice Herbaceous Perennials, Grasses & Shrubs.
MAP PAGE: **5**

MChe **Cheshire Herbs,** Fourfields, Forest Road, Nr Tarporley, Cheshire, CW6 9ES
TEL: (01829) 760578 *FAX:* (01829) 760354 *CONTACT:* Mr & Mrs Ted Riddell
◆ *OPENING TIMES:* 1000-1700 daily 3rd Jan-24th Dec.
No mail order
CAT. COST: 20p *W/SALE or RETAIL:* Both *CREDIT CARDS:* None
SPECIALITIES: Display Herb garden & Elizabethan knot garden. See also SEED Index.
MAP PAGE: **7**

MCli **Clipston Nursery,** Naseby Road, Clipston, Market Harborough, Leicestershire, LE16 9RZ
TEL: (01858) 525567 *CONTACT:* Kate Hayward
OPENING TIMES: 1000-1800 daily Mar-Sep.
No mail order
CAT. COST: 2 x 2nd class *W/SALE or RETAIL:* Retail *CREDIT CARDS:* None
SPECIALITIES: Perennials including many unusual varieties. *MAP PAGE:* **5/7**

MCLN **Country Lady Nursery,** Lilac Cottage, Chapel Lane, Gentleshaw, Nr Rugeley, Staffordshire, WS15 4ND
TEL: (01543) 675520 *CONTACT:* Mrs Sylvia Nunn
OPENING TIMES: 1000-1700 Wed-Sun & Bank Hols Mar-Oct. Other times by appt.
No mail order
CAT. COST: A5 Sae + 2 x 1st class *W/SALE or RETAIL:* Retail *CREDIT CARDS:* None
SPECIALITIES: Wide range of unusual Perennials, incl. Hardy Geranium, Campanula, Penstemon. 1 acre show garden. *MAP PAGE:* **7**

MCol **Collinwood Nurseries,** Mottram St. Andrew, Macclesfield, Cheshire, SK10 4QR
TEL: (01625) 582272 *CONTACT:* A Wright
OPENING TIMES: 0830-1730 Mon-Sat 1300-1730 Sun. Closed Sun in Jan-Mar, July & Aug.
MIN. MAIL ORDER UK: No minimum charge *MIN. VALUE EC:*
CAT. COST: 1 x 1st class *W/SALE or RETAIL:* Retail *CREDIT CARDS:* None
SPECIALITIES: Chrysanthemums (Dendranthema). *MAP PAGE:* **7**

MDHE **DHE Plants,** (Off.) Rose Lea, Darley House Estate, Darley Dale, Matlock, Derbyshire, DE4 2QH
TEL: (01629) 732512 *CONTACT:* Peter M Smith
OPENING TIMES: 1000-1700 Tue-Sat, 1030-1630 Sun. Advance telephone call desirable - see note below.
MIN. MAIL ORDER UK: No minimum charge* *MIN. VALUE EC:*
CAT. COST: 2 x 1st class *W/SALE or RETAIL:* Retail *CREDIT CARDS:* None
SPECIALITIES: Alpines; esp. Erodium, Helianthemum, Saxifraga & Sisyrinchium. *Note: mail order Oct-Mar only. Nursery stock at Robert Young GC, Bakewell Rd, Matlock. *MAP PAGE:* **7**

MDun **Dunge Valley Gardens,** Windgather Rocks, Kettleshulme, High Peak, SK23 7RF
TEL: (01663) 733787 *FAX:* (01663) 733787 *CONTACT:* David Ketley
OPENING TIMES: 1030-1800 daily 1st Apr-31st Aug or by appt.
No mail order
CAT. COST: A4 Sae *W/SALE or RETAIL:* Retail *CREDIT CARDS:* None
SPECIALITIES: Rhododendron species & hybrids. Trees, Shrubs & Perennials, some rare & wild collected. Meconopsis & Trillium. *MAP PAGE:* **7**

MEas **Eastfield Country Gardens,** Eastfield, Sherwood Avenue, Hope, Sheffield, S30 2RQ
TEL: (01433) 621750 *CONTACT:* Isobel Anderson
OPENING TIMES: Daily by appt. please, Easter to Oct.
MIN. MAIL ORDER UK: £5.00 + p&p* *MIN. VALUE EC:*
CAT. COST: Sae *W/SALE or RETAIL:* Retail *CREDIT CARDS:* None
SPECIALITIES: Hardy & Tender Perennials: Salvia, Scabious, scented-leaf Pelargonium. *Note: mail order to UK only. *MAP PAGE:* **7**

◆ **See also Display Advertisements**

MECR **English Cottage Roses Ltd, The Nurseries, Stapleford Lane, Toton, Beeston, Nottinghamshire, NG9 5FD**
TEL: (0115) 949 1100 *CONTACT:* Clive Jobbins
OPENING TIMES: Mail Order only.
MIN. MAIL ORDER UK: £4.50 (One rose) *MIN. VALUE EC:* £4.50 *EXPORT:* Yes
CAT. COST: Free *W/SALE or RETAIL:* Both *CREDIT CARDS:* None
SPECIALITIES: All types of Rose tree, some exclusive to English Cottage Roses Ltd.

MFie **Field House Nurseries, Leake Road, Gotham, Nottinghamshire, NG11 0JN**
TEL: (0115) 9830278 *CONTACT:* Doug Lochhead & Valerie A Woolley
OPENING TIMES: 0900-1700 Fri-Wed or by appt.
MIN. MAIL ORDER UK: No minimum charge* *MIN. VALUE EC:* Nmc *EXPORT:* Yes
CAT. COST: 4 x 1st or IRCs *W/SALE or RETAIL:* Retail *CREDIT CARDS:* Visa, Access
SPECIALITIES: Auriculas, Primula, Alpines & Rock plants. *Note: mail order for Auriculas, Primula & Seeds ONLY. See also SEED Index. *MAP PAGE:* **7**

MFir **The Firs Nursery,** Chelford Road, Henbury, Macclesfield, Cheshire, SK10 3LH
TEL: (01625) 426422 *CONTACT:* Fay J Bowling
OPENING TIMES: 1000-1700 Mon, Tue, Thu, Fri, Sat Mar-Sep.
No mail order
CAT. COST: 2 x 1st class *W/SALE or RETAIL:* Retail *CREDIT CARDS:* None
SPECIALITIES: Herbaceous Perennials, some unusual & alpines. *MAP PAGE:* **7**

MFos **Fosse Alpines, 33 Leicester Road, Countesthorpe, Leicestershire, LE8 5QU**
TEL: (0116) 2778237 *FAX:* (0116) 2778237 *CONTACT:* T K West
OPENING TIMES: By appt. only
MIN. MAIL ORDER UK: £8.00 + p&p *MIN. VALUE EC:* £8.00 + p&p
CAT. COST: 2 x 1st class *W/SALE or RETAIL:* Retail *CREDIT CARDS:* None
SPECIALITIES: Alpines including specialist species in small quantities. *MAP PAGE:* **7**

MFry **Fryer's Nurseries Ltd, Manchester Road, Knutsford, Cheshire, WA16 0SX**
TEL: (01565) 755455 *FAX:* (01565) 653755 *CONTACT:* Gareth Fryer
OPENING TIMES: 0900-1730 Mon-Sat & 1030-1630 Sun & 1000-1730 Bank Hols.
MIN. MAIL ORDER UK: No minimum charge *MIN. VALUE EC:* Nmc *EXPORT:* Yes
CAT. COST: Free *W/SALE or RETAIL:* Both *CREDIT CARDS:* Visa, Access, Switch
SPECIALITIES: Extensive Rose Nursery & Garden Centre producing over half a million bushes annually. Rose fields in bloom Jun-Oct. *MAP PAGE:* **7**

MGam **Gamesley Fold Nursery,** Gamesley Fold Cottage, 10 Gamesley Fold, Glossop, Derbyshire, SK13 9JJ
TEL: (01457) 867856 *CONTACT:* Sarah Wood
OPENING TIMES: Most days. Please phone before visiting.
No mail order
CAT. COST: None issued *W/SALE or RETAIL:* Both *CREDIT CARDS:* None
SPECIALITIES: Wild Flowers (British native plants). *MAP PAGE:* **9**

MGan **Gandy's (Roses) Ltd, North Kilworth, Nr Lutterworth, Leicestershire, LE17 6HZ**
TEL: (01858) 880398 *FAX:* (01858) 880433 *CONTACT:* Miss R D Gandy
OPENING TIMES: 0900-1700 Mon-Sat & 1400-1700 Sun.
MIN. MAIL ORDER UK: No minimum charge *MIN. VALUE EC:* £25.00 + p&p
CAT. COST: Free *W/SALE or RETAIL:* Both *CREDIT CARDS:* None
SPECIALITIES: 580 Rose varieties. *MAP PAGE:* **5/7**

MGos ◆ **Goscote Nurseries Ltd, Syston Road, Cossington, Leicestershire, LE7 4UZ**
OPENING TIMES: 0800-1630 Mon-Fri, 0900-1630 Sat, 1000-1630 Sun (1700 closing Apr-Oct).
MIN. MAIL ORDER UK: £10.00 + p&p *MIN. VALUE EC:* £50.00 + p&p
CAT. COST: 4 x 1st class *W/SALE or RETAIL:* Retail *CREDIT CARDS:* Visa, Access, MasterCard, Delta, Switch
SPECIALITIES: Rhododendron, Azalea, Trees, Shrubs, Heathers, Conifers, Alpines, Herbaceous. Especially Ericaceae. *MAP PAGE:* **7**

MGra **Grange Cottage Herbs, 4 Grange Cottages, Nailstone, Nuneaton, Warwicks, CV13 0QN**
TEL: (01530) 262072 *CONTACT:* Alec Duthie
OPENING TIMES: 1000-1700 Fri-Sun Apr-Jun. Other times by arrangement.
MIN. MAIL ORDER UK: £10.00 + p&p *MIN. VALUE EC:* Tba.
CAT. COST: Phone for details *W/SALE or RETAIL:* Both *CREDIT CARDS:* None
SPECIALITIES: Herbs - Culinary, Medicinal & Aromatic. Wild Flowers. *MAP PAGE:* **7**

MGrG **Granby Gardens,** Granby House, 8 Long Acre, Bingham, Nottinghamshire, NG13 8BG
TEL: (01949) 837696 *FAX:* (01949) 837696 *CONTACT:* Maureen Gladwin
OPENING TIMES: 1000-1630 Sun-Wed & Fri, other times please phone first.
No mail order
CAT. COST: W/SALE or RETAIL: Retail *CREDIT CARDS:* None
SPECIALITIES: A wide range of Herbaceous Perennials, Shrubs & Climbers. Some rare & unusual. *MAP PAGE:* **7**

MHar **Harts Green Nursery,** 89 Harts Green Road, Harborne, Birmingham, B17 9TZ
TEL: (0121) 427 5200 *CONTACT:* B Richardson
OPENING TIMES: 1400-1730 Wed Apr-July & Sep. Closed Aug. Other times by appt.
No mail order
CAT. COST: 2 x 1st class *W/SALE or RETAIL:* Retail *CREDIT CARDS:* None
SPECIALITIES: Alpines & Hardy Perennials. *MAP PAGE:* **5/7**

MHay **F Haynes & Partners Ltd,** (Off.) 56 Gordon Street, Kettering, Northamptonshire, NN16 0RX
TEL: (01536) 519836 *CONTACT:* Mr Maple
OPENING TIMES: 0800-1530 daily.
MIN. MAIL ORDER UK: No minimum charge *MIN. VALUE EC:*
CAT. COST: Free *W/SALE or RETAIL:* Retail *CREDIT CARDS:* Access, Diners, EuroCard, MasterCard, Switch, Visa
SPECIALITIES: Roses, especially exhibition & miniature. NOTE: Nursery at Main Street, Slipton, Nr Kettering. *MAP PAGE:* **6/8**

MHel **Heldon Nurseries, Ashbourne Road, Spath, Uttoxeter, Staffordshire, ST14 5AD**
TEL: (01889) 563377 *FAX:* (01889) 563377 *CONTACT:* Mrs J H Tate
OPENING TIMES: 1000-sunset daily.
MIN. MAIL ORDER UK: £2.00 + p&p *MIN. VALUE EC:* £50.00 + p&p *EXPORT:* Yes
CAT. COST: Sae *W/SALE or RETAIL:* Retail *CREDIT CARDS:* None
SPECIALITIES: Carnivorous plants, Cactus & Succulents. *MAP PAGE:* **7**

MHew **Hewthorn Herbs & Wild Flowers, 82 Julian Road, West Bridgford, Nottingham, NG2 5AN**
TEL: (0115) 981 2861 *CONTACT:* Julie Scott
OPENING TIMES: By appt, only.
MIN. MAIL ORDER UK: No minimum charge *MIN. VALUE EC:* £10.00 + p&p
CAT. COST: 3 x 1st class *W/SALE or RETAIL:* Retail *CREDIT CARDS:* None
SPECIALITIES: Native Wild Flowers. Culinary & Aromatic Herbs, Dye Plants, Native Medicinals. All organically grown. *MAP PAGE:* **7**

MHFP **Hill Farmhouse Plants,** Hill Farmhouse, Cottingham, Market Harborough, Leicestershire, LE16 8XS
TEL: (01536) 770994 *CONTACT:* R Cain
OPENING TIMES: 0930-1800 Sats only from 1st Mar-31st Jul & 1st Sep-30th Sep. Other times by appt.
No mail order
CAT. COST: 2 x 1st class *W/SALE or RETAIL:* Retail *CREDIT CARDS:* None
SPECIALITIES: Hardy Geraniums & Cottage Garden plants. *MAP PAGE:* **7/8**

◆ **See also Display Advertisements**

MHig **Highgates Nursery,** 166a Crich Lane, Belper, Derbyshire, DE56 1EP
TEL: (01773) 822153 *CONTACT:* R E & D I Straughan
OPENING TIMES: 1030-1630 Mon-Sat mid Mar-mid Oct. Closed Sun.
No mail order
CAT. COST: 2 x 1st class *W/SALE or RETAIL:* Retail *CREDIT CARDS:* None
SPECIALITIES: Alpines. *MAP PAGE:* **7**

MHlr **The Hiller Garden,** Dunnington, Nr Alcester, Warwickshire, B49 5PD
TEL: (01789) 490991 *FAX:* (01789) 490439 *CONTACT:* David Carvill & Brian Meredith
◆ *OPENING TIMES:* 1000-1700 daily.
No mail order
CAT. COST: 2 x 1st class *W/SALE or RETAIL:* Retail *CREDIT CARDS:* Visa, Access, Switch
SPECIALITIES: Two acre garden displaying Herbaceous Perennials, Old-fashioned & Shrub Roses, & Shrubs. All available for sale during the season. *MAP PAGE:* **5**

MHul **Diana Hull, Fog Cottages, 178 Lower Street, Hillmorton, Rugby, Warwickshire, CV21 4NX**
TEL: (01788) 536574 after 1600 *CONTACT:* Diana Hull
OPENING TIMES: By appt. only.
MIN. MAIL ORDER UK: No minimum charge *MIN. VALUE EC:* Nmc
CAT. COST: Sae or IRC for list. *W/SALE or RETAIL:* Retail *CREDIT CARDS:* None
SPECIALITIES: Pelargonium species. See also SEED Index. *MAP PAGE:* **5**

MInt **Intakes Farm,** Sandy Lane, Longsdon, Stoke-on-Trent, Staffordshire, ST9 9QQ
TEL: (01538) 398452 *CONTACT:* Mrs Kathleen Inman
OPENING TIMES: By appt. only.
No mail order
CAT. COST: None issued *W/SALE or RETAIL:* Retail *CREDIT CARDS:* None
SPECIALITIES: Double, Variegated & unusual forms of British natives & Cottage Garden plants. *MAP PAGE:* **7**

MJac **Jackson's Nurseries,** Clifton Campville, Nr Tamworth, Staffordshire, B79 0AP
TEL: (01827) 373307 *FAX:* (01827) 373307 *CONTACT:* N Jackson
OPENING TIMES: 0900-1800 Mon Wed-Sat, 1000-1700 Sun.
No mail order
CAT. COST: 2 x 1st class *W/SALE or RETAIL:* Both *CREDIT CARDS:* None
SPECIALITIES: Fuchsia. *MAP PAGE:* **7**

MJon **C & K Jones, Golden Fields Nurseries, Barrow Lane, Tarvin, Cheshire, CH3 8JF**
TEL: (01829) 740663 *FAX:* (01829) 741877 *CONTACT:* Keith Jones/P Woolley
OPENING TIMES: 0800-1700 daily Mar-Sep, 0900-1600 daily Oct-Feb.
MIN. MAIL ORDER UK: 1 plant + p&p *MIN. VALUE EC:* 1 plant + p&p *EXPORT:* Yes
CAT. COST: £1.00 *W/SALE or RETAIL:* Both *CREDIT CARDS:* not for telephone orders
SPECIALITIES: Roses. *MAP PAGE:* **7**

MLan **Lane End Nursery,** Old Cherry Lane, Lymm, Cheshire, WA13 0TA
TEL: (01925) 752618 *FAX:* (01925) 752618 *E-MAIL:* sawyer@laneend.u-net.com
CONTACT: I Sawyer
OPENING TIMES: 0930-1800 Thu-Tue Feb-Dec.
No mail order
CAT. COST: None issued *W/SALE or RETAIL:* Retail *CREDIT CARDS:* None
SPECIALITIES: Award of Garden Merit plants with a wide range of choice & unusual Shrubs, Trees, Perennials & Ferns. *MAP PAGE:* **7**

MLea **Lea Rhododendron Gardens Ltd, Lea, Matlock, Derbyshire, DE4 5GH**
TEL: (01629) 534380/534260 *FAX:* (01629) 534260 *CONTACT:* Jon Tye
OPENING TIMES: 1000-1900 daily.
MIN. MAIL ORDER UK: £15.00 + p&p *MIN. VALUE EC:* £15.00 + p&p *EXPORT:* Yes
CAT. COST: 30p + Sae *W/SALE or RETAIL:* Retail *CREDIT CARDS:* None
SPECIALITIES: Rhododendron, Azalea & Kalmia. *MAP PAGE:* **7**

MLLN **Lodge Lane Nursery & Gardens,** Lodge Lane, Dutton, Nr Warrington, Cheshire, WA4 4HP
TEL: (01928) 713718 *CONTACT:* Rod or Diane Casey
OPENING TIMES: 1000-1700 Wed-Sun & Bank Hols, 1300-1700 Tue mid Mar-early Oct.
No mail order
CAT. COST: 2 x 1st class *W/SALE or RETAIL:* Retail *CREDIT CARDS:* None
SPECIALITIES: Unusual hardy & tender Perennials, Herbs & Shrubs. *MAP PAGE:* **7**

MLsm **Landsmith,** 18 Green Platt, Cotgrave, Nottingham, Nottinghamshire, NG12 3HZ
TEL: (0115) 989 2405 *CONTACT:* Linda Smith
OPENING TIMES: By appt. only for collection of postal or telephone orders.
MIN. MAIL ORDER UK: No minimum charge* *MIN. VALUE EC:*
CAT. COST: Sae + 2 x 1st class *W/SALE or RETAIL:* Retail *CREDIT CARDS:* None
SPECIALITIES: Hardy Perennials, many unusual, esp. Digitalis. *Note: mail order to UK only.
MAP PAGE: **7**

MMat **Mattock's Roses, The Rose Nurseries, Nuneham Courtenay, Oxford, Oxfordshire, OX44 9PY**
TEL: (01865) 343265 *FAX:* (01865) 343267 *CONTACT:* Mr Mark W Mattock
◆ *OPENING TIMES:* 0900-1730 Mon-Sat, 1100-1700 Sun. Closes 1700 Nov-Feb.
MIN. MAIL ORDER UK: No minimum charge *MIN. VALUE EC:* Nmc *EXPORT:* Yes
CAT. COST: Free *W/SALE or RETAIL:* Both *CREDIT CARDS:* Visa, MasterCard
SPECIALITIES: Roses. *MAP PAGE:* **5**

MMea **Mears Ashby Nurseries Ltd,** Glebe House, Glebe Road, Mears Ashby, Northamptonshire, NN6 0DL
TEL: (01604) 812371/811811 *FAX:* (01604) 812353 *E-MAIL:* 106612.1047@compuserve.com
CONTACT: John B & J E Gaggini
OPENING TIMES: 0800-1700 Mon-Fri (Wholesale & Retail). 0930-1730 Sat & Sun (Retail only).
No mail order
CAT. COST: * *W/SALE or RETAIL:* Both *CREDIT CARDS:* Visa, Access, Switch, MasterCard, Diners
SPECIALITIES: Specialist growers of container Trees, Shrubs, Conifers & Fruit, esp. Wisteria.
*Note: Please state Retail or W/sale Catalogue. *MAP PAGE:* **5/6**

MMil **Mill Hill Plants,** Mill Hill House, Elston Lane, East Stoke, Newark, Nottinghamshire, NG23 5QJ
TEL: (01636) 525460 *CONTACT:* G M Gregory
◆ *OPENING TIMES:* 1000-1800 Wed-Sun & Bank Hols Mar-Sep, Fri-Sun in Oct & by appt.
MIN. MAIL ORDER UK: No minimum charge* *MIN. VALUE EC:*
CAT. COST: Sae for Iris list. *W/SALE or RETAIL:* Retail *CREDIT CARDS:* None
SPECIALITIES: Hardy Perennials - many unusual & Bearded Iris. *Note: mail order Iris only, UK only. *MAP PAGE:* **7**

MMiN **Millfield Nurseries, Mill Lane, South Leverton, Nr Retford, Nottinghamshire, DN22 0DA**
TEL: (01427) 880422 *FAX:* (01427) 880422 *CONTACT:* Mr S G Clark
OPENING TIMES: By appt. only.
MIN. MAIL ORDER UK: £10.00 + p&p *MIN. VALUE EC:* £25.00 + p&p
CAT. COST: 3 x 1st class *W/SALE or RETAIL:* Both *CREDIT CARDS:* None
SPECIALITIES: Hosta. *MAP PAGE:* **7**

MMor **F Morrey & Son,** Forest Nursery, Kelsall, Tarporley, Cheshire, CW6 0SW
TEL: (01829) 751342 *FAX:* (01829) 752449 *CONTACT:* D F Morrey
OPENING TIMES: 0830-1730 Mon-Sat.
No mail order
CAT. COST: 20p *W/SALE or RETAIL:* Both *CREDIT CARDS:* Visa, Access, Switch
SPECIALITIES: Azalea, Rhododendron, Acer, Camellia, Conifers & ornamental Trees.
MAP PAGE: **7**

MNes **Ness Gardens,** Univ. of Liverpool Botanic Gdns., Ness, Neston, South Wirral, Cheshire, L64 4AY

TEL: (0151) 353 0123 *FAX:* (0151) 353 1004 *E-MAIL:* sorbus@liv.ac.uk *CONTACT:* D Maher
OPENING TIMES: 0930-1700 Apr-Oct, 1000-1600 Nov-Mar daily.
No mail order
CAT. COST: None issued *W/SALE or RETAIL:* Retail *CREDIT CARDS:* Delta, Switch, Visa
SPECIALITIES: Rhododendron, Primula, Meconopsis & Penstemon. *MAP PAGE:* **7**

MNFA **The Nursery Further Afield,** Evenley Road, Mixbury, Nr Brackley, Northamptonshire, NN13 5YR

TEL: (01280) 848808/848539 *FAX:* (01280) 848864 *CONTACT:* Gerald Sinclair
OPENING TIMES: 1000-1700 Wed-Sat & Bank Hol Mons Apr-early Oct. Closed 18th-31st Aug 1997.
MIN. MAIL ORDER UK: £15.00 + p&p* *MIN. VALUE EC:*
CAT. COST: Sae *W/SALE or RETAIL:* Retail *CREDIT CARDS:* None
SPECIALITIES: Hardy Perennials esp. Geranium, Hemerocallis, Aster & Anemone. *Note: mail order Hemerocallis within UK only. *MAP PAGE:* **5**

MNrw **Norwell Nurseries,** Woodhouse Road, Norwell, Newark, Nottinghamshire, NG23 6JX

TEL: (01636) 636337 *CONTACT:* Dr Andrew Ward
◆ *OPENING TIMES:* 1000-1700 daily exc. Sat & Mon (except May & Jun Tue-Sun). Aug & 20th Oct-1st Mar by appt.
MIN. MAIL ORDER UK: £10.00 + p&p *MIN. VALUE EC:*
CAT. COST: 3 x 1st class *W/SALE or RETAIL:* Both *CREDIT CARDS:* None
SPECIALITIES: New nursery with increasing range of unusual & choice herbaceous Perennials & Alpines. Esp. Penstemon, hardy Geranium, Campanula, Primula & Grasses. *MAP PAGE:* **7**

MOke **Okell's Nurseries,** Duddon Heath, Nr Tarporley, Cheshire, CW6 0EP

TEL: (01829) 741512 *FAX:* (01829) 741587 *CONTACT:* Gary & Donna Okell
OPENING TIMES: 0900-1730 daily.
No mail order
CAT. COST: Free *W/SALE or RETAIL:* Both *CREDIT CARDS:* Visa, Access
SPECIALITIES: Heathers. *MAP PAGE:* **7**

MOne **One House Nursery,** Buxton New Road, Macclesfield, Cheshire, SK11 0AD

TEL: (01625) 427087 *CONTACT:* Miss J L Baylis
◆ *OPENING TIMES:* 1000-1700 daily.
MIN. MAIL ORDER UK: No minimum charge* *MIN. VALUE EC:*
CAT. COST: 3 x 1st class *W/SALE or RETAIL:* Retail *CREDIT CARDS:* None
SPECIALITIES: Alpines & Perennials. Good range of Primula, Sempervivum, Dwarf Rhododendron, Dwarf Conifers, Bulbs & Gentians *Note: mail order for Sempervivum only. *MAP PAGE:* **7**

MPhe **Phedar Nursery, Bunkers Hill, Romiley, Stockport, Cheshire, SK6 3DS**

TEL: (0161) 430 3772 *FAX:* (0161) 430 3772 *CONTACT:* Will McLewin
OPENING TIMES: Frequent, esp. in Spring but very irregular. Please telephone to arrange appt.
MIN. MAIL ORDER UK: No minimum charge *MIN. VALUE EC:* Nmc *EXPORT:* Yes*
CAT. COST: A5 Sae + 1 x 1st class *W/SALE or RETAIL:* Both *CREDIT CARDS:* None
SPECIALITIES: Helleborus, Paeonia, Erythronium. *Note: exports subject to destination. See also SEED Index. *MAP PAGE:* **7/9**

MPla **E L F Plants,** Cramden Nursery, Harborough Road North, Northampton, Northamptonshire, NN2 8LU

TEL: (01604) 846246 Eve. *CONTACT:* E L Fincham-Nichols
OPENING TIMES: 1000-1700 Thu-Sat ex Nov, Dec & Jan.
No mail order
CAT. COST: 3 x 1st class *W/SALE or RETAIL:* Retail *CREDIT CARDS:* None
SPECIALITIES: Dwarf and slow growing Shrubs & Conifers, many unusual. Some Alpines, Daphne & Heathers. *MAP PAGE:* **5**

MRav **Ravensthorpe Nursery, 6 East Haddon Road, Ravensthorpe, Northamptonshire, NN6 8ES**
TEL: (01604) 770548 *FAX:* (01604) 770548 *CONTACT:* Jean & Richard Wiseman
OPENING TIMES: 1000-1800 (dusk if earlier) Tue-Sun. Also Bank Hol Mons.
MIN. MAIL ORDER UK: No minimum charge *MIN. VALUE EC:* Nmc
CAT. COST: 4 x 1st class *W/SALE or RETAIL:* Retail *CREDIT CARDS:* Visa, Access
SPECIALITIES: Over 2,600 different Trees, Shrubs, & Perennials with many unusual varieties. Search & delivery service for large orders - winter months only. *MAP PAGE:* **5**

MRPP **R P P Alpines, 6 Bentley Road, Bushbury, Wolverhampton, West Midlands, WV10 8DZ**
TEL: (01902) 784508 *CONTACT:* R Smallwood
◆ *OPENING TIMES:* 1100-1700 Wed-Sun, Mon & Tue by appt. only. Open Bank Hols.
MIN. MAIL ORDER UK: No minimum charge *MIN. VALUE EC:* £35.00 + p&p
CAT. COST: 2 x 1st class *W/SALE or RETAIL:* Retail *CREDIT CARDS:* None
SPECIALITIES: Rare & choice Alpines from Europe, Himalaya & other regions. A selection of Bulbs & Hardy Perennials. All in small quantities but ever changing. *MAP PAGE:* **7**

MS&S **S & S Perennials,** 24 Main Street, Normanton Le Heath, Leicestershire, LE67 2TB
TEL: (01530) 262250 *CONTACT:* Shirley Pierce
OPENING TIMES: Afternoons only - otherwise please telephone.
No mail order
CAT. COST: 2 x 1st class *W/SALE or RETAIL:* Retail *CREDIT CARDS:* None
SPECIALITIES: Erythronium, Fritillaria, hardy Cyclamen, Iris, dwarf Narcissus & Hepatica. *MAP PAGE:* **7**

MSal **Salley Gardens, 32 Lansdowne Drive, West Bridgford, Nottinghamshire, NG2 7FJ**
TEL: (0115) 9233878 evenings *CONTACT:* Richard Lewin
OPENING TIMES: Mail Order only.
MIN. MAIL ORDER UK: No minimum charge *MIN. VALUE EC:* Nmc *EXPORT:* Yes
CAT. COST: Sae *W/SALE or RETAIL:* Retail *CREDIT CARDS:* None
SPECIALITIES: Medicinal plants, esp. from North America & China. Dye plants. See also SEED Index.

MSCN **Stonyford Cottage Nursery,** Stonyford Lane, Cuddington, Northwich, Cheshire, CW8 2TF
TEL: (01606) 888128 *CONTACT:* F A Overland
OPENING TIMES: 1000-1730 Tues-Sun & Bank Hol Mons 1st Mar-30th Nov.
No mail order
CAT. COST: 4 x 1st class *W/SALE or RETAIL:* Both *CREDIT CARDS:* None
SPECIALITIES: Wide range of Herbaceous Perennials, Diascia, Salvia & Hardy Geranium. *MAP PAGE:* **7**

MSta **Stapeley Water Gardens Ltd, London Road, Stapeley, Nantwich, Cheshire, CW5 7LH**
TEL: (01270) 623868 *FAX:* (01270) 624919 *CONTACT:* Mr R G A Davies (Chairman)
◆ *OPENING TIMES:* Open 0900 Mon-Fri, 1000 Sat, Sun & Bank Hols all year. Please check closing times (Closed Xmas day).
MIN. MAIL ORDER UK: £15.00 + p&p *MIN. VALUE EC:* No minimum charge *EXPORT:* Yes
CAT. COST: £1.00 *W/SALE or RETAIL:* Both *CREDIT CARDS:* Visa, Access
SPECIALITIES: World's largest Water Garden Centre. Full range of Hardy & Tropical Water Lilies, Aquatic, Bog & Poolside plants. Also large general stock. Curators of National Collection of Nymphaea (UK & France). *MAP PAGE:* **7**

MSte **Steventon Road Nurseries,** Steventon Road, East Hanney, Wantage, Oxfordshire, OX12 0HS
TEL: (01235) 868828 *CONTACT:* John Graham
OPENING TIMES: 1000-1630 Wed-Fri, 1000-1700 Sat & Sun. 7th Mar-26th Oct 1997.
No mail order
CAT. COST: 4 x 1st class *W/SALE or RETAIL:* Retail *CREDIT CARDS:* None
SPECIALITIES: Tender & Hardy Perennials. *MAP PAGE:* **5**

◆ **See also Display Advertisements**

MSto **Richard Stockwell, 64 Weardale Road, off Hucknall Road, Sherwood, Nottinghamshire, NG5 1DD**
TEL: (0115) 969 1063 *FAX:* (0115) 969 1063 *CONTACT:* Richard Stockwell
OPENING TIMES: Any time, by appt., for collection of postal or telephone orders only.
MIN. MAIL ORDER UK: No minimum charge *MIN. VALUE EC:* Nmc *EXPORT:* SO
CAT. COST: 4 x 2nd class or 2 x IRC *W/SALE or RETAIL:* Retail *CREDIT CARDS:* None
SPECIALITIES: Very rare climbing species, also dwarf species. Available in small numbers. See also SEED Index. *MAP PAGE:* **7**

MTho **A & A Thorp,** Bungalow No 5, Main Street, Theddingworth, Leicestershire, LE17 6QZ
TEL: (01858) 880496 *CONTACT:* Anita & Andrew Thorp
OPENING TIMES: Dawn to Dusk all year.
No mail order
CAT. COST: 50p + Sae *W/SALE or RETAIL:* Retail *CREDIT CARDS:* None
SPECIALITIES: Unusual plants or those in short supply. *MAP PAGE:* **7**

MTis **Tissington Nursery,** Tissington, Nr Ashbourne, Derbyshire, DE6 1RA
TEL: (01335) 390650 *CONTACT:* Mrs Sue Watkins
OPENING TIMES: 1000-1800 Wed-Sun Mar-Oct & Bank Hols.
No mail order
CAT. COST: 2 x 1st class *W/SALE or RETAIL:* Retail *CREDIT CARDS:* Visa, Access
SPECIALITIES: Perennials, Shrubs & Climbers incl. unusual varieties. *MAP PAGE:* **7**

MTol **Tollgate Cottage Nursery,** Ladbroke, Leamington Spa, Warwickshire, CV33 0BY
TEL: (01926) 814020 *FAX:* (01926) 814020 *CONTACT:* Brenda Timms
OPENING TIMES: By appt. only.
No mail order
CAT. COST: None issued. *W/SALE or RETAIL:* Retail *CREDIT CARDS:* None
SPECIALITIES: Hardy Herbaceous, some unusual. *MAP PAGE:* **5**

MUlv **Ulverscroft Grange Nursery,** Priory Lane, Ulverscroft, Markfield, Leicestershire, LE67 9PB
TEL: (01530) 243635 *CONTACT:* Ted Brown
OPENING TIMES: From 1000 Wed-Sun Mar-Nov. Other times by appt.
No mail order
CAT. COST: None issued *W/SALE or RETAIL:* Both *CREDIT CARDS:* None
SPECIALITIES: Herbaceous & Shrubs, many unusual *MAP PAGE:* **7**

MWar **Ward Fuchsias,** 5 Pollen Close, Sale, Cheshire, M33 3LS
TEL: (0161) 282 7434 *CONTACT:* K Ward
OPENING TIMES: 0930-1800 Tue-Sun Feb-Jun incl Bank Hols.
MIN. MAIL ORDER UK: No minimum charge *MIN. VALUE EC:*
CAT. COST: Free* *W/SALE or RETAIL:* Retail *CREDIT CARDS:* None
SPECIALITIES: Fuchsia. *Includes cultural leaflet. *MAP PAGE:* **7/9**

MWat **Waterperry Gardens Ltd, Waterperry, Nr Wheatley, Oxfordshire, OX33 1JZ**
TEL: (01844) 339226/254 *FAX:* (01844) 339883 *CONTACT:* Mr R Jacobs
OPENING TIMES: 0900-1730 Mon-Fri, 0900-1800 Sat & Sun Summer. 0900-1700 Winter.
MIN. MAIL ORDER UK: No minimum charge* *MIN. VALUE EC:* Nmc
CAT. COST: 75p *W/SALE or RETAIL:* Retail *CREDIT CARDS:* None
SPECIALITIES: General plus National Reference Collection of Saxifraga (Porophyllum). *Note: ltd mail order, please phone for further information and credit card facilities. *MAP PAGE:* **5**

MWhe **A D & N Wheeler,** Pye Court, Willoughby, Rugby, Warwickshire, CV23 8BZ
OPENING TIMES: 1000-1630 daily mid Feb-late Jun. Other times please phone first for appt.
MIN. MAIL ORDER UK: £6.00 + p&p *MIN. VALUE EC:*
CAT. COST: 3 x 1st class *W/SALE or RETAIL:* Retail *CREDIT CARDS:* None
SPECIALITIES: Fuchsia, Pelargonium & Hardy Geranium. *MAP PAGE:* **5**

MWoo **Woodfield Bros,** Wood End, Clifford Chambers, Stratford-on-Avon, Warwickshire, CV37 8HR
TEL: (01789) 205618 *CONTACT:* B Woodfield
OPENING TIMES: 1000-1630 Mon-Fri, 1000-1600 Sat & 0900-1200 Sun for plant collection ONLY.
MIN. MAIL ORDER UK: See list for details *MIN. VALUE EC:*
CAT. COST: Sae *W/SALE or RETAIL:* Both *CREDIT CARDS:* None
SPECIALITIES: Carnations, Lupins & Delphinium. UK Mail Order for Carnations only. *MAP PAGE:* **5**

MYat **R J Yates, The Gardens, Roecliffe Manor, Woodhouse Eaves, Leicestershire, LE12 8TN**
TEL: (0116) 230 3422 *CONTACT:* R J Yates
OPENING TIMES: 0930-1630 Sat & Sun only. Please phone before visit.
MIN. MAIL ORDER UK: £10.00 + p&p *MIN. VALUE EC:* £20.00 + p&p
CAT. COST: Large (A4) Sae *W/SALE or RETAIL:* Retail *CREDIT CARDS:* None
SPECIALITIES: Primula & Kabschia Saxifrages. *MAP PAGE:* **7**

NArc **Arcadia Nurseries Ltd, Brasscastle Lane, Nunthorpe, Middlesborough, Cleveland, TS8 9EB**
TEL: (01642) 310782 *FAX:* (01642) 300817 *CONTACT:* Mrs M E Phillips
OPENING TIMES: Garden Centre 0900-1700 Spring-Autumn, 0900-1500 Winter. Mail Order office 0900-1700 all year.
MIN. MAIL ORDER UK: £7.95 *MIN. VALUE EC:* £7.95 + p&p *EXPORT:* Yes
CAT. COST: 3 x 1st class *W/SALE or RETAIL:* Retail *CREDIT CARDS:* Visa, Access, EuroCard, Switch
SPECIALITIES: Fuchsia. *MAP PAGE:* **9**

NBat **Battersby Roses, Peartree Cottage, Old Battersby, Great Ayton, Cleveland, TS9 6LU**
TEL: (01642) 723402 *FAX:* (01642) 723402 *CONTACT:* Eric & Avril Stainthorpe
OPENING TIMES: 1000-dusk most days.
MIN. MAIL ORDER UK: n/a *MIN. VALUE EC:* No min. charge
CAT. COST: Sae *W/SALE or RETAIL:* Both *CREDIT CARDS:* None
SPECIALITIES: Exhibition Roses. *MAP PAGE:* **9**

NBea **Beamish Clematis Nursery,** Burntwood Cottage, Stoney Lane, Beamish, Co. Durham, DH9 0SJ
TEL: (0191) 370 0202 *FAX:* (0191) 370 0202 *CONTACT:* Colin Brown or Jan Wilson
OPENING TIMES: 0900-1700 daily Feb-Nov.
No mail order
CAT. COST: None issued* *W/SALE or RETAIL:* Both *CREDIT CARDS:* None
SPECIALITIES: Clematis, Climbers, Shrubs & ornamental Trees. *Please phone first for plant availability. *MAP PAGE:* **10**

NBee **Beechcroft Nurseries,** Bongate, Appleby-in-Westmorland, Cumbria, CA16 6UE
TEL: (01768) 351201 *FAX:* (01768) 352546 *CONTACT:* Roger Brown
◆ *OPENING TIMES:* 0800-1800 Mon-Sat, 1100-1800 Sun.
MIN. MAIL ORDER UK: No minimum charge* *MIN. VALUE EC:*
CAT. COST: £2.50* *W/SALE or RETAIL:* Retail *CREDIT CARDS:* None
SPECIALITIES: Hardy field-grown Trees & Shrubs. *Note: mail order Trees Nov-Mar only. *Sae for Tree list only. *MAP PAGE:* **9**

NBir **Birkheads Cottage Garden Nursery,** Birkheads Lane, Nr Sunniside, Newcastle upon Tyne, Tyne & Wear, NE16 5EL
TEL: (01207) 232262 *FAX:* (01207) 232262 *CONTACT:* Mrs Christine Liddle
OPENING TIMES: 1000-1800 Sat & Sun & Bank Hols Apr-mid Oct & by appt.
No mail order
CAT. COST: None issued *W/SALE or RETAIL:* Retail *CREDIT CARDS:* None
SPECIALITIES: Allium, Campanula, Digitalis, Euphorbia, Hardy Geraniums, Meconopsis, Primula & Herbs. *MAP PAGE:* **10**

NBrk **T H Barker & Sons,** Baines Paddock Nursery, Haverthwaite, Ulverston, Cumbria, LA12 8PF
TEL: (015395) 58236 *E-MAIL:* mjsullivan@enterprise.net *CONTACT:* W E Thornley
◆ *OPENING TIMES:* 0930-1730 Wed-Mon all year.
MIN. MAIL ORDER UK: 2 plants + p&p *MIN. VALUE EC:*
CAT. COST: £1.00 (Clematis & Climbers) *W/SALE or RETAIL:* Retail *CREDIT CARDS:* None
SPECIALITIES: Clematis, Lonicera, Passiflora & other climbers; Cottage Garden Plants esp. Hardy Geranium, Aster, Ranunculus, Iris & Viola. Many rare. Most stock grown on the nursery.
MAP PAGE: **9**

NBro **Brownthwaite Hardy Plants,** Fell Yeat, Casterton, Kirkby Lonsdale, Lancashire, LA6 2JW
TEL: (015242) 71340* *CONTACT:* Chris Benson
OPENING TIMES: Tue-Sun 1st Apr-30th Sep.
No mail order
CAT. COST: 3 x 1st class *W/SALE or RETAIL:* Retail *CREDIT CARDS:* None
SPECIALITIES: Herbaceous Perennials & Grasses. *Note: Tel. No. (015242) 71340 after 1800.
MAP PAGE: **9**

NBus **Bush Green Cottage Nursery,** Foxfield Road, Broughton-in-Furness, Cumbria, LA20 6BY
TEL: (01229) 716724 *CONTACT:* Jim Haunch
OPENING TIMES: 1000-1700 Tues, Sun & Bank Hols. Garden open at same time.
MIN. MAIL ORDER UK: No minimum charge *MIN. VALUE EC:*
CAT. COST: 4 x 1st class *W/SALE or RETAIL:* Both *CREDIT CARDS:* None
SPECIALITIES: Hardy Geraniums, Hostas, interesting hardy perennials. See also SEED index.
MAP PAGE: **9**

NCat **Catforth Gardens,** Roots Lane, Catforth, Preston, Lancashire, PR4 0JB
TEL: (01772) 690561/690269 *CONTACT:* Judith Bradshaw & Chris Moore
OPENING TIMES: 1030-1700 15th Mar-14th Sep 1997.
No mail order
CAT. COST: 5 x 1st class *W/SALE or RETAIL:* Retail *CREDIT CARDS:* None
SPECIALITIES: National Collection of Hardy Geraniums. Garden open every day. Over 1500 varieties of Herbaceous plants. *MAP PAGE:* **9**

NCGP **The Cottage Garden Plant Centre,** Seven Acres, Thorn Road, Hedon, North Humberside, HU12 8HN
TEL: (01482) 891434 *CONTACT:* Pat Pinnock
OPENING TIMES: 0900-1700 daily all year
MIN. MAIL ORDER UK: No minimum charge *MIN. VALUE EC:*
CAT. COST: 3 x 1st class *W/SALE or RETAIL:* Retail *CREDIT CARDS:* None
SPECIALITIES: Herbaceous Perennials & Herbs. *MAP PAGE:* **9**

NChi **Chipchase Castle Nursery,** Chipchase Castle, Wark, Hexham, Northumberland, NE48 3NT
TEL: (01434) 230083 *CONTACT:* Suzanne Newell & Janet Beakes
OPENING TIMES: 1000-1700 Thu-Sun & Bank Hol Mons from Easter-mid Oct.
No mail order
CAT. COST: A5 Sae for list *W/SALE or RETAIL:* Retail *CREDIT CARDS:* None
SPECIALITIES: Unusual Herbaceous. Esp. Campanula, Codonopsis, Dianthus, Eryngium, Erysimum, Geranium, Penstemon & Viola. *MAP PAGE:* **10**

NCLN **Crags Lewisia Nursery, Rosley, Wigton, Cumbria, CA7 8DD**
TEL: (016973) 42527 *FAX:* (016973) 42527 *CONTACT:* E & E Parkinson
OPENING TIMES: 1000-dusk daily May-Sep.
MIN. MAIL ORDER UK: £10.00 + p&p *MIN. VALUE EC:* £10.00 + p&p
CAT. COST: 2 x 2nd class *W/SALE or RETAIL:* Both *CREDIT CARDS:* None
SPECIALITIES: Lewisia Cotyledon Crags hybrids. *MAP PAGE:* **9/10**

NCra Craven's Nursery, 1 Foulds Terrace, Bingley, West Yorkshire, BD16 4LZ
TEL: (01274) 561412 *CONTACT:* S R Craven & M Craven
OPENING TIMES: By appt. only.
MIN. MAIL ORDER UK: £10.00 + p&p *MIN. VALUE EC:* £50.00 + p&p *EXPORT:* Yes
CAT. COST: £1.00 *W/SALE or RETAIL:* Both *CREDIT CARDS:* None
SPECIALITIES: Show Auricula, Primula, Pinks, Alpines and specialist Seeds. See also SEED Index. *MAP PAGE:* **9**

NCut Cutting Edge Nursery, Highfield Farm, Knowle Road, off Upper Sheffield Road, Barnsley, Yorkshire, S70 4AW
TEL: (01226) 730292 *CONTACT:* Brian B Cockerline
◆ *OPENING TIMES:* 0900-1700 daily all year round,
No mail order
CAT. COST: 2 x 1st class *W/SALE or RETAIL:* Retail *CREDIT CARDS:* None
SPECIALITIES: Wide selectionof Perennials & Shrubs, many uncommon. *MAP PAGE:* **9**

NDal Daleside Nurseries Ltd, Ripon Road, Killinghall, Harrogate, North Yorks, HG3 2AY
TEL: (01423) 506450 *FAX:* (01423) 527872 *CONTACT:* Messrs Darley & Townsend
OPENING TIMES: 0900-1700 Mon-Sat, 1000-1200 & 1330-1630 Sun.
No mail order
CAT. COST: None issued *W/SALE or RETAIL:* Retail *CREDIT CARDS:* Visa, Access
SPECIALITIES: Many plants & trees not generally available. Container grown Fruit, Apples, Pears & Soft Fruit. *MAP PAGE:* **9**

NDea Deanswood Plants, Potteries Lane, Littlethorpe, Ripon, North Yorkshire, HG4 3LF
TEL: (01765) 603441 *CONTACT:* Jacky Barber
OPENING TIMES: 1000-1700 Tue-Sun 1st Apr-30th Sep.
No mail order
CAT. COST: List 2 x 25p *W/SALE or RETAIL:* Retail *CREDIT CARDS:* None
SPECIALITIES: Pond, Marginals & Bog plants. *MAP PAGE:* **9**

NEgg Eggleston Hall, Barnard Castle, Co. Durham, DL12 0AG
TEL: (01833) 650403 *FAX:* (01833) 650378 *CONTACT:* Mrs R H Gray
OPENING TIMES: 1000-1700 daily
No mail order
CAT. COST: £1.50 + Sae *W/SALE or RETAIL:* Retail *CREDIT CARDS:* None
SPECIALITIES: Rare & Unusual plants with particular emphasis to Flower Arrangers. *MAP PAGE:* **9**

NFai Fairy Lane Nurseries, Fairy Lane, Sale, Greater Manchester, M33 2JT
TEL: (0161) 905 1137 *CONTACT:* John B Coxon
OPENING TIMES: 1000-1730 Wed-Mon Summer, 1000-1600 Wed-Mon Winter. Closed 22nd Dec-2nd Jan 1998.
MIN. MAIL ORDER UK: No minimum charge *MIN. VALUE EC:*
CAT. COST: 4 x 1st class *W/SALE or RETAIL:* Retail *CREDIT CARDS:* Access, Visa
SPECIALITIES: Hardy & tender Perennials, Herbs, Hebe & less usual Shrubs. *MAP PAGE:* **7/9**

NFla Flaxton House Nursery, Flaxton, York, North Yorkshire, Y06 7RJ
TEL: (01904) 468753 *CONTACT:* Mrs H Williams
OPENING TIMES: 1000-1700 Tues-Sun 1st Mar-31st Oct.
No mail order
CAT. COST: 3 x 2nd class *W/SALE or RETAIL:* Retail *CREDIT CARDS:* None
SPECIALITIES: Wide General Range of Shrubs & Herbaceous with many unusual plants. *MAP PAGE:* **9**

◆ See also Display Advertisements

NGar **Gardenscape, (Off.) Fairview, Summerbridge, Nr Harrogate, North Yorkshire, HG3 4DH**

TEL: (01423) 780291 *FAX:* (01423) 780291 *CONTACT:* Michael D Myers
OPENING TIMES: By appt. only.
MIN. MAIL ORDER UK: No minimum charge *MIN. VALUE EC:* £10.00 + p&p
CAT. COST: 3 x 2nd class. Available from Autumn 1997. *W/SALE or RETAIL:* Both *CREDIT CARDS:* None
SPECIALITIES: National Collections of Wood Anemones, Hepaticas & Primula marginata. Also Galanthus, Colchicums & unusual dwarf Bulbs, Ferns, Grasses, Alpines & Perennials.
MAP PAGE: **9**

NGno **Gnostic Garden, PO Box 1ED, Newcastle Upon Tyne, NE99 1ED**

TEL: CONTACT: Dan Gibson
OPENING TIMES: Mail order only
MIN. MAIL ORDER UK: No minimum charge *MIN. VALUE EC:* Nmc *EXPORT:* Yes
CAT. COST: 5 x 2nd class (refundable) *W/SALE or RETAIL:* Retail *CREDIT CARDS:* None
SPECIALITIES: Ethnobotanical plants & seeds. Hardy Subtropical and Tropical.

NGre **Greenslacks Nurseries, Ocot Lane, Scammonden, Huddersfield, Yorkshire, HD3 3FR**

TEL: (01484) 842584 *CONTACT:* Mrs V K Tuton
OPENING TIMES: 1000-1600 Wed-Sun 1st Mar-31st Oct.
MIN. MAIL ORDER UK: No minimum charge *MIN. VALUE EC:* £20.00 + p&p *EXPORT:* Yes
CAT. COST: 4 x 1st class or 2 x IRCs *W/SALE or RETAIL:* Retail *CREDIT CARDS:* None
SPECIALITIES: Unusual & Hardy plants esp. Succulents - Sedum, Sempervivum, Lewisia, Saxifraga & Primula. *MAP PAGE:* **9**

NHal **Halls of Heddon, (Off.) West Heddon Nurseries, Heddon-on-the-Wall, Newcastle-upon-Tyne, Northumberland, NE15 0JS**

TEL: (01661) 852445 *CONTACT:* Judith Lockey
OPENING TIMES: 0900-1700 Mon-Sat 1000-1700 Sun.
MIN. MAIL ORDER UK: No minimum charge* *MIN. VALUE EC:* £25.00 + p&p*
EXPORT: Yes
CAT. COST: 2 x 2nd class *W/SALE or RETAIL:* Retail *CREDIT CARDS:* None
SPECIALITIES: Chrysanthemum & Dahlia. Wide range of Herbaceous. *Note: Mail Order Dahlia & Chrysanthemum only. *EC & Export Dahlia tubers ONLY. *MAP PAGE:* **10**

NHar **Hartside Nursery Garden, Nr Alston, Cumbria, CA9 3BL**

TEL: (01434) 381372 *FAX:* (01434) 381372 *CONTACT:* S L & N Huntley
OPENING TIMES: 0900-1630 Mon-Fri, 1230-1600 Sat, Sun & B/Hols, 1st Mar-31st Oct. By appt. 1st Nov-28th Feb.
MIN. MAIL ORDER UK: No minimum charge *MIN. VALUE EC:* Nmc
CAT. COST: 4 x 1st class or 3 x IRC *W/SALE or RETAIL:* Retail *CREDIT CARDS:* Visa, Access, AmEx
SPECIALITIES: Alpines grown at altitude of 1100 feet in Pennines. Primula, Ferns, Gentian & Meconopsis. *MAP PAGE:* **9/10**

NHaw **The Hawthornes Nursery,** Marsh Road, Hesketh Bank, Nr Preston, Lancashire, PR4 6XT

TEL: (01772) 812379 *CONTACT:* Irene & Richard Hodson
OPENING TIMES: 0900-1800 daily 1st Apr-30th Jun, Thurs & Fri July-Sep. Gardens open for NGS.
No mail order
CAT. COST: W/SALE or RETAIL: Both *CREDIT CARDS:* None
SPECIALITIES: Bedding & Basket plants. Fuchsia, Clematis, Diascia, Penstemon, Argyranthemum, Osteospermum & other Perennials. *MAP PAGE:* **9**

NHed **Hedgerow Nursery, 24 Braithwaite Edge Road, Keighley, West Yorkshire, BD22 6RA**
TEL: (01535) 606531 *CONTACT:* Nigel Hutchinson
OPENING TIMES: 1000-1700 Wed-Sun & Bank Hols.
MIN. MAIL ORDER UK: No minimum charge *MIN. VALUE EC:* Nmc *EXPORT:* Yes
CAT. COST: 4 x 2nd class *W/SALE or RETAIL:* Both *CREDIT CARDS:* None
SPECIALITIES: NCCPG Collection of dwarf Hebe. Saxifraga, Primula, Rhododendron & Conifers. *MAP PAGE:* **9**

NHex **Hexham Herbs,** Chesters Walled Garden, Chollerford, Hexham, Northumberland, NE46 4BQ
TEL: (01434) 681483 *CONTACT:* Susie & Kevin White
◆ *OPENING TIMES:* 1000-1700 Mar-end Oct daily. Please phone for Winter opening times.
No mail order
CAT. COST: £1.50 inc. p&p *W/SALE or RETAIL:* Retail *CREDIT CARDS:* None
SPECIALITIES: Extensive range of Herbs & National Collections of Thymus & Origanum. Wild flowers, Grasses & unusual Perennials, esp. Geranium, Epilobium & Variegated plants.
MAP PAGE: **10**

NHHG **Hardstoft Herb Garden,** Hall View Cottage, Hardstoft, Pilsley, Nr Chesterfield, Derbyshire, S45 8AH
TEL: (01246) 854268 *CONTACT:* Lynne & Steve Raynor
OPENING TIMES: 1000-1800 daily, 1st Mar-30th Sep.
No mail order
CAT. COST: Free *W/SALE or RETAIL:* Retail *CREDIT CARDS:* None
SPECIALITIES: Very wide range of Herb Plants. Over 40 Lavenders & 12 Rosemary. Scented Pelargoniums. *MAP PAGE:* **7**

NHlc **Halecat Garden Nurseries,** Witherslack, Grange over Sands, Cumbria, LA11 6RU
TEL: (015395) 52229 *CONTACT:* Mrs M Stanley
◆ *OPENING TIMES:* 0900-1630 Mon-Fri, 1400-1600 Sun & parties by appointment.
No mail order
CAT. COST: 2 x 2nd class *W/SALE or RETAIL:* Retail *CREDIT CARDS:* Visa
SPECIALITIES: Hosta, Hydrangea, Euphorbia, grey foliage and perennial border plants.
MAP PAGE: **9**

NHol **Holden Clough Nursery, Holden, Bolton-by-Bowland, Clitheroe, Lancashire, BB7 4PF**
TEL: (01200) 447615 *FAX:* (01200) 447615 *CONTACT:* P J Foley
◆ *OPENING TIMES:* 0900-1630 Tue-Sat all year (closed some Fri), 0900-1630 B/Hol Mons, 1300-1630 Easter Sun + 1 Sun in Apr & 1 in May each year.
MIN. MAIL ORDER UK: No minimum charge *MIN. VALUE EC:* Nmc *EXPORT:* Yes
CAT. COST: £1.40 *W/SALE or RETAIL:* Both *CREDIT CARDS:* None
SPECIALITIES: Large general list incl. Primula, Saxifraga, Pulmonaria, Astilbe, Gentiana, Grasses, Hosta & Rhododendron. NOTE: Closed 24th Dec-1st Jan 1998. *MAP PAGE:* **9**

NLak **Lakes' Hardy Plants,** 4 Fearns Building, Penistone, Sheffield, South Yorkshire, S30 6BA
TEL: (01226) 370574 *CONTACT:* Dr P A Lake
OPENING TIMES: 1000-1700 Mon-Sat 1st Mar-31st Oct. Other times by appt. Please phone first if making long journey.
MIN. MAIL ORDER UK: No minimum charge *MIN. VALUE EC:*
CAT. COST: 4 x 1st class/Sae for list *W/SALE or RETAIL:* Retail *CREDIT CARDS:* Visa, Access
SPECIALITIES: Unusual Herbaceous & Cottage garden plants esp. Diascia, Digitalis, Eryngium, Euphorbia & Penstemon. *MAP PAGE:* **9**

NLan **Landlife Wildflowers Ltd,** The Old Police Station, Lark Lane, Liverpool, Lancashire, L17 8UU
TEL: (0151) 728 7011 *FAX:* (0151) 728 8413 *E-MAIL:* info@landlife.u-net-com
CONTACT: Gillian Watson
OPENING TIMES: By appt. for collection only.
MIN. MAIL ORDER UK: £12.80 *MIN. VALUE EC:*
CAT. COST: Sae + 2 x 2nd class *W/SALE or RETAIL:* Both *CREDIT CARDS:* Visa, AmEx
SPECIALITIES: Wild herbaceous plants. See also SEED Index. *MAP PAGE:* **7/9**

NLee **Lees Lane Nurseries, Lees Lane, Dalton, Nr Parbold, Wigan, Lancashire, WN8 7RB**
TEL: (01257) 464601 *FAX:* (01257) 464601 *CONTACT:* M Henshall
OPENING TIMES: 1030-1600 daily, closed Sat 23rd Dec 1996-2nd Jan 1997.
MIN. MAIL ORDER UK: £50.00 + p&p *MIN. VALUE EC:* £500.00 + p&p *EXPORT:* Yes
CAT. COST: 1 x 1st class *W/SALE or RETAIL:* Both *CREDIT CARDS:* None
SPECIALITIES: Lavenders. *MAP PAGE:* **9**

NMar **J & D Marston,** Culag, Green Lane, Nafferton, Driffield, East Yorkshire, YO25 0LF
TEL: (01377) 254487 *CONTACT:* J & D Marston
◆ *OPENING TIMES:* 1350-1700 Easter-mid Sep, Sat, Sun & other times by appt.
MIN. MAIL ORDER UK: £15.00 + p&p *MIN. VALUE EC:*
CAT. COST: 5 x 1st class *W/SALE or RETAIL:* Retail *CREDIT CARDS:* None
SPECIALITIES: Hardy & Greenhouse Ferns only. *MAP PAGE:* **9**

NMen **Mendle Nursery, Holme, Scunthorpe, DN16 3RF**
TEL: (01724) 850864 *FAX:* (01724) 850864 *CONTACT:* Mrs A Earnshaw
OPENING TIMES: 1000-1600 daily
MIN. MAIL ORDER UK: No minimum charge *MIN. VALUE EC:* Nmc
CAT. COST: 2 x 1st class *W/SALE or RETAIL:* Retail *CREDIT CARDS:* None
SPECIALITIES: Many unusual Alpines esp. Primula, Saxifraga & Sempervivum. *MAP PAGE:* **9**

NMGW **MGW Plants,** 45 Potovens Lane, Lofthouse Gate, Wakefield, Yorkshire, WF3 3JE
TEL: (01924) 820096 *CONTACT:* Michael G Wilson
◆ *OPENING TIMES:* 1000-dusk Wed-Sat all year.
MIN. MAIL ORDER UK: £10.00 + p&p *MIN. VALUE EC:*
CAT. COST: 2 x 1st class *W/SALE or RETAIL:* Retail *CREDIT CARDS:* None
SPECIALITIES: Alpines incl. Campanula & Geranium. Bulbs incl. Colchicum & Crocus. Herbaceous incl. Geranium & Iris. *MAP PAGE:* **9**

NMir **Mires Beck Nursery, Low Mill Lane, North Cave, Brough, North Humberside, HU15 2NR**
TEL: (01430) 421543 *CONTACT:* Irene Tinklin & Martin Rowland
OPENING TIMES: 1000-1600 Thur-Sat 1st Mar-31st July. 1000-1500 Thur-Fri 1st Aug-28th Feb & by appt.
MIN. MAIL ORDER UK: £15.00 + p&p *MIN. VALUE EC:* £15.00 + p&p
CAT. COST: 3 x 1st class *W/SALE or RETAIL:* Both *CREDIT CARDS:* None
SPECIALITIES: Wild flower plants of Yorkshire provenance. See also SEED index.
MAP PAGE: **9**

NMos **Stanley Mossop, Boonwood Garden Centre, Gosforth, Seascale, Cumbria, CA20 1BP**
TEL: (01946) 821817 *FAX:* (019467) 25829 *CONTACT:* Stanley & Gary Mossop.
OPENING TIMES: 1000-1700 daily.
MIN. MAIL ORDER UK: No minimum charge *MIN. VALUE EC:* £50.00 + p&p *EXPORT:* Yes
CAT. COST: Free *W/SALE or RETAIL:* Both *CREDIT CARDS:* None
SPECIALITIES: Achimenes, Achimenantha, Eucodonia, Gloxinia (incl. species) & Smithiantha.
MAP PAGE: **9**

NMun **Muncaster Castle, Ravenglass, Cumbria, CA18 1RQ**
TEL: (01229) 717357 *FAX:* (01229) 717010 *CONTACT:* Susan Clark
OPENING TIMES: 1000-1700 daily 1st Apr-31st Oct. All other times by appt.
MIN. MAIL ORDER UK: £20.00 + p&p *MIN. VALUE EC:* £50.00 + p&p *EXPORT:* Yes
CAT. COST: 3 x 1st class *W/SALE or RETAIL:* Retail *CREDIT CARDS:* Access, Visa, not for telephone orders
SPECIALITIES: Rhododendron & Azalea. *MAP PAGE:* **9**

NNor **Northumbria Nurseries, Castle Gardens, Ford, Berwick-upon-Tweed, Northumberland, TD15 2PZ**
TEL: (01890) 820379 *FAX:* (01890) 820594 *CONTACT:* Hazel M Huddleston & Lynda Storm
◆ *OPENING TIMES:* 0900-1800 Mon-Fri all year, & 1000-1800 Sat-Sun & Bank Hols Mar-Oct & by appt. (Or till dusk).
MIN. MAIL ORDER UK: Nmc* *MIN. VALUE EC:* No minimum charge
CAT. COST: £2.30 PO/Chq. *W/SALE or RETAIL:* Both *CREDIT CARDS:* Visa, Access
SPECIALITIES: Over 1600 different species of container grown hardy ornamental Shrubs, Perennials & Alpines. *Please phone for further info. on mail order prices. *MAP PAGE:* **10**

NNrd **Norden Alpines, Hirst Road, Carlton, Nr Goole, Humberside, DN14 9PX**
TEL: 01405 861348 *CONTACT:* Norma & Denis Walton
OPENING TIMES: 100-1700 all year but please ring first in the winter months.
MIN. MAIL ORDER UK: £10.00 + p&p *MIN. VALUE EC:* £10.00 + p&p
CAT. COST: 3 x 2nd class *W/SALE or RETAIL:* Both *CREDIT CARDS:* None
SPECIALITIES: Many unusual Alpines - over 2000 esp. Auricula, Campanula, Primula, Saxifraga & dwarf Iris. *MAP PAGE:* **9**

NOak **Oak Tree Nursery,** Mill Lane, Barlow, Selby, North Yorkshire, YO8 8EY
OPENING TIMES: 1000-1630 Tue-Sun mid Feb-mid Oct.
No mail order
CAT. COST: 2 x 1st class *W/SALE or RETAIL:* Retail *CREDIT CARDS:* None
SPECIALITIES: Cottage Garden plants. *MAP PAGE:* **9**

NOrc **Orchard House Nursery,** Orchard House, Wormald Green, Nr Harrogate, North Yorks, HG3 3PX
TEL: (01765) 677541 *FAX:* (01765) 677541 *CONTACT:* Mr B M Corner
OPENING TIMES: 0900-1700 Mon-Sat.
No mail order
CAT. COST: £1.00 *W/SALE or RETAIL:* Both *CREDIT CARDS:* None
SPECIALITIES: Herbaceous, Ferns, Grasses & unusual cottage garden plants. *MAP PAGE:* **9**

NPal **The Palm Farm, Thornton Hall Gardens, Station Road, Thornton Curtis, Nr Ulceby, Humberside, DN39 6XF**
TEL: (01469) 531232 *FAX:* (01469) 531232 *CONTACT:* W W Spink
OPENING TIMES: 1400-1700 daily ex Winter when advised to check by phone first.
MIN. MAIL ORDER UK: £11.00 + p&p *MIN. VALUE EC:* £25.00 + p&p *EXPORT:* Yes
CAT. COST: 1 x 2nd class *W/SALE or RETAIL:* Both *CREDIT CARDS:* None
SPECIALITIES: Hardy & half-Hardy Palms, unusual Trees, Shrubs & Conservatory plants. *MAP PAGE:* **9**

NPer **Perry's Plants,** The River Garden, Sleights, Whitby, North Yorkshire, YO21 1RR
TEL: (01947) 810329 *FAX:* (01947) 810329 *CONTACT:* Pat & Richard Perry
◆ *OPENING TIMES:* 1000-1700 Easter to October.
No mail order
CAT. COST: Large (A4) Sae *W/SALE or RETAIL:* Retail *CREDIT CARDS:* None
SPECIALITIES: Lavatera, Malva, Erysimum, Euphorbia, Anthemis, Osteospermum & Hebe. Also uncommon Hardy & Container plants. *MAP PAGE:* **9**

NPin **Pinks & Carnations, 22 Chetwyn Avenue, Bromley Cross, Bolton, Lancashire, BL7 9BN**
TEL: (01204) 306273 *FAX:* (01204) 306273 *CONTACT:* R & T Gillies
◆ *OPENING TIMES:* Appt. only.
MIN. MAIL ORDER UK: No minimum charge *MIN. VALUE EC:* £15.00 + p&p
CAT. COST: 1 x 1st class *W/SALE or RETAIL:* Both *CREDIT CARDS:* Visa, Access
SPECIALITIES: Pinks, Perpetual Flowering Carnations. See also SEED Index. *MAP PAGE:* **9**

NPla **Plantations Perennials,** Cicely's Cottage, 43 Elmers Green, Skelmersdale, Lancashire, WN8 6SG
TEL: (01695) 720790/724448 *CONTACT:* Maureen Duncan/Jennifer Madeley
OPENING TIMES: By appt. only. Please phone.
No mail order
CAT. COST: 4 x 1st class *W/SALE or RETAIL:* Retail *CREDIT CARDS:* None
SPECIALITIES: Perennials & Shrubs incl. Argyranthemum, Diascia, Osteospermum, Penstemon, Viola, Hedera & Hebe. *MAP PAGE:* **9**

NPri **Primrose Cottage Nursery,** Ringway Road, Moss Nook, Wythenshawe, Manchester, M22 5WF
TEL: (0161) 437 1557 *FAX:* (0161) 499 9932 *CONTACT:* Caroline Dumville
◆ *OPENING TIMES:* 0815-1800 Mon-Sat, 0930-1730 Sun.
No mail order
CAT. COST: 1 x 1st class *W/SALE or RETAIL:* Retail *CREDIT CARDS:* Visa, Access, Switch
SPECIALITIES: Hardy Herbaceous Perennials, Alpines, Herbs, Roses, Patio & Hanging Basket Plants. *MAP PAGE:* **7**

NPro **ProudPlants,** Shadyvale Nurseries, Ainstable, Carlisle, Cumbria, CA4 9QN
TEL: (01768) 896604 *CONTACT:* Roger Proud
OPENING TIMES: 0800-1800 daily Mar-Nov. Other times by appt.
No mail order
CAT. COST: None issued *W/SALE or RETAIL:* Retail *CREDIT CARDS:* None
SPECIALITIES: Interesting & unusual Shrubs & Perennials esp. Dwarf & Ground cover plants. *MAP PAGE:* **9/10**

NPSI **Plants of Special Interest,** 4 High Street, Braithwell, Nr Rotherham, South Yorkshire, S66 7AL
TEL: (01709) 812328 *FAX:* (01709) 790342 *CONTACT:* Rita Anna Dunstan
◆ *OPENING TIMES:* 1000-1700 Tue-Sun Mar-Nov.
No mail order
CAT. COST: 3 x 1st class *W/SALE or RETAIL:* Retail *CREDIT CARDS:* Access
SPECIALITIES: Wide selection of Herbaceous plants, esp. Aquilegia, Zantedeschia & Ferns. *MAP PAGE:* **9**

NRai **Rainbow's End Nursery, 37 Melbourn Road, Crookes, Sheffield, S10 1NR**
TEL: (0114) 268 1700 *FAX:* (0114) 268 1700 *E-MAIL:* k@seedsearch.demon.co.uk
CONTACT: Karen Platt
OPENING TIMES: 7th & 8th Jun, 6th & 7th Sep 1997. Please check first.
MIN. MAIL ORDER UK: No minimum charge *MIN. VALUE EC:* Nmc
CAT. COST: 3 x 1st class *W/SALE or RETAIL:* Retail *CREDIT CARDS:* None
SPECIALITIES: Black & White forms ie. Ophiopogon planiscarpus nigrescens, Alcea rosea nigra, Dianthus barbatus 'Sooty' etc. *MAP PAGE:* **7/9**

NRar **Rarer Plants,** Ashfield House, Austfield Lane, Monk Fryston, Leeds, North Yorkshire, LS25 5EH
TEL: (01977) 682263 *CONTACT:* Anne Watson
OPENING TIMES: 1000-1600 Sun & Mon 1st Feb-1st Jun.
No mail order
CAT. COST: Sae *W/SALE or RETAIL:* Retail *CREDIT CARDS:* None
SPECIALITIES: Helleborus & unusual plants. *MAP PAGE:* **9**

NRog **R V Roger Ltd, The Nurseries, Pickering, North Yorkshire, YO18 7HG**
TEL: (01751) 472226 *FAX:* (01751) 476749 *E-MAIL:* ian@clivia.demon.co.uk
CONTACT: J R, A G & I M Roger
OPENING TIMES: 0900-1700 Mon-Sat, 1300-1700 Sun. Closed Dec 25th-Jan 2nd each year.
MIN. MAIL ORDER UK: No minimum charge *MIN. VALUE EC:* Nmc *EXPORT:* Yes
CAT. COST: £1.50 *W/SALE or RETAIL:* Both *CREDIT CARDS:* Visa, Access
SPECIALITIES: General list, hardy in North of England. Co-holders of National Erodium & Erythronium Collection. See also SEED Index. *MAP PAGE:* **9**

NRoo **Rookhope Nurseries,** Rookhope, Upper Weardale, Co. Durham, DL13 2DD
TEL: (01388) 517272 *CONTACT:* Karen Blackburn
OPENING TIMES: 0900-1600 mid Mar-mid Oct.
MIN. MAIL ORDER UK: No minimum charge *MIN. VALUE EC:*
CAT. COST: 3 x 1st class *W/SALE or RETAIL:* Retail *CREDIT CARDS:* Visa, Access, MasterCard
SPECIALITIES: Wide range of Hardy plants grown at 1,100 feet in the northern Pennines.
MAP PAGE: **9/10**

NRya **Ryal Nursery, East Farm Cottage, Ryal, Northumberland, NE20 0SA**
TEL: (01661) 886562 *FAX:* (01661) 886562 *CONTACT:* R F Hadden
OPENING TIMES: 1300-1700 Tue, 1000-1700 Sun Mar-Jul & by appt.
MIN. MAIL ORDER UK: £5.00 + p&p *MIN. VALUE EC:* £5.00 + p&p
CAT. COST: Sae *W/SALE or RETAIL:* Both *CREDIT CARDS:* None
SPECIALITIES: Alpine & Woodland plants. *MAP PAGE:* **10**

NSla **Slack Top Alpines,** Hebden Bridge, West Yorkshire, HX7 7HA
TEL: (01422) 845348 *CONTACT:* M R or R Mitchell
OPENING TIMES: 1000-1800 Wed-Sun & Bank Hol Mons 1st Mar-31st Oct.
No mail order
CAT. COST: Sae *W/SALE or RETAIL:* Both *CREDIT CARDS:* None
SPECIALITIES: Alpine & Rockery plants. *MAP PAGE:* **9**

NSpr **Springwood Pleiones, 35 Heathfield, Leeds, W Yorkshire, LS16 7AB**
TEL: (0113) 261 1781 *CONTACT:* Ken Redshaw
OPENING TIMES: By appt. only.
MIN. MAIL ORDER UK: £2.00 + p&p *MIN. VALUE EC:* £2.00 + p&p *EXPORT:* Yes
CAT. COST: 1 x 1st class *W/SALE or RETAIL:* Retail *CREDIT CARDS:* None
SPECIALITIES: Pleione. *MAP PAGE:* **9**

NSti **Stillingfleet Lodge Nurseries,** Stillingfleet, Yorkshire, YO4 6HW
TEL: (01904) 728506 *FAX:* (01904) 728506 *CONTACT:* Vanessa Cook
OPENING TIMES: 1000-1600 Tue Wed Fri & Sat 1st Apr-18th Oct.
MIN. MAIL ORDER UK: No minimum charge *MIN. VALUE EC:*
CAT. COST: 7 x 2nd class *W/SALE or RETAIL:* Retail *CREDIT CARDS:* None
SPECIALITIES: Foliage & unusual perennials. Hardy Geraniums, Pulmonaria, variegated plants & Grasses. Holder of National Pulmonaria Collection. *MAP PAGE:* **9**

NSty **Stydd Nursery, Stonegate Lane, Ribchester, Nr Preston, Lancashire, PR3 3YN**
TEL: (01254) 878797 *FAX:* (01254) 878254 *CONTACT:* Mrs C Walker
OPENING TIMES: 1330-1700 Tue-Fri, 1330-1700 Sat. Please check first.
MIN. MAIL ORDER UK: No minimum charge *MIN. VALUE EC:* £50.00 + p&p
CAT. COST: (£1) 4 x 1st class *W/SALE or RETAIL:* Retail *CREDIT CARDS:* None
SPECIALITIES: Old Roses & ornamental foliage. Half-hardy Perennials, Conservatory Plants.
MAP PAGE: **9**

NTay **Taylors Nurseries,** Sutton Road, Sutton, Doncaster, Yorkshire, DN6 9JZ
TEL: (01302) 700716 *FAX:* (01302) 708415 *CONTACT:* John Taylor
◆ *OPENING TIMES:* 0800-1800 Summer, 0800-1700 Winter daily. Closed Xmas & Boxing day & New Year's day.
MIN. MAIL ORDER UK: 2 plants + p&p *MIN. VALUE EC:*
CAT. COST: 2 x 1st class *W/SALE or RETAIL:* Retail *CREDIT CARDS:* Visa, Access
SPECIALITIES: Clematis (over 150 varieties) & Herbaceous Perennials. *MAP PAGE:* **9**

◆ See also Display Advertisements

NTow **Town Farm Nursery,** Whitton, Stillington, Stockton on Tees, Cleveland, TS21 1LQ
TEL: (01740) 631079 *CONTACT:* F D Baker
◆ *OPENING TIMES:* 1000-1800 Fri-Mon Mar-Oct.
MIN. MAIL ORDER UK: £5.00 + p&p *MIN. VALUE EC:*
CAT. COST: Sae *W/SALE or RETAIL:* Retail *CREDIT CARDS:* None
SPECIALITIES: Unusual Alpines, Border Perennials & Shrubs. *MAP PAGE:* **9**

NVic **The Vicarage Garden,** Carrington, Urmston, Manchester, M31 4AG
TEL: (0161) 775 2750 *FAX:* (0161) 775 3679 *CONTACT:* Mr R Alexander
OPENING TIMES: 1000-1800 Fri-Wed Apr-Sept. 1030-1700 Fri-Wed Oct-Mar.
MIN. MAIL ORDER UK: £10.00 + p&p* *MIN. VALUE EC:*
CAT. COST: 5 x 1st class *W/SALE or RETAIL:* Both *CREDIT CARDS:* Visa, Access
SPECIALITIES: Herbaceous. *Note: mail order to UK only. *MAP PAGE:* **9**

NWCA **White Cottage Alpines,** Sunnyside Nurseries, Hornsea Road, Sigglesthorne, East Yorkshire, HU11 5QL
TEL: (01964) 542692 *FAX:* (01964) 542692 *CONTACT:* Sally E Cummins
◆ *OPENING TIMES:* 1000-1700 (or dusk) Thu-Sun & Bank Hol Mons. Closed Dec & Jan.
MIN. MAIL ORDER UK: £7.50 + p&p *MIN. VALUE EC:*
CAT. COST: 4 x 1st class *W/SALE or RETAIL:* Retail *CREDIT CARDS:* None
SPECIALITIES: Alpines. *MAP PAGE:* **9**

NWea **Weasdale Nurseries, Newbiggin-on-Lune, Kirkby Stephen, Cumbria, CA17 4LX**
TEL: (01539) 623246 *FAX:* (01539) 623277 *CONTACT:* Andrew Forsyth
OPENING TIMES: 0900-1700 Mon-Fri.
MIN. MAIL ORDER UK: No minimum charge *MIN. VALUE EC:* Nmc
CAT. COST: £2.50* *W/SALE or RETAIL:* Retail *CREDIT CARDS:* None
SPECIALITIES: Hardy forest trees, hedging, broadleaved & conifers. Specimen Trees & Shrubs grown at 850 feet. Mail Order a speciality. *Or 10 x 1st class stamps. *MAP PAGE:* **9**

NWes **Westwinds Perennial Plants, Filpoke Lane, High Hesleden, Hartlepool, Cleveland, TS27 4BT**
TEL: (0191) 518 0225 *E-MAIL:* harryb@hartmail.demon.co.uk *CONTACT:* Harry Blackwood
OPENING TIMES: Dawn until Dusk Sun & Mon and by appt.
MIN. MAIL ORDER UK: * *MIN. VALUE EC:* £20.00 + p&p
CAT. COST: 2 x 1st class *W/SALE or RETAIL:* Retail *CREDIT CARDS:* None
SPECIALITIES: Penstemon, Hosta, Geranium, Phygelius plus a range of specimen size Shrubs & Climbers. NB Mail order for Hostas only. *MAP PAGE:* **9/10**

NWoo **Woodlands Cottage Nursery,** Summerbridge, Harrogate, North Yorkshire, HG3 4BT
TEL: (01423) 780765 *FAX:* (01423) 780765 *CONTACT:* Mrs Ann Stark
OPENING TIMES: 1100-1800 Mon, Wed, Fri, Sat & Sun, mid Mar-end Sep.
No mail order
CAT. COST: 3 x 1st class *W/SALE or RETAIL:* Retail *CREDIT CARDS:* None
SPECIALITIES: Herbs, plants for Shade & Hardy Perennials. *MAP PAGE:* **9**

NYoL **Yorkshire Lavender, Sideways, Terrington, York, N Yorks, YO6 4QB**
TEL: (01653) 648430 *CONTACT:* Nigel W B Goodwill
OPENING TIMES: By appt. only.
MIN. MAIL ORDER UK: No minimum charge *MIN. VALUE EC:* Nmc *EXPORT:* Yes
CAT. COST: Free *W/SALE or RETAIL:* Retail *CREDIT CARDS:* None
SPECIALITIES: Lavandula. *MAP PAGE:* **9**

NYor **Yorkshire Garden World, West Haddlesey, Nr Selby, North Yorkshire, YO8 8QA**
TEL: (01757) 228279 *CONTACT:* Carole Atkinson
OPENING TIMES: 0930-1730 daily Mar-Oct. 0930-dusk daily Nov-Feb.
MIN. MAIL ORDER UK: £20.00 + p&p *MIN. VALUE EC:* £20.00 + p&p
CAT. COST: 6 x 1st class *W/SALE or RETAIL:* Both *CREDIT CARDS:* Visa, Access, AmEx
SPECIALITIES: 450 Herbs, 200 Heathers & 100 Conifers. National Collection of Santolina. 4 acre display garden, admission charge - please phone for details. *MAP PAGE:* **9**

NZep **Zephyrwude Irises, 48 Blacker Lane, Crigglestone, Wakefield, West Yorkshire, WF4 3EW**
TEL: (01924) 252101 *CONTACT:* Richard L Brook
OPENING TIMES: Viewing only 0900-dusk daily May-June, peak late May. Phone first, 0900-2300.
MIN. MAIL ORDER UK: £15.00 + p&p *MIN. VALUE EC:* £20.00 + p&p
CAT. COST: 1 x 1st class *W/SALE or RETAIL:* Both *CREDIT CARDS:* Visa, Access, AmEx
SPECIALITIES: Bearded Iris, 1970s-80s hybrids only. Mainly 12" dwarf & intermediate, some tall. 300 variety display garden. Cat. available Apr-Sep 15th. Deliv. Aug-Oct only. *MAP PAGE:* **9**

SAga **Agar's Nursery,** Agars Lane, Hordle, Lymington, Hampshire, SO41 0FL
TEL: (01590) 683703 *CONTACT:* Mrs Diana Tombs
OPENING TIMES: 1000-1600 Fri-Wed 1st Feb-20th Dec.
No mail order
CAT. COST: None issued *W/SALE or RETAIL:* Retail *CREDIT CARDS:* None
SPECIALITIES: Penstemon, Salvia & Iris. Also wide range of Hardy plants inc. Shrubs & Climbers. *MAP PAGE:* **2**

SAll **Allwood Bros, Mill Nursery, Hassocks, West Sussex, BN6 9NB**
TEL: (01273) 844229 *FAX:* (01273) 846022 *CONTACT:* Sue James
OPENING TIMES: 0900-1600 Mon-Fri.
MIN. MAIL ORDER UK: No minimum charge *MIN. VALUE EC:* Nmc *EXPORT:* SO
CAT. COST: 2 x 1st class *W/SALE or RETAIL:* Both *CREDIT CARDS:* Access, Visa
SPECIALITIES: Dianthus, incl Hardy Border Carnations, Pinks, Perpetual & Allwoodii. Gypsophila some available as Seed. See also SEED Index. *MAP PAGE:* **3**

SAlw **Always Alpines,** Priors Leaze Lane, Hambrook, Chichester, W Sussex, PO18 8RQ
TEL: (01243) 773629* *CONTACT:* Mrs S Reynolds
OPENING TIMES: 1000-1500 Tues/Wed, 1200-1600 Fri, 1000-1600 Sun, Mar-Oct.
No mail order
CAT. COST: Sae *W/SALE or RETAIL:* Retail *CREDIT CARDS:* None
SPECIALITIES: Alpines & Dwarf Perennials for rock gardens, alpine house, scree, troughs, walls & front of border. *NOTE Phone out of opening hours. *MAP PAGE:* **2/3**

SApp **Apple Court, Hordle Lane, Hordle, Lymington, Hampshire, S041 0HU**
TEL: (01590) 642130 *FAX:* (01590) 644220 *E-MAIL:* applecourt@btinternet.com
CONTACT: Diana Grenfell & Roger Grounds
◆ *OPENING TIMES:* Open daily (Closed 1300-1400) Jul-Aug. Thu-Mon Feb-Oct. Closed Nov-Jan.
MIN. MAIL ORDER UK: £15.00 + p&p *MIN. VALUE EC:* £50.00 + p&p
CAT. COST: 4 x 1st class *W/SALE or RETAIL:* Retail *CREDIT CARDS:* None
SPECIALITIES: Hosta, Grasses, Ferns, Hemerocallis. National Collection Woodwardia, Rohdea, & Hosta. *MAP PAGE:* **2**

SApu **Apuldram Roses, Apuldram Lane, Dell Quay, Chichester, Sussex, PO20 7EF**
TEL: (01243) 785769 *FAX:* (01243) 536973 *E-MAIL:* d.sawday@virginnet
CONTACT: Mrs Sawday
OPENING TIMES: 0900-1700 Mon-Sat, 1030-1630 Sun & Bank Hols. ex. Dec 23rd-Jan 5th.
MIN. MAIL ORDER UK: £4.50 + p&p *MIN. VALUE EC:* £4.50 + p&p
CAT. COST: 2 x 1st class *W/SALE or RETAIL:* Both *CREDIT CARDS:* Switch, MasterCard, Visa
SPECIALITIES: Roses. *MAP PAGE:* **2/3**

SArc **Architectural Plants, Cooks Farm, Nuthurst, Horsham, West Sussex, RH13 6LH**
TEL: (01403) 891772 *FAX:* (01403) 891056
CONTACT: Angus White/Christine Shaw/Sarah Chandler
◆ *OPENING TIMES:* 0900-1700 Mon-Sat.
MIN. MAIL ORDER UK: £14.00 + p&p *MIN. VALUE EC:* £150.00 + p&p *EXPORT:* Yes
CAT. COST: Free *W/SALE or RETAIL:* Both *CREDIT CARDS:* Visa, Access, EuroCard, Switch, Delta, Electron, JCB
SPECIALITIES: Architectural plants & hardy Exotics. *MAP PAGE:* **3**

◆ See also Display Advertisements

SAsh **Ashenden Nursery,** Cranbrook Road, Benenden, Cranbrook, Kent, TN17 4ET
TEL: (01580) 241792 *CONTACT:* Kevin McGarry
OPENING TIMES: By appt. Please telephone.
No mail order
CAT. COST: Sae + 1 x 1st class *W/SALE or RETAIL:* Retail *CREDIT CARDS:* None
SPECIALITIES: Rock garden & perennials. *MAP PAGE:* **3**

SAWi **Anthony Archer-Wills Ltd,** Broadford Bridge Road, West Chiltington, West Sussex, RH20 2LF
TEL: (01798) 813204 *FAX:* (01798) 815080 *CONTACT:* Anthony Archer-Wills
OPENING TIMES: By appt. only - please telephone.
MIN. MAIL ORDER UK: £15.00 + p&p *MIN. VALUE EC:*
CAT. COST: £1.00 + 2 x 2nd class *W/SALE or RETAIL:* Both *CREDIT CARDS:* None
SPECIALITIES: Ponds, Lakes & Water garden plants. *MAP PAGE:* **3**

SAxl **Axletree Nursery, Starvecrow Lane, Peasmarsh, Rye, East Sussex, TN31 6XL**
TEL: (01797) 230470 *FAX:* (01797) 230470 *CONTACT:* D J Hibberd
OPENING TIMES: 1000-1700 Wed-Sat mid Mar-end Sep.
MIN. MAIL ORDER UK: No minimum charge *MIN. VALUE EC:* Nmc
CAT. COST: 4 x 1st class *W/SALE or RETAIL:* Retail *CREDIT CARDS:* None
SPECIALITIES: Extensive range of Perennials, esp. Hardy Geraniums. *MAP PAGE:* **3**

SBai **Steven Bailey Ltd, Silver Street, Sway, Lymington, Hampshire, SO41 6ZA**
TEL: (01590) 682227 *FAX:* (01590) 683765 *CONTACT:* Fiona Whittles
OPENING TIMES: 1000-1300 & 1400-1630 Mon-Fri all year. 1000-1300 & 1400-1600 Sat Mar-Jun ex Bank Hols.
MIN. MAIL ORDER UK: Quotation *MIN. VALUE EC:* Quotation *EXPORT:* Yes
CAT. COST: 2 x 2nd class *W/SALE or RETAIL:* Both *CREDIT CARDS:* Visa, Access
SPECIALITIES: Carnations, Pinks & Alstroemeria. *MAP PAGE:* **2**

SBam **Bamboo Nursery Ltd, Kingsgate Cottage, Wittersham, Tenterden, Kent, TN30 7NS**
TEL: (01797) 270607 *FAX:* (01797) 270825 *CONTACT:* A Sutcliffe
OPENING TIMES: Appt. only.
MIN. MAIL ORDER UK: No minimum charge *MIN. VALUE EC:* £50.00 + p&p *EXPORT:* Yes
CAT. COST: Sae *W/SALE or RETAIL:* Both *CREDIT CARDS:* None
SPECIALITIES: Bamboo. *MAP PAGE:* **3**

SBar **Barnhawk Nursery,** Little Barn, Woodgreen, Fordingbridge, Hampshire, SP6 2QX
TEL: (01725) 512213 *FAX:* (01725) 512213 *CONTACT:* R & V Crawford
◆ *OPENING TIMES:* 1000-1700 Fri & Sat (other days please phone first) Feb-Oct.
No mail order
CAT. COST: 3 x 1st class *W/SALE or RETAIL:* Both *CREDIT CARDS:* None
SPECIALITIES: Choice plants for peat and scree, dwarf shrubs. Two acre garden to visit during opening times. *MAP PAGE:* **2**

SBid **Biddenden Nursery at Garden Crafts, Sissinghurst Road, Biddenden, Kent, TN27 8EJ**
TEL: (01580) 292100 *FAX:* (01580) 292 097 *CONTACT:* Gerald Bedrich
◆ *OPENING TIMES:* 0900-1700 Mon-Fri, 1000-1700 Sat & Sun.
MIN. MAIL ORDER UK: No minimum charge *MIN. VALUE EC:* Nmc *EXPORT:* Yes
CAT. COST: 3 x 1st class *W/SALE or RETAIL:* Both *CREDIT CARDS:* Visa, Access, AmEx, Switch
SPECIALITIES: Wide range of unusual Shrubs, esp. Ceanothus, Hydrangea & Viburnum. Rare & unusual Herbaceous. Comprehensive range of 'Sissinghurst' plants. *MAP PAGE:* **3**

SBir **Birchfleet Nursery, Nyewood, Petersfield, Hampshire, GU31 5JQ**
TEL: (01730) 821636 *FAX:* (01730) 821636 *CONTACT:* John & Daphne Gammon
OPENING TIMES: By appt. only. Please telephone.
MIN. MAIL ORDER UK: £20.00 + p&p *MIN. VALUE EC:* £30.00 + p&p *EXPORT:* Yes
CAT. COST: Sae *W/SALE or RETAIL:* Both *CREDIT CARDS:* None
SPECIALITIES: Oaks incl. many hybrids, and other rare trees. *MAP PAGE:* **2/3**

SBla **Blackthorn Nursery,** Kilmeston, Alresford, Hampshire, SO24 0NL
TEL: 01962 771796 *FAX:* 01962 771071 *CONTACT:* A R & S B White
OPENING TIMES: 0900-1700 Fri & Sat Mar-last weekend of June
No mail order
CAT. COST: 3 x 1st class *W/SALE or RETAIL:* Retail *CREDIT CARDS:* None
SPECIALITIES: Choice Perennials & Alpines, esp. Daphne, Epimedium & Helleborus.
MAP PAGE: **2**

SBod **Bodiam Nursery,** Ockham House, Bodiam, Robertsbridge, East Sussex, TN32 5RA
TEL: (01580) 830811/830649 *FAX:* (01580) 830071 *CONTACT:* Richard Biggs
OPENING TIMES: 0900-1800 or dusk.
MIN. MAIL ORDER UK: £30.00 + p&p *MIN. VALUE EC:*
CAT. COST: 4 x 1st class *W/SALE or RETAIL:* Both *CREDIT CARDS:* Visa, MasterCard, EuroCard
SPECIALITIES: Heathers, herbaceous Perennials, Conifers, Azalea, Camellia & Climbers.
MAP PAGE: **3**

SBra ◆ **J Bradshaw & Son, Busheyfield Nursery, Herne, Herne Bay, Kent, CT6 7LJ**
OPENING TIMES: 1000-1700 Tue-Sat 1st Mar-31st Oct. Other times by appt. only.
MIN. MAIL ORDER UK: 2 plants + p&p* *MIN. VALUE EC:* 2 plants + p&p
CAT. COST: Sae + 2 x 1st class *W/SALE or RETAIL:* Both *CREDIT CARDS:* None
SPECIALITIES: Clematis & Climbers. Mainly wholesale. NCCPG Collection of climbing Lonicera & Clematis montana. *Note: Lonicera only by mail order. *Trade export ONLY. *MAP PAGE:* **3**

SChu **Church Hill Cottage Gardens,** Charing Heath, Ashford, Kent, TN27 0BU
TEL: (01233) 712522 *CONTACT:* Mr M & J & Mrs M Metianu.
OPENING TIMES: 1000-1700 1st Feb-30th Nov Tue-Sun & Bank Hols Mon. Other times by appt.
MIN. MAIL ORDER UK: £10.00 + p&p *MIN. VALUE EC:*
CAT. COST: 3 x 1st class *W/SALE or RETAIL:* Retail *CREDIT CARDS:* None
SPECIALITIES: Unusual hardy plants, Dianthus, Hosta, Ferns & Viola. Alpines & Shrubs.
MAP PAGE: **3**

SCit **The Citrus Centre, West Mare Lane, Marehill, Pulborough, West Sussex, RH20 2EA**
TEL: (01798) 872786 *FAX:* (01798) 874880 *CONTACT:* Amanda & Chris Dennis
OPENING TIMES: 0930-1730 Wed-Sun & Bank Hols. Closed Xmas & Boxing Day.
MIN. MAIL ORDER UK: No minimum charge *MIN. VALUE EC:* Nmc *EXPORT:* Yes
CAT. COST: Sae *W/SALE or RETAIL:* Both *CREDIT CARDS:* Visa, Access
SPECIALITIES: Citrus & Citrus relatives. *MAP PAGE:* **3**

SCog **Coghurst Nursery, Ivy House Lane, Near Three Oaks, Hastings, East Sussex, TN35 4NP**
TEL: (01424) 756228 *CONTACT:* J Farnfield, L A & D Edgar
OPENING TIMES: 1200-1630 Mon-Fri, 1000-1630 Sun.
MIN. MAIL ORDER UK: No minimum charge *MIN. VALUE EC:* Nmc
CAT. COST: 2 x 2nd class *W/SALE or RETAIL:* Both *CREDIT CARDS:* None
SPECIALITIES: Camellia, Rhododendron, Azalea & Eucryphia. *MAP PAGE:* **3**

SCoo **Cooling's Nurseries Ltd,** Rushmore Hill, Knockholt, Sevenoaks, Kent, TN14 7NN
TEL: (01959) 532269 *FAX:* (01959) 534092 *CONTACT:* M Hooker
OPENING TIMES: 0900-1700 Mon-Sat & 1000-1630 Sun.
No mail order
CAT. COST: 3 x 1st class *W/SALE or RETAIL:* Retail *CREDIT CARDS:* Visa, Access, Switch, Electron, Delta
SPECIALITIES: Large range of Perennials, Conifers & Bedding plants. Some unusual Shrubs.
MAP PAGE: **3**

SCou **Coombland Gardens, Coombland, Coneyhurst, Billingshurst, West Sussex, RH14 9DG**
TEL: (01403) 741727 *FAX:* (01403) 741079 *CONTACT:* David Browne
◆ *OPENING TIMES:* 1400-1600 Mon-Fri Mar-end Oct. Bank Hols & other times by appt. only.
MIN. MAIL ORDER UK: £20.00 + p&p* *MIN. VALUE EC:* 8 plants + p&p*
CAT. COST: 5 x 1st class *W/SALE or RETAIL:* Retail *CREDIT CARDS:* None
SPECIALITIES: Hardy Geranium, Erodium and choice Herbaceous. *Note: Hardy Geraniums only to EC. See also SEED Index. *MAP PAGE:* **3**

SCro **Croftway Nursery, Yapton Road, Barnham, Bognor Regis, West Sussex, PO22 0BH**
TEL: (01243) 552121 *FAX:* (01243) 552125 *E-MAIL:* croftway@aol.com
CONTACT: Graham Spencer
OPENING TIMES: 0900-1730 daily. Closed 1st Dec- 14th Feb except by appt.
MIN. MAIL ORDER UK: No minimum charge* *MIN. VALUE EC:* Nmc*
CAT. COST: 4 x 1st class *W/SALE or RETAIL:* Both *CREDIT CARDS:* Visa, Access
SPECIALITIES: Wide general range, emphasis on Perennials. Specialists in Iris & Hardy Geranium. *Note: mail order for Iris & Geranium only. *MAP PAGE:* **3**

SDad **J Dadswell,** 4 Marle Avenue, Burgess Hill, West Sussex, RH15 8JG
TEL: (01444) 232874 *CONTACT:* Judith Dadswell
OPENING TIMES: By appt. only
No mail order
CAT. COST: 3 x 1st class *W/SALE or RETAIL:* Retail *CREDIT CARDS:* None
SPECIALITIES: Geranium. *MAP PAGE:* **3**

SDay **A La Carte Daylilies, Little Hermitage, St. Catherine's Down, Nr Ventnor, Isle of Wight, PO38 2PD**
TEL: (01983) 730512 *CONTACT:* Jan & Andy Wyers
◆ *OPENING TIMES:* By appt. only
MIN. MAIL ORDER UK: No minimum charge *MIN. VALUE EC:* Nmc
CAT. COST: 3 x 1st class *W/SALE or RETAIL:* Retail *CREDIT CARDS:* None
SPECIAL!TIES: Hemerocallis *MAP PAGE:* **2**

SDea **Deacon's Nursery, Moor View, Godshill, Isle of Wight, PO38 3HW**
TEL: (01983) 840750 (24 hrs), (01983) 522243 *FAX:* (01983) 523575
CONTACT: G D & B H W Deacon
◆ *OPENING TIMES:* 0800-1600 Mon-Fri May-Sep, 0800-1700 Mon-Fri 0800-1300 Sat Oct-Ap
MIN. MAIL ORDER UK: No minimum charge *MIN. VALUE EC:* Nmc *EXPORT:* Yes
CAT. COST: Stamp appreciated. *W/SALE or RETAIL:* Both *CREDIT CARDS:* Visa, Access
SPECIALITIES: Over 250 varieties of Apple, old & new. Pears, Plums, Gages, Damsons, Cherries etc. Fruit & Nut trees, triple Peaches, Ballerinas. Modern Soft Fruit. Grapes, Hops. Family Trees - Blueberries. *MAP PAGE:* **2**

SDeJ **De Jager & Sons, The Nurseries, Marden, Kent, TN12 9BP**
TEL: (01622) 831235 *FAX:* (01622) 832416 *CONTACT:* Mrs M Guiney
OPENING TIMES: 0900-1700 Mon-Fri.
MIN. MAIL ORDER UK: £15.00 + p&p *MIN. VALUE EC:* £15.00 + p&p *EXPORT:* Yes
CAT. COST: Free *W/SALE or RETAIL:* Both *CREDIT CARDS:* Visa, Access
SPECIALITIES: Wide general range, esp. Bulbs. Lilium, Tulipa, Narcissus species & miscellaneous. Large range of Perennials. *MAP PAGE:* **3**

SDen **Denmead Geranium Nurseries, Hambledon Road, Denmead, Waterlooville, Hampshire, PO7 6PS**
TEL: (01705) 240081 *CONTACT:* I H Chance
OPENING TIMES: 0800-1300 & 1400-1700 Mon-Fri, 0800-1230 Sat (ex Aug), 1400-1700 Sat May-Jun. Closed Sun & B/Hol Mons.
MIN. MAIL ORDER UK: 6 plants + p&p *MIN. VALUE EC:* 6 plants + p&p
CAT. COST: 3 x 2nd class *W/SALE or RETAIL:* Both *CREDIT CARDS:* None
SPECIALITIES: Pelargoniums - Zonals, Ivy-leaved, Scented, Unique, Rosebud, Stellars, Miniature, Dwarf, Swiss Balcony, Mini Cascade, Ornamental, Regals & Angels. *MAP PAGE:* **2**

SDix **Great Dixter Nurseries, Northiam, Rye, East Sussex, TN31 6PH**
TEL: (01797) 253107 *FAX:* (01797) 252879 *CONTACT:* K Leighton
OPENING TIMES: 0900-1230 & 1330-1700 Mon-Fri, 0900-1200 Sat all year. Also 1400-1700 Sat, Sun & Bank Hols Apr-Oct.
MIN. MAIL ORDER UK: £15.00 + p&p *MIN. VALUE EC:* £15.00 + p&p
CAT. COST: 4 x 1st class *W/SALE or RETAIL:* Retail *CREDIT CARDS:* Access, Switch, Visa
SPECIALITIES: Clematis, Shrubs and Plants. (Gardens open). *MAP PAGE:* **3**

SDow **Downderry Nursery, 649 London Road, Ditton, Aylesford, Kent, ME20 6DJ**
TEL: (01732) 840710 *FAX:* (01732) 840710 *CONTACT:* Dr S J Charlesworth
OPENING TIMES: By appt. only.
MIN. MAIL ORDER UK: No minimum charge *MIN. VALUE EC:* Nmc *EXPORT:* Yes
CAT. COST: 2 x 1st class *W/SALE or RETAIL:* Both *CREDIT CARDS:* None
SPECIALITIES: Lavandula (NCCPG Collection Holder). *MAP PAGE:* **3**

SDry **Drysdale Garden Exotics, Bowerwood Road, Fordingbridge, Hampshire, SP6 1BN**
TEL: (01425) 653010 *CONTACT:* David Crampton
OPENING TIMES: 0930-1730 Wed-Fri, 1000-1730 Sun. Closed 24th Dec-2nd Jan incl.
MIN. MAIL ORDER UK: £10.00 + p&p *MIN. VALUE EC:* £15.00 + p&p
CAT. COST: 3 x 1st class *W/SALE or RETAIL:* Retail *CREDIT CARDS:* None
SPECIALITIES: Plants for exotic & foliage effect. Plants for Mediterranean gardens. National Reference Collection of Bamboos. *MAP PAGE:* **2**

SEas **Eastfield Plant Centre,** Paice Lane, Medstead, Alton, Hampshire, GU34 5PR
TEL: (01420) 563640 *FAX:* (01420) 563640 *CONTACT:* D M & P Barton
OPENING TIMES: 0900-1700 daily 1st Mar-20th Dec or by appt.
No mail order
CAT. COST: None issued *W/SALE or RETAIL:* Retail *CREDIT CARDS:* None
SPECIALITIES: General range. *MAP PAGE:* **2**

SEND **East Northdown Farm,** Margate, Kent, CT9 3TS
TEL: (01843) 862060 *FAX:* (01843) 860206 *CONTACT:* Louise & William Friend
◆ *OPENING TIMES:* 0900-1700 Mon-Sat, 1000-1700 Sun all year. Closed Xmas week & Easter Sun.
No mail order
CAT. COST: 4 x 1st class *W/SALE or RETAIL:* Both *CREDIT CARDS:* Visa, Access
SPECIALITIES: Chalk & Coast-loving plants. *MAP PAGE:* **3**

SExb **Exbury Enterprises Ltd,** Exbury, Nr Southampton, Hampshire, SO45 1AZ
TEL: (01703) 898625 *FAX:* (01703) 243380 *CONTACT:*
OPENING TIMES: 0900-1700 Plant Centre seasonal.
MIN. MAIL ORDER UK: £15.00 + p&p *MIN. VALUE EC:*
CAT. COST: Sae *W/SALE or RETAIL:* Both *CREDIT CARDS:* Visa, Access
SPECIALITIES: Rhododendron, Azalea, Camellia & Pieris. *MAP PAGE:* **2**

SFam **Family Trees, PO Box 3, Botley, Hampshire, SO3 2EA**
TEL: (01329) 834812 *CONTACT:* Philip House
◆ *OPENING TIMES:* 0930-1230 Wed & Sat mid Oct-mid Apr,
MIN. MAIL ORDER UK: £40.00 + p&p *MIN. VALUE EC:* £300.00 + p&p
CAT. COST: Free *W/SALE or RETAIL:* Retail *CREDIT CARDS:* None
SPECIALITIES: Fruit & Ornamental trees. Trained Fruit trees. Also Standards & Old Roses. *MAP PAGE:* **2**

SHam **Hamptons Nurseries,** Pillar Box Lane, Hadlow, Nr Tonbridge, Kent, TN11 9SW
TEL: (01732) 810633 *FAX:* (01732) 810633 *CONTACT:* Mrs J Pazowski
OPENING TIMES: 1000-1700 every day Mar-Oct, Nov-Feb please phone first.
No mail order
CAT. COST: None issued *W/SALE or RETAIL:* Retail *CREDIT CARDS:* Access, MasterCard, Visa
SPECIALITIES: Unusual Perennials, Shrubs & Ferns plus plants for baskets & tubs. *MAP PAGE:* **3**

SHar **Hardy's Cottage Garden Plants, Priory Lane, Freefolk, Whitchurch, Hampshire, RG28 7NJ**
TEL: (01256) 896533 *FAX:* (01256) 896572 *CONTACT:* Rosy Hardy
OPENING TIMES: 0900-1730 daily 1st Mar-31st Oct.
MIN. MAIL ORDER UK: No minimum charge *MIN. VALUE EC:* Nmc
CAT. COST: 4 x 1st class. From May 1997. *W/SALE or RETAIL:* Both *CREDIT CARDS:* Visa, Access
SPECIALITIES: Penstemon, Hardy Geranium, & other Herbaceous both old & new.
MAP PAGE: **2**

SHay **Hayward's Carnations, The Chace Gardens, Stakes Road, Purbrook, Waterlooville, Hampshire, PO7 5PL**
TEL: (01705) 263047 *FAX:* (01705) 263047 *CONTACT:* A N Hayward
OPENING TIMES: 0930-1700 Mon-Fri.
MIN. MAIL ORDER UK: £10.00 + p&p *MIN. VALUE EC:* £50.00 + p&p
CAT. COST: 1 x 1st class *W/SALE or RETAIL:* Both *CREDIT CARDS:* None
SPECIALITIES: Hardy Pinks & Border Carnations. Greenhouse perpetual Carnations.
MAP PAGE: **2**

SHBN **High Banks Nurseries,** Slip Mill Road, Hawkhurst, Kent, TN18 5AD
TEL: (01580) 753031 *FAX:* (01580) 753031 *CONTACT:* Jeremy Homewood
OPENING TIMES: 0800-1700 daily
No mail order
CAT. COST: £1 + (A4) Sae *W/SALE or RETAIL:* Both *CREDIT CARDS:* Access, Visa
SPECIALITIES: Wide general range with many unusual plants. *MAP PAGE:* **3**

SHDw **Highdown Nursery, New Hall Lane, Small Dole, Nr Henfield, West Sussex, BN5 9YH**
TEL: (01273) 492976 *FAX:* (01273) 492976 *CONTACT:* A G & J H Shearing
OPENING TIMES: 0900-1700 daily
MIN. MAIL ORDER UK: £10.00 + p&p *MIN. VALUE EC:* £10.00 + p&p *EXPORT:* Yes
CAT. COST: 3 x 1st class *W/SALE or RETAIL:* Both *CREDIT CARDS:* None
SPECIALITIES: Herbs. *MAP PAGE:* **3**

SHel **Hellyer's Garden Plants,** Orchards, Rowfant, Nr Crawley, Sussex, RH10 4NJ
TEL: (01342) 718280 *CONTACT:* Penelope Hellyer
◆ *OPENING TIMES:* 1000-1600 Fri, Sat & Sun Mar-Sep (closed Aug) & by prior appt.
No mail order
CAT. COST: List 3 x 1st + Sae *W/SALE or RETAIL:* Retail *CREDIT CARDS:* None
SPECIALITIES: Unusual hardy & half-hardy plants incl. Salvia, Penstemon & small selection of Climbers, Shrubs & Rock plants. Over 90 varieties of hardy Geranium. *MAP PAGE:* **3**

SHFr **Sue Hartfree,** 25 Crouch Hill Court, Lower Halstow, Nr Sittingbourne, Kent, ME9 7EJ
TEL: (01795) 842426 *CONTACT:* Sue Hartfree
OPENING TIMES: Any time by appt. Please phone first.
No mail order
CAT. COST: Sae + 1 x 1st class *W/SALE or RETAIL:* Both *CREDIT CARDS:* None
SPECIALITIES: Unusual & interesting Shrubs, Hardy & Half-hardy Perennials incl. Salvia, Lobelia & Lysimachia. All can be seen growing in the garden. *MAP PAGE:* **3**

SHhN **Hartshill Nurseries,** Thong Lane, Gravesend, Kent, DA12 4AD
TEL: (01474) 357653 *FAX:* (01474) 321587 *CONTACT:* N Gibson
OPENING TIMES: 0900-1700 Mon-Fri.
No mail order
CAT. COST: Wholesale cat. only. *W/SALE or RETAIL:* Both *CREDIT CARDS:* None
SPECIALITIES: Trees, Shrubs, Perennials. *MAP PAGE:* **3**

SHHo **Highfield Hollies,** Highfield Farm, Hatch Lane, Liss, Hampshire, GU33 7NH
TEL: (01730) 892372 *FAX:* (01730) 894853 *CONTACT:* Mrs Louise Bendall
◆ *OPENING TIMES:* By appt.
MIN. MAIL ORDER UK: No minimum charge *MIN. VALUE EC:*
CAT. COST: 2 x 1st class *W/SALE or RETAIL:* Retail *CREDIT CARDS:* None
SPECIALITIES: Ilex. Over 70 species & cultivars incl. many specimen trees & topiary.
MAP PAGE: **2/3**

SHig **Higher End Nursery,** Hale, Fordingbridge, Hampshire, SP6 2RA
TEL: (01725) 512243 *CONTACT:* D J Case
OPENING TIMES: 1000-1700 Wed-Sat 1400-1700 Sun Apr-Aug.
No mail order
CAT. COST: 2 x 1st class *W/SALE or RETAIL:* Retail *CREDIT CARDS:* None
SPECIALITIES: Water Lilies, Bog & Marginal, Helleborus, Rodgersia, Trollius, Bergenia.
MAP PAGE: **2**

SHya **Brenda Hyatt, 1 Toddington Crescent, Bluebell Hill, Chatham, Kent, ME5 9QT**
TEL: (01634) 863251 *CONTACT:* Mrs Brenda Hyatt
OPENING TIMES: Appt. only.
MIN. MAIL ORDER UK: No minimum charge *MIN. VALUE EC:* Nmc
CAT. COST: £1.00 *W/SALE or RETAIL:* Retail *CREDIT CARDS:* None
SPECIALITIES: Show Auricula. *MAP PAGE:* **3**

SIde **Iden Croft Herbs, Frittenden Road, Staplehurst, Kent, TN12 0DH**
TEL: (01580) 891432 *FAX:* (01580) 892416 *E-MAIL:* idencroft.herbs@dial.pipex.com
CONTACT: Rosemary & D Titterington
◆ *OPENING TIMES:* 0900-1700 Mon-Sat all year. 1100-1700 Sun & Bank Hols 1st Mar- 30th Sep.
MIN. MAIL ORDER UK: No minimum charge *MIN. VALUE EC:* Nmc
CAT. COST: A4 Sae for list* *W/SALE or RETAIL:* Retail *CREDIT CARDS:* Visa, Access, AmEx, Delta, JCB, EuroCard, Switch
SPECIALITIES: Herbs & Aromatic plants. National Mentha & Origanum collection. Export orders undertaken for dispatch during Spring months. See also SEED index. *8x1st class for descriptive list. *MAP PAGE:* **3**

SIgm **Tim Ingram,** Copton Ash, 105 Ashford Road, Faversham, Kent, ME13 8XW
TEL: (01795) 535919 *CONTACT:* Dr T J Ingram
OPENING TIMES: 1400-1800 Tue-Thur & Sat-Sun Mar-Oct. Nov-Feb by appt.
MIN. MAIL ORDER UK: £8.00 + p&p* *MIN. VALUE EC:*
CAT. COST: 4 x 1st class *W/SALE or RETAIL:* Retail *CREDIT CARDS:* None
SPECIALITIES: Unusual Perennials, alpines & plants from Mediterranean-type climates incl. Lupins, Penstemons, Salvias & Umbellifers. Fruit & ornamental Trees. *NOTE: Only Fruit Trees by Mail Order (Nov-Mar). *MAP PAGE:* **3**

SIng **W E Th. Ingwersen Ltd,** Birch Farm Nursery, Gravetye, East Grinstead, West Sussex, RH19 4LE
TEL: (01342) 810236 *CONTACT:* M P & M R Ingwersen
OPENING TIMES: 0900-1300 & 1330-1600 daily 1st Mar-30th Sep. 0900-1300 & 1330-1600 Mon-Fri Oct-Feb.
No mail order
CAT. COST: 2 x 1st class *W/SALE or RETAIL:* Retail *CREDIT CARDS:* None
SPECIALITIES: Very wide range of hardy plants mostly alpines. See also SEED Index.
MAP PAGE: **3**

SJus **Just Roses, Beales Lane, Northiam, Nr Rye, East Sussex, TN31 6QY**
TEL: (01797) 252355 *FAX:* (01797) 252355 *CONTACT:* Mr J Banham
OPENING TIMES: 0900-1200 & 1300-1700 Tue-Fri & 0900-1200 & 1300-1600 Sat & Sun.
MIN. MAIL ORDER UK: 1 plant + p&p *MIN. VALUE EC:* No minimum charge
CAT. COST: Free *W/SALE or RETAIL:* Retail *CREDIT CARDS:* None
SPECIALITIES: Roses. *MAP PAGE:* **3**

◆ See also Display Advertisements

SKee **Keepers Nursery,** Gallants Court, Gallants Lane, East Farleigh, Maidstone, Kent, ME15 0LE
TEL: (01622) 726465 *FAX:* (01622) 726465 *CONTACT:* Hamid Habibi
◆ *OPENING TIMES:* All reasonable hours by appt.
MIN. MAIL ORDER UK: £10.00 + p&p *MIN. VALUE EC:*
CAT. COST: 2 x 1st class *W/SALE or RETAIL:* Retail *CREDIT CARDS:* None
SPECIALITIES: Old & unusual Top Fruit varieties. Top Fruit propagated to order.
MAP PAGE: **3**

SKen **Kent Street Nurseries,** Sedlescombe, Battle, East Sussex, TN33 0SF
TEL: (01424) 751134 *FAX:* (01424) 751134 *CONTACT:* Mrs D Downey
OPENING TIMES: 0900-1800 daily all year.
No mail order
CAT. COST: A5 Sae* *W/SALE or RETAIL:* Both *CREDIT CARDS:* None
SPECIALITIES: Fuchsia, Pelargonium, Bedding & Perennials. *Note: Separate Fuchsia & Pelargonium lists, please specify which required. *MAP PAGE:* **3**

SLan **Langley Boxwood Nursery, Rake, Nr Liss, Hampshire, GU33 7JL**
TEL: (01730) 894467 *FAX:* (01730) 894703 *CONTACT:* Elizabeth Braimbridge
◆ *OPENING TIMES:* Weekdays; Sat by appt. only. Please phone first for directions.
MIN. MAIL ORDER UK: £20.00 + p&p *MIN. VALUE EC:* £100.00 + p&p *EXPORT:* Yes
CAT. COST: 4 x 1st class *W/SALE or RETAIL:* Both *CREDIT CARDS:* None
SPECIALITIES: Buxus species, cultivars & hedging. Good range of topiary. *MAP PAGE:* **2/3**

SLBF **Little Brook Fuchsias,** Ash Green Lane West, Ash Green, Nr Aldershot, Hampshire, GU12 6HL
TEL: (01252) 29731 *FAX:* (01252) 29731 *CONTACT:* Carol Gubler
OPENING TIMES: 0900-1700 Wed-Sun 1st Jan-6th Jul.
No mail order
CAT. COST: 40p + Sae *W/SALE or RETAIL:* Both *CREDIT CARDS:* None
SPECIALITIES: Fuchsia old & new. *MAP PAGE:* **3**

SLeo **Leonardslee Gardens Nurseries, Market Garden, Lower Beeding, West Sussex, RH13 6PX**
TEL: (01403) 891412 *FAX:* (01403) 891336 *CONTACT:* Chris Loder
OPENING TIMES: Daily BY APPOINTMENT ONLY.
MIN. MAIL ORDER UK: No minimum charge *MIN. VALUE EC:* £100.00 + p&p *EXPORT:* Yes
CAT. COST: 2 x 1st class *W/SALE or RETAIL:* Both *CREDIT CARDS:* Visa, Access
SPECIALITIES: Rhododendron & Azalea in all sizes. Internet Web site: http://www.pavilion.co.uk/cmc/pcat. *MAP PAGE:* **3**

SLim **Lime Cross Nursery,** Herstmonceux, Hailsham, East Sussex, BN27 4RS
TEL: (01323) 833229 *FAX:* (01323) 833944 *CONTACT:* J A Tate, G Monk
◆ *OPENING TIMES:* 0830-1700 Mon-Sat & 0930-1700 Sun.
No mail order
CAT. COST: Free *W/SALE or RETAIL:* Both *CREDIT CARDS:* Access, Visa
SPECIALITIES: Conifers. *MAP PAGE:* **3**

SLMG **Long Man Gardens,** Lewes Road, Wilmington, Polegate, East Sussex, BN26 5RS
TEL: (01323) 870816 *CONTACT:* O Menzel
OPENING TIMES: 0900-1800 (or dusk if sooner) Tue-Sun. Please check day before visit.
No mail order
CAT. COST: Free list *W/SALE or RETAIL:* Retail *CREDIT CARDS:* None
SPECIALITIES: Mainly Conservatory plants. *MAP PAGE:* **3**

SLod **The Lodge Nursery,** Cottage Lane, Westfield, Nr Hastings, East Sussex, TN35 4RP
TEL: (01424) 870186 *CONTACT:* Mrs Sandra Worley
OPENING TIMES: 1030-1700 Wed-Sun mid Mar-end Oct.
MIN. MAIL ORDER UK: No minimum charge* *MIN. VALUE EC:*
CAT. COST: 4 x 1st class *W/SALE or RETAIL:* Retail *CREDIT CARDS:* None
SPECIALITIES: Small nursery with a wide variety of mainly Herbaceous Perennials. *Note: mail order to UK only. *MAP PAGE:* **3**

SLPl **Landscape Plants, Cattamount, Grafty Green, Maidstone, Kent, ME17 2AP**
TEL: 01622 850245 *FAX:* 01622 858063 *CONTACT:* Tom La Dell
OPENING TIMES: By appt. only.
MIN. MAIL ORDER UK: £50.00 + p&p *MIN. VALUE EC:* 100.00 + p&p *EXPORT:* Yes
CAT. COST: 2 x 1st class *W/SALE or RETAIL:* Both *CREDIT CARDS:* None
SPECIALITIES: Low maintenance Shrubs. *MAP PAGE:* **3**

SMac **MacGregors Plants,** Kestrels, Carters Clay Road, Lockerley, Romsey, Hampshire, SO51 0GL
TEL: (01794) 340256 *FAX:* (01794) 341828 *CONTACT:* Irene & Stuart Bowron
OPENING TIMES: 1000-1600 Fri-Sun Mar-Oct & at other times by appt.
MIN. MAIL ORDER UK: £10.00 + p&p *MIN. VALUE EC:*
CAT. COST: 2 x 1st class *W/SALE or RETAIL:* Both *CREDIT CARDS:* None
SPECIALITIES: Phygelius (National Collection) and less common Shrubs & Perennials, particularly for Shade. *MAP PAGE:* **2**

SMad **Madrona Nursery, Pluckley Road, Bethersden, Kent, TN26 3DD**
OPENING TIMES: 1000-1700 Sat-Tue 22nd Mar-2nd Nov.
MIN. MAIL ORDER UK: No minimum charge *MIN. VALUE EC:* Nmc
CAT. COST: Free *W/SALE or RETAIL:* Retail *CREDIT CARDS:* None
SPECIALITIES: Unusual Shrubs, Conifers & Perennials. *MAP PAGE:* **3**

SMer **Merryfield Nurseries (Canterbury) Ltd,** Stodmarsh Road, Canterbury, Kent, CT3 4AP
TEL: (01227) 462602 *CONTACT:* Mrs A Downs
OPENING TIMES: 1000-1600 Mon, 0900-1730 Tue-Sat, 1000-1700 Sun, & Bank Hol Mons.
MIN. MAIL ORDER UK: £10.00 + p&p* *MIN. VALUE EC:*
CAT. COST: 4 x 1st class *W/SALE or RETAIL:* Retail *CREDIT CARDS:* Access, Visa
SPECIALITIES: Herbaceous, Fuchsia. *Note: mail order to UK only. *MAP PAGE:* **3**

SMrm **Merriments Gardens,** Hawkhurst Road, Hurst Green, East Sussex, TN19 7RA
TEL: (01580) 860666 *FAX:* (01580) 860324 *CONTACT:* Mark & Amanda Buchele
OPENING TIMES: 0900-1730 daily.
No mail order
CAT. COST: £1.00 + 2 x 1st class *W/SALE or RETAIL:* Retail *CREDIT CARDS:* Visa, Access, AmEx
SPECIALITIES: Unusual Shrubs. Tender & Hardy Perennials. *MAP PAGE:* **3**

SMur **Murrells Plant & Garden Centre,** Broomers Hill Lane, Pulborough, West Sussex, RH20 2DU
TEL: (01798) 875508 *FAX:* (01798) 872695 *CONTACT:* Clive Mellor
OPENING TIMES: 0900-1730 summer, 0900-1700 winter, 1000-1600 Sun.
No mail order
CAT. COST: 3 x 1st class *W/SALE or RETAIL:* Retail *CREDIT CARDS:* Switch, MasterCard, Electron, Visa
SPECIALITIES: Shrubs, Trees & Herbaceous Plants incl. many rare & unusual varieties. *MAP PAGE:* **3**

SNut **Nutlin Nursery,** Crowborough Road, Nutley, Nr Uckfield, Sussex, TN22 3BG
TEL: (01825) 712670 *CONTACT:* Mrs Morven Cox
OPENING TIMES: Ring in the evening before visiting.
No mail order
CAT. COST: 3 x 1st class *W/SALE or RETAIL:* Retail *CREDIT CARDS:* None
SPECIALITIES: Hydrangea & Wisteria. *MAP PAGE:* **3**

SOgg **Stuart Ogg, Hopton, Fletching Street, Mayfield, East Sussex, TN20 6TL**
TEL: (01435) 873322 *CONTACT:* Stuart Ogg
OPENING TIMES: Appt. only, unless advertised in local press.
MIN. MAIL ORDER UK: No minimum charge *MIN. VALUE EC:* Nmc *EXPORT:* Yes*
CAT. COST: Sae *W/SALE or RETAIL:* Retail *CREDIT CARDS:* None
SPECIALITIES: Delphinium. *Seed only for export.

◆ **See also Display Advertisements**

SOkh **Oakhurst Nursery,** Mardens Hill, Crowborough, East Sussex, TN6 1XL
TEL: (01892) 653273 *FAX:* (01892) 653273 *CONTACT:* Stephanie Colton
OPENING TIMES: 1100-1700 most days mid Apr-mid Sep. Other times and if travelling please phone first, especially at weekends.
No mail order
CAT. COST: 2 x 1st class *W/SALE or RETAIL:* Retail *CREDIT CARDS:* None
SPECIALITIES: Common & uncommon Herbaceous Perennials. *MAP PAGE:* **3**

SOWG **The Old Walled Garden,** Oxonhoath, Hadlow, Kent, TN11 9SS
TEL: (01732) 810012 *FAX:* (01732) 810012 *CONTACT:* John & Heather Angrave
OPENING TIMES: 0900-1700 Mon-Fri. Weekends by appt.
MIN. MAIL ORDER UK: £10.00* *MIN. VALUE EC:*
CAT. COST: 2 x 1st class *W/SALE or RETAIL:* Both *CREDIT CARDS:* None
SPECIALITIES: Many rare & unusual Shrubs. Wide range of Conservatory plants esp. Australian. *Note: mail order within UK only. *MAP PAGE:* **3**

SPan **Pandora Nursery,** The Walled Garden, Bury Lodge Estate, West Street, Hambledon, Hampshire, PO7 4QL
TEL: (01705) 632746 *CONTACT:* Paul & Amanda O'Carroll
OPENING TIMES: By appt. only, please ring first. Ring for show list.
No mail order
CAT. COST: 3 x 1st class *W/SALE or RETAIL:* Retail *CREDIT CARDS:* None
SPECIALITIES: Cistus & Euphorbia plus expanding selection of Shrubs, Climbers & Hardy Perennials. *MAP PAGE:* **2**

SPer **Perryhill Nurseries,** Hartfield, East Sussex, TN7 4JP
TEL: (01892) 770377 *FAX:* (01892) 770929 *CONTACT:* P J Chapman (Manager)
OPENING TIMES: 0900-1700 daily March 1-Oct 31. 0900-1630 Nov 1-Feb 28.
No mail order
CAT. COST: £1.65 *W/SALE or RETAIL:* Retail *CREDIT CARDS:* Visa, Access, MasterCard, EuroCard, Switch
SPECIALITIES: Wide range of Trees, Shrubs, Conifers, Rhododendron etc. Over 1000 Herbaceous varieties, 400 shrub & climbing Roses. *MAP PAGE:* **3**

SPla **Plaxtol Nurseries, The Spoute, Plaxtol, Sevenoaks, Kent, TN15 0QR**
TEL: (01732) 810550 *FAX:* (01732) 810550 *CONTACT:* Tessa, Donald & Jenny Forbes
OPENING TIMES: 1000-1700 daily. Closed two weeks from Xmas eve.
MIN. MAIL ORDER UK: £10.00 + p&p* *MIN. VALUE EC:* £30.00 + p&p
CAT. COST: 2 x 1st class *W/SALE or RETAIL:* Retail *CREDIT CARDS:* Visa, AmEx, MasterCard
SPECIALITIES: Hardy Shrubs & Herbaceous esp. for Flower Arranger. Old-fashioned Roses, Ferns & Climbers. *Note: mail order Nov-Mar ONLY. *MAP PAGE:* **3**

SReu **G Reuthe Ltd, Crown Point Nursery, Sevenoaks Road, Ightham, Nr Sevenoaks, Kent, TN15 0HB**
TEL: (01732) 810694 *FAX:* (01732) 862166 *CONTACT:* C Tomlin & P Kindley
OPENING TIMES: 0900-1630 Mon-Sat (1000-1630 Sun & Bank Hols during Apr & May ONLY. Occasionally in June; please check.)
MIN. MAIL ORDER UK: £25.00 + p&p *MIN. VALUE EC:* £500.00* *EXPORT:* Yes
CAT. COST: £2.00 *W/SALE or RETAIL:* Retail *CREDIT CARDS:* Visa, Access
SPECIALITIES: Rhododendron, Azalea, Trees, Shrubs & Climbers. *Note: Certain plants only to EC & Export. *MAP PAGE:* **3**

SRGP **Rosie's Garden Plants, Rochester Road, Aylesford, Kent, ME20 7EB**
TEL: (01622) 715777 *FAX:* (01622) 715777 *CONTACT:* J C Heptinstall
OPENING TIMES: By appt. only.
MIN. MAIL ORDER UK: No minimum charge *MIN. VALUE EC:* Nmc *EXPORT:* Yes
CAT. COST: 2 x 1st class *W/SALE or RETAIL:* Both *CREDIT CARDS:* None
SPECIALITIES: Hardy Geranium. *MAP PAGE:* **3**

SRms **Rumsey Gardens, 117 Drift Road, Clanfield, Waterlooville, Hampshire, PO8 0PD**
TEL: (01705) 593367 *CONTACT:* Mr N R Giles
◆ *OPENING TIMES:* 0900-1700 Mon-Sat & 1000-1700 Sun & Bank Hols.
MIN. MAIL ORDER UK: No minimum charge *MIN. VALUE EC:* Nmc
CAT. COST: None issued *W/SALE or RETAIL:* Retail *CREDIT CARDS:* None
SPECIALITIES: Wide general range. National Collection of Cotoneaster. *MAP PAGE:* **2**

SRos **Rosewood Daylilies,** 70 Deansway Avenue, Sturry, Nr Canterbury, Kent, CT2 0NN
TEL: (01227) 711071 *CONTACT:* Chris Searle
OPENING TIMES: By appt. only. Please telephone.
MIN. MAIL ORDER UK: No minimum charge *MIN. VALUE EC:*
CAT. COST: 2 x 1st class *W/SALE or RETAIL:* Retail *CREDIT CARDS:* None
SPECIALITIES: Hemerocallis, mainly newer American varieties. *MAP PAGE:* **3**

SRum **Rumwood Nurseries, Langley, Maidstone, Kent, ME17 3ND**
TEL: (01622) 861477 *FAX:* (01622) 863123 *CONTACT:* Mr R Fermor
OPENING TIMES: 0900-1700 Mon-Sat 1000-1700 Sun.
MIN. MAIL ORDER UK: No minimum charge *MIN. VALUE EC:* Nmc
CAT. COST: Sae *W/SALE or RETAIL:* Both *CREDIT CARDS:* Visa, Access, AmEx, Switch
SPECIALITIES: Roses & Trees. *MAP PAGE:* **3**

SSad **Mrs Jane Sadler,** Ingrams Cottage, Wisborough Green, Billingshurst, West Sussex, RH14 0ER
TEL: (01403) 700234 *FAX:* (01403) 700234 *CONTACT:* Mrs Jane Sadler
OPENING TIMES: Irregular. Please phone first.
No mail order
CAT. COST: Sae *W/SALE or RETAIL:* Retail *CREDIT CARDS:* None
SPECIALITIES: Small nursery specialising in less common varieties, esp. Auriculas, Lavenders & Pelargoniums. *MAP PAGE:* **3**

SSca **Scalers Hill Nursery,** Scalers Hill, Cobham, Nr Gravesend, Kent, DA12 3BH
TEL: (01474) 822856, (0468) 906770 *CONTACT:* Mrs Ann Booth
OPENING TIMES: 1000-1600 Wed-Sat or by appt. Mid Mar-end Oct.
No mail order
CAT. COST: 2 x 1st class *W/SALE or RETAIL:* Retail *CREDIT CARDS:* None
SPECIALITIES: Unusual Perennials & Alpines. *MAP PAGE:* **3**

SSea **Seale Nurseries,** Seale Lane, Seale, Farnham, Surrey, GU10 1LD
TEL: (01252) 782410 *FAX:* (01252) 783038 *CONTACT:* David May
◆ *OPENING TIMES:* 0900-1700 daily
No mail order
CAT. COST: 2 x 2nd class *W/SALE or RETAIL:* Retail *CREDIT CARDS:* Visa, Switch, Access
SPECIALITIES: Pelargonium, Fuchsia, Herbaceous. *MAP PAGE:* **3**

SSmi **Alan C Smith,** 127 Leaves Green Road, Keston, Kent, BR2 6DG
TEL: (01959) 572531 *FAX:* (01959) 572531 *CONTACT:* Alan C Smith
OPENING TIMES: Appt. only.
MIN. MAIL ORDER UK: No minimum charge *MIN. VALUE EC:*
CAT. COST: 50p *W/SALE or RETAIL:* Retail *CREDIT CARDS:* None
SPECIALITIES: Sempervivum & Jovibarba. *MAP PAGE:* **3**

SSmt **Peter J Smith, Chanctonbury Nurseries, Rectory Lane, Ashington, Pulborough, Sussex, RH20 3AS**
TEL: (01903) 892870 *FAX:* (01903) 893036 *CONTACT:* Peter J Smith
OPENING TIMES: By appt. only
MIN. MAIL ORDER UK: £6.00 + p&p *MIN. VALUE EC:* £30.00 + p&p
CAT. COST: 1 x 1st class *W/SALE or RETAIL:* Both *CREDIT CARDS:* Visa, Access, MasterCard
SPECIALITIES: The Princess & Little Princess range of hybrid Alstroemeria for conservatory & garden. Also hybrid Limonium & Freesias.

SSoC **Southcott Nursery,** Southcott, South Street, Lydd, Romney Marsh, Kent, TN29 9DQ
TEL: (01797) 321848 *FAX:* (01797) 321848 *CONTACT:* Suzy Clark
◆ *OPENING TIMES:* 1000-1730 Tue-Sat Mar-Nov & Bank Hol w/ends.
No mail order
CAT. COST: 3 x 1st class *W/SALE or RETAIL:* Retail *CREDIT CARDS:* None
SPECIALITIES: Unusual Hardy & Half Hardy Perennials & Shrubs. *MAP PAGE:* **3**

SSpe **Speldhurst Nurseries,** Langton Road, Speldhurst, Tunbridge Wells, Kent, TN3 0NR
TEL: (01892) 862682 *FAX:* (01892) 863338 *CONTACT:* Christine & Stephen Lee
OPENING TIMES: 1000-1700 Wed-Sat excl. Jan. 100-1600 Sun Mar-Jul & Sep-Oct.
No mail order
CAT. COST: 4 x 1st class for list. *W/SALE or RETAIL:* Retail *CREDIT CARDS:* MasterCard, Visa
SPECIALITIES: Herbaceous, Grasses. *MAP PAGE:* **3**

SSpi **Spinners Garden,** Boldre, Lymington, Hampshire, SO41 5QE
TEL: (01590) 673347 *CONTACT:* Peter Chappell
OPENING TIMES: 1000-1700 Tue-Sat, Sun & Mon by appt. only.
No mail order
CAT. COST: 3 x 1st class *W/SALE or RETAIL:* Retail *CREDIT CARDS:* None
SPECIALITIES: Less common Trees and Shrubs esp. Acer, Magnolia, species & lace-cap Hydrangea. Woodland & Bog Plants. *MAP PAGE:* **2**

SSpr **Springbank Nurseries, Winford Road, Newchurch, Sandown, Isle of Wight, PO36 0JX**
TEL: (01983) 865444 *FAX:* (01983) 868688 *CONTACT:* K Hall
OPENING TIMES: Daily Sept & Oct. Collections by appt. Specific open days to be advertised.
MIN. MAIL ORDER UK: £10.00 + p&p *MIN. VALUE EC:* £25.00 + p&p *EXPORT:* Yes
CAT. COST: 2 x 1st class *W/SALE or RETAIL:* Retail *CREDIT CARDS:* None
SPECIALITIES: Nerine sarniensis hybrids (over 600 varieties), & some species. Interesting reference collection. *MAP PAGE:* **2**

SSta **Starborough Nursery, Starborough Road, Marsh Green, Edenbridge, Kent, TN8 5RB**
TEL: (01732) 865614 *FAX:* (01732) 862166 *CONTACT:* C Tomlin & P Kindley
OPENING TIMES: 1000-1600 Mon-Sat. Closed Jan & Jul.
MIN. MAIL ORDER UK: £25.00 + p&p* *MIN. VALUE EC:* £500.00 *EXPORT:* Yes
CAT. COST: £2.00 *W/SALE or RETAIL:* Retail *CREDIT CARDS:* Visa, Access
SPECIALITIES: Rare and unusual Shrubs especially Daphne, Acer, Rhododendron, Azalea, Magnolia & Hamamelis. *Note: certain plants only to EC & Export. *MAP PAGE:* **3**

SSte **Stenbury Nursery,** Smarts Cross, Southford, Nr Whitwell, Isle of Wight, PO38 2AG
TEL: (01983) 840115 *CONTACT:* Tony Bradford
OPENING TIMES: 0930-1700 Summer, 1000-1530 Winter Thu-Tue.
No mail order
CAT. COST: 3 x 1st class *W/SALE or RETAIL:* Retail *CREDIT CARDS:* None
SPECIALITIES: Hemerocallis, Geranium, Penstemon & Osteospermum. *MAP PAGE:* **2**

SSto **Stone Cross Nurseries & Garden Cen.,** Rattle Road, Pevensey, Sussex, BN24 5EB
TEL: (01323) 763250 *FAX:* (01323) 763195 *CONTACT:* Mr & Mrs G F Winwood
◆ *OPENING TIMES:* 0830-1730 Mon-Sat & 1000-1600 Sun & Bank Hols.
No mail order
CAT. COST: 50p refundable *W/SALE or RETAIL:* Both *CREDIT CARDS:* Visa, Access, Switch
SPECIALITIES: Hebe & Clematis, Evergreen Shrubs. Lime tolerant & coastal Shrubs & Plants. *MAP PAGE:* **3**

SSvw **Southview Nurseries,** Chequers Lane, Eversley Cross, Basingstoke, Hampshire, RG27 0NT
TEL: (01734) 732206 *E-MAIL:* tink@sprynet.co.uk *CONTACT:* Mark & Elaine Trenear
◆ *OPENING TIMES:* 0900-1300 & 1400-1630 Thu-Sat 1st Feb-31st Oct. Nov-Jan by appt. only.
MIN. MAIL ORDER UK: No minimum charge* *MIN. VALUE EC:*
CAT. COST: Free *W/SALE or RETAIL:* Retail *CREDIT CARDS:* None
SPECIALITIES: Unusual Hardy plants, specialising in Old Fashioned Pinks & period plants. NCCPG Collection of Old Pinks. *Note: mail order to UK only. *MAP PAGE:* **2/3**

STil **Tile Barn Nursery, Standen Street, Iden Green, Benenden, Kent, TN17 4LB**
TEL: (01580) 240221 *CONTACT:* Peter Moore
OPENING TIMES: 0900-1700 Wed-Sat.
MIN. MAIL ORDER UK: £10.00 + p&p *MIN. VALUE EC:* £25.00 + p&p *EXPORT:* Yes
CAT. COST: Sae *W/SALE or RETAIL:* Both *CREDIT CARDS:* None
SPECIALITIES: Cyclamen species. *MAP PAGE:* **3**

STre **Peter Trenear, Chantreyland, Chequers Lane, Eversley Cross, Hampshire, RG27 0NX**
TEL: 0118 9732300 *CONTACT:* Peter Trenear
OPENING TIMES: 0900-1630 Mon-Sat.
MIN. MAIL ORDER UK: £5.00 + p&p *MIN. VALUE EC:* £10.00 + p&p
CAT. COST: 1 x 1st class *W/SALE or RETAIL:* Retail *CREDIT CARDS:* None
SPECIALITIES: Trees, Shrubs, Conifers & Pinus. *MAP PAGE:* **2/3**

SUsu **Usual & Unusual Plants,** Onslow House, Magham Down, Hailsham, East Sussex, BN27 1PL
TEL: (01323) 840967 *FAX:* (01323) 844725 *CONTACT:* Jennie Maillard
OPENING TIMES: 0930-1730 daily Mar-31st Oct. Closed Tues. Thu-Sun only during Aug.
No mail order
CAT. COST: 1 x 1st + Sae *W/SALE or RETAIL:* Retail *CREDIT CARDS:* None
SPECIALITIES: Small quantities of a wide variety of unusual perennials, esp. Diascia, Erysimum, Euphorbia, Hardy Geranium, Penstemon & Salvia. *MAP PAGE:* **3**

SVen **Ventnor Botanic Garden,** Undercliff Drive, Ventnor, Isle of Wight, PO38 1UL
TEL: (01983) 855397 *FAX:* (01983) 856154 *E-MAIL:* simon@vbgidemon.co.uk
CONTACT: Simon Goodenough & Jan Wyers
OPENING TIMES: 1000-1700 7 days a week Mar-Oct.
MIN. MAIL ORDER UK: MIN. VALUE EC:
CAT. COST: Sae for list *W/SALE or RETAIL:* Retail *CREDIT CARDS:* MasterCard, Visa
SPECIALITIES: MAP PAGE: **2**

SWas **Washfield Nursery,** Horn's Road (A229), Hawkhurst, Kent, TN18 4QU
TEL: (01580) 752522 *CONTACT:* Elizabeth Strangman & Graham Gough
OPENING TIMES: 1000-1700 Wed-Sat. Closed December.
No mail order
CAT. COST: 4 x 1st class *W/SALE or RETAIL:* Retail *CREDIT CARDS:* None
SPECIALITIES: Alpine, Herbaceous & Woodland, many unusual & rare. Helleborus, Epimedium, Hardy Geranium. *MAP PAGE:* **3**

SWat **Water Meadow Nursery, Cheriton, Nr Alresford, Hampshire, SO24 0QB**
TEL: (01962) 771895 *FAX:* (01962) 771895 *CONTACT:* Mrs Sandy Worth
OPENING TIMES: 0900-1700 Fri & Sat, 1400-1700 Sun, Mar-Nov.
MIN. MAIL ORDER UK: £10.00 + p&p *MIN. VALUE EC:* £50.00 + p&p *EXPORT:* Yes
CAT. COST: 3 x 1st class *W/SALE or RETAIL:* Both *CREDIT CARDS:* None
SPECIALITIES: Water Lilies, extensive Water Garden plants, unusual Herbaceous Perennials, aromatic & hardy Shrubs & Climbers. *MAP PAGE:* **2**

SWCr **Wych Cross Nurseries,** Wych Cross, Forest Row, East Sussex, RH18 5JW
TEL: (01342) 822705 *FAX:* (01342) 825329 *CONTACT:* J Paisley
OPENING TIMES: 0900-1730 Mon-Sat.
No mail order
CAT. COST: Free list *W/SALE or RETAIL:* Retail *CREDIT CARDS:* Visa, MasterCard, Delta, Switch
SPECIALITIES: Roses. *MAP PAGE:* **3**

SWes **Westwood Nursery, 65 Yorkland Avenue, Welling, Kent, DA16 2LE**
TEL: (0181) 301 0886 *CONTACT:* Mr S Edwards
OPENING TIMES: Not open.
MIN. MAIL ORDER UK: No minimum charge *MIN. VALUE EC:* £50.00 + p&p
CAT. COST: Sae *W/SALE or RETAIL:* Retail *CREDIT CARDS:* None
SPECIALITIES: Pleiones & Hardy Orchids. Alpine House & Garden Orchids.

◆ **See also Display Advertisements**

SWyc Wychwood Waterlily & Carp Farm, Farnham Road, Odiham, Hook, Hampshire, RG29 1HS
TEL: (01256) 702800 *FAX:* (01256) 701001 *E-MAIL:* 101536.576@compuserve.com
CONTACT: Reg, Ann & Clair Henley
OPENING TIMES: 1000-1800 daily
MIN. MAIL ORDER UK: £1.00 + p&p *MIN. VALUE EC:* £1.00 + p&p *EXPORT:* Yes
CAT. COST: 1 x 1st class *W/SALE or RETAIL:* Retail *CREDIT CARDS:* Visa, Access
SPECIALITIES: Aquatics. Nymphaea, Moisture loving, Marginals & Oxygenating plants. Moist & Water Iris inc. American ensata. *MAP PAGE:* **2/3**

WAbb Abbey Dore Court Gardens, Abbeydore, Nr Hereford, Herefordshire, HR2 0AD
TEL: (01981) 240419 *FAX:* (01981) 240279 *CONTACT:* Mrs C Ward
OPENING TIMES: 1100-1800 Thu-Tue from Mar-3rd Sun Oct.
No mail order
CAT. COST: None issued *W/SALE or RETAIL:* Retail *CREDIT CARDS:* None
SPECIALITIES: Shrubs & hardy Perennials, many unusual, which may be seen growing in the garden. Some Seeds available from garden. *MAP PAGE:* **5**

WAbe Aberconwy Nursery, Graig, Glan Conwy, Colwyn Bay, Conwy, Wales, LL28 5TL
TEL: (01492) 580875 *CONTACT:* Dr & Mrs K G Lever
OPENING TIMES: 1000-1700 Tue-Sun.
No mail order
CAT. COST: 2 x 2nd class *W/SALE or RETAIL:* Retail *CREDIT CARDS:* Access, Visa
SPECIALITIES: Alpines, including specialist varieties, esp. Autumn Gentian, Saxifraga & dwarf ericaceous. Shrubs, Conifers & Woodland plants. *MAP PAGE:* **4**

WAct Acton Beauchamp Roses, Acton Beauchamp, Worcester, Hereford & Worcester, WR6 5AE
TEL: (01531) 640433 *FAX:* (01531) 640802 *CONTACT:* Lindsay Bousfield
OPENING TIMES: 1000-1700 Wed-Sat Apr-Jul & Oct-Dec. 1000-1700 B/Hol Mons. Also by appt.
MIN. MAIL ORDER UK: No minimum charge *MIN. VALUE EC:* Nmc *EXPORT:* Yes
CAT. COST: 3 x 1st class *W/SALE or RETAIL:* Retail *CREDIT CARDS:* Access, Visa
SPECIALITIES: Species Roses, Old Roses, modern shrub, English, climbers, ramblers & ground-cover Roses. *MAP PAGE:* **5**

WAlt Alternatives, The Brackens, Yorkley Wood, Nr Lydney, Gloucestershire, GL15 4TU
TEL: (01594) 562457 *CONTACT:* Mrs Rosemary Castle
OPENING TIMES: 14th Apr-end Sep, by prior arrangement only.
MIN. MAIL ORDER UK: £5.00 + p&p* *MIN. VALUE EC:*
CAT. COST: 3 x 1st class *W/SALE or RETAIL:* Retail *CREDIT CARDS:* None
SPECIALITIES: Unusual forms & varieties of British Native Plants. *Note: mail order to UK only. *MAP PAGE:* **5**

WApp Applegarth Nursery, The Elms, Maesbrook, Oswestry, Shropshire, SY10 8QF
TEL: (01691) 831577 *FAX:* (01691) 831577 *CONTACT:* Cathy Preston
OPENING TIMES: Please ring.
No mail order
CAT. COST: 1 x 1st class *W/SALE or RETAIL:* Both *CREDIT CARDS:* None
SPECIALITIES: Herbs & Wild Flowers with particular speciality in plants with a wildlife value. *MAP PAGE:* **7**

WASP All Seasons Plants, Greenmount, Abbotswood, Evesham, Worcestershire, WR11 4NS
TEL: (01386) 41550 *CONTACT:* Mrs A Sparkes
OPENING TIMES: By appt. only - please telephone first.
No mail order
CAT. COST: 2 x 1st class *W/SALE or RETAIL:* Retail *CREDIT CARDS:* None
SPECIALITIES: Hebe, Parahebe, climbing Honeysuckle & other choice plants. *MAP PAGE:* **5**

WBcn **Beacon's Nurseries,** Tewkesbury Road, Eckington, Nr Pershore, Worcestershire, WR10 3DE
OPENING TIMES: 0900-1300 & 1400-1700 Mon-Sat & 1400-1700 Sun.
No mail order
CAT. COST: 2 x 1st class *W/SALE or RETAIL:* Retail *CREDIT CARDS:* None
SPECIALITIES: Shrubs, Camellias, Herbaceous, Aquatics, Conifers, Heathers, climbing plants & Roses. *MAP PAGE:* **5**

WBea **Beacon's Botanicals,** Garth Madryn, Church Road, Penderyn, Nr Hirwaun, Mid Glamorgan, Wales, CF44 9JP
TEL: (01685) 811298 *CONTACT:* Mrs S H Williams
OPENING TIMES: Almost always - but please check by telephone first.
No mail order
CAT. COST: None issued *W/SALE or RETAIL:* Retail *CREDIT CARDS:* None
SPECIALITIES: Hardy Geraniums, Aquilegia, Campanula, Polemonium, Rubus. Extensive range of rare & unusual Herbaceous plants. *MAP PAGE:* **4**

WBod **Bodnant Garden Nursery Ltd, Tal-y-Cafn, Colwyn Bay, Clwyd, Wales, LL28 5RE**
TEL: (01492) 650731 *FAX:* (01492) 650863 *E-MAIL:* ianshutes@enterprise.net
CONTACT: Mr Ian Shutes
OPENING TIMES: All year.
MIN. MAIL ORDER UK: No minimum charge *MIN. VALUE EC:* Nmc *EXPORT:* Yes
CAT. COST: 3 x 1st class *W/SALE or RETAIL:* Retail *CREDIT CARDS:* Visa, MasterCard, Switch, Connect
SPECIALITIES: Rhododendron, Camellia & Magnolia. Wide range of unusual Trees and Shrubs. *MAP PAGE:* **4**

WBon **S & E Bond,** (Off.) 10 Courtlands, Winforton, Herefordshire, HR3 6EA
TEL: (01544) 328422 after 1800 *CONTACT:* Miss S Bond
OPENING TIMES: 1000-1730 Wed-Sun & Bank Hol Mons 1st Mar-31st Oct.
MIN. MAIL ORDER UK: No minimum charge *MIN. VALUE EC:*
CAT. COST: A5 Sae *W/SALE or RETAIL:* Retail *CREDIT CARDS:* None
SPECIALITIES: Shade plants. *Note: nursery at Lemore Manor, Eardisley, Hereford. *MAP PAGE:* **5**

WBou **Bouts Cottage Nurseries, Bouts Lane, Inkberrow, Worcestershire, WR7 4HP**
TEL: (01386) 792923 *CONTACT:* M & S Roberts
OPENING TIMES: Not open to the public.
MIN. MAIL ORDER UK: No minimum charge *MIN. VALUE EC:* Nmc
CAT. COST: Sae *W/SALE or RETAIL:* Retail *CREDIT CARDS:* None
SPECIALITIES: Viola.

WBro **Brook Farm Plants,** Boulsdon Lane, Newent, Gloucestershire, GL18 1JH
TEL: (01531) 822534 *CONTACT:* Mrs S E Keene
OPENING TIMES: 1000-1400 Tues & Thurs & 1400-1800 Sat, Apr-Oct. Most other times by appt.
MIN. MAIL ORDER UK: No minimum charge *MIN. VALUE EC:*
CAT. COST: 2 x 2nd class *W/SALE or RETAIL:* Retail *CREDIT CARDS:* None
SPECIALITIES: Digitalis, Papaver, Campanula & other unusual Perennials. *MAP PAGE:* **5**

WByw **Byeways,** Daisy Lane, Whittington, Oswestry, Shropshire
TEL: (01691) 659539 *CONTACT:* Barbara Molesworth
OPENING TIMES: By appt. only. Please phone first.*
No mail order
CAT. COST: Sae + 1 x 2nd class *W/SALE or RETAIL:* Retail *CREDIT CARDS:* None
SPECIALITIES: Aster, Campanula, Hardy Geranium & Pulmonaria. *NOTE: Also at Newtown Market on Tue. *MAP PAGE:* **7**

WCel **Celyn Vale Eucalyptus Nurseries, Carrog, Corwen, Clwyd, LL21 9LD**
TEL: (01490) 430671 *FAX:* (01490) 430671 *CONTACT:* Andrew McConnell
◆ *OPENING TIMES:* 0900-1715 Mon-Fri Mar-end Oct. Please telephone first outside these days.
MIN. MAIL ORDER UK: 3 Plants + p&p *MIN. VALUE EC:* 3 plants + p&p *EXPORT:* Yes
CAT. COST: 2 x 1st class *W/SALE or RETAIL:* Both *CREDIT CARDS:* Visa, Access
SPECIALITIES: Hardy Eucalyptus & Acacia. *MAP PAGE:* **4**

WCer **Cerney House Gardens,** North Cerney, Cirencester, Gloucestershire, GL7 7BX
TEL: (01285) 831205 *FAX:* (01285) 831676 *CONTACT:* Barbara Johnson
OPENING TIMES: 1400-1800 Tue, Wed & Fri Apr-Sep.
No mail order
CAT. COST: A4 Sae + 4 x 1st class *W/SALE or RETAIL:* Retail *CREDIT CARDS:* None
SPECIALITIES: Herbs, Hardy Geraniums, Ajuga, Pulmonaria, Vinca, Tradescantia & Symphytum.
MAP PAGE: **5**

WCHb **The Cottage Herbery,** Mill House, Boraston, Nr Tenbury Wells, Worcestershire, WR15 8LZ
TEL: (01584) 781575 *FAX:* (01584) 781483 *CONTACT:* K & R Hurst
OPENING TIMES: 1000-1800 Sun and by appt, May-end July.
No mail order
CAT. COST: 4 x 2nd class *W/SALE or RETAIL:* Retail *CREDIT CARDS:* None
SPECIALITIES: Over 400 varieties of Herbs. Aromatic & scented foliage plants, esp. Symphytum, Pulmonaria, Lamium, Monarda, Ajuga, Salvia, Lobelia & Crocosmia. See also SEED Index.
MAP PAGE: **5**

WChe **Checkley Waterplants,** The Knoll House, Checkley, Herefordshire, HR1 4ND
TEL: (01432) 860672 *CONTACT:* Mrs M P Bennett
OPENING TIMES: By appt. only.
MIN. MAIL ORDER UK: No minimum charge *MIN. VALUE EC:*
CAT. COST: Sae *W/SALE or RETAIL:* Both *CREDIT CARDS:* None
SPECIALITIES: Pond, Bog and moisture loving plants. *MAP PAGE:* **5**

WChr **Paul Christian - Rare Plants, PO Box 468, Wrexham, Clwyd, LL13 9XR**
TEL: (01978) 366399 *FAX:* (01978) 366399 *E-MAIL:* paul@rareplants.co.uk
CONTACT: Dr. P Christian
OPENING TIMES: Not open.
MIN. MAIL ORDER UK: No minimum charge *MIN. VALUE EC:* Nmc *EXPORT:* Yes
CAT. COST: 3 x 1st or $3 (notes not cheques, or equiv. currency) *W/SALE or RETAIL:* Retail
CREDIT CARDS: Visa, Access, Switch, Delta
SPECIALITIES: Bulbs, Corms, Tubers, especially Arisaema, Colchicum, Crocus, Erythronium, Fritillaria, Iris, Rhodohypoxis & Trillium. Also Greenhouse bulbs & ground orchids.

WCla **John Clayfield,** Llanbrook Alpine Nursery, Hopton Castle, Clunton, Shropshire, SY7 0QG
TEL: (01547) 530298 *CONTACT:* John Clayfield
OPENING TIMES: Daily - but please check first.
No mail order
CAT. COST: None issued *W/SALE or RETAIL:* Both *CREDIT CARDS:* None
SPECIALITIES: Alpines & Wildflowers. Cottage garden & Herbaceous plants. *MAP PAGE:* **5/7**

WCoo **Mrs Susan Cooper,** Firlands Cottage, Bishop Frome, Worcestershire, WR6 5BA
TEL: (01885) 490358 *CONTACT:* Mrs Susan Cooper
OPENING TIMES: Appt. only.
MIN. MAIL ORDER UK: £20.00 + p&p* *MIN. VALUE EC:*
CAT. COST: Small Sae *W/SALE or RETAIL:* Retail *CREDIT CARDS:* None
SPECIALITIES: Rare & unusual Trees & Shrubs. Provenances on request at time of order. *Note: mail order to UK only. *MAP PAGE:* **5**

WCot Cotswold Garden Flowers, 1 Waterside, Evesham, Worcestershire, WR11 6BS
TEL: (01386) 47337 (Off.*) *FAX:* (01386) 47337
CONTACT: Bob Brown/Vicky Parkhouse/John McLeod
OPENING TIMES: 0800-1630 Mon-Fri all year. 1000-1800 Sat & Sun Mar-Sep, Sat & Sun Oct-Feb by appt.
MIN. MAIL ORDER UK: No minimum charge *MIN. VALUE EC:* Nmc *EXPORT:* Yes
CAT. COST: Free *W/SALE or RETAIL:* Both *CREDIT CARDS:* None
SPECIALITIES: Easy & unusual Perennials for the Flower Garden. *NOTE: Nursery at Sands Lane, Badsey. Tel: (01386) 833849. *MAP PAGE:* **5**

WCra Cranesbill Nursery, White Cottage, Stock Green, Nr Redditch, Worcestershire, B96 6SZ
TEL: (01386) 792414 *CONTACT:* Mrs S M Bates
OPENING TIMES: 1000-1700 Fri-Tue 15th March-mid Oct. August by appt. only.
MIN. MAIL ORDER UK: No minimum charge *MIN. VALUE EC:* Nmc
CAT. COST: 4 x 1st class *W/SALE or RETAIL:* Retail *CREDIT CARDS:* None
SPECIALITIES: Hardy Geraniums. NOTE:- Mail Order Autumn only. *MAP PAGE:* **5**

WCru Crûg Farm Plants, Griffith's Crossing, Nr Caernarfon, Gwynedd, Wales, LL55 1TU
TEL: (01248) 670232 *FAX:* (01248) 670232 *E-MAIL:* bleddyn&sue@crug-farm.demon.co.uk
CONTACT: Mr B Wynn-Jones
◆ *OPENING TIMES:* 1000-1800 Thu-Sun 22nd Feb-28th Sep & Bank Hols.
No mail order
CAT. COST: Sae + 2 x 2nd class *W/SALE or RETAIL:* Both *CREDIT CARDS:* Visa, Access
SPECIALITIES: Shade plants, climbers, Hardy Geranium, Pulmonaria, rare Shrubs, Tropaeolum, Herbaceous & bulbous incl. self-collected new introductions from the far East. *MAP PAGE:* **4**

WDav Kim W Davis, Lingen Nursery & Garden, Lingen, Nr Bucknell, Shropshire, SY7 0DY
TEL: (01544) 267720 *CONTACT:* Kim W Davis
OPENING TIMES: 1000-1700 daily Feb-Oct. Fri-Sun Nov-Jan by appt.
MIN. MAIL ORDER UK: No minimum charge *MIN. VALUE EC:* Nmc
CAT. COST: 3 x 1st class *W/SALE or RETAIL:* Both *CREDIT CARDS:* None
SPECIALITIES: Alpines, Rock Plants & Herbaceous esp. Androsace, Aquilegia, Campanula, Iris, Primula & Penstemon. *MAP PAGE:* **5**

WDib Dibley's Nurseries, Llanelidan, Ruthin, Clwyd, LL15 2LG
TEL: (01978) 790677 *FAX:* (01978) 790668 *CONTACT:* R Dibley
◆ *OPENING TIMES:* 0900-1700 daily Apr-Sept.
MIN. MAIL ORDER UK: No minimum charge *MIN. VALUE EC:* £20.00 + p&p
CAT. COST: Large (A4) Sae *W/SALE or RETAIL:* Both *CREDIT CARDS:* Visa, Access, Switch, Delta
SPECIALITIES: Streptocarpus, Columnea, Solenostemon & other Gesneriads & Begonia. *MAP PAGE:* **4**

WDin Dingle Nurseries, Welshpool, Powys, Wales, SY21 9JD
TEL: (01938) 555145 *FAX:* (01938) 555778 *CONTACT:* Kerry Hamer
OPENING TIMES: 0900-1700 Wed-Mon. (Wholesale Mon-Sat only).
No mail order
CAT. COST: Free plant list *W/SALE or RETAIL:* Both *CREDIT CARDS:* None
SPECIALITIES: Trees, Shrubs & Conifers. Herbaceous, Forestry & Hedging Trees. *MAP PAGE:* **4/7**

WEas Eastgrove Cottage Garden Nursery, Sankyns Green, Nr Shrawley, Little Witley, Worcestershire, WR6 6LQ
TEL: (01299) 896389 *CONTACT:* Malcolm & Carol Skinner
OPENING TIMES: 1400-1700 Thu-Mon 1st Apr-31st July. Closed Aug. 1400-1700 Thu, Fri & Sat 1st Sep-18th Oct. Also 1400-1700 Sun 14th & 28th Sep & 12th Oct.
No mail order
CAT. COST: 5 x 2nd class *W/SALE or RETAIL:* Retail *CREDIT CARDS:* None
SPECIALITIES: Outstanding country flower garden from which exceedingly wide range of well grown hardy & half-hardy plants are produced. *MAP PAGE:* **5**

WElm **The Garden at the Elms Nursery,** Frenchlands Lane, Lower Broadheath, Worcestershire, WR2 6QU
TEL: (01905) 640841 *FAX:* (01905) 640675 *CONTACT:* Mrs E Stewart
OPENING TIMES: 1000-1700 Tue & Wed 1st Apr-30th Sept.
No mail order
CAT. COST: 3 x 1st class *W/SALE or RETAIL:* Retail *CREDIT CARDS:* None
SPECIALITIES: Unusual hardy plants & cottage garden favourites, most grown on the nursery from stock in an old farmhouse garden. *MAP PAGE:* **5**

WFar **Farmyard Nurseries,** Llandysul, Dyfed, Wales, SA44 4RL
TEL: (01559) 363389 *FAX:* (01559) 362200 *CONTACT:* R A Bramley
◆ *OPENING TIMES:* 1000-1700 daily except Christmas, Boxing & New Years Day.
MIN. MAIL ORDER UK: No minimum charge *MIN. VALUE EC:*
CAT. COST: 4 x 1st class *W/SALE or RETAIL:* Both *CREDIT CARDS:* None
SPECIALITIES: Excellent general range, esp. Helleborus & Herbaceous. *MAP PAGE:* **4**

WFib **Fibrex Nurseries Ltd, Honeybourne Road, Pebworth, Stratford-on-Avon, Warwickshire, CV37 8XT**
TEL: (01789) 720788 *FAX:* (01789) 721162 *CONTACT:* H M D Key & R L Godard-Key
OPENING TIMES: 1200-1700 Mon-Fri Jan-Mar & Sept-Nov, Tue-Sun Apr-Aug, closed Dec. Office hours 0900-1700 Mon-Fri all year.**
MIN. MAIL ORDER UK: £10.00 + p&p* *MIN. VALUE EC:* £20.00 + p&p
CAT. COST: 2 x 2nd class *W/SALE or RETAIL:* Both *CREDIT CARDS:* MasterCard, Visa
SPECIALITIES: Ivies (Hedera), Ferns & Pelargonium & Helleborus. *Note: Hellebores not available by mail order. **Plant collections subject to time of year; please check by phone. *MAP PAGE:* **5**

WFoF **Flowers of the Field,** Field Farm, Weobley, Herefordshire, HR4 8QJ
TEL: (01544) 318262 *CONTACT:* Kathy Davies
OPENING TIMES: 0900-1900 daily
No mail order
CAT. COST: 2 x 1st class *W/SALE or RETAIL:* Both *CREDIT CARDS:* None
SPECIALITIES: Traditional & unusual Perennials, Shrubs, Trees & Herbs. Summer & winter Bedding. Cut Flowers & Ornamental Grasses. *MAP PAGE:* **5**

WFox **Foxbrush Gardens,** Portdinorwic, Gwynedd, Wales, LL56 4JZ
TEL: (01248) 670463 *CONTACT:* Mrs J Osborne
OPENING TIMES: Apr-end Sep by prior arrangement only.
No mail order
CAT. COST: Sae *W/SALE or RETAIL:* Retail *CREDIT CARDS:* None
SPECIALITIES: Acer & Camellia. Conifers & hardy Perennials. *MAP PAGE:* **4**

WFro **Fron Nursery, Fron Issa, Rhiwlas, Oswestry, Shropshire, SY10 7JH**
TEL: (01691) 600605 evenings *CONTACT:* Thoby Miller
OPENING TIMES: By appt. only. Please phone first.
MIN. MAIL ORDER UK: £20.00 + p&p *MIN. VALUE EC:* £50.00 + p&p *EXPORT:* Yes
CAT. COST: 1 x 1st class *W/SALE or RETAIL:* Both *CREDIT CARDS:* None
SPECIALITIES: Rare and unusual Trees, Shrubs & Perennials. *MAP PAGE:* **4/7**

WGer **Gerddi Fron Goch,** Pant Road, Llanfaglan, Caernarfon, Gwynedd, LL54 5RL
TEL: (01286) 672212 *FAX:* (01286) 678912 *CONTACT:* RA & Mrs V Williams
OPENING TIMES: 0900-1800 daily, all year.
No mail order
CAT. COST: None issued *W/SALE or RETAIL:* Retail *CREDIT CARDS:* None
SPECIALITIES: Wide range of Trees, Shrubs, Conifers and Herbaceous Perennials, some Ferns & Grasses; emphasis on plants for coastal & damp sites *MAP PAGE:* **4**

WGle **Glebe Garden Nursery,** Kidnappers Lane, Leckhampton, Cheltenham, Gloucestershire, GL53 0NR
TEL: (01242) 521001 *CONTACT:* Miss T K Budden
OPENING TIMES: 0900-1700 daily.
MIN. MAIL ORDER UK: No minimum charge *MIN. VALUE EC:*
CAT. COST: 1 x 2nd class *W/SALE or RETAIL:* Both *CREDIT CARDS:* None
SPECIALITIES: Herbaceous, incl. unusual Hemerocallis, Liriope, Paeonia & Heuchera.
MAP PAGE: **5**

WGor **Gordon's Nursery,** 1 Cefnpennar Cottages, Cefnpenner, Mountain Ash, Mid Glamorgan, Wales, CF45 4EE
TEL: (01443) 474593 *FAX:* (01443) 475835 *E-MAIL:* 101716.2661@compuserve.com
CONTACT: D A Gordon
OPENING TIMES: 1000-1800 1st Mar-31st Oct daily. 1100-1600 1st Nov-28th Feb Sat & Sun only.
No mail order
CAT. COST: 3 x 1st class *W/SALE or RETAIL:* Retail *CREDIT CARDS:* Visa
SPECIALITIES: Conifers, Alpines especially Lewisias and perennials. *MAP PAGE:* **4**

WGre **Greenacres Nursery,** Bringsty, Worcestershire, WR6 5TA
TEL: (01885) 482206 *FAX:* (01885) 482206 *CONTACT:* Daphne Everett
OPENING TIMES: By appt. only.
No mail order
CAT. COST: Sae *W/SALE or RETAIL:* Both *CREDIT CARDS:* None
SPECIALITIES: Heathers. *MAP PAGE:* **5**

WGwG **Gwynfor Growers,** Gwynfor, Pontgarreg, Llangranog, Llandysul, Dyfed, Wales, SA44 6AU
TEL: (01239) 654360 *FAX:* (01239) 654360 *CONTACT:* David & Hilary Pritchard
OPENING TIMES: 1000-1600 Wed-Sun Spring & Summer. 1000-1600 Sat only Autumn & Winter. Please phone first.
No mail order
CAT. COST: 4 x 1st class *W/SALE or RETAIL:* Retail *CREDIT CARDS:* None
SPECIALITIES: Good general range specialising in Herbaceous plants esp. Geranium & Primula.
MAP PAGE: **4**

WGWT **Grafted Walnut Trees,** Bramley Cottage, Wyck Rissington, Cheltenham, Glos, GL54 2PN
TEL: (01451) 822098 *CONTACT:* George Latham
OPENING TIMES: Not open.
MIN. MAIL ORDER UK: No minimum charge *MIN. VALUE EC:*
CAT. COST: 3 x 1st class *W/SALE or RETAIL:* Both *CREDIT CARDS:* None
SPECIALITIES: Grafted Walnut Trees incl. nut bearing varieties of English Walnut, ornamental forms of English & black Walnut, most minor Walnut species & hybrids. *MAP PAGE:* **5**

WGwy **Gwydir Plants,** Plas Muriau, Betws-y-coed, North Wales, LL24 0HD
TEL: (01690) 710201 *FAX:* (01690) 750379 *CONTACT:* Mrs D Southgate & Mrs L Schärer
OPENING TIMES: 1000-1730 Tue-Sat & Bank Hols, 1400-1730 Sun, Mar-Oct.
No mail order
CAT. COST: 2 x 1st class *W/SALE or RETAIL:* Retail *CREDIT CARDS:* None
SPECIALITIES: Herbs, Wild flowers, native Shrubs & Cottage Garden plants incl. many for damp soils. *MAP PAGE:* **4**

WHal **Hall Farm Nursery,** Vicarage Lane, Kinnerley, Nr Oswestry, Shropshire, SY10 8DH
TEL: (01691) 682135 *CONTACT:* Mrs C Ffoulkes-Jones
OPENING TIMES: For 1997: 1000-1700 Tue-Sat only, 1st Mar-25th Oct. 1998 may differ.
No mail order
CAT. COST: 4 x 1st class *W/SALE or RETAIL:* Retail *CREDIT CARDS:* None
SPECIALITIES: Unusual Herbaceous plants incl. Hardy Geranium, Penstemon, Grasses & many others. *MAP PAGE:* **7**

◆ **See also Display Advertisements**

WHar **Harley Nursery,** Harley, Shropshire, SY5 6LP
TEL: (01952) 510241 *CONTACT:* Duncan Murphy
OPENING TIMES: 0900-1730 Mon-Sat, 1000-1750 Sun & Bank Hols.
No mail order
CAT. COST: 2 x 1st class *W/SALE or RETAIL:* Retail *CREDIT CARDS:* Visa, Access
SPECIALITIES: Wide range of own grown Shrubs, Climbing & Hedging plants. Many unusual varieties. *MAP PAGE:* **7**

WHCG **Hunts Court Garden & Nursery,** North Nibley, Dursley, Gloucestershire, GL11 6DZ
TEL: (01453) 547440 *FAX:* (01453) 547440 *CONTACT:* T K & M M Marshall
◆ *OPENING TIMES:* Nursery & Garden 0900-1700 Tue-Sat ex Aug. Also by appt.*
No mail order
CAT. COST: 3 x 2nd class *W/SALE or RETAIL:* Retail *CREDIT CARDS:* None
SPECIALITIES: Old Rose species & climbers. Hardy Geraniums. Shrubby Potentilla, Penstemon & unusual shrubs. *See Display Advert for Charity openings. *MAP PAGE:* **5**

WHCr **Hergest Croft Gardens,** Kington, Herefordshire, HR5 3EG
TEL: (01544) 230160 *FAX:* (01544) 230160 *CONTACT:* Stephen Lloyd
OPENING TIMES: 1330-1830 daily Apr-Oct.
No mail order
CAT. COST: None issued *W/SALE or RETAIL:* Retail *CREDIT CARDS:* None
SPECIALITIES: Acer, Betula & unusual woody plants. *MAP PAGE:* **5**

WHen **Henllys Lodge Plants,** Henllys Lodge, Beaumaris, Anglesey, Gwynedd, Wales, LL58 8HU
TEL: (01248) 810106 *CONTACT:* Mrs E Lane
OPENING TIMES: 1100-1700 Mon, Wed, Fri, Sat, Sun & by appt. Apr-Oct.
No mail order
CAT. COST: 2 x 1st class *W/SALE or RETAIL:* Retail *CREDIT CARDS:* None
SPECIALITIES: Hardy Geranium, Ground cover & cottage style Perennials. See also SEED Index. *MAP PAGE:* **4**

WHer **The Herb Garden,** Plant Hunter's Nursery, Capel Ulo, Pentre Berw, Gaerwen, Anglesey, Gwynedd, Wales, LL60 6LF
TEL: (01248) 421064 *CONTACT:* Corinne & David Tremaine-Stevenson
OPENING TIMES: 0900-1700 daily exc. Tues. Open all Bank Hols. (Please ring first out of season).
MIN. MAIL ORDER UK: £15.00 + p&p *MIN. VALUE EC:*
CAT. COST: List £1.50 in stamps *W/SALE or RETAIL:* Retail *CREDIT CARDS:* None
SPECIALITIES: Wide range of Herbs, rare Natives & Wild flowers; rare & unusual Perennials, Scented Pelargoniums & Old Roses. *MAP PAGE:* **4**

WHil **Hillview Hardy Plants, Worfield, Nr Bridgnorth, Shropshire, WV15 5NT**
TEL: (01746) 716454 *FAX:* (01746) 716454 *E-MAIL:* hillview_hardy_plants@compuserve.com
CONTACT: Ingrid Millington
OPENING TIMES: 0900-1700 Mon-Sat Mar-mid Oct. By appt. mid Oct-Feb.
MIN. MAIL ORDER UK: £10.00 + p&p *MIN. VALUE EC:* £10.00 + p&p *EXPORT:* Yes
CAT. COST: 4 x 2nd class *W/SALE or RETAIL:* Both *CREDIT CARDS:* None
SPECIALITIES: Hardy Perennials & Alpines incl. Auriculas. Contract growing for Wholesale. *MAP PAGE:* **7**

WHoo **Hoo House Nursery,** Hoo House, Gloucester Road, Tewkesbury, Gloucestershire, GL20 7DA
TEL: (01684) 293389 *FAX:* (01684) 293389 *CONTACT:* Robin & Julie Ritchie
◆ *OPENING TIMES:* 1400-1700 Mon-Sat.
No mail order
CAT. COST: 3 x 1st class *W/SALE or RETAIL:* Both *CREDIT CARDS:* None
SPECIALITIES: Wide range of Herbaceous & Alpines - some unusual. *MAP PAGE:* **5**

WHow **How Caple Court Gardens,** How Caple Court, How Caple, Herefordshire, HR1 4SX
TEL: (01989) 740626 *FAX:* (01989) 740611 *CONTACT:* R L Lee
OPENING TIMES: 0900-1700 Mon-Sat all year also Sun 1st May-31st Oct.
No mail order
CAT. COST: 1 x 2nd class *W/SALE or RETAIL:* Retail *CREDIT CARDS:* None
SPECIALITIES: English & old Rose varieties. Old Apples varieties. Herbaceous Perennials. *MAP PAGE:* **5**

WHut **Hutchings & Son,** (Off.) 6 Willow Road, Evesham, Worcestershire, WR11 6YW
TEL: (01386) 765835 *FAX:* (01386) 423347 *CONTACT:* Matt Hutchings
OPENING TIMES: Please telephone to arrange visit. Evening calls welcome.
No mail order
CAT. COST: Free *W/SALE or RETAIL:* Both *CREDIT CARDS:* None
SPECIALITIES: Field grown ornamental Trees. Personal delivery South Midlands. Planting service. *Note: Nursery at Knowle Hill, Badsey, Evesham. *MAP PAGE:* **5**

WIvy **Ivycroft Plants,** Upper Ivington, Leominster, Herefordshire, HR6 0JN
OPENING TIMES: Please phone for opening times.
No mail order
CAT. COST: 2 x 1st class *W/SALE or RETAIL:* Retail *CREDIT CARDS:* None
SPECIALITIES: Cyclamen, Violas, Alpines and Herbaceous. *MAP PAGE:* **5**

WJas **Paul Jasper - Fruit & Ornamental Trees, The Lighthouse, Bridge Street, Leominster, Herefordshire, HR6 8DU**
TEL: FAX only for orders. *FAX:* (01568) 616499 *E-MAIL:* pjasper253@aol.com
CONTACT: Paul Jasper
OPENING TIMES: Not open for Retail sales.
MIN. MAIL ORDER UK: £20.00 + p&p *MIN. VALUE EC:* £50.00 + p&p
CAT. COST: 2 x 1st class *W/SALE or RETAIL:* Both *CREDIT CARDS:* None
SPECIALITIES: Full range of Fruit & Ornamental Trees. Over 100 modern and traditional apple varieties plus 120 other varieties all direct from the grower. *MAP PAGE:* **5**

WJek **Jekka's Herb Farm, Rose Cottage, Shellards Lane, Alveston, Bristol, Avon, BS12 2SY**
TEL: (01454) 418878 *FAX:* (01454) 411988 *CONTACT:* Jekka McVicar
OPENING TIMES: By appt. only
MIN. MAIL ORDER UK: No minimum charge *MIN. VALUE EC:* Nmc* *EXPORT:* Yes
CAT. COST: 4 x 1st class *W/SALE or RETAIL:* Both *CREDIT CARDS:* None
SPECIALITIES: Culinary, Medicinal, Aromatic Decorative Herbs, Native Wild Flowers. *Individual quotations for EC Sales. See also SEED Index. *MAP PAGE:* **5**

WJun **Jungle Giants, Plough Farm, Wigmore, Herefordshire, HR6 9UW**
TEL: (01568) 770708 *FAX:* (01568) 770383 *CONTACT:* Michael Brisbane & Paul Lickorish
OPENING TIMES: Daily - by appt. only please.
MIN. MAIL ORDER UK: £20.00 + p&p *MIN. VALUE EC:* £25.00 + p&p *EXPORT:* Yes
CAT. COST: £5.75* *W/SALE or RETAIL:* Both *CREDIT CARDS:* None
SPECIALITIES: Bamboo. *Full descriptive information pack incl. p&p. *MAP PAGE:* **5**

WKen **Kenchester Water Gardens, Church Road, Lyde, Hereford, HR1 3AB**
TEL: (01432) 270981 *FAX:* (01432) 342243 *CONTACT:* M R Edwards
OPENING TIMES: 0900-1730 daily
MIN. MAIL ORDER UK: £5.00 + p&p *MIN. VALUE EC:* £50.00 + p&p
CAT. COST: 3 x 1st class *W/SALE or RETAIL:* Both *CREDIT CARDS:* Access, Visa
SPECIALITIES: Nymphaea (over 140 varieties). Hardy Aquatics, Marginal, Bog and moisture plants. NCCPG Collection of Water Lilies (Nymphaea) *MAP PAGE:* **5**

◆ **See also Display Advertisements**

WKif **Kiftsgate Court Gardens,** Kiftsgate Court, Chipping Camden, Gloucestershire, GL55 6LW

TEL: (01386) 438777 *FAX:* (01386) 438777 *CONTACT:* Mrs J Chambers
OPENING TIMES: 1400-1800 Wed, Thu & Sun Apr 1st-Sep 30th & Bank Hol Mons. Also Sats in Jun & Jul.
No mail order
CAT. COST: None issued *W/SALE or RETAIL:* Retail *CREDIT CARDS:* None
SPECIALITIES: Small range of unusual plants. *MAP PAGE:* **5**

WLeb **Leba Orchard - Green's Leaves,** Lea Bailey, Nr Ross-on-Wye, Herefordshire, HR9 5TY

TEL: (01989) 750303 *CONTACT:* Paul Green
OPENING TIMES: By appt. only, weekends preferred.
MIN. MAIL ORDER UK: £10.00 + p&p *MIN. VALUE EC:*
CAT. COST: 2 x 2nd class *W/SALE or RETAIL:* Both *CREDIT CARDS:* None
SPECIALITIES: Ivies, ornamental Grasses & Sedges. Increasing range of rare & choice Shrubs, also some Perennials. *MAP PAGE:* **5**

WLRN **Little Rhyndaston Nurseries,** Hayscastle, Haverfordwest, Pembrokeshire, SA62 5PT

TEL: (01437) 710656 *CONTACT:* D A & P Baster
OPENING TIMES: 0900-1700 Mon-Sat, 1100-1700 Sun. Closed August.
No mail order
CAT. COST: None issued *W/SALE or RETAIL:* Retail *CREDIT CARDS:* Visa, MasterCard, Switch
SPECIALITIES: Herbaceous Perennials, Conifers, Shrubs, Alpines, Climbers, Patio plants, many suitable for coastal locations. *MAP PAGE:* **4**

WMal **Marshall's Malmaison, 4 The Damsells, Tetbury, Gloucestershire, GL8 8JA**

TEL: (01666) 502589 *CONTACT:* J M Marshall
OPENING TIMES: By appt. only.
MIN. MAIL ORDER UK: £16.00 incl. p&p *MIN. VALUE EC:* £16.00 incl p&p *EXPORT:* Yes
CAT. COST: 1st class Sae *W/SALE or RETAIL:* Both *CREDIT CARDS:* None
SPECIALITIES: Malmaison Carnations.

WMaN **The Marches Nursery, Presteigne, Powys, Wales, LD8 2HG**

TEL: (01544) 260474 *FAX:* (01544) 260474 *CONTACT:* Jane Cooke
OPENING TIMES: Mail Order only.
MIN. MAIL ORDER UK: No minimum charge *MIN. VALUE EC:* Nmc
CAT. COST: 2 x 1st class *W/SALE or RETAIL:* Retail *CREDIT CARDS:* None
SPECIALITIES: Cottage garden Perennials, some uncommon incl. Campanula, Dendranthema, Penstemon & Phlox. See also SEED Index.

WMAq **Merebrook Water Plants,** Merebrook Farm, Hanley Swan, Worcester, Worcestershire, WR8 0DX

TEL: (01684) 310950 *FAX:* (01684) 310034 *E-MAIL:* lily@merebrk.demon.co.uk
CONTACT: Roger Kings
OPENING TIMES: 1000-1700 Thu-Tue Easter-Sep.
MIN. MAIL ORDER UK: No minimum charge *MIN. VALUE EC:*
CAT. COST: 1 x 2nd class *W/SALE or RETAIL:* Retail *CREDIT CARDS:* None
SPECIALITIES: Nymphaea (Water Lilies) & other Aquatic plants. *MAP PAGE:* **5**

WMer **Merton Nurseries,** Holyhead Road, Bicton, Shrewsbury, Shropshire, SY3 8EF

TEL: (01743) 850773 *FAX:* (01743) 850773 *CONTACT:* Jessica Pannett
OPENING TIMES: 0900-1730 daily ex. Christmas & New Year
No mail order
CAT. COST: 2 x 1st class *W/SALE or RETAIL:* Retail *CREDIT CARDS:* Access, Visa
SPECIALITIES: Hardy Perennials & Clematis. *MAP PAGE:* **7**

WMEx Marston Exotics, Brampton Lane, Madley, Herefordshire, HR2 9LX
TEL: (01981) 251140 *FAX:* (01981) 251649 *CONTACT:* Paul Gardner
OPENING TIMES: 0800-1630 Mon-Fri all year, 1300-1700 Sat & Sun Mar-Oct.
MIN. MAIL ORDER UK: See list for details *MIN. VALUE EC:* £100.00 + p&p *EXPORT:* Yes
CAT. COST: list 1 x 1st class* *W/SALE or RETAIL:* Both *CREDIT CARDS:* Visa, MasterCard, Switch
SPECIALITIES: Carnivorous plants. *Price list & Growers Guide £1.80. See also SEED Index.
MAP PAGE: **5**

WMou Mount Pleasant Trees, Rockhampton, Berkeley, Gloucestershire, GL13 9DU
TEL: 01454 260348 *CONTACT:* P & G Locke
OPENING TIMES: By appt. only.
No mail order
CAT. COST: 3 x 2nd class *W/SALE or RETAIL:* Both *CREDIT CARDS:* None
SPECIALITIES: Wide range of Trees for forestry, hedging, woodlands & gardens esp. Tilia, Populus & Sequoiadendron. *MAP PAGE:* **5**

WNdy Nordybank Nurseries, Clee St Margaret, Craven Arms, Shropshire, SY7 9EF
TEL: (01584) 823322 *CONTACT:* P J Bolton
OPENING TIMES: 1200-1800 Mon, Wed & Sun Easter-mid Oct.
No mail order
CAT. COST: 2 x 1st class *W/SALE or RETAIL:* Retail *CREDIT CARDS:* None
SPECIALITIES: Native & Hardy Herbaceous plants esp. Geranium, Campanula & Aquilegia varieties. *MAP PAGE:* **5/7**

WNor Norfields, Lower Meend, St Briavels, Gloucestershire, GL15 6RW
TEL: (01594) 530134 *FAX:* (01594) 530113 *CONTACT:* Andrew Norfield
OPENING TIMES: Not open.
MIN. MAIL ORDER UK: £3.00 + p&p *MIN. VALUE EC:* £3.00 + p&p *EXPORT:* Yes
CAT. COST: 1 x 1st class *W/SALE or RETAIL:* Retail *CREDIT CARDS:* None
SPECIALITIES: Wide range of Tree seedlings for growing on. Acer, Betula, Stewartia & pregerminated seed. See also SEED Index.

WOak Oak Cottage Herb Garden, Nesscliffe, Nr Shrewsbury, Shropshire, SY4 1DB
TEL: (01743) 741262 *FAX:* (01743) 741262 *CONTACT:* Jane & Edward Bygott.
◆ *OPENING TIMES:* Usually 1150-1750 weekdays, most weekends & Bank Hols. Best to ring first.
MIN. MAIL ORDER UK: £5.00 *MIN. VALUE EC:* £10.00
CAT. COST: 3 x 2nd class *W/SALE or RETAIL:* Retail *CREDIT CARDS:* None
SPECIALITIES: Herbs, Wild flowers & Cottage plants. Design of Herb Gardens. *MAP PAGE:* **7**

WOld Old Court Nurseries, Colwall, Nr Malvern, Worcestershire, WR13 6QE
TEL: (01684) 540416 *FAX:* (01684) 565314 *CONTACT:* Paul & Meriel Picton
OPENING TIMES: 1000-1300 & 1415-1730 Wed-Sun Apr-Oct. 2nd week Sep-2nd week Oct only 1000-1730 daily.
MIN. MAIL ORDER UK: No minimum charge* *MIN. VALUE EC:* Nmc
CAT. COST: £2.50. Price list free. *W/SALE or RETAIL:* Retail *CREDIT CARDS:* None
SPECIALITIES: National collection of Michaelmas Daisies. Herbaceous Perennials. *Note: mail order for Aster only. *MAP PAGE:* **5**

WOMN The Old Manor Nursery, Twyning, Gloucestershire, GL20 6DB
TEL: (01684) 293516 *FAX:* (01684) 293516 *CONTACT:* Mrs Joan Wilder
OPENING TIMES: 1400-1700, or dusk if earlier, Mons 1st Mar-31st Oct EXCEPT B/Hols. Winter visits by appt.
No mail order
CAT. COST: 30p + A5 Sae *W/SALE or RETAIL:* Retail *CREDIT CARDS:* None
SPECIALITIES: Predominantly Alpines, small supply of unusual and rare varieties of other Perennial plants. *MAP PAGE:* **5**

WOrn **Ornamental Tree Nurseries,** Broomy Hill Gardens, Cobnash, Kingsland, Herefordshire, HR6 9QZ
TEL: (01568) 708016 *FAX:* (01568) 709022 *CONTACT:* Russell Mills
OPENING TIMES: 0800-1700 Thu-Tue.
No mail order
CAT. COST: Sae *W/SALE or RETAIL:* Both *CREDIT CARDS:* None
SPECIALITIES: Ornamental Trees. *MAP PAGE:* **5**

WOve **Overcourt Garden Nursery,** Sutton St Nicholas, Hereford, HR1 3AY
TEL: (01432) 880845 *CONTACT:* Nicola Harper
OPENING TIMES: 0930-1630 Tues-Sat 1st Mar-31st Oct. If travelling please phone first.
No mail order
CAT. COST: 3 x 2nd class *W/SALE or RETAIL:* Retail *CREDIT CARDS:* None
SPECIALITIES: Hardy Perennials, many unusual which may be seen growing in the garden. *MAP PAGE:* **5**

WOVN **The Old Vicarage Nursery,** Lucton, Leominster, Herefordshire, HR6 9PN
TEL: (01568) 780538 *FAX:* (01568) 780818 *CONTACT:* Mrs R M Flake
◆ *OPENING TIMES:* 1000-1700 most days, but please telephone first to be sure.
No mail order
CAT. COST: 2 x 1st class *W/SALE or RETAIL:* Retail *CREDIT CARDS:* None
SPECIALITIES: Roses - old roses, climbers & ramblers, species & ground cover. Euphorbia & half-hardy Salvia. *MAP PAGE:* **5**

WPat **Chris Pattison,** Brookend, Pendock, Gloucestershire, GL19 3PL
TEL: (01531) 650480 *FAX:* (01531) 650480 *CONTACT:* Chris Pattison
OPENING TIMES: 0900-1700 Mon-Fri. Weekends by appt. only.
No mail order
CAT. COST: 3 x 1st class *W/SALE or RETAIL:* Both *CREDIT CARDS:* None
SPECIALITIES: Choice & rare Shrubs and Alpines. Grafted Stock esp. Japanese Maples, Liquidambars & Daphne. *MAP PAGE:* **5**

WPbr **Perrybrook Nursery,** Brook Cottage, Wykey, Ruyton XI Towns, Shropshire, SY4 1JA
TEL: (01939) 261120 *FAX:* (01939) 261120 *CONTACT:* Gayle Williams
OPENING TIMES: By appt. most afternoons but please ring first.
No mail order
CAT. COST: 4 x 1st class *W/SALE or RETAIL:* Both *CREDIT CARDS:* None
SPECIALITIES: Herbaceous Perennials. Many unusual varieties available in small numbers esp. Tricyrtis, Epimedium & Centaurea. *MAP PAGE:* **7**

WPen **Penpergwm Plants,** Penpergwm Lodge, Abergevenny, Gwent, Wales, NP7 9AS
TEL: (01873) 840422/840208 *FAX:* (01873) 840470/840208 *CONTACT:* Mrs J Kerr/Mrs S Boyle
OPENING TIMES: 27th Mar-30th Sep.
No mail order
CAT. COST: 2 x 1st class *W/SALE or RETAIL:* Retail *CREDIT CARDS:* None
SPECIALITIES: Hardy Perennials. *MAP PAGE:* **5**

WPer **Perhill Nurseries,** Worcester Road, Great Witley, Worcestershire, WR6 6JT
TEL: (01299) 896329 *FAX:* (01299) 896990 *CONTACT:* Duncan & Sarah Straw
OPENING TIMES: 0900-1700 Mon- Sat, 1000-1600 Sun, 1st Feb-15th Oct & by appt.
MIN. MAIL ORDER UK: No minimum charge* *MIN. VALUE EC:*
CAT. COST: 6 x 2nd class *W/SALE or RETAIL:* Both *CREDIT CARDS:* None
SPECIALITIES: Over 2500 varieties of rare & unusual Alpines & Herbaceous Perennials. Old fashioned Dianthus, Penstemon, Campanula, Salvia, Thyme, Herbs & Veronica. *Note: mail order to UK only. *MAP PAGE:* **5**

WPGP **Pan-Global Plants,** Spoonbed Nursery, Rococo Garden, Painswick, Glos, GL6 6TH
TEL: (01452) 814242 *FAX:* (01452) 813204 *CONTACT:* N Macer
◆ *OPENING TIMES:* 1100-1700 Wed-Sun 8th Jan-30th Nov. Daily July & Aug. Also Bank Hols.
MIN. MAIL ORDER UK: £100.00 + p&p *MIN. VALUE EC:*
CAT. COST: 3 x 1st class *W/SALE or RETAIL:* Retail *CREDIT CARDS:* None
SPECIALITIES: Rare, Unusual & hard to find Trees, Shrubs & Herbaceous esp. Paeonia sp. & Hydrangea. *MAP PAGE:* **5**

WPhl **Just Phlomis, Sunningdale, Grange Court, Westbury-on-Severn, Gloucestershire, GL14 1PL**
TEL: (01452) 760268 *FAX:* (01452) 760268 *E-MAIL:* phlomis@aol.com
CONTACT: J Mann Taylor
OPENING TIMES: Appt. only.
MIN. MAIL ORDER UK: £7.50 + p&p *MIN. VALUE EC:* £7.50 + p&p
CAT. COST: 2 x 2nd class *W/SALE or RETAIL:* Retail *CREDIT CARDS:* None
SPECIALITIES: Phlomis from the National Collection. *MAP PAGE:* **5**

WPLl **Plas Lluest Nursery,** Llanbadarn Fawr, Aberystwyth, Dyfed, Wales, SY23 3AU
TEL: (01970) 612101 *FAX:* (01970) 612101 *CONTACT:* David Webber
◆ *OPENING TIMES:* 1000-1630 Mon-Fri, 1100-1500 Sat, Summer only.
MIN. MAIL ORDER UK: No minimum charge* *MIN. VALUE EC:*
CAT. COST: 4 x 1st class *W/SALE or RETAIL:* Both *CREDIT CARDS:* None
SPECIALITIES: Herbaceous Perennials. *Note: mail order to UK only. *MAP PAGE:* **4**

WPnn **The Perennial Nursery, Rhosygilwen, Llanrhian Road, Sr Davids, Pembrokeshire, SA62 6DB**
TEL: (01437) 721954 *FAX:* (01437) 721954 *CONTACT:* Mrs Philipa Symons
OPENING TIMES: 0930-1730 Wed-Mon Mar-Oct. Nov-Apr by appt.
MIN. MAIL ORDER UK: £10.00 + p&p *MIN. VALUE EC:* £20.00 + p&p
CAT. COST: 1 x 1st class *W/SALE or RETAIL:* Retail *CREDIT CARDS:* None
SPECIALITIES: Herbaceous Perennials & Alpines, esp. Erodium. *MAP PAGE:* **4**

WPri **Priory Plants,** (Off.) 5 Nursery Road, Malvern, Worcs, WR14 1QY
TEL: (01684) 565246 *CONTACT:* Debbie Davies
OPENING TIMES: 1000-1400 Mon, Wed, Thurs, Fri & 1000-1600 weekends, Mar-Oct.
No mail order
CAT. COST: Sae + 1st class for plant list. *W/SALE or RETAIL:* Retail *CREDIT CARDS:* None
SPECIALITIES: Cottage Garden Plants & Unusual Perennials. *Nursery at 12 Priory Rd, Malvern. *MAP PAGE:* **5**

WPyg **The Pygmy Pinetum,** Cannop Crossroads, Nr Coleford, Forest of Dean, Gloucestershire, GL15 7EQ
TEL: (01594) 833398 *FAX:* (01594) 810815 *CONTACT:* Keith Parker
OPENING TIMES: 0900-1800 daily all year.
No mail order
CAT. COST: 3 x 2nd class *W/SALE or RETAIL:* Retail *CREDIT CARDS:* Visa, MasterCard, Switch
SPECIALITIES: Unusual Shrubs, Alpines & Herbaceous. Wide range of Trees, Heathers, Ferns, Top Fruit, Water plants & Climbers. *MAP PAGE:* **5**

WRha **Rhandirmwyn Plants,** (Off.) 8 Pannau Street, Rhandirmwyn, Nr Llandovery, Carmarthenshire, Wales, SA20 0NP
TEL: (01550) 760220 *CONTACT:* Sara Fox/Thomas Sheppard
OPENING TIMES: 1000-1700 Sat & Sun Apr-end Oct, or by appt.
No mail order
CAT. COST: None issued *W/SALE or RETAIL:* Retail *CREDIT CARDS:* None
SPECIALITIES: Old-fashioned Cottage Garden plants, over 400 varieties. *Nursery is at Pwyllpriddog Farm, Rhandirmwyn. *MAP PAGE:* **4**

◆ **See also Display Advertisements**

WRHF **Red House Farm,** Flying Horse Lane, Bradley Green, Nr Redditch, Worcestershire, B96 6QT
TEL: (01527) 821269 *FAX:* (01527) 821674 *CONTACT:* Mrs Maureen Weaver
OPENING TIMES: 0900-1700 daily all year.
No mail order
CAT. COST: 2 x 1st class *W/SALE or RETAIL:* Retail *CREDIT CARDS:* None
SPECIALITIES: Cottage garden Perennials. *MAP PAGE:* **5**

WRic **Rickard's Hardy Ferns, Kyre Park, Kyre, Tenbury Wells, Worcestershire, WR15 8RP**
TEL: (01885) 410282 *FAX:* (01885) 410398 *CONTACT:* Hazel & Martin Rickard
OPENING TIMES: Wed-Mon all year but appt. advisable Nov-Feb.
MIN. MAIL ORDER UK: £15.00 + p&p *MIN. VALUE EC:* £30.00 + p&p
CAT. COST: 5 x 1st class* *W/SALE or RETAIL:* Retail *CREDIT CARDS:* None
SPECIALITIES: Ferns, hardy & half-hardy, Tree-ferns. National Reference Collection of Polypodium, Cystopteris & Thelypteroid ferns. *Descriptive list. *MAP PAGE:* **5**

WRil **Rileys Plants Ltd, The Plant Centre, Knowle Hill, Evesham, Worcestershire, WR11 5EN**
TEL: (01386) 833022 *FAX:* (01386) 832915 *E-MAIL:* 100326.34@compuserve.com
CONTACT: John Woolman
OPENING TIMES: 0900-1700 Mon-Sun.
MIN. MAIL ORDER UK: No minimum charge *MIN. VALUE EC:* Nmc
CAT. COST: Free *W/SALE or RETAIL:* Both *CREDIT CARDS:* Access, Visa
SPECIALITIES: Chrysanthemum, Dahlias, Hanging Basket & Patio Plants. *MAP PAGE:* **5**

WRTC **Rose Tree Cottage Plants, Popes Hill, Newnham-on-Severn, Gloucestershire, GL14 1JX**
TEL: (01594) 826692 *CONTACT:* Stephen Bishop
OPENING TIMES: 1400-1800 (dusk if earlier) Mon-Fri or by appt.
MIN. MAIL ORDER UK: No minimum charge *MIN. VALUE EC:* Nmc
CAT. COST: 4 x 1st class *W/SALE or RETAIL:* Both *CREDIT CARDS:* None
SPECIALITIES: Unusual Shrubs, Herbaceous & Alpines. *MAP PAGE:* **5**

WRus **Rushfields of Ledbury,** Ross Road, Ledbury, Herefordshire, HR8 2LP
TEL: (01531) 632004 *CONTACT:* B & J Homewood
OPENING TIMES: 1100-1700 Wed-Sat. Other times by appt.
No mail order
CAT. COST: A5 Sae 29p + £1.00 *W/SALE or RETAIL:* Both *CREDIT CARDS:* Visa, Access, AmEx
SPECIALITIES: Unusual Herbaceous, incl. Euphorbia, Hardy Geranium, Helleborus, Hosta, Osteospermum, Penstemon, Primroses & Grasses. *MAP PAGE:* **5**

WSan **Sandstones Cottage Garden Plants,** 58 Bolas Heath, Great Bolas, Shropshire, TF6 6PS
TEL: (01952) 541657 *CONTACT:* Joanne Brelsforth
OPENING TIMES: By appt.
MIN. MAIL ORDER UK: £10.00 + p&p *MIN. VALUE EC:*
CAT. COST: 4 x 1st class *W/SALE or RETAIL:* Retail *CREDIT CARDS:* None
SPECIALITIES: Unusual & interesting Hardy Perennials. Also large range of variegated varieties. *MAP PAGE:* **7**

WSel **Selsley Herb Farm,** Waterlane, Selsley, Stroud, Gloucestershire, GL5 5LW
TEL: (01453) 766682 *FAX:* (01453) 753674 *CONTACT:* Rob Wimperis
OPENING TIMES: 1000-1700 Tue-Sat, 1400-1700 Sun & Bank Hols Apr-Sep.
MIN. MAIL ORDER UK: No minimum value *MIN. VALUE EC:*
CAT. COST: 4 x 1st class *W/SALE or RETAIL:* Retail *CREDIT CARDS:* None
SPECIALITIES: Herbs, also Lavandula, Penstemon & Rosemary. *MAP PAGE:* **5**

WSHC **Stone House Cottage Nurseries,** Stone, Nr Kidderminster, Worcestershire, DY10 4BG
TEL: (01562) 69902 *FAX:* (01562) 69902 *CONTACT:* J F & L N Arbuthnott
OPENING TIMES: 1000-1730 Wed-Sat. For Sun opening see NGS 'Yellow Book'. Appt. only mid-Oct-Mar.
No mail order
CAT. COST: Sae *W/SALE or RETAIL:* Retail *CREDIT CARDS:* None
SPECIALITIES: Small general range, especially wall Shrubs, Climbers and unusual plants.
MAP PAGE: **5**

WShi **John Shipton (Bulbs), Y Felin, Henllan Amgoed, Whitland, Dyfed, Wales, SA34 0SL**
TEL: (01994) 240125 *E-MAIL:* bluebell@connect-wales.co.uk *CONTACT:* John Shipton
OPENING TIMES: By appt. only.
MIN. MAIL ORDER UK: No minimum charge *MIN. VALUE EC:* Nmc *EXPORT:* Yes
CAT. COST: Sae *W/SALE or RETAIL:* Both *CREDIT CARDS:* None
SPECIALITIES: Native British Bulbs & Bulbs and Plants for naturalising. See also SEED Index.
MAP PAGE: **4**

WSPU **Specialist Plant Unit,** Pershore Colleg of Hort., Avonbank, Pershore, Worcestershire, WR10 3JP
TEL: (01386) 561385 *FAX:* (01386) 555601 *CONTACT:* Julia Sanders
OPENING TIMES: 0900-1700 Mon-Sat, 1000-1600 Sun.
No mail order
CAT. COST: £1.00 *W/SALE or RETAIL:* Both *CREDIT CARDS:* Visa, Access
SPECIALITIES: National Collection of Penstemon. Also South African plants. *MAP PAGE:* **5**

WStI **St Ishmael's Nurseries,** Haverfordwest, Pembrokeshire, SA62 3SX
TEL: (01646) 636343 *FAX:* (01646) 636343 *CONTACT:* Mr D & Mrs H Phippen
OPENING TIMES: 0900-1730 daily Summer. 0900-1700 daily Winter.
No mail order
CAT. COST: None issued *W/SALE or RETAIL:* Retail *CREDIT CARDS:* Visa, Diners, Access, Switch, Delta, MasterCard, EuroCard
SPECIALITIES: Wide general range. *MAP PAGE:* **4**

WSuF **Sunnybank Farm, Llanveynoe, Herefordshire, HR2 0NL**
OPENING TIMES: Mail Order only.
MIN. MAIL ORDER UK: £5.00 incl. p&p *MIN. VALUE EC:* * *EXPORT:* Yes
CAT. COST: Sae *W/SALE or RETAIL:* Both *CREDIT CARDS:* None
SPECIALITIES: Vines. *EC sales by arrangement.

WThi **39 Steps,** Grove Cottage, Forge Hill, Lydbrook, Gloucestershire, GL17 9QS
TEL: (01594) 860544 *CONTACT:* Graham Birkin
OPENING TIMES: By appt. only.
No mail order
CAT. COST: 3 x 1st class *W/SALE or RETAIL:* Retail *CREDIT CARDS:* None
SPECIALITIES: Shade lovers, Helleborus & Iris. *MAP PAGE:* **5**

WTre **Treasures of Tenbury Ltd, Burford House Gardens, Tenbury Wells, Worcestershire, WR15 8HQ**
TEL: (01584) 810777 *FAX:* (01584) 810673 *CONTACT:* Mrs P A Cox & Mr Charles Chesshire
OPENING TIMES: 1000-1800 daily. Until dusk in Winter
MIN. MAIL ORDER UK: No minimum charge *MIN. VALUE EC:* Nmc
CAT. COST: Free Clematis list *W/SALE or RETAIL:* Retail *CREDIT CARDS:* Visa, Access, Switch
SPECIALITIES: Clematis and Herbaceous, Conservatory plants, Bamboos, Trees & Shrubs.
MAP PAGE: **5**

WTus **Martin Tustin,** Bowers Hill Nursery, Willersey Road, Badsey, Nr Evesham, Worcestershire, WR11 5HG

TEL: (01386) 832124 *FAX:* (01386) 832124 *CONTACT:* Martin Tustin
OPENING TIMES: 0900-1800 daily ex Xmas week.
No mail order
CAT. COST: Free *W/SALE or RETAIL:* Both *CREDIT CARDS:* None
SPECIALITIES: Lavenders. *MAP PAGE:* **5**

WTyr **Ty'r Orsaf Nursery,** Maentwrog Road (A470), Ty Nant, Nr Gellilydan, Gwynedd, Wales, LL41 4RB

TEL: (01766) 590233 *CONTACT:* A G & M Faulkner
OPENING TIMES: 0900-1800 daily Summer, 0930-1530 daily Winter.
No mail order
CAT. COST: 4 x 2nd class *W/SALE or RETAIL:* Retail *CREDIT CARDS:* None
SPECIALITIES: Hardy herbaceous, Shrubs & Alpines incl. Astilbe, Campanula, Geranium, Sidalcea, Potentilla, Scabiosa etc. *MAP PAGE:* **4**

WUnd **Under the Greenwood Tree, Shrub & Wildflower Nursery, The Art Studio, Clee Liberty, Clee St. Margaret, Craven Arms, Shropshire, SY7 8EF**

TEL: (01584) 823396 *CONTACT:* David Stoves
OPENING TIMES: Mail order only.
MIN. MAIL ORDER UK: No minimum charge *MIN. VALUE EC:* Nmc
CAT. COST: 1 x 1st class *W/SALE or RETAIL:* Both *CREDIT CARDS:* None
SPECIALITIES: Complete British Flora excl. legally protected plants. Plants & seeds of known British origin. *MAP PAGE:* **5,7**

WWat **Waterwheel Nursery, Bully Hole Bottom, Usk Road, Shirenewton, Chepstow, Gwent, Wales, NP6 6SA**

TEL: (01291) 641577 *FAX:* (01291) 641577 *CONTACT:* Desmond & Charlotte Evans
◆ *OPENING TIMES:* 0900-1800 Tue-Sat. Best to phone first for directions. Also open Bank Hol Mons.
MIN. MAIL ORDER UK: No minimum charge* *MIN. VALUE EC:* £50.00 + p&p
CAT. COST: 2 x 1st class *W/SALE or RETAIL:* Retail *CREDIT CARDS:* None
SPECIALITIES: Wide range of Trees, Shrubs & Perennials etc. many unusual. *Note: mail order from Oct, last orders by end Jan. PLEASE NOTE NO EXPORT OUTSIDE EC. *MAP PAGE:* **5**

WWeb **Webbs of Wychbold,** Wychbold, Droitwich, Worcestershire, WR9 0DG

TEL: (01527) 861777 *FAX:* (01527) 861284 *CONTACT:* David Smith/Oliver Spencer
◆ *OPENING TIMES:* 0900-1800 Mon-Fri Winter. 0900-2000 Mon-Fri Summer. 0900-1800 Sat & 1030-1630 Sun all year.
No mail order
CAT. COST: None issued *W/SALE or RETAIL:* Both *CREDIT CARDS:* Visa, Access, AmEx
SPECIALITIES: Hardy Trees & Shrubs, Climbers, Conifers, Alpines, Heathers, Herbaceous, Herbs, Roses & Fruit. *MAP PAGE:* **5**

WWes **Westonbirt Arboretum,** (Forest Enterprise), Tetbury, Gloucestershire, GL8 8QS

TEL: (01666) 880544 *FAX:* (01666) 880559 *CONTACT:* Glyn R Toplis
OPENING TIMES: 1000-1800 daily Summer, 1000-1700 Winter.
MIN. MAIL ORDER UK: No minimum charge* *MIN. VALUE EC:*
CAT. COST: Free *W/SALE or RETAIL:* Retail *CREDIT CARDS:* Visa, Access
SPECIALITIES: Trees & Shrubs, many choice & rare. *Note: mail order Nov-Mar only.
MAP PAGE: **5**

WWhi **Whimble Nursery,** Kinnerton, Presteigne, Powys, LD8 2PD

TEL: (01547) 560413 *CONTACT:* Liz Taylor
OPENING TIMES: 1300-1700 Thur, Fri & Sun mid Apr-end June, & by appt.
No mail order
CAT. COST: £2.50* *W/SALE or RETAIL:* Both *CREDIT CARDS:* None
SPECIALITIES: Mainly Herbaceous, some unusual; small collections of Aquilegia, Campanula, Dianthus, Geranium, Penstemon, Viola. * Send SAE for plant list (no descriptions).
MAP PAGE: **5**

WWin **Wintergreen Nurseries, Bringsty Common, Worcestershire, WR6 5UJ**
TEL: (01886) 821858 eves. *CONTACT:* S Dodd
OPENING TIMES: 1000-1730 Wed-Sun 1st Mar-31st Oct & by appt.
MIN. MAIL ORDER UK: £30.00 + p&p *MIN. VALUE EC:* £30.00 + p&p
CAT. COST: 2 x 2nd class *W/SALE or RETAIL:* Both *CREDIT CARDS:* None
SPECIALITIES: General, especially Alpines & Herbaceous. *MAP PAGE:* **5**

WWol **Woolmans Plants Ltd, The Plant Centre, Knowle Hill, Evesham, Worcestershire, WR11 5EN**
TEL: 01386 833022 *FAX:* 01386 832915 *E-MAIL:* 100326.34@compuserve.com
CONTACT: John Woolman
OPENING TIMES: 0900-1700 Mon-Sun.
MIN. MAIL ORDER UK: No minimum charge *MIN. VALUE EC:* Nmc
CAT. COST: Free *W/SALE or RETAIL:* Both *CREDIT CARDS:* Access, Visa
SPECIALITIES: Chrysanthemum, Hanging Basket & Patio Plants, Dahlias. *MAP PAGE:* **5**

WWoo **Woodlands Nurseries,** Woodlands View, Blakemere, Herefordshire, HR2 9PY
TEL: (01981) 500306 *FAX:* (01981) 500184 *CONTACT:* Larry & Mal Lowther
OPENING TIMES: By appt. only.
No mail order
CAT. COST: 2 x 1st class *W/SALE or RETAIL:* Both *CREDIT CARDS:* None
SPECIALITIES: Common & unusual herbaceous Perennials. Shrubs, Ferns & Trees.
MAP PAGE: **5**

WWtk **Watkins Nurseries,** Ffridd-y-Gog, Corwen, Clwyd, LL21 9NP
TEL: (01490) 412524 *CONTACT:* D G & L M Watkins
OPENING TIMES: 1000-1800 Sat & Sun. Weekdays by appt.
No mail order
CAT. COST: 2 x 2nd class *W/SALE or RETAIL:* Retail *CREDIT CARDS:* None
SPECIALITIES: Herbaceous & Alpines. *MAP PAGE:* **4**

WWye **Wye Valley Herbs,** The Nurtons, Tintern, Chepstow, Gwent, Wales, NP6 7NX
TEL: (01291) 689253 *CONTACT:* Adrian & Elsa Wood
◆ *OPENING TIMES:* 1030-1700 daily 1st Mar-mid Oct. Other times by appt.
No mail order
CAT. COST: 3 x 1st class *W/SALE or RETAIL:* Retail *CREDIT CARDS:* None
SPECIALITIES: A range of herbaceous Perennials, some unusual. Aromatic, Culinary, Medicinal & Dye Herbs, Salvia, Grasses & Sedges. *MAP PAGE:* **5**

◆ **See also Display Advertisements**

Additional Nursery Index

Please note that all these nurseries are listed in ascending order of their numeric Codes.
All nurseries are listed in alphabetical order of their name in the **Nursery-Code Index** on page 703.
Addresses printed in **bold type** provide a Mail Order Service to the EU.

1 **Foliage Scented & Herb Plants,** Walton Poor Cottage, Crocknorth Road, Ranmore Common, Dorking, Surrey, RH5 6SX

TEL: (01483) 282273 *FAX:* (01483) 282273 *CONTACT:* Mrs Prudence Calvert
OPENING TIMES: 1000-1700 Wed-Sun Apr-Sep & Bank Hols. 1000-1700 Thu & Fri or by appt. remainder of year.
No mail order
CAT. COST: 3 x 2nd class *W/SALE or RETAIL:* Retail *CREDIT CARDS:* None
SPECIALITIES: Herbs, aromatic & scented plants. *MAP PAGE:* **3**

2 **Jasmine Cottage Gardens,** 26 Channel Road, Walton St. Mary, Clevedon, North Somerset, BS21 7BY

TEL: (01275) 871850 *E-MAIL:* baron@bologrew.demon.co.uk *CONTACT:* Mr & Mrs M Redgrave
OPENING TIMES: Thurdays & daily by appt.
No mail order
CAT. COST: None issued *W/SALE or RETAIL:* Retail *CREDIT CARDS:* None
SPECIALITIES: Rhodochiton, Asarina, Isotoma. Seed also available. *MAP PAGE:* **2**

3 **Ballagan Nursery,** Gartocharn Road, Nr Balloch, Alexandria, Strathclyde, G83 8NB

TEL: (01389) 752947 *FAX:* (01389) 711288 *CONTACT:* Mr G Stephenson
OPENING TIMES: 0900-1800 daily.
No mail order
CAT. COST: None issued *W/SALE or RETAIL:* Retail *CREDIT CARDS:* Visa, Access, Switch
SPECIALITIES: Home grown bedding and general nursery stock. *MAP PAGE:* **10**

4 **Clonmel Garden Centre,** Glenconnor House, Clonmel, Co. Tipperary, Rep. of Ireland

TEL: 00 353 (0)5223294 *FAX:* 00 353 (0)5229196 *CONTACT:* C E & T Hanna
OPENING TIMES: 0900-1800 Mon-Sat, 1200-1800 Sun & Public Hols.
No mail order
CAT. COST: *W/SALE or RETAIL:* Both *CREDIT CARDS:* Visa, Access
SPECIALITIES: Wide range of plants incl. many less common varieties. The Garden Centre is situated in the grounds of a Georgian Country House with extensive gardens. *MAP PAGE:* **11**

5 **Beetham Nurseries,** Pool Darkin Lane, Beetham, Nr Milnthorpe, Cumbria, LA7 7AP

TEL: (01539) 563630 *FAX:* (01539) 564487 *CONTACT:* S J Abbit or Asst. Manager
OPENING TIMES: 0900-1800 Summer, 0900-dusk Winter.
No mail order
CAT. COST: None issued *W/SALE or RETAIL:* Retail *CREDIT CARDS:* Visa, AmEx, Switch
SPECIALITIES: Comprehensive range of Trees, Shrubs & Herbaceous Plants. Many unusual varieties. *MAP PAGE:* **9**

7 **Liscahane Nursery,** Ardfert, Tralee, Co. Kerry, Rep. of Ireland

TEL: 00 353 (0)6634222 *FAX:* 00 353 (0)6634600 *CONTACT:* Dan Nolan/Bill Cooley
◆ *OPENING TIMES:* 0900-1800 Tue-Sat & 1400-1800 Sun Summer. 0830-1300 & 1400-1730 Winter. Closed Mon.
No mail order
CAT. COST: None issued *W/SALE or RETAIL:* Retail *CREDIT CARDS:* Visa, Access
SPECIALITIES: Coastal shelter plants, Eucalyptus & Pines. *MAP PAGE:* **11**

9 **Bretby Nurseries,** Bretby Lane, Burton-on-Trent, Staffordshire, DE15 0QR

TEL: (01283) 703355 *FAX:* (01283) 704035 *CONTACT:* Mr David Cartwright
◆ *OPENING TIMES:* 0900-1700 Mon-Sat, 1030-1630 Sun.
No mail order
CAT. COST: Info. on request *W/SALE or RETAIL:* Both *CREDIT CARDS:* Visa, AmEx, Diners, EuroCard, Switch, Delta, Electron
SPECIALITIES: Wide range of shrubs. *MAP PAGE:* **7**

See note on Mail Order, EC sales & Export on page 11

10 **Kingfisher Nurseries,** Catshill, Bromsgrove, Worcestershire, B61 0BW

TEL: (01527) 835084 *FAX:* (01527) 578070 *CONTACT:* Gary Booker
OPENING TIMES: 0900-1730 Mon-Sat, (0900-2000 Wed), 1000-1700 Sun all year.
No mail order
CAT. COST: None issued *W/SALE or RETAIL:* Retail *CREDIT CARDS:* Visa, Access, Switch
SPECIALITIES: Half-hardy Perennials for Patio gardening. Annual flowering plants.
MAP PAGE: **5**

12 **Banff & Buchan Nurseries Ltd, Lintmill Nursery, Cullen, Buckie, Scotland, AB56 4XN**

TEL: (01542) 841841 *FAX:* (01542) 841212 *CONTACT:* D Paterson
OPENING TIMES: 0900-1700 Mon-Fri
MIN. MAIL ORDER UK: At cost *MIN. VALUE EC:* At cost *EXPORT:* Yes
CAT. COST: 1 x 1st class *W/SALE or RETAIL:* Both *CREDIT CARDS:* None
SPECIALITIES: Hardy nursery stock. NOTE: Wholesale export only. *MAP PAGE:* **10**

14 **Seaside Nursery,** Claddaghduff, Co. Galway, Rep. of Ireland

TEL: 00 353 (0)954 4687 *FAX:* 00 353 (0)954 4761 *CONTACT:* Charles Dyck
OPENING TIMES: 0900-1300 & 1400-1800 Mon-Sat, 1400-1800 Sun.
No mail order
CAT. COST: £2.00 *W/SALE or RETAIL:* Both *CREDIT CARDS:* Visa, AmEx
SPECIALITIES: Plants & Hedging suitable for seaside locations. Rare plants originating from Australia & New Zealand, esp Phormiums. *MAP PAGE:* **11**

16 **Parkinson Herbs, Barras Moor Farm, Perran-ar-Worthal, Truro, Cornwall, TR3 7PE**

TEL: (01872) 864380 *FAX:* (01872) 864380 *CONTACT:* Elizabeth Parkinson
OPENING TIMES: 0900-1700 daily.
MIN. MAIL ORDER UK: £5.00 + p&p *MIN. VALUE EC:* £5.00 + p&p
CAT. COST: Free *W/SALE or RETAIL:* Retail *CREDIT CARDS:* None
SPECIALITIES: Herbs. Scented-leaf Geraniums & Violets, named varieties. *MAP PAGE:* **1**

17 **Old Manor Nurseries,** South Leverton, Retford, Nottinghamshire, DN22 0BX

TEL: (01427) 880428 *FAX:* (01427) 881101 *CONTACT:* Rebecca Vickers
OPENING TIMES: 1000-1700 Fri-Mon Mar-Oct.
No mail order
CAT. COST: None issued *W/SALE or RETAIL:* Retail *CREDIT CARDS:* None
SPECIALITIES: General range of hardy Perennials. *MAP PAGE:* **7**

19 **Denmans Garden, (John Brookes Ltd),** Clock House, Denmans, Fontwell, Nr Arundel, West Sussex, BN18 0SU

TEL: (01243) 542808 *FAX:* (01243) 544064 *CONTACT:* John Brookes
OPENING TIMES: 0900-1700 daily 4th Mar-15th Dec.
No mail order
CAT. COST: £2.50 *W/SALE or RETAIL:* Retail *CREDIT CARDS:* Visa, Diners
SPECIALITIES: Rare and unusual plants. *MAP PAGE:* **3**

22 **Elly Hill Herbs,** Elly Hill House, Barmpton, Darlington, Co. Durham, DL1 3JF

TEL: (01325) 464682 *CONTACT:* Mrs Nina Pagan
OPENING TIMES: By appt. only
No mail order
CAT. COST: 50p + large Sae *W/SALE or RETAIL:* Retail *CREDIT CARDS:* None
SPECIALITIES: Herbs. *MAP PAGE:* **9**

24 **Woodborough Garden Centre,** Nursery Farm, Woodborough, Nr Pewsey, Wiltshire, SN9 5PF

TEL: (01672) 851249 *FAX:* (01672) 851249 *CONTACT:* Els M Brewin
OPENING TIMES: 0900-1700 Mon-Sat, 1100-1700 Sun.
No mail order
CAT. COST: None issued *W/SALE or RETAIL:* Retail *CREDIT CARDS:* None
SPECIALITIES: Wide range of Shrubs, Trees, Herbaceous, Alpines & Herbs. Large selection of Climbers, esp. Clematis, & spring Bulbs. *MAP PAGE:* **2**

◆ **See also Display Advertisements**

25 Houghton Farm Plants, Houghton (B2139), Arundel, West Sussex, BN18 9LW
TEL: (01798) 831327* *FAX:* (01798) 831183 *CONTACT:* M J & R Lock
OPENING TIMES: 1000-1700 Mon-Fri & 1000-1200 Sat Apr-Oct.
MIN. MAIL ORDER UK: £10.00 + p&p *MIN. VALUE EC:*
CAT. COST: 3 x 1st class *W/SALE or RETAIL:* Retail *CREDIT CARDS:* None
SPECIALITIES: Euphorbia, Geranium & unusual Herbaceous. *Answer Phone (01798) 831100.
MAP PAGE: **3**

◆

26 The Flower Centre, 754 Howth Road, Raheny, Dublin 5, Rep. of Ireland
TEL: 00 353-1-8327047 *FAX:* 00 353-1-8327251 *CONTACT:* Eugene Higgins
OPENING TIMES: 1000-1300 & 1430-1800 Summer, 1000-1300 & 1430-1700 Winter daily. Mon-Sat only Jan & Feb.
No mail order
CAT. COST: None issued *W/SALE or RETAIL:* Retail *CREDIT CARDS:* None
SPECIALITIES: Impatiens, Universal pansies, Fuchsia & hanging baskets. *MAP PAGE:* **11**

27 Chennels Gate Gardens & Nursery, Eardisley, Herefordshire, HR3 6LJ
TEL: (01544) 327288 *CONTACT:* Mark Dawson
OPENING TIMES: 1000-1700 Mon, Fri & Sat Apr-Sep.
No mail order
CAT. COST: None issued *W/SALE or RETAIL:* Retail *CREDIT CARDS:* None
SPECIALITIES: Interesting & unusual Cottage Garden plants. *MAP PAGE:* **5**

28 Linda Gascoigne Wild Flowers, 17 Imperial Road, Kibworth Beauchamp, Leicestershire, LE8 0HR
TEL: 0116 2793959 *CONTACT:* Linda Gascoigne
OPENING TIMES: By appt. only.
MIN. MAIL ORDER UK: £5.00 + p&p *MIN. VALUE EC:* £10.00 + p&p
CAT. COST: 3 x 1st class *W/SALE or RETAIL:* Retail *CREDIT CARDS:* None
SPECIALITIES: Wide range of attractive Wild Flowers & Wildlife plants. No peat used.
MAP PAGE: **7**

30 Nanney's Bridge Nursery, Church Minshull, Nantwich, Cheshire, CW5 6DY
TEL: (01270) 522239 *FAX:* (01270) 522523 *CONTACT:* C M Dickinson
OPENING TIMES: By appt. only.
No mail order
CAT. COST: 3 x 1st class *W/SALE or RETAIL:* Both *CREDIT CARDS:* None
SPECIALITIES: Erysimums, Geraniums, Penstemons, Salvias & Ornamental Grasses.
MAP PAGE: **7**

31 Cold Harbour Nursery, (Off.) 19 Hilary Road, Poole, Dorset, BH17 7LZ
TEL: 01202 696875 evenings *CONTACT:* Steve Saunders
OPENING TIMES: 1400-1800 Sat, 1000-1800 Sun & Bank Hols (dusk if earlier) Mar-Oct. Other times by appt.
No mail order
CAT. COST: 2 x 2nd class *W/SALE or RETAIL:* Retail *CREDIT CARDS:* None
SPECIALITIES: Herbaceous Perennials, incl. hardy Geraniums & Grasses. NOTE:- Nursery at Bere Road, (opp. Silent Woman Inn), Wareham, Dorset. *MAP PAGE:* **2**

32 Grange Farm Nursery, Guarlford, Malvern, Worcestershire, WR13 6NY
TEL: (01684) 562544 *CONTACT:* Mrs C Nicholls
◆ *OPENING TIMES:* 0900-1730 daily Summer. 0900-1700 daily Winter. ex Xmas & 2 weeks in Jan.
No mail order
CAT. COST: Free pamphlet *W/SALE or RETAIL:* Retail *CREDIT CARDS:* Visa, Access, Switch
SPECIALITIES: Wide general range of container grown hardy Shrubs, Trees, Conifers, Heathers, Alpines & Herbaceous. Shrub, climbing & bush Roses. *MAP PAGE:* **5**

See note on Mail Order, EC sales & Export on page 11

33 Birchwood Farm Nursery, Portway, Coxbench, Derbyshire, DE21 5BE
TEL: (01332) 880685 *CONTACT:* Mr & Mrs S Crooks
◆ *OPENING TIMES:* 0900-1700 Mon, Tue, Thu, Fri, Sat Mar-Oct or by appt.
No mail order
CAT. COST: None issued *W/SALE or RETAIL:* Retail *CREDIT CARDS:* None
SPECIALITIES: Unusual Hardy Perennials & Shrubs. *MAP PAGE:* **7**

34 Bradley Nursery and Gardens, Sled Lane, Wylam, Northumberland, NE41 8JL
TEL: (01661) 852176 *E-MAIL:* yp@dial.pipex.com *CONTACT:* Chris Potter
OPENING TIMES: 0900-1700 daily Mar-Oct.
No mail order
CAT. COST: None issued *W/SALE or RETAIL:* Retail *CREDIT CARDS:* MasterCard, Visa
SPECIALITIES: Herbs & Cottage Garden plants. Herbaceous Perennials & Shrubs.
MAP PAGE: **10**

36 Herterton House Garden Nursery, Hartington, Cambo, Morpeth, Northumberland, NE61 4BN
TEL: (01670) 774278 *CONTACT:* Mrs M Lawley & Mr Frank Lawley
OPENING TIMES: 1330-1730 Mon Wed Fri-Sun 1st April-end Sep. (Earlier or later in the year weather permitting).
No mail order
CAT. COST: None issued *W/SALE or RETAIL:* Retail *CREDIT CARDS:* None
SPECIALITIES: Achillea, Aquilegia, Geum, Geranium, Polemonium. *MAP PAGE:* **10**

40 Layham Garden Centre, Lower Road, Staple, Canterbury, Kent, CT3 1LH
TEL: (01304) 611380 (off.), (01304) 813267 (gdn. centre) *FAX:* (01304) 615349
CONTACT: L W Wessel
OPENING TIMES: 0900-1700 Mon-Sat 0900-1700 Sun.
MIN. MAIL ORDER UK: £10.00 + p&p *MIN. VALUE EC:* £25.00 + p&p
CAT. COST: Free *W/SALE or RETAIL:* Both *CREDIT CARDS:* Visa, AmEx, Switch
SPECIALITIES: Roses, Herbaceous, Shrubs, Trees, Conifers, Liners & Whips. Aquatic plants.
MAP PAGE: **3**

41 Littlewood Farm Nursery, Cheddleton, Nr Leek, Staffordshire, ST13 7LB
TEL: (01538) 360478 *CONTACT:* Nanette Bloore
OPENING TIMES: 1000-1800 Tue-Sun & Bank Hols Apr-Oct
No mail order
CAT. COST: 3 x 1st class *W/SALE or RETAIL:* Retail *CREDIT CARDS:* None
SPECIALITIES: Unusual Hardy Herbaceous plants, incl. Hardy Geranium, Campanula, Hosta & Pulmonaria. Also Grasses & Alpines. *MAP PAGE:* **7**

43 Marle Place Plants & Gardens, Marle Place, Brenchley, Nr Tonbridge, Kent, TN12 7HS
TEL: (01892) 722304 *FAX:* (01892) 724099 *CONTACT:* Mrs L M Williams
OPENING TIMES: Easter-end Oct. Gardens open 1000-1730.
MIN. MAIL ORDER UK: No minimum charge *MIN. VALUE EC:* Nmc
CAT. COST: 1 x 1st class *W/SALE or RETAIL:* Retail *CREDIT CARDS:* None
SPECIALITIES: Herbs, Wild Flowers, Aromatics, Santolina & Calamintha. *MAP PAGE:* **3**

45 Field House Gardens, Field House, Clee St Margaret, Craven Arms, Shropshire, SY7 9DT
TEL: (01584) 823242 *FAX:* (01584) 823242 *CONTACT:* John & Pam Bell
OPENING TIMES: 1200-1700 first Sat & Sun in month 5th Apr-5th Oct 1997, or by appt.
No mail order
CAT. COST: 4 x 2nd class *W/SALE or RETAIL:* Retail *CREDIT CARDS:* None
SPECIALITIES: Hardy herbaceous Perennials esp. Campanulas, Geranium & Penstemon all propagated from the attached garden. *MAP PAGE:* **5**

46 Cilwern Plants, Cilwern, Talley, Llandeilo, Dyfed, Wales, SA19 7YH
TEL: (01558) 685526 *CONTACT:* Anne Knatchbull-Hugessen
◆ *OPENING TIMES:* 1100-1800 daily Apr-Sept, 1100-dusk daily Oct-Mar.
MIN. MAIL ORDER UK: £10.00 + p&p *MIN. VALUE EC:* £30.00 + p&p
CAT. COST: Sae for list *W/SALE or RETAIL:* Retail *CREDIT CARDS:* None
SPECIALITIES: Hardy Perennials, esp. Geraniums & Penstemon. *MAP PAGE:* **4**

◆ **See also Display Advertisements**

Additional Nursery Index

47 Sue Robinson, 21 Bederic Close, Bury St Edmunds, Suffolk, IP32 7DN
TEL: (01284) 764310 *FAX:* (01284) 764310 *CONTACT:* Sue Robinson
OPENING TIMES: By appt. only.
No mail order
CAT. COST: None issued *W/SALE or RETAIL:* Retail *CREDIT CARDS:* None
SPECIALITIES: Variegated & Foliage plants. Garden open. Lectures at Clubs & Societies, group bookings welcome.

53 The Priory, Kemerton, Tewkesbury, Gloucestershire, GL20 7JN
TEL: (01386) 725258 *FAX:* (01386) 725258 *CONTACT:* Mrs P Healing
OPENING TIMES: 1400-1900 Thurs afternoons.
No mail order
CAT. COST: None issued *W/SALE or RETAIL:* Retail *CREDIT CARDS:* Visa, Access, AmEx, Diners
SPECIALITIES: Daturas, Rare & unusual plants. *MAP PAGE:* **5**

54 Bucknell Nurseries, Bucknell, Shropshire, SY7 0EL
TEL: (01547) 530606 *FAX:* (01547) 530699 *CONTACT:* A N Coull
OPENING TIMES: 0800-1700 Mon-Fri & 1000-1300 Sat.
No mail order
CAT. COST: Free *W/SALE or RETAIL:* Both *CREDIT CARDS:* None
SPECIALITIES: Bare rooted hedging Conifers & forest Trees. *MAP PAGE:* **5**

56 Ryans Nurseries, Lissivigeen, Killarney, Co. Kerry, Rep. of Ireland
TEL: 00 353 (0)6433507 *FAX:* 00 353 (0)6433507 *CONTACT:* Mr T Ryan
OPENING TIMES: 0900-1800 Mon-Sat 1400-1800 Sun.
No mail order
CAT. COST: None issued *W/SALE or RETAIL:* Retail *CREDIT CARDS:* Visa
SPECIALITIES: Camellia, Pieris, Azalea, Acacia, Eucalyptus, Dicksonia & many tender & rare plants. *MAP PAGE:* **11**

60 Muckross Garden Centre, Muckross, Killarney, Co. Kerry, Rep. of Ireland
TEL: 00 353 (0)6434044 *FAX:* 00 353 (0)6431114 *CONTACT:* John R Fuller B.Ag.Sc.(Hort.)
OPENING TIMES: 1000-1800 Tue-Sat & 1415-1800 Sun. Jan & Feb please check first.
MIN. MAIL ORDER UK: IR£20.00 + p&p *MIN. VALUE EC:* IR£20.00 + p&p
CAT. COST: Free *W/SALE or RETAIL:* Retail *CREDIT CARDS:* Visa, Access
SPECIALITIES: Many rare & unusual plants. Azalea, Hydrangea, Rhododendron & Camellia *MAP PAGE:* **11**

61 Wards Nurseries (Sarratt) Ltd, Dawes Lane, Sarratt, Nr Rickmansworth, Hertfordshire, WD3 6BQ
TEL: (01923) 263237 *FAX:* (01923) 270930 *CONTACT:* M F Rawlins
OPENING TIMES: 0800-1700 Mon-Sat, 1030-1630 Summer Suns, 1000-1600 Winter Suns.
No mail order
CAT. COST: Sae* *W/SALE or RETAIL:* Both *CREDIT CARDS:* Visa, Access, AmEx
SPECIALITIES: Shrubs & Climbers, fragrant & aromatic plants. *State interest when asking for lists. *MAP PAGE:* **6**

63 Kayes Garden Nursery, 1700 Melton Road, Rearsby, Leicestershire, LE7 4YR
TEL: (01664) 424578 *CONTACT:* Hazel Kaye
OPENING TIMES: 1000-1700 Tues-Sat & Bank Hols 1000-1200 Sun Mar-Oct. 1000-1600 Fri & Sat Nov, Dec & Feb. Closed Jan.
No mail order
CAT. COST: 2 x 1st class *W/SALE or RETAIL:* Retail *CREDIT CARDS:* None
SPECIALITIES: Herbaceous inc. Campanula, Nepeta, Potentilla, Pulmonaria, Sedum, Digitalis, Euphorbia, Geranium, Lathyrus, Veronica etc. *MAP PAGE:* **7**

See note on Mail Order, EC sales & Export on page 11

73 Newton Hill Alpines, 335 Leeds Road, Newton Hill, Wakefield, Yorkshire, WF1 2JH

TEL: (01924) 377056 *CONTACT:* Sheena Vigors
OPENING TIMES: 0900-1700 Fri-Wed all year. Closed Thur. Please phone first.
No mail order
CAT. COST: 2 x 1st class *W/SALE or RETAIL:* Both *CREDIT CARDS:* None
SPECIALITIES: Alpines, esp. Saxifraga, also Erica, Conifers & dwarf Shrubs. *MAP PAGE:* **9**

77 The Old Mill Herbary, Helland Bridge, Bodmin, Cornwall, PL30 4QR

TEL: (01208) 841206 *FAX:* (01208) 841206 *CONTACT:* Mrs B Whurr
OPENING TIMES: 1000-1700 Thurs-Tues Apr-19th Oct
No mail order
CAT. COST: 6 x 1st class *W/SALE or RETAIL:* Retail *CREDIT CARDS:* None
SPECIALITIES: Culinary, Medicinal & Aromatic Herbs, Shrubs, Climbing & Herbaceous plants. *MAP PAGE:* **1**

78 Bloomers Nurseries, Nash Road, Thornborough, Nr Buckingham, MK18 2DR

TEL: (01280) 815987 *CONTACT:* Caroline Gilchrist
OPENING TIMES: 0900-1700 Mon-Fri, 1000-1700 Sat & Sun. Closed 1st Nov-1st Mar.
No mail order
CAT. COST: 4 x 1st class *W/SALE or RETAIL:* Retail *CREDIT CARDS:* None
SPECIALITIES: Herbaceous & Shrub Roses. *MAP PAGE:* **5**

84 Crocknafeola Nursery, Killybegs, Co. Donegal, Rep. of Ireland

TEL: 00 353 (0)73 51018 *FAX:* 00 353 (0)73 51018 *CONTACT:* Andy McKenna
OPENING TIMES: 0900-2000 Mon-Sat & 1200-1800 Sun in Summer, until dusk in Winter; closed Dec-Feb.
No mail order
CAT. COST: None issued *W/SALE or RETAIL:* Retail *CREDIT CARDS:* None
SPECIALITIES: Hardy Shrubs, Trees & Hedging suitable for exposed areas. *MAP PAGE:* **11**

86 R F Beeston, (Office) 294 Ombersley Road, Worcester, Worcestershire, WR3 7HD

TEL: (01905) 453245 *CONTACT:* R F Beeston
OPENING TIMES: By appt. only Mon-Fri 1st Mar-31st Oct.
MIN. MAIL ORDER UK: No minimum charge *MIN. VALUE EC:* £50.00 + p&p
CAT. COST: Sae *W/SALE or RETAIL:* Retail *CREDIT CARDS:* None
SPECIALITIES: Rare Alpines, esp. Androsace, Dionysia, Primula, Saxifraga, Gentiana. NOTE: Nursery at Bevere Nursery, Bevere, Worcester. *MAP PAGE:* **5**

87 Walled Garden Nursery, Helwith Cottage, Marske, Richmond, North Yorkshire, DL11 7EG

TEL: (01748) 884774 *FAX:* (01748) 884774 *CONTACT:* Howard Leslie
OPENING TIMES: 1000-1800 Wed-Sun. Also by appt. NOTE: Nursery at Barningham, nr Barnard Castle.
MIN. MAIL ORDER UK: £2.00 + p&p *MIN. VALUE EC:*
CAT. COST: 3 x 2nd class *W/SALE or RETAIL:* Both *CREDIT CARDS:* None
SPECIALITIES: Less common Hardy Herbaceous plants, esp. Corydalis. *MAP PAGE:* **9**

88 Goldsmith Trees & Landscape Ltd, Crown Nursery, High Street, Ufford, Woodbridge, Suffolk, IP13 6EL

TEL: (01394) 460755 *FAX:* (01394) 460142 *CONTACT:* Jill Proctor
◆ *OPENING TIMES:* 0900-1700 Mon-Sat
MIN. MAIL ORDER UK: No minimum charge* *MIN. VALUE EC:*
CAT. COST: Free *W/SALE or RETAIL:* Both *CREDIT CARDS:* Visa, Delta, MasterCard, EuroCard, JCB, Switch
SPECIALITIES: Mature & semi-mature Native & Ornamental Trees. *Note: mail order to UK only. *MAP PAGE:* **6**

◆ **See also Display Advertisements**

99 Earlstone Nursery, Earlstone Manor Farm, Burghclere, Newbury, Berkshire, RG15 9NG

TEL: (01635) 278648 *FAX:* (01635) 278672 *E-MAIL:* ginsberg@dial.pipex.com
CONTACT: B C Ginsberg
OPENING TIMES: By appt.
MIN. MAIL ORDER UK: £50.00 + p&p* *MIN. VALUE EC:*
CAT. COST: Free *W/SALE or RETAIL:* Both *CREDIT CARDS:* None
SPECIALITIES: Buxus sempervirens. *Note: UK export only. *MAP PAGE:* **2**

100 Newington Nurseries, Newington, Wallingford, Oxfordshire, OX10 7AW

TEL: (01865) 400533 *FAX:* (01865) 891766 *E-MAIL:* new.nurse@btinternet.com
CONTACT: Mrs A T Hendry
OPENING TIMES: 1000-1700 Tues-Sun Mar-Oct, 1000-1600 Tues-Sun Nov-Feb.
No mail order
CAT. COST: 4 x 1st class *W/SALE or RETAIL:* Retail *CREDIT CARDS:* Access, MasterCard, Visa
SPECIALITIES: Unusual cottage garden plants, old-fashioned Roses, Conservatory Plants & Herbs. *MAP PAGE:* **5**

101 Wharf Nurseries, Wharf House, The Wharf, Leicester Road, Market Harborough, Leicestershire, LE16 7BH

TEL: (01858) 468201, (01858) 431465 *FAX:* (01858) 431465 *CONTACT:* Tom Isaac/Wayne Hyde
OPENING TIMES: 0900-1700 Mon-Fri Apr-Sept
No mail order
CAT. COST: 2 x 2nd class *W/SALE or RETAIL:* Both *CREDIT CARDS:* None
SPECIALITIES: Aptenia cordifolia. *MAP PAGE:* **7**

102 S & N Brackley, 117 Winslow Road, Wingrave, Aylesbury, Buckinghamshire, HP22 4QB

TEL: (01296) 681384 *CONTACT:* Mrs S Brackley/Mrs K Earwicker
OPENING TIMES: Please phone for appt.
MIN. MAIL ORDER UK: No minimum charge* *MIN. VALUE EC:* Nmc *EXPORT:* Yes
CAT. COST: 1st class Sae. *W/SALE or RETAIL:* Both *CREDIT CARDS:* None
SPECIALITIES: Sweet Pea Plants (for collection only). *Note: Onion & Leek Plants by mail order. Seeds only by mail to EC. See also Seed Supplier Index. *MAP PAGE:* **5/6**

103 Castle Gardens, New Road, Sherborne, Dorset, DT9 3SA

TEL: (01935) 817747 *FAX:* (01935) 817427 *CONTACT:* Geoff Cooney
OPENING TIMES: 0900-1800 every day exc. Christmas & Boxing Day.
MIN. MAIL ORDER UK: £15.00 + p&p *MIN. VALUE EC:* £20.00 + p&p
CAT. COST: £3.00 in stamps *W/SALE or RETAIL:* Retail *CREDIT CARDS:* MasterCard, Visa, Switch, Delta
SPECIALITIES: Wide general range. Strong in Shrubs, Herbaceous, Roses & Clematis. *MAP PAGE:* **2**

104 Eggesford Gardens, Eggesford, Chulmleigh, Devon, EX18 7QU

TEL: (01769) 580250 *FAX:* (01769) 581041 *CONTACT:* Jonathon Parrish
OPENING TIMES: 0900-1800 every day exc. Christmas & Boxing Day.
MIN. MAIL ORDER UK: £15.00 + p&p *MIN. VALUE EC:* £20.00 + p&p
CAT. COST: £3.00 in stamps *W/SALE or RETAIL:* Retail *CREDIT CARDS:* MasterCard, Visa, Switch, Delta
SPECIALITIES: Wide General Range. Strong in Shrubs, Herbaceous, Roses & Clematis. *MAP PAGE:* **1**

105 Tickenham Gardens, Clevedon Road, Tickenham, Clevedon, BS21 6SD

TEL: (01275) 858015 *FAX:* (01275) 858290 *CONTACT:* Tim Hanley
OPENING TIMES: 0900-1800 every day exc. Christmas & Boxing Day.
MIN. MAIL ORDER UK: £15.00 + p&p *MIN. VALUE EC:* £20.00 + p&p
CAT. COST: £3.00 in stamps *W/SALE or RETAIL:* Retail *CREDIT CARDS:* MasterCard, Visa, Switch, Delta
SPECIALITIES: Wide General Range. Strong in Shrubs, Herbaceous, Roses & Clematis. *MAP PAGE:* **2**

See note on Mail Order, EC sales & Export on page 11

106 Brimsmore Gardens, Tintinhull Road, Yeovil, Somerset, BA21 3NU

TEL: (01935) 411000 *FAX:* (01935) 411129 *CONTACT:* Malcolm Mills
OPENING TIMES: 0900-1800 every day exc. Christmas & Boxing Day.
MIN. MAIL ORDER UK: £15.00 + p&p *MIN. VALUE EC:* £20.00 + p&p
CAT. COST: £3.00 in stamps *W/SALE or RETAIL:* Retail *CREDIT CARDS:* MasterCard, Visa, Switch, Delta
SPECIALITIES: Wide general range. Strong in Shrubs, Herbaceous, Roses & Clematis.
MAP PAGE: **2**

107 MapleAsh Plants, Ashcombe Cottage, Ranmore Common, Dorking, Surrey, RH5 6SP

TEL: (01306) 881599 *CONTACT:* Beryl Davis
OPENING TIMES: By appt.
No mail order
CAT. COST: None issued *W/SALE or RETAIL:* Retail *CREDIT CARDS:* None
SPECIALITIES: Less usual Hardy Perennials. Garden open. *MAP PAGE:* **3**

108 Tinpenny Plants, Tinpenny Farm, Fiddington, Tewkesbury, Glos, GL20 7BJ

TEL: (01684) 292668 *CONTACT:* Elaine Horton
OPENING TIMES: 1200-1700 Wed, or by appt.
No mail order
CAT. COST: 2 x 1st class *W/SALE or RETAIL:* Retail *CREDIT CARDS:* None
SPECIALITIES: Wide range of Hardy garden worthy plants esp. Helleborus, Iris & Sempervivum.
MAP PAGE: **5**

109 Brogdale Horticultural Trust, Brogdale Road, Faversham, Kent, ME13 8XZ

TEL: (01795) 535286 *FAX:* (01795) 531710 *CONTACT:* G Oughton
OPENING TIMES: 0930-1730
MIN. MAIL ORDER UK: No minimum charge* *MIN. VALUE EC:*
CAT. COST: 50p + p&p *W/SALE or RETAIL:* Both *CREDIT CARDS:* None
SPECIALITIES: Fruit Trees & Bushes. *Note: mail order to UK only. *MAP PAGE:* **3**

110 Morton Hall Gardens, Morton Hall, Ranby, Retford, Nottingham, DN22 8HW

TEL: (01777) 702530 *CONTACT:* Gill McMaster
◆ *OPENING TIMES:* 0900-1600 Mon-Fri, 1400-1700 Sat-Sun & Bank Hols, Mar-Nov incl.
MIN. MAIL ORDER UK: £5.00 + p&p *MIN. VALUE EC:* £10.00 + p&p
CAT. COST: 3 x 1st class *W/SALE or RETAIL:* Retail *CREDIT CARDS:* None
SPECIALITIES: Shrubs & Perennials. *MAP PAGE:* **7**

111 Bressingham Plant Centre, Elton, Peterborough, PE8 6SH

TEL: (01832) 280058 *FAX:* (01832) 280081 *CONTACT:* Tom Green
◆ *OPENING TIMES:* 0900-1730 daily. (Direct retail Plant Centre).
No mail order
CAT. COST: None issued *W/SALE or RETAIL:* Retail *CREDIT CARDS:* AmEx, Delta, Switch, MasterCard
SPECIALITIES: Very wide general range. Many own varieties. Focus on Hardy Ornamental plants & Grasses. *MAP PAGE:* **8**

112 Bressingham Plant Centre, Dorney, Windsor, Buckinghamshire, SL4 6QP

TEL: (01628) 669999 *FAX:* (01628) 669693 *CONTACT:* Peter Freeman
◆ *OPENING TIMES:* 0900-1730 daily. (Direct retail Plant Centre).
No mail order
CAT. COST: None issued *W/SALE or RETAIL:* Retail *CREDIT CARDS:* AmEx, Delta, Switch, MasterCard
SPECIALITIES: Very wide general range. Many own varieties. Focus on Hardy Ornamental plants & Grasses. *MAP PAGE:* **3/6**

Seed Suppliers

Agroforestry Research Trust, 46 Hunters Moon, Dartington, Totnes, Devon, TQ9 6JT

TEL: *CONTACT:* Martin Crawford *CAT. COST:* 3 x 1st class
MIN. ORDER: No minimum charge *CREDIT CARDS:* None
SPECIALITIES: Trees, Shrubs & Perennials. See also in Nursery Index under Code 'CAgr'.

Allwood Bros, Hassocks, West Sussex, BN6 9NB

TEL: (01273) 844229 *FAX:* (01273) 846022 *CONTACT:* Sue James *CAT. COST:* 2 x 1st class
MIN. ORDER: No minimum charge *CREDIT CARDS:* MasterCard, Visa, Switch
SPECIALITIES: Carnations, Pinks & Dianthus. See also in Nursery Index under Code 'SAll'.

Ashwood Nurseries, Greensforge, Kingswinford, West Midlands, DY6 0AE

TEL: (01384) 401996 *FAX:* (01384) 401108 *CONTACT:* John Massey & Philip Baulk
CAT. COST: 4 x 1st class
MIN. ORDER: No minimum charge *CREDIT CARDS:* Visa, Access, AmEx
SPECIALITIES: Lewisias, Cyclamen, Hellebores & Auriculas. See also in Nursery Index under Code 'MAsh'.

B & T World Seeds, Paguignan, 34210 Olonzac, France

TEL: 33 0468912963 *FAX:* 33 0468913039 *CONTACT:* David Sleigh *CAT. COST:* £10 (Europe)*
MIN. ORDER: £5.00 *CREDIT CARDS:* Visa, Access
SPECIALITIES: Master list contains over 37,000 items. *£14 to non-European destinations. 187 Sub-lists available. Lists to specification.

Blackmore & Langdon Ltd, Pensford, Bristol, Avon, BS18 4JL

TEL: (01275) 332300 *FAX:* (01275) 332300 *CONTACT:* J S Langdon *CAT. COST:* Sae
MIN. ORDER: No minimum charge *CREDIT CARDS:* None
SPECIALITIES: Delphinium, Begonia. See also in Nursery Index under Code 'CBla'.

S & N Brackley, 117 Winslow Road, Wingrave, Aylesbury, Buckinghamshire, HP22 4QB

TEL: (01296) 681384 *CONTACT:* S Brackley & K Earwicker *CAT. COST:* 1st class Sae
MIN. ORDER: No minimum charge *CREDIT CARDS:* None
SPECIALITIES: Wholesale & Retail suppliers of Gold Medal Sweet Peas & Exhibition Vegetables. Seeds & plants. See also in Additional Nursery Index under Code 102.

Bush Green Cottage Nursery, Foxfield Road, Broughton-in-Furness, Cumbria, LA20 6BY

TEL: (01229) 716724 *CONTACT:* Jim Haunch *CAT. COST:* 2 x 2nd class
MIN. ORDER: No minimum charge *CREDIT CARDS:* None
SPECIALITIES: Hardy Geraniums and Perennials. See also in Nursery Index under Code 'NBus'.

Carters Seeds Ltd, Hele Road, Torquay, Devon, TQ2 7QJ

TEL: (01803) 616156 *FAX:* (01803) 615747 *CONTACT:* Customer Services *CAT. COST:* n/a
MIN. ORDER: *CREDIT CARDS:* None
SPECIALITIES: General range available from retail stockists.

Chadwell Seeds, 81 Parlaunt Road, Slough, Berkshire, SL3 8BE

TEL: (01753) 542823 *CONTACT:* Chris Chadwell *CAT. COST:* 3 x 2nd class
MIN. ORDER: No minimum charge *CREDIT CARDS:* None
SPECIALITIES: Seed collecting expedition to the Himalaya. Separate general Seed list of Japanese, N. America & Himalayan plants.

Chase Organics (GB) Ltd, Coombelands House, Addlestone, Weybridge, Surrey, KT15 1HY

TEL: (01932) 820958 *FAX:* (01932) 829322 *CONTACT:* M Hedges *CAT. COST:* Free
MIN. ORDER: 75p p&p under £14.00 *CREDIT CARDS:* Visa, Access
SPECIALITIES: 'The Organic Gardening Catalogue' offers Vegetable, Herb & Flower seeds & garden sundries especially for Organic gardeners.

Cheshire Herbs, Fourfields, Forest Road, Little Budworth, Cheshire, CW6 9ES

TEL: (01829) 760578 *FAX:* (01829) 760354 *CONTACT:* Mr & Mrs Ted Riddell *CAT. COST:* 20p
MIN. ORDER: No minimum charge *CREDIT CARDS:* None
SPECIALITIES: Herbs. See also in Nursery Index under Code 'MChe'.

Chiltern Seeds, Bortree Stile, Ulverston, Cumbria, LA12 7PB
TEL: (01229) 581137 *FAX:* (01229) 584549 *E-MAIL:* 101344.1340@compuserve.com *CONTACT:*
CAT. COST: 3 x 2nd class
MIN. ORDER: No minimum charge *CREDIT CARDS:* Visa, Access, AmEx, Switch, MasterCard, EuroCard

Coombland Gardens, Coombland, Coneyhurst, Billingshurst, West Sussex, RH14 9DG
TEL: (01403) 741727 *FAX:* (01403) 741079 *CONTACT:* David Browne *CAT. COST:* £1.00
MIN. ORDER: £10.00 incl. p&p *CREDIT CARDS:* None
SPECIALITIES: Extensive list. See also in Code Nursery Index under 'SCou'.

The Cottage Herbary, Mill House, Boraston, Nr Tenbury Wells, Worcestershire, WR15 8LZ
TEL: (01584) 781575 *FAX:* (01584) 781483 *CONTACT:* K & R Hurst *CAT. COST:* List free
MIN. ORDER: No minimum charge *CREDIT CARDS:* None
SPECIALITIES: Herbs. See also in Nursery Index under Code 'WCHb'.

Craven's Nursery, 1 Foulds Terrace, Bingley, West Yorkshire, BD16 4LZ
TEL: (01274) 561412 *CONTACT:* S R & M Craven *CAT. COST:* £1.00
MIN. ORDER: £5.00 *CREDIT CARDS:* None
SPECIALITIES: Seeds of Show Auriculas, Primulas, Pinks & Alpines. See also in Nursery Index under Code 'NCra'.

CTDA, 174 Cambridge Street, London, SW1V 4QE
TEL: (0171) 976 5115 *FAX:* (01432) 820337 *CONTACT:* Basil Smith *CAT. COST:* Free
MIN. ORDER: No minimum charge *CREDIT CARDS:* None
SPECIALITIES: Hardy Cyclamen & Hellebores. See also in Nursery Index under Code 'LCTD'.

Seed Suppliers

Samuel Dobie & Sons Ltd, Broomhill Way, Torquay, Devon, TQ2 7QW
TEL: (01803) 616281 *FAX:* (01803) 615150 *CONTACT:* Customer Services *CAT. COST:* Free
MIN. ORDER: No minimum charge *CREDIT CARDS:* Visa, MasterCard
SPECIALITIES: Wide selection of popular Flower & Vegetable seeds. Also includes young Plants, summer flowering Bulbs & garden sundries.

Jack Drake, Inshriach Alpine Nursery, Aviemore, Invernesshire, Scotland, PH22 1QS
TEL: (01540) 651287 *FAX:* (01540) 651656 *CONTACT:* J C Lawson *CAT. COST:* £1.00
MIN. ORDER: No minimum charge *CREDIT CARDS:* None
SPECIALITIES: Rare & unusual Alpines & Rock Plants especially Primulas, Gentians & many others. See also in Nursery Index under Code 'GDra'.

John Drake, Hardwicke House, Fen Ditton, Cambridgeshire, CB5 8TF
TEL: (01223) 292246 *CONTACT:* John Drake *CAT. COST:* 70p*
MIN. ORDER: £12.50 *CREDIT CARDS:* None
SPECIALITIES: Aquilegia. *Note: Seed Catalogue available Aug.

Equatorial Plants, 7 Gray Lane, Barnard Castle, Co. Durham, DL12 8PD
TEL: (01833) 690519 *FAX:* (01833) 690519 *CONTACT:* Richard Warren PhD. *CAT. COST:* Free
MIN. ORDER: £5.00 *CREDIT CARDS:* Visa, Access
SPECIALITIES: Orchid seed.

Field House Nurseries, Leake Road, Gotham, Nottinghamshire, NG11 0JN
TEL: (0115) 9830278 *CONTACT:* Doug Lochhead & Valerie A Woolley *CAT. COST:* 4 x 1st or IRCs
MIN. ORDER: No minimum charge *CREDIT CARDS:* Visa, Access
SPECIALITIES: Primulas & Alpines. See also in Nursery Index under Code 'MFie'.

Mr Fothergill's Seeds Ltd, Gazeley Road, Kentford, Newmarket, Suffolk, CB8 7QB
TEL: (01638) 751887 *FAX:* (01638) 751624 *CONTACT:* *CAT. COST:* Free
MIN. ORDER: No minimum charge *CREDIT CARDS:* Visa, Access, MasterCard, Switch
SPECIALITIES: Annuals, Biennials, Perennials, Herbs, Vegetables, plus Plants, soft Fruit and Garden Sundries. Overseas orders on application.

Glenhirst Cactus Nursery, Station Road, Swineshead, Nr Boston, Lincolnshire, PE20 3NX
TEL: (01205) 820314 *CONTACT:* N C & S A Bell *CAT. COST:* 2 x 1st class
MIN. ORDER: No minimum charge *CREDIT CARDS:* None
SPECIALITIES: Extensive range of Cacti & Succulent seeds. Mail order all year. See also under Cactus & Succulent Specialists Index.

Elisabeth Goodwin Nurseries, The White Gate, 86 Cambridge Road, Girton, Cambridgeshire, CB3 0PJ
TEL: (01223) 276013 *CONTACT:* Elisabeth Goodwin *CAT. COST:* 50p coin/2x1st class
MIN. ORDER: No minimum charge *CREDIT CARDS:* None
SPECIALITIES: Drought tolerant plants. The Nursery is moving in 1997, all orders will be forwarded. See also in Nursery Index under Code 'EGoo'.

Peter Grayson (Sweet Pea Seedsman), 34 Glenthorne Close, Brampton, Chesterfield, Derbyshire, S40 3AR
TEL: (01246) 278503 *FAX:* (01246) 566918 *CONTACT:* Peter Grayson *CAT. COST:* Sae
MIN. ORDER: No minimum charge *CREDIT CARDS:* None
SPECIALITIES: Lathyrus species & cultivars. World's largest collection of Old-Fashioned Sweet Peas.

Harvest Nurseries, Harvest Cottage, Boonshill Farm, Iden, Rye, E Sussex, TN31 7QA
TEL: (0181) 325 5420 *CONTACT:* D A Smith *CAT. COST:* 2 x 1st class
MIN. ORDER: No minimum charge *CREDIT CARDS:* None
SPECIALITIES: Epiphyllums & wide range of Succulents. Descriptive catalogue. See also under Cactus & Succulent Specialists Index.

James Henderson & Sons, Kingholm Quay, Dumfries, DG1 4SU
TEL: (01387) 252234 *FAX:* (01387) 262302 *CONTACT:* J H & R J Henderson *CAT. COST:* Sae
MIN. ORDER: 3kgs *CREDIT CARDS:* None

Henllys Lodge Plants, Henllys Lodge, Beaumaris, Anglesey, Gwynedd, Wales, LL58 8HU
TEL: (01248) 810106 *CONTACT:* Mrs E Lane *CAT. COST:* 2 x 2nd class
MIN. ORDER: No minimum charge *CREDIT CARDS:* None
SPECIALITIES: Small range of hardy Perennials, esp. hardy Geraniums. See also in Nursery Index under Code 'WHen'.

Holly Gate Cactus Nursery, Billingshurst Road, Ashington, West Sussex, RH20 3BA
TEL: (01903) 892 930 *CONTACT:* Mr T M Hewitt *CAT. COST:* 2 x 1st class
MIN. ORDER: £2.00 + p&p *CREDIT CARDS:* None
SPECIALITIES: Cacti & Succulents.

Home Meadows Nursery Ltd, Martlesham, Woodbridge, Suffolk, IP12 4RD
TEL: (01394) 382419 *CONTACT:* S D & M I O'Brien Baker & I D Baker *CAT. COST:* Sae
MIN. ORDER: No minimum charge *CREDIT CARDS:* None
SPECIALITIES: See also in Nursery Index under Code 'EHMN'.

Hopleys Plants Ltd, High Street, Much Hadham, Hertfordshire, SG10 6BU
TEL: (01279) 842509 *FAX:* (01279) 843784 *CONTACT:* Aubrey Barker *CAT. COST:* 5 x 1st class
MIN. ORDER: No minimum charge *CREDIT CARDS:* Visa, Access, Switch
SPECIALITIES: See also in Nursery Index under Code 'LHop'.

Diana Hull, Fog Cottages, 178 Lower Street, Hillmorton, Rugby, Warwickshire, CV21 4NX
TEL: (01788) 536574 after 1600 *CONTACT:* Diana Hull *CAT. COST:* Sae or IRC for list
MIN. ORDER: No minimum charge *CREDIT CARDS:* None
SPECIALITIES: Pelargonium species. See also in Nursery Index under Code 'MHul'.

Iden Croft Herbs, Frittenden Road, Staplehurst, Kent, TH12 0DN
TEL: (01580) 891432 *FAX:* (01580) 892416 *E-MAIL:* idencroft.herbs@dial.pipex.com
CONTACT: Rosemary & D Titterington *CAT. COST:* A4 Sae for list
MIN. ORDER: No minimum charge *CREDIT CARDS:* Visa, Access, AmEx, Delta, JCB, EuroCard, Switch
SPECIALITIES: Herbs - aromatic, wildflower, for bees/butterflies & hardy herbaceous. See also in Nursery Index under Code 'SIde'.

W E Th. Ingwersen Ltd, Birch Farm Nursery, Gravetye, E. Grinstead, West Sussex, RH19 4LE
TEL: (01342) 810236 *CONTACT:* M P & M R Ingwersen *CAT. COST:* Sae
MIN. ORDER: No minimum charge *CREDIT CARDS:* None
SPECIALITIES: Alpines & rock garden plants. See also in Nursery Index under Code 'SIng'.

Jekka's Herb Farm, Rose Cottage, Shellards Lane, Alveston, Bristol, Avon, BS12 2SY
TEL: (01454) 418878 *FAX:* (01454) 411988 *CONTACT:* Jekka McVicar *CAT. COST:* 4 x 1st class
MIN. ORDER: No minimum charge *CREDIT CARDS:* None
SPECIALITIES: Herb seed (NO wild flower seed). See also in Nursery Index under Code 'WJek'.

Landlife Wildflowers Ltd, The Old Police Station, Lark Lane, Liverpool, Merseyside, L17 8UU
TEL: (0151) 728 7011 *FAX:* (0151) 728 8413 *E-MAIL:* info@landlife.u-net-com
CONTACT: Gillian Watson *CAT. COST:* Sae + 2 x 2nd class
MIN. ORDER: No minimum charge *CREDIT CARDS:* Visa, AmEx
SPECIALITIES: Native Herbaceous plants. See also in Nursery Index under Code 'NLan'.

The Marches Nursery, Presteigne, Powys, LD8 2HG
TEL: (01544) 260474 *FAX:* (01544) 260474 *CONTACT:* Jane Cooke *CAT. COST:* Sae
MIN. ORDER: No minimum charge *CREDIT CARDS:* None
SPECIALITIES: Hardy Perennials. See also in Nursery Index under Code 'WMaN'.

Marston Exotics, Brampton Lane, Madley, Herefordshire, HR2 9LX
TEL: (01981) 251140 *FAX:* (01981) 251649 *CONTACT:* Paul Gardner *CAT. COST:* List 1 x 1st class
MIN. ORDER: See list for details *CREDIT CARDS:* MasterCard, Switch, Visa
SPECIALITIES: Carnivorous plants. Price list & Growers Guide £1.80. See also in Nursery Index under Code 'WMEx'.

S M McArd (Seeds), 39 West Road, Pointon, Sleaford, Lincolnshire, NG34 0NA
TEL: (01529) 240765 *FAX:* (01529) 240765 *CONTACT:* Susan McArd *CAT. COST:* 2 x 2nd class
MIN. ORDER: No minimum charge *CREDIT CARDS:* None
SPECIALITIES: Unusual & giant Vegetables. Seeds & Plants.

Mires Beck Nursery, Low Mill Lane, North Cave, Brough, North Humberside, HU15 2NR
TEL: (01430) 421543 *CONTACT:* Martin Rowland & Irene Tinklin *CAT. COST:* 3 x 1st class
MIN. ORDER: No minimum charge *CREDIT CARDS:* None
SPECIALITIES: Wild Flower Plants of Yorkshire Provenance (only avail. from Autumn 1997). See also in Nursery Index under Code 'NMir'.

Monksilver Nursery, Oakington Road, Cottenham, Cambridgeshire, CB4 4TW
TEL: (01954) 251555 *FAX:* (01954) 202666 *E-MAIL:* monksilver@dial.pipex.com
CONTACT: Joe Sharman & Alan Leslie *CAT. COST:* 6 x 1st class
MIN. ORDER: £10.00 *CREDIT CARDS:* None
SPECIALITIES: Seed of some plants available. See also in Nursery Index under Code 'EMon'.

Monocot Nursery, Jacklands, Jacklands Bridge, Tickenham, Clevedon, Avon, BS21 6SG
TEL: (01275) 810394 *CONTACT:* M R Salmon *CAT. COST:* Sae
MIN. ORDER: No minimum charge *CREDIT CARDS:* None
SPECIALITIES: Rare & unusual Bulbous & Tuberous plants. See also in Nursery Index under Code 'CMon'.

◆ **See also Display Advertisements**

Seed Suppliers

Natural Selection, 1 Station Cottages, Hullavington, Chippenham, Wiltshire, SN14 6ET
TEL: (01666) 837369 *CONTACT:* Martin Cragg-Barber *CAT. COST:* Sae
MIN. ORDER: No minimum charge *CREDIT CARDS:* None
SPECIALITIES: Unusual British natives. See also in Nursery Index under Code 'CNat'.

Andrew Norfield Seeds, Lower Meend, St Briavels, Gloucestershire, GL15 6RW
TEL: (01594) 530134 *FAX:* (01594) 530113 *CONTACT:* Andrew Norfield *CAT. COST:* 1 x 1st class
MIN. ORDER: No minimum charge *CREDIT CARDS:* None
SPECIALITIES: Germinated & pretreated Seed of hardy Trees, Shrubs, Herbaceous & House plants. See also in Nursery Index under Code 'WNor'.

North Green Seeds, 16 Wilton Lane, Little Plumstead, Norwich, Norfolk, NR13 5DL
TEL: FAX: (01603) 714661 *CONTACT:* John Morley *CAT. COST:* 4 x 1st class
MIN. ORDER: £5.00 + p&p *CREDIT CARDS:* None
SPECIALITIES: Small specialist range of Galanthus, Allium & Fritillaria Seed. See also in Nursery Index under Code 'EMor'.

Orchard Nurseries, Tow Lane, Foston, Grantham, Lincolnshire, NG32 2LE
TEL: (01400) 281354 *FAX:* (01400) 281354 *CONTACT:* R & J Blenkinship *CAT. COST:* Sae
MIN. ORDER: No minimum charge *CREDIT CARDS:* None
SPECIALITIES: Helleborus orientalis hybrids. See also in Nursery Index under Code 'EOrc'.

Paradise Centre, Twinstead Road, Lamarsh, Bures, Suffolk, CO8 5EX
TEL: (01787) 269449 *FAX:* (01787) 269449 *CONTACT:* Cees & Hedy Stapel-Valk
CAT. COST: 5 x 1st class
MIN. ORDER: £7.50 + p&p *CREDIT CARDS:* Visa, other
SPECIALITIES: Unusual bulbous & tuberous plants, incl. Bog & Shade species. See also in Nursery Index under Code 'EPar'. *NB Credit cards accepted for orders over £17.50.

Passiflora (National Collection), Lampley Road, Kingston Seymour, Clevedon, North Somerset, BS21 6XS
TEL: (01934) 833350 *FAX:* (01934) 877255 *E-MAIL:* passion@3wa.co.uk *CONTACT:* John Vanderplank
CAT. COST: 3 x 1st class
MIN. ORDER: £6.00 *CREDIT CARDS:* Visa, Access, EuroCard
SPECIALITIES: Over 200 Passiflora. See also in Nursery Index under Code 'WGre'.

Phedar Nursery, Bunkers Hill, Romiley, Stockport, Cheshire, SK6 3DS
TEL: (0161) 430 3772 *FAX:* (0161) 430 3772 *CONTACT:* Will McLewin *CAT. COST:* Saes for lists.
MIN. ORDER: No minimum charge *CREDIT CARDS:* None
SPECIALITIES: Helleborus species seed wild collected & hybrids seed in categories; available Aug. Paeonia species seed wild coll. Nov. See also in Nursery Index under Code 'MPhe'.

Alan Phipps Cacti, 62 Samuel White Road, Hanham, Bristol, BS15 3LX
TEL: (0117) 960 7591 *CONTACT:* A Phipps *CAT. COST:*
MIN. ORDER: £5.00 *CREDIT CARDS:* None
SPECIALITIES: See also in Cactus & Succulent Specialists Index. NB Minimum order is for mixed species or single genera.

Pinks & Carnations, 22 Chetwyn Avenue, Bromley Cross, Nr Bolton, Lancashire, BL7 9BN
TEL: (01204) 306273 *FAX:* (01204) 306273 *CONTACT:* Ruth & Tom Gillies *CAT. COST:* 1 x 1st class
MIN. ORDER: No minimum charge *CREDIT CARDS:* Visa, Access
SPECIALITIES: Perpetual Flowing Carnations, Border Carnations, Allwoodii Alpinus. See also in Nursery Index under Code 'NPin'.

Plant World Botanic Gardens, Seed Dept. (PF), St Marychurch Road, Newton Abbot, Devon, TQ12 4SE
TEL: (01803) 872939 *FAX:* (01803) 872939 *CONTACT:* Ray Brown
CAT. COST: 3 x 1st class/ $2/ 3 x IRC
MIN. ORDER: £8 UK, £20 o/s *CREDIT CARDS:* Visa, Access, MasterCard, EuroCard
SPECIALITIES: Meconopsis, Gentiana, Primula, Aquilegia, Campanula, Viola, Geranium, Salvia, Eryngium. See also in Nursery Index under Code 'CPla'. No plants by Mail Order.

Pleasant View Nursery, Two Mile Oak, Nr Denbury, Newton Abbot, Devon, TO12 6DG
TEL: Write with Sae *CONTACT:* Mrs B D Yeo *CAT. COST:* 2 x 2nd class
MIN. ORDER: £10.00 + p&p *CREDIT CARDS:* None
SPECIALITIES: Salvia seed only. See also in Nursery Index under Code 'CPle'.

Potterton & Martin, The Cottage Nursery, Moortown Road, Nettleton, Caistor, Lincolnshire, LN7 6HX
TEL: (01472) 851792 *FAX:* (01472) 851792 *CONTACT:* *CAT. COST:* 50p in stamps only
MIN. ORDER: No minimum charge *CREDIT CARDS:* Visa, Access, MasterCard, EuroCard
SPECIALITIES: Alpines & dwarf Bulbs. Seed list sent out in November. See also in Nursery Index under Code 'EPot'.

Poyntzfield Herb Nursery, Nr Balblair, Black Isle, Dingwall, Ross & Cromarty, Highland, Scotland, IV7 8LX
TEL: (01381) 610352* *FAX:* (01381) 610352 *CONTACT:* Duncan Ross *CAT. COST:* Sae + 3 x 1st class
MIN. ORDER: £5.00 + p&p *CREDIT CARDS:* None
SPECIALITIES: *Note: Phone 1200-1300 & 1800-1900. See also in Nursery Index under Code 'GPoy'.

W Robinson & Sons Ltd, Sunny Bank, Forton, Nr Preston, Lancashire, PR3 0BN
TEL: (01524) 791210 *FAX:* (01524) 791933 *CONTACT:* Miss Robinson *CAT. COST:* Free
MIN. ORDER: No minimum charge *CREDIT CARDS:* Visa, Access, AmEx
SPECIALITIES: Mammoth Vegetable seed. Onions, Leeks, Tomatoes & Beans.

R V Roger Ltd, The Nurseries, Pickering, North Yorkshire, YO18 7HG
TEL: (01751) 472226 *FAX:* (01751) 476749 *E-MAIL:* ian@clivia.demon.co.uk
CONTACT: J R Roger, S Peirson & A G & I M Roger *CAT. COST:* Sae
MIN. ORDER: No minimum charge *CREDIT CARDS:* Visa, Access
SPECIALITIES: Bulbs & Seed Potatoes. See also in Nursery Index under Code 'NRog'.

Rougham Hall Nurseries, Ipswich Road, Rougham, Bury St Edmunds, Suffolk, IP30 9LZ
TEL: (01359) 270577 *FAX:* (01359) 271149 *CONTACT:* A A & K G Harbutt *CAT. COST:* Sae
MIN. ORDER: No minimum charge *CREDIT CARDS:* None
SPECIALITIES: Delphinium mixed varieties & wide range of Hardy Perennials.

Salley Gardens, 32 Lansdowne Drive, West Bridgford, Nottinghamshire, NG2 7FJ
TEL: (0115) 9233878 evngs *CONTACT:* Richard Lewin *CAT. COST:* Sae
MIN. ORDER: No minimum charge *CREDIT CARDS:* None
SPECIALITIES: Wildflower & Medicinal Herbs. See also in Nursery Index under Code 'MSal'.

The Seed House, 9a Widley Road, Cosham, Portsmouth, PO6 2DS
TEL: (01705) 325639 *CONTACT:* Mr R L Spearing *CAT. COST:* 4 x 1st class or 4 x IRA
MIN. ORDER: £5.00 *CREDIT CARDS:* None
SPECIALITIES: Australian seeds suitable for the European climate incl. Acacia, Banksia, Callistemon, & Eucalypts etc.

Seeds by Size, 45 Crouchfield, Boxmoor, Hemel Hempstead, Hertfordshire, HP1 1PA
TEL: (01442) 251458 *E-MAIL:* johnrobertsize@seeds-by-size.co.uk *CONTACT:* Mr John Robert Size
CAT. COST: Sae
MIN. ORDER: No minimum charge *CREDIT CARDS:* None
SPECIALITIES: Flowers & Vegetables. 1,400 varieties of Vegetable, (175 Cabbage, 99 Cauliflower, 70 Onion, 80 Tomatoes) & 4,500 flowers such as 290 varieties of Sweet Pea.

John Shipton (Bulbs), Y Felin, Henllan Amgoed, Whitland, Dyfed, Wales, SA34 0SL
TEL: (01994) 240125 *E-MAIL:* bluebell@connect-wales.co.uk *CONTACT:* John Shipton
CAT. COST: Sae
MIN. ORDER: No minimum charge *CREDIT CARDS:* None
SPECIALITIES: Species native to the British Isles. See also in Nursery Index under Code 'WShi'.

◆ **See also Display Advertisements**

Seed Suppliers

Sino-Himalayan Plant Association, 81 Parlaunt Road, Slough, Berkshire, SL3 8BR

TEL: (01753) 542823 *CONTACT:* Chris Chadwell *CAT. COST:*
MIN. ORDER: *CREDIT CARDS:* None
SPECIALITIES: Seed available for exchange to Members. Please apply for membership.

Stewart's (Nottingham) Ltd, 3 George Street, Nottingham, NG1 3BH

TEL: (0115) 9476338 *CONTACT:* Brenda Lochhead *CAT. COST:* 2 x 1st class
MIN. ORDER: No minimum charge *CREDIT CARDS:* Visa, MasterCard, Switch
SPECIALITIES: Large general range esp. Vegetables. Also seed Potatoes & Grasses.

Richard Stockwell, 64 Weardale Road, Sherwood, Nottingham, NG5 1DD

TEL: (0115) 969 1063 *FAX:* (0115) 969 1063 *CONTACT:* Richard Stockwell
CAT. COST: 4 x 2nd class or 2 x IRC
MIN. ORDER: No minimum charge *CREDIT CARDS:* None
SPECIALITIES: Very rare climbing species, also dwarf species. See also in Nursery Index under Code 'MSto'.

Suttons Seeds Ltd, Hele Road, Torquay, Devon, TQ2 7QJ

TEL: (01803) 614455 *FAX:* (01803) 615747 *CONTACT:* Customer Services *CAT. COST:* Free
MIN. ORDER: No minimum charge *CREDIT CARDS:* Visa, MasterCard
SPECIALITIES: Wide general range of Flower & Vegetable Seed, plus young Plants & summer flowering Bulbs. See also in Nursery Index under Code 'CSut'.

Thompson & Morgan (UK) Ltd, Poplar Lane, Ipswich, Suffolk, IP8 3BU

TEL: (01473) 688821 *FAX:* (01473) 680199 *CONTACT:* Martin Thrower *CAT. COST:* Free
MIN. ORDER: No minimum charge *CREDIT CARDS:* Visa, Access, Switch
SPECIALITIES: Largest illustrated Seed catalogue in the world.

Edwin Tucker & Sons, Brewery Meadow, Stonepark, Ashburton, Newton Abbot, Devon, TQ13 7DG

TEL: (01364) 652403 *FAX:* (01364) 654300 *CONTACT:* Geoff Penton *CAT. COST:* Free
MIN. ORDER: No minimum charge *CREDIT CARDS:* Visa, Access
SPECIALITIES: Over 70 varieties of Seed Potatoes. Wide range of Vegetables, Flowers, Green Manures & sprouting seeds in packets. All not treated.

Unwins Seeds Ltd, Mail Order Dept., Histon, Cambridge, Cambridgeshire, CB4 4ZZ

TEL: (01945) 588522 *FAX:* (01945) 475255 *CONTACT:* Customer Services Dept. *CAT. COST:* Free
MIN. ORDER: No minimum charge *CREDIT CARDS:* Visa, Access
SPECIALITIES: Wide general range. Over 50 varieties of Sweet Peas.

Jill White, 6 Edward Avenue, Brightlingsea, Essex, CO7 0LZ

TEL: (01206) 303547 *CONTACT:* Jill White *CAT. COST:* Sae or 2 x IRC
MIN. ORDER: No minimum charge *CREDIT CARDS:* None
SPECIALITIES: Cyclamen. See also in Nursery Index under Code 'EJWh'.

Y.S.J Seeds, Kingsfield Conservation, Broadenham Lane, Winsham, Chard, Somerset, TA20 4JF

TEL: (01460) 30070 *FAX:* (01460) 30070 *CONTACT:* Mrs M White *CAT. COST:* 31p stamps
MIN. ORDER: No minimum charge *CREDIT CARDS:* None
SPECIALITIES: British Wild Flowers seeds from native stock plants. See also in Nursery Index under Code 'CKin'.

Roy Young Seeds, 23 Westland Chase, West Winch, King's Lynn, Norfolk, PE33 0QH

TEL: (01553) 840867 *FAX:* (01553) 840867 *CONTACT:* Mr Roy Young
CAT. COST: UK 20p, o/s 3 x IRCs
MIN. ORDER: No minimum charge* *CREDIT CARDS:* None
SPECIALITIES: Cactus & Succulent SEEDS only. 24pg Cat. listing app. 2,000 species, varieties & forms (Retail). 10 pg A4 listing (Wholesale). *£25 min Wholesale order charge.

Cactus & Succulent Suppliers

Bradley Batch Nursery, 64 Bath Road, Ashcott, Bridgwater, Somerset, TA7 9QJ
TEL: (01458) 210256 *CONTACT:* J E White
OPENING TIMES: 1000-1800 Tue-Sun. *W/SALE or RETAIL:* Both
No mail order *CAT. COST:* None issued *CREDIT CARDS:* None
SPECIALITIES: Echeveria, Haworthia, Lithops & Cacti.

Bridgemere Nurseries, Bridgemere, Nr Nantwich, Cheshire, CW5 7QB
TEL: (01270) 520381/520239 *FAX:* (01270) 520215 *CONTACT:* Carol Adams
OPENING TIMES: 0900-2000 Mon-Sat, 1000-2000 Sun, in summer, until 1700 winter.
W/SALE or RETAIL: Retail
No mail order *CAT. COST:* None issued *CREDIT CARDS:* Visa, Access, MasterCard, Switch
SPECIALITIES: General range of Cacti & other Succulents incl. specimen plants. See also in ORCHID Index and Nursery Index under Code 'MBri'

Brookside Nursery, Elderberry Farm, Bognor Road, Rowhook, Horsham, West Sussex, RH12 3PS
TEL: (01403) 790996 *FAX:* (01403) 790195 *CONTACT:* A J Butler
OPENING TIMES: 1000-1700 Thur-Sun; open Bank Hol Mons. Please phone first.
W/SALE or RETAIL: Both
MIN. VALUE: No minimum charge *CAT. COST:* 1 x 1st class *CREDIT CARDS:* None
SPECIALITIES: Cacti, Succulents & Carnivorous plants

Connoisseurs' Cacti, (Off.) 51 Chelsfield Lane, Orpington, Kent, BR5 4HG
TEL: (01689) 837781 *FAX:* (01689) 837781 *CONTACT:* John Pilbeam
OPENING TIMES: 1030-1430 but please phone first. *W/SALE or RETAIL:* Both
MIN. VALUE: No minimum charge *CAT. COST:* Sae or IRC *CREDIT CARDS:* None
SPECIALITIES: Mammillaria, Sulcorebutia, Gymnocalycium, Rebutia, Haworthia, Asclepiads etc. NOTE: Nursery at Woodlands Farm, Shire Lane, Nr Farnborough, Kent.

Croston Cactus, 43 Southport Road, Eccleston, Chorley, Lancashire, PR7 6ET
TEL: (01257) 452555 *CONTACT:* John Henshaw
OPENING TIMES: 0930-1700 Wed-Sat & by appt. *W/SALE or RETAIL:* Retail
MIN. VALUE: No minimum charge *CAT. COST:* 2 x 1st or 2 x IRCs *CREDIT CARDS:* None
SPECIALITIES: Mexican Cacti, Echeveria hybrids & some Bromeliads & Tillandsia.

Cruck Cottage Cacti, Cruck Cottage, Cliff Road, Wrelton, Pickering, North Yorkshire, YO18 8PJ
TEL: (01751) 472042 *CONTACT:* R J A Wood/D Wood
OPENING TIMES: 0900-sunset. Closed Sat a.m. & Mon. Please ring first. *W/SALE or RETAIL:* Both
No mail order *CAT. COST:* None issued *CREDIT CARDS:* None
SPECIALITIES: Large range of Cacti & Succulents especially Caudiciforms - Euphorbia & Astrophytum. Exhibition area of mature plants - entrance FREE. Nursery in a garden setting.

W G Geissler, Winsford, Kingston Road, Slimbridge, Gloucestershire, GL2 7BW
TEL: (01453) 890340 *FAX:* (01453) 890340 *CONTACT:* W G Geissler
OPENING TIMES: 0900-1700 (2000 in summer) Mar-Nov. *W/SALE or RETAIL:* Retail
No mail order *CAT. COST:* Sae *CREDIT CARDS:* None
SPECIALITIES: Hardy Cacti & Succulents & related books.

Glenhirst Cactus Nursery, Station Road, Swineshead, Nr Boston, Lincolnshire, PE20 3NX
TEL: (01205) 820314 *CONTACT:* N C & S A Bell
OPENING TIMES: 1000-1700 Thu, Fri, Sun & Bank Hols 1st Apr-30th Sep. Mail order all year.
W/SALE or RETAIL: Both
MIN. VALUE: No minimum charge *CAT. COST:* 2 x 1st class *CREDIT CARDS:* None
SPECIALITIES: Extensive range of Cacti & Succulent plants & seeds, inc. Christmas Cacti & Orchid Cacti. Hardy & half-hardy desert plants. All stock fully described on lists.

◆ **See also Display Advertisements**

Harvest Nurseries, Harvest Cottage, Boonshill Farm, Iden, Nr Rye, E Sussex, TN31 7QA
TEL: (0181) 325 5420 *CONTACT:* D A Smith
OPENING TIMES: Mail Order ONLY *W/SALE or RETAIL:* Retail
MIN. VALUE: No minimum charge *CAT. COST:* 2 x 1st class *CREDIT CARDS:* None
SPECIALITIES: Epiphyllums & wide range of Succulents. Descriptive catalogue. See also SEED index.

Holly Gate Cactus Nursery, Billingshurst Road, Ashington, West Sussex, RH20 3BA
TEL: (01903) 892 930 *CONTACT:* Mr T M Hewitt
OPENING TIMES: 0900-1700 daily. *W/SALE or RETAIL:* Both
MIN. VALUE: £5.00 + p&p *CAT. COST:* 3 x 1st class *CREDIT CARDS:* Visa, Access, AmEx
SPECIALITIES: Cactus, Succulents & Pelargoniums.

Kent Cacti, (Off.) 35 Rutland Way, Orpington, Kent, BR5 4DY
TEL: (01689) 836249 *FAX:* (01689) 830157 *CONTACT:* Mr D Sizmur
OPENING TIMES: 1000-1700 most days. Please phone first. *W/SALE or RETAIL:* Retail
MIN. VALUE: No minimum charge *CAT. COST:* A5 Sae *CREDIT CARDS:* None
SPECIALITIES: Agave, Astrophytum, Conophytum, Crassula, Echeveria, Echinocereus, Mammillaria etc.
NOTE: Nursery at Woodlands Farm, Shire Lane, Farnborough, Kent.

Long Man Gardens, Lewes Road, Wilmington, Polgate, East Sussex, BN26 5RS
TEL: (01323) 870816 *CONTACT:* O Menzel
OPENING TIMES: 0900-1800 (or dusk if sooner) Tue-Sun. Please check before visiting. Viewing charge £2. *W/SALE or RETAIL:* Retail
No mail order *CAT. COST:* Free list *CREDIT CARDS:* None
SPECIALITIES: Agave, Echeveria, Euphorbia etc.

Pete & Ken Cactus Nursery, Saunders Lane, Ash, Nr Canterbury, Kent, CT3 2BX
TEL: (01304) 812170 *CONTACT:* Ken Burke
OPENING TIMES: 0900-1800 daily. *W/SALE or RETAIL:* Retail
MIN. VALUE: £3.00 + p&p *CAT. COST:* Sae for list *CREDIT CARDS:* None
SPECIALITIES: Cactus, Succulents, Lithops (Living stones).

Alan Phipps Cacti, 62 Samuel White Road, Hanham, Bristol, BS15 3LX
TEL: (0117) 9607591 *CONTACT:* A Phipps
OPENING TIMES: All times, but prior phone call ESSENTIAL to ensure a greeting.
W/SALE or RETAIL: Both
MIN. VALUE: £5.00 + p&p *CAT. COST:* Sae or 2 x IRC (EC) *CREDIT CARDS:* None
SPECIALITIES: Rebutia, Mammillaria & Astrophytum. See also SEED index.

The Plant Lovers, Candesby House, Candesby, Spilsby, Lincolnshire, PE23 5RU
TEL: (01754) 890256 *CONTACT:* Tim Wilson
OPENING TIMES: Daily - but please phone first. *W/SALE or RETAIL:* Both
No mail order *CAT. COST:* None issued *CREDIT CARDS:* None
SPECIALITIES: Sempervivum (Houseleeks) & wide range of Cacti and other Succulents. Brochure available.

Robert Scott Cacti, 78 Bousley Rise, Ottershaw, Surrey, KT16 0LB
TEL: (01932) 872667 *FAX:* (01932) 872667 *E-MAIL:* 100552.736@compuserve.com
CONTACT: Robert Scott
OPENING TIMES: By appt. only. *W/SALE or RETAIL:* Both
MIN. VALUE: £10.00 + p&p *CAT. COST:* 4 x 1st class *CREDIT CARDS:* None
SPECIALITIES: Cactaceae & Mesembryanthemaceae. Seed raised plants from many families & large specimen plants. National Collection holder of Haworthia, Asphodelaceae.

Southfield Nurseries, Bourne Road, Morton, Nr Bourne, Lincolnshire, PE10 0RH
TEL: (01778) 570168 *CONTACT:* Mr & Mrs B Goodey
OPENING TIMES: 1000-1230 & 1330-1600 daily (ex Xmas & New Year). *W/SALE or RETAIL:* Both
MIN. VALUE: No minimum charge *CAT. COST:* 1 x 1st class *CREDIT CARDS:* None
SPECIALITIES: A wide range of Cacti & Succulents including some of the rarer varieties all grown on our own nursery.

See note on Mail Order, EC sales & Export on page 11

Toobees Exotics, 20 Inglewood, St Johns, Woking, Surrey, GU21 3HX
TEL: (01483) 722600 *FAX:* (01483) 751995 *CONTACT:* Bob Potter
OPENING TIMES: Please phone for opening times. *W/SALE or RETAIL:* Retail
MIN. VALUE: No minimum charge *CAT. COST:* Sae *CREDIT CARDS:* None
SPECIALITIES: South African & Madagascan Succulents. Many rare & unusual species.

Westfield Cacti, Kennford, Exeter, Devon, EX6 7XD
TEL: (01392) 832921 *CONTACT:* Ralph & Marina Northcott
OPENING TIMES: 1000-1700 daily. *W/SALE or RETAIL:* Both
MIN. VALUE: £5 + p&p *CAT. COST:* 3 x 1st class *CREDIT CARDS:* Access, Visa, MasterCard, EuroCard
SPECIALITIES: Epiphytes.

Whitestone Gardens Ltd, The Cactus Houses, Sutton-under-Whitestonecliffe, Thirsk, Yorkshire, YO7 2PZ
TEL: (01845) 597467 *FAX:* (01845) 597035 *E-MAIL:* roy@whitestn.demon.co.uk
CONTACT: Roy Mottram
OPENING TIMES: Daylight hours Sat-Thu. *W/SALE or RETAIL:* Retail
MIN. VALUE: No minimum charge *CAT. COST:* 4 x 2nd class *CREDIT CARDS:* Visa
SPECIALITIES: Cacti & other Succulents, Books & Sundries.

H & S Wills, 2 St Brannocks Park Road, Ilfracombe, Devon, EX34 8HU
TEL: (01271) 863949 *FAX:* (01271) 863949 *CONTACT:* H Wills
OPENING TIMES: Appt. only *W/SALE or RETAIL:* Retail
MIN. VALUE: £3.00 + p&p *CAT. COST:* 3 x 1st class *CREDIT CARDS:* None
SPECIALITIES: Sempervivum, Jovibarba & Rosularia.

Roy Young Seeds, 23 Westland Chase, West Winch, King's Lynn, Norfolk, PE33 0QH
TEL: (01553) 840867 *FAX:* (01553) 840867 *CONTACT:* Mr Roy Young
OPENING TIMES: Not open. Mail Order ONLY. *W/SALE or RETAIL:* Both
MIN. VALUE: Nmc* *CAT. COST:* UK 20p, o/s 3 x IRC *CREDIT CARDS:* None
SPECIALITIES: Cactus & Succulent SEEDS only. 24pg cat. listing approx. 2000 species, varieties & forms (retail). 10pg A4 listing (wholesale). *Minimum Wholesale order £25.00

◆ See also Display Advertisements

Orchid Suppliers

Bridgemere Nurseries, Bridgemere, Nr Nantwich, Cheshire, CW5 7QB

TEL: (01270) 520381/520239 *FAX:* (01270) 520215 *CONTACT:* Carol Adams
OPENING TIMES: 0900-2000 Mon-Sat, 1000-2000 Sun in Summer, until 1700 in Winter.
W/SALE or RETAIL: Retail
No mail order *CAT. COST:* None issued *CREDIT CARDS:* Visa, Access, MasterCard, Switch
SPECIALITIES: Cymbidium, Paphiopedilum, Phalaenopsis, Miltonia, Odontoglossum.

Burnham Nurseries, Forches Cross, Newton Abbot, Devon, TQ12 6PZ

TEL: (01626) 52233 *FAX:* (01626) 62167 *CONTACT:* Brian Rittershausen
OPENING TIMES: 0900-1700 Mon-Fri & 1000-1600 Sat & Sun. *W/SALE or RETAIL:* Both
MIN. VALUE: No minimum charge *CAT. COST:* Large Sae + 31p stamp *CREDIT CARDS:* Visa, Access
SPECIALITIES: All types of Orchid.

Equatorial Plant Co., 7 Gray Lane, Barnard Castle, Co. Durham, DL12 8PD

TEL: (01833) 690519 *FAX:* (01833) 690519 *CONTACT:* Richard Warren PhD
OPENING TIMES: By appt. only. *W/SALE or RETAIL:* Both
MIN. VALUE: No minimum charge *CAT. COST:* Free *CREDIT CARDS:* Visa, Access
SPECIALITIES: Laboratory raised Orchids only.

Flora Exotica, Pasadena, South-Green, Fingringhoe, Colchester, Essex, CO5 7DR

TEL: (01206) 729414 *CONTACT:* J Beddoes
OPENING TIMES: Not open to the public *W/SALE or RETAIL:* Both
MIN. VALUE: No minimum charge *CAT. COST:* 6 x 1st class *CREDIT CARDS:* None
SPECIALITIES: Insectivorous plants, esp. Pinguicula & rare & exotic Flora incl. Orchids. See also in Nursery Index under Code 'EFEx'.

Greenaway Orchids, Rookery Farm, Puxton, Nr Weston-super-Mare, N Somerset, BS24 6TL

TEL: (01934) 820448 *FAX:* (01934) 820209 *CONTACT:* Robert Dadd
OPENING TIMES: 0800-1800 Tue-Sun *W/SALE or RETAIL:* Retail
No mail order *CAT. COST:* None issued *CREDIT CARDS:* Visa, MasterCard
SPECIALITIES: Large selection of tropical Orchid species & hybrids. Flask seed raising, seedling to flowering size including endangered species.

Hardy Orchids Ltd, New Gate Farm, Scotchey Lane, Stour Provost, Gillingham, Dorset, SP8 5LT

TEL: (01747) 838308 *FAX:* (01747) 838308 *CONTACT:* N J Heywood
OPENING TIMES: 0800-1300 & 1400-1700 Mon-Fri, by appt. only. *W/SALE or RETAIL:* Both
MIN. VALUE: £10.00 + p&p *CAT. COST:* 4 x 1st class *CREDIT CARDS:* Visa, Access
SPECIALITIES: Hardy Orchids.

Mansell & Hatcher Ltd, Cragg Wood Nurseries, Woodlands Drive, Rawdon, Leeds, LS19 6LQ

TEL: (0113) 250 2016 *CONTACT:* Mr Allan Long
OPENING TIMES: 0900-1700 Mon-Fri. *W/SALE or RETAIL:* Both
MIN. VALUE: No minimum charge *CAT. COST:* 3 x 1st class *CREDIT CARDS:* Visa, Access
SPECIALITIES: Odontoglossum, Masdevallia, Miltonia & Cattleya & species Orchids.

McBeans Orchids, Cooksbridge, Lewes, Sussex, BN8 4PR

TEL: (01273) 400228 *FAX:* (01273) 401181 *CONTACT:* Jim Durrant
OPENING TIMES: 1030-1600 daily ex. Xmas & Boxing day, New Year & Good Friday.
W/SALE or RETAIL: Both
MIN. VALUE: £50.00 + p&p *CAT. COST:* Free *CREDIT CARDS:* Visa, AmEx, Access
SPECIALITIES: Orchids - Cymbidium, Odontoglossum, Phalaenopsis, Paphiopedilum, Miltonia, Cattleya & other genera.

Uzumara Orchids, 9 Port Henderson, Gairloch, Rosshire, Scotland, IV21 2AS

TEL: (01445) 741228 *CONTACT:* Mrs I F La Croix
OPENING TIMES: By appt ONLY. *W/SALE or RETAIL:* Retail
MIN. VALUE: No minimum charge *CAT. COST:* Sae *CREDIT CARDS:* None
SPECIALITIES: African & Madagascan Orchids.

Westwood Nursery, 65 Yorkland Avenue, Welling, Kent, DA16 2LE

TEL: (0181) 301 0886 *FAX:* (0181) 301 0886 *CONTACT:* Mr S Edwards
OPENING TIMES: Not open *W/SALE or RETAIL:* Retail
MIN. VALUE: No minimum charge *CAT. COST:* Sae *CREDIT CARDS:* None
SPECIALITIES: Pleione, Hardy Orchids & Australian Terrestrial Orchids.

Woodstock Orchids, Woodstock House, 50 Pound Hill, Great Brickhill, Buckinghamshire, MK17 9AS

TEL: (01525) 261352 *FAX:* (01525) 261724 *CONTACT:* Joan & Bill Gaskell
OPENING TIMES: STRICTLY by appt ONLY. *W/SALE or RETAIL:* Both
MIN. VALUE: See Cat. for details *CAT. COST:* Sae *CREDIT CARDS:* Visa, Access
SPECIALITIES: Orchids & Exotic House plants.

Fruit and Vegetable Index

Reverse Synonyms

The following list of reverse synonyms is intended to help users find from which genus an unfamiliar plant name has been cross-referred. For a fuller explanation see page 10

Acacia - Racosperma
Acanthocalyx - Morina
Acca - Feijoa
× *Achicodonia - Eucodonia*
Achillea - Anthemis
Acinos - Calamintha
Acinos - Micromeria
Aethionema - Eunomia
Agapetes - Pentapterygium
Agarista - Leucothoe
Agastache - Cedronella
Aichryson - Aeonium
Ajania - Chrysanthemum
Ajania - Eupatorium
Albizia - Acacia
Alcea - Althaea
Allardia - Waldheimia
Allocasuarina - Casuarina
Aloysia - Lippia
Althaea - Malva
Alyogyne - Hibiscus
Alyssum - Ptilotrichum
× *Amarygia - Amaryllis*
Amaryllis - Brunsvigia
Amomyrtus - Myrtus
Amsonia - Rhazya
Anaphalis - Gnaphalium
Anchusa - Lycopsis
Androsace - Douglasia
Anemone - Eriocapitella
Anisodontea - Malvastrum
Anomatheca - Lapeirousia
Anredera - Boussingaultia
Antirrhinum - Asarina
Aphanes - Alchemilla
Arctanthemum - Chrysanthemum
Arctostaphylos - Arbutus
Arctotis - × *Venidioarctotis*
Arctotis - Venidium
Arenga - Didymosperma
Argyranthemum - Anthemis
Argyranthemum - Chrysanthemum
Armoracia - Cochlearia
Arundinaria - Pseudosasa
Asarina - Antirrhinum
Asclepias - Gomphocarpus
Asparagus - Smilax
Asperula - Galium
Asphodeline - Asphodelus
Asplenium - Camptosorus
Asplenium - Ceterach
Asplenium - Phyllitis
Asplenium - Scolopendrium
Aster - Crinitaria
Aster - Microglossa
Asteriscus - Pallenis
Astilboides - Rodgersia
Atropanthe - Scopolia
Aurinia - Alyssum
Austrocedrus - Libocedrus
Azorella - Bolax
Azorina - Campanula
Bambusa - Arundinaria
Bashania - Arundinaria
Bellevalia - Muscari
Bellis - Erigeron
Blechnum - Lomaria
Bolax - Azorella
Borago - Anchusa
Bothriochloa - Andropogon
Boykinia - Telesonix
Brachyglottis - Senecio
Bracteantha - Helichrysum
Brimeura - Hyacinthus
Brugmansia - Datura
Brunnera - Anchusa
Buglossoides - Lithospermum
Bulbine - Bulbinopsis
Buphthalmum - Inula
Cacalia - Adenostyles
Caiophora - Loasa
Caladium - Xanthosoma
Calamagrostis - Agrostis
Calamintha - Clinopodium
Calliergon - Acrocladium
Callisia - Phyodina
Callisia - Tradescantia
Calocedrus - Libocedrus
Calocephalus - Leucophyta
Calomeria - Humea
Caloscordum - Nothoscordum
Calytrix - Lhotzkya
Camellia - Thea
Cardamine - Dentaria
Carpobrotus - Lampranthus
Cassiope - Harrimanella
Catapodium - Desmazeria
Cayratia - Parthenocissus
Centaurium - Erythraea
Centella - Hydrocotyle
Centranthus - Kentranthus
Centranthus - Valeriana
Cephalaria - Scabiosa
Ceratostigma - Plumbago
Cercestis - Rhektophyllum
Cestrum - Iochroma
Chaenomeles - Cydonia
Chaenorhinum - Linaria
Chamaecyparis - Cupressus
Chamaecytisus - Cytisus
Chamaedaphne - Cassandra
Chamaemelum - Anthemis
Chasmanthium - Uniola
Cheilanthes - Notholaena
Chiastophyllum - Cotyledon
Chimonobambusa - Arundinaria
Chimonobambusa - Gelidocalamus
Chimonobambusa - Quiongzhuea
Chionohebe - Pygmea
× *Chionoscilla - Scilla*
Chlorophytum - Diuranthera
Chondrosum - Bouteloua
Cicerbita - Lactuca
Cionura - Marsdenia
Cissus - Ampelopsis
Cissus - Parthenocissus
× *Citrofortunella - Citrus*
Citronella - Villaresia
Clarkia - Eucharidium
Clarkia - Godetia
Clavinodum - Arundinaria
Claytonia - Calandrinia
Claytonia - Montia
Clematis - Atragene
Cleyera - Eurya
Clinopodium - Acinos
Clinopodium - Calamintha
Clytostoma - Bignonia
Clytostoma - Pandorea
Cnicus - Carduus
Codonopsis - Campanumoea
Colobanthus - Arenaria
Consolida - Delphinium
Cordyline - Dracaena
Cornus - Chamaepericlymenum
Cornus - Dendrobenthamia
Coronilla - Securigera
Cortaderia - Gynerium
Corydalis - Fumaria
Corydalis - Pseudofumaria
Cosmos - Bidens
Cotinus - Rhus
Cotula - Leptinella
Crassula - Rochea
Crassula - Sedum
Crassula - Tillaea
Cremanthodium - Ligularia
Crinodendron - Tricuspidaria
Crocosmia - Antholyza
Crocosmia - Curtonus
Crocosmia - Montbretia
Cruciata - Galium

Ctenanthe - Calathea
Ctenanthe - Stromanthe
× Cupressocyparis - Chamaecyparis
Cyathodes - Leucopogon
Cyathodes - Styphelia
Cyclosorus - Pneumatopteris
Cymbalaria - Linaria
Cynara - Scolymus
Cyperus - Mariscus
Cypripedium - Criogenes
Cyrtanthus - Anoiganthus
Cyrtanthus - Vallota
Cyrtomium - Phanarophlebia
Cyrtomium - Polystichum
Cytisus - Argyrocytisus
Cytisus - Genista
Cytisus - Lembotropis
Cytisus - Spartocytisus
Daboecia - Menziesia
Dacrycarpus - Podocarpus
Dactylorhiza - Orchis
Danae - Ruscus
Darmera - Peltiphyllum
Dasypyrum - Haynaldia
Datura - Brugmansia
Datura - Datura
Davallia - Humata
Delairea - Senecio
Delosperma - Lampranthus
Delosperma - Mesembryanthemum
Dendranthema - Ajania
Dendranthema - Chrysanthemum
Dendrocalamus - Bambusa
Derwentia - Hebe
Desmodium - Lespedeza
Dichelostemma - Brodiaea
Dicliptera - Barleria
Dicliptera - Justicia
Dietes - Moraea
Disporopsis - Polygonatum
Distictis - Phaedranthus
Distylium - Sycopsis
Dolichothrix - Helichrysum
Dracaena - Pleomele
Dracunculus - Arum
Dregea - Wattakaka
Drepanostachyum - Arundinaria
Drepanostachyum - Thamnocalamus
Drepanostachyum - Chimonobambusa
Drimys - Tasmannia
Duchesnea - Fragaria
Dunalia - Acnistus
Echeveria - Cotyledon
Echinacea - Rudbeckia
Edraianthus - Wahlenbergia
Egeria - Elodea
Elatostema - Pellionia
Eleutherococcus - Acanthopanax
Elliottia - Botryostege
Elliottia - Cladothamnus
Elymus - Agropyron
Elymus - Leymus
Ensete - Musa
Epilobium - Chamaenerion
Epipremnum - Philodendron
Epipremnum - Scindapsus
Episcia - Alsobia
Eranthis - Aconitum
Erigeron - Aster
Erigeron - Haplopappus
Erysimum - Cheiranthus
Eucodonia - Achimenes
Eupatorium - Ageratina
Eupatorium - Ajania
Eupatorium - Ayapana
Eupatorium - Bartlettina
Euphorbia - Poinsettia
Euryops - Senecio
Fallopia - Bilderdykia
Fallopia - Polygonum
Fallopia - Reynoutria
Farfugium - Ligularia
Fargesia - Arundinaria
Fargesia - Sinarundinaria
Fargesia - Thamnocalamus
Fatsia - Aralia
Felicia - Agathaea
Felicia - Aster
Fibigia - Farsetia
Filipendula - Spiraea
Foeniculum - Ferula
Fortunella - Citrus
Furcraea - Agave
Galium - Asperula
Galtonia - Hyacinthus
Gaultheria - Chiogenes
Gaultheria - × Gaulnettya
Gaultheria - Pernettya
Gelasine - Sisyrinchium
Genista - Chamaespartium
Genista - Cytisus
Genista - Echinospartum
Genista - Teline
Gentianopsis - Gentiana
Gladiolus - Acidanthera
Gladiolus - Homoglossum
Gladiolus - Petamenes
Glechoma - Nepeta
Gloxinia - Seemannia
Gomphocarpus - Asclepias
Goniolimon - Limonium
Graptopetalum - Sedum
Graptopetalum - Tacitus
Greenovia - Sempervivum
Gymnospermium - Leontice
Habranthus - Zephyranthes
Hacquetia - Dondia
× Halimiocistus - Cistus
× Halimiocistus - Halimium
Halimione - Atriplex
Halimium - Cistus
Halimium - × Halimiocistus
Halimium - Helianthemum
Halocarpus - Dacrydium
Hechtia - Dyckia
Hedychium - Brachychilum
Hedyscepe - Kentia
Helianthella - Helianthus
Helianthemum - Cistus
Helianthus - Heliopsis
Helichrysum - Gnaphalium
Helictotrichon - Avena
Helictotrichon - Avenula
Heliopsis - Helianthus
Hepatica - Anemone
Herbertia - Alophia
Hermodactylus - Iris
Heterocentron - Schizocentron
Heterotheca - Chrysopsis
Hibbertia - Candollea
Hieracium - Andryala
Himalayacalamus - Arundinaria
Himalayacalamus - Drepanostachyum
Hippocrepis - Coronilla
Hippolytia - Achillea
Hippolytia - Tanacetum
Hoheria - Plagianthus
Homalocladium - Muehlenbeckia
Howea - Kentia
Hyacinthoides - Endymion
Hyacinthoides - Scilla
Hymenocallis - Elisena
Hymenocallis - Ismene
Hyophorbe - Mascarena
Hypochaeris - Hieracium
Incarvillea - Amphicome
Indocalamus - Sasa
Ipheion - Tristagma
Ipheion - Triteleia
Ipomoea - Mina
Ipomoea - Pharbitis
Ipomopsis - Gilia
Ischyrolepis - Restio
Isolepis - Scirpus
Jeffersonia - Plagiorhegma
Jovibarba - Sempervivum
Juncus - Scirpus
Jurinea - Jurinella
Justicia - Beloperone
Justicia - Jacobinia
Justicia - Libonia
Kalanchoe - Bryophyllum
Kalanchoe - Kitchingia
Kalimeris - Aster
Kalimeris - Asteromoea
Kalimeris - Boltonia
Kalopanax - Eleutherococcus
Keckiella - Penstemon
Knautia - Scabiosa
Kniphofia - Tritoma

Kohleria - Isoloma
Kunzea - Leptospermum
Lablab - Dolichos
Lagarosiphon - Elodea
Lagarostrobos - Dacrydium
Lallemantia - Dracocephalum
Lamium - Galeobdolon
Lamium - Lamiastrum
Lampranthus - Mesembryanthemum
Lampranthus - Oscularia
Laurentia - Hippobroma
Lavatera - Malva
Ledebouria - Scilla
× Ledodendron - Rhododendron
Lepechinia - Sphacele
Lepidothamnus - Dacrydium
Leptinella - Cotula
Leptodactylon - Gilia
Leucanthemella - Chrysanthemum
Leucanthemella - Leucanthemum
Leucanthemopsis - Chrysanthemum
Leucanthemopsis - Tanacetum
Leucanthemum - Chrysanthemum
Leucochrysum - Helipterum
Leucophyta - Calocephalus
Leucopogon - Cyathodes
× Leucoraoulia - Raoulia
Leuzea - Centaurea
Leymus - Elymus
Ligularia - Senecio
Ligustrum - Parasyringa
Lilium - Nomocharis
Limonium - Statice
Linanthus - Linanthastrum
Lindelofia - Adelocaryum
Lindera - Parabenzoin
Liriope - Ophiopogon
Lithocarpus - Quercus
Lithodora - Lithospermum
Littorella - Plantago
Lophomyrtus - Myrtus
Lophomyrtus - Myrtus
Lophospermum - Asarina
Lophospermum - Maurandya
Lophostemon - Tristania
Lotus - Dorycnium
Lotus - Tetragonolobus
Ludwigia - Jussiaea
Luma - Myrtus
× Lycene - Lychnis
Lychnis - Agrostemma
Lychnis - Silene
Lychnis - Viscaria
Lycianthes - Solanum
Lytocaryum - Cocos
Lytocaryum - Microcoelum
Macfadyena - Bignonia
Macfadyena - Doxantha
Machaeranthera - Xylorhiza
Mackaya - Asystasia
Macleaya - Bocconia
Mahonia - Berberis
Mandevilla - Dipladenia
Mandragora - Atropa
Marrubium - Ballota
Matricaria - Chamomilla
Matricaria - Tripleurosperum
Maurandella - Asarina
Maurandella - Maurandya
Maurandya - Asarina
Melicytus - Hymenanthera
Melinis - Rhynchelytrum
Mentha - Preslia
Merremia - Ipomoea
Mimulus - Diplacus
Minuartia - Arenaria
Modiolastrum - Malvastrum
Moltkia - Lithodora
Moltkia - Lithospermum
Morina - Acanthocalyx
Mukdenia - Aceriphyllum
Muscari - Hyacinthus
Muscari - Leopoldia
Muscari - Leopoldia
Muscari - Muscarimia
Muscari - Pseudomuscari
Myricaria - Tamarix
Myrteola - Myrtus
Naiocrene - Claytonia
Naiocrene - Montia
Nectaroscordum - Allium
Nematanthus - Hypocyrta
Nemesia - Diascia
Neopaxia - Claytonia
Neopaxia - Montia
Neoregelia - Guzmania
Neoregelia - Nidularium
Nepeta - Dracocephalum
Nepeta - Origanum
Nephrophyllidium - Fauria
Nipponanthemum - Chrysanthemum
Nipponanthemum - Leucanthemum
Nymphoides - Villarsia
Oemleria - Osmaronia
Olearia - Pachystegia
Olsynium - Phaiophleps
Olsynium - Sisyrinchium
Onixotis - Dipidax
Ophiopogon - Convallaria
Orchis - Dactylorhiza
Oreopteris - Thelypteris
Orostachys - Sedum
Osmanthus - × Osmarea
Osmanthus - Phillyrea
Osteospermum - Dimorphotheca
Othonna - Hertia
Othonna - Othonnopsis
Ozothamhus - Helichrysum
Pachyphragma - Cardamine
Packera - Senecio
Paederota - Veronica
Papaver - Meconopsis
Parahebe - Derwentia
Parahebe - Hebe
Parahebe - Veronica
Paraserianthes - Albizia
Paris - Daiswa
Parthenocissus - Ampelopsis
Parthenocissus - Vitis
Passiflora - Tetrapathaea
Paxistima - Pachystema
Pecteilis - Habenaria
Pelargonium - Geranium
Peltoboykinia - Boykinia
Penstemon - Chelone
Pentaglottis - Anchusa
Pentalinon - Urechites
Pericallis - Senecio
Persea - Machilus
Persicaria - Aconogonon
Persicaria - Bistorta
Persicaria - Polygonum
Persicaria - Tovara
Petrocoptis - Lychnis
Petrophytum - Spiraea
Petrorhagia - Tunica
Petroselinum - Carum
Phegopteris - Thelypteris
Phoenicaulis - Parrya
Photinia - Heteromeles
Photinia - Stransvaesia
Photinia - × Stravinia
Phuopsis - Crucianella
Phyla - Lippia
Phymosia - Sphaeralcea
Physoplexis - Phyteuma
Physostegia - Dracocephalum
Pieris - Arcterica
Pilosella - Hieracium
Piper - Macropiper
Pisonia - Heimerliodendron
Plagiomnium - Mnium
Plecostachys - Helichrysum
Plectranthus - Solenostemon
Pleioblastus - Arundinaria
Pleioblastus - Sasa
Podranea - Tecoma
Polianthes - Bravoa
Polygonum - Persicaria
Polypodium - Phlebodium
Polystichum - Phanerophlebia
Poncirus - Aegle
Potentilla - Comarum
Pratia - Lobelia
Prumnopitys - Podocarpus
Prunus - Amygdalus
Pseudocydonia - Chaenomeles
Pseudopanax - Metapanax
Pseudopanax - Neopanax
Pseudopanax - Nothopanax
Pseudosasa - Arundinaria

Pseudotsuga - Tsuga
Pseudowintera - Drimys
Pterocephalus - Scabiosa
Ptilostemon - Cirsium
Pulicaria - Inula
Pulsatilla - Anemone
Pushkinia - Scilla
Pyrethropsis - Argyranthemum
Pyrethropsis - Chrysanthemum
Pyrethropsis - Leucanthemopsis
Pyrethropsis - Leucanthemum
Reineckea - Liriope
Retama - Genista
Rhapis - Chamaerops
Rhodanthe - Helipterum
Rhodanthemum - Chrysanthemopsis
Rhodanthemum - Chrysanthemum
Rhodanthemum - Leucanthemopsis
Rhodanthemum - Pyrethropsis
Rhodiola - Rosularia
Rhodiola - Sedum
Rhododendron - Azalea
Rhododendron - Azaleodendron
Rhododendron - Rhodora
Rhodophiala - Hippeastrum
Rosularia - Cotyledon
Rosularia - Sempervivella
Rothmannia - Gardenia
Ruellia - Dipteracanthus
Ruschia - Mesembryanthemum
Saccharum - Erianthus
Sagina - Minuartia
Salvia - Salvia
Sanguisorba - Dendriopoterium
Sanguisorba - Poterium
Sasa - Arundinaria
Sasa - Pleioblastus
Sasaella - Arundinaria
Sasaella - Pleioblastus
Sasaella - Sasa
Sasamorpha - Sasa
Sauromatum - Arum
Saussurea - Jurinea
Scadoxus - Haemanthus
Schefflera - Brassaia
Schefflera - Dizygotheca
Schefflera - Heptapleurum
Schizachyrium - Andropogon
Schizostachyum - Arundinaria
Schizostachyum - Thamnocalamus
Schoenoplectus - Scirpus
Scirpoides - Scirpus
Scirpus - Eriophorum
Sedum - Hylotelephium
Sedum - Rhodiola
Sedum - Sedastrum
Sedum - Villadia
Semiaquilegia - Aquilegia
Semiaquilegia - Paraquilegia
Semiarundinaria - Arundinaria
Senecio - Cineraria
Senecio - Kleinia
Senecio - Ligularia
Senna - Cassia
Seriphidium - Artemisia
Shortia - Schizocodon
Sibbaldiopsis - Potentilla
Sieversia - Geum
Silene - Lychnis
Silene - Melandrium
Silene - Saponaria
Sinacalia - Ligularia
Sinacalia - Senecio
Sinarundinaria - Semiarundinaria
Sinningia - Gesneria
Sinningia - Rechsteineria
Sisymbrium - Hesperis
Sisyrinchium - Phaiophleps
× *Smithicodonia* - × *Achimenantha*
Solanum - Lycianthes
Soleirolia - Helxine
Solenopsis, - Isotoma
Solenostemon, - Coleus
× *Solidaster - Aster*
× *Solidaster - Solidago*
Sorbaria - Spiraea
Sparaxis - Synnotia
Sphaeralcea - Iliamna
Sphaeromeria - Tanacetum
Spirodela - Lemna
Spraguea - Calyptridium
Stachys - Betonica
Steirodiscus - Gamolepis
Stenomesson - Urceolina
Stenotus - Haplopappus
Steptocarpus - Streptocarpella
Stewartia - Stuartia
Stipa - Achnatherum
Stipa - Lasiagrostis
Strobilanthes - Pteracanthus
Succisa - Scabiosa
Sutera - Bacopa
Syagrus - Arecastrum
Syagrus - Cocos
Tanacetum - Achillea
Tanacetum - Balsamita
Tanacetum - Chrysanthemum
Tanacetum - Matricaria
Tanacetum - Pyrethrum
Tanacetum - Spathipappus
Tanacetum - Sphaeromeria
Tecoma - Tecomaria
Telekia - Buphthalmum
Tephroseris - Senecio
Tetradium - Euodia
Tetraneuris - Actinella
Tetraneuris - Hymenoxys
Tetrapanax - Fatsia
Thamnocalamus - Arundinaria
Thamnocalamus - Sinarundinaria
Thlaspi - Hutchinsia
Thlaspi - Noccaea
Thuja - Platycladus
Thuja - Thujopsis
Thymus - Origanum
Tonestus - Haplopappus
Toona - Cedrela
Trachelium - Diosphaera
Trachycarpus - Chamaerops
Tradescantia - Rhoeo
Tradescantia - Setcreasea
Tradescantia - Tradescantia
Tradescantia - Zebrina
Trichopetalum - Anthericum
Tripetaleia - Elliottia
Tripleurospermum - Matricaria
Tripogandra - Tradescantia
Tristagma - Beauverdia
Tristaniopsis - Tristania
Triteleia - Brodiaea
Tritonia - Crocosmia
Tropaeolum - Nasturtium hort.
Tuberaria - Helianthemum
Tulipa - Amana
Tweedia - Oxypetalum
Ugni - Myrtus
Ursinia - Euryops
Uvularia - Oakesiella
Vaccinium - Oxycoccus
Verbascum - Celsia
Verbascum - × *Celsioverbascum*
Verbena - Glandularia
Verbena - Lippia
Veronicastrum - Veronica
Vigna - Phaseolus
Villadia - Sedum
Viola - Erpetion
Vitaliana - Androsace
Vitaliana - Douglasia
Weigela - Diervilla
Weigela - Macrodiervilla
Xanthorhiza - Zanthorhiza
Yushania - Arundinaria
Yushania - Sinarundinaria
Yushania - Thamnocalamus
Zantedeschia - Calla
Zauschneria - Epilobium
Zephyranthes - × *Cooperanthes*
Zephyranthes - Cooper

Plant Deletions

Plants marked with an '87', '88', '89', '90', '91', '92', '93', '94', '95', or '96' were listed in the 1987, '88, '89, '90/91, '91/92, '92/93, '93/94, '94/95, '95/96 or '96/97 editions respectively.
Back editions of **THE RHS PLANT FINDER** may be obtained by writing to
The Administrator, The RHS Plant Finder, RHS Gardens, Wisley, Woking, Surrey GU23 6QB
Price £6.00 each inclusive of p&p. Please make cheques payable to RHS Enterprises Ltd.

ABELIA
96 x ***grandiflora*** dwarf form

ABELMOSCHUS
90 ***esculentus***
92 ***moschatus*** 'Mischief'

ABIES
96 ***alba*** 'Green Spiral'
96 – 'Pendula'
91 x ***arnoldiana***
96 ***chensiensis***
87 – subsp. ***chensiensis***
90 ***cilicica***
96 ***concolor*** 'Argentea'
89 – 'Aurea'
92 – var. ***lowiana***
96 ***delavayi***
92 – var. ***smithii***
95 ***densa*** S&L 5538
87 ***durangensis*** var. ***coahuilensis***
92 ***fargesii***
92 – var. ***faxoniana***
94 ***firma***
87 x ***insignis*** 'Beissneriana'
96 ***koreana*** 'Blauer Pfiff'
96 ***lasiocarpa***
92 ***magnifica*** 'Glauca'
90 ***nebrodensis***
94 ***nephrolepis***
94 ***nordmanniana*** 'Barabits' Compact'
94 – subsp. ***equi-trojani***
96 – 'Reflexa'
95 ***numidica*** 'Lawrenceville'
95 ***pinsapo*** 'Pendula'
88 ***procera*** 'Noble's Dwarf'
95 – 'Prostrata'
87 ***recurvata***
96 – var. ***ernestii***
93 ***sachalinensis***
87 x ***shastensis***
93 ***sibirica***
96 ***spectabilis***
95 ***vejarii***

ABROTANELLA
90 ***emarginata***
90 ***forsterioides***

ABUTILON
92 'Cynthia Pike' (v)
95 'Imp'
93 ***indicum***
96 'Lemon Queen'
89 'Lopen Red'
93 ***megapotamicum*** 'Compactum'
93 – 'Joy Bells'
92 ***ochsenii***
95 'Orange Glow' (v) 🏆
95 'Orange Vein'
95 'Oxon Red'
94 ***pictum variegatum***
91 x ***suntense*** 'Gorer's White'
95 – 'White Charm'
94 ***vitifolium*** 'Wild Forest'
87 'White Swan'

ACACIA
90 ***adunca***
95 ***beckleri***
96 ***boormanii***
95 ***brachybotrya***
95 ***burkittii***
95 ***chlorophylla***
95 ***extensa***
93 ***genistifolia***
96 ***gillii***
94 ***glaucocarpa***
87 ***implexa***
89 ***jonesii***
89 ***myrtifolia***
90 ***neriifolia***
94 ***pendula***

ACAENA
94 ***acris***
95 ***argentea***
95 sp. RB 94004

ACALYPHA
90 ***godseffiana***
96 ***reptans***
93 ***wilkesiana***
93 – 'Can-can'
93 – 'Gold Cant'
93 ***wilkesiana pudsiana***

ACANTHOLIMON
92 ***acerosum***
95 – var. ***acerosum***
88 ***confertiflorum***
95 ***hypochaerum***
96 ***litvinovii***

ACANTHUS
94 ***australis***

ACER
94 ***buergerianum*** subsp. ***ningpoense***
96 ***campestre*** 'Autumn Red'
95 – 'Nanum'
95 – 'Queen Elizabeth'
96 – 'Rockhampton Red Stem'
96 – 'Weeping'
96 ***cappadocicum*** subsp. ***sinicum*** var. ***tricaudatum***
96 ***caudatum***
96 x ***coriaceum***
96 x ***dieckii***
96 ***distylum***
96 ***forrestii*** TW 348
96 x ***freemanii*** 'Elegant'
93 ***griseum*** 'Tilgates'
96 ***japonicum*** 'Viride'
93 ***maximowiczianum morifolium***
96 ***miyabei***
89 ***morifolium***
96 ***nipponicum***
96 ***palmatum*** 'Crippsii'
90 – 'Hamaotome'
92 – 'Maimori'
96 – 'Mizu-kuguri'
96 – 'Monzukushi'
95 – 'Ogon-sarasa'
89 – 'Sango-nishiki'
96 – 'Shichihenge'
96 – 'Tatsuta-gawa'
94 – 'Tsukomo'
96 – 'Wada's Flame'
93 – 'Yasemin'
94 – 'Yezo-nishiki'
96 ***pectinatum***
95 – 'Sparkling'
94 ***pentapotamicum***
94 ***platanoides*** 'Erectum'
96 – 'Reitenbachii'
91 ***rubrum*** 'Columnare'
95 – 'Tridens'
95 ***saccharum*** 'Aureum'
94 – 'Newton Sentry'
88 ***shirasawanum*** 'Junihitoe'
96 ***sieboldianum*** 'Kinugasayama'
93 – 'Miyami-nishiki'
94 ***sinopurpurascens***
95 ***stachyanthum***
94 ***takesimense***
89 ***tataricum*** subsp. ***ginnala*** 'Durand Dwarf'
96 ***tetramerum***
87 ***truncatum*** 'Akaji-nishiki'

ACHILLEA
96 ***ageratifolia*** subsp. ***ageratifolia*** NS 692
93 ***distans*** subsp. ***tanacetifolia***
92 'Forncett Tapestry'
88 x ***hausmanniana***
90 'Heidi'
94 ***holosericea***
96 'Little Beauty'
94 ***millefolium*** var. ***borealis***
93 – 'Kelwayi'
89 – 'Purpurea'
91 – 'Rougham Beauty'
95 'Moonbeam'
96 ***nana***
95 'Obristii'
96 ***odorata***
90 ***oxyloba***
96 'Peach Queen'
87 x ***prichardii***
93 ***ptarmica*** (The Pearl Group) 'The Pearl' (clonal) (d)
91 'Rougham Salmon'
95 'Theo Ploeger'

ACHIMENES
94 'Admiration'
92 ***antirrhina***
92 – 'Redcap'
92 'Ballerina'
92 'Blue John'
92 'Bright Jewel'
91 'Cameo Lilac'
92 'Camille Pink'
92 'Carmencita'
92 'Carnelian'
92 ***cettoana***
92 – 'Tiny Blue'
92 'Coral Cameo'
92 'Crystal'
92 'Diadem'
92 ***erecta*** 'Mexican Dwarf'
92 ***erecta rosea***
92 'Erlkönig'
92 'Fascination'
92 'Flamboyant'
92 'Garnet'
94 'Germanica'
92 'Glacier'
91 ***grandiflora***
92 'India Hybrid'
92 'Jewel Glow'
92 'Lady Lyttelton'
94 'Lake City'
92 'Lavender Jade'
92 'Leonora'
92 'Madame Gehune'
92 'Mair's White'
96 'Margaret White'
92 'Margarita'
94 'Master Ingram'
92 'Mauve Delight'
95 'Mauve Queen'
92 ***mexicana***
92 'Miniata'
94 'Minute'
95 'Miss Blue'
92 'National Velvet'
94 'Nessida'
92 'Opal'
92 'Painted Lady'
91 'Pearly Grey'
92 ***pedunculata***
92 'Purple Queen'
92 'Purple Triumph'
92 'Red Riding Hood'
95 'Ruby'
92 ***skinneri***
92 'Sunburst'
89 'Tetra Altrote Charm'
92 'Tetra Blauer Planet'
89 'Tetra Dark Violet Charm'
92 'Tetra Orange Star'
92 'Tetra Purpur Elfe'
89 'Tetra Rokoko Elfe'
92 'Tetra Rosa Queen'
92 'Tetra Verschaffelt'
92 'Tetra Weinrote Elfe'
92 'The Monarch'
92 'Tiger Eye'
92 'Topaz'
92 'Tresco'
96 'Violetta'
92 ***warscewicziana***
92 'White Giant'
92 'White Knight'
92 'White Marvel'
92 'Yellow Beauty'

ACHLYS
96 ***triphylla***

ACIPHYLLA
90 ***congesta***

92 *crenulata*
90 *ferox*
93 *glacialis*
95 *lamondii*
88 *lecomtei*
96 *procumbens*
92 *similis*
89 *spedenii*

ACOELORRHAPHE
94 *wrightii*

ACOKANTHERA
94 *oblongifolia*

ACONITUM
94 *anthora*
95 x *cammarum* 'Franz Marc'
91 *carmichaelii* (Wilsonii Group) 'Kelmscott Variegated'
89 *chasmanthum*
96 *elliotii*
96 *falconeri*
96 *hookeri*
92 *kirinense*
95 *smithii*
89 *spicatum*

ACTAEA
94 *rubra* subsp. *arguta*

ACTINIDIA
95 'Ananasnaya' (f)
91 *arguta* 'Meader No. 2' (f)
95 – 'Stamford' (f)
88 *deliciosa* 'Abbott' (f)
96 – 'Boskoop'
93 – 'Bruno' (f/F)
93 – hermaphrodite (F)
88 – 'Matua'
92 *giraldii*

ACTINOTUS
93 *helianthi*

ADENOCARPUS
96 *foliolosus*

ADENOPHORA
96 *coelestis*
92 *kurilensis*
94 *potaninii* dark form
96 – 'Lilacina Flora Plena'

ADIANTUM
94 *monochlamys*
90 *raddianum* 'Goldelse'
92 – 'Lady Geneva'
92 *tenerum* 'Scutum Roseum'
91 *trapeziforme*

ADONIS
92 *chrysocyathus*

AECHMEA
90 *blumenavii*
96 *chantinii* 🏆
90 *cylindrata*
90 *fulgens* var. *discolor* 🏆
96 'Grand Prix'
90 *lueddemanniana*
95 *nudicaulis* 🏆
95 *orlandiana* 🏆
89 *recurvata*
96 'Romero'
92 *servitensis*

AEONIUM
93 *arboreum* 'Albovariegatum'
95 – var. *rubrolineatum*
93 *lindleyi*

AESCHYNANTHUS
93 'Greensleeves'
94 'Little Tiger'

AESCULUS
95 *hippocastanum* 'Memmingeri'
95 – 'Monstrosa'
95 – 'Pyramidalis'

AETHIONEMA
89 *armenum* 'Mavis Holmes'
96 *caespitosum*
93 *diastrophis*
95 *glaucum*
93 *saxatile*
88 *stylosum*
93 *thomasianum*

AGAPANTHUS
94 *africanus minor*
96 'Apple Court'
96 'Ben Hope'
96 'Bicton Hybrid'
96 'Blue Star'
93 *campanulatus* 'Ultramarine'
95 'Dawnstar'
96 giant hybrids
96 'Kew White'
93 'Marjorie'
95 'Moonstar'
96 'Peter Pan' American
95 'Podge Mill'
95 *praecox* subsp. *orientalis* 'Mount Thomas'
96 'Sky Star'
96 'Spode'
96 'Super Star'
96 'White Giant'
96 'White Star'
96 'White Starlet'

AGASTACHE
96 *cana* variegated
96 *mexicana* 'Carminea'
95 *pallidiflora*
95 *palmeri*
96 *urticifolia* 'Alba Variegata'

AGAVE
95 *americana* 'Mediopicta Alba' 🏆
94 *angustifolia* var. *rubescens*
96 *bovicornuta*
94 *cerulata* subsp. *nelsonii*
94 – subsp. *subcerulata*
91 *colorata*
94 *deserti* subsp. *deserti*
94 – subsp. *pringlei*
93 *ellemeetiana*
96 *ferdinandi-regis*
96 *franzosinii*
91 *funkiana*
94 *ghiesbreghtii*
94 *kerchovei*
94 *lurida*
94 *mckelveyana*
91 *mitriformis*
94 *pachycentra*
89 *parviflora*
95 *potatorum* 🏆
96 *sebastiana*
90 *shawii*
96 – subsp. *goldmaniana*
91 *sobria*
95 *striata rubra* 🏆
94 *titanota*
91 *toumeyana*
91 – var. *bella*
96 *utahensis* var. *eborispina*
96 – subsp. *kaibabensis*
92 – var. *nevadensis*
94 *vilmoriniana*
94 *weberi*

AGLAONEMA
90 *commutatum* var. *maculatum*
90 – 'Pseudobracteatum'
90 *nitidum* 'Curtisii'
91 'Silver King'

AGROSTOCRINUM
91 *scabrum*

AINSLIAEA
94 *latifolia* S&SH 103
95 *paucicapitata* B&SWJ 103

AIPHANES
95 *caryotifolia*

AJANIA
95 *pacifica* 'Hakai'
94 *tibetica*

AJUGA
91 *chamaepitys*
95 *genevensis* 'Pink Beauty'
96 *reptans* 'Cavalier'
96 – 'Jungle Bronze'
96 – 'Silver Carpet'
95 – 'Tortoiseshell' (v)

ALANGIUM
91 *platanifolium* var. *macrophyllum*

ALBUCA
91 *setosa*
90 *spiralis*

ALCEA
96 *rosea* double white
95 – Powder Puff Group
96 – single white
90 – 'Sutton's Single Brilliant'
96 *rugosa* 'Caucasian Yellow'

ALCHEMILLA
91 *bulgarica*
95 *falklandica*
96 *hoppeana* Della Torre
94 *mollis* 'Grandiflora'
95 *plicatula*
93 *scalaris*
95 aff. *venosa*

ALETRIS
96 *farinosa*

ALLAMANDA
96 *blanchetii*
96 *cathartica* 'Stansill's Double'

ALLARDIA
95 *tomentosa*
95 *tridactylites*

ALLIUM
95 *aflatunense* Fedtschenko
93 *amphibolum*
90 *auctum*
91 *barszczewskii*
94 *bucharicum*
96 *carolinianum* CC 322
94 *cernuum* var. *neomexicanum*
94 *chamaemoly*
94 *cyaneum album*
93 *cyaneum* 'Cobalt Blue'
88 *douglasii*
96 *fimbriatum* var. *purdyi*
96 *fistulosum* red
94 *flavum* forms
96 *goodingii*
92 'Laxton Sunset'
96 *libonicum*
94 *mairei* var. *amabile* red
95 *narcissiflorum* Villars pink
94 *pskemense*
95 *rosenbachianum* 'Akbulak'
96 *roseum* var. *carneum*
89 *rubellum*
95 *rubrovittatum* CDB 292
94 *schmitzii*
96 *schoenoprasum* 'Shepherds Crooks'
96 *sessiliflorum*
96 sp. ACE 1745
92 *splendens*
96 *subhirsutum*
94 *subvillosum*
96 *thunbergii* 'Nanum'

ALLOCASUARINA
95 *distyla*

ALNUS
89 *acuminata* subsp. *arguta*
94 *cremastogyne*
94 *fauriei*
96 *formosana*
94 *fruticosa*
94 *glutinosa* var. *barbata*
87 *hirsuta* var. *sibirica*
96 *jorullensis*
90 *lanata*
95 *oblongifolia*
95 *pendula*
95 *pinnatisecta*
94 *tenuifolia*

ALOCASIA
90 x *argyraea*
90 x *chantrieri*
90 *cuprea*
90 'Green Velvet'
90 *korthalsii*
90 *longiloba*
90 *macrorrhiza*
94 *sanderiana*
90 *watsoniana*
90 *wentii*

ALOE
95 *bakeri* 🏆
94 *descoingsii*

95 ***melanacantha*** ♀
96 ***mitriformis***
95 ***rauhii*** ♀
95 ***somaliensis*** ♀
94 ***variegata*** ♀

ALONSOA
92 ***incisifolia***
92 ***meridionalis*** 'Shell Pink'

ALOPECURUS
95 ***arundinaceus***
93 ***geniculatus***

ALPINIA
96 ***purpurata***
96 ***vittata*** (v)
96 ***zerumbet***

ALSTROEMERIA
91 Butterfly hybrids
96 ***diluta***
95 ***exserens***
94 – F&W 7207
91 'Furie'
95 ***hookeri*** subsp. ***cummingiana***
95 – subsp. ***hookeri***
91 'Joli Coeur'
96 ***magnifica***
95 'Ohio'
96 ***pallida*** JJA 12497
95 ***presliana***
96 Princess Margarita
96 'Purple Joy'
95 ***revoluta***
96 'Rosy Wings'
95 'Saffier'
95 'Saxony'
96 'Sovereign'
95 sp. Wr 8893
95 ***spathulata***
90 Canaria = 'Stagelb'
89 Appelbloesem = 'Stakaros'
89 Annabel = 'Stalan'
90 Libelle = 'Stalbel'
90 Jubilee = 'Stalilas'
90 Isabella = 'Stalis'
90 Monika = 'Stalmon'
90 Atlas = 'Stalrama'
90 Mandarin = 'Stalrin'
91 Rosello = 'Stalrobu'
90 Samora = 'Stalsam'
90 Tango = 'Staltang'
90 Red Sunset = 'Stamarko'
90 Pink Triumph = 'Stapink'
90 Ramona = 'Stapiram'
90 Rosita = 'Starosello'
90 Zebra = 'Stazeb'
95 'Sunrise'
91 'Sweetheart'
95 ***umbellata***
96 'Vanitas'
96 ***versicolor***
91 Walter Fleming
96 'White Knight'
90 Rita = 'Zelido'

ALYSSUM
94 ***longistylum***
96 ***moellendorfianum***
94 ***ovirense***
95 ***poderi***
95 ***scardicum***
96 ***sphacioticum***
96 ***tenium***
89 ***troodii***

AMARYLLIS
91 ***belladonna*** 'Bloemfontein'
91 ***belladonna*** 'Hathor'
91 – 'Windhoek'

AMELANCHIER
92 ***alnifolia*** var. ***semi-integrifolia***
95 ***asiatica***
89 – var. ***sinica***

AMOMUM
96 ***compactum***

AMORPHA
93 ***nana***

AMORPHOPHALLUS
93 ***rivierei***

AMPELOPSIS
92 ***glandulosa*** var. ***brevipedunculata*** f. ***citrulloides***

ANAGALLIS
93 ***arvensis*** var. ***latifolia***
91 ***monellii*** 'Caerulea'
96 – red

ANANAS
90 ***comosus***

ANAPHALIS
89 ***keriensis***
96 ***nepalensis***
94 ***subrigida***
94 ***trinervis***

ANCHUSA
93 ***azurea*** 'Italian Pride'

ANDROMEDA
93 ***glaucophylla*** 'Latifolia'
88 ***polifolia*** var. ***angustifolia***
92 – 'Compacta Alba' ♀
96 – 'Hayachine'
93 – 'Iwasugo'
95 – 'Red King'

ANDROSACE
89 ***alpina***
96 ***bisulca*** var. ***aurata*** ACE 1750
96 ***bulleyana*** ACE 2198
96 ***carnea*** subsp. ***brigantiaca*** Myer's form
96 – subsp. ***rosea*** × ***carnea*** subsp. ***laggeri***
93 ***chaixii***
92 ***chamaejasme***
88 – subsp. ***lehmanniana***
94 ***elongata***
93 ***globifera*** × ***muscoidea***
90 × ***heeri*** pink
96 ***helvetica***
93 ***kochii tauricola***
95 ***lanuginosa*** CC 1271
96 ***lehmannii*** EMAK 951
94 ***obtusifolia***
94 ***occidentalis***
95 × ***pedemontana***
96 ***rotundifolia*** 'Elegans'
96 ***sarmentosa monstrosa***
92 ***sempervivoides*** dark form
94 ***septentrionalis*** var. ***puberulenta***
96 – 'Stardust'
96 ***strigillosa***
90 ***tapete***
96 ***tridentata***
91 ***uliginosa***
93 ***villosa*** var. ***taurica*** 'Palandoken'
88 ***wulfeniana***

ANEMONE
96 ***apennina*** 'Petrovac' CE&H 538
90 ***biflora***
94 ***blanda*** 'Blue Mist'
90 – 'Blue Pearl'
96 – 'Blue Star'
88 – var. ***scythinica***
92 ***bucharica***
96 ***caucasica***
96 ***cernua***
96 ***coronaria*** 'Blue Moon'
91 – (De Caen Group) 'Excelsior'
88 ***elongata***
92 ***eranthoides***
89 'French Hill'
96 × ***hybrida*** 'Alba Dura'
93 – 'King George V'
90 ***lithophila***
94 ***mexicana***
93 ***multifida*** pink
94 ***narcissiflora*** subsp. ***biarmiensis***
94 ***nemorosa*** 'Bracteata, New Zealand'
94 – 'Celestial'
91 – 'Currie's Pink'
95 – 'Green Dream'
93 – 'Parlez Vous'
93 – 'Purity'
90 ***nikoensis***
87 ***obtusiloba*** f. ***patula***
94 ***pavonina*** var. ***ocellata*** JCA 161.901
92 ***petiolulosa***
94 ***pseudoaltaica***
96 ***raddeana***
93 ***reflexa***
96 ***riparia***
94 ***tomentosa*** 'September Glanz'
96 – 'Serenade'
96 ***trifolia*** pink
94 ***tschernjaewii***

ANEMONELLA
94 ***thalictroides*** 'Atlas Double'

ANGELICA
96 ***pinnata***
94 ***sylvestris*** pink
96 ***triquinata***
93 ***ursina***

ANIGOZANTHOS
91 ***bicolor***
96 ***flavidus*** green
91 – grey
91 – orange
91 ***gabrielae***
96 ***preissii***
91 ***viridis***

ANISOTOME
92 ***aromatica***
92 ***flexuosa***

ANNONA
94 ***cherimola***

ANODA
95 ***crenatiflora***
96 ***cristata***

ANOMATHECA
96 ***laxa*** Blue Form
95 ***laxa viridiflora***
96 ***moisii***

ANTENNARIA
93 ***alpina***
95 ***dimorpha***

ANTHEMIS
94 ***tinctoria*** 'Powis White'

ANTHOCERCIS
91 ***littorea***

ANTHURIUM
90 ***andraeanum*** 'Album'
90 'Aztec'
90 'Brazilian Surprise'
93 ***clarinervium***
90 ***crystallinum***
90 × ***ferrierense***
93 – 'Roseum'
90 ***leuconeurum***
90 ***magnificum***
90 'Nova'
90 ***scherzerianum album***
90 ***scherzerianum minimum***
90 ***scherzerianum*** 'Rothschildianum'
90 – 'Wardii'
90 ***veitchii***
89 ***warocqueanum***

ANTHYLLIS
89 ***barba-jovis***
94 ***hermanniae*** prostrate form
96 ***montana*** 'Rubra Compacta'

ANTIRRHINUM
96 ***barrellieri***
93 ***majus***

APHELANDRA
90 'Snow Queen'

APONOGETON
90 ***desertorum***

AQUILEGIA
96 ***alpina*** 'Carl Ziepke'
96 – German form
93 ***bertolonii*** var. ***australis***
93 'Betty Barton'
94 'Blue Spurs'
91 ***brevistyla***
88 ***caerulea*** var. ***daileyae***
95 ***chrysantha*** double dark red
91 – var. ***hinckleyana***
93 'Coronato'
94 ***dinarica***
94 'Dove'
87 'Edelweiss'
96 ***eximia***
96 ***flabellata*** double white
94 – var. ***pumila*** from Mount Hakkoda, Japan
96 ***formosa*** × ***longissima***
92 – Nana Group

94 ***glandulosa*** var. ***jucunda***
91 Harbutt's Hybrids
96 ***karelinii***
96 ***kurdistanica***
88 Langdon's Rainbow Hybrids
90 ***longissima*** 'Flore Pleno'
96 Lowdham strain
96 x ***maruyamana***
96 'Maxi Star'
96 ***microphylla***
94 'Modra Pisen'
94 'Mrs Shaw's Double'
95 ***ottonis*** subsp. ***ottonis***
96 ***rockii***
96 sp. from Zigana Pass, Turkey
94 ***viscosa***
89 – subsp. ***hirsutissima***
96 ***vulgaris*** 'Anne Calder'
96 – 'Belhaven Blue'
92 – 'Crystal Star'
96 – 'Double Pleat'
95 – var. ***flore-pleno*** green
93 – – 'Warwick'
96 – from Brno, Czech Republic
96 – from Rize, Turkey
96 – 'Gisela Powell'
94 – var. ***hispanica***
89 – 'Millicent Bowden'
95 – subsp. ***nevadensis***
94 – 'Reverend E. Baty'
96 – 'Ruth Steer'
96 – scented
96 – tall form
94 – 'Tom Fairhurst'
96 – 'Warwick'

ARABIS
95 ***alpina*** subsp. ***caucasica*** 'Gillian Sharman' (v)
96 – – 'Snow White'
87 – – 'Snowflake'
92 ***blepharophylla*** 'Alba'
89 ***breweri***
95 ***caerulea***
91 ***collina***
95 ***cypria***
91 ***ferdinandi-coburgi*** 'Reversed'
95 ***koehleri***
96 ***microphylla***
96 'Pink Snow'
91 ***procurrens***
89 ***pumila***
91 ***scopoliana***
91 ***serrata*** var. ***japonica***
96 ***soyeri***
94 – subsp. ***coriacea***
94 – 'Variegata'
94 ***sparsiflora rubra***
94 ***stelleri*** var. ***japonica***
91 ***turrita***

ARACHNIODES
93 ***aristata***
96 ***simplicior*** C&L 236

ARALIA
95 ***decaisneana*** CC 1925
96 ***elata*** 'Silver Umbrella'

ARAUCARIA
94 ***columnaris***

ARBUTUS
91 ***unedo*** 'Merriott'

ARCHONTOPHOENIX
92 ***alexandrae***
95 ***cunninghamiana*** 🏆

ARCTOSTAPHYLOS
88 ***auriculata***
90 ***densiflora*** 'Emerald Carpet'
92 ***manzanita***
95 ***patula***
93 ***pumila***
93 ***stanfordiana***
93 ***uva-ursi*** 'Clyde Robin'
94 – 'Point Reyes'

ARCTOTIS
96 ***grandiflora***
95 x ***hybrida*** 'Champagne'
95 – cream
93 – cream and green
96 – 'Harlequin'
96 – 'Irene'
96 – orange
95 – 'Pollen'
95 – 'White'

ARECA
92 ***aliceae***
92 ***triandra***

ARENARIA
93 ***aggregata***
96 – subsp. ***erinacea***
93 ***canescens***
95 ***fendleri***
94 ***festucoides*** CC&McK 405
96 ***hookeri*** subsp. ***desertorum***
96 ***lithops***
95 ***longifolia***
93 ***ludoviciana*** 'Valerie Finnis'
96 ***procera***
95 ***saxosonum***
93 ***scariosa***
95 sp. CC 1368
95 ***tetraquetra*** JJA 188.450

ARENGA
89 ***caudata***

ARGEMONE
90 ***platyceras***

ARGYRANTHEMUM
91 ***adauctum***
91 – subsp. ***gracile***
91 'Brontes'
95 'Donington Hero' 🏆
96 double yellow
94 ***frutescens*** subsp. ***pumilum***
94 ***maderense*** 'Forde Abbey'
94 'Pink Silver Queen'
96 'Rosali' (d)
96 'Stydd Rose'
91 ***sundingii***
95 'Whiteknights' 🏆

ARISAEMA
95 ***elephas***
96 ***griffithii*** var. ***pradhanii***
96 ***jacquemontii*** SEP 263
95 ***longilaminum***

ARISTOLOCHIA
94 ***brasiliensis***
93 ***contorta***
92 ***heterophylla***

ARMERIA
89 ***alliacea*** 'Grandiflora'
87 ***arctica***
89 'Bloodgood'
90 Carlux Hybrids
93 ***filicaulis***
94 ***juniperifolia*** 'Ardenholme'
96 ***leucocephala***
90 ***maritima*** 'Birch Pink'
93 – 'La Pampa'
87 – subsp. ***sibirica***
93 – 'Splendens Alba'

ARNICA
95 ***angustifolia***
92 – subsp. ***alpina***
93 ***longifolia***
95 ***louisiana***
92 ***unalaschkensis***

ARRHENATHERUM
92 ***elatius***

ARTEMISIA
87 ***absinthium*** 'Poland's Variety'
96 ***campestris***
92 ***genipi***
92 ***judaica***
96 aff. ***parviflora*** CLD 1531
96 ***rupestris***
95 sp. B&SWJ 088
94 ***splendens*** Willdenow var. ***brachyphylla***

ARTHROPODIUM
89 ***cirratum*** bronze
92 – pink
95 – 'Three Knights'
95 – 'White Knights'

ARUM
90 ***byzantinum***
94 ***creticum*** white
95 ***euxinum***
95 ***italicum*** subsp. ***italicum*** 'Tiny'
93 – subsp. ***neglectum***
96 ***rupicola***
96 – var. ***rupicola***
96 – var. ***virescens***

ARUNCUS
96 ***dioicus*** var. ***kamtschaticus*** AGSJ 59
96 sp. CLD 718

ASARINA
94 ***procumbens*** dwarf form

ASARUM
92 ***hartwegii*** 'Silver Heart'

ASCLEPIAS
93 ***albicans***
95 ***amplexicaulis***
95 ***cryptoceras***
95 ***exaltata***
96 ***incarnata*** 'Alba'
95 ***rubra***
96 ***speciosa***
93 ***subulata***
93 ***viridiflora***

ASPARAGUS
91 ***scandens***

ASPERULA
96 ***perpusilla***
95 ***purpurascens***
95 ***taygetea*** NS 758

ASPLENIUM
94 ***cuneifolium***
90 ***dalhousieae***
94 ***lepidum***
95 ***marinum***
95 ***onopteris***
95 ***rhizophyllum***
94 ***ruta-muraria*** subsp. ***dolomiticum*** var. ***eberlei***
90 ***scolopendrium*** 'Apple Court'
95 – (Crispum Group) 'Horning'
93 – 'Crispum Robinson'
95 – 'Crispum Variegatum Bolton'
94 – 'Digitatum'
90 ***squamulatum***
95 ***trichomanes*** subsp. ***pachyrachis***

ASTER
94 ***alpinus*** 'Beechwood'
90 – var. ***dolomiticus***
95 – 'Roseus'
92 ***amellus*** 'Danzig'
94 – 'Glücksfund'
95 – 'Praecox Junifreude'
88 – 'Rotfeuer'
92 ***asteroides***
96 ***bellidiastrum***
95 ***ericoides*** 'Blue Heaven'
94 – 'Ideal'
94 – 'Novembermyrte'
94 – 'Perfection'
92 – 'Schneetanne'
94 – 'Vimmer's Delight'
90 ***falconeri***
95 ***flaccidus***
94 ***flaccidus albus***
96 ***himalaicus*** BM&W 12
96 – EMAK 0952
94 ***ibericus***
92 ***laevis*** 'Blauschleier'
95 ***nepaulensis***
95 ***novae-angliae*** 'Ernie Moss'
95 – 'Lye End Companion'
90 ***novi-belgii*** 'Amethyst'
91 – 'Ashwick'
89 – 'Autumn Princess'
92 – 'Barker's Double'
94 – 'Beechwood Beacon'
92 – 'Beechwood Lady'
94 – 'Belmont Blue'
94 – 'Blue Gem'
90 – 'Blue Jacket'
90 – 'Blue Orb'
94 – 'Blue Plume'
94 – 'Borealis'
94 – 'Bridgette'
91 – 'Camerton'
90 – 'Candelabra'
90 – 'Catherine Chiswell'
90 – 'Charmwood'
94 – 'Chilcompton'
94 – 'Colin Bailey'
94 – 'Crimson Velvet'

90 – 'Desert Song'
94 – 'Dora Chiswell'
94 – 'Dorothy Bailey'
90 – 'Dunkerton'
93 – 'Dymbro'
91 – 'Emma'
94 – 'Ernie Moss'
90 – 'Fair Trial'
94 – 'Felicity'
93 – 'Festival'
94 – 'Flair'
96 – 'Flamingo'
94 – 'Gayborder Beauty'
94 – 'Gayborder Blue'
88 – 'Gayborder Rapture'
88 – 'Gayborder Rose'
94 – 'Gayborder Spire'
91 – 'Gayborder Supreme'
89 – 'Glorious'
90 – 'Goblin Coombe'
90 – 'Grey Lady'
91 – 'Happiness'
94 – 'Heather'
94 – 'Hey Day'
94 – 'Janice Stephenson'
92 – 'Jezebel'
92 – 'Jugendstil'
94 – 'Juliet'
94 – 'Karen'
92 – 'Kassel'
91 – 'Kilmersdon'
91 – 'Leona'
94 – 'Leuchtfeuer'
93 – 'Lilakönigin'
95 – 'Little Blue Baby'
91 – 'Lucille'
91 – 'Maid of Athens'
94 – 'Margaret Murray'
94 – 'Mars'
94 – 'Mary'
94 – 'May Louise'
94 – 'Melbourne'
94 – 'Melbourne Lad'
94 – 'Melbourne Mauve'
94 – 'Melbourne Sparkler'
94 – 'Michelle'
90 – 'Minster'
94 – 'Miranda'
94 – 'Miss Muffet'
94 – 'Mistress Ford'
91 – 'Mittelmeer'
90 – 'Moderato'
90 – 'Monkton Coombe'
94 – 'Mrs J. Sangster'
94 – 'My Smokey'
94 – 'Nancy'
92 – 'Nesthäkchen'
94 – 'Nightfall'
92 – 'Norma Chiswell'
94 – 'Norman Thornely'
94 – 'Orchid Pink'
91 – 'Owen Tudor'
91 – 'Owen Wells'
91 – 'Peaceful'
94 – 'Peerless'
91 – 'Penelope'
94 – 'Pensford'
94 – 'Perry's White'
92 – 'Petunia'
90 – 'Pink Bonnet'
96 – 'Pink Buttons'
91 – 'Pink Cascade'
93 – 'Pink Perfection'
93 – 'Pink Profusion'
91 – 'Pitcote'
90 – 'Powder Puff'
90 – 'Princess Marie Louise'
93 – 'Priory Maid'
94 – 'Purple Emperor'
89 – 'Queen of Sheba'
94 – 'Rachel Ballard'
94 – 'Raspberries and Cream'
91 – 'Real Pleasure'
93 – 'Rebecca'
94 – 'Red Greetings'
90 – 'Red King'
96 – 'Rembrandt'
94 – 'Robert'
94 – 'Rosie Nutt'
90 – 'Rosy Dreams'
94 – 'Royal Violet'
94 – 'Royalty'
90 – 'Ruby Glow'
94 – 'Sailing Light'
94 – 'Saturn'
93 – 'Silberblaukissen'
94 – 'Silver Mist'
94 – 'Sir Edward Elgar'
94 – 'Sputnik'
94 – 'Stella Lewis'
94 – 'Strawberries and Cream'
94 – 'Sussex Violet'
94 – 'Symbol'
91 – 'Taplow Spire'
91 – 'The Urchin'
94 – 'True Blue'
91 – 'Vice Regal'
90 – 'Walkden's Pink'
94 – 'Wickwar Crimson'
94 – 'Winford'
91 – 'Winsome Winnie'
93 ***oblongifolius***
94 ***perfoliatus***
94 ***procumbens***
94 ***sedifolius*** 'Roseus'
96 ***shortii***
89 ***trinervius*** subsp. ***ageratoides***
96 ***yunnanensis***

ASTERISCUS
93 ***intermedius***
96 ***spinosus***

ASTILBE
96 x ***arendsii*** 'Lilli Goos'
89 – 'Purple Splendour'
95 ***biternata***
90 x ***crispa rosea***
91 ***koreana***
94 ***microphylla*** var. ***saisuensis***
96 'Möwe' (*japonica* hybrid)
95 'Nana' (*simplicifolia* hybrid)
90 'Robinson's Pink'
96 ***simplicifolia*** 'Sheila Haxton'

ASTRAGALUS
95 ***amphioxys***
89 ***crassicarpus*** var. ***paysonii***
91 ***kentrophyta*** subsp. ***implexus***
96 ***penduliflorus***
96 ***purpureus***
92 ***purshii***
95 ***thompsoniae***
96 ***utahensis***
91 ***vexilliflexus nobilis***
95 ***whitneyi leucophyllus***
93 ***whitneyi sonneanus***

ASTRANTIA
94 ***carniolica***
94 ***major*** 'Prockter'

ASYNEUMA
96 ***limonifolium***
90 ***linifolium***
89 – subsp. ***eximium***
95 ***trichostegium***

ATHAMANTA
94 ***cretensis***
96 ***macedonica***
94 – subsp. ***arachnoidea***

ATHYRIUM
90 ***distentifolium***
93 ***filix-femina*** 'Clarissimum'
94 – Percristatum Group
95 ***frangulum***
94 ***palustre***
96 ***strigulosum***

ATRAPHAXIS
90 ***billardierei*** var. ***tournefortii***

AUBRIETA
96 'Alida Vahli'
92 'Aurea'
92 'Barker's Double'
96 'Bonfire'
87 'Bridesmaid'
91 'Bright Eyes'
94 'Britannia'
94 'Carnmenellis'
94 'Church Knowle'
93 'Claret Cascade'
88 'Crimson Bedder'
87 'Crimson Queen'
96 'Cumulus'
94 ***deltoidea*** (Variegata Group) 'Shaw's Red'
87 'Eileen Longster'
89 Eversley Hybrids
95 'Henslow Purple'
94 'Lucy'
93 ***mastichina***
94 'Pink Gem'
89 'Rose Cascade'
96 'Rosea Plena'
92 'Vindictive'
92 'Violet Queen'
94 Wisley hybrid

AUCUBA
89 ***japonica*** 'Dentata'
95 – 'Fructu Albo'
96 – 'Latiomaculata' (v)

AURINIA
96 ***petraea***
93 ***saxatilis*** 'Argentea'
91 – 'Nelly Reuben' (v)

AVENA
94 ***sterilis***

AZORELLA
95 Sydamerik form

BACCHARIS
94 ***crispa***
91 ***patagonica*** prostrate form

BAECKEA
92 ***virgata***

BALLOTA
89 ***frutescens***
94 ***nigra*** 'Dingle Gold'
94 – 'Dingle Gold Variegated'

BAMBUSA
91 ***multiplex*** var. ***riviereorum***

BANKSIA
94 ***baueri***
94 ***baxteri***
93 ***benthamiana***
94 ***blechnifolia***
93 ***canei***
94 ***dryandroides***
93 ***hookeriana***
92 ***occidentalis***
93 ***ornata***
93 ***petiolaris***
93 ***praemorsa***
93 ***repens***
94 ***saxicola***
91 ***serratifolia***
93 ***violacea***

BAPTISIA
95 ***alba***
93 ***sphaerocarpa***

BARBAREA
93 ***vulgaris***

BARTSIA
92 ***alpina***

BAUERA
90 ***rubioides***

BAUHINIA
94 x ***blakeana***
95 ***monandra***

BEGONIA
91 'Amoena' (T)
93 ***annulata***
91 'Bali Hi' (T)
96 'Bertinii' (T)
91 'Bertinii Compacta'
90 'Black Velvet'
90 'Bow-Mag'
90 ***burle-marxii***
90 'Camouflage'
93 x ***cheimantha*** 'Gloire de Lorraine'
90 'Chimbig'
91 'City of Ballarat' (T)
91 'Corona' (T)
91 'Dorothy White' (T)
91 'Elaine Tarttelin' (T)
91 'Falstaff' (T)
96 ***fimbriata***
91 'First Love' (T)
96 'Gloire de Lorraine'
94 ***grandis***
93 – dark form
91 'Guardsman' (T)
92 x ***hiemalis*** 'Aida'
92 – 'Aphrodite Pink'
92 – 'Arosa'
92 – 'Barbara'
92 – 'Christel'
92 – 'Elatior'
92 – 'Elfe'
92 – 'Heidi'
92 – 'Ilona'

92 – 'Korona'
92 – 'Lara'
92 – 'Lorina'
92 – 'Mandela'
92 – 'Mark Rosa'
92 – 'Nelly'
92 – 'Nelson'
92 – 'Nixe'
92 – 'Nymphe'
92 – 'Pia Elise'
92 – 'Radiant'
92 – 'Rosalea'
92 – 'Schwabenland'
92 – 'Schwabenland Mini'
92 – 'Schwabenland Red'
92 – 'Schwabenland Rose'
92 – 'Schwabenland White'
92 – 'Schwabenland Yellow'
92 – 'Sirène'
92 – 'Sylvia'
92 – 'Tora'
91 'Joy Towers' (T)
90 'Mac MacIntyre'
95 ***maculata*** ♀
93 'Madame Richard Gallé' (T)
91 'Mrs T. White' (T)
91 'Peach Melba' (T)
90 ***plagioneura***
94 'Purpurea' (R)
91 'Rose Princess' (T)
95 'Sandersonii'
90 'Silbreen'
91 'Snow Bird' (T)
91 'Sunburst' (T)
90 Superba Group (C)
92 'Tigerlash'
91 'Zoe Colledge' (T)

BELLEVALIA
96 ***forniculata*** JCA 227.770

BELLIS
95 ***perennis*** 'Aucubifolia' (v)
92 – 'Bunter Teppich'
92 – 'Chevreuse'
92 – 'Double Bells'
92 – 'Lilliput Rose'
92 – 'Pink Buttons'
89 – 'Red Alice'
92 – 'Roggli'
92 – 'Shrewley Gold' (v)
92 – 'String of Pearls'
92 – 'Tuberosa Monstrosa'
95 – 'White Pearl'
89 ***sylvestris***

BERBERIS
91 ***amurensis latifolia***
95 'Blenheim'
91 ***brachypoda***
91 ***brevipaniculata*** Schneider
92 x ***carminea*** 'Bountiful'
92 ***dictyophylla*** var. ***approximata***
89 ***dumicola***
89 ***francisci-ferdinandii***
92 x ***frikartii*** 'Mrs Kennedy'
94 ***gracilis***
92 'Haalboom'
92 ***hakeoides***
94 ***hookeri***
89 – var. ***viridis***
96 x ***hybridogagnepainii*** 'Robin Hood'
90 ***ilicifolia***
92 x ***interposita***
91 ***koreana*** 'Harvest Fire'
92 ***linearifolia*** 'Jewel'
92 x ***mentorensis***
92 ***montana***
89 ***orthobotrys*** var. ***canescens***
94 x ***ottawensis*** 'Lombart's Purple'
87 ***poiretii***
93 ***sargentiana*** 'Nana'
95 x ***stenophylla*** 'Corallina'
89 – 'Pendula'
92 – 'Prostrata'
87 – 'Semperflorens'
92 ***thunbergii*** 'Coronita'
87 – 'Dart's Red Devil'
93 – 'Green Ring'
90 – 'Pearly Queen'
96 – 'Vermilion'
89 ***valdiviana*** x ***darwinii***
92 ***wilsoniae*** var. ***stapfiana***
93 – var. ***subcaulialata***
92 ***yunnanensis***

BERGENIA
95 ***afghanica***
95 'Borodin'
95 'Croesus'
95 'Distinction'
96 'Eroica'
87 'Perfect'
95 x ***spathulata***
96 ***stracheyi*** red
95 'Summer Mountain'
87 'White Dwarf'

BESSEYA
93 ***ritteriana***
95 ***wyomingensis***

BETA
96 ***vulgaris*** 'Bull's Blood'

BETULA
94 ***aetnensis***
95 ***austrosinensis***
94 ***borealis***
93 ***calcicola***
95 ***delavayi***
90 ***fontinalis*** 'Inopina'
89 ***nana*** 'Walter Ingwersen'
94 ***neoalaskana***
93 ***ovalifolia***
95 ***papyrifera*** var. ***minor***
95 ***pendula arvii***
96 ***pendula*** var. ***pendula*** 'Dissecta'
95 ***schmidtii***
95 sp. CLD 407
94 ***szechuanica*** W 983
94 ***utilis*** 'Buckland'
94 – SS&W 4382
94 – 'Trinity College'

BIARUM
95 ***carratracense***
95 ***dispar***
95 ***ochridense***
95 ***tenuifolium*** var. ***abbreviatum***
95 – var. ***zeleborii***

BIDENS
96 ***ferulifolia*** 'Golden Goddess'
96 ***triplinervia*** var. ***macrantha***

BILLARDIERA
94 ***longiflora*** 'Rosea'

BILLBERGIA
94 x ***albertii***
90 ***bucholtzii***
90 ***chlorosticta***
90 ***distachya***
90 ***leptopoda***
90 'Santa Barbara' (v)

BLACKSTONIA
93 ***perfoliata***

BLANDFORDIA
96 ***punicea***

BLECHNUM
96 ***auriculatum***
96 ***fluviatile***

BLOOMERIA
96 ***crocea***
96 – var. ***aurea*** JCA 13091

BOEHMERIA
93 ***nivea***

BOISDUVALIA
94 ***densiflora***

BOMAREA
95 ***multiflora***
96 ***sasilla***
93 ***volubilis***

BOSCIA
95 ***albitrunca***

BOTHRIOCHLOA
93 ***saccharoides***

BOUGAINVILLEA
96 'Albo d'Ora'
92 'Alison Davey'
95 'Indha' (*glabra* hybrid)
92 'Jawhuri'
92 Manila Red
91 'Maureen Hatten'
91 'Roy Walker'
95 'Royal Bengal Red' (v)
95 'Sea Foam'
91 ***spectabilis*** 'Lateritia'
95 – 'Royal Bengal Orange' (v)
91 – 'Speciosa Floribunda'
92 'Sunfire Jennifer'
96 'White Empress'

BOUVARDIA
93 ***bouvardioides***
96 x ***domestica***
91 'Jourhite'
91 'Lichtrose'
91 'Roxane'
95 ***scabrida***
95 ***ternifolia***
91 'Torosa'
91 'Zywerden'

BOYKINIA
96 ***major***

BRACHYGLOTTIS
94 ***hectorii***
90 ***kirkii*** 'Variegata'
94 'New Zealand'
95 ***repanda*** 'Purpurea'

BRACHYSCOME
90 ***diversifolia***
95 'Lemon Drops'
91 ***stolonifera***

BRACTEANTHA
95 ***bracteata*** 'Golden Beauty'
93 ***subundulata***

BRAYA
96 ***alpina***

BREYNIA
92 ***nivosa***
94 – 'Rosea Picta'

BRIZA
96 ***minor***
87 ***subaristata***

BROCCHINIA
93 ***reducta***

BROMUS
95 ***commutatus***
94 ***lanceolatus***

BRUGMANSIA
96 ***aurea***
93 x ***candida*** 'Variegata'
96 'La Fleur Lilas'
96 ***suaveolens*** yellow

BRUNSVIGIA
96 ***herrei***
96 ***natalensis***
95 ***orientalis*** 'Alba'

BRYANTHUS
96 ***gmelinii***

BRYUM
96 ***truncorum***

BUDDLEJA
96 ***abbreviata***
94 ***bhutanica***
88 ***caryopteridifolia*** 'Variegata'
92 ***crispa*** 'Variegata'
91 ***davidii*** 'Bluegown'
96 – 'Calanadrina'
96 – 'Charming'
94 – 'Dubonnet'
87 – 'Opéra'
94 – 'Operetta'
89 – 'Pink Pearl'
94 – 'Royal Red Variegated'
92 – 'Salicifolia'
87 – 'Southcombe Splendour'
95 – 'Variegata'
87 – 'Widecombe'
87 – 'Windtor'
88 ***latiflora***
96 ***lewisiana*** x ***asiatica***
89 'Town Foot'
95 'West Hill'
87 x ***weyeriana*** 'Golden Tassels'
93 'White Butterfly'

BULBINE
96 ***alooides*** S&SH 74
95 ***annua***

BULBINELLA
93 ***caudata***
92 ***setosa***

BUPLEURUM
96 ***longifolium roseum***
89 ***triradiatum***

BUTIA
94 ***yatay***

BUXUS
95 ***microphylla*** 'Green China'
93 ***natalensis***
91 ***sempervirens*** 'Bullata'
89 – 'Elegans'
93 – 'Lawson's Golden'
96 – 'Tropical Garden'

CACALIA
96 ***glabra***

CAESALPINIA
92 ***decapetala*** var. ***japonica***
93 ***sappan***

CAIOPHORA
96 ***horrida***
96 ***lateritia***

CALADIUM
94 ***bicolor*** forms
90 – 'John Peel'
90 – 'June Bride'
90 – 'Mrs Arno Nehrling'
90 – 'Pink Beauty'
90 – 'Postman Joyner'
90 – 'Rosebud'
90 'Candidum'

CALAMAGROSTIS
94 × ***acutiflora*** 'Stricta'

CALANDRINIA
95 ***caespitosa*** P&W 6229
95 ***ciliata*** var. ***menziesii***
94 ***colchaguensis*** F&W 7210
94 ***compressa***
96 ***dianthoides***
92 ***discolor***
95 ***feltonii***
96 'Neon'
95 ***rupestris***
95 ***skottsbergii***
95 sp. JCA 12317

CALANTHE
95 ***alismifolia***
95 ***argenteostriata***
95 ***cardioglossa***
95 ***kintaroi***
95 ***okinawensis***
95 ***triplicata***

CALATHEA
94 ***bachemiana***
96 ***bella***
96 ***burle-marxii***
90 ***elliptica*** 'Vittata'
90 ***eximia***
90 ***fasciata***
90 ***lancifolia*** ♈
90 ***leopardina***
90 ***louisae***
90 ***majestica*** 'Sanderiana'
90 ***micans***
90 ***musaica***
93 ***pendula***
90 ***rufibarba***

CALCEOLARIA
96 ***alba*** RB 94025
93 'Brownii'
89 ***corymbosa***
95 ***integrifolia*** 'Gaines' Yellow'
95 – 'Sunshine' ♈
95 ***lanigera*** RB 94026
94 ***montana*** F&W 7225
95 ***picta***
94 'Sir Daniel Hall'

CALLIANDRA
91 ***eriophylla***
94 ***houstoniana***
94 ***selloi***

CALLIANTHEMUM
89 ***angustifolium***
91 ***kernerianum***

CALLICARPA
90 ***mollis***
95 × ***shirasawana***

CALLIERGON
96 ***giganteum***

CALLISTEMON
90 ***citrinus*** purple
89 ***montanus***
90 ***pallidus*** lilac
92 ***shiressii***

CALLUNA
88 ***vulgaris*** f. ***alba***
96 – 'Ashgarth Shell Pink'
92 – 'Baby Wicklow'
88 – 'Beoley Crimson Variegated'
95 – 'Bronze Hamilton'
96 – 'Cape Wrath'
95 – 'Catherine'
96 – 'Corrie's White'
94 – 'Elizabeth'
88 – 'Gnome'
89 – 'Goldsworth Purple'
88 – 'Gynodioica'
96 – 'Jochen'
95 – 'Kees Gouda'
96 – 'Mick Jamieson' (d)
88 – 'Monstrosa'
89 – 'Orange Beauty'
88 – 'Procumbens'
95 – 'Red Hugh'
96 – 'Rote Oktober'
88 – 'Spicata Nana'
96 – 'Summer Gold'
88 – 'Tomentosa'
96 – 'Wollmers Weisse' (d)

CALOCEDRUS
95 ***formosana***

CALOCHORTUS
96 ***albus*** J&JA 13053
96 ***ambiguus***
96 ***apiculatus***
93 ***catalinae***
96 ***exilis***
96 ***venustus*** Cuddy Valley reds
96 – J&JA 13288
92 ***weedii***

CALOPOGON
96 ***tuberosus***

CALTHA
95 ***polypetala*** Hochst.

CALYCANTHUS
92 ***floridus*** var. ***glaucus***

CALYDOREA
96 ***xiphioides***

CALYSTEGIA
93 ***hederacea***

CALYTRIX
93 ***alpestris***
89 ***glutinosa***
91 ***tetragona***

CAMASSIA
92 ***cusickii*** 'Zwanenburg'
92 – subsp. ***suksdorfii*** Atroviolacea Group

CAMELLIA
96 'Arbutus Gum' (*reticulata* × *japonica*)
96 'Autumnal White'
95 'Bellbird'
94 'Bernadette Karsten' (*reticulata* × *japonica*)
96 ***caudata***
96 'Chandleri'
88 'Cornish Cream' (*saluenensis* × *cuspidata*)
95 'Cornish Pink'
96 'Debut' (*reticulata* × *japonica*)
95 'Doctor Louis Polizzi' (*saluenensis* × *reticulata*)
87 'Dorothy James' (hybrid)
89 'Dream Castle' (*reticulata* × *japonica*)
96 'Dream Girl' (*sasanqua* × *reticulata*)
96 'Elizabeth Bolitho'
94 'Elsie Dryden' (*reticulata* × *japonica*)
95 'Emmy'
94 ***euphlebia***
95 'Fascination'
96 'Flower Girl' (*sasanqua* × *reticulata*)
94 ***forrestii***
96 ***fraterna***
96 'Grace Caple' (*pitardii* × *japonica*)
94 'Harold L. Paige' (*japonica* × *reticulata*)
95 ***hiemalis*** 'Pink Snow'
94 'Interval' (*reticulata* hybrid)
94 ***japonica***
89 – 'Alba Superba'
96 – 'Alex Blackadder'
89 – 'Alta Gavin'
93 – 'Angela Cocchi'
89 – 'Anna Bruneau'
89 – 'Anna M. Page'
89 – 'Anne Smith'
92 – 'Apollo 14'
91 – 'Auguste Delfosse'
90 – 'Australis'
93 – 'Azumakagami'
91 – 'Baronne Leguay'
96 – 'Beau Harp'
96 – 'Belle of the Ball'
95 – 'Benten-kagura'
96 – 'Betty Sheffield Pink'
89 – 'Billie McCaskill'
94 – 'Billie McFarland'
90 – 'Bride's Bouquet'
95 – 'Bright Buoy'
96 – 'Bryan Wright'
96 – 'Burgundy Gem'
96 – 'Caleb Cope'
87 – 'Candy Stripe'
89 – 'Captain Folk'
87 – 'Cardinal Variegated'
89 – 'Centenary'
89 – 'Charlotte Bradford'
93 – 'Christmas Beauty'
96 – 'Clarissa'
89 – 'Clarke Hubbs'
94 – 'Cleopatra'
89 – 'Coccinea'
93 – 'Contessa Samailoff'
87 – 'Coral Pink Lotus'
87 – 'Coral Queen'
95 – 'Coronation'
96 – 'Daphne du Maurier'
93 – 'Daviesii'
92 – 'De Notaris'
94 – 'Deep Secret'
92 – 'Diddy Mealing'
96 – 'Dona Jane Andresson'
93 – 'Doris Ellis'
89 – 'Drama Girl Variegated'
94 – 'Edelweiss'
91 – 'Edith Linton'
87 – 'Elena Nobili'
93 – 'Elizabeth Le Bey'
93 – 'Ellen Sampson'
89 – 'Emmett Barnes'
95 – Emmett Pfingstl™ (v)
91 – 'Etherington White'
91 – 'Etoile Polaire'
96 – 'Eugène Lizé'
93 – 'Evalina'
87 – 'Evelyn'
93 – 'Eximia'
91 – 'Ezo-nishiki'
89 – 'Fanny Bolis'
93 – 'Fimbriata'
95 – 'Firebird'
95 – 'Flora'
90 – 'Fortune Teller'
95 – 'Fran Homeyer'
94 – 'Frances Council'
96 – 'Funny Face Betty'
96 – 'Furo-an'
93 – 'Gay Chieftain'
89 – 'Gay Marmee'
96 – 'Geisha Girl'
92 – 'Général Leclerc'
94 – 'George Orman'
89 – 'Goshoguruma'
87 – 'Grand Prix Variegated'
89 – 'Grand Sultan'
87 – 'Gus Menard'
89 – 'Hassaku-shibori'
87 – 'Helen Bower'
94 – 'Henry Turnbull'
89 – 'High, Wide 'n' Handsome'
89 – 'Hishikaraito'
93 – 'Ice Queen'
93 – 'Ichisetsu'
92 – 'Iwane-shibori'
94 – 'James Allan'
89 – 'Jennifer Turnbull'
89 – 'Judge Solomon'
87 – 'Julia Drayton'
96 – 'Just Darling'
93 – 'Kate Thrash'
87 – 'Katherine Nuccio'
92 – 'King Size'

91 – 'Koyoden'
96 – 'Kumasaka'
89 – 'La Belle France'
92 – 'La Pace'
89 – 'Lady Kay'
93 – 'Lady Mackinnon'
93 – 'Lady McCulloch Pink'
92 – 'Latifolia Variegated'
95 – 'Laura Walker'
92 – 'Leonora Novick'
89 – 'Lillian Rickets'
89 – 'Louise Wilson'
87 – 'Mabel Blackwell'
95 – 'Magic Moments'
91 – 'Marchioness of Exeter'
87 – 'Margaret Rose'
96 – 'Margaret Short'
87 – 'Marian Mitchell'
96 – 'Martha Brice'
88 – 'Mary Agnes Patin'
93 – 'Mary Charlotte'
87 – 'Masterpiece'
95 – 'Melinda Hackett'
95 – 'Mikado'
94 – 'Minnie Maddern Fiske'
89 – 'Miss Anaheim'
89 – 'Miss Betty'
95 – 'Miss Frankie'
93 – 'Miya'
91 – 'Moonlight'
96 – 'Moonlight Sonata'
95 – 'Morning Glow'
93 – 'Moshio'
89 – 'Mrs Baldwin Wood'
89 – 'Mrs George Bell'
89 – 'Mrs Swan'
87 – 'Mrs Tingley'
91 – 'Mrs William Thompson'
95 – 'Nanbankô'
89 – 'Nancy Bird'
94 – 'Olive Honnor'
95 – 'Otome'
95 – 'Owen Henry'
95 – 'Paul Jones Supreme'
89 – 'Paulette Goddard'
91 – 'Pearl Harbor'
93 – 'Pearl Maxwell'
91 – 'Pink Ball'
93 – 'Pink Diddy'
96 – 'Platipetala'
90 – 'Premier'
95 – 'Press's Eclipse'
95 – 'Prince Eugène Napoléon'
88 – 'Prince Murat'
93 – 'Prince of Orange'
89 – 'Princess Lear'
95 – 'Priscilla Brooks'
89 – 'Purple Swirl'
90 – 'Queen's Escort'
93 – 'Rebel Yell'
95 – 'Red Cardinal'
89 – 'Red Elephant'
95 – 'Red Rogue'
89 – 'Richard Nixon'
90 – 'Richfield'
95 – 'Rosa Perfecta'
89 – 'Rosemary Elsom'
90 – 'Rosina Sobeck'
91 – 'Sacco Vera'
96 – 'Sarah Frost'
87 – 'Sawada's Dream'
96 – 'Sea Foam'
95 – 'Senator Duncan U. Fletcher'
89 – 'Sheridan'
93 – 'Shiragiku'
89 – 'Shiro Chan'
89 – 'Simeon'
88 – 'Snow Chan'
95 – 'Speciosissima'
87 – 'Spring Fever'
91 – 'Suibijin'
94 – 'Sundae'
95 – 'Sunset Glory'
92 – 'Sunset Oaks'
96 – 'Sweet Delight'
95 – 'Tama-ikari'
95 – 'Tarô'an'
93 – 'Tick Tock'
89 – 'Touchdown'
95 – 'Virginia Robinson'
89 – 'Waverley'
90 – 'White Giant'
89 – 'Wildwood'
91 – 'William Bull'
95 – 'Winter Cheer'
89 'Lois Shinault' (*reticulata* X *granthamiana*)
94 ***lutchuensis***
94 'Mandalay Queen' (*reticulata* hybrid) 🏆
96 'Marjorie Miller'
94 X 'Maud Messel' (X *williamsii* X *reticulata*)
94 'Otto Hopfer' (*reticulata* X *japonica*)
89 'Phyl Doak' (*saluenensis* X *reticulata*)
89 'Pink Sparkle' (*reticulata* X *japonica*)
94 ***pitardii*** X ***cuspidata***
90 'Quercifolia'
96 ***reticulata*** 'Arch of Triumph' 🏆
96 – 'Brilliant Butterfly'
94 – 'Eden Roc'
89 – 'Hody Wilson'
94 – 'K.O. Hester'
89 – 'Lisa Gael'
90 – 'Mary Williams'
89 – 'Mildred Pitkin'
94 – 'Miss Tulare'
94 – 'Overture'
94 – 'Samantha'
94 – 'Songzilin'
93 – 'Tongzimian'
89 – 'Wild Silk'
95 ***rosiflora*** 'Cascade'
96 ***sasanqua*** 'Apple Blossom'
95 – 'Azuma-beni'
96 – 'Bert Jones'
96 – 'Fragrans'
96 – 'Momozono-nishiki'
94 – 'Navajo'
91 – 'Shin-azuma-nishiki'
94 – 'Shinonome'
95 – 'Yae-arare'
94 'Shiro-wabisuke' (Wabisuke)
94 'Shôwa-wabisuke' (Wabisuke)
89 'Terrell Weaver' (*reticulata* X *japonica*)
95 'Tiny Princess' (*japonica* X *fraterna*)
94 'Valentine Day' (*reticulata* X *japonica*)
90 X ***vernalis***
93 – 'Ginryû'
94 X ***williamsii*** 'Blue Danube'
87 – 'Charlean Variegated'
95 – 'Coral Delight'
96 – 'Dresden China'
94 – 'Elizabeth de Rothschild'
95 – 'Free Style'
95 – 'Jury's Sunglow'
92 – 'Lady Gowrie'
95 – 'Lady's Maid'
95 – 'Little Lavender'
94 – 'Perfecta'
91 – 'Pink Cherub'
95 – 'Red Dahlia'
96 – 'Rose Holland'
95 – 'Rose Quartz'
93 – 'Rosie Anderson'
95 – 'Shimna'
95 – 'Twinkle Star'
87 – 'Waltz Time'
94 ***yuhsienensis***

CAMPANULA

87 'Abundance'
90 ***alliariifolia*** X ***makaschvilii***
96 ***alpestris*** 'Rosea'
96 ***alpina*** var. ***bucegiensis***
95 ***andrewsii*** subsp. ***andrewsii*** NS 705
96 – subsp. ***hirsutula***
95 – – NS 724
91 ***argaea***
96 ***arvatica*** X ***cochleariifolia***
90 ***barbata*** deep blue
89 ***carpatica*** 'Albescens'
94 – 'Bees' Variety'
89 – 'Jingle Bells'
87 – 'Loddon Bell'
96 – 'Queen of Sheba'
87 – var. ***turbinata*** 'Grandiflora'
96 ***celsii*** subsp. ***carystea***
95 ***cochleariifolia*** 'Annie Hall'
93 – X ***arvatica***
87 – 'Patience Bell'
96 ***colorata***
94 ***coriacea***
93 ***crispa***
89 ***davisii***
89 ***glomerata*** 'Wisley Supreme'
96 ***grossheimii***
96 ***hakkiarica***
92 ***hypopolia***
87 'Iceberg'
96 ***isophylla*** X ***fragilis***
95 – 'Pamela'
88 ***lactiflora*** 'Superba' 🏆
94 ***latifolia*** 'Arthur Wood'
91 – 'Lavender'
93 ***lusitanica***
96 ***modesta***
92 ***morettiana***
92 – 'Alba'
96 ***pelviformis***
94 ***persicifolia*** Ashfield double ice blue
96 – 'China Blue'
90 – 'Curiosa'
96 – 'Grandiflora'
95 ***portenschlagiana*** 'Bavarica'
90 ***pyramidalis*** 'Aureovariegata'
95 ***radchensis***
96 ***rotundifolia*** 'Flore Pleno'
95 ***rupestris*** NS 401
95 ***rupicola*** NS 798
96 sp. ex Furze
95 ***sporadum*** K 92.162
92 ***stevenii***
94 ***topaliana*** subsp. ***cordifolia*** NS 409
95 – subsp. ***delphica*** NS 829
87 'Warley Gem'
93 ***witasekiana***

CAMPHOROSMA

94 ***monspeliaca***

CAMPSIS

95 X ***tagliabuana*** 'Guilfoylei'

CAMPYLOTROPIS

88 ***macrocarpa***

CANNA

96 'China Lady'
93 'City of Portland'
96 ***flaccida***
96 ***indica*** X ***generalis***
95 ***indica variegata***
96 'La Bohème'

CAPPARIS

92 ***spinosa***

CARAGANA

91 ***pygmaea***

CARDAMINE

95 ***pratensis*** 'Improperly Dressed'

CARDIOSPERMUM

96 ***halicacabum***

CARDUNCELLUS

91 ***mitissimus***
96 ***rhaponticoides***

CARDUUS

96 ***nutans***

CAREX

93 ***berggrenii*** narrow-leaved
90 ***buxbaumii***
96 ***cyperus***
96 ***flaccosperma***
91 ***fraseri***
93 ***pendula*** 'Variegata'
93 ***saxatilis*** 'Variegata'
92 ***solandri***
93 sp. from Chile
96 ***spicata***

CARICA

94 ***chrysopetala***
93 ***pubescens***

CARLINA

94 ***vulgaris*** 'Silver Star'

CARPENTERIA

94 ***californica*** 'Bodnant'

CARPINUS

95 ***betulus*** 'Quercifolia'
95 – 'Variegata'

88 ***caroliniana*** var. ***virginiana***
96 ***tschonoskii***

CARYA
96 ***aquatica***
96 ***laciniosa***
96 ***pallida***
96 ***texana***

CASSINIA
96 ***leptophylla*** subsp. ***vauvilliersii*** CC 570
89 ***quinquefaria***
91 ***sturtii***

CASSIOPE
95 ***fastigiata***
91 ***hypnoides***
96 'Inverleith'
96 ***lycopodioides*** var. ***crista-pilosa***
96 – var. ***globularis***
93 – 'Major'
96 ***lycopodioides minima***
96 ***mertensiana*** var. ***californica***
92 – var. ***ciliolata***
96 ***selaginoides***
96 – McB 1124

CASUARINA
95 ***glauca***
95 ***muelleriana***
93 ***torulosa***

CATALPA
94 ***fargesii*** f. ***duclouxii***

CAYRATIA
92 ***thomsonii***

CEANOTHUS
90 ***burfordiensis***
96 ***coeruleus***
96 ***depressus***
96 ***fendleri***
91 ***griseus***
96 – var. ***horizontalis***
89 x ***pallidus*** 'Plenus'
96 ***papillosus*** x ***thyrsiflorus***
96 x ***regius***

CEDRUS
95 ***deodara*** 'Deep Cove'
91 – 'Golden Jubilee'
92 – 'Inversa Pendula'
94 – 'Nana Aurea'
90 – Paktia Group
90 – 'Polar Winter'
92 – 'Prostrata'
96 – 'Robusta'
91 ***libani*** subsp. ***brevifolia*** 'Horizon'
96 – subsp. ***libani*** 'De Creffe'

CELASTRUS
92 ***hypoleucus***
96 ***loeseneri*** (f)
96 – (m)
96 ***scandens*** (f)
96 – (m)
96 sp. KR 1269

CELMISIA
90 ***armstrongii***
96 ***ceracophyllus***
96 ***haastii***
96 ***lyallii***
90 ***spectabilis argentea***
96 ***spectabilis major***

CELTIS
96 ***biondii***
96 ***bungeana***
96 ***glabrata***
96 ***jessoensis***
96 ***reticulata***
96 ***tetrandra***

CENTAUREA
91 ***babylonica***
91 ***chilensis***
94 ***chrysantha***
89 ***cineraria*** 'Colchester White'
95 ***jacea***
95 ***montana purpurea***
95 ***nigra*** 'Breakaway' (v)
87 ***triumfettii*** subsp. ***stricta alba***
95 ***uniflora*** subsp. ***nervosa*** JCA 287.000

CENTRADENIA
94 ***inaequilateralis***
93 – 'Mini Cascade'

CEPHALOTAXUS
96 ***fortunei*** 'Prostrate Spreader'
93 ***harringtonia*** 'Gnome'
96 – 'Nana'

CERASTIUM
88 ***biebersteinii***

CERATOSTIGMA
96 ***minus*** SF 95001

CERATOTHECA
93 ***triloba alba***

CERCIS
87 ***chingii***
94 ***griffithii***
94 ***racemosa***
93 ***siliquastrum*** 'Bodnant'
89 – 'Rubra'

CERCOCARPUS
95 ***montanus***
93 – var. ***paucidentatus***

CEROPEGIA
94 ***armandii***
95 ***sandersoniae***

CESTRUM
96 ***diurnum***

CHAENACTIS
89 ***alpina***

CHAENOMELES
91 ***speciosa*** 'Atrococcinea Plena'
92 – 'Brilliant'
96 – 'Phylis Moore'
90 x ***superba*** 'Alba'
92 – 'Ernst Finken'
95 – 'Red Trail'
91 – 'Vesuvius'

CHAENORHINUM
94 'Blue Pygmy'
95 ***origanifolium*** 'Blue Sceptre'

CHAETACANTHUS
93 ***setiger*** 'White Lady'

CHAMAEBATIARIA
96 ***millefolium***

CHAMAECRISTA
96 ***nictitans***

CHAMAECYPARIS
94 ***lawsoniana*** 'Allumii Green'
89 – 'Annesleyana'
91 – 'Barry's Bright'
89 – 'Booth'
87 – 'Boy Blue'
89 – 'Darleyensis'
95 – 'Dow's Gem'
95 – 'Drinkstone Gold'
94 – 'Elfin'
90 – 'Ellwoodii Glauca'
88 – 'Ellwood's Prize'
95 – 'Erecta Argenteovariegata'
90 – 'Gold Lace'
92 – 'Gold Pyramid'
94 – 'Goldgren'
91 – 'Grayswood Bronze'
88 – 'Green Monarch'
88 – 'Holden Gold'
90 – 'Juvenalis Stricta'
95 – 'Kilbogget Gold'
90 – 'Lemon Pillar'
92 – 'Merrist Wood'
90 – 'Moerheimii'
95 – 'Naberi'
96 – 'Nivea'
96 – 'Parsons'
94 – 'Pendula Vera'
93 – 'Rock Gold'
90 – 'Shawii'
95 – 'Snowgold'
88 – 'Suffolk Belle'
96 – 'Summerford Spire'
87 – 'Tilgate'
87 – 'Trentham Gold'
89 – 'Van Eck'
88 – 'Watereri'
92 ***nootkatensis*** 'Aurea'
89 – 'Tatra'
91 ***obtusa*** 'Bronze Elegance'
94 – 'Filicoides'
89 – 'Goldspire'
90 – 'Heinrich'
96 – 'Verdon'
95 ***pisifera*** 'Filifera Gracilis'
88 – 'Floral Arts'
92 – 'Teddy Bear'
92 – 'Tsukumo'
96 ***thyoides***
95 – 'Heatherbun'
88 – 'Marwood'

CHAMAEDOREA
90 ***elegans*** 'Bella'
94 ***microspadix***

CHASMANTHIUM
90 ***latifolium*** 'Variegatum'

CHEILANTHES
96 ***alabamensis***
94 ***argentea***
96 ***bonariensis***
90 ***distans***
94 ***farinosa***
92 ***guanchica***
96 ***hirta*** var. ***ellisiana***
96 ***kaulfussii***
96 ***lendigera***
94 ***myriophylla***
96 ***pulchella***

CHENOPODIUM
89 ***bonus-henricus*** 'Variegatum'
92 ***foliosum***

CHEVREULIA
90 ***lycopodioides***

CHIMONANTHUS
91 – 'Mangetsu'
94 ***zhejiangensis***

CHIONOCHLOA
93 ***beddiei***
96 ***flavicans***

CHIONODOXA
91 ***albescens***
92 ***forbesii*** 'Tmoli'

CHIONOHEBE
91 ***ciliolata***
95 x ***petrimea*** 'Margaret Pringle'

CHOISYA
96 ***mollis***

CHORISIA
91 ***speciosa***

CHRYSOLEPIS
92 ***chrysophylla***

CHRYSOTHAMNUS
90 ***nauseosus***

CHUNIOPHOENIX
95 ***hainanensis***

CHUQUIRAGA
95 ***straminea***

CIBOTIUM
96 ***barometz***
96 ***glaucum***
96 ***schiedei***

CICHORIUM
96 'Rosso di Verona'

CICUTA
89 ***virosa***

CIMICIFUGA
93 ***heracleifolia***
93 ***japonica compacta***

CIRSIUM
95 ***candelebrum***
94 ***eriophorum*** subsp. ***britannicum***
95 ***falconeri***
94 ***forrestii*** CLD 1000
95 ***japonicum***
95 – 'Snow Beauty'
96 – 'Strawberry Ripple'
96 – 'White Beauty'
95 – 'White Victory'
95 ***mexicanum***
95 ***spinosissimum***

CISTUS
94 'Chelsea Pink'
94 x ***dansereaui*** unblotched
90 'Elma Colicte'
90 x ***glaucus***
90 ***heterophyllus***
93 x ***laxus***
92 ***ochreatus***
94 ***populifolius*** subsp. ***major***
91 ***salviifolius*** 'Sienna'

96 'Snowflake'
90 ***varius***

CITHAREXYLUM

95 ***ilicifolium***

× CITROFORTUNELLA

90 ***floridana***

× CITRONCIRUS

89 ***webberi***
93 'Zehnder' (*paradisi* hybrid)

CITRUS

96 × ***reticulata*** Mandarin Group (F)
94 – 'Variegata'
94 ***sinensis*** 'Arnci Alberetto' (F)
96 × ***tangelo*** 'Mapo' (F)

CLADRASTIS

92 ***sinensis***

CLARKIA

93 ***amoena***
96 ***breweri***

CLAYTONIA

92 ***megarhiza***

CLEMATIS

96 'Acton Pride'
95 'Ajisai' (LxJ)
96 ***akebioides*** CLD 0601/12
96 ***alpina*** 'Alba Belsay'
96 – 'Blush Queen'
95 – 'Inshriach'
96 – 'Linava'
95 – 'Maria'
96 – 'Ria'
96 – 'Wisley Purple'
96 ***apiifolia*** var. ***biternata*** GR 0008
92 ***armandii*** Trengwainton form
95 ***atrata***
89 'Blue Diamond'
95 'Boskoop Glory'
95 ***brevicaudata***
95 ***buchananiana*** De Candolle
96 ***campaniflora*** × ***viticella***
96 × ***cartmanii*** 'Joe' × 'Sharon' (Fo)
96 'Cherry Brandy'
96 ***chrysocoma*** ACE 1093
96 – B&L 12324
96 ***cirrhosa*** 'Ourika Valley'
96 'Darlene'
95 ***delavayi*** var. ***spinescens*** KGB 283
95 ***denticulata*** P&W 6287
96 'Dilly Dilly'
96 'Doctor Label'
96 'Donna'
95 ***drummondii***
96 'East Sunset'
90 'Elizabeth Foster'
96 'Farrago'
96 ***fremontii***
90 ***grata*** var. ***argentilucida*** Wallich
95 – CC&McK 185
95 'Green Parrot'
96 'Hainton Ruby' (P)
96 'Halina Nell' (Fl)
96 'Harlequin'
96 'Heirloom'
95 ***heracleifolia*** B&SWJ 812
96 – CC 612
95 'Hint of Pink'
95 ***hirsuta***
96 'Iola Fair' (P)
95 'Joan Baker' (Vt)
96 'Kyllus' (L)
89 ***lanuginosa***
96 ***macropetala*** 'Pearl Rose' (A/d)
96 – 'Rödklokke' (A/d)
95 'Marinka'
92 'Mercurius' (J)
96 'Morning Glory'
95 ***occidentalis*** subsp. ***grosseserrata***
96 'Paala'
89 ***parviflora*** var. ***depauperata***
96 'Pat Ann'
93 'Patricia Ann Fretwell'
90 'Perryhill Pearl'
96 ***petriei*** × ***cartmanii*** 'Joe' (Fo)
88 'Prairie River' (A)
95 'Princess'
91 'Pruinina' (A)
96 'Radiant'
95 ***reticulata***
96 ***songarica*** 'Sundance'
96 sp. B&L 12329
96 sp. B&SWJ 1423
96 sp. B&SWJ 1668
96 sp. B&SWJ 292
96 sp. B&SWJ 599
96 sp. CC&McK 1011
96 sp. CC&McK 1099
96 ***tangutica*** 'Warsaw'
96 'Zato'

CLEMATOPSIS

96 ***scabiosifolia***

CLEOME

93 ***spinosa*** Jacquin

CLERODENDRUM

91 ***cyrtophyllum***
94 ***spectabile***
94 – 'Variegatum'

CLETHRA

95 ***alnifolia*** 'Fingle Dwarf'
90 – 'Nana'
93 ***tomentosa***

CLEYERA

96 ***japonica*** 'Tricolor' (v)

CLITORIA

96 ***mariana***
96 ***ternatea***
96 – 'Blue Sails'

CLUSIA

89 ***major***

COCOS

96 ***nucifera*** 'Dwarf Golden Malay'

CODIAEUM

90 ***variegatum*** var. ***pictum*** (v)
90 – – 'Excellent' (v)
90 – – 'Gold Star' (v)
93 – – 'Nervia' (v)
90 – – 'Norma' (v)

× CODONATANTHUS

93 'Aurora'
91 'Fiesta'
92 'Vista'

CODONOPSIS

96 ***benthamii***
95 ***dahurica***
93 ***thalictrifolia***
96 ***viridiflora*** CLD 156

COLCHICUM

96 ***alpinum***
93 ***autumnale*** pink
95 ***boissieri*** CE&H 628
96 ***burttii***
93 'Darwin'
95 ***giganteum*** AC&W 2337
96 'Jarka'
89 'Lilac Bedder'
95 ***parlatoris***
96 ***psaridis***
94 ***pusillum***
96 ***speciosum*** 'Ordu'
91 ***szovitsii***

COLEONEMA

96 ***aspalathoides***
93 ***virgatum***

COLOBANTHUS

96 ***acicularis***
94 ***muscoides***
96 ***quitensis***
90 ***strictus***
90 ***subulatus***

COLUMNEA

94 'Early Bird'
91 ***fendleri***
93 'Flamingo'
93 ***hosta***
93 'Mary Ann'
90 ***microphylla***

COLUTEA

90 ***arborescens*** 'Variegata'
95 ***multiflora***

COLUTEOCARPUS

95 ***vesicaria***

COMMELINA

96 ***tuberosa*** 'Axminster Lilac'

COMPTONIA

94 ***peregrina***

CONANTHERA

94 ***sabulosa***

CONIUM

92 ***maculatum***

CONOCEPHALUM

96 ***supradecompositum***

CONRADINA

95 ***canescens***

CONVALLARIA

93 ***majalis*** 'Berlin Giant'

CONVOLVULUS

96 ***assyricus***
96 ***capensis***
94 ***cataonnicus***
94 ***chilensis***
96 ***compactus***
94 ***humilis***

COPROSMA

89 ***ciliata***
93 'Green Globe'
96 ***quadrifida***
93 ***rigida*** (f)
90 ***serrulata***
90 ***spathulata*** (m)
90 ***viridis*** (f)

COPTIS

92 ***laciniata***

CORDYLINE

90 ***banksii*** 'Purpurea'
90 ***fruticosa***
90 – 'Negri'
89 ***pumilio***
95 'Red Mountain'

COREOPSIS

94 'Gold Child'

CORETHROGYNE

96 ***californica***

CORIANDRUM

96 ***sativum*** 'Morocco'

CORIARIA

90 ***angustissima***
96 'Pictons'

CORIS

91 ***monspeliensis***

CORNUS

90 ***asperifolia*** var. ***drummondii***
92 ***bretschneideri***
94 ***controversa*** French variegated
90 ***florida*** 'Barton's White'
93 ***glabrata***
94 ***hongkongensis***
92 ***kousa*** 'Robert'
93 – 'Tilgates'
90 – 'Variegata'
96 ***linifolia***
95 ***paucinervis***
95 'Porlock' ♕
94 ***stolonifera*** 'Baileyi'

COROKIA

91 × ***virgata*** 'Pink Delight'

CORREA

88 'Kane's Hybrid'

CORTADERIA

95 ***chathamica***

CORTUSA

95 ***brotheri*** C&R
96 – ex KBE 141
95 ***turkestanica***

CORYDALIS

92 ***afghanica***
91 ***aitchisonii***
96 ***atrata***
96 ***aurea***
89 ***cava*** subsp. ***cava***
95 – subsp. ***marschalliana***
92 ***darwasica***
95 ***decumbens***
93 ***diphylla***
95 ***ecristata***
93 ***fargesii***
96 ***lindleyana***
92 ***lineariloba***
96 ***paczoskii*** RS 12180
95 ***pallida***
94 – B&SWJ 395
95 ***petrophila*** KGB 432
95 ***sempervirens*** 'Cream Beauty'

96 ***solida*** from Penza
96 – PJC 214
93 – subsp. ***tauricola***
96 ***tashiroi***
93 ***unifolia***
89 ***vittae***
94 ***wendelboi*** 'Kartal Tepe'

CORYLOPSIS
87 ***coreana***
89 ***himalayana*** var. ***griffithii***

CORYLUS
96 ***colurna*** variegated
92 ***maxima*** 'Garibaldi' (F)
92 – 'Waterloo' (F)
94 ***sieboldiana***

CORYMBIUM
96 ***africanum***

COSMOS
94 ***bipinnatus*** 'Sonata' 🏆

COSTUS
96 ***curvibracteatus***

COTINUS
89 ***coggygria*** 'Drinkstone Form'

COTONEASTER
94 ***congestus*** 'Menai'
94 ***conspicuus*** 'Red Pearl'
95 ***declinatus***
95 ***integerrimus*** Mac&W 5916
96 ***lacteus*** 'Variegatus'
92 ***microphyllus*** 'Inermis'
94 ***nagaensis***
95 ***nivalis***
94 ***parneyi***
90 'Saldam'
91 ***salicifolius*** 'Klampen'
89 – 'Perkeo'
90 ***schlechtendalii*** 'Eastleigh'
92 ***sikkimensis*** Lowndes
94 ***splendens*** 'Glasnevin'
89 × ***suecicus*** 'Greensleeves'
88 – 'Jürgl'
92 'Valkenburg'
87 × ***watereri*** 'Inchmery'

COTULA
92 ***coronopifolia*** 'Cream Buttons'

COTYLEDON
94 ***orbiculata*** var. ***oblonga***

COWANIA
92 ***mexicana***

CRAMBE
93 ***filiformis***

CRASPEDIA
94 ***glauca***
92 ***incana***
96 ***lanata***

CRASSULA
96 ***exilis*** subsp. ***cooperi***
90 ***lactea***
94 ***milfordiae nana***
96 ***milfordiae*** 'Silver Stars'
95 ***moschata***
95 ***multicaulis***
94 ***sarcocaulis*** dark form

+ CRATAEGOMESPILUS
96 'Jules d'Asnières'

CRATAEGUS
94 ***chlorosarca***
94 ***chungtienensis*** CLD 117
89 ***laevigata*** 'Cheal's Crimson'
96 – 'Masekii' (d)
89 – 'Rosea'
96 ***monogyna*** 'Pendula Rosea'
93 ***opaca*** (F)
93 'Red Italian' (F)
91 ***stipulacea***

CRAWFURDIA
96 ***crawfurdioides***

CREMANTHODIUM
89 ***oblongatum***
96 ***pinnatifidum***
92 ***reniforme***
96 sp. ACE 1420

CREPIS
96 ***paludosa***

CRINUM
90 ***campanulatum***
94 ***moorei*** f. ***album***

CRISTARIA
95 ***grandidentata*** RB 94042

CROCOSMIA
96 × ***crocosmiiflora*** 'A.E. Amos'
96 – 'Brightest and Best' J.E. Fitt
92 – 'Météore'
96 'Golden Fleece' M. Wickenden
89 'Orange Flame'
96 ***pottsii*** CC 1077

CROCUS
94 ***ancyrensis*** 'Golden Bunch'
94 ***banaticus*** 'John Marr'
91 ***biflorus*** 'Bowles' Blue'
92 – subsp. ***melantherus***
94 – sulphur
91 ***candidus***
96 ***carpetanus*** B&S 399
96 ***caspius***
96 – PF 5036
94 ***chrysanthus*** 🏆
94 – 'Jeannine'
93 – 'Snowwhite'
91 ***corsicus albus***
94 ***gargaricus*** subsp. ***gargaricus***
96 ***gargaricus minor*** JRM 3299/75
94 ***hadriaticus*** AM form
96 – f. ***hadriaticus***
93 – 'Tom Blanchard'
96 ***imperati*** 🏆
93 – subsp. ***imperati***
94 'Keith Rattray'
89 ***korolkowii*** 'Unicoloratus'
91 ***kotschyanus*** subsp. ***hakkariensis***
93 – subsp. ***suworowianus***
94 ***laevigatus*** white
96 ***michelsonii***
96 ***nevadensis*** AB&S 4415
96 – SB&L 62
90 ***niveus*** 'Cape Matapan'
94 ***olivieri*** subsp. ***istanbulensis***
93 ***pallasii*** subsp. ***pallasii***
91 ***reticulatus*** subsp. ***hittiticus***
96 ***scardicus*** JCA Sar Planina 1985
92 ***sieberi*** subsp. ***sublimis***
89 ***speciosus*** 'Globosus'
95 – subsp. ***ilgazensis***
93 – subsp. ***xantholaimos***
89 ***vernus*** 'Early Perfection'
93 – 'Glory of Limmen'
93 – 'Kathleen Parlow'
89 – 'King of the Striped'
94 – 'Little Dorrit'
94 – 'Negro Boy'

CROTALARIA
92 ***grevei***

CROWEA
91 ***angustifolia***
88 ***exalata*** × ***saligna***

CRYPTANTHA
95 ***flava***
95 ***johnstonii***
95 – NNS 93-178
95 ***paradoxa***
95 – NNS 93-181

CRYPTANTHUS
90 ***acaulis***
92 – var. ***ruber***
92 – – 'New Coster's Favorite' (v)
92 ***beuckeri***
90 ***bivittatus*** 'Minor'
92 Black Mystic Group
90 ***bromelioides*** var. ***tricolor*** (v) 🏆
92 Carnival Group
92 Feuerzauber Group
92 ***fosterianus*** 🏆
92 'It' (v) 🏆
92 Italy Group
90 'Luddemannii'
92 'Red Star'
92 Silber Lila Group
90 'Zebrinus'
92 ***zonatus*** 🏆
93 ***zonatus argyraeus***

× CRYPTBERGIA
90 'Rubra'

CRYPTOMERIA
95 ***japonica*** 'Aurea'
91 – 'Dacrydioides'
89 – 'Elegantissima'
92 – 'Fasciata'
90 – 'Knaptonensis'
96 – 'Lobbii'
91 – 'Tansu'
89 – 'Viridis'

CRYPTOSTEGIA
95 ***grandiflora***

CTENANTHE
90 ***kummeriana***
90 ***oppenheimiana*** 'Tricolor' 🏆

CUNILA
91 ***origanoides***

CUNNINGHAMIA
88 ***lanceolata*** 'Glauca'

CUPHEA
94 ***aequipetala***
94 ***bracteata*** CD&R 1205
94 ***maculata***
90 'Mickey Mouse'
96 × ***purpurea***
91 – 'Firefly'
96 ***viscosissima***

× CUPRESSOCYPARIS
94 ***leylandii*** 'Golden Sun'
92 – 'Haggerston Grey' 🏆
90 – 'Leighton Green'
93 ***notabilis*** 🏆
93 – 'Brookhill'

CUPRESSUS
91 ***arizonica*** var. ***glabra*** 'Silver Smoke'
91 – 'Variegata'
96 ***goveniana*** var. ***abramsiana***
92 ***guadalupensis*** var. ***forbesii***
96 ***lusitanica***
94 ***macnabiana***
91 ***macrocarpa*** 'Coneybearii Aurea'
94 – 'Crippsii'
96 – 'Gold Spire'
91 – 'Golden Flame'
91 – 'John Keown'
89 – 'Pendula'
94 ***sargentii***
94 ***sempervirens*** 'Green Spire'
91 – 'Stricta Aurea'
88 ***torulosa***
95 – CLD 1031
88 – 'Vladivostock'

CYANANTHUS
96 ***delavayi***
96 – ACE 2449
96 ***incanus*** ACE 1700
88 ***lobatus*** 'Inshriach Blue'
96 sp. ACE 1813

CYANELLA
95 ***hyacinthoides***

CYATHEA
96 ***baileyana***
94 ***dealgardii***
90 ***kermadecensis***
96 ***nova-caledoniae***
96 ***robusta***

CYATHODES
96 ***empetrifolia***

CYCLAMEN
90 ***cilicium*** patterned leaf
93 ***coum*** 'Boothman's'
89 – subsp. ***caucasicum album***
96 – subsp. ***coum*** magenta
91 – 'Dazzle'
94 – Elegans Group from Iran
94 – from Russia
94 – from Turkey
89 ***hederifolium*** × ***africanum***
94 – 'Antiochus'
90 – Corfu form

96 – 'Cotswold White'
94 – 'Daley Thompson'
95 – 'Elsie Thomas'
94 ***hederifolium minimum***
96 ***hederifolium*** 'San Marino Silver'
96 – 'Stargazer'
96 ***intaminatum*** 'E.K. Balls'
96 – 'Silver Cloud'
96 ***trochopteranthum*** 'Speckles'

CYCLOSORUS

94 ***pennigerus***

CYDONIA

91 ***oblonga*** 'Broadview'

CYMBALARIA

96 ***muralis*** 'Rosea'

CYMBIDIUM

89 ***goeringii***

CYMBOPOGON

90 ***flexuosus***

CYMOPTERUS

95 ***terebinthinus***

CYNARA

91 ***cardunculus*** (Scolymus Group) 'Brittany Belle'
94 – (Scolymus Group) 'Gigante di Romagna'
90 – (Scolymus Group) 'Glauca'

CYNOGLOSSUM

92 ***amabile*** 'Album'
96 ***creticum***
93 ***germanicum***
96 ***glochidiatum***
95 – CC 718
95 ***nervosum roseum***
95 ***wallichii***

CYPELLA

92 ***coelestis*** 'Platensis'

CYPERUS

94 ***involucratus*** 'Flabelliformis'
95 – 'Variegatus'

CYPHANTHERA

94 ***tasmanica***

CYPRIPEDIUM

96 x ***barbeyi***
95 'Gisela'
94 ***henryi*** x ***flavum***
95 ***hispidula***

CYRTANTHUS

96 'Atalanta'
96 ***flanaganii*** S&SH 11
95 ***flavidus***
96 ***ochroleucus***

CYRTOSPERMA

90 ***johnstonii***

CYSTOPTERIS

94 ***montana***
96 ***regia***

CYTISUS

89 'Baronscourt Amber'
95 x ***beanii*** 'Osiris'
96 'C.E. Pearson'
87 'Charmaine'
96 'College Girl'
94 'Crimson King'
87 'Donard Seedling'
95 'Enchantress'
93 'Garden Magic'
92 'Johnson's Crimson'
89 'Lady Moore'
96 'Luna' 🏆
96 'Miki'
94 'Mrs J. Rodgers'
96 'Mrs Norman Henry'
94 ***multiflorus*** 'Toome's Variety'
95 'Newry Seedling'
87 'Orange Arch'
87 x ***praecox*** 'Buttercup'
96 'Radiance'
96 'Royal Standard'
96 ***scoparius*** f. ***indefessus***
87 'Southcombe Apricot'
89 ***subspinescens***
96 'Sunset'
96 'Sunshine'
92 ***supranubius***

DABOECIA

88 ***azorica***
96 ***cantabrica*** 'Clifden'
88 – 'Heraut'
96 – 'Hookstone Pink'

x DACTYLOGLOSSUM

95 ***Dactylorhiza saccifera*** x ***Coeloglossum viride***

DACTYLORHIZA

95 ***cordigera***
96 ***elata*** 'Lydia'
95 – x ***majalis***
95 ***foliosa*** x ***praetermissa***
95 – x ***purpurella***
96 – x ***romana***
95 – x ***saccifera***
96 ***fuchsii*** 'Bressingham Bonus'
95 ***incarnata*** subsp. ***coccinea*** x ***elata***
95 – – x ***majalis***
95 – – x ***praetermissa***
96 – x ***foliosa***
95 ***larissa*** x ***foliosa***
95 ***maderensis*** x ***majalis***
95 'Madonna'
95 ***majalis*** x ***elata***
96 ***nieschalkiorum***
96 ***pindica***
96 ***praetermissa*** subsp. ***junialis*** var. ***junialis***
95 ***purpurella*** x ***incarnata*** subsp. ***coccinea***
90 ***sambucina***
95 ***urvilleana***

DAHLIA

95 'Abingdon Ace' (SD)
92 'Abridge Ben' (MinD)
96 'Abridge Bertie' (MinD)
92 'Abridge Fox' (MinD)
92 'Abridge Taffy' (MinD)
91 'Ace of Hearts' (Col)
93 'Adelaide Fontane' (LD)
96 'Akita' (Misc)
90 'Aladdin' (SD)
88 'Alfred C' (GS-c)
92 'Alltami Alpine' (MD)
95 'Alltami Apollo' (GS-c)
89 'Alltami Coral' (MS-c)
89 'Alltami Ruby' (MS-c)
89 'Amaran Guard' (LD)
92 'Amaran Pico' (MD)
96 'Amber Banker' (MC)
88 'Amelisweerd' (MS-c)
87 'Anchorite' (SD)
93 'Andrew Lockwood' (Pom)
95 'Ann'
88 'Ann Hilary' (SD)
88 'Anniversary Doc' (SD)
93 'Appenzell' (MS-c)
92 'Appetizer' (SS-c)
89 'Apple Blossom' (MC)
95 'Apricot Honeymoon Dress' (SD)
88 'Armgard Coronet' (MD)
89 'Arthur Lashlie' (MC)
93 'Autumn Fairy' (D)
95 'Aylett's Dazzler' (MinD) 🏆
92 'Bacchus' (MS-c)
89 'Bach' (MC)
96 'Banker' (MC)
87 'Barbara Schell' (GD)
95 'Barbarry Climax' (SBa)
96 'Barbarry Epic' (SD)
92 'Barbarry Flush' (MinD)
96 'Barbarry Glamour' (SBa)
96 'Barbarry Lavender' (MinD)
96 'Barbarry Oracle' (SD)
95 'Barbarry Standard' (MinD)
95 'Barbarry Trend' (MinD)
90 'Baseball' (MinBa)
91 'Bassingbourne Beauty' (SD)
92 'Bella Rose' (SS-c)
92 'Belle Epoque' (MC)
89 'Belle of Barmera' (GD)
90 'Bettina' (SS-c)
95 'Betty Ann' (Pom)
94 'Betty Bowen' (SD)
87 'Birchwood' (Pom)
87 'Bitsa' (MinBa)
93 'Black Jack' (SD)
90 'Blaisdon Red' (SD)
87 'Bob Fitzjohn' (GS-c)
96 'Bonanza' (LD)
94 'Bonny Blue' (SBa)
95 'Border Triumph' (DwB)
92 'Bright'
89 'Brookfield Dierdre' (MinBa)
92 'Brunton' (MinD)
89 'Bull's Pride' (GD)
89 'Bushfire' (Pom)
91 'Café au Lait' (LD)
95 'Camano Choice' (SD)
88 'Cantab Symbol' (MS-c)
88 'Carol Channing' (GS-c)
89 'Caroussel' (MC)
96 'Carstone Sunbeam' (SD)
95 'Catherine Ireland' (MinD)
88 'Cefn Glow' (SS-c)
88 'Centenary Symbol' (MS-c)
96 'Charlie Kenwood' (MinD)
95 'Charmant' (MinBa)
93 'Cheerio' (SS-c)
88 'Cherida' (MinBa)
93 'Cherry Fire' (S-c)
95 'Chiltern Amber' (SD)
87 'Chinese Lantern' (SD)
90 'Chorus Girl' (MinD)
91 'Christine' (SD)
88 'Claire' (Misc)
95 'Clarence' (S-c)
95 'Clint's Climax' (LD)
95 'Cloverdale' (SD)
95 ***coccinea palmeri***
96 – CD&R 1367
90 'Cocktail' (S-c)
89 'Color Spectacle' (LSD)
91 'Coral Puff'
87 'Corfu'
88 'Corrine'
87 'Cortez Silver' (MD)
93 'Cream Alva's' (GD)
92 'Cream Klankstad' (SC)
92 'Cream Linda' (SD)
90 'Cream Pontiac' (SC)
91 'Crichton Cherry' (MinD)
95 'Crichton Honey' (SBa)
90 'Crossfield Sceptre' (MS-c)
93 'Croydon Supreme' (LD)
89 'Cryfield Jane' (MinBa)
89 'Cryfield Max' (SC)
87 'Cryfield Rosie' (SBa)
87 'Daleko Adonis' (GS-c)
93 'Daleko Gold' (MD)
95 'Daleko National' (MD)
93 'Daleko Olympic' (LD)
90 'Daleko Tangerine' (MD)
89 'Daleko Venus' (MS-c)
88 'Dana Audrey' (MinC)
88 'Dana Judy' (SS-c)
93 'Dana Louise' (MD)
89 'Dana Peerless' (SS-c)
93 'Danum Cream' (MS-c)
87 'Danum Cupid' (MinBa)
93 'Danum Pinky' (MS-c)
92 'Dauntless' (GS-c)
95 'Davar Donna' (SS-c) 🏆
96 'Davenport Pride' (MS-c)
88 'Dedham' (SD)
95 'Deepest Yellow' (MinBa)
92 'Defile' (MD)
89 'De-la-Haye' (MS-c)
89 'Delectus' (SD)
93 'Denise Willow' (Pom)
91 'Diamant' (MD)
92 'Diana Gregory' (Pom)
95 'Diane Nelson' (SD)
95 'Doc van Horn' (LS-c)
93 'Doctor Caroline Rabbitt' (SD)
90 'Doctor John Grainger' (MinD)
90 'Donald van de Mark' (GD)

90 'Dorothy Whitney Wood' (SS-c)
96 'Duncan'
95 'Dusky Lilac' (SWL)
93 'Dutch Baby' (Pom)
90 'Early Bird' (SD)
90 'Eastwood Pinky' (MS-c)
87 'Eastwood Star' (MS-c)
88 'Eden Marc' (SC)
93 'Edith Arthur' (SS-c)
95 'Edna C' (MD)
92 'Eileen Denny' (MS-c)
90 'Elizabethan' (SD)
90 'Elmbrook Rebel' (GS-c)
95 'Emmental' (SD)
92 'Emmerdale' (SS-c)
96 'Evelyn Rumbold' (GD)
95 'Evening Mail' (GS-c) 🏆
93 'Extase' (MD)
92 'Fernhill Champion' (MD)
95 'Feu Céleste' (Col)
93 'Fille du Diable' (LS-c)
89 'Flying Picket' (SD)
89 'Formby Perfection' (MD)
95 'Frank Holmes' (Pom)
93 'Frank Hornsey' (SD)
90 'Fred Sheard' (MinD)
90 'Free Lance' (MS-c)
96 'Freestyle' (SC)
93 'Frits' (MinBa)
95 'G.F. Hemerik' (Sin)
89 'Gale Lane' (Pom)
92 'Garden News' (MD)
95 'Gateshead Galaxy' (DwB)
95 'Geerlings Queeny' (SC) 🏆
90 'Gerald Grace' (LS-c)
93 'Gilt Edge' (MD)
94 'Gina Lombaert' (MS-c)
90 'Ginger Nut' (Pom)
88 'Ginger Willo'
93 'Giraffe' (Misc)
88 'Glenafton' (Pom)
88 'Glenbank Honeycomb' (Pom)
93 'Gloria Romaine' (SD)
93 'Glorie van Naardwijk' (SD)
95 'Gold Diable' (SS-c) 🏆
92 'Golden Festival'
90 'Golden Fizz' (MinBa)
90 'Golden Hope' (MinD)
96 'Golden Symbol' (MS-c)
93 'Golden Willo' (Pom)
96 'Good Intent' (LD)
95 'Gordon Lockwood' (Pom)
92 'Hallmark' (Pom)
95 'Hamari Fiesta' (SD)
90 'Hamari Saffron' (MS-c)
90 'Hamari Sunset' (MS-c)
92 'Hamilton Lillian' (SD) 🏆
90 'Haseley Cameo' (SD)
90 'Haseley Pearl' (DBa)
90 'Haseley Triumph' (SD)
90 'Hazel's Surprise' (SD)
94 'Helga' (MS-c)
91 'Heljo's Flame' (S-c)
94 'Herbert Smith' (D)
88 'Higherfield Crown' (SC)
90 'Highgate Lustre' (MS-c)
88 'Highgate Torch' (MS-c)
95 'Hillcrest Blaze' (SS-c) 🏆
96 'Hindu star' (MinBa)
96 'Holland Festival' (GD)
90 'Holland Herald' (LS-c)
87 'Horn of Plenty' (MinD)
90 'Hot Spot' (MinD)
95 'Ice Cream Beauty' (SWL)
88 'Ice Queen' (SWL)
93 'Inca Matchless' (MD)
87 'Inca Metropolitan' (LD) 🏆
96 'Inland Dynasty' (GS-c)
89 'Invader' (SC)
94 'Irene van der Zwet' (Sin)
93 'Jacqueline Tivey' (SD)
92 'Jaldec Jerry' (GS-c)
95 'Jaldec Joker' (SC) 🏆
89 'Jancis' (MinS-c)
88 'Janet Clarke' (Pom)
93 'Janet Goddard' (SD)
92 'Jean Bailiss' (MS-c)
90 'Jescot Jim' (SD)
88 'Jescot Nubia' (SS-c)
95 'Jessica Crutchfield' (SWL) 🏆
89 'Jill Doc' (MD)
95 'Jo Anne' (MS-c)
89 'Joy Bennett' (MD)
89 'Joyce Green' (GS-c)
93 'Just Julia' (MS-c)
93 'Just Mary' (SD)
93 'Katisha' (MinD)
96 'Kelvin Floodlight' (GD)
88 'Kenora Carousel' (MS-c)
88 'Kenora Sunburst' (LS-c)
92 'Kenora Valentine' (LD) 🏆
92 'Kenora Wildfire' (GD)
96 'Key West' (LD)
89 'Kiwi Nephew' (SS-c)
93 'Kung Fu' (SD)
95 'La Gioconda' (Col)
90 'Lady Orpah' (SD)
95 'Laura Marie' (MinBa)
90 'Laurence Fisher' (MS-c)
90 'Lavendale' (MinD)
87 'Lavender Leycett' (GD)
92 'Lavender Nunton Harvest' (SD)
94 'Lavender Perfection' (GD)
90 'Lavender Pontiac' (SC)
95 'Lavender Symbol' (MS-c)
95 'Lavengro' (GD)
92 'Le Vonne Splinter' (GS-c)
88 'Lemon Hornsey' (SD)
96 'Lemon Puff' (Anem)
90 'Leverton Chippy' (SD)
92 'Leycett' (GD)
93 'Liberator' (GD)
93 'Life Force'
95 'Life Size' (LD)
92 'Lilac Athalie' (SC)
95 'Lilian Ingham' (SS-c)
87 'Limited Edition' (LS-c)
93 'Linda Lusardi' (SS-c)
92 'Lipoma' (MinBa)
95 'Lismore Peggy' (Pom)
88 'Little Conn' (Pom)
95 'Little Laura' (MinBa)
89 'Lloyd Huston' (GS-c)
87 'Louise Bailey' (MinD)
89 'Love's Dream' (SWL)
89 'Lula Pattie' (GD)
87 'Madelaine Ann' (GD)
92 'Magic Moment' (MS-c)
92 'Magnificat' (MinD)
92 'Majestic Athalie' (SC)
92 'Majjas Symbol' (MS-c)
87 'Margaret Duross' (GD)
87 'Margaret Jean' (GD)
88 'Mariposa' (Col)
93 'Mark Lockwood' (Pom)
92 'Mark Willo' (Pom)
95 'Masons' (SWL)
93 'Match' (SS-c)
93 'Matterhorn' (SWL)
88 'Mauvine' (Pom)
88 'Meiktila' (SWL)
93 'Meiro' (SD)
90 'Melanie Jane' (MS-c)
89 'Melton' (MinD)
96 ***merckii*** gold-leaved
96 – 'Hadspen Star'
89 'Merriwell Topic' (MD)
94 'Midnight Fire' (Misc)
93 'Mies' (Sin)
90 'Millbank Inferno' (SD)
93 'Minder' (GD)
92 'Miramar' (SD)
90 'Miranda' (MS-c)
93 'Miss Blanc' (SD)
91 'Miss Swiss' (SD)
92 'Mistill Beauty' (SC)
95 'Mistill Delight' (MinD)
89 'Morley Lady' (SD)
90 'Morley Lass' (SS-c)
87 'Mrs Silverston' (SD)
93 'Mummies Favourite' (SD)
93 'Nationwide' (SD) 🏆
93 'Nellie Birch' (MinBa)
89 'Nescio' (Pom)
90 'Nettie' (MinBa)
88 'Neveric' (LS-c)
90 'Newby' (MinD)
94 'Nicolette' (MWL)
92 'Night Editor' (GD)
93 'Nijinsky' (SBa)
88 'Norm Williams'
95 'Nunton Harvest' (SD)
87 'Onslow Linda Ann' (MinD)
95 'Onslow Michelle' (SD)
95 'Orange Nugget' (MinBa)
88 'Pamela' (SD)
90 'Pastel Pontiac' (SC)
90 'Pat Seed' (MD)
90 'Patti-pink' (SS-c)
95 'Paul Damp' (MS-c)
92 'Paul's Delight' (SD)
89 'Peace Pact' (SWL)
90 'Peach Pontiac' (SC)
90 'Pearl Hornsey' (SD)
89 'Pearl Sharowean' (MS-c)
95 'Pensford Marion' (Pom)
92 'Pensford Willo' (Pom)
94 'Peter' (LD)
89 'Peters Glorie' (MD)
95 'Phill's Pink' (SD) 🏆
93 'Pied Piper' (MinBa)
95 'Pink Cloud' (SS-c)
93 'Pink Frank Hornsey' (SD)
93 'Pink Giraffe' (O)
95 'Pink Honeymoon Dress' (SD)
93 'Pink Katisha' (MinD)
95 'Pink Kerkrade' (SC)
89 'Pink Leycett' (GD)
95 'Pink Paul Chester' (SC) 🏆
93 'Pink Risca Miner' (SBa)
92 'Pink Vaguely Noble' (MinBa)
90 'Pink Worton Ann' (MinD)
93 'Pioneer' (MS-c)
93 'Playboy' (GD)
92 'Polar Sight' (GC)
92 'Polyand' (LD)
87 'Pop Stretton' (GS-c)
87 'Poppa Jim' (SD)
89 'Pot Black' (MinBa)
93 'Prefect' (MS-c)
95 'Pretty Little Princess' (SS-c) 🏆
88 'Primrose Bryn' (SS-c)
95 'Primrose Rustig' (MD)
94 'Procyon' (SD)
90 'Promise' (MS-c/Fim)
92 'Purbeck Lydia' (LS-c)
90 'Purple Doris Day' (SC)
87 'Purple Joy' (MD)
93 'Quel Diable' (LS-c)
88 'Rachel's Place' (Pom)
92 'Raisa' (LD)
88 'Rani' (Pom)
88 'Red Admiral' (MinBa)
93 'Red Alert' (LBa)
93 'Red and White' (SD)
88 'Red Delight' (Col)
89 'Red Lotus'
88 'Red Schweitzer' (MinD)
95 'Red Sensation' (MD)
88 'Regal Kerkrade' (SC)
95 'Requiem' (SD)
95 'Reverend P. Holian' (GS-c)
87 'Richard Nash' (SD)
90 'Robbie Huston' (LS-c)
88 'Roberta' (LD)
93 'Robin Hood' (SBa)
88 'Rokesly Mini' (MinC) 🏆
96 'Rosalie' (Pom)
91 'Rosalinde' (S-c)
92 'Rose Cupid' (MinBa)
89 'Rose Newby' (MinD)
87 'Rose Symbol' (MS-c)
88 'Rose Willo' (Pom)

94 'Rosella' (MD)
88 'Rosewood' (SS-c)
95 'Rothesay Castle' (DwB)
95 'Rothesay Robin' (SD)
88 'Rotonde' (SC)
95 'Royal Ivory' (SWL)
94 ***rupicola***
95 'Ruskin Dynasty' (SD)
89 'Ruskin Emil' (SS-c)
88 'Ruskin Melody'
93 'Ruskin Petite' (MinBa)
95 'Rustig' (MD)
93 'Rusty Hope' (MinD)
89 'Saint Croix' (GS-c)
93 'Saiva'
87 'Salmon Kokarde' (MinD)
92 'Salmon Symbol' (MS-c)
90 'Sandra Chapman' (MS-c)
90 'Sango' (MinBa)
88 'Scarborough'
95 'Scarlet Beauty' (SwL)
89 'Scaur Princess' (SD)
95 'Schweitzer's Kokarde' (MinD)
96 'Scottish Relation' (SS-c) 🏆
89 'Scott's United' (MinD)
87 'Senzoe Jenny' (MinD)
89 'Sharowean Pride' (MS-c)
93 'Sherwood Monarch' (GS-c)
89 'Sherwood Sunrise' (SD)
91 'Shoreline' (D)
92 'Shy Lass' (SC)
89 'Shy Princess' (MC)
93 'Silver Slipper' (SS-c)
93 'Sky High' (SD)
95 'Sneezy' (Sin)
95 'Snowflake' (SWL)
91 'Spencer' (SD)
89 'Stoke Festival '86' (SS-c)
88 'Stoneleigh Joyce' (Pom)
88 'Strawberry Gem' (Pom)
87 'Stump Cross'
93 'Stylemaster' (MC)
88 'Sue Willo' (Pom)
95 'Suffolk Bride' (MS-c)
96 'Suffolk Spectacular' (MD)
90 'Sugar Candy' (MS-c)
91 'Sultan'
88 'Sunburst' (Col)
94 'Sunny Boy' (MinBa)
95 'Sunray Glint' (MS-c)
92 'Sunray Symbol' (MS-c)
90 'Supermarket' (MS-c)
89 'Sure Thing' (MC)
87 'Swallow Falls' (SD)
95 'Sweet Content' (SD)
92 'Sweet Symbol' (MS-c)
96 'Symbol' (MS-c)
87 'Symbol Jim'
93 'Syston Sophia' (LBa)
93 'Syston Zone' (MS-c)
93 'Tahiti Sunrise' (MS-c)
91 'Tango' (SD)
88 'Teatime' (MS-c)
93 'Thais' (Col)
90 'The Bride' (SC)
93 'Thelma Clements' (LD)
93 'Tiger Tiv' (MD)
90 'Tinker's White' (SD)
89 'Topaz Puff'
90 'Tourbillon' (LC)
90 'Trelawny' (GD)
95 'Trengrove Summer' (MD)
87 'Twiggy' (SWL)
92 'Twilight Time' (MD)
93 'Union Jack' (Sin)
90 'Val Saint Lambert' (MC)
95 'Vantage' (GS-c)
93 'Venlo' (D)
87 'Vicky Jackson' (SWL)
89 'Vidal Rhapsody' (MS-c)
88 'Vidal Tracy' (SS-c)
90 'Vigor' (SWL)
93 'Violet'
93 'Violet Davies' (MS-c)
95 'W.J.N.' (Pom)
88 'Walter Hardisty' (GD) 🏆
93 'Wanda's Sunshine' (GD)
95 'Wandy' (Pom) 🏆
95 'Welcome Guest' (MS-c)
88 'Weston Aramac' (SS-c)
89 'Weston Forge' (SC)
92 'Whale's Rhonda' (Pom)
92 'White Aster' (Pom)
95 'White Hornsey' (SD)
88 'White Lady Linda' (SD)
87 'White Marc' (SC)
95 'White Rustig' (MD)
92 'William 'B'' (GD)
88 'William Gregory'
95 'William John' (Pom)
88 'Willo's Fairy' (Pom)
88 'Willo's Flame' (Pom)
95 'Willo's Flecks' (Pom)
95 'Willo's Night' (Pom)
95 'Willo's Violet' (Pom)
96 'Winter Dawn' (SWL)
92 'Wittem' (MD)
89 'Wood Plumpton' (MC)
88 'Wootton Amber'
93 'Wootton Carol' (SD)
92 'Worton Ann' (MinD)
87 'Worton Ruth' (SD)
87 'Wyndal Horizon' (MS-c)
95 'Yellow Frank Hornsey' (SD)
88 'Yellow Jubilee'
93 'Yes Sir' (MD)
94 'Zingaro' (SD)

DALEA

96 ***gattingeri***

DAPHNE

92 ***aurantiaca***
95 ***caucasica* x *petraea***
89 ***cneorum*** 'Major'
92 – 'Ruby Glow'
91 – var. ***verlotii***
92 ***euboica***
93 ***gnidioides***
92 ***gnidium***
92 ***kamtschatica***
90 ***kiusiana***
95 ***laureola*** 'Margaret Mathew'
90 'Louis Mountbatten'
95 ***mezereum*** var. ***autumnalis***
94 ***papyracea***
91 ***petraea*** 'Flore Pleno'
89 'Rossetii'
92 'Silver Y'
91 ***tangutica*** 'Aureomarginata'
95 – 'Rajah'
96 'Warnford'

DAPHNIPHYLLUM

95 ***humile*** JR 902

DASYLIRION

94 ***leiophyllum***
92 ***texanum***

DASYPYRUM

93 ***villosum***

DATURA

96 ***ceratocaula***
94 ***signata***

DAVALLIA

95 ***solida***

DELOSPERMA

93 ***lehmannii***
89 ***ornatulum***
93 ***pallidum***
95 'Wilson'

DELPHINIUM

96 'After Midnight'
96 'Alie Duyvensteyn'
88 'Antares'
88 'Aphrodite'
91 'Apollo'
96 'Atholl'
91 'Baby Doll'
91 (Belladonna Group) 'Blue Bees'
91 (Belladonna Group) 'Lamartine'
91 (Belladonna Group) 'Orion'
94 (Belladonna Group) 'Wendy'
91 ***bellamania***
96 ***biternatum***
93 'Blue Mirror'
88 'Ceylon'
88 ***cheilanthum***
90 'Cinderella'
96 'Cream Cracker'
91 'Dairymaid'
89 ***denudatum***
96 'Diana Grenfell'
96 'Dorothy Ash'
96 'Dunsdon Green'
94 'Eastgrove White'
96 'Elisabeth Sahin'
96 'Evita'
96 'Florestan'
96 'Foxhill Eileen'
96 'Foxhill Lady'
96 'Foxhill Oscar'
96 'Foxhill Pinta'
96 'Foxhill Roseanna'
95 'Giotto' 🏆
91 ***grandiflorum*** 'Azure Fairy'
96 – 'White Butterfly'
88 Great Expectations Group
91 'Hilda Lucas'
90 'Horizon'
96 'Iceman'
90 'Jennifer Langdon'
96 'Jill Curley'
90 'Jo-Jo'
92 'Julia Medcalf'
90 'Jumbo'
90 'Lady Eleanor'
93 'Layla'
96 'Loch Katrine'
88 'Loch Lomond'
90 'Loch Maree'
90 'Loch Morar'
96 'Loch Torridon'
90 'Magic Moment'
88 Moody Blues Group
92 'Mount Everest'
94 ***parishii*** JJA 12737
90 'Patricia'
91 'Patricia, Lady Hambleden'
90 'Peacock'
95 Percival Group
90 'Peter Pan'
93 'Radiance'
96 'Rakker'
90 'Reverend E. Lascelles'
96 'Romany'
91 'Rosina'
88 Rosy Future Group
90 'Round Table'
91 'Royal Wedding'
95 x ***ruysii*** 'Piccolo'
91 'Sarabande'
90 'Savrola'
91 'South Seas'
96 Southern Countrymen Group 🏆
96 Southern Noblemen Group
96 sp. CC&McK 123
93 sp. CLD 1476
93 ***stachydeum***
91 'Stardust'
91 'Summer Wine'
92 'Taj Mahal'
93 ***tatsienense*** 'Blue Ice'
96 'Thamesmead' 🏆
91 'Thelma Rowe' 🏆
92 'Tiny Tim'
94 ***trolliifolium***
91 'Turiddu'
88 'Wheatear'
91 'William Richards'
93 ***xantholeucum***
91 'Xenia Field'
96 Zeeland Series light blues 🏆
88 'Zeus'

DENDRANTHEMA

95 'Abbygates' (25b)
89 'Alf Price' (25b)
96 'Alfreton Cream' (5b)
87 'Alice Fitton' (7b)
89 'Alison McNamara' (3b)
91 'Allison '88' (29Rub)
91 'Allswell' (24b)
87 'Amanda' (11)

88 'Amber Chessington' (25a)
87 'Amber Leading Lady' (25b)
95 'Amber Yvonne Arnaud' 🏆
87 'Amy Fitton' (4a)
88 'Ann Dickson' (25a)
96 'Apricot Cassandra' (5b)
96 'Apricot Enbee Wedding' (29d)
87 'Apricot Harry Gee' (1)
95 'Apricot Madeleine' (29c)
91 'Apricot New Stylist' (24b)
95 'Apricot Vedova' (6a)
90 'Arcadian' (24b)
89 'Ark Royal' (24b)
89 'Arkle' (25a)
87 'Arnold Fitton' (1)
90 'Arthur' (25a)
95 'Arthur Hawkins' (24b)
96 'Artic Beauty' (4b)
95 'Aucklander' (23b)
96 'Aurora' (4a)
91 'Bambi' (24b)
89 'Bambino' (29c)
87 'Barbara Hall' (23a)
93 'Barbara Ward' (7b)
87 'Barker's Wine' (24c)
87 'Barnsley' (5a)
88 'Batley Centenary' (25b)
87 'Beaujolais' (24b)
87 'Bergerac' (24b)
89 'Betty Saxton' (24a)
92 'Bill Florentine' (3b)
96 'Bill Sands' (3a)
92 'Birchwood' (24b)
87 'Birmingham' (2)
87 'Blanche Poitevine' (5b)
95 'Bob Dawsey' (25a)
95 'Bonigold'
88 'Bonus' (24a)
87 'Bowers Jim'
87 'Breakaway'
96 'Brendon' (9c)
92 'Brideshead' (13b)
95 'Bridget' (6b)
96 'Brierton Celebration' (7b)
95 'Brierton Festival' (7b)
93 'Brierton Lad' (7b)
88 'Brighton' (25b)
87 'Broadway Flare' (29c)
87 'Broadway Magic' (19e)
87 'Broadway Peach' (29c)
87 'Broadway Royal' (29c)
93 'Broadway Sovereign' (29c)
95 'Bronze Bridget' (6b)
87 'Bronze Eda Fitton' (23a)
88 'Bronze Emilia' (29c)
95 'Bronze Fairweather' (3b)
89 'Bronze Juweeltje'
94 'Bronze Majestic' (2)
87 'Bronze Miss World' (24a)
89 'Bronze Nathalie' (29c)
95 'Bronze Pamela'
87 'Bronze Shoesmith Salmon' (4a)
90 'Bronze Venice' (24b)
91 'Bronze Wessex Charms' (29d)
92 'Bronze World of Sport' (25a)
91 'Buckland' (25c)
92 'Buff Courtier' (24a)
87 'Candy' (7a)
95 'Canopy' (24a)
96 'Cappa' (9a)
89 'Capulet' (3b)
88 'Carmine Margaret' (24b)
89 'Carol Moonlight' (29b)
87 'Carrie' (25a)
94 'Chaffinch' (22a)
92 'Chamoirose'
87 'Chanelle' (25a)
95 'Charles Fraser' (25a)
90 'Chatsworth' (29c)
87 'Cheltenham Show' (25a)
91 'Chempak Crimson' (24b)
89 'Cherry Chintz' (24a)
96 'Cherry Dynasty' (14a)
94 'Cherry Venice' (24b)
87 'Chesswood Beauty' (7b)
88 'Chintz' (24b)
88 'Chippendale' (24a)
89 'Christina' (25b)
96 'Christine'
95 'Christmas Carol' (5a)
96 'Christmas Wine' (5a)
88 'Clarette'
92 'Cloth of Gold' (24b)
95 'Cloudbank' (9a)
87 'Conderton' (15a)
95 'Connie Meyhew' (5a)
91 'Contour' (24a)
95 'Copeland' (14b)
93 'Copper Hedgerow' (7b)
90 'Copper Rylands Gem' (24b)
88 'Copper Spoon'
95 'Coral Rynoon' (9d)
94 'Cornish' (25b)
89 'Countdown' (5a)
87 'Countryman' (24b)
87 'Cranforth' (24b)
95 'Cream Allouise' (25b)
91 'Cream Pennine Pink' (29c)
96 'Cream Pennine Serene'
96 'Cream Pennine Thrill' (29)
89 'Crimson Daily Mirror' (5a)
90 'Crimson Purple Glow' (5a)
89 'Crimson Venice' (24b)
87 'Crimson Woolman's Glory' (7a)
96 'Cropthorne'
90 'Crown Derby' (15a)
96 'Cygnet' (24b)
89 'Daily Mirror' (5a)
96 'Dark Corfu'
87 'Dark Eve Gray' (24b)
88 'Dark Pennine Pink' (29c)
91 'Darlington Jubilee' (25a)
92 'David Higgins' (3b)
96 'Deane Joy' (9a)
96 'Deane Snow' (9a)
94 'Dee Lemon' (24c)
91 'Dee Prince' (29c)
92 'Denise Oatridge' (5a)
96 'Diamond Wedding' (25a)
92 'Distinction' (3b)
92 'Dolly' (9c)
90 'Doreen Bircumshaw' (24a)
94 'Dorridge Candy' (4b)
94 'Dorridge Choice' (5b)
93 'Dorridge Dream' (23b)
96 'Dorridge Gem' (24b)
88 'Dorridge Jewel' (15a)
91 'Dorridge Lady' (24b)
91 'Dorridge Snowball' (3b)
91 'Dorridge Sun' (3b)
95 'Duke of Kent' (1)
89 'Early Red Cloak' (24b)
95 'East Riding' (25a)
95 'Eastleigh' (24b)
87 'Eda Fitton' (23a)
94 'Eddie Wilson' (25b)
87 'Edith Goodall' (24a)
95 'Edwin Painter' (7b)
96 'Elizabeth Burton' (5a)
89 'Elsie Prosser' (1)
96 'Embleton' (24a)
88 'Emilia' (29c)
87 'Enid Whiston' (4b)
95 'Epic' (6b)
95 'Ernie Lapworth' (25b)
91 'Eugene' (25b)
89 'Eve Gray' (24b)
91 'Evelyn' (25a)
93 'Fair Lady' (5a)
89 'Fairisle' (24b)
87 'Far North' (5a)
90 'Fiona Lynn' (24a)
89 'Flambard' (24b)
93 'Flash Point'
89 'Flo Cooper' (25a)
93 'Folk Song' (4b)
87 'Forest Flare' (24b)
96 'Formcast' (24a)
96 'Fortune' (24b)
91 'Frank Taylor' (15a)
94 'Fred Brocklehurst' (25a)
87 'Fred Raynor'
96 'Frederick Thompson'
89 'Gemma Jones' (5b)
87 'Gerrie Hoek' (29c)
92 'Gerry Milner' (23b)
92 'Gillette' (23b)
87 'Gillian Gore' (23b)
95 'Gladys Homer' (24a)
92 'Gladys Sharpe' (25a)
89 'Glorie'
92 'Glorietta' (4b)
91 'Gold Coin' (7b)
89 'Goldcrest' (25b)
96 'Golden Allouise' (25b)
89 'Golden Echo' (4a)
95 'Golden Fred Shoesmith' (5a)
95 'Golden Gigantic' (1)
96 'Golden Lady' (3b)
96 'Golden Orfe' (29c)
89 'Golden Oyster' (25b)
95 'Golden Pennine Pink' (29c)
89 'Golden Percy Salter' (24b)
93 'Golden Queen' (3b)
95 'Golden Quill Elegance' (9f)
87 'Golden Shoesmith Salmo' (4a) 🏆
90 'Golden Stardust' (24b)
87 'Golden Woolman's Glory' (7a)
94 'Goldmarianne'
95 'Goldmine'
87 'Goldway' (25b)
95 'Gordon Taylor' (7b)
95 'Grace Lovell' (25a)
89 'Granny Gow' (29d)
89 'Graphic' (23b)
95 'Green Chartreuse' (5b)
89 'Green Goddess' (1)
95 'Green Nightingale' (10)
89 'Greensleeves' (11)
90 'Hamburg' (25a)
96 'Hardwick Bronze'
96 'Hardwick Lemon' (29c)
96 'Hardwick Primrose' (29c)
96 'Hardwick Yellow' (19b)
88 'Harford'
96 'Harold Lawson' (5a)
96 'Harry Gee' (1)
96 'Harry James' (25a)
96 'Harry Lawson'
87 'Harry Whiston' (1)
95 'Harvest Bounty'
94 'Harvest Dawn' (25)
92 'Havelsonne'
89 'Hayley Boon' (25b)
93 'Helmsman' (24b)
96 'Hesketh Crystal' (5b)
89 'Highland Skirmish' (29d)
89 'Honey Margaret' (29e)
96 'Illusion'
95 'Inkberrow' (24b)
92 'International' (3a)
95 'Iris Coupland' (5a)
91 'Isabel' (15b)
92 'Isabellrosa' (29K)
92 'Jack Wood' (25a)
90 'James Hall' (5a)
95 'Jan Okum' (24b)
96 'Jan Wardle' (5a)
96 ***japonense*** var. ***ashizuriense***
87 'Jessie Gilmour' (23a)
89 'Jessie Habgood' (1)
92 'Jessie Raynor'
91 'Jill Collins' (24b)
87 'Jinx' (7b)
95 'John Austin' (25a)
96 'John Murray'
92 'John Statham' (23b)
87 'John Wood' (5a)
91 'Joy Hughes' (4b)
95 'Joy Smith' (24b)
91 'Joyce Stevenson' (24b)
91 'Jubilee' (9c)
87 'Julie Ann' (25b)
91 'Juliet' (24b)
87 'Just Tom' (24b)
92 'Kampfhahn'
93 'Kento-homari' (9f)
96 'Kingfisher' (12a)

95 'Kismet' (4c)
87 'Kissy'
94 'Kleiner Bernstein'
93 'Kokinran' (9f)
93 'Komaki-zukura' (9f)
88 'Lady Anna' (25a)
94 'Lady Clara' (29Rub)
87 'Lapley Blush' (29b)
87 'Lapley Bracken' (29d)
87 'Lapley Hallmark' (29c)
87 'Lapley Princess' (29c)
87 'Lapley Rose' (29b)
87 'Lapley Snow' (29d)
87 'Lapley Sunset'
96 'Lemon Blanket'
90 'Lemon Drop' (23a)
96 'Lemon Hawaii' (9c)
92 'Lemon Rynoon' (9d)
91 'Lemon Tench' (29K)
93 'Len Futerill' (25b)
92 'Liberty' (15a)
87 'Linda Young' (5b)
87 'Lipstick' (28)
87 'Littleton'
95 'Lorraine' (24b)
95 'Louise Etheridge' (23a)
89 'Lovely Charmer' (7b)
96 'Lucida' (29c)
87 'Lydia' (25a)
89 'Madge Welby' (25b)
95 'Mancetta Bride' 🏆
90 'Manito'
87 'Margaret Fitton' (23b)
96 'Margaret Patricia' (24b)
95 'Margaret Riley' (25b)
90 'Marian Gosling' (24b)
89 'Marie Taylor' (29c)
91 'Mark Slater' (2)
96 'Marlene Jones' (25b)
94 'Martin Walker' (25b)
96 'Martina' (24b)
92 'Mary Blomfield' (4a)
90 'Mary Dyer' (24a)
87 'Mason's Golden'
96 'Maudie Hodgson' (24b)
93 'Mauve Mist' (29K)
92 'Medallion' (9c)
88 'Michael Fish' (25b)
87 'Michael Pullom' (25a)
95 'Michael Woolman'
96 'Michelle Walker' (24b)
94 'Midnight' (24b)
93 'Milltown' (24b)
87 'Mosquito' (28b)
94 'Mottram Lady' (29d)
94 'Mottram Melody' (29d)
88 'Mrs Farley'
88 'Munsel'
89 'Muriel Foster' (29d)
96 'Muriel Vipas' (25b)
87 'My Jeanie' (25a)
93 'Myako-no-suki' (9f)
95 'Myssy Angie' (29c) 🏆
87 'Naden Pound'
95 'Nathalie' (19c) 🏆
89 'Ned Holdaway' (25b)
95 'New Stylist' (24b)
95 'Niederschlesien'
87 'Nora Brook'
93 'Noshi-no-nuki' (9f)
95 'Oakfield Bride' (24b)
96 'Ogmore Vale' (12a)
95 'Olga Patterson' (5b)
88 'Olga Williams' (25b)
87 'Olwyn' (4b)
96 'Orange Corfu'
95 'Orange Fair Lady' (5a)
95 'Orange Pennine Pink' (29c)
90 'Orchid Helen'
88 'Orlando' (25a)
96 'Orno' (29b)
96 'Overbury'
89 'Oyster' (25b)
91 'Oyster Fairweather' (3b)
92 'Pacific' (15a)
88 'Paint Box' (24b)
87 'Pandora' (5a/12a)
96 'Pat' (6b)
95 'Pat Addison' (24b)
87 'Pat Amos' (23a)
96 'Patricia'
96 'Pavilion' (25a)
95 'Payton Glow' (29c)
95 'Payton Plenty' (29c)
95 'Payton Prince' (29c)
95 'Payton Rose' (29c)
89 'Peach Chessington' (25a)
89 'Peach Juweeltje'
87 'Pelsall Lady' (25a)
93 'Pennine Ace' (29f)
90 'Pennine Air' (29d)
89 'Pennine Alfie' (29f)
95 'Pennine Amber' (29c)
91 'Pennine Angel' (29a)
89 'Pennine Ann' (29a)
96 'Pennine Autumn' (29c)
89 'Pennine Belle' (29d)
89 'Pennine Brandy' (29c)
95 'Pennine Brenda' (29d)
96 'Pennine Bride' (29c)
88 'Pennine Brighteye' (29c)
88 'Pennine Bronze' (29c)
89 'Pennine Cadet' (29a)
93 'Pennine Calypso' (29b) 🏆
92 'Pennine Cameo' (29a)
88 'Pennine Champ' (29c)
89 'Pennine Chorus' (29c)
89 'Pennine Chum' (29d)
96 'Pennine Clarion' (29c)
93 'Pennine Copper' (29c)
95 'Pennine Crimson' (29c)
96 'Pennine Cupid' (29c)
90 'Pennine Dandy' (29c)
89 'Pennine Darkeye' (29c)
89 'Pennine Dew' (29c)
89 'Pennine Dixie' (29d)
95 'Pennine Dove' (29d)
89 'Pennine Dream' (29d)
88 'Pennine Echo' (29d)
89 'Pennine Elf' (29c)
91 'Pennine Ember' (29d)
88 'Pennine Fairy' (29c)
89 'Pennine Flirt' (29b)
92 'Pennine Flute' (29f) 🏆
93 'Pennine Gambol' (29a) 🏆
89 'Pennine Gem' (29c)
89 'Pennine Globe' (29a)
88 'Pennine Gloss' (29d)
87 'Pennine Gold' (29c)
95 'Pennine Harmony' (29f)
92 'Pennine Ivory' (29d)
90 'Pennine Jewel' (29f)
93 'Pennine Jude' (29a)
95 'Pennine Lace' (29f)
92 'Pennine Lemon' (29c)
93 'Pennine Light' (29d)
92 'Pennine Lotus' (29c) 🏆
93 'Pennine Magic' (29c)
89 'Pennine Marvel' (29c)
92 'Pennine Mary' (29d)
95 'Pennine Mavis' (29f)
92 'Pennine Mist' (29c)
88 'Pennine Model' (29c)
95 'Pennine Nectar' (29c)
91 'Pennine Orchid' (29d)
88 'Pennine Penny' (29d)
91 'Pennine Pet' (29f)
92 'Pennine Phyllis' (29b) 🏆
96 'Pennine Pink' (29c)
89 'Pennine Plume' (29d)
88 'Pennine Polka' (29c)
91 'Pennine Poppet' (29a)
89 'Pennine Prince' (29c)
89 'Pennine Prize' (29a)
89 'Pennine Quiver' (29d)
93 'Pennine Rascal' (29c)
89 'Pennine Rave' (29a)
87 'Pennine Red' (29c)
96 'Pennine Robe' (29c)
89 'Pennine Rose' (29c)
90 'Pennine Salute' (29d)
88 'Pennine Sand' (29c)
96 'Pennine Serene' (29d)
95 'Pennine Sergeant' (29c)
87 'Pennine Shell' (29c)
89 'Pennine Shield' (29c)
93 'Pennine Signal' (29d) 🏆
93 'Pennine Silk' (29c)
92 'Pennine Silver' (29c)
88 'Pennine Smile' (29c)
93 'Pennine Smoke' (29d)
88 'Pennine Solo' (29d)
92 'Pennine Spice' (29c)
95 'Pennine Sugar' (29)
96 'Pennine Sun' (29d) 🏆
90 'Pennine Sweetheart' (29c)
89 'Pennine Tan' (29c)
96 'Pennine Tango' (29d)
96 'Pennine Thrill' (29d)
89 'Pennine Torch' (29d)
95 'Pennine Trill' (29c)
92 'Pennine Trinket' (29c)
88 'Pennine Tune' (29a)
94 'Pennine Twinkle' (29a)
91 'Pennine Vista' (29c)
96 'Pennine Waltz' (29c)
96 'Pennine Wax' (29)
94 'Pennine Whistle' (29f) 🏆
95 'Pennine White' (29c)
93 'Pennine Wine' (29c)
87 'Penny Lane' (25b)
89 'Peter Pan' (24b)
90 'Phil Oultram' (5b)
87 'Pilsley Queen' (29c)
96 'Pink Chempak Rose' (14b)
92 'Pink Chessington' (25a)
89 'Pink Gambit' (24a)
96 'Pink Gin' (9c)
87 'Pink Mason' (7b)
96 'Pink Sands' (9d)
96 'Pink Windermere' (24a)
95 'Plessey Snowflake' (29d)
87 'Plushred' (4b)
91 'Polar Queen' (3b)
96 'Pomander' (25b)
87 'Poppet' (28a) 🏆
90 'Port Stanley' (5b)
92 'Primrose Doreen Bircumshaw' (24a)
96 'Primrose Dorridge Crystal' (24a)
92 'Primrose Fairweather' (3b)
91 'Primrose Heide' (29c)
95 'Primrose Muriel Vipas' (25b)
87 'Primrose Olwyn' (4b)
94 'Primrose Polaris' (9c)
96 'Primrose Sam Vinter' (5a)
96 'Primrose Tennis' (25b)
93 'Primrose World of Sport' (25a)
91 'Pure Silk' (14b)
96 'Purple Gerrie Hoek'
95 'Purple Payton Lady' (29c)
92 'Purple Pennine Wine' (29c) 🏆
93 'Purple-pink'
95 'Quill Elegance' (9f)
95 'Rachel Fairweather' (3a)
91 'Ralph Lambert' (1)
90 'Rebecca Walker' (25a)
95 'Red Admiral' (6b)
92 'Red Cassandra' (5b)
89 'Red Claire Louise' (24b)
88 'Red Cropthorne'
87 'Red Fair Lady' (5a)
87 'Red Glory' (7a)
96 'Red Hoek' (29c)
95 'Red Keystone' (25a)
91 'Red Lilian Hoek' (29c)
96 'Red Margaret'
92 'Red Pennine Jade' (29d)
91 'Red Resilient' (4b)
96 'Red Windermere' (24a)
89 'Redwing' (4b)
92 'Reg Pearce' (15a)
91 'Resilient' (4b)
91 'Rheingold' (29c)
94 'Ringdove' (12a)
92 'Robert Earnshaw' (3b)
96 'Roblaze' (9c)
95 'Roblush' (9c)
95 'Rockwell' (14b)
95 'Rolass' (9c)
96 'Romark' (9c)
94 'Ron Eldred' (15a)
95 'Ron James' (4a)
87 'Ronald Rowe' (24b)
95 'Rose'
88 'Rose Madeleine' (29c)
95 'Rose Payton Lady' (29c)
96 'Rose Windermere' (24a)
87 'Rosedew' (25a) 🏆
91 'Rosette' (29c)
96 'Royal Hawaii' (9c)
90 'Rutland' (24a)
87 'Rychart' (9d)

87 'Rychoice' (9d)
90 'Ryfire' (9d)
96 'Ryred'
91 'Rystar' (9d) 🏆
89 'Sally Ball' (29a)
90 'Sally Duchess' (25a)
90 'Salmon Allouise' (25b)
87 'Salmon Chessington' (25a)
94 'Salmon Fairweather' (3b)
92 'Salmon Margaret Riley' (25a)
96 'Salmon Nu Rosemary' (9d) 🏆
90 'Salmon Orpheus' (1)
95 'Salmon Payton Dale' (29c)
92 'Salmon Pennine Gambol' (29a) 🏆
91 'Salmon Pennine Pink' (29c)
92 'Salmon Pennine Wine' (29c) 🏆
87 'Salmon Primrose'
88 'Salmon Rutland' (24a)
93 'Salmon Shirley McMinn' (15a)
95 'Salmon Talbot Parade' (29c) 🏆
94 'Salmon Tracy Waller' (24d)
96 'Salmon Woolley Pride' (24b)
95 'Sam Oldham' (24a)
93 'Samuri Bronze' (29Rub)
95 'Sandra Burch' (24b)
90 'Sassen'
96 'Satin Pink Gin' (9c)
90 'Scarlet Pennine Crimson' (29c)
92 'Schaffhausen'
94 'Seagull'
95 'Sefton' (4a)
91 'Sentry' (24b)
87 'Seychelle' (2)
90 'Sheffield Anniversary' (24a)
91 'Sheffield Centenary' (3b)
91 'Sheila Morgan' (5b)
89 'Sherwood Forester' (24a)
95 'Shirley Glorious' (24a)
89 'Shirley Imp' (3b)
94 'Shirley McMinn' (15a)
95 'Shirley Model' (3a)
95 'Shirley Primrose' (1)
91 'Shirley Sunburst' (3a)
91 'Shirley Victoria' (25a)
95 'Shoesmith's Salmon' (4a) 🏆
93 'Sid Griffiths' (29c)
87 'Sierra' (25b)
95 'Silver Gigantic' (1)
95 'Silver Jubilee' (24a)
94 'Silver Stan Addison' (5b)
91 'Skater's Waltz' (5a)
89 'Skylark'
92 'Snooker' (23b)
94 'Snow Bunting'
87 'Snow Elf' (28)
89 'Snowcap' (14a)
87 'Snowdon' (5b/9c)
94 'Snowflake' (24a)
95 'Snowshine' (5a)
90 'Soccer' (25a)
92 'Solitaire' (24a)
96 'Southway Sacy' (29d)
90 'Southway Seville' (29c)
96 'Southway Sovereign' (29d)
88 'Spartan Bronze' (29c)
96 'Spartan Crest'
96 'Spartan Fire'
95 'Spartan Flame' (29c)
96 'Spartan Legend' (29c)
96 'Spartan Leo' (29c)
95 'Spartan Orange' (29d)
96 'Spartan Pearl'
93 'Spartan Pink' (29c)
96 'Spartan Royal'
96 'Spartan Sunrise' (29c)
95 'Spartan Sunset' (29d)
93 'Spartan Wendy' (29c)
92 'Spartan Yellow' (29c)
94 'Springtime' (24a)
95 'Stan Addison' (5b)
89 'Standby' (24b)
95 'Star Centenary' (3b)
90 'Stardust' (24b)
95 'Stoika' (9d)
96 'Stuart Lawson' (5b)
91 'Stuart Shoesmith' (4b)
89 'Sun Blaze' (29a)
90 'Suncharm Orange' (22a)
96 'Suncharm White' (22a)
96 'Sunflash' (5b/12a)
95 'Sunny Margaret' (29c)
88 'Sunset Rylands Gem' (24b)
96 'Susan Dobson' (25b)
90 'Susan Freestone' (24b)
89 'Susan Pullom' (25a)
95 'Susan Riley' (23a)
96 'Sussex County' (15a)
93 'Swallow'
95 'Swalwell' (25b) 🏆
95 'Swansdown' (25b)
89 'Sydenham Girl' (24b)
95 'Talbot Bouquet' (29a) 🏆
92 'Talbot Classic' (29c)
95 'Talbot Jo' (29d)
93 'Tanaga'
94 'Tenerife' (23b)
96 'Tennis' (25b)
96 'Terry Ball' (29c)
87 'Terry Morris' (7b)
96 'Thacker's Joy' (24a)
87 'Tiara' (28a)
96 'Tim Woolman' (25a)
94 'Tinkerbelle' (24b/12a)
93 'Tolima'
89 'Tom Stillwell'
92 'Tone Dragon' (29a)
91 'Tone Girl' (29a)
89 'Tone Glow' (29a)
92 'Tone Tints' (29a)
92 'Tone Yellow' (29a)
92 'Trudie Bye' (3b)
95 'Truro' (24a)
92 'Twinkle' (28)
92 'Vanessa Lynn' (24b)
90 'Vanity Apricot'
90 'Vanity Yellow'
96 'Vedova' (6a)
93 'Vesuvius'
91 'Violet Lawson' (15a)
94 'Vision On' (24b)
91 'Vitax Victor' (25a)
89 'Wagtail' (22a)
95 'Wessex Amber' (29d)
91 'Wessex Charms' (29d)
95 'Wessex Cream' (29d)
95 'Wessex Glory' (29d)
95 'Wessex Gold' (29d)
95 'Wessex Melody' (29d)
92 'Wessex Opal' (29d)
91 'Wessex Pearl' (29d)
92 'Wessex Prince' (29d)
92 'Wessex Royal' (29d)
90 'Wessex Sentry' (29d)
90 'Wessex Shell' (29d) 🏆
96 'Wessex Solo' (29d)
95 'Wessex Tang' (29d)
92 'Wessex Tune' (29d)
96 'White Fiji' (9c)
96 'White Gerrie Hoek' (29c)
88 'White Len Futerill' (25a)
95 'White Lilac Prince' (1)
95 'White Margaret Riley' (25b)
93 'White Pamela' (29c)
94 'White Pearl Celebration' (24a)
90 'White Sally Duchess' (25a)
96 'Winchcombe' (29c)
89 'Woody's Choice' (5b)
96 'Woolley Pride' (14b)
92 'Woolman's Celebration' (23b)
96 'Woolman's Century' (1)
95 'Woolman's Giant'' (14a)
95 'Woolman's Glory' (7a)
95 'Woolman's Highlight' (3b)
95 'Woolman's Queen' (24a)
89 'Worcester' (14b)
91 'Xenia Noelle' (4b)
95 'Yellow Balcombe Perfection' (5a)
90 'Yellow Broadway Sovereign' (29c)
91 'Yellow Cassandra' (15b)
89 'Yellow Chessington' (25a)
92 'Yellow Cornish' (25b)
87 'Yellow Cricket' (25b)
93 'Yellow Dorridge Crown' (25b)
94 'Yellow Duke' (1)
96 'Yellow Egret' (23b)
88 'Yellow Emilia' (29c)
92 'Yellow Fair Lady' (5a)
95 'Yellow Fairweather' (3b)
92 'Yellow Jack Wood' (25a)
89 'Yellow Jemma Wilson' (23b)
88 'Yellow Juweeltje'
96 'Yellow Margaret Riley' (25b)
90 'Yellow Pamela' (29c)
91 'Yellow Pennine Pink' (29c)
96 'Yellow Pinocchio' (29c)
94 'Yellow Polaris' (9c)
91 'Yellow Resilient' (5b)
87 'Yellow Sam Vinter' (5a)
92 'Yellow Shirley Imp' (3b)
96 'Yellow Tennis' (25b)
92 'Yellow Vitax Victor' (25a)
94 'Yellowmoor' (25b)
89 'Yorkshire Television' (5a)
96 ***zawadskii*** var. ***latilobum***

DERMATOBOTRYS

93 ***saundersii***

DESCHAMPSIA

89 ***cespitosa*** 'Tardiflora'
89 – 'Tauträger'
96 ***flexuosa*** 'Peter David'

DESMOSCHOENUS

95 ***spiralis***

DEUTZIA

95 ***discolor*** 'Major'
94 ***hookeriana*** KW 6393
91 x ***hybrida*** 'Reuthe's Pink'
95 ***longifolia***
88 – 'Vilmoriniae'
95 x ***magnifica*** 'Nancy'
93 – 'Staphyleoides'
91 x ***maliflora***
90 – 'Avalanche'
94 ***ningpoensis*** 'Pink Charm'
92 x ***rosea*** 'Rosea'
96 ***scabra*** 'Watereri'
95 ***staminea***

DIANELLA

96 ***revoluta*** var. ***revoluta***

DIANTHUS

92 'Achievement' (p)
93 'Ada Wood' (pf)
96 'Albus'
95 'Alder House' (p)
95 'Aldersey Rose' (p)
95 'Alfred Galbally' (b)
89 'Alfriston' (b) 🏆
96 'Alick Sparkes' (pf)
92 'Allspice Sport' (p)
89 ***alpinus*** 'Ascreavie Form'
90 – x ***callizonus***
91 – 'Cherry Beauty'
94 – Correvon's form
95 – 'Drake's Red'
89 – 'Ruby Venus'
95 – salmon
90 ***angulatus***
91 'Anna' (pf)
94 'Anna Wyatt' (p)
89 'Anne Jones' (b)
95 'Ann's Lass' (pf)
95 'Anthony' (p)
89 'Apollo' (b)
94 'Apricale' (pf)
93 'Arbel' (pf)
94 'Ariel' (p)
93 x ***arvernensis*** 'Albus'
92 'Autumn Glory' (b)
88 'Avoca Purple' (p)

95 'Bailey's Splendour' (pf)
89 'Barbara Norton' (p)
96 ***barbatus albus***
89 'Barton's Pink' (p)
96 'Bath's Pink'
95 'Becky's Choice' (p)
87 'Beryl Giles' (pf)
95 'Betty Webber' (p)
91 ***biflorus***
95 'Blaby Joy'
92 Black and White Minstrels Group
92 'Bookham Beau' (b)
93 'Bookham Heroine' (b)
92 'Bookham Prince' (b)
96 'Brecas' (pf)
89 'Bressingham Pink' (p)
96 'Bridesmaid' (p)
89 'Brilliance' (p)
96 'Brymos' (p)
95 'Bryony Lisa' (b) 🏆
91 'Buckfast Abbey' (p)
90 ***carthusianorum*** Atrorubens Group
94 – var. ***humilis***
91 – 'Nanus'
91 'Castleroyal Princess' (p)
92 'Celestial' (b)
94 'Chelsea Pink' (p)
87 'Cherry Heldenbrau' (pf)
89 'Cherry Pie' (p)
95 'Christopher Tautz' (b) 🏆
95 'Cindy' (p)
94 'Clara Lucinda' (pf)
91 'Clarabelle' (b)
94 'Clara's Choice' (pf)
95 'Clara's Glow' (pf)
91 'Coleton Fishacre'
96 'Cornish Snow' (p)
92 'Countess of Lonsdale' (b)
89 'Cranborne Seedling' (p)
89 'Crimson Clove' (p)
89 'Crimson Treasure' (p)
93 ***cruentus***
90 'Crusader' (b)
92 'Dainty' (b)
96 'Dainty Dance'
95 'Daisy Hill Scarlet' (b)
95 'Dark Pierrot' (pf)
94 'Dawn' (pf)
92 'Delicata'
91 ***deltoides*** 'Hilltop Star'
96 – red
94 – 'Samos'
89 – 'Steriker' (p)
92 – 'Vampir'
96 – 'Wisley Variety'
95 – 'Zwolle'
95 'Devon Blossom' (p)
96 'Devon Pink Pearl'
87 'Diane Marie' (pf)
89 'Dianne' (pf)
93 'Dianne Hewins' (pf)
89 'Dicker Clove' (b)
95 'Dinkirk Spirit' (pf)
90 'Doctor Danger'
88 'Donizetti' (p)
91 'Dot Clark' (b)
90 'Double Devon' (p)
91 'Douglas Fancy' (b)
93 'Downs Glory' (b)
89 'Downs Souvenir' (b)
89 'Downs Unique' (b)
96 'Duchess of Fife' (p)
95 'Duke of Argyll'
92 'Dusty Sim' (pf)
94 ***echiniformis***
96 'Edan Lady' (pf)
89 'Edenside Glory' (b)
96 'Edith Johnson' (pf)
96 'Edward' (p)
89 'Eileen Neal' (b)
95 'Elizabeth Anne' (pf)
95 'Eliza's Choice'
95 'Emma Sarah' (b)
95 ***eretmopetalus***
96 'Esperance' (pf)
92 'Eve' (p)
96 'Faith Raven' (p)
91 'Fancy Monarch' (b)
96 'Fascination' (b)
94 'Fashino' (pf)
94 'Favourite Lady' (p)
89 'Fay' (p)
95 ***ferrugineus***
90 'Firefly' (b)
96 'Firewitch'
89 'Flanders' (b) 🏆
91 'Fragrans' (pf)
95 'Fragrant Lace' (p)
92 'Fred Sutton' (pf)
89 'Gaiety' (p)
95 Gala (pf)
88 'George Vernon' (pf)
95 'Gertrude' (p)
89 'Glenda' (p)
96 'Gloriosa' (p)
89 'Glory'
89 'Goblin' (p)
96 'Gold Dust'
89 'Grace How' (b)
90 'Grace Mather' (p)
91 ***gracilis***
87 'Grandad' (p)
95 ***gratianopolitanus*** 'Albus'
90 – 'Compactus Eydangeri' (p)
90 – × ***subacaulis***
91 'Green Lanes' (p)
89 'Grey Dove' (b)
92 'Greystone' (b)
89 'Grome' (p)
94 'Gypsy Lass'
92 'Hambledon' (p)
95 'Happiness' (b)
87 'Hardwicke's Pink' (p)
93 'Harvest Moon' (pf)
96 'Heath' (b)
89 'Heldenbrau' (pf)
89 'Helen Keates' (b)
89 'Helga' (p)
95 'Henry of Essex' (p)
94 'Highland Chieftain' (p)
89 'Highland Gem' (p)
96 'Hollycroft Fragrance' (p)
92 'Hollycroft Rose' (p)
93 'Horton'
91 'Hound Tor'
88 'Houston House' (p)
96 'Iceberg' (p)
96 'Imperial Clove' (b)
94 ***integer*** subsp. ***minutiflorus***
96 'Ipswich Crimson' (p)
90 'Irish Pink' (p)
92 'Isobel Templeton' (b)
88 'Jack Wood' (pf)
89 'Jack's Lass' (pf)
90 'Jacqueline's Delight' (p)
94 'Jaffa' (pf)
95 'James' (pf)
89 'Jane Bowen' (p)
91 'Janet' (p)
92 'Jester' (p)
95 'Jewel'
93 'Joanne Taylor' (pf)
89 'John Malcolm' (p)
89 'Katy' (b)
91 'Kitty Jay'
92 'Kobusa' (pf)
92 'Laddie Sim' (pf)
94 'Lady Diana' (p)
92 'Lancing Lass' (p)
93 'Le Rêve' (pf)
94 'Leatham Pastel' (pf)
92 'Lena' (pf)
93 'Lilian' (p)
89 'Lily Lesurf' (b)
89 'Little Beauty' (pf)
93 'Little Gem' (pf)
95 'Lord Chatham' (b)
96 'Lord Grey' (b)
89 'Lord Nuffield' (b)
93 'Louise's Choice' (p) 🏆
95 'Maggie' (p)
89 'Maisie Neal' (b) 🏆
89 'Margaret Curtis' (p)
92 'Mark' (p)
96 'Martin Nest'
92 'Mary Livingstone' (b)
92 'Mary Murray' (b)
92 'Maurice Prichard' (p)
94 'May Jones' (p)
92 'Melody' (pf)
89 'Messines White' (p)
96 'Microchip' (p)
94 'Milley' (p)
96 'Miss Sinkins' (p)
95 ***monspessulanus*** subsp. ***sternbergii***
89 'Mrs Blarney's Old Pink' (p)
88 'Mrs Dunlop's Old Pink'
96 'Muriel Wilson' (pf)
91 'Murton' (p)
96 'Nancy Lindsay' (p)
94 'Neptune' (pf)
95 'Nicola Jane Mannion' (pf)
95 'Nina' (pf)
91 'Nora Urling Clark' (pf)
96 'Norman Hayward' (b)
96 'Oakfield Clove' (b)
92 'Oakwood Bill Ballinger' (p)
95 'Oakwood Billy Boole' (p)
87 'Oakwood Dainty' (p)
89 'Oakwood Dorothy' (p)
92 'Oakwood Sparkler' (p)
93 'Old Fringed Pink' (p)
96 'Old Irish' (p)
96 'Old Red Clove' (p)
89 'Orchid Lace' (p,a)
92 'Pallas' (b)
91 ***pavonius albus***
89 ***pavonius*** 'Roaschia'
89 'Peter Adamson' (b)
89 'Peter Wood' (b) 🏆
89 'Petula' (p)
93 'Phyllis Marshall' (b)
96 'Picture' (b)
91 'Pink Baby' (p)
89 'Pink Bouquet' (p)
90 'Pink Delight' (p)
96 'Pink Devon Pearl'
94 'Pink Galil' (pf)
90 'Plum Diadem' (p)
89 'Pluto' (p)
89 'Portrait Sim' (pf)
92 'Portsdown Sunset' (b)
92 'Prichard's Variety' (p)
88 'Pride of Ayrshire' (p)
94 'Prince of Wales'
96 'Pummelchen' (p)
94 ***pungens***
95 'Queen's Reward' (pf)
89 'Raspberry Ripple' (p)
93 'Red Denim' (p)
92 ***repens***
96 'Rhian's Choice' (p) 🏆
89 'Richard Pollak' (b)
96 'Robert Allwood' (pf)
89 'Robert Douglas' (b)
89 'Robert Smith' (b)
92 'Rose Bradwardine' (b)
93 'Ruffles' (p)
93 'Rupert Lambert'
95 'Ruth' (p)
96 'Sabra' (pf)
89 'Sacha' (pf)
92 'Sally's Mauve'
89 'Salmon Fragrant Ann' (p)
89 'Salmon Queen' (b)
93 'Samantha Holtom' (pf)
92 'Sandra' (p)
95 'Scaynes Hill' (p)
95 'Sean Hitchcock' (b)
91 'Sevilla' (pf)
92 'Shaston Delight' (b)
89 'Shaston Supreme' (b)
94 'Shegange' (pf)
89 'Sheila Short' (pf)
90 'Sheila Weir' (b)
93 'Sheila's Choice' (p) 🏆
94 'Shocking Pink Sim' (pf)
89 'Show Ideal' (p)
89 'Shrimp' (b)
94 'Snowflake' (p)
96 'Solway Sovereign' (pf)
94 'Sonata' (p)
93 sp. NS 643
93 'Spark' (p)
92 ***spiculifolius***
96 'Spindrift' (b)
95 'Spinfield Happiness' (b) 🏆
93 'Spotty' (p)
92 'Sprite' (b)
93 ***subacaulis*** subsp. ***brachyanthus***
92 'Surrey Clove' (b)
92 'Sway Breeze' (p)
95 'Sway Lass' (p)
89 'Syston Beauty' (p)
95 'Tamsin Fifield' (b) 🏆
94 'Taunton' (p)
93 ***tianschanicus***
91 'Timothy' (p)
91 'Tom Bradshaw' (pf)
89 'Tom Welborn' (p)
89 'Tony Cutler' (b)

95 'Tony Langford' (pf)
93 'Trisha's Choice' (p)
91 'Truly Yours' (pf)
93 'Valerie' (p)
92 'Vanda' (p)
93 'Victoria' (p)
96 'Violet Carson' (b)
92 'Water Nymph' (b)
91 'Welland' (p)
95 'Wells-next-the-Sea' (p)
88 'Welwyn' (p)
96 'Whatfield Polly Anne' (p)
91 'White Bouquet' (p)
92 'William Newell' (b)
89 'William of Essex' (p)
94 'Winnie Lesurf' (b)
89 'Wisp' (p)
90 ***xylorrizus***
94 'Young Marie' (pf)
89 'Zephyr' (b)
96 'Zoe's Choice' (p)

DIASCIA
95 'Blue Mist'
91 ***capensis***
95 'Christine'
96 'Coral Cloud'
96 ***denticulata***
95 'Katherine Sharman' (v)
94 ***purpurea***
94 ***rigescens*** 'Forge Cottage'
92 – 'Variegata'
92 ***stricta***

DICENTRA
95 'Adrian Bloom Variegated'
96 'Cherub'
94 ***formosa*** 'Paramount'
92 – 'Sweetheart'
95 'Paramount'
91 ***pauciflora***
95 ***peregrina alba***
94 'Silver Beads'
95 ***torulosa***
96 – CLD 685
95 'Tsuneshige Rokujo'
96 ***uniflora***

DICHORISANDRA
94 ***thyrsiflora***

DICKSONIA
96 ***herbertii***
95 ***lanata***
96 ***youngiae***

DICOMA
92 ***zeyheri***

DIEFFENBACHIA
90 x ***bausei*** (v)
95 'Camille' (v)
95 'Candida' (v)
95 'Compacta' (v)
90 'Janet Weidner' (v)
95 'Jeanette' (v)
95 'Jupiter' (v)
95 'Mars' (v)
95 'Neptune' (v)
95 'Saturnus' (v)
95 'Schott Gitte' (v)
95 ***seguine*** 'Amoena' (v)
95 – 'Carina' (v)
90 – 'Exotica' (v)
90 – 'Jenmanii' (v)
95 – 'Katherine' (v)
95 – 'Tropic Snow' (v)
95 'Triumph' (v)
95 'Tropic Sun' (v)
95 'Tropic White' (v)
95 'Veerie' (v)
90 'Wilson's Delight' (v)

DIERAMA
96 ***ambiguum***
96 'Coral Pink'
96 ***luteoalbidum*** CD&R 1025
95 ***ochroleucum***
94 ***pulcherrimum*** 'Peregrine'
96 sp. CD&R 96

DIGITALIS
96 cream hybrids
89 ***lutea*** 'Sarah'
96 ***nervosa***
94 ***obscura*** dwarf form
96 – JCA 409.401
96 ***purpurea*** 'Campanulata'
95 ***stewartii***

DIONYSIA
90 ***bryoides***
90 ***curviflora***
90 ***denticulata***
90 ***janthina***
90 ***michauxii***
90 ***revoluta***
90 – subsp. ***canescens***
96 ***tapetodes*** 'Peter Edwards' (Hewer 1164)

DIOSCOREA
93 ***japonica***

DIOSPYROS
87 ***glaucifolia***

DIPCADI
94 ***fulvum***

DIPLAZIUM
93 ***japonicum***

DIPSACUS
91 ***laciniatus***

DISCARIA
90 ***toumatou***

DISPORUM
95 ***sessile***
88 – var. ***yakushimense***
95 ***trachycarpum***

DISTYLIUM
95 ***racemosum tutcheri***

DIURIS
96 ***longifolia***

DODECADENIA
95 ***grandiflora***

DODECATHEON
96 ***alpinum*** JCA 9542
91 ***alpinum purpureum***
96 ***dentatum*** subsp. ***dentatum***
95 ***hendersonii*** 'Inverleith' 🏆
95 x ***lemoinei***
94 ***meadia*** 'Alpenglow'
93 – 'Queen Victoria'
96 – 'Rose Farben'
95 – 'Splendidum'
96 ***pulchellum*** subsp. ***macrocarpum***
92 – 'Sooke's Variety'

DORONICUM
96 ***catatactarum***
96 ***orientale*** 'Goldzwerg'
95 ***plantagineum***

DORYANTHES
91 ***excelsa***

DRABA
88 ***alpina***
95 ***arabisans*** var. ***canadensis***
92 ***asprella***
93 ***athoa***
94 ***aurea*** var. ***leiocarpa***
94 ***balcanica***
91 ***borealis***
96 ***breweri***
95 ***bruniifolia*** subsp. ***heterocoma*** var. ***nana***
96 – subsp. ***olympica***
94 ***cappadocica*** JCA 419.500
91 ***carinthiaca***
96 ***caucasica***
94 ***crassifolia***
88 ***fladnizensis***
93 ***glabella***
95 ***hispanica*** var. ***brevistyla***
93 – var. ***segurensis***
96 ***igarishii***
96 ***incerta***
96 ***lasiocarpa*** Compacta Group
92 ***mollissima*** x ***longisiliqua***
94 ***norvegica***
93 ***oreades***
90 ***oreibata***
91 ***paysonii*** var. ***paysonii***
94 ***rigida*** var. ***rigida***
90 ***setosa***
91 ***sibirica***
94 ***sierrae***
96 sp. ACE 1382
96 sp. from Mt Bross
96 sp. JHH 9309139
91 ***stellata***

DRACAENA
96 ***cincta*** 'Tricolor' (v)
96 ***draco***
90 ***fragrans*** (Compacta Group) 'Compacta'
90 – 'Lindenii'
95 – 'Warneckei' 🏆
90 ***reflexa***
95 – 'Variegata' 🏆
96 ***surculosa*** 'Florida Beauty' ***surculosa*** (v)
96 – 'Wit' (v)

DRACOCEPHALUM
94 ***bullatum***
96 aff. ***forrestii*** ACE 2465
90 ***heterophyllum***
89 ***integrifolium***
96 ***rupestre***
96 sp. CLD 551

DRACOPHYLLUM
91 ***fiordense***
92 ***pronum***

DREGEA
94 ***sinensis*** 'Variegata'

DREPANOSTACHYUM
96 ***khasianum***

DRIMYS
95 ***winteri*** 'Glauca'

DROSANTHEMUM
96 ***speciosum***

DROSERA
94 x ***beleziana***
94 ***bicolor***
95 ***binata*** T form
94 ***burmannii***
94 ***callistos***
94 ***closterostigma***
96 ***dilatatopetiolaris***
95 ***erythrogyne***
96 ***falconeri***
96 ***fulva***
93 ***heloides***
96 ***indica***
96 ***lanata***
94 ***leucoblasta***
94 ***lovelliae***
95 ***macrantha*** subsp. ***eremaea***
94 ***macrophylla***
95 ***macrophylla marchantii***
95 ***macrophylla monantha***
94 x ***nagamotoi*** 'Nagamoto'
94 – 'Watari'
94 ***natalensis***
95 ***neesii*** subsp. ***neesii***
96 ***nitidula***
94 x ***obovata***
94 ***occindentalis***
96 ***ordensis***
94 ***oreopodion***
93 ***paleacea***
94 ***prostratoscaposa***
96 ***pygmaea***
95 ***radicans***
94 ***scorpioides***
93 ***subhirtella subhirtella***
93 ***whittakeri***

DRYANDRA
93 ***obtusa***
94 ***polycephala***
94 ***pteridifolia***

DRYAS
89 ***octopetala*** var. ***argentea***

DRYOPTERIS
94 ***affinis*** 'Crispa Barnes'
93 – 'Crispa Cristata'
94 – 'Cristata Ramosissima Wright'
96 – 'Revoluta'
95 ***aitoniana***
95 ***buschiana***
96 ***carthusiana*** x ***oreades***
96 ***cristata***
94 ***dilatata*** 'Crispa'
96 – 'Jimmy Dyce'
96 ***filix-mas*** 'Decomposita'
93 – Grandiceps Group
95 ***fuscipes***
93 ***lepidopoda***
94 ***stenolepis***
93 ***sublacera***

DRYPIS
96 ***spinosa***
DUDLEYA
91 ***brittonii***
93 ***cymosa***
96 – JCA 11777
DUMORTIERA
96 ***hirsuta***
DYCKIA
96 ***fosteriana***
94 ***remotiflora***
DYSCHORISTE
94 ***rogersii***
ECHINACEA
95 ***laevigata***
96 ***purpurea*** dark stemmed form
ECHINOPS
96 ***chantavicus***
96 ***giganteus***
95 ***humilis***
95 ***niveus***
95 ***ritro*** Linnaeus 'Charlotte'
95 – Linnaeus ACL 149/75
91 ***tournefortii*** 'Albus'
ECHIUM
96 ***pininana* x *wildpretii***
EDRAIANTHUS
95 ***dalmaticus albus***
94 ***graminifolius*** subsp. ***niveus***
95 – NS 785
95 ***serpyllifolius*** 'Major'
95 ***tenuifolius***
EHRETIA
96 ***dicksonii***
ELAEAGNUS
90 ***angustifolia*** var. ***orientalis***
88 x ***ebbingei*** 'Tricolor' (v)
ELAEOCARPUS
89 ***decipiens***
91 ***hookerianus***
ELATOSTEMA
95 ***carneum***
ELEUTHEROCOCCUS
89 ***henryi***
ELLIOTTIA
93 ***pyroliflora***
89 ***racemosa***
ELMERA
96 ***racemosa***
ELODEA
93 ***callitrichoides***
ELYMUS
91 ***interruptus***
94 ***nutans***
ELYTROPUS
96 ***chilensis***
EMILIA
93 ***coccinea***
EMINIUM
94 ***lehmannii***
96 ***rauwolffii***
91 ***stipitatum***
EMMENOPTERYS
95 ***henryi***
EMPETRUM
88 ***nigrum*** 'Compactum'
88 – subsp. ***hermaphroditum***
88 – 'Smaragd'
96 ***rubrum***
96 – 'Tomentosum'
ENCEPHALARTOS
95 ***lebomboensis***
ENGELMANNIA
90 ***pinnatifida***
ENKIANTHUS
93 ***campanulatus*** Nymans form
90 ***cernuus***
89 ***serrulatus***
93 ***tectus***
EPACRIS
93 ***impressa***
90 ***pauciflora***
EPHEDRA
96 ***glauca***
96 ***intermedia***
95 sp. RB 94052
EPIDENDRUM
94 ***ibaguense***
EPILOBIUM
94 ***arizonicum*** K 92.460
95 ***brunnescens***
95 ***caucasicum***
90 ***glabellum*** 'Roseum'
89 ***gunnianum***
94 ***rostratum***
EPIMEDIUM
90 ***grandiflorum*** 'Rose Glow'
91 – 'White Beauty'
96 ***sempervirens***
EPIPREMNUM
95 ***pinnatum*** 'Aztec' ♀
EQUISETUM
94 ***ramosissimum***
89 ***telmateia***
ERANTHIS
94 ***hyemalis*** 'Flore Pleno'
93 ***longistipitata***
EREMAEA
91 ***purpurea***
EREMURUS
92 Himrob Group
ERICA
88 ***andevalensis***
94 ***australis aragonensis***
92 ***baccans***
96 ***carnea*** 'Kramer's Rubin'
88 – 'Mayfair White'
88 – 'Mr Reeves'
92 – 'Netherfield Orange'
96 – Red Jewel = 'Rotes Juwel'
92 – 'Sneznick'
88 – 'Winter Red'
96 – 'Winter Sports'
93 ***cerinthoides***
93 ***ciliaris***
96 – 'Egdon Heath'
93 ***cinerea***
89 – 'Creel'
90 – 'Electra'
89 – 'Hutton Pentreath'
87 – 'Lankidden'
90 – 'Lilian Martin'
91 – 'Pink Lace'
93 ***colorans***
93 ***conspicua***
94 ***densifolia***
95 ***erigena*** 'Mrs Parris' Red'
93 ***glandulosa***
93 ***gracilis*** red
96 x ***griffithsii*** 'Ashlea Gold'
96 x ***hiemalis*** 'Dusky Maid'
93 – 'Limelight'
88 ***maderensis***
96 ***manipuliflora*** subsp. ***anthura*** 'Waterfall'
93 ***mauritanica***
93 ***mollis***
91 ***multiflora***
88 ***oatesii***
88 ***perlata***
93 ***persoluta***
93 ***perspicua***
90 ***scoparia***
93 – subsp. ***platycodon*** 'Lionel Woolner'
93 ***sessiliflora***
95 ***subdivaricata***
88 ***taxifolia***
93 ***transparens***
94 ***vagans*** f. ***alba***
88 – 'Bianca'
88 – 'Elegant Spike'
88 ***vestita***
91 x ***watsonii***
92 x ***williamsii***

ERIGERON
91 ***allocatus***
93 ***annuus***
95 'Birch Hybrid'
96 ***borealis*** Arctic form
92 ***caespitosus***
91 ***chrysopsidis*** var. ***brevifolius***
96 ***compositus*** JCA 8911
94 – 'Lavender Dwarf'
92 ***delicatus***
95 'Doctor Worth'
95 ***elegantulus***
96 'Festivity'
96 'Gaiety'
96 ***glabellum yukonensis***
95 ***glabellus***
91 ***glaucus*** 'Sennen'
93 'Goliath'
93 'H.E. Beale'
91 ***humilis***
95 ***hyssopifolius***
89 ***myosotis***
93 'Nachthimmel'
93 'Pamela'
96 'Profusion'
95 ***pulchellus*** 'Meadow Muffin'
95 ***pumilus intermedius***
93 ***radicatus***
88 ***roylei***
93 ***rydbergii***
96 'Sincerity'
96 'Snow Queen'
89 ***speciosus*** 'Roseus'
94 ***thunbergii***
92 'Viridis'
ERINUS
94 ***alpinus*** dark purple
92 – 'Roseus'
ERIOGONUM
96 ***argophyllum***
96 ***breedlovei***
91 ***flavum*** var. ***xanthum***
89 ***giganteum***
94 ***gracilipes*** JCA 11718
94 ***kelloggii***
93 ***kennedyi***
90 – subsp. ***gracilipes***
95 ***latifolium***
94 ***lobbii*** K 92.214
95 – var. ***robustum***
93 ***multiceps***
93 ***ovalifolium*** var. ***depressum***
96 – var. ***nivale***
94 ***soredium***
95 ***umbellatum*** 'Kannah Creek'
94 ***ursinum*** var. ***nervulosum***
96 ***wrightii***
95 – subsp. ***wrightii*** K 92.224
ERIOPHORUM
90 ***brachyantherum***
91 ***scheuchzeri***
ERIOPHYLLUM
96 ***lanatum achilleifolium***
93 ***lanatum*** var. ***integrifolium***
ERITRICHIUM
96 ***howardii***
ERODIUM
95 ***chium*** Guitt 88042202
95 ***ciconium*** Guitt 85051602
96 ***corsicum*** dark pink
92 'Crimson Glow'
94 x ***lindavicum***
94 ***malviflorum***
93 ***petraeum*** 'Burgundy'
94 – hybrids
92 – subsp. ***petraeum***
92 ***sibthorpianum***
95 x ***variabile*** dwarf white
ERYNGIUM
95 x ***allionii*** ♀
93 ***alpinum*** 'Violet Lace'
96 ***aquifolium***
95 ***billardierei***
92 'Calypso' (v)
95 ***humile*** JCA 13912
96 'Jos Eijking'
94 ***spinalba*** 'Silbermannstreu'
87 x ***zabelii*** 'Spring Hills'
ERYSIMUM
94 ***arenicola***
91 ***bicolor***
94 ***capitatum capitatum***
94 ***carniolicum***
95 'Changeling'
96 ***cheiri*** 'Chevithorne'

94 – 'Malmesbury' (v)
96 'Devon Cream'
96 'Emm's Variety'
94 'New Zealand Limelight'
93 'Newark Park'
92 ***nivale***
89 ***odoratum***
94 ***pusillum*** NS 727

ERYTHRINA
96 ***caffra***
96 ***corallodendron***
95 ***herbacea***
96 ***livingstoneana***

ERYTHRONIUM
93 ***dens-canis*** 'Pajares Giant'
92 ***grandiflorum*** f. ***chrysandrum***
92 – var. ***pallidum***
95 ***hendersonii*** × ***citrinum***
95 ***idahoense***
92 ***mesochoreum***
92 'Miss Jessopp'
95 ***montanum***
96 ***revolutum*** 'Rose Beauty'
96 ***umbilicatum***

ESCALLONIA
92 'Bantry Bay'
96 'Compacta Coccinea'
93 'Donard Gem'
92 'Donard Glory'
95 'Donard Scarlet'
95 'Donard White'
95 'Glasnevin Hybrid'
92 'Greenway'
95 'Lanarth Hybrid'
90 'Lord Headfort's Seedling'
95 ***pulverulenta***
90 'Red Guard'
95 'Rose Queen'
95 ***rubra***
95 – 'Hybrida'
90 – var. ***macrantha*** 'Sanguinea'
95 'Saint Keverne'
96 × ***stricta*** 'Harold Comber'
90 'William Watson'
90 'Wintonensis'

EUCALYPTUS
94 ***acaciiformis***
92 ***alpina***
95 ***barberi***
92 ***bridgesiana***
94 ***foecunda***
95 ***globulus*** subsp. ***bicostata***
88 ***maculata***
92 ***moorei***
94 ***muelleriana***
89 ***populnea***
88 ***preissiana***
96 ***radiata***

EUCODONIA
92 ***ehrenbergii***
92 ***verticillata***

EUCOMIS
96 ***comosa*** purple-leaved
95 'Frank Lawley'

EUCROSIA
94 ***bicolor***

EUCRYPHIA
91 × ***hillieri***

EUGENIA
94 ***smithii***
93 ***uniflora***

EUONYMUS
92 ***americanus***
93 ***bungeanus*** var. ***semipersistens***
88 × ***buxifolius*** 'Nanus'
92 ***europaeus*** 'Brilliant'
90 – 'Chrysophyllus'
96 ***fortunei***
92 – 'Carrierei'
95 – 'Dart's Cardinal'
90 – 'Dart's Covergirl'
92 – 'Emerald Charm'
91 – 'Sarcoxie'
96 – 'Variegatus' EM '85
89 ***hamiltonianus maackii***
95 ***hamiltonianus*** subsp. ***sieboldianus*** Semiexsertus Group
94 ***japonicus*** 'Macrophyllus'
96 – 'Silver King'
95 – 'Viridivariegatus'
93 ***wilsonii***

EUPATORIUM
95 ***coelestinum*** forms
96 ***fortunei***
95 ***glechonophyllum***
95 ***hildalgense***
94 ***xylorhizum*** JJH 95059

EUPHORBIA
95 ***britzensis***
95 ***characias*** subsp. ***characias*** 'Little Court'
96 – 'Whistleberry Gold'
96 – 'Whistleberry Jade'
95 – subsp. ***wulfenii*** 'Jayne's Golden Giant'
96 – – 'Red House'
95 – – Ulverscroft form
96 ***cyparissias*** 'Ashfield'
94 ***franchetii***
90 'Goldburst'
91 ***marginata***
89 ***millotii***
95 ***nereidum***
95 ***palustris*** 'Zauberflöte'
96 ***polychroma*** 'Vic's Purple'
92 ***regis-jubae***
91 ***tenuissima***

EURYOPS
92 ***linearis***
95 ***tenuissimus***

EVOLVULUS
91 ***passerinoides***
95 ***pilosus***

EXOCHORDA
93 × ***macrantha*** 'Irish Pearl'

FABIANA
96 ***imbricata alba***

FAGUS
90 × ***moesiaca***
96 ***sylvatica*** Cuprea Group
92 – f. ***latifolia***
95 – 'Nana'
95 – f. ***tortuosa***
93 – 'Trompenburg'
92 – var. ***variegata***

FALLUGIA
89 ***paradoxa***

FARGESIA
89 ***nitida*** 'Chennevières'

FELICIA
94 ***amelloides*** 'Blue Eyes'
96 – 'Santa Anita Variegated' 🏆
94 ***echinata***
95 ***filifolia*** blue
95 – pink
95 – white

FERULA
91 ***communis*** Purpurea Group

FESTUCA
93 ***glauca*** 'Blausilber'
94 ***ochroleuca***
94 ***rubra*** 'Variegata'
93 ***vivipara glauca***

FICUS
94 ***aspera***
96 ***benjamina*** 'Flandriana'
96 – 'Golden Princess'
96 – 'Green Gem'
94 ***capensis***
93 ***elastica*** 'Belgica'
91 – 'Schrijveriana' (v) 🏆
96 – 'Zulu Shield'
90 ***natalensis*** subsp. ***leprieurii***
96 ***palmata***
90 ***religiosa***
94 ***rubiginosa*** 🏆
93 – 'Variegata'

FILIPENDULA
95 ***multijuga*** B&SWJ 789
94 ***palmata*** miniature
94 ***purpurea splendens***
95 sp. from Chirisan, B&SWJ 605
95 sp. from Odesan, B&SWJ 930

FITTONIA
96 ***albivenis*** Argyroneura Group 🏆
95 – (Argyroneura Group) 'Nana'
96 – Verschaffeltii Group 🏆

FOENICULUM
93 ***vulgare*** black

FORSYTHIA
94 ***europaea***
94 × ***intermedia***
96 – Goldzauber
94 – 'Mertensiana'
89 – 'Phyllis'
94 – 'Vitellina'
94 ***japonica*** var. ***saxatilis***
95 ***suspensa*** 'Hewitt's Gold'

94 – var. ***sieboldii***

FORTUNEARIA
91 ***sinensis***

FRAGARIA
95 × ***ananassa*** 'Cambridge Rival' (F)
92 – 'Cantata' (F)
96 – 'Domanil' (F)
92 – 'Gento' (F)
91 – 'Grandee'
94 – 'Harvester'
91 – 'Hedley'
95 – 'Idil' (F)
96 – 'Pantagruella' (F)
92 – 'Rabunda' (F)
91 – 'Sweetheart'
96 – 'Talisman' (F)
91 – 'Tantallon'
96 – 'Tenira' (F)
95 ***nipponica***
92 ***vesca*** 'Delicious' (F)
88 – 'Reine des Vallées'

FRASERA
92 ***speciosa***

FRAXINUS
89 ***bungeana***
87 ***cuspidata***
92 ***dipetala***
96 ***excelsior*** 'Altena'
89 – 'Argenteovariegata'
96 – 'Atlas'
95 – 'Eureka'
95 ***lanuginosa*** Koidz 0131
95 ***latifolia***
94 ***mandshurica***
96 ***ornus*** 'Fastigiata Pyramidalis'
94 – 'Messek'
90 ***paxiana***
89 ***pennsylvanica*** var. ***subintegerrima***
94 ***sogdiana*** Potamophila Group

FREESIA
96 'Ballerina'
96 'Melanie' (d)
96 'Oberon'
96 'Royal Blue'
96 'Royal Gold'

FREMONTODENDRON
94 'Ken Taylor'
93 'San Gabriel'

FREYLINIA
94 ***rosmarinifolia***

FRITILLARIA
95 ***affinis*** var. ***tristulis***
93 ***agrestis***
95 ***alfredae*** subsp. ***glaucoviridis***
88 – subsp. ***platyptera***
95 × ***argolica***
89 ***ariana***
95 ***camschatcensis*** green
95 ***camschatcensis multiflora***
93 ***camschatcensis*** yellow
90 ***caucasica caucasica***
93 ***cirrhosa***
95 ***collina***
94 ***drenovskyi***
91 ***eduardii***
96 ***epirotica***

91 ***gibbosa***
94 ***imperialis*** 'Argenteovariegata'
93 – 'Blom's Orange Perfection'
91 ***japonica***
94 ***kotschyana***
89 ***meleagris*** 'Poseidon'
89 – 'Purple King'
89 – 'Saturnus'
96 ***minuta***
92 ***olgae***
92 ***orientalis***
93 ***persica*** 'Senkoy'
95 ***pontica*** Pras 1276
95 ***tuntasia***
95 ***walujewii***

FUCHSIA
93 'A 1'
90 'Aad Franck'
96 'Abbey Kilner'
89 'Aber Falls'
89 'Abt. Koloman Holzinger'
93 'Abundance'
96 'Achilles'
93 'Admiration'
89 'Airball'
92 'Al Stettler'
90 'Aladna's Marina'
96 'Aladna's Rosy'
91 'Alan's Joy'
96 'Albert H'
90 'Albertina'
94 'Albion'
91 'Alexandra Dyos'
96 'Alice Sweetapple'
93 'Alice Topliss'
93 'Allegra'
93 'Alsa Garnett'
91 'Althea Green'
96 'Altmark'
94 'Amber Supreme'
90 'American Prelude'
96 'American Spirit'
89 ***americana elegans***
94 'Andromeda'
89 'Angela'
94 'Angeline'
91 'Ann Margaret'
90 'Ann Pacey'
95 'Ann Porter'
93 'Anne Smith'
90 'Anneek Geerlings'
96 'Annie Johnson'
93 'Ann's Beauty'
90 'Anthea Bond'
91 'Antonella Merrills'
93 'Antonia'
94 'Apollo'
93 'Arabella'
90 'Arc en Ciel'
89 'Architect Ludwig Mercher'
90 'Arel's Fleur'
93 'Ark Royal'
93 'Arlendon'
95 'Art Nouveau'
93 'Arthur Cope'
93 'Ashley and Isobel'
96 'Ashwell'
92 'Aubrey Harris'
93 'Auntie Maggie'
92 'Averil Lunn'
90 'Axel of Denmark'
92 'Baby Lilac'
90 'Baby Love'
95 'Baby Neerman'
90 'Baby Veerman'
93 'Balcony Queen'
96 'Bali Hi'
93 'Ballerina'
94 'Banstead Bell'
91 'Barbara Anne'
91 'Barbara Edwards'
96 'Barbara Hallett'
95 'Barbara Hassey'
96 'Barbara Pountain'
96 'Barnsdale'
96 'Barry Sheppard'
91 'Beacon Kon'
93 'Beauty Queen'
93 'Bedford's Park'
95 'Begame Kiekeboe'
90 'Belinda Allen'
95 'Bella'
92 'Bella Madina'
93 'Bella Mia'
93 'Bellbottoms'
95 'Belle de Lisse'
93 'Belvoir Elf'
93 'Belvoir Lakes'
91 'Benjamin Pacey'
96 'Ben's Ruby'
90 'Berbanella'
91 'Berba's Delight'
90 'Berba's Fleur'
90 'Berba's Frances Femke'
90 'Berba's Impossible'
94 'Berba's Inge Mariel'
90 'Berba's Love'
95 'Berba's Trio'
90 'Bernard Rawdin'
92 'Bernisser Stein'
89 'Beryl's Jewel'
90 'Betma Whitison'
92 'Betty Wass'
93 'Beverley Baby'
93 'Biddy Lester'
96 'Big Charles'
93 'Bill Kennedy'
95 'Billie Roe'
96 'Blackberry Ripple'
93 'Blaze'
93 'Blue Anchor'
94 'Blue Anne'
93 'Blue Bonnet'
93 'Blue Boy'
90 'Blue Ranger'
93 'Bob Armbruster'
95 'Bob Brown'
96 'Bohémienne'
93 'Bonanza'
94 'Bonnie Berrycloth'
93 'Born Free'
89 'Bosun's Superb'
91 'Boy Blue'
93 'Bravo'
95 'Brenda Megan Hill'
90 'Brunette'
96 'Buena Maria'
96 'Buenos Aires'
96 'Buttons and Bows'
93 'Caetar'
95 'Callaly Pink'
94 'Calverley'
93 'Cameron Ryle'
96 'Cannenburch Floriant'
93 'Carefree'
96 'Carole Hardwick'
96 'Carole Scott'
90 'Caroline Imp'
90 'Cecil Glass'
90 'Cees van Braunschott'
94 'Centenary'
89 'Chance Encounter'
96 'Chancellor'
95 'Chaos'
93 'Charleston'
95 'Chartwell'
90 'Chatsworth'
90 'Checkmate'
91 'Cherry Pie'
93 'Cheviot Princess'
90 'Chris van der Linden'
90 'Christine Clements'
92 'Christine Pugh'
95 'Christine Truman'
93 'Christine Windsor'
96 Christmas Candy
93 'Christmas Holly'
95 'Churchtown'
93 'Cicely Ann'
90 'Cinnamon'
90 'Cissbury Gem'
93 'City of Derby'
94 'Classic Jean'
96 'Claudine Sanford'
92 'Cliff's Supreme'
96 'Clifton Belle'
94 'Clouds'
94 'Cloverdale Delight'
94 'Cloverdale Pride'
95 'Cloverdale Star'
96 'Col'.
92 'Concord'
95 'Concorde'
92 'Contamine'
93 'Contramine'
93 'Cookie'
91 'Coral Rose'
94 'Cornelian Fire'
89 'Country Girl'
93 'Cracker'
96 'Croix d'Honneur'
93 'Cropwell Butler'
90 'Crown Derby'
93 'Cyndy Robyn'
96 'Danielle'
90 'Dark Spider'
95 'Dawn Redfern'
93 'De Bono's Pride'
96 'Deben'
96 'Deborah'
91 'Deborah Louise'
92 'Deborah Young'
94 'Debra Hampson'
92 'Debra Imp'
96 'Dedham Vale'
96 'Delta's Drop'
90 'Delta's Fellow'
95 'Delta's Flame'
92 'Delta's Glorie'
92 'Delta's Rien'
90 'Delta's Robyn'
93 'Deltaschön'
95 'Denis Bolton'
90 'Derby Belle'
90 'Derby Countess'
94 'Desmond Davey'
92 'Diabolo'
94 'Diamond Fire'
89 'Diana's Calypso'
91 'Diane Christiansen'
96 'Diann Goodwin'
90 'Didi'
93 'Dirk van Delen'
93 'Doctor Manson'
89 'Donauweibchen'
93 'Doreen Stroud'
96 'Doris Birchell'
96 'Doris Deaves'
94 'Doris Yvonne'
95 'Dorothy M. Goldsmith'
89 'Dorothy Woakes'
92 'Dove Cottage'
93 'Drama Girl'
96 'Dreamy Days'
95 'Drifter'
92 'Drooping Lady'
89 'Duchess of Petitport'
96 'Dunrobin Bedder'
90 'Dutch Firebird'
90 'Dutch Flamingo'
90 'Dutch Geertien'
94 'Dutch Girl'
93 'Dutch Pearl'
93 'Dutch Shoes'
93 'E.J. Goulding'
94 'Ecstasy'
91 'Eden Dawn'
94 'Edie Lester'
96 'Edith Jack'
96 'Edith of Kimbolton'
93 'Edna'
95 'Edna May'
91 'Edwin Miles'
93 'Eelco Brinkman'
90 'El Matador'
93 'Elanor Grace'
94 'Elf'
89 'Elisabeth Nutzinger'
96 'Elizabeth Anne'
92 'Elizabeth Brown'
93 'Elizabeth Burton'
93 'Elsie Johnson'
90 'Elsine'
96 'Elsstar'
92 'Emile Zola'
96 'Eric Cooper Taylor'
92 'Erich Mehlis'
93 'Eschott Elf'
94 'Esme Tabraham'
93 'Esther'
93 'Ethel'
94 'Ethel May Lester'
95 'Ethel Weeks'
89 'Ethel Wilson'
90 'Eva Watkins'
94 'Exeter'
95 'Expo '86'
92 'Fairplay'
95 'Fan Tan'
93 'Fancy Sockeye'
90 'Fatima'
96 'Feather Duster'
93 'Felixstowe Display'
93 'Feltham's Pride'
92 'Fernrother Fairy'
93 'Fire Lady'
93 'Firebird'
96 'Firecracker'
90 'Firenzi'
92 'First Kiss'
96 'First Lord'
96 'First Love'
93 'Fizzy Lizzy'
89 'Flamingo'
89 'Flarepath'
89 'Flim Flam'
90 'Flirt'
93 'Florence Taylor'

93 'Florrie Bambridge'
96 'Flowerdream'
93 'Fluffy Ruffles'
96 'Fondant Cream'
93 'Foxtrot'
90 'Francois Villon'
90 'Franz Veerman'
90 'Fred Standen'
89 'Fred's First'
90 'Freestyle'
96 'Frosted Amethyst'
90 'Frosty Bell'
95 ***fulgens*** × ***splendens***
91 'Gabriel Rose'
90 'Garden Beauty'
96 'Gazebo'
90 'Gazette'
90 'Geertje'
90 'Général Negrier'
96 'Geoff Amos'
90 'Geoff Barnett'
92 'George Bunstead'
94 'George Humphrey'
93 'George 'n' Jo'
92 'George Robinson'
90 'George Roe'
95 'Giant Falls'
90 'Gidding'
90 'Gillian Shepherd'
96 'Gladys Lorimer'
92 'Glendale'
89 'Gleneagles'
94 'Gold Foil'
94 'Golden Guinea Pig'
91 'Golden Lustre'
90 'Golden Lye's Favourite'
90 'Golden Spade'
94 'Golden Spangles'
96 'Golden Spring Classic'
90 'Gondolier'
91 'Goose Girl'
90 'Grace'
89 'Grace Groom'
93 'Grady'
91 'Granada'
93 'Grange Farm'
93 'Gray Dawn'
93 'Hampshire Leonora'
90 'Harbour Bridge'
89 'Harlequin'
94 'Harold Smith'
90 'Harriet Lye'
96 'Harry Lye'
93 'Harvest Glow'
93 'Hay Wain'
91 'Haylettes Gold'
90 'Heather'
95 'Heathfield'
92 'Helen McDermott'
90 'Helene Houwen Claessen'
96 'Hendrik Schwab'
95 'Henning Becker'
88 'Henriette Ernst'
93 'Heydon'
91 'High Peak'
93 'Highland Beauty'
92 'Hilda Fitzsimmons'
91 'Hill Top'
90 'HMS Victorious'
89 'Hobson'
93 'Honnepon'
91 'Humpty Dumpty'
96 'Hungarton'
93 'Ice Festival'
96 'Imagination'
93 'Improved Hanna'
90 'Ina Buxton'
96 'Ina Jo Marker'
93 'Indian Princess'
92 'Irish Wedding'
94 'Isabel Ryan'
90 'Ivan Gadsby'
91 'Ivor Moore'
95 'Jaap Brummel'
94 'Jack Coast'
91 'Jack Horner'
90 'Jack King'
91 'Jack Sprat'
89 'James Shurvell'
90 'Jan Houtsma'
95 'Jandel'
92 'Jane Elizabeth'
91 'Janet Williams'
96 'Janice Revell'
93 'Janneke'
92 'Jason Slaney-Welch'
90 'Jaspers Donderstraal'
95 'Jaunty'
96 'Javelin'
95 'Jayne Rowell'
90 'Je Maintiendrai'
89 'Jean Burton'
94 'Jean Dawes'
91 'Jean Ewart'
96 'Jean Muir'
94 'Jennette Marwood'
96 'Jessie Pearson'
92 'Jewel'
95 'Jezebel'
96 'Jill Whitworth'
96 'Jim Dodge'
93 'Jim Dowers'
94 'Joan Leach'
90 'Joanne'
90 'Joan's Delight'
94 'Joe Browning'
90 'Johannes Novinski'
93 'John Baker'
91 'John Waugh'
96 'John Yardell'
90 'Joker'
90 'Jolanda Weeda'
92 'Jolly Jorden'
91 'Joseph Holmes'
94 'Joy White'
94 'Judi Spiers'
95 'Judith Coupland'
96 'Judith Mitchell'
93 'Julia Ditrich'
92 'Julie Adams'
90 'Julie Horton'
96 'Kabibi'
90 'Karan'
90 'Kathleen'
95 'Kathleen Colville'
94 'Kathleen Saunders'
96 'Kathy Scott'
93 'Kay Louise'
96 'Kay Riley'
93 'Kegworth Clown'
89 'Kentish Belle'
90 'Kentish Maid'
96 'Kevin Stals'
91 'Kim Hampson'
92 'King of Siam'
90 'Klein Beekestein'
89 'Kocarde'
90 'Kolibrie'
89 'Komeet'
92 'Kursal'
92 'La Bergère'
90 'Lady Bower'
89 'Lady Dorothy'
94 'Lady Pamela Mountbatten'
96 'Laing's Hybrid'
96 'Laleham'
95 'Lambaba'
90 'Larissa'
93 'Larksfield Skylark'
94 'Laurie'
94 'Lavender Blue'
96 'Lavender Cascade'
90 'Lavender Thumb'
89 'Lechlade Fairy'
93 'Lemacto'
90 'Leo Goetelen'
96 'Leonhart von Fuchs'
96 'Libra'
89 'Liemers Lantaern'
95 'Lilac Dainty'
91 'Lilac Sceptre'
90 'Lilian Windsor'
93 'Linda Copley'
89 'Linda Pratt'
93 'Lindy'
90 'L'Ingénue'
95 'Linsey Brown'
89 'Little One'
93 'Loni Jane'
90 'Lonneke'
90 'Look East'
92 'Lord Leverhulme'
91 'Lorna Doone'
96 'Lorna Hercherson'
90 'Love in Bloom'
89 'Love It'
96 'Love Knot'
93 'Lucerowe'
91 'Lucie Harris'
93 'Lucinda'
94 'Lumière'
93 'Lunter's Glorie'
91 'Lunter's Klokje'
93 'Lunter's Roehm'
89 'Lustre Improved'
96 'Lye's Favourite'
90 'Lye's Perfection'
90 'Lyndhurst'
94 'Lynne Marshall'
92 'Mabel Grey'
90 'Madame Danjoux'
90 'Madame Lanteime'
91 'Madame Theobald'
93 'Madame van der Strasse'
96 'Maddy'
90 'Madurodam'
89 ***magellanica*** var. ***molinae*** 'Enstone'
96 – – 'Enstone Gold'
88 – var. ***myrtifolia***
94 ***magellanica purpurea***
96 'Magenta Flush'
93 'Maggie Little'
96 'Mardale'
93 'Margaret Swales'
96 'Margaret Tebbit'
90 'Margaret Thatcher'
96 'Margarita'
93 'Margharitte'
89 'Margie'
91 'Marie Julie'
90 'Marja'
94 'Marjorie Coast'
93 'Marlies'
95 'Marshside'
91 'Marta Frädrich'
96 'Martha Brown'
90 'Martha Franck'
90 'Martyn Smedley'
96 'Mary Ellen'
93 'Mary Kipling'
95 'Mary Rose'
95 'Mary Stilwell'
93 'Maryn'
92 'Matthew Welch'
92 'Maudena'
95 'Maureen Munro'
91 'Mazarine'
95 'Mazda'
96 'Medalist'
92 'Mediterranean'
89 'Medusa'
90 'Melissa Heavens'
90 'Mendocino Rose'
95 'Meols Cop'
87 'Mephisto'
89 'Mercurius'
90 'Mia van der Zee'
94 'Michele Wallace'
90 'Millie Butler'
93 'Mini Skirt'
96 ***minutissima***
93 'Minx'
92 'Miranda Morris'
93 'Miss Leucadia'
91 'Miss Muffett'
96 'Misty Morn'
90 'Mon Ami'
89 'Monsieur Joule'
94 'Montezuma'
96 'Moon Glow'
93 'Mordred'
90 'Mosedale Hall'
96 'Mother's Day'
93 'Mounbatten'
94 'Mount Stewart'
95 'Mrs Minnie Pugh'
96 'Muirfield'
96 'My Beauty'
89 'My Love'
95 'Myra Baxendale'
90 'Nanne de Jong'
89 'Naomi Adams'
90 'Nemerlaer'
92 'New Constellation'
92 'Nicola White'
90 'Nicolina'
95 'Nikki'
93 'Noblesse'
95 'O Sole Mio'
96 'Oakham'
93 'Old Rose'
94 'Oldbury'
95 'Oldbury Delight'
94 'Oldbury Galore'
94 'Oldbury Gem'
94 'Oldbury Pearl'
90 'Olympiad'
92 'Omar Giant'
95 'Omeomy'
95 'Onna'
96 'Orange Bell'
91 'Orange Cocktail'
94 'Orange Flame'
94 'Orange Flash'
93 'Orange Pip'
93 'Orangy'
95 'Oranje Boven'
96 'Orchid Princess'
93 'Oriental Lace'

95 'Orientalis'
96 'Oso Sweet'
96 'Ovation'
91 'Pale Beauty'
94 'Palford'
90 'Panylla Prince'
96 'Pa's Princess'
95 'Passing Cloud'
90 'Patricia Bardgett'
90 'Patricia Ewart'
94 'Paul Pini'
91 'Paula Baylis'
91 'Pauline Flint'
93 'Pearl Farmer'
96 'Pearly Gates'
96 'Pebble Mill'
89 'Pèredrup'
89 'Petit Point'
91 'Phyllis Stevens'
95 'Piet Hein'
96 'Pink Campanella'
94 'Pink Claws'
89 'Pink Cornet'
96 'Pink Galaxy'
91 'Pink Haze'
95 'Pink Most'
96 'Pink Pineapple'
93 'Pink Ruffles'
96 'Pink Snow'
89 'Pink Trumpet'
92 'Pink Veil'
90 'Piquant'
90 'Playboy'
94 'Pluto'
91 'Pole Star'
91 'Polly Flinders'
94 'Poppet'
89 'Präsident Walter Morio'
93 'Pretty Belinda'
93 'Pretty Grandpa'
96 'Pride and Joy'
93 'Priest Land'
89 'Prince Syray'
92 'Princess Saranntoe'
90 'Pukkie'
96 'Purple Ann'
94 'Purple Lace'
89 'Puttenden Manor'
93 'Queen of Hearts'
90 'Rachel Catherine'
96 'Rahnee'
96 'Rainbow'
92 'Ratae Beauty'
91 'Rebecca Louise'
96 'Rebecca Williams'
90 'Recy Holmes'
93 'Red Petticoat'
90 'Red Rain'
90 'Red Rover'
90 'Regina van Zoeren'
95 'Reisken Boland'
94 'Renate'
90 'Revival'
90 'Rhanee'
94 'Ri Mia'
93 'Richard Livesy'
92 'Rigoletto'
93 'Rika'
94 'Ringwood Gold'
95 'River Plate'
95 'Robert Bruce'
90 'Robert Hall'
92 'Robin Pacey'
92 'Rolts'
94 'Ron Holmes'
91 'Ron's Pet'
90 'Rosabell'
96 'Rose Bower'
90 'Rosedale'
91 'Rosetta'
96 'Rosy Bows'
95 'Rothbury Beauty'
96 'Royal Mosaic'
89 'Royal Ruby'
89 'Royal Sovereign'
92 'Royal Splendour'
95 'Rubens'
91 'Ruby Glow'
93 'Ruthie'
96 'Rutti Tutti'
93 'Sacramento Bells'
96 'Sahara'
96 'Sally Gunnell'
93 'San Pasqual'
94 'Sangria'
96 'Santa Barbara'
91 'Santa Claus'
95 'Sarah Ann'
95 'Sarah Louise'
93 'Sarina'
94 'Satchmo'
90 'Saxondale Sue'
95 'Scarlet Ribbons'
93 'Schnabel'
95 'Sensation'
93 'Serendipity'
90 'Shady Blue'
89 'Sheila Hobson'
92 'Sheila Joy'
96 'Shepard's Delight'
96 'Sherborne Las'
90 'Sherwood'
90 'Shower of Stars'
93 'Shuna'
93 'Shuna Lindsay'
90 'Shy Look'
92 'Silver Jubilee'
94 'Silver Pink'
91 'Simple Simon'
96 'Siobhan'
96 'Skylight'
90 'Skyway'
90 'Slender Lady'
89 'Snowcap Variegated'
91 'Snowfall'
90 'Snowflake'
92 'Soldier of Fortune'
88 'Spangles'
93 'Sparks'
93 'Spellbound'
93 'Sportsknight'
89 'Spotlight'
92 'Spring Bells'
96 'Spring Classic'
96 'Springtime'
93 'Saint Andrews'
96 'Stad Elburg'
95 'Stathern Surprise'
93 'Stephanie'
96 'Stephanie Morris'
89 'Steve Wright'
93 'Stevie Doidge'
91 'Storm'
90 'Storm Petrel'
96 'Strawberry Fizz'
96 'Student Prince'
93 'Sugar Plum'
90 'Summer Mist'
90 'Summer Night'
92 'Summer Snow'
90 'Sundance'
92 'Sunny Jim'
96 'Sunny Skies'
96 'Sunsrise First'
95 'Supersport'
90 'Susan Allen'
95 'Susan Daley'
93 'Susan Jill'
96 'Susan Joy'
96 'Suzy'
96 'Swanland Candy'
90 'Sweet Revenge'
93 'Sweetie Dear'
93 'Swiss Miss'
95 'Sylvia Dyos'
96 'Tabatha'
92 'Tahiti'
93 'Tahoe'
93 'Tamar Isobel'
96 'Tammy'
96 'Tartan'
89 'Ted's'
88 'Telegraph'
91 'Temple Bells'
96 'Texas Star'
95 'Thames Valley'
92 'The Observer'
93 'The Phoenix'
96 'The Red Arrows'
93 'The Speedbird'
96 'The Spoiler'
95 'Think Pink'
90 'Thomos'
90 'Tina Head'
92 'Tolemac'
93 'Tom Hobson'
92 'Tom Silcock'
91 'Tommy Tucker'
96 'Top Score'
90 'Topsin'
92 'Torotino'
93 'Tortorina'
96 'Tosca'
96 'Tour Eiffel'
89 'Tourtonne'
90 'Toven'
94 'Tower of London'
96 'Trabant'
96 'Tradewinds'
96 'Tranquility'
89 'Tresco'
96 'Trish Dewey'
93 'Trisha'
93 'Trixie Coleman'
92 'Troutbeck'
90 'Trubell'
93 'Twiggy'
90 'Ultra Light'
95 'Uncle Jinks'
93 'Unique'
96 'Uppingham Lass'
91 'Valamay'
93 'Valerie'
90 'Valerie Cotterell'
95 'Varty's Pride'
94 'Venus'
92 'Vera Stuart'
93 'Vespa'
93 'Victoria Louise'
96 'Violacea'
91 'Violet Lace'
92 'Violet Mist'
91 'Vivien Harris'
90 'Waltraud Strumper'
90 'Walz Bugel'
90 'Walz Gong'
90 'Walz Hobo'
90 'Walz Kalebas'
90 'Walz Kattesnoor'
90 'Walz Knipperbol'
90 'Walz Meermin'
90 'Walz Piano'
90 'Walz Ratel'
90 'Walz Toeter'
95 'Walz Trompet'
90 'Walz Viool'
96 'Washington Centennial'
96 'Water Baby'
89 'Waveney Unique'
93 'Waxen Beauty'
92 'Wee One'
92 'Wendy Blythe'
96 'Wendy Brooks'
90 'Wentelwiek'
94 'Wentworth'
92 'Westergeest'
90 'Whistling Rufus'
93 'White Bride'
93 'White Fairy'
88 'White Gem'
91 'White Haven'
94 'White Lace'
93 'White Loeky'
94 'White Surprise'
91 'White Swan'
93 'White Water'
88 'Wicked Lady'
89 'Wild Glove'
90 'Wilf Tolley'
96 'William C. Dodson'
93 'Willie Lott'
91 'Willy Winky'
90 'Wilma Versloot'
93 'Wilson's Joy'
93 'Wingfield Sheppard'
90 'Wise Choice'
96 'Wm's Las'
90 'Yankee Clipper'
90 'Zaanlander'
95 'Zeeuwse Parel'

FURCRAEA

96 ***foetida***

GAHNIA

90 ***grandis***
94 ***setifolia***

GAILLARDIA

95 ***aristata*** Pursch JCA 11449
89 'Aurea'
89 'Chloe'
89 'Croftway Yellow'
91 'Golden Queen'
88 x ***grandiflora*** 'Ipswich Beauty'
93 'Kahome'
96 Kelway's Hybrids
95 Monarch Group
96 'Summer Sun'

GALANTHUS

96 'April Fool'
92 ***caucasicus*** late form
95 ***elwesii poculiformis***
96 'Ermine Street'
95 green-tipped Greatorex
93 'Mrs Backhouse Number Twelve'
96 ***nivalis*** 'Appleby One'
95 – 'Boyd's Double'
96 – subsp. ***imperati***
96 – 'Maximus'
96 – 'Tiny Tim'

96 ***peshmenii***
92 ***plicatus*** 'Beth Chatto'
94 – subsp. ***byzantinus*** 'Greenpeace'
95 – – 'Trym'
93 – 'Silverwells'
96 – 'Upcher'
96 ***reginae-olgae*** subsp. ***reginae-olgae*** 'Cambridge' ♀
94 'Warley Belles'
94 'Warley Duo'
94 'Warley Longbow'

GALIUM
96 ***arenarium***
92 ***firmum***

GALPHIMIA
93 ***glauca***

GALTONIA
89 ***princeps*** 'Praecox'
95 ***viridiflora*** S&SH 3

GAMOCHAETA
94 ***nivalis***

GARDENIA
90 ***augusta*** 'Belmont'
94 – 'Gold Magic'
96 – 'Radicans Variegata'
94 ***cornuta***
93 ***spatulifolia***

GARRYA
93 x ***issaquahensis***
90 ***laurifolia*** var. ***macrophylla***
92 x ***thuretii***

GAULTHERIA
89 ***cordifolia***
92 ***coriacea***
92 ***cumingiana***
92 ***depressa*** var. ***novae-zelandiae***
94 – pink
89 ***erecta***
93 ***eriophylla***
95 ***forrestii***
94 ***leucocarpa***
92 ***mucronata*** var. ***angustifolia***
93 – Davis's Hybrids
89 – 'Goldsworth Pink'
89 – 'Goldsworth Red'
94 – 'White Magic' (f)
95 ***myrsinoides*** 'Geoffrey Herklots'
93 ***parvula*** 'Ohau'
93 – 'Rough Creek'
90 ***procumbens*** 'Dart's Red Giant'
92 ***semi-infera***
94 sp. P&W 6142
93 ***tetramera***
93 ***trichophylla*** red
90 ***wardii***

GAZANIA
96 'Blackberry Split'
95 'Blaze of Fire'
95 Flesh Tones Group
96 'Flore Pleno'
95 'Harlequin'
95 'Hazel'
94 ***madeira***
95 'Michael' ♀
95 'Mini Star White'
93 'New Magic'
96 ***rigens*** 'Aureovariegata'
88 – 'Torquay Silver'
95 'Slate'
95 'Snuggle Bunny'
95 'Sunbeam'
91 'Vimmer's Variegated'

GENISTA
95 ***albida***
96 ***anglica***
88 ***berberidea***
90 ***falcata***
93 ***florida***
93 ***horrida***
95 ***involucrata*** Spach
93 ***januensis***
89 ***maderensis magnifoliosa***
95 ***pilosa*** 'Superba'
93 ***radiata***
92 ***sericea***
95 x ***spachiana*** ♀
95 ***tenera***
92 ***tinctoria*** 'Golden Plate'
96 – 'Moesiaca'
96 – var. ***virgata***

GENNARIA
96 ***diphylla***

GENTIANA
92 ***acaulis*** 'A.G. Week's Form'
96 – 'Coelestina'
94 – 'Gedanensis'
96 – 'Harlin'
89 – 'Leith Vale'
88 – 'Nora Bradshaw'
96 – 'Trotter's Variety'
96 ***affinis***
90 ***algida*** f. ***igarishii***
94 ***alpina***
89 – Trotter's form
92 ***altaica***
96 ***asclepiadea*** 'Whitethroat'
96 ***bisetaea***
96 'Black Boy'
94 'Blauer Edelstein'
96 ***brachyphylla***
94 – subsp. ***favratii***
88 'Bucksburn Azure'
89 ***burseri***
94 – var. ***villarsii***
94 ***calycosa***
93 x ***caroli*** 'Coronation'
92 ***clusii alba***
92 ***clusii corbariensis***
88 ***clusii*** 'Mount Rax'
95 ***clusii rochelii***
96 'Coronation'
88 ***cruciata*** subsp. ***phlogifolia***
94 ***dendrologi***
92 ***dinarica*** 'Harlin'
92 ***divisa***
92 'Drumcairn White'
88 'Elizabeth Brand'
94 'Excelsior'
94 'Exploi'
94 'Fasta Highlands'
96 ***fetisowii***
91 ***frigida***
95 ***gracilis***
94 'Ida K'
90 'Inverdevon'
96 'John Aitken'
96 ***kolalowskyi***
95 ***ligustica***
94 ***loderi***
96 ***macrophylla*** 'Alba'
94 'Magnificent'
94 ***makinoi*** 'Royal Blue'
94 'Maryfield'
96 'Merlin'
94 'Midnight'
89 'Mount Everest'
96 ***obconica*** RH 61
89 ***occidentalis***
96 ***ornata***
96 'Orva'
95 ***patula***
96 ***platypetala***
96 ***prolata*** K 214
94 ***puberulenta***
96 ***punctata***
89 ***pyrenaica***
87 'Queen of the Blues'
96 ***sceptrum***
96 ***septemfida*** var. ***lagodechiana*** 'Latifolia'
96 ***setigera***
96 ***sikokiana***
95 ***sino-ornata*** 'Autumn Frolic'
94 – 'Blauer Dom'
95 sp. C 183
95 sp. C 201
95 sp. C 24
95 sp. C 77
96 sp. Olga's pale
94 'Susan'
87 'The Souter'
94 'Thunersee'
90 ***tianschanica***
94 ***trichotoma*** CLD 429
96 ***trinervis***
93 ***triptosperma japonica***
89 'Utterby Seedling'
96 'Veora'
96 ***verna*** subsp. ***pontica***
96 – – 'Alba'
91 – subsp. ***tergestina***
91 ***villosa***
96 ***walujewii***
91 'Wendy Jean'
89 ***wilsonii***
94 'Zauberland'

GENTIANOPSIS
90 ***crinita***

GEOGENANTHUS
90 ***poepigii***

GERANIUM
95 'Ann Folkard' x ***psilostemon***
96 ***antrorsum***
95 ***argenteum***
95 'Blue Pearl'
92 ***caeruleatum***
96 ***cataractarum*** subsp. ***pitardii***
95 ***dahuricum***
89 ***divaricatum***
91 ***drakensbergense***
96 'Eva'
95 ***grandistipulatum***
94 ***kotschyi***
94 ***krameri***
96 ***macrostylum*** JCA 6000
96 x ***magnificum*** 'Wisley Variety'
96 ***magniflorum*** S&SH 32
89 ***mascatense***
91 'Maxwelton'
96 'Nora Bremner'
95 ***palcaense*** F&W 7851
96 ***palustre*** 'Plus'
96 ***phaeum aureum***
96 ***phaeum*** 'Joan Grey'
94 – Mrs Gardener's Selection
94 ***platypetalum*** Fischer & Meyer 'Album'
95 ***pratense*** 'Alboroseum'
96 – 'Catforth Cadense'
96 – CC 806
96 – 'Fiona'
94 – x ***himalayense***
94 – pale form
96 – 'Striatum Akaton'
96 – 'Summer Skies' (d)
96 'Priestley's Pink'
95 ***renardii roseum***
94 'Robert Burns'
94 ***rubicaule***
94 'Sally'
89 ***sanguineum*** 'Hadspen'
96 'Scheherezade'
96 ***schlechteri***
94 ***sessiliflorum*** subsp. ***brevicaule*** Glabrum Group
95 ***shikokianum***
95 'Silver Pink'
93 'Southcombe Beauty'
95 sp. from Central Asia
96 sp. from Chile
95 ***subulatostipulatum***
96 ***swatense*** SEP 131
94 ***sylvaticum*** 'Meran'
96 ***traversii*** 'Sugar Pink'
96 ***versicolor*** 'Bill Baker'
95 ***weddellii*** F&W 7890

GEUM
96 ***aleppicum*** subsp. ***strictum***
96 'Birkhead's Creamy Lemon'
96 ***calthifolium***
92 – var. ***nipponicum***
94 ***capense*** S&SH 33
91 ***elatum***
96 – CC&McK 390
96 'Gordon Cooper'
96 x ***heldreichii***
91 ***japonicum***
96 ***leiospermum***
96 ***macrophyllum*** var. ***sachalinense***
96 'Orangeman'
94 ***pseudochinense***
96 ***pseudococcineum***
89 ***rivale*** cream
94 – 'Variegatum'
91 ***rossii***
95 'Two Ladies'

GIBASIS
89 ***linearis***

GIGASPERMUM
94 ***repens***

GILIA
96 ***caespitosa***

GINKGO
94 ***biloba*** 'Heksenbezen Leiden'
96 – 'Lakeview'
96 – 'Mayfield' (m)

GLADIOLUS
87 'Ali Baba' (B)
92 'Andorra' (B)
92 'Anglia' (B)
94 'Anitra' (P)
95 'Apricot Queen' (L)
94 ***atroviolaceus***
89 'Blue Conqueror' (L)
95 'Blue Star'
93 'Blushing Bride' (N)
94 Butterfly hybrids
92 'Campanella' (B)
92 'Carmen' (L)
89 'Chanson'
95 'Charm Glow'
94 'Cindy' (B)
92 'Confetti' (B)
96 'Dancing Doll'
92 'Deciso' (L)
93 'Desirée' (B)
92 Dream Party (L)
91 'Dutch Parade' (L)
95 'Edward van Beinum' (L)
92 'Erin' (Min)
96 'Essex' (P/S)
94 'Esta Bonita' (G)
95 'Firebird'
96 'Friendship' (L)
96 'Gillian' (L)
92 'Greenland' (S)
91 'Gypsy Baron' (G)
95 'Helene' (P/B)
95 'Her Majesty' (L)
93 'Herman van der Mark'
94 'High Style' (L)
94 'Hypnose' (B)
92 'Introspection' (L)
89 'Invitation'
95 'Jessica' (L)
93 'Joyeuse Entrée' (L)
96 'Jupiter'
96 'Liebelei'
92 'Little Darling' (P/S)
92 ***longicollis***
92 'Lorena' (B)
91 Love Letter (M)
89 'Lovely Day' (G)
92 'Madrilene' (B/S)
93 Maestro (L)
93 'Mandy'
95 'Marvinka' (M)
94 'Mascagni' (M)
89 'Merry'
92 'Misty Eyes' (L)
95 'Nicole'
95 'Ovation' (L)
92 'Pandion' (G)
94 ***papilio*** 'Grey Ghost'
94 'Passion' (L)
93 'Peach Blossom' (N)
95 'Pegasus' (P/Min)
92 'Piccolo' (B)
95 'Picture' (P)
92 'Pink Lady' (L)
89 'Pink Pearl' (S)
91 Pink Perfection (L)
94 'Piquant' (P)
89 'Prince Carnival' (L)
93 Promise (M)
89 'Prosperity'
92 'Queen of the Night' (L)
95 'Red Beauty'
95 'Red Jewel' (P/S)
96 'Robin' (P)
94 'Rose Delight' (L)
95 'Rose Supreme' (G)
92 'Royal Beauty' (L)
96 'Royal Dutch' (L)
92 'Royal Violet' (L)
96 'Sabu'
92 Sancerre (B/L)
96 'Saxony' (P)
89 'Scout'
94 'Shakespeare' (L)
92 'Shamrock' (L)
89 'Shell Pink'
89 'Shocking Pink'
96 'Spic and Span' (L)
93 'Spitfire' (N)
89 'Spring Gem'
92 'Storiette' (B)
92 Sundance (L)
93 'Tangerine' (P)
96 'Theresa'
92 'Treasure' (P)
93 Up to Date
93 'Vidi Napoli'
95 'White Prosperity' (L)
96 'Wine and Roses' (L)
96 'Wise Cracks'
92 'Yellow Special' (P)
94 'Ziegennerbaum'

GLAUCIDIUM
96 ***palmatum*** var. ***leucanthum***

GLAUCIUM
96 ***squamigerum***

GLEDITSIA
89 ***sinensis***
92 ***triacanthos*** 'Bujotii'
94 – 'Elegantissima' (v)

GLOBULARIA
96 ***albiflora***
95 ***bisnagarica***

GLORIOSA
95 ***caramii***
96 ***superba*** 'Carsonii'

GLOXINIA
93 'Tessa'

GLUMICALYX
96 aff. ***goseloides*** JJ&JH 9401347

GLYCERIA
93 ***fluitans***
93 ***notata***

GLYCYRRHIZA
96 ***lepidota***
93 ***missouriensis***

GLYPTOSTROBUS
94 ***pensilis***

GMELINA
93 ***arborea***

GNAPHALIUM
90 ***andicola***
93 ***mackayi***

GNIDIA
96 aff. ***aberrans*** JJ&JH 940178

GOMPHOCARPUS
96 ***fruticosus***
95 ***physocarpus*** S&SH 67

GONIOLIMON
96 ***tataricum***
96 – 'Woodcreek'

GOODENIA
95 ***humilis***
89 ***lunata***
92 ***repens***

GOSSYPIUM
91 ***sturtianum***

GRAPTOPETALUM
91 ***paraguayense*** subsp. ***bernalense***

GRATIOLA
92 ***nana***

GREVILLEA
89 ***aspleniifolia*** 'Robin Hood'
95 ***banksii*** f. ***albiflora***
95 – var. ***forsteri***
91 ***bipinnatifida***
87 'Claret'
94 'Desert Flame'
91 ***fasciculata***
87 ***jephcottii***
94 ***juniperina*** 'Rubra'
91 ***pilulifera***
92 'Red Cloud'

GREWIA
96 ***biloba***

GRINDELIA
93 ***integrifolia***
93 ***lanceolata***
93 ***oregana***

GRISELINIA
92 ***littoralis*** 'Gold Edge' (v)
93 – 'Milkmaid'
89 ***lucida*** 'Variegata'
95 ***racemosa***
96 ***ruscifolia***

GUICHENOTIA
92 ***ledifolia***
92 ***macrantha***

GUNNERA
96 ***magellanica*** (f)
95 × ***mixta***
95 ***prorepens*** small form

GUZMANIA
92 'Atilla'
92 Carine Group
92 'Claudine'
92 ***conifera***
92 ***donnellsmithii***
92 Gisela Group
92 'Golden King'
92 ***lingulata*** var. ***cardinalis***
92 – var. ***minor*** 'Red'
92 – – 'Vella'
92 Muriel Group
92 ***musaica*** 🏆
92 'Nellie'
92 Rana Group
92 'Remembrance'
92 'Ruby'
92 ***scherzeriana***
92 ***wittmackii***

GYMNADENIA
94 ***camtschatica***

GYMNOCARPIUM
93 ***jessoense***

GYPSOPHILA
93 ***libanotica***
92 × ***monstrosa***
93 'Pacific Rose'
96 ***paniculata*** 'Pink Star' (d)

HAASTIA
87 ***sinclairii***

HABERLEA
96 ***rhodopensis austinii***

HACQUETIA
96 ***epipactis*** 'Variegata'

HAEMANTHUS
90 ***carneus***
95 'König Albert'

HAKEA
92 ***francisiana***
88 ***macraeana***
88 ***nitida***
88 ***platysperma***
91 ***stenocarpa***
96 ***suaveolens***
88 ***victoriae***

HALESIA
94 ***diptera*** var. ***magniflora***

× HALIMIOCISTUS
94 ***revolii*** (Coste) Dansereau

HALIMIUM
96 ***atriplicifolium***

HAMAMELIS
95 × ***intermedia*** 'Advent'
95 – 'Allgold'
95 – Hillier's clone
93 – 'Nina'
93 – 'Perfume'
95 – 'Winter Beauty'
95 ***mollis*** Henry form
95 – 'James Wells'
94 – 'Jermyns Gold'
95 – Renken form
95 ***vernalis*** 'January Pride'
95 – 'Lombart's Weeping'
95 – 'New Year's Gold'
95 – 'Squib'

HAPLOCARPHA
94 ***cheilanthifolia***

HAPLOPAPPUS
89 ***clementis***
96 ***foliosus***
91 ***hirsutus***
95 sp. P&W 6545
96 sp. RB 94063
94 ***suffruticosus***

HEBE
96 'Amethyst'
92 × ***andersonii***
95 'April Joy'
91 ***armstrongii*** × ***selaginoides***
88 'Barnettii'

94 'Blue Streak'
87 'Brian Kessell'
90 ***buchananii*** 'Major'
87 'Cilsouth'
91 'Croftway Emberglow'
92 ***cupressoides*** 'Glauca'
93 – 'Neil's Choice'
96 'Diamond'
96 'Diana'
89 ***diosmifolia*** 'Variegated'
88 'Ettrick Shepherd'
94 ***formosa***
88 'Gillanders'
89 ***giselli***
88 'Greenway Purple'
87 'Harlequin'
96 'Kewensis'
96 'Lewisii'
95 'Lilac Wand'
88 'Lycing'
92 'Marlene'
93 'Mauvena'
96 'Miss Lowe'
96 'Mont Blanc'
95 'Mrs E. Tennant'
87 'Obora Gold'
92 ***parviflora*** (Vahl) Ckn. & Allan
93 – 'Christine Eggins'
96 'Paula'
94 'Perryhill White'
96 'Perry's Bluey'
87 ***planopetiolaris***
91 ***propinqua*** var. ***major***
96 'Royal Blue'
92 ***rupicola***
96 ***salicifolia*** 'Variegata'
87 'Southcombe Pink'
96 'Southlandii'
96 ***speciosa*** 'Kapiti'
95 'Spring Glory'
96 ***stricta macroura*** 'Cookiana'
96 ***subsimilis***
88 ***tetragona*** 'Southcombe Dwarf'
88 ***treadwellii***
96 'Violet Queen'
96 'Violet Wand'
87 'Wakehurst'
90 'Wendy'
95 'White Spires'
87 'Widecombe'
96 'Wootten'

HEBENSTRETIA

93 ***dentata***

HECHTIA

96 ***argentea***
96 ***montana***

HECTORELLA

88 ***caespitosa***

HEDERA

94 ***azorica*** 'São Miguel'
90 ***colchica*** 'Dendroides' Arborescent
94 ***helix*** '238th Street'
96 – 'Arborescens Variegata'
90 – 'Arrowhead'
94 – 'Bates'
93 – 'Blarney'
93 – 'Bulgaria'
94 – f. ***caucasigena***
93 – – 'Telavi'
90 – 'Cavendishii Latina'
96 – 'Clouded Gold'
93 – 'Compacta'
93 – 'Dark Knight'
93 – 'Digitata-Hesse'
93 – 'Dorado' (v)
93 – 'F.C. Coates'
93 – 'Feenfinger'
95 – 'Fiesta'
92 – 'Finger Point'
93 – 'Galaxy'
94 – 'Garland'
93 – 'Glacier Improved' (v)
93 – 'Gladiator' (v)
93 – 'Gold Dust' (v)
96 – 'Gold Knight'
93 – 'Golden Arrow'
93 – 'Golden Emblem'
93 – 'Golden Envoy'
93 – 'Golden Fleece'
94 – 'Golden Pittsburgh' (v)
93 – 'Goldtobler' (v)
93 – 'Good's Self-branching'
93 – 'Green Heart'
93 – 'Green Survival'
93 – 'Guenevere'
93 – 'Hahn's Variegated'
93 – 'Hebron'
93 – 'Holly'
93 – 'Imp'
93 – 'Irish Lace'
93 – 'Itsy Bitsy'
93 – 'Jersey Doris' (v)
93 – 'Knobby Eight'
93 – 'Kobold'
93 – 'Konsforth'
93 – 'Laubfrosch'
93 – 'Lee's Silver' (v)
96 – 'Limelight'
93 – 'Lise' (v)
91 – 'Little Eve'
93 – 'Lucida Aurea'
93 – 'Manda's Star'
94 – 'Marilyn' (v)
94 – 'Microphylla Picta' (v)
93 – 'Milford'
92 – 'Minature Needlepoint'
93 – 'Minigreen'
93 – 'Mount Vernon'
93 – 'Nebulosa'
93 – 'Obscura'
93 – 'Old English'
93 – 'Old Lace'
93 – 'Peppermint'
93 – 'Perfection'
93 – 'Permanent Wave'
93 – 'Plattensee'
93 – 'Plimpton'
93 – 'Rochester'
93 – 'Rubáiyát'
93 – 'Rumania'
93 – 'Schäfer Four' (v)
95 – 'Schäfer One' (v)
90 – 'Schimmer'
93 – 'Silver Kolibri' (v)
93 – 'Star'
93 – 'Star Dust' (v)
93 – 'Sterntaler'
93 – 'Stiftpark'
93 – 'Student Prince' (v)
90 – 'Teena'
93 – 'Tomboy'
93 – 'Transit Road'
93 – 'Tribairn'
93 – 'Triloba'
93 – 'Welsomii'
93 – 'Wilson'
93 – 'Wingertsberg'
93 – 'Yalta'
94 ***hibernica*** 'Aran'
94 – 'Helford River'
94 – 'Hibernica Variegata'
94 – 'Rottingdean'
94 – 'Sark'
94 ***rhombea*** var. ***rhombea***

HEDYCHIUM

96 ***coronarium*** var. ***chrysoleucum***
94 ***horsfieldii***
96 ***pradhanii***
96 'Shamshiri'
95 ***spicatum*** CC 1215

HEDYSARUM

96 ***coronarium*** 'Album'
90 ***hedysaroides*** subsp. ***exaltatum***
96 ***nitidum***
94 ***varium***

HEDYSCEPE

95 ***canterburyana***

HELENIUM

95 'Baronin Linden'
96 'Bressingham Gold'
91 'Gartensonne'
95 'Goldlackzwerg'
93 'Helena'
93 'Königstiger'
94 'Margot'
92 'Rubinkuppel'
88 'Tawny Dwarf'

HELIANTHEMUM

94 'Ben Attow'
93 'Brilliant'
87 'Cherry Pink'
90 'Cupreu'
93 'Etna'
93 'Firefly'
96 'Gaiety'
95 'Gloiriette'
90 'Harlequin'
88 'Low Yellow'
90 'Loxbeare Gold'
88 ***nummularium*** subsp. ***grandiflorum***
90 – subsp. ***obscurum***
93 ***oblongatum***
93 'Orange Surprise'
88 'Peach'
88 'Prima Donna'
95 'Rose Perfection'
94 ***scardicum***
95 × ***sulphureum***
88 Trenear's Hybrids
95 'Westfield Wonder'
88 'Wisley Yellow'

HELIANTHUS

95 ***divaricatus***
96 ***occidentalis***

HELICHRYSUM

96 ***aggregatum***
93 ***amorginum***
91 – 'Pink Bud'
91 – 'White Bud'
91 – 'Yellow Bud'
95 ***arenarium*** subsp. ***aucheri***
94 ***baxteri***
89 ***bellidioides*** var. ***gracile***
89 ***cooperi***
87 'Darwin Gold'
94 ***dasyanthum***
89 ***dealbatum***
96 ***depressum***
96 ***foetidum***
88 ***frigidum*** 'Miffy Beauty'
96 ***gunnii***
95 ***maginatum***
96 ***pagophyllum***
89 ***retortum***
93 'Silver Princess'
93 'Silver Streams'

HELICONIA

96 ***mariae***

HELICTOTRICHON

94 ***alopecuroides***

HELIOPSIS

96 ***helianthoides*** 'Bressingham Doubloon' (d)
94 – 'Gigantea'
88 – 'Mid West Dream'
94 – var. ***scabra*** 'Ballerina'
93 – – 'Desert King'
91 – – 'Patula'
92 – 'Sonnenschild'
96 ***orientalis***

HELIOTROPIUM

96 ***arborescens*** 'Album'
93 ***europaeum***
90 × ***hybridum***
95 'Marine'

HELLEBORUS

96 ***argutifolius*** × ***sternii***
95 ***dumetorum*** Slovenia WM 9214/9301
95 ***foetidus*** compact form
96 – 'Melle'
95 – 'Pontarlier'
95 – scented form
95 – 'Tros-os-Montes'
96 – 'Yorkley'
94 ***lividus*** dwarf
96 ***multifidus*** subsp. ***hercegovinus***
96 – – WM 9011/9105
95 – subsp. ***istriacus*** WM 9002/9222
96 – – WM 9321/22/24
95 – subsp. ***multifidus*** WM 9010/9104
95 ***niger*** 'Higham's Variety'
94 – 'Trotter's Form'
95 – WM 9227
95 ***orientalis*** hort. 'Amethyst'
92 – 'Apple Blossom'
90 – 'Blowsy'
91 – 'Blue Showers'
90 – 'Blue Spray'
87 – 'Blue Wisp'
91 – 'Button'
93 – 'Christmas Lantern'
89 – 'Cosmos'
92 – 'Darley Mill'
89 – 'Dick Crandon'

87 – 'Dotty'
89 – 'Ernest Raithby'
92 – 'Freckleface'
89 – 'Garnet'
94 – 'Hades'
91 – 'Hazel Key'
95 – 'Hercules'
96 – ivory spotted
89 – 'John Cross'
90 – 'Laura'
95 – 'Lavinia Ward'
95 – 'Lilliwhite'
89 – 'Lynne'
88 – 'Mercury'
91 – 'Mystery'
91 – 'Nancy Ballard'
89 – 'Nocturne'
89 – 'Parrot'
90 – 'Patchwork'
89 – 'Peggy Ballard'
91 – 'Rembrandt'
91 – 'Richard Key'
89 – 'Rosa'
89 – 'Rossini'
91 – 'Sarah Ballard'
91 – 'Saturn'
94 – 'Sirius'
91 – 'Tom Wilson'
92 – 'Tommie'
90 – 'Upstart'
92 – 'Vulcan'
89 – 'Yellow Button'
96 x ***sternii*** Ashfield strain
95 – dwarf form
91 ***torquatus*** 'Pluto'
95 ***vesicarius***
96 ***viridis*** from Spain

HELWINGIA

95 ***himalaica***

HEMEROCALLIS

88 'A la Mode'
94 'Added Dimensions'
96 'Admiral'
88 'After Glow'
96 'Amazon Amethyst'
95 x ***andersonii*** 'Nancy Saunders'
88 'Angel Face'
96 'Angel Flight'
96 'Ann Kelley'
95 'Antarctica'
87 'Apollo'
88 'Applause'
96 'Apple Court Damson'
95 'Apple Tart'
89 'Ariadne'
92 'Arkansas Post'
94 'Asian Pheasant'
89 'Atlas'
89 'Atomic Age'
88 'August Pink'
93 ***aurantiaca***
95 'Aurora'
92 'Avanti'
95 'Azor'
95 'Back Bay'
96 'Barbara Corsair'
96 'Battle Hymn'
90 'Bees Rose'
88 'Belinda'
88 'Bellringer'
95 'Beloved Returns'
95 'Berlin Lemon' 🏆
95 'Berlin Red Velvet' 🏆
93 'Black Falcon'
96 'Black Prince'
92 'Blaze of Fire'
88 'Bold Ruler'
88 'Bonnie Rose'
95 'Boulderbrook Serenity'
88 'Bourbon Prince'
96 'Brass Buckles'
94 'Brass Cup'
94 'Bright Banner'
88 'Bright Charm'
88 'Brilliant Red'
89 'Broad Ripples'
96 'Button Box'
95 'By Jove'
91 'By Myself'
95 'Cadence'
96 'Camden Ballerina'
89 'Candle Glow'
88 'Candy Fluff'
88 'Capri'
96 'Captured Heart'
88 'Carriage Trade'
96 'Catherine Wheel'
95 'Caviar'
94 'Charlie Brown'
88 'Charlotte Holman'
94 'Cheek to Cheek'
93 'Cherry Smoke'
96 'Chestnut Lane'
88 'Chetco'
91 'Chicago Cameo'
91 'Chicago Sugar Plum'
95 'Child of Fortune'
89 'Claret Cup'
95 'Claudine'
94 'Constitutional Island'
88 'Coquinna'
96 'Corsican Bandit'
93 'Cosmic Flash'
94 'Crumpet'
87 'Cuddlesome'
91 'Curls'
94 'Curly Ripples'
96 'Dainty Dreamer'
95 'Daisy MacCarthy'
95 'Dancing Dwarf'
95 'Danity Dreamer'
96 'Dark Elf'
88 'Dauntless'
88 'Dawn Supreme'
89 'Delft Rose'
92 'Delicate Splendor'
96 'Delightsome'
88 'Demure'
90 'Deva'
95 'Dorcas'
96 'Double Coffee'
90 'Double Firecracker'
92 'Double Grapette'
95 'Double Pink Treasure'
95 'Down Town'
94 'Dresden Gleam'
88 'Dynamo'
88 'Eden'
95 'Elf's Cap'
95 'Elsie Spalding'
96 'Enchanting Blessing'
89 'Esther Murray'
96 'Fairy Delight'
96 'Fairy Jester'
95 'Fairy Wings'
88 'Far Afield'
92 'Far East'
96 'Feelings'
88 'Finlandia'
96 'Fire Music'
88 'First Romance'
87 'Flair'
95 'Folklore'
88 'Fond Caress'
96 ***forrestii***
88 'Fortyniner'
89 'Fox Grape'
96 'French Porcelain'
95 'Fresh Air'
94 'Frosty White'
96 'Full Reward'
95 'Gateway'
94 'Gay Nineteen'
88 'Georgia Peach'
94 'Glowing Gold'
92 'Gold Dust'
95 'Golden Chance'
89 'Golden Dewdrop'
89 'Golden Glory'
88 'Goldensong'
95 'Graceful Eye'
96 'Grape Velvet'
88 'Grecian Gift'
96 'Green Magic'
92 'Green Puff'
94 'Gusto'
95 'Hadspen Samphire'
96 'Heartthrob'
94 'Heaven Knows'
95 'Helle Berlinerin'
91 'Hemlock'
88 'High Glory'
95 'High Time'
88 'Hippity Hop'
95 'Holiday Harvest'
93 'Home Run'
95 'House of Lords'
90 'How about That'
94 'Ice Castles'
96 'Ice Cool'
88 'Illinois'
92 'Indian Serenade'
88 'Inlaid Gold'
88 'Irene Felix'
94 'Iron Gate Glacier'
94 'Iron Gate Iceberg'
88 'Jack Frost'
89 'Jake Russell'
88 'Janet'
88 'Joan Durelle'
96 'Journey's End'
96 'Jovial'
88 'July Gold'
88 'June Royalty'
91 'Kathleen Ormerod'
92 'Kecia'
94 'Kelway's Gold'
96 'Killer Purple'
92 'Kinfolk'
89 'King Haiglar'
96 'Lady Inora Cubiles'
95 'Lady Limelight'
96 'Lady Mischief'
91 'Late Advancement'
88 'Late Date'
88 'Laurel Anne'
95 'Lemon Ice'
88 'Lester Pastel'
87 'Lilac Chiffon'
87 'Lilly Dache'
96 'Lilting Lady'
93 'Little Greenie'
94 'Little Men'
95 'Little Sally'
96 'Little Showoff'
94 'Little Toddler'
92 'Littlest Angel'
93 'Lively Set'
96 'Louis McHargue'
95 'Loving Memories'
96 'Lowenstine'
96 'Lukey Boy'
96 'Luna Danca'
95 'Lusty Leland'
93 'Magic Dawn'
89 'Mantra'
91 'Marcus Perry'
90 'Margaret Perry'
88 'Mary Anne'
89 'Mascot'
88 'Melotone'
96 'Midnight Magic'
96 'Misty'
96 'Mokan Cindy'
88 'Momento'
96 'Mormon Spider'
94 'Mount Joy'
89 'Mrs B.F. Bonner'
89 'Multnomah'
94 'My Happy Valentine'
88 'Nehoiden'
93 'New Swirls'
91 'Night Hawk'
96 'Nile Plum'
96 'Nina Winegar'
88 'Northfield'
96 'Nova'
96 'Nutmeg Elf'
87 'Old Vintage'
95 'Open Hearth'
91 'Ophir'
91 'Oriontio'
94 'Ozark Lass'
94 'Party Partner'
94 'Pastel Accent'
93 'Patricia Fay'
95 'Peaceful'
92 'Peach Supreme'
95 'Peacock Maiden'
88 'Pecheron'
87 'Pink Perfection'
96 'Pink Snowflake'
88 'Polar Bear'
88 'Powder Puff'
96 'Prairie Sunset'
89 'Precious'
93 'Precious Treasure'
94 'Premier'
90 'President'
96 'Prince Redbird'
95 'Pumpkin Face'
96 'Rare China'
91 'Raspberry Pixie'
96 'Raspberry Sundae'
94 'Revolute'
93 'Right On'
94 'Rosavel'
89 'Rose Motif'
88 'Rosetta'
88 'Roseway'
96 'Royal Ruby'
96 'Royal Saracen'
94 'Ruffled Pinafore'
94 'Saladin'
96 'Sari'
96 'Sariah'
88 'Satin Glass'
87 'Sawanne Belle'
87 'Sea Gypsy'
95 'Seductress'
88 'Shell Cameo'
88 'Sherwood'

96 'Show Amber'
96 'Silent World'
94 'Siloam Queen's Toy'
96 'Siloam Rose Queen'
88 'Sleeping Beauty'
96 'Smoky Mountain Autumn'
88 'Snappy Rhythm'
94 'Snow Elf'
95 'So Excited'
91 'Soft Whisper'
96 'Solano Bulls Eye'
92 'Soledad'
96 'Solid Scarlet'
95 'Sound of Music'
96 'Spanish Gold'
89 'Star Ruby'
92 'Stolen Hours'
96 'Summer Interlude'
93 'Sun Pixie'
93 'Sure Thing'
88 'Sweetheart Supreme'
96 'Taffy Tot'
89 'Taj Mahal'
96 'Telstar'
88 'Temple Bells'
93 'Thelma Perry'
88 'Theresa Hall'
96 'Thy True Love'
87 'Tiny Tex'
94 'Tom Collins'
96 'Tootsie'
93 'Turkish Turban'
96 'Twenty Third Psalm'
96 'Veiled Beauty'
94 'Vesper Song'
93 'Walt Disney'
88 'War Clouds'
96 'War Paint'
88 'Whirl of Lace'
94 'Whiskey on Ice'
96 'Wind Song'
95 'Windsong'
94 'Winnetka'
95 'Winnie the Pooh'
96 'World of Peace'
88 'Yellow Beacon'
94 'Young Countess'

HEMIPHRAGMA
89 ***heterophyllum***

HEMIZYGIA
96 ***obermeyerae***

HEPATICA
94 ***maxima***
94 ***nobilis*** 'Elkofener Heidi'
94 – 'Elkofener Micky'
94 – 'Elkofener Resi'
94 – 'Elkofener Schrei'
95 – 'Landquart Marble'
93 – 'Little Abington'
91 – 'Tabby'
92 ***transsilvanica*** 'Ada Scott'
95 – 'Nivea'
94 – pink

HEPTACODIUM
95 ***miconioides***

HERACLEUM
96 ***nepalense*** B&SWJ 2105
93 ***stevenii***

HERBERTIA
96 ***pulchella***

HERMANNIA
95 ***depressa*** S&SH 12
96 ***pinnata***

HERPOLIRION
93 ***novae-zealandiae***

HESPEROCHIRON
95 ***californicus***

HEUCHERA
96 'Apple Blossom'
93 'Baby's Breath'
87 'Damask'
96 'Dingle Amber'
96 'Dingle Mint Chocolate'
87 'Freedom'
91 'Gloriana'
96 ***hallii***
93 'Ibis'
94 ***maritima***
96 'Mary Rose'
94 ***micrantha*** var. ***diversifolia***
96 'Moondrops'
90 'Oakington Superba'
96 ***parvifolia***
88 'Pruhoniciana'
88 ***sanguinea*** 'Variegata'
91 'Shere Variety'
95 'Sparkler' (v)

HEXAGLOTTIS
95 ***longifolia***

HIBISCUS
91 ***diversifolius***
94 'Dixie Belle'
94 ***fallax***
96 ***geranioides***
94 'Hawaiian Girl'
93 ***militaris***
96 'Morning Glory'
88 ***moscheutos*** subsp. ***palustris***
96 – Southern Belle Group
94 ***pedunculatus***
93 ***purpureus*** 'Variegatus'
94 ***rosa-sinensis*** 'American Beauty'
94 – 'Brilliant'
90 – 'Colombo'
90 – 'Nairobi'
90 – 'Paramaibo'
94 – 'Ross Estey'
94 ***sinosyriacus*** 'Autumn Surprise'
96 – 'Red Centre'
94 ***storckii***
89 ***syriacus*** 'Caeruleus Plenus'
92 – 'Hinomaru' (d)
90 – 'Violet Clair Double'
94 ***tiliaceus***

HIERACIUM
96 ***alpinum***
93 ***candidum***
96 ***glabrum***
96 ***mixtum***
95 ***pannosum*** NS 399
88 × ***rubrum***

× HIPPEASPREKELIA
96 'Mystique'

HIPPEASTRUM
91 'Amadeus'
94 'Bouquet'
91 'Bright Red'
91 'Cantate'
94 'Fire Dance'
94 ***gracile*** 'Donau'
95 – 'Pamela'
96 'King of the Stripes'
96 'Lucky Strike'
94 'Maria Goretti'
91 'Minerva'
91 'Orange Souvereign' 🏆
91 'Orange Star'
94 ***phycelloides***
96 'Rosy Queen'
91 'Salmon Beauty'
96 'Spotty'
94 'Striped Vlammenspel'
91 'Valentine'
96 'Vera'
96 'White Snow'
91 'Wonderful'
96 'Wonderland'

HIRPICIUM
95 ***armerioides*** S&SH 6

HOHERIA
92 ***populnea*** 'Alba Variegata'
87 – var. ***sinclairii***
94 ***sexstylosa*** var. ***crataegifolia***

HOLODISCUS
95 ***discolor*** var. ***ariifolius***

HOMALOTHECA
94 ***supina***

HOMERIA
95 ***comptonii***

HOOKERIA
96 ***lucens***

HORDEUM
96 ***murinum***

HORKELIA
96 ***fusca capitata***

HOSTA
92 'Anne Arett' (v)
95 'Apple Pie'
91 'Besançon' (*ventricosa*)
93 'Big John' (*sieboldiana*)
91 'Blue Fan Dancer'
91 'Blue Piecrust'
95 ***capitata***
96 'Chelsea Ore' (*plantaginea*) (v)
91 'Claudia'
92 'Dark Victory'
94 'Devon Cream'
96 'Devon Giant'
95 'Emma Foster' (*montana*)
95 'Eunice Choice'
93 ***fortunei*** var. ***albopicta*** f. ***viridis***
91 'Freising' (*fortunei*)
95 'Gingee'
95 'Golden Giboshi'
91 'Green Formal'
92 'Green Ripples'
95 'Green Smash'
91 'Grenfell's Greatest' (*sieboldiana*)
92 'Hadspen Nymphaea'
93 'Harvest Moon'
95 'Kath's Gold'
96 ***kikutii*** var. ***pruinosa***
96 'Lime Krinkles'
94 ***longipes*** var. ***longipes***
96 'Maculata'
93 'Maple Leaf' (*sieboldiana*) (v)
96 'Midwest Gold'
92 ***minor*** f. ***alba*** Maekawa
96 ***opipara***
95 'Parker Jervis Blue'
88 'Pixie Power'
92 'Primrose' (*kikutii*)
95 'Rosanne'
91 'Royal Lady' (*sieboldii*)
91 'Royal Tiara' (*nakaiana*) (v)
92 ***sieboldii*** f. ***spathulata***
92 – f. ***subcrocea***
91 'Susy'
91 (Tardiana Group) 'Baby Blue'
92 ***tardiflora*** 'Gold Streak'
89 ***tsushimensis***
96 'Wheaten Gold'
91 'Willy Nilly'

HOUSTONIA
87 ***serpyllifolia***

HOVENIA
94 ***acerba***

HOWEA
94 ***belmoreana***

HOYA
96 ***archboldiana***
93 ***carnosa*** 'Nana'
96 – 'Prolifica'
96 ***crassicaulis***
96 ***curtisii***
96 ***ischnopus***
96 ***kenejiana***
96 ***meredithii***
96 ***obovata***
96 ***parasitica*** var. ***citrina***
96 ***pottsii***
96 ***serpens***
96 ***uncinata***

HUGUENINIA
89 ***tanacetifolia***

HUMULUS
96 ***lupulus*** (f)
96 – (m)
95 – 'Northdown'
95 – 'Target'
91 – variegated

HYACINTHELLA
96 ***acutiloba***
94 ***heldreichii***
90 ***leucophaea***
94 ***lineata***
94 ***pallens***

HYACINTHOIDES
93 ***hispanica*** 'Azalea'
93 – 'Mount Everest'
93 – 'Myosotis'
94 – 'Queen of the Pinks'
94 – 'White City'
93 ***non-scripta*** white bell

HYACINTHUS
94 ***orientalis***
93 – 'Apollo'
91 – 'Blue Ice'
93 – 'Blushing Dolly'

93 – 'Cherry Blossom'
95 – 'Chestnut Flower' (d)
89 – 'Côte d'Azur'
93 – 'Debutante'
89 – 'Eros'
93 – 'Fireball'
91 – 'General Köhler' (d)
93 – 'Grace Darling'
93 – 'Indian Prince'
92 – 'Madame Sophie' (d)
93 – 'Maryon'
93 – 'Morning Star'
93 – 'Orange Queen'
93 – 'Paul Hermann'
96 – 'Pink Surprise'
93 – 'Princess Victoria'
93 – 'Sky Jacket'
92 – 'Tubergen's Scarlet'
89 – 'Yellow Hammer'

HYBANTHUS
95 ***floribundus***

HYDRANGEA
89 ***arborescens*** subsp. ***discolor***
94 – 'Hills of Snow'
90 – subsp. ***radiata*** 'Robusta'
93 ***aspera*** 'Rocklon'
96 ***cordifolia***
92 ***heteromalla wilsonii***
95 ***hirta***
91 ***macrophylla*** 'Adria'
93 – 'Aduarda'
89 – 'Draps Pink' (H)
89 – 'Fargesii'
94 – 'Khudnert'
96 – 'Le Cygne' (H)
96 – 'Magic Light'
88 – 'Max Löbner'
88 – 'Mousseline' (H)
88 – 'Oamacha'
90 – 'Queen Elizabeth'
96 – 'Red Lacecap'
93 – 'Rheinland' (H)
93 – 'Rotdrossel' (L)
95 – 'Schadendorffs Perle'
96 – 'Tödi' (H)
89 – 'Yodogawa'
96 ***paniculata*** 'Touchard'
94 – 'Vera'
94 ***scandens*** subsp. ***chinensis***
93 ***serrata*** 'Amagyana'
92 – 'Impératrice Eugénie'
92 ***serrata koreana***

HYDROCLEYS
91 ***nymphoides***

HYDROPHYLLUM
96 ***appendiculatum***

HYMENOCALLIS
95 ***amancaes***

HYMENOSPORUM
95 ***flavum***

HYMENOXYS
96 ***lapidicola***
96 ***torreyana***

HYOPHORBE
94 ***verschaffeltii***

HYOSCYAMUS
96 ***aureus***

HYPERICUM
93 ***acmosepalum***
96 'Archibald'
93 ***armenum***
96 ***bellum*** pale form
93 ***calycinum aureum***
88 ***canariense***
92 ***cerastioides*** subsp. ***meuselianum***
93 ***delphicum***
92 'Eastleigh Gold'
95 ***empetrifolium*** subsp. ***empetrifolium*** NS 615
93 ***ericoides***
96 'Gemo'
95 ***henryi*** subsp. ***hancockii*** FSP 047
95 × ***inodorum***
89 – 'Hysan'
94 ***leschenaultii*** Choisy
95 ***maclarenii***
91 ***nanum***
91 ***patulum***
96 ***pseudohenryi***
88 ***pulchrum*** f. ***procumbens***
96 ***subsessile***
89 'Summer Sunshine'
89 ***xylosteifolium***

HYPOCHAERIS
94 ***acaulis*** F&W 7208
95 ***tenuifolia odorata*** F&W 7204

HYPOLEPIS
96 ***punctata***
92 ***rugulosa***

HYPOXIS
96 ***krebsii***

HYPSELA
89 ***rivalis***

HYSSOPUS
96 ***officinalis decussatus***
90 ***officinalis officinalis***
95 ***seravshanicus***

IBERIS
90 'Correifolia'
87 ***sempervirens*** 'Garrexiana'
88 – 'Gracilis'
93 – 'Variegata'

ILEX
87 × ***altaclerensis*** 'Balearica'
94 – 'Camelliifolia Variegata' (f)
89 – 'Maderensis'
91 – 'Moria' (f/v)
92 – 'Mundyi' (m)
91 ***aquifolium*** 'Apricot' (f)
91 – 'Cookii' (f)
93 – 'Donningtonensis' (m)
91 – 'Grandis'
91 – 'Green Sentinel' (f)
91 – 'Heterophylla Aurea Marginata' (m)
87 – 'Ovata' (m)
96 – 'Samuel Foster'
93 – 'Scotica' (f)
96 – 'Silver Wedding' (f/v)
93 ***attenuata*** × ***opaca***
92 ***buergeri***
96 ***cassine***
93 – var. ***angustifolia*** (f)
96 – yellow-berried
94 'Clusterberry' (f)
94 ***cornuta*** 'Burfordii' (f)
95 – Korean form
96 – 'Rotunda' (f)
96 ***crenata*** 'Bennett's Compact' (m)
93 – 'Congesta'
93 – 'David Ellis'
88 – 'Dwarf Pagoda' (f)
91 – 'Firefly' (m)
96 – 'Green Dragon'
93 – 'Green Lustre' (f)
96 – 'Ivory Hall' (f)
93 – 'Ivory Tower' (f)
94 – f. ***microphylla***
91 – var. ***paludosa***
93 – 'Piccolo' (f)
96 – 'Rotundifolia'
96 – 'Sentinel' (f)
94 – 'Twiggy' (f)
93 – f. ***watanabeana*** (f)
95 ***decidua*** 'Warren Red' (f)
92 ***dipyrena***
93 ***georgei***
93 ***glabra***
94 – 'Ivory Queen' (f)
91 – f. ***leucocarpa***
91 – 'Nana'
94 'Good Taste' (f)
96 ***hookeri***
91 ***integra***
94 'Jim'
90 ***leucoclada***
96 ***macrocarpa***
95 × ***meserveae*** 'Blue Boy' (m)
95 – 'Blue Girl' (f)
91 – Blue Stallion (m)
95 – 'Goliath' (f)
96 – 'Red Darling' (f)
96 ***myrtifolia*** yellow-berried
91 ***opaca*** 'Natalie Webster' (f)
93 – 'Villanova' (f)
92 ***pernyi*** 'Jermyns Dwarf' (f)
95 ***purpurea***
93 'Shin Nien' (m)
94 ***verticillata*** 'Christmas Cheer' (f)

ILLICIUM
93 ***anisatum laurifolium***
94 ***verum***

ILYSANTHES
95 ***floribunda***

IMPATIENS
94 ***burtonii***
93 ***congolensis***
95 'Damask Rose'
93 'Dan White'
93 'Danbee'
93 'Dandin'
93 'Danova'
93 'Danrose'
93 'Danshir'
93 'Dansky'
96 'Diamond Orange'
89 ***glandulifera*** white
93 'Lambada'
95 'Orange Delight'
93 'Samba'
92 ***scabrida***
92 'Strawberry Ripple'

INCARVILLEA
95 ***arguta*** CC&McK 117
96 ***compacta*** CLD 0233
93 ***emodi***
96 ***mairei multiflora*** var. ***mairei*** f. ***multifoliolata***
96 ***mairei*** pink
96 ***sinensis***

INDIGOFERA
89 ***decora*** f. ***alba***

INULA
96 ***candida***
95 ***ensifolia*** 'Compacta'
95 ***heterolepis***
95 ***montbretiana***
89 ***obtusifolia***
92 ***rhizocephala*** var. ***rhizocephaloides***
93 ***viscosa***

IOCHROMA
96 ***coelestis***
91 ***purpurea***

IPOMOEA
96 ***aculeata***
96 ***brasiliensis***
94 ***cairica***
96 ***costata***
95 ***hederacea***
96 ***leptotoma***
96 ***violacea*** Linnaeus

IPOMOPSIS
95 ***aggregata*** subsp. ***arizonica***
92 ***aggregata macrosiphon***
94 ***rubra***
95 – K 92.249
96 ***spicata*** var. ***orchidacea***
95 ***stenothyrsa***

IRESINE
94 ***lindenii*** 'Formosa'

IRIS
89 'Ablaze' (MDB)
95 ***acutiloba***
91 – subsp. ***lineolata***
95 'Agnes James' 🏆
89 'Airy Fancy' (Spuria)
96 ***aitchisonii*** var. ***chrysantha***
91 ***albomarginata***
96 'Alizes' (TB)
95 'All the Way' (AB)
93 'Alsterquelle' (SDB)
94 'Amazon Princess' (SDB)
87 'Amber' (TB)
95 'American Heritage' (TB)
93 'Amiquita' (CH)
96 'Amsterdam' (TB)
93 'Angel Eyes' (MDB)
96 'Angel's Kiss' (SDB)
96 'Annikins' (IB)
96 'Antarctic' (TB)
96 'Antique Ivory' (TB)
96 'April Accent' (MDB)
93 'April Sweetheart' (SDB)
96 'Apropos' (TB)
96 'Aquilifer' (AB)
96 'Arabic Night' (IB)

96 'Arctic Snow'
94 'Arctic Wine' (IB)
96 'Art Gallery' (IB)
92 'Astralite' (SDB)
93 'Auburn Valley' (SDB)
90 'Autumn Primrose' (TB)
95 'Azure Excho' (IB)
91 ***babadagica***
94 'Babe' (SDB)
91 'Ballerina'
95 'Banbury Velvet' 🏆
96 'Barbara's Kiss' (Spuria)
96 'Barletta' (TB)
92 'Barnett Anley'
89 ***barnumae*** f. ***urmiensis***
94 'Bay Ruffles' (SDB)
96 'Bedtime Story' (IB)
96 'Bel Azur' (IB)
89 'Bellboy' (MTB)
96 'Belle Meade' (TB)
96 'Bengal Tiger' (TB)
88 'Benton Yellow' (TB)
95 'Berry Rich' (BB)
96 'Bewick Swan' (TB)
88 'Bibelot' (BB)
96 'Big Money' (TB) 🏆
96 'Big Wheel' (CH)
91 'Black Forest' (TB)
93 'Black Ink' (TB)
92 'Black Onyx' (TB)
93 'Black Star' (SDB)
96 'Blackberry Brandy' (BB)
96 'Blackfoot'
96 'Blockley' (SDB)
93 'Blood Dance' (SDB)
93 'Blue Admiral' (TB)
95 'Blue Asterisk' (IB)
90 'Blue Beret' (MDB)
95 'Blue Chip Pink' (TB)
94 'Blue Elegance' (Dutch)
96 'Blue Eyed Brunette' (TB) 🏆
92 'Blue Frost' (IB)
96 'Blue Icing' (IB)
95 'Blue Mascara' (SDB)
96 'Blue Neon' (SDB)
95 'Blue Owl' (TB)
92 'Blue Petticoats' (TB)
94 'Blue Sapphire' (TB)
96 'Blue Sparks' (SDB)
88 'Blue Valley' (TB)
96 'Bluebird in Flight' (IB)
94 'Bluebird Wine' (TB)
96 'Blues Singer' (TB)
96 'Border Town' (Spuria)
95 'Bright Chic' (SDB)
91 'Bright Spring' (DB)
88 'Britomas' (TB)
95 'Bronze Perfection' (Dutch)
95 'Bronze Queen' (Dutch)
93 'Brown Chocolate'
96 'Brown Doll' (IB)
96 'Bubbly Blue' (IB)
95 ***bucharica*** × ***aucheri***
95 'Buckden Pike' 🏆
93 'Buckeye Blue' (SDB)
96 ***bulleyana*** ACE 1819
96 – ACE 1890
95 'Bunny Hop' (SDB)
88 'Buster Brown' (DB)
90 'Butter Cookie' (IB)
96 'Buttered Chocolate' (Spuria)
96 'Buttermilk'
93 'Buttertubs' (TB)
96 'Cabaret Royale' (TB)
89 'Calypso Clown' (AB)
94 'Camelot Rose' (TB)
95 'Canary Frills' (TB)
92 'Candy Apple' (SDB)
88 'Candy Cane' (BB)
96 'Can't Stop' (SDB)
92 'Cape Town' (TB)
92 'Cappucino' (CH)
94 'Captive Heart' (SDB)
96 'Caress' (SDB)
95 'Carmel Mission' (CH)
96 'Carnival Glass' (BB)
90 'Catani' (SDB)
96 ***caucasica***
95 'Center Ring' (TB)
96 'Champagne Music' (TB)
94 'Char True' (Spuria)
95 'Charter Member' (CH)
94 'Cherry Pop' (SDB)
93 'Chickee' (MTB)
96 'Chico Maid' (TB)
95 'Childsong' (AB)
94 'Chinese Coral' (TB)
91 'Chione' (Aril)
93 'Chippendale' (TB)
91 'Christmas Rubies' (TB)
92 ***chrysographes*** 'Black Magic'
93 – 'Rob'
93 – 'Rubens'
93 'Chubby Cheeks' (SDB)
91 'Chubby Cherub' (MDB)
89 'Cinnamon Roll' (Spuria)
89 'Cinnamon Stick' (Spuria)
89 'Circlette' (SDB)
96 'Circus Stripes' (TB)
95 'Cirrus' (TB)
94 'City Girl' (SDB)
89 'City of Lincoln' (TB)
95 'Classy Babe' (SDB)
96 'Clever Devil' (CH)
94 'Closed Circuit' (TB)
88 'Clotho' (Aril)
93 'Cloud Fluff' (IB)
96 'Colonial Gold' (TB)
95 'Comma' (SDB)
96 'Concord Touch' (SDB)
96 'Confederate Soldier' (IB)
88 'Constance Meyer' (TB)
96 'Copper Pot' (TB)
93 'Coquette Doll' (SDB)
96 'Cotati' (BB)
94 'Court Magician' (SDB)
88 'Craithie' (TB)
96 'Cranberry Crush' (TB)
93 ***crenata*** 'Lady Gem'
93 'Crimson Velvet' (SDB)
92 'Crispette' (TB)
94 'Crispin' (SDB)
96 ***cristata*** 'Abbey's Violet'
95 'Crocus' (MDB)
96 'Crushed Velvet' (TB)
92 'Crystal Bright' (SDB)
96 'Curio' (MDB)
96 'Curlew' (IB)
96 'Cyanea' (DB)
96 'Cycles' (TB)
91 'Dainty Belle' (MDB)
92 'Daisy Powell' (TB)
96 'Dardanus' (Aril)
95 'Daring Eyes' (MDB)
92 'Dark Fairy' (SDB)
92 'Dark Fury' (TB)
93 'Dash Away' (SDB)
92 'Debra Jean' (TB)
96 'Deep Space' (TB)
95 'Deepening Shadows' (CH)
93 ***delavayi*** 'Didcot'
96 'Deltaplane' (TB)
96 'Derry Down' (SDB)
96 'Diligence' (SDB)
96 'Disco Jewel' (MTB)
94 'Ditto' (MDB)
94 'Dixie Pixie' (SDB)
92 'Doll Dress' (BB)
92 'Dotted Swiss'
94 'Douglas 402' (TB)
89 ***douglasiana*** 'Apple Court White'
96 'Dragonsdawn' (AB)
95 'Dream Builder' (TB)
93 'Dumpling' (MDB)
93 'Dusky Dancer' (TB)
96 'Dutch Chocolate' (TB)
96 'Early Frost' (IB)
93 'Early Snowbird' (TB)
94 'Easy Grace' (TB)
94 'Eccentric' (SDB)
93 'Echo Pond' (MTB)
92 'Ecstatic Night' (TB)
96 'Edale' (TB)
92 'Egret Snow' (MDB)
95 'Elegans' (TB)
96 'Elisa Renee' (TB)
96 'Elizabeth of England' (TB)
92 'Ellen Manor' (TB)
92 'Elusive Quest' (IB)
92 'Emerald Fountain' (TB)
94 'Emphasis' (TB)
94 'Empress of India' (TB)
96 'Encanto' (SDB)
96 'Enchanted Blue' (SDB)
96 'Encircle' (CH)
96 ***ensata*** 'Aoigata'
96 – 'Beni Renge'
95 – 'Benokohji'
89 – 'Buri-cho'
89 – 'Chidori'
89 – 'Chigesyo'
95 – 'Continuing Pleasure' 🏆
95 – 'Flying Tiger' 🏆
96 – 'Geisha Gown'
96 – 'Geisha Obi'
96 – 'Hoyden'
96 – 'Imperial Velvet'
95 – 'Katy Mendez' 🏆
92 – 'Koko-no-iro'
89 – 'Murakumo'
96 – 'Prairie Glory'
96 – 'Prairie Noble'
96 – 'Royal Banner'
96 – 'Royal Game'
95 – 'Sapphire Star'
96 – 'Sorceror's Triumph'
95 – 'Southern Son' 🏆
93 – 'Springtime Showers'
96 – 'White Chiffon'
95 – 'Winged Sprite'
96 – 'World's Delight' 🏆
92 'Esther Fay' (TB)
90 'Ethel Hope' (Spuria)
94 'Evening Pond' (MTB)
96 'Ever After' (TB)
96 'Exotic Gem' (TB)
94 'Eye Shadow' (SDB)
96 'Fall Primrose' (TB)
94 'Fancy Caper' (IB)
92 'Fantasy Faire' (TB)
96 'Fantasy World' (IB)
94 'Fashion Fling' (TB)
92 'Fashion Show' (TB)
93 'Fiji Dancer' (TB)
95 'Fine Line' (CH)
96 'First Chapter' (AB)
96 'First Lilac' (IB)
93 'First Step' (SDB)
96 'Flammenschwert' (TB)
93 'Flareup' (TB)
96 'Flash'
95 'Flight of Cavalry' (IB)
93 'Forte' (SDB)
96 'Foxcote' (IB)
94 'Foxfire' (TB)
93 'Fracas' (SDB)
89 'Frenchii' (BB)
93 'From the Heart' (IB)
96 'Frosted Angel' (SDB)
96 'Frosty Crown' (SDB)
95 'Funny Face' (MDB)
93 'Funtime' (SDB)
96 'Gala Gown' (TB)
95 ***galatica***
92 'Galilee' (TB)
96 'Gallant Moment' (TB)
94 'Galleon Gold' (SDB)
93 'Garden Gnome' (MDB)
95 'Gelee Royal' (AB)
92 'Gemini' (BB)
89 'Gentle Grace' (SDB)
92 'Gilston Guitar' (TB)
94 'Gilston Gulf' (TB)
92 'Gingerbread Castle' (TB)
96 'Gleaming Gold' (SDB)
94 'Glee Club' (IB)
95 'Going West' (CH)
96 'Gold Intensity' (BB)
89 'Golden Chocolate' (Spuria)
92 'Golden Chord' (TB)
93 'Golden Emperor' (Dutch)
94 'Golden Eyelet' (MDB)
93 'Golden Forest' (TB)
89 'Golden Glow' (TB)
95 'Golden Hind' (TB)
94 'Good Morning America' (TB)
96 'Goring Ace' (CH) 🏆
92 'Gosau' (TB)
93 'Gossamer Steel' (TB)
88 'Grace Sturtevant' (TB)
93 'Graclac'
96 'Granada Gold' (TB)
95 'Grape Orbit' (SDB)
94 'Gringo' (TB)
91 'Gudrun' (TB)
91 'Gypsy Eyes' (SDB)
92 'Gypsy Jewels' (TB)
88 'Gypsy Smoke' (IB)

96 'Gyro' (TB)
96 'Halo in Pink' (TB)
96 'Halo in Yellow' (TB)
95 'Hands On' (CH)
96 'Happy Mood' (IB) 🏆
96 ***hartwegii***
96 – subsp. ***columbiana***
95 'Harvest Festival' (SDB)
88 ***haynei***
93 'Heather Hawk' (TB)
96 'Heavenly Days' (TB)
96 'Hedge'
92 'Helen Traubel' (TB)
88 ***hermona***
94 'High Barbaree' (TB)
94 'Highland Cascade' (TB)
95 'Hildegarde' (Dutch)
88 'Hipermestra' (Aril)
96 ***histrioides***
95 – 'Angel's Eye'
93 – var. ***sophenensis***
95 'Holiday Flame' (IB)
96 'Honey Dip' (SDB)
96 'Hoodwink' (SDB)
89 ***hoogiana*** 'Noblesse'
95 'Hot Number' (CH)
96 'Hugh Miller' (TB)
95 'Ice Dancer' 🏆
96 'Ice White'
95 'Idylwild' (CH)
90 'I'm Yellow' (SDB)
96 ***imbricata***
92 'Immortal Hour'
91 'Impelling' (BB)
96 'Imperial Sun' (Spuria)
90 'In the Buff' (IB)
96 'Indiscreet' (TB)
96 'Inferno' (TB)
91 'Instructor'
94 'Interpol' (TB)
92 'Invisible Ink' (MDB)
91 'Iris King' (IB)
92 'Irish Lullaby' (TB)
96 'Irish Spring' (TB)
96 'Ivor Knowles' (CH)
94 'Ivory Gown' (TB)
96 'Jana White' (MTB)
94 'Janice Ruth' (TB)
93 ***japonica*** 'Rudolph Spring'
91 'Jill Welch' (MTB)
95 'Jillaroo' (SDB)
93 'Jillian Mason' (IB)
95 'Jitterbug' (TB)
96 'Joan Lay' (TB)
95 'Joanna' (TB)
96 'Joyce McBride' (SDB)
95 'Jungle Warrior' (SDB)
92 'Just So' (SDB)
94 'Kansas' (TB)
96 'Kashmir White' (TB)
95 'Kate Izzard' (TB)
95 'Katie-Koo' 🏆
96 'Kildonan' (TB)
95 ***kirkwoodii***
94 'Kiwi Slices' (SDB)
94 'Knotty Pine' (SDB)
94 ***kolpakowskiana***
93 ***korolkowii***
89 – 'Concolor'
95 'La Selva Beach' (CH)
92 'La Senda' (Spuria)
96 'Lace Jabot' (TB)
96 'Lady Ilse' (TB)
96 'Lady River' (TB)
96 'Lamorna' (TB)
93 'Langport Carnival' (IB)
95 'Langport Dawn' (IB)
96 'Langport Dolly' (IB)
96 'Langport Finch' (IB)
96 'Langport Flash' (IB)
94 'Langport Girl' (IB)
96 'Langport Judy' (IB)
96 'Langport Kestrel' (IB)
96 'Langport Lady' (IB)
95 'Langport Pansy' (IB)
96 'Langport Secret' (IB)
96 'Langport Smoke' (IB)
96 'Langport Snow' (IB)
96 'Langport Tartan' (IB)
95 'Las Olas' (CH)
95 'Laura' (TB)
96 'Lavanesque' (TB)
91 'Lavender Ribbon'
96 'Lavender Royal' (CH) 🏆
94 'Lemon Blossom' (SDB)
91 'Lemon Charm' (SDB)
92 'Lemon Duet' (TB)
93 'Lemon Lark' (SDB)
93 'Lemon Queen' (Dutch)
95 'Lenzschnee' (TB)
94 'Licorice Stick' (TB)
96 'Light Laughter' (IB)
95 'Lighted Window' (TB)
91 'Lighten Up' (SDB)
96 'Likiang' (Chrysographes)
92 'Lilac Festival' (TB)
95 'Lilac Lulu' (SDB)
93 'Lilac Mist' (TB)
92 'Lima Colada' (SDB)
92 'Lime Ripples' (IB)
95 'Lincoln Imp' (CH) 🏆
96 'Lindis' (AB)
94 'Liquid Smoke' (TB)
94 'Little Bishop' (SDB)
96 'Little Jewel' (DB)
95 'Little Miss' (BB)
96 'Little Sir Echo' (BB)
94 'Little Suki' (SDB)
89 'Little Swinger' (BB)
95 'Little Tilgates' 🏆
96 'Little Vanessa' (SDB)
92 'Little Wonder' (IB)
88 'L'lita' (TB)
93 'Logo' (IB)
95 'Lollipop' (SDB)
94 'Lorna Lee' (TB)
91 ***lortetii***
88 – var. ***samariae***
94 'Louise Hopper' (MTB)
94 'Love Chant' (TB)
94 'Love Lisa' (SDB)
94 'Lovely Me' (SDB)
93 'Love's Allure' (TB)
96 'Lucinda' (TB)
93 'Lunar Fire' (TB)
94 ***lutescens*** 'Jackanapes'
91 – 'Nancy Lindsay'
93 'Lynn Hall' (TB)
95 'Lynwood Gold' (IB)
95 ***maackii***
96 ***macrosiphon***
96 'Magharee' (TB)
95 'Maiden Blush' (TB)
96 'Main Sequence' (AB)
95 'Mama Hoohoo' (IB)
96 'Maori King' (TB)
95 'Mar Monte' (CH)
96 'Margrave' (TB)
89 'Mariposa Tarde' (Spuria)
96 'Marmot' (MDB)
94 'Maroon Caper' (IB)
90 'Mary B' (MDB)
89 'Masked Ball' (TB)
92 'May Thirty-first' (SDB)
96 'Meadow Moss' (SDB)
93 'Memphis Delight' (TB)
96 'Merry Madrigal' (TB)
96 'Midas Kiss' (IB)
96 ***milesii*** CC&McK 357
92 'Mill Pond' (MDB)
96 'Mini Dynamo' (SDB)
90 'Mini Plic' (MDB)
94 'Mirror Image' (TB)
93 'Miss Banbury' (TB)
95 'Mission Santa Cruz' (CH)
93 'Mockingbird' (MTB)
96 'Modern Classic' (TB)
96 'Moon Shadows' (SDB)
92 'Morning Sunlight' (TB)
93 'Mulberry Rose' (TB)
96 'Music Caper' (SDB)
93 'Music Maker' (TB)
96 'Mute Swan' (TB)
96 'Myra's Child' (SDB)
90 'Nancy's Khaki' (TB)
95 'Naranja' (TB)
93 'Narnia' (SDB)
96 'Navy Doll' (MDB)
96 'New Wave' (MTB)
96 'Night Affair' (TB)
96 'Night Edition' (TB)
95 'Night Shift' (IB)
93 'Nightfall'
95 'Nineveh' (AB)
94 'Normandie' (TB)
95 'Norton Sunlight' (Spuria)
95 'Nuggets' (MDB)
95 ***nusairiensis***
89 'Of Course' (IB)
94 'Oh Jay' (SDB)
94 'Ohio Belle' (SDB)
96 'Oktoberfest' (TB)
95 'Old Monterey' (CH)
96 'On Fire' (SDB)
88 'Oracle' (BB)
91 'Orangerie'
95 'Orchid Flare' (MDB)
95 'Oriental Baby' (IB)
96 'Oroville' (Spuria)
95 'Ouija' (BB) 🏆
96 'Outline' (AB)
96 'Outstep' (SDB)
93 'Owlet' (SDB)
94 'Pagan Princess' (TB)
96 'Painted Rose' (MTB)
96 ***pallida*** JCA 589.800
93 – × ***tectorum***
94 'Palomino' (TB)
91 ***pamphylica***
91 'Panda' (MTB)
96 'Paradise Pink' (TB)
94 ***paradoxa***
95 'Parakeet' (MTB)
91 ***parvula***
94 'Passport' (BB)
93 'Patacake' (SDB)
96 'Patina' (TB)
93 'Peach Float' (TB)
96 'Peach Melba' (TB)
94 'Peaches ala Mode' (BB)
94 'Pecan Spot' (SDB)
96 'Penny Bunker' (Spuria)
96 'Penny Candy' (MDB)
89 'Pepper Mill' (SDB)
93 'Perry Hill' (TB)
93 'Persian Fancy' (TB)
95 'Petite Polka' (SDB)
95 'Phillida' 🏆
88 'Pink Charm' (TB)
95 'Pink Pleasure' (TB)
95 'Piper's Tune' (IB)
96 'Pippi Longstockings' (SDB)
94 'Piroska' (TB)
96 'Pixie' (DB)
96 'Pixie Plum' (SDB)
94 'Pixie Princess' (SDB)
94 ***planifolia***
96 ***plicata***
93 'Poet' (TB)
96 'Popinjay' (CH)
93 'Powder Rock' (TB)
93 'Prairie Sunset' (TB)
95 'Prairie Warbler' (Chrysographes)
92 'Primrose Drift' (TB)
92 'Princely' (TB)
90 'Princess of Love' (SDB)
93 'Privileged Character' (SDB)
95 'Prodigy' (MDB)
96 'Prophetic Message' (AB)
96 'Proud Land' (TB)
96 ***pseudacorus*** 'Kimboshi' × ***ensata***
91 – 'Mandshurica'
96 – 'Tiger Brother'
95 ***pumila aequiloba***
94 ***pumila lutea***
96 ***purdyi***
96 – × ***tenuissima***
96 'Purple Dream' (CH)
92 'Pussycat' (MDB)
94 'Pussytoes' (MDB)
95 'Quip' (MDB)
94 'Rabbit's Foot' (SDB)
95 'Rainbow Connection' (CH)
91 'Rainbow Rock'
93 'Rainbow Sherbet' (SDB)
95 'Raindance Kid' (IB)
95 'Raku' (CH)
92 'Raspberry Ripples' (TB)
94 'Raspberry Rose' (IB)
94 'Raven Hill' (TB)
88 'Real Gold' (AB)
92 'Red Atlast' (MDB)
96 'Red Kite' (TB)
93 'Red Oak' (Spuria)
94 'Red Tempest' (IB)
93 'Red Ward' (TB)
92 'Redwood Falls' (Spuria)
96 'Reflection'
92 'Regal Splendor' (TB)
94 ***regis-uzziae*** S&L 133

93 'Reluctant Dragon' (SDB)
89 'Reuthe's Bronze' (CH)
92 'Revved Up' (IB)
96 'Rickshaw' (SDB)
96 'Ride Joy' (TB)
96 'Right Royal' (TB)
95 'Ring o'Roses' (CH) 🏆
95 'Rio del Mar' (CH) 🏆
93 'Rio Tulare'
89 'Ripe Wheat' (Spuria)
92 'Risque' (TB)
95 'Roaring Camp' (CH) 🏆
96 'Rose Caress' (TB)
96 'Roseplic' (TB)
94 'Rosie Lulu' (SDB)
95 'Royal Blue' (Reticulata)
95 'Royal Elf' (SDB)
96 'Royal Eyelash' (SDB)
96 'Royal Ruffles' (TB)
93 'Royal Sparks' (SDB)
95 'Royal Velours'
92 'Rumbling Thunder' (TB)
92 'Runaway' (IB)
93 'Rushing Stream' (TB)
96 'Ruth Nies Cabeen' (Spuria)
96 'Safari Boy' (IB)
93 'Saffron Charm' (AB)
96 'Sailor's Dance' (TB)
92 'Saint Teresa' (IB)
92 'Saintbury' (SDB)
94 'Sam Carne'
91 x ***sambucina***
95 'San Andreas' (CH)
96 'San Jose' (TB)
92 'San Leandro' (TB)
96 'Sandy Caper' (IB)
96 'Santa Clarita' (CH)
94 'Sass with Class' (SDB)
95 'Saturnus' (Dutch)
94 ***schachtii***
95 'School Boy' (CH)
95 'Sea Gal' (CH)
96 'Sea Urchin' (SDB)
93 'Seawolf' (TB)
93 'Serena' (TB)
95 ***setosa major***
95 'Shaft of Gold' (TB)
91 'Shawsii'
95 'Sheer Class' (SDB)
95 'Sheik' (AB)
92 'Sherborne' (SDB)
96 'Short Distance' (IB)
95 ***sibirica*** 'Ashfield Clementine'
95 – 'Berlin Ruffles' 🏆
95 – 'Cleeton Double Chance' 🏆
96 – 'Feathered Giant'
95 – 'Hubbard'
87 – 'Jirovette'
96 – 'Lavender Bonanza'
94 – 'Letitia'
91 – 'Mabel Coday'
96 – 'Marshmallow Frosting'
88 – 'Miss Underwood'
87 – 'Mountain Lake'
91 – 'Mrs Perry'
96 – 'Nora Distin'
91 – 'Pearl Queen'
95 – 'Polly Dodge'
92 – 'Roanoke's Choice'
96 – 'Shrawley'
94 – 'Signals Blue'
88 – 'Snow Princess'
95 – 'Splash Down' 🏆
89 – 'Steve'
90 – 'Tetra-white Rose'
89 – 'Turquoise Cup'
93 – 'White Sails'
89 – 'Wine Wings'
95 – 'Zakopane' 🏆
93 'Sigh' (SDB)
88 'Silver Shower' (TB)
95 'Simply Wild' (CH)
93 'Sindpers' (Juno)
93 ***sintenisii*** subsp. ***brandzae***
93 'Sky Bolt' (SDB)
96 'Sky Search' (TB)
95 'Skylaser' (CH)
96 'Smiling Gold' (TB)
95 'Smoky Valley' (BB)
93 'Snappie' (IB)
96 'Snow Festival' (IB)
94 'Snow Gambit' (MTB)
96 'Snow Troll' (SDB)
95 'Snowcone' (IB)
95 'Snowy River' (MDB)
95 'Solar Song' (SDB)
93 'Somerset Girl' (TB)
93 'Something Special' (BB)
96 'Song of Spring' (TB)
96 'Sounder' (BB)
90 'Southcombe Velvet'
96 sp. CLD 1399
94 'Space Odyssey' (TB)
95 'Spanish Don' (CH)
90 'Sparkling Waters' (TB)
90 'Spartan'
93 'Speckled Bird' (AB)
92 'Spring Fern' (SDB)
89 'Spring Reverie' (Spuria)
96 'Spring Wine' (IB)
96 ***spuria*** subsp. ***demetrii***
96 'Stability' (Spuria)
94 'Star Shower' (SDB)
93 'Stardate' (SDB)
93 'Starlight Waltz' (SDB)
96 'Starlit River' (TB)
95 ***stenophylla***
96 'Stepping Little' (BB)
92 'Sterling Silver' (TB)
96 ***stolonifera*** 'George Barr'
92 'Strawberry Sundae' (TB)
93 'Striking Gold' (MTB)
93 'Strum' (IB)
96 'Stylish' (DB)
88 'Sugar Pie' (BB)
94 'Sugar Please' (SDB)
96 'Sullom Voe' (TB)
96 'Sultry Sister' (TB)
93 'Summer Pearl' (TB)
93 'Sun King' (TB)
93 'Sun Miracle' (TB)
96 'Sun Symbol' (SDB)
94 'Sunbrella' (SDB)
94 'Sunlit Trail' (SDB)
96 'Sunny Side' (Spuria)
95 'Sunny Smile' 🏆
92 'Sunrise Point' (TB)
96 'Sunset Fires' (TB)
96 'Sunset Trail' (AB)
94 'Surprise Blue' (MTB)
95 'Surprise Sultan' (TB)
96 'Suspense' (Spuria)
96 'Svelte' (IB)
96 'Swahili' (TB)
94 'Sweet Lavender' (TB)
94 'Sweet Treat' (SDB)
96 'Sylvia Murray' (TB)
96 'Symphony' (Dutch)
94 'Tanex'
92 'Tea Rose' (TB)
92 'Techny Chimes' (TB)
96 'Tell Fibs' (SDB)
91 'Tender Tears' (SDB)
96 'Tequila Sunrise' (TB)
93 'The Desert' (TB)
94 'Thor' (Aril)
88 'Three Oaks' (TB)
94 'Threepio' (SDB)
96 'Thrice Blessed' (SDB)
93 'Tic Tac' (MDB)
95 'Tid-bit' (DB)
96 'Tidle de Winks' (BB)
93 'Tillamook' (TB)
91 ***timofejewii***
92 'Ting-a-ling' (MTB)
94 ***tingitana***
93 – var. ***fontanesii***
95 'Tintinara' (TB)
94 'Toasty' (SDB)
90 Tol-Long
96 'Tom Tit' (TB)
94 'Torchy' (SDB)
96 'Tornado' (AB)
96 'Transcribe' (SDB)
96 'Treasure' (TB)
93 'Tricks' (SDB)
91 'Triple Crown'
93 'Trout River'
91 'Tulare' (BB)
95 'Tupelo Honey' (TB)
96 'Turkish Warrior' (AB)
95 'Twin Lakes' (CH)
93 'Twist of Lemon' (MDB)
92 'Two Bits' (MTB)
92 'Ultrapoise' (TB)
96 ***unguicularis*** JCA 600.412
95 'Ursula Vahl' (TB)
96 'Vague a l'Ame' (TB)
93 'Valimar' (TB)
95 ***variegata alba***
94 ***variegata*** var. ***reginae***
94 'Velvet Robe' (TB)
91 'Velvet Toy' (MDB)
91 ***versicolor alba***
96 'Vim' (SDB)
95 'Vinho Verde' 🏆
96 'Violet Zephyr' (Spuria)
96 'Violetta' (DB)
90 ***virginica***
93 'Virtue' (IB)
94 'Wake Up' (SDB)
95 'Wampum' (IB)
95 'Warl-sind' (Juno)
96 'Watchman' (AB)
94 'Waterboy' (SDB)
94 'Wedding Vow' (TB)
94 'Wee Doll' (MDB)
95 'Welfenprinz' 🏆
94 'Well Suited' (SDB)
95 'Wensleydale' 🏆
95 'Westerlies' (CH)
95 'Wharfedale' 🏆
93 'Whisky' (MDB)
96 'White Superior' (Dutch)
95 'White Wedgwood' (Dutch)
92 'Wild Ginger' (TB)
92 'Winkieland' (IB)
95 'Wirral Gold' 🏆
90 'Witch Doctor' (TB)
96 'Woodling' (SDB)
93 'Worlds Beyond' (TB)
92 ***xiphium*** 'Lusitanica'
92 'Yellow and White'
95 'Yellow Apricot' (Chrysographes)
95 'Yellow Court' (Chrysographes)
89 'Yellow Queen' (Dutch)
96 'Yvonne Pelletier' (TB)
96 'Zipper' (MDB)

ISOPYRUM

93 ***affine-stoloniferum***

IXIA

93 ***conferta***
93 'Hubert'
93 ***rapunculoides***
93 'Uranus'

JABOROSA

96 ***magellanica***

JASIONE

89 ***crispa*** subsp. ***amethystina***
88 ***laevis*** subsp. ***orbiculata***
96 sp. from Spain
89 ***tuberosa***

JASMINUM

91 ***dispermum***
96 ***humile*** B&L 12086
95 – KR 709
96 ***simplicifolium*** subsp. ***suavissimum***
95 x ***stephanense*** 'Variegatum'

JEFFERSONIA

92 ***dubia*** 'Alba'

JOVIBARBA

94 ***allionii*** from Estang x *hirta* from Biele
94 – x ***hirta*** subsp. ***glabrescens*** from Smeryouka
95 ***arenaria*** 'Opiz'
92 ***heuffelii*** 'Blaze'
92 – 'Bolero'
94 – 'Brocade'
96 – 'Bronze King'
90 – 'Cameo'
92 – 'Capricorn'
92 – 'Cinnabar'
94 – 'Cloverdale'
94 – 'Hystyle'
92 – 'Iobates'
92 – var. ***patens***
92 – 'Purple Light'
92 – 'Starlight'
96 – 'Sundancer'
89 – 'Wotan'
90 – 'Xanthoheuff'
94 ***hirta*** from Col d'Aubisque
92 x ***kwediana*** 'Pickwick'
92 x ***nixonii*** 'Stefan'
92 x ***smithii*** 'Ritz'

JUANIA
90 ***australis***

JUANULLOA
91 ***mexicana***
94 – 'Gold Finger'

JUGLANS
96 ***regia*** 'Corne du Périgord' (F)
93 – 'Fords Farm'
93 – 'Northdown Clawnut'
95 – 'Red Leaf'

JUNCUS
93 ***effusus*** 'Aureostriatus'
90 ***pusillus***

JUNIPERUS
94 ***ashei***
90 ***chinensis*** 'Belvedere'
95 – 'Iowa'
96 – 'Keteleeri'
95 – 'Mas'
96 ***communis*** 'Clywd'
90 – 'Edgbaston'
88 – 'Effusa'
87 – 'Gimborn'
94 – 'Goldenrod'
87 – 'Inverleith'
96 – 'Mayer'
89 – 'Nana Aurea'
93 – 'Nana Prostrata'
90 – f. ***oblonga***
91 – 'Oblonga Pendula'
92 – 'Prostrata'
92 – 'Repanda' Waddon clone
93 – 'Silver Lining'
90 – 'Windsor Gem'
92 ***drupacea***
95 ***excelsa*** var. ***polycarpos***
88 ***flaccida***
92 ***horizontalis*** 'Coast of Maine'
96 – 'Golden Carpet'
91 – 'Jade Spreader'
91 – 'Prostrata'
90 – 'Schoodic Point'
89 × ***pfitzeriana*** 'Arctic'
91 – 'Mathot'
94 – 'Milky Way' (v)
94 – 'Nelson's Compact'
91 ***pinchotii***
87 ***pingii*** 'Forrestii'
96 ***procera***
95 ***recurva***
91 ***sabina*** 'Von Ehren'
90 ***saltuaria***
95 ***scopulorum***
90 – 'Hilborn's Silver Globe'
88 – 'Lakewood Globe'
96 – 'Silver Globe'
92 – 'Tolleson's Blue Weeping'
90 ***silicicola***
88 ***squamata*** 'Blue Spreader'
94 ***virginiana*** 'Canaertii'
93 – 'Compressa'
93 ***wallichiana***

JURINEA
96 ***moschus*** subsp. ***moschus***

JUSTICIA
91 ***plumbaginifolia***
94 ***polianthor robusta***

KAEMPFERIA
94 ***parishii***

KALANCHOE
92 ***blossfeldiana*** 'Annetta'
92 – 'Attraction'
92 – 'Bali'
92 – 'Beta'
92 – 'Calypso'
92 – 'Caprice'
92 – 'Charm'
92 – 'Cinnabar'
92 – 'Flores'
92 – 'Fortyniner'
92 – 'Inspiration'
92 – 'Lucky Island'
92 – 'Pollux'
92 – 'Regulus'
92 – 'Sensation'
92 – 'Sentosa'
92 – 'Seraya'
92 – 'Siam'
92 – 'Singapore'
92 – 'Yellow Nugget'
93 ***fedtschenkoi*** 'Variegata'
94 ***marmorata***
94 ***synsepala***
94 ***synsepala laciniata***
88 ***uniflora***

KALMIA
93 ***latifolia*** 'Candy'
93 – f. ***myrtifolia***
93 – 'Nancy'
93 – 'Olympic Wedding'
96 – 'Pinwheel'
93 – 'Raspberry Glow'
96 – 'Richard Jaynes'
96 – 'Shooting Star'
93 – 'Willowcrest'
93 – 'Yankee Doodle'
96 ***pygmaea***

KALMIA × RHODODENDRON
95 'No Suchianum'

KECKIELLA
96 ***antirrhinoides antirrhinoides***
91 ***antirrhinoides*** 'Microphylla'
94 ***lemmonii*** JCA 13004
95 ***ternata*** JLS 86304LACA

KENNEDIA
90 ***eximia***
95 ***prostrata***
90 – West Australian form
90 – West Coast form

KERNERA
89 ***saxatilis***

KNIPHOFIA
96 ***caulescens*** BH 5020
91 'Comet'
96 'Cream Flame'
87 'David' 🏆
96 'Dr E.M. Mills'
89 'Firefly'
95 'Fireking'
96 'Minister Verschuur'
96 'Pencil'
89 'Ross Sunshine'
91 'Rougham Beauty'
88 'Saturn'
94 ***schimperi***
95 sp. from Ethiopia
93 'Strawberry Split'
88 'Sunset'

KOBRESIA
89 ***simpliciuscula***

KOELERIA
92 ***alpina***

KOHLERIA
92 'Linda'
91 'Longwood'
94 'Success'

KUMMEROWIA
88 ***stipulacea***

KUNZEA
91 ***ericifolia***

LABICHEA
91 ***punctata***

LABLAB
96 ***purpureus***

LABURNUM
95 ***alpinum***
96 × ***watereri*** 'Alford's Weeping'

LACCOSPADIX
92 ***australasica***

LACHENALIA
96 ***aloides*** 'Nelsonii'
95 – 'Pearsonii'
90 ***arbuthnotiae***
90 ***bachmanii***
95 ***mediana***
92 ***orchioides*** var. ***glaucina***
96 ***reflexa***
95 × ***regeliana***
89 ***unifolia***
89 'Violet Queen'
94 ***zeyheri***

LACTUCA
90 ***macrantha***
91 ***sibirica***
88 ***tenerrima***

LAGENOPHORA
96 ***pinnatifida***
89 ***pumila***
93 ***stipitata***

LAGERSTROEMIA
95 ***chekiangensis***
87 ***fauriei***
90 ***indica*** 'Berlingot Menthe'
94 – 'forms'
91 – Little Chief Hybrids
91 – Petite Orchid™
93 – 'Petite Pinkie'
91 – Petite Red™
91 – 'Watermelon Red'

LALLEMANTIA
95 ***canescens***

LAMARCKIA
92 ***aurea***

LAMIUM
92 'Alan Leslie'
95 ***album*** 'Ashfield Variegated'
96 ***garganicum*** 'Golden Carpet' (v)
96 ***maculatum*** 'Silver Dollar'

LAMPRANTHUS
96 ***amoenus***
96 ***falciformis***
96 ***primavernus***
96 ***stayneri***
96 ***zeyheri***

LANTANA
92 ***camara*** 'Arlequin'
90 – 'Miss Tibbs'
92 – 'Naide'
92 'Sunkiss'

LAPAGERIA
94 ***rosea*** 'Penheale'
93 – 'Picotee'

LARIX
90 ***griffithii***
92 ***kaempferi*** 'Blue Haze'
95 – 'Dervaes'
94 ***potaninii*** CLD 123
92 ***principis-rupprechtii***
93 ***sieboldii***

LASER
96 ***trilobum***

LASERPITIUM
93 ***halier***

LATHYRUS
94 ***chrysanthus***
96 ***clymenum***
96 ***filiformis***
94 ***gmelinii***
95 ***hookeri***
95 ***latifolius*** Rollinson's form
96 ***macrocarpus*** F&W 7737
95 ***multiceps*** F&W 7192
96 ***odoratus*** 'America'
96 – 'Captain of the Blues'
96 – 'Countess Cadogan'
96 – 'Cupani'
96 – 'Quito'
96 – 'The Busby Pea'
96 – 'Violet Queen'
95 ***roseus***
95 ***sativus alboazureus***
96 ***sativus*** var. ***albus***
90 ***sativus caeruleus***
95 ***tingitanus*** red and white
96 ***tingitanus roseus***

LAURENTIA
93 ***longiflora***

LAVANDULA
96 ***angustifolia*** 'Heacham Blue'
91 – 'Jackman's Dwarf'
87 – 'Nana Rosea'
96 – No. 9
94 – 'Norfolk'
96 'Cambridge Lady'
95 ***dentata*** forms
96 × ***intermedia*** 'Mitcham Blue'
95 ***stoechas*** subsp. ***sampaioana***
93 ***viridis*** white-bracted

LAVATERA
96 ***arborea*** 'Ile d'Hyères'
89 ***cretica***
96 ***tauricensis***

LEDEBOURIA
94 ***ovalifolia***

LEDUM
96 ***glandulosum***
96 ***palustre*** subsp. ***decumbens***
94 – f. ***dilatatum***
93 – var. ***diversipilosum***
94 – 'Minus'

LEEA
90 ***rubra*** Blume ex Sprengel

LEIOPHYLLUM
96 ***buxifolium*** 'Compactum'
93 – 'Nanum'
94 – var. ***prostratum***

LEONOTIS
93 ***ocymifolia*** var. ***albiflora***
94 – var. ***ocymifolia***

LEONTICE
92 ***leontopetalum***
91 – subsp. ***ewersmannii***

LEONTOPODIUM
95 ***alpinum*** subsp. ***nivale***
94 ***alpinum pirinicum***
91 ***discolor***
95 ***hayachinense*** AJS/J 111
94 ***himalayanum*** EMAK 605
92 ***leontopodioides***
95 ***ochroleucum***
96 ***souliei***

LEOPOLDIA
96 ***brevipedicellata***

LEPECHINIA
91 ***chamaedryoides***

LEPTARRHENA
96 ***pyrolifolia***

LEPTINELLA
96 ***dendyi*** forms
92 ***goyenii***
94 ***pectinata*** subsp. ***villosa***

LEPTODACTYLON
91 ***pungens***

LEPTOSPERMUM
92 ***liversidgei*** x ***scoparium***
88 ***micromyrtus***
93 ***scoparium*** 'Album'
87 – 'Big Red'
88 – 'Flore Pleno'
89 – 'Gaiety'
95 – 'Gaiety Girl' (d)
95 – Jervis Bay form
91 – 'Karekare'
87 ***scoparium nanum*** 'Elizabeth Jane'
89 – 'Ruru'
95 ***scoparium*** 'Nichollsii Grandiflorum'
94 – 'Pink Damask'
89 – 'Pink Pearl'
92 – 'Roland Bryce'
96 – 'Wiri Amy'

LESCHENAULTIA
95 ***biloba***
96 ***formosa***
96 – orange

LESPEDEZA
93 ***davurica***
92 ***juncea***

LESQUERELLA
95 ***arizonica***
95 ***fendleri***
96 ***kingii sherwoodii***
91 ***multiceps***

LEUCADENDRON
93 ***sessile***

LEUCAENA
95 ***latisiliqua***

LEUCANTHEMOPSIS
87 ***pallida*** subsp. ***spathulifolia***

LEUCANTHEMUM
95 ***discoideum***
95 x ***superbum*** 'Flore Pleno'
90 – 'Juno'
91 – 'Marion Collyer'
89 – 'Moonlight'
93 – 'Wirral Pride'
95 ***vulgare*** 'Corinne Tremaine'
95 – 'Maistern'

LEUCOCHRYSUM
94 ***albicans*** subsp. ***albicans*** var. ***tricolor***

LEUCOGENES x HELICHRYSUM
96 ***Leucogenes grandiceps*** x ***Helichrysum bellidioides***

LEUCOJUM
95 ***longifolium***

LEUCOPOGON
89 ***collinus***

LEUCOSCEPTRUM
96 ***canum***

LEUCOSPERMUM
92 ***cordifolium*** yellow

LEUCOTHOE
96 ***axillaris***
90 ***keiskei*** 'Minor'
95 'Zebonard'

LEWISIA
96 ***brachycalyx*** pink
88 'Chastity'
92 ***cotyledon*** var. ***cotyledon***
94 – 'Harold Judd'
92 'Joyce Halley'
92 'Karen'
94 'L.W. Brown'
95 ***oppositifolia*** ex JCA 11835
96 – 'Richeyi'
96 'Oxstalls Lane'
94 'Paula'
91 ***stebbinsii***
92 'Susan'
92 ***tweedyi*** Mount Wenatchee form

LIATRIS
96 ***cylindracea***
95 ***elegans***
95 ***microcephala***
96 ***scariosa*** 'Alba'
91 'Snow Queen'

LIBERTIA
96 sp. from New Zealand
94 ***stolonifera***

LICUALA
90 ***spinosa***

LIGULARIA
96 ***alpigena***
95 ***jacquemoniana***
94 ***moorcroftiana***

LIGUSTICUM
94 ***ferulaceum***

LIGUSTRUM
94 x ***ibolium*** 'Midas'
92 ***japonicum*** 'Macrophyllum'
95 ***lucidum*** 'Aureovariegatum'
90 – 'Macrophyllum'
96 ***obtusifolium*** var. ***regelianum***
94 ***sempervirens***
94 ***strongylophyllum***

LILAEOPSIS
94 ***macloviana***

LILIUM
91 'Achilles' (Ia)
96 'Admiration' (Ia)
96 'Aladdin' (Ia)
96 'Allright' (VIIb/d)
92 'Amber Gold' (Ic)
91 ***amoenum*** (IX)
89 'Anne Boleyn' (Ia)
89 'Apricot' (Ia)
89 'Apricot Beauty' (Ib)
94 ***argenteum***
93 ***auratum*** 'Cinnabar' (IX)
94 – 'Golden Ray'
92 – Red Band Group (IX)
96 Aurelian Hybrids (VIIa)
93 'Ballade' (Ia)
92 'Beckwith Tiger' (Ic)
92 Bellmaid Group (IV)
96 'Blitz' (Ia)
92 'Bright Beauty' (Ia)
94 'Bronwen North' (Ic)
93 ***bulbiferum*** var. ***croceum*** (IX) 🏆
91 'Bull's Eye' (Ib)
94 Bullwood hybrids (IV)
91 Burgundy Group (Ic)
92 'Cambridge' (Ic)
93 'Canasta' (Ia)
93 'Carla Luppi' (Ia)
96 'Charmeur' (7c)
94 'Cherrywood' (IV)
94 'Coachella' (IV)
94 'Cocktail' (Ia)
94 'Commodore' (Ia)
94 'Compass' (Ia)
88 ***concolor*** (IX)
92 'Connecticut Yankee' (Ic)
96 'Connection' (Ia)
91 'Crimson Sun' (VIb)
89 'Damson' (VIa)
96 'Dandy' (Ia)
95 ***davidii*** (IX) 🏆
93 'Discovery' (Ic)
96 'Domination'
94 'Dream' (Ia)
94 'Dreamland' (Ia)
89 'Escapade' (Ia)
92 'Esther' (Ia)
92 'Eurovision' (Ia)
95 Everest Group (VIId)
93 'Feuerzauber' (Ia)
96 'Fiesta Gitana' (Ia)
96 'Fire Star' (VIIc/d)
94 'Firebrand' (I)
94 'Firecracker' (Ia)
96 'Flamenco' (Ib)
93 ***formosanum*** 'Snow Queen' (IX)
93 'Fuga' (Ic)
92 'Genève' (Ia)
96 'Gibraltar' (Ia)
92 'Gold Medal' (Ia)
90 Golden Clarion Group (VIa)
94 'Gran Sasso' (Ia)
94 ***grayi***
95 'Green Dragon' (VIa) 🏆
92 'Hallmark' (Ic)
95 'Harmony' (Ia)
94 'Harvest' (Ia)
96 'Her Grace' (Ia)
94 'Hornback's Gold' (Ic)
92 Imperial Crimson Group (VIIc)
90 x ***imperiale*** (VIa)
94 'Iona' (Ic)
95 'Jacques S. Dijt' (II)
95 Jamboree Group (VIId)
94 'Jan de Graaf'
96 'Jazz' (Ia)
92 'Joanna' (Ia)
96 'Kyoto' (VIId)
94 'Lady Bowes Lyon' (Ic)
94 'Lake Tahoe' (IV)
94 'Lake Tulare' (IV)
94 ***lancifolium*** var. ***flaviflorum***
90 'Langtry' (Ic)
94 'Laura' (VII)
95 ***ledebourii*** (IX)
96 ***leichtlinii*** 'Delta' (IX)
96 'Levant' (Ic)
94 'Lilliput' (Ia)
96 'Little Girl' (VIIb)
96 'Little Kiss' (Ia)
96 ***longiflorum*** 'Casa Rosa'
95 ***lophophorum*** CLD 1061 (IX)
94 'Lotus' (VI)
92 Mabel Violet Group (VIa)
94 'Magic Eye' (Ia)
89 'Magic Fire' (VId)
95 'Make Up' (Ia)
91 'Manuella' (Ia)
94 'Maria Callas' (Ia)
92 'Marilyn Monroe' (Ia)
95 'Marseille' (Ia)
91 ***martagon*** x ***hansonii*** (II)
96 – 'Inshriach' (IX)
93 – var. ***pilosiusculum*** (IX)
96 – pink
93 'Massa'
92 'Maxwill' (Ic)
90 Mid-Century hybrids (Ia)

91 'Monte Negro' (Ia)
95 Moonlight Group (VIa)
96 'Mrs R.O. Backhouse' (II) 🏆
94 ***nanum*** deep purple (IX)
94 – McBeath's form (IX)
92 'Nell Gwyn'
96 'Nivea' (I)
93 'Orange Sensation'
94 'Orange Wattle' (Ic)
91 'Orestes' (Ib)
93 Oriental Superb Group
96 Paisley Group (II)
91 'Pan' (Ic)
93 'Paprika' (Ib)
96 'Parisienne' (Ia)
94 ***parryi*** dwarf form (IX)
96 'Passage' (VIIc)
92 'Passat' (Ia)
96 'Peau Douce'
95 'Perugia' (VIId)
92 'Phoebus' (Ia)
96 'Picture' (VIId)
96 'Pink Beauty' (VIIc)
93 'Pink Panther'
92 Pink Pearl Trumpets Group (VIa)
96 'Polka'
91 ***polyphyllum***
94 'Preference' (Ia)
94 'Primavera' (Ia)
92 'Prins Constantijn' (Ib)
96 'Providence'
91 'Purple Sensation' (Ia)
96 ***pyrenaicum*** var. ***albanicum***
96 – var. ***pyrenaicum*** (IX)
96 – var. ***rubrum*** (IX)
94 'Rangoon' (Ia)
91 'Red Fox' (Ic)
93 'Red Marvel'
93 'Redstart' (Ib)
90 ***regale*** yellow (IX)
96 'Rosefire' (Ia)
94 'Rosemary North' (I) 🏆
92 Rosepoint Lace Group (Ic)
96 'Sahara' (Ia)
94 'Scentwood' (IV)
96 'Shuksan' (IV)
96 'Silhouette' (Ia)
92 'Sirocco' (Ia)
94 'Snowstar' (Ia)
96 'Sorisso' (Ia)
95 'Sorrento' (Ia)
95 ***speciosum*** 🏆
95 – 'Elite' (IX)
93 – 'Ida Uchida' (IX)
93 – 'Rosemede' (IX)
91 – 'Twinkle' (IX)
89 'Staccato' (Ia)
94 'Stardrift' (VIId)
94 'Starfish' (I)
92 'Sunset' (Ia)
96 'Symphony' (Ib)
93 'Tabasco' (Ia)
96 'Taptoe' (Ia)
93 'Tiger White' (Ic)
92 'Tropicana' (Ia)
93 'Troubadour' (VIIc)
91 'Unique' (Ia)
96 'Ventoux' (Ia)
89 'Vermilion Brilliant' (Ia)
94 'Vino' (VII)
94 'Wattle Bird' (Ia)
94 'White Cloud' (Ia)
93 'White Lady' (VIa)
92 'White Prince' (Ia)
96 'White Star Gazer' (VII)
95 'Yellow Present'
94 'Yellow Star' (Ib)
93 'Yellowhammer'

LIMONIUM
96 ***binervosum***
87 ***chilwellii***
96 ***dregeanum***
95 ***perezii***
95 – 'Atlantis'
93 ***platyphyllum*** 'Grandiflorum'
96 ***ramosissimum***

LINARIA
96 ***bipunctata***
96 'Blue Pygmy'
94 ***canadensis***
92 x ***dominii***
87 ***lilacina***
95 ***lobata alba***
88 ***nobilis***
93 'Parham Variety'
95 ***purpurea*** 'Dwarf Canon Went'
96 – Harbutt's hybrids
95 ***tristis***
90 – var. ***lurida***
88 ***vulgaris*** 'Flore Pleno'

LINDELOFIA
91 ***longiflora*** 'Hartington White'

LINDERA
96 ***megaphylla***

LINUM
96 ***hirsutum***
96 ***mongolicum***
93 ***mucronatum*** subsp. ***armenum***
89 ***narbonense album***
90 ***perenne*** dwarf
96 – 'Himmelszelt'
96 ***spathulatum***
91 ***usitatissimum***

LIPPIA
96 sp. RB 94075

LIQUIDAMBAR
96 ***styraciflua*** 'Moraine'

LIRIOPE
93 ***minor***
93 ***muscari*** 'Curley Twist'
92 – 'Paul Aden'
94 – 'Purple Bouquet'

LITHOCARPUS
92 ***henryi***
96 ***pachyphyllus***

LITHODORA
92 ***oleifolia*** 'Barker's Form'

LITHOPHRAGMA
94 ***glabrum*** JCA 10514

LITHOSPERMUM
93 ***arvense***

LIVISTONA
90 ***rotundifolia***

LLOYDIA
96 ***flavonutans***

LOASA
89 ***nana***

LOBELIA
92 ***alata***
89 ***begoniifolia***
95 ***cardinalis*** JLS 88010WI
92 x ***gerardii*** 'Alba'
96 'Hadspen Royal Purple'
92 'Huntsman'
96 ***kalmii***
89 ***linnaeoides*** 'Dobson'
96 ***longiflora*** RB 94066
93 ***minorescens***
91 ***nicotinifolia***
96 ***oligodon***
96 'Pope's Velvet'
95 ***richardsonii*** red
96 ***sessilifolia*** B&L 12396
96 ***siphilitica*** 'Nana'
96 ***surrepens***
91 ***tenuior***
90 ***villosa***

LOBELIA × PRATIA
96 ***Lobelia linnaeoides*** x ***Pratia macrodon***

LOMATIA
96 ***silaifolia***

LOMATIUM
95 ***canbyi***
94 ***macrocarpum***

LONICERA
95 ***arizonica***
90 ***discolor***
95 ***glaucescens***
96 'Hidcote'
93 ***hispida***
95 ***hispidula***
93 ***japonica***
96 – 'Peter Adams'
96 – 'Soja'
89 ***myrtillus***
91 ***obovata***
96 ***periclymenum clarkii***
96 ***periclymenum*** 'Cottage Beauty'
96 – 'Cream Cascade'
96 – var. ***glaucohirta***
96 sp. CLD 1451
96 sp. D Fox 89251
87 ***trichosantha***
89 ***utahensis***
95 ***vesicaria***
93 ***webbiana***
93 ***xylosteum***

LOPHOMYRTUS
91 'Pinkalina'
93 x ***ralphii*** 'Lilliput'
94 – 'Traversi'

LOPHOSPERMUM
91 ***erubescens*** white

LOTUS
94 ***rectus***

LUDWIGIA
91 ***longifolia***
91 ***octovalvis***

LUMA
93 ***apiculata*** 'Penwith' (v)
87 – purple

LUNARIA
94 ***annua*** 'Croftacre Purple Pod'
95 – 'Golden Spire'
90 – purple stem

LUPINUS
92 ***albifrons collinus***
96 ***albifrons*** var. ***douglasii***
93 – var. ***emineus***
94 ***arboreus albus***
95 'Beryl, Viscountess Cowdray'
95 'Blushing Bride'
93 'Boningale Lass'
95 ***breviscapus***
93 'Catherine of York'
89 'Cherry Pie'
96 'Clifford Star'
89 'Comet'
96 'Daydream'
93 'Fred Yule'
90 'Freedom'
96 'Gold Dust'
89 'Guardsman'
91 'Halina'
89 'Harlequin'
89 'Harvester'
90 ***hirsutissimus***
89 'Joy'
93 'Lady Fayre'
89 'Lilac Time'
89 'Limelight'
90 ***longifolius***
93 'Loveliness'
95 'Moonraker'
89 'Mystic Charm'
93 'Nellie B. Allen'
91 'Orangeade'
89 'Pat Baird'
94 ***princei***
92 ***rivularis***
88 'Rougham Beauty'
96 'Royal Parade' 🏆
89 'Serenade'
95 'Troop the Colour' 🏆
94 ***varius*** subsp. ***orientalis***
96 'Walton Lad'

LUZULA
95 ***alopecurus***
95 ***alpinopilosa*** subsp. ***candollei***
90 ***banksiana***
95 ***celata***
91 – from Ohau, New Zealand
91 'Mount Dobson'
95 ***sibirica***
95 ***sylvatica*** 'Tatra Gold'

× LYCENE
95 ***kubotae***

LYCHNIS
95 ***alpina*** subsp. ***americana***
96 ***coronaria*** 'Blych' (d)
94 ***kiusiana***
95 ***punctata*** dwarf
96 ***viscaria*** 'Splendens Rosea'
94 – subsp. ***viscaria***

LYCIUM
88 ***pallidum***

LYCORIS
95 ***aurea***

88 ***radiata***
88 ***squamigera***

LYGODIUM
93 ***japonicum***

LYONIA
89 ***lucida***
91 ***mariana***

LYSIMACHIA
95 ***congestiflora*** 'Golden Falls'
96 ***mauritiana***
96 ***nummularia nana***

LYTHRUM
91 ***salicaria*** 'Red Gem'
95 x ***salmonea***

MACHAERANTHERA
89 ***bigelovii***
94 ***glabriuscula***

MAGNOLIA
96 ***acuminata*** 'Golden Glow'
93 – 'Kobandori'
95 – var. ***subcordata***
93 'Albatross'
96 'Andre Harvey'
93 'Anne Rosse'
93 x ***brooklynensis*** 'Evamaria'
93 – 'Hattie Cartham'
96 'Butterflies'
91 'Caerhays Surprise'
92 ***campbellii*** var. ***alba*** 'Ethel Hillier'
92 – 'Darjeeling'
92 – (Raffillii Group) 'Wakehurst'
87 – 'Visa'
93 'Cecil Nice'
89 ***dawsoniana*** 'Caerhays'
93 – 'Clarke'
93 – 'Ruby Rose'
93 ***denudata*** late form
93 'Emma Cook'
93 'Fourteen Carat'
95 ***fraseri***
91 'Freeman'
96 ***grandiflora*** 'Charles Dickens'
90 – 'Rosemoor'
93 – 'Saint George'
92 x ***highdownensis***
95 'Judy' 🏆
96 'Kerr van Ann'
93 'Ko-1'
93 'Koban Dori'
93 ***liliiflora*** 'Doris'
93 – 'Mini Mouse'
87 x ***loebneri*** 'Spring Snow'
93 'Mag's Pirouette'
92 'Michael Rosse'
93 'Mossman's Giant'
87 ***nitida***
96 ***obovata***
93 ***officinalis*** var. ***biloba*** 🏆
92 'Orchid'
96 'Pickard's Charm'
94 'Pickard's Firefly'
94 'Pickard's Garnet'
94 'Pickard's Glow'
91 'Pickard's Maime'
91 'Pickard's Pearl'
96 'Pickard's Stardust'
92 'Princess Margaret'
91 x ***proctoriana*** 'Slavin's Snowy'
92 'Purple Eye'
93 'Randy' 🏆
95 'Rouged Alabaster'
95 ***salicifolia*** 'Jermyns'
93 ***sargentiana*** 'Nymans'
96 x ***soulangeana*** 'Coimbra'
87 – 'Deep Purple Dream'
96 – 'Just Jean'
91 – 'Rose Superb'
89 – 'Triumphans'
93 ***sprengeri*** var. ***diva*** 'Claret Cup'
93 'Tina Durio'
93 ***tripetala*** 'Woodlawn'
93 'Ursula Grau'
95 x ***veitchii*** 'Isca'
93 'Wada's Snow White'
93 ***zenii***

MAGNOLIA × MICHELIA
93 Yuchelia No. 1

× MAHOBERBERIS
92 ***neubertii***

MAHONIA
92 ***aquifolium*** 'Donewell'
90 – dwarf form
93 – 'Scallywag'
92 'Cantab'
92 ***higginsiae***
96 ***keiskei***
92 x ***media*** 'Arthur Menzies'
91 – 'Hope'
95 ***napaulensis***
92 – 'Maharajah'
93 ***trifoliolata***
90 x ***wagneri***
92 – 'Hastings Elegant'
90 – 'Vicaryi'

MAIANTHEMUM
96 ***bifolium*** British form
91 – Yakushima form

MALPIGHIA
93 ***coccigera***
89 ***glabra*** 'Fairchild'

MALUS
96 x ***adstringens*** 'Almey'
96 – 'Purple Wave'
96 ***baccata*** 'Dolgo'
96 – 'Gracilis'
95 – var. ***mandshurica***
89 'Bonfire'
93 ***brevipes***
91 'Coralburst'
96 ***coronaria*** 'Elk River'
96 ***domestica*** 'Alderman' (C)
96 – 'Alford' (Cider)
96 – 'Ananas Reinette' (D)
96 – 'Andrew Johnson' (F)
96 – 'Anne-Marie' (C)
96 – 'Arthur W. Barnes' (C)
96 – 'Backwell Red' (Cider)
96 – 'Baron Ward' (C)
96 – 'Beauty of Stoke' (C)
96 – 'Belle-fille Normande' (C)
96 – 'Belle-fleur de France' (C)
92 – 'Bolingbroke Beauty' (D)
96 – 'Bulmer's Chisel Jersey' (Cider)
96 – 'Bulmer's Crimson King' (Cider)
96 – 'Bulmer's Fillbarrel' (Cider)
96 – 'Bulmer's Foxwhelp' (Cider)
96 – 'Bulmer's Norman' (Cider)
96 – 'Buxted Favorite' (F)
96 – 'Calagolden Elbee' (D)
93 – 'Calville Rouge d'Hiver' (C)
96 – 'Charles Eyre' (C)
94 – 'Cinderella' (F)
92 – 'Compact Mac' (F)
92 – 'Compact Sue' (F)
96 – 'Cortland' (C)
96 – 'Cox's Red Sport' (D)
96 – 'Crimson Bramley' (C)
96 – 'Crimson Peasgood' (C)
96 – 'Early Crimson' (F)
96 – 'Edwin Beckett' (D)
96 – 'Feltham Beauty' (D)
96 – 'First and Last' (D)
93 – 'Foxwhelp' (Cider)
96 – 'Franklyn's Golden Pippin' (D)
96 – 'Frederick' (Cider)
94 – 'Friandise' (D)
96 – 'Frogmore Prolific' (C)
95 – 'Geneva'
95 – 'George Favers' (F)
96 – 'Golden Nonpareil' (D)
96 – 'Grange's Pearmain' (C)
96 – 'Gulval Seedling' (F)
96 – 'Harry Master's Dove' (Cider)
94 – 'Harry Master's Lambrook' (Cider)
94 – 'Harry Master's Red Streak' (Cider)
96 – 'Hormead Pearmain' (C)
93 – 'Invicta' (D)
96 – 'James Lawson' (D)
96 – 'John Broad' (F)
96 – Jubilee (Delbards) (F)
95 – 'Lady Bacon' (F)
96 – 'Lady Williams' (D)
96 – 'Lady's Delight' (C)
96 – 'Laxton's Pearmain' (D)
96 – 'Laxton's Reward' (D)
96 – 'Leeder's Perfection' (F)
96 – 'Lodgemore Nonpareil' (D)
96 – 'Lord of the Isles' (F)
96 – 'Lord Rosebery' (D)
96 – 'Mabbott's Pearmain' (D)
96 – 'Maiden's Blush' (D)
96 – 'Maidstone Favourite' (D)
96 – 'Mannington's Pearmain' (D)
96 – 'Marriage-maker' (D)
96 – 'Mead's Broading' (C)
96 – 'Mère de Ménage' (C)
96 – 'Merton Beauty' (D)
96 – 'Merton Charm' (D) 🏆
96 – 'Merton Joy' (D)
96 – 'Monarch Advanced' (C)
96 – 'Mrs Crittenden' (F)
96 – 'Nehou' (Cider)
95 – 'New German' (D)
94 – 'Niemans Neiburger' (F)
94 – 'Norfolk Royal Russet' (D)
96 – 'Norman's Pippin' (D)
96 – 'Nutmeg Pippin' (D)
95 – 'Paroquet' (D)
95 – 'Patricia' (D)
96 – 'Powell's Russet' (D)
96 – 'Puckrupp Pippin' (D)
96 – 'Queen Caroline' (C)
95 – 'Queenie' (D)
92 – 'Red Bramley' (C)
92 – 'Red Jonagold' (F)
96 – 'Red Melba' (D)
96 – 'Red Newton Wonder' (C)
95 – 'Red Superb' (D)
96 – 'Reinette d'Obry' (Cider)
96 – 'Rosamund' (D)
96 – 'Scarlet Crofton' (D)
96 – 'Scarlet Pimpernel' (D)
96 – 'Schweizer Orange' (F)
95 – 'Shortymac' (D)
96 – 'Starking Red Delicious' (D)
96 – 'Stark's Earliest' (D)
96 – 'Stembridge' (Cider)
96 – 'Summergold' (F)
96 – 'Taunton Cream' (F)
93 – 'Tenroy' (D)
96 – 'The Queen' (F)
95 – 'Transparente de Bois Guillaume' (D)
96 – 'Tyler's Kernel' (C)
94 – 'Vilberie' (Cider)
96 – 'Wellspur Delicious' (D)
96 – 'White Jersey' (Cider)
96 – 'Yellowspur' (D)
89 'Elise Rathke'
95 'Gardener's Gold'
96 ***halliana***
95 x ***hartwigii*** 'Katherine' 🏆
90 ***hupehensis*** 'Rosea'
96 ***mahonia***
93 'Makamik'
93 Pom'Zai
94 'Prince Georges'
95 ***rufiensis***
95 'Stellata'
96 'Strathmore'
96 ***toringo*** 'Rosea'
95 – 'Wintergold'
96 x ***zumi*** 'Professor Sprenger'

MALVA
96 'Harry Hay'
93 ***pyramidalis***
96 ***robusta***
91 ***sylvestris*** 'Alba'
95 – 'Cottenham Blue'
90 – 'Mest'
95 – Wallace Blues Group

MALVASTRUM
95 ***lateritium*** 'Hopley's Variegated'
94 ***latifolium***

MANDEVILLA
96 'White Delite'

MANDRAGORA
93 ***arborescens***

MANGIFERA
94 'Heidi'

MANGLIETIA
93 ***insignis***

MANIHOT
94 ***esculenta***

MARANTA
95 ***bicolor***
90 ***leuconeura*** 'Massangeana'

MARCHANTIA
96 ***calcarea***
96 ***palmatoides***
96 sp. from Tristan da Cunha

MARKHAMIA
94 ***lutea***

MARRUBIUM
96 ***vulgare*** variegated

MATTHIOLA
88 East Lothian
95 ***fruticulosa*** 'Alba'
94 'Les Merriennes' (d)

MAURANDELLA
96 ***antirrhiniflora***

MAURANDYA
96 ***wislizenii***

MAYTENUS
95 ***boaria*** 'Worplesdon Fastigiate'
92 ***magellanica***

MAZUS
89 ***miquelii***

MECONOPSIS
93 ***betonicifolia*** 'Glacier Blue'
96 ***grandis*** EMAK 473
92 ***horridula alba***
94 ***impedita*** KGB 303
96 ***integrifolia*** ACE 1732
96 Kingsbarns Hybrids
96 ***latifolia***
96 ***pseudointegrifolia***
96 x ***sheldonii*** 'Corrennie'
95 – 'Glen Tough'
92 ***sherriffii***
96 sp. ACE 1875
94 ***speciosa*** KGB 316
90 'White Swan'

MEDICAGO
91 ***falcata*** 'Cambot'
89 ***intertexta***

MELALEUCA
96 ***acuminata***
91 ***biconvexa***
94 ***bracteata*** 'Golden Revolution'
93 ***capitata***
89 ***citrina***
91 ***ericifolia nana***
91 ***glaberrima***
94 ***quinqenervia***
91 ***scabra***
91 ***striata***

MELANTHIUM
96 ***virginicum***

MELILOTUS
94 ***altissimus***

MELINIS
94 ***repens***

MELIOSMA
87 ***cuneifolia***
96 ***dilleniifolia*** subsp. ***flexuosa***
95 – subsp. ***tenuis***
92 ***parviflora***
91 ***pinnata*** var. ***oldhamii***

MENTHA
91 ***angustifolia*** 'Variegata'
96 x ***piperita*** f. ***citrata*** orange
94 ***pulegium*** Greek form
93 x ***villosa alopecuroides*** 'Cae Rhos Lligwy' (v)

MENZIESIA
95 ***ciliicalyx***
95 ***pentandra*** AGS J 317

MERENDERA
94 ***hissarica***
94 ***nivalis***
91 ***robusta***

MERTENSIA
88 ***alpina***
95 ***pulmonarioides*** 'Alba'

MERYTA
93 ***sinclairii*** 'Moonlight' (v)

MESEMBRYANTHEMUM
96 ***hispidum***

MESPILUS
94 ***germanica*** 'Autumn Blaze' (F)
93 – 'Westerveld' (F)

METASEQUOIA
92 ***glyptostroboides*** 'Emerald Feathers'
95 – 'Waasland'

METROSIDEROS
96 ***collinus***
93 'Mistral'

MIBORA
93 ***mimima***

MICHELIA
90 ***champaca***
93 ***crassipes***
96 ***doltsopa*** 'Silver Cloud'
87 ***maudiae***
96 ***sinensis***
93 'Touch of Pink'

MICROMERIA
95 ***caerulea***
90 ***cristata***
95 ***varia***

MICROSERIS
91 ***lanceolatus alpinus***

MICROSTROBOS
93 ***niphophilus***

MILLIGANIA
88 ***densiflora***

MIMULUS
96 ***aridus***
95 ***aurantiacus*** red
94 'Bees' Scarlet'
94 ***boydii***
96 'Burgess'
92 'Caribbean Cream'
93 'Doreen's Delight'
89 'Fire King'
88 'Firedragon'
95 ***longiflorus saccharatus***
95 'Magnifique'
96 'Malibu Ivory'
94 'Malibu Red'
89 ***minimus***
96 ***moschatus*** 'Variegatus'
96 'Plymtree'
91 'Shep'
95 sp. CW 5233
96 'Tigrinus Queen's Prize'
96 ***tilingii*** var. ***caespitosus***
96 'Western Hills'
87 'Wildwood's'

MINUARTIA
94 ***biflora***
92 ***imbricata***
92 ***juniperina***
92 ***kashmirica***
96 ***obtusiloba***
91 ***verna*** subsp. ***caespitosa***
95 – subsp. ***verna***

MISCANTHUS
91 ***litoralis*** 'Zuneigung'
96 ***sinensis***
96 – 'Dixieland'
96 – 'Hinjo'
96 – 'Rigoletto'
96 – 'Tiger Cub'

MITELLA
94 ***diphylla***
89 ***pentandra***

MITRASACME
95 ***pilosa***

MITRIOSTIGMA
96 ***axillare***

MODIOLA
94 ***caroliniana***

MODIOLASTRUM
87 ***peruvianum***

MOEHRINGIA
96 ***glaucovirens***

MONADENIUM
94 ***ritchiei***

MONARDA
96 ***didyma*** 'Variegata'
95 'Maiden's Pride'
95 'Meereswogen'
94 'Morgenröte'
94 'Purple Ann'
91 ***russeliana***

MONARDELLA
96 ***macrantha***
94 ***villosa***
93 – 'Sheltonii'

MONOTOCA
94 ***glauca***

MONSTERA
90 ***obliqua***
90 ***obliqua expilata***

MONTIA
91 ***chamissoi***

MORAEA
96 ***natalensis***
96 ***papilionacea***
96 ***ramosissima***
96 ***schimperi***
96 ***stricta***
96 ***tripetala***
96 ***vegeta***

MORINA
92 ***alba***
89 ***coulteriana***
91 ***ramallyi***

MORUS
96 ***alba*** 'Black Tabor'
96 – 'Laciniata'
94 – 'Macrophylla'
92 – 'Nana'
91 ***australis***
94 ***rubra***

MUHLENBERGIA
96 ***dumosa***

MUNDULEA
93 ***sericea***

MURBECKIELLA
94 ***pinnatifida***

MUSA
95 ***acuminata*** 'Dwarf Cavendish' 🏆
95 ***ornata*** 🏆
96 'Rojo'

MUSCARI
93 ***armeniacum*** 'Blue Pearl'
95 – 'New Creation'
96 ***azureum*** 'Amphibolis'
91 ***bourgaei***
95 ***caucasicum***
93 'Dark Eyes'
94 ***muscarimi*** 'Major'
88 ***parviflorum***

MUSSCHIA
93 ***aurea***

MUTISIA
92 ***brachyantha***
95 ***ilicifolia*** RB 94087
96 ***subspinosa***

MYOSOTIS
96 ***alpestris***
88 – 'Nana'
88 ***azorica***
95 ***elderi***
90 ***forsteri***
92 ***macrantha***
96 ***persicifolia*** 'Coronata'
89 ***petiolata***

95 – var. ***pottsiana***
95 ***pulvinaris***
91 ***pygmaea***
92 ***saxosa***
95 ***suavis***
89 ***symphytifolia***

MYOSURUS
96 ***minimus***

MYRCEUGENIA
92 ***exsucca***

MYRICARIA
92 ***germanica***

MYRIOPHYLLUM
92 ***elatinoides***

MYRTUS
94 ***communis citrifolia***

NANDINA
90 ***domestica*** 'Little Princess'
89 – 'Umpqua Chief'
96 – 'Wood's Dwarf'

NARCISSUS
94 'Acclamation' (4)
95 'Accolade' (3)
93 'Akala' (1)
93 'Alba Pax' (2)
89 'Albacrest' (3)
89 'Aldringham' (2)
96 'Algarve' (2)
93 'Alice's Pink' (2)
96 'Allafrill' (2)
94 ***alpestris*** MS 571
94 'Alpha' (9)
89 'Alray' (1)
96 'Amber Light' (2)
89 'Andrew Marvell' (9)
89 'Ann Cameron' (2)
89 'April Message' (1)
89 'Arctic Flame' (2)
94 'Ardbane' (2)
93 'Arie Hoek' (2)
93 'Armagh' (1)
94 'Armynel' (2)
96 'Arndilly' (2)
92 'Arragon' (2)
95 'Ashwell' (3)
94 ***asturiensis*** 'Fuente De'
94 – 'Giant'
93 'Aurum' (1)
94 'Ayston' (2)
89 'Backchat' (6)
96 'Badanloch' (3)
93 'Ballintoy' (2)
89 'Ballyroan' (2)
94 'Ballytrim' (2)
96 'Balvraid Lass' (2)
89 'Bandolier' (2)
89 'Bar None' (1)
93 'Barley Cove' (2)
91 'Barnby Moor' (3)
96 'Barnsdale Wood' (2)
93 'Barnwell Alice' (2)
93 'Beauticol' (11)
95 'Beersheba' (1)
96 'Ben Bhraggie' (2)
96 'Ben Loyal' (2)
89 'Ben Rinnes' (3)
93 'Benvarden' (3)
94 'Bermuda' (2)
96 'Berry Gorse' (3)
92 'Big Cycla' (6)
96 'Big John' (1)
89 'Birdalone' (2)
96 'Birichen' (2)
93 'Birkdale' (2)
96 'Birthday Girl' (2)
93 'Bit o'Gold' (2)
94 'Bithynia' (3)
94 'Bizerta' (2)
93 'Bovagh' (2)
94 'Braddock' (3)
89 'Brave Adventure' (2)
96 'Brierglass' (2)
89 'Bright Spark' (3)
95 'Brilliant Star' (11)
90 'Brindisi' (2)
93 'Broadway Rose' (2)
93 'Brookfield' (2)
93 'Broughshane' (1)
93 ***bulbocodium*** subsp. ***bulbocodium*** var. ***nivalis***
96 'Buncrana' (2)
94 'Burgemeester Gouverneur' (1)
96 'Burning Heart' (11)
93 'Burning Torch' (2)
93 'Canby' (2)
91 'Canford' (3)
94 ***cantabricus*** forms
89 'Capstan' (2)
89 'Carrara' (3)
89 'Carrickmannon' (2)
93 'Carrigeen' (2)
95 'Caruso' (2)
89 'Celtic Gold' (2)
96 'Celtic Song' (2)
96 'Chablis' (11)
93 'Cha-cha' (6)
93 'Chagall' (2)
93 'Chapeau' (2)
93 'Charade' (2)
92 'Charity Fair' (6)
93 'Checkmate' (2)
93 'Chelsea Derby' (2)
96 'Chinese Sacred Lily' (8)
93 'Chungking' (3)
93 'Church Bay' (2)
89 'City Lights' (2)
93 'Clare Park' (2)
96 'Clashmore' (2)
93 'Cloudcap' (2)
96 'Cloud's Hill' (4)
93 'Cloyfin' (2)
89 'Cold Overton' (2)
96 'Colloggett' (2)
94 'Coloratura' (3)
95 'Colston Bassett' (3)
93 'Comal' (1)
95 'Como' (9)
96 'Coquille' (2)
95 'Coral Fair' (2)
89 'Coral Ribbon' (2)
93 'Coralline' (6)
94 'Corinthian' (1)
96 'Cornish Cream' (12)
96 'Coverack Perfection' (2)
89 'Coylum' (3)
93 'Craigtara' (2)
93 'Cranborne' (2)
89 'Crater' (2)
96 'Crenver' (3)
92 'Curly' (2)
96 'Cushendall' (3)
91 'Cushendun' (3)
91 'Cyclope' (1)
89 'Dalinda' (1)
96 'Darlow Dale' (2)
94 'Davlyn' (2)
96 'Davochfin Lass' (1)
89 'Dawncrest' (2)
89 'Debbie Rose' (2)
93 'Debrett' (2)
93 'Delamont' (2)
89 'Delightful' (3)
93 'Derg Valley' (1)
94 'Descanso' (1)
89 'Deseado' (1)
95 'Desert Orchid' (2)
93 'Dilemma' (3)
89 'Dorada Dawn' (2)
93 'Double Event' (4) 🏆
93 'Downhill' (3)
93 'Dramatis' (9)
89 'Dress Circle' (3)
96 'Drop o' Gold' (5)
93 'Drumadoon' (2)
93 'Drumnasole' (3)
93 'Drumragh' (1)
93 'Drumtullagh' (2)
93 'Duke of Windsor' (2)
91 'Dulcie Joan' (2)
89 'Dumbleton' (1)
93 'Dundarave' (2)
91 'Dunlambert' (2)
93 'Durango' (6)
89 'Earlicheer' (4)
96 'Edwalton' (2)
89 'El Camino' (6)
94 'Eleanor Rose' (2)
94 ***elegans*** var. ***fallax*** S&L 324
96 'Embo' (2)
96 'Eribol' (2)
96 'Eriskay' (4)
93 'Ernevale' (3)
94 'Estio Pinza' (2)
96 'Evelix' (2)
93 'Exception' (1)
96 'Explosion' (8)
96 'Fairlight Glen' (2)
91 'Fairmaid' (3)
95 'Fairmile' (3)
95 'Faraway' (3)
96 'Fellowship' (2)
94 'Fergie' (2)
89 'Fiery Flame' (2)
96 'Finchcocks' (2)
94 'Fire Flash' (2)
94 'Firgrove' (3)
94 'First Date' (3)
95 'Flowerdream'
90 'Fontmell' (1)
95 'Fount' (2)
91 'Fourways' (3)
94 'Gainsborough' (2)
89 'Galahad' (1)
89 'Gambler's Gift' (2)
94 'Ganaway' (3)
96 'Gay Challenger' (4)
89 'Gay Record' (4)
89 'Gay Symphony' (4)
94 'Gilford' (3)
96 'Gimli' (6)
94 'Gipsy Moth' (2)
93 'Glacier' (1)
94 'Glad Day' (2)
89 'Glandore' (2)
96 'Glen Cassley' (3)
95 'Glencraig' (2)
96 'Glenmorangie' (2)
95 'Glorious' (8)
96 'Glory of Lisse' (9)
94 'Glowing Embers' (2)
96 'Gold Medallion' (1)
93 'Gold Quest' (1)
95 'Golden Ranger' (2)
91 'Golden Rupee' (1)
91 'Golden Sand' (1)
96 'Golden Showers' (1)
96 'Grapillon' (11)
95 'Great Expectations' (2)
95 'Green Howard' (3)
93 'Green Ice' (2)
95 'Green Orchid'
91 'Green Peace' (3)
94 'Green Rival' (2)
93 'Greenholm' (2)
95 'Greenvale' (2)
96 'Greeting' (2)
89 'Gunsynd' (2)
96 'Hazel Rutherford' (2)
96 'Hazel Winslow' (2)
93 'Heart Throb' (2)
92 'High Church' (2)
89 'High Tower' (3)
96 'Holbeck' (4)
95 'Holly Berry' (2)
95 'Home Fires' (2)
93 'Hoodsport' (11)
91 'Hot Sun' (3)
95 'Howard's Way' (3)
95 'Ibberton' (3)
96 'Ibis' (6)
91 'Ida May' (2)
94 'Innisfree' (3)
94 'Interim' (2)
91 'Irish Charm' (2)
89 'Ivory Crown' (2)
94 'Ivy League' (1)
96 'Jane France' (1)
96 'Jane MacLennan' (4)
96 'Jane van Kralingen' (3)
94 'Jeannine Hoog' (1)
94 'Jolly Roger' (2)
96 'Juanito'
94 'Kanchenjunga' (1)
91 'Karelia' (1)
96 'Kathleen Munro' (2)
89 'Kelpie' (6)
89 'Kentucky Cardinal' (2)
94 'Kildavin' (2)
94 'Kilmorack' (2)
89 'King's Ransom' (1)
89 'Kipling' (3)
96 'Kitten' (6)
94 'Knockstacken' (1)
89 'Knowehead' (2)
95 'La Riante' (3)
93 'Ladybank' (1)
95 'Lalique' (3)
89 'Lancelot' (1)
94 'Langford Grove' (3)
89 'Leader' (2)
96 'Leading Light' (2)
94 'Lemnos' (2)
96 'Lemon Candy' (2)
93 'Lemon Drops' (5)
96 'Lemon Express' (1)
94 'Lemon Meringue' (1)
94 'Lemon Sherbet' (2)
89 'Leonora' (3)
95 'Letty Green' (4)
94 'Limeade' (2)
89 'L'Innocence' (8)
91 'Lisbane' (3)
96 'Little Jazz' (6)
96 'Loch Coire' (3)

95 'Loch Garvie' (2)
93 'Loch Loyal' (2)
95 'Loch Owskeich' (2) 🏆
96 'Loch Tarbert' (2)
95 'Loth Lorien' (3)
92 'Louise de Coligny' (2)
89 'Lucky Star' (3)
94 'Lusky Mills' (3)
96 'Lydwells' (2)
93 'Lyles' (2)
94 'Lynwood' (1)
96 'Madrigal' (2)
96 'Magic Maiden' (2)
94 'Mahmoud' (3)
89 'Maid of Ulster' (2)
96 'Maiden Over' (2)
96 'Mairead' (2)
96 'Majestic Gold' (1)
89 'Mandolin' (2)
93 'Mantle' (2)
94 'March Madness' (2)
94 'Marcola' (2)
94 'Marshfire' (2)
96 'Mary Schouten' (2)
89 'Matapan' (3)
89 'May Queen' (2)
94 'Medalist' (2)
93 'Melancholy' (1)
94 'Melody Lane' (2)
95 'Mermaid's Spell' (2)
94 'Merrymaker' (4)
89 'Milestone' (2)
89 'Mill Grove' (2)
95 'Minikin' (3)
96 ***minor*** 'Douglasbank'
90 'Mint Julep' (3)
89 'Modest Maiden' (2)
94 'Moina' (3)
94 'Mondaine' (2)
94 'Moneymore' (2)
96 'Monksilver' (3)
94 'Montalto' (2)
96 'Montclair' (2)
93 'Monterrico' (4)
94 'Monument' (2)
96 'Moon Goddess' (1)
94 'Moon Orbit' (2/1)
89 'Moonlight Sonata' (1)
93 'Morag MacDonald' (2)
94 'Mount Ida' (2)
94 'Mount Vernon' (2)
95 'Mountpleasant' (2)
89 'Mrs Ernst H. Krelage' (1)
96 'Muirfield' (1)
89 'Music Hall' (1)
89 'My Love' (2)
89 'Navarone' (1)
93 'Nevta' (2)
93 'New Generation' (1)
94 'Northern Light' (2)
89 'Norval' (2)
94 'Noweta' (3)
93 'Nymphette' (6)
96 'Oakham' (2)
89 'Ocean Spray' (7)
95 'Old Satin' (2)
94 'Oneonta' (2)
93 'Orange Lodge' (2)
93 'Orange Queen' (3)
94 'Orange Sherbet' (2)
94 'Orator' (2)
94 'Pacific Princess' (3)
92 ***pallidiflorus***
89 'Park Royal' (2)
89 'Parkdene' (2)
89 'Parkridge' (2)
93 'Pearl Wedding' (4)
91 'Pearly King' (1)
96 'Pennyghael' (2)
89 'Perky' (6)
95 'Petsamo' (1)
89 'Pimm' (2)
95 'Pink Dawn' (2)
95 'Pink Mink' (2)
93 'Pink Silhouette' (2)
95 'Pink Whispers' (2)
96 'Piquant' (3)
94 'Playboy' (2)
96 'Polglass' (3)
89 'Polonaise' (2)
94 'Pontresina' (2)
94 'Portavo' (2)
94 'Pretty Polly' (2)
96 'Primrose Beauty' (4)
96 'Printal' (11)
89 'Privateer' (3)
96 'Proska' (2)
95 x ***pulchellus***
93 'Pzaz' (3)
95 'Queen of Bicolors' (1)
89 'Queen of Spain' (10)
89 'Queensland' (2)
96 'Radical' (6)
95 'Rathgar' (2)
91 'Rathowen Flame' (2)
89 'Rathowen Gold' (1)
94 'Red Bay' (2)
89 'Red Curtain' (1)
93 'Red Devon' (2) 🏆
94 'Red Hall' (3)
89 'Red Mars' (2)
93 'Red Rascal' (2)
89 'Red Rum' (2)
95 'Redlands' (2)
94 'Reliance' (2)
91 'Revelry' (2)
89 'Revenge' (1)
89 'Rich Reward' (1)
91 'Richhill' (2)
89 'Right Royal' (2)
89 'Rimster' (2)
96 'Ringmer' (3)
91 'Ringway' (3)
95 'Rival'
94 'Roman Tile' (2)
96 ***romieuxii*** AB&S 4656
94 – forms
94 'Rosapenna' (2)
91 'Rose Noble' (2)
93 'Rosedew' (2)
93 'Rotarian' (3)
93 'Roulette' (2)
93 'Rousillon' (11)
95 'Royal Ballet' (2)
96 'Royal Dornoch' (1)
91 'Royal Oak' (1)
94 'Royal Viking' (3)
89 'Rubythroat' (2)
94 'Rushlight' (2)
95 'Ryan Son' (3)
92 'Sabik' (2)
94 'Sacramento' (3)
94 'Safari' (2)
96 'Saint Duthus' (1)
94 'Salmon Leap' (2)
93 'Salmon Spray' (2)
93 'Sammy Boy' (2)
89 'Santa Rosa' (2)
89 'Scarlet Thread' (3)
95 'Scoreline' (1)
95 'Scotney Castle' (1)
91 'Sea Princess' (3)
89 'Sealed Orders' (3)
89 'Sedate' (2)
93 'Shandon' (2)
94 'Sheik' (2)
89 'Shell Bay' (2)
96 'Shepherd's Hey' (7)
94 'Showboat' (2)
93 'Shuttlecock' (6)
95 'Shy Face' (2)
95 'Sigrid Undset' (3)
89 'Silent Cheer' (3)
89 'Silent Morn' (3)
93 'Silver Shell' (11)
96 'Silvermere' (2)
96 'Silversmith' (2)
95 'Sinopel' (3)
89 'Sir Ivor' (1)
96 'Sligachan' (1)
93 'Slowcoach' (3)
94 'Snow Dream' (2)
93 'Snow Gleam' (1)
89 'Snow Magic' (3)
96 'Snug' (1)
95 'Solferique' (2)
96 'Southease' (2)
91 'Southgrove' (2)
94 'Space Age' (2)
93 'Spey Bay' (3)
89 'Spring Fashion' (2)
94 'Spring Valley' (3) 🏆
94 'Springston Charm' (2)
93 'Springwood' (2)
93 'Sputnik' (6)
94 'Stainless' (2)
89 'Standfast' (1)
95 'Stanley Park'
93 'Starship' (2)
93 'Strangford' (3)
94 'Strephon' (1)
96 'Suilven' (3)
93 'Sun Chariot' (2)
93 'Sun Salver' (2)
94 'Sunbather' (2)
92 'Sunlover' (2)
94 'Super Star' (2)
93 'Svenska Bojan' (2)
96 'Swallowcliffe' (6)
94 'Swallownest' (1)
92 'Sweet Harmony' (2)
96 'Symphonette' (2)
95 'Syracuse' (3)
94 'Tanera' (2)
96 ***tazetta*** subsp. ***lacticolor***
94 'Tekapo' (2)
89 'The Prince' (2)
94 'Theano' (2)
89 'Timandaw' (3)
91 'Tingford' (3)
91 'Tollymore' (2)
89 'Tomphubil' (2)
94 'Top Gallant' (3)
94 'Top Notch' (2)
89 'Torch Bearer' (2)
94 'Torrish' (3)
94 ***tortifolius*** MS 540
89 'Touch of Silver' (2)
89 'Trelay' (3)
93 'Trillick' (3)
93 'Trilune' (11)
90 'Troon' (2)
93 'Tudor Rose' (2)
93 'Tullybeg' (3)
95 'Tullycore' (2)
94 'Tullyglass' (2)
95 'Tullynakill' (2)
92 'Tweedsmouth' (9)
94 'Ulster Prince' (1) 🏆
96 'Una Bremner' (2)
96 'Uncle Ben' (1)
93 'Undertone' (2)
96 'Upper Broughton' (2)
94 'Vantage' (2)
95 'Verdant' (1)
89 'Verve' (2)
89 'Viennese Rose' (4)
92 'Vincent van Gogh' (1)
94 'Vinsky' (3)
96 'Virgil' (9)
93 'Vital' (2)
93 'Vocation' (2)
95 'Wahkeena' (2)
96 'War Dance'
96 'Webster' (9)
94 'Welvan' (3)
96 'Westholme' (2)
94 'White Empress' (1)
95 'White Ermine' (2)
94 'White Majesty' (1)
89 'White Prince' (1)
94 'White Spray' (2)
94 'Woodland Glade' (3)
89 'Woodland Splendour' (3)
95 'Woolsthorpe' (2)
93 'Xanthin Gold' (1)
96 'Yellow Tresamble' (5)
94 'Zeus' (2)

NECTAROSCORDUM
94 ***tripedale***

NEILLIA
96 ***thyrsiflora***

NEMATANTHUS
91 'Bijou'
93 'Black Gold'
93 'Jungle Lights'

NEMESIA
96 'Hermione'

NEMOPANTHUS
88 ***mucronatus***

NEOLITSEA
90 ***caerulea***
95 ***parviflora***

NEOMARICA
94 ***gracilis***

NEOPAXIA
92 ***australasica*** 'Arthur'
92 – 'Lomond'

NEOREGELIA
92 ***carolinae*** Meyendorffii Group
92 – f. ***tricolor*** 'Perfecta' (v)
90 ***concentrica*** 'Plutonis'
89 ***cyanea***
94 'Fireball'
92 Picta Group
90 ***spectabilis*** 🏆
90 ***tristis***

NEPENTHES
91 ***alata*** x ***merrilliana***
91 – x ***ventricosa***
91 ***albomarginata***
91 ***ampullaria***
91 ***bicalcarata***
91 ***hirsuta***
91 x ***hookeriana***

91 ***leptochilia***
96 ***macfarlanei***
91 ***merrilliana***
91 ***rafflesiana gigantea***
90 ***stenophylla***
91 – x ***reinwardtiana***

NEPETA
91 ***floccosa***
96 'Gottfried Kühn'
93 ***longiflora***
95 ***nepetella*** subsp. ***amethystina***
96 'Pink Dawn'
90 'Valerie Finnis'

NEPHROLEPIS
92 ***cordifolia*** 'Plumosa'
92 ***exaltata*** 'Whitmanii'

NERINE
94 ***bowdenii*** 'Alba'
96 ***breachiae***
95 'Curiosity'
95 'Fairyland'
95 'Hera'
94 'Hertha Berg'
91 'Joan'
90 'Lady de Walden'
94 'Lady Eleanor Keane'
92 'Lady Llewellyn'
94 'Maria'
95 'Miss France Clarke'
90 'Mrs Cooper'
95 'Mrs Dent Brocklehurst'
94 'Mrs Graham Vivien'

NERIUM
93 ***oleander*** 'Cardinal'
93 – double apricot
95 – double white
94 – 'Emile Sahut'
94 – 'Madame Léon Brun' (d)
96 – 'Marie Gambetta'
96 – 'Mont Blanc'
96 – 'Oportum'

NICOTIANA
91 'Hopley's'
90 'Sissinghurst Green'
94 ***trigonophylla***

NIDULARIUM
90 ***billbergioides*** 'Flavum'
90 ***burchellii***
90 ***fulgens***
90 ***regelioides***

NIEREMBERGIA
96 ***repens*** 'Violet Queen'

NIVENIA
96 ***stokoei***

NOLANA
96 ***humifusa*** 'Little Bells'
94 ***paradoxa***

NOLINA
96 ***bigelowii***
96 ***humilis***
96 ***microcarpa***

NOMOCHARIS
96 ***aperta*** ACE 2271
96 – CLD 229
91 x ***finlayorum***
96 ***pardanthina*** CLD 1490

NOTHOFAGUS
91 ***antarctica*** 'Benmore'
95 ***betuloides***
95 ***fusca***
95 ***truncata***

NOTHOSCORDUM
94 ***bivalve***
93 ***bonariense***
93 ***gracile***

NUPHAR
95 ***japonica***
96 ***variegata***

NYMPHAEA
95 'August Koch' (T/D)
95 ***capensis*** (T/D)
95 – var. ***zanzibariensis*** (T)
92 'Emily Grant Hutchings' (T/N)
94 'Guy Maurel'
95 'Martin E. Randig'
93 'Maxima' (H)
95 'Perry's Red Volunteers'
93 'Pumila Rubis'
93 'Souvenir de Fridolfing' (H)
95 'Trudy Slocum' (T)
93 ***tuberosa*** 'Alba' (H)

NYSSA
96 ***ogeche***
94 ***sylvatica*** 'Jermyns Flame'

OENOTHERA
95 ***californica***
94 ***chicaginensis***
94 ***elata*** subsp. ***hirsutissima***
96 ***fruticosa*** cream
95 – 'Cuthbertson'
89 – 'Sundrops'
94 ***macrocarpa alba***
94 ***nuttallii***
95 ***serrulata*** K 92.296
95 ***suaveolens***

OLEARIA
92 ***bidwellii***
95 ***ilicifolia*** x ***moschata***
89 ***megalophylla***
89 ***minor***
89 ***phlogopappa*** 'Comber's Mauve'
94 ***pleniflora***
95 'Talbot de Malahide'

OLSYNIUM
96 ***biflorum***
96 ***junceum***
96 ***scirpoideum*** F&W 776

OMPHALODES
91 ***cappadocica*** 'Bridget Bloom'
92 ***luciliae alba***
94 ***luciliae*** var. ***cilicica***

OMPHALOGRAMMA
96 ***delavayi*** KGB 600
96 – KGB 800
89 ***elegans***
87 ***minus***
96 ***vinciflorum***

ONCOBA
94 ***spinosa***

ONIXOTIS
93 ***triquetra***

ONONIS
87 ***crispa balearica***
95 ***cristata***
92 ***fruticosa***
95 ***natrix***

ONOPORDUM
91 ***acaule***
95 ***argolicum***
94 ***salteri***

ONOSMA
92 ***albopilosa***
94 ***armena***
90 ***aucheriana***
95 ***montana***
95 ***pyramidalis***
96 ***tornensis***

ONYCHIUM
96 ***japonicum*** L 1649

OPHIOPOGON
96 ***intermedius*** 'Compactus'
96 ***planiscapus*** 'Silvershine'

OPITHANDRA
91 ***primuloides***

OREOBOLUS
88 ***pauciflorus***

ORIGANUM
95 ***acutidens*** JCA 735.000
92 x ***applei***
93 'Emma Stanley'
90 'French'
93 ***laevigatum*** 'Dingle'
96 'Pink Cloud'
96 'Purple Cloud'
89 'Roding'
90 ***vulgare*** 'Curly Gold'
94 – subsp. ***gracile***
93 – 'Tracy's Yellow'
96 'White Cloud'

ORNITHOGALUM
95 ***woronowii***

OROSTACHYS
95 ***erubescens***
92 ***furusei***

ORTHOSIPHON
96 ***labiatus***

ORYZOPSIS
92 ***hymenoides***

OSBECKIA
95 ***stellata***

OSMANTHUS
94 ***decorus*** 'Angustifolius'
93 ***heterophyllus*** 'Dodd and Zinger's Variegated'
96 – 'Latifolius Variegatus'
96 – 'Myrtifolius'
91 ***suavis***

OSMORHIZA
94 ***claytonii***

OSMUNDA
91 ***regalis*** 'Gracilis'
94 – var. ***spectabilis***

OSTEOSPERMUM
95 'Basutoland'
91 'Cannington Sally'
93 'Cannington Vernon'
93 'Croftway Blush'
95 'Croftway Coconut-ice'
93 'Croftway Eveningstar'
93 'Croftway Goldback'
93 'Croftway Hall'
93 'Croftway Halo'
93 'Croftway Humbug'
93 'Croftway Silverspoons'
95 'Croftway Snow'
93 'Croftway Tufty'
93 'Croftway Velvetspoons'
90 'Croftway Whirlydots'
93 'Croftway Wonderwhirls'
90 ***ecklonis*** x ***jucundum***
93 'Falmouth'
91 'Goulds'
95 'Hampton Court Purple'
88 'Lilac Beauty'
96 Merriments Dark Seedling
96 'Mrs Reside's Purple'
94 'Perhill Purple'
94 'Perhill White'
90 'Pink Whirls' low form
95 'Prostrate Sparkler'
92 'Trailing Whirl'
91 'Valerie Finnis'

OSTROWSKIA
92 ***magnifica***

OTANTHUS
92 ***maritimus***

OTHONNA
87 ***coronopifolia***

OURISIA
89 ***breviflora***
88 ***macrocarpa***
96 ***microphylla***
95 ***racemosa***
95 ***vulcanica***

OXALIS
95 ***acetosella subpurpurascens***
92 ***enneaphylla*** 'Ruth Tweedie'
96 ***japonica*** 'Picta'
90 ***laciniata*** blue
92 ***latifolia***
96 ***ortgiesii***
91 ***pes-caprae***
96 'Royal Velvet'
90 ***rubra***

OXYLOBIUM
96 ***lancelolatum***
90 ***parviflorum***

OXYTROPIS
92 ***adamsiana***
96 ***campestris***
93 – var. ***gracilis***
96 ***chankaensis***
94 ***halleri***
93 ***jacquinii***
92 ***lagopus***
92 ***lambertii***
95 ***persica***
92 ***splendens***

92 ***todomoshiriensis***
91 ***uralensis***
96 ***viscida***
94 ***williamsii***

OZOTHAMNUS
91 ***diosmifolius***
93 ***purpurascens***
90 ***selaginoides***
96 ***selago*** 'Major'
92 – var. ***tumidus***

PACHYLAENA
95 ***atriplicifolia*** JCA 12522

PACKERA
94 ***werneriifolius***

PAEONIA
89 ***anomala*** var. ***intermedia***
95 'Auten's Red'
96 ***bakeri***
96 ***cypria***
95 ***delavayi*** Potaninii Group (S)
94 – Trollioides Group (S)
95 – 'Yellow Queen'
95 'Early Windflower'
95 'Ellen Cowley'
95 'Flame'
93 'Friendship'
87 ***japonica*** (Mak.) Miyabe & Tak.
92 'Jenny'
96 ***lactiflora*** 'Alice Graemes'
90 – 'Amo-no-sode'
95 – 'Augustin d'Hour'
95 – 'Augustus John'
93 – 'Aureolin'
92 – 'Auten's Pride'
95 – 'Balliol'
96 – 'Bridal Gown'
95 – 'Bright Era'
94 – 'Bright Knight'
96 – 'Butter Ball'
96 – 'Canarie'
90 – 'Carolina Moon'
95 – 'Cecilia Kelway'
95 – 'Dandy Dan'
90 – 'Do Tell'
95 – 'Duc de Wellington'
93 – 'Duchess of Kent'
96 – 'Duchess of Marlborough'
95 – 'Elegant Lass'
90 – 'Emma Klehm'
95 – 'Empress of India'
95 – 'English Elegance'
94 – 'Eva'
96 – 'Fairy's Petticoat'
93 – 'Fedora'
96 – 'Fire Flower'
91 – 'François Ortegat'
90 – 'Fuji-no-mine'
95 – 'Full Moon'
95 – 'Gannymede'
96 – 'Globe of Light'
90 – 'Gloriana'
90 – 'Glory Hallelujah'
94 – 'Hiawatha'
95 – 'His Majesty'
95 – 'John Howard Wigell'
93 – 'Kelway's Gorgeous'
93 – 'Kelway's Perfection'
95 – 'Kelway's Rosemary'
90 – 'King Midas'
93 – 'La Lorraine'
95 – 'Lady Mary Dashwood'
90 – 'Lake of Silver'
90 – 'Largo'
96 – 'Le Cygne'
95 – 'Limosel'
95 – 'Love Mist'
95 – 'Lowell Thomas'
92 – 'Madame Lemoine'
90 – 'Marietta Sisson'
95 – 'Matilda Lewis'
91 – 'Minnie Shaylor'
95 – 'Mistral'
95 – 'Moon River'
90 – 'Moonglow'
90 – 'Mr Thim'
96 – 'Mrs Edward Harding'
96 – 'Octavie Demay'
95 – 'Persier'
96 – 'Philippe Rivoire'
95 – 'Pink Cream'
96 – 'Pink Giant'
95 – 'Poetic'
94 – 'Queen Alexandra'
95 – 'Queen of Hearts'
95 – 'Queen of Sheba'
96 – 'Queen Wilhelmina'
95 – 'R.W. Marsh'
96 – 'Raoul Dessert'
95 – 'Red Champion'
95 – 'Red Flag'
96 – 'Rhododendron'
94 – 'Richard Carvel'
95 – 'Rose of Silver'
96 – 'Ruigegno'
95 – 'Sante Fe'
95 – 'Snow Cloud'
91 – 'Snow Mountain'
95 – 'Souvenir d'A. Millet'
95 – 'Starlight'
95 – 'Suzette'
96 – 'Tamate-boko'
95 – 'The Moor'
94 – 'The Nymph'
94 – 'Thura Hires'
90 – 'Victoria'
92 'Laddie'
96 x ***lemoinei*** 'Alice Harding' (S)
93 ***mascula*** subsp. ***arietina*** 'Purple Emperor'
95 – 'Immaculata'
96 – subsp. ***russoi***
95 'Moonrise'
95 ***officinalis*** 'Crimson Globe'
94 – subsp. ***officinalis***
96 'Paladin'
95 ***peregrina*** 'Fire King'
96 'Polindra'
95 'Postilion'
94 ***rhodia***
93 'Rose Gem'
95 ***suffruticosa*** Great Gold Powder = 'Da-jin-fen' (S)
95 – False Kudzu Purple = 'Jia-ge-jin-zi' (S)
95 – subsp. ***Rockii*** (S)
96 – Top Table Red = 'Sho-an-hong' (S)
91 – 'Yatsu-kazishi' (S)
96 – Best-shaped Red = 'Zhuan-yuan-hong' (S)
96 – Diamond Dust = 'Zuan-fen' (S)
93 'Tango'
94 ***veitchii*** 'Alba'
94 'Walter Mains'

PALISOTA
94 ***barteri***

PALIURUS
90 ***ramosissimus***

PANDANUS
90 ***veitchii*** 🏆

PANICUM
96 ***miliaceum*** 'Violaceum'

PAPAVER
94 ***alpinum*** Linnaeus ***album***
87 ***apokrinomenon***
96 ***fauriei***
93 'French Grey'
94 ***kerneri***
87 ***kwanense***
87 ***nudicaule*** Meadhome Strain
94 – Oregon Rainbow Group
91 ***orientale*** 'Constance Finnis'
95 – 'Forncett Banner'
95 – 'Forncett Post'
95 – 'Forncett Summer'
96 – 'Garden Gnome'
90 – 'Lavender Girl'
89 – 'Lighthouse'
95 – 'Mrs George Stobart'
96 – 'Pink Chiffon'
87 – 'Salome'
87 – 'Snowflame'
95 ***palaestinum***
90 ***pyrenaicum*** subsp. ***degenii***
94 ***rhaeticum*** JCA 752.500
90 ***rhoeas*** Whispering Fairies Group
96 ***somniferum*** 🏆
94 ***suaveolens***
89 ***thianschanicum***

PARAHEBE
92 x ***bidwillii*** 'Rosea'
91 ***birleyi***
91 ***catarractae*** 'Tiny Tot'
94 ***peltata***
94 ***spathulata***

PARAQUILEGIA
95 ***anemonoides*** Gothenburg Strain

PARKINSONIA
96 ***aculeata***

PAROCHETUS
94 ***communis*** summer-flowering

PARONYCHIA
93 ***argyroloba***
88 ***cephalotes***

PARROTIA
91 ***persica*** 'Prostrata'

PARTHENOCISSUS
93 ***semicordata***
96 sp. KR 708

PASITHEA
96 ***caerulea***

PASSIFLORA
96 ***adulterina***
92 ***bryonioides***
92 ***caerulea rosea***
94 x ***caeruleoracemosa*** 'Lilac Lady'
92 x ***caponii*** 'John Innes'
92 ***cirrhiflora***
96 ***cissifolia***
92 ***edulis*** 'Alice'
94 – f. ***edulis*** (F)
94 ***eichleriana***
94 'Golden Glow'
92 'Hartwiesiana'
96 ***iralda***
96 ***jamesonii***
96 'Lucia'
96 ***luismanvelii***
96 ***ornitheura***
96 ***pilosa***
96 ***quadriglandulosa***
92 ***trifoliata***
92 ***truxillensis***
91 'Wilcrowl'

PAULOWNIA
94 ***tomentosa*** 'Lilacina'

PEDICULARIS
94 ***canadensis***
95 ***verticillata***

PELARGONIUM
91 'Ada Sutcliffe' (Min)
95 'Ade's Elf' (Z/St)
95 'Admiral Bouvant' (I)
95 'Aerosol Improved' (Min)
92 'Aida' (R)
95 'Ainsdale Beauty' (Z)
95 'Ainsdale Glasnost' (Z)
95 'Ainsdale Happiness' (Z/d)
95 'Ainsdale Sixty' (Z)
95 Alba (Z/d)
96 'Albert Sheppard' (Z/C/d)
95 'Alex Kitson' (Z)
96 'Alice Greenfield' (Z)
93 'Aloe' (Z)
95 'Amelia' (Min)
91 'Amour' (R)
95 'Amy Parmer' (Min)
92 'Andenken an Emil Eschbach' (I/d)
96 'Angela' (Min)
95 'Angela Mitchell' (Z/C/d)
95 'Annabelle' (Dw)
95 'Anne Mitchell' (Min)
89 'Annette Kellerman' (Z)
95 'Antony Ayton' (R)
95 ***appendiculatum***
95 'Arthur Mitchell' (Min)
95 'Ashdown Forest' (Dw)
92 'Avenida' (Z)
95 'Baby Clare' (Min)
95 'Baby Doll' (Min/d)
96 'Ballerina' (R)
95 'Ballet Dancer' (Min/d)
92 'Barbara Rice' (Z/d)
95 'Barcelona' (R)
95 'Barham' (Min/d)
96 Barock (I)
96 'Beatrix Little' (Dw)

94 'Beauty of Coldwell' (Z/C)
95 'Belstead' (Min)
92 'Belvedere' (R)
95 'Benedict' (Min)
94 'Bengal Fire' (Z/C)
96 'Bernina' (I)
95 'Betsy Trotwood' (Dw)
95 ***bijugum***
95 'Black Top' (R)
95 'Blanchland Cerise' (Dw)
95 'Blanchland Dazzler' (Min)
94 'Blisworth Mrs Mappin' (Z/v)
96 'Blizzard'
96 'Blizzard Cascade'
92 'Blossomtime' (Z/d)
95 'Blushing Bell' (Dw)
93 'Bold Appleblossom' (Z)
95 'Bold Romance' (Z)
90 'Bovey Beauty'
95 'Brett' (Min)
95 'Brettenham' (Min)
95 'Brialyn Star' (A)
92 'Brick Giant'
95 'Bridal Veil' (Min/C) 🏆
95 'Bristol Dandy' (Z/C/d)
95 'Brixworth Gold' (Min/C/d)
94 'Brixworth Serenade' (Min/C/d)
96 'Brookside Abigail'
96 'Brookside Arundel'
95 'Brookside Jupiter' (Z)
95 'Brownie' (Min)
91 'Burge' (R)
93 'C.Z.' (Ca)
95 'Calando' (I)
95 'Cally' (Min/d)
95 'Canasta' (Z)
91 'Carol Cooper' (Fr/d)
96 'Carol Plumridge' (Dw/C)
96 'Carol West' (Z/v)
92 'Carol's Treasure' (Z/C)
95 'Carolyn' (Min)
95 'Cassio' (Min/d)
95 Century Series (Z) 🏆
94 'Cerise' (I/d)
95 'Cézanne' (I/d)
95 'Champion' (R/d)
91 'Chang' (Z)
96 'Charles Gounod' (Z/d)
95 'Chattisham' (Min)
95 'Cheerio' 🏆
95 'Cherie' (Z) 🏆
95 'Cherie Mitchell' (Min)
93 'Cherie Salmon'
94 'Cherry Blossom' (Z/d)
94 'Cherry Galilee' (I/d)
96 'Chessington' (Z/C)
95 'Chic'
95 'Chiltern Beacon' (Min/d)
94 'Chinese Red' (Z/d)
93 'Christine Read' (Dw)
95 'Christopher Mitchell' (Min)
95 'Clare' (Min)
96 'Clevedon Joy' (Z/c)
96 Coco-Rico (I)
95 'Colour Sergeant' (Min)
95 'Confetti' (R)
95 'Congestum'
90 'Copper Flair' (Z/C)
96 'Coral Island' (Z/d)
96 'Coral Reef' (Z/d)
90 'Corot' (I/d)
96 'Corvina' (R)
92 'County Girl' (Z)
95 ***crassipes***
95 'Credo' (Z)
95 'Crestfield Pink' (Min)
95 'Crimson Glow' (Dw/d)
93 'Crimson Nosegay'
95 ***crithmifolium***
96 ***cucullatum*** subsp. ***strigifolium***
92 'Danielle' (Z)
96 'Dark Mabel' (R)
94 'Dark Pink Sugar Baby' (I)
90 'David Gamble' (Z)
95 'David Mitchell' (Min/Ca/C/d)
95 'Dawn Bonanza' (R)
96 'Daydream' (Z/C/d)
92 'Delilah' (Z)
95 'Della' (Min/d)
90 'Desert Dawn' (Z/C)
95 'Devon Cream'
96 'Dewit's' (Dw)
95 'Di' (Min/d)
95 'Dick's White' (Dw/d)
96 'Didden's Improved Picardy' (Z/d)
95 ***dipetalum***
95 'Doctor Coralit' (I)
95 'Dondo' (Dw/d)
95 'Don's Agnes Brown' (Min)
95 'Don's Diamond Jubilee' (Z/C/v)
95 'Don's Seagold'
95 'Don's Sunkissed' (Dw/v)
95 'Don's Swanland Girl' (Min)
90 'Double Skies of Italy' (Z/C/d)
95 ***drummondii***
94 'Duchess' (I)
95 'Dutch Vermillion' (Min)
96 'Earth Magic' (Z/v)
91 'Edgar Chisnall' (Z)
92 'Elizabeth Iris' (Dw)
96 'Elmscfi' (Dw)
95 'Elsie' (Z/C/d)
95 'Emilia Joy' (A)
90 'Emily De Sylva' (I/d)
95 'Emma' (Min/C/d)
95 'Empress Irene' (Z)
95 'Expo' (I/d)
90 'Fabel' (Z)
91 'Faircop' (Sc)
95 'Fairy Princess' (Min)
95 'Fairy Storey' (Min/v)
95 'Falkenham' (Min)
96 'Fantasy' (R)
96 'Felix' (I)
95 ***fergusoniae***
94 'Feu d'Amour' (I/d)
95 'Filigree' (Dw/v)
95 'Finger'
95 'Fireworks' (Dw)
96 'First Ladies'
92 'Flamboyant' (I/d)
95 'Flamenco' (R)
95 'Flamingo Dancer' (Z/Ca)
96 'Flarepath' (Z/C/v)
95 'Flash' (Min)
92 Flirtpel (Z/d)
95 'Florence Mitchell' (Dw)
93 'Flynn' (Min)
92 'Fortuna' (Z)
91 Fortuna (Z)
96 'Francis Parmenter' (MinI/v)
89 'Fraulein Gruss' (R)
91 'Friesian Beauty' (Z)
92 'Gallant' (Z/d)
95 'Gama' (Min)
95 'Ganymede' (Z)
95 'Garland' (Dw/d)
89 'Gaudy' (Z)
95 'Gauguin' (I/d)
93 'Gemma Pride' (R)
93 'Gemma Rose' (R)
95 'Geratus' (Min/Ca/d)
95 'Gerona' (I)
92 'Gilda' (Z)
95 'Gina' (Min)
92 'Gladys Washbrooke' (Z/d)
92 'Glen' (Z/d)
92 'Glenys Carey' (Z/d)
96 Gloria (Z/d)
95 'Golden Chance' (Min/C/v)
95 'Golden Fireball' (Z/C)
96 'Golden Flora'
96 'Golden Gleam' (Z/C)
96 'Golden Lilac Mist'
91 'Golden Magaluf' (I/d/C/v)
93 'Golden Oriole' (Dw/C)
91 'Gottweig' (Z)
95 'Granada' (R)
95 'Grand Prix'
91 'Grasmere Beauty' (Z)
95 'Greco' (Z)
96 Gregor (Z/d)
94 'Grenada' (R)
96 'Grenche Belle' (I/d)
95 'Greta Garbo' (Z)
92 'Grollie's Cream'
95 'GTI'
91 'Guernsey'
95 'Guido' (Z)
96 'Guitari' (I)
96 'Gwen' (Min/v)
96 'H. Walker' (R)
95 'Haidee' (Min)
95 'Harlequin' (Dw)
94 'Harlequin Hilda Day' (I)
96 'Harmony' (R)
90 'Harvest Moon' (Z)
91 'Hayley Clover'
91 'Hazel Candy' (R)
91 'Hazel Dream' (R)
91 'Hazel Fire' (R)
96 'Hazel Frances' (R)
96 'Hazel Frills' (R)
91 'Hazel Orchid' (R)
90 'Hazel White' (R)
96 'Helena Hall' (R)
96 'Henley' (Min/d)
95 'Henri Joignot' (Z/C/d)
93 'Henry Jacoby' (Z)
92 'Henry's Rose' (Z/C)
91 'High Glow' (R)
96 'Highfields Came' (Z/d)
94 'Highfields Concerto' (Z)
96 'Highfields Fashion' (Z)
90 'Highfields Fiesta' (Z)
96 'Highfields Flair' (Z/d)
96 'Highfields Flash' (Z/d)
89 'Highfields Glory' (Z)
94 'Highfields Glow' (Z/d)
92 'Highfields Harmony' (Z)
92 'Highfields Jazz' (Z/d)
92 'Highfields Peerless' (Z)
92 'Highfields Progress' (Z)
92 'Highfields Romance' (Z)
96 'Highfields Salmon' (Z/d)
92 'Highfields Sensation' (Z)
95 'Highland Princess' (Dw)
94 'Hollywood Star' (Z) 🏆
91 'Honeywood Margaret' (R)
93 ***hystrix***
95 'Ice Cap' (Min)
92 'Improved Goertz'
94 'Improved Rubin' (Z/d)
96 'Inka'
94 'Ione' (Z/d)
96 'Irene Hardy' (Z/d)
96 'Irene Lollipop' (Z/d)
96 'Irene Toyon' (Z) 🏆
95 'Isaac Read' (Dw)
95 'Jack Cox' (Dw/d)
96 'Jack of Hearts' (I)
94 'Jan Portas' (Min/C)
96 'Jane Shoulder' (Min)
96 'Janet James'
95 'Jay' (Dw)
95 'Jayne' (Min/d)
92 'Jean Viaud' (Z/d)
91 'Jennifer Strange' (R)
96 'Jewel' (Z/d)
95 'Jilly Mitchell' (Dw/d)
91 'Jim Small' (Z/C)
95 'Jim's Delight' (Z/C)
95 'Joan Sharman' (Min)
96 'John's Dilys'
94 'John's Valerie'
96 'John's Wishy-washy'
91 'Joy Thorp' (I)
95 'Joyce Headley' (Dw/C)
95 'Joyful' (Min)
89 'Joyrider' (Z/d)
95 'Karen' (Dw/C)
92 'Karen Gamble Improved' (Z)
96 'Kari Anne'
95 ***karrooense*** Knuth
95 'Kath Parmer' (Dw/C)
92 'Kathleen Gamble Improved' (Z)
96 'Kathleen Mott' (Z/C)
90 'Katina' (Z)
95 'Kelly' (I)
89 'Kelly's Eye' (Z/C)
89 'Kelvendon Wonder' (Min)
96 'Kewense' (Z)
95 'Koora' (Min/d)
95 'Kosset' (Min/d)
96 'Laced Belle Notte' (I)

96 'Laced Sugar Baby' (DwI)
96 'Lady Lexington' (I)
96 'Lady Mavis Pilkington' (Z/d)
95 'Lakeland' (I)
96 'Lara Ballerina'
96 'Lee Gamble' (Z)
91 'Legende' (R)
95 'Lemore' (Min/d)
96 'Lerchenmuller' (Z/d)
95 'Lesando' (Z)
90 'Lesley Kefford' (Z)
91 'Lilac Gemma' (R)
96 'Lilac Ricard' (Z/d)
96 'Lilett'
96 'Lilian Lilett'
92 'Lilian Woodberry' (Z)
91 'Little Dandy'
95 'Little Dazzler' (Min)
95 'Little Love' (A)
95 'Little Witch' (Z/St)
93 ***longifolium***
95 'Lorraine' (Dw)
91 'Loveliness' (Z)
96 'Lulu' (I)
93 'Luscious' (Min)
95 ***luteolum***
90 'Lyrik' (Z/d)
95 'M.A.F.F.' (Min)
95 'Mac's Red' (Z/C)
96 ***madagascariense***
92 'Madame Irene' (Z/d)
91 'Madeline Crozy'
95 'Madison'
95 'Manta' (Min)
95 'Mantilla' (Min)
96 'Margaret Bryan' (Z/C)
95 'Market Day' (R)
95 'Martina' (I)
96 'Mary Godwin' (Z)
95 'Mary Lee' (Min)
89 'Mary Screen' (Min)
95 'Master Paul' (Z/v)
96 'Maverick Star'
96 'Meadowside Dark and Dainty'
91 'Meill Jamison' (Min)
96 'Mercia' (R)
96 'Mercia Glory' (R)
95 'Mercia Prince' (R)
96 'Mere Ripon' (R)
91 'Mere Seville' (Z)
95 'Mexican Girl' (I)
95 'Mia' (Min/d)
92 'Mickey' (R)
92 'Mikado' (R)
90 'Milka' (R)
94 'Mill Purple' (I)
91 'Mill Wine' (I/d)
95 Minipel Karminrot (Dw)
95 Minipel Orange (Dw)
95 Minipel Red (Dw)
95 Minipel Rosa (Dw)
95 Minipel Scharlach (Dw)
95 'Miss Prim' (Min)
94 'Mission Dubonnet' (R)
95 'Mitzi' (Min)
95 'Mixed Blessings' (Min/C)
96 'Molly Malone'
96 'Momo'
93 'Monkwood Beacon' (R)
93 'Monkwood Bonanza' (R)
93 'Monkwood Jester' (Z/d)
95 'Montevideo'
96 'Monty' (I/d)
93 'More Mischief' (Dw/Ca/d)
95 'Mosaic Bella Notte' (I)
96 'Mosaic Silky' (Z/v)
94 'Mozart' (R)
93 'Mrs Brock' (Z)
96 'Mrs H.J. Jones' (I)
96 'Mrs L.R. Bodey' (R)
95 'Mrs Mavis Colley' (Z/v)
91 'Mrs Mayne'
95 ***multicaule*** subsp. ***multicaule***
94 'Mustang'
95 'Nanette' (Z)
95 'Nella' (Min)
95 'New Dawn Rose Form' (I)
95 'Night and Day' (Dw)
96 'Nina West' (Z)
95 ***oblongatum***
96 'Occold Tangerine' (Dw)
95 ***ochroleucum***
96 'Oldbury Cascade' (I/v)
92 'Orange' (Z/St)
95 'Orange Embers' (Dw)
95 'Orange Glow' (Dw/d)
95 'Orange Ruffy' (Min)
95 'Orwell' (Min)
91 'Ostergruss' (R)
95 'Otley' (Min)
90 'Otley Slam' (R)
90 'Our Jim' (Z)
95 'Oyster Maid' (Min)
89 'Pam Screen'
95 'Paradise Moon' (Min/d)
95 'Peggy Franklin' (Min)
96 'Persian Queen' (R)
96 'Phyllis Brooks' (R)
96 'Picardy' (Z/d)
95 Picasso
93 'Pico'
95 'Picotee'
95 'Pier Head' (Z)
95 'Pink Bridal Veil' (Z/C)
91 'Pink Delight' (Z/d)
95 'Pink Elizabeth Read' (Dw)
95 'Pink Floral Cascade' (Fr/d)
94 'Pink Fringed Aztec' (R)
95 'Pink Golden Ears' (Dw/St/C)
92 'Pink Lady' (Z)
91 'Pink Lady Harold' (Z)
93 'Pink Moon'
95 'Pink Nosegay'
91 'Pink Pandora' (T)
95 'Pink Profusion' (Min)
96 'Pink Slam' (R)
93 'Pink Snowdrift' (I/d)
95 'Pink Splendour' (Min/d)
95 'Pink Startel' (Z/St)
95 ***pinnatum***
96 'Pioneer'
95 'Pixie Glow' (Z/St)
95 'Pixie Prince' (Z/St)
95 'Playboy Blush' (Dw)
95 'Playboy Candy' (Dw)
95 'Playboy Cerise' (Dw)
95 'Playboy Coral' (Dw)
95 'Playboy Coral Orange' (Dw)
95 'Playboy Mauve' (Dw)
95 'Playboy Powder Pink' (Dw)
95 'Playboy Salmon' (Dw)
95 'Playboy Salmon Eyed' (Dw)
95 'Playboy Scarlet' (Dw)
95 'Playboy White' (Dw)
95 'Playford' (Dw)
90 'Poetic' (Z)
95 'Polaris' (Min)
92 Polka (Z/d)
96 'Posey' (Min/d)
92 Prelude (Z)
94 'Prince Harry' (I)
94 'Princess Margaretha' (Z)
94 'Princess Pink' (Z)
95 'Prudence' (Min)
95 ***punctatum***
95 'Purple Gem' (Min)
95 'Purple Pat' (Min/d)
93 'Purple Rogue' (R)
96 'Ragtime' (St)
92 'Raola Lemon'
96 'Ravensbeck'
96 'Rebecca' (R)
95 'Red Beauty' (Z/d)
96 'Red Brooks Barnes' (Dw/C)
92 'Red Capri' (Sc)
95 'Red Comet' (Min)
95 'Red Devil' (Z/St)
89 'Red Doll'
94 'Red Dollar' (Z/C)
95 'Red Dwarf' (Min/d)
95 'Red Elmsett' (Z/C/d)
95 'Red Grace Wells' (Min)
90 'Red Grande' (I)
90 'Red Patricia Andrea' (T)
95 'Red Pearl' (Min)
94 'Red Star' (Z)
96 'Red Streak' (Min/Ca)
95 'Red Sybil Holmes' (I)
95 'Reg 'Q'' (Z/C)
91 'Ric-Rac'
94 'Ringo Rose' (Z)
92 Rio (Z)
90 'Robin Hood' (Dw/d)
96 'Robinson Crusoe' (Dw/C)
91 'Roi des Balcons Rouge' (I)
95 'Roller's Pearly Lachs' (I)
90 'Ron' (R)
90 'Ron's Delight' (R)
95 'Ron's Elmsett' (Dw/C/d)
95 'Ron's Semer' (Min)
95 'Ron's Shelley' (Dw)
95 Rosais (I/d)
95 'Rose Crousse' (I/d)
91 'Rose Lady Lexington' (I/v)
90 'Rose Star' (Z/d)
93 'Rosebud' (Z/d)
91 'Rouge' (R)
89 'Royal Pageant'
96 'Royal Parade' (R)
93 'Ruben' (Z/d)
95 'Ruben' (I/d)
91 'Rubin' (Z/d)
92 'Sabrina' (Z/d)
96 'Saint Catherine'
96 'Saint Malo'
96 'Salmon Grozser Garten' (Dw)
90 'Salmon Kovalevski' (Z)
93 'Salmon Nosegay'
92 'Salmon Satisfaction' (Z)
95 'Sarah Mitchell' (Min)
95 'Sarkie' (Z/d)
96 'Saturn' (Z)
93 ***scabroide***
94 'Scarlet Breakway' (Z)
96 'Scarlet Crousse' (I/C)
92 'Scarlet Galilee' (I/d)
96 'Scarlet Gem' (St)
95 'Scarlet Shelley' (Dw)
95 'Scarlett O'Hara' (Min)
92 'Schwarzwalderin' (I)
90 'Sea Mist' (Min)
92 'Serenade' (Z/d)
95 'Sheila Thorp' (Dw/d)
94 'Shiraz' (R)
95 'Silas Marner' (Dw)
92 'Silvia' (R)
95 'Snow Witch' (Z/St)
96 'Snowmite'
95 'Snowstar' (Z)
96 'Sofie Cascade' (I)
96 'Solent Sunrise' (Z/C)
96 'South American Delight' (R)
95 'Southampton' (Z)
95 'Sparkle' (Dw)
95 'Speckled Egg' (Dw)
95 'Speckled Hen' (Dw)
95 'Speckled Orange' (Dw)
96 'Splendour' (R) 🏆
95 'Sporwen' (Min)
89 'Spray Paint' (Min)
96 'Springfield Lilac' (R)
96 'Springfield Rose' (R)
95 ***staphysagrioides***
96 'Starbust'
95 'Stella May' (Dw)
90 'Stellar Pixie Rose' (St)
90 'Stellar Red Devil' (Z/St/d)
96 'Stellar Snowflake' (Z/St)
92 'Stuart Gamble' (Z/d)
89 'Sugar Plum Fairy' (I)
91 'Summer Idyll'
95 'Sunbeam' (Dw/d)
95 'Sundance Orange Scarlet' 🏆
91 'Sunday's Child'
91 'Sundridge Surprise' (Z)
95 'Sunset Marble' (I)
95 'Suntrap' (Z/C)
96 'Susan' (Dw)
92 'Susan Jane' (Z/d)
92 'Susie' (Z/C)
95 'Sussex Surprise' (Dw/v)
91 'Swan Song' (Z)
91 'Sweet Miriam' (Sc)
95 'Swing' (Z)
96 'Sylvia' (R)
95 'Tanya' (Min)

95 'Tattoo' (Min)
96 'Ten of Hearts' (I)
95 'Terry' (I)
91 'The Mary Rose' (R)
94 'Thea' (R)
95 'Timmy Griffin' (Min)
95 'Tina Vernon' (Dw/C)
95 'Tiny Tim'
96 'Titan' (Z)
95 'Tom Tit' (Dw)
95 'Toni' (Min)
95 'Tracery' (Dw/St)
95 'Travira' (I)
96 'Treasure Trove' (Z/v)
95 'Trumps' (Min)
93 'Tutti Frutti' (Z)
96 'Twist' (Z)
92 Twist (ZxI)
96 'Vagabond' (R)
96 'Valerie' (Z/d)
96 'Valley Court' (I)
91 'Variegated Oak' (Sc/v)
90 'Velley Court' (I/v)
91 Velvet (I)
96 'Vera Vernon' (Z/v)
96 'Vesuvius' (Z)
95 'Vida' (Min)
95 'Video Red' (Min)
95 'Video Rose' (Min)
95 'Video Salmon' (Min)
96 'Violetta' (Z/d)
95 ***vitifolium***
92 'Volcano' (Z)
95 'Vulcano Fire' (Dw)
91 'Wallace's Pink' (Fr)
94 'Waltz' (Z)
91 'Wembley Gem' (Z)
95 'Westerfield' (Min)
95 'Weston Triumph' (Z/C/v)
95 'Wherstead' (Min)
90 'Whistling Dancer' (Z/C)
96 'White Nosegay'
95 'White Roc' (Min/d)
90 'White Startel' (Z)
95 'White Swaine' (Min)
96 'White Wooded Ivy'
95 'Wiener Blut'
95 'Wilf Vernon' (Min/d)
95 'Wine Red'
96 'Winford Festival'
96 'Winford Winnie'
91 'Wirral Cascade' (Fr/d)
95 'Wirral Supreme' (Z)
96 'Wordsworth'
95 'Yellow Snowball' (Z/C/d)
90 'Zoe Washbrooke' (Z/d)

PELLAEA
95 ***atropupurea***
95 ***ternifolia***

PENNISETUM
96 ***alopecuroides*** black
96 – 'Little Bunny'
96 – 'Weserbergland'
93 ***americanum***
94 ***setaceum*** 'Rubrum'

PENSTEMON
91 ***acaulis***
94 ***albertinus*** K 92.315
94 'Alice Howarth'
93 ***ambiguus***
94 ***anguineus***
95 ***angustifolius*** K 92.3128
93 ***australis***
94 ***baccharifolius***
95 ***barbatus*** 'Rose Elf'
94 'Barbelles'
92 ***berryi***
95 'Beverley'
94 'Blue Eye'
95 'Blue King'
96 Broken Tops Mountain, USA
94 ***cardinalis***
96 ***cardinalis regilis***
96 ***caryi***
88 'Claret'
94 ***clutei***
94 ***comarrhenus***
91 ***compactus***
96 'Delaware'
90 ***digitalis*** 'Nanus'
91 ***dissectus***
93 ***ellipticus***
88 'Eva'
92 'Fairy Bouquet'
91 ***frederici-augusti***
88 ***fruticosus*** var. ***scouleri*** 'Boulder'
94 – – f. ***roseus***
94 – – f. ***ruber***
93 ***gairdneri*** subsp. ***oreganus***
94 'Gletsjer'
96 ***globosus***
96 ***grahamii***
96 ***grandiflorus*** 'Prairie Snow'
88 'Greencourt Purple'
95 ***grinnellii***
96 ***heterophyllus*** 'Perhill Purple'
96 'Heythrop Park'
94 'Hillview Pink'
89 ***hirsutus*** 'Darnley Violet'
92 ***humilis*** 'Albus'
91 ***impressus***
94 'Jeannie'
92 ***labrosus***
94 ***laevis***
92 ***lanceolatus***
92 ***laricifolius*** subsp. ***exilifolius***
91 ***leonardii***
95 ***leonensis***
90 'Lilactime'
93 ***mensarum***
88 ***mexicanus***
92 ***mucronatus***
88 'Newbury Gem'
96 'Old Silk'
96 ***oliganthus***
96 ***ophianthus***
92 ***pachyphyllus***
96 'Papal Purple' x 'Evelyn'
96 'Park Garden'
95 ***parryi***
92 ***paysoniorum***
96 ***petiolatus***
95 pink and cream
94 'Plum Beauty'
94 ***procerus*** subsp. ***formosus***
93 ***procurrens***
92 ***pseudospectabilis***
93 'Purpurglocken'
94 ***ramaleyi***
93 ***sanguineus***
94 'Scarlet 'n' White'
92 ***speciosus***
94 ***spectabilis***
92 ***stenophyllus***
96 ***subserratus***
92 ***subulatus***
94 'Tapestry'
96 ***thompsoniae***
92 ***thurberi***
92 ***virens*** pale blue
96 ***virgatus*** subsp. ***asa-grayi***
95 – subsp. ***virgatus***
88 'Waterloo'
95 ***whippleanus*** K 92.353

PENTALINON
96 ***luteum***

PENTAS
90 ***lanceolata*** 'Kermesina'
90 – 'Quartiniana'

PENTASCHISTIS
93 sp. SH 44

PEPEROMIA
92 – 'Luna'
93 – 'Variegata'
92 ***columbiana***
92 – 'Carnival'
92 ***deppeana***
90 ***fraseri***
92 'Green Valley'
94 ***incana***
92 ***maculosa***
92 ***miqueliana***
90 ***obtusifolia*** 'Variegata'
92 'Pauline'
92 ***pereskiifolia***
92 ***puteolata***
92 ***rubella***
92 'Teresa'
92 'Tine'
92 ***tristachya***

PERICALLIS
96 ***appendiculata***
95 ***multiflora***

PERILLA
96 ***frutescens*** green

PERROTTETIA
95 ***racemosa***

PERSEA
95 ***ichangensis***
95 ***indica***
94 ***lingue***

PERSICARIA
95 ***affinis*** 'Hartswood'
96 – Kew form
95 ***amplexicaulis*** 'Clent Rose'
95 – 'Eggins Pink'
90 ***amplexicaulis oxyphylla***
91 ***emodi*** 'George Taylor'
95 ***regeliana***
96 sp. from Taiwan B&SWJ 1765

PETASITES
91 ***japonicus***
96 ***kablikianus*** AL&JS 90170YU

PETREA
96 ***volubilis*** 'Albiflora'

PETROCOPTIS
94 ***grandiflora***
94 ***pyrenaica rosea***

PETROMARULA
90 ***pinnata***

PETRORHAGIA
96 ***velutina***

PHACELIA
88 ***sericea***

PHAGNALON
96 ***helichrysoides***

PHALARIS
96 ***canariensis***

PHANEROPHLEBIA
94 ***macrosora***

PHELLODENDRON
94 ***amurense*** var. ***sachalinense***
93 ***chinense***
95 ***japonicum***

PHILADELPHUS
93 'Albâtre'
91 ***argyrocalyx***
92 'Atlas'
90 ***coronarius*** Threave form
89 'Etoile Rose'
92 'Falconeri'
96 'Galahad'
96 ***incanus***
95 ***intectus***
92 x ***lemoinei*** 'Lemoinei'
96 ***lewisii***
90 ***microphyllus*** 'Superbus'
90 'Mrs Reid'
87 'Norma'
91 'Pentagon'
89 ***pubescens***
91 x ***purpureomaculatus***
93 'Rosace'
91 ***satsumi***
89 ***schrenkii***
90 ***sericanthus***
93 'Silver Slipper'
92 'Snowbelle'
92 ***tenuifolius***

PHILODENDRON
93 ***bipennifolium*** ♈
90 – 'Variegatum'
96 ***erubescens*** 'Valeria'
90 ***ilsemannii***
90 ***imbe*** 'Variegatum'
94 ***ornatum***
90 'Painted Lady'

PHLEUM
89 ***alpinum***
95 ***montanum***

PHLOMIS
95 ***herba-venti*** subsp. ***pungens***
94 'Nova'
91 ***orientalis***
96 ***purpurea*** dark form

PHLOX
96 ***bifida*** 'Onsted Gem'
94 – 'Starcleft'
88 'Boris'
93 ***caerulea*** x ***aleutica***

93 *caespitosa* subsp. *pulvinata*
90 'Chequers'
96 *chonela* 'Nana'
90 *diffusa* 'Octopus'
94 *douglasii* 'Blue Mist'
94 – 'Lilac Cloud'
96 – 'Millstream Laura'
90 – 'Petra'
96 – 'Pink Chint'
91 – 'Star Dust'
96 – 'White Drift'
93 *drummondii*
91 'Geddington Cross'
92 *hoodii* subsp. *glabra*
89 'Lee Raden'
95 'Minima Colvin'
88 'Moonlight'
95 *multiflora*
95 *nana*
94 – 'Arroya'
93 – 'Chameleon'
93 – 'Denver Sunset'
91 – 'Lilacina'
93 – f. *lutea*
96 – 'Manzano'
96 – 'Mary Maslin'
94 – 'Paul Maslin'
93 – 'Tangelo'
96 – 'Vanilla Cream'
94 *ovata*
87 *paniculata* 'Ann'
92 – 'Blue Mist'
96 – 'Boy Blue'
91 – 'Buccaneer'
91 – 'Cherry Pink'
89 – 'Denny'
95 – 'Elizabeth Campbell'
92 – 'Frau Antonin Buchner'
96 – 'Gaiety'
87 – 'Glow'
91 – 'Inspiration'
93 – 'Kelway's Cherub'
90 – 'Little Lovely'
93 – 'Marlborough'
91 – 'Pink Gown'
93 – 'Purpurkuppel'
94 – 'Shenstone'
93 'Pleu de Pervanche'
93 x *procumbens*
88 'Snowflake'
90 *subulata* 'Brilliant'
87 – 'Jill Alexander'
94 – 'Lavinia'
87 – 'Pink Delight'
90 – pink seedling
96 – 'Rose Mabel'
93 – 'Sarah'
90 – 'White Drift'
96 – 'Winifred'
93 – 'Woodside'
93 x *weseli*

PHOEBE
95 *sheareri*

PHORMIUM
91 'Burgundy'
94 'Gold Spike'
95 'Purple Queen'
95 'Smiling Morn' (v)

PHOTINIA
90 *lasiogyna* Hangzhou 11818
93 *lindleyana*
90 *villosa longipes*
94 *villosa* f. *maximowicziana*

PHRAGMITES
92 *australis* subsp. *altissimus*
94 – var. *pseudodonax*

PHYGELIUS
96 *aequalis* 'Apricot Trumpet'
93 *capensis albus*
95 x *rectus* 'Logan's Pink'

PHYLICA
96 *arborea* 'Superba'

x PHYLLIOPSIS
96 *hillieri*

PHYLLODOCE
96 *caerulea* Norwegian form
96 *tsugifolia*

PHYLLOSTACHYS
95 *aurea* 'Albovariegata'
95 *aurea formosana*
88 *bambusoides* 'Kronberg'
95 – 'Slender Crookstem'
87 *elegans*
94 *nidularia* Smooth Sheath
95 *nigra* 'Han-chiku'

PHYSALIS
95 *peruviana* (F)

PHYSARIA
94 *alpestris*
90 *alpina*
91 *bellii*
92 *chambersii*
91 *didymocarpa*
94 *floribunda*
91 *vitulifera*

PHYSOCARPUS
96 *bracteatus*
96 *capitatus*

PHYTOLACCA
94 *heteropetala*

PICEA
94 *abies* 'Dumosa'
94 – 'Frohburg Prostrata'
94 – 'Gregoryana Veitchii'
93 – 'Kámon'
90 – 'Mariae Orffiae'
87 – 'Parsonsii'
90 – 'Pseudoprostrata'
95 – 'Pyramidata'
96 – 'Remontii'
92 – 'Rubrospicata'
96 – 'Saint Mary's Broom'
96 *alcockiana*
95 *asperata* 'Blue Sky'
92 *glauca* 'Elf'
92 *glehnii*
94 – 'Yatsubusa'
96 *koraiensis* Beijing 176
95 *mariana*
90 – 'Beissneri'
96 x *mariorika* 'Gnom'
96 – 'Machala'
95 *meyeri*
91 *morrisonicola*
91 *omorika* 'Glauca'
93 *orientalis* 'Aureospicata'
96 – 'Early Gold'
94 – 'Gracilis'
92 – 'Skylands Prostrate'
95 – 'Wittboldt'
96 *pungens* 'Blue Trinket'
89 – 'Compacta'
96 – 'Corbet'
96 – 'Endtz'
93 – 'Glauca Pendula'
93 – 'Mrs Cesarini'
96 – 'Oldenburg'
95 – 'Pendula'
94 – 'Prostrate Blue Mist'
92 – 'Rovelli's Monument'
92 – 'Spek'
94 *purpurea* 🏆
96 *retroflexa*
91 *schrenkiana* var. *tianschanica*
96 *smithiana* CC&McK 363
92 *spinulosa*
92 *wilsonii*

PICRASMA
96 *quassioides*

PIERIS
93 'Brouwer's Beauty'
92 *floribunda* 'Elongata'
92 *formosa* var. *forrestii* 'Ball of Fire'
96 – – 'Charles Michael'
92 *japonica* 'Crystal'
95 – 'Daisy Hill'
93 – 'Green Pillar'
94 – 'Hino Crimson'
93 – 'Kakashima'
95 – pink
95 – 'Rosamund'
96 – 'Silver Sword'
90 – 'Stockman'
93 – 'Weeping Bride'
93 – 'Weeping Groom'
89 'Valley Fire'

PILEA
95 *cadierei* 'Minima' 🏆
93 *depressa*
92 *involucrata*
92 – 'Bronze'
92 – 'Moon Valley' 🏆
93 – 'Norfolk' 🏆
93 *microphylla*
93 'Silver Tree'

PILOSELLA
96 *aurantiaca* subsp. *carpathicola*

PIMELEA
94 *argentea*
92 *ferruginea* 'Magenta Mist'

PIMENTA
94 *dioica*

PIMPINELLA
95 *flahaultii*
93 *minima rosea*

PINGUICULA
94 *alpina*
96 'Ayantla'
94 *caerulea*
96 *crassifolia*
94 *cyclosecta*
95 'Fraser Beaut'
95 'George Sargent'
95 'Hamburg'
95 'Hameln'
94 *ionantha*
94 *lusitanica*
94 *lutea*
92 *oaxaca*
95 *oblongiloba*
94 *orchidioides*
94 'Pachuca'
94 *planifolia*
93 *primulifolia*
95 *rayonensis*
96 *rosea*
96 *santiago* 'Nuyoo Pass'
96 'Sargent'
95 'Tina'
95 'Vera Cruz'
96 *villosa*

PINUS
93 *ayacahuite* var. *veitchii*
87 *balfouriana*
87 *banksiana* 'Schoodic'
95 – 'Uncle Fogy'
88 *bhutanica*
95 *cembra* 'Glauca'
93 – subsp. *sibirica*
95 *cembroides*
87 *densata*
96 *engelmannii*
96 *flexilis* 'Vanderwolf's Pyramid'
87 *gordoniana*
95 *halepensis* subsp. *brutia*
92 x *holfordiana*
92 x *hunnewellii*
96 *kesiya* TW 333
94 *koraiensis* 'Compacta Glauca'
90 – 'Silver Mop'
92 *kwangtungensis*
95 *lawsonii*
91 *luchuensis*
87 *mugo* 'Hesse'
87 – 'Spingarn's Form'
92 – 'Trompenburg'
91 – 'Yellow Tip'
90 *nigra* var. *caramanica* 'Pyramidata'
87 – 'Globosa'
93 – subsp. *laricio* 'Aurea'
96 – subsp. *salzmannii*
94 – 'Semeriana'
87 – 'Strypemonde'
95 *oaxacana*
92 *parviflora* 'Blue Giant'
95 – 'Gimborn's Pyramid'
96 – 'Janome'
90 – 'Shikoku-goyo'
87 *peuce* 'Nana'
94 *pinaster* subsp. *hamiltonii*
91 *ponderosa* subsp. *scopulorum*
94 *pungens* 'Glauca'
96 *radiata* 'Nana'
90 *resinosa*
96 *roxburghii*
89 *rudis*
87 *strobus* 'Compacta'
96 – 'Contorta'
92 – 'Prostrata'
87 – 'Pumila'
93 – 'Radiata Aurea'
87 – 'Umbraculifera'
94 *sylvestris* 'Bonna'
87 – 'Corley'

90 – 'Iceni'
92 – var. ***mongolica***
92 – 'Prostrata'
93 – 'Sei'
87 – 'Umbraculifera'
92 – 'Vera Hayward'
92 – 'Viridis Compacta'
87 ***tabuliformis*** var. ***mukdensis***
87 ***wincesteriana***

PIPER
92 ***ornatum***

PITTOSPORUM
89 ***chathamicum***
92 ***cuneatum***
91 'Green Flame'
90 ***heterophyllum aculeatum***
93 ***moluccanum***
93 ***omeiense***
93 ***patulum***
94 ***ralphii*** 'Variegatum'
92 ***tenuifolium*** 'All Gold'
95 – 'Churchills'
94 – 'Nutty's Leprechaun'
90 – 'Silver Sheen'
89 – 'Snowflake'

PITYROGRAMMA
92 ***chrysophylla***

PLAGIANTHUS
87 ***divaricatus***
96 ***regius*** var. ***chathamicus***

PLAGIOMNIUM
96 ***affine***

PLANERA
92 ***aquatica***

PLANTAGO
91 ***arborescens*** subsp. ***maderensis***
91 ***barbata***
96 ***lanceolata*** 'Freaky'
96 ***major*** B&L 12649

PLATANUS
95 'Augustine Henry'
95 × ***hispanica*** 'Bloodgood'
95 – 'Liberty'
95 – 'Tremonia'
95 ***orientalis*** 'Autumn Glory'
95 – var. ***insularis***
93 ***wrightii***

PLATYCODON
94 ***grandiflorus apoyama*** 'Fairy Snow'
96 ***grandiflorus*** 'Axminster Streaked'
95 – blue
93 – double blue
93 – 'Flore Pleno'

PLECTOCOLEA
96 ***hyalina***

PLEIOBLASTUS
88 'Chigogasa'

PLEIONE
93 ***formosana*** 'Lilac Jubilee'
93 – 'Polar Star'
94 – 'Ruby Throat'
96 g. **Sajama**
95 g. **Shantung** 'Pixie'
95 – 'Silver Wedding'
96 g. **Tolima** 'Nightingale'
96 – 'Tufted Duck'
95 g. **Vesuvius** 'Linnet'

PLEUROCHAETE
96 ***luteoalba***

PLEXIPUS
96 ***cuneifolius***

PLUMERIA
96 forms

POA
93 ***alpina***
93 ***buchananii***
89 ***flabellata***

PODOCARPUS
87 ***macrophyllus*** 'Aureus'
92 ***nubigenus***

PODOLEPIS
94 ***jaceoides***

PODOPHYLLUM
96 ***hexandrum*** ACE 1894

POGOSTEMON
92 ***heyneanus***

POLEMONIUM
96 ***caeruleum*** subsp. ***amygdalinum***
94 – – 'Album'
96 – dwarf form
96 – 'Idylle'
94 – 'Lewdon Farm Pink'
93 – subsp. ***nipponicum*** f. ***album***
96 – subsp. ***villosum***
88 ***lanatum***
96 ***mexicanum***
90 ***pulcherrimum*** subsp. ***calycinum***
95 – subsp. ***pulcherrimum***
96 ***reptans*** 'Firmament'
90 × ***richardsonii*** 'Album'

POLYGONATUM
95 ***hookeri*** AGS/ES 523
89 × ***hybridum*** 'Nanum'
89 ***involucratum***
89 ***oppositifolium***
89 ***orientale***
94 sp. SS&W

POLYMNIA
90 ***sonchifolia***

POLYPODIUM
96 'Addison'
94 ***aureum*** ♀
90 – 'Glaucum'
90 – 'Undulatum'
94 ***cambricum*** 'Macrostachyon'
94 – (Pulcherrimum Group) 'Pulcherrimum May'
94 – (Pulcherrimum Group) 'Pulchritudine'
94 × ***font-queri***
94 ***interjectum*** 'Glomeratum Mullins'
94 × ***shivasiae***
94 ***vulgare*** 'Elegantissimum'

POLYPOGON
92 ***monspeliensis***
94 ***viridis***

POLYSCIAS
90 ***filicifolia***

POLYSTICHUM
96 ***braunii*** × ***proliferum***
95 ***discretum***
95 ***fallax***
95 ***interjectum***
96 ***lonchitis***
89 ***lonchitoides***
96 ***munitum*** 'Incisum'
96 ***setiferum*** Congestum Cristatum Group
95 – Conspicuolobum Group
94 – (Divisilobum Group) 'Divisilobum Grandiceps'
88 – (Divisilobum Group) 'Oakfield'
94 – 'Foliosum'
94 – 'Imbricatum'
94 – Perserratum Group
89 – (Perserratum Group) 'Schroeder'
96 – (Plumosodivisilobum Group) 'Baldwinii'
93 – Revolvens Group
89 – 'Thompsoniae'
94 – 'Vivien Green'
96 ***yunnanense***

POMADERRIS
93 ***kumeraho***

POPULUS
90 × ***canescens*** 'Macrophylla'
89 ***ciliata***
93 ***deltoides*** 'Cordata' (f)
92 × ***generosa***
89 ***grandidentata***
89 ***koreana***

POTENTILLA
95 ***anserina*** 'Ortie' (v)
95 – 'Variegata'
92 ***bifurca***
91 ***brauniana***
95 ***coriandrifolia***
94 ***cuneata aurea***
89 'Cyril'
89 'Daphne'
94 ***fruticosa*** 'Barnbarroch'
93 – var. ***dahurica*** 'Farrer's White'
89 – 'Daisy Hill Variety'
96 – 'Donard Gold'
94 – 'Golden Charm'
96 – 'Goldrush'
93 – 'Honey'
94 – var. ***parvifolia***
95 – 'Pastel Pink'
96 – 'Perryhill'
96 – var. ***pyrenaica***
90 – 'Yellow Dome'
94 – 'Yellow Star'
96 ***gracilis*** var. ***pulcherrima***
88 ***lignosa***
95 ***lineata***
94 'Master Floris'
96 ***millefolia klamathensis***
89 ***multifida***
93 ***nepalensis*** 'Flammenspiel'
92 – 'Salmon Seedling'
91 ***neumanniana aurea***
92 ***nitida*** 'Alannah'
93 ***nivalis***
88 'Orange Glow'
88 ***pensylvanica***
96 'Pheasant Eye'
89 'Roulette'
94 ***salesoviana***
94 'Songbird'
88 'Southcombe White'
95 sp. CLD 286

PRATIA
89 ***angulata*** 'Tennyson'
89 ***pedunculata*** 'Tunnack'
90 ***physaloides***

PRIMULA
91 ***allionii*** 'Clarkes' (2)
96 – 'Crystal' KRW 69/425 (2)
94 – 'E.K. Balls' (2)
92 – 'Jane' (2)
96 – 'Jouster' (2)
96 – KRW 1962/324 (2)
93 – Lismore P45/16 (2)
95 – 'Nymph' KRW 282/51 (2)
96 – 'Pink Gin' (2)
95 – × ***pubescens*** (2)
96 – × ***pubescens*** 'Rosalie' (2)
95 – R C E form (2)
95 – 'Superba'
91 'American Pink Hose-in-hose' (Prim)
91 'Amethyst' (Poly)
94 ***angustifolia*** (20)
92 ***apennina*** (2)
92 'April Snowflake' (Prim)
91 ***aureata*** subsp. ***fimbriata*** (21)
93 – 'R.B. Cooke' (21)
91 ***auricula*** hort. 'A. Delbridge' (A)
92 – A74 (A)
93 – 'Admiral'
96 – 'Alan' (A)
91 – var. ***albocincta*** (2)
94 – 'Alice' (d)
89 – 'Alpine Violet' (A)
93 – 'Amethyst' (S)
93 – 'Ann Hill' (S)
92 – 'Archer' (d)
94 – 'Ashcliffe Gem' (A)
89 – 'Aubergine' (B)
95 – 'Avocet' (S)
95 – 'Balbithan' (B)
91 – 'Balihai' (S)
96 – 'Banana Split'
89 – 'Barnhill' (d)
93 – 'Bartle's Cross' (S)
94 – 'Baupaume' (S)
93 – 'Beauty of Bath' (S)
96 – 'Beckjay' (S)
96 – 'Bernard Smith' (d)
93 – 'Betty Sheriff' (B)
93 – 'Big Ben' (S)
91 – 'Black Ice' (S)
89 – 'Blackcock' (S)
93 – 'Blakeney' (d)
91 – 'Blue Bonnet' (A)
95 – 'Blue Garden'

90 – 'Blue Lagoon' (S)
95 – 'Blue Mist' (B)
96 – 'Blue Ridge' (A)
93 – 'Bluebird' (S)
93 – 'Bookham Star' (S)
95 – 'Border Stripe' (B)
96 – 'Bramshill' (S)
92 – 'Brass Dog' (S)
94 – 'Bright Ginger' (S)
94 – 'Café au Lait' (A)
92 – 'Carcerot' (A)
89 – 'Carolina Duck' (S)
95 – 'Chantilly Cream' (d)
91 – 'Cherie' (S)
93 – 'Chirichua' (S)
92 – 'Citron' (S)
95 – 'Coll' (A)
96 – 'Commander' (A)
93 – 'County Park' (B)
93 – 'County Park Cream' (B)
89 – 'Crackley Seashell' (d)
93 – 'Crackley Tagetes' (d)
92 – 'Cream Blush' (d)
95 – 'Crimson Cavalier'
89 – 'Desert Dawn' (A)
89 – 'Desert Magic' (A)
89 – 'Desert Peach' (A)
89 – 'Desert Queen' (A)
89 – 'Desert Rose' (A)
89 – 'Desert Sands' (A)
89 – 'Desert Star' (A)
94 – 'Dogan' (S)
93 – 'Douglas Blue' (S)
94 – 'Douglas Rose' (S)
94 – 'Douglas Salmon' (S)
92 – 'Downlands' (S)
92 – 'Dunlin' (S)
93 – 'Durness' (S)
89 – 'Elizabeth Saunders' (d)
94 – 'Elsinore' (S)
94 – 'Emerald' (S)
96 – 'Enismore'
96 – 'Envy' (S)
93 – 'Esso Blue' (S)
96 – 'Eventide' (S)
94 – 'Everest Green' (S)
96 – 'Faro' (S)
94 – 'Fawsley's Favourite' (S)
89 – 'Firecrest' (S)
94 – 'Foreign Affairs' (S)
94 – 'Frank Bailey' (d)
94 – 'Frank Edger' (d)
95 – 'Freda' (S)
96 – 'Frittenden Yellow' (B)
94 – 'Gem' (A)
93 – 'George Edge' (B)
93 – 'George Harrison' (B)
92 – 'Girlguide' (S)
96 – 'Gold Blaze' (S)
94 – 'Golden Fleece' (S)
96 – 'Golden Gleam' (A)
94 – 'Golden Hill' (S)
93 – 'Golden Lilliput' (S)
94 – 'Golden Meadow' (S)
96 – 'Goldilocks' (S)
96 – 'Gooseberries and Cream'
96 – 'Grace' (S)
95 – 'Gracie' (A)
92 – 'Graisley' (S)
93 – 'Green Mansions' (S)
92 – 'Green Woodpecker' (S)
91 – green-edged pin eye
92 – 'Greenfinch' (S)
95 – 'Greenough Stripe'
91 – 'Grey Edge'
89 – 'Grey Lady' (S)
94 – 'Grey Seal' (S)
93 – 'Grey Yellow' (S)
94 – 'Gwen Baker' (d)
93 – 'Hardley' (S)
95 – 'Hermia'
89 – 'Holne' (A)
96 – 'Hurstwood Majesty' (S)
91 – 'Ida' (A)
95 – 'Joan Goalby' (d)
95 – 'John' (S)
95 – 'John Gledhill' (A)
94 – 'Jungfrau' (d)
89 – 'King Cole' (S)
94 – 'Kinloch' (A)
93 – 'Lee' (A)
94 – 'Lemon White Eye' (B)
92 – 'Light Sussex' (S)
96 – 'Lime 'n' Lemon'
95 – 'Lisa's Red' (S)
94 – 'Lochlands' (S)
95 – 'Lockyer's Gem' (B/Sc)
96 – 'Lyn' (A)
96 – 'Magpie' (S)
95 – 'Mandan' (S)
93 – 'Margot' (S)
95 – 'Marsco' (S)
93 – 'Martin's Red'
96 – 'Matley' (S)
91 – 'McWatt's Blue' (B)
94 – 'Mersey Tiger' (S)
90 – 'Milk Chocolate' (S)
96 – 'Milkmaid' (A)
94 – 'Minsmere' (S)
92 – 'Monoglow' (S)
96 – 'Moonbeam' (S)
90 – 'Moonlight' (S)
94 – 'Mrs A. Harrison' (B)
92 – 'Mrs C. Warne'
94 – 'Mrs Dargan' (d)
95 – 'Mrs Harris' (B)
95 – 'Nathan Silver' (A)
96 – 'New Baby' (A)
95 – 'Night Heron' (S)
95 – 'Norah' (A)
96 – 'Nordean'
95 – 'Nubian' (S)
95 – 'Old Pink Lace'
93 – 'Ower' (A)
92 – 'Parchment' (S)
93 – 'Party Time' (S)
92 – 'Pat Berwick' (A)
90 – 'Pathan' (A)
96 – 'Paula Lewis'
90 – 'Peach Blossom'
89 – 'Pennant's Parakeet' (S)
92 – 'Philip Green' (S)
94 – 'Pioneer Stripe' (S)
93 – 'Proctor's Yellow' (B)
93 – 'Prospero' (A)
95 – 'Purple Emperor' (A)
96 – 'Purple Frills'
89 – 'Purple Heron' (S)
89 – 'Purple Lake' (S)
96 – 'Quality Chase' (A)
87 – 'Queen Alexandra' hort. (B)
93 – 'Queen of Sheba' (S)
96 – 'Radiance' (A)
96 – 'Ray Brown' (v)
95 – 'Redstart' (B)
94 – 'Rose Kaye' (A)
94 – 'Rover Stripe' (Sc)
92 – 'Ruffles' (S)
95 – 'Ruth Steed' (S)
90 – 'Sam Gordon'
89 – 'Scarlet Ibis' (S)
89 – 'Scarlet Lancer' (S)
92 – 'Senorita' (A)
89 – 'Shaheen' (S)
92 – 'Shako' (A)
96 – 'Shergold' (A)
92 – 'Shogun' (A)
88 – 'Show Red' (S)
96 – 'Sir Robert Ewbank' (d)
94 – 'Sphinx' (A)
93 – 'Spinney Lane' (A)
92 – 'Spitfire' (S)
94 – 'Stan's Grey' (S)
96 – 'Stoney Cross' (S)
94 – 'Stratton' (A)
89 – 'Sunburst' (S)
89 – 'Sungold' (S)
92 – 'Sunny Boy' (S)
94 – 'Swale' (A)
95 – 'Tavistock' (S)
90 – 'Tiphareth' (A)
95 – 'Tomdown' (S)
91 – 'Tony Murloch'
92 – 'Turnbull' (A)
89 – 'Velvet Knight' (B)
89 – 'Violetta' (S)
93 – 'Vivien' (S)
95 – 'Waincliffe Yellow' (S)
94 – 'Westcott Pride' (d)
92 – 'Wexland' (S)
89 – 'Woodpigeon' (S)
95 – 'Wye Lemon' (S)
95 – 'Wye Orange' (S)
92 – 'Yellow Hammer' (S)
95 – 'Young Rajah' (S)
96 ***auriculata*** (11)
94 'Barbara Barker' (2)
94 'Barnard's Crimson' (Prim)
91 'Barrowby Gem' (Poly)
95 'Belinda Red Shades' 🏆
95 'Belle Watling' (dPrim)
92 x ***berninae*** (2)
90 'Blue Diamond'
93 'Blue Rhapsody'
92 'Blue Triumph'
91 'Bon Accord Cerise' (dPoly)
95 'Bon Accord Elegance' (dPoly)
95 'Bon Accord Gem' (dPoly)
91 'Bon Accord Lavender' (dPoly)
91 'Bon Accord Lilac' (dPoly)
95 'Bonfire' (Poly)
93 Bootheosa Group (21)
96 ***boothii*** (21)
95 'Boudicca' (Prim)
91 Bressingham (4)
94 'Buckland Enchantress'
96 x ***bulleesiana*** Asthore Hybrids (4)
96 ***bulleyana*** ACE 2478 (4)
95 – CLD 920 (4)
89 'Butter-pat' (Prim)
93 'Caerhays Ruby' (Prim)
95 ***capitata*** subsp. ***capitata*** (5)
96 – KEKE 497 (5)
96 – subsp. ***sphaerocephala*** ACE 2092 (5)
92 ***capitellata*** (11)
96 ***carniolica*** (2)
92 x ***caruelii*** (2)
92 ***cawdoriana*** (8)
92 'Charlotte' (Prim)
89 'Charmian' (dPrim)
89 'Cheerleader'
89 'Cherry Pie' (Prim)
95 'Chevithorne Pink' (Poly)
96 'Cluny'
93 ***clusiana*** 'Murray-Lyon' (2)
95 ***cockburniana*** hybrids (4)
89 'Coerulea' (Prim)
96 Cottage Mixed (Prim)
93 Cowichan Red Group (Poly)
92 'Crimson Beauty' (dPrim)
91 'Crispii' (Prim)
96 'Dales Red'
91 dark scarlet (Prim)
96 ***deflexa*** (17)
88 ***denticulata*** 'Prichard's Ruby' (9)
87 ***deuteronana*** (21)
96 'Doctor Lemon's White'
91 'Doctor Molly' (Prim)
91 'Double Red' (dPoly)
88 ***duthieana*** (18)
95 'E.R. Janes' (Prim)
91 'Eastgrove's Gipsy' (Poly)
96 ***elatior*** JCA 785.150 (30)
96 – subsp. ***pallasii*** JCA 786.500 (30)
95 – – JJH 9192145 (30)
91 – subsp. ***ruprechtii*** (30)
91 'Elizabeth Dickey' (dPoly)
90 ***ellisiae alba*** (21)
91 'Enchantress' (Poly)
90 ***erythrocarpa*** (9)
91 'Evonne' (dPoly)
92 'Exhilaration'
89 x ***facchinii*** (2)
90 ***fedtschenkoi*** (11)
91 'Finesse' (Prim)
91 x ***floerkeana*** f. ***biflora*** (2)
96 ***forrestii*** ACE 1427* (3)
96 – CLD 1242 (3)
96 – CLD 738 (3)
96 ***glauca*** ML form
91 'Gloria' (Prim)
95 ***gracilipes*** 'Heathpool' (21)
96 – L&S form (21)
94 – mid form (21)
92 ***griffithii*** 'Fantail' (21)
93 'Hall Barn White'
94 ***hazarica*** JCA (11)
89 ***hidakana*** (24)

90 'Highland Jewel' (dPrim)
91 'Hipperholme'
93 ***hirsuta*** 'Dyke's Variety' (2)
96 ***hirsuta nivea*** (2)
96 ***integrifolia*** JCA 787.502 (2)
89 'Jubilee' (dPrim)
93 'Julian'
92 'Ladybird' (Prim)
89 'Lambrook Peach' (Poly)
91 'Lambrook Pink' (Poly)
95 'Lambrook Yellow' (Poly)
90 ***latifolia*** f. ***cynoglossifolia*** (2)
92 'Lemon Soufflé' (Prim)
91 lilac purple (dPoly)
94 'Lizzie Green' (Prim)
96 'Lopen Red' (Poly)
94 ***macrophylla*** var. ***moorcroftiana*** (18)
93 'Madame Pompadour' (dPoly)
93 ***marginata*** 'Alpbach' (2)
95 – cut-leaved (2)
93 – 'Gold Plate' (2)
96 – 'Hurstwood' (2)
95 – KND seedling (2)
91 – 'Longifolia' (2)
95 – 'Miss Savory' (2)
91 – 'Sharp's Variety' (2)
95 – 'Shipton' (2)
92 'Matthew Pixton'
96 ***minima*** JCA 788.900 (2)
95 ***minkwitziae*** (7)
89 ***minutissima*** (16)
94 ***miyabeana*** B&SWJ 153 (4)
96 'Moulin Rouge' (Prim)
89 x ***murettiana dinyana*** (2)
96 ***nana*** (21)
92 – f. ***alba*** (21)
92 ***nipponica*** (8)
95 'Peggy Fell'
91 'Penlan Cream' (dPoly)
95 'Peter's Red'
95 'Peter's Violet'
91 'Pink Lady'
89 'Pink Ruffles' (Prim)
96 ***poissonii*** ACE 2407 (4)
96 – CLD 1404 (4)
96 – CLD 485 (4)
94 x ***polyantha*** (30)
96 x ***pubescens*** 'Gnome' (2)
95 – 'Moonlight' (2)
93 – 'Nivea' (2)
92 – 'Old Rose' (2)
93 – 'Paul' (2)
87 – 'The Fawn' (2)
93 – yellow (2)
95 ***pulchra*** (21)
90 Pyramid Pinks Group (4)
96 x ***pumila*** (2)
89 'Quarry Wood' (4)
91 'Queen of the Whites' (Prim)
94 'Red Paddy' (dPrim/Poly)
91 'Red Warbler' (Prim)
92 ***reidii*** hybrids (28)
96 ***reptans*** (16)
92 'Rhapsody' (dPrim)
93 ***rosea*** var. ***elegans*** (11)
95 – 'Micia Visser-de Geer' (11)
89 'Royal Purple' (Prim)
89 'Ruby Button' (Prim)
96 ***scapigera*** (21)
90 'Schneekissen Improved' (Prim)
94 'Sea Way' (Prim)
96 ***secundiflora*** ACE 1518 (26)
96 – ACE 1820 (26)
95 – CLD 363/488 (26)
91 'Shocking Pink'
91 ***sieboldii*** 'Cherokee' (7)
90 – 'Chinese Mountain' (7)
94 – 'Colin' (7)
87 – 'Deechin' (7)
87 – 'Hakutsuri' (7)
87 – 'Harunuyuki' (7)
94 – 'Joan Jervis' (7)
89 – 'Shironyi' (7)
87 – 'Sunrokumare' (7)
89 – 'Tsu-no-motana' (7)
94 – 'Wrangle Blush' (7)
94 – 'Wrangle Snowflake' (7)
94 – 'Wrangle White' (7)
89 – 'Ykiguruma' (7)
91 ***sikkimensis*** var. ***hopeana*** (26)
95 – 'Phokphey' (26)
94 – var. ***pudibunda*** (26)
91 Silver Dollar Group (Poly)
91 'Silverwells' (4)
91 single green (Prim)
92 'Sir Galahad' (Prim)
93 ***soldanelloides*** (28)
91 ***sonchifolia*** Tibetan form (21)
94 'Soup Plate' (21)
96 sp. CLD 1217 (4)
95 sp. CLD 183
96 sp. CLD 487 (4)
94 ***specuicola*** (11)
96 Springtime Group (Prim)
89 'Stardust' (Prim)
94 'Stradbrook Dream'
94 'Strawberries and Cream'
96 ***stricta*** (11)
93 'Sunrise' KRW 220/49 (2)
96 Sunset Group
95 ***takedana*** (24)
96 'Tantallon' (21)
92 Tartan Reds Group (Prim)
96 'Techley Red' (Prim)
89 'The Bride' (Poly)
95 'The Grail' (Prim)
90 'Tina' (Prim)
89 'Tinney's Apple Blossom' (21)
87 'Tinney's Dairymaid' (21)
95 x ***truncata*** (2)
93 'Tyrian Purple' (dPoly)
90 ***tyrolensis*** (2)
92 x ***venusta*** Askival Hybrids (2)
94 ***veris*** subsp. ***columnae*** (30)
93 – subsp. ***macrocalyx*** (30)
96 Victorian shades (Poly)
92 ***villosa*** var. ***commutata*** (2)
94 ***vulgaris*** 'Brendon Hills' (30)
94 – Cornish pink (30)
95 – double red (30)
93 – 'Lutea' (30)
92 'Wanda Cherry Red' (Prim)
92 Wanda Group (Prim)
91 'Wanda Improved' (Prim)
91 'Westmorland Blue' (Prim)
92 'Whipped Cream'
91 ***whitei*** 'Arduaine' (21)
96 'Wisley Red' (Prim)

PRINSEPIA
87 ***utilis***

PRITCHARDIA
92 ***pacifica***

PROBOSCIDEA
96 ***fragrans***

PROSOPIS
92 ***glandulosa***
94 ***pubescens***

PROSTANTHERA
87 ***caerulea***
89 ***chlorantha***
92 ***eurybioides***
96 'Poorinda Pixie'
94 ***rotundifolia alba***
88 ***stricta***

PROTEA
92 ***burchellii***
94 ***compacta***
95 ***neriifolia***

PRUNELLA
94 ***vulgaris*** var. ***lilacina***

PRUNUS
88 ***americana***
92 x ***amygdalopersica***
90 ***armeniaca*** var. ***ansu*** 'Flore Pleno'
96 ***avium*** 'Alba'
96 – 'Black Heart' (F)
96 – 'Caroon' (F)
96 – 'Emperor Francis' (F)
96 – 'Frogmore Early' (F)
96 – 'Kent Bigarreau' (F)
96 – 'Merton Bounty' (F)
96 – 'Nabella' (F)
96 – 'Strawberry Heart' (F)
94 – 'Summit' (F)
96 'Beni-higan'
96 ***besseyi***
96 ***campanulata***
90 ***cerasifera*** 'Mirage'
95 – 'Vesuvius'
88 – 'Woodii'
94 'Collingwood Ingram'
87 ***davidiana*** 'Alba'
87 – 'Rubra'
96 ***domestica*** 'Black Prince' (C)
96 – 'Blaisdon Red' (C)
96 – 'Bountiful' (C)
95 – German Prune Group (C)
96 – 'Late Transparent Gage' (D)
96 – 'Laxton's Supreme' (C/D)
95 – 'Monsieur Hâtif' (C)
96 – 'Olympia' (C/D)
96 – 'Peach Plum' (D)
91 – 'Pixy' (F)
95 – 'Ruth Gerstetter' (C)
96 – 'Thames Cross' (D)
95 ***dulcis*** 'Praecox'
92 'Edo-zakura'
96 'Fudan-zakura'
96 'Hilling's Weeping'
95 ***hirtipes*** 'Semiplena'
96 'Hokusai'
96 'Horinji'
96 'Imose'
95 ***incisa*** 'Boten'
95 – 'Pendula'
90 – 'Rubra'
95 ***insititia*** (F)
93 – 'Black Bullace' (F)
94 – 'Mirabelle de Metz' (C)
96 x ***juddii***
91 ***laurocerasus*** 'Barmstedt'
95 – 'Caucasica'
91 – 'Goldglanz'
92 – 'Greenmantle'
95 – 'Herbergii'
91 – 'Holstein'
96 ***litigiosa***
93 ***mandshurica***
94 ***mume*** 'Alphandii' (d)
93 x ***nigrella*** 'Muckle'
96 'Ojôchin'
94 ***pendula*** 'Stellata'
91 ***persica*** 'Alboplena'
91 – 'Cardinal' (d)
87 – 'Crimson Cascade' (F)
96 – 'Early Alexander' (F)
92 – 'Eros' (F)
89 – 'Foliis Rubris' (F)
96 – 'Miriam' (F)
95 – var. ***nectarina*** 'Fuzalode' (F)
94 – 'Nemarquard' (F)
90 – 'New Award' (F)
90 – 'Pink Peachy' (F)
95 – 'Red Peachy' (F)
90 – 'Weeping Flame' (F)
95 – 'White Peachy' (F)
93 – 'Windle Weeping' (d)
96 ***pseudocerasus*** 'Cantabrigiensis'
94 'Rhexlicer'
92 ***salicifolia***
96 ***serrulata***
96 x ***sieboldii*** 'Caespitosa'
96 ***spinosa*** 'Plena'
96 'Taki-nioi'
92 'Uzu-zakur'
87 ***virginiana***
91 x ***yedoensis*** 'Erecta'
96 – 'Moerheimii'

PSEUDOMERTENSIA
89 ***moltkioides***

PSEUDOPANAX
92 ***laetivirens***

PSEUDOTSUGA
87 ***guinieri***
92 ***macrocarpa***
92 ***menziesii*** var. ***flahaultii***
89 – 'Knap Hill'
88 – 'Oudemansii'
96 – Pendula Group
87 ***rehderi***

PSILOSTROPHE
96 ***tagentinae***

PSORALEA
94 ***corylifolia***

PTELEA
91 ***nitens***

PTERIS
92 ***cretica*** 'Major'
90 – 'Wilsonii'
90 ***longifolia*** 'Mariesii'
93 ***wallichiana***

PTEROSTYLIS
95 ***acuminata ingens***
96 ***revoluta***

PTILOSTEMON
92 ***diacantha***

PTYCHOSPERMA
94 ***elegans***
94 ***macarthurii***

PULMONARIA
96 'Lambrook Silver'
95 'Oxford Blue'
95 'Red Freckles'
95 'Regal Ruffles'
90 ***saccharata*** 'White Barn'
94 'Salmon Glow'
94 'Wendy Perry'

PULSATILLA
94 ***albana*** var. ***albana***
90 – subsp. ***armena***
96 x ***gayeri***
89 ***halleri*** 'Budapest'
93 – subsp. ***rhodopaea***
94 – subsp. ***styriaca***
94 – subsp. ***taurica***
93 ***pratensis*** subsp. ***hungarica***
93 ***sibirica***
91 ***vulgaris*** Balkan form
92 – 'Mrs Van der Elst'

PURSHIA
95 ***tridentata***

PUSCHKINIA
96 ***scilloides***
96 – var. ***libanotica*** S&L 113

PUYA
92 ***lanata***
96 ***mitis***
96 sp. G&P 5036

PYRACANTHA
95 ***atalantioides*** 'Nana'
90 ***angustifolia*** 'Variegata'
94 ***coccinea*** 'Kasan'
95 ***crenulata***
92 'Fiery Cascade'
95 ***fortuneana*** B&L 12398
92 ***koidzumii*** 'Victory'
92 'Lavinia Rutgers'
95 'Orange Cadence'
95 'Red Delight'

x **PYRACOMELES**
88 ***vilmorinii***

PYRROSIA
94 ***serpens***

PYRUS
93 ***caucasica***
96 ***communis*** 'Abbé Fétel' (D)
96 – 'Admiral Gervais' (D)
96 – 'Alexandrina Bivort' (D)
96 – 'Bellissime d'Hiver' (C)
96 – 'Beurré Bachelier' (D)
96 – 'Beurré de Jonghe' (D)
96 – 'Beurré Diel' (D)
94 – 'Beurré Giffard' (D)
96 – 'Beurré Jean van Geert' (D)
96 – 'Buckland' (F)
96 – 'Butt' (Perry)
96 – 'Charles Ernest' (D)
96 – 'Duchesse de Bordeaux' (D)
96 – 'Fertility' (D)
92 – 'Gros Blanquet' (D)
96 – 'Hellen's Early' (Perry)
93 – 'Jeanne d'Arc' (D)
96 – 'Laxton's Early Market' (D)
95 – 'Longueville' (D)
96 – 'Louise Marillat' (F)
95 – 'Marie Louise d'Uccle' (D)
91 – 'Marquise' (D)
92 – 'Messire Jean' (D)
96 – 'Muirfield Egg' (D)
96 – 'Nouvelle Fulvie' (D)
96 – 'Ovid' (D)
96 – 'Parsonage' (Perry)
91 – 'Pierre Corneille' (D)
96 – 'Précoce de Trévoux' (D)
96 – 'Red Pear' (Perry)
94 – 'Starkrimson' (D)
96 – 'Taynton Squash' (Perry)
92 – 'Windsor' (D)
93 ***pashia***
94 – CC&McK 369
94 – CLD 114
94 ***pyrifolia***
93 – 'Hosui' (F)
96 – 'Nijisseiki' (F)
95 – 'Shinko' (F)
93 – 'Yakumo' (F)

QUERCUS
93 'Columna'
95 ***durifolia***
95 ***graciliformis***
93 x ***hickelii*** 'Gieszelhorst'
92 ***hypoleucoides***
92 x ***lucombeana*** 'Ambrozyana'
90 Macon
96 ***macrocarpa*** x ***turbinella***
96 ***mongolica***
94 ***oxyodon***
93 ***pungens***
95 ***pyrenaica*** 'Argenteomarginata'
93 ***robur*** 'Albomarmorata'
94 – 'Aureobicolor' (v)
93 – 'Kassel'
92 – f. ***variegata***
94 x ***schochiana***

QUESNELIA
90 ***liboniana***

RACOPILUM
96 ***robustum***

RAMONDA
94 ***serbica*** 'Alba'

RANUNCULUS
95 ***abnormis*** JCA 809.500
89 ***amplexicaulis*** 'Grandiflorus'
92 ***anemoneus***
96 x ***arendsii***
93 ***bilobus***
96 ***brotherusii*** CC&McK 745
91 ***cadmicus***
95 ***caucasicus*** subsp. ***caucasicus***
96 ***eschscholtzii oxynotus***
96 ***eschscholtzii trisectus***
95 ***ficaria*** double red (d)
91 – 'Hoskin's Spider'
92 – 'Wyatt's White'
96 x ***flahaultii***
96 ***glacialis***
90 ***hirtellus***
89 ***lappaceus***
96 ***macaulayi***
91 ***pygmaeus***
94 ***pyrenaeus***
93 ***seguieri***
90 ***traunfellneri***

RANZANIA
96 ***japonica***

RAOULIA
96 ***bryoides***
96 ***hookeri*** var. ***apice-nigra***
94 – var. ***hookeri***
96 ***parkii***

RAUVOLFIA
96 ***verticillata***

REEVESIA
89 ***pubescens***

REGELIA
91 ***cymbifolia***
91 ***inops***
91 ***megacephala***

RELHANIA
94 ***acerosa***

RESEDA
91 ***odorata***

RESTIO
96 ***tetraphyllus***

RETAMA
93 ***sphaerocarpa***

RHAMNUS
92 ***citrifolia***
94 ***imeretina***
92 ***procumbens***

RHAPIS
95 ***humilis*** 🏆

RHEUM
96 ***compactum***
95 ***delavayi***
91 'Green Knight'
92 x ***hybridum*** 'Early Albert'
94 ***moorcroftianum*** CC&McK 813
96 ***nobile***
95 ***reticulatum*** JJH 9209375
92 ***webbianum***

RHINANTHUS
93 ***minor***

RHIPSALIS
94 ***baccifera***

RHODIOLA
96 ***himalensis*** (D. Don) Fu EMAK 331
91 ***hirsuta***
91 – Baetica Group
90 ***komarovii***
95 sp. CLD 1329
95 sp. JJH 392
91 ***wallichiana stephanii***

RHODODENDRON
96 'Abbot' (EA)
92 'Abe Arnott'
95 ***aberconwayi*** dwarf form
96 – McLaren U35A
96 'Adamant'
96 Adelaide Group & cl.
89 'Agamujin' (EA)
94 'Ageeth' (EA)
95 'Ahren's Favourite'
96 'Airy Fairy'
93 Akbar Group & cl.
90 ***alabamense*** (A)
92 'Albatross Townhill White'
96 ***albertsenianum*** F 14195
91 'Album'
89 'Alice de Stuers' (M)
96 'Alice Gilbert'
89 'Alice Martineau'
91 Alix Group & cl.
94 'Allen's Surprise'
95 ***amagianum*** x ***reticulatum*** (A)
96 Amalfi Group & cl.
91 ***ambiguum*** best form
95 – dwarf form
95 – 'Keillour Castle'
94 'Ambrosia' (EA)
89 'Ambush'
95 'Anah Kruschke'
94 'Anchorage'
94 'Andrew Elphinstone' (EA)
92 (Angelo Group) 'Solent Queen'
96 'Angelo Solent Queen'
93 'Angelus' (EA)
93 'Anilin'
91 'Ann Aberconway'
92 'Anne Dring'
88 'Anne van Hoeke'
95 'Anne's Delight'
91 'Annette'
91 'Anthony Koster' (M)
96 ***anthosphaerum*** Eritimum Group
95 'Antoon van Welie'
95 ***aperantum*** F 27020

Plant Deletions

89 'Apollo' (EA)
96 'Apotrophia'
96 'Apple Blossom'
93 'Apricot Lady Chamberlain'
96 'April Chimes'
96 Arblact Group
95 ***arboreum*** subsp. ***delavayi*** var. ***peramoenum***
96 – 'Goat Fell'
89 – 'Patterson'
96 – Sch 1111
95 Arbutifolium Group
92 'Arctic Snow'
92 'Ardeur'
96 ***argipeplum*** Bhutan form
96 – Eastern form
95 ***argyrophyllum*** 'Sichuan'
89 'Arlie'
96 Armia Group
96 'Arthur J. Ivens'
95 'Atalanta' (EA)
95 Atroflo Group
96 ***augustinii*** subsp. ***augustinii*** Vilmorinianum Group
96 – subsp. ***chasmanthum*** white C&Cu 9407
96 – Dartington Form
96 – Reuthe's dark form
95 – subsp. ***rubrum*** F 25914
96 ***auriculatum*** compact form
93 Aurora Group & cl.
94 ***austrinum*** (A) 🏆
96 Avocet Group
91 Ayesha Group
96 'Ayton'
93 'B. de Bruin'
89 'B.Y. Morrison' (EA)
93 'Babeuff' (M)
91 'Babylon'
92 'Bach Choir'
95 'Bad Eilsen'
93 'Bali'
89 'Balta'
95 'Barbecue' (K)
93 Baron Philippe de Rothschild Group & cl.
96 'Basilisk' (K)
96 'Bastion'
93 Bauble Group
96 'Beaulieu' (K)
95 'Beautiful Day'
90 'Beefeater'
93 'Ben Morrison' (EA)
95 'Ben Moseley'
95 'Benigasa' (EA)
94 'Bernstein'
96 Berryrose Group & cl.
96 'Bert's Own'
94 'Betty Arrington'
93 'Betty Kelly' (K)
94 'Betty Robertson'
96 Bibiani Group & cl.
91 'Bishopsgate'
89 'Black Beauty'
96 Blanc-mange Group & cl.
96 'Blue Ensign'
96 'Blue Jay'
95 'Blueshine Girl'
93 'Blurettia'
96 Boadicea Group
93 'Bob White' (EA)
94 ***bodinieri***
94 'Bravo' (EA)
90 'Bray'
95 'Bremen'
94 'Bridesmaid White'
91 'Brightwell'
93 'Brinny'
96 'Brookside'
93 'Broughtonii Aureum' (Ad)
96 Bulbul Group & cl.
90 'Bulstrode' (EA)
92 ***bureaui*** 'Berg'
96 Burning Bush Group
96 'C.B. van Nes' 🏆
93 'Cadis'
96 ***caesium*** F 26798
96 ***callimorphum*** var. ***myiagrum***
96 ***calophytum*** Grieg's form
95 ***calostrotum*** subsp. ***riparioides***
91 Calrose Group
92 ***campanulatum*** subsp. ***campanulatum*** 'Roland Cooper'
96 – SS&W 9108
96 – TSS 44
96 – TW 27
95 'Campfire' (EA)
91 Campirr Group
96 ***campylocarpum*** TSS 43
90 ***campylogynum*** Brodick form
96 – Celsum Group
96 – copper
95 – (Cremastum Group) 'Thimble'
90 – 'Crushed Strawberry'
91 – 'Hillier's Pink'
95 – 'New Pink'
95 – 'Plum Brandy'
93 – yellow
91 ***camtschaticum*** Murray-Lyon form
95 'Canadian Beauty'
90 'Candi'
95 'Candida'
96 ***canescens*** (A)
91 'Caperci Special'
96 Cardinal Group & cl.
90 'Carex White'
92 'Carita Charm'
92 'Carmel' (EA)
94 'Carnival' (EA)
93 'Caroline'
96 ***carringtoniae*** (V)
96 'Castle of Mey'
95 ***catacosmum*** F 21727
96 'Catalode'
96 ***catawbiense*** 'Powell Glass'
96 Cauapo Group
89 ***caucasicum*** 'Cunningham's Sulphur'
96 'Cavalcade'
92 'Cavalier' (EA)
94 Cavalier Group
95 ***cephalanthum*** subsp. ***cephalanthum*** Crebreflorum Group KW 8337
90 'Challenger' (EA)
91 Chanticleer Group
94 ***charitopes*** subsp. ***tsangpoense*** KW 5844
93 'Charlemagne' (G)
95 'Cheapside'
90 'Chelsea'
93 'Chelsea Manor'
92 'Cherokee'
93 'Cherry Pink'
90 'Chichibu' (EA)
93 'Chinmar'
92 'Chinsai' (EA)
95 ***ciliatum*** BL&M 324
96 ***ciliicalyx***
96 ***cinnabarinum*** Caerhays John Group
87 – 'Caerhays Yellow'
91 – 'Magnificum'
91 – subsp. ***xanthocodon*** Exbury AM form
96 – – KW 6026
94 'Circus'
91 'Citroen'
96 ***coelicum***
91 'Colleen' (EA)
96 ***collettianum***
95 'Colyer' (EA)
96 'Commodore' (EA)
89 'Comte de Gomer' (M)
89 'Comte de Papadopoli' (M)
91 'Con Amore' (EA)
91 'Concerto'
93 'Concessum'
91 'Conversation Piece' (EA)
92 'Cool Haven'
90 'Coquille'
95 'Coral Redwing' (EA)
95 'Coral Wing' (EA)
96 Cornsutch Group
96 Coronet Group
93 'Corot'
96 'Cotton Candy'
95 'Crater Lake'
93 Cremorne Group & cl.
89 'Crepello'
96 ***crinigerum*** bicolored form
96 'Crown Jewel' (EA/d)
91 'Crown Supreme'
95 'Crushed Strawberry'
90 'Crystal Violet'
90 'Cunningham's Album Compactum'
93 'Cytherea' (EA)
94 'Daisetsuzan'
93 'Dame Edith Evans'
92 'Dandy' (EA)
91 'Daphne' (EA)
95 'Darkness' (EA)
87 'Dart' (K)
95 ***dauricum*** dwarf
93 – × ***formosum***
94 'David Rockefeller'
94 'Davidson'
94 ***davidsonianum*** 'Serenade'
90 'Dawn's Chorus' (K)
96 'Dawn's Glory'
95 'Dayan'
89 ***degronianum*** subsp. ***heptamerum*** var. ***kyomaruense***
89 ***degronianum heptamerum*** 'Oki Island'
90 – 'Wada'
95 'Delectable' (K)
96 ***dendricola*** Taronense Group
95 ***denudatum***
91 × ***detonsum*** Edinburgh select form
89 'Devon' (K)
89 Diamant Group salmon pink (EA)
96 'Diana Colville'
96 Dicharb Group
94 ***dichroanthum*** subsp. ***septentroniale***
96 'Dido'
94 ***dilatatum leucanthum*** (A)
91 'Directeur Moerlands' (M) 🏆
90 'Director Dorsman'
96 Diva Group & cl.
92 'Doctor Reichenbach' (M)
95 'Doctor Rieger'
91 'Dollar Princess'
93 'Dorothy Gish' (EA/d)
91 'Dorothy Rees' (EA)
95 'Dorothy Swift'
96 'Douglas McEwan'
96 'Duchess of Portland'
89 Duke of Cornwall Group & cl.
95 Dusky Maid Group
96 'Early Gem'
92 'Easter Parade' (EA)
95 'Eastertide' (EA/d)
94 'Eddisbury' (K)
95 'Edith Bosley'
96 'Edith Mackworth Praed'
93 'Edmond Amateis'
92 'Edward M. Boehm' (EA)
92 'Eisenhower' (K)
96 'Elegant Bouquet' (V)
90 Elena Group
93 'Elsa Crisp'
96 'Emanuela'
89 'Embley Crimson' (K)
96 'Emma Williams'
91 'Endsleigh Pink'
90 'Esveld Select'
91 'Eucharis' (EA)
94 'Everest White'
93 'Everything Nice'
91 Exburiense Group
96 'Exbury Lady Chamberlain'
90 'Exbury Matador'
92 'Explorer' (EA)
91 'Fabia Roman Pottery'
92 'Fabia Waterer'
93 'Falkner Alison'
93 Fancy Free Group & cl.
96 Fandango Group
91 'Favor Major' (K)
96 'Fawley' (K)
89 'Feespite'
94 'Fénelon' (G)
91 'Ferndown Beauty' (EA)
96 ***ferrugineum*** f. ***album***
94 – Atrococcineum Group
88 – 'Plenum'
92 'Feuerwerk' (K)
93 'Fiesta' (EA/d)

95 Fine Feathers Group
95 'First Love'
90 ***fittianum***
93 'Fittra'
90 'Flaire' (K)
96 Flamingo Group
96 'Flare'
95 'Flautando'
95 'Flavour'
96 aff. ***flinckii*** KR 1755
89 'Flip'
96 'Flirt'
95 ***floribundum*** 'Swinhoe'
95 ***formosum*** Chamberlain 109
90 ***fortunei*** 'Lu-Shan'
96 – McLaren S146
95 'Frans van der Bom' (M)
94 'Fraseri' (M)
95 'Fridoline' (EA)
93 'Frieda' (EA)
96 'Frill'
94 'Frühlingstraum'
96 'Frühlingszauber'
90 ***fulgens*** Leonardslee form
96 Full House Group
96 ***fulvum*** F 17636
93 'Galloper Light' (A/d)
87 'Garden Beauty' (EA)
92 'Gardenia' (EA)
96 'Garnet'
93 Gaul Group & cl.
93 'Gemstone'
96 'General Sir John du Cane'
96 ***genestierianum***
96 'Georg Arends'
96 Gibraltar Group
91 'Gill's Crimson'
96 Gipsy King Group
94 'Gipsy King Memory'
94 'Girard's Pink' (EA)
94 'Girard's Scarlet' (EA)
90 'Glacier' (EA)
90 'Gladys Rose'
93 Glamour Group & cl.
90 ***glaucophyllum*** 'Prostratum'
96 'Gleam'
94 'Glen's Orange'
94 'Gletschernacht'
93 'Glon Komachi' (EA)
94 'Gloria Mundi' (G)
96 'Gloriana'
93 'Glory of Littleworth' (A/d)
92 'Gnome' (EA)
96 Goblin Group & cl.
95 'Golden Dream'
92 'Golden Hind'
96 'Golden Queen'
91 'Golden Spur'
91 Goldfinch Group
95 'Goldstrike'
95 'Goldsworth Orange' x ***insigne***
96 'Goldtopas' (K)
89 'Good News'
94 'Goosander'
94 'Gorbella'
91 'Gosho-zakura' (EA)
96 'Gossamer White' (V)
95 'Graf Lennart'
96 'Grafton'
95 'Grand Pré'
96 'Green Eye'
92 'Greenwood Yukon' (EA)
92 'Greeting' (EA)
96 Grenadier Group & cl.
91 Grenadine Group & cl. 🏆
90 'Gretchen' (EA)
91 'Gretia'
96 'Grilse'
95 'Gumpo' x ***nakaharae*** (EA)
93 'Gwen Bell'
89 'Gwynidd Lloyd' (EA)
93 'Gypsy' (EA)
95 'H.O. Carre' (EA)
91 'Hachika-tsugi' (EA)
96 'Hachmann's Bananaflip'
94 'Hachmann's Diadem'
94 'Hachmann's Violetta'
96 ***haematodes*** subsp. ***chaetomallum*** KW 5431
87 'Halopeanum'
93 'Hanah-fubuki' (EA)
91 ***hanceanum*** x ***lutescens***
89 'Hanio-no-shion' (EA)
90 'Hansel'
95 'Happy Occasion'
92 'Harkwood Orange'
94 'Haru-no-hikari' (EA)
94 'Haru-no-sono' (EA)
92 'Haru-no-yuki'
89 'Harwell' (K)
90 Hawk Group & cl.
88 (Hawk Group) 'Hawk Buzzard'
96 (Hawk Group) 'Hawk Falcon'
93 (Hawk Group) 'Hawk Merlin'
93 'Hazel'
96 Hebe Group
89 'Helen Johnson'
91 'Helena' (EA)
96 ***heliolepis*** var. ***brevistylum***
90 ***hemsleyanum*** x Polar Bear Group
95 Hermes Group
89 'Hershey's Bright Red'
96 Hesperides Group
93 'Hiawatha' (K)
96 'Highland White Jade'
89 'Hikkasen' (EA)
96 'Hill Ayah'
88 'Hillcrest'
91 'Hinode-no-taka' (EA)
93 'Hino-red' (EA)
96 ***hippophaeoides*** var. ***hippophaeoides*** Fimbriatum Group
92 – – 'Sunningdale'
92 ***hippophaëoides*** 'Inshriach'
89 'Hollandia' (G)
96 ***hookeri*** 'Golden Gate'
95 'Hopeful' (EA)
94 'Horizon'
88 'Hotspur Orange' (K)
92 'Hugh Wormald' (K)
89 Huntsman Group
95 'Hyde Park' (K)
91 'Hydon Harrier'
96 'Hydon Snowflake'
96 Icarus Group
95 'Ightham Pink'
96 'Ightham Purple'
90 'Ightham White'
89 'Igneum Novum' (G)
90 'Imazuma' (EA)
91 ***imberbe***
96 ***impeditum*** 'Harry White's Purple'
91 – Litangense Group
89 'Imperator' (M)
93 Inamorata Group
96 Indiana Group
90 'Inshriach Blue'
91 Intrepid Group
96 Iola Group
92 'Irene'
96 ***irroratum*** subsp. ***kontumense*** KR 3282
96 – KW 5002A
93 Isabella Group & cl.
93 Ispahan Group
94 'Issho-no-haru' (EA)
95 'Ivan D. Wood'
94 'Ivory Coast'
94 'J. Jennings' (K)
92 'J.H. Agnew'
91 'J.H. van Nes'
95 Jacquetta Group
96 Jaipur Group
96 'Jalisco Janet'
95 'Jalisco Jubilant'
89 'Jan Steen' (M)
94 'Jancio'
92 Janet Group
95 'Janet Baker'
91 'Jasper Pimento'
93 'Jerez'
89 Joanita Group
96 'John Keats'
95 'John Marchand'
96 'Johnson's Impeditum'
95 ***johnstonneanum*** Parryae Group 🏆
90 'Joho-ngodor-akako'
95 'Joseph Haydn' (EA)
96 'Joseph Whitworth'
93 Josephine Group
93 'Joyful'
90 'July Fragrance'
95 'June Fire'
96 'Jungfrau'
92 Jutland Group
96 ***kaempferi*** 'Eastern Fire' (EA)
89 – 'Hall's Red'
95 – f. ***latisepalum*** (EA)
91 Karkov Group & cl.
92 'Kasumi-gaseki'
92 'Kathleen'
95 'Katsura-no-hana' (EA)
93 ***keiskei*** x Carolinianum Group
91 – Windsor Great Park form
96 Keiskrac Group
96 'Kentucky Minstrel' (K)
96 'Keston Rose'
89 Kiev® Group & cl.
93 'Kilauea' (K)
94 'Killarney' (EA)
93 'King's Red' (K)
96 ***kiusianum*** 'Benichidori' (EA)
90 – 'Chidori'
96 – 'Mountain Pride' (EA)
91 – 'Tenshi'
93 'Kojo-no-hikari' (EA)
92 'Kormesing'
91 'Krishna'
89 'Kumoidori' (EA)
95 'Kumo-no-ito' (EA)
91 'Kurai-no-himo' (EA)
89 'La France' (EA)
95 Lady Berry Group & cl.
96 Lady Jean Group
95 'Lady Malmesbury'
96 Lady Montagu Group & cl.
94 'Lady of Spain'
91 'Lady Robin' (EA)
93 'Laurie'
95 'Le Havre'
94 'Leibnitz' (G/d)
90 'Lemon Grass'
95 'Lem's 121'
88 'Leonard Messel'
96 ***lepidotum*** CC&McK 530
90 – Obovatum Group
96 ***leptanthum*** (V)
96 'Lewis Monarch'
95 'Lillian Peste'
90 'Limbatum'
96 'Lincill'
95 ***lindleyi*** 'Geordie Sherriff'
90 Linswegeanum Group
92 'Litany' (EA)
96 'Little Ginger' (V)
96 'Littlest Angel' (V)
95 'Llenroc'
95 'Lobster Pot' (K)
94 'Loch Tay'
94 'Lotte' (EA)
94 'Louis B. Williams'
87 'Louisa Hill'
92 'Louise Gable' (EA)
91 'Lucy Lockhart'
95 ***lutea*** 'Batami Gold'
96 ***lutescens*** 'Exbury'
96 – pink
93 ***lysolepis***
92 – 'Woodland Purple'
95 ***macgregoriae*** yellow (V)
96 ***macrosepalum*** (A)
88 'Madame Carvalho'
96 ***maddenii*** pink
96 'Mademoiselle Masson'
93 'Madison Snow'
93 'Madrigal' (EA)
96 'Maestro'
96 'Magic Flute' (V)
93 'Mah Jong'
91 'Mahler' (EA)
96 Mai Group
95 ***maius*** Herklots
92 Major Group
93 'Malemute'
93 'Manderley'
94 'Mannheim'
91 'March Sun'
90 Margaret Findlay Group & cl.
96 Marie Antoinette Group
91 'Marina' (K)
92 'Mariner'
94 'Marionette'
96 'Marmot' (EA)
96 Marshall Group
95 'Mary Belle'
90 'Matsukasa Pink'
95 'Matsuyo' (EA)

90 'Mayfair'
96 Medea Group
89 'Medway' (K)
94 ***mekongense***
mekongense 'Yellow Fellow'
94 ***mekongense*** var. ***melinanthum*** Semilunatum Group
90 'Melpomene'
89 'Melville'
95 'Mephistopheles' (K)
96 Merops Group
95 Metis Group
96 ***microgynum*** Gymnocarpum Group
89 'Midsummer Beauty' (EA)
89 'Midsummer Snow'
96 'Mikado'
91 ***minus*** var. ***chapmanii***
89 – var. ***minus*** (Carolinianum Group) 'Album'
89 'Miyagino' (EA)
92 'Modesty' (EA)
96 Mohamet Group & cl.
91 'Moira' (EA)
95 'Moira Pink' (EA)
96 'Molly Buckley'
95 'Molly Fordham'
91 'Molly Miller'
96 'Monica Wellington'
91 'Montreal'
96 'Moonstone Pink'
91 'Mortimer'
94 'Mosaique'
96 'Motherly Love'
96 'Mountain Dew'
91 ***moupinense*** white
92 'Mrs A.M. Williams'
92 'Mrs Alfred Taubman'
94 'Mrs Chitton'
96 'Mrs John Kelk'
89 'Mrs Mary Ashley'
95 'Mrs Peter Koster' (M)
89 'Mrs Tom Agnew'
90 ***mucronulatum*** best form (EA)
96 – var. ***chejuense*** 'Dwarf Cheju'
96 – 'Crater's Edge'
91 – Reuthe's form
96 – 'Winter Brightness' ♀
92 'Multatuli' (M)
96 ***multicolor*** (V)
94 'Multiflorum'
88 'Multimaculatum'
89 'Mum'
95 ***myrtifolium*** 'Kotscaki'
96 'Mystic'
90 ***nakaharae*** 'Benenden'
93 – x 'Kin-no-zai' (EA)
95 – Starborough form
96 'Nancy Buchanan' (K)
90 'Nancy Fortescue'
91 'Naniwagata' (EA)
94 'Naomi Hope'
95 'Naomi Nautilus'
94 'Naomi Pink Beauty'
96 'Naomi Stella Maris'
91 'Natalie Coe Vitetti' (EA)
95 Neda Group
93 Nehru Group
96 ***neriiflorum*** subsp. ***neriiflorum*** Euchaites Group KW 6854
96 – – 'Lamellen'
92 'Nero'
93 'Nicholas'
95 'Night Light' (K)
94 'Nihon-no-hana' (EA)
89 'Nimrod Scheherezade'
91 'Niphetos' (EA)
96 ***nivale***
95 – subsp. ***boreale***
92 – – Nigropunctatum Group
92 ***niveum*** 'Clyne Castle'
95 'Noble Fountain'
91 'Noordtianum' (EA)
93 'Normandy'
94 'Noyo Brave'
93 'Nuccio's Allegro' (EA/d)
94 'Nuccio's Bit o' Sunshine' (EA)
93 'Nuccio's Carnival' (EA)
93 'Nuccio's Carnival Blaze' (EA)
93 'Nuccio's Carnival Candy' (EA)
93 'Nuccio's Carnival Clown' (EA)
93 'Nuccio's Carnival Jackpot' (EA)
93 'Nuccio's Carnival Magic' (EA)
93 'Nuccio's Dew Drop' (EA)
93 'Nuccio's Dream Clouds' (EA/d)
93 'Nuccio's Feathery Touch' (EA)
93 'Nuccio's Garden Party' (EA/d)
93 'Nuccio's Happy Days' (EA/d)
93 'Nuccio's Harvest Moon' (EA)
93 'Nuccio's High Society' (EA)
93 'Nuccio's Magnificence' (EA/d)
93 'Nuccio's Mama Mia' (EA)
93 'Nuccio's Masterpiece' (EA/d)
93 'Nuccio's Melody Lane' (EA)
93 'Nuccio's Mexicali Rose' (EA)
93 'Nuccio's Misty Moon' (EA)
93 'Nuccio's Pink Bubbles' (EA/d)
93 'Nuccio's Pink Champagne' (EA/d)
93 'Nuccio's Pink Snow' (EA)
93 'Nuccio's Pink Tiger' (EA)
93 'Nuccio's Polka' (EA)
93 'Nuccio's Primavera' (EA)
93 'Nuccio's Rain Drops' (EA)
93 'Nuccio's Snow Storm' (EA)
93 'Nuccio's Spring Triumph' (EA)
93 'Nuccio's Sunburst' (EA/d)
93 'Nuccio's Wild Cherry' (EA)
91 ***oblongifolium*** (A)
93 Oklahoma Group
96 'Omurasaki' (EA)
93 'Ooh Gina'
92 'Opal' (EA)
94 'Ophelia'
89 'Oporto'
95 'Orange King' (EA)
96 'Orangeade' (K)
96 ***orbiculare*** x ***decorum***
89 'Orchid Lights'
96 Oregonia Group
96 ***oreotrephes*** R/USDA 59593/ R11300
89 Orestes Group
93 'Organdie'
93 'Orient' (K)
90 'Ostbo's Low Yellow'
91 'Otome' (EA)
93 'Otome Zakura' (EA)
96 'Our Marcia' (V)
90 'Overstreet'
95 'P.G. Puddle'
95 ***pachytrichum*** (Monosematum Group) 'Blackhills'
91 'Panaché'
95 Pandora Group
92 'Papineau' (EA)
96 'Paradise Pink' (EA)
91 ***parryae***
92 'Parsons' Gloriosum'
91 'Patricia's Day'
96 ***pauciflorum*** (V)
93 'Paul Vossberg'
93 'Peach Blow' (EA)
93 'Peach Glow' (K)
94 'Pearl Bradford' (EA)
95 'Peekaboo'
94 'Peking'
93 'Pelopidas'
96 'Pematit Oxford'
96 'Pennywhistle' (V)
96 ***pentaphyllum*** (A)
96 ***peregrinum*** 'Wilson'
88 'Perfection' (EA)
88 'Peter Koster' (M)
96 'Pettychaps' (EA)
94 ***phaeochrysum*** Glendoick form
96 – var. ***phaeochrysum***
96 'Philomene'
91 'Pickard's Gold'
90 'Picotee' (EA)
96 'Pillar Box'
93 'Pink Beauty'
93 'Pink Cameo'
91 'Pink Lady Rosebery'
92 'Pink Mimosa' (Vs)
94 'Pink Petticoats'
89 'Pink Treasure' (EA)
94 'Pioneer Silvery Pink'
96 'Piquante'
89 'Platinum Pearl'
89 'Polly Clarke'
93 'Polonaise' (EA)
91 ***polycladum*** Compactum Group
91 ***ponticum*** 'Gilt Edge'
91 Portia Group & cl.
95 'Pratt's Hybrid'
96 Prelude Group & cl.
93 'Primula'
95 'Princess Elizabeth'
95 'Princess Elizabeth' (M)
88 'Prinses Marijke'
90 'Prosti'
96 ***pseudochrysanthum*** AM 1956 form AM
90 – dwarf form
92 'Psyche' (EA)
96 ***pubescens*** 'Fine Bristles'
96 'Pucella' (G) ♀
88 'Pure Gold' (K)
96 'Purple Carpeter'
96 'Purple Lace'
94 'Purple Split'
91 'Purple Velvet'
89 'Purpureum Grandiflorum'
96 ***quadrasianum*** var. ***rosmarinifolium*** (V)
89 Quaker Girl Group
92 'Quaker Maid' (K)
95 'Queen Louise' (K)
95 'Queen's Wood'
91 'R.W. Rye' ♀
93 ***racemosum*** 'Forrest'
95 'Radistrotum'
93 'Radmosum'
94 'Raeburn'
89 'Raoul Millais'
95 'Rasputin'
89 'Red Bells'
96 Red Cap Group
95 'Red Elf'
94 'Red Walloper'
96 Remus Group
96 'Rennie' (EA)
96 Review Order Group
96 ***rex*** subsp. ***arizelum*** 'Brodick'
96 – – F 21861
96 – – KW 20922
95 – 'Quartz' ♀
92 'Rhapsody' (EA)
91 'Rijneveld'
93 'Rimini'
94 'Rio'
96 ***ririei*** W 5254A
90 'River Belle'
96 'Rivulet'
93 'Robert Louis Stevenson'
91 'Robin Hill Congo' (EA)
87 'Rogue River Belle' (O)
91 'Rosa Regen'
92 'Rosalie' (EA)
91 Rosalind Group & cl.
94 'Rosalinda' (EA)
95 'Rose Plenum' (G)
93 'Rose Queen'
89 'Rosella' (K)
96 'Rosevallon'
89 Rouge Group & cl.
96 Royal Flush Group pink
96 Royal Flush Group yellow
91 'Royal Purple'
90 'Royal Windsor'
95 Royalty Group
92 'Rubinstern' (EA)
91 ***russatum album***
95 ***russatum*** 'Collingwood Ingram'

89 – 'Hill of Tarvit'
89 – 'Keillour'
92 – tall form
96 Russautinii Group
96 'Russellianum'
95 'Sabina'
96 'Saint Keverne'
96 'Saint Kew'
96 'Saint Wenn'
93 'Sakuragata' (EA)
93 'Salmon King' (EA)
89 'Salmon Queen' (M)
96 'Salmon Sander' (EA)
96 'Salmon Trout'
94 ***saluenense*** subsp. ***chameunum*** F 25560
94 – hairy form
93 'Salute'
94 ***sanguineum*** subsp. ***sanguineum*** var. ***himertum*** R 10906
96 'Santa Claus'
91 ***sargentianum*** Leonardslee form
89 'Satrap' (EA)
96 ***scabrifolium*** SBEC K 160
91 'Scandinavia'
95 'Scarlatti' (K)
96 'Scarlet Pimpernel' (K)
96 ***schistocalyx*** F 17637
90 'Schneebukett'
93 'Schneewolke'
96 ***scopulorum*** Magor's hardy form
93 'Seattle Gold'
91 ***seinghkuense***
96 ***selense*** subsp. ***selense*** Probum Group
90 'Serena'
91 ***serrulatum*** (A)
96 'Seville'
96 Shepherd's Delight Group
91 'Sherbrook' (EA)
96 ***sherriffii*** AM 1966 clone
94 'Shiho' (EA)
94 'Shiko' (EA)
93 'Shiko-no-kagami' (EA)
87 'Shinto' (EA)
91 'Shin-utena' (EA)
93 'Shinyomo-no-haru' (EA)
93 'Shira-fuji' (EA/v)
96 'Silvetta'
96 ***simiarum*** SF 92304
94 'Simmond's Classic'
91 ***simsii*** double form
96 ***sinofalconeri*** KR 1992
90 ***sinogrande*** Trewithen form
96 'Sir George Sansom'
96 'Sir John Tremayne'
96 'Sirius'
96 Smithii Group
92 Snow White Group
94 'Soft Lips' (K)
91 Soulking Group
90 'Souvenir de D.A. Koster'
95 'Spek's Brilliant' (M)
96 'Spellbinder'
96 ***sphaeroblastum*** F 17110
89 'Spinoza' (M)
96 ***spinuliferum*** 'Jack Hext'
96 – TW 413
96 – TW 418
90 'Splendens' (EA)
96 'Spring Dawn'
93 'Spring Glory'
94 'Spring Parade'
95 'Spring Song'
96 'Springday'
94 'Star of Zaffelare'
94 'Stephanie'
87 Stonehurst Group
94 'Stour' (K)
96 'Strategist'
96 ***succothii*** KW 13666
90 'Sui-yohi' (EA)
93 'Sumer Snow'
95 'Sun Charm'
96 'Sunny'
88 'Sunset Boulevard' (K)
89 'Susan Everett'
96 'Sweet Beatrice' (V)
93 'Swen'
95 'Sword of State' (K)
96 'Sylvetta'
96 ***taggianum***
95 – Headfortianum Group
89 'Tamarind'
91 ***tanastylum*** var. ***pennivenium***
96 Tasco Group
91 'Tebotan' (EA/d)
90 ***telmateium*** Drumonium Group
88 ***temenium***
94 – x ***eclecteum***
95 'Tender Heart' (K)
91 'Tensing'
91 Tessa Group pink
95 Thais Group
93 'The Lizzard'
96 'The Warrior'
96 Thomdeton Group
94 ***thomsonii*** 'Balbirnie'
91 'Tiger'
95 'Tinsmith' (K)
96 'Top Brass'
94 'Top of the Rockery'
96 'Topaz'
96 'Tortoiseshell Biscuit'
90 'Tottenham' (Ad)
93 'Toucan' (K)
93 'Tow Head'
94 'Trent' (K)
96 ***trichanthum*** W 1342
96 ***trichocladum*** KW 21079
92 ***trichostomum*** deep form
89 'Tyrian Rose' (EA)
93 'Uta-maru'
96 Valaspis Group & cl.
95 'Valley Sunrise'
92 'Van'
96 'Van Heka'
92 'Van Weerden Poelman'
95 Vanguard Group
95 Varna Group
91 'Veesprite'
91 Vega Group
93 'Vellum'
91 'Venapens'
94 ***vialii*** (A)
93 'Victoria de Rothschild'
93 'Vienna'
96 'Vinecrest'
87 'Violette'
91 ***virgatum album***
88 ***virgatum*** subsp. ***oleifolium*** 'Penheale Pink'
90 'Virgo'
90 'Viscosepalum' (G)
93 'Vivacious'
94 'Voodoo'
89 'Wadai-akasuba' (EA)
89 'Wada's Pink Delight'
91 'Wantage'
90 'Wavertree'
91 'Wee Willie' (EA)
94 'White Gold'
91 'White Moon' (EA)
96 'White Perfume'
93 'White Prince' (EA/d)
96 'White Swan' (K)
95 'Whitney's Best Yellow'
90 'William Fortescue'
91 ***williamsianum*** 'Exbury White'
92 – x ***martinianum***
96 Wilsonii Group
89 'Windle Brook'
94 'Windsor Apple Blossom' (K)
91 'Windsor Hawk'
94 'Windsor Peach Glow' (K)
94 'Windsor Sunbeam' (K)
95 'Woodchat'
90 'Wye' (K)
96 'Xenophile'
94 ***yakushimanum*** x ***recurvoides***
95 – 'Snow Mountain'
96 – Tremeer tall form
94 'Yamato-no-hikari'
91 'Yaye-giri' (EA)
92 'Yaye-hiryu' (EA)
90 ***yedoense*** var. ***poukhanense***
90 – var. ***poukhanense album***
90 'Yellow'
95 'Yellow by Trailer'
89 'Yokohama' (EA)
90 'Yokora'
91 'Yorozuyo' (EA)
96 Yuncinn Group
92 ***yungningense*** Glomerulatum Group
96 ***yunnanense*** 'Diana Colville'
96 – Hormophorum Group
94 – selected form
96 – 'Tower Court'
96 Yvonne Group
93 'Yvonne Opaline'
93 'Yvonne Pride'
96 ***zaleucum***

RHODOHYPOXIS
94 ***milloides*** 'Super Milloides'
96 'True'

RHODOPHIALA
92 ***rosea***

RHODOTHAMNUS
96 ***chamaecistus***

RHOICISSUS
90 ***capensis*** 🏆

RHOPALOBLASTE
91 ***ceramica***

RHUS
95 ***aromatica***
94 ***succedanea***

RIBES
90 ***alpinum*** 'Pumilum'
92 ***burejense***
95 ***fasciculatum*** var. ***chinense***
93 ***glandulosum***
92 ***henryi***
89 ***leptanthum***
96 ***macabeanum***
94 ***magellanicum***
91 ***menziesii***
96 ***nigrum*** 'Black Reward' (F)
95 – 'Green's Black' (F)
95 – 'Loch Ness' (F) 🏆
91 – 'Tsema' (F)
91 ***roezlii*** var. ***cruentum***
89 ***sanguineum*** 'Atrorubens'
89 – 'Carneum'
96 – 'Elk River Red'
96 – 'Giant White'
91 – var. ***glutinosum***
91 ***uva-crispa*** var. ***reclinatum*** 'Angler' (F)
91 – – 'Antagonist' (F)
91 – – 'Beauty' (F)
91 – – 'Beauty Red' (D)
91 – – 'Belle de Meaux' (F)
91 – – 'Berry's Early Giant' (C)
91 – – 'Black Seedling' (F)
91 – – 'Bobby' (F)
91 – – 'British Oak' (D)
91 – – 'Brown's Red' (D)
91 – – 'Champion' (F)
91 – – 'Coiner' (F)
91 – – 'Colossal' (F)
91 – – 'Conquering Hero' (F)
91 – – 'Early Green Hairy' (D)
91 – – 'Echo' (D)
91 – – 'Emerald' (D)
91 – – 'Faithful' (C)
91 – – 'Fascination' (F)
91 – – 'Forever Amber' (D)
91 – – 'Gautrey's Earliest' (F)
91 – – 'Gem' (D)
91 – – 'Glencarse Muscat' (D)
91 – – 'Globe Yellow' (F)
91 – – 'Golden Lion' (F)
91 – – 'Green Overall' (C)
91 – – 'Green Walnut' (F)
91 – – 'Grüne Flashen Beere' (F)
91 – – 'Grüne Kugel' (C)
91 – – 'Grüne Reisen' (C)
91 – – 'Guy's Seedling' (D)
91 – – 'Helgrüne Samtbeere' (C)
91 – – 'Highlander' (D)
91 – – 'Höning Früheste' (D)
91 – – 'Hot Gossip' (F)
91 – – 'Hough's Supreme' (F)

91 – – 'Hue and Cry' (C)
91 – – 'Improved Mistake' (F)
91 – – 'Independence' (F)
91 – – 'Ingal's Prolific Red' (C)
91 – – 'Jenny Lind' (F)
91 – – 'Jolly Angler' (F)
91 – – 'Jolly Potter' (F)
91 – – 'Katherina Ohlenburg' (C)
91 – – 'Kathryn Hartley' (C)
91 – – 'Lady Delamere' (C)
91 – – 'Lady Haughton' (D)
91 – – 'Lady Leicester' (D)
91 – – 'Langley Green' (C)
91 – – 'Lauffener Gelbe' (F)
91 – – 'Leader' (C)
91 – – 'Lily of the Valley' (F)
91 – – 'Lloyd George' (F)
91 – – 'Lord Audley' (D)
91 – – 'Lord Elcho' (F)
91 – – 'Lord George' (F)
91 – – 'Marmorierte Goldkugel' (D)
91 – – 'Maurer's Seedling' (D)
91 – – 'Mertensis' (F)
91 – – 'Mischief' (F)
91 – – 'Monarch' (D)
91 – – 'Montgomery' (F)
91 – – 'Mrs Westlon' (F)
91 – – 'Muttons' (D)
91 – – 'Nailer' (F)
91 – – 'Napoléon le Grand' (D)
91 – – 'Norden Hero' (D)
91 – – 'Ostrich' (C)
91 – – 'Pixwell' (F)
91 – – 'Plain Long Green' (F)
91 – – 'Postman' (F)
91 – – 'Pottage' (F)
91 – – 'Preston's Seedling' (D)
91 – – 'Profit' (F)
91 – – 'Railway' (F)
91 – – 'Ries von Kothen' (C)
91 – – 'Roaring Lion' (F)
91 – – 'Robustenda' (F)
91 – – 'Rushwick Seedling' (C)
91 – – 'Sensation' (C)
91 – – 'Shiner' (F)
91 – – 'Slap Bang' (C)
91 – – 'Smaragdbeere' (C)
91 – – 'Smiling Beauty' (C)
91 – – 'Snow' (F)
91 – – 'Souter Johnny' (F)
91 – – 'Stockwell' (F)
91 – – 'Sulphur' (D)
91 – – 'Talfourd' (D)
91 – – 'Thatcher' (F)
91 – – 'Viper' (C)
91 – – 'Weisse Riesen' (F)
91 – – 'Weisse Volltriesen' (C)
91 – – 'Werdersche Frühemarkt' (D)
91 – – 'White Fig' (C)
91 – – 'White Swan' (C)

RICINUS

92 ***communis***

ROBINIA

96 × ***ambigua*** 'Bellarosea'
96 – 'Decaisneana'
95 ***fertilis*** 'Monument'
96 ***luxurians***
92 × ***margaretta***
93 ***pseudoacacia*** 'Semperflorens'

RODGERSIA

96 ***pinnata*** CLD 432
96 – 'Maurice Mason'
92 ***podophylla*** 'Pagode'

ROMANZOFFIA

94 ***californica***
92 ***suksdorfii***

ROMULEA

91 ***bulbocodium*** var. ***leichtliniana***
94 – white

ROSA

93 'Aberdonian' (F)
91 'Abundance' (F)
94 Acey Deucy (F)
96 ***acicularis*** var. ***engelmannii***
94 'Akebono' (HT)
89 'Alamein' (F)
93 'Alison Wheatcroft' (F)
92 Allotria (F)
90 'Amarillo' (HT)
95 'Amberlight' (F)
90 'Amorette' (Patio)
96 Anabell (F)
94 'Andrea' (Min)
90 'Andrew's Rose' (F)
92 Anneka (F)
90 'Appreciation' (HT)
92 Apricot Spice (HT)
92 'Arabesque' (F)
96 Arctic Sunrise (Min/GC)
95 ***arkansana***
96 – × ***moyesii***
94 Arnold Greensitt (HT)
94 'Arthur Hillier' (S)
90 'Artistic' (F)
89 'Ascot' (F)
96 'Avignon' (F)
94 'Baby Princess' (Min)
91 Baccará (HT)
95 'Bambino' (Min)
94 ***banksiae*** 'Lutescens' (Ra)
95 'Barbara Richards' (HT)
92 Baron Meillandina (Min)
96 Beauty Queen (F)
92 'Beauty Secret' (Min)
91 'Bel Ange' (HT)
92 Benevolence (HT)
89 'Berlin' (S)
92 Beryl Bach (HT)
95 'Bharami' (Min)
92 Bill Slim (F)
92 Bischofsstadt Paderborn (S)
92 'Blaze Away' (F)
95 Bob Grieves
93 'Bold Bells' (S)
95 'Born Free' (Min)
90 'Bountiful' (F)
90 'Brandy Butter' (HT)
92 'Bridgwater Pride' (F)
92 Bright Eyes (F)
94 'Bristol Post' (HT)
95 'Brownie' (F)
92 'Buccaneer' (HT)
91 'Burning Love' (F)
96 Canadian White Star (HT)
90 'Capistrano' (HT)
96 'Carol Amling' (Gn)
91 Carol Ann (F)
95 Caroline Davison (F)
94 ***caudata***
93 'Centurion' (F)
95 ***cerasocarpa*** (Ra)
94 'Chami' (HM)
93 'Chaplin's Pink Companion' (Cl)
92 Charles de Gaulle (HT)
94 'Charley's Aunt' (HT)
96 'Charlotte Elizabeth' (F)
92 'Charm of Paris' (HT)
92 'Chatterbox' (F)
94 'Cherry Pie' (HT)
94 Chorus (F)
92 Christingle (F)
91 'Chuckles' (F)
94 'City of Bath' (HT)
92 City of Bradford (F)
94 'City of Glasgow' (HT)
95 'City of Gloucester' (HT)
91 'Climbing Andrea' (ClMin)
89 'Climbing Blue Peter' (ClMin)
91 'Climbing Dornröschen' (Cl)
91 'Climbing Ellinor LeGrice' (ClHT)
90 'Climbing Firecrest' (ClF)
91 'Climbing Korona' (ClF)
92 'Climbing Madame Jules Bouché' (ClHT)
93 'Climbing Orangeade' (ClF)
95 Climbing Soraya (ClHT)
93 'Climbing Wendy Cussons' (ClHT)
96 Clive Lloyd (HT)
96 Clydebank Centenary (F/Min)
94 'Clytemnestra' (HM)
93 'Coalite Flame' (HT)
89 'Cologne Carnival' (HT)
96 ***colvillei***
95 Colwyn Bay (F)
96 'Commemoration'
91 'Comtesse d'Oxford' (HP)
92 'Comtesse O'Gorman' (HP)
95 'Conchita' (Poly)
92 Conqueror's Gold (F)
91 'Coral Star' (HT)
93 'Coronet' (F)
92 Corsair (F)
96 'Corso' (HT)
93 Country Heritage (HT)
92 'Countryman' (S)
92 'Crarae' (HT)
96 'Creme'
91 Crimson Wave (F)
90 'Culverbrae' (Ru)
92 'Dale Farm' (F/Patio)
92 'Dame de Coeur' (HT)
92 Dame Vera Lynn (F)
96 ***davurica***
96 Dee Bennett (Min)
89 'Dekorat' (HT)
96 'Devon Maid' (Cl)
91 Diamant (F)
93 'Dian' (Min)
95 'Dimples' (F)
89 'Doctor F.L. Skinner'
96 Dollie B (Min)
95 'Double Joy' (Min)
96 'Dukat' (Cl)
92 Dwarf Favourite (Patio)
95 Dwarf Queen '82 (Min)
96 'Egyptian Treasure' (F)
91 'Eiffel Tower' (HT)
90 'Eleanor'
92 Elegant Pearl (Min/Patio)
96 ***elegantula*** (S)
95 Elfin (Min)
92 'Ellen Mary' (HT)
92 'Ellinor LeGrice' (HT)
96 'Elsa' (HT)
89 'Else Poulsen' (Poly)
94 'Embassy' (HT)
92 'Embassy Regal' (HT)
92 'Emily Carter'
91 Eminence (HT)
94 'English Estates' (HT)
92 Esperanto Jubileo (HT)
95 Esther's Baby (Patio)
94 Estima (Min)
96 'Ethel' (Ra)
94 'Etude' (Cl)
96 'Eurydice'
89 'Eve Allen' (HT)
96 'Evelyn Taylor' (F)
93 'Evening Sentinel' (F)
92 'Fairlight' (F)
92 'Fairy Prince' (GC)
95 Fantan (HT)
91 'Fashion' (F)
89 ***fedtschenkoana*** 'Flore Pleno'
96 Fifi (F)
91 'Fillette' (F)
90 'Firecrest' (F)
96 Flaming Rosamini (Min)
92 Flanders Field (F)
89 'Flashlight' (F)
94 'Fleet Street' (HT)
91 'Florida von Scharbeutz' (F)
94 Fontainebleau (HT)
93 'Fosse Way' (HT)
96 'Frau Eva Schubert' (Ru)
96 Freddy (F)
94 Free Spirit (Min)
92 Friction Lights (F)
89 'Frost Fire' (Min)
94 'Frosty' (Min)
95 'Fyfield Princess' (F)
96 ***gallica*** 'Beckett's Single' (G)
91 'Garden Princess'

96 'Gardener's Delight' (Ra)
92 'Garnette Rose' (Gn)
91 'Garnette Salmon' (Gn)
92 'Garnette Yellow' (Gn)
95 'Gay Gordons' (HT)
93 'Gay Vista' (S)
92 Gentle Maid (F/Patio)
95 'Geranium Red' (F)
96 'Geschwinds Orden'
96 'Geschwinds Schönste' (Ra)
94 Gilda (F)
96 'Ginsky' (F)
91 Glowing Embers (F)
94 'Godfrey Winn' (HT)
92 'Gold Coin' (Min)
92 'Gold Marie' (F)
95 'Gold Pin' (Min)
91 Gold Topaz (F)
93 'Golden Angel' (Min)
90 'Golden Autumn' (HT)
95 'Golden Penny' (Min)
96 'Golden Treasure' (F)
94 'Goliath' (HT)
89 'Grace Kimmins' (F)
91 'Granadina'
92 'Grandpa's Delight' (F)
96 Green Snake (S/GC)
92 'Grey Dawn' (F)
94 Guiding Spirit (Min/Patio)
95 'Gypsy Jewel' (Min)
96 'Gypsy Moth' (F)
90 'Hadspen Arthur'
90 'Hadspen Eleanor'
92 'Halley's Comet' (F)
93 'Hamburg Love' (F)
94 'Hansestadt Lübeck' (F)
90 x ***hardyi***
96 Harkness Marigold (F)
96 Harold Macmillan (F)
92 'Harriny' (HT)
92 'Harry Edland' (F)
95 Harvest Home (Ru)
93 'Harvester' (HT)
91 'Hazel Le Rougetel' (Ru)
93 'Heather' (Min)
92 Heidelberg (S)
92 Heidi (MinMo)
92 Helga (HT/F)
91 'Help the Aged' (HT)
90 ***hemsleyana***
96 'Hiawatha Recurrent' (Ra)
96 'High Noon' (Cl)
95 High Spirits (Min)
93 'Highlight' (F)
96 'Himmelsauge' (Ra)
92 Hiroshima's Children (F)
96 Hollie Roffey (Min)
94 'Honeysweet' (F)
94 'Hot Pewter' (HT)
94 Hotline (MinMo)
96 ***hypoleuca***
92 Ice Fairy (GC)
92 'Ice White' (F)
95 'Ideal' (Poly)
96 'Ideal Home' (HT)
91 IGA '83 München (GC)
92 ***iliensis***
89 'Incense' (HT)
90 Indian Song (HT)
96 'Inspiration' (Cl)
92 Iris Webb (F)
95 'Irish Brightness' (HT)
96 Irish Mist (F)
92 'Isabel de Ortiz' (HT)
96 'Isobel' (HT)
92 'Isobel Harkness' (HT)
94 'Ivory Tip Top' (F)
92 'Janice Tellian' (Min)
92 'Jean Thomson Harris' (F)
94 Jim Dandy (Min)
92 Jimmy Savile (F)
96 Joan Ball (Min)
96 'Johanna Röpcke' (Ra)
92 'John Abrams' (F)
96 'John Cabot' (S)
94 John Hughes (F)
95 'John Waterer' (HT)
95 'Joybells' (F)
96 Joyfulness (F)
92 'Jules Margottin' (HP)
92 Juliet Anne (Min)
91 'June Bride' (F)
91 'June Park' (HT)
94 'June Time' (Min)
89 'Junior Miss' (F)
90 'K of K' (HT)
96 'Kerrygold' (F)
92 'Korp' (F)
89 'Kumbaya' (F)
93 'La Jolla' (HT)
96 'La Plus Belle des Ponctuées' (G)
95 'Lady Helen' (HT)
92 Lady Meillandina (Min)
92 Lady Mitchell (HT)
90 Lakeland Princess (HT)
91 'Laure Davoust' (Ra)
96 'Lavender Lace' (Min)
92 'Lemon Delight' (MinMo)
91 'Lemon Yellow' (F)
93 Letchworth Garden City (F)
91 'Liberty Bell' (HT)
95 Lichtkönigin Lucia (S)
92 Lilac Airs (HT)
96 'Lily de Gerlache' (HT)
94 'Linda Guest' (HT)
94 'Little Girl' (ClMin)
92 Little One
94 'Little Stephen' (HT)
92 'Lively Lady' (F)
96 Lloyds of London (F)
92 Lolita (HT)
96 ***longicuspis*** Bertoloni B&L 12386 (Ra)
92 Lordly Oberon (S)
92 'Love Affair' (Min)
95 'Luis Brinas' (HT)
95 ***macrophylla*** SF 16/131
94 'Madame Bérard' (ClT)
96 'Mademoiselle Marie Dirvon' (Bb)
94 'Maid Marion'
91 'Mainzer Wappen' (HT)
93 'Mala Rubinstein' (HT)
92 'Malmesbury' (HT)
92 Mandy (HT)
93 Mannheim (S)
92 'Marchioness of Salisbury' (HT)
93 'Marianne Powell' (HT)
92 Marion Harkness (HT)
92 Maritime Bristol (HT)
92 Marty (F)
92 'Mary Barnard' (F)
96 Mary Campbell (F)
96 Mary Hayley Bell (S)
92 Mary Jean (HT)
92 Mary Sumner (F)
96 ***maximowicziana***
94 May Lyon (HT)
96 'May Woolley' (F)
95 'Mehbronze' (Patio)
96 'Meitosier' (Cl)
92 Midas (HT)
89 'Midget' (Min)
94 Millie Walters (Min)
94 'Miranda Jane' (F)
92 'Mission Supreme' (HT)
94 Modern Art (HT)
95 'Modern Times' (HT)
96 Molly McGredy (F)
91 'Montezuma' (HT)
92 'Mood Music' (Min)
94 Mother and Baby (HT)
90 ***moyesii*** 'Nassau' (S)
90 'Mrs Reynolds Hole' (T)
90 'Mrs Wakefield Christie-Miller' (HT)
90 'Mrs Wemyss Quin' (HT)
94 ***multiflora*** 'Wilsonii'
93 'Munster' (S)
96 ***muriculata***
92 Muriel (F/Patio)
93 'My Guy' (HT)
92 'Naomi' (HT)
96 Nevertheless (F)
93 Neville Gibson (HT)
91 'Nikki' (F)
92 Nimbus (F)
92 ***nitida*** 'Kebu'
96 'Non Plus Ultra' (Ra)
92 Nona (F)
94 'Norah Cruickshank' (HT)
95 'Northumberland WI' (HT)
96 'Norwich Salmon' (Cl)
89 'Nymph'
96 'Octet' (S)
96 x ***odorata*** 'Bengal Crimson' (Ch)
91 – 'Miss Willmott's Crimson China' (Ch)
94 'Oh La La' (F)
90 'Ohio' (S)
96 Old Glory (Min/Patio)
92 Olive (F)
96 Olympiad (HT)
92 Olympic Spirit (F)
92 'Only You' (HT)
92 'Opera' (HT)
91 'Orange Goliath' (HT)
90 Orange Minimo (Min)
90 'Orange Mother's Day' (F)
96 Orange Star (Min)
94 'Over the Rainbow' (Min)
94 'Oxfam' (HT)
92 Pacemaker (HT)
94 Pacesetter (HT)
92 Paint Box (F/Min)
92 Pallas (Min)
96 Pandora (Min)
92 Pat James (F)
93 'Peaches 'n' Cream' (Min)
94 'Peachy' (HT)
92 'Penny' (F)
93 'Percy Thrower' (HT)
94 Peter Frankenfeld (HT)
96 Petite Folie (Min)
89 'Petula Clarke' (HT)
94 'Phoebe' (S)
92 Phoenix (Min)
96 'Pilgrim' (S)
90 ***pimpinellifolia*** 'Lady Hamilton'
93 'Pineapple Poll' (F)
89 'Pink Cloud' (ClHT)
92 'Pink Fountain' (F)
93 'Pink Heather' (Min)
91 'Pink Meteor' (F)
94 Pink Nevada (S)
96 'Pink Petticoat' (Min)
93 'Pink Showers' (ClHT)
96 ***pisocarpa***
92 Playboy (F)
96 Playtime (F)
95 Potter and Moore (S)
92 Potton Heritage (HT)
90 'Poulbright' (F)
95 'Poulgold' (Min/Patio)
96 ***prattii***
92 Pride of Maldon (F)
95 Pride of Park (F)
96 'Primevère'
92 'Prince Charming' (Min)
94 Prince Sunblaze (Min)
96 'Princess Michiko' (F)
91 Prins Claus (HT)
92 Proud Titania (S)
96 Prunella (F)
94 Pucker Up (Min)
96 'Purezza' (Ra)
96 'Purity' (Ra)
91 'Purple Elf' (Min)
92 'Queen Esther' (HT)
90 'Queenie' (F)
96 Rainbow's End (Min)
92 'Ralph Tizzard' (F)
96 'Red Beauty' (Min)
95 'Red Empress' (Cl)
92 'Red Maid' (F)
94 Red Minimo (Min)
90 'Red Planet' (HT)
93 'Red Queen' (HT)
96 Red Splendour (F)
91 'Red Sprite' (Min)
92 'Redcliffe' (F)
91 Rediffusion Gold (F)
92 'Redland Court' (F)
93 x ***reversa*** white
92 'Ripples' (F)
92 'Robin' (Min)
92 Rochester Cathedral (S)
92 Roddy McMillan (HT)
91 'Rosamini Gold' (Patio)
91 'Rosamini Orange' (Patio)
91 'Rosamini Pink' (Patio)
91 'Rosamini Red' (Patio)
91 'Rosamini White' (Patio)
92 'Rose of Clifton' (F)
91 'Rose of Tralee' (F)
94 Rosie (Min)
93 'Rosmarin' (Min)
96 Rosy Gem (Min)

96 'Rotkäppchen' (Poly)
92 'Royal Bath and West' (F)
90 'Royal Conquest' (F)
95 Royal Flush (F/Patio)
92 'Royal Lavender' (ClHT)
96 Royal Meillandina (Min/Patio)
96 Royal Sunblaze (Min)
96 ***rugosa*** var. ***ventenatiana*** (Ru)
96 Rumba (F)
93 'Ruth Woodward' (Fl)
91 'Saga' (F)
93 Saint Hugh's (HT)
96 ***salictorum***
96 Salita (Cl)
92 'Salmon Sprite' (F)
90 'Sandra Marie' (HT)
90 'Santa Catalina' (FCl)
91 'Saul' (HT)
92 Save the Children (F/Patio)
96 Scherzo (F)
96 Sea Foam (S)
96 'Sea of Fire' (F)
92 Seafarer (F)
96 Seaspray (F)
96 ***sempervirens*** (Ra)
96 Sentimental (HT)
92 ***serafinii***
91 'Serenade' (HT)
92 ***sericea*** subsp. ***omeiensis*** f. ***pteracantha*** 'Atrosanguinea' (S)
96 'Serratipetala' (Ch)
90 Shalom (F)
92 Sheila Macqueen (F)
96 'Sheldon'
95 Shell Beach (Min)
91 'Shepherdess' (F)
92 Shire County (HT)
92 Showman (HT)
92 'Silver Charity' (F)
96 'Silver Charm'
94 Sir Harry Pilkington (HT)
94 'Snow Bride' (Min)
91 'Snowgoose' (Min)
95 'Soleil d'Or' (S)
92 'Sonatina' (F)
96 sp. CDC 262
91 'Spartan' (F)
94 'Special Guest' (HT)
95 Spek's Centennial (F)
89 'Spica Red'
92 Spirit of Pentax (F)
94 Spot Minijet (Min)
95 'Stacey Sue' (Min) ♀
91 'Stanley Duncan' (Min)
92 'Stephen Langdon' (F)
92 'Stirling Castle' (F)
95 'String of Pearls' (Poly)
91 'Stromboli' (F)
92 'Sugar Sweet' (F)
91 'Summer Song' (F)
93 'Sun Blush' (HT)
93 'Sunbeam' (Min)
91 'Sunday Times' (F)
89 'Sunny Queen'
91 'Sunny South' (HT)
95 Super Dorothy (Ra)
95 Super Excelsa (Ra)
92 Suspense (HT)
95 'Swedish Doll' (Min)
96 'Sweet Honesty' (Min)
92 'Swinger' (Min)
89 'Sylvian Dot'
95 Tatjana (HT)
96 Telford's Promise (GC/S)
95 Temptation (F/Patio)
91 Tender Night (F)
96 Tennessee (Min)
96 The Daily Telegraph (F)
92 The Fisherman's Cot (F)
93 'The Friar' (S)
94 'The Havering Rambler'
95 'The Miller' (S)
92 'The Queen Alexandra' (Ra)
92 'The Yeoman' (S)
91 'Tinker Bell' (Min)
96 Tiny Tot (Min)
89 'Toddler' (F)
93 'Tom Brown' (F)
94 'Tom Tom' (F)
92 Tonight (HT)
94 Torch of Liberty (Min)
95 'Toy Clown' (Min)
92 'Tricia's Joy' (Cl)
96 Paint-pot = 'Trobglow' (Min)
96 'Truly Yours' (HT)
96 'Turkestan'
92 'Twinkles' (Min)
92 'Typhoo Tea' (HT)
91 'Tyrius' (HT)
89 'Tzigane' (HT)
96 ***ultramontana***
89 'Una' (Ra)
92 'Uncle Joe' (HT)
95 'Vagabonde' (F)
91 'Vanda Beauty'
92 'Velvet Hour' (HT)
92 Velvia (F)
92 'Vesper' (F)
96 'Vesuvius' (HT)
92 Volunteer (F)
91 Wagbi (F)
91 ***webbiana*** var. ***microphylla***
94 'Wee Man' (Min)
96 'Welcome Guest' (HT)
93 'Whippet' (HT)
89 'White Dick Koster'
93 'White Flight' (Ra)
91 'White Sunblaze' (Min)
95 'Wickham Highway' (F)
96 'Wild Flower' (S)
91 'Winefred Clarke' (HT)
94 Winsome (Min/Patio)
89 'Wisbech Gold' (HT)
91 'Woburn Gold' (F)
95 Woodlands Lady (Min/Patio)
96 ***yainacensis***
94 'Yellow Beauty' (Min)
94 'Yellow Petals' (HT)
93 'Yellow Pixie' (Patio)
93 'Yellow Queen Elizabeth' (F)
94 'Zola' (S)
91 'Zorina' (F)
96 'Zwergkönig' (Min)

ROSCOEA
96 ***cautleyoides*** pink

ROSMARINUS
95 'Compactus Albus'
89 ***creticus***
96 ***officinalis*** 'Alderney'
95 ***officinalis brevifolius***
96 ***officinalis*** 'Eden'
95 – Israeli
96 – 'Mrs Harding'
87 – 'Pat Vlasto'
89 – 'Suffolk Blue'

ROSULARIA
96 ***adenotricha*** subsp. ***adenotricha***
96 ***alpestris*** subsp. ***alpestris***
96 – CC 327
95 ***globulariifolia***
96 ***haussknechtii***
90 ***libanotica*** from Kaypak
90 ***radiciflora*** subsp. ***glabra*** from Beyas Dag
90 ***radiciflora radiciflora*** from Bitlis
96 ***sempervivum*** subsp. ***amanensis***
92 ***serpentinica*** from Sandras Dag
96 ***serrata***
94 – from Crete, Greece
90 ***stylaris***

RUBUS
96 ***canadensis***
93 ***coreanus*** 'Dart's Mahogany'
95 ***deliciosus***
95 ***fruticosus*** 'Kotata'
94 'Hildaberry' (F)
94 ***idaeus*** 'Glen Garry' (F)
94 ***lambertianus***
89 ***lasiostylus***
94 ***trilobus***
90 ***ulmifolius***

RUDBECKIA
95 ***grandiflora*** var. ***alismifolia***
91 ***hirta*** 'Irish Eyes'
96 ***nitida***
96 'Toto'
96 ***viridis***

RUELLIA
94 ***colorata***

RUMEX
93 ***acetosa*** 'Hortensis'
89 ***alpestris*** 'Rubra'

RUMOHRA
96 ***adiantiformis*** ♀

RUSCHIA
96 ***putterillii***
93 ***schollii*** pale pink

RUSCUS
93 ***aculeatus*** andromonoecious

RUTTYA
92 ***fruticosa***

SAGINA
93 ***subulata***

SAINTPAULIA
92 'Alexander'
91 'Alma'
92 'Barnados'
91 'Bella'
91 'Bertini'
91 'Blue Nymph'
92 'Bright Eyes' ♀
92 'Celebration'
92 'Centenary'
92 'Colorado' ♀
94 ***confusa***
92 'Delft' ♀
92 'Emma Louise'
95 'Fancy Trail' ♀
92 'Fred'
91 'Fusspot'
92 'Garden News' ♀
92 'Gisela'
95 'Granger's Wonderland' ♀
92 'Gredi' ♀
92 'Ice Maiden' ♀
92 'Iona'
92 'Jupiter'
92 'Kim'
91 'Lotte'
92 'Lupus'
91 'Ma Chérie'
92 'Maria' ♀
92 'Meteor Trail'
95 'Midget Valentine' ♀
92 'Midnight Trail'
91 'Miki'
95 'Moon Kissed' ♀
92 'Orion'
92 'Phoenix' ♀
92 'Porcelain'
92 'Rococo Pink' ♀
91 'Sarah'
91 'Silver Milestone Star'
92 'Starry Trail' ♀
92 'Susi'
95 'Tomahawk' ♀
95 ***velutina***
91 'Wonderland'

SALIX
93 'Aegma Brno' (f)
96 ***alba*** 'Cardinalis' (f)
94 – 'Richmond'
96 ***aurita***
92 ***babylonica*** var. ***pekinensis***
94 x ***balfourii***
93 ***bebbii*** x ***hastata***
95 ***bicolor*** Willdenow
96 ***burjatica***
93 – 'Germany'
93 – 'Korso'
93 x ***calodendron*** (f)
95 ***candida***
91 ***caprea*** 'Weeping Sally' (f)
94 ***cascadensis***
96 ***cinerea*** 'Variegata'
89 ***cordata***
92 ***daphnoides*** 'Oxford Violet'
93 x ***dasyclados***
90 x ***erdingeri***
90 ***eriocephala*** 'American Mackay'
94 x ***finnmarchica***
90 x ***gillotii***
90 ***glabra***
90 ***gooddingii***
87 'Harlequin'
92 ***humilis***
96 ***japonica*** Thunberg

90 ***kitaibeliana***
96 × ***laurina*** (f)
91 ***lucida***
90 ***mackenzieana***
89 × ***meyeriana***
92 'Micrugosa' (m)
93 ***myrsinites***
89 ***pendulina*** var. ***elegantissima***
93 ***purpurea*** subsp. ***lambertiana***
94 ***pyrifolia***
95 ***reinii***
90 ***repens*** 'Pygmaea'
93 ***retusa*** 'Pygmaea'
90 ***retusoides***
94 × ***sadleri***
90 ***schwerinii***
94 × ***sepulcralis*** 'Salamonii'
93 × ***sericans***
90 × ***sirakawensis***
93 'The Hague'
87 ***thibetica***
93 ***triandra*** 'Champion'
95 – 'Rouge d'Orléans'
96 ***udensis***
91 ***waldsteiniana***

SALVIA
96 ***amgiana***
93 ***angustifolia*** Salisbury
96 ***azurea*** subsp. ***pitcheri***
95 ***brandegeei***
96 ***brevilabra***
96 ***cadmica***
96 ***caespitosa anatolica***
96 ***coccinea*** 'Desert Blaze'
95 ***dorrii***
92 ***farinacea*** 'Porcelain'
95 ***guaranitica*** 'Black Knight'
96 ***henryi***
96 ***hirtella*** JCA 13800
95 ***huberi***
94 ***hydrangea***
95 ***jurisicii*** 'Alba'
96 ***lanigera***
96 ***macellaria***
96 ***macrosiphon***
96 ***mexicana*** var. ***major***
96 ***microphylla alba***
95 ***napifolia***
91 ***nelsonii***
95 ***nemorosa*** 'Brightness'
94 – 'Mariosa'
93 ***ningpo***
91 ***officinalis*** 'Cedric'
96 – 'Minor'
96 ***pomifera***
95 ***potentillifolia***
94 'Powis Castle'
93 'Rosentraum'
92 ***rosifolia***
96 ***scorodoniifolia***
92 ***sessei***
88 × ***sylvestris***
96 ***urticifolia***

SALVINIA
89 ***auriculata***

SAMBUCUS
92 ***alba*** 'Variegata'
95 ***caerulea*** var. ***neomexicana***
91 ***canadensis*** 'Hidden Springs'
91 – 'John's'
93 – 'Rubra'
94 ***javanica***
91 ***mexicana***
95 ***nigra*** 'Bimble' (v)
92 – 'Fructu Luteo'
96 – 'Golden Locks'
96 – 'Hadspen'
95 – 'Nana'
96 – 'Party Girl'
95 – 'Viridis'
96 ***sieboldiana*** var. ***coreana***
95 sp. SF 92305

SANCHEZIA
93 ***nobilis*** Hooker

SANGUISORBA
96 ***dodecandra***

SANICULA
96 ***arctopoides***

SANSEVIERIA
95 ***trifasciata*** 'Bantel's Sensation' 🏆
95 – 'Craigii' 🏆
96 – 'Gigantea' (v)
95 – 'Hahnii' 🏆
93 – 'Moonshine' 🏆

SAPINDUS
96 ***drummondii***

SAPONARIA
92 × ***boissieri***
87 ***ocymoides*** 'Splendens'

SARCOCOCCA
93 ***hookeriana*** var. ***hookeriana***

SARCOPOTERIUM
89 ***spinosum***

SARRACENIA
96 × ***ahlesii***
89 ***alata*** × ***minor***
96 – × ***oreophila***
93 – pubescent form
96 × ***catesbyi*** (× ***catesbyi*** × ***flava***)
96 – × ***popei***
96 – red
96 – × ***rubra***
96 × ***comptonensis***
96 'Evendine'
96 × ***excellens*** × ***wrigleyana***
89 ***flava*** × ***alata***
93 – copperlid form
93 – heavy veined form
96 × ***formosa*** × ***excellens***
89 × ***gilpinii***
96 'Gulf Rubra'
96 ***leucophylla*** × ***catesbyi***
96 – × ***oreophila***
96 – × ***popei***
93 ***minor*** × ***oreophila***
96 – × ***wrigleyana***
96 × ***moorei*** 'Marston Select'
96 – (× ***moorei*** × ***catesbyi***)
96 – × ***moorei*** × ***readii***
96 ***oreophila*** × ***minor***
96 × ***popei*** (× ***popei*** × ***flava***)
96 – × purpurea subsp. venosa
89 ***psittacina*** × ***alata***
96 ***purpurea*** 'Louis Burke'
96 × ***readii*** × ***excellens***
96 'Red Burgundy'
96 – × ***excellens***
96 – subsp. ***gulfensis***
93 – subsp. ***wherryi***
96 ***willisii*** × ***flava***
96 – × ***minor*** 'Giant'

SASA
96 ***chrysantha***

SASAELLA
95 ***ramosa*** 'Tsuyu-zasa'

SASSAFRAS
93 ***tzumu***

SATUREJA
95 ***cuneifolia***
93 ***spinosa***

SATYRIUM
93 ***nepalense***

SAUSSUREA
94 ***alpina***
92 ***ceratocarpa***
96 – var. ***depressa***
96 ***chionophylla***
94 ***discolor***
94 ***hypoleuca***
96 ***spathulifolia*** ACE 1344

SAXIFRAGA
92 'Alan Hayhurst' (7)
96 'Anagales Sunset'
96 ***androsacea*** (12)
93 ***aquatica***
92 'Arabella' (× *edithiae*) (8)
90 'Armida' (× *boeckleri*) (8)
94 ***armstrongii***
96 'Aurantiaca' (× *luteopurpurea*) (6)
92 'Avoca Gem'
96 'Backhouseana' (*paniculata*) (7)
92 'Beauty of Letchworth'
90 'Bellisant' (× *hornibrookii*) (8)
91 'Ben Lawers' (*oppositifolia*) (9)
94 'Berenika' (× *bertolonii*) (8)
94 'Biegleri' (8)
88 'Big Mö' (*andersonii*) (8)
93 'Blanik' (× *borisii*) (8)
94 'Blanka' (× *borisii*)
95 'Bornmuelleri' (8)
92 ***bronchialis***
91 'Buchholzii' (× *fleischeri*) (8)
90 'Buster' (× *hardingii*) (8)
94 ***caucasica***
92 'Cervinia' (*oppositifolia*) (9)
94 ***cespitosa*** var. ***emarginata*** (12)
90 'Chelsea Pink' (× *urbium*) (3)
95 ***cherlerioides pseudoburseriana***
94 × ***churchillii*** (7)
92 ***cinerea***
95 'Claudia' (× *borisii*) (8)
95 'Cleo' (× *boydii*) (8)
93 'Coningsby Queen' (× *hornibrookii*) (8)
94 'Cordata' (*burseriana*) (8)
92 'Crinkle' (3)
95 ***crispa*** (4)
94 ***cuneifolia*** subsp. ***cuneifolia*** (3)
95 'Cwm Idwal' (*rosacea*) (12)
93 ***decumbens***
92 'Diana' (× *lincoln-fosteri*) (8)
87 ***diversifolia***
96 'Dorothy Milne' (8)
90 'Dulcimer' (× *petraschii*) (8)
95 'Eleanora Francini Corti' (8)
93 ***erioblasta*** (12)
94 'Eriophylla' (7)
90 'Felicity' (× *anglica*) (8)
95 ***flagellaris***
96 – subsp. ***crassiflagellata*** CC 298 (2)
87 'Forsteriana' (*petraea*)
95 ***fortunei*** var. ***incisilobatum*** CDC 135
94 ***fragilis*** (12)
93 'Gaertneri' (*mariae-theresiae*) (8)
94 × ***gaudinii*** (7)
95 'Glowing Ember'
92 'Grandiflora' (*burseriana*) (8)
87 'Grandiflora' (*oppositifolia*) (9)
92 'Harry Marshall' (× *irvingii*) (8)
94 × ***hausmannii*** (7x6)
88 ***hirsuta*** subsp. ***paucicrenata***
94 × ***hornibrookii*** (8)
90 'Intermedia' (*marginata*) (8)
94 ***jacquemontii*** CC&McK 414
95 'Jan Palach' (× *krausii*) (8)
87 'Jenkinsii' (× *salmonica*) (8)
90 'Jubilee' (× *edithiae*) (8)
93 'Kelso' (× *boydii*) (8)
92 'Kew Green'
92 'Knapton Red' (12)
93 'Knebworth' (7)
96 ***kotschyi*** (8)
94 'Krákatit' (× *megaseiflora*) (8)
91 ***latepetiolata*** (11)
95 'Lemon Spires' (8)
92 'Loeflingii' (× *grata*) (8)
90 ***lolaensis***
90 'London Cerise' (× *urbium*) (3)
93 'Louise' (*marginata*) (8)
95 ***lowndesii***
95 × ***luteopurpurea*** (8)
92 ***lyallii*** (1)
94 × ***macnabiana*** (7)
93 'Magdalena' (× *thomasiana*) (8)
94 'Magna' (*burseriana*) (8)
93 'Major' (*paniculata* subsp. *Cartilaginea*) (7)
92 'Mangart' (*burseriana*) (8)

92 ***marginata rocheliana*** 'Balkan' (8)
92 × ***mariae-theresiae*** (8)
88 ***michauxii*** (1)
92 'Midas' (× *elisabethae*) (8)
91 'Minor' (*marginata* var. *coriophylla*) (8)
95 'Mondscheinsonate' (× *boydii*) (8)
92 'Monika' (*webrii*) (8)
87 ***mucronulata*** (2)
92 'Muffet' (*burseriana*) (8)
91 'Multipunctata' (*paniculata*) (7)
96 ***mutata*** (7)
89 'Nana' (*bronchialis*) (5)
94 'Nepal' (*andersonii*) (8)
87 ***nipponica*** (4)
93 'Oberon' (8)
96 ***obtusa*** (8)
93 'Old Britain' (× *boydii*) (8)
90 ***oppositifolia*** Iceland form (9)
92 – subsp. ***rudolphiana*** (9)
92 ***paniculata*** var. ***punctata*** (7)
91 × ***patens*** (6x7)
95 ***pedemontana*** (12)
90 – subsp. ***cervicornis*** (12)
95 – subsp. ***cymosa*** (12)
95 – – NS 674 (12)
93 ***pentadactylis***
95 ***petraea***
87 'Pike's Primrose' (12)
87 'Pike's White' (12)
95 'Planegg' (8)
94 'Popelka' (*marginata*) (8)
96 ***porophylla*** × ***sempervivum*** (8)
93 ***portosanctana***
91 'Priestwood White' (12)
92 × ***pseudoforsteri*** (3)
92 × 'Pseudofranzii' (× *paulinae*) (8)
91 'Pseudokellereri' (8)
92 × 'Pseudopaulinae' (× *paulinae*) (8)
96 'Pseudopungens' (× *apiculata*) (8)
90 ***pulvinaria***
94 'Redsox' (*marginata*) (8)
92 'Romeo' (× *hornibrookii*) (8)
95 'Ronald Young' (8)
93 ***rosacea***
95 'Rosamunda' (8)
95 'Roy Clutterbuck' (8)
95 'Rubra' (*paniculata*) ♀
92 'Russell Vincent Prichard' (× *irvingii*) (8)
96 × ***salmonica***
95 ***sempervivum*** f. ***sempervivum***
96 'Skye' (*oppositifolia*) (9)
92 ***squarrosa***
88 'Subluteiviridis' (× *gusmusii*) (8)
96 aff. ***subsessiliflora*** (8)
95 'Tábor' (× *schottii*) (8)
94 ***tenella*** (12)
87 'Theresia' (× *mariae-theresiae*)
95 ***trifurcata***
89 'Valerie Keevil' (× *anglica*) (8)
88 ***vandellii***
91 'Variegata' (*exarata moschata*) (12)
94 'Volgeri' (× *hofmannii*) (8)
87 'Wargrave Rose' (12)
88 'Waterperry' (*sempervivum*) (8)
95 'Wheatley Gem' (8)
92 'White Imp' (8)
93 'Witham's Compact' (12)
89 'Zita' (*sempervivum*) (8)

SCABIOSA
92 ***atropurpurea*** dark form
94 – 'Sunburst'
89 ***caucasica*** 'Backhouse'
96 – 'Moonstone'
95 ***columbaria*** var. ***webbiana***
96 ***cretica***
96 'Dingle Lilac'
96 ***fischeri***
92 ***japonica*** 'Alba'
96 ***lacerifolia***
96 ***mansenensis***
96 ***olgae***
89 ***pseudograminifolia***
92 ***speciosa***
96 ***vestita***

SCABIOSA × CEPHALARIA
95 ***Scabiosa cinerea*** × ***Cephalaria alpina***

SCADOXUS
95 ***multiflorus*** subsp. ***katherinae*** ♀
96 ***rigidus***

SCAEVOLA
91 'Blue Jade'
93 ***calendulacea***

SCHEFFLERA
93 ***arboricola*** 'Beauty'
93 – 'Diane'
93 – 'Henriette'
93 – 'Milena'
93 – 'Worthy'
91 ***elegantissima*** 'Castor'
91 – 'Castor Variegata'
90 'Starshine'

SCHIMA
89 ***yunnanensis***

SCHISANDRA
96 ***henryi***

SCHISTOSTEGA
96 ***pennata***

SCHIVERECKIA
96 ***podolica***

SCHIZANTHUS
95 ***hookeri*** JCA 12492

SCHIZOLOBIUM
94 ***excelsum***

SCHIZOPETALON
96 ***walkeri***

SCHIZOSTYLIS
93 ***coccinea*** 'Madonna'
95 – 'Mary Barnard'
96 – 'Molly Gould'
95 – 'Pink Ice'
88 – 'Rosalie'
88 – 'Rose Glow'

SCILLA
90 ***bifolia*** subsp. ***danubialis***
96 ***greilhuberi***
95 ***haemorrhoidalis***
95 – MS 923
95 ***hohenackeri***
95 ***mischtschenkoana*** 'Tubergeniana' ♀
95 – 'Zwanenburg' ♀
92 ***monanthos***
88 ***nivalis***
92 ***siberica*** var. ***taurica***
91 ***vvedenskyi***

SCINDAPSUS
90 ***pictus argyraeus*** ♀

SCLERANTHUS
96 ***brockiei***

SCLEROCHITON
96 ***harveyanus***

SCOLIOPUS
93 ***hallii***

SCOPOLIA
96 ***anomala***
96 ***carniolica*** from Slovenia
93 ***stramoniifolia***

SCROPHULARIA
95 ***coccinea***
92 ***grandiflora***
95 ***macrantha***

SCUTELLARIA
90 ***albida***
96 ***alpina*** 'Alba'
96 ***baicalensis*** 'Coelestina'
93 ***hyssopus***
91 ***ovata***
96 ***repens***
96 ***scordiifolia*** 'Seoul Sapphire'
92 ***ventenatii***

SEDUM
93 ***acre*** subsp. ***neglectum***
96 – tetraploid
93 ***adolphi***
91 ***album*** subsp. ***album*** var. ***balticum***
91 – 'Ibiza'
91 – subsp. ***teretifolium*** var. ***turgidum***
91 ***alfredii*** var. ***nagasakianum***
91 ***allantoides***
91 ***alsinifolium*** var. ***fragrans***
91 × ***amecamecanum***
91 ***anglicum*** subsp. ***anglicum*** var. ***sibernicum***
91 – var. ***microphyllum***
91 – subsp. ***pyrenaicum***
91 ***apoleipon***
92 × ***battandieri***
96 ***beyrichianum*** Masters
91 ***borissovae***
91 ***borschii***
91 ***brevifolium*** var. ***induratum***
91 – var. ***novum***
91 ***brissemoretii***
91 ***burrito***
91 ***caducum***
91 ***cepaea*** var. ***gracilescens***
91 ***chontalense***
91 ***clavatum***
95 ***cockerellii*** K 92.401
91 ***commixtum***
91 ***compactum***
91 ***compressum***
93 ***confusum***
91 ***craigii***
93 ***dasyphyllum*** subsp. ***oblongifolium*** var. ***riffense***
91 – var. ***suendermannii***
91 ***decumbens***
91 ***dendroideum***
91 ***diffusum***
91 ***ewersii*** var. ***cyclophyllum***
92 ***ewersii hayesii***
91 ***frutescens***
91 ***furfuraceum***
91 ***fusiforme***
91 ***greggii***
91 ***grisebachii*** subsp. ***kostovii***
93 ***gypsicola glanduliferum***
91 ***hemsleyanum***
94 ***hirsutum***
91 ***hispanicum*** 'Pewter'
91 ***indicum*** var. ***densirosulatum***
91 – var. ***yunnanense***
91 ***japonicum*** var. ***senanense***
91 ***laconicum***
91 ***lancerottense***
94 ***laxum*** subsp. ***laxum***
94 ***laxum retusum*** JCA 11601
91 ***liebmannianum***
89 ***lineare*** 'Major'
91 'Little Gem'
91 ***longipes***
91 ***lucidum***
91 – 'Obesum'
91 × ***luteolum***
91 × ***luteoviride***
91 ***magellense***
96 ***makinoi***
93 ***middendorfianum*** 'Striatum'
91 ***moranii***
91 ***multiflorum***
91 ***nanifolium***
91 ***nussbaumerianum***
91 ***nutans***
91 ***oaxacanum***
89 ***obtusatum*** subsp. ***boreale***
96 ***ochroleucum***
91 – subsp. ***montanum***
92 ***oreades***
93 ***oreganum*** 'Variegatum'
91 ***oxycoccoides***
91 ***oxypetalum***
93 ***pachyphyllum***
93 – × ***treleasei***
92 ***parvum***
96 'Philip Houlbrook'
91 ***potosinum***
91 ***reptans***
91 ***rosulatobulbosum***

91 ***rubens***
91 – var. ***praegeri***
91 x ***rubrotinctum*** 'Aurora'
89 ***rupestre albescens***
88 ***rupestre*** 'Major'
91 – 'Viride'
91 ***rupifragum***
91 ***ruwenzoriense***
89 ***sediforme*** 'Gran Canaria'
91 ***serpentinii***
91 ***sexangulare*** var. ***sexangulare*** f. ***elatum***
91 ***sieboldii ettyuense***
96 ***spathulifolium*** var. ***majus***
91 ***spectabile*** 'Carmen'
92 – 'Green Ice'
91 – 'Humile'
91 ***spurium*** 'Bronze Carpet'
91 – 'Carneum'
95 – 'Fool's Gold' (v)
91 – 'Salmoneum'
93 ***stahlii***
91 ***stefco***
91 ***stelliforme***
96 ***stevenianum***
91 ***subtile***
91 ***treleasei***
89 ***tschernokolevii***
91 ***tuberiferum***
91 ***urvillei***
91 – Hillebrandtii Group
91 – Sartorianum Group
91 – Stribrnyi Group
91 ***versadense***
91 – var. ***villadioides***
95 ***viviparum***
90 ***yabeanum***
91 ***zentaro-tashiroi***

SELAGINELLA
92 ***lepidophylla***
95 ***martensii*** 🏆
96 – 'Variegata'
95 ***uncinata*** 🏆

SELAGO
92 ***thunbergii***

SELINUM
96 ***candollei***
96 sp. EMAK 886

SEMPERVIVUM
91 'Alaric'
95 'Amtmann Fischer'
94 ***arachnoideum cristatum***
96 ***arachnoideum*** var. ***glabrescens*** 'Album'
95 – x ***grandiflorum***
96 – 'Mole Harbord'
95 – x ***montanum***
94 'Arlet'
96 ***armenum***
94 – var. ***insigne*** from Akyarma Gecidi
95 'Aymon Correvon'
95 ***ballsii*** from Kambeecho
95 'Banyan'
89 'Big Red'
95 'Bold Chick'
94 'Bronze Tower'
95 'Burgundy'
96 ***calcareum*** 'Benz'
96 – from Ceuze
94 – from La Mata de la Riba
94 – 'Nigricans'
94 – 'Spinulifolium'
94 ***cantabricum*** subsp. ***cantabricum*** from Someido No 1
96 – from Lago de Enol
94 – subsp. ***guadarramense*** from Morcuera No 1
94 – – from Morcuera No 3
94 – subsp. ***urbionense*** from Picos de Urbión, Spain
95 'Carluke'
94 'Celon'
96 ***ciliosum*** from Alí Butús
88 – x ***leucanthum***
94 – x ***marmoreum*** from Sveta Peta
88 'Clipper'
94 'Dame Arsac'
90 ***davisii***
95 'Delta'
94 'Dragoness'
90 'Dunstan'
95 'Educator Wollaert'
95 ***erythraeum*** from Rila, Bulgaria
91 – 'Red Velvet'
94 ***excelsum***
95 'Fat Jack'
95 'Fusilier'
96 'Gambol'
92 ***glabrifolium***
90 ***globiferum***
94 'Godaert'
95 ***grandiflorum*** x ***montanum***
94 – x ***tectorum***
94 'Gruaud Larose'
95 'Hayter's Red'
95 'Hekla'
94 'Highland Mist'
96 'Hullabaloo'
95 'Hyacintha'
94 ***ingwersenii*** x ***marmoreum*** from Sveta Peta
89 'Jubilation'
89 'Jungle Shadows'
96 'Kerneri'
96 'Kimono'
88 'Kolagas Mayfair'
89 'Kristina'
91 'Kubi'
94 ***lacktugum*** 'Metaoicum'
91 Le Clair's Hybrid No 4
90 ***leucanthum***
94 'Liliane'
94 ***marmoreum*** var. ***angustissimum***
94 – var. ***blandum***
88 – x ***dinaricum*** from Karawanken
95 'Mauvine'
95 'Merkur'
90 ***minus***
96 'Missouri Rose'
89 'Mors'
88 'Mount Usher'
94 'Moyin'
90 'Mrs Elliott'
94 ***nevadense*** from Puerto de San Francisco
96 'Pink Lemonade'
95 'Pompeon'
95 x ***praegeri***
87 ***pumilum*** x ***arachnoideum***
95 'R.H.I.'
95 'Red Cap'
95 'Red Giant'
89 'Red Planet'
91 x ***roseum***
95 'Rotsand'
95 'Rubellum'
88 'Ruby'
94 'Rule Britannia'
95 'Ruth'
88 'Samba'
95 'Smaragd'
94 'Soul'
95 sp. from Mont Cenis
94 'Sparkle'
89 'Sponnier'
95 'Strawberry Sundae'
96 'Sunkist'
95 ***tectorum*** 'Atrorubens'
88 – subsp. ***cantalicum***
96 – from Andorra
96 – from Mont Ventoux
94 – from Neuvéglise
94 – 'Robustum'
94 'Theo'
95 'Verdo'
89 'Wega'
89 'Witchery'
95 'Zackenkrone'
95 ***zeleborii***
90 – x ***kosaninii*** from Koprivnik

SENECIO
90 ***adonidifolius***
95 ***amplectens holmii***
94 ***argyreus*** JJA 12431
91 ***canus***
94 ***chilensis***
95 ***cineraria*** 'Silver Dust' 🏆
94 – 'Silver Filigree'
95 – 'Sleights Hardy'
95 ***crassulifolius***
95 ***formosus***
93 ***gillesii***
96 ***gilliesii*** JJA 12379
93 ***gnaphaloides***
94 ***harbourii*** K 92.410
90 ***hypochionaeus*** var. ***argaeus***
95 ***incanus***
95 – subsp. ***carniolicus***
91 ***jacquemontianus***
89 ***littoralis***
92 ***natalensis***
92 ***pectinatus***
95 ***populnea***
94 ***soldanella***
96 ***speciosus***
93 ***tamoides***

SENNA
94 ***candolleana***
95 ***floribunda*** 🏆
94 ***multiglandulosa***
94 ***polyantha***
94 ***procumbens***
91 ***retusa***
94 ***splendida***
95 ***sturtii***

SERENOA
90 ***repens***

SERIPHIDIUM
94 ***canum nanum***

SETARIA
94 ***chevarlaria***

SHORTIA
90 ***galacifolia brevistyla***
89 x ***interdexta*** 'Wimborne'
93 ***soldanelloides*** dwarf form
93 – var. ***ilicifolia*** 'Askival'
90 – var. ***minima***
91 ***uniflora***
89 – var. ***kantoensis***

SIBBALDIA
95 ***cuneata***
95 ***procumbens***

SIBBALDIOPSIS
92 ***tridentata***
96 – 'Lemon Mac'

SIBIRAEA
95 ***laevigata*** CLD 781

SIDA
93 ***napaea***

SIDALCEA
94 'Mrs Cadman'
96 'Paramount'
96 'Puck'

SIDERITIS
95 ***dasygnaphala***
93 ***scardica***
95 ***syriaca*** NS 551

SILENE
96 ***acaulis*** 'Correvoniana'
94 – from Pfiezujoch
90 ***acaulis variegata***
91 ***altaica***
95 ***andicola***
91 'Bill MacKenzie'
95 ***burchellii***
95 ***californica***
93 ***californica alba***
91 ***caryophylloides***
93 ***dioica*** 'Perkin' (v)
94 – 'Rosea Plena Variegata'
90 – 'Tresevern Gold'
93 ***flavescens***
94 ***foliosa***
96 ***fortunei***
94 ***frivaldskyana*** HH&K 214
89 ***hookeri bolanderi***
94 ***keiskei*** var. ***akaisialpina***
95 – pale pink
94 ***laciniata***
96 ***nigrescens***
96 aff. – ACE 1391
94 ***pendula rosea***
94 ***petersonii*** var. ***petersonii***
88 'Pink Bells'
95 ***pygmaea***
96 ***rotundifolia***
96 ***rupestris***
89 ***saxifraga***
96 ***schafta*** 'Brilliant'
88 – 'Robusta'
91 ***scouleri***

96 sp. ACE 1320
95 sp. CDB 13013
95 ***tatarica***
93 ***undulata***
96 ***virginica***
96 ***wrightii***

SILPHIUM
96 ***trifoliatum***

SILYBUM
96 ***eburneum***

SINNINGIA
92 'Brilliant Scarlet'
93 'Foxy Blue'
93 ***leucotricha***
92 'Royal Purple'

SINOJACKIA
94 ***rehderiana***
92 ***xylocarpa***

SISYMBRIUM
89 ***officinale***

SISYRINCHIUM
92 ***californicum*** from British Columbia
96 ***macrocarpum***
96 ***narcissiflorum***
96 ***striatum*** 'Rushfields'
93 'Wisley Blue'
94 ***yuccifolium***

SKIMMIA
96 ***japonica*** 'Keessen'
94 – 'Pigmy' (f)
94 – 'Red Riding Hood'
96 – 'Stoneham Red'
95 ***japonica viridis***
95 ***mica***
90 ***multinervia***

SMELOWSKIA
96 ***calycina*** var. ***americana***

SMILAX
93 ***china***

SMYRNIUM
89 ***perfoliatum*** subsp. ***rotundifolium***

SOLANUM
91 ***aculeatissimum***
90 ***capsicastrum*** 'Variegatum'
95 ***dulcamara*** var. ***album***
90 ***elaeagnifolium***
95 ***muricatum*** 'Pepino Gold' (F)
91 – 'Ryburn'
93 ***nigrum***
93 ***pseudocapsicum*** 'Mandarin'
96 – 'Thurino'
95 ***umbelliferum***
90 ***valdiviense***
91 – 'Variegatum'

SOLDANELLA
96 ***austriaca***
92 × ***ganderi***
96 ***pusilla alba***
95 'Tinkerbell'

SOLENOMELUS
96 ***lechleri***

SOLENOPSIS
91 ***erianthum***
94 ***laurentia***
96 sp. white

SOLENOSTEMON
93 'Brightness' (v)
94 'Bronze Queen'
93 'Charles Rudd'
96 'Jean Falmouth'
93 'Midnight'

SOLIDAGO
95 ***bicolor***
95 ***canadensis*** var. ***scabra***
96 'Golden Falls'
89 'Goldenplume'
95 'Goldstrahl'
92 'Goldwedel'
95 'Leda'
88 'Leraft'
96 'Lesden'
96 'Loddon'
96 'Mimosa'
96 ***multiradiata*** var. ***scopulorum***
92 'Septembergold'
95 ***spathulata***
90 ***ulmifolia***
96 ***virgaurea*** pale yellow

SONCHUS
95 ***oleraceus***

SOPHORA
95 ***alopecuroides***
89 ***japonica*** 'Violacea'
96 ***microphylla*** 'Goldilocks'
95 ***mollis***
92 ***tetraptera*** 'Grandiflora'

SORBUS
94 × ***arnoldiana*** 'Schouten'
96 ***arranensis***
93 ***aucuparia*** gold
96 ***cascadensis***
95 ***cashmiriana*** pink
95 ***croceocarpa***
96 ***dentata***
92 'Ethel's Gold'
96 ***glabrescens***
95 'Guardsman'
91 ***hupehensis*** var. ***obtusa*** 'Rufus'
96 ***kurzii*** KR 1501
96 ***microphylla***
95 ***obtusa aureus***
96 ***pogonopetala***
96 ***poteriifolia*** KW 6968
92 'Red Marbles'
95 ***reducta*** B&L 12091
96 'Rowancroft'
94 ***sinensis***
96 sp. SEP 492
92 'Tundra'
93 ***vexans***
96 ***vilmorinii*** 'Pendula'

SPARRMANNIA
96 ***ricinocarpa***

SPARTINA
91 ***pectinata*** 'Variegata'

SPATHICARPA
90 ***sagittifolia***

SPATHIPHYLLUM
96 'Adagio'
90 ***cannifolium***
90 ***cochlearispathum***
90 ***cuspidatum***
90 ***floribundum***
90 'Mauna Loa' 🏆
90 'McCoy'
90 ***patinii***

SPERGULARIA
95 ***marina***

SPHAERALCEA
93 Dixfield hybrids
95 ***parvifolia***
94 ***rivularis***

SPHAGNUM
96 ***fuscum***
96 ***magellanicum***
96 ***pulchrum***

SPHENOTOMA
91 ***gracilis***

SPILANTHES
96 ***acmella***
96 ***oleracea***

SPIRAEA
94 ***calcicola***
96 'County Park'
96 'Dingle Apricot'
96 'Dingle Gold'
87 ***japonica*** 'Bumalda'
95 – 'Coccinea'
94 – var. ***fortunei*** 'Ruberrima'
93 ***nipponica*** 'Rotundifolia'
96 ***vacciniifolia***
95 ***wilsonii***

STACHYS
95 ***balansae***
93 ***byzantina*** 'Margery Fish'
87 ***corsica***
96 ***heraclea***
96 'Hopleys Variegated'
96 ***macrantha*** 'Rosea Compacta'
96 – 'Violacea'
93 ***niveum***
96 ***tmolea***

STACHYTARPHETA
91 ***jamaicensis***

STACHYURUS
95 ***salicifolius***
89 ***spinosus***

STAEHELINA
93 ***uniflosculosa***

STANLEYA
90 ***pinnata***
88 ***pinnatifida***

STAPHYLEA
96 ***pringlei***

STEGNOGRAMMA
96 ***pozoi***

STELLARIA
96 ***ruscifolia***

STENANTHIUM
95 ***occidentale***
89 ***robustum***

STENOGLOTTIS
96 ***longifolia***
96 ***plicata***

STENOTUS
88 ***andersonii***

STEPHANANDRA
95 ***incisa*** 'Dart's Horizon'

STERNBERGIA
96 ***sicula*** 'John Marr' ex JRM 3186/75

STIPA
91 ***atropurpurea***
93 ***calensis***
94 ***krylovii***
94 ***spartea***
95 ***tirsa***
94 ***turkestanica***
94 ***zalesskyi***

STREPTOCARPUS
93 'Anna'
95 ***baudertii***
95 'Blue Angel' 🏆
95 ***buchananii***
95 ***compressus***
94 ***confusus***
96 'Constant Nymph' seedling'
94 ***cooksonii***
95 ***cooperi***
95 ***cyanandrus***
95 ***daviesii***
92 'Eira'
94 ***eylesii***
94 – subsp. ***silvicola***
95 ***fanniniae***
95 ***fasciatus***
94 ***galpinii***
94 ***goetzei***
96 ***grandis***
94 ***haygarthii***
95 'Holiday Blue' 🏆
93 hybrids
95 ***johannis*** 🏆
95 ***kentaniensis***
95 ***kirkii***
95 ***kungwensis***
94 ***latens***
93 'Lesley'
95 ***meyeri***
94 ***molweniensis***
93 'New Buckenham'
95 ***parviflorus***
95 ***pole-evansii***
95 ***polyanthus***
95 ***porphyrostachys***
95 ***primulifolius***
94 ***prolixus***
95 'Royal Mixed' 🏆
95 ***saundersii***
95 ***solenanthus***

STREPTOPUS
90 ***axillaris***
91 ***simplex***

STROBILANTHES
92 ***urticifolius***

STROMANTHE
90 ***porteana***
95 ***sanguinea*** var. ***spectabilis*** 🏆

STROPHANTHUS
93 ***divaricatus***

STYLIDIUM
94 ***caespitosum***
95 ***crassifolium*** 🏆

91 ***graminifolium***
STYLOMECON
93 ***heterophylla***
STYRAX
92 ***dasyanthus***
94 – var. ***cinerascens***
96 ***formosanus***
90 ***officinalis***
94 ***serrulatus***
92 ***wilsonii***
SUCCISA
93 sp. Orkney dwarf form
SUTERA
95 ***cordata*** 'Eight Bells'
94 ***diffusa***
92 ***pristisepala***
SWAINSONA
96 ***maccullochiana***
91 ***procumbens***
SWERTIA
95 ***komarovii*** JJH 93091003
90 ***longifolia***
91 ***petiolata***
SYMPHORICARPOS
96 ***albus*** 'Turesson'
92 x ***doorenbosii*** 'Erect'
SYMPHYANDRA
95 ***campanulata***
95 ***ossetica*** hybrids
SYMPHYTUM
94 ***ibericum*** variegated form
91 ***officinale*** 'Bohemicum'
SYNADENIUM
94 ***grantii***
94 – 'Rubrum'
SYNEILESIS
91 ***palmata***
SYNGONIUM
96 'Jenny'
SYNTHYRIS
95 ***missurica***
96 ***pinnatifida laciniata***
SYRINGA
95 x ***diversifolia*** 'William H. Judd'
94 ***emodi*** 'Aurea'
95 'Fountain'
92 x ***henryi***
87 x ***hyacinthiflora*** 'Alice Eastwood'
92 – 'Blue Hyacinth'
88 – 'Buffon'
92 – 'Clarke's Giant'
90 'Minuet'
90 'Miss Canada'
89 ***oblata***
89 x ***persica*** 'Gigantea'
91 x ***prestoniae*** 'Coral'
89 – 'Hiawatha'
91 – 'James Macfarlane'
93 – 'Kim'
91 – 'Nocturne'
92 ***pubescens*** subsp. ***julianae***
91 ***reticulata*** 'Ivory Silk'
94 ***sweginzowii*** 'Superba'
91 ***villosa***
89 ***vulgaris*** 'Alphonse Lavallée' (d)
89 – 'Ambassadeur'
95 – 'Aucubifolia'
89 – 'Charles X'
95 – 'Dingle Variegated'
89 – 'Etna'
89 – 'General John Pershing' (d)
87 – 'Lavaliensis'
89 – 'Maréchal de Bassompierre' (d)
89 – 'Maréchal Foch' (d)
90 – 'Marie Legraye'
87 – 'Monique Lemoine' (d)
87 – 'Night'
96 – 'Paul Deschanel' (d)
87 – 'Réaumur'
89 – 'Ruhm von Horstenstein'
89 – 'Souvenir d'Alice Harding' (d)
90 – 'William Robinson' (d)
90 ***wolfii***
96 ***yunnanensis*** 'Rosea'
SYZYGIUM
94 ***paniculatum***
TABERNAEMONTANA
96 ***divaricata***
TAIWANIA
92 ***cryptomerioides***
TALINUM
91 ***okanoganense*** pink-stemmed
92 ***parviflorum***
95 ***spinescens***
TANACETUM
89 ***bipinnatum***
95 ***coccineum*** 'Alfred'
93 – 'J.N. Twerdy'
92 – 'Jubilee Gem'
90 – 'Marjorie Robinson'
93 – 'Peter Pan'
95 – 'Red Dwarf'
88 – 'Red King'
91 – 'Sam Robinson'
87 – 'Silver Challenger'
89 ***dolichophyllum***
95 ***griffithii***
94 ***huronense***
95 ***nuttallii***
93 ***parthenium*** 'Golden Moss'
93 – 'Selma Tetra'
92 – 'Snowball' (d)
92 – 'Spirit'
92 – 'Sundew'
TAPEINOCHILOS
96 ***ananassae***
TARAXACUM
94 ***pamiricum***
TAXODIUM
93 ***distichum*** var. ***imbricatum***
95 – 'Pendens'
95 – 'Pendulum'
TAXUS
95 ***baccata*** f. ***adpressa***
91 – 'Cheshuntensis'
96 – 'David'
94 – 'Decora'
91 – 'Glauca'
93 – 'Gracilis Pendula'
92 – 'Grayswood Hill'
96 – 'Icicle'
96 – 'Judith'
92 – 'Lutea'
87 – 'Nana'
89 – 'Prostrata'
90 – 'Pyramidalis'
87 ***cuspidata*** 'Densa'
93 – 'Golden Jubilee'
95 – 'Luteobaccata'
91 – 'Minima'
90 x ***hunnewelliana*** 'Richard Horsey'
90 x ***media*** 'Halloriana'
91 – 'Kelseyi'
91 – 'Skalborg'
TECOMA
96 ***capensis*** 'Apricot'
94 – 'Lutea'
TELLIMA
95 ***grandiflora*** Alba Group
95 – 'Perky' JLS 86282SCCA
90 – 'Pinky'
TELOPEA
94 ***oreades***
TEPHROSERIS
92 ***takedanus***
TETRACLINIS
95 ***articulata***
TETRANEURIS
96 ***acaulis*** var. ***caespitosa*** K 92.258
90 – var. ***glabra***
92 ***acaulis ivesiana***
TETRATHECA
95 ***hirsuta***
TEUCRIUM
94 ***cossonii***
94 ***creticum***
94 ***parviflorum***
89 ***polium*** f. ***pii-fontii***
93 ***scoridifolia***
96 ***scorodonia*** 'Cae Rhos Lligwy' (v)
88 ***subspinosum roseum***
THALICTRUM
95 ***chelidonii***
88 ***delavayi*** 'Amethystine'
95 ***javanicum***
88 ***petaloides***
92 ***reniforme***
96 sp. B&SWJ 2159
THELYMITRA
96 ***antennifera***
THELYPTERIS
89 ***dentata***
THEMEDA
96 ***triandra*** subsp. ***japonica***
THERMOPSIS
96 ***barbata*** ACE 2298
THEVETIA
94 ***peruviana*** 'Alba'
THLASPI
96 ***alpestre***
89 ***alpinum*** subsp. ***auerswaldii***
94 – subsp. ***brevicaule***
96 ***cepaeifolium*** subsp. ***cenisium***
94 ***densiflorum***
96 ***montanum***
94 ***nevadense***
96 ***ochroleucum***
THRINAX
90 ***parviflora***
94 ***radiata***
THUJA
95 ***occidentalis*** 'Baurmanii'
87 – 'Cloth of Gold'
88 – 'Columbia'
95 – 'Cristata Argenteovariegata'
93 – 'Cuprea'
92 – 'Globosa Compacta Nana'
92 – 'Indomitable'
91 – 'Madurodam'
92 – 'Malonyana'
90 – 'Mastersii'
95 – 'Perk Vlaanderen' (v)
94 – 'Pumila Sudworth'
90 – 'Robusta'
88 – 'Semperaurea'
96 – 'Smaragd Variegated'
92 – 'Vervaeneana'
91 ***orientalis*** 'Berckman'
94 – 'Filiformis Erecta'
96 – 'Golden Ball'
93 – 'Golden Sceptre'
91 – 'Green Cone'
89 – 'Hillieri'
93 – 'Minima Aurea'
95 ***plicata*** 'Brabant'
92 – 'Extra Gold'
88 – 'Savill Gardens'
95 – 'Windsor Gold'
96 ***standishii***
THYMUS
92 ***carnosus*** 'Argenteus'
90 ***corsicus***
94 ***epiroticus***
91 ***hirsutus***
91 ***hyemalis*** 'Albus'
94 ***insertus***
87 ***serpyllum*** 'Little Heath'
92 – 'Silver Dew'
88 – 'Winter Beauty'
87 'Southcombe Spreader'
89 ***striatus***
96 'Valerie Finnis'
96 'Widecombe'
88 'Wintergold'
THYSANOTUS
96 ***patersonii***
96 ***tuberosus***
TIARELLA
95 'Maple Leaf'
96 ***polyphylla*** 'Axminster Variegated'
TIGRIDIA
94 ***douglasii***
96 ***durangense***
95 – dwarf form
92 ***van-houttei***
TILIA
93 ***cordata*** 'Dainty Leaf'

91 x *flavescens*
93 *koreana*

TILLANDSIA
92 *achyrostachys*
92 *aëranthos*
92 *albertiana*
95 *albida*
92 *anceps*
92 *andreana*
92 *andrieuxii*
92 *araujei*
92 *arhiza*
92 *atroviridipetala*
92 *bartramii*
92 *bergeri*
92 *cacticola*
92 *capitata* 'Peach'
92 – 'Rubra'
92 *carlsoniae*
92 *chiapensis*
92 *complanata*
92 *compressa*
92 *concolor*
92 *crocata*
92 *disticha*
92 *duratii*
92 *ehlersiana*
92 *elizabethiae*
92 *erubescens*
92 *exserta*
92 *fasciculata*
92 *festucoides*
92 *flexuosa*
92 *floribunda*
92 *funckiana*
95 *gardneri*
92 *gymnobotrya*
92 *hammeri*
92 *harrisii*
93 *himmorum*
92 *incarnata*
93 *ionantha* 'Blushing Bride'
93 – 'Fireball'
93 – 'Fuego'
95 – var. *ionantha*
92 *ionantha stricta*
92 *ionantha* var. *vanhyningii*
92 *ixioides*
92 *jaliscomonticola*
92 *kautskyi*
92 *kirchhoffiana*
93 *lampropoda*
92 *latifolia* var. *divaricata*
92 *leiboldiana*
95 *lindenii* ♀
92 *loliacea*
92 *lucida*
92 *macdougallii*
92 *makoyana*
92 *mallemontii*
92 *massiliense* var. *vivipara*
92 *mauryana*
95 *melanocrater tricolor*
92 *meridionalis*
92 *mima*
92 *mitlaensis*
92 *monadelpha*
92 *multicaulis*
92 *multiflora*
92 *myosura*
92 *neglecta*
92 *paleacea*
92 *paucifolia*
92 *paucifolia prolifera*
92 *plagiotropica*
92 *plumosa*
93 x *polita*
93 *prodigiosa*
95 *pruinosa*
92 *pseudobaileyi*
92 *pueblensis*
92 *purpurea*
92 *recurvata*
92 *roland-gosselinii*
92 *schatzlii*
92 *schiedeana* subsp. *glabrior*
92 *schiedeana major*
92 *setacea*
92 *straminea*
92 *streptocarpa*
92 *streptophylla*
95 *stricta*
92 *tectorum*
92 *tenuifolia*
92 – var. *saxicola*
92 – var. *tenuifolia*
92 *tricholepis*
92 *tricolor*
95 *usneoides*
93 *utriculata*
92 *variabllis*
92 *vernicosa*
93 *vicentina* var. *glabra*
92 *viridiflora*

TINANTIA
94 *undulata*

TIPUANA
94 *tipu*

TITHONIA
92 *rotundifolia*

TOFIELDIA
95 *glutinosa* var. *brevistyla*
96 *pusilla*

TONESTUS
91 *pygmaeus*

TORREYA
93 *californica*
90 *grandis*
94 *nucifera*
90 – 'Spreadeagle'

TORTULA
96 *princeps*
96 *ruralis* subsp. *ruraliformis*

TOWNSENDIA
94 'Boulder'
96 *eximia*
96 *glabella*
94 *grandiflora*
90 *hirsuta*
96 *jonesii* var. *tunulosa*

TRACHYMENE
90 *humilis*

TRADESCANTIA
90 x *andersoniana* 'Lilacina Plena'
88 – 'Purple Glow'
89 – 'Taplow Crimson'
87 *brevicaulis caerulea*
95 *cerinthoides* 'Variegata' ♀
93 *chilensis*
95 *fluminensis* 'Tricolor Minima' ♀
90 *spathacea*
95 – 'Vittata' ♀
92 *tabulaemontana*
93 *zebrina* 'Purpusii' ♀
93 – 'Quadricolor' (v) ♀

TRAGOPOGON
90 *ruber*

TREVESIA
89 *palmata* 'Micholitzii'

TRICHOCOLEA
96 *tomentella*

TRICHOPHORUM
96 *cespitosum*

TRICYRTIS
94 *flava*
89 *formosana* 'Variegata'
90 *hirta* dwarf form
91 *japonica* 'Kinkazan'
93 *lambertii*
93 *puberula*

TRIDENS
95 *flavus*

TRIENTALIS
96 *borealis*

TRIFOLIUM
93 *pratense* 'Harlequin' (v)
93 – 'Purple Velvet'
93 *repens* 'Variegatum'
95 *stellatum*
96 *uniflorum*

TRILLIUM
94 *chloropetalum* white
96 *decumbens*
92 *discolor*
92 *erectum roseum*
96 'Hokkaido'
93 *lancifolium*
92 *nervosum*
92 *pusillum*
92 *rugelii* pink

TRIOSTEUM
91 *erythrocarpum*

TRIPLEUROSPERMUM
93 *maritimum*

TRIPTEROSPERMUM
96 *cordifolium*
96 *lanceolatum*
96 *taiwanense*

TRITELEIA
94 *bridgesii*

TRITICUM
92 *spelta*

TRITONIA
95 *deusta*
95 *hyalina*
95 'Lynette'

TROCHOCARPA
96 *gunnii*
96 *thymifolia*

TROLLIUS
88 x *cultorum* 'Byrne's Giant'
90 – 'Empire Day'
90 – 'Glory of Leiden'
94 – 'John Rider'
90 – 'Meteor'
90 – 'Orange Glow'
90 – 'Orangekönig'
90 – 'Oranje Nassau'
90 – 'T. Smith'
94 – 'Taleggio'
90 – 'Yellow Beauty'
95 *riederianus*

TROPAEOLUM
94 *majus* 'Crimson Velvet'
96 – 'Indian Chief'
94 *peregrinum*
95 x *tenuirostre*

TSUGA
93 *canadensis* 'Ammerland'
94 – 'Compacta'
87 – 'Dawsonia'
87 – 'Essex'
87 – 'Gentsch White' (v)
92 – 'Gracilis'
87 – 'Greenwood Lake'
96 – 'Minima'
92 *caroliniana*
94 *chinensis*
87 – var. *tchekiangensis*
87 *dumosa*
92 *heterophylla* 'Green Mantle'
92 – 'Laursen's Column'
93 *mertensiana*
96 – dwarf form
92 – 'Glauca'
90 *sieboldii*
89 *yunnanensis*

TUBERARIA
89 *globulariifolia*

TULBAGHIA
91 *capensis* 'Variegata'

TULIPA
89 'Aga Khan' (2)
91 'Akela' (5)
95 'Amulet' (3)
95 'Anneke' (3)
89 'Annie Salomons' (14)
93 'Arie Alkemade's Memor' (2)
94 'Arlington' (5)
94 'Asta Nielsen' (5)
91 'Astarte' (3)
92 *aximensis* (15)
91 'Baby Doll' (2)
94 'Bandoeng' (3)
91 'Baronesse' (5)
91 Beauty Queen (1)
91 'Bird of Paradise' (10)
91 'Black Diamond' (5)
93 'Black Swan' (5)
93 'Blizzard' (3)
89 'Blushing Beauty' (5)
89 'Blushing Bride' (5)
95 'Bruno Walter' (3)
91 *buhseana* (15)
94 'Cabaret' (6)
95 'Caland' (10)
95 'Capri' (4) ♀
95 'Cashmir' (5)
94 'Charles Needham' (5)
89 'Chatham' (5)
91 'China Lady' (14) ♀
91 'Christmas Dream' (1)
95 *clusiana* f. *clusianoides* (15)

94 'Compliment' (6)
89 'Compostella' (14)
94 'Copland's Purple' (5)
95 'Coriolan' (3)
94 'Corrie Kok' (3)
94 'Crispa Pink' (7)
89 'Dante' (2)
93 'Daydream' (4)
94 'Delano' (3)
89 'Demeter' (3) 🏆
91 'Diplomate' (4)
94 'Doctor James Parkinson' (3)
95 'Dover' 🏆
89 'Dreamboat' (14)
91 'Dreamland' (5)
95 'Duke of Wellington' (5)
89 'Dutch Princess' (3)
91 'Early Glory' (3)
94 'Early Light' (1)
94 'Easter Fire' (5)
94 'El Toreador' (2)
89 'Ellen Willmott' (6)
95 'Engadin' (14) 🏆
95 'Esther' (5)
94 'Etude' (3)
93 'Fidelio' (3) 🏆
91 'Fire Queen' (3)
94 'Floradale' (4)
95 'Florosa' (8)
91 'Françoise' (3)
94 'Frankfurt' (3)
94 'G.W. Leak' (5)
95 'Garanza' (2)
91 'Gerbrand Kieft' (11)
95 'Golden Eagle' (13)
94 'Golden Eddy' (3)
94 'Golden Show' (3)
94 'Goldenes Deutschland' (4)
88 ***goulimyi*** (15)
95 'Goya' (2)
94 'Graceful' (14)
95 'Hadley' (1)
94 'Henry Ford' (5)
93 'Hermione' (11)
93 'High Society' (3)
95 ***hissarica*** (15)
89 'Hocus Pocus' (5)
95 ***humilis*** 'Pallida' (15)
93 – 'Violet Queen' (15)
94 'Humoresque' (13)
95 ***iliensis*** (15)
94 'Inglescombe Yellow' (5)
91 'Ivory Floradale' (4)
94 'James V. Forrestal' (10)
94 'Jan Vermeer' (2)
91 'Jenny' (1)
93 'Johann Gutenberg' (7)
91 ***julia*** (15)
91 'Juri Gagarin' (14)
93 ***karabaghensis*** (15)
93 'Koningin Wilhelmina' (4) 🏆
93 'Kryptos' (5)
91 'Lady Montgomery' (11)
91 'Laverock' (7)
94 'Libretto' (3)
93 'Lighting Sun' (4)
93 'Lilac Perfection' (11)
94 'Longfellow' (14)
89 'Lutea Major' (10)
91 'Majestic' (14)
93 'Marjolein' (6) 🏆
94 'Marquette' (2)
94 'Maskerade' (5)
93 'Meissner Porzellan' (3)
93 'Mirella' (3) 🏆
95 'Mirjoran' (3)
91 'Modern Style' (5)
94 'Most Miles' (3) 🏆
96 'Mrs John T. Scheepers' (5) 🏆
95 'Murillo Maxima' (2)
89 'Musical' (3)
89 'Niphetos' (5)
91 'Noranda' (7)
93 'Olympic Flame' (4)
93 'Olympic Gold' (4)
88 'Orange Boy' (12)
95 'Orange Cassini' (3)
94 'Orange Goblet' (4)
91 'Orange King' (5)
94 'Orange Monarch' (3)
96 'Orange Toronto' (14)
95 'Orange Wonder' (3)
94 'Ornament' (3)
90 ***orphanidea*** 'Splendens' (15)
91 'Oscar' (3)
94 'Pandit Nehru' (3)
95 'Paul Crampel' (2)
89 Peacock strain (*greigii* × *kaufmanniana*)
95 'Peer Gynt' (3)
93 'Perfecta' (10)
89 'Pink Emperor' (13)
90 ***planifolia*** (15)
94 'Polo' (13)
89 'Primrose' (12)
89 'Prince Charles' (3)
94 'Princess Elizabeth' (5)
92 'Princesse Charmante' (14)
93 'Prinses Margriet' (3)
94 'Red Present' (3)
91 'Red Reflection' (14)
95 'Red Surprise' (14) 🏆
94 'Rheingold' (2)
92 'Rhodos' (5)
93 'Robinea' (3)
95 'Rockery Master' (14)
91 'Rococo' (10)
91 'Rosanna' (14)
91 'Rosella' (3)
91 'Rosy Queen' (2)
91 'Salmon Parrot' (10)
93 'San Marino' (5)
89 'Show Girl' (5)
94 'Sint Maarten' (1)
91 'Smyrna' (14)
93 'Snow Queen' (2)
95 ***sosnowskyi*** (15)
94 'Sothis' (7)
94 'Spalding' (3)
91 'Sun Dance' (14)
94 'Sunkist' (5)
93 'Sussex' (5)
92 'Sylvia Warder' (14)
89 'Tambour Maître' (3)
89 'Tarakan' (5)
95 'Teheran' (3)
94 'Thule' (3)
89 'Timay'
95 'Topscore' (3)
91 'Treasure' (14)
91 'Trendsetter' (3)
88 ***vvedenskyi*** 'Josef Marks' (15)
90 – 'Orange Sunset' (15)
95 'Wallflower' (5)
89 'Water Lily'
94 'White Alba' (7)
91 'Wienerwald' (3)
94 'Wilhelm Kordes' (2)
94 'Wim van Est' (5)
91 'Wirosa' (11)
91 'Yellow Parrot' (10)
89 'Yellow River' (3)

TUTCHERIA
89 ***spectabilis***

TYPHA
96 ***minima*** var. ***gracilis***

UGNI
90 ***molinae*** 'Variegata'

ULEX
92 ***europaeus*** 'Dubloon'
95 – 'Strictus'
93 ***gallii***
96 ***minor***

ULMUS
89 ***glabra*** 'Lutescens'
92 'Louis van Houtte'
90 ***minor*** 'Sarniensis'
95 ***procera***
95 – 'Argenteovariegata'
95 'Regal'

UNCINIA
96 ***divaricata***
93 ***egmontiana***
95 ***ferruginea***
94 ***rubra*** var. ***phallax***

UNGNADIA
87 ***speciosa***

URSINIA
92 ***chrysanthemoides***
91 ***sericea***

URTICA
96 ***pilulifera dodartii***

UTRICULARIA
93 ***aurea***
93 ***caerulea***
93 ***fibrosa***
94 ***pusilla***
94 ***simplex***

UVULARIA
95 ***caroliniana***

VACCARIA
96 ***hispanica***

VACCINIUM
92 ***angustifolium***
93 – Newfoundland form
94 ***bracteatum***
90 ***consanguineum***
93 ***constablei***
92 ***corymbosum*** 'Blue Ray' (F)
89 – 'Tifblue' (F)
89 – 'Woodward' (F)
94 ***delavayi*** 'Drummondii'
93 ***deliciosum***
95 ***eriophyllum***
94 ***erythrinum***
94 ***erythrocarpum***
95 ***griffithianum***
92 ***membranaceum***
92 ***myrsinites***
91 ***nubigenus***
96 ***ovalifolium***
96 ***oxycoccos*** var. ***intermedium***
96 ***parvifolium***
92 ***sprengelii***
94 ***uliginosum***

VALLEA
93 ***stipularis***

VEITCHIA
92 ***merrillii***

VELLA
95 ***spinosa***

VERBASCUM
94 'Bill Bishop'
94 ***blattaria*** 'Pink Beauty'
96 'Bold Queen'
95 (Cotswold Group) 'Bridal Bouquet'
96 (Cotswold Group) 'C.L. Adams'
92 (Cotswold Group) 'Hartleyi'
96 ***elegantissimum***
89 'Golden Bush'
89 ***pestalozzae***
96 ***phoeniceum*** 'Candy Spires'
94 'Turkey'
95 ***undulatum***
96 ***virgatum***

VERBENA
92 ***bipinnatifida***
96 ***canadensis***
92 'Cardinal'
95 'Cleopatra'
96 'Cupido'
95 ***litoralis***
95 'New Ophelia'
95 'Ophelia'
94 'Othello'
96 'Peaches and Cream'
91 ***peruviana*** Japanese form
96 'Red Cascade'
93 ***rigida*** 'Lilacina'
95 'Romance Silver'
94 'Rose du Barry'
95 Sandy Series 🏆
96 ***scabridoglandulosa***
95 ***stricta*** JLS 88008WI
94 ***tenera***

VERNONIA
95 ***baldwinii***
93 ***mespilifolia***
95 ***nudiflora***

VERONICA
87 ***armena rosea***
96 ***austriaca*** subsp. ***teucrium*** 'Blue Fountain'
88 ***cusickii***
87 × ***cynarium***
94 ***dabneyi***
90 'Green Mound'
95 ***longifolia*** 'Incarnata'
96 ***orientalis***
93 ***prostrata*** 'Pavlava Hills'
95 ***schmidtiana*** var. ***bandaiana***
93 ***spicata*** 'Mori's Form'
94 ***subsessilis***

94 – 'Blau Pyramide'
96 ***sumilensis***
90 ***tauricola*** from Ala Dag
93 ***teucrioides***
96 ***thessalonica***
94 ***thymoides***
93 ***virense***
88 ***virgata***
95 ***waldsteiniana***

VIBURNUM

87 'Aldenhamensis'
91 ***calvum***
91 ***dentatum*** var. ***pubescens*** 'Longifolium'
89 ***dilatatum*** 'Erie'
94 – f. ***xanthocarpum***
95 ***grandiflorum***
92 – Foetens Group
92 ***hupehense***
91 ***ichangense***
91 ***kansuense***
93 ***koreanum***
96 ***lantana*** 'Xanthocarpum'
94 ***nudum***
91 ***opulus*** 'Andrews'
91 – 'Apricot'
92 – 'Flore Pleno'
91 – 'Hans'
92 – 'Harvest Gold'
95 – 'Summer Gold'
89 – 'Wentworth'
91 ***parvifolium***
92 ***plicatum*** 'Rosace'
92 – 'Roseum'
92 ***propinquum***
92 ***prunifolium***
95 ***purdomii***
94 ***sargentii*** 'Susquehanna'
93 ***sempervirens***
92 ***setigerum sulcatum***
93 ***sieboldii*** 'Seneca'
92 ***tinus*** 'Little Bognor'
94 – 'Prostratum'
94 – 'Strictum'
96 ***trilobum***
91 ***veitchii***

VICIA

89 ***bithynica***

VICTORIA

90 ***amazonica***
90 ***cruziana***

VILLADIA

91 ***ramossisima***

VINCA

92 ***difformis argentea***
96 ***major*** 'Sissinghurst'
96 – 'Starlight'
94 ***minor*** 'Spring Morning'

VIOLA

90 'Adam's Gold' (Va)
92 'Agnes Susannah'
94 'Alys' (Va)
95 'Ann Robb' (ExV)
89 'Arlington' (C)
92 'Avalanche' (Va)
95 'Baby Blue'
92 'Baby Franjo'
92 'Bambini' (Va)
90 'Barbara Swan' (ExV)
95 'Bates Green Purple'
95 'Beatrice' (Vtta)
95 'Benjie' (Va)
94 'Berna'
90 'Beth'
90 ***betonicifolia*** white
95 'Betty Grace' (Va)
94 'Black Diamond' (Va)
94 'Black Velvet'
89 ***blanda***
95 'Blue Haze'
92 'Blue Heaven' (Va)
95 'Blue Lace' (Va)
92 'Blue Perfection' (Va)
96 'Blue Princess'
91 'Blue Ripple'
92 'Blue Skies' (C)
90 'Blue Waves'
87 'Bob's Bedder'
91 'Bonnie Heather' (Va)
95 ***bubanii***
89 ***camschatalorum***
95 ***canadensis***
89 ***canina*** subsp. ***montana***
89 'Captivation'
96 ***cazorlensis***
92 'Cendrillon' (Vt)
89 ***cenisia***
95 'Chameleon'
90 'Cheekie Chappie'
94 'Cindy' (Va)
92 'Colwall' (C)
96 'Comte de Chambord' (dVt)
92 'Constellation'
96 Cornish indigenous mauve
96 ***cornuta compacta***
94 ***cornuta*** 'Foliis Aureis'
90 – pale blue
95 – 'Violacea'
96 'Coronation'
94 ***crassa***
89 ***crassiuscula***
95 'Cream Sensation' (Va)
92 'Cuty' (Va)
92 CW 5021
94 ***delphinantha***
93 'Dirty Molly'
92 'Double Blue' (dVt)
92 'Double Russian' (dVt)
95 'Dulcie Rhoda' (Va)
95 'Ednaston Gem'
93 'Elizabeth Robb' (FP)
91 'Evelyn Jackson' (Va)
95 ***eximia***
90 'Fairy Tales' (Va)
96 ***flettii***
94 'Gemma' (Va)
95 'George Lee'
93 'George Rowley' (FP)
93 'Gloriole'
95 ***gracilis*** 'Major'
90 'Haze' (Va)
95 'Hazel Jean' (Va)
94 'Helen' (Va)
94 'Highland Night'
94 'Honey' (Va)
91 'Horrie' (Va)
93 'Hyacintha' (C)
95 ***incisa***
93 'Irene Missen'
94 'Ivory'
94 'Jack Frost' (FP)
96 'Jack Simpson'
93 'James Christie' (FP)
94 'Jamie' (Va)
88 'Jane' (Va)
94 'Jeannie' (Va)
90 'Jenny Wren' (Va)
93 'Joan Christie' (FP)
96 'Jodie' (Va)
93 'Joe Millet' (FP)
95 'John Fielding' (Va)
96 'John Raddenbury' (Vt)
91 'John Rodger' (SP)
95 Joker Series (P) ♀
96 'June' (SP)
95 'Kadischa' (Va)
94 'Karen' (Va)
96 'Kathleen Hoyle' (ExV)
90 'Kathleen Williams' (ExV)
94 'Kizzy' (Va)
95 'Lady Finnyoon' (Va)
96 'Lady Jane' (Vt)
88 'Lady May'
96 'Lavender Lady'
95 'Lee' (Va)
92 'Lindy'
91 'Lizzie's Favourite' (Va)
96 'Love Duet'
94 'Lulu' (Va)
96 'Macgregor's Moth' (Va)
94 ***maculata***
89 'Magic Lantern'
87 'Major'
96 ***mandshurica***
95 – 'Bicolor'
94 – 'Ikedaeana'
90 ***mandshurica triangularis bicolor***
90 'Mandy Miller' (Va)
95 'Margaret' (Va)
92 'Marquis de Brazais' (Vt)
96 'Mary Dawson' (Va)
94 'Mattie' (Va)
93 'Mavis Tuck'
93 'May Roberts' (ExV)
92 'Melita'
93 'Midnight' (Va)
89 'Moonshadow'
92 'Moonshine'
91 'Moseley Bedder'
96 'Mother's Day'
90 'Mrs Alex Forrest' (ExV)
96 'Mrs Pinehurst' (Vt)
93 'Mrs Reid's French'
94 'Nancy Jean' (Va)
87 'Nickie's Blue' (C)
95 'Nimrod' (Va)
96 'Noni' (Vt)
93 'Nora May' (Va)
93 ***nuttallii vallicola***
93 ***odorata*** 'Aurea'
90 – blue double
90 – 'Caerulea Plena'
96 – 'Wellsiana' (Vt) ♀
89 'Old Blue'
88 'Old Jordans'
96 'Orchid Pink' (Vt)
92 'Oxbrook Cream'
94 'Pamela' (Va)
96 'Pam's Fancy' (ExV)
90 'Peggy Brookes' (FP)
95 'Penny Black' (Va)
94 ***perinensis*** JCA 992.600
94 'Piglets' (Vt)
95 'Piper' (Va)
94 'Pixie' (Va)
96 'Prince Henry' (T)
96 'Princess Alexandra' (Vt)
95 Princess Series ♀
94 'Purple Radiance'
96 'Quatre Saisons' (Vt)
96 'Rawson's White' (Vt)
93 ***riviniana*** 'Autumn White'
90 'Roem van Aalsmeer'
92 'Royal Picotee'
95 ***rupestris***
96 – blue
93 ***scariensis***
95 ***schariensis*** JCA 993.150
96 'Scottish Yellow' (Va)
96 ***sempervirens***
94 ***septentrionalis*** 'Rubra'
93 ***sheltonii***
94 ***sororia*** 'Red Sister'
91 'Spey' (C)
93 'Spode Blue'
93 'Stewart William' (FP)
92 'Sulphur Queen'
96 'Sunshine' (Va)
96 'Susan' (SP)
92 'Sybil Cornfield'
94 'Tamberti' (Vt)
91 'The Clevedon Violet' (Vt)
96 'Tina Whittaker' (Vt)
96 'Toulouse'
96 'Translucent Blue'
96 ***tricolor*** subsp. ***macedonica***
89 – subsp. ***subalpina***
89 'Triumph' (Vt)
91 'Tropical Waves'
96 'Tuscany' (Vt)
95 Ultima Series ♀
94 'Vignette' (Va)
92 x ***visseriana***
95 x ***visseriana lutea***
96 'Wendy' (SP)
95 'Wheatley White'
96 'White Czar' (Vt)
91 'White Waves'
93 'Woodlands Gold' (Va)
95 'Yellow Snowdon'
95 'Yoyo' (Va)

VITALIANA

92 ***primuliflora*** subsp. ***cinerea***
95 – subsp. ***praetutiana compacta***

VITEX

87 ***agnus-castus*** 'Albus'
94 – 'Blue Spire'
92 ***incisa***
91 ***negundo*** var. ***heterophylla***

VITIS

93 'Alden' (O/W)
93 'Aris' (O/W)
92 ***betulifolia***
93 'Canadice'
94 ***coignetiae*** cut-leaved
96 – Soja 457
92 ***davidii***
91 – var. ***cyanocarpa***
95 'Espiran' (G)
96 ***flexuosa***
93 'Glenora' (F)
88 'Isabella' (O/B)
88 ***piasezkii***

93 'Ramdas' (O/W)
93 'Vanessa'
93 'Venus'
93 ***vinifera*** 'Alzey Red' (O/R)
95 – 'Angers Frontignan' (G/O/B)
95 – 'Ascot Citronelle' (G/W)
95 – 'Auvergne Frontignan' (G/O/W)
95 – 'Black Prince' (G/B)
95 – 'Cote House Seedling' (O/W)
93 – 'Emerald Riesling' (O/W)
95 – 'Grizzley Frontignan' (G/R)
91 – 'Madame Mathias Muscat'
95 – 'Madeira Frontignan' (G/R)
96 – 'Melon de Bourgogne' (O/W)
93 – 'Nobling' (O/W)
93 – 'Pinot Meunier' (O/B)
95 – 'Regner' (O/W)
93 – 'Rotberger' (O/G/B)
93 – 'Traminer' (O/W)
91 – 'Wabetta'
95 – 'West's St Peter's' (G/B)
93 ***wilsoniae***

VITTADINIA
94 ***australis***

VRIESEA
92 ***barclayana*** var. ***barclayana***
92 – var. ***minor***
92 ***cereicola***
95 ***duvaliana*** 🏆
92 ***espinosae***
92 'Favorite'
90 ***fenestralis***
90 ***fosteriana*** 🏆
90 – 'Red Chestnut'
90 ***gigantea***
92 Hitchcockiana Group
92 'Margot'
90 ***platynema***
90 – 'Variegata'
95 ***psittacina*** 🏆
92 ***rauhii***
91 ***splendens*** 'Fire'
92 ***tequendamae***
92 Tiffany Group
92 ***zamorensis***

WAHLENBERGIA
91 ***gloriosa*** white
92 ***lobelioides***
94 'Tasmanian Skies'

WASHINGTONIA
90 ***lindenii***

WATSONIA
96 'Indian Orange'
91 ***marginata alba***
96 peach hybrid
94 ***socium***
96 sp. SH 89
87 'Starspike'
96 ***stenosiphon***
92 Tresco Hybrids

WEIGELA
96 'Abel Carrière Golden'
89 'Conquête'
96 'Duet'
95 'Féerie'
95 'Fiesta' 🏆
94 ***florida*** 'Albovariegata'
94 – 'Langtrees'
96 – 'Magee'
96 – 'Pink Princess'
92 – var. ***venusta***
91 ***lonicera***
95 'Majestueux'
96 'Olympiade' (v)
92 ***praecox***
90 'Stelzneri'
89 ***subsessilis***
89 'Van Houttei'

WIGANDIA
93 ***caracasana***

WISTERIA
94 ***russelliana***
96 ***sinensis*** 'Prematura Alba'

WOODSIA
96 ***ilvensis***
93 ***mollis***

WOODWARDIA
94 ***obtusa***
90 ***orientalis***
96 sp. from Emei Shan, China
93 ***virginica***

WULFENIA
92 ***amherstiana***
92 ***baldaccii***
92 × ***suendermanii***

XANTHORRHOEA
94 ***quadrangulata***
94 ***thorntonii***

XANTHOSOMA
90 ***violaceum***

YUCCA
90 ***aloifolia*** 'Purpurea'
92 ***filamentosa*** 'Schneefichte'
95 ***flaccida*** striated cultivar
89 ***gloriosa*** 'Albovariegata'
95 ***recurvifolia*** 'Marginata'
96 – 'Variegata'
94 ***treculeana***
95 'Vomerensis'
96 ***whipplei*** var. ***caespitosa***
95 – JLS 86188LACA

ZAMIOCULCAS
90 ***zamiifolia***

ZANTEDESCHIA
96 ***aethiopica*** 'Childsiana'
91 ***angustiloba***
92 'Aztec Gold'
94 'Candy'
93 'Carmine Red'
94 'Christina'
94 'Dominique'
92 'Dusky Pink'
91 'Galaxy'
94 'Garnet'
92 'Golden Affair'
91 'Golden Sun'
94 'Jubilee'
91 'Lady Luck'
96 'Little Suzy'
93 'Monique'
94 'Number 13'
94 'Oriental Sun'
94 'Pink Opal'
94 'Yvonne'

ZANTHOXYLUM
95 ***ailanthoides***
92 ***schinifolium***

ZAUSCHNERIA
89 ***californica*** subsp. ***cana*** 'Splendens Plena'
96 ***californica etteri***
96 ***californica*** subsp. ***latifolia*** RMRF 93-0443

ZEPHYRANTHES
96 'Panama Pink'
96 ***traubii***

ZIERIA
88 ***arborescens***

ZIGADENUS
93 ***fremontii***
89 ***glaberrimus***
93 ***leimanthoides***
91 ***muscitoxicus***

ZINNIA
91 ***grandiflora***

ZIZIA
96 ***aptera***

ZIZIPHORA
93 ***pamiroalaica***

Hardy Plant Society Search List

The following plants, for which no source is known in the British Isles, are being sought by the Hardy Plant Society for its members and for collections held by other societies and individuals. If any one knows the whereabouts of any items, seed or plant, on this list, in the British Isles or overseas, would they please contact:-

Mrs Jean Sambrook, Garden Cottage, 214 Ruxley Lane, West Ewell, Surrey KT19 9EZ

ABRONIA
umbellata
ACAENA
caesiiglauca 'Frikart'
ACONITUM
delavayi
fletcherianum
pulchellum
ADONIS
dahurica 'Pleniflora'
AESCULUS
'Autumn Splendor'
x ***carnea*** 'O'Neill'
parviflora var. ***serotina***
– – 'Rogers'
pavia var. ***flavescens***
– 'Humilis'
AGAPANTHUS
'Dorothy Palmer'
nutans
praecox 'Aureovariegatus'
'Rosemary'
'Victoria'
AGERATUM
orientale 'Leichtlinii'
– 'Pallidum'
AJUGA
pyramidalis 'Metallica Crispa Purpurea'
– 'Metallica Crispa Rubra'
reptans 'Bronze Beauty'
– 'Burgundy Lace'
– 'Compacta'
– 'Cristata'
– 'Gaiety'
– 'Jungle Beauty Improved'
– 'Mini Crisp Red'
– 'Nana Compacta'
– 'Pink Beauty'
– 'Pink Silver'
– 'Purple Brocade'
– 'Royalty'
– 'Silver Beauty'
AKEBIA
quinata 'Alba'
– 'Rosea'
– 'Shirobana'
– 'Variegata'
ALLIUM
protensum
ALSTROEMERIA
'Afterglow'
'Ballerina'
caryophyllea 'Alba'
haemantha 'Parigo Charm'
'Sonata'
AMARYLLIS
belladonna 'Barberton'
– 'Cape Town'
– 'Elata'
– 'Jagersfontein'
– 'Maxima'
– 'Rosea'
– 'Rosea Perfecta'
– Spectabilis Tricolor = 'Spectabilis'
AMELANCHIER
x ***grandiflora*** 'Autumn Sunset'
– 'Cumulus'
– 'Prince Charles'
– 'Prince William'
– 'Princess Diana'
ANEMONE
glauciifolia
x ***hybrida*** 'Beauté Parfait'
– 'Brilliant'
– 'Collerette'
– 'Herbstrose'
– 'Herzblut'
– 'Lady Ardilaun'
– 'Lord Ardilaun'
– 'Magdalena Uhink'
– 'Magenta'
– 'Mignon'
– 'Stuttgard'
– 'Treasure'
– 'Turban'
– 'Vase d'Argent'
nemorosa 'Rubra Plena'
tenuifolia
ANTHEMIS
tinctoria 'Moonlight'
– 'Perry's Variety'
ARISAEMA
angustina
ARISTOLOCHIA
moupinensis
ARMERIA
maritima white foliage
ARTEMISIA
ifranensis
ARUM
longispathum
orientale subsp. ***danicum***
ASCLEPIAS
tuberosa 'Gerbe d'Or'
ASPARAGUS
tenuifolius
ASPHODELINE
amurensis 'Flore Pleno'
lutea 'Flore Pleno'
ASTER
amellus 'Bessie Chapman'
paternus
thomsonii 'Winchmore Hill'
ASTILBE
x ***arendsii*** 'Mars'
japonica 'Aureoreticulata'
ASYNEUMA
campanuloides
AUBRIETA
'Aileen'
'King of the Purples'
'Purple Splendour'
BAPTISIA
perfoliata
BELLIS
perennis 'Bunter Teppich'
– 'Chevreuse'
– 'Double Bells'
– 'Eliza'
– 'Helichrysiflora'
– 'Lilliput Rose'
– 'Lutea'
– 'Madame Crousse'
– 'Mavourneen'
– 'Mount Etna'
– 'Pink Buttons'
– 'Rubriflora'
– 'Shrewley Gold' (v)
– 'String of Pearls'
– 'Tuberosa Monstrosa'
– 'Victoria'
sylvestris
BERGENIA
crassifolia 'Variegata'
'Walter Kienli'
BERKHEYA
macrophylla
BETA
vulgaris 'Variegata'
BOMAREA
andimarcana
carderi
BRASSICA
Four Seasons Cabbage
BRUNNERA
macrophylla 'Blaukuppel'
BULBINELLA
modesta
BUPLEURUM
ranunculoides 'Canalease'
CACCINIA
macrantha
CALCEOLARIA
integrifolia white
CALTHA
laeta var. ***alpestris***
leptosepala 'Grandiflora'
– var. ***leptosepala*** blue flowered
novae-zelandiae
palustris Elata Group
– 'Pallida Plena'
– 'Pleurisepala'
– 'Purpurascens'
– 'Semiplena'
– Silvestris Group
CALYSTEGIA
gigantea
CAMPANULA
'Fergusonii'
'Gremlin'
'Pamela'
persicifolia 'Spetchley'
'Profusion'
rapunculoides 'Plena'
trachelium 'Versicolor'
'Woodstock'
zoysii f. ***alba***
CANNA
'Feuerzauber'
x ***generalis*** 'America'
'Liebesglut'
CARDAMINE
nemorosa 'Plena'
CARPINUS
betulus 'Albovariegata'
– 'Variegata'
caroliniana 'Pyramidalis'
CARYOPTERIS
x ***clandonensis*** 'Blue Mist'
– 'Dark Knight'
CATANANCHE
caerulea 'Perry's White'
CENTAUREA
atropurpurea 'Alba'
CENTRANTHUS
ruber 'Bragg's Variety'
CERCIS
canadensis 'Appalachian Red'
– 'Pinkbud'
– 'Royal White'
– 'Silver Cloud'
– 'Wither's Pink Charm'
CHAEROPHYLLUM
hirsutum 'Rubriflorum'
CHASMANTHE
intermedia
CHELONE
obliqua 'Praecox Nana'
CIMICIFUGA
simplex 'Braunlaub' variegated form
CLEMATIS
recta 'Plena'
CLETHRA
alnifolia 'Creel's Calico'
COCHLEARIA
officinalis 'Variegata'
COLCHICUM
callicymbium 'Danton'
guadarramense
'Mr Kerbert'
'President Coolidge'
triphyllum
CONVALLARIA
majalis 'Gigantea'
– 'Robusta'
– 'Rosea Plena'
COREOPSIS
bigelovii
'Double Sunburst'

gigantea
grandiflora 'Perry's Variety'
lanceolata 'Mahogany'
maritima
pubescens
pulchra

CORNUS
mas 'Spring Glow'

CORTADERIA
selloana 'Bertini'

COSMOS
scabiosoides

COTINUS
coggygria 'Daydream'
– 'Nordine Red'

CRAMBE
pinnatifida

CRINUM
x *powellii* 'Krelagei'
– 'Variegatum'

CROCOSMIA
'Mephistopheles'

CROCUS
'Albidus'
chrysanthus 'Al Jolson'
– 'Andromeda'
– 'Atom'
– 'Aubade'
– 'Belle Jaune'
– 'Bloemfontein'
– 'Blue Beauty'
– 'Blue Bonnet'
– 'Blue Butterfly'
– 'Blue Jacket'
– 'Blue Jay'
– 'Blue Princess'
– 'Blue Rock'
– 'Blue Throat'
– 'Bullfinch'
– 'Bumble-bee'
– 'Buttercup'
– 'Constellation'
– 'Crescendo'
– 'Cum Laude'
– 'Cupido'
– 'Curlew'
– 'Dandy'
– 'Distinction'
– 'Golden Pheasant'
– 'Golden Plover'
– 'Goldene Sonne'
– 'Grand Gala'
– 'Grey Lady'
– 'Harlequin'
– 'Ivory Glory'
– 'Ivory Glow'
– 'Jester'
– 'Johan Cruyff'
– 'Khaki'
– 'Koh-i-Nor'
– 'Lemon Queen'
– 'Lentejuweel'
– 'Lilette'
– 'Lilliputaner'
– 'Magic'
– 'Mannequin'
– 'Mariette'
– 'Marion'
– 'Marlene'
– 'Morning Star'
– 'Mrs Moon'
– 'Mystic'
– 'Nanette'
– 'Olympiade'
– 'Opal'
– 'Palette'
– 'Parade'
– 'Paradiso'
– 'Plaisir'
– 'Reverence'
– 'Rising Sun'
– 'Ruby Gown'
– 'Shot'
– 'Siskin'
– 'Solfatare'
– 'Solo'
– 'Sorrento'
– 'Spotlight'
– 'Spring Song'
– 'Sulphur Glory'
– 'Sunset'
– 'Sunshine'
– 'Susie'
– 'Symphonia'
– 'Topolino'
– 'Trance'
– 'White Egret'
– 'White Splendour'
– 'Winter Gold'
– 'Yellow Gem'
– 'Yellow Hammer'
– 'Yellow Queen'
vernus 'Blue Ribbon'

CUNNINGHAMIA
lanceolata 'Chason's Gift'

CYPRIPEDIUM
arietinum
candidum
montanum
x *ventricosum*

DACTYLIS
glomerata 'Aurea'

DACTYLORHIZA
elata white
majalis 'Glasnevin'

DAHLIA
'Emperor Franz-Joseph'

DEINANTHE
caerulea f. *alba*

DELPHINIUM
brachycentrum

DENDRANTHEMA
'Anna Hay' (30)
'Ceres'
'Jean Harlowe'
'Tiny'

DIANTHUS
'Beverley Pink' (p)
'Black Prince' (p)
'Evelyn'
'Granado' (b)
'Lambrook Beauty' (p)
'Lincolnshire Lass' (p) 🏆
'Lucy Glendill' (b)
'Old Man's Head' (p)
'Ruth Fischer' (p)

DICENTRA
'Appleblossom'
'Queen of Hearts'

DISPORUM
menziesii

DORONICUM
pardalianches 'Goldstrauss'

DRACOCEPHALUM
isabellae
tanguticum

ECHINACEA
purpurea 'Abendsonne'

ECHINOPS
exaltatus f. *albus*

ENKIANTHUS
campanulatus 'Renoir'
– 'Showy Lantern'

EPILOBIUM
angustifolium var. *variegatum*

EPIMEDIUM
x *youngianum* Yenomoto form

EREMURUS
afghanicus
aitchisonii 'Dawn'
x *isabellinus* 'Highdown Dwarf'
– 'Highdown Gold'
kaufmannii
'Lady Falmouth'
'Primrose'
robustus var. *tardiflorus*
'Sunset'

ERIGERON
'Double Beauty'
glaucus 'B. Ladhams'

ERYNGIUM
floribundum
lassauxii
x *zabelii* 'James Ivory'

ERYSIMUM
'Miss Massey' (d)

EUPATORIUM
fistulosum 'Gateway'
purpureum 'Album'

FRAGARIA
vesca 'Alpina Scarletta'

FRANCOA
rupestris

FRITILLARIA
imperialis 'Flore Pleno'

GAILLARDIA
x *grandiflora* 'Ipswich Beauty'

GALANTHUS
'Allen's Perfection'
'Cupid'
'Jenny Wren'
'Rebecca'
'Romeo'
'Tomtit'
'Valentine'
'White Swan'

GALEGA
officinalis var. *compacta*

GENTIANA
asclepiadea 'Caelestina'
– 'Phaeina'
x *japonica*

GERANIUM
sanguineum double

GEUM
x *ewenii*
pentapetalum 'Plenum'

GLADIOLUS
x *brenchleyensis*

GLYCERIA
maxima 'Pallida'

HEDYCHIUM
'F.W. Moore'

HELENIUM
autumnale 'Aurantiacum'
'Baronin Linden'
'Brilliant'
'Chanctonbury'
'Flammenrad'
'Goldreif'
'Kugelsonne'
'September Gold'
'Spätrot'
'Tawny Dwarf'

HELIANTHUS
gracilentus
'Hallo'
hirsutus
longifolius
schweinitzii
simulans
tomentosus
'Zebulon'

HELIOPSIS
helianthoides 'Gigantea'
– 'Mid West Dream'
– var. *scabra* 'Desert King'
– – 'Patula'

HELLEBORUS
niger 'Mr Poë's Variety'

HEMEROCALLIS
'Aurantiaca Major'
'E.A. Bowles'
fulva var. *rosea*
'Gay Music'

HEUCHERA
'Baby's Breath'
'Crimson Cascade'
'Damask'
'Freedom'
'Gaiety'
'Gloriana'
'Honeybells'
'Ibis'
'June Bride'
'Lady Warwick'
'Montrose'
'Mount St Helens'
'Oakington Jewel'
'Oakington Superba'
'Oxfordii'
'Rose Cavalier'
'Rufus'
'Scarlet Beauty'
'Tattletale'

HIDALGOA
wercklei

HYDRANGEA
macrophylla 'Merritt's Beauty'
– 'Pink 'n' Pretty'

- 'Red 'n' Pretty'
- 'Red Star'
- 'Revelation'
- 'Trophy'
quercifolia 'Alice'
- 'Alison'
- 'PeeWee'

HYPERICUM
olympicum f. ***minus*** 'Schwefelperle'

IBERIS
sempervirens 'Plena'

ILEX
vomitoria 'Folsom's Weeping' (f)
- 'Grey's Little Leaf'
- 'Jewel' (f)
- 'Nana'
- f. ***pendula***
- 'Shadow's Female' (f)
- 'Straughn's'
- 'Wiggin's Yellow' (f)
- 'Will Fleming'
- 'Yellow Berry' (f)

ILLICIUM
floridanum 'Album'
- 'Halley's Comet'

IMPERATA
cylindrica 'Major'

INDIGOFERA
'Rose Carpet'

IRIS
'Barcarole' (Regeliocyclus)
'Camilla' (Regeliocyclus)
'Clara' (Regeliocyclus)
'Dorothea'
'Dress Circle' (Spuria)
'Emily Grey'
ensata 'Benibotan'
- 'Kegoromo'
- 'Kumazumi'
- 'Lady in Waiting'
- 'Pin Stripe'
- 'Reign of Glory'
- 'Sky Mist'
- 'Tinted Cloud'
- 'Warei Hotei'
'Ice Blue'
'Lutetas' (Regeliocyclus)
'Medea' (Regeliocyclus)
'Mercurius' (Regeliocyclus)
'Myddelton Blue'
orientalis 'Snowflake'
pseudacorus 'Gigantea'
sibirica 'Big Blue'
- 'Blue Reverie'
tectorum 'Lilacina'
Tollong Group
Toltec Group
unguicularis 'Bowles' White'
- 'Ellis's Variety'

ITEA
virginica 'Sarah's Eve'
- 'Saturnalia'

JEFFERSONIA
dubia 'Flore Pleno'

JUNIPERUS
horizontalis 'Argentea'
- 'Blue Horizon'
- 'Heidi'
- 'Lime Glow'
- 'Watnong'

KADSURA
japonica 'Chirimen' (v)
- 'Fukurin' (v)
- 'Shiromi'

KNIPHOFIA
'Adam'
'Amberlight'
'Bees' Orange'
'Bees' Yellow'
'Bressingham Glow'
'Bressingham Torch'
'Burnt Orange'
'Buttercrunch'
'Canary Bird'
'Chartreuse'
'Cleopatra'
'Cool Lemon'
'Enchantress'
'Florella'
'Green Lemon'
'Honeycomb'
'Hortulanus Laren'
'Indian'
leichtlinii 'Aurea'
'Lemon Queen'
'Maxima'
parviflora
'Primulina' hort.
rogersii
'Russell's Gold'
'Slim Coral Red'
'Slim Orange'
'Snow Maiden'
'Spanish Gold'
'The Rocket'

KNOWLTONIA
capensis

LATHYRUS
latifolius violet
ornatus

LAVANDULA
'Backhouse Purple'
'Glasnevin Variety'

LEONTOPODIUM
haplophylloides

LEUCANTHEMUM
× ***superbum*** 'Beauté Anversoise'

LIATRIS
pycnostachya 'Alba'
scariosa 'White Spire'
spicata 'Picador'
- 'Snow Queen'

LIGULARIA
altaica

LIGUSTICUM
mutellina

LILIUM
arboricola
candidum 'Peregrinum'
× ***princeps*** 'Myddelton House'

LIMONIUM
platyphyllum 'Blue Cloud'

LINARIA
aeruginea 'Aureopurpurea'

LINUM
narbonense 'June Perfield'
- 'Six Hills'

LOBELIA
'Mrs Humbert'

LONICERA
sempervirens 'Cedar Lane'

LOROPETALUM
chinense 'Blush'

LUPINUS
'Betty Astell'
'Blue Jacket'
'City of York'
'George Russell'

LYCHNIS
chalcedonica 'Alba Plena'
flos-cuculi 'Adolph Muss'

LYSIMACHIA
leschenaultii

MAGNOLIA
grandiflora 'Bracken's Brown Beauty'
- 'Gloriosa'
- 'Majestic Red'
- 'Ruff'
virginiana 'Henry Hicks'

MATELEA
carolinensis

MECONOPSIS
× ***cookei***
grandis 'Keillour Crimson'
- 'Miss Dickson'
× ***sheldonii*** 'Archie Campbell'
torquata

MELITTIS
melissophyllum 'Variegata'

MIMULUS
lewisii 'Albus'
- 'Sunset'

MISCANTHUS
floridulus 'Nippon Summer'
sinensis 'Arabesque'
- 'Autumn Red'
- 'Blondo'
- 'Gracillimus Nanus'
- 'Gracillimus Variegatus'
- 'Interstate'
- 'November Sunset'
- 'Positano'

MONARDA
'Falls of Hill's Creek'
'Gardenview Red'
'Gardenview Select'
'Gardenway Red'
'Magnifica'
'Ohio Glow'
'Raspberry Wine'
'Red Explosion'
'Souris'
'Stone's Throw Pink'
'Sunset'
'Violet Queen'

MULGEDIUM
giganteum

MYOSOTIS
dissitiflora 'Elegantissima' (v)

NARCISSUS
'Alpha of Donard' (1)
'Astron' (2)
'Gog'
'Golden Miller' (1)
'Golden Thought'
'Green Mantle' (3)
'Lucinda'
'Magistrate' (1)
'Precentor' (1)
'Red Light' (2)
'Saint Dorothea' (1)
'Slieve Bernagh' (1)
'Slieve Donard' (1)
'Solid Gold' (1)

NEPETA
racemosa 'Blue Wonder'
- 'White Wonder'

OENOTHERA
fruticosa 'Best Red'

ORIGANUM
vulgare 'Bury Hill'

PAEONIA
'Argosy'
'Black Douglas'
'Black Pirate'
'Chalice'
'Constance Spry'
'Cytherea'
'Daystar'
'Early Bird'
'Early Windflower'
'Good Cheer'
lactiflora 'Coral Charm'
- 'Doris Cooper'
- 'Jean Bockstoce'
- 'Sea Shell'
- 'Sword Dance'
'Legion of Honour'
'Little Dorrit'
mascula subsp. ***arietina*** 'Hilda Milne'
'Moonrise'
officinalis 'Phyllis Prichard'
- 'Red Ensign'
- 'Splendens'
'Roman Gold'
'Rose Garland'
suffruticosa 'Bijou de Chusan'
- 'Elizabeth'
'Sybil Stern'
'Victoria Lincoln'
'White Innocence'
wittmanniana var. ***nudicarpa***

PANICUM
'Squaw'

PAPAVER
orientale 'Atrosanguineum Maximum'
- 'Australia's Orange'
- 'Barr's White'
- 'Blush Queen'
- 'Bobs'
- 'Border Beauty'
- 'Brightness'
- 'Burgundy'

– 'Cavalier'
– 'Cerise Bedder'
– 'Colonel Bowles'
– 'Countess of Stair'
– 'Crimped Beauty'
– 'Crimson Pompon'
– 'Curtis's Strain'
– 'Delicatum'
– 'Dengas'
– 'Duke of Teck'
– 'E.A. Bowles'
– 'Edna Perry'
– 'Enchantress'
– 'Enfield Beauty'
– 'Ethel Swete'
– 'Fire King'
– 'Fringed Beauty'
– 'Gibson's Salmon'
– 'Goldschmidt'
– 'Grenadier'
– 'Henri Cayeux Improved'
– 'Humphrey Bennett'
– 'Ida Brailsford'
– 'Immaculatum'
– 'Iris Perry'
– 'Ivy Perry'
– 'Jeannie Mawson'
– 'Joyce'
– 'Lady Haig'
– 'Lady Haskett'
– 'Lady Roscoe'
– 'Lavender Glory'
– 'Little Prince'
– 'Lovely'
– 'Magnificence'
– 'Mahony'
– 'Margherite'
– 'Marie Studholme'
– 'Masterpiece'
– 'Max Leichtlin'
– 'May Curtis'
– 'Medusa'
– 'Menelik'
– 'Minimum'
– 'Miss Julia'
– 'Mogul'
– 'Mrs Carl Skinner'
– 'Mrs John Harkness'
– 'Mrs Lockett Agnew'
– 'Mrs M. Bevan'
– 'Mrs Marsh'
– 'Orange Queen'
– 'Oriental King'
– 'Oriental Queen'
– 'Oriflamme'
– 'Pale Face'
– 'Parkmanii'
– 'Perry's Blush'
– 'Perry's Favorite'
– 'Perry's Pigmy'
– 'Perry's Unique'
– 'Persepolis'
– 'Peter Pan'
– 'Princess Ena'
– 'Princess Mary'
– 'Purity'
– 'Queen Alexandra'
– 'Royal Prince'
– 'Royal Scarlet'
– 'Ruby Perry'
– 'Salmon Beauty'
– 'Salmon Perfection'
– 'Salmon Queen'
– 'Sass Pink'
– 'Semiplenum'
– 'Silberblick'
– 'Silver Queen'
– 'Silverblotch'
– 'Snoflame'
– 'Sonata'
– 'Souvenir'
– 'Splendens'
– 'Sungold'
– 'Surprise'
– 'The King'
– 'The Queen'
– 'Thora Perry'
– 'Tom Tit'
– 'Toreador'
– 'Van der Glotch'
– 'Vuurkogel'
– 'Winnie'
– 'Wurtemburgia'

PENSTEMON
'Prairie Dawn'

PHLEUM
pratense 'Aureum'

PHLOX
buckleyi
carolina forms
caryophylla
dolichantha
floridana
– subsp. ***bella***
glaberrima
idahoensis
paniculata 'Antoine Mercier'
– 'Hochgesang'
× ***procumbens*** 'Pinstripe'
– 'Snowdrift'
– 'Vein Mountain'
stansburyi

PHORMIUM
'Aurora'
tenax 'Goliath'
– 'Purple Giant'

PHYTOLACCA
variegated forms

PIMPINELLA
saxifraga 'Rosea'

POLEMONIUM
carneum 'Rose Queen'
laxiflorum

POLYGONUM
coriaceum

POTENTILLA
alba 'Snow White'
'Arc-en-ciel'
'Congo'
'Hamlet'
ovalis

PRIMULA
'Donard Gem'

PRUNUS
persica var. ***nectarina*** 'White Glory'
× ***yedoensis*** 'Afterglow'
– 'Pink Shell'
– 'Snow Fountains'

PULMONARIA
officinalis var. ***immaculata***

RANUNCULUS
aconitifolius 'Luteus Plenus'
alpestris 'Flore Pleno'
parnassiifolius 'Semiplenus'

RESEDA
odorata 'Parson's White'

RHEUM
'Dr Baillon'
palmatum 'Atropurpureum Dissectum'

RHODODENDRON
prunifolium 'Cherry-bomb' (A)
– 'Coral Glow' (A)
– 'Lewis Shortt' (A)
– 'Peach Glow' (A)
– 'Pine' (A)

RIGIDELLA
flammea
orthantha

ROMNEYA
coulteri 'Butterfly'

ROSCOEA
cautleyoides 'Bees' Dwarf'

RUDBECKIA
laciniata 'Foliis Variegatis'
nitida 'Autumn Glory'
serotina

RUTA
graveolens 'Blue Beauty'

SACCHARUM
strictum

SALVIA
beckeri
ceratophylla
cryptantha
dichroa
eichleriana
formosa
'Glory of Stuttgart'
guaranitica 'Costa Rica'
– 'Indigo Blue'
– 'Purple Splendor'
ianthina
pinnata
teddii
valentina
yunnanensis

SANGUISORBA
officinalis 'Shiro-fukurin'

SAXIFRAGA
'Flore Pleno' (*virginiensis*)

SCABIOSA
caucasica 'Blue Mountain'
– 'Constancy'
– 'Diamond'
– 'Loddon White'
– 'Mrs Isaac House'
– 'Penhill Blue'
– 'Rhinsburg Glory'

SENECIO
cineraria 'Hoar Frost'

SIDALCEA
'Donard Queen'
'H. Blanchard'
malviflora 'Pompadour'
'Scarlet Beauty'

SILPHIUM
'Carpenter's Cup'

SOPHORA
japonica 'Violacea'

TAMARIX
ramosissima 'Cheyenne Red'

TANACETUM
coccineum 'A.M. Kelway'
– 'Allurement'
– 'Avalanche'
– 'Beau Geste'
– 'Bishop of Salisbury'
– 'Bridal Pink'
– 'Bright Boy'
– 'Charming'
– 'China Rose'
– 'Comet'
– 'Countess Poulett'
– 'Duke of York'
– 'Kelway's Lovely'
– 'Kelway's Magnificent'
– 'Langport Scarlet'
– 'Lorna'
– 'Mrs Bateman Brown'
– 'Progression'
– 'Radiant'
– 'Somerset'
– 'White Madeleine'

TEUCRIUM
polium 'Album'

TIARELLA
cordifolia 'Montrose'

TILIA
americana 'Dakota'
– 'Douglas'
– 'Legend'
– 'Rosehill'
cordata 'DeGroot'
– 'Glenleven'
– 'Green Globe'
– 'Handsworth'
heterophylla 'Continental Appeal'
tomentosa 'Sterling'

TRILLIUM
catesbyi f. ***album***
– f. ***cahnae***
– f. ***polymerum***
japonicum
ovatum 'Edith'
petiolatum
reliquum

TROLLIUS
asiaticus var. ***aurantiacus***

ULMUS
alata 'Lace Parasol'

VERATRUM
stenophyllum
yunnanense

VERNONIA
angustifolia

VERONICA
spicata 'Gina's Pale Blue'

VIOLA
'Red Giant'

VITEX
agnus-castus 'Rosea'

The National Council For The Conservation Of Plants & Gardens (NCCPG) Collections

All or part of the following Genera are represented by a National Collection.
Full details of these collections are contained in the National Plant Collections Directory 1997 available from: NCCPG, The Pines, c/o Wisley Gardens, Woking, Surrey GU23 6QB.
Price £3.50 including post and packing.

Abelia
Abies
Abutilon
Acacia
Acanthus
Acer
Achillea
Actinidia
Adenophora
Adiantum
Aechmea
Aesculus
Agapanthus
Alchemilla
Allium
Alnus
Alstroemeria
Amelanchier
Ampelopsis
Anemone
Aquilegia
Arabis
Araceae
Aralia
Arbutus
Argyranthemum
Artemisia
Arundinaria
Asplenium
Aster
Astilbe
Athyrium
Aubrieta
Aucuba
Azara
Bambusa
Begonia
Berberis
Bergenia
Betula
Borago
Borzicactinae
Brachyglottis
Buddleja
Buxus
Calamintha
Calathea
Calceolaria
Calluna
Caltha
Camassia
Camellia
Campanula
Canna
Carpinus
Carya
Caryopteris
Cassiope
Castanea
Catalpa
Catasetum
Cattleya
Ceanothus
Celmisia
Ceratostigma
Cercidiphyllum
Chamaecyparis
Chionodoxa
Chusquea
Cimicifuga
Cistus
Citrus
Clematis
Codiaeum
Colchicum
Coleus
Conifers
Conophytum
Convallaria
Coprosma
Cordyline
Coreopsis
Coriaria
Cornus
Cortaderia
Corylopsis
Corylus
Cotinus
Cotoneaster
Crocosmia
Crocus
× *Cupressocyparis*
Cyclamen
Cymbidium
Cystopteris
Cytisus
Daboecia
Dahlia
Daphne
Davallia
Delphinium
Dendranthema
Dendrobium
Deutzia
Dianella
Dianthus
Diascia
Dicentra
Dicksoniaceae
Diervilla
Digitalis
Dodecatheon
Doronicum
Dracaena
Dryopteris
Echeveria
Echinocereus
Elaeagnus
Embothrium
Enkianthus
Epimedium
Erica
Erigeron
Erodium
Eryngium
Erysimum
Erythronium
Escallonia
Eucalyptus
Eucryphia
Euonymus
Euphorbia
Fagus
Ferns
Ficus
Fragaria
Fraxinus
Fritillaria
Fuchsia
Galanthus
Garrya
Gaultheria
Gentiana
Geranium
Geum
Gladiolus
Grevillea
Griselinia
Halimium
Hamamelis
Haworthia
Hebe
Hedera
Hedychium
Helenium
Helianthemum
Helianthus
Helichrysum
Heliopsis
Helleborus
Hemerocallis
Hepatica
Hesperis
Heuchera

Hibiscus
Hillier Plants
Hoheria
Hosta
Hoya
Hyacinthus
Hydrangea
Hypericum
Ilex
Inula
Iris
Jasminum
Juglans
Juniperus
Kalmia
Kniphofia
Laburnum
Lamium
Lathyrus
Lavandula
Leptospermum
Leucanthemum
Leucojum
Lewisia
Libertia
Ligustrum
Linum
Liriodendron
Liriope
Lithocarpus
Lithops
Lobelia
Lonicera
Lupinus
Lycaste
Lychnis
Lysimachia
Magnolia
Mahonia
Malus
Meconopsis
Mentha
Monarda
Monsonia
Narcissus
Nepeta
Nerine
Nerium
Nothofagus
Nymphaea
Oenothera
Olearia
Ophiopogon
Opuntia
Origanum
Osmunda
Osteospermum
Ourisia
Oxalis
Paeonia
Papaver
Paphiopedilum
Parahebe
Parthenocissus
Passiflora
Pelargonium
Penstemon
Pernettya
Philadelphus
Phlomis
Phlox
Phormium
Photinia
Phygelius
Phyllodoce
Phyllostachys
Picea
Pieris
Pinguicula
Pinus
Pittosporum
Pleioblastus
Platanus
Platycodon
Pleione
Pleurothallidinae
Polemonium
Polygonum
Polypodium
Polystichum
Populus
Potentilla
Primula
Prunus
Pseudopanax
Pulmonaria
Pyracantha
Pyrus
Quercus
Ranunculus
Rheum
Rhododendron
Rhus
Ribes
Rodgersia
Rohdea
Rosa
Rosmarinus
Rubus
Rudbeckia
Ruscus
Salix
Salvia
Sambucus
Sansevieria
Santolina
Sarcocaulon
Sarcococca
Sarracenia
Sasa
Saxifraga
Scabiosa
Scilla
Sedum
Semiaquilegia
Sempervivum
Sisyrinchium
Skimmia
Slieve Donard Plants
Sorbaria
Sorbus
Spiraea
Sir F Stern
Stewartia
Streptocarpus
Styracaceae
Symphyandra
Symphytum
Syringa
Tanacetum
Taxus
Thalictrum
Thelypteridaceae
Thuja
Thymus
Tilia
Trillium
Trollius
Tropaeolum
Tulbaghia
Tulipa
Vaccinium
Variegated Plants
Veratrum
Verbascum
Veronica
Viburnum
Vinca
Viola
Vitis
Watsonia
Weigela
Wisteria
Woodwardia
Yucca
Zelkova

BIBLIOGRAPHY

INTERNATIONAL PLANT FINDERS

Canada

The Canadian Plant Source Book. (1996/97). Anne & Peter Ashley, 93 Fentiman Avenue, Ottawa, ON, Canada K1S OT7. 21,000 hardy plants available at retail and wholesale nurseries across Canada, including those who ship to US. English common names & English & French cross-indexes. $20 (Canadian or US). inc. p&p. Add $5 for airmail.

Germany

Pflanzen-Einkaufsführer. (1995). Anne & Walter Erhardt. Verlag Eugen Ulmer, PO Box 70 05 61, D-70574 Stuttgart. ISBN 3-8001-6544-9. Some 60,000 plants from 460 European nurseries, **includes CD-ROM**.

Italy

Il Cercapiante. (1996). Filippo Cerrina Feroni & Tiziana Volta, Ed. Giorgio Mondadori. Via Andrea Ponti 10, 20143 Milano. Italy. 1st edition listing 15,000 plants from 400 nurseries including 100 specialist suppliers; 100 European nurseries; all Italian botanical and professional Associations, all Italian Garden Clubs, wide Bibliography.

Netherlands

Plantenvinder voor de Lage Landen. (1997/98). ed. Sarah Hart. Uitgeverij TERRA, Postbus 188, 7200AD Zutphen, Netherlands. ISBN 90-6255-732-5. Approx. 50,000 plants and 140 nurseries.

United Kingdom

Find That Rose! The 15th annual publication covers Autumn 1997 & Spring 1998 and lists approx. 2,800 varieties with basic type, colour and fragrance code together with full details of approx. 70 growers. Send Sae for further info. or £2.25 payment to The Editor, Angela Pawsey, British Rose Growers' Association, 303 Mile End Road, Colchester, Essex CO4 5EA.

The Fruit and Veg Finder. HDRA, Ryton-on-Dunsmore, Coventry CV8 3LG. Produced in association with Brogdale Horticultural Trust. The 5th edition lists sources and descriptions for more than 3000 vegetable varieties and almost 1,300 fruits, from a total of about 200 suppliers. ISBN 0-905343-20-4.

The Seed Search. (1997). 1st edition. Karen Platt, 37 Melbourn Road, Crookes, Sheffield S10 1NR. Email k@seedsearch.demon.co.uk. A directory of over 33,000 seeds with details and essential information on suppliers from around the world. Lists all types of seed - trees, flowers, vegetables, herbs. Also lists English common names and hazardous plants/seeds. ISBN 0-9528810-0-4.

USA

The Andersen's Horticultural Library's Source List of Plants and Seeds. Andersen Horticultural Library, Minnesota Landscape Arboretum, 3675 Arboretum Drive, Box 39, Chanhassen, MN 55317 USA. Compiled by Richard Isaacson. (4th ed. 1996). Approx. 59,000 plants and seeds from 450 retail & wholesale outlets in the US & Canada. All are prepared to ship interstate. Does not include Orchids, Cacti or Succulents. $34.95 US currency only.

Combined Rose List. (1996). Beverly R Dobson & Peter Schneider, PO Box 677, Mantua, Ohio 44255. Lists over 9,500 roses from 222 nurseries In US, Canada & Overseas.

Cornucopia - A Source Book of Edible Plants. (1990). Stephen Facciola, Kampong Publications, 1870 Sunrise Drive, Vista, California 92084. A very substantial and comprehensive volume (678 pages), which documents 3,000 species of edible plants & 7,000 cultivars available in the US and abroad. ISBN 0-9628087-0-9. A software version for Microsoft Windows is available ISBN 0-9628087-1-7.

Gardening by Mail. (1994). 4th ed. Barbara J. Barton. Houghton Mifflin Co., 222 Berkeley Street, Boston, MA 02114, USA. 5th ed., completely updated with email and WWW addresses, due for publication Nov. 1997. A directory of mail order resources for gardeners in the USA and Canada, including seed companies, nurseries, suppliers of all garden necessaries and ornaments, horticultural and plant societies, magazines, libraries and books.

Sources of Propagated Native Plants and Wildflowers. New England Wild Flower Society, Garden in the Woods, 180 Hemenway Road, Framingham, MA 01701-2699. Over 200 native North American wild flowers, ferns, grasses and shrubs. Details of 60 nurseries

Hortus West: A Western North America Native Plant Directory & Journal. (Volume 8: Issues 1&2, 1997). ed. Dale Shank. Hortus West, PO Box 2870, Wilsonville, OR 97070-2870. Published twice annually. Directory lists 2,050 western native species commercially available through 190 native plant vendors in 11 Western United States and two Canadian provinces. Annual (two-issue) subscription: $12.00 postpaid (outside US add $3.00).

Perennials: A Nursery Source Manual. (1989). ed. Barbara Pesch. Brooklyn Botanic Garden, 1000 Washington Avenue, Brooklyn, NY 11225-1099. ISBN 0 945352 48 4. Lists 320 nurseries and some 4000 perennials.

Taylor's Guide to Speciality Nurseries. (1993). Barbara R Barton ed. Houghton Mifflin Co., 222 Berkeley Street, Boston, MA 02114, USA. Over 300 nurseries in the US selling ornamental garden plants, all of which will ship.

GENERAL

The following list of bibliographic sources and references is by no means exhaustive but lists some of the more useful and available works used in the preparation of ***The RHS Plant Finder***.

The New Plantsman and *The Garden* are published regularly by the Royal Horticultural Society, Vincent Square, London SW1P 2PE.

Altwegg, A, Fortgens, G & Siebler, E (eds). (1996). *ISU Yearbook 1965-95*. Internationale Stauden-Union, Windisch, Germany.

Armitage, A M (1989). *Herbaceous Perennial Plants*. Varsity Press, Athens, Georgia.

Bailey, L H, Bailey, E Z et al. (1976). *Hortus Third*. Macmillan, New York.

Bean, W J (1970-1988). *Trees and Shrubs Hardy in the British Isles*. (8th ed. edited Sir George Taylor & D L Clarke & Supp. ed. D L Clarke). John Murray, London.

Beckett, K A (ed.) (1993-94). *Encyclopaedia of Alpines*, **1 & 2**. Alpine Garden Society, Pershore, Worcs.

Beckett, K A (1987). *The RHS Encyclopaedia of House Plants*. Century Hutchinson, London.

Blundell, M (1992). *Wild Flowers of East Africa*. Collins, London.

Bond, P & Goldblatt, P (1984). Plants of the Cape Flora. *Journal of South African Botany*, supp. vol. 13. Kirstenbosch.

Bramwell, D & Z (1974). *Wild Flowers of the Canary Islands*. Stanley Thomas, London.

Brickell, C D (ed.). (1989). *RHS Gardeners' Encyclopedia of Plants and Flowers*. Dorling Kindersley, London.

Brickell, C D (ed.). (1996). *RHS A-Z Encyclopedia of Garden Plants*. Dorling Kindersley, London.

Brummitt, R K & Powell, C E (1992). *Authors of Plant Names*. Royal Botanic Gardens, Kew.

Brummitt, R K (1992). *Vascular Plant Families and Genera*. Royal Botanic Gardens, Kew.

Chittenden, F J (ed.). (1965). 2nd ed. *The Royal Horticultural Society Dictionary of Gardening*. Oxford University Press.

Clausen, R R & Ekstrom, N H (1989). *Perennials for American Gardens*. Random House, New York.

Clement, E J & Foster, M C (1994). *Alien Plants of the British Isles*. Botanical Society of the British Isles, London.

Davis, B & Knapp, B (1992). *Know Your Common Plant Names*. MDA Publications, Newbury, Berks.

Davis, P H et al. (ed.). (1965-1988). *Flora of Turkey*, vols 1-10. University Press, Edinburgh.

Flora of New Zealand, vols 1-3. (1961-80). Wellington, New Zealand.

Eggli, U & Taylor, N (1994). *List of Names of Succulent Plants other than Cacti Published 1950-92*. Royal Botanic Gardens, Kew.

Forrest, M (ed. Nelson, E C). (1985). *Trees and Shrubs Cultivated in Ireland*. Boethius Press for An Taisce, Dublin.

Galbraith, J (1977). *Field Guide to the Wild Flowers of South-East Australia*. Collins, London.

Graf, A B (1981). 2nd ed. *Tropica*. Roehrs, New Jersey.

Greuter, W et al. (ed.). (1994). *International Code of Botanical Nomenclature (Tokyo Code)*. Koeltz Scientific Books, Königstein, Germany.

Greuter, W, Brummitt, R K, Farr, E et al. (1993). *N.C.U.3 Names in Current Use for Extant Plant Genera*. Koeltz Scientific Books, Königstein, Germany.

Grierson, A J C & Long D G (1983-91) vol. 1 pts 1-3 & vol. 2 pt 1; Noltie, H J (1994) vol. 3 pt 1. *Flora of Bhutan*. Royal Botanic Garden Edinburgh.

Griffiths, M (ed.) (1994). *RHS Index of Garden Plants*. Macmillan, London.

Harkness, M G (1993). 2nd ed. *The Bernard E. Harkness Seedlist Handbook*. Batsford, London.

Heath, R E (1981). *Collectors Alpines*. Collingridge, Twickenham, UK.

Hillier Manual of Trees and Shrubs. (1991). 6th ed. David & Charles, Newton Abbot, Devon.

Hogg, R (1884). 5th ed. *The Fruit Manual*. Journal of Horticulture Office, London.

Huxley, A (ed.). (1992). *The New Royal Horticultural Society Dictionary of Gardening*. Macmillan, London.

Index Kewensis, vols 1-4 & supps 1-19. 1893-1991. Clarendon Press, Oxford.

Jacobsen, H (1973). *Lexicon of Succulent Plants*. Blandford, London.

Jellitto, L & Schacht, W (1990). 3rd ed. Schacht, W & Fessler, A *Hardy Herbaceous Perennials*. Timber Press, Portland, Oregon, USA.

Kelly, J (ed.). (1995). *The Hillier Gardener's Guide to Trees and Shrubs*. David & Charles, Newton Abbot, Devon.

Krüssmann, G (English ed. trans. M E Epp). (1984-1986). *Manual of Cultivated Broadleaved Trees & Shrubs*, vols 1-3. Batsford, London.
Laar, H J van de. (1989). *Naamlijst van Houtige Gewassen*. Proefstation voor de Boomteelt en het Stedelijk Groen, Boskoop, Holland.
Laar, H J van de & Fortgens, Ing. G (1988). *Naamlijst van Vaste Planten*. Proefstation voor de Boomkwekerij, Boskoop, Holland.
Leslie, A C, (1993). *New Cultivars of Herbaceous Perennial Plants 1985-1990*. Hardy Plant Society.
Mabberley, D J (1987). *The Plant-Book*. Cambridge University Press.
McGregor, R L, Barkley, T M et al. (1986). *Flora of the Great Plains*. University Press of Kansas, USA.
Metcalf, L J (1987). *The Cultivation of New Zealand Trees and Shrubs*. Reed Methuen, Auckland, New Zealand.
Ohwi, J (ed F G Meyer & E H Walker). (1965). *Flora of Japan*. Smithsonian Institution, Washington.
Phillips, R & Rix, E M *Shrubs*. (1989). Pan Books, London.
Phillips, R & Rix, E M (1991/2). *Perennials*. Pan Books, London.
Phillips, R & Rix, E M (1993). *Vegetables*. Pan Books Ltd, London.
The New Plantsman. The Royal Horticultural Society, London.
Polunin, O & Stainton, A (1984). *Flowers of the Himalaya*. Oxford University Press.
Press, J R & Short, M J (1994). *Flora of Madeira*. Natural History Museum, London.
Rehder, R (1940). 2nd ed. *Manual of Cultivated Trees & Shrubs Hardy in North America*. Macmillan, New York.
Stace, C A (1992). *New Flora of the British Isles*. St Edmundsbury Press, Bury St Edmunds, Suffolk.
Stainton, A (1988). *Flowers of the Himalaya: A Supplement*. Oxford University Press.
Stearn, W T (1973). 2nd ed. *Botanical Latin*. David & Charles. Newton Abbot, England.
Stearn, W T (1992). *Stearn's Dictionary of Plant Names for Gardeners*. Cassell, London.
Taffler, S (1988-97). *The Sport*. Hardy Plant Society Variegated Plant Group, South Petherton, Somerset.
Thomas, G S (1990). 3rd ed. *Perennial Garden Plants*. J M Dent & Sons, London.
Trehane, R P (1989). *Index Hortensis* (Vol. 1: Perennials). Quarterjack Publishing, Wimborne, Dorset.
Trehane, R P (1995). *International Code of Nomenclature for Cultivated Plants - 1995*. Quarterjack Publishing, Wimborne, Dorset.
Tutin, T G (1964-1980). *Flora Europaea*, vols 1-5. Cambridge University Press.
Tutin, T G et al. (1993). 2nd ed. *Flora Europaea*, vol 1. Cambridge University Press.
Van der Werff, D (ed.). (1995-97). *New, Rare and Elusive Plants*, vols 1(1-4) & 2(1-4). Aquilegia Publishing, Hartlepool, Co. Durham.
Walters, S M (ed.). et al. (1984, 1986, 1989 & 1995). *The European Garden Flora*, vols 1-4. Cambridge University Press, UK.
Willis, J C (1973). 8th ed. revised Airy Shaw, H K *A Dictionary of the Flowering Plants and Ferns*. (8th ed.). Cambridge University Press.
Wilson, H D (1978). *Wild Plants of Mount Cook National Park*. Christchurch, New Zealand.
Zander, R (1993). *Handwörterbuch der Pflanzennamen*. Ulmer, Stuttgart, Germany.

GENERA

Acacia
Beckett, K A (1993). *The Plantsman*, **15(3)**: 131-47.
Simmons, M H (1987). 2nd ed. *Acacias of Australia*. Nelson, Melbourne, Australia.
Acaena
Yeo, P F (1972). The species of *Acaena* with Spherical Heads Cultivated and Naturalized in the British Isles. *Plants Wild and Cultivated* (ed. Green, P S). Botanical Society of the British Isles, Middlesex.
Acer
De Jong, P C et al. *International Dendrology Society Year Book 1990*: 6-50. London.
Gelderen, D M van, De Jong, P C & Oterdoom, H J (1994). *Maples of the World*. Timber Press, Portland, Oregon.
Harris, J G S (1983). *The Plantsman*, 5(1): 35- 58.
Vertrees, J D (1978). *Japanese Maples*. Timber Press, Oregon.
Adiantum
Goudry, C J (1985). *Maidenhair Ferns in Cultivation*. Lothian, Melbourne, Australia.
Aeschynanthus
Dates, J D *The Gesneriad Register 1990*: Check List of Aeschynanthus. American Gloxinia and Gesneriad Society, Galesburg, Illinois.
Aesculus
Wright, D (1985). *The Plantsman*, **6(4)**: 228-47.
Agapetes
Argent, G C G & Woods, P J B (1988). *The Plantsman*, **8(2)**: 65-85.
Ajuga
Adam, C G (1982). *Alpine Garden Society Bulletin*, **50(1)**: 82-84.
Allium
Davies, D (1992). *Alliums*. Batsford, London.
Mathew, B (1996). *A Review of* Allium *section* Allium. Royal Botanic Gardens, Kew.
Alnus
Ashburner, K (1986). *The Plantsman*, **8(3)**: 170- 88.
Androsace

Smith, G F & Lowe, D B (1977). *Androsaces.* Alpine Garden Society.

Anemone, Japanese

McKendrick, M (1990). *The Plantsman*, **12(3)**: 140- 51.

Anemone nemorosa

Toubøl, U (1981). *The Plantsman*, **3(3)**: 167- 74.

Aquilegia

Munz, P A (1946). *Aquilegia:* The Cultivated and Wild Columbines. *Gentes Herbarum*, **7(1)**. Bailey Hortorium, New York.

Araceae

Bown, D (1988). *Aroids*. Century Hutchinson, London.

Arecaceae/Palmae (Palms)

Uhl, N J & Dransfield, J (1987). *Genera Palmarum.* Alan Press, Lawrence, Kansas, USA.

Argyranthemum

Cheek, R (1993). *The Garden*, **118(8)**: 350-55.

Humphries, C J (1976). A Revision of the Macaronesian Genus *Argyranthemum. The Bulletin of the British Museum (Natural History), Botany,* **5(4)**.

Arisaema

Mayo, J J (1982). *The Plantsman*, **3(4)**: 193-209.

Pradhan, U C (1990). *Himalayan Cobra-lilies* (Arisaema): *Their Botany and Culture*. Primulaceae Books, Kalimpong, West Bengal, India.

Arum

Boyce, P (1993). *The Genus* Arum. HMSO, London.

Asplenium

Rickard, M (1997). *The Garden*, **122(2)**: 86-92.

Aster

Ranson, E R (1947). *Michaelmas Daisies*. Garden Book Club.

Aubrieta

International Registration Authority Checklist Weihenstephan.

Begonia

Ingles, J (1990). *American Begonia Society Listing of Begonia Cultivars*. (Revised Edition Buxton Checklist).

Wall, B (1989). *The Plantsman*, **11(1)**: 4-14.

Thompson, M L & Thompson, E J (1981). *Begonias: The Complete Reference Guide*. Times Books, New York.

Betula

Ashburner, K (1980). *The Plantsman*, **2(1)**: 31-53.

Ashburner, K & Schilling, A D (1985). *The Plantsman*, **7(2)**: 116-25.

Hunt, D (ed). (1993). Betula*: Proceedings of the IDS Betula Symposium.* International Dendrology Society, Richmond, Surrey.

Bougainvillea

Bor, N L & Raizada, M B (1982). 2nd ed. *Some Beautiful Indian Climbers and Shrubs*: 291-304. Bombay Natural History Society.

Gillis, W T (1976). Bougainvilleas of Cultivation. *Baileya* **20(1)**: 34-41. New York.

Iredell, J (1990). *The Bougainvillea Grower's Handbook*. Simon & Schuster, Brookvale, Australia.

Iredell, J (1994). *Growing Bougainvilleas*. Cassell, London.

MacDaniels, L H (1981). A Study of Cultivars in *Bougainvillea. Baileya* **21(2)**: 77-100. New York.

Swithinbank, A (1995). *The Garden*, **120(10)**: 634- 37.

Bromeliaceae

Beadle, D A (1991). *A Preliminary Listing of all the Known Cultivar and Grex Names for the Bromeliaceae.* Bromeliad Society, Corpus Christi, Texas, USA.

Luther, H E & Sieff, E (1991). *An Alphabetical List of Bromeliad Binomials*. Bromeliad Society, Orlando, Florida, USA.

Rauh, W (1979). *Bromeliads*. Blandford Press, Dorset.

Buddleja

Maunder, M (1987). *The Plantsman*, **9(2)**: 65-80.

Bulbs

Bryan, J E (1989). *Bulbs*, vols 1 & 2. Christopher Helm, Bromley, Kent.

Du Plessis, N and Duncan, G (1989). *Bulbous Plants of Southern Africa*. Tafelberg, Cape Town, South Africa.

Grey-Wilson, C & Matthew, B (1981). *Bulbs*. Collins, London.

Rix, M & Phillips, R (1981). *The Bulb Book.* Pan Books, London.

Scheepen, J van (ed.). (1991). *International Checklist for Hyacinths and Miscellaneous Bulbs*. KAVB, Hillegom, Netherlands.

Buxus

Batdorf, L R (1989). *Checklist of Buxus*. American Boxwood Society.

Braimbridge, E (1994). *The Plantsman*, **15(4)**: 236-54.

Callistemon

Mitchem, C M (1993). *The Plantsman,* **15(1)**: 29- 41.

Calochortus

Martinelli, S (1995). *Alpine Garden Society Bulletin*, **63(1 & 2)**: 71-92, 180-99. Pershore, Worcestershire.

Camellia

Savige, T J (1993, corrected 1994). *The International Camellia Register*. The International Camellia Society, Wirlinga, Australia.

Campanula

Lewis, P & Lynch, M (1989). *Campanulas*. Christopher Helm, Bromley, Kent.

Carnivorous Plants

Pietropaulo, J & Pietropaulo, P (1986). *Carnivorous Plants of the World*. Timber Press, Oregon.

Slack, A (1988). Rev. ed. *Carnivorous Plants*. Alphabooks, Sherborne, Dorset.

Carpinus

Rushforth, K (1986). *The Plantsman*, **7(3 & 4)**: 173-91 & 212-16.

Caryopteris

Pattison, G (1989). *The Plantsman*, **11(1)**: 15-18.

Cassiope

Blake, F S (1985). *Alpine Garden Society Bulletin*, **53(1)**: 61-65.

Starling, B (1989). *The Plantsman*, **11(2)**: 106- 16.

Cestrum

Beckett, K A (1987). *The Plantsman*, **9(3)**: 129- 32.

Chaenomeles

Weber, C (1963). Cultivars in the Genus *Chaenomeles*. *Arnoldia*, **23(3)**: 17-75. Arnold Arboretum, Harvard, Massachusetts.

Cimicifuga

Compton, J (1992). *The Plantsman*, **14(2)**: 99-115.

Compton, J (1997). *Botanical Journal of the Linnean Society*, **123(1)**: 1-23.

Cistus

Page, R G (1991). *The Plantsman*, **13(3)**: 143-56.

Page, R G (1996). *The New Plantsman*, **3(3)**: 184-89.

Citrus

Davies, F S & Albrigo, L G (1994). *Citrus*. CAB International, Wallingford, Oxon.

Saunt, J (1990). *Citrus Varieties of the World*. Sinclair International Ltd., Norwich, England.

Clematis

Evison, R & Matthews, V (1994). *The New Plantsman*, **1(2)**: 95-101.

Fisk, J (1989). *Clematis, the Queen of Climbers*. Cassell, London.

Fretwell, B (1989). *Clematis*. Collins, London.

Grey-Wilson, C (1986). *The Plantsman*, **7(4)**: 193- 204.

Hutchins, G (1990). *The Plantsman*, **11(4)**: 193- 208.

Lloyd, C & Bennett, T H (1989). *Clematis*. Viking, London.

Oviatt-Ham, M (1996). *The Garden*, **121(3)**: 140- 45.

Snoeijer, W (1991). *Clematis Index*. Fopma, Boskoop, Netherlands.

Snoeijer, W (1996). *Checklist of Clematis Grown in Holland*. Fopma, Boskoop, Netherlands.

Codonopsis

Matthews, Y S (1980). *Alpine Garden Society Bulletin*, **48(2)**: 96-108.

Grey-Wilson, C (1990). *The Plantsman*, **12(2)**: 65- 99.

Grey-Wilson, C (1995). *The New Plantsman*, **2(4)**: 213-25.

Conifers

Krüssmann, G (English trans. M E Epp). (1985). *Manual of Cultivated Conifers*. Batsford, London.

Lewis, J ed. Leslie, A C (1987 & 1989). *The International Conifer Register*, pt 1 (*Abies* to *Austrotaxus*), pt 2 (*Belis* to *Pherosphaera* (excluding Cypresses and Junipers) & pt 3 (Cypresses). Royal Horticultural Society, London.

Ouden, P den & Boom, B K (1965). *Manual of Cultivated Conifers*. Martinus Nijhorff, The Hague, Netherlands.

Welch, H J (1979). *Manual of Dwarf Conifers*. Theophrastus, New York.

Welch, H J (1990). *The Conifer Manual*, **1**. Kluwer Academic Publishers, Dordrecht, Holland.

Welch, H J (1993). *The World Checklist of Conifers*. Landsman's Bookshops Ltd, Bromyard, Herefordshire.

Coprosma

Hutchins, G (1995). *The New Plantsman*, **2(1)**: 12- 37.

Cornus

Howard, R A (1961). Registration Lists of Cultivar Names in *Cornus* L., *Arnoldia*, **21(2)**: 9-18. Arnold Arboretum, Harvard, Massachusetts.

Corokia

Hutchins, G (1994). *The Plantsman*, **15(4)**: 225- 35.

Corydalis

Lidén, M and Zetterlund, H (1988). *Alpine Garden Society Bulletin*, **56(2)**: 146-69.

Rix, E M (1993). *The Plantsman*, **15(3)**: 129-30.

Corylopsis

Wright, D (1982). *The Plantsman*, **4(1)**: 29-53.

Corylus

Game, M (1995). *The Garden*, **120(11)**: 674-77.

Cotoneaster

Fryer, J (1996). *The Garden*, **121(11)**: 709-15.

Crocosmia

Kostelijk, P J (1984). *The Plantsman*, **5(4)**: 246- 53.

Crocus

Kerdorff, H & Pasche, E (1996). *Alpine Garden Society Bulletin*, **64(3)**: 296-312.

Kerdorff, H & Pasche, E (1996). *Alpine Garden Society Bulletin*, **64(4)**: 459-67.

Mathew, B (1982). *The Crocus*. Batsford, London

Cyclamen

Grey-Wilson, C (1988). *The Genus* Cyclamen. Christopher Helm, Bromley, Kent.

Grey-Wilson, C (1991). *The Plantsman*, **13(1)**: 1- 20.

Cynara

Wiklund, A (1992). *The Genus* Cynara. *Botanical Journal of the Linnean Society*, **109(1)**: 75-123.

Cyrtanthus

Holford, F (1989). *The Plantsman*, **11(3)**: 170-75.

Dahlia

Pycraft, D (1969-95) & Hedge, R (1996). *International Register of Dahlia Names 1969* & supps 1-7. Royal Horticultural Society, London.

Daphne
Brickell, C D & Mathew, B (1976). *Daphne*. Alpine Garden Society.
Delphinium
Leslie, A C (1996). *The International* Delphinium *Register Cumulative Supplement 1970-1995*. The Royal Horticultural Society, London.
Dendranthema (Chrysanthemum)
British National Register of Chrysanthemums. National Chrysanthemum Society. (1964-1993).
Deutzia
Taylor, J (1990). *The Plantsman*, **11(4)**: 225-40.
Dianthus
Leslie, A C (1983-93). 2nd ed. & supps 1-12. *The International* Dianthus *Register*. The Royal Horticultural Society, London.
Diascia
Benham, S (1987). *The Plantsman*, **9(1)**: 1-17.
Harrison, H (1996). *The Hardy Plant*, **18(1)**: 41- 48. Hardy Plant Society.
Lord, W A (1996). *The Garden*, **121(4)**: 192-94.
Dierama
Hilliard, O M & Burtt, B L (1990). *The Plantsman*, **12(2)**: 106-12.
Hilliard, O M and Burtt, B L (1991). Dierama. Acorn Books CC. Johannesburg, South Africa.
Dionysia
Grey-Wilson, C (1988). *The Plantsman*, **10(2)**: 65- 84.
Grey-Wilson, C (1989). *The Genus* Dionysia. Alpine Garden Society, Woking, Surrey.
Dodecatheon
Mitchem, C M (1991). *The Plantsman*, **13(3)**: 157- 70.
Dracaena
Bos, J J, Graven, P, Hetterscheid, W L A & van de Wege, J J (1992). *Edinburgh Journal of Botany*, **10(3)**: 311-31.
Drosera
Cheek, M (1993). *Kew Magazine*, **10(3)**: 138-44. Blackwell, Oxford.
Epimedium
Barker, D G (1996). *Epimediums and Other Herbaceous Berberidaceae*. Hardy Plant Society, Pershore, Worcs.
Stearn, W T (1995). *Curtis's Botanical Magazine*, **12(1)**: 15-25. Royal Botanic Gardens, Kew.
White, R (1996). *The Garden*, **121(4)**: 208-14.
Episcia
Arnold, P *The Gesneriad Register 1977*: Episcia. American Gloxinia and Gesneriad Society, Binghamton, New York.
Eriogonum
Elliott, J (1993). *Alpine Garden Society Bulletin*, **61(2)**: 200-14.
Erodium
Addyman, M & Clifton, R (1992). *Erodiums in Cultivation.* N.C.C.P.G., Wisley, Surrey.
Bacon, L (1990). *Alpine Garden Society Bulletin*, **58(1)**: 65-83.
Leslie, A C (1980). *The Plantsman*, **2(2)**: 117-26.
Erythronium
Mathew, B (1992). A Taxonomic and Horticultural Review of *Erythronium*. *Botanical Journal of the Linnean Society*, **109(4)**: 453-71.
Eucomis
Compton, J (1990). *The Plantsman*, **12(3)**: 129-39.
Eucryphia
Wright, D (1983). *The Plantsman*, **5(3)**: 167-85.
Euonymus
Brown, N (1996). *The New Plantsman*, **3(4)**: 238-43.
Lancaster, R (1981). *The Plantsman*, **3(3)**: 133- 66.
Euphorbia
Turner, R (1995). *Euphorbias*. Batsford, London.
Fagus
Wyman, D (1964). Registration List of Cultivar Names of *Fagus* L., *Arnoldia*, **24(1)** 1-8. Arnold Arboretum, Harvard, Massachusetts.
Ferns
Kaye, R (1968). *Hardy Ferns*. Faber & Faber, London.
Johns, R J (1991). *Pteridophytes of Tropical East Africa*. Royal Botanic Gardens, Kew.
Jones, D L (1987). *Encyclopaedia of Ferns*. Lothian, Melbourne, Australia.
Rush, R (1984). *A Guide to Hardy Ferns*. The British Pteridological Society, London.
Festuca
Wilkinson, M J & Stace, C A (1991). A new taxonomic treatment of the *Festuca ovina* aggregate in the British Isles. *Botanical Journal of the Linnean Society*, **106(4)**: 347-97.
Fragaria
Day, D (ed.). (1988, revd 1993). *Grower Digest 3: Strawberries*. Nexus Business Communications, London.
Fremontodendron
McMillan Browse, P (1992). *The Plantsman*, **14(1)**: 41-44.
Fritillaria
Turrill, W B & Seely, J R (1980). Studies in the Genus *Fritillaria. Hooker's Icones Plantarum*, **39(1 & 2)**. Royal Botanic Gardens, Kew.
Fuchsia
Bartlett, G (1996). *Fuchsias - A Colour Guide*. Crowood Press, Marlborough, Wiltshire.
Boullemier, L B (1991). 2nd ed. *The Checklist of Species, Hybrids & Cultivars of the Genus* Fuchsia. Blandford Press, Dorset, UK.
Nijhuis, M (1994). *1000 Fuchsias*. Batsford, London.
Nijhuis, M (1996). *500 More Fuchsias*. Batsford, London.
***Gaultheria* (inc. *Pernettya*).**
Middleton, D J (1990/91). *The Plantsman*, **12(3)**: 167-77 & **13(3)**: 188-89.
Middleton, D J (1991). Infrageneric Classification of the Genus *Gaultheria. Botanical Journal of the Linnean Society*, **106(3)**: 229-58.

Gentiana
Bartlett, M (1975). *Gentians*. Blandford Press, Dorset.
Wilkie, D (1950). 2nd ed. *Gentians*. Country Life, London.
Geranium
Abbott, P (1994). *A Guide to Scented Geraniaceae*. Hill Publicity Services, Angmering, W Sussex.
Bath, T, & Jones, J (1994). *The Gardener's Guide to Growing Hardy Geraniums*. David & Charles, Newton Abbot, Devon.
Clifton, R T F (1992). *Geranium Family Species Checklist*, **4(2)**: Geranium. The Geraniaceae Group of the British Pelargonium and Geranium Society, Kent.
Jones, J et al. (1992). *Hardy Geraniums for the Garden*. Hardy Plant Society, Pershore, Worcs.
Yeo, P F (1992). 2nd ed. *Hardy Geraniums*. Croom Helm, London.
Gesneriaceae
Dates, J D *The Gesneriad Register* 1986: *Check List of Intergeneric Hybrids in the tribe Gloxinieae*. American Gloxinia and Gesneriad Society, Sugar Grove, Illinois.
Dates, J D The Gesneriad Register 1987: *Check List of* Bucinellina, Columnea, Dalbergaria, Pentadenia, Trichantha *and Intergeneric Hybrids*. American Gloxinia and Gesneriad Society, Galesburg, Illinois.
Dates, J D *The Gesneriad Register 1990: Appendix C: Registered Gesneriads 1957-90*. American Gloxinia and Gesneriad Society, Galesburg, Illinois.
Gladiolus
Lewis, G J & Obermeyer, A A & Barnard, T T (1972). A Revision of the South African Species of *Gladiolus. Journal of South African Botany*, **supp. vol. 10**. Purnell, Cape Town.
List of Gladiolus Cultivars. The British Gladiolus Society.
Gleditsia triacanthos
Santamour, F S Jr & McArdle, A J (198?). *Checklist of Cultivars of Honeylocust*. USA.
Grevillea
Olde, P & Marriott, N (1995). *The Grevillea Book (3)*. Kangaroo Press, Kenthurst, NSW, Australia.
Haemanthus
Snijman, D (1984). A Revision of the Genus *Haemanthus. Journal of South African Botany*, **supp. vol. 12**. National Botanic Gardens, Kirstenbosch, Republic of South Africa.
Hamamelidaceae
Wright, D (1982). *The Plantsman*, **4(1)**: 29-53.
Hamamelis
Coombes, A J (1996). *The Garden*, **121(1)**: 28-33.
Heathers
Small, D and Small, A (1992). *Handy Guide to Heathers*. Denbeigh Heather Nurseries, Suffolk.
Underhill, T (1990). *Heaths and Heathers*. David & Charles, Newton Abbot, Devon.
Hebe
Hayter, T (ed.). (1986-97). *Hebe News*. 20 Beech Farm Drive, Macclesfield, Cheshire.
Hutchins, G (1979). Hebe *and* Parahebe *Species in Cultivation*. County Park Nursery, Essex.
Chalk, D (1988). *Hebes and Parahebes*. Christopher Helm, London.
Hedera
McAllister, H (1988). *The Plantsman*, **10(1)**: 27- 29.
McAllister, H A & Rutherford, A (1990). *Hedera helix & H. hibernica* in the British Isles. *Watsonia*, **18**.
Rose, P Q (1980). *Ivies*. Blandford Press, Dorset.
Rose, P Q (1996). *The Gardener's Guide to Growing Ivies*. David & Charles, Newton Abbot, Devon.
Rutherford, A, McAllister, H A & Rill, R R (1993). *The Plantsman*, **15(2)**: 115-28.
Hedychium
Schilling, A D (1982). *The Plantsman*, **4(3)**: 129- 49.
Spencer-Mills, L (1996). *The Garden*, **121(12)**: 754-59.
Helichrysum
Hilliard, O M & Burtt, B L (1987). *The Garden*, **112(6)**: 276-77.
Heliconia
Berry, F & Kress, W J (1991). Heliconia: *An Identification Guide*. Smithsonian Institution Press, Washington.
Helleborus
Mathew, B (1981). *The Plantsman*, **3(1)**: 1-10.
Mathew, B (1989). *Hellebores*. Alpine Garden Society, Woking, Surrey.
McLewin, W & Mathew, B (1995). *The New Plantsman*, **2(2)**: 112-22.
McLewin, W & Mathew, B (1996). *The New Plantsman*, **3(1)**: 50-60.
McLewin, W & Mathew, B (1996). *The New Plantsman*, **3(3)**: 170-77.
Rice, G & Strangman, E (1993). *The Gardener's Guide to Growing Hellebores*. David & Charles, Newton Abbot, Devon.
Hemerocallis
Erhardt, W (1988). Hemerocallis *Daylilies*. Batsford, London.
Kitchingman, R M (1985). *The Plantsman*, **7(2)**: 68-89.
Munson, R W (1989). Hemerocallis, *The Daylily*. Timber Press, Oregon.
Webber, S (ed.). (1988). *Daylily Encyclopaedia*. Webber Gardens, Damascus, Maryland.
Hibiscus
Beers, L & Howie, J (1990). 2nd ed. *Growing Hibiscus*. Kangaroo Press, Kenthurst, Australia.
Dickings, I (1995). *The Garden*, **120(8)**: 487-91.
Hippeastrum
Alfabetische Lisjt van de in Nederland in cultuur

zijnde Amaryllis (Hippeastrum) *Cultivars*. (1980). Koninklijke Algemeene Veereniging voor Bloembollencultur, Hillegom, Netherlands.

Hosta

Grenfell, D (1985). *The Plantsman*, **7(4)**: 251-54.
Grenfell, D (1990). Hosta. Batsford, London.
Grenfell, D (1993). *Hostas*. The Hardy Plant Society, Pershore, Worcs.
Grenfell, D (1996). *The Gardener's Guide to Growing Hostas*. David & Charles, Newton Abbot, Devon.
Grenfell, D (1993). *The Plantsman*, **15(3)**: 168- 84.
Hensen, K J W (1985). *The Plantsman*, **7(1)**: 1-35.
Schmid, W G (1991). *The Genus* Hosta. Timber Press, Oregon.

Hoya

Innes, C (1988). *The Plantsman*, **10(3)**: 129-40.

Hyacinthus orientalis

Stebbings, G (1996). *The Garden*, **121(2)**: 68-72.

Hydrangea

Haworth-Booth, M (1975). *The Hydrangeas*. Garden Book Club, London.
Lawson-Hall, T & Rothera, B (1995). *Hydrangeas*. Batsford, London.
Mallet, C (1992 & 1994). *Hydrangeas*, **1 & 2**. Centre d'Art Floral, Varengeville-sur-Mer, France

Hypericum

Robson, N K B (1980). *The Plantsman*, **1(4)**: 193- 200.

Ilex

Andrews, S (1983). *The Plantsman*, **5(2)**: 65-81.
Andrews, S (1984). *The Plantsman*, **6(3)**: 157-66.
Andrews, S (1985). *The Garden*, **110(11)**: 518-22.
Andrews, S (1994). *The Garden*, **119(12)**: 580-83.
Dudley, T R & Eisenbeiss, G K 1973 & (1992). *International Checklist of Cultivated* Ilex **1**: *Ilex opaca*; **2**: *Ilex crenata*. US Department of Agriculture, US National Arboretum, Washington.

Impatiens

Grey-Wilson, C (1983). *The Plantsman*, **5(2)**: 65- 81.

Incarvillea

Grey-Wilson, C (1994). *The New Plantsman*, **1(1)**: 36-52.

Iridaceae

Innes, C (1985). *The World of Iridaceae*. Holly Gate International, Sussex.

Iris

Hoog, M H (1980). *The Plantsman*, **2(3)**: 141-64.
Mathew, B (1981). *The Iris*. Batsford, London.
Mathew, B (1993). *The Plantsman*, **15(1)**: 14-25.

***Iris* (Series *Unguiculares*).**

Service, N (1990). *The Plantsman*, **12(1)**: 1-9.

Kniphofia

Taylor, J (1985). *The Plantsman*, **7(3)**: 129-60.

Kohleria

Dates, J D (ed.). *The Gesneriad Register 1985: Check List of* Kohleria. American Gloxinia and Gesneriad Society, Lincoln Acres, California.

Lachenalia

Duncan, G D (1988). The *Lachenalia* Handbook. *Annals of Kirstenbosch Botanic Gardens*, **17**. Republic of South Africa.

Lantana

Howard, R A (1969). A Check List of Cultivar Names used in the Genus *Lantana*. *Arnoldia* **29(11)**: 73-109. Arnold Arboretum, Harvard, Massachusetts.

Larix

Horsman, J (1988). *The Plantsman*, **10(1)**: 37-62.

Lathyrus

Norton, S (1994). *The Garden*, **119(5)**: 216-21.
Norton, S (1994). *The New Plantsman*, **1(2)**: 78- 83.
Norton, S (1996). Lathyrus. NCCPG, Woking, Surrey.

Lavandula

Tucker, A O & Hensen, K J W (1985). The Cultivars of Lavender and Lavandin. *Baileya*, **22(4)**: 168-177. New York.

Leguminosae

Lock, J M (1989). *Legumes of Africa*. Royal Botanic Gardens, Kew.
Lock, J M & Heald, J (1994). *Legumes of Indo-China*. Royal Botanic Gardens, Kew.
Lock, J M & Simpson, K (1991). *Legumes of West Asia*. Royal Botanic Gardens, Kew.

Leptospermum

Nomenclature Committee of the Royal New Zealand Institute of Horticulture. (1963). Check List of *Leptospermum* Cultivars. *Journal of the Royal New Zealand Institute of Horticulture*, **5(5)**: 224-30. Wellington, New Zealand.

Leucojum

Elliott, J (1992). *The Plantsman*, **14(2)**: 70-79.

Lewisia

Elliott, R (1978). *Lewisias*. Alpine Garden Society, Woking.
Mathew, B (1989). *The Genus* Lewisia. Christopher Helm, Bromley, Kent.

Liliaceae sensu lato

Mathew, B (1989). *The Plantsman*, **11(2)**: 89-105.

Lilium

Leslie, A C (1982-96). 3rd ed. & supps 1-14. *The International Lily Register*. The Royal Horticultural Society, London.

Liriodendron

Andrews, S (1993). *IDS Yearbook 1992*: 15-19. London.

Lonicera

Bradshaw, D (1991). *The Plantsman*, **13(2)**: 106-10.
Bradshaw, D (1995). *The Garden*, **120(7)**: 406-11.
Wright, D (1983). *The Plantsman*, **4(4)**: 236-55.

Magnolia

Calaway, D J (1994). *Magnolias*. Batsford, London.

Holman, N (1979). *The Plantsman*, **7(1)**: 36-39.
Treseder, N G (1978). *Magnolias*. Faber & Faber, London.

Malus

Fiala, J L (1994). *Flowering Crabapples*. Timber Press, Portland, Oregon.
Morgan, J & Richards, A (1993). *The Book of Apples*. Ebury Press, London.
Parfitt, B (1965). *Index of the Apple Collection at the National Fruit Trials*. Ministry of Agriculture, Fisheries and Food, Faversham, Kent.
Taylor, H V (1948). *The Apples of England*. Crosby Lockwood, London.

Meconopsis

Cobb, J L S (1989). *Meconopsis*. Christopher Helm, Bromley, Kent.
Grey-Wilson, C (1992). *The Plantsman*, **14(1)**: 1- 33.
Grey-Wilson, C (1996). *The New Plantsman*, **3(1)**: 22-39.
Cox, P (1996). *The New Plantsman*, **3(2)**: 80-83.

Moraea

Goldblatt, P (1986). *The Moraeas of Southern Africa*. National Botanic Gardens of South Africa.

Narcissus

Blanchard, J W (1990). Narcissus. Alpine Garden Society, Woking, Surrey.
Kington, S (1989-95). 2nd ed. & supps 14-21. *The International Daffodil Checklist*. The Royal Horticultural Society, London.
Throckmorton, T D (ed.). (1985). *Daffodils to Show & Grow and Abridged Classified List of Daffodil Names*. The Royal Horticultural Society and American Daffodil Society, Hernando, Mississippi.

Nematanthus

Arnold, P *The Gesneriad Register 1978: Check List of* Nematanthus. American Gloxinia and Gesneriad Society.

Nerium

Pagen, F J J (1987). *Oleanders*. Agricultural University, Wageningen, Holland.

Nothofagus

Hill, R S & Read, J (1991). *Botanical Journal of the Linnean Society*, **105(1)**: 37-72.

Nymphaea

Davies, R (1993). *Identification of Hardy* Nymphaea. Stapeley Water Gardens Ltd (for the International Water Lily Society), Cheshire.
Swindells, P (1983). *Waterlilies*. Croom Helm, London.

Orchidaceae

Cribb, P & Bailes, C (1989). *Hardy Orchids*. Christopher Helm, Bromley, Kent.

Origanum

Paton, A (1994). *Kew Magazine*, **11(3)**: 109-17.

Ostrya

Rushforth, K (1986). *The Plantsman*, **7(3) & (4)**: 173-91 & 212-16.

Paeonia

Harding, A, & Klehm, R G (1993). *The Peony*. Batsford, London.
Haw, S G (1991). *The Plantsman*, **13(2)**: 94-97.
Haworth-Booth, M (1963). *The Moutan or Tree Peony*. Garden Book Club, London.
Kessenich, G M (1976). *Peonies*. (Variety Check List, pts 1-3). American Peony Society.
Rogers, A (1995). *Peonies*. Timber Press, Portland, Oregon.

Papaveraceae

Grey-Wilson, C (1993). *Poppies*. Batsford, London.

Parahebe

Heads, M (1994). *Botanical Journal of the Linnean Society*, **115(1)**: 65-89.

Passiflora

Vanderplank, J (1996 2nd ed.). *Passion Flowers*. Cassell, London.

Pelargonium

Abbott, P G (1994). *A Guide to Scented Geraniaceae*. Hill Publicity Services, Angmering, W. Sussex.
Baggust, H (1988). *Miniature and Dwarf Geraniums*. Christopher Helm, Bromley, Kent.
A Checklist and Register of Pelargonium Cultivar Names, pt 1 (1978) & pt 2 (1985). Australian Geranium Society, Sydney.
Clifford, D (1958). *Pelargoniums*. Blandford Press, London.
Complete Copy of the Spalding Pelargonium *Checklist*. Unpublished. USA.
Miller, D (1996). *Pelargoniums*. Batsford, London.
Van der Walt, J J A et al. (1977-88). *Pelargoniums of South Africa*, **1-3**. National Botanic Gardens, Kirstenbosch, Republic of South Africa.

Penstemon

Charlesworth, G (1994). *Alpine Garden Society Bulletin*, **62(2 & 4)**: 158-80 & 465-75.
Lindgren, D T (1992). *List and Description of Named Cultivars in the Genus* Penstemon. University of Nebraska.
Lord, W A (1994). *The Garden*, **119(7)**: 304-09.

Philadelphus

Taylor, J (1990). *The Plantsman*, **11(4)**: 225-40.
Wright, D (1980). *The Plantsman*, **2(2)**: 104-16.

Phlox

Wherry, E T (1955). *The Genus* Phlox. Morris Arboretum Monographs III, Philadelphia, Penn.

Phormium

Heenan, P B (1991). *Checklist of* Phormium *Cultivars*. Royal New Zealand Institute of Horticulture, Canterbury, New Zealand.

Phygelius

Coombes, A J (1988).*The Plantsman*, **9(4)**: 233-46.

Phyllostachys

Renvoize, S (1995). *Curtis's Botanical Magazine*, **12(1)**: 8-15. Royal Botanic Gardens, Kew.

Pieris

Bond, J (1982). *The Plantsman*, **4(2)**: 65-75.
Wagenknecht, B.L. 1961. Registration List of

Names in the Genus *Pieris*. *Arnoldia*, 21(8). Arnold Arboretum, Harvard, Massachusetts.
Pinus
Muir, N (1992). *The Plantsman*, **14(2)**: 80-98.
Poaceae/Gramineae (Grasses)
Clayton, W D & Renvoize, S A (1986). *Genera Graminum*. HMSO, London
Grounds, R (1979). *Ornamental Grasses*. Pelham Books, London.
Poaceae (Bambusoideae)
Chao C S (1989). *A Guide to Bamboos Grown in Britain*. Royal Botanic Gardens, Kew.
McClintock, D (1992). *The Plantsman*, **14(3)**: 169- 77.
Wang D & Shen S-J (1987). *Bamboos of China*. Timber Press, Oregon.
Zhu S, Ma N & Fu M (eds.). (1994) *A Compendium of Chinese Bamboo*. China Forestry Publishing House.
Podocarpus
Hutchins, G (1991). *The Plantsman*, **13(2)**: 98- 105.
Polypodium
Leslie, A C (1993). *The Garden*, **118(10)**: 450-52.
Potentilla
Brearley, C (1991). *The Plantsman*, **13(1)**: 42-53.
Brearley, C (1992). *Alpine Garden Society Bulletin*, **60(3) & (4)**: 321-28 & 428-35.
Davidson, C G, Enns, R J & Gobin, S (1994). *A Checklist of* Potentilla fruticosa: *The Shrubby Potentillas*. Agriculture and Agri-Food Canada Research Centre, Morden, Manitoba, Canada.
Davidson, C G & Lenz, L M (1989). Experimental Taxonomy of *Potentilla fruticosa*. *Canadian Journal of Botany*, **67(12)**: 3520-28.
***Potentilla* (Shrubby)**
Brearley, C (1987). *The Plantsman*, **9(2)**: 90-109.
Primula
Baker, G & Ward, P (1995). *Auriculas*. Batsford, London.
Fenderson, G K (1986). *A Synoptic Guide to the Genus* Primula. Allen Press, Lawrence, Kansas.
Green, R (1976). *Asiatic Primulas*. The Alpine Garden Society, Woking.
Halda, J J (1992). *The Genus* Primula. Tethys Books, Colorado.
Hecker, W R (1971). *Auriculas & Primroses*. Batsford, London.
Richards, J (1993). Primula. Batsford, London.
Smith, G F, Burrow, B & Lowe, D B (1984). *Primulas of Europe and America*. The Alpine Garden Society, Woking.
Wemyss-Cooke, T J (1986). *Primulas Old and New*. David & Charles, Newton Abbot.
Primula allionii
Marcham, A J (1992). *Alpine Garden Society Bulletin*, **60(3)**: 255-67.
Prunus
Bultitude, J *Index of the Plum Collection at the National Fruit Trials*. Ministry of Agriculture, Fisheries & Food, Faversham, Kent.
Crawford, M (1996). *Plums*. Agroforestry Research Trust, Dartington, Devon.
Grubb, N H (1949). *Cherries*. Crosby Lockwood, London.
Index of the Cherry Collection at the National Fruit Trials. 1986. Ministry of Agriculture, Fisheries & Food, Faversham, Kent.
Jacobson, A L (1992). *Purpleleaf Plums*. Timber Press, Portland, Oregon.
Jefferson, R M & Wain, K K (1984). *The Nomenclature of Cultivated Flowering Cherries* (Prunus): *The Sato-zakura Group*. USDA
Smith, M W G (1978). *Catalogue of the Plums at the National Fruit Trials*. Ministry of Agriculture, Fisheries & Food, Faversham, Kent.
Taylor, H V (1949). *The Plums of England*. Crosby Lockwood, London.
Pulmonaria
Hewitt, J (1994). *Pulmonarias*. The Hardy Plant Society, Pershore, Worcs.
Mathew, B (1982). *The Plantsman*, **4(2)**: 100-11.
Pyracantha
Egolf, D R & Andrick, A O (1995). *A Checklist of* Pyracantha *cultivars*. US Department of Agriculture, Washington.
Pyrus
Crawford, M (1996). *Directory of Pear Cultivars*. Agroforestry Research Trust, Dartington, Devon.
Parfitt, B (1981). *Index of the Pear Collection at the National Fruit Trials*. Ministry of Agriculture, Fisheries & Food, Faversham, Kent.
Smith, M W G (1976). *Catalogue of the British Pears*. Ministry of Agriculture, Fisheries & Food, Faversham, Kent
Quercus
Miller, H A & Lamb, S H (1985). *Oaks of North America*. Naturegraph Publishers, Happy Camp, California.
Mitchell, A (1994). *The Plantsman*, **15(4)**: 216- 24.
Muir, N (1996). *The New Plantsman*, **3(4)**: 216-36.
Ranunculus ficaria
Carter, J R L (1996). *The Garden*, **121(2)**: 90-95.
Raoulia
Hutchins, G (1980). *The Plantsman*, **2(2)**: 100-03.
Rhododendron
Argent, G, Fairweather, G & Walter, K (1996). *Accepted Names in* Rhododendron *Section* Vireya. Royal Botanic Garden Edinburgh.
Chamberlain, D F (1982). *Notes from the Royal Botanic Garden, Edinburgh*, **39(2)**. HMSO, Edinburgh.
Chamberlain, D F & Rae, S J (1990). A Revision of *Rhododendron* IV Subgenus *Tsutsusi*. *Edinburgh Journal of Botany,* **47(2)**. HMSO, Edinburgh.
Cox, P A & Cox, K N E (1988). *Encyclopaedia of*

Rhododendron *Hybrids*. Batsford, London.
Cullen, J (1980). *Notes from the Royal Botanic Garden, Edinburgh*, **39(1)**. HMSO, Edinburgh.
Davidian, H H (1982, 1989, 1992 & 1995). *The* Rhododendron *Species*, **1-4.** Batsford, London.
Galle, F C (1987). *Azaleas*. Timber Press, Portland, Oregon.
Lee, F P (1958). *The Azalea Book*. D Van Nostrand, New York.
Leslie, A C (compiler). (1980). *The Rhododendron Handbook*. The Royal Horticultural Society, London.
Leslie, A C (1989-96). *The International* Rhododendron *Register: Checklist of Rhododendron Names & supps 28-36*. The Royal Horticultural Society, London.
Salley, H E & Greer, H E (1986). Rhododendron *Hybrids*. Batsford, London.

Rhus

Coombes, A J (1994). *The New Plantsman*, **1(2)**: 107-113.

Ribes

Index of the Bush Fruit Collection at the National Fruit Trials. 1987. Ministry of Agriculture, Fisheries & Food, Faversham, Kent.

Romneya

McMillan Browse, P (1989). *The Plantsman*, **11(2)**: 121-24.

Rosa

Austin, D (1988). *The Heritage of the Rose*. Antique Collectors' Club, Woodbridge, Suffolk.
Beales, P (1992). *Roses*. Harvill, London.
Bean, W J (1900-1988). 8th ed. rev. D L Clarke & G S Thomas. *Rosa* in *Trees and Shrubs Hardy in the British Isles*, **4** & supp.
Dickerson, B C (1992). *The Old Rose Advisor*. Timber Press, Portland, Oregon.
Haw, S G (1996). *The New Plantsman*, **3(3)**: 143-46.
McCann, S (1985). *Miniature Roses*. David & Charles, Newton Abbot, Devon.
Pawsey, A (1996). 14th ed. *Find That Rose!* British Rose Growers' Association, Colchester, Essex.
Phillips, R & Rix, M (1988). *Roses*. Macmillan, London.
Phillips, R & Rix, M (1993). *The Quest for the Rose*. BBC Books, London.
Thomas, G S (1995). *The Graham Stuart Thomas Rose Book*. John Murray, London

Rosularia

Eggli, U (1988). A monograph study of the genus *Rosularia. Bradleya*, **6 suppl**. British Cactus & Succulent Society, Bury, Lancashire.

Salix

Newsholme, C (1992). *Willows*. Batsford, London.

Salvia

Compton, J (1994). *The Plantsman*, **15(4)**: 193-215.

Saxifraga

Horn, R Webr, K M & Byam-Grounds, J (1986). *Porophyllum Saxifrages*. Byam-Grounds Publications, Stamford, Lincolnshire, UK.
Kohlein, F (1984). *Saxifrages and Related Genera*. Batsford, London.
McGregor, M (1995). *Saxifrages: The Complete Cultivars and Hybrids (International Register of Saxifrages, ed. 1)*. The Saxifrage Society.
Webb, D A & Cornell, R J (1989). *Saxifrages of Europe*. Christopher Helm, Bromley, Kent.

Saxifragaceae

Stocks, A (1995). *Saxifragaceae*. Hardy Plant Society.

Sedum

Evans, R L (1983). *Handbook of Cultivated Sedums*. Ivory Head Press, Motcombe, Dorset.
Hensen, K J W & Groendijk-Wilders, N.(1986). *The Plantsman*, **8(1)**: 1-20.
Stephenson, R (1994). Sedum. Timber Press, Portland Oregon.

Sempervivum

Mitchell, P J (1985). *International Cultivar Register for* Jovibarba, Rosularia, Sempervivum. The Sempervivum Society, W Sussex.

Shortia

Barnes, P G (1990). *The Plantsman*, **12(1)**: 23-34.

Sinningia

Dates, J D *The Gesneriad Register 1988: Check List of* Sinningia. American Gloxinia and Gesneriad Society, Galesburg, Illinois.

Skimmia

Brown, P D (1980). *The Plantsman*, **1(4)**: 224-59.

Solenostemon

Pedley, W K & Pedley, R (1974). *Coleus - A Guide to Cultivation and Identification*. Bartholemew, Edinburgh.

Sophora

Hutchins, G (1993). *The Plantsman*, **15(1)**: 1-13.

Sorbus

McAllister, H (1985). *The Plantsman*, **6(4)**: 248- 55.
McAllister, H (1996). *The Garden*, **121(9)**: 561-67.
Rushforth, K (1991). *The Plantsman*, **13(2)**: 111- 24.
Rushforth, K (1992). *The Plantsman*, **13(4)**: 226- 42 **&** **14(1)**: 54-62.
Wright, D (1981). *The Plantsman*, **3(2)**: 65-98.

Streptocalyx

Innes, C (1993). *The Plantsman*, **15(2)**: 73-81.

Streptocarpus

Arnold, P *The Gesneriad Register 1979: Check List of* Streptocarpus. American Gloxinia and Gesneriad Society, Binghamton, New York.

Sutherlandia

Schrire, B D & Andrews, S (1992). *The Plantsman*, **14(2)**: 65-69.

Syringa

Fiala, Fr J L (1988). *Lilacs*. Christopher Helm, Bromley, Kent.
Rogers, O M (1976). *Tentative International Register of Cultivar Names in the Genus*

Syringa. University of New Hampshire.
Taylor, J (1990). *The Plantsman*, **11(4)**: 225-40.
Vrugtman, F (1976-83). *Bulletin of the American Association of Botanical Gardens and Arboreta.*

Tilia

Muir, N (1984). *The Plantsman*, **5(4)**: 206-42.
Muir, N (1988). *The Plantsman*, **10(2)**: 104-27.

Tillandsia

Kiff, L F (1991). *A Distributional Checklist of the Genus* Tillandsia. Botanical Diversions, Encino, California.

Tricyrtis

Chesters, J & Lanyon, J (1996). *The Garden*, **121(9)**: 536-39.
Matthew, B (1985). *The Plantsman*, **6(4)**: 193-224.

Trillium

Mitchell, R J (1989-92). *The Plantsman*, **10(4)**: 216-31, **11(2 & 3)**: 67-79 & 132-51, **12(1)**: 44-60, **13(4)**: 219-25.

Tulbaghia

Benham, S (1993). *The Plantsman*, **15(2)**: 89-110.

Tulipa

Scheepen, J van (ed.). *Classified List and International Register of Tulip Names*. (1996). Royal General Bulbgrowers' Association, Hillegom, Holland.

Ulmus

Green, P S (1964). Registration of the Cultivar Names in *Ulmus. Arnoldia*, **24(608)**. Arnold Arboretum, Harvard, Massachusetts.

Umbelliferae

Ingram, T (1993). *Umbellifers*. Hardy Plant Society, Pershore, Worcs.
Pimenov, M G & Leonov, M V (1993). *The Genera of the Umbelliferae*. Royal Botanic Gardens, Kew.

Veratrum

Mathew, B (1989). *The Plantsman*, **11(1)**: 34-61.

Viola

Coombs, R E 1981 *Violets*. Croom Helm, London.
Farrar, E (1989). *Pansies, Violas & Sweet Violets*. Hurst Village Publishing, Reading.
Fuller, R (1990). *Pansies, Violas & Violettas*. Crowood Press, Marlborough, Wiltshire.
Perfect, E G (1996). *Armand Millet and his Violets*. Park Farm Press, High Wycombe, Bucks.

Vitis

Pearkes, G (1989). *Vine Growing in Britain*. Dent, London.
Robinson, J (1986). *Vines, Grapes and Wines*. Mitchell Beazley, London.

Watsonia

Goldblatt, P (1989). *The Genus* Watsonia. National Botanic Gardens, Republic of South Africa.

Weigela

Howard, R A (1965). A Check-list of Cultivar Names in *Weigela. Arnoldia*, **25(9-11)**. Arnold Arboretum, Harvard, Massachusetts.
Taylor, J (1990). *The Plantsman*, **11(4)**: 225-40.

Wisteria

McMillan-Browse, P (1984). *The Plantsman*, **6(2)**: 109-22.
Valder, P (1995). *Wisterias*. Florilegium, Balmain, NSW, Australia.

Zauschneria (Epilobium)

Raven, P H (1976). *Annals of the Missouri Botanical Garden*, **63** 326-340.

Zelkova

Ainsworth, P (1989). *The Plantsman*, **11(2)**: 80-86.
Hunt, D (1994). *I.D.S. Yearbook 1993*, 33-41. International Dendrology Society, Sherborne, Dorset.
Muir, N (1991). *The Plantsman*, **13(2)**: 125-26.

INDEX MAP

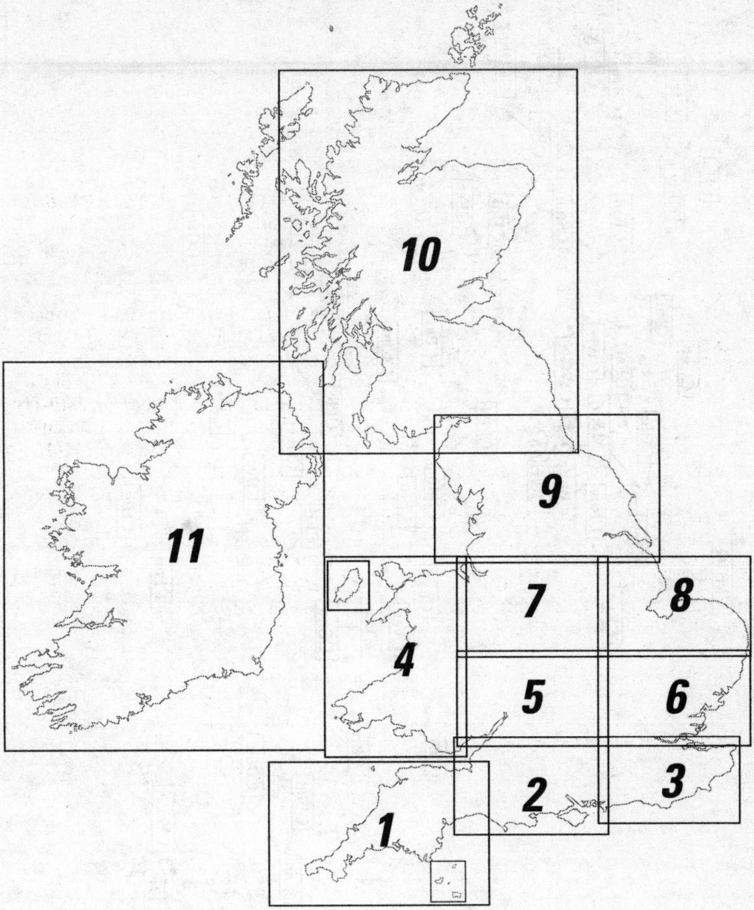

Motorways

Primary routes

Other 'A' roads

The maps on the following pages show the approximate location of the nurseries whose details are listed in this directory.

Details of nurseries with letter Codes in boxes are given in the CODE-NURSERY Index. CRow

Details of nurseries with number Codes in circles are given in the ADDITIONAL NURSERY Index. (20)

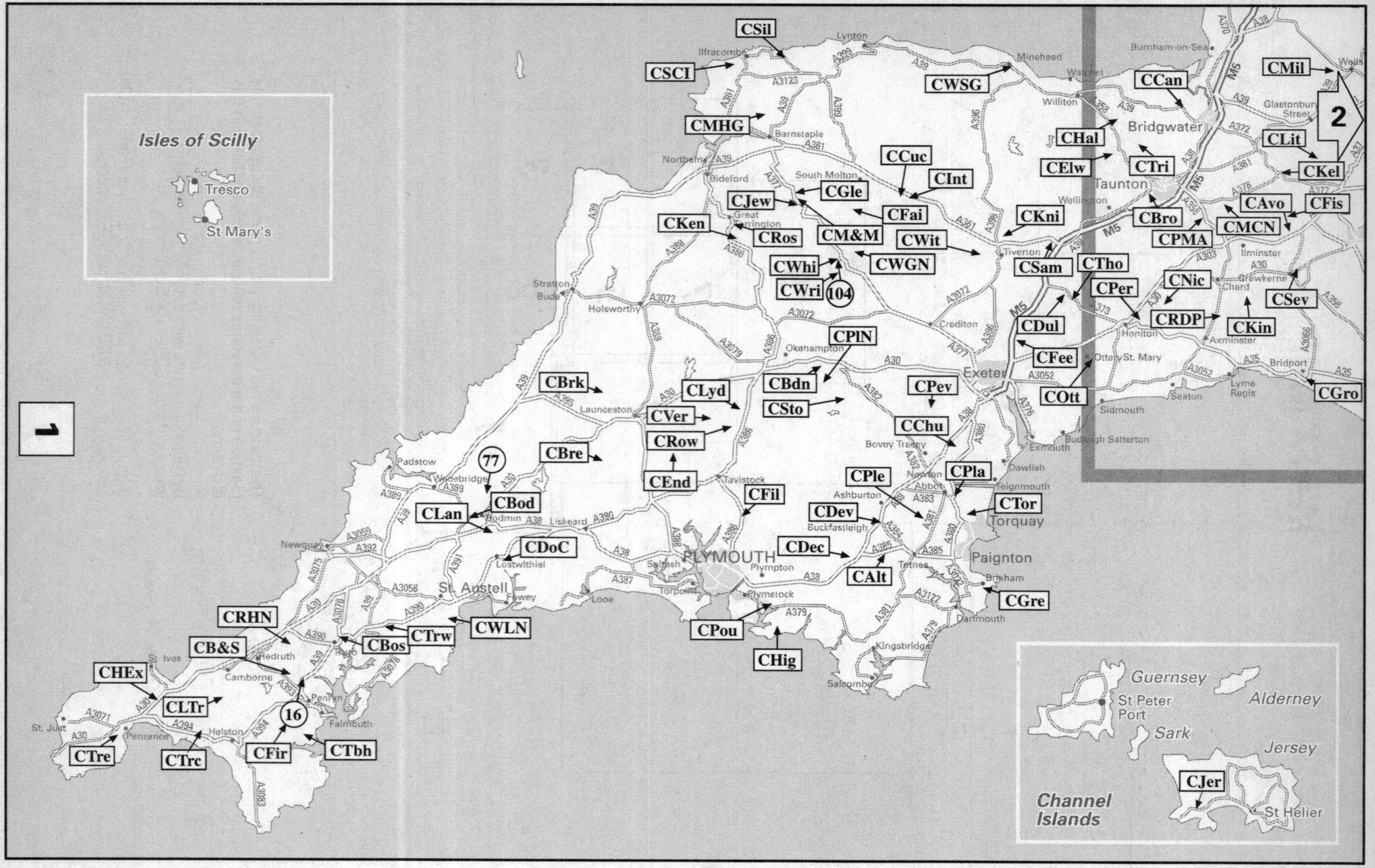
1
2
Isles of Scilly
Tresco
St Mary's
Channel Islands
Guernsey
St Peter Port
Alderney
Sark
Jersey
St Helier
CJer
CSil
CSCI
CMHG
CWSG
CCan
CMil
CHal
CElw
CTri
CLit
CKel
CCuc
CInt
CJew
CGle
CFai
CKen
CRos
CM&M
CWit
CKni
CBro
CAvo
CFis
CMCN
CPMA
CWhi
CWGN
CWri
104
CSam
CTho
CNic
CPer
CSev
CDul
CRDP
CKin
CPlN
CFee
CBdn
COtt
CGro
CBrk
CLyd
CPev
CVer
CSto
CChu
CRow
CBre
77
CEnd
CPle
CPla
CTor
CBod
CLan
CFil
CDev
CDoC
CDec
CAlt
CGre
CRHN
CWLN
CTrw
CPou
CBos
CB&S
CHig
CHEx
CLTr
16
CTre
CTrc
CFir
CTbh
Ilfracombe
Lynton
Minehead
Watchet
Burnham-on-Sea
Wells
Williton
Glastonbury
Street
Bridgwater
Barnstaple
Northam
Bideford
South Molton
Great Torrington
Taunton
Wellington
Tiverton
Ilminster
Crewkerne
Chard
Stratton
Bude
Holsworthy
Crediton
Honiton
Axminster
Okehampton
Exeter
Ottery St. Mary
Bridport
Lyme Regis
Seaton
Sidmouth
Launceston
Budleigh Salterton
Exmouth
Bovey Tracey
Padstow
Wadebridge
Tavistock
Dawlish
Newton Abbot
Teignmouth
Ashburton
Bodmin
Liskeard
Torquay
Buckfastleigh
Newquay
Plymouth
Plympton
Paignton
Lostwithiel
Saltash
Totnes
St. Austell
Fowey
Looe
Torpoint
Brixham
Plymstock
Dartmouth
Truro
Redruth
St Ives
Kingsbridge
Camborne
Penryn
Salcombe
Falmouth
St. Just
Penzance
Helston
M5
A30
A38
A39
A303
A361
A396
A386
A388
A3072
A3079
A3123
A399
A377
A382
A385
A380
A379
A381
A390
A391
A394
A3083
A3071
A3075
A3058
A3059
A3052
A35
A358
A370
A372
A378
A3066
A356
A37
A376
A395
A389
A392
A393
A3076
A3078
A383
A3022
A3122
A387

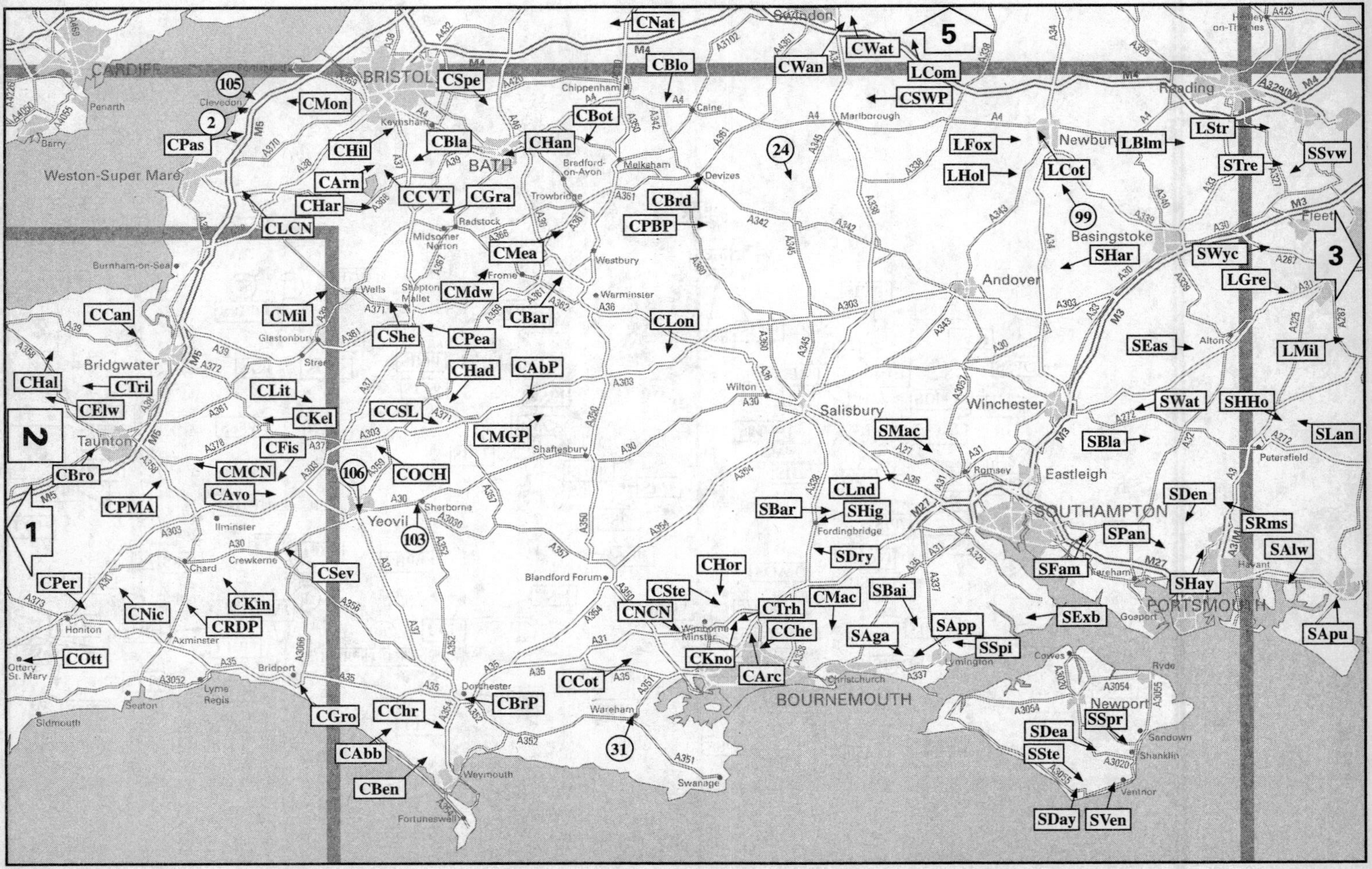

CARDIFF
BRISTOL
BATH
Weston-Super Mare
Swindon
Reading
Newbury
Basingstoke
Andover
Salisbury
Winchester
Eastleigh
SOUTHAMPTON
PORTSMOUTH
BOURNEMOUTH
Bridgwater
Taunton
Yeovil
Penarth
Barry
Clevedon
Chippenham
Marlborough
Caine
Devizes
Melksham
Bradford-on-Avon
Trowbridge
Keynsham
Radstock
Midsomer Norton
Frome
Westbury
Warminster
Wells
Shepton Mallet
Glastonbury
Street
Burnham-on-Sea
Wilton
Shaftesbury
Sherborne
Ilminster
Crewkerne
Chard
Honiton
Axminster
Ottery St. Mary
Sidmouth
Seaton
Lyme Regis
Bridport
Dorchester
Weymouth
Fortuneswell
Blandford Forum
Wimborne Minster
Wareham
Swanage
Christchurch
Lymington
Fordingbridge
Romsey
Fareham
Gosport
Havant
Petersfield
Alton
Fleet
Henley on-Thames
Cowes
Ryde
Newport
Sandown
Shanklin
Ventnor
1
2
3
5
105
2
24
99
106
103
31
CNat
CBlo
CWan
CWat
LCom
CSWP
CSpe
CMon
CPas
CBot
CHan
CBla
CHil
CArn
CCVT
CGra
CHar
CLCN
CBrd
CPBP
CMea
CMdw
CBar
CMil
CShe
CPea
CCan
CHal
CTri
CElw
CLit
CKel
CHad
CAbP
CCSL
CMGP
CFis
CMCN
COCH
CAvo
CBro
CPMA
CSev
CKin
CNic
CRDP
CPer
COtt
CGro
CChr
CAbb
CBen
CBrP
CCot
CLon
CHor
CSte
CNCN
CTrh
CChe
CKno
CArc
CMac
CLnd
SBar
SHig
SDry
SMac
SBai
SAga
SApp
SSpi
SExb
SFam
SPan
SDen
SRms
SHay
SAlw
SApu
SLan
SHHo
SWat
SBla
SEas
LMil
LGre
SWyc
SHar
STre
SSvw
LStr
LBlm
LCot
LFox
LHol
SDea
SSte
SSpr
SDay
SVen
M4
M5
M3
M27
A4
A34
A303
A30
A36
A350
A338
A31
A35
A37
A39

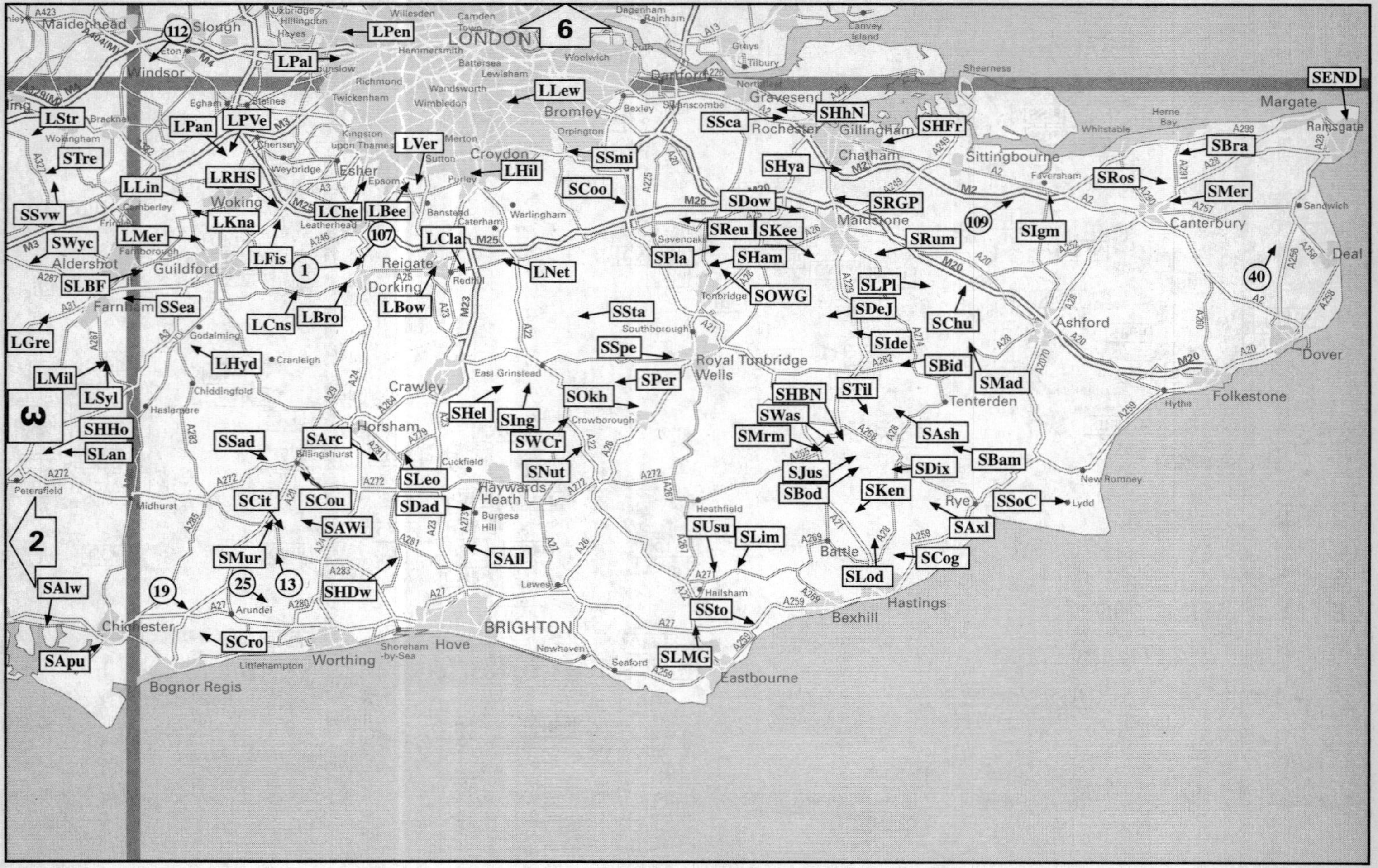

6
3
2
LONDON
Maidenhead
Slough
Windsor
Uxbridge
Hillingdon
Hayes
Willesden
Camden Town
Hammersmith
Battersea
Lewisham
Woolwich
Dagenham
Rainham
Grays
Tilbury
Canvey Island
Dartford
Richmond
Twickenham
Wandsworth
Wimbledon
Bromley
Bexley
Swanscombe
Gravesend
Rochester
Gillingham
Chatham
Sheerness
Sittingbourne
Faversham
Whitstable
Herne Bay
Margate
Ramsgate
Sandwich
Canterbury
Deal
Dover
Folkestone
Hythe
New Romney
Lydd
Rye
Ashford
Tenterden
Maidstone
Sevenoaks
Tonbridge
Southborough
Royal Tunbridge Wells
Crowborough
East Grinstead
Crawley
Horsham
Billingshurst
Cuckfield
Haywards Heath
Burgess Hill
Lewes
Heathfield
Hailsham
Battle
Hastings
Bexhill
Eastbourne
Seaford
Newhaven
BRIGHTON
Hove
Shoreham -by-Sea
Worthing
Littlehampton
Arundel
Bognor Regis
Chichester
Midhurst
Petersfield
Haslemere
Chiddingfold
Cranleigh
Godalming
Guildford
Farnham
Aldershot
Farnborough
Frimley
Camberley
Bracknell
Wokingham
Egham
Staines
Chertsey
Weybridge
Woking
Kingston upon Thames
Esher
Epsom
Leatherhead
Sutton
Merton
Croydon
Purley
Banstead
Caterham
Warlingham
Orpington
Reigate
Redhill
Dorking
M4
M3
M25
M26
M20
M23
M2
A404(M)
A329(M)
A423
A327
A287
A31
A3
A246
A25
A24
A29
A264
A281
A272
A283
A285
A286
A27
A280
A23
A273
A22
A26
A267
A21
A225
A20
A229
A228
A262
A274
A268
A265
A28
A2070
A259
A269
A2
A249
A252
A257
A290
A291
A299
A256
A258
A260
A13
A226
LPen
LPal
LLew
LStr
LPan
LPVe
LVer
LHil
STre
LRHS
LLin
SSvw
LKna
LChe
LBee
LMer
SWyc
LFis
LCla
SLBF
SSea
LCns
LBro
LBow
LNet
LGre
LHyd
LMil
LSyl
SHHo
SLan
SSad
SArc
SLeo
SCit
SCou
SAWi
SDad
SMur
SHDw
SAll
SAlw
SApu
SCro
SHel
SIng
SWCr
SNut
SOkh
SPer
SSpe
SSta
SSmi
SCoo
SSca
SHhN
SHFr
SHya
SDow
SReu
SKee
SPla
SHam
SOWG
SRGP
SRum
SLPl
SDeJ
SIde
SChu
SBid
SMad
SIgm
SRos
SMer
SBra
SEND
SHBN
SWas
SMrm
STil
SAsh
SBam
SJus
SBod
SDix
SKen
SSoC
SAxl
SCog
SLod
SUsu
SLim
SSto
SLMG
112
107
1
109
40
19
25
13

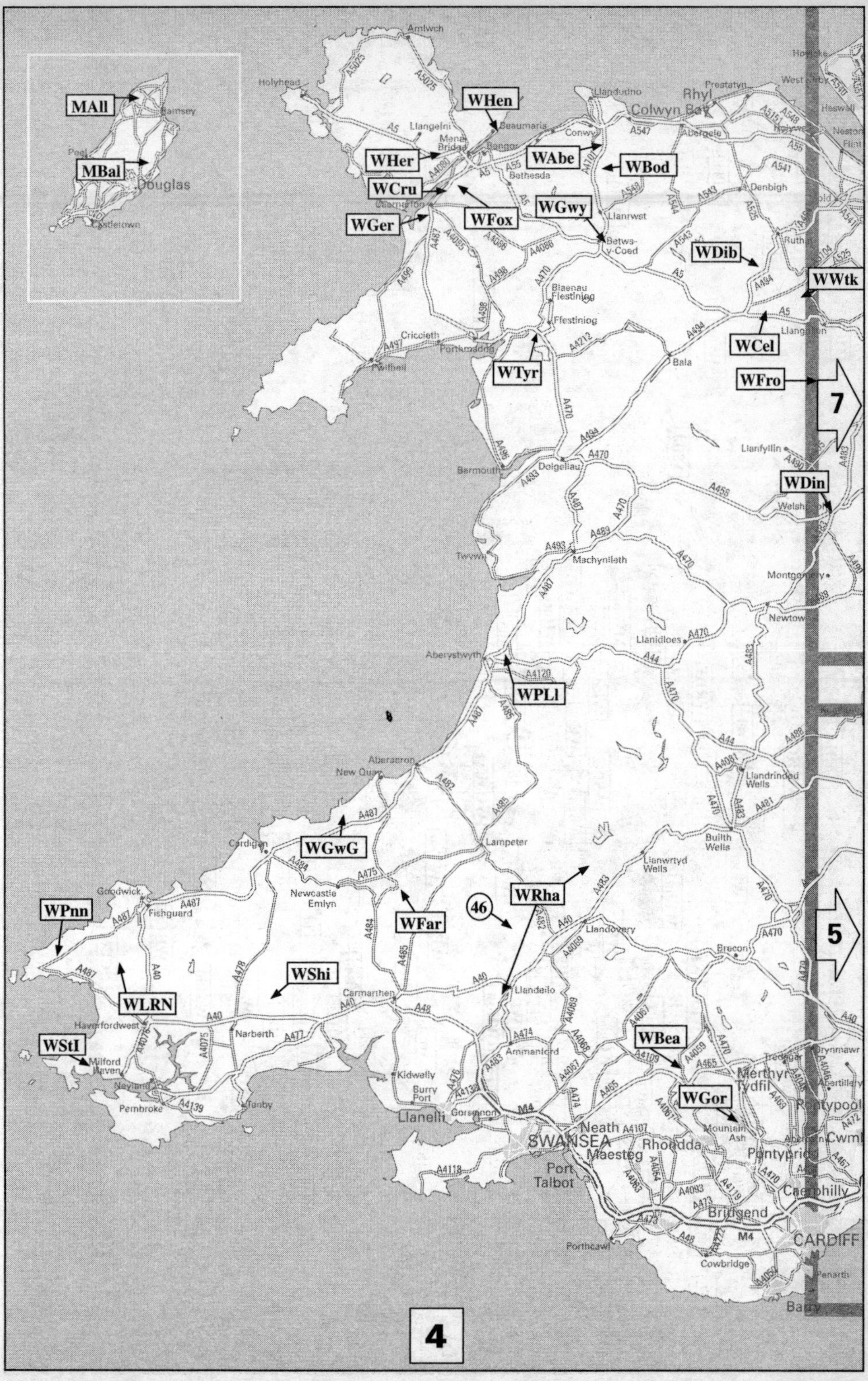
MAll
MBal
Ramsey
Peel
Douglas
Castletown
Amlwch
Holyhead
Llangefni
Menai Bridge
Beaumaris
Bangor
Caernarfon
Bethesda
Llandudno
Conwy
Colwyn Bay
Rhyl
Prestatyn
Abergele
Denbigh
Llanrwst
Betws-y-Coed
Ruthin
Blaenau Ffestiniog
Ffestiniog
Criccieth
Porthmadog
Pwllheli
Bala
Llangollen
Barmouth
Dolgellau
Tywyn
Machynlleth
Llanfyllin
Welshpool
Montgomery
Newtown
Llanidloes
Aberystwyth
Aberaeron
New Quay
Llandrindod Wells
Builth Wells
Llanwrtyd Wells
Lampeter
Cardigan
Newcastle Emlyn
Goodwick
Fishguard
Llandovery
Brecon
Llandeilo
Carmarthen
Haverfordwest
Narberth
Milford Haven
Neyland
Pembroke
Tenby
Kidwelly
Burry Port
Llanelli
Gorseinon
Ammanford
SWANSEA
Neath
Port Talbot
Maesteg
Rhondda
Merthyr Tydfil
Mountain Ash
Pontypridd
Caerphilly
Pontypool
Cwmbran
Abertillery
Brynmawr
Tredegar
Bridgend
Porthcawl
Cowbridge
CARDIFF
Penarth
Barry
WHen
WHer
WCru
WGer
WFox
WAbe
WBod
WGwy
WDib
WWtk
WCel
WTyr
WFro
7
WDin
WPLl
WGwG
WRha
46
WFar
WPnn
WLRN
WShi
WStI
WBea
WGor
5
4

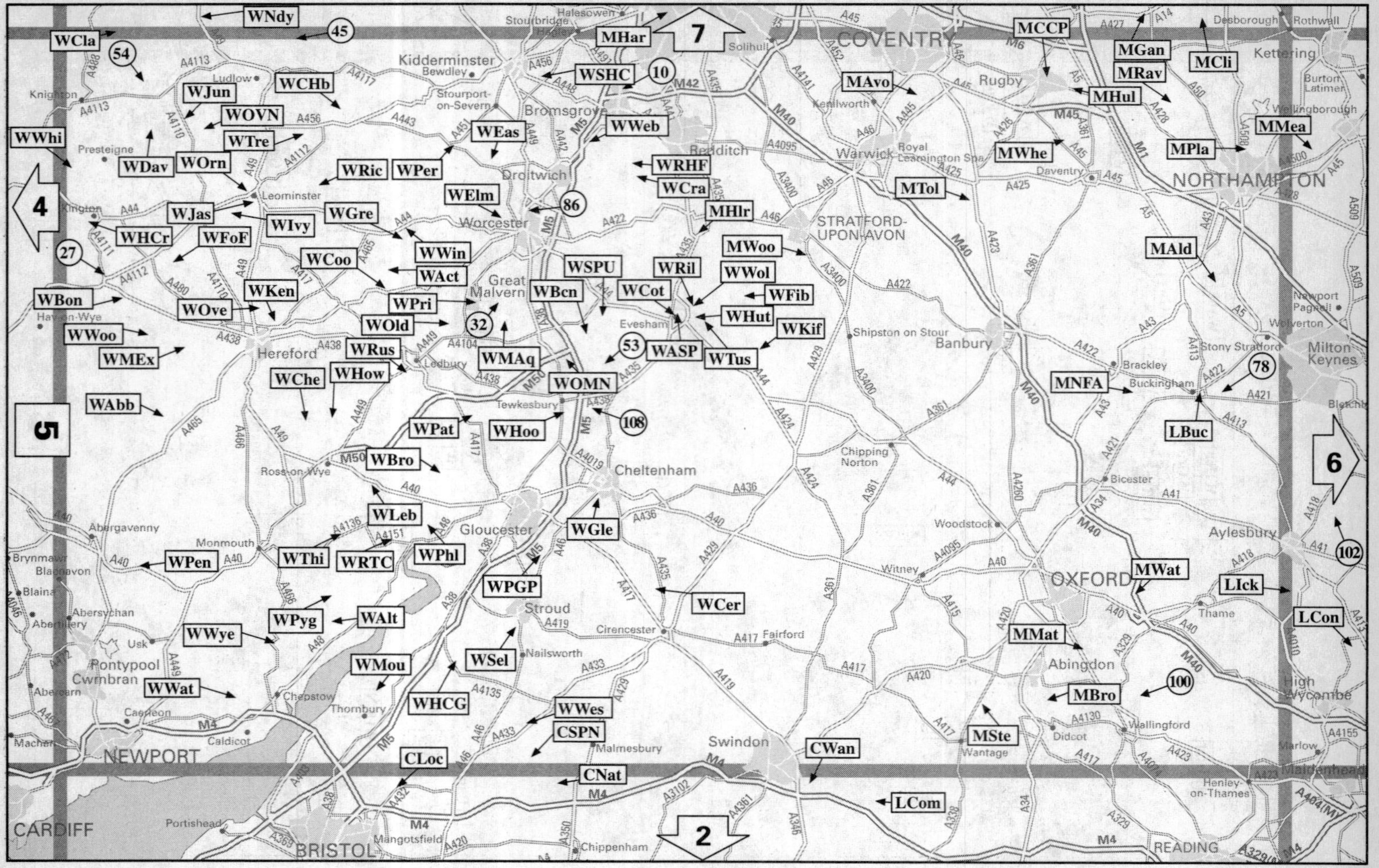

7
6
5
4
2
WNdy
45
WCla
54
MHar
10
WSHC
WCHb
WJun
WOVN
WTre
WWhi
WDav
WOrn
WEas
WWeb
WRic
WPer
WRHF
WCra
WElm
86
WJas
WIvy
WGre
WHCr
WFoF
MHlr
27
WCoo
WWin
WAct
WSPU
WRil
WCot
WBcn
WKen
WOve
WPri
WOld
32
WBon
WWoo
WMEx
WRus
WMAq
53
WASP
WTus
WHut
WFib
WKif
WWol
MWoo
WChe
WHow
WOMN
WAbb
WPat
WHoo
108
WBro
WLeb
WGle
WThi
WRTC
WPhl
WPen
WPGP
WCer
WPyg
WAlt
WWye
WMou
WSel
WHCG
WWat
WWes
CSPN
CLoc
CNat
CWan
LCom
MSte
MMat
MBro
100
MWat
LIck
LCon
102
LBuc
78
MNFA
MAld
MTol
MWhe
MAvo
MCCP
MGan
MRav
MHul
MCli
MPla
MMea
COVENTRY
NORTHAMPTON
STRATFORD-UPON-AVON
OXFORD
Kidderminster
Bromsgrove
Droitwich
Worcester
Redditch
Warwick
Royal Leamington Spa
Rugby
Kettering
Daventry
Hereford
Leominster
Ludlow
Great Malvern
Evesham
Tewkesbury
Cheltenham
Gloucester
Stroud
Cirencester
Banbury
Chipping Norton
Witney
Bicester
Aylesbury
Abingdon
Swindon
Newport
Cardiff
Bristol
Reading
Milton Keynes
Buckingham
Monmouth
Chepstow
Ross-on-Wye

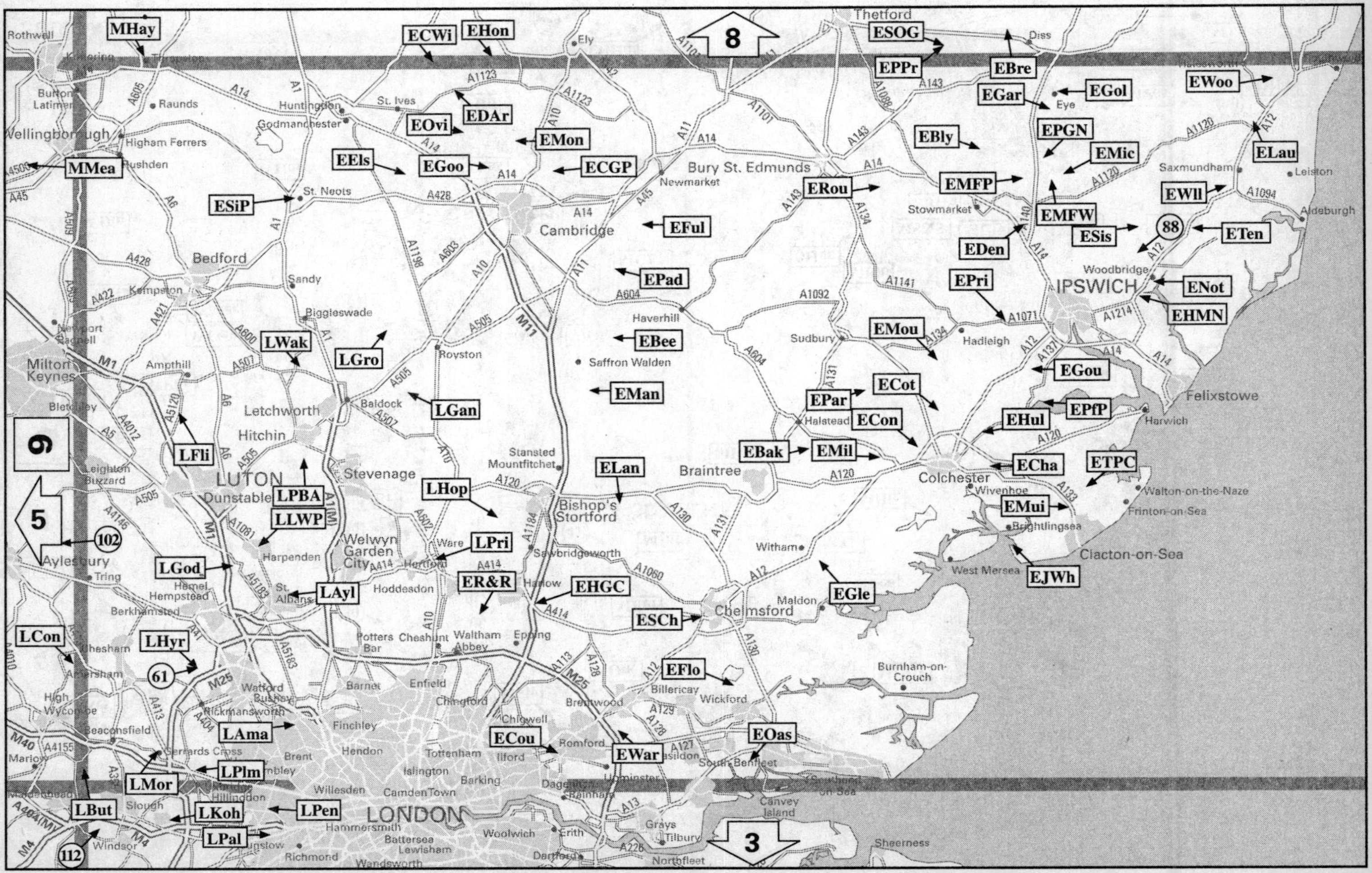
8
6
5
3
MHay
ECWi
EHon
ESOG
EPPr
EBre
EGar
EGol
EWoo
EDAr
EOvi
EMon
EEls
EGoo
ECGP
MMea
ESiP
ERou
EMFP
EBly
EPGN
EMic
ELau
EWll
EMFW
ESis
88
ETen
EDen
EFul
EPad
EPri
ENot
EHMN
EBee
EMou
EGou
EMan
ECot
EPar
ECon
EPfP
EHul
LWak
LGro
LGan
LFli
LPBA
LLWP
EBak
EMil
ELan
ECha
ETPC
LHop
EMui
LPri
LGod
102
ER&R
EHGC
LAyl
EJWh
EGle
ESCh
LCon
LHyr
61
EFlo
LAma
ECou
EWar
EOas
LPlm
LMor
LBut
LKoh
LPen
LPal
112
Thetford
Diss
Ely
Eye
Rothwell
Kettering
Thrapston
Burton Latimer
Raunds
Wellingborough
Higham Ferrers
Rushden
Huntingdon
Godmanchester
St. Ives
St. Neots
Bury St. Edmunds
Newmarket
Stowmarket
Saxmundham
Leiston
Aldeburgh
Cambridge
Bedford
Kempston
Sandy
Biggleswade
Newport Pagnell
Milton Keynes
Bletchley
Ampthill
Royston
Haverhill
Saffron Walden
Sudbury
Hadleigh
Woodbridge
IPSWICH
Felixstowe
Harwich
Letchworth
Baldock
Hitchin
Stevenage
Halstead
Stansted Mountfitchet
Braintree
Colchester
Wivenhoe
Walton-on-the-Naze
Frinton-on-Sea
Brightlingsea
Clacton-on-Sea
Leighton Buzzard
LUTON
Dunstable
Bishop's Stortford
Harpenden
Welwyn Garden City
Ware
Hertford
Sawbridgeworth
Witham
West Mersea
Aylesbury
Tring
Hemel Hempstead
Berkhamsted
St. Albans
Hoddesdon
Harlow
Maldon
Chelmsford
Chesham
Amersham
Potters Bar
Cheshunt
Waltham Abbey
Epping
Burnham-on-Crouch
Watford
Bushey
Barnet
Enfield
Billericay
Wickford
High Wycombe
Rickmansworth
Chingford
Brentwood
Beaconsfield
Finchley
Chigwell
Marlow
Gerrards Cross
Brent
Hendon
Tottenham
Ilford
Romford
Basildon
South Benfleet
Hillingdon
Islington
Barking
Upminster
Willesden
Camden Town
Dagenham
Rainham
Canvey Island
Slough
LONDON
Hammersmith
Grays
Tilbury
Windsor
Battersea
Lewisham
Woolwich
Erith
Richmond
Wandsworth
Dartford
Northfleet
Sheerness

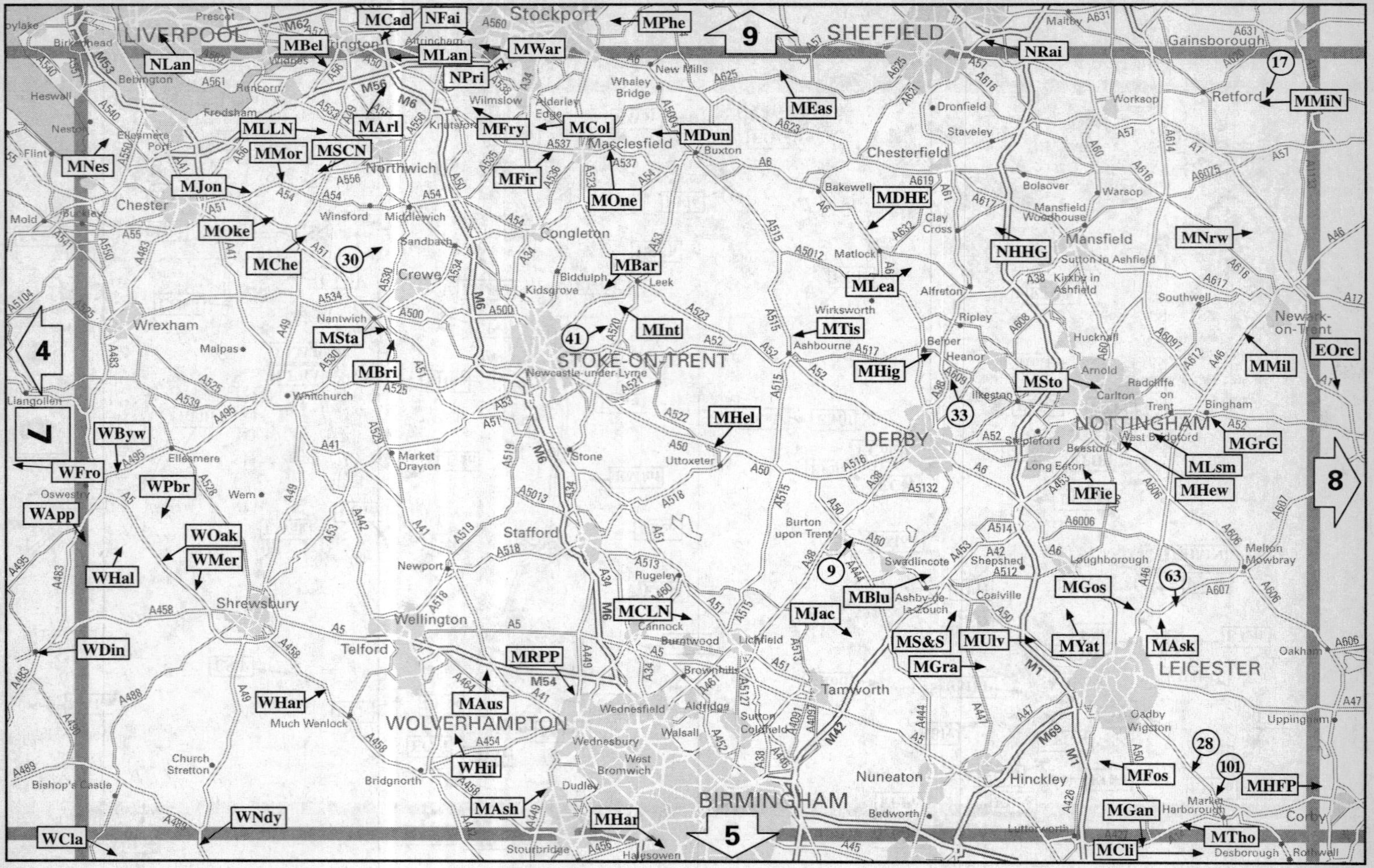

7
4
9
8
5
LIVERPOOL
SHEFFIELD
STOKE-ON-TRENT
DERBY
NOTTINGHAM
LEICESTER
BIRMINGHAM
WOLVERHAMPTON
Stockport
Chester
Wrexham
Shrewsbury
Telford
Wellington
Stafford
Crewe
Congleton
Macclesfield
Buxton
Chesterfield
Mansfield
Newark-on-Trent
Gainsborough
Retford
Worksop
Tamworth
Nuneaton
Hinckley
Lichfield
Burton upon Trent
Loughborough
Melton Mowbray
Oakham
Uttoxeter
Ashbourne
Matlock
Bakewell
Northwich
Nantwich
Oswestry
Llangollen
Market Harborough
Corby
NLan
MBel
MCad
NFai
MLan
MWar
NPri
MPhe
NRai
MEas
MMiN
MLLN
MArl
MFry
MCol
MDun
MNes
MMor
MSCN
MJon
MFir
MOne
MDHE
MOke
MChe
MBar
NHHG
MNrw
MLea
MInt
MSta
MBri
MTis
MHig
MSto
MMil
EOrc
MHel
MGrG
MLsm
MHew
MFie
WByw
WFro
WPbr
WApp
WOak
WMer
WHal
MBlu
MJac
MGos
MAsk
MCLN
MS&S
MUlv
MYat
MGra
MRPP
WDin
WHar
MAus
WHil
MFos
MHFP
MAsh
MHar
MGan
MTho
MCli
WNdy
WCla

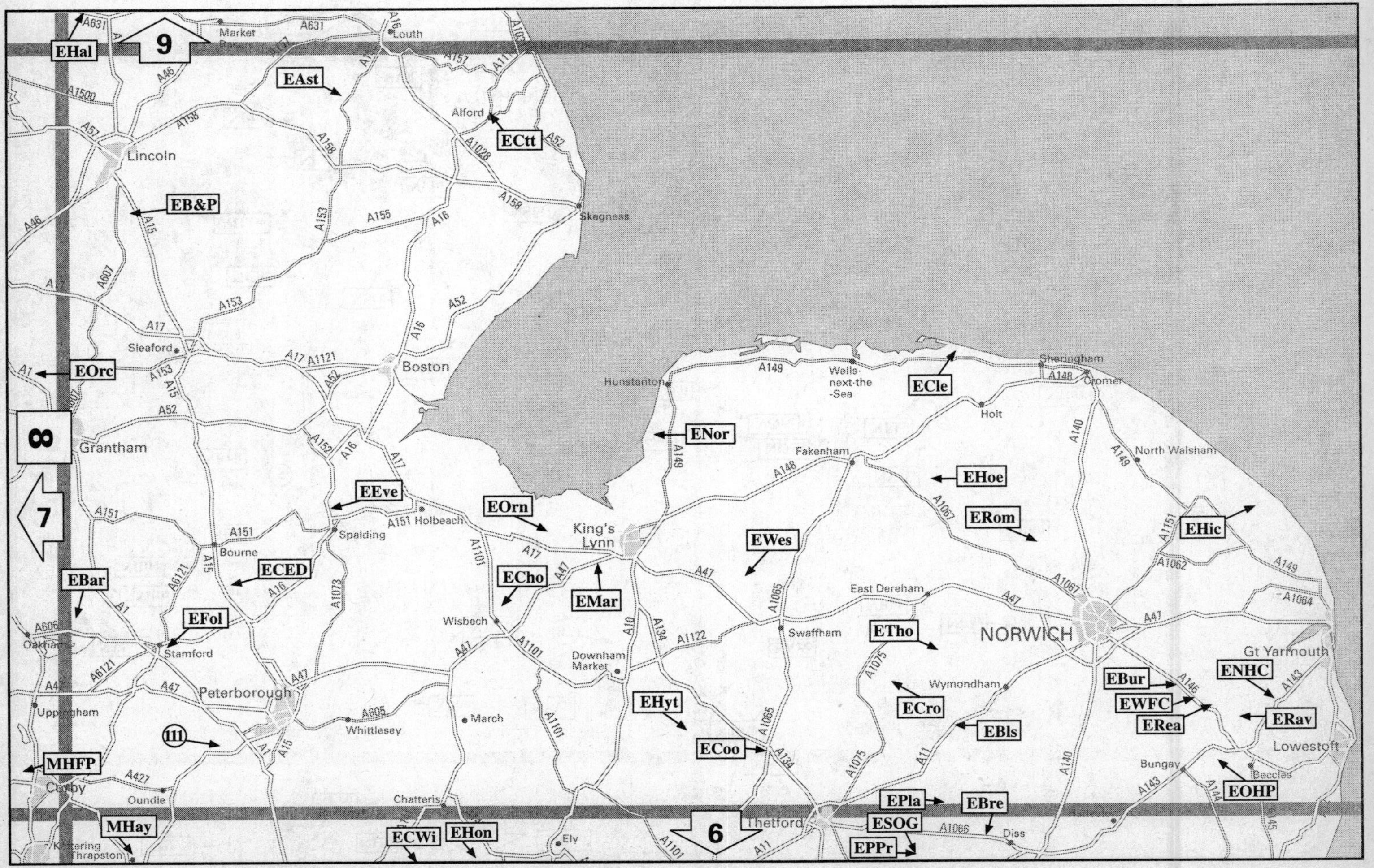
9
8
7
6
Lincoln
Market Rasen
Louth
Alford
Skegness
Boston
Sleaford
Grantham
Spalding
Holbeach
Bourne
Stamford
Oakham
Uppingham
Peterborough
Whittlesey
March
Wisbech
Chatteris
Ely
Oundle
Corby
Kettering
Thrapston
King's Lynn
Hunstanton
Wells-next-the-Sea
Sheringham
Cromer
Holt
Fakenham
North Walsham
Downham Market
Swaffham
East Dereham
NORWICH
Wymondham
Thetford
Diss
Gt Yarmouth
Lowestoft
Beccles
Bungay
EHal
EAst
ECtt
EB&P
EOrc
EEve
EOrn
ECED
EBar
EFol
ECho
EMar
ENor
ECle
EHoe
ERom
EWes
EHic
ETho
ECro
EBls
EHyt
ECoo
EPla
EBre
ESOG
EPPr
ECWi
EHon
MHFP
MHay
EBur
EWFC
ERea
ENHC
ERav
EOHP
111

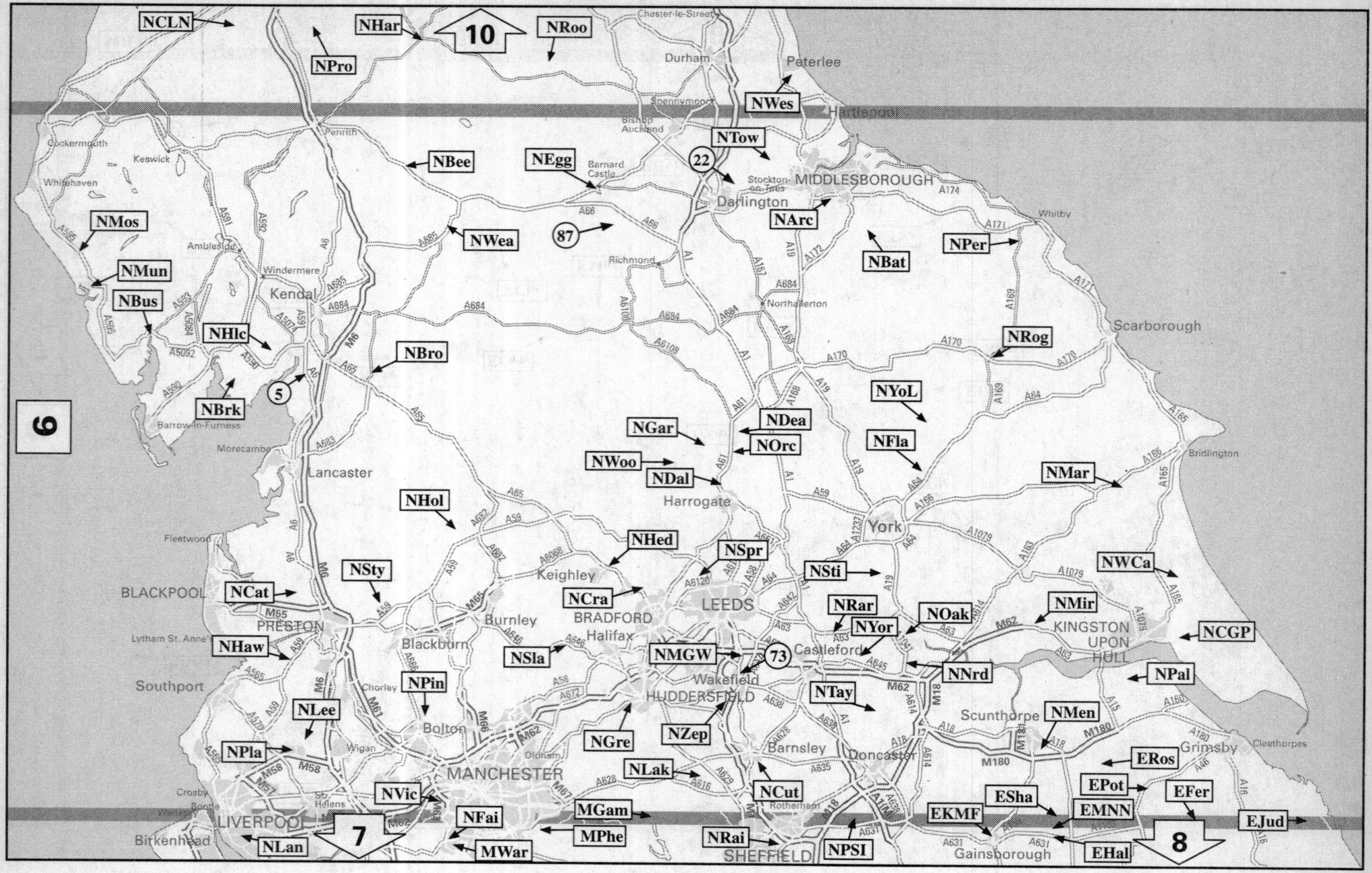
9
10
7
8
NCLN
NHar
NPro
NRoo
NWes
NTow
22
NEgg
NBee
NWea
87
NArc
NBat
NPer
NMos
NMun
NBus
NHlc
NBro
5
NBrk
NRog
NYoL
NGar
NDea
NOrc
NWoo
NDal
NFla
NMar
NHol
NHed
NSpr
NSti
NWCa
NSty
NCat
NCra
NRar
NOak
NMir
NYor
NCGP
NHaw
NSla
NMGW
73
NNrd
NPal
NPin
NLee
NTay
NGre
NZep
NMen
NPla
NLak
NCut
ERos
EPot
EFer
NVic
MGam
ESha
EMNN
EKMF
EJud
NFai
MPhe
NRai
NPSI
EHal
NLan
MWar
Chester-le-Street
Durham
Peterlee
Spennymoor
Hartlepool
Bishop Auckland
Penrith
Cockermouth
Keswick
Whitehaven
Barnard Castle
Stockton-on-Tees
MIDDLESBOROUGH
Darlington
Whitby
Ambleside
Windermere
Kendal
Richmond
Northallerton
Scarborough
Barrow-in-Furness
Morecambe
Lancaster
Bridlington
Harrogate
York
Fleetwood
Keighley
BLACKPOOL
LEEDS
PRESTON
Burnley
BRADFORD
Halifax
KINGSTON UPON HULL
Lytham St. Anne's
Blackburn
Castleford
Wakefield
Southport
Chorley
HUDDERSFIELD
Bolton
Scunthorpe
Wigan
Oldham
Barnsley
Doncaster
Grimsby
Cleethorpes
MANCHESTER
Crosby
Bootle
St. Helens
Rotherham
LIVERPOOL
Birkenhead
SHEFFIELD
Gainsborough
M6
M55
M61
M62
M65
M66
M67
M18
M180
M181
M58
M57
A1
A1(M)
A6
A19
A59
A61
A64
A65
A66
A170
A171
A174
A165
A166
A169
A168
A167
A172
A684
A6108
A1079
A163
A15
A18
A16
A180
A46
A631
A614
A638
A635
A628
A616
A629
A58
A672
A646
A6068
A682
A595
A591
A592
A593
A5084
A5092
A590
A5074
A685
A683
A565
A570
A580
A6120
A642
A63
A645
A1041
A1237
A160
A1033

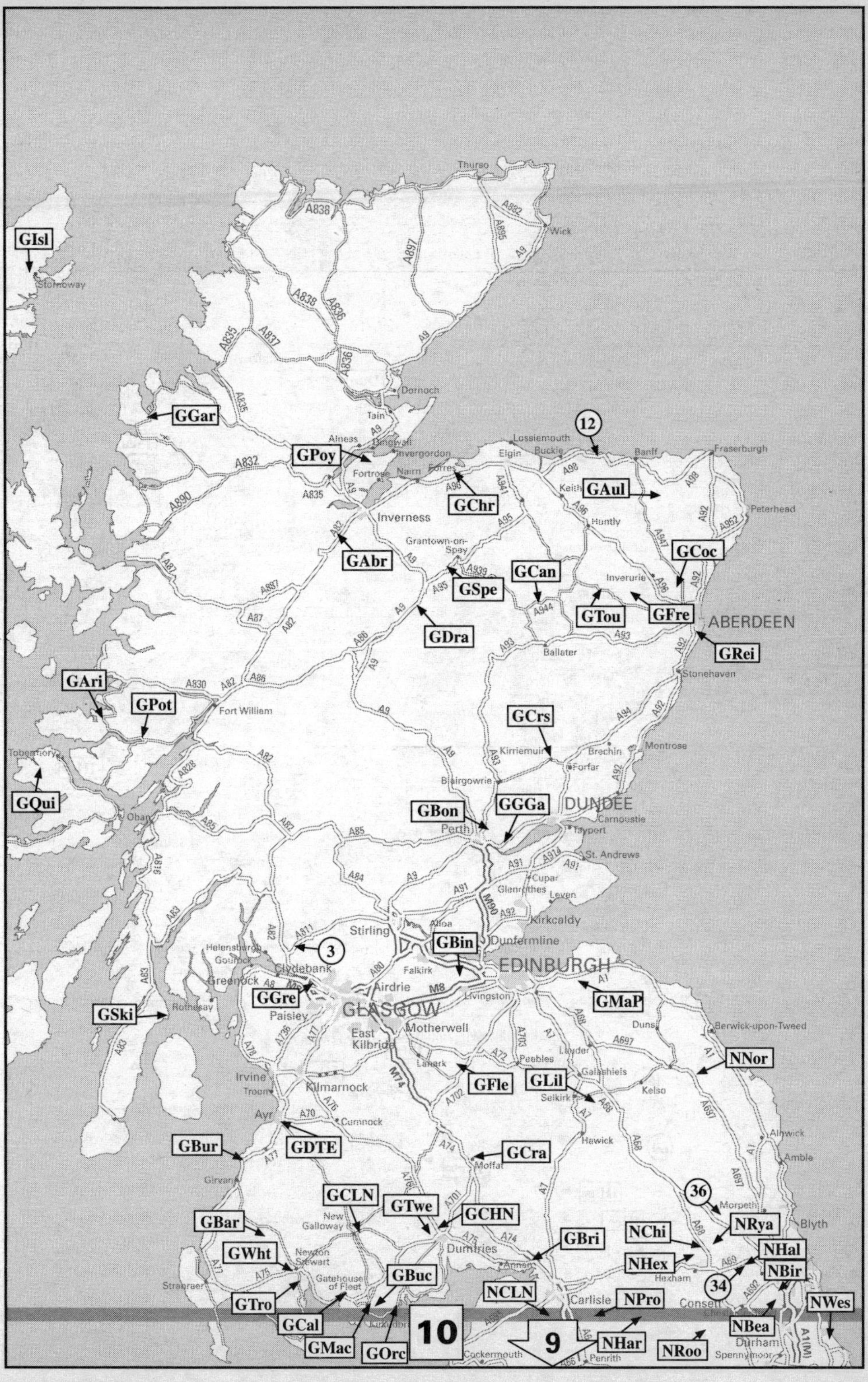
GIsl
Stornoway
Thurso
Wick
A838
A882
A895
A897
A9
A836
A835
A837
Dornoch
GGar
Tain
Alness
Dingwall
Invergordon
GPoy
A832
Fortrose
Nairn
Forres
A890
Inverness
GChr
A96
A941
Elgin
Lossiemouth
Buckie
12
Banff
Fraserburgh
A98
GAul
Keith
Huntly
Peterhead
A92
A952
A947
GAbr
A82
Grantown-on-Spey
A95
A939
GCan
GCoc
Inverurie
GSpe
A944
GTou
GFre
ABERDEEN
A87
A887
GDra
A93
GRei
Ballater
Stonehaven
A86
GAri
GPot
A830
Fort William
GCrs
A94
Kirriemuir
Brechin
Forfar
Montrose
Tobermory
GQui
A828
Oban
Blairgowrie
GBon
GGGa
DUNDEE
Carnoustie
Tayport
Perth
St. Andrews
A85
A84
A91
A914
A816
Cupar
Glenrothes
Leven
M90
Kirkcaldy
A83
Stirling
Alloa
Dunfermline
GBin
A811
3
Helensburgh
Gourock
Clydebank
Greenock
EDINBURGH
A80
Falkirk
Airdrie
M8
A1
Livingston
GGre
GMaP
GSki
Rothesay
GLASGOW
Paisley
Motherwell
East Kilbride
A736
A77
A78
A703
A68
Duns
Berwick-upon-Tweed
A697
NNor
A72
Lanark
Peebles
Lauder
Galashiels
GFle
GLil
Selkirk
Kelso
M74
Irvine
Troon
Kilmarnock
A76
A702
A7
Ayr
A70
Cumnock
GDTE
GBur
Hawick
A74
GCra
Moffat
Alnwick
Amble
Girvan
GCLN
GTwe
GCHN
A701
36
Morpeth
NRya
Blyth
GBar
New Galloway
NChi
A75
NHal
Dumfries
GBri
GWht
Newton Stewart
NHex
A69
Hexham
NBir
A692
34
Stranraer
Annan
GBuc
Gatehouse of Fleet
GTro
NCLN
Carlisle
NPro
Consett
NWes
GCal
Kirkcudbright
10
NBea
9
NHar
NRoo
Durham
GMac
GOrc
Cockermouth
Penrith
A66
Spennymoor
A1(M)

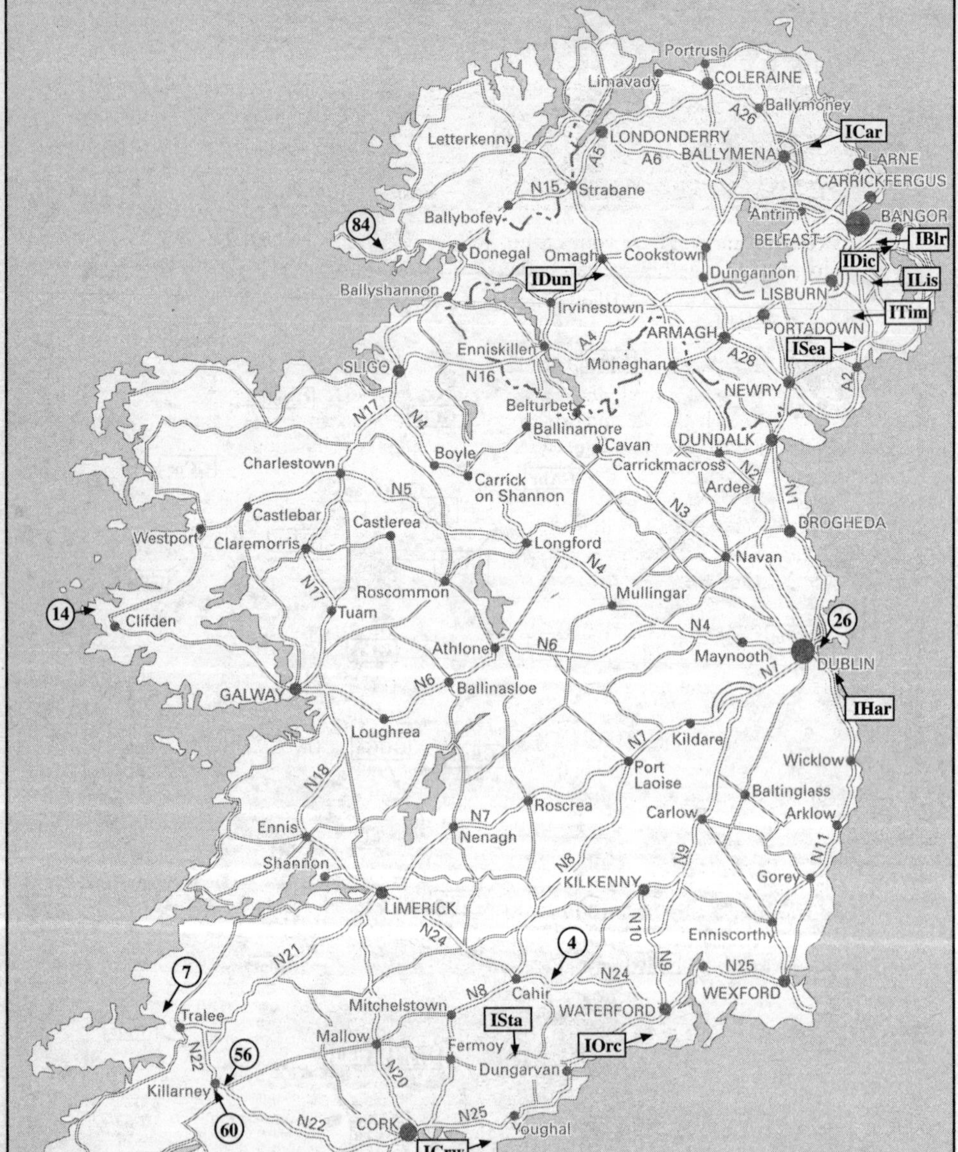
Portrush
COLERAINE
Limavady
Ballymoney
A26
ICar
Letterkenny
LONDONDERRY
A6
BALLYMENA
LARNE
A5
CARRICKFERGUS
N15
Strabane
84
Ballybofey
Antrim
BANGOR
BELFAST
IBlr
Donegal
Omagh
Cookstown
IDic
IDun
Dungannon
ILis
Ballyshannon
LISBURN
Irvinestown
ITim
A4
ARMAGH
PORTADOWN
Enniskillen
ISea
SLIGO
A28
Monaghan
N16
A2
NEWRY
Belturbet
N17
N4
Ballinamore
DUNDALK
Cavan
Boyle
Carrickmacross
Charlestown
N2
Carrick on Shannon
N5
Ardee
N1
Castlebar
N3
Castlerea
DROGHEDA
Westport
Claremorris
Longford
Navan
N4
N17
Roscommon
Mullingar
14
Tuam
Clifden
N4
26
Athlone
N6
Maynooth
DUBLIN
N7
N6
Ballinasloe
GALWAY
IHar
Loughrea
Kildare
N7
N18
Wicklow
Port Laoise
Baltinglass
Roscrea
Carlow
Arklow
N7
Ennis
Nenagh
N9
N11
N8
Shannon
KILKENNY
Gorey
LIMERICK
N10
N24
Enniscorthy
4
N21
N9
N25
7
N24
N8
Cahir
WEXFORD
Mitchelstown
WATERFORD
ISta
Tralee
Mallow
IOrc
N22
Fermoy
56
N20
Dungarvan
Killarney
N25
60
N22
CORK
Youghal
ICrw
IHos
IDee

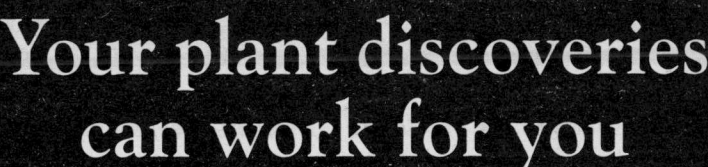

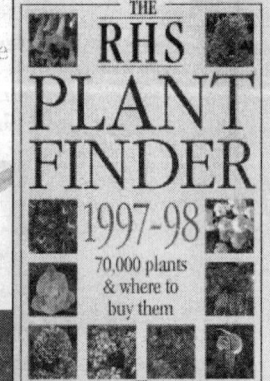

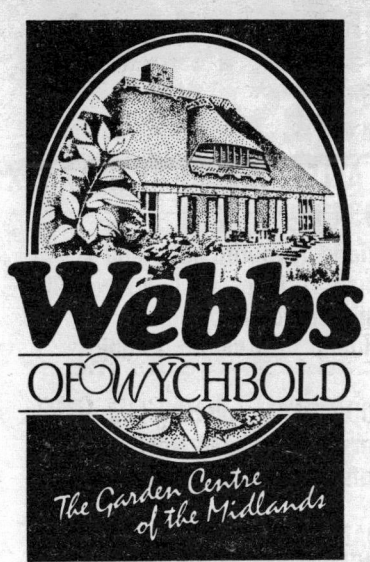

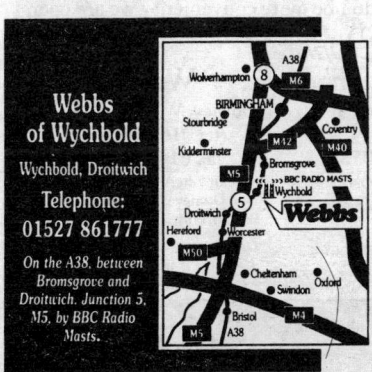

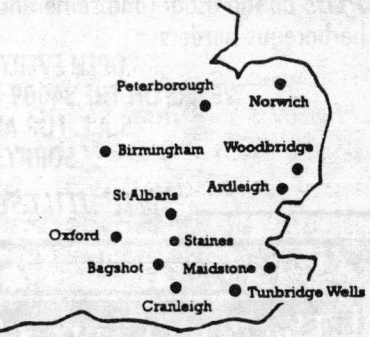

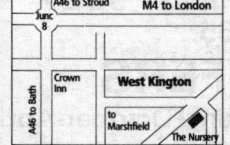

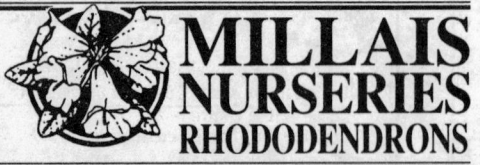

HALEcat GARDEN · NURSERIES

Witherslack
Nr. Grange-over-Sands
Cumbria. Tel: 015395 52229

INTERESTING PLANTS

Hostas • Heathers • Grey Foliage Plants Euphorbias • Ground Covers • Border Perennials

Mature examples of many of our plants may be seen in the Main Garden adjoining the Nursery which is open at all opening times with no obligation to buy. Evening Coach Parties by appointment.

Over 80 species and varieties of hydrangea available

OPEN THROUGHOUT THE YEAR.
Monday-Friday 9.00am-4.30pm. Sunday (April-Sept 2.00pm-4.00pm).Closed on Saturdays.
Follow Brown Daisy sign off A590 through Witherslack village

Par-ham

Elizabeth House & Gardens
Pulborough
Tel: 01903 744888

Visit this beautiful house and gardens in a peaceful Downland setting, in the heart of an ancient deer park

Church; Shop; Plant Sales; Teas in Big Kitchen; Picnic Area;
Registered Charity 276673

1997 PARHAM GARDEN WEEKEND: 19TH & 20TH JULY

UNUSUAL HOUSEPLANTS

Streptocarpus, Columneas, Begonias, Gesneriads and Solenostemons (Coleus)

See us at all the major flower shows or visit our nurseries. We despatch mail order and we also supply over 120 Garden Centres throughout Britain. We hold the National Collection of Streptocarpus.

LARGE SAE (A4) FOR COLOUR CATALOGUE

DIBLEYS NURSERIES (WDib)

LLANELIDAN, RUTHIN, NORTH WALES, LL15 2LG
Tel Number 01978 790677 Fax Number 01978 790668

Access VISA SWITCH

Kenwith Nursery

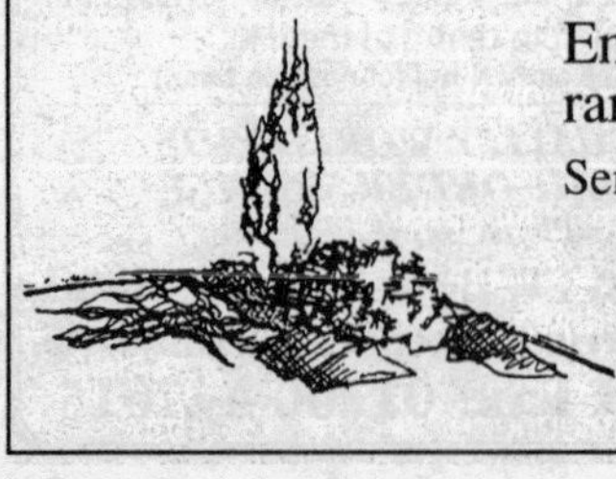

England's leading postal and retail dwarf and rare conifer specialists

Send 3 x 1st class stamps for catalogue to:

Gordon Haddow
Kenwith Nursery, Blinsham, Nr. Torrington,
Beaford, Winkleigh, North Devon EX19 8NT
Tel: 01805 603274 Fax: 01805 603663

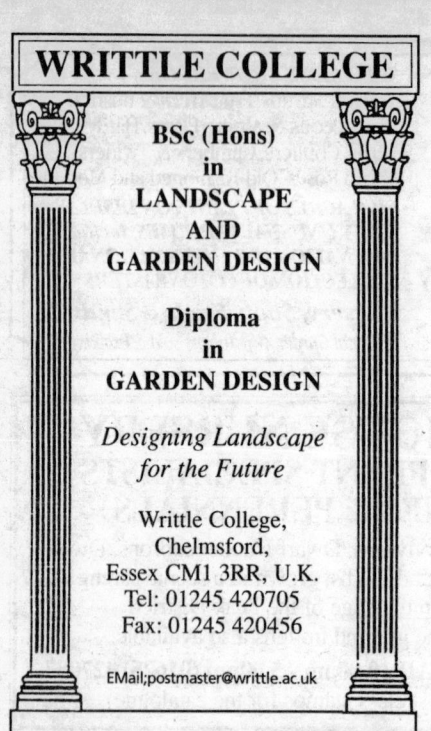

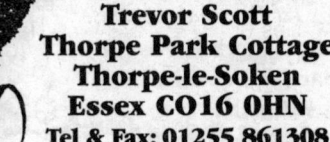

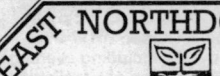

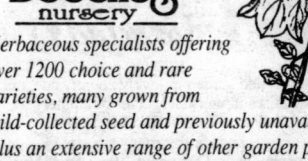

INDEX OF ADVERTISERS

THE HARDY PLANT SOCIETY

The Hardy Plant Society was formed to foster interest in hardy herbaceous plants on the widest possible scale. It aims to give its members information about the wealth of both well known and little known hardy plants, how to grow them to the best advantage and where they may be obtained. It also aims to ensure that all worthy hardy plants remain in cultivation and have the widest possible distribution.

Regional and Local Groups

Members may join any of the growing number of local groups organising many events in their own area including plant sales, garden visits, demonstrations and lectures. Most groups issue their own newsletter. the Groups form a basis for friendly exchange of information and plants and are an invaluable way of meeting other keen plantsmen locally. There is also a Correspondents Group for those not able to get out and about.

Genus and special Groups

Members may also join any of the specialised groups within the Society which will put them in touch with other members having similar interests. At present there are five such groups covering 'Variegated plants', 'Hardy Geraniums', 'Grasses', 'Paeony' & 'Pulmonarias'.

Publications and Slide Library

The Society's Journal 'The Hardy Plant' is currently issued twice a year containing major illustrated articles on a wide variety of plants and gardens. Regular newsletters keep members informed of current events. A central collection of slides is available for loan to members wishing to compile illustrated lectures.

Seed Distribution

Each year members are encouraged to collect seed from plants in their gardens for the seed Distribution which produces a printed list of all available seed, much of which comes from overseas. This currently lists over 2,500 varieties of seed, the majority of which is not available from commercial sources and, for a nominal sum members may select a number of packets from this.

Plant Sales and Shows

At organised meetings, both national and local, members bring interesting and unusual plants which are sold to aid the Society's funds. The Society puts on displays at the Royal Horticultural Society and other shows around the country and members can be involved by helping with the stands or by supplying plants to be shown.

Propagation and Wants scheme

This is run by the Southern Counties Group which propagates material from rarer or more difficult plants to ensure that the plants have the widest possible distribution. Some groups regularly issue lists of plants that members want but have been unable to locate. Word of mouth often helps locate wanted plants.

Conservation

The Society is most concerned about the conservation of garden plants. Countless fine plants have totally disappeared from cultivation and remain but a memory. In close cooperation with the National Council for the Conservation of Plants and gardens, the Society is making efforts to ensure that all worthy plants are kept in cultivation.

For further information or Membership Application Form please write to:

The Administrator
Mrs Pam Adams
Little Orchard
Great Comberton
Pershore
Worcs WR10 3DP
Tel No 01386 710317

HARDY PLANT SOCIETY

MEMBERSHIP APPLICATION FOR 1997

The Annual Subscriptions are as follows:

Single Membership **£10.00**

Joint Membership (any two members living at the same address) **£12.00**

Subscriptions are renewable annually on **1 January**. Subscriptions of members joining after 1 October are valid until the end of the following year.

Overseas members are requested to remit by International Money Order in **Sterling** or by Credit Card. (Visa/Master Card/Eurocard/Access).

APPLICATION FORM

I/We wish to apply for membership for 1997

NAME/S ....

ADDRESS ....

....

.... POST CODE ....

and would like to apply for the following type of membership

SINGLE	£10.00	....
JOINT (2 members at one address)	£12.00	....
Airmail postage (outside Europe)	£6.00	....
	TOTAL	

I enclose a cheque in Pounds Sterling payable to **THE HARDY PLANT SOCIETY**.
(Please **DO NOT** send cheques in Foreign Currency)

OR

Please debit my Visa / Master Card / Eurocard / Access

CARD NUMBER ☐☐☐☐ ☐☐☐☐ ☐☐☐☐ ☐☐☐☐

EXPIRY DATE

☐☐ ☐☐

Your name as on Card ....

Signature .... Date ....

Please print name and address clearly, tear out page and send to:

THE ADMINISTRATOR, Mrs Pam Adams,
Little Orchard, Great Comberton,
Pershore, Worcs. WR10 3DP. ENGLAND

For further details of the Society please see previous page